THE OXFORD GUIDE TO
UNITED STATES HISTORY

THE OXFORD GUIDE TO
UNITED STATES HISTORY

Editor in Chief

Paul S. Boyer

Editors

Melvyn Dubofsky, Eric H. Monkkonen,
Ronald L. Numbers, David M. Oshinsky, Emily S. Rosenberg

OXFORD
UNIVERSITY PRESS

Oxford New York
Auckland Cape Town Dar es Salaam Hong Kong Karachi
Kuala Lumpur Madrid Melbourne Mexico City
Nairobi New Delhi Shanghai Taipei Toronto

and an associated company in
Berlin

Originally published in 2001 as *The Oxford Companion to United States History*.

Published by Oxford University Press, Inc.
198 Madison Avenue, New York, New York, 10016-4314

ISBN: 978-0-19-534091-4

CONTENTS

INTRODUCTION

~

The hundreds of historians who have collaborated in the creation of *The Oxford Companion to United States History* have done so out of a shared conviction that history matters. A sense of the past makes civilization possible and helps us all grasp the larger meaning and context of our individual lives. Along with our knowledge of our personal ancestry, our family histories, and our individual experiences, we all acquire a sense of identity from the histories of groups that are also a part of our past. Whether they be racial, religious, ethnic, regional, or professional, such groups and interlocking social networks help make us who we are. Among these groups, the largest that shapes the sense of personal identity for most of us—along with our membership in the global human family—is citizenship in a nation-state.

The history of a nation, in turn, is a complex mosaic of many smaller bits of history. Included in this mosaic are a dizzying array of diverse historical components:

- Notable men and women—presidents and protesters; inventors, business innovators, religious leaders—whose lives have made a difference;
- Great dramatic events such as wars and economic depressions;
- Ideas, ideologies, and faiths that have won the allegiance of millions;
- Long-term historical processes such as immigration and urbanization;
- Innovations in science and medicine, including the conquest of deadly killer diseases of the past such as typhoid, smallpox, and tuberculosis;
- Technological changes such as the factory system, railroads, the automobile, television, and the computer;
- Economic developments from the rise of the stock market in the early nineteenth century to the multinational enterprises and global economy.

The Oxford Companion to United States History offers in convenient, readily accessible form a rich treasure house of information about, and interpretations of, all these historical factors that have gone into making the United States what it is today, and thus into making individual Americans what they are. For users in other parts of the world, this reference work contributes to your understanding of a nation that, for better or worse, looms large on the world stage as the twenty-first century dawns. This is, in short, not only a work about the past; it is a work that illuminates the present as well.

BACKGROUND AND GOALS OF THE BOOK

This monumental reference work has been some nine years in the making. Or, taking a longer view, it is part of a tradition of scholarly publishing extending back to the year 1478—fourteen years before Christopher Columbus's first voyage of discovery—when a German printer named Thomas Rood published the first scholarly book at Oxford and, in effect, founded Oxford University Press. Oxford's history of publishing in the field of American history began with one of the first accounts of England's North American colonies, John Smith's annotated *Map of Virginia* (1612). (The entry on John Smith in the present Oxford University Press volume thus represents a link with the past reaching back nearly 400 years!) The first "Oxford Companion"—to English literature—appeared in 1932. In the decades that followed, a long succession of "Companions" on a wide variety of subjects, including wine, women, and song, have been trusted and beloved by generations of users, and won for Oxford University Press a premier place in the field of scholarly reference works. The present long-awaited and entirely new volume is the first Oxford Companion to United States history in more than a generation.

The over-riding goal of everyone associated with this project has been, quite simply, to produce the best possible reference work available covering the entire sweep of American history—and we believe we have succeeded. To prepare such a work requires detailed preliminary planning, thoughtful selection of entries by an experienced team of editors, knowledgeable choice of contributors, and long hours of editorial work and guiding the work through the final stages of production. The planning began with a November 1992 meeting of the editorial team in New York City with the experienced Trade Reference staff from Oxford University Press, to formulate the project's broad goals and guiding principles and to sketch out the range of entries essential to a work of the depth and quality we were determined to achieve.

The challenge at that meeting was particularly great because the study of American history—like American society itself—had been transformed in recent decades. The old days when "American history" meant primarily political, diplomatic, and military history—with perhaps a token gesture toward social and cultural history—were, happily, long behind us. Any up-to-date reference work in American history had to give extensive, in-depth coverage to African American history; women's history; economic history; religious history; cultural history ("high," "popular," and "mass"); and the history of science, medicine, and technology. Such a work had to give full coverage of many different subgroups of Americans and a broad array of topics in the social and cultural realms. Even a quick glance through the book that is now in your hands, from "Abortion" and "Acquired Immunodeficiency Syndrome" (AIDS) to "Yellow Fever" and "Zakrzewska, Marie" (a pioneering woman physician) will make clear that *The Oxford Companion to United States History* meets this criterion of breadth with flying colors.

At the same time, we were aware that such a work had to give full attention to the political, military, and diplomatic topics that remain crucial to an understanding of the American experience—but from a modern vantage point that placed these events and developments within their larger social context. The *Oxford Companion to United States History* has accomplished this goal as well, with entries on the nation's leading political, military, and diplomatic figures, events, and treaties from a fully contemporary perspective. The editors and authors have also kept at the forefront of their attention the fact that a definitive reference work like this must also give full and comprehensive coverage to every time period, from the pre-Columbian era to the present. This goal, too, has been accomplished, with a discussion of the earliest inhabitants of North America in the essay "Indian History and Culture: Migration and Pre-Columbian Era" to such essays as "Internet and World Wide Web," "Clinton, Bill," and "Human Genome Project."

We have been particularly careful to give appropriate coverage to the Colonial Era, before the United States existed as a nation. This long span of American history is covered not only in a major overview "Colonial Era" essay, and in many entries on specific events, topics, and individuals, but also in the early parts of general essays such as "Literature," "Painting," "Religion," and so forth. In short, the more than 1,400 essays in this work encompass the great sweep of American history in all its rich complexity and its many eras and aspects.

Still another central goal has been to make this a "state of the art" work incorporating the best and most up-to-date historical scholarship. We have chosen contributors who are authorities on the subjects they write about, and who in many cases are themselves the authors of books and essays that have shaped contemporary understanding of the topics they write about. Whether established senior scholars or young historians on the threshold of their careers, all the contributors brought a special expertise and competence to the writing of their essays.

Simply because a reference work is comprehensive and authoritative, it need not be dry and dull! The contributors have paid attention to the quality of their prose as well as the accuracy of their facts, and throughout the editorial process we have concentrated on making every essay clear, readable, and interesting, as well as accurate and thorough. Learning about history need not be like taking medicine, and it is our hope that the essays in *The Oxford Companion to United States History* will give pleasure as well as provide information.

From Theodore Parker to Charlie Parker; Cotton Mather to the Cotton Industry; Martha Graham to Billy Graham; Sitting Bull to the 1930s Sit-Down Strikes; from the Bay Psalm Book to the Internet; from Racism, the Nativist Movement, and the Wounded Knee Massacre to Philanthropy, the Civil Rights Movement, and Cultural Pluralism—this is America's story in as comprehensive a form as can be gathered between the covers of a single volume. The book also includes a carefully chosen selection of historically and culturally significant maps that provide a valuable cartographic and visual perspective on this story.

We have kept constantly in mind the wide array of users who turn to a work like *The Oxford Companion to United States History*, whether on their own shelves, in a public-library reference room, or in their school library. We understand that reference works like this serve many purposes, from settling an argument, checking a quick fact, or gleaning a biographical detail to preparing a research paper or gaining a comprehensive overview understanding of an entire time period such as the Antebellum Era, the Civil War, or the New Deal, or a broad topic such as Agriculture, Labor Movements, Indian History and Culture. We have selected the entries, from the broadest to the most specific, and pitched the level of coverage, with these various uses in mind. This is a work for many purposes and many users, from the high-school student perhaps approaching American history for the first time to the seasoned historian suffering a momentary memory lapse to the individual seeking a specific bit of information or simply curious about the past.

HOW TO USE THIS WORK

The Oxford Companion to United States History has been planned for maximum usefulness. This is a work to be thumbed and worn out, not a book to be put behind glass on a shelf!

The straightforward **alphabetical arrangement**, rather than a potentially confusing topical grouping or chronological structure, permits the user to go easily and immediately to the desired essay. In addition, each essay concludes with a brief bibliography listing key works relevant to that topic, for the user who wishes a more detailed treatment.

Within this alphabetical structure, entry terms are often arranged by **key words** rather than by the first word. Individuals, of course, are alphabetized by their last names (DiMaggio, Joe), and other entries are typically listed by the most important word in the title, as in "Land Policy, Federal" and "Pearl Harbor, Attack on." Book titles are listed by the first substantive word in the title, rather than the article: "*Grapes of Wrath, The*." A moment's thought about the logic of titling entry terms should facilitate the search process.

In most essays, you will notice that certain names or terms are preceded by an **asterisk**. This means that you will find a separate essay on that individual, event, or topic elsewhere in the volume. The multi-part Civil War essay, for example, contains many asterisks to specific battles (Antietam, Gettysburg, Vicksburg); prominent individuals (Abraham Lincoln, Jefferson Davis, Ulysses S. Grant, Thomas [Stonewall] Jackson, Robert E. Lee, etc.); and other relevant topics (Confederate States of America; Draft Riots, Civil War; Railroads; Slavery; the South; and so forth).

At the end of most essays you will also find an entry beginning with the phrase "**See also. . . .**" These "See also" entries direct you to other essays in the work that are relevant to the topic at hand, even though these entries are not mentioned by name in the body of the essay.

Another very important user aid is the **Blind Entry**. This is an entry term, at the appropriate point in the alphabetical sequence, that directs you to an essay or essays on that topic that for one reason or another appear under a different title. Blind entries serve a variety of purposes. Some help you find essays on topics or events that are known by different terms. For example, a blind entry for "French and Indian War" directs you to the essay entitled "Seven Years' War"—another name for the same conflict. Similarly, a blind entry for "G.I. Bill of Rights" steers you to the official name of this important World War II law: "Servicemen's Readjustment Act." A blind entry for "Automobile" directs you to essays entitled "Motor Vehicles" and "Automotive Industry" that cover the history of the automobile in great detail. We have also provided blind entries for entry terms that are alphabetized by a key word rather than by first word, or for subjects that appear as part of a compound entry term. Thus the blind entry "Steel Industry" steers the user to the essay entitled "Iron and Steel Industry." Still other blind entries identify specific topics that are covered in larger, more comprehensive essays. For example, the blind entry "Amana Community" directs the user to the essay on "Utopian and Communitarian Movements," while the blind entry "Central Park" suggests that the researcher consult the essays entitled "Parks, Urban," and "Olmsted, Frederick Law," both of which deal with Central Park.

All of these aids are designed with a single purpose in mind: to make *The Oxford Companion to American History* just as helpful as it can possibly be to all the users of the work.

ACKNOWLEDGMENTS

Perhaps more than any other form of scholarship, a reference work such as this is the product of many individuals collaborating toward a single end. The Associate Editors whose names appear on the title page played key roles at every stage, from the initial choices of entries and the selection of contributors to editing the final essays. The work would hardly have been possible without the cheerful, conscientious labors of this team of historians. Each editor took responsibility for a general category of essays. These areas are as follows:

Paul S. Boyer: Cultural and Intellectual History
Melvyn Dubofsky: Business, Labor, and Economic History
Eric H. Monkkonen: Social History
Ronald L. Numbers: Medicine, Science, and Technology
David M. Oshinsky: Political and Legal History
Emily S. Rosenberg: Diplomatic and Military History

The members of the Advisory Board listed on page ii provided wise counsel in the initial planning stages, suggested names of potential contributors, and in some cases agreed to write essays themselves.

The expertise and experience, as well as the calm and good humor, of the dedicated editorial staff in the Trade Reference Division at Oxford University Press–New York were absolutely essential to this project at every stage, from the initial planning to the sometimes hectic last-minute details. Shepherding an "Oxford Companion" through the successive stages of conception, gestation, and birth is a monumental task at which the professional editors at Oxford have become amazingly proficient. (If one may pursue the analogy, the conception stage is probably the most fun.) Thanks, then, to Linda Halvorson Morse, Executive Editor of Trade Reference, who wrote the initial letter of invitation that started the ball rolling; Development Editors John Drexel and Liz Sonneborn; Nancy Toff, Vice President and Editorial Director, who provided wise oversight and inspiration; two ever-optimistic, unfailingly cheerful, and remarkably gifted project editors, Hannah Borgeson and Catherine Carter; the awesome William McCormack, indefatigable phoner of potential contributors and prodder of laggard authors; editorial assistants Amy Strong and Christopher Stahl; copyeditors Hannah Borgeson, Margaret A. Hogan, and Marion T. Brady; and production editor Aimee Chevrette. Ann Boyer provided invaluable proofreading assistance under last-minute time pressures. All of these exceptionally talented and dedicated individuals were crucial to the success of this undertaking.

Finally, of course, this work represents the achievement of the more than nine hundred authors whose names appear on pages xiii–xliii. It is they who wrote the essays—and who thus are the authors of the book. These contributors—ranging from talented doctoral dissertators and busy young assistant professors to established and well-known historians in mid-career to distinguished retired scholars—took on their assignments willingly, wrote their essays with skill and care, and bore cheerfully (for the most part) the sometimes niggling editorial process and the inevitable delays in a project of this magnitude. My thanks to them all.

Best wishes as you use *The Oxford Companion to the United States History.* I do hope you will find it of value as you explore the American past in all its rich complexity.

September 2000
Paul S. Boyer
Editor in Chief

ABOUT THE EDITORS

~

EDITOR IN CHIEF

Paul S. Boyer (Ph.D., Harvard 1966) is Merle Curti Professor of History at the University of Wisconsin-Madison, where he also directs the Institute for Research in the Humanities. His books include *Purity in Print: The Vice Society Movement and Book Censorship in America* (1968); *Notable American Women, 1600–1950* (asst. ed., 3 vols., 1971), *Salem Possessed: The Social Origins of Witchcraft* (co-author with Stephen Nissenbaum, 1974); *Urban Masses and Moral Order in America, 1820–1920* (1978); *By the Bomb's Early Light: American Thought and Culture at the Dawn of the Atomic Age* (1985); *When Time Shall Be No More: Prophecy Belief in Modern American Culture* (1992); and *Fallout: A Historian Reflects on America's Half Century Encounter with Nuclear Weapons* (1998). *Salem Possessed* won the American Historical Association's Dunning Prize; *When Time Shall Be No More* received the Wisconsin Library Association's Banta Award. An elected member of the American Academy of Arts and Sciences, Boyer has served on the executive board of the Organization of American Historians. His essays have appeared in the *Journal of American History, American Quarterly, New Republic, Nation, Chronicle of Higher Education,* and many other periodicals.

EDITORS

Melvyn Dubofsky is Distinguished Professor of History and Sociology, Binghamton University, SUNY. His books include *We Shall Be All: A History of the Industrial Workers of the World* (1969; 1988); *John L. Lewis: A Biography* (in collaboration with Warren W. Van Tine, 1977); *The State and Labor in Modern America* (1994); and the essay collection *Hard Work: The Making of Labor History* (2000). He has held Fulbright Professorships and Guest Professorships at the University of Tel Aviv, Israel, and the University of Salzburg, Austria and served as the John Adams Professor of American History at the University of Amsterdam. Dubofsky has directed NEH Summer Seminars for Professionals and for College Teachers (1980, 1981, and 1996), and is a member of the Philip Taft Labor History Prize Committee, served as a member and chair the American Historical Association's Committee on the Littleton-Griswold Prize, and is on the editorial board of the journal *Labor History.*

Eric H. Monkkonen is Professor of History and Policy Studies at UCLA. Former president of the Urban History Association, and the Social Science History Association, he has published five books, edited three more, and written over fifty research articles. His most recent book, *Murder in New York City* (2000) examines the major social shifts affecting homicide. These include the effects of mass immigration, urban growth, the Civil War, demographic changes, and Prohibition. This work ethnographically reconstructs ordinary violence, showing how gender roles and weapons shaped fatal individual conflicts. By comparing New York City to London and Liverpool, Monkkonen sets American violence in an international context.

Ronald L. Numbers is Hilldale and William Coleman Professor of the History of Science and Medicine and chair of the Department of the History of Medicine at the University of Wisconsin-Madison. He has written or edited more than two dozen books, including *The Creationists* (1992) and *Darwinism Comes to America* (1998). A former editor of *Isis,* he is co-editing, with David C. Lindberg, the eight-volume *Cambridge History of Science.* He is a past president of the American Society of Church History, the current president of the History of Science Society, and a fellow of the American Academy of Arts and Sciences.

David M. Oshinsky, the Board of Governors Professor of History at Rutgers, received his doctorate from Brandeis University. His books include *A Conspiracy So Immense: The World of Joe McCarthy,* which won the Hardeman Prize in 1984 for the best book about the history of Congress and *"Worse Than Slavery": Parchman Farm and the Ordeal of Jim Crow Justice,* which was awarded the Robert F. Kennedy Prize in 1996 for the year's most distinguished contribution to the field of human rights. Oshinsky's articles and reviews appear regularly in the *New York Times, Washington Post,* and *Chronicle of Higher Education.* In 1987, he was awarded Rutgers' highest classroom honor, the Warren I. Susman Award for Excellence in Teaching.

Emily S. Rosenberg, DeWitt Wallace Professor of History at Macalester College, specializes in United States foreign relations in the twentieth century. She is the author of the widely used book *Spreading the American Dream: American* Economic and Cultural Expansion, 1890–1945 and, most recently, of *Financial Missionaries to the World: The Politics and Culture of Dollar Diplomacy, 1900–1930,* which won the Ferrell Senior Book award from the Society for Historians of American Foreign Relations in 2000. She has co-authored several textbooks, among them *In Our Times: America Since 1945* and *Liberty, Equality, Power: A History of the American People,* and written numerous articles on international finance, gender issues, and foreign relations. She has served on the board of the Organization of American Historians, on the board of editors of the *Journal of American History* and *Diplomatic History,* and as president of the Society for Historians of American Foreign Relations.

DIRECTORY OF CONTRIBUTORS

Susan Ariel Aaronson, *Senior Fellow, National Policy Association, Washington, D.C.*
GROUP OF SEVEN CONFERENCES

Pnina Abir-Am, *Visiting Assistant Professor in the History of Science and Technology, University of California, Berkeley*
WATSON, JAMES D.

Henry J. Abraham, *James Hart Professor Emeritus of Government and Foreign Affairs, University of Virginia, Charlottesville*
FEDERAL GOVERNMENT, JUDICIAL BRANCH

Paul P. Abrahams, *Professor Emeritus of History and Humanities, University of Wisconsin—Green Bay*
FOREIGN TRADE, U.S.; GLOBAL ECONOMY, AMERICA AND THE; TARIFFS

W. Andrew Achenbaum, *Professor of History and Dean, College of Humanities, the Arts, and Communication, University of Houston, Texas*
AMERICAN ASSOCIATION OF RETIRED PERSONS; SOCIAL SECURITY

Marsha E. Ackermann, *Independent Scholar, Ann Arbor, Michigan*
REFRIGERATION AND AIR CONDITIONING

Willi Paul Adams, *Professor of North American History, John F. Kennedy Institute for North American Studies, Free University of Berlin, Germany*
COMMON SENSE; PAINE, THOMAS

Jeffrey S. Adler, *Associate Professor of History and Criminology, University of Florida, Gainesville*
CRIME

Thomas P. Adler, *Professor of English, Purdue University, West Lafayette, Indiana*
PULITZER PRIZES

Tanya Agathocleous, *Ph.D. candidate in English, Rutgers University, New Brunswick, New Jersey*
HUGHES, LANGSTON; JOHNSON, JAMES WELDON

Ginette Aley, *Instructor in History, Iowa State University, Ames*
AGRICULTURE: THE "GOLDEN AGE" (1890s–1920); GRAIN PROCESSING INDUSTRY

Michael Allen, *Professor of History, University of Washington, Tacoma*
MISSISSIPPI RIVER

Deborah J. Anderson, *Assistant Professor of Economics, University of New Mexico, Albuquerque*
PERKINS, FRANCES (co-author)

Margo A. Anderson, *Professor of History, University of Wisconsin—Milwaukee*
CENSUS, FEDERAL

Rima D. Apple, *Professor in the School of Human Ecology and the Women's Studies Program, University of Wisconsin—Madison*
HOME ECONOMICS MOVEMENT

Joyce Appleby, *Professor of History, University of California, Los Angeles*
INDIVIDUALISM

Jerold W. Apps, *Professor Emeritus of Education and Rural Sociology, University of Wisconsin—Madison*
BREWING AND DISTILLING

Thomas J. Archdeacon, *Professor of History, University of Wisconsin—Madison*
IMMIGRATION LAW

Raymond O. Arsenault, *John Hope Franklin Professor of Southern History, University of South Florida, St. Petersburg*
CIVIL RIGHTS MOVEMENT; CLINTON, BILL; LONG, HUEY; *SWANN* v. *CHARLOTTE-MECKLENBURG BOARD OF EDUCATION*

Milton B. Asbell, *Adjunct Assistant Professor in the Department of Dental Care Systems, School of Dental Medicine, University of Pennsylvania, Philadelphia*
DENTISTRY

Gary Ashwill, *Ph.D. candidate in English, Duke University, Durham, North Carolina*
LITERATURE: EARLY NATIONAL AND ANTEBELLUM ERAS

Jeremy Atack, *Professor of Economics and History, Vanderbilt University, Nashville, Tennessee; Research Associate, National Bureau of Economic Research, Cambridge, Massachusetts*
PRODUCTIVITY

Erik W. Austin, *Director of Archival Development, Inter-University Consortium for Political and Social Research, University of Michigan, Ann Arbor*
PUBLIC OPINION

Edward L. Ayers, *Hugh P. Kelly Professor of History, University of Virginia, Charlottesville*
ANTEBELLUM ERA

Simon Baatz, *Independent scholar*
AMERICAN PHILOSOPHICAL SOCIETY; SCIENCE: COLONIAL ERA

Reid Badger, *Professor Emeritus of American Studies, University of Alabama, Tuscaloosa*
RAGTIME

Jean Harvey Baker, *Professor of History, Goucher College, Baltimore, Maryland*
DEMOCRATIC PARTY; PIERCE, FRANKLIN; VAN BUREN, MARTIN

Ross K. Baker, *Professor of Political Science, Rutgers University, New Brunswick, New Jersey*
BAKER v. *CARR*; FEDERAL GOVERNMENT, LEGISLATIVE BRANCH: HOUSE OF REPRESENTATIVES

Alexander Balinky, *Professor Emeritus of Economics, Rutgers University, New Brunswick, New Jersey*
GALLATIN, ALBERT

Randall Balmer, *Ann Whitney Olin Professor of American Religion, Barnard College, Columbia University, New York, New York*
TELEVANGELISM

Lois W. Banner, *Professor of History, University of Southern California, Los Angeles*
NATIONAL AMERICAN WOMAN SUFFRAGE ASSOCIATION; STANTON, ELIZABETH CADY

Lance Banning, *Professor of History, University of Kentucky, Lexington*
LIBERTY; REVOLUTION AND CONSTITUTION, ERA OF

Robert C. Bannister, *Scheuer Professor of History Emeritus, Swarthmore College, Swarthmore, Pennsylvania*
PARSONS, TALCOTT; SOCIAL DARWINISM; SOCIOLOGY

Martha Banta, *Professor Emeritus of English, University of California, Los Angeles*
MIDDLETOWN

John Barnard, *Professor Emeritus of History, Oakland University, Rochester, Michigan*
REUTHER, WALTER

William C. Barnett, *Ph.D. candidate in History, University of Wisconsin—Madison*
YOSEMITE NATIONAL PARK

Richard A. Bartlett, *Professor Emeritus of History, Florida State University, Tallahassee*
LEWIS AND CLARK EXPEDITION

James L. Baughman, *Professor of Journalism and Mass Communication, University of Wisconsin—Madison*
FEDERAL COMMUNICATIONS COMMISSION; LUCE, HENRY R.; TELEVISION

Martha Bayles, *Independent scholar; Contributing correspondent, "Religion and Ethics News Weekly" (PBS); Visiting Scholar, Claremont McKenna College, Claremont, California*
POPULAR CULTURE

E. M. Beck, *Professor of Sociology, University of Georgia, Athens*
LYNCHING (co-author)

Ronald Becker, *Head, Special Collections, Rutgers University Libraries, New Brunswick, New Jersey*
LIBRARY OF CONGRESS

Mary Farrell Bednarowski, *Professor of Religious Studies, United Theological Seminary of the Twin Cities, New Brighton, Minnesota*
NEW AGE MOVEMENT

Richard Beeman, *Professor of History, University of Pennsylvania, Philadelphia*
HENRY, PATRICK

Laura A. Belmonte, *Assistant Professor of History, Oklahoma State University, Stillwater*
UNITED STATES INFORMATION AGENCY; VOICE OF AMERICA

John Belohlavek, *Professor of History, University of South Florida, Tampa*
CLAYTON-BULWER TREATY; SEWARD, WILLIAM

Doron Ben-Atar, *Associate Professor of History, Fordham University, New York, New York*
EMBARGO ACTS

Michael Les Benedict, *Professor of History, Ohio State University, Columbus*
FOURTEENTH AMENDMENT; IMPEACHMENT; JOHNSON, ANDREW

Ludy T. Benjamin Jr., *Professor of Psychology, Texas A & M University, College Station*
PSYCHOLOGY

David Harry Bennett, *Professor of History, Syracuse University, Syracuse, New York*
NATIVIST MOVEMENT

Susan Porter Benson, *Associate Professor of History, University of Connecticut, Storrs*
DEPARTMENT STORES; WANAMAKER, JOHN

Thomas J. Bergin, *Professor of Computer Science and Information Systems, American University, Washington, D.C.*
VON NEUMANN, JOHN; WIENER, NORBERT

Christopher Berkeley, *Independent scholar*
BOSTON; MCDONALD'S; PLYMOUTH; REVERE, PAUL

Jonathan M. Berkey, *Ph.D. candidate in American History, Pennsylvania State University, University Park*
ANTIETAM, BATTLE OF; BULL RUN, BATTLE OF; DRAFT RIOTS, CIVIL WAR

Edward Berkowitz, *Professor of History, George Washington University, Washington, D.C.*
AMERICANS WITH DISABILITIES ACT

Charles E. Beveridge, *Series Editor, Frederick Law Olmsted Papers, American University, Washington, D.C.*
OLMSTED, FREDERICK LAW

M. Langley Biegert, *Editor, Holt, Rinehart and Winston, Austin, Texas*
SCOUTING

Lindy Biggs, *Associate Professor of History, Auburn University, Auburn, Alabama*
"AMERICAN SYSTEM" OF MANUFACTURES; MASS PRODUCTION

Roger E. Bilstein, *Professor Emeritus of History, University of Houston—Clear Lake, Texas*
AVIATION INDUSTRY; MISSILES AND ROCKETS

Henry C. Binford, *Charles Deering McCormick Professor of Teaching Excellence, Northwestern University, Evanston, Illinois*
SLUMS

Günter Bischof, *Professor of History, University of New Orleans, Louisiana*
MARSHALL PLAN

Katharine Bjork, *Community Faculty Member, Metropolitan State University, Minneapolis, Minnesota*
PROTECTORATES AND DEPENDENCIES; PUERTO RICO

Sarah J. Blackstone, *Associate Professor of Theater, Southern Illinois University, Carbondale*
CODY, WILLIAM ("BUFFALO BILL")

Karen J. Blair, *Professor of History, Central Washington University, Ellensburg*
WOMEN'S CLUB MOVEMENT

Francine D. Blau, *Frances Perkins Professor of Industrial and Labor Relations, Cornell University, Ithaca, New York*
PERKINS, FRANCES (co-author)

Michael Bliss, *Professor of History, University of Toronto, Ontario, Canada*
OSLER, WILLIAM

Jack S. Blocker Jr., *Professor of History, Huron College, University of Western Ontario, London, Ontario Canada*
TEMPERANCE AND PROHIBITION

Geoffrey Blodgett, *Robert Danforth Professor of History Emeritus, Oberlin College, Oberlin, Ohio*
ELIOT, CHARLES WILLIAM

Martin Blumenson, *Independent scholar*
PATTON, GEORGE S., JR.

Edith L. Blumhofer, *Director, Institute for the Study of American Evangelicals, Wheaton College, Illinois*
McPHERSON, AIMEE SEMPLE; REVIVALISM

Stuart M. Blumin, *Professor of American History, Cornell University, Ithaca, New York*
SOCIAL CLASS

Howard Bodenhorn, *Associate Professor of Economics, Lafayette College, Easton, Pennsylvania*
BANKING AND FINANCE

Charles C. Bolton, *Director, Center for Oral History and Cultural Heritage and Associate Professor of History, University of Southern Mississippi, Hattiesburg*
STATES' RIGHTS PARTY

Gerald Bordman, *Independent scholar*
MUSICAL THEATER; THEATER

David Bordwell, *Jacques Ledoux Professor of Film Studies, University of Wisconsin—Madison*
DISNEY, WALT; GRIFFITH, D. W.

Hannah Borgeson, *Department of History, City College, City University of New York*
BICYCLES AND BICYCLING

Eileen Boris, *Professor of Studies in Women and Gender, University of Virginia, Charlottesville*
HOMEWORK

Charlotte G. Borst, *Associate Professor of History, Saint Louis University, Missouri*
MIDWIFERY

Daniel H. Borus, *Associate Professor of History, Rochester University, Rochester, New York*
HOWELLS, WILLIAM DEAN; *LOOKING BACKWARD: 2000–1887*

Shearer Davis Bowman, *Associate Professor of History, University of Texas at Austin*
KANSAS-NEBRASKA ACT; NULLIFICATION

Jeanne Boydston, *Professor of History, University of Wisconsin—Madison*
WOMEN IN THE LABOR FORCE

Horace Clarence Boyer, *Associate Director, Fine Arts Center and Professor of Vocal Jazz and African American Music (ret.), University of Massachusetts, Amherst*
SPIRITUALS

Paul S. Boyer, *Merle Curti Professor of History, University of Wisconsin—Madison*
EDUCATION: OVERVIEW; LEISURE; MITCHELL, MARIA; PRINTING AND PUBLISHING

William H. Brackney, *Professor of Historical Theology and Principal of the Divinity College, McMaster University, Hamilton, Ontario, Canada*
ANTISLAVERY; BAPTISTS; GRIMKÉ, SARAH AND ANGELINA

James C. Bradford, *Associate Professor of History, Texas A & M University, College Station*
KING, ERNEST J.; MAHAN, ALFRED THAYER; PEARL HARBOR, ATTACK ON; PERRY, OLIVER HAZARD AND MATTHEW

Ronald Brashear, *Curator, Science and Technology Rare Books, Smithsonian Institution Libraries, Washington, D.C.*
HALE, GEORGE ELLERY

Holly Beachley Brear, *Adjunct Professor of Anthropology, George Mason University, Fairfax, Virginia*
ALAMO, BATTLE OF THE

Joseph Brent, *Professor Emeritus of American History, University of the District of Columbia, Washington, D.C.*
PEIRCE, CHARLES SANDERS

Susan A. Brewer, *Associate Professor of History, University of Wisconsin—Stevens Point*
PROPAGANDA

Alan Brinkley, *Allan Nevins Professor of History, Columbia University, New York, New York*
EMPLOYMENT ACT OF 1946; KENNEDY, JOHN F.

Robert H. Brinkmeyer Jr., *Professor of American Literature and Southern Studies, University of Mississippi, University*
FAULKNER, WILLIAM

Simon J. Bronner, *Professor of American Studies and Folklore, Pennsylvania State University, Harrisburg*
FOLK ART AND CRAFTS; FOLKLORE

D. Clayton Brown, *Professor of History, Texas Christian University, Fort Worth*
COTTON INDUSTRY

Kathleen M. Brown, *Associate Professor of History, University of Pennsylvania, Philadelphia*
BACON'S REBELLION

Roger H. Brown, *Professor Emeritus of History, American University, Washington, D.C.*
HARTFORD CONVENTION; WHISKEY REBELLION

Blaine A. Brownell, *President, Ball State University, Muncie, Indiana*
SOUTH, THE

W. Elliot Brownlee, *Professor of History, University of California, Santa Barbara*
TAXATION

Matthew J. Bruccoli, *Jeffries Professor of English, University of South Carolina, Columbia*
FITZGERALD, F. SCOTT

Robert V. Bruce, *Professor Emeritus of History, Boston University, Massachusetts*
BELL, ALEXANDER GRAHAM

C. D. B. Bryan, *Independent scholar*
MAYO CLINIC

Rex C. Buchanan, *Associate Director, Kansas Geological Survey, Lawrence*
EARTH SCIENCES; GEOLOGICAL SURVEYS

Kerry W. Buckley, *Independent scholar*
BEHAVIORISM; HALL, G. STANLEY

Thomas R. Buecker, *Curator, Fort Robinson Museum, Nebraska State Historical Society, Lincoln*
CRAZY HORSE

John D. Buenker, *Professor of History and Ethnic Studies, University of Wisconsin—Parkside, Kenosha*
PROGRESSIVE PARTY OF 1912–1924; PURE FOOD AND DRUG ACT; SECURITIES AND EXCHANGE COMMISSION; SIXTEENTH AMENDMENT; WAGNER, ROBERT F.

Paul Buhle, *Visiting Associate Professor of American Civilization, Brown University, Providence, Rhode Island*
COMMUNISM; RADICALISM; SOCIALIST PARTY OF AMERICA

John J. Bukowczyk, *Professor of History, Wayne State University, Detroit, Michigan*
POLISH AMERICANS

John L. Bullion, *Professor of History, University of Missouri—Columbia*
COMMITTEES OF CORRESPONDENCE; SONS OF LIBERTY; STAMP ACT

Steven C. Bullock, *Associate Professor of History, Worcester Polytechnic Institute, Worcester, Massachusetts*
FRATERNAL ORGANIZATIONS

Vern L. Bullough, *Distinguished Professor Emeritus in History and Sociology, State University of New York, Buffalo; Professor Emeritus of History, California State University, Northridge; Clinical Professor of Nursing, University of Southern California, Los Angeles*
NURSING; SEXUAL MORALITY AND SEX REFORM; VENEREAL DISEASE

Steven Dedalus Burch, *Visiting Assistant Professor of Communication Arts, Allegheny College, Meadville, Pennsylvania*
HAYES, HELEN

David Burner, *Professor of History, State University of New York, Stony Brook*
COOLIDGE, CALVIN; GOLDWATER, BARRY

John C. Burnham, *Professor of History, Ohio State University, Columbus*
TOBACCO PRODUCTS (co-author)

William Burr, *Senior Analyst, The National Security Archive, Washington, D.C.*
NUCLEAR STRATEGY

Larry Burt, *Associate Professor of History, Southwest Missouri State University, Springfield*
AMERICAN INDIAN MOVEMENT

Sargent Bush Jr., *John Bascom Professor of English, University of Wisconsin—Madison*
BYRD, WILLIAM, II

W. Michael Byrd, *Senior Research Scientist and Instructor of Public Health Practice, Harvard School of Public Health, Boston, Massachusetts*
NATIONAL MEDICAL ASSOCIATION (co-author)

Timothy A. Byrnes, *Associate Professor of Political Science, Colgate University, Hamilton, New York*
SPELLMAN, FRANCIS CARDINAL

John F. Callahan, *Morgan S. Odell Professor of Humanities, Lewis and Clark College, Portland, Oregon*
ELLISON, RALPH

Randolph B. Campbell, *Regents Professor of History, University of North Texas, Denton*
HOUSTON, SAM

Stanley W. Campbell, *Professor Emeritus of History, Baylor University, Waco, Texas*
FUGITIVE SLAVE ACT

Tracy Campbell, *Associate Professor of History, University of Kentucky, Lexington*
TOBACCO INDUSTRY

Charles Capper, *Associate Professor of History, University of North Carolina at Chapel Hill*
FULLER, MARGARET

W. Bernard Carlson, *Associate Professor, Division of Technology, Culture, and Communications, University of Virginia, Charlottesville*
ELECTRICAL INDUSTRY; WESTINGHOUSE, GEORGE

Lois Green Carr, *Historian, Historic St. Mary's City, St. Mary's City, Maryland; Adjunct Professor of History, University of Maryland, College Park*
BRENT, MARGARET

Noël Carroll, *Monroe C. Beardsley Professor of Philosophy, University of Wisconsin—Madison*
POSTMODERNISM

John Carson, *Assistant Professor of History, University of Michigan, Ann Arbor*
INTELLIGENCE, CONCEPTS OF

Fred V. Carstensen, *Professor of Economics, University of Connecticut, Storrs*
McCORMICK, CYRUS

Dan T. Carter, *Educational Foundation University Professor, University of South Carolina, Columbia*
SCOTTSBORO CASE; WALLACE, GEORGE C.

Evan Carton, *Professor of English, University of Texas at Austin*
HAWTHORNE, NATHANIEL

Nicholas Casner, *Professor of History, Boise State University, Boise, Idaho*
BURR, AARON; MASON-DIXON LINE

Joan Cass, *Independent scholar*
DANCE

Norman Caulfield, *Associate Professor of History, Fort Hays State University, Hays, Kansas*
GADSDEN PURCHASE

Mary Kupiec Cayton, *Professor of History and American Studies, Miami University, Oxford, Ohio*
EMERSON, RALPH WALDO; TRANSCENDENTALISM

Claude Cernuschi, *Associate Professor of Art History, Boston College, Chestnut Hill, Massachusetts*
POLLOCK, JACKSON

Leon Chai, *Professor of English and Comparative Literature, University of Illinois at Urbana-Champaign*
ROMANTIC MOVEMENT

John Whiteclay Chambers II, *Professor of History, Rutgers University, New Brunswick, New Jersey*
CONSCIENTIOUS OBJECTION

Stephanie A. Carpenter Chan, *Assistant Professor of History, Murray State University, Kentucky*
AGRICULTURE: 1770s TO 1890

Alfred D. Chandler Jr., *Isidor Straus Professor of Business History Emeritus, Harvard Business School, Boston, Massachusetts*
DU PONT, PIERRE

David A. Chappell, *Associate Professor of Pacific Islands History, University of Hawai'i at Manoa, Honolulu*
HAWAI'I

David L. Chappell, *Associate Professor of History, University of Arkansas, Fayetteville*
STATES' RIGHTS

E. Charles Chatfield, *H. Orth Hirt Professor of History Emeritus, Wittenberg University, Springfield, Ohio*
ANTIWAR MOVEMENTS; KELLOGG-BRIAND PACT; PACIFISM; PEACE MOVEMENTS

Ellen Chesler, *Senior Fellow/Director of Programming, Open Society Institute, New York, New York*
SANGER, MARGARET

Eric Howard Christianson, *Associate Professor of History with a joint appointment in the College of Pharmacy, University of Kentucky, Lexington*
MEDICINE: COLONIAL ERA

Gene Clanton, *Emeritus Professor of History, State University of Washington, Pullman*
POPULIST PARTY

Christopher Clark
CONSCRIPTION

Clifford E. Clark Jr., *M.A. and A.D. Hulmgs Professor of American Studies and Professor of History, Carleton College, Northfield, Minnesota*
ARCHITECTURE: DOMESTIC ARCHITECTURE; BEECHER, HENRY WARD; DONNER PARTY; HILL, JAMES J.; HOUSING

Bruce Clayton, *Harry A. Logan Sr., Professor of History, Allegheny College, Meadville, Pennsylvania*
BOURNE, RANDOLPH

Lawrence A. Clayton, *Professor of History, University of Alabama, Tuscaloosa*
SOTO, HERNANDO DE

Linda A. Clayton, *Senior Research Scientist and Instructor of Public Health Practice, Harvard School of Public Health, Boston, Massachusetts*
NATIONAL MEDICAL ASSOCIATION (co-author)

Paul G. E. Clemens, *Professor of History, Rutgers University, New Brunswick, New Jersey*
DARTMOUTH COLLEGE CASE; *FLETCHER* V. *PECK*; HAMILTON, ALEXANDER; *MARBURY* v. *MADISON*; NORTHWEST ORDINANCE

Kendrick A. Clements, *Professor of History, University of South Carolina, Columbia*
WILSON, WOODROW

J. Garry Clifford, *Professor of Political Science, University of Connecticut, Storrs*
BULGE, BATTLE OF THE (1944–1945); D-DAY; WORLD WAR II: CAUSES; WORLD WAR II: CHANGING INTERPRETATIONS; WORLD WAR II: MILITARY AND DIPLOMATIC COURSE; WORLD WAR II: POSTWAR IMPACT

Alan Clive, *FEMA—Federal Emergency Management Agency, Washington, D.C.*
JOHNSTOWN FLOOD

Charles L. Cohen, *Professor of History, University of Wisconsin—Madison*
BAY PSALM BOOK; COLONIAL ERA; HALF-WAY COVENANT; CAPTIVITY NARRATIVES, INDIAN; CORONADO, FRANCISCO VASQUEZ DE; INDIAN HISTORY AND CULTURE: FROM 1500 TO 1800; PILGRIMS; POCAHONTAS; PURITANISM

Greta L. Cohen, *Professor of Sport Sociology, University of Rhode Island, Kingston*
ZAHARIAS, MILDRED DIDRIKSON ("BABE")

Michael P. Cohen, *Professor of English, Southern Utah University, Cedar City*
SIERRA CLUB

Jon T. Coleman, *Ph.D. candidate in History, Yale University, New Haven, Connecticut*
ARNOLD, BENEDICT; JONES, JOHN PAUL

Jerald A. Combs, *Professor of History, San Francisco State University, California*
JAY, JOHN; JAY'S TREATY; PINCKNEY'S TREATY; QUASI-WAR WITH FRANCE; XYZ AFFAIR

David Conrad, *Professor Emeritus of History, Southern Illinois University, Carbondale*
AGRICULTURE: SINCE 1920; AGRICULTURAL ADJUSTMENT ADMINISTRATION; JAMES, JESSE; LONDON ECONOMIC CONFERENCE; MacARTHUR, DOUGLAS; OREGON TRAIL

Dennis M. Conrad, *Editor, Papers of General Nathanael Greene, Rhode Island Historical Society, Providence*
GREENE, NATHANAEL

David R. Contosta, *Professor of History, Chestnut Hill College, Philadelphia, Pennsylvania*
ADAMS, HENRY

Blanche Wiesen Cook, *Distinguished Professor of History, John Jay College of Criminal Justice, City University of New York*
ROOSEVELT, ELEANOR

Susan C. Cook, *Professor of Music, University of Wisconsin—Madison*
IVES, CHARLES

Carolyn C. Cooper, *Research Affiliate, Yale University, New Haven, Connecticut*
WHITNEY, ELI

Anthony H. Cordesman, *Senior Fellow and Co-Director, Middle East Studies Program, Center for Strategic and International Studies, Washington, D.C.*
PERSIAN GULF WAR; POWELL, COLIN

Saul Cornell, *Associate Professor of History, Ohio State University, Columbus*
WARREN, MERCY OTIS

David Cortes, *Independent scholar*
BLALOCK, ALFRED

George Cotkin, *Professor of History, California Polytechnic State University, San Luis Obispo*
SECULARIZATION

Robert J. Cottrol, *Professor of Law and History and Harold Paul Green Research Professor of Law, George Washington University School of Law, Washington, D.C.*
CIVIL RIGHTS CASES

David T. Courtwright, *Professor of History, University of North Florida, Jacksonville*
DRUGS, ILLICIT

Francis G. Couvares, *Professor of History and American Studies, Amherst College, Amherst, Massachusetts*
CENSORSHIP

Thomas R. Cox, *Professor Emeritus of History, San Diego State University, California*
LUMBERING

Robert Cozzolino, *Ph.D. candidate in Art History, University of Wisconsin—Madison*
CALDER, ALEXANDER

Michael J. Crawford, *Head, Early History Branch, Naval Historical Center, Washington, D.C.*
GREAT AWAKENING, FIRST AND SECOND; WILKES EXPEDITION

Donald T. Critchlow, *Founding Editor,* Journal of Policy History
BIRTH CONTROL AND FAMILY PLANNING

Paul Jerome Croce, *Associate Professor of American Studies, Stetson University, Deland, Florida*
JAMES, WILLIAM

Ruth Crocker, *Associate Professor of History, Auburn University, Auburn, Alabama*
ADDAMS, JANE; SETTLEMENT HOUSES; SOCIAL WORK

Alfred W. Crosby, *Professor Emeritus of History, University of Texas at Austin*
COLUMBIAN EXCHANGE; INFLUENZA

Shane Crotty, *Andino Laboratory, University of California, San Francisco*
BIOTECHNOLOGY INDUSTRY

James L. Crouthamel, *Professor Emeritus of History, Hobart & William Smith Colleges, Geneva, New York*
HEARST, WILLIAM RANDOLPH; PULITZER, JOSEPH

Charles L. Crow, *Professor Emeritus of English, Bowling Green State University, Bowling Green, Ohio*
SPIRITUALISM

*Robert M. Crunden
ARMORY SHOW; LEWIS, SINCLAIR; O'NEILL, EUGENE; PROGRESSIVE ERA

Noble E. Cunningham Jr., *Curators' Professor Emeritus of History, University of Missouri, Columbia*
JEFFERSON, THOMAS

Thomas J. Curran, *Associate Professor of History, St. John's University, Jamaica, New York*
KNOW-NOTHING PARTY

Charles G. Curtis Jr., *Partner, Foley & Lardner, Madison, Wisconsin*
RULE OF REASON

Wayne Cutler, *Research Professor of History, University of Tennessee, Knoxville*
POLK, JAMES KNOX

Jane E. Dabel, *Post-doctoral Fellow, Center for the Study of Gender and Women, University of California, Berkeley*
COLONIZATION MOVEMENT, AFRICAN; NAT TURNER'S UPRISING

Matthew Dallek, *Independent scholar*
AFFIRMATIVE ACTION

Helen Damon-Moore, *Director of Volunteer Services and Service Learning and Adjunct Professor of Women's Studies, Cornell College, Mt. Vernon, Iowa*
MAGAZINES

Cletus Daniel, *Professor of Collective Bargaining, Labor Law, and Labor History, School of Industrial and Labor Relations, Cornell University, Ithaca, New York*
CHAVEZ, CESAR

Pete Daniel, *Curator, National Museum of American History, Washington, D.C.*
SHARECROPPING AND TENANTRY

Eric D. Daniels, *Ph.D. candidate in History, University of Wisconsin—Madison*
DEMOCRACY IN AMERICA; FILLMORE, MILLARD; FREE SOIL PARTY; TYLER, JOHN; WHIG PARTY

Norman Daniels, *Goldthwaite Professor of Philosophy, Tufts University, Medford, Massachusetts*
RAWLS, JOHN

Roger Daniels, *Charles Phelps Taft Professor of History, University of Cincinnati, Ohio*
INCARCERATION OF JAPANESE AMERICANS

David Dary, *Professor of Journalism and Director, H.H. Herbert School of Journalism and Mass Communication, University of Oklahoma, Norman*
COWBOYS

Sheri I. David, *Professor of History, Northern Virginia Community College, Manassas*
MEDICARE AND MEDICAID

Thomas E. Davidson, *Senior Curator, Jamestown-Yorktown Foundation, Williamsburg, Virginia*
JAMESTOWN

Colin J. Davis, *Associate Professor of History, University of Alabama at Birmingham*
AMERICAN FEDERATION OF LABOR; HARRIMAN, E. H.

Janet Davis, *Assistant Professor of American Studies and History, University of Texas at Austin*
CIRCUSES

Ronald L. Davis, *Professor of History, Southern Methodist University, Dallas, Texas*
COLTRANE, JOHN; GERSHWIN, GEORGE; MUSIC: POPULAR MUSIC; PARKER, CHARLIE

David De Leon, *Associate Professor of History, Howard University, Washington, D.C.*
DYLAN, BOB

Don De Nevi, *Lecturer in Criminal Justice, San Francisco State University, California*
SERRA, JUNIPERO

James M. Dennis, *Professor of Art History, University of Wisconsin—Madison*
O'KEEFFE, GEORGIA; PAINTING: SINCE 1945; WARHOL, ANDY

Michael Aaron Dennis, *Assistant Professor of Science and Technology Studies, Cornell University, Ithaca, New York*
BUSH, VANNEVAR; SCIENCE: SINCE 1945

Alan Derickson, *Professor of Labor Studies and History, Pennsylvania State University, University Park*
INDUSTRIAL DISEASES AND HAZARDS

William Deverell, *Associate Professor of History, California Institute of Technology, Pasadena*
CALIFORNIA

Leah Dilworth, *Associate Professor of English, Long Island University, Brooklyn, New York*
INDIAN HISTORY AND CULTURE: THE INDIAN IN POPULAR CULTURE

Leonard Dinnerstein, *Professor of American History, University of Arizona, Tucson*
ANTI-SEMITISM

Robert A. Divine, *George W. Littlefield Professor Emeritus in American History, University of Texas at Austin*
JOHNSON, LYNDON B.; LIMITED NUCLEAR TEST BAN TREATY

John Dizikes, *Professor of American Studies and Fellow, Cowell College, University of California, Santa Cruz*
HORSE RACING; OPERA

L. Mara Dodge, *Assistant Professor of History, Westfield State College, Westfield, Massachusetts*
JUVENILE DELINQUENCY

Justus D. Doenecke, *Professor of History, New College of the University of Southern Florida, Sarasota*
AMERICA FIRST; ISOLATIONISM; NEUTRALITY; NEUTRALITY ACTS

Jay P. Dolan, *Professor of History, University of Notre Dame, Notre Dame, Indiana*
ROMAN CATHOLICISM

Bobby J. Donaldson, *Assistant Professor of History and African American Studies, University of South Carolina, Columbia*
DAVID WALKER'S APPEAL

Arthur Donovan, *Professor of History, U.S. Merchant Marine Academy, Kings Point, New York*
MARITIME TRANSPORT

Kendall J. Dood, *Independent scholar*
PATENT AND COPYRIGHT LAW

Jacob H. Dorn, *Professor of History, Wright State University, Dayton, Ohio*
RAUSCHENBUSCH, WALTER; SOCIAL GOSPEL

Erika Doss, *Professor of Fine Arts and Director, American Studies Program, University of Colorado at Boulder*
ABSTRACT EXPRESSIONISM

George H. Douglas, *Professor of English, University of Illinois at Urbana-Champaign*
MENCKEN, H. L.; MUCKRAKERS

Gregory Evans Dowd, *Associate Professor of History, University of Notre Dame, Notre Dame, Indiana*
McGILLIVRAY, ALEXANDER; PONTIAC; YAMASEE WAR

Joan E. Draper, *Associate Professor of Architecture, University of Colorado, Denver*
LANDSCAPE DESIGN

Karen Dubinsky, *Associate Professor of History, Queen's University, Kingston, Ontario, Canada*
RAPE

Thomas Dublin, *Professor of History, State University of New York, Binghamton*
DOMESTIC LABOR; FACTORY SYSTEM; LOWELL MILLS

Melvyn Dubofsky, *Distinguished Professor of History and Sociology, State University of New York, Binghamton*
SLAVERY: OVERVIEW

Ellen C. DuBois, *Professor of History, University of California, Los Angeles*
ANTHONY, SUSAN B.; EQUAL RIGHTS AMENDMENT; GENDER; NATIONAL WOMAN'S PARTY; NINETEENTH AMENDMENT; SENECA FALLS CONVENTION; WOMAN SUFFRAGE MOVEMENT

Lynn Dumenil, *Professor of History, Occidental College, Los Angeles, California*
AMERICAN LEGION; MASONIC ORDER; SACCO AND VANZETTI CASE; TWENTIES, THE

Colleen A. Dunlavy, *Professor of History, University of Wisconsin—Madison*
RAILROADS; TECHNOLOGY

Ellen Dwyer, *Associate Professor of Criminal Justice and History, Indiana University, Bloomington*
MENTAL HEALTH INSTITUTIONS; MENTAL ILLNESS

Charles W. Eagles, *Professor of History, University of Mississippi, University*
KENT STATE AND JACKSON STATE

Wilton E. Eckley, *Professor Emeritus of Liberal Arts and International Studies, Colorado School of Mines, Golden*
BARNUM, P. T.

R. David Edmunds, *Watson Professor of American History, University of Texas at Dallas, Richardson*
TECUMSEH; WOVOKA

Diane D. Edwards, *Independent scholar*
INDIAN HEALTH SERVICE; OPTOMETRY

Marc Egnal, *Professor of History, York University, Toronto, Ontario, Canada*
PROCLAMATION OF 1763

Carolyn Woods Eisenberg, *Professor of History, Hofstra University, Hempstead, New York*
BERLIN BLOCKADE AND AIRLIFT (1948–1949)

Sarah Elbert, *Professor of History and Women's Studies, State University of New York, Binghamton*
ALCOTT, LOUISA MAY

Ward E. Y. Elliott, *Burnet C. Wohlford Professor of American Political Institutions, Claremont McKenna College, Claremont, California*
SUFFRAGE

Richard E. Ellis, *Chair, Department of History, State University of New York, Buffalo*
CLINTON, DEWITT

James W. Ely Jr., *Professor of Law and History and Milton R. Underwood Chair in Free Enterprise, Vanderbilt University School of Law, Nashville, Tennessee*
ADKINS v. *CHILDREN'S HOSPITAL*

Everett Emerson, *Alumni Distinguished Professor Emeritus of English, University of North Carolina at Chapel Hill*
LITERATURE: COLONIAL ERA; WHEATLEY, PHILLIS

Stanley L. Engerman, *John H. Munro Professor of Economics and Professor of History, University of Rochester, Rochester, New York*
CAPITALISM; ECONOMICS; SLAVERY: THE SLAVE TRADE

J. Nicholas Entrikin, *Professor of Geography, University of California, Los Angeles*
PARK, ROBERT; REGIONALISM

Elizabeth W. Etheridge, *Professor Emeritus of History, Longwood College, Farmville, Virginia*
CENTERS FOR DISEASE CONTROL

John D. Fairfield, *Professor of History, Xavier University, Cincinnati, Ohio*
CITY PLANNING

Candace Falk, *Editor/Director, Emma Goldman Papers, University of California, Berkeley*
GOLDMAN, EMMA

*Byron Farwell
JACKSON, THOMAS J. ("STONEWALL")

Elizabeth Faue, *Associate Professor of History, Wayne State University, Detroit, Michigan*
WORKING-CLASS LIFE AND CULTURE

Carol Faulkner, *Assistant Professor of History, State University of New York, Geneseo*
AMERICAN ANTI-SLAVERY SOCIETY; EMANCIPATION PROCLAMATION

Douglas J. Feeney, *Ph.D. candidate in History, State University of New York, Binghamton*
STRIKES AND INDUSTRIAL CONFLICT

Henry L. Feingold, *Professor Emeritus of History, Baruch College and the Graduate School and University Center, City University of New York; Director, Jewish Resource Center of Baruch College*
JUDAISM

Cynthia Lee Felando, *Lecturer in Film Studies, University of California, Santa Barbara*
VALENTINO, RUDOLPH

Georgina Feldberg, *Associate Professor of Social Science and Director, Centre for Health Studies, York University, Toronto, Ontario, Canada*
TUBERCULOSIS

James W. Feldman, *Ph.D. candidate in History, University of Wisconsin—Madison*
PONY EXPRESS

Daniel Feller, *Professor of History, University of New Mexico, Albuquerque*
JACKSON, ANDREW

John Ferling, *Professor of History, State University of West Georgia, Carrollton*
ADAMS, JOHN; IMPERIAL WARS; SEVEN YEARS' WAR

Robert H. Ferrell, *Professor Emeritus of History, Indiana University, Bloomington*
TRUMAN, HARRY S.

John Ferris, *Professor of History, University of Calgary, Alberta, Canada*
CENTRAL INTELLIGENCE AGENCY; INTELLIGENCE GATHERING AND ESPIONAGE; OFFICE OF STRATEGIC SERVICES

James F. Findlay Jr., *Professor Emeritus of History, University of Rhode Island, Kingston*
MOODY, DWIGHT L.; NATIONAL COUNCIL OF CHURCHES

John E. Findling, *Professor of History, Indiana University Southeast, New Albany*
WORLD'S FAIRS AND EXPOSITIONS

Sidney Fine, *Andrew Dickson White Professor of History, University of Michigan, Ann Arbor*
LAISSEZ-FAIRE; SIT-DOWN STRIKE, FLINT

Leon Fink, *Zachary Smith Professor of History, University of North Carolina at Chapel Hill*
KNIGHTS OF LABOR

Paul Finkelman, *Chapman Distinguished Professor of Law, University of Tulsa, Tulsa, Oklahoma*
CHARLES RIVER BRIDGE v. *WARREN BRIDGE; GIBBONS* v. *OGDEN; KOREMATSU* v. *UNITED STATES; SCOTT* v. *SANDFORD;* ZENGER TRIAL

Margaret Finnegan, *Independent scholar*
CONSUMER CULTURE; CONSUMER MOVEMENT

Jon W. Finson, *Professor of Music and Adjunct Professor of American Studies, University of North Carolina at Chapel Hill*
FOSTER, STEPHEN

Claude S. Fischer, *Professor of Sociology, University of California, Berkeley*
TELEPHONE

Roger A. Fischer, *Professor Emeritus of History, University of Minnesota, Duluth*
HARRISON, WILLIAM HENRY

Price Fishback, *Frank and Clara Kramer Professor of Economics, University of Arizona, Tucson*
MINING

James Rodger Fleming, *Professor of Science, Technology, and Society, Colby College, Waterville, Maine*
SCIENCE: REVOLUTIONARY WAR TO WORLD WAR I

Marvin E. Fletcher, *Professor of History, Ohio University, Athens*
BROWNSVILLE INCIDENT

Wayne Flynt, *Distinguished University Professor and Professor of History, Auburn University, Auburn, Alabama*
POPULIST ERA; RURAL LIFE

Gerald P. Fogarty, S. J., *William R. Kenan Jr., Professor of Religious Studies and History, University of Virginia, Charlottesville*
GIBBONS, JAMES CARDINAL; HUGHES, JOHN [ARCHBISHOP]

Joyce C. Follet, *Public historian, Sophia Smith Collection, Smith College, Northampton, Massachusetts*
NATIONAL ORGANIZATION FOR WOMEN

George B. Forgie, *Associate Professor of History, University of Texas at Austin*
DOUGLAS, STEPHEN A.; LINCOLN-DOUGLAS DEBATES

Todd Forney, *Instructor in History, Ohio State University, Columbus*
MILITARY SERVICE ACADEMIES

Lawrence Foster, *Professor of American History, Georgia Institute of Technology, Atlanta*
NOYES, JOHN HUMPHREY

Robert Booth Fowler, *Professor of Political Science and Integrated Liberal Studies, University of Wisconsin—Madison*
CATT, CARRIE CHAPMAN

Richard Wightman Fox, *Professor of History, University of Southern California, Los Angeles*
NIEBUHR, REINHOLD

Stephen Fox, *Independent scholar*
MUIR, JOHN

Abraham H. Foxman, *National Director, Anti-Defamation League*
ANTI-DEFAMATION LEAGUE

Benis M. Frank, *Chief Historian of the Marine Corps (ret.), Marine Corps History and Museums Division, Washington, D.C.*
IWO JIMA, BATTLE OF

Libbie J. Freed, *Ph.D. candidate in the History of Science, University of Wisconsin—Madison*
HEATING

Joshua B. Freeman, *Associate Professor of History, Queens College, City University of New York*
BROOKLYN BRIDGE; DEBS, EUGENE V.; LA GUARDIA, FIORELLO

Tony A. Freyer, *University Research Professor of History and Law, University of Alabama, Tuscaloosa*
ANTITRUST LEGISLATION; *NORTHERN SECURITIES* CASE; *SLAUGHTERHOUSE CASES*

Robert H. Freymeyer, *Professor of Sociology, Presbyterian College, Clinton, South Carolina*
MOBILITY

J. William Frost, *Jenkins Professor of Quaker History, Swarthmore College, Swarthmore, Pennsylvania*
AMERICAN FRIENDS SERVICE COMMITTEE

Jennifer Frost, *Assistant Professor of History, University of North Colorado, Greeley*
STUDENTS FOR A DEMOCRATIC SOCIETY

Vivien Green Fryd, *Associate Professor of Fine Arts, Vanderbilt University, Nashville, Tennessee*
SCULPTURE

Donna R. Gabaccia, *Charles H. Stone Professor of American History, University of North Carolina at Charlotte*
IMMIGRANT LABOR

David W. Galenson, *Professor of Economics, University of Chicago, Illinois*
INDENTURED SERVITUDE

Stuart Galishoff, *Professor of History Emeritus, Georgia State University, Atlanta*
PUBLIC HEALTH

Trudy Garfunkel, *Independent scholar*
GRAHAM, MARTHA

Thomas P. Gariepy, *Professor of the History of Medicine, Stonehill College, Easton, Massachusetts*
SURGERY

Tim Alan Garrison, *Assistant Professor of History, Portland State University, Oregon*
CHEROKEE CASES; SEQUOYAH

Patrick M. Garry, *Director, Center for Constitutional Studies, Minneapolis, Minnesota*
CIVIL LIBERTIES; *NEAR* V. *MINNESOTA; SCHENCK* V. *UNITED STATES*

Roger L. Geiger, *Professor of Higher Education, Pennsylvania State University, University Park*
EDUCATION: THE RISE OF THE UNIVERSITY; MORRILL LAND GRANT ACT

Charles Geisst, *Professor of Finance, Manhattan College, Riverdale, New York*
ASTOR, JOHN JACOB; NEW YORK STOCK EXCHANGE; STOCK MARKET; VANDERBILT, CORNELIUS

Donald B. Gibson, *Professor of American Literature, Rutgers University, New Brunswick, New Jersey*
WASHINGTON, BOOKER T.; WRIGHT, RICHARD

Paula Giddings, *Research Professor of Women's Studies, Duke University, Durham, North Carolina*
BETHUNE, MARY MCLEOD; WELLS-BARNETT, IDA B.

Mark T. Gilderhus, *Professor of History and Lyndon Baines Johnson Chair, Texas Christian University, Fort Worth*
FOREIGN RELATIONS: U.S. RELATIONS WITH LATIN AMERICA; GOOD NEIGHBOR POLICY; ORGANIZATION OF AMERICAN STATES; PAN AMERICAN UNION

Paul A. Gilje, *Professor of History, University of Oklahoma, Norman*
RIOTS, URBAN

Howard Gillette Jr., *Professor of American Civilization and History, George Washington University, Washington, D.C.*
WASHINGTON, D.C.

Michael L. Gillette, *Independent scholar*
GREAT SOCIETY

William Gillette, *Professor of History, Rutgers University, New Brunswick, New Jersey*
FIFTEENTH AMENDMENT

Steven M. Gillon, *Carol Elizabeth Young Professor and Dean of the Honors College, University of Oklahoma, Norman*
HUMPHREY, HUBERT

W. Clark Gilpin, *Professor of the History of Christianity, University of Chicago, Illinois*
WILLIAMS, ROGER

Jo Gladstone, *Independent scholar*
JACOBI, MARY PUTNAM

Nathan Godfried, *Associate Professor of History, University of Maine, Orono*
AGENCY FOR INTERNATIONAL DEVELOPMENT; FOREIGN AID

Ron Goeken, *Research Associate, Minnesota Population Center, University of Minnesota, Minneapolis*
LIFE STAGES

David Gollaher, *President and CEO, California Healthcare Institute, La Jolla*
DIX, DOROTHEA

Juan Gomez-Quinones, *Professor of History, University of California, Los Angeles*
HISPANIC AMERICANS; PUEBLO REVOLT

Susan Gonda, *Instructor of History, Grossmont College, El Cajon, California; Co-President, Women's History Reclamation Project, San Diego, California*
MOTT, LUCRETIA

Walter Goodman, *Critic, The New York Times*
HOUSE COMMITTEE ON UN-AMERICAN ACTIVITIES

Judith R. Goodstein, *University Archivist and Faculty Associate in History, California Institute of Technology, Pasadena*
MILLIKAN, ROBERT A.; SCIENCE: FROM 1914 TO 1945

Colin Gordon, *Associate Professor of History, University of Iowa, Iowa City*
CHAMBERS OF COMMERCE; NATIONAL ASSOCIATION OF MANUFACTURERS; NATIONAL CIVIC FEDERATION

*David M. Gordon, *Former Director of Center for Economic Policy Analysis, New School for Social Research, New York, New York*
WORK

Linda Gordon, *Professor of History, New York University*
DOMESTIC VIOLENCE; SOCIAL SECURITY ACT; WELFARE, FEDERAL

Elliott J. Gorn, *Associate Professor of History, Purdue University, West Lafayette, Indiana*
BOXING; JOHNSON, JACK

Patricia Peck Gossel, *Curator, History of Biology and Medicine, National Museum of American History, Smithsonian Institution, Washington, D.C.*
WELCH, WILLIAM H.

Lewis L. Gould, *Eugene C. Barket Centennial Professor Emeritus in American History, University of Texas at Austin*
BALLINGER-PINCHOT CONTROVERSY; GILDED AGE; HAY, JOHN; HUNTINGTON, COLLIS P.; MCKINLEY, WILLIAM; PARIS, TREATY OF; ROOSEVELT, THEODORE; TAFT, WILLIAM HOWARD

Norman A. Graebner, *Randolph P. Compton Professor of History and Public Affairs Emeritus, University of Virginia, Charlottesville*
EXPANSIONISM; SAN FRANCISCO CONFERENCE; UNITED NATIONS

William Graebner, *Professor of History, State University of New York, Fredonia*
BABY AND CHILD CARE

Harvey J. Graff, *Professor of History, University of Texas at San Antonio*
LITERACY

Henry F. Graff, *Professor Emeritus of History, Columbia University, New York, New York*
FEDERAL GOVERNMENT, EXECUTIVE BRANCH: THE PRESIDENCY

J. L. Granatstein, *Director and CEO, Canadian War Museum, Ottawa, Ontario*
FOREIGN RELATIONS: U.S. RELATIONS WITH CANADA

Mark A. Granquist, *Assistant Professor of Religion, St. Olaf College, Northfield, Minnesota*
LUTHERANISM

James Grant, *Editor, Grant's Interest Rate Observer, New York, New York*
BARUCH, BERNARD

Julie Greene, *Associate Professor of History, University of Colorado at Boulder*
VOLUNTARISM

Paul R. Greenough, *Professor of History, University of Iowa, Iowa City*
WORLD HEALTH ORGANIZATION

Donald J. Greiner, *Carolina Distinguished Professor of English, Associate Provost, and Dean of Undergraduate Affairs, University of South Carolina, Columbia*
UPDIKE, JOHN

Philip Greven, *Professor Emeritus of History, Rutgers University, New Brunswick, New Jersey*
WINTHROP, JOHN

Donald A. Grinde Jr., *Professor of History, University of Vermont, Burlington*
BRANT, JOSEPH; INDIAN HISTORY AND CULTURE: SINCE 1950; INDIAN REMOVAL ACT; INDIAN REORGANIZATION ACT

Gerald N. Grob, *Henry E. Sigerist Professor of the History of Medicine, Institute for Health, Health Care Policy, and Aging Research, Rutgers University, New Brunswick, New Jersey*
DISEASE

Dean Grodzins, *Visiting Scholar, Charles Warren Center for Studies in American History, Harvard University, Cambridge, Massachusetts*
BROWN, JOHN

Peter Grose, *Research Fellow, Belfer Center for Science and International Affairs, John F. Kennedy School of Government, Harvard University, Cambridge, Massachusetts*
COUNCIL ON FOREIGN RELATIONS

James A. Gross, *Professor of Industrial and Labor Relations, Cornell University, Ithaca, New York*
NATIONAL LABOR RELATIONS ACT; NATIONAL LABOR RELATIONS BOARD; TAFT-HARTLEY ACT

Laurence F. Gross, *Associate Professor of Regional Economics and Social Development, University of Massachusetts, Lowell*
TEXTILE INDUSTRY

Robert A. Gross, *Forrest D. Murden Jr. Professor of History and American Studies, College of William and Mary, Williamsburg, Virginia*
SHAYS'S REBELLION

James Grossman, *Vice President for Research and Education, The Newberry Library, Chicago, Illinois*
DALEY, RICHARD J.

Carl J. Guarneri, *Professor of History, Saint Mary's College of California, Moraga*
UTOPIAN AND COMMUNITARIAN MOVEMENTS

Catherine Gudis
CLOTHING AND FASHION

Samuel Haber, *Professor Emeritus of American History, University of California, Berkeley*
PROFESSIONALIZATION

Barton C. Hacker, *Curator, Armed Forces History Collections, Smithsonian Institution, Washington, D.C.*
NUCLEAR WEAPONS

Thomas Hager, *Director of Communications, University of Oregon, Eugene*
PAULING, LINUS

Peter L. Hahn, *Associate Professor of History, Ohio State University, Columbus*
EISENHOWER DOCTRINE

Michael Haines, *Banfi Vintners Professor of Economics, Colgate University, Hamilton, New York*
LIFE EXPECTANCY

Peter Bacon Hales, *Professor of Art History and Director, The American Studies Institute, University of Illinois at Chicago*
BOURKE-WHITE, MARGARET; PHOTOGRAPHY; STEICHEN, EDWARD JEAN; STIEGLITZ, ALFRED

Kermit L. Hall, *Provost and Vice Chancellor for Academic Affairs, North Carolina State University, Raleigh*
ENGEL v. *VITALE;* FIELD, DAVID DUDLEY; LEGAL PROFESSION; MUNICIPAL JUDICIAL SYSTEMS; *PLESSY* v. *FERGUSON;* STATE GOVERNMENTS; STONE, HARLAN FISKE; STORY, JOSEPH

Stephen S. Hall, *Contributing Writer,* The New York Times Magazine*; Columnist,* Technology Review *("Biology, Inc.")*
GENETICS AND GENETIC ENGINEERING

Mark H. Haller, *Professor of History and Criminal Justice, Temple University, Philadelphia, Pennsylvania*
CAPONE, AL; GAMBLING AND LOTTERIES; ORGANIZED CRIME

Pekka Hämäläinen, *Ph.D. candidate in History, University of Helsinki, Finland*
FUR TRADE

Neil W. Hamilton, *Trustees Professor of Regulatory Policy, William Mitchell College of Law, St. Paul, Minnesota*
ACADEMIC FREEDOM

Richard F. Hamm, *Associate Professor of History and Public Policy, State University of New York, Albany*
EIGHTEENTH AMENDMENT

Thomas D. Hamm, *Associate Professor of History and Humanities and Curator of the Friends Archives, Earlham College, Richmond, Indiana*
SOCIETY OF FRIENDS

David J. Hancock, *Associate Professor of History, University of Michigan, Ann Arbor*
NAVIGATION ACTS

Lilian Handlin, *Independent scholar*
BANCROFT, GEORGE

Fraser J. Harbutt, *Associate Professor of History, Emory University, Atlanta, Georgia*
CONTAINMENT; YALTA CONFERENCE

Victoria A. Harden, *Historian, National Institutes of Health and Director, DeWitt Stetten Jr. Museum of Medical Research, Bethesda, Maryland*
ACQUIRED IMMUNODEFICIENCY SYNDROME; NATIONAL INSTITUTES OF HEALTH

Keith J. Hardman, *Professor of Philosophy and Religion, Ursinus College, Collegeville, Pennsylvania*
FINNEY, CHARLES G.

Tamara Hareven, *Unidel Professor of Family Studies and History, University of Delaware, Newark*
FAMILY

Anthony A. Harkins, *Instructor in History, Iowa State University, Ames*
GRAPES OF WRATH, THE; HUMOR; PUBLIC BROADCASTING

David Edwin Harrell Jr., *Daniel E. Breeden Eminent Scholar in the Humanities, Auburn University, Auburn, Alabama*
PENTECOSTALISM

Trudier Harris, *J. Carlyle Sitterson Professor of English, University of North Carolina at Chapel Hill*
BALDWIN, JAMES

Ellis W. Hawley, *Professor Emeritus of History, University of Iowa, Iowa City*
CORPORATISM; FEDERAL TRADE COMMISSION; HOOVER, HERBERT; NATIONAL RECOVERY ADMINISTRATION; TEAPOT DOME SCANDAL

John Heidenry, *Editor in Chief,* ThePostion.com
WALLACE, DEWITT AND LILA

Christina Dallett Hemphill, *Professor of History, Ursinus College, Collegeville, Pennsylvania*
ETIQUETTE AND MANNERS

Rickey L. Hendricks, *Independent scholar*
HEALTH MAINTENANCE ORGANIZATIONS

Gregg Herken, *Historian and Curator, Space History Division, National Air and Space Museum, Smithsonian Institution, Washington, D.C.*
TELLER, EDWARD

George C. Herring, *Alumni Professor of History, University of Kentucky, Lexington*
GULF OF TONKIN RESOLUTION; PENTAGON PAPERS; TET OFFENSIVE; VIETNAM WAR

Leo Hershkowitz, *Professor of History, Queens College, City University of New York*
ELLIS ISLAND; MORGAN, J. P.; NEW YORK CITY; STATUE OF LIBERTY; STRAUSS, LEVI; TWEED, WILLIAM M. AGEAR

Lawrence Lee Hewitt, *Professor of History (retired), Southeastern Louisiana University, Hammond*
VICKSBURG, SIEGE OF

John Higham, *John Martin Vincent Professor of History Emeritus, The Johns Hopkins University, Baltimore, Maryland*
HISTORIOGRAPHY, AMERICAN

Lee R. Hiltzik, *University Archivist, Rockefeller University, New York, New York*
ROCKEFELLER INSTITUTE

Andrea Hinding, *Curator, YMCA Archives, University of Minnesota, St. Paul*
YMCA AND YWCA

Arnold R. Hirsch, *Research Professor of History, University of New Orleans, Louisiana*
NEW ORLEANS

Jeffrey D. Hockett, *Associate Professor of Political Science, University of Tulsa, Tulsa, Oklahoma*
BLACK, HUGO; FRANKFURTER, FELIX; *SCHECHTER POULTRY CORP.* v. *UNITED STATES*

Lillian Hoddeson, *Professor of History, University of Illinois at Urbana-Champaign*
BARDEEN, JOHN; MANHATTAN PROJECT

Steven Hoelscher, *Assistant Professor of American Studies and Geography, University of Texas at Austin*
MARDI GRAS

J. David Hoeveler, *Professor of History, University of Wisconsin—Milwaukee*
BUCKLEY, WILLIAM F., JR.; CONSERVATISM

Joan Hoff, *Director, Contemporary History Institute and Professor of History, Ohio University, Athens*
NIXON, RICHARD M.

Sylvia D. Hoffert, *Professor of Women's Studies and History, University of North Carolina at Chapel Hill*
CHILDBIRTH

Elizabeth Cobbs Hoffman, *Dwight E. Stanford Professor of American Foreign Relations, San Diego State University, California*
PEACE CORPS

Margaret A. Hogan, *Ph.D. candidate in History, University of Wisconsin—Madison*
PEALE, NORMAN VINCENT

Peter C. Holloran, *Assistant Professor of History, Worcester State College, Worcester, Massachusetts*
ORPHANAGES; WILLARD, FRANCES

William F. Holmes, *Professor of History, University of Georgia, Athens*
FREE SILVER MOVEMENT

Ari Hoogenboom, *Professor Emeritus of History, Brooklyn College and the Graduate School and University Center, City University of New York*
CIVIL SERVICE REFORM; INTERSTATE COMMERCE ACT

Gerald Horne, *Professor of Communications Studies and Afro-American Studies and Director, Sonja Haynes Stone Black Cultural Center, University of North Carolina at Chapel Hill*
NATION OF ISLAM

Joseph Horowitz, *Independent scholar*
BERNSTEIN, LEONARD; MUSIC: CLASSICAL MUSIC; THOMAS, THEODORE; TOSCANINI, ARTURO

Reginald Horsman, *Professor Emeritus of History, University of Wisconsin—Milwaukee*
BEAUMONT, WILLIAM

Fred Howard, *Aeronautics librarian (retired); Co-editor, The Papers of Wilbur and Orville Wright*
WRIGHT, WILBUR AND ORVILLE

Daniel Walker Howe, *Rhodes Professor of American History, Oxford University, Oxford, England*
CHANNING, WILLIAM ELLERY; CLAY, HENRY; UNITARIANISM AND UNIVERSALISM

Suellen Hoy, *Independent historian; Guest Professor, University of Notre Dame, Notre Dame, Indiana*
HYGIENE, PERSONAL

Margaret Humphreys, *Associate Professor of History and Associate Clinical Professor of Medicine, Duke University, Durham, North Carolina*
MALARIA; YELLOW FEVER

Jane H. Hunter, *Associate Professor of History, Lewis and Clark College, Portland, Oregon*
MISSIONARY MOVEMENT

Daniel Hurewitz, *Ph.D. candidate in History, University of California, Los Angeles*
GAY AND LESBIAN RIGHTS MOVEMENT

R. Douglas Hurt, *Professor and Director, Graduate Program in Agricultural History and Rural Studies, Iowa State University, Ames; Editor,* Agricultural History
FARM MACHINERY

John F. Hutchinson, *Professor of History, Simon Fraser University, Burnaby, British Columbia, Canada*
RED CROSS, AMERICAN

Gordon Hutner, *Professor of English, University of Kentucky, Lexington*
LITERARY CRITICISM; LITERATURE: CIVIL WAR TO WORLD WAR I

Joseph Illick, *Professor of History, San Francisco State University, California*
PENN, WILLIAM

John C. Inscoe, *Professor of History, University of Georgia, Athens; Editor,* Georgia Historical Quarterly
MISSOURI COMPROMISE

Nancy Isenberg, *Associate Professor of History and Co-holder of the Mary Frances Barnard Chair in 19th-century American History, University of Tulsa, Tulsa, Oklahoma*
WOMEN'S RIGHTS MOVEMENTS

Paul Israel, *Managing Editor,* Thomas A. Edison Papers, *Rutgers University, New Brunswick, New Jersey*
ATLANTIC CABLE; MORSE, SAMUEL F. B.; TELEGRAPH

William Issel, *Professor of History, San Francisco State University, California*
SAN FRANCISCO

Maurice Isserman, *William R. Kenan Jr. Professor of History, Hamilton College, Clinton, New York*
OTHER AMERICA, THE

Donald C. Jackson, *Associate Professor of History, Lafayette College, Easton, Pennsylvania*
DAMS AND HYDRAULIC ENGINEERING; HYDROELECTRIC POWER

*Wilbur R. Jacobs
PARKMAN, FRANCIS

Peter L. Jakab, *Curator, Aeronautics Department, National Air and Space Museum, Smithsonian Institution, Washington, D.C.*
LINDBERGH, CHARLES

John A. James, *Professor of Economics, University of Virginia, Charlottesville*
MONETARISM; MONETARY POLICY, FEDERAL

Robert F. Jefferson, *Assistant Professor of History and African American World Studies, University of Iowa, Iowa City*
SEGREGATION, RACIAL

John W. Jeffries, *Professor of History, University of Maryland, Baltimore County*
WORLD WAR II: DOMESTIC EFFECTS

Reese V. Jenkins, *Professor of History, Rutgers University, New Brunswick, New Jersey*
EDISON, THOMAS

Richard Jensen, *Professor Emeritus of History, University of Illinois, Chicago*
HANNA, MARK

T. Christopher Jespersen, *Assistant Professor of American Diplomatic History, School of International Affairs and Development, Clark Atlanta University, Atlanta, Georgia*
FOREIGN RELATIONS: U.S. RELATIONS WITH ASIA; INSTITUTE FOR PACIFIC RELATIONS; "OPEN DOOR" POLICY

Claudia Durst Johnson, *Professor Emeritus of English, University of Alabama, Tuscaloosa*
ANDERSON, MARIAN; DRAMA

Loch K. Johnson, *Regents Professor of Political Science, University of Georgia, Athens*
U-2 INCIDENT; WAR POWERS ACT

Robert David Johnson, *Associate Professor of History, Brooklyn College, City University of New York*
ANTI-IMPERIALIST LEAGUE; CARNEGIE ENDOWMENT FOR INTERNATIONAL PEACE; FEDERAL GOVERNMENT, EXECUTIVE BRANCH: DEPARTMENT OF STATE

Susan Lee Johnson, *Assistant Professor of History, University of Colorado at Boulder*
GOLD RUSHES

Dorothy V. Jones, *Scholar-in-residence, The Newberry Library, Chicago, Illinois; History Department Associate, Northwestern University, Evanston, Illinois*
HUMAN RIGHTS, INTERNATIONAL

Howard Jones, *University Research Professor of History, University of Alabama, Tuscaloosa*
MONROE DOCTRINE; WEBSTER-ASHBURTON TREATY

James H. Jones, *Alumni Distinguished Professor of History, University of Arkansas, Fayetteville*
KINSEY, ALFRED; TUSKEGEE EXPERIMENT

Patrick D. Jones, *Ph.D. candidate in History, University of Wisconsin—Madison*
SOUTHERN CHRISTIAN LEADERSHIP CONFERENCE; STUDENT NON-VIOLENT COORDINATING COMMITTEE

Susan D. Jones, *Assistant Professor of History, University of Colorado, Boulder*
VETERINARY MEDICINE

William Jordan, *Instructor in History, Philips Exeter Academy, Exeter, New Hampshire*
DU BOIS, W. E. B.; GARVEY, MARCUS

Winthrop D. Jordan, *William F. Winter Professor of History, Professor of Afro-American Studies, and F. A. P. Barnard Distinguished Professor, University of Mississippi, University*
SLAVE UPRISINGS AND RESISTANCE

James C. Juhnke, *Professor of History, Bethel College, North Newton, Kansas*
MENNONITES AND AMISH

Carl F. Kaestle, *University Professor and Professor of Education, History, and Public Policy, Brown University, Providence, Rhode Island*
CARNEGIE FOUNDATION FOR THE ADVANCEMENT OF TEACHING; EDUCATION: THE PUBLIC SCHOOL MOVEMENT; MANN, HORACE; McGUFFEY READERS; NATIONAL EDUCATION ASSOCIATION

Jennifer L. Kalish, *Ph.D. candidate in History, University of California, Los Angeles*
AFFLUENT SOCIETY, THE; LONELY CROWD, THE; SUBURBANIZATION

Lilikala Kame'leihiwa, *Director, Center for Hawaiian Studies, University of Hawaii at Manoa, Honolulu*
LILI'OKALANI

John P. Kaminski, *Director, The Center for the Study of the American Constitution, University of Wisconsin—Madison*
ARTICLES OF CONFEDERATION; BILL OF RIGHTS; CONSTITUTION; CONSTITUTIONAL CONVENTION OF 1787; FEDERALIST PAPERS

Yale Kamisar, *Clarence Darrow Distinguished University Professor of Law, University of Michigan Law School, Ann Arbor*
MIRANDA v. *ARIZONA*

Walter D. Kamphoefner, *Professor of History, Texas A&M University, College Station*
GERMAN AMERICANS

Edward R. Kantowicz, *Independent scholar*
CULTURAL PLURALISM

Justin Kaplan, *Independent scholar*
CLEMENS, SAMUEL L.; STEFFENS, LINCOLN

Lawrence S. Kaplan, *University Professor Emeritus of History, Kent State University, Kent, Ohio*
FOREIGN RELATIONS: U.S. RELATIONS WITH EUROPE; NORTH ATLANTIC TREATY ORGANIZATION

Carolyn L. Karcher, *Professor of English, American Studies, and Women's Studies, Temple University, Philadelphia, Pennsylvania*
CHILD, LYDIA MARIA

Michael B. Katz, *Sheldon and Lucy Hackney Professor of History, University of Pennsylvania, Philadelphia*
ALMS HOUSES; POVERTY

Wendy J. Katz, *Assistant Professor of Art History, University of Nebraska, Lincoln*
EAKINS, THOMAS; HOMER, WINSLOW; WHISTLER, JAMES MCNEILL

Bruce E. Kaufman, *Professor of Economics, Georgia State University, Atlanta*
INDUSTRIAL RELATIONS

Russell A. Kazal, *Assistant Professor of History, Beaver College, Glenside, Pennsylvania*
ASSIMILATION

Steven J. Keillor, *Fellow, MacLaurin Institute, Minneapolis, Minnesota*
SCANDINAVIAN AMERICANS

Evelyn Fox Keller, *Professor of the History and Philosophy of Science, Massachusetts Institute of Technology, Cambridge*
MCCLINTOCK, BARBARA

Robin D. G. Kelley, *Professor of History and Africana Studies, New York University, New York*
MALCOLM X

Karen M. Kennelly, *President, Mount St. Mary's College, Los Angeles, California*
SETON, MOTHER ELIZABETH ANN

Paul Kens, *Associate Professor of Political Science and History, Southwest Texas State University, San Marcos*
LOCHNER v. *NEW YORK*

Ben Keppel, *Associate Professor of History, University of Oklahoma, Norman*
AMERICAN DILEMMA, AN; BUNCHE, RALPH

Andrea Moore Kerr, *Independent scholar*
STONE, LUCY

Daniel J. Kevles, *Koepfli Professor of the Humanities, California Institute of Technology, Pasadena*
CARSON, RACHEL; EUGENICS

Richard B. Kielbowicz, *Associate Professor of Communications, University of Washington, Seattle*
POSTAL SERVICE, U.S.

Jon T. Kilpinen, *Associate Professor of Geography, Valparaiso University, Valparaiso, Indiana*
ROCKY MOUNTAINS

Barbara A. Kimmelman, *Associate Professor of History, Philadelphia University, Pennsylvania*
AGRICULTURAL EXPERIMENT STATIONS

Harvey Klehr, *Andrew W. Mellon Professor of Politics and History, Emory University, Atlanta, Georgia*
COMMUNIST PARTY—USA

Daniel Lee Kleinman, *Associate Professor of Rural Sociology, University of Wisconsin—Madison*
NATIONAL ACADEMY OF SCIENCES; NATIONAL SCIENCE FOUNDATION

Mark L. Kleinman, *Senior Account Executive, Crocker/Probasco/Flanagan, Sacramento, California; formerly Associate Professor of History, University of Wisconsin—Oshkosh*
AMERICANS FOR DEMOCRATIC ACTION; HISS, ALGER; PROGRESSIVE PARTY OF 1948

James T. Kloppenberg, *Professor of History, Harvard University, Cambridge, Massachusetts*
EQUALITY; PRAGMATISM; REPUBLICANISM

Bettina L. Knapp, *Professor Emerita of Romance Languages and Comparative Literature, Hunter College and the Graduate School and University Center, City University of New York*
POE, EDGAR ALLAN

Dale T. Knobel, *President, Denison University, Granville, Ohio*
IRISH AMERICANS

Thomas J. Knock, *Associate Professor of History, Southern Methodist University, Dallas, Texas*
FOURTEEN POINTS; INTERNATIONALISM; LEAGUE OF NATIONS; VERSAILLES, TREATY OF; WORLD WAR I

Peter B. Knupfer, *Associate Professor of History, Kansas State University, Manhattan*
COMPROMISE OF 1850

Lyle Koehler, *Independent scholar*
HUTCHINSON, ANNE

Sally Gregory Kohlstedt, *Professor of History of Science, University of Minnesota, Minneapolis*
AMERICAN ASSOCIATION FOR THE ADVANCEMENT OF SCIENCE; MUSEUMS: MUSEUMS OF SCIENCE AND TECHNOLOGY; SMITHSONIAN INSTITUTION

Gerd Korman, *Professor Emeritus of Industrial and Labor Relations, Cornell University, Ithaca, New York*
HILLMAN, SIDNEY

Robert Korstad, *Assistant Professor of Public Policy and History, Duke University, Durham, North Carolina*
DUKE, JAMES

J. Morgan Kousser, *Professor of History and Social Science, California Institute of Technology, Pasadena*
RECONSTRUCTION

Michael P. Kramer, *Associate Professor of English, Bar-Ilan University, Ramat-Gan, Israel*
LANGUAGE, AMERICAN

Paul Krause, *Associate Professor of History, University of British Columbia, Vancouver, Canada*
CARNEGIE, ANDREW; HOMESTEAD LOCKOUT; IRON AND STEEL INDUSTRY

Stephen Kretzmann, *Instructor, Masters of Arts in Community Development Program, North Park University, Chicago, Illinois*
GALVESTON HURRICANE AND FLOOD

Gretchen Kreuter, *Honorary Fellow, Institute for Research in the Humanities, University of Wisconsin—Madison*
AMERICAN ASSOCIATION OF UNIVERSITY WOMEN

David Krieger, *President, Nuclear Age Peace Foundation, Santa Barbara, California*
NUCLEAR ARMS CONTROL TREATIES

Donald D. Kummings, *Professor of English, University of Wisconsin—Parkside, Kenosha*
POETRY

Bruce Kuniholm, *Vice Provost for Academic and International Affairs and Professor of Public Policy and History, Duke University, Durham, North Carolina*
FOREIGN RELATIONS: U.S. RELATIONS WITH THE MIDDLE EAST

Diane B. Kunz, *Adjunct Professor of International Relations and History, School of International and Public Affairs, Columbia University, New York, New York*
BRETTON WOODS CONFERENCE; GENERAL AGREEMENT ON TARIFFS AND TRADE; INTERNATIONAL MONETARY FUND; WORLD BANK

Karen Ordahl Kupperman, *Professor of History, New York University, New York*
POWHATAN; SMITH, JOHN

Kenneth Franklin Kurz, *Independent scholar*
WHITE HOUSE; WORKS PROGRESS ADMINISTRATION

Peter J. Kuznick, *Associate Professor of History and Director, Nuclear Studies Institute, American University, Washington, D.C.*
CONANT, JAMES B.

Benjamin Labaree, *Professor Emeritus of History and Environmental Studies, Williams College, Williamstown, Massachusetts*
BOSTON TEA PARTY (1773)

Paul Lack, *Vice President for Academic Affairs, McMurry University, Abilene, Texas*
TEXAS REPUBLIC AND ANNEXATION

Walter LaFeber, *The Marie Underhill Noll Professor of American History, Cornell University, Ithaca, New York*
IRAN-CONTRA AFFAIR

Marcel C. LaFollette, *Independent scholar*
SCIENCE: SCIENCE AND POPULAR CULTURE

Eric E. Lampard, *Professor Emeritus of Economic History, State University of New York, Stony Brook*
DAIRY INDUSTRY AND DAIRY PRODUCTS

Gary Land, *Professor of History, Andrews University, Berrien Springs, Michigan*
SEVENTH-DAY ADVENTISM

David J. Langum, *Professor of Law, Cumberland School of Law, Samford University, Birmingham, Alabama*
PROSTITUTION AND ANTIPROSTITUTION

John A. Larkin, *Professor of History, State University of New York, Buffalo*
PHILIPPINES

Edward J. Larson, *Richard B. Russell Professor of History and Law, University of Georgia, Athens*
SCOPES TRIAL

Roger D. Launius, *NASA Chief Historian, National Aeronautics and Space Administration, Washington, D.C.*
NATIONAL AERONAUTICS AND SPACE ADMINISTRATION; SATELLITE COMMUNICATION; SPACE PROGRAM

William M. Leary, *Coulter Professor of History, University of Georgia, Athens*
AIRPLANES AND AIR TRANSPORT

Susan E. Lederer, *Assistant Professor of History of Medicine, Yale University School of Medicine, New Haven, Connecticut*
BIOETHICS; REED, WALTER

Jean B. Lee, *Associate Professor of History, University of Wisconsin—Madison*
MOUNT VERNON

R. Alton Lee, *Professor Emeritus of History, University of South Dakota, Vermillion*
LANDRUM-GRIFFIN ACT

Mark H. Leff, *Associate Professor of History, University of Illinois at Urbana-Champaign*
INCOME TAX, FEDERAL

Donald R. Lennon, *Associate Professor Emeritus, East Carolina University, Greenville, North Carolina*
BUNKER HILL, BATTLE OF

Thomas M. Leonard, *Distinguished Professor of History, University of North Florida, Jacksonville*
PANAMA CANAL

Harvey Levenstein, *Professor Emeritus of History, McMaster University, Hamilton, Ontario, Canada*
FOOD AND DIET

David O. Levine, *Executive Director, Touch American History Foundation, Marina Del Rey, California*
EDUCATION: COLLEGIATE EDUCATION

David W. Levy, *David Ross Boyd Professor of History, University of Oklahoma, Norman*
CROLY, HERBERT

Peter B. Levy, *Associate Professor of History, York College, York, Pennsylvania*
NEW LEFT

Walter Licht, *Professor of History, University of Pennsylvania, Philadelphia*
INDUSTRIALIZATION

Alex Lichtenstein, *Associate Professor of History, Florida International University, Miami*
SOUTHERN TENANT FARMERS' UNION AND NATIONAL FARM LABOR UNION

Alan Lichtman, *Professor of History, American University, Washington, D.C.*
HARDING, WARREN G.

Susan Lindee, *Associate Professor of History and Sociology of Science, University of Pennsylvania, Philadelphia*
HUMAN GENOME PROJECT

James M. Lindgren, *Professor of History, State University of New York, Plattsburgh*
HISTORIC PRESERVATION

Diane Lindstrom, *Professor of History, University of Wisconsin—Madison*
BANK OF THE UNITED STATES, FIRST AND SECOND; DEPRESSIONS, ECONOMIC; MULTINATIONAL ENTERPRISES; STOCK MARKET CRASH OF 1929

Edward Linenthal, *Edward M. Penson Professor of Religion and American Culture, University of Wisconsin—Oshkosh*
STRATEGIC DEFENSE INITIATIVE

Richard Lingeman, *Senior Editor,* The Nation
DREISER, THEODORE

Alan Lizotte, *Professor of Criminal Justice, State University of New York, Albany*
GUN CONTROL (co-author); NATIONAL RIFLE ASSOCIATION (co-author)

Michael A. Lofaro, *Professor of American Literature and American Studies, University of Tennessee, Knoxville*
BOONE, DANIEL; CROCKETT, DAVY

Christopher Losson, *Adjunct Professor of History, Missouri Western State College, St. Joseph*
SHILOH, BATTLE OF

Spencie Love, *Independent Scholar*
DREW, CHARLES RICHARD

*David S. Lovejoy
GLORIOUS REVOLUTION IN AMERICA

Richard Lowitt, *Professor of History (ret.), University of Oklahoma, Norman*
McNARY-HAUGEN BILL; OKLAHOMA CITY BOMBING; SUBSIDIES, AGRICULTURAL

Richard Magat, *Visiting Fellow, Program on Non-Profit Organizations, Yale University, New Haven, Connecticut*
FORD FOUNDATION

John K. Mahon, *Professor Emeritus of History, University of Florida, Gainesville*
SEMINOLE WARS

John Majewski
ECONOMIC DEVELOPMENT; ROADS AND TURNPIKES, EARLY

Charles J. Maland, *Lindsay Young Professor of English, University of Tennessee, Knoxville*
CHAPLIN, CHARLIE

James L. Mallery
SAN FRANCISCO EARTHQUAKE AND FIRE

Bill C. Malone, *Professor Emeritus of History, Tulane University, New Orleans, Louisiana*
MUSIC: TRADITIONAL MUSIC

Margaret M. Manchester, *Assistant Professor of History, Providence College, Providence, Rhode Island*
CAMP DAVID ACCORDS

Elizabeth Mancke, *Associate Professor of History, University of Akron, Akron, Ohio*
EXPLORATION, CONQUEST, AND SETTLEMENT, ERA OF EUROPEAN (co-author)

Howard Markel, *Associate Professor of Pediatrics and Communicable Diseases, Associate Professor of History, and Director, Historical Center for the Health Sciences, University of Michigan, Ann Arbor*
CHOLERA

Harry M. Marks, *Associate Professor, The Elizabeth Treide and A. McGehee Harvey Professorship in the History of Medicine, The Johns Hopkins University, Baltimore, Maryland*
MEDICINE: FROM THE 1870s TO 1945; MEDICINE: SINCE 1945

Karal Ann Marling, *Professor of Art History and American Studies, University of Minnesota, Minneapolis*
FAIRS, COUNTY AND STATE; PRESLEY, ELVIS; ROUTE 66; SHOPPING CENTERS AND MALLS

Alice Goldfarb Marquis, *Visiting Scholar, Department of History, University of California, San Diego, La Jolla*
NATIONAL ENDOWMENTS FOR THE ARTS AND THE HUMANITIES

Cora Bagley Marrett, *Senior Vice Chancellor for Academic Affairs and Provost, University of Massachusetts, Amherst*
THREE MILE ISLAND

John F. Marszalek, *William L. Gales Distinguished Professor of History, Mississippi State University, Mississippi State*
SHERMAN, WILLIAM T.

Judith A. Martin, *Professor of Geography, and Director, Urban Studies, University of Minnesota, Minneapolis*
CHICAGO

William Martin, *Harry and Hazel Chavanne Professor of Religion and Public Policy, Rice University, Houston, Texas*
GRAHAM, BILLY

Martin E. Marty, *The Fairfax M. Cone Distinguished Service Professor Emeritus, University of Chicago, Illinois*
ECUMENICAL MOVEMENT; PROTESTANTISM

Theodore O. Mason Jr., *John B. McCoy-Bank One Distinguished Teaching Professor of English, Kenyon College, Gambier, Ohio*
ROBESON, PAUL

Robert E. May, *Professor of History, Purdue University, West Lafayette, Indiana*
MEXICAN WAR

Robert N. Mayer, *Professor of Family and Consumer Studies, University of Utah, Salt Lake City*
NADER, RALPH

Lawrence J. McCaffrey, *Professor Emeritus of History, Loyola University of Chicago, Illinois*
ANTI-CATHOLIC MOVEMENT

Carole R. McCann, *Director of Women's Studies and Associate Professor of American Studies, University of Maryland, Baltimore County*
ABORTION

Robert McCarter, *Director, School of Architecture and Professor of Architecture, University of Florida, Gainesville*
WRIGHT, FRANK LLOYD

Joseph A. McCartin, *Associate Professor of History, Georgetown University, Washington, D.C.*
NEW DEAL ERA, THE; POWDERLY, TERENCE

Bernadette McCauley, *Associate Professor of History, Hunter College, City University of New York*
HOSPITALS

Wilfred M. McClay, *SunTrust Chair of Excellence in Humanities and Professor of History, University of Tennessee, Chattanooga*
POLITICAL SCIENCE

Bruce McConachie, *Professor of Theater Arts, University of Pittsburgh, Pennsylvania*
MINSTRELSY; VAUDEVILLE

Stuart McConnell, *Professor of History, Pitzer College, Claremont, California*
GRAND ARMY OF THE REPUBLIC; NATIONALISM

Brendon McConville, *Associate Professor of History, State University of New York, Binghamton*
CONTINENTAL CONGRESS; REVOLUTIONARY WAR

Richard P. McCormick, *University Professor of History Emeritus, Rutgers University, New Brunswick, New Jersey*
ELECTORAL COLLEGE

Thomas K. McCraw, *Isidor Straus Professor of Business History, Harvard Business School, Boston, Massachusetts*
BUSINESS; ECONOMIC REGULATION; FEDERAL REGULATORY AGENCIES

David McDowall, *Professor of Criminal Justice, State University of New York, Albany*
GUN CONTROL (co-author); NATIONAL RIFLE ASSOCIATION (co-author)

Robert S. McElvaine, *Elizabeth Chisholm Professor of Arts and Letters and Professor of History, Millsaps College, Jackson, Mississippi*
BONUS ARMY; HOPKINS, HARRY; ROOSEVELT, FRANKLIN DELANO

Georgiary Bledsoe McElveen, *Mary Lou Williams Instructor of Music and Ph.D. candidate in Musicology, Duke University, Durham, North Carolina*
GOSPEL MUSIC, AFRICAN AMERICAN

Gerald W. McFarland, *Professor of History, University of Massachusetts, Amherst*
GREENWICH VILLAGE; MUGWUMPS

Nellie Y. McKay, *Professor of Afro-American Studies, University of Wisconsin—Madison*
HURSTON, ZORA NEALE; MORRISON, TONI

Elizabeth McKillen, *Associate Professor of History, University of Maine, Orono*
NORTH AMERICAN FREE TRADE AGREEMENT

Sally G. McMillen, *Professor of History, Davidson College, Davidson, North Carolina*
CHILD REARING; MARRIAGE AND DIVORCE

Kim McQuaid, *Professor of Social Science, Lake Erie College, Painesville, Ohio*
BUSINESS ROUNDTABLE

Clay McShane, *Professor of History, Northeastern University, Boston, Massachusetts*
AUTOMOBILE RACING; MOTOR VEHICLES

Jeffrey L. Meikle, *Professor of American Studies and Art History, University of Texas at Austin*
INDUSTRIAL DESIGN; PLASTICS

Curt Meine, *Research Associate, International Crane Foundation, Baraboo, Wisconsin*
LEOPOLD, ALDO

Marcia L. Meldrum, *Research Fellow, National Institutes of Health, Bethesda, Maryland*
ALZHEIMER'S DISEASE

Russell R. Menard, *Professor of History, University of Minnesota, Minneapolis*
AGRICULTURE: COLONIAL ERA

Dennis Merrill, *Professor of History, University of Missouri, Kansas City*
FOREIGN RELATIONS: THE ECONOMIC DIMENSION

Thomas Mertes, *Administrator, Center for Social Theory and Comparative History, University of California, Los Angeles*
INSURANCE

Timothy Messer-Kruse, *Assistant Professor of Labor History, University of Toledo, Toledo, Ohio*
SMITH ACT; SOCIALISM

Melissa L. Meyer, *Associate Professor of History, University of California, Los Angeles*
INDIAN HISTORY AND CULTURE: FROM 1800 TO 1900; INDIAN HISTORY AND CULTURE: OVERVIEW

Joanne Meyerowitz, *Professor of History, Indiana University, Bloomington*
FEMININE MYSTIQUE, THE

Robert L. Middlekauff, *Preston Hotchkiss Professor Emeriti of American History, University of California, Berkeley*
MATHER, INCREASE AND COTTON

Andre Millard, *Professor of History and Director of American Studies, University of Alabama at Birmingham*
RESEARCH LABORATORIES, INDUSTRIAL

Angela Miller, *Associate Professor of History, Art History, and Archaeology, Washington University, St. Louis, Missouri*
PAINTING: TO 1945

Donald L. Miller, *John Henry MacCracken Professor of History, Lafayette College, Easton, Pennsylvania*
MUMFORD, LEWIS

*Lillian B. Miller
MUSEUMS: MUSEUMS OF ART

Wilbur R. Miller, *Professor of History, State University of New York, Stony Brook*
POLICE

Kenneth P. Minkema, *Executive Editor,* Works of Jonathan Edwards *and Lecturer in American Religious History, Yale University, New Haven, Connecticut*
EDWARDS, JONATHAN

Max M. Mintz, *Professor Emeritus of History, Southern Connecticut University, New Haven*
SARATOGA, BATTLE OF

Wilson D. Miscamble, *Associate Professor of History, University of Notre Dame, Norte Dame, Indiana*
ACHESON, DEAN; KENNAN, GEORGE

Greg Mitchell,
SINCLAIR, UPTON

Nancy Mitchell, *Associate Professor of History, North Carolina State University, Raleigh*
FOREIGN RELATIONS: U.S. RELATIONS WITH AFRICA

Gregory Mixon, *Assistant Professor of History, University of North Carolina at Charlotte*
TROTTER, WILLIAM MONROE

Douglas Monroy, *Professor of History, Colorado College, Colorado Springs*
SPANISH SETTLEMENTS IN NORTH AMERICA

Peter Moogk, *Associate Professor of History, University of British Columbia, Vancouver, Canada*
CARTIER, JACQUES

Jesse T. Moore Jr., *Associate Professor of History and Associate Dean, University of Rochester, Rochester, New York*
URBAN LEAGUE, NATIONAL

Leonard J. Moore, *Associate Professor of History, McGill University, Montreal, Quebec, Canada*
JOHN BIRCH SOCIETY; KU KLUX KLAN; LIBERTARIAN PARTY

Jeffrey P. Moran, *Assistant Professor of History, University of Kansas, Lawrence*
SEX EDUCATION

Richard Moran, *Professor of Sociology, Mount Holyoke College, South Hadley, Massachusetts*
CAPITAL PUNISHMENT

H. Wayne Morgan, *George Lynn Cross Research Professor of History Emeritus, University of Oklahoma, Norman*

ARTHUR, CHESTER A.; BLAINE, JAMES G.; BRYAN, WILLIAM JENNINGS; GARFIELD, JAMES; HAYES, RUTHERFORD

Edward T. Morman, *Associate Librarian for Historical Collections and Programs, New York Academy of Medicine, New York*
DIPHTHERIA; TYPHOID FEVER

James M. Morris, *Professor of History, Christopher Newport University, Newport News, Virginia*
SHIPBUILDING

Sylvia Jukes Morris, *Independent scholar*
LUCE, CLARE BOOTHE

Charles T. Morrissey, *Oral History Consultant, Baylor College of Medicine, Houston, Texas*
DEBAKEY, MICHAEL; HEART DISEASE

Richard Moser, *National Field Representative, American Association of University Professors (AAUP), Washington, D.C.*
MY LAI MASSACRE

Wilson J. Moses, *Professor of American History, Pennsylvania State University, University Park*
NATIONAL ASSOCIATION FOR THE ADVANCEMENT OF COLORED PEOPLE

Richard J. Moss, *John J. and Cornelia V. Gibson Professor of History, Colby College, Waterville, Maine*
WEBSTER, NOAH

Albert E. Moyer, *Professor of History, Virginia Polytechnic Institute and State University, Blacksburg*
NEWCOMB, SIMON; PHYSICAL SCIENCES

Malcolm Muir Jr., *Professor of History, Austin Peay University, Clarksville, Tennessee*
LEYTE GULF, BATTLE OF

Theresa D. Napson-Williams, *Ph.D. candidate in History, Rutgers University, New Brunswick, New Jersey*
TUBMAN, HARRIET

Roderick Frazier Nash, *Professor History and Environmental Studies, University of California, Santa Barbara*
GRAND CANYON

Claus-M. Naske, *Professor of History, University of Alaska, Fairbanks; Executive Director, University of Alaska Press*
ALASKA

Victor S. Navasky, *Publisher and Editorial Director,* The Nation
KENNEDY, ROBERT

Anna Kasten Nelson, *Distinguished Adjunct Historian in Residence, American University, Washington, D.C.*
NATIONAL SECURITY ACT OF 1947; NATIONAL SECURITY COUNCIL; NATIONAL SECURITY COUNCIL DOCUMENT #68

Daniel Nelson, *Professor of History, University of Akron, Akron, Ohio*
FIRESTONE, HARVEY; NATIONAL INDUSTRIAL CONFERENCE BOARD; SCIENTIFIC MANAGEMENT

Keith L. Nelson, *Professor of History, University of California, Irvine*
KISSINGER, HENRY; PREPAREDNESS CONTROVERSY (1914–1917)

Julie R. Newell, *Associate Professor of History, Southern Polytechnic State University, Marietta, Georgia*
SILLIMAN, BENJAMIN

David K. Nichols, *Associate Professor of Political Science, Montclair State University, Upper Montclair, New Jersey*
FEDERAL GOVERNMENT, EXECUTIVE BRANCH: OVERVIEW

Roger L. Nichols, *Professor of History, University of Arizona, Tucson*
BLACK HAWK; SOUTHWEST, THE

Stephen Nissenbaum, *Professor of History, University of Massachusetts, Amherst*
NEW ENGLAND; SALEM WITCHCRAFT

David W. Noble, *Professor of American Studies and History, University of Minnesota, Minneapolis*
BEARD, CHARLES A.

Alan T. Nolan, *Trustee, Indiana Historical Society, Indianapolis*
LEE, ROBERT E.

Mark A. Noll, *Professor of History, Wheaton College, Wheaton, Illinois*
BIBLE, THE; RELIGION

Norman Nordhauser, *Professor of History, Southern Illinois University, Edwardsville*
AMERICAN BANKERS' ASSOCIATION, PETROLEUM INDUSTRY

Sherwin B. Nuland, *Clinical Professor of Surgery, Yale School of Medicine, New Haven, Connecticut*
HALSTED, WILLIAM

Ronald L. Numbers, *Hilldale and William Coleman Professor of the History of Science and Medicine, University of Wisconsin—Madison*
EVOLUTION, THEORY OF; GRAY, ASA; HEALTH INSURANCE; MEDICINE: OVERVIEW; PSEUDOSCIENCE AND QUACKERY; SCIENCE: OVERVIEW; SCIENCE: SCIENCE AND RELIGION

David E. Nye, *Professor of American Studies, Odense University, Odense, Denmark*
ELECTRICITY AND ELECTRIFICATION; ILLUMINATION

Barbara B. Oberg, *Lecturer in History, Princeton University, Princeton, New Jersey*
DECLARATION OF INDEPENDENCE; FRANKLIN, BENJAMIN

Anthony Patrick O'Brien, *Professor of Economics, Lehigh University, Bethlehem, Pennsylvania*
BUSINESS CYCLE

Sharon O'Brien, *James Hope Caldwell Professor of American Cultures and Professor of English and American Studies, Dickinson College, Carlisle, Pennsylvania*
CATHER, WILLA

Arnold A. Offner, *Cornelia F. Hugel Professor of History, Lafayette College, Easton, Pennsylvania*
TRUMAN DOCTRINE

Kathy J. Ogren, *Director, Johnson Center for Integrative Studies, University of Redlands, Redlands, California*
ARMSTRONG, LOUIS; BASIE, WILLIAM ("COUNT")

John Kennedy Ohl, *Professor of History, Mesa Community College, Mesa, Arizona*
WHEELER, EARLE G.

Gary Y. Okihiro, *Professor of International and Public Affairs and Director, Center for the Study of Ethnicity and Race, Columbia University, New York, New York*
RACE AND ETHNICITY

Robert Oliver
MEDICAL EDUCATION; WILLIAMS, DANIEL HALE

Michael L. Olsen, *Professor of History, New Mexico Highlands University, Las Vegas*
SANTA FE TRAIL

Alison G. Olson, *Professor of History, University of Maryland, College Park*
ALBANY CONGRESS

Keith W. Olson, *Professor of History, University of Maryland, College Park*
VETERANS ADMINISTRATION

William L. O'Neill, *Professor of History, Rutgers University, New Brunswick, New Jersey*
STEVENSON, ADLAI

John Opie, *Distinguished Professor of History Emeritus, New Jersey Institute of Technology, Newark*
HOMESTEAD ACT

Michael Oriard, *Distinguished Professor of American Literature and Culture, Oregon State University, Corvallis*
GRANGE, RED

Annelise Orleck, *Associate Professor of History, Dartmouth College, Hanover, New Hampshire*
TRIANGLE SHIRTWAIST COMPANY FIRE

Andrew J. O'Shaughnessy, *Associate Professor, University of Wisconsin—Oshkosh*
ADAMS, SAMUEL; MAYFLOWER COMPACT

Lisa Turner Oshins, *Administrative Specialist, Office of the Executive Vice Chancellor, University of California, Santa Barbara*
QUILTS AND QUILTING

David M. Oshinsky, *Board of Governors Professor of History, Rutgers University, New Brunswick, New Jersey*
ARMY-MCCARTHY HEARINGS; FORD, GERALD; MCCARTHY, JOSEPH

Gary B. Ostrower, *Professor of History, Alfred University, Alfred, New York*
COLLECTIVE SECURITY; HUGHES, CHARLES EVANS; WASHINGTON NAVAL ARMS CONFERENCE

David S. Painter, *Associate Professor of History, School of Foreign Service, Georgetown University, Washington, D.C.*
COLD WAR

Nell Irvin Painter, *Edwards Professor of American History, Princeton University, Princeton, New Jersey*
SOJOURNER TRUTH

Bruce Palmer, *Professor of History, University of Houston—Clear Lake, Texas*
FARMERS' ALLIANCE MOVEMENT

Michelle Lee Park, *Independent scholar*
NATIONAL PARK SYSTEM

Donald L. Parman, *Professor of History, Purdue University, West Lafayette, Indiana*
DAWES SEVERALTY ACT

Herbert S. Parmet, *Distinguished Professor Emeritus of History, City University of New York*
BUSH, GEORGE; EXECUTIVE PRIVILEGE

Karen Hunger Parshall, *Professor of History and Mathematics, University of Virginia, Charlottesville*
MATHEMATICS AND STATISTICS

J'Nell L. Pate, *Professor of History, Tarrant County College, Fort Worth, Texas*
LIVESTOCK INDUSTRY

Thomas G. Paterson, *Professor Emeritus of History, University of Connecticut, Storrs*
BAY OF PIGS; CUBAN MISSILE CRISIS

David S. Patterson, *Deputy Historian and General Editor of the Foreign Relations Series, U.S. Department of State, Washington, D.C.*
PERMANENT COURT OF INTERNATIONAL JUSTICE

Tiffany Ruby Patterson, *Assistant Professor of History, State University of New York, Binghamton*
WALKER, MADAME C. J.

Philip J. Pauly, *Associate Professor of History, Rutgers University, New Brunswick, New Jersey*
BIOLOGICAL SCIENCES

Elizabeth Anne Payne, *Director, McDonnell-Barksdale Honors College and Professor of History, University of Mississippi, University*
WOMEN'S TRADE UNION LEAGUE

Barry Lee Pearson, *Professor of English, University of Maryland, College Park*
BLUES

James Lal Penick Jr., *Professor Emeritus, University of Alabama at Birmingham*
CONSERVATION MOVEMENT

Burton W. Peretti, *Assistant Professor of History, Western Connecticut State University, Danbury*
DAVIS, MILES; JAZZ

Elisabeth Israels Perry, *John Francis Bannon Professor of History and American Studies, Saint Louis University, Missouri*
SMITH, ALFRED E.

Tom F. Peters, *Professor of Architecture and History and Director, Building and Architectural Technology Institute, Lehigh University, Bethlehem, Pennsylvania*
SKYSCRAPERS

John Pettegrew, *Assistant Professor of History, Lehigh University, Bethlehem, Pennsylvania*
GILMAN, CHARLOTTE PERKINS

Sarah K. A. Pfatteicher
CHALLENGER DISASTER

Paula F. Pfeffer, *Professor of History, Loyola University of Chicago, Illinois*
RANDOLPH, A. PHILIP

Jane M. Picker, *Professor of Law, Cleveland Marshall College of Law, Cleveland State University, Ohio*
INTERNATIONAL LAW

G. Kurt Piehler, *Assistant Professor of History and Director, Center for the Study of War and Society, University of Tennessee, Knoxville*
ARLINGTON NATIONAL CEMETERY; LINCOLN MEMORIAL; MOUNT RUSHMORE; STILWELL, JOSEPH; TOMB OF THE UNKNOWNS; VIETNAM VETERANS MEMORIAL

Harold L. Platt, *Professor of History, Loyola University of Chicago, Illinois*
INSULL, SAMUEL

Brenda Gayle Plummer, *Professor of History, University of Wisconsin—Madison*
BROWN v. *BOARD OF EDUCATION*

Howard J. Pollack, *Professor of Music, Moores School of Music, University of Houston, Texas*
COPLAND, AARON

Jonathan Z. S. Pollack, *Instructor in History, Madison Area Technical College, Madison, Wisconsin*
ELLINGTON, EDWARD ("DUKE"); FITZGERALD, ELLA; GOODMAN, BENNY

Robert Pool, *Science writer,* Discover *and* New Science
INTERNET AND WORLD WIDE WEB

Daniel A. Pope, *Associate Professor of History, University of Oregon, Eugene*
ADVERTISING

*E. B. Potter, *Professor of History Emeritus, U.S. Naval Academy, Annapolis, Maryland*
NIMITZ, CHESTER

Richard Gid Powers, *Professor of History, College of Staten Island, City University of New York*
ANTICOMMUNISM; FEDERAL BUREAU OF INVESTIGATION; ROSENBERG CASE

Marla Prather, *Curator of Post-War Art, Whitney Museum of American Art, New York, New York*
DE KOONING, WILLEM

Walter F. Pratt Jr., *Associate Dean and Professor of Law, Notre Dame Law School, Notre Dame, Indiana*
INSULAR CASES

Robert N. Proctor, *Distinguished Professor of the History of Science, Pennsylvania State University, University Park*
CANCER

Stephen Prothero, *Assistant Professor of Religion, Boston University, Massachusetts*
ISLAM

Francis Paul Prucha, *Professor Emeritus of History, Marquette University, Milwaukee, Wisconsin*
BUREAU OF INDIAN AFFAIRS

Carroll W. Pursell, *Adeline Barry Davee Distinguished Professor of History, Case Western Reserve University, Cleveland, Ohio*
STEAM POWER

Stephen G. Rabe, *Professor of History, University of Texas at Dallas, Richardson*
ALLIANCE FOR PROGRESS

*Howard N. Rabinowitz
GOLF

Patrick Rael, *Assistant Professor of History, Bowdoin College, Brunswick, Maine*
DOUGLASS, FREDERICK

Nicole Hahn Rafter, *Professor, Law, Policy, and Society Program, Northeastern University, Boston, Massachusetts*
NATIONAL PRISON ASSOCIATION

Judith R. Raftery, *Associate Professor of History, California State University, Chico*
AMERICANIZATION MOVEMENT

Stephen Railton, *Professor of English, University of Virginia, Charlottesville*
COOPER, JAMES FENIMORE

James A. Rawley, *Carl Adolph Happold Distinguished Professor of History Emeritus, University of Nebraska, Lincoln*
LINCOLN, ABRAHAM

Leslie J. Reagan, *Associate Professor of History and Medical Humanities, University of Illinois at Urbana-Champaign*
ROE v. *WADE*

Steven L. Rearden, *Joint History Office, Washington, D.C.*
FEDERAL GOVERNMENT, EXECUTIVE BRANCH: DEPARTMENT OF DEFENSE

Carol Reardon, *Associate Professor of American History, Pennsylvania State University, University Park*
GETTYSBURG, BATTLE OF

Tim Redman, *Professor of Studies in Literature, University of Texas at Dallas*
POUND, EZRA

Merl E. Reed, *Professor Emeritus of History, Georgia State University, Atlanta*
FAIR EMPLOYMENT PRACTICE COMMITTEE

William J. Reese, *Professor of Educational Policy Studies and Professor of History, University of Wisconsin—Madison*
AMERICAN ASSOCIATION OF UNIVERSITY PROFESSORS (co-author); EDUCATION: EDUCATION IN CONTEMPORARY AMERICA

Gary W. Reichard, *Associate Vice President for Academic Affairs and Professor of History, California State University, Long Beach*

EISENHOWER, DWIGHT D.; TAFT, ROBERT; WATERGATE

Joseph P. Reidy, *Professor of History, Howard University, Washington, D.C.*
SLAVERY: DEVELOPMENT AND EXPANSION OF SLAVERY

Janice L. Reiff, *Associate Professor of History, University of California, Los Angeles*
PULLMAN STRIKE AND BOYCOTT

Harold C. Relyea, *Specialist in American National Government, Congressional Research Service, Washington, D.C.*
FREEDOM OF INFORMATION ACT

Lex Renda, *Associate Professor of History, University of Wisconsin—Milwaukee*
ANTI-MASONIC PARTY

David S. Reynolds, *Distinguished Professor of American Literature and American Studies, Baruch College, City University of New York*
WHITMAN, WALT

Douglas M. Reynolds
SLOAN, ALFRED P.

Michael Reynolds, *Independent scholar, Former Associate Dean and Professor of English, North Carolina State University, Raleigh*
HEMINGWAY, ERNEST

Terry S. Reynolds, *Professor of History and Chair, Department of Social Sciences, Michigan Technological University, Houghton*
ENGINEERING

Leo P. Ribuffo, *Society of Cincinnati George Washington Distinguished Professor of History, George Washington University, Washington, D.C.*
CARTER, JIMMY; ENERGY CRISIS OF THE 1970s; REAGAN, RONALD

Barry D. Riccio, *Associate Professor of History, Eastern Illinois University, Charleston*
LIPPMANN, WALTER

Julian Rice, *Independent Scholar*
BLACK ELK

Leonard L. Richards, *Professor of History, University of Massachusetts, Amherst*
ADAMS, JOHN QUINCY; SHAW, LEMUEL

Robert D. Richardson Jr., *Independent scholar*
THOREAU, HENRY DAVID

Martin Ridge, *Senior Research Associate, The Huntington Library, San Marino, California*
TURNER, FREDERICK JACKSON

Andrew Chamberlin Rieser, *Assistant Professor of History, St. Cloud State University, St. Cloud, Minnesota*
CHAUTAUQUA MOVEMENT; LIBERALISM; *THEORY OF BUSINESS ENTERPRISE, THE; THEORY OF THE LEISURE CLASS, THE;* VEBLEN, THORSTEIN; WARD, LESTER

Steven A. Riess, *Professor of History, Northeastern Illinois University, Chicago*
BASKETBALL; FOOTBALL; SPORTS: AMATEUR SPORTS AND RECREATION; SPORTS: PROFESSIONAL SPORTS

John S. Rigden, *Director of Special Projects, American Institute of Physics, College Park, Maryland*
RABI, ISIDOR I.

Oliver A. Rink, *Professor of American History, California State University, Bakersfield*
DUTCH SETTLEMENTS IN NORTH AMERICA

Antonio Rios-Bustamante, *Director, Chicano Studies Program and Professor of History, University of Wyoming, Laramie*
LOS ANGELES

Norman K. Risjord, *Professor Emeritus of History, University of Wisconsin—Madison*
EARLY REPUBLIC, ERA OF THE; FEDERALIST PARTY

Jon H. Roberts, *Professor of History, University of Wisconsin—Stevens Point*
HODGE, CHARLES; PSYCHOTHERAPY

David R. Roediger, *Professor of History, University of Minnesota, Minneapolis*
INDUSTRIAL WORKERS OF THE WORLD; RAILROAD STRIKES OF 1877

Naomi Rogers, *Lecturer in Women and Gender Studies Program, Yale University, New Haven, Connecticut*
MEDICINE: ALTERNATIVE MEDICINE; POLIOMYELITIS

Andrew Rolle, *Research Scholar, The Huntington Library, San Marino, California; Cleland Professor of History Emeritus, Occidental College, Los Angeles, California*
FRÉMONT, JOHN CHARLES

Carl Rollyson, *Professor of English, Baruch College, City University of New York*
MONROE, MARILYN

Charles Romney, *Fellow, The Huntington Library, San Marino, California*
FIFTIES, THE

James D. Rose
STEEL STRIKE OF 1919

Ruth Rosen, *Professor of History, University of California, Davis*
FEMINISM

Emily S. Rosenberg, *DeWitt Wallace Professor of History, Macalester College, St. Paul, Minnesota*
DOLLAR DIPLOMACY; FOREIGN RELATIONS: OVERVIEW; FOREIGN RELATIONS: THE CULTURAL DIMENSION; GOLD STANDARD; POTSDAM CONFERENCE

Norman L. Rosenberg, *DeWitt Wallace Professor of History, Macalester College, St. Paul, Minnesota*
ABRAMS v. *UNITED STATES;* ALIEN AND SEDITION ACTS; SEDITION; SIXTIES, THE

Joshua L. Rosenbloom, *Associate Professor of Economics, University of Kansas, Lawrence; Research Associate, National Bureau of Economic Research, Cambridge, Massachusetts*
LABOR MARKETS

Theodore Rosenof, *Professor of History, Mercy College, Dobbs Ferry, New York*
KEYNESIANISM

Steven J. Ross, *Professor of History, University of Southern California, Los Angeles*
SINGLE-TAX MOVEMENT

Marc Rothenberg, *Editor, Joseph Henry Papers Project, Smithsonian Institution Archives, Washington, D.C.*
BARTRAM, JOHN AND WILLIAM; BOWDITCH, NATHANIEL; HENRY, JOSEPH

David J. Rothman, *Bernard Schoenberg Professor of Social Medicine and Professor of History, Columbia University, New York, New York*
DEATH AND DYING; PRISONS AND PENITENTIARIES

William G. Rothstein, *Professor of Sociology, University of Maryland, Baltimore County*
FLEXNER REPORT

Joan Shelley Rubin, *Professor of History, University of Rochester, Rochester, New York*
BOOK-OF-THE-MONTH CLUB

Cameron L. Saffell, *Center for Agricultural History and Rural Studies, Iowa State University, Ames; Curator of Agriculture, New Mexico Farm and Ranch Heritage Museum, Las Cruces*
AMERICAN FARM BUREAU FEDERATION

Nancy A. Sahli, *Independent scholar*
BLACKWELL, ELIZABETH

Kirkpatrick Sale, *Independent scholar*
COLUMBUS, CHRISTOPHER

Neal Salisbury, *Professor of History, Smith College, Northampton, Massachusetts*
KING PHILIP'S WAR; PEQUOT WAR

John A. Salmond, *Pro Vice-Chancellor and Professor of American History, La Trobe University, Bundoora, Victoria, Australia*
CIVILIAN CONSERVATION CORPS

Jonathan D. Sarna, *Joseph H. and Belle R. Braun Professor of American Jewish History, Brandeis University, Waltham, Massachusetts*
WISE, ISAAC MAYER

Jonathan D. Sassi, *Assistant Professor of History, College of Staten Island, City University of New York*
NATIVE AMERICAN CHURCH

John E. Sauer, *Independent scholar*
TOBACCO PRODUCTS (co-author)

Udo Sautter, *Professor of North American History, University of Tübingen, Germany*
UNEMPLOYMENT

Todd L. Savitt, *Professor of Medical Humanities, Brody School of Medicine, East Carolina University, Greenville, North Carolina*
SICKLE-CELL ANEMIA

Richard C. Sawyer, *Teacher of Science and Mathematics, Newton Senior High School, Newton, Iowa*
FEDERAL GOVERNMENT, EXECUTIVE BRANCH: DEPARTMENT OF AGRICULTURE

Gary Scharnhorst, *Professor of English, University of New Mexico, Albuquerque*
ALGER, HORATIO

Thomas H. Schaub, *Professor of English and American Literature, University of Wisconsin—Madison*
LITERATURE: SINCE WORLD WAR I

William J. Scheick, *J. R. Millikan Centennial Professor of American Literature, University of Texas at Austin*
BRADSTREET, ANNE

Timothy E. Scheurer, *Professor of Humanities, Franklin University, Columbus, Ohio*
BERLIN, IRVING

Emily Schiller, *Lecturer in English and UCLA Writing Programs, University of California, Los Angeles*
CRÈVECOEUR, J. HECTOR ST. JOHN; WOOLMAN, JOHN

A. Gregory Schneider, *Professor of Behavioral Science, Pacific Union College, Angwin, California*
METHODISM

Dorothee Schneider, *Graduate College Scholar in Sociology, University of Illinois at Urbana-Champaign*
GOMPERS, SAMUEL

John C. Schneider, *Director, Corporate and Foundation Relations and Senior Adjunct Lecturer in History, Tufts University, Medford, Massachusetts*
HOMELESSNESS AND VAGRANCY

Richard Schneirov, *Professor of History, Indiana State University, Terre Haute*
HAYMARKET AFFAIR

Rennie B. Schoepflin, *Associate Professor of History, La Sierra University, Riverside, California*
CHRISTIAN SCIENCE; HEALTH AND FITNESS

Ann Schofield, *Professor of American Studies and Women's Studies, University of Kansas, Lawrence*
JONES, MARY ("MOTHER")

Michael S. Schudson, *Professor of Communication and Adjunct Professor of Sociology, University of California, San Diego, La Jolla*
JOURNALISM

Robert J. Schulmann, *Associate Professor of History and Director, Einstein Papers Project, Boston University, Massachusetts*
EINSTEIN, ALBERT

Stanley K. Schultz, *Professor of History, University of Wisconsin—Madison*
URBAN RENEWAL

Carlos Arnaldo Schwantes, *Professor of History, University of Idaho, Moscow*
WEST, THE

*Bernard Schwartz, *Chapman Distinguished Professor of Law, University of Tulsa, Tulsa, Oklahoma*
JUDICIAL REVIEW

Roy V. Scott, *Professor Emeritus of History, Mississippi State University, Mississippi State*
AGRICULTURAL EDUCATION AND EXTENSION; GRANGER LAWS; GRANGER MOVEMENT; WALTON, SAM

Randolph Scully, *Ph.D. candidate in History, University of Pennsylvania, Philadelphia*
VIRGINIA DECLARATION OF RIGHTS

Judith Sealander, *Professor of History, Bowling Green State University, Bowling Green, Ohio*
PHILANTHROPY AND PHILANTHROPIC FOUNDATIONS

John F. Sears, *Associate Editor, Eleanor Roosevelt Papers; Independent scholar and consultant*
NIAGARA FALLS

Bruce E. Seely, *Professor of History, Michigan Technological University, Houghton*
HIGHWAY SYSTEM

Howard P. Segal, *Adelaide and Alan Bird Professor of History, University of Maine, Orono*
AUTOMATION AND COMPUTERIZATION

Robert W. Seidel, *Professor and Director, Charles Babbage Institute Center for the History of Computing, University of Minnesota, Minneapolis*
COMPUTERS; FERMI, ENRICO; GATES, WILLIAM H.; LAWRENCE, ERNEST O.

Terry L. Seip, *Associate Professor of History, University of Southern California, Los Angeles*
FREEDMEN'S BUREAU

Harold E. Selesky, *Associate Professor of History and Director, Maxwell Program in Military History, University of Alabama, Tuscaloosa*
YORKTOWN, BATTLE OF

Christopher Sellers, *Associate Professor of History, State University of New York, Stony Brook*
ENVIRONMENTAL PROTECTION AGENCY

Milton C. Sernett, *Professor of African American Studies, Syracuse University, Syracuse, New York*
AFRICAN AMERICAN RELIGION

Todd A. Shallat, *Professor of History, Boise State University, Boise, Idaho*
ARMY CORPS OF ENGINEERS; CANALS AND WATERWAYS

Ronald E. Shaw, *Professor Emeritus of History, Miami University, Oxford, Ohio*
ERIE CANAL

Janann Sherman, *Assistant Professor of History, University of Memphis, Memphis, Tennessee*
RANKIN, JEANNETTE

Michael S. Sherry, *Professor of History, Northwestern University, Evanston, Illinois*
HIROSHIMA AND NAGASAKI, ATOMIC BOMBING OF

Kenneth E. Shewmaker, *Professor of History, Dartmouth College, Hanover, New Hampshire*
WEBSTER, DANIEL

Crandall Shifflett, *Professor of History, Director of Graduate Studies, and Project Director, Virtual Jamestown, Virginia Polytechnic Institute and State University, Blacksburg*
APPALACHIA

Jan Shipps, *Professor Emeritus of History and Religious Studies, Indiana University-Pudue University, Indianapolis*
MORMONISM

Philip Shoemaker
OBSERVATORIES

James R. Shortridge, *Professor of Geography, University of Kansas, Lawrence*
MIDDLE WEST, THE

Richard M. Shusterman, *Professor of Philosophy, Temple University, Philadelphia, Pennsylvania*
RORTY, RICHARD

John W. Shy, *Professor Emeritus of History, University of Michigan, Ann Arbor*
CLARK, GEORGE ROGERS

David B. Sicilia, *Assistant Professor of History, University of Maryland, College Park*
CHEMICAL INDUSTRY

Joel H. Silbey, *President White Professor of History, Cornell University, Ithaca, New York*
BUCHANAN, JAMES; LIBERTY PARTY; POLITICAL PARTIES; REPUBLICAN PARTY

Bryant Simon, *Assistant Professor of History, University of Georgia, Athens*
TENNESSEE VALLEY AUTHORITY

James F. Simon, *Martin Professor of Law, New York Law School, New York*
DOUGLAS, WILLIAM O.

John Y. Simon, *Professor of History, Southern Illinois University, Carbondale*
GRANT, ULYSSES S.

Daniel J. Singal, *Professor of History, Hobart and William Smith Colleges, Geneva, New York*
MODERNIST CULTURE

Amritjit Singh, *Professor of English, Rhode Island College, Providence*
HARLEM RENAISSANCE

Kathryn Kish Sklar, *Distinguished Professor of History, State University of New York, Binghamton*
BEECHER, CATHARINE; KELLEY, FLORENCE; LYON, MARY; *MULLER* v. *OREGON;* NATIONAL CONSUMERS' LEAGUE

Robert Sklar, *Professor of Cinema Studies, New York University, New York*
FILM

Theda Skocpol, *Victor S. Thomas Professor of Government of Sociology, Harvard University, Cambridge, Massachusetts*
PENSIONS, CIVIL WAR

Robert A. Slayton, *Associate Professor of History, Chapman University, Orange, California*
JUNGLE, THE

Hugh Richard Slotten,
COAST AND GEODETIC SURVEY, U.S.

Carl Smith, *Franklyn Bliss Snyder Professor of English and American Studies and Professor of History, Northwestern University, Evanston, Illinois*
CHICAGO FIRE; JORDAN, MICHAEL

Daniel Scott Smith, *Professor of History, University of Illinois at Chicago*
DEMOGRAPHY

Elbert B. Smith, *Professor Emeritus of History, University of Maryland, College Park*
TAYLOR, ZACHARY

Erin A. Smith, *Assistant Professor of American Studies and Literature, University of Texas at Dallas, Richardson*
LITERATURE, POPULAR

Jane S. Smith, *Visiting Scholar, Institute for Health Services Research and Policy Studies and Adjunct Professor of History, Northwestern University, Evanston, Illinois*
SALK, JONAS

Mark C. Smith, *Associate Professor of American Studies and History, University of Texas at Austin*
SOCIAL SCIENCE

Richard V. Smith, *Professor Emeritus of Geography, Miami University, Oxford, Ohio*
TOURISM

Ronald A. Smith, *Professor Emeritus of Kinesiology, Pennsylvania State University, University Park*
NATIONAL COLLEGIATE ATHLETIC ASSOCIATION

Dean R. Snow, *Professor of Anthropology, Pennsylvania State University, University Park*
INDIAN HISTORY AND CULTURE: DISTRIBUTION OF MAJOR GROUPS, CIRCA 1500; INDIAN HISTORY AND CULTURE: MIGRATION AND PRE-COLUMBIAN ERA; IROQUOIS CONFEDERACY

Jean R. Soderlund, *Professor of History, Lehigh University, Bethlehem, Pennsylvania*
ADAMS, ABIGAIL

Rickie Solinger, *Independent historian*
ILLEGITIMACY

Richard D. Sonn, *Associate Professor of History, University of Arkansas, Fayetteville*
ANARCHISM

Jennifer M. Spear, *Assistant Professor of History, Dickinson College, Carlisle, Pennsylvania*
FRENCH SETTLEMENTS IN NORTH AMERICA; LA SALLE, RENE-ROBERT CAVELIER, SIEUR DE

Allan Burton Spetter, *Professor of History, Wright State University, Dayton, Ohio*
HARRISON, BENJAMIN

Robert J. Spitzer, *Distinguished Service Professor of Political Science, State University of New York, Cortland*
VETO POWER

Paul E. Sprague, *Professor Emeritus of Architectural History, University of Wisconsin—Milwaukee*
SULLIVAN, LOUIS

J.C.A. Stagg, *Professor of History and Editor in Chief of the Papers of James Madison, University of Virginia, Charlottesville*
MADISON, JAMES, MONROE, JAMES

Paul J. Staiti, *Alumnae Foundation Professor of Fine Arts, Mount Holyoke College, South Hadley, Massachusetts*
COPLEY, JOHN SINGLETON

Maren Stange, *Associate Professor of American Studies, The Cooper Union, New York, New York*
HOW THE OTHER HALF LIVES

John M. Staudenmaier, S.J., *Professor of Technology, University of Detroit Mercy, Detroit, Michigan; Editor in Chief,* Technology and Culture: International Journal of the Society for the History of Technology
FORD, HENRY

David L. Stebenne, *Associate Professor of History, Ohio State University, Columbus*
WATSON, THOMAS, SR.

Stephen J. Stein, *Chancellors' Professor of Religious Studies, Indiana University, Bloomington*
SHAKERISM

Anders Stephanson, *Associate Professor of History, Columbia University, New York, New York*
MANIFEST DESTINY

Christopher H. Sterling, *Professor of Media and Public Affairs, and of Telecommunications, Columbian School of Arts and Sciences, George Washington University, Washington, D.C.*
PALEY, WILLIAM; RADIO; SARNOFF, DAVID

James Brewer Stewart, *James Wallace Professor of History, Macalester College, St. Paul, Minnesota*
CIVIL WAR: CAUSES; CIVIL WAR: CHANGING INTERPRETATIONS; CIVIL WAR: DOMESTIC EFFECTS; CIVIL WAR: MILITARY AND DIPLOMATIC COURSE; GARRISON, WILLIAM LLOYD

Jesse Stiller, *Historian, Office of the Comptroller of the Currency, Department of the Treasury, Washington, D.C.*
FEDERAL GOVERNMENT, EXECUTIVE BRANCH: DEPARTMENT OF THE TREASURY

Francis N. Stites, *Professor Emeritus of History, San Diego State University, California*
MARSHALL, JOHN; *McCULLOCH* v. *MARYLAND*

Mark A. Stoler, *Professor of History, University of Vermont, Burlington*
MARSHALL, GEORGE; STIMSON, HENRY

Ronald Story, *Professor of History, University of Massachusetts, Amherst*
BASEBALL; COBB, TY; DIMAGGIO, JOE; RUTH, GEORGE HERMAN ("BABE")

Paul Street, *Assistant Professor of American History, Northern Illinois University, DeKalb*
MEATPACKING AND MEAT PROCESSING INDUSTRY; SWIFT, GUSTAVUS

Sharon Hartman Strom, *Professor of History and Women's Studies, University of Rhode Island, Kingston*
OFFICE TECHNOLOGY

Shelton Stromquist, *Professor of History, University of Iowa, Iowa City*
GREENBACK LABOR PARTY; LABOR MOVEMENTS

Sterling Stuckey, *Professor of History and Presidential Chair, University of California, Riverside*
RACISM; SLAVERY: HISTORIANS AND SLAVERY

William Stueck, *Professor of History, University of Georgia, Athens*
KOREAN WAR

Roger H. Stuewer, *Professor of the History of Science and Technology, University of Minnesota, Minneapolis*
COMPTON, ARTHUR H.

Thomas J. Sugrue, *Bicentennial Class of 1940 Professor of History and Sociology, University of Pennsylvania, Philadelphia*
URBANIZATION

Robert B. Sullivan, *Traducteurs Clio/Clio Translations, Ottawa, Ontario, Canada*
RUSH, BENJAMIN

Daniel E. Sutherland, *Professor of History, University of Arkansas, Fayetteville*
CONFEDERATE STATES OF AMERICA

William R. Swagerty, *Associate Professor of History, University of Idaho, Moscow*
EXPLORATION, CONQUEST, AND SETTLEMENT, ERA OF EUROPEAN (co-author)

John P. Swann, *Historian, Food and Drug Administration, Rockville, Maryland*
PHARMACEUTICAL INDUSTRY

Andrew Szanton, *Freelance writer and Former Oral Historian, Smithsonian Institution, Washington, D.C.*
WIGNER, EUGENE

William R. Tanner, *Professor Emeritus of History, Humboldt State University, Arcata, California*
INTERNAL SECURITY ACT (McCARRAN ACT)

John Tauranac, *Writer and map maker, New York, New York*
EMPIRE STATE BUILDING

Joseph E. Taylor III, *Assistant Professor of History, Iowa State University, Ames*
FISHERIES

R. E. Taylor, *Professor of Anthropology, University of California, Riverside*
UREY, HAROLD C.

Jon C. Teaford, *Professor of History, Purdue University, West Lafayette, Indiana*
MUNICIPAL AND COUNTY GOVERNMENTS

Richard S. Tedlow, *Class of 1957 Professor of Business Administration, Harvard Business School, Boston, Massachusetts*
MASS MARKETING

Athan Theoharis, *Professor of History, Marquette University, Milwaukee, Wisconsin*
HOOVER, J. EDGAR

J. Mark Thompson
BOSTON MASSACRE

Russell Thornton, *Professor of Anthropology, University of California, Los Angeles*
INDIAN HISTORY AND CULTURE: FROM 1900 TO 1950

Daniel J. Tichenor, *Assistant Professor of Political Science, Rutgers University, New Brunswick, New Jersey*
FEDERAL GOVERNMENT, EXECUTIVE BRANCH: OTHER DEPARTMENTS

Neal Tolchin, *Associate Professor of English, Hunter College and the Graduate School and University Center, City University of New York*
MELVILLE, HERMAN

Stewart E. Tolnay, *Professor of Sociology, State University of New York, Albany*
LYNCHING (co-author)

David A. Tomlin, *Independent scholar*
GIBBS, JOSIAH WILLARD

Elizabeth Toon, *Visiting Assistant Professor of Science and Technology Studies, Cornell University, Ithaca, New York*
AMERICAN MEDICAL ASSOCIATION

Jose Torre
ROCKEFELLER, JOHN D.

Stanley Trachtenberg, *Professor Emeritus of English, Texas Christian University, Fort Worth*
BELLOW, SAUL

Sarah W. Tracy, *Assistant Professor of Honors, History of Science, and Medicine, Honors College, University of Oklahoma, Norman*
ALCOHOL AND ALCOHOL ABUSE

David F. Trask, *Consulting historian*
MILITARY, THE; SPANISH-AMERICAN WAR; SUBMARINES

Walter I. Trattner, *Professor Emeritus of History, University of Wisconsin—Milwaukee*
CHILD LABOR

Thomas Trautmann, *Marshal Sahlins Collegiate Professor of History and Anthropology, University of Michigan, Ann Arbor*
MORGAN, LEWIS HENRY

Lorett Treese, *College Archivist, Bryn Mawr College, Bryn Mawr, Pennsylvania*
VALLEY FORGE

James W. Trent, *Professor of Social Work, Southern Illinois University, Edwardsville*
MENTAL RETARDATION

William Vance Trollinger Jr., *Associate Professor of History, University of Dayton, Dayton, Ohio*
CHRISTIAN COALITION; FUNDAMENTALIST MOVEMENT; MORAL MAJORITY; SUNDAY, BILLY

Anthony Troncone, *Assistant Professor of History, Dominican College, Orangeburg, New York*
WAR INDUSTRIES BOARD

Carole J. Trone, *Ph.D. candidate in Educational Policy Studies, University of Wisconsin—Madison*
AMERICAN ASSOCIATION OF UNIVERSITY PROFESSORS (co-author)

Joe W. Trotter Jr., *Mellon Professor of History, Carnegie Mellon University, Pittsburgh, Pennsylvania*
AFRICAN AMERICANS

Arleen Marcia Tuchman, *Associate Professor of History, Vanderbilt University, Nashville, Tennessee*
ZAKRZEWSKA, MARIE

Maxine Turner, *Professor Emerita of Communication, Georgia Institute of Technology, Atlanta*
FARRAGUT, DAVID

Mark Tushnet, *Carmack Waterhouse Professor of Constitutional Law, Georgetown University Law Center, Washington D.C.*
CIVIL RIGHTS; CIVIL RIGHTS LEGISLATION; FEDERALISM; MARSHALL, THURGOOD

William M. Tuttle Jr., *Professor of History and American Studies, University of Kansas, Lawrence*
SERVICEMEN'S READJUSTMENT ACT

Dorothy Twohig, *Associate Professor Emeritus of History, University of Virginia, Charlotte; Editor-in-Chief Emeritus,* Papers of George Washington
WASHINGTON, GEORGE; WASHINGTON'S FAREWELL ADDRESS

Jules Tygiel, *Professor of History, San Francisco State University, California*
ROBINSON, JACKIE

Ian Tyrrell, *Associate Professor of History, University of New South Wales, Sydney, Australia*
WOMAN'S CHRISTIAN TEMPERANCE UNION

Timothy B. Tyson, *Associate Professor of Afro-American Studies, University of Wisconsin—Madison*
KING, MARTIN LUTHER, JR.

Frank Uhlig Jr., *Editor Emeritus,* Naval War College Review, *Naval War College, Newport, Rhode Island*
MIDWAY, BATTLE OF

Melvin I. Urofsky, *Professor of History and Public Policy, Virginia Commonwealth University, Richmond*
SUPREME COURT, U.S.; *WEST COAST HOTEL COMPANY* v. *PARRISH*; *WISE,* STEPHEN S.

Jonathan G. Utley, *Professor Emeritus of History, University of Tennessee, Knoxville*
HULL, CORDELL

Robert M. Utley, *Historian*
CHIEF JOSEPH; GERONIMO; INDIAN WARS; LITTLE BIGHORN, BATTLE OF THE; SITTING BULL; WOUNDED KNEE TRAGEDY

William L. Van Deburg, *Professor of Afro-American Studies, University of Wisconsin—Madison*
BLACK NATIONALISM; BLACK PANTHERS

Bailey Van Hook, *Associate Professor of Art History, Virginia Polytechnic Institute and State University, Blacksburg*
CASSATT, MARY

Warren Van Tine, *Professor of American History, Ohio State University, Columbus*
LEWIS, JOHN L.

William E. Van Vugt, *Professor of History, Calvin College, Grand Rapids, Michigan*
BRITISH AMERICANS

Frank E. Vandiver, *Distinguished University Professor and Sarah and John Lindsey Chair in Humanities, Texas A & M University, College Station*
PERSHING, JOHN J.

Rudolph J. Vecoli, *Professor of American History and Director of the Immigration History Research Center, University of Minnesota, Minneapolis*
IMMIGRATION; ITALIAN AMERICANS

Marga Vicedo, *Associate Professor of Philosophy, Arizona State University West, Phoenix*
MORGAN, THOMAS HUNT

Wendy Wagner, *Assistant Professor of English, Bates College, Lewiston, Maine*
UNCLE TOM'S CABIN

J. Samuel Walker, *Historian, U.S. Nuclear Regulatory Commission, Washington, D.C.*
ATOMIC ENERGY COMMISSION; NUCLEAR POWER; NUCLEAR REGULATORY COMMISSION

Samuel Walker, *Professor of Criminal Justice, University of Nebraska, Omaha*
AMERICAN CIVIL LIBERTIES UNION

Alan Wallach, *Ralph H. Wark Professor of Art and Art History and Professor of American Studies, College of William and Mary, Williamsburg, Virginia*
COLE, THOMAS

Altina Waller, *Professor of History, University of Connecticut, Storrs*
HATFIELD-McCOY FEUD

Karen Walloch, *Ph.D. candidate in the History of Science, University of Wisconsin—Madison*
SMALLPOX

Kerry S. Walters, *Professor of Philosophy, Gettysburg College, Gettysburg, Pennsylvania*
DEISM

Eric H. Walther, *Associate Professor of History, University of Houston, Texas*
CALHOUN, JOHN C.; DAVIS, JEFFERSON

Susan Ware, *Editor,* Notable American Women, vol. 5, *Radcliffe Institute for Advanced Study, Cambridge, Massachusetts*
LEAGUE OF WOMEN VOTERS

John Harley Warner, *Professor of the History of Medicine, American Studies, and History, Yale University, New Haven, Connecticut*
MEDICINE: FROM 1776 TO THE 1870s

Frank A. Warren, *Professor of History, Queens College, City University of New York*
THOMAS, NORMAN

Joan Waugh, *Associate Professor of History, University of California, Los Angeles*
CHARITY ORGANIZATION MOVEMENT

Devra Weber, *Associate Professor of History, University of California, Riverside*
MIGRATORY AGRICULTURAL WORKERS

Timothy P. Weber, *Dean and Professor of Church History, Northern Baptist Theological Seminary, Lombard, Illinois*
MILLENNIALISM AND APOCALYPTICISM

William Earl Weeks, *Lecturer in History, San Diego State University, California*
ADAMS-ONÍS TREATY; BARBARY WARS; GHENT, TREATY OF; LOUISIANA PURCHASE; NEW ORLEANS, BATTLE OF; WAR OF 1812

Gerhard L. Weinberg, *William Rand Kenan Jr., Professor of History Emeritus, University of North Carolina at Chapel Hill*
WAR CRIMES TRIALS, NUREMBERG AND TOKYO

Anne Sharp Wells, *Journal of Military History, Lexington, Virginia*
JOINT CHIEFS OF STAFF; LEAHY, WILLIAM D.

Camille Wells, *Distinguished Lecturer in Architectural History, University of Virginia, Charlottesville*
MONTICELLO

Christopher W. Wells, *Instructor of History, Northland College, Ashland, Wisconsin*
AUDUBON, JOHN JAMES; AUTOMOTIVE INDUSTRY; COURTSHIP AND DATING; HOUSEHOLD TECHNOLOGY

Mark K. Wells, *Permanent Professor and Head, Department of History, United States Air Force Academy, Colorado Springs, Colorado*
MITCHELL, BILLY

Wyatt C. Wells, *Assistant Professor of History, Auburn University, Montgomery, Alabama*
FEDERAL RESERVE ACT; FEDERAL RESERVE SYSTEM

Simon Wendt
CONGRESS OF RACIAL EQUALITY

Marilyn Wessel, *Dean and Director, Museum of the Rockies, Montana State University, Bozeman*
4-H CLUB MOVEMENT (co-author)

Thomas Wessel, *Professor of History, Montana State University, Bozeman*
4-H CLUB MOVEMENT (co-author)

Mark I. West, *Professor of English and American Studies Coordinator, University of North Carolina at Charlotte*
MENNINGER, KARL AND WILLIAM

Robert B. Westbrook, *Professor of History, University of Rochester, Rochester, New York*
DEWEY, JOHN

Dana F. White, *Professor of Urban Studies, Emory University, Atlanta, Georgia*
ATLANTA

G. Edward White, *University Professor and John B. Minor Professor of Law and History, University of Virginia, Charlottesville*
HARLAN, JOHN MARSHALL; HOLMES, OLIVER WENDELL, JR.; JURISPRUDENCE; O'CONNOR, SANDRA DAY; WARREN, EARL

Lawrence J. White, *Arthur E. Imperatore Professor of Economics, Stern School of Business, New York University, New York*
SAVINGS AND LOAN DEBACLE

Neil L. Whitehead, *Associate Professor of Anthropology, University of Wisconsin—Madison*
ANTHROPOLOGY

Stephen J. Whitfield, *Max Richter Professor of American Civilization, Brandeis University, Waltham, Massachusetts*
MURROW, EDWARD R.

Lee H. Whittlesey, *Archivist, National Park Service, Yellowstone National Park, Wyoming*
YELLOWSTONE NATIONAL PARK

William M. Wiecek, *Congdon Professor of Public Law and Legislation, Syracuse University College of Law, and Professor of History, Maxwell School, Syracuse University, Syracuse, New York*
BRANDEIS, LOUIS; CHURCH AND STATE, SEPARATION OF; TANEY, ROGER B.

Wayne A. Wiegand, *Professor of Library and Information Studies, University of Wisconsin—Madison*
LIBRARIES

Joseph Wiesenfarth, *Professor Emeritus of English, University of Wisconsin—Madison*
JAMES, HENRY

David K. Wiggins, *Professor of Physical Education, George Mason University, Fairfax, Virginia*
ALI, MUHAMMED; KING, BILLIE JEAN; LOUIS, JOE; OWENS, JESSE

Carolyn Williams, *Associate Professor of History, University of North Florida, Jacksonville*
AMISTAD CASE

Michael Williams, *Professor of Geography and Fellow, Oriel College, Oxford University, Oxford, England*
FORESTS AND FORESTRY

R. Hal Williams, *Professor of History, Southern Methodist University, Dallas, Texas*
CLEVELAND, GROVER

Vernon J. Williams Jr., *Professor of History and American Studies, Purdue University, West Lafayette, Indiana*
BOAS, FRANZ

Garry Wills, *Cultural historian and Adjunct Professor of American History, Northwestern University, Evanston, Illinois*
GETTYSBURG ADDRESS

Don B. Wilmeth, *Asa Messer Professor and Professor of Theatre and English, Brown University, Providence, Rhode Island*
AMUSEMENT PARKS AND THEME PARKS

Daniel J. Wilson, *Professor of History, Muhlenberg College, Allentown, Pennsylvania*
PHILOSOPHY

R. Jackson Wilson, *Sydenham Clark Parsons Professor of History, Smith College, Northampton, Massachusetts*
DICKINSON, EMILY

Robert J. Wilson III, *Professor of History, Georgia College and State University, Milledgeville*
PARKER, THEODORE; SEWALL, SAMUEL

Theodore A. Wilson, *Professor of History, University of Kansas, Lawrence*
ATLANTIC CHARTER

Allan M. Winkler, *Professor of History, Miami University, Oxford, Ohio*
CIVIL DEFENSE; LA FOLLETTE, ROBERT; POST-COLD WAR ERA

Mary Pickard Winsor, *Professor of History of Science, Institute for the History and Philosophy of Science and Technology, University of Toronto, Ontario, Canada*
AGASSIZ, LOUIS

Lawrence S. Wittner, *Professor of History, State University of New York, Albany*
ANTINUCLEAR PROTEST MOVEMENTS

Stephanie Grauman Wolf, *Senior Research Fellow, Library Company of Philadelphia and the McNeil Center for Early American Studies, University of Pennsylvania, Philadelphia*
PHILADELPHIA

Cynthia Griffin Wolff, *Class of 1922 Professor of Humanities, Massachusetts Institute of Technology, Cambridge*
WHARTON, EDITH

Wendy Wolff, *Historical Editor, Senate Historical Office, Washington, D.C.*
FEDERAL GOVERNMENT, LEGISLATIVE BRANCH: OVERVIEW; FEDERAL GOVERNMENT, LEGISLATIVE BRANCH: SENATE

Nancy Woloch, *Adjunct Professor of History, Barnard College, Columbia University, New York, New York*
BEARD, MARY; EARHART, AMELIA; SEXUAL HARRASSMENT

Peter H. Wood, *Professor of History, Duke University, Durham, North Carolina*
SLAVERY: SLAVE FAMILIES, COMMUNITIES, AND CULTURE

*C. Vann Woodward, *Historian*
COMPROMISE OF 1877

William Worley, *Research Associate in History, University of Missouri, Kansas City*
KANSAS CITY

Donald Worster, *Hall Professor of American History, University of Kansas, Lawrence*
DUST BOWL; ENVIRONMENTALISM; LAND POLICY, FEDERAL

Ben Yagoda, *Associate Professor of English, University of Delaware, Newark*
ROGERS, WILL

Virginia Yans-McLaughlin, *Professor of History, Rutgers University, New Brunswick, New Jersey*
MEAD, MARGARET

Terence Young, *Lecturer, University of Southern California, Los Angeles*
PARKS, URBAN

Henry Yu, *Assistant Professor of History, University of California, Los Angeles*
ASIAN AMERICANS

Craig Zabel, *Associate Professor of Art History, Pennsylvania State University, University Park*
ARCHITECTURE: PUBLIC ARCHITECTURE; BULFINCH, CHARLES; JOHNSON, PHILIP; PEI, I. M.

Thomas W. Zeiler, *Associate Professor of History, University of Colorado, Boulder*
TRADING WITH THE ENEMY ACT; TRILATERAL COMMISSION

John J. Zernel, *Adjunct Professor of the History of Science, Distance and Continuing Education, Oregon State University, Corvallis*
POWELL, JOHN WESLEY

Robert H. Zieger, *Distinguished Professor of History, University of Florida, Gainesville*
CONGRESS OF INDUSTRIAL ORGANIZATIONS; MEANY, GEORGE

Olivier J. Zunz, *Commonwealth Professor of History, University of Virginia, Charlottesville*
DETROIT

*deceased

LIST OF HISTORICAL MAPS

THE OXFORD GUIDE TO

UNITED STATES HISTORY

A

ABM TREATY. *See* Nuclear Arms Control Treaties.

ABOLITIONISM. *See* Antislavery.

ABORTION. The legal status of abortion in the United States has undergone dramatic shifts but its practice has been consistent: Throughout American history, many women have relied on abortion to control their fertility. Before the mid–nineteenth century, abortion induced prior to quickening (the moment when the pregnant woman feels fetal movement) was a legal and accepted practice, especially for young, unmarried women. By midcentury, the commercialization of abortion gave greater visibility to its prevalence among married, white, native-born women. This increased visibility coincided with growing agitation by women for fuller inclusion in public life and with increased *immigration of ethnically diverse people, both of which provoked concern about the nation's changing character. Thus when physicians pursued the criminalization of abortion in an effort to stabilize their professional standing through laws restraining their competitors, especially midwives, their proposals resonated with legislators' gender, ethnic, and nationalist fears. In the twenty years between 1860 and 1880, with little public debate, every state made abortion illegal, except when performed by a licensed physician to save the life of the pregnant woman. In this same period, federal and state laws also prohibited the distribution of contraceptive information and devices.

At times during the one hundred years when abortion was illegal, police allowed its practice to continue undisturbed; at times it was repressed. Throughout the period, many women continued to procure abortions despite the risks, and juries often refused to convict abortionists, indicating continued public acceptance of the practice. During the 1930s, abortion clinics run by licensed physicians operated quite openly, contributing to an estimated 800,000 abortions a year. However, the procedure was still quite risky; induced abortions accounted for 14 percent of maternal mortality. After *World War II, *hospitals tightened the practice of therapeutic abortion by establishing physician review boards, leading to a dramatic reduction in hospital abortions. Police raids on the illegal clinics that had thrived in the 1930s made abortion even more difficult and dangerous to obtain. Abortion death rates doubled between 1951 and 1962, with the risk falling most heavily on women of color who were four times more likely than white women to die from abortion.

Political challenges to abortion laws were rare before the 1960s. The birth control movement led by Margaret *Sanger did not contest abortion restrictions, instead pointing to the high rates of injury and death from criminal abortion as a compelling reason to decriminalize contraception. As repression of abortion increased through the 1950s, leading women to take more desperate risks, physicians and women began to seek reform of abortion laws. By 1973, through legislative and court actions, the abortion reform/repeal movement won changes in nineteen state laws. At the same time, networks were organized to provide women with access to safe and affordable illegal abortions. In *California, the Society for Humane Abortion inspected facilities, bargained over fees, and referred thousands of women to clean and inexpensive illegal abortions in Mexico. In *Chicago, self-trained women organized an abortion service called Jane that performed twelve thousand abortions between 1969 and 1973 without a single fatality. These referral networks were part of the resurgent women's movement, which also pushed beyond reform to seek repeal of abortion laws. They argued that the decision to abort a pregnancy involved the fundamental right of women to control their bodily processes.

This activism ended in 1973 with the *Supreme Court's *Roe* v. *Wade* landmark decision. Grounded in the 1965 decision *Griswold* v. *Connecticut,* which had established the right to privacy in contraceptive decision-making, *Roe* established a fundamental right to abortion. Under *Roe,* except to ensure maternal health, states could not restrict abortion before fetal viability. (Viability is the point in pregnancy when the fetus is "capable of meaningful life outside the womb," roughly the end of the second trimester.) After *Roe,* maternal mortality rates dropped by almost one half.

Efforts to undercut *Roe* began almost immediately. Small groups opposed to abortion reform blossomed into the "pro-life" movement, arguing that abortion violated the fetus's right to life. Initially led by the American Roman Catholic church, the movement expanded as social conservatives and Protestant fundamentalists (some intent on rebuilding the *Republican party after *Watergate) took up the issue. Early successful restrictions centered on ending federal funding of abortion for poor women and requiring parental consent and notification laws for teenagers. Outside the courtroom and legislature, organized efforts emerged to disrupt the practice of abortion. Harassment of clinic patients and abortion providers became common. In the late 1980s and early 1990s, Operation Rescue, led by Randall Terry, blockaded abortion clinics in cities nationwide. The goal of this activity was to publicize the pro-life cause and make abortion difficult, if not impossible, to obtain. Between 1982 and 1998, there were more than 150 bombings and 5 murders associated with anti-abortion activity.

While not recriminalizing abortion, the Supreme Court in 1992 retreated from its holding in *Roe.* In the *Casey* v. *Planned Parenthood* decision, which upheld mandatory waiting periods and state-mandated counseling, the Court ruled that the state's interest in protecting potential life permitted some restrictions on abortion throughout pregnancy, as long as the restrictions did not impose an undue burden on women. Thus, abortion was no longer a fundamental right; the lower standard of "undue burden" gave legislators greater leeway to limit abortion. As the twentieth century ended, abortion remained legal, but practical access was increasingly problematic. Harassment, violence, and restrictions led many hospitals and practitioners to stop providing abortion. An estimated 83 percent of U.S. counties had no abortion provider. At the same time, however, federal and state laws protecting women's access to clinics, and the innovative use of antiracketeering laws against organizers of clinic blockades, continued to hinder efforts to stop abortion completely.

[*See also* Birth Control and Family Planning; Medicine; Roman Catholicism; Women's Rights Movements.]

• James Mohr, *Abortion in America*, 1978. Laurence Tribe, *Abortion: The Clash of Absolutes*, 1990. Janet Farrell Brodie, *Abortion and Contraception in Nineteenth Century America*, 1994. David Garrow, *Liberty and Sexuality: The Right to Privacy and the Making of Roe v. Wade*, 1994. Leslie Reagan, *When Abortion Was a Crime*, 1997. Rickie Solinger, *Abortion Wars: A Half Century of Struggle 1950–2000*, 1998.

—Carole R. McCann

ABRAMS* v. *UNITED STATES (1919). This *Supreme Court case from the *World War I era involved Russian-born anarchists convicted under the 1918 Sedition Act of distributing leaflets denouncing U.S. military intervention against Russia's new Bolshevik government. Writing for the majority, Justice John Clarke followed recent rulings by Justice Oliver Wendell *Holmes Jr. in **Schenck* v. *United States* and *Debs* v. *United States* upholding the conviction of socialists for making antiwar statements on the grounds that such statements posed a "clear and present danger" in wartime America. The *Abrams* case involved the same principle, Clarke held, because the anarchists' leaflets created a "clear and present danger" of causing "the substantive evils that Congress has a right to prevent."

Justice Holmes, joined by Justice Louis *Brandeis, dissented. Although Holmes denied that he was shifting ground, recent scholarship has shown that in his *Abrams* dissent, Holmes—stung by criticism from libertarian friends such as Zechariah Chafee of Harvard Law School and Harold J. Laski—did indeed seek to rework the *Schenck* and *Debs* test. In those cases, Holmes had linked the "clear and present danger" test to the broader claim that speech need not produce action in order to carry criminal liability. But in *Abrams*, he narrowed the "clear and present danger" test to make it more protective of First Amendment, free-speech rights in hopes that, first, the courts would adopt it as a test of fundamental *constitutional* law and, second, that it might protect speech, such as that of the *Abrams* defendants, which had little likelihood of producing dangerous consequences. The *Abrams* dissent made Holmes a libertarian hero and propelled his "clear and present danger" test to the center of First Amendment discourse.

[*See also* Bill of Rights; Censorship; Civil Liberties; Sedition; Socialist Party of America].

• Richard Polenberg, *Fighting Faiths: The Abrams Case, the Supreme Court, and Free Speech*, 1987. G. Edward White, *Justice Oliver Wendell Holmes: Law and the Inner Self*, 1993.

—Norman L. Rosenberg

ABSTRACT EXPRESSIONISM, a dominant style of art in America from the end of *World War II to the early 1960s. Abstract Expressionism included the gestural painting of Jackson *Pollock, Willem *de Kooning, and Helen Frankenthaler (1928–); the improvisatory nonobjective metal-welded sculpture of Herbert Ferber (1906–1991), David Smith (1906–1965), and Seymour Lipton (1903–1986); and the tonal studies of Mark Rothko (1903–1970). Sometimes called "The New York School" because of the many Abstract Expressionist artists centered there from the late 1940s through the 1950s, the style simultaneously erupted in the San Francisco Bay area in the paintings and sculptures of Clyfford Still (1904–1980), Richard Diebenkorn (1922–), and Manuel Neri (1930–), and was subsequently embraced by artists across America. Concurrent with U.S. global ascendancy in politics and industrial production, Abstract Expressionism was critically acclaimed as a uniquely American form of modern art, and *New York City declared the capital of contemporary art.

In 1945, art critic Robert Coates of the *New Yorker* magazine first reported that a style of abstract art, largely devoid of representational subject matter and painted in a gestural and expressionist manner, was gaining ascendancy in America. Abstract Expressionists rejected the narrative and representational styles, widespread public appeal, and political views of 1930s *New Deal Era and social realist artists such as Thomas Hart Benton (1889–1975) and Ben Shahn (1898–1969), as well as the hard-edged abstract art of interwar modernists like Stuart Davis (1894–1964). Instead, they pioneered improvisational modes of art focused on the physicality of media and personal expression. Pollock's much-publicized "drip paintings" (1947–1950), dubbed "action painting" by critic Harold Rosenberg, were made by placing unprimed canvases on the floor and pouring and dripping paints in precise patterns onto their surfaces. David Smith similarly experimented with materials, techniques, and composition in his abstract metal sculptures of the 1950s. Abstract Expressionist art embodies profound disaffection with the postwar political climate of consensus, *Cold War, and nuclear menace, as well as artistic yearning for self-determination. Some Abstract Expressionist artists retained identifiable subjects as in de Kooning's *Woman I*, 1950–1952, for example, while others, including Barnett Newman (1905–1970), pursued flatter, nongestural styles.

Despite their differing stylistic preferences, Abstract Expressionist artists were generally allied in aesthetic and technical experimentation, a focus on the creative process, the use of art as a means of self-realization, the separation of art and popular culture, and the rejection of art for public or social purposes.

The stylistic origins of Abstract Expressionism can be found in Surrealist art (many European artists, such as Hans Hoffman, André Masson, and Max Ernst, as well as the Chilean painter Roberto Matta Echaurren, found refuge in the United States during World War II); the indigenous arts of North America (represented in several exhibits at the Museum of Modern Art in the 1930s and 1940s); and renewed interest in nineteenth-century American transcendentalist landscape painting. The movement's cultural and intellectual underpinnings include the psychological theories of Sigmund Freud and C. G. Jung; existential philosophy (Jean-Paul Sartre's *Existentialism and Humanism* was translated into English in 1948); and Joseph Campbell's *The Hero with a Thousand Faces* (1949), a study of myth and the importance of modern mythmakers. The context of Abstract Expressionism also includes such diverse forms of postwar cultural experimentation as the Beat movement in literature; the *jazz of John *Coltrane, Miles *Davis, and Charlie *Parker; avant-garde *dance and composition; the rock-and-roll movement in popular music; and the rebellious youth-culture films of James Dean and Marlon Brando.

Critics such as Clement Greenberg championed Abstract Expressionism as evidence of American cultural superiority and heroic individualism. Later cultural historians explored the ways it illuminated the interconnections of Cold War art and politics. Although succeeded by other art styles such as Pop and Minimalism, Abstract Expressionism remained a major point of departure for artistic and critical explorations, from the process art of Eva Hesse (1936–1970) to the 1980s movement of Neo-Expressionism.

[*See also* Fifties, The; Painting: To 1945; Painting: Since 1945.]

• Dore Ashton, *The New York School, A Cultural Reckoning*, 1972. Michael Auping, ed., *Abstract Expressionism: The Critical Developments*, 1987. Erika Doss, *Benton, Pollock, and the Politics of Modernism: From Regionalism to Abstract Expressionism*, 1991. Stephen Polcari, *Abstract Expressionism and the Modern Experience*, 1991. Michael Leja, *Reframing Abstract Expressionism: Subjectivity and Painting in the 1940s*, 1993. Ann Eden Gibson, *Abstract Expressionism: Other Politics*, 1997.

—Erika Doss

ACADEMIC FREEDOM. The American tradition of academic freedom drew inspiration from the German concept of *Lehr-*

freiheit, the statutory rights of professors in state universities to teach and do research freely. Ultimately, the tradition is rooted in the Enlightenment conviction that reason, if left free, could discover useful knowledge and foster human progress. The liberal intellectual system that grew from this conviction was understood as a social community with indefinite possibilities created by human intellectual diversity, but also one that recognized the inherent fallibility of human thought.

In this system, knowledge is the evolving critical consensus of a decentralized community that adheres to the principle that all knowledge claims, regardless of the source, must be capable of being checked. The professoriate saw a unique opportunity to contribute to the progress of knowledge as a community of checkers with specialized training, information, and skills.

For many years after the initial founding of institutions of higher education in colonial America, professors labored under the prevailing assumption that employees had no control over the conditions placed upon them, including restrictions on free expression. As the modern university and its research mission developed in the late 1800s, and as professors increasingly challenged the cherished beliefs of the time, the lack of protection for academic speech became a critical problem.

At the turn of the twentieth century, as social scientists began a critical analysis of the economic order, wealthy members of some governing boards sought to coerce academic speech. For example, in 1900, Jane Lathrop Stanford, the sole trustee of Stanford University, forced Professor Edward Ross to resign because of his support of the *free silver movement and his criticism of the corporate and political order. A second faculty member was dismissed for defending Ross, and seven others resigned, including Professor Arthur Lovejoy, who joined the faculty at Johns Hopkins University. Lovejoy in 1913 drafted a letter to colleagues at nine other leading universities, signed by seventeen professors at Johns Hopkins, proposing a professional association, the *American Association of University Professors (AAUP). With the founding of the AAUP in 1915, the professoriate sought to pressure university employers to protect the freedom of academic speech.

As the American tradition of academic freedom evolved, university employers, acknowledging the university's unique mission of creating and disseminating knowledge, granted rights of exceptional vocational freedom of speech to professors in teaching, research, and extramural utterance without interference, so long as they met the obligation of professional competence and ethical conduct. The faculty as a collegial body also assumed the duty of peer review to enforce the obligations imposed upon individual professors and to defend the academic freedom of colleagues. Peer review is in fact, an essential corollary of academic freedom in the United States.

Building on this tradition, the U.S. *Supreme Court in *Sweezy* v. *New Hampshire* (1957) expanded the First Amendment's free speech guarantees to protect academic decisions by universities and individual professors from coercion by the government (ruling that interrogatories by New Hampshire's attorney general about the content of a course were unlawful). In *Pickering* v. *Board of Education* (1968), the Court also expanded the First Amendment to protect the speech of government employees, including professors employed in public universities (ruling that a teacher's newspaper editorial criticizing the school board was protected speech).

Since the formation of the AAUP, academic freedom has been threatened repeatedly by waves of zealotry from outside the university, including strident patriotism during *World War I, *anticommunism prior to *World War II, and McCarthyism in the early 1950s. The two most recent waves have come from inside the university: student activism in the 1960s and the "political correctness" standards of the academic left in the 1990s.

[*See also* Bill of Rights; Civil Liberties; Education: Rise of the University; McCarthy, Joseph.]

• Lewis Joughin, ed., *Academic Freedom and Tenure*, 1969. American Association of University Professors, *Policy Documents and Reports*, 8th ed., 1994. Neil W. Hamilton, *Zealotry and Academic Freedom: A Legal and Historical Perspective*, 1995.

—Neil W. Hamilton

ACHESON, DEAN (1893–1971), statesman. Born to a privileged background, Acheson attended Groton, Yale, and Harvard Law School. After a clerkship with Justice Louis *Brandeis, he joined the Washington law firm of Covington and Burling in 1921.

A conservative Democrat, Acheson joined Franklin Delano *Roosevelt's administration in 1933 as undersecretary of the treasury but resigned quietly that same year in disagreement over monetary policy. With the onset of war in Europe he became a fervent interventionist and pushed for measures supporting Great Britain. Named assistant secretary of state for economic affairs in 1941, he played an important role at the *Bretton Woods Conference (1944), which established the *International Monetary Fund and the *World Bank.

Promoted to undersecretary of state in 1945, Acheson served until 1947, helping to shape U.S. policies in the early *Cold War, including the *Truman Doctrine and the *Marshall Plan. Appointed secretary of state in 1949 by President Harry S. *Truman, Acheson proved the key builder of political, economic, and military structures to contain the Soviet Union—a Cold War strategy codified in *National Security Council Document 68 in 1950. The *North Atlantic Treaty Organization, the decision to build the hydrogen bomb, the American military response to North Korean aggression, the substantial defense build-up, and the incorporation of West Germany and Japan into the western alliance all bear his strong imprint. Despite his anticommunist policies and convictions, Acheson was mercilessly criticized by the right wing of the *Republican party, especially Senator Joseph *McCarthy. A man of great self-assurance and caustic wit, he dismissed such assailants as "primitives."

Acheson returned to his law practice in 1953 but remained involved in foreign policy issues and vigorously defended the *containment strategy and policies he had helped to fashion. When presidents John F. *Kennedy and Lyndon B. *Johnson sought his advice, he consistently counseled a tough line until 1968, when he abruptly urged U.S. disengagement from the *Vietnam War. His aptly titled memoir *Present at the Creation* won the Pulitzer Prize in 1970.

[*See also* Federal Government, Executive Branch: Department of State; Korean War; New Deal Era, The; World War II.]

• Douglas Brinkley, *Dean Acheson: The Cold War Years, 1953–1971*, 1992. James Chace, *Acheson: The Secretary of State Who Created the American World*, 1998.

—Wilson D. Miscamble

ACQUIRED IMMUNODEFICIENCY SYNDROME (AIDS), a *disease caused by the human immunodeficiency virus (HIV). In 1981, medical reports first described unusual infections and *cancer previously seen only in severely immunosuppressed patients, such as those undergoing organ transplants. By mid-1982, epidemiological evidence indicated that the disease was probably caused by a virus transmissible via sexual intercourse, transfusion of contaminated blood or blood products, and intravenous drug injections. Later, it was also determined that AIDS could be passed from mother to baby during delivery or in breast milk.

Homosexual males, including many affluent urban professionals, were the largest initial group affected by the disease in the United States and in other developed countries. After some initial resistance to lifestyle changes recommended by public-health officials, this group mounted an aggressive response to AIDS, organizing to provide medical care, disseminating information about prevention, raising money, and becoming politically active. In developing countries, especially in Africa and

Asia where it has taken a very heavy toll, AIDS afflicts men and women equally and is transmitted primarily by heterosexual intercourse.

In 1984, researchers in Robert C. Gallo's laboratory at the National Cancer Institute (NCI) of the U.S. *National Institutes of Health published papers demonstrating causation by a retrovirus described the previous year by scientists at the Pasteur Institute in Paris. Laboratory tests were quickly developed to confirm individual diagnoses and to screen blood donations for contamination. Subsequent research showing the rapid mutation of the causative microorganism dimmed hope for speedy development of a preventive vaccine.

In 1986, a drug known as azidothymidine (AZT) was identified by NCI researchers as inhibiting HIV activity in laboratory studies. Clinical trials by the drug's manufacturer, Burroughs Wellcome, Inc., proved encouraging, and in record time the Food and Drug Administration approved AZT for AIDS treatment. For nearly a decade, with a few other similar drugs, AZT stood as the only antiviral therapy available. During this time, however, treatment of the opportunistic infections and cancers that characterized AIDS advanced significantly. By 1996, a decade of medical research on AIDS began to produce new therapies that raised hopes that AIDS need not lead inexorably to death.

Because AIDS can be transmitted by sexual contact or intravenous drug use and because of its association with the homosexual community, some conservative religious and political groups in American society stigmatized the disease as shameful or as retribution for sin. During the presidency of Ronald *Reagan, these groups blocked federal action to promote the use of condoms for safe sex. They also opposed the creation of needle-exchange programs to protect intravenous drug abusers. Widespread fear of the disease prompted some parents to insist that infected children be denied entry into public schools. On occasion, health-care, police, and fire-department personnel refused to respond to emergencies that involved infected people. A few insurance companies canceled health policies for persons diagnosed with AIDS, and some employers fired infected employees. In the worst cases, infected people experienced violence against themselves or their property. By contrast, C. Everett Koop, surgeon general of the United States Public Health Service in the Reagan administration, spoke out forcefully about safe sex to prevent AIDS and, in October 1986, mailed a brochure about AIDS written in lay language to every U.S. household.

By 1986, leadership at a national level, knowledge that AIDS could not be casually transmitted, and public statements by prominent people infected with HIV were helping to mitigate societal fears. Tennis professional Arthur Ashe, basketball star Magic Johnson, and AIDS activist Elizabeth Glaser were among celebrities infected with AIDS who spoke publicly about the disease. Actress Elizabeth Taylor led the theater and film communities in efforts to raise money to combat AIDS. Playwrights and filmmakers addressed the social issues raised by AIDS. The Names Project encouraged the friends and families of AIDS victims to create a national quilt in memory of those who had died.

By 2000, AIDS deaths in the United States had surpassed 420,000, and an estimated 650,000–900,000 were living with HIV/AIDS. Along with its direct human cost, the epidemic also forced a reassessment of the sexual revolution that had advocated a variety of sexual practices without fear of disease. Furthermore it illustrated how social attitudes such as homophobia can have important public-health implications.

[*See also* Public Health.]

• Randy Shilts, *And the Band Played On: Politics, People, and the AIDS Epidemic*, 1987. Mirko D. Grmek, *History of AIDS: Emergence and Origin of a Modern Pandemic*, trans. Russell C. Maulitz and Jacalyn Duffin, 1990. National Research Council, Committee on AIDS Research and the Behavioral, Social, and Statistical Sciences, *AIDS: The Second Decade*, eds. Heather G. Miller, Charles F. Turner, and Lincoln E. Moses, 1990. Virginia Berridge and Philip Strong, *AIDS and Contemporary History*, 1993. National Research Council, Committee on AIDS Research and the Behavioral, Social, and Statistical Sciences, Panel on Monitoring the Social Impact of the AIDS Epidemic, *The Social Impact of AIDS in the United States*, eds. Albert R. Jonsen and Jeff Stryker, 1993. Caroline Hannaway, Victoria A. Harden, and John Parascandola, eds., *AIDS and the Public Debate: Historical and Contemporary Perspectives*, 1995.

—Victoria A. Harden

ADAMS, ABIGAIL (1744–1818), wife of John *Adams, the second president of the United States; mother of John Quincy *Adams, the sixth president; correspondent. Born in Weymouth, Massachusetts, to Congregational minister William Smith and his wife Elizabeth Quincy Smith, Abigail received no formal schooling yet educated herself in literature, history, and French. Abigail and John Adams, within a decade of their marriage in 1764, had five children, of whom four (Abigail, John Quincy, Charles, and Thomas Boylston) survived childhood. During the *Revolutionary War Era, when John served as delegate to the *Continental Congress and diplomat in Europe, Abigail managed the family farm, purchasing land and livestock and negotiating with laborers and tenants. Even after she was reunited with her husband in Europe in 1784, as well as during his terms as vice president and president, Abigail took primary responsibility for the family's business. She also served as John's confidante and adviser in public affairs.

Abigail Adams is best known for her copious, perspicacious correspondence, in which she discussed politics as well as domestic concerns. She expressed opinions on a wide variety of issues, including her renowned advice to John in 1776 that Congress revise the Anglo-American laws subordinating married women to their husbands. In private letters, Abigail Adams hailed women's actions to support American independence, heralded the strength of female patriotism, and called for improved female education. Nevertheless, throughout her life, she conformed to the roles expected of a high public official's wife in the late eighteenth century. Only her correspondents, and later generations who have read her letters, could appreciate Adams's advanced thinking on women's rights.

[*See also* Colonial Era; Women's Rights Movements.]

• L. H. Butterfield et al., eds., *Adams Family Correspondence*, vols. 1–6, 1963–1993. Edith B. Gelles, *Portia: The World of Abigail Adams*, 1992.

—Jean R. Soderlund

ADAMS, HENRY (1838–1918), historian, social critic, man of letters. Born in *Boston, the son of Charles Francis Adams, a U.S. congressman and diplomat, and Abigail Brooks Adams, he was also the great-grandson and grandson of two presidents, John *Adams and John Quincy *Adams. Henry grew up in Boston, summering at the Adams homestead in nearby Quincy. Following graduation from Harvard College in 1858 he embarked on an extensive European tour, returning to the United States late in 1860. When President Abraham *Lincoln appointed Charles Francis Adams the U.S. minister to Great Britain in 1861, Henry accompanied his father to London where he served as private secretary.

Adams wrote his first serious articles on history and politics while in Great Britain during the *Civil War. Upon his return to the United States in 1868 he set himself up as a freelance journalist in *Washington, D.C., writing blistering attacks on postwar political corruption. *Chapters of Erie and Other Essays* (1871), written with his brother Charles Francis Adams Jr., deals with fraud and bribery in the railroad industry. In 1870 he accepted an offer to teach history at Harvard and concurrently to edit the prestigious *North American Review*. While teaching, editing, and writing more articles on current American politics, Adams also worked on his *Life of Albert Gallatin* (1879). He married Marian "Clover" Hooper in 1872.

Adams resigned his teaching position in 1877 and returned to Washington, D.C. Soon thereafter he commenced his nine-volume *History of the United States during the Administrations of Thomas Jefferson and James Madison* (1889–1891), as he and his wife presided over a celebrated salon from their home on Lafayette Square, across from the White House. Here they entertained a select group of friends including the statesman John Hay, the geologist Clarence King, and the artist John LaFarge. His anonymous novel *Democracy* (1880) summed up his disgust with *Gilded Age Washington politics. Marian Adams's suicide in 1885 deepened Adam's already pessimistic and negative outlook on many aspects of modern life.

In 1890–1892, Adams took a round-the-world voyage with LaFarge. Breaking his trip in Paris, he began a custom of spending part of each year in the French capital. While in France Adams became fascinated with the Middle Ages and wrote his *Mont-Saint-Michel and Chartres* (1905, 1913). Contrasting the unity of medieval culture with the seeming multiplicity of the early twentieth century, he proposed to use his own life story to portray what he liked to call the acceleration of history and the breakdown of philosophical and moral certainty. The result was his *Education of Henry Adams* (1904, 1918), a brilliant but often distorted autobiography written in the third person.

Adams's eloquent and often biting criticisms of American life have made him one of the nation's most important observers. He was also a pathbreaker in historical scholarship, offering the country's first graduate seminar in history while teaching at Harvard. His own historical writings were exhaustively researched. After more than a century, they remain of value, though later historians found him somewhat biased against Thomas *Jefferson and the whole Jeffersonian program.

[*See also* Historiography, American.]

• David R. Contosta, *Henry Adams and the American Experiment*, 1980. Ernest Samuels, *Henry Adams*, 1989.

—David R. Contosta

ADAMS, JOHN (1735–1826), second president of the United States. As a young man in pre-Revolutionary *Boston, John Adams summed up his hopes: a modest fortune, and officer's rank in the militia, and election to the upper house of the Massachusetts assembly. He never grew wealthy or soldiered, but he succeeded in public life beyond his wildest expectations.

Born in Braintree, Massachusetts, to parents of modest means, Adams graduated from Harvard College in 1755, studied law, and in 1758 opened a legal practice in Boston. He had only one client during his first year and did not win a case before a jury for three years. In 1764, Adams married Abigail Smith of nearby Weymouth, a formidable figure in her own right. Four of their five children survived to adulthood, including the future president John Quincy *Adams.

In 1770, representing the British soldiers charged in the *Boston Massacre, Adams won significant legal victories for his clients and himself. At first he remained in the background of the protest movement against British imperial policies, writing anonymous essays and covert propaganda. After 1773, however, now convinced of a British conspiracy to suppress colonial liberties, he played an open and active role in the protest campaign, and emerged as a leader in the *Continental Congress. He not only chaired the Board of War and Ordnance, but served on more than sixty other committees, including one that prepared guidelines for America's first diplomats and another that drafted the *Declaration of Independence. Thomas *Jefferson called him "our colossus" in the independence struggle.

Adams also gained a reputation as an expert on political theory. His pamphlets *Novanglus* (1774) and *Thoughts on Government* (1776) furthered the independence cause and influenced the earliest state constitutions. As U.S. Commissioner to France during the *Revolutionary War, Adams battled tenaciously to induce France to make greater military contributions to the American cause, while also securing recognition and an urgently needed loan from Holland. As a member of the U.S. delegation that negotiated the Treaty of Paris ending the war, Adams was instrumental in gaining boundary and fishing-rights concessions from the British.

After serving as U.S. minister to Great Britain (1785–1788) and as vice president under George *Washington, Adams defeated Jefferson in the 1796 presidential election. His presidency was consumed with the so-called *Quasi-War with France, an undeclared naval war involving violations of U.S. shipping rights arising from the general European conflict spawned by the French Revolution. Fearing that war would be disastrous for the fragile American union, Adams pursued peace with honor, a policy that rankled many bellicose members of his own *Federalist party. Although Adams was grudgingly respected even by his political enemies for his integrity and stubborn honesty, his identification with the Federalists, and with the *Alien and Sedition Acts of 1798 (repressive measures about which he had personal reservations), stirred growing animosity among Thomas Jefferson's followers.

Adams's peace initiatives, plus his long-standing feud with Alexander *Hamilton, so divided the Federalist party that Jefferson defeated Adams in 1800. Yet his policies kept the peace, leading him to characterize his presidential diplomacy as the "most splendid diamond in my crown."

Retiring to his farm in Braintree, Adams wrote his memoirs and essays on his wartime diplomacy and conducted a voluminous correspondence with Thomas Jefferson and others on political theory and the American Revolution. Like Jefferson, he died on the fiftieth anniversary of Independence, 4 July 1826.

[*See also* Adams, Abigail; Early Republic, Era of the; Federal Government, Executive Branch: The Presidency; Foreign Relations: U.S. Relations with Europe; Revolution and Constitution, Era of.]

• John Ferling, *John Adams: A Life*, 1992. Joseph J. Ellis, *Passionate Sage: The Character and Legacy of John Adams*, 1993.

—John Ferling

ADAMS, JOHN QUINCY (1767–1848), sixth president of the United States. Born in Quincy, Massachusetts, the son of John *Adams and Abigail *Adams, John Quincy Adams graduated from Harvard College in 1787. Apart from a brief interlude practicing law in Massachusetts, he spent almost his entire adult life in public service and politics. Beginning at age fourteen as the secretary to the U.S. minister to Russia, Francis Dana, he subsequently held overseas posts in England, the Netherlands, Prussia, Russia, Ghent, and again in England before becoming President James *Monroe's secretary of state in 1817. A tough, belligerent negotiator, he seemed like "a bulldog among spaniels," according to one English diplomat.

As secretary of state, Adams was an aggressive advocate of *expansionism. He not only supported Andrew *Jackson's invasion of Spanish Florida in 1819, but used it to bully Spain into negotiating a transcontinental settlement, the *Adams-Onís Treaty (1819), which gave Florida to the United States and ended Spanish claims to the Pacific Northwest. In 1823, when the British foreign secretary suggested a joint Anglo-American manifesto against further European intervention in Latin America, Adams successfully urged President Monroe to issue such a pronouncement unilaterally and wrote much of what became known as the *Monroe Doctrine.

In the four-way presidential race of 1824, Adams finished second in both the popular vote and in the *electoral college. Since none of the candidates received a majority of the electoral votes, the election went to the House of Representatives where Henry *Clay threw his support to Adams over the front runner Andrew Jackson. When President Adams subsequently made Clay secretary of state, Jackson denounced the appointment as a "corrupt bargain," resigned his Senate seat, and began organizing for the next election. Adams, never popular in the slave states, made Jackson's task easier by laying out a program of national planning that infuriated Thomas *Jefferson's strict constructionist followers, violated the concept of *states' rights, and thus drove virtually the entire *South into Jackson's camp. With most of his nationalistic proposals mocked by the opposition and rejected by Congress, Adams was denied a second term in 1828—the same ignominy his father had experienced in 1800. Jackson defeated him handily, winning 92 percent of the electoral vote in the slave states, 49 percent in the free states.

In 1830, Adams won election to the House of Representatives from the Plymouth district of Massachusetts. Serving until his death in 1848, he led the long (1836–1844) fight against the "gag rule," a House rule that automatically tabled *antislavery petitions and barred Congress from discussing the sensitive *slavery issue. He also led the battle against the annexation of Texas (1836) and against the *Mexican War (1846–1848). His sharp tongue and tactical dexterity made him a powerful figure in Congress and a folk hero to much of the North, earning him the sobriquet "Old Man Eloquent."

[*See also* *Amistad* Case; Early Republic, Era of the; Expansionism; Federal Government, Executive Branch: The Presidency; Federal Government, Executive Branch: Department of State; Federal Government, Legislative Branch: House of Representatives; Foreign Relations: U.S. Relations with Europe; Texas Republic and Annexation.]

• Mary W. M. Hargreaves, *The Presidency of John Quincy Adams*, 1985. Leonard L. Richards, *Life and Times of Congressman John Quincy Adams*, 1986.

—Leonard L. Richards

ADAMS, SAMUEL (1722–1803), radical patriot and political agitator, described by Thomas *Jefferson as "truly the *Man of the revolution.*" A *Boston native and Harvard graduate (1740), Adams, after several business failures and an interlude as a tax collector, gained prominence as a brilliant polemicist and popular leader in opposition to the *Stamp Act (1765–1766) and the Townshend Duties (1767–1770). He was elected a member (1765–1774) and then clerk (1766–1780) of the Massachusetts legislature. Instrumental in drafting the Circular Letter of 1768, Adams energized the revolutionary movement during the so-called years of quiet by helping form the *Committees of Correspondence (1772) and selectively publishing the incriminating correspondence of colonial officials including Massachusetts Governor Thomas Hutchinson. A planner of the *Boston Tea Party in 1773, Adams led the opposition to the Coercive Acts and supported the radical Suffolk Resolves endorsed by the Second *Continental Congress in 1774. Acknowledging his central role, General Thomas Gage, the military governor of Boston, excluded him from the general amnesty he issued in 1774.

A member of the Continental Congress from 1774 to 1781, Adams signed the *Declaration of Independence. His influence diminished thereafter, although he served in the convention that drafted the Massachusetts state constitution in 1779–1780, and was lieutenant governor (1789–1794) and then governor of Massachusetts (1794–1797). His neglect among the pantheon of revolutionary heroes might be explained by his prominence in state rather than national politics. More agitator than statesman, Samuel Adams was nevertheless a preeminent early leader in the independence movement. He gained posthumous celebrity in the late twentieth century when a popular Boston beer bore his name.

[*See also* Revolution and Constitution, Era of.]

• John C. Miller, *Sam Adams: Pioneer in Propaganda*, 1936. Pauline Maier, *The Old Revolutionaries: Political Lives in the Age of Samuel Adams*, 1980.

—Andrew J. O'Shaughnessy

ADAMS-ONÍS TREATY (1819), also known as the Transcontinental Treaty, established the United States' first transcontinental boundary and acquired Florida. The treaty arose from a long-standing territorial dispute between the United States and Spain over the precise boundaries of the *Louisiana Purchase of 1803. Spanish officials, citing a prior agreement with France, first contested the legitimacy of Napoleon's sale of the Louisiana territory and then attempted to define its boundaries as the eastern bank of the *Mississippi River (effectively nullifying the purchase) and excluding the province of West Florida, claimed by the United States. The Napoleonic Wars delayed negotiations until 1817, when they quickly became deadlocked.

Andrew *Jackson's invasion of Florida during the First *Seminole War of 1817–1818 broke the deadlock. Spain's minister to the United States and chief negotiator Don Luis de Onís, confronted by the prospect of losing Florida to American conquest, agreed to Secretary of State John Quincy *Adams's proposed treaty, which ceded both East and West Florida to the United States and established a transcontinental boundary extending to the Oregon coast. In exchange, Adams gave up a dubious claim to Texas and assumed five million dollars in American citizens' claims against the Spanish government.

By resolving the dispute with Spain, the Adams-Onís Treaty finalized the Louisiana Purchase. By conceding the claim to Texas, the agreement contributed to later agitation for the "reannexation of Texas," which proslavery expansionists alleged had been wrongly given away. The western boundary established by the treaty acknowledged *California and the *Southwest as Mexican territory, setting the stage for the conquest of those lands by the United States in 1848.

[*See also* Early Republic, Era of the; Expansionism; Foreign Relations: U.S. Relations with Europe; Texas Republic and Annexation.]

• Samuel Flagg Bemis, *John Quincy Adams and the Foundations of American Foreign Policy*, 1949. William Earl Weeks, *John Quincy Adams and American Global Empire*, 1992.

—William Earl Weeks

ADDAMS, JANE (1860–1935), settlement-house leader. Addams was born in Cedarville, Illinois. Her mother died when she was three; her father, a Quaker businessman and state legislator, subsequently remarried. Graduating from Rockford (Illinois) Female Seminary in 1881, Addams entered the Woman's Medical College of Pennsylvania but dropped out because of illness. Eight years of foreign travel, vocational uncertainty, and unfocused anxiety ended when Addams and her friend Ellen Gates Starr purchased Hull House in 1889 as a "settlement house," or neighborhood social center on *Chicago's Halsted Street.

Supported by wealthy Chicagoans, especially Addams's longtime partner Mary Rozet Smith, Hull House offered its working-class immigrant neighborhood educational and cultural programs as well as practical help and even material aid. It also became a political and intellectual center for a group of women intellectuals excluded from university and governmental careers. Florence *Kelley began her reform career at Hull House. Pursuing the agendas of Progressivism, Addams and her colleagues fought prostitution and saloons and lobbied for sweatshop regulation, health and housing codes, and worker-protection laws, especially for women. Addams encouraged women social experts and helped bring into politics the influence of organized women, whom she viewed as "social housekeepers" with different political priorities from men.

Addams was notably successful in shaping her own image. Her two memoirs, *Twenty Years at Hull-House* (1910) and *Second Twenty Years* (1930), created a benevolent, all-knowing persona. Although remembered as a social worker, Addams was primarily a public intellectual who lectured widely and published extensively on reform issues. *Democracy and Social Ethics* (1902) offers the most comprehensive statement of her social thought. She was active in the *woman suffrage movement, and in 1912 backed Theodore *Roosevelt's *Progressive party candidacy. John *Dewey often visited Hull House during his years at the University of Chicago.

A lifelong pacifist, Addams broke with Dewey and other *Progressive Era reformers to oppose America's entry into *World War I. During the war she lectured for Herbert *Hoover's Food Administration, which supplied food to war refugees. She described her wartime experiences in *Peace and Bread in Time of War* (1922). From 1919 to her death she was president of the Women's International League for Peace and Freedom. In the 1920s, Addams's *pacifism and her support for the Sheppard-Towner Act of 1921 (providing federally funded health care for mothers and children) made her a target of Redbaiters. But by 1931, when she won the Nobel Peace Prize, her reputation had recovered. While scholars have noted the race and class limitations of the settlement movement, Addams is widely recognized as an advocate for social citizenship and leader in the Progressive Era reform movement.

[*See also* Immigration; Prostitution and Antiprostitution; Settlement Houses; Society of Friends; Twenties, The.]

• Allen F. Davis, *American Heroine: The Life and Legend of Jane Addams,* 1973. Ruth Crocker, *Social Work and Social Order: The Settlement Movement in Two Industrial Cities,* 1992.

—Ruth Crocker

ADKINS* v. *CHILDREN'S HOSPITAL (1923). During the early twentieth century, Progressives sought to ameliorate the consequences of *industrialization by enacting minimum wage laws. Conservatives and business groups challenged these laws in the courts. In *Adkins*, the U.S. *Supreme Court, by a vote of five to three, struck down a 1918 congressional statute setting a minimum wage for women in the District of Columbia. The 1918 law, the Court held, violated the liberty of contract protected by the due process clause of the Fifth Amendment. Writing for the Court, Justice George Sutherland emphasized that under the *Constitution, freedom of contract was the general rule and restraint the exception. Minimum wage laws, he argued, foisted on employers a welfare function that properly belonged to society as a whole. Moreover, Sutherland insisted, in light of the *Nineteenth Amendment, women could not be more restricted in the exercise of contractual freedom than men.

Chief Justice William Howard *Taft and Justice Oliver Wendell *Holmes Jr. wrote dissenting opinions. Taft maintained that legislators could regulate the hours of work or minimum wages of women under the government's police powers. Holmes expressed doubt about the constitutional basis for the liberty-of-contract doctrine.

The *Adkins* decision stands as a classic expression of the Court's commitment to contractual freedom. It made clear the Court's determination to keep wages and prices free of regulatory interference. During the *New Deal Era of the 1930s, however, the Supreme Court moderated its long-standing commitment to economic liberty and freedom of contract. *Adkins* was overruled in **West Coast Hotel Company* v. *Parrish* (1937), in which the justices, on a five–four vote, sustained a Washington State minimum wage law.

[*See also* Bill of Rights; Progressive Era.]

• Hadley Arkes, *The Return of George Sutherland: Restoring a Jurisprudence of Natural Rights,* 1994. James W. Ely Jr., *The Guardian of Every Other Right: A Constitutional History of Property Rights,* 2d ed., 1998.

—James W. Ely Jr.

ADOLESCENCE. *See* Life Stages.

ADOPTION. *See* Childbirth; Child Rearing; Family.

ADVERTISING. From its origins in colonial handbills, signboards, and newspaper announcements, American advertising by the late twentieth century had grown into a multi-billion dollar industry. Its transformations reflect both the course of American *business and the shifting patterns of American culture. For most of its history, observers have seen advertising as a central feature of the American social landscape and have considered the United States the "promised land" of advertising. For example, historian David Potter (*People of Plenty*, 1954) treated advertising as emblematic of American abundance and a pervasive means of democratic social control.

In the *Colonial Era, where production for market was constrained, currency in short supply, and goods rarely identified with their producers, advertising remained small scale and intermittent. Yet by the eighteenth century a network of shopkeepers and craftsmen sought customers among the growing number of colonists who could afford manufactured amenities and luxuries such as pottery, books, furniture, and musical instruments. Sellers trumpeted the wide range of choices available and portrayed their goods as appropriate for refined and fashionable men and women. Benjamin *Franklin's *Pennsylvania Gazette* introduced innovations such as headlines, illustrations, and advertising notices placed next to news items. At times, more than half of the newspaper was devoted to advertising. While it may be an exaggeration to speak of an eighteenth-century Anglo-American "consumer revolution," the spread of advertising impressed observers on both sides of the Atlantic.

Nevertheless, down to the *Civil War, advertising developed slowly. Steam-powered presses and cheap newsprint allowed the emergence of a "penny press" in the 1830s, but most of these innovations limited attractive displays and confined advertisements within column rules. Display advertising became common only in the 1870s. *Magazines generally segregated advertisements in the back pages and barred eye-catching display. "Announcement" remained a near-synonym for "advertisement."

There were exceptions. P. T. *Barnum's promotions usually involved finding free publicity, but he wrote accurately in his autobiography, "I thoroughly understood the art of advertising." Jay Cooke's marketing of Union bonds during the Civil War entailed vivid advertisements in papers across the North. The pioneers of persuasive advertising copy, however, were usually medicine makers. Employing a range of media, these "Toadstool Millionaires" (the title of a 1961 book by James Harvey Young) won customers for their nostrums with emotional appeals to fear and faith.

The appearance of mass retailers, in particular downtown *department stores, and the rise of mass-produced, brand-named consumer goods after 1880 gave advertising much of its modern form. Volney Palmer, generally considered the nation's first advertising agent, and his successors solicited advertisers to fill space in the newspapers and magazines they represented. By the 1890s, advertising agencies were taking over the preparation of advertising copy and design, and being compensated through a discount for the space they purchased from publishers. Freelance copywriters gave way to a new generation of agency employees. In the early 1900s, agencies increasingly boasted of their broad competence as sales and marketing professionals. The 1912 introduction of Procter & Gamble's shortening, Crisco, involved a multifaceted marketing campaign. Meanwhile, new general-interest magazines provided a medium for advertising to a professional and managerial middle-class market. By *World War I, the institutional triad of advertisers, agencies, and media had assumed roles that largely endure today. Meanwhile, the industry developed voluntary associations to tighten standards and win popular respect. The leading trade journal, *Printer's Ink*, and the Associated Advertising Clubs of America launched an energetic, if self-serving, "Truth in Advertising" movement to upgrade ethical standards.

Although President Calvin *Coolidge in 1926 proclaimed advertising "part of the greater work of the regeneration and redemption of mankind," advertising experts thought of themselves in less exalted terms. They hoped to entice ill-informed and manipulable consumers into acceptance of modern, corporate-dominated society. In the 1930s, Depression Era advertising turned shrill, playing upon Americans' economic worries and matching the industry's combative response to *New Deal Era consumer-protection proposals. As they had in 1917–1918, advertising leaders in *World War II sought legitimation through contributions to the war effort. The War Advertising Council, founded in 1942, lived on after 1945 as the Advertising Council, usually promoting uncontroversial causes like forest fire prevention. The subtexts consistently touted advertising's social benefits and the industry's service to the nation.

Advertising in the postwar era both facilitated and reflected economic prosperity and a culture of consumption. Expenditures grew from under $3 billion in 1945 to about $187 billion in 1997. *Television advertising accounted for approximately one-quarter of this. TV's combination of visual appeals, motion, and sound gave advertisements new dimensions and greater power. Although postwar advertising generally emphasized conformity through consumption of standardized products, by the 1960s segmentation was becoming a dominant marketing strategy. Product distinctions proliferated, mass media gave way to specialized ones, and advertisements "positioned" products for targeted "niche markets." Advertising agencies diversified as well. A younger generation of men and women, often from ethnic minorities, undertook what they liked to call a creative revolution: elements of fantasy, humor, irony, and even self-mockery assumed a larger place in the repertoire of persuasion. However, advertising remained a business; agencies knew that clients' sales constituted the bottom line. Geographic expansion also characterized late twentieth-century advertising. While New York's Madison Avenue still symbolized the industry, large firms were increasingly multinational, and agencies from Richmond, Virginia, to Poland, Oregon, gained industry acclaim.

As it became more ubiquitous, advertising attracted scholarly and critical attention. While some scholars pointed out the uncertainties and limits of its sway, a host of cultural critics including Vance Packard (*The Hidden Persuaders*, 1957) warned of its persuasive powers and of the materialism and consumerism it was said to promote. Yet despite the attacks, at the end of the century, advertising remained central to the nation's economy and culture. With its ever-changing forms and styles, its omnipresence seemed assured for the foreseeable future.

[*See also* Consumer Culture; Consumer Movement; Fifties, The; Gilded Age; Journalism; Mass Marketing; Post–Cold War Era.]

• Otis A. Pease, *The Responsibilities of American Advertising*, 1958. Stuart Ewen, *Captains of Consciousness*, 1976. Daniel Pope, *The Making of Modern Advertising*, 1983. Stephen R. Fox, *The Mirror Makers: A History of American Advertising and Its Creators*, 1984. Roland Marchand, *Advertising the American Dream*, 1985. Richard S. Tedlow, *New and Improved: The Story of Mass Marketing in America*, 1990. T. J. Jackson Lears, *Fables of Abundance: A Cultural History of Advertising in America*, 1994.

—Daniel A. Pope

AFFIRMATIVE ACTION. The term "affirmative action" first appeared in a legislative context in the 1935 *National Labor Relations Act and was later written into state laws prohibiting racial discrimination in employment. But the phrase, implying simply that government agencies should try to prevent discrimination against *African Americans, initially attracted little notice. Prior to the 1960s, virtually no one saw affirmative action as a way of giving minorities preferential treatment in hiring, promotions, and admissions.

More than anything else, the *civil rights movement helped change the meaning of affirmative action. In 1964, after years of black protest, Congress passed the landmark Civil Rights Act, which among other things created new agencies run by officials eager to bring minorities into the mainstream of American life. By 1965, with the passage of the Voting Rights Act, the legal barriers to integration began to crumble and government and civil rights leaders began to confront a new, more difficult issue: how to give underprivileged minorities a fair shot at economic and social equality.

One answer was affirmative action. In 1965 President Lyndon B. *Johnson issued an executive order establishing the Office of Federal Contract Compliance, which, along with the Equal Employment Opportunity Commission, began requiring companies for the first time to set numerical racial hiring goals. The trend toward quotas, goals, and timetables continued into the late sixties, as the Richard M. *Nixon administration supported this new, more radical interpretation of affirmative action.

The nation's major institutions, under pressure from consumers, employees, students, and federal bureaucrats, and aware of recent U.S. *Supreme Court decisions supporting race and gender preferences, quickly began devising their own affirmative action programs. By 1978, when the Supreme Court ruled in *Bakke* v. *University of California* that universities could use race as a plus factor in admissions, affirmative action had become deeply entrenched in American society.

By the late twentieth century, affirmative action had become a source of great controversy. Opponents tended to see racial preferences as unjust—an unfair government program that exacerbated an already large racial divide, harming whites while stigmatizing blacks as needing preferential treatment. Opponents also contended that affirmative action mainly aided more privileged African Americans and did little to help poor blacks.

In the 1990s, *Republican party politicians and activists lobbied hard against affirmative action, helping pass Proposition 209, a 1996 California initiative to abolish racial and gender preferences, and backing the Regents of the University of California who in 1995 voted to end affirmative action in hiring and admissions. That same year, President Bill *Clinton tried to stake out a middle ground on the issue, arguing that affirmative action was a flawed though necessary response to centuries of discrimination against women, blacks, and other groups.

Many in the civil rights community went further in their defense of affirmative action, arguing that white males still held a disproportionate number of powerful positions in society, and that laws and programs mandating preferences were one way to combat that imbalance. These supporters also argued that *racism and sexism were still rampant, and that affirmative action was a small but just part of national social policy. As the twentieth century ended, the debate over affirmative action appeared unlikely to end anytime soon.

[*See also* Civil Rights Legislation; Post–Cold War Era; Sixties, The.]

• Hugh Davis Graham, *The Civil Rights Era: Origins and Development of National Policy, 1960–1972*, 1990. Steven M. Cahn, ed., *The Affirmative Action Debate*, 1995.

—Matthew Dallek

AFFLUENT SOCIETY, THE (1958). In response to *World War II, the *Cold War, and the global economic preeminence of the United States during the 1940s and 1950s, many intellectuals reassessed the benefits of American democracy and *capitalism. John Kenneth Galbraith's *The Affluent Society* emerged as one of the most influential texts of this genre. A Harvard economist and *Democratic party political adviser, the Canadian-born Galbraith questioned the efficacy of Americans' support for Keynesian economic practices in an age of material abundance. Tax and fiscal policies aimed at promoting constant economic growth had made sense during a time of deprivation (as in the Great Depression of the 1930s), but in the booming postwar years, Galbraith argued, a policy of economic liberalism would ultimately lead to financial and moral instability.

Specifically, Galbraith criticized the United States's focus on economic production. Corporations committed to growth deliberately manufactured consumer demand for products the public neither needed nor wanted. Such a system, Galbraith predicted, would create debt, inflation, and overproduction, and thus ultimately lead to economic depression. He further contended that consumer spending had created a horrible social imbalance. As Americans feverishly invested in cars, televisions, and a multitude of other consumer goods, public services and public resources such as parks and other facilities serving the common good were neglected and impoverished. To redress this imbalance, Galbraith proposed a program to reduce private spending and increase government investment in social programs. Although few followed Galbraith's prescription for change, *The Affluent Society* represented an important voice of dissent at a time when most intellectuals and policy makers uncritically celebrated American capitalism.

[*See also* Consumer Culture; Depressions, Economic; Economics; Fifties, The; Keynesianism.]

• Richard H. Pells, *The Liberal Mind in a Conservative Age: American Intellectuals in the 1940s and 1950s*, 2d ed., 1989.

—Jennifer L. Kalish

AFL-CIO. *See* Labor Movements; American Federation of Labor (AFL); Congress of Industrial Organizations (CIO).

AFRICA, U.S. RELATIONS WITH. *See* Foreign Relations: U.S. Relations with Africa.

AFRICAN AMERICAN RELIGION. The religious odyssey of peoples of African descent in British North America began as a complex interplay of forced acculturation, voluntary adaptation, and assimilation to the dominant European Protestant Christian culture. After the *Revolutionary War, African American Christians in the newly founded United States increased in number as the result of the evangelical *revivalism of the era. Slaves voiced their longing for freedom in the preached word and spirituals, and met secretly for worship in what has been called "the invisible institution." Independent black churches, mostly *Baptist, began in the *South in the mid–eighteenth century, though few survived the restrictions on freedom of assembly imposed following the Denmark Vesey insurrection in 1822 and *Nat Turner's uprising in 1831. Approximately one in seven of the nearly four million *African Americans held in *slavery as the *Civil War began belonged to the predominantly white and Protestant denominations. Celebrating emancipation as divine providence, African Americans established their own churches in the post–Civil War South.

Independent black denominations began in the North with the establishment of the African Methodist Episcopal Church in 1816 under the leadership of Richard Allen of *Philadelphia. In *New York City another group of black Christians in 1822 organized what became the African American Episcopal Zion Church. The third of the three major black Methodist traditions, the Christian Methodist Episcopal Church, formerly the Colored Methodist Episcopal Church, was founded in 1870 at Jackson, Tennessee, by ex-slaves. The earliest independent black Baptist congregations in the North, appeared in *Boston and New York in the early 1800s. The National Baptist Convention, U.S.A., Inc., became the first truly national organization in 1895, but a major schism in 1915 produced the rival National Baptist Convention of America. Pentecostal and Holiness churches appeared among African Americans in significant numbers around *World War I and multiplied as their members became urbanized and migrated northward. Charles Harrison Mason built up the Church of God in Christ, which emphasized glossalalia (speaking in tongues), while Charles Price Jones led the Church of Christ (Holiness), U.S.A., which stressed the doctrine of personal sanctification. African American religious diversity increased in the interwar period with the appearance of black Jewish and black Muslim groups.

Small-town and rural churches, mostly southern, were typical of African Americans in the nineteenth century. Migration to northern industrial centers during and after World War I transplanted the folk religious legacy of the ex-slaves to the city. Ecstatic worship services and new musical styles, notably gospel, flourished alongside the more sedate services of the seminary-trained northern preachers. Women found greater opportunities for religious leadership in the storefront churches and prayer groups that proliferated in northern cities in the wake of the Great Migration. By the late twentieth century, women occupied the pulpit in growing numbers of African American churches, though some conservative black denominations still restricted the ordained ministry to men. Women have been the mainstays of African American church-based missionary, educational, and service societies and outnumber men when congregations gather for worship and religious education.

Serving multiple functions in black communities, African American churches have been places of protest and praise, forums for political discussion, and revival meetings focused on personal salvation. Black churches have assisted with housing, employment, education, recreation, and health care. Black churchgoers marched, sang, and prayed in support of the *civil rights movement led by Martin Luther *King Jr., himself a Baptist preacher and member of the Progressive National Convention of America, organized in 1961. In the 1960s theologians debated the meaning of the Black Power movement and some fashioned a Black Theology emphasizing social and economic issues and the distinctive aspects of African American ritual traditions.

By strict interpretation, there is no single "black church" or uniform expression of "black religion." A rich and varied tapestry of religious expression and religious institutions has flourished among African Americans in the United States. While most religiously affiliated African Americans belong to one of the black Protestant denominations mentioned above, predominantly white denominational traditions, such as the Methodists, Baptists, and Roman Catholics, claim significant numbers of African American Christians as well. Black churches cooperate in local and national ecumenical organizations and remain important centers for religious growth and community assistance. That African American religious institutions continue to thrive and expand bears witness to the multicultural texture of the American experience.

[*See also* Black Nationalism; Emancipation Proclamation; Gospel Music, African American; Islam; Methodism; Nation of Islam; Pentecostalism; Religion; Roman Catholicism; Slave Uprisings and Resistance; Slavery: Slave Families, Communities, and Culture.]

• Ethel L. Williams and Clifton F. Brown, eds., *The Howard University Bibliography of Afro-American Religious Studies: With Locations in American Libraries*, 1977. Milton C. Sernett, ed., *Afro-American Religious History: A Documentary Witness*, 1985. C. Eric Lincoln and Lawrence H. Mamiya, *The Black Church in the African American Experience*, 1990. Larry G. Murphy, J. Gordon Melton, and Gary L. Ward, eds., *Encyclopedia of African American Religions*, 1993. Wardell J. Payne, ed., *Directory of African American Religious Bodies*, 2d ed., 1995.

—Milton C. Sernett

AFRICAN AMERICANS. The African American community had its roots in the great migration of peoples from the Old World to the New. Unlike European, Asian, and Latino Americans, however, Africans entered the New World in chains. Despite the *Revolutionary War and the emergence of the United States as an independent republic, most African Americans remained in bondage until the *Civil War and the First *Reconstruction. In the 1860s and 1870s, African Americans gained freedom and citizenship, but the rise of racial *segregation soon undercut this achievement. By *World War I, the United States had institutionalized new patterns of class and racial inequality in its politics, culture, and economy. The Jim Crow system, as it was called, persisted through the mid–twentieth century.

As the nation instituted different forms of inequality and as African Americans confronted ongoing status and *social class conflicts within their own communities, they nonetheless staged both individual and collective resistance to discrimination, and shaped the nation's history in the process. The black freedom struggle culminated in the rise of the modern *civil rights movement and gave rise to what has been called the Second Reconstruction in the 1950s and 1960s. While the civil-rights struggle demolished the legal underpinnings of Jim Crow, it failed to fully translate such changes into material improvements in the lives of poor and working-class blacks. As these gaps in the civil-rights agenda became clearer, black activists launched the Black Power movement and advocated new and more autonomous strategies for social change. With the demise of the industrial economy in the 1970s and 1980s, whites intensified their resistance to the gains of the Second Reconstruction as well as to the Black Power movement. By the close of the twentieth century, African Americans again searched for appropriate strategies to counteract new forms of inequality.

The Era of Enslavement. When Europeans arrived on the West African coast during the fifteenth and sixteenth centuries, they had already established the economic and technological foundations for the international slave trade. Between 1433 and 1488, Portuguese mariners used new knowledge of ocean currents to navigate Africa's western coast, establish trade relations on the so-called Gold Coast, and set up sugar plantations on the northwest African islands of Madeira, Principe, and Sao Tomé. Portugal was soon importing some 500 to 1,000 Africans per year to work its island plantations. As early as 1502, the Spanish imported Africans to work on their New World sugar plantations in Hispaniola (today's Haiti). By century's end, the Spanish colonies imported an average of about 80,000 Africans each year. Following a brief decline during the 1790s, the number of slave imports peaked during the early nineteenth century. No less than 10 million Africans landed in the Americas during the era of the slave trade. Another 2 million died in the infamous Middle Passage en route to the New World. The European colonies of the Caribbean and Latin America absorbed over 90 percent of these Africans.

Although some Africans had entered the present-day United States with Spanish explorers and helped to establish St. Augustine, Florida (the first permanent non-Indian community in North America), the British colonies became the center of African American settlement in North America. The first Africans entered British North America in 1619, when a Dutch man-of-war deposited some twenty Africans at *Jamestown. Initially, the black population increased only slowly, comprising no more than 170 in 1640. Until the late seventeenth century, *indentured servitude rather than enslavement "for life" defined the labor system of the tobacco-growing Chesapeake colonies of Virginia and Maryland. Early Africans like Anthony and Richard Johnson won their freedom, legally married, purchased property, gained redress in courts of law, and sometimes imported their own black and white servants. By the early eighteenth century, however, both Virginia and Maryland had passed statutes pronouncing Africans or black servants "Durante Vita" or "slaves for life." The rice- and indigo-producing colonies of South Carolina and Georgia soon followed suit. By the late eighteenth century, the black population had grown through a combination of imports and natural increase to nearly 800,000.

As Africans made the transition from a less rigid form of servitude to bondmen and bondwomen "for life," colonial authorities reinforced their enslavement with "Slave Codes." Borrowing from Caribbean precedents, the new legislation redefined human beings as property by eliminating the right of blacks to bear arms, engage in trade, own property, move about freely, peaceably assemble, or seek legal redress. Such codes also legalized the maiming and even killing of enslaved persons as part of the owners' "property right." Although such laws were most prevalent in the *South, the northern colonies also enacted statutes restricting the lives of bondmen and bondwomen, including laws mandating the whipping of blacks who "attempted to strike" a white person.

Technological changes and the opening of new agricultural land in the Deep South intensified the demand for slave labor in the early national era. The cotton gin enabled planters to increase production from under 300,000 bales in 1820 to nearly 4.5 million in 1860. Slave-produced cotton dominated the nation's foreign exports and fueled the early *industrialization of Great Britain and New England milltowns like Lowell and Waltham, Massachusetts. Under the impact of cotton production, nearly a million blacks experienced forced migration from the declining tobacco-growing states of the Upper South to the booming Deep South states of Georgia, South Carolina, Alabama, Mississippi, and Louisiana. Whereas the majority of blacks had lived in the Chesapeake region during the eighteenth century, the Deep South claimed nearly 60 percent of all African Americans by 1860.

From the outset of their enslavement in the New World, Africans and their American descendants acted in their own behalf. As bondmen and bondwomen, they built formal and informal religious, social, and political networks, ran away, rebelled, and plotted to rebel. Such revolts and plots include the Stono Rebellion (1739), Gabriel Prosser's Plot (1800), Denmark Vesey's Plot (1822) and Nat Turner's Rebellion (1831). African Americans also shaped the advent and outcome of the American Revolution and the Civil War. Some 180,000 blacks, enslaved and free, served in the Union forces and helped transform the war between the states into a war of liberation.

Civil War to World War II. Following the Civil War, some four million African Americans gained their freedom and made the transition from "slave" to "citizen." The Thirteenth, *Fourteenth, and *Fifteenth Amendments to the *Constitution granted blacks citizenship and equal rights under the law. Yet in the late nineteenth and early twentieth centuries, African Americans experienced what the historian Rayford Logan called the "nadir" of their history—economic exploitation under the *sharecropping, crop-lien, and convict lease systems; *lynchings; disfranchisement; and institutional segregation. Southern white-supremacist groups like the Knights of the White Camelia and the *Ku Klux Klan encouraged and carried out mob attacks on African Americans and their communities. In 1896, the *Supreme Court upheld racial segregation in its landmark **Plessy* v. *Ferguson* decision. Jurists, scholars, and popular writers justified the subordination of blacks, further undermining the promise of the First Reconstruction. Racist publications and portrayals of black life proliferated, culminating in D. W. *Griffith's racist film *The Birth of a Nation* (1915).

As the promise of freedom faded, black leaders Booker T. *Washington and W. E. B. *Du Bois offered divergent strategies for action. Ordinary African Americans, meanwhile, used their newly won geographical *mobility to resist limitations on their rights as citizens and workers. Beginning gradually during the late nineteenth and early twentieth centuries, black population movement turned into the Great Migration during World War I and its aftermath. The proportion of blacks living in cities rose from about 2.6 million, or 27 percent, in 1910, to 6.4 million (49 percent) in 1940 and over 18 million, or over 80 percent, in 1970—10 percent higher than the figure for the population at large.

Although African Americans improved their lot by taking jobs in urban industries, they nonetheless entered the industrial economy at the lowest rungs of the occupational ladder. Moreover, as their numbers increased in northern and western cities, they faced growing residential and educational restrictions and limitations on access to social services and public accommodations. Responding to the impact of such class and racial restrictions, African Americans intensified their institution-building and their cultural, political, economic, and civil rights activities. They founded mutual aid societies, fraternal orders,

MAP 1: THE DISTRIBUTION OF THE AFRICAN-AMERICAN POPULATION OF NEW YORK CITY IN 1934

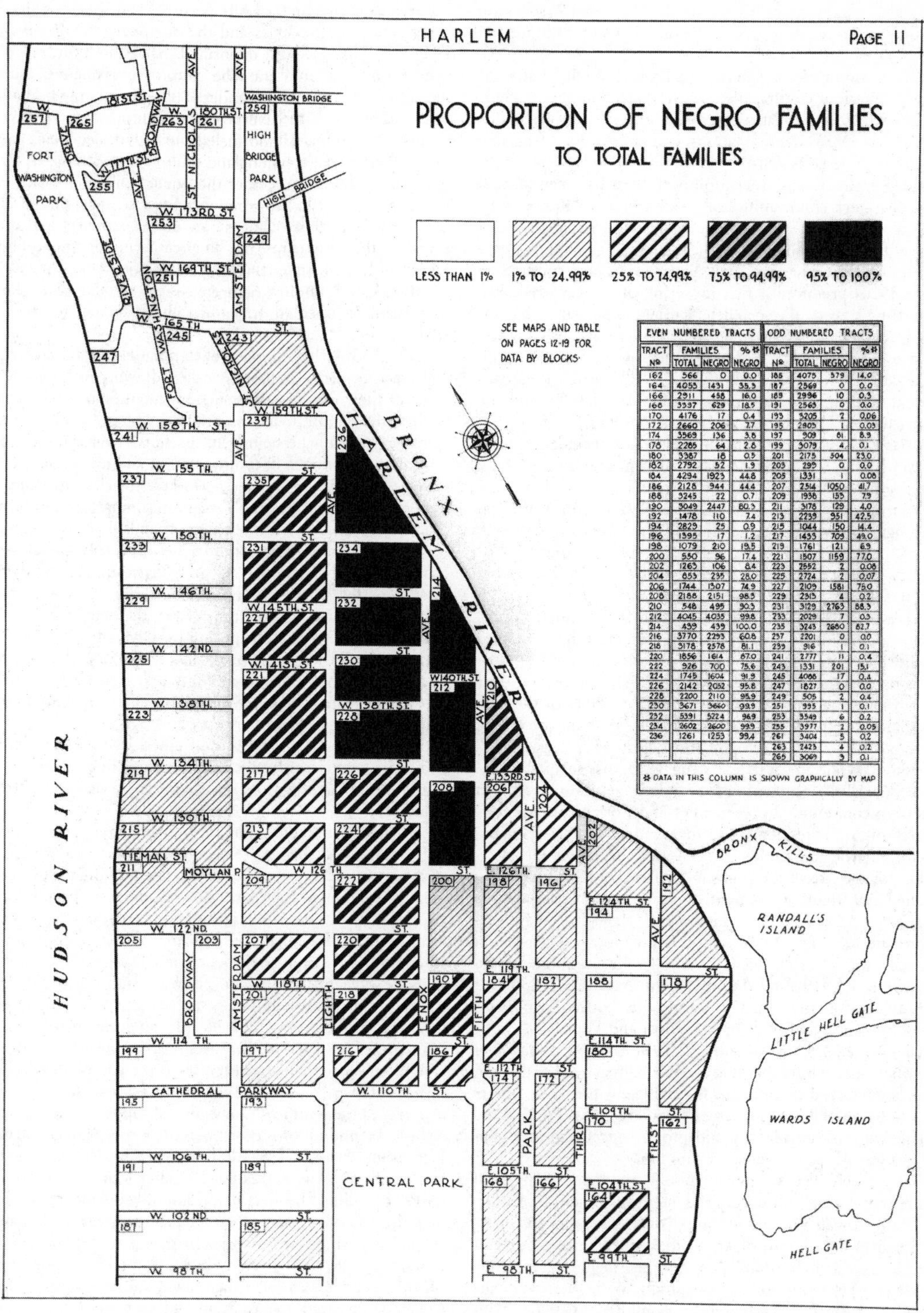

EVEN NUMBERED TRACTS				ODD NUMBERED TRACTS			
TRACT Nº	FAMILIES TOTAL	FAMILIES NEGRO	% # NEGRO	TRACT Nº	FAMILIES TOTAL	FAMILIES NEGRO	% # NEGRO
162	566	0	0.0	185	4075	579	14.0
164	4055	1431	35.3	187	2569	0	0.0
166	2911	458	16.0	189	2996	10	0.3
168	3397	629	18.5	191	2565	0	0.0
170	4176	17	0.4	193	3205	2	0.06
172	2660	206	7.7	195	2905	1	0.03
174	3569	136	3.8	197	909	81	8.9
178	2285	64	2.8	199	3079	4	0.1
180	3387	18	0.5	201	2175	504	23.0
182	2792	52	1.9	203	299	0	0.0
184	4294	1923	44.8	205	1331	1	0.08
186	2128	944	44.4	207	2514	1050	41.7
188	3245	22	0.7	209	1938	155	7.9
190	3049	2447	80.3	211	3178	129	4.0
192	1478	110	7.4	213	2239	951	42.5
194	2829	25	0.9	215	1044	150	14.4
196	1395	17	1.2	217	1433	709	49.0
198	1079	210	19.5	219	1761	121	6.9
200	550	96	17.4	221	1507	1159	77.0
202	1263	106	8.4	223	2552	2	0.08
204	853	235	28.0	225	2724	2	0.07
206	1744	1307	74.9	227	2109	1581	75.0
208	2188	2151	98.3	229	2313	4	0.2
210	548	495	90.3	231	3129	2763	88.3
212	4045	4035	99.8	233	2029	7	0.3
214	439	439	100.0	235	3243	2680	82.7
216	3770	2293	60.8	237	2201	0	0.0
218	3178	2578	81.1	239	916	1	0.1
220	1856	1614	87.0	241	2777	11	0.4
222	926	700	75.6	243	1331	201	15.1
224	1745	1604	91.9	245	4088	17	0.4
226	2142	2052	95.8	247	1827	0	0.0
228	2200	2110	95.9	249	505	2	0.4
230	3671	3660	99.9	251	995	1	0.1
232	5391	5224	96.9	253	3549	6	0.2
234	2602	2600	99.9	255	3977	2	0.05
236	1261	1253	99.4	261	3404	5	0.2
				263	2423	4	0.2
				265	3069	3	0.1

DATA IN THIS COLUMN IS SHOWN GRAPHICALLY BY MAP

Prepared by the Federal Housing Administration, a New Deal agency, this map shows the pattern of African American settlement on Manhattan Island north of Central Park and along the Harlem River in the early 1930s. In the 1920s, this part of the city was the center of the vibrant literary and cultural movement known as the Harlem Renaissance and of the mass movement of African Americans led by Marcus Garvey.

[*See* African Americans; Demography; Garvey, Marcus; Harlem Renaissance; New York City; Urbanization.]

and social clubs; established a range of new business and professional services; and launched diverse political, labor, and civil rights organizations, including the *National Association for the Advancement of Colored People (NAACP), founded in 1909.

*Urbanization and northern migration profoundly affected African American cultural life as well. Black churches, including those of the *Baptist, Pentecostal, and African Methodist Episcopal (AME) denominations, ranging from struggling storefronts to large establishments with thousands of members, provided spiritual and social support to urban newcomers. From the black communities of *New Orleans, *Kansas City, *Chicago, and other cities emerged vibrant new adaptations of musical traditions rooted in the past, including *ragtime, *gospel, the *blues, and *jazz. *New York City's black community of the 1920s produced a rich flowering of literary, dramatic, and artistic activity, the so-called *Harlem Renaissance, including such writers, performers, and intellectuals as Langston *Hughes, Zora Neale *Hurston, Paul *Robeson, and Alain Locke (1885–1954). In *Native Son* (1940), novelist Richard *Wright offered a searing picture of race relations and life among the black underclass in Depression-era Chicago.

African American activism in these years included Marcus *Garvey's mobilization of the urban black masses in the 1920s; participation in the *Democratic party's *New Deal Era coalition during the 1930s; and A. Philip *Randolph's March on Washington movement demanding an end to discrimination in defense industries and the NAACP's "Double V" campaign (for military victory abroad and victory over racism at home) before and during *World War II.

Partly because of blacks voters' overwhelming support of the New Deal, President Franklin Delano *Roosevelt in 1941 issued Executive Order 8802 banning racial discrimination in industries with government contracts and setting up the federal *Fair Employment Practice Committee (FEPC) to monitor the process. For the first time, African Americans broke the job ceiling and moved into jobs above the "unskilled" and "semiskilled" categories. While the wartime struggle against inequality entailed substantial tensions and conflicts within the African American community between elites and workers, urban newcomers and older residents, and men and women, it nevertheless formed the communal, institutional, and leadership foundation for the rise of the postwar *civil rights movement.

The Civil Rights Movement. Building upon their wartime militancy, African Americans moved their struggle to the streets during the 1950s and 1960s, adopting nonviolent direct-action strategies for social change. Grassroots organizations like the Montgomery (Alabama) Improvement Association initiated boycotts, sit-ins, freedom rides, and voter education projects across the South and parts of the North and West.

The Supreme Court's landmark 1954 **Brown* v. *Board of Education* decision outlawing racial segregation in public schools intensified the impetus for change, while black writers such as Ralph *Ellison and James *Baldwin contributed to the heightened sense of identity and group consciousness within the postwar African American community.

While their actions were rooted in their own local community-based institutions and national organizations like the *Southern Christian Leadership Conference, African Americans gained the support of white allies in federal agencies and diverse peace and freedom organizations, including the New York-based Fellowship of Reconciliation. With their white allies, African Americans achieved a Second Reconstruction with passage of the Civil Rights Acts of 1964, 1965, and 1968. This legislation demolished the legal pillars of discrimination in employment, housing, and the voting booth, and sought to reverse centuries of inequality by setting up affirmative action programs in employment and institutions of higher education.

While the Second Reconstruction destroyed the legal foundations of the segregationist system, it also highlighted the further and more difficult challenge of translating legal victories into real change. Moreover, the 1968, assassination of Martin Luther *King Jr. removed a key symbol and source of unity in the nonviolent freedom struggle. According to one activist, King was "the one man of our race that this country's older generations, the militants, and the revolutionaries and the masses of black people would still listen to." As the limitations of the Civil Rights movement became more apparent, growing numbers of young African Americans advocated Black Power as an alternative to nonviolent direct-action strategies. Partly because revolutionary black organizations like the *Black Panther party (formed in 1966) emphasized the mass mobilization of poor and working-class blacks, armed struggle, and opposition to the *Vietnam War, they came under the combined assault of federal, state, and local authorities. Under the weight of official and unofficial white resistance, the Black Power movement fragmented and gradually dissipated by the early 1970s.

Late Twentieth Century Developments. As the civil rights and Black Power movements weakened, white resistance to the gains of the Second Reconstruction intensified. Opposition to *affirmative action policies in employment and education were closely related to the deindustrialization of the nation's economy. The loss of jobs to mechanization and low-wage overseas factories affected all industrial workers, black and white, but the persistence of overt and covert discriminatory employment practices rooted in white kin and friendship networks made black workers and their communities especially vulnerable to economic down swings. African American *unemployment rates persisted at well over the white rate, especially among young black males. At the same time, the beneficiaries of existing affirmative action programs—the middle class and better-educated members of the black working class—experienced a degree of upward mobility and moved into outlying urban and suburban neighborhoods. They left working-class and poor blacks, disproportionately single women with children, concentrated in the central cities, where violence, drug addiction, and class-stratified social spaces intensified, causing acute tensions in day-to-day intraracial as well as interracial relations.

Perhaps even more than in the industrial era, the post-industrial age challenged African Americans to develop new strategies for coping with social change and the persistence of inequality. Some of their emerging responses built upon earlier struggles. Institution-building, marches, participation in electoral politics, and migration in search of better opportunities all continued to express black activism and resistance to social injustice. Yet, much had changed in the nation and in African American life, and such time-tested strategies took on different meanings in the 1980s and 1990s. Rising numbers of southern-born blacks returned to the South during the 1970s. After declining for more than a century, the proportion of blacks living in the South increased by 1980. Other African Americans rallied behind the Rainbow Coalition and supported the Reverend Jesse Jackson's bid for the Democratic party's presidential nomination in 1984 and 1988. Still others endorsed *Nation of Islam minister Louis Farrakhan's Million Man March (MMM) in 1994. Calling the march a "day of atonement" for black men, leaders of the MMM encouraged black men to earn and reclaim a position of authority in their families and communities. Four years later, many black women responded to the MMM's gender bias with their own Million Woman March, which emphasized the centrality of women in the ongoing black freedom struggle. Through these various actions and many more, African Americans continued to resist shifting forms of inequality and gave direction to their own lives as a new century began.

These same years saw the emergence a new generation of African American academics, musicians, performers, sports figures, and writers. Such diverse men and women as the scholars and public intellectuals Henry Louis Gates, Cornel West, and Stephen L. Carter; basketball superstar Michael *Jordan and track-and-field athlete Jackie Joyner-Kersee; film actors Eddie Murphy and Denzel Washington; jazz musicians Joshua Redman, Herbie Hancock, and Wynton and Bradford Marsalis; television celebrity Oprah Winfrey; and an array of novelists and writers including Maya Angelou, Alice Walker, and Toni *Morrison enriched American life and gave voice to the black experience.

By the 1990s, the nation's more than 30 million African Americans, representing about 12 percent of the total population, had transformed themselves from a predominantly rural people into an overwhelmingly urban people; from a southern regional group to a national population living in every part of the nation; and, perhaps most importantly, from a group confined to southern agriculture, domestic service, and general labor to a work force with representation in every sector of the nation's economy.

[*See also* African American Religion; Ali, Muhammed; *Amistad* Case; Anderson, Marian; Antislavery; Armstrong, Louis; Basie, William ("Count"); Black Nationalism; Brownsville Incident; Bunche, Ralph; *Civil Rights Cases;* Civil Rights Legislation; Coltrane, John; Cotton Industry; Davis, Miles; Douglass, Frederick; Drew, Charles Richard; Ellington, Edward ("Duke"); Freedmen's Bureau; Fugitive Slave Act; Johnson, James Weldon; Johnson, Jack; Louis, Joe; Lowell Mills; Malcolm X; Nat Turner's Uprising; Owens, Jesse; Parker, Charlie; Pentecostalism; Powell, Colin; Racism; Race, Concept of; Robinson, Jackie; Sickle-Cell Anemia; Slave Uprisings and Resistance; Slavery; Sojourner Truth; Spirituals; Student Non-Violent Coordinating Committee; Tobacco Industry; Trotter, William Monroe; Tubman, Harriet; Tuskegee Experiment; Urban League, National; Wheatley, Phillis.]

• Lerone Bennett Jr., *Before the Mayflower: A History of Black America,* 5th ed., 1982. Mary Frances Berry and John W. Blassingame, *Long Memory: The Black Experience in America,* 1982. John Hope Franklin and A. Moss Jr., *From Slavery to Freedom: A History of African Americans,* 7th ed., 1994. Charles M. Christian, *Black Saga: The African American Experience,* 1995. Darlene Clark Hine and Kathleen Thompson, *A Shining Thread of Hope: The History of Black Women in America,* 1998. James Oliver Horton and Lois E. Horton, eds., *A History of the African People: The History, Traditions & Culture of African Americans,* 1995. Arwin D. Smallwood and Jeffrey M. Elliot, *The Atlas of African-American History and Politics: From the Slave Trade to Modern Times,* 1998. Robin D. G. Kelley and Earl Lewis, eds., *To Make Our World Anew,* 2000. Joe W. Trotter, *The African American Experience,* forthcoming 2001.

—Joe W. Trotter Jr.

AGASSIZ, LOUIS (1807–1873), zoologist. Born in Switzerland, Agassiz earned degrees in zoology (1829) and medicine (1830) from the University of Munich. Encouraged by Georges Cuvier and Alexander von Humboldt, he studied fossil fish at the Muséum d'histoire naturelle in Paris for eight months. In 1832, he became director of a museum in Neuchâtel. Agassiz's Ice Age theory, which held that northern Europe had once been covered by a mass of ice, made him famous. In 1846, burdened by debt, he came to the United States to lecture and was lionized. Harvard gave him a professorship in 1850. His claim that human races were distinct creations, not descended from Adam and Eve, was welcomed by some supporters of *slavery, but his belief that science should be independent of the *Bible alienated religious conservatives. In his 1857 "Essay on Classification," Agassiz argued that taxonomic categories, classes as well as species, reflect the Divine Intellect, as do links among embryos, fossils, and biogeography. When Charles Darwin's *Origins of Species* appeared in 1859, Agassiz contested it vigorously; he never accepted the theory of *evolution. His greatest legacy was Harvard's Museum of Comparative Zoology (known as "the Agassiz Museum"), founded in 1859. With other leading men of science, he sought to make American science more professional. To that end, he promoted the creation of the *National Academy of Sciences in 1863. His tactic of leaving students alone with a single fish, telling them to "study nature, not books!", became legendary. He went by steamer up the Amazon River in 1865–1866, and in 1872 sailed to San Francisco. His 1873 summer school on Penikese Island proved a model for others. Agassiz's first wife, Cécile Braun, who bore three children, died in 1848. In 1850, he married Elizabeth Cary, who later founded Radcliffe College, the women's college associated with Harvard.

[*See also* Science: Revolutionary War to World War 1.]

• Edward Lurie, *Louis Agassiz,* 1960. Mary P. Winsor, *Reading the Shape of Nature: Comparative Zoology at the Agassiz Museum,* 1991.

—Mary Pickard Winsor

AGENCY FOR INTERNATIONAL DEVELOPMENT. The Foreign Assistance Act of 1961 created the Agency for International Development (AID), a semi-autonomous organization within the State Department which became the central bureaucracy responsible for economic aid programs. The agency's predecessors included the Economic Cooperation Administration, which implemented the *Marshall Plan; the Mutual Security Administration (1951), which continued economic and military assistance to Western Europe and began addressing the needs of underdeveloped states; and the International Cooperation Administration (1955). Using loans, food assistance, and technology transfers, among other methods, AID sought to enhance the productivity and overall market expansion of less developed nations. By the 1990s, the agency operated in more than one hundred countries, with two thousand employees in the field, and nearly ten thousand contractors.

Although concerned with the economic growth of poor nations, agency policies also reflected the real and perceived needs of the American political economy. AID officials proclaimed that their programs sought to foster a thriving private sector in the Third World and to guarantee an open door in recipient nations to foreign private investment, particularly from the United States. The agency's efforts to build a strong private business community in the less developed world contributed to the larger U.S. strategy of creating stable governments capable of resisting communist or economic nationalist movements that were anticapitalist.

AID programs sought the integration of developing countries into the global marketplace. The agency often pushed these countries to limit their social spending, increase privatization, and promote the export economy. Starting in the 1980s, for example, AID urged recipient nations to develop nontraditional, capital-intensive crops for export. This policy of promoting export-led growth aimed at alleviating the crushing levels of international debt that many third world countries had incurred during the oil-price rises of the 1970s. Critics pointed out, however, that it destabilized traditional farming in many places, increasing poverty while simultaneously creating new markets for U.S. and other petrochemical and agribusiness corporations.

[*See also* Federal Government, Executive Branch: Department of State; Foreign Aid; Foreign Relations; Foreign Trade, U.S.]

• Frances Moore Lappe, Rachel Schurman, and Kevin Danaher, *Betraying the National Interest,* 1987. Vernon W. Ruttan, *United States Development Assistance Policy: The Domestic Politics of Foreign Economic Aid,* 1996.

—Nathan Godfried

AGRICULTURE ADJUSTMENT ADMINISTRATION. In 1933, American agriculture neared collapse as farm bankruptcies and foreclosures multiplied and agricultural prices fell below the cost of production. President Franklin Delano *Roosevelt instructed his agricultural experts to draft legislation. The result was the Agricultural Adjustment Act (AAA) of May 1933.

The law's fundamental goal was "parity": raising basic farm prices until they were in balance with the general economy. One way was to eliminate existing commodity surpluses by taking farm acreage out of production and inducing farmers to produce only what was needed for domestic consumption. The government paid benefits to farmers who contracted to reduce acreage and also offered "parity" payments on the crops actually grown. To finance these payments, the secretary of agriculture taxed the domestic processors of basic commodities—wheat, cotton, tobacco, corn-hogs, and milk products. Since pork and milk production could not be controlled effectively by reducing acreage, the government negotiated agreements among the meat packers and dairy companies to regulate markets and fix prices.

The law created the Agricultural Adjustment Administration to administer the new system. The first administrator was George N. Peek, a businessman and agricultural reformer. Because Peek assumed power in 1933 after crops had been planted and sows were bearing litters of pigs, his agency contracted with farmers to plow under nearly half of their crops and to slaughter baby pigs. Although calculated to increase prices and raise farm income, the destruction of crops and livestock stirred widespread dismay.

By late 1935, the AAA had enabled agriculture to approach a parity position. AAA payments especially benefited larger commercial farmers and southern planters. Acreage reduction, however, hurt tenant farmers and sharecroppers, many thousands of whom were evicted or received pitifully small payments.

The AAA saved agriculture from collapse, but as the crisis eased, constitutional questions arose. In 1936 the U.S. *Supreme Court struck down the act for exceeding the government's interstate commerce powers. To keep the AAA operating, Congress passed a new law that preserved AAA programs under the pretext of soil conservation. In 1938 Congress passed a second AAA that emphasized price supports and subsidies. Congress ended the AAA during *World War II as agricultural prices rose sharply and demand exceeded supply; the Department of Agriculture assumed many of the AAA's programs and implemented them as the core of post–World War II agricultural policy.

[*See also* Agriculture: Since 1920; Cotton Industry; Dairy Industry; Federal Government, Executive Branch: Department of Agriculture; Livestock Industry; New Deal Era, The; Sharecropping and Tenantry; Tobacco Industry.]

• Edwin Nourse, Joseph Davis, and John D. Black, *Three Years of the Agricultural Adjustment Administration*, 1937. David E. Conrad, *The Forgotten Farmers: The Story of Sharecroppers in the New Deal*, 1965.

—David E. Conrad

AGRICULTURAL EDUCATION AND EXTENSION. The system of agricultural education and extension consists of the land-grant colleges with their associated *agricultural experiment stations and cooperative extension services, and secondary schools that offer vocational instruction in agriculture. The sixty-nine land-grant colleges that existed by the end of the twentieth century were established under the provisions of the *Morrill Land Grant Act of 1862, which required that they offer residential instruction in agriculture.

The Hatch Act of 1887 appropriated federal funds for the establishment in each state of one or more experiment stations to undertake systematic study of agricultural problems and to formulate scientific knowledge that could be presented in college classrooms. The stations were usually located at the land-grant colleges and commonly shared faculty with them.

The experiment stations were required to disseminate their findings among farmers, but the printed word proved to be an ineffective form of communication as also were farmers' institutes. In 1903, Seaman A. Knapp introduced in Texas the demonstration method by which farmers learned improved agricultural practices under the direction of a skilled adviser, later to be known as a county agent. Success with this teaching innovation led to boys' and girls' corn and tomato clubs, which developed into the *4-H club movement for farm youth, and to home-demonstration work with rural women. The Smith-Lever Act of 1914 provided additional federal support for a nationwide educational program for all members of the farm family.

Vocational instruction in agriculture began around 1897 with nature study in the public schools of New York State and elsewhere. In the first decade of the twentieth century, some states authorized the establishment of agricultural high schools. These institutions disappeared when public high schools began to employ graduates of the land-grant colleges to offer courses in vocational agriculture and home economics. The Smith-Hughes Act of 1917 funded such educational programs. This system of agricultural education contributed greatly to the development of the United States in the twentieth century. By increasing dramatically agricultural productivity, it permitted a sharp reduction in farm population while providing abundant and low-cost food and fiber.

[*See also* Agriculture: 1770s to 1890; Agriculture: The "Golden Age" (1890s–1920); Agriculture: Since 1920; Education: Collegiate Education.]

• Edward D. Eddy, *Colleges for Our Land and Time: The Land-Grant Idea in American Education*, 1957. Alan I. Marcus, *Agricultural Science and the Quest for Legitimacy: Farmers, Agricultural Colleges, and Experiment Stations*, 1985.

—Roy V. Scott

AGRICULTURAL EXPERIMENT STATIONS. By the 1880s, *industrialization and *urbanization in America were generating increasing demands for farm products, while the plains and western states were producing surpluses for a developing international market. At the same time, farmers were targeting the nation's *railroads, banks, and capitalists as sources of economic destabilization and proposing a range of moderate to radical actions. The Hatch Act (1887) was part of the government's response to that challenge. This measure allotted funds, initially fifteen thousand dollars annually, to establish agricultural research stations in every state addressing the needs of growers. An Office of Experiment Stations within the U.S. Department of Agriculture coordinated this decentralized system.

Expectations concerning the role of the agricultural stations generated tensions, since their constituency included such diverse groups as farmers, agricultural businesses, and state and federal legislators. Moreover, the close geographical and structural relationship many of them had with the land-grant colleges placed strong educational demands on station personnel. The most effective late nineteenth-century agricultural experiment station administrators, such as William A. Henry of Wisconsin, Eugene Davenport of Illinois, and Liberty Hyde Bailey of New York, balanced these potentially conflicting demands while strengthening their states' agricultural economies and allocating some resources for scientific work. The 1906 Adams Act, for which these leading agricultural administrators strongly lobbied, provided each state with additional funds exclusively to support fundamental agricultural research. The Smith-Lever Extension Act (1914) provided funds to each state to pay county extension agents who would bring farmers the fruits of station work, while simultaneously strengthening the stations as sites of basic research by freeing station researchers from time-consuming extension work.

Most station research was directed toward increasing U.S. agricultural *productivity. Plant pathology and economic entomology focused on reducing production losses to diseases and pests, while research on culture methods, fertilizers, and breeding sought to improve production directly by increasing yield. Chemistry, nutrition, genetics, and agricultural technologies were prominent research areas as well.

Over the years, station research revealed close links between basic and applied research and between science and industry. For example, concern for the *dairy industry in the 1880s inspired chemist Stephen M. Babcock's research into the butterfat content of milk at the Wisconsin experiment station, resulting in a butterfat test that enabled producers to provide a richer, more standardized product. The discovery of vitamin A by Elmer V. McCollum at the Wisconsin station and by T. B. Osborne and L. B. Mendel at the Connecticut station originated in research on livestock nutrition. The genetics of corn was studied as both a basic and applied science at various stations beginning in the 1910s. At the New York station in the 1920s, geneticist Rollins A. Emerson trained future Nobelists George W. Beadle and Barbara *McClintock. At the Illinois station the development of hybrid corn, perhaps the single most important contribution of the experiment stations to American agriculture, bettered the yield and uniformity of the corn crop while increasing growers' dependence on the seed companies that had collaborated closely with the experiment station on the development of hybrids. Later technological innovations—such as the mechanical tomato picker and cotton picker, developed cooperatively among experiment stations and manufacturers—fostered more efficient cultivation and harvesting by the larger producers while throwing many farm laborers out of work.

From the mid–twentieth century on, critics of the agricultural research system, pointing to such developments, argued that experiment-station research had come to serve corporate needs more than those of American farmers. Such criticism, in turn, provoked many station scientists and government administrators to defend the station system's contributions to world agricultural production.

[*See also* Agricultural Education and Extension; Agriculture: 1770s to 1890; Agriculture: The "Golden Age" (1890s–1920); Agriculture: Since 1920; Cotton Industry; Federal Government, Executive Branch: Department of Agriculture; Livestock Industry.]

• Lawrence Bush and William B. Lacy, *Science, Agriculture, and the Politics of Research,* 1983. Charles E. Rosenberg, *No Other Gods: On Science and American Social Thought,* rev. ed., 1997.

—Barbara A. Kimmelman

AGRICULTURE

AGRICULTURE: COLONIAL ERA

Agriculture dominated the colonial economy, and the great majority of the population lived in the countryside. The agricultural practices of colonial farmers often earned the scorn of European contemporary observers, and their reputation fared little better at the hands of later historians. They were portrayed as wasteful and slovenly farmers who abused the land, neglected their livestock, accepted small yields and low incomes, used primitive tools, and resisted useful innovations, preferring customary practices and constrained by the dead hand of tradition. Recently historians have challenged that view for two reasons. First, the denigration of colonial agriculture often arose from an inappropriate comparison with European farmers, who faced a much different situation. In America, where land was relatively cheap and labor costly, following the "best" European practices seldom made sense. Farm practices that appeared wasteful to Old World observers often reflected efforts to save labor in a region of high wages. Second, the critics of colonial farmers often underestimated their impressive accomplishments, most evident in the creation of what might be called a "mestizo" agriculture. At its best, colonial agriculture wove together crops and farming techniques from America, Africa, and Europe to produce a unique system of husbandry more productive than any of its individual sources. American agriculture was mestizo in another, more sinister sense. It combined labor stolen from Africa with land stolen from Native Americans to produce commodities, and sometimes luxuries, for European consumers.

Agricultural Crops and Practices. Colonial agriculture was strikingly diverse. The plantation districts of the coastal South, where slaves, often working on large units with one hundred or more laborers, produced rice, indigo, and tobacco for export to Europe, differed radically from the southern backcountry and the northern colonies, where small family farms produced a diverse range of products for their own subsistence and small surpluses for export or sale in local markets. Agriculturally, the colonies represent a spectrum ranging from north to south, from farm region to plantation district. While agriculture in the farming regions of the backcountry and northern colonies appears relatively homogeneous, one should distinguish between *New England, where thin soils and a short growing season limited the size of surpluses available for export, and the Mid-Atlantic colonies, where a warmer climate and richer soils yielded much larger crops for export.

By the end of the eighteenth century, wheat cultivation was well established in the Mid-Atlantic colonies, where it had expanded into the Hudson, Mohawk, Delaware, and Susquehanna river valleys. Plows drawn by oxen or increasingly by horses were in common use. Corn, barley (used in beer making), and oats for feed were raised as well. Sheep were common in New England, and cattle were raised for export in Delaware, New Jersey, and Massachusetts. Livestock grazed on English grasses imported and planted for the purpose. Farmers in New England and New York raised flax as a commercial crop.

The plantation *South, too, was far from homogeneous, as different principal crops with differing labor and capital requirements led to sharply differing agricultural practices and contrasting social systems and cultures. In the lower South (the coastal portions of Georgia and South Carolina) the major export crops were rice and indigo, plantations were large, planters wealthy, and a majority of the population enslaved. In the upper South colonies of Maryland and Virginia around the Chesapeake Bay, where tobacco was the main crop, plantations were smaller (indeed, much tobacco was grown on family farms), planters less rich, and the slave presence, while still substantial, less overwhelming.

Another source of diversity (and another much-debated topic among historians) was the degree to which farmers produced surpluses for market, a distinction that tended to reinforce and deepen the plantation-farm dichotomy. Plantations, especially the largest ones, were highly commercialized, often engaged in single-crop production, and imported from abroad much of what they needed for consumption. Yet even the largest, most commercialized operations grew some of the food their workers consumed, while even the smallest, most self-sufficient farms sold some surplus on the market and purchased some consumer goods.

Despite its diversity, all colonial agriculture did share common characteristics. The first was its relatively high *productivity, and the high incomes it generated for farm residents, especially in the eighteenth century, when farm prices rose steadily as trade patterns shifted in favor of agriculture. This high productivity had several sources, including colonial farmers' creativity, evident in the mestizo system they created; the abundance and fertility of land; and the hard work of farm families, including farm wives, who often helped in the fields, did dairying and kept a garden, in addition to performing the household work traditionally associated with women. The high productivity and incomes generated by colonial agriculture meant that the free population in rural areas lived quite well by early modern standards, as is evident in their diet and material culture. The quality of the colonial diet is revealed in the height of the population: By the time of the *Revolutionary

War, American-born men of European ancestry were, on average, just over 5'8" tall, about 3.5 inches taller than their English counterparts and about the same height as American males who served in the military during *World War II.

Further evidence of the vitality of agriculture in the colonial North comes from recent research challenging the conventional wisdom that *industrialization in America began in the cities and was imported from England. Recent scholarship points to the domestic origins of America's industrial revolution and argues that agriculture provided the labor force, capital, and much of the expertise that made industrialization possible.

The Plantation Workforce. Before about 1680, most unfree workers on colonial plantations were indentured servants recruited to the colonies from Britain. In the eighteenth century, most unfree workers were slaves of African ancestry. Initially, high mortality and a shortage of women kept the slave population from reproducing itself, so planters had to rely on continual imports to maintain their workfore. American-born slaves experienced lower death rates and had a balanced sex ratio, so as the native-born share of the population rose, the rate of natural population growth increased as well. By the 1720s in the Chesapeake colonies, though much later in the lower South, the colonial slave population was growing by reproduction. When most slaves were African-born, slaves were largely confined to fieldwork: with the rise of an American-born slave population, however, the occupations available to slaves diversified, and they took over much of the skilled work on plantations.

[*See also* Colonial Era; Food and Diet; Indentured Servitude; Indian History and Culture: From 1500 to 1800; Livestock Industry; Slavery: The Slave Trade; Slavery: Development and Expansion of Slavery; Tobacco Industry; Women in the Labor Force.]

• James T. Lemon, *The Best Poor Man's Country: A Geographical Study of Early Pennsylvania,* 1976. Paul G. E. Clemens, *The Atlantic Economy and Colonial Maryland's Eastern Shore: From Tobacco to Grain,* 1980. John J. McCusker and Russell R. Menard, *The Economy of British America, 1607–1789,* 1985. Lois Green Carr, Russell R. Menard, and Lorena S. Walsh, *Robert Cole's World: Agriculture and Society in Early Maryland,* 1991. Allan Kulikoff, *The Agrarian Origins of American Capitalism,* 1992. Winifred Barr Rothenberg, *The Transformation of Rural Massachusetts, 1750–1850,* 1992. Joyce E. Chaplin, *An Anxious Pursuit: Agricultural Innovation and Modernity in the Lower South, 1730–1815,* 1993. Daniel Vickers, *Farmers and Fishermen: Two Centuries of Work in Essex County, Massachusetts, 1630–1830,* 1994. Stanley L. Engerman and Robert E. Gallman, eds., *The Cambridge Economic History of the United States, Volume I: The Colonial Era,* 1996.

—Russell R. Menard

AGRICULTURE: 1770s to 1890

Following the *Revolutionary War, the new nation built its economy largely on the marketing of agricultural products. New crops and technologies, plus territorial expansion, fostered agricultural growth in the nineteenth century. The cotton kingdom founded on *slavery, developed in the southern United States, producing the era's most important cash crop and principal U.S. export. In the North, the agricultural economy flourished by marketing its grain crops and livestock. The new lands acquired through the *Louisiana Purchase and the *Mexican War spread the market economy of agriculture to the Pacific Coast, as rivers, canals, and *railroads linked farmers, distributors, and consumers. The largest contributor to economic growth in the first half of the nineteenth-century, antebellum American agriculture was marked by regional distinctions. Cotton characterized the *South, and wheat, corn, beef, and pork, the *Middle West (and soon the Great Plains). Farmers of the Northeast, with its large urban concentrations, supplied the cities with perishable commodities such as fruit, vegetables, and dairy products.

In the aftermath of the Revolution, it took time to reestablish domestic commodity markets and open new international ones. The federal government, initially under the *Articles of Confederation, promoted an economy built on small family farms. The Land Ordinance of 1785, followed by the *Northwest Ordinance of 1787, established a system of land distribution and rapid territorial transition to statehood. Vermont, Kentucky, Tennessee, and Ohio became states as settlers sought out new farmland—a process that would continue throughout the nineteenth century.

Several economic problems beset small farmers, including tight credit, the lack of hard currency, and an inability to pay taxes. In 1786, under the leadership of Daniel Shays, debt-ridden farmers in western Massachusetts organized militias and closed courts to forestall being penalized for failing to pay bills and taxes. Only military repression ended *Shays's Rebellion. Federal taxation spurred a comparable rural rebellion in 1791. Opposed to excise taxes on whiskey, a primary money-making product, farmers in the Mid-Atlantic and Upper South regions fueled the *Whiskey Rebellion. President George *Washington sent federal troops to end the uprising.

Other events in the 1790s, especially the cotton-gin patent secured by Eli *Whitney in 1793, had a more lasting impact. Whitney's relatively simple machine spread the cultivation of short-staple cotton across the South. By 1860, the region produced as much as 6 million bales of cotton, accounting for two-thirds of the nation's exports. While the southern states continued to grow tobacco, rice, and sugar cane, and raise livestock, the cotton gin accelerated the spread of the cotton economy, and with it, the expansion of slavery and the plantation system. This, in turn, gave rise to a two-tier southern agricultural system consisting of a small minority of wealthy plantation owners and a vast majority of slaves and poor white subsistence farmers.

In the North, early–nineteenth–century agriculture was characterized by the production of livestock (sheep, hogs, and cattle) and such grains as wheat and corn. Roads and trails, rivers and canals, and eventually railroads connected farmers to their markets. For the most part, transportation improvements were funded by state, local, or private monies. Except for the National Road, Congress did not fund such improvements in the *Antebellum Era. In 1825, the *Erie Canal, built by New York State, connected eastern markets with the newer western states and territories. Discovering the dual advantages of available land and cheap transportation, farmers flocked west, often displacing Indian settlements and violating Indian treaty rights in the process. By the 1850s, they were moving as far as *California and Oregon. Single men, families, and entire communities migrated west for many reasons, but most went in search of new farmland and new beginnings.

The rapid geographical expansion of agriculture stimulated new farm *technology. Farmers quickly discovered that implements that worked in the east failed on midwestern and western soils. Hence the invention of new agricultural implements—including Hiram and John Pitts's threshing machines, John Deere's cast-iron plows, and Cyrus *McCormick's reapers—became vitally important in the early- to mid-nineteenth century. Hiram Moore pioneered in the development of the combine, which could perform both harvesting and threshing operations, and in 1886 George S. Berry patented a steam-powered and self-propelled combine that could cut as much as fifty acres of wheat per day. The introduction of steam- and gasoline-powered farm equipment significantly increased per-capita productivity and laid the groundwork for the later emergence of large-scale agribusinesses.

Following the *Civil War, agriculture continued to spread. The *Homestead Act, the *Morrill Land Grant Act, the Pacific Railroad Act, and the creation of the U.S. Department of Agriculture (USDA) in 1862, all promoted agricultural expansion. While cotton remained king in the South, a new system of labor replaced slavery: *sharecropping. Combining sharecropping and other forms of farm tenantry with a crop lien system, southern planters kept their impoverished labor force tied to the land. In the North, agricultural specialization grew apace.

Dairy and truck farming (raising fruits and vegetables for urban markets) grew ever more specialized and standardized. Midwestern farms continued to flourish on a base of corn, hogs, and beef, while Wisconsin emerged as a leader in dairy products.

The greatest changes occurred on the Great Plains and beyond, where cattle and wheat produced on bonanza farms and ranches financed by eastern and foreign investment became the key commodities. With the arrival of railroads and the establishment of the first cattle town in Kansas by Joseph McCoy in 1867, the Great Plains and *Rocky Mountain regions soon dominated cattle ranching. Large herds, large ranches, and large-scale investments characterized the *livestock industry's growth in the 1870s and 1880s. Absentee investors who purchased ranches in the hopes of making a quick profit soon transformed centuries-old Spanish, Mexican, and Native American modes of livestock culture into a modern, market-driven industry based on the labor of *cowboys, who eventually became the stuff of myth and legend. But drought and harsh winters bled the profits out of the livestock industry in the late 1880s, dashing the hopes of the speculative investors. Wheat cultivation followed a similar pattern, as climatic and market changes brought failure to those who had gambled on bonanza farms. By 1900, the production of both these commodities had been reorganized and reestablished on a smaller scale.

If most of the nineteenth century was the farmer's age, the century's last twenty-five years proved agriculture's testing time. Unfavorable terms of trade—that is, the ratio of farm products to effective demand—caused falling prices. As their income fell, farmers found it increasingly difficult to pay their mortgages, taxes, and other debts. Bankruptcies increased, farm tenancy grew, and sharecropping spread among white as well as black farmers as cultivation expanded into Texas and Oklahoma. Hence, the late nineteenth century was characterized by farmer organization and action. The Patrons of Husbandry, or the Grange, organized by Oliver Kelley in the late 1860s, soon gave rise to more politically active movements in rural America. Southern farmers' alliances under the leadership of Charles McCune, organized in the late 1870s and 1880s, allied with farm groups in the North and Middle West, led by Milton George, to form a national confederation. Never cohesive, the alliances put aside their economic and ideological differences to form the *Populist party in the early 1890s. Although the Populist insurgency faded after William Jennings *Bryan's unsuccessful presidential bid in 1896, many of the political reforms sought by farmers later became law. More importantly, after 1897 the terms of trade shifted back in favor of agriculture, bring a new prosperity to farmers.

[*See also* Canals and Waterways; Cotton Industry; Dairy Industry; Expansionism; Farmers' Alliance Movement; Federal Government, Executive Branch: Department of Agriculture; Food and Diet; Foreign Trade, U.S.; Gilded Age; Granger Movement; Greenback Labor Party; Indian History and Culture: From 1800 to 1900; Land Policy, Federal; Livestock Industry; Populist Era; Roads and Turnpikes, Early; Urbanization.]

• Alan Bogue, *From Prairie to Corn Belt: Farming on the Illinois and Iowa Prairies in the Nineteenth Century,* 1963. Gilbert C. Fite, *The Farmers' Frontier, 1865–1900,* 1966. John Blassingame, *The Slave Community,* 1972. David P. Szatmary, *Shays' Rebellion: The Making of Agrarian Insurrection,* 1980. R. Douglas Hurt, *American Farm Tools from Hand-Power to Steam-Power,* 1982. Howard S. Russell, *A Long Deep Furrow: Three Centuries of Farming in New England,* 1982. Thomas Slaughter, *The Whiskey Rebellion: Frontier Epilogue to the American Revolution,* 1986. Terry G. Jordan, *North American Cattle-Ranching Frontiers,* 1993. R. Douglas Hurt, *American Agriculture: A Brief History,* 1994.

—Stephanie A. Carpenter Chan

AGRICULTURE: THE "GOLDEN AGE" (1890s–1920)

A brief era of rare prosperity and hopes fulfilled, the so-called golden age of American agriculture was a time when most everything went right for the nation's farmers. Historians generally situate this period between the *Spanish-American War and *World War I, or, more precisely, from 1909 to 1914, when strong agricultural prices translated into parity, a boost in purchasing power for farm men and women that matched or surpassed that of other economic sectors. A period characterized by optimism and modernization, it was summed up by one contemporary as an era of "corn, cattle, and contentment." Of lasting consequence, notes R. Douglas Hurt in *American Agriculture: A Brief History* (1994), is the concept of parity prices and income, which soon became the basis of American agricultural policy.

What sets this "golden age" apart from other periods in American agricultural history is the absence of the hard times and agrarian discontent characteristic of other eras. After the *Civil War, many farmers suffered from mortgage indebtedness, high *railroad rates, and surplus production. To increase their *productivity, farm men and women invested more capital in implements and machinery, such as improved plows, reapers, and threshing machines. Moreover, the movement to settle and cultivate western lands, which doubled the number of farms in the United States between 1870 and 1890, contributed significantly to the surplus crop production. As agricultural expansion outpaced consumer demand, foreign and domestic, farm prices fell.

The growing plight of farmers was lost on a larger American society in the midst of shifting from a predominantly rural agricultural basis to an urban industrial one. To resist social, economic, and political marginalization, agriculturists from the late 1860s through the 1890s formed organizations such as the Grange, the Farmers' Alliance, and the People's or *Populist party. Through these, the farm sector voiced its discontent and sought economic improvement, and, ultimately, political change, all of which typified this period of agrarian revolt.

As conditions improved for the farm sector by the early twentieth century, the angry voices partially faded away. A favorable combination of factors related to crop yields, farm prices, land values, and an expanded domestic market precipitated the dawn of agriculture's golden age. Agricultural expansion slowed around 1890, as most of the new land being brought under cultivation was marginal, in need of irrigation, and not conducive to surplus crop and livestock production. As production stabilized by the late 1890s, the output of farm goods, unlike previous decades, better matched consumer demand, bringing farmers higher prices.

Land values rose, in some cases dramatically, as rising farm prices increased the demand for good land. One estimate puts the average price increase of farmland from 1900 to 1910 at between 200 and 300 percent. Industrialization and the rapid *urbanization that accompanied it expanded the domestic market and consumer demand for farm goods. *Chicago and Cleveland, Ohio, grew by 55 percent and 46 percent, respectively, between 1890 and 1900, while *Los Angeles and *Atlanta swelled by 211 percent and 72 percent, respectively, in 1900–1910. Such phenomenal urban growth, rather than foreign markets, stimulated and sustained the era of agricultural prosperity.

For farm men and women, the new prosperity manifested itself in several significant ways. A mood of optimism, propagated by the press, popular magazines, and public discourse, enlarged the sense that all was well with farmers, especially in the *Middle West. References to the "new agriculture" implied that more modern methods and equipment had replaced the outmoded practices of pioneer days. Prosperity was especially apparent in the improved credit position of many farmers, who now enjoyed unequaled borrowing and purchasing power.

This enhanced purchasing power reflected the advantageous price relationship between farm goods and nonfarm goods. With nonfarm prices increasing far more slowly than farm prices, argues Gilbert C. Fite in *American Farmers* (1981), farmers received substantially higher prices for the goods they sold than they paid for the goods they purchased. The United States Department of Agriculture (USDA), later determining that the years 1909–1914 represented a time of price parity for farmers—an economic relationship in which farm goods could be exchanged for a fair amount of nonfarm goods—designated this period as the baseline for formulating future policy regarding agricultural prices.

However, the prosperity associated with the golden age of agriculture was neither ubiquitous nor synonymous with satisfaction or respect. While the Midwest seemed to bask in good times, the *South experienced little of the period's well-being. Most of that region's sharecroppers and tenant farm families lived amid abject *poverty and would long continue to do so, largely because of landowners' reluctance to abandon cotton as the primary cash crop and adopt diversified agriculture. Further, despite the farm sector's overall prosperity, rural life still presented hardship with few amenities, and many young people left the family farm for the city.

This trend alarmed a group of mainly urban professionals and social reformers affiliated with the *Progressive party. Their concern with the quality of rural life and the promotion of efficient farming practices formed the core of the Country Life movement. To these urban reformers, David B. Danbom contends in *Born in the Country: A History of Rural America* (1995), farm men and women seemed out of step with an industrialized society and thus represented a problem to be studied. Once seen as the backbone of American society, rural America and its institutions now appeared more like a backwater. In 1908, President Theodore *Roosevelt appointed a Country Life Commission to propose ways to improve rural life and keep young people from leaving the farm. The commission's 1909 report identified substandard schools, poor roads, inadequate communication, and social isolation as significant problems in life and community leadership in farming regions.

While a number of the Country Lifers' objectives were achieved, neither the larger American society nor rural and agricultural people in general participated in the movement. Instead, rural and farm people determined their own response to the prosperity of the age. Enjoying enhanced purchasing power, they became uncharacteristically consumption oriented. Some reinvested their profits in farm operations; even more purchased items that made their homes more comfortable, modern, and pleasant, such as carpets, drapes, wallpaper, and kitchen conveniences. Farm men and women also invested in the era's new technologies and amenities, installing hand pumps as well as plumbing, *electricity, and *telephones when they became available. They also bought automobiles, which substantially altered patterns of rural life. Their communities benefited from the prosperity as well, as farmers paid to improve rural roads, schools, and churches, and sought rural free delivery of mail.

The prosperity and increased consumer spending during agriculture's golden age opened the door for changes on many levels. In 1920, the average farm family produced only 40 percent of what it consumed, as opposed to 60 percent twenty years earlier. Store-bought items increasingly supplanted traditional patterns of home production. Modernization of farms and the purchase of machine *technology, some historians argue, led to shifts in *gender, *family, and community relations. Inasmuch as the family farm was part of a complex web of community ties, modernization disrupted traditional practices of interdependence often found in rural areas.

American's entrance into World War I in 1917 marked the beginning of the end of America's golden age of agriculture. The stabilized production levels that had contributed to farmers' prosperity now seemed a problem to be overcome as the Woodrow *Wilson administration concluded that successful prosecution of the war depended on America's ability to feed not only its citizens but those of its British and French allies as well. Acting under the 1917 Food Production Act and Food Control Act, Wilson named Herbert *Hoover as food administrator. Slogans such as "Food will win the war" and government assistance in providing seed, fertilizer, machinery, and even capital induced farmers to produce more food. The end of the war, however, shattered the mood of optimism. In May 1920, the government ended its wartime subsidies. Agricultural exports fell as European nations recovered from the war and soon were growing enough to feed themselves. The falling farm prices that followed spelled trouble for the nation's farm sector where too many farmers had heeded the patriotic call to produce more by borrowing money to expand production. As the agricultural depression of the 1920s descended upon America's farm men and women and agrarian discontent erupted once again, the golden age of agriculture collapsed with a thud.

[*See also* Business Cycle; Consumer Culture; Cotton Industry; Farmers' Alliance Movement; Federal Government, Executive Branch: Department of Agriculture; Foreign Trade, U.S.; Granger Movement; Motor Vehicles; Populist Era; Progressive Era.]

• Earle D. Ross, *Iowa Agriculture: An Historical Survey,* 1951. D. Jerome Tweton, "The Golden Age of Agriculture: 1897–17," *North Dakota History* 37 (1970): 41–55. David B. Danbom, *The Resisted Revolution: Urban America and the Industrialization of Agriculture, 1900–1930,* 1979. Gilbert C. Fite, *Cotton Fields No More: Southern Agriculture, 1865–1980,* 1984. R. Douglas Hurt, *Agricultural Technology in the Twentieth Century,* 1991. Mary Neth, *Preserving the Family Farm: Women, Community, and the Foundations of Agribusiness in the Midwest, 1900–1940,* 1995. Dorothy Schwieder, *Iowa: The Middle Land,* 1996.

—Ginette Aley

AGRICULTURE: SINCE 1920

In the 1920s American agriculture entered hard times economically and politically, and for the first time in the nation's history, the number of farmers and farms declined absolutely. Yet production increased dramatically thanks to mechanization, new plant strains, better grades of livestock, more scientific cultivation practices, more potent insecticides, and increased use of fertilizer. These innovations raised the costs of farming; encouraged the growth of large commercial farms; and reduced the number of small subsistence farms.

In the upper *Middle West, tractor-drawn equipment, combines, and farm trucks facilitated large wheat farming operations. Cotton remained king in the *South, but continued to be grown and harvested largely by tenant farmers and sharecroppers. Tobacco, a labor-intensive crop produced mostly in the upper South, was cultivated on small holdings with a high percentage of tenant farmers. Corn, the most universal crop, benefited from improved practices, but its harvesting was not yet fully mechanized. Increasingly, midwestern corn growers developed hog production in large-scale operations. Irrigated citrus farming and truck farming in Florida, California, and Texas's Rio Grande valley developed rapidly in the 1920s.

Severe depression struck American agriculture in 1921 and became chronic. Largely the result of excess production, dwindling foreign demand for U.S. farm products, and rising overseas competition, the economic contraction was aggravated by inefficient and disorganized domestic marketing. Since the agricultural depression occurred amidst a booming general economy, it stimulated political protest by farmers. A group in Congress known as the farm bloc sought to enact legislation to assist farmers economically. A few modest measures were passed, but President Calvin *Coolidge vetoed the major one, the *McNary-Haugen Bill.

When Herbert *Hoover became president in 1929, he promised to aid agriculture. The result was the Agricultural Marketing Act, which facilitated the formation of cooperative marketing organizations for each principal commodity. This measure also provided for government-operated stabilization corporations that could buy domestic surpluses at higher than market prices and dispose of them on the world market.

The new law coincided with the *stock market crash of 1929. As the general economy plunged into depression, farm surpluses mounted alarmingly and the stabilization corporations lacked the funds to absorb them. By 1931, the Hoover administration abandoned the stabilization effort and farm prices plunged.

The Depression of the 1930s worsened the agricultural crisis, as consumers had less and less money to buy food and clothing. When Franklin Delano *Roosevelt entered the White House in 1933, agricultural markets faced collapse. Roosevelt's advisers urgently drafted an emergency farm bill, which became the Agricultural Adjustment Act of 1933. This sweeping measure created broad new government powers and agricultural programs. Its basic idea was to give farmers a "fair exchange value" for their products in relation to the general economy. In practice, this became known as "parity."

This landmark law embodied several new concepts. One was domestic allotment, an attempt to limit the production of basic agricultural commodities to the quantity needed for domestic use. This approach was predicated on the belief that if commodity production fell substantially prices would rise, benefiting farmers and the entire economy.

A new government agency, the *Agricultural Adjustment Administration (AAA), received extraordinary powers to administer the act. The domestic allotment plan mandated acreage-reduction programs. The government offered farmers contracts whereby they received payments for reducing their planted acreage by as much as 40 percent. For perishable commodities, New Deal administrators negotiated marketing agreements among processors to raise prices to parity levels.

By 1935, the AAA had raised agricultural prices to near parity levels and saved many farmers from ruin. Opposition arose among conservatives, however, to this vast expansion of government powers. The *Supreme Court in 1935 held the Agricultural Adjustment Act unconstitutional, but Congress quickly passed legislation reinstating many AAA programs, and a changed Court upheld it. In 1938 another Agricultural Adjustment Act revived many of the early programs, including price supports. In the cotton South, an unintended consequence of the New Deal's acreage-reduction program was to displace thousands of poor tenant farmers and sharecroppers. Overall, however, by the end of the *New Deal Era, American agriculture had regained a near-parity position. In the process, farmers had become a protected class, insulated by the government from free-market forces.

*World War II brought global food shortages. American farmers were exhorted to produce as much as possible, and the risks of overproduction were quickly forgotten. As farmers met the challenge by growing bumper crops, farm income tripled between 1939 and 1945, far outpacing the increases in industrial wages and corporate profits. American agriculture played a vital role in the Allied victory and thereby prospered.

As farmers continued to produce at high levels after the war, the problem of surpluses predictably returned. Despite government price supports, farm income declined. The "farm problem" became a burning political question, forcing Congress to act. Agricultural legislation in 1948 and 1949 made feeble efforts to address the problem with "flexible" (lowered) price supports, but these measures had little effect. By late 1963, parity stood at 76 percent, the lowest since 1934.

With the nation plagued by agricultural surpluses, Congress in 1956 enacted a "soil bank" program that took entire farms out of production. Still later, in 1985, the Conservation Reserve Program eliminated thirty-seven million acres of erodible land from cultivation. Yet both measures failed to decrease overall farm output, and the problems of overproduction and low prices persisted.

In the 1960s and 1970s, the focus of agriculture programs changed from eliminating surpluses to stimulating production for foreign markets. Government price supports for basic commodities encouraged farmers to produce single crops for export. In the process, diversified farming virtually disappeared. Improved technology and knowledge, much of it gained from land-grant universities and government extension programs, increased production dramatically.

Often, farmers took the money they received for not cultivating their land and bought or leased more land to put into production. Those who were successful as agricultural entrepreneurs used government loans and subsidies to expand their operations, and above all they played the markets well. Fortunately, growing world demand for American farm products worked in their favor. As farmers put more land into cultivation, however, protests by environmental groups prompted Congress to pass laws in 1977, 1981, and 1985 denying benefits to farmers who did not comply with the conservation programs.

In the 1980s declining world markets produced great surpluses, forcing the government to lower loan and price-support levels. Several laws, including the Farm Act of 1990, continued the trend toward world market orientation, and renewed exports after 1987 gave farmers record incomes.

Post–1920 American agriculture has also seen great demographic changes. Government programs, market forces, and the dynamics of modern life gave rise to large agribusinesses and a new farmer elite while worsening the prospects for small farmers and stimulating a dramatic rural-to-urban movement. From 1920 to 1995, the U.S. farm population fell from 31.5 million to 5 million. In 1990, only one in ten sons and daughters of farmers could hope to become farmers themselves.

While issues related to overproduction persisted, the nation's chronic "farm problem" gained added complexity in the late twentieth century. Dietary changes, health concerns, the rise of giant supermarket chains and fast-food outlets, and the increased use of synthetic fabrics affected specific agricultural sectors such as the *livestock and *dairy industries, poultry, tobacco, and cotton. The rise of a global economy, the worldwide marketing agricultural goods, the creation of a European free-trade zone, and the *North American Free Trade Agreement all had important implications for U.S. agriculture. Controversies surrounding *migratory agricultural workers, pesticide use (an issue highlighted by Rachel *Carson's 1962 *Silent Spring*), the environmental hazards posed by some agribusinesses, and the genetic engineering of crops and livestock raised complex policy issues. Yet late twentieth-century American agricultural abundance made possible food stamps for low-income families, school-lunch programs, food for the elderly and Indian reservations, and unparalleled nutritional levels for the general populace. With its vast fertile lands and efficiencies of food production, processing, and marketing, America, as a new century dawned, faced agricultural "problems" that would delight many other nations.

[*See also* Agricultural Education and Extension; Agricultural Experiment Stations; Cotton Industry; Depressions, Economic; Environmentalism; Federal Government, Executive Branch: Department of Agriculture; Foreign Trade, U.S.; Genetics and Genetic Engineering; Global Economy, America and the; Mass Marketing; Sharecropping and Tenantry; Tobacco Industry; Twenties, The; Urbanization.]

• A. B. Genung, *A Brief Survey of 35 Years of Government Aid to Agriculture Beginning in 1920*, 1960. Edward Higbee, *Farms and Farmers in an Urban Age*, 1963. Leonard Kyle, *The Economics of Large Scale Crop Farming*, 1970. Gilbert C. Fite, *American Farmers: The New Minority*, 1981. Hiram M. Drache, *History of U.S. Agriculture and Its Relevance to Today*, 1996.

—David E. Conrad

AIDS. *See* Acquired Immunodeficiency Syndrome.

AID TO FAMILIES WITH DEPENDENT CHILDREN. *See* Welfare, Federal.

AIR CONDITIONING. *See* Refrigeration and Air Conditioning.

AIR FORCE. *See* Military, The.

AIR FORCE ACADEMY. *See* Military Service Academies.

AIRPLANES AND AIR TRANSPORT. The centuries-old dream of powered, heavier-than-air, controllable flight became reality on 17 December 1903, when Orville Wright lifted his fragile biplane off the sands of Kill Devil Hill, North Carolina, and traveled 120 feet in twelve seconds. Orville, his brother Wilbur, and other pioneer aviators quickly recognized and exploited the military and commercial potential of the new means of transport. The first air express delivery in the United States took place in November 1910, when a department store in Columbus, Ohio, flew a bolt of silk to Dayton, Ohio. The following year, on 25 September, Earle Ovington flew the first Post Office–sanctioned airmail as part of an aerial meet at Garden City, New York. The first sustained effort to carry passengers came in 1914. Operating from January to March, the St. Petersburg–Tampa Airboat Line safely carried some twelve hundred people between the Florida cities in a two-seat (pilot and one passenger) Benoist flying boat.

Single-passenger airline operations, obviously, were not economically viable. With their limited lifting capacity and unreliable engines, airplanes could best be employed in carrying lightweight, high-value cargo. The U.S. Post Office early recognized the advantages and limitations of air transport. In 1918, farsighted postal officials established the U.S. Air Mail Service. Over the next nine years, this government-operated adjunct of the Post Office established a transcontinental air route from New York to San Francisco, inaugurated systematic night flying, and experimented with radio and instrument navigation. Between 1918 and 1927, postal airmen flew more than 13.7 million miles and carried over 300 million letters, setting a standard of excellence for bad-weather and night flying unmatched in the world and laying the foundations for U.S. commercial aviation.

The outstanding performance of the Air Mail Service drew the attention of private investors. Congress facilitated their entry into aviation by passing the Air Mail Act of 1925 and the Air Commerce Act of 1926, measures that assured profit and established the essential regulatory structure for the early development of commercial aviation. Encouraged by Charles *Lindbergh's dramatic transatlantic solo flight in May 1927, an event that brought enormous public attention to aviation, the private sector began to make substantial investments in air-transport enterprises.

By the early 1930s, four major domestic airlines that would dominate the industry for the next forty years had emerged. All were headed by dynamic individuals: William A. Patterson of United Air Lines, Edward V. Rickenbacker of Eastern Air Lines, C. R. Smith of American Airlines, and Jack Frye of TWA. One airline, meanwhile, came to monopolize international travel. Pan American Airways, the government's "chosen instrument" for international service, established long-distance operations throughout Latin America and across two oceans. Under the adroit leadership of Juan Trippe, this superbly run company also flew a series of impressive flying boats, culminating in the four-engine Boeing 314. The federal government underwrote the development expenses for Pan American's international routes by providing generous postal subsidies. Between 1929 and 1940, Pan American received $47.2 million in mail payments, compared to the $59.8 million received by all domestic airlines. This funding enabled Pan American not only to expand worldwide but also to turn a modest profit.

In an effort to lessen their dependency on federal subsidies, the domestic airlines emphasized passenger travel in the 1930s. Their transition from reliance on mail contracts to passenger operations was facilitated by a series of technological developments that produced a new generation of airlines. Important advances in airframe design led to the adoption of stressed-skin metal wings and fuselages in place of the previous fabric-covered, wood-framed construction. At the same time, improved cylinder heads and pistons, plus better fuel, resulted in more efficient, reliable, and powerful engines.

The first modern passenger transport, the twin-engine Boeing 247, went into service with United Air Lines in 1933. A streamlined, all-metal stressed-skin plane powered by two 550-horsepower Pratt & Whitney engines mounted into nacelles on the wing, the 247 could carry ten passengers at a cruising speed of approximately 160 miles per hour. The Douglas DC-3 appeared in 1936. The 21-passenger DC-3, which within three years was carrying 80 percent of all U.S. air travelers, gave airlines the first real opportunity to make a profit from flying passengers.

The federal government promoted airline-industry growth before *World War II not only by providing subsidies but also by licensing airmen and aircraft and by constructing and operating the ground facilities that made possible safe point-to-point navigation. In addition to its existing responsibility for radio aids to navigation, Washington expanded its regulatory activities in 1936, by taking over three air-traffic-control centers that had been set up by the airlines six months earlier to deal with expanding air traffic. In 1938, the Air Commerce Act established the framework for government policy toward aviation that would last for the next forty years, creating a regulatory structure that encompassed strict economic control, safety oversight, and federal operation of the nation's airways and air-traffic-control facilities.

America's entry into World War II temporarily ended the rapid growth of the airline industry, which carried 3.4 million passengers—primarily business travelers—in 1941. By June 1942, the army had requisitioned 200 airplanes out of the industry's total of 360. The war years saw a dramatic increase in aircraft utilization as the airlines struggled to meet the demands for priority air travel. Despite the sharp reduction in equipment, the airlines, by filling most seats carried nearly as many passengers in 1942 and 1943 as they had in 1941.

The U.S. air-transport industry underwent rapid expansion during the 1950s, reflecting partly the nation's vibrant economic growth. The decade witnessed two watershed events. Flying larger, pressurized four-engine Douglas DC-6s and Lockheed Constellations that could carry more than fifty passengers from San Francisco to New York in ten hours, domestic airlines boarded 38 million passengers in 1955, marking the first year that airlines hauled more people than railroads. Three years later, international airlines took more travelers to Europe than steamship companies did.

The explosive growth of the air-transport industry during the 1950s imposed an intolerable strain on an air-traffic-control system designed for DC-3s. Following a series of midair collisions, Congress passed the Federal Aviation Act in 1958. The new law created the Federal Aviation Agency, which united all the government's principal safety-related functions in a single, powerful organization that reported directly to the president.

The new regulatory structure was in place in time for the jet revolution of the 1960s, which saw piston-engine and turboprop airplanes give way to faster, more efficient jet transports. At the same time, changes in airline fare structures lured leisure travelers away from trains and buses. By the mid-1960s, some 50 percent of airline passengers were traveling for pleasure rather than business, a pattern that would remain constant for the rest of the century.

The 1960s were golden years for the air-transport industry. The major trunk carriers grew larger, regional airlines prospered, and scheduled air-taxi lines brought air service to small communities. By the end of the decade, few people were outside the aerial network that was coming to dominate intercity transportation. The number of passengers carried by scheduled airlines rose from 56.3 million in 1960 to 158.5 million in 1969. At the same time, the net operating income of domestic airlines averaged $255.4 million a year, while international airlines averaged $139.4 million.

The good times ended in the early 1970s. The appearance of the wide-bodied "jumbo jets"—the Boeing 747, Douglas DC-10, and Lockheed L-1011 Tristar—added capacity at a time when demand was leveling off. The oil crisis of 1973–1974 quadrupled airline fuel prices. Finally, in 1974 the nation entered a period of inflation and economic stagnation that the press labeled "stagflation."

As the airlines struggled, the federal government abandoned the regulatory structure in place since 1938. In October 1978, President Jimmy *Carter signed the landmark Airline Deregulation Act, by which Washington gave up the control over routes and fares that it had exercised since 1938. Airlines now were free to add or drop routes as market conditions dictated and to charge whatever fares they pleased.

Deregulation could not have come at a worse time. Another round of cost increases occurred in 1979 and 1980, together with a deep recession that lasted into 1982. In the midst of these economic woes, the Professional Air Traffic Controllers Organization began an illegal strike, crippling the nation's air-traffic system. President Ronald *Reagan fired eleven thousand strikers, breaking both the strike and the union. Several years passed before the air traffic control system fully recovered.

New airlines proliferated in the unregulated environment, increasing from thirty-six in 1978 to ninety-six in 1983 (although only two survived the decade). At the same time, the industry's costs doubled. Between 1979 and 1983, the domestic airline industry suffered a staggering net loss of $1.2 billion.

The later 1980s witnessed a wave of mergers and bankruptcies as the air-transport industry struggled to adjust to the new deregulated era. Not until the mid-1990s did a measure of stability and profitability return to an industry once again dominated by a handful of giant carriers.

In June 1995, the industry carried its ten billionth passenger since the St. Petersburg–Tampa Airboat Line began flying in 1914. Over the years, air travel had changed from an individual adventure to a routine feature of the national scene. By the end of the century, with U.S. airlines carrying some 750 million passengers a year, plus a significant portion of small parcel traffic, the industry clearly had become a vital component of the nation's transportation infrastructure. For both business and leisure travel, Americans had come to rely on air transport no less than earlier generations had depended on railroads, buses, and steamships. Air travel, however, brought a speed that had not been possible previously, contributing to the accelerated pace of life that characterized the second half of the twentieth century in the United States.

[*See also* Aviation Industry; Energy Crisis of the 1970s; Federal Regulatory Agencies; Military, The; Postal Service, U.S.; Technology; Wright, Wilbur and Orville.]

• Ronald Miller and David Sawers, *The Technical Development of Modern Aviation,* 1970. Nick A. Komons, *Bonfire to Beacons: Federal Civil Aviation Policy under the Air Commerce Act, 1926–1938,* 1978. W. David Lewis and Wesley P. Newton, *Delta: The History of an Airline,* 1979. Marylin Bender and Selig Altschul, *The Chosen Instrument: Pan Am, Juan Trippe—the Rise and Fall of an American Entrepreneur,* 1982. R. E. G. Davies, *Airlines of the United States since 1914,* 1982. Roger E. Bilstein, *Flight in America, 1908–1983,* 1984. William M. Leary, *Aerial Pioneers: The U.S. Air Mail Service, 1918–1927,* 1985. Henry Ladd Smith, *Airways: The History of Commercial Aviation in the United States,* reprint, 1991. Roger E. Bilstein, *The American Aerospace Industry,* 1996.

—William M. Leary

ALAMO, BATTLE OF THE. The most famous battle of the Texas Revolution occurred at a Spanish mission compound known as the Alamo in San Antonio. At this site on 6 March 1836 the Mexican army led by General Antonio López de Santa Anna defeated 189 troops inside the compound under Colonel William Barrett Travis; all the Alamo defenders were killed. As the Texas Revolution proceeded, the words "Remember the Alamo" became a battle cry.

Although there were skirmishes in 1835 between the Mexican government and colonists in the Texas province, the battle at the Alamo was the first encounter of the Texas Revolution, coming four days after colonists officially declared independence from Mexico. San Antonio was taken from Mexican troops in December 1835 when colonists stormed the town. In January 1836, General Sam *Houston sent James Bowie to destroy the Alamo and move the remaining troops east. Upon arriving in San Antonio, however, Bowie opted to fortify the compound and defend the area. Travis joined him later that month.

After the Alamo battle, Santa Anna led his forces east in pursuit of the rest of the Texas army. On 21 April 1836, the Mexican army was defeated at the Battle of San Jacinto by the Texas army under Houston. Texas became independent and later applied to the United States for statehood.

As a site commemorating Texas's unique identity and its separation from Mexico, the Alamo is currently the top Texas tourist attraction. It is also a favorite target of groups protesting ethnic and racial discrimination, especially during the annual Fiesta Week.

[*See also* Texas Republic and Annexation.]

• Stephen L. Hardin, *Texian Iliad: A Military History of the Texas Revolution,* 1994. Holly Beachley Brear, *Inherit the Alamo: Myth and Ritual at an American Shrine,* 1995.

—Holly Beachley Brear

ALASKA. In March 1867, U.S. Secretary of State William Henry *Seward negotiated the purchase of Alaska from Russia for $7.2 million, including the property of the Russian American Company. Ridiculed by some as "Seward's Folly" but approved by most, the treaty added to the United States a vast arctic and subarctic subcontinent of grandeur and substantial natural resources. The purchase encompassed 586,412 square miles, one-fifth the size of the present contiguous United States.

After a period of military government, Congress passed in 1884 the first Organic Act, which made Alaska a judicial district with a severely restricted form of territorial government. Meanwhile, in 1880, Richard T. Harris and Joseph Juneau discovered gold near the present site of Juneau. Soon, Juneau, the first American town in Alaska, developed into a booming mining community. In 1896, George W. Carmack and his Indian companions discovered gold on the Klondike, a tributary of the Yukon River, in Canada's Yukon Territory. The discovery triggered a massive gold rush in 1897 with thousands of men and women converging on the Klondike. Many of those people eventually drifted into Alaska where some discovered gold in various localities. Congress granted Alaska a voteless delegate to Congress in 1906 and six years later, with the second Organic Act, gave Alaska a limited form of territorial government.

By 1940, Alaska's population, dependent on seasonal salmon fishing and *mining, stood at approximately 72,000, of whom more than 34,000 were Native peoples. During *World War II, the federal government spent more than two billion dollars to fortify Alaska and built the Alaska Highway connecting the territory with the contiguous states. During the war, the Japanese briefly occupied two islands in the Aleutian Chain, Attu and Kiska. By 1950, Alaska's population had reached nearly 130,000.

The statehood movement, launched in 1943, culminated in 1958, when Congress admitted Alaska as the forty-ninth state. Much of the state's subsequent history has revolved around issues of land and natural resources. To put the new state on a solid economic footing, Congress granted Alaska the right to select more than 100 million acres of land from the vacant, unappropriated, and unreserved public domain and 800,000 acres from the National Forests for community expansion. Soon, state land selections alarmed Alaska's Natives, who claimed much of the lands and resources by ancestral rights. The *Tundra Times,* founded in 1962 and edited by Howard

Rock, an Eskimo artist, championed Native land claims as did the Alaskan Federation of Natives, established in 1966. In 1966, Secretary of the Interior Stewart Udall halted all land conveyances in Alaska until the Native land claims were settled.

In 1968, the Atlantic Richfield Company (ARCO) and Humble Oil and Refining Company (now Exxon), prospecting at Prudhoe Bay on Alaska's North Slope, discovered what proved to be the largest oilfield ever found in North America. In 1969, a consortium of eight oil companies proposed an eight hundred-mile pipeline from Prudhoe Bay to the ice-free port of Valdez on Prince William Sound. Since the pipeline would cross public domain lands, the oil companies sought a waiver from the land freeze. The new secretary of the interior in the Richard M. *Nixon administration, Walter J. Hickel, a promoter of economic development and former governor of Alaska, attempted to lift the land freeze but Congress resisted.

In 1970, five Native villages filed suit, claiming land the proposed pipeline would traverse. After difficult negotiations, Congress in 1971 passed, and the president signed, the Alaska Native Claims Settlement Act (ANCSA). In return for the extinguishment of aboriginal title, including hunting and fishing rights and any pending statutory claims, the Natives received $962.5 million and 40 million acres in fee simple title. Twelve regional corporations and 220 village corporations were to manage this settlement for the Natives and their descendants. The trans-Alaska pipeline was built, and in June 1977 the first oil flowed southward to Valdez.

In 1980, Congress passed the Alaska National Interest Lands Conservation Act (ANILCA), which added 104.3 million acres to conservation systems. As oil revenues soared, Alaska's economy boomed. By 1982, fully 86.5 percent of state revenues came from the *petroleum industry. In 1976, Alaskans amended their state constitution to place at least 25 percent of all mineral lease bonuses, royalties, and rentals into a permanent fund, to be used only for "income-producing investments." The idea was to convert a part of the state's nonrenewable oil wealth into a renewable source of wealth for future generations. In 1980, the legislature enacted into law the innovative concept of "permanent fund dividends," to distribute a portion of the earnings of the permanent fund directly to Alaska's citizen shareholders. After several court battles, Alaskan shareholders received their first permanent fund dividend check in 1982. In 1997, with the market value of the Alaskan Permanent Fund standing at $22.1 billion, the dividend checks amounted to $1,296.54. A major oil spill by the tanker *Exxon Valdez* in 1989 revived the controversy over Alaska's oil industry and its impact on the state.

Heavily dependent on *tourism; federal, state, and local government spending; and income from its natural resources (many of them nonrenewable), Alaska in the 1990s faced an uncertain economic future. Once the oil ran out, many feared, the boom-and-bust economic cycles would return.

[*See also* Conservation Movement; Federal Government, Executive Branch: Other Departments; Gold Rushes; Indian History and Culture.]

• Claus-M. Naske and Herman E. Slotnick, *Alaska: A History of the 49th State,* 2d ed., 1987. Morgan B. Sherwood, *Exploration of Alaska, 1865–1900,* 1992. Nikolai N. Bolkhovitnov, *Russian-American Relations and the Sale of Alaska, 1834–1867,* trans. and ed. Richard A. Pierce, 1996.

—Claus-M. Naske

ALBANY CONGRESS. Representatives of seven American colonies meeting in Albany, New York, in the summer of 1754 drew up a plan to unite the American colonies under a federal government. The Albany Congress had initially been convened by the English Board of Trade, which was concerned about the weakness of intercolonial defense at the beginning of the *Seven Years' War, as well as about growing friction between the colonists and the Iroquois.

The plan, derived largely from the ideas of Benjamin *Franklin and Governor William Shirley of Massachusetts, provided for a chief military executive and a commissioner for Indian affairs, both to be paid by the Crown. A grand council of delegates would be drawn from the thirteen mainland colonies, the size of each colony's delegation being proportional to its share of taxes. The delegates, to be elected every three years and to meet every year, were charged with negotiating Indian treaties that would bind all the colonies, and with providing for intercolonial defense to be paid for by indirect taxes. The proposed Grand Council would have had more powers than the provincial assemblies vis-à-vis the imperial executives, but fewer powers than Parliament enjoyed in relation to the king.

Nothing immediately came of the Albany Plan. It was not supported by the colonial assemblies, which distrusted one another. And it was never presented for authorization in Parliament because the English ministry hesitated to introduce a plan for an intercolonial assembly that might facilitate American resistance to imperial authority. An early blueprint for colonial union, the Albany Plan showed that, in the mid-1750s, intercolonial cooperation was not yet a viable option.

[*See also* Colonial Era; Indian History and Culture: From 1500 to 1800; Revolution and Constitution, Era of.]

• Robert C. Newbold, *The Albany Congress and Plan of Union of 1754,* 1955.

—Alison G. Olson

ALCOHOL AND ALCOHOL ABUSE. Alcohol looms large in American history, and attitudes toward it have been linked to myriad reformist causes; reflected many social concerns; and mirrored the prevailing cultural, political, and economic climate of successive eras.

Alcoholic beverages, whether rum distilled from West Indian sugar, home-brewed beer, or imported wines, were widely consumed in colonial America, and the physician-statesman Benjamin *Rush targeted them in his widely reprinted *Inquiry into the Effects of Ardent Spirits upon the Human Body and Mind* (1784). Fearful for the new republic, Rush recoiled at the prospect of intoxicated voters shaping its destiny—no small concern at a time when elections often featured heavy drinking. Annual per capita consumption of absolute alcohol when Rush wrote ranged between four and six gallons (twice the rate in 2000), and evidence suggests a further sharp rise between 1800 and 1830. The profitability of corn whiskey, heavy frontier drinking, the spread of saloons in cities, and the *immigration of beer-drinking Germans and whiskey-swilling Irish all encouraged the nation's bibulous tendencies.

These tendencies elicited a reaction within the Protestant churches, however, which linked salvation with temperance and other reforms. The American Society for the Promotion of Temperance (ASPT), founded by Evangelical clergymen in 1826, also gained support from farmers, industrialists, and homemakers. Indeed, the temperance campaign—really a series of reform drives—comprised the nineteenth century's longest and largest social-reform movement. Alcohol was seen as imperiling capitalist enterprise, domestic tranquility, and the national virtue. By 1836 the ASPT, renamed the American Temperance Society, advocated total abstinence. In the early 1840s, Americans thronged to temperance rallies, "took the pledge" for sobriety, and in record numbers lobbied to end the licensing of saloons. The Washingtonian movement, a grassroots total-abstinence campaign, sponsored parades and speeches; offered recruits financial and moral assistance; and established institutions for inebriates—Washingtonian Homes—that relied on moral suasion to keep residents sober. The Washingtonian enthusiasm soon gave way to better-organized temperance fellowships, such as the Good Templars and the Blue Ribbon societies. The late *Antebellum Era also saw renewed middle-class drives for local and state prohibition. In the 1850s, eleven states passed prohibitory legislation, although most were soon repealed.

The *brewing and distilling industries expanded after the *Civil War, and alcohol consumption, especially in the immigrant cities, remained high. But the temperance movement revived as well, linking "Demon Rum" to concerns about immigration, workplace efficiency, social welfare, and urban political corruption. Frances *Willard's *Woman's Christian Temperance Union (WCTU) redefined temperance, along with other reforms, as a women's issue involving home protection. At the WCTU's prompting, Congress mandated the inclusion of "scientific" temperance instruction in high-school physiology texts.

This era of social reorganization and professionalization also brought the first widespread attempt to medicalize drunkenness. The American Association for the Cure of Inebriates (AACI), founded in 1870 by physicians and reformers, promoted the concept of inebriety as a hereditary disease exacerbated by chronic debauchery. As their drinking progressed, the AACI contended, inebriates lost control of their actions and required restorative medical and moral treatment. Envisioning a new medical speciality to address this ailment, the AACI built a network of private institutions to treat habitual drunkards. California, Iowa, Massachusetts, New York, and other states followed suit. In this age of industrial *capitalism, the goal was to restore inebriates' economic productivity as well as their willpower. The AACI faded as the prohibition movement grew, however; by 1920, most of the inebriate institutions had closed, and habitual drunkenness was again viewed as primarily a moral, political, and legal issue.

The church-based Anti-Saloon League (ASL), meanwhile, founded in 1895 and supported by industrialists like Henry *Ford and Pierre *du Pont, spearheaded the prohibition drive. Under superintendent Wayne Wheeler, the ASL's innovative bipartisan lobbying approach secured prohibitory state legislation and, in 1919, ratification of the *Eighteenth Amendment, establishing nationwide prohibition. A *World War I reaction against German American–owned breweries and fears that alcohol would undermine the nation's military contributed to this success.

But many Americans, especially in the cities, rejected prohibition; speakeasies flourished and bootleg liquor flowed freely in many municipalities. With repeal in 1933, the nation entered what some scholars have called an "Age of Ambivalence" about alcohol. The reopened breweries and distilleries advertised heavily to win new customers. As old taboos faded, alcohol consumption spread widely. In the later twentieth century, wine connoisseurship spread and U.S. wine production flourished in *California and elsewhere. While the major breweries dominated the beer market, imported brands and local microbreweries also flourished.

Simultaneously, however, antialcohol sentiment remained powerful in evangelical Protestantism; in such organizations as Alcoholics Anonymous (AA, 1935) and Mothers Against Drunk Driving (MADD), founded in 1980 and boasting some six hundred chapters nationwide by 2000; and in heightened concern about college binge drinking, alcohol-related domestic abuse, and fetal alcohol syndrome. Beginning in the early 1980s, these efforts, coupled with *health and fitness concerns, spurred a slow decline in per capita alcohol consumption.

These years also saw renewed debate over the nature of alcoholism. AA founders William Wilson and Robert Smith, a physician, along with the National Committee for Education on Alcoholism, led a crusade to treat alcoholism as a disease. In the 1950s, the biostatistician E. M. Jellinek of the Yale Center of Alcohol Studies promoted a multistage model of alcohol addiction based on his research on AA members. But the disease concept met criticism as well. The *American Medical Association in the 1960s and 1970s encouraged physicians to treat alcoholism's "medical aspects" but argued that labeling alcoholism a disease did not relieve individuals of responsibility for their intoxicated behavior. The *Supreme Court concurred, declining to exonerate persons for actions committed while drunk. Although the National Institute for Alcohol Abuse and Alcoholism (NIAAA) was established in 1971, lending federal support and funding to alcoholism studies, some social scientists, including ones funded by the NIAAA, mustered evidence discrediting the disease model. The 1970s and 1980s witnessed the emergence of a broad-based *public-health approach oriented toward preventing excessive drinking.

As the century ended, what some called a neotemperance movement gained momentum, linked to the antitobacco and antidrug campaigns. In the mid-1990s, however, the nation still had nearly thirty thousand liquor stores, many supermarkets and convenience outlets sold beer and wine, and more than half of adult Americans regularly drank alcoholic beverages. Alcohol's central role in American culture, if somewhat diminished, seemed firmly entrenched.

[*See also* Advertising; Drugs, Illicit; Leisure; Mass Marketing; Medicine; Popular Culture; Temperance and Prohibition; Tobacco Products; Twenties, The; Working-Class Life and Culture.]

• American Association for the Cure of Inebriates, *Proceedings, 1870–1875,* 1981. Mark Lender and James Kirby Martin, *Drinking in America: A History,* rev. ed., 1987. Craig Reinarman, "The Social Construction of an Alcohol Problem: The Case of Mothers against Drunk Drivers and Social Control in the 1980s," *Theory and Society* 17 (1988): 91–120. Jack Blocker, *American Temperance Movements: Cycles of Reform,* 1989. Peter Conrad and Joseph Schneider, "Alcoholism: Drunkenness, Inebriety, and the Disease Concept," in *Deviance and Medicalization: From Badness to Sickness,* rev. ed., 1992, pp. 73–109. William L. White, *Slaying the Dragon: The History of Addiction Treatment and Recovery in America,* 1998.

—Sarah W. Tracy

ALCOHOLICS ANONYMOUS. *See* Alcohol and Alcohol Abuse; Temperance and Prohibition.

ALCOHOLISM. *See* Alcohol and Alcohol Abuse; Temperance and Prohibition.

ALCOTT, LOUISA MAY (1832–1888), author. Alcott grew up in Concord, Massachusetts, where her parents, Bronson and Abigail May Alcott, championed *transcendentalism, abolitionism, women's rights, and educational reform. The family lived in poverty as the impecunious Bronson Alcott pursued a series of reform activities, including a short-lived Utopian experiment in 1843. Louisa worked as a seamstress, servant, and governess, and in the 1850s published, often anonymously or pseudonymously, more than thirty thrillers in weekly story papers. Briefly a *Civil War nurse, she wrote her experiences into *Hospital Sketches* (1863) and published several abolitionist interracial romances as war stories.

In 1868–1869 Alcott published as a two-part serial the novel that would make her famous, *Little Women*, based on her own family and her Concord circle, including the Emerson and Thoreau families. *Little Women* and its sequels, *Little Men* (1871) and *Jo's Boys* (1886), popularized various reform causes while offering toasty, tragic-comic domestic dramas. Alcott never married and like her heroine, Jo March, the endearing militant sister of *Little Women*, struggled against the constraints of poverty and Victorian ideas of womanhood. Her biographer Madeleine B. Stern, in documenting Alcott's "double literary life," has suggested that the Civil War romances connect the thrillers and the later domestic fictions and uncover radical subtexts in *Little Women*. Stern also argues that the success of *Little Women* may have constricted the range of Alcott's later fiction. Alcott's *Work: A Story of Experience* (1873), her 1864 novel *Moods*, and her letters and journals were published or reissued in the 1990s, part of a renewed interest in her life and work.

[*See also* Antislavery; Emerson, Ralph Waldo; Literature: Civil War to World War I; Literature, Popular; Thoreau, Henry David; Utopian and Communitarian Movements.]

• Madeleine B. Stern, *Louisa May Alcott*, 1985. Sarah Elbert, *A Hunger for Home: Louisa May Alcott's Place in American Culture*, 1987. Madeleine B. Stern, ed., *Louisa May Alcott Unmasked: Collected Thrillers*, 1995. Sarah Elbert, ed., *Louisa May Alcott on Race, Sex and Slavery*, 1997.

—Sarah Elbert

ALGER, HORATIO (1832–1899), writer. After graduating Phi Beta Kappa from Harvard College in 1852, Alger completed a ministerial course at Harvard Divinity School in 1860. In 1864 he became minister of a Unitarian church in Brewster, Massachusetts. Dismissed from the Unitarian ministry in 1866 on charges of pederasty, he moved to *New York City to earn his living as a writer. *Ragged Dick: or, Street Life in New York*, his most popular juvenile story, appeared in book form the following year. In this novel, Alger first used the basic elements of his standard formula: a young hero who rises from rags to middle-class respectability, and adult patrons who aid his rise, often rewarding the hero with a job, a new suit, or a watch. Employed as a tutor in the homes of several prominent New York families, including the Seligmans and Cardozos, while establishing his literary career, he toured Europe in 1873. Alger traveled to the West to gather local color for his juveniles in 1877, 1878, and 1890. In all, Alger wrote 103 books for juvenile readers including biographies of Daniel *Webster, James *Garfield, and Abraham *Lincoln, before his retirement in 1896.

A reform-minded Republican, Alger often criticized unfair or corrupt business practices, including stock-market manipulation and exploitive wages. He avoided factory settings; his heroes were newsboys, bootblacks, and clerks. Despite his modern reputation as an apologist for *capitalism, he was essentially a didactic moralist whose appeal was fundamentally nostalgic and whose melodramas affirmed the virtues of honesty, frugality, education, and filial piety.

[*See also* Gilded Age; Literature: Civil War to World War I; Literature, Popular.]

• Gary Scharnhorst with Jack Bales, *The Lost Life of Horatio Alger, Jr.*, 1985. Carol Nackenoff, *The Fictional Republic: Horatio Alger and American Political Discourse*, 1994.

—Gary Scharnhorst

ALI, MUHAMMAD (1942–), boxer and three-time heavyweight champion. Born as Cassius Clay in Louisville, Kentucky, Muhammad Ali first gained international attention when he won the gold medal in the light heavyweight division at the 1960 Rome Olympics. In 1964 he captured the heavyweight championship for the first time in a surprising sixth-round technical knockout of Sonny Liston. Shortly after that fight, Ali announced that he had joined the *Nation of Islam (Black Muslims), the black separatist religious group led by Elijah Muhammad. Ali's religious conversion provoked much controversy in America, especially among whites who abhorred his membership in a group that spoke of "white devils" and the superiority of the black race. He further infuriated many Americans when he refused induction into the armed forces in 1967, during the *Vietnam War, on religious grounds. His stand resulted in the revoking of his heavyweight crown and conviction for draft evasion. In 1970 the U.S. *Supreme Court unanimously reversed his conviction and Ali resumed his boxing career.

Over the next decade Ali fought several memorable bouts, including three legendary fights with Joe Frazier, a victory over George Foreman in a title bout in Zaire, two championship fights with Leon Spinks, and a humiliating defeat at the hands of Larry Holmes. In 1981 Ali retired from the ring after suffering a loss to the relatively unknown Trevor Berbick. After his retirement, Ali spent time raising money to combat Parkinson's syndrome for which he was diagnosed in 1984, making promotional appearances and doing missionary work for the Nation of Islam, and participating in various sports tributes and fundraisers.

[*See also* Boxing; Sports: Professional Sports.]

• Thomas Hauser, *Muhammad Ali: His Life and Times*, 1991. Elliot J. Gorn, *Muhammad Ali: The People's Champ*, 1995.

—David K. Wiggins

ALIEN AND SEDITION ACTS (1798). The term "Alien and Sedition Acts" refers to four controversial laws enacted by the Federalist-controlled Congress in 1798 in response to fears about imminent war with France and about the loyalty of pro-French Irish immigrants. The Alien Enemies Act empowered the president to restrain or expel any "alien enemy" immigrant from a nation with which the United States was at war; the Alien Act authorized expulsion of *any* alien, without a hearing, considered "dangerous to the peace and safety" of the United States; and the Naturalization Act extended to fourteen years (from five) the waiting time required for immigrants to become citizens. The passing of the war scare rendered the first measure meaningless; President John *Adams never invoked the second; and the third only encouraged many Irish immigrants, eager to vote for the Federalists' Jeffersonian-Republican opponents, to become citizens before the fourteen-year requirement went into effect.

The fourth of these measures, the Sedition Act, a national seditious libel law that was to expire automatically in 1800, targeted supporters of the Jeffersonian-Republican party by declaring it a crime to make defamatory statements about the government or the president. Although it permitted persons charged to plead truth as a defense and allowed juries to determine if a statement was actually seditious, these safeguards proved meaningless when Jeffersonian critics appeared before Federalist judges and juries in more than a dozen libel prosecutions.

The Alien and Sedition Acts deepened partisan political passions. While Federalists defended them as a measured, appropriate response to legitimate concerns about how disloyal aliens and licentious criticism might endanger the nation's safety, Jeffersonians claimed that all four laws exceeded the limited constitutional powers delegated to the national government. The Virginia and Kentucky Resolutions (1798–1779), secretly drafted by James *Madison and Thomas *Jefferson and passed by their respective state legislatures, contended that these acts upset the balance of power between the states and the national government and argued that the national union rested on a compact among the states. Jefferson's Kentucky Resolution even vaguely implied that an individual state could decide if a national law invaded its sovereign rights.

Jeffersonians also charged that the Sedition Act muzzled legitimate political dissent in violation of the First Amendment. Government rightly rested on the opinion of the citizenry, they argued, and public discussion could not proceed in the face of the kind of legal obstructions posed by libel prosecutions such as those conducted under the Sedition Act. The Alien and Sedition Acts rebounded against the Federalists. Prosecutions for seditious libel failed to silence their Jeffersonian critics, and Adams lost the presidency to Jefferson in 1800. A decade later, the Jeffersonian-Republicans dominated national politics, and the *Federalist party was moribund.

Although the political passions of the late 1790s soon cooled, the Alien and Sedition Acts episode raised issues that would reappear over the course of U.S. history, including the regulation of *immigration, determining the balance of power between the national and state governments, and drawing the constitutional limits of political dissent.

[*See also* Bill of Rights; Censorship; Early Republic, Era of the; Immigration Law; Nullification; Quasi-War with France; Sedition; States' Rights.]

• Norman Rosenberg, *Protecting the "Best Men": An Interpretive History of the Law of Libel*, 1986. Stanley Elkins and Eric McKitrick, *The Age of Federalism: The Early American Republic, 1788–1800*, 1993. Saul Cornell, *The Other Founders: Anti-Federalism and the Dissenting Tradition in America, 1788–1828*, 1999.

—Norman L. Rosenberg

ALLIANCE FOR PROGRESS. On 13 March 1961, President John F. *Kennedy announced the Alliance for Progress, an economic assistance program to promote political democracy, economic growth, and social progress in Latin America. The United States and Latin American nations formally agreed to the alliance at a conference held that August at Punta del Este, Uruguay. U.S. delegates promised that Latin America would receive over twenty billion dollars in public and private capital from the United States and international lending authorities during the 1960s. The money would arrive in the form of grants, loans, and direct private investments. When combined with an expected eighty billion dollars in internal investment, this new money was projected to stimulate an economic growth rate of not less than 2.5 percent a year. This economic growth, it was hoped, would facilitate significant improvements in employment, and in infant mortality, life expectancy, and literacy rates. In agreeing to the alliance, Latin American leaders pledged to work for equality and social justice by promoting agrarian reform and progressive income taxes.

The Kennedy administration developed this so-called *Marshall Plan for Latin America because it judged the region susceptible to social revolution and communism. Fidel Castro had transformed the Cuban Revolution into a strident anti-American movement and had allied his nation with the Soviet Union. U.S. officials feared that the lower classes of Latin America, mired in poverty and injustice, might follow similarly radical leaders.

Although the alliance helped raise outside capital, it failed to transform Latin America. During the 1960s, Latin American economies performed poorly, usually falling below the 2.5 percent target. The region witnessed few improvements in health, education, or welfare. Latin American societies remained unfair and authoritarian. Extraconstitutional changes of government repeatedly unsettled the region.

The Alliance for Progress fell short of its goals for several reasons. Latin America had formidable obstacles to change: elites resisted land reform, equitable tax systems, and social programs; new credits often brought greater indebtedness rather than growth. And the Marshall Plan experience served as a poor guide to solving the problems of a region that was far different from Western Europe. The United States also acted ambiguously, calling for democratic progress and social justice but worried that communists would take advantage of the instability caused by progressive change. Further, Washington provided wholehearted support only to those Latin American governments and organizations, like the military, that pursued fervent anticommunist policies.

[*See also* Cold War; Foreign Relations: U.S. Relations with Latin America; Vietnam War.]

• Jerome Levinson and Juan de Onís, *The Alliance That Lost Its Way: A Critical Report on the Alliance for Progress*, 1970. L. Ronald Scheman, ed., *The Alliance for Progress: A Retrospective*, 1988. Stephen G. Rabe, *The Most Dangerous Area in the World: John F. Kennedy Confronts Communist Revolution in Latin America*, 1999.

—Stephen G. Rabe

ALMS HOUSES. From the early nineteenth century to the *New Deal Era, alms houses dominated the structure of public welfare in America. Once the cutting edge of public policy, by the early twentieth century alms houses (also known as poorhouses) had drifted into the backwaters of social policy. Nonetheless, they still inspired dread among the poor, who used them only as refuges of last resort.

In the *Colonial Era, alms houses were one of four ways that public authorities helped persons who could not support themselves. (Authorities also auctioned the care of the poor to the lowest bidder; contracted their care to private individuals; and gave them small amounts of food, fuel, or cash—a practice known as outdoor relief.) Although alms houses existed in a few large cities as early as the seventeenth century, their numbers became significant only in the early nineteenth century when state legislatures required, encouraged, or permitted county governments to construct them. Two influential legislative documents encouraging the spread of alms houses were the Quincy Report (1821) in Massachusetts and the Yates Report (1824) in New York.

The early nineteenth-century founding of many novel institutions—alms houses, mental hospitals, reformatories, and penitentiaries, for instance—reflected a new faith in the power of formal institutions to reform individuals and ameliorate social problems. In an era of *urbanization and *immigration, alms houses were thought the least expensive and most effective way to care for the poor. Alms houses would benefit from economies of scale, inmates could be made to earn part of their support, and the threat of institutionalization would deter persons from asking for help.

Alms houses failed to reach any of their goals, and they never eliminated outdoor relief, which continued to serve many more people than alms houses. From the start, alms houses remained crippled by a contradiction in goals between deterrence and compassion. They sought simultaneously to deter poor persons from asking for relief and to provide them with humanitarian care. Alms houses were undercut, too, by insufficient funds, the lack of capable staff, and unrealistic expectations about the capacity of inmates to work. Alms houses proved much more expensive than predicted—far more costly than outdoor relief—and conditions within them deteriorated badly.

Alms house inmates proved a varied lot. At first, families frequently entered together, but with the great Irish immigration of the 1830s and 1840s, alms houses more often served as refuges for unattached or widowed persons, men more than women. Young men temporarily out of work used them as short-term refuges; poor, single women turned to them as maternity homes; and the destitute elderly ended their lives in alms houses. Throughout the nineteenth century, state governments removed special categories of inmates from alms houses. First came the sick and mentally ill, then, starting in the 1870s, children. By the early twentieth century, most short-term residents, mainly young men, also were gone. Thus, by *World War I most alms houses had acquired their present identity as public old-age homes.

[*See also* Antebellum Era; Early Republic, Era of the; Irish Americans; Mental Health Institutions; Orphanages; Poverty; Prisons and Penitentiaries.]

• David J. Rothman, ed., *The Almshouse Experience: Collected Reports*, 1971. Michael B. Katz, *In the Shadow of the Poorhouse: A Social History of Welfare in America*, 10th anniversary ed., 1996.

—Michael B. Katz

ALZHEIMER'S DISEASE, a progressive neural disorder that gradually degrades the cognitive system and culminates in death. Once considered a rare *disease of middle age, Alzheimer's came to be viewed in the 1970s as a major *public-health problem in the United States, estimated to be the fourth or fifth leading cause of death in those over sixty-five.

Alois Alzheimer of Munich first described the disease in 1906, after dissecting the brain of a woman who had died in her fifties from a progressive dementia and observing cortical atrophy, cellular plaques, and neurofribrillary "tangles." Other physicians who verified these lesions in similar patients recognized the disease as a cause of dementia and premature senility. Nevertheless, for decades thereafter, most physicians continued to believe that memory loss and functional deterioration in the elderly were characteristic of the normal aging process. However, electron-microscopic studies at Albert Einstein College of Medicine, by Robert Terry in the 1960s and Robert Katzman in the 1970s, identified Alzheimer's plaques and tangles in the brains of 50 to 60 percent of all elderly patients suffering from progressive dementia. In a brief but influential editorial in the *Archives of Neurology* in April 1976,

Katzman argued that senility should be recognized not as normal aging, but as an organic disease that would significantly impact American families financially and emotionally as more of the population lived past the age of seventy.

In 1977, Katzman and Terry wrote to Donald Tower, director of the National Institute of Neurological and Communicative Disorders and Stroke (NINCDS), explaining the need for further research on Alzheimer's disease. Tower collaborated with Robert Butler, director of the newly created National Institute on Aging (NIA), collaborated with staff of the National Institute of Mental Health in sponsoring a major Alzheimer's conference, which presented current research findings and encouraged scientists to develop new projects. Establishing a Neurobiology on Aging program within the NIA in 1977, Butler and others successfully promoted the funding and expansion of Alzheimer's research. The Health Research Services Act of 1985 established ten Centers of Excellence across the country to define diagnostic standards for the disease and to coordinate basic, clinical, and social research projects. By 1993, federal grant support for Alzheimer's research had grown from less than $5 million to more than $300 million a year.

Butler, Tower, and Katzman sought grassroots support from lay groups across the country, formed by relatives and caregivers of Alzheimer's patients. Local groups met in Washington, DC, in 1979 to organize the Alzheimer's Disease and Related Disorders Association (ADRDA). In the years that followed, ADRDA lobbied actively for federal research funding and significantly increased public interest in and concern about Alzheimer's disease.

Although the cause of Alzheimer's disease remains unknown, some researchers have hypothesized that chemical changes in certain proteins found in the brain, perhaps the result of genetic mutations or brain injury, may be the keys to its etiology. Despite significant research progress, Alzheimer's disease remains a tragic scourge and public-health challenge, as families watch beloved relatives deteriorate, while struggling to find the resources for their care.

• Patrick Fox, "From Senility to Alzheimer's Disease: The Rise of the Alzheimer's Disease Movement," *Milbank Quarterly* 67 (1989): 58–102. Robert Katzman, "Current Research on Alzheimer's Disease in a Historical Perspective," in *Alzheimer's Disease: Causes, Diagnosis, Treatment, and Care*, eds. Zaven S. Khachaturian and Teresa Radebaugh, 1996, pp. 15–29.

—Marcia Meldrum

AMANA COMMUNITY. *See* Utopian and Communitarian Movements.

AMERICA FIRST. When Germany invaded Poland in September 1939, thereby unleashing *World War II, President Franklin Delano *Roosevelt sought to aid the Allies by such means as cash-and-carry (September 1939) and the exchange of fifty American destroyers for eight British bases in the Western hemisphere (September 1940). In the summer of 1940, amid rumors of increased shipments of American ships, tanks, and aircraft to Britain, Yale law student R. Douglas Stuart Jr. organized the Emergency Committee to Defend America First, which late in August renamed itself the America First Committee (AFC). The AFC was the primary "isolationist" organization that led opposition to Roosevelt's interventionist measures during 1940 and 1941.

Chaired by Sears Roebuck executive Robert E. Wood, the AFC included such diverse members as journalist John T. Flynn, retired diplomat William R. Castle, former New Dealer Hugh Johnson, advertising executive Chester Bowles, textile manufacturer William H. Regnery, and Chicago financier Sterling Morton. Stuart became executive secretary. Aviator Charles *Lindbergh, who joined the AFC national committee in April 1941, was its chief drawing card, though he dealt the committee a severe blow that September by publicly claiming that Jews as a group sought full-scale American participation in the war. A staff composed of socialists, pacifists, and liberals prepared its position papers. At its peak in 1941, the AFC had 450 chapters, a membership of 850,000, and an income of $370,000 donated by 25,000 contributors. Huge AFC rallies featured such speakers as Lindbergh, Flynn, Senator Burton K. Wheeler (Dem.–MT), Senator Gerald P. Nye (Rep.–ND), Representative Hamilton Fish (Rep.–NY), and socialist leader Norman *Thomas. Although unable to defeat Roosevelt on any specific issue, the AFC undoubtedly caused him to be more circumspect on such matters as extending terms for draftees and convoying British vessels. The AFC disbanded after Japan's attack on *Pearl Harbor in December 1941.

[*See also* Isolationism.]

• Wayne S. Cole, *America First: The Battle against Intervention, 1940–1941*, 1953. Justus D. Doenecke, ed., *In Danger Undaunted: The Anti-Interventionist Movement as Revealed in the Papers of the America First Committee*, 1990.

—Justus D. Doenecke

AMERICAN RED CROSS. *See* Red Cross, American.

AMERICAN ANTI-SLAVERY SOCIETY. The American Anti-Slavery Society (AASS) was founded in 1833 by a small group of radicals calling for the immediate abolition of *slavery. The leading spirit was William Lloyd *Garrison, whose interaction with black abolitionists inspired him to reject colonization as a means of eradicating slavery. The founders of the AASS did not condone a violent overthrow of the slave system, but believed that moral suasion would convince slaveholders of its evils.

Abolitionists soon came to disagree over the necessity of violence, the position of women in the movement, and the role of politics and organized religion in the *antislavery cause. These divisions reached a critical point in 1839 when a majority in the AASS voted to allow women to serve as delegates to antislavery conventions. Led by Lewis Tappan, opponents of Garrison's approach to abolitionism, with its exclusive emphasis on moral suasion and its interest in other reforms as well as antislavery, formed a new organization, the American and Foreign Anti-Slavery Society, in 1840.

The violence of the 1850s caused many AASS members to rethink their commitment to moral suasion. Frederick *Douglass rejected Garrisonian abolitionism in favor of political abolitionism. By the eve of the *Civil War, Garrison and others endorsed the *Republican party and supported John *Brown's raid. While some Garrisonians continued to oppose violence, most endorsed the war as a means to end slavery.

Garrison retired in 1865 after ratification of the Thirteenth Amendment ended slavery, but Wendell Phillips, Sallie Holley, and others maintained the AASS. As the interests of abolitionists fragmented, the AASS could no longer sustain its activities or newspaper, the *National Anti-Slavery Standard*, and it disbanded in 1870 after the *Fifteenth Amendment extended the franchise to freedmen. The AASS had witnessed the abolition of slavery, but had not been directly instrumental in its demise. Nevertheless, its members recognized that *racism and the exploitation of black labor remained problems, and their principal legacy was a strong commitment to racial equality.

[*See also* Antebellum Era; Civil War: Causes; Colonization Movement, African; Peace Movements; Women's Rights Movements.]

• Benjamin Quarles, *Black Abolitionists*, 1991. Jean Fagan Yellin and John C. Van Horne, eds., *The Abolitionist Sisterhood: Women's Political Culture in Antebellum America*, 1994.

—Carol Faulkner

AMERICAN ASSOCIATION FOR THE ADVANCEMENT OF SCIENCE. The American Association for the Advancement of Science (AAAS) was founded in 1848 to facilitate communication among scientists and to establish an authoritative public presence for science in the larger community.

Growing out of the Association of American Geologists and Naturalists (1840), the early AAAS drew inspiration from the British Association for the Advancement of Science (1832). Its peripatetic annual meetings and published *Proceedings* soon made it the most distinguished national scientific organization. Leadership came from such eminent scientists as Joseph *Henry of the *Smithsonian Institution, Alexander Dallas Bache of the U.S. Coast Survey, William Barton Rogers of the Massachusetts Institute of Technology, and Louis *Agassiz of Harvard University, all of whom shared a commitment to positioning scientific research in the foreground of public culture.

The growing sectional crisis and other factors led to a decline in membership and the cancellation of the 1861 meeting. The creation of the *National Academy of Sciences (1863) and the growth of specialized scientific organizations, such as the American Chemical Society (1874), made postwar recovery difficult. Restructured and incorporated in the 1870s, the AAAS increased its membership and created a research fund. The psychologist James McKeen Cattell merged his journal *Science* into the AAAS in 1900 and in other aspects revitalized the organization. In 1907 the Smithsonian Institution provided office space and in 1945 the AAAS acquired its own headquarters in *Washington, D.C. In Cattell's vision, the elitist National Academy of Sciences would be the upper house of American science, while the AAAS would serve as the lower house, accessible to all scientists and responsive to the public. In the 1920s, to create a united scientific front on matters of mutual concern, the AAAS encouraged the affiliation of specialized societies. During the late twentieth century the AAAS advocated scientific education, encouraged racial and gender diversity in the scientific community, and addressed issues of public policy and scientific ethics.

[*See also* Coast and Geodedic Survey, U.S.; Science: Revolutionary War to World War I; Science: From 1914 to 1945; Science: Since 1945.]

• Robert H. Kargon, *The Maturing of American Science: A Portrait of Science in Public Life Drawn from the Presidential Addresses of the American Association for the Advancement of Science*, 1974. Sally Gregory Kohlstedt, Michael A. Sokal, and Bruce V. Lewenstein, *The Establishment of Science in America: 150 Years of the American Association for the Advancement of Science*, 1999.

—Sally Gregory Kohlstedt

AMERICAN ASSOCIATION OF RETIRED PERSONS (AARP). The American Association of Retired Persons arose out of an effort by a prominent Los Angeles high school principal to improve the status of retired school teachers. Dr. Ethel Percy Andrus founded the National Retired Teachers Association (NRTA) in 1947 to lobby for *health-insurance coverage and increases in state pensions for retired educators. NRTA's membership, twenty thousand in 1955, soared after Andrus arranged with Leonard Davis, an insurance agent, to offer NRTA members insurance coverage; the pair established AARP so others might be eligible. Chartered in 1958, NRTA–AARP retained separate boards of directors but shared office space and staff.

Membership grew from 150,000 to 1,000,000 between 1959 and 1969. By 1982, the American Association of Retired Persons had outgrown its parent organization, and NRTA became a division within AARP. More than 33 million members belonged to AARP by the mid-1990s, making it, after the Roman Catholic Church, the nation's second largest voluntary association.

The AARP offers members a variety of services, from travel advice and discounts on mail-order prescriptions to auto, life, and *insurance programs. Concern over its ties to Leonard Davis's Colonial Penn Insurance Company in the late 1970s led AARP to choose other underwriters for its insurance plans. By the end of the twentieth century, AARP had become a key voice for older Americans in Washington, lobbying against age discrimination and for health-care reform. Its influence, however, was mixed, as it experienced difficulty in mobilizing its membership in a consistent manner.

• David D. Van Tassel and Jimmy Elaine Wilkinson Meyer, eds., *U.S. Aging Policy Interest Groups*, 1992. Henry J. Pratt, *Gray Agendas: Interest Groups and Public Pensions in Canada, Britain and the United States*, 1993.

—W. Andrew Achenbaum

AMERICAN ASSOCIATION OF UNIVERSITY PROFESSORS (AAUP). The late nineteenth-century growth of the university and of academic specialization triggered notable clashes between academics and administrators. William Graham Sumner's controversial use of Herbert Spencer's *The Study of Sociology* at Yale in the late 1870s, the economist Richard T. Ely's 1894 quarrel with the University of Wisconsin regents over his support for labor *strikes and boycotts, and Stanford University's dismissal of the economist Edward Ross in 1900 under pressure from Mrs. Leland Stanford underscored the threats facing *academic freedom. In 1915, after the outbreak of *World War I, John *Dewey of Columbia University and the historian Arthur O. Lovejoy of Johns Hopkins University called a meeting at Columbia of academics concerned about academic freedom. Those attending founded the AAUP, the first professional organization for protecting academic freedom and tenure, with Dewey as first president. The organization's inaugural statement, issued by a committee of well-known academics, defended the freedom of inquiry and research, of teaching, and of academics' public statements and actions.

Academic freedom remained the association's cornerstone principle, reflecting the belief that scholarly excellence depends on unfettered intellectual inquiry. To this end, the organization developed guidelines for tenure procedures and due-process requirements in personnel cases, including peer review of charges prior to dismissal. Through various committees, the AAUP compiled academic statistics, investigated complaints of unfair dismissal, and censured institutions that violated its standards. In the 1990s it also targeted the erosion of tenure through the increasing use of adjunct and part-time faculty, arguing that job security is essential to true academic freedom. With a $4 million budget in 1999, the AAUP had some 45,000 members organized in thirty state associations and some five hundred local chapters.

[*See also* Beard, Charles A.; Civil Liberties; Education: Collegiate Education; Education: Rise of the University; Education: Education in Contemporary America; Professionalization.]

• Walter P. Metzger, "Origins of the Association," *AAUP Bulletin* 51.3 (1965): 229–37. Louis Joughin, ed., *Academic Freedom and Tenure: A Handbook of the American Association of University Professors*, 1969.

—Carole J. Trone and William J. Reese

AMERICAN ASSOCIATION OF UNIVERSITY WOMEN (AAUW). In 1881, seventeen women met at the Massachusetts Institute of Technology at the invitation of Marion Talbot, a Boston University graduate, and her mother, also college educated, and formed the Association of Collegiate Alumnae, forerunner of the AAUW. In the 1890s, the new organization established graduate fellowships to encourage women to pursue science careers. By the 1920s, it pursued equity in education, *equality for women, and *internationalism. During *World War II, led by Helen C. White of the University of Wisconsin, AAUW women performed community leadership and public service. In the *Cold War, however, AAUW's progressive stance on women's rights, international cooperation, and educational reform brought charges of disloyalty. Nonetheless, the AAUW Educational Foundation (1955) expanded the organization's fellowship program; by 1967, nearly 100 fellowships were awarded annually from an endowment of some $3.5 million.

The post–1970 women's movement brought significant changes. Active in Washington on women's and family issues, the AAUW endorsed the *Equal Rights Amendment and reproductive rights in 1971, and joined the coalition that promoted Title IX of the Education Act of 1972, mandating gender equity in higher-education athletic programs. *The AAUW Report: How Schools Shortchange Girls* (1992) and *Hostile Hallways: The AAUW Survey on Sexual Harassment in America's Schools* (1994), based on extensive research, showed the prevalence of gender bias in public schools and its link to adolescent girls' drop in self-esteem, and proposed strategies for improvement. While never abandoning its initial goals, the AAUW has steadily expanded its agenda, from supporting graduate education for women to addressing the needs of public school girls and young women.

[*See also* Education: Rise of the University; Feminism; Women's Rights Movements.]

• Marion Talbot and Lois Kimball Mathews Rosenberry, *The History of the American Association of University Women, 1881–1931*, 1931. Susan Levine, *Degrees of Equality: The American Association of University Women and the Challenge of Twentiety Century Feminism*, 1995.

—Gretchen Kreuter

AMERICAN BANKERS' ASSOCIATION (ABA). Organized at a meeting of bankers in Saratoga Springs, New York, in 1875, the American Bankers' Association is one of the oldest national trade associations, engaged in lobbying, public relations, and educational programs. Historically, the association has attempted to present a unified voice for a diverse financial industry comprising national banks, state banks, savings banks, private banks, and trust companies. The ABA coordinates the activities of fifty state banking associations. By the 1950s about 98 percent of American banks belonged to the ABA.

In its early days the association lobbied for resumption of specie payment on U.S. currency and repeal of *Civil War taxes on bank deposits and checks. The early ABA also worked to develop uniform and efficient local banking practices. After the financial panics of 1893 and 1907, the ABA joined in the call for a more flexible money supply controlled by a central bank and based on commercial borrowing. Although the *Federal Reserve Act of 1913 differed somewhat from these proposals, the ABA found much to praise in the new system.

During the Great Depression and *World War II, the ABA approved of a larger role for the federal government in the creation of financial credit for industry and agriculture. After initial opposition, it also supported the federal guarantee of bank deposits provided for by the 1933 act creating the Federal Deposit Insurance Corporation. After the emergency was over, however, the ABA demanded a reduction in government spending and a less active federal role in credit expansion. The association criticized government regulations that favored its rivals, the savings and loan institutions and credit unions. When brokerage firms and credit card companies in the 1970s offered checking and savings accounts to the public, the ABA lobbied for deregulation that would allow banks to compete in a full range of financial services. In 1996 the association contributed about $1.6 million to election campaigns to assure that its position on issues affecting banking would be heard.

[*See also* Banking and Finance; Depressions, Economic; Gold Standard.]

• Wilbert M. Schneider, *The American Bankers' Association, Its Past and Present*, 1956. Benjamin Joseph Klebaner, *American Commercial Banking: A History*, 1990.

—Norman Nordhauser

AMERICAN BAR ASSOCIATION. The American Bar Association (ABA) was founded in 1878 in Saratoga Springs, New York, as a voluntary, national organization of the *legal profession. Its initial membership totaled 289 lawyers, and its purposes included advancing *jurisprudence, elevating professional standards, promoting the administration of justice and uniformity of law, improving legal education, and facilitating exchanges among lawyers. The principal founder was Simeon Eben Baldwin, a distinguished attorney from New Haven, Connecticut, who served as a state supreme court justice and as governor of Connecticut. The ABA's early accomplishments included proposing intermediate courts of appeal, which relieved the *Supreme Court of the United States of a long backlog of cases, and creating the National Conference of Commissioners on Uniform State Laws.

During the early decades of the twentieth century, the ABA expanded its membership, adopted codes of ethics for lawyers and judges, established standards for professional legal education, promoted the independence of the judiciary, and, in 1936, adopted a new constitution making it a more representative organization. ABA presidents during these years included Elihu Root, secretary of war under President Theodore *Roosevelt; President William Howard *Taft; and Charles Evans *Hughes.

Experiencing rapid growth in the mid-1900s, the ABA addressed issues ranging from President Franklin Delano *Roosevelt's controversial Supreme Court reorganization plan to the *civil rights movement. During this time, the ABA also began reviewing the qualifications of federal judicial nominees and supporting newly created federal legal-services programs. Robert G. Story (executive trial counsel at the Nuremberg war crimes trials), and Supreme Court Justice Lewis F. Powell were among the ABA presidents of this era.

In the later twentieth century, the ABA functioned as a strong advocate for the rule of law at home and abroad, and ABA representatives provided free legal assistance to emerging democracies in central and eastern Europe. During the *Watergate controversy, the ABA emphasized the supremacy of the law, even in cases involving the nation's highest public officials. Other critical issues addressed during this period included tort reform, alternative means of dispute resolution, and judicial independence. ABA presidents in these years included Leon Jaworski and Lawrence Walsh, special prosecutors in the *Watergate and *Iran-Contra Affair investigations, respectively, and Roberta Cooper Ramo, the first woman to head the organization. In 1998, the ABA elected Robert Grey as the first African American to chair its policy-making body, the House of Delegates. As the twentieth century ended, the ABA's membership approached 400,000.

• James Grafton Rogers, *American Bar Leaders: Biographies of Presidents of the American Bar Association, 1878–1928*, 1932. Gerald Carson, *A Good Day at Saratoga*, 1978.

—Norman Gross

AMERICAN CIVIL LIBERTIES UNION (ACLU), a nonprofit membership association devoted to the defense of individual rights under the U.S. *Constitution. Founded in 1920 as a successor to the National Civil Liberties Bureau, which defended the rights of dissidents and conscientious objectors during *World War I, the ACLU established a reputation as the defender of unpopular causes. Its most famous early case involved the defense of John T. Scopes, who was tried in 1925 for violating a Tennessee law prohibiting the teaching of the theory of *evolution in public schools. During *World War II, the ACLU challenged the federal government's program of placing Japanese Americans in internment camps. In the 1970s, the organization successfully defended the right of a domestic Nazi group to hold a demonstration in the heavily Jewish community of Skokie, Illinois—a controversial case that cost it some support.

Molded by Roger Baldwin, the organization's executive director from 1920 to 1950, the ACLU participated in an estimated 80 percent of the landmark cases on individual rights decided by the U.S. *Supreme Court. The ACLU's agenda includes First Amendment rights of free speech and religious liberty, due process of law, equal protection of the law, and the right to privacy. The ACLU has traditionally relied on volunteer attorneys representing clients without charge. Beginning in the late 1960s, however, it began to employ full-time staff attorneys to handle cases in specialized areas such as prisoners' rights. The organization's membership grew from about 1,000 in 1920 to over 275,000 in the 1990s. The ACLU maintains a national office in *New York City, a legislative office in *Washington, D.C., and affiliate chapters in every state.

[*See also* Bill of Rights; Civil Liberties; Conscientious Objection; Incarceration of Japanese Americans; Scopes Trial.]

• Samuel Walker, *In Defense of American Liberties: A History of the ACLU*, 1990.

—Samuel Walker

AMERICAN COLONIZATION SOCIETY. *See* Colonization Movement, African.

AMERICAN DILEMMA, AN (1944). Gunnar Myrdal's *An American Dilemma: The Negro Problem and Modern Democracy* ranks among the most important studies of American race relations. The "American Negro Problem," Myrdal argued, lay not in *African Americans' imagined inferiority, but in white Americans' inability to reconcile the contradiction between a generalized belief in *equality and a powerful "group prejudice" against blacks. For twenty years, this two-volume work represented the conventional wisdom of the American political establishment about the nation's "race problem." It is cited prominently in **Brown* v. *Board of Education*, the U.S. *Supreme Court's 1954 decision outlawing racial *segregation in public education.

The impact of *An American Dilemma* was enhanced by the sponsorship of the Carnegie Foundation, which in 1938 had commissioned Myrdal, a distinguished Swedish sociologist, to conduct a study of racial issues in America. Along with his scholarly reputation, Myrdal's most important qualification was that, like Alexis de Tocqueville a century earlier, he was an outsider who could presumably analyze American race relations with greater objectivity than an American could.

After 1964, as the civil rights and Black Power movements gained strength, some critics came to agree with the African American writer Ralph *Ellison that Myrdal's analysis had been flawed. In their view, *An American Dilemma* considered African Americans primarily in their role as the victims of white racism rather than as full-fledged participants in the creation of American culture.

[*See also* African Americans; Black Nationalism; Civil Rights Movement; *Democracy in America*; Racism; Social Science; World War II.]

• David W. Southern, *Gunnar Myrdal and Black-White Relations: The Use and Abuse of "An American Dilemma," 1944–1969*, 1987. Walter A. Jackson, *Gunnar Myrdal and America's Conscience: Social Engineering and Racial Liberalism, 1938–1987*, 1990.

—Ben Keppel

AMERICAN FARM BUREAU FEDERATION. The American Farm Bureau Federation promotes the economic and educational interests of farmers. Coordinating a network of state and county bureaus, the Farm Bureau has helped shape American agricultural practices and policies since its formation in 1919. With about four million members, it is the nation's largest general farm organization. The most active support comes from the *Middle West, where many of its original members resided. The organization's policies are generally conservative.

The Farm Bureau developed alongside the federal government's county *agricultural education and extension system in the 1920s and 1930s. Both institutions sought to bring the latest scientific and technical advances to American agricultural producers. In many areas the bureau underwrote the cost of county extension agents who demonstrated new methods to farmers. This direct cooperation between the Farm Bureau and the government was strongest in the 1930s under the *New Deal Era's *Agricultural Adjustment Administration. Critics charged that this arrangement unfairly benefited only "modern," capital-intensive farmers. The Farm Bureau responded that it was aiding the work and educational efforts of land-grant colleges and state *agricultural experiment stations for the benefit of all farmers. While continuing to support the government's farmer education programs, the federation from the early 1940s on promoted its own educational efforts.

The federation also has acted as a major lobbying organization for agricultural legislation. During the Great Depression and the New Deal it developed or supported farm legislation that emphasized soil and water conservation, rural electrification, price supports, protective tariffs, and acreage-control regulations. After *World War II the Farm Bureau recommended measures to reduce farmers' dependence on federal programs and to eliminate production quotas—a position rooted in its traditional belief in minimal government interference and control in a free-market agricultural economy.

The American Farm Bureau Federation has historically worked to open or expand markets for farm products as the best way to relieve farmers' economic problems, maintain high demand for American agricultural goods, and reduce crop surpluses. For many years the federation has urged local farmers to form marketing cooperatives to sell their products and to operate supply cooperatives, such as those for fuel or electricity, to reduce costs. The Farm Bureau also promotes farm safety and funds research for new uses of farm products.

[*See also* Agriculture: Since 1920.]

• Grant McConnell, *The Decline of Agrarian Democracy*, 1953. Christiana McFadyen Campbell, *The Farm Bureau: A Study of the Making of National Farm Policy 1933–40*, 1962.

—Cameron L. Saffell

AMERICAN FEDERATION OF LABOR. Formed in 1886 as an umbrella organization to represent craft unions, the American Federation of Labor (AFL) emphasized practical "bread and butter" unionism, promoted the integity of its affiliates, and upheld the sanctity of union contracts. Apart from one two-year interval (1893–1895), Samuel *Gompers served as president from 1886 to 1924. Early on, its leaders mediated jurisdictional conflicts among affiliates and promoted legislation considered beneficial to organized labor, including *immigration restriction. It also sought to establish powerful city and state federations.

The burgeoning strength of its member unions in the early twentieth century created a vibrant AFL and solidified trade union power. The Woodrow *Wilson presidential administration bestowed critical recognition on the AFL by establishing a separate Department of Labor in 1913. An alliance between labor and the *Democratic party took shape during *World War I when the administration created a National War Labor Board empowered to encourage trade union recognition. A grateful Gompers worked tirelessly for Wilson's war programs, promoting the American Alliance for Labor and Democracy and attacking more radical labor organizations. Stimulated by the AFL's alliance with the administration, trade union membership expanded from 1,562,000 in 1910 to 4,125,000 in 1919. The war's end brought an employer backlash, however, and subsequent unsympathetic Republican administrations weakened the AFL still more.

The Great Depression of the 1930s brought further strains as the industrial unions within the AFL's ranks, most notably John L. *Lewis's United Mine Workers of America, challenged it to organize mass-production workers. Refusing to devote scarce resources to a risky endeavor, the more cautious members of the AFL executive board balked. This strategy backfired in 1938 when eleven industrial unions created the rival *Congress of Industrial Organizations (CIO).

Although the AFL had initially failed to organize the millions of nonunion workers seeking representation rights, it competed aggressively for new members throughout *World War II and the postwar years, growing more rapidly than the CIO. Diluting their craft principles, AFL affiliates accepted masses of new members regardless of skill or job title. By the mid–1950s the AFL had 50 percent more members that the CIO (9 million to 6 million). In 1952 the incumbent presidents of the two rival labor organizations died, clearing the way for a merger. The merged AFL-CIO held its first convention in December 1955.

[*See also* Federal Government, Executive Branch: Other Departments (Department of Labor); Gilded Age; Industrialization; Labor Movements; New Deal Era, The.]

• Philip Taft, *The A.F.L.*, 2 vols., 1957–1959.

—Colin J. Davis

AMERICAN FRIENDS SERVICE COMMITTEE, relief organization seeking to implement the Quaker peace testimony. Many American Quaker Yearly Meetings joined in 1917 to create the American Friends Service Committee (AFSC) as a place for conscientious objectors to war to demonstrate patriotism and love of God by engaging in relief and reconstruction. During *World War I, the AFSC sent to France 550 young men and 50 women to join the ongoing relief work of English Quakers.

The Service Committee continues to operate under a pattern developed before 1920. The organization is not a missionary body and does not proselytize. Those who receive aid are not subjected to religious or political tests. Originally most staff were Quakers but in the 1960s the AFSC sought to recruit personnel of similar ethnic background to those it sought to help, and by the 1990s less than 15 percent were members of the *Society of Friends. Most funding has always come from non-Quaker sources. Those Friends who are fundamentalist or Conservative evangelicals oppose its sole emphasis upon material improvements. From its inception, the AFSC has also faced criticism from political conservatives who opposed its *pacifism and efforts for domestic social reform.

By 1920 the AFSC had supervised the feeding of one million German children and undertaken relief projects in Poland, Serbia, and Russia. In its first domestic program during the 1920s, the AFSC began feeding children of striking coal miners. In the 1930s it promoted a homestead program for unemployed coal miners. Programs on behalf of *civil rights and migrant workers have been a continuing theme. Peace education, another major domestic program, has taken many forms, including work camps, news releases, conferences, and demonstrations. After *World War II, the AFSC commissioned groups of experts to produce a series of books with policy recommendations on major issues of foreign and domestic policy.

The AFSC has consistently criticized U.S. military policies and supported disarmament and international organizations. In World War II, it raised money for and ran Civilian Public Service camps for conscientious objectors. Until the 1940s the AFSC worked closely with the government; indeed, its chief administrator, Clarence Pickett, was a friend of Eleanor *Roosevelt. After experiencing official restrictions during World War II and red-baiting during the *Cold War, the AFSC drew back from close governmental cooperation. The AFSC opposed American military intervention in all Cold War conflicts and sought to foster cultural contacts with peace groups in the U.S.S.R. During the *Vietnam War, it disobeyed a U.S. embargo and sent medical supplies to North Vietnam, worked with wounded civilians and refugees in South Vietnam, and joined with other peace groups in antiwar demonstrations. The AFSC has sought incremental changes by improving the lives of the poor and oppressed through nonviolent social change.

[*See also* Civil Rights Movement; Conscientious Objection; Philanthropy and Philanthropic Foundations.]

• The archives of the AFSC are at its headquarters in Philadelphia, Pa. John Forbes, *The Quaker Star under Seven Flags, 1917–1927*, 1962. J. William Frost, " 'Our Deeds Carry Our Message': The Early History of the American Friends Service Committee," *Quaker History* 81 (Spring 1992): 1–51.

—J. William Frost

AMERICAN INDEPENDENT PARTY. *See* Wallace, George C.

AMERICAN INDIAN MOVEMENT. Of the various forms of ethnic and racial nationalism in the 1960s and 1970s, the American Indian Movement (AIM) emerged as the best-known "Red Power" organization. AIM got its start in 1968 when charges of police brutality in Indian neighborhoods in Minneapolis led Chippewas Dennis Banks and George Mitchell to assemble "red patrols" to follow police and witness arrests.

AIM soon evolved into a national group patterned after the *Black Panthers, with chapters appearing in many cities. Especially popular among urban Indians, it quickly became a powerful force in the politics of many reservations as well. Members styled themselves as traditional warriors but drew on tactics of the larger *civil rights movement. Russell Means, an Oglala Sioux, became AIM's principal spokesperson by staging attention-grabbing actions, such as the 1972 demonstrations in Gordon, Nebraska, to protest the murder of Raymond Yellow Thunder, and the Trail of Broken Treaties caravan that same year, which concluded in a six-day occupation of the *Bureau of Indian Affairs (BIA) offices in *Washington, D.C. In 1973, Means was involved in AIM's dramatic seventy-one–day siege of the village of Wounded Knee Creek, South Dakota, site of an 1890 massacre of Indians, as well as a fracas between AIM members and police in the Custer County, South Dakota, courthouse. In 1975, armed AIM members took over an electronics factory on the Navajo reservation.

By the late 1970s, AIM's popularity was fading as its militant, sometimes violent tactics became increasingly controversial. The government cracked down, imprisoning key leaders, and internal dissension split the ranks. Nonetheless, AIM's long-term influence far surpassed its short lifespan. AIM not only contributed to a sense of pan-Indian unity and to pride in Indian identity and heritage, but also drew national attention to Indian issues.

[*See also* Indian History and Culture: Since 1950; Sixties, The; Wounded Knee Tragedy.]

• Peter Matthiessen, *In the Spirit of Crazy Horse*, 1991.

—Larry Burt

AMERICANIZATION MOVEMENT. The effort to transform immigrants into patriotic citizens began with the nation's founding, but peaked in the late nineteenth and early twentieth centuries. Initially, Americans generally assumed that immigrants, most of whom came from Protestant northern and western Europe, would easily be absorbed into the population. By the 1880s, however, as Catholics and Jews from southern and eastern Europe arrived in great numbers, civic, religious, and settlement workers tried by various means to assimilate these "new immigrants." Education took on new importance, both for children and adults. Night schools offered English and civics classes, and industries often required that their foreign-born workers attend.

The outbreak of *World War I in 1914 accelerated nativism and fears of subversion. Frances Kellor and the Committee for Immigrants in America established immigrant-education programs within the federal Bureau of Education and organized National Americanization Day on 4 July 1915. Later, the National Americanization Committee launched campaigns linking naturalization and military preparedness. Its mottoes—"American First," "100 percent Americanism," and "English First"—underscored the movement's nativist cast. The federal Bureau of Education, the Immigration and Naturalization Service, the General Federation of Women's Clubs, and the U.S. *Chambers of Commerce joined forces for Americanization work. Although women far outnumbered men as Americanization teachers, most efforts targeted men; programs for women emphasized child-rearing and domesticity rather than citizenship.

After the war, the fear of Bolshevism fueled the movement. Yet it lacked a core. No federal agency had the power to institute the kind of programs favored by the proponents of Americanization. Moreover, most recent immigrants worked in industries where their introduction to American life, coming through unions and leisure activities, often differed from the principles taught in civic classes. After the patriotic frenzy of the 1919 Red Scare, many native-born Americans concluded that Americanization could not transform undesirable aliens. They focused instead on immigrant restriction, a movement that led to the restrictive and discriminatory Immigration Act of 1924.

[*See also* Anticommunism; Education: The Public School Movement; Immigration; Immigration Law; Nativist Movement; Settlement Houses.]

• John F. McClymer, "The Americanization Movement and the Education of the Foreign Born," in *American Education and the European Immigrant: 1840–1940*, ed. Bernard J. Weiss, 1982, pp. 96–116. Ellen Fitzpatrick, *Endless Crusade: Women Social Scientists and Progressive Reform*, 1990. James R. Barrett, "Americanization from the Bottom Up: Immigration and the Remaking of the Working Class in the United States, 1880–1930," *Journal of American History* 79 (December 1992): 996–1020.

—Judith R. Raftery

AMERICAN LEAGUE. *See* Baseball.

AMERICAN LEGION. The American Legion, an organization open to all military war-time veterans, was founded in 1919 by a handful of *World War I officers, including Theodore Roosevelt Jr. Within a year, the organization boasted 840,000 former officers and enlisted men—mostly middle-class whites—and was well on its way to becoming a highly influential association. Espousing a rhetoric of love of country and duty to uphold the nation's principles, it became a nationalistic defender of "100 percent Americanism." During the 1919–1921 Red Scare, Legionnaires promised to be "the greatest bulwark against Bolshevism and anarchy." Legion posts throughout the country helped to institute loyalty oaths for teachers and prevented individuals whom they viewed as radicals from speaking in their local communities, sometimes by running the offender out of town.

The Legion pursued its mission as the self-proclaimed protector of American "Justice, Freedom, and Democracy" throughout the twentieth century. During *World War II, Legionnaires were active in organizing local *civil defense. In addition, the Legion became officially associated with the *Federal Bureau of Investigation, assisting government agents in investigating enemy aliens. At war's end, an infusion of new veterans swelled the membership roster to 3.5 million. In keeping with their anticommunist stance, Legionnaires during the *Cold War adamantly insisted upon the need to roust "subversives" from government service and other positions of authority, and it vehemently supported the U.S. anti-Soviet foreign policy.

In addition to promoting nationalistic patriotism, the Legion has been one of the most powerful lobbying agencies in the nation's history. It was instrumental in the establishment in 1921 of the Veterans Bureau, the predecessor of the *Veterans Administration. The *Servicemen's Readjustment Act of 1944, the so-called G.I. Bill of Rights, the government's generous package of benefits to veterans, was drafted by former Legion Commander Harry W. Colmery and vigorously supported by Legion lobbyists. In 1999, the American Legion had nearly three million members in almost fifteen thousand posts worldwide.

[*See also* Anticommunism; Twenties, The.]

• William Pencak, *For God and Country: The American Legion, 1919–1941*, 1989.

—Lynn Dumenil

AMERICAN MEDICAL ASSOCIATION. The American Medical Association (AMA) was formed in 1847 by elite physicians hoping to improve the stature of their profession. This was no small task in the crowded and chaotic nineteenth-century medical marketplace, where homeopaths and other practitioners of alternative medicine challenged orthodox physicians' claims to authority and patients. Although AMA leaders aimed to improve standards of *medical education and practice, regulate relations among physicians, represent the profession to the public, and promote "the usefulness, honor and interests of the medical profession," in its first fifty years the AMA won only lackluster support from physicians and possessed little public visibility or political power.

In 1901, the association reorganized itself, instituting a proportional representation system that gave state and local associations a voice in a newly created House of Delegates, which approved the association's policies and positions. Led by J. N. McCormack, national AMA representatives helped state and local medical societies reorganize themselves as constituent units in the national organization. As a result, membership increased dramatically, from fewer than ten thousand in 1900 to around seventy thousand in 1910.

A more active and public profile accompanied this growth. The AMA's Council on Medical Education, for instance, monitored medical schools and their facilities, making the association a *de facto* arbiter of national standards governing medical education. The *Journal of the American Medical Association (JAMA)* became one of the world's preeminent medical journals, and the association began publishing specialized journals as well. AMA bureaus endeavored to safeguard the public's health by debunking quackery and so-called miracle cures, permitting approved food and drug advertisers to use the AMA seal, and sponsoring educational programs for the general public.

Historians of medicine have focused much attention on the association's objections to what its leaders termed "socialistic tendencies" in the organization of medical care. An AMA committee endorsed compulsory health insurance at the state level in the late 1910s, but the association soon recanted. Over the next three decades, the AMA (often represented by *JAMA*'s vocal editor Morris Fishbein) condemned advocates of federal health programs, government-sponsored health insurance, and other initiatives that threatened to disrupt the traditional physician-patient relationship or provide alternatives to fee-for-service medical practice. These battles peaked in the late 1940s when the AMA helped mobilize opposition to President Harry S. *Truman's national health insurance plan and lent its support to private plans instead. This stance held through the 1960s and after, as the AMA leadership fought—and then reluctantly accepted—Medicare, Medicaid, and other programs considered government intrusions into medical practice.

The AMA grew slightly less conservative in the last quarter of the twentieth century, as the balance of power shifted among the medical profession, the federal government, commercial insurers, and advocates of health-care reform. Nevertheless, with its substantial membership and tradition of vigorous advocacy, the association remained an important player in American health-care politics, widely regarded as "the voice of the American medical profession."

[*See also* Health Insurance; Health Maintenance Organizations; Medicare and Medicaid; Medicine.]

• James G. Burrow, *AMA: Voice of American Medicine*, 1963. Paul Starr, *The Social Transformation of American Medicine*, 1982.

—Elizabeth Toon

AMERICAN PARTY. *See* Know-Nothing Party.

AMERICAN PHILOSOPHICAL SOCIETY. Benjamin *Franklin organized the American Philosophical Society (APS) in 1743, but failure to attract wider support led to its collapse in 1745. Throughout the 1750s and 1760s, a small group of Philadelphians met intermittently to discuss science, and in 1766 they organized themselves into the American Society for Promoting and Propagating Useful Knowledge. Led by Charles Thomson, the membership consisted principally of liberal members of the *Society of Friends (Quakers) who supported the Assembly party in Pennsylvania politics. In 1767 a rival group, mostly Anglicans and Presbyterians, aligned with Pennsylvania's Proprietary party, organized an American Philosophical Society. Franklin, elected president of the latter body in 1768, oversaw the merger of the two groups and on 2 January 1769 presided over the first meeting of the American Philosophical Society, held at *Philadelphia, for Promoting Useful Knowledge. Later that year the APS, with the financial support of the Provincial Assembly, made eleven sets of observations of the Transit of Venus. These were published in 1771 in the society's *Transactions*, winning international recognition for American science. From the society's inception, it usually recruited its officers from the University of Pennsylvania faculty and its active members from the city of Philadelphia; yet until the 1840s, the APS served as a national scientific society, acting as a resource for the federal government and disseminating the research of American scientists through its *Transactions.*

With the emergence of specialized scientific societies and the creation of official national organizations for American science, the APS lost its national role and transformed itself into a general learned society. In 1917 the society helped organize the American Council of Learned Societies. Since the 1950s the APS has been a major archival repository of collections in early American history and the history of science; it awards approximately $600,000 each year in research grants.

[*See also* Science: Colonial Era; Science: Revolutionary War to World War I.]

• Brooke Hindle, *The Pursuit of Science in Revolutionary America, 1735–1789*, 1956. Edward C. Carter II, *"One Grand Pursuit": A Brief History of the American Philosophical Society's First 250 Years, 1743–1993*, 1993.

—Simon Baatz

AMERICAN PROTECTIVE ASSOCIATION. *See* Anti-Catholic Movement.

AMERICAN SAMOA. *See* Protectorates and Dependencies.

AMERICANS FOR DEMOCRATIC ACTION (ADA) was founded in January 1947 by the liberal leadership of a *World War II–era interventionist group, the Union for Democratic Action. The ADA's creation marked the culmination of a crucial breach in American liberal ranks between the anticommunist or "*Cold War" liberals who rallied to the ADA and the more communist-tolerant liberals of the Progressive Citizens of America (eventually the *Progressive party of 1948). Among the ADA's founding members were leading anticommunist liberals from academe, politics, and labor, including Reinhold *Niebuhr, historian Arthur M. Schlesinger Jr. (1917–), Walter *Reuther, Eleanor *Roosevelt, lawyer Joseph Rauh, and Hubert *Humphrey. Although it generally worked to influence the *Democratic party, the ADA was officially an independent political organization. Its founders hoped to bring a significant degree of progressive, pragmatic, noncommunist influence to mainstream politics, embodying Schlesinger's concept of a "vital center" in American political culture formulated in his 1949 book of that title.

The ADA helped President Harry S. *Truman retain the liberal vote in the 1948 presidential election, in part by pushing Truman leftward on issues such as *civil rights, but also by leading a full-scale attack on Progressive party presidential candidate Henry A. Wallace, portraying him and his colleagues as dupes of the *Communist party. Ironically, in the early 1950s, the ADA itself came under similar attack by McCarthyite forces. In the following years the organization was active in various progressive liberal causes, ranging from civil rights to President Lyndon B. *Johnson's *Great Society reforms. Reflecting American liberalism generally, by the mid-1960s the ADA was badly split over American involvement in Vietnam, although it officially supported Johnson's war policy. By early 1968, however, the group had come to oppose the war. It endorsed Hubert Humphrey's presidential candidacy that year, but with barely concealed ambivalence. With Richard M. *Nixon's election to the presidency in 1968, the ADA was pushed to the political margins, never having fully attained the level of influence its founders envisioned.

[*See also* Anticommunism; Civil Rights Movement; Liberalism; McCarthy, Joseph; Vietnam War.]

• Steven M. Gillon, *Politics and Vision: The ADA and American Liberalism, 1947–1985*, 1987. Mark L. Kleinman, *A World of Hope, A World of Fear: Henry A. Wallace, Reinhold Niebuhr, and American Liberalism*, 2000.

—Mark L. Kleinman

AMERICANS WITH DISABILITIES ACT. The Americans with Disabilities Act (1990) brought *civil rights protections enjoyed by other minority groups to people with disabilities. An earlier law, the Rehabilitation Act of 1973, had made it illegal for organizations receiving federal funds to discriminate against the handicapped. Implementation of this act created an awareness of people with disabilities as a minority group and led to efforts to extend civil rights protections for the disabled into the workplace and other areas. In 1986 the National Council on the Handicapped, a presidential advisory group, suggested that Congress enact a comprehensive law requiring equal opportunity for people with disabilities. Because of the vagaries of presidential and congressional politics, it took until 26 July 1990 for President George *Bush, a leading proponent of the measure, to sign the measure into law. Senators Edward Kennedy (Dem.–MA), Robert Dole (Rep.–KS), and Tom Harkin (Dem.–IA) played the key roles in Congress. Among the issues that complicated passage were business fears of excessive litigation and costs, the concerns regarding degree of protections that people with *acquired immunodeficiency syndrome (AIDS) would receive, and debate over the penalties for job discrimination against the disabled.

The law contained four significant titles, or sections. Title I prohibited discrimination in hiring or promotion against qualified individuals with disabilities. Title II outlawed discrimination in government and public activities, including public transportation. Title III required that such entities as hotels and shops be accessible to people with disabilities. Title IV sought to ensure that telecommunication relay systems were available for use by speech- and hearing-impaired individuals.

The act did not engender much controversy in the first years of its existence, although litigation did arise over certain legal technicalities. To the disappointment of its advocates, the rate of employment among people with disabilities did not increase nor did the level of welfare receipt among people with disabilities fall significantly.

• Edward Berkowitz, "A Historical Preface to the Americans with Disabilities Act," *Journal of Policy History* 6 (1994): 96–119.

—Edward D. Berkowitz

"AMERICAN SYSTEM" OF MANUFACTURES. American manufacturers stole the show at London's 1851 Crystal Palace Exposition. Several American products especially impressed the British, among them Cyrus *McCormick's reaper, Alfred C. Hobbs's unpickable lock, and most of all the guns: Samuel Colt's revolver and the Robbins and Lawrence rifle. These items impressed exposition visitors not only because of their excellence, but also because they were produced in large quantities, and in the case of the guns, with interchangeable parts.

While historians debate the precise meaning of the American system of manufactures, most define it as the system of production that originated in the arms industry to manufacture guns with interchangeable parts. In nineteenth-century America, this system was often called the "armory system." The process was dubbed the "American System" by a British commission sent to the United States in 1853 to learn about the system that produced the articles displayed at the 1851 exposition.

The idea of parts' interchangeability, which originated in France, was novel at the beginning of the nineteenth century and not important to most manufacturers. The American government, however, recognized the potential advantages of guns with interchangeable parts that could be easily repaired on the battlefield. At the urging of several presidents and secretaries of war, the Ordnance Department and Congress supported efforts by inventors and entrepreneurs to manufacture such arms. A number of armsmakers claimed to achieve interchangeability in the early nineteenth century, but as historian Merritt Roe Smith has shown (*Harpers Ferry Armory and the New Technology,* 1977), the first truly interchangeable arms were the rifles made by John Hall at his shop at the federal arsenal at Harpers Ferry, Virginia.

The American system of manufactures is vital to an understanding of the development of U.S. industry. Precision manufacture of interchangeable parts led to greater and greater division of labor and the invention of self-acting machines that could be operated by workers with less training and experience than traditional craftsmen. The system of modern *mass production first introduced by Henry *Ford at the Ford Motor Company can be traced directly to the armory system.

[*See also* Factory System; Industrialization.]

• Nathan Rosenberg, ed., *The American System of Manufactures: The Report of the Committee on the Machinery of the United States 1855 and the Special Reports of George Wallis and Joseph Whitworth*, 1969. Otto Mayr and Robert C. Post, eds., *Yankee Enterprise: The Rise of the American System of Manufactures,* 1981. David A. Hounshell, *From the American System to Mass Production,* 1984.

—Lindy Biggs

AMISH. *See* Mennonites and Amish.

***AMISTAD* CASE.** In 1839, in violation of Spanish law, Spanish slave traders transported over forty enslaved Africans to Cuba. Here they were transferred to another vessel, the *Amistad.* After a mutiny led by an African named Cinque from the Mendi tribe in Nigeria, the blacks seized the vessel and ordered surviving crew members to return to Africa. Instead, a U.S. warship seized the vessel off Long Island and towed it to New London, Connecticut. Spain demanded the return of the mutineers to Cuba for trial; the *Amistad*'s owners, citing *Pinckney's Treaty of 1795 between the United States and Spain, demanded the return of the vessel and its cargo, including the Africans.

Abolitionists formed an *Amistad* committee and hired lawyer Roger Baldwin to defend the Africans. A federal judge in Hartford declared the blacks free, since the slave traders' action had been illegal, and instructed President Martin *Van Buren to return them to Africa. Van Buren, however, who favored extraditing the slaves to Cuba for trial, did not comply. On appeal, the case went to the U.S. *Supreme Court, headed by Chief Justice Roger B. *Taney.

The former president John Quincy *Adams, arguing for the defense, declared that, based on the *Declaration of Independence, the *Amistad* mutineers were free persons and justified in defending their freedom. In an 1841 decision written by Justice Joseph *Story (*U.S.* v. *The Amistad*), the high court ruled for the defense, finding that Pinckney's Treaty did not apply, and that since Spain had banned the slave trade, the Africans had been enslaved illegally. Abolitionists, while pleased, had hoped for a broader ruling based on natural law. Private contributions financed the slaves' return to Africa. Although the Taney court in the 1857 *Dred Scott* decision eroded the impact of the *Amistad* verdict, it nevertheless stands as a historic milestone in the struggle against slavery and racial oppression.

[*See also* Antislavery; *Scott* v. *Sandford*; Slavery: The Slave Trade.]

• Howard Jones, *Mutiny on the Amistad*, 1987. Karen Zeinert, *The Amistad Slave Revolt and American Abolition*, 1997.

—Carolyn Williams

AMUSEMENT PARKS AND THEME PARKS. Elements of the American amusement and theme park go back to antiquity. More direct antecedents include various European traditions, ranging from medieval fairs and carnivals to seventeenth-century pleasure gardens such as London's Vauxhall, Ranelagh, and Cremorne. These gardens featured pyrotechnics, games, live entertainment, promenading and dancing, and even primitive versions of amusement rides. Prior to the American Revolution, several modest versions of such gardens opened on the East Coast.

These were initially largely pastoral environments that catered to an essentially rural culture. They began to change in the late nineteenth century, however, reflecting the new urban industrial age. Spurring this change were profit-minded entrepreneurs, hotel and resort operations, and the electric traction or trolley companies established following the *Civil War. To meet the flat fees charged for *electricity by utility companies, trolley concerns sought ways to stimulate weekend business. One effective method was to build a park at the end of the trolley line, thus creating an early version of the amusement park. In addition, by the mid-nineteenth century, numerous seaside resorts had begun to appear along the upper eastern seaboard. These resorts initially catered to the wealthy, but easy access via public transportation rapidly changed their status.

Despite the many precursors of the modern amusement park, including mechanical rides dating back to 1800, the immediate impetus was the 1893 World's Columbian Exposition in *Chicago and its "Midway Plaisance." This amusement area, consciously separated from the fair's more "serious" exhibits, became the prototype of amusement parks for the next sixty years with its enticing array of concessions, shows, and rides, including the first Ferris Wheel, designed by the civil engineer George Washington Gale Ferris (1859–1896). Costing $350,000 (recovered quickly), the original Ferris Wheel stood 264 feet high, weighed 1,200 tons, had 36 pendulum cars, and accommodated 2,160 riders.

Inspired by the success of the "Midway Plaisance," Paul Boynton opened "Water Chutes" on Chicago's south side, arguably the first modern amusement park. Turning eastward, Boynton in 1895 opened a similar venue, "Sea Lion Park," on New York's Coney Island. Boynton's addition to what had been simply a beach resort dating from the 1870s marked the beginning of the traditional amusement park's golden era—a period of massive *immigration and explosive urban growth.

Between 1895 and 1903, three additional amusement parks were built on Coney Island: "Steeplechase Park" (1897), spearheaded by George C. Tilyou; "Luna Park" (1903), constructed by Elmer "Skip" Dundy and Frederic Thompson on the site of the unsuccessful "Sea Lion Park"; and, within a year, across from "Luna," the $3.5 million "Dreamland," created by real estate speculator William H. Reynolds. Even though the parks initially attracted enormous crowds (one million on one day in 1914), Coney Island's decline began before *World War I: "Dreamland" burned down, "Luna" went bankrupt, and Tilyou died. By *World War II, Coney Island's heyday was over, with fewer patrons making the subway trip from Brooklyn. By the late 1990s, only one park, Astroland, remained as a sad reminder of Coney Island's glory days.

Nevertheless, Coney Island served as a model for most subsequent "traditional" amusement parks, many built by transportation companies following the 1904 St. Louis World's Fair. The number of such parks peaked in 1919, with 1,500 in operation. The 1920s saw a dramatic upsurge in the development of mechanical rides, followed by initial prosperity during the early Great Depression as patrons sought inexpensive entertainment and a vicarious escape from hard times. By 1935, however, only four hundred amusement parks remained. World War II further battered the industry, taking for the war effort materials needed by the aging parks, contributing to their deterioration.

Postwar prosperity initially revived the amusement park business, swelling attendance and revenues, and stimulating the construction of new parks. Beginning in the 1960s, however, urban amusement parks again struggled to survive and many of the more historic parks closed, including Palisade Park in New Jersey, Chicago's Riverview, Cleveland's Euclid Beach, and North Dartmouth, Massachusetts's Lincoln Park.

Ironically, the savior of the outdoor amusement business, and at the same time a major factor in the demise of the older-style traditional parks, was the theme park, a creative example of advertising packaging and organizational savvy. Walt *Disney's concept of organizing amusement areas around one or more themes was revolutionary. "Disneyland," which opened in Anaheim, California, in 1955, set the pattern with its five distinct, themed areas replacing the old midway. Although originally scoffed at, the theme park idea gained momentum quickly. The first successful park after Disneyland, "Six Flags Over Texas," opened in 1961; by the late 1990s, Six Flags owned twelve parks and the corporation claimed that 85 percent of Americans lived within a day's drive of a Six Flags park. Just as the urban amusement parks had flourished in an era of trolleys and subways, the theme park, tapping a regional and national market, was a product of the age of the interstate highway system and commercial air travel. In 1971 the Disney organization opened Walt Disney World Resort in Orlando, Florida, still the World's largest theme park a quarter century later. EPCOT (Experimental Prototype Community of Tomorrow), one of several additions to Disney World, opened in 1982.

The American theme park spread around the world in the 1980s and remained in the 1990s a global success. Although escalating costs and a saturated market slowed the growth of theme parks in the 1990s, business remained healthy. In 1996, for example, Disneyland attracted a record fifteen million patrons and some two dozen other major parks set similar attendance records. Entrepreneurs constantly seek innovations, including the Indoor Family Entertainment Center phenomenon of the 1990s, most notably represented by "Camp Snoopy" (1992), a seven-acre theme park inside Minneapolis's giant Mall of America, which boasts sixteen rides (including a log chute and a roller coaster). As the twentieth century ended, the United States boasted approximately six hundred parks, large and small, with fixed-site amusement rides.

[*See also* Barnum, P. T.; Circuses; Consumer Culture; Foreign Relations: The Cultural Dimension; Highway System; Leisure; Shopping Centers and Malls; Tourism; Urbanization; World's Fairs and Expositions.]

• Richard W. Flint, "Meet Me in Dreamland: The Early Development of Amusement Parks in America," in *Victorian Resorts and Hotels: Essays from a Victorian Society Autumn Symposium*, ed. Richard Guy Wilson, 1982, pp. 99–107. Robert W. Rydell, *All the World's a Fair: Visions of Empire at American International Expositions*, 1984. Judith A. Adams, *The American Amusement Park Industry: A History of Technology and Thrills*, 1991. David Nasaw, *Going Out: The Rise and Fall of Public Amusements*, 1993. Don B. Wilmeth, "Amusement and Theme Parks," in *Encyclopedia of American Social History*, eds. Mary Kupiec Cayton, Elliott J. Gorn, and Peter W. Williams, 1993, pp. 1705–12. Steven Watts, *The Magic Kingdom: Walt Disney and the American Way of Life*, 1997.

—Don B. Wilmeth

ANARCHISM. Anarchist rejection of centralized government and preference for direct democracy and voluntary associations is deeply rooted in American historical experience. Idealization of nature as an alternative to the depravity of modern civilization runs equally deep, as in the work of Henry David *Thoreau, for example.

Most native-born, individualist anarchists of the nineteenth century shared the Jeffersonian preference for artisans and small farmers over an industrial economy. Some tried to supplant the state with utopian communities. Benjamin Tucker (1854–1939), whose journal *Liberty* (1881–1908) espoused total individual sovereignty, illustrates this tradition. Also an anarchist, Tucker rejected violence and favored education to spread his ideas.

The *Haymarket affair of 1886 was a watershed event marking the shift from individualist to European-inspired collectivist and revolutionary anarchism associated with such figures as the Russian Mikhail Bakunin (1814–1876). The Haymarket affair, in which eight men (mostly German immigrants) were condemned on little evidence for complicity in the throwing of a bomb at an anarchist-sponsored labor rally that killed seven Chicago policemen, galvanized the anarchist movement. The Russian-Jewish immigrant Emma *Goldman, editor of *Mother Earth* (1906–1917), dated her conversion to the cause from this event. The execution of labor organizer Joe Hill in 1915 and of Sacco and Vanzetti in 1927 furnished further martyrs for the movement. At the same time, these events, as well as Alexander Berkman's attempted assassination of Carnegie Steel executive Henry Clay Frick during the 1892 *Homestead lockout and the assassination of President William *McKinley in 1901, linked anarchism with terrorism in most Americans' minds. In 1903, Congress barred "persons opposed to all organized governments" from entering the United States.

The *Industrial Workers of the World (IWW), founded in 1905, was part of a trend away from terrorism and toward organizing anarchist unions. The IWW enjoyed some success organizing miners and textile workers, but government repression during and after *World War I took its toll. IWW leader Bill Haywood was imprisoned and in 1921 fled to Bolshevik Russia, following Goldman, Berkman, and other radicals already deported as radicals.

The counterculture of the 1960s showed the persistence of many anarchist values: direct democracy, back-to-nature communalism, alternative education, sexual liberation, and opposition to war and the draft. After the 1960s, radical environmentalists such as Earth First! demonstrated anarchists' preference for direct action, and anarcha-feminists exposed the patriarchal nature of power.

[*See also* Sacco and Vanzetti Case; Sixties, The; Utopian and Communitarian Movements.]

• David De Leon, *The American as Anarchist: Reflections on Indigenous Radicalism*, 1978. Paul Avrich, *The Modern School Movement: Anarchism and Education in the United States*, 1980. Paul Avrich, *Anarchist Portraits*, 1988.

—Richard D. Sonn

ANDERSON, MARIAN (1902–1993), contralto. Born in *Philadelphia, Anderson sang in a church choir and at age nineteen began formal voice training. At twenty-three, she made her debut with the New York Philharmonic Orchestra. She later toured in concert in many European and South American capitals. Her foreign acclaim prompted an invitation to tour in the United States, where for two decades she was in demand as a performer of *opera and *spirituals. In 1939, because she was an *African American, Anderson was barred by the Daughters of the American Revolution from performing in Constitution Hall in *Washington, D.C., an event that exposed the depth of *racism in America. Her open-air *Lincoln Memorial concert that Easter, arranged by Eleanor *Roosevelt and Secretary of the Interior Harold Ickes, drew an audience of 75,000 and was broadcast nationally. On 7 January 1955, Anderson became the first African American to sing with the New York Metropolitan Opera Company in its seventy-five year history. Also the first African American to perform at the White House, Anderson sang at the inaugurations of presidents Dwight D. *Eisenhower and John F. *Kennedy. Her many honors included, in 1963, the Presidential Medal of Freedom.

• Marian Anderson, *My Lord, What a Morning*, 1956, reissued in 1992. Shirlee Petkin Newman, *Marian Anderson: Lady from Philadelphia*, 1965.

—Claudia Durst Johnson

ANTEBELLUM ERA. Every period of American history, unfortunately, could be considered "antebellum." A war has seemed to await the end of each era, defining in retrospect what came before. Yet in all U.S. history only the decades between 1815 and 1861 take their defining identity from the war that followed. That is understandable: Not only did the *Civil War alter the fundamental character of the nation but it grew entirely from conflicts within America itself, within Americans themselves. The notion of the "antebellum era" promises to make sense of what was at once the nation's greatest failure and its most important step toward fulfilling its founding words of freedom.

Precisely because the antebellum label is so convenient, however, other names for this period, other ways of grasping its history, invite consideration. By putting the end of the story first, "antebellum" both compresses too much and leaves out too much. By making everything point toward the bloodshed and redemption of the Civil War, it prevents us from seeing the circuitous paths the sectional conflict followed. The unimaginable slaughter and the unanticipated emancipation that accompanied the Civil War grew from many roots, all of them entangled.

People at the time, ironically, saw their era as fundamentally *post*bellum. They viewed themselves as living in the shadow of the *Revolutionary War, trying to measure up to the standards of the new nation and the sacrifices of their ancestors. The names of their towns and cities, their public buildings and holidays, their politics and schools, all were defined by their vision of what the founders had intended. Even arguments about *slavery, the fundamental division in the country, drew on the Revolutionary Era both for defense and attack. Americans looked backward as much as forward, not knowing that later generations would see their half century as prologue to war rather than as a culmination of the founding.

Continental Expansion and Warfare. A hopeful interpretation might call this time the Era of American Expansion. In 1815 the young nation included only eighteen states, with Louisiana standing exposed at the western boundary, Florida in the hands of the Spanish, and an unsettled line floating between Canada and the United States. The western half of the continent remained only vaguely known to Anglo Americans and seemed far too distant to be of importance any time soon. Even within the country's sketchy borders, American Indians populated large and rich areas in both the North and the *South. But over the next four decades the nation's continental boundaries expanded beyond recognition. A new state entered the Union about every two and a half years, and by the end of the 1850s thirty-three states—including two on the Pacific coast—claimed a place.

A less hopeful interpretation might call these years the Era of Continental Warfare. Expansion occurred because the young country repeatedly seized, bought, or negotiated territory, often with force. The years of expansion began with the end of British influence on the Western frontier following the *War of 1812, soon followed by Spain's abandonment of Florida. In the 1820s and 1830s, the Cherokee, Choctaw, Sac, Fox, Seminole, and Chickasaw nations, deprived of European allies, faced expulsion from the eastern half of the continent. In the 1840s, the United States provoked a war with Mexico that yielded a territory of unknown possibility stretching from Texas to the Pacific Ocean. Negotiation with Great Britain defined the northern boundary from Maine to Oregon and, after a bit more fine-tuning with the *Gadsden Purchase, the external boundaries of the current continental United States had been fixed, all in a remarkably short time and on a scale people could barely have imagined only a few decades earlier. The military conflict that made this possible proved easy for the United States, leading many Americans to imagine it their *manifest destiny to expand without limitation. The United States, in fact, claimed the entire western hemisphere as a place under its jurisdiction and protection. In a sense, this period was defined by almost continuous warfare, and not merely by the Civil War at its end.

Social and Technological Trends. Meanwhile, the population grew relentlessly. The number of Americans increased from 8.4 million in 1815 to 31.4 million by 1860. Not only did men and women marry young and raise large families, but three million additional people crossed the Atlantic from Europe in a mixture of hope and desperation. People of all backgrounds spread out across the vast expanse of the burgeoning country, establishing farms and towns far from the older cities of the east. They were a restless people, with about half the population of any town moving every ten years. By the end of the period, the United States claimed 5 million more people than England and the new nation boasted 8 cities of over 150,000 inhabitants, more than any other country in the world.

Not only did ever-expanding boundaries and population encourage people to move, but machines changed the scale of life in what historians have come to call the Transportation Revolution. Steamboats transformed water transportation in the 1810s, *canals and waterways boomed in the 1820s, and *railroads arrived in the 1830s. The capacity of ships docking in American ports doubled every decade between 1820 and 1860. American vessels plied the Atlantic with cargoes of cotton and wheat for England and Europe. Clipper ships sailed around South America and into the Pacific, carrying prospectors and immigrants.

A revolution in communication accompanied this revolution in transportation. Newspapers, confined to just a few major cities in 1815, became staples of American life in the 1830s and 1840s, read and published in hundreds of communities of every size. Daguerreotypes and colorful lithographs decorated homes that had been empty of pictures a generation earlier. In the 1840s, the first *telegraph wires carried information from one city to another; by the late 1850s, telegraph cables connected the United States and Europe. Novels sold tens of thousands of copies in a few months. Some of the greatest American writers—James Fenimore *Cooper, Ralph Waldo *Emerson, Nathaniel *Hawthorne, Herman *Melville, Edgar Allan *Poe, and Walt *Whitman, among them—flourished in the new environment, defining and reaching large audiences with bold acts of imagination. Later generations would think of the era as the American Renaissance.

Some historians have argued that the decades of the first half of the nineteenth century brought a market revolution in which American life became newly bound up in the values, opportunities, and constraints of commercial exchange. A class of working people of both genders emerged in the cities of the eastern seaboard. Political conflict polarized around issues of *banking and finance, *tariffs, unions, and corporations. Farmers and merchants more finely tuned their labors to prices established far away. How much change these patterns marked from earlier generations remains a matter of dispute, but without doubt, buying and selling encompassed much of American life in the mid–nineteenth century.

Women's lives took on a new texture in these same years. While difficult labor in the household, on the farm, and in *childbirth continued to consume the energies of most American women, a new ideal of separate spheres emerged. Women were especially suited for nurturance, this notion held, because they were more sensitive, moral, and pure than men. Accordingly, women were urged to separate themselves as much as possible from the hurly-burly of the marketplace, the street, and the crowd, focusing their energies and talents on their children and others who would benefit from their tender attentions. The ideal woman became both elevated and isolated.

Enabled, heartened, and worried by the many kinds of changes around them, Americans made these years an Age of Reform. *Revivalism flourished as *Baptists, Methodists, and Presbyterians vied for converts. Reform groups emerged to stamp out alcohol and war, to encourage education and humane treatment of the unfortunate, to improve diet and health. Most importantly, black and white abolitionists launched a decades-long struggle to bring an end to slavery, risking their lives in the process. Women accounted for many members of these organizations, lending their energy and intelligence to activities beyond the home, using the separate-spheres creed to the advantage of themselves and others and laying the groundwork of the *women's rights movements. These reform organizations electrified Americans with the sense that society could be fundamentally altered and improved, that evil could be overcome with sufficient effort and God's help.

Reform Movements and Party Politics. These years have also been known as the Era of the Common Man. Andrew *Jackson typified the aspirations of many white men, common or not: independence, pride, and self-determination, built on control of female, black, and Native dependents. Political parties—*Democratic, *Whig, *Free Soil, *Know-Nothing, and *Republican—mobilized nearly all white men, who swore allegiance to their parties, expressing their passions and beliefs in slogans, songs, and parades. On election days, as many as eight out of ten eligible voters went to the polls. The modern world had never seen such a vibrant—if messy, coarse, and sometimes corrupt—democracy.

Slavery and the Coming of the Civil War. The modern world had also never seen such a vast and powerful slave society. In the fundamental tragedy of this time, this era of revolutions in politics, transportation, and reform was also a period when an empire for slavery extended across a quarter of the new nation. Slavery, propelled by the same territorial expansion and technological innovation that drove so much else in the new country, spread like a hemorrhage. Over 300,000 slaveowners held nearly 4 million people in bondage by 1860. Slavery, contrary to the expectations of virtually everyone in 1815, grew stronger with each passing decade, embracing an ever larger part of the continent to the *South and *West, holding more people within its bonds, accounting for a larger share of the nation's exports. Cotton and slavery created a per capita income for white southerners higher than that of any country in Europe except England.

The discussions in the churches, the reform organizations, and the political parties turned repeatedly, if fitfully and sometimes obliquely, to the morality of slavery and the sectional conflict it bred. Rivalry and distrust between the North and the South came to infect everything in public life. Each section viewed the other as aggressive and expansionist, intent on making the nation all one thing or another. The North claimed that the slaveholder South would destroy the best government on earth rather than accept the results of a fair election. The white South claimed that the arrogant and greedy North would destroy the nation rather than tolerate a labor system the *Constitution itself had acknowledged. Both sides were filled with righteous rage, accepting violence to gain the upper hand, whether that involved capturing fugitive slaves or applauding John *Brown's failed insurrection. Americans could not stop the momentum they themselves had created.

What most Americans thought of as progress brought on the Civil War. Had the nation not expanded so relentlessly, the elaborate compromises of 1820, 1850, and 1854 might have held. Had the nation not been made so aware of itself through newspapers, novels, and sermons; through political parties and reform organizations; and through railroads and telegraphs, the bargains and evasions of the Revolutionary generation might have endured. Had cotton not been so in demand and so crucial to the prosperity of the nation and Europe, slavery might have faded rather than growing stronger. No one sought a war that would kill 630,000 Americans, but the killing came on the heels of many changes people did desperately seek. The war that broke out, suddenly and irrevocably defining this era, bore the marks of the emerging modern world. It would rage with terrifying efficiency and far-reaching consequences, forever, changing the way Americans thought of the years that had come before.

[*See also* Agriculture: 1770s to 1890; Anti-Catholic Movement; Antislavery; Bank of the United States, First and Second; Cherokee Cases; Compromise of 1850; Cotton Industry; Education: The Public School Movement; Expansionism; Immigration; Indian History and Culture: From 1800 to 1900; Journalism; Labor Movements; Literature: Early National and Antebellum Eras; Lowell Mills; Methodism; Mexican War; Nativist Movement; Painting: To 1945; Prisons and Penitentiaries; Romantic Movement; Science: Revolutionary War to World War I; Steam Power; Texas Republic and Annexation; Transcendentalism; Utopian and Communitarian Movements; Working-Class Life and Culture.]

• George Rogers Taylor, *The Transportation Revolution, 1815–1860*, 1951. Eric Foner, *Free Soil, Free Labor, Free Men: The Ideology of the Republican Party before the Civil War*, 1970. Kathryn Kish Sklar, *Catharine Beecher: A Study in American Domesticity*, 1973. Eugene Genovese, *Roll, Jordan, Roll: The World the Slaves Made*, 1974. David M. Potter, *The Impending Crisis, 1848–1861*, 1976. Kerby A. Miller, *Emigrants and Exiles: Ireland and the Irish Exodus to North America*, 1985. David S. Reynolds, *Beneath the American Renaissance: The Subversive Imagination in the Age of Emerson and Melville*, 1988. Harry L. Watson, *Liberty and Power: The Politics of Jacksonian America*, 1990. Charles G. Sellers, *The Market Revolution: Jacksonian America, 1815–1846*, 1991. Ronald Walters, *American Reformers, 1815–1860*, 1996.

—Edward L. Ayers

ANTHONY, SUSAN B. (1820–1906), women's rights activist. Born in Adams, Massachusetts, Anthony was influenced by her father's Quakerism as well as his independence in marrying Lucy Read, a *Baptist. When his business failed in 1837, Susan became a teacher. She never married and was a lifelong believer in the importance of self-support for women. In 1850, she met Elizabeth Cady *Stanton and became a passionate subscriber to Stanton's women's rights ideas. The Stanton-Anthony partnership sustained American *feminism for the next half-century. Starting in 1854, they focused on the denial of basic economic rights to married women. For six years, Anthony collected petitions to the New York state legislature, which in 1860 passed a comprehensive Married Women's Property Act. Simultaneously, she worked for the *American Anti-Slavery Society, viewing women's rights and abolitionist sentiments as closely related. In 1863, she and Stanton collected a half million women's signatures petitioning Congress to abolish *slavery.

After the *Civil War, following the lead of the *antislavery movement, Stanton and Anthony concentrated on equal citizenship and political rights for women. They tried but failed to convince Congress to include women in the *Fourteenth and *Fifteenth Amendments. Now committed to a focus on political *equality and the *Constitution as the source of those rights, they formed the National Woman Suffrage Association in 1869, precipitating a split with Lucy *Stone and other women's rights activists not willing to break with longtime abolitionist and *Republican party allies. For the next half decade, they advanced the argument that the Fourteenth Amendment included women when it bestowed federal citizenship on "all persons born in the United States." Since the vote was patently a fundamental right of citizenship, they contended, woman suffrage was already constitutional. Accordingly, in November 1872 Anthony took the most famous act of her life: She convinced election officials to allow her to vote for president. For this she was found guilty of illegal voting in U.S. District Court and fined $100, which she refused to pay. Two years later, the U.S. *Supreme Court ruled against the suffragists' line of argument.

From this point on, Anthony realized the necessity of a separate woman suffrage amendment and dedicated herself to that goal. In 1876, she presented a militant "Woman's Declaration of Rights" at Fourth of July ceremonies held at the Centennial Exposition in *Philadelphia. In 1880, she began to compile and publish the multivolume *History of Woman Suffrage*, an act of historical consciousness unequalled in American reform. In 1890, she oversaw the unification of the suffrage movement, split since 1869, and the election of Stanton as the first president of the *National American Woman Suffrage Association. In 1892, Anthony succeeded Stanton as president. Throughout the 1890s, despite advancing age, Anthony traveled to California, Kansas, South Dakota, and Colorado to work for state suffrage referenda, and to England and France to organize suffragists internationally. She retired in 1900. By the time the *Nineteenth Amendment passed in 1920, no name was more identified with woman suffrage than that of Susan B. Anthony.

[*See also* Society of Friends; Woman Suffrage Movement; Women's Rights Movements.]

• Kathleen Barry, *Susan B. Anthony: A Biography of a Singular Feminist*, 1988. Lynn Sherr, *Failure Is Impossible: Susan B. Anthony in Her Own Words*, 1995.

—Ellen C. DuBois

ANTHROPOLOGY. Anthropology in the United States had its professional inception around 1900 with the foundation of the first chair in this field at Columbia University. Its intellecutal origins were closely wedded to an evolutionary paradigm, as in the nineteenth century works of Edward Burnett Tylor and Lewis Henry *Morgan. By treating human differences as correlates of evolutionary stages, instead of analyzing them deductively from a universal human nature, they offered a way of reformulating the notion of human unity; cultural differences represented different stages of one evolutionary process. The critical conceptual difference that distinguishes these early ethnologists from the professional anthropology that followed was their view of "culture" as a unitary human product, rather than as a token of human diversity.

In the United States, the legacy of evolutionism continued almost unbroken through the twentieth century, particularly through the works of Julian Steward and Leslie White in the 1930s and 1940s. Alert to the "unfashionable" nature of the idea of cultural evolution, Steward therefore largely promoted it as a way to achieve conceptual rigor with regard to the classification of phenomena and as a means to picture historical change or process. Both Steward and White were concerned to show conceptual differences with biological evolution and the superior explanatory potential of cultural evolution as compared to cultural relativism. The critical contrast with biological evolution was held to be the attribution of qualitative difference to successive evolutionary stages, and the concept of "multilinear evolution," that is, the search for parallels of limited occurrence, not universals of human history.

Early on, evolutionist ideas were challenged by more particularist and relativist notions of anthropology. The internal colonialism of Native peoples that was still being practiced at the turn of the century was the backdrop against which ethnography was initially undertaken in the United States, in order to salvage knowledge of cultural forms before they disappeared. As a result, the close analysis of specific cultures, evinced in the works of Karl Kroeber, Franz *Boas, Margaret *Mead, and Robert Lowie during the 1920s and 1930s, was seen as the proper realm of anthropology, which was thereby restricted to in-depth description of particular ethnographic contexts, rather than the comparative and diachronic project that evolutionary theories had implied.

Until the 1960s this remained the intellectual agenda of U.S. anthropology, which largely ignored the emergence of both functionalism and structuralism in Europe. Steward's ideas about cultural evolution were fruitfully married to the notion of ecology by a number of anthropologists, notably Robert Netting, Roy Rappaport, and Andrew Vayda. Intellectual connections with archaeological anthropology were very strong among such theorists since archaeologists had always been concerned with the longer time scales in which evolutionary theorists tend to deal.

Evolutionary theories also influenced cultural materialist anthropologists, who espoused a depoliticized version of Marxist theory that gave causal primacy to the productive "base" over the contingent expression of those economic relationships as society and culture, or "superstructure." Morton Fried, Elman Service, and Marshall Sahlins all produced major works on the political evolution of bands, tribes, and states, while Marvin Harris provided both a critique of anthropological theory and a didactic demonstration of how cultural materialism could explain the "riddles" of culture, such as food taboos.

Anthropology was central to the wider intellectual changes in the academy at the end of the twentieth century, both as exemplar of the limitations of social science, as in the critique of modernism, and as an innovative practitioner of the humanities, as in the critique of ethnographic writing and representation. The integration of history with anthropology occurred through recognition of the ways global colonial encounters had already induced fundamental social and cultural changes in the non-European world that preceded ethnographic recording. Culture change and its relation to western colonialism was therefore much emphasized, as in the work of Eric Wolf, but with a new stress on the symbiotic nature of cultural encounters, and an interest in delineating the role of individual agency in such processes.

This stress on the individual also engendered interest in the notion of "performance." Myth, ritual, history, and society are actually witnessed ethnographically as particular performances. An appreciation of the way such discrete performances feed structural changes provided a key conceptual link with earlier theory, as in the work of Sahlins. In sum, the process of colonialism produced mutually entangled histories that the old small-scale, village-based ethnographies could not witness or describe. At the same time came an increased emphasis on individual agency within sociocultural structures that are also to be understood in the actors', not the observers', own terms.

The idea of symbolic structure was retained to explicate the coordination of cultural proclivities and historical actions, as in the work of Victor Turner on "communitas." But Emiko Ohnuki-Tierney showed that symbolic transformation itself cannot be adequately explained without reference to wider historical transformations, especially colonialism. The relation between these symbolic and historical transformations was stressed by Sahlins who demonstrated the importance of knowing the actual impact of different ways of symbolizing history on historical actions.

From literary and political critiques of the genre of ethnographic writing, as in the work of George Marcus, Michael Fisher, and Clifford Geertz, it became apparent that anthropology needed to recognize more generally that nonwestern forms of cultural and historical consciousness were present in the performance of myth, ritual, and the plastic arts. The legacy of European structuralism was the canard that nontextual societies were historically "cold," but among Africanists dealing with an extant indigenous historiography this was not the case, as Jan Vansina had already shown in his work on the oral transmission of historical data.

With the issue of "representation" to the fore, literary and epistemological analyses of ethnographic writing, and its relation to colonialism, increasingly influenced debate. The works of Sherry Ortner, Richard Price, Michael Taussig, and Michael Herzfield displayed just this mix of a theoretical concern with the lingering intellectual legacy of colonialism and the need for new forms of ethnographic and historiographic representation in order fully to slough it off. So, too, the interest in performance led to a productive line of enquiry that dealt with the nature of discourse as a symbolic and semiotic act, as in the works of Ellen Basso, Jonathan Hill, and Greg Urban. Trends as the century closed suggested that this phase of experimentation had given way to the confident practice of a more historically alert and humanistic anthropology.

[*See also* Education: Rise of the University; Evolution, Theory of; Modernist Culture; Postmodernism; Social Science.]

• Julian Steward, *Basin-Plateau Aboriginal Socio Political Groups,* 1938. Roy Rappaport, *Pigs for the Ancestors,* 1968. Marshall Sahlins, *Stone Age Economics,* 1972. Clifford Geertz, *The Interpretation of Culture,* 1973. G. Marcus and M. Fisher, *Anthropology as Cultural Critique,* 1986. Richard Price, *Alabi's World,* 1991.

—Neil L. Whitehead

ANTI-BALLISTIC MISSILE TREATY (1972). *See* Nuclear Arms Control Treaties.

ANTI-CATHOLIC MOVEMENT. Inherited from British sectarianism, anti-Catholicism became the core ingredient in the American *nativist movement. Like English, Scottish, Welsh, and Irish Protestants, many Anglo-Americans considered popery a subversive culture as well as an alien creed. They were convinced that Catholics, submissive to papal authority and beset by superstition, could never be loyal or productive citizens. Before 1820, with Catholics few in number, nativist worries were more fantasy than reality. After that date, massive Irish *immigration provided a large, visible enemy and intensified fears for American institutions and values. These anxieties inspired vicious anti-Catholic propaganda with pornographic overtones, such as Maria Monk's *Awful Disclosures* (1836); triggered attacks on Catholic neighborhoods and churches; increased demands for limitations on immigration and more rigid qualifications for citizenship; and in the 1850s produced the American (*Know-Nothing) party with an anti-Catholic agenda.

Reflecting economic conditions, nativism waxed and waned during the nineteenth and twentieth centuries. Inspired by *Social Darwinism, it took on racist and anti-Semitic dimensions, but anti-Catholicism remained a key ingredient. Immigration brought large numbers of Catholics from Italy and Eastern Europe into urban America and Irish American control of a rapidly expanding Catholic church with a large institutional structure, including parochial schools; political domination in many cities; and labor movement leadership. All this frightened nativists. The religious factor in American prejudice was particularly noticeable in rural areas and small towns. But even in more sophisticated environments such as business, the professions, and academia, Catholics as well as Jews often faced either exclusion or quotas.

In the late nineteenth and early twentieth centuries, the American Protective Association, the Guardians of Liberty, the American Minute Men, Covenanters, the Knights of Luther, and especially the revived *Ku Klux Klan all appealed to anti-Catholic bigotry. The Klan mobilized against Catholic presidential candidates Alfred E. *Smith in 1928 and John F. *Kennedy in 1960.

Conditions improved as the twentieth century moved along. The favorable presentation of priests in 1930s and 1940s movies, Catholic patriotism during *World War II, economic and social *mobility after it, growing religious tolerance, and the popularity of John F. Kennedy all helped to diminish anti-Catholicism and open doors of opportunity to its former victims. In the late 1960s, academics were the last important segment of the population to abandon their prejudice.

Although most Catholics felt comfortable in the United States by century's end, some still complained that they experienced more media criticism and ridicule than other racial or religious minorities. What remained of anti-Catholicism was often directed at the church's official condemnation of contraception and *abortion. A majority of the American Catholic laity has rejected the former and has reservations concerning the latter.

[*See also* Anti-Semitism; Immigration Law; Irish Americans; Italian Americans; Labor Movements; Protestantism; Roman Catholicism; Urbanization.]

• Ray Allen Billington, *The Protestant Crusade,* 1800–1860, 1938, rpt. 1964. John Higham, *Strangers in the Land: Patterns of American Nativism,* 1860–1925, 1955, rpt. 1965.

—Lawrence J. McCaffrey

ANTICOMMUNISM. Anticommunism was one of the most significant forces in twentieth-century American politics. While its enemies saw anticommunism as dictating U.S. foreign and domestic policy, anticommunists viewed themselves as a derided minority ignored by decision-makers dedicated to policies of coexistence and détente that legitimized communist totalitarianism.

American anticommunism emerged from the Palmer raids: the roundup of alien communists organized in December 1919 and January 1920 by J. Edgar *Hoover, then a twenty-five-year-old Justice Department attorney, with the backing of Attorney General A. Mitchell Palmer. From these raids arose a tradition of countersubversive anticommunism rooted in the conviction that a Red network linked the American reform movement to the Communist International in Moscow. Also thanks to the Palmer raids, all American anticommunists, in a guilt-by-association process, were identified with conspiracy-hunting countersubversives eager to smear groups and ideas they hated.

In reality, anticommunism reflected the diversity of American society; its activists brought to the movement the distinct and often antagonistic interests of the communities that produced them. Countersubversive anticommunists like Hoover, Hamilton Fish, Martin Dies, Richard M. *Nixon, Joseph *McCarthy, and Robert Welch of the *John Birch Society, who regarded Soviet espionage and government subversion as the essence of the communist threat, were the most vocal. Far more numerous, however, were responsible anticommunists possessing accurate knowledge about domestic and foreign *communism and sincerely concerned about the threat it posed to their own communities, the nation, and the world. This group included Catholics like Father Edmund Walsh of Georgetown University, Patrick Scanlon, editor of the *Brooklyn Tablet,* Francis Cardinal *Spellman, and William F. *Buckley Jr.; *New Deal Era liberals like the theologian Reinhold *Niebuhr and Arthur Schlesinger Jr.; Jewish anticommunists of such varied political convictions as Louis Marshall of the American Jewish Committee, George Sokolsky of the Hearst newspaper chain, and Norman Podhoretz of *Commentary*; socialists like Abraham Cahan of the *Forward*; labor-union officials like Samuel *Gompers, David Dubinsky, Sidney Hillman, George *Meany, and Albert Shanker; and black anticommunists such as the columnist George Schuyler. The press tycoon Henry R. *Luce, publisher of *Time, Life,* and *Fortune* magazines, represented another powerful anticommunist voice. Excommunists and ex–fellow travelers like Whittaker Chambers, Sidney Hook, Eugene Lyons, and Jay Lovestone were especially important for the insights and experience they brought to the movement. United only in their hatred of communism, these individuals often warred as fiercely among themselves as against the common enemy.

American anticommunism exerted its greatest influence during the late 1940s and early 1950s, when it provided the moral and intellectual basis for the *containment policies that underlay the Western alliance against the Soviet Union and other communist regimes. During those *Cold War years, anticommunists created a widespread grassroots movement that mobilized millions of Americans in opposition to Soviet policies. The mass base of American anticommunism was weakened, however, by the collapse of McCarthy's irresponsible career in 1954. After that, outspoken anticommunism was often equated with the right-wing extremism of demonized groups like the John Birch Society, and blamed for the disastrous policies of the John F. *Kennedy, Lyndon B. *Johnson, and Richard Nixon administrations in Southeast Asia.

Moribund by the late 1970s, anticommunism enjoyed a remarkable revival during the Ronald *Reagan administration, led by a president whose anticommunist career began as a labor-union leader in Hollywood. Under Reagan, anticommunists from Walt Rostow and Paul Nitze's Committee on the Present Danger directed an anticommunist foreign policy aimed at dismantling what Reagan termed the Soviet Union's "Evil Empire." The collapse of that empire brought to an end the momentous history of American anticommunism. The debate over its role in American history, however, showed no sign of abating.

[*See also* Communist Party—USA; Hiss, Alger; House Committee on Un-American Activities; Rosenberg Case.]

• *Newsletter of the Historians of American Communism,* 1982–present. Kenneth O'Reilly, *Hoover and the Un-Americans,* 1983. John Earl Haynes, *Communism and Anti-Communism in the United States: An Annotated Guide to Historical Writings,* 1987. M. J. Heale, *American Anticommunism: Combating the Enemy Within, 1830–1970,* 1990. John E. Haynes, *Red Scare or Red Menace,* 1996. Richard Gid Powers, *Not without Honor: The History of American Anticommunism,* 1997.

—Richard Gid Powers

ANTI-DEFAMATION LEAGUE (ADL). Founded in 1913 by the Chicago Lawyer Sigmund Livingston with the sponsorship of the Jewish service organization B'nai B'rith "to stop the defamation of the Jewish people and to secure justice and fair treatment to all citizens alike," ADL fights *anti-Semitism and bigotry, defends democratic ideals, and protects *civil rights for all Americans. With national headquarters in *New York City, the organization at the end of the twentieth century encompassed thirty regional offices in the United States and maintained sites in Jerusalem, Vienna, and Moscow.

ADL was founded amid the atmosphere of pervasive anti-Semitism that culminated in the 1915 lynching in Georgia of Leo Frank, a Jew falsely accused of murder. In its early years, ADL worked to eradicate negative stereotypes of Jews in newspapers, on stage, and in the movies. The league later expanded to investigate and expose the *Ku Klux Klan and other hate groups, foster interreligious and intergroup understanding, bridge cultural differences through antibias training and education, and file legal briefs challenging discrimination. After the establishment of the State of Israel in 1948, ADL spearheaded efforts to counter anti-Zionism and Arab anti-Jewish sentiment. It also engaged in Holocaust education and exposed myths perpetrated by Holocaust deniers.

The ADL's model hate-crimes statute, upheld by the U.S. *Supreme Court and enacted by forty states and the District of Columbia, provides for enhanced penalties when crimes are committed because of a victim's race, religion, ethnicity, sexual orientation, gender, or national origin. The league also monitors hate on the *Internet and World Wide Web; and tracks extremists, from neo-Nazi skinhead groups to international terrorists, and seeks to break the cycle of hatred through programs designed for schools and the workplace.

[*See also* Judaism; Racism.]

• Maryanne Wagner and Ralph Carlson, *American Jewish Desk Reference,* 1999. http://www.adl.org.

—Abraham H. Foxman

ANTIETAM, BATTLE OF (1862). In the late summer of 1862, as the *Civil War raged on, simultaneous Confederate invasions of Kentucky and Maryland led England's leaders to consider recognizing the independence of the *Confederate States of America. Invading Maryland, Robert E. *Lee divided his forty thousand–man army into four parts to capture Harpers Ferry, Virginia, held by Union forces. After Union General George B. McClellan, commanding 87,000 soldiers, cautiously probed the Confederate position at South Mountain on 14 September, Lee collected most of his army along the banks of Antietam Creek, near Sharpsburg, Maryland.

The battle of Antietam commenced on 17 September when Federal troops began a series of uncoordinated attacks against the Confederate left. By late morning the Federal attack had shifted to the Confederate center. Here the Confederates took cover in a sunken farm road, later known as "Bloody Lane." By midafternoon, the battle had shifted to the Confederate right. After taking Rohrbach or "Burnside's" bridge, the Federals advanced toward Sharpsburg. Only the timely arrival of Ambrose Powell Hill's Confederates from Harpers Ferry saved the rebel army's line of retreat. The Confederates abandoned the field on the 18th.

The date 17 September 1862 has the dubious distinction of being the bloodiest day of the Civil War, indeed, of all American history; total casualties amounted to 22,719 killed, wounded, or missing. In the aftermath of the battle of Antietam, England abandoned its consideration of Confederate independence. Following the battle, Abraham *Lincoln issued the *Emancipation Proclamation, which freed all slaves in areas of rebellion as of 1 January 1863. What had begun as a war for the Union now became a war for freedom.

• Stephen W. Sears, *Landscape Turned Red: The Battle of Antietam,* 1983. Gary W. Gallagher, ed., *Antietam: Essays on the 1862 Maryland Campaign,* 1989.

—Jonathan M. Berkey

ANTI-IMPERIALIST LEAGUE. Founded in 1899 to oppose U.S. annexation of the *Philippines following the *Spanish-American War, the Anti-imperialist League was the largest lobbying organization on a U.S. foreign-policy issue through the end of the nineteenth century. The league, strongest in the Northeast, was an ideological heir of both the antebellum abolitionist movement and *Mugwump critics of *Gilded Age political corruption. Although the league attracted such notables as Andrew *Carnegie, Jane *Addams, William *James, and the editor E. L. Godkin, its fate underscored the awkward nature of dissent against President William *McKinley's policy toward the Philippines. Struggling to articulate a consistent message, league officials such as Erving Winslow, George Boutwell, and Edwin Burritt Smith offered a variety of arguments against annexation. These ranged from the contention that acquiring colonies would violate the *Constitution and betray traditional American anti-imperial ideals to charges that McKinley had exceeded his executive authority. This diffuse approach hampered the league's efforts to win support within the *Republican party, where proponents of expansion, such as Theodore *Roosevelt and Alfred Thayer *Mahan, maintained a strong following. After a scant two-thirds majority in the Senate approved the Treaty of Paris, thus confirming the annexation, the league declined in strength, especially once war broke out between American forces and Filipino nationalists headed by Emilio Aguinaldo. Politically, the leadership's partisan affiliation prevented a working alliance with anti-expansionist Democrats. Although presidential nominee William Jennings *Bryan promised to transform his 1900 campaign into a referendum on imperialism, his views on financial and racial issues differed from those of many Republican anti-imperialists and divided league activists. Meanwhile, the drawn-out conflict in the Philippines exposed league activists to charges of treason, causing a further decline in their political support and intensifying internal divisions about how forcefully to oppose McKinley's policy.

[*See also* Expansionism; Hawai'i; Protectorates and Dependencies.]

• E. Berkeley Tompkins, *Anti-Imperialists in the United States: The Great Debate, 1890–1920,* 1970. Richard Welch Jr., *Response to Imperialism: The United States and the Philippine-American War, 1899–1902,* 1979.

—Robert David Johnson

ANTI-MASONIC PARTY. This political party arose in New York in response to the 1826 disappearance of William Morgan, a Mason. His lodge was suspected of murdering him in revenge for his publication of the organization's secrets. When state and local officials, mostly proto-Democrats, procrastinated in the investigation, angry citizens formed a political party and in 1827 won several New York legislative seats. By 1829 Anti-Masonry had spread throughout much of the Northeast, with its greatest political impact in Pennsylvania. Between 1828 and 1838, Anti-Masons elected seventy-six candidates to Congress. In 1832, Anti-Masonic party candidates won 10 percent of all House races, and the party's presidential candidate, William Wirt, carried Vermont and won almost 8 percent of the popular vote nationally.

Anti-Masons owed some of their popularity to the religious *revivalism of the 1820s. The role of economic factors is more problematic. While some studies show that the party had the support of the emerging middle class, others indicate that economically declining groups voted for it. By 1836, most Anti-Masons had joined the *Whig party because Democratic President Andrew *Jackson had vigorously defended the *Masonic order. In addition, Anti-Masons opposed his Sunday mail transportation policies. Anti-Masons gave the Whigs an evangelical, populist dimension, as well as gifted leaders and political operatives such as Thaddeus Stevens of Pennsylvania and Thurlow Weed of New York. Anti-Mason inspired social policies favored by Whigs, such as liquor and sabbatarian legislation, funding of educational and reformatory institutions, and to some extent the *antislavery impulse of the party's northern wing.

[*See also* Antebellum Era; Temperance and Prohibition.]

• Kathleen S. Kutolowski, "Antimasonry Reexamined: Social Bases of the Grassroots Party," *Journal of American History* 71 (1984): 269–93. Paul Goodman, *Towards a Christian Republic: Antimasonry and the Great Transition in New England, 1826–1836*, 1988. Michael F. Holt, *Political Parties and American Political Development from the Age of Jackson to the Age of Lincoln*, 1992.

—Lex Renda

ANTINUCLEAR PROTEST MOVEMENTS. After the U.S. government's atomic bombing of *Hiroshima and Nagasaki in August 1945, a recognition of the dangers that nuclear war posed to human survival sparked the development of an antinuclear movement in the United States and abroad. *Manhattan Project scientists—some of whom had opposed the use of *nuclear weapons during *World War II—organized the Federation of Atomic Scientists (which later became the Federation of American Scientists) and the Emergency Committee of Atomic Scientists, with Albert *Einstein, Leo Szilard, and Eugene Rabinowitch playing leading roles in a crusade for nuclear disarmament. A burgeoning world government movement also warned of the menace of nuclear war, as did pacifist groups like the Fellowship of Reconciliation, the War Resisters League, and the Women's International League for Peace and Freedom. A communist-led antinuclear campaign, focused on the Stockholm peace petition, surfaced as well. With the deepening of the *Cold War, however, American attitudes grew more hawkish and the protest movement dwindled.

In 1954, though, another wave of protest began, stimulated by the terrible destructiveness of the newly developed hydrogen bomb and by the atmospheric testing of this weapon, which showered the planet with radioactive fallout. Joining with British philosopher Bertrand Russell, Einstein issued a dramatic appeal to world leaders to halt the nuclear arms race. Subsequently, meeting in Pugwash, Nova Scotia, scientists launched the periodic Pugwash conferences of scientists from East and West to discuss nuclear issues, while chemist Linus *Pauling began a scientists' petition calling for an end to nuclear testing. In 1957, Norman Cousins, editor of the *Saturday Review*, and other nuclear critics organized the National Committee for a SANE Nuclear Policy (SANE), a group that placed antinuclear ads in newspapers, held public meetings and demonstrations, initiated petition drives, and soon had 25,000 members. Established in 1959, the Student Peace Union mobilized college students against the nuclear menace and introduced Britain's nuclear disarmament symbol in America. Two years later, Women Strike for Peace, founded by Dagmar Wilson and other concerned mothers, brought thousands of women into the streets, demonstrating for an end to nuclear testing and the nuclear arms race. These dramatic protests played an important role in convincing previously reluctant governments to negotiate the *Limited Nuclear Test Ban Treaty (1963), banning atmospheric tests. Reassured, many concerned citizens turned to other issues.

Nevertheless, the revival of the Cold War in the early 1980s—symbolized by the advent of the hawkish administration of President Ronald *Reagan and the deployment of a new generation of nuclear missiles in Europe—led to a new and more powerful wave of popular protest. Organizations like SANE, Mobilization for Survival, and Physicians for Social Responsibility organized a mammoth antinuclear effort, with the largest political demonstrations in American history. The Nuclear Weapons Freeze Campaign garnered the support of the major churches, unions, the *Democratic party, and—according to polls—70 percent or more of the public. This movement, too, ebbed in subsequent years, as national political leaders responded to popular antinuclear sentiment and negotiated significant arms control and disarmament agreements. But nuclear dangers remained, raising the possibility of future antinuclear protest campaigns.

[*See also* Antiwar Movements; Nuclear Strategy; Nuclear Weapons; Pacifism; Peace Movements; Science: Since 1945.]

• Lawrence S. Wittner, *One World or None: A History of the World Nuclear Disarmament Movement through 1953*, 1993. Lawrence S. Wittner, *Resisting the Bomb: A History of the World Nuclear Disarmament Movement, 1954–1970*, 1998.

—Lawrence S. Wittner

ANTISALOON LEAGUE. *See* Alcohol and Alcohol Abuse; Temperance and Prohibition.

ANTI-SEMITISM. A term coined in Germany in 1879, "Anti-Semitism" means hostility toward Jews. Rooted in Christian teachings, this antagonism dates back almost two thousand years. Assumptions about "Jewish" responsibility for the death of Jesus pervaded Christian theology well into the twentieth century. The worst manifestations of European anti-Semitism occurred during crisis times when people blamed Jews for social ills. These malevolent ideas were based not only on theological beliefs but also on erroneous assumptions about Jewish religious, economic, and political predilections. Jews were believed to kill gentile children and use their blood for religious ceremonies; in different centuries they were censured as usurers, "blood-sucking" economic predators, and plotters against Christian governments.

European immigrants brought anti-Semitism to America as early as the seventeenth century. In 1654, Peter Stuyvesant, the Dutch governor of New Amsterdam, sought to prevent Jews from settling in what is now *New York City. Throughout the *Colonial Era, authorities limited the economic and political activities of Catholics and non-Christians. In some colonies, Jews could not become lawyers or physicians. In most they could not vote. Jews gradually gained legal rights after the *Revolutionary War, but not until 1877 did New Hampshire become the last state to lift its ban on non-Christian voting.

Although anti-Semitism to a degree remained part of the cultural baggage of successive waves of Christian immigrants from Europe, these prejudices were both molded and softened as the newcomers encountered a culturally diverse society and American commitments to the idea of tolerance. But while the restrictions on Jews in the United States were never as stringent as they had been in Europe, individual Jews often found themselves the targets of prejudice and ancient cultural stereotypes portraying them as cold-hearted, cunning, and loathsome.

While anti-Semitic attitudes have waxed and waned

throughout American history, they were especially strong during the *Civil War and the periods of heavy *immigration in the late nineteenth and early twentieth centuries. *The Passing of the Great Race* (1916) by the prominent New York lawyer and civic leader Madison Grant purveyed a virulent anti-Semitism. The national-quota provisions of the immigration acts of 1921, 1924, and 1952 aimed to limit the number of Jewish (and Asian) immigrants.

Anti-Semitism in America peaked between 1918 and 1945. The 1917 Bolshevik revolution in Russia led to a "Red scare" targeting aliens, especially Jews, who were thought to harbor subversive attitudes. Auto magnate Henry *Ford ran a series in his *Dearborn Independent* newspaper, throughout the 1920s on "The International Jew." The articles blamed every evil and moral failing in the United States on Jews and charged that Jews were plotting to overthrow existing governments. In the same decade housing and employment discrimination increased, colleges and universities established Jewish quotas, and leaders of society harbored a chilling animosity that contributed to the ostracism of Jews in many spheres.

During the Depression-wracked 1930s, the presence of Jews among President Franklin Delano *Roosevelt's advisers resulted in opponents of the New Deal labeling it the "Jew Deal." In 1938, as Hitler's power increased in Germany, a Roman Catholic radio priest, Father Charles Coughlin, denounced Jews and encouraged his followers to join him in a "Christian Front." Coughlin's attacks intensified over the next four years. In 1942, after the United States had entered *World War II, Roosevelt threatened to jail Coughlin for *sedition and Coughlin's superiors silenced him. But Coughlin was not alone. Anti-Semitism in the State Department, the corporate world, and the public at large played a role in Washington's hesitant response to the desperate plight of European Jews persecuted by the Nazis.

American anti-Semitism declined precipitously after World War II. The horror of the Holocaust, Hitler's genocidal program to exterminate European Jews, served to discredit the pronouncements of anti-Semites. The 1947 film *Gentleman's Agreement*, starring Gregory Peck, exposed anti-Jewish discrimination in American society. Civil rights organizations challenged various forms of discrimination. The American Jewish Committee, the American Jewish Congress, the *Anti-Defamation League (ADL) of B'nai B'rith monitored incidents of anti-Semitism and sought legislation minimizing its impact. The AJ Committee also engaged in extensive study on the causes of anti-Semitism, worked behind the scenes with elected political officials, and sponsored uplifiting radio programs designed to present Jews in a favorable light. The AJ Congress actively challenged existing institutional prejudices through the legal system, while the ADL both engaged in serious research on the causes of anti-Semitism and sought media publicity to expose bigotry. By the end of the twentieth century, expressions of anti-Semitism were quickly disavowed by leaders in religion, government, and business. But though much diminished, anti-Semitism persisted, peddled by alienated, marginal organizations obsessed with conspiratorial theories, and exploited by some leaders of disadvantaged minorities as a focus for their anger and resentment.

[*See also* Cultural Pluralism; Immigration Law; Judaism; New Deal Era, The; Twenties, The.]

• Bertram Korn, *American Jewry and the Civil War*, 1951. Robert G. Weisbord and Robert Stein, *Bittersweet Encounter: The African American and the American Jew*, 1970. Michael Barkun, *Religion and the Racist Right: The Origins of the Christian Identity Movement*, 1994. Leonard Dinnerstein, *Antisemitism in America*, 1994. Fred Jaher, *A Scapegoat in the Wilderness*, 1994.

—Leonard Dinnerstein

ANTISLAVERY. The American antislavery crusade was a multifaceted, long-term social reform movement that persisted from the mid-eighteenth century through Emancipation in 1864. Over the years, the movement evolved from religious protest and colonization efforts to political organization, abolitionism, violent protest, and, finally, emancipation.

Beginnings of Antislavery Agitation. Antislavery originated as a moral and religious issue. Various Protestant denominations—*Mennonites and Amish, Presbyterians, Congregationalists, *Baptists, and the *Society of Friends (Quakers)—all contributed, with Quakers the early leaders. Eighteenth-century Quakers George Keith, John *Woolman, and Anthony Benezet each attacked *slavery on the basis of moral principle: namely, the equality of all persons before God. Among Baptists, local associations resolved to oppose the extension of slavery; some writers even called for its abolition. By the second decade of the nineteenth century, religious activists had formed antislavery societies that held public meetings and distributed literature to raise consciousness about the moral issues involved.

An early effort to achieve the progressive elimination of slavery was the African *colonization movement. As a "gradualist" compromise between the moral issue of human bondage and the racial prejudices of white society, national leaders like Bushrod Washington, Thomas *Jefferson, James *Monroe, and Henry *Clay advocated manumitting (freeing) slaves and returning them to Africa, with the costs—including compensation to the owners—to be paid from a combination of public and private funds. The American Colonization Society, established in 1817, founded Monrovia (later Liberia) on the West African coast in 1822 as a colony for freed slaves. By 1860, some twelve thousand *African Americans had returned to Africa. The colonization movement stirred hostility, however, from southerners opposed to manumission; from those who disapproved of spending public monies on the project; and from persons truly interested in the slaves' well-being, who saw repatriation to Africa as simply a further injustice to persons of color.

By the late 1820s, rising public indignation in the North, called by some "ultraism," strengthened antislavery sentiments. Local societies began to appear, particularly in New England. Leaders like Lewis and Arthur Tappan in *New York City, William Lloyd *Garrison in *Boston, and Theodore Dwight Weld in Ohio founded a national organization, the *American Anti-Slavery Society (AAS), in 1833. Garrison, regarded as a fanatic by some and, worse yet, an incendiary by others, brought to the cause a sense of urgency; a genuine threat to slaveholders; and an uncompromising periodical, *The Liberator*, founded in 1831. An organizational genius, Garrison created a system whereby paid AAS agents fanned out across the North to lecture, debate, distribute tracts, sell *Liberator* subscriptions, and assist free blacks and fugitive slaves wherever possible. Through the AAS, the antislavery leadership combined careful planning and organization with the zeal of an evangelical religious crusade. Among the most effective AAS lecturers were the *Grimké sisters of South Carolina, Sarah and Angelina, who had embraced Quakerism and moved North. In 1839 the Grimkés and Weld (whom Angelina had married) published *American Slavery as It Is*, a powerful documentary record of brutal abuses.

The religious dimension of antislavery found expression as well in the ministry of the Charles G. *Finney and at two Ohio schools founded in 1833: Lane Theological Seminary in Cincinnati and Oberlin College. Lane, a Presbyterian school, was situated in close proximity to a large population of free blacks. Its faculty and students included many antislavery firebrands, and a series of public lyceum debates soon gave Lane such a reputation as a hotbed of activism that in 1834 the trustees forbade further discussion of the matter. Fifty-one Lane students, called "the Rebels," withdrew and enrolled at Oberlin, an antislavery center where Finney was professor of theology. Through various forms of ministry and activism, Oberlin students and faculty infused the antislavery cause with new energy and momentum, making the college one of the movement's major leadership resources.

The Turn to Politics. In 1840, Theodore Dwight Weld, the Tappan brothers, and other antislavery leaders turned to political organization. They were encouraged by the British Parliament's abolition of slavery throughout the British Empire in 1833. Forming the *Liberty party (also known as the Human Rights party), they nominated James G. Birney, a slaveowner turned abolitionist, for president. In part a reaction against Garrison (who was displaying increasingly radical and anarchist tendencies), the Liberty party stressed natural rights and political action. In 1840, too, these same individuals founded the American and Foreign Anti-Slavery Society, which challenged Garrison for leadership of the movement. (The issue of equality for women in the antislavery campaign, which Garrison supported and more conservative antislavery leaders opposed, figured in this split as well.) Although Birney received only about seven thousand votes, his candidacy brought national attention to the antislavery cause—and sharpened the proslavery defenses of southern whites. Running again in 1844, Birney received 62,300 votes.

Congress's defeat in 1846 of the Wilmot Proviso (a resolution barring slavery in any territories other than Texas acquired in the *Mexican War), coupled with the failure of either national party to take an unequivocal stand against slavery, further energized the effort to oppose slavery at the ballot box. In 1848 the *Free Soil party took up the antislavery banner, nominating former president Martin *Van Buren on a platform opposed to the expansion of slavery into the territories, summed up in the slogan "Free Soil, Free Labor, Free Men." While Van Buren ran third behind the *Whig party candidate Zachary *Taylor (who won) and the Democrat Lewis Cass of Michigan, he did garner nearly 300,000 votes. Within a few years, many Free Soil voters would join the new *Republican party, a coalition of antislavery enthusiasts, religious leaders, and former Whigs.

Abolitionism. Meanwhile, "abolition" had become the cry of the more ardent antislavery advocates and "action-men." Radical activity ensued. Abolitionists flooded the South with inflammatory pamplets. Free northern blacks and escaped slaves like Frederick *Douglass, William Wells Brown, and William and Ellen Craft played an important role in the movement. Douglass became a major abolitionist spokesman, particularly with the publication of his *Narrative of the Life of Frederick Douglass, an American Slave* (1845). Abolitionists organized and operated the so-called Underground Railroad, a complex network of antislavery households that spirited runaway slaves to the North and *West, the Caribbean, and Canada. The 1850 *Fugitive Slave Act, a victory for slaveholders, heightened abolitionist fervor and directly inspired the most famous of all antislavery works, Harriet Beecher Stowe's 1852 novel **Uncle Tom's Cabin*. The *Kansas-Nebraska Act (1854) and the *Supreme Court's *Dred Scott* (**Scott* v. *Sandford*) decision (1857), representing further victories for the slave power, added fuel to the abolitionist cause. Most radical of all were the ultraists like John *Brown, who were prepared to wage armed conflict to achieve their objectives. Brown's career of antislavery violence, first in Kansas and then at Harpers Ferry, Virginia, in 1859, won the support of Douglass and other prominent abolitionist leaders. Within two years the *Civil War, which would finally end slavery in America, was underway.

From its inception, the antislavery movement benefited greatly from the evangelical energies unleashed in the Second *Great Awakening, and from the many voluntary associations generated within the Protestant community. Countless antislavery leaders and supporters had roots in the evangelical missionary and revivalist traditions, and many also participated in other reform arenas, from Anti-Masonry and adventism to the *temperance and *women's rights movements. Such leading women's rights advocates as Lucretia *Mott, the Grimké sisters, and Elizabeth Cady *Stanton got their start in the antislavery movement. Antislavery was the first great human rights crusade in American history. A sustained campaign lasting more than a century, it not only helped bring about the emancipation of the slaves, but it also inspired a long tradition of social reform.

[*See also* Antebellum Era; Anti-Masonic Party; Protestantism; Revivalism.]

• P. J. Staudenraus, *The African Colonization Movement, 1816–1865*, 1961. Bertram Wyatt-Brown, *Lewis Tappan and the Evangelical War against Slavery*, 1971. James B. Stewart, *Holy Warriors: The Abolitionists and American Slavery*, 1977. Ronald G. Walters, *The Antislavery Appeal: American Abolitionism after 1830*, 1978. Lewis Perry and Michael Fellman, eds., *Antislavery Reconsidered: New Perspectives on the Abolitionists*, 1979. Robert Abzug, *Passionate Liberator: Theodore Dwight Weld and the Dilemma of Reform*, 1980. Lawrence J. Friedman, *Gregarious Saints: Self and Community in American Abolitionism*, 1982. Aileen S. Kradotir, *Means and Ends in American Abolitionism: Garrison and His Critics on Strategy and Tactics, 1834–1850*, 1989. Jean Fagan Yellin, *Women and Sisters: The Antislavery Feminists in American Culture*, 1989.

—William H. Brackney

ANTITRUST LEGISLATION. Opposition to concentrated corporate power occupies a noteworthy if ambiguous place in American history. Ever since Congress passed the Sherman Antitrust Act of 1890, public consensus supported antitrust values in principle, even as repeated disputes arose over their application in particular cases. Such inconsistency paralleled the nation's unfolding experience with big government and managerial *capitalism; the shifting significance of small business and organized labor; the growing importance of economic experts; and the central policy-making role of lawyers and courts, particularly the U.S. *Supreme Court. A popular faith in competition governed antitrust development. What "competition" meant, however, and who benefited, was subject to change.

Gilded Age Beginnings. The antitrust movement originated as managerial capitalism burgeoned near the end of the nineteenth century. Following the *Civil War, technological innovation and *mass marketing fostered the development of large-scale corporate combinations, leading to a separation between owners and managers. In this new form of corporate enterprise, managers increasingly acted as the principal decision-makers. The rise of big business spawned corporate mergers as well as loose cartel arrangements and other trade restraints. (A cartel is a secret agreement among supposedly competing businesses to establish a monopoly by price fixing or other means.) While some states successfully limited both forms of combination, New Jersey enacted a law in 1889 permitting the formation of holding companies and facilitating the formation of corporate combinations controlled by managers. Because the New Jersey law conflicted with other states' laws, its critics demanded federal action.

The Sherman Act was a product of countervailing market and political pressures. Small business and farm groups, eager to limit the growth of large corporate combinations, supported federal action in principle. Big business interests and their lawyers, by contrast, were divided over the possible results of a more uniform national antitrust policy. Fearing that federal power might be used against it, organized labor opposed federal antitrust legislation. Popular opinion, at the time and ever since, reflected these divergent sentiments. Americans profoundly distrusted giant concentrations of corporate wealth and power, while at the same time they yearned for the consumer benefits that bigness often seemed to facilitate; people were also anxious about the apparent lack of legal accountability of huge, "soulless" corporations. Congress responded to those conflicting desires and interests with a law embodying several general provisions: Section 1 of the Sherman Act banned "[e]very contract, combination . . . or conspiracy" that restrained interstate or foreign trade of commerce; Section 2 prohibited individual firms from monopolization and attempted monopolization. The act's enforcement relied upon the state and federal courts.

Federal or state prosecutors, as well as private litigants, could win treble damages by proving violations of the law.

The Sherman Act's general provisions invited diverse interpretation. During the first decade of the law's operation, the Supreme Court encouraged corporations to adopt the holding company approach. (A holding company is a corporation that owns a controlling share of the stock of one or more other firms.) In 1895 the high court held that the E. C. Knight Company, a holding company that monopolized sugar production in the United States, did not violate the antitrust law. The Supreme Court and state courts also decided, however, that loose cartel practices were illegal under both the Sherman Act and state laws. The Court's simultaneous enforcement of rules against cartel practices and its toleration of holding companies facilitated a great turn-of-the-century merger wave. By 1903 most of the nation's largest firms were holding companies in which decisions were generally left to managers. Meanwhile, the Supreme Court and lower federal judges increasingly applied the Sherman Act against organized labor, enabling employers to defeat strikes and boycotts.

The Progressive Era. After 1900, demands for stricter antitrust enforcement increased. In the **Northern Securities Case* (1904), Theodore *Roosevelt's administration became the first to prosecute successfully a holding company. This victory brought an end to the first merger wave. Federal officials, corporate leaders, economists, Wall Street lawyers, and Supreme Court justices soon concluded that a more flexible "*rule of reason" should govern merger cases. Adopting a rule of reason as the basic doctrine governing merger cases, the Supreme Court in 1911 struck down predatory pricing practices that Standard Oil and American Tobacco were using to crush smaller firms.

Louis *Brandeis, a prominent lawyer who championed small business and opposed big corporations, favored employing the rule of reason to allow for loose collusion among small enterprises, while urging the breakup of giant corporations. In taking this position, Brandeis adopted an Americanized version of European cartel policy. But in 1911 the Supreme Court frustrated Brandeis's hopes, outlawing loose cartel arrangements even among smaller companies.

Woodrow *Wilson's victory in the 1912 presidential election brought the enactment of two new antitrust laws. The *Federal Trade Commission Act of 1914 created an administrative agency with broad powers to prevent "unfair methods of competition." The terms "unfair" and "competition" remained sufficiently general, however, that judicial interpretation was inevitable. Similarly, the 1914 Clayton Act included provisions condemning the anticompetitive implications of price discrimination, exclusive arrangements, interlocking directorates, and stock-purchase mergers, particularly holding companies. The Clayton Act also contained language that seemed to prohibit injunctions against labor. However, the Supreme Court construed both laws so narrowly that the advocates of more vigorous antitrust enforcement grew frustrated. The Justice Department prosecuted single-firm monopolies, oligopolistic competition among a few managerially centralized big corporations characterized most leading industries. Still, the federal government's persistent prosecution of price fixing violations did enhance competitive opportunities for small businesses. Farmer cooperatives and exporters, by contrast, benefited from antitrust legislation.

The New Deal Era and Beyond. As the twentieth century progressed, antitrust legislation achieved mixed results. The Norris-LaGuardia Anti-Injunction Act of 1932 decisively exempted labor organizations from the antitrust laws. Yet following the early New Deal's unsuccessful experiment with federally authorized cartelization under the *National Recovery Administration, antitrust enforcement became more vigorous. Small business benefited from various fair-trade laws. In antitrust cases heard by the Supreme Court under Chief Justice Earl *Warren (1953–1969), the Court favored smaller business as it curtailed many horizontal and vertical mergers. Simultaneously, however, corporate managers, created conglomerates of competitively unrelated firms joined together primarily for investment purposes. The Hart-Scott-Rodino Act of 1976 added antitrust provisions that permitted the Justice Department's Antitrust Division to pursue a more proactive policy against mergers with antitrust implications. The Supreme Court's and the Antitrust Division's embrace of free-market theories during Ronald *Reagan's administration in the 1980s, however, turned the Hart-Scott-Rodino Act to the benefit of new forms of financially driven vertical mergers. The court, moreover, expanded the application of the rule of reason to permit what previously had been treated as clear-cut violations of the antitrust laws. By the 1990s a reaction against the more extreme free-market enthusiasm of the 1980s arose, creating new possibilities for the future of antitrust enforcement.

Bringing antitrust law into the computer age, the Department of Justice won a landmark case against the software giant Microsoft in 2000. Microsoft appealed, however, and the final outcome remained uncertain.

[*See also* Business; Corporatism; Federal Government, Executive Branch: Other Departments (Department of Justice); Gilded Age; Industrialization; Labor Movements; Laissez-faire; New Deal Era, The; Petroleum Industry; Progressive Era.]

• Thomas K. McCraw, *Prophets of Regulation: Charles Francis Adams, Louis D. Brandeis, James M. Landis, and Alfred E. Kahn*, 1984. James May, "Antitrust in the Formative Era: Political and Economic Theory in Constitutional and Antitrust Analysis, 1880–1918," *Ohio State Law Journal* 50 (1987): 257–395. Martin J. Sklar, *The Corporate Reconstruction of American Capitalism, 1890–1916: The Market, the Law, and Politics*, 1988. Neil Fligstein, *The Transformation of Corporate Control*, 1990. Tony Freyer, *Regulating Big Business: Antitrust in Great Britain and America, 1880–1990*, 1992. Rudolph J. R. Peritz, *Competition Policy in America, 1888–1992*, 1996.

—Tony A. Freyer

ANTIWAR MOVEMENTS. Organized opposition has accompanied most American wars. Sometimes dissent came from broader *peace movements, which sought to supplant national wars with *internationalism and nonviolent resolution of conflict, but peace advocates often supported particular wars. Sometimes war resistance derived from *pacifism, understood as the repudiation of organized violence, but pacifists in that sense usually dissented as individual conscientious objectors (COs) or withdrew into sectarian communities. Sometimes opposition came from political, class, or sectional interests that were reinforced by broad principles.

In the nineteenth century, an organized and growing peace movement called for the arbitration of international disputes, but opposition to particular wars primarily reflected sectional and class interests. Thus New Englanders who belonged to the *Federalist party motivated by economic and political interests, challenged the constitutional legitimacy of the *War of 1812. Similarly, the *Mexican War was challenged in the North, where interest in western expansion reinforced *antislavery principles. Opposition to the *Civil War in the border states and the Ohio River valley fused local economic and cultural interests with a principled defense of states' rights. Finally, the U.S. subjugation of the *Philippines in 1899–1901 was opposed mainly by members of a cultural elite who believed that the war was eroding the anticolonial foundations of U.S. foreign policy. A few absolute pacifists resisted all those wars, but regional interests or class-based opposition predominated.

This pattern changed during *World War I. During the period of U.S. neutrality, 1914–1917, a principled opposition formed against any increase in military budgets and against any intervention in the European struggle. The strongest, most political antiwar group, the American Union against Militarism (1915), mobilized progressives to challenge both Woodrow *Wilson's preparedness budget and his subsequent break with

Germany. After U.S. entry into the war, opposition continued among many religious COs, progressive pacifists, and antiwar socialists like Eugene V. *Debs, as well as within some ethnic communities, especially *Irish Americans. The ostracizing and persecution of dissenters only strengthened their organizational ties, so that the principle of war resistance emerged from the war upheld by such groups as the Fellowship of Reconciliation (FOR, 1915) and the War Resisters League (WRL, 1921). Some, like the *American Friends Service Committee (1917), had a progressive orientation, and all of them, especially the Women's International League for Peace and Freedom (1919), were related to international networks. Thus the organizational base was created for a recurrent antiwar movement.

Given the prevailing antiwar mood of post–World War I society, these organizations found ready constituencies for political activism against military spending and military training in the schools, as well as for constructive internationalism. In the 1930s they spearheaded support for legislative measures calling for strict neutrality and, after 1939, lobbied against so-called collective-security programs. They were joined and eventually led by the socialist leader Norman *Thomas in the Keep America Out of [the European] War Organization. From the political right came support from the isolationist *America First movement, and from the far left (until Germany invaded Bolshevik Russia in June 1941), the *Communist party. Organized opposition to war virtually dissolved after the attack on *Pearl Harbor.

The institutional framework of war resistance remained, however, and the WRL especially came to harbor a number of COs who objected to both war and conscription. Steeped in Gandhian principles, they experimented with nonviolent direct action in the prisons and Civilian Public Service (CPS) camps housing conscientious objectors. Nonviolence was also applied to race relations during and after *World War II. Further developed in both the *civil rights movement and the *antinuclear protest movements of the 1950s, nonviolent direct action and civil disobedience were frequently employed tactics among opponents of the *Vietnam War after 1965.

Opposition to the Vietnam War, scarcely visible during the period of initial involvement and escalation, eventually became widespread. Antiwar activism was often spontaneous and local. Nonetheless, shifting national coalitions also provided focal points for public antiwar information and agitation. The most visible forms of activism were mass demonstrations, large-scale civil disobedience, and countercultural images; less public, but at least as important, was quiet, hard work in electoral and legislative politics. The Vietnam Veterans Against the War organization (1967) helped to legitimize antiwar activism. By 1970 antiwar sentiment pervaded national institutions, including Congress; by 1972 it was dominant.

Adopting similar strategies in the post–Vietnam War era, a Latin American Solidarity movement helped to check the Ronald *Reagan administration's support of the "Contras" in Nicaragua and of military regimes elsewhere in Central America. An effective Washington lobby mobilized legislative opposition to the United States-sponsored Contra war. Simultaneously, a decentralized, grassroots citizens' movement made contact with Nicaraguans and Salvadorans and publicized their causes. The *Persian Gulf War of 1991 stirred considerable opposition, which was ultimately ineffectual and aborted, given the brevity of the campaign.

In summary, recurrent antiwar activism—grounded in a continuous peace movement; marked by ever shifting organizational bases, tactics, and philosophies; and growing or waning in relation to prevailing issues—has frequently been a factor influencing foreign and military policy-making, especially in twentieth-century America.

[*See also* Anti-imperialist League; Conscientious Objection; Isolationism; Preparedness Movement Controversy (1914–1917).]

• Samuel Eliot Morison, Frederick Merk, and Frank Freidel, *Dissent in Three American Wars,* 1970. Charles DeBenedetti, *The Peace Reform in American History,* 1980. Lawrence Wittner, *Rebels against War: The American Peace Movement, 1933–1983,* 1984. Charles DeBenedetti and Charles Chatfield, *An American Ordeal,* 1990. Charles Howlett, *The American Peace Movement: References and Resources,* 1991. Charles Chatfield, *The American Peace Movement: Ideals and Activism,* 1992. Frances Early, *A World without War: How U.S. Feminists and Pacifists Resisted World War I,* 1997.

—E. Charles Chatfield

APARTMENT HOUSES. *See* Housing.

APPALACHIA. Geographically, Appalachia includes the mountains and valleys of states eastward from the Ohio River to the piedmont and northward from Georgia to Maine. Appalachia most often refers to the more populated southern Alleghenies, Blue Ridge, Appalachian, Ozarks, and Great Smoky mountains, a land inhabited by a people with a distinct history, memory, and culture.

Appalachian settlement constituted part of the fourth great migration wave (ca. 1717–1775) from Europe to America. Over 60 percent of the settlers came from England's borderlands region surrounding the Irish Sea: the Scottish lowlands, northern Ireland, and the six northern counties of England. The numbers averaged 5,000 per year or about 285,000 total. Largely Presbyterians at first, many were converted to more evangelical forms of Christianity by Methodist and *Baptist missionaries. From the Palatinate of southwestern Germany about 100,000 German Protestants (Lutherans, Quakers, Moravians, Calvinists, Dunkers, and *Mennonites and Amish) came to British America in a series of waves that began in 1683 and continued until the *Revolutionary War. The number who settled in Appalachia is unknown, but at the first census in 1790, they composed only 5 percent of the population of the Carolinas, Georgia, Tennessee, and Kentucky, compared to 90 percent who were English, Irish, or lowland Scots.

Demographically, one of Appalachia's most arresting features has been the fertility rate. Beginning in the nineteenth century and continuing for roughly 150 years, the birthrate of Appalachia exceeded the national average. If the reasons are unclear, the consequences are obvious. In a region of narrow valleys, steep mountainsides, and rocky ridges, continuous population growth and practices of partible inheritance over time produced overpopulation, land scarcity, and rural *poverty. Consequently, throughout its history, *mobility has been another distinctive feature of Appalachian life. The need to find supplementary work to preserve the family in a kinship-based society has been called "the stable ideal." Such conditions also bred a patriarchal family structure with strong male authority over women and children in the household.

Poverty and isolation, often mistakenly associated with Appalachia's entire history, actually arose in distinct periods of its development. Between 1850 and 1900, as turnpikes and *railroads diverted traffic around Appalachia, the region grew isolated. Overpopulation led to increasing landlessness. Sectionalism and the *Civil War exacerbated these conditions, giving rise to xenophobia and a more introverted society.

Simultaneously, beginning in the 1880s, local-color writers began to paint literary pictures of a "strange land and a peculiar people." The "hillbilly" genre they created persisted into the late twentieth century as the source of misunderstandings and caricatures of regional history and culture. Over eight hundred movies, from the early nickelodeon one-reelers to late twentieth-century films like *Deliverance, Thelma and Louise,* and *Raising Arizona,* depicted hillbillies as "cultural others." Other twentieth-century writers and folklorists such as Altina Waller, Durwood Dunn, and David Whisnant, provided correctives to these distorted images, however.

Between the 1890s and the 1930s, migration to nearby rural industries such as quarrying, coal *mining, *lumbering, and iron making provided some respite from chronic rural poverty.

In Appalachia's version of the New South, local and state governments, legislatures, and politicians transformed themselves into propagandists for the region and invented tax incentive schemes to encourage industrial development. Outside capital flowed into the region and, together with inside help from a small commercially minded urban elite of lawyers, bankers, and merchants, stimulated rapid urban and industrial growth. With the coming of alternative fuels in the 1920s and the Great Depression of the 1930s, the boom decades ended. Racial *segregation, as seen, for example, in Coe Ridge, Kentucky, and Piedmont, West Virginia, and higher rates of *lynching than in the non-Appalachian South during these years shattered the illusion of racial harmony in the region.

Between 1940 and 1970, New Deal programs, the *World War II draft, and out-migration brought more contact with other Americans. Many fled to the "Appalachian ghettos" in Baltimore, Cleveland, Dayton, Cincinnati, Chicago, and Detroit. The 1960 census revealed a regional population decrease for the first time since the area was settled by Europeans. John F. *Kennedy focused attention on poverty in Appalachia in his 1960 campaign for the *Democratic party's presidential nomination, as did Michael Harrington in *The *Other America* (1962). The 1970s saw a reversal, demographically and economically, as out-migrants returned, young people chose to remain, and many older Americans decided to retire in Appalachia.

[*See also* Folklore; Methodism; New Deal Era, The; Regionalism.]

• Henry D. Shapiro, *Appalachia on Our Mind: The Southern Mountains and Mountaineers in the American Consciousness*, 1978. Ronald D. Eller, *Miners, Millhands, and Mountaineers: Industrialization of the Appalachian South, 1880–1930*, 1982. Altina L. Waller, *Feud: Hatfields, McCoys, and Social Change in Appalachia, 1860–1900*, 1988. David Hackett Fischer, *Albion's Seed: Four British Folkways in America*, 1989. Crandall A. Shifflett, *Coal Towns: Life, Work, and Culture in Company Towns of Southern Appalachia, 1880–1960*, 1991. Henry Louis Gates Jr., *Colored People*, 1995.

—Crandall Shifflett

ARCHITECTURE

Public Architecture
Domestic Architecture

ARCHITECTURE: PUBLIC ARCHITECTURE

The first public architecture in America were places of ceremonial significance to Native Americans, from the great earth mound at Cahokia, Illinois, to Pueblo kivas. In the early *Colonial Era, religious structures were typically the most prominent public buildings. Puritan meetinghouses in *New England usually stood on central commons and served not only for religious services, but also for town meetings. In the eighteenth century, church spires were challenged as public landmarks only by symbols of colonial governance, such as the Pennsylvania State House (Independence Hall, 1731–1753) in *Philadelphia. Less formal, but of equal significance to the public realm, were the public markets and taverns. The Raleigh Tavern in Williamsburg, a principal social center of the capital, became the site for political meetings on the eve of the *Revolutionary War.

The establishment of the United States through revolution against the colonial power of Britain called for an immediate creation of public architecture asserting the new nation's democratic values. This is best reflected in the dome-crowned U.S. Capitol in *Washington, D.C., designed primarily by William Thornton, Benjamin Latrobe, and Charles *Bulfinch from 1793 to 1829, and greatly expanded by Thomas U. Walter from 1851 to 1865. The dome emerged in American governmental architecture as a symbol of democratic gathering for political discourse to foster civic betterment and unity. Thomas *Jefferson in his design for the University of Virginia (1817–1826) in Charlottesville as an "academical village," created an architectural microcosm for the new republic of individual diversity—through the separation and variety of the pavilions, united into a community by Neoclassical colonnades and headed by the library rotunda, a secular temple of enlightened and rational thought. During the early nineteenth century, Neoclassical revival styles held strong associations with the *Romantic movement. William Strickland's Second Bank of the United States (1818–1824) in Philadelphia, a Greek Revival adaptation of the Parthenon, evokes a new beginning for Western civilization through a revivification of the democracy and architecture of the ancient Greeks.

During the *Gilded Age, civic structures became larger, reflecting the growth of governmental bureaucracy as well as local boosterism; A grand new city hall or county courthouse could assert a locality's primacy over its rivals. One of the most prominent examples is Philadelphia City Hall (1871–1901) by John McArthur Jr., an enormous Second Empire picturesque mass placed on the center square of Philadelphia and topped with a 548-foot tower. A popular style of American public architecture in the late nineteenth century was the Richardsonian Romanesque, which proclaimed monumentality through massive walls and simple, strong arches, as popularized by architect Henry Hobson Richardson (1838–1886) with such buildings as the Allegheny County Courthouse and Jail (1884–1888) in Pittsburgh.

The new city that arose after the *Chicago fire of 1871 was not dominated by the traditional landmarks of public architecture, but by commercial skyscrapers. Even a major public space like Dankmar Adler and Louis *Sullivan's Auditorium (1886–1890) was cloaked in commercial facades containing a hotel and offices. Yet commercial buildings sometimes provided the grandest and most inviting public spaces of the day, such as the interior courts of Daniel H. Burnham's Marshall Field Store (1902–1914). In capitalist America, the private sector has built some of the most notable architecture for the public. Toward the end of his career, Sullivan attempted to define an American democratic architecture through such small-town banks as the National Farmers Bank (1906–1908) at Owatonna, Minnesota.

The 1893 World's Columbian Exposition in Chicago presented the more imperial image of Beaux-Arts Classicism to the public. The City Beautiful Movement arose creating ensembles of public buildings as the focus of urban plans. Washington, D.C., in particular was transformed into an ordered procession of Classical Revival government buildings, *museums, and monuments. Some of America's greatest public buildings were created during this American Renaissance, such as the Boston Public Library (1887–1895), designed by the firm of Charles Follen McKim, William R. Mead, and Stanford White; Richard Morris Hunt's entrance wing (1895–1902) to the Metropolitan Museum of Art in New York; Henry Bacon's *Lincoln Memorial (1912–1922) in Washington, D.C., and several archetypical domed state capitols from Rhode Island to Utah. Millionaire capitalists turned philanthropists endowed the nation with many new public buildings, most notably Andrew *Carnegie's funding of hundreds of public *libraries. Large railroad stations offered the public noble entrances into cities with central halls on a scale to please an emperor, as still can be seen in New York's Grand Central Terminal (1903–1913) by the firms of Reed and Stem, Warren and Wetmore.

During the *New Deal Era the Public Works Administration (1933–1939) constructed many new public buildings, from small-town post offices to college libraries, often in a stripped classical style suggesting stability in austere times. After *World War II, new art museums were often the most dramatic and timeless definitions of architecture for the public, such as Frank Lloyd *Wright's Guggenheim Museum (1956–1959) in New York and Louis I. Kahn's Kimbell Art Museum (1966–1972) in Fort Worth, Texas. The triumph of modernism and the growth of government led to *urban renewal projects that eradicated older sections of cities in preference for anonymous *skyscrapers and vacuous plazas, as epitomized by the Nelson A. Rockefeller Empire State Plaza (1962–1978) in Albany, by Wallace K. Harrison and Max Abramovitz. By the 1970s, *postmodernism began a reexamination of the traditional symbolism of public architecture. James Hammond, Thomas H. Beeby, and Bernard Babka's Harold Washington Library Center in Chicago (1987–1991) reasserts an ornamented monumentality and traditional grandeur for a major public building.

The automobile profoundly affected traditional notions of public space. In the decades after World War II, *shopping centers and malls replaced Main Street and the town square as the center of most American communities. This development can be particularly traced in the suburbs of Minneapolis from Southdale Shopping Center (1956) to the Mall of America (1992). As the twentieth century ended, public life for some Americans was perhaps no better represented than by the artificial, controlled, and fantastic domains of theme parks, particularly Walt Disney World Resort (1971) near Orlando, Florida. Yet American public architecture still has moments of greatness, such as Maya Lin's *Vietnam Veterans Memorial (1981–1982) in Washington, D.C., where two angled, partially subterranean walls of dark granite bearing the names of the war dead become a vortex for the fractured public feelings of a nation.

[*See also* Architecture: Domestic Architecture; City Planning; Indian History and Culture: Migration and Pre-Columbian Era; Modernist Culture; Puritanism; Sculpture; World's Fairs and Expositions.]

• Henry-Russell Hitchcock and William Seale, *Temples of Democracy: The State Capitols of the U.S.A.*, 1976. Lois Craig and the Staff of the Federal Architecture Project, *The Federal Presence: Architecture, Politics, and Symbols in United States Government Building*, 1978. Diane Maddex, ed., *Built in the U.S.A.: American Buildings from Airports to Zoos*, 1985. Craig Zabel and Susan Scott Munshower, eds., *American Public Architecture: European Roots and Native Expressions*, 1989. Alan Gowans, *Styles and Types of North American Architecture: Social Function and Cultural Expression*, 1992. Pamela Scott, *Temple of Liberty: Building the Capitol for a New Nation*, 1995.

—Craig Zabel

ARCHITECTURE: DOMESTIC ARCHITECTURE

Since the *Colonial Era, house building in America has been characterized by three qualities: a persistent use of the traditional European housing forms and styles; a gradual but significant increase in the amount of space allocated to each person; and, despite growing population and ecological pressures, a continued interest in free-standing, single-family houses. From the eighteenth century on, single-family housing has also been considered a badge of social status and a form of art.

Archaeological evidence indicates that the first colonists often built thatched huts and wigwams, modeled after Native American forms. As soon as possible, however, they turned to traditional European structures. Settlers in St. Mary's City, Maryland, for example, erected medieval-style houses, thirty feet long and eighteen feet wide, constructed on poles embedded in the earth, that resembled the timber-framed houses they had known in England.

More permanent house forms, supported by rock foundations, supplanted pole houses by the early eighteenth century. Many were "hall-and-parlor" houses, like the Fairbanks house in Dedham, Massachusetts (1636), the oldest surviving wooden frame building in America. These houses often had two equal-sized rooms, about sixteen feet square or one "bay," to either side of a central hallway and a massive seven-foot fireplace for heat. Built with small windows and heavy doors, these structures displayed a fortresslike appearance.

By the early eighteenth century, simple clapboard-sided timber-framed houses, now two stories high and three bays wide, were a familiar sight on the eastern seaboard. Although a wide variety of other house styles, ranging from the log cabins of Germans and Scandinavians to the earth-walled adobe homes of Hispanic settlers in the Southwest, also dotted the landscape, by the 1730s the simple rectangular structures (sometimes also called I-houses, each two rooms wide and one room deep) had become commonplace.

The I-house never became either a totally dominant or a static and unchanging style, however. The regional variants of log houses, adobe structures, and other ethnic housing forms persisted far into the twentieth century, and almost every conceivable variation of the I-house form was also built. In the southern tidewater, front porches and rear sections were added. In *New England, the roof sometimes extended back down to cover a rear kitchen, creating a "salt-box" look. And Dutch settlers in the cities of New York and New Jersey favored parapeted roofs where the gable end of the house extended above the roof line, or (after 1750) distinctive gambrel roofs, which start at one pitch or downward slant for a few feet and then change to a steeper pitch.

By the 1750s, colonial prosperity had created an upper class that sought to raise its status by adopting British classicism. Refined by English architects Inigo Jones, Christopher Wren, and James Gibbs, this style was popularized in pattern books that provided drawings of window moldings, flattened classical columns (pilasters), and gable decorations. These Georgian-style houses were built often in a symmetrical five-bay pattern (two windows, a door, two windows). The Georgian style modernized the traditional I-house form by adding stylish decorative detailing.

American fondness for wooden classical house style resulted in the adoption, between the 1770s and 1850s, of a number of variations of this design, including the more delicate Adamesque style (including a prominent front door with fanlight and delicate roof moldings), named for the Scottish architectural brothers Robert and James Adams; the Roman Revival (with a two-story front porch supported by columns); and the Greek Revival (with a low-pitched roof and cornice lines emphasized by wide, divided bands of trim).

Whether built in the North or *South, classical revival houses added a quality of simple elegance to the westward expanding frontier settlements. They also fit well with the popular commitment to democratic politics that contemporaries associated with the Roman and Greek empires. Long a recognizable feature of the East Coast landscape, colonial styles enjoyed revivals in the 1890s, 1930s, and 1950s.

In the middle decades of the nineteenth century, the classical revival's dominance was undercut by the architectural planbook writer Andrew Jackson Downing, who helped popularize Gothic, Italianate, and other historical revival housing forms. This *Romantic movement, which endowed house design with moral significance, portrayed the house as a symbol of intellectual achievement and social status.

While wealthy industrialists in Newport, Rhode Island, built huge homes patterned after Italian villas, Americans of more modest means took advantage of the availability of mass-produced windows, doors, and two-by-four-inch interior framing (called the balloon frame), and the invention of central heating, electric lighting, and indoor plumbing, to increase the convenience and space in their homes as well. In the *Middle West, Frank Lloyd *Wright and other architects created their own distinctly American style, the Prairie School, characterized by its prominent, overhanging roof line and horizontal bands of windows.

From the 1890s on, middle-class Americans also built smaller, more efficient houses. These were located in new residential suburbs, connected to nearby cities first by train and later by automobile freeways. From the turn of the century until the 1930s, small one- or two-story bungalows, with large front porches, sprang up in many of these suburbs.

After *World War II, one-story ranch or Cape Cod houses

superseded bungalows in popularity. But even these small structures were often enlarged. Where each family member in the 1790s enjoyed between 67 and 169 square feet of space, family members in 1991 could expect to enjoy an average of 674 square feet.

Although Modernism, with its square forms, use of steel and glass, and flat roofs was popularized in the 1950s by the German expatriate architects Ludwig Mies Van der Rohe (1886–1969) and Walter Gropius (1883–1969), the style remained most popular among the wealthy. Despite the persistent interest of architects, most domestic housing has been designed and constructed by local builders in small, suburban developments, following styles available in popular magazines and plan books. Strong, well-built, and full of conveniences, these comfortable structures are testimony to the persistence of traditional housing forms in America.

[*See also* Architecture: Public Architecture; Housing; Modernist Culture; Suburbanization.]

• Lester Walker, *American Shelter: An Illustrated Encyclopedia of the American Home*, 1981. Gwendolyn Wright, *Building the Dream*, 1981. Virginia and Lee McAlester, *A Field Guide to American Houses*, 1984. Clay Lancaster, *The American Bungalow, 1880–1930*, 1985. Clifford E. Clark Jr., *The American Family Home, 1800–1960*, 1986. Alan Gowans, *The Comfortable House, North American Suburban Architecture, 1890–1930*, 1986.

—Clifford E. Clark Jr.

ARLINGTON NATIONAL CEMETERY. Administered by the U.S. Army, this military cemetery across the Potomac River from *Washington, D.C., is one of the nation's most important memorial sites. In 1864, in an act of retribution against Confederate general Robert E. *Lee, the War Department confiscated his estate in Arlington, Virginia, and turned it into an army cemetery. After the war, this temporary burial ground became part of a network of federal military cemeteries administered by the U.S. Army.

In the late 1890s and early 1900s, U.S. presidents promoted reconciliation between the North and *South by honoring the Confederate cause at the cemetery. In 1900, President William *McKinley signed legislation establishing a Confederate burial section at Arlington for the southern *Civil War dead buried in scattered cemeteries around Washington. In 1914, the United Daughters of the Confederacy built a Confederate War Memorial at Arlington. In 1925, Congress made Lee's former home a national memorial, and eight years later the National Park Service took custody of the structure.

Arlington holds the graves of over 150,000 veterans who served in every American war from the *Revolutionary War to the *Persian Gulf War. The grounds also contain such national memorials as the Arlington Memorial Amphitheater and the *Tomb of the Unknowns. Military or veteran's status is required for burial at Arlington, but the cemetery contains the graves of many prominent civilian leaders. The decision of the Kennedy family in 1963 to inter the remains of President John F. *Kennedy at Arlington, and five years later those of his brother, Senator Robert *Kennedy, enhanced the cemetery's importance as a national site of mourning.

[*See also* Military, The; National Park System.]

• Dean W. Holt, *American National Cemeteries*, 1992. G. Kurt Piehler, *Remembering War the American Way*, 1995.

—G. Kurt Piehler

ARMORY SHOW. The International Exhibition of Modern Art, initially intended to boost new American art and challenge conservative critics and curators, opened in mid-February 1913 at the 69th Regiment Armory in *New York City and continued to mid-March. It then moved in abbreviated form to *Chicago and *Boston. The sponsoring organization, the Association of American Painters and Sculptors, led by artists Arthur B. Davies, Walt Kuhn, and Walter Pach, took their chief inspiration from the Cologne Sonderbund Show (1912) and the Orphist circle around the Duchamp family in Paris. Exposing large numbers of untutored Americans to the Cubist work of Pablo Picasso, the Fauvist work of Henri Matisse, and other unconventional paintings and sculptures, the show excited hostile criticism and parody as it won unprecedented publicity for modernism in art (one critic compared Marcel Duchamp's *Nude Descending a Staircase, No. 2* to "an explosion in a shingle factory"). Some found it morally and politically threatening. Although it included some 1,600 works, the show omitted much that was happening on the contemporary art scene, especially in Germany and Italy, and presented a seriously skewed notion of the new artistic movements then maturing. Few noticed the American works at all. A triumph of promotion rather than taste, the Armory Show intimidated mature realistic painters and convinced many younger artists that to succeed they had to study in Paris. It had a more beneficent impact in drawing such major French artists as Marcel Duchamp and Francis Picabia to visit New York for extended periods, during which they exercised great influence on such opinion leaders as the photographer Alfred *Stieglitz and the painter and art patron Katherine Dreier.

[*See also* Modernist Culture; Painting: To 1945; Progressive Era.]

• Milton W. Brown, *The Story of the Armory Show*, 1963. Robert M. Crunden, *American Salons: Encounters with European Modernism, 1885–1917*, 1993.

—Robert M. Crunden

ARMS CONTROL. *See* Nuclear Strategy; Nuclear Arms Control Treaties; Washington Naval Arms Conference.

ARMSTRONG, LOUIS (1900?–1971), jazz trumpeter, band leader, vocalist. One of the twentieth century's premier *jazz musicians, Louis Armstrong was born in poverty in *New Orleans. He first learned to play brass instruments in Joseph Jones's Colored Waifs' Home. His skills matured in settings where ensemble jazz improvisation first evolved, including street parades, dance halls, and Fate Marable's Mississippi riverboat band. Armstrong's considerable influence as a jazz pioneer began with membership in the bands of Edward ("Kid") Ory (1918) and Joseph ("King") Oliver (1922), with whom he first recorded in 1923. Armstrong also collaborated with *blues musicians like Bessie Smith.

A virtuoso trumpet soloist, Armstrong through his Hot Five and Hot Seven recordings (1925–1928) disseminated jazz improvisation to a wide audience. His initial success was followed by fame as a band leader and vocalist; beginning in 1929, he fronted his own bands, including Louis Armstrong's All Stars (1947). Armstrong's world tours earned him recognition as the ambassador of American jazz. The State Department sent him on tour to Europe, Japan, South America, and Africa during the 1960s. Armstrong brought his talents to film in *Pennies from Heaven* (1936), *New Orleans* (1947), *High Society* (1956), and some twenty other movies. Popular songs became an increasingly important part of Armstrong's repertoire; "Hello Dolly" (1963) reached the top of *Billboard*'s charts in 1964.

Armstrong's performances, often accompanied by his use of exaggerated facial expressions characteristic of black *vaudeville, generated controversy when younger jazz musicians complained that this behavior reinforced negative racial stereotypes. Ironically, conservatives also criticized Armstrong for his defense of *civil rights activists in the Little Rock, Arkansas, school desegregation struggle of 1957. Armstrong's most influential work, from 1920 to 1940, exemplified the dynamic possibilities of jazz solo improvisation, innovative rhythmic phrasing, and mastery of the blues tradition. Despite his resistance to later jazz forms such as bebop, Armstrong's work remained a creative standard against which many later musicians—including Miles *Davis and Wynton Marsalis—would measure their craft.

[*See also* Foreign Relations: The Cultural Dimension; Music: Popular Music.]

• James Lincoln Collier, *Louis Armstrong: An American Genius,* 1983. Gerald Early, " 'And I Will Sing of Joy and Pain for You': Louis Armstrong and the Great Jazz Traditions," in *Tuxedo Junction: Essays on American Culture,* 1989, pp. 291–300.

—Kathy J. Ogren

ARMY. *See* Military, The.

ARMY CORPS OF ENGINEERS. The Corps of Engineers, founded in 1802, is the nation's oldest and largest construction agency: a builder of dams, canals, ports, roads, forts, airfields, missile emplacements, and space-exploration facilities as well as a diverse organization with a military command and a vast responsibility for water resources.

Combat engineers emerged from a mix of European traditions. During the *Revolutionary War, British-trained surveyors staffed a small geographers department in General George *Washington's army. French fort engineers planned the siege at the Battle of *Yorktown and commanded the short-lived U.S. Corps of Artillerists and Engineers, founded in 1794. Congress endorsed a French-style force of scientific technicians in the 1802 legislation that created the Corps and its engineering school, the U.S. Military Academy at West Point. Expanded after the *War of 1812, the Corps planned coastal defenses through the Board of Engineers for Fortifications (1816–1831). U.S. Topographical Engineers—a bureau of the Corps in 1818, made an independent command from 1831 to 1863—mapped roads, waterways, and rail routes into the *West. With the General Survey Act of 1824, Congress loaned Corps engineers to canal companies and launched an ambitious program of army-directed navigation improvement.

Dam building for flood control, a twentieth-century mission, evolved from the levee work of the Mississippi River Commission, a Corps-led organization founded in 1879. Army engineers also pioneered iron framing, flood modeling, underwater explosives, floating bridges, atomic bomb facilities for the *Manhattan Project, and enormous lock-and-dam projects such as the *Panama Canal; the Saint Lawrence Seaway project, completed in 1959; the 434-mile McClellan-Kerr waterway along the Arkansas River; and the ten-state Pick-Sloan project of the Missouri River basin. The Clean Water Act of 1972 made the Corps a protector of wetlands, a role frequently at odds with its development mission. Often controversial, the Corps grew with the nation, evolving from fort-building to space exploration, from combat to water science and monumental public works.

[*See also* Canals and Waterways; Dams and Hydraulic Engineering; Engineering; Environmental Protection Agency; Military, The; Military Service Academies.]

• Forest Hill, *Roads, Rail, and Waterways: The Army Engineers and Early Transportation,* 1957. Todd Shallat, *Structures in the Stream: Water, Science, and the Rise of the U.S. Army Corps of Engineers,* 1994.

—Todd A. Shallat

ARMY-McCARTHY HEARINGS (1954). On 22 April 1954, a huge crowd packed the Senate Caucus Room for the opening session of the Army-McCarthy hearings. At least forty million people followed the action on radio and television. In a narrow sense, the hearings focused on two distinct questions: First, did Republican Senator Joseph *McCarthy of Wisconsin and his top aide, Roy M. Cohn, exert improper pressure on the U.S. Army to win preferential treatment for Private G. David Schine, a part-time member of McCarthy's staff who had been drafted the previous year? Second, did army officials use Schine as a "hostage" in an effort to sabotage McCarthy's ongoing investigation of "communist influence" in the armed forces?

In a larger sense, however, the issues ranged from the threat of domestic subversion to the constitutional separation of powers, from the integrity of the *military to McCarthy's political future. As chairman of the Senate Committee on Government Operations and its powerful Subcommittee on Investigations, McCarthy had generated enormous publicity by charging that communists infested the government, including the U.S. Army. In response, military officials claimed that Cohn had threatened to "wreck the army" through reckless investigations if his close friend Schine did not receive special favors, such as extra weekend passes and an assignment near Washington.

The controversy infuriated President D. Dwight *Eisenhower, a five-star general, who deeply resented McCarthy's public assaults upon army personnel. It was Eisenhower who convinced Senate Republicans to televise the hearings, thereby bringing the senator into the living rooms of millions of Americans who had never seen his behavior at close range. McCarthy's day-to-day performance, marred by petulant outbursts and crude personal attacks, amply confirmed his critics' portrait of him as a bully and a fraud. The highlight of the hearings occurred on 9 June, when army counsel Joseph Welch berated the senator—"Have you no sense of decency, sir?"—to thunderous applause. The hearings ended on 17 June. In December, the Senate censured McCarthy for bringing that body "into dishonor and disrepute." Although McCarthy remained in office until his death in 1957, the Army-McCarthy hearings effectively ended his political career.

[*See also* Anticommunism; Cold War.]

• Michael Straight, *Trial by Television,* 1954. David M. Oshinsky, *A Conspiracy So Immense: The World of Joe McCarthy,* 1983.

—David M. Oshinsky

ARNOLD, BENEDICT (1741–1801), Continental army general and traitor. Born in Norwich, Connecticut, Arnold at fourteen ran away from home and joined the colonial militia. The tedium of service during the *Seven Years' War soon drained soldiering of its glory and Arnold deserted, establishing a pattern of abandoning allegiances when they failed to produce wealth, status, or fame. A prominent New Haven merchant, Arnold fought in the *Revolutionary War as leader of a Connecticut militia company. In 1775, he participated with Ethan Allen, the Vermont militia leader, in the capture of Fort Ticonderoga and led an army through Maine toward Quebec. The conquest of Canada failed, but Arnold's wilderness march enhanced his reputation. Injured in the Battle of Bemis Heights, Arnold was given command of *Philadelphia in 1778. Here he married Peggy Shippen, daughter of a wealthy family with Loyalist ties. Rampant corruption in Arnold's command, coupled with disputes with local officials, led to his court-martial in 1779. Acquitted on most charges, he was given command of the military fort at West Point on the Hudson River north of *New York City. The Philadelphia debacle, coupled with resentment over earlier slights and a desperate need for money to support a lavish lifestyle, led Arnold to plot with Sir Henry Clinton, the British commander in New York, to betray West Point to the British for twenty thousand pounds and a military commission. The plot unraveled in 1780 when the Americans captured (and later hanged) John André, a British go-between. Fleeing to the British, Arnold subsequently commanded a 1,200-man force in Virginia and led a raid on New London, Connecticut. He died in England, his name forever equated with treason in the United States.

[*See also* Military Service Academies.]

• Matilda A. Gocek, *Benedict Arnold: A Reader's Guide and Bibliography,* 1973. James Kirby Martin, *Benedict Arnold, Revolutionary Hero: An American Warrior Reconsidered,* 1997.

—Jon T. Coleman

ARTHUR, CHESTER A. (1829–1886), twenty-first president of the United States. Born in North Fairfield, Vermont, where his father was a *Baptist minister, Chester Alan Arthur graduated from Union College in 1848 and entered the bar. Practicing law in *New York City, he gained prominence in the 1850s for his *antislavery views and leadership in the emerging *Republican party. He married Ellen Herndon of Virginia in 1859; they had a son and daughter.

Arthur served with efficiency as quartermaster-general for New York during the *Civil War. He was a member of the Republican party's Stalwart faction, which New York Senator Roscoe Conkling led. President Ulysses S. *Grant appointed him collector of the Port of New York in 1871. In this lucrative post he distributed many patronage jobs, rewarding party loyalists while also seeking to recognize merit. President Rutherford *Hayes, an opponent of the Stalwart faction, removed him in 1878. His selection as James *Garfield's vice presidential running mate in 1880 reflected the party's effort to heal its internal division. He became president upon Garfield's assassination in 1881.

A conscientious and dignified chief executive, Arthur attempted to curb wasteful congressional "pork" spending. He yielded to pressure from *California, where Chinese workers were arriving in great numbers to work in the mines, and signed the 1882 Chinese Exclusion Act forbidding Chinese immigration for ten years. He had vetoed an earlier bill barring Chinese immigrants altogether. He appointed a Tariff Commission that recommended lower rates, but thanks to heavy lobbying, the so-called "Mongrel Tariff" of 1883 changed little. His secretary of state James G. *Blaine promoted U.S. commercial and trade interests with Latin America and Korea. Although identified with the patronage system, Arthur supported *civil service reform. He signed the 1883 Pendleton Act, which established the Civil Service Commission and launched the move toward a nonpartisan, expert civil service.

Arthur's wife died of pneumonia in 1880, so his widowed sister served as his White House hostess. Courtly and fashionable, he was nicknamed "Elegant Arthur." He sought the 1884 Republican nomination, but the Stalwarts considered him a turncoat while party reformers doubted his conversion to their cause, and he lost to Blaine. Arthur did not publicly support Blaine, who went on to lose New York, and the presidency, to Grover *Cleveland. Resuming his legal practice in New York, Arthur died of Bright's disease in 1886. Having upheld the authority of the presidency in an era of congressional dominance, Arthur was a transitional figure in the long movement toward enhanced federal activity.

[*See also* Federal Government, Executive Branch: The Presidency; Foreign Relations: U.S. Relations with Latin America; Gilded Age; Immigration Law; Tariffs.]

• Thomas C. Reeves, *Gentleman Boss: The Life of Chester A. Arthur*, 1975. Justus Doenecke, *The Presidencies of James A. Garfield and Chester A. Arthur*, 1981.

—H. Wayne Morgan

ARTICLES OF CONFEDERATION. On 7 June 1776, Richard Henry Lee of Virginia moved in the Second *Continental Congress that the thirteen American colonies declare their independence from Great Britain, and that Congress establish a committee to draft articles of confederation to bind the colonies together. Five days later, Congress created such a committee composed of one delegate from each colony with John Dickinson of Pennsylvania as chair. Congress approved the final version of the Articles of Confederation on 15 November 1777 and sent the document to the states for ratification. On 9 July 1778, delegates from eight states signed the Articles. Maryland, the last state to ratify, did so on 1 March 1781, at which time Congress declared "the Confederation of the United States" completed and perpetual.

The Articles provided for a unicameral Congress with no separate executive or judiciary. Congress, which could act only on the states, not on individuals, was to be elected annually in a manner determined by each state legislature. States could send up to seven delegates, with a minimum of two delegates needed for a state to be represented officially. Despite wide differences in population, each state had but one vote.

Congress had the sole power of determining war and peace, sending and receiving ambassadors, negotiating treaties, settling boundary disputes between states, regulating coinage, borrowing money, managing affairs with Indians, establishing and regulating a post office, regulating the army and navy, appointing courts for the trial of piracy and felonies on the high seas, and for dealing with cases concerning captured ships. The vote of nine states was required for most important matters. Congress did not have the power to regulate foreign or interstate commerce, to levy and collect taxes, or to raise an army. It could only request the states to pay their share of federal expenses and supply soldiers for the Continental army.

Canada was specifically allowed to join the confederation, but all other colonies needed the approval of nine states to enter. Every state was to abide by the determination of Congress on questions delegated to Congress by the Articles, and the Articles were to be inviolably observed by every state. Amendments to the Articles had to be ratified by the legislature of every state.

Even before adoption of the Articles, Congress observed most of their provisions. The British military danger encouraged the states to meet their obligations to Congress. After peace returned, however, the Articles' inherent weakness became apparent and, after several attempts to strengthen Congress by amending them failed because of the unanimity requirement, a *Constitutional Convention was called in 1787 to revise the Articles. In one of its first acts, the Convention voted to abandon the Articles altogether and draft a new constitution.

Congress under the Articles had three great successes: it obtained an advantageous peace treaty ending the *Revolutionary War, it acquired a huge public domain from state cessions of their western lands, and it enacted the *Northwest Ordinance, which established the pattern for the administration of federal territories.

[*See also* Colonial Era; Constitution; Federalism; Foreign Trade, U.S.; Revolution and Constitution, Era of; States' Rights; Taxation.]

• Merrill Jensen, *The Articles of Confederation: An Interpretation of the Social-Constitutional History of the American Revolution, 1774–1781*, 1940. Jack N. Rakove, *The Beginnings of National Politics: An Interpretive History of the Continental Congress*, 1979. Richard B. Morris, *The Forging of the Union, 1781–1789*, 1987.

—John P. Kaminski

ASIAN AMERICANS. American economic, military, and missionary activities profoundly affected the pattern of Asian and Pacific islanders' emigration to the United States. U.S. imperial expansion in the Pacific, the Yankee clipper trade with China, the annexation of *Hawai'i and the *Philippines, *World War II, the *Korean War, and the *Vietnam War all helped determine which Asian groups came to America and their treatment once here. When Americans colonized the Hawaiian islands in the nineteenth century, they brought in Asian workers for their sugar plantations. American labor contractors, together with recruiters from South America, Australia, and Canada, created a diaspora of Asian laborers all around the Pacific basin.

Used on the West Coast as labor competition to drive down wages in railroad construction, *mining, and *agriculture, Chinese and then Japanese immigrant workers were portrayed by European Americans as a "yellow peril." Asian workers were recruited in three successive waves—Chinese (1850–1882), Japanese (1890–1924), and Filipino (1900–1935)—as cheap laborers and then excluded or discriminated against as they came to be perceived as a threat. As West Coast nativists demonized "Orientals," labor organizers created unions that excluded Asians. Anti-Asian nativism and violence in the 1870s and 1890s drove Chinese Americans out of most industries and from small towns into large urban ghettos in Seattle and *San Francisco.

Congress excluded Chinese immigrants in 1882—a ban that continued until 1943. West Coast citizens started a "Japanese and Korean Exclusion League" in 1905, and in 1906 San Francisco's school board segregated Asian children. When the board reversed this action under pressure from President Theodore

*Roosevelt, Japan voluntarily agreed to halt the emigration of Japanese laborers to America. California restricted Japanese Americans' rights to own or lease farmland, and the Immigration Act of 1924 barred Asian immigrants entirely. The Great Depression of the 1930s, World War II, and the *Cold War halted the Asian diaspora, but millions of Asian migrants remained in their adopted homelands.

*Gender has played an important role in Asian American history. Asian manual laborers who came to the United States in the nineteenth century were overwhelmingly male. The few women who did emigrate to America (less than 10 percent of the roughly 100,000 Chinese emigrants) were harassed through legislation and stereotyped as prostitutes or objects of white male sexual fantasies. Because of Japan's greater diplomatic power, Japanese American male laborers could send for brides from Japan. Male Chinese and Filipino laborers found it much more difficult to bring wives to America, and these immigrants lived in almost exclusively male social worlds. Confronting racist housing and job discrimination, most Asian Americans endured a difficult and marginal existence.

World War II proved the most dramatic example of America's hypocritical treatment of Asian Americans. The United States forcibly interned over 110,000 Japanese Americans, of whom two thirds were American citizens. Ostensibly motivated by security fears, this action underscored the continuing power of *racism. In contrast, American propaganda heroicized America's wartime allies China and the Philippines, enhancing the standing of Chinese Americans and Filipino Americans. Despite discrimination, Filipino Americans, Chinese Americans, and Japanese Americans volunteered in high numbers for military service. Troops of the 442nd Regimental Combat Team, made up solely of Japanese Americans, many of whose families were interned, distinguished themselves for valor. After the war, Asian American veterans demanded that they be allowed to bring wives to the United States. The War Brides Act of 1947 allowed a small number of Asian American wives to enter the country. For veterans, the postwar period brought rising prosperity and *civil rights gains. Reflecting U.S. Cold War foreign-policy considerations, the 1952 McCarren-Walter Immigration Act removed the 1924 ban on Asian immigration.

In late twentieth-century America, native-born Asian Americans combined with extensive new Asian immigration to create one of the fastest growing segments of the U.S. population. A clause of the Immigration Act of 1965 encouraging the emigration of professionals proved pivotal, not only increasing Asian immigration, but changing the profile significantly from the earlier bachelor laborers. By the 1970s, many migrants from the Philippines, Taiwan, Korea, and India were emigrating to America to fill jobs in the burgeoning economy. Often coming as family units, large numbers of highly educated and skilled immigrants proved a boon to the U.S. economy, especially in high-tech industries. These professionals joined a growing number of second- and third-generation Chinese and Japanese Americans in white-collar jobs that had previously barred Asians. By the 1980s, the two most numerous Asian immigrant groups were South Koreans and Filipinos. Their paths to the United States paralleled that of migrants from Pacific islands with U.S. military bases, such as Samoa, Okinawa, and Guam. From 1980 to 1990, the number of Asians and Pacific Islanders in the United States grew by 80 percent, from 3.8 million to an estimated 6.9 million, comprising by 1990 just under 3 percent of the population.

Some post–World War II Asian immigrants were political refugees. For example, the U.S. government allowed Chinese students to stay in America after the Chinese communists came to power in 1949. After the Vietnam War, tens of thousands of refugees who had been identified with the American cause came to the United States from South Vietnam, Cambodia, and Laos. Although many of the Vietnamese were from the United States–supported Saigon government and military elite, they had difficulty finding work in anything except menial labor. Worse off were the Hmong, nomadic hill tribes recruited by the *Central Intelligence Agency to fight the North Vietnamese. Products of a village culture and ill-equipped for life in urban-industrial America, the Hmong found their exile particularly difficult.

Equated with a mythical "Orient" and cast as foreign and exotic, Asian Americans have historically suffered from the perception that they were not fully American. Even late twentieth-century positive representations of Asian Americans as a model minority—hard working, highly educated, and well paid—often attributed their success to supposedly "Confucian" values, further reinforcing their "otherness." As the twentieth century ended, Asians and Pacific Islanders made up an important and diverse group of American citizens. Their experiences shaped by extravagant dreams that clashed with harsh realities, they continued to seek opportunities in a nation that too often failed to live up to its promise.

[See also Foreign Relations: U.S. Relations with Asia; Immigration; Immigration Law; Incarceration of Japanese Americans; Missionary Movement; Nativist Movement.]

• Roger Daniels, *Asian America: Chinese and Japanese in the United States since 1850*, 1988. Gary Okihiro, *Margins and Mainstreams: Asian Americans in American History and Culture*, 1994. Ronald Takaki, *Strangers from a Different Shore*, 1989. Sucheng Chan, *Asian Americans: An Interpretive History*, 1991. William O'Hare and Judy Felt, *Asian Americans: America's Fastest Growing Minority Group, Population Trends and Public Policy*, 1991. Alexander Saxton, *The Indispensable Enemy*, 2d ed., 1996.

—Henry Yu

ASIA, U.S. RELATIONS WITH. *See* Foreign Relations: U.S. Relations with Asia.

ASSIMILATION, refers to processes that lead to greater homogeneity in a society. The term commonly describes the weakening of ethnic ties, cultures, and identities among members of an immigrant ethnic group, who in turn forge links to, and adopt the identities and cultural traits of, the larger society or its dominant ethnic group. Assimilation can also describe cases where members of different, nondominant ethnic groups find common ground. Understanding assimilation requires knowledge of what an individual or group is assimilating to.

Americans have discussed assimilation in terms of three main stances toward immigrants. "Anglo-conformity" was the assumption that newcomers and their children would adopt the culture of the nation's self-defined "Anglo-Saxon core." The "melting pot" stance (the term is from a popular 1908 play by Israel Zangwill) foresaw a mixing of peoples that would produce a new American culture. From the eighteenth century on, the third stance, *cultural pluralism, envisaged immigrant groups retaining their separate social worlds within a common political framework. This approach has nineteenth-century antecedents, but intellectuals such as Randolph *Bourne and Horace Kallen (1882–1974), a German-Jewish immigrant who later taught philosophy at the New School for Social Research in *New York City, articulated it most fully in the 1910s. Significantly, until the mid–twentieth century, most European American proponents of these stances envisioned no role for non-Europeans. European newcomers likewise have historically been the main reference point for most scholarly theories of assimilation; this has hampered understanding of how non-European immigrants have or have not assimilated.

The first sustained scholarly treatment of assimilation came from University of Chicago sociologists who developed a set of influential concepts in the early twentieth century. One cast migration as a process involving the "disorganization" of peasant communities and their members' journeys to the more individualized world of the city. Another concept broke social interaction into stages running from competition to assimilation. The concept of "ecological succession" depicted immigrant city-dwellers as moving from ethnic "colonies" through new districts, until they became absorbed into a hazily defined "American" population.

When immigration history became a professional subfield beginning in the 1920s, its practitioners made assimilation a central theme. They also adopted Chicago concepts. The historian Oscar Handlin's *The Uprooted* (1951), for example, described European immigrants as dislocated peasants who Americanized by becoming individuals. But scholars also began to define more clearly assimilation's social setting. Marcus Lee Hansen, arguing that third-generation immigrants showed renewed interest in their heritage, suggested in 1937 that ethnic identity might reemerge. Ruby Jo Reeves Kennedy proposed in 1944 that assimilation was occurring along religious lines, within a "triple-melting-pot" structure. Writing in 1956, Will Herberg saw these Protestant, Catholic, and Jewish melting pots as stemming from the third generation's discovery of religion as a permissible version of ethnic identity. Sociologist Milton Gordon's *Assimilation in American Life* (1964) found cultural assimilation to the "core subsociety" of white, middle-class Protestants, but not structural assimilation into its institutions. The result was a society centered around the "core" but retaining religious subdivisions, unassimilated racial groups, and some European ethnic "vestiges."

The 1960s saw a rejection of assimilation theory and a stress on ethnic group persistence. This approach, presaged by Gordon, was heralded by Nathan Glazer and Daniel Patrick Moynihan's *Beyond the Melting Pot* (1963) and Rudolph J. Vecoli's 1964 critique of Handlin's *The Uprooted.* The decade's turbulent politics fueled the shift, underlining the discrimination historically suffered by non-Europeans and encouraging a European American "ethnic revival." Beginning in the early 1980s, however, historians cautiously revisited assimilation. Some depicted a pluralistic America with room for assimilative processes between ethnic groups. Others examined how European ethnics claimed a common "white" identity; how second-generation Mexican and Japanese immigrants underwent a measure of acculturation even as they contended with *racism; and how 1930s unionism brought greater unity to an ethnically divided working class. By the end of the century, assimilation had reemerged as an acknowledged factor in ethnic history.

[*See also* Americanization Movement; Immigration; Labor Movements; Nativist Movement; Religion; Sixties, The; Sociology; *and entries on specific immigrant groups:* Irish Americans, etc.]

• Milton M. Gordon, *Assimilation in American Life: The Role of Race, Religion, and National Origins,* 1964. Harold J. Abramson, "Assimilation and Pluralism," in *Harvard Encyclopedia of American Ethnic Groups,* ed. Stephan Thernstrom, 1980, pp. 150–60. Philip Gleason, *Speaking of Diversity: Language and Ethnicity in Twentieth-Century America,* 1992. George J. Sánchez, *Becoming Mexican American: Ethnicity, Culture, and Identity in Chicano Los Angeles, 1900–1945,* 1993. Ewa Morawska, "In Defense of the Assimilation Model," *Journal of American Ethnic History* 13 (Winter 1994): 76–87. Russell A. Kazal, "Revisiting Assimilation: The Rise, Fall, and Reappraisal of a Concept in American Ethnic History," *American Historical Review* 100 (April 1995): 437–71.

—Russell A. Kazal

ASSOCIATIONISM. *See* Corporatism; Utopian and Communitarian Movements.

ASTOR, JOHN JACOB (1763–1848), fur trader, real-estate developer, financier. Born in Germany, Astor emigrated to the United States in 1783. A chance shipboard conversation with a fellow passenger familiar with the Pacific Northwest led to his decision to enter the *fur trade. Organizing fur trading expeditions with the Indians of the Northwest, he founded several trading posts including Astoria, Oregon, at the mouth of the Columbia River, the first American settlement west of the Rocky Mountains. In 1808 he established the American Fur Company. The fur trade proved immensely profitable, encompassing China, the United States, and Europe. Known for exchanging liquor for furs, Astor gained an unsavory reputation in some quarters. He invested much of his large fortune in real estate in and around *New York City. He also became a financier, joining with Stephen Girard, a Philadelphia banker, during the *War of 1812 to raise sixteen million dollars for the U.S. Treasury, at a substantial profit to themselves. This episode would later be cited by politicians as an example of the business elite taking advantage of the Treasury in times of crisis.

In contrast to his earlier reputation for sharp dealings and cutthroat trade with the Indians, Astor in his later years became a well-known philanthropist. He contributed $350,000 to found the Astor Library, forerunner of the New York Public Library. At his death he was the richest man in America, with a fortune estimated at $20 million. His wealth founded a family dynasty that would remain prominent through the nineteenth and early twentieth centuries.

[*See also* Banking and Finance; Indian History and Culture: From 1800 to 1900; Libraries; Philanthropy and Philanthropic Foundations.]

• Washington Irving, *Astoria, or Anecdotes of an Enterprise beyond the Rocky Mountains,* ed. Richard Dilworth, 1976. John D. Haeger, *John Jacob Astor: Business and Finance in the Early Republic,* 1991.

—Charles Geisst

ASTRONOMY. *See* Earth Sciences.

ASYLUMS. *See* Mental Health Institutions; Orphanages; Alms Houses.

ATLANTA. Established in 1836 as a regional railroad hub, "Terminus" (briefly, "Marthasville") was incorporated as the city of Atlanta in 1847. As late as 1860, its population stood at just 9,554. The *Civil War Union general William T. *Sherman brought this municipality to national attention in 1864. The Atlanta that Sherman's Army of the Tennessee occupied on 2 September 1864 had served as the nerve center of the Confederacy, but the smoldering city that he evacuated on 15 November was a burned-out ruin. It would not remain so for long.

On 21 December 1886, *Atlanta Constitution* editor Henry Grady, addressing the New England Society of New York, singled out General Sherman and assured him that he was "considered an able man in our parts, though some people think he is a kind of careless man about fire, and that from the ashes he left us in 1864 we have raised a brave and beautiful city." In 1881, 1887, and 1895, Atlanta boosters promoted their city's rebirth with a series of international expositions; during the 1920s and again in the 1960s, its commercial leadership launched "Forward Atlanta" campaigns to attract new businesses to the city. These manifestations of the "Atlanta Spirit," together with its development as a transportation center—first rail, then air and automotive—meant growth and expansion, resulting in population bursts from 37,409 in 1880 to more than 200,000 in 1920 and nearly 500,000 in 1970. By the early 1990s, when Atlanta was advertising its "internationality" and successfully advancing itself as host city for the 1996 Summer Olympics, the municipality served as the focal point for a metropolitan region of more than three million inhabitants.

As the transportation and communications center for the Southeast, Atlanta by the late twentieth century provided regional offices for most major American corporations and was also corporate headquarters for Coca-Cola, Delta Airlines, and the Turner Communications division of Time-Warner Corporation. Its major research universities included Emory, Georgia State, the Georgia Institute of Technology, and the six-member Atlanta University Center, the world's largest concentration of historically black institutions of higher learning.

Through the late nineteenth and early twentieth centuries, Atlanta promoted itself ceaselessly, some said shamelessly, as the capital of a new—albeit segregated—*South. Booker T. *Washington's apparent acceptance of this "separate but equal" doctrine in his address at the 1895 Cotton States Exposition came to be called the "Atlanta Compromise." But many black Atlantans—from Washington's contemporary W. E. B. *Du Bois to the Reverend Martin Luther *King Jr.—rejected this policy of accommodation, challenged it in the courts and in the streets, and eventually overturned racial *segregation. Their long struggle earned for Atlanta the title of "Civil Rights Capital."

As the *civil rights movement unfolded, Atlanta presented itself to the nation as "The City Too Busy to Hate." Unlike other southern cities, its leadership preached and practiced controlled change. Atlanta could embrace relatively progressive racial policies because, as political scientist Clarence N. Stone demonstrated in *Regime Politics: Governing Atlanta, 1946–1988* (1989), a tight coalition of business leaders and governmental officials assumed leadership during the 1940s, expanded its base during the 1960s and 1970s, and survived into the post–civil rights era. Maintaining its regional leadership in the face of increasing competition from other New South cities loomed as Atlanta's challenge for the twenty-first century.

[*See also* Railroads.]

• Ronald Bayor, *Race and the Shaping of Twentieth-Century Atlanta*, 1996. Darlene R. Roth and Andy Ambrose, *Metropolitan Frontiers: A Short History of Atlanta*, 1996.

—Dana F. White

ATLANTIC CABLE. A cable *telegraph link between the United States and Great Britain was conceived soon after the first telegraph systems were developed in those countries in the 1840s. Little progress was made until 1854, however, when the *New York City paper merchant Cyrus W. Field (1819–1892) became the principal promoter of the project. With a group of his wealthy New York friends, Field formed an American company to undertake the project. After completing construction of the Newfoundland–New York overland route and organizing the American Telegraph Company to control telegraph lines along the eastern seaboard, Field was unable to convince American investors to back the Atlantic cable. Accompanied by Samuel F. B. *Morse, inventor of the first American telegraph, he traveled to London to raise the necessary funds by forming the Atlantic Telegraph Company (1856) and winning the support of the British government. Work began in August 1857, but the cable broke while being laid. Raising additional capital, Field completed the cable in August 1858 between Newfoundland and Ireland. (Transatlantic messages were then relayed to England via an England–Ireland cable.) People on both sides of the Atlantic celebrated the cable's success, and Queen Victoria sent a celebratory message to President James *Buchanan, but after operating for only about a month, the cable failed. Unable to raise sufficient capital in America for a third attempt, especially after the outbreak of the *Civil War, Field once again turned to British investors. The first permanent Atlantic Cable, completed in 1866, was largely a British project, and British investors, cable companies, and engineers would continue to dominate the world's cable industry.

• Samuel Carter, *Cyrus Field: A Man of Two Worlds*, 1968. Vary T. Coates and Bernard Finn, *A Retrospective Technology Assessment: Submarine Telegraphy: The Transatlantic Cable of 1866*, 1979.

—Paul Israel

ATLANTIC CHARTER. On 9–12 August 1941, President Franklin Delano *Roosevelt and British Prime Minister Winston Churchill met secretly aboard U.S. and British warships anchored in Placentia Bay, Newfoundland. The two leaders and their respective staffs brought divergent agendas to their Newfoundland rendezvous. The British sought active American participation in the military effort to block Axis threats in North Africa, the Atlantic islands, and Southeast Asia. Roosevelt hoped to obtain a statement of "peace aims" to counteract *isolationism back home and to get on record Britain's commitment to such traditional American goals as open agreements, self-determination, and multilateral trade.

Both sides partially achieved their goals. Roosevelt confirmed his policy of all-out American aid for Britain and Russia, and the two leaders agreed on a statement of war and peace aims soon termed the "Atlantic Charter." The dramatic circumstances of the conference ensured that the document would be celebrated—and endlessly debated—as an epochal event in the struggle for individual freedom and group rights. Five of the Charter's eight principles dealt with individual and group rights: self-determination, freedom from want and fear, improved economic and social conditions for all, renunciation of territorial expansion, and protection against forced territorial changes. The remaining three embodied liberal internationalist thinking about the causes of war and the foundations of world peace. These were freedom of the seas, open access to markets and raw materials, and disarmament of aggressor nations pending the establishment of a permanent structure to assure world peace. The Atlantic Charter reflected American ideals embodied in President Woodrow *Wilson's *Fourteen Points of 1918 and FDR's "Four Freedoms" proclamation of January 1941, and it strongly implied the universal applicability of these principles.

Long after the immediate circumstances that led to the Atlantic Conference had faded, the charter remained a living document. Beginning as an assertion of the aspirations of the nations opposing the Axis powers, the charter became the statement of Allied war aims after the United States entered *World War II in December 1941. In 1945 it served as the guiding manifesto of the new *United Nations, and indeed was formally incorporated in a "Declaration by the United Nations" as a "common programme of purposes and principles." The Atlantic Charter is today included in the U.S. State Department's listing of treaties still in force, with all the nations adhering to the United Nations Declaration as its signatories. Initially no more than a press release by the leader of a belligerent power and the head of a neutral nation, the Atlantic Charter has come to be considered a pivotal document in the long campaign for universal principles of international *human rights and justice.

• Theodore A. Wilson, *The First Summit: Roosevelt and Churchill at Placentia Bay, 1941*, rev. ed., 1991. David Facey-Crowther and Douglas Brinkley, eds., *The Atlantic Charter: Retrospect and Prospect*, 1994.

—Theodore A. Wilson

ATOMIC BOMB. *See* Hiroshima and Nagaski, Atomic Bombing of; Manhattan Project; Nuclear Strategy; Nuclear Weapons; Oppenheimer, J. Robert; World War II.

ATOMIC ENERGY COMMISSION. The Atomic Energy Commission (AEC), made up of five members appointed by the president of the United States, was created by Congress in 1946. Establishing the principle of civilian control of atomic energy, Congress assigned the new agency responsibility for developing and testing *nuclear weapons and for encouraging peaceful uses of the new *technology. David E. Lilienthal (1899–1981), a former director of the *Tennessee Valley Authority, became its first chairman. As the *Cold War progressed, the agency focused its resources on weapons, expanding the U.S. stockpile, and, after January 1950, undertaking a crash program to build a hydrogen bomb. The agency's military emphasis proved a source of frustration an disappointment for Lilienthal, whose interests lay in the nonmilitary uses of atomic energy. But Cold War tensions and the still-rudimentary state of the technology prevented major strides in civilian applications.

Although the AEC stood at the center of numerous controversies in its early years, the most divisive occurred in 1954 when it stripped J. Robert *Oppenheimer, leader of the scientific effort to build the atomic bomb during *World War II, of his security clearance for alleged communist associations. The chairman of the AEC, Lewis L. Strauss took the lead, for both personal and political reasons, in ending Oppenheimer's career as a scientific adviser to the AEC. At about the same time the AEC's atmospheric testing of nuclear weapons set off a major public debate over the health effects of the radioactive fallout they produced. The AEC's claims that fallout posed no significant health hazard aroused much dissent, permanently undermining the agency's credibility.

By the mid-1960s, the AEC was devoting increasing attention to promoting the peaceful uses of atomic energy. Its encouragement of the *nuclear power industry helped stimulate a boom in reactor construction. But public faith in the AEC was further shaken by its dual mandate to promote and regulate nuclear power. By the early 1970s, controversies over reactor safety, radiation standards, environmental protection, waste disposal, and nuclear weapons proliferation had severely damaged confidence in the AEC. In response to widespread criticism, Congress abolished the AEC in 1974, dividing its functions between the Energy Research and Development Administration (later a part of the Department of Energy) and the *Nuclear Regulatory Commission.

[*See also* Federal Government, Executive Branch: Other Departments (Department of Energy); Manhattan Project; Nuclear Arms Control Treaties.]

• Richard G. Hewlett and Francis Duncan, *Atomic Shield, 1947–1952,* 1969. Richard G. Hewlett and Jack M. Holl, *Atoms for Peace and War, 1953–1961,* 1989.

—J. Samuel Walker

AUDUBON, JOHN JAMES (1785–1851), artist, naturalist, and ornithologist. Born in Haiti, the illegitimate son of a French naval officer and a Haitian chambermaid, Audubon grew up in France and moved to *Philadelphia in 1803. In 1807 he relocated to Kentucky and became a shopkeeper, and in 1808 married Lucy Bakewell. He neglected business in favor of drawing and studying local birds, however, and after a series of setbacks found himself bankrupt and in debtor's prison in 1819.

In 1820 he moved to Cincinnati to paint portraits and work as a taxidermist for the Western Museum. Four years later he went to Philadelphia to seek funding for an ambitious project to document all known American birds. He failed, but found success after traveling to England in 1826. Delighting his European patrons, Audubon played the part of the American woodsman with relish, slicking his hair with bear grease, wearing rough wool pants and a buckskin jacket, and claiming to have hunted with Daniel *Boone.

His four-volume masterwork, *The Birds of America* (1827–1838), combined unprecedented scope with unusual quality of execution and detail. Printed on "double elephant" folio pages (40 × 30 inches), Audubon's life-size, full-color engravings of 435 species were immediately hailed as a masterpiece in both Europe and America. In 1838 he published a popular octavo version of *Birds* in the United States and later, with his son John Wodehouse Audubon and John Bachman, *The Viviparous Quadrupeds of North America* (1842–1854).

Although self-taught, Audubon was a great stylist, combining skilled draftsmanship based on extensive field and laboratory work with an awareness of profile and motion that made the work of other ornithologist-artists seem stiff and inert. Unparalleled in his accomplishment, Audubon was praised by the Parisian scientist Georges Cuvier for having created "the greatest monument ever erected by art to nature."

• Alice Ford, *John James Audubon: A Biography*, 1988. Shirley Streshinsky, *Audubon: Life and Art in the American Wilderness,* 1993.

—Christopher W. Wells

AUTOMATION AND COMPUTERIZATION. Automation and computerization are related but separate phenomena. Automation means the mechanization—and usually the speeding up—of production, not only in manufacturing but also in service. Computerization is an advanced form of automation. Fantasies and anxieties about automation predate the nation's founding. The golem of Jewish legend, for example, is a powerful automaton. But Americans' historic receptivity to technological innovation and their need for machines to compensate for scarcity of labor have made the United States a center for automation.

American automation began in the early *New England textile mills and other communities of the 1820s and 1830s, where workers labored amid rows of complex, noisy, and dangerous machines, and in the pioneering Midwestern slaughterhouses of the 1840s and 1850s, where workers butchered, divided into parts, and packed hogs in "disassembly" lines. In both enterprises employees stood in place while the work came to them and repeated their respective assigned tasks day after day. By contrast, in the much smaller early American craft and machine shops, employees had moved about more freely from task to task as the work itself remained stationary. Automation severely limited workers' physical movement and occupational diversity alike.

Nevertheless, automation does not inevitably result in "deskilling," or the steady loss of skills, both technical and intellectual, to machines. In the *iron and steel industry, new machines may have diluted skills, but in textiles and other industries, the number of semiskilled workers actually increased as employers required a labor force with the knowledge and dexterity to operate complex machinery. Mere physical strength mattered ever less. Hence the irrelevance to industries not dependent on sheer manual labor of Frederick Taylor's system of *scientific management (Taylorism)—the elimination of allegedly extraneous work motions and the acceleration of others.

Although scientific management, as conceived by Taylor, and automation were thus two quite different concepts, Taylorism provided ideological justification for subsequent automation in industry. For Taylor, workers as well as machines lacked intelligence and performed most efficiently when controlled completely by engineers and managers.

Automation usually means the substitution of machines for workers, causing "technological unemployment." The term became popular during the economic *depression and mass *unemployment of the 1930s, when for the first time the American public singled out President Herbert *Hoover and other engineers for being as responsible as greedy industrialists for the efficient large-scale manufacturing machines hitherto lauded as engines of prosperity and job creation. Although America has never experienced anything comparable to England's eighteenth-century Luddites, or "machine breakers," both white-collar citizens and industrial workers of the 1930s did finally associate automated machinery and job losses.

Automation need not, however, always mean fewer workers. At Henry *Ford's pioneering Michigan automobile assembly lines at Highland Park (1910s) and River Rouge (1920s), low-cost *mass production and increased efficiency created thousands of new jobs. In fact, the process of mass production characterized much of the American industrial landscape. Yet these two huge Ford plants came to epitomize automation in *popular culture, technological history, and scholarly discourse under the rubric "Fordism." They were also the models for the classic critique of automation in Charlie *Chaplin's 1936 movie *Modern Times.*

Recovery from the Great Depression through *World War II military production, followed by postwar prosperity, lessened concern about automation until the mid–1950s, when another wave of technological innovation arose. Now the threat that *computers might replace white-collar workers, even intellectual workers like librarians, generated growing unease. The 1957 movie *Desk Set,* starring Spencer Tracy as an efficiency expert computerizing a corporate research department headed by Katharine Hepburn, popularized postwar anxiety about technological unemployment.

Similarly, Kurt Vonnegut's novel *Player Piano* (1952) envisioned the United States as a prosperous welfare state dependent on one huge computer for all major decisions. In Vonnegut's technological dystopia, only a few engineers and managers hold meaningful jobs while most citizens resent their menial daily tasks despite the domestic comforts provided by technological progress. Significantly, the term "computer," hitherto applied to men and women skilled in numerical calculations, was now applied to the mechanical devices that replaced them. (Years later, automatic programming codes would replace human computer programmers.) Congressional hearings on automation in 1955, which revealed that substantial numbers of blue- and white-collar workers alike were being displaced by machines, made automation a public issue.

Not until the radical critiques of American *technology of the 1960s and 1970s, however, did earlier piecemeal condemnations of automation and computerization become parts of a broader indictment of the overall quality of work. Harvey Swados's pathbreaking 1957 essay in *The Nation*, "The Myth of the Happy Worker," vigorously argued that assembly-line workers' high pay and good benefits hardly compensated for their daily grind and loss of autonomy.

White-collar workers less threatened by technological unemployment, particularly those in presumably lifetime corporate positions, often thought themselves immune to the ills endured by production workers. Studs Terkel's *Working* (1972) and the Department of Health, Education, and Welfare's *Work in America* (1973) amply demonstrated otherwise. In the 1980s and 1990s America's largest corporations discharged large numbers of managerial and white-collar employees. Technological innovation now seemed to threaten even more educated employees, though blue-collar workers lost still more jobs owing to automation. Half as many factory positions existed in 1996 as in 1966.

By the 1990s, the computerization of America had become a fact of life. In the 1940s and 1950s, computer pioneers like John Mauchly and John Von Neumann never anticipated more than a few giant computers that would be operated by skilled programmers employed by the largest national and international institutions to solve the most complex quantitative problems. By the 1980s, computers had become available to ordinary Americans and embedded in their lives in countless ways.

At the end of the twentieth century, many Americans anticipated an ever more automated and computerized high-tech utopia. But other citizens, aware of actual and potential technological and environmental disasters, retreated from the nation's historically uncritical embrace of technological progress and saw automation and computerization as, at best, profoundly mixed blessings. For them, chess champion Gary Kasparov's 1997 loss to International Business Machine's (IBM's) Deep Blue computer symbolized the human implications of technological triumphs.

[*See also* Automotive Industry; Business; Fifties, The; Global Economy, America and the; Industrialization; Industrial Relations; Labor Markets; Meatpacking and Meat Processing Industry; Sixties, The; Textile Industry.]

• Harry Braverman, *Labor and Monopoly Capital: The Degradation of Work in the Twentieth Century*, 1974. James B. Gilbert, *Work without Salvation: America's Intellectuals and Industrial Alienation, 1880–1910*, 1977. David F. Noble, *Forces of Production: A Social History of Industrial Automation*, 1984. Paul Ceruzzi, "An Unforeseen Revolution: Computers and Expectations, 1935–1985," in *Imagining Tomorrow: History, Technology, and the American Future*, ed. Joseph J. Corn, 1986, pp. 188–201. David Montgomery, *The Fall of the House of Labor: The Workplace, the State, and American Labor Activism, 1865–1925*, 1987. Harvey Swados, *On the Line*, 1957; rpt. 1990. Amy Sue Bix, *Inventing Ourselves Out of Jobs? America's Debate over Technological Unemployment, 1929–1981*, 2000.

—Howard P. Segal

AUTOMOBILE RACING. The American love affair with the automobile quickly translated into an enthusiasm for automobile racing. Indeed, many Americans first learned of the *automotive industry through the widely publicized 1895 *Chicago Times-Herald* race from Jackson Park to Waukegan, Illinois. Automakers Henry *Ford and Louis Chevrolet both took the lead in sponsoring racers. The Vanderbilt Cup road races on Long Island (begun in 1904) soon attracted 200,000 spectators, but dangerous, expensive road racing became primarily a European, not an American, sport.

Americans preferred oval track racing. Ray Harroun won the first Indianapolis 500 in 1912 in a Marmon Wasp with a rear-view mirror, one of the few innovations to move from racers to production cars. Led by Ford in 1913, American automakers abandoned racing, a policy they have pursued inconsistently. They saw few technical benefits, feared bad publicity from accidents, and did not want to compete with European cars. Except at Indianapolis, oval track racing declined by the 1930s.

After *World War II, however, drag racing and stock-car racing rejuvenated American competition. Drag racing had roots in the *Los Angeles area. Adolescents could afford to buy and modify used Ford Model Ts and V-8s (introduced in 1932) for quarter-mile races. In 1951 *Hot Rod Magazine* editor Wally Parks founded the National Hot Rod Association (NHRA), which soon attracted over fifteen thousand amateur hot rodders. The NHRA-sanctioned track races became quite sophisticated technically. By 1952 methane-fueled dragsters could reach 150 miles per hour in a quarter of a mile. Exciting professional duels on drag-race tracks, hyped by a "gender war" theme between "Big Daddy" Garlits and the first woman racer, Shirley Muldowney, enlivened the 1970s. Street drag racing dwindled in popularity in the 1970s, however, hedged in by environmental restrictions and hard-to-modify computerized cars.

Stock car racing became popular because NASCAR (a racing organization founded in 1948) insisted that the races it sponsored involve standard car models stocked at dealerships. Restrictions on modifications guaranteed close races. The stock-car format proved well adapted to the emerging medium of *television, enjoying special popularity in the *South, where many early racers were said to have gotten their start during the Prohibition Era transporting moonshine liquor.

[*See also* Motor Vehicles.]

• H. F. Moorhouse, *Driving Ambitions: A Social Analysis of the American Hot Rod Enthusiasm*, 1991. Robert C. Post, *High Performance: The Culture and Technology of Drag Racing, 1950–1990*, 1994.

—Clay McShane

AUTOMOBILES. *See* Automotive Industry; Motor Vehicles.

AUTOMOTIVE INDUSTRY. Dynamism and uncertainty characterized the early American automotive industry. Its scores of tinkerers and entrepreneurs typically assembled rather than manufactured their products, subcontracting for parts from carriage builders, bicycle manufacturers, and machinists. Most companies catered to wealthy consumers until 1908, when Henry *Ford's Model T permanently changed the industry.

Sturdy, powerful, and inexpensive, the Model T combined innovative engineering with revolutionary manufacturing methods to become the first mass-produced car. Ford and his employees introduced economies of scale, creating the world's first assembly line by 1914. That same year, to address the absenteeism and turnover problems of the assembly line, Ford doubled his already competitive wages to five dollars a day. As other manufacturers struggled to keep pace, a wave of mergers swept the industry. Before *World War I interrupted production, the industry had expanded its operations, boosted production, cut prices, and made important technological advances.

Automobiles pervaded American life in the 1920s, embodying both the tensions and the flash of the era's developing *consumer culture. The decade's volatile market caused 60 percent of all auto manufacturers to fail, and the remainder—based mainly in *Detroit—to struggle. While Henry Ford solidified his personal control over the Ford Motor Company, Alfred P. *Sloan brought professional management, market forecasting, and basic technical research to General Motors (GM). As cheap used cars challenged the Model T in the low-priced market, new car sales flattened after 1923 at roughly 3.6 million per year. Ford responded by further cutting Model T prices, while Sloan introduced the annual model change—an innovation Ford adopted in 1927 with his Model A.

Though automobile sales slipped even before Wall Street crashed in 1929, the Depression of the 1930s failed to break America's automotive habit. Cars outnumbered *telephones and bathtubs throughout the decade, and if stagnant sales forced GM, Chrysler, and Ford temporarily to halt production in 1932, all three companies again earned profits in 1933, solidifying their dominance as waves of independents went bankrupt. The "Little Five"—Nash, Hudson, Packard, Willys-Overland, and Studebaker—battled insolvency, watching their market-share erode over the decade from twenty-five to ten percent.

Hefty paychecks had always helped Detroit sustain an open (non-union) shop, but the Depression divided management and labor. Speed-ups, slashed wages, and layoffs generated unrest, unionization, strikes, and violence. The *National Labor Relations Act of 1935 guaranteed unions the right to organize, precipitating an often brutal struggle between Detroit manufacturers and the United Automobile Workers (UAW) of the *Congress of Industrial Organizations (CIO). The UAW's forty-four-day *sit-down strike against GM in Flint, Michigan, forced the industry to recognize the union in February 1937. Only Ford resisted, though after a strike in which the National Labor Relations Board (NLRB) intervened in 1941, Ford signed the most generous union contract in the industry.

After the United States entered *World War II, Detroit became the nation's primary armaments producer. Americans temporarily suppressed their desire for new cars, but the war's end unleashed a flood of pent-up demand. In the five years after 1945, Americans purchased 21.4 million vehicles, nearly doubling the number of cars in the country. While the UAW "set its house in order" under Walter *Reuther, Americans transformed their landscape to accommodate their automobiles, constructing a 41,000-mile interstate *highway system and thronging to new suburban developments. GM, Chrysler, and Ford prospered, but of the Little Five, only Nash survived. Even well-financed and innovative newcomers like Preston Tucker and Kaiser-Frazer failed to crack the market, going bankrupt by the mid-1950s.

New problems plagued the industry in the 1960s. While Ralph *Nader publicized the "designed-in dangers" of American cars, new labor tensions emerged, foreign competition grew, and Congress instituted the first national emissions controls. GM's problems were emblematic: averaging under twelve miles per gallon, its line provoked consumer dissatisfaction when the 1973 OPEC oil embargo raised gasoline prices by 30 percent. Big-car sales plummeted as small foreign imports penetrated the market, (imports had an 18.3 percent market share by 1975), prompting the industry to pledge—and the government to require—improved fuel efficiency.

After clamoring for smaller, fuel-efficient cars in the 1970s, Americans again embraced large cars in the 1980s and 1990s as fuel prices dropped. Foreign manufacturers that had broken into the American market in the 1970s joined Detroit in supplying less fuel-efficient minivans, pickups, and sports utility vehicles to eager buyers. Powerful, entrenched, and increasingly global, the automotive industry by 2000 barely resembled its early predecessor, though throughout the century the industry had been instrumental in establishing patterns of life, economy, and mobility.

[*See also* Bicycles and Bicycling; Depressions, Economic; Energy Crisis of the 1970s; Industrialization; Labor Movements; Mass Production; Motor Vehicles; Suburbanization; Twenties, The.]

• Allan Nevins and Frank Ernest Hill, *Ford,* 3 vols., 1954–1963. James J. Flink, *The Car Culture,* 1975. Stephen Meyer, *The Five Dollar Day: Labor Management and Social Control in the Ford Motor Company, 1908–1921,* 1981. David A. Hounshell, *From the American System to Mass Production, 1800–1932,* 1985. James J. Flink, *The Automobile Age,* 1989. Paul Ingrassia and Joseph B. White, *Comeback: The Rise and Fall of the American Automobile Industry,* 1995.

—Christopher W. Wells

AVIATION INDUSTRY. At the time of the first flight by Wilbur and Orville *Wright in 1903, aircraft builders in the United States constituted a disparate group of amateurs. During 1908 and 1909, Orville Wright completed a series of highly publicized flights in America for the U.S. Army; overseas, his brother Wilbur dazzled European royalty and enthusiastic crowds. Against this backdrop of public acclaim and investor interest, the Wrights formed a manufacturing company in 1909, followed by dozens of other entrepreneurs. Military contracts represented the core market, and the outbreak of *World War I in 1914 brought additional orders from Europe. When the United States declared war in 1917, Congress authorized massive aircraft contracts for domestic production. Although subsequent investigations revealed widespread fraud, the wartime effort provided valuable experience in high-volume production and the manufacture of myriad basic components such as engines, propellers, magnetos, and instrumentation.

During the 1920s and 1930s, manufacturers successfully incorporated numerous technological innovations developed by the National Advisory Committee for Aeronautics. The military services also carried on practical research, and new curricula in aeroengineering at major universities contributed to an expanding population of trained engineers. Trade associations and professional societies appeared. Government regulatory agencies, such as the Civil Aeronautics Authority (1938) and the later Federal Aviation Administration (1958), helped stabilize the industry, which encouraged airlines and private pilots alike to order new aircraft. Douglas Aircraft Company launched the historic DC–3 airliner in 1935 and builders of light planes for private pilots delivered classic designs like the two-seat Piper Cub and Beechcraft's twin-engine models for executive travel.

The success of the American aviation industry during the interwar years rested on a mix of corporate innovation, federal research and development, and the contribution of such emigres from Europe such as Igor Sikorsky (flying boats and helicopters), Theodore von Karman (theorist and educator), and others in both the private and public sectors. A late 1930s wave of orders from European air forces, accelerated by the Lend Lease program, had a significant impact on the aviation industry's record production during *World War II, totaling 300,000 aircraft. Development of planes like the complex Boeing B–29 bomber rested on sophisticated management and production procedures, including the coordination of thousands of suppliers. At the same time, the introduction of jet propulsion engines and aircraft by Britain and Germany proved crucial in subsequent American progress, as did German developments.

After 1945, *Cold War antagonisms intensified the wartime concentration of aviation industries in the Northeast and along the Pacific coast, including the Seattle-based Boeing Company, although diversification in the *South and *Middle West occurred as well. Electronics became a major component of both civil and military aircraft, increasing their costs. Postwar prosperity and business expansion created a strong demand for postwar airliners, and vast production resources gave U.S. manufactures the lead in global sales. During the 1960s, American jet transports dominated the world market. The light plane industry also soared, turning out 18,000 planes in the record year 1978, compared to 240 civil transports and 1,000 military aircraft. During the 1990s despite financial difficulties and the end of the Cold War, manufacturers continued to produce annually 900 light planes, 500 transports, and 700 military planes. Exports remained crucial to the industry, and multinational agreements proliferated. Although American manufacturers led the world, corporate mergers reduced the number of domestic firms, which faced strong challenges from European consortia.

[*See also* Airplanes and Air Transport; Engineering; Military, The; Technology; Weaponry, Nonnuclear.]

• Jacob Vander Meulen, *The Politics of Aircraft: Building an American Military Industry*, 1991; Roger Bilstein, *The American Aerospace Industry: From Workshop to Global Enterprise*, 1996.

—Roger E. Bilstein

B

BABY AND CHILD CARE, the most widely read and influential *child-rearing manual of the second half of the twentieth century. Written during *World War II by the pediatrician Dr. Benjamin Spock, with the assistance of his first wife, Jane Cheney Spock, *The Common Sense Book of Baby and Child Care* by the mid-1990s had more than 46 million copies in six editions (1946, 1957, 1968, 1977, 1985, 1992). The book's success owed much to Spock's readable prose; his precise and accessible advice; and his effort, not always successful, to convince anxious parents that good child rearing was a matter of "common sense."

Despite its popularity, *Baby and Child Care* proved controversial after 1968, when the Reverend Norman Vincent *Peale and others charged Spock (then a leader of the anti–*Vietnam War peace movement) and his "permissive" approach to child rearing with having produced a generation of spoiled, radical youths. In the 1970s, Gloria Steinem led feminists in casting the Freudian Spock as an oppressor of women. With good reason, Spock disputed the charge of permissiveness, insisting that *Baby and Child Care* championed a flexible approach encompassing either "moderate strictness" or "moderate permissiveness." Spock met some of the feminist objections in 1977 and later editions by adopting nonsexist language, advocating an expanded parenting role for fathers, and acknowledging the existence of two-career families and their need for day care.

Scholars generally rejected the view that *Baby and Child Care* was responsible for the upheavals of the 1960s. The historian William Graebner presented Spock as a social engineer whose "democratic" approach to child rearing, based on *Progressive Era educational theory, reflected interwar anxieties about aggression and totalitarianism. While Michael Zuckerman argued that Spock's advocacy of a confident parent presiding over frictionless parent-child relationships prepared children to be cooperative and amicable adults in a postwar corporate order, Nancy Pottishman Weiss contended that Spock's advocacy of unfailing maternal confidence was burdensome and counterproductive for many women readers.

[*See also* Family; Feminism; Sixties, The.]

• Michael Zuckerman, "Dr. Spock: The Confidence Man," in *The Family in History*, ed. Charles E. Rosenberg, 1975, pp. 179–207. Nancy Pottishman Weiss, "Mother, the Invention of Necessity: Dr. Benjamin Spock's *Baby and Child Care*," *American Quarterly* 29 (Winter 1977): 519–46. William Graebner, "The Unstable World of Benjamin Spock: Social Engineering in a Democratic Culture, 1917–1950," *Journal of American History* 67 (Dec. 1980): 612–29.

—William Graebner

BACON, NATHANIEL. *See* Bacon's Rebellion.

BACON'S REBELLION (1676). This Virginia uprising, beginning with vigilante actions by frontier residents who opposed Governor William Berkeley's Indian policy, quickly escalated into a struggle that left Berkeley disgraced and the colony tightly in the grip of the Stuart monarchs. The leader, twenty-nine-year-old Nathaniel Bacon, a well-born English immigrant with substantial property holdings and close ties to Berkeley, mobilized disgruntled frontier planters, small property holders, white servants, and African slaves against both Indians and the governor.

Although granted a council seat by Berkeley, Bacon shared his wealthy neighbors' conviction that the governor's policies left them vulnerable to Indian attack and excluded from the Indian *fur trade. The large planters' discontents, worsened by falling tobacco prices, might have remained confined to name-calling, lawsuits, and duels had not the small property holders also decried Berkeley's alleged failure to protect them from Indians. Under Bacon's leadership, a frontier force disobeyed Berkeley's orders and in April 1676 brutally attacked a nearby settlement of peaceful Susquehannock Indians.

Under challenge, Berkeley called the first election in fifteen years. Bacon won election to the burgesses, Virginia's upper house, but was arrested when he tried to take his seat. Soon released and commissioned by Berkeley to fight Indians, he rallied a force of some thirteen hundred men for more attacks that killed hundreds of Indians along the Potomac and Rappahannock Rivers. When Berkeley reversed himself and declared Bacon a traitor, Bacon's army marched on *Jamestown, the capital, which they burned on 19 September. As Berkeley raised his own force, the conflict became colonywide, with combatants gutting their opponents' houses and seizing their property.

Bacon's followers complained of overtaxation, political exclusion, religious persecution, and economic restrictions. A handful of influential white women supported Bacon's cause, as did many servants and some four hundred slaves who, promised their freedom by the rebels, were the last to surrender to Berkeley's troops. With Bacon's death from dysentery on 26 October and the arrival of a royal commission to investigate the rebellion, the uprising dissipated, leaving Virginia under tighter royal control and in the grip of a conservative reaction that restricted both the public influence of white women and the de facto freedom of enslaved people. Although scholars continue to debate the significance of this short-lived rebellion, there is agreement that this upheaval came just as Virginia fully embraced slavery. Thus might the political wounds left by Bacon's Rebellion have been partially healed, inadvertently or intentionally, by the racial imperatives of *slavery.

[*See also* Colonial Era; Indian History and Culture: From 1500 to 1800; Indian Wars; Tobacco Industry.]

• Wilcomb Washburn, *The Governor and the Rebel: A History of Bacon's Rebellion,* 1957. Edmund Morgan, *American Slavery, American Freedom: The Ordeal of Colonial Virginia,* 1975.

—Kathleen M. Brown

BACTERIOLOGY. *See* Biological Sciences.

BAKER* v. *CARR (1962). In this 6–2 decision, the U.S. *Supreme Court established that the Federal courts could decide cases involving the malapportionment of state legislatures. Previously, in *Colegrove* v. *Green* (1946), the Court held that matters relating to the fair apportionment of state legislative seats were a "political question" that should be considered only by elected officials.

Baker v. *Carr* involved the wide discrepancy in the numbers of voters living in different state legislative districts in Tennessee, which had ignored a state constitutional provision requiring periodic redistricting. Voters in the less populous rural districts enjoyed disproportionate political power, while those in larger urban districts had their voting power diluted and were thus denied the equal protection of the law guaranteed by the *Fourteenth Amendment.

By taking the case, and thereby overruling the *Colegrove* decision, the Supreme Court opened the door to litigation to equalize the size of constituencies for all elective offices and established the principle of "one person, one vote." In *Wesberry* v. *Sanders* (1964), the Court held that U.S. congressional districts within a state must consist of roughly equal populations. The same year, the Court in *Reynolds v. Sims* extended the ruling to both the lower and upper houses of state legislatures.

[*See also* Equality; Federalism; Suffrage.]

• David M. O'Brien, *Storm Center,* 2d ed., 1990. Melvin I. Urofsky, *The Continuity of Change,* 1991.

—Ross K. Baker

BALDWIN, JAMES (1924–1987), writer. Baldwin was born in *New York City's Harlem to Emma Berdis Jones, who later married David Baldwin, a migrant from New Orleans. The elder Baldwin, a preacher who resented his stepson's illegitimacy, tried to crush the young Jimmy's imaginative spirit. The problematic nature of their relationship would recur in Baldwin's works. The precocious Baldwin haunted Harlem's libraries; such authors as Harriet Beecher Stowe profoundly influenced him. As a teenager, he preached in his father's Pentecostal church.

Racist rebuffs when he sought employment in New Jersey, along with fellowship support, contributed to Baldwin's decision to emigrate to Paris in 1948. His first and best-received novel, *Go Tell It on the Mountain* (1953), drew on his own experience. Returning frequently to the United States during the era of the *civil rights movement, he marched; wrote *Blues for Mister Charles* (1964), a play about the movement; and, in 1963, with other black activists and artists, met with Attorney General Robert *Kennedy to seek solutions to the racial crisis.

Baldwin offered seminal statements on America's burdened racial history in two influential collections of essays, *Notes of a Native Son* (1955) and *The Fire Next Time* (1963). He returned to these themes in *Going to Meet the Man* (1965) and *Evidence of Things Not Seen* (1981), on a series of child murders in Atlanta. He offered groundbreaking treatments of homosexuality in his novels *Giovanni's Room* (1956) and *Another Country* (1962).

Of African American writers who substantially shaped American culture, Baldwin ranks near the top. During almost forty years of writing and lecturing, he encouraged Americans to live up to their ideals, to make democracy a reality, to live and work in harmony, and to turn their profession of Christianity into reality.

[*See also* African Americans; Gay and Lesbian Rights Movement; Literature: Since World War II; Pentecostalism.]

• David Leeming, *James Baldwin: A Biography,* 1994. Trudier Harris, ed., *New Essays on* Go Tell It on the Mountain, 1996.

—Trudier Harris

BALLINGER-PINCHOT CONTROVERSY. The main actors in this bitter *Progressive Era dispute over the future of conservation policy during the presidency of William Howard *Taft (1909–1913) were Secretary of the Interior Richard A. Ballinger and Chief Forester Gifford Pinchot. At issue was the federal government's role in overseeing natural resources. From his post in the Department of Agriculture, Pinchot wanted to continue the forest-management and coal-land policies of Theodore *Roosevelt that involved a large role for the federal government. Under Roosevelt, Pinchot had enjoyed wide discretion in setting priorities about western land, water, and *mining issues. Ballinger, a westerner from Seattle, Washington, sought to shift power back to the states and to allow localities to develop their own resources. He also believed that Pinchot had often failed to follow the letter of government policy or to observe appropriate legal procedures.

The resulting controversy spilled into the press in the fall of 1909. Taft's critics argued that he and Ballinger had repudiated the conservation goals of Roosevelt. Spurred by overblown charges against Ballinger provided by Louis Glavis, a Department of the Interior official, Pinchot pressed his case in the newspapers with sensational, exaggerated allegations that Ballinger had approved the sale of valuable coal lands in *Alaska to a consortium of Seattle businessmen, who had in turn sold the land to J. P. *Morgan and other New York bankers. When Pinchot in January 1910 wrote a public letter criticizing Ballinger to a U.S. senator, Taft fired him. In the congressional inquiry that followed, the Republican majority exonerated Ballinger, and the Democrats sided with Pinchot.

A discredited Ballinger left office in the spring of 1911. The controversy became a decisive element in the split between Roosevelt and Taft that led Roosevelt to challenge Taft for the Republican presidential nomination in 1912, and then to launch his independent candidacy on the *Progressive party ticket.

[*See also* Conservation Movement; Federal Government, Executive Branch: Department of Agriculture; Federal Government, Executive Branch: Other Departments (Department of the Interior); Forests and Forestry; Land Policy, Federal; States' Rights.]

• Samuel P. Hays, *Conservation and the Gospel of Efficiency: The Progressive Conservation Movement, 1890–1920,* 1958. James L. Penick Jr., *Progressive Politics and Conservation: The Ballinger-Pinchot Affair,* 1969.

—Lewis L. Gould

BANCROFT, GEORGE (1800–1891) historian, politician, diplomat. Educated at Exeter Academy and Harvard College (B.A., 1817; M.A. in divinity, 1818), Bancroft then pursued philological studies in Germany and received a Ph.D. from Göttingen in 1820. Following a continental tour, Bancroft returned to America in 1822 to serve at Harvard as a Latin tutor and an occasional preacher. His simultaneous literary ventures made him a leading magazine writer, translator, and poet. Bancroft also joined Joseph Cogswell in founding the Round Hill School (1823), where he served as headmaster, fund-raiser, and educational reformer. In 1827, Bancroft married Sarah Dwight. She died in 1837; and in 1838 Bancroft married Elizabeth Davis Bliss. Involvement in Dwight family economic enterprises transformed an impecunious intellectual into a gentleman of means.

Bancroft's belief that a democracy required the guidance of men of letters encouraged political involvement; his assumption that history revealed God's plan for humanity encouraged inquiries into the nation's past. In 1834, the first volume of his *History of the United States* appeared, establishing Bancroft's reputation as the nation's leading contemporary historian. The democratic ethos shaped Bancroft's scholarship as much as his political allegiances. Neither conflicted with his immersion in western land speculation, Dwight banking activities, Washington lobbying, or Massachusetts politics. Bancroft helped cement Democratic party alliances with workingmen's organizations, disaffected national Republicans, and Anti-Masons. His reward was the collectorship of the Boston Customhouse, a growing national reputation, and ties to successive Democratic administrations in Washington. Bancroft's role at the national Democratic convention in 1849 led to his appointment as secretary of the navy in President James Knox *Polk's cabinet. Bancroft played a pivotal role in the *Mexican War, firmly espoused *Manifest Destiny, and was instrumental in establishing the Naval Academy in Annapolis, Maryland. After a term as U.S. ambassador to Great Britain (1846–1849), Bancroft settled in *New York City, where he continued his historical work. Appointed minister plenipotentiary to Prussia by President Andrew *Johnson in 1867, he lived in Berlin for the next seven years. Returning to the United States, he settled in *Washington, D.C., where the tenth and final volume of *History of the United States* appeared in 1874. A six-volume revised edition appeared in 1876, followed by *The History of the Formation of the Constitution of the United States* in 1882. Despite advancing age, Bancroft remained a presence on the Washington political and social scene as an elder dignitary and statesman who had witnessed the nation's transformation in the course of nearly a century and had brilliantly recorded its complex social and political evolution.

[*See also* Anti-Masonic Party; Historiography, American; Military, The; Military Service Academies.]

• Russel B. Nye, *George Bancroft, Brahmin Rebel*, 1944. Lilian Handlin, *George Bancroft: The Intellectual as Democrat*, 1984.

—Lilian Handlin

BANKING AND FINANCE. Encouraged by Alexander *Hamilton, Robert Morris persuaded the *Continental Congress to charter the Bank of North America in 1781. It lent money to the cash-strapped Revolutionary government as well as to private citizens and served as a model for later commercial banks. Like the Bank of North America, most early banks lent money conservatively. Most such banks, which were chartered by the states to serve the public interest, were also partly state-owned.

Banking grew in tandem with population and trade, and the post–1800 period witnessed an explosion of banks. By 1818, 338 banks provided short-term credit for merchants, artisans, and farmers. By then banks had lost much of their public-interest function, and had become instead primarily profit-making enterprise. Political leaders, while bowing to the public's clamor for more credit, grew concerned over the monetary consequences of easy money. Many banknotes traded at substantial discounts, and some were not accepted at any price, leaving many citizens with worthless paper.

The First and Second Banks of the United States. The first *Bank of the United States (BUS) mitigated some monetary problems. Granted a twenty-year charter by Congress in 1791, it acted as both a commercial bank and the government's fiscal agent. Proposed by Hamilton, the bank was based in *Philadelphia with branches in eight other cities; it was well managed but widely criticized by those seeking easier credit for unduly restraining state bank lending. Opponents succeeded in defeating the bank's recharter in 1811.

Difficulties in financing the *War of 1812 demonstrated the value of a national bank, and in 1816, granted the second BUS a twenty-year charter. Modeled after its predecessor, the Second BUS also engaged in commercial and central bank activities. Philadelphia's Nicholas Biddle, assuming leadership of the bank in 1823, built it into a powerful institution by requiring each of its branches to play a defined role within a national economy as determined by the central bank in Philadelphia. The second BUS also proved an effective regulator of note issues and lending by the 464 existing state banks. But Biddle's policies roused opposition, and by 1832, when the *Whig party leader Henry *Clay, a BUS supporter, ran for president opposing Andrew *Jackson's reelection bid, the bank's recharter became a political flashpoint. Congress approved the renewal, but Jackson vetoed it in July 1832 and interpreted his reelection that November as broad support for his antibank stance. He removed federal deposits from the BUS, and its charter expired in 1836.

The resulting void in financial markets was filled by the rapid expansion of state banks. By 1860, the nation's 1,562 banks held $422 million in capital. This era, commonly referred to as the "free banking era," ended in 1863 with passage of the National Bank Act. Proposed by treasury secretary Salmon P. Chase, the act invited state banks to obtain a federal charter. Designed to assist *Civil War finance and end currency chaos, the act required national banks to buy government bonds and deposit them with the U.S. Treasury, which issued banknotes equal to 90 percent of the value of the collateral bonds. The act generated a uniform national currency, nicknamed greenbacks, and protected banknote holders from loss. When a bank failed, the treasury sold its bonds and reimbursed banknote holders. The act also imposed reserve requirements and minimum capital requirements on member banks.

Because the high costs of a national charter, many state banks remained independent, and the system grew slowly. In 1865, Congress imposed a 10 percent tax on state banknotes, leading more state banks to accept national charters. Although the number of national banks increased after 1865, state banks continued to outnumber national banks, and the aggregate volume of deposits in each remained nearly equal. A federal charter imposed other liabilities on member banks, including a prohibition on real-estate lending; an arbitrary ceiling on aggregate note issues; and rules preventing banks from increasing note issues in a timely manner in response to short-term changes in the demand for currency. The last two features created an inelastic currency; seasonal pressures in the money market; and a proclivity to financial panics, bank runs, and suspension of payments.

The Federal Reserve Act and the Glass-Steagall Act. Following a financial panic in 1907, Congress commissioned studies of contemporary and historical banking systems. Most of these studies criticized systems lacking a strong central bank. In response, Congress passed the *Federal Reserve Act in 1913. The *Federal Reserve System divided the country into twelve districts, each with a Reserve Bank and one or more branches. Reserve Banks were organized as federally chartered corporations owned by member banks. Members included all national banks and those state institutions that chose to join.

The Reserve Banks became the principal medium for carrying out the credit and monetary policies of the Federal Reserve System, as well as its general regulatory policies and supervisory powers. Reserve Banks hold the required reserves of member banks and provide check-clearing and settlement services for them. The Reserve Banks also act as fiscal agents and depositories for the U.S. Treasury and other federal government units. A seven-member Board of Governors of the Federal Reserve System, appointed by the president and located in Washington, D.C., administers the twelve Reserve Banks and their branches. The system's prime policy arm is the Federal Open Market Committee, which meets about twenty times each year to set monetary policies designed to combat inflation, limit unemployment, and promote economic growth.

The Federal Reserve's inability to prevent banking panics and widespread closings during the Great Depression of the 1930s exposed several weaknesses. President Franklin Delano *Roosevelt provided a stopgap solution by declaring a national bank holiday in March 1933, which slowed internal drains of reserves. Banks were not allowed to reopen until they had been inspected and recertified by state or federal auditors. Roosevelt also suspended the *gold standard to halt the external drain of reserves.

The failure of several thousand banks and the loss of millions to bank depositors during the Depression prompted Congress to pass legislation designed to recapitalize and restore public confidence in the nation's financial intermediaries. The Federal Home Loan Bank System and the Federal Savings and Loan Insurance Corporation (FSLIC), both established in 1932, assisted the savings and loan industry and promoted home ownership. More significant, perhaps, was the Glass-Steagall Act of 1933, which established the Federal Deposit Insurance Corporation (FDIC). The FDIC protects depositors against bank failures. All national banks and member banks of the Federal Reserve System are required to join. State banks that meet prescribed conditions may be admitted.

Banking in the Late Twentieth Century. Until the early 1980s, the federal regulatory system in conjunction with bank and thrift insurance limited bank failure to just a handful each year. In the 1980s, however, the failure of about five hundred savings and loans as well as several large commercial banks effectively bankrupted the FSLIC, and its unmet obligations required taxpayers to subsidize its shortfall of more than $100 billion.

The Financial Institutions Reform, Recovery, and Enforcement Act of 1989 reformed and recapitalized the federal deposit insurance programs. The FSLIC was closed and its supervisory powers transferred to the Office of Thrift Supervision. Its insurance function was shifted to the FDIC, which became the principal regulator of the nation's banks.

By 1998, the nation's 10,481 commercial banks and 1,687 savings banks held deposits of more that $5 trillion. The two largest U.S. banks were Citigroup, Inc., of *New York City and BankAmerica Corporation of *San Francisco, with assets of $6.8 billion and $6.2 billion, respectively. As in other areas of the economy, a series of mergers and acquisitions, producing ever-larger banking conglomerates, characterized the industry in the late twentieth century. The rise of the computer and electronic data transfer, as well as the economic globalization and the growth of *multinational enterprises, had profound effects for banking as well. A major piece of reform legislation, the Financial Services of 1999, repealed parts of the Glass-Steagall Act and enabled banks to provide a broader array of financial services and more easily to merge with insurance and securities companies.

[*See also* Antebellum Era; Depressions, Economic; Early Republic, Era of the; Economic Development; Federal Government, Executive Branch: Department of Treasury; Free Silver Movement; Greenback Labor Party; Monetary Policy, Federal; Morgan, J. P.; New Deal Era, The; Populist Era; Populist Party; Progressive Era; Savings and Loan Debacle.]

• Bray Hammond, *Banks and Politics in America from the Revolution of the Civil War,* 1957. Milton Friedman and Anna J. Schwartz, *A Monetary History of the United States, 1867–1960,* 1963. Richard Sylla, *The American Capital Market, 1846–1914,* 1975. John A. James, *Money and Capital Markets in Postbellum America,* 1978. Eugene Nelson White, *The Regulation and Reform of the American Banking System, 1900–1929,* 1983. Edward J. Kane, *The S&L Insurance Mess,* 1989. Naomi R. Lamoreaux, *Insider Lending,* 1994. Elmus Wicker, *The Banking Panics of the Great Depression,* 1996. Howard Bodenhorn, *A History of Banking in Antebellum America,* 2000.

—Howard Bodenhorn

BANKS OF THE UNITED STATES, FIRST AND SECOND. Between 1791 and 1811 and again from 1816 to 1836, the U.S. government created and operated a national bank that by most historical assessments met the nation's financial needs effectively. But the banks' size and scope led to political controversy.

The first Bank of the United States (BUS) served the economic policies of Alexander *Hamilton, the nation's first secretary of the treasury. In his "Report on a National Bank" (1790), Hamilton argued that the nation needed a federally chartered bank to establish the public credit, attract foreign investment, serve as an administrative arm of the federal treasury, and draw the support of wealthier citizens to the new government. Despite the opposition of Thomas *Jefferson, President George *Washington signed the bill authorizing a national bank after it passed both houses of Congress by solid majorities. The U.S. government held one-fifth of the ten million dollars of stock offered; individuals purchased the remaining four-fifths. The BUS served as the fiscal agent for the U.S. treasury: It held federal funds, transferred them throughout the United States, and disbursed these funds to pay interest and principal on the national debt. Its bank notes, which functioned much like today's paper currency, acted as legal tender in payment of U.S. debts. This gave the BUS unusual power, for it enjoyed access to government receipts, and it could and did establish branches throughout the country.

Although the first Bank of the United States fulfilled Hamilton's intentions, a bill to recharter the BUS was tabled in 1811 by a one-vote margin in both houses of Congress. This reaction arose largely from the fact that the *Federalist party had established the BUS and Federalists served as directors and officers of the bank and its branches. For many Jeffersonian Republicans, however, the question transcended politics; they were wary of the bank's inordinate power over state and local *economic development.

The second Bank of the United States was created by Congress in 1816 on much the same terms as had governed the first, although the law authorizing its establishment raised its capitalization to $35 million and required the BUS to pay a bonus of $1.5 million to the federal government. After a rocky start, the second BUS met the needs of the government and its stockholders while promoting the nation's economic development. Nicholas Biddle (1786–1844), a Philadelphia financier who assumed the bank presidency in 1823, deserved credit for much of this success.

But again the BUS became entangled in national politics. In 1829, President Andrew *Jackson declared his opposition to the BUS. Noting that it was by far the largest bank in the nation, he accused the BUS of using monopoly power and exclusive privileges to deny common citizens access to credit and economic opportunity. Angered by Jackson's veto of the bill to recharter the bank in 1832, Biddle used the bank's power to seek support in Congress and the press. Jackson retaliated by removing federal deposits from the BUS, which he had begun to call "the Monster." With compromise no longer possible the federal charter of the BUS lapsed in 1836.

[*See also* Banking and Finance; Federal Government, Executive Branch: Department of the Treasury; Federal Reserve System; *McCulloch* v. *Maryland;* Monetary Policy, Federal.]

• John Thom Holdsworth and Davis R. Dewey, *The First and Second Banks of the United States,* 1910 (U.S. Senate, 61st Cong. 2d sess., Doc. 571). Bray Hammond, *Banks and Politics in America from the Revolution to the Civil War,* 1957.

—Diane Lindstrom

BAPTISTS. In general, Baptists are evangelical Protestant Christians who hold to the authority of the *Bible, the lordship of Jesus Christ, the independence of local congregations, the necessity of a conversion experience and a believer's baptism by immersion, and evangelism and missionary outreach. Most Baptists are at least mildly Calvinistic, but smaller groups uphold the theologically Arminian (freewill) position. The Baptist movement originated as a sect of dissenters in seventeenth-century England. The first Baptists emigrated to North America in the 1630s, settling mostly in *New England and by the 1680s in the Middle Colonies. The first congregation was established by Roger *Williams at Providence, Rhode Island, in 1638–1639. Regionally, Baptists held association meetings of churches as early as the 1670s, the most prominent becoming the Philadelphia Baptist Association, formed in 1707. Early Baptists were often severely persecuted by the established denominations.

The eighteenth century was a time of rapid growth for Baptists in America. No other group received more impetus from the First Great Awakening. Baptist churches were formed from Congregationalist churches, and evangelism gave rise to new church throughout the colonies. In 1764, James Manning opened the first Baptist institution of higher learning, the Rhode Island College, which later became Brown University. During the *Revolutionary War period, such prominent Baptist leaders as Isaac Backus of Massachusetts and John Leland of Virginia formulated the principles of separation of *church and state, and through their connections successfully made the case to both national and state constitution writers. As the new nation developed, Baptists conducted overseas and domestic missions through voluntary societies. By 1840, Baptists were numerous in every state and territory, with over twenty educational institutions and missions in Asia, Africa, the Caribbean, and Europe. Beginning in the 1840s, division erupted among Baptists in America. Northern antislavery churches formed a dissenter mission society in 1843; Baptists in the South in 1845 formed the Southern Baptist Convention. Some Baptists opposed mission and benevolence societies altogether. Leading Baptists in the urban North under William Colgate even formed an independent American Bible Union to foster a Baptist version of Scripture. Beginning in 1838, black Baptists established their own associations and later national conventions: German, Swedish, Danish, and Norwegian emigrants formed ethnic conventions that would later become separate Baptist denominations.

In the twentieth century, Baptists grew to over 25 million members in the United States. The largest group, the Southern Baptist Convention, maintained associations and conventions in every state and most countries overseas. The National Baptist Convention in the U.S.A., along with the National Baptist Convention of America and the Progressive National Baptist Convention, organized most African American Baptists. The oldest national group, the American Baptist Churches in the U.S.A., formed in 1907, continued the work of the Northern Baptist Convention. The many smaller Baptist bodies included the Primitive Baptists, the Missionary Baptists, and the Freewill Baptists. Theological differences produced several conservative or fundamentalist Baptist bodies of churches, such as the General Association of Regular Baptists (1932), the Conservative Baptist Association (1943), the Baptist Bible Fellowship (1950), and the Liberty Baptist Fellowship (1977). Continuing ethical and theological debate within the Southern Baptist Convention over such matters as women in the ministry, freedom of conscience, ecumenism, scriptural interpretation, and issues of human sexuality produced the Southern Baptist Alliance (1986) and the Cooperative Baptist Fellowship (1991).

Baptists contributed leaders to various avenues of American life, including four U.S. presidents (Warren *Harding, Harry S. *Truman, Jimmy *Carter, and Bill *Clinton), Chief Justice Charles Evans *Hughes; the *Social Gospel theologian Walter *Rauschenbush; and the *civil rights leader Martin Luther *King Jr.

[*See also* African American Religion; Antislavery; Bill of Rights; Great Awakening, First and Second; Missionary Movement; Protestantism; Religion; Revivalism.]

• Edwin S. Gaustad, *Historical Atlas of Religion in America,* 1962. William H. Brackney, *The Baptists,* 1988. Kate Penfield, ed., *Into a New Day: Exploring a Baptist Journey of Division, Diversity and Dialogue,* 1997.

—William H. Brackney

BARBARY WARS (1801–1816). The term "Barbary Wars" refers to a series of limited military clashes between the United States and the North African kingdoms of Tunis, Tripoli, Algeria, and Morocco, collectively known as the Barbary Coast. Precipitated by attacks on American merchant vessels and the ransoming of American citizens and cargoes by Barbary Coast pirates, the conflict led to the rebirth of the U.S. Navy and Marine Corps.

The crisis began in 1784 as a by-product of American independence. Deprived of the protection of the British Navy, American merchant shipping fell prey to piracy by the North African kingdoms. In 1787, the *Continental Congress ratified a treaty with Morocco providing for the payment of tribute in exchange for a cessation of the attacks. Depredations by Tripoli and Algiers continued. *New England merchants, irked by ship seizures and rising insurance rates, pushed Congress to pass the Naval Act of 1794, which reestablished the U.S. Navy and authorized the construction of six naval frigates to defend U.S. interests in the Mediterranean.

In 1801, President Thomas *Jefferson, without consulting Congress, dispatched a naval squadron to the Mediterranean to protect American lives and commerce. The campaign suffered a setback in 1803 when Tripoli seized the USS *Philadelphia* and captured its three hundred–man crew. In 1804, Lieutenant Commander Stephen Decatur led sixty men on a daring raid into Tripoli harbor to board and burn the *Philadelphia,* although its crew remained hostage. In March 1805, Lieutenant William Eaton led a squad of seven Marines and four hundred mercenaries to victory at Derna, on the shores of Tripoli. The pasha of Tripoli soon agreed, in exchange for a sixty-thousand-dollar payment, to release the American prisoners and to commit no further acts of piracy against American vessels. The Barbary Wars concluded in 1816 when a naval squadron commanded by Decatur shelled Algiers into submission, thereby ending U.S. conflicts with the North African states until the later twentieth century.

[*See also* Military, The.]

• Ray W. Irwin, *The Diplomatic Relations of the United States with the Barbary Powers, 1776–1816,* 1931. Michael L. S. Kitzen, *Tripoli and the United States at War,* 1993.

—William Earl Weeks

BARDEEN, JOHN (1908–1991), theoretical physicist. Bardeen was born in Madison, Wisconsin, where his father, George Russell Bardeen, was dean of the University of Wisconsin Medical School. After earning an M.A. in electrical *engineering at Wisconsin, Bardeen worked for three years at Gulf Research Laboratory in Pittsburgh and then entered Princeton University's graduate program in mathematics, where he embarked on a study of electron interactions in solids. As a junior fellow at Harvard (1935–1938) he consolidated his characteristic experimentally grounded pragmatic approach to physics. While an assistant professor of physics at the University of Minnesota (1938–1941) he began work on superconductivity, the phenomenon in which certain metals and alloys abruptly lose all electrical resistance below a certain temperature—a phenomenon that had baffled physicists since its discovery in 1911.

After directing an engineering group at the Naval Ordnance Laboratory in Washington, D.C., during *World War II, Bardeen joined William Shockley's new semiconductor research group at Bell Telephone Laboratories in New Jersey. Here he launched the group on a program of basic research that in December 1947 led to his invention, with the experimental physicist Walter Brattain, of the first transistor, a key component in the electronics revolution. For this achievement he shared the 1956 Nobel Prize for physics.

Conflicts with Shockley over further transistor research at Bell Labs led Bardeen in 1951 to move to the University of Illinois where, with Leon Cooper and J. Robert Schrieffer, he solved the puzzle of superconductivity by 1957. Central to their theory was the attractive interaction between electrons inside superconductors resulting from the coupling of electrons to quantized sound waves in the solid. For this he shared a second Nobel Prize in 1972, making him the first person ever awarded two Nobel Prizes in the same field.

Bardeen continued to consult for businesses after his return to academia, including Haloid (which became Xerox) and General Electric. He served on numerous high-level government scientific-advisory bodies under Presidents Eisenhower, Kennedy, and Reagan. As a member of Reagan's White House Science Council, he strongly opposed the *Strategic Defense Initiative. Bardeen remained active in cutting-edge research until his death.

[*See also* Physical Sciences; Science: Since 1945.]

• Lillian Hoddeson et al., eds., *Out of the Crystal Maze: A History of Solid State Physics, 1900–1960,* 1992. Michael Riordan and Lillian Hoddeson, *Crystal Fire: The Birth of the Information Age,* 1997.

—Lillian Hoddeson

BARNUM P. T. (1810–1891), show man, politician, circus owner, one of America's premier show-business entrepreneurs. Born on a farm in Bethel, Connecticut, Phineas Taylor Barnum in 1836 went on the road, selling tickets for Aaron Turner's traveling show. Tiring of itinerant show business, he in 1841 purchased a museum in *New York City, where he featured a menagerie and such attractions as the dwarf Charles Stratton (1838–1883), better known as Tom Thumb. In 1850, he successfully promoted the American tour of the singer Jenny Lind, the "Swedish Nightingale." In 1865, he won a seat in the Connecticut legislature. During his term, his American Museum in New York was destroyed by fire; and he was more than ready in 1870 to join William Coup and Dan Costello in the circus business.

Eventually buying out his partners, he combined his circus with that of James Bailey in 1881 to form the Barnum and Bailey Combined Circus, a touring show, taking advantage of the nation's growing network of *railroads, that could justifiably lay claim to being the "Greatest Show on Earth"—indeed, one big enough to present Jumbo, "the world's largest elephant," among its many attractions. Jumbo made over one million dollars for Barnum before he was hit by a train in 1885. Ever the innovator, Barnum continued to display Jumbo's hide in the menagerie of the circus. A showman to the end, Barnum lived in Bridgeport, Connecticut, where he had built a lavish mansion, Iranistan. A man who could take the smallest and the largest and turn them into wonders for young and old, Barnum enlivened and enriched nineteenth-century America.

[*See also* Antebellum Era; Circuses; Gilded Age; Leisure; Minstrelsy; Vaudeville.]

• Irving Wallace, *The Fabulous Showman*, 1967. Wilton Eckley, *The American Circus*, 1984.

—Wilton E. Eckley

BARTRAM, JOHN (1699–1777), botanist, father of **WILLIAM** (1739–1823), naturalist. Born on a farm near Darby, Pennsylvania, John Bartram spent most of his adult life on his farm at Kingsessing, four miles from *Philadelphia. By 1730 his interest in botany had attracted the attention of Philadelphia's scientific community, through which he met Peter Collinson, a London merchant and naturalist who became his mentor and patron. Collinson and other British plant enthusiasts purchased seeds and plants from Bartram, thereby helping finance his botanical exploration of Pennsylvania, New Jersey, New York, Virginia, and Delaware. He returned with specimens and observations valued by the European scientific community. Named king's botanist (George III) in 1765, Bartram used his stipend to finance an expedition to South Carolina, Georgia, and Florida.

William Bartram, the son of John and his second wife, Ann Mendenhall, while still a teenager accompanied his father on botanical collecting trips. After failing as a planter and a merchant, William followed his father's footsteps by spending four years (1773–1777) exploring the Carolinas, Georgia, and Florida with the financial support of John Fothergill, a London physician. His account of his travels, *Travels through North and South Carolina, Georgia, East and West Florida* (1791), influenced English romantic writers such as William Wordsworth and Samuel Taylor Coleridge. In 1778 he returned to the family farm at Kingsessing, now owned by his brother John, where he provided encouragement and training to the succeeding generation of American naturalists, including Thomas Say and Alexander Wilson. The careers of the Bartrams, father and son, demonstrate the importance of European patronage for American *science during the *Colonial Era.

• Edmund Berkeley and Dorothy Smith Berkeley, *The Life and Travels of John Bartram: From Lake Ontario to the River St. John*, 1982. Thomas P. Slaughter, *The Natures of John and William Bartram*, 1996.

—Marc Rothenberg

BARUCH, BERNARD (1870–1965), venture capitalist, investor, government official. Born in Camden, South Carolina, and reared in *New York City, Bernard Mannes Baruch graduated from the City College of New York in 1889. His first job on *Wall Street, at the brokerage firm of A. A. Housman & Co., paid $3 a week, but he became a millionaire by the time he was thirty. He was a governor of the *New York Stock Exchange, a leader in mining finance, and an occasional investor in properties controlled by the Guggenheim family. Although he did not sell out just before the *stock market crash of 1929, as legend has it, he did salvage the bulk of his fortune.

Bernard Baruch's government service came in *World War I and *World War II. In March 1918, President Woodrow *Wilson named him chairman of the *War Industries Board. Granted sweeping powers, he effectively marshaled the U.S. economy for war. In 1919, he served in a senior capacity with the U.S. peace delegation at Versailles. During World War II he performed a variety of services, including the drafting of an influential report on rubber rationing. In 1946, President Harry S. *Truman named the seventy-five-year-old Baruch to present to the *United Nations the U.S. plan for the international control of atomic energy drafted by Dean *Acheson and David E. Lilienthal. Despite a dramatic opening speech by Baruch, the negotiations came to naught.

Six feet four inches tall, Baruch was a prototypical twentieth-century celebrity, cultivating his press image as "adviser to presidents" and "park bench statesman." In fact, the advice he eagerly offered a succession of presidents was only selectively accepted. His mastery of public relations is suggested by the fact that the *New York Times* devoted a paragraph-length news story in 1947 to his sprained ankle.

[*See also* Cold War; Depressions, Economic; Nuclear Arms Control Treaties; Nuclear Weapons; Stock Market; Versailles, Treaty of.]

• Jordan A. Schwartz, *The Speculator: Bernard M. Baruch in Washington, 1917–65*, 1981. James Grant, *Bernard M. Baruch: The Adventures of a Wall Street Legend*, 1997.

—James Grant

BASEBALL. Americans had played bat-and-ball games for decades when, in 1845, Alexander Cartwright of New York devised the rules—foul lines, nine innings, three outs, ninety-foot basepaths—that created modern baseball. Cartwright's game quickly became popular with young clerks and urban craftsmen. By 1860, baseball had spread throughout the Northeast, and by 1870 to the rest of the nation.

The first teams were amateur, organized by men's clubs, the games ending with dinner and drinks. Some players earned good money from ambitious clubs, which charged admission in order to pay the players. The first wholly professional team was the Cincinnati (Ohio) Red Stockings of 1869, whose manager, Harry Wright, hired every player. Taking advantage of the burgeoning railroad system to tour the country, they challenged and defeated all teams they faced that year. In 1876, entrepreneurs formed the National League (NL), with salaried players and profit-seeking owners.

Baseball exploded in popularity in the 1880s as Irish and German immigrants embraced it. A new American Association (AA) challenged the NL with cheap tickets, Sunday games, and liquor. From 1884 to 1891 the champions of the NL and AA staged an early "World Series" featuring such luminaries as Cap Anson of the Chicago White Stockings, King Kelly of the Boston Red Stockings, and Charles Comiskey of the St. Louis (Missouri) Browns. Minor-league clubs proliferated, newspapers covered baseball avidly, and sporting-goods companies prospered manufacturing baseball equipment. Baseball now became what club owners and equipment manufacturers called it, the national pastime. Wanting their fair share, players formed a union and then, in 1890, the Players League. Both the Players League and the AA soon collapsed, however, leaving the NL standing alone through the 1890s, able to keep salaries low and players tied to their teams through a reserve clause.

In 1900, as player discontent grew and fan interest revived, a regional organization, the Western League, renamed itself the American League (AL). With such former NL greats as Comiskey, John McGraw, and Connie Mack as managers or owners, the AL stole dozens of NL players, including the era's greatest hitter, Napoleon Lajoie. By 1903, when the modern World Series was inaugurated, the new league was well established, as was a professional agreement to control players' movements and major-minor–league relations. Pitchers dominated this so-called dead ball era. Christy Mathewson of the New York Giants and "Three-Fingered" Brown of the Chicago Cubs hurled their clubs to repeated pennants. Connie Mack's Philadelphia Athletics, with the goofy left-hander Rube Waddell, and the Boston Red Sox, led by the brilliant young pitcher George Herman ("Babe") *Ruth, dominated the AL. Other stars included Detroit's hard-hitting Ty *Cobb, the game's fiercest competitor, and the Pittsburgh shortstop Honus Wagner.

Two developments ushered in the "golden age" of the 1920s. First, eight members of Comiskey's Chicago White Sox conspired with gamblers to lose the 1919 World Series. The resulting trial and publicity sullied the reputation of baseball, whose owners created the office of baseball commissioner and filled it with the strong-willed judge Kenesaw Mountain Landis. Landis banned the eight "Black Sox" for life and ruled organized baseball with an iron hand for three decades. Second, Babe Ruth, now a full-time outfielder with the New York Yankees, started to hit home runs as no one ever had. As the Yankee owner Jacob Ruppert built a championship team around Ruth and a huge new stadium for his fans, the Yankees became a dynasty. Lively baseballs, sluggers, and big ballparks lifted baseball's popularity to new heights. Ruth retired in 1935 after setting career and season home-run records. The 1930s witnessed the first All Star Game, the first major-league night game (in Cincinnati), the opening of the Baseball Hall of Fame at Cooperstown New York, and Branch Rickey's creation of a "farm system" for the St. Louis Cardinals. In 1936, Joe *DiMaggio first appeared in the Yankee outfield, continuing the dynasty.

Organized baseball had been segregated since the 1880s, forcing *African Americans to form the Negro National and American Leagues. These leagues had such Hall-of-Fame players as the pitcher Satchel Paige and the catcher Josh Gibson, but playing conditions were poor and paychecks uncertain. All this changed when Branch Rickey moved from St. Louis, where his farm system had produced champions, to the Brooklyn (New York) Dodgers during *World War II. Rickey found talent in the Negro leagues, signing UCLA athlete Jackie *Robinson, who became the first black major leaguer in 1947 and led the Dodgers to six NL pennants in ten years. By 1960, the Negro leagues had collapsed, and every major-league club had black players on its roster, including Willie Mays, the brilliant New York Giants centerfielder, and Hank Aaron of the Milwaukee (Wisconsin) Braves, who hit more career homers than Babe Ruth. The 1950s also witnessed the first franchise movements in decades, including, with the advent of jet air travel, the move of the Brooklyn Dodgers and New York Giants to *California, and televised baseball, which seriously damaged the minor leagues. Meanwhile, the Yankees rolled on. Hall of Famer Mickey Mantle replaced DiMaggio; manager Casey Stengel raised relief pitching and platooning to new heights; Roger Maris broke Ruth's season home-run record; and the catcher Yogi Berra was the AL's most valuable player three times. New York won a staggering fourteen pennants and ten world championships in seventeen years.

Several developments highlighted baseball's evolution after 1970. First, clubs discovered a new source of talent in Latin American players, including such greats as Juan Marichal and Felipe Alou of San Francisco. Second, clubs built parks with artificial turf, which made line-drive hitters and speedsters such as Cincinnati's Pete Rose and St. Louis's Lou Brock more valuable. Third, the players formed a strong union, achieving, among other things, free agency, or the right to market themselves to the highest bidder, and salary arbitration, which drove salaries sharply higher and distributed talent more evenly among clubs. Owner-union clashes also produced the sport's first strikes. Finally, more clubs moved and more cities gained franchises, necessitating intraleague playoffs to determine pennant winners.

By the 1990s, television—including "superstations" broadcasting local games nationwide, and television advertising—had come to influence baseball, as had competing sports, making franchises astonishingly valuable and producing a shift to corporate rather than family ownership. A team with superstation revenues, the Atlanta Braves, dominated the NL in the 1990s, not least through the efforts of Greg Maddox, the greatest pitcher of the decade. Live attendance flourished as well, thanks partly to the construction of "old-fashioned" stadiums with suburban amenities. Fans were rewarded in 1998 by the New York Yankees, who won 114 games, a new regular-season AL record, and Mark McGuire of the St. Louis Cardinals, who crashed seventy home runs, shattering Roger Maris's home-run record and besting the Chicago Cubs' Sammy Sosa, whose sixty-six homers also broke Maris's record.

[*See also* Sports.]

• Harold Seymour, *Baseball*, 2 vols., 1960–1971. Jules Tygiel, *Baseball's Great Experiment*, 1983. Lawrence Ritter, *The Glory of Their Times*, 1985. Daniel Okrent, *Nine Innings*, 1989. Joseph L. Reichler, ed., *The Baseball Encyclopedia*, 1990. Andrew Zimbalist, *Baseball Billions*, 1992.

—Ronald Story

BASIE, WILLIAM ("COUNT") (1904–1984), *jazz pianist, arranger, band leader. Basie was born in Red Bank, New Jersey, where he received early musical training, including inspiration from the stride pianist "Fats" Waller. Basie developed a distinctive piano style that pared down the cascading notes of his predecessors. His sound—rooted in polyrhythmic intensity and *blues changes—eventually came to epitomize *Kansas City jazz.

Basie performed in *vaudeville and accompanied the blues singers Clara Smith and Maggie Jones. In Kansas City, he played for silent movies (1927) and joined Walter Page's Blue Devils (1928) and Benny Moten's Kansas City Orchestra (1929). After Moten's death in 1935, Basie and Buster Smith reorganized Moten's band, which became Count Basie's Orchestra. A leading swing-era ensemble, it produced such hits as "Jumpin' at the Woodside" (1938) and "Taxi War Dance" (1939), which perfectly suited the athletic new dances of the day. Basie's music attracted radio and ballroom audiences and featured such jazz greats as Lester Young and Jo Jones.

Basie's band first recorded on the Decca label in 1937, thanks in part to the promoter John Hammond. Basie's bands remained the standard-bearer of swing music, even after the *World War II craze for the music abated. His ensembles toured Europe, Asia, South America, and the United States. Basie performed at President John F. *Kennedy's Inaugural Ball in 1961, and twenty years later received a Kennedy Center Achievement Award. Basie and his wife Catherine had two children, Aaron Woodward (adopted) and Diane Basie. He died in Hollydale, New York.

• Raymond Horricks, *Count Basie and His Orchestra: Its Music and Musicians*, 1957. Ross Russell, *Jazz Style in Kansas City and the Southwest*, 1971. Chris Sheridan, *Count Basie: A Bio-Discography*, 1986.

—Kathy J. Ogren

BASKETBALL. James Naismith, an instructor at the YMCA Training School at Springfield College in Massachusetts, invented basketball in 1891 as an indoor winter game. The object was to throw a soccer ball into an elevated peach basket (the "goal"). Players could not run with the ball (which led to dribbling) and received a "foul" for rule violations. Play resumed after each goal with a "jump ball." By 1895, field goals were two points and foul shots one, and backboards were added to prevent fans from interfering with shots. Two years later the number of players on a team was fixed at five. They wore knee pads because play was rough, with frequent fights over balls that went out of bounds. Cages were built around the court to keep the ball in play and prevent fan interference.

Basketball quickly gained popularity across the nation. At YMCAs, *settlement houses, and school yards social workers believed that it improved morals, promoted teamwork, reduced juvenile delinquency, and Americanized recent immigrants. By the 1920s, it had become a cornerstone of interscholastic sports in the small towns of Kentucky, Illinois, and Indiana, where high school basketball symbolized hometown pride.

Basketball was well liked by women college students. In 1892, the Smith College gymnasium director, Senda Berenson, modified the rules to make it more appropriate for young ladies. She curtailed physical play by forbidding grabbing of the ball and promoted teamwork by permitting no one to hold it more than three seconds or dribble more than three times. Berenson redesigned the court, placing three women in the offensive zone, three in the defensive, and two in midcourt to reduce fatigue (reflecting contemporary views of women's limited physical capacity) and encourage team play. In 1895, Stanford University defeated the University of California–Berkeley, 2–1, in the first women's intercollegiate contest. However, the game was soon deemphasized by women's physical educators who opposed female competitive sports. In the 1930s and 1940s industrial league teams dominated women's play. Not until the era of Title IX in the 1970s did the game regain its popularity on campus. Renewed interest led to the rise of two women's pro leagues in 1996: the Women's National Basketball League and the defunct American Basketball League.

In the first male college game, also in 1895, Minnesota State topped Hamline University 9–3. However, basketball did not become a major sport until the 1930s. In 1938, New York sports writers organized the National Invitational Tournament at New York's Madison Square Garden. The *National Collegiate Athletic Association (NCAA) tournament followed in 1939. A major college-basketball scandal, involving gambling, point shaving, and thrown games, occurred in 1951, causing Madison Square Garden to drop big-time basketball, ruining New York City's college programs, and harming New York's status as the game's mecca. College basketball regained its luster in the 1960s, abetted by UCLA's ten championships between 1964 and 1975. By the end of the century, NCAA tournament had become a premier American sporting event.

Professional men's basketball began in 1898 with metropolitan Philadelphia's short-lived National Basketball League. In the 1920s, the touring New York Original Celtics and the black New York Rens were the dominant clubs. Top white teams also played in regional semipro leagues like the American Basketball League (1933–1946) and the National Basketball League (1937–1948). In 1946, owners of major urban sports arenas formed the Basketball Association of America (BAA) to augment use of their facilities. In 1949 it merged with the NBL to form the National Basketball Association (NBA), which became racially integrated in 1950. Several franchises failed, and smaller cities' teams relocated to larger metropolises. The Boston Celtics dominated the NBA for several years, with eleven championships between 1957 and 1969. Rule innovations, talented performers, flashy play, and *television helped build attendance from under two million in 1960 to ten million in 1980. Such NBA superstars as Michael *Jordan of the Chicago Bulls became multimillionaires through their salaries and product endorsements and enjoyed widespread celebrity.

[*See also* Sports; YMCA and YWCA.]

• Neil D. Isaacs, *All the Moves: A History of College Basketball*, 1975. Robert Peterson, *Cages to Jumpshots: Pro Basketball's Early Years*, 1990.

—Steven A. Riess

BAY OF PIGS, site in Cuba of the failed April 1961 invasion by Cuban exiles trained by the *Central Intelligence Agency (CIA). U.S. leaders ranked Premier Fidel Castro's growing ties with the Soviet Union; his radical, anti-Yankee Cuban Revolution; and his call for revolutions elsewhere as major threats to U.S. interests in Latin America. In late 1959, U.S. officials recruited anti-Castro Cubans in Florida to overthrow Castro's government. On 17 March 1960, President Dwight D. *Eisenhower approved the creation of a covert "paramilitary force." While hatching plots to assassinate Castro, the CIA opened a camp in Guatemala to train the anti-Castro recruits.

President John F. *Kennedy, who took office in January 1961, shared the *Cold War assumptions that fueled U.S. hostility toward Castro. In the 1960 presidential campaign, he had vowed to expunge communism from Cuba. CIA planners, particularly Richard Bissell, recalling the CIA's toppling of an unfriendly government in Guatemala in 1954, predicted triumph for the exile expedition. The *Joint Chiefs of Staff (JCS), Secretary of State Dean Rusk, and some other advisers harbored doubts about the plan but muted their criticism of an operation they knew the president basically endorsed. Kennedy approved an assault at two Bay of Pigs beaches, insisting that Washington's role be concealed and that no U.S. military forces be committed.

Planners assumed that the expedition would spark an anti-Castro uprising. On 15 April, B-26 bombers attacked Cuba's air bases, only partially disabling Castro's air force. Sensitive to the international protest that erupted, Kennedy canceled further U.S. air strikes, rejecting CIA advice that air superiority was essential. The invasion, carried out on 16–17 April, soon went awry. Cuban aircraft disabled freighters carrying radio gear, equipment malfunctioned, and a coral reef undetected by the CIA wrecked boats. Local people and militia pinned down the brigade until Castro's army arrived. Despite CIA assurances otherwise, brigade members could not easily escape to the mountains, eighty miles away. No popular uprisings occurred.

Of some 1,400 brigade invaders, more than 1,100 were captured and 114 died. Castro's forces suffered about 150 fatalities. Castro released the brigade prisoners in December 1962, in exchange for U.S. medical supplies. A postinvasion study by General Maxwell Taylor, as well as documents later declassified, revealed the reasons for failure: logistical breakdowns, poor understanding of conditions in Cuba, insufficient interagency coordination, CIA and presidential wishful thinking, timid counsel from presidential advisers, a pervasive overestimation of both the brigade's chances for victory and a mass uprising, and an underestimation of Castro's ability to rally his armed forces and militia.

After the debacle, Washington's anti-Castro effort continued in a plan called Operation Mongoose. It included new assassination plots, sabotage raids, economic sanctions, and contingency plans for a U.S. military invasion. The Bay of Pigs crisis pushed Cuba closer to the Soviet Union. The subsequent Cuban–Soviet agreement to deploy nuclear-capable weapons on the island sparked the frightening October 1962 *Cuban missile crisis.

[*See also* Foreign Relations: U.S. Relations with Latin America.]

• Thomas G. Paterson, *Contesting Castro: The United States and the Triumph of the Cuban Revolution*, 1994. Piero Gleijeses, "Ships in the Night: The CIA, the White House, and the Bay of Pigs," *Journal of Latin American Studies* 27 (Feb. 1995): 1–42.

—Thomas G. Paterson

BAY PSALM BOOK. *The Whole Booke of Psalmes Faithfully Translated into English Metre* (1640), familiarly called the *Bay Psalm Book*, was the first book published in Anglo-America, which underlines the importance that singing played in Puritan devotion. The Massachusetts clergy undertook the project because they judged the current most popular Psalter, Thomas Sternhold and John Hopkins's *Whole Book of Psalms* (1562), an insufficiently literal translation of the Hebrew, and Henry Ainsworth's more accurate *Book of Psalms* (1612) problematic because of the author's separation from the Church of England. Thomas Welde, John Eliot, and Richard Mather penned most of the verses, while John Cotton wrote the preface. A consensus that the text warranted artistic improvement led Henry Dunster, president of Harvard College, and Richard Lyon to publish a revision, differently titled, in 1651.

The *Bay Psalm Book* played a central role in both public services and domestic devotions for over a century, since Puritans sang psalms to praise God, comfort the afflicted, admonish the wicked, urge sinners to Christ, and vivify their sense of heaven's imminent glory. Some scholars derogated the poetry's quality, calling attention to its forced rhymes and the inverted order of phrases, but its "singsong" cadences aided memorization, a useful means for increasing worshipers' participation in an age when books were scarce and many individuals could not read. The volume lost favor in the mid-eighteenth century as congregations' musicianship improved and ministers accepted scriptural paraphrases as liturgically sound; still, the twenty-seventh (and last) New England edition appeared as late as 1762.

[*See also* Bible, The; Colonial Era; Literature: Colonial Era; Puritanism.]

• Zoltán Haraszti, *The Enigma of the Bay Psalm Book.*, 1956. Charles Hambrick-Stowe, *The Practice of Piety: Puritan Devotional Disciplines in Seventeenth-Century New England,* 1982, pp. 111–16.

—Charles L. Cohen

BEARD, CHARLES A. (1874–1948), historian, political scientist. Born in Indiana, Beard was reared in the political culture of civic *republicanism, which found economic virtue in the widespread ownership of productive private property. Graduating from DePauw University in 1898, he came to maturity in a decade of crisis associated with the depression of the 1890s and the closing of the frontier, proclaimed by historian Frederick Jackson *Turner in 1893, with dire implications for small landholders. Turner foresaw an urban-industrial future of economic dependency. Beard, however, after a year at Oxford University (1898–1899), became convinced that industrial workers, as a democratic majority, could escape dependency by using the national government to curb corporate power. This was the hopeful message of his first book, *The Industrial Revolution* (1901).

Earning a Ph.D. from Columbia University in 1904, Beard joined Columbia's history faculty that year. His best-known work, *Economic Interpretation of the Constitution* (1913), contrasted virtuous owners of private property who respected the national interest with capitalists who were committed to self-interest and a rootless international marketplace. He sought to demonstrate that the Founding Fathers were capitalists who had designed the checks and balances of the *Constitution to frustrate majority rule and to protect economic hierarchy. He hoped this analysis would help Progressives like Theodore *Roosevelt to regulate the great corporations. If the reformers succeeded, Beard believed, democracy and national interest would replace hierarchy and self-interest.

Beard also believed that *industrialization, as the product of a universal evolutionary process, would spread democracy worldwide. He supported the Allied cause in *World War I, convinced that the war would liberate the German people, made democratic by industrialization, from their reactionary political leaders. But in 1917, when Columbia under President Nicholas Murray Butler dismissed several faculty members for their antiwar views, Beard resigned in protest. He never again held a permanent academic position, though he lectured widely, dividing his time between Washington, D.C., and a farm in Connecticut. He was president of the American Political Science Association in 1926 and the American Historical Association in 1933. With his wife, Mary *Beard, he wrote the four-volume *Rise of American Civilization* (1927). In the tradition of civic republicanism, the Beards contrasted virtuous, public-spirited, private-property owners with a corrupt capitalist class that pursued economic gain worldwide at the expense of the national interest. This corporate class, Beard now concluded, had pushed America into war in 1917.

Rejecting *internationalism, Beard concluded that industrialism supported democracy only in nations with democratic traditions, as the United States. In 1939–1941, he opposed U.S. entrance into *World War II as a threat to America's democratic tradition. His final book, *President Roosevelt and the Coming of the War 1941* (1948), argued that Franklin Delano *Roosevelt had maneuvered Japan into the attack on *Pearl Harbor.

Beard's influence waned after his death, as a younger generation of historians rejected his nationalistic and class-based views in favor of a "consensus" model that saw international *capitalism as a necessary economic foundation for democracy. As historians explored America's racial and ethnic diversity, the absence of *cultural pluralism in the work of Beard (and Turner) became painfully evident; other historians attacked Beard's *Economic Interpretation of the Constitution* for various methodological flaws. Some radical historians of the 1960s praised Beard as an intellectual forerunner, however, and his seminal influence was widely acknowledged as the twentieth century ended.

[*See also* Academic Freedom; Historiography, American; Isolationism; Political Science; Progressive Era.]

• Ellen Nore, *Charles A. Beard*, 1983. Peter Novick, *That Noble Dream: The Objectivity Question and the American Historical Profession,* 1988.

—David Noble

BEARD, MARY (1876–1958), historian. Born in Indianapolis, Mary Ritter attended DePauw University and in 1900 married the future historian Charles A. *Beard. Their children were born in 1901 and 1907. After 1902 the Beards lived in New York, where Mary Beard briefly studied sociology at Columbia University. She also became active in the *Women's Trade Union League and the *woman suffrage movement. She edited *The Woman Voter,* a publication of the Woman Suffrage party of New York; started a suffragist organization for working women; and joined the Congressional Union, a militant suffragist faction led by Alice Paul that became the National Woman's party. (NWP). In the 1920s, Mary Beard split with the NWP over its proposal for an *equal rights amendment; she supported protective legislation for working women, which the proposed amendment threatened.

Mary Beard's interest in reform led to her career as a scholar. Her early books were *Women's Work in Municipalities* (1915); *A Short History of the American Labor Movement* (1920); and, with her husband, *The Rise of American Civilization* (1927), a widely read synthesis of American history. Her books on women include *On Understanding Women* (1931) and *America through Women's Eyes* (1933), a documentary collection.

An iconoclastic feminist, Mary Beard tackled issues central to twentieth-century *feminism, such as the tension between egalitarianism and *gender identity. In her best-known book, *Woman as Force in History* (1946), she denied that women had been historically victimized by male domination, assailed feminism for devaluing women's contributions, and opposed the trend among feminists to reshape women according to criteria developed by men.

[*See also* Historiography, American; Labor Movements; Progressive Era; Women in the Labor Force.]

• Nancy F. Cott, ed., *A Woman Making History: Mary Ritter Beard through Her Letters,* 1991.

—Nancy Woloch

BEAUMONT, WILLIAM (1785–1853), physician and scientist, the first American physiologist to achieve international renown. A native of Lebanon, Connecticut, Beaumont earned a license to practice medicine in 1812 after an apprenticeship with a physician in northern Vermont. From 1812 to 1839, Beaumont mostly served in the medical department of the United States

Army: on the Canadian border during the *War of 1812 and at various frontier posts in the Great Lakes region during the 1820s and 1830s. After his retirement from the army, Beaumont established a successful private practice in St. Louis, Missouri, where he lived until his death.

Beaumont achieved permanent fame for his research on human digestion. In June 1822, while at Fort Mackinac in Michigan Territory, Beaumont treated a French-Canadian voyageur, Alexis St. Martin, who had been shot in the stomach. The wound healed in such a manner as to leave a permanent gastric fistula, or opening. This enabled Beaumont to insert food into St. Martin's stomach, observe the digestive process, and remove gastric juice for analysis. At different times over the next decade, working in extremely difficult conditions, Beaumont pursued his experiments. Much of his most valuable work was carried out in Fort Crawford at Prairie du Chien, Wisconsin. Beaumont's book, *Experiments and Observations on the Gastric Juice and the Physiology of Digestion* (1833), established that digestion was a chemical process, a finding quickly accepted in both in the United States and Europe.

[*See also* Medicine: From 1776 to the 1870s.]

• Jesse D. Myer, *Life and Letters of Dr. William Beaumont,* 1912. Reginald Horsman, *Frontier Doctor: William Beaumont, America's First Great Medical Scientist,* 1996.

—Reginald Horsman

BEECHER, CATHARINE (1800–1878), educator and social reformer. Beecher was born in East Hampton, New York, the oldest child of Lyman Beecher, a prominent Evangelical clergyman, and the sister of Henry Ward *Beecher and Harriet Beecher Stowe, author of the antislavery classic **Uncle Tom's Cabin.* Catharine Beecher's writings gained a wide readership in the decades before the *Civil War because they so cogently expressed new views about the expanded power of middle-class women in modern family life.

Beecher's career flourished in the dynamic cultural environment of the *Antebellum Era. In 1823, she founded one of the new nation's most rigorous academies for women, the Hartford Female Seminary, and hitched her own star to the rising status of women as educators. In 1832, she followed her father and siblings to Cincinnati, Ohio, where, like them, she championed *New England Evangelicalism in the multicultural environment of the American *West.

Although she did not use the term, Beecher advocated "domestic feminism"—that is, expanded power for women within domestic life and ancillary power in the wider society. She was best known for *Treatise on Domestic Economy* (1841), which was reprinted annually through 1856 and greatly expanded in a widely reprinted version coauthored with Harriet Beecher Stowe, *The American Woman's Home; or, Principles of Domestic Science* (1869). Beecher's advice to women reflected contemporary economic changes that were relocating male labor and much of what had formerly been domestic production outside the household. She advised married women to exercise greater control over home life, including family finances, and to value their work as an honorable calling of great significance for the future of American democracy.

[*See also* Domestic Labor; Feminism; Women's Rights Movements; Work.]

• Kathryn Kish Sklar, *Catharine Beecher: A Study in American Domesticity,* 1973. Jeanne Boydston, Mary Kelley, and Anne Margolis, *The Limits of Sisterhood: The Beecher Sisters on Women's Rights and Woman's Sphere,* 1988.

—Kathryn Kish Sklar

BEECHER, HENRY WARD (1813–1887), minister and social reformer. Few mid–nineteenth century preachers enjoyed greater popularity than Henry Ward Beecher. Actively involved in the temperance, *antislavery, and *women's right movements, Beecher was a charismatic preacher who helped shape the Evangelical Protestant position on the political issues of his day.

Son of Lyman Beecher, a leader of the Second Great Awakening, Henry was born in Litchfield, Connecticut, the eighth of thirteenth children. After graduating from Amherst College in 1834 and attending Lane Seminary in Cincinnati, he served as a minister in Indiana, and, from 1847 to 1887, as pastor to the Plymouth Congregational Church in Brooklyn, New York. Stressing the regenerative power of God's love for man, Beecher promoted a romantic Christian gospel that stressed social activism and the restorative power of nature.

Although he wrote for the *Independent,* a Congregational newspaper, and lectured on the lyceum circuit, Beecher was perhaps best known for his prominent role in the abolitionist movement in the 1850s. Conducting mock auctions of "slave girls" in his church and sending rifles (nicknamed "Beecher's Bibles") to antislavery settlers in the contested Kansas territory, Beecher and his sister, Harriet Beecher Stowe, the author of **Uncle Tom's Cabin,* mobilized northern opposition to slavery. During the *Civil War, he lectured in England and helped swing public opinion against the *South.

After the war, he published a successful novel, *Norwood* (1867), and edited a new magazine, the *Christian Union.* But accusations of adultery tarnished his career in 1874. The heavily publicized trial, involving Beecher's alleged relationship with his parishioner Elizabeth Tilton, resulted in a hung jury and his exoneration; historians remain divided over whether he was guilty. Henry Ward Beecher influenced a generation of preachers and served as a role model for Washington Gladden and other proponents of the *Social Gospel who sought a more political, socially activist role for the ministry.

[*See also* Beecher, Catharine; Great Awakening, First and Second; Kansas-Nebraska Act; Protestantism; Romantic Movement; Temperance and Prohibition.]

• William G. McLoughlin, *The Meaning of Henry Ward Beecher: An Essay on the Shifting Values of Mid-Victorian America, 1840–1870,* 1970. Clifford E. Clark Jr., *Henry Ward Beecher: Spokesman for a Middle-Class America,* 1978. Altina L. Waller, *Reverend Beecher and Mrs. Tilton: Sex and Class in Victorian America,* 1982.

—Clifford E. Clark Jr.

BEHAVIORISM. The school of experimental *psychology known as behaviorism was first articulated by John B. Watson (1878–1958) in a 1913 article in *Psychological Review* entitled "Psychology as a Behaviorist Views It." Rejecting the notion of consciousness, Watson viewed all behavior as conditioned by external experience that could be observed, measured, and controlled. As espoused by its founder, however, behaviorism had more to do with defining psychology's purpose and function than with any specific methodology beyond a seemingly rigorous empiricism. Watson belonged to the first generation of American-trained psychologists—a cohort determined to make psychology no longer a stepchild of *philosophy but an empirical science.

Watson's formulation of behaviorism characterized psychology as a science whose primary objective was to predict and control human behavior. Accordingly, he promoted behaviorism as a management tool, a pedagogical method, an *advertising technique, and a *child-rearing method. (Watson's own child-rearing manual, *Psychological Care of Infant and Child* [1928], enjoyed considerable influence.) In this sense, Watson's behaviorism, which characterized *Homo sapiens* as "organic machines," belonged on the spectrum of *Progressive Era social thought along with *scientific management and technocracy linked to the work of Thorstein *Veblen.

Behaviorists promised to unlock the mechanism that governed human action. Their notion of a malleable human nature inspired the new professional managerial classes that saw the intractability of the "human factor" as the last obstacle to a rationally managed society. The 1920s witnessed the transformation of large foundations from charitable trusts to professionally managed enterprises. As foundation support became more problem-oriented, it increasingly focused on scientific research related to social conduct and behavior. Within this context, human behavior became the focus of a new synthesis in an increasingly integrated research community. The "social and behavioral sciences" became invariably linked.

Behaviorism, emphasizing the primacy of environment over instincts, held special appeal for reformers. Watson, however, never contended that all human beings were equal, only that they were the same. By denying the existence of consciousness, behaviorism desanctified both the outer world of nature and the realm of inner experience, reducing both to manipulable objects. If behaviorism represented the freedom to remake the individual, it also raised the specter of conditioning human behavior into predetermined channels. Behaviorism, wrote the social philosopher Horace Kallen, made human beings "as equal as Fords."

As a popularizer of self-help psychology, Watson made behaviorism a household word in the 1920s. Behaviorism's claims to demystify psychology and to simplify the complexities of modern life appealed strongly to middle-class Americans. By the 1930s, it had become the dominant paradigm in American experimental psychology. Although few psychologists accepted the more radical aspects of Watson's extreme materialism, behaviorism's objective methodology powerfully influenced the direction of American psychology. Influenced by Watson's popular writings, B. F. Skinner, of Harvard University, became the preeminent behaviorist of the post–*World War II generation. Skinner's major achievement, the development of operant conditioning, was based on the notion of designing an environment so controlled that the subject conditioned itself to behave in ways predetermined by the experimenter. Though his experimental subjects were pigeons, Skinner promoted a vision of human social engineering and scientific management in his utopian novel *Walden Two* (1948).

Behaviorism helped legitimize experimental psychology among the natural sciences and provided scientific underpinning to the belief in American exceptionalism that characterized American *social science in the twentieth century. Behaviorism's ascendancy reflected a preoccupation with order and efficiency among the shapers of modernist America.

[*See also* Professionalization; Twenties, The.]

• John M. O'Donnell, *The Origins of Behaviorism: American Psychology, 1870–1920*, 1985. Kerry W. Buckley, *Mechanical Man: John Broadus Watson and the Beginnings of Behaviorism*, 1989. Daniel W. Bjork, *B. F. Skinner: A Life*, 1993.

—Kerry W. Buckley

BELL, ALEXANDER GRAHAM (1847–1922), inventor of the *telephone and educator of the deaf. Born in Edinburgh, Scotland, the son and grandson of speech teachers, Bell immigrated to Canada with his parents in 1870 and then moved to *Boston as a teacher of speech to the deaf. Driven to match his father's prominence as a speech analyst, he undertook research in acoustics and speech with the aid of electrical and mechanical devices. In 1873 he was appointed professor of vocal physiology at Boston University. This position gave him standing in scientific circles, and Boston's leadership in American *technology gave him access to technical expertise.

His combined work in sound and *electricity led him to devise a means of transmitting several telegraphic messages at once over a single wire by superimposing intermittent currents of differing frequencies. In 1874, while struggling to perfect his multiple or "harmonic" *telegraph, he experimented with a continuous but varying or "undulatory" current and suddenly saw that it possessed not only the varying frequencies but also the varying amplitudes essential to the reproduction of speech and all other sounds. On 7 March 1876, he patented the telephone. Three days later, he addressed to his assistant the famous first intelligible sentence transmitted by telephone: "Mr. Watson, come here, I want to see you."

Thomas A. Watson came, and so did fame and fortune. In 1877 Bell and three others organized a voluntary association, incorporated in 1878 as the Bell Telephone Company. After decisively defeating a swarm of litigants claiming priority of conception he pursued a multitude of ideas and causes. Sometimes chided for scattering his energies too widely, he nevertheless followed a consistent goal, that of furthering communication and community. He also strove to overcome his own lifelong tendency toward solitude. He organized and campaigned for the teaching of lipreading and speech to the deaf, always stating his vocation as "teacher of the deaf" on official forms. He invented the audiometer to measure hearing, and his name entered the language in the word "decibel," a standard unit of sound volume. The deaf and blind Helen Keller (1880–1968) dedicated her autobiography to him as a mentor and protector. He led in promoting the method of teaching small children developed by the Italian educator Maria Montessori (1870–1952).

As an inventor, he abandoned telephony in the 1880s after inventing the "photophone," which transmitted speech by means of light rays but was of little use without lasers and fiber optics. The death of his newborn son from respiratory failure in 1881 moved him to invent a "vacuum jacket" that anticipated the "iron lung" of the polio era, and the shooting of President James *Garfield that same year prompted him to devise a "telephone probe" that sounded when it encountered metal—such as a bullet—in flesh. The probe saved many soldiers' lives before X rays superseded it. In the 1890s and early 1900s, Bell organized research that advanced aviation and hydrofoil boats. In designing aircraft his use of tetrahedral structural elements inspired him to develop and patent a system of space frame architecture. In 1883 Bell and his father-in-law rescued the weekly journal *Science* from financial collapse and continued to subsidize it until 1894. In 1900 it became the official journal of the *American Association for the Advancement of Science, which it remains to this day. He also served as a guiding spirit of the National Geographic Society and its phenomenally successful magazine.

When Bell died of diabetes at the age of seventy-five, his erstwhile rival and later friend Thomas *Edison praised him as having "brought the human family in closer touch." Bell's brilliant coupling of sound waves and electrical pulsations had given rise to the telecommunications revolution.

• Robert V. Bruce, *Bell: Alexander Graham Bell and the Conquest of Solitude*, 1973; reprints 1990, 1995, 1998.

—Robert V. Bruce

BELLAMY, EDWARD. *See Looking Backward: 2000–1887.*

BELLOW, SAUL (1915–), writer, teacher. A writer who grounded his work in the urban American experience, Bellow was born in Lachine, Quebec, Canada, the fourth child of Russian Jewish parents. In 1924, the family moved to *Chicago, the background for much of Bellow's fiction. A novelist of ideas, Bellow in his work work puts in comic perspective the split between personal ambition and the claims of the spirit.

His first published novel, *Dangling Man* (1944), whose protagonist is waiting to be drafted during *World War II, explores the conflict between the real world of compromised action and the ideal one of thought and feeling. *The Victim* (1947) addresses the issue of *anti-Semitism and the nature of moral accountability. *The Adventures of Augie March* (1953) marked a breakthrough to a freewheeling style combining elevated philosophy, slang, and esoteric allusion that translates the American myth into contemporary linguistic and social possibilities. It received the National Book Award, as did the self-lacerating *Herzog* (1964) and *Mr. Sammler's Planet* (1970). Other notable

Bellow works are *Henderson the Rain King* (1959), *Humboldt's Gift* (1975), and the novella *Seize the Day* (1956), in all of which striving heroes, often aided by teachers in the guise of confidence men, come to recognize the obligations of love and the sustaining power of family. *The Dean's December* (1982) and *More Die of Heartbreak* (1987) moved away from the earlier exuberant comedy toward a more somber assessment of contemporary culture. He also published several collections of short fiction, including *Mosby's Memoirs and Other Stories* (1968) and *Him with His Foot in His Mouth and Other Stories* (1984), and three late novellas: *The Bellarosa Connection* (1989), *A Theft* (1989), and *The Actual* (1997). He returned to the full-length novel form with *Ravelstein* (2000). *It All Adds Up: From the Dim Past to the Uncertain Future* (1994) is a selection of his nonfiction. He taught at the University of Minnesota (1946–1949) and, beginning in 1963, at the University of Chicago. Saul Bellow received the Nobel Prize for literature in 1976.

[*See also* Literature: Since World War I.]

• Stanley Trachtenberg, ed., *Critical Essays on Saul Bellow,* 1979. Peter Hyland, *Saul Bellow,* 1992.

—Stanley Trachtenberg

BERLIN BLOCKADE AND AIRLIFT (1948–1949). On 24 June 1948, the Soviet Union cut off rail, highway, and water access routes from the western zones of Germany into Berlin. In reaction, the three Western occupying powers—the United States, Great Britain, and France—blocked supplies going into the eastern zone and instituted an airlift of food and coal for the western sectors of the city. This dramatic *Cold War confrontation raised international fears of a third world war.

The Soviets acted in Berlin in response to the London decisions of June 1948, in which six Western nations, including the United States, agreed to the formation of a separate West German government. With a West German constituent assembly scheduled for the fall, the Western powers on 20 June introduced a new currency for the western zones and on 23 June made that currency legal tender in Berlin. The Soviet military governor Vassily Sokolovsky first explained the blocking of Berlin's access routes as arising from the need to protect the eastern zone's currency, but he quickly emphasized the impending division of the country.

At the February 1945 *Yalta Conference, the *World War II Allies had agreed to divide Germany into four zones of occupation and to administer them through a quadripartite Allied Control Council. Although Berlin was inside the eastern zone, the city was similarly divided into four occupation sectors. In July 1945, when the Western armies entered Berlin, Deputy Military Governor Lucius D. Clay had been instructed to negotiate a permanent agreement over access routes, but he had neglected to do so.

In halting traffic into West Berlin, the Soviets maintained that Western rights in the city were predicated on the promise of German unity. During a series of negotiations in Moscow and at the *United Nations, the Soviets' most consistent demand was that the Western powers halt the formation of a separate West German government. Buoyed by the surprising success of the airlift, the Americans and British refused. By 25 April 1949, the West German constituent assembly had drafted a new Basic Law, thereby defeating Soviet aims. An agreement was made to end the blockade and counterblockade by 12 May 1949. The massive airlift of supplies, operated by Great Britain and the United States, continued until 30 September 1949, delivering two million tons of goods through 250,000 flights and winning popular support for a separate West German government.

With the conclusion of the Berlin crisis, the division of Germany and of Europe remained frozen for four decades. The confrontation convinced President Harry S. *Truman of the importance of a possessing a credible nuclear arsenal and the need for a military alliance with Western Europe. Accordingly, the birth of West Germany coincided with the creation of the *North Atlantic Treaty Organization.

[*See also* Containment; Foreign Relations: U.S. Relations with Europe; Nuclear Strategy.]

• Avi Shlaim, *The United States and the Berlin Blockade: A Study in Crisis Decision-Making,* 1983. William Stivers, "The Incomplete Blockade: Soviet Supply of West Berlin," *Diplomatic History* 21 (Fall 1997): 569–602.

—Carolyn Woods Eisenberg

BERLIN, IRVING (1888–1989), songwriter and music publisher. Born Israel Baline in Temun, Siberia, Berlin moved with his family to *New York City when he was four; he began his music career at sixteen as a singing waiter. His first hit tune, "Marie from Sunny Italy" (1907), written to compete with a rival bar, set him on a career path wherein art and commerce were inextricably linked. His "Alexander's Ragtime Band" (1911) helped transform *ragtime into a national craze and enabled him to start his own publishing company. In the 1920s, he built and operated his own theater. His shows *Yip, Yip Yaphank* (1918) and *This Is the Army* (1942), and the song "God Bless America" (1938) boosted American morale and patriotism during the two world wars; some even suggested that "God Bless America" replace the "Star-Spangled Banner" as the national anthem.

Berlin's hit songs like "All Alone" (1942), "Heat Wave" (1933), "White Christmas" (1942), and "There's No Business Like Show Business" (1946) drew upon diverse strands in American music, including various ethnic styles and *jazz and swing rhythms, as well as European-influenced harmonies. His folklike simplicity in melody and straightforward language articulated deeply held myths and beliefs, making him the epitome of the Tin Pan Alley composer of the first half of the twentieth century. His determination to control completely the production and distribution of his artistic output was widely emulated in the popular-music industry.

[*See also* Music: Popular Music.]

• Alec Wilder, "Irving Berlin," in *American Popular Song: The Great Innovators, 1900–1950,* ed. James T. Maher, 1972, pp. 91–120. Lawrence Bergreen, *As Thousands Cheer: The Life of Irving Berlin,* 1990.

—Timothy E. Scheurer

BERNSTEIN, LEONARD (1918–1990), composer, conductor, teacher, pianist. He was the first American-born and -trained symphonic conductor to achieve peak international celebrity as an interpreter of the mainstream European repertoire. As a composer, he combined American popular influences (including Broadway and *jazz) with European forms and genres. As an educator, he tutored a mass public and inspired legions of gifted young musicians. His mentors included the Boston Symphony's Serge Koussevitzky, who inculcated both a belief in America and a pedagogic bent.

Born in Lawrence, Massachusetts, Bernstein attended Harvard College and Philadelphia's Curtis Institute of Music. Becoming assistant conductor of the New York Philharmonic Symphony in 1943, at twenty-five, he won notice that November by stepping in at the last moment for the ailing Bruno Walter. Bernstein's early compositions included the Serenade for Violin, Strings, and Harp (1954), perhaps his finest concert work, and such Broadway fare as *On the Town* (1944); *Wonderful Town* (1953); *Candide* (1956); and his crowning creative achievement, *West Side Story* (1957). In 1958 he became the first American music director of the New York Philharmonic. In this capacity, he enduringly championed the music of Charles *Ives and Gustav Mahler (with whose polyglot synthesis or fragmentation he strongly identified). Building on an ingenious series of television "specials" beginning in 1954, he invigorated the Philharmonic's Young People's Concerts as a nationally televised medium for music education. Breaking with traditional "music appreciation," he refused to sanctify famous music; rather, he dismantled it to see how it worked, or juxtaposed it with popular songs he adored. He campaigned for contemporary music and American music.

After leaving the New York Philharmonic in 1969, Bernstein increasingly based his career in Europe. With the Vienna Philharmonic, he consolidated his reputation as a performer of Beethoven, Brahms, and other European masters. His identification with American music faded; his boyish optimism, which he had retained into middle age, gave way to Old World gravitas and gloom. And yet he is bound to be remembered as a defining American cultural icon, signifying energy, enthusiasm, irreverence, versatility, and eclecticism.

[*See also* Music: Classical Music; Music: Popular Music; Musical Theater.]

• Leonard Bernstein, *The Joy of Music,* 1959. David Schiff, "Re-Hearing Bernstein," *Atlantic,* June 1993. Humphrey Burton, *Leonard Bernstein,* 1994. Joseph Horowitz, "The Teachings of Leonard Bernstein," in *The Post-Classical Predicament,* 1995.

—Joseph Horowitz

BETHUNE, MARY MCLEOD (1875–1955), school founder, government administrator, leader of African American women. Born in Mayesville, South Carolina, and educated at a Presbyterian school in North Carolina and *Chicago's Moody Bible Institute, Bethune in 1904 founded the Daytona Normal and Industrial Institute for girls in Florida; she was its president until 1942. Merged with Cookman Institute in 1923, it was subsequently known as Bethune-Cookman College—the only extant historically black college founded by a black woman. In 1935, she founded the National Council of Negro Women, which united the major black women's organizations, including the National Association of Colored Women, of which she had been president (1924–1928). She was also active in several interracial civil rights organizations.

Bethune's service on the advisory committee of the New Deal's National Youth Administration (1936–1943) extended her influence, particularly after she became director of its Negro Affairs Division in 1939. Her access to the White House and her alliance with First Lady Eleanor *Roosevelt facilitated her efforts to bring more black men and women into New Deal agencies and to combat racial discrimination in federal social welfare programs. Organizing the blacks in New Deal agencies into the Federal Council of Negro Affairs in 1936, she initiated two government-sponsored National Negro Conferences (1937 and 1939), which delineated the plight of *African Americans and offered policy recommendations. In 1949, Bethune retired to Daytona Beach to live with her son, Albert, born in 1899 during her marriage (1898–1909) to Albertus Bethune.

[*See also* New Deal Era, The.]

• B. Joyce Ross, "Mary McLeod Bethune and the National Youth Administration: A Case Study of Power Relationships in the Black Cabinet of Franklin D. Roosevelt," *Journal of Negro History* (Jan. 1975): 1–28. Elaine M. Smith, "Mary McLeod Bethune and the National Youth Administration," in *Clio Was a Woman: Studies in the History of American Women,* ed. Mabel E. Deutrich and Virginia C. Purdy, 1980.

—Paula Giddings

BIBLE, THE. The Bible has been a nearly universal presence in American history. Christopher *Columbus thought his voyages had been foretold in Scripture (specifically Isaiah 46:11). Printing began in England's North American colonies with the **Bay Psalm Book* of 1640. Since its founding in 1816, the American Bible Society (ABS) has been a leader in promoting the Scriptures, distributing about four billion complete Bibles, testaments, or selections. The Bible's conspicuous place in American public life is illustrated in Abraham *Lincoln's second inaugural address, which ascribed much of the tragedy of the *Civil War to the fact that both North and *South "read the same Bible." Even in the more secular twentieth century, biblical allusions frequently appeared in the speech of the famous, including Presidents Wilson, Carter, Reagan, and Clinton.

Through much of American history, the Bible was available in the 1611 King James Version, the Catholic Douay Version (1582–1610), or in foreign-language translations favored by immigrants. The English Revised Version appeared in 1881 and the Revised Standard Version in 1952. By the late twentieth century, numerous translations and paraphrases stood alongside the still-beloved King James Version.

From the beginning, the Bible provided themes for Americans to define themselves as a people, and then as a nation. New England Puritans believed themselves in covenant with God just like the Hebrews of the Old Testament. During the sectional strife that led to the Civil War, both North and South mined the Scriptures for support. Defenders of *slavery favored Old Testament passages like Leviticus 25:45, which defined conditions for servitude, while *antislavery advocates favored New Testament texts like Galatians 5:1, with its paean to liberty in Christ. If anything, the Bible was more obviously at work in the popular culture of *African Americans than among whites. Blacks sang and preached about Adam and Eve; Moses and the Exodus from Egypt; Daniel in the lions' den; Jonah in the belly of the fish; and Jesus's birth, death, and future return. With profound symbolism, grateful African Americans from Baltimore in September 1864 presented President Lincoln with a pulpit Bible bound in velvet, furnished in gold, with a raised design depicting the emancipation of a slave.

The Bible has penetrated all forms of culture. Composers like William Billings (1746–1800) and John Knowles Paine (1839–1906) wrote musical settings for the Psalms. Novelists have regularly drawn on biblical materials, as in the plotting of Lew Wallace's *Ben Hur* (1880), the opening line of Herman *Melville's 1851 *Moby Dick* ("Call me Ishmael"), or in titles like William *Faulkner's *Absalom, Absalom!* (1936) and John Steinbeck's *East of Eden* (1952). Ever since religious objects began to be mass-marketed in the mid–nineteenth century, both Catholics and Protestants have purchased immense quantities of pictures, statues, games, children's toys, refrigerator magnets, jewelry, T-shirts, greeting cards, and calendars decorated with biblical motifs.

The heart of the biblical presence in America is religious. The Bible has been the focus of private meditations; regular reading by families; and informal study in *Methodist cell groups, Catholic retreats, and a multitude of other gatherings. Above all, the meaning of the Bible in America is rooted in the sermon, that ubiquitous vehicle by which for centuries, week in and week out, in churches across the land, biblical language, values, and culture have worked their way into the fabric of everyday life.

[*See also* African American Religion; Gospel Music, African American; Protestantism; Puritanism; Religion; Revivalism; Roman Catholicism.]

• Margaret T. Hills, *The English Bible in America: A Bibliography of Editions of the Bible and the New Testament Published in America, 1777–1957,* 1961. Nathan O. Hatch and Mark A. Noll, eds., *The Bible in America,* 1982. Bruce M. Metzger and Michael D. Coogan, eds., *The Oxford Companion to the Bible,* 1993.

—Mark A. Noll

BICYCLES AND BICYCLING. The "dandy horse" or "swiftwalker," powered by its rider pushing against the ground, gained popularity in East Coast cities around 1819 but was soon banned from sidewalks as dangerous to pedestrians. Pedal power was introduced to the United States at the 1868 New York Athletic Games in the form of the French-developed "velocipede," with a metal frame, rubber tires, and front-wheel pedals. It, too, enjoyed a brief vogue but was then banned from many roads. The Bostonian Albert Pope introduced steel frames; brakes; and, by the 1880s, front wheels up to six feet high. "High wheelers" were thus faster than their ancestors and even more dependent on pavement. Approximately 100,000 were on the road in 1887.

The "safety" bicycle, first manufactured in the United States by Pope in 1889, featured same-sized wheels, the rear one connected to pedals under the rider by a chain; ball bearings; and pneumatic tires (invented by the Scotsman John Dunlop). These bikes could move twice as fast as a horse and carriage and were relatively affordable. More than four million Americans owned safeties by 1896, making the 1890s bicycling's golden age. So pervasive was the 1890s craze that the government opened a separate patent office just for bicycle-related innovations. While bike manufacturers, repairers, and accessory-makers thrived, and playwrights and songwriters celebrated the bicycle, everyone from tailors to barkeepers complained of declining business as their customers took up cycling. Even church attendance was said to have dropped. Despite warnings of moral depravity and such maladies as "bicycle hump" and "bicycle twitch," cyclists of all ages and classes took to the roads. Promoted by feminists such as Frances *Willard, the bicycle allowed women independent mobility and gave them reason to wear bloomers rather than sweeping skirts.

After the first recorded bicycle races in East Coast cities in the 1860s and 1870s, amateur and professional road and especially track racing quickly became favorite spectator sports. In 1899, drafting behind a train, Charles M. Murphy biked the world's first subminute mile. The athletic color line was broken that year by the African American Marshall "Major" Taylor, who won the world championship. In the 1920s, velodrome races—where men rode continuously for six days, stopping only when absolutely necessary for physical or mechanical reasons—drew tens of thousands of fans. The American Bicycle League's national championships first included women in 1937, but by then public interest in competitive cycling had waned, not to be renewed until U.S. cyclists performed well at the 1971 Pan American games. The first Americans competed in the grueling Tour de France in 1981, but it was Greg LeMond's 1983 world-championship victory that brought competitive cycling back into the public imagination. Lance Armstrong, racing for the U.S. Postal Service team after recovering from nearly fatal testicular *cancer, became the first American on a U.S. team to win the Tour de France in 1999. With a follow-up victory in 2000, Armstrong and his team further boosted the popularity and visibility of competitive cycling.

Advances in bicycle technology in the golden age contributed, ironically, to the machine's decline. Techniques pioneered by bike manufacturers such as the assembly line, planned obsolescence, and marketing incentives were readily adopted by the *automotive industry. Bicycle organizations, notably the League of American Wheelmen (now Bicyclists), founded in 1880, supported the "good roads" movement that quite literally paved the way for automobiles. Responding to the bicycle craze, *New York City passed the nation's first comprehensive traffic code in 1897, requiring, for example, that cyclists use hand signals; by 1909, partly because of stricter regulations, cyclists had almost disappeared from roadways and the automobile's "golden age" was under way. As the century wore on, most highways were built without provision for nonautomotive transportation, and bicycling ceased to be perceived as a serious endeavor.

Mountain bikes, invented in the West in the 1970s and mass-marketed beginning in the 1980s, are probably the United States' greatest recent contribution to cycling; Americans dominated competition, and the bikes broadened cycling's appeal. By the 1990s, numerous types of specialized bikes existed, but just 1 percent of all trips made in the United States involved bikes. Still, according to one estimate, nearly half of all adult Americans had bicycled at least once in 1990. Because of bicycling's health and environmental benefits, numerous grassroots organizations and some government agencies were working as the twentieth century ended to make roads and attitudes friendlier toward cyclists.

[*See also* Mass Production; Sports: Amateur Sports and Recreation.]

• Frances Willard, *A Wheel within a Wheel: How I Learned to Ride the Bicycle,* 1895; reprint, 1997. Marshall "Major" Taylor, *The Fastest Bicycle Rider in the World: The Story of a Colored Boy's Indomitable Courage and Success against Great Odds,* 1928; reprint, 1972. Robert A. Smith, *A Social History of the Bicycle: Its Early Life and Times in America,* 1972; revised edition, *Merry Wheels and Spokes of Steel: A Social History of the Bicycle,* 1995. Peter Nye, *Hearts of Lions: The Story of American Bicycle Racing,* 1988. Clay McShane, *Down the Asphalt Path: The Automobile and the American City,* 1994, esp. pp. 54–56 and 116–118. David B. Perry, *Bike Cult: The Ultimate Guide to Human-Powered Vehicles,* 1995. Frank J. Bertho, *The Birth of Dirt: Origins of Mountain Biking,* 1999.

—Hannah Borgeson

BILL OF RIGHTS (1791), the first ten amendments of the *Constitution. Although elements of the Bill of Rights can be traced back to ancient Greece, the Roman Republic, the *Bible, medieval Germany, the Reformation, the Renaissance, and the Enlightenment, its more immediate origins are found in English history and in the colonial and revolutionary experiences of Americans themselves. Magna Carta (1215) proclaimed a commitment to limited government and legal process. The seventeenth-century Whig ideology that developed during the struggles against Stuart absolutism in England was revived in the political literature of the American revolutionaries a century later to warn against governmental abuse of power. Both eras ended in monumental enunciations of rights.

Background. English and colonial American rights were rooted in the unwritten doctrines of the common law. On rare occasions, usually in response to specific violations of rights by the monarch, Englishmen specified some rights in documents such as Magna Carta, the Petition of Right (1628), the Nineteen Propositions (1642), the Habeas Corpus Act (1679), and the Bill of Rights (1689). Americans in every colony, however, codified their rights in detail in dozens of documents limiting government. The fullest such assertion of rights appeared as early as 1641, in the Massachusetts Body of Liberties. In both England and America, written statements were viewed as tangible manifestations of rights already in existence.

As the movement toward independence advanced, Americans added the natural-rights philosophy to their common-law foundation of *liberty. The *Declaration of Independence abandoned the common law and based liberty exclusively upon natural rights by stating "these truths to be self-evident, that all men are created equal, that they are endowed by their Creator with certain unalienable Rights, that among these are Life, Liberty and the pursuit of Happiness."

When they created their state constitutions, Americans either prefaced these documents with a bill of rights or incorporated various protections within the body of their constitution. The Massachusetts Declaration of Rights (1780), for example, declared "All men are born free and equal, and have certain natural, essential and unalienable rights." Interpreting this fundamental tenet, the state supreme court declared an end to *slavery in Massachusetts.

On occasion, state legislatures protected specific rights thought to be endangered, confirmed earlier enactments of rights, or even enacted full-fledged bills of rights as statutes. All of these guarantees were based upon the social-compact theory in which people surrendered some rights to government but retained certain rights essential to liberty. Government was supposed to protect these retained rights, but frequently during the Revolutionary era, state legislatures violated their bills of rights with impunity.

Because the Confederation Congress acted directly only on states and not on people, the *Articles of Confederation contained no bill of rights. The *Northwest Ordinance (1787, reconfirmed in 1789), however, contained a limited bill of rights because Congress could indirectly act on people through its appointed territorial governor, secretary, and judges.

The *Constitutional Convention of 1787 included a limited

number of specific protections of rights in its draft constitution. Near its conclusion, however, the Convention by a vote of ten states to none defeated a motion to appoint a committee to draft a bill of rights. This omission, which Antifederalists asserted endangered liberties, proved to be the single most powerful argument raised against ratifying the Constitution. Federalists maintained that a bill of rights was unnecessary because the federal government would have only delegated powers that would not threaten liberties. In fact, they suggested, an incomplete bill of rights would be dangerous since it would imply the abandonment of rights not listed. Furthermore, the Constitution itself was said to be a bill of rights, especially Article I, sections 9 and 10 that specifically prohibited the state and federal governments from actions violating rights. Only with the Federalists' promise that amendments to the Constitution, including a bill of rights, would be advocated in the first Congress, was ratification achieved.

Despite their promises, most Federalists ran for election to Congress opposed to any immediate amendments. Therefore, although President George *Washington endorsed a bill of rights in his inaugural address and James *Madison vigorously advocated a bill of rights in the House of Representatives in June 1789, most members of Congress opposed even discussing the matter. Madison, however, persevered and obtained the necessary two-thirds vote to send draft amendments to the Senate. The Senate modified the amendments and eliminated some key provisions, particularly limitations on the states. On 25 September 1789, Congress agreed to twelve amendments, and by 15 December 1791, two years later, the necessary three-quarters of the states had ratified ten of these amendments, which have become known as the Bill of Rights.

Contents of the Bill of Rights. The first eight amendments in the Bill of Rights protect freedom of religion, speech, and the press and the right to petition the government, to assemble, to bear arms, and to be entitled to a jury trial in civil cases. Quartering troops in peacetime and unreasonable searches and arrests are prohibited. Common-law protections are provided in criminal cases including "due process of law" and the right to counsel. Excessive bail and fines, and cruel and unusual punishments are forbidden.

The Ninth Amendment provides that the enumeration of certain rights in the Constitution or in subsequent amendments does not deny the existence of other rights that remain with the people. The Tenth Amendment explains that powers not delegated to the federal government by the Constitution are reserved to the states or to the people.

Later Court Rulings and Controversies. In *Barron* v. *Baltimore* (1833) the U.S. *Supreme Court ruled that the Bill of Rights applied only to the federal government, not to state or local governments. The *Fourteenth Amendment (1868) added language that allowed later courts, beginning with *Gitlow* v. *New York* (1925), to apply the federal Bill of Rights to restrict the powers of state and local governments (the doctrine of incorporation). How far this incorporation extends the Bill of Rights is still a matter of debate.

Certain of the amendments in the Bill of Rights have proven particularly contentious and have generated much litigation, judicial interpretation, and public discussion. The First Amendment's ban on an "establishment of religion," coupled with its prohition against any restrictions on the "free exercise" of religion, has been the basis of many court challenges involving the separation of *church and state. Similarly, the First Amendment's guarantee of freedom of speech and freedom of the press has led to numerous judicial pronouncements on issues relating to *censorship, obscenity, and attempts to silence political dissidents or to curtail publications deemed seditious or dangerous, particularly in wartime. The Second Amendment's guarantee of "the right of the people to keep and bear Arms" remains deeply controversial, pitting *gun-control advocates against individuals and groups such as the *National Rifle Association suspicious of any governmental restraints in this area. The Fifth Amendment's "due process" protections, including protection against self-incrimination, have inspired many *civil liberties battles and was the basis of the Supreme Court's landmark 1966 decision, **Miranda* v. *Arizona*, spelling out the rights of persons in police custody. The Tenth Amendment, reserving to the states or to the people "all powers not delegatated to the United States by the Constitution" has often been invoked by opponents of "big government" alarmed over what they see as the unwarranted expansion of federal power.

The Fourth Amendment's protection against unreasonable searches and seizures (along with other amendments) has been interpreted by the Courts to protect the right to privacy in cases involving *birth control, *abortion, and homosexuality.

[*See also Abrams* v. *United States*; Alien and Sedition Acts; Civil Rights; Colonial Era; Early Republic, Era of the; Federalist Party; Holmes, Oliver Wendell, Jr.; Revolution and Constitution, Era of; *Schenck* v. *United States*; Sedition; Smith Act; Virginia Declaration of Rights.]

• Irving Brant, *The Bill of Rights: Its Origin and Meaning,* 1967. Paul L. Murphy, *The Historic Background of the Bill of Rights,* 1990. Kermit L. Hall, ed., *By and For the People: Constitutional Rights in American History,* 1991. Bernard Schwartz, *The Great Rights of Mankind: A History of the American Bill of Rights,* Expanded Edition, 1992. Patrick T. Conley and John P. Kaminski, eds., *The Bill of Rights and the States: The Colonial and Revolutionary Origins of American Liberties,* 1992. Leonard W. Levy, *Origins of the Bill of Rights,* 1999.

—John P. Kaminski

THE BILL OF RIGHTS

Article I Congress shall make no law respecting an establishment of religion, or prohibiting the free exercise thereof; or abridging the freedom of speech, or of the press; or the right of the people peaceably to assemble, and to petition the government for a redress of grievances.

Article II A well-regulated militia being necessary to the security of a free State, the right of the people to keep and bear arms shall not be infringed.

Article III No soldier shall, in time of peace, be quartered in any house without the consent of the owner, nor in time of war, but in a manner to be prescribed by law.

Article IV The right of the people to be secure in their persons, houses, papers, and effects, against unreasonable searches and seizures, shall not be violated, and no warrants shall issue but upon probable cause, supported by oath or affirmation, and particularly describing the place to be searched, and the persons or things to be seized.

Article V No person shall be held to answer for a capital, or otherwise infamous crime, unless on a presentment or indictment of a grand jury, except in cases arising in the land or naval forces, or in the militia, when in actual service in time of war or public danger; nor shall any person be subject for the same offense to be twice put in jeopardy of life or limb; nor shall be compelled in any criminal case to be a witness against himself, nor be deprived of life, liberty, or property, without due process of law; nor shall private property be taken for public use without just compensation.

Article VI In all criminal prosecutions, the accused shall enjoy the right to a speedy and public trial, by an impartial jury of the State and district wherein the crime shall have been committed, which district shall have been previously ascertained by law, and to be informed of the nature and cause of the accusation; to be confronted with the witnesses against him; to have compulsory process for obtaining witnesses in his favor, and to have the assistance of counsel for his defense.

Article VII In suits at common law, where the value in controversy shall exceed twenty dollars, the right of trial by jury shall be preserved, and no fact tried by a jury shall be otherwise reexamined in any court of the United States, than according to the rules of the common law.

Article VIII Excessive bail shall not be required, nor excessive fines imposed, nor cruel and unusual punishments inflicted.

Article IX The enumeration in the Constitution, of certain rights, shall not be constructed to deny or disparage others retained by the people.

Article X The powers not delegated to the United States by the Constitution, nor prohibited by it to the States, are reserved to the States respectively, or to the people.

BIOCHEMISTRY. *See* Biological Sciences.

BIOETHICS is the study of the moral dimensions of the life sciences and health care, including *medicine, *nursing, and the allied health professions. As an academic discipline, bioethics emerged in the 1960s and 1970s amid public controversies involving the misuse of human subjects in medical research and disquiet about the morality and safety of recombinant DNA research. Subsequent media coverage of such issues as xenografting and human cloning made bioethics and bioethicists familiar to many Americans.

Before the advent of bioethics (a term coined in 1970–1971), such ethical issues as truth-telling and the confidentiality of the doctor–patient relationship comprised part of a tradition of medical ethics going back to the Hippocratic oath of ancient Greece. In the United States, physicians had adopted ethical codes to guide practitioners in their relations with one another, with their patients, and with society. When physicians established the *American Medical Association (AMA) in 1847, they followed the example of such earlier medical societies as the Boston Medical Association and the College of Physicians of Philadelphia in ratifying ethics codes for their members. Based on the ethical code written by the English physician Thomas Percival in 1792, the AMA code particularly addressed the relationships among physicians and offered explicit rules for consultations with nonorthodox practitioners, who actively competed for patients with AMA members.

In the nineteenth and early twentieth centuries, the ethical dimensions of medicine received little attention outside the medical profession. The clergy, especially Catholic theologians, occasionally offered ethical analyses of such practices as *abortion and contraception. In the 1910s and 1920s, the leaders of the medical profession grew concerned about public accusations against physicians who performed experiments on such vulnerable groups as orphans and inmates of *mental-health institutions. But proposals to restrict such practices, introduced at both the state and federal levels, generally failed because most Americans trusted the medical profession to protect patients' interests and well-being. Buoyed by startling medical breakthroughs—insulin (1920s) and penicillin (1940s)—the American medical profession continued to enjoy popular esteem and respect.

During the 1960s and 1970s, this trust eroded. In this era of the *civil rights movement and the *women's rights movement, proponents of the rights of patients challenged the medical profession's traditional authority to oversee patients' interests and to police itself. Revelations of scandalous abuses in human-subject research, especially the forty-year study of untreated syphilis in four-hundred African American men (the *Tuskegee Experiment) shocked the public and the U.S. Congress. In the wake of public hearings, President Richard M. *Nixon in July 1974 signed the National Research Act, requiring institutions receiving federal aid to form institutional review boards to monitor proposals involving human research subjects. The act also created a National Commission for the Protection of Human Subjects of Biomedical and Behavioral Research to develop guidelines to protect human participants in biomedical research. Including physicians, lawyers, clergy, philosophers, and social scientists, the commission issued several reports from 1975 through 1978.

The broad spectrum of bioethical concerns in the 1970s and 1980s, including issues relating to brain death, severely "defective" newborns, and the maintenance of comatose patients on respirators prompted Congress to authorize a second commission. The President's Commission for the Study of Ethical Problems in Medicine and Biomedical and Behavioral Research, appointed by President Jimmy *Carter in 1978, produced a series of papers between 1980 and 1983 on such issues as health-care decision-making, defining brain death, genetic screening, and decisions involving life-sustaining treatment. In 1995, in the wake of revelations of human radiation experiments sponsored by the federal government during the *Cold War, President Bill *Clinton formed the National Bioethics Advisory Commission. Reflecting the growing interdisciplinary nature of bioethics, the eighteen-member board comprised people trained in medicine, law, nursing, religious studies, history, and bioethics, as well as an advocate for the mentally ill. As one of its first duties, the board reviewed the ethical and legal implications of human cloning, prompted by the successful cloning of an adult sheep by Scottish researchers.

As an academic discipline, bioethics flourished in American medical schools and in such private institutions as the Hastings Center for Bioethics in Briarcliff Manor, New York, during the last quarter of the twentieth century. As interest in bioethics burgeoned, the courts increasingly played a role in medical decision-making; between 1976 and 1988, for example, U.S. courts addressed fifty-four cases involving the right to refuse life-prolonging therapies. Another measure of the growing status of bioethics was its prominence in the media; by the 1990s, journalists routinely consulted bioethicists for pronouncements on biomedical issues.

[*See also* Biotechnology Industry; Birth Control and Family Planning; Genetics and Genetic Engineering; Medical Education.]

• Donald E. Konold, *A History of American Medical Ethics, 1847–1912*, 1962. Ruth R. Faden and Tom L. Beauchamp, *A History and Theory of Informed Consent*, 1986. George Weisz, ed., *Social Science Perspectives on Medical Ethics*, 1990. David J. Rothman, *Strangers at the Bedside: A History of How Law and Bioethics Transformed Medical Decision Making*, 1991. Susan E. Lederer, *Subjected to Science: Human Experimentation in America before the Second World War*, 1995. Robert Baker et al., eds., *The American Medical Ethics Revolution*, 1999.

—Susan E. Lederer

BIOLOGICAL SCIENCES. The biological sciences encompass a wide range of objects and problems—from cells to whales, from eating to evolution. The degree to which these studies have been perceived as a cohesive science, or even as a federation of sciences, has varied greatly over time. Americans participated significantly in the shaping of many biological sciences from the early nineteenth century to the end of the twentieth. Some areas of biology were among the first regions of science in which Americans became world leaders. Knowledge imported and developed by American biologists had substantial impact, both through its application in medical and agricultural technologies and through its influence on ways that Americans thought about themselves and their relations with the natural world.

Colonial and Antebellum Eras. Prior to 1800, no coherent conception of "biological science" existed in either England or its North American colonies. If we set aside modern categories, however, we can find relevant knowledge and discussion among both physicians and a loosely defined group of collectors and writers known as naturalists. Colonial physicians, for the most part, sought to absorb the theories about the human body and its ills that were prominent in European medical circles—particularly at the University of Edinburgh, where leading American doctors such as Benjamin *Rush completed their education. The real biological novelties of North America were its plants and animals. Early European travelers reported on the organisms of the New World, and in the early 1700s European naturalists such as Mark Catesby and Peter Kalm traversed the Eastern Seaboard and described uniquely American organisms according to the new standards of scientific taxonomy. Colonials such as the Pennsylvania nurseryman John *Bartram collected plants and seeds for the growing network of botanists and plant enthusiasts in Europe.

After the *Revolutionary War, natural history significantly enhanced American *nationalism. Government explorers, beginning with the *Lewis and Clark Expedition, collected plants as part of their efforts to reinforce U.S. claims of sovereignty over western territories; at the same time, they sought to assess the agricultural potential of these areas and to determine the abundance of animal species that could be exploited for profit. Eastern naturalists showcased distinctively American plants and animals to heighten national self-consciousness and to demonstrate that Americans could participate in the cosmopolitan world of science. Charles Willson Peale's museum, established on the second floor of Philadelphia's Independence Hall in 1802, linked a mounted bald eagle and the skeleton of the "American mastodon," excavated and reconstructed by Peale, with his paintings of George *Washington, Thomas *Jefferson, and other national heroes.

By the mid–nineteenth century, U.S. naturalists controlled the study of the organisms of North America. Beginning in the late 1830s, the Harvard botanist Asa *Gray coordinated efforts to describe and classify the continent's plants. The zoologist Louis *Agassiz, who emigrated from Switzerland to teach at Harvard in 1846, sought to do the same with animals but was supplanted after about 1860 by a network of collectors led by the *Smithsonian Institution's Spencer Baird (1823–1887). After the *Civil War, a network of scientists associated with the Smithsonian's National Museum, the U.S. Commission of Fish and Fisheries, and the Department of Agriculture sought to manage the organisms of North America. Although too late to save the passenger pigeon, which became extinct in 1914, they preserved the bison. They also introduced a vast number of new species and varieties into American *agriculture but experienced mixed success in keeping out insects and weeds.

American naturalists thought about the implications of their science for religion and ethics. A number of scientists delivering the prestigious Lowell Lectures in Boston in the mid–nineteenth century, for example, emphasized the existence and wisdom of the Creator and the prevalence of progressive change. These commonplaces took a new turn with the publication of Charles Darwin's *Origin of Species* in 1859 and with the new prominence of materialistic ideas among such British scientific intellectuals as Thomas H. Huxley (1825–1895) and Herbert Spencer (1820–1903). American scientists soon agreed that evolution was a fact, but few saw it as random or amorally competitive. Some, such as Edward Drinker Cope (1840–1897) and Lester *Ward, argued explicitly for the "neo-Lamarckian" view of evolution as the progressive emergence of intelligence in the living world. Most American biologists had a looser expectation—that some progressive, or "orthogenetic," force guided life in certain directions, most notably toward humanity and Anglo-American civilization. This evolutionary message was conveyed to mass audiences in the decades around 1900 through museums, world's fairs, and the new secondary-school subject of biology. Protestant fundamentalists responded by pressing for laws restricting the teaching of evolution. The resulting 1925 *Scopes trial in Tennessee publicized the tensions between fundamentalist Christians and scientists but had relatively little impact on the teaching of biology; science educators may have eliminated the word "evolution" from their texts, but they continued to teach the principles of progressive development.

Civil War to World War II. The emergence of research universities after 1870 produced a significant increase in the number of trained biological scientists and reinforced the idea that the biological sciences formed a single major scientific unit. The new Johns Hopkins University in Baltimore established the first academic biology department in 1876, and similar programs arose during the next two decades at the University of Pennsylvania, Clark University, Columbia University, and the University of Chicago. In 1883, biological scientists took the lead in creating the American Society of Naturalists. One of the first American organizations limited to professional scientific specialists, it had become by the 1890s a federation of yet more specialized societies created by, among others, morphologists, anatomists, physiologists, and psychologists. The most important center for academic biology was the Marine Biological Laboratory established in Woods Hole, Massachusetts, in 1888. Directed by Charles Otis Whitman (1842–1910), this scientific summer colony became a locus for both basic biological research and for the informal interactions of a vibrant scientific community.

The first generation of academic biologists focused primarily on the study of cells and embryonic development. They hoped to gain a unified understanding of metabolism, development, reproduction, heredity, and evolution. Among the notable discoveries of this period were Jacques Loeb's 1899 demonstration of artificial parthenogenesis, and Edmund Beecher Wilson and Nettie Stevens's recognition in 1904 that chromosomes play a major role in determining sex. The most important American advance in biology, however, came from a project begun at Columbia University by Thomas Hunt *Morgan in 1910 to map the locations of genes on chromosomes, using the fruit fly *(Drosophila)*. By the 1920s a confederation of zoologists, botanists, and agricultural researchers were developing genetics as both a fundamental science and as the basis for improving such crops as corn.

These academic developments were paralleled by activities in America's rapidly modernizing medical schools. In the 1880s and 1890s, Harvard and Johns Hopkins made laboratory research integral to their medical programs. The Hopkins anatomist Franklin P. Mall fostered the work of Florence Sabin (1871–1953), Herbert Evans (1882–1971), and George Corner (1889–1981) on human embryology, sex hormones, and reproduction. The new science of bacteriology developed at both medical schools and research centers such as the *Rockefeller Institute for Medical Research (later Rockefeller University) in New York. Influential medical scientists such as the Johns Hopkins pathologist William Welch (1850–1934) and the Harvard physiologist Walter Cannon (1871–1945) fended off the attacks of anti-vivisectionists by publicizing the laboratory origins of new therapies against infectious diseases, most notably *diphtheria.

In the early twentieth century, some leading biologists extended their interest in improving human life to include "race betterment," or *eugenics. The most prominent of these, Charles B. Davenport (1866–1944), established the Eugenics Record Office in 1910 to collect data on human heredity and to demonstrate what he believed to be the ill effects of miscegenation, the inferiority of recent immigrant groups, and the value of laws to sterilize the "unfit." By the end of the 1930s, however, declining *immigration, advances in genetics, the expansion of the *social sciences, and the rise of Nazism had discredited the eugenics movement and the more general ambition to explain human social phenomena in biological terms. Biologists turned instead to *birth control and family planning, population policy, and circumscribed problems in medical genetics. In their place, social scientists and psychiatrists came to the fore as interpreters of "human nature."

Post–World War II Developments. The scientific boom triggered by *World War II proved less important for biology than for a number of other disciplines. Biological scientists did important war work, most notably in the development of antibiotics and in the prevention of *malaria and other tropical diseases through insect control. But the war did not lead to "big science" in biology and it did not give biologists the public visibility that the physicists acquired through their role in the development of the atomic bomb. Nevertheless, postwar federal funding for the biological sciences came from the *Atomic Energy Commission (which supported major initiatives in genetics and ecology), the *National Institutes of Health (whose support for biomedical research grew dramatically beginning around 1957), the Department of Agriculture, and the *National Science Foundation. Private organizations, ranging from the Rockefeller Foundation to the March of Dimes, which raised money for *poliomyelitis research, also provided significant funding. In the long run, this pattern of gradual growth and diversified patronage proved advantageous for biologists.

The development of molecular biology, spurred by the determination of the structure of DNA (deoxyribonucleic acid) in 1953 by the American James D. *Watson and the Englishman Francis Crick, was the most important early postwar event in the biological sciences. The antipolio vaccines developed by Jonas *Salk and Albert Sabin (1906–1993) seemed the culmination of biomedical researchers' efforts to eliminate the major infectious diseases in the United States. The oral contraceptive, based on a drug synthesized by the chemist Carl Djerassi (1923–) in 1951, and on the research of the endocrinologist Gregory Pincus (1903–1967) and others in the 1950s, was marketed in 1960 by the G. D. Searle Company. It was the most visible of the many important drugs introduced by an alliance of biologists, chemists, and corporations. Plant geneticists responded to concerns about overpopulation and famine by developing more productive varieties of tropical crops, thereby making possible the so-called green revolution.

Biologists also played important roles in assessing the problems resulting from scientific-industrial developments. In the 1950s, the biochemist Linus *Pauling and geneticist Hermann J. Muller (1890–1967) participated prominently in scientific-political campaigns against fallout from atmospheric nuclear testing. Rachel *Carson's *Silent Spring* (1962) indicted the indiscriminate use of pesticides. The microbiologist René Dubos (1901–1982) emerged as the philosopher of the environmental movement. Within this activist context, biologists became sufficiently confident to make evolution an explicit part of the secondary-school curricula they developed in the 1960s.

Late twentieth-century changes in the biological sciences were so rapid and substantial that a brief sketch must suffice. Numbers tell an important story: while the annual production of Ph.D.s in the *physical sciences remained about the same in 1995 as in 1970, recruitment of biological scientists increased by two-thirds during that period. Much of this growth occurred in molecular biology. The development of recombinant-DNA technology in the mid-1970s led, after an initial controversy about safety, to the creation of a major new science-based *biotechnology industry. Geneticists working through the Department of Energy and the National Institutes of Health obtained funding in 1990 for a fifteen-year "big science" project to map the human genome. A looser network of scientists introduced a series of technologies, ranging from amniocentesis to in vitro fertilization, that transformed the possibilities for human reproduction. The emergence of *Acquired Immunodeficiency Syndrome (AIDS) in the 1980s stimulated research in immunology and cell biology while simultaneously ending the widespread belief that the battle against infectious *diseases had been won.

During this same period, issues involving organisms and their evolution once again became prominent. In the 1970s, the new discipline of sociobiology, led by the Harvard entomologist Edward O. Wilson, challenged the primacy of social scientists as interpreters of human behavior. Wilson also addressed the problem of declining global biodiversity. The argument that dinosaurs were warm-blooded social animals, and the claim that they had been wiped out by a meteorite, increased public attention to evolutionary history. In 1987, the U.S. *Supreme Court upheld science educators' claim that evolution, but not creationism, should be taught in public schools.

By the 1990s, biology had replaced physics as the most important and visible of the natural sciences in America. Through their activities in *medicine and agriculture, biologists were transforming the conditions of people's lives; through their investigations into genetics, ecology, and evolutionary history, they were redefining the meaning of life.

[*See also* Agricultural Experiment Stations; Antinuclear Protest Movements; Bioethics; Chemical Industry; Education: Rise of the University; Environmentalism; Evolution, Theory of; Federal Government, Executive Branch: Department of Agriculture; Fundamentalist Movement; Genetics and Genetic Engineering; Human Genome Project; Medical Education; Psychology; World's Fairs and Expositions.]

• Charles E. Rosenberg, *No Other Gods: On Science and American Social Thought,* 1976. Horace Freeland Judson, *The Eighth Day of Creation,* 1979. Ronald Rainger, Keith R. Benson, and Jane Meienschein, eds., *The American Development of Biology,* 1988. Donna J. Haraway, *Primate Visions,* 1989. Jane Maienschein, *Transforming Traditions in American Biology, 1880–1915,* 1991. Gregg Mitman, *The State of Nature,* 1992. Lily E. Kay, *The Molecular Vision of Life,* 1993. Robert E. Kohler, *Lords of the Fly,* 1994. Adele E. Clarke, *Disciplining Reproduction,* 1998. Toby A. Appel, *Shaping Biology,* 2000. Philip J. Pauly, *Biologists and the Promise of American Life,* 2000.

—Philip J. Pauly

BIOLOGY. *See* Biological Sciences.

BIOPHYSICS. *See* Biological Sciences.

BIOTECHNOLOGY INDUSTRY. Robert Swanson and Herbert Boyer founded the Genentech Corporation in South San Francisco, California, in April 1976, giving birth to the biotechnology industry. In a broad sense, biotechnology has a long history. People have modified plants and animals for millennia by selective breeding to generate better agricultural plants and more productive livestock. Makers of wine, beer, and cheese have long relied on fermentation with microorganisms. However, the term "biotechnology" in the late twentieth century came to denote procedures involving genetic engineering and the tools of molecular biology. Genetic engineering became possible in 1973 when Stanley Cohen at Stanford University and Herbert Boyer at the University of California–San Francisco accomplished the first recombinant DNA experiment. Joining together two independent pieces of DNA, they introduced that hybrid DNA molecule into an *E. coli* bacterium, where the DNA was inherited as part of the bacterium's genetic material. Genes, discrete pieces of DNA that commonly code for specific proteins, could now be manipulated. The next important discovery showed that it was possible to put a human gene in bacteria, and express the protein that the gene encoded. This feat was accomplished when Genentech expressed human somatostatin protein in bacteria in 1977. Genentech then cloned the gene for human insulin into bacteria and, in 1982, marketed human insulin purified from the genetically engineered bacteria as the first recombinant DNA technology-based drug.

By the early 1980s, numerous biotechnology companies, including Biogen, Cetus, Genex, and Amgen had appeared. Biotechnology gave rise to an independent industry, while at the same time contributing to other more established industries—pharmaceutical, agricultural, and medical—and to the manufacture of various industrial and consumer goods (e.g., oil-eating bacteria and enzymes that are high-grade detergents). The major pharmaceutical companies all purchased biotechnology companies in the 1980s and 1990s and established multibillion-dollar research-and-development divisions using the tools of biotechnology. The resulting pharmaceutical products included human growth hormone (somatropin), erythropoietin (EPO), tissue plasminogen activator (tPA), interferon-alpha (INF-α), GM-CSF, the hepatitis B vaccine, and Herceptin, as well as human insulin.

Major agribusiness companies used biotechnology to engineer better crops. The first genetically modified crop was a virus-resistant tobacco plant, produced in 1983. The first genetically modified whole food marketed to consumers was the rot-resistant Flavr-Savr tomato, introduced in 1994. Many other genetically modified plants (cotton, soybeans, and corn, among others) were made in the 1980s and 1990s. Most were resistant to viruses, insects, or herbicides. Genetically modified foods sometimes led to controversy, particularly in Europe, where some people feared that the genetic modification might be hazardous to human beings, plants, or animals. However, most short-term field trials of such foods showed them safe for both human beings and the environment.

Biotechnology, particularly in the *pharmaceutical industry, could be very expensive. To bring a product to market sometimes cost upwards of $100 million and ten years of effort. Approximately nine out of ten biotechnology products failed commercially because of patent, production, efficacy, or side-effect problems.

The future of the industry at the beginning of the twenty-first century looked promising, but advances came slowly. Three major scientific developments—the cloning of Dolly the lamb in Scotland in 1997, the first successful gene-therapy trials (2000), and the complete mapping of the human genome (2000)—generated particular excitement. The cloning of a lamb by Ian Wilmut was important less because of the cloning per se, than because the technology paved the way for more rapid and extensive transgenic livestock development. Gene therapy—the process of introducing a gene into a human being to remedy a genetic *disease—offered hope to persons suffering from such diseases as hemophilia, cystic fibrosis, and diabetes. The mapping of the full human-genome sequence, the molecular blueprint for human life, was simultaneously completed by the *National Institutes of Health *Human Genome Project and the biotechnology company Celera Genomics. Although the mapping of the human genome seemed unlikely to lead to immediate medical breakthroughs, it promised substantially to influence biotechnology and *medicine for many years to come.

[*See also* Agriculture: Since 1920; Bioethics; Biological Sciences; Food and Diet; Medicine: Since 1945; Science: Since 1945; Watson, James D.]

• James Watson, Michael Gilman, Jan Witkowski, and Mark Zoller, *Recombinant DNA*, 1992. Robert Bud, *The Uses of Life*, 1993. Cynthia Robbins-Roth, *From Alchemy to IPO: The Business of Biotechnology*, 2000. Shane Crotty, *Ahead of the Curve, David Baltimore's Life in Science*, 2001.

—Shane Crotty

BIRTH CONTROL AND FAMILY PLANNING. Americans have practiced birth control throughout their history. Women in the *Colonial Era, relying on centuries-old techniques, used sponges and suppositories to prevent pregnancy. Traditional folk medicine offered recipes for abortifacient brews of aloes, pennyroyal, and extracts from wild juniper bushes that so poisoned or irritated the system that miscarriages occurred as a side effect. Mechanical *abortions, performed without anesthesia or antibiotics, were rare, painful, and dangerous.

The Nineteenth Century. In the nineteenth century, the fertility rate of American women fell from around 7 children per mother in 1800 to 3.5 in 1900. This decline can be attributed to periodic abstinence from sexual intercourse, coitus interruptus (male withdrawal before ejaculation), placing objects in the vagina to create a barrier between sperm and uterus, and inducing abortion through drugs or mechanical means. While all such methods violated official standards of sexual conduct, a few freethinkers began in the 1830s to argue for family limitation to restrict the labor supply and ease the economic burdens of the poor. Also contributing to changing attitudes was the fact that marriage began to be seen as an expression of romantic love rather than merely an economic alliance.

As the century wore on, the declining fertility of native-born white women alarmed social leaders. Francis A. Walker, director of the 1870 U.S. Census, in noting the higher fertility of immigrant newcomers compared to native-born couples, called for restriction on *immigration. Concerns about "race suicide" and exhortations to native-born couples of Anglo-Saxon origins to have more children persisted into the *Progressive Era. This preoccupation, in turn, affected attitudes toward abortion. Prior to 1840, U.S. law, drawn from English common law, generally allowed abortion before quickening (the first fetal movement felt by the mother). At midcentury, however, physicians campaigned successfully to outlaw all induced abortions. This campaign allowed the medical profession to extend its authority while also addressing disturbing demographic trends. By the 1880s, most states had outlawed induced abortion except for therapeutic purposes. The 1873 Comstock Law, a federal obscenity law named for Anthony Comstock (1844–1915) of New York's Society for the Suppression of Vice, prohibited the mailing of abortifacients, contraceptives, or information about abortion or contraception.

From 1900 to World War II. The modern American family-planning movement emerged from three distinct although overlapping forces: the early twentieth century birth-control advocacy of Margaret *Sanger and other feminists; a Progressive Era *eugenics campaign; and a post–*World War II population-control movement. Sanger, a nurse active in New York's socialist and radical labor movements, became increasingly concerned about the plight of working-class mothers who bore the burden of uncontrolled fecundity. Her 1914 pamplet "Family Limitation" forced her to flee to Europe to avoid prosecution under the Comstock Law. Upon her return she launched the *Birth Control Review* (1917), organized the American Birth Control Conference (1921), and otherwise devoted herself to the cause. Meanwhile, Sanger's rival Mary Ware Dennett (1872–1947) had formed the Voluntary Parenthood League, which campaigned for the repeal of federal laws against birth control. In 1925, Dr. Robert Latou Dickinson (1861–1950), concerned that birth control was acquiring a "bad name," organized the Committee on Maternal Health to sponsor research on fertility and sterility. In 1939, facing financial difficulties, these three groups merged to form the Birth Control Federation of America. Renamed the Planned Parenthood Federation in 1942, it pursued the cautious goal of providing contraceptive services to married women in physician-directed clinics.

By 1937, Americans spent $38 million on condoms and more than $200 million on "feminine hygiene" (contraceptive douching). Despite liberalization by some state and lower federal courts, however, contraceptives—many unsafe and defective—could still be purchased only with a prescription, and at inflated prices. Through the efforts of Clarence J. Gamble, an heir to the Ivory Soap fortune, the Food and Drug Administration (FDA) began to test condoms and other contraceptive devices in the late 1930s. The birth-control movement took heart from federal judge Augustus Hand's 1937 ruling in *United States* v. *One Package* that Congress in enacting the Comstock law had lacked crucial information about the risks of pregnancy and the usefulness of contraceptives. Nevertheless, complete birth-control bans remained in effect in Connecticut and Massachusetts into the 1960s. In a landmark victory for reproductive rights, the *Supreme Court in *Griswold* v. *Connecticut* (1965) struck down the Connecticut law banning the distribution of contraceptive devices or information as a violation of married couples' right to privacy. The same principle, extended to unmarried persons in *Eisenstadt* v. *Baird* (1972), later formed the basis for **Roe* v. *Wade* (1973), which established a constitutional right to abortion.

Post–World War II Developments. Meanwhile, the post–

World War II concerns about overpopulation led philanthropic foundations and activist organizations, including the Population Council, the *Ford Foundation, and the Population Crisis Committee, to join Planned Parenthood in calling for federal support for international and domestic birth-control programs and reproductive services. In 1951, the chemist Carl Djerassi and his team at Syntex, a small Mexico City chemical company, synthesized a drug that would prove effective as an oral contraceptive. The endocrinologist and biotechnology entrepreneur Gregory Pincus (1903–1967) of Worcester, Massachusetts, and others conducted the experiments that established the drug's effectiveness and appropriate use. Thanks to Pincus's research, financed by Sanger and Katharine Dexter McCormick, the drug gained FDA approval and was marketed in 1960 by G. D. Searle and Company. The "pill," along with effective intrauterine devices (IUDs), transformed contraceptive practices in the United States.

By linking birth control to the War on Poverty, the Lyndon B. *Johnson administration initiated federally supported family-planning programs in the mid-1960s. The Family Planning Service and Population Research Act of 1970 gave legislative support for such programs. The Roman Catholic hierarchy opposed federal involvement in family planning, however, favoring instead the "rhythm method" by which married couples abstained from sexual intercourse during the fertile period of the woman's menstrual cycle. Pope Paul VI's 1968 encyclical *Humanae Vitae* indicated the divisiveness of the issue even within the Catholic church, however.

The family-planning debate was transformed in the late 1960s as feminists defined abortion as a women's rights issue. The abortion-reform movement, led by women's groups and such organizations as Planned Parenthood, Zero Population Growth (founded 1968), and the National Abortion and Reproductive Action League (known as NARAL), secured liberalized legislation in many states. The landmark *Roe* v. *Wade* decision, however, also mobilized the anti-abortion forces. Congress restricted Medicaid funds for abortion, and many states placed stringent restrictions on abortion procedures. Although the federal courts overturned many of these state regulations, others were upheld. While most anti-abortion activists confined themselves to rallies and peaceful demonstrations, a few violence-prone loners on the movement's fringes bombed abortion clinics and even murdered physicians and other providers of abortion services.

By the 1990s, about 60 percent of American women used artificial contraception, with little difference among Protestants, Catholics, and Jews, and the federal government was spending $700 million annually on family-planning programs that included oral and mechanical birth control, sterilization, and abortion. While the abortion controversy raged on, the debate over contraception appeared largely settled as the twentieth century ended.

[*See also* Biological Sciences; Biotechnology Industry; Censorship; Feminism; Marriage and Divorce; Medicare and Medicaid; Roman Catholicism.]

• David M. Kennedy, *Birth Control in America: The Career of Margaret Sanger,* 1970. Linda Gordon, *Woman's Body, Woman's Right: Birth Control in America,* 1976; rev. ed. 1990. James Mohr, *Abortion in America: The Origins and Evolution of National Policy,* 1978. James Reed, *From Private Vice to Public Virtue: The Birth Control Movement and American Society since 1830,* 1978. Ellen Chesler, *Woman of Valor: Margaret Sanger and the Birth Control Movement in America,* 1992. David Garrow, *Liberty and Sexuality: The Right to Privacy and the Making of "Roe v. Wade,"* 1994. Donald T. Critchlow, *Intended Consequences: Birth Control, Abortion, and the Federal Government,* 1999.

—Donald T. Critchlow

BLACK, HUGO (1886–1971), associate justice of the U.S. *Supreme Court (1937–1971). A police court judge and attorney in his native Alabama, Black served as a U.S. senator from 1925 to 1937, strongly supporting President Franklin Delano *Roosevelt's New Deal. For this loyalty, Roosevelt selected Black as his first Supreme Court nominee in 1937.

Black's appointment was marred by reports that he had belonged to the *Ku Klux Klan. While admitting past Klan involvement, Black repudiated the Klan's *racism and religious bigotry. Known as one of the Court's greatest civil libertarians, Black participated in the unanimous desegregation ruling, **Brown* v. *Board of Education* (1954). Yet he also wrote—and never renounced—the majority opinion in **Korematsu* v. *United States* (1944), which sustained the federal government's forcible relocation of Japanese Americans during *World War II on grounds of national security.

Black contended that judges should strictly follow the original intention behind the *Constitution's provisions. Most strikingly, Black concluded that the First Amendment protects virtually all forms of speech and press, including obscenity, libel, and seditious utterances, which must be protected from government *censorship. This constitutional absolutism was rooted in his affinity for Populism, the nineteenth-century agrarian movement (especially strong in Alabama) that emphasized the need to combat government's tendency to serve powerful interests at the expense of the less fortunate.

[*See also* Bill of Rights; Civil Liberties; Incarceration of Japanese Americans; New Deal Era, The; Populist Era; Sedition.]

• Hugo L. Black, *A Constitutional Faith,* 1968. Jeffrey D. Hockett, *New Deal Justice: The Constitutional Jurisprudence of Hugo L. Black, Felix Frankfurter, and Robert H. Jackson,* 1996.

—Jeffrey D. Hockett

BLACK ELK (1863–1950), Lakota (Sioux) spiritual leader and spokesperson. In John G. Neihardt's *Black Elk Speaks* (1932), Black Elk presented an account of his childhood and youth on the pre-reservation plains. The memoir recalls children's games, courting customs, skirmishes with enemy tribes, the Battle of the *Little Bighorn, the death of *Crazy Horse, a trip to Europe with Buffalo Bill's Wild West Show, and the Ghost Dance. However, the most influential chapter was the introductory description of the "Great Vision," a dream he experienced at the age of nine. It describes his journey to the home of the "six grandfathers" (the cosmic powers of the four directions, the sky, and the earth) and their prophecy of Black Elk's role in the dissolution and restoration of Lakota culture. Through *Black Elk Speaks,* the Great Vision helped stimulate a revival of Indian spirituality throughout North America. It also inspired later environmentalists with its expression of kinship among spirits, animals, plants, and human beings.

In 1944, Black Elk granted Neihardt additional interviews concerning Sioux history, social structures, and oral narratives. Transcripts of these as well as the 1931 interviews used for *Black Elk Speaks* were published in Raymond J. DeMallie's *The Sixth Grandfather* (1984). The transcripts revealed that Neihardt changed many of Black Elk's statements. Black Elk also described seven Lakota religious ceremonies in *The Sacred Pipe,* edited and posthumously published 1963 by Joseph Epes Brown. Although here, too, the editor's voice occasionally intrudes, Black Elk does present an extraordinarily detailed and thoughtful account of Sioux belief and ritual.

[*See also* Cody, William ("Buffalo Bill"); Environmentalism; Indian History and Culture.]

• Joseph Brown, ed., *The Sacred Pipe: Black Elk's Account of the Seven Rites of the Oglala Sioux,* 1963. Raymond J. DeMallie, ed. *The Sixth Grandfather: Black Elk's Teachings Given to John G. Neihardt,* 1984.

—Julian Rice

BLACK HAWK (1767?–1838), Illinois Sauk war leader. Born in the village of Saukenuk at the confluence of the Rock and Mississippi Rivers in western Illinois, Black Hawk was respected within Sauk society for his bravery and his conservative views. Though not a chief, he offered leadership for a sizable part of the tribe. Bitterly anti-American, Black Hawk during the *War of 1812 led many Sauks in fighting for the British in Ohio, Indiana, Illinois, and Missouri. In Black Hawk's absence, the defense of Saukenuk fell to young Keokuk, who became the recognized war chief, setting off a bitter rivalry between the two men. With the return of peace, white settlers poured into the Sauks' fertile homeland. After repeated minor clashes, the government in 1831 forcibly moved the Sauks beyond the Mississippi into Iowa.

Determined to return to Illinois, Black Hawk in April 1832 led dissident Sauks, Mesquakies, and Kickapoos back across the Mississippi, setting off the short-lived Black Hawk War. He soon recognized that his cause was hopeless, but when his peace emissary was murdered, he renewed the attack and moved into present-day Wisconsin. The conflict ended in the virtual annihilation of Black Hawk's four hundred warriors and their families as they tried to recross the Mississippi. After touring in the East and dictating his autobiography, Black Hawk died in Iowa in 1838. His career illustrates the difficulties eastern and midwestern tribes confronted as the United States expanded. Whether they tried diplomacy or warfare, the results were the same: They lost their homelands and were forced to move west.

[*See also* Expansionism; Indian History and Culture: From 1800 to 1900.]

• Donald Jackson, ed., *Black Hawk: An Autobiography,* 1955. Roger L. Nichols, *Black Hawk and the Warrior's Path,* 1992.

—Roger L. Nichols

BLACK HAWK UPRISING. *See* Indian Wars.

BLACK NATIONALISM. An important ideology in African American history, black nationalism is grounded in the belief that efforts to operate within a political system deemed racist and unresponsive to black needs are doomed to failure. Adapting traditional nationalist tenets to their own situation as members of a racially defined minority population, most African American nationalists have equated "racial" with "national" identities and goals. Joined by ties of history, kinship, and culture, they have viewed themselves as wholly differentiated from competing social and ethnic groups. These common racial ties have been manifested in political movements arguing for the creation of an autonomous nation-state or a transnational union of states; in the creation of race-based economic, educational, and religious entities; and in the promotion of distinctive cultural productions. Seeking to turn alleged racial deficits (skin color, cultural traits) into wellsprings of strength, black nationalists have worked to enhance in-group values while shunning those promoted by the larger society. Critics of these efforts to encourage black sociocultural autonomy have charged that black nationalism's separatist orientation has discouraged interracial cooperation and hindered the creation of pluralistic society in which each component supports and enriches all others. Nationalists countered by noting many *African Americans' continued lack of material progress and the persistence of *racism in American life. They also cited the beneficial effects on black self-esteem of the words and programmatic innovations of black nationalists such as the slave-era activists Martin Delany (1812–1885) and Henry Highland Garnet (1815–1882), who advocated a return to Africa; early twentieth-century Pan-African nationalist Marcus *Garvey; and the *Nation of Islam's *Malcolm X and Louis Farrakhan. At the end of the twentieth century, black nationalism seemed likely to continue to provide an ideological and symbolic basis for group unity as long as politically disaffected and economically disadvantaged African Americans perceived a need to employ it against the forces of white racism and cultural diffusion.

• Jeremiah Moses Wilson, ed., *Classical Black Nationalism: From the American Revolution to Marcus Garvey,* 1996. William L. Van Deburg, ed., *Modern Black Nationalism: From Marcus Garvey to Louis Farrakhan,* 1997.

—William L. Van Deburg

BLACK PANTHERS. Founded in Oakland, California, in 1966 by Huey P. Newton and Bobby Seale, the Black Panther Party for Self-defense soon became the best-known revolutionary, nationalist organization of the Black Power Era. Rejecting the *civil rights movement's integrationist goals and nonviolence, Panthers advocated self-help, community control, and armed defense against police brutality. The party's youthful, urban constituency organized citizens' patrols in black neighborhoods; wore paramilitary uniforms featuring black berets and leather jackets; and operated health clinics, food pantries, "liberation schools," and children's breakfast programs. Newton's 1967 imprisonment after his conviction (later reversed) for killing a policeman spurred a nationwide "Free Huey" campaign.

Addressing *African Americans' specific problems, party leaders freely modified classical Marxism-Leninism, moving from a black-nationalist stance to revolutionary *socialism to intercommunalism. In this revolutionary vision, a Black Power vanguard would overcome the tyrannies of race and class; lead the masses in seizing the means of production; and redistribute wealth, *technology, and political power. To this end, the Panthers forged alliances with nonblack leftists and established trade-union caucuses.

Black Panther militance frightened white America and many black moderates. The *Federal Bureau of Investigation (FBI) and local police targeted the Panthers in a campaign against so-called black nationalist hate groups. A joint FBI-police raid in Chicago in 1969 left dead the head of the Illinois Black Panthers, Fred Hampton, and an associate, Mark Clark. Other Black Panthers died in police shoot-outs, and many were imprisoned. Bobby Seale was among the "Chicago Eight" radicals tried for conspiracy in 1969. The party's minister of information, Eldridge Cleaver, fled the United States to Cuba and then to Algiers. Bitter internal division and ideological disputes with other nationalist groups further weakened the party. Fading by 1972, the Panthers nevertheless inspired latter-day activists by proving that class consciousness and the concept of black self-rule need not be mutually exclusive.

[*See also* Black Nationalism; Radicalism; Sixties, The; Vietnam War.]

• Bobby Seale, *Seize the Time: The Story of the Black Panther Party and Huey P. Newton,* 1970. Huey P. Newton, *To Die for the People,* 1972. William L. Van Deburg, *New Day in Babylon: The Black Power Movement and American Culture, 1965–1975,* 1992.

—William L. Van Deburg

BLACK POWER MOVEMENT. *See* Black Nationalism.

BLACKWELL, ELIZABETH (1821–1910), first woman medical school graduate in the United States, key figure in opening the medical profession to women. Born in England, Blackwell came to the United States in 1832, part of a family that, through marriage, came to include such feminist pioneers as her sister-in-law Lucy *Stone and Antoinette Brown Blackwell (1825–1921), the first ordained woman minister in the United States. Following considerable effort and difficulty, including opposition from the medical establishment, Elizabeth Blackwell was admitted to Geneva Medical College in New York, from which she graduated in 1849. After postgraduate study in London and Paris, she returned to *New York City, where she and her sister Emily (1826–1910) established the New York Infirmary for Women and Children (1857) and its school of medicine for women (1868).

Tension between the two physician sisters over the management of the infirmary led to Elizabeth's 1869 decision to return to England. Although she initially remained active in the women's medical movement, she soon became attracted to other causes. Indeed, her interest in such topics as moral reform, *spiritualism, hygiene, and animal welfare soon overshadowed her medical interests. She became a prolific author of works on reform topics, writing such books as *The Human*

Element in Sex (1880) and *Counsel to Parents on the Moral Education of Their Children* (1880). Her memoirs, *Pioneer Work in Opening the Medical Profession to Women* (1895), focus on her early life and medical career in the United States. Blackwell's historical significance derives less from her contributions to medical practice than from the example she set for women interested in the medical profession.

[*See also* Feminism; Medical Education; Medicine: From 1776 to the 1870s; Women's Rights Movements.]

• Nancy Ann Sahli, *Elizabeth Blackwell, M.D. (1821–1910): A Biography*, 1982.

—Nancy A. Sahli

BLAINE, JAMES G. (1830–1893), *Republican party leader. Blaine was born in Pennsylvania but moved to Maine in the mid-1850s, where he edited a newspaper before entering politics. His service in the U.S. House of Representatives (1863–1876), included three terms as Speaker (1869–1875). A moderate on *Reconstruction policy, Blaine was known for his support of the *gold standard and of international reciprocity agreements to promote trade. A contender for the Republican presidential nomination in 1876, he lost his bid because of accusations that as Speaker he had facilitated the award of a land grant to a railroad and then profited financially from his action. Blaine served in the Senate from 1876 until he became secretary of state in 1881 under President James *Garfield—a brief tenure that ended in December 1881, three months after Garfield's assassination. Blaine won the Republican presidential nomination in 1884 but narrowly lost to Grover *Cleveland. As secretary of state under President Benjamin *Harrison, 1889–1892, he worked for a *Pan American Union, or reciprocal trade area, and for trade agreements with other nations. These efforts proved largely unsuccessful, but they did establish an important precedent for the future.

Blaine was a charismatic politician known to his admirers as the "Plumed Knight" and the "Magnetic Man." Despite his ability to galvanize his followers, however, he could never overcome the suspicions of political reformers within and outside his party, who questioned his financial dealings and his *internationalism. He presciently understood that the Republican party needed to address the new industrial order, especially by promoting international trade, as the issues relating to the *Civil War and Reconstruction faded. In this sense he was a politician of the future more than of his time. He left an indelible imprint on his followers, who saw him as a foresighted leader and a constructive party guide.

[*See also* Federal Government, Executive Branch: Department of State; Federal Government, Legislative Branch: Senate; Federal Government, Legislative Branch: House of Representatives; Gilded Age; Industrialization; Railroads; Tariffs.]

• David Saville Muzzey, *James G. Blaine: A Political Idol of Other Days*, 1934. Morton Keller, *Affairs of State: Public Life in Late Nineteenth Century America*, 1977. Edward P. Crapol, *James G. Blaine: Architect of Empire*, 2000.

—H. Wayne Morgan

BLALOCK, ALFRED (1899–1964), surgeon, professor, pioneer of the so-called blue baby operation. A native of Culloden, Georgia, Blalock graduated from the University of Georgia and earned an M.D. at Johns Hopkins Medical School in 1922. He served as an intern and assistant resident at the Johns Hopkins Hospital until 1925, when he became a resident surgeon at Vanderbilt University Hospital. Blalock taught *surgery at the medical schools of Vanderbilt and Johns Hopkins and held numerous appointments as a visiting lecturer at other universities. During his twenty-two-year career at Johns Hopkins, Blalock occupied the posts of director of surgery and surgeon in chief. He died in Baltimore, Maryland, survived by his wife, Mary Chambers O'Bryant, and their three children.

Blalock's research focused on the physiological effects of diminished blood volume. He also conducted the first successful canine transplant of a kidney. His procedure, connecting the organ's vascular supply to a cervical artery, served as a model for the surgical treatment of pulmonary stenosis, a narrowing of the pulmonary artery that causes diminished circulation and a bluish complexion among infants. In 1944, at Johns Hopkins, Blalock and Dr. Helen Taussig conducted the first "blue baby" operation by connecting one end of the left subclavian artery to the left pulmonary artery of a fifteen-month-old girl.

[*See also* Medical Education; Medicine: From the 1870s to 1945; Medicine: Since 1945.]

• Alfred Blalock, *Principles of Surgical Care: Shock and Other Problems*, 1940. Mark M. Ravitch, *Alfred Blalock, 1899–1964*, 1966.

—David Cortes

BLUE CROSS/BLUE SHIELD. *See* Health Insurance.

BLUES. During the first decade of the twentieth century, a new African American social song form called blues spread throughout the *South and along the *Mississippi and Ohio Rivers. This form was similar to other nineteenth-century music, including *spirituals, work songs, hollers, ballads, and reels, but the term "blues"—meaning a type of vocal song with instrumental accompaniment for dancing—arose after 1900. Rooted in oral tradition, blues by 1912 had entered *popular culture through sheet music. W. C. Handy (1873–1958), one of the first professionally trained musicians to transcribe blues into printed notation and composer of such works as "Memphis Blues" (1911) and "St. Louis Blues" (1914), became its first popularizer and spokesperson. In 1920, "Crazy Blues" by Mamie Smith (1883–1946) convinced the recording industry that selling African American music performed by African American artists to African American consumers could be profitable. Ma Rainey (1886–1939) and Bessie Smith (1894–1937), along with other women vocalists, dominated blues recordings in the early 1920s performing an urbane style sometimes called *vaudeville blues.

In 1926, the Texas songster Blind Lemon Jefferson (1897–1929) began a successful recording career, encouraging record companies to seek out other southern guitar or piano players such as the Mississippi Delta's Charlie Patton (1891–1934) and Robert Johnson (1911–1938), whose recordings influenced three generations of blues and rock musicians.

Through the 1930s and 1940s, waves of southern migrants flooded into *Detroit, and St. Louis, Missouri. Although *World War II temporarily halted recording activity, the war's end brought a demand for music consistent with postwar affluence and optimism. Post–World War II blues drew on big-band *jazz, gospel, boogie-woogie, and regional blues styles reflecting demographic changes related to wartime job opportunities. West Coast labels recorded such Texas-born artists as T-Bone Walker (1910–1975), who popularized the electric guitar, while East Coast labels recorded Carolina- and Virginia-born musicians. The exodus from Mississippi continued to affect Midwest blues, as exemplified by Muddy Waters (1915–1983), whose hard-edged electric Chicago blues influenced musicians in America and Britain. Initially called "rhythm and blues," much the same music by the mid-1950s was targeted to an integrated audience and called rock and roll. Beginning in the late 1970s, a so-called blues revival brought traditional blues to a worldwide audience. By the 1990s, African American audiences continued to support traditional or soul blues, and contemporary rhythm and blues continued to draw on a blues-based aesthetic.

As a major form of oral literature, blues influenced a wide range of African American art, including the poetry of Langston *Hughes, Amiri Baraka, Sherley Anne Williams, and Sterling Brown; the visual art of Romare Bearden; the novels of Zora Neale *Hurston, Albert Murray, and Ralph *Ellison, and the plays of August Wilson. Because of its influence on

American music, including jazz, country, and rock, as well as its larger cultural impact, blues ranks as twentieth-century America's most important musical innovation and a central component of the African American cultural heritage.

[*See also* African Americans; Gospel Music, African American; Music: Popular Music; Music: Traditional Music.]

• Albert Murray, *Stomping the Blues,* 1976. Lawrence Cohn, ed., *Nothing but the Blues: The Music and the Musicians,* 1993.

—Barry Lee Pearson

BOAS, FRANZ (1858–1942), founder of modern American cultural *anthropology. Born in Minden, Westphalia, Germany, into a freethinking Jewish household, Boas attended Heidelberg, Bonn, and Kiel universities, receiving his doctorate in physics from Kiel in 1881. After a year in the German army and another two years of reading, Boas went to Baffin Island on an expedition to study the cultural geography of the Eskimos. His experiences among the Eskimos created in him a desire to understand the laws of human nature and prompted him to make a gradual transition from cultural geography to ethnology.

In 1887, hoping for career opportunities denied him in the conservative, anti-Semitic climate of Bismarck's Germany, Boas immigrated to the United States. Yet for almost a decade after his arrival, he confronted serious obstacles in securing and holding professional positions, primarily because of the virulent *anti-Semitism that pervaded the nation. In 1896, Frederic W. Putnam appointed him assistant curator at the American Museum of Natural History in *New York City; he advanced to the curatorship in 1901. He was simultaneously serving as a lecturer at Columbia University, where he became professor of anthropology in 1899, a position he held until his death. Before 1920, Boas had trained such prominent anthropologists as Alfred L. Kroeber, Robert H. Lowie, Edward Sapir, and Alexander A. Goldenweiser. Students trained after 1920 included Melville J. Herskovits, Ruth Benedict, Margaret *Mead, and Otto Klineberg. So great was Boas's impact on American anthropology that by the 1950s virtually all the anthropologists in America had studied under him or one of his students.

Boas's scholarship—especially his pathbreaking *The Mind of Primitive Man* (1911)—profoundly influenced the concepts of "race" and "culture." Debunking the concepts of cultural hierarchies and of "race" as a supraindividual organic entity, Boas almost single-handedly ushered in the modern conceptions of *race and cultural relativism.

All too aware of the insidious implications of *racism during *World War II, Boas suffered a fatal heart attack while denouncing Nazi propaganda in 1942.

[*See also* Cultural Pluralism; Social Science.]

• George W. Stocking Jr., *Race, Culture, and Evolution,* 1968. Vernon J. Williams Jr., *Rethinking Race,* 1996.

—Vernon J. Williams Jr.

BONUS ARMY. In 1932, with the nation mired in depression, thousands of unemployed *World War I veterans traveled to *Washington, D.C., to petition Congress for the immediate payment of thousand-dollar bonuses that 1924 legislation had promised to pay them in 1945. Styling themselves the "Bonus Expeditionary Force" (a takeoff on the American Expeditionary Forces of 1918), these protestors, many with their families, set up camp in vacant federal buildings and in shacks on the Anacostia Flats a few miles from the Capitol.

The House approved the Bonus Bill, but in June the Senate decisively rejected it. Yet many members of the "Bonus Army" stayed in Washington. In July, the Herbert *Hoover administration ordered the veterans' eviction from the federal buildings. During this operations, police gunfire killed one veteran. Hoover sent in troops under the command of General Douglas *MacArthur to restore calm. Exceeding his orders, MacArthur employed his forces, complete with a machine-gun squadron and several tanks, to drive the veterans out of the District of Columbia entirely. Using tear gas and bayonets, the troops cleared the petitioners and their families from their makeshift homes, which were then burned.

The spectacle of U.S. troops forcibly driving from the nation's capital peaceful, unarmed citizens who were themselves veterans illustrated the gap that had opened between the government and Great Depression victims by the end of Hoover's presidency. MacArthur insisted that the "mob" was "animated by the essence of revolution" and bent on taking over the government. In fact, the rout of the nonresisting Bonus Army demonstrated that government officials were more fearful of a revolution in 1932 than the unemployed were interested in fomenting one.

[*See also* Depressions, Economic; New Deal Era, The.]

• Roger Daniels, *The Bonus March,* 1971. Donald J. Lisio, *The President and the Protest,* 1974.

—Robert S. McElvaine

The **BOOK-OF-THE-MONTH CLUB,** founded in 1926 by the advertising executive Harry Scherman and two partners, sells recently published books by mail to subscribers who contract to purchase its monthly recommendations or alternate selections. In 1927, the club pioneered the marketing technique known as the "negative option," automatically shipping goods unless customers instructed them not to. To determine its offerings, the club employed a board of well-known literary figures, including Henry Seidel Canby, William Allen White, Dorothy Canfield Fisher, and, after 1944, Clifton Fadiman. Initially, subscribers bought at least four books a year at full price plus postage; subsequently, the club introduced discounts, free "book-dividends," and its own editions. By 1945, it had 768,000 members. Typical "books-of-the-month" prior to *World War II included Pearl S. Buck's *The Good Earth*, Erich Maria Remarque's *All Quiet on the Western Front*, and James Truslow Adams's *The Epic of America.* A host of other book-marketing ventures following the same formula soon arose, beginning with the Literary Guild (1927), many catering to special reading interests such as religion, history, mysteries, or science fiction.

The club's initial practices remained essentially intact until 1977, when Time, Inc. (later Time Warner) acquired the company. After 1988 (with membership around three million), management gradually eliminated the judges, centralized operations, and shifted book selection from its editorial to its marketing staff.

In cultural terms, the organization before 1950 appealed to Americans anxious to cultivate both refinement and the personality necessary for social success. Assailed by critics as a "middlebrow" enterprise that vulgarized art, the club might better be understood as the product of mediations between competing values of social performance and the cultivation of autonomy, as well as among authors, publishers, and audiences. At the end of the twentieth century, its aesthetic system generally favored "serious" fiction that promised to help middle-class readers gain power over their lives.

[*See also* Literature: Since World War I; Mass Marketing; Twenties, The.]

• Joan Shelley Rubin, *The Making of Middlebrow Culture,* 1992. Janice A. Radway, *Reading with the Book-of-the-Month Club,* 1997.

—Joan Shelley Rubin

BOOK PUBLISHING. *See* Printing and Publishing.

BOONE, DANIEL (1734–1820), explorer and pioneer. Boone was born in Berks County, Pennsylvania, and in 1752 his family settled in North Carolina. In 1755 he enlisted as a volunteer in General Edward Braddock's unsuccessful campaign against the French at Fort Duquesne (Pittsburgh, Pennsylvania). He married Rebecca Bryan in 1756 and in 1765 explored as far south as Pensacola, Florida. Two years later, Boone and two companions crossed the Cumberland Mountains and kept winter camp, but returned home without realizing that they had reached Kentucky.

On 1 May 1769, with his acquaintance John Findley and four other men, Boone once more set out for the West and again reached Kentucky. Boone explored and hunted for two years before returning to North Carolina. He finally succeeded in settling in Kentucky in 1775 under Richard Henderson's Transylvania Company, having cut the Wilderness Road with thirty other backwoodsmen and founded the town of Boonesborough (now Boonesboro, Kentucky).

In July 1776 Boone's daughter Jemima and Betsy and Fanny Callaway were captured by a small Shawnee and Cherokee war party. Their rescue by Boone and his men caused a sensation on the frontier. James Fenimore *Cooper used the adventure in *The Last of the Mohicans* (1826).

On 7 February 1778, Boone and thirty salt makers were captured by Shawnee Indians. Adopted into the tribe, Boone was given the name "Shel-tow-ee" or "Big Turtle." He escaped to warn Boonesborough of an impending Shawnee attack, which came on 7 September. Though heavily outnumbered by Shawnee warriors, Boonesborough's defenders withstood the eleven-day siege. Four years later, Daniel's son, Israel, was killed at the Battle of Blue Licks, the last major engagement of the *Revolutionary War.

The publication of "The Adventures of Col. Daniel Boon" in John Filson's *The Discovery, Settlement and Present State of Kentucke* (1784) ensured the now wealthy Boone's fame. But in 1799, having previously lost nearly all his 100,000 acres of land in Kentucky through lawsuits, he gladly accepted an invitation from the Spanish governor of Missouri to settle in the Femme Osage district. Given 850 acres of land and the position of syndic (magistrate), Boone gained 8,500 acres more by bringing one hundred new families to Missouri but again lost all his land in 1803 when his Spanish title was voided by the *Louisiana Purchase. In 1814, Congress awarded the penniless pioneer 850 acres for his services in opening the West, but he sold the land to pay his debts. Even at his advanced age, Boone continued to hunt, explore, and trap.

No one is perhaps more central to the frontier experience than Daniel Boone. He was involved in the exploration and settlement of the western frontier for nearly seventy years, and he became the prototype of the frontier hero. For many Americans, Daniel Boone's pioneering adventuresome spirit best exemplified the American way of life.

[*See also* Early Republic, Era of the; Expansionism; Indian History and Culture: From 1500 to 1800; Land Policy, Federal; Revolution and Constitution, Era of the; Spanish Settlements in North America.]

• Richard Slotkin, *Regeneration through Violence: The Mythology of the American Frontier, 1600–1860,* 1973. Michael A. Lofaro, *The Life and Adventures of Daniel Boone,* 1978; 2d ed., 1986. John M. Faragher, *Daniel Boone: The Life and Legend of an American Pioneer,* 1992.

—Michael A. Lofaro

BOSTON. Located on a peninsula the Indians called Shawmut and now the capital of Massachusetts, Boston was settled in 1630 by Puritans led by John *Winthrop. Winthrop set the tone for Boston's tradition of civic responsibility when, aboard the *Arbella* en route to *New England, he urged the settlers to build a harmonious, godly community that would be "a city upon a hill" and "a beacon to all nations." As Boston prospered as a maritime center, Puritan ministers like Increase and Cotton *Mather struggled to preserve Winthrop's vision.

England interfered only sporadically in Massachusetts's affairs, so when imperial policy tightened after 1763, Bostonians reacted strongly. Urban unrest culminated in the *Boston Tea Party (1773), which led to the Coercive Acts and to the First *Continental Congress (1774), putting Boston in the forefront of the American Revolution.

Boston's economic development, already eclipsed by that of *New York City by the 1770s, was further stunted by the postwar depression, New England's agricultural decline, and trade disruptions associated with the *War of 1812. Ultimately, however, the war spurred domestic manufacturing to replace imported goods. A group of businessmen known as the Boston Associates helped bring *industrialization to America by building textile mills in nearby Waltham, Lowell, and Lawrence.

Amid shifting economic fortunes, Boston thrived as an intellectual and cultural center. The artist John Singleton *Copley and the architect Charles *Bulfinch were Boston natives. The transcendentalist utopian experiment Brook Farm (1841–1847) was located nearby. Many leading lights of the American literary renaissance including Ralph Waldo *Emerson, Henry David *Thoreau, and Nathaniel *Hawthorne, lived in Boston or such nearby towns as Concord and Salem. The city was a major publishing center, and across the Charles River in Cambridge was Harvard College. Winthrop's "city on a hill" became the poet Oliver Wendell Holmes's "hub of the solar system." Boston was home to many *Antebellum Era reformers, including William Lloyd *Garrison, publisher of the abolitionist journal *Liberator.* The reformist impulse drew strength from the liberal Protestant movement exemplified by Unitarianism, also rooted in Boston. The later nineteenth century saw the establishment of the Massachusetts Institute of Technology (1865), the Museum of Fine Arts (1870), and the Boston Symphony Orchestra (1881). The *Christian Science "Mother Church" was dedicated in Boston in 1895.

The nineteenth century also brought great demographic changes, as the native-born "Brahmin" elite confronted successive waves of immigrants, including French Canadians, Irish (especially after Ireland's 1840s famine years), and, by the turn of the century, Italians and eastern European Jews. A growing African American community included William Monroe *Trotter, editor of a black newspaper, the *Boston Guardian.* The Irish gained political power through such colorful figures as James Michael Curley (1874–1958) and John F. "Honey Fitz" Fitzgerald (1863–1950), grandfather of President John F. *Kennedy.

*Suburbanization and a decline in manufacturing caused economic problems and population losses through much of the twentieth century. The 1960s saw racial conflicts over school busing between black and white ethnic neighborhoods. But beginning around the same time, Boston experienced dynamic economic growth based a on high-tech electronics industry, finance, medicine, education, and publishing. As the century ended, thanks to these knowledge-based industries and its rich history, Boston retained its cachet as an intellectual and cultural mecca.

[*See also* Civil Rights Movement; Colonial Era; Early Republic, Era of the; Immigration; Irish Americans; Italian Americans; Literature: Early National and Antebellum Eras; Puritanism; Revolutionary War; Revolution and Constitution, Era of the; Sixties, The; Textile Industry; Transcendentalism; Unitarianism and Universalism; Utopian and Communitarian Movements.]

• Shaun O'Connell, *Imagining Boston: A Literary Landscape,* 1990. Thomas H. O'Connor, *Bibles, Brahmins, and Bosses: A Short History of Boston,* 3d ed., 1991.

—Christopher Berkeley

BOSTON MASSACRE (1770). The Boston Massacre, a pivotal event of the Revolutionary Era, grew out of Great Britain's attempts after the *Seven Years' War to tighten control over its North American colonies and to defray the enormous costs associated with them. After customs officials complained about unruly colonists, and cabinet members concluded that the frontier constabulary was ineffective and too expensive, the

MAP 2: BOSTON IN THE 1770s

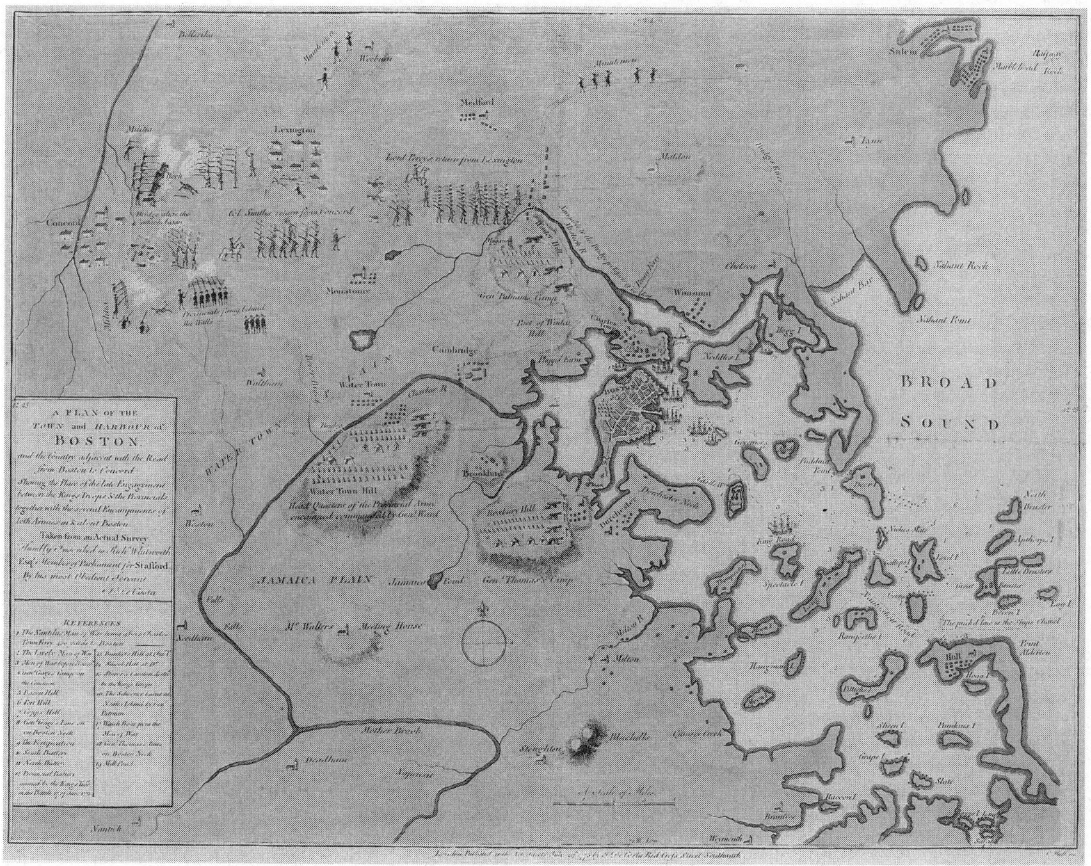

Prepared in England, this map illustrates the fighting at Lexington and Concord on 19 April 1775, which proved deadly for the British troops involved. The map shows many features of Boston and its environs, including the harbor and nearby Cambridge on the Charles River, home of Harvard College. The large inlet lying just west of Boston and nearly cutting it off from the mainland, called Back Bay, was dredged in the late nineteenth century and became a district of elite townhouses and cultural institutions.

[*See* Boston; Colonial Era; New England; Puritanism; Revolutionary War.]

Crown redirected troops from the interior to the seaboard, with two regiments stationed among captious Bostonians. Rather than stifling dissent, the soldiers' arrival in October 1768 increased tensions. Soldiers and civilians maintained a strained but generally peaceful relationship until 5 March 1770, when nervous redcoats fired into a threatening crowd. Five townspeople died, and in prints and orations they were eulogized as martyrs to British tyranny.

Even though General Thomas Gage removed the troops from *Boston and a local jury acquitted all but two of the soldiers involved, the consequences proved significant. The "massacre" embarrassed the British ministry, heightened colonial resentment, and galvanized a growing anti-army sentiment in America. To many colonists, the episode proved the tyrannical designs of the British ministry, the corrupting influence of standing armies, and the ever-present danger that free governments could succumb to tyranny—themes repeated in annual "massacre orations." Pro-British Loyalists, on the other hand, contended that scheming radicals, not abusive officials, had provoked the incident.

[*See also* Adams, John; Colonial Era; Revolution and Constitution, Era of; Revolutionary War.]

• John Shy, *Toward Lexington: The Role of the British Army in the Coming of the American Revolution*, 1965. Hiller Zobel, *The Boston Massacre*, 1970.

—J. Mark Thompson

BOSTON TEA PARTY (1773). The Boston Tea Party was a catalyst that precipitated the *Revolutionary War. On the night of 16 December 1773, as a crowd gathered on Boston's Griffin's Wharf, a group of about fifty men lightly disguised as Indians boarded the ships *Dartmouth, Beaver,* and *Eleanor*. In the next three hours, they broke open 340 chests of tea and dumped their contents into the water, destroying cargo worth nearly ten thousand pounds sterling belonging to Great Britain's East India Company. This dramatic action stemmed from a running controversy over Parliament's power to raise revenue by placing duties on imports into America. Colonists protested "taxation without representation," but Parliament retained the duty on tea as a symbol of its taxing authority. In 1773, ignoring warnings of a colonial reaction, Parliament authorized the East India Company to reduce its massive surplus by shipping thousands of pounds of dutied tea to *Boston, *New York City, *Philadelphia, and Charleston, South Carolina.

At the other ports the tea ships were either turned back or their cargo seized by customhouse officials, but at Boston, Governor Thomas Hutchinson insisted that the tea be landed and the duties paid. His longtime adversary Samuel *Adams adamantly opposed such payment. When negotiations broke down, Adams rallied his supporters at Boston's Old South Church, from where they marched to Griffin's Wharf. The event's larger importance lay in Great Britain's reaction. Instead of seeking reconciliation, the ministry passed the Coercive Acts (1774), closing the port of Boston, altering the colony's charter, and ordering British troops under General Thomas Gage to occupy the town. As colonists elsewhere rallied behind the beleaguered Bostonians, the First *Continental Congress approved a stringent boycott of British goods. With neither side willing to back down, the final crisis was at hand.

[*See also* Revolution and Constitution, Era of.]

• Benjamin W. Labaree, *The Boston Tea Party*, 1964; reprints 1968, 1981.

—Benjamin W. Labaree

BOTANY. *See* Biological Sciences.

BOURKE-WHITE, MARGARET (1904–1971), photographer. One of America's most flamboyant, ambitious, and successful photojournalists, Margaret Bourke-White remains a controversial figure. Born in *New York City to a bluestocking mother and an engineering-inventor father, Bourke-White married in her teens, divorced, took up *photography while attending several different colleges, and decided on a career in commercial photography even before she graduated from Cornell in 1927. First as an architectural photographer and then as a photographer of industrial subjects in the *Middle West, Bourke-White drew upon the technical expertise of others to make dazzling photographs of previously impossible subjects—steel mill interiors alight with molten metal, crane-and-derrick aerial views of architectural interiors, and the like. These pictures endeared her to clients and to Henry R. *Luce, who after 1929 made her the principal photographic force at *Fortune* magazine, his paean to *capitalism.

During the 1930s, Bourke-White published a photodocumentary on the Soviet Union, *Eyes on Russia* (1931); documented *Dust Bowl conditions (*Fortune*, October 1934); collaborated with the novelist Erskine Caldwell (whom she later briefly married) on a documentary-like study of rural southern poverty, *You Have Seen Their Faces* (1937); and saw her photograph of the Fort Peck Dam project in Montana on the cover of the first issue of Luce's *Life* magazine (23 November 1936), while simultaneously inventing *Life's* trademark genre, the picture-essay. Bourke-White aggressively and courageously covered *World War II in Czechoslovakia, the Soviet Union, North Africa, and Germany; afterward, she returned to the Luce publishing empire, photographing such plum subjects as Japanese life, the *Korean War, and the peaceful revolution—and tragic assassination—of Mahatma Gandhi. From the mid-1950s on, Parkinson's disease curtailed her career. Bourke-White's technically masterful, dramatically composed photojournalism chronicled not just the events but the attitudes of an American era.

• Margaret Bourke-White, *Portrait of Myself*, 1963. Vicki Goldberg, *Margaret Bourke-White: A Biography*, 1986. Sean Gallahan, *Margaret Bourke-White: Photographer*, 1998.

—Peter Bacon Hales

BOURNE, RANDOLPH (1886–1918), essayist, social critic, dissenter during *World War I. A New Jersey native educated at Columbia University (B.A., 1912; M.A., 1913), Bourne came under the influence of John *Dewey's *pragmatism and ideas clustered around the Progressive movement. He made his mark quickly in *New York City's liberal intellectual community by contributing prolifically to the *Atlantic*, the *New Republic*, the *Seven Arts*, and the *Dial* magazines. His books—*Youth and Life* (1913), *The Gary Schools* (1916), the posthumous *History of a Literary Radical* (1920) and others—spoke eloquently for youthful idealism, a cosmopolitan cultural community, a vital literary tradition, progressive education, and an ethnic diversity he called "trans-National America."

Although physically handicapped from birth, his face twisted, his back deformed, his growth stunted, Bourne was rich in friends and wrote movingly about the value of friendship. Women appreciated his sensitivity and *feminism. In 1918, at the time of his early death from the worldwide *influenza epidemic, he was engaged to a beautiful actress, Esther Cornell. During World War I, his conscience and insights into the role of power and wartime hysteria compelled him to dissent from the prevailing wisdom that an Allied victory would further peace and democracy. Bourne's searing wartime dissents ensured the demise of the *Seven Arts*; made him anathema to Dewey and many former editors and friends; and forced him to turn his attention to noncontroversial literary themes and to an overview of "The State," a work unfinished at his death.

[*See also* Cultural Pluralism; Progressive Era.]

• Bruce Clayton, *Forgotten Prophet: The Life of Randolph Bourne*, 1984.

—Bruce Clayton

BOWDITCH, NATHANIEL (1773–1838), astronomer and mathematician. Born in Salem, Massachusetts, Nathaniel Bowditch ended his formal education at age ten. Between 1795 and 1803 he made five voyages on merchant ships, serving on the last voyage as master and part owner. He became head of the Essex Fire and Marine Insurance Company in 1804. In 1823, he became actuary of the Massachusetts Hospital Life Insurance Company of Boston, a position he held until his death.

Self-educated, Bowditch mastered mathematics, celestial mechanics, French, and German, and familiarized himself with the scientific research underway in Europe. Although initially known for his *New American Practical Navigator* (1802), a manual for mariners, he also published extensively on celestial mechanics, mathematics, and physics, establishing himself as the leading American celestial mechanician and mathematician of the first quarter of the nineteenth century and becoming one of the few American men of science with an international reputation.

Bowditch's greatest contribution to American science, however, was his translation and annotation of Pierre Simon Laplace's *Traite de mécanique céleste* (1799–1825), a five-volume summary of the progress of physical astronomy since Isaac Newton. Between 1814 and 1817 Bowditch translated into English and annotated the four volumes published to that point. Publication of Bowditch's work began in 1829 and was completed posthumously in 1839. Adding the missing steps in Laplace's demonstrations, reporting recent improvements and discoveries in mathematics, and providing the sources from which Laplace had drawn, Bowditch's commentary proved crucial in the education of the next generation of American astronomers and mathematicians.

[*See also* Insurance; Mathematics and Statistics; Science: Revolutionary War to World War I.]

• Henry Ingersoll Bowditch, *Memoir of Nathaniel Bowditch*, 1839. John C. Greene, *American Science in the Age of Jefferson*, 1984.

—Marc Rothenberg

BOXING. Prizefighting began in England, where by the late eighteenth century it was acknowledged as the "national sport" but was also illegal. Boxers fought with bare knuckles, most forms of wrestling and hitting were permitted, and fights lasted until one or both contestants quit or could not continue. Tom Molineaux, a free black, was the first great American fighter. In two matches in England in 1810 and 1811, Molineaux came close to defeating the English champion Tom Cribb. Becoming famous in England, Molineaux remained virtually unknown to Americans, who initially showed little interest in the prize ring. This changed in the mid–nineteenth century as a modern working class, including many immigrants from England and Ireland, arose in American cities. A series of matches culminated with an 1849 championship fight, tinged with ethnic antipathy, between James "Yankee" Sullivan, an Irish immigrant, and the native-born Tom Hyer. Hyer's victory began a wave of spectacular fights in the 1850s. These illegal events—fighters and fans boarded steamboats and trains to stage battles beyond the reach of the law—received heavy newspaper coverage but were especially popular among working-class men, who saw reflected in them their own rough-cut masculine culture centered around saloons, political wards, and volunteer fire companies. Prizefighting declined after the *Civil War, partly owing to fixed fights and fans' violence, but also because the middle class prosecuted fighters more vigilantly. But in the 1880s, Boston's John L. Sullivan (1858–1918) circumvented the laws against prizefighting by wearing gloves and adhering to the new Marquis of Queensberry rules that mandated three-minute rounds and imposed other restrictions. Attracting a widening audience, Sullivan earned over one million dollars and became America's first great sports celebrity.

Boxing's modern era dates from 1892, when James J. Corbett (1866–1933), fighting under the Queensberry rules, defeated the aging Sullivan. Boxing now appealed to a broader spectrum of men seeking an elusive sense of masculinity in an era of economic change. Rapidly developing media—mass-circulation newspapers, *radio, and finally *television—connected the sport to a growing cult of celebrity characteristic of *consumer culture. Fighters like Jack Dempsey (1895–1983), who reigned as heavyweight champion through most of the 1920s, enjoyed enormous popularity.

Perhaps more than any other sport, boxing in the twentieth century developed a reputation as an ethnic ladder, as first the Irish, then Jews, Italians, *African Americans, and Latinos gained prominence. But prizefighting was not, in fact, a major avenue of social mobility. Despite the occasional champion who amassed riches, most fighters came from extremely poor families, and they remained poor. Although boxing audiences included numerous well-to-do fans, the fighters themselves continued to come from socially oppressed or stigmatized groups. Nonetheless, great fighters were idolized by their people as exemplars of male toughness in a world where poverty was taken as a badge of masculine failure, so that African American champions like Jack *Johnson, Joe *Louis, and Muhammad *Ali were extremely influential in their day.

[*See also* Gender; Immigration; Journalism; Popular Culture; Sports; Working-Class Life and Culture.]

• Elliott J. Gorn, *The Manly Art: Bare-Knuckle Prize Fighting in America*, 1986. Jeffrey Sammons, *Beyond the Ring: The Role of Boxing in American Society*, 1988.

—Elliot J. Gorn

BOY SCOUTS OF AMERICA. *See* Scouting.

BRADFORD, WILLIAM. *See* Pilgrims.

BRADSTREET, ANNE (c. 1612–1672), first published colonial American poet. The daughter of Dorothy Yorke and Thomas Dudley (a relative of Sir Philip Sidney), Anne was born in Northampton, England. At the age of sixteen, she married Simon Bradstreet, with whom she migrated to Massachusetts Bay in 1630. She bore eight children from 1633 to 1652 in the course of various resettlements, which ended in Andover, Massachusetts, where she lived for the last twenty-seven years of her life. Without her knowledge, her brother-in-law Reverend John Woodbridge published the first edition of her verse in London as *The Tenth Muse Lately Sprung up in America* (1650). Although this book was well received, Bradstreet felt ambivalent about it. Referring to it as an "ill-formed offspring" taken "by friends less wise than true," she deplored its imperfections. The publication of this book also appears to have occasioned a shift of artistic perception, for her subsequent poetry was more personal, original, experimental, and aesthetic than the exercises in the first edition. These later manuscript poems, with authorial revisions of the earlier printed verse, first appeared in the posthumous American edition *Several Poems Compiled with Great Variety of Wit and Learning* (1678), which circulated widely in *New England. Bradstreet's writings are sometimes informed by anxieties and discontents reflecting the restricted experience of colonial women. "Contemplations," a sequence of thirty-three stanzas emblematically configuring in its imagery and structure the cross-like intersection of the temporal and the eternal, is arguably her best work.

[*See also* Colonial Era; Literature: Colonial Era; Poetry.]

• Elizabeth Wade White, *Anne Bradstreet: The Tenth Muse*, 1971. Anne Stanford, *Anne Bradstreet: The Wordly Puritan*, 1974.

—William J. Scheick

BRANCH DAVIDIANS. *See* Millennialism and Apocalyptacism; Religion.

BRANDEIS, LOUIS (1856–1941), attorney, reformer, associate justice of the U.S. *Supreme Court. Born in Louisville, Kentucky, Brandeis graduated from Harvard Law School in 1877 and for thirty-seven years practiced law in Boston. His eminent reputation in commercial practice rested on his mastery of facts and spacious vision of law. Drawn to many of the reform causes of the *Progressive Era, he became a confidant and adviser to President Woodrow *Wilson, shaping much of Wilson's "New Freedom" program. Brandeis spoke for the strand of Progressivism that feared corporate bigness and concentration and put its faith in local forms of self-government as "laboratories of democracy." In **Miller* v. *Oregon* (1908), Brandeis pioneered the "Brandeis brief," an argument relying more on facts and social science evidence than on legal precedent or syllogism. In 1914, Brandeis espoused Zionism and became a leader of the American wing of the movement.

In 1916, Wilson nominated Brandeis to the Supreme Court. Despite unprecedented conservative and anti-Semitic attacks on Brandeis, he was confirmed and served for twenty-three years. He advocated judicial self-restraint in cases involving state *economic regulation, urging deference to legislative policy judgments. Usually in dissent during the chief justiceships of William Howard *Taft (1921–1930) and Charles Evans *Hughes (1930–1941), he repeated his Brandeis-brief technique, amassing facts and statistics to demonstrate that the legislative judgment was reasonable. Believing that the diversity-of-citizenship jurisdiction of the federal courts permitted large corporations to evade state regulation, Brandeis required federal judges to follow state substantive law in *Erie Railroad* v. *Tompkins* (1938).

On issues of personal *liberty, however, Brandeis was a vigilant judicial activist, hostile to laws that inhibited speech and press. His demand for a speech-protective reading of the "clear and present danger" test articulated by Justice Oliver Wendell *Holmes Jr. in **Schenck* v. *United States* (1991), eventually prevailed in *Brandenburg* v. *Ohio* (1969). His eloquent call in the *Whitney* v. *California* (1927) concurrence for civic courage in defense of First Amendment rights similarly gained canonical status in *Dennis* v. *United States* (1951). In a seminal 1890 law-review article, Brandeis had developed the concept of a right of privacy protected by the *Bill of Rights, a position he adopted in his *Olmstead* v. *United States* (1928) dissent. This, too, the Court later affirmed in *Griswold* v. *Connecticut* (1964) and **Roe* v. *Wade* (1973).

Though critical of the use of judicial power to frustrate state economic regulation, Brandeis had a profound reverence for the Supreme Court and for the rule of law. He therefore strenuously opposed President Franklin Delano *Roosevelt's 1937 court-packing plan as an assault on both.

[*See also* Anti-Semitism; Censorship; Civil Liberties; Corporatism; Judaism.]

• Melvin I. Urofsky, *A Mind of One Piece: Brandeis and American Reform* 1971. Philippa Strum, *Louis D. Brandeis: Justice for the People*, 1984.

—William M. Wiecek

BRANT, JOSEPH, or Thayendanegea (1742–1807), pro-British Mohawk chief. The son of the Mohawk chief Niklaus Brant and grandson of Sa Ga Yean Qua Prah Ton (one of four Indian leaders to visit London in 1710), Joseph Brant grew up in the household of Sir William Johnson (1715–1774), a fur trader, superintendent of Indian affairs north of the Ohio River 1755–1774, and proprietor of a vast estate on the Mohawk River near present-day Amsterdam, New York. Brant's sister Molly was Johnson's common-law wife and bore him eight children. In 1758, during the *Seven Years' War, young Joseph Brant guided the expedition of Colonel John Bradstreet to the French Fort Frontenac on Lake Ontario, which fell to the British.

Educated at the Indian Charity School in Lebanon, Connecticut, Brant served in the late 1760s and 1770s as a translator and diplomat who helped the British negotiate with the *Iroquois Confederacy. After the death of his first wife, Margaret, daughter of the Oneida sachem Skenandoah, Brant married Catherine Croghan, the Mohawk daughter of a British agent.

In 1775, as the *Revolutionary War began, Brant allied with the British. He visited England and was commissioned a colonel in the British army. Recruiting Iroquois allies for the Loyalist cause, Brant led ruinously effective Iroquois raids against American settlements in the Mohawk Valley, northern Pennsylvania, and the Ohio Valley in 1777 and 1778. In retaliation, American forces devastated Iroquois villages in 1779. After the Revolution, Brant ignored the American-Iroquois peace treaties and continued to raid the frontier.

For his military services, the British awarded him a pension and land along the Grand River in Ontario. In his last years, Brant translated the *Bible into Mohawk. He died near his estate at Brantford, Ontario.

[*See also* Indian History and Culture: From 1500 to 1800.]

• Isabel Thompson Kelsay, *Joseph Brant*, 1984. Donald A. Grinde Jr. and Bruce E. Johansen, *Exemplar of Liberty: Native America and the Evolution of Democracy*, 1991.

—Donald A. Grinde Jr.

BRENT, MARGARET (c. 1601–1671), leader in colonial Maryland. Brent, a Roman Catholic, arrived in Maryland with her sister Mary and two brothers in 1638. Unmarried and hence legally able to control property, she established herself as a landowner and entrepreneur. Her business and diplomatic skills proved crucial after a raid on the Catholic-led colony early in 1645 by a ship captain armed with letters of marque from England's Protestant Parliament. Governor Leonard Calvert fled but returned with soldiers to reclaim the Maryland government in December 1646. He found his colony in a shambles, most of its inhabitants gone. At his death in June 1647, Calvert named Brent his executor with instructions to pay his debts. These included the soldiers' wages which he had pledged, if necessary, to pay himself or pay from the estate of his brother, the absentee proprietor, Lord Baltimore. The governor's property proved insufficient and Brent had to contend with threats of mutiny. Without time to gain Lord Baltimore's consent, Maryland's Provincial Court granted her power of attorney over his Maryland assets. On 21 January 1648, before risking use of this property, Brent—probably hoping to persuade the Maryland assembly to raise taxes to pay the soldiers—"requested to have vote in the howse for herselfe and voyce" as Lord Baltimore's attorney. In an era when women were excluded from politics, the assembly denied the request. Brent then paid the soldiers with Lord Baltimore's cattle, thereby averting a crisis that might have destroyed the colony and its policy of religious toleration. Lord Baltimore, in England, was outraged at her actions, even though the assembly advised him that she had saved the colony and "deserved favour and thanks from your Honour . . . [rather than] bitter invectives." To escape the proprietor's anger Brent and her sister joined their brother Giles in Virginia, where the family established a thriving plantation called Peace. Here Margaret Brent died in 1671.

[*See also* Colonial Era; Roman Catholicism.]

• Lois Green Carr, "Brent, Margaret," in Edward T. James, et al., eds., *Notable American Women, 1607–1950: A Biographical Dictionary*, 3 vols., 1971, pp. 236–37. Lois Green Carr, "Margaret Brent: A Brief History," electronic publication by the Maryland State Archives, 1998: http://www.mdsa.net

BRETTON WOODS CONFERENCE (1944). The breakdown of the world economic system during the 1930s Great Depression convinced American and British planners of the need for a new international economic framework as part of the postwar settlement. Anglo-American discussions led by U.S. Assistant Secretary of the Treasury Harry Dexter White and the British Treasury representative John Maynard Keynes began in 1942. These talks as well as intragovernmental planning in both countries led to an international conference held in Bretton Woods, New Hampshire, in July 1944. Attended by representatives of forty-five nations, the conclave produced the blueprints for two new institutions, the *International Monetary

Fund (IMF) and the International Bank for Reconstruction and Development (or *World Bank), as well as discussions of a third, the International Trade Organization.

The underlying principles of the Bretton Woods agreements followed American, not British preferences, hardly surprising since the United States at the end of *World War II owned half of the world's supply of monetary gold and produced half of global gross national product. Embracing the capitalist ethos of the United States, the Bretton Woods system assumed that prosperity brought peace and that the best guarantee of prosperity was an international economic system based on the freest possible flow of money and goods.

American planners had hoped that the wartime participation of the Soviet Union in the Grand Alliance with the United States and Great Britain would convince the Soviet government to join the new international economic order. Soviet attendance at the Bretton Woods conference seemed to augur well, but the following year the Soviet dictator Joseph Stalin vetoed Soviet participation in the Bretton Woods organizations. Although operational arrangements of the Bretton Woods institutions evolved in the decades after 1944, the agreements nonetheless provided the basic framework for the capitalist economic system during the *Cold War and after.

[*See also* Capitalism; Depressions, Economic; Foreign Relations: U.S. Relations with Europe; Foreign Trade, U.S.; General Agreement on Tariffs and Trade; Tariffs.]

• Richard Gardner, *Sterling-Dollar Diplomacy: The Origins and the Prospects of Our International Economic Order,* 1969. Randall Bennett Woods, *A Changing of the Guard: Anglo-American Relations 1941–1947,* 1990.

—Diane B. Kunz

BREWING AND DISTILLING. Adrian Block and Hans Christensen established the first brewery in British North America in 1612 in New Amsterdam (now *New York City). Others soon followed, although many taverns brewed their own beer, making it difficult for commercial breweries to succeed. In 1793, *Philadelphia was the brewing center of the colonies. By 1810, 132 U.S. breweries produced 185,000 barrels (31 gallons each) of beer.

Rum, distilled from molasses produced by slaves on West Indian sugar plantations, figured prominently in the economy of England's mainland colonies. In the early nineteenth century, settlers moving into Kentucky and Tennessee began making whiskey, which became beer's major competitor. Whiskey, distilled from wheat, rye, and corn, soon became a lucrative alternative to selling grain. Noted early distillers included Dr. James C. Crow, Jasper Newton, "Jack" Daniel, and James Beam. Bourbon, acorn-based whiskey, was first distilled in Bourbon County, Kentucky.

The brewing industry, meanwhile, moving west with the settlers, responded to the influx of European immigrants, especially Germans. Jacob Best, a German immigrant, established the Best Brewery in Milwaukee in 1844, four years before Wisconsin became a state. Renamed Pabst Brewery, it was the country's leading brewer by 1874. A second Milwaukee brewery, started by John Braun in 1846, became the Blatz Brewery when Valentine Blatz, a former employee, married Braun's widow shortly after his death. August Krug started a brewery in Milwaukee in 1849, which later became the Schlitz Brewery. A St. Louis brewery launched by George Schneider in 1850 became the Anheuser-Busch Brewery when Eberhard Anheuser bought the company and four years later was joined by Adolphus Busch. In 1855, the German-born Frederick E. Miller of Milwaukee purchased a local brewery and renamed it the Miller Brewing Company. By 1860, the nation's 1,269 breweries produced more than one million barrels of beer, 85 percent of it still brewed in New York and Pennsylvania. In 1873, 4,131 U.S. breweries (an all-time high) produced nine million barrels of beer. The years 1880 to 1910 saw a decline in brewery numbers as improvements in production and distribution enabled fewer plants to produce more beer. The number of breweries fell to 1,500 by 1910.

Americans' taste in distilled spirits, meanwhile, had expanded to include mixed drinks or cocktails (an American slang coinage) utilizing imported Scotch and Irish whiskey; gin, a grain-based, juniper-flavored liquor invented by the Dutch; and vodka, a flavorless but potent drink made from rye and barley malt or sometimes potatoes, that originated in Russia, Scandinavia, and eastern Europe. The bourbon-based mint julep enjoyed particular popularity in the *South.

The *Eighteenth Amendment (1919) forced all breweries and distilleries to stop making beer and spirits. Some breweries continued by producing candy, soft drinks, and near-beer (no more than 0.5 percent alcohol). Prohibition ended in 1933, but by 1934 only 756 breweries were back in operation. The number of U.S. breweries reached a low of 80 in 1983, but with interest in microbreweries and pub breweries (on-site breweries) the total increased thereafter. By 1996, more than 1,500 breweries (many of them small, local enterprises) were operating in the United States. The leading national breweries at century's end were Anheuser-Busch, Miller, Coors, and Stroh.

Consumption of distilled drinks declined in the late twentieth century owing to *health and fitness concerns and the growing popularity of specialty beers and domestic and imported wines. From 1980 to 1995, U.S. production of distilled spirits fell from 236 to 104 million gallons, including a 20-percent drop in whiskey production. Mixed drinks remained important in American drinking patterns, however, as evidenced by the more than $2 billion in distilled spirits imported in 1996.

[*See also* Alcohol and Alcohol Abuse; Colonial Era; German Americans; Immigration; Mass Production; Temperance and Prohibition; Twenties, The; Working-Class Life and Culture.]

• Stanley Wade Baron, *Brewed in America: A History of Beer and Ale in the United States,* 1972. William L. Downard, *Dictionary of the History of the American Brewing and Distilling Industries,* 1980. Jerry Apps, *Breweries of Wisconsin,* 1992.

—Jerry Apps

BRITISH AMERICANS. British Americans (including the English, Scots, Welsh, and Scotch-Irish) began to settle North America permanently in 1607. They dominated *immigration in the *Colonial Era, bringing with them the English language and Protestant Christianity, as well as the legal system and political, cultural, and economic values that shaped the nation. Arriving from distinct parts of Britain and settling in distinct parts of America, they laid the foundations of America's regional cultures. By 1776, with about half the white population consisting of English immigrants and their descendents, America was overwhelmingly a British world. Through the twentieth century, Britons continued to constitute a substantial though diminishing share of immigrants.

Between 1820 and 1930, at least five million Britons (including Canadians of British origins) permanently settled in the United States. These immigrants were "invisible" in the sense that they blended into the dominant culture and society more readily than other immigrant groups. Generally they did not form ethnic settlements, nor were they seen as "foreigners." In the *Antebellum Era, many Britons came seeking farmland and helped push the frontier westward; by the 1880s, more settled in cities. Throughout the nineteenth century, British Americans loomed large in *literature and the arts; in *banking and finance; and in the *industrialization process, especially in the *textile industry, the *iron and steel industry, *mining, *railroads, and *engineering. In the twentieth century, though spread across the economic spectrum, British Americans figured prominently in the skilled and professional ranks, continuing to blend in with American society and to contribute to its development. Despite the nation's growing ethnic diversity,

British Americans dominated national politics, the judiciary, and higher education well into the twentieth century.

• Charlotte Erickson, *Invisible Immigrants: The Adaptation of English and Scottish Immigrants in Nineteenth-Century America,* 1972. David Hackett Fischer, *Albion's Seed: Four British Folkways in America,* 1989.

—William E. Van Vugt

BROOK FARM. *See* Utopian and Communitarian Movements.

BROOKLYN BRIDGE. When it opened on 24 May 1883, the Brooklyn Bridge was the longest suspension bridge in the world and among the most celebrated creations of the nineteenth century. In 1867, the New York State legislature chartered a company to build a bridge across the East River, between Brooklyn and Lower Manhattan, to provide more reliable transportation than the existing ferries for a growing stream of commuters. John Augustus Roebling (1806–1869), a German-born wire manufacturer, designed a span that incorporated many innovations, including extensive use of steel. When Roebling died of injuries in 1869, as construction was about to begin, his son, Washington Roebling (1837–1926), took over as chief engineer. Though crippled by the bends while supervising excavation for the bridge towers, the younger Roebling conquered innumerable technical problems during the long course of construction.

The Brooklyn Bridge helped pave the way for the consolidation of the cities of Brooklyn and New York in 1898. Its success spurred a national wave of bridge building. Though the bridge carried massive vehicular traffic, generations of New Yorkers found its elevated walkway a haven from the city's bustle.

From its opening, the Brooklyn Bridge served as a symbol of the new industrial America. Though the novelist Henry *James deemed it a "monster" obliterating the city of his youth, the cultural critic Lewis *Mumford judged it an artistic success as "a fulfillment and a prophecy" of the Machine Age. The painters John Marin and Joseph Stella saw the bridge as embodying modernity, while the poet Hart Crane in "The Bridge" (1930) viewed it as an affirmation of faith in the possibilities of America. As the twentieth century ended, the Brooklyn Bridge continued to move commuters into and out of *New York City's downtown business district while conjuring up hope and harmony.

• Alan Trachtenberg, *Brooklyn Bridge: Fact and Symbol,* 1965. David McCullough, *The Great Bridge,* 1972.

—Joshua B. Freeman

BROWN, JOHN (1800–1859), northern white abolitionist whose attempt to start a slave uprising at Harpers Ferry, Virginia (now West Virginia), helped bring on the *Civil War. Brown, a businessman with a checkered career, joined the *antislavery movement in the 1830s. He helped fugitive slaves escape via the Underground Railroad; befriended black leaders, notably Frederick *Douglass; and eventually quit business to take up arms against the "Slave Power." In 1855–1857, Brown fought against proslavery militia in the guerrilla war for control of Kansas territory, winning a national reputation for courage but local notoriety for the "Pottawatomie massacre" (23–24 May 1856) in which he supervised the lynching of five proslavery men.

In 1857–1859, his focus shifted to the *South and to inciting servile insurrection. With the secret support of prominent abolitionists, he organized an interracial "army" of twenty-one men and led them in an assault on the federal arsenal at Harpers Ferry (16–17 October 1859), expecting to seize weapons and arm the slaves. Instead, state and federal troops (the latter commanded by Lieutenant Colonel Robert E. *Lee), crushed his force. Brown himself was captured; hastily tried for treason in a Virginia court; convicted; and, on 2 December 1859, hanged. The bravery of the "old man" during this ordeal, as well as his eloquence in defending his actions, made a powerful impression on the country. Many northerners hailed him as a martyr for freedom, while white southerners excoriated him as the embodiment of northern aggression. In this charged political atmosphere, compromise between the sections became increasingly impossible.

[*See also* Antebellum Era; Civil War: Causes; Kansas-Nebraska Act; Slave Uprisings and Resistance.]

• Stephen B. Oates, *To Purge This Land with Blood: A Biography of John Brown,* 1970. Paul O. Boyer, *The Legend of John Brown: A Biography and a History,* 1972.

—Dean Grodzins

BROWNSVILLE INCIDENT (1906). In the summer of 1906, despite local white protest, the U.S. Army garrisoned Fort Brown in Brownsville, Texas, with three companies of the Twenty-fifth Infantry, a regiment whose enlisted personnel were all African American. Racial tension became intense. Around midnight on 13 August 1906, eight to ten men marched through the town's streets firing their rifles. They killed one man, wounded another, and throughly terrified the townspeople. White Texans concluded that the raiding party came from the fort. After several investigations, the army reached the same conclusion. President Theodore *Roosevelt authorized the army to present the soldiers with an ultimatum: The guilty men in the regiment must come forward or all would suffer punishment. No one responded, and all 156 men were discharged. Booker T. *Washington tried but failed to change Roosevelt's mind. In 1909, Congress authorized an Army Court of Inquiry into the claims of the discharged soldiers. Eventually, fourteen were readmitted into the service. In 1972, the army changed the discharges to honorable, and Congress authorized a payment to the one living survivor. The controversy can be viewed from several perspectives. At the time, many whites accepted the notion that *African Americans would naturally attack whites and join in a conspiracy of silence, while most blacks deemed the lack of due process typical of white justice. Though some of the African American soldiers probably were guilty of the shooting, a different standard of justice clearly prevailed for African Americans; all were presumed guilty and had to prove their innocence. Booker T. Washington's inability to achieve justice despite his long-established policy of racial acquiescence became clear. Southern whites continued for many years to cite the Brownsville Incident to reinforce their fear of armed African Americans taking justice into their own hands.

[*See also* Military, The; Progressive Era; Racism.]

• Marvin E. Fletcher, *The Black Soldier and Officer in the United States, 1891–1917,* 1974. Garna L. Christian, *Black Soldiers in Jim Crow Texas, 1899–1917,* 1995.

—Marvin E. Fletcher

BROWN v. BOARD OF EDUCATION (1954), U.S. *Supreme Court decision holding racially segregated schools unconstitutional. Linda Brown, a black elementary-school student in Topeka, Kansas, could not attend classes near her home because state law mandated racial separation in public schools. Attorneys for the *National Association for the Advancement of Colored People (NAACP) in 1951 filed suit in federal court on behalf of Brown and several other plaintiffs, seeking a ruling on the constitutionality of racially segregated schools. The NAACP had decided to test the prevailing legal doctrine that racially segregated schooling did not violate the equal protection clause of the *Fourteenth Amendment if equal resources were provided to blacks and whites. This doctrine, embodied in the Supreme Court's 1896 **Plessy* v. *Ferguson* decision, governed all aspects of domestic race relations and legitimated the pervasive segregation that banished *African Americans and other racial minorities to the margins of society. The challenge to school *segregation thus indirectly bucked powerful legal precedent and generations of social practice.

Brown was distinguished by the plaintiffs' use of testimony from social scientists who argued that segregation psychologically damaged black children. The U.S. District Court upheld segregation in its August 1951 decision in the case but attached to its opinion a statement supporting *social science claims. The NAACP continued this approach when the case reached the Supreme Court. The high court heard *Brown* with four companion cases brought against segregating school districts.

Commentators opposed to overturning *Plessy* argued that the abolition of school segregation required congressional passage of a law specifically prohibiting it. NAACP attorneys argued that the Fourteenth Amendment banned any discrimination by the states and required no further articulation. Attorneys for the segregationist states held that inferior conditions in black schools were correctable, that their clients had already begun reforms, and that the high court should not confuse the practical difficulties of equalizing black and white schools with the principle of separate-but-equal itself. Segregationists denied the wide scope claimed for the Fourteenth Amendment by their adversaries. If segregation psychologically injured black children, they contended, the children would suffer further during the integration process.

Overturning the *Plessy* doctrine, the Supreme Court unanimously ruled on 17 May 1954, that segregated schools are "inherently unequal." The opinion, prepared by Chief Justice Earl *Warren, reiterated the argument about the psychological harm of segregation. After the decision, concern about the practical aspects of implementing desegregation and fear that violence would accompany desegregation efforts, led the Court to hear arguments in *Brown* that specifically addressed implementation issues. Historians referred to these 1955 hearings as *Brown II.* Predisposed to let district courts arrange the details of desegregation, the Supreme Court sent the school-segregation cases back to the original districts with instructions to execute its mandate "with all deliberate speed."

Brown featured the participation of several noted figures. Chief Justice Warren, named by President Dwight D. *Eisenhower to the Court after the sudden death of Chief Justice Fred M. Vinson in 1953, presided over an increasingly activist Court. Thurgood *Marshall, leader of the NAACP defense team, had argued several major cases before the Supreme Court. A Howard University Law School graduate, he was himself appointed to the Supreme Court in 1967 by President Lyndon B. *Johnson, the first African American so honored. The psychologist Kenneth Clark of the City College of New York, one of the expert witnesses, was known for his study of African American children's response to black and white dolls. When black children rejected dolls that most resembled them, Clark believed, they revealed an internalized a sense of inferiority. While his thesis was (and remains) controversial, Clark, an African American, subsequently became a highly influential academic and public intellectual.

Immediate popular reaction to *Brown* was mixed. Technically, the Court's decision bound only the specific school districts in litigation, but its broader application was clear. Reaction in the Deep *South was negative. So-called citizens councils, devoted to upholding white supremacy, originating in Mississippi in July 1954, soon spread throughout the region. In 1956, more than one hundred congressmen and senators signed the "Southern Manifesto" endorsing segregation.

Some southern whites resisted violently. They rioted when Autherine Lucy, a black student, enrolled at the University of Alabama in 1956. A 1957 confrontation between President Eisenhower and Arkansas governor Orval Faubus over integrating Little Rock Central High School resulted in federal military intervention for the first time since *Reconstruction.

Separate schools also existed in northern communities, often because of demography rather than law. Considerable friction developed over implementation issues in these areas, especially regarding busing to achieve racial balance. Few northerners openly defended segregation, but the racial composition of public schools subsequently became a divisive national issue.

Brown was preceded by nearly twenty years of litigation before the Supreme Court. Thurgood Marshall and other NAACP attorneys exposed the limitations of the separate-but-equal doctrine in cases involving graduate school education. They thus laid the groundwork for ending segregation by gradually eroding the legal foundations on which it rested.

The court's decision also had deep implications for the equal protection clause of the Fourteenth Amendment. Plaintiffs in *Brown* had argued that segregation singled out citizens by race. The justices accepted the view that only a belief in the inferiority of blacks, which they found untenable, could validate such distinctions.

The abandonment of segregation accelerated by the *Brown* decision coincided with the *Cold War effort to present the United States to the world as a showcase of democracy. The Supreme Court decision legitimated the claims of African Americans and other racial minorities to participate in national life and set the stage for the emerging *civil rights movement.

[*See also* Civil Rights Legislation; Federal Government, Judicial Branch; Fifties, The; Race, Concept of; Racism.]

• Richard Kluger, *Simple Justice,* 1975. Raymond Wolters, *The Burden of Brown,* 1984. Mark V. Tushnet, *The NAACP's Legal Strategy against Segregated Education, 1925–1950,* 1987. Mark V. Tushnet, *Making Civil Rights Law,* 1994.

—Brenda Gayle Plummer

BRYAN, WILLIAM JENNINGS (1860–1925), populist leader, presidential candidate, secretary of state. A powerful orator first elected to Congress from Nebraska in 1890, Bryan won the *Democratic party's 1896 presidential nomination after delivering his electrifying "Cross of Gold" speech at the party convention in *Chicago. The *Populist party also nominated him, and he ran on a platform endorsing free silver and other reforms. He personified the agrarian values of individualism, equality, and Protestant morality in an urban-industrial era of deepening class and ethnic divisions. His opposition to corporate power mirrored the spirit of discontent pulsing through the nation's heartland, but he failed to rally the urban working class and lost to the Republican William *McKinley.

In foreign affairs, Bryan opposed overseas *expansionism after the *Spanish-American War as dangerous to republican institutions. Although losing again to McKinley in 1900, he retained national visibility through his newspaper, the *Commoner,* advocating trust control, prohibition, and political reform. Again the Democratic candidate in 1908, he lost to William Howard *Taft.

President Woodrow *Wilson named him secretary of state in 1913. Bryan sought to keep America out of the European war that began in August 1914. Considering Wilson's notes to Germany protesting the sinking of the British liner *Lusitania* in 1915 as too hostile, he resigned. In the 1920s, Bryan promoted Florida real estate, supported the *fundamentalist movement, and battled the theory of *evolution. At the celebrated 1925 *Scopes trial, he testified as a prosecution witness. To the end, Bryan represented an America of small towns and consensual values—an older American under assault in the new industrial age.

[*See also* Agriculture: The "Golden Age" (1890s–1920); Federal Government, Executive Branch: Department of State; Free Silver Movement; Gold Standard; Populist Era; Protestantism; Social Class; Temperance and Prohibition; World War I.]

• Paolo Coletta, *William Jennings Bryan,* 3 vols., 1964–1969. Robert Cherny, *Righteous Cause: The Life of William Jennings Bryan,* 1985.

—H. Wayne Morgan

BUCHANAN, JAMES (1791–1868), fifteenth president of the United States. Born in Lancaster County, Pennsylvania, the son of a storekeeper and farmer, Buchanan was a successful lawyer who soon turned to politics. Originally a Federalist, he became a Jacksonian Democrat, serving successively as a state legislator, congressman, minister to Russia (1832–1834), U.S. Senator (1834–1845), secretary of state under James Knox *Polk (1845–1849), and ambassador to Great Britain (1853–1856). Like other antebellum Democrats, Buchanan distrusted federal power, favored popular sovereignty, and remained largely indifferent to *slavery. Elected president in 1856 with significant southern backing, Buchanan faced a sectional crisis inflamed by the struggle for control of the Kansas territory and the *Republican party's emergence as a northern party opposed to slavery's expansion. Despite his efforts at conciliation, tensions intensified throughout his presidency. Buchanan's prosouthern tilt on the Kansas issue, based on his hatred of the Republicans and his sympathy for southern fears, provoked a split with the powerful Illinois senator Stephen A. *Douglas, who believed that Buchanan and his southern-dominated cabinet had leaned too far to placate the *South. This split and the bloodshed in Kansas increased both northern resistance to southern demands and the South's determination to preserve the slave system.

Buchanan did not seek renomination in 1860 (nor would he have succeeded had he tried). As the *Democratic party fragmented, the election of the Republican Abraham *Lincoln led seven southern states to secede and to seize federal property within their borders. Buchanan, still president, opposed secession and insisted on federal rights, but he did not believe that he could compel the seceding states to return, and his term ended in futility. His distinguished career of public service irretrievably tarnished by a failed presidency, Buchanan consistently ranks low in scholarly assessments of presidential greatness. A Jacksonian in outlook who lacked Old Hickory's willingness to use the presidency to accomplish great ends, he is remembered primarily for weakness and ineffectiveness.

[*See also* Antebellum Era; Antislavery; Federalist Party; Jackson, Andrew; Kansas-Nebraska Act.]

• Philip S. Klein, *President James Buchanan,* 1962. Elbert B. Smith, *The Presidency of James Buchanan,* 1975.

—Joel H. Silbey

BUCKLEY, WILLIAM F., JR. (1925–), conservative journalist and intellectual. Buckley grew up in Sharon, Connecticut, one of ten children of William Frank Buckley and Aloise Steiner Buckley. The father had grown wealthy in the oil business, and both parents had strong Roman Catholic loyalties. After service in *World War II and graduation from Yale University, Buckley won notoriety with his book *God and Man at Yale* (1951), an attack on his alma mater's liberal economic thinking and religious agnosticism. Buckley inherited much of his *conservatism from his father, particularly the *anticommunism. He befriended Whittaker Chambers, a protagonist in the Alger *Hiss case, and published their letters in *Odyssey of a Friend* (1964). With L. Brent Bozell, Buckley wrote *McCarthy and His Enemies* (1954), a defense of Joseph *McCarthy's anti-Communist investigations.

Founding the *National Review* magazine in 1955, Buckley brought together the disparate strands of American conservatism—free-market and libertarian, religious and traditionalist, elitist and populist. It became America's leading conservative journal. Buckley also became known through his long-running National Public Television program *Firing Line.* There and in his writings, Buckley displayed his wit and sarcasm, his ample lexicon, and his erudition. Buckley himself did not develop a consistent intellectual conservatism; his opinions could reflect any of the varieties he welcomed in his magazine. Usually, however, he saw American conservatives as a beleaguered minority standing against a dominant and privileged liberal establishment. Against this ascendancy, Buckley defended a conservative counterculture and its tribal loyalists. Through his longevity, sustained productivity, and public visibility, Buckley served the conservative intellectual movement as a paterfamilias.

[*See also* Cold War; Fifties, The; Liberalism; Roman Catholicism.]

• Mark Royden Winchell, *William F. Buckley, Jr.,* 1984. John B. Judis, *William F. Buckley, Jr.: Patron Saint of the Conservatives,* 1988.

—J. David Hoeveler

BUFFALO BILL. *See* Cody, William ("Buffalo Bill").

BULFINCH, CHARLES (1763–1844), architect. Born to privilege in colonial *Boston, Bulfinch attended Harvard College and then made a grand tour of Europe, 1785–1787. He was especially impressed by contemporary British architecture, particularly the government buildings of William Chambers and the refined and delicate early neoclassicism of Robert Adam. Returning to Boston, Bulfinch designed buildings as an amateur architect, the pleasurable pursuit of a gentleman. However, his ambitious and architecturally progressive Tontine Crescent (1793–1794) brought his financial ruin. Thenceforth, Bulfinch supported himself as a professional architect. In 1799, he became Boston's superintendent of police (with a regular salary) and was named chair of the board of selectmen. Bulfinch played a major role in reshaping Boston's image through his many buildings, notably his domed Massachusetts State House (1795–1798), as well as making the city more livable through his administrative duties. Building mostly in brick, he designed elegantly conceived buildings with Adamesque motifs, forms, and proportions, while exhibiting the restraint and economy characteristic of the Federal style. Bulfinch moved to *Washington, D.C., when in 1818 he was officially appointed architect of the U.S. Capitol, a building that had been under construction since 1793. By 1829, Bulfinch had brought the Capitol to completion. His most notable contribution to earlier designs was the creation, under political pressure, of a taller and more distinctive central dome (replaced in later expansion). Although he relied primarily upon British sources, Charles Bulfinch established some of the most compelling early architectural expressions of the new republic.

[*See also* Architecture; Early Republic, Era of the.]

• Harold Kirker and James Kirker, *Bulfinch's Boston, 1787–1817,* 1964. Harold Kirker, *The Architecture of Charles Bulfinch,* 1969.

—Craig Zabel

BULGE, BATTLE OF THE (1944–1945). In mid-December 1944, as the Allied armies stood poised to invade Germany, came Adolf Hitler's last, desperate gamble for victory in *World War II, a thrust through the Ardennes Forest in Belgium intended to split Allied forces and retake the port of Antwerp. Hitler hoped that the American home front would crack after such a crushing defeat. With bad weather preventing U.S. air reconnaissance, German forces under Field Marshal Gerd von Rundstedt achieved surprise along a fifty-mile front on 16 December, as fourteen infantry divisions, backed by five panzer (tank) divisions, crashed through the Allied lines and created a huge "bulge" toward Liège and Antwerp. English-speaking German commandos wearing U.S. uniforms and dog tags disrupted communications and panicked GIs unable to distinguish friend from foe. Some 7,500 men in the 106th Infantry Division surrendered, the largest U.S. surrender in the European theater. German SS troops later massacred American soldiers captured at Malmédy.

The heaviest fighting was around Bastogne, a vital road junction. Defended by General Troy Middleton's Eighth Corps and General Anthony McAuliffe's 101st Airborne Division, some 18,000 Americans held off superior German forces for over a week. With stormy weather preventing aerial reinforcement, the American position appeared hopeless, but on 22 December, McAuliffe made his memorable reply to a German surrender demand: "Nuts!" Clearing weather the following day enabled planes to drop supplies. Meanwhile, responding to General

Dwight D. *Eisenhower's orders, General George S. *Patton Jr. made a "left turn" of his 250,000-man Third Army, then on the Moselle River eighty miles away, and drove northward; Patton's Fourth Armored Division broke through the German encirclement on 26 December and saved Bastogne. Finally, after constant urgings from Eisenhower, the British general Bernard Montgomery mounted a counterattack from the north that flattened the "bulge" by early January.

The war's largest single battle on the Western front, the Battle of the Bulge cost the United States. Nearly 70,000 soldiers were killed, captured, or wounded. At a cost to Germany of 30,000 battle deaths, 40,000 wounded, 30,000 prisoners of war, 277 planes, and most of its remaining armor, the offensive delayed the Allied advance for a month. By concentrating his reserves in the west, Hitler enabled the Soviets—advancing in the east—to capture Berlin. "The failure of the Ardennes offensive," the German armaments minister Albert Speer later wrote, "meant that the war was over."

• Russell F. Weigley, *Eisenhower's Lieutenants*, 1981. Charles B. MacDonald, *The Battle of the Bulge*, 1984.

—J. Garry Clifford

BULL MOOSE PARTY. *See* Progressive Party of 1912–1924.

BULL RUN, BATTLE OF (1861). The first major battle of the *Civil War occurred on 21 July 1861 at Bull Run (or Manassas), Virginia, some thirty miles from *Washington, D.C. Confederate general P. G. T. Beauregard deployed his force of twenty thousand along a stream called Bull Run. On 18 July, the Confederate general Joseph E. Johnston was ordered to join Beauregard. The Confederates used railroads strategically for the first time in the history of warfare, sending Johnston's twelve thousand men sixty miles from the Shenandoah Valley to reinforce Beauregard's army.

Under intense public pressure to capture Richmond, Union general Irvin McDowell planned to move from Centreville, Virginia, with 30,000 men to turn the Confederate left flank. On the morning of 21 July, the Union forces attacked. During one intense moment of fighting, General Bernard E. Bee rallied his Alabamians by declaring, "There is Jackson standing like a stone wall," giving General Thomas J. Jackson his familiar nickname. At around 4 PM, newly arrived Confederate troops attacked the Federal right flank. The Union units withdrew despite attempts to rally them and retreated in panicked disarray all the way to Washington. The losses in the battle were considered heavy, though they would soon seem insignificant: The confederates suffered 1,982 casualties, the Union 2,896. For Southerners, the victory rebuilt confidence after earlier, dispiriting setbacks, but did not prompt the European recognition they sought. For many Northerners, the humiliating defeat spurred a renewed sense of purpose, and Congress vastly increased the size of the volunteer army.

• William C. Davis, *Battle at Bull Run*, 1977.

—Jonathan M. Berkey

BUNCHE, RALPH J. (1904–1971), political scientist, diplomat, the first *African American to win the Nobel Peace Prize. Born in Detroit, the son of a barber, Bunche graduated summa cum laude from the University of California at Los Angeles in 1927 and went on to earn a Ph.D. in government from Harvard in 1934. His dissertation, "French Administration in Togoland and Dahomey," won an award as the best political science dissertation produced at Harvard that year. Bunche founded the political science department at Howard University, where he taught from 1928 to 1950. His book *A World View of Race* (1936) saw racial conflict as a product of class conflict. He was an influential adviser to the Swedish social scientist Gunnar Myrdal on his classic 1944 study of U.S. race relations, *An *American Dilemma*. Bunche married Ruth Ethel Harris, a Washington, D.C., schoolteacher, in 1930. They had three children.

During *World War II, Bunche served in the *Office of Strategic Services, heading the Africa section of its Research and Analysis Branch. As a State Department specialist in postwar planning (1944–1946), he helped draft the *United Nations (UN) charter. Turning to international diplomacy, Bunche served from 1946 to 1971 as a high-ranking UN official, concentrating on international peacekeeping. He won the Nobel Peace Prize in 1950 for negotiating armistice agreements between Israel and its Arab neighbors.

Bunche's achievements brought many accolades but also controversy. Accused in 1954 of having been a communist in the 1930s, he was publicly cleared after an investigation. He actively supported the early *civil rights movement, marching with Martin Luther *King Jr. in 1965, but in 1967 he criticized King's anti–*Vietnam War position.

• Brian Urquhart, *Ralph Bunche: An American Life*, 1993. Ben Keppel, *The Work of Democracy: Ralph Bunche, Kenneth B. Clark, Lorraine Hansberry and the Cultural Politics of Race*, 1995.

—Ben Keppel

BUNKER HILL, BATTLE OF (1775). The Battle of Bunker Hill, fought on 17 June 1775, helped to dispel the British view that rebellious American colonists would flee when faced with British army professionals. After the engagements at Lexington and Concord, volunteer forces assembled around *Boston, headquarters of the British army. Fearing that the British would fortify strategic locations adjoining the city, Boston's Committee of Safety on 16 June ordered New England troops into the Charlestown peninsula north of Boston, to fortify Bunker Hill. This promontory, overlooking the narrow neck joining the peninsula to the mainland, constituted a protected yet strategic location. Instead of fortifying Bunker Hill, however, the party dug entrenchments on nearby Breed's Hill, farther south and closer to Boston.

When the British command discovered the works, General William Gage insisted on a frontal assault. On the afternoon of the seventeenth, General William Howe led 2,200 Redcoats against a colonial force of equal number. During two consecutive British attacks up Breed's Hill, the Americans held their fire until the last moment. Although the devastating patriot barrages forced the Redcoats to retreat with heavy losses, Howe re-formed his decimated ranks for a third attack. With their ammunition exhausted, the Americans withdrew. However, this British "victory" so depleted the Redcoat ranks that they could not pursue the fleeing colonials. British casualties reached 1,054, while the Americans lost about 440.

Bunker Hill, arguably the bloodiest battle of the *Revolutionary War, showed the courage and tenacity of the citizen-soldier and left a lasting impression on the British command. It also, however, undermined future efforts to build a more professionalized Continental Army based on long-term commitments.

[*See also* Revolution and Constitution, Era of.]

• Richard M. Ketchum, *Decisive Day: The Battle of Bunker Hill*, 1974. W. J. Wood, *Battles of the Revolutionary War, 1775–1781*, 1990.

—Donald R. Lennon

BUREAU OF INDIAN AFFAIRS. The federal agency responsible for dealing with American Indians, the Bureau of Indian Affairs (BIA) was created within the War Department in 1824. In 1832, Congress authorized a commissioner of Indian affairs to direct it. The BIA shifted to the Department of the Interior when that department was established in 1849. The creation of area offices (eventually twelve in number) decentralized the bureau in 1949, and in 1977 an assistant secretary of the interior for Indian affairs replaced the commissioner.

As the nation's relations with Indian tribes grew more complex, the bureau's responsibilities multiplied. The Washington, D.C., office directed the work of Indian superintendents and Indian agents in the field, arranged treaty negotiations, and distributed annuity goods and money mandated by the treaties as payment for land cessions and handled claims of white citizens for depredations by Indians. Later, the BIA organized a national Indian school system, provided health services, and directed forestry and irrigation projects. The BIA held tribal lands in trust and managed the assets of individual Indians held in trust by the federal government.

Although sharply criticized for mismanagement and inefficiency, and for perpetuating Indian dependency by dominating Indians' lives, the BIA survived. Indians denounced it but were unwilling to see it disappear, for it provided a special connection with the federal government. Moreover, under preferential hiring practices, the BIA's staff by the end of the twentieth century was nearly all Indian. Since 1966, every BIA head has been of Indian heritage.

From the mid-twentieth century on, many of the BIA's operations were assumed by other federal departments, by the states, or most important, by the tribal governments themselves. By the 1990s, the BIA, once the controlling force in reservation life, had become a service agency for the increasingly autonomous tribes while still remaining the chief federal agency concerned with federal trust responsibility.

[*See also* Federal Government, Executive Branch: Other Departments; Indian History and Culture: From 1800 to 1900; Indian History and Culture: From 1900 to 1950; Indian History and Culture: Since 1950.]

• Donald J. Berthrong, "Nineteenth-Century United States Government Agencies," and Philleo Nash, "Twentieth-Century United States Government Agencies," both in *Handbook of North American Indians,* ed. William C. Stuyvesant, vol. 4, *History of Indian-White Relations,* ed. Wilcomb E. Washburn, 1988, pp. 255–75.

—Francis Paul Prucha

BURR, AARON (1756–1836), political leader, vice president, conspirator. Best remembered for his duel with Alexander *Hamilton and the failed attempt to create a separate empire in the western United States, Burr remains one of the more enigmatic figures in a generation of revolutionaries and nation-builders. Born in Newark, New Jersey, the son and namesake of a prominent Presbyterian minister and grandson of Jonathan *Edwards, Burr graduated from the College of New Jersey (Princeton) at the age of sixteen and began legal studies. In 1775, he joined the Continental Army, serving with distinction under Benedict *Arnold and George *Washington. After the *Revolutionary War, he practiced law in New York and entered politics, holding office as the state's attorney general and a U.S. senator (1791–1797). His long-term rivalry with Hamilton crystallized in the presidential election of 1800. When Burr tied Thomas *Jefferson in the *electoral college presidential vote, throwing the election into the House of Representatives, Hamilton influenced Federalist congressmen to vote for Jefferson, making Burr vice president. In 1804, during Burr's unsuccessful campaign for governor of New York, Hamilton portrayed him as "a dangerous man, and one who ought not be trusted with the reins of government." This led to a duel at Weehawken, New Jersey, on 11 July 1804, in which Burr killed Hamilton.

In 1805–1806, Burr plotted with General James Wilkinson, Jonathan Dayton, and others to create an empire encompassing the Mississippi Valley, Mexico, and the American West. The nebulous scheme disintegrated, and Burr was indicted for treason. The 1807 trial, presided over by Chief Justice John *Marshall in the U.S. Circuit Court in Richmond, Virginia, ended with Burr's acquittal on the grounds that he had not committed overt treasonable acts. Nevertheless, Burr's political influence faded and he lived in European exile for several years before resuming his New York law practice. His 1833 marriage to a younger widow, Eliza Jumel, soon ended in divorce. His beloved daughter, Theodosia, the child of an earlier marriage, had died in 1813.

[See also Early Republic, Era of the; Federalist Party; Revolution and Constitution, Era of.]

• Thomas Perkins Abernathy, *The Burr Conspiracy,* 1954. Milton Lomask, *Aaron Burr: The Years from Princeton to Vice President, 1756–1805,* 1979.

—Nicholas Casner

BURR CONSPIRACY. *See* Burr, Aaron.

BUSH, GEORGE (1924–), forty-first president of the United States. George Herbert Walker Bush was born in Milton, Massachusetts, to Dorothy Pierce Bush and Prescott Bush Sr. a businessman and later (1953–1963) a U.S. Senator from Connecticut. After graduating from Philips Andover Academy, Bush served as a naval pilot in the Pacific, flying fifty-eight missions during *World War II. On his return, he married Barbara Pierce of Rye, New York, and then attended Yale College, playing on the baseball team and graduating in 1948.

Rejecting a career on Wall Street (where his father was a partner in the brokerage firm of Brown Brothers Harriman), Bush moved to West Texas, where he formed a successful oil-exploration company before moving to Houston and entering politics. Running as a Republican, he campaigned unsuccessfuly to unseat incumbent Senator Ralph Yarborough in 1964. Two years later, Bush was elected to the U.S. House of Representatives from Texas's Seventh District. After losing another Senate race to Democrat Lloyd Bentsen in 1970, Bush served as the U.S. Ambassador to the *United Nations during the Richard M. *Nixon administration, and then as chair of the Republican National Committee during the *Watergate scandals and Nixon's resignation in August 1974.

Under President Gerald Ford, Bush headed the U.S. Liaison Office in Beijing, China, before returning to Washington to run the *Central Intelligence Agency (CIA). As CIA director, Bush helped to revive the agency's morale, which had been damaged by embarrassing exposés of its covert operations. Leaving the CIA in 1977 when Democrat Jimmy *Carter became president, Bush launched his campaign for the White House. After unsuccessfully contesting Ronald *Reagan for the Republican presidential nomination in 1980, Bush accepted the vice-presidential slot. Following the landslide Republican victory that fall, Bush served President Reagan loyally and participated in the secret arms-for-hostages trade with the Islamic fundamentalist government of Iran. Attempting to minimize damage to his political career, Bush alleged that he had been "out of the loop" during the most intense dealings of the so-called *Iran-Contra affair.

Bush won the presidency in 1988 by defeating his Democratic opponent, Governor Michael Dukakis of Massachusetts, with a sweep of forty states and 53.4 percent of the popular vote. Facing Democratic majorities in both houses of Congress, the Bush administration achieved its most notable successes in foreign affairs, the area of Bush's primary interest and preparation. Bush worked skillfully with President Mikhail Gorbachev during the collapse of the Soviet Union, and he responded forcefully to Iraq's invasion of Kuwait in August 1990 by organizing economic and military resistance through the United Nations and the Arab League. In early 1991, a U.S.-led coalition ejected Saddam Hussein's forces from Kuwait, thereby preserving a favorable balance of power in the oil-rich Persian Gulf. Bush also promoted U.S. interests in Central America by overseeing an end to Sandinista control in Nicaragua following free elections, and by forcibly removing dictator Manuel Noriega from power in Panama and extradicting him to the United States to face drug-smuggling charges.

The Bush domestic record proved less impressive. The president's few achievements included the *Americans with Disabilities Act (1990) and a bipartisan five-year budget agreement (1991) that attempted to tame the spiraling federal deficits of the 1980s. The budget agreement forced Bush to renounce his "Read my lips: No new taxes" pledge. That, combined with a lingering economic downturn, contributed to his reelection defeat in 1992. A favorable public opinion rating of 89 percent reached during of the Persian Gulf crisis could not be sustained, as Bush faced the additional complication of Texas billionaire H. Ross Perot's independent candidacy and the skillful campaigning of his Democratic opponent, Governor Bill *Clinton of Arkansas. The distribution of the popular vote—Clinton 43 percent, Bush 38 percent, Perot 18 percent—demonstrated the significance of the third-party candidate in the final outcome.

Highly popular at its peak, George Bush's administration made an effective transition to what Bush called "a new world order," and, despite the prolonged recession, contributed to long-term stability at home.

Of the Bushes' five surviving children, two entered politics. John E. ("Jeb") Bush (1953–) won the Florida governorship in 1998, while George W. Bush (1946–) was elected Texas governor in 1994 and reelected in 1998. In 2000, in a very close and disputed election, he defeated Democrat Al Gore to win the presidency with running mate Dick Cheney, resulting in the first father-son presidential succession since John *Adams and John Quincy *Adams.

[*See also* Cold War; Foreign Relations: U.S. Relations with Latin America; Persian Gulf War; Post–Cold War Era.]

• David Mervin, *George Bush and the Guardianship Presidency*, 1994. Herbert S. Parmet, *George Bush: The Life of a Lone Star Yankee*, 1997. George W. Bush and Brent Scowcroft, *A World Transformed*, 1998.

—Herbert S. Parmet

BUSH, VANNEVAR (1890–1974), inventor, engineer, wartime administrator. Armed with a dual Harvard–Massachusetts Institute of Technology (MIT) doctorate in *mathematics and electrical *engineering, Bush, a native of Everett, Massachusetts, became a pioneering designer of analog *computers as a professor of engineering (and later dean) at MIT from 1919 to 1938. The differential analyzer (1928), a mechanical array of precisely machined gears, cams, and shafts capable of solving previously unsolvable differential equations of interest to the *electrical industry and researchers in many specialized fields, brought Bush public attention as the inventor of a "mechanical brain."

Arriving in Washington, D.C., in January 1939 as president of the Carnegie Institution (1939–1953) and chair of the National Advisory Committee for Aeronautics, Bush soon began the work of organizing American science for the coming war. In June 1940, with President Franklin Delano *Roosevelt's approval, he established the National Defense Research Committee (NDRC) to mobilize researchers. In June 1941, the NDRC became part of a new and larger organization, the Office of Scientific Research and Development (OSRD), also led by Bush. Carving out a space between the *military, which would use the new weapons developed under OSRD contract in academic and industrial *research laboratories, and the corporations building these weapons, Bush helped facilitate a profound transformation in military attitudes. When *World War II began, the U.S. armed services were bastions of technological conservatism; by war's end they were technological enthusiasts. Among the weapons Bush championed were radar and the atomic bomb.

In *Science—the Endless Frontier* (1945), an OSRD report to Roosevelt articulating the federal government's duty to fund basic research in American universities, Bush called for a new federal agency, a National Research Foundation. In 1950, after years of debate, President Harry S. *Truman established the *National Science Foundation (NSF). The NSF, however, was not the organization envisioned in Bush's report. Indeed, Bush had by then concluded that the armed services had taken over American science; his *Modern Arms and Free Men* (1949) called on the nation's political leaders to reassert control of the military. By the time of his death, Bush had become a severe critic of the very world of government-science relations he had helped bring into existence.

[*See also* Cold War; Education: Rise of the University; Education: Education in Contemporary America; Nuclear Weapons; Science: Since 1945; Technology.]

• Larry Owens, "Vannevar Bush and the Differential Analyzer: The Text and Context of an Early Computer," *Technology and Culture* 27 (1986): 63–95. G. Pascal Zachary, *Endless Frontier: Vannevar Bush, Engineer of the American Century*, 1977.

—Michael A. Dennis

BUSINESS. Modern capitalist economic progress began during the seventeenth and eighteenth centuries, just when the thirteen colonies that would form the United States were being settled. Such corporate enterprises as the Massachusetts Bay Company, the Virginia Company of London, and the Royal African Company even brought immigrants to the New World. This latter corporation's commerce in human beings constituted only a small fraction of the transatlantic slave trade, but it symbolized the extent to which businesspeople on both sides of the Atlantic were willing to go to make a profit. Most white immigrants to America during the eighteenth and early nineteenth centuries came as indentured servants. In this business transaction, the would-be immigrant exchanged three to seven years of service for passage to a land of enhanced opportunity. Mostly self-selected risk takers, indentured servants embraced an entrepreneurial culture once their terms of servitude ended.

Statistical Gauges of Business Success. The modern capitalist era marked a profound historical discontinuity. For the 8,000 years of recorded human experience up to around 1700, most people lived on the edge of survival. Their incomes grew slowly, if at all. But beginning the First Industrial Revolution in about 1760, business growth accelerated. Between 1820 and 2000, per-capita incomes in the United States doubled every forty-two years—a phenomenal business achievement and "miracle" of economic growth.

Only a few major countries attained such growth, and all were organized around capitalist economies. Of the twenty-five nations classified as "high-income" countries by the early twenty-first century, the United States had long occupied a special position. Its economy was the world's largest—double that of the runner up, Japan. The per-capita purchasing power of Americans ranked first among major countries. The volume of U.S. industrial production also ranked first, as it had since the 1880s. So too, during much of this period, had its *productivity (value of output per hour of work) in manufacturing, distribution, services, construction, *mining, and most other business activities.

The Ongoing Role of Immigrants. People of many nationalities and ethnic groups made fundamental contributions to American business throughout the nation's history. The early Treasury secretaries Alexander *Hamilton (from the West Indies) and Albert *Gallatin (from Switzerland) played vital roles in shaping a national economy hospitable to entrepreneurship. Immigrant businessmen formed companies that became internationally leading firms. In 1837, for example, William Procter, a candlemaker from England, and James Gamble, a soap boiler from Ireland, founded Procter and Gamble, which became the world's largest consumer-products company. John Jacob *Astor, a poor immigrant from Germany, amassed a vast fortune in the *fur trade, transoceanic commerce, and *New York City real estate. Daniel McCallum (Scotland), general superintendent of the New York and Erie Railroad, published the earliest known treatise on business administration in 1855. In the 1870s, while working for the Louisville and Nashville Railroad, Albert Fink (Germany) devised such an ingenious method of separating fixed costs from variable costs (a distinction vital in accounting and business planning) that he later became known as the "Father of Railway Economics." Andrew *Carnegie, who emigrated from Scotland, became the world's greatest steel magnate.

Twentieth-century immigrants continued to make vital contributions to American business. David *Sarnoff, born in a Russian shtetl, emigrated to the United States as a boy.

Without formal education beyond the eighth grade, he became the architect and chief executive officer of the Radio Corporation of America (RCA), a leader in *radio network broadcasting (NBC, 1926) and *television research and development. Other Jewish immigrants from Eastern Europe, such as Samuel Goldwyn (Poland) and Louis B. Mayer (Russia), built movie studios that made Hollywood the world's entertainment capital.

During the 1970s, An Wang (China) innovated in producing mini-computers and office workstations. In the 1980s, Roberto Gouizeta (Cuba) became chief executive officer (CEO) of the Coca-Cola Company and led it to unprecedented growth. In the 1990s, Alex Trotman (Scotland) served as CEO of the Ford Motor Company and presided over its "globalization."

Just as the "American" business achievement drew freely on the abilities of diverse immigrants, so did business-related American *science and *technology. In the 1790s, during the First Industrial Revolution, Samuel Slater (England) brought the power loom to the budding American *textile industry. The du Pont family (France) founded a small gunpowder firm in 1802 that eventually became the world's leading chemical company. In the early twentieth century, Charles Steinmetz (Germany), the resident inventive genius at General Electric, led that company's move into high-tech products.

In the 1930s and 1940s, a cadre of brilliant physicists, chemists, and mathematicians fleeing Nazi Europe, including as Albert *Einstein (Germany), Enrico *Fermi (Italy), Niels Bohr (Denmark), Hans Bethe (Germany), and John *von Neumann (Hungary), advanced the frontiers of American *science. Augmenting this distinguished group were immigrant German rocket scientists who had worked for the Nazi regime, the best-known of whom was Werner von Braun. Much of late-twentieth-century American leadership electronics, nuclear, and aerospace derived from the scientific and entrepreneurial talents of immigrants. Andrew Grove (Hungary), a key figure in the rise of Intel Corporation, played such a key role in the development of microprocessors that *Time* magazines named him its "Person of the Year" for 1997. Intel and hundreds of other information-technology firms, including Hewlett-Packard, Apple Computer, Sun Microsystems, Oracle, and Cisco Systems, set up their headquarters in California's Silicon Valley, southeast of *San Francisco. Collectively, these companies spearheaded American economic growth at the turn of the twenty-first century—and became a powerful magnet for still another flood of immigrant talent, notably from East Asia and South Asia.

Attitudes and Ideologies. From the start, many American businesspeople were unabashedly ambitious about increasing their fortunes. Benjamin *Franklin wrote in his *Autobiography* that as a young *Philadelphia printer he had taken care "not only to be in reality industrious and frugal but to avoid all appearances to the contrary." In *The Protestant Ethic and the Spirit of Capitalism* (1904–1905), the German sociologist Max Weber declared that Franklin's sentiments expressed "above all the idea of a duty of the individual toward the increase of his capital, which is assumed as an end in itself." In earlier times, Weber added, that this new way of thinking, which "called forth the applause of a whole [American] people, would . . . have been proscribed as the lowest sort of avarice and as an attitude entirely lacking in self-respect."

Yet even in the *Colonial and Early National Eras, a large proportion of Americans fervently embraced the opportunities afforded by the North American continent's rich resources. They also benefited from a pro-business legal system inherited from the British, particularly rules protecting property rights. Taking the sanctity of contracts almost for granted, they started thousands of proprietorships and partnerships in cities along the eastern seaboard: *Boston, Newport, New York, Philadelphia, Baltimore, and Charleston. Moving westward, they not only established farms, but also opened innumerable small businesses.

Early nineteenth-century Americans enacted laws to promote this business growth, such as general incorporation laws, very low tax rates, and liberal bankruptcy proceedings. Relying on this latter advantage, which shifted part of the risk of doing business from entrepreneurs to creditors, Americans showed themselves singularly willing to traffic in personal and business credit. This trait, fully evident by the mid-nineteenth century, has remained a hallmark of the nation's business and *consumer culture. By 2000, business and consumer debt stood at several trillion dollars each, and Americans possessed well over a billion credit cards.

Throughout the nation's history, most of the American electorate endorsed the business system. They took political action to restrain it less frequently than did voters in other democratic capitalist countries, not to mention socialist ones. They tolerated the gyrations of the *business cycle more willingly, including dozens of recessions and several deep economic *depressions. The worst of all business downturns, the worldwide Great Depression of the 1930s, hit the United States harder than almost any other nation, but resulted in less political turmoil than occurred in Germany, Japan, Britain, France, Italy, and many other countries.

The individualistic *laissez-faire ideology embraced by most Americans promoted a high degree of entrepreneurial effort and released an immense amount of business energy. But the social and environmental cost of business success sometimes proved woefully high. Up until the *New Deal Era of the 1930s, and in many ways beyond that, business exploited children, women, minorities, and laborers of all types. The United States consistently had a lower percentage of unionized workers than did comparable countries. Even in the early twenty-first century, American business and its political allies—in contrast to Great Britain, France, Germany, and Japan—did a relatively ineffectual job of protecting those who found it hard to compete within the system. By 2000, the gap between rich and poor had become greater in the United States than in any other developed country, reversing both a national commitment to *equality and a sixty-year statistical trend. Some CEOs of large American firms were receiving 400 times the earnings of the lowest-paid members of their own companies. This multiple far exceeded the averages in Europe or Japan, and was ten times the rate in the United States itself as recently as 1975.

African Americans and Women. The extraordinary mixture of cultures and nationalities resulting from mass *immigration became the defining trait of the American business system. The 1900 census revealed that a majority of the nation's seventy-six million people were either nonwhite, immigrants, or second-generation Americans. Despite the record of economic exploitation, one of the signal triumphs of American society and its business system was to absorb the best contributions of a myriad of cultures without disintegrating under the stress of racial and ethnic strife. The great exception, of course, was the *Civil War. But while that conflict ended *slavery and gave millions of *African Americans a chance to participate in the business opportunities available to their fellow citizens, progress proved slow for a century after emancipation. Open racism prevailed in business up until the post–*World War II *civil rights movement and the landmark voting rights and public-accommodation laws enacted during the 1960s. Equality in employment opportunity was the last barrier to fall, and in mainstream American business it did not begin to come down until about the 1970s. Despite significant progress, latent racism continued to plague American business into the twenty-first century.

Discrimination also hampered most American women who attempted business careers. In 1900, females comprised only 4.5 percent of all U.S. managers, proprietors, and other business officials, and by 1940 only 11 percent. But women's business opportunities grew markedly after 1970, epitomized by the careers of Estée Lauder, Mary Kay Ash, Oprah Winfrey, Margaret Whitman, and other entrepreneurs. By 2000, about 40 percent of all new firms were being started by women, and women had made extraordinary gains in business-related professions such as law and accounting. In big business, however, the "glass ceiling" remained formidable. In 2000, only three of America's 500 largest firms had female chief executive officers, and only two were headed by African Americans.

Even so, entrepreneurial activity by African American, Asian, and Hispanic businesspeople—both men and women—has historically been far greater than is commonly recognized. Devoting their energies to enterprises often overlooked by historians who have tended to focus on large firms, members of these groups operated service businesses such as insurance companies, small stores, dressmaking and millinery boutiques, barber and beauty salons, and shoe repair shops, catering primarily to members of their own ethnic or gendered clienteles.

The First Industrial Revolution. Scholars disagree over whether the term "industrial revolution" is applicable to business. Critics point out that economic growth seldom occurs in tumultuous spurts analogous to violent political upheavals. Instead, business typically evolves through the steady accretion and dissemination of small and medium-sized gains in technology and organizational design.

Yet, breakthroughs such as the *telegraph, *railroad, electric motor, internal combustion engine, *computer, polymerization of chemicals, and the mapping of the human genome do tend to accelerate business growth. And even in normal times, business never stands still. Entrepreneurial energies and competitive pressures promote what the economist Joseph Schumpeter aptly termed a "perennial gale of creative destruction." A constant succession of new products, new firms, and new forms of business organizations are forever sweeping away old ones. So the idea of industrial revolutions, though flawed, does offer a useful framework for understanding the evolution of American business.

During the First Industrial Revolution, from about 1760 to 1840, the new roads and canals markedly improved American business productivity. In a few industries, factories first appeared, *steam power began to replace water and animal power, and work was regulated by the clock rather than by the sun and seasons. Machine-based *mass production was adopted for some products, most notably cotton textiles, and prices of these products dropped precipitously.

Most businesses remained small in these years, employing at most a few hundred workers and never more than a thousand. An artisanal and mercantile economy predominated, as opposed to a full-fledged industrial one. Thousands of modest proprietorships and partnerships—grocers, blacksmiths, fabric merchants, printers, tailors, dressmakers, milliners—sold specialized goods. Most remained local, and almost no products were branded. Kinship and religious affiliations, by enforcing commercial commitments through non-economic sanctions, figured significantly in financing and maintaining business relationships, because they helped to enforce commerical commitments through non-economic sanctions. The same had been true in colonial times for *New England's Puritan merchants and for southern planters marketing their products.

The largest companies of the First Industrial Revolution, measured by their market value, were *banking, *insurance, and canals. Some of these firms survived into the twenty-first century as big businesses, such as Citigroup, Fleet Financial Group, and Cigna Corporation (insurance). Through special acts passed by state legislatures, a few hundred such firms operated as corporations. (To put this early nineteenth-century figure in perspective, tens of thousands of corporations were doing business by 1900, and 4.5 million by 2000.) Still, most American enterprises have always been small proprietorships or partnerships, of which there were more than 15 million in 2000.

The Second Industrial Revolution. The corporate form accelerated the progress of business during this crucial era, roughly 1850–1950. Practically all states stopped requiring special acts of incorporation and instead passed general laws permitting groups to incorporate for any legitimate business purpose. Some states vied with each other in offering generous terms. This "charter mongering" led to the incorporation of many prominent firms' headquarters in New Jersey and Delaware, each of which offered low fees for incorporation and permitted holding companies to own subsidiary corporations.

The advantages of corporations over proprietorships and partnerships included limited liability, easier financing, and institutional permanence. Most important, corporations afforded far more efficient means of governance, through stockholder oversight and hierarchical management structures based on merit rather than family connection or social standing.

The 1880s proved an especially portentous decade for the development of American business. As the commercialization of *electricity, the *telephone, and the internal combustion engine began in earnest, entrepreneurs founded scores of important new companies. Among the firms started in this decade (some with different names originally) one finds Scott Paper, the Times Mirror Company, Kroger, Dresser Industries, Consolidated Edison, Eastman Kodak, Chiquita Brands, Honeywell, Johnson and Johnson, Tyco International, Avon Products, Coca-Cola, Sears Roebuck, Sun Oil, Union Carbide, Unisys, Upjohn, US West, Hershey Foods, Westinghouse, Merck, Alcoa, Abbott Laboratories, Amoco, Pennzoil, and Berkshire Hathaway.

During the Second Industrial Revolution, the telegraph and then the telephone made instantaneous communication possible on a broad scale. Between 1840 and 1890, railroad firms laid down more than 200,000 miles of new tracks. Around 1900, the automobile, truck, and airplane all materialized in a remarkably brief time. Both the Ford Motor Company and General Motors were founded during the first decade of the new century; Boeing in 1916; and Chrysler, Lockheed, Douglas Aircraft, Yellow Freight, Delta Airlines, and United Airlines during the 1920s.

Meanwhile, alongside mass production, most of the modern institutions of *mass marketing—*department stores, franchised outlets, catalogue stores, and chain retailers—appeared during this era as well. Numerous companies, including many of those listed above, "integrated vertically"—that is, they both produced and marketed goods. In some cases they also procured raw materials and conducted research and development in-house.

This multifunctional approach gave rise to the "multidivisional structure" in the governance of firms, as several large corporations began to organize their divisions along product lines rather than functional ones, giving bottom-line responsibility to division heads who oversaw both the production and marketing of particular products. The older functional system, under which sets of executives handled production, sales, and purchasing of all items across the company, made it difficult to pinpoint responsibility when problems arose. The new multidivisional system, by contrast, carved giant companies into smaller segments categorized by individual products, and gave aspiring managers a clear path up the corporate ladder. Created in the early 1920s almost simultaneously by Alfred P. *Sloan Jr. at General Motors and by several DuPont executives, the multidivisional structure proved to be the most influential organizational innovation of the twentieth century. Companies in the United States and worldwide emulated it, particularly after World War II, when many firms began offering different lines of products.

Although the vast majority of Second Industrial Revolution businesses remained small or medium-sized, a few became giants. The Pennsylvania Railroad employed more than 100,000 people by the 1890s, General Motors several hundred thousand by the 1940s, and the American Telephone and Telegraph Company about one million before its breakup under antitrust pressures during the 1980s. Some companies (Singer Sewing Machines, H. J. Heinz, Ford Motor Company) grew large through internal expansion. Others (United States Steel, International Harvester, General Electric) resulted from major mergers. Prominent financiers such as the investment banker J. P. *Morgan organized several large combinations. But in the United States during the Second Industrial Revolution, finance proved less important as a source of business innovation than in other major economies, notably those of Germany and Japan.

Most companies that became "big businesses" shared certain common characteristics, all of which differed from conventional business practices during the First Industrial Revolution. They tended to be capital-intensive, and vertically integrated, and to serve national (and sometimes international) mass markets with standardized, machine-manufactured products. They typically generated enormous cash flows and financed their operations through retained earnings more than by issuing stocks and bonds. These Second Industrial Revolution firms employed large staffs of professional managers organized in formal hierarchies.

The Third Industrial Revolution: 1950s and Beyond. In this fertile business era, the percentage of jobs in the service sector came to exceed the total in manufacturing, mining, construction, and *agriculture combined. Beginning in the 1980s, many corporations downsized their staffs, flattened their hierarchies, and outsourced their non-core functions. These steps derived from intensified competition both domestically and from overseas challengers such as Japanese automobile and consumer electronics companies. A third trend in business growth, and in the long run the most important, was the driving force of science and technology. This was not an altogether new phenomenon, of course. The steam engine had symbolized the First Industrial Revolution and the electric motor and internal combustion engine the Second. But the Third Industrial Revolution brought unparalleled levels of scientific knowledge readily applicable to business: jet engines, rocket power, *nuclear power, satellite communications, lasers, computer hardware and software, robotics, and a dazzling array of new chemicals based on polymer science and of pharmaceuticals based on genetic research and development.

A simple listing of representative new companies and their founding dates illustrates the nature of the Third Industrial Revolution. Note the preponderance of service firms, high-tech companies, and marketers of international scope. In the 1940s, Wal-Mart, Mattel, Toys "Я" Us, *McDonald's, and Circuit City; in the 1950s, Eckerd Drugs, Caldor, and Service Merchandise; in the 1960s, MCI Communications, Turner Broadcasting, Nike, Intel, The Gap, The Limited, and Columbia HCA Healthcare; in the 1970s, Federal Express, Microsoft, Apple Computer, and Home Depot; in the 1980s, Compaq, Sun Microsystems, Dell Computer, and Gateway; in the 1990s, an explosion of Internet-based firms such as eBay and amazon.com.

The "Information Age" component of the Third Industrial Revolution seemed to peak at the turn of the twenty-first century, with its multitudinous startups of "dot.com" and *biotechnology businesses. The term "IPO" (initial public offering of a company's common stock) entered the vernacular. As a means of measuring the value and prospects of firms and the health of the national economy, the NASDAQ Composite Index, consisting mostly of high-tech stocks, began to rival the venerable Dow Jones Industrial Average, which originated in 1884 for railroads and 1897 for industrial corporations. In several high-tech industries, venture *capitalism displaced traditional investment banking as the quickest route to personal fortunes for both founding entrepreneurs and their financial backers.

As firms that grew out of the Second and Third Industrial Revolutions internationalized their operations and moved much of their manufacturing to offshore sources of inexpensive labor, the number of well-paid jobs in American manufacturing declined. Simultaneously, franchised service operations such as McDonald's, Kinko's copy centers, and 7-Eleven convenience stores proliferated. These companies typically paid low initial wages, but they offered masses of immigrants first-time jobs and numerous students entry into the workforce as part-time employees. They also provided entrepreneurial opportunities for owner-operator franchisees, of which there were nearly one million by the early twenty-first century.

How all of these changes would ultimately turn out remained unknowable. But throughout its history, the American business system had exhibited a remarkable resilience and adaptability. So it seemed likely that Schumpeter's "perennial gale of creative destruction" would remain a fitting metaphor for its future course.

[*See also* Advertising; Airplanes and Air Transport; Antitrust Legislation; Automotive Industry; Business Roundtable; Canals and Waterways; Chemical Industry; Child Labor; Cotton Industry; du Pont, Pierre; Economic Regulation; Electrical Industry; Factory System; Foreign Trade, U.S.; Human Genome Project; Indentured Servitude; Industrialization; Industrial Diseases and Hazards; Industrial Relations; Iron and Steel Industry; Labor Markets; Labor Movements; Multinational Enterprises; Pharmaceutical Industry; Social Darwinism; Petroleum Industry; Roads and Turnpikes, Early; Rockefeller, John D.; Stock Market; Stock Market Crash of 1929; Strikes and Industrial Conflict; Tobacco Industry; Unemployment; Women in the Labor Force.]

• Bernard Bailyn, *The New England Merchants in the Seventeenth Century,* 1955. Jonathan R. T. Hughes, *The Vital Few: American Economic Progress and Its Protagonists,* 1965. Alfred D. Chandler Jr., *The Visible Hand: The Managerial Revolution in American Business,* 1977. David A. Hounshell, *From the American System to Mass Production, 1800–1932: The Development of Manufacturing Technology in the United States,* 1984. Stuart Bruchey, *Enterprise: The Dynamic Economy of a Free People,* 1990. Richard S. Tedlow, *New and Improved: The Story of Mass Marketing in America,* 1990. Mansel G. Blackford, *A History of Small Business in American Life,* 1991. Naomi R. Lamoreaux, *Insider Lending: Banks, Personal Connections, and Economic Development in Industrial New England,* 1994. Philip Scranton, *Endless Novelty: Specialty Production and American Industrialization, 1865–1925,* 1997. Angel Kwolek-Folland, *Incorporating Women: A History of Women and Business in the United States,* 1998. Juliet E. K. Walker, *The History of Black Business in America: Capitalism, Race, Entrepreneurship,* 1998. Thomas K. McCraw, *American Business, 1920–2000: How It Worked,* 2000.

—Thomas K. McCraw

BUSINESS CYCLE. As far back as reliable statistics for the American economy exist, periods of expanding output and employment have alternated with periods when output and employment have contracted. This pattern has also characterized the economies of the other industrial nations. Although such fluctuating "cycles" have been irregular in amplitude and duration, the word "cycle" does emphasize their recurring nature.

Systematic research into the U.S. business cycle dates to the early and mid-twentieth century work of Wesley C. Mitchell, Arthur F. Burns, and others associated with the National Bureau of Economic Research (NBER), a private organization whose widely used dating of business cycle peaks and troughs has been accepted by the U.S. Department of Commerce. The NBER considers a recession to have occurred when output, employment, and trade have declined for at least six months.

A particularly severe recession has been termed a depression, although no formal definition of depression exists.

Because of the paucity of data for earlier periods, the NBER began its business-cycle chronology with the recession that followed the cyclical peak of December 1854. Significant economic downturns clearly occurred before the 1850s, however. Major recessions, perhaps severe enough to be called depressions, took place in 1819 and 1837. The close linkages between the U.S. and foreign economies was evident in these early contractions. The 1819 downturn followed a decline in U.S. exports, particularly cotton. The protracted downturn that began in 1837 was set off when the Bank of England tightened credit. Because statistics on prices for these years are more readily available than data on production and employment, some economic historians have argued that the pre–*Civil War cycles mainly affected prices and wages and not the real productive economy. Contemporary accounts, however, establish that noticeable increases in *unemployment occurred in urban areas during contractions; soup kitchens for the jobless, for example, appeared as early as 1819.

In the *Gilded Age, major recessions came during the 1870s, 1880s, and 1890s. The downturn that began with the cyclical peak of January 1893 was particularly severe, causing high unemployment through the remainder of the decade. The pace of industrialization exposed more workers to unemployment during these downturns. During the 1890s' depression, unemployment probably peaked at well above 10 percent of the labor force and may have exceeded 15 percent. As the fraction of the workforce experiencing unemployment during business-cycle contractions increased, so did agitation for reform. The most visible manifestation of the pressure for government action during these years was the march of the unemployed on *Washington, D.C., in 1894, led by Jacob Coxey of Ohio and popularly known as Coxey's Army. Local governments and private agencies, however, provided the bulk of assistance to the unemployed during the nineteenth century by expanding existing programs of poor relief and sometimes creating public-works programs.

Most recessions in the post–Civil War period also brought financial panics during which banks, unable to satisfy their depositors' demands, suspended withdrawals, thereby exacerbating the crisis. For this reason, after a particularly severe panic and recession in 1907, influential figures demanded reform of the banking system. The 1913 *Federal Reserve Act was designed to moderate recessions by providing a lender of last resort to banks experiencing liquidity problems. Although a brief but severe recession occurred in 1920–1921, economists attributed it to demobilization problems following *World War I. Most observers were thus surprised by the length and severity of the downturn that began in 1929.

According to the NBER, the Great Depression of the 1930s began with the cyclical peak of August 1929 and reached its trough in March 1933, at which point the unemployment rate probably exceeded 25 percent. Unemployment remained high until 1941, when the reinstatement of the military draft and increased military spending stimulated the economy and expanded job opportunities. Economists continue to debate the causes of the Great Depression, some blaming the 1929 *stock market crash, others the Smoot-Hawley Tariff of 1930, and still others the series of bank panics during 1930–1933. President Franklin Delano *Roosevelt's New Deal (building in some respects on initiatives dating to the Herbert *Hoover administration) represented the first significant attempt by the federal government to ameliorate the impact of the business cycle.

Although many public figures and scholars feared that depression would return after *World War II, the postwar business cycle proved relatively mild. The long expansion during the 1960s led many to declare the business cycle "dead," but severe recessions in 1974–1975 and 1981–1982 revived concern about macroeconomic stability. Subsequently, however, the long expansion of the 1990s once more stimulated discussion about whether business cycles were inevitable in modern economic life.

Many explanations for the business cycle have been advanced. In earlier agricultural economies, some observers linked contractions to sunspots, which occur in fairly regular cycles. In the nineteenth century, Karl Marx proposed that cycles resulted from the tendency of capital accumulation to cause an overproduction of goods relative to the purchasing power of the working class. The British economist John Maynard Keynes provided the most influential explanation. In *The General Theory of Employment, Interest, and Money* (1936), Keynes attributed business cycles to fluctuations in total spending or aggregate demand. Controversy long raged between supporters of Keynes's theory and proponents of its main rival, *monetarism or the neo-quantity theory of money. Monetarists, led by Milton Friedman (1912–) of the University of Chicago, ascribed business cycles to fluctuations in the money stock. Toward the end of the twentieth century, many economists embraced a theory that saw the business cycle as an expression of the rational response of workers and firms to the economic impact of underlying technological transformations.

[*See also* Agriculture; Antitrust Legislation; Banking and Finance; Business; Capitalism; Cotton Industry; Depressions, Economic; Economic Development; Economic Regulation; Employment Act of 1946; Foreign Trade, U.S.; Keynesianism; Mass Production; Monetary Policy, Federal; Multinational Enterprises; New Deal Era, The; Stock Market; Tariffs.]

• Arthur F. Burns and Wesley C. Mitchell, *Measuring Business Cycles*, National Bureau of Economic Research, Studies in Business Cycles, No. 2, 1946. Milton Friedman and Anna Jacobson Schwartz, *A Monetary History of the United States, 1867–1960*, 1963. David Glasner, ed. *Business Cycles and Depressions: An Encyclopedia*, 1997. Michael D. Bordo, Claudia Goldin, and Eugene N. White, eds., *The Defining Moment: The Great Depression and the American Economy in the Twentieth Century*, 1998.

—Anthony P. O'Brien

BUSINESS ROUNDTABLE. The Business Roundtable, an elite lobbying and advisory organization of chief executive officers (CEOs) from two hundred of the nation's largest business enterprises, was established in 1972 in response to a surge of regulatory legislation that began in the mid-1960s. New laws that protected the environment, affected consumer goods, regulated energy use, secured worker safety and health, and guaranteed equal employment opportunity, combined to increase production costs and diminish business profits. Big business reacted aggressively to defend its interests.

During the 1975–1985 decade of relatively slow economic growth, income polarization, intense foreign competition, divisive social issues, and rising *conservatism, the roundtable's influence grew steadily. Its initial victories, however, were defensive. The roundtable defeated the AFL-CIO's efforts to reform federal labor law and Ralph *Nader's campaign to create a Consumer Protection Agency. Subsequently, roundtable committees learned to influence the national political agenda and to achieve legislative and administrative victories that climaxed in multibillion-dollar corporate tax reductions and selective business deregulation during and after the presidency of Ronald *Reagan. By the 1980s and 1990s, roundtable representatives regularly participated in broad coalitions of corporate and noncorporate groups to affect legislation in such diverse areas as *civil rights, liability law reform, and health-care cost reduction. The roundtable proved especially effective at lobbying legislators representing congressional districts and states where its corporate members had large investments and employee payrolls.

Accommodating itself to the party in power, the roundtable rarely resorted to open confrontation. More often than not, it succeeded in convincing the government to promote the interests of big business in an increasingly global economy in which high-technology development and subsidized trade increased corporate profits. Tax incentives, export promotion programs, federally insured overseas investment, and the privatization of formerly public services all improved corporate balance sheets. Hence, most big business executives saw federal power as a permanent presence in the economic marketplace and utilized the roundtable to defend their interests in Washington.

[*See also* Business; Corporatism; Economic Regulation; Keynesianism; Multinational Enterprises; National Association of Manufacturers; National Industrial Conference Board; Taxation.]

• Sar A. Levitan and Martha J. Cooper, *Business Lobbies: The Public Good and the Bottom Line,* 1984. Kim McQuaid, *Uneasy Partners: Big Business in American Politics, 1945–1990,* 1994, esp. pp. 125–185.

—Kim McQuaid

BYRD, WILLIAM, II (1674–1744), Virginia landowner, political leader, writer, diarist. Born in Henrico County, Virginia, Byrd was sent to Felsted School in England at age seven. He mastered several languages, studied law, and was admitted to the bar and even to the Royal Society, England's premier scientific organization, by age twenty-two. Between 1692 and 1705, and again from 1714 to 1726, he was often in London as Virginia's agent on mercantile and political issues. In 1704, Byrd inherited the estate Westover on the James River, with other plantations and many slaves. Here he and Lucy Parke Byrd shared an affectionate but often tempestuous marriage from 1706 until Lucy's death in 1716. In 1724, he married Maria Taylor. He built an elegant brick manor house; planned the city of Richmond on a part of his land; and won respect as a gentleman tobacco planter and political leader, serving in Virginia's House of Burgesses and Council of State. At his death he owned more than 100,000 acres and one of America's two largest private libraries.

A lifelong author, Byrd wrote two posthumously published accounts of a 1728 expedition to establish the North Carolina–Virginia line: the entertaining *Secret History of the Line* (1929), composed in cipher with satiric names for all characters, and the longer, less ribald *History of the Dividing Line* (1841), sometimes called a Virginia "epic." Besides poems, travel narratives, natural history, and extensive correspondence, Byrd's most intriguing literary product is his cipher-encoded secret diary, which survives for 1709–1712, 1717–1721 ("the London Diary"), and 1739–1741. Although repetitive and formulaic, it reveals much about Byrd and about gentry life in England and colonial Virginia.

[*See also* Colonial Era; Literature: Colonial Era; Slavery: Development and Expansion of Slavery; Tobacco Industry.]

• Pierre Marambaud, *William Byrd of Westover, 1674–1744,* 1971. Kenneth A. Lockridge, *The Diary, and Life, of William Byrd II of Virginia, 1674–1744,* 1987.

—Sargent Bush

C

CALDER, ALEXANDER (1898–1976), sculptor, painter, illustrator, printmaker, designer. Born in *Philadelphia into an artistic family, Calder had his own cellar workshop by age eight. In 1919 he graduated from Stevens Institute of Technology in Hoboken, New Jersey, with a mechanical engineering degree. After studying painting under John Sloan and Guy Pène du Bois at the Art Students League of New York (1923–1925), Calder went to Europe in 1926, where he was warmly received by the avant-garde. In Paris he began constructing miniature "toys" with movable parts that developed into the legendary *Cirque Calder* (1926–1932), a performance diorama admired by Calder's peers and patrons for its magical artist-controlled interactive shows.

After visiting Piet Mondrian's studio in 1930, Calder committed himself to a constructivist-surrealist form of abstraction. In 1931 he produced motorized and manual kinetic sculptures that Marcel Duchamp famously called "mobiles." Calder balanced diverse elements in innovative works that enabled separate and multiple movements controlled by random air currents. In these works, Calder introduced into modern *sculpture a sense of time, immediacy, and chance that inspired subsequent generations experimenting with abstract, installation, environmental, and performance art.

Purchasing a farm in Roxbury, Connecticut, in 1938, Calder thereafter divided his time between Europe and the United States. From the 1950s until his death, he produced massive mobiles and nonmobiles, called "stabiles," commissioned internationally for public spaces. Like his delicate mobiles, the most graceful stabiles absorb and incorporate their environment; they remain still while the viewer revolves around their ever-changing open shapes.

[*See also* Abstract Expressionism; Modernist Culture; Twenties, The.]

• Katharine Kuh, "Alexander Calder," in *The Artist's Voice: Talks with Seventeen Artists,* 1960, pp. 38–51. Marla Prather, *Alexander Calder: 1898–1976,* 1998.

—Robert Cozzolino

CALHOUN, JOHN C. (1782–1850), politician and *states'-rights champion. For over a generation John Caldwell Calhoun dominated politics both in his native South Carolina and the entire *South, and exerted a powerful national influence. Born near Abbeville on the South Carolina frontier, Calhoun graduated from Yale in 1804, entered the bar in 1807, served in the state legislature, and in 1810 was elected to Congress. Marriage to his cousin Floride in 1811 brought him a large plantation. Early in his congressional career Calhoun exhibited strong nationalism, ranking as a leading "war hawk," supporting the *War of 1812 and thereafter advocating federal internal improvements, a national bank, and the protective tariff of 1816. As James *Monroe's secretary of war (1817–1825), Calhoun reorganized and modernized the department. By the time he served as vice president (under both John Quincy *Adams and Andrew *Jackson), Calhoun had shifted to a states' right position. His influential *South Carolina Exposition and Protest* (1828), an attack on the tariff of 1818, argued that protective *tariffs were unconstitutional, and that states retained their sovereignty when they entered the Union. The rise of *antislavery sentiment and northern voting power profoundly influenced his thinking; realizing that white southerners lacked the votes to override the North, he hoped to find a mechanism to preserve southern rights and interests within the Union. His theories of *nullification and state interposition offered a third path between unconditional unionists and secessionists. During the Nullification Crisis of 1828–1833, Calhoun resigned the vice presidency (1832) and took a seat in the U.S. Senate to advocate his state's views. Briefly serving as secretary of state under John *Tyler (1844–1845), Calhoun helped secure the annexation of Texas as a slave state. Returning to the Senate in 1845, he vigorously opposed the *Compromise of 1850, seeing it as a thinly veiled attack on slaveholders, and came ominously close to advocating secession in the days preceding his death.

[*See also* Bank of the United States, First and Second; Civil War: Causes; Federal Government, Executive Branch: Department of State; Federal Government, Legislative Branch: Senate; Slavery: Development and Expansion of Slavery; Texas Republic and Annexation.]

• Robert L. Meriwether and Clyde Wilson, eds., *The Papers of John C. Calhoun,* 23 vols. to date, 1959–. John Niven, *John C. Calhoun and the Price of Union,* 1988.

—Eric H. Walther

CALIFORNIA. America's most populous state, with some 32 million people in 1996, and the third largest in area (almost 160,000 square miles), California displays enormous variety in climate and landscape, from the Mojave Desert in the south to the Sierra Nevada Mountains in the central region to a thousand-mile-long Pacific coastline. This natural diversity is matched by California's complex human history. The first migrants arrived between thirty thousand and fifteen thousand years ago, likely crossing into North America during the Ice Age. The explorer Juan Rodríguez Cabrillo sailed along the Southern California coast in 1542. Sir Francis Drake may have landed near present-day *San Francisco in 1579. The Spanish explorer and administrator Gaspar de Protola established small colonies beginning in 1769. Beginning with San Diego (1769), Franciscan missionaries, initially led by Junípero *Serra, founded twenty-one missions along the Pacific coast. With Mexican independence (1821), California became a Mexican possession. The Mexican government secularized the missions in the 1830s, theoretically freeing California Indians from the missions' control.

Anglo-Americans came in large numbers by the early 1840s, mostly to farm in the north. Some settled in the community surrounding the Austrian John Sutter's ranching, farming, and lumber enterprises along the American River in the Sacramento Valley. By the mid-1840s, they clashed with the dominant Mexican or Spanish ranching class, the "Californios." The Anglo-Americans' Bear Flag Revolt (1846) established a short-lived California Republic. The Treaty of Guadalupe Hidalgo (1848) following the *Mexican War transferred California, with the rest of the *Southwest, from Mexico to the United States.

The 1848 discovery of gold in Sutter's millrace made California famous, but the *gold rush also brought violence, a

MAP 3: MAP OF CALIFORNIA BY EUSEBIO FRANCISCO KINO (1705)

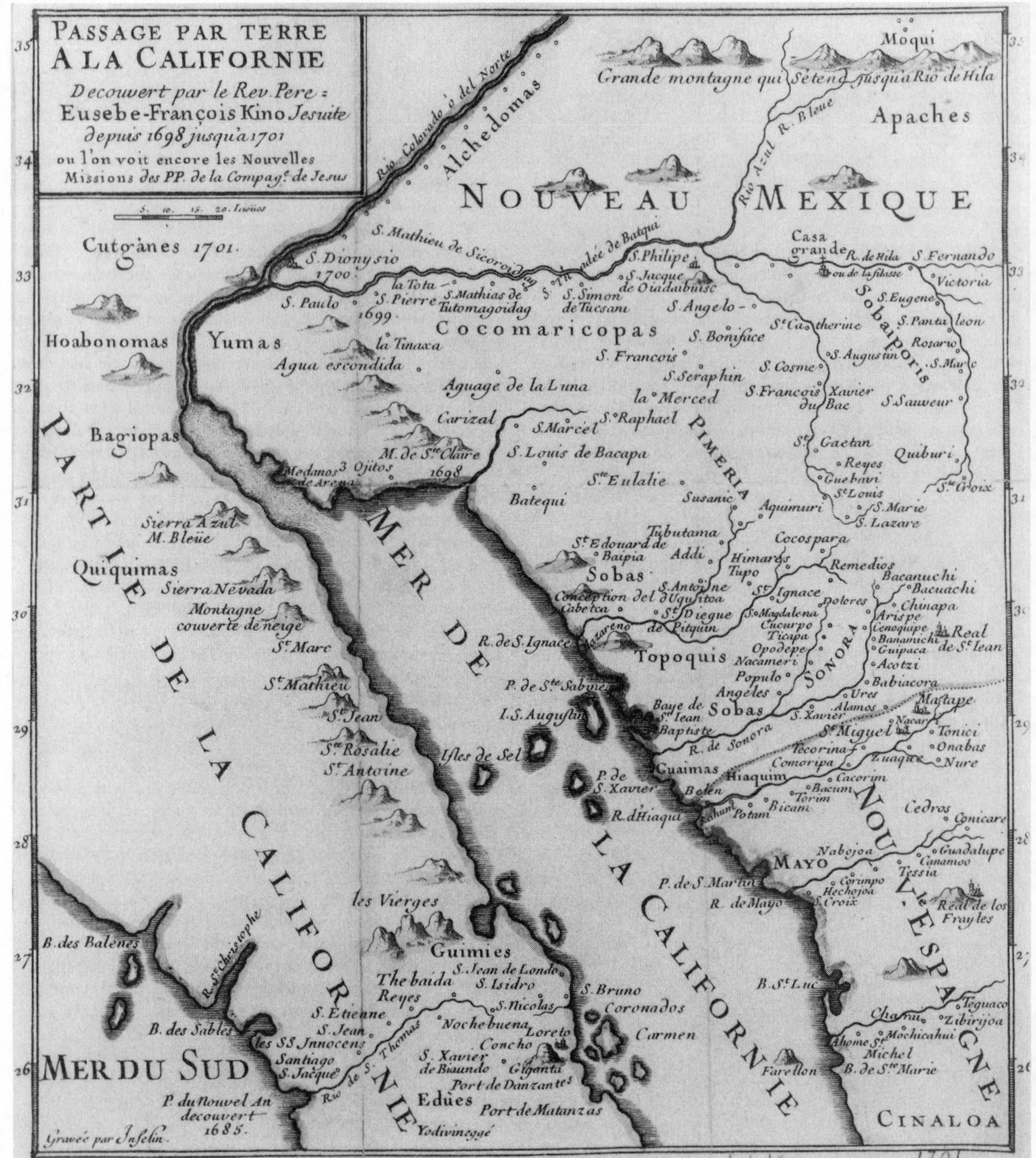

Kino (ca. 1644–1711) was a mathematician, astronomer, Jesuit missionary, and explorer of the American Southwest. His exploration of California in 1701–02 established that the region was part of the North American mainland, and not, as was widely believed, an island. This map, drawn in 1701 and published in Paris in 1705, remained the basis of California maps until the early nineteenth century. The Colorado River, separating present-day California and Arizona, appears at the top center of the map (labeled "Rio Colorado à del Norte").

[*See* California; Exploration, Conquest, and Settlement, Era of; Mexican War; Spanish Settlements in North America.]

gender ratio heavily skewed toward men, and discrimination against foreigners and people of color. Nonetheless, the gold rush hastened California's entry into the Union as the thirty-first state (1850). Under the *Compromise of 1850, California joined as a free state.

With gold and population growth came *urbanization, especially of San Francisco, whose expansion the 1906 earthquake and fire only briefly interrupted. The Central Pacific Railroad, built largely by Chinese labor, completed a transcontinental link in 1869. The economically vital tourist market initially consisted of wealthy easterners attracted by the state's climate and natural beauty. The conservationist John *Muir campaigned for *Yosemite National Park (established 1890) and founded the environmentalist *Sierra Club in 1892. The expanding citrus economy of the late nineteenth century lured settlers to Southern California and provided capital for urban and industrial growth. By the early twentieth century, Southern California's oil and its *film industry, centered in Hollywood, stimulated the state's economy.

*Racism and discrimination stain California's history. The Foreign Miners' Tax of the gold rush era was accompanied by violence against Chinese, Mexicans, and Indians. California's congressional delegation strongly supported the federal Chinese exclusion law enacted in 1882. The state's 1913 Alien Land Act prohibited noncitizens from owning farmland. The Great Depression of the 1930s exacerbated social tensions and brought violence against Mexican farmworkers trying to unionize. The novelist John Steinbeck chronicled the plight of California's *Dust Bowl migrants in *The *Grapes of Wrath* (1939). In Southern California, Mexican and Mexican American workers faced forced repatriation. *World War II brought the *incarceration of Japanese Americans, *Los Angeles riots targeting Mexican Americans, and discriminatory hiring practices against *African Americans and other minorities.

World War II and its aftermath also launched a period of booming prosperity, population growth, and economic diversification. Aircraft manufacturing, shipbuilding, and armaments manufacturing all surged during the 1940s. A swelling postwar migration to Southern California produced the burgeoning subdivisions and proliferating freeways that became synonymous with the region. *Tourism increased with the 1955 opening of Disneyland in Anaheim, near Los Angeles. San Francisco, meanwhile, became not only a mecca for the 1950s Beat poets and the 1960s counterculture, but also headquarters for such corporate giants as the Bank of America (founded by A. P. Giannini as the Bank of Italy in 1904). Beginning in the 1970s, "Silicon Valley" south of San Francisco emerged as a leader of the *computer industry. Post–Cold War military spending cuts brought a downturn, but recovery was swift, and as the 1990s ended, California enjoyed global economic power.

With population growth came increasing political clout. The California senator Hiram Johnson was a *Progressive Era luminary. The former California governor Earl *Warren served as chief justice of the U.S. *Supreme Court from 1953 to 1969. Richard M. *Nixon and Ronald *Reagan, both Californians, occupied the White House much of the time between 1969 and 1989. By 1998, California had fifty-two congresspersons, far more than any other state. With a richly diverse population of Hispanics, African Americans, whites, and Asians, California epitomized both the problems and the promise of a multicultural, multiethnic society as the twenty-first century began.

[*See also* Asian Americans; Depressions, Economic; Disney, Walt; Hispanic Americans; Immigration Law; Indian History and Culture; Railroads; San Francisco Earthquake and Fire; Spanish Settlements in North America.]

• Kevin Starr, *Americans and the California Dream, 1850–1915,* 1986. Albert Camarillo, *Chicanos in California: A History of Mexican Americans in California,* 1990. Norris Hundley Jr., *The Great Thirst: Californians and Water, 1770s–1990s,* 1992. William Deverell and Tom Sitton, eds., *California Progressivism Revisited,* 1994. Richard Candida Smith, *Utopia and Dissent: Art, Poetry, and Politics in California,* 1995.

—William Deverell

CAMP DAVID ACCORDS (1978). After negotiations at Camp David, the presidential retreat in Maryland, the Egyptian president Anwar Sadat and the Israeli prime minister Menachem Begin, with President Jimmy *Carter looking on, signed the accords at the White House on 17 September 1978. The Camp David Accords consisted of two basic agreements. The "Framework for the Conclusion of a Peace Treaty between Egypt and Israel" called for full recognition and diplomatic relations between the two states, the withdrawal of Israeli forces from the Sinai Peninsula (occupied since the Six-Day War of 1967), and Israeli right of passage through the Suez Canal. "A Framework for Peace in the Middle East" called for implementation of UN Resolutions 242 and 338 and was intended to constitute a framework for ongoing peace negotiations between Israel and its other neighbors. Negotiations on the problem of a Palestinian homeland would continue during a five-year transitional period.

The United States hoped to promote peace and to reduce Soviet influence in the vital Middle East region. President Sadat gambled that his efforts would result in increased American aid and investment in Egypt's failing economy. The government of Israel sought to end hostilities with Egypt (ongoing since 1948), given the increase in frequency and intensity of Palestinian terrorist attacks launched from within Lebanon during the Lebanese civil war.

While Sadat, Begin, and President Carter were widely hailed as heroes, Arab reaction was mixed. The Arab League and Palestinian Liberation Organization (PLO) condemned Egypt for having violated an agreement made at Khartoum in September 1967 calling for Arab unity in dealing with Israel and for leaving the Palestinian problem unresolved. Islamic revivalists condemned the lack of mention of Jerusalem, the third holiest city of Islam. Ultimately, the accords contributed to the isolation of Egypt within the Arab world and to Sadat's assassination in 1981. They did, however, continue to serve as the framework for further negotiations, including between Israel and the PLO in Madrid in 1991. They also came to symbolize President Carter's style of personal peacemaking, an asset he would employ frequently during his postpresidential years.

[*See also* Foreign Relations: U.S. Relations with the Middle East.]

• William B. Quandt, *Camp David: Peacemaking and Politics,* 1986. Dan Tschirgi, *The American Search for Mideast Peace,* 1989.

—Margaret M. Manchester

CANADA, U.S. RELATIONS WITH. *See* Foreign Relations: U.S. Relations with Canada.

CANALS AND WATERWAYS. The first waterway engineers in the Americas were the prehistoric builders who constructed fish weirs and ditches. Europeans encountered snags, sandbars, and rapids. In 1785, George *Washington organized a company that cleared rocks from the Potomac. Canal builders also developed the Santee, James, Delaware, Susquehanna, Schuylkill, and Merrimack Rivers.

Canals in the *Antebellum Era were typically semipublic stock corporations supported by state and municipal bonds. In 1808, Secretary of the Treasury Albert *Gallatin asked Congress to supplement local investment with twenty million dollars for roads and canals. John C. *Calhoun's "Bonus Bill," an elaborate attempt to implement Gallatin's concept, was vetoed by President James *Madison in 1817. New Yorkers, twice denied federal assistance, raised seven million dollars in state revenues and bonds for the 364-mile *Erie Canal, completed in 1825.

The Erie Canal inspired an enthusiastic "canal era" of state and federal waterway projects. Encouraged by the U.S. *Supreme Court's outspoken nationalism in *Gibbons* v. *Ogden* (1824), Congress purchased $300,000 in canal stock to finance a cut through the Delaware Peninsula. Virginians chartered a larger enterprise, the Chesapeake and Ohio Canal. By 1830, New Jersey, Ohio, Indiana, and Illinois had launched ambitious projects, and Pennsylvania spanned the Alleghenies with the Main Line Canal from *Philadelphia to Pittsburgh, opened in 1834.

Antebellum canal engineers were mostly millwrights, surveyors, mechanics, or masons, some field-trained on the Erie Canal and others formally schooled at the U.S. Military Academy at West Point. Construction fell to dollar-a-day laborers, increasingly *Irish Americans. The financial panic of 1837 hurt canal investors, pushing Maryland, Ohio, Michigan, Indiana, and Illinois to the brink of bankruptcy. In 1838, as the nation's attention shifted to *railroads and steamboats, Congress suspended federal aid to canal corporations. From 1815 to 1861 the total U.S. expenditure on canal construction was about $195 million dollars—two-thirds of it public money.

After the *Civil War, the federal investment in waterways focused on levees, jetties, locks, and dams. One popular project was the deepwater shipping channel that opened the *Mississippi River below *New Orleans. Serious flooding in Louisiana, meanwhile, led to the 1879 establishment of a levee-oversight bureau called the Mississippi River Commission. In 1902, Congress extended federal financing through the U.S. Reclamation Service, later renamed the Bureau of Reclamation. Senator George W. Norris of Nebraska, a crusader for public hydropower, sponsored the 1933 law that created the *Tennessee Valley Authority (TVA).

Rural demand for electricity helped justify massive construction. One *engineering triumph was Boulder Dam (renamed Hoover Dam in 1947) on the Colorado River, finished in 1935. The 1936 Flood Control Act greatly expanded the *Army Corps of Engineers' jurisdiction with $310 million for some 250 projects. Flood control became a primary justification for the corps' basinwide dam and canal projects such as the St. Lawrence Seaway, opened in 1959, the Pick-Sloan project on the Missouri River, and the Tennessee-Tombigbee Waterway. In all, about 75,000 large dams have been built in the nation's rivers.

A major twentieth-century waterway project was the St. Lawrence Seaway. This joint Canadian–U.S. engineering project was authorized by Canada in 1951 and by the U.S. Congress in 1954. The seaway opened in 1959. By a system of canals, dams, and locks extending over 2,300 miles westward from Montreal, the St. Lawrence Seaway links the Great Lakes to the St. Lawrence River and the Atlantic Ocean by a twenty-seven-foot-deep channel that can accommodate freighters with a capacity of nearly 30,000 tons. The seaway proved an economic boon to such ports as Buffalo, Cleveland, *Detroit, *Chicago, Milwaukee and Duluth, enabling the agricultural and industrial products of the upper *Middle West to reach world markets, and bringing imported goods and raw materials to the American heartland.

Once widely praised as monuments to American know-how, dams, ecologists now maintain, have degraded water quality and killed migrating fish. In 1997, the Federal Energy Regulatory Commission (FERC) responded to environmental protest by calling for the removal of Edwards Dam in Maine. In the Pacific Northwest, meanwhile, a Corps study concluded that the most effective way to restore sea-going salmon and steelhead was to breach Snake River dams.

[*See also* Roads and Turnpikes, Early.]

• Ellis L. Armstrong, *History of Public Works in the United States, 1776–1976*, 1976. Richard A. Bartlett, *Rolling Rivers: An Encyclopedia of America's Rivers*, 1984.

—Todd A. Shallat

CANCER. Cancers are malignant tumors or malignancies that arise in bone marrow or lymph nodes and spread to other tissues or organs. The oldest cancers in the Americas are those found in the bones of fossilized dinosaurs; cancers no doubt also afflicted the earliest human beings on the continent, who arrived about twelve thousand years ago. Little is known about cancer rates prior to the nineteenth century, though lip and lung cancers were probably not uncommon among native smokers of tobacco. Natural sources of radiation—like radon or ultraviolet solar radiation—must also have contributed to the occasional lung or skin cancer, though cancer rates as a whole were probably lower than those for subsequent generations of European colonists.

John Le Conte (1818–1891), a professor of physics at the University of California after the *Civil War, was one of the first Americans to suggest that cancer was on the rise. Le Conte portrayed cancer as a "disease of civilization," though it did not surpass *tuberculosis as a cause of U.S. mortality until the 1920s. (*Heart disease was already in first place, a position it held through the twentieth century.) One reason for the transition was that *life expectancy was increasing, pushing more people into the cancer-prone years. Age-adjusted mortality rates began to be calculated about this time, though statistical record-keeping remained rudimentary. Federal mortality statistics did not distinguish among different kinds of cancer until the early twentieth century; the first population-based registry was not established until 1937, in Connecticut.

Cancer rates grew rapidly after *World War II, bucking the trend of diseases—like syphilis and *poliomyelitis—that were succumbing to scientific medicine. Funding for the U.S. National Cancer Institute, established in 1937, increased dramatically in the 1950s, but environmental or lifestyle causes of cancer received little attention. Wilhelm Hueper's *Occupational Tumors and Allied Diseases* (1942) set the stage for the view that "the environment"—including diet and tobacco products—was responsible for most human cancers, a view later endorsed by the *World Health Organization (*Prevention of Cancer*, 1964).

Rachel *Carson's widely read *Silent Spring* (1962)—based partly on Hueper's work—fueled the idea that environmental pollution might be partly to blame for increasing cancer rates, though epidemiological studies by Richard Doll, A. Bradford Hill, and Ernst Wynder in the early 1950s showed that cigarettes bore responsibility for most of the increase. The U.S. surgeon general in 1964 identified tobacco as a major cause of cancer; smoking rates for men peaked at about that time, though lung-cancer rates would continue to rise for another quarter of a century. Lung cancer had become the leading cause of cancer death among males by the early 1950s; among women, mortality from lung cancer did not surpass breast cancer mortality until the 1980s.

President Richard M. *Nixon in his 1971 State of the Union address declared a "war on cancer"; the National Cancer Act of that same year signaled major increases in research funds devoted to cancer. The National Cancer Institute became the largest single unit of the *National Institutes of Health, reporting directly to the president, with an annual budget that surpassed two billion dollars by the 1990s. Many scientists hoped that a cancer vaccine might be found to eliminate the disease, as had been the case with polio and *smallpox.

In the 1970s, labor and environmental activists such as Samuel Epstein (*The Politics of Cancer*, 1978) began to protest the failure of the National Cancer Institute to address the causes of cancer in a manner that might lead to effective prevention. Lung cancers and other internal tumors began to appear in tens of thousands of asbestos workers, especially shipyard workers who had sprayed the mineral inside ships in World War II. Widely publicized cases of cancers caused by vinyl chloride, benzene, dry-cleaning fluids, hair dyes, and other petrochemicals gave rise to the widespread and controversial notion that the modern chemical environment was causing unprecedented numbers of cancers.

Cancer rates continued to climb until the early 1990s, by which time the decline in smoking was resulting in lower cancer rates. Cancer mortality rates fell by about 3 percent from 1990 to 1995, the first clear drop since data had begun to be recorded. Cancer rates remained particularly high for *African Americans, though most observers believed the inequality had more to do with environmental factors relating to *poverty than with race-specific organic factors. As the twentieth century ended, cancer rates had still not fallen as much as deaths from heart attack, apparently because treatments for heart failure had improved much more rapidly than treatments for cancer. Projections suggested that cancer would become the number-one cause of U.S. deaths sometime early in the twenty-first century.

[*See also* Disease; Environmentalism; Food and Diet; Medicine; Tobacco Industry; Tobacco Products.]

• Richard Doll and Richard Peto, *The Causes of Cancer,* 1981. James T. Patterson, *The Dread Disease: Cancer and Modern American Culture,* 1987. Robert N. Proctor, *Cancer Wars: How Politics Shapes What We Know and Don't Know about Cancer,* 1995.

—Robert N. Proctor

CAPITALISM. The term "capitalism" has frequently been used to describe the American economy. The general usage of the term, however, dates to the late nineteenth century and was largely drawn from the multivolume work *Das Kapital (Capital)* by Karl Marx. Initially used mainly by Marxist critics of capitalism, it came to mean an economic system with private ownership of land and capital, an individual's right to his or her own labor, and the existence of competitive markets that determine prices and quantities for goods and services and for factors of production (land, raw materials, labor, capital). Often it has been defined as free enterprise, or *laissez-faire, describing an economy in which government plays a limited role. Capitalism is, however, a term more frequently used and debated than clearly defined; its precise meaning has seldom been widely agreed upon.

Capitalism has often been contrasted with other basic types of economic systems that preceded or coexisted with it. In the Marxist scheme, all societies followed, or will follow, a predictable set of economic stages. First comes the transition from feudalism to capitalism, leading to freer markets and freer labor, thus permitting rapid economic growth. Capitalism, in turn, would lead to *communism, as a result of labor revolt, Marx predicted. In the *Cold War Era, social scientists and government leaders drew a sharp political contrast between the capitalist world (the United States and, in some cases, western Europe), and the communist bloc (the Soviet Union, its eastern European allies, and the People's Republic of China), a comparison based on the two blocs' relative economic development and differences in political freedoms. Capitalism's supporters credited it with generating more rapid growth and greater political freedoms than communism.

Some scholars assert that capitalism itself passes through successive stages, reflecting changing economic structures. In the early stages of merchant or commercial capitalism in western Europe, from the sixteenth to the eighteenth centuries, expanding commerce, especially overseas trade with colonial empires, drove the economic system. Industrial capitalism, based on a manufacturing sector and factory production using free labor, followed as the next stage. The final stage, finance capitalism, characterized by V. I. Lenin and others as the highest stage of capitalism, was marked by excess production and savings that needed foreign outlets. Hence, according to this interpretive scheme, imperialism arose in the late nineteenth century to preserve domestic capitalist economies from collapse. Such divisions into stages have been applied more easily to England and to western Europe than to the United States, where, by contrast, capitalism's different stages have generally revolved around changes in the relation of government to business.

American capitalism began with English colonial policy, which established basically free markets internally, combined with mercantilistic regulations to control international trade. Mercantilism, however, under which governments sought to promote home industry and maximize exports, existed alongside most elements of capitalism, such as individual freedoms and the role of markets in internal and external trade. That mercantilism as conventionally defined was not inconsistent with capitalism is apparent from the fact that the newly independent United States adopted a form of mercantilism, using state power to promote economic growth. In the late nineteenth century, the government began to regulate businesses through *antitrust legislation and related measures, but throughout the century governments had played an important, positive role in the economy through expenditures to build transportation, *tariffs to protect industries, banking controls to police the financial system, and public *education to improve human capital. The late nineteenth-century rise of government *economic regulation, however, represented a shift away from earlier governmental stress on the promotion of *business and economic growth. Both positive and negative government-business relationships characterized capitalism, despite the significant shift in the government's role. Even with the growth of regulation, considerable room for competitive markets and freedom of individual choice existed within the economic sphere. Thus, the often proclaimed end of capitalism in the United States has (apparently) not yet occurred.

The term "capitalism" has carried both positive and negative connotations: The positive connotation, as suggested by the title of Carl Snyder's 1940 book, *Capitalism: The Creator,* celebrates the alleged link between capitalism and political freedom. The negative connotations are clearly conveyed in such terms as "capitalist exploiter," "capitalist imperialist," or simply "filthy capitalist." Praise of capitalists and capitalism has been a central theme among those who desire to limit public restrictions on business behavior, while many reformers and reform movements in U.S. history have emphasized the social costs of "unfettered" or "unbridled" capitalism. Capitalism's critics have focused on how it unevenly distributes income and wealth and also on how the market system trivializes culture.

Capitalism's long-term survival prospects have been much discussed. During the Great Depression of the 1930s, commentators frequently proclaimed capitalism's decline or demise, often in contrast to the ability of the communist economies to avoid such severe economic collapse. By contrast, the economic revival of the capitalist economies in the post–*World War II era, particularly through the 1970s, a period of unusually rapid growth by any historical standard, elicited praise. Social scientists extolled the post–*World War II economies alternatively as a return to capitalist principles or as the development of a new economic system with an enlarged governmental role and the introduction of elements of *socialism—a hybrid economic system with only some capitalistic elements surviving. Some labeled this "managed capitalism," reflecting an enhanced government commitment to influence macroeconomic policy (monetary and fiscal policies) as well as to regulate microeconomic behavior of markets. Whether this system will come to be regarded as a new stage of economic and political development or as another example of capitalism's basic adaptability and flexibility remains to be seen.

[*See also* Banking and Finance; Depressions, Economic; Economic Development; Expansionism; Fifties, The; Gilded Age; Industrialization; New Deal Era, The; Progressive Era; Stock Market.]

• Werner Sombart, "Capitalism," in *Encyclopedia of the Social Sciences,* ed. E. R. A. Seligman, 1930, vol. 3, pp. 195–208. Louis Hacker, *The Triumph of American Capitalism,* 1940. Joseph A. Schumpter, *Capitalism,*

Socialism, and Democracy, 1942. Carter Goodrich, *Government Promotion of American Canals and Railroads, 1800–1890,* 1960. Milton Friedman, *Capitalism and Freedom,* 1962. Jonathan R. T. Hughes, *The Govermental Habit Redux,* 1991.

—Stanley L. Engerman

CAPITAL PUNISHMENT. Since George Kendall's execution in *Jamestown in 1608, about twenty thousand people have been legally put to death in America—more than seven thousand of them in the twentieth century. All thirteen colonies mandated public hanging for certain crimes against the state, person, or property. When the *Bill of Rights was adopted in 1791, the Eighth Amendment's prohibition against "cruel and unusual" punishment was understood to outlaw torture and the intentional infliction of pain, not the death penalty itself. Over the next two centuries, however, the criminal law gradually reduced the number of crimes punishable by death while introducing other reforms that lowered the number of executions. In 1793, for example, Pennsylvania introduced a distinction between murder and manslaughter and limited the death penalty to offenders convicted of the former. By the 1830s, five states (Pennsylvania, New York, New Jersey, Rhode Island, and Massachusetts) had outlawed public executions, and in the 1840s states began to grant juries the discretion to impose life imprisonment in capital cases. In the early twentieth century, states further restricted capital statutes, eliminating horse thievery, cattle rustling, assaults, and, finally, *rape. By 1977, only murder could result in capital punishment.

The number of executions began to drop in the 1950s, and the years from 1968 to 1976 saw a moratorium on executions. Executions resumed thereafter, although the average time served under death sentence grew to more than ten years, owing mainly to the expanding role of federal appellate courts. In 1990, the *Supreme Court limited appeals to the federal courts by death row inmates.

The issue of deterrence long dominated the debate concerning capital punishment. By the late twentieth century, concerns about arbitrariness, racial discrimination, costs, and conviction of the innocent had taken center stage. In the 1972 case *Furman* v. *Georgia,* the Supreme Court temporarily ended the death penalty in America, deeming its application arbitrary and capricious. In response, thirty-eight states and the federal government enacted new capital punishment laws designed to pass constitutional muster. These laws typically separated the guilt-or-innocence phase of the trial from the sentencing phase, mandated a statutory list of "aggravating" and "mitigating" factors to guide juries in capital trials, and required automatic review by state courts of all death sentences and convictions. Many scholars, however, believed that these reforms failed to eliminate arbitrariness, and that the administration of the death penalty remained no less inconsistent and arbitrary in the mid-1990s than it had been in 1972.

Some scholars contended that capital punishment involved racial discrimination. In *Equal Justice and the Death Penalty* (1990), David C. Baldus and his associates demonstrated that the victim's race was a significant factor in predicting which convicted murderers received the death penalty. Killers of whites were 4.3 times more likely to be sentenced to death than killers of *African Americans. In *McCleskey* v. *Kemp* (1987), however, the Supreme Court held that such statistical patterns were insufficient to prove violation of the *Fourteenth Amendment's equal protection clause in specific cases; proof of intentional discrimination against a particular defendant had to be provided.

The cost of death-penalty cases became an important issue as well, as the "super due process" requirements made the prosecution of capital cases extraordinarily expensive. In New Jersey, for example, capital trials cost about $750,000 in the 1990s, whereas noncapital murder trials cost around $50,000. Since only 15 percent of capital trials end in a death sentence, in 85 percent of the cases taxpayers pay the cost of both a capital trial and life imprisonment. Consequently, the cost of sending a single person to death row in New Jersey in the 1990s was a staggering $7.3 million.

Finally, the conviction of the innocent became an important issue in the late twentieth-century debate over capital punishment. According to one study (Bedau and Radelet), 350 people in the twentieth century were wrongly convicted of offenses punishable by death, and 25 were actually executed. Further, this study found that many of the wrongful convictions were not good-faith errors but resulted from conspiracies by the police, prosecutors, defense attorneys, judges, witnesses, and even jurors. The problems of human fallibility and malfeasance, neither of which can be effectively remedied, remained central in the continuing capital punishment debate as the twentieth century ended.

[*See also* Crime; Jurisprudence; Prisons and Penitentiaries; Racism.]

• William J. Bowers, Glenn L. Pierce, and John F. McDevitt, *Death as Punishment in America, 1864–1982,* 1984. Franklin E. Zimring and Gordon Hawkins, *Capital Punishment and the American Agenda,* 1986. H. A. Bedau and Michael L. Radlet, "Miscarriages of Justice in Potentially Capital Cases," *Stanford Law Review* 41 (Nov. 1987): 161–70. David Baldus, Charles Pulaski Jr., and George G. Wentworth, *Equal Justice and the Death Penalty: A Legal and Empirical Analysis,* 1990. Robert Johnson, *Death Work: A Study of the Modern Execution Process,* 1990. Hugo Adam Bedau, *The Death Penalty in America,* 1997.

—Richard Moran

CAPONE, AL (1899–1947), major *Chicago bootlegger who symbolized the supposed lawlessness of the 1920s Prohibition Era. Alphonse Capone was born in Brooklyn, New York, left school at fourteen, and joined the street life of the city. Around 1919 or 1920, Capone moved to Chicago, where he aided John Torrio in building a major bootlegging operation. In 1925, after Torrio was shot and decided to leave Chicago, four individuals became joint partners in overseeing the expanding operations: Capone, his brother Ralph, their cousin Frank Nitti, and Jack Guzik. They entered into agreements with other entrepreneurs to coordinate a highly decentralized system for distributing liquor, managing gambling houses and slot machines, and operating various nightclubs and brothels. In 1928, Capone purchased a mansion near Miami on Palm Island, visiting Chicago only occasionally thereafter. In 1929–1930, he spent nearly a year in a *Philadelphia jail after an arrest for carrying a concealed weapon.

The media creation of a notorious and largely fictional Capone stemmed from two main factors. First, bootlegging in Chicago received national and international attention because of the unusual violence that characterized the struggles among bootleggers, including the notorious St. Valentine's Day Massacre of 1929. Second, Capone courted media attention, held press conferences, and reveled in the attention that he received. Out of the articles, books, movies, and television dramas, there eventually emerged a fictional master criminal who was given the nickname "Scarface" and portrayed as one who helped create "*organized crime" in America and controlled the city of Chicago during his heyday.

Al Capone was convicted of income tax evasion in October 1931. Serving time in the Atlanta Penitentiary and then in *San Francisco's Alcatraz, he was released in 1939 suffering from syphilis of the brain. He retired with his wife and son to Palm Island, where he died of a stroke. Although his criminal career was brief, the fictional Capone has continued to shape not only America's vision of the 1920s but also the power of criminals in American society.

[*See also* Crime; Prostitution and Antiprostitution; Temperance and Prohibition; Twenties, The.]

• Laurence Bergreen, *Capone,* 1994. David E. Ruth, *Inventing the Public Enemy: The Gangster in American Culture, 1918–1934,* 1996.

—Mark H. Haller

CAPTIVITY NARRATIVES, INDIAN. An archetypal genre recounting an innocent's descent into, and redemption from, an alien world, Indian captivity narratives were both a product and a representation of the American historical experience. Emerging from real conflicts between indigenous peoples and encroaching Euroamericans, they also served ideological and political needs. Tropes of captivity appear in sixteenth-century accounts of discovery and exploration, but not until 1682, with the publication of Mary Rowlandson's extremely popular *The Soveraignty and Goodness of God,* did a distinctive genre emerge. (Living in Lancaster, on the Massachusetts frontier, Rowlandson had spent three months in captivity in 1676, during *King Philip's War.) During the next two centuries, Indian captivity narratives gained such popularity that many editions have disappeared because they were literally read to pieces.

Captivity narratives ran the gamut from fact to fiction, but the plot remained consistent: the protagonist is ripped from family and friends, initiated into native society, and comes home ineffably changed. Most willingly returned when they could, but a few preferred to stay, becoming (as did Mary Jemison in James Seaver's prototypical narrative of 1824) fully transculturated. (In 1758, during the *Seven Years' War, the fifteen-year-old Jemison was captured by Shawnees at her family's farm in Pennsylvania. She spent most of her long life among the Senecas in New York State, marrying twice, bearing eight children, and rejecting all suggestions of repatriation.) Some accounts portrayed Indians as kindly people who adopted hostages into their families or as moral paragons who showed up white society's sins, but most depicted them as ignorant, barbaric, and devilish, or, at worst, as subhumans deserving extirpation.

The captivity narratives' messages changed more than their plots. Self-consciously religious, most of the early tracts exemplified God's providence and believers' faith. Eighteenth-century works tended toward propaganda in which natives served first as cruel proxies for the French or British, then as themselves epitomes of evil. Imbued with romanticism, eastern antebellum audiences idealized natives as noble relics of a national past now sadly expiring, but westerners, still living under the tomahawk's chop, saw only bloody threats and linked the extermination of Indians to America's *Manifest Destiny.

The genre declined as the 1800s ebbed, its tropes no longer resonant in an urbanizing culture seemingly devoid of aborigines. It enjoyed a long fictional afterlife in American *popular culture, however, as in Alan Le May's 1954 novel *The Searchers,* which was made into a film in 1956 by John Ford, starring John Wayne in a quest to recover his niece (played by Natalie Wood), kidnapped by a Comanche chief.

The narratives' highly stereotyped representations of Indians reflect Euroamerican attitudes toward natives more accurately than they portray frontier life, although, read carefully, they can reveal valuable ethnographic information. They are significant in American literary history as one of the first bodies of work to feature women, sometimes as authors, most usually as subjects. Focused, as one critic has remarked, on a "domestic drama" of abduction that foregrounds female sentiments and actions, captivity narratives developed a version of America's "rise to greatness" in which women played a major role.

[*See also* Colonial Era; Indian History and Culture: The Indian in Popular Culture; Literature: Colonial Era; Literature: Early National and Antebellum Eras; Literature, Popular.]

• Kathryn Zabelle Derounian-Stodola and James Arthur Levernier, *The Indian Captivity Narrative, 1550–1900,* 1993. June Namias, *White Captivities: Gender and Ethnicity on the American Frontier,* 1993. John Demos, *The Unredeemed Captive: A Family Story from Early America,* 1994.

—Charles L. Cohen

CARNEGIE, ANDREW (1835–1919), industrial entrepreneur and philanthropist whose life embodied the rags-to-riches myth of the self-made man. Born to a working-class family in Dunfermline, Scotland, Carnegie immigrated to America in 1848 and settled near Pittsburgh, Pennsylvania. Soon after his arrival, he began work in a textile mill for $1.20 per week. Five decades later, he stood at the pinnacle of the U.S. steel industry, the richest man in the world.

Carnegie rose rapidly, by 1853 becoming the personal assistant to Thomas A. Scott (1823–1881), the future head of the Pennsylvania Railroad. In 1856, Carnegie invested his savings in a sleeping-car company that netted him five thousand dollars in annual dividends. That same year he assisted Scott in suppressing union organizers, winning for himself the superintendency of the Pennsylvania Railroad's western division.

Carnegie's investments grew throughout the 1860s. Aided by a loan from Scott, Carnegie founded the Keystone Bridge Company in 1867 and within a year controlled assets in excess of $400,000. By then, his earnings were so large that he pledged to retire from business and pursue scholarship and philanthropy because, he feared, the quest for wealth would inevitably lead to personal degradation.

But Carnegie did not keep his promise. He continued to invest heavily in the iron business he had purchased in the 1860s and by 1872 was planning the world's most advanced steel mill. Over the course of the next three decades, Carnegie competed ruthlessly against his rivals in the steel industry while also resisting the initiatives of organized labor. He became a trailblazer in reducing production costs and extending managerial control over workers. In 1875, Carnegie's new steel mill, the Edgar Thomson Works near Pittsburgh, ushered in a revolution in industrial production and organization. He rid the mill of union workers and produced rails at a lower cost and earned more money than any other U.S. metal maker. The Bessemer process of steelmaking—which Carnegie was the first to use—produced vast quantities of hard, durable metal at low cost. In combining the essential stages of metal production (smelting, refining, and rolling), Carnegie achieved a new level of automation and technological integration.

Carnegie's profits, investments, and fame continued to expand during the 1880s, when he found new sources of personal fulfillment as well. He married Louise Whitfield, with whom he later had one child, Margaret; he began to dispense his wealth by donating money for thousands of Carnegie libraries; and he summed up his social thought in *Triumphant Democracy* (1886). In several influential essays, notably "Wealth" (*North American Review,* 1889), he defended the theoretical right of workers to join unions and proclaimed the responsibility of the wealthy to redistribute their money for the good of the community. In 1892, however, Carnegie and his close business associate Henry Clay Frick (1849–1919) chose to maximize profits rather than respect their workers' right to a union. The result was the violence-ridden Homestead Steel strike that thwarted unionism in the steel industry until the 1930s.

Carnegie paid dearly for his victory at Homestead in the arena of public opinion, but he remained active publicly. In the late 1890s, he campaigned against the *Spanish-American War and opposed the annexation of the *Philippines. In 1901, he sold the Carnegie Steel Company to J. P. *Morgan for $480 million, freeing himself to pursue such philanthropic ventures as the *Carnegie Foundation for the Advancement of Teaching, the Carnegie Hero Fund, and the *Carnegie Endowment for International Peace. His total benefactions—including more than 2,800 Carnegie libraries—amounted to $350 million.

In his declining years, Carnegie served as a kind of ambassador-at-large for world peace. From the late 1880s on, he spent much of each year at his estate in Scotland. *World War I seemed to crush his otherwise undaunted spirit, and he died in 1919 at Shadowbrook, his estate in the Berkshire Hills of Massachusetts.

[*See also* Gilded Age; Homestead Lockout; Industrialization; Iron and Steel Industry; Labor Movements; Libraries; Peace

Movements; Philanthropy and Philanthropic Foundations; Railroads.]

• Burton J. Hendrick, *The Life of Andrew Carnegie,* 1932. Joseph Frazier Wall, *Andrew Carnegie,* 1970; reprint 1989.

—Paul Krause

CARNEGIE ENDOWMENT FOR INTERNATIONAL PEACE. Founded in 1910 with a ten-million-dollar grant from the industrialist Andrew *Carnegie, the Carnegie Endowment for International Peace was the most prominent of a number of *Progressive Era organizations that encouraged a more academic approach to peace activism. Specifically, the endowment's leaders envisioned a scientific approach through which impartial research would yield recommendations for a more stable international order. This agenda represented a marked shift from the traditional American approach to peace, which more often relied upon religious, moral, and pacifist appeals.

Carnegie himself believed that arbitration treaties and closer ties between the United States and Great Britain would ensure international stability, but the endowment's ideological foundations were shaped more by figures such as Elihu Root (1845–1937), Theodore *Roosevelt's secretary of state; Nicholas Murray Butler (1862–1947), president of Columbia University; and James Brown Scott (1866–1993) of the American Society of International Law. All three were conservatives whose previous experience with peace activism had centered not on issues like disarmament and self-determination but rather on codifying *international law as the most realistic way to avoid war among the great powers. The organization's distance from more established peace groups increased with the outbreak of *World War I. The endowment's key leaders all emerged as unabashed proponents of the Allied cause, with many urging U.S. intervention. Root and Butler became prominent members of the wartime League to Enforce Peace, which called for a postwar international organization with sufficient military strength to suppress threats to the peace.

Since World War I, the endowment has continued to champion international law and arbitration and has concentrated on sponsoring scholarly studies of international law and foreign policy. It publishes the journal *Foreign Policy* and, in 1993, established a public-policy research center in Moscow.

[*See also* Internationalism; League of Nations; Pacifism; Peace Movements; Philanthropy and Philanthropic Foundations.]

• Sondra Herman. *Eleven against War: Studies in American Internationalist Thought, 1898–1921,* 1969. C. Roland Marchand, *The American Peace Movement and Social Reform, 1898–1918,* 1973.

—Robert D. Johnson

CARNEGIE FOUNDATION FOR THE ADVANCEMENT OF TEACHING, created by Andrew *Carnegie in 1905. Its board chose Henry Pritchett as the first president. The foundation's immediate purpose was to provide pensions for college faculty members. But Pritchett, devoted to *Progressive Era principles of *professionalization, standardization, and efficiency, had a larger agenda in mind. The foundation conducted several studies of professional education, most notably Abraham Flexner's landmark *Medical Education in the United States and Canada* (1910), which advocated higher, clearer standards. It also created, in 1918, the Teachers Insurance and Annuity Association (TIAA) to assume the pension obligation, which had grown too large for the foundation to carry. After Pritchett's retirement in 1930, the foundation advocated more standardized testing in schools and colleges, highlighted by its role in founding the Educational Testing Service (1947).

From 1955 until 1979, the foundation was governed by two presidents of the Carnegie Corporation of New York, John Gardner (1955–1965) and Alan Pifer (1965–1979). Under them, it was redirected and revitalized, chiefly through the establishment of the Carnegie Commission on Higher Education, chaired by Clark Kerr. Kerr, former president of the University of California, produced a series of influential studies on the status and needs of higher education.

In 1979, the foundation appointed Ernest Boyer as president, once again separating the administration of the foundation from that of the larger Carnegie Corporation. Boyer, a former U.S. commissioner of education, produced several influential studies, including *High School* (1983), in which he supported the 1980s reform agenda of higher academic standards but also urged more student-centered learning and public-service activities. In *College* (1987) and *Scholarship Reconsidered* (1990), Boyer explored the tensions between the research and teaching missions of American higher education. Boyer died in 1995, and in 1997 Lee Shulman, a professor of education at Stanford University, became the foundation's eighth president. Shulman's research on teaching at all levels of American education reinforced his determination to maintain the foundation's balanced attention to elementary, secondary, and higher education.

[*See also* Education; Flexner Report; Medical Education.]

• Ellen Condliffe Lagemann, *Private Power for the Public Good: A History of the Carnegie Foundation for the Advancement of Teaching,* 1983.

—Carl F. Kaestle

CARSON, RACHEL (1907–1964), nature writer, environmentalist. Raised on a farm in western Pennsylvania, Carson attended the Pennsylvania College for Women and earned a master's degree in zoology from Johns Hopkins University. In 1935, she went to work at the U.S. Fish and Wildlife Service, producing numerous publications for the agency until she left in 1953 to write independently.

Carson's *The Sea Around Us* (1951), a hugely successful book about the oceans, was at once scientifically knowledgeable and compellingly lyrical. She is best known for *Silent Spring* (1962), an impassioned defense of unspoiled nature for its own sake and a powerful warning that the chemical despoliation of the environment, especially by the insecticide DDT, threatened human health. An international best-seller, the book eloquently popularized the idea that human beings must recognize themselves as part of nature rather than purely as masters of it.

In *Silent Spring,* which first appeared in the *New Yorker* magazine, Carson lucidly explained the intricate interconnectedness of nature and how chemical herbicides or insecticides applied by spraying the earth or the air could diffuse through the local soil, then be carried through ground and surface water to distant areas and accumulate in the wild food chain. Her book roused a barrage of ridicule and denunciation from the *chemical industry, parts of the food industry, academic scientists allied with both, and some powerful sectors of the media. However, *Silent Spring*'s carefully documented analyses were reviewed and endorsed by the President's Science Advisory Committee, and Carson's views helped inspire the environmental protection movement that began in the 1960s.

[*See also* Agriculture: Since 1920; Environmentalism.]

• Martha Freeman, ed., *Always, Rachel: The Letters of Rachel Carson and Dorothy Freeman, 1952–1964,* 1995. Paul Brooks, *The House of Life: Rachel Carson at Work, with Selections from Her Writings Published and Unpublished,* 1972.

—Daniel J. Kevles

CARTER, JIMMY (1924–), thirty-ninth president of the United States. James Earl Carter Jr., was born in Plains, Georgia, the son of a conservative agribusinessman and a liberal nurse. Growing up in a prosperous but demanding family, Carter graduated from the U.S. Naval Academy at Annapolis in 1946. The high point of his naval career was service in the nuclear submarine corps under Admiral Hyman Rickover (1900–1986), who reinforced Carter's commitment to self-discipline and efficiency. Returning to Plains following his father's death in

1953, Carter established himself as a civic leader and was elected to the Georgia State Senate in 1962. Defeat in the 1966 Democratic gubernatorial primary plunged him into a brief depression that ended with a spiritual rebirth. He won the governorship in 1970 and attracted national attention by repudiating racial *segregation in his inaugural address. Winning the Democratic presidential nomination in 1976, he narrowly defeated the Republican Gerald *Ford by courting diverse constituencies and by emphasizing different sides of himself: farmer, fiscally conservative small businessman, nuclear engineer, and "born again" *Baptist. In the aftermath of the *Watergate scandal, he insisted on his honesty.

Carter entered the presidency with two major handicaps. First, he not only lacked experience dealing with Congress but also, viewing himself as an ethical "outsider" untainted by Washington corruption, doubted the propriety of making any deals. Second, while most congressional Democrats wanted to expand the welfare state, Carter stressed efficiency and limited government instead.

Nonetheless, Carter did record several major achievements. In keeping with his relatively conservative economic philosophy, he deregulated the airline and trucking industries and took steps to decontrol the prices of natural gas and oil. An advocate of *civil rights, he appointed many *African Americans to federal office. His campaign to protect human rights abroad, which he considered both sound national policy and a personal Christian duty, placed the issue firmly on the American agenda. At great political cost, he secured ratification of treaties returning the Canal Zone to Panama, mediated the *Camp David Accords between Egypt and Israel, and rejected military intervention in both the Nicaraguan civil war and the Iranian revolution.

In 1979–1980, Carter's presidency was disabled by deteriorating economic conditions, the collapse of Soviet-American détente, and his decision to allow the exiled Shah of Iran into the United States for medical treatment. The oil shortages and rising fuel prices that accompanied the Iranian revolution worsened the "stagflation" (a combination of stagnation and inflation) already afflicting the economy. Carter's unsuccessful effort in July 1979 to rally the country with an inspirational address was ridiculed as a lamentation over the nation's "malaise." The Shah's arrival in November provoked Islamic militants to seize the U.S. embassy in Iran and take American hostages. Soviet–American relations, acrimonious from the start of Carter's term, plummeted when the Soviets invaded Afghanistan in December 1979 and remained there despite the sanctions Carter imposed. Similarly, neither negotiations nor an inept rescue attempt in April 1980 managed to free the Americans held hostage in Iran. Having satisfied neither liberals nor conservatives, Carter narrowly won renomination but then lost the 1980 election to Ronald *Reagan. In a final blow, Iran released the hostages hours after Carter left office.

Carter returned to Plains depressed and facing financial insecurity. He recuperated quickly by pursuing diverse activities with his customary discipline. Establishing the Carter Center at Atlanta's Emory University as his base, he continued to mediate Arab–Israeli differences, supervised foreign elections, focused attention on disease and starvation in poor and unstable nations, and volunteered with Habitat for Humanity, a program to build houses for the poor. In 1994, he defused a confrontation between the United States and North Korea and helped arrange the peaceful end of Haiti's military dictatorship. Although critics still questioned his diplomatic judgment and administrative style, Carter's postpresidential years largely restored his reputation.

[*See also* Cold War; Federal Government, Executive Branch: The Presidency; Foreign Relations: U.S. Relations with Latin America; Foreign Relations: U.S. Relations with the Middle East; Energy Crisis of the 1970s; Panama Canal.]

• Burton I. Kaufman, *The Presidency of James Earl Carter, Jr.*, 1993. Peter Bourne, *Jimmy Carter: A Comprehensive Biography from Plains to the Presidency*, 1997.

—Leo P. Ribuffo

CARTIER, JACQUES (1491–1557), French explorer. A Breton pilot from St-Malo, Cartier had already visited Brazil before receiving King Francis I's order in 1534 to locate "certain islands and lands" blessed with gold "and other precious things" and, evidently, to find a passage to Asia. Of the three accounts of his voyages, dictated to a secretary or based upon Cartier's log books, two survived in incomplete English and Italian translations. His expeditions helped establish French claims to territory in the New World.

Cartier's 1534 expedition explored and charted the Gulf of St. Lawrence. The 1535 expedition surveyed the St. Lawrence Valley as far as Montreal Island. This expedition wintered near present Quebec City and kidnapped local Iroquoian people to be exhibited as trophies in France. Regarding the native peoples as another of the New World's curiosities, Cartier used force and deception in dealing with them. Appointed in 1541 to assist La Rocque de Roberval in locating a mythical, wealthy kingdom reported by natives and to establish a farming settlement above Quebec, Cartier was diverted by the discovery of quartz crystals and iron pyrites, which he mistook for diamonds and gold. Ignoring de Roberval, he rushed back to France in 1542 to profit from the "treasures" he had found. Cartier's booty proved worthless, and he entered private business and retired to an estate near St-Malo. Cartier's fame rests on his discovery of the St. Lawrence, an avenue into the continent's interior rivaled only by the *Mississippi. The fertile St. Lawrence Valley would be the core of the later colony of New France.

[*See also* Exploration, Conquest, and Settlement, Era of European; French Settlements in North America.]

• Henry P. Biggar, ed., *The Voyages of Jacques Cartier, Published from the Originals with Translations*, 1924. H. P. Biggar, ed., *A Collection of Documents Relating to Jacques Cartier and the Sieur de Roberval*, 1930.

—Peter Moogk

CARTOGRAPHY. *See* Earth Sciences.

CASSATT, MARY (1844–1926), artist and member of the Impressionist movement. Born into an upper-class Pennsylvania family, Cassatt as a child spent four years in France and Germany. She enrolled in the Pennsylvania Academy of the Fine Arts at age sixteen but was determined to seek training abroad. She traveled to Europe with her mother in 1865 and, except for a brief return to the United States in 1870–1871 and several short trips home, remained there for the rest of her life, moving permanently to Paris in 1874. Cassatt studied with the conservative artists Jean-Léon Gérôme and Charles Chaplin but became dissatisfied with submitting her work for exhibition to the Paris Salon, perceiving that its juries were prejudiced against women artists. She accepted Edgar Degas's invitation to join the Impressionists in 1877 and first exhibited with them in 1879.

Cassatt belonged to a cultured intellectual circle in Paris, although her gender and class prevented her from close interaction with her contemporaries in the cafés of Paris, the symbol of modern life for some impressionist artists. Her first painting of a mother and child, in 1888, announced a theme with which she became increasingly identified. Cassatt continued to paint until 1915, when poor eyesight forced her to stop. Cassatt also served as art adviser to her friends Louisine and Henry O. Havemeyer, whose collection of Impressionist and old master paintings was eventually donated to New York's Metropolitan Museum of Art.

[*See also* Painting: To 1945.]

• Nancy Mowll Mathews, *Mary Cassatt: A Life*, 1994. Judith Barter et al., *Mary Cassatt: Modern Woman*, 1998.

—Bailey Van Hook

CATHER, WILLA (1873–1947), writer. Although associated with the midwestern landscape she celebrated in her fiction, Cather was born in a small farming community in the Shenandoah Valley of Virginia and emigrated to Nebraska with her family in 1883. She attended the University of Nebraska and went on to jobs in teaching and publishing, becoming managing editor of *McClure's Magazine* in 1908. Her ambition was to be a writer, however, and she found support for her creativity from women friends and lovers, notably Sarah Orne Jewett (1849–1909), author of *The Country of the Pointed Firs* (1896); Isabelle McClung; Edith Lewis; and Elizabeth Sergeant. S. S. McClure published her first book of short fiction, *The Troll Garden,* in 1905, and in 1911 Cather took a leave of absence from *McClure's* to write fiction. Her first novel, *Alexander's Bridge* (1912), was heavily influenced by Henry *James, but in *O Pioneers!* (1913) she returned to her familiar Nebraska prairies for inspiration. Finding increasing literary and economic success, Cather over the next three decades published fourteen novels or collections of stories, including *My Ántonia* (1918), *The Professor's House* (1925), and *Death Comes for the Archbishop* (1927).

Cather's early novels were hailed by such prominent critics as Henry Louis *Mencken and Edmund Wilson. Her critical reputation soared throughout the 1920s, but in the 1930s, when left-wing critics favored socially conscious fiction, she was attacked by Granville Hicks and others for "escapism." But she never lost her wide readership, and by the 1990s she was reinstated as a major American novelist. Once viewed as a simple celebrator of the American past, she came to be recognized as an explorer of the darker tones of American life—change, loss, diminishment. Yet she also provided an unsentimental counterpoint to this underside of the American dream: the human desire to make meaning through creative work, family, religion, art, domestic crafts, and—most important to Willa Cather—through storytelling.

[*See also* Literature: Civil War to World War I; Literature: Since World War I; Magazines; Twenties, The.]

• Sharon O'Brien, *Willa Cather: The Emerging Voice,* 1987; reprint 1997. James Woodress, *Willa Cather,* 1987. Hermione Lee, *Willa Cather: A Life Saved Up,* 1989.

—Sharon O'Brien

CATT, CARRIE CHAPMAN (1859–1947), woman suffrage leader. Born in Wisconsin and reared mostly in Iowa, Catt by the early 1880s was already a widely traveled suffragist. By the late 1880s, recognized as a tireless campaigner, keen strategist, and skilled political tactician, she was a major figure in the *National American Woman Suffrage Association (NAWSA). Succeeding Susan B. *Anthony as head of NAWSA, she served from 1900 to 1904 and again in 1915–1920, a period that brought victory in New York state in 1917 and final ratification of the *Nineteenth Amendment (granting woman suffrage) in 1920. A single-minded, disciplined leader who considered herself a political realist, Catt employed whatever strategies she believed necessary, including placating white racists in the *South. While supporting U.S. involvement in *World War I, she always kept the suffrage goal paramount.

In 1919–1920, Catt helped launch the *League of Women Voters, to enable newly enfranchised women to exert real political influence. She envisioned the league as a nonpartisan organization that would promote a different politics from the partisan struggle she had come to detest. Catt became active in the international peace movement before and after World War I, but world peace proved a more elusive goal than woman suffrage.

Catt was twice widowed; the 1905 death of her second husband, a successful civil engineer, left her financially independent. In her later years she cultivated close personal relationships with many women. Childless, she nurtured friendships as she had earlier honed her skills at devising the political strategies that made woman suffrage a reality.

[*See also* Peace Movements; Woman Suffrage Movement.]

• Robert Booth Fowler, *Carrie Catt: Feminist Politician,* 1988.

—Robert Booth Fowler

CATTLE INDUSTRY. *See* Livestock Industry.

CENSORSHIP. From the *Colonial Era to the present, struggles over censorship have loomed large in American life, figuring in the history of *antislavery and abolitionism, *labor movements, antiwar protests, radical politics, gay rights advocacy, public education debates, controversies over sex and reproduction, and many other issues.

Although John Peter Zenger's 1735 acquittal did not eliminate seditious libel from American jurisprudence, it did make government censorship attempts more difficult. Though the founders' commitment to wholly unfettered speech remains in dispute, the First Amendment's guarantee of free speech and freedom of the press erected a strong barrier against censorship, and Americans of the era clearly valued free political discourse. While common-law ideas of libel, blasphemy, *sedition, and obscenity persisted, radical ideas of free expression thrived as well, as groups and individuals asserted their interests in the public arena. But although the *Bill of Rights seemed a bulwark in defense of free speech, the 1798 *Alien and Sedition Acts revealed its continued vulnerability.

Like the *Federalist party in the 1790s, subsequent leaders during the *Civil War, the two world wars, and the *Cold War would insist that the nation's fate depended on the government's capacity to censor its critics. Confronted with antiwar and pro-South agitation during the Civil War, President Abraham *Lincoln suspended the writ of habeas corpus in 1863 and authorized the arrest of southern sympathizers, war opponents, and persons engaged in "any disloyal practice." In *World War I, under the 1917 Espionage Act and the 1918 Sedition Amendment, the Woodrow *Wilson administration suppressed antiwar periodicals and arrested numerous war critics, including the socialist leader Eugene V. *Debs. During the 1918–1920 Red Scare, officials imprisoned and deported many labor activists and radicals. During *World War II and the early *Cold War the government again engaged in censorship, monitoring wartime movie scripts and, later, removing books by politically suspect authors from *United States Information Agency libraries abroad.

But anticensorship sentiment remained strong. The Wilson administration's abuses led Roger Baldwin and others in 1920 to found what became the *American Civil Liberties Union (ACLU). The *Supreme Court Justice Oliver Wendell *Holmes's dissent in *Abrams* v. *United States* (1919) sharply criticized censorship, as did the Harvard Law professor Zechariah Chafee in his critique of wartime censorship, *Freedom of Speech* (1920). The ACLU-Holmes-Chafee approach insisted that the First Amendment was meant primarily to serve the social good, by assuring a hearing for unpopular political views, not to protect individual liberty. This approach gave short shrift to traditional libertarianism, represented by Theodore Schroeder of the National Free Speech League, for example, which insisted on the individual's freedom of expression, political, sexual, or otherwise. In a tactically shrewd move, *Progressive Era intellectuals offered their socially based argument for free speech in an era not particularly receptive to libertarian ideas. However, this argument made it harder to defend nonpolitical forms of expression, such as "obscene" books, "indecent" movies, and birth-control information.

Following Holmes's lead, the Supreme Court in *Near* v. *Minnesota* (1931) overturned governmental efforts to impose prior restraint on a newspaper. In *New York Times* v. *Sullivan* (1964), the high court rejected a libel suit against the *Times* for a political ad, even though the ad contained certain inaccuracies. In 1971, the justices turned back President Richard M. *Nixon's efforts to prevent publication of the *Pentagon Papers. The liberalizing trend gradually extended to sexually explicit material, in such cases as *United States* v. *Ulysses* (1933); *Roth* v. *United States* and *Alberts* v. *California* (1957); and a 1966 case involving John Cleland's *Memoirs of a Woman of Pleasure.* Signaling a conservative turn, however, the Supreme Court in *Miller* v. *California* (1973) made it somewhat easier for local authorities to suppress sexually explicit material deemed obscene by local community standards.

Throughout American history, censorship battles have unfolded within a larger cultural context. For example, the expansion of First Amendment protection reflected the efforts of successive generations of artists, writers, and "sex radicals," from nineteenth-century advocates of "free love" to twentieth-century proponents of *abortion and gay rights. Conversely, in times of rapid social change, threatened social groups have used censorship as an instrument of social control. Amid the social upheavals of the *Gilded Age, elite groups like the New England Watch and Ward Society and Anthony Comstock's New York Society for the Suppression of Vice, relying on local statutes and on an 1873 federal law barring obscene material from the mails, sought to suppress dime novels, crime magazines, books deemed indecent, and contraceptive information. In the early twentieth century, as immigrants transformed urban America, as women surged into the workplace and the voting booths, as Victorian sexual mores eroded, and as movies and other new amusements captivated mass audiences, reformers condemned the stage, the press, and motion pictures for corrupting the young.

Would-be censors especially targeted motion pictures. As local and state censorship boards pressured studios to produce more decorous movies, the Supreme Court in *Mutual* v. *Ohio* (1915) denied the film industry First Amendment protection. Catholic pressure forced Hollywood to accept a production code under Will H. Hays in 1930, and a Catholic censor, Joseph Breen, in 1934. Though the code was technically voluntary, Hollywood understood that the alternative was consumer boycotts and censorship. As oligopolies controlling production, distribution, and exhibition, the studios could enforce self-censorship. The comic-book industry, accused of promoting *juvenile delinquency, copied the Hollywood model, adopting an almost identical code and enforcement mechanism. The movie-censorship tide turned in 1952, however, when the Supreme Court in *Burstyn* v. *Wilson* (a case involving Roberto Rossellini's film *The Miracle,* denounced by New York's Francis Cardinal *Spellman) reversed its 1915 position and gave the film First Amendment protection. Local and state censorship boards disbanded, and Hollywood abandoned the production code in 1966, adopting a rating system instead.

Censorship pressures revived, however, amid the culture wars of the late twentieth century. Evangelical Christians and conservative politicians defending "family values" demanded legal measures against sexually explicit movies, TV shows, rock lyrics, and *Internet websites. The 1996 Communications Decency Act (CDA), which barred "indecent" materials from the Internet, was challenged by the ACLU and others, and in 1997 the Supreme Court struck it down on First Amendment grounds. Congress responded with the Child Online Protection Act (dubbed "CDA-II"), and the legal jousting continued. At the local level, conservatives sought to purge objectionable books from school libraries and curricula. On the political left, meanwhile, activists and feminists called for legal action against "hate speech" denigrating ethnic or racial groups, and against pornography considered degrading to women. Issues of censorship and free speech, in short, once again loomed large as a new century began.

[*See also* Anticommunism; Christian Coalition; Conservatism; Education: Education in Contemporary America; Feminism; Film; Gay and Lesbian Rights Movement; Hoover, J. Edgar; Moral Majority; Post–Cold War Era; Radicalism; Roman Catholicism; *Schenck* v. *United States;* Sexual Morality and Sex Reform; Socialism; Socialist Party of America; Television; Twenties, The; Zenger Trial.]

• Leonard W. Levy, *Emergence of a Free Press,* 1985. John D'Emilio and Estelle B. Freedman, *Intimate Matters: A History of Sexuality in America,* 1988. Samuel Walker, *In Defense of American Liberties: A History of the ACLU,* 1990. Donna Lee Dickerson, *The Course of Tolerance: Freedom of the Press in Nineteenth-Century America,* 1990. Mark E. Neely Jr., *The Fate of Liberty: Abraham Lincoln and Civil Liberties,* 1991. Frank Walsh, *Sin and Censorship: The Catholic Church and the Motion Picture Industry,* 1996. David M. Rabban, *Free Speech in Its Forgotten Years,* 1997.

—Francis G. Couvares

CENSUS, FEDERAL. The decennial population census originated in the 1787 federal *Constitution as a mechanism for determining each state's political representation in the House of Representatives and *electoral college. The Constitution (art. 1, sec. 2) specifies that representatives and direct taxes are "apportioned among the several States which may be included within this Union, according to their respective Numbers" and goes on to require a census every ten years to determine those numbers. The census counted everyone in the country, except "Indians not taxed." The Constitution reduced the slave population count in each state to three-fifths of the total before adding it to the free population count for purposes of representation (the Three-Fifths Compromise). These provisions embedded race classifications in the census. The United States thus became the first nation to conduct a regular population census and use it to apportion legislative seats.

The nation successfully managed the allocation of political representation as it grew from thirteen states with 3.9 million people in 1790 to fifty states with a quarter of a billion people in 1990. From 1790 to 1840, the State Department conducted the census, sending U.S. marshals' assistants to all households to tally the number of persons in the household, in broad demographic categories of age, sex, and social status. From 1850 to 1900, a Census Office in the Interior Department conducted the census. In 1850, Congress mandated an individual-level count that collected detailed information on Americans' demographic, social, and economic situations. Since 1910, the Bureau of the Census, housed in the Commerce Department, has taken the census. In 1890, a system of machine tabulation automated much of the work. UNIVAC, the first nondefense *computer, tabulated the 1950 census. Today, the census is taken primarily by mail. In 1990, the bureau introduced the TIGER (Topologically Integrated Geographic Encoding and Referencing) system to provide maps and a list of every address in the United States.

Government, the private sector, and scholars use census data for planning; market forecasting; and social, economic and political analysis. By the late twentieth century, these uses were as important as the original political functions and congressional interests still shaped the questions asked and the data reported.

At times, the census became enmeshed in political controversies of such magnitude that it was challenged. When the Thirteenth Amendment to the Constitution abolished slavery, it also abolished the Three-Fifths Compromise and gave southern states full representation for the newly freed African American population in Congress. After the *Civil War, Northerners realized that white Southerners would not permit the freed slaves to vote unless further federal protections were put in place. Hence Congress wrote provisions to guarantee voting rights into the *Fourteenth and *Fifteenth Amendments of the Constitution. In 1920, members of Congress from rural states that were slated to lose representation to states with growing urban populations attacked the census. For the first and only time, Congress did not reapportion itself after the 1920 census. From the late 1960s, big-city mayors and civil rights leaders charged that the census undercounted minorities and the poor.

As the 2000 census loomed, partisan wrangling erupted over the Census Bureau's proposal to use statistical sampling techniques to supplement traditional counting techniques. As the census became politicized, ironically, this mechanism designed to defuse the contentiousness surrounding the allocation of political representation itself became embroiled in broader controversies about the distribution of power in American society.

[*See also* Civil Rights Movement; Demography; Federal Government, Legislative Branch: House of Representatives; Urbanization.]

• Margo Anderson, *The American Census: A Social History*, 1988. Harvey Choldin, *Looking for the Last Percent: The Controversy over Census Undercounts*, 1994. Margo Anderson and Stephen E. Fienberg, *Who Counts? The Politics of Census Taking in Contemporary America*, 1999.

—Margo Anderson

CENTERS FOR DISEASE CONTROL. The Centers for Disease Control and Prevention, founded in Atlanta, Georgia, in 1946, is the world's premier public health institution. It evolved from a *World War II unit of the U.S. Public Health Service—Malaria Control in War Areas—which was charged with keeping the *South, where many troops were trained, *malaria free. Originally called the Communicable Disease Center, its purpose was to control communicable *diseases throughout the United States. Several name changes reflected its expanding mission, but the acronym CDC continued.

Dr. Joseph W. Mountin, founder of the CDC, envisioned an institution that would assist state health departments in disease control through laboratory work and epidemiology. The "disease detectives" of its Epidemic Intelligence Service, organized in 1951, quickly achieved fame. This unit, conceived by Dr. Alexander Langmuir, introduced the concept of disease surveillance, first used effectively against *poliomyelitis and *influenza in the 1950s. Routine disease surveillance would become the cornerstone of *public-health practice.

The CDC played a vital role in the global elimination of *smallpox and discovered the Legionnaires' disease bacterium, the hantavirus (agent of a serious respiratory disease outbreak in the American *Southwest), and the causes of toxic shock syndrome and Lassa and Ebola fevers. In 1981, the CDC first identified a new fatal disease, subsequently named AIDS (*acquired immunodeficiency syndrome). Among its successes in environmental health were the removal of lead from gasoline and the development of a serum test for dioxin, used to detect exposure to Agent Orange among *Vietnam War veterans. The CDC's massive swine flu inoculation campaign of 1976 elicited bitter criticism when the expected epidemic never materialized and serious side effects from the vaccine came to light. In the 1980s, the CDC added accidents, violence, and lifestyle issues to its concerns. Disease prevention, a requisite to achieving the goal of a healthy people in a healthy world, became the CDC's emphasis in the 1990s.

[*See also* Environmentalism; Medicine: Since 1945.]

• Elizabeth W. Etheridge, *Sentinel for Health: A History of the Centers for Disease Control*, 1992.

—Elizabeth W. Etheridge

CENTRAL INTELLIGENCE AGENCY. The *National Security Act of 1947 created the *National Security Council (NSC), a presidential advisory body. This act also created the Central Intelligence Agency (CIA) as successor to the *World War II *Office of Strategic Services, with responsibility for recruiting and controlling agents, conducting covert actions, and providing intelligence assessments. General Walter Bedell Smith, Dwight D. *Eisenhower's wartime chief of staff, was director from 1950 to 1953. Director Allen Dulles (1953–1961) enjoyed broad leeway from President Eisenhower, who respected the agency's intelligence assessments and authorized a wide range of covert actions, including coups in Iran and Guatemala to overthrow regimes viewed as hostile to U.S. interests.

Beginning in the 1960s, the CIA faced rising criticism. Failures like the shooting down of a U-2 spy plane over Russia in 1960 and the disastrous *Bay of Pigs operation in 1961 shook official confidence. Conservatives attacked it as a bastion of the liberal establishment—President Richard M. *Nixon derided it as "a muscle-bound bureaucracy" drawn from the "Ivy League and Georgetown set." Liberals and radicals criticized the CIA's covert actions against Third World states, including its role in recruiting a secret army in Laos and in the overthrow and assassination of Salvadore Allende, the leftist president of Chile, in 1973. A congressional committee under Senator Frank Church of Idaho documented the agency's failures and excesses, while presidents marginalized it and slashed its staff. In violation of the law, the CIA also carried out various domestic operations that figured in the Nixon Era *Watergate scandals. Under director William Casey in the Ronald *Reagan administration, the CIA participated in the secret and illegal support of the Nicaraguan contras and thus figured in the *Iran-Contra Affair. The arrest of several double agents operating within the agency did further damage.

From the 1970s to the 1990s, the CIA faced persistent attacks for inadequate security; recruitment failures; assessment errors; illegal domestic operations; and the politicization of intelligence, both in overrating Russia's strength and failing to anticipate Soviet actions. In fact, the CIA's record in recruiting agents was respectable, and its officers generally tried to be law-abiding even when pressured otherwise. Many of the CIA's more dubious undertakings, such as the far-fetched schemes to assassinate or discredit Cuban premier Fidel Castro, were initiated on instructions from higher up. The CIA often carried out covert operations effectively and resisted efforts to politicize its intelligence assessments, which were often quite good, involving not only agents but also data analysis and technical means such as photographic satellites. An understanding of the CIA is crucial to understanding *Cold War America, both at home and abroad.

[*See also* Foreign Relations: U.S. Relations with Latin America; Foreign Relations: U.S. Relations with the Middle East; Intelligence Gathering and Espionage.]

• John Ranelagh, *The Agency*, 1986. Christopher Andrews, *For the President's Eyes Only*, 1995.

—John Ferris

CENTRAL PARK. *See* New York City; Olmsted, Frederick Law; Parks, Urban.

CHALLENGER DISASTER (1986). On 28 January 1986, in the skies over Cape Canaveral, Florida, the space shuttle *Challenger* exploded seventy-three seconds after liftoff, killing all seven astronauts on board: Greg Jarvis, Christa McAuliffe, Ron McNair, Ellison Onizuka, Judy Resnick, Dick Scobee, and Mike Smith. Although shuttle launches had become almost routine in the five years and twenty-four trips since the first liftoff, *Challenger* flight STS 51-L stood out for carrying the high-school teacher McAuliffe. As a result, millions of Americans watched the launch and explosion live on television. The Teacher in Space program was intended to boost the *National Aeronautics and Space Administration's declining budget and public interest. Instead, the disaster highlighted budget and management troubles at NASA.

President Ronald *Reagan appointed former secretary of state William Rogers to head a scientific commission to investigate the explosion. The commission's report, issued two months later, traced the cause to the rubber O-rings used to seal the joints in the shuttle's solid rocket boosters. The unusually cold weather on the morning of the launch stiffened the O-rings, allowing fuel to leak from the boosters and ignite a deadly fireball. The Rogers Commission also discovered that NASA managers had not heeded warnings by engineers at both Morton-Thiokol and the Rockwell Corporation on the evening of 27 January 1986, that a launch in temperatures of less than fifty degrees was likely to be hazardous. Nearly three years and $2.4 billion later, NASA relaunched the U.S. *space program with its next shuttle, *Discovery.*

• U.S. Senate, *Rogers Commission Report,* 1986. Malcolm McConnell, *Challenger: A Major Malfunction,* 1987.

—Sarah K. A. Pfatteicher

CHAMBERS, WHITTAKER. *See* Hiss, Alger.

CHAMBERS OF COMMERCE, organizations representing a broad range of *business interests in a given city or state, often led by bankers, realtors, and representatives of other service industries. Such organizations were formed as early as the 1780s, but their numbers and their political role blossomed in the *Gilded Age in response to the challenges of rapid economic growth, labor unrest, and urban political reform. Unlike more narrowly focused employers' or trade associations, local and regional chambers focused on such issues as property taxes, zoning and regulation, and business promotion.

In 1912, a group of leading municipal chambers and trade associations formed the United States Chamber of Commerce (USCC) to unite business interests on public policy issues. Through the middle years of the twentieth century, the USCC was less confrontational than organizations like the *National Association of Manufacturers and more likely to encourage its members to accommodate to changing patterns of labor relations and political regulation. The USCC cooperated closely with the federal government in mobilizing the economy for *World War I and with Herbert *Hoover's Commerce Department during the 1920s. The USCC initially attempted to work with the New Deal but, like the larger business community that it represented, grew increasingly disenchanted with many of President Franklin Delano *Roosevelt's policies. While the USCC participated in the postwar business backlash against the New Deal, it also acted as a leading business advocate for a limited welfare state built on public spending and the "politics of growth." After the 1930s, the USCC was led by a loose coalition of internationalists, shippers, exporters, bankers, and natural-resource interests. Through political lobbying; informational services to members; and its magazine, *Nation's Business,* the USCC proved a moderate and politically pragmatic vehicle for business opinion and influence.

[*See also* Business Roundtable; National Industrial Conference Board; New Deal Era, The.]

• Richard Hume Werking, "Bureaucrats, Businessmen and Foreign Trade: The Origins of the United States Chamber of Commerce," *Business History Review* 52.3 (1978): 321–41. Robert M. Collins, *The Business Response to Keynes, 1929–1964,* 1981.

—Colin Gordon

CHANNING, WILLIAM ELLERY (1780–1842), clergyman and author, leader of American Unitarianism. Born in Newport, Rhode Island, Channing graduated from Harvard College in 1793. In 1803, he was ordained minister of the Federal Street Church (now the Arlington Street Church) in *Boston. He engaged in theological debates with the Calvinist Congregationalists; his *Unitarian Christianity* (1819) was widely circulated. During the 1820s, he led in the development of a distinct Unitarian denomination, which he hoped would remain a branch of Christianity. Channing accepted the *Bible as divine revelation and strongly believed in free will.

Channing wrote on a wide variety of subjects, and his essays won international attention. His social views, derived from his religious principles, called for the full development of the potential of every human being; "Self-Culture" (1838) expressed this belief. Channing supported many reform causes; his *antislavery statements offended conservatives, even within his own congregation.

Channing synthesized *Protestantism's moralism with the Enlightenment's commitment to human dignity. The transcendentalists admired him, although he never became one of them. He influenced such contemporaries as Ralph Waldo *Emerson, Margaret *Fuller, Senator Charles Sumner, Horace *Mann, Lydia Maria *Child, and Dorothea *Dix. As a result, his cultural significance far transcends the small Unitarian denomination he helped found.

[*See also* Religion; Transcendentalism; Unitarianism and Universalism.]

• Jack Mendelsohn, *Channing: The Reluctant Radical,* 1971.

—Daniel Walker Howe

CHAPLIN, CHARLIE (1889–1977), movie actor, director. Born in London, Charles Spencer Chaplin survived a difficult childhood to win early success as an English music-hall performer. In 1913, he signed a movie contract with Keystone Studios. He soon developed his tramp persona, using a familiar costume and brush mustache, and began to direct his own movies, appearing in thirty-five for Keystone (1914), fourteen for Essanay (1915–1916), and twelve for Mutual (1916–1917). Most were two-reel comedies. Blending comedy, romance, and pathos in his films, Chaplin became an internationally popular *film star and generated increasingly lucrative contracts, which enabled him to build his own studio and in 1919 to cofound United Artists. *The Kid* (1921), *The Gold Rush* (1925), and *City Lights* (1931) are among his most famous nondialogue comic features.

The Great Depression awakened Chaplin's social conscience. *Modern Times* (1936) criticized industrial efficiency at the expense of human needs, while *The Great Dictator* (1940) satirized Hitler. During the *Cold War, conservative groups attacked Chaplin for his leftist political involvements, his dalliances with very young women, and his failure to become a U.S. citizen; their boycotts helped doom *Monsieur Verdoux* (1947) and *Limelight* (1952) at the box office. In September 1952, after Chaplin left the United States for a trip to London, the U.S. attorney general revoked his reentry permit, stating that Chaplin, still a British citizen, would have to defend himself against political and morals charges before an immigration board if he desired readmission. In this hostile political climate, Chaplin settled in Switzerland, where he remained until his death, returning to America only briefly in 1972 to receive a special Academy Award in Los Angeles. In 1975, he was knighted by Queen Elizabeth II.

• David Robinson, *Chaplin: His Life and Art,* 1985. Charles J. Maland, *Chaplin and American Culture,* 1989.

—Charles J. Maland

CHARITY ORGANIZATION MOVEMENT. The charity organization movement was a late nineteenth-century philanthropic reform that sought to bring rich and poor together even as the forces of *immigration, *industrialization, and *urbanization drove them apart. Beginning in England in 1869, the movement quickly crossed the Atlantic and established a beachhead in numerous American cities with the formation of local charity organization societies. The practitioners of charity organization tackled *poverty by making charity more professional, efficient, and "scientific" while retaining the humanitarian basis by recruiting "friendly visitors." These trained charity workers, usually female, pioneered the case method of *social work. The methods of scientific charity—organization, coordination, and investigation—brought private resources to bear upon the lives of the urban poor. With its network of local societies, the charity organization movement soon established influential journals, participated actively in the National Conference of Charities and Corrections, and in 1898 established the first professional training school for social work—the New York School of Philanthropy. These elements provided the basis for twentieth-century approaches to poverty and dependency.

The American charity organization movement drew ideological nourishment from many sources, including English poor-law reform, Puritan ideology, *social Darwinism, and liberal Christian philanthropy as embodied in the *Social Gospel. According to the movement's leaders, the aim of charity was not primarily to assuage suffering but rather to uplift and transform the recipients into productive and independent members of society. As the movement progressed, women played an important role as leaders and workers. In the 1880s and 1890s, Josephine Shaw Lowell (1843–1905) of New York and Boston's Annie Adams Fields (1834–1915) moved their organizations from repressive measures to more positive programs stressing environmental conditions. After the devastating depression of 1893–1896, a new generation of leaders such as Edward T. Devine (1867–1948) of New York and Mary Richmond (1861–1928) of Baltimore, Maryland, promoted innovations that ensured the continued influence of charity organization ideas and practices in the twentieth century.

Charity organization had numerous critics, including ministers and settlement house workers who chastised it for being all head and no heart. Historians who view the movement as little more than a handmaiden to industrial *capitalism, however, ignore its role in initiating such reforms as tenement house regulation and *tuberculosis-prevention programs. Charity organization's greatest legacy was in facilitating the move from volunteerism to professional social work. The movement outlived its usefulness by the 1920s, as government agencies took over many of its most successful programs. The Great Depression of the 1930s brought a massive federal presence in areas previously dominated by private charities.

[*See also* Depressions, Economic; Gilded Age; Settlement Houses.]

• Frank Dekker Watson, *The Charity Organization Movement in the United States,* 1922; reprint, 1971. Michael Katz, *In the Shadow of the Poor House: A Social History of Welfare in America,* 1986. Joan Waugh, *Unsentimental Reformer: The Life of Josephine Shaw Lowell,* 1997.

—Joan Waugh

CHARLES RIVER BRIDGE v. WARREN BRIDGE (1837), *Supreme Court ruling relating to corporate development. In 1650, the Massachusetts legislature gave Harvard College an exclusive right to operate a ferry from *Boston across the Charles River to Charlestown. Under acts of 1785 and 1792, Massachusetts transferred all rights of Harvard's monopoly to the Charles River Bridge Company and gave that company a seventy-year charter to operate a toll bridge between Charlestown and Boston. In 1828, the legislature chartered the Warren Bridge Company to build a new bridge that would revert to the state within six years after its completion. The stock owners of the Charles River Bridge complained that the charter for the new Warren Bridge violated its contract with the state. The Charles River Bridge Company argued that its original monopoly to operate the ferry included the bridge and that, in effect, the state had granted the company an exclusive right to operate a bridge between the two cities. The Charles River Bridge Company sued, citing the contracts clause of the U.S. *Constitution (art. 1, sec. 9), which bars states from "impairing the Obligations of Contracts."

By a vote of 4–3, the U.S. Supreme Court in 1837 upheld Massachusetts's right to charter the Warren Bridge. Writing for the Court, Chief Justice Roger B. *Taney ruled that the charter granted to the Charles River Company should be read strictly; it did not include the promise of a monopoly, and therefore the state had the power to charter a new company.

This ruling allowed new industries to develop alongside—and even to supplant—existing technologies and companies. It gave states flexibility in developing public policy toward industries and utilities. It encouraged more competitive enterprise yet allowed states to grant monopolies to enterprises that served the public interest. Adhering to the logic of *Charles River Bridge,* however, states often included contract clauses enabling them to revoke all or some of the charter rights.

[*See also* Business; Capitalism; Economic Development; Industrialization.]

• Stanley I. Kutler, *Privilege and Creative Destruction: The Charles River Bridge Case,* 1971. Elizabeth B. Monroe, "Abridging Vested Interest: The Battle of the Masschusetts Bridge," in *Historic Supreme Court Cases: 1690–1990,* ed. John Johnson, 1992, pp. 174–81.

—Paul Finkelman

CHAUTAUQUA MOVEMENT. Begun with the modest objective of training Methodist Sunday school teachers, Chautauqua soon emerged as a national movement with broad cultural implications. In 1874, Bishop John Heyl Vincent (1832–1920) and the industrialist Lewis Miller (1829–1899) converted a Methodist camp meeting on the shores of Lake Chautauqua in western New York into an "outdoor university" combining *Bible study with courses in science, history, literature, and the arts. By the 1880s, Chautauqua had evolved into the foremost advocate for adult education. Its eight-week summer program featured *Social Gospel–minded academics, politicians, preachers, prohibitionists, and reformers. Embracing the summer vacation as a fact of modern life, Vincent and Miller adapted it to their broader mission of spiritual and social renewal.

Through correspondence courses, university extension, journals like The *Chautauquan,* and especially reading circles, Chautauqua's influence spread widely. In 1878, Vincent inaugurated the Chautauqua Literary and Scientific Circle (CLSC). Under the leadership of director Kate F. Kimball (1860–1917), 264,000 people—75 percent of them women—had enrolled in the CLSC by the century's end. Students completing the four-year reading program received official (if symbolic) diplomas. Criticized by some as superficial, the CLSC nevertheless gave thousands of mostly white, Protestant, middle-class women opportunities to develop stronger public voices and organizational experience. Many CLSC women established independent Chautauqua assemblies in their own communities. By 1904, more than one hundred towns, mainly in the *Middle West, held assemblies on grounds patterned on the original Chautauqua. Local boosters, *railroads, and interurban lines supported these assemblies as profitable (yet moral) tourist attractions.

In 1904, for-profit lyceum organizers introduced a network of mobile Chautauquas, or "circuits." Using aggressive sales tactics, one-sided contracts, and a tightly scheduled booking system, circuit Chautauquas hastened the decline of the independent assemblies (many of which later became residential subdivisions). To modernists like Sinclair *Lewis, the circuit Chautauqua, with its "animal and bird educators" (i.e., pet tricks), uplifting lectures, sentimental plays, and heavy-handed wartime patriotism, symbolized the shallowness of middle-class culture. Despite ridicule from the avant-garde, however, the circuits launched the careers of many performers and linked some six thousand small towns to the larger world. In the mid-1920s, the rise of commercial *radio, movies, automobiles, and an expanded *consumer culture signaled the end of the circuits' popularity in rural America. The last tent show folded in 1933. The original assembly on Lake Chautauqua still thrives.

[*See also* Gilded Age; Leisure; Methodism; Popular Culture; Progressive Era; Protestantism; Social Class; Tourism; Twenties, The; Women's Club Movement.]

• Theodore Morrison, *Chautauqua: A Center for Education, Religion, and the Arts in America,* 1974. Alan Trachtenberg, " 'We Study the Word and Works of God': Chautauqua and the Sacralization of Culture in America," *Henry Ford Museum and Greenfield Village Herald* 13.2 (1984): 3–11.

—Andrew Chamberlin Rieser

CHAVEZ, CESAR (1927–1993), labor activist, founder and president of the United Farm Workers of America. Chavez spent his early childhood on his grandfather's homestead near Yuma, Arizona. After losing the farm in the late 1930s, the Chavez family joined *California's migratory farm-labor force. Following military service, Chavez in 1945 resumed work as a farm laborer in California. After marrying in 1948, Chavez and his family relocated to San Jose's notorious "Sal Si Puedes" (literally "get out if you can") barrio. Becoming involved in Mexican-American political and social action, Chavez established the National Farm Workers Association in Delano, California, in 1962 (it was rechristened the United Farm Workers Organizing Committee in 1966 and the United Farm Workers of America [UFW] in 1972). His new union gained prominence in 1965, when, together with another union of Filipino farmworkers backed by the AFL-CIO, it embarked on a campaign to organize growers of table grapes in California. The five-year campaign became a cause célèbre in the United States and abroad, bringing Chavez to national and international prominence.

Chavez's approach to worker activism sought social and racial justice and employed not only strikes and boycotts but also mass marches, fasts, and nonviolent civil disobedience. He won a fiercely dedicated following of young Chicano and Anglo organizers and the support of Hollywood celebrities, political luminaries, and social reformers. Unprecedented union victories against leading wineries and table-grape producers caused anti-union employers, in collusion with the teamsters' union, to block Chavez's further advance. In response, Chavez turned to political action. In 1975, with the help of a sympathetic liberal governor, Chavez won passage of the California Agricultural Labor Relations Act granting the state's farmworkers the organizing rights long denied them under federal law. By the late 1970s, UFW membership approached fifty thousand. By the early 1980s, however, employer opposition, surplus labor, and internal dissension diluted most of the UFW's earlier gains. Increasingly insular and eccentric, Chavez invested the UFW's dwindling resources in ineffectual boycotts and direct-mail fund-raising efforts. He nevertheless ranks as the most influential Mexican-American leader of his generation and arguably the most important in the nation's history.

[See also Agriculture: Since 1920; Hispanic Americans; Labor Movements; Migratory Agricultural Workers.]

• Jacques E. Levy, *Cesar Chavez: Autobiography of La Causa,* 1975. Richard Griswold del Castillo and Richard A. Garcia, *Cesar Chavez: A Triumph of Spirit,* 1995.

—Cletus Daniel

CHEMICAL INDUSTRY. The largest industry in America, the chemical industry supplies roughly a quarter of the world's chemicals, more than any other nation. In the *Colonial Era, chemical manufacturing was confined to such rudimentary products as indigo dyes, naval stores, leather, glass, soap, and candles. In the early 1800s, producers relied heavily on imports of alkalies (especially soda ash, caustic soda, and bleach) from Great Britain. The typical nineteenth-century American chemical manufactory was owner-managed, employed eight to twelve workers, and served local markets. *Philadelphia, an industry center, hosted the first professional organization (Chemical Society of Philadelphia, 1792) and publication (*American Journal of Pharmacy,* 1825). The DuPont Corporation, a giant in the chemical industry, had its origins in 1802, when E. I. du Pont started a gunpowder company near Wilmington, Delaware.

In the late nineteenth century, American producers excelled at prospecting, *mining, smelting, and refining iron ore, coal, copper, lead, zinc, tungsten and other inorganic minerals into fertilizers, explosives, nitric acid, and sulfuric acid. Progress with dyestuffs, coal-tar compounds, and other organics accelerated after the adoption of the Solvay process, a commercial technology for the manufacture of sodium carbonate, in the 1880s. Some American firms, exploiting abundant *hydroelectric power, became large producers of electrochemicals. In 1914, inorganic chemicals accounted for roughly half of U.S. production; organics for about one-quarter; and acids and electrochemicals for one-quarter.

American producers made significant progress in advanced technologies (pharmaceuticals, dyestuffs, and fine chemicals) in the early twentieth century. Vital to the *World War I military effort, the industry was supported by *tariffs and the government's confiscation and licensing of key German technologies, especially dyestuffs and the Haber-Bosch process for nitrogen fixation. Between 1900 and 1930, the U.S. chemical industry's growth far outstripped that of Germany or Great Britain. Rapid expansion of the *automotive industry in the 1920s spurred demand for thermoplastics, protective coatings, and petroleum products. A merger wave in that decade created Allied Chemical and Dye and Union Carbide and Carbon, which joined Du Pont and American Cyanamid as the nation's largest producers. Robust sales of rayon, cellophane, pesticides, fertilizers, and other key products in the 1930s earned the industry a reputation as "depression proof." Leading firms invested heavily in research and development, opening some 430 new laboratories between 1918 and 1945.

*World War II brought heavy government involvement through an enormously successful synthetic-rubber program; aggressive investment in government-owned, company-operated plants; and a new round of German technology confiscation. The postwar decades brought both a petrochemicals "revolution" and new challenges. Exploiting abundant oil and natural gas sources, American chemical and petroleum companies mass-produced such "miracle" *plastics as polyester, polyethylene, polypropylene, and polyvinylchloride. Foreign competition and the *energy crisis of the 1970s led to overcapacity and falling profits. Meanwhile, the industry confronted new regulatory controls in the early 1970s, following public outcry over the health and environmental risks of agricultural chemicals and water-and airborne wastes. In 1984, methyl isocymate gas escaping from a Union Carbide plant in Bhopal, India, killed more than three thousand people and injured thousands more. Despite its problems, however, the American chemical industry was one of the few key sectors of the American economy to retain its global dominance at the end of the twentieth century.

[*See also* Carson, Rachel; du Pont, Pierre; Environmentalism; Factory System; Mass Production; Petroleum Industry; Research Laboratories, Industrial.]

• Williams Haynes, *American Chemical Industry,* 6 vols., 1945–1954. Ashish Arora, Ralph Landau, and Nathan Rosenberg, *Chemicals and Long-Term Economic Growth,* 1998.

—David B. Sicilia

CHEMISTRY. *See* Physical Sciences.

CHEROKEE CASES (1831 and 1832). The U.S. *Supreme Court's decisions in *Cherokee Nation* v. *Georgia* (1831) and *Worcester* v. *Georgia* (1832), often referred to as the *Cherokee Cases,* considered the status of Indian tribes within the American constitutional framework. In an attempt to drive the Cherokee Indians from Georgia, the state legislature in 1828 extended the state's jurisdiction over the Cherokee Nation, annexed its land, and abolished its laws, government, and judiciary. In 1830, with Congress and President Andrew *Jackson also intent on removal, Cherokee officials asked the Supreme Court to strike down the Georgia law and recognize the Cherokee Nation as an independent state. In *Cherokee Nation,* Chief Justice John *Marshall wrote that the Cherokee Nation was not a foreign nation under article 3 of the Constitution but a "domestic, dependent nation" with a relationship to the federal government that resembled that "of a ward to his guardian." A year later, Georgia convicted a Congregational missionary named Samuel Worcester of violating a law that prohibited "white persons" from entering Cherokee territory without a license from the state. Removal proponents had enacted the law to muzzle missionaries suspected of encouraging Cherokees to resist expulsion. Before the Supreme Court in *Worcester* v. *Georgia,* Worcester's attorneys contended that Georgia's actions interfered with Congress's constitutional authority to regulate

MAP 4: WESTERN LANDS OCCUPIED BY THE CHEROKEE INDIANS (1884)

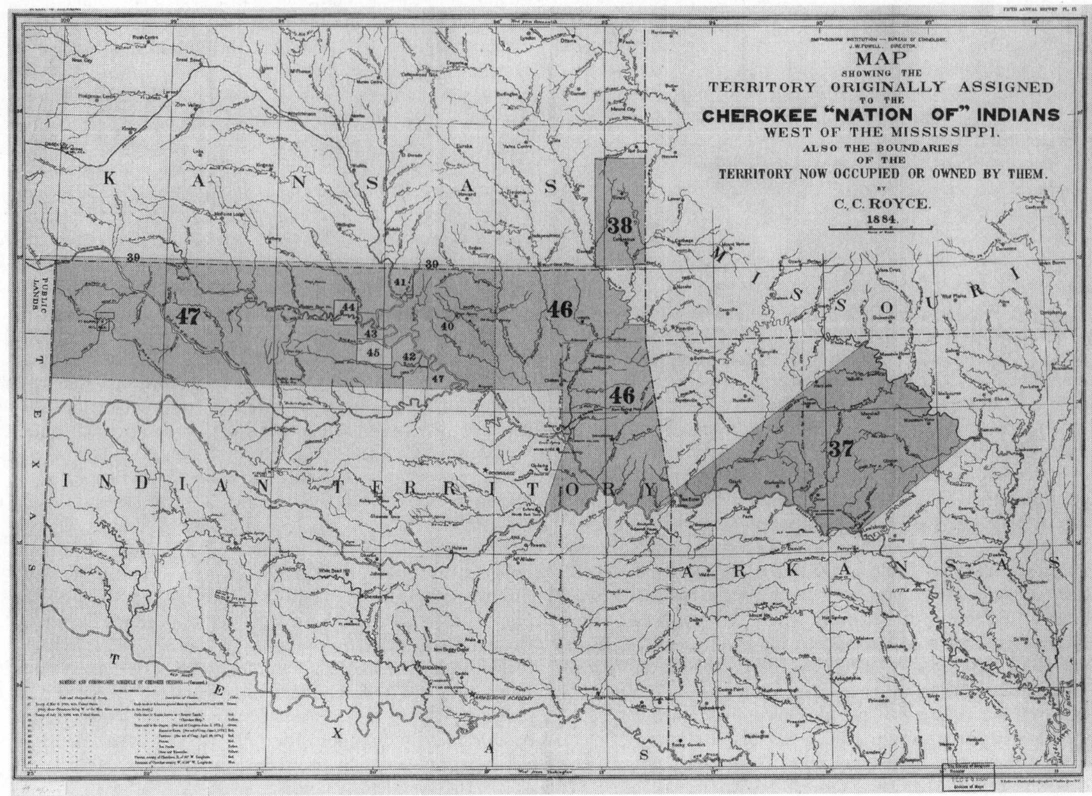

The Cherokee Indians and other tribes expelled from Georgia in the 1830s were granted land in the Indian Territory, beyond the Mississippi River. This government map shows the land in present-day Oklahoma, as well as tracts in Missouri and Kansas, occupied by Cherokees in the 1880s. As farmers and ranchers followed the railroads west after the Civil War, the Indian Territory came under heavy pressure. The government opened the western part of the Territory to settlement by non-Indians in 1889, and Oklahoma entered the Union in 1907, further eroding Indian land rights.

[*See* Agriculture: 1770s to 1890; *Cherokee Cases*; Dawes Severalty Act; Expansionism; Indian History and Culture: From 1800 to 1900; Livestock Industry.]

Indian affairs, illegally obstructed federal treaties with the Cherokees, and trespassed upon the rights of a sovereign nation. This time Marshall and the Court struck down the Georgia laws and declared the Cherokees a sovereign nation with legitimate title to their lands. Georgia repudiated the decision, and President Jackson refused to enforce it against the state. Consequently, in 1838, the United States forcibly removed most of the Cherokee population to the Indian territory in Oklahoma. *Worcester,* however, would be recognized in the twentieth century as a foundation of tribal powers.

[*See also* Antebellum Era; Expansionism; Indian History and Culture: From 1800 to 1900; Indian Removal Act.]

• Jill Norgren, *The Cherokee Cases: The Confrontation of Law and Politics,* 1991. Stephen Breyer, "For Their Own Good," *The New Republic,* Aug. 7, 2000, pp. 32–8.

—Tim Alan Garrison

CHICAGO. Founded in 1833 on Lake Michigan's swampy shores, Chicago rebounded from a devastating fire in 1871 to become America's fastest-growing city. Surpassing the one-million population mark by 1890, it ranked for years as the nation's second-largest metropolis. Long a railroad hub, it would later claim one of the world's busiest airports, O'Hare International. A *meatpacking and industrial powerhouse, late nineteenth-century Chicago was not only "hog butcher to the world" (Carl Sandburg) but also a manufacturing and printing center and home to the retailing giants Sears, Roebuck and Montgomery Ward. The social elite, led by tycoons like the meatpacker Philip Armour, the industrialist George Pullman, the hotelier Potter Palmer, and the merchant Marshall Field, inhabited a different world from that of the immigrants portrayed in William Stead's *If Christ Came to Chicago* (1894) and Upton *Sinclair's *The *Jungle* (1906). *Gilded Age Chicago was a hotbed of unionism and radical activism, epitomized by the *Haymarket Affair (1886) and the *Pullman Strike (1894). The *Progressive Era reformers John *Dewey and Jane *Addams and the revivalist Dwight L. *Moody shaped the urban culture as well.

Chicago is known for architectural innovation. The first steel-frame skyscrapers arose after the 1871 fire. The University of Chicago (1892), funded by John D. *Rockefeller, favored the Gothic style. Local boosterism combined with a civic-space ideology to create the "White City" at the 1893 World's Columbian Exposition. The Architect Daniel Burnham (1846–1912), overseer of this project, also pioneered regional planning with his *Plan of Chicago* (1909). Chicago inspired such architects as Louis *Sullivan and Frank Lloyd *Wright and, later, the International Style landmarks of Walter Gropius and Mies van der Rohe. For much of the late twentieth century, it boasted the world's tallest structure, the Sears Tower. The city also developed an extensive park system along the lakefront and in the neighborhoods.

From the 1870s on, Chicago lured immigrants: Irish, Germans, Italians, Poles, and others from Eastern Europe; later, Mexicans, Puerto Ricans, and Asians. From the *Reconstruction Era on, thousands of *African Americans migrated to Chicago. All these groups helped define the self-contained character of the city's neighborhoods, each with its distinctive ethnic, religious, and cultural institutions. Most neighborhoods had commercial cores at major streetcar intersections, featuring ornate movie theaters and branches of department stores like Marshall Field's and Carson Pirie Scott. After 1900, Chicago's neighborhoods acquired a definable look: brick bungalows and flats and large masonry courtyard apartments. White flight to the suburbs paralleled a post-1950s surge in the minority population. Misconceived *urban renewal efforts produced high-rise (and often high-crime) housing projects such as Robert Taylor Homes and Cabrini-Green. The contrast between Chicago's quiet neighborhood life and the sometimes violent intrusion of larger social and political realities was epitomized in the Prohibition Era lawlessness of the gangster Al *Capone and again in the racial unrest of the 1960s and the violence of the 1968 Democratic Convention.

Known for its brash politics, Chicago produced one of the nation's enduring political machines, extending through the mayoralties of Republican Big Bill Thompson (1915–1923, 1928–1932) and Democrats Anton Cermak (1932–1937), Richard J. *Daley (1954–1976), and his son Richard M. Daley (1989–). Harold Washington (1922–1987), elected in 1984, was the city's first black mayor.

Chicago's musical culture extends from *jazz and *blues clubs to the Chicago Symphony and the Lyric Opera. The Art Institute leads an array of cultural institutions. Chicago has produced such diverse writers as Theodore *Dreiser, Sherwood Anderson, Harriet Monroe, Richard *Wright, Saul *Bellow, and Studs Terkel. Professional baseball, football, and basketball teams vie for Chicagoans' loyalty. Like other major cities, Chicago lost population after 1960, while "Chicagoland"—the larger metropolitan area beyond the city limits—grew dramatically.

[*See also* Architecure; Chicago Fire; Department Stores; Immigration; Literature: Civil War to World War I; Literature: Since World War I; Printing and Publishing; Railroads; Sixties, The; Skyscrapers; Suburbanization; Thomas, Theodore; Twenties, The; World's Fairs and Expositions.]

• Irving Cutler, *Chicago: Metropolis of the Mid-Continent,* 1982. Dominic A. Pacyga and Ellen Skerrett, *Chicago: City of Neighborhoods,* 1986.

—Judith A. Martin

CHICAGO FIRE. The Chicago fire of 8–10 October 1871 is perhaps the most famous urban disaster in American history. Its exact cause is unknown, notwithstanding the legend that it was started by Mrs. Catherine O'Leary's cow kicking over a lantern. Whatever the conflagration's origin, the combination of a long drought, high winds, a delay in the alarm system, and an overmatched fire department assured catastrophe for the new metropolis, which was constructed almost entirely of wood. The flames destroyed a third of the city, including the entire commercial downtown and the homes of about 100,000 of *Chicago's 334,000 residents. The fire claimed remarkably few lives (estimates range in the low hundreds), however, and it spared most of Chicago's factories and railroad facilities.

Striking a city that seemed to embody the spirit of modernity in the United States, the disaster drew worldwide attention and evoked a massive outpouring of charity. No less impressive than Chicago's destruction was the astonishing rapidity with which it was rebuilt, a testimony not only to the grit and energy of its citizens but also to the young city's strategic location between the industrial East and the agricultural West which made it a major center of communications, transportation, manufacturing, and trade. The heroic story of Chicago's triumphant resurrection from the ashes, endlessly retold, overlooks many social divisions accentuated by the whole experience, but the city's recovery does reveal the resilience of the individual spirit and the force of *urbanization in nineteenth-century America.

• Karen Sawislak, *Smoldering City: Chicagoans and the Great Fire, 1871–1874,* 1995. Carl Smith, *Urban Disorder and the Shape of Belief: The Great Chicago Fire, the Haymarket Bomb, and the Model Town of Pullman,* 1995.

—Carl Smith

CHICAGO SCHOOL OF ECONOMICS. *See* Economics.

CHIEF JOSEPH (1840–1904), Nez Perce Indian chief (upon his father's death in 1871), leader of a band living in the Wallowa Valley of eastern Oregon. Neither father nor son had subscribed to the treaties that established and then reduced the Nez Perce reservation in Idaho. When in 1877 the federal government ordered all Nez Perces to settle on the reservation,

Joseph complied, but en route some young men committed depredations that set off the Nez Perce War of 1877. In subsequent battles with the U.S. Army, and in the famed trek of eight hundred Nez Perces in a desperate bid for Canadian refuge, Joseph was one of several chiefs. Others, war chiefs, played a larger military role. However, after the final battle at Bear Paw Mountain, Montana (5 October 1877), with other leading chiefs dead or escaping to Canada, Joseph surrendered with the famous speech ending, "From where the sun now stands, I will fight no more forever." Thus in white perceptions, Chief Joseph became the "Red Napoleon" who had repeatedly outwitted American generals and conducted a humane war. Confined with his people in the Indian Territory (later Oklahoma), he endeared himself to Americans and in 1893 was allowed to move to a reservation in Washington State, where he passed his remaining years.

[*See also* Indian History and Culture: From 1800 to 1900; Indian History and Culture: The Indian in Popular Culture; Indian Wars.]

• Merrill D. Beal, *"I Will Fight No More Forever": Chief Joseph and the Nez Perce War,* 1963. Alvin M. Josephy Jr., *The Nez Perce Indians and the Opening of the Northwest,* 1965.

—Robert M. Utley

CHILD, LYDIA MARIA (1802–1880), novelist, journalist, *antislavery reformer. One of nineteenth-century America's most influential writers and activists, Child, the daughter of a Medford, Massachusetts, baker, was largely self-educated. After making her literary debut with a novel of interracial marriage, *Hobomok, A Tale of Early Times* (1824), she won popularity by editing the nation's first children's magazine (*Juvenile Miscellany,* 1826–1834) and publishing two best-selling domestic advice manuals, *The Frugal Housewife* (1829) and *The Mother's Book* (1831). Upon her marriage in 1828 to the *Whig newspaper editor David Lee Child, the two agitated against the forced removal of the Cherokees from Georgia and soon against *slavery as well, joining forces with William Lloyd *Garrison in 1831.

Child produced more than a dozen books and many articles and short stories for the abolitionist cause, besides editing the *National Anti-Slavery Standard* (1841–1843). Of these works, the most enduring is *An Appeal in Favor of That Class of Americans* (1833), which sets U.S. slavery in an international historical context, denounces all forms of racial discrimination, and refutes theories of African inferiority. *An Appeal* helped recruit such stalwarts as William Ellery *Channing, Wendell Phillips, Thomas Wentworth Higginson, and Charles Sumner to the antislavery banner.

Child's pioneering *History of the Condition of Women, in Various Ages and Nations* (1835) influenced such feminist theorists as Sarah *Grimké, Margaret *Fuller, and Elizabeth Cady *Stanton. Her *Letters from New York* (1843–1845), which publicized the plight of the city's poor, launched a new school of urban journalism. And her *Progress of Religious Ideas, through Successive Ages* (1855) combated bigotry and dogmatism by highlighting the commonalities between Christianity and other faiths.

[*See also* Antebellum Era; *Cherokee Cases*; Feminism; Indian History and Culture: The Indian in Popular Culture; Indian Removal Act; Racism; Women's Rights Movements.]

• Deborah Pickman Clifford, *Crusader for Freedom: A Life of Lydia Maria Child,* 1992. Carolyn L. Karcher, *The First Woman in the Republic: A Cultural Biography of Lydia Maria Child,* 1994.

—Carolyn L. Karcher

CHILDBIRTH. Women controlled the childbirth experience in the *Colonial Era. At the onset of labor, the expectant mother sent for her midwife and called upon her female friends and relatives to attend her in her home. They offered moral support and assisted the midwife during labor and delivery. While childbirth was acknowledged as potentially dangerous to both mother and child, birthing was viewed as a natural process, and midwives intervened as little as possible. After the birth of the baby, friends and relatives assisted the new mother during her convalescence, which was typically short if the birth was normal and free of complications.

The first major change in childbirth practices for white women began after 1750 when affluent colonists in urban areas began to call upon male doctors to attend them in their homes during delivery. Regularly trained physicians assured these women that knowledge of anatomy and access to ergot (a medicinal substance that promotes uterine contractions) and obstetrical forceps could ensure faster labors and safer deliveries. By 1850, ether and chloroform were available to reduce labor pains. Unfortunately, hiring doctors did not necessarily guarantee safety. Medical intervention was accompanied by concern over the incidence of puerperal (childbed) fever, a bacterial infection of the womb, as well as the misapplication of forceps.

Besides choosing doctors over midwives, those who could afford to do so also began hiring monthly nurses to assist during delivery and to provide postnatal services. Women who aspired to social prominence extended the confinement period before birth and the lying-in period afterward to testify to their affluence and physical delicacy.

Economic status, geography, ethnicity, and race significantly influenced the way women experienced childbirth. The obstetrical services available to poor women depended on where they lived. Those who resided in small towns, rural areas, or urban ethnic neighborhoods continued to use midwives and to depend on their female support network for services. Urban women utterly without resources could seek obstetrical care in almshouses or charity hospitals. The prevalence of *malaria and other diseases complicated the birth process for southern women, and before the *Civil War they had little access to anesthesia. Slave owners had an economic interest in managing the fertility of slave women. Pioneer women delivered their own babies or sought help from whomever was available. Throughout the nineteenth century, Native American women tried to maintain their own culturally prescribed birth rituals.

In the early twentieth century, childbirth began to move from the home to the *hospital. Doctors encouraged this development because hospital births centralized obstetric care, enabled them to combat infection, and provided a regular supply of patients for the clinical education of medical students. Women accepted this change in the conviction that hospitals could provide safety in the form of specialized services in cases of premature or complicated deliveries. Extended hospital stays also offered respite from household responsibilities.

The increase in hospital births resulted in a further shift in the balance of power between doctors and their obstetrical patients over who would control the childbirth experience. Doctors increasingly looked for pathology in their obstetrics cases and intervened in the childbirth process by routinely performing episiotomies and cesarean sections and using forceps. They also began to experiment with new forms of anesthesia such as scopolamine, a drug with amnesiac properties that suppressed a patient's memory of painful contractions, as well as various forms of spinal anesthetic.

Continuing concern about maternal and infant mortality prompted Congress to pass the Sheppard-Towner Act in 1921 to provide programs for prenatal, obstetric, and postnatal care for poor women. By the mid-1950s, the mortality rate for childbearing women had declined, partly as a result of the availability of antibiotic drugs, blood banks, safer forms of anesthesia, and X rays.

In the 1940s, women began opposing the medicalization of childbirth and demanding more control over the procedures associated with the experience. Following the lead of Dr. Grantly Dick-Read, who argued that pain in childbirth resulted as much from anxiety as from physiology, they opposed the routine use of anesthesia, called for less medical intervention, and advocated a return to what they called "natural childbirth." By the 1960s, reformers were promoting such innovations as Lamaze breathing techniques, birthing at home, the presence of fathers during birth, and the utilization of nurse-midwives instead of doctors. Nevertheless, most American women continued to experience childbirth in a medicalized context over which they had only limited control.

[*See also* Medical Education; Medicine; Midwifery; Slavery: Development and Expansion of Slavery; Slavery: Slave Families, Communities, and Culture.]

• Richard W. Wertz and Dorothy C. Wertz, *Lying-in: A History of Childbirth in America,* 1977. Jane B. Donegan, *Women & Men Midwives: Medicine, Morality, and Misogyny in Early America,* 1978. Judy Barrett Litoff, *American Midwives, 1860 to the Present,* 1978. Judith Walzer Leavitt, *Brought to Bed: Childbearing in America, 1750–1950,* 1986. Sylvia D. Hoffert, *Private Matters: American Attitudes toward Childbearing and Infant Nurture in the Urban North, 1800–1860,* 1989. Sally G. McMillen, *Motherhood in the Old South: Pregnancy, Childbirth and Infant Rearing,* 1990.

—Sylvia D. Hoffert

CHILDHOOD. *See* Life Stages.

CHILD LABOR. Child labor, long a feature of American rural life, grew enormously and changed character with the *industrialization of the late nineteenth century. On farms and in coal mines, on city streets and in tenements, in mills and canneries, almost two million children, some as young as five and six years old, worked long hours for a pittance, often under harsh conditions.

In response, some people began to fight the evil of child labor. In 1901, Edgar Gardner Murphy, a clergyman, organized the Alabama Child Labor Committee, the first organization of its kind in the United States. A year later, Florence *Kelley, Lillian Wald, and Robert Hunter created the New York Child Labor Committee. In the early twentieth century, twenty-eight states restricted child labor by law, but most of the laws were vaguely worded, full of exemptions, and laxly enforced. To achieve better enforcement of these laws on a national basis, reformers in 1904 created the National Child Labor Committee (NCLC). The NCLC, under the leadership of such reformers as Felix Adler, Samuel McCune Lindsay, Alexander McKelway, and Owen R. Lovejoy, led the fight against child labor.

By 1909, despite further success in securing state regulation of child labor, the NCLC sought federal legislation. Despite vigorous opposition from various groups, Congress in 1916 passed, and President Woodrow *Wilson signed into law, the Keating-Owen Child Labor Act, the first federal law addressing the issue. Two years later, however, in *Hammer* v. *Dagenhart,* the U.S. *Supreme Court ruled the measure unconstitutional as an unwarranted exercise of the power to regulate interstate commerce granted to the federal government in the *Constitution. When Congress quickly passed a second federal child-labor statute, using its taxing power, the Supreme Court again invalidated that measure as well.

For the reformers, the only remaining course appeared to be a constitutional amendment. Winning broad public support, the proposed amendment sailed through both houses of Congress in 1924 by large majorities. Opponents, however, organized an aggressive counterattack, led by big business (especially the *National Association of Manufacturers) in alliance with conservative organizations and publications. Some Catholic church leaders, moreover, opposed the amendment as a threat to parental rights and parochial education. Falling eight states short of ratification, the proposed amendment died.

In June 1938, however, Congress passed, and President Franklin Delano *Roosevelt signed into law, the Fair Labor Standards Act, which effectively prohibited child labor. The Supreme Court unanimously upheld the act in February 1941. Even before the 1938 law, however, the use of machines on farms and in factories had diminished the need for unskilled manual labor. As a result, by the 1950s child labor had been largely eliminated in America.

At the end of the twentieth century, however, the practice reappeared. An influx of immigrants from Asia and Latin America, including illegal aliens, gave new life to tenement sweatshops; the fast-food industry employed masses of young workers. Simultaneously, a rise in both school-dropout rates and *juvenile delinquency prompted many people to promote paid employment for youngsters as a positive good. Thus, despite legislative and judicial victories, the issue of child labor remained troubling and unresolved.

[*See also* Immigration; New Deal Era, The; Progressive Era.]

• Walter I. Trattner, *Crusade for the Children: The National Child Labor Committee and Child Labor Reform in America,* 1970.

—Walter I. Trattner

CHILD REARING. The history of child rearing has no exact chronological markings. Stages and cultural traditions blend and overlap, yet changes and trends are perceptible.

Native American parenting struck early settlers as overly indulgent. Tribal parents showered affection on their children and rarely scolded them. These youngsters had far more freedom than did European children. Adolescent boys and girls came of age by engaging in tribal rituals suited to their future adult roles.

During the early *Colonial Era, many parents were relatively unself-conscious about child rearing; survival was paramount. Laws and community beliefs upheld paternal authority. *New England Puritans demanded strict obedience from their offspring and often employed a heavy hand, both at home and school, to restrain children, whom they believed to be born in sin. Parents sometimes used the apprenticeship system, sending out offspring in order to reform adolescents' character or because destitution made it difficult to keep them at home. Southern colonists, by contrast, tended to be more affectionate and indulgent toward children. A high death rate, especially in the Chesapeake region, meant that many children were raised by stepparents or kin. *Orphanages and orphan courts in the *South looked after parentless children.

Until the twentieth century, children's health proved a major worry for parents; infant and child mortality was high. Because medical caregivers lacked basic knowledge about diseases and their treatment, natural immunities and preventive medicine offered the best assurances of good health. To this end, mothers breast-fed their babies and often used home cures and folk remedies. Slave children were especially vulnerable to sickness and death; immediately before the *Civil War, slave infants and children experienced twice the mortality rates of white infants and children nationwide.

The premodern family functioned as an economic unit; children, especially among immigrants and the poor, contributed to family survival by working in field or factory. As farming declined and public education expanded, laws began to limit *child labor, and children's economic contributions to the family gradually diminished.

Child rearing has usually been a shared responsibility. In the past eras, parenting was less intensive than it would become, owing in part to mothers' demanding domestic chores coupled with an endless cycle of bearing, feeding, and nursing children. In large families, older children often served as deputy parents to younger siblings. Adult slaves, whose primary duty was to their master, often had to depend on kin or members of the slave community to help raise their offspring.

A shift in middle-class attitudes toward child rearing occurred by the second quarter of the nineteenth century. Parenting became more affectionate and intensive, influenced by Enlightenment ideas, by the ideology of the *Romantic Movement and by advice manuals that depicted children as innocent creatures needing to be molded. Parent–child relationships were now more personal and private. With most fathers working outside the home, mothers became the primary parent, celebrated for their domestic role. By the end of the century, mothers and fathers had grown more emotionally tied to their children, for better or worse. With declining fertility and smaller families, child rearing became more self-conscious; the focus shifted from survival to preoccupation with youngsters' emotional health and moral well-being.

Outside agencies and institutions also began to play a greater role in child rearing by the late nineteenth century. The medical and *public-health professions addressed children's health issues. Public and parochial schools offered academic subjects as well as exposure to technical trades, social skills, health issues, and physical education. Sunday schools, nursery schools, athletic teams, and children's organizations also contributed to child rearing.

Less is known about child rearing among the poor than among the more privileged. Parents in destitute households struggled to insure family survival, leaving little time for attentive nurturing. Children who had to work for wages had little extra time for socializing or even attending school. City streets became the place where many immigrant children were socialized.

In the 1950s and after, many middle-class parents relied upon Benjamin Spock's popular **Baby and Child Care* (first edition, 1946). Spock urged parents to create a democratic family and treat the children as equals. Initially, he promoted mothers as the principal nurturers, but later editions encouraged fathers to contribute as well.

With rapidly rising divorce rates from the 1960s through the 1980s, more children were reared in single-parent households, typically with their mother. By the end of the twentieth century, with both parents often working outside the home, experts warned of the implications for child rearing and of the many youngsters who spent hours each day in front of a *television or computer screen, lacking adult supervision and acquiring cultural and behavioral norms from sources unconnected to the nuclear family.

[*See also* Education: The Public School Movement; Family; Immigration; Indian History and Culture; Industrialization; Marriage and Divorce; Poverty; Puritanism; Slavery: Slave Families, Communities, and Culture; Social Class.]

• Edmund Morgan, *The Puritan Family,* 1966. Robert Bremner, *Children and Youth in America,* 3 vols., 1970–1974. Carl N. Degler, *At Odds: Women and the Family in America from the Revolution to the Present,* 1980. John Demos, *Past, Present and Personal: The Family and the Life Course in American History,* 1986. Stephanie Coontz, *The Social Origins of Private Life: A History of American Families, 1600–1900,* 1988. Brenda Stevenson, *Life in Black and White: Family and Community in the Slave South,* 1996.

—Sally G. McMillen

CHINESE-AMERICANS. *See* Asian Americans.

CHOLERA. No *disease, with the possible exception of *yellow fever, aroused more fear in nineteenth-century America than cholera, a deadly affliction that attacks the gastrointestinal system and causes a copious, watery diarrhea. Before the development of intravenous fluids in the twentieth century, cholera victims could dehydrate and die within a matter of hours after an attack. Although long present in Asia, cholera remained relatively rare in America until 1832. After that date, the Atlantic Ocean ceased to play its traditional role of buffer to the spread of epidemic diseases, as steamships transported growing numbers of emigrants from impoverished and unhealthful regions of the world to the United States. Domestic *industrialization and *urbanization, as well as the rudimentary nature of *public health institutions, also contributed to the propagation of cholera.

The major U.S. epidemics occurred in 1832, 1849, and 1866, when thousands died from the disease. The 1849 epidemic claimed more than 5,000 lives in *New York City alone. The last visitation came in 1892, when fewer that 150 deaths resulted nationwide. Prior to the advent of the germ theory of disease, which gained widespread credibility after the identification in 1882 of the tubercle bacillus as the cause of *tuberculosis, physicians and laypersons alike attributed cholera to such factors as air polluted with rotting organic waste and refuse (called miasma), imbalances in the equilibrium of bodily fluids, and divine punishment. Well-off Americans who escaped the disease often targeted particular social groups as the source of the scourge: the intemperate, the wicked (particularly in 1832), and the impoverished (especially Irish immigrants in 1849 and 1866 and East European Jews and southern Italians in 1892).

In 1866, the newly created Metropolitan Board of Health in New York City blunted an impending cholera epidemic by imposing sanitary measures on the city and thereby slowing the spread of the disease through the food and water chain. New York's success inspired other cities to create their own permanent boards of health. In 1883, the German bacteriologist Robert Koch discovered the etiologic agent of cholera, *Vibrio cholerae,* and its mode of transmission. In 1887, the Americans T. Mitchell Prudden and Hermann Biggs applied this knowledge at the Quarantine Station of the Port of New York to prevent the entry of the disease into the United States. That same year, William T. Sedgwick used improved water-filtering methods to ensure a clean supply of pure and safe water in Lowell, Massachusetts. By the early twentieth century, most urban areas claimed a modern filtered water system and a sanitary sewage works, both bulwarks against the spread of cholera. By the end of the twentieth century, cholera was virtually unknown in the United States and other developed countries.

[*See also* Medicine: From 1776 to the 1870s; Medicine: From the 1870s to 1945.]

• Charles E. Rosenberg, *The Cholera Years: The United States in 1832, 1849, and 1866,* 1962. Howard Markel, *Quarantine! East European Jewish Immigrants and the New York City Epidemics of 1892,* 1997.

—Howard Markel

CHRISTIAN COALITION. Emerging from the failed bid of Pat Robertson, (1930–), a prominent television evangelist, for the *Republican party's 1988 presidential nomination, the Christian Coalition by the early 1990s had become the flagship institution of the religious right. Much of its success was attributable to Ralph Reed, who was handpicked by Robertson in 1989 to establish a new organization of political conservatives dedicated to mobilizing opposition to *abortion, homosexuality, and pornography, and supporting tax cuts, "parental rights," and prayer in the schools. Learning from and building upon the Reverend Jerry Falwell's defunct *Moral Majority, Reed created a politically savvy organization with strong grassroots support. By 1997 the coalition claimed 1.9 million members. But Reed enjoyed less success in constructing a broad-based conservative coalition: white Protestant charismatics, fundamentalists, and evangelicals dominated his organization.

The Christian Coalition waged many campaigns at the local level, in school board, city council, and mayoral elections. But it also wielded substantial clout national by helping boost the arch-conservative victory in the North Carolina senatorial election in 1990 and mobilizing public support for the confirmation of Clarence Thomas to the *Supreme Court in 1991. The Christian Coalition's most visible success came in 1994, when it contributed much to the Republican sweep of congressional elections.

Reed stepped down in 1997 to launch his own political consulting firm. Whatever the Christian Coalition's future, its key role in the political maturation of the religious right was indisputable.

[*See also* Conservatism; Fundamentalist Movement; Gay and

Lesbian Rights Movement; Pentecostalism; Protestantism; Reagan, Ronald; Religion.]

• William Martin, *With God on Our Side: The Rise of the Religious Right in America*, 1996. Justin Watson, *The Christian Coalition: Dreams of Restoration, Demands for Recognition*, 1997.

—William Vance Trollinger Jr.

CHRISTIAN SCIENCE. Mary Baker Eddy (1821–1910) "discovered" Christian Science in 1866, when she spontaneously recovered from a severe injury after embracing the beliefs that reality is completely spiritual and that evil—especially sickness and death—is only an illusion. Eddy's understanding of the mind-body relationship and her healing techniques owed much to the principles of homeopathy and the practice of Phineas Parkhurst Quimby (1802–1866), a *New England mentalist (mind reader) and magnetic healer. However, the power of Eddy's personality, her authoritative textbook *Science and Health* (1875; to which she added *Key to the Scriptures* in 1883), and her effective organization of the Church of Christ, Scientist, turned Christian Science into a successful worldwide movement.

Joined by a handful of followers, Eddy founded the first Church of Christ, Scientist, in Lynn, Massachusetts, in 1879. Strife hounded the movement's early years as such influential former students as Emma Curtis Hopkins, Luther M. Marston, and Ursula N. Gestefeld challenged Eddy's originality and prophetic authority, withdrew from the movement, and dispensed their own brand of Christian Science. To protect Christian Scientists from heterodoxy, Eddy established in 1883 the monthly *Journal of Christian Science* (renamed the *Christian Science Journal* in 1885) and encouraged the formation of a National Christian Scientist Association in 1886.

In the 1890s, Eddy centralized her new religion, establishing *Boston's Mother Church (1892), an official board of directors, and the Christian Science Publishing Society (1898). Through these organizational structures and a newfound evangelistic zeal, membership grew rapidly—from 8,724 in 1890 to about 55,000 (72 percent of whom were women) by 1906—and the movement spread to Europe and Asia. The *Christian Science Monitor,* a national newspaper sponsored by the church, was founded in 1908. The 1936 federal census reported 268,915 Christian Scientist adherents. By the mid-1990s churches numbered about three thousand worldwide, although the vast majority of members were in the United States and membership had been declining steadily for decades.

Christian Science attracted converts primarily because it promised to heal their bodies and souls. Although dramatic physical cures attracted the most public attention, healing often simply involved a process of growth and enlightenment that slowly transformed a person into the spiritual image of God's ideal. All Christian Scientists practiced healing by "demonstrating" over (that is, curing) "false claims" (sickness, sin, and death), but some devoted themselves professionally to full-time service as practitioners. To expand the healing mission of practitioners, Eddy chartered the Massachusetts Metaphysical College in 1881, formalized the curriculum, and established institutes of healing and instruction across the United States. Through lectures and class instruction, such key nineteenth- and early twentieth-century leaders as Augusta Stetson, Edward Kimball, Carol Norton, and Bicknell Young influenced Christian Science practice and the interpretation of Eddy's writings.

Turn-of-the-century legal and legislative struggles among clergy, physicians, and Christian Scientists over the practice of religious healing reflected a larger contest for religious and medical authority in the United States. With an uneasy truce in this conflict, Christian Scientists came to represent for many Americans the most urbane and sedate examples of the often marginalized yet perennial practice of religious healing.

[*See also* Medicine: Alternative Medicine; Religion.]

• Stephen Gottschalk, *The Emergence of Christian Science in American Religious Life*, 1973. Rennie B. Schoepflin, *Lives on Trial: Christian Science Healers in Progressive America*, 2001.

—Rennie B. Schoepflin

CHRYSLER CORP. *See* Automotive Industry.

CHURCH AND STATE, SEPARATION OF. The separation of church and state in the United States is a constantly evolving ideal that emerged out of struggles for disestablishment of established churches in the new states during the era of the *Revolutionary War. The concept reflected the thought of the eighteenth-century Enlightenment, which in turn was influenced by the Protestant Reformation. Americans like Thomas *Jefferson and James *Madison considered religious influence in politics to be divisive and potentially repressive.

Not an end in itself, separation of church and state is a means of protecting religious liberty, securing the freedom of individuals in their choice, practice, and support of religious affiliation or nonaffiliation. The ideal has reflected the religious diversity of the American people and has adapted itself to vast changes in American society.

Separation was originally mandated by the religious-freedom provisions of the early state constitutions and in the First Amendment, which declares: "Congress shall make no law respecting an establishment of religion, or prohibiting the free exercise thereof." Scant evidence exists regarding the framers' intentions. At a minimum they clearly meant to preclude the federal government from interfering in religious matters, but equally clearly they did not intend to disestablish state churches or authorize the federal government to do so. This, however, is the narrowest possible reading of the framers' intent—a reading that perforce ignores two centuries of national experience.

Nineteenth-century struggles over religious policy merely identified problems of separation, rather than providing solutions for them. Litigation over schisms in the Congregational churches, prosecutions for blasphemy and Sabbath-breaking, persecution of Mormons for polygamy, efforts of Catholic prelates to obtain public funds for religious education, the *Kulturkampf* waged by mainline Protestant clergy to "Americanize" the new Roman Catholic, Jewish, and Christian Orthodox immigrants from eastern and southern Europe all fueled religious controversy without clarifying any definitive meaning of the separation of church and state principle.

In the twentieth century, the federal judiciary, particularly the U.S. *Supreme Court, assumed responsibility for defining and enforcing separation. In *Cantwell* v. *Connecticut* (1940), the Court interpreted the religion clause of the First Amendment as a restriction on state power. Thenceforth, the content of separation became largely a matter of judicial debate.

The "free exercise" principle developed without much controversy at first. Numerous cases in the 1940s involving *Jehovah's Witnesses, most notably the second case involving Witnesses' refusal to salute the American flag, *West Virginia Board of Education* v. *Barnette* (1943), imposed severe constraints on the states' abilities to dictate or prohibit religious observance. But in *Employment Division* v. *Smith* (1990), a case involving the sacramental use of peyote by members of the *Native American Church, the Court determined that states could enforce laws of general applicability no matter how drastically such laws inhibited an individual's religious practice. Recognizing that the *Smith* principle could lead to discrimination and impermissible state interference with religious practices, especially those of minority groups, Congress in 1993 passed the Religious Freedom Restoration Act, repudiating *Smith*'s permissive approach to state authority. The Court responded to this unusual initiative by holding the statute unconstitutional as an intrusion on its powers of judicial review (*Boerne* v. *Flores* [1997]).

Issues involving the "establishment" clause generally proved more controversial, however, evoking efforts for constitutional amendments to overturn Supreme Court rulings. Questions of state aid to parochial schools and released time for religious education ignited the controversy. In *Everson* v. *Board of Education* (1947), Justice Hugo *Black adopted a strict interpretation of separation and imposed Jefferson's metaphor of "a wall of separation" as a canonical reading of the First Amendment. Establishment controversies nevertheless continued, involving school prayer (**Engel* v. *Vitale* [1962], *Abington School District* v. *Schempp* [1963]), federal and state financial subventions for religious schools; and, finally, the constitutional flashpoint, cases involving the display of religious symbols such as crèches and menorahs on government property. In *Lemon* v. *Kurtzman* (1971), the Supreme Court tried unsuccessfully to resolve establishment-clause controversies by adopting the so-called three-part *Lemon* test, requiring a secular legislative purpose for government involvement in religious matters, forbidding governmental promotion or inhibition of religion, and barring excessive government entanglement with religion.

Chief Justices Warren Burger and William H. Rehnquist articulated the principal alternative to the Black-Jefferson view of strict separation, calling for a policy of "accommodation" of religious practice and rejecting impartial neutrality between religion and secularism (*Lynch* v. *Donnelly*, 1984). As the twentieth century ended, strict separation and accommodation vied for dominance in public debate. As religious practice became both more pervasive and more diverse in American society, issues of separation of church and state seemed likely to continue to roil understandings of the First Amendment.

[*See also* Bill of Rights; Federalism; Islam; Judaism; Mormonism; Protestantism; Religion; Roman Catholicism.]

• Paul G. Kauper, *Religion and the Constitution*, 1964. Mark De Wolfe Howe, *The Garden and the Wilderness: Religion and Government in American Constitutional History*, 1965. Sydney E. Ahlstrom, *A Religious History of the American People*, 1972. Laurence H. Tribe, *American Constitutional Law*, 2d ed., 1988, pp. 1154–301. Leonard W. Levy, *The Establishment Clause: Religion and the First Amendment*, 1994. Stephen M. Feldman, *Please Don't Wish Me a Merry Christmas: A Critical History of the Separation of Church and State*, 1997.

—William M. Wiecek

CHURCHES. *See* Religion; Specific religious groups.

CHURCH OF JESUS CHRIST OF LATTER-DAY SAINTS. *See* Mormonism.

CIO. *See* Congress of Industrial Organizations (CIO); American Federation of Labor (AFL); Labor Movements.

CIRCUSES. The circus arrived in America in 1793, when the English rider John Bill Ricketts and his troupe held a show in an enclosed arena in *Philadelphia. Ricketts brought jugglers, acrobats, ropewalkers, clowns, and trained animals together into one circular arena for the first time in the United States, in front of an audience that included President George *Washington. Soon other European artists were performing in permanent wooden buildings at major population centers along the eastern seaboard. These early one-ring shows bore little resemblance to the sprawling three-ring circus of the 1890s; they had no parade, nor did they perform in canvas tents. But, like their successors, these first American circuses provided audiences with an exciting window into the world.

In the early nineteenth century, circuses moved slowly by horseback or boat. Wagon travel began in 1825, when circuses started using the canvas tent, an innovation borrowed from the itinerant animal menagerie shows. With their tents quickly erected and disassembled, circuses became increasingly nomadic. No longer dependent upon urban markets to cover the costs of constructing wooden arenas, showmen could now play in rural areas. As a traveling amusement, circuses, became notorious as hotbeds of gambling and vice. Several states banned the *Antebellum Era circus, which was often shunned by "respectable" middle-class families.

During the nineteenth century, the growth of circuses mirrored the physical expansion of the American republic. The circus's development depended upon internal improvements such as roads and canals and inventions like the steamship and especially *railroads. Just weeks after the final spike of the transcontinental railroad was hammered home at Promentory Point, Utah, in 1869, Dan Castello's Circus and Menagerie made the first transcontinental railroad tour in American circus history. As railroad companies constructed more miles of track, *Gilded Age railroad circuses grew rapidly. By the 1890s, many proprietors had adopted from other popular amusement, such as the freak show and the world's fairs features like the sideshow and the "ethnological congress." (i.e., exhibitions of tribal peoples in exotic settings and native garb). On "circus day," showmen conducted a free parade to attract paying customers.

The Museum proprietor P. T. *Barnum, entering the railroad circus business in 1870, contributed significantly to the industry. With partners W. C. Coup, Dan Castello, and, later, James A. Bailey, Barnum made *advertising a priority. Barnum and Bailey's circus employed scores of "advance men" who plastered thousands of lithograph posters throughout a town weeks beforehand. By 1890, their vast big top contained three rings, two stages, a peripheral hippodrome track, and space for ten thousand spectators. An outspoken temperance advocate, Barnum banned liquor from his shows and trumpeted his circus as "moral" entertainment that attracted middle-class families. Competitors like the Ringling Brothers echoed Barnum's claims with their self-styled "Sunday School" circus. Yet circuses remained venues for fights, gambling, and drunkenness.

In 1900, nearly one hundred circuses roamed the country—the highest number in American history. The Ringling Brothers' organization became a huge circus conglomerate. Circuses shaped Americans' views about race, *gender, and contemporary politics. Employing hundreds of people and assembling animals from around the globe, railroad circuses brought the world to small-town America. Displaying exotic people and animals as representatives of a racial and zoological hierarchy, circuses helped popularize scientific theories concerning racial difference. Displaying reenactments of recent foreign battles and peace treaties, circuses celebrated American nationalism and involvement in world affairs. Muscular circus performers embodied the physical fitness ideals of President Theodore *Roosevelt and other practitioners of the "strenuous life."

By the 1920s, circus parades had mostly disappeared because towns were too clogged with cars to accommodate them. During the Depression, John Ringling North, owner of the Ringling Brothers and Barnum & Bailey Circus (and nephew of the original Ringling Brothers), attempted to make the circus more appealing to current public taste by hiring industrial designer Norman Bel Geddes to modernize the midway. In 1956, beset by rising labor and transportation costs as well as by the after effects of a tragic 1944 circus-tent fire in Hartford, Connecticut, that took 168 lives, the Ringling Brothers and Barnum and Bailey circus abandoned the canvas tent in favor of air-conditioned urban arenas that dramatically diminished the circus's presence. Furthermore, the advent of *radio and *television eroded the circus's authority as an educational amusement. With its elephant pyramids and dancing tigers, the circus came to seems anachronistic when one could easily see animals in their native habitat on television. However, the shared experience of watching live animals and human beings perform astounding feats still continued to draw countless Americans to the circus each year. The Circus World Museum in the Ringling Brothers' hometown of Baraboo, Wisconsin, preserves the history of this long-lived popular-culture institution.

[*See also* Canals and Waterways; Leisure; Popular Culture; Race, Concept of; Racism; World's Fairs and Expositions.]

• Neil Harris, *Humbug: The Art of P. T. Barnum,* 1973. Fred Dahlinger Jr., "The Development of the Railroad Circus" (4 parts), *Bandwagon: Journal of the Circus Historical Society* 27–28 (Nov/Dec. 1983–May/June 1984): 6–11, 16–27, 28–36. 29–36. A. H. Saxon, *P. T. Barnum, The Legend and the Man,* 1989. Stuart Thayer, *Travelling Showmen: The American Circus before the Civil War,* 1997.

—Janet Davis

CITY PLANNING. City planning arose early in American life. European colonizers designed St. Augustine (Spain, 1565), New Amsterdam (Holland, 1625–1626), Williamsburg (England, 1699), and *New Orleans (France, 1722) as commercial and administrative centers. England began to lose its empire when it allowed colonists to plan their own cities. New Haven (1638), Charleston (1680), *Philadelphia (1682–1683), and Savannah (1733) became organizing forces for colonial life, regional development, and ultimately revolution. While their prominent public spaces and buildings bespoke civic ambitions, expanding commercial streets and wharves underscored the primacy of economic interests. Civic purpose would predominate only in *Washington, D.C. (1791).

As urban rivalries drove commercial expansion in the *Antebellum Era, city planning became a form of speculation. To facilitate the "buying, selling, and improving of real estate," the *New York City Commissioners' Plan of 1811 extended a gridiron of streets throughout Manhattan, offering a model for the nation. Speculation in standardized building lots encouraged rapid, chaotic growth. Driven by concerns about public health and moral order, sanitarians, lawyers, engineers, and landscape architects enlarged the scope of city planning beginning at midcentury. An expanding body of municipal law limited property rights and addressed the health, safety, and welfare of city residents. New water, sewer, transit, and park systems reduced mortality rates and, by 1900, provided Americans with the finest public services in the world.

The expansion of public services was part of an effort to construct an urban culture modeled on the middle-class home. The "moral influence" of sewers and parks depended upon the cult of domesticity and the feminized ideal of Christian nurture. "Municipal housekeeping" included an urge to purify and compartmentalize city life that gained force from the separation of business and culture implicit in the notion of male and female spheres. Zoning, the most important tool of modern planners, was the logical culmination. In *Euclid* v. *Ambler Realty Co.* (1926) the *Supreme Court declared the creation of building zones with height, bulk, and use restrictions a legitimate use of the police power to preserve residence sections "of a certain desired type." Zoning's legal defense relied upon the same faith in middle-class domesticity that supported municipal housekeeping.

The modern planning profession arose from *Chicago's 1893 World's Columbian Exposition, the exemplar of municipal engineering and moral uplift. Daniel Burnham (1846–1912), the fair's director, helped popularize the City Beautiful movement. Combining innovative traffic solutions with inspiring civic spaces, Burnham's *Plan of Chicago* (1909) offered a watered-down but alluring alternative to the plan of Henry George (1839–1897), elaborated in *Progress and Poverty* (1877–1879), to ease congestion and improve public services with a single tax on speculative realty values. Charging that the City Beautiful hid civic decay behind superficial splendor, the Georgists organized the First National Conference on City Planning (1909). Uniting *settlement-house workers, *housing advocates, architects, engineers, and realtors committed to both *Progressive Era social reform and social efficiency, the NCCP became the organizational vehicle for the emerging planning profession.

In the booming 1920s, planners' focus on the technical problems of zoning and traffic won them powerful allies and professional status while insulating them from popular demands. Maximizing realty values and managing the conflicting needs of commerce and industry, zoning protected exclusive retail and residential districts and streamlined industrial production. Improved roads, traffic regulations, and parking facilitates subsidized motorists and the automotive and allied industries. After the 1929 *stock market crash, city planners mourned the collapse in realty values and rediscovered urban blight. The profession revived, however, when the New Deal employed planners to design and administer public works. While some planners recaptured a reforming spirit, federal programs geared to banking and construction interests received greater support than greenbelt towns or public housing.

The 1949 Housing Act, promising "a decent home" for every American, exemplified postwar federal planning that promoted *suburbanization at the expense of cities. While federal mortgage insurance and highway construction subsidized suburban growth, public housing remained underfunded, segregated, and concentrated in the inner city. After 1954, urban renewal cleared "slums" and handed the land over, at bargain prices, to private developers of luxury apartments and office towers. By the late 1960s, the destruction of the urban fabric by public authority had created such social and political problems that such urban initiatives were abandoned.

Long planned as centers of business and havens of domesticity, many American cities at the end of the twentieth century were plagued with economic decline and homelessness. As the city's economic and residential functions were partially supplanted by "technoburbs" and "gated communities," its future appeared to depend upon a restoration of neglected civic functions. In revitalizing civic life, future planners may recapture the possibilities that have always drawn people to cities. If planning can reconnect culture to *business, it might even revive the civic cooperation essential to both prosperity and social justice.

[*See also* Architecture: Public Architecture; Automotive Industry; Highway System; Landscape Design; New Deal Era, The; Parks, Urban; Segregation, Racial; Urbanization; World's Fairs and Expositions.]

• Jane Jacobs, *The Death and Life of Great American Cities,* 1961. John W. Reps, *The Making of Urban America: A History of City Planning in the United States,* 1965. Mel Scott, *American City Planning Since 1890,* 1969. Robert Caro, *The Power Broker: Robert Moses and the Fall of New York,* 1974. Stanley K. Schultz, *Constructing Urban Culture: American Cities and City Planning, 1800–1920,* 1989. John D. Fairfield, *The Mysteries of the Great City: The Politics of Urban Design, 1877–1937,* 1993. Zane L. Miller and E. Bruce Tucker, *Changing Plans for America's Inner Cities: Cincinnati's Over-the-Rhine and Twentieth Century Urbanism,* 1998.

—John D. Fairfield

CIVIL DEFENSE, the protection of American citizens from foreign attack, became a governmental objective in 1941, as *World War II began, when President Franklin Delano *Roosevelt appointed former *New York City mayor Fiorello *La Guardia to head the U.S. Office of Civil Defense. After the war, the *Cold War and the nuclear arms race led Washington to explore ways of safeguarding citizens from nuclear attack. The Federal Civil Defense Administration, created by President Harry S. *Truman in 1951, pursued a variety of approaches, including population dispersal. For example, the government urged military contractors to locate factories in remote areas less vulnerable to an urban-based attack. The Truman administration also supported a shelter program until the costs began to appear prohibitive. The administration then began cajoling citizens to "Duck and Cover"—drop to their knees and cover their heads—in an atomic attack. With the development of the hydrogen bomb in the 1950s, the Dwight D. *Eisenhower administration promoted a policy of emergency evacuation, changing the orientation, the *Bulletin of the Atomic Scientists* commented, "from 'Duck and Cover' to 'Run like Hell.' "

As scientists reported deadly radioactive fallout from hydrogen bomb tests in the mid-1950s, policy-makers offered a new rationale for shelters: protection not from a nuclear blast, but from fallout. Shelter building flourished in the later Eisenhower and early Kennedy years. The Office of Civil and Defense Mobilization, established in 1958, distributed free copies of *Family Fallout Shelter,* a booklet offering protection advice. Some experts advocated deep underground shelters accommodating up to a thousand people. Others proposed more modest basement or backyard shelters. Civil-defense preoccupations peaked in the early 1960s. As the confrontation between President John F. *Kennedy and the Soviet leader Nikita Khrushchev over Berlin reached a crisis level, Kennedy urged Americans to build fallout shelters and asked Congress for an additional $208 million for an expanded shelter program. Interest waned as the confrontation passed, however, and the 1962 *Cuban Missile Crisis prompted sober reflections on both sides. The 1963 *Limited Nuclear Test Ban Treaty prohibiting atmospheric nuclear tests minimized the fallout danger, further reducing concern with civil defense. Interest increased in the early 1980s, however, as fears of nuclear holocaust revived and the Ronald *Reagan administration promoted a "crisis relocation" program of population dispersal if nuclear war seemed imminent. In the 1990s, as the Cold War ended and the threat of full-scale nuclear war diminished, civil-defense planning shifted to the hazards of isolated missile attacks or chemical-biological assaults from rogue states or terrorist groups.

[*See also* Nuclear Arms Control Treaties; Nuclear Weapons; Sixties, The.]

• Allan M. Winkler, "A Forty-Year History of Civil Defense," *Bulletin of the Atomic Scientists* 40.6 (June–July 1984). Allan M. Winkler, *Life under a Cloud: American Anxiety about the Atom,* 1993.

—Allan M. Winkler

CIVIL DISOBEDIENCE. *See* Thoreau, Henry David.

CIVILIAN CONSERVATION CORPS. The Civilian Conservation Corps (CCC) was created in March 1933, during the first "hundred days" of President Franklin Delano *Roosevelt's New Deal, the first of a number of agencies designed to combat massive unemployment among youth. It bore Roosevelt's personal stamp, reflecting his concern about the destruction of America's natural resources, a theme he had stressed during the 1932 campaign.

Given the urgency of the crisis, the Roosevelt administration decided to operate the CCC through existing federal departments. The Department of Labor selected young men between eighteen and twenty-five years of age from public-relief rolls. The War Department transported them to camps of two hundred men each and administered these, while the Departments of Agriculture and the Interior supervised the specific conservation tasks. Director Robert Fechner and a small central staff coordinated the program. Enrollees earned thirty dollars a month, twenty-five dollars of which was sent home to their families. The initial enrollment period was six months, renewable for up to two years. Black youths were enrolled according to population ratio, almost always in segregated camps.

The CCC proved enormously popular and effective, lasting until June 1942. Though the nearly three million enrollees performed a wide variety of conservation tasks, the CCC was best known for its reforestation work. Of all the trees planted on public lands between 1776 and 1942, 75 percent were planted by the corps.

[*See also* Forests and Forestry; New Deal Era, The.]

• John A. Salmond, *The Civilian Conservation Corps 1933–1942: A New Deal Case Study,* 1967.

—John A. Salmond

CIVIL LIBERTIES. The term "civil liberties" refers to those individual freedoms protected by the *Constitution, particularly by the *Bill of Rights. These are liberties that, when the Constitution was adopted, had come to be seen as natural rights.

Revolutionary War through the Civil War. In the years leading up to the *Revolutionary War, the colonists began voicing their opposition to British policies in the language of natural rights. Having earlier based their rights claims on royal charters and the English common law, they now asserted, in the language of John Locke's *Two Treatises on Civil Government* (1690), that government could not infringe on certain natural, inalienable rights. This new natural-rights view of civil liberty later inspired both the *Declaration of Independence and the Bill of Rights.

As a public-policy issue, civil liberties rarely surfaced prior to *World War I. Throughout the nation's first 130 years, few occasions arose for suspension of the habeas corpus privilege, press *censorship, regulation of the right of assembly, or the imposition of loyalty oaths. Consequently, the law regarding civil liberties remained ill-defined until well into the twentieth century.

During America's *Quasi-War with France in 1798, the Federalists in Congress enacted the *Alien and Sedition Acts, which, under the guise of war-justified controls, criminalized seditious libel and sought to suppress the activities of the Jeffersonian Republican political opposition. These laws also aimed to subdue the violent political partisanship that threatened the Federalists' vision of a stable society. But the *Federalist party's unpopularity doomed it, and with Thomas *Jefferson's electoral victory in 1800, the politics of civil liberty remained quiescent until 1861.

When the *Civil War began, President Abraham *Lincoln imposed a series of measures (e.g., suspending the writ of habeas corpus and barring all "treasonable correspondence" from the mails) aimed at silencing opponents of the war. Using a rationale that would often be employed in the next century, Lincoln insisted that restrictions on civil liberties were needed to address the perceived threat of disloyal activities.

World War I through World War II. As these instances illustrate, attacks on civil liberties have usually coincided with periods of turmoil and insecurity. During *World War I and its aftermath, civil liberties were subjected to greater restrictions than ever before in American history, typified by the repressive Espionage and Sedition Acts passed by Congress in 1917–1918 and emulated by many states. In the immediate postwar period, an economic depression and a surge of strikes threatened the economy, creating problems that many Americans blamed on radicals and aliens. The 1917 Bolshevik Revolution in Russia and increasing *radicalism among certain immigrant groups in the United States spawned a Red Scare that led to the notorious Palmer raids of 1919–1920. These raids, led by President Woodrow *Wilson's attorney general, A. Mitchell Palmer, and the young J. Edgar *Hoover of the Justice Department's countersubversion division, resulted in the arrest of hundreds of suspected communists and radicals, and the deportation of 249 Russian-born aliens.

In ruling on the constitutionality of the wartime espionage and *sedition acts, the U.S. *Supreme Court for the first time interpreted the First Amendment as a limitation on governmental power. Although the Court in two noteworthy 1919 cases, **Schenck* v. *United States* and **Abrams* v. *United States,* did not adopt a pro–civil liberties stance, these cases remain landmarks in the development of First Amendment doctrine, in part because of the eloquent dissent by Justice Oliver Wendell *Holmes Jr. in the *Abrams* case.

As the Red Scare subsided, federal measures directed against dissenters faded as well. During the *New Deal Era, as tyrannical governments assaulted individual freedom elsewhere in the world, the Supreme Court expanded the constitutional protection of civil liberties. Incorporating the Bill of Rights into the *Fourteenth Amendment, the Court thereby applied these restraints to the states as well as to the federal government. The 1930s Supreme Court also downgraded the traditional primacy of property rights in the constitutional hierarchy. For instance, under then existing law, picketing by union members could be outlawed because of its harmful effect on private property. But in *Senn* v. *Tile Layers Union* (1937), a majority of the justices, recognizing the free speech aspect of this activity, prohibited any outright bans on picketing. Furthermore, by protecting the civil liberties of political dissidents, the Court encouraged the atmosphere of social experimentation central to the New Deal.

Even America's entry into *World War II did not disrupt the Supreme Court's focus on enlarging the scope of individual liberty. The great exception, of course, involved the relocation and detention of 125,000 people of Japanese ancestry, most of whom were citizens of the United States. The Supreme Court did not seriously intervene. In *Hirabayashi* v. *United States* (1943), it upheld a curfew ordinance against Japanese-Americans in Seattle on the grounds that wartime conditions sometimes justified measures that "place citizens of one ancestry in a different category from others." In **Korematsu* v. *United States* (1944), the Court upheld the evacuation of Japanese-Americans, but added, in *Endo* v. *United States* (1944), that the War Relocation Authority should attempt to separate "loyal" internees from "disloyal" ones, and release the former.

Cold-War Era Retrenchment. The early postwar era saw considerable retrenchment in the area of civil liberties. The conservative mood in the country brought a shift in political priorities from a concern for individual freedom to a desire for stability, order, and security. This mood found its way into the Supreme Court's civil-liberties decisions. The notions of "judicial restraint" and "balancing individual and community rights" facilitated this retrenchment. Under this new approach, First Amendment liberties no longer had an absolute or preferred position in constitutional adjudication, but had to be balanced against other concerns, such as public safety.

The most difficult civil-liberties questions of this period involved the *Cold War crusade against domestic *communism. With the nation in the grip of McCarthyism, the federal government used the 1940 *Smith Act to prosecute Communist party officials. At the same time, loyalty programs directed at federal employees were implemented by both the Harry S. *Truman and Dwight D. *Eisenhower administrations. Congress also passed a series of anticommunist measures, including the McCarran Internal Security Act (1950) and the Communist Control Act (1954). In addition, the *House Committee on Un-American Activities embarked on its notorious investigation of persons suspected of a communist taint. For the most part, the Court supported this postwar anticommunist crusade. In *Dennis* v. *United States* (1951), for instance, the Court upheld the conviction of eleven Communist party officers under the Smith Act for advocating (rather than actively planning) the overthrow of the U.S. government; in so ruling, the Court weakened the "clear and present danger" test established in *Schenck*.

A similar retrenchment occurred in the Court's approach to a variety of other civil-liberties questions. On the issue of picketing, for instance, the Court pulled back from its 1937 position that peaceful picketing represents a form of speech enjoying First Amendment protection. In *International Brotherhood of Teamsters* v. *Hanke* (1950), the Court held that picketing could also be a tool of economic coercion and restraint of trade, and hence could be regulated.

After this period of postwar retrenchment, however, the pendulum soon swung in the other direction. The rise of the *civil rights movement and the anti– *Vietnam War crusade of the 1960s brought a dramatic expansion of civil liberties that, in turn, helped fuel the era's political activism. In *Shelton* v. *Tucker* (1960), for instance, the Court struck down restrictions aimed at discouraging membership in the *National Association for the Advancement of Colored People.

The Warren Court and Beyond. A series of precedent-breaking Supreme Court decisions under Chief Justice Earl *Warren (1953–1969) created a powerful body of libertarian-oriented constitutional law in the field of civil liberties. In *Albertson* v. *Subversive Activities Control Board* (1965), for example, the Court overturned the registration requirements aimed at the Communist party and, for the first time, the Warren Court consistently supported the First Amendment rights of those protesting U.S. involvement in a foreign war (Vietnam). In so doing, the justices recognized a social interest in free speech. More than simply an individual right, free speech was now seen as essential to the open debate needed for the maintenance of democracy. Long viewed as a threat to social stability, civil liberties were now seen as making a positive social contribution.

The Warren Court also reformed the law dealing with the civil liberties of criminal defendants. The Sixth Amendment guarantee of counsel was now interpreted to mean that the states must provide lawyers for indigent defendants. And in **Miranda* v. *Arizona* (1966), the Court ruled that the Fifth Amendment privilege against self-incrimination required police to inform all suspects of their right to remain silent and to have an attorney present during interrogation.

The Warren Court's civil-liberties activism also led it to carve out a new constitutional right of privacy. In *Griswold* v. *Connecticut* (1965), the Court used this privacy right to strike down state legislation prohibiting the use of contraceptives and the dispensing of *birth control and family planning information to married couples.

This judicial activism was significantly tempered during the tenure of Chief Justice Warren Burger (1969–1986), named to that position by President Richard M. *Nixon. The Burger Court shifted rightward in its treatment of some civil-liberties issues. The Court's law-and-order stance, for instance, weakened certain criminal-procedure protections, including the *Miranda* precedent. Yet most of the First Amendment protections and privacy rights articulated by the Warren Court were sustained. Indeed, it was the Burger Court, in **Roe* v. *Wade* (1973), that used the constitutional right of privacy to guarantee *abortion rights.

The Court's commitment to First Amendment and privacy rights continued through the presidency of Ronald *Reagan. During the 1980s and 1990s, however, calls for censorship came from political liberals advocating speech codes and advertising restrictions on "politically incorrect" speech. Perhaps the most heated and controversial of civil-liberties issues in the 1990s were ones involving the First Amendment's establishment-of-religion clause, such as crèches on public property, secular books for parochial school students, and prayer at public events. Yet despite public pressures, the strict church-state separation laid down by the Warren Court survived.

The end of the twentieth century brought one significant change in the area of civil liberties. Whereas dissent in wartime and national-security concerns had once produced the disputes and conflicts, *technology now became the First Amendment battleground, involving such issues as free speech on the *Internet and world wide web, and the privacy of information relating to citizens' genetic profiles.

[*See also* Anticommunism; Antiwar Movements; Church and State, Separation of; Communist Party—USA; Debs, Eugene V.; Genetics and Genetic Engineering; Goldman, Emma; Incarceration of Japanese Americans; McCarthy, Joseph; Sixties, The; Strikes and Industrial Conflict.]

• Zechariah Chafee, *Free Speech in the United States*, 1948. O. K. Frankel, *The Supreme Court and Civil Liberties*, 1960. Leonard Levy, *Legacy of Suppression: Freedom of Speech and Press in Early America*, 1960. Barnard Bailyn, *The Ideological Origins of the American Revolution*, 1967. Leo

Pfeffer, *Church, State and Freedom,* 1967. Paul L. Murphy, *World War I and the Origin of Civil Liberties in the United States,* 1979. Nat Hentoff, *The First Freedom: The Tumultuous History of Free Speech in America,* 1980. John Stevens, *Shaping the First Amendment,* 1982. Kermit L. Hall, ed., *Civil Liberties in American History,* 1987.

—Patrick M. Garry

CIVIL RIGHTS. The concept of civil rights has changed dramatically since it first became a central idea in political discussions in the nineteenth century. Initially referring to a limited class of rights to which all people were entitled, the term has come to refer to a general guarantee against differential treatment in all areas of social life on the basis of what society deems to be an arbitrary grounds.

The Revolutionary War and Antebellum Eras. The idea of natural rights played an important role in the *Revolutionary War Era. Natural rights were those rights people enjoyed in a state of nature, independent of any organized society: the right to life and *liberty and the right to attempt to procure property. Civil rights were the rights people possessed once they organized a society. The idea of civil rights came into its own during the abolitionist campaign against *slavery. For abolitionists, one fatal characteristic of slavery was that slaves were denied civil rights. They could not own property, enter into contracts, or testify in court. These and a few other rights were what abolitionists understood to be civil rights. Typically the justification was that these rights distinguished organized—civil—society from the state of nature: People organized society so that they could have stable property holdings and secure contractual agreements, and a person's property and contracts could not be protected unless the person could testify about them.

Through the mid–nineteenth century, political activists and theorists sharply distinguished between civil rights, on the one hand, and political and social rights, on the other. Civil rights were associated with all organized societies, whereas political rights were rooted in the particular arrangements of specific societies. Abolitionists believed that freed slaves had a right to own property, but they did not think that emancipation automatically entailed the right to vote or to serve on juries. They could imagine societies in which voting played a small role and in which juries played no role at all; it followed, they believed, that the rights to vote and to serve on juries were political rather than civil rights. The point was perhaps clearest in connection with women, who generally had the right to own property and make contracts, but the view that women had the right to vote was far from the mainstream in the mid–nineteenth century.

The Reconstruction Era through the 1930s. Congress's first venture into the area of protecting civil rights came with the Civil Rights Act of 1866, passed to enforce the Thirteenth Amendment's abolition of slavery. The act granted all citizens equal rights to sue and testify; enter into contracts; and purchase, sell, or inherit property. The act was adopted over President Andrew *Johnson's veto, in which he expressed concern that the Thirteenth Amendment did not give Congress the power to enact it. In part because of that concern, Congress proceeded to propose, and the states to ratify, the *Fourteenth Amendment, which guaranteed "equal protection of the laws." To the extent that the Fourteenth Amendment was designed to place the 1866 Civil Rights Act on a secure constitutional footing, it protected core civil rights but did not deal with political rights such as the right to vote. The importance of the distinction was driven home by the perceived need to adopt the *Fifteenth Amendment, securing the right to vote against efforts to restrict it on the basis of race.

The distinction between civil rights and political rights came under increasing pressure toward the end of the century. The *Supreme Court held that the Fourteenth Amendment barred states from denying *African Americans the opportunity to serve on juries (*Strauder* v. *West Virginia,* 1880). An amendment designed primarily to protect *civil* rights was thus interpreted to protect one of the central *political* rights. The increasing activism of woman-suffrage advocates further strained the distinction between civil and political rights.

In contrast, the distinction between civil rights and social rights survived. In a sense, the category of social rights was simply residual: Everything not encompassed within civil or political rights implicated social rights. In part, the category identified the ways in which politically organized societies arranged their nonpolitical institutions. The Supreme Court in **Plessy* v. *Ferguson* (1896), upholding a state statute mandating racial *segregation on privately owned railroads, asserted that the statute's challengers were claiming that they had a right to associate with whomever they chose. But that claim was mistaken, the Court's holding implied, because the right to associate was a social right, subject to regulation by ordinary legislative decision-making.

Advocates for African Americans continued to press the claim that racial segregation and discrimination denied their civil rights. The core of their claim was that civil rights were denied whenever race discrimination affected any activity that society deemed fundamental, including education and employment. The *National Association for the Advancement of Colored People (NAACP), organized in 1909, proved particularly effective in promulgating this broadened notion of civil rights, through political advocacy and support of legal challenges to segregation.

By the 1930s, the older distinctions among civil, political, and social rights had largely been obliterated. For the next decades, civil rights activists struggled to obtain legal protection for civil rights as they had come to be understood. Challenges to state-mandated segregation culminated in **Brown* v. *Board of Education* (1954), which repudiated the idea that education was not a civil right. During *World War II, the national government created a *Fair Employment Practice Committee, which attempted, without much success, to ensure that defense contractors refrained from discriminating in employment on the basis of race. Civil rights statutes enacted in 1957 and 1960 made modest efforts to overcome race discrimination in voting practices in the South.

The Era of the Civil Rights Movement and Beyond. The full transformation of the idea of civil rights occurred in the 1960s. Civil rights acts adopted in 1964 and 1965 banned race discrimination in employment and in public accommodations such as restaurants and hotels and responded to persistent discrimination in voting by displacing the authority of southern states to adopt voter-qualification standards. The effects of these two statutes were dramatic. Voter registration in the *South expanded, and African Americans became important participants in politics there. Gains in employment were achieved more slowly, as employers resisted hiring and especially promoting workers they believed to be unqualified.

Beyond the 1960s, the idea of civil rights underwent further development. It expanded past the realm of race discrimination to include a significant number of other "protected" classes. Since the early twentieth century, some women's rights activists had pressed for a ban on gender-based discrimination in employment. That proposal met with resistance from organized labor and from some other women's rights activists, who thought it important to ensure the survival of state laws that they believed protected women against exploitative employment practices. In part to divide the liberal coalition supporting the proposed Civil Rights Act of 1964, the Virginia representative Howard Smith introduced an amendment that would expand the coverage of the proposal's ban on employment discrimination to include discrimination based on gender. This portion of the 1964 act became one of the most important vehicles for gender equality over the following decade. Similar expansions of the notion of civil rights occurred as older Americans obtained protection in the Age Discrimination in Employment Act (1967), and the physically handicapped established their right to accommodation of their disabilities through the *Americans with Disabilities Act (1990) and other statutes. The list of protected classes continued to increase as gays and lesbians sought protection against discrimination in employment and housing.

By the late twentieth century, the expanded notion of civil rights had begun to develop new elaborations. From the early years of the *civil rights movement, activists had divided over whether they sought treatment for African Americans as individuals or as members of a distinctive social group. In employment, this produced strategic divisions over whether to seek a legal regime of nondiscrimination or one of proportional hiring. The strategic disagreements mattered little until the civil rights movement began to succeed. After the adoption of the 1964 and 1965 Civil Rights Acts, however, the differences became important. Proponents of *affirmative action and race-conscious apportionment of election districts contended that their approaches were the best way to ensure that African Americans would obtain fair treatment and the resources to which they were entitled, and that they were effective ways of securing a stable, self-determining African American community. Their opponents argued that race-conscious approaches undermined the focus on individual rights that had been the hallmark of previous struggles for civil rights.

The expansion of the concept of civil rights generated concern among some observers. Critics suggested that the discourse of civil rights produced an escalation of rhetoric that made it increasingly difficult to reach accommodations among competing interests. Others expressed concern that the concept had come to cover such a wide range of social life that its moral force had become diluted. These concerns, plus persistent conflicts over affirmative action and continued efforts to claim civil rights by groups that believed themselves to be disadvantaged, ensured that the concept of civil rights would continue to evolve as a new century began.

[*See also* Antislavery; *Civil Rights Cases;* Civil Rights Legislation; Constitution; Gay and Lesbian Rights Movement; Republicanism; Woman Suffrage Movement; Women's Rights Movements.]

• Hugh Davis Graham, *The Civil Rights Era: Origins and Development of National Policy, 1960–1972,* 1990. Richard Kluger, *Simple Justice: The History of* Brown v. Board of Education *and Black America's Struggle for Equality,* 1976. Daniel T. Rodgers, *Contested Truths: Keywords in American Politics since Independence,* 1987. Mary Ann Glendon, *Rights Talk: The Impoverishment of Political Discourse,* 1991. Andrew Kull, *The Color-Blind Constitution,* 1992.

—Mark Tushnet

CIVIL RIGHTS CASES (1883). In the *Civil Rights Cases,* the *Supreme Court declared unconstitutional provisions of the Civil Rights Act of 1875 that prohibited racial discrimination in public accommodations. The decision would severely curtail Congressional efforts to protect *African Americans from private discrimination until the passage of the Civil Rights Act of 1964.

Justice Joseph P. Bradley's majority opinion represented a conservative view of the Thirteenth and *Fourteenth Amendments. In this view the Thirteenth Amendment simply abolished *slavery while the Fourteenth granted former slaves citizenship and relief only from *state* abridgement of individual rights, not from other forms of discrimination. In writing for the majority, Bradley characterized the Civil Rights Act of 1875 as an impermissible attempt by Congress to create a municipal code regulating the private conduct of individuals in the area of racial discrimination. Even private interference with such rights as voting, jury service, or appearing as witnesses in state court, he further asserted, lay outside Congress's power to control. An individual faced with such interference had to look to state government for relief. Bradley also rejected the contention that the Thirteenth Amendment allowed Congress to pass the 1875 legislation, declaring that denial of access to public accommodations did not constitute a badge or incident of slavery. Such a broad construction, he argued, would make blacks "the special favorite of the laws."

In his dissent, Justice John Marshall *Harlan, a former slaveholder, declared that the decision rested on "narrow and artificial" grounds. Harlan argued that the Thirteenth Amendment gave Congress broad powers to legislate to insure the rights of former slaves. The freedom conferred by that amendment, he contended, went beyond the simple absence of bondage: it encompassed freedom from all "badges of slavery."

Along with the Supreme Court's earlier decisions in the **Slaughterhouse* and *Cruikshank* cases (1873 and 1876), the *Civil Rights Cases* sharply limited the Fourteenth Amendment as a vehicle for protecting the newly freed black population and, many scholars believe, helped to usher in the era of Jim Crow.

[*See also* Civil Rights; Civil Rights Legislation; Civil Rights Movement; Reconstruction; Segregation, Racial; Suffrage.]

• Eugene Gressman, "The Unhappy History of Civil Rights Legislation," *Michigan Law Review* 50 (1952): 1323, 1329–30.

—Robert J. Cottrol

CIVIL RIGHTS LEGISLATION. America's first civil rights legislation came during *Reconstruction. The *Fourteenth and *Fifteenth Amendments extended citizenship to all persons born or naturalized in the United States, granted all citizens equal protection of the laws, and outlawed the denial of citizens' rights on the basis of race. Empowered by these amendments, Congress passed a civil rights act in 1870 providing remedies against state officials who violated citizens' constitutional rights, and another in 1875 requiring equal treatment of all in places of public accommodation. The *Supreme Court interpreted the 1870 act narrowly, however, and in the **Civil Rights Cases* (1883) held the 1875 act unconstitutional, ruling that Congress's power did not extend to cases of private discrimination.

More than eighty years would pass before Congress again addressed the issue of civil rights. As *African Americans became part of the New Deal coalition, they increasingly pressed for more effective civil rights legislation, but southern white politicians blocked all such bills until the enactment of the Civil Rights Act of 1957. Prodded by northern Republicans, the Dwight D. *Eisenhower administration proposed a civil rights bill designed in part to divide the *Democratic party's liberal and southern wings. Senate Majority Leader Lyndon B. *Johnson, viewing the bill as a vehicle for his presidential ambitions, maneuvered to get a watered-down version enacted. The act created a Civil Rights Commission to investigate and report on civil rights issues and set up a cumbersome method of enforcing federal voting-rights guarantees. A modest extension of the act in 1960 did not increase its effectiveness.

The Civil Rights Act of 1964, by contrast, inaugurated a new era of civil rights legislation. John F. *Kennedy had made civil rights an issue during his presidential campaign, but as president he was reluctant to expend substantial political capital on the issue. His successor, Lyndon Johnson, however, forcefully pushed a comprehensive civil rights bill and used his influence to break a Senate filibuster. The act's major provisions banned racial discrimination in public accommodations and prohibited discrimination by employers and unions. The act also authorized the federal government to deny public funds to segregated schools.

The Supreme Court ruled the 1964 act constitutional, finding that Congress could use its power to regulate interstate commerce to ban racial discrimination. Desegregation of many restaurants and hotels followed quickly. The threatened loss of federal funding sped the pace of school desegregation.

The Voting Rights Act of 1965 dramatically expanded federal

power over voting, invalidating literacy tests and other practices used to exclude African Americans from the franchise. It also required southern cities and states, and some northern ones, to secure permission from the Justice Department or a federal court for changes in their voter-registration laws. The 1965 act dramatically expanded the numbers of African American voters. Originally in effect for a limited period, it was regularly extended and eventually made permanent. Under the act, some states created race-based electoral districts designed to increase blacks' legislative representation—a practice that became intensely controversial in the 1990s.

The Civil Rights Act of 1968 banned race discrimination in *housing, including renting. To prevent acts of violence against civil rights advocates, the act also expanded federal laws making interference with a citizen's civil rights a federal crime. And, responding to urban upheavals, the act made it a federal crime to cross state lines to incite a riot.

As the political climate became more conservative after 1970, the Supreme Court became increasingly skeptical of expansive applications of civil rights legislation. A series of decisions in the late 1980s narrowing the scope of civil rights laws provoked counter efforts in Congress to extend the laws' scope. President George *Bush vetoed a civil rights bill in 1990, asserting that it permitted racial quotas in hiring to increase minority representation in business and education. Extended negotiations produced a bill with some cosmetic changes, which Bush then signed as the Civil Rights Act of 1991.

By the 1980s, a comprehensive set of civil rights laws was in place, producing a general culture of civil rights. The 1964 Civil Rights Act included a provision, long sought by women's rights advocates, outlawing employment discrimination on the basis of sex. Later statutes applied the nondiscrimination principle to older citizens (the Age Discrimination in Employment Act, 1967) and the handicapped (the *Americans with Disabilities Act, 1990). Although proposals to extend the principle to homosexuals stirred controversy, the civil rights culture had transformed the embattled proponents of minority rights into powerful interest groups capable of placing their concerns at the center of public debate.

[*See also* Affirmative Action; Civil Rights; Civil Rights Movement; Gay and Lesbian Rights Movement; New Deal Era, The; Segregation, Racial; Sixties, The; Women's Rights Movements.]

• Robert F. Burk, *The Eisenhower Administration and Black Civil Rights,* 1985. Hugh Davis Graham, *The Civil Rights Era: Origins and Development of National Policy,*1990. Mark Stern, *Calculating Visions: Kennedy, Johnson, and Civil Rights,* 1992. Robert Mann, *The Walls of Jericho: Lyndon Johnson, Hubert Humphrey, Richard Russell, and the Struggle for Civil Rights,* 1996.

—Mark Tushnet

CIVIL RIGHTS MOVEMENT. The American civil rights movement encompasses more than three centuries of struggle against racial discrimination, and is best understood in this broad context.

Revolutionary Era through the Civil War. The movement that culminated in the organized protests and *civil rights legislation of the 1950s and 1960s drew upon the traditions and experiences of uncooperative and fugitive slaves, black and white abolitionists, and free blacks who resented second-class citizenship. During the second half of the eighteenth century, the egalitarian rhetoric of the American and French Revolutions and Quaker (*Society of Friends) religious doctrines produced a nascent *antislavery movement that led to wholesale emancipation in the North and doubts about the future of slavery in the *South. The outlawing of American involvement in the international slave trade in 1808 and the creation of the American Colonization Society in 1817 anticipated the abolitionist movement that arose in the 1820s and 1830s. Abolitionist activity, in turn, focused attention on the issue of *civil rights, especially in northern cities where free black communities, many sustained by strong independent black churches, sheltered fugitive slaves, nurtured black abolitionist leaders such as Frederick *Douglass, and agitated for equal treatment for themselves.

By the 1840s several elements that would characterize the post–*World War II civil rights movement were already in place: interracial cooperation and conflict, patterns of community-based protest, the political salience of black religious institutions, a reliance on Northern-based national organizations, and the use different tactics in the North and South. The *Fugitive Slave Act of 1850 intensified civil-rights activism, as did the 1857 Dred Scott decision (**Scott* v. *Sandford*) and John *Brown's 1859 raid on Harpers Ferry.

The *Civil War itself posed new challenges for the civil rights struggle. In its early stages abolitionists failed in their efforts to infuse the war effort with antislavery or civil rights zeal. While the Abraham *Lincoln administration eventually acknowledged that the war for the Union was also a war of emancipation, it generally resisted consideration of the broader implications of black citizenship. Nevertheless, blacks' service in the Union Army, the *Emancipation Proclamation, and radical Republican proposals for a postwar *reconstruction of the South ultimately forced reconsideration of the traditional and legal limitations on civil rights.

Civil War through World War II. The Thirteenth Amendment abolished *slavery in 1865, but the actual meaning of emancipation remained vague. The struggle over the Civil Rights Act of 1866 convinced some Republican leaders that the Thirteenth Amendment provided an inadequate Constitutional foundation for civil rights; accordingly, they drafted the *Fourteenth Amendment, ratified in 1868, strengthening the equal protection and due process protections, and encouraged Congress to enact additional civil rights acts in 1870, 1871, and 1875. In 1883, however, the *Supreme Court declared the 1875 Civil Rights Act unconstitutional, confirming white America's waning interest in civic equality. The generation that had ended slavery passed from the scene without resolving, or even honestly addressing, the underlying problems of white *racism, discrimination, and inequality.

During the 1890s, black participation in the Populist revolt briefly revived the civil rights cause, but the demise of the *Populist party left *African Americans more vulnerable than ever. In the North, African American communities were too small to influence a political culture more concerned with immigrants than with native blacks. In the Jim Crow South, home to the vast majority of African Americans, a reign of terror inhibited challenges to the racial status quo. A few scattered civil rights protests occurred, including several boycotts of segregated streetcars, but most southern blacks adjusted to the indignities of disfranchisement, debt peonage, and rigid system of racial *segregation reinforced by the "separate but equal" doctrine of the 1896 **Plessy* v. *Ferguson* decision.

In the early twentieth century Booker T. *Washington's accommodationist philosophy dominated discussions of racial progress. But as white supremacist violence mounted, an alternative philosophy rooted in racial pride and earlier protest traditions reemerged. Following the 1906 *Atlanta race riot and a racial massacre in Springfield, Illinois, in 1908, African American and liberal white intellectuals founded the *National Association for the Advancement of Colored People (NAACP). Two years later, a somewhat more conservative group formed the National *Urban League (NUL). Although several decades passed before these organizations became fully effective, they provided an embryonic organizational base for the modern civil rights movement. The NAACP proved especially influential, primarily through the activities of W. E. B. *Du Bois, the outspoken editor of *Crisis* magazine, and James Weldon *Johnson, the NAACP's first black executive secretary. While the organizational center of the civil rights struggle remained in the

North, the seeds of a southern movement were germinating, especially among railroad porters and other black union members, black teachers and professionals, and ministers.

During the 1920s, the civil rights cause attracted diverse supporters, including the black nationalist Marcus *Garvey, writers and artists of the *Harlem Renaissance, socialist and communist politicians, and black labor leaders such A. Philip *Randolph. The struggle entered a new phase during the depression decade of the 1930s, setting the stage for a future national movement. President Franklin Delano *Roosevelt's political dependence on white southern Democrats and his single-minded focus on the economic crisis left little room for attention to racial discrimination. But the New Deal's social-justice orientation offered a measure of hope to civil rights activists who, for the first time since Reconstruction, regarded the federal government as a potential ally. The NAACP devoted almost all of its scanty resources to judicial and legislative reform. While Charles Houston, Thurgood *Marshall, and other NAACP attorneys attacked the legal structure of racial segregation, executive secretary Walter White campaigned, for federal antilynching legislation.

The 1940s proved a pivotal decade. By threatening a mass march on Washington in 1941, A. Philip Randolph forced Roosevelt to create the *Fair Employment Practice Committee (FEPC), empowered to combat racial discrimination in wartime employment. As black servicemen and industrial workers proved critical to the war effort, Randolph and others promoted the "Double V campaign" for victory against both foreign enemies and racial discrimination at home. The campaign yielded mixed results. The armed forces remained rigidly segregated throughout the war, and interracial violence erupted in *Detroit and other northern cities. Hints of change ahead, however, included a government propaganda campaign to discredit Nazi racial theories, a shift in racial attitudes among intellectuals, some influenced by Gunnar Myrdal's 1944 study of American race relations *An *American Dilemma*; and *Smith* v. *Allwight*, a 1944 Supreme Court decision outlawing white primaries.

For most civil rights advocates, the Supreme Court's increasingly liberal trajectory validated the NAACP's legal approach. For a small but vocal minority, however, the rising expectations of wartime inspired more militant tactics, such as sit-ins, economic boycotts, and protest marches. The emergence of direct action as a significant component of the civil rights struggle dates to the war years. The NAACP's Youth Councils and the *Communist Party—USA fostered some direct action, but more important was the *Congress of Racial Equality (CORE), an interracial organization of northern pacifists, labor activists, and left-wing intellectuals founded in 1942.

World War II to 1968. Civil-rights activism intensified in the immediate postwar era. Jackie *Robinson broke the color line in major-league *baseball, a CORE "Freedom Ride" through the upper South challenged segregation in interstate buses, the Supreme Court issued a series of encouraging rulings, and President Harry S. *Truman desegregated the armed services and convened a presidential commission on civil rights. The NAACP, meanwhile, expanded its legal assault on Jim Crow, culminating in the 1954 **Brown* v. *Board of Education* school desegregation decision. Legal backsliding and political demagoguery, however, soon slowed the pace of the civil rights revolution. In a 1955 follow-up to the *Brown* decision, the Supreme Court proposed an ambiguous timetable, allowing southern school districts to desegregate "with all deliberate speed." As segregationist White Citizens Councils spread across the South and as the *lynching of Emmett Till, a black boy from Chicago visiting relatives in Mississippi, dominated the headlines, the prospects for civil rights seemed dim.

But the movement revived in December 1955, when an act of courage galvanized an entire black community. In Montgomery, Alabama, the arrest of Rosa Parks (1913–), a seamstress and NAACP activist who violated a local segregation ordinance by refusing to move to the back of a city bus, sparked a thirteen-month bus boycott that attracted national and international attention. Led by the Reverend Martin Luther *King Jr., who promoted a Gandhian strategy of nonviolent resistance, the Montgomery Improvement Association (MIA) became the touchstone of the subsequent movement. A testing ground for differing theories of racial adjustment and social change, Montgomery demonstrated the economic and moral vulnerability of segregation, the inability of even moderate segregationists to compromise, the resolute courage of many Southern blacks, the political importance and emotional power of *African-American religion, and the viability of nonviolent direct action.

In 1957 the movement seemed to gain momentum, with King's formation of the *Southern Christian Leadership Conference (SCLC), President Dwight D. *Eisenhower's use of federal troops to desegregate Little Rock's Central High School, and the passage of the first federal civil rights law since Reconstruction. But the later 1950s proved disappointing, as the pace of school desegregation slowed and the weakness of the 1957 Civil Rights Act became apparent. *Cold War politics dominated American public life, frustrating efforts to refocus national attention on civil rights.

Then in February 1960, four black college students staged an impromptu sit-in at a segregated Woolworth's lunch counter in Greensboro, North Carolina. The movement soon spread to more than a hundred southern cities, prompting the founding of the *Student Nonviolent Coordinating Committee (SNCC). Although many NAACP and SCLC leaders were wary of SNCC's confrontational style, King's endorsement and the wise counsel of longtime activist Ella Baker helped sustain the new organization, which drew support from black college and high school students across the South.

In 1961, CORE sponsored another "freedom ride" testing a recent Supreme Court decision prohibiting segregation on interstate buses. When CORE suspended the action following white-supremacist violence in Anniston and Birmingham, Alabama, SNCC activists vowed to complete the ride. Confrontations with state officials and other white supremacists in Alabama and Mississippi, prompted additional freedom rides, a full-scale mobilization of the civil rights movement, and the belated intervention of the John F. *Kennedy administration, which assured the riders' safe passage into Mississippi—although not their protection from imprisonment.

The Freedom Ride crisis deepened the Kennedy administration's fears of an uncontrolled mass movement. Attorney General Robert *Kennedy urged civil rights leaders to redirect their efforts toward voter registration. But most, including King, refused to abandon an approach that enhanced the struggle's emotional energy and moral power, while providing a dramatic focus of media attention.

The nonviolent direct action strategy suffered a serious setback in Albany, Georgia, in 1962. Not only did Albany officials confound SCLC's efforts to fill the jails with protesters, but persistent tensions between SCLC leaders and local activists eventually convinced King to abandon the campaign. Later in the year, James Meredith's attempt to desegregate the University of Mississippi provoked such violence by white supremacists that some observers feared mass civil conflict in the Deep South. While applauding the Kennedy administration for enforcing the law at the University of Mississippi, civil rights advocates worried about the increasingly violent resistance.

The opposition reached a fever pitch in 1963, with the murder of Mississippi NAACP leader Medgar Evers, Alabama governor George *Wallace's demagogic "stand in the schoolhouse door," Birmingham public-safety commissioner Eugene

("Bull") Connor's use of attack dogs and fire hoses against SCLC-sponsored demonstrations, and the death of four black children in a Birmingham church bombing. But such excesses only strengthened a movement that relied on the public perception that the civil rights demonstrators possessed the courage and moral integrity to outlast their opponents. The movement's rising power was confirmed by a successful mass march on Washington in August and the Kennedy administration's long-awaited endorsement of a comprehensive civil rights bill. Following President Kennedy's assassination in November, Lyndon B. *Johnson used his legislative skills and the image of a martyred president to push through a civil rights act that outlawed state-supported racial discrimination.

While the 1964 Civil Rights Act proved a milestone in the movement's history, King and other leaders continued to demand an end to the remaining vestiges of Jim Crow, especially black disfranchisement. A 1964 "Freedom Summer" voter-registration campaign in Mississippi involving hundreds of college students and other volunteers revealed the depth of opposition to the movement—a harsh reality highlighted by the murder of three civil rights workers and by the failure of the Mississippi Freedom Democratic Party to supplant the state's all-white delegation at the Democratic National Convention. After continued agitation, however, including the Selma-to-Montgomery march of March 1965, Congress approved the Voting Rights Act of 1965, outlawing legally sanctioned disfranchisement and voter intimidation.

The euphoria did not last long. Among African Americans, the protracted struggle for equality brought a revolution of rising expectations that inevitably gave way to frustration and disillusionment. The growing realization that civil rights legislation did not end racial prejudice or alter the structural realities of race and *social class exacerbated tensions within the movement. The limitations of the civil rights revolution became painfully clear in 1966 and 1967 when the focus shifted northward to cities such as *Chicago and *Detroit, where *poverty, urban blight, and de facto segregation bred despair and rage. As the movement failed to make much headway in the North, many African Americans, especially the young, found the politics of racial pride and *Black Nationalism increasingly attractive. A series of inner-city riots in 1965–1968 exacerbated racial polarization and white backlash. As the commitment to nonviolence waned, the politics of law and order displaced the white *liberalism that had been an important element of the civil rights coalition. At the same time, civil rights leaders differed sharply over King's efforts to broaden the movement to include anti-poverty campaigns, opposition to the *Vietnam War, and international agitation for *human rights.

The Enduring Legacy. By 1968, the year of King's assassination and the public's growing preoccupation with the Vietnam War, the classic phase of the civil rights movement was over, leaving its fragmented remnants to struggle over such issues as *affirmative action, court-ordered busing, economic inequality, and de facto segregation. They did so, however, in the political and cultural context of the "rights revolution"—an ever-expanding struggle by a wide variety of groups seeking civic and social equality. At the end of the twentieth century and beyond, feminists, *Hispanic Americans, *Asian Americans, homosexuals, older Americans, abortion opponents, persons with disabilities, and other groups continued to draw upon the experiences, strategies, and rhetoric of the African-American civil rights movement whose powerful legacy of civic activism and political empowerment continues to influence American culture.

[*See also Civil Rights Cases*; Colonization Movement, African; Democratic Party; Feminism; Fifties, The; Gay and Lesbian Rights Movement; Malcolm X; New Deal Era, The; Riots, Urban; Sixties, The; Socialist Party of America; Suffrage; Trotter, William Monroe; Wells-Barnett, Ida B.; Women's Rights Movements.].

• C. Vann Woodward, *The Strange Career of Jim Crow,* 3d ed., 1974. Richard Kluger, *Simple Justice,* 1975. Howell Raines, ed., *My Soul Is Rested: Movement Days in the Deep South Remembered,* 1977. Sara M. Evans, *Personal Politics: The Roots of Women's Liberation in the Civil Rights Movement and the New Left,* 1979. Clayborne Carson, *In Struggle: SNCC and the Black Awakening of the 1960s,* 1981. David J. Garrow, *Bearing the Cross: Martin Luther King, Jr., and the Southern Christian Leadership Conference,* 1986. Taylor Branch, *Parting the Waters: America in the King Years, 1954–1963,* 1988. Peter J. Albert and Ronald Hoffman, eds., *We Shall Overcome: Martin Luther King, Jr., and the Black Freedom Struggle,* 1990. Charles Payne, *I've Got the Light of Freedom: The Organizing Tradition and the Mississippi Freedom Struggle,* 1995. John Lewis, with Michael D'Orso, *Walking with the Wind: A Memoir of the Movement,* 1998.

—Raymond O. Arsenault

CIVIL SERVICE REFORM. Early nineteenth-century Americans, with the widest suffrage in the world and many offices to be filled by election, invented mass-based *political parties to nominate and elect candidates. Since electioneering required time and money that few Americans could spare, political leaders recruited civil servants (or would-be civil servants) to perform party work and contribute to the party a percentage of their salary (called a political assessment). Local, state, and federal civil officers accepted this arrangement, because not to do so would jeopardize their jobs. If reelected, the patron could replace a recalcitrant civil servant; if the patron was defeated, his victorious opponent would distribute the spoils of office (the patronage) among his party workers. This spoils system, critics maintained, had a deleterious effect on the civil service and on politics. Government service suffered from frequent turnover and low morals among workers more loyal to their patron than to their agency. And the patronage system enabled political bosses to control party machinery and determine the fate of aspiring politicians.

After the *Civil War, merchants angered by customhouse irregularities and corruption; urban professionals in the Northeast; and intellectuals (especially editors and writers) embraced civil service reform. Leaders of the National Civil-Service Reform League included such figures as Carl Schurz (1829–1906), a Republican senator and journalist; Edwin L. Godkin (1831–1902), editor of *The Nation;* and George William Curtis (1824–1892), editor of *Harper's Weekly.* These reform-minded Republicans deplored their party's crassness and corruption in the era of Ulysses S. *Grant and James G. *Blaine.

Civil service reformers advocated open, competitive examinations for government work and a ban on political assessments. Since this reform was modeled on British experience and would deprive the political parties of money and workers, politicians of both parties attacked it as antidemocratic and monarchical. Supporters claimed that this reform would introduce efficient business practices in the civil service and raise the level of party politics. Although civil service reform was introduced in the New York Customhouse (the nation's largest office) in 1879 during the Rutherford *Hayes administration, it was the shocking assassination of President James *Garfield in 1881 by a mentally deranged disappointed office-seeker that spurred reform on the federal level. After the *Republican party lost the midterm election of 1882, a lame-duck Congress passed the 1883 Pendleton Civil Service Reform Act. While that act initially applied to (classified) only 10 percent of federal workers, outgoing presidents, to freeze their partisans in office, gradually extended the ranks of classified workers. By the *Progressive Era, most important nonpolicy-making positions were classified.

Civil service reform profoundly affected American society and politics. By laying the base for professional bureaucracies, it enabled twentieth-century government on all levels to play a larger role in American society. But this innovation, by depriving political parties of a dependable source of funds and workers, also forced politicians to rely on, and become beholden to, corporations and political-action committees to finance soaring campaign costs in the age of television.

[*See also* Antebellum Era; Gilded Age; Jackson, Andrew; Roosevelt, Theodore.]

• Ari Hoogenboom, *Outlawing the Spoils: A History of the Civil Service Reform Movement, 1865–1883*, 1961.

—Ari Hoogenboom

CIVIL WAR

Causes
Military and Diplomatic Course
Domestic Effects
Changing Interpretations

CIVIL WAR: CAUSES

Modern historians agree that the problem of *slavery was central in causing the American Civil War, and that this problem first emerged as a result of the *Revolutionary War. Although the use of enslaved black laborers had been common throughout the British colonies, the impact of the Revolution began a complicated process of legislated emancipation in the North that had no equivalent in the *South. As the new nation emerged after 1776, so did the recognition that it contained two contrasting regions that possessed potentially conflicting understandings of such values as "*liberty," "rights," and "*equality."

When framing the U.S. *Constitution in 1787, the founders demonstrated their eagerness to compromise on such conflicts. Consequently, they granted so many concessions to all parties that later generations were to find themselves arguing endlessly over the Constitution's "true" meaning. Defenders of slavery could point to clauses that defined a slave as three-fifths of a free person for purposes of apportioning representatives to Congress, that provided for the enactment of a federal fugitive slave law, and that obliged the federal government to quell slave insurrections. Opponents of the institution could counter that the Constitution never referred directly to "slavery," that it allowed for the prohibition of the international slave trade, and that its Tenth Amendment relieved the federal government of any support for slavery in the states. The point is not that these differing interpretations led to Civil War, but instead that the Constitution's ambiguity left it incapable of providing authoritative guidance in subsequent decades when sectional animosities grew dangerous. Southern planters who constantly espoused *states' rights and abolitionists who insisted that the federal government must legislate against slavery had equally plausible constitutional grounds for their conflicting points of view.

During the first four decades of the nineteenth century, disagreements over slavery were never absent. In Congress, in 1820, serious North-South divisions developed over the proposed admission of Missouri as a slave state, a conflict that was finally mitigated by legislation known as the *Missouri Compromise. Maine was admitted as a free state to balance the addition of Missouri, and further legislation provided that no slave states could subsequently be created north of 36°30 north latitude within the territory acquired, as Missouri had been, in the 1803 *Louisiana Purchase. A decade later, well-organized northern groups of black and white abolitionists began voicing militant opposition to slaveholding, thereby increasing southern whites' fears of slave insurrection and the frequency of North-South disagreements in Congress.

Yet for all their disruptiveness, these early debates over slavery did little to weaken ties between North and South. By the 1830s, the southern *cotton industry had become integral to an expanding national economy. In the political realm, the establishment of universal white male *suffrage encouraged voters from both sections to join one of two broadly based political parties, the *Whig party or the *Democratic party which debated important but sectionally neutral economic issues such as the banking system, federally funded internal improvements, trade and monetary policy, and the sale of federally owned western lands. Members of the two parties in all parts of the country also agreed that their "white" skin was what most qualified them for citizenship, thereby expressing a shared antipathy toward *African Americans that further cemented ties between North and South.

As long as voters and politicians focused on these national issues and remained united by race and party preferences, North-South disagreements over slavery were subordinated. But once sectional loyalties as "Northerners" or "Southerners" began to be substituted for national loyalties as "Whigs," "Democrats," and "white" Americans, interregional ties of economy and politics frayed, party structures crumbled, and war drew closer.

The outlines of this disruptive process emerged in the later 1840s, when the federal government embarked on a policy of rapid westward expansion and conquest through the annexation of *Texas (1845), the *Mexican War (1846–1848), and the settlement of boundary disputes with Great Britain over Oregon (1846). After the federal government acquired the territories that today comprise *California, Washington, Oregon, New Mexico, Arizona, Nevada, and Utah, the question of slaveholders' constitutional rights to extend their labor system into these areas suddenly became paramount. As congressional debate turned to the southern demand for unlimited slavery expansion versus the increasing northern insistence on "free soil," voters and politicians took increasingly hostile sectional positions.

Behind this intransigence lay southern whites' belief that slavery would decline as an economic system unless it was allowed to expand westward, resentment at the prospect of being excluded from national expansion, and suspicion that meddlesome "Yankees" were conspiring to challenge slavery in the existing slave states. From northern points of view, the planters' demands for the unlimited expansion of slavery threatened to populate new western states with "degraded" blacks and their "autocratic" masters, a situation that would make white, free-labor homesteading unthinkable and transform the republic into a "slaveocracy."

The nation's political system ultimately proved incapable of reconciling these concerns. In the *Compromise of 1850, congressional leaders sought to fashion a comprehensive settlement of conflicting claims over slavery's expansion into territories conquered from Mexico, and other points at issue relating to slavery, but this arrangement proved short-lived once the prospect arose in 1854 of admitting two additional new states, Kansas and Nebraska. Since both territories were located north of 36°30°, the limit for slavery's expansion established by the Missouri Compromise, slaveholding interests insisted that this earlier legislation be repealed. Passed by a deeply divided Congress, the *Kansas-Nebraska Act did exactly this, thereby inaugurating six years of escalating violence and sectional polarization that destroyed the two-party system and drove the South toward secession. Meanwhile, the publication of Harriet Beecher Stowe's **Uncle Tom's Cabin*, written in response to the 1850 *Fugitive Slave Act, deepened the moral revulsion against slavery spreading across the North.

Both northern and southern partisans began moving into Kansas after the passage of the 1854 act, seeking to dictate the legal status of slavery in the territory's constitution. As bloody guerrilla warfare erupted, the intersectional ties undergirding the two-party system began to rupture. As politicians divided over "bleeding Kansas," the Whig party collapsed, and its northern members joined a large minority of northern Democrats to form a new, exclusively northern political party unalterably opposed to slavery's further expansion—the *Republican party—which competed strongly in the 1856 elections.

After the U.S. *Supreme Court decreed in **Scott* vs. *Sandford* (1857) that citizens possessed unlimited rights to hold slaves as property throughout the Union, Republicans' power in the North grew even more rapidly. Meanwhile, the Democrats became ever more closely tied to slaveholders' interests and southern votes. By late 1859, after the U.S. Army crushed John *Brown's attempt to foment a slave insurrection by capturing the federal arsenal at Harpers Ferry, Virginia, the nation's political culture polarized almost completely.

Hence when the Republican Abraham *Lincoln captured the presidency in 1860 by pledging unbending hostility to slavery's further expansion, he attracted not a single southern electoral vote. His election did, however, lead an increasing number of influential slaveholders to conclude that secession constituted the only alternative to living under a wholly unrepresentative government dedicated to the overthrow of slavery and to the extinction of "southern rights." At this point, secession movements took power in the Deep South and moved to occupy the federal military installations. Though Lincoln made clear his intention to defend the Union with force if necessary, South Carolina's secessionists on 12 April 1861 turned their cannons against Fort Sumter, and the war began.

[*See also* Antebellum Era; Antislavery; Calhoun, John C.; Early Republic, Era of the; Free Soil Party; Racism.]

• Eric Foner, *Free Soil, Free Labor, Free Men: The Ideology of the Republican Party before the Civil War*, 1970. David M. Potter, *The Impending Crisis, 1848–1861*, 1976. Richard H. Sewell, *Ballots for Freedom: Antislavery Politics in the United States, 1837–1860*, 1976. William Cooper, *The South and the Politics of Slavery, 1828–1856*, 1978. James Brewer Stewart, *Holy Warriors: The Abolitionists and American Slavery*, 1997. Michael F. Holt, *The Political Crisis of the 1850s*, 1978.

—James Brewer Stewart

CIVIL WAR: MILITARY AND DIPLOMATIC COURSE

In retrospect, it may seem surprising that during the Civil War the *South was able to endure for four years against so much stronger a military foe. In fact, each side had important strengths and liabilities.

North and South Compared. The North's population dwarfed the South's by a ratio of more than two to one (22 million to 9 million), and 3.5 million of the South's population comprised slaves whom the Confederacy refused to arm. In industry, transportation, and the financial capacity to provision armies, the South was far outdistanced, even before the North's Union Navy effectively blockaded the Confederacy's Atlantic trade routes.

Yet the South did possess advantages, especially during the war's first two years. Robert E. *Lee and Thomas J. ("Stonewall") *Jackson were more skillful military leaders than those the Union initially brought forward. The South also had the advantage of fighting a largely defensive war on its own soil, terrain its armies knew well and within which they could maneuver advantageously. Then, too, most of the war's important battles in the eastern theater were fought in the hundred-mile corridor between the Northern and Southern capitals, *Washington, D.C., and Richmond, Virginia, a setting easier for Confederates to defend than for Union armies to occupy.

1861: Military Stalemate and Diplomatic Maneuverings. Whatever the balance of comparative strengths and weaknesses, neither side anticipated a war of such complexity, ferocity, or duration. The young men who eagerly responded to President Abraham *Lincoln's 1861 call for 75,000 volunteers expected an easy march to Richmond and a rapid end to the war, not the rout they experienced at Confederate hands in July 1861 at the Battle of *Bull Run, in Virginia's Shenandoah Valley. Now realizing the urgency of developing a consolidated military strategy, Lincoln appointed George B. McClellan (1826–1885) as overall commander of Union forces and furnished him support to develop an army, quartered outside Washington, D.C., of close to 80,000 and requiring unprecedented levels of provisioning and armament.

While McClellan's army amassed matériel and maneuvered for advantage in Virginia in late 1861 and early 1862, Unionists also struggled successfully for control in the Confederacy's various border regions. These areas included slave states that had not seceded, such as Maryland, Kentucky, and Missouri, and strategic areas such as northern Virginia (admitted to the Union during the war as present-day West Virginia) and eastern Tennessee. Despite strong pro-Confederate sympathies, these locales by 1862 had all been at least partially secured by pro-Union governments, making possible a concerted military strategy for the war's western theater. The abiding hostility to abolition among whites in these border regions, however, influenced President Lincoln's resistance to the idea of attacking *slavery, especially during the war's first two years.

The Lincoln administration also worked to build diplomatic support abroad. Secretary of State William *Seward, a diplomat of unusual acumen, immediately warned the European powers, Great Britain in particular, that the war was a domestic conflict in which other nations should not become involved; above all, they must refuse diplomatic recognition to the *Confederate States of America. The Confederate urgently sought such recognition to gain international legitimacy and to facilitate trade, credit, and arms purchases abroad. Confederates hoped that European, and particularly British, dependence on Southern-grown cotton would work in their favor. During the 1850s, as much as 80 percent of the region's total crop had been exported to England's textile industry. If faced with idle factories and an angry working class, Confederates reasoned, British textile interests would surely insist that the Confederacy be recognized.

Several factors weighed against this strategy. British textile factories possessed large raw cotton inventories, precluding immediate shortages. British public opinion showed no marked preference for the Confederate over the Union cause. And most important to the British government, the potential benefit of Confederate recognition never outweighed the risks of alienating Washington. Accordingly, although response did not fully satisfy the Lincoln administration, it clearly fell short of Confederate expectations. While refusing diplomatic recognition to the Confederacy, Britain did recognize the South's status as a belligerent. This halfway measure, with its nod of sympathy to the Confederacy cause, denied Washington's contention that the war was simply a civil uprising of domestic traitors and upheld the Confederacy's use of privateers against the Union's shipping. Yet the withholding of recognition made it harder for the Confederacy to obtain credit and arms and easier for Great Britain and France to honor the Union blockade of Southern ports.

Most important, this arrangement also enabled the United States and Great Britain to weather subsequent wartime diplomatic crises. One such crisis was provoked in late 1861 when Captain Charles Wilkes violated British sovereignty by capturing and returning to the United States two Confederate emissaries, James M. Mason and John Slidell, who were traveling to Europe aboard the *Trent*, a British vessel. This action, plainly illegal under international law, drew official British protests and threats to send troops to Canada should the United States refuse to apologize. Valuing Britain's continuing refusal to recognize the Confederacy, Lincoln and Seward quickly admitted the error and permitted the two Confederates to continue their mission to Europe. The successful resolution of the "*Trent* Affair" helped the two powers to resolve subsequent controversies involving Confederate privateers that relied on British outfitters and operated out of British ports.

1862–Early 1863: Battlefront Frustration and Homefront Tensions. Though military stalemate prevailed in the East through 1862, the Union Army and Navy did capture large swaths of the Atlantic coastline from North Carolina to Florida, including the rich cotton-growing regions of South Carolina and Georgia. In April 1862, Fort Pulaski fell, exposing approaches to Savannah, Georgia. Less than a month later, Admirals David *Farragut and David D. Porter captured *New

Orleans and the entire Gulf Coast. The Civil War's most spectacular naval battle took place on 9 March 1862, the historic but inconclusive clash between iron-clad warships, the Union's *Monitor* and the Confederacy's *Merrimack,* off Hampton Roads, Virginia.

The *Mississippi River Valley also saw Union initiatives as Commander Henry W. Halleck (1815–1872) began to engage his Confederate counterpart, Albert Sidney Johnston (1803–1862). Two of Halleck's subordinates, Generals Ulysses S. *Grant and Don Carlos Buell, collaborated to capture Fort Henry and Fort Donaldson on the Mississippi, which in turn led to the occupation of Nashville, Tennessee, a major Cumberland River port and an important strategic objective. Seeking to recoup these losses, Johnston mounted a deadly but inconclusive counteroffensive against Grant and Buell at the Battle of Shiloh (6–7 April 1862), which Union armies countered with victories at Corinth and Memphis, two river towns that gave them control over much of the Mississippi.

President Lincoln, meanwhile, was struggling to develop an understanding of grand strategy and to identify generals who could implement such a vision. Turning to an overly cautious McClellan, Lincoln demanded action on the eastern front, and by early April a huge Union army was camped ten miles from Richmond. Robert E. Lee and Stonewall Jackson moved quickly to relieve this threat in late June with a series of battles (the so-called Seven Days) that all but drove the defeated McClellan out of Virginia. Lincoln replaced him with the impetuous John Pope (1822–1892), who marched once more on Richmond, only to be defeated by Lee and Jackson at the Second Battle of Bull Run.

By late August 1862, a thoroughly frustrated Lincoln had reluctantly reappointed McClellan, who now faced a crisis as the armies of Lee and Jackson marched through Maryland in an all-out effort to capture Washington, D.C. At the Battle of *Antietam, on 17 September, McClellan stopped Lee's invasion at a cost of 12,000 Union casualties, which, combined with a Confederate toll of 9,000, constituted the bloodiest single day of the war. When McClellan refused to pursue this dearly bought advantage, Lincoln again dismissed him, this time in favor of Ambrose E. Burnside (1824–1881), who declared himself unprepared for the task and then confirmed the truth of this self-appraisal by sacrificing 12,500 men in a failed offensive at Fredericksburg, Virginia. As 1862 ended, the Confederates had proven themselves exceptional defensive tacticians, and Lincoln had yet to achieve a grand strategy.

In both North and South, domestic politics influenced battlefield events. Confederate President Jefferson *Davis, although able and dedicated, found his efforts to support the war effort on the home front blocked by obstruction from zealous defenders of "*states' rights." The Confederacy's 1862 Conscription Act proved nearly unenforceable in numerous locales. Worse still, Confederate governors like Joseph Brown in Georgia and Zebulon Vance in North Carolina refused to share supplies and soldiers with armies that were not defending their respective states. Pockets of Unionist resistance to the war effort compounded these organizational problems, as did inflation, which spiraled out of control despite the best efforts of Confederate Secretary of the Treasury Judah P. Benjamin (1811–1884).

Lincoln's political critics, by contrast, included those who called for stronger central government, particularly for powers appropriate for abolishing slavery. His own cabinet represented a wide diversity of opinion, ranging from the abolitionist Salmon P. Chase (1808–1873), secretary of the treasury, to the staunchly proslavery Montgomery Blair (1812–1883), the postmaster general. Lincoln's adroitness in managing this diverse group, however, did not transfer easily to congressional politics, where abolitionist-minded Republican critics demanded military emancipation of the slaves while conservative "war" Democrats decried the administration's "tyranny." In dealing with his domestic opponents, Lincoln jealously guarded his powers as commander in chief, sometimes using them to stifle pro-Confederacy dissent with military courts-martial, denials of bail, and suppressions of "subversive" publications.

When Congress formed a Joint Committee on the Conduct of the War, Lincoln initially resisted the efforts of its Radical Republican members to push him toward emancipation. As his prewar speeches had made clear, Lincoln hated slavery, regarding it as antithetical to the republican spirit of the *Declaration of Independence. He considered *African Americans as fully human as he but saw no necessary argument for intellectual, political, or social *equality. These views, combined with his preoccupation with retaining the loyalty of the proslavery border states, caused him to respond warily to emancipationist pressures. Hence when abolitionist military commanders issued field orders in 1861 emancipating the slaves of pro-Confederate masters, Lincoln countermanded them.

Seeking alternatives to general emancipation, Lincoln attempted in 1861 and 1862 to persuade border-state slaveholders to accept gradual, compensated emancipation and embarked on an ill-starred attempt to colonize freed slaves outside the United States. Of the 450 blacks who attempted to settle on an island off Haiti, for example, at least 80 died from disease and starvation before returning to the United States. Abandoning the colonization idea, Lincoln began to implement military measures that incrementally favored general emancipation, such as permitting Union commanders to grant refuge—and de facto freedom—to slaves who fled to army camps. He also chose not to veto congressional legislation known as the Confiscation Acts, which sanctioned the seizure of Confederate sympathizers' property, including their slaves.

By the summer of 1862, Union military reversals made Radical Republicans even more vocal about the need to destroy the Confederacy by uprooting slavery. At the same time, the British and French governments, sensing Union military weakness, signaled that they might now be willing to extend diplomatic recognition to the Confederacy. After considerable deliberation, and following the Union victory at Antietam, Lincoln announced on 22 September 1862 that if the rebellion continued, the slaves of the South would be freed as of 1 January 1863. Though the *Emancipation Proclamation freed no slaves when it was announced, it transformed the Union Army into an army of liberation that abolished slavery as it conquered Confederate territory. Lincoln's action also opened the Union Army to African American soldiers, a step he authorized when he issued the final proclamation on New Year's Day, 1863.

May 1863–April 1865: Chancellorsville to Appomattox. Though the North's war to preserve the Union had now been recast into a war for emancipation, the military momentum in the vital eastern theater remained with the Confederates. At the Battle of Chancellorsville, Virginia (1–4 May 1863), Lee's army so roundly defeated the Union forces under General Joseph Hooker (1814–1879) that Lee decided to carry the war for the first time into the North by invading Pennsylvania. Lee hoped to secure provisions, achieve strategic surprise, and stimulate Confederate sympathizers to rise up in *Philadelphia and Harrisburg. As Lee moved into Pennsylvania, Union General George Meade (1815–1872) followed, and the two clashed at the Battle of *Gettysburg, in an epic three-day engagement (2–4 July) that produced over 43,000 casualties and a Union victory. Gettysburg proved it was a decisive turning point in the East; thereafter, as Lee fought defensively, his armies ever more weakened by death, desertion, and hunger.

The war in the West also turned in the Union's favor in July 1863 as Grant and his subordinate William T. *Sherman successfully concluded a siege of the Mississippi River town of Vicksburg. This victory, together with Grant's conquest of Jackson, Mississippi, opened the entire Mississippi Valley to Union domination. Turning his attention to Tennessee, the last significant Confederate presence in the West, Grant defeated General Braxton Bragg (1817–1876) at Lookout Mountain and Missionary Ridge.

With the Confederacy in slow retreat everywhere as 1864 opened, Lincoln, having finally established his grand strategy, appointed Ulysses S. Grant general in chief of all the Union armies. During May, Grant's forces pushed deep into Virginia, vanquishing Lee's armies in a brutal series of battles in the wilderness, at Cold Harbor, and at Petersburg. Farther West, Sherman moved inexorably toward Atlanta, Georgia, which fell just before Lincoln's reelection victory in November 1864. In a devastating scorched-earth campaign, Sherman's forces marched on to the sea, reaching Savannah by Christmas.

Though hostilities continued through March 1865, the Confederate cause was clearly lost. On 9 April, unable to hold out any longer, Lee surrendered to Grant at Appomattox Courthouse. The war's human toll: some 360,000 Union dead, 275,000 wounded; 258,000 Confederate dead, at least 100,000 wounded. Prisoners of war on both sides suffered severely, especially at the notorious Confederate camp at Andersonville, Georgia, where many thousands of Union soldiers died. The bloodletting ended at last, but neither sectional reconciliation nor full equality for the freedmen were necessarily to follow.

[*See also* Cotton Industry; Vicksburg, Siege of; Weaponry, Nonnuclear.]

• Bruce Catton, *The Centennial History of the Civil War*, 3 vols., 1961–1965. Willie Lee Rose, *Rehearsal for Reconstruction: The Port Royal Experiment*, 1965. Hans L. Trefousse, *The Radical Republicans: Lincoln's Vanguard for Racial Justice*, 1969. David Crook, *The North, the South and the Powers, 1861–1865*, 1974. Leon Litwack, *Been in the Storm So Long: The Aftermath of Slavery*, 1979. James L. Roark, *Masters without Slaves: Southern Planters in the Civil War and Reconstruction*, 1979. Herman Hattaway and Archer Jones, *How the North Won*, 1988. James M. McPherson, *Battle Cry of Freedom: The Civil War Era*, 1988. Garry Wills, *Lincoln at Gettysburg: Words That Remade America*, 1992.

—James Brewer Stewart

CIVIL WAR: DOMESTIC EFFECTS

The Civil War's domestic impact was so extensive and varied that it almost defies description. Total casualties on both sides (360,000 Union, 258,000 Confederate) equal the number lost in all other American wars combined. The percentage of the eligible population mobilized (50 percent in the North, 75 percent in the *South) remains unsurpassed in Western military history. The nearly four million African American slaves liberated by the war represent a process of emancipation unequaled in the Western Hemisphere in scope and degree of governmental coerciveness. The war also had deep and enduring impacts on civilians; on women and families; on various ethnic groups; and on the nation's economy, government, and law.

Initially regarded as a specialized exercise conducted by traditional rules, the war soon came to be understood, especially in the North, as a comprehensive process demanding the resources and involvement of the entire society. While the Union and Confederate governments both sought unprecedented new powers when organizing their war efforts, it was the federal government in *Washington, D.C., that ultimately mobilized its total resources in a rationalized fashion, and, in the process, began to assume the functions of a modern administrative state.

Powerful new agencies in the War and Treasury Departments, designed to fund and supply the Northern war effort, signaled this expansion of federal power. So did unprecedented government-run systems of surveillance and intelligence. The close cooperation ultimately achieved between army and navy operations marked the emergence of integrated command structures and strategic planning. Given the North's strong and well-organized industrial base, government agencies also worked closely with private interests in standardizing railway systems, multiplying *telegraph networks, stimulating inventions, and industrializing the *technology of warfare. By war's end, it was the North's industrial capacity and *railroad networks that powered a Union Army built for invasion and conquest.

This consolidating further emerged in nonmilitary legislation passed by Congress during the war: the Legal Tender and National Banking Acts, which established new national currency and credit systems; the *Homestead Act, which capitalized national *agriculture through federal land sales to individual buyers; and the *Morrill Land Grant Act, which helped fund the nation's embryonic system of state universities.

In a further manifestation of centralized state power, the Lincoln administration suppressed *civil liberties. To combat draft resistance and antiwar opinion, particularly among northern "peace Democrats" (nicknamed by their opponents "Copperheads," after the poisonous snake), Lincoln in 1863 suspended the writ of habeas corpus. Some fifteen thousand civilians were arrested, though most were quickly released.

In the Confederacy, by contrast, political and economic localism stifled such consolidating tendencies. Instead, deeply embedded traditions of slaveholding and family hierarchy fostered suspicions of concentrated power and stimulated conflicts between various levels of government. As a result, authorities financed the war not by fostering economic innovation, as in the North, but by printing inflationary amounts of paper money that seriously disrupted the economy and the lives of ordinary people. Because the Confederate government never succeeded in asserting its authority over state and local governments, systems of supply and communications remained uncertain and military command structures divided, leaving Confederate soldiers to struggle with inadequate provisions, limited armaments, and confusing orders. Again in contrast to the North, the war's impact ultimately reinforced the white South's ingrained distrust of social innovation and its hostility to centralized power.

Whatever their contrasting situations, ordinary Northerners and Southerners shared equally in the pains of deprivation, separation, and death and bereavement, experiences that would influence changes in *family structures and *gender roles. In both regions, homemaking women assumed the work responsibilities of their absent menfolk in farming, plantation management, factory labor, and commercial activity, thereby moving outside the traditional constraints of the "domestic sphere."

In addition, a tide of sick and wounded soldiers drew impressive numbers of women into voluntary efforts to provide medical care. Since roughly two soldiers died of disease and infection for every one killed in battle, the need for nurses was obvious. In both North and South, thousands of women of all ages volunteered, thereby creating new opportunities in the rapidly professionalizing field of *medicine. Many women also volunteered with the U.S. Sanitary Commission, a private agency that held fund-raising events to supply sanitary supplies, bandages, blankets, and canned fruits and vegetables to the Union troops. Because of this wartime volunteering and the competencies they developed while performing "men's work," middle- and upper-class women in both regions also found themselves empowered to assume leadership roles in postwar reform associations and charitable bureaucracies such as the American *Red Cross, the *Woman's Christian Temperance Union, and the *National American Woman Suffrage Association.

The Civil War's most profound consequences, however, were experienced by the South's nearly four million slaves, their masters, and *African Americans in the North. During the first two years of fighting, President Abraham *Lincoln spoke for most Northern whites when he insisted that the war be fought exclusively to preserve the Union, not to emancipate slaves. Slowly, however, Lincoln revised this opinion, thanks to the combined actions of abolitionists in the North and escaping slaves in the South.

The large numbers of slaves who fled to the Union Army quickly proved their value to the military effort as soldiers, day laborers, and skilled workers. Meanwhile, militant African Americans across the North agitated successfully for the right to enlist in the Union Army. By 1863, as the North's military fortunes improved, regiments made up of Northern free blacks and Southern escapees were fighting very effectively. Military emancipation, viewed in this way, resulted as much from armed African Americans asserting their equality in a white nation's civil war as from Union victories. Put into force on 1 January 1863, the *Emancipation Proclamation reflected these battlefield realities while adding President Lincoln's crucial assurance that the Union Army's southward march to victory guaranteed an unconditional end to *slavery.

The draft riots that targeted *New York City's African American communities in July 1863 thus expressed white racist opposition to black emancipation as well as anger over inequitable methods of military conscription.

From most Southern whites' point of view, the end of the war revealed a region turned upside down, economically ruined, peopled by independent-minded former slaves, stripped by plundering invaders, and dominated by Northern occupiers. The continuing struggle for African American equality and for political *Reconstruction would thus unfold against the intransigent opposition of an embittered Southern white majority.

[*See also* Banking and Finance; Confederate States of America; Davis, Jefferson; Draft Riots, Civil War; Education: Collegiate Education; Education: Rise of the University; Federal Government, Executive Branch: The Presidency; Industrialization; Land Policy, Federal; Monetary Policy, Federal; Nursing; Racism; Railroads; Women in the Labor Force; Woman Suffrage Movement.]

• Charles W. Ramsdell, *Behind the Lines in the Southern Confederacy*, 1944. Clarence L. Mohr, "Southern Blacks in the Civil War: A Century of Historiography," *Journal of Negro History* 69 (Apr. 1974), 177–95. James M. McPherson, *Ordeal by Fire: The Civil War and Reconstruction*, 1987, pp. 386–403. Patrick O'Brien, *The Economic Effects of the American Civil War*, 1988. David W. Blight, *Frederick Douglass' Civil War: Keeping Faith in Jubilee*, 1989. Drew Gilpin Faust, *Mothers of Invention: Women of the Slaveholding South in the American Civil War*, 1996.

—James Brewer Stewart

CIVIL WAR: CHANGING INTERPRETATIONS

Historical interpretations of the Civil War were initially defined by writers whose views reflected the values of the victors. From the 1860s through the 1880s, New England historians such as James Ford Rhodes presented the Civil War as a noble crusade by patriotic Northerners to preserve the Union from secessionist traitors and to rid the republic of the moral blight of slaveholding.

Such views, however, were supplanted at the close of the nineteenth century by a new generation of scholars who sympathized with the defeated *South and saw *African Americans as innately inferior. By viewing *slavery as well-suited for an inferior and dependent people, scholars such as Woodrow *Wilson, John W. Burgess, and John Spencer Bassett reflected contemporary anthropological theories of "scientific" *racism as well as their own southern roots. Accordingly, they defended slaveholders' "*states' rights" arguments and condemned abolitionists and *Republican party politicians for their aggressions against an unoffending South that led to a tragic war of conquest.

In the 1920s, confronting the devastating consequences of *World War I, a new generation of historians deepened this "pro-Confederacy" interpretation but also modified it with condemnations of warfare in general. Viewed in the disillusioning aftermath of the 1914–1918 war, the Civil War, too, appeared unjustifiable to historians such as James G. Randall and Avery Craven, who condemned "extremist" abolitionists and irresponsible secessionists alike for this presumed unnecessary catastrophe. Slavery, from this point of view, should have presented no moral or political problems since it was demonstrably beneficial to racially "inferior" African Americans and was also unsuited to westward expansion—a system fated to slow economic extinction had not a "blundering generation" needlessly drifted into war. Though white supremacism dominated all these interpretations, a few egalitarian dissenters such as W. E. B. *Du Bois, Carter G. Woodson (1875–1950), Herbert Aptheker, and Dwight Lowell Dumond argued during the 1930s that slavery, a moral abomination, had fostered unspeakable cruelty and the righteous crusade required to destroy it.

A minority view at the time, this interpretation was embraced by most historians after *World War II, for a number of compelling reasons. By the later 1940s, Nazism had utterly discredited academic *racism, and racial *segregation seemed to mock the nation's moral posture in the emerging *Cold War. The first phase of a militant *civil rights movement had begun to take shape. By the mid-1960s, a new generation of scholars led by Kenneth Stampp, John Hope Franklin, and Arthur Schlesinger Jr. reflected these influences when they passionately insisted that the moral issues of slavery and abolition lay at the heart of the Civil War's meaning and justified its human costs.

After the 1970s, this *Cold War emphasis on the moral centrality of slavery was modified on several broad fronts. Neo-Marxist historians such Eugene Genovese and Eric Foner argued that fundamental differences in political economy underlay irreconcilable sectional disagreements over slavery's westward expansion. A second group of scholars, typified by James Rawley and Michael Holt and stressing the underlying white supremacism and anti-Catholicism in the free states, argued that these biases, as much as hatred of slavery, inspired the spread of disruptive sectional feelings among voters North and South. A third school of thought, represented by James McPherson and Richard H. Sewell, continued to emphasize slavery's immorality as the fundamental cause of the Civil War.

[See also Historiography, American; Race, Concept of.]

• Thomas J. Pressley, *Americans Interpret Their Civil War*, 1962. Eric Foner, "The Causes of the American Civil War: Recent Interpretations and New Directions," *Civil War History* (Mar. 1974): 197–214.

—James Brewer Stewart

CLARK, GEORGE ROGERS (1752–1818), frontiersman, *Revolutionary War military leader in the Ohio River Valley. Born on a farm in piedmont Virginia, Clark came to Kentucky as a surveyor. An aggressive, charismatic young man, he soon led Kentucky settlers unhappy with their proprietors into Virginia's political orbit. Patrick *Henry and Thomas *Jefferson were among his allies. With the outbreak of the Revolutionary War, Clark as Virginia's local commander defended the small, vulnerable Kentucky settlements by boldly attacking. In 1777, his small force captured the French-speaking towns of southern Illinois and Indiana. When a British force recaptured Vincennes on the Wabash River in 1778, Clark led a heroic winter march to retake it in 1779. His strategic vision—strike westward to defend against an Indian threat from north of the Ohio—never wavered, but his ultimate goal of seizing the British base at *Detroit was beyond his resources. As help waned from Virginia—itself under direct British attack in 1781—Clark's gains slipped away, and Kentucky lapsed into a more passive defense.

By age thirty, Clark had lost his health and some of his influence and was drinking too much. A classic Indian-hater, he nevertheless consciously imitated what he saw as the Indian leadership style—bluff mixed with terrorism and calibrated kindness, undergirded by absolute fearlessness. Postwar flirtations with Spanish and French ventures in the Mississippi Valley further sullied his reputation, and even before his death his significance for regional and American history was being debated.

[*See also* Burr, Aaron; French Settlements in North America; Indian History and Culture: 1500 to 1800; Indian Wars; Middle West, The; Revolution and Constitution, Era of.]

• John Bakeless, *Background to Glory: The Life of George Rogers Clark,* 1957; reprint 1992.

—John Shy

CLAY, CASSIUS. *See* Ali, Muhammed.

CLAY, HENRY (1777–1852), statesman and *Whig party leader in the second-party system. Born in Virginia, Clay read law and in 1797 moved to Lexington, Kentucky. After serving in the Kentucky legislature and teaching law at Transylvania University, he won election in 1810 to the U.S. House of Representatives, where he served, apart from brief intervals, until 1825, usually as Speaker. An unsuccessful presidential candidate in 1824, he participated in the congressional maneuvering that brought John Quincy *Adams to the White House. When Adams appointed him secretary of state, the supporters of Andrew *Jackson charged a "corrupt bargain." After two early appointive terms in the U.S. Senate (1806–1807, 1810–1811), he won election to the Senate in 1831, serving until 1842 and again from 1849 until his death. A perennial presidental candidate, Clay ran four more times between 1832 and 1848, but it was as a master legislator, eloquent orator, and the *West's magnetic "Prince Hal" that his reputation lives.

While Speaker of the House in 1812, Clay was among the "War Hawks" who favored declaring war on Britain, but he also served as a peace negotiator at Ghent (1814) and thereafter pursued conciliation in both domestic and foreign affairs. He became known as "the Great Compromiser" for his role in the *Missouri Compromise of 1820, the Tariff Compromise of 1833, and the sectional *Compromise of 1850. Coming from the border state of Kentucky, Clay hoped desperately to avoid a civil war. Although a slaveholder, he favored the slaves' gradual emancipation and their removal to Africa. He argued in vain for the right of Native Americans to retain their lands in the Southeast. He warned, correctly, that the 1845 annexation of *Texas would worsen sectional tensions and lead to war with Mexico.

As a Whig leader, Clay battled for national economic development through a program he called "the American System." This included protective *tariffs, a national bank, and federal subsidies to "internal improvements" (transportation projects like highways and canals). His *Democratic party opponents, fearing the expansion of federal power at the expense of the states, frustrated the plan's adoption. Although Clay ended on the losing side of many controversies, the *Republican party that arose after his death implemented much of his economic program.

[*See also* Antebellum Era; Bank of the United States, First and Second; Calhoun, John C.; Canals and Waterways; Colonization Movement, African; Federal Government, Legislative Branch: House of Representatives; Federal Government, Legislative Branch: Senate; Political Parties; Roads and Turnpikes, Early; War of 1812.]

• Merrill Peterson, *The Great Triumvirate: Webster, Clay, and Calhoun,* 1987. Robert Remini, *Henry Clay,* 1991.

—Daniel Walker Howe

CLAYTON ACT. *See* Antitrust Legislation.

CLAYTON-BULWER TREATY (1850). America's expanded trade in the Far East and acquisition of Oregon and *California in the 1840s heightened U.S. policy-makers' interest in a Central American canal. Further, President Zachary *Taylor and Secretary of State John M. Clayton hoped to restrict English hegemony to British Honduras (Belize), foreclosing any other British claims in the region. These U.S. interests, however, threatened Great Britain's presence and ambitions. In late 1849, Foreign Secretary Lord Palmerston dispatched to Washington a new minister, Sir Henry Bulwer, to avert a crisis. Bulwer sought to protect British interests—focusing upon Honduras, the adjoining Bay Islands, the Atlantic (Mosquito) coast of Nicaragua, and the remainder of the isthmus—from American *expansionism.

Clayton and Bulwer signed an ambiguous treaty on 19 April 1850, declaring that neither country would build a canal in Central America without mutual consent or cooperation. If a canal were built, both nations would guarantee its neutrality. Each power also pledged neither to fortify nor to establish colonies in the region.

Although the agreement blocked further British expansion, it infuriated many Americans, who realized that it had compromised America's exclusive opportunity to build a canal and likely violated the *Monroe Doctrine. Moreover, the British refused to withdraw from Honduras or Nicaragua. For the next half-century, differing interpretations of the treaty caused friction between the two countries. Finally, in 1901, the Hay-Pauncefote Treaty abrogated Clayton-Bulwer and gave the United States sole rights to build and maintain a canal.

[*See also* Foreign Relations: U.S. Relations with Latin America; Hay, John; Panama Canal.]

• Mary W. Williams, *Anglo-American Isthmian Diplomacy, 1815–1915,* 1914; reprint, 1965. Wilbur D. Jones, *The American Problem in British Diplomacy, 1841–1861,* 1974.

—John M. Belohlavek

CLEMENS, SAMUEL L. [Mark Twain] (1835–1910), author. Samuel Langhorne Clemens was born in the hamlet of Florida, Missouri, and raised in Hannibal, Missouri, a thriving commercial town on the *Mississippi River. His father, a slave owner and justice of the peace, went bankrupt as a shopkeeper and land speculator. Young Samuel ended his formal schooling at the age of twelve and at seventeen left home for good. His imagination, however, continued to dwell in Hannibal and along the river and ultimately created the most memorable boyhood in American literature. He served as an itinerant typesetter, a river pilot (fulfilling a boyhood ambition), a Confederate irregular (for a grim two weeks) in the *Civil War, and a prospector and journalist in the Nevada territory and *California.

In 1865, at the age of thirty, Clemens published his first nationally recognized story, then titled "The Notorious Jumping Frog of Calaveras County." He had finally settled on his vocation, describing it in a letter to his brother Orion as "seriously scribbling to excite the *laughter* of God's creatures." As a sign and instrument of this new purpose he took the public identity "Mark Twain" (a pseudonym derived from the river leadsman's call meaning twelve feet of navigable depth), although, as he soon discovered, this public identity laid claims on him to be a professional funny man that often collided with the private imperatives of Samuel Clemens.

Just turned thirty-one, he left California to seek fame and fortune in the East. His first success, *The Innocents Abroad* (1869), a humorous and satirical travel book based on a summer-long excursion to Europe and the Middle East, sold an estimated 100,000 copies in its first two years, a considerable figure for the time. A major attraction on the lecture circuit and part owner of a Buffalo, New York, newspaper, he completed his transition from sagebrush bohemianism to respectability by his 1870 marriage to Olivia Langdon, daughter of an upstate New York coal baron. They moved from Buffalo to Hartford, Connecticut, where, with Harriet Beecher Stowe as neighbor, he built for his growing family an extravagant, eye-catching mansion that saw two decades of domestic happiness.

With essayist and *Hartford Courant* editor Charles Dudley Warner, Clemens collaborated on a topical novel, *The Gilded Age* (1873), the title of which supplied an enduring label for the post–*Civil War era. *The Adventures of Tom Sawyer* (1876) prepared the way for his masterpiece, *The Adventures of Huckleberry Finn* (1885), a classic of world literature. No other American work has been so highly praised for its originality and brilliance—Ernest *Hemingway called it "the best book we've had"—or so widely abused, for its ironic, at times ambivalent treatment of the refractory issues of race and *slavery, its use of the racial slur "nigger," and its controversial plot resolution. *Roughing It* (1872), *A Tramp Abroad* (1880), and *Life on the Mississippi* (1883) helped consolidate Clemens's reputation. He was an international literary celebrity as much at home in London, Paris, Vienna, and Berlin as in Hartford and New York.

Clemens's considerable prosperity, derived from book sales and fees from lectures and readings, allowed him to live and entertain on the scale of a merchant prince. But it also tempted him into business ventures—a publishing house and an automatic typesetting machine—that promised greater wealth but in 1894 bankrupted him. His 1889 novel *A Connecticut Yankee in King Arthur's Court* was a turning point in his faith in progress, *technology, and his confidence in himself as a writer. A later novel, the somber *Tragedy of Pudd'nhead Wilson* (1894), dealt once again with the subject of race and blood in America. To pay his debts and recoup his fortunes, he traveled in 1895–1896 to Australia, New Zealand, India, and South Africa on a round-the-world lecture tour that also supplied material for his final travel book, *Following the Equator* (1897). His business reverses together with the death (in 1896) of his favorite daughter, Susy, had put an end to the Hartford idyll. At times he believed that his rags-to-riches, obscurity-to-fame history, which reminded his friend William Dean *Howells of *The Arabian Nights,* had been only a dream, from which he awakened to the reality of failure.

Restored to financial health with the aid of Standard Oil tycoon Henry H. Rogers, Mark Twain after a period of self-exile returned to the United States in 1900 and to public celebrity that continued to his death. He was as conspicuous for his cigars and white suits, shock of white hair, and Fifth Avenue promenades as for his ability to express a quotable opinion on virtually any topic. In addition to autobiography, the literary form he found most congenial in his final years was the polemic. These he directed against orthodox religion, Mary Baker Eddy's *Christian Science, William Shakespeare, imperialism, *racism, *lynching, patriotism, the martial spirit, and conventional wisdom in general. Such late works as *The Man That Corrupted Hadleyburg* (1900), *What Is Man?* (1906), and *The Mysterious Stranger* (published 1916) reveal the depth of his pessimism. He died in Redding, Connecticut, at an Italianate villa built with proceeds from his serialized autobiography.

Mark Twain's life and career bridge the eras of the *Pony Express and the motor car, the river raft and the steam yacht, the open frontier and the modern metropolis. The twenty-nine volumes of his collected works demonstrate the latitude of the designation "author." He wrote novels, short stories, travel books, humorous and satirical sketches, social and literary commentary, essays, philosophic argument, autobiography, speeches, and polemics. Almost as many volumes have been devoted to publishing his letters, notebooks, journalism, fugitive pieces, stage plays, and poetry. What unifies this half-century-long body of work is a dazzling and dominating authorial personality together with a distinctive voice, stance, and style—at once quizzical, celebratory, lyric, vernacular, ironic, and unmistakably native—that have influenced American writing ever since.

[*See also* Gilded Age; Literature: Civil War to World War I.]

• William Dean Howells, *My Mark Twain,* 1910. Albert Bigelow Paine, *Mark Twain: A Biography,* 3 vols., 1912. James M. Cox, *Mark Twain: The Fate of Humor,* 1966. Justin Kaplan, *Mr. Clemens and Mark Twain,* 1966. Jeffrey Steinbrink, *Getting to Be Mark Twain,* 1991. Shelley Fisher Fishkin, *Was Huck Black? Mark Twain and African-American Voices,* 1993.

—Justin Kaplan

CLEVELAND, GROVER (1837–1908), twenty-second and twenty-fourth president of the United States. Born in Caldwell, New Jersey, Cleveland spent most of his early life in Buffalo, New York, where he practiced law and held minor offices. (He also fathered a child out of wedlock, an indiscretion that his political opponents would later use against him.) In 1881, running as a Democrat, he won election as mayor of Buffalo. The following year he was elected governor of New York, establishing in both positions a reputation for honesty and courage. Elected president in 1884, narrowly defeating James G. *Blaine, he became the first Democrat to serve in that office since the *Civil War. As president, he worked for *civil service reform and *tariff reform. Seeking to restrain governmental expansion, he vetoed over two-thirds of the bills passed by Congress, more than all his predecessors combined.

Losing a close reelection race to the Republican Benjamin *Harrison in 1888, Cleveland returned to his legal practice. He regained the presidency in 1892, defeating Harrison and the *Populist party candidate James B. Weaver, thereby becoming the only president to serve two nonconsecutive terms. In response to a devastating depression that began in 1893, Cleveland persuaded Congress to repeal the Sherman Silver Purchase Act of 1890, which he believed undermined the government's economic stability. In 1894, he vetoed a compromise silver measure, led an inept attempt at tariff reform, and sent federal troops to Illinois to put down the Pullman railroad strike. Leaving office under a cloud of unpopularity, he retired to Princeton, New Jersey, where he died in 1908.

Cleveland's stature rose posthumously, boosted in 1932 by Allan Nevins's *Grover Cleveland: A Study in Courage,* which praised his honesty and forthrightness. While historians in 1948 and 1962 ranked him "near great," subsequent scholarly assessments, dwelling on his ineffective handling of the crises of the 1890s, placed him in the "average" category.

If not a great president, Cleveland was nonetheless an important one. In initiatives like the repeal of the Tenure of Office Act in 1887 (an act, passed in 1867, that prohibited a president from removing appointed officials without the approval of the Senate), his brisk use of the *veto power, reforms in federal land and Indian policy, and efforts at tariff reform, he recaptured for the presidency some of the powers it had lost during *Reconstruction. Although not closely involved with its passage, Cleveland signed into law the *Interstate Commerce Act of 1887, a pioneering federal regulatory measure. Establishing important precedents, he used a sweeping court injunction to end the Pullman strike and sent federal troops to Illinois without a request from the governor. Cleveland also asserted presidential authority in foreign policy, giving it a moral dimension akin to Woodrow *Wilson's. He tried unsuccessfully to reverse the 1893 revolution that overthrew the Hawaiian monarchy, citing wrongful involvement by U.S. officials and business interests in *Hawai'i. In settling an 1895 border dispute between Great Britain and Venezuela, he gave the *Monroe Doctrine additional force in U.S. foreign policy.

Cleveland, however, showed little understanding of the large forces of *industrialization and *urbanization unfolding in the late nineteenth century. Following the Democratic philosophy of *states' rights and limited government, he devoted himself principally to maintaining the *gold standard. His actions during the depression of the 1890s split the *Democratic party, heightened the influence of its agrarian wing, and strengthened the *Republican party.

[*See also* Depressions, Economic; Federal Government, Executive Branch: The Presidency; Foreign Relations: U.S. Relations with Latin America; Free Silver Movement; Gilded Age; Monetary Policy, Federal; Populist Era; Pullman Strike and Boycott.]

• Robert McElroy, *Grover Cleveland: The Man and the Statesman,* 2 vols., 1923. Horace Samuel Merrill, *Bourbon Leader: Grover Cleveland and the Democratic Party,* 1957. J. Rogers Hollingsworth, *The Whirligig of Politics: The Democracy of Cleveland and Bryan,* 1963. Rexford G. Tugwell, *Grover Cleveland,* 1968. H. Wayne Morgan, *From Hayes to McKinley: National Party Politics, 1877–1896,* 1969. John F. Marszalek, ed., *Grover Cleveland: A Bibliography,* 1988. Richard E. Welch Jr., *The Presidencies of Grover Cleveland,* 1988.

—R. Hal Williams

CLINTON, BILL, (1946–), forty-second president of the United States. Born in Hope, Arkansas, William Jefferson Clinton was raised by his mother, Virginia Dwire Clinton, and his stepfather, Roger Clinton, a Hot Springs, Arkansas, car salesman. Clinton's natural father, William Jefferson Blythe III, died in an automobile accident before his son's birth. Graduating from Georgetown University in 1968, Clinton attended Oxford University as a Rhodes Scholar (1968–70) and graduated from Yale Law School in 1973. He returned to Arkansas to run for Congress, but lost to a popular Republican incumbent. In 1976, following his marriage to fellow lawyer Hillary Rodham, he was elected state attorney general. Two years later, at thirty-two, he won the Arkansas governorship. Defeated for reelection in 1980 after raising gasoline taxes and licensing fees, he made a comeback in 1984, winning a second term. Reelected in 1986 and 1990, he helped found the Democratic Leadership Council, an organization devoted to moving the party closer to the political center.

As the Democrats' most visible advocate of pragmatic, centrist politics, Clinton sought the party's 1992 presidential nomination. Though dogged by charges of sexual impropriety and draft-dodging in the *Vietnam War Era, he won the nomination, choosing Tennessee senator Al Gore (1948–) as his running mate. Stressing economic recovery amidst a nagging recession and styling himself a "New Democrat" blending fiscal moderation with social concern, Clinton pledged to overhaul the nation's health, *welfare, and *education systems while also reducing budget deficits. Opposing the Republican incumbent George *Bush and independent H. Ross Perot (1930–), a Texas billionaire, Clinton won with 43 percent of the popular vote.

During his first two years in office, Clinton won approval for a family-leave law, a motor-votor registration act, the *North American Free Trade Agreement (negotiated by the Bush administration), the Brady *gun-control act, and a deficit-reducing federal budget. His biggest disappointment came on health care, as Congress rebuffed a sweeping reform plan drafted by a team headed by First Lady Hillary Clinton.

Despite limited diplomatic experience, Clinton enjoyed considerable foreign policy succcess. His administration under Secretary of State Warren Christopher helped negotiate peace accords in the Middle East and Northern Ireland and dispatched peacekeeping missions to Haiti and Bosnia. But Clinton's enhanced stature abroad failed to mollify domestic opponents of "Clintonism," defined by conservatives as a blend of cleverly disguised "tax and spend" *liberalism, political opportunism, and private immorality. Religious and cultural conservatives assailed Clinton on issues ranging from *abortion to gays in the *military. Ironically, liberal Democrats also criticized Clinton, accusing him of forsaking the social justice causes vital to racial minorities, organized labor, and the poor. Despite an improving economy, Republicans brandishing a conservative, anti-Clinton "Contract with America" won both houses of Congress, for the first time in forty years, in the 1994 midterm election.

Despite this setback, the likeable, articulate, and charismatic Clinton retained his personal popularity. A celebrity "Baby Boomer" and popular culture icon riding the crest of a booming economy, he dominated the political center. Sensing the electorate's rightward shift, Clinton embraced welfare reform, a favorite Republican cause, and in 1996 signed a landmark bill slashing welfare spending, limiting benefits, and shifting the major welfare program from Washington to the states. A consummate campaigner and fund-raiser, Clinton easily defeated his 1996 Republican challenger, Kansas senator Robert Dole (1923–). (Ross Perot ran again also, but garnered far fewer votes than in 1992.) As Clinton's second term began, few doubted his capacity for political survival.

This capacity was soon sorely tested. In 1994, Republicans had initiated an investigation of the Clintons' alleged involvement in the Whitewater scandal, a 1980s Arkansas real estate swindle. However, Special Prosecutor Kenneth Starr (appointed by Attorney General Janet Reno) failed to find evidence of illegality by either Clinton. Starr turned to other alleged presidential wrongdoings, however, and his inquiry gained momentum in 1998 with the disclosure of a sexual liaison between Clinton and a young White House intern, Monica Lewinsky. As the scandal unfolded, Clinton's initial denials gave way to a stunning public admission that he had not told the whole truth about the matter. Since Clinton had also denied the relationship in sworn testimony in an Arkansas sexual harrassment lawsuit, Starr presented this evidence of perjury to Congress in September 1998. In December, by a partisan vote, the House forwarded to the Senate two articles of *impeachment. Clinton, however, mobilized enough Senate support to avoid removal from office. Both Congress and the public divided sharply over the gravity and "impeachability" of the president's offenses. He retained broad popular support, polls revealed, even among those who questioned his integrity.

Prosperity and Clinton's skillful handling of the ceremonial and symbolic aspects of presidential leadership helped him weather the storm, but public expectations of the presidency remained low in his final two years. Focusing on foreign affairs, trade, and strategic issues, Clinton with Secretary of State Madeleine Albright (1997–), Defense Secretary William Cohen, and Trade Representative Charlene Barshefsky pursued trade agreements with China, Vietnam, and other nations; urged support for the controversial World Trade Organization; sought to revive the stalled Mideast peace process; and promoted a scaled-down version of the controversial missile-defense system first proposed by President Ronald *Reagan. On the domestic front, he continued to press for a financial restructuring of the nation's Medicaid and *Social Security systems, and convened a high-profile Presidential Initiative on Race chaired by historian John Hope Franklin. The Clinton scandals remained in the public eye, however, thanks to the president's continuing legal problems, including the threat of disbarment; Hillary Clinton's bid for a U.S. Senate seat from New York; and Republican attempts to link Vice President Gore—the Democrats' 2000 presidential candidate—to Clinton's political and ethical failings, particularly campaign finance irregularities in the 1996 election.

Confronting the disjunction between Clinton's public accomplishments and private shortcomings, citizens pondered the issue of character in public life; the boundaries between the public and the private spheres; and the nature of presidential leadership in a *post–Cold War era of media-driven politics, material abundance, and moral uncertainty. These debates seemed likely to represent Bill Clinton's primary contribution to American political history.

[*See also* Democratic Party; Federal Government, Executive Branch: The Presidency; Foreign Relations; Foreign Trade, U.S.; General Agreement on Tariffs and Trade; Medicare and Medicaid; Strategic Defense Initiative; Welfare, Federal.]

• Elizabeth Drew, *On the Edge: The Clinton Presidency,* 1995. David Maraniss, *First in His Class: A Biography of Bill Clinton,* 1995. David Maraniss, *The Clinton Enigma,* 1998. Richard Posner, *An Affair of the State: The Investigation, Impeachment, and Trial of President Clinton,* 1999. Joe Conason and Gene Lyons, *The Hunting of the President,* 2000. Mark Rozell, ed., *The Clinton Scandal and the Future of American Government,* 2000.

—Raymond O. Arsenault

CLINTON, DEWITT (1769–1828), political leader and key figure in the building of the *Erie Canal. Born in Little Britain, New York, Dewitt Clinton was the son of James Clinton, a *Revolutionary War general, and the nephew of George Clinton, a powerful governor of New York (1777–1795). Following his graduation from Columbia College in 1786, Clinton read law, became his uncle's private secretary, was elected to the state assembly in 1795, and served in the state senate from 1798 to 1802.

Appointed the U.S. Senate in 1802, Clinton played a significant role in the framing of the Twelfth Amendment, which separated the voting for president and vice president. Unhappy in national politics, he resigned from the Senate in 1803 to become mayor of *New York City, a post he held off and on until 1815. His most important mayoral accomplishments were expanding the public-school system and establishing an orphan asylum and a hospital. A learned man with broad interests, Clinton also helped establish the New-York Historical Society, the American Academy of the Arts, and the Literary and Philosophical Society.

Increasingly unhappy with President James *Madison's handling of diplomatic relations with Great Britain in the events leading up to the *War of 1812 and Virginia's domination of national politics, he put together a coalition of antiwar Republicans and Federalists and ran for president in 1812. Madison won reelection, but the contest was very close; had Clinton carried Pennsylvania, he would have won.

As governor of New York in 1817–1822 and 1825–1828, Clinton promoted and oversaw the building of the Erie Canal and played a prominent role in the ceremonies marking its completion in 1825. Arrogant and vindictive, Clinton relentlessly pursued his political enemies, leading those enemies to form an opposition group, the Albany Regency, whose most important member was the future president Martin *Van Buren.

[*See also* Antebellum Era; Canals and Waterways; Early Republic, Era of the; Education: The Public School Movement; Federalist Party.]

• Steven E. Siry, *DeWitt Clinton and the American Political Economy: Sectionalism, Politics, and Republican Ideology, 1787–1828,* 1990. Craig Hanyan and Mary Hanyan, *DeWitt Clinton and the Rise of the People's Men,* 1996. Evan Cornog, *The Birth of Empire: DeWitt Clinton and the American Experience, 1769–1828,* 1998.

—Richard E. Ellis

CLOTHING AND FASHION. Clothing and fashion are cultural expressions of individuals' understanding of, and participation in, the social and economic life of their communities and nation. In America, frequently changing fashions and aesthetic play have characterized the history of clothing, enabling people of different races, classes, and sexual persuasions to express their individual and collective identities and escape the constraints of tradition.

To Europeans at first contact, the draped furs, tattoos, and ornaments of shell, stone, feather, and hemp worn by Native Americans indicated their uncivilized state, contrasting with the processed cloth and leather from which European garments were machine- and hand-sewn. While a few Europeans may have adopted native garb—skins, furs, and moccasins—settlers more typically conformed to Old World rather than New World styles of dress. Native Americans wore European garb only selectively and purposefully, usually to communicate friendliness to traders and missionaries or to help them pass unnoticed through hostile territory during wars.

Puritan settlers abided by English sumptuary laws that prohibited extravagance and regulated clothing styles according to trade, rank, and wealth. Thus, a miller in apron and shirtsleeves would not be confused with a magistrate in frock coat, knee breeches, and silk stockings. During the *Revolutionary War Era, colonists boycotted British goods and produced their own cloth and clothing—called homespun—demonstrating republican self-sufficiency, frugality, and industry. The patriotic rejection of British imports, coupled with the invention of the cotton gin and the rise of the *textile industry in the Northeast, stimulated cloth manufacture in the new nation and hastened the shift from home production to commercially produced goods. By the mid–nineteenth century, mail-order catalogs and the establishment of dry-goods and *department stores helped nationalize the distribution of cloth, trim, and ready-made clothing. The rise of standardized sizing, stimulated by the *Civil War demand for uniforms, allowed manufacturers to employ women, immigrants, and children to assemble garments by the piece in their homes. Sweatshop labor accounted for nearly half of all clothing manufactured in the United States from 1870 to 1900.

As early as the 1820s, the suit—a dark and simple coat, waistcoat, and trousers (the latter said to derive from English sportsmen and French Revolutionary workmen's costumes)—had become the standard garb of urban upper-class and middle-class men as well as some skilled craftsmen. Women had no such utilitarian and comfortable attire. Dress reformers and women's rights advocates in the 1850s advocated simpler dress, but outfits such as Amelia Bloomer's loose-fitting Turkish-style trousers and short dress failed to gain currency. Though Quakers, Shakers, and other religious sectarians abandoned corsets and layers of petticoats in favor of plain dress or a form of trousers, urban women did not customarily wear pants until the 1930s and 1940s.

*Magazines featuring colored lithographic fashion plates, notably *Godey's Lady's Book* (1830–1898), along with sewing machines (developed in 1846) and paper clothing patterns (devised by Ebenezer Butterick in 1863) communicated women's fashion trends widely. One pale and sylphlike ideal of female beauty was dubbed the "steel-engraving lady" after the print technology that popularized it. Her bell-shaped skirt, sloped shoulders, crimped waist, and muted colors obscured the genteel lady's sexuality and stressed her delicacy and virtuous morality.

By midcentury, a more voluptuous figure came into fashion, perhaps owing to the influence of immigrant women, for whom weight offered a cultural gauge of wealth. Both men and woman nipped their waists with corsets and enhanced their rears with padding and bustles to create a nature-defying shape called the "Grecian Bend." This fashion was satirized on stage by the "British Blondes," a touring company that entertained burlesque and *vaudeville houses with their comically over-adorned, buxom, and bustle-enhanced characters.

The British Blondes' stage antics spoofed what economist Thorstein *Veblen described in *The *Theory of the Leisure Class* (1899) as "conspicuous consumption"—the elaborate fashions by which leisure-class women exhibited their husbands' wealth and status. Wealthy Americans' demand for fashions that would distinguish them from the masses was fulfilled in part by Parisian haute couture, the art of hand-sewn, high-style fashions initiated by Charles Frederick Worth, the first to use live fashion models. Reflecting the elegance of Second Empire France (1852–1870), Worth's lavish gowns were widely emulated by fashion-conscious Americans.

Changing roles for women and the craze for outdoor activities led to new fashion trends captured by Charles Dana Gibson (1867–1944) in his 1890s magazine illustrations of the statuesque "Gibson Girl," an emancipated figure costumed for golf course or office. Her shirtwaist and flowing skirt, easy to manufacture and appropriate to different classes, resembled a man's suit. Women's hemlines rose steadily, first during the dance craze of the 1910s and then going knee-length in the "flapper" fashion of the 1920s. The silent-screen actresses Mary Pickford and Clara Bow typified this youthful ideal: small and boyish, with understressed breasts (sometimes achieved through tight wrapping) and hips.

More sober fashions for both sexes prevailed during the Great Depression of the 1930s and *World War II. In 1943, servicemen in *Los Angeles attacked Mexican-American youths for wearing "zoot suits": exaggerated drape-shaped jackets with outrageously padded shoulders and fiercely tapered trousers, illustrating how fashion may constitute a form of cultural resistance.

Postwar youth similarly used clothing to defy convention—the blue jeans and leather jacket style popularized by the movie rebels James Dean and Marlon Brando in the 1950s, the hippies in bell-bottoms and miniskirts in the 1960s, the ripped T-shirt and safety-pin adorned punks of the late 1970s. Post-1960s clothing styles became more androgynous, reflecting a pastiche of global influences. Thrift-store and secondhand clothing was recycled as high style. Cross-dressing and fashion fetishism (as with sadomasochistic gear of leatherwear, whips, and chains) influenced mainstream fashion design, exhibiting the ways clothing can express diverse ideas about gender and sexuality.

Fashion became a fast-moving international enterprise in the 1980s and 1990s. Styles that originated with inner-city youth and hip-hop and rap-music cultures demonstrated global appeal. So did the clothing or footwear endorsed by high-visibility sports stars. High turnover and pressures for product variety in the retail industry, combined with economic globalization, contributed to the reemergence of sweatshops in the United States, Asia, and Central and Latin America. As consumption, technological sophistication, and marketing savvy became concentrated in developed countries, and labor and production in poorer countries, a garment might be designed in America, sewn in China, assembled in Mexico, and then marketed to a consumer public avid for the latest offering of the ever-changing, kaleidoscopic world of fashion.

[*See also* Child Labor; Consumer Culture; Cotton Industry; Domestic Labor; Fifties, The; Film; Foreign Relations: The Cultural Dimension; Gender; Global Economy, America and the; Mass Marketing; Puritanism; Sixties, The; Twenties, The; Women's Rights Movements.]

• Lois Banner, *American Beauty,* 1983. Valerie Steele, *Fashion and Eroticism: Ideals of Feminine Beauty from the Victorian Era to the Jazz Age,* 1985. Stuart Cosgrove "The Zoot Suit and Style Warfare," in *Zoot Suits and Second-Hand Dresses,* ed. Angela McRobbie, 1989. Diana de Marly, *Dress In North America: The New World, 1492–1800,* 1990. Marjorie Garber, *Vested Interests: Cross Dressing and Cultural Anxiety,* 1992. Anne Hollander, *Sex and Suits,* 1994.

—Catherine Gudis

COAST AND GEODETIC SURVEY, U.S. The U.S. Coast Survey, authorized by Congress in 1807 to map and chart the country's coastline, is the oldest scientific institution of the federal government. After a decision in the 1870s to connect the surveys on the Atlantic and Pacific coasts by a triangulation across the continent, the official title became the Coast and Geodetic Survey. In 1970, after the establishment of the National Oceanic and Atmospheric Administration (NOAA), the name was again changed to the National Ocean Survey. Twelve years later, it became the National Ocean Service. In 1991, a separate office within the Ocean Service of NOAA was retitled the Coast and Geodetic Survey. Finally, a 1994 reorganization of NOAA reestablished an office called the U.S. Coast Survey.

This government institution played an especially important role in the development of the United States during the period when Alexander Dallas Bache served as superintendent (1843–1867). Under Bache's command, the coast survey not only supported the country's dramatic economic and commercial growth but also became its preeminent scientific institution. Bache, the great-grandson of Benjamin *Franklin, utilized the survey's resources to promote scientific research and to influence or dominate other prominent institutions, including the *American Association for the Advancement of Science and the *National Academy of Sciences.

To perform the practical task of mapping with great exactness and precision, Bache's coast survey completed extensive scientific research, from astronomical and geophysical studies to observations of the Gulf Stream and studies of microscopic animals from the ocean bottom. Bache successfully mobilized popular support for the survey and convinced politicians that the scientific research was compatible with commercial interests.

Compared to other federal agencies encouraging science in the early and mid–nineteenth century, the coast survey had by far the largest budget. By the late 1850s, the expenditures had topped the half-million-dollar mark, a level of sponsorship not exceeded until the mid-1880s by the U.S. Geological Survey. The coast survey under Bache also supported more scientists—either directly or indirectly, through his practice of employing consultants—than any other American institution. As the most prominent scientific institution in this period, the coast survey helped shape a geographical style for nineteenth-century American science. One of the first scientist-entrepreneurs in the United States, Bache helped to recast modern science from an individualistic enterprise to the highly structured social activities of contemporary "Big Science."

[*See also* Antebellum Era; Geological Surveys; Physical Sciences; Science: Revolutionary War to World War I.]

• Thomas G. Manning, *U.S. Coast Survey vs. Naval Hydrographic Office: A Nineteenth-Century Rivalry in Science and Politics,* 1988. Hugh Richard Slotten, *Patronage, Practice, and the Culture of American Science: Alexander Dallas Bache and the U.S. Coast Survey,* 1994.

—Hugh Richard Slotten

COAST GUARD. *See* Federal Government, Executive Branch: Department of the Treasury; Military, The.

COBB, TY (1886–1961), *baseball player. Born in small-town Georgia to ambitious, domineering parents. Tyrus Raymond Cobb played professionally for Augusta in 1904 before joining the Detroit Tigers in 1905. He retired twenty-four years later holding forty-three league records, including a .367 lifetime batting average, 892 stolen bases, and 2,234 runs scored. Cobb, a great bunter with a tricky split grip, perfected the slap-and-run style of the pre–Babe *Ruth era. He won twelve batting titles, hit over .400 three times, and once led the league in every offensive category except home runs. Incomparably famous and wealthy for an athlete of the time, Ty Cobb led the voting for charter membership in the Baseball Hall of Fame at Cooperstown, New York.

A fiercely aggressive competitor, Cobb dominated games through sheer force of will. He slid with his spikes up, ran over fielders, snarled at pitchers, and fought with his fists at the slightest provocation. One of the first Southerners in the majors, a bitter racist and sectionalist, he was hypersensitive to hazing and bristled when northern blacks failed to show deference. Most of all, he could not bear to fail. At-bats were "a crusade," baseball "a kind of war" that only the red-blooded could win. Ty Cobb personified the *social Darwinism of the age.

A loner, unpopular with teammates and opponents alike, Cobb abhorred the power-hitting and good humor that Ruth brought to baseball in the 1920s. As a player-manager after 1921, he played well but handled people poorly, finally retiring in 1928 at age forty-one, when he hit .323. He spent his final years an isolated alcoholic. Few mourned his passing.

• Ty Cobb with Al Stumpf, *My Life in Baseball*, 1961. Charles C. Alexander, *Ty Cobb*, 1984.

—Ronald Story

CODY, WILLIAM ("BUFFALO BILL") (1846–1917), scout and showman. Born in Iowa, Cody moved with his family to Kansas in 1854. With his father's death in 1857, he went to work for a freight company. The claim that he rode for the *Pony Express cannot be documented. In the 1860s he served as a scout with Kansas cavalry and U.S. Army units fighting the Comanche and Kiowa Indians. Cody married Louisa Frederici in 1866. In 1867, the Kansas Pacific Railroad employed him to supply buffalo meat to railroad construction crews, giving rise to his nickname, Buffalo Bill. During these years he was also an army scout with the Fifth Cavalry under General Philip Sheridan, the former *Civil War leader now engaged in subduing the Plains Indians. An expert rider and marksman, Cody possessed an uncanny sense of direction.

Cody's acting career began in *Chicago in 1872 when he produced and starred in a Western melodrama by the popular writer Ned Buntline (E. Z. C. Judson). In 1876, during the Sioux War, he briefly rejoined the Fifth Cavalry. From 1883 until 1916, he toured with Buffalo Bill's Wild West Show, an open-air production that indelibly engraved elements of the mythic American West in the national imagination and that proved equally popular in Britain and Europe. He also operated cattle ranches, first in Nebraska and then near Cody, Wyoming, the town named for him. Countless dime novels contributed to his celebrity, as did his showmanship, familiar buckskin costume, and fanciful 1879 autobiography. He made the *cowboy an American hero, the Sioux the symbol of all Native Americans, and "Buffalo Bill" the quintessential frontiersman. For all his entrepreneurial ventures, he died penniless.

[*See also* Circuses; Indian History and Culture: From 1800 to 1900; Indian Culture and History: The Indian in Popular Culture; Indian Wars; Literature, Popular; Popular Culture; Railroads; West, The.]

• Don Russell, *The Lives and Legends of Buffalo Bill*, 1960. Nellie Irene Snyder Yost, *Buffalo Bill: His Family, Friends, Fame, Failures, and Fortunes*, 1979.

—Sarah J. Blackstone

COLD WAR. For almost forty-five years (1945–1989), the Cold War dominated international relations and loomed large on the American homefront. Beginning after *World War II, the Cold War arose from the interaction of a chaotic postwar international situation and the foreign policies of the United States, the Soviet Union, and other nations. Characterized by high tension between the United States and the Soviet Union, the polarization of domestic and international politics, the division of the world into economic and military spheres, conflict in the Third World, and a dangerous arms race, the Cold War left its imprint on the history of the twentieth century.

Historiography. Historians have offered conflicting explanations of the Cold War's outbreak, its persistence, and its ultimate demise, explanations often grounded in deep, if unacknowledged, ideological and philosophical differences. Defenders of U.S. policies blame the Cold War on an expansionist and ideologically-motivated Soviet Union, while critics argue that expansionist U.S. policies also played an important role in starting and sustaining the Cold War. Some critics, known as revisionists, stress the long history of American economic *expansionism and argue that economic interests as well as ideological beliefs shaped U.S. policies. Others stress the importance of a global conception of U.S. national security interests that emerged during World War II and dominated U.S. policy throughout the Cold War. According to this view, U.S. leaders sought to prevent any power or coalition of powers from dominating Europe and/or Asia, to maintain U.S. strategic supremacy, to fashion an international economic environment open to U.S. foreign trade and investment, and to integrate the Third World nations of Asia, Africa, and Latin America into the world economy in an era of decolonization and national liberation. This expansive assertion of U.S. interests clashed with Soviet security concerns.

Since the limited availability of Soviet foreign policy archives makes Soviet motives difficult to discern, the influence of the Soviet system on the Soviet Union's foreign policy remains contested. While many scholars still see Joseph Stalin and his successors as incorrigible ideologues and expansionists, others question the long-assumed links between the Soviet Union's repressive internal regime and Moscow's foreign policy. Instead, they highlight bureaucratic differences within the Soviet decision-making elite and security concerns rooted in Russian history and geography. Most scholars agree, however, that the Soviet Union's Cold War objectives were to maintain safeguards against future German aggression, including secure borders and a buffer zone in eastern Europe; to build up the Soviet Union's industrial base; and to maintain a powerful military. Most also concur that these objectives clashed with Western ideals, economic objectives, and security requirements.

The scholarly debates survived the Cold War's end in 1989. Some analysts argue that victory in the Cold War vindicates U.S. policies during the conflict. Others, emphasizing the Cold War's high costs, argue that less confrontational U.S. policies could have achieved the same or a better outcome earlier and less expensively. Similarly, while some scholars seize on newly released Soviet and other communist records to argue that the foreign policy of the Soviet Union and other communist regimes was ideologically motivated and aggressively expansionist, others point out that the available documents are too limited and ambiguous to draw such sweeping conclusions. (Full documentation on some aspects of U.S. Cold War policy, especially covert action, remains unavailable as well.)

Rather than rehash these debates, this essay focuses on the interaction of international systemic factors and national politics and policies and offers an international, as opposed to a national or binational, perspective. Although the Soviet-American rivalry loomed large, the Cold War encompassed much more than U.S.–Soviet relations. It also involved changes in the global distribution of power; ideological conflict within and among states; shifts in the world economy; political, social, and economic change in the Third World; and a dangerous and destabilizing arms race. To understand the Cold War, attention to all these factors is necessary.

Global Balance of Power. Throughout the Cold War, the global distribution of power influenced American and Soviet perceptions of their national interests and, consequently, their actions. In 1939, there were six great powers: Great Britain, France, Germany, the Soviet Union, Japan, and the United States. By 1945, the United States stood alone, its power magnified by its wartime mobilization, its rivals' destruction, and its allies' exhaustion. In 1945, the United States had the world's most powerful navy and air force; was the sole possessor of atomic weapons; and controlled around half of the world's manufacturing capacity, most of its food surpluses, and a large portion of its financial reserves. The United States also held extensive domestic oil reserves and controlled access to vast oil fields in Latin America and the Middle East.

Despite an upsurge in Soviet military power in the 1970s and a relative decline in U.S. economic strength, the global distribution of power remained tilted against the Soviet Union throughout the Cold War. If popular support, industrial infrastructure, skilled manpower, and technological prowess are factored into the definition of power, the postwar era was bipolar only in a narrow military sense. In reality, the Soviet Union remained an "incomplete superpower" throughout the Cold War.

This imbalance becomes even starker when the Western alliance is measured against the Soviet bloc. To be sure, the Soviet Union and its Warsaw Pact allies maintained more ground forces in central Europe, and Soviet and Chinese communist troops outnumbered any possible opponent in northeast Asia during the 1950s. In the 1970s, the Soviet Union also achieved rough parity in strategic nuclear weapons. But the loyalty of Moscow's Warsaw Pact partners always remained in doubt, and after the Sino-Soviet split, which began in the late 1950s and was complete by the mid-1960s, almost a third of Soviet ground forces had to be deployed along their border with the People's Republic of China (PRC). In assessing the nuclear balance, the Soviets had to weigh the arsenals of the other nuclear powers—Great Britain, France, and the PRC—as well as that of the United States.

Although the wartime defeat of Germany and Japan and the decline of Britain and France initially improved the Soviet Union's relative strategic position, these same developments left undisputed leadership of the noncommunist world to the United States. The rapid reconstruction of western Europe, facilitated by the *Marshall Plan, and its incorporation into a U.S.-led alliance, the *North Atlantic Treaty Organization, and Japan's economic recovery and security pact with the United States, meant that four of the world's five centers of industrial might (the United States, Great Britain, western Europe, the Soviet Union, and Japan) stayed outside Soviet control. Economic recovery and political stability in Germany and Japan and their alignment with the West were huge victories for the United States. The Sino-Soviet split had an equally important impact on the global balance of power. Chinese hostility greatly complicated Soviet strategic dilemmas and ended any possibility of communism constituting an alternative world system that could compete with the capitalist West.

Transnational Ideological Conflict. The Cold War was a political, social, and economic as well as a military and strategic phenomenon, and a regime's internal ideological underpinnings often determined its alignment. The impact of internal politics on the global balance of power invested domestic political struggles with international strategic significance.

After Nazi Germany's invasion of the Soviet Union in June 1941 broke up the Nazi-Soviet alliance, World War II, both internationally and within nations, pitted the extreme right (Germany, Italy, and Japan) against an uneasy alliance of the center (Britain and the United States) and the communist left (the Soviet Union). With the defeat of the right, the major fault line in postwar international relations, and within most industrial nations, shifted to the left, reflecting and underpinning the emerging superpower tension.

Depression and global war accentuated existing social and political divisions and generated popular demands for economic reform. Among the Western powers, only the United States failed to shift leftward after the war. But while the *Republican party captured both houses of Congress in the 1946 midterm elections, it proved unable to roll back the *New Deal.

While the Western economies suffered periods of stagnation and glaring inequities, they experienced unprecedented economic growth from the late 1940s to the early 1970s and functioned sufficiently well thereafter to sustain their military might, expand welfare benefits, and legitimize Western political and economic institutions. The prosperity associated with the long boom redressed the failures of prewar capitalism, undercut the appeal of anticapitalist parties, supported the ascendancy of moderate elites who associated their own well-being with that of the United States, and sustained the cohesion of the Western alliance. The defeat of the extreme right in World War II reduced divisions among noncommunist elements, facilitating, at least in western Europe and Japan, the emergence of a consensus supporting some form of welfare-state capitalism and alignment with the United States. In addition, the Cold War provided a justification for the repression of indigenous communist and other radical groups in the name of national security.

The Soviet Union entered the postwar era with enormous prestige because of the key role it played in defeating Nazi Germany. Within the Soviet Union, victory in the war consolidated the Communist party's control, and throughout Europe and in important parts of the Third World Communist parties gained ground thanks to their participation in wartime resistance movements and to chaotic economic, social, and political conditions. In France, Italy, Greece, China, Vietnam, and elsewhere, communists and their allies appeared poised to take power. In addition, for many in the Third World, the Soviet Union seemed to offer a model for the rapid transition from a backward agrarian society to a modern industrial power.

The appeal of *communism and the Soviet model of development declined sharply as the Cold War progressed. Repression in the Soviet Union, Eastern Europe, and the PRC tarnished communism's image. In the 1960s and 1970s some reform-minded European Communist parties attempted to divorce communism from the harsh reality of Soviet (and Chinese) practice, but these efforts failed to wrest leadership of world communism from the Soviet Union and the PRC. The faltering Soviet economy further discredited communism's appeal, as did growing international awareness of human rights and environmental abuses in the communist world.

World Economy. Transnational ideological conflict was closely related to the development of national economies and the evolution of the global economy. Economic changes restructured power relationships among, as well as within, nations. The reconstruction, reform, and relative resilience of the world capitalist system contrasted sharply with the failure of communism. *Capitalism, on the defensive in 1945 owing to the Great Depression and its association with fascism, staged a remarkable comeback. U.S. aid programs like the Marshall Plan supported the reconstruction of Western Europe and Japan, promoted European economic integration, helped forge a stable global financial order at the *Bretton Woods Conference (1944), and through the *General Agreement on Tariffs and Trade (GATT) encouraged the lowering of tariffs and the removal of other impediments to the free flow of goods and capital. These changes, and high levels of military spending, helped fuel the extended period of economic growth.

Even though U.S technological and financial dominance and share of world production decreased over time, the vitality of the West German and Japanese economies and the emergence of such Western-oriented "newly industrializing countries" as Taiwan and South Korea ensured the West's economic supremacy. While the *energy crisis of the 1970s caused economic difficulties in the West, the Soviets gained no lasting advantages from it. As an oil exporter, the Soviet Union benefited briefly from higher oil prices, but the windfall distracted attention from the need for structural reforms. In the mid-1980s, when the Soviet Union finally had a government interested in fundamental reform, international oil prices collapsed.

Although the roots of Soviet economic problems date at least to the emergence of the Stalinist system in the late 1920s, military competition with the United States and the PRC forced the Soviets to devote a much larger share of their smaller gross national product to defense, and siphoned off resources needed for economic development. The diversion of investment from productive sectors and consumer goods undermined the Soviet Union's willingness and ability to compete with the United States and to maintain its empire. Soviet bloc economic growth, which had soared in the late 1940s and the 1950s, slowed in the early 1970s and never recovered. The inability of the Soviet Union's economy to compete with the West restricted its citizens' standard of living, threatened its national security, and ultimately eroded support for the communist system.

Third World. The Cold War overlapped the era of decolonization and national liberation in the Third World, and these two momentous processes had a profound reciprocal effect. The Cold War made decolonization more difficult and more violent, and in Latin America and other already independent societies, it polarized efforts at social, economic, and political change. Although most Third World conflicts were indigenous in origin, and their eventual outcome owed more to their internal histories and characteristics than to U.S. and Soviet policies, Soviet-American rivalry exacerbated instability and conflict in the Third World.

Decolonization represented opportunity for the Soviet Union and vulnerability for the United States and its allies. The desire of Third World nationalist movements to liberate their countries and their economies from foreign control, to overthrow repressive internal power structures sustained by outside forces, and to challenge the West's cultural hegemony at times aligned some movements against the United States and its allies and with the Soviet Union. The diffusion of military technology lessened the power gap between the industrial nations and the Third World, and nationalist elites were able to organize Third World peasants into formidable fighting forces that could hold their own against Western armies on their home ground. This proved particularly important in Asia, where the Chinese, Korean, and Vietnamese communists utilized both guerrilla tactics and large-unit warfare against Western forces.

Western leaders feared that revolutionary nationalism in the Third World could cut off raw materials, oil, food sources, and markets needed to rebuild the economies of western Europe and Japan and to ensure continued U.S. prosperity. They also worried that the Soviet Union would form alliances with national liberation movements or benefit from the turmoil accompanying the end of Western control.

The Soviets proved unable to exploit conditions in the Third World, however. Although Communist parties eventually came to power in some Third World countries (often the poorest ones), these gains proved ephemeral as most national liberation movements resisted outside control. Soviet involvement in the Third World also galvanized Western counteractions including economic and military assistance for pro-Western governments and groups; covert action against anti-Western governments and groups as in Iran, Guatemala, Cuba, and Chile; direct challenges to the Soviets as in the 1962 *Cuban Missile Crisis; and massive military intervention as in the *Vietnam War. As the declining competitiveness of the Soviet economy and unpromising experiences with Soviet-style planning left Third World countries little choice but to abide by the economic rules set by the Western-dominated *International Monetary Fund and *World Bank and to look to the United States and its allies for capital, *technology, and markets, the threat that Third World radicalism would add to Soviet power dissipated.

Arms Race. The arms race was one of the Cold War's most dynamic aspects, as technological advances threatened to give an edge to one superpower or the other, thereby triggering vigorous countermeasures and increasing the risk of nuclear disaster. This pattern of action and counteraction continued throughout the Cold War, resulting in ever higher levels of military spending, destabilizing technological competition, and expanding nuclear arsenals. Moreover, military expenditures created constituencies with an economic interest in perpetuating Cold War tensions.

During World War II, the systematic application of science to warfare resulted in new technologies and improved weapons—long-range bombers, aircraft carriers, radar, the jet engine, long-range rockets, and the atomic bomb—that extended the scale and scope of death and destruction. The atomic bomb was especially terrifying because it vastly magnified the destructive force of warfare and concentrated it in time.

The atomic bomb's potential to revolutionize warfare unleashed an arms race as the Soviet Union, Great Britain, and subsequently other nations developed their own nuclear arsenals, and the United States sought to maintain its lead. The development of hydrogen bombs and ballistic missiles exposed most of the globe to potential devastation.

Although the superpowers sporadically attempted to control the arms race, it continued until the end of the Cold War, exacerbated by the different structures of the U.S. and Soviet nuclear forces, which in turn led each side to seek different solutions to the objective of mutual deterrence: discouraging an adversary's attack by maintaining an invulnerable retaliatory capacity. Whereas the United States relied heavily on a deterrence "triad" of intercontinental ballistic missiles (ICBMs), submarine-launched ballistic missiles, and manned bombers, Soviet planners looked to large numbers of ICBMs.

Technological change—especially improved accuracy and multiple warheads—further complicated arms control efforts by magnifying each side's ability to destroy the other's strategic forces, or at least its ICBMs, and hence its retaliatory capacity. This potential counterforce capability raised the possibility (and temptation) of a successful first strike, and thus undermined mutual deterrence.

The United States predicated its strategy of extended deterrence on overall strategic superiority. According to this view, the function of U.S. strategic forces was to deter not only a Soviet attack on the United States but also Soviet advances anywhere in the world. Nuclear superiority, U.S. strategists believed, was needed to compensate for assumed Soviet conventional superiority in Europe and to discourage Soviet "adventurism" elsewhere. Although the United States reluctantly accepted the principle of nuclear parity with the Soviets in the 1970s, U.S. strategists continued to worry that mutual deterrence at the global level would give the Soviets greater freedom on the regional level, especially in Europe. For their part, Soviet strategists, convinced that parity was necessary to discourage an attack on the Soviet Union, tried to match each and every U.S. advance.

Although some analysts have argued that nuclear weapons and the near certainty of retaliation may have prevented a war between the superpowers, these factors did not prevent dangerous crises, like the one over Cuba in 1962, or numerous nonnuclear conflicts in the Third World. In addition, the safety procedures built into the command and control systems of both superpowers were not foolproof, and the necessity of maintaining readiness to respond instantaneously to a nuclear attack pushed safety to the limit. With both sides' nuclear forces geared to "launch on warning," an accidental nuclear war became a dangerous possibility.

In the mid-1980s, Soviet leaders, recognizing that military expenditures were crippling the country's economy, concluded that fewer nuclear weapons would provide sufficient security. They also recognized that maintaining coercive control of eastern Europe, an imperative of a competitive security strategy, was incompatible with democratic and economic reform in the Soviet Union. Accordingly, the Soviets made concessions that led to important arms-control agreements that reduced tensions with the West and helped end the Cold War.

The history of the arms race underscores what international relations scholars call the security dilemma. Actions taken by one nation to enhance its own security can easily be construed by its adversary as threatening, and lead to countermeasures that reduce both sides' security. The security dilemma had especially stark implications for the Soviet Union. Most of the measures the Soviets adopted to improve their security provoked countermeasures by the more powerful United States and its allies that preserved or increased Western supremacy and thus diminished Soviet security.

The Cold War's Impact. The Cold War was central to the history of the second half of the twentieth century. It shaped the foreign policies of the United States and the Soviet Union and deeply affected their societies and their political, economic, and military institutions. By justifying the projection of U.S. power and influence all over the world, the Cold War facilitated the assertion of global leadership by the United States. The doctrine of containment, the overarching principle of U.S. Cold War foreign policy, not only aimed at limiting Soviet power and influence but also facilitated the expansion of U.S. power and influence. By providing Soviet leaders with an external enemy to justify their repressive internal regime and external empire, the Cold War helped the Soviet Communist party maintain its grip on power.

In addition to its impact on the superpowers, the Cold War both caused and perpetuated the post–World War II division of Europe, and, within Europe, of Germany. It also facilitated the postwar reconstruction and reintegration into the international system of Germany, Italy, and Japan. Its impact proved especially great in the Third World, where it interacted with decolonization and sweeping social and economic changes. The Cold War led to the division of Vietnam and Korea and to costly wars in both nations, and it escalated conflicts throughout the Third World. Indeed, nearly 99 percent of the more than 20 million people who died in wars between 1945 and 1990 perished in the Third World. In addition, apart from periodic crises over the flash-point city of Berlin, most of the crises that threatened to escalate into nuclear war occurred in the Third World.

The Cold War also had a profound impact on domestic politics in the United States. Early postwar Washington's anticommunist agenda found its domestic echo in a preoccupation with subversion and disloyalty, expressed in the *Rosenberg and Alger *Hiss cases and the investigations of Senator Joseph *McCarthy and the *House Committee on Un-American Activities. Martin Luther *King Jr. and other *civil rights movement leaders, meanwhile, effectively exploited Cold War concerns, warning that *racism damaged the image of the United States abroad. Cold War preoccupations and nuclear fears pervaded 1950s *popular culture, while 1960s campus protesters and New Leftists criticized their country's hegemonic ambitions and the Cold War mind-set underlying the Vietnam War.

The Cold War preoccupied every president from Harry S. *Truman and Dwight D. *Eisenhower to Ronald *Reagan and George *Bush, and fueled the careers of such policy-makers as George *Kennan, Dean *Acheson, John Foster *Dulles, and Henry *Kissinger. It gave rise to vastly increased federal military and security institutions and stimulated levels of defense spending that energized the economies of entire regions in the *South, *Southwest, and Pacific Coast; produced major population shifts; and promoted the rise of think tanks and new information technologies such as *computers. The interstate *highway system, the *space program, consumerist culture, increased religiosity, and expanded federal spending on *education were all linked to the Cold War. In short, the homefront history of the United States in the later twentieth century, no less than its international role and strategic politics, can be understood only in a Cold War context.

[*See also* Americans for Democratic Action; Anticommunism; Bay of Pigs; Berlin Blockade and Airlift; Carter, Jimmy; Central Intelligence Agency; Democratic Party; Fifties, The; Ford, Gerald; Foreign Relations; Hiroshima and Nagasaki, Atomic Bombing of; Johnson, Lyndon B.; Kennedy, John F.; Korean War; Military, The; National Security Act of 1947; National Security Council; National Security Council Document #68; Nixon, Richard M.; Nuclear Arms Control Treaties; Nuclear Strategy; Nuclear Weapons; Post–Cold War Era; Progressive Party of 1948; Sixties, The; Students for a Democratic Society; Truman Doctrine; U-2 Incident.]

• Michael McCGwire, *Perestroika and Soviet National Security,* 1991. Melvyn P. Leffler, *A Preponderance of Power: National Security, the Truman Administration, and the Cold War,* 1992. R. Craig Nation, *Black Earth, Red Star: A History of Soviet Security Policy, 1917–1991,* 1992. Woodrow Wilson International Center for Scholars, *Cold War International History Project Bulletin,* 1992–. Raymond L. Garthoff, *Détente and Confrontation: American-Soviet Relations from Nixon to Reagan,* rev. ed., 1994. Raymond L. Garthoff, *The Great Transition: American-Soviet Relations and the End of the Cold War,* 1994. Melvyn P. Leffler and David S. Painter, eds., *Origins of the Cold War: An International History,* 1994. Thomas J. McCormick, *America's Half-Century: United States Foreign Policy in the Cold War,* 2d ed., 1995. James E. Cronin, *The World the Cold War Made: Order, Chaos, and the Return of History,* 1996. Walter LaFeber, *America, Russia, and the Cold War, 1945–1996,* 8th ed., 1996. Vladislav Zubok and Constantine Pleshakov, *Inside the Kremlin's Cold War: From Stalin to Khrushchev,* 1996. John Lewis Gaddis, *We Now Know: Rethinking Cold War History,* 1997. David S. Painter, *The Cold War: An International History,* 1999. Geoffrey Roberts, *The Soviet Union in World Politics: Coexistence, Revolution, and Cold War, 1945–1991,* 1999.

—David S. Painter

COLE, THOMAS (1801–1848), America's leading landscape painter during the second quarter of the nineteenth century. Cole was born in Bolton-le-Moors, England. Trained as an engraver, he immigrated to the United States in 1818 and, after seven years as an artistic jack-of-all-trades in Pennsylvania and Ohio, arrived in New York, where his paintings of Hudson Valley landscapes brought him almost instant success. During his relatively brief career, he painted European and American landscapes as well as historical works and allegories of which The Course of Empire series and The Voyage of Life series are the best known.

Cole's landscapes were generally naturalistic. Adapting European artistic forms and aesthetic theories to American scenery, he often depicted a pristine American wilderness, as in his well-known *Kaaterskill Falls* (1827). He also painted pastoral scenes, for example, *View on the Catskill, Early Autumn* (1837), a vision of a peaceful valley as yet undisturbed by industry. Traveling to Europe in 1829–1832 and again in 1841–1842, Cole added subjects from the grand tour to his repertory.

Cole is remembered primarily as a romantic landscapist and as founder of the Hudson River school, which also included Asher B. Durand (1796–1886), his frequent painting companion, and Frederick Edwin Church (1826–1900), his student. Yet even before his first European sojourn, Cole was preoccupied with history painting. An able poet and talented essayist—his 1836 "Essay on American Scenery" is a classic statement of American landscape aesthetics—he employed texts of his own devising for his major historical allegories. Highly critical of democracy and fearful of the effects of *industrialization, he believed that American society was irrevocably headed for disaster. His Course of Empire series was a thinly veiled attack on Jacksonian Democracy, while the moralizing Voyage of Life and unfinished Cross and the World series proclaimed a religious alternative to the futility of secular history.

[*See also* Early Republic, Era of the; Jackson, Andrew; Painting: To 1945; Romantic Movement.]

• Louis Legrand Noble, *The Life and Works of Thomas Cole,* 1853; reprint, ed. Elliot S. Vesell, 1964. William C. Truettner and Alan Wallach, eds., *Thomas Cole: Landscape into History,* 1994.

—Alan Wallach

COLLECTIVE BARGAINING. *See* Industrial Relations; Labor Movements; Strikes and Industrial Conflict.

COLLECTIVE SECURITY. Before 1914, many observers believed that the international balance of power had made a general European war improbable. *World War I proved them wrong; its carnage persuaded many statesmen, led by U.S. President Woodrow *Wilson and British Viscount Robert Cecil, to craft a new collective-security system that would align against an aggressor the combined might of the rest of the world. The *League of Nations in 1920 became the world's first "collective-security" organization, although the term itself was not commonly used until the mid-1930s. No aggressor would threaten war, the league's founders believed, if faced with overwhelming collective force. In reality, the new system failed to prevent Japan from occupying Manchuria in 1931, Italy from invading Ethiopia in 1935, or Germany from precipitating *World War II when it attacked Poland in 1939.

Although the breakdown of peace in the 1930s discredited the League of Nations, the allies incorporated collective security into the *United Nation's Charter in 1945. To improve upon the league, the UN's founders permitted five states, including the United States and the Soviet Union, an absolute veto over collective action. Intended to revitalize collective security, the veto nearly killed it once Washington and Moscow became *Cold War adversaries. The absence of genuine collective security during the Cold War did not prevent misuse of the term. For instance, the organizers of the *North Atlantic Treaty Organization (NATO) used the rhetoric of collective security even though NATO and similar organizations, like the Soviet-sponsored Warsaw Pact, were for the most part old-style alliances.

Only twice did the U.N. come close to implementing collective security. When the *Korean War began in 1950, the Security Council (with the Soviets absent and unable to exercise their veto) authorized armed resistence against North Korea. During the Persian Gulf Crisis of 1990, a post–Cold War Security Council endorsed military measures to end Iraq's occupation of Kuwait. Otherwise, collective security remained more an ideal than a reality as the twentieth century ended.

[*See also* Internationalism; Persian Gulf War.]

• David Armstrong, Lorna Lloyd, and John Redmond, *From Versailles to Maastrict: International Organization in the Twentieth Century,* 1996.

—Gary B. Ostrower

COLLEGES. *See* Education: Collegiate Education.

COLONIAL ERA. Perceptions of the "Colonial Era of the United States" are often Anglo-centric and teleological. The most usual periodization—from 1607 to either 1763 or 1775—enshrines an English (after 1707, British) frame of reference: the first permanent settlement at *Jamestown, the *Proclamation of 1763 securing British hegemony over eastern North America, and the outbreak of the *Revolutionary War. This perspective is defensible, since the polities that coalesced into the United States had all been provinces of the British empire, but it understates the roles other European nations played: from a Spanish standpoint, for example, the era might date from 1565, the year St. Augustine was founded, to 1821, when the future American *Southwest won its independence from Spain as part of Mexico. Moreover, restricting the story only to components of the American republic-to-be implies that its formation was preordained, whereas in the mid–eighteenth century, Britain's thirteen North American colonies were not collectively distinguishable from its other imperial jurisdictions, and their future identity was in no way predictable. The Colonial Era, in short, should be understood on its own terms and not as the preface to a national historical narrative.

Interpretations of the era have changed markedly since nineteenth-century patriots viewed the colonies as nascent states built by refugees from a tyrannical homeland to secure their liberty and property. As the twentieth century opened, scholars like Charles Andrews adopted a "scientific" methodology that substituted "objectivity" for nationalist apologetics, propounding that Britain had ruled the colonies benignly, encouraging commerce and representative government. At mid-century, Perry Miller's declension thesis—that the unraveling of *New England *Puritanism under the pressure of adapting to the New World was paradigmatic for understanding the fundamental theme of American history—dominated the literature. The next generation of students, attuned to social scientific theory and benefiting from advances in quantification and computer technology, criticized Miller for limiting his sources to texts published by an educated elite and assuming that theological polemics accurately mirrored social realities. Aggregating court records, wills, and vital statistics, they reconstructed the mundane doings of individuals, families, and communities, contending that the southern or Mid-Atlantic colonies forecast social developments in the United States far more closely than did New England. Meanwhile, contemporary movements for minority rights, highlighting Anglo-America's ethnic and racial heterogeneity, focused historians' attention on African slaves, Amerindians, and non-English migrants. Tracking their movements reinvigorated transatlantic analyses. By the end of the twentieth century, connections between Britain and the colonies were again in favor, but the spotlight shone on consumption patterns, the cult of gentility, and evangelical communications instead of political institutions. Historians knew far more about colonial Anglo-America than they did a century ago, but greater knowledge had lessened confidence that a single comprehensive synthesis was possible.

Beginnings of Settlement. Anglo-America was planted where the Spanish did not reach and where competing European powers, notably France and the Netherlands, trod lightly. England could not contemplate colonization until the reign of Elizabeth I (1558–1603), when the national faith and the resolution of long-standing agitations over the dynastic succession afforded the requisite internal stability, and the emergence of an outward-looking merchant class supplied the necessary capital. By then Spain had explored the Gulf of Mexico's rim and the French the St. Lawrence Valley, leaving England to contest the mainland between roughly 32° and 45° north latitude, an expanse whose fertile soils and temperate climate could sustain high agricultural productivity. North America attracted the English Crown as a forward base to attack Spain's possessions, and the Church of England fitfully heeded biblical imperatives to proselytize the heathen. But private, not public, parties underwrote English ventures, and personal motives for migration—obtaining land and/or worshiping God as conscience dictated—predominated.

The colonies were molded by the continuing encounter with the Eastern Woodland aborigines, whose villages usually contained a few hundred members. Individual bands were extremely autonomous, and supertribal entities like the Five Nations of the Iroquois exceptional. Amerindians could facilitate or threaten a colony's survival: In Virginia, for example, the Powhatans taught planters how to grow tobacco, but in 1622 they attempted to annihilate the plantation, killing a quarter of the inhabitants. Interaction between them and the English was not uniformly hostile: They showed colonists how to survive in the wilderness and exchanged furs for textiles, pots, guns, and alcohol; occasionally they slept with European lovers or worshiped the Christian God. Inexorably, however, as colonists intruded on native lands, relations worsened. For most of the seventeenth century conflicts involved only particular colonies and bands, as in the *Pequot War and *King Philip's War, but as English claims collided with those of France and Spain, Amerindians were inextricably drawn into imperial wars, although their own objectives always dictated how, when, and with whom they fought. The native impact on colonial life was immense: As producers and consumers, they expanded markets; as healers, farmers, hunters, and pharmacists, they offered specialized knowledge; as allies to reward or enemies to placate, they engendered political debate; as darkly imagined presences, they embodied a putative savagery against which Europeans could pronounce their own civility; and as woodland warriors, they contributed to the militarization of a colonial society in which virtually all adults knew how to handle a gun.

Hoping to profit from commerce (and privateering), the Virginia Company of London inaugurated English colonization in 1607. The first years proved disastrous: Political factionalism, class conflict, native hostility, drought, and lack of a salable export stunted the colony until experiments with tobacco gave planters a merchandisable good, and the company's concession to let settlers own land gave them incentive to grow it. Tobacco proceeds encouraged inhabitants to regard Virginia as home, not as a field of dreams, and slowly the colony evolved from an outpost of transients into a settled society with a representative assembly and an established church. In 1634, the Old Dominion gained a neighbor on the Chesapeake. George and

Cecilius Calvert, first and second Lords Baltimore, founded Maryland to advance the family fortune and erect a haven for Roman Catholics. The effort to encourage a mixed polity of Catholics and Protestants, purposefully articulated by the Act Concerning Religion (1649) allowing liberty of conscience for Christian Trinitarians, made Maryland unique in the Western Hemisphere.

Religious forces were likewise instrumental in forming New England. Within the Anglican church, a Puritan minority complained about the lack of moral discipline and the retention of Catholic "superstitions." When the Crown and bishops stymied protest, handfuls of Separatists, who denied that the church was a true body of Christ, fled to the Netherlands. Dissatisfied with life under the Dutch and fearing renewed warfare with Spain, the *Pilgrims, a fragment of one congregation, settled *Plymouth, Massachusetts, in 1620. The so-called Great Migration, singular among seventeenth-century English folk-wanderings for the high percentage of family groups involved, commenced a decade later, composed of Puritans like John *Winthrop who perceived ecclesiastical corruptions, moral decay, social dislocation, economic slowdowns, and the king's personal rule as providential warnings to escape God's wrath against England. Expressing through the *Mayflower Compact their hope of erecting a godly society in Massachusetts, they yoked church and state as separate but coordinate agencies to uphold religious orthodoxy and good behavior. Political disputes, doctrinal disagreements, and personal ambitions caused malcontents to "hive out": Connecticut was founded by townsfolk who thought the Massachusetts church-state complex a bit too strict and their lands inadequate, New Haven by a circle who thought the Bay Colony too lax and its prime commercial sites taken, and Rhode Island by Roger *Williams and other religious dissidents expelled by the orthodox. Rhode Island never erected a church establishment, but with that exception the New England colonies were cut from the same cultural cloth, modeling their governments on those of English trading companies, marketing their crops and fish around the Atlantic, and promoting Calvinist brands of moralism. The speedy erection of political and religious institutions, a demographic regime that facilitated *family formation, an economy that allowed most households a competence, and a shared ethical system enabled New England to achieve political and social stability more quickly than the Chesapeake.

The English Civil Wars, which erupted in 1642, ended the Great Migration and the initial phase of colonization. No new settlements were chartered until after Charles II assumed the throne in 1660. By that date, the Chesapeake and New England colonies had become embryonic regions, internally similar and externally distinctive. Their existence secured England's claim to North America.

Integration into the Empire. Colonization after Charles II's Restoration in 1660 took place under the Crown's watchful eye. With mercantile companies no longer inclined to wager large sums for uncertain returns, leadership passed to prominent nobles and gentry on whom the king bestowed generous proprietary grants. Such gifts provided a cheap way for the king to liquidate his political debts while extending England's occupation of the North Atlantic littoral, although they risked diluting royal control by giving powerful men nearly complete control over their domains. One proprietorship resulted from the capture of New Netherland, originally chartered by the Dutch West India Company in 1624. Primarily a trading outpost, New Netherland featured a polyglot populace of merchants and farmers when the English seized it in 1664 and Charles II transferred it to his brother, James, Duke of York. Almost immediately the duke passed holdings west of the Hudson onto two lords. Wrangles over titles dragged on for decades, until the Crown united the properties as New Jersey in 1702. Grandiose schemes of social engineering, reminiscent of Lord Baltimore's plan to erect feudal baronies, propelled two other proprietorships. Devising Pennsylvania as simultaneously a sanctuary for the *Society of Friends (Quakers) and a commercial center, William *Penn provided his "holy experiment" with a popularly elected assembly while expecting residents to acquiesce in laws he drew up. To attract an ideal balance of large and small property holders, the lords of Carolina dreamed of introducing a hereditary nobility while soliciting small freeholders and guaranteeing liberty of conscience. Neither experiment worked as planned: Pennsylvania's Quaker-dominated assembly in *Philadelphia challenged Penn's policies and authority, while the Carolinians never conferred a single title. Nonetheless, both colonies prospered, Pennsylvania challenging New York's provision trade, and Carolina exporting timber, foodstuffs, naval stores, and deerskins.

The abundance of land forced entrepreneurs to utilize bound labor, since most freemen preferred to own a homestead rather than hire themselves out. Virginians pioneered *indentured servitude, by which persons deeded their labor in return for passage to America. Because servants contracted for only a limited number of years, however, masters had constantly to replace them, and when competition from English and other colonial *labor markets cut the available supply, Virginians turned to importing African slaves, who could be held in perpetuity. The English first fully exploited *slavery on Barbados, where by 1660 planters had transformed forests into cane fields and built immensely profitable sugar refineries. The conversion to slave labor was not accomplished blithely, for many English regarded Africans as brutish, heathen, and ignorant outlanders, a characterization that helped rationalize enslaving them but raised concerns about how to assimilate them. Nevertheless, the profitability of harnessing a permanently bound labor force won out. Between 1685 and 1720, Virginia converted to a slave-labor system, and as early as 1708 South Carolina, many of whose founders brought slaves with them from Barbados, had a black majority. While slaves labored in every mainland colony, 80 percent of them were in the *South.

For half a century, England lacked both a coherent colonial program and the bureaucracy to implement one. Kings chartered plantations according to circumstances, not plans, and the distance to North America hindered communication. As a result, the Crown exercised little effective oversight. During the interregnum following the beheading of Charles I in 1649, Parliament forced the submission of governments that supported the displaced Stuart monarchy. After the Restoration in 1660, England's realization that its control over its possessions was tenuous and that losing them would compromise national security stimulated efforts to integrate the colonies into the empire. Imperial policy was designed to benefit the British metropolis principally and its subordinate provinces secondarily. Parliament regulated colonial currencies, inhibited crafts that might compete with metropolitan industries, and passed *Navigation Acts to make England the imperial hub, exclude foreign trade, guarantee stocks of military stores, and secure colonial markets. The Crown attempted to standardize political forms and royalize colonial governments by attacking charters and buying out proprietors. In the most radical effort, James II in 1686 collected the provinces from New Hampshire to New Jersey into the Dominion of New England under a single governor-general and eliminated their assemblies. The colonists, fearful that closer imperial oversight would curtail their trade and liberties, sought to hold officials at arm's length. When the *Glorious Revolution deposed James in 1689, rebellions in Massachusetts and New York overthrew the Dominion of New England and unseated the proprietary government in Maryland. Over time, however, England's imperial policies took hold. Trade flowed substantially according to the Navigation Acts, with little damage to merchants' pocketbooks, as it turned out. Political structures were never completely standardized, but by the early eighteenth century eight of the twelve extant colonies had a royal governor, assemblies convened annually in every province, and a stable imperial polity had crystallized. There would be no further armed revolts against an imperial governor until the American Revolution.

A Complex Social Order. By around 1715, all of the colonies had also achieved substantial communal stability: family-formation had reached levels that allowed for self-sustaining growth, and ruling elites had cohered. Over the next fifty years, burgeoning size would catalyze increasingly complex social orders. Enjoying ample harvests, adequate fuel supplies, and a favorable *disease environment, colonial populations multiplied at nearly the maximum possible rate of natural increase. Their density in some coastal areas reduced the size of landholdings, cutting family income, but the availability of land limited the extent of overcrowding. Regional patterns of agriculture and agricultural exports intensified. The South specialized in staples cultivated mainly by slaves: tobacco (the mainland's leading export in 1770) from the Chesapeake, rice (the third most important commodity) from the Carolina-Georgia tidewater, and indigo (the fifth) from the Carolina piedmont. Family members supplied the bulk of labor in the North, which evolved a more mixed agricultural regime. Mid-Atlantic farmers grew wheat, which in raw or processed forms comprised the second leading export in 1770. With horticulture constrained by rocky soils, New Englanders exported fish (the Northern colonies' third most valuable commodity) and whale products along with foodstuffs, livestock, and rum. Southern commodities, valued as reexports or military necessities, fell under British control. The Navigation Acts mandated shipping them to England, and British merchants owned the ships enlisted. Northern goods were less vital, hence less regulated and carried more often in colonial hulls. Long before 1775, the South and North were following different developmental trajectories. Southerners reinvested their profits in land and slaves without diversifying their holdings; northerners invested in various enterprises, triggering economic differentiation.

As wealth accumulated, *social class structures became more articulated, with the greatest stratification in coastal and riverine areas linked to transatlantic markets. Slaves comprised the lowest social rank, their manumission a virtual impossibility. In the South, they frequently lived in gangs of twenty or more; in the North, they more often worked as individuals who staffed the elite's townhouses, advertising a family's wealth rather than generating it. Perhaps one in five Euramericans resided at or close to the subsistence level, but the majority resided in yeomen or artisan families that earned a competent livelihood. As their disposable income rose and ocean transportation improved, middling households bought British consumer goods. Upper-class whites, who owned the most lucrative plantations or counting houses, held more than half the total value of property. Aspiring to the status and power of the British upper classes, they purchased metropolitan luxuries and manuals of gentility to distinguish themselves from the lower orders materially and morally. Eighteenth-century American society increasingly resembled Britain's, but with significant differences: *Mobility was greater, property-holding more widespread, and, elite pretensions notwithstanding, the patronage networks that governed social advancement in Britain virtually nonexistent. The population was also more ethnically and racially heterogeneous. Fleeing poverty, war, and religious persecution, most voluntary migrants came from Germany, Scotland, Ireland, and (by way of England) France. By 1775, 20 percent of the colonies' 2.5 million non-Indian people were African or African American, and half of the inhabitants south of New England were not ethnically English.

The religious structure differed markedly as well, most notably in its denominational diversity and in the Church of England's failure to become a universally exclusive establishment. Dissenters occupied many colonies before the church gained a foothold. The Church of England never ordained an American bishop, and even in the South it neither monopolized ecclesiastical tax revenues nor limited political officeholding to its members. The Congregationalists gained hegemony over New England, while in the Mid-Atlantic colonies Presbyterians, Dutch and German Reformed, Lutherans, *Mennonites and other German sectarians, Catholics, and Jews joined Quakers, who held meetings throughout the colonies, and *Baptists, who gained converts in the South after 1750. Pluralism diluted the power of religious establishments, facilitated the growth of religious liberty, and, combined with settlers' tendency to move beyond clerical oversight, exploded the presumption that everyone in a vicinity had to (or would) join a particular church. In the face of voluntary church membership, ministers engineered revivals to recruit congregants. One type of revival, typified by Jonathan *Edwards's ministry in Northampton, Massachusetts, emerged from Congregationalist attempts to regenerate the piety of their ancient communities. A second issued from the peregrinations of George Whitefield, an Anglican minister who touched off the so-called *Great Awakening (1739–1745), accelerating the number of church admissions while fracturing the Congregationalists and Presbyterians. The awakening's immediate impact can be exaggerated—rates of conversion soon declined to previous levels—but the process of organizing new churches with believers who had experienced a spiritual new birth became the centerpiece of nineteenth-century American evangelicalism.

The conditions of colonial society encouraged a politically active citizenry. Widespread property holding allowed most white adult males—certainly a far greater percentage than in Britain—to meet *suffrage requirements, and relatively unrestrictive religious tests barred few from voting or from holding office. Convinced that their property gave them a stake in political decisions, and quick to voice opinions shaped by weekly newspapers and gossip, householders regarded their legislators as agents for promoting local interests. Instructed by engaged constituents and claiming that provincial assemblies were miniature Houses of Commons, representatives repeatedly faced off against the governor and his council, gaining power to initiate revenue bills, determine the salaries of imperial officials, control their own internal organization, and, on occasion, exercise executive prerogatives. Legislative battles frequently involved allocating military expenses, since between 1689 and 1763 the colonies participated in four worldwide struggles for empire among Britain, France, and Spain. The first two (King William's War, 1689–1697; Queen Anne's War, 1702–1713) had little long-term impact on them except for the communities disrupted—mainly in New England—and the individuals killed, but the second pair (King George's War, 1739–1748; the French and Indian War, 1754–1763) eventuated in Britain's making good its claims to the Ohio Valley and expelling France from the North American mainland.

Conclusion. By 1763, characteristic patterns distinguished colonial regions from each other. New England's town meetings, Congregational establishment, and ethnocentrism earned it a reputation for egalitarianism, moralism, and xenophobia. The Mid-Atlantic colonies remained the most ethnically and religiously heterogeneous, their diverse interest groups forcing the appearance of long-term partisan political blocs in Pennsylvania and New York earlier than elsewhere. In the South, monoculture, slave labor, and guaranteed British markets supported the largest population, the highest per-capita income, and the wealthiest, most powerful mainland elite. From all regions, families moved into the interior, less a distinctive cultural enclave than a transient zone in which migrants, having outstripped organized institutions and thrust themselves upon native tribes, concocted out of custom and exigency societies less hierarchical and more violent than coastal communities, though by no means lastingly so. At the same time, certain similarities were everywhere apparent. Habits of enterprise had erected transatlantic commercial networks yielding one of the world's highest standards of living. The European system of state churches failed to materialize, the Reformed tradition influenced worship, and, although adherents of *Protestantism's different stripes competed for power and place, they united in identifying Britain as the champion of true religion against the superstition and tyranny of *Roman Catholicism. Jealous of their English rights (even as, and perhaps because, they deprived slaves of them), citizens regarded their representative assemblies as bulwarks against monarchical prerogatives and as protectors of their liberties. Triumph over France fired colonists' pride in the empire and themselves.

None of these conditions made the American Revolution inevitable. Some historians have argued that the prevalence of ecclesiastical schisms, class conflicts, and sectional antagonisms amounted to a "crisis" that propelled rebellion, but confrontations were ordinarily resolved without resort to violence, and in any case how or why such tensions might have been displaced onto British authorities is not clear. The Colonial Era's legacy was one of finite contingencies, framed by the elaborated cultural rules of England and adorned by those of northwest Europe, from which the future of Anglo-America would emerge. In creating the United States, the American Revolution actualized one possibility out of many.

[*See also* African Americans; Agriculture; Albany Congress; Bacon's Rebellion; *Bay Psalm Book*; Bible, The; Boston; Byrd, William, II; Captivity Narratives, Indian; Columbian Exchange; Economic Development; Exploration, Conquest, and Settlement, Era of European; French Settlements in North America; Fur Trade; German Americans; Half-way Covenant; Hutchinson, Anne; Immigration; Indian History and Culture: From 1500 to 1800; Indian Wars; Iroquois Confederacy; Literacy; Literature: Colonial Era; Mather, Increase and Cotton; Medicine: Colonial Era; New York City; Pocahontas; Powhatan; Religion; Revolution and Constitution, Era of; Salem Witchcraft; Science: Colonial Era; Seven Years' War; Smith, John; Spanish Settlements in North America; Tobacco Industry; Zenger Trial.]

• Charles Andrews, *The Colonial Period of American History,* 4 vols., 1934–1938. Perry Miller, *The New England Mind,* 2 vols., 1939–1953. Wesley Frank Craven, *The Colonies in Transition 1660–1713,* 1968. Winthrop Jordan, *White over Black: American Attitudes toward the Negro 1550–1812,* 1968. Edmund Morgan, *American Slavery, American Freedom: The Ordeal of Colonial Virginia,* 1975. John J. McCusker and Russell R. Menard, *The Economy of British America, 1607–1789,* 1985. Bernard Bailyn, *The Peopling of British North America,* 1986. Patricia Bonomi, *Under the Cope of Heaven: Religion, Society, and Politics in Colonial America,* 1986. Jack P. Greene, *Peripheries and Center: Constitutional Development in the Extended Polities of the British Empire and the United States, 1607–1789,* 1986. Jack P. Greene, *Pursuits of Happiness: The Social Development of Early Modern British Colonies and the Formation of American Culture,* 1988. Edmund S. Morgan, *Inventing the People: The Rise of Popular Sovereignty in England and America,* 1988. David Hackett Fischer, *Albion's Seed: Four British Folkways in America,* 1989.

—Charles L. Cohen

COLONIALISM. *See* Expansionism.

COLONIZATION MOVEMENT, AFRICAN. Efforts to colonize *African Americans to Africa began at the time of the *Revolutionary War. In 1777, the Virginia legislature discussed Thomas *Jefferson's proposal for the colonization of the state's free blacks. Proponents of colonization represented diverse interest groups, including blacks and whites, northerners and southerners, as well as proslavery advocates and *antislavery leaders. Some colonization supporters believed that whites and African Americans could never live together peacefully in the United States and that African Americans should therefore return to Africa. A number of *slavery's advocates wished to relocate the southern free black population to Africa in order to create a southern society comprised exclusively of enslaved blacks and free whites. Some abolitionists supported the movement because they believed that colonization would result in the gradual emancipation of slaves by proving that African Americans were self-reliant. Other colonization supporters argued that American blacks could go to Africa to spread the gospel as Christian missionaries.

The founding of the American Colonization Society (ACS) in 1816 by Robert Finley, a white clergyman, institutionalized the colonization effort. Finley wished to settle free blacks in Africa and hoped that colonization would hasten the end of slavery. The society garnered the support of prominent slaveowners eager to remove the free black population. At the same time, most free blacks opposed this movement, fearing that it would result in widespread deportation of free people of color. In 1822, the ACS founded a colony in Liberia on Africa's west coast, it attracted more than ten thousand colonists before 1865. The ACS appointed Liberia's agents and governors until the colony gained independence in 1847.

Interest in colonization among blacks increased with passage of the *Fugitive Slave Act in 1850 as fears of kidnapping and enslavement escalated in northern states. Martin R. Delany (1812–1885), a northern black leader, developed his own colonization effort in the 1850s, arguing that African Americans could never attain equality in the United States. Delany hoped to create a self-reliant nation along the African coast where free American blacks would farm their own land and establish trading networks. In spite of Delany's advocacy, most free blacks continued to oppose colonization. Frederick *Douglass, a prominent African American leader, resisted colonization because he believed that blacks could eventually achieve equality with whites. The abolitionist William Lloyd *Garrison also rejected the colonization effort, agitating instead for the immediate emancipation of American slaves. President Abraham *Lincoln proposed a plan for the colonization of contraband slaves who fled to Union Army camps during the *Civil War.

The postwar passage of the Thirteenth, *Fourteenth, and *Fifteenth Amendments to the *Constitution, guaranteeing African Americans' freedom and citizenship and granting African American men the vote, ended any widespread attempts to colonize American blacks. Colonization schemes were promoted in the 1890s by Bishop Henry M. Turner (1834–1915) of the African Methodist Episcopal Church and in the 1920s by the black nationalist leader Marcus *Garvey, but without notable success.

[*See also* Antebellum Era; Black Nationalism; Early Republic, Era of the; Missionary Movement.]

• P. J. Staundenraus, *The African Colonization Movement, 1816–1865,* 1961. Floyd John Miller, *The Search for Black Nationality: Black Emigration and Colonization, 1787–1863,* 1975.

—Jane E. Dabel

COLTRANE, JOHN (1926–1967), *jazz saxophonist and leader in the "hard bop" style of the late 1950s and 1960s. Born in Hamlet, North Carolina, Coltrane later moved to *Philadelphia, where he became acquainted with rhythm and blues and was influenced by the bop revolution that emerged in jazz during *World War II. Playing with Eddie Vinson's band after his release from the navy in 1946, he was convinced by Vinson to change from alto to tenor saxophone. In 1949, Coltrane joined the big band of Dizzy Gillespie (1917–1993), but in 1953 he shifted to Johnny Hodges's smaller band. Coltrane first won serious attention and achieved a major stylistic breakthrough when he joined Miles *Davis's quintet in 1955. He became the saxophonist in the quartet of Thelonious Monk (1917–1982) two years later, but soon returned to Davis's group. For a time he flirted with the sonorities and subtle lyricism of cool jazz, but he felt a growing need to develop a more personal approach.

In 1960, Coltrane formed his own group with the intent of exploring different jazz sounds. Intent upon moving beyond notes and creating pure sound, he borrowed from African, Indian, and Middle Eastern sources. His tone tended to be hard and harsh and lacked the varied coloration of the bop innovator Charlie *Parker. Although Coltrane was not politically a black nationalist, the statement he made did have social implications. Coltrane's playing changed substantially during his lifetime, since his musical search was based on a spiritual quest that persisted until his death.

• Cuthbert Ormond Simpkins, *Coltrane,* 1975. Eric Nisenson, *Ascension: John Coltrane and His Quest,* 1993.

—Ronald L. Davis

COLUMBIAN EXCHANGE. As of 1492, the Americas and Eurasia-Africa, except for occasional connections via the Bering Strait, had been separated for millions of years. During this time, organisms diverged in their evolution, and human beings on either side of the Atlantic developed their own ways of life, including their own crops, domesticated animals, and *diseases. When the voyages of Christopher *Columbus and other European sailors established contacts between these great land masses, they triggered an exchange of life-forms with massive consequences for the human populations and for the entire biosphere. Weeds, crops, animals, and germs comprised some of the categories of significant exchange.

The Old World had more species of what we call weeds, that is, plants equipped to spread swiftly on disturbed soils, because it was much larger in area and because it had more species of grazing animals, particularly of domesticated ones, to whose teeth and hooves Eurasian and African grasses and herbs had been obliged to adapt. Thus, many of America's most aggressive weeds, especially in the temperate zones, come from European origins: dandelions, crabgrass, wild oats, sow thistle, kudzu, tumbleweed, plantain, cheat grass, and many others. Only a few weeds—armaranth and Canadian water weed, for example—went the other way and established themselves east of the Atlantic.

In 1492, the native crops of the Old and New Worlds were entirely different, with the exception of cotton, which was cultivated on both sides of the Atlantic. The most important Native American cultivars were maize, white potatoes, sweet potatoes, and manioc or cassava. By the late twentieth century these crops accounted for roughly one-third of the world's food production. Among the more important Eurasian-African crops (a longer list, as would be expected of a much larger area) were wheat, barley, rice, sugarcane, oats, rye, soybeans, bananas, carrots, cabbage, and oranges.

The Eastern and Western Hemispheres also exchanged many kinds of wild animals. For instance, black and brown rats were brought to America, and gray squirrels and muskrats to Eurasia. The exchange of domesticated animals, however, was more important. Amerindians were much less effective as animal domesticators than their European counterparts, possibly because they had fewer domesticable animals to work with. Their livestock—llamas, guinea pigs, turkeys, and dogs—included none that were ridden, pulled heavy loads, provided hides or fertilizer in significant amounts beyond the local level, or supplied large quantities of nourishment (i.e., meat and milk) for human consumption. The domesticated animals of Eurasia-Africa, which included horses, cattle, sheep, goats, pigs, donkeys, and chickens, were a major source of nourishment, leather, fiber, power, and fertilizer. After 1492, these domesticated animals were gradually introduced in the Americas.

Most of the troublesome human diseases originated in the Old World. America had its own, like Chagas's disease and something akin to syphilis, but nothing as appalling and influential as the Old World's *smallpox, measles, whooping cough, chicken pox, bubonic plague, *malaria, *yellow fever, *diphtheria, amoebic dysentery, and *influenza. With its greater area and bigger animal and human populations, Eurasia-Africa was also home to more kinds of germs. In addition, human beings had lived in dense populations, seedbeds for germs, for much longer in Eurasia-Africa than in the Americas. They had practiced irrigation agriculture for much longer, creating conditions for the propagation of waterborne infections, and had traded longer and more intensively, ensuring the wide diffusion of infections. Above all, they had for thousands of years lived among domesticated animals and vermin-carrying creatures like rats, with which they shared and mutually cultivated a great number of pathogens. The germs of smallpox, measles, influenza, plague, and other of humanity's historically most important maladies are very similar to those carried by Old World animals or even, in the case of plague, exactly the same.

No American disease figured importantly in the Old World, with the possible exception of syphilis, a *venereal disease that many claim Europeans acquired from the Amerindians of the West Indies during the first Columbian expeditions. Skeletal evidence indicates that syphilis, or some infection like it, was indeed present in the pre-Columbian Americas. Evidence for it before 1492 in the Old World is not so clear, but the question remains unresolved. Some scholars hold that the appearance of syphilis in war-torn Italy soon after the first Columbian voyages was entirely a coincidence.

The effects of the Columbian Exchange on the size and distribution of human populations is clear and spectacular. Even more than that of direct efforts at extermination or subjugation, the impact of Old World diseases on Amerindians radically reduced their number, conceivably by as much as 90 percent, opening their two continents and nearby islands to massive shifts of Europeans and Africans across the Atlantic. The exchange of cultivated plants and livestock increased food production on both sides of the Atlantic, making possible the enormous world population growth of recent centuries. American white potatoes, for instance, enabled farmers in cool, rainy northern Europe to extract more nourishment from the soil than ever before. Hundred of millions of Chinese are dependent on the New World's maize, sweet potatoes, and even such lesser American crops as the peanut. Multitudes of Africans depend on maize, peanuts, and, especially, manioc. It is difficult to imagine how the Americas could support their hundreds of millions and export foodstuffs as well without wheat, rice, beef, chicken, and other foodstuffs of European origin.

The full significance of the Columbian Exchange cannot even now be fully measured, because it reversed more than 100 million years of divergent evolution. What may be described as approximate balances of nature within the ecosystems of the Eastern and Western Hemispheres were radically upset by the additions from overseas of new organisms such as those mentioned here, as well as numerous others.

[*See also* Agriculture: Colonial Era; Cotton Industry; Exploration, Conquest, and Settlement, Era of European; Food and Diet; Indian History and Culture: Migration and Pre-Columbian Era; Indian History and Culture: Distribution of Major Groups, Circa 1500; Indian History and Culture: From 1500 to 1800.]

• Alfred W. Crosby, *The Columbian Exchange,* 1972. Redcliffe Salaman, *The History and Social Influence of the Potato,* 2d ed., 1985. Alfred W. Crosby, *Ecological Imperialism,* 1986. Russell Thornton, *American Indian Holocaust and Survival,* 1987. William M. Denevan, ed., *The Native Population of the Americas in 1492,* 2d ed., 1992. Jared Diamond, *Guns, Germs, and Steel,* 1996.

—Alfred W. Crosby

COLUMBUS, CHRISTOPHER (c.1450–1506), explorer. About the life of the man the English-speaking world knows as Christopher Columbus (and the Spanish-speaking as Cristóbal Colón), almost nothing is known before the fateful year 1492. He was probably born in Genoa, Italy, sometime between 1450 and 1452, and probably spent some years as a merchant seaman before coming to Spain around 1485 seeking royal support for a sailing journey westward into the Ocean Sea. Sponsored by the Spanish monarchs, Queen Isabela and King Ferdinand, Columbus set sail with three ships from Palos, in southwestern Spain, on 3 August 1492, and made landfall on 12 October at an island he called San Salvador, somewhere (but no one knows where) in what are now the Bahamas. The admiral "took possession" of that island and its people (the Tainos) in the name of the Spanish sovereigns and in the next ninety-six days went on to claim three other small coral islands as well as two large forested islands that he named Española and Cuba.

Columbus returned to Spain in March 1493 and presented to his sponsors a half-dozen kidnapped Tainos, considerable gold treasure, and promises of more of both. This served to assure royal backing for a second voyage, in September 1493, this one consisting of seventeen ships and some fourteen hundred colonists ready to establish Spain's new empire. On arriving back in Española, Columbus created a colonial outpost from which he acted as governor of the island for the next seven years. His disastrous misrule of the colony led, in 1500, to his being shipped back to Spain in chains. After two years of disgrace, Columbus convinced the Spanish sovereigns to allow him one last voyage, in May 1502, provided he stayed away from Española. When this voyage, too, ended in disaster, Columbus returned to Spain for good. He died in Valladolid on 19 May 1506, a largely forgotten man. Deeply interested in biblical prophecy, he had always seen his voyages as steps in the fulfillment of God's divine plan.

Although Columbus himself knew what he had achieved—the discovery (for Europeans) of a fantastically rich New World and the routes to it—it would be another generation before he would be credited with actually discovering the Americas (which is why the Italian navigator Amerigo Vespucci [1454–1512] got his name on them in 1507), and another century before Europe would truly comprehend the historical magnitude of his feat. Five hundred years after Columbus landed in San Salvador, his reputation was tinged by the recognition that his true legacy included the exploitation and depletion of nature and the enslavement and near extinction of the peoples he encountered.

[*See also* Columbian Exchange; Exploration, Conquest, and Settlement, Era of European; Indian History and Culture: Migration and Pre-Columbian Era; Indian History and Culture: Distribution of Major Groups, Circa 1500; Indian History and Culture: From 1500 to 1800; Spanish Settlements in North America.]

• Samuel Eliot Morison, *Admiral of the Ocean Sea: A Life of Christopher Columbus,* 1942. Oliver Dunn and James W. Kelley Jr., *The Diario of Christopher Columbus's First Voyage to America,* 1989. Kirkpatrick Sale, *The Conquest of Paradise: Christopher Columbus and the Columbian Legacy,* 1990.

—Kirkpatrick Sale

COMMITTEES OF CORRESPONDENCE. Throughout the eighteenth century, colonial assemblies designated some of their members as committees of correspondence to communicate with their agents in Britain and with other assemblies. Merchants used similar bodies to keep in touch and to lobby politicians. The most significant committee of correspondence, however, had different purposes and a more crucial impact.

In 1772, at the urging of Samuel *Adams and others, *Boston's Town Meeting created a committee of correspondence to maintain contacts with the selectmen of every Massachusetts town and, through them, with every town meeting. Its goals were to defeat Governor Thomas Hutchinson's efforts to create a proadministration faction; to rally support for Boston's resistance to imperial taxation; to educate townspeople about their constitutional rights and the threats to those rights; and, finally, to habituate the townspeople to concern themselves with larger political and constitutional issues. The committee's efforts proved spectacularly successful. Even before the 1774 crisis over the Coercive Acts, many Massachusetts towns were becoming more unified in resistance to Britain and had developed a nascent *republicanism that would animate the populace as the revolutionary crisis unfolded. As Samuel Adams exulted in 1776, the Boston Committee of Correspondence had "raised the Spirits of the People, drawn their attention from *picking up pins,* and directed their Views to great objects."

Loyalists such as Hutchinson claimed that the Boston Committee of Correspondence tricked gullible country folk into rebellion, but the reality was quite different. Encouraged to express their own ideas, the towns developed more radical democratic ideals than Boston itself. The committee of correspondence diffused and decentralized thought about the nature and structure of government, producing by late 1774 in the critical colony of Massachusetts a more unified and fiercer resistance to Britain and a more sophisticated ideology of republicanism, than had hitherto existed.

[*See also* Colonial Era; Revolution and Constitution, Era of; Revolutionary War.]

• Richard D. Brown, *Revolutionary Politics in Massachusetts: The Boston Committee of Correspondence and the Towns, 1772–1774,* 1976.

—John L. Bullion

COMMON SENSE (1776), Revolutionary Era pamphlet. American independence had not yet been publicly discussed when on 10 January 1776 the *Philadelphia printer Robert Bell published a forty-seven–page pamphlet whose title page only hinted at its explosive contents: *COMMON SENSE: addressed to the inhabitants of AMERICA, on the following interesting subjects: I. Of the Origin and Design of Government in general, with concise Remarks on the English Constitution. II. Of Monarchy and Hereditary Succession. III. Thoughts on the present State of American Affairs. IV. Of the present ability of America.* Ominously, the epithet proclaimed: "Man knows no Master save creating Heaven, or those whom choice and common Good ordain." The author, Thomas *Paine, had only recently immigrated from England and initially remained anonymous. An expanded second edition went through at least thirteen printings; total sales, estimated at 150,000 copies within three months, eventually reached half a million. A German translation was published in February by the Philadelphia printers Melchior Steiner and Carl Cist. This wide distribution, together with newspaper excerpts, made *Common Sense* the single most influential pamphlet of the *Revolutionary War.

In rousing agitator's rhetoric, Paine dispelled as a myth the "balanced," liberty-protecting character of the British constitution. Hereditary monarchy and aristocracy were absurd, Paine argued, and irreconcilable with the natural equality of human beings. The colonists could not seriously hope for a permanent reconciliation with "the Royal brute of Britain." The day had arrived for them to declare their independence. Paine did not specify how the future republican American government should be organized, nor did he advocate social leveling. He argued only that Americans had good reason and the material resources to assert their independence, if only they would join in support of "the rights of mankind and of the FREE AND INDEPENDENT STATES OF AMERICA." Public and private reaction to *Common Sense* was overwhelming. The taboo had been broken, and debate did not cease until independence was declared.

[*See also* Revolution and Constitution, Era of; Republicanism.]

• Gregory Claeys, *Thomas Paine: Social and Political Thought,* 1989. Thomas Paine, *Collected Writings,* ed. Eric Foner, 1995.

—Willi Paul Adams

COMMUNISM. Whether in its religious, utopian, or Marxist form, communism has played a muted yet significant role in American history. To a vision (or recollection) of common property-holding originating in antiquity, modern thinkers and activists added a detailed social rationale and many examples of state leadership. In the process, "communism" lost most of its religious and voluntary quality, yet it remained a key marker for twentieth century life even where, as in the United States, its popular appeal proved short-lived.

"Communism," for millennia an imagined memory of some distant Golden Age, came alive in the early sixteenth century in the Radical Reformation uprising against monarchy and church, from England to Central Europe. Brutally suppressed, these millennialist movements were carried in a small way through disciples to the New World. Colonial and post-revolutionary Pennsylvania alone saw dozens of largely Germanic communal experiments. Amish and particularly Hutterite settlements carried on communal traditions for centuries after.

The American Shakers, similar to the German-American religious idealists in their search for a comprehensively ordered collective life, had a remarkable impact upon the American scene, from music to furniture design, even as their celibate colonies dwindled through the nineteenth and twentieth centuries. Assorted other *Antebellum-Era experiments drew outstanding intellectuals (the geologist Robert Dale Owen, travel writer and labor reformer Frances Wright, newspaper publisher Horace Greeley, and novelist Nathaniel *Hawthorne, to name only a few) to projects whose scant practical success belied their greater literary popularity. Edward Bellamy's wildly popular novel **Looking Backward: 2000–1887* (1888), induced the last major burst of enthusiasm for communal living until the 1960s. These efforts had, however, long since abandoned the word "Communism" to the political Communists.

Karl Marx and Friedrich Engels' *Communist Manifesto* (1848), named to distinguish their "scientific" doctrine from what they contemptuously dismissed as utopian *socialism, came to life when the Paris Commune of 1871 dissolved the political "state" in favor of a council of citizens. Amid the American *railroad strikes of 1877, a similar body ruled St. Louis for one week, making major decisions in the name of working people until occupying troops recaptured authority. But only in Russia in 1917, when workers' councils ("Soviets") briefly took over large sections of the nation's industry, did such direct popular rule become more than a dream of left-wing socialists. As a civil war raged, the Bolshevik party steadily exerted its authority over the Soviets. Soon the State ruled absolutely, and the very meaning of "Communism" had been in many ways reversed. Although the Communist International, appealing for workers' solidarity worldwide, rapidly became a mechanism of Russian foreign policy, the promise of revolution inspired allies in various nations; strong, admiring Communist parties in central and southern Europe; and a much weaker Communist party in the United States.

In the 1930s, the rise of fascism, the impending threat of world war, and the devastating effects of the Depression gave the Communist cause a temporary but significant appeal to hundreds of thousands of Americans. Although the *Communist Party–USA won only a miniscule vote in presidential elections (80,181 in 1936), some immigrant workers, industrial unionists, reformers, intellectuals, writers, and artists embraced the Communists' Popular Front (a coalition of antifascist forces) until the Hitler-Stalin Pact of 1939, and again during *World War II, when the United States and the Soviet Union were allies. The *Cold War atmosphere of intimidation, as well as disillusionment with the Soviet Union, eclipsed the American Communist party. Its surrounding milieu and faithful political descendants, however, continued, in various degrees, to influence the social movements of the 1960s and 1970s, the Third World "support movements" of the 1980s, and even the revived labor movement of the 1990s.

[*See also* Anarchism; Anticommunism; Depressions, Economic; Hiss, Alger; Hoover, J. Edgar; Industrial Workers of the World; Labor Movements; McCarthy, Joseph; Mennonites and Amish; Millennialism and Apocalypticism; New Deal Era, The; Noyes, John Humphrey; Radicalism; Rosenberg Case; Shakerism; Sixties, The; Socialist Party; Strikes and Industrial Conflict; Utopian and Communitarian Movements.]

• Friedrich Engels, *Socialism: Utopian and Scientific,* trans., Edward Averling, 1892; new ed., 1975. Donald Bell, *Marxian Socialism in the United States,* 1967. Robert Fogarty, ed., *Dictionary of American Communal and Utopian History,* 1980. Carl J. Guarneri, *The Utopia Alternative: Fourierism in Nineteenth Century America,* 1991. Stephen J. Stein, *The Shaker Experience in America,* 1992. Donald E. Pitzer, ed., *America's Communal Utopias,* 1997. Mari Jo Buhle, Paul Buhle, and Dan Georgakas, eds., *Encyclopedia of the American Left,* 1998.

—Paul Buhle

COMMUNIST PARTY—USA. Two American communist parties were founded in 1919: one by non–English speaking immigrants, the other led by the journalist John Reed (1887–1920), author of an admiring history of the Bolshevik Revolution, *Ten Days That Shook the World* (1919). Forced to unify by the Communist International, the Communist Party–USA (CPUSA) spent the 1920s as a marginal force in American life. Dominated by Finnish, Slavic, and Eastern European Jewish immigrants, the party was torn by factional warfare between Charles Ruthenberg and Jay Lovestone, on the one hand, and William Z. Foster, a radical trade union leader, on the other. Frequent Comintern mediation culminated in 1929 with Lovestone's deposition as party leader through Joseph Stalin's personal intervention.

In the early 1930s, the CPUSA led militant strikes and protests from Gastonia, North Carolina, to California's Imperial Valley. The party's ultrarevolutionary posture did not lead to substantial membership growth, however; in 1934, after five years of economic depression, it had only 26,000 members. Membership grew once the Comintern adopted the Popular Front against fascism in 1935, reaching nearly 100,000 by 1939, many of them native-born Americans. The CPUSA became a political force in several states, notably New York, Minnesota, and California. Communists were influential in several of the newly organized CIO unions, as well as in groups representing *African Americans, immigrants, writers, and intellectuals.

The Nazi-Soviet Pact of 1939 reduced communist influence, but the CPUSA rebounded during the American-Soviet alliance of *World War II. In 1945, however, party leader Earl Browder was deposed after Moscow denounced his policy of cooperation with American *capitalism. Party members rallied behind Henry Wallace's 1948 *Progressive party presidential campaign. As the *Cold War gathered momentum and American communists faced legal attack and became pariahs, the party created an underground organization and sent many members into hiding. Events abroad completed the party's decimation. Revelations of Stalin's crimes, Soviet *anti-Semitism, and the Russian invasion of Hungary in 1957 reduced the CPUSA to fewer than three thousand members by 1958. The crisis of *communism in the Soviet Union led to still another factional war in 1989 that left Gus Hall, party leader since 1959, as head of an organization with barely one thousand members.

[*See also* Anticommunism; Federal Bureau of Investigation; Hiss, Alger; Labor Movements; McCarthy, Joseph; New Deal Era, The; Rosenberg Case; Scottsboro Case; Smith Act; Socialism; Twenties, The.]

• Irving Howe and Lewis Coser, *The American Communist Party,* 1957. Harvey Klehr and John Haynes, *The American Communist Movement,* 1992.

—Harvey Klehr

COMMUNITARIANISM. *See* Utopian and Communitarian Movements.

COMPROMISE OF 1850, a series of laws passed by Congress to settle issues arising from the deepening sectional conflict over *slavery. Although enacted separately, the laws followed a tradition of complex federal compromises over slavery's expansion designed to obtain concessions from all parties. A tough new *Fugitive Slave Act, designed to stop interference by northerners with the capture and return of fugitive slaves, empowered federal marshals to deputize bystanders to assist in seizing runaways and permitted the settlement of cases without jury trials. Legislation to organize the new territories of New Mexico and Utah permitted the settlers to introduce or ban slavery when they sought statehood. (This legislation also permitted suits directly to the *Supreme Court over the status of slaves in the territories, thereby laying the groundwork for the 1857 *Scott* v. *Sandford* case. *California was admitted as a free state over the protests of southerners fearful of a free-state majority in the Senate. Congress also banned public slave-trading in *Washington, D.C., a compromise between *antislavery forces demanding total abolition in the district and southerners who viewed any restriction as unconstitutional. Finally, the slave state *Texas relinquished its claims on much of neighboring New Mexico territory in exchange for the federal government's assumption of Texas's preannexation debts.

The final shape of the legislation was hammered out during months of rancorous congressional debate. Although each element of the compromise garnered a majority vote, the entire package never attracted a solid majority in either house. Arguing for a comprehensive compromise were leaders of the aging Jacksonian generation, including Henry *Clay of Kentucky and Daniel *Webster of Massachusetts, joined by a group of younger politicians like Stephen A. *Douglas of Illinois, who drew upon party loyalty to forge agreements on individual bills. Opposing compromise were powerful militants from both sections, including the northerners William *Seward of New York and Salmon P. Chase of Ohio, and the southerners John C. *Calhoun and Jefferson *Davis.

The Compromise of 1850 briefly muted sectional antipathies and delayed civil war for a decade. But the controversial enforcement of the Fugitive Slave Act proved deeply divisive, and the settlement finally unraveled in 1854, when an overconfident Douglas, in the *Kansas-Nebraska Act, engineered the reversal of the 1820 *Missouri Compromise and opened Kansas to slavery on the basis of the local-option principle. Northerners, furious at this use of one compromise to overturn another, abandoned the *Democratic party in droves and flocked to the new *Republican party.

[*See also* Antebellum Era; Civil War: Causes; Mexican War.]

• Holman Hamilton, *Prologue to War: The Compromise of 1850,* 1964. David M. Potter, *The Impending Crisis, 1848–1861,* comp. and ed. Don E. Fehrenbacher, 1976. William W. Freehling, *The Road to Disunion,* vol. 1, *Secessionists at Bay, 1776–1854,* 1990. Mark J. Stegmaier, *Texas, New Mexico and The Compromise of 1850: Boundary Dispute & Sectional Crisis,* 1996.

—Peter B. Knupfer

COMPROMISE OF 1877. One of four nineteenth-century political compromises designed to hold the states together without resort to force, the Compromise of 1877 was the last and in some respects the most successful. Unlike the previous compromises, that of 1877 was framed in secrecy. The occasion was the disputed presidential election of 1876 in which each candidate—the Republican Rutherford *Hayes and the Democrat Samuel J. Tilden (1814–1886), the governor of New York—claimed a majority of electoral votes. The traditional account by historians told of a last-minute bargain in which the Republicans agreed to abandon the two remaining Republican state governments in the *South and their protection of freedmen's rights in exchange for a pledge by southern Democrats to support Hayes.

In reality, negotiations had gone on for months and involved many more interests than electoral politics. The *Democratic party in the South and the *Republican party in the North had both fallen under the dominance of conservatives, often former Whigs. Negotiations between these two groups were conducted by the nonpartisan Western Associated Press, to which belonged all important newspapers of the Mississippi Valley, South and North. Confederate Colonel Andrew Jackson Keller of the *Memphis Avalanche* and Union General Henry Van Ness Boynton of the *Cincinnati Gazette* did most of the bargaining. They found a South battered first by the war and then by severe depression, desperately demanding federal subsidies for new or deteriorated *railroads, fallen bridges, destroyed public buildings, and blocked harbors. Bills for such subsidies flooded Congress, supported in large measure by powerful corporate lobbies. Hayes, working closely with Keller and Boynton, promised that "to restore peace and prosperity to the South," he would be "exceptionally liberal" about internal improvements. As expected, enough southern Democratic congressmen opposed the pro-Tilden filibuster plan of northern Democrats to thwart it. The electoral commission ruled in favor of Hayes, who was peacefully inaugurated.

While Hayes's promise of federal subsidies went largely unfulfilled, disappointing southern capitalists, the principal losers in the compromise were the ex-slaves, abandoned by the Republican party. But Radical *Reconstruction was already on the wane, and Tilden would probably have wiped out what remained of it even more quickly than did Hayes.

[*See also* African Americans; Civil War; Gilded Age; Whig Party.]

• Keith Ian Polakoff, *The Politics of Inertia: The Election of 1876 and the End of Reconstruction,* 1973.

—C. Vann Woodward

COMPTON, ARTHUR H. (1892–1962), physicist. Born in Wooster, Ohio, Compton received his B.S. from the College of Wooster and his Ph.D. from Princeton University (1916), after which he taught for a year at the University of Minnesota; worked as a research engineer in the Westinghouse Research Laboratories in Pittsburgh, Pennsylvania (1917–1919); studied on a fellowship at the Cavendish Laboratory in Cambridge, England (1919–1920); and became professor of physics at Washington University in St. Louis, Missouri (1920–1923). In 1916, he married Betty Charity McCloskey; they had two sons.

In 1922, while doing research on X rays, Compton discovered what came to be called the Compton effect, for which in 1927 he shared the Nobel Prize in physics. X rays were long known to behave like ordinary electromagnetic waves under various experimental conditions. Compton now showed that when X rays collide with electrons in a substance like carbon, they behave like particles. This discovery at long last established the validity of Albert *Einstein's light-quantum hypothesis of 1905 and became a milestone in the creation of quantum mechanics.

Compton moved to the University of Chicago in 1923, where in the 1930s he carried out important cosmic-ray research. During *World War II, he directed the *Manhattan Project's Metallurgical Laboratory in Chicago, where Enrico *Fermi achieved the first nuclear chain reaction on 2 December 1942. In 1945, he became chancellor of Washington University and taught there until his retirement in 1961. The deeply religious son of a Presbyterian minister, Compton in his public lectures and writings always insisted upon the compatability of science and religious faith.

[*See also* Science: From 1914 to 1945; Science: Since 1945.]

• Marjorie Johnson, ed., *The Cosmos of Arthur Holly Compton,* 1967. Roger H. Stuewer, *The Compton Effect: Turning Point in Physics,* 1975.

—Roger H. Stuewer

COMPUTERS. Electronic computers came into widespread use during and after *World War II. Analog and electromechanical computers, anticipated by the nineteenth-century English mathematician Charles Babbage, had existed earlier, including the differential analyzer built by Vannevar *Bush at the Massachusetts Institute of Technology (MIT) in 1928.

World War II and Early Postwar Developments. Howard H. Aiken at Harvard constructed the Automatic Sequence Controlled Calculator (called the Mark I), a behemoth at eight feet tall and fifty-one feet long, in 1939–1944. Wartime electronic computers constructed to calculate tables of ballistic trajectories and to decipher enemy codes were anticipated by the experiments of John Atanasoff, Wallace Eckert, and Conrad Zuse. The Electronic Numerical Integrator and Computer (ENIAC) at the Moore School of Engineering at the University of Pennsylvania was the font of postwar computer development. Designed by J. Presper Eckert Jr. and John Mauchly and put into operation in 1946, it inspired the mathematician John von Neumann at Princeton's Institute for Advanced Study to formulate a fundamental design, or architecture, of a stored-program computer named EDVAC. This machine architecture became the standard for electronic digital computers.

Because of their great size and cost, computers required governmental or industrial support. Mauchly and Eckert's attempts to develop a commercial computer, the UNIVAC, succeeded only after they had won contractual support from the government. In 1951, their company was purchased by the Remington Rand Corporation, which also purchased Engineering Research Associates, a company spun out the navy's cryptographic establishment.

Early Governmental and Industrial Applications. UNIVAC's success persuaded IBM (International Business Machines Corporation), a manufacturer of electromechanical office equipment, to invest heavily in a series of scientific and business computers in the 1950s, including the 700 series, the IBM 650, and the IBM 1401. IBM also won the contract to manufacture the networked computers of the air force's semi-automatic ground environment (SAGE) defense system. These were developed in MIT's Project Whirlwind. The SAGE system provided IBM with a large computer market, as well as access to the extensive software developments of the Systems Development Corporation, and the magnetic core computer memories developed by MIT. Going on to develop the SABRE airline ticket-reservation system and the 360 series of computers, IBM soon dominated the computer marketplace. Among other industrial spin-offs of Project Whirlwind was the minicomputer, developed by Kenneth Hogan of the Digital Equipment Corporation. It would eventually make computing power available to individuals who did not require the speed or power of a mainframe computer.

Early computers at military and nuclear laboratories solved scientific problems that had previously been intractable because of the time-consuming calculations required. New techniques such as the Monte Carlo method provided numerical simulations when analytical solutions were not available. Large amounts of experimental data could be analyzed automatically by computer programs. Other computationally intensive fields such as fluid mechanics benefited enormously from the computer. In the aerospace industry, the use of computers grew rapidly in the 1950s, and computer modeling supplemented, and in some cases, replaced, more expensive and time-consuming tests of aerodynamic design. The *space program provided additional applications (and resources) for computers, as well as demands for miniaturization that inspired greater use of transistors and integrated circuits, developed in the late 1950s by Jack Kilby of Texas Instruments and Robert Noyce of Fairchild Semiconductor. By 1964, the number of individual circuits that could be integrated on a single silicon chip was doubling every eighteen to twenty-four months (a fact noted by Gordon Moore in 1965 and later called "Moore's Law"). A spin-off of the avionics and space electronic fields, very large integrated circuits would prove important for consumer electronics. Computer-aided design and manufacture, important first in the aerospace industry and then in many other *engineering applications, had by the 1990s largely replaced other design techniques.

The substitution of computers for clerical and accounting personnel appealed to federal agencies that processed large amounts of data or financial transactions. By 1958, three-quarters of the Department of Defense computers, which accounted for half of all government machines, were devoted to supply and logistics functions such as cataloging; inventory control and distribution; requirements forecasting; and other management, budgetary, and financial processes. The federal government's need to process 25 billion individual pieces of paper annually increased demands for automation. Not only the Defense Department, but also the *Social Security Administration's wage-record operations; the Treasury Department's check accounting; the Department of Agriculture's commodity-stabilization operations; the Census Bureau's statistical program; the Internal Revenue Service's tax collections; and the Department of Health and Human Services' massive medical and federal *welfare record-keeping all came to rely heavily on computers. Computers hastened the growth of government at all levels, especially the federal.

Social and Cultural Concerns. The appearance of automated data-processing facilities in government raised concerns about job loss and stimulated popular fears of invasion of privacy and control of government by these giant electronic brains. The democratic process found uses for computers in applications such as automated vote tabulation, but when UNIVAC accurately predicted the outcome of the 1952 presidential election on the basis of a small sample of the vote, the voice of the people seemed as amendable to computer analysis as any other process. Deepening apprehensions about the social implications of computers found expression in such works as Norbert Wiener's *Cybernetics* (1947) and *The Human Uses of Human Beings* (1950); Joseph Weizenbaum's *Computer Power and Human Reason* (1976); and science-fiction stories by Ray Bradbury, Isaac Asimov, and many others.

Commercial, Medical, and Academic Uses. In the world of commerce, *insurance, *banking, and process industries led the way in adopting computers. Industrial-process engineering, which planned flow-intensive techniques such as those pioneered in the *chemical, *petroleum, and *nuclear-power industries, as well as in the *nuclear-weapons complex, found early applications for computers to synchronize and automatically adjust the flows of materials. Attempts in the machine-tool industry to replace skilled laborers with the numerically controlled tools, however, showed computers' limits as labor-replacing devices, since skilled laborers had to monitor computer performance to prevent errors.

In other industries where flow was important, industrial robotics proved more successful, for example, on assembly lines for automobiles and other mass-produced goods, where the volume of output justified a heavy investment in computers and programming. As service and information industries eclipsed industrial manufacturing, the use of computers extended into almost every area of *business, creating what many viewed as a Second Industrial Revolution. The invention of the laser and the universal product code enabled retailers to record sales, adjust inventories, and track markets automatically. The most dramatic displacement of labor by computers occurred in the *telephone industry, where human operations were almost completely replaced by computerized switching facilities. Both the promise of vastly more *leisure time and the early fears of widespread *unemployment in the computer age, however, remained unrealized at the end of the twentieth century. Moreover, *productivity studies in service industries found little evidence for a positive impact by computers, while in the 1990s defects in computer programs that prevented them from recognizing the turn of a century—the so-called Y2K phenomenon—cost much time and money to correct.

In *medicine, computers transformed diagnostic procedures, enabled physicians and the general public to access information and research data more rapidly, and made possible new therepeutic and prosthetic devices. In *education, their impact was mixed. Like the phonograph *radio, and *television before it, the computer was widely heralded as a revolutionary education technology. Although many colleges and universities added computer-science programs in the 1960s, early attempts at computer-aided instruction in primary and secondary education, such as the $2 billion Plato project, proved disappointing. Computer manufacturers routinely gave machines to schools at a discount or without cost, but adapting them to educational purposes proved difficult. As the twentieth century ended, the advent of worldwide computer networks via the *Internet (itself an offspring of government support) reawakened enthusiasm for computer-based education as well as skepticism about its value.

Miniturization and the Era of the Personal Computer. The miniaturization of electronic components made possible the use of computers in automobiles, appliances, automatic teller machines (ATMs), card-reader systems, digital recording and playback equipment, handheld computer games, and many other applications. As more and more control processes became automated, this "smart" technology, initially developed in military and space programs, pervaded many spheres of human activity, leading some to label the last quarter of the twentieth century the "information age."

Computer-related businesses exerted enormous economic clout as the twentieth century ended. In 1998, IBM had revenues of $81 billion; the computer-based data provider Electronic Data Systems, $17 billion; and the Seattle-based software giant Microsoft, founded by the now multibillionaire Bill *Gates, $14 billion. The *stock-market boom of the 1990s was sustained largely by surging computer and information technology stocks.

The most visible feature of the computer revolution at century's end was the rapid spread of personal computers. By 1998, 47 percent of American households owned computers, and the rate was increasing every year. These computers had widespread applications, from video games, word processing, and record-keeping to instant, worldwide communication via e-mail and access to a vast array of information on the world wide web. Like the earlier mainframes, the ubiquitous personal computer gave rise to social concerns, from Internet pornography and the effects of video games on children to the disparity in computer access between the poor and the affluent. Whatever the apprehensions, the computer was clearly here to stay. Having so radically transformed American life in the later twentieth century, it seemed certain—in tandem with other communications technologies—to exert even greater influence in the twenty-first.

[*See also* Automation and Computerization; Business Cycle; Census, Federal; Cold War; Electronics; Federal Government, Executive Branch; Department of Defense; Intelligence Gathering and Espionage; Mass Marketing; Mass Production; Nuclear Strategy; Post–Cold War Era; Technology.]

• James W. Cortada, *The Computer in the United States: From Laboratory to Market, 1930 to 1960,* 1993. Martin Campbell-Kelly and William Aspray, *The Computer: A History of the Information Machine,* 1996. Arthur L. Norberg and Judy E. O'Neill, *Transforming Computer Technology: Information Processing for the Pentagon, 1962–1986,* 1996.

—Robert W. Seidel

CONANT, JAMES B. (1893–1978), president of Harvard University, science administrator, diplomat. Born in Dorchester, Massachusetts, Conant received his B.A. and Ph.D. from Harvard, where he taught organic chemistry from 1916 until he became Harvard's president in 1933. Active in poison-gas research in *World War I, Conant in *World War II oversaw the military application of science as head of the National Defense Research Committee and deputy director of the Office of Scientific Research and Development (OSRD). As chairman of OSRD's *Manhattan Project executive committee and a member of President Franklin Delano *Roosevelt's top policy group and President Harry S. *Truman's interim committee, Conant participated in crucial decisions regarding the development and use of atomic weapons. In 1946, troubled by criticism of the U.S. atomic bombings of Japan, Conant played a central role, with McGeorge Bundy, in preparing Secretary of War Henry *Stimson's influential essay, "The Decision to Use the Atomic Bomb" (*Harper's*, Feb. 1947).

Subsequently, fearing the nuclear destruction of civilization, Conant sought international control of atomic weapons, opposed development of the hydrogen bomb, and questioned the benefits of *nuclear power. A typical *Cold War liberal, he championed expanded defense spending and military preparedness while nevertheless opposing the militarization of academic research and trying to shield academia from McCarthyism. While defending *civil liberties, he believed that communist teachers should be banned from America's schools.

Leaving Harvard in 1953, Conant served as high commissioner for Germany (1953–1955) and as the first U.S. ambassador to the German Federal Republic (1955–1957). He devoted his final years to educational reform. His influential book *The American High School Today* (1959), a response to the Soviet Union's 1957 launch of its *Sputnik* space satellite, called for more rigorous instruction in science, mathematics, and foreign languages.

[*See also* Education: Rise of the University; Education: Education in Contemporary America; Hiroshima and Nagasaki, Atomic Bombing of; McCarthy, Joseph; Nuclear Arms Control Treaties; Nuclear Weapons; Science: From 1914 to 1945; Science: Since 1945.]

• James G. Hershberg, *James B. Conant,* 1993.

—Peter J. Kuznick

CONFEDERATE STATES OF AMERICA. When Abraham *Lincoln was elected president in November 1861, many southern whites feared that their economic security and cultural identity, especially as represented by the institution of *slavery, would be threatened by a government dominated by the *Republican party. Between 20 December 1860 and 1 February 1861, seven southern states—South Carolina, Mississippi, Florida, Alabama, Georgia, Louisiana, and Texas—seceded from the Union in protest. On 4 February, their representatives met at Montgomery, Alabama, to form the Confederate States of America (CSA). Four additional states—Virginia, Tennessee, Arkansas, and North Carolina—joined the Confederacy in April and May after Lincoln called for troops to quell the rebellion, and the *Civil War began. This doubled the white population of the would-be new nation, to 5.5 million (plus 3.7 million blacks, mostly slaves), and enabled the Confederacy to fight for its independence. Kentucky and Missouri sent representatives to the Confederate Congress, but these two states' legislatures never officially recognized the new government. The CSA's capital was moved to Richmond, Virginia, in July 1861.

The most rabid secessionists, known as "fire–eaters," had been agitating for a separate southern nation for years, but with secession now accomplished, these radicals gave way to more moderate leaders like Jefferson *Davis, who became president of the Confederacy. Initially, all Confederates agreed that the government should adhere to a doctrine of *states' rights. However, Davis soon realized that his government must wield more power, even at the expense of the states, if it hoped to win independence. His decision to institute military conscription (a first in American history), suspend habeas corpus, and nationalize segments of the economy angered both powerful state political leaders and many common folk. In addition, perhaps as high as 40 percent of white Southerners had opposed secession. Thousands of these "unionists" created turmoil by enlisting in the U.S. Army, organizing peace movements within the South, and resisting Confederate authority. As casualty lists grew, hope of foreign intervention faded, and inflation drove down the value of the Confederate dollar, even many loyal rebels became alienated from the government.

A revolutionary political experiment in many respects, the

Confederacy finally collapsed in April and May 1865, with the fall of Richmond, the surrender of the CSA's armies, and the capture or flight of its political leaders. Some southern whites would long romanticize the "Lost Cause" of the Confederacy, but its legacies were chiefly involuntary; slavery was abolished and secession was decisively discredited as a viable political option.

[*See also* South, The.]

• Emory M. Thomas, *The Confederate Nation, 1861–1865,* 1979. George C. Rable, *The Confederate Republic: A Revolution against Politics,* 1994.

—Daniel E. Sutherland

CONFEDERATION ERA. *See* Articles of Confederation; Revolution and Constitution, Era of.

CONFERENCE BOARD. *See* National Industrial Conference Board.

CONGRESS. *See* Federal Government, Legislative Branch.

CONGRESS OF INDUSTRIAL ORGANIZATIONS. John L. *Lewis of the United Mine Workers (UMW) and other unionists created the Committee for Industrial Organization (CIO) in November 1935, as a means of encouraging industrial unionism within the *American Federation of Labor (AFL). The early CIO, with the financial support of Lewis's UMW, exhibited a high degree of rank-and-file activism. Lewis and his associates, most notably Sidney Hillman (1887–1946) of the Amalgamated Clothing Workers, broke with the traditions of the AFL by embracing political action, working with communists and other radicals, and welcoming *African American workers.

Victories in key *Middle West strikes in 1936–1937 established the United Rubber Workers and the United Automobile Workers (UAW) as major CIO affiliates. When the U.S. Steel Company signed a contract with the Steel Workers Organizing Committee in March 1937, this bolstered the CIO's prestige and appeal. The CIO also benefited from its support of Franklin Delano *Roosevelt in the 1936 presidential election. Defeat in the bloody "Little Steel" strike of 1937 and the recession of 1937–1939 slowed the CIO's momentum. In 1938, the CIO formalized its break with the AFL, holding its first constitutional convention and adopting its permanent name, the Congress of Industrial Organizations.

In 1940, Lewis departed the CIO, which was now led by Steelworkers' chief Philip Murray (1886–1952), and in 1942 Lewis, with no formal announcement, severed the tie between the UMW and the CIO. Also that year, as the United States entered *World War II, CIO leaders issued a no-strike pledge, relying on their influence in the National War Labor Board for advances in wages and union recognition. Extensive wartime strikes by CIO members, however, compromised this strategy. Thanks to the wartime boom and a tight labor market, CIO membership approached 5 million.

After the war, CIO leaders sought partnership with business and government. The strike wave of 1946, however, along with *Republican party gains in the 1946 elections, curbed these ambitions. CIO efforts to bring large-scale organization to the *South ("Operation Dixie") failed, but the CIO-affiliated UAW and the steelworkers achieved impressive economic contract gains that set new standards for American workers. The CIO also continued its operations in an effort to strengthen liberal forces in the *Democratic party.

In 1949–1950, long-simmering ideological conflict led to the ouster of eleven allegedly procommunist affiliates. Murray's death in 1952 brought other internal conflicts into the open. The new CIO president Walter *Reuther concluded that a merger with the older AFL represented the CIO's best hope of institutional survival. This merger took place in 1955.

The CIO brought union organization and improved working conditions and living standards to millions of workers; it also integrated the labor movement into mainstream American liberal politics. Its inability to expand geographically and into white-collar and service sectors, however, limited its postwar effectiveness.

[*See also* Automotive Industry; Communist Party—USA; Depressions, Economic; Iron and Steel Industry; Labor Movements; Liberalism; Mass Production; New Deal Era, The; Strikes and Industrial Conflict.]

• Robert H. Zieger, *The CIO, 1935–1955,* 1995.

—Robert H. Zieger

CONGRESS OF RACIAL EQUALITY. The Congress of Racial Equality (CORE), one of the most important national organizations of the post-*World War II African American freedom movements, was founded by an interracial group of pacifists in 1942. Committed to nonviolent direct action and interracial activism, CORE first launched protests against racial *segregation in public accommodations in the North. In 1947, CORE activists undertook the Journey of Reconciliation, riding buses into the *South to test a recent U.S. *Supreme Court decision outlawing segregation in interstate travel facilities. Although mob violence stopped the trip in Chapel Hill, North Carolina, the project served as a model for CORE's 1961 Freedom Rides.

Initially a mostly white organization in the Northeast and Midwest, CORE expanded into the South after the Montgomery Bus Boycott of 1955–1956. The charismatic leadership of James Farmer, appointed national director in 1961, and increased media attention surrounding the Freedom Rides enabled CORE to launch a wide range of campaigns in the South during the 1960s. The experience of CORE organizers, the influence of southern blacks, and the impact of black nationalists like Robert F. Williams and *Malcolm X, led to a growing radicalization. In 1966, under the leadership of Floyd McKissick, CORE endorsed the "Black Power" slogan and the following year deleted the term "multi-racial" from its constitution, forcing whites from the organization. In 1968, new national director Roy Innis promoted black separatism and "black capitalism." Although CORE had lost most of its national influence and vitality by the end of the 1960s, it had for nearly three decades played an influential role in the struggle to topple America's formal racial caste system and to create a new black sense of self.

[*See also* Black Nationalism; Civil Rights; Civil Rights Movement; Pacifism; Racism.]

• Inge Powell Bell, *CORE and the Strategy of Nonviolence,* 1968. August Meier and Elliot Rudwick, *CORE: A Study in the Civil Rights Movement,* 1975. James Farmer, *Lay Bare the Heart: An Autobiography of the Civil Rights Movement,* 1985. William L. Van Deburg, *New Day in Babylon: The Black Power Movement and American Culture, 1965–1975,* 1992.

—Simon Wendt

CONSCIENTIOUS OBJECTION. Conscientious objection—the principled refusal to bear arms—was brought to England's North American colonies by pacifist Protestant sects, especially *Mennonites, Brethren, and the *Society of Friends (Quakers), who believed that biblical commandments and Jesus's teachings prohibited them from engaging in war or any violence against other human beings. Since these religious faiths were comparatively small, economically productive, and otherwise law-abiding, most colonial governments eventually exempted them from bearing arms.

Some objectors were forced into militia service during the *Revolutionary War, but several of the new states recognized religious conscientious objection. Indeed, James *Madison sought to include protection for religious objectors in the *Bill of Rights, but this amendment, after passing in the House of Representatives in 1790, failed in the Senate.

Both North and South adopted national conscription in the

*Civil War, and some objectors suffered severely, but ultimately both sides recognized the objectors' sincerity and determination. The Abraham *Lincoln administration eventually allowed conscripted pacifists to assist wounded soldiers and former slaves.

The Selective Service Act of 1917 recognized only members of the historic peace churches as "conscientious objectors" (COs), the first official use of the term, and required them to serve in the military in nonarmsbearing roles. Some 64,700 men, including many who were not members of the historic peace churches, claimed CO status on religious or political grounds in *World War I, and 20,900 COs were inducted into the army. The *military treated many harshly, and 450 "absolutists," who refused any cooperation, went to military prisons.

More liberal, the Selective Service Act of 1940, on the eve of *World War II, authorized CO status for all religious objectors and allowed them to choose either nonarms-bearing military service or alternative civilian service. Of the 50,000 COs drafted in 1940–1945, most served in the army's medical corps; 12,000 performed alternative work in Civilian Public Service (CPS), and 5,000 absolutists were imprisoned.

Of the 35,000 COs who performed alternative service between 1951 and 1965, the *Cold War's peak, most worked in hospitals or mental institutions, the CPS camps having been abolished. During the *Korean War, nearly 1.5 percent of inductees were exempted as COs, compared with .15 percent in each world war.

In the *Vietnam War, large numbers of young men, both secular and religious, applied for CO status or simply refused to cooperate with the Selective Service System. These new COs received support from mainline religious bodies as well as antiwar and antidraft groups. The *Supreme Court, in the *Seeger* (1965) and *Welsh* (1970) decisions, expanded the criteria for CO status to include secular ethical beliefs. More than 170,000 registrants were classified as COs between 1965 and 1970, and CO exemptions soared from 8 percent of actual inductions in 1967 to 43 percent in 1971. Additionally, between 1965 and 1973, 17,500 members of the armed forces applied for noncombatant status or discharge as COs.

Conscription ended in 1973, but even in an all-volunteer military, conscientious objection remained an issue. In 1990–1991, during the *Persian Gulf War, between 1,500 and 2,000 persons in military units applied for discharge as COs. Tensions between the freedom-of-conscience principle and America's citizen-soldier tradition continue to define the evolution of conscientious objection in America.

[*See also* Conscription; Pacifism; Peace Movements.]

• Lillian Schlissel, ed., *Conscience in America: A Documentary History of Conscientious Objection in America, 1757–1967,* 1968. Charles C. Moskos and John Whiteclay Chambers II, eds., *The New Conscientious Objection: From Sacred to Secular Resistance,* 1993. James W. Tollefson, *The Strength Not to Fight: An Oral History of Conscientious Objectors of the Vietnam War,* 1993.

—John Whiteclay Chambers II

CONSCRIPTION, known in the United States as "the draft," is the act of compelling citizens into military service. Long used in Europe as a means of raising armies quickly and cheaply, it was not employed in the United States until the *Civil War, when both sides introduced conscription to fill their manpower needs. In the North, the Conscription Act of March 1863 exempted men who could hire a substitute or pay a three-hundred–dollar fee. These provisions stirred growing protest that culminated in the New York City Draft Riots of 13–16 July 1863. For four days, until federal troops restored order, rioting Irish immigrants targeted the city's elite as well as *African Americans, whom they blamed for the war. As a result, the Conscription Act was amended to limit exemptions to conscientious objectors opposed to military service on moral or religious grounds. The Confederacy experienced analogous problems with its conscription law, adopted in April 1862, which favored wealthy slave owners.

Upon U.S. entry into *World War I, Congress passed the Selective Service Act of 1917, which required all male citizens between twenty-one and thirty years of age (later changed to eighteen and forty-five) to register for military service. Over 2.8 million males were drafted in 1917–1918. Only men with a verified family hardship, the physically disabled, and conscientious objectors were exempt.

Conscription was again imposed on the eve of *World War II, with the Selective Service Act of 1940. Although not initially popular, this first peacetime draft facilitated rapid military mobilization after the U.S. declaration of war in December 1941. More than ten million males were drafted between 1940 and 1947. Once again, the only exemptions were for family hardship, disability, or *conscientious objection to war. Owing to the manpower needs of U.S. occupation forces in Germany and Japan, and to the beginnings of the *Cold War, conscription continued after the war's end. It was further extended by the Universal Military Training and Service Act of June 1951, a congressional response to the *Korean War, which was periodically extended thereafter. The *Vietnam War prompted passage of the Military Selective Service Act of 1967, which differed from its predecessors in permitting educational deferments for males between the ages of eighteen and twenty-six. The social inequality of this provision, combined with the growing unpopularity of the war, caused riots and demonstrations. This act expired in 1973, and in 1974 President Gerald *Ford granted clemency to many thousands of Vietnam Era draft resisters, provided they took an oath of allegiance and performed two years of public service. Draft registration resumed in 1980 for all males when they reached the age of eighteen, but at least through the end of the century, no inductions were needed.

[*See also* Confederate States of America; Draft Riots, Civil War; Military, The.]

• George Q. Flynn, *The Draft, 1940–1973,* 1993.

—Christopher Clark

CONSERVATION MOVEMENT. Launched in 1908 as a national crusade, the conservation movement involved the wide range of concerns later embraced by the environmental movement. Its intellectual origins date to the western land surveys of the nineteenth century, but it belongs to the realm of politics as much as to science. In the *Progressive Era, two main branches, utilitarian and preservationist, emerged. Gifford Pinchot (1865–1946), a wealthy Pennsylvania forester who in 1898 became head of the federal government's small division of forestry (renamed the U.S. Forest Service in 1905), led the utilitarian wing. He advocated multiple-purpose use of the national forests. An astute strategist, he won the support of industries and interest groups eager to exploit the forests for profit by proposing a system of government regulation that eliminated wasteful competition and conflict. Close to President Theodore *Roosevelt, Pinchot spearheaded an expanding program focused on "wise use" of natural resources, coordinated with other departments and agencies concerned with federal lands. The National Reclamation Act of 1902, establishing a federal agency to oversee irrigation projects in the *Southwest, exemplified this objective.

Opposition to these policies arose in the western states most affected by them, and congressional opposition soon followed. The "conservation movement" was, in effect, Pinchot's public-relations crusade to create broad popular support for policies that until then had been promoted by narrow interest groups and bureau chiefs like himself—policies that western opponents identified with eastern corporations and elitist eastern bureaucrats. Through magazine articles and a 1908 White House conference, Pinchot crafted a public constituency for conservation.

The forest service's timber doctrine—of continual yield management (cutting no more timber than annual growth replaced)—became the foundation for a wildlife-preservation policy and the central doctrine of the U.S. Fish and Wildlife

Service. A former forest service ranger, Aldo *Leopold, carried over from forestry the notion that game populations were an agricultural crop to be harvested periodically to prevent overpopulation and preserve their range and food supply. Leopold also learned from Pinchot to cultivate an interlocking coalition of support groups constituting an effective wildlife lobby.

The preservationist wing of the movement, originally a part of Pinchot's grand concert of interests, split off after the Hetch Hetchy controversy (1913). This conflict focused on whether the Hetch Hetchy Valley, a part of *Yosemite National Park, should be used as a water reservoir for *San Francisco—the position Pinchot supported—or preserved for its natural beauty, as advocated by John *Muir, a nature writer and activist well-known to readers of mass-circulation magazines. Although the Hetch Hetchy Valley became a reservoir, disappointed preservationists helped in 1916 to establish the *National Park Service, a federal bureau that rivaled the utilitarian forest service. The first director, Stephen Mather, proved as adept as Pinchot at buttressing his agency with the support of friendly industries and interest groups whose managers understood the commercial benefits awaiting those who helped meet the *leisure needs of a rapidly growing urban middle class.

[*See also* Ballinger-Pinchot Controversy; Environmentalism; Forests and Forestry.]

• A. Hunter Dupree, *Science in the Federal Government: A History of Policies and Activities to 1940,* 1957. James Lal Penick Jr., "The Progressives and the Environment: Three Themes from the First Conservation Movement," in *The Progressive Era,* ed. Louis L. Gould, 1974, pp. 115–131.

—James Lal Penick Jr.

CONSERVATISM. The term "conservatism" did not gain parlance in American politics until the middle of the twentieth century. The United States has never had a national party bearing that label, in contrast to Great Britain and Canada, for example. When Peter Viereck published *Conservatism Revisited* in 1949, and Russell Kirk *The Conservative Mind* in 1953, they invoked an understanding of that term that had clear European antecedents, especially in Edmund Burke, British statesman of the late eighteenth century. Burke, particularly in his criticism of the French Revolution, evoked tradition and the mystique of history to countervail any present generation's fascination with newness and change. He urged a discriminate but not implacable defense of the standing order, with its rank and hierarchy. Burke's conservatism appreciated folkways and local color, but it especially celebrated the symbols of unity, in crown and state, that preserved the organic quality of the nation.

In the United States, this brand of conservatism had to compete with other forms. The revolutionary spirit that fostered American independence often expressed hostility to Old World social and political institutions and located a contrasting American identity in the new nation's youth and republican simplicity. In the first political party system, the *Federalist party espoused an early form of American conservatism. Alexander *Hamilton's economic program envisioned an alliance of the federal government with the *business classes, but the Federalists also found a religious constituency in the established churches of *New England. The *Whig party generally continued this alliance. Henry *Clay's "American System" looked to the federal government to assist in the nation's economic growth. At the same time, Whigs tended to support a moral politics, embracing such causes as *temperance and *antislavery. In antebellum America, rival elements in the *Democratic party often complained of both the social elitism and the "moral imperialism" of the Whigs. A number of writers and artists of the *Antebellum Era, including the novelists James Fenimore *Cooper and Nathaniel *Hawthorne and the painter Thomas *Cole, offered a distinctly conservative perspective in their work.

The *Republican party, arising in the mid-1850s, inherited the Whigs' moral fervor and became an *antislavery party. Its sponsorship of homestead legislation, construction of a national railroad, and creation of land-grant colleges continued the economic nationalism of the Federalists and Whigs. The party, however, came increasingly under the influence of business interests that made defense of property rights a major priority. In the *Gilded Age, conservatism came to be associated with *laissez-faire minimal-government principles and found its major voice in the judicial branch of government as it became a bulwark against state regulation of business activity. This libertarian and free-market brand of conservatism gained in theoretical and rhetorical significance thereafter. It found expression in such antistatist and elitist proponents as H. L. *Mencken and Albert J. Nock (1870–1945), and in economic theorists like Friedrich von Hayek, whose *The Road to Serfdom* (1941) challenged *Keynesianism. Later, the monetary theories of the University of Chicago economist Milton Friedman (1912–), gave free-market economics more theoretical persuasiveness and solidified that philosophy in American conservative ideology.

The *Cold War added another component to American conservatism: *anticommunism. In 1950, the Wisconsin senator Joseph *McCarthy launched his campaign to expose communists in the State Department. The investigation of Alger *Hiss, a former department official accused of communist affiliation by Whittaker Chambers (1901–1961), lent drama to the anticommunist movement. Chambers's autobiography, *Witness* (1952), an emotional center for a large conservative readership, described *communism as a deadly challenge to Western civilization and especially to its religious tradition. Like Chambers, a remarkable number of anticommunist conservative intellectuals, in fact, came from the political left. They included Max Eastman, Will Herberg, Frank S. Meyer, and the novelist John Dos Passos (1896–1970). William F. *Buckley Jr.'s *National Review*, launched in 1955, provided a forum for free-market, anticommunist, and religious conservatives.

These conditions gave rise to a new kind of conservatism that became dominant in the later twentieth century: populist conservatism. In 1964, a movement in the Republican party took control from its moderate eastern wing and nominated Senator Barry *Goldwater of Arizona for president. Goldwater, supported by conservative intellectuals and the many college chapters of Buckley's Young Americans for Freedom, campaigned against union shops, compulsory *Social Security, and government projects such as the *Tennessee Valley Authority. He appealed to Americans troubled by the Cold War stalemate and called for decisive action against the communist threat. Goldwater's defeat helped open the way for a more emphatically populist conservative, George C. *Wallace of Alabama. Wallace first gained national attention by defying court-ordered desegregation, but in campaigns for the presidency, his attacks on government officials and the social elites that he believed controlled them proved to have wide appeal.

Ronald *Reagan inherited the momentum of populist conservatism and rode it to political success. Intellectually, Reaganism also owed much to a new group of "neoconservatives" made up of former leftists, including Jewish New Yorkers, such as Norman Podhoretz and Irving Kristol. Their disaffection with *liberalism often derived from issues like *affirmative action and school busing to achieve racial balance. The neoconservatives charged that liberalism had moved from a legitimate concern with *equality of opportunity to an illegitimate preoccupation with equality of results. Neoconservatives, furthermore, often registered populist prejudices in their attacks on liberal elites, whom they saw as dominant in academe, the media, and government.

Winning the presidency in 1980 thanks to the populist wing of the Republican party (and many disaffected New Deal Democrats), Reagan combined important strands of American conservatism in a significant new way, employing populist rhetoric while working in the interests of corporate America and the wealthier classes. Insisting that "the problem is government," he saw a great economic future for America once business enterprise was liberated from government restraint. At the same time expressing conservatives' recoil from the countercultural movements of the 1960s and 1970s, Reagan invoked a traditional America rooted in the religious and patriotic values of earlier times. He thus garnered support from religious conservatives affiliated with such groups as the *Moral Majority of the televangelist Jerry Falwell. Finally, Reagan expressed an unrelenting hostility toward the Soviet Union, describing it as an "evil empire." The collapse of communism and the demise of the Cold War at the end of the 1980s set the stage for a new configuration of American conservatism.

[*See also* Christian Coalition; Early Republic, Era of the; Fundamentalist Movement; New Deal Era, The; Republicanism; Sixties, The; Temperance and Prohibition.]

• Ronald Lora, *Conservative Minds in America,* 1972. George H. Nash, *The Conservative Intellectual Movement: Since 1945,* 1976. Robert M. Crunden, ed., *The Superfluous Men: Conservative Critics of American Culture,* 1900–1945, 1977. John P. East, *The American Conservative Movement: The Philosophical Founders,* 1986. Jerome L. Himmelstein, *To the Right: The Transformation of American Conservatism,* 1990. J. David Hoeveler Jr., *Watch on the Right: Conservative Intellectuals in the Reagan Era,* 1992. Mark Gerson, *The Neoconservative Vision: From the Cold War to the Culture Wars,* 1996.

—J. David Hoeveler

CONSTITUTION. The Constitution of 1787 is the basic governing document of the United States.

Intellectual Antecedents. The origins of the Constitution extend back centuries into Judeo-Christian culture, drawing upon the *Bible (the Hebrew scriptures far more than the Christian); the political culture of the classical world, particularly the five-hundred-year history of the Roman republic; natural law and natural rights doctrines formulated by ancient, medieval, and early modern writers; the rhetoric and philosophy of the Renaissance, Reformation, and Enlightenment; social contract theory; and English constitutional history, including common law, Whig libertarian tradition, and the formal enunciations in the Magna Carta (1215), Petition of Right (1628), Habeas Corpus Act (1679), and Bill of Rights (1689). Writers cited during the debate over the ratification of the Constitution included first and foremost the Baron de Montesquieu, followed by Sir William Blackstone, John Locke, Sir Edward Coke, Jean Louis DeLolme, James Harrington, Thomas Hobbes, David Hume, Richard Price, and Algernon Sidney. Frequently mentioned ancient writers included Aesop, Horace, Polybius, Socrates, Tacitus, and Virgil. The three most widely cited literary writers were Alexander Pope, William Shakespeare, and Jonathan Swift.

Historical Background. Despite the impressive breadth of these antecedents, the founders drew most heavily on their own experiences in America as colonists, rebels, and constitution-writers. Beginning with their colonial charters, the New World settlers had embodied their English common-law rights in over two hundred written documents. Only on rare occasions in England, and after repeated abuses by the monarch, had rights been asserted in writing. In America, however, as a matter of course, colonists wrote charters and sometimes adopted statements of rights based on English common law. In some colonies these guarantees were offered willingly by the crown or benevolent founders or proprietors as in Rhode Island, Pennsylvania, New Jersey, and the Carolinas. In others, rights had to be wrested from arbitrary or incompetent governors who tried to preserve the prerogatives of the crown or proprietors.

During the *Colonial Era, governments developed in each colony with a governor, judiciary, and (usually) bicameral legislature. Governors controlled appointments to the judiciary and to their council, which often served as the upper house of the legislature. Largely left to develop on their own before 1764, colonial governments had come to an accommodation in which assemblies, the lower houses of the legislatures, developed a degree of self-government through their control over all tax measures and appropriations, including the salaries of governors and the rest of the civil list. Assemblies effectively used this fiscal authority as a check on their governors.

After the end of the *Seven Years' War in 1763, Parliament pursued a new activist imperial policy toward its American colonies. One tax after another provoked vehement responses from colonial dissenters. When Parliament repealed the *Stamp Act in response to colonial protests, the Declaratory Act (1766) unequivocally asserted Parliament's undisputed authority to pass any legislation for the colonies: self-government was a grant, not a right. The colonists never accepted this absolutist position, and after a decade of friction, Americans declared their independence and embarked on an unprecedented period of constitution writing at both the state and national levels.

Between 1776 and 1780, Americans drafted and adopted state constitutions that, with few exceptions, created similar governments. Structurally the new state governments resembled their colonial predecessors with governors, bicameral legislatures (except for Pennsylvania, Georgia, and the self-proclaimed republic of Vermont), and judiciaries. Despite the commitment to the concept of separation of powers, real political power shifted almost exclusively to the assemblies. Assemblymen were elected annually. Governors, often elected by the legislatures for one-year terms, were denied the veto, and senates (the new upper houses) were not allowed to amend money bills. Most appointments, including the judiciary, were made annually by the assemblies. Judicial review of legislative acts hardly existed.

At the national level, the *Continental Congress, after more than a year of deliberation, submitted a draft constitution, the *Articles of Confederation, to the state legislatures for the requisite unanimous ratification. The Articles created a unicameral Congress in which each state had one vote, and delegates to Congress could serve only three years in any six-year period. Congress could act only on the states, not directly on the people. The Articles did not provide for a separate executive or judiciary, and according to Article II, the states retained their "sovereignty, freedom and independence" and Congress possessed only those powers "expressly delegated" to it. Lacking the power to regulate foreign or interstate commerce or levy taxes, Congress raised revenue by asking the states for money. Most important matters needed the approval of nine states in Congress. Amendments to the Articles required the approval of Congress and the unanimous ratification of the state legislatures.

Repeated efforts to strengthen Congress by amending the Articles or by persuading the states to grant specific additional powers failed. Congress could not pay its wartime debt and the states failed to pay their congressionally apportioned requisitions. When a postwar economic depression began in late 1784, most of the state legislatures enacted debtor-relief measures that sometimes violated the property rights of creditors. Sporadic violence by debtors, such as *Shays's Rebellion in Massachusetts, erupted in several states. Unable to address adequately these economic, political, social, and diplomatic crises, Congress on 21 February 1787 called a Constitutional Convention to meet in *Philadelphia in May "for the sole and express purpose of revising the Articles of Confederation" so they would be "adequate to the exigencies of government and the preservation of the Union."

In fact, when the *Constitutional Convention of 1787 convened, the delegates voted immediately to abandon the Articles of Confederation and to draft a new constitution that would create a national government. The Virginia Plan, based mainly on the ideas of James *Madison, served as the Convention agenda. After four months, thirty-nine delegates signed the document on 17 September 1787. Every part of the new Constitution was found either in a state constitution, the Articles of Confederation, or the *Northwest Ordinance (passed two months earlier by Congress). Despite this apparent lack of originality, the new Constitution was unique in the way it married the concepts of separation of powers, checks and balances, and *federalism.

Provisions of the Constitution. The Constitution consisted of seven articles introduced by a preamble setting forth the aims of the American people. The first seven words of the preamble heralded a profound change: "We the People of the United States." The people—not the states—entered into this new compact to "form a more perfect Union, establish Justice, insure domestic Tranquility, provide for the common defence, promote the general Welfare, and secure the Blessings of Liberty to ourselves and our Posterity."

The first article—half of the entire document—dealt with the legislative branch of the new government. All legislative power was given to a bicameral Congress composed of a Senate and House of Representatives. Each state was to have two senators elected for a six-year term by the state legislatures. The vice president of the United States served as the Senate's president and could vote only to break ties.

Members of the House of Representatives, elected for two-year terms, were to be apportioned among the states on the basis of population, counting each slave as three-fifths of a person. Individuals qualified to vote for the lower house of their state's legislature were eligible to vote for that state's federal representatives. Every ten years a federal census would be taken, after which Congress would reapportion representatives among the states. All revenue bills had to originate in the House but the Senate could offer amendments.

The regulations for electing Congress were left to each state legislature, but Congress could alter such rules. Congress had to assemble at least once a year. Each house elected its own officers, adopted its own rules, kept its own journals, and judged the elections and qualifications of its members. Recall and mandatory term limits were eliminated. Members' salaries were to be set by law and paid by the federal treasury. No member could hold another federal office.

Congress was specifically empowered to lay and collect taxes, borrow money, regulate foreign and interstate commerce, establish rules for naturalization and uniform bankruptcy laws, coin money, fix the standard of weights and measures, punish counterfeiters, establish a post office, grant copyrights and patents, create inferior judicial courts, define and punish piracy and crimes at sea, declare war, raise and maintain an army and navy, provide rules for the state militias, exercise complete jurisdiction over the federal capital and other federal properties, and "make all Laws which shall be necessary and proper for carrying into Execution the foregoing Powers." The president had *veto power over any bill passed by Congress, subject to a congressional override by a two-thirds vote of each house.

The Constitution specifically prohibited Congress from passing bills of attainder, ex post facto laws, and export duties; granting titles of nobility; suspending the writ of habeas corpus except in emergencies; and prohibiting the foreign slave trade before 1808. The states, too, were prohibited from passing bills of attainder, ex post facto laws, and laws impairing the obligation of contracts; coining money; issuing paper money; declaring anything but gold and silver legal tender; entering into treaties or alliances; or laying import or export duties without the consent of Congress.

Article II vested the executive power of the federal government in a president and vice president, both elected for four-year terms by specially chosen electors. The electors themselves were to be elected in a manner decided by each state legislature. The president, who had to be a natural-born citizen of the United States, was to be commander-in-chief of the military and the state militias when brought into federal service. He or she could grant pardons and reprieves, and, with the advice and consent of the Senate, make appointments and enter into treaties, subject to the approval of two-thirds of the senators present. The president, vice president, and all civil officers of the United States are removable from office on *impeachment by the House of Representatives and conviction by the Senate for "Treason, Bribery, or other High Crimes and Misdemeanors." When the president is impeached, the Chief Justice of the United States presides over the trial in the Senate.

The third branch of government—the judiciary—is the least defined in the Constitution. Article III provides for one *Supreme Court and such inferior courts as Congress shall create. Federal judges hold their appointments during good behavior and their salaries cannot be diminished during their tenure. The jurisdiction of the federal judiciary extends to all cases of law and equity arising under the Constitution, federal laws, and treaties; and to cases involving the United States, cases between citizens of different states, and other cases where a national venue was considered important. The original jurisdiction of the U.S. Supreme Court was spelled out; in all other cases the Court could exercise appellate jurisdiction in law and fact, with such exceptions as Congress might by law direct.

Jury trial was guaranteed in all criminal cases (except impeachments) and these trials had to be held in the state where the crime was committed. Treason was defined narrowly as waging war against the United States or adhering to, or giving aid and comfort to, the enemies of the United States. Conviction for treason needed the testimony in open court of two witnesses to the same overt act. Punishment for treason could not extend to family or friends of the guilty party.

Article IV provided that each state give "full faith and credit" to the public acts, records, and judicial proceedings of every other state. Citizens of each state were to be entitled to all of the "privileges and immunities of Citizens in the several States." States were required to extradite persons wanted for crimes in other states, and slaves who escaped to another state could not be freed. Congress was authorized to make rules and regulations for federal territories and to admit new states into the Union. The United States guaranteed every state a republican form of government, protection from foreign invasion, and (upon application of the state legislature or executive) assistance against domestic violence.

Unlike the Articles of Confederation, the Constitution provided for a realistic (though difficult) method of amendment. According to Article V, amendments to the Constitution could be proposed by two-thirds of both houses of Congress or by a constitutional convention that Congress must call at the request of two-thirds of the state legislatures. Proposed amendments could be adopted by the agreement of three-fourths of either the state legislatures or state ratifying conventions, whichever method Congress directs.

Article VI validated all debts and engagements entered into by the United States before the adoption of the Constitution and declared the Constitution, all laws made in pursuance of it, and all treaties to be the supreme law of the land, notwithstanding anything in the constitution or laws of any state. Article VI also required all federal and state officials to take an oath to support the Constitution, but prohibited any religious test for federal officeholding.

Ratification. Unlike the Articles of Confederation, unanimous ratification by the state legislatures was not required to adopt the Constitution. Article VII provided that the ratification of nine state conventions would be sufficient to establish the Constitution among the ratifying states.

The Constitutional Convention sent the engrossed manuscript Constitution to Congress, which transmitted the new form of government to the states for their ratification in specially elected conventions. An intense public debate over the Constitution raged for almost a year. In June 1788 New Hampshire became the ninth state to ratify, followed quickly by Virginia and New York. A key issue in this debate focused on the kind of government to be created by the Constitution: Did Article I, section 8, grant Congress power to do anything necessary to promote the general welfare and national defense, or did it grant to Congress only limited, enumerated powers? In other words, would the new government be a consolidated national government that would eliminate the sovereignty of the states or would it be a limited government of specified powers that would leave the states sovereign and free to act in all other matters? Coupled with this issue was the debate over the omission of a federal bill of rights, which supporters of the Constitution argued was unnecessary because the Constitution's internal checks on government would prevent any violation of rights.

In several states, ratification was achieved only with a promise that amendments to the Constitution, especially a bill of rights, would be proposed in the first Congress. Largely through the efforts of James Madison, the first Congress in September 1789 proposed a *Bill of Rights, which was adopted with little public debate in December 1791.

A Living Document. The debate over the breadth of federal power was renewed soon after the establishment of the new federal government. In essence, the question was how to interpret the "necessary and proper" clause. Should the Constitution be broadly or strictly interpreted? The followers of Alexander *Hamilton advocated a broad interpretation, which President George *Washington endorsed. The election of Thomas *Jefferson as president in the "Revolution of 1800" heralded a shift to a stricter interpretation that circumscribed the actions of the federal government. The *Civil War and the three constitutional amendments adopted in its aftermath, particularly the *Fourteenth Amendment, allowed the federal government in the twentieth century to expand the protections embodied in the Bill of Rights to include actions by state and municipal governments. Over the years, ebbs and flows occurred in how the branches of the federal government viewed their constitutional powers and responsibilities. Not until the *New Deal Era and *World War II did the expansion of federal power through a broad reading of the Constitution's national defense, commerce, and general-welfare clauses overwhelmingly change the nature of the relationship between the states and the federal government. As the twentieth century ended, the debate over federalism continued.

[*See also* Albany Congress; Early Republic, Era of the; Federal Government; Republicanism; Revolution and Constitution, Era of; Slavery: Development and Expansion of Slavery; States' Rights; Suffrage; Taxation.]

• Robert Allen Rutland, *The Ordeal of the Constitution: The Antifederalists and the Ratification Struggle of 1787–1788,* 1966. Gordon S. Wood, *The Creation of the American Republic, 1776–1787,* 1969. Merrill Jensen, John P. Kaminski, and Gaspare J. Saladino, eds., *The Documentary History of the Ratification of the Constitution,* 15 vols. to date, 1976–. Willi Paul Adams, *The First American Constitutions: Republican Ideology and the Making of the State Constitutions in the Revolutionary Era,* 1980, expanded ed., 2000. Forrest McDonald, *Novus Ordo Seclorum: The Intellectual Origins of the Constitution,* 1985. Richard B. Morris, *The Forging of the Union, 1781–1789,* 1987. Patrick T. Conley and John P. Kaminski, eds., *The Constitution and the States: The Role of the Original Thirteen in the Framing and Adoption of the Federal Constitution,* 1988. Bernard Schwartz, *The Great Rights of Mankind: A History of the American Bill of Rights,* expanded ed., 1992. Gordon S. Wood, *The Radicalism of the American Revolution,* 1992.

—John P. Kaminski

CONSTITUTIONAL CONVENTION OF 1787. By late 1786, only three years after the end of the *Revolutionary War, most Americans had concluded that the Confederation Congress was too weak to deal with the social, economic, political, and diplomatic problems confronting the nation. Minimally, Congress needed power to tax through a tariff and to regulate foreign and interstate commerce. Repeated attempts to amend the *Articles of Confederation or to persuade the states to grant Congress special powers had failed to obtain the required unanimous approval of the state legislatures. Finally, on 21 February 1787, Congress called for a convention in *Philadelphia to revise the articles.

Fifty-five delegates from twelve states attended at one time or another between May and September 1787. Only Rhode Island refused to send delegates. Prominent Revolutionary leaders among the delegates included George *Washington and George Mason of Virginia, Benjamin *Franklin and Robert Morris of Pennsylvania, Roger Sherman of Connecticut, and Delaware's John Dickinson. James *Madison and Edmund Randolph of Virginia, Alexander *Hamilton of New York, James Wilson and Gouverneur Morris of Pennsylvania, and South Carolina's Charles Pinckney also played crucial roles. Absent were Confederation Secretary for Foreign Affairs John *Jay and Secretary at War Henry Knox, Thomas *Jefferson and John *Adams (both on diplomatic assignment in Europe), Patrick *Henry and Richard Henry Lee of Virginia (both refused appointments), and Governors George Clinton of New York and John Hancock of Massachusetts. Indeed, only two sitting governors served as delegates. The delegates were generally far wealthier and better educated than the average American of the day. The convention rules granted each state one vote. Sessions were held in Pennsylvania's state house (now Independence Hall), and delegates were sworn to secrecy.

Ignoring their instructions only to amend the Articles of Confederation, the delegates planned a completely new national government. James Madison's "Virginia Plan," reflecting the interest of the three largest states (Virginia, Massachusetts, and Pennsylvania), proposed a bicameral legislature, with representation in each house proportional to population. The smaller states rallied around the "New Jersey Plan," which preserved the unicameral Congress of the Articles, with equal state representation. After the convention rejected this plan in mid-June, a consensus formed around the "Connecticut Compromise" providing for a bicameral system, with equal state representation in the upper house and proportional representation in the lower house.

A five-man Committee of Detail organized the agreed-upon provisions into a draft constitution, which, after further revision, was put in final form by a five-man Committee of Style, appointed on 8 September. Gouverneur Morris was the primary author. As adjournment neared, the convention considered and rejected both a *Bill of Rights and a follow-up convention to consider amendments. Jacob Shallus prepared a four-page engrossed *Constitution on parchment, and thirty-nine delegates signed it on 17 September 1787. Three delegates in attendance—the Virginians Randolph and Mason, and Elbridge Gerry of Massachusetts—refused to sign.

The proposed Constitution radically changed the federal government's structure and its relationship with the states and the people, transferring many powers from the states to the central government. Abandoning the forbidding amendment procedure of the Articles of Confederation, the document provided that adoption by nine state conventions would establish the Constitution among the ratifying states. After almost a year of intense public debate, eleven states ratified the new Constitution.

[*See also* Revolution and Constitution, Era of.]

• Max Farrand, ed., *The Records of the Federal Convention of 1787,* 3 vols., 1911; reprint 1966. Carl Van Doren, *The Great Rehearsal,* 1948.

—John P. Kaminski

CONSUMER CULTURE. The term "consumer culture" refers to cultures in which mass consumption and production both fuel the economy and shape perceptions, values, desires, and constructions of personal identity. Economic developments, demographic trends, and new technologies profoundly influence the scope and scale of consumer culture. *Social class, *gender, ethnicity, region, and age all affect definitions of consumer identity and attitudes about the legitimacy of consumer-centered lifestyles.

The intellectual roots of consumer culture date to seventeenth-century Western Europe and the antimercantilist idea that domestic markets could adequately sustain national economies. By the 1770s, as early capitalist ideology and early *industrialization took hold in England, a widespread culture of consumption arose. This early English consumer culture influenced life in colonial America. Colonists acquired English-made goods as markers of status and respectability. Despite Jeffersonian Republican and religious protests against luxury and aristocratic emulation, the ties between gentility and commodity consumption grew after the *Revolutionary War, especially as early industrialization and commercial and transportation revolutions made consumer goods more easily available and less expensive. These developments led white women in middle-class, urban communities to relinquish many familiar tasks of *domestic labor, such as making soap. By the 1830s, consumption had become central to how middle-class women defined themselves as wives and mothers.

Consumer culture began to assume its modern contours after the *Civil War. The explosive growth of industrialization and its accompanying techniques of mass distribution made the consumption of ready-made goods possible on an unprecedented scale. *Urbanization and population growth broadened markets for consumption. By 1900, *department stores, mail-order catalogs, and mass-circulated *magazines made consumer culture broadly accessible. As *mass production pushed prices down, and as department stores offered cheap knockoffs of expensive goods, immigrants and working-class Americans got their own taste of consumerism. Consumer culture had also expanded beyond its urban base. Mass magazines and catalogs kept the remotest corners of the nation abreast of new styles and merchandise.

Some Americans resisted consumerism. In 1899, the cultural critic Thorstein *Veblen derided what he called the "conspicuous consumption" of luxury goods. Progressives both condemned the "profligate" consuming patterns of workers and immigrants and reacted politically when corporate monopolies, inflation, and unsafe merchandise threatened their own increasingly commodity-centered lifestyles. Some, like Florence *Kelley, sought to organize a *consumer movement as a force for reform, but most middle-class Americans simply took consumerism for granted.

The rise of national "brand name" products added a new dynamic to consumer culture. During the early 1900s, merchandisers began promoting brand names in order to gain leverage in marketing and distributing their wares. By the 1920s, much of this promotional work had passed to *advertising agencies. Using dramatic graphics and carefully honed copy to associate brand name products with desirable personality traits and social values, advertising agencies became cultural arbiters of style and taste.

Some historians suggest that brand names, national advertising campaigns, the movies, and, by the 1930s, chain stores and *radio led to a homogenization of American culture. But ethnic enclaves, unions, and competing values contributed to distinct cultures of consumption. During the 1950s, however, economic prosperity, *suburbanization, and a *Cold War emphasis on Americanism and idealized nuclear families undermined these distinctions. With the advent of *television and ubiquitous commercial icons like Holiday Inn and *McDonald's, and the spread of *shopping centers and malls, Americans absorbed a larger set of shared cultural references and consumer-centered aspirations.

Critics like Vance Packard (*The Hidden Persuaders,* 1957) and cultural subgroups like the Beat poets and writers of the 1950s and the 1960s counterculture rejected what they saw as the homogenizing effects of mass consumer culture. But even in the postwar era, demographically distinct cultures of consumption existed—in part, because marketers increasingly relied upon market segmentation. Women's consumerism continued to revolve primarily around home and family. *Leisure and entertainment industries, in particular, triumphed by targeting previously untapped markets. Record companies focused on the ascendant youth culture and its growing access to disposable income. Sporting-goods makers and magazines like *Playboy* profited by exploiting the consumer interests of men. African-American entrepreneurs succeeded by meeting the needs and interests of black shoppers. Other manufacturers courted consumers abroad. U.S. foreign policy-makers encouraged this globalization of American consumer culture as a weapon in the Cold War.

Consumer culture's ability to nurture common bonds while appealing to the interests of distinct groups continues. By meaning different things to different people, while nonetheless upholding the centrality of commodity consumption, consumer culture managed to deflect critics and become a powerful presence in American society.

[*See also* Capitalism; Fifties, The; Foreign Relations: The Cultural Dimension; Sixties, The.]

• Daniel Horowitz, *The Morality of Spending,* 1985. Elaine Tyler May, *Homeward Bound,* 1988. Elaine Abelson, *When Ladies Go A-Thieving: Middle-Class Shoplifters in the Victorian Department Store,* 1989. Susan Strasser, *Satisfaction Guaranteed: The Making of the American Mass Market,* 1989. Lizabeth Cohen, *Making a New Deal,* 1990. William Leach, *Land of Desire,* 1993.

—Margaret Finnegan

CONSUMER MOVEMENT. The modern consumer movement arose in the *Progressive Era, as citizens concerned about unsafe products and environmental hazards used lobbying, voting, and journalistic exposés to press for government protection. In the same vein, the Consumers Union (1936), publisher of *Consumer Reports,* tests products for safety, economy, and reliability, to give consumers an objective basis for choice.

Some Progressive reformers espoused a different kind of consumer activism, however, mobilizing shoppers' purchasing power to promote social change. Florence *Kelley's *National Consumers' League (1899), emphasizing the social link between middle-class women shoppers and the workers who produced the goods they bought, mobilized consumer pressure to champion protective legislation for workers, especially women and children. Woman suffragists, likewise, used consumer pressure to demand respect and support from businesses that needed their patronage. Such socially engaged consumerism actually had long historical antecedents, including Revolutionary Era patriots who had boycotted English tea and textiles and abolitionists who had refused to purchase goods made of slave-produced cotton.

Consumer activism revived in the late 1960s, flourished in the 1970s, and, despite a conservative backlash against government regulation, survived in diminished form in the 1990s. A by-product of 1960s social activism, consumer advocates insisted on citizens' rights to safe and reasonably priced goods and services and to the full disclosure of product information. The lawyer Ralph *Nader gained fame for *Unsafe at Any Speed* (1965), which detailed safety hazards plaguing General Motors' (GM) Corvair automobile. Using $425,000 won in an invasion-of-privacy suit against GM in 1970, Nader founded numerous consumer groups, nicknamed "Nader's Raiders," that pursued legal challenges to unsafe products and demanded greater government protection for consumers. The formation of the Consumer Federation of America (1968), the Occupational Safety and Health Administration (1970), and the Consumer Product Safety Commission (1972) attested to the movement's success but also to its regulatory and legalistic bent. Focused on consumers' rights, the modern movement downplayed the power of consumers to effect social change.

But while the idea of mobilizing purchasing power to achieve larger social goals was not a hallmark of the post-1960 consumer movement, it did survive. Many Americans boycotted grapes in the 1970s to support *migratory agricultural workers' unionization campaign. In the 1980s and 1990s, religious groups organized boycotts of corporations that produced movies, TV shows and records they considered offensive; labor unions called for boycotts of nonunion companies; and activists urged consumers to reject products made in unsafe Third World factories paying starvation wages or employing *child labor.

[*See also* Consumer Culture.]

• David Bollier, *Citizen Action and Other Big Ideas: A History of Ralph Nader and the Modern Consumer Movement,* 1989. Margaret Finnegan, *Selling Suffrage: Consumer Culture and Votes for Women,* 1998.

—Margaret Finnegan

CONTAINMENT. The term "containment" signifies the fundamental American politico-military strategy of the *Cold War: resistance, in association with compatible allies, to the perceived expansionary tendencies of the Soviet Union, and later of other communist states. Containment's parentage could be traced to Thucydides' accounts of the Peloponnesian War. More immediately, Winston Churchill, Britain's *World War II prime minister, called privately for resistance to Soviet expansionism in 1944–1945, repeating the theme publicly in his 5 March 1945, "Iron Curtain" speech at Fulton, Missouri. George *Kennan, a U.S. diplomat and Soviet expert, made a similar case in his "long telegram" of 22 February 1946 and gave it authoritative definition as director of the State Department's policy-planning staff in a July 1947 *Foreign Affairs* article. Soviet expansionism, he warned, born of historical, ideological, and political impulses, must be contained by an American-led coalition until time and events forced an internal transformation.

These ideas received institutional expression in the *Truman Doctrine, promulgated by President Harry S. *Truman in March 1947, pledging support for Greece and Turkey and for freedom generally; in the *Marshall Plan of 1948, committing the United States to the politico-economic reconstruction of Western Europe; and decisively in the formation of the *North Atlantic Treaty Organization in 1949.

The containment doctrine was always controversial. In *The Cold War* (1947), the influential columnist Walter *Lippmann criticized Truman's excessively open-ended promises to strengthen regimes against communism. Kennan himself soon came to regret the universalist and militaristic twist his formulation received. Left-wing politicians, beginning with former vice president Henry A. Wallace, typically saw it as provocative or as a cover for capitalist exploitation, while the right (most memorably in the *Republican party's 1952 call for the "liberation" of countries behind the Iron Curtain) frequently condemned it as too passive.

Receiving an enlarged definition in the *National Security Council's April 1950 document (NSC-68), containment underpinned the globalization of American diplomacy that began with the *Korean War in 1950 and continued with bilateral treaties and regional pacts like the Southeast Asia Treaty Organization (1954) and the Central Treaty Organization (1959). Defensively conceived, containment steadily became a more aggressive, multifaceted response to complex postcolonial crises in many unstable countries, notably Vietnam. In Vietnam, as in other ex-colonial nations, nationalism was often confused with communism, and containment rhetoric based on European precedents applied uncritically to incomparable situations.

After 1972, containment seemed vindicated by the era of détente and *nuclear arms control treaties. However, the Soviet invasion of Afghanistan in 1979 and the confrontational stance of President Ronald *Reagan's first term, led to renewed tensions until 1985, when Mikhail Gorbachev inaugurated, and Reagan progressively encouraged, the Soviet retreat that ended the *Cold War in 1989.

Encompassing an array of shifting concepts and policy variations, containment was, essentially, a creative compromise by successive U.S. administrations determined to resist Soviet/communist expansionism but understanding the fundamental need to avoid nuclear war.

[*See also* Anticommunism; Foreign Relations; National Security Council Document #68; Progressive Party of 1948.]

• John Lewis Gaddis, *Strategies of Containment,* 1982. Michael S. Sherry, *In the Shadow of War,* 1995.

—Fraser J. Harbutt

CONTINENTAL CONGRESS (1774–1776). The ten years between the *Stamp Act crisis and the closing of the port of *Boston in 1774 saw an erosion of British authority throughout the thirteen mainland colonies. In particular, the colonists' efforts to avoid British taxation led to a fatal crisis within the imperial order. When neither rioting nor royal petitions won for the colonists the political settlement they wished, provincials inspired by members of the Boston Whig movement began to systematically destroy taxed tea or otherwise impede its sale. The resulting crisis led Parliament to pass the Boston Port Bill (Coercive Acts), which in turn led to the calling of the First Continental Congress. This body, drawn from the provincial gentry, was primarily a last-ditch effort to seek legal redress and reform within the empire. Meeting in *Philadelphia on 5 September 1774, the fifty-five delegates from all the colonies except Georgia elected Peyton Randolph of Virginia president of the congress; denounced the Coercive Acts; toyed with the Pennsylvanian Joseph Galloway's "Plan of Union," which would have kept the colonies in the empire; and formulated an address to George III. Adjourning on 26 October, the delegates agreed to reassemble the following year to set a course of action.

The Second Continental Congress, which convened in May 1775, contained both a conservative element, headed by John *Jay of New York and Pennsylvania's John Dickinson (1732–1808), and a radical group leaning toward independence. The Battles of Lexington and Concord, in April 1775, and the subsequent siege of the British army in Boston by a provincial militia army, drove the majority of congressional delegates into the radical camp, where John *Adams, Thomas *Jefferson, Richard Henry Lee (1732–1794), and others advocated the end of the imperial relationship. In mid-June 1775, Congress voted to raise an army and named George *Washington to lead it. In July 1776, the delegates issued the *Declaration of Independence, proclaiming the colonies free from Great Britain, a move widely celebrated across America. By the *Articles of Confederation, debated for months and finally adopted on 15 November 1777, the delegates constituted themselves as a unicameral legislative body that functioned as the central authority of the new nation until 1788. These representatives faced a host of domestic, military, and diplomatic problems. Foremost among these were raising and maintaining a Continental Army to fight the *Revolutionary War, finance and money-supply issues, and launching overseas diplomatic initiatives. Factional fighting magnified these issues. Although the Continental Congress provided sufficient political leadership for the colonists to win the war, the financial and diplomatic problems faced by the new nation ultimately led to the *Constitutional Convention of 1787 and a new government.

[*See also* Albany Congress; Boston Tea Party; Bunker Hill, Battle of; Committees of Correspondence; Constitution; Revolution and Constitution, Era of.]

• Jack Rakove, *The Beginnings of National Politics: An Interpretive History of the Continental Congress,* 1979. Calvin Jillson and Rick K. Wilson, *Congressional Dynamics: Structure, Coordination, and Choice in the First American Congress, 1774–1789,* 1994.

—Brendan McConville

CONTRACEPTION. *See* Birth Control and Family Planning.

COOLIDGE, CALVIN (1872–1933), thirtieth president of the United States. Born in Plymouth, Vermont, John Calvin Coolidge graduated from Amherst College and worked as an attorney before entering politics as a Republican. After holding various local and state offices, he was elected governor of Massachusetts in 1918. He won national attention in 1919 by using state troops against striking *Boston police. Elected vice president in 1920, he became president upon Warren *Harding's death in 1923. He won election in his own right in 1924, easily defeating the Democrat John W. Davis and the Progressive Robert *La Follette. Choosing not to seek an additional term, he left the White House in 1929, assuring the nation that continued prosperity lay ahead. As his successor Herbert *Hoover coped with the Great Depression, Coolidge confined himself to writing articles extolling conservative principles.

When he was in office, Coolidge's dour Yankee taciturnity became the target of humorists. In contrast to the scandal-ridden Harding administration, Coolidge symbolized the older virtues of honesty and sober practicality. In domestic affairs, Coolidge embraced the complementary ideologies of Treasury Secretary Andrew Mellon (1855–1937) and Commerce Secretary Hoover. Combining Mellon's belief in unrestricted *capitalism with Hoover's philosophy of corporate cooperation and voluntaristic effort for humane purposes, Coolidge presided over the most conservative administration in modern American history—an administration committed to freeing business from governmental restraints, raising *tariffs to benefit industry, lowering taxes for the wealthy, and suppressing labor unions. He twice vetoed the *McNary-Haugen Bill designed to raise agricultural prices to help economically depressed farmers.

In foreign policy, the *Washington Naval Arms Conference of 1922, an early arms-control effort negotiated by Secretary of State Charles Evans *Hughes, temporarily slowed an arms race among the world's naval powers. In general, however, Coolidge continued the nation's post–*World War I retreat from world affairs. Accepting a plan devised by Vice President Charles G. Dawes (1865–1951), the Coolidge administration somewhat scaled back the disastrous reparation payments that the 1919 Versailles treaty had imposed on defeated Germany, but the effect was neutralized by high U.S. tariffs and Germany's worsening economy. In Latin America, the government under Coolidge somewhat modified the aggressive interventionism of previous years, while encouraging the expanding economic penetration of U.S. corporations. Although the *Kellogg-Briand Pact of 1928, signed by the United States and France along with many other nations, renounced war as an instrument of national policy, its benign optimism and lack of enforcement provisions marked an appropriate end to an administration based on the premise that government functioned best when it functioned least.

[*See also* Conservatism; Depressions, Economic; Foreign Relations: U.S. Relations with Latin America; Isolationism; Republican Party; Twenties, The.]

• Robert Ferrell, *The Presidency of Calvin Coolidge*, 1994.

—David Burner

COOPER, JAMES FENIMORE (1789–1851), novelist. Brought up in Cooperstown, New York, a pioneer settlement presided over by his father, Cooper was thirty when he published his first novel, *Precaution* (1820). That it seemed English to its readers offers a gauge to Cooper's larger significance: In 1820, Americans tended to associate literature exclusively with the Old World. His second novel, *The Spy* (1821), was aggressively American and a popular success. This tale of the *Revolutionary War launched a career that produced thirty more novels as well as histories and travel books.

America's first professional novelist, Cooper helped prove that America could sustain an imaginative writer, both economically and aesthetically. Although his work relied on conventions established by British writers, especially Sir Walter Scott, he created American scenes and characters, dramatized the nation's history, and embodied what he took to be republican principles. During the 1820s and 1830s, he was one of the world's best-selling writers. He largely invented the genre of sea fiction. Ten of his novels describe settling the continent; these often explore the moral and political conflicts that arose from the imposition of the forms of European civilization on the New World wilderness and the Native Americans. Cooper's greatest achievement was the Leather-Stocking series: *The Pioneers* (1823), *The Last of the Mohicans* (1826), *The Prairie* (1827), *The Pathfinder* (1840), and *The Deerslayer* (1841). The hero of these tales is Natty Bumppo, hunter, scout, and warrior of the wilderness. Accompanied by his Delaware friend Chingachgook, Natty became one of the nation's first and most enduring mythic archetypes.

[*See also* Indian History and Culture: The Indian in Popular Culture; Literature: Early National and Antebellum Eras.]

• James Grossman, *James Fenimore Cooper*, 1949.

—Stephen Railton

COPLAND, AARON (1900–1990), composer, pianist, conductor, and writer. Born in Brooklyn, the son of Russian-Jewish immigrants, Copland found his most important teacher, Nadia Boulanger, in Paris (1921–1924). She helped guide his understanding of Europe's master composers while encouraging his inclination to assert his American identity.

On his return to the States, he won important friends, including, notably, the conductor Serge Koussevitzky. The modernity of Copland's *Music for the Theatre* (1925), *Piano Concerto* (1926), and *Piano Variations* (1930) perplexed some listeners and delighted others. Even as he continued to write challenging pieces like the *Piano Sonata* (1941), some more accessible works—including *El Salón México* (1936); ballet scores for Eugene Loring (*Billy the Kid*, 1938), Agnes de Mille (*Rodeo*, 1942), and Martha *Graham (*Appalachian Spring*, 1944); the patriotic *Fanfare for the Common Man* and *Lincoln Portrait* (both 1942); and film music for *Our Town* (1940) and *The Red Pony* (1948)—made him by midcentury the best-known American concert composer of his time. For some of his later scores—including the *Piano Fantasy* (1957), *Connotations* (1962), and *Inscape* (1967)—he adapted Arnold Schoenberg's twelve-tone method of composition.

Working within the tradition of European art music, though indebted as well to *jazz and the folk musics of the Americas, Copland produced a vibrant body of work resonant of American life in style and content. His writings include *What to Listen for in Music* (1939) and *Our New Music* (1941, rev. 1968). Exceptionally generous, he also helped the careers of numerous composers as teacher, benefactor, concert organizer, critic, and friend.

[*See also* Dance; Music: Classical Music.]

• Aaron Copland and Vivian Perlis, *Copland: 1900 through 1942*, 1984. Aaron Copland and Vivian Perlis, *Copland since 1943*, 1989. Howard Pollack, *Aaron Copland: The Life and Work of an Uncommon Man*, 1999.

—Howard J. Pollack

COPLEY, JOHN SINGLETON (1738–1815), leading painter of colonial *Boston. Of Irish immigrant origins, Copley spent his early childhood in the commercial district of Long Wharf, where his parents sold tobacco. After his father's death and his mother's remarriage in 1748 to the English-born printmaker Peter Pelham, he moved to Lindel's Row near the Town House, an area of small business trade as well as artisans' studios and shops. Pelham introduced Copley to English artistic culture through books on theory and his own prints. After Pelham's death in 1751, Copley supported his mother and half-brother Henry by portrait painting, in which he was largely self-trained. In 1769, he married Susanna Clarke.

Copley painted approximately 350 pictures that gratified the expanding American taste for high style and anglicized images. In the new *consumer culture of Boston, Copley portrayed merchants, landowners, and professionals clothed in expensive silks and surrounded by Chippendale furniture, pedigree dogs, and cultivated flowers that collectively evoked their elite status. His sitters included John Hancock, Paul *Revere, Jeremiah Lee, Joseph Warren, Samuel *Adams, Dorothy Quincy, Mercy Otis *Warren, and members of the Boylston and Amory families. His characteristically precise style resulted in crisply defined images and compositions in which objects, whether significant or insignificant, are assigned equal importance. That aesthetic practice elicited the critical attention of the London artists Sir Joshua Reynolds and the Pennsylvania-born Benjamin West (1738–1820), who urged him to emigrate, which the politically nonpartisan Copley did in 1774.

After a year of studying and painting in Italy, Copley by 1776 was living with his family in London's Leicester Square. In England he turned to large historical subjects, such as *Watson and the Shark* (1778), *The Death of the Earl of Chatham* (1779), *The Death of Major Peirson* (1782–1784), and *The Siege of Gibraltar* (1787–1791).

[*See also* Colonial Era; Painting: To 1945.]

• Jules Prown, *John Singleton Copley,* 2 vols., 1966. Carrie Rebora and Paul Staiti, *John Singleton Copley in England,* 1995.

—Paul Staiti

CORONADO, FRANCISCO VÁZQUEZ DE (1510–1554), explorer. A minor noble from Salamanca, Spain, Coronado sought his fortune in Mexico at age twenty-five, married Beatríz de Estrada within two years, and in 1538 became provincial governor of Nueva Galicia. Viceroy Antonio de Mendoza, spurred by tales of marvelous realms to the north, commissioned him to locate the Seven Cities of Cíbola and take over their wealth. Coronado risked much of his wife's estate to help finance the expedition, which included approximately 350 Spaniards, 1,000 Amerindian "volunteers," and 1,500 animals. Departing Culiacán on 22 April 1540, the reconnaissance party reached contemporary Arizona, *California, New Mexico, Texas, Oklahoma, and Kansas, revealing Cíbola as Zuñi pueblos and the fabulous Kingdom of Quivira as a Wichita village. Discouraged by the lack of gold, worried about maintaining the army, and debilitated by a head injury, Coronado ordered the force home in early spring 1542. Accounting the mission a failure, the Crown charged him with incompetence and mistreatment of native peoples, but the Audiencia of Mexico exonerated him. Removed from the governorship, he held municipal office in Mexico City, where he died.

Coronado's excursion forewarned the pueblo peoples about Spanish intentions to subjugate and convert them even as his unenthusiastic reports about the American *Southwest soured New Spain's interest in the region for forty years. Coronado demonstrated the vast expanse of the North American landmass, information readily assimilated into sixteenth-century maps, but his knowledge of the interior did not circulate widely, and cartographers remained ignorant of its details until the eighteenth century.

[*See also* Exploration, Conquest, and Settlement, Era of European; Spanish Settlements in North America.]

• Herbert E. Bolton, *Coronado: Knight of Pueblos and Plains,* 1949; reprint 1990. George P. Hammond and Agapito Rey, eds., *Narratives of the Coronado Expedition 1540–1542,* 1940.

—Charles L. Cohen

CORPORATION FOR PUBLIC BROADCASTING. *See* Public Broadcasting.

CORPORATISM refers both to a distinctive institutional structure and a body of political thought. Its central characteristic is a system of governance exercised through an established set of private associations linking business, labor, agriculture, and other functional groups with each other and with the state for purposes of achieving political stability and harmonious economic and social development. In most versions of corporatism, business, labor, agricultural, and professional societies have representation in joint councils that share power with public agencies and theoretically serve all legitimate interests.

Modern corporatist thought, originating in response to nineteenth-century *liberalism and *socialism, called in essence for modernized guilds and estates that could recreate a harmonious moral order grounded in organic social relationships. Its first theorists were primarily Roman Catholics and aristocrats. By the end of *World War I, however, secular, laboristic, and technocratic versions had appeared as well, some of whose advocates discerned a modern corporatism in the institutional machinery produced by war mobilization. Subsequently, fascist theorists in Europe urged that the state itself be turned into a corporative apparatus, but efforts purporting to do this, notably in Italy and Germany, were mostly a camouflage for dictatorships.

Fascist-style corporatism had little appeal in liberal democracies. But new forms of governance through state-society partnerships did attract supporters who produced designs for a corporative apparatus operating alongside the liberal state. In the United States, where reformers and businesspeople desire to remedy market failures while minimizing governmental growth, the result was a "Progressivism" stressing public-spirited private "associational action" rather than expanded public administration. Such was the approach advocated by the *National Civic Federation (founded in 1900) and later by Herbert *Hoover, who, as secretary of commerce (1921–1928) and then as president, sought to establish an associational structure that would make state bureaucratic growth unnecessary.

The United States came closest to being "corporatized" during the Great Depression of the 1930s, when President Franklin Delano *Roosevelt's initial alternative to a failed Hooverism, the *National Recovery Administration (NRA), a more coercive associationalism under which the state would force noncooperators into line. In practice, however, the NRA worked badly, and following its invalidation by the *Supreme Court in 1935, the New Deal moved toward the creation of an enlarged welfare and regulatory state as more appropriate to liberal economic governance. Only in a few select industries and in special cases like defense mobilization did the Roosevelt administration's flirtation with corporatist solutions continue.

Still, *World War II and the postwar recovery undermined antibusiness liberalism, and associationalism again won support as the best way to meet economic and social needs without undue governmental expansion. A limited corporatism found new champions in the war-spawned Committee for Economic Development and a new array of government-established industrial councils. It was also central to the Dwight D. *Eisenhower administration's vision of a "corporate commonwealth" working to curb "socialism" by entrusting a share of the nation's governance to responsible wielders of private economic power. During the 1950s, America did not erect the corporatist institutions that were helping to guide European economic development, yet even in the United States development, the "cooperative mode" then in vogue meant an enlarged role for private organizations.

In the 1960s and 1970s, new critiques of the political economy altered the functions of both the federal government and the private intermediaries sharing in national governance. Still, some critics alleged that the new policies failed to achieve the balance between planning and freedom that highly developed capitalist economies required. The United States, so an articulate group of "reindustrializers" and "industrial policy" advocates argued, needed its own version of the corporatist machinery that was achieving such a balance abroad. Moreover, a growing body of academic theory held that corporatism was evolving spontaneously in advanced capitalist societies everywhere and could take forms compatible with liberal-democratic values.

In the 1980s and 1990s, agitation for making America more

"competitive" through corporatist policies continued but enjoyed little success. Serious presidential support ended with Ronald *Reagan's inauguration, and Americans repeatedly showed their unwillingness to embrace corporatist forms of state building. In the polity at large, corporatism encountered potent opposition from populist republican, and entrepreneurial forces that invoked historical experience and the persisting divisiveness of government, business, and labor as reasons why joint public–private planning could never work in the United States. Limited forms of corporatism did exist, however, in state-level development commissions and in partnerships for technical research.

Corporatism has been more at home in western Europe, Latin America, and Asia than in the United States. But variations of it entered into twentieth-century American political discourse, and recurring attempts at "corporatization" left an institutional residue and proved useful for certain public regulatory and promotional tasks.

[*See also* Capitalism; Depressions, Economic; Economic Development; New Deal Era, The; Progressive Era; Republicanism.]

• Eugene O. Golob, *The "Isms": A History and Evaluation,* 1954. James Weinstein, *The Corporate Ideal in the Liberal State, 1900–1918,* 1968. Philippe C. Schmitter and Gerhard Lembruch, eds., *Trends toward Corporatist Intermediation,* 1979. Robert Griffith, "Dwight D. Eisenhower and the Corporate Commonwealth," *American Historical Review* 87 (Feb. 1982): 87–122. Peter J. Williamson, *Corporatism in Perspective: An Introductory Guide to Corporatist Theory,* 1989. Ellis W. Hawley, "Society and Corporate Statism," in *Encyclopedia of American Social History,* eds. Mary K. Cayton, Elliott J. Gorn, and Peter W. Williams, 1993, pp. 621–36.

—Ellis W. Hawley

COTTON INDUSTRY. Cotton, the world's chief natural fiber for textile manufacturing and the principal ingredient in a variety of other products including foods and building materials, has figured prominently in American history. It played an important role in the growth of *slavery in the American *South and was the major export earner for the United States until around 1920. Since cotton requires semi-tropical growing conditions, it was grown exclusively in the southern states until the early twentieth century, when it expanded westward into Arizona and *California, and New Mexico.

The settlers of *Jamestown brought cottonseed to the New World, but they were unable to produce the fiber in significant quantities. The lack of a technology able to separate the seed from the lint retarded the production of cotton. Planters along the southeastern tidewater belt grew small amounts of long-staple "sea island" cotton, a variety with a longer fiber, but not enough for economic significance. When Eli *Whitney invented the cotton gin in 1793, short-staple cotton cultivation became economically feasible because farmers and planters could grow short-staple or "upland" varieties in large quantities and supply the modernized textile industry in Europe, particularly Britain, the world leader in cotton-textile production. By the early nineteenth century, cotton became so lucrative a crop that it was known as "white gold." Settlers and planters spread across the South seeking fertile land. Planters used slaves to supply the intensive hand labor essential to cultivating the crop, and cotton growing became synonymous with slavery. The South produced much of the cotton that went into British and European textiles and brought much wealth to southern planters.

The *Civil War ended slavery, but not cotton production. Indeed, cotton acreage increased, and by 1900 the U.S. production was over 10 million bales, twice the number grown in 1860. Cotton still created prosperity for large farmers and planters, but it too often caused poverty for small landowners, tenants, and sharecroppers. Small, self-sufficient farmers typically devoted some acres to cotton as a meager source of cash, but most tenants and sharecroppers fared even worse because they had too little land. As world production increased in the late nineteenth century, cotton prices declined and profits became harder to achieve, even for many large landowners. Adding to cotton growers' woes, the boll weevil, and destructive boring beetle, migrated from Mexico to Texas in the 1890s and gradually invaded the entire cotton belt. Production fell, many cotton workers were displaced, and southern agriculture diversified, but cotton remained the predominant crop. Insecticides and other control methods helped, but boll weevil depredations remained a chronic problem.

The economics of cotton cultivation worsened after *World War I as U.S. production expanded owing to improved varieties and cultivation practices as well as the greater production in California, Arizona, New Mexico, and especially Texas. By 1932 world production surpassed 23,000,000 bales, of which the U.S. portion was 13,000,000, glutting the cotton market. The price for American cotton fell below 10 cents per pound, the lowest level since the 1890s, and growers suffered severe hardship. Producers of other agricultural staples such as wheat and corn also faced saturated markets, but the severity of the economic depression in southern cotton-growing areas created the greatest human distress. To alleviate these conditions, the *Agricultural Adjustment Act of 1933 offered subsidized cotton prices in exchange for mandatory crop reduction to limit supply. Surpluses persisted, however, thanks to greater foreign production and the increased use of synthetics in textile manufacturing.

Post–*World War II changes further transformed cotton cultivation. Mechanization, particularly in weed control and harvesting, displaced great numbers of cotton laborers and sharecroppers, spurring southern *urbanization and the migration of millions of white and black southerners to the North and *West. The number of landowning cotton farmers also fell, from over 1 million in 1945 to approximately 30,000 by 2000. Yet total U.S. production at the end of the twentieth century remained high because of improved seed genetics and machinery, the expansion of irrigation, and new technologies to control the boll weevil and other insects.

At century's end, overproduction remained the cotton industry's fundamental problem. Growers continued to wrestle with low prices and to rely heavily on exports. Synthetics still held a large share of the fabric market, and cotton textile imports reduced the domestic market for raw cotton. While continuing to rely on various forms of federal support, the industry also conducted research and engaged in promotion activities to expand its market. Despite the industry's problems, cotton remained a viable crop and an important component of U.S. *agriculture as the new century began.

[*See also* African Americans; Clothing and Fashion; Foreign Trade, U.S.; Industrialization; Lowell Mills; New England; Sharecropping and Tenantry.]

• Harry Brown, *Cotton: History, Species, Varieties, Morphology, Breeding, Culture, Disease, Marketing, and Uses,* 1938. Gilbert C. Fite, *Cotton Fields No More: Southern Agriculture, 1865–1980,* 1984. Pete Daniel, *Breaking the Land: The Transformation of Cotton, Tobacco, and Rice Cultures since 1880,* 1985. Devra Weber, *Dark Sweat, White Gold: California Farmworkers, Cotton and the New Deal,* 1994. C. Wayne Smith and J. Tom Cothren, eds., *Cotton: Origin, History, Technology, and Production,* 1999.

—D. Clayton Brown

COUNCIL ON FOREIGN RELATIONS, nongovernmental policy institute established in 1921. Returning from the 1919 Paris Peace Conference, the scholars and diplomats advising President Woodrow *Wilson sought to perpetuate their association. In New York they found a community of bankers, lawyers, and investors hungry for expert knowledge of foreign conditions. This partnership of government officials, academics, and business leaders gave rise to the Council on Foreign Relations. Over time, it became a model for private public-affairs research institutes the world over.

In an isolationist era, the council invited to membership prominent Americans concerned with international affairs. Unabashedly elitist, the council nonetheless sought to stimulate public debate, primarily through its influential journal, *Foreign Affairs*.

Though independent of the government, the council led the campaign for U.S. engagement in combating fascism in the 1930s, supplied policy ideas during *World War II, and became a source of foreign-policy analysis and innovation as the *Cold War began. George *Kennan defined the policy of *containment in *Foreign Affairs* (under the pseudonym "X") in 1947; Dwight D. *Eisenhower led a council study group before becoming president; and Henry *Kissinger used a sabbatical year at the council's townhouse campus in New York to write his influential *Nuclear Weapons and Foreign Policy* (1957). From the business community, the banker David Rockefeller (1915–) guided the council's growth as chair and benefactor.

The *Vietnam War fractured the American consensus on foreign policy, and the council's preeminence suffered accordingly; new centers of expertise and deliberation sprang up outside the traditional East Coast establishment. The council became a flashpoint for ideological criticism from the right and left alike. The end of the Cold War in 1989 opened an array of new issues for research and analysis. Gradually adapting to these altered circumstances, the council established branches in Washington and around the country, enlarging its invited membership (close to three thousand by the 1990s) to include widely diverse viewpoints and opening many of its study and discussion groups to public *television and the *Internet.

[*See also* Foreign Relations; Internationalism; Isolationism.]

• Robert D. Schulzinger, *The Wise Men of Foreign Affairs,* 1984. Peter Grose, *Continuing the Inquiry: The Council on Foreign Relations at Seventy-five,* 1996.

—Peter Grose

COUNTRY MUSIC. *See* Music: Traditional Music.

COUNTY GOVERNMENTS. *See* Municipal and County Governments.

COURTS. *See* Federal Government, Judicial Branch; Municipal Judicial Systems.

COURTSHIP AND DATING. Colonial Americans generally cared more about the suitability of their marriage partners than about love, which they expected to develop after marriage. As a result, couples courted publicly and received aid and advice from families and neighbors. Premarital pregnancy rates were low during the seventeenth and early eighteenth centuries, and premarital sexual relations, even if pregnancy did not result, produced strong social and even legal pressures for marriage. Toward the end of the *Colonial Era, however, the ideal of romantic love gained wide currency. Many families allowed "bundling"—the controversial practice of letting courting couples spend an evening in bed together fully clothed, sometimes with a board placed between them. In the same period, the number of couples producing children before eight and a half months of marriage rose to nearly 30 percent.

By the early nineteenth century, couples began to consider romantic love prerequisite for marriage and based their unions on companionship. The era's fiction frequently drew on love themes, while articles, essays, and public orations stressed mutual respect, reciprocity, and romance as ingredients of good marriages. Young courting couples chose their own partners, and their letters focused on romance rather than on the practical matters that had dominated the correspondence of earlier generations. As romanticism developed, so did a new "separate spheres" ideology, which held that a woman's proper sphere of influence was in the home, and a man's in the public realm. As men and women increasingly occupied separate spheres, romance and candor became the strongest links between people living in different worlds.

As families and neighbors lost influence over couples, genteel standards of propriety came to guide courting behavior. Particularly after the *Civil War, an elaborate system of rules governing courting emerged. On a woman's invitation, men conducted formal "calls" to her home, during which couples might converse, read aloud, play parlor games, or give a piano recital. Parents gave their children privacy to court alone, often removing themselves from the parlor, trusting that decorum would prevent improper behavior. As the century progressed, however, new opportunities for interacting outside the home emerged. College enrollments rose, and students developed their own rules governing relationships. More women entered the workforce, particularly as schoolteachers. And especially in urban areas, new public diversions like dance halls, *amusement parks, theaters, and *parks enticed courting couples away from the safety of their parlors.

*World War I accelerated the disintegration of *etiquette based on the separate-spheres ideology, but popular magazines and advice columns quickly outlined new rules to replace the old. By 1925, traditional courtship had fallen out of fashion. Instead, young couples began to go on "dates," which differed significantly from courting: They cost money, focused less on long-term commitment, took place in public, and were initiated and paid for by men. Standards of sexual morality also changed, and the terms "necking" and "petting"—the former referring to kisses and caresses above the neck, the latter to the same below it—entered public discussion, giving names to previously unspoken private activities. In some circles, young people dated widely, rather than with one exclusive partner, since status hinged on being seen regularly with different desirable dates. During this period, for example, people considered dancing all evening with one partner a social failure: the "belle of the ball" was the young woman who danced with more partners than anyone else.

After *World War II, "going steady"—two people dating exclusively—partially replaced the competitive system of the interwar years. For one man to cut in on another at a dance, once considered flattering to the young woman, came to be deemed rude. A profusion of articles, columns, and even marriage classes defined the new dating etiquette: Boys "protected" girls, exercising control by opening car doors, ordering in restaurants, and taking responsibility for asking girls for dates, while girls behaved submissively to help their dates feel like men. Americans began marrying younger and more often that at any point in the century, and married couples had more children.

In the late 1960s and early 1970s, however, the sexual revolution—more a revolution in mores than in actual sexual behavior—turned this whole system on its head. Few of the carefully elaborated rules of the 1940s and 1950s still held. Couples still dated—some going steady—but women began to ask men on dates, many men stopped automatically reaching for the check, and living together became a widely accepted step toward marriage. The social norms governing sexuality fractured, with no unifying set of rules filling the void. "Singles" clubs and bars proliferated, and people of all ages sought congenial partners through dating services, the "personals" sections of magazines and newspapers, and Internet sites. Couples conducted courting on their own terms, as both men and women assumed more individual responsibility and initiative in finding a mate than at any previous time, while also exercising greater freedom in the process.

[*See also* Gender; Family; Illegitimacy; Internet and World-wide Web; Marriage and Divorce; Romantic Movement; Sexual Morality and Sex Reform; Urbanization.]

• E. S. Turner, *A History of Courting,* 1954. Ellen K. Rothman, *Hands and Hearts: A History of Courtship in America,* 1984. Kathy Peiss, *Cheap Amusements: Working Women and Leisure in Turn-of-the-Century New York,* 1986. Beth L. Bailey, *From Front Porch to Back Seat: Courtship in*

Twentieth-Century America, 1988. Karen Lystra, *Searching the Heart: Women, Men, and Romantic Love in Nineteenth-Century America,* 1989.

—Christopher W. Wells

COWBOYS. The American cowboy descended from the Spanish and Mexican *vaquero*, who evolved in New Spain after the arrival of cattle in the Western Hemisphere. As cattle ranching spread northward into *California and Texas, Americans adopted the tools and techniques of the *vaquero*. Texas cowboys watched over cattle, branded them, and rounded them up before herding them to markets first in *New Orleans and by the 1850s northward to Missouri and beyond. As *railroads pushed westward following the *Civil War and the demand for beef increased in the East, Texas cowboys began to drive cattle herds north to railheads in Kansas and later Nebraska. By the late 1870s, cowboys, including many of *African-American and Hispanic descent, were found in cattle-raising regions throughout the *West. After the invention of barbed wire and the fencing of ranches, the cowboy became a hired man on a horseback, repairing fences, doctoring cattle, and participating in cattle-branding roundups. By 1900, the golden age of the American cowboy was over.

Compared to his counterpart south of the Rio Grande, the American cowboy played a regional and relatively short-lived role. Yet he found his place in the history and mythology of the *West, celebrated for fairness, justice, and courage, as exemplified by the hero of Owen Wister's enduring novel *The Virginian* (1902). Dime novels, folk songs, motion pictures, television series, and the fashion and advertising industries all helped to create the mythic version of the American cowboy that survives today.

[*See also* Folklore; Hispanic Americans; Livestock Industry; Southwest, The.]

• David Dary, *Cowboy Culture: A Saga of Five Centuries,* 1982.

—David Dary

CRAZY HORSE (c. 1840–1877), warrior-chieftain of the Oglala band of the Lakota (Western) Sioux. Born along the east slope of the Black Hills, Crazy Horse took his father's name after displaying bravery in wars with the Crow, Shoshoni, and other tribes. Increasingly suspicious of white encroachment as he witnessed the growing conflict on the plains between Indians and white settlers, Crazy Horse built a reputation as a great warrior against the whites. He served briefly as one of the four shirt-wearers of the Oglalas, an important honor.

Resistant to change, Crazy Horse preferred the traditional life of hunting and war. By the mid-1870s, the U.S. government recognized him as a head of the nontreaty element of the Lakotas. He joined the Hunkpapa Lakota leader *Sitting Bull, and together their camps, in the Powder River country in northern Wyoming, became a mecca for Sioux tribesmen opposed to government control. Crazy Horse was an important leader in the Great Sioux War (1876–1877) and a key figure in the Indian victory at the Battle of the *Little Bighorn (1876). A target of subsequent army campaigns, he was forced to surrender his band at Red Cloud Agency, Nebraska, in May 1877. That September, when military authorities feared he would lead an outbreak, he was fatally stabbed while resisting arrest on 5 September. A modest, generous, spiritual man of a somewhat morose nature, and much esteemed by his followers, Crazy Horse symbolizes the resistance of nineteenth-century Plains Indians to domination by white culture.

[*See also* Indian History and Culture: From 1800 to 1900; Indian Wars.]

• Eleanor H. Hinman, ed., "Oglala Sources on the Life of Crazy Horse," *Nebraska History* 57 (Spring 1976): 1–51. Richard G. Hardorff, *The Oglala Lakota Crazy Horse,* 1985.

—Thomas R. Buecker

CRÈVECOEUR, J. HECTOR-ST. JOHN DE (1735–1813), agronomist, cartographer, and author whose *Letters from an American Farmer* (1782) has often been embraced as an early testament to America as the land of opportunity and a melting pot of classes and nationalities. Born Michel-Guillaume Jean de Crèvecoeur near Caen in Normandy, Crèvecoeur fought for the French in the *Seven Years' War. Later, he traveled throughout the American colonies, and in 1769 he settled in Orange County, New York, where he farmed and raised a family. During the *Revolutionary War, he suffered persecution by the Patriots for his Loyalist leanings and then was jailed for three months by Loyalists who suspected that he was a Patriot spy. He returned for a time to the intellectual salons of Paris and then served as French consul in *New York City from 1783 to 1790, after which he returned permanently to France.

In *Letters from an American Farmer,* James, the fictionalized narrator, describes to a London gentleman his experiences as a third-generation farmer in Pennsylvania. Although the much-anthologized third letter, "What Is an American?" appears to argue for a new agrarian democracy, the later letters reveal that Crèvecoeur's "perfect society" endorses *slavery and *social class distinction and even fosters lawlessness, violence, and revolution. As the self-indulgence and cruelty of southern slaveowners undermine the atmosphere of peaceful industry, the narrative fabric of this land of promise begins to unravel. In the final letter, the Revolutionary War brings chaos and destruction, betraying James's American dream. Additional essays, later assembled as *Sketches of Eighteenth-Century America* (1925), paint an even darker picture of the suffering brought about by the Revolution.

[*See also* Republicanism; Revolution and Constitution, Era of.]

• Thomas Philbrick, *St. John de Crèvecoeur,* 1970. Gay Wilson Allen and Roger Asselineau, *St. John de Crèvecoeur: The Life of an American Farmer,* 1987.

—Emily Schiller

CRIME. During the mid–seventeenth century, public officials in Puritan Massachusetts expressed fears that crime and disorder were tearing apart the fabric of society. Nearly three and a half centuries later, prominent observers made similar claims, reporting that crime was surging and undermining public order. For Puritans, however, the criminality consisted not of mugging, murder, and crack-cocaine use, but of fornication, Sabbath-breaking, and tippling (excessive drinking). Although commentators in virtually every era have insisted that crime had reached epidemic proportions, the history of crime in America is not the story of ever-increasing rates of disorder. Rather, both the level and the character of crime have changed along with America society. Shifting patterns of crime, therefore, provide an important perspective on the development of American society.

Over time, levels of criminal behavior have waxed and waned. Homicide, for instance, has been far more common in some periods of American history than in others, and the contexts that sparked lethal violence have changed dramatically during the four centuries since Europeans established settlements in North America. Similarly, urban *riots have punctuated some eras and virtually disappeared in others.

Even the definition of criminal behavior has proved to be malleable. Some forms of conduct have been criminalized, as policy-makers have sought to use the legal system to establish or to reinforce social norms. In seventeenth-century *New England, for instance, gossiping and lying were criminal offenses. Anxious to bolster the authority of elders and thus to promote stability in new settlements, lawmakers in Connecticut in 1650 made disobedience to parents a capital offense. Conversely, cursing, witchcraft, and *abortion have been decriminalized over the course of American history.

Finally, the standards for discretionary law enforcement have changed markedly over time. White law-enforcers and jurors in the nineteenth-century *South, for instance, typically overlooked dueling and the *lynching of *African Americans, although both activities violated the law. Likewise, for much of American history law enforcers ignored domestic violence, and until well into the twentieth century policemen seldom arrested parents who killed their newborn children. In 1908, for example, a *Chicago newspaper reported the discovery of the body of a one-day-old infant in the Chicago river, found with a rope tied around its neck. "The body was wrapped in a cloth and bore no marks of violence," the newspaper noted, "beyond the bruises made by the rope." Neither the police nor the county coroner treated the death as a criminal act. Although laws concerning the murder of infants have changed little since 1908, such a discovery would surely trigger a homicide investigation in modern America, reflecting shifting social values.

In short, as values and ideologies changed, standards of acceptable behavior, definitions of crime, and patterns of enforcement shifted accordingly. Thus, criminality must be understood and analyzed in historical context.

Early America. The ideologies and social conditions of the *Colonial Era shaped assumptions about deviant behavior and the nature of crime. Because the criminal-justice systems of particular colonies reflected the values of the early settlers, crime—and ideas about crime—varied from colony to colony. Perhaps nowhere was this process more apparent than in Puritan New England.

The religious intensity of Puritan settlers infused every facet of life in seventeenth-century *New England, including criminality. Puritans believed that moral weakness and Satanic influence posed the greatest challenges to the survival of their society. Thus, they viewed sin and crime in similar—and nearly interchangeable—terms and relied on Mosaic law to undergird their legal system. As a consequence, Puritans made adultery and blasphemy capital offenses. Furthermore, such moral offenses as fornication (premarital sexual relations) and such offenses against public order as drunkenness, which threatened to undermine the religious focus of town life, became the targets for law enforcers and emerged as the most common crimes in Puritan society. Devout New England Puritans were not unusually promiscuous or intemperate. Rather, their values made them particularly sensitive to sexual relations, and patterns of crime reflected Puritan ideas about evil more than actual patterns of conduct. Over time, however, the religious zeal of New Englanders faded, and policy-makers and law enforcers came to view such behavior as less menacing and less worthy of prosecution. By the late eighteenth century, New England law enforcers arrested few fornicators or adulterers, though premarital and extramarital sex had hardly disappeared.

Settlers in other colonies had migrated in search of wealth and status—rather than religious goals—and, therefore, devoted less attention to moral offenses. Rates of prosecution for Sabbath-breaking in Virginia counties during the mid–seventeenth century, for example, were one-eighth those of Essex County, Massachusetts, during the same era. Law enforcement and criminality in the Chesapeake region focused greater attention on property crimes, particularly those affecting the cash crop of the area, tobacco. Maryland lawmakers, for instance, made it a capital offense to break into and rob a tobacco house.

Despite sharp variations in the emphases of law enforcers and in patterns of arrest, in colonial America the combination of relative cultural homogeneity, powerful pressures for conformity, modest *social class divisions, and general prosperity resulted in few murders and little extreme violence. The legal development and expansion of *slavery, however, produced one significant—and difficult to measure—category of violent behavior. As lawmakers degraded the legal status of Africans and *African Americans, making them slaves and, therefore, chattel, violence against slaves ceased to be illegal behavior, except in the most egregious cases. Just as assessments of crime in early America failed to include most forms of violence against Native Americans, the relative absence of serious crime in British colonies must be qualified by the recognition that the use of violence to maintain order and hierarchy in areas with slave populations was not ordinarily considered criminal conduct.

Industrial America. *Urbanization and *immigration redefined crime during the early nineteenth century, producing a surge in disorder and violence during the decades before the *Civil War and a dramatic reduction in disorder and violence during the late nineteenth century until the mid–twentieth century. Early *industrialization strained social relations in the North, particularly in urban centers. In addition, millions of European immigrants and native-born farmers concentrated in cities during the *Antebellum Era. This rapid influx of newcomers exaggerated group loyalties and triggered ethnic, religious, and political tensions that erupted into nearly eighty major riots, with a death toll of close to one thousand people. Cities such as Baltimore, Maryland, *Philadelphia, and *New York City each experienced close to a dozen large riots and hundreds of smaller gang wars between 1820 and 1865. The rioting peaked in the New York City draft riots of July 1863, when a protest against the conscription of local men into the Union Army exploded into a torrent of violence against African Americans that claimed more than one hundred lives.

During the mid–nineteenth century, middle-class northerners forged new ideas about the nature of crime and criminality. Moving away from narrowly religious assumptions about the roots of crime, they increasingly believed that individuals had the power to resist temptation; strong people possessed the self-control to resist the evils and pitfalls that plagued urban society. Relying first on "moral suasion," such as temperance pledges, and later on institutional and legal forces, such as the common school and the municipal *police, middle-class city dwellers struggled to inculcate such discipline in workers and immigrants. As a consequence of this crusade to "uplift" the poor and the foreign born, law enforcers devoted new attention to discouraging rowdy and undisciplined behavior, resulting in a wave of arrests for drunkenness, vagrancy, and disorderly conduct.

Middle-class pressures for conformity, however, were undercut by other social trends in mid-nineteenth-century northern society. If employers and moral reformers celebrated emotional restraint and eschewed passionate behavior, plebeian culture—blending ethnic-, class-, and gender-based traditions—prized aggressiveness. In working-class areas with a high proportion of unattached newcomers, young men reveled in visiting brothels, attending bare-knuckle *boxing matches, engaging in drinking rituals, and affirming their status through demonstrations of toughness; raucous behavior emerged as a badge of cultural independence from the suffocating strictures of proper society. Within plebeian society, therefore, pressures for conformity produced a surge in disorderly behavior and violence during the decades preceding the Civil War. The typical brawl, which contributed to soaring rates of assault and homicide in antebellum cities, involved young, immigrant workers who had been drinking, who belonged to the same ethnic group, and who used their fists or knives to settle trivial disputes.

Although this surge in crime sparked fears about a "dangerous class" lurking in the city, it was short-lived. During the final third of the nineteenth century, arrest rates for drunkenness, disorderly conduct, and assault fell sharply in most cities, despite the heightened sensitivity of law enforcers. In Oakland, California, for instance, the overall arrest rate dropped by nearly 50 percent between 1875 and 1900. Some forms of disorder became more discreet, as law enforcers concentrated brothels in red-light districts and compelled madams to shield *prostitution from public view. But the transformation was not merely one of appearances. Homicide rates plummeted during the late nineteenth century, falling by as much as 50 percent in cities such as Philadelphia and *Boston, despite high levels of *unemployment and *poverty and the arrival of millions of immigrants. The decline in rates of violence is particularly significant since handguns became inexpensive and readily available—for the first time—late in the century, and since law enforcers began to arrest those who engaged in hitherto accepted or overlooked forms of *domestic violence, such as child abuse and wife beating.

Overlapping cultural, institutional, and legal forces contributed to this process. Demands for sobriety, punctuality, and discipline in the workplace discouraged rowdiness among workers. Public schools inculcated similar habits, using classroom discipline to encourage children to develop self-control; police campaigns to arrest disorderly and transient young men for violating vagrancy and tramp laws reinforced this message. Moreover, changing *gender ideologies weakened the bachelor subculture that had earlier exalted aggressive behavior. Such a trend toward social order, however, was not unique to American cities; rates of violence had been falling in much of western Europe for at least two centuries.

This decline in arrest rates and in levels of disorder and personal violence is doubly remarkable in view of the demographic and intellectual changes of the era. Immigration from southern and eastern Europe surged during these years. Experiencing discrimination by law enforcers and employers, many of the newcomers, suspicious of the legal system, settled their scores themselves. Nonetheless, rates of assault and homicide generally fell. During the same period, policy-makers, influenced by the work of the Italian physician Cesare Lombroso and the New York prison reformer Richard L. Dugdale (1841–1883), searched for genetic sources of crime. The so-called savage tendencies of Mediterranean peasants and the widely circulating reports of the Italian Mafia, particularly after the assassination of David Hennessey, the New Orleans police chief, in 1890, made native-stock Americans fear the newcomers.

Three exceptions to this trend underscore the ways in which urbanization and industrialization generated order. First, in the Deep South, an area with modest levels of industrial development and relatively few cities, rates of violence remained extremely high. According to one study, South Carolina had more homicides in 1878 than the combined total of homicides in Maine, New Hampshire, Vermont, Massachusetts, Rhode Island, Connecticut, Michigan, and Minnesota. Second, levels of violence among African Americans, who faced systematic exclusion from the jobs and schools that encouraged order in northern cities, soared, while they plummeted for other groups. Homicide rates for African Americans during the early twentieth century, for example, were three times higher than the rate for the general population in New York City, six times higher in Chicago, and fourteen times higher in Omaha, Nebraska, and this gap would grow larger over the course of the century. Third, newly settled western areas experienced high rates of disorder and violence. Such disorder, ranging from drunkenness to vigilantism and violence, however, waned when sex ratios evened, public institutions matured, and the economy of western cities grew. In short, in regions where the influence of middle-class—or bourgeois—values was less pronounced and among groups denied the rewards of urban, industrial society, levels of violence remained high. Industrial society was neither harmonious nor crime-free, though its dictates discouraged public disorder and thus reduced some forms of crime.

Modern America. Despite numerous short-term fluctuations, the trend toward lower levels of disorder and violence persisted until the 1960s. The United States then experienced a dramatic surge in crime that lasted for nearly two decades. Unlike earlier shifts in criminal activity, during the modern wave both property crime and violent crime exploded. Reported robberies and burglaries, for example, increased approximately threefold. Violent crime followed a similar trajectory as riots erupted in major cities and rates of homicide doubled in many areas, peaking around 1980 and falling during the next twenty years. The character of crime changed as well. Although violent crime touched all of American society, it became particularly concentrated in inner cities, among teenagers, and among African Americans; during the early 1970s, for instance, urban centers with more than one million residents experienced homicide rates twice as high as cities with between 100,000 and 250,000 residents.

Numerous explanations, none wholly sufficient, have been offered to account for this crime wave. The relative decline of the industrial economy simultaneously robbed poor city dwellers of stable employment, challenged the reward system that encouraged delayed gratification, and weakened inner-city schools. Demographic forces may also partially account for the crime wave. Just as disorder and violence rose during the early nineteenth century, when American society included a disproportionate number of young and unmarried people, the more recent wave coincides roughly with the baby boomers entering their teenage years. Persistent racial discrimination and crime related to illicit *drugs, particularly crack cocaine, contributed to the surge as well.

As in earlier eras, crime assumed a distinctive character in late twentieth-century America. The post-1960 crime surge hit much of the world and virtually every European nation. Although rates of property crime, such as burglary, tended to be similar in the United States and western Europe, levels of violent crime remained, as in the past, significantly higher in the United States. In 1900, for example, the homicide rates for New York City and Chicago were approximately ten times that of London. At the close of the century, the gap persisted and perhaps even widened. In the mid-1980s, the homicide rate in the United States was more than five times that of western Europe nations, and the robbery rate was more than four times higher; late twentieth-century America possessed one of the highest rates of violent crime in the world. Such extraordinary and long-standing levels of violent crime, in fact, suggest one realm in which American social development has been distinctive—or exceptional.

In the later 1990s, as the economy boomed, overall violent crime rates declined markedly, reversing several decades of upward trends. In 1999, for example, the violent crime rate dropped 7 percent from 1998. Rates for the minority population of inner cities, however, and especially for inner-city youth under the age of eighteen, remained for higher than the national average. These data again underscored the complex fluctuations in patterns of crime—chronologically, regionally, and demographically.

[*See also* Draft Riots, Civil War; Education: The Public School Movement; Eugenics; Gun Control; Organized Crime; Prisons and Penitentiaries; Temperance and Prohibition; Working-Class Life and Culture.]

• Michael Stephen Hindus, *Prison and Plantation: Crime, Justice, and Authority in Massachusetts and South Carolina, 1767–1878*, 1980. Lawrence M. Friedman and Robert V. Percival. *The Roots of Justice: Crime and Punishment in Alameda County, California, 1870–1910*, 1981. Eric H. Monkkonen, "A Disorderly People?: Urban Order in the Nineteenth and Twentieth Centuries," *Journal of American History* 68 (Dec. 1981): 539–59. Bradley Chapin, *Criminal Justice in Colonial America, 1606–1660*, 1983. Roger D. McGrath, *Gunfighters, Highwaymen, and Vigilantes*, 1984. Elizabeth Pleck, *Domestic Tyranny: The Making of American Social Policy against Family Violence from Colonial Times to the Present*, 1987. Ted Robert Gurr, ed., *Violence in America: The History of Crime*, 1989. Lawrence M. Friedman, *Crime and Punishment in American History*, 1993. Roger Lane, *Murder in America: A History*, 1997.

—Jeffrey S. Adler

CROCKETT, DAVY (1786–1836), frontiersman, congressman, folk hero. David Crockett was born in Tennessee where, in 1806, he married Mary (Polly) Finley. She died in 1815, and a year later he married Elizabeth Patton. Although he served as a militia officer, justice of the peace, town commissioner of

Lawrenceburg, and a volunteer in the Creek War (1813–1814), Crockett was a relatively unknown backwoods hunter and storyteller when he was elected to the Tennessee legislature in 1821. There he took an active interest in land policies relating to western settlement. In 1827, he won election to the U.S. House of Representatives. Serving two terms (1827–1831), he split with his fellow Tennessean, President Andrew *Jackson, on land issues and Indian removal. Crockett was defeated for a third term in 1831, when he openly opposed Jackson's policies, but was reelected in 1832 as a *Whig party candidate. As the 1836 election approached, some Whig leaders touted Crockett as their alternative to Jackson's handpicked successor, the Democrat Martin *Van Buren. However, President Jackson and Tennessee governor William Carroll helped engineer Crockett's 1835 congressional defeat. "You may all go to hell," he proclaimed, "and I will go to Texas." His last letters reveal that he hoped to rejuvenate his political career in Texas and make his fortune as a land agent.

Arriving in Texas in February 1836 amid the movement for Texan independence from Mexico, Crockett joined Colonel William B. Travis at San Antonio de Bexar. On 20 February, Mexican General Antonio López de Santa Anna laid siege to the Alamo, a San Antonio mission occupied by Travis and his forces. During Santa Anna's first shelling of the Alamo, Travis wrote, Crockett was everywhere "animating the men to do their duty." On 6 March, the Alamo was overrun. According to Lieutenant José Enrique de la Peña, Crockett and five or six other survivors were captured and executed on Santa Anna's orders.

Crockett was celebrated in humorous stories based on his adventures, and by the early 1830s he had already become the subject of fanciful exploits and tall tales. The mythmaking was enhanced by his heavily publicized tour of eastern cities in 1834, by his autobiography, and by other "autobiographical" books and almanacs actually written by others. For many Americans his stand at the Alamo completed the union of history and legend that made Davy Crockett a premier representative of frontier individualism.

[*See also* Alamo, Battle of the; Folklore; Indian Removal Act; Indian Wars; Texas Republic and Annexation.]

• James Adkins Shackford, *David Crockett: The Man and the Legend,* 1956; rev. ed., 1986. Michael A. Lofaro and Joe Cummings, eds., *Crockett at Two Hundred: New Perspectives on the Man and the Myth,* 1989.

—Michael A. Lofaro

CROLY, HERBERT (1869–1930), political philosopher and editor. Croly was born in *New York City, the son of two prominent journalists. Entering Harvard College in 1886, he studied intermittently for fourteen years but eventually left without earning a degree. He worked for the *Architectural Record,* a New York trade journal, until 1906. A close and thoughtful observer of politics, he was moved by the early stirrings of American Progressivism to write his most important book, *The Promise of American Life* (1909). The work criticized the Jeffersonian ideal of a weak central government and advocated an expanded government role in social reform and business regulation. Theodore *Roosevelt's praise of the book established Croly's reputation as an insightful analyst of American political culture. His second work of political commentary, *Progressive Democracy,* appeared in 1914.

Two wealthy admirers, Dorothy and Willard Straight, provided Croly with funds to found and edit the *New Republic,* a weekly magazine of political and cultural commentary. From 1914 until he suffered a debilitating stroke in 1928, Croly—together with a remarkable collection of editors and writers, including Walter *Lippmann, John *Dewey, and Randolph *Bourne—produced a literate, highly influential journal of liberal opinion and commentary on foreign affairs, domestic policy, literature, art, politics, and religion.

Painfully bashful, reticent, and modest, Croly nevertheless gathered a circle of admiring friends who respected his intelligence, integrity, and seriousness of purpose. He was one of that group of American intellectuals who transformed American *liberalism at the turn of the century.

[*See also* Progressive Era.]

• David W. Levy, *Herbert Croly of the New Republic: The Life and Thought of an American Progressive,* 1985. Edward A. Stettner, *Shaping Modern Liberalism: Herbert Croly and Progressive Thought,* 1993.

—David W. Levy

CUBA. *See* Protectorates and Dependencies.

CUBAN MISSILE CRISIS, October 1962 confrontation between the United States and the Soviet Union over Soviet nuclear-capable missiles in Cuba. Fidel Castro's radical Cuban government alarmed U.S. officials because it advocated revolution throughout Latin American and built economic and military ties with the Soviet Union, the United States's primary *Cold War adversary. Since 1959, the Eisenhower and Kennedy administrations had sought to overthrow Castro through the failed *Bay of Pigs expedition and other hostile measures.

In summer 1962, Cuba and the Soviet Union secretly agreed to deploy in Cuba forty-eight SS-4 ballistic missiles with a range of 1,020 miles, thirty-two SS-5s with a range of 2,200 miles, twenty–four surface-to-air missiles (SAMs), antiaircraft batteries with 144 launchers, and forty-two bombers with a 600-mile range. While seeking to defend Cuba, Soviet Premier Nikita Khrushchev also wanted to counter the American Jupiter missiles in Turkey targeted against the Soviet Union and bolster Moscow's leadership of the communist world, currently under challenge from Mao Zedong's China.

As *Republican party partisans criticized President John F. *Kennedy for failing to unseat Castro, the *Central Intelligence Agency monitored Cuba through U-2 reconnaissance flights. On 14 October, a U-2 spy plane photographed missile sites. The CIA predicted that some Soviet missiles could shortly become operational, perhaps even with nuclear warheads. On 16 October, an alarmed President Kennedy assembled key advisers, soon designated the Executive Committee (ExComm), and debated how to respond. ExComm advisers ruled out an air strike because it might leave missiles untouched. Kennedy readied U.S. forces for an invasion but hesitated because of potential high casualties and possible Soviet retaliation, perhaps against Berlin. (Unbeknownst to Kennedy, Soviet tactical nuclear weapons were already deployed in Cuba to blunt an invasion, and about 42,000 Soviet troops, not 10,000 as thought, guarded the island.) ExComm shelved the negotiations option because U.S. officials refused to talk with Castro, and they feared that Khrushchev would simply stall until missiles were operational. In the end, ExComm endorsed a naval blockade, or "quarantine," to stop further Soviet military shipments and to force Khrushchev to retreat in the face of superior U.S. power in the region.

Kennedy announced the blockade on 22 October. U.S. war vessels patrolled the Caribbean to intercept ships, and 140,000 U.S. troops in Florida prepared for an assault against Cuba. Nervous observers sketched doomsday scenarios, but the president received widespread bipartisan support. Moscow denounced the blockade as a violation of *international law and an intrusion into Soviet–Cuban affairs. On 26 October, in one of several letters he exchanged with Kennedy during the crisis, Khrushchev proposed to remove the "defensive" Soviet missiles if the United States pledged not to invade Cuba. The next day, Khrushchev asked for more: removal of the Jupiter missiles from Turkey. Meanwhile, the president's brother Robert *Kennedy met privately with Soviet Ambassador Anatoly Dobrynin, exploring the missile-swap option. That day, 27 October, the crisis escalated when a SAM shot down a U-2 over Cuba and an Alaska-based U.S. spy plane strayed into Soviet territory.

The crisis seemed about to "[spin] out of control," recalled National Security Adviser McGeorge Bundy.

Deciding to strike a deal, President Kennedy publicly agreed to the no-invasion pledge and privately, through Robert Kennedy, assured Dobrynin that the Jupiters would be withdrawn. Khrushchev, fearing a loss of control over events and the unpredictable Castro, accepted these terms. Not until mid-November, however, did the Soviets agree to pull out the bombers (the SS-5s had never arrived). Castro bitterly resented the settlement and rejected *United Nations on-site inspections to confirm missile removal. Although the missiles and bombers departed Cuba, a formal Soviet-American agreement was never signed, and Kennedy's no-invasion pledge was highly qualified.

Taking credit for effective crisis management, Kennedy enhanced his image for boldness and courage. In retrospect, Kennedy's handling looks less impressive, as Secretary of Defense Robert McNamara later put it, because of the "misinformation, miscalculation, misjudgment, and human fallibility" that dogged all leaders in the crisis. Soviet leaders in 1964 deposed Khrushchev, apparently believing he had undertaken a reckless gamble. The outcome of the crisis both slowed and accelerated the Cold War. In its aftermath, Washington and Moscow worked to soothe tensions, installed a "hot line" or teletype link between the White House and the Kremlin, and signed the *Limited Nuclear Test Ban Treaty in 1963. Still, some analysts argue that Kennedy's success in driving the missiles from Cuba may have emboldened him to become more interventionist in Vietnam. U.S. policy toward Cuba remained hard-line, with new assassination plots and CIA sabotage. The Soviets vowed to end their nuclear inferiority by building more weapons, thus escalating the nuclear arms race. With its potential for thermonuclear exchange, the Cuban missile crisis ranks as perhaps the Cold War's most perilous moment.

[*See also* Foreign Relations: U.S. Relations with Latin America; Nuclear Strategy; Nuclear Weapons.]

• Laurence Chang and Peter Kornbluth, eds., *The Cuban Missile Crisis, 1962,* 1992. James Nathan, ed., *The Cuban Missile Crisis Revisited,* 1992. James Blight et al., *Cuba on the Brink,* 1993. Thomas G. Paterson, *Contesting Castro,* 1994. Aleksandr Fursenko and Timothy Naftali, *"One Hell of a Gamble": Khrushchev, Castro, and Kennedy, 1958–1964,* 1997. Mark J. White, *Missiles in Cuba: Khrushchev, Castro, and the 1962 Crisis,* 1997.

—Thomas G. Paterson

CULTURAL PLURALISM is both a social reality and a social theory that emphasizes the retention of ethnic culture and customs by the diverse ethnic groups making up American society. Cultural pluralists are typically second- or third-generation offspring of immigrants who feel at home speaking English and are comfortable with American economic life and democratic politics yet still wish to retain their ancestral language, religion, and customs as well as an emotional attachment to their ancestral country. As a theory, cultural pluralism was not systematically formulated, or even given a name, until the twentieth century. America's native-born Anglo-Saxon intellectuals generally emphasized the importance of homogeneity, unity, and assimilation, leaving the pluralist position to immigrant leaders. German Americans employed a phrase that summed up the cultural pluralism ideal in commonsense fashion: "Germania meine Mutter, Columbia meine Braut" (Germany my mother, America my bride). Just as individuals do not usually renounce allegiance to their parents and ancestral family when they marry, despite occasional friction and tension, the metaphor suggests, so too with ethnic groups.

Horace Kallen (1882–1974), a German-Jewish philosopher who taught at *New York City's New School for Social Research, first used the term "cultural pluralism" in *Culture and Democracy in the United States,* 1924. While Kallen continued for nearly half a century to champion the notion of dual cultural loyalties, arguing that this would enrich American culture, not endanger it, he also endowed the concept with a rigidity that was absent in the nineteenth-century, commonsense notion. He often argued polemically that "people cannot change their grandparents," thereby confusing ethnic or cultural loyalties with biological, genetic, or racial inheritance. Men and women cannot change their grandparents, but they can and do change their language and cultural values. Extreme assertions of diversity, such as Kallen's, imply a kind of racial or ethnic essentialism and separatism, not merely cultural pluralism.

The theory of cultural pluralism remained a defensive, minority position until the later twentieth century. After the African American *civil rights movement and the white ethnic revival of the 1960s and 1970s, however, pluralism became the mainstream intellectual position in the United States. It still remained controversial, however. Many argued that dual loyalties could distort American foreign policy, since members of an ethnic group may lobby for policies favoring their ancestral country. Others contended that bilingual education—one by-product of the cultural-pluralism ideal—retards the economic progress of immigrant children and weakens the American social fabric. Since the United States remains an immigrant-receiving country, some form of cultural pluralism will likely continue to describe the American reality, even if the theory is modified or falls out of fashion.

[*See also* Ethnicity; Immigration; Nativist Movement.]

• John Higham. *Send These to Me: Jews and Other Immigrants in Urban America,* 1975. Arthur Mann. *The One and the Many: Reflections on the American Identity,* 1979. David A. Hollinger, *Postethnic America: Beyond Multiculturalism,* 1995.

—Edward R. Kantowicz

CUSTER, GEORGE ARMSTRONG. *See* Little Bighorn, Battle of the.

D

DAIRY INDUSTRY AND DAIRY PRODUCTS. Dairying in North America began with the earliest European invasions. Spaniards brought cattle to Veracruz (Mexico) in 1525; English cattle reached *Jamestown in 1611.

Colonial Era and Nineteenth Century. From colonial times the dairy remained women's work, including butter churning and cheese pressing, well into the nineteenth century, long after commercial sales flourished in the public markets of seaports and river towns. Dairying acquired more than local significance in parts of New York, Pennsylvania, and *New England, when farmers could no longer compete with wheat shipped by *canals and *railroads, from newly settled lands further west. Dairy farming eventually took hold in part of the "Old Northwest" as wheat culture followed the westward-moving "frontier" beyond the Mississippi Valley.

From the 1850s cheese making was reorganized into small "factory" associations where the more adept cheesemakers (women and men) could work on greater volumes of milk gathered from neighboring farms. By the early 1900s, almost all cheese was made in factories and Wisconsin had displaced New York as the banner cheese state. Butter making lingered on farms until the 1880s when, despite the threats from oleomargarine, De Laval's steam-driven cream separator from Sweden first led to an expansion of cooperative "creamery" associations and large-scale "centralizer" plants, especially in the *Middle West. Not before *World War I did creameries supply more than half the nation's huge butter output, with Minnesota the banner state. Gail Borden (1801–1874) patented condensed milk (concentrated and sterilized under heat in a vacuum pan) in 1856 and by 1899 twenty-four condenseries were manufacturing condensed and evaporated milk countrywide. By that time sanitary bottling procedures and pasteurization techniques (partial sterilization by heat) were making milk products safer and ending the dreadful sequence of nineteenth-century urban epidemics associated with tainted milk.

Dairy farming remained a seasonal and, *California excepted, a family enterprise. Milk yields increased somewhat owing to more ample feed and better cow barns but the "dairy quality" of the stock improved little before importations of Shorthorns, Ayrshires, Holstein-Friesians, and Channel Islands breeds after the mid-nineteenth century. Under competitive pressures to preserve the fertility of their soil and raise the return on its use, dairymen sought a more balanced crop program and more nutrient-rich diet (including unripened maize, alfalfa, and clover preserved in airtight silos from the 1880s) in order to extend lactation further into the winter months. The Babcock Test (1890), developed by Stephen M. Babcock at the University of Wisconsin, provided a more accurate test of milk quality based on butterfat content, and stimulated cooperative herd improvement through selective breeding; official animal testing and disease eradication programs (especially Bovine Tuberculosis) followed under sponsorship of state agricultural colleges. By the middle of the nineteenth century, annual milk yields per cow had nearly doubled, averaging 3,883 lbs. by 1900.

Technical advances in milk processing and distribution brought hand-separators, milking machines, cooling equipment, and storage tanks to commercial dairy farms, while refrigerated tank trucks and glass-lined railcars by the 1930s carried milk to processing plants and profitable metropolitan markets. Ice cream, offered by confectioners in *New York City and *Philadelphia in the 1770s, was first manufactured for wholesale delivery in Baltimore in 1851 and gained popularity after the introduction of waffle-cones at the Louisiana Purchase Exposition in St. Louis, 1904. The recovery of U.S. cheese production from the loss of lucrative foreign markets, following export of substandard "skim" and "filled" cheese, was facilitated from the late 1890s by the regulatory enforcement of state dairy and food commissions and by laboratory investigations of enzyme action in the "cold curing" of natural cheddar type cheese. It was the introduction of J. L. Kraft's patented "processed" cheese in *Chicago after 1916, however, that changed the United States into a "nation of cheese eaters."

Twentieth-Century Developments. The thrust of technological development in dairying, as in other industries, has been toward continuous production for mass markets and away from "batch" and "bulk" operations. From the 1920s, when dairying was already a $4 billion industry, such tendencies were driven by the imperatives of "big business" toward growth and restructuring. Private bankers determined that mergers and acquisitions, rather than direct investments, were the most economical modes of expansion and in 1923 the National Dairy Products Company set off a "merger mania" by absorbing the small margins of independent wholesalers, and soon displaced the Borden Company as the largest dairy corporation in capitalization and sales. Between 1921 and 1948, eight large dairy corporations emerged while thousands of local mergers occurred among smaller corporations. Over 500 of these local mergers involved cooperatives exempted from federal *antitrust legislation by the Capper-Volstead Act, 1922. The agricultural crises of the 1930s eventually brought federal dairy price supports and cartel-like agreements to equalize prices paid to producers of milk used either for fluid or manufacturing purposes.

After 1900, the number of farms with dairy cattle barely increased, but many had become specialized dairy enterprises. From the 1930s, innovations in cattle breeding and feeding, including artificial insemination by proven sires and commercial availability of hybrid-corn seed (maize), continuously raised milk output, but it was "genetically engineered" capacity rather than scientifically enhanced rations that accounts for spiraling milk yields. By 1980, high-yield, low-fat Holsteins constituted 80 percent of the national herd. By 1995, the herd, comprising only 9.46 million cows, averaged 16,451 lbs. of milk per head, compared with the peak herd of 27.7 million in 1945, averaging but 4,375 lbs. per head.

Although mechanization and the purchase of feed and specialized services had reduced the intensive labor of farm families as the twentieth century ended, more than 80 percent of dairy farms in the 1990s continued to be held by family or individual proprietors, 15.5 percent were partnerships that included family members, and 3.5 percent were family corporations. The trend in milk production, as in other agricultural sectors, was toward fewer but larger operations; only 6 percent of all farms reported milk animals in 1992, with California now the largest milk producer.

The post–*World War II popularity of store sales of ice cream (earlier a soda fountain item), the rise of "Italian-style" cheese pizza, and the conversion of yogurt from a "health food" into a fruit-flavored dessert, as well as such marketing novelties as prepackaged sliced natural cheese introduced by Kraft in the 1950s, all boosted dairy consumption. Most fluid milk, along with an array of branded and packaged dairy products, was now retailed in self-service supermarkets or convenience stores in wax paper cartons (1930s) or molded plastic jugs (1960s). Home deliveries had virtually disappeared.

On the manufacturing and marketing sides of dairying, the process of consolidation intensified in the 1970s when the $20 billion business industry became a target of Wall Street mergers, acquisitions, and divestitures in which giant food corporations took over divisions of large dairy conglomerates. By the 1990s transnational food conglomerates such as Philip Morris, Unilever, Nestlé, Con Agra, and Groupe Danone S.A. were major players in the dairy industry, which, however, represented only a fraction of their total food sales. The huge Minnesota-based Land O' Lakes Co. (1921) and other regional cooperatives, in contrast, selling chiefly bulk milk and low-branded dairy goods, had meanwhile raised their market share to 42 percent of corporate sales.

In 1996 the federal government began a phased termination of dairy price supports and greatly reduced milk marketing regulations with a view to lowering the public costs of handling vast milk surpluses in a deregulated market environment. The Agricultural Improvement and Reform Act of 1996 retained the restrictions on dairy imports permitted under the *General Agreement on Trade and Tariffs (GATT), while seeking to promote maximum allowable exports of U.S. dairy products to global markets. Such changes introduced a higher degree of price volatility in domestic markets, where dairymen already faced a perilous future from changing consumption patterns related to health and dietary concerns (per capita consumption of all dairy products fell from a peak of 838 lbs. milk equivalent in 1931 to barely 517 lbs. by 1994, with butter the principal victim) and public uneasiness over the genetic manipulation of cattle and the increased use of antibiotics and bovine sumatropin growth hormone (BGH).

[*See also* Agriculture; Food and Diet; Health and Fitness; Livestock Industry.]

• H. S. Perloff et al., *Regions, Resources, and Economic Growth,* 1960. Eric E. Lampard, *Rise of the Dairy Industry in Wisconsin, 1820–1920,* 1963. Ralph Selitzer, *Dairy Industry in America,* 1976. Sally McMurry, *Transforming Rural Life: Dairying Families and Agricultural Change, 1820–1885,* 1995. A. C. Manchester and D. P. Blayney, *Structure of Dairy Markets,* 1997.

—Eric E. Lampard

DALEY, RICHARD J. (1902–1976), mayor of *Chicago. The grandson of Irish immigrants, Daley grew up in the Irish Catholic world of Chicago's South Side, attending daily mass and parochial schools. After high school he worked part-time in the nearby stockyards, did clerical work in the afternoon, and spent his evenings in law classes and at the Hamburg Athletic Club, which was run by the local Democratic organization.

Elected to the Illinois legislature in 1936, Daley was a hard-working, clean-living exception to the carousing lifestyle of the state's legislative culture. His honesty and financial acuity led Governor Adlai *Stevenson to appoint him revenue director in 1948, but he soon returned to Chicago as Cook County Clerk, a position notable for its three hundred patronage jobs. Becoming chairman of the Cook County Democratic party in 1953, he won election as mayor two years later.

A master of budgets and patronage, Daley parlayed his control of city government and local Democratic politics into an organization that outlasted nearly all its peers in midcentury American cities. Like New York's governor Nelson Rockefeller, Daley recognized the economic and political value of huge construction projects. During his twenty-two years as mayor, the city vastly expanded O'Hare Airport, the mass-transit system, and the expressways; constructed the University of Illinois–Chicago; revitalized the downtown; transformed the South Side through *urban renewal; and built a cavernous convention center on Lake Michican. These projects, along with efficiently delivered municipal services, gave Chicago a reputation as "The City that Works." They also provided jobs for party stalwarts, bond issues for lawyers and bankers, development for the business community, and many ribbon-cutting opportunities for the mayor.

Daley emerged as a national power after his notorious manipulation of Cook County votes helped elect John F. *Kennedy in 1960. But his autocratic style proved ill adapted to the turbulence of the 1960s. Accustomed to winning black votes with petty favors and patronage, Daley could not negotiate effectively with *African Americans protesting school segregation and housing discrimination. His reactionary "law and order" response to social upheaval was cemented when Chicago police brutally attacked antiwar demonstrators at the 1968 Democratic National Convention.

As America's "last big-city boss," Daley saw himself as harnessing the power of downtown business and the federal government on behalf of ordinary Chicagoans. In truth, he remained rooted in the political culture of an earlier era. Cronyism and corruption were part of the grease that made the city work. The "second ghetto" of massive African American housing projects, separated from Daley's beloved Bridgeport and other white neighborhoods by fourteen-lane expressways, symbolized Daley's Chicago no less than its breathtaking downtown skyline.

[*See also* Democratic Party; Irish Americans; Municipal and County Governments; Roman Catholicism; Racism; Segregation, Racial; Sixties, The; Urbanization.]

• Milton L. Rakove, *Don't Make No Waves, Don't Back No Losers: An Insider's Analysis of the Daley Machine,* 1975. Roger Biles, *Richard J. Daley: Politics, Race, and the Governing of Chicago,* 1995. Adam Cohen and Elizabeth Taylor, *American Pharaoh: Mayor Richard J. Daley,* 2000.

—James Grossman

DAMS AND HYDRAULIC ENGINEERING. In colonial America, small streams powered rural grist mills and sawmills. In the early nineteenth century, entrepreneurs built factories powered by the flow of large rivers; the *Lowell mills in Massachusetts, where capitalists diverted the Merrimack River to energize the textile looms, became a particularly famous example of this. Builders also erected dams to inundate rocky stretches of rivers and enhance the operation of canals. By mid-century, the *Army Corps of Engineers was actively removing "snags" and otherwise improving river navigability.

Urban growth prompted large-scale dam construction. In 1887 *San Francisco began receiving water from a dam 146 feet high; in the 1890s *New York City began building a 297-foot dam. In the *West, privately financed canal and reservoir projects led the way in "reclaiming" and cultivating desert land through irrigation. In 1902 the U.S. Reclamation Service (later renamed the Bureau of Reclamation) started building large western dams. As *hydroelectric power systems grew in the 1890s, corporations began transmitting electricity from remote waterpower sites to distant, urban "load centers." *Niagara Falls became the site of a renowned early hydroelectric power plant. By 1910 such systems were operating throughout America.

During Theodore *Roosevelt's presidency, plans for "conserving" water resources became a prominent component of Progressivism. Despite conflicts over the proper roles of government and private enterprise, Congress by the mid-1920s had authorized the Corps of Engineers to devise multiple-use strategies for developing America's rivers. "Multipurpose" planning garnered additional attention because of southern *California's desire to dam the Colorado River for irrigation, power generation, and municipal water supply. In 1928 Congress authorized $177 million to build the 726-foot-high Boulder (later Hoover) Dam on the Colorado and to fund other improvements desired by California legislators. Catastrophic floods along the *Mississippi River in 1927 also encouraged federal support for water projects.

Large dams constituted an important part of President Franklin Delano *Roosevelt's New Deal; starting in 1933 with the *Tennessee Valley Authority (a government agency that supplanted private electric companies), the Roosevelt administration championed water projects nationwide. These included the Bureau of Reclamation's Grand Coulee Dam in Washington State and the Corps of Engineers' Fort Peck Dam in Montana. During the 1940s and 1950s, dam building emerged as a staple of the national economy. Although sometimes decried as "pork-barrel" waste, water projects proved politically effective in infusing federal funds into local economies.

By the 1960s, thousands of dams impounded rivers throughout America, prompting fears that too many wild rivers and fragile wetlands had been destroyed by reservoirs of limited social value. As early as 1909, naturalist John *Muir had (unsuccessfully) opposed construction of the Hetch Hetchy Dam in *Yosemite National Park. By the time *environmentalism became a political force in the 1970s, dams were no longer considered an unalloyed public good. By the turn of the century, efforts to reduce water consumption were superseding interest in new water projects, and the demolition of dams to aid spawning fish was gaining support. Dams remained an important part of the American landscape, but little new construction was planned.

[*See also* Canals and Waterways; Electrical Industry; Engineering; Factory System; Progressive Era.]

• Louis C. Hunter, *A History of Industrial Power in the United States, 1780–1930: Water Power*, 1979. Donald C. Jackson, *Building the Ultimate Dam: John S. Eastwood and the Control of Water in the West*, 1995.

—Donald C. Jackson

DANCE. Dance has always been part of the American scene, but except for Indian ritual dances, early dance was imported. George *Washington and others of the Virginia aristocracy ran "dancing assemblies" as venues for upper-class courtship. Steps, music, and teachers came from England and France. The American "square dances" evolved from English reels. Immigrant groups brought folk dancing. Black slaves preserved ancient dances from Africa. African American dance swept through white America in waves. From 1912 to 1914, the Bunny Hug, Turkey Trot, and other dilutions of vernacular dance invaded fashionable ballrooms. The 1930s jitterbug era saw teenagers Lindy-Hopping (a dance named for Charles *Lindbergh) in movie theaters. The 1930s also brought a craze for Caribbean and South American dances originated by African slaves, including the Rumba and Conga from Cuba and the Brazilian Samba. The 1950s brought Elvis *Presley and rock-and-roll which in turn launched the Twist, popularized in the early 1960s by Chubby Checker. Tap dance, with its buck and wing, soft shoe, and eccentric improvisations, developed from the syncopated foot-stamping and hand-clapping of slaves in religious ecstasy, mixed with Irish clog dancing.

American professional dance falls into three categories: ballet, modern, and *jazz. All forms spotlight highly energized, charismatic individuals. John Durang (1768–1822), America's first professional dancer, learned his craft by watching foreigners, mostly French. Like performers on colonial stages, Durang mastered specialty numbers suitable for comic opera, farce, melodrama, or *circus programs. Parisian Paul Hazard taught Philadelphian George Washington Smith and ballerinas Augusta Maywood and Mary Ann Lee, who made a joint 1837 debut in a French opera-ballet. Maywood moved to Europe. Lee also went abroad to study, but returned to America with the ballet *Giselle*. Smith had a long career as a *danseur noble*, partnering Lee and the visiting Viennese ballerina Fanny Elssler, who profoundly impressed nineteenth-century American audiences.

Because dance centers on the body, many preachers denounced it as sinful. The Utah Mormons were exceptions, however. Brigham Young, believing that dance was desirable, built a theater in Salt Lake City to present touring ballet performers and the Mormons' own well-trained troupe, from 1848 to 1868.

American ballet came into its own in the 1930s, when Russian-born George Balanchine (1903–1983), creator of a large repertory in "Neoclassicism," arrived in 1934 and started the New York City Ballet Company. "Classicism" denotes a ballet technique, with the female on point. "Neo" refers to modern styling—the legs perhaps parallel, instead of turned out, or the omission of plots. Choreographing famous musical scores, Balanchine alternated fast, flashy leg-work with languorous adagio movements.

The American Ballet Theater also arose in the 1930s, featuring classic revivals along with works by great choreographers like Agnes de Mille (1905–1993), Antony Tudor, Jerome Robbins, and Eliot Feld. During the same decade, William Christensen fostered the San Francisco Ballet. In the 1960s, Robert Joffrey (with Gerald Arpino) created the Joffrey Ballet and Arthur Mitchell founded the Dance Theater of Harlem. The main center of dance was New York, but the Pennsylvania Ballet, the Boston Ballet, the Atlanta Ballet, and other regional companies flourished as well.

In the first half of the twentieth century, modern dancers condemned ballet as a decadent European form, demanding significant content instead. Each leading modernist was inspired differently: Isadora Duncan (1878–1927) by ancient Greek art and musical visualizations; Ruth St. Denis by Hinduism and sacred Christian themes; Ted Shawn by masculine pursuits; Martha *Graham by Freudian tragedies; Doris Humphrey by humanistic grandeur; Anna Sokolow by grim realty; and José Limón by his Mexican heritage.

Dancers who took African American jazz onto the stage were led by Katherine Dunham (1912–), who came to dance from anthropology in the 1940s. Dunham's technique blended head and neck movements from the Pacific Islands, torso and arm movements from Africa and the West Indies, and toe and foot movements from Haiti. During the 1960s and 1970s, Alvin Ailey popularized jazz dance with an electrifying repertory. After his death in 1989, Judith Jamison continued Ailey's American Dance Theater.

Postmodern choreographers, beginning in the 1950s, turned against the modernists' emphasis on content to concentrate on art materials. Merce Cunningham explored motion in time and space. Alwin Nikolais placed bodies in gorgeous mixed-media scenes. Paul Taylor took a fresh approach to every aspect of dance. They were succeeded by artists like Trisha Brown, Mark Morris, Twyla Tharp, and Bill T. Jones who combined dance styles; used plain, everyday movement; or investigated concepts like "slow." By the end of the twentieth century, the balance of dance trade had been reversed. The United States was recognized as the fount of neoclassic ballet, postmodern dance, and above all jazz, and American choreography and performers were exported to companies throughout the world.

[*See also* Modernist Culture; Musical Theater.]

• Olga Maynard, *The American Ballet*, 1959. Marshall and Jean Stearns, *Jazz Dance*, 1968. Lincoln Kirstein, *Movement and Metaphor*, 1970. Joseph H. Mazo, *Prime Movers: The Makers of Modern Dance in America*, 1977. Sally Banes, *Terpsichore in Sneakers*, 1980. Joan Cass, *Dancing through History*, 1993.

—Joan Cass

***DARTMOUTH COLLEGE* CASE** (1819). In *Dartmouth College v. Woodward*, the U.S. *Supreme Court extended the scope of the contract clause of the *Constitution (article 1, section 10). In 1769, the royal governor of New Hampshire, acting in the name of the English crown, granted Dartmouth College a charter to operate as a private institution under the administration of a group of trustees. In 1816, however, the New Hampshire legislature passed several laws that transformed Dartmouth from a private to a public college, subject to inspection by the state.

The college, claiming that its charter rights had been violated, took the case to court, with Daniel *Webster, a Dartmouth graduate, as its chief attorney. At this time, it was understood that state legislatures could regulate corporations, but that private property could not be taken from individuals by state action without proper compensation. Writing for the majority, Chief Justice John *Marshall ruled that the college was a "private eleemosynary institution" and that the 1769 charter was a valid contract between the state and the original donors to the institution. By voiding the legislation that had transformed Dartmouth into a public institution, Marshall not only strengthened the contract clause of the Constitution, but also expanded the federal judiciary's role in overseeing state legislative action affecting property rights.

[*See also* Economic Regulation.]

• G. Edward White, *The Marshall Court and the Culture of Change, 1815–1835*, 1988.

—Paul Clemens

DATING. *See* Courtship and Dating.

DAVID WALKER'S *APPEAL* (1829). David Walker's *An Appeal to the Coloured Citizens of the World*, a seminal work of black nationalist doctrine, called for violent resistance against *slavery and white supremacy. Evoking a spirit of race pride, the pamphlet challenged all *African Americans to overcome their apathy and rise up in defense of their rights and freedoms. Walker (1785–1830), born free in Wilmington, North Carolina, moved to *Boston in 1827. There he opened a second-hand clothing store and worked as an agent of the *Freedom's Journal*, the first black weekly newspaper. Walker privately published his pamphlets, scholars believe, and clandestinely transported them to southern ports with the aid of northern seaman.

Divided into a preamble and four articles, Walker's *Appeal* culled ideas from the *Declaration of Independence, the U.S. *Constitution, and the *Bible. It denounced slavery as antithetical to the precepts of Christianity and *republicanism, refuted notions of black inferiority proffered by Thomas *Jefferson, and sharply attacked the American Colonization Society.

Walker's pamphlet evoked fear and insecurity throughout the *South and prompted legislative measures to thwart the circulation of "seditious" documents. In the North, few white abolitionists publicly endorsed the apocalyptic themes of Walker's writings. Although no slave uprisings were tied directly to Walker's effort, his pamphlet continued to confound the slave South and inspire generations of black nationalist thinkers.

[*See also* Antebellum Era; Antislavery; Black Nationalism; Colonization Movement, African; Racism.]

• Herbert Aptheker, *"One Continual Cry": David Walker's* Appeal to the Colored Citizens of the World *(1829–1830)*, 1965. Sterling Stuckey, *Slave Culture: Nationalist Theory and the Foundations of Black America*, 1987. Peter Hinks, *To Awaken My Afflicted Brethren: David Walker and the Problem of Antebellum Slave Resistance*, 1997.

—Bobby Donaldson

DAVIS, JEFFERSON (1808–1889), president of the *Confederate States of America. Born in Kentucky, raised in Mississippi, and educated at Transylvania College and the U.S. Military Academy at West Point, Davis early settled upon a military career. In 1832, he served in the Black Hawk War and received *Black Hawk's surrender. In 1835, shattered by the death of his wife of three months, he resigned his commission and sought seclusion at his Briarfield plantation at Davis Bend, Mississippi. Entering Congress in 1845, he resigned in 1846 to serve in the *Mexican War. Rising to the rank of colonel, he fought with distinction, especially at the Battle of Buena Vista. As a U.S. senator (1847–1851), he grew more radical politically, advocating the expansion of *slavery and of southern power. After an unsuccessful campaign for the governorship of Mississippi (1851), he served as Franklin *Pierce's secretary of war (1853–1857). He returned to the Senate in 1857 but resigned when Mississippi seceded in 1861.

Hoping for a high military command in the Confederacy, he was disappointed by his selection as president of the Confederate States, but he pressed vigorously to establish and protect the infant nation. His insistence on strong centralized power to conduct the *Civil War alienated many *states'-rights Southerners, and his detailed oversight of military strategy irritated Confederate generals. His rigid personality and inability to build consensus compounded his problems. Fleeing the Confederate capital at Richmond in April 1865 as the Union forces closed in, he was captured in Georgia. Imprisoned for two years but never tried, Davis spent his postwar years largely in literary efforts to justify the course of secession and war.

[*See also* South, The.]

• Haskell M. Monroe et al., eds. *The Papers of Jefferson Davis*, 9 vols. to date, 1971–. William C. Davis, *Jefferson Davis: The Man and His Hour, a Biography*, 1991.

—Eric H. Walther

DAVIS, MILES (1926–1991), musician. Born in Alton, Illinois, a dentist's son, Miles Davis began playing the trumpet professionally in his teens. In 1944 he enrolled in a New York conservatory but gravitated to Harlem's *jazz nightclubs. He soon was recording with Charlie *Parker and working with big bands. Davis began leading groups, and in 1949 his nonet recorded the *Birth of the Cool* arrangements, helping to introduce the impressionistic "cool" jazz style. Slowed by heroin addiction, Davis resurfaced in 1955 with an acclaimed quintet (including John *Coltrane). It recorded *Milestones, Kind of Blue*, and other albums, roaming from a classic bebop style to modal explorations. Davis also created *Porgy and Bess* and *Sketches of Spain* (1958–1960) with arranger Gil Evans. These albums were among the most influential in jazz history. Into the 1960s, Davis made numerous appearances and created albums and film scores. In 1968 he controversially incorporated electronic instruments and soul motifs in *In a Silent Way* and *Bitches Brew*. His jazz-rock "fusion" experiments continued until 1975, when illnesses forced a retirement. In the 1980s Davis returned, blending contemporary pop trends into his performances.

Davis's tight, dynamic range; hard-edged lyricism; and astringent trumpet timbre created one of jazz's most distinctive voices. His uncompromising "cool" persona, fired by racial pride and mistrust of the music business and the mass audience, made him a rebellious role model for African American men for four decades. Above all, Davis was the most restless and influential stylistic innovator in jazz's first century.

• Jack Chambers, *Milestones: The Music and Times of Miles Davis*, 2 vols., 1983, 1985. Miles Davis and Quincy Troupe, *Miles: The Autobiography*, 1989.

—Burton W. Peretti

DAWES SEVERALTY ACT (1887), an important law relating to Indian affairs. Sponsored by Senator Henry Dawes of Massachusetts, its central purposes included ending tribal title to land in favor of individual holdings, transforming Native Americans into farmers, and assimilating Indians into white society. The ideological roots of the legislation lay in the post–*Civil War public faith in *laissez-faire, private property, citizenship, and the "Americanization" of immigrants and minorities. The Women's National Indian Association, the Indian Rights Association, and the Lake Mohonk Conferences, important eastern reform groups, were largely responsible for passage of the legislation. Western settlers and economic interests had little influence on passage, although they benefited greatly afterward.

The Dawes Severalty Act applied to all Indians except a few groups in New York, Nebraska, and Indian Territory. Major provisions included assignment of 160 acres to each family head, 80 acres to unmarried Indians over eighteen and to orphans, and 40 acres to those under eighteen. Title to allotments was held in trust by the government for twenty-five years, during which time the land could not be sold or encumbered. Citizenship was granted to all allottees and to others who adopted the "habits of civilized life." Unallotted land was declared surplus and could be purchased by the federal government for subsequent settlement by non-Indians.

The act proved disastrous to Native Americans. Legislation approved in 1891 permitted the leasing of allotments, and by 1916 over one-third of such land was rented to non-Indians. Other measures, most notably the Burke Act of 1906, allowed Indians to sell their allotments. The checkerboarding that resulted when allotments became intermingled with non-Indian holdings on reservations created major obstacles to proper land management and produced serious jurisdictional problems that persisted more than a century later. Many arid reservations were allotted that should have been left in common title to permit ranching. Allotments commonly became so fractionalized by heirship that they were virtually worthless except for leasing. Most importantly, the sale of surplus land and allotments reduced Indian land holdings from 156 million acres in 1881, when allotment of individual tribes started, to 53 million acres in 1933. The *Indian Reorganization Act of 1934 prohibited further allotment, but did little to restore Indian land holdings. Allotment and citizenship did not "free the Indian" as promised, but led to increased federal control, *poverty, and reduced agricultural production. What started as well-intended legislation produced a major disaster.

[*See also* Americanization Movement; Homestead Act; Indian History and Culture: From 1800 to 1900; Indian History and Culture: From 1900 to 1950.]

• D. S. Otis, *The Dawes Act and the Allotment of Indian Lands*, ed. Francis Paul Prucha, 1973. Michael R. McLaughlin, "The Dawes Act, or Indian General Allotment Act of 1887: The Continuing Burden of Allotment. A Selective Bibliography," *American Indian Culture and Research Journal* 20, no. 2 (1996): 59–105.

—Donald L. Parman

D-DAY (1944). At 6:30 A.M. on 6 June 1944, after foul weather had postponed the operation for a day, forty-seven Allied divisions invaded Normandy in the largest amphibious assault in history. Under Supreme Allied Commander General Dwight D. *Eisenhower, the invasion armada constituted some 4,400 ships and landing craft, carrying 154,000 troops and 1,500 tanks, supported by some 11,000 aircraft. The invasion force included twenty-one American divisions, plus British, Canadian, and Polish troops. Of sixty German divisions in France and the Low Countries, only six infantry divisions and one armored division defended Normandy, in part because Allied deception and disinformation pointed to Pas de Calais as the likely invasion site. Still, Germany's formidable coastal defenses included underwater obstacles and mines, concrete pillboxes, tank traps, artillery emplacements, and other hazards. To secure bridges and airfields, British and U.S. airborne divisions had dropped behind German lines in a predawn parachute-glider assault.

The invasion targeted forty miles of coastline between the Orne River and the Cotentin peninsula, with British forces assigned the eastern sector and American troops the west. On Utah Beach, the American right, Major General J. Lawton Collins's VII Corps suffered only light casualties and quickly made contact with units of the Eighty-second Airborne Division. At Omaha Beach, however, where the Germans had moved in a first-rate division at the last minute, withering fire from machine gun emplacements on coastal cliffs cost more than two thousand casualties before General L. T. Gerow's troops dislodged the enemy. The British and Canadians suffered fewer casualties. The British Third Division repelled an armored counterattack northwest of Caen, throwing the Germans on the defensive. By the end of D-Day, approximately 150,000 Allied troops and accompanying materiel had successfully landed. Within a week the build-up had reached a half million men.

The German failure to grasp that the invasion was really taking place proved decisive to the successful Allied invasion at a time of overwhelming German superiority in troops, guns, and tanks. The German High Command, viewing the Normandy attack as a feint, failed until too late to commit their armored reserves. The largest German army remained in the Pas de Calais area, poised to resist an invasion that never occurred. Allied air power and sabotage by the French resistance impeded German movements and enabled the Allies to outpace the Germans in replenishing their forces. The Allied capture of the port of Cherbourg at the end of June set the stage for the American break-out at St. Lô on 25 July. Fierce fighting lay ahead, but victory in Normandy helped end *World War II within a year.

• Stephen E. Ambrose, *D-Day, June 6, 1944: The Climatic Battle of World War II*, 1994. Theodore A. Wilson, ed., *D-Day 1944*, 1994.

—J. Garry Clifford

DEATH AND DYING. Starting in the 1980s, social historians began to trace the history of death in America, a subject once considered outside the realm of historical analysis. Their contributions rescued the subject from oversimplification and clichés, including the stereotype—reinforced by such books as Jessica Mitford's *The American Way of Death* (1963)—of Americans as a death-denying people, too optimistic, energetic, or youth-obsessed to accept its finality. Instead, this new scholarship established critical phases in the history of death and demonstrated the links between this history and broader themes in the nation's development.

The Colonial and Antebellum Eras. Although Americans experienced death in very different ways over the course of two hundred years—pioneering families did not respond to death on the nineteenth-century frontier in the same way as immigrant families responded in early twentieth-century urban ghettos—two distinct stages mark the history of death in America. In the first stage, death was a religious and communal event, part of a shared experience. In the second, death was a medical event, isolated and hidden behind institutional walls. The experience in antebellum *New England under the influence of evangelical Christianity well represents the first stage. The experience of death in the modern, scientifically based, twentieth-century hospital captures the second.

Many of the precepts of *Puritanism survived well into the nineteenth century, particularly in New England, and these precepts, even in modified form, framed the society's fundamental encounter with death and dying. Religious doctrine established the definition of the good death: one that was fully and consciously prepared for. The bad death, as the injunction in the Anglican Book of Common Prayer declared, was the unexpected and quick death: "From sudden death, good Lord deliver us." No document better expresses the need for preparation than Cotton *Mather's 1710 treatise addressed to pregnant women (*Elizabeth in Her Holy Retirement*). Its essential message was that the pregnant woman should prepare herself for her death. This was not only because of the actual risks involved, but also because preparation for death was so vital a task that any occasion, and especially one as fundamental as *childbirth, was made to serve this purpose. Indeed, well into the nineteenth century, textbooks for young children carried such exhortations as: "Look in the graveyard and you shall see, Children buried there shorter than thee."

Early nineteenth-century physicians as well as clergymen shared this outlook. Thus, one noted *Boston physician advised a patient suffering from *tuberculosis that it was time for her to prepare for death, not to combat it through more visits to doctors. "Submit and be content," he counseled. Such medical reliance upon the influence of *religion persisted through much of the nineteenth century. "In serious illness," a leading medical textbook instructed doctors, "you can very properly prepare the way for the introduction of the clergy. We are physicians of the physical body, the temporary life. They are the physicians of the soul, ... the eternal life. Never belittle anything that your patients earnestly believe."

Death in antebellum New England was a communal event. The dying person called in neighbors, made formal farewells, distributed personal effects, and selected those who would watch over his or her final hours. In this same spirit, the actual moment of death was critically important. The dying person was to pass over "without struggle." This constituted the most telling sign that salvation and a heavenly reunion could be anticipated. Thus, the religious-communal death, with the two features very much interconnected, was the central feature in pre-modern America. Death was not hidden and death was not the enemy. It was the testing ground of faith, to be witnessed by family and a wide circle of friends.

From the Civil War to the End of the Twentieth Century. The transition to a second and very different encounter with death came in the *Civil War, because death in war contradicted all the inherited religious and social definitions of the good death. Soldiers died alone on the battlefield, violently, often without witnesses, or in military hospitals, far from family and friends. The enormous effort made by both the Union and Confederate armies to locate the bodies of dead soldiers and transport them home—an effort that gave rise to the practice of embalming—testified to just how radically death in war violated prevailing beliefs and conventions.

However atypical the war experience, it became the prototype of the modern experience of death, that is, death in the hospital. This institution took death out of the home, away from the family, and gave it over to strangers. Why did *hospitals over the course of the twentieth century assume a monopoly over death? Part of the reason was their growing ability to treat illness; since their therapeutic efforts were not always successful, the patient under care sometimes turned into the dying patient. Some of the hospital's centrality also reflected the facts of urban life, including smaller apartments, scattered families, and weakened community relationships. Whatever the cause, the results were unequivocal. The hospital sequestered death and rendered it nearly invisible, not only from the community and friends, but from family as well.

William *Osler of the Johns Hopkins University Medical School, a giant of early twentieth-century clinical medicine, was highly critical of the change. "The tender mother, the loving wife, the devoted sister, the faithful friend and the old servant ... all are gone ...," Osler observed: "Now you [health-care professionals] reign supreme and have added to every illness a domestic complication of which our fathers knew nothing. You have upturned an inalienable right in displacing those who I have just mentioned. You are intruders, innovators and usurpers." Osler's critique remained equally valid in the post-*World War II period. Studying death in public hospitals in the 1960s, the sociologist David Sudnow found that institutional routines enforced the separation of dying patients from their social support network. "While patients in critical conditions technically have the right to round the clock visitors," he noted, "nurses ... strove to separate relatives from those patients about to die. They urged family members to go home or insisted that they wait outside in the corridors, not in the patient's room. Why? If a relative was present then it was necessary for someone from the staff to be present to demonstrate continuing concern which was inefficient as well as futile." And what was true for nurses was still more true for physicians.

Although the demographics of death had changed in many ways by the closing decades of the twentieth century—men living, on average, well into their seventies and women, almost to their eighties—the most central social development related to death in these years was the broad-based effort to recapture death from the hospital and the health-care professional. The rise of hospices, the emergence of advanced directives and living wills, and even the movement for physician-assisted suicide, all represent a rebellion against the prevailing system. The goal was now to facilitate death at home among family and friends and give decisionmaking about death to the patient. As a new century dawned, neither religion nor organized *medicine commanded the authority they once did and many Americans appeared determined to sieze control over the process of dying, even if biology ultimately placed that goal beyond reach.

[*See also* Demography; Health and Fitness; Life Stages; Nursing; Urbanization.]

• David Sudnow, *Passing On: the Social Organization of Dying*, 1967. Philippe Ariès, *The Hour of Our Death*, 1974. David E. Stannard, *The Puritan Way of Death: A Study in Religion, Culture and Social Change*, 1977. Norbert Elias, *The Loneliness of Dying*, 1985. Ruth Richardson, *Death, Dissection, and the Destitute*, 1987, 2d ed., 2000. Gary Laderman, *The Sacred Remains: American Attitudes toward Death, 1799–1883*, 1996.

—David J. Rothman

DEATH PENALTY. *See* Capital Punishment.

DEBAKEY, MICHAEL (1908–), cardiovascular surgeon. Heart surgery was not feasible when Michael DeBakey, a native of Lake Charles, Louisiana, earned his M.D. from Tulane University in 1932. After teaching surgery at Tulane (1937–1948), he became professor of surgery at the Baylor College of Medicine in Houston in 1948. As president of this institution (1969–1979), he led it from fiscal crisis to major stature. He became chancellor in 1979. DeBakey was concurrently senior attending surgeon at Houston's Methodist Hospital.

A pioneer in his field, DeBakey by 1996 had performed more than sixty thousand cardiovascular procedures. His innovations varied from Dacron artificial arteries (1953) to the development of a left ventricular bypass pump (1968). Other pace-setting achievements included patch-graft angioplasty and aorto-coronary bypass using vein grafts from the leg. He developed more than seventy surgical instruments and other technology for cardiovascular surgery and treatment, published in excess of 1,500 professional articles, and trained more than 1,000 surgeons. A public advocate of federal support of biomedical research, education, and better health care, he chaired President Lyndon B. *Johnson's Commission on Heart Diseases, Cancer, and Stroke; endorsed the federal Medicare system when practicing physicians overwhelmingly opposed it; and championed the establishment of the National Library of Medicine in 1956. To help laypersons understand the heart and heart disease, he coauthored two bestsellers, *The Living Heart* (1977) and *The New Living Heart Diet* (1984). When DeBakey in 1996 conferred in Moscow with Russian physicians who performed quintuple coronary bypass surgery on President Boris Yeltsin, media coverage portrayed him as America's most prominent cardiovascular surgeon.

[*See also* Heart Disease; Medicare and Medicaid; Medicine: Since 1945.]

• William C. Roberts, "Michael Ellis DeBakey: A Conversation with the Editor," *American Journal of Cardiology* 79, no. 7 (1 April 1997): 929–50.

—Charles T. Morrissey

DEBS, EUGENE V. (1855–1926), labor leader, socialist, and presidential candidate. The son of Alsatian immigrants, Eugene Victor Debs became a *railroad worker at age fourteen in his native Terre Haute, Indiana. After four years as a railway fireman, he took a job as a clerk but remained active in the Brotherhood of Locomotive Firemen, becoming its secretary-treasurer and editor of its journal. In 1893 he broke with the craft-union tradition by helping found the American Railway Union, which organized both skilled and unskilled workers. The following year, he led a boycott of the Pullman Palace Car Company, which tied up the nation's railroad system but ultimately failed.

After six months in jail for his role in the Pullman boycott, Debs began a career as a lecturer and journalist. Embracing *socialism, he ran as the Socialist party's candidate for president five times, beginning in 1900. His best showing came in 1912 when he won nearly 6 percent of the popular vote. In 1905 Debs helped found the *Industrial Workers of the World, a radical alternative to the *American Federation of Labor. Debs served two years in prison (1919–1921) for a 1918 speech denouncing the federal government's repressive wartime policies. Even behind bars, he polled nearly 920,000 votes in the 1920 presidential election. Afterward, he returned to Terre Haute, still committed to socialism but hampered by ill health.

Debs looms large in American labor history as an eloquent spokesperson for workers' rights and an early advocate of industrial unionism. Later, he became the most influential socialist in the nation's history. A spellbinding orator, he used the language of Christianity and American *radicalism to argue for revolutionary change, widening socialism's appeal beyond the immigrant circles where it first won favor. Even after government repression and factionalism crippled the Socialist party, Debs remained a popular symbol of dissent and egalitarianism.

[*See also* Labor Movements; Pullman Strike and Boycott; Socialist Party of America; Thomas, Norman.]

• Ray Ginger, *The Bending Cross, A Biography of Eugene Victor Debs*, 1949. Nick Salvatore, *Eugene V. Debs: Citizen and Socialist*, 1982.

—Joshua B. Freeman

DECLARATION OF INDEPENDENCE. When the Second *Continental Congress met in *Philadelphia in May 1775, only a minority of delegates favored independence from Great Britain. Just a year later, however, sentiment for complete separation was strong enough to make a movement toward independence politically feasible. By that time George III had declared the colonies to be in rebellion, and Parliament had pronounced them beyond the protection of the Crown and forbidden all trade with them. Thomas *Paine's **Common Sense*, published in January 1776 and widely circulated, forcefully and convincingly argued for a complete political and emotional break with the mother country.

By the spring of 1776 the delegates to the Continental Congress from the two largest colonies, Massachusetts and Virginia, strongly advocated independence. On 15 May, the delegates adopted John *Adams's radical resolution that the colonies assume full powers of self-government and that all exercise of British authority be suppressed. On 7 June, Richard Henry Lee moved (and Adams seconded) that the colonies were "and of right ought to be, free and independent States." Four days later, Congress appointed a committee consisting of John Adams, Benjamin *Franklin, Thomas *Jefferson, Robert R. Livingston (1746–1813), and Roger Sherman (1721–1793) to draft a preamble to Lee's resolution. This preamble is what we know as the Declaration of Independence.

Jefferson, the youngest member of the committee and, according to John Adams, one with "reputation of a masterly pen," was chosen to prepare the document. Influenced by George Mason's draft of the *Virginia Declaration of Rights and using the opening of his own first draft of the Virginia Constitution, Jefferson prepared a rough draft of the Declaration of Independence. He submitted it first to Adams and then to Franklin and other members of the committee for suggestions. They proposed some stylistic alterations and on 28 June the revised version was presented to Congress. On 2 July the Congress meeting as a committee of the whole adopted the Lee resolution, declaring independence without a negative vote (the New York delegation, waiting for new instructions, abstained). Between 2 and 4 July the committee's preamble, the Declaration, was debated. The congressional delegates, again meeting as a committee of the whole, further revised the document. The preamble was changed only in minor stylistic ways but major deletions were made in the list of grievances (see below). The Declaration was adopted on 4 July, and on the 15th, Congress directed that the word "Unanimous" be added to the document's official title, "Declaration of the Thirteen United States of America." After the official engrossed parchment copy was signed on 2 August, broadsides were distributed throughout the country.

Seeking not to set forth a new theory of government but to justify and publicize the American cause, and to provide a philosophical rationale and political justification for independence, Jefferson turned to ideas that were the conventional wisdom of the day. He sought consensus, not originality. Among the ideas upon which he drew were those of natural law philosophy, the British Whig revolutionary tradition, and the Scottish enlightenment. Among these were the writings of John Locke, Algernon Sidney, John Trenchard, and Thomas Gordon. The Declaration proclaimed "self-evident truths": that all men are created equal and that they possess certain God-given rights by virtue of being human beings. Among these natural, "unalienable" rights are "Life, Liberty, and the pursuit of Happiness." The corollary of Jefferson's premise was that government is instituted only to secure these rights and that whenever government fails in this duty, the people have the right "to alter or to abolish it" and institute a new one. Such a change, however, is not to be undertaken "for light and transient Causes."

The longest section of the document offered a catalog of grievances leveled not against Parliament but directly and personally at the Crown, to which, the colonists maintained, their loyalty was exclusively owed. These "facts submitted to a candid world" were systematically enumerated to demonstrate how patient the colonists had been in the face of repeated injury. Most of the accusations had been anticipated in earlier documents that Jefferson penned or contributed to (*A Summary View of the Rights of British America, Declaration of the Causes and Necessity for Taking Up Arms*, and the Preamble to the Virginia Constitution). Nineteen grievances, one of which is divided into eight parts, were included in the final version of the Declaration of Independence. Among the offenses of the king were refusing his assent to laws necessary for the public good, dissolving properly elected legislatures, creating a multitude of new offices "to harass our People," quartering armed troops in the colonies, imposing taxes without the consent of the people, ravaging coasts and burning towns, and inciting "domestic Insurrections." The repetition of the phrase "He has" before each of George III's misdeeds made a rhetorically powerful summary of "repeated Injuries and Usurpations" that could serve as useful propaganda for attracting support from other countries.

Most of the revisions that Congress made to the document tightened and improved the prose in this list of grievances. The most notable excision was a lengthy paragraph condemning the slave trade and holding George III responsible for its continuation by opposing all legislative efforts to halt it. Congress also softened Jefferson's strident criticism of the British electorate for failing to object to the abuses being heaped upon their compatriots in North America.

In the immediate post-revolution period, little attention seems to have been paid to the Declaration or its authorship. In the 1790s, a period of intense partisanship, however, the Republicans were eager to establish a connection between their party leader, Jefferson, and the nation's founding document. Federalists understandably played down the association. John Adams insisted that Jefferson had merely put a collaborative effort on paper.

Contemporary scholars tend to emphasize the social and cultural context of the document rather than the evolution of its text and the political ideas expressed in it. Criticized today for excluding blacks and women from its ringing assertion of equality, the Declaration of Independence nonetheless inspired the language and ideology of later social and political reform charters, including the declaration of the 1848 Seneca Falls woman's rights convention which Elizabeth Cady *Stanton explicitly modeled on the 1776 document.

[*See also* Colonial Era; Committees of Correspondence; Constitution; Equality; Republicanism; Revolution and Constitution, Era of; Revolutionary War; Seneca Falls Convention; Slavery: The Slave Trade; Women's Rights Movements.]

• Carl Becker, *The Declaration of Independence: A Study in the History of Political Ideas,* 1922. Garry Wills, *Inventing America,* 1978. Jay Fliegelman, *Declaring Independence: Jefferson, Natural Language & the Culture of Performance,* 1993. Pauline Maier, *American Scripture: The Declaration of Independence,* 1997. Julian P. Boyd, *The Declaration of Independence: The Evolution of a Text,* rev. ed., 1999. Robert M. S. McDonald, "Thomas Jefferson's Changing Reputation as Author of the *Declaration of Independence*: The First Fifty Years," *Journal of the Early Republic* 19 (Summer 1999), 169–95.

—Barbara B. Oberg

DEFENSE DEPARTMENT. *See* Federal Government, Executive Branch: Department of Defense.

DEFENSE INDUSTRY. *See* Federal Government, Executive Branch: Department of Defense; Military, The; Weaponry, Nonnuclear; World War I; World War II.

DEISM, a generic term for the "rational" religion that challenged orthodox Christianity from the middle *Colonial Era through the era of the *Early Republic. Essentially an Enlightenment phenomenon, American deism was inspired by British free thought; Newtonian physics; the empiricist psychology of John Locke; and, in the later eighteenth century, French revolutionary thought. American thinkers in the early eighteenth century were moderately influenced by deism, but by the 1780s it had become popular and militant. Both Ethan Allen (1738–1789) in *Reason the Only Oracle of Man* (1784) and Thomas *Paine in *The Age of Reason* (1794) publicly and notoriously endorsed it. Deism reached its highpoint in the 1790s under the radical leadership of Elihu Palmer (1764–1806). A number of deistical societies, "temples of reason," and newspapers devoted to rational religion were launched.

Deists rejected Christian belief in scriptural inerrancy, miracles, Jesus's divinity, and revelation. Some also condemned Christianity on moral grounds, arguing that it encouraged intolerance, superstition, and irrationality. As an alternative, deism posited an impersonal First Cause whose rationality is reflected in physical laws and human intellect, and lauded the exercise of virtue and reason as the truest form of worship. As notorious for their radical *republicanism as for their religious heterodoxy, deists defended free speech and universal tolerance, opposed *slavery and the conservative principles of the *Federalist party, and enthusiastically endorsed the radical ideology of the French Revolution. Thomas *Jefferson, a deist sympathizer, was vilified during his first presidential campaign in 1800 as a libertine infidel. Rational religion and radical republicanism remained associated in the public mind throughout the next few decades.

Deism waned as the Enlightenment gave way to the *Romantic movement and a resurgent Christian evangelism in the early nineteenth century. But its ideal of rational religion inspired liberal versions of Christianity such as *Unitarianism and Universalism. Moreover, its advocacy of religious freedom and separation of *church and state helped enshrine these two principles in the American mind.

• Kerry S. Walters, *The American Deists: Voices of Reason and Dissent in the Early Republic,* 1992. Kerry S. Walters, *Rational Infidels: The American Deists,* 1992. Kerry S. Walters, *Benjamin Franklin and His Gods,* 1999.

—Kerry S. Walters

DE KOONING, WILLEM (1904–1997), painter. Born in Rotterdam, Willem de Kooning studied at the Rotterdam Academy of Fine Arts and Techniques from age twelve. He immigrated to the United States in 1926 and settled in New York the following year, initially supporting himself as a housepainter and commercial artist. He became a full-time artist around 1936, first making portraits of unidentified men and then of women. His first solo exhibition, at New York's Charles Egan Gallery in 1948, consisted of painterly abstractions mostly in black and white. By 1950, de Kooning had emerged as a key figure in the *Abstract Expressionism movement or "New York School," although much of his work is arguably not abstract. He is best known for the large paintings of women he first exhibited in 1953. These depictions of women with exaggerated breasts and terrifying, toothy grins were realized with slashing brushstrokes that some critics read as violent assaults on the subjects. These works gave way to abstract urban landscapes in the mid-1950s, made with strident tones and thick, gouged paint that evokes the gritty textures of *New York City streets. By the late 1950s de Kooning had developed a distinctive gestural style that significantly influenced a subsequent generation of painters. In 1963 he moved permanently to East Hampton, Long Island, where he made paintings of women and landscapes inspired by the light of the Atlantic coast. In 1969 de Kooning began to make *sculptures; he was also a supremely gifted draftsman. He developed *Alzheimer's disease in the mid-1980s.

[*See also* Painting: Since 1945.]

• Harold Rosenberg, *Willem de Kooning,* 1974. Marla Prather, Richard Shiff, and David Sylvester, *Willem de Kooning: Paintings* (exhibition catalog), 1994.

—Marla Prather

DEMOCRACY. *See* Constitution; Republicanism; Suffrage.

DEMOCRACY IN AMERICA (1835–1840). Alexis de Tocqueville's two-volume *Democracy in America* has endured as a classic study of American society and institutions. While nineteenth-century intellectuals read Tocqueville hoping his insight into American life would supplement their debates over the democratic and nationalistic revolutions sweeping Europe, the work's searching analysis of the social impact of democratic institutions underlies its continuing influence. From the *Cold War Era, when Americans sought reassurance about their political system, to the radical 1960s, when many citizens' confidence in democracy faltered, to the multiculturalist debates of the late twentieth century, Tocqueville has offered Americans illuminating criticisms of and theories about their society.

Although born to an aristocratic Parisian family, Tocqueville (1805–1859) embraced the French Enlightenment. As a judicial official, he cultivated a keen interest in liberal institutions. Securing a commission in 1831 to study American prisons with another young nobleman, Gustave de Beaumont, he set out for a nine-month tour of the United States. Tocqueville interviewed prison officials, *Supreme Court justices, businessmen, farmers, and *Whig party leaders. Returning to France, he and Beaumont published their study of American prisons, leaving Tocqueville free to compose *Democracy in America.*

America, Tocqueville argued, offered Europeans an opportunity to learn how the excesses of majority rule might be tempered. Expecting to find that popular passions had run amok without an aristocracy, the Frenchman instead discovered the stabilizing effects of American law, *religion, and the *family. While he addressed topics ranging from race relations to women's roles in society, Tocqueville's underlying theme remained the balance between *equality and *liberty. He feared that Americans would both abuse and erode their *individualism—a term he coined to describe Americans' independence and self-reliance. But in the voluntary associations he found throughout the United States, Tocqueville saw hope that America would endure.

[*See also* Antebellum Era; Early Republic, Era of the; Prisons and Penitentiaries; Voluntarism.]

• George Wilson Pierson, *Tocqueville and Beaumont in America*, 1938. Abraham S. Eisenstadt, ed., *Reconsidering Tocqueville's* Democracy in America, 1988.

—Eric D. Daniels

DEMOCRATIC PARTY. No certain date marks the beginning of the Democratic party, but its intellectual heritage can be traced to Thomas *Jefferson and James *Madison, both of whom shunned parties even as they shaped the policies and sensibility of the so-called Democratic-Republican political movement during the 1790s. Opposing the centralizing programs of Secretary of the Treasury Alexander *Hamilton, who urged a revenue system based on *tariffs, excise taxes, a federal bank, and funding of the national debt, Jefferson and Madison established enduring party themes. Champions of the common people, especially small farmers, they spoke for small and frugal government, of *states' rights, and the people's sovereignty. In their presidential administrations from 1801 until 1817, the two Virginians sought to retire the national debt, remove the government from the nation's economic life, and rely on state militias rather than a federal army.

While the Democrats had leaders, a program, and an ideology, they had no organization or loyal following until after 1828 when Andrew *Jackson was elected president. The Democrats, who now embraced the name their enemies had employed to tarnish them as radicals, held national presidential nominating conventions beginning in 1832, making this the world's oldest continuing political party. Coalescing around the popular Jackson, they started campaign newspapers, organized local and state committees, and built support through barbecues and partisan clubs.

Jackson, in turn, using presidential patronage to solidify support, defined national issues—especially in his opposition to a national bank and to federally funded internal improvements. These positions linked Democrats throughout the country to an organization with a national identity distinct from the *Whig party (and later the *Know-Nothing and *Republican parties) in a competitive two-party system. By 1836 when master party-builder Martin *Van Buren won the presidency, nearly 80 percent of white males were voting in national elections, with the Democrats the majority party controlling Congress and many state legislatures.

From 1840 to 1860, the Democrats displayed considerable resiliency. While they elected presidents James Knox *Polk, Franklin *Pierce, and James *Buchanan in this period, they faced a bitter sectional crisis. Recruiting urban German and Irish immigrants into their ranks, they achieved a nationwide constituency, only to see it shattered in the 1850s by congressional divisions over *slavery in the territories and the emergence of a powerful Republican party in the North. On the eve of the *Civil War, as party realignments shuffled the support of all political parties, the Democrats' power and programs tilted toward the *South.

From 1860, when a divided Democratic party offered the electorate two sectional candidates—Stephen A. *Douglas of Illinois and Kentucky's John Breckinridge (1821–1875)—until the end of *Reconstruction in 1877, the Democrats were a minority party. During the Civil War many leaders and supporters joined the Confederacy, and the majority Republicans tarred northern Democrats as disloyal copperheads. Still, even as Democrats opposed Emancipation and such popular Republican legislation as the *Homestead Act and support for higher education, they continued to hold a third of the voters as well as a few northern governorships and legislatures.

After the war, Democrats came to embody white *racism as they opposed the Reconstruction amendments granting freedmen citizenship and voting rights. White southerners' disproportionate power in the party was perpetuated by a party rule that presidential nominations must be approved by two-thirds, not just a majority, of convention delegates. Using voting-precinct surveys and door-to-door leafletting (a campaign strategy developed by New York's Samuel Tilden), Democrats captured the House of Representatives in 1874, stunningly demonstrating their durability. As Reconstruction collapsed and the South returned to white domination, the party's future was assured, albeit with a dependence on the South and the increasingly Democratic border states that lasted until after *World War II. Urban ethnic voters and white southerners formed the party's core constituencies. Although failing to win the presidency apart from Grover *Cleveland's two victories in 1884 and 1892, the late nineteenth-century Democratic party elected significant numbers of congressmen and senators who, given seniority rules, dominated important committees.

From 1896 to 1932, Republicans overwhelmingly controlled the federal government. Even William Jennings *Bryan, who sounded like a Jacksonian with his agrarian appeals and complaints about monopolies, could not win the presidency in 1896, 1900, or 1908. But Bryan marked a watershed in party thinking when he championed an activist government. The 1908 Democratic platform espoused regulation of trusts and *railroads, a federal *income tax, and a national health bureau. In keeping with the party themes of equal rights and opportunities for all, liberal Democrats came to accept government intervention as a necessity for the well-being of citizens in an industrial society.

Woodrow *Wilson, in his successful presidential campaign of 1912, picked up on these themes with his New Freedom concept grounded in individual freedom achieved with the aid of the national government. Although Wilson won in 1912 primarily owing to a split in Republican ranks, he pursued a popular legislative agenda that included *child-labor reform, aid to *agriculture, federal income taxes, corporate regulations, and banking reform. In his second term (until incapacitated by a stroke in 1919) he identified the Democratic party with an internationalist perspective sustained by party leaders throughout the remainder of the twentieth century.

The Democrats' long electoral drought in the 1920s ended in 1932 with the election of Franklin Delano *Roosevelt. As the Republicans failed to meet the challenges of the Great Depression, the Democrats, led by the masterful coalition-builder Roosevelt, used the government to alleviate economic and social problems. For the first time, the party became popular among *African Americans, historically attached to the party of Lincoln. The New Deal coalition of urban ethnic voters, blacks, farmers, union members, and (increasingly restive) white southerners enabled Roosevelt's successor Harry S. *Truman to win election in his own right in 1948, sustained Democratic strength in Congress in the 1950s even as the Republicans regained the presidency, and undergirded the 1960s administrations of John F. *Kennedy and Lyndon B. *Johnson.

On foreign affairs, Democrats had historically differed widely, from Polk's *expansionism to Bryan's *pacifism and anti-imperialism to Wilson's *internationalism. From the late 1930s through the *Cold War, the party firmly espoused internationalism, military strength, and America's mission to resist totalitarianism of the right or left. Roosevelt stiffened the nation's resolve to battle fascism, and the Truman administration embraced America's postwar global role in the struggle against communism in Europe, Korea, and elsewhere. By the 1960s, the party's Cold War liberalism focused on Asia, as President Johnson, while championing social *welfare and *civil rights at home, also plunged the nation into full-scale war in Vietnam.

The late 1960s and 1970s brought a broad-based reaction against the Democrats, not only because of the *Vietnam War's bitter legacy, but also because of the party's identification with welfare spending, school busing, racial preferences, and a series of volatile social issues from *abortion to gay rights unpopular with conservatives. The party struggled to represent the interests of various minority constituencies while simultaneously offering a national vision, but Republican Richard M. *Nixon defeated the liberal stalwart Hubert *Humphrey in the 1968 presidential race and crushed the 1972 Democratic candidate, liberal senator George McGovern (1922–) of South Dakota. The southern Democrat Jimmy *Carter narrowly won in 1976, in the aftermath of *Watergate, but by the 1980s, as many white middle-class and working-class voters concluded that the party had abandoned "mainstream" values, millions of Roosevelt Democrats became Reagan Democrats.

As the twentieth century ended, Democratic and Republican leaders alike struggled to adapt in an era of diminished party loyalty, voter fractiousness, personalized over-organized politics, and the dominance of *television. Divided government became the pattern: Democrats in the 1980s generally controlled Congress, the Republicans the presidency; in the 1990s, the situation was reversed.

Amid growing voter cynicism and apathy, Democratic neoliberals in Congress, organized as the Democratic Leadership Council, sought to erase the party's identification with big government and deficit spending. Adopting a centrist approach, Arkansas governor Bill *Clinton proved a charismatic campaigner, returning the Democrats to the White House in 1992. Embracing deficit reduction and welfare reform, and aided by a buoyant economy, Clinton won reelection in 1996—only to endure the ignominy of an *impeachment trial on charges arising from his efforts to conceal an affair with a White House intern. In the Cold War's aftermath, Clinton continued the tradition of Democratic internationalism, focusing now on regional peacekeeping, combating threats from rogue states, and promoting world trade.

[*See also* Affirmative Action; Antitrust Legislation; Bank of the United States, First and Second; Compromise of 1877; Depressions, Economic; Federal Government, Executive Branch: The Presidency; Federal Government, Legislative Branch: House of Representatives; Federal Government, Legislative Branch: Senate. Foreign Relations; Gay and Lesbian Rights Movement; German Americans; Irish Americans; Liberalism; New Deal Era, The; Political Parties; Populist Era; Populist Party; Progressive Era; Progressive Party of 1912–1924; Progressive Party of 1948; Sixties, The.]

• David Cohn, *The Fabulous Democrats*, 1956. Ralph Goldman, *The Democratic Party in American Politics*, 1966. Richard Wade, "The Democratic Party, 1960–1972," in *History of U.S. Political Parties*, ed. Arthur Schlesinger Jr., 1973, pp. 2827–68. Dewey Grantham, *The Life and Death of the Solid South*, 1979. Robert Rutland, *The Democrats: From Jefferson to Carter*, 1979. Alan Ware, *The Breakdown of the Democratic Party Organization*, 1985. Murray Fisher, ed., *Of the People: The 200-Year History of the Democratic Party*, 1992. Peter Kovler, ed., *Democrats and the American Idea*, 1992.

—Jean Harvey Baker

DEMOGRAPHY. Demography examines the sources and consequences of population increases or decreases. This, in turn, involves assessing the rates of birth, death, and geographic movement—fertility, mortality, and migration. Historically, American demography fits into a three-stage progression characteristic of societies that now have low birth and death rates. Convenient labels for these three stages are Malthusian-frontier, neo-Malthusian, and post-Malthusian. (The term "Malthusian" comes from Thomas Robert Malthus, a pioneering English theorist of demography). Originating in the theory of demographic transition, this periodization scheme locates a turbulent transitional era, between two periods of relative stability, when a demographic pattern of roughly balanced *high* birth and death rates gives way to one of relatively equal *low* birth and death rates.

While "demographic transition" theorists once portrayed the decline in fertility as a response to a reduction in mortality, this theory is today usually seen as a useful description, or first approximation, of historical experience rather than a guide to cause and effect or a detailed blueprint that adequately captures all of the features of the demographic history of the United States or any other society. In comparative terms, the most distinctive feature of American demographic history is the extremely rapid growth of people of European and African origins, from 250,000 in 1700 to a projected 275 million by the year 2000—a thousandfold increase. Over these same three hundred years, the population of Europe multiplied only fivefold.

The human impact of this demographic transition is profound. Before 1800, in the traditional or pretransitional era of high fertility, the average woman who survived to age fifty had seven children; in the 1990s, the average was two children. The high fertility of the traditional era produced a very young aggregate population. About half of the pre-1800 population was under age sixteen; by the 1990s, the median age was thirty-three years. Only one in forty Americans in 1800 was over sixty-five, compared to one in eight at the end of the twentieth century.

Mortality rates have changed dramatically as well. Until about the 1870s, the average *life expectancy in the United States was around forty-five years, compared to seventy-six years in the 1990s. The impact of mortality decline is somewhat misleading if portrayed in terms of averages, however, since relatively few individuals actually die around the average age at death. Instead, infants and young children once died at radically higher rates than today, pulling the average down. In the pre-1870s period, about one in six infants died before his or her first birthday, and one in four died before age five. In the 1990s, fewer than 2 percent of American infants died before their fifth birthday. Instead of infectious diseases, which took a heavy toll on the young, the major killers at the end of the twentieth century were chronic *diseases related to aging, especially cardiovascular disease and *cancer, which together accounted for nearly two-thirds of all deaths.

Three elements characterize the demography of the earliest stage of American population history: (1) an extremely high rate of overall growth that, despite a substantial contribution of *immigration, was mostly due to natural increase—the difference between birth and death rates; (2) high fertility caused by markedly younger marriage ages for women than in western Europe; and (3) mortality that was high compared to the late twentieth century, but moderate in comparison to contemporary death rates in Europe.

The term "Malthusian-frontier" summarizes the larger economic and cultural context of this demographic regime of rapid natural increase in early America. Writing in 1798, Malthus linked mortality rates and marriage age to the tenuous but ultimately equilibrating relationship between population size and food supply. Because Malthus lived in an era when sustained growth of economic *productivity was nearly inconceivable, long-term population growth seemed impossible. Demographic expansion, he theorized, would ultimately be halted by what he called the "positive check" of higher mortality caused by famine and malnutrition.

Malthus, however, viewed eighteenth-century America as an exception to his general rule that resource constraints would limit population growth. America's seemingly boundless frontier and low population density meant that land was cheap and labor expensive. Because couples could acquire land relatively easily, they could, Malthus reasoned (as had Benjamin *Franklin a half-century earlier), marry earlier than their counterparts in Europe. This relaxation of what Malthus called the "preventive check" of late marriage spurred American population growth.

Over the course of the nineteenth century, couples married later and, more significantly, began to practice family limitation. Fertility fell by 50 percent, even though few couples apparently made use of contraceptive devices. These nineteenth-century trends can be attributed in part to the declining availability of agricultural land as the frontier moved toward

MAP 5: MAP OF THE UNITED STATES BY POPULATION DENSITY (1941)

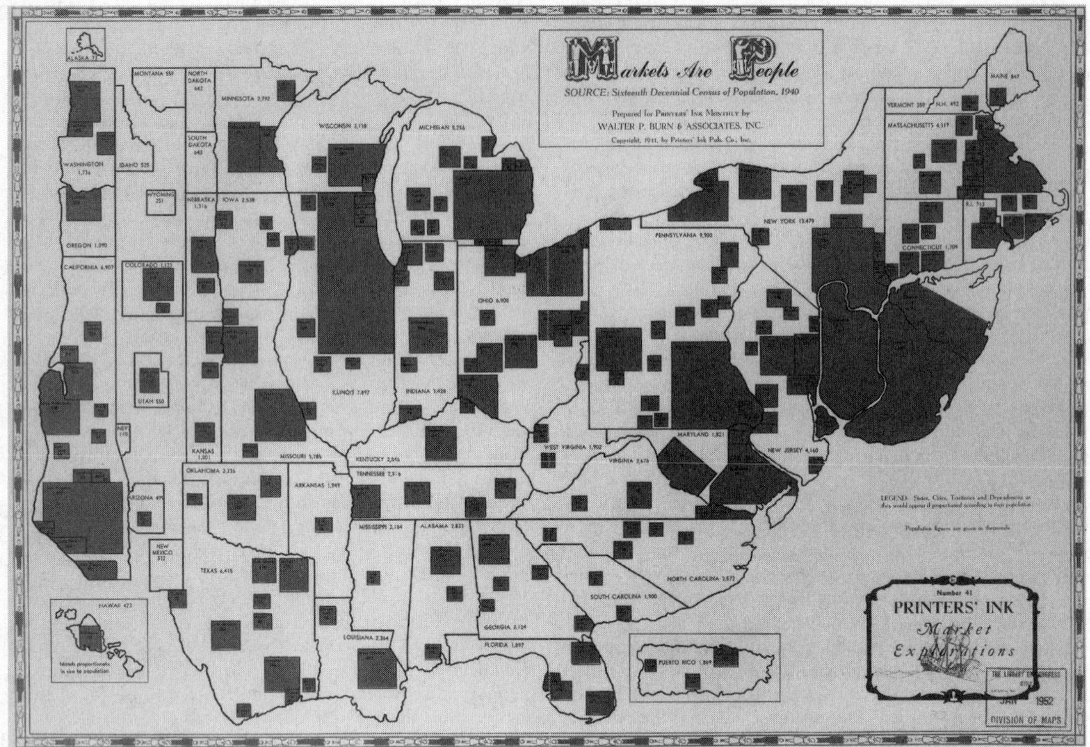

The interests of marketers and advertisers helped stimulate the demographic study of the U.S. population in the twentieth century, since businesses wished to concentrate their efforts where potential customers were most numerous. This cartogram, prepared by a marketing firm and based on the 1940 census, dramatically shows the heavy concentration of population along the northern Atlantic seaboard; the Upper Middle West, in a corridor including Cleveland, Detroit, Chicago, and Milwaukee; and along the Pacific Coast, particularly around Los Angeles and San Francisco.

[*See* Advertising; Demography; Mass Marketing.]

closure. *Urbanization also played a role in this large-scale demographic transition. Before 1800, during the "Malthusian-frontier" era, only one in twenty Americans lived in a town or city. Since 1970, with the process of urbanization nearly complete, about three-fourths of Americans have resided in places with populations over 2,500. While large numbers of foreigners arrived in the United States from 1840 to 1920, in no decade did immigration account for more than one-third of total population increase. High (though declining) rates of natural increase continued as a distinctive feature of American demographic history during this transitional stage.

The third phase of American demographic history, the closing decades of the twentieth century, was characterized by the increasing irrelevance of marriage, demographically speaking. The wide gap between fertility rates of married and unmarried women shrank dramatically in this period. By the 1990s, further, Americans were marrying later than at any time in the nation's history.

The three-period framework fits the historical experience of *African Americans as well. As with the population as a whole, rapid rates of aggregate growth characterized the early historical demography of the American black population, especially in the era of *slavery. Of the 10 to 11 million Africans brought to the New World in the slave trade, some 600,000 to 650,000 were imported into the area that became the United States. During the nineteenth century, annual natural increase among American slaves was over 2 percent, only slightly under the rate for the white population. Compared to slaves in other regions of the Americas, the enslaved population in the United States had both higher fertility and lower mortality. Since emancipation, blacks and whites have experienced the same trends in mortality and fertility, although both rates have been consistently higher for blacks. The black-white difference in life expectancy at birth was six years in 1990 compared to eight years in 1900.

Prior to the twentieth century, the indigenous Indian population experienced a radically different demographic trajectory from that of European and African Americans. Instead of rapidly increasing, the numbers of Indians declined precipitously, a demographic catastrophe owing largely to extremely high death rates from diseases of European origin—most importantly *smallpox, typhus, and measles. Having no previous experience with these diseases, whole populations were nearly wiped out by epidemics. Estimates of the numbers of Indians in North America before European contact are varied and disputed. One conjecture places the figure at more than 5 million in the conterminous U.S. area in 1492. By 1800, the Indian population was about 600,000. It reached its nadir of 250,000 in the 1890s. The Indian population rebounded after 1900, however, reaching nearly 1.9 million in the 1990 census.

The public discussion of population-related issues over the course of American history has typically reflected these broad trends. During the *Colonial Era, Americans exulted in, and British officials worried about, the colonies' exploding population. Central to nineteenth-century demographic thinking were the relationships among land availability, population, and the social order. Thomas *Jefferson and James *Madison believed that territorial expansion would sustain the egalitarian economic basis of republican political institutions. During the *Antebellum Era, both southern and northern writers tied the eventual extinction of slavery to a limitation of its territorial expansion into cheap lands. At century's end, historian Frederick Jackson *Turner saw the closing of the frontier as the end of an epoch in American history.

Differential fertility among various groups attracted considerable comment during the period of transition to lower birth rates. Native-born New Englanders, the vanguard group in the control of fertility within marriage, were thought to be on a path toward "race suicide." By the close of the twentieth century, population questions often intertwined with value debates over such issues as *abortion, women's status, and intergenerational equity.

Even in the third stage of relative demographic stability, important changes still occurred. The baby boom of the post–*World War II era, peaking in 1957, nearly doubled total fertility rates. A "baby bust" of equal magnitude then surprised the experts. These fluctuations gave rise to the prospect of the nation's having too few people of working age to fund the retirement of the baby boomers beginning in the second decade of the twenty-first century. A new wave of immigration, principally from Latin America and Asia, was another important development of the late twentieth century with demographic implications.

Despite these changes, by the late twentieth century, fertility fluctuated narrowly around replacement levels, mortality was declining at a markedly lower pace than in the three-quarters of a century after 1880, urbanization had nearly ended, and Americans had become less residentially and geographically mobile. With only 3 percent of the workforce engaged in *agriculture, it was obvious that the long-term shift from farm to city was over. As a new century approached, demographic phenomena were much more stable than they had been during the previous century and a half.

[*See also* Birth Control and Family Planning; Columbian Exchange; Heart Disease; Indian History and Culture; Life Stages; Marriage and Divorce.]

• Robert V. Wells, *Revolutions in Americans' Lives: A Demographic Perspective on the History of Americans, Their Families, and Their Society*, 1982. Samuel H. Preston and Michael R. Haines, *Fatal Years: Child Mortality in Late Nineteenth-Century America*, 1991. Massimo Livi-Bacci, *A Concise History of World Population*, 1992. Douglas L. Anderton, Richard E. Barrett, and Donald L. Bogue, *The Population of the United States*, 3d. ed., 1997. Michael R. Haines, "The Population of the United States, 1790–1920," in *The Cambridge Economic History of the United States*, vol. II, *The Long Nineteenth Century*, eds. Stanley Engerman and Robert Gallman, 2001.

—Daniel Scott Smith

DENTISTRY. Throughout the *Colonial Era, Americans suffered from extremely poor dental health. Dental decay and soft-tissue disease were rampant, and people typically relied on their own resources for dental care. Toothbrushes were rare, but many owned a "tooth forcep" to pull rotting teeth. Domestic dental care prevailed until the later eighteenth century, when European-trained "operators for the teeth" arrived to seek their fortune. These operators (later called surgeon-dentists) not only introduced the formal practice of dentistry but served as preceptors to local folk, usually skilled mechanics, who wished to learn the trade.

Early nineteenth-century dental practice consisted largely of tooth restoration and extraction and the construction of artificial dentures. In 1846 the Hartford, Connecticut, dentist Horace Wells launched a revolution in dental (and general) *surgery with his successful demonstration of the use of nitrous oxide as a general anesthetic. At about the same time, William T. G. Morton of Boston began using sulfuric ether for the same purpose.

The *Gilded Age saw the emergence of dentistry as a distinctive profession, with its own schools, societies, and journals. Dentists organized the American Dental Association in 1866, the American Academy of Dental Science in 1876, and the National Association of Dental Examiners in 1883. By 1900, some one hundred dental schools were scattered throughout the country, most of them of inferior quality. In 1926, William J. Gies completed a survey of the state of American dental education, analogous to the more famous *Flexner Report of 1910 on *medical education. As Gies saw it, dentists had two choices for upgrading their profession: making dentistry a medical specialty and requiring an M.D. degree, or bringing dental schools up to the quality of medical schools. American dentists chose the latter course.

In the early twentieth century, dental practice became increasingly specialized. Orthodontics (preventing and correcting irregularities of the teeth) became a recognized specialty in 1901, thanks to the efforts of Edward H. Angle, the first American dentist to limit his practice to a particular area of expertise. Periodontics (which focused on the gums) followed in 1918, oral surgery in 1918. Oral pathology (1936), dental *public health (1937), and endodontics (which focused on the roots of teeth, 1959) eventually emerged as dental specialties as well. Twentieth-century dentists continued to devote much of their practice to prosthetics, replacing missing parts of the mouth and jaw with artificial devices such as dentures and bridges.

In 1919 the U.S. Department of Public Health established a dental division to call attention to the needs of the indigent, the disabled, and minorities; in 1948 the *National Institutes of Health created the National Institute for Dental Research. Among these agencies' most successful programs were fluoridating public drinking water to prevent cavities, screening for oral cancer, and encouraging the use of mouth protectors by athletes.

Twentieth-century dental practice was greatly influenced by the increasing presence of dental hygienists and assistants. In 1908, Alfred C. Fones established the first school for dental hygienists; by midcentury, every state recognized and regulated hygienists. During the second half of the century, dental technicians, often working independently in laboratories, fabricated various forms of tooth replacements. The economics of dental practice changed as well, with fewer and fewer patients needing cavities to be filled and more and more of them covered by dental insurance.

[*See also* Medicine; Professionalization.]

• Robert Koch, *A History of Dental Surgery,* 1909. Bernhard W. Weinberger, *An Introduction to the History of Dentistry,* 1948. Malvin E. Ring, *Dentistry: An Illustrated History,* 1985. Milton B. Asbell, *Dentistry: A Historical Perspective,* 1988.

—Milton B. Asbell

DEPARTMENT OF AGRICULTURE. *See* Federal Government, Executive Branch: Department of Agriculture.

DEPARTMENT OF DEFENSE. *See* Federal Government, Executive Branch: Department of Defense.

DEPARTMENT OF STATE. *See* Federal Government, Executive Branch: Department of State.

DEPARTMENT OF THE TREASURY. *See* Federal Government, Executive Branch: Department of the Treasury.

DEPARTMENT OF VETERANS AFFAIRS. *See* Veterans Administration.

DEPARTMENT STORES. Between 1850 and 1890, urban growth spawned giant emporiums that sold vast arrays of merchandise at fixed prices and provided services and amenities that encouraged customers to linger and browse. Rowland H. Macy in *New York City (1858), John *Wanamaker in *Philadelphia (1861), and Marshall Field in *Chicago (1865) led this retailing revolution. During their golden age between 1890 and 1940, department stores supplanted small specialized shops in cities large and small. Elaborate store buildings attracted the public with their sheer size, luxurious appointments, and technological innovations. Highly successful as both businesses and cultural institutions, department stores nonetheless wrestled with troubling contradictions.

Resisting the corporate merger movements of the late nineteenth and early twentieth centuries, they tended to remain locally oriented, family-identified businesses loosely linked through buying and information-sharing groups as well as trade associations such as the National Retail Dry Goods Association (1911) and the Retail Research Association (1916). Even when department stores merged, as in the formation of Federated Department Stores in 1929, separate stores retained their individual identities and management autonomy. Attractive, ever-changing merchandise and attentive services combined with functional structures and management innovations, such as systematic data gathering, to make department stores enormously profitable.

Persistent operating problems nevertheless shadowed the giant stores' successes. Buyers who headed merchandise departments insisted that their expertise required autonomy, but the stores' functional organization challenged their authority by subordinating them to managers in charge of service, merchandising, advertising, and accounting. While close supervision hampered buyers' abilities to respond to fashion trends and customer demand, loose control threatened the store's overall image and financial health. Time-and-motion studies and employee bonuses enhanced efficiency, but efficiency sometimes undermined customer service. Statistical data failed to enhance predictability and regularity, as the flow of customers fluctuated wildly according to hour, day of the week, season, and weather.

Class and gender differences created other tensions. Male managers struggled to control the behavior of salesclerks and customers who were predominantly female. Working-class saleswomen, hired as cheap labor yet expected to sell skillfully, might offend or ignore more upper-class customers. Wealthy female customers used their class prerogatives to push stores into expensive and wasteful practices. Department stores appealed primarily to an affluent minority, but their heavy fixed operating costs compelled them to court working-class consumers in price-segregated departments and bargain basements. Sensual appeals encouraged customers to buy but also seduced some into shoplifting or reckless overuse of credit.

The combination of internal contradictions and the decay of central cities after *World War II weakened the department store as the flagship institution in the twentieth century's *consumer culture. Self-service replaced skilled selling. Suburban branch stores, rare and small before 1940, proliferated and even eclipsed downtown stores. Beginning in the 1980s, a rash of mergers, bankruptcies, and closings undermined department stores' power as local institutions. Specialty stores, mall-based chains, discount stores, and catalog merchants grabbed greater market share. Dethroned from their former glory, department stores nonetheless maintained a presence in many downtowns and in *shopping centers and malls, wielding a significant if reduced economic and cultural power.

[*See also* Gender; Mass Marketing; Social Class; Urbanization.]

• Susan Porter Benson, *Counter Cultures: Saleswomen, Managers, and Customers in American Department Stores, 1890–1940,* 1986. William Leach, *Land of Desire: Merchants, Power, and Rise of a New American Culture,* 1993.

—Susan Porter Benson

DEPRESSIONS, ECONOMIC. Depressions are sustained troughs in the *business cycle characterized by declines in output, employment, income, and trade. Their spreading effects can be traced through declining prices, profits, interest rates, wages, consumer spending, and capital investment. Depressions date from the earliest years of American history, but the paucity of data precludes evaluation of them in the *Colonial Era. Before 1815, depressions were caused primarily by exogenous shocks, that is, by forces external to the economy such as wars, widespread crop failures, or other disasters. With the growth of *capitalism, however, depressions became more pervasive, in part because the market held sway over more economic production and exchange, and also because of the dramatic increase in capital formation that accompanied *economic development and *industrialization. While economists agree on the correlation between business cycles and capitalism, they are unable to offer a simple consistent explanation as to why depressions occur.

The United States experienced depressions after the onset of severe economic contractions in 1818–1819, 1836–1837, 1856–1857, 1872–1873, 1884–1885, 1892–1893, 1920–1921, 1929–1933, and 1937–1938. While most began with *stock-market panics or banking crises, these events did not determine either the severity or length of the contraction: each depression had its own unique history.

Depressions draw attention because of their pervasive effect upon the economy, politics, and society. First of all, *unemployment and the decline in income creates human misery. As the economy matured, the urban unemployed found it increasingly difficult to supplement the family's income, since they could no longer fish, hunt, or garden to fill the family's larder. Part-time jobs for the breadwinner or the breadwinner's family disappeared. With modest savings, families quickly faced destitution. Even for those retaining jobs, the decline in prices led to a demand for wage cuts. Labor unions faced insurmountable challenges. If workers resisted wage cuts and struck, firms could hire replacements from the mass of the unemployed. Deprived of effective economic means of protest, workers and their allies increasingly sought political solutions.

*Business enterprises suffered during extended downturns as well. Not only did they postpone new investments in plants and equipment, but they also faced the prospect of substantial losses. In the early nineteenth century, industrial firms confronted depressions by suspending activity. But by the end of the century, the *mass-production industries, such as steel, oil, and cigarettes, changed tactics; rather than reduce production and maintain prices, they slashed prices and maintained production. This ignited competitive wars that were often resolved by mergers and other anticompetitive activities. For banks, depressions presented some of the most daunting challenges. Savings tended to flow out, while repayments on loans slowed. Banks cut back on lending, making it even more difficult for businesses to survive. Deprived of working capital (short-term loans to cover raw materials, wages, and goods in transit), firms went bankrupt.

Panics of 1819, 1837, and 1857; Depression of 1839–1843. While the *Antebellum Era witnessed severe business cycles, especially in the late 1810s, the 1830s, and the 1850s, only the downturn of the 1830s and early 1840s has attracted much scholarly attention. Even here, considerable debate exists as to the extent of the decline in production. Part of the difficulty in describing the effects of the antebellum depressions lies in the fact that the economy was not fully integrated. For example, the Panic of 1857 brought hard times in the North, while the southern *cotton industry enjoyed unprecedented prosperity. Secondly, the economy remained flexible; it could adjust quickly to price declines. This can be seen in the Panic of 1819. Despite a sudden and sharp decline in output and prices, a wave of bankruptcies, and widespread unemployment, recovery came quickly after 1822 as wages and interest rates adjusted to the price shock.

The depression of 1839–1843 had its origins in international trade and investment. Rapid increases in British investment in the United States encouraged a boom in the mid-1830s. As British silver flowed into the United States, it was deposited in banks, which then increased their lending. Prices soared. But in 1836, the British government raised interest rates, making British investment more attractive than American, and silver flowed back to England. This caused the short-lived Panic of 1837. The economy recovered briefly, but with the Panic of 1839 (again abetted by rising British interest rates), prices did not bounce back. Indeed, they fell some 46 percent between 1839 and 1843. But output actually rose 16 percent during this period, leading some experts to argue that this was not a depression.

Nevertheless, the monetary contraction of 1839–1843 wrought considerable havoc on individuals and their governments. Debtors, particularly landowners, turned to their state legislatures seeking relief from creditors. It came in the form of stay laws, restrictions upon forced sales, and freedom from attachment for debt for certain classes of property. In the cities, thousands were thrown out of work. Workers' trade unions, having grown rapidly in good times, disappeared. Aside from some outdoor relief, cities did little to address the needs of the poor. Governments were reluctant to become involved in relief, and even had they wanted to, their finances were in disarray. Revenues dried up, leaving cities to impose wage cuts, lay off employees, and seek additional loans. States fared even worse. In the 1830s, states, especially in the Middle Atlantic and *Middle West, had undertaken huge debts to build canals and *railroads. By the 1840s, many were on the edge of bankruptcy. In the wave of constitutional revision after the depression, more than half of the states wrote into their constitutions prohibitions against further debt for internal improvements.

Depressions of 1873–1879, 1882–1885, and 1893–1896. Some historians have described the period from 1873 to 1896 as the long depression, but this is inaccurate. While prices did fall during this period, output rose on average 4 percent a year. Each decade, however, brought a sharp economic contraction, or depression, in 1873–1879 (the longest in American history), 1882–1885, and 1893–1896. The first two had their origins in the collapse of railroad booms. After the *Civil War, the nation constructed thousands of miles of railroads. In a race to get the most profitable routes and feeders, railroads sold billions of dollars worth of bonds and stocks. When they discovered that their profit estimates had been too high, they could not pay their debts on the bonds or dividends on their stocks. This led to a financial panic. Banks curtailed credit and foreigners stopped buying American assets. Prices fell some 25 percent, creating havoc for industrial workers and farmers. In the depression of the 1870s, unemployment in construction and manufacturing climbed to perhaps 10 percent, while those who kept their jobs faced wage cuts. In farming, by the mid-1880s, wheat sold for sixty-four cents a bushel, half its normal price. Debt-burdened farmers in newly settled areas faced bankruptcy. Nonfarming businesses that depended upon railroads, construction, and *agriculture failed. At the bottom of the depression in the 1870s and again in the 1880s, some ten thousand firms filed for bankruptcy, citing liabilities of almost a quarter of a billion dollars.

Widespread hardship brought demands for relief. Cities again expanded their soup kitchens. Charity organization societies formed in some twenty-five cities to coordinate relief. But many leaders worried that such assistance would undermine citizens' self-reliance. Most assistance came in the form of helping the unemployed find work through employment exchanges or public works projects. In 1894, a "Commonwealth Army" of some five hundred jobless workers, organized by Jacob S. Coxey (1854–1951) of Massillon, Ohio, marched to *Washington, D.C., in support of Coxey's bold but not revolutionary demand: the creation of $500,000,000 in paper money by the federal government to be distributed to the states so that they could hire the unemployed to build roads. While Coxey's plan failed, the cycle of repeated depressions led to a growing discontent with *laissez-faire policies. Religious leaders and intellectuals, in particular, insisted that the government become more deeply involved in ensuring the material well-being of its citizens.

Facing wage cuts and layoffs, workers responded with waves of strikes. The most dramatic took place in the railroad industry, which had sought economies in the wake of bankruptcy. In July 1877, workers staged major strikes against the transappalachian railroads. Violence erupted in several places, but the bloodiest battles occurred in Pittsburgh, taking the lives of some fifty civilians and five militiamen. Again in 1894, workers struck *Chicago's Pullman Company when it announced wage cuts and layoffs. Eugene V. *Debs led his American Railway Union in a sympathetic boycott, refusing to pull Pullman cars. Fourteen thousand state and federal troops were called out by the Grover *Cleveland administration and the Justice Department issued an injunction against Debs. Again violence ensued: In Chicago, twenty were killed and thousands of railroad cars destroyed. The workers lost, as they usually did in the major strikes, and their unions witnessed precipitous declines in membership.

Finally, the depressions of the late nineteenth century had political consequences. Although farmers and workers lobbied for a number of reforms, the most pressing issue was the money supply. After the Civil War, the United States slowly moved toward adoption of a *gold standard of monetary valuation. This required bringing down wartime inflation and then, as gold discoveries lagged behind the pace of economic growth, prices fell still further. In 1893, a financial panic occurred when foreign investors and American businessmen liquidated their paper assets and demanded gold. Facing huge drains, banks curtailed credit, the economy slowed, unemployment mounted, and the depression of the mid-1890s settled in. Many demanded relief through the coinage of silver, which, by increasing the monetary supply, would cause prices to rise and hasten recovery. Others argued that in a growing global economy, the nation must adhere to a gold standard. The monetary issue reached its climax in the presidential election of 1896, when the Republican "gold-bug" William *McKinley decisively defeated the Populist and Democratic "free silver" candidate, William Jennings *Bryan. *Radicalism had been repudiated; political power had been consolidated in the hands of the more prosperous.

Depression of 1920–1921; the Great Depression of the 1930s. The twentieth century experienced two depressions, both closely associated with public policy. The first occurred in 1920–1921. After *World War I, with strong consumer demand from Europe and at home, U.S. firms maintained high levels of production and even increased inventories. But a sudden contraction in demand, as the U.S. government slashed spending and European production recovered, burst this speculative inventory bubble. Real gross national product fell some 6 percent, unemployment spiked to 12 percent, and wholesale prices fell by 37 percent. Prices returned to prewar levels by July 1921, however, and the economy began to rebound.

The Great Depression that began in 1929 did not witness such rapid recovery. Indeed, it proved to be the worst depression in American history. The real gross national product fell 30 percent, prices declined 23 percent, net investment became negative (that is, new capital investment did not equal the depreciation of the existing stock of capital), and unemployment became a fact of life for 24 percent and more of the labor force. Recovery from such an economic catastrophe was slow and difficult. The gross national product did not return to 1929 levels until 1937, and then in 1937–1938 the economy experienced a "depression within a depression." Unemployment remained high. As late as 1941, even as the war in Europe stimulated the U.S. economy, more than 10 percent of Americans were still seeking work.

The causes of the Great Depression remain a matter of intense debate. Most scholars argue that a combination of factors led to the downturn in 1929, including changes in Federal Reserve policy, a decline in consumption, and diminished investment. The 1929 *stock market crash did not cause the depression, but stock speculation on Wall Street had encouraged the Federal Reserve to raise interest rates. Losses in the stock market diminished consumer spending by investors, while poor harvests and low agricultural prices restrained farm spending. After record years of residential construction, investment peaked in 1926 but fell thereafter, dropping to one-half its 1926 level by 1929. What made this depression so devastating, however, was not the downturn in 1929, but the great skid thereafter, as the economy declined at an accelerating rate into 1933.

Recently, economists have highlighted the international nature of the depression of the 1930s and the role of the *gold standard in spreading its misery. During *World War I, most nations had gone off gold; that is, they would not redeem their currency for gold at the prewar rate. During the 1920s the leading industrial nations returned to the gold standard. However, the system suffered from serious flaws. Among the most important was the fact that the United States and France held a disproportionate share of the world's gold, reducing the flexibility of other nations. To remain on the gold standard when faced with demands for their gold, these nations would have to raise interest rates, slowing their economies and creating unemployment. In an era of mass politics this proved impossible, and nations began to abandon the gold standard, culminating with Great Britain and the British Commonwealth nations in 1931. Recovery generally came quickly to nations that devalued their currencies.

The United States, however, remained committed to the gold standard, and as other countries devalued, Americans faced tremendous pressure. Offered the choice of American goods or American gold, holders of U.S. dollars preferred gold, believing that the United States would not stay on the gold standard forever. This constrained the *Federal Reserve System. It could not expand the monetary supply, since this would increase the potential claims on its gold stocks. Instead, to conserve what gold it had, the Federal Reserve raised interest rates, driving the economy deeper into depression.

Recovery began when Franklin Delano *Roosevelt became president in March 1933. While depressions usually brought a change in presidential administrations, Roosevelt won in a landslide and used this mandate to secure passage of an amazing slate of legislation during his first hundred days. Most importantly, he devalued the dollar, increasing the value of gold from slightly more than twenty to thirty-five dollars an ounce. At these prices, and with political unrest rising in Europe, gold flowed into the United States. Since the money stock in the United States was a function of gold holdings, the money supply grew rapidly, increasing by some 11 or 12 percent a year until 1937. As their reserves grew, banks were encouraged to lend, businesses to build inventories, and consumers to spend in anticipation of further price increases. But given the depth of the depression, the public demanded more than monetary measures. The New Deal, the label given to Roosevelt's policies between 1933 and 1938, brought a host of programs that altered fundamentally the relationship between the government and the economy. Among the most important programs were regulation of securities, trucking, banking, and utilities; federal deposit insurance; agricultural price supports; minimum-wage and maximum-hour legislation; collective bargaining for unions; *Social Security; unemployment *insurance; and public *housing. The federal government matched state spending (on a 1:1 or 2:1 ratio, depending on the program) for relief, assistance to the elderly and disabled, and destitute mothers with dependent children.

In 1937, the federal government's decision to increase required bank reserves and to cut spending, coupled with the withholding of Social Security taxes from workers' paychecks, again sent the economy into depression. The stock market fell 50 percent, industrial production 38 percent, and the number of unemployed doubled. The government immediately shifted course, increasing bank reserves and undertaking more spending on public works and work relief. While *Keynesianism would not be adopted as explicit policy until after *World War II, the 1937–1938 debacle proved that government would no longer stand by while the economy sank.

Post–World War II Era. From World War II to the end of the twentieth century, the United States did not experience a depression. The business cycle did not disappear, however, as the era witnessed a number of recessions. Growth slowed noticeably in 1954–1955, 1957–1958, 1960–1961, 1969–1970, 1974–1975, 1980–1982, and 1990–1992. The sources of these recessions varied, but all were mercifully brief, thanks in some measure to government policy. First of all, government spending soared in this era, rising from one-fifth to two-fifths of the gross national product between 1940 and 1990. Further, postwar governmental activities had a much greater effect upon the level of economic activity. Specifically, fiscal policy worked to moderate economic cycles through automatic stabilizers. When the economy moved into recession, government tax revenues fell, while its expenditures rose. The resulting fiscal deficit stimulated economic recovery.

In the early 1960s, *Democratic party policy-makers moved beyond these built-in countercyclical effects. Embracing Keynesian economics in 1963, President John F. *Kennedy assumed explicit responsibility for macroeconomic performance. The Kennedy tax cuts (passed shortly after his assassination) consciously produced a government budget deficit designed to stimulate the economy and prevent an anticipated recession. The *Republican party, by contrasts, led by President Ronald *Reagan in the 1980s, tried to reduce the federal government's role. Explicitly repudiating Keynesian economics, Reagan's advisors sought to slash government by means of tax and spending cuts and to reassert the primacy of markets in determining the pace and pattern of economic activity. But while they secured modest tax cuts, spending soared, producing huge fiscal deficits. As Keynesians would have predicted, this brought a sturdy if not spectacular recovery from the 1980–1982 recession. And much to the chagrin of Reaganites, Americans still expected the government to take responsibility for macroeconomic performance. When President George *Bush called for fiscal restraint and higher taxes during a recession, he was voted out of office in 1992.

[*See also* Banking and Finance; Canals and Waterways; Charity Organization Movement; Economic Regulation; Foreign Relations: The Economic Dimension; Hoover, Herbert; Labor Movements; Monetarism; Monetary Policy, Federal; New Deal Era, The; Pullman Strike and Boycott; Railroad Strikes of 1877; Securities and Exchange Commission; Strikes and Industrial Conflict; Van Buren, Martin; Works Progress Administration.]

• Rendings Fels, *American Business Cycles 1865–1897*, 1959. Samuel Reznick, *Business Depressions and Financial Panics*, 1968. Peter Temin, *The Jacksonian Economy*, 1969. Lester V. Chandler, *America's Greatest Depression*, 1970. Geoffrey H. Moore, "Business Cycles, Panics, and Depressions," in *Encyclopedia of American Economic History*, ed. Glenn Porter, 1980, II, pp. 151–6. Nicolas Spulber, *Managing the American Economy, from Roosevelt to Reagan*, 1989. Peter Temin, *Lessons from the Great Depression*, 1989. Barry Eichengreen, *Golden Fetters: The Gold Standard and the Great Depression*, 1992. David Glasner, ed., *Business Cycles and Depressions*, 1997.

—Diane Lindstrom

DETROIT. Founded by Antoine de la Mothe Cadillac in 1701 as a French fur-trading outpost and fort, Detroit passed into British control in 1763 and to the Americans in 1796. The *Erie Canal (1825), improvements in Great Lakes navigation, and the railroad allowed Detroit to capitalize on its site and natural resources through tobacco and cigar production, copper smelting, and iron making. In 1880, it was America's eighteenth largest city; by 1920, now totally industrialized, with nearly a million inhabitants, it ranked fourth. When Henry *Ford introduced assembly-line production in his Highland Park plant, the city (as its nickname "Motown" suggests) became closely tied to the *automotive industry. The Great Depression of the 1930s brought labor unrest, but in 1950 Walter *Reuther of the United Automobile Workers signed with the General Motors Corporation a major wage-and-benefit agreement heralded by *Fortune* magazine as the "Treaty of Detroit."

Despite hopeful moments, Detroit often experienced racial tension. The movement of black tenants into a federally funded housing project prompted a race riot in 1943. Twenty years later, Martin Luther *King Jr. marked the anniversary by leading a peaceful march through the city. Race riots and arson in the summer of 1967, however, left forty-three dead and burned large sections of the city. Detroit suffered as the *energy crises of the 1970s and Japanese competition battered the automobile companies. Although the industry gradually regained *productivity and market share, the shift of production abroad resulted in declining corporate investment in the city and region. Despite an *urban renewal effort symbolized by a downtown convention complex called the Renaissance Center (1977), hard times lingered. From 1970 to 1990, Detroit's population dropped by one-third.

[*See also* Civil Rights Movement; Depressions, Economic; French Settlements in North America; Riots, Urban.]

• Nelson Lichtenstein, *The Most Dangerous Man in Detroit: Walter Reuther and the Fate of American Labor*, 1995. Thomas J. Sugrue, *The Origins of the Urban Crisis: Race and Inequality in Postwar Detroit*, 1996.

—Olivier J. Zunz

DEWEY, JOHN (1859–1952), philosopher, educator, reformer. Over a long and diverse career, John Dewey established himself as the most significant American philosopher of the first half of the twentieth century and a leading voice among reformers struggling to extend democracy at home and abroad. At the heart of his thinking lay an expansive moral vision of democracy as not merely a political ideal but a wider way of life. As a philosopher, he sought compelling arguments for his democratic ideals, while as an activist he tried to give these ideals practical expression in the school, the workplace, and the polity.

Born in Burlington, Vermont, the son of a storekeeper, Dewey graduated from the University of Vermont in 1879. Among the first graduate students in *philosophy in an American university, he received his Ph.D. from Johns Hopkins University in 1884, and began his college teaching career at the University of Michigan. In 1894 he moved to the recently founded University of Chicago. While at Michigan, Dewey gained prominence as a proponent of neo-Hegelian idealism, but at Chicago he moved toward Darwinian naturalism and *pragmatism. Adopting the functional *psychology of William *James's *Principles of Psychology* (1890), Dewey developed an instrumental view of human intelligence that saw it not as the repository of transcendent reason or a mere receptacle of sense impressions but as the means by which a uniquely purposive creature addressed the problems that confronted it in a struggle for a fruitful existence.

*Chicago was also the site of Dewey's earliest ventures into educational reform. Recognizing the pedagogical implications of his new philosophy and psychology, he established a Laboratory School, in which to test his ideas. In the curriculum of this school, as well as in such widely read books as *The School and Society* (1899), *The Child and the Curriculum* (1902), and later *Democracy and Education* (1916), Dewey called for a pedagogy that would build on the inherent interests of children, while leading them to the accumulated wisdom of adults embodied in the established subjects. He urged teachers to structure the classroom as a cooperative community of inquiry, thereby fostering in children both the skills of scientific investigation and the character essential for a democratic society.

Dewey left Chicago for Columbia University in 1904, following a bitter dispute with university president William Rainey Harper (1856–1906) over control of the Laboratory School Dewey had founded, and he remained at Columbia for the remainder of his career. Prior to *World War I, he devoted much of his energy as a philosopher to the defense of pragmatism from its idealist and realist critics, while urging his fellow philosophers to turn their attention from the epistemological conundrums that philosophers had created for themselves to the ethical "problems of men." In the major books of his later phase—*Experience and Nature* (1925), *The Quest for Certainty* (1929), *Art as Experience* (1934), and *Logic: The Theory of Inquiry* (1938)—Dewey himself pursued this project by developing a philosophy designed to provide the moral ideals of democracy with what he termed "an encouraging nod." At the same time, in his only work of formal political theory, *The Public and Its Problems* (1927), he offered a vigorous, if ultimately wistful, defense of participatory democracy against critics such as Walter *Lippmann, who were eager to shrink government by the people to minimal dimensions.

Beginning with his strong support of American intervention in World War I, Dewey also functioned as a public intellectual, speaking out on a wide range of controversial issues not only in the United States but in Japan, China, Turkey, Mexico, and the Soviet Union. He played a leading role in the Outlawry of War movement in the 1920s, radical third-party politics in the 1930s, and anti-Stalinist agitation in the 1940s. A long-time critic of *capitalism, Dewey advanced his own brand of democratic *socialism in *Individualism Old and New* (1930), *Liberalism and Social Action* (1935), and *Freedom and Culture* (1939).

Dewey's posthumous reputation went into eclipse among academic philosophers increasingly preoccupied with technical problems of analysis, as well as in a political culture inclined to the kind of skeptical "realism" about the possibilities of democracy that he had spent his life combating. The final years of the twentieth century, however, which witnessed the emergence of schools of "neopragmatism" in philosophy, literature, and legal theory, brought a rekindled interest in Dewey's philosophy, if not a revitalization of his extraordinary democratic hope.

[*See also* Bourne, Randolph; Education; Evolution, Theory of; Intelligence, Concepts of; Liberalism; Progressive Era; Rorty, Richard.]

• George Dykhuizen, *The Life and Mind of John Dewey,* 1973. Neil Coughlan, *Young John Dewey,* 1975. Steven C. Rockefeller, *John Dewey: Religious Faith and Democratic Humanism,* 1991. Robert B. Westbrook, *John Dewey and American Democracy,* 1991. James Campbell, *Understanding John Dewey,* 1995. Alan Ryan, *John Dewey and the High Tide of American Liberalism,* 1995.

—Robert B. Westbrook

DICKINSON, EMILY (1830–1886), poet. Emily Dickinson was one of the two finest American poets of the nineteenth century. She managed this extraordinary achievement despite powerful obstacles, many of them self-imposed. She had little of what normally counts as "experience," and whatever wisdom she displayed about the world's ways resulted from keen self-awareness and hard thought, rather than close encounters with life. Except for a year at nearby Mount Holyoke Female Seminary in 1847–1848, she lived out her life in Amherst, Massachusetts, in houses belonging to her father, Edward, a prominent lawyer. Toward the end, she rarely even ventured onto the few streets of Amherst. She never married or bore a child, and she probably never had carnal knowledge of another human body, male or female. If she loved, it was brief, furtive, and incomplete. She never earned any money or held any sort of "job"; she listed herself in local records as "at home"—the era's term for "housewife."

Her subjects were conventionally Victorian: flowers and birds, death and dying, immortality, and the travail of religious faith, love and loss. Her models were equally conventional: poets much less talented than herself, like Robert Burns and Elizabeth Barrett Browning. She avoided the other truly fine American poet of her time, Walt *Whitman, because her father told her that Whitman's *Leaves of Grass* was naughty. For her cadences, she went mainly to Protestant hymns, with their steady iambic lines of eight or ten syllables. Instead of audiences that might have given her encouragement or useful commentary, she shared her work with only a couple of relatives—her sister, Lavinia; her sister-in-law, Susan, wife of her brother, Austin—and a few friends. Almost none of it was published in her lifetime; a complete scholarly edition first appeared in 1955.

But out of this seeming dearth of possibility and these potentially inhibiting choices, she wrung a large and remarkable body of *poetry—thousands of poems with such stunning opening lines as "It would have starved a Gnat—/ to live so small as I," "I felt a Funeral in my Brain," "I heard a fly buzz when I died," or "My business is circumference—/ A fairer house than prose." The most concentrated frenzy of work came in her thirty-third year, 1862, when she wrote more than three hundred poems, turning out brilliant pieces at the astonishing rate of almost one a day.

In the spring of that critical year, she confronted the possibility of publishing her work. She initiated a correspondence with Thomas Wentworth Higginson (1823–1911) of Boston, who had published "Letter to a Young Contributor" in the *Atlantic Monthly.* The situation seemed perfect: Higginson was a successful professional author and editor who had offered friendly advice to novice writers; the *Atlantic Monthly,* found in most upper-middle-class *New England homes, regularly published poetry by women and men whose abilities were meager compared to Dickinson's. Sending carefully chosen samples of her work, she asked Higginson for his editorial judgment—was her poetry "alive"?

A series of letters ensued in which Higginson offered cautious encouragement, trying all the while to penetrate the mystery in which his curious correspondent wrapped herself. When he suggested that she might eventually publish her work, Dickinson replied, "That is as foreign to my thought as Firmament to Fin." With that richly alliterative and perfectly iambic sentence, she transformed what had been mere hesitation into principaled refusal. In so doing, she created the one fact of mythic proportions that still clings to her: the poet of enormous talent who disdained to do anything so tawdry with her art as to put it into print.

But she did know how to put the disdain into verse:

> Publication—is the Auction
> Of the Mind—of Man—
> Poverty—be justifying
> For so foul a thing
>
> Possibly. . . .

These lines resonated with generations of admirers who made Dickinson into something of a cult figure, celebrated as much for her refusal to allow her art to become merchandise as for the art itself, and revered as much for the oddments of her personality as for her poetry. But the deeper meaning of the way Dickinson justified her refusal to publish lies in the way it reveals how completely, by the mid–nineteenth century, literature had in fact become a commodity, poetry a species of intellectual property with a cash value.

[*See also* Literature: Early National and Antebellum Eras; Literature: Civil War to World War I.]

• Thomas H. Johnson, ed., *The Poems of Emily Dickinson,* 3 vols., 1955. Richard B. Sewall, *The Life of Emily Dickinson,* 1974. R. Jackson Wilson, *Figures of Speech: American Writers and the Literary Marketplace from Benjamin Franklin to Emily Dickinson,* 1989.

—R. Jackson Wilson

DIET. *See* Food and Diet.

DIMAGGIO, JOE (1914–1999), *baseball player. Born into a California immigrant family that spoke only Italian, Joseph Paul DiMaggio quit high school to work and play baseball. In 1936 the New York Yankees bought him, hoping to replace Babe *Ruth. He finished that year with a .323 batting average, 29 home runs, and the nickname "Joltin' Joe." In 13 seasons with the Yankees, DiMaggio hit .325 with 361 homers, easily becoming the first *Italian American elected to the Hall of Fame.

To contemporaries, DiMaggio was not just great but special. First, he was consistent. He led the league in major categories in nine seasons and, in 1941, hit safely in fifty-six straight games. He was also versatile. Equally skilled at hitting, fielding, and base running, he led the Yankees to ten pennants and eight world championships. And he performed with a grace, self-possession, and poise that astounded sportswriters and made him the most charismatic athlete of his generation.

Moreover, though reserved and uncomfortable in crowds, DiMaggio enjoyed meeting celebrities and beautiful women at Toots Shor's and other *New York City nightspots, where he learned to hold his liquor and his tongue. The immigrant's son thus became "Broadway Joe" as well as the "Yankee Clipper," a gossip-column favorite and the subject, however dignified and distant, of mass adoration. Fittingly, after divorcing his first wife, he married Hollywood's reigning sex symbol, Marilyn *Monroe, in 1954. The marriage lasted a year. When Monroe died in 1962, DiMaggio had roses placed thereafter at the crypt holding her ashes. To the turbulent 1960s, he came to symbolize a lost grace and stability. In the commercial 1980s, he appeared, dignity intact, in *television commercials, adding "Mr. Coffee" to his list of affectionate nicknames.

[*See also* Sports: Professional Sports.]

• Maury Allen, *Where Have You Gone, Joe DiMaggio?*, 1975. George DeGregorio, *Joe DiMaggio: An Informal Biography*, 1981.

—Ronald Story

DIPHTHERIA, a bacterial *disease of children, spread most frequently by person-to-person contact, is characterized by the formation of a pseudomembrane in the throat that can lead to death by suffocation. The diphtheria bacillus also secretes an exotoxin that can cause other symptoms such as inflammation of the heart.

Diphtheria has probably existed since classical antiquity, but it was not identified as a specific disease until 1819. During the 1880s, scientists in Germany and France isolated the pathogen, the bacillus that caused the disease; developed means of laboratory diagnosis; and discovered the exotoxin. This disease is especially significant in modern medical history because diphtheria antitoxin, produced in a Berlin laboratory in 1890 and available on a commercial scale shortly thereafter, was the first effective therapeutic developed through bacteriological research.

The earliest notable diphtheria epidemic in America was probably the New England "throat distemper" of 1735–1740. Samuel Bard of New York reported another outbreak in 1771. In the 1850s diphtheria established itself as an endemic disease, and it emerged as the leading killer of children in the 1880s. Fear of the disease then justified measures ranging from placarding houses to forced isolation of patients in special institutions.

In 1892, the bacteriologist Hermann Biggs (1859–1923) established the New York City Health Department's laboratory of pathology and bacteriology, the first such facility in the world. Here, under the direction of William H. Park, diphtheria diagnosis and antitoxin production and distribution soon became the principal activities, and this innovation was quickly adopted elsewhere. The development of the diphtheria antitoxin also spurred the growth of the American *pharmaceutical industry.

Although contemporaries had reason to question the efficacy of antitoxin in its early years, product standardization and further scientific developments soon led to dramatic declines, first in case mortality and later in the incidence of diphtheria itself. For most of the twentieth century, diphtheria in the United States was successfully controlled by childhood immunization and the availability of effective antibiotics.

[*See also* Medicine; Public Health.]

• Ernest Caulfield, *A True History of the Terrible Epidemic Vulgarly Called the Throat Distemper: Which Occurred in His Majesty's New England Colonies between the Years 1735 and 1740*, 1939. Terra Ziporyn, *Disease in the Popular American Press: The Case of Diphtheria, Typhoid Fever, and Syphilis*, 1988. Evelynn Hammonds, *Childhood's Deadly Scourge: The Campaign to Control Diphtheria in New York City, 1880–1930*, 1999.

—Edward T. Morman

DISEASE. As in all human societies, disease has played a profound but ever-changing role throughout American history.

The Columbian Encounter and the Early Colonial Era. When Europeans first reached the New World, they encountered a hitherto unknown indigenous population as well as a novel natural and biological environment. Amerindians probably had migrated from Asia to *Alaska across a land bridge produced by a lowering of the oceans during the last Ice Age. Many pathogens responsible for infectious diseases that took a heavy toll in Asia, Europe, and Africa probably did not survive the migration through the harsh climate of Siberia and Alaska. New World peoples were thus isolated from many of the epidemic and endemic diseases that had profoundly shaped population structures elsewhere. The absence of contact with diverse populations also gave them a far more homogeneous genetic inheritance.

These and other factors gave precolumbian America a unique disease environment. Many Old World diseases—*malaria, *smallpox, bubonic plague, and some of the infectious diseases associated with childhood—were unknown. The greatest risks to the Amerindian population involved accidents, wildlife diseases associated with hunting and food-gathering, warfare, and sporadic famines and food shortages. The relative absence of domesticated livestock minimized zoonotic (animal-transmitted) diseases, and low population density and the absence of commercial contacts among tribes reduced the potential dangers of epidemic infectious disease. Nevertheless, *life expectancy at birth for Native Americans—as well as Europeans—was generally in the low thirties on the eve of colonization, even though the causes of morbidity and mortality among both varied sharply.

The migration of Europeans to the Americas beginning at the end of the fifteenth century had a catastrophic impact on the indigenous population. The introduction of new diseases into a population often lacking immunological defenses led to extraordinarily high mortality rates. Infants lacked antibodies from their mothers, who had never been exposed to these new diseases. Children and adults often did not receive the kind of care that might have mitigated the impact of disease; neither custom, tradition, nor religion provided any guide. Genetic homogeneity may have also enhanced vulnerability. Whatever the reasons, the Amerindian population suffered a precipitous decline in the period following the first contacts with Europeans. Diseases such as smallpox, measles, whooping cough, chicken pox, and malaria—to cite only a few—exacted a heavy toll. On the eve of colonization the population of the future contiguous United States was between two and twelve million. When the nadir was reached in the early twentieth century, the number of Native Americans had fallen to about 250,000. Disease and the ensuing social demoralization, not military conquest, played the major role in this demographic disaster.

The colonists, meanwhile, faced their own novel health problems. The Atlantic crossing, which could last three or four months, posed its own risks. Within the new environment the settlers faced rigorous conditions. The construction of adequate housing, securing an uncontaminated water supply, and the development of an adequate and varied food supply took time. During the period of adjustment (often aptly described as a process of "seasoning"), many new settlements experienced extraordinarily high mortality and morbidity rates that, if unchecked, threatened their very existences.

The period of seasoning varied from place to place. In *New England the process of adjustment was brief; within a short time, mortality rates dropped and inhabitants enjoyed unprecedented levels of health. In seventeenth-century Andover, Massachusetts, the average age of death among the first generation was nearly seventy-one, and infant and child mortality was correspondingly low. Nor was Andover unique. Consequently, New England's population grew rapidly in the seventeenth century.

The southern colonies, by contrast, remained dangerous places. The importation of such tropical diseases as malaria and *yellow fever into a region with a warm and moist climate proved devastating; mortality rates in the *South exceeded those of New England, the Middle Atlantic colonies, and even Great Britain. On average, seventeenth-century white male New Englanders who survived to the age of twenty outlived their Maryland counterparts by more than two decades. The greater resistance of *African Americans to the ravages of imported tropical diseases undoubtedly contributed to the growth of *slavery in the South. This pattern of regional variation in mortality and morbidity would persist until well into the twentieth century.

The Era of Infectious Diseases and Epidemics. The eighteenth century brought changes to the disease ecology of the American colonies. Natural population growth, high rates of *immigration, and the geographic *mobility that accompanied the growth in trade and commerce enhanced the movement of infectious pathogens. Smallpox and yellow fever epidemics appeared in growing port cities. Since many infectious diseases had not gained a foothold in the American colonies, the population included a disproportionately high number of susceptible persons. The result was the partial replication of the harsh disease environment characteristic of England and Europe. Although the colonial population continued to grow, its curve resembled a saw-tooth shape on an upward gradient because of the impact of epidemic disease. However hard hit by infectious diseases, colonial America nonetheless had lower mortality rates than those of England and Europe.

Mortality rates among the young from such diseases as measles, mumps, whooping cough, and a variety of respiratory and intestinal disorders rose dramatically during the eighteenth century, particularly in more densely populated towns. Although the spectacular epidemics of yellow fever and smallpox were the most feared, the worst killers were intestinal disorders, including *typhoid fever and various forms of dysentery.

Seasonal patterns as well as population density shaped morbidity and mortality patterns. Intestinal diseases were most frequent in warmer months because of stagnant water, contaminated food, and large insect populations that could transmit malaria and yellow fever. Respiratory and pulmonary diseases peaked in cold weather. Because infectious diseases that killed the young were by far the dominant cause of morbidity and mortality, the proportion of aged persons in the population remained low; chronic and degenerative diseases were relatively rare.

The morbidity and mortality patterns in place by the late eighteenth century persisted in one form or another for much of the nineteenth century. Nevertheless, a changing social and physical environment as well as population movements both to and within the United States contributed to a significant modification of the earlier disease environment, especially in urban areas. The *immigration of destitute groups such as the Irish into densely populated neighborhoods where squalor and unhygienic conditions prevailed dramatically increased health risks. Infants and young children were particularly susceptible to infectious diseases. Intestinal disorders continued to take the highest toll, but other diseases associated with population density and unsanitary conditions—typhus, typhoid, smallpox, and respiratory disorders—also loomed large. Population growth exceeded the ability of municipal governments to provide a safe water supply or a sanitation system to remove organic waste and to ensure clean streets (which were usually covered with heaps of animal wastes). *Housing codes were all but absent; inadequate ventilation and crowding quickly transmitted infectious diseases. *Tuberculosis emerged as the leading cause of death. Occupations that posed a threat to health went largely unregulated. Urban areas also continued to experience periodic epidemics related to the quickened pace of trade and commerce. *Cholera became an international disease during the nineteenth century as rapid ocean transportation magnified the ability to move pathogens. Southern cities experienced both cholera and yellow fever epidemics. Recent scholarship indicates a decline in the life expectancy of Americans in the nineteenth century. Indeed, only in-migration from abroad and from rural areas assured urban growth.

Rural areas and small towns, by contrast, often escaped the infectious diseases that plagued urban areas even though health indicators declined during the first half of the nineteenth century. In 1830, for example, urban death rates were between two and three times higher than rural areas; small-town rates tended to fall midway between. Under certain circumstances, however, the advantage conferred upon rural inhabitants became a liability. During the *Civil War, young men recruited from rural areas, lacking the immunity of their urban counterparts who had survived the infectious diseases of infancy and childhood, died in large numbers when they encountered unhygienic conditions and dangerous pathogens in the military camps. Indeed, the overwhelming number of Civil War deaths occurred not from battlefield wounds, but from respiratory and enteric disorders as well as smallpox, measles, malaria, and other diseases.

Although infectious diseases remained the major causes of mortality, their distribution varied by region and class. Malaria, yellow fever, and hookworm, for example, were largely confined to the South. (Malaria had been present in the Northeast and upper Mississippi Valley, but an inhospitable environment contributed to its eventual disappearance.) *Social class and race were important factors as well. Lower-class and minority ethnic and racial groups tended to have higher mortality rates. Nutritional levels and sanitary conditions undoubtedly exacerbated the impact of infectious diseases on these groups. But more prosperous groups did not escape the threat of infectious disease; infant mortality remained high at all levels of the population. Hidden from public view, severe *mental illness and other chronic diseases often resulted in dependency.

The Era of Chronic and Infectious Diseases. Beginning in the second half of the nineteenth century, the United States, as well as England and many European nations, experienced what has become known as the second "epidemiological transition." The first, which occurred perhaps ten thousand or more years ago, involved the development of agriculture, which created a more stable food supply. The result was a more sedentary population that increased in both size and density. Population growth in turn heightened the potential for epidemic and infectious diseases. During the second epidemiological transition, infectious diseases began a period of sustained decline as a cause of mortality, to be replaced by chronic and degenerative diseases. This unparalleled transformation had a profound impact on virtually all human beings.

Slowly but surely, infectious diseases declined as major elements in mortality in the late nineteenth century. By 1940 most of the infectious diseases associated with childhood—viral diseases such as measles, mumps, whooping cough, and chicken pox, and bacterial diseases that included scarlet and rheumatic fever—were insignificant in mortality rates, while *heart disease and *cancer loomed much larger. What caused this massive shift in morbidity and mortality? Most scholars agree that medical interventions played virtually no role. Before *World War II, the function of *medicine was primarily the diagnosis of disease. With the exception of a few surgical procedures and antitoxins, such as the *diphtheria antitoxin, physicians had few effective therapies. Antibiotic therapy against bacterial diseases did not become common until after 1945, and the development of vaccines for most viral infectious diseases still lay in the future. Yet in 1945 infectious diseases had ceased to be a major element in shaping mortality patterns.

It is easier to describe the decline of mortality from infectious diseases than to explain it. Many scholars have attributed it to economic growth and a rising standard of living. The difficulty with such global explanations is that they are not based on empirical data that shed light on the precise mechanisms responsible for the mortality decline for specific diseases. Some have pinpointed dietary improvements as the most important factor. Yet the relationship between diet—excluding severe malnutrition, which rarely existed in the United States—and most infectious diseases is tenuous at best. Moreover, economic growth involves more than living standards; it includes rising levels of *literacy and *education and a variety of other complex social changes. Some of these changes and their interactions—including housing arrangements, population density, water and food purity, personal hygiene, individual behavioral patterns, and public-health activities—may have had a more direct influence on mortality levels. Although the importance of economic development in the reduction in mortality is generally recognized, no consensus exists on the precise role of specific factors.

In some cases the reduction in mortality followed specific public-health interventions. Typhoid fever, for example, was generally disseminated by contaminated water. The building of central sewer systems did not seem to have a major impact, but reduced mortality did follow the introduction of water filtration. The reduction in mortality from tuberculosis, on the other hand, presents far greater complexities. Mortality began to fall well before overt efforts were made to contain the disease. Improved diet and a reduction in exposure thanks to better housing and the building of sanitoriums may account for growing resistance to the disease, but the evidence for these explanations remains inconclusive. The fall in infant and child mortality from diarrheal diseases probably followed changes in baby-feeding practices, improvement in the milk supply, and public-health authorities' efforts to sensitize parents to more effective means of care and prevention. Whatever the precise reasons, the mortality decline was clearly a function of reduced exposure and greater resistance among the population.

The mortality decline that began in the late nineteenth century also reflected a dramatic increase in survival rates among infants and children. Longevity among the elderly increased as well, but not as spectacularly. As infant and child mortality fell, more Americans survived to adulthood and old age, and the median age and the proportion of elderly in the population increased commensurately.

The change in the age distribution of the population mirrored a shift in the causes of mortality. In the nineteenth century, infectious diseases were the major causes of mortality; death stalked infants and children. In the twentieth century, by contrast, the major causes of death were chronic and degenerative diseases, and death in old age became the norm. Indeed, the longer individuals survived, the more likely they were to die from cancer or cardiovascular, cerebrovascular, or pulmonary diseases. In 1993, heart disease, cancer, strokes, and pulmonary disease accounted for 67 percent of all deaths. Although the etiology of these diseases remains unclear, the presumption is that they involve a complex blend of genetic, environmental, and behavioral factors. To be sure, mortality within each category has not remained constant. Deaths from *heart disease peaked in the first half of the twentieth century and declined in the second half. Similarly, the mix of types of cancers has changed even while the overall mortality rate has remained relatively stable. Moreover, mortality within all these categories differs by class, race, ethnicity, and gender. But given the aging of the population and the fact that human beings may have a determinant life span, chronic and degenerative diseases seem likely to remain major elements in mortality.

The decline in mortality from infectious disease and the development of effective antibiotic therapy after 1945 encouraged a belief that such diseases no longer posed a threat. Yet neither past nor present experience justified such optimism. The rapidity of modern transportation and the opening of hitherto uninhabited regions raised the possibility of new viral and bacterial diseases immune to available therapies. The indiscriminate use of antibiotics also led to the emergence of resistant mutant strains that posed major threats to life. *Influenza—an old viral disease—periodically reemerged, often in virulent form. The influenza pandemic of 1918–1919 killed more than half a million Americans, and subsequent experience demonstrated that its recurrence remained a distinct possibility. Other viral, bacterial, and rickettsial diseases (such as Rocky Mountain Spotted Fever) have also created a niche for themselves in response to behavioral and environmental changes. The emergence of *acquired immunodeficiency syndrome (AIDS), a new disease that became the major cause of mortality among the 25–44-year-old age group in the 1990s, demonstrated the importance of changing behavioral patterns, while Lyme disease, a tick-borne infection first observed in the 1970s, mirrored a novel kind of ecology. Whatever the future brings, disease and death—whatever forms they take—remain inevitable concomitants of life itself.

[*See also* Alzheimer's Disease; Columbian Exchange; Death and Dying; Food and Diet; Hospitals; Indian History and Culture: Migration and Pre-Columbian Era; Industrial Diseases and Hazards; Life Stages; Poliomyelitis; Poverty; Public Health; Race and Ethnicity; Sickle-Cell Anemia; Surgery; Urbanization; Venereal Disease.]

• John Duffy, *Epidemics in Colonial America*, 1953. Alfred W. Crosby Jr., *The Columbian Exchange: Biological and Cultural Consequences of 1492*, 1972. John B. and Sonja M. McKinlay, "The Questionable Contribution of Medical Measures to the Decline of Mortality in the United States in the Twentieth Century," *Milbank Memorial Fund Quarterly* 55 (1977): 405–428. Abdel R. Omran, "Epidemiologic Transition in the U.S.: The Health Factor in Population Change," *Population Bulletin* 32 (1977): 3–42. Henry F. Dobyns, *Their Numbers Become Thinned: Native American Population Dynamics in Eastern North America*, 1983. Gretchen A. Condran, Henry Williams, and Rose A. Cheney, "The Decline in Mortality in Philadelphia from 1870 to 1930: The Role of Municipal Services," *Pennsylvania Magazine of History and Biography* 108 (1984): 153–77. Stephen J. Kunitz, "Mortality Change in America, 1620–1920," *Human Biology* 56 (1984): 559–82. Samuel H. Preston, *Fatal Years: Child Mortality in Late Nineteenth-Century America*, 1991. Charles Merbs, "A New World of Infectious Disease," *Yearbook of Physical Anthropology* 35 (1992): 3–42.

—Gerald N. Grob

DISNEY, WALT (1901–1966), motion picture producer, director, major innovator in U.S. film animation. Born in *Chicago, Walt Disney attended the Chicago Academy of Fine Arts, drove an ambulance in France in 1918, and worked as a commercial artist in Kansas City before moving to Hollywood in 1923. Here he founded an animation studio with his older brother Roy. After several efforts, the studio found success with Mickey Mouse and the first sound cartoon, *Steamboat Willie* (1928). Disney created the first full-color cartoon (*Flowers and Trees*, 1932) and the first animated feature (*Snow White and the Seven Dwarfs*, 1937). A shrewd entrepreneur, he pioneered the use of merchandising, launched a *television series when most producers avoided the new medium, and created theme parks.

Disney's productions became the most popular motion pictures in history. The short cartoons starring Mickey and Donald Duck played in theaters around the world. The features after *Snow White*—chiefly *Pinocchio* (1940), *Fantasia* (1940), *Bambi* (1942), *Song of the South* (1947), *Cinderella* (1950), and *Peter Pan* (1953)—proved ageless. Although many were not financially successful at first, all eventually became immensely profitable through constant rereleases. With their sumptuous color, meticulous backgrounds, and detailed character movement, the films remain dazzling cinematic achievements. The stories blend songs, slapstick, sentiment, and relentless optimism with a dash of sheer childhood terror. Although criticized for homogenizing their literary sources, Disney's cartoons struck a universal emotional chord.

Disney had little talent for drawing, but he inspired his brilliant staff with his infectious enthusiasm, his dedication to technical advancements, and his skill in building vivid gags and stories. In the 1950s Disney turned to the lucrative arena of live-action filming for family audiences. His weekly television show (1954–1981) served as a display case and promotional tool. Disneyland, a theme park, opened in Anaheim, California, in 1955, followed by Walt Disney's World in Florida in 1971.

Although Disney's company was riven with conflicts after his death, the firm emerged in the mid-1980s as the prototype of a successful international media conglomerate. Late twentieth-century Hollywood, relying on "synergies" among movies, video games, product tie-ins, and theme parks, has fulfilled Disney's vision of cinema as an all-pervading entertainment environment.

[*See also* Amusement Parks and Theme Parks; Film; Foreign Relations: The Cultural Dimension; Leisure; Mass Marketing; Multinational Enterprises; Popular Culture.]

• Richard Schickel, *The Disney Version: The Life, Times, Art, and Commerce of Walt Disney*, rev. ed., 1985. Eric Smoodin, *Disney Discourse: Producing the Magic Kingdom*, 1994.

—David Bordwell

DISTILLING INDUSTRY. *See* Brewing and Distilling.

DIVORCE. *See* Marriage and Divorce.

DIX, DOROTHEA (1802–1887), asylum movement leader. Dorothea Dix was born in Hampden, Maine, the daughter of an alcoholic Methodist preacher who was the black sheep of a wealthy merchant family. In 1836–1837, her career as a schoolmistress thwarted by ill health, she suffered a nervous breakdown. Traveling to England seeking a cure, she encountered leading reformers, including the Quaker Samuel Tuke, head of the well-known York Retreat for the mentally disordered. Returning to the United States, Dix in 1841–1842 undertook an exhaustive survey of the appalling treatment of Massachusetts's indigent insane, confined in jails and almshouses, often in chains. She was supported by prominent reformers and by the Unitarian leader William Ellery *Channing, a close friend. In 1843, in response to her scathing report, the Massachusetts legislature appropriated funds to expand the state mental hospital in Worcester. This set the pattern for her successful advocacy of similar reforms in many states, from New York to Mississippi. She was now well-known, but her long campaign (1847–1854) to win federal funding for state asylums for the mentally ill proved unsuccessful. When the *Civil War began, Dix, inspired by the British heroine Florence Nightingale, sought to become America's supreme nurse. Appointed superintendent of army nurses, she proved a domineering, inept administrator and was gradually relieved of power. Dix also supported prison reform, but otherwise generally ignored the other reform movements of the day, including women's rights and *antislavery. Yet her single-minded focus allowed her to accomplish more in politics than any other woman of her era.

[*See also* Alms Houses; Mental Illness; Prisons and Penitentiaries.]

• David Gollaher, *Voice for the Mad: The Life of Dorothea Dix*, 1995. Thomas J. Brown, *Dorothea Dix: New England Reformer*, 1998.

—David Gollaher

DIXIECRATS. *See* States' Rights Party.

DOLLAR DIPLOMACY. The term "dollar diplomacy" is associated primarily with the foreign policy of President William Howard *Taft (1909–1913). Taft and his secretary of state, Philander C. Knox, believed that bringing financial stability to debt-ridden but strategically important countries would promote both international progress and U.S. interests. They sought to expand upon President Theodore *Roosevelt's actions in the Dominican Republic, where American bankers refunded defaulted loans and the U.S. government established a customs receivership to guarantee the bankers' repayments. Wider use of similar U.S. private bank loans, Taft and Knox hoped, could leverage the acceptance of financial advisers and fiscal reform, encouraging *gold-standard currencies, honest and efficient revenue collection, modern banking and tax systems, and stable democratic governments. Taft and Knox tried to institute dollar diplomacy arrangements in China, Liberia, and several Central American nations. China persistently refused American loans linked to advisers. Nicaragua and Liberia, along with the Dominican Republic, became prime examples of dollar-diplomacy dependencies, but the expected stability and prosperity never materialized, and U.S. economic influence became increasingly heavy-handed and exploitative. Critics of American *capitalism abroad turned the phrase "dollar diplomacy" into a pejorative term portraying the U.S. government as a bill collector for American banking and corporate interests, and connoting a general corruption of public diplomacy for private profit.

Still, Taft's strategy, using loans to discipline nations into fiscal responsibility, survived in various forms under his successors. President Woodrow *Wilson and the Republican regimes of the 1920s all cooperated with bankers and professional financial advisers to facilitate loan and advising arrangements in many nations. And the Bretton Woods system, established after 1944, institutionalized the practice of attaching "conditionalities" to projected loans—the basic formula of dollar diplomacy. In short, the Taft administration's assumptions about using loans to accomplish certain goals of international policy, although criticized, became a normal part of U.S. policymaking in the twentieth century.

[*See also* Bretton Woods Conference; Expansionism; Foreign Relations: U.S. Relations with Africa; Foreign Relations: U.S. Relations with Asia; Foreign Relations: U.S. Relations with Latin America; Foreign Trade, U.S.; Good Neighbor Policy; Multinational Enterprises.]

• Emily S. Rosenberg, *Financial Missionaries to the World: The Politics and Culture of Dollar Diplomacy, 1900–1930*, 1999.

—Emily S. Rosenberg

DOMESTIC LABOR. Since the *Colonial Era, domestic labor has been a significant contributor to economic production and development in America. While domestic labor encompasses a wide range of market and nonmarket activities, this essay will focus on three major productive elements: household manufactures for home consumption; industrial outwork, a form of waged labor conducted in the home; and independent production within the home for sale in wider commodity markets.

Household manufactures for home consumption prevailed as a system of domestic labor in rural areas prior to the era of *industrialization. With the emergence of mechanized textile, shoe, and garment production after 1830, household manufactures declined steadily. With the growth of the *factory system in the nineteenth century (initially concentrated in *New England and the Middle Atlantic states), household manufactures declined in those regions, while remaining substantial in the *South and *Middle West. The rapid expansion of commercial markets for items previously produced within the home substantially reduced household manufacturing across the United States. American families after *World War II rarely produced goods at home for their own consumption.

Independent production within the home for sale in broader markets declined at the same time. Such independent production was more commonly concentrated in cities than in rural areas. In the first half of the nineteenth century, independent male weavers or shoemakers often worked in their own homes, drawing upon the unpaid labor of family members for certain steps in the production process. Women dressmakers and laundry workers also brought work home and commonly sold their services to a varied clientele. Technological developments and the steady commodification of goods and services undermined independent production within the home. Increasingly individuals who performed such work at home were displaced by wage workers employed in urban factories and shops that took advantage of machinery or economies of scale to undersell homeworkers.

Industrial outwork, by contrast, has had a much longer and more significant history. For almost 150 years, a substantial share of industrial wage work was performed in workers' homes. From the emergence of the first factories in the 1790s until the passage of the Fair Labor Standards Act in 1938, employers found it economical to give out work to be performed outside of factories or workshops. Rural and urban residents alike were drawn into a system of dispersed contracting out, earning wages for domestic labor performed with raw materials owned by their employers and producing goods for sale in distant markets.

Industrial outwork flourished initially in rural communities, as wives and daughters in farming families supplemented farm income by laboring for textile mills, storekeepers, or middlemen who distributed raw materials throughout the countryside and sold the finished cloth, hats, and shoes in widely dispersed markets. The first water-powered cotton spinning mills typically expanded production by putting out yarn to be woven by members of farming families. Handloom weaving on an outwork basis grew significantly in New England in the early nineteenth century, but declined after the mid-1820s with the adoption of the power loom. Farm women turned to braided straw hats and palm-leaf hats as an outwork occupation, and by 1837 more than fifty thousand women and children were employed on a part-time basis in Massachusetts alone. At about the same time, farm women also worked at binding and stitching shoe uppers. By mid-century a decentralized hybrid system had developed with much of shoebinding done by women in their own homes while male artisans working in small urban shops did the shoemaking itself. Domestic labor in boot and shoe manufacturing declined sharply after the *Civil War with the more complete mechanization of shoemaking and the adoption of *steam power in urban factories.

In the *Gilded Age, the garment industry became the leading employer of homeworkers. In *Boston, for instance, clothing manufacturers put cut goods into rural communities; by 1870, Boston employers paid some two million dollars in wages to a workforce of about fifty thousand New England farm women. By then, however, urban *homework in the garment industry dwarfed its rural cousin. In Boston, *New York City, and *Philadelphia, home employment in the needle trades came to be known as the "sweating" system, as women and children in urban immigrant families earned meager wages from employers whose exploitative practices led them to be known as "sweaters." By the early twentieth century, the impoverishment of immigrant families and the squalid conditions within which they worked and lived concerned *Progressive Era reformers who lobbied to outlaw tenement-house production and *child labor in manufacturing.

While rural outwork had been a part-time occupation for members of farming families in the *Antebellum Era, its later urban counterpart was full-time and highly exploitative, depending on a system of underpaid subcontracting that forced workers to put in long hours during peak seasons simply to survive. The low wages and long hours of homeworkers, in turn, undermined wages and employment in factories and workshops. State and local efforts to regulate or outlaw homework were typically stymied by court rulings, such as *Lochner v. New York* (1905), which protected workers' putative right to "freedom of contract" under the *Fourteenth Amendment. Only when Congress enacted the Fair Labor Standards Act in the *New Deal Era did industrial outwork become largely unprofitable. Afterward, the federal government's enforcement of wage and hours regulations on homeworkers and the outright ban of homework in a number of industries sharply limited these practices.

Industrial outwork, while exploitative, has nonetheless had a certain appeal for individuals and families that have sought to work within its bounds. In an economic system in which the wages of male household heads were (and often still are) insufficient to support a family, outwork permitted the employment of children and married women to supplement family income. Homework has also permitted women homemakers to combine housekeeping, cooking, and *child rearing with wage-earning activities. Homework has had a certain rationality for urban immigrant families in the United States for the past century, but it has been a logic based on the inadequacy of state regulation of wages and hours of labor.

At the end of the twentieth century industrial outwork made a comeback with the growth of an underground, largely immigrant economy in the garment trades of New York, *Los Angeles, and other large cities. In the 1980s, the Ronald *Reagan administration rescinded the laws against homework in several industries and cut back on regulatory enforcement. These steps, coupled with the growth of telecommuting among white-collar clerical workers, led to a resurgence of homework. Whether this form of domestic labor will see continued growth depends on future technological changes and legal struggles. Homework, then, is an issue that refuses to go away.

[*See also* Agriculture: 1770s to 1890; Clothing and Fashion; Consumer Movement; Early Republic, Era of the; Economic Regulation; Homework; Immigration; Kelley, Florence; Labor Markets; Mass Marketing; Textile Industry; Women in the Labor Force.]

• Rolla Tryon, *Household Manufactures in the United States, 1640–1860*, 1917, reprint ed. 1966. Eileen Boris and Cynthia R. Daniels, eds., *Homework: Historical and Contemporary Perspectives on Paid Labor at Home*, 1989. Gregory Nobles, "Merchant Middlemen in the Outwork Network of Rural New England," in *Merchant Credit and Labour Strategies in Historical Perspective*, ed. Rosemary E. Ommer, 1990, pp. 333–47. Thomas Dublin, "Rural Putting-Out Work in Early Nineteenth-Century New England: Women and the Transition to Capitalism in the Countryside," *New England Quarterly* 64 (1991): 531–73. Eileen Boris, *Home to Work: Motherhood and the Politics of Industrial Homework in the United States*, 1994. Thomas Dublin, *Transforming Women's Work: New England Lives in the Industrial Revolution*, 1994.

—Thomas Dublin

DOMESTIC PRODUCTION. *See* Homework.

DOMESTIC VIOLENCE. In the late twentieth century, a revived feminist movement forced "domestic violence" into public view. Previously called "wife-beating," the newer, somewhat oblique term reflected the understanding that many victims are not wives but girlfriends, and very occasionally husbands or boyfriends. "Domestic violence" consists primarily of violence against women.

Inasmuch as male domination appears virtually universal in human history, violence against women has probably been equally universal. In most patriarchal societies, husbands were customarily entitled to "chastise" their wives, although women resisted what they considered unacceptable levels of violence. But until the birth of modern *feminism, a woman's defenses were limited to whatever personal resistance she could mount with the help of kinfolk. Feminists initially approached the problem circuitously and euphemistically, calculating that a frontal attack on this male privilege would elicit a backlash. In the United States, women activists began even before the creation of a *women's rights movement to embed criticism of male violence in the temperance crusade, using the battered woman as the archetypical victim of the drunkard and rendering drinking a gendered (male) vice. By the mid–nineteenth century, feminists were invoking domestic violence as an argument for divorce and maternal custody of children. In the 1870s women reformers organized a movement against child abuse, again highlighting male violence. Mothers often reported their husbands to the new anti–child abuse societies to draw attention to their own victimization, advancing the then novel idea that violence against women harmed children; this campaign helped deflate the Victorian romanticism about the family that veiled it from investigation.

The leaders of these campaigns were mainly elite and white, but less privileged women also resisted violence against women. In the 1890s African American leader Ida B. *Wells-Barnett inaugurated her crusade against *lynching by challenging white southern lies about black men's rapes of white women. Wells-Barnett publicized instead the widespread real *rape of black women by white men. At the same time, employed, mainly poor, women protested workplace abuse, ranging from harassment to rape.

A major advance in public policy against domestic violence, however inadvertent, was Aid to Dependent Children (ADC), a part of the *Social Security Act of 1935. ADC (later AFDC) offered battered women economic help if they left abusive men. Battered-women's advocates generally considered the repeal of AFDC in 1996 a setback for the cause of stopping domestic violence.

In the 1970s a revived women's movement challenged domestic violence directly. Demanding prosecution of batterers and founding battered-women's shelters, activists argued that domestic violence was not only a personal but also a social and even a political practice that contributed to subordinating all women. By the late twentieth century, the overwhelming majority of Americans believed that nothing justifies domestic violence. As if to symbolize these achievements, President Bill *Clinton in 1994 established for the first time a Violence against Women Office in the Justice Department.

[*See also* Family; Gender; Marriage and Divorce; Temperance and Prohibition.]

• Elizabeth Pleck, *Domestic Tyranny: The Making of American Social Policy against Family Violence from Colonial Times to the Present*, 1987. Linda Gordon, *Heroes of Their Own Lives: The Politics and History of Family Violence*, 1988.

—Linda Gordon

DONNER PARTY. Of all the tragedies on the migration west in the mid–nineteenth century, none has earned more notoriety than the ill-fated Donner Party whose eighty-seven members were trapped by snow in *California's Sierra Nevada Mountains in 1846 and reduced to cannibalism. Part of a large wagon train that had left Springfield, Illinois, in April, the Donner Party, named for the family of wealthy George and Tamsen Donner who owned three of the twenty wagons, split off from the main party to try an untested shortcut through the Wasatch Mountains and across the Great Salt Lake Desert. The party reached Truckee (now Donner) Lake just east of the summit of the Sierra Nevada mountains on 31 October only to be caught by a blizzard. After the first death on 16 December, ten men and five women set out on makeshift snowshoes to get help. In their thirty-three-day trek, eight members, all males who either died or were murdered, were eaten by the remainder. When a rescue party reached the surviving members of the group that had remained behind, they, too, reported that they had resorted to cannibalism to survive. All told, forty members of the party died before the last one was brought out in April 1847. Although the trek westward reveals many examples of personal sacrifice and sharing, the Donner Party's fate highlights the ambitiousness, folly, recklessness, and ruthlessness that also marked the westward movement.

• Jared Diamond, "Living through the Donner Party," *Discover* (March 1992): 100–7. Joseph A. Kind, *Winter of Entrapment: A New Look at the Donner Party*, 1992.

—Clifford E. Clark Jr.

DOUGLAS, STEPHEN A. (1813–1861), U.S. senator, presidential candidate. Arriving in Illinois as a young man from his native Vermont, Stephen A. Douglas practiced law and played a key role in building the state *Democratic party. Serving in the U.S. House of Representatives (1843–1847) and the Senate (1847–1861), he attained a party leadership role and a command of the legislative process unsurpassed in his generation. Called "the Little Giant" for his short height and towering reputation, he worked indefatigably to promote his region's interests, especially geographic expansion and railroad construction. Reluctantly addressing the issue of *slavery in the territories, Douglas adopted the formula known as "popular sovereignty"—that is, leaving the issue to local control—as he engineered passage of the *Compromise of 1850.

If Douglas adopted popular sovereignty as an expedient, he embraced it thereafter as a principle, with ironic effects. His application of the doctrine in the *Kansas-Nebraska Act (1854), which abandoned the geographic restraints on slavery written into the *Missouri Compromise (1820), led directly to the creation of the *Republican party. His use of the doctrine to block Kansas's admission as a slave state alienated the *South and hastened the sectional split of the Democratic party. His defense of popular sovereignty in his famous debates with Abraham *Lincoln in the 1858 Illinois senatorial race, while securing his reelection, served mainly to boost the fame of his Republican rival. Douglas won the presidential nomination of the northern Democrats in 1860, but was defeated by Lincoln and the Republicans, which in turn triggered secession. Although Douglas venerated the Union, he figured prominently in many of the events leading to its disruption.

[*See also* Antebellum Era; Civil War: Causes; Federal Government, Legislative Branch: House of Representatives; Federal Government, Legislative Branch: Senate; Lincoln-Douglas Debates; Railroads.]

• Robert W. Johannsen, *Stephen A. Douglas*, 1973.

—George B. Forgie

DOUGLAS, WILLIAM O. (1898–1980), associate justice of the U.S. *Supreme Court. A native of Minnesota, Douglas graduated from Columbia Law School in 1925 and later taught at Yale Law School. A New Deal Democrat, he served on the *Securities and Exchange Commission from 1935 to 1939, the final years as chairman. President Franklin Delano *Roosevelt appointed him to the Supreme Court in 1939. Douglas promoted the causes of human dignity and individual liberties, most often grounding his decisions in the *Bill of Rights. His judicial positions sought, in the words of a 1968 opinion, "to take the government off of the backs of the people." For Douglas, that meant full constitutional protection for all, including the despised and defenseless. His 1953 stay of execution for the convicted spies Julius and Ethel Rosenberg triggered one of four congressional impeachment efforts. His most famous opinion, in *Griswold* v. *Connecticut* (1965), established a constitutional right to privacy and laid the foundation for the controversial **Roe* v. *Wade* decision (1973) upholding a woman's constitutional right to an *abortion.

Douglas wrote more than a dozen books, providing lively narratives of his world travels and wilderness expeditions and promoting his cherished causes, particularly *environmentalism and protection of *civil liberties. He was married four times and his freewheeling lifestyle coupled with his outspoken libertarianism outraged conservatives. Even his supporters sometimes found the willful, irascible Douglas easier to admire than to like. But for them, he stood as a symbol of the unwavering belief that individuals could improve the nation and the world.

[*See also* New Deal Era, The; Rosenberg Case.]

• William O. Douglas, *Go East, Young Man,* 1974. William O. Douglas, *The Court Years,* 1980. James F. Simon, *Independent Journey: The Life of William O. Douglas,* 1980.

—James F. Simon

DOUGLASS, FREDERICK (1818–1895), abolitionist, reformer, author. Born Frederick Bailey in rural Maryland to an enslaved woman and her master, he spent his youth alternately as a field hand and household servant in Baltimore, where his mistress gave him an aborted education. Returned to farm labor when his Baltimore master died, he attempted to flee, resulting in an often-recounted showdown with the slave breaker Edward Covey, whom he vanquished. Douglass recorded his slave experiences in three autobiographies: *Narrative of the Life of Frederick Douglass* (1845), *My Bondage and My Freedom* (1855), and *Life and Times of Frederick Douglass* (1881).

In 1838 he fled North, married a free black, and worked on the docks in New Bedford, Massachusetts. He met the abolitionist-leader William Lloyd *Garrison in 1839; in 1841, after an impromptu *antislavery speech in Nantucket, Massachusetts, he became an agent of the Massachusetts Anti-Slavery Society. He lectured widely, and his *Narrative* sold more than any other autobiography by a former slave. Only **Uncle Tom's Cabin* rivaled its impact. After two years in the British Isles (1845–1847), Douglass broke with Garrison over the latter's rejection of political means to end *slavery. Purchasing his freedom and settling in Rochester, New York, he edited a series of antislavery periodicals: *North Star* (1847–1851), renamed *Frederick Douglass' Paper* (1851–1860), and *Douglass' Monthly* (1859–1863). His writings, urging the nation to return to first principles and warning of the dangers of apostasy, exemplify the jeremiad (an allusion to the biblical prophet Jeremiah), a literary genre stretching from Cotton Mather to Martin Luther *King Jr. His autobiographies embody another long American literary tradition extolling the individual's capacity for self-fashioning and social mobility through the cultivation of moral virtue. His thought never represented a consensus, however. His advocacy of racial *assimilation, his rejection of *black nationalism as impractical, and his support for the *woman suffrage movement all roused criticism, as did his 1884 marriage to a white woman.

Douglass viewed the *Civil War as a millennial struggle between liberty and tyranny. Through his wartime writings and his role in recruiting two black regiments (the Massachusetts Fifty-fourth and Fifty-fifth), he sought to transform a war to preserve the Union into one to abolish slavery—a goal achieved with the Thirteenth Amendment (1865). Douglass continued his journalistic efforts with the *New National Era* (1870–1874), but the promise of the post-slavery era quickly faded as reformers encountered entrenched *racism in the *Reconstruction Era South. As the North's commitment to biracial democracy gave way to efforts at sectional reconciliation, Douglass's faith in the nation waned. As race relations reached their nadir, he consoled himself with a series of minor government posts: U.S. marshal (1877–1881) and recorder of deeds (1881–1886) in Washington, D.C., and consul general in Haiti (1889–1891). Like many of his generation, he had attributed the evils of racism to the institution of slavery. The post–Civil War Era exposed the fallacy of that view as well as the limits of his self-help ideology as a vehicle for racial equality and African American social mobility.

[*See also* African Americans; Antebellum Era; Civil War: Causes; Gilded Age; Literature: Early National and Antebellum Eras; Literature: Civil War to World War I; Mather, Increase and Cotton; Slave Uprisings and Resistance.]

• David W. Blight, *Frederick Douglass' Civil War: Keeping Faith in Jubilee,* 1989. William S. McFeely, *Frederick Douglass,* 1991.

—Patrick Rael

DRAFT RIOTS, CIVIL WAR. By late 1862, as *Civil War casualties mounted in costly military campaigns, the patriotic fervor that had inspired many northern men to enlist was waning. The *Emancipation Proclamation further eroded support for the war in some quarters. Accordingly, in March 1863, Congress passed the Conscription Act to draft men into military service. Racial animosity, dissatisfaction with the Abraham *Lincoln administration, and labor unrest all helped fuel draft opposition. Most odious to many was the commutation clause, which enabled a draftee to avoid service by hiring a substitute or paying a $300 fee. Draft resistance erupted across the *Middle West, but was concentrated in Ohio, Indiana, and Iowa. *New England resistance was centered mainly in *Boston, Vermont, New Hampshire. Violent opposition also broke out in the Pennsylvania coal regions.

The most serious outburst arose in July 1863 in *New York City, where *Irish American immigrants bitterly resented the draft and feared job competition from free blacks. Violence erupted on 13 July and continued for four days, as mobs attacked draft offices, public buildings, the homes of city officials and *Republican party leaders, and *African Americans. Many blacks were lynched and an African American orphanage was destroyed. The rioting ended only after Lincoln dispatched to New York City Union troops from General George Meade's army, which was pursuing the Confederates after the Battle of *Gettysburg. Overall, the violence claimed at least 105 lives.

The draft riots had several aftereffects. Draft resistance continued, but on a lesser scale after the New York City riot. In 1864, Congress repealed the commutation clause. Federal authorities vigorously enforced later drafts, employing sufficient military force to quell any resistance. In politics, Tammany Hall, the *Democratic party's New York City machine, arose from the ashes of the riots by balancing the interests of immigrants and workers with those of the conservative elite.

[*See also* Civil War: Domestic Effects; Conscription; Lynching; Riots, Urban.]

• Adrian Cook, *The Armies of the Streets: The New York City Draft Riots of 1863,* 1974. Iver Bernstein, *The New York City Draft Riots: Their Significance for American Society and Politics in the Age of the Civil War,* 1990.

—Jonathan M. Berkey

DRAFT, THE. *See* Conscription.

DRAMA. The history of *theater in the United States can be divided into three parts: the first 150 years, marked by efforts to break free of English cultural domination; the richly productive period from 1920 to 1950; and the last half of the twentieth century, shaped by the effects of *television and *film and a general sense of decline.

In the first period, down to 1920, the nation's struggle for a broader democracy and cultural independence was reenacted on the stage by American types in native dramas. Taking center stage, as performers and characters, were the dispossessed of Europe, the disenfranchised, and the powerless, all of whom endeavor to come to terms with tradition and authority: the Indian, the youthful freethinker, the *African American, the rustic, the frontiersman, and, above all, the young woman, whom the stage rewarded with decent work and equal opportunity.

Many of those barred from the corridors of power turned to the theater, which was itself an outcast subculture, attacked by the pious as the devil's drawing room, a counterforce of evil plotting to compete with the church for time, money, and souls.

William Dunlap (1766–1839), the eighteenth-century father of American drama, turned to the *Revolutionary War for his materials. His successors found inspiration in Native American culture and frontier life. Few dramas of this first period have endured, but two merit attention: P. T. *Barnum's production of *The Drunkard* and George Aikin's **Uncle Tom's Cabin* (from Harriet Beecher Stowe's novel). Their themes of temperance and Christian *antislavery sentiment brought religious people into the theater for the first time, a trend that suffered a momentary reversal in 1865 with the assassination of President Abraham *Lincoln in a Washington, D.C., theater by an actor, John Wilkes Booth.

In this formative period, American *theater* was far more exciting than American *plays.* Despite religious disapproval and the paucity of native-written drama, theater flourished in resident professional companies in every major city and in rural settlements from South Carolina to *California, reached by many touring companies. The period produced few well-known playwrights but many legendary performers, including Edwin Booth (John Wilkes Booth's brother), Joseph Jefferson, Edwin Forrest, Anna Cora Mowatt, and Lotta Crabtree.

One American type of drama that embodied democratic, working-class ideals was the burlesque or travesty, in great demand from the 1840s until around 1910. These parodies of serious drama and upper-class society were incorporated into an entertainment original to the United States, the formulaic minstrel show. The minstrel tradition and the show-girl extravaganza (like the British import, *The Black Crook*) evolved into the *vaudeville shows of the early twentieth century.

Beginning in the 1880s, American playwrights generally moved away from melodrama toward realism, laying the groundwork for the post-1920 blossoming of American drama. These authors included Steele Mackaye, James A. Herne, Bronson Howard, Clyde Fitch, and William Vaughn Moody.

The second period of American theater, beginning in 1920 with the production of Eugene *O'Neill's *Beyond the Horizon* and continuing for four decades, was unquestionably its greatest. This era was made grand not by actors (though there were many of considerable talent) but by playwrights, whose work continues to live in revivals on professional, community, and university stages; in adaptations for other mediums such as television and film; and in printed anthologies.

Although O'Neill dominated this period, several other American playwrights achieved distinction in world theater, notably Tennessee Williams (1911–1983) and Arthur Miller (1915–), but also Clifford Odets, Thornton Wilder, Lillian Hellman, William Inge, and Edward Albee, among others. Wilder's *Our Town* (1938), an evocation of small-town *New England, became an enduring favorite.

The range of successful dramatic forms during these years is impressive, including naturalistic-psychological dramas, historical romances, proletarian dramas, domestic Gothics, allegories, and realistic, middle-class tragedies. Although an eclectic period stylistically, realism dominated.

The American stage from the 1920s to the 1960s responded to the cultural turbulence of the times—the modernist disillusionment following *World War I; the Great Depression of the 1930s; the fascist menace and *World War II; and the consumerist, conformist *Cold War culture of the 1950s.

Even in the sometimes frivolous 1920s, playwrights addressed economic injustice and social upheaval. Elmer Rice's *The Adding Machine* (1923) satirized *capitalism. Maxwell Anderson and Laurence Stalling's antiwar, antifascist play *What Price Glory?* appeared the following year. But Eugene O'Neill, the preeminent playwright of the 1920s who joined classical themes and Freudian psychology in his domestic tragedies, usually ignored the issues of the day in favor of a more universal stance. A possible exception, *The Great God Brown* (1928), offers an allegory of the clash of the creative spirit with capitalism. This grim picture was not entirely alleviated by *Show Boat* (1927), a romantic musical by Jerome Kern and Oscar Hammerstein II (based on an Edna Ferber novel), in which the issue of racial injustice looms large.

In the Depression-ridden 1930s, more plays of social relevance came to the fore. These included Clifford Odets's *Waiting for Lefty* (1935), which wed radical politics and radical stylistics, the play being presented as if the audience were present at a labor-union meeting. In 1933, one of the longest runs in theatrical history began with the production of Erskine Caldwell's *Tobacco Road,* a play based on his novelistic stereotyping of poor southern whites. Two Depression-Era dramas exposed the assault on the human spirit by capitalistic greed. John Steinbeck's long-running *Of Mice and Men* (1937) dealt with *migratory agricultural workers excluded from the American dream. Lillian Hellman's *The Little Foxes* (1939) deromanticized an aristocratic but self-destructive southern family obsessed with money. Despite Hellman's success, women playwrights and directors were rare. Similarly, with the exception of actor-singer Paul *Robeson, African Americans' theatrical participation was limited to small, often demeaning roles or to occasional experimental productions usually staged far from Broadway.

The 1930s also brought a brief interval of government funding for dramatic art: the Federal Theatre Project, a division of the New Deal's *Works Progress Administration, employed over 1,200 theatre professionals nationwide. Its tendency to produce controversial, socially critical plays, like Marc Blitzstein's *The Cradle Will Rock,* caused Congress to end the program in 1939.

These decades also saw the development of the musical—a particularly American contribution to dramatic entertainment. The developing tradition of staged musical dramas reached a pinnacle in 1935 with an American opera, *Porgy and Bess,* with script and music by Ira and George *Gershwin. Based on a novel and play by Dubose and Dorothy Heywood, it chronicled African American life in Charleston, South Carolina. Not until 1957 with Leonard *Bernstein's *West Side Story,* which recast the Romeo and Juliet tale in the violent world of New York street gangs, did a work in this genre reach a similar level of success. Many musicals followed in the next decades, making this genre America's chief contribution to world theater. Some of the most successful over the years included *Guys and Dolls, Brigadoon, Camelot, My Fair Lady, The King and I, The Fantasticks, Hello, Dolly, Hair,* and *A Chorus Line.*

A series of memorable productions made the 1940s the single most important decade in the history of American theater. Four plays by O'Neill were produced, including one of his greatest, *The Iceman Cometh* (1946). Tennessee Williams and Arthur Miller made their Broadway debuts with two plays each: Williams's *The Glass Menagerie* (1945) and *A Streetcar Named Desire* (1947), and Miller's *All My Sons* (1947) and *Death of a Salesman* (1949). In addition, two classic American musicals, Richard Rodgers and Oscar Hammerstein's *Oklahoma* (1943) and *South Pacific* (1949), alleviated O'Neill's grim philosophical explorations, Miller's social warnings, and the Gothic despair of Williams.

The third period of theater in the United States, beginning around 1950, was marked by several developments: the growing influence on actors and directors of Lee Strasberg's Actors' Studio, with its psychological, naturalistic style called "the Method"; a tendency to eliminate barriers between audience and performers (with arena stages, audience participation, and a diminished theatricality in staging); the continued impact of film and television (more accessible dramatic forms that drained both talent and audiences from the stages and fostered a star system based on popularity rather than talent); and, finally, the growth of a less commercially driven off-Broadway theatrical tradition.

Among the playwrights who energized the theater as the twentieth century ended were the prolific Neil Simon, whose *Brighton Beach Memoirs* (1983), the first play in an autobiographical cycle, tempered his usual light comedies; David Mamet, the controversial author of *American Buffalo* (1996) and other works; Wendy Wasserstein, whose first highly acclaimed play was *Uncommon Women and Others* (1977); African American playwright August Wilson, author of *Ma Rainey's Black Bottom* (1984); and Tony Kushner, whose play on the subject of *acquired immunodeficiency syndrome (AIDS), *Angels in America,* premiered in 1993. In addition, for over forty years, from *West Side Story* to *Into the Woods* (1987), lyricist Stephen Sondheim strongly influenced *musical theater. Although the Broadway musical was invigorated by British playwright Andrew Lloyd Webber (among his biggest hits were *Cats* [1981] and *Phantom of the Opera* [1986]), his influence intensified pressures for large and costly cinematic productions.

The 1990s found the American theater more decentralized and open to women and minority playwrights and a wider array of cultural themes. For example, Lorraine Hansberry's *A Raisin in the Sun* (1959) provided audiences with a rare theatrical experience: a play by an African American playwright, about racial integration in the North, with African American characters. Not until August Wilson in the 1980s did an African American playwright have such a profound impact.

The end of the twentieth century also brought evidences of decline, marked by ephemera, bombastic spectacle, revivals from better times, and periodic infusions of life from Europe and England.

[*See also* Depressions, Economic; Early Republic, Era of the; Indian History and Culture: The Indian in Popular Culture; Minstrelsy; New Deal Era, The; Popular Culture.]

• Gerald Weales, *American Drama since World War II,* 1962. Helen Krich Chinoy and Linda Walsh Jenkins, *Women in the American Theatre,* 1981. Ethan Mordden, *The American Theatre,* 1981. Gerald Boardman, *American Musical Comedy,* 1982. Gary Larson, *The Reluctant Patron: The United States Government and the Arts, 1943–1965,* 1983. Claudia D. Johnson, *American Actress: Perspective on the Nineteenth Century,* 1984. Errol Hill, ed., *The Theatre of Black Americans,* 1987. C. W. E. Bigsby, *Modern American Drama, 1945–1990,* 1994.

—Claudia Durst Johnson

DRED SCOTT CASE. *See Scott* v. *Sandford.*

DREISER, THEODORE (1871–1945), novelist. Born in Terre Haute, Indiana, the son of German-American parents, Theodore Dreiser endured poverty and ostracism as a boy. The popular songwriter Paul Dresser (1857–1911) was his brother. Dreiser worked as a reporter in *Chicago, St. Louis, Pittsburgh, and New York, absorbing impressions of urban crime and vice, wealth and poverty. His journalistic experience, Balzac's novels, and Herbert Spencer's *social Darwinism turned him toward determinism and fictional realism. His first novel, *Sister Carrie* (1900), a tale of a young woman's career in the city, was attacked as immoral or found shocking and grim by most critics. *Jennie Gerhardt* (1911), the story of an impoverished young woman driven by family poverty to become a rich man's mistress, was championed by young writers rebelling against the Victorian idealism dominating American fiction and criticism. In *The Financier* (1912) and *The Titan* (1914) Dreiser chronicled the rise of the fictional robber baron Frank Cowperwood, modeled on the Chicago financier and traction magnate Charles Yerkes (1837–1905). Dreiser's autobiographical novel *The "Genius"* (1915) was banned for nearly a decade. His masterpiece, *An American Tragedy* (1925), is a powerfully documented narrative about a young man impelled by ambition and dreams of wealth to plot the murder of his pregnant sweetheart. In the 1930s Dreiser was sporadically active in radical politics. *The Bulwark* (1946) tells of a Quaker whose faith is tested, and *The Stoic* (1947) concluded the Cowperwood trilogy.

[*See also* Literature: Civil War to World War I; Literature: Since World War I.]

• Ellen Moers, *Two Dreisers,* 1969. Richard Lingeman, *Theodore Dreiser: At the Gates of the City (1871–1910),* 1986. Richard Lingeman, *Theodore Dreiser: An American Journey (1910–1945),* 1990.

—Richard Lingeman

DREW, CHARLES RICHARD (1904–1950), pioneering blood plasma scientist, surgeon, teacher. Born in *Washington, D.C., Charles Drew graduated from McGill University Medical School in Montreal in 1933, ranking second in a class of 137. During a two-year fellowship at Columbia University's medical school (1938–1940), he did research on blood banking, setting up Presbyterian Hospital's first blood bank, and became the first African American to receive the doctor of science degree. Drew served as medical director of the Blood for Britain Project in 1940 and also of a 1941 American *Red Cross pilot project involving the mass production of dried plasma. Drew's work proved pivotal to the success of the Red Cross's blood-collection program, a major life-saving agent during *World War II. In 1941 Drew became chairman of Howard University's department of surgery and chief surgeon at Freedmen's Hospital, where he worked tirelessly to build Howard's surgical residency program. Between 1941 and 1950, he trained more than half of the black surgeons certified by the American Board of Surgery. During the war years, Drew had spoken out against the Red Cross's blood segregation policy. When he died at the age of forty-five after an auto accident in North Carolina, a legend sprang up that he had bled to death after being turned away from a whites-only hospital. Although the legend was false, persisting medical discrimination against *African Americans perpetuated it. Throughout his career, Drew was committed to making medical care and training available to citizens of all races and economic levels.

[*See also* Medical Education; Medicine: Since 1945; Segregation, Racial; Surgery.]

• Charles E. Wynes, *Charles Richard Drew: The Man and the Myth,* 1988. Spencie Love, *One Blood: The Death and Resurrection of Charles R. Drew,* 1996.

—Spencie Love

DRUGS, ILLICIT. In the beginning there were no illicit drugs. From the seventeenth through the early nineteenth centuries, narcotics were simply part of medical practice, as they had been for millennia. A few patients—and doctors—exhibited symptoms of what would today be called addiction, but they were never numerous and posed no threat to the social order. The one controversial drug, alcohol, was cheap, ubiquitous, and liberally prescribed as a "stimulant."

Concerns about opium centered on overdose and adulteration. Imported from the Middle East, opium often contained sand, fruit pulp, flour, beeswax, lead, and the like. Indeed, the first national drug law, enacted in 1848, was intended to bar *adulterated* foreign drugs, not drugs per se.

In the later nineteenth century, narcotic addiction took on a more visible and sinister aspect. Morphine, the principal alkaloid of opium, available commercially after 1827, came into wide use with the spread of hypodermic medication in the 1860s and 1870s. Morphine injected hypodermically was much more powerful and potentially addictive than opium taken orally. By 1900 there were perhaps as many as 220,000 medical addicts. Contrary to legend, most of these addicts were not *Civil War veterans, but rather ailing women introduced to morphine by their physicians or through patent medicines, which often contained narcotics and alcohol.

They were joined by as many as ninety thousand opium smokers, mostly Chinese laborers and members of the white underworld. Habitués of the opium pipe, regarded much less sympathetically than medical addicts, were subject to restrictive local and state legislation, typically designed to outlaw public opium dens. The possibility of sexual relations between white women and Chinese men in the dens stirred fears, though in fact Chinese smokers usually kept to themselves.

Sexual anxieties also surrounded the nonmedical use of cocaine. Like morphine, cocaine began as a promising new alkaloid drug. In the mid-1880s Parke, Davis, its leading U.S. manufacturer, promoted it for a range of illnesses, from hay fever to alcoholism. Sigmund Freud relayed these glowing American reports to a European audience in his 1884 paper, "Über Coca." Cocaine's outstanding therapeutic property, that of local anesthesia, first noted by Carl Koller, helped to revolutionize *surgery and *dentistry. But overdose cases soon appeared in the medical literature and, as early as 1886, warnings of addiction resulting from medical treatment.

In the 1890s, concern shifted to underworld sniffing and injection of cocaine. Alcohol, cigarettes, and opium smoking were well established among prostitutes, pimps, and gamblers, and now cocaine, reputedly a potent aphrodisiac and stimulant, joined the list. In 1900, half the prostitutes in the Fort Worth, Texas, jail were said to be cocaine addicts.

With the wholesale price fluctuating at about two dollars an ounce in the late 1890s, cocaine was affordable by ordinary laborers, including *African Americans who toiled in work camps throughout the *South. Although the actual extent of its use remains uncertain, a racially charged folklore linked cocaine use by African Americans to violent rampages and "increased and perverted" sexual desires.

Alarmed city councils and state legislatures passed laws restricting cocaine's purchase to those holding a prescription from a licensed physician—a provision increasingly applied to opiates as well. Had this legislation succeeded, the emerging drug subculture might have been thwarted. But economic and competitive considerations tempted physicians, particularly older and marginal practitioners, to continue to prescribe liberally. Pharmacists criticized such overprescribing but shared the blame for the problem. Retail sales were highly profitable, though "certainly the most disagreeable feature of the apothecary's business," as one New York pharmacist lamented.

Sales to addicts were rationalized by the realization that spurned customers could simply go to another druggist—or a street dealer. Drugs diverted from legal sources were resold illegally by peddlers to those underage and without prescription. Teenage boys were avid customers for "decks" of cocaine and heroin (a semisynthetic derivative of morphine) peddled in *slums and vice districts. Opium prepared for smoking was also available, though more often supplied by smugglers and illegal manufacturers who dodged the heavy customs duty. The cliché that the 1914 Harrison Narcotic Act created the black market and drug subcultures of twentieth-century America is a political myth. Illegal sales, smuggling, and underworld use flourished decades before the Harrison Act. Drug abuse and trafficking spawned legislation, not the other way around.

The catalyst for national legislation, however, was the diplomatic situation in the Far East. American missionaries, notably Episcopal bishop Charles Henry Brent, had long deplored the British opium trade in China. In 1905 they helped secure a policy of suppressing opium smoking in the *Philippines, which had become a U.S. possession. In 1906 Brent asked for President Theodore *Roosevelt's help in setting up an international opium conference, which finally convened in Shanghai in February 1909. Representing the United States were Brent; Charles Tenney, a missionary and educator; and Hamilton Wright, a physician who subsequently became the chief architect of federal drug laws.

But while the U.S. government was calling for suppression of the Asian opium traffic, it continued to tolerate (and tax) opium smoking at home. To refute charges of hypocrisy, Roosevelt's secretary of state, Elihu Root, persuaded Congress to prohibit imports of smoking opium. (A later amendment also forbade its domestic manufacture.) This legislation, signed into law a week after the opening of the 1909 Shanghai conference, represented the first nationwide ban on a particular type of drug. In this sense, smoking opium was America's first "illicit drug."

In 1910, Hamilton Wright turned his attention to a comprehensive narcotic control bill, which he wanted passed before the Hague Opium Commission, a follow-up to the Shanghai conference, convened in 1911. Wright missed the deadline by three years, owing to prolonged negotiations and compromises with medical groups, the *pharmaceutical industry, and patent-medicine manufacturers. The 1914 Harrison Narcotic Act, named for its sponsor, Congressman Francis Harrison of New York, was a watered-down version of what Wright sought. It required dealers in opiates and cocaine to register, pay a nominal tax, and keep accurate records of their transactions. Unregistered dealers faced prosecution. Thus narcotic distribution would be confined to legitimate medical channels and made a matter of public record.

The Harrison Act was ambiguous on a key point: whether registered doctors and pharmacists could maintain a supply of drugs for those who were addicted. In 1919 the U.S. *Supreme Court, in the five-to-four *Webb* decision, ruled that they could not. This was the key precedent for the antimaintenance policy. It would have lasting implications, particularly after the Treasury Department quickly closed more than thirty experimental public clinics designed to provide a legal supply of drugs for addicts, forcing them into the black market.

In the 1920s, street drugs, mostly diverted from surplus European manufactures, were still relatively pure. However, international agreements in 1925 and 1931 made the large-scale diversion of legally manufactured drugs more difficult. Smuggled and adulterated heroin became the mainstay of the black market, which centered on *New York City, home to approximately half the nation's nonmedical narcotic addicts. In 1924 Congress effectively outlawed heroin, which, like smoking opium, was associated with vice and crime.

The Bureau of Narcotics, under the direction of Harry J. Anslinger from 1930 to 1962, was the federal agency most responsible for suppressing the illicit drug traffic. Anslinger was a hardliner who wanted traffickers behind bars and addicts in jail or in institutional treatment programs. Two large prison-hospitals, at Lexington, Kentucky, and Fort Worth, Texas, were built in the 1930s for the latter purpose. A skilled bureaucrat and lobbyist, Anslinger increased the scope and penalties of drug laws during his long tenure. He played a key role in passage of the 1937 Marijuana Tax Act, which added a national ban to state and local legislation. This legislation was inspired by the fear that marijuana use was spreading, as indeed it was among *jazz musicians, Mexican laborers, Caribbean sailors, and soldiers returning from Panama. Unknown before 1910, marijuana smoking became a subcultural ritual by the 1930s. It was a cheap high: fifteen cents a "reefer" in Harlem "tea pads." Anslinger and other authorities condemned it for inciting wild violence. This rationale, never plausible, was later replaced by the stepping-stone hypothesis. "Over 50 percent of ... young addicts started on marijuana smoking," Anslinger testified in 1951, and "graduated to heroin ... when the thrill of marijuana was gone."

Concern over the post–*World War II resurgence of heroin trafficking and addiction prompted Congress to enact the 1951 Boggs Act and 1956 Narcotic Control Act, which provided progressively stiffer mandatory sentences, all the way up to the death penalty for selling heroin to minors. States followed suit. Texas made marijuana possession punishable by life imprisonment. The prison-mindedness of drug policy provoked a reaction among those who viewed addiction as a *public health problem. In 1958 a joint committee of the *American Bar Association and the *American Medical Association criticized the police approach and suggested the possibility of a controlled legal supply. In the 1960s, two physicians, Vincent Dole and Marie Nyswander, showed that heroin addicts could be maintained indefinitely on oral methadone, a synthetic narcotic. Their work challenged both the antimaintenance policy and the reigning explanation of addiction, popularized in the 1920s by Lawrence Kolb, a physician with the U.S. Public Health Service. Kolb and his disciples held that addicts suffered from defective, even psychopathic, personalities. But for Dole and Nyswander, addicts were more or less normal persons whose drug use triggered a permanent metabolic change. They needed narcotics the way a diabetic needed insulin. Methadone maintenance satisfied that need and kept them out of the illicit market.

Methadone maintenance was, and remains, a cost-effective treatment for narcotic addiction. Its heyday came during the heroin epidemic of the late 1960s and early 1970s, when the country had an estimated half-million addicts. After 1974 methadone's star faded, owing to restrictive federal regulations, local resistance to clinics, and its irrelevance to other popular countercultural drugs. Among these were marijuana, a revival of cocaine sniffing, and experimentation with lysergic acid diethylamide (LSD), a powerful hallucinogen. The causes of the drug explosion of the 1960s and 1970s were various: affluence; Vietnam; paraphernalia shops; media coverage; youthful disenchantment with mainstream culture; proselytizing gurus like poet Allen Ginsberg, novelist Ken Kesey, and one-time Harvard psychologist Timothy Leary; growing consumption of alcohol and other "gateway" drugs; new sources of supply in Asia and Latin America; and, not least, the entry of tens of millions of baby boomers into their teens and twenties, the prime drug experimenting years.

The Richard M. *Nixon administration responded with a multifaceted drug war. International enforcement efforts increased, with notable successes in Turkey and France. More funds were appropriated for research and new treatment approaches, including therapeutic communities modeled on California's Synanon Foundation. Federal antidrug spending increased from $80 million in 1969 to $730 million in 1973. Six decades of piecemeal legislation was rationalized by the 1970 Controlled Substances Act, which sorted drugs into five schedules, depending on their abuse potential and therapeutic value. Drugs commonly regarded as "illicit" fell into either Schedule I (heroin, marijuana, LSD, peyote, and other hallucinogens) or Schedule II (cocaine, methamphetamine, morphine). Schedule I drugs were forbidden to everyone, doctors included. Schedule II drugs were allowed in medicine but tightly regulated. Other therapeutically useful drugs such as barbiturates and tranquilizers were placed in Schedules III through V and subject to looser controls.

Most post-1970 federal legislation took the form of incremental amendments to the Controlled Substances Act, as when the synthetic hallucinogen MDMA (Schedule I) or anabolic steroids (Schedule III) were added to the list. More far-reaching amendments were enacted in 1986 and 1988, in the midst of the crack epidemic. An inexpensive, smokable form of cocaine, crack exploded in the inner cities in the mid-1980s, culminating a sustained fifteen-year increase in cocaine consumption. Like heroin, crack had pronounced ethnic and class overtones and was associated with prostitution, sexual degradation, and violence. The 1986 and 1988 legislation, centerpieces of the Ronald *Reagan administration's drug war, substantially increased criminal and civil penalties. Crack was singled out for the heaviest punishment. Possessing five grams with intention to distribute brought a mandatory minimum sentence of five years, the same penalty prescribed for five hundred grams of powder cocaine. Federal penitentiaries became crowded with crack dealers, 95 percent of whom were black or Latino.

As in the 1950s, the vogue of imprisonment sparked a counterattack. Libertarians proposed "controlled legalization" as an alternative to the fifty-billion-dollar black market and a ballooning federal antidrug budget that reached fifteen billion dollars by 1997. The idea was to replace the costly and intrusive "drug war" with a regulated adult market in psychoactive drugs. Liberals and public health advocates espoused less radical harm-reduction measures, such as needle-exchange programs, which proliferated during the 1990s. Drug courts, a means of diverting nonviolent drug offenders into mandatory treatment, also became more common. The basic policy of the Bill *Clinton administration (1993–2001) nevertheless remained that of its predecessors: drug abuse was defined, suppressed, and managed principally, if no longer exclusively, by criminal statutes and law enforcement.

[*See also* Alcohol and Alcohol Abuse; Foreign Relations: U.S. Relations with Asia; Foreign Relations: U.S. Relations with Latin America; Medicine; Prisons and Penitentiaries; Progressive Era; Prostitution and Antiprostitution; Sexual Morality and Sex Reform; Sixties, The; Tobacco Products.]

• Charles C. Terry and Mildred Pellens, *The Opium Problem*, 1928. Richard J. Bonnie and Charles H. Whitebread II, *The Marijuana Conviction: A History of Marijuana Prohibition in the United States*, 1974. Edward M. Brecher et al., *Licit and Illicit Drugs*, 1974. David T. Courtwright, *Dark Paradise: Opiate Addiction in America before 1940*, 1982. David F. Musto, *The American Disease: Origins of Narcotic Control*, 3d ed., 1999. David Courtwright, Herman Joseph, and Don Des Jarlais, *Addicts Who Survived: An Oral History of Narcotic Use in America, 1923–1965*, 1989. John Burnham, *Bad Habits: Drinking, Smoking, Taking Drugs, Gambling, Sexual Misbehavior, and Swearing in American History*, 1993. Jill Jonnes, *Hep-Cats, Narcs, and Pipe Dreams: A History of America's Romance with Illegal Drugs*, 1996. Joseph Spillane, *Cocaine: From Medical Marvel to Modern Menace in the United States, 1884–1920*, 2000.

—David T. Courtwright

DU BOIS, W. E. B. (1868–1963), African-American scholar, polemicist, activist, and intellectual. Born and reared in Great Barrington, Massachusetts, Du Bois graduated from Fisk University in 1888. Enrolling as a junior at Harvard, he remained to earn a Ph.D. in history in 1895, with two years of study (1892–1894) at the University of Berlin. In 1896, Harvard published his dissertation on the suppression of the African slave trade. That same year, during a brief teaching stint at Wilberforce University in Ohio, he married a student, Nina Gomer; they had two children. A fellowship at the University of Pennsylvania (1896–1897) resulted in a pathbreaking sociological study, *The Philadelphia Negro* (1899). From 1897 to 1910, he taught sociology at Atlanta University.

At this time, most southern blacks could not vote and faced racial *segregation in public facilities; scores were lynched each year. Before 1900, Du Bois tended to agree with Booker T. *Washington, who advised blacks not to protest social and political inequality but instead to focus on vocational training and economic advancement. However, in *The Souls of Black Folk* (1903), a collection of essays on race that included one on Washington, Du Bois rejected accommodationism and sided with the growing ranks of Washington's opponents. He soon emerged as leader of the Niagara Movement, an organization that opposed Washington and promoted political activism. When this organization broke up, Du Bois in 1910 joined with a group of liberal whites to form an organization with similar aims, the New York-based *National Association for the Advancement of Colored People (NAACP). As editor of its journal, *The Crisis*, Du Bois exerted great influence as the NAACP's public voice. In monthly unsigned editorials he demanded social, economic, and political *equality for all blacks and an end to *lynching; promoted his idea of a "talented tenth" of liberally educated black leaders; and encouraged the development of African-American arts and the preservation of black folk culture.

During the 1920s, Du Bois focused increasingly on Pan-Africanism, *socialism, and economic issues while questioning the NAACP's exclusive focus on legal challenges to segregation. Increasingly at odds with the NAACP leadership, he resigned in 1934 and returned to Atlanta University. He rejoined the NAACP staff in 1944, but his increasingly radical politics ran counter to the postwar climate of *anticommunism and led to his resignation again, in 1948. He ran unsuccessfully for the U.S. Senate in New York in 1950 on the Progressive party ticket and the following year stood trial on charges of acting as an unregistered agent of a foreign power in connection with his activities in a peace organization. Though acquitted, Du Bois was banned from traveling abroad (1952–1958). Upon retrieving his passport, he visited Eastern Europe, China, and the Soviet Union, where he received the Lenin Peace Prize. In 1961, having officially joined the Communist Party, Du Bois left the United States for good. He spent his remaining years in Ghana, assembling an "Encyclopedia Africana."

The author of seventeen books, including five novels and one masterpiece of American literature, *The Souls of Black Folk,* Du Bois contributed significantly to many fields as an activist, scholar, critic, sponsor of African-American letters, and, above all, spokesman for African-American rights. At a time when Booker T. Washington's accommodationism seemed the most viable response to systematic racial oppression, Du Bois eloquently and persuasively described an alternative. He became the leading advocate of racial justice in the early twentieth century, helping to assure the victory of militant protest over accommodationism.

Yet Du Bois's legacy is complicated by the complexity of his thought and his later radicalism. Some historians characterize Du Bois's thinking as riddled with contradiction. Indeed, he championed the NAACP's campaign for integration, equality, and color-blind institutions while also promoting black cultural nationalism and even positing racial essentialism, most strikingly in his 1897 essay "The Conservation of the Races." His 1934 break with the NAACP came after he had begun to promote economic nationalism for blacks. Some see this break, and his increased interest in racial separatism, Pan Africanism, and Marxism, as at odds with his earlier liberal integrationism. Yet through most of his career, Du Bois was attracted to socialism, grappled with ideological dilemmas, and sought to balance competing ideas and approaches, taking intermediate positions between idealism and pragmatism, integration and separation, self-help and demands for reparation, liberal education and vocational training. He often concluded that such dilemmas could never be fully resolved. As he put it in a much-quoted statement on African-American identity in an 1897 *Atlantic Monthly* essay reprinted in *The Souls of Black Folk*: "One ever feels his two-ness—an American, a Negro; two souls, two thoughts, two unreconciled strivings; two warring ideals in one dark body, whose dogged strength alone keeps it from being torn asunder."

[*See also* African Americans; Black Nationalism; Civil Rights Movement; Communist Party—USA; Garvey, Marcus; Progressive Party of 1948; Race, Concept of; Racism.]

• Elliott Rudwick, *W. E. B. Du Bois: A Study in Minority Group Leadership,* 1960. Arnold Rampersad, *The Art and Imagination of W. E. B. Du Bois,* 1976. Gerald Horne, *Black and Red: W. E. B. Du Bois and the Afro-American Response to the Cold War, 1944–1963,* 1986. Manning Marable, *W. E. B. Du Bois: Black Radical Democrat,* 1986. David Levering Lewis, *W. E. B. Du Bois: Biography of a Race, 1868–1919,* 1993. David Levering Lewis, *W. E. B. Du Bois: The Fight for Equality and the American Century, 1919–1963,* 2000. William Jordan, *"Getting America Told": Black Newspapers and America's War for Democracy, 1914–1920,* 2001.

—William Jordan

DUKE, JAMES (1856–1925), manufacturer of *tobacco products, philanthropist. James "Buck" Duke, the son of Washington Duke and Artelia Roney Duke, was born on the family's farm in Orange County, North Carolina. After the *Civil War, Washington Duke and his sons began manufacturing and selling smoking tobacco under the brand name "Pro Bono Publico." The family moved to nearby Durham and opened a factory. Under James's leadership, the company began making hand-rolled cigarettes in New York. Securing exclusive rights to the Bonsack cigarette-making machine in 1885, the firm soon gained dominance in the industry. Duke's imaginative advertising enlarged markets for his mass-produced cigarettes, but his real genius lay in creating a corporate structure that integrated purchasing, manufacturing, marketing, and distribution. Organizing the American Tobacco Company (known to its detractors as the "American Tobacco Trust") in 1890, he consolidated control over the entire *tobacco industry. Ruthlessly cutting prices to undermine competitors, American and its affiliates dominated the production of cigarettes, pipe tobacco, snuff, chewing tobacco, and every tobacco product except cigars. The Trust became so dominant that the U.S. *Supreme Court ordered its dissolution in 1911 under *antitrust legislation.

James Duke increasingly devoted himself to Duke Power Company, which figured prominently in the *industrialization of the Carolina Piedmont region. He also became involved in philanthropic causes, primarily the Methodist church and Trinity College, which moved from Randolph County, North Carolina, to Durham in 1892. Creating the family philanthropic foundation, the Duke Endowment, in 1924, Duke specified that its annual income be distributed among colleges, *hospitals, and *orphanages in North and South Carolina. The endowment provided for the transformation of Trinity College into Duke University.

[*See also* Education: Rise of the University; Mass Marketing; Mass Production; Methodism; Philanthropy and Philanthropic Foundations.]

• Robert F. Durden, *The Dukes of Durham, 1865–1929,* reprint 1987. Robert F. Durden, *The Launching of Duke University, 1924–1949,* 1993.

—Robert Korstad

DULLES, JOHN FOSTER (1888–1959), secretary of state, 1953–1959. The grandson of Benjamin *Harrison's secretary of state John W. Foster, John Foster Dulles attended Princeton University and George Washington University Law School. A long-time lawyer with the blue-ribbon law firm Sullivan and Cromwell, he was also legal counsel at the 1919 Versailles peace conference, negotiator for the *United Nations Charter and the Japanese peace treaty of 1951, and a prominent Presbyterian layman. As secretary of state, he was widely viewed as the dominant force in shaping U.S. foreign policy—an assessment that frequently came with a critical bite given the era's *Cold War tensions. Although the Dwight D. *Eisenhower administration did end the *Korean War and inch toward détente with the Soviet Union, it remained deeply hostile to the People's Republic of China (contributing to two crises involving islands off the Chinese mainland), took the first direct U.S. steps into the Vietnam quagmire, and conducted problematic covert operations in eastern Europe, Iran, Guatemala, Indonesia, and Cuba led by the *Central Intelligence Agency under Dulles's brother Allen (1893–1969).

Assessments of Dulles's significance have changed as declassified archival records made clear that Eisenhower exercised more behind-the-scenes policy-making authority than many had thought at the time. In addition, Dulles's views are now seen as more complex than once imagined. His fervent public antagonism to "godless" *communism was only one wellspring of a sophisticated worldview. In private deliberations, Dulles revealed a typically American blend of realpolitik and liberal, essentially Wilsonian reform impulses. His enthusiasm for European integration, for example, emerged in part from attentiveness to the kind of economic interests he had protected as a corporate lawyer. But it also reflected his conviction that Europe must unite if another war were to be avoided—a conviction shared by close friends like Jean Monnet, a founding father of the European Common Market. Similarly mixed calculations shaped Dulles's approach to the Middle East. His response to the 1956 Suez Crisis, for example, combined a concern for Western oil interests with the judgment that a Eurocentric colonial mentality would no longer serve this purpose.

[*See also* Anticommunism; Federal Government, Executive Branch: Department of State; Fifties, The; Foreign Relations; Nuclear Strategy; Versailles, Treaty of; Vietnam War.]

• Ronald W. Pruessen, *The Road to Power: John Foster Dulles, 1888–1953,* 1982. Frederick W. Marks, *Power and Peace: The Diplomacy of John Foster Dulles,* 1993.

—Ronald Pruessen

DU PONT, PIERRE (1870–1954), corporate executive. Born near Wilmington, Delaware, Pierre du Pont graduated from the Massachusetts Institute of Technology in 1890. In 1902 he and two cousins purchased the century-old family firm, E. I. du Pont de Nemours Powder Company, from their elders. Through mergers and acquisitions, he and his cousin Coleman du Pont soon transformed the small-scale and competitive explosives industry, gaining control of 70 percent of the industry's productive capacity. Concentrating production in a small number of large works, they also established an international marketing and distribution network, a central purchasing office, and a research and development department. As treasurer (1904), du Pont developed new methods of asset counting, capital allocation, financial forecasting, and determining the rate of return on investment—techniques that became standard procedures in American industry. Under his leadership as president (1915) and board chairman (1919–1940), the firm produced a full line of chemicals.

Du Pont also played a central role in the General Motors Corporation, of which he became board chairman in 1915. During the recession of 1920, the DuPont Company acquired a substantial block of GM stock to save the company from bankruptcy. As president (1920) and board chairman (1926–1929), Pierre du Pont, with his deputy Alfred *Sloan, devised a creative organizational structure and marketing strategy to produce *motor vehicles "for every purse and person"—a strategy that made GM a market leader worldwide. As the key creator of what became America's largest chemical company and its largest automobile enterprise, du Pont pioneered in establishing methods of twentieth-century corporate management.

[*See also* Automotive Industry; Business; Chemical Industry; Foreign Relations: The Economic Dimension; Industrialization; Mass Marketing; Multinational Enterprises.]

• Alfred D. Chandler Jr. and Stephen Salsbury, *Pierre S. du Pont and the Making of the Modern Corporation,* 1971. Joseph Frazier Wall, *Alfred I. du Pont, The Man and His Family,* 1990.

—Alfred D. Chandler Jr.

DUPONT CORPORATION. *See* Chemical Industry; du Pont, Pierre.

DUST BOWL, the name applied to the high plains of Texas, Oklahoma, New Mexico, Colorado, and Kansas during the later 1930s as immense dust storms blew across the region, darkening the sky and depositing soil hundreds of miles to the east. At its peak the Dust Bowl covered nearly 100 million acres, with similar conditions extending northward into Canada. In 1938, the worst year for erosion, farmers lost an estimated 850 million tons of topsoil.

Severe wind erosion led to a precipitous drop in farm income, impaired health, and caused widespread damage to houses and machinery. Those conditions, combined with national economic depression, turned many people into refugees; in the worst-hit counties, one-third to one-half of the population left, many migrating to *California. For those who stayed, bankruptcies were common in both town and country.

The causes of this environmental catastrophe are disputed. Some historians see the farmers as innocent victims of drought; others argue that agricultural practices were heavily to blame. During *World War I and the 1920s, wheat farming expanded rapidly into the windy, drought-prone plains. Native grasses that had evolved a high degree of climatic resilience abruptly disappeared under the plow. For a while crops were abundant and profits high, but then began a record-breaking drought that withered the fields and left them bare.

Severe but short-lived droughts recurred in the decades after the 1930s, but none had the impact of the Dust Bowl years, leading many observers to conclude that farmer ingenuity and improved technology had made another disaster impossible. In truth, while a constant flow of federal dollars along with irrigation from deep aquifers managed to stave off a repeat catastrophe, the future of the region remains volatile and uncertain.

[*See also* Agriculture: Since 1920; Depressions, Economic; Migratory Agricultural Workers; New Deal Era, The; Southwest, The.]

• Donald Worster, *Dust Bowl,* 1979. R. Douglas Hurt, *The Dust Bowl,* 1981.

—Donald Worster

DUTCH SETTLEMENTS IN NORTH AMERICA. The Dutch claim to North America derived from the voyage of Henry Hudson, who in 1609 set sail in the *Half Moon* on behalf of the Dutch East India Company in an attempt to find a northeast passage to China above Norway. When halted by ice, Hudson decided to cross the Atlantic and search for a northwest passage. Hudson's search led him to explore the North American coast from Delaware Bay to the headwaters of the river that would bear his name.

Between 1614 and 1618 private merchants from Amsterdam exploited the region and established a *fur trade in the area they christened "New Netherland." Private trade ended with the chartering of the West India Company in 1621. Within its chartered domain (from the Cape of Good Hope to the *Philippines), the West India Company, a national joint-stock company, was authorized to trade, colonize, and wage war in the name of the United Provinces.

In 1624, the company settled some three hundred Walloons (French-speaking Protestant refugees from the southern Netherlands) at the mouth of the Delaware River, on the Hudson River near present-day Albany, at the mouth of the Connecticut River, and on Manhattan Island. Within two years the settlements were consolidated at New Amsterdam (on Manhattan Island, purchased from the local Indians for forty guilders in 1626 by Pieter Minuit) and Fort Orange (present-day Albany).

The small settlements survived on farming and the fur trade. Meanwhile, in 1629, the directors of the West India Company hatched a plan to establish feudal estates in the colony. The company soon abandoned the plan, however, and in 1640 opened the colony to *vrij burghers* (free citizens), promising two hundred acres for each head of household. The 1640s witnessed hard times for the colony. *Indian wars, called the "Kieft Wars" after Willem Kieft, the director general at the time, threatened Europeans with annihilation and nearly led to the abandonment of New Netherland. The company directors responded by replacing Kieft in 1647.

Peter Stuyvesant (ca. 1610–1672), immortalized as the one-legged tyrant in Washington Irving's satirical *Knickerbocker History of New York* (1809), ruled New Netherland with an iron fist as director general from 1646 to 1664. His administration brought political stability even while his enforcement of a strict Calvinistic orthodoxy made him a symbol of intolerance. He aggressively defended Dutch colonial rights wherever they were challenged. In 1655, he led a military expedition to capture the colony of New Sweden on the Delaware River, and he prepared for a siege when the English *Navigation Acts precipitated a series of commercial wars between Great Britain and the United Provinces. By the early 1660s New Netherland had become a target of English imperialist ambitions.

In September 1664 an attack financed by England's Duke of York forced the capitulation of New Netherland. The invasion was the opening round in the Second Anglo-Dutch War (1664–1666). At war's end a grateful Charles II bequeathed "New York" to his brother, the Duke. New Amsterdam became *New York City. A Dutch naval squadron recaptured New York in the third Anglo-Dutch War (1673–1674), but the United Provinces surrendered it once again in the Treaty of Westminister (1674).

[*See also* Colonial Era; Exploration, Conquest, and Settlement, Era of European; Indian History and Culture: From 1500 to 1800.]

• Charles R. Boxer, *The Dutch Seaborne Empire, 1600–1850,* 1965, reprint 1990. Oliver A. Rink, *Holland on the Hudson: An Economic and Social History of Dutch New York,* 1986.

—Oliver A. Rink

DYLAN, BOB (1941–), singer, songwriter, 1960s cultural icon who reinvented himself over several decades. Born Robert Allen Zimmerman to middle-class Jewish parents and reared mainly in Hibbing, Minnesota, he played in high-school bands such as his Golden Chords, embraced the music of *African Americans and marginalized groups labeled "hillbillies" and "poor white trash," and delivered screaming imitations of Little Richard (Richard Wayne Penniman). In three semesters at the University of Minnesota (1959–1960), he absorbed the social and musical subcultures of the Twin Cities; worked on the harmonica, guitar, and piano; and honed his vocal timing and style. He came to *New York City in January 1961, an unknown lacking even a place to stay. But his evolving music, combining elements of folk, *blues, country, and rock and roll, sung in an "Okie" voice heavily influenced by his beloved Woody Guthrie (1912–1967), quickly attracted attention in the *Greenwich Village coffeehouses patronized by Beatniks, folk-song aficianados, and gawking tourists.

Legally changing his name in 1962, he became in succession a traditional acoustic guitar folksinger (*Bob Dylan,* 1962); a protest folksinger championing *civil rights ("Blowin' in the Wind," 1962; *Freewheelin' Bob Dylan,* 1963; *The Times They Are a-Changin',* 1964); an amplified-sound folksinger (*Bringing It All Back Home,* 1965) and hero of campus antiwar protesters; a depoliticized rock star (*John Wesley Harding,* 1968); a born-again Christian (*Slow Train Coming,* 1979); and an admirer of Orthodox *Judaism—among other identities.

During an unpredictable, continuously productive career, Dylan inspired many and disappointed many others. In the 1990s he toured regularly, won the French government's highest cultural award (1990), gave a massive thirtieth-anniversary concert (1992), won three Grammy Awards (1991, 1994, 1998), was honored by the Kennedy Center for the Performing Arts (1997), and produced one of his best records in years (*Time out of Mind,* 1997).

[*See also* Antiwar Movements; Civil Rights Movement; Music: Popular Music; Music: Traditional Music; Sixties, The; Vietnam War.]

• Robert Shelton, *No Direction Home: The Life and Music of Bob Dylan,* 1997. Clinton Heylin, *Bob Dylan: Behind the Shades,* 2000.

—David De Leon

E

EAKINS, THOMAS (1844–1916), painter and portraitist. Thomas Eakins rarely enjoyed critical or popular success during his lifetime, but a 1930 Museum of Modern Art exhibition featuring his work together with that of Winslow *Homer and Albert P. Ryder helped establish his reputation as a major American artist precisely because of his status outside cosmopolitan artistic and social circles. Born in *Philadelphia, Eakins studied art and anatomy in that city before leaving in 1866 for Jean-Léon Gérôme's studio at the École des Beaux-Arts in Paris. He settled in Philadelphia in 1870, where he painted just under three hundred works, mostly of eminent professionals, nearly all without a commission. A scientific model of objective observation underpinned his style. In portraits of rowers like *Max Schmitt in a Single Scull* (1871), for example, Eakins calculated wave movement and light refraction, drew perspective grids, and sketched rudder positions. *William Rush Carving his Allegorical Figure of the Schuylkill River* (1877) emphasized a palpably real and respectable nude female model, underscoring the importance of the body in artistic production, regardless of genteel proprieties. An interest in *photography, including assisting in Eadweard Muybridge's 1883 University of Pennsylvania study of human and animal motion, stemmed from the same aim of empirical analysis. His paintings of the nude male body in action, such as *Swimming Hole* (1883) or *Salutat* (1898), helped redefine masculinity away from the genteel toward an ideal of muscular physical fitness.

Eakins's commitment to scientific detachment affronted contemporary artistic decorum. The *Gross Clinic* (1875), a portrait of Dr. Samuel Gross, foregrounded the surgeon's bloodied hands and scalpel. The jury at Philadelphia's 1876 Centennial Exhibition rejected it, though Jefferson Medical College bought it three years later. Eakins returned to the theme in *Agnew Clinic* (1889). As director of instruction at the Pennsylvania Academy of the Fine Arts, Eakins thoroughly revised the curriculum, but in 1886, the directors forced his resignation for using a nude male model in a mixed-sex drawing class. Eakins's later portraits, such as *Amelia Van Buren* (1891), increasingly showed tired, aging, or isolated figures, in shadowy light or slumping postures, again underscoring his disdain for artistic or social conventions.

[*See also* Gilded Age; Painting: To 1945.]

• Elizabeth Johns, *Thomas Eakins: The Heroism of Modern Life*, 1983. Kathleen Foster, *Thomas Eakins Rediscovered*, 1997.

—Wendy J. Katz

EARHART, AMELIA (1897–1937), aviator. Born in Kansas, Amelia Earhart learned to fly in California and made her first solo flight in 1921. In 1926 she became a social worker and resident in Denison House, a Boston *settlement house. Two years later, at the urging of publisher George Palmer Putnam, she became the first woman to cross the Atlantic by air. The 1928 flight, made with a pilot and mechanic (Earhart kept the log), brought her acclaim, not least because of her uncanny resemblance to aviator Charles *Lindbergh, who had made the first transatlantic flight one year before. After 1928, as an author, lecturer, and airline executive, Earhart publicized the aviation industry. She also headed an organization of women pilots. In 1931, Earhart married Putnam, who managed her career. In 1932 she became the first woman to fly the Atlantic solo and in 1935 she made the first solo flight from Honolulu to California. The same year she became an aviation consultant and career counselor for women at Purdue University. In 1937 Earhart embarked on a round-the-world flight with navigator Fred Noonan. On 2 July, as their plane headed east from New Guinea to tiny Howland Island in the Pacific, it vanished. Extensive searches revealed no sign of fliers or plane. Theories and legends abound about Earhart's fate; it is generally assumed that the plane ran out of fuel and sank in the Pacific somewhere near Howland Island. A celebrity of the late 1920s and 1930s, Earhart promoted commercial aviation, the adventure of flying, and women's achievement.

[*See also* Airplanes and Air Transport; Feminism; Twenties, The.]

• Muriel Earhart Morrissey, *Courage is the Price*, 1963. Susan Ware, *Still Missing: Amelia Earhart and the Search for Modern Feminism*, 1993.

—Nancy Woloch

EARLY REPUBLIC, ERA OF THE (1789–1828). Elections for the new federal government established by the *Constitution were held in the winter of 1788–1789. Supporters of the Constitution, calling themselves Federalists, won control of both houses of Congress and George *Washington was elected president. Even those who had opposed the Constitution, it appeared, were willing to give it a try. The First Congress gathered in New York in March 1789, and Washington was inaugurated on 30 April. The president's dress for the ceremony—a dark suit of American manufacture adorned with an elegant dress sword—bespoke his desire to retain republican simplicity while commanding respect for the office.

Establishing the New Government. The government's first need was revenue. In May, James *Madison, the *Federalist party's floor leader in the House of Representatives, introduced a bill levying customs duties on imports. The rates were generally low, but a protective duty of 50 percent was placed on a few products, such as steel and cloth, to encourage their domestic manufacture.

Fleshing out the constitutional outlines for the executive and judiciary, Congress next created three executive departments: state, treasury, and war. Washington appointed Thomas *Jefferson secretary of state and named thirty-two-year-old Alexander *Hamilton, an experienced financier who had helped organize the Bank of New York in the mid-1780s, to head the treasury. Although courts and lawyers were unpopular among American's debt-ridden farmers, and the Constitution mentioned only a *Supreme Court, Congress nevertheless boldly established federal district courts in each state and circuit courts of appeal, capped by a six-member Supreme Court. The centrality of the Supreme Court was established during John *Marshall's long tenure as chief justice (1801–1835). In a series of landmark rulings, the Marshall court upheld the supremacy of national over state power, free economic competition, and judicial review of legislative actions.

The question of public credit proved especially troublesome. The *Continental Congress, lacking the power to tax, had financed the *Revolutionary War by issuing paper money and other IOUs that quickly depreciated in value, most ending in the hands of speculators. Hamilton nevertheless proposed to pay off the nation's debt at its face value, exchanging the depreciated IOUs for interest-bearing government bonds. Only by paying its past debts in full, Hamilton argued, could the government restore its credit for future borrowing.

Hamilton further proposed a bank to help the Treasury Department fund the national debt and collect and disperse funds. The resulting *Bank of the United States, chartered by Congress in 1791, allied business and government. The government owned one-fifth of the stock, and the president appointed one-fifth of the directors. Its notes, accepted by the government as legal tender, were intended to function as a national currency.

Hamilton believed that the support of the wealthy was essential to the new government's survival. Jefferson and Madison, however, longtime allies in Virginia politics, were increasingly uneasy about the ties Hamilton was forging between the government and northern businessmen, fearing that national policy was being shaped by a moneyed elite unconcerned about the common people. In addition, since the Constitution made no mention of banks among the delegated powers of Congress, Jefferson and Madison argued that the Bank of the United States was unconstitutional.

As a republic with an elected head, the United States stood almost alone in a world of monarchies, and many feared that the wealthy few might turn to a king to protect their interests. By 1791, Jefferson and Madison were referring to themselves and their allies as Republicans, implying that Hamilton and his Federalist supporters secretly favored a monarchy. From this developing rift emerged the first political parties. Although President Washington generally sided with Hamilton and the Federalists, the Republicans dared not criticize him, and he won reelection without opposition in 1792.

The French Revolution, which broke out in 1789, reinforced the symbolic differences between the parties in the United States. Republicans rejoiced at the formation of a fellow republic in Europe; Federalists were alarmed at the bloodshed and violence that attended the revolution. When Great Britain formed a coalition of monarchies to contain the revolution and the French declared war, Republicans in America sympathized with the French, while Federalists regarded Britain as a bastion of stability. Although both sides agreed that America must not become involved in the conflict, *neutrality proved difficult to sustain. France attempted to commission warships in American ports, and Britain angered Americans by seizing any vessel caught trading with the French. Under Washington's successor, John *Adams, the United States and France engaged in an undeclared naval war. Napoleon's rise to power in France in 1799 calmed relations for a time, since Napoleon's ambitions for recovering France's North American empire required mending fences with the United States. The election of Jefferson as president in 1800 also brought a change in American policy.

Jefferson, Madison, and the War of 1812. Jefferson's philosophy of government, known to historians as "*liberalism," involved limiting the government activities; cutting costs; and, in contrast to Hamilton's approach, keeping business interests at arm's length. His ideal, as expressed in his inaugural address was "a wise and frugal government which shall restrain men from injuring one another, which shall leave them otherwise free to regulate their own pursuits of industry and improvement, and shall not take from the mouth of labor the bread it has earned." Implementing this policy, Secretary of the Treasury Albert *Gallatin cut government expenses and virtually extinguished the national debt by 1806.

Although Jefferson limited the government's domestic role, he took an active part in foreign affairs. When the Barbary pirates in the Mediterranean seized U.S. vessels and held American sailors for ransom, Jefferson dispatched a naval squadron to the region and after a brief, though undeclared, war wrested treaties from the North African city-states that allowed American merchant ships to cruise the Mediterranean unmolested. Jefferson also used the powers of the federal government (and stretched the Constitution in so doing) to acquire foreign territory, notably with the *Louisiana Purchase. The port of *New Orleans was crucial to the commerce of the Trans-Appalachian West, and when Spain in 1802, anticipating an imminent French takeover of New Orleans, closed the port to American shipping, western frontiersmen screamed for war. Jefferson sent James *Monroe and Robert R. Livingston to France with instructions to purchase New Orleans and the Gulf Coast. Napoleon, his dream of New World empire having evaporated when *yellow fever wiped out a French army in the West Indies, and ever in need of money, agreed to the American proposal. Indeed, he sold not only New Orleans but the vast territory between the *Mississippi River and the *Rocky Mountains for fifteen million dollars, doubling the size of the nation. Jefferson and Secretary of State Madison contended that West Florida was also included in the purchase, and in 1810, taking advantage of Spain's weakness, the United States annexed the Gulf Coast territory.

Jefferson proved less successful in pursuing America's policy of neutrality in the European war, particularly after 1805 when Great Britain and France, having battled to a draw, shifted to commercial warfare. While both sides seized U.S. ships, American wrath was primarily directed at the British, who impressed American seamen into the Royal Navy and intrigued with Indians of the interior. In 1807–1809, Jefferson and his successor, Madison, attempted an embargo that halted all American trade, but British policy remained unaffected. After the Battle of Tippecanoe in November 1811 exposed a British plot to arm American Indians, Congress declared war on Britain.

Except for several naval engagements, won by America's superbly built frigates, the *War of 1812 went badly from the outset, when an American army in *Detroit surrendered to a British-Indian force and left the British and their Indian allies in possession of the western Great Lakes. American efforts in 1812 and 1813 to invade upper Canada turned into bloody fiascoes. In 1814 a British amphibious force seized *Washington, D.C., burning the *White House and other public buildings. However, American pride surged albeit belatedly in January 1815, when General Andrew *Jackson's Tennessee volunteers repulsed a British invasion of New Orleans. The Treaty of *Ghent (December 1814) ended the war, but the issues that had brought it on were resolved only by Napoleon's defeat at Waterloo in June 1815 and the end of the war in Europe.

Nationalism and Sectionalism in post–1815 America. The War of 1812, fought essentially to uphold U.S. honor, revealed flaws in the national fabric. The difficulties of transporting and supplying armies demonstrated the need for interstate roads and canals. The vexations of wartime finance showed the value of the Bank of the United States, whose charter had expired in 1811. And when the war ended, a deluge of cheap British goods threatened the American manufacturing that had sprung up during the period of embargo and war. Congress, abetted by a postwar spirit of national unity, responded with a series of measures reminiscent of the Federalist philosophy of energetic government.

In 1816, Congress chartered a Second Bank of the United States empowered to establish branches throughout the country and to issue notes that would serve as a national currency. Next came new *tariffs whose rates on textiles, iron, and other imports were high enough to shield American manufacturers from foreign competition. In 1817, Congress capped its effort to promote a national economy with a bill appropriating funds for the construction of a nationwide system of roads and canals. President Madison, balking at this use of federal power, vetoed the bill as unconstitutional on his last day in office. Nevertheless, these three issues—bank, tariff, and internal improvements—would dominate the nation's domestic politics for a generation.

The postwar spirit of nationalism carried over into foreign policy where the administration of Madison's successor, James Monroe, and his secretary of state, John Quincy *Adams, resumed the quest for westward expansion. The *Lewis and Clark Expedition (1804–1806) had strengthened America's claim to the territory (vaguely known as "Oregon") between *California and *Alaska. Great Britain also claimed this region, as did Russia, which had already colonized Alaska. In 1818, Adams negotiated a convention with Britain by which the two countries would jointly occupy and govern Oregon (then inhabited by Indians and a few fur traders) until settlement resolved the question of ownership. In the 1819 *Adams-Onís Treaty with Spain, the United States purchased Florida and confined Spanish claims on the Pacific Coast to California by drawing a boundary line across the continent from the Gulf Coast of Louisiana to the forty-second parallel (the present northern boundary of Utah, Nevada, and California). Adams's vision thus laid the foundation for a continental republic. In private discussions with British and Russian emissaries, Adams insisted on Americans' right to settle in the Pacific Northwest and made clear that the United States would eventually claim title to Oregon.

In 1823, Adams's attention was directed to South America. While Spain was distracted by the Napoleonic wars, a number of Spanish colonies in Latin America had rebelled and become independent and in 1821 Mexico won its independence. These fledgling nations presented a new market for American manufacturers and traders. Monroe and Adams were not deeply concerned that Spain might attempt to recover Latin America, but they were anxious about possible intervention by other European powers. Acting on these apprehensions, President Monroe in his annual message to Congress on 2 December 1832, in a passage drafted by Adams, reiterated the "doctrine of the spheres," a keystone of American policy since *Washington's Farewell Address in 1796. The two halves of the earth, Monroe explained, were separated by both geography and systems of government. They might exchange goods, but neither hemisphere had a right to intervene in the affairs of the other. Any European intervention in the Latin American republics, he warned, would be viewed as a "manifestation of an unfriendly disposition toward the United States." With Oregon in mind, Adams also inserted into Monroe's address an additional warning that the American continents were "henceforth not to be considered as subjects for future colonization by any European power." A statement of America's commercial as well as territorial ambitions, the so-called *Monroe Doctrine marked the climax of the postwar spirit of nationalism.

Even at that triumphant moment, however, a countervailing spirit of self-conscious regionalism was spreading among southerners who saw little benefit to themselves in the federal programs established by Congress. Blessed with a magnificent river system to carry their heavy staples to market, southerners had little need for roads and canals. Southern planters eyed the Bank of the United States with deep suspicion and viewed the tariff as a parasitical drain on their cotton profits. One southerner revealed still another reason to be wary of federal power: "If Congress can make canals," he muttered, "they can emancipate [the slaves]." This concern stemmed from an effort by northern congressmen a few years earlier to restrict *slavery in the territory of Missouri. The Missouri controversy, when for the first time blunt criticism of the "peculiar institution" of slavery was expressed on the floor of Congress, generated a mood of sectional defensiveness.

The War of 1812 had diminished Indian resistance to white settlement east of the Mississippi River, and after the war settlers poured into the Ohio and Tennessee valleys. Four new states entered the Union between 1816 and 1819—Indiana and Illinois in the North, Alabama and Mississippi in the *South. Pioneers, many of them southern slaveholders, had also crossed the Mississippi into the Missouri Territory. When Missouri applied for statehood in 1819, some northern congressmen proposed a prohibition on the further introduction of slaves into Missouri and the freeing of slaves already there. Northerners reasoned that Congress had the power to regulate slavery in land it had purchased. In creating the Northwest Territory in 1787, the Continental Congress had prohibited slavery north of the Ohio River, and the northern congressmen argued that the same regulatory principle should apply to the land acquired in the Louisiana Purchase, including the Missouri Territory.

The effort to restrict slavery in Missouri ignited a fierce debate that ended in a compromise in 1820 with the admission of Missouri as a slave state and Maine as a free state, and a prohibition on slavery in the remainder of the Louisiana Purchase north of 36°30' north latitude—Missouri's southern boundary. The Missouri controversy began a forty-year sectional dispute over slavery that ended in the *Civil War.

With the Federalist party's collapse after the War of 1812, the postwar decade brought a period of one-party rule commonly called the "era of good feelings." In fact, this misnamed era saw much ill feeling, as the Missouri controversy illustrates. By the mid-1820s, amid growing mistrust of the federal government among southerners and westerners, the dominant Jeffersonian-Republican party had split into two factions—National Republicans, led by such nationalists as Henry *Clay and the former Federalist Daniel *Webster, and Democratic Republicans, who eventually fastened onto the military hero Andrew Jackson. (The latter became the *Democratic party after Jackson's election as president in 1828.) The birth of this "second party system" was attended by political instability and animosity, wreaking havoc with the presidency of Monroe's successor, John Quincy Adams, elected in 1824.

Jackson actually received the most popular votes in 1824, but with four candidates in the field, no one received a majority. In this situation the Constitution requires the House of Representatives to select a president. When Speaker of the House Henry Clay engineered the selection of fellow nationalist John Quincy Adams, Jackson was understandably outraged; when Adams named Clay secretary of state, Jackson's followers accused Adams of gaining office through a "corrupt bargain."

As the "corrupt bargain" cry reverberated, Adams and Clay were pictured as old-fashioned aristocrats clinging to power by backstairs bargaining that thwarted the will of the people. Jackson was thus portrayed as the leader of the "common man," even though his political ideology remained unknown. An appeal to the "common man" resonated in the 1820s, for most states had revised their Revolutionary Era constitutions to extend the vote to all adult white males.

Politics, Society, and Culture in Jacksonian America. The 1828 presidential campaign, which Jackson won handily, was fought not on issues but on personalities, with each candidate playing a symbolic role: Adams the eastern aristocrat, Jackson the western democrat. The contest between Jackson and Adams and the birth of the second party system was staged against a backdrop of dramatic social and economic change. The population was growing at a breathtaking pace, doubling every twenty-three years. Although the birthrate had begun to decline (and would continue to do so into the twentieth century), a flood of immigrants ensured a rapid peopling of the land. In the economic realm, the introduction of water-powered spinning and weaving machines in the *textile industry heralded a coming industrial revolution. As mill towns sprang up at every waterfall in the northeastern states, the move from farm to city began. In 1790, more than 90 percent of Americans lived on farms or in small villages. That figure fell to 80 percent by 1820 and to 55 percent by 1860.

Rapid economic growth presented new opportunities for northern white women. Previously limited to *homework or to household-related jobs like cleaning and cooking, some young women now became school teachers or mill workers. One destination for young farm women was the *Lowell mills in Massachusetts, at the falls of the Merrimac River. An unnamed rural crossroads in 1823, Lowell by 1830 boasted ten mills and three thousand operatives, nearly all of them female.

Southern agriculture burgeoned as tobacco culture spread westward, and the *cotton industry boomed thanks to Eli *Whitney's cotton gin and the rise of textile mills. As cotton plantations spread across the lower South, output surged from 178,000 bales in 1810 to 732,000 in 1830. This agriculture boom rested on slave labor. In 1810–1830, the number of slaves in the South grew from 1.2 million to 2 million. Post-Revolutionary *antislavery sentiment in the South, expressed in the *colonization movement, faded as slavery became more important economically. As an abortive revolt in Charleston, South Carolina, in 1822 and Nat *Turner's 1831 uprising in Virginia underscored the slaves' desire for freedom, southern states retaliated with harsh slave codes.

These decades saw efforts to achieve cultural independence to match political independence. A group of post-Revolutionary poets known as the "Hartford Wits" produced some works of note, while the nation's first professional novelist, Charles Brockden Brown, published four flawed but ambitious gothic novels in 1798–1799. Washington Irving's *The Sketch-Book* (1819–1820) included such classic tales as "Rip Van Winkle" and "The Legend of Sleepy Hollow," while James Fenimore *Cooper launched his series of Leatherstocking novels of frontier life with *The Pioneers* (1823) and *The Last of the Mohicans* (1826). Noah *Webster's patriotic *American Dictionary of the English Language* (1828) included thousands of American usages. In the visual arts, Gilbert Stuart and other post-Revolutionary painters offered portraits of Washington, Jefferson, and other founders, while younger artists such as Thomas *Cole found inspiration in the American landscape.

Irving's "Rip Van Winkle," in which Rip awakens from a twenty-year sleep to find his world transformed, evoked the unsettling social changes of the era. The burgeoning cities, still without professional *police, fire, or *public-health departments, seethed with *crime, occasional riots, and periodic epidemics. Protestant Christianity, long viewed as a pillar of stability and continuity, was in ferment, as liberal rationalists went in one direction, Evangelicals in another. *Religion was becoming democratized: frontier revivals led by untutored preachers broke out in Kentucky and Tennessee in 1801–1802; Charles G. *Finney conducted vastly successful urban revivals in the 1820s and 1830s; a young farmer in upstate New York, Joseph Smith, having proclaimed a new revelation from God, founded the Church of Jesus Christ of Latter-Day Saints (Mormons) in 1830.

In 1819, the Boston minister William Ellery *Channing, in a series of sermons in Baltimore, Maryland, set forth the principles of Unitarianism. Ralph Waldo *Emerson, the leading intellectual of his generation, left the Unitarian ministry in 1832, charging that the church had become a hollow shell. Viewing American society with a troubled eye, Emerson sought to improve it through the leadership of principled, free, and self-reliant individuals.

Other reformers looked to benevolent societies and even government. Temperance groups sought to curb drinking and urban violence. Tax-supported public schools arose to tame unruly youth and immigrants. The urban poor were encouraged to attend Sunday schools to learn reading, writing, and self-improvement. The result, in the decades after 1820, was a soul-searching reform movement intent on improving every facet of American society. It would ultimately address the greatest evil of all, human slavery.

[*See also* African Americans; Agriculture: 1770s to 1890; Antebellum Era; Architecture; Canals and Waterways; *Charles River Bridge* v. *Warren Bridge*; Cholera; Demography; Depressions, Economic; Disease; Education: The Public School Movement; Education: Collegiate Education; Expansionism; Factory System; Federal Government; Foreign Relations; Immigration; Indian History and Culture: From 1800 to 1900; Indian Removal Act; Industrialization; Iron and Steel Industry; Labor Movements; Literature: Early National and Antebellum Eras; *Marbury* v. *Madison*; *McCulloch* v. *Maryland*; Medicine: From 1776 to the 1870s; Missouri Compromise; Monetary Policy, Federal; Mormonism; Music: Popular Music; Music: Traditional Music; Painting: To 1945; Poetry; Quasi-War with France; Republicanism; Revolution and Constitution, Era of; Roads and Turnpikes, Early; Romantic Movement; Science: Revolutionary War to World War I; Slave Uprisings and Resistance; Taxation; Temperance and Prohibition; Textile Industry; Tobacco Industry; Tobacco Products; Urbanization; Women in the Labor Force; Unitarianism and Universalism; Work.]

• George Dangerfield, *The Awakening of American Nationalism, 1815–1828,* 1965. Nobel E. Cunningham Jr., *The Process of Government under Jefferson,* 1978. Joseph J. Ellis, *After the Revolution: Profiles of Early American Culture,* 1979. Robert W. Tucker and David C. Hendrickson, *Empire of Liberty: The Statecraft of Thomas Jefferson,* 1990. Larzer Ziff, *Writing in the New Nation: Prose, Print, and Politics in the Early United States,* 1991. Stanley Elkins and Eric McKitrick, *The Age of Federalism,* 1993. Peter S. Onuf, ed., *Jeffersonian Legacies,* 1993. Norman K. Risjord, *Jefferson's America, 1760–1815,* 1993. Edwin S. Gaustad, *Sworn on an Altar of God: A Religious Biography of Thomas Jefferson,* 1995. Joseph J. Ellis, *American Sphinx: The Character of Thomas Jefferson,* 1997.

—Norman K. Risjord

EARTH SCIENCES. The science of geology in the United States developed almost simultaneously with the exploration of the continent, and the continent's geology profoundly affected the scientists who studied it. Geologists pondered such basic questions as the age and nature of the rocks, how they had been deposited, and the meaning of the fossils they contained. But geologists were also driven by the need to understand the rocks for *mining and, later, petroleum exploration. In short, the history of geology in America is rooted in the physical context of the land and its natural resources.

After the first wave of European exploration, mapping, particularly geologic mapping, provided the benchmark for later study. Much of that early mapping was based on European ideas and methods; the Englishman William McClure completed the first widely published geologic map of the United States in 1809. Early geology was, for the most part, a subset of natural history, and much of the groundwork was done by faculty who taught natural history at American colleges. Yale's Benjamin *Silliman established the *American Journal of Science* (1818), known colloquially as *Silliman's Journal,* and published extensively on geology. His student and son-in-law James Dwight Dana later took over the editorship of the journal and wrote books that helped to systematize mineralogy. Parker Cleaveland of Bowdoin College became famous for his landmark *Elementary Treatise on Mineralogy and Geology* (1816).

Gradually, geology emerged as a separate discipline. In 1840 the Association of American Geologists and Naturalists held its first annual meeting; eight years later it became the *American Association for the Advancement of Science. Another sign of maturation was the establishment of state *geological surveys, an early example of government-supported *science in the United States. The North Carolina survey, launched in 1823, was first. Several prominent geologists of the early nineteenth century worked with these surveys, including James Hall of New York, David Dale Owen of Indiana, and William Barton Rogers of Virginia.

The accomplishments of these and other figures derived in part from the development of the nation's infrastructure. The construction of bridges, roads, *canals and waterways, and *railroads—combined with scientific curiosity and the economic importance of locating minerals such as salt and coal—provided ample motivation for detailed geological research. Pre–*Civil War exploring expeditions set an example for the great federal surveys of the American *West after the war. These surveys provided a wealth of knowledge about regional geology and often captured the public's imagination. Clarence King studied the mountain country of California, Nevada, and Utah. Ferdinand V. Hayden made detailed geologic studies in Colorado, Wyoming, and Nebraska, and did much to bring about the creation of *Yellowstone National Park in 1872. George M. Wheeler took stock of Arizona and Nevada. The best-known of these intrepid early geologists, John Wesley *Powell, a one-armed Civil War veteran, explored the Colorado Plateau and led a celebrated 1869 trip through the *Grand Canyon. From all this activity grew the U.S. Geological Survey, created in 1879, with first King and then Powell as its head. Under Powell it became the premier example of government-sponsored science in America. In retrospect, this post–Civil War era assumed heroic status in American geology. With expansion across the West came a host of new natural knowledge, not only about mineral resources but about the history of the earth and life as well.

Fossil discoveries by such figures as Edward Drinker Cope, Othniel Charles Marsh, and Joseph Leidy contributed to American leadership in vertebrate paleontology and provided compelling evidence of organic evolution. The studies of Utah's ancient Lake Bonneville by Grove Karl Gilbert advanced the science of geomorphology. With hard-rock mining and especially the growth of the *petroleum industry came extensive new information about subsurface geologic structures, such as anticlines. Studies of the *Rocky Mountains and the Appalachian Mountains led to new theories of mountain formation. Examination of interbedded limestones and shales on the Great Plains improved understanding of sedimentation. Later, in the first half of the twentieth century, geophysical techniques, such as seismic reflection, became especially important, and various subdisciplines of geology, such as geochemistry, stratigraphy, sedimentology, and geohydrology, matured and grew.

The most notable development in twentieth-century geology was plate tectonics: the realization that the land could move. Building on the ideas of Germany's Alfred Wegener, geologists marshalled new evidence, such as that supplied by Americans Maurice Ewing and Harry Hess concerning sea-floor spreading, to support the concept and pave the way for the theory's general acceptance. After the 1960s and the advent of plate tectonics, geology became increasingly quantified and computerized. Geologists used a variety of new methods, such as deep-ocean drilling, planetary and space science, and remote sensing, to learn more about the earth. Late twentieth-century geologists faced issues of large social import: supplying energy and natural resources, dealing with environmental contamination, and mitigating geologic hazards such as earthquakes and volcanoes. They also encountered questions of popular interest, such as meteor-impact theories and the demise of the dinosaurs. And they continued to confront the basic intellectual challenges of understanding the earth's past and its deep subsurface, pondering places in the planet that no one had ever been to or seen.

[*See also* Coast and Geodetic Survey, U.S.; Roads and Turnpikes, Early.]

• Richard A. Bartlett, *Great Surveys of the American West*, 1962. Mary C. Rabbitt, *Minerals, Lands, and Geology for the Common Defence and General Welfare*, 3 vols., 1979–1986. Cecil J. Schneer, ed., *Two Hundred Years of Geology in America: Proceedings of the New Hampshire Bicentennial Conference on the History of Geology*, 1979. Henry Faul and Carol Faul, *It Began with a Stone: A History of Geology from the Stone Age to the Age of Plate Tectonics*, 1983. Ellen T. Drake and William M. Jordan, eds., *Geologists and Ideas: A History of North American Geology*, 1985. Mott T. Greene, "History of Geology," *Osiris* 1, 2d series (1985) 97–116.

—Rex C. Buchanan

ECOLOGY. *See* Environmentalism.

ECONOMIC CYCLES. *See* Business Cycle; Depressions, Economic.

ECONOMIC DEVELOPMENT. Economists define economic development as a sustained increase in per-capita income. While this definition is a good starting point, historians generally conceive economic development as a broader set of social and political changes. In the context of U.S. history, those changes include the settlement of a capacious frontier, the growth of large cities, a vast influx of immigrants, and the rapid spread of new *technology. The complexity of these changes notwithstanding, the course of U.S. development can be traced through three major periods: the extensive growth of the colonial and revolutionary periods; the expansion of commerce during the first half of the nineteenth century; and the emergence of "managerial *capitalism" after the *Civil War.

The Colonial and Revolutionary Periods. The economy of colonial America grew rapidly because of sustained population growth and profitable cultivation of staple crops. Massive free and unfree *immigration from Europe and Africa—coupled with a moderate climate, relatively high nutritional levels, and high fertility rates—resulted in extraordinarily rapid population growth. Between 1650 and 1770, the population of Britain's mainland North American colonies increased from 55,000 to more than 2.2 million. Most colonists participated in a vibrant agricultural economy. High prices for wheat and tobacco—British North America's two main staples—encouraged the particularly rapid settlement of the middle and southern colonies in the eighteenth century. White colonists in the slave *South—benefiting from slave labor and high staple prices—ranked as the wealthiest of the colonists.

Rapid population growth produced substantial economic development. Because no sweeping technological or organizational advances dramatically stimulated *productivity, per-capita income grew quite modestly by modern standards, increasing anywhere from .3 to .6 percent per year. Yet colonists built an increasingly sophisticated commercial infrastructure that resulted in the growth of towns and cities. Such development was particularly important in *New England and the Middle Colonies, where cities became major market centers. By 1770 such cities as *Boston, *New York, and *Philadelphia provided an impressive array of mercantile services that induced future economic growth.

Government policy, both in Britain and the colonies, also aided colonial development. Unlike France or Spain, British authorities did not seek to regulate overseas migration, thus abetting the population explosion in the North American colonies. British mercantilist policies, designed to further the interests of the imperial center, sometimes impeded colonial trade with other nations. Colonists, however, successfully evaded the most onerous regulations, while the British mercantile system enabled American merchants to export grains, lumber, livestock, and other goods. The *Revolutionary War, in fact, initially had devastating economic consequences because American merchants lost many of the trading privileges they had enjoyed under the British empire.

Expansion of Commerce between the Revolution and the Civil War. Most export *agriculture in the colonial and revolutionary period was confined to areas with access to water transportation. Transporting bulky crops over the nation's rutted and muddy roads was prohibitively expensive. In the period 1800–1820, private turnpike companies—which improved roads in order to collect tolls—alleviated the worst problems of overland transport, but grains and other bulky commodities remained too expensive to ship over roads. Hence proponents of economic development avidly improved rivers and built canals to extend the nation's system of waterways. The *Erie Canal, completed in 1825, was by far the most important of these improvements. Built through the gently rolling landscape of upstate New York, the Erie Canal connected the Great Lakes to the Hudson River. It transformed such cities as Buffalo, Rochester, and Syracuse into major transport, mercantile, and manufacturing hubs. Canal systems in Ohio and other Midwestern states extended the reach of the Erie system, providing farmers throughout the *Middle West with an all-water connection to New York City. The steamboat, meanwhile, facilitated trade on the *Mississippi and Ohio River systems, providing yet another avenue of commerce.

*Steam power soon had an even larger impact when applied to overland carriage. Areas in which water transportation was either unavailable or prohibitively expensive turned to the railroad. First built in the late 1820s, *railroads rapidly spread across the county. By 1860, Americans had built approximately 30,000 miles of track, with four separate roads penetrating the Appalachian Mountain barrier. Railroads not only accelerated the growth of cities on the eastern seaboard, but also transformed Pittsburgh, *Chicago, and other Midwestern cities into major marketing and manufacturing centers.

Although historians have discarded the view that the railroad single-handedly accounted for American *industrialization, it nevertheless contributed to the dramatic expansion of commerce in everyday life. In the North and Midwest, the expansion of the railroad network created a self-reinforcing cycle of growth. As transportation improved, farmers produced more grains, dairy products, and other produce for urban centers. With more cash to spend on consumer goods, farm families demanded textiles, shoes, furniture, and other manufactured products. Manufacturers and merchants, responding to the larger agrarian market, increased their output and improved productivity. Firms producing such goods as ready-made apparel, hats and caps, and boots and shoes, for example, increased productivity through specialization and greater division of labor. Incremental technological advances—usually the result of tinkering by rather ordinary mechanics—further increased manufacturing productivity.

The South lagged far behind in inventive activity and other measures of economic development. Its slave-based economy, to be sure, produced enormous profits for many planters and farmers. The southern economy did especially well in the 1850s, when the price of cotton, tobacco, and other staples soared. Yet in almost every other measure of development—*urbanization rates, inventive activity, manufacturing output, population growth—the North far outstripped the South. As the *Civil War approached, the regional disparities grew. In 1860, the value of manufactured goods produced in New York City alone exceeded the combined production of the eleven southern states that would form the Confederacy. Underlying the South's failure was a lack of adequate demand to spur *industrialization. Plantation *slavery restrained population growth among free farmers and an unequal distribution of rural income undermined the earnings and consumption habits of farm families that had provided northern entrepreneurs with lucrative markets. However profitable to southern planters, slavery seriously impeded southern industrial development.

The limitations of southern development notwithstanding, the U.S. economy grew impressively between 1800 and 1860. Historians debate to what extent federal and state government action contributed to this remarkable economic expansion. State governments frequently intervened in the economy in the early nineteenth century, especially when, as in New York and Pennsylvania, they operated their own canal systems. Although New York's Erie Canal succeeded, most other state-owned canals failed. State and federal governments provided *engineering expertise, land grants, and other subsidies to the railroads, but private investors supplied most of the capital. The most important government intervention was enforcing a stable set of property rights (including a patent system) that encouraged economic expansion and technological innovation. State governments made it easier for entrepreneurs to obtain corporate charters for banks, factories, and other enterprises, while the federal courts protected interstate commerce and used law to validate corporate charters and contracts. With a strong legal foundation in place, national markets and national enterprises came to dominate the economy.

Managerial Capitalism and the Modern Economy. The post-Civil War expansion of the railroad network—including the construction of the first transcontinental lines—enabled entrepreneurs to establish national corporations. While a few large firms had flourished earlier during the market revolution, especially in the New England *textile industry, these firms paled compared to the corporate giants of the late nineteenth and early twentieth century. By 1910, Standard Oil, U.S. Steel, Armour and Co., and the American Tobacco Company were among the firms with assets in excess of $200 million. Another round of technological change soon added such newer businesses as Ford Motor Company and General Motors to the list of industrial giants. These enterprises tended to be capital intensive, using their large size to forge substantial economies of scale. Technological advances became even more important. Many large firms organized research divisions and departments that institutionalized technological change.

Borrowing from the experience of the railroads, these large industrial firms also developed complex administrative bureaucracies heavily stocked with middle managers and upper-echelon executives. Entrepreneurs such as John D. *Rockefeller and Andrew *Carnegie used these new administrative forms to ascertain precise production costs, enabling them to identify and then to eliminate expensive bottlenecks. Rockefeller's Standard Oil Company, in particular, ruthlessly cut production costs, enabling the company to buy out or destroy less efficient competitors. By 1890, Standard Oil—which owned 20,000 oil wells, 4,000 miles of pipeline, and 5,000 specialty railroad cars—controlled more than 90 percent of the American oil and kerosene market. Whereas large corporations tended to dominate industries with relatively homogenous output (oil, steel, and tobacco), smaller firms thrived in sectors that produced specialty goods, ranging from complex machinery to such consumer goods as furniture. By the early twentieth century, America's combination of large and small firms encouraged the birth of new industries, including automobiles and electrical manufacturing.

*Mass production made the marketing and distribution of consumer goods extraordinarily important. To insure a constant demand for their products, businesses invested heavily in *advertising, first in print publications, later on *radio and *television. Innovative retailers devised new ways of selling both basic necessities and luxury goods. *Department stores, fashionable retail districts, and, eventually, supermarkets as well as *shopping centers and malls indelibly shaped the American landscape. By the early twentieth century, a number of firms expanded the scale of consumer borrowing (especially through installment plans) that allowed a broad range of families to purchase automobiles and other consumer durables.

By 1900, the United States possessed the basic elements of a developed economy: growing per capita income, rapidly evolving technologies, increasingly efficient industrial producers, and sophisticated marketing and distribution channels. Although certain regions of the country—most notably *Appalachia and other parts of the South—continued to lag, rapid economic development made the United States the world's largest economy for much of the twentieth century and laid the material foundations for what publisher Henry *Luce called "The American Century."

Because economic development is so complicated, scholars continue to debate the ultimate source of U.S. success. Some stress the availability of such abundant natural resources as fertile soils and rich supplies of iron, coal, and oil. Others underscore the emergence of a national, integrated market that encompassed most of North America. While political and geographic barriers hindered development elsewhere, these scholars argue, U.S. businesses grew in tandem with an expanding home market. Finally, many scholars have emphasized the importance of distinctive American cultural and political attitudes, including a devotion to private property and free enterprise, and a corresponding suspicion of *economic regulation that might hinder *business success.

Despite widespread support of economic development, many Americans have nevertheless feared that the growing power of big business might subvert democracy. These fears, coupled with deep swings in the *business cycle, have created important political movements, especially in the *Populist, *Progressive and *New Deal Eras, that raised important questions about economic development. Should the federal government encourage certain industries with *tariffs and other subsidies? Should state and federal governments dissolve or regulate corporations that threaten to become monopolies? How should government mediate conflicts among labor, business, and consumers? What kinds and levels of *taxation best encourage economic development while also promoting other social goods? These and similar questions relating to economic development remained divisive as the twentieth century ended.

The advent of the desktop computer in the 1980s and the *Internet and World Wide Web in the 1990s opened a new era of U.S. economic development. The "information age" also exemplified many of the same characteristics of earlier changes, including the rapid adaptation of new technologies; a complex mix of both large corporation (including giants such as Microsoft and Intel) and smaller, more flexible firms; and attitudes and regulations generally favorable to free enterprise and hostile to government regulation. Yet despite these links to the past, the new economy also raised new questions. Would the rapid transmission of information make global markets the driving force of continued growth? Would the new information technologies transform *consumer culture? How would new technologies affect the managerial structure of "old economy" stalwarts such as the steel, *automotive, and *chemical industries? While these issues remained unresolved, the rapid emergence of "new economy" industries did once again illustrate the self-reinforcing nature of economic development. The earlier success of the U.S. economy created deep pools of capital, high levels of per-capita income, and a strong commitment to research and development that allowed new enterprises to flourish. Clearly the history of economic development remains unfinished, as it continues to influence society, politics, and culture.

[*See also* Antitrust Legislation; Canals and Waterways; *Charles River Bridge* v. *Warren Bridge;* Computers; Cotton Industry; Ford, Henry; Foreign Trade, U.S.; Global Economy, America and the; Iron and Steel Industry; Labor Markets; Laissez-faire; Multinational Enterprises; Office Technology; Patent and Copyright Law; Research Laboratories, Industrial; Roads and Turnpikes, Early; Stock Market; Tobacco Industry.]

• George Rogers Taylor, *The Transportation Revolution, 1815–1860,* 1951. Alfred D. Chandler, *The Visible Hand: The Managerial Revolution in American Business,* 1977. Diane Lindstrom, *Economic Development in the Philadelphia Region, 1810–1850,* 1978. John J. McCusker and Russell R. Menard, *The Economy of British America, 1607–1789,* 1985. William Robert Fogel, *Without Consent or Contract: The Rise and Fall of American Slavery,* 1989. Stuart Bruchey, *Enterprise: The Dynamic Economy of a Free People,* 1990. Stanley L. Engerman and Robert E. Gallman, *The Cambridge Economic History of the United States, Volume I: The Colonial Period,* 1996. Philip Scranton, *Endless Novelty: Specialty Production and American Industrialization, 1865–1925,* 1997.

—John Majewski

ECONOMIC REGULATION. The objectives of economic regulation are usually mixed: to achieve an appropriate balance between efficiency and equity, to steer acquisitive human urges into productive channels, and to strike reasonable trade-offs between economic growth and environmental protection. The United States has had an uneven history of regulation, one that was relatively good in comparison to many other countries. For most of its history, the United States featured the world's most entrepreneurially "free" economy with the least amount of public regulation. Such generalizations, however, disguise a more complex reality.

In the *Colonial Era, religious considerations limited entrepreneurial impulses, yet the spread of a pervasive market economy in the eighteenth and nineteenth centuries worked a dramatic change. Although such old customs as the "just price" (the maximum allowable price for a basic necessity) ended, that did not preclude all regulation. The developing American capitalist economy still required a strong regulatory framework. Commercial transactions depended on a system of contract law enforced through courts. Other public and private regulatory mechanisms were essential as well.

The Monetary System and the Capital Markets. All cash-and-credit economies, including the American one, also require a monetary authority—typically a central bank—to regulate the supply and value of money. In colonial America, banks were almost nonexistent, but after independence Alexander *Hamilton's First Bank of the United States (1791–1811) served some functions of a central bank until its twenty-year charter expired. The Second Bank of the United States (1816–1836) was even more successful, but it too fell victim to politics and its charter was not renewed. Thereafter, the United States had no central bank until the creation of the *Federal Reserve System in 1913. During those three generations, the government generally maintained the *gold standard, state authorities regulated banking haphazardly, and the nation experienced a chronically deficient money supply. All of these conditions changed under the *Federal Reserve System. By the 1930s the "Fed," assisted by other bodies and officials such as state banking commissions and the Controller of the Currency, had become a modern regulatory agency overseeing the monetary system.

The nation's securities (stock and bond) markets, which developed during the nineteenth century and then blossomed in the twentieth, have benefited from one of the world's most modern and effective regulatory systems. A series of laws passed during the 1930s (including the Securities Act of 1933, the Securities Exchange Act of 1934, the Public Utility Holding Company Act of 1935, and the Trust Indenture Act of 1939) created a system in which regulation was overseen by the *Securities and Exchange Commission and the federal courts, but implemented largely through third parties. These included hundreds of thousands of private lawyers and accountants, officials of the *New York Stock Exchange and other exchanges, plus the National Association of Securities Dealers (NASD).

Labor Markets and Conditions of Work. Efficient, equitable, and flexible *labor markets require systematic wage scales, rules for the number of hours and days to be worked, and numerous other regulations. In America, some of these had long been enforced through apprenticeship systems. With industrialization, however, the exploitation of factory labor became commonplace, and it lasted for many decades. During the *Progressive Era, most states instituted workers' compensation laws and some enacted unemployment insurance, but effective national resolution of the labor question awaited the *New Deal Era. The *National Labor Relations Act of 1935 gave organized labor the power to bargain collectively; other laws passed during the 1930s ended *child labor, set maximum hours, and established minimum wage levels.

By the 1990s some aspects of the American labor market were heavily regulated through antidiscrimination laws designed to protect women, minorities, the handicapped, and others. But in areas such as layoff policies and paid vacation time for employees, American practice granted fewer benefits to workers than those of some other countries, especially in Western Europe.

Product Markets and Competition. The United States has always had one of the world's most intensely competitive economies. There are many reasons why. For one thing, the entrepreneurial spirit of its ethnically mixed population has been remarkably vigorous. Also, for the first 150 years of the nation's history few countervailing forces existed to challenge business interests. The United States had no strong guild tradition, no established church, no hereditary aristocracy, and no powerful peacetime military. Until the mid–twentieth century, it had only a minuscule government. All of these conditions interacted to intensify *business competition.

With the rise of "big business" in the 1870s and 1880s, state legislatures responded by enacting *antitrust legislation. In 1890, Congress passed the landmark Sherman Antitrust Act, which outlawed cartels and monopolies. Since then, the Sherman Act, in combination with the *Federal Trade Commission Act and the Clayton Antitrust Act (both passed in 1914), has had mixed results. But on balance, economists conclude that these antitrust measures have increased the level of competition within the American economy. Perhaps the truest index of the effectiveness of U.S. antitrust laws has been their widespread emulation by other nations since *World War II.

The Economic Infrastructure. Active economic regulation has been most conspicuous in the areas of transportation, electric utilities, and telecommunications, where conventional competition seemed inadequate to achieve its usual function of automatically regulating prices and quality. The years from the 1870s through the New Deal saw a proliferation of state and federal commissions charged with regulating these industries. First *railroads, then gas and electric utilities, streetcars, pipelines, *telephones, trucking, and finally airlines came under regulation by public commissions, which oversaw prices and sometimes actually set them. Almost every state established a railroad and utility commission. The most prominent federal agencies were the Interstate Commerce Commission (created in 1887), which regulated first railroads, then pipelines and trucking; the Federal Power Commission (established in 1920, strengthened in 1930, and in the 1980s renamed the Federal Energy Regulatory Commission), which oversaw gas and electric utilities; the *Federal Communications Commission (1934, *radio, telephones, and *television); and the Civil Aeronautics Board (1938, airlines). This complex regulatory structure proved controversial, however, in part because the "cost-plus" formula employed by regulators in some of these agencies provided little incentive for efficiency for cost cutting, and in part because some of the industries regulated (trucking, for example) had few of the "natural monopoly" characteristics of early railroads and electric utilities. During the years after World War II, and particularly after the economic downturn of the 1970s, the "cost-plus" type of economic regulation began to be discredited.

Deregulation. The deregulation movement began in a serious way during the presidential administration of Jimmy *Carter. It rapidly gathered force in many industries and spread to other countries as well. During the 1980s, the election of such "free market"–oriented politicians as Ronald *Reagan in the United States, Margaret Thatcher in the United Kingdom, and Helmut Kohl in Germany underscored the apparent popularity of deregulation. "Privatization" schemes moreover, marched alongside deregulation, as governments in Great Britain, Germany, Japan, and several other countries sold nationalized industries to private investors. In the United States, "privatization" often meant spinning off what had been public functions (such as garbage collection) to private contractors. Meanwhile, deregulation in the federal government included the outright abolition of several agencies, such as the Civil Aeronautics Board and the Interstate Commerce Commission. By the end of the twentieth century some of the industries mentioned above (railroads, trucking, airlines, radio, and television) were scarcely regulated at all, and others, such as electric power and telephones, were being moved toward deregulation.

Toward the end of the 1980s, as if to underscore the apparent triumph of free-market economics, the collapse of socialist economies and the breakup of the Soviet bloc seemed to complete the cycle of deregulation and privatization. This development, coupled with the superior growth performance of capitalist economies, seemingly demonstrated once and for all the virtues of minimal regulation.

Conclusion. But it would be a serious mistake to pronounce an end to the need for economic regulation, let alone regulation applying to health, safety, and the environment. At the end of the 1990s experience with deregulated industries remained brief by historical standards, and economic history has a way of taking unexpected turns. Even so, several general conclusions concerning the history of economic regulation in the United States seem warranted:

First, the United States has regulated its economy less than most industrialized countries have done, although it has created large numbers of regulatory agencies. Second, the onset of regulation in America was usually associated with periods of political reform: the Progressive Era, the New Deal, and the New Frontier and *Great Society Era of the 1960s. Finally, and paradoxically, the enactment of consumer protection, health and safety, and environmental laws accelerated during the 1970s and 1980s, an era of economic deregulation. Regulatory bodies such as the *Environmental Protection Agency (1970), the Occupational Safety and Health Administration (1970), and the Consumer Product Safety Commission (1972) were created during the Richard M. *Nixon administration. These latter laws differed from traditional economic regulation despite their powerful economic impacts. In some respects they resembled Progressive-Era legislation such as the *Pure Food and Drug Act and the Meat Inspection Act (both passed in 1906), and similar measures having to do with *forestry and other environmental concerns. They represented a nonpartisan consensus that people and the environment must be protected from the excesses of the unfettered market.

[*See also* Airplanes and Air Transport; Banking and Finance; Bank of the United States, First and Second; Capitalism; Environmentalism; Factory System; Industrial Diseases and Hazards; Industrialization; Interstate Commerce Act; Laissez-faire; Monetary Policy, Federal; Stock Market.]

• Ellis W. Hawley, *The New Deal and the Problem of Monopoly: A Study in Economic Ambivalence,* 1966. Alfred E. Kahn, *The Economics of Regulation,* 1971. Jonathan R. T. Hughes, *Social Control in the Colonial Economy,* 1976. James Q. Wilson, ed., *The Politics of Regulation,* 1980. Stephen Breyer, *Regulation and Its Reform,* 1982. Thomas K. McCraw, *Prophets of Regulation: Charles Francis Adams, Louis D. Brandeis, James M. Landis, Alfred E. Kahn,* 1984. Martha Derthick and Paul J. Quirk, *The Politics of Deregulation,* 1985. Morton Keller, *Regulating a New Economy: Public Policy and Economic Change in America, 1900–1933,* 1990. Richard H. K. Vietor, *Contrived Competition: Regulation and Deregulation in America,* 1994.

—Thomas K. McCraw

ECONOMICS. Writings about economic matters developed in the United States before the emergence of an academic discipline devoted to political economy and economics. As in Britain, U.S. authors devoted an extensive pamphlet literature to the advocacy of economic policies and actions, most particularly as related to monetary issues, employment, and international trade.

Economic Thought in the Early Republic. Despite the early influence of Adam Smith's *The Wealth of Nations* (1776), his major policies did not become the basis for the organization of the U.S. economy after independence. Instead the programs associated with Alexander *Hamilton introduced a system of mercantilism, discarding free trade in favor of tariff protection for manufactured goods. The federal *Constitution and related legislation defined the government's power over monetary and banking issues, *immigration, and land distribution. Differences between the Hamiltonians and the more agrarian followers of Thomas *Jefferson on economic policy seem minor compared to their general acceptance of Smithian principles about *individualism, choice, and markets. Although economic arguments about the path of economic growth and the distribution of income remained central in the early national era, no discipline emerged in the United States that could be described as economics.

Prior to 1820, colleges subsumed political economy (as it was generally called until about 1900) into their concern with moral philosophy and the moral study of social problems. The central readings were based on treatises written by Europeans, whether British, such as by Adam Smith and John Ramsay McCulloch, or, more importantly in the first half of the nineteenth century, by the Frenchman Jean-Baptiste Say. American editions of European texts often used footnotes to describe how American conditions differed. These references, and the emerging school of American writers of texts or monographs on economics, substantially revised British economic theory. Few American economists believed in the accuracy of the pessimistic theories about population growth and land rents associated with Thomas Malthus and David Ricardo. American economics reflected the seemingly unlimited amount of land available in the United States, and thus evinced a greater optimism concerning the effects of population growth on land rent. Perhaps the most sophisticated of these "optimists" was the Pennsylvanian Henry Charles Carey, who followed his father Matthew Carey by advocating protective *tariffs and using the American experience to invert the principles of Ricardian rent. Carey argued that population density and *urbanization offered significant economic returns, presenting a case for reducing the pace of western migration in order to encourage the development of cities and manufacturing industries.

Elements of Political Economy (1837) by Reverend Francis Wayland, president of Brown University, was the first influential economics textbook published in the United States. Wayland regarded political economy as basically an extension of Christian moral philosophy, which aimed to influence social action by its impact on popular audiences. While Wayland exemplified the predominant approach down to the *Civil War, there was also a Pennsylvania school of protectionists and a southern school, exemplified by Thomas Cooper, that extolled free trade, anticapitalism, and (under certain conditions of land availability and climate) *slavery.

Economics as a University-Based Discipline. The professionalization of economics as an academic subject came in the last third of the nineteenth century, under the influence of scholars who had studied in Germany, often with members of the Germany Historical School. These scholars, the most important of whom in influencing the direction taken by economists was Richard T. Ely of Johns Hopkins University and, after 1892, the University of Wisconsin, maintained the antebellum interest in social reform, which they now based on Christian *socialism. They also maintained the goal of educating the masses, and often involved themselves in nonacademic organizations to reach a wider audience. When the American Economic Association was formed in 1885, with Francis A. Walker of the Massachusetts Institute of Technology as president and Ely as secretary, its founders attempted to broaden the membership to include businessmen, government officials, and other members of the public. While more professional economists emphasized empirical research, most aimed the research to advance social reforms they advocated.

In the late nineteenth century, many colleges and universities introduced programs in economics. Subsequently, programs in *political science (government) emerged as a separate academic discipline. Academic journals devoted to economics appeared in the 1880s. An increasing concern with empirical research, theory, and scientific approaches did not mean a loss of interest in social reform, but rather a shift in the strategy of influencing public policy toward bringing the presumed expertise of the academic economists to bear upon public officials. Economists now served on government regulatory agencies, testified before legislative and investigative bodies, and designed state and municipal tax structures. In the years before *World War I, academic economists were central in the drafting of the *Federal Reserve System, tariff policy and its implementation, and other forms of national economic regulation. At the state level, University of Wisconsin economist John R. Commons promoted the "Wisconsin Idea," by which economists and other specialists would work with legislators in the shaping of public policy. World War I saw an expanded use of economists in the national government, particularly at the *War Industries Board.

In the first three decades of the twentieth century the discipline of economics assumed its present shape. Economics became mainly an academic discipline, with teaching and research primarily at colleges and universities, although, as befit a field dealing with real-world issues, a nonacademic fringe of policy advocates always existed. Economists developed a standard corpus of microeconomic theory, first in prose, then geometrically, and later mathematically. They gave more attention to collecting empirical and quantitative data concerning the economy, a trend boosted by the formation of the National Bureau of Economic Research (NBER) in 1920, under the leadership of Edwin F. Gay, a Harvard economic historian. Its director of research, the Columbia University economist Wesley C. Mitchell, whose major research focused on the economic problem of the *business cycle, led the NBER to collect and analyze large bodies of quantitative data. Despite a new emphasis on theoretical and empirical matters, economists still sought to influence public policy by demonstrating their importance to political elites. Economists often participated in government economic commissions in the 1920s.

From the Great Depression to the Post–Cold War Era. The depression of the 1930s led to some disillusionment with the standard economic models, particularly as the decline persisted for longer than had earlier economic downturns. Thus the analysis of the British economist John Maynard Keynes attracted considerable attention, and under the influence of the Harvard economist Alvin Hansen and his students, including Paul Samuelson, *Keynesianism dominated macroeconomic theory in the 1940s and 1950s. Keynes modified the standard classical model, but more important for policy purposes, he presented an argument for an activist government role in the economy, including the use of government tax and expenditure changes to influence the economy. It is unclear whether or not Keynes actually influenced U.S. economic policy in the 1930s, but the "Keynesian Revolution" clearly had a major impact upon the discipline.

The interest in using the government as an active agent in influencing the economy placed a premium on the acquisition of reliable information about economic conditions. While data of various types had long been collected by government agencies and as part of the decennial censuses, the 1930s saw the beginnings of the government's collection of monthly data on *unemployment and prices, and quarterly data on national income and output. While the concept of national income was long known, and several American writers presented estimates in the nineteenth century, only with the work of Simon Kuznets in the 1930s was the concept clarified and detailed methods of implementation and measurement devised. The government's measures of national income subsequently featured in wartime debates about military mobilization. The 1930s thus saw a marked increase in the number of government regulatory agencies and statistical collection organizations, often using economists, a tendency further accelerated during *World War II. Economists continued the time-honored tradition of disagreeing with each other, at times causing negative public and political reactions. Some criticized economists for being too certain about their arguments, while others, like President Harry S. *Truman, expressed frustration over their equivocation, preferring what he referred to as "a one-armed economist" (one who would never say "on the other hand"!).

At the end of World War II, reflecting Keynesian influence, Congress passed the *Employment Act of 1946, which included a provision for a Council of Economic Advisers to collect and prepare data for the president and issue an annual economic report. The precise nature and impact of this council has changed over time, reflecting political and personal factors, but it did make economists (who in most cases served only briefly, on leave from academic positions) central to policy debates, and, over time, led to more positions for economists in governmental agencies. Although microeconomic theory continued to become more mathematical and abstract, in the years after 1950 economists and economic knowledge became more highly valued by business, governments, and international agencies, while economics came to play a role in the study of political science and law. Under the theoretical and empirical critiques of Milton Friedman and others, especially at the University of Chicago, macroeconomics shifted away from the Keynesianism of the 1950s toward a focus on monetary forces and the ability of markets to adapt to changing conditions. Despite disagreements among economists about theory and policy, economics continues to influence public policy and adjust its principles in accord with what has been established as basic empirical reality.

[*See also* Banking and Finance; Demography; Depressions, Economic; Economic Development; Economic Regulation; Education: Rise of the University; Monetarism; Monetary Policy, Federal; Social Gospel; Social Science; Sociology.]

• Michael Joseph Lalor O'Connor, *Origins of Academic Economics in the United States*, 1944. Joseph Dorfman, *The Economic Mind in American Civilization*, 5 vols., 1946–1959. John B. Parrish, "Rise of Economics as an Academic Discipline: The Formative Years to 1900," *Southern Economic Journal* 34 (July 1967): 1–16. Herbert S. Stein, *The Fiscal Revolution in America*, 1969. Robert L. Church, "Economists as Experts: The Rise of an Academic Profession in America 1870–1917," in *The University in Society*, ed. Lawrence Stone, vol. II, 1974, pp. 571–609. Mary O. Furner, *Advocacy and Objectivity*, 1975. Paul K. Conkin, *Prophets of Prosperity*, 1980. William J. Barber, *From New Era to New Deal*, 1985. William J. Barber, ed., *Breaking the Academic Mould*, 1988. Mary O. Furner and Barry Supple, eds., *The State and Economic Knowledge*, 1990. William J. Barber, *Designs within Disorder*, 1996.

—Stanley L. Engerman

ECUMENICAL MOVEMENT. The ecumenical movement is the formal endeavor by Christians to achieve unity in the face of denominational differences. A worldwide phenomenon, it has particularly flourished in the United States, where the wide diversity of competing denominations eventually impelled leaders to promote cooperation and even merger between previously separated church bodies.

Until the Second Vatican Council (1962–1965) freed American Catholics for ecumenical activity, most of the movement in the United States was Protestant. An Evangelical Alliance, formed in London in 1846, attracted many Americans, who organized their own version of it in 1867. It promoted allied activities by "evangelicals," which then meant the mainstream of Protestant churches. The alliance remained largely an effort of clergy leaders and did not grasp the imagination of most lay people.

The International Missionary Conference at Edinburgh, Scotland, presided over by the young American Methodist John R. Mott in 1910, is usually seen as the beginning of modern ecumenism. However, already in 1908 mainstream American Protestants had organized a Federal Council of Churches. Its successor, the *National Council of Churches of Christ in the U.S.A., founded in 1950, originally included twenty-five Protestant and four Orthodox churches. Expanding thereafter, it became a major voice of cooperative moderate-to-liberal non–Roman Catholic Christianity.

Meanwhile, state and local councils and federations of churches also engaged in common activities, often including theological discussion. Various denominations, as part of the movement, moved to end longstanding divisions. The twentieth century brought mergers of separate Presbyterian, Methodist, Lutheran, and other bodies. Most notable was a merger of the Congregational Christian and Evangelical and Reformed churches into the United Church of Christ in 1957.

Despite setbacks in formal organization, the ecumenical movement changed the spirit of American mainstream Protestantism. Meanwhile, the more conservative Protestants, through the National Association of Evangelicals after 1942, also expressed an ecumenical spirit, as did Catholics after 1965. By the end of the twentieth century the ecumenical spirit was undimmed, even as leaders looked for new forms by which the movement might express itself.

[*See also* Lutheranism; Methodism; Protestantism; Religion; Roman Catholicism.]

• Ruth Rouse et al., eds., *A History of the Ecumenical Movement*, 2 vols., 1967, 1970. Russell Richey, ed., *Denominationalism*, 1977.

—Martin E. Marty

EDDY, MARY BAKER. *See* Christian Science.

EDISON, THOMAS (1847–1931), inventor and business entrepreneur. Thomas Alva Edison was born in Milan, Ohio, but moved with his family to Port Huron, Michigan, at age seven. He was educated mostly at home by his mother, a former schoolteacher. At twelve, he organized a team of boys to sell sandwiches and newspapers on the train to *Detroit. Learning telegraphy, he worked in various midwestern cities as a *telegraph and presswire operator. This experience immersed him in this new *technology and shaped his career-long creative strategies. In the late 1860s he published articles in the leading national telegraph journal describing his new designs.

Moving to Boston in 1868 Edison launched a series of businesses based on these innovative telegraph designs. These ventures led him to New York and, in 1870, to Newark, New Jersey, where he designed and, with a shop partner, produced stock tickers and related equipment. By the mid-1870s the already sophisticated inventor enjoyed close relations with officers of the Western Union Telegraph Company and financial leaders on Wall Street. He organized an experimental laboratory at Newark in 1875 and, with the aid of a Western Union contract, opened a laboratory at Menlo Park, New Jersey, in 1876.

During the next five years he and a small group of assistants made a series of remarkable inventions related to the telegraph, *telephone, phonograph, incandescent light bulb, and an associated electric power generating system. His invention of the phonograph in 1877 attracted worldwide attention. His success in 1879 in developing a practical incandescent lighting system, supported by New York financiers, won him further public attention and stimulated an eight-year period of intense inventive and entrepreneurial effort promoting and installing urban electric generating stations across America. Edison and his closest technical associates also started key companies for the production of electric generating equipment, electrical distribution supplies, and even indoor electrical fixtures. With the involvement of the financier J. P. *Morgan, these companies merged in 1889 into Edison General Electric and in 1892 into the General Electric Company.

In 1887 Edison built a new research laboratory—ten times the size of the Menlo Park shop—in rural Orange, New Jersey.

Here Edison and his numerous associates continued with electric lighting research, but, more importantly, started new projects, including improvement and commercialization of the phonograph, production of cylinder recordings, development of motion-picture equipment, production of movie films, and installation of a massive iron-ore concentration works in northern New Jersey. The successful phonograph and motion-picture projects prompted construction of large-scale production facilities surrounding the laboratory, but the failing ore-concentration project devoured much of Edison's time (and money) during the 1890s.

After 1900 Edison continued with production and improvements associated with the phonograph and motion pictures but also initiated commercial manufacture of electric storage batteries and portland cement. (Portland cement is a hydraulic cement that can set underwater or in high humidity conditions. His company was the "Edison Portland Cement Company.") He engaged in chemical production and research on underwater sonic detection devices during *World War I and in the 1920s marketed a line of small electrical appliances. His friends Henry *Ford and Harvey *Firestone supported his last project, a search for a natural substitute for rubber. Edison married twice (his first wife died) and had a daughter and two sons in each marriage.

With 1,093 U.S. patents, Thomas Edison stands as America's most prolific inventor. His innovations contributed to the establishment of at least a half-dozen important new industries. This pioneer in collaborative industrial research persistently carried his patented inventions and improvements into the marketplace. His laboratories in Newark, Menlo Park, and Orange, New Jersey, foreshadowed later American industrial *research laboratories such as those of General Electric, DuPont, Eastman Kodak, and AT&T.

Edison extended his patenting, licensing, production, and marketing efforts to Europe and Latin America (he held patents in twenty-four countries), participating in America's emergence as a world industrial power. Prolific inventor, entrepreneur, and pioneer in industrial research, Edison helped to illuminate the night, electrify the world, lay the foundation for technical creativity in modern corporate enterprise, and, with his introduction of recorded sound and the movies, create the visual-aural communications revolution that reshaped twentieth-century *popular culture.

[*See also* Electrical Industry; Electricity and Electrification Film.]

• Matthew Josephson, *Edison: A Biography*, 1959, reprint 1992. Wyn Wachhorst, *Thomas Alva Edison: An American Myth*, 1981. Robert Friedel, Paul Israel, and Bernard S. Finn, *Edison's Electric Light: Biography of an Invention*, 1986. *The Papers of Thomas A. Edison*, Reese V. Jenkins et al., eds., vols. 1–4, 1989–1998. William S. Pretzer, ed., *Working at Inventing: Thomas A. Edison and the Menlo Park Experience*, 1989. Andre Millard, *Edison and the Business of Innovation*, 1990.

—Reese V. Jenkins

EDUCATION

EDUCATION: OVERVIEW

From the founding of Harvard College in 1636 and Massachusetts's public-school law of 1647 to America's vast and diverse modern-day educational system, education has been a central thread in the national experience, a focus of reform effort, and a subject of urgent public debate. The founders and early leaders of the new nation viewed an educated electorate as crucial to their republican experiment. As nineteenth-century municipalities expanded their public-school systems, religious bodies founded colleges to educate and nurture their young. While some turn-of-the-century reformers looked to the public schools to "Americanize" the immigrant masses, the philosopher John *Dewey viewed the schools as incubators of a more just and humane social order. In the same era, research universities arose to promote scientific inquiry, scholarly endeavor, and professional training. In the 1944 *Servicemen's Readjustment Act, Congress granted generous educational benefits to returning *World War II veterans. When the Russians launched the space satellite *Sputnik* in 1957, Congress responded with increased funds for education, especially in math and science. When the *civil rights movement arose in the 1950s, schools became a prime battleground. **Brown* v. *Board of Education,* the *Supreme Court's landmark 1954 civil rights decision, outlawed racial *segregation in the public schools. Soon, women and other disadvantaged groups would also demand equal access to educational opportunities. As the twentieth century ended, politicians vied to propose strategies for improving American education. The underlying point is clear: There are few better ways to approach American history as a whole than to examine the nation's centuries-long effort to educate its citizens.

—Paul S. Boyer

EDUCATION: THE PUBLIC SCHOOL MOVEMENT

The people who devised the U.S. *Constitution and wrote about the nature of republican government often emphasized the importance of education. However, proposals to create state systems of common schools, such as those put forward by Thomas *Jefferson in Virginia and Benjamin *Rush in Pennsylvania, did not succeed in the early national period. New state legislatures resisted both governmental innovation and increased taxes. Still, by comparison with other countries, local primary schools were widely available. They were funded locally by a patchwork of tuition payments, property taxes, in-kind contributions, endowments, and church support. Thus, the rhetoric of *republicanism did not translate into a movement to create free public schools.

Beginnings of the Public School Movement. By the 1840s conditions were more auspicious for such a reform. *Industrialization and *urbanization led to visible social problems. The *immigration of large numbers of Roman Catholics led native-born Protestants to worry about how to assimilate newcomers while maintaining the hegemony and institutions they had created. By this time state governments had become more active in shaping institutions and the economy. The *Whig party in particular advocated such state activism and thus championed legislation that required towns to provide free education through property taxes. In many states, Whigs also promoted legislation to consolidate small, rural districts into town-level school systems, and they created state school boards and superintendents to oversee the creation of rudimentary state systems of public schools. Into these superintendencies came some of the famous school reformers, like Horace *Mann of Massachusetts, Henry Barnard of Connecticut, and John Pierce of Michigan. They worked to consolidate district schools and promoted longer school terms, normal schools for teacher training, higher school expenditures per pupil, and innovations in curriculum and pedagogy.

By 1860 such systems were the general rule in the Northeast and the *Middle West, while they failed, after considerable debate, in the *South. During the postwar *Reconstruction period, southern legislatures created fledgling public school systems, and by the late nineteenth century they were mostly tax-supported. However, harshly unequal per-pupil expenditures for segregated black schools forced *African Americans to provide supplementary funds from their meager resources.

Gilded Age to the 1950s. The public school movement in the nation as a whole went through a period of consolidation in the *Gilded Age. The teaching force had become largely female, and normal schools proliferated; a male-dominated profession of school administration was emerging; city school systems with age-graded classes became the model; and the public high school surpassed the private academy as the predominant provider of secondary education.

Late nineteenth-century immigration, urbanization, labor strife, and the depression of the 1890s helped launch another period of reform. Like the *Antebellum Era, this was a time of accelerated population movement, transformative economic reorganization, and cultural anxiety. In education, this turbulence led to reform proposals that varied greatly in their assumptions and goals. Some, following John *Dewey, believed that schools should recognize the individuality of children, appeal to their interests, make learning an active process, and produce citizens who were good critical thinkers. Others, like David Snedden, looked more to teaching of specific content and attitudes, tailoring programs to categories of children and training them for specific roles, depending upon predictions about their likely occupational destinations. These predictions were often made on the basis of family background and, increasingly, standardized tests scores. The *Progressive-Era values of efficiency and scientific measurement prevailed. In school policy the progressive administrators adopted a corporate model of school-board governance and a hierarchical model for school systems, with a superintendent firmly in charge of all activity.

Some of the features of child-centered progressive education made their way into the public schools. Surviving records suggest increasing concern for the interests of children, widespread use of the project method, and somewhat more active classrooms. As Robert and Helen Lynd said of the schools of Muncie, Indiana, in the 1930s, however, "in the struggle between quantitative administrative efficiency and qualitative educational goals in an era of strain like the present, the big guns" were all on the side of efficiency. (*Middletown in Transition*, p. 241).

By 1940 most children aged five to sixteen were enrolled in school for at least a part of the year; 73 percent of high-school aged youths were in school. In the hundred years since the beginning of the common school reform movement, the states had created public school systems quite similar from state to state. Local school districts were governed by the states on such matters as the length of the school year, teacher certification, and some basic curriculum requirements. Schools were otherwise governed locally. They were inclusive, with less than 10 percent of school children in private schools. Still, the public schools were often Protestant in outlook and in some of their religious practices, like *Bible reading and daily prayers. Furthermore, the public schools were highly segregated by race, either formally or informally, not just in the South and not only for African Americans, but more generally across the nation, with regard to all people of color. Finally, financial resources for public schools varied greatly from state to state and district to district.

New Currents of Reform, 1960–2000. A new phase of public school reform addressed some of these remaining issues. Tackling problems like equity of funding, racial integration, and other group rights was the hallmark of educational reform in the 1960s and 1970s, and it coincided with the expansion of the federal role in education. The *Supreme Court's **Brown* v. *Board of Education* (1954), declaring legalized school segregation unconstitutional, laid the groundwork for racial integration, but it gained momentum only when subsequent cases, beginning in the mid-1960s, defined the demands on local school systems and provided mechanisms for enforcement. Bolstered by the Civil Rights Act of 1964 and the Elementary and Secondary Education Act of 1965, the Lyndon B. *Johnson administration launched a "War on Poverty," which attempted to promote equality of opportunity through compensatory education, Head Start for preschool-aged children, school integration, and job training programs. Court decisions and executive activism led to substantial integration of southern schools, and the legislation that aimed at equalizing opportunity proved popular despite ambiguous evidence of the programs' effectiveness.

The quest to secure group rights expanded in the 1970s. Federal legislation defined and made mandatory the recognition of educational rights of women, language minorities, and children with disabilities. The Supreme Court (in *San Antonio Independent School District* v. *Rodriguez*, 1973) ruled that equalization of resources across districts was not required by the Constitution. However, many states had voluntarily implemented partial equalization formulas, and in the 1980s and 1990s several state supreme courts demanded such equalization, citing specific language regarding equal educational opportunity in their state constitutions.

While the ambitious federal agenda eventually encountered a backlash from weary bureaucrats and defenders of various traditions, it also installed a new recognition of diversity in the practices, procedures, and expectations of local school systems, much of it reinforced by new state laws and regulations. Integration efforts also encountered backlash from both whites and blacks, when the negative aspects of busing children were often not matched with improved school achievement by minorities. This disappointment, coupled with the heavy concentration of nonwhite citizens in many large cities, hindered the government's efforts to bring school integration to the North and West. In the face of these obstacles, aggressive, liberal school reform declined. The shift of mood was reflected in the election of Ronald *Reagan in 1980. Public school reformers changed their emphasis from equity and inclusion to concerns about the content of the curriculum and the quality of learning across all groups. Reforms were implemented in many states to require more and better coursework from high school students, recruit and train better teachers, and change the structure of school systems to enhance professional control by principals and teachers in local schools.

Some educators and parents concluded that it was too little, too late. Disillusionment with the public schools grew. Many people called for school reform outside the structure of the public school system, either through "voucher" payments to private schools or the creation of "charter" schools, variously regulated in different states but everywhere freed from some of the supervision and rules of public systems. The popularity of free-market models, as well as the growing proportion of the population without school-aged children, contributed to the sense of crisis. Supporters of public schools worried that the civic and integrative purposes of schools would founder if people abandoned a common, public system.

The "public school movement" of the previous century and a half had, in truth, been many movements, many efforts to reform public schools, which had become a focal point for debates about America's values, its children, and its future. The twenty-first century would face the question of whether there would be a public school system, and, if so, how it would restore public confidence in its ability to provide high-quality education and assist in the imperative task of unifying a diverse population, those twin mandates established in the 1840s.

[*See also* Americanization Movement; Americans with Disabilities Act; Civil Rights Legislation; Civil Rights Movement; Depressions, Economic; Education: Collegiate Education; Education in Contemporary America; Education: The Rise of the University; Intelligence, Concepts of; Poverty; Protestantism; Segregation, Racial; Taxation.]

• Lawrence A. Cremin, *American Education*, 3 vols. 1970–1988. David B. Tyack, *The One Best System: A History of Urban Education in America*, 1974. Carl Kaestle, *Pillars of the Republic: Common Schools and American Society, 1780–1860*, 1983. Diane Ravitch, *The Troubled Crusade: American Education, 1945–1980*, 1983. James D. Anderson, *The Education of Blacks in the South, 1860–1935*, 1988.

—Carl F. Kaestle

EDUCATION: COLLEGIATE EDUCATION

Since the founding of Harvard College in 1636, American colleges have responded to society's perceived needs. From the late nineteenth century on, American institutions of higher learning have focused on three goals: the transmission of knowledge, especially of Western civilization; the creation of new knowledge in an increasing array of academic disciplines; and the integration of young people into the upper economic and social strata through training and socialization. Young people attended college not just to further their education, but to learn the elite's values and mores and to make the connections considered vital to success.

These broad academic and social aims have been met at a variety of diverse institutions, which mirrored American society itself: public and private institutions, small colleges and large universities, rural residential and urban commuter schools, secular and denominational colleges, as well as women's and historically black colleges. In their myriad admissions procedures, faculty recruitment, and curricular approaches, American colleges have expressed America's democratic ideals as well as its overt and subtle patterns of class and racial discrimination.

Colonial and Antebellum Era Beginnings. The European university was a model for American higher education, but a distinctive American tradition emerged as early as the eighteenth century. By the time of the *Revolutionary War, nine colleges had been established, primarily to provide denominational education for future ministers and upper-class gentlemen. However, the College of Philadelphia and King's College in New York (later the University of Pennsylvania and Columbia University, respectively), founded in the 1750s, embraced nonsectarian and utilitarian principles and soon introduced such "practical" subjects as English literature and legal and *medical education.

In the *Antebellum Era, even the most conservative colleges confronted the conflict between classical and contemporary American influences: What role did the past and its tradition of education for the clergy and for "gentlemen" have in a dynamic society bent on progress? What was education's function in a society geared to individual opportunity and *mobility? Balancing meritocratic and democratic values, the traditional curriculum was soon augmented by scientific and other modern studies, though often after considerable internal debate. The Rensselaer Polytechnic Institute, the nation's first technical college, started in 1824. By contrast, the Yale College faculty defended the classical curriculum in an 1828 report. Still, with fewer than one hundred students graduating annually, Yale by 1847 had established a School of Applied Chemistry, soon renamed the Sheffield School after a benefactor, thereby opening the door to instruction in *science, modern languages, history, and other popular subjects.

Beginning in the *Colonial Era, both public and private colleges solicited government support. After the Revolution, the *Northwest Ordinance of 1787 promoted broad educational opportunity through the allocation of federal land grants to schools and colleges. The *Morrill Land Grant Act (1862) and the Hatch Act (1887) stimulated the creation of state land-grant colleges and universities and other publicly funded agricultural, technical, and teachers' colleges. In the later nineteenth century, the state-university movement was led by midwestern and western institutions such as the state universities of Michgan, Wisconsin, and California. At the same time, philanthropists such as Leland Stanford and Ezra Cornell founded private colleges and universities where, in Cornell's words, "any person [could] find instruction in any study."

Throughout the 1800s, the United States became a "land of colleges" as religious-sponsored institutions, from rural Protestant denominational colleges in the *Middle West to urban Catholic colleges, were formed to cater to local, first-generation students. In Indiana, for example, between 1835 and 1844, Presbyterians formed Wabash College, the Methodists started Indiana Asbury (now DePauw University), and the Baptists established Franklin College. Typical of the evolution of Jesuit higher education was the Loyola University of Chicago, which began as St. Ignatius College in 1870. Over time these schools deemphasized the parochial impulses of their founders to satisfy their students' social and professional aspirations. Nevertheless, higher education remained the prerogative of a small minority of the population. In 1915, fewer than one in twenty young people went to college.

1865–1920. Women's colleges and the historically black colleges, which provided opportunity and training to women and minorities excluded from, or made to feel unwelcome at, private and public colleges and universities, grew rapidly in the *Gilded Age. Vassar, Smith, and Wellesley colleges were the first of the so-called Seven Sisters women's liberal arts colleges. Predominantly white benevolent societies and missionary bodies, black religious organizations, and wealthy individuals and corporate philanthropic foundations started and maintained private black liberal arts colleges, such as Fisk and Howard universities, to prepare an educated leadership class as well as to enable individual students to move into the mainstream, national culture.

In the late nineteenth and early twentieth centuries, especially during the *Progressive Era, entrepreneurial academic leaders, research-focused faculty, and ambitious young people transformed the traditional college into the forward-looking university, the stepping-stone to respectability and individual success, by expanding the curriculum and stimulating increased enrollment. Subject areas formerly considered inappropriate to a liberal education, such as *agriculture and *social work, now became accepted courses of study as colleges and universities sought to meet the increasing demand for more practical education and training. The nation's first undergraduate business school, the Wharton School of Finance and Commerce, was founded at the University of Pennsylvania in 1881.

Since 1920. By the 1920s, the day of the so-called self-made man had passed; the college-educated fraternity man became the arbiter of taste and training in American life. The boom in college enrollment after *World War I forced Americans to confront the contradiction between their belief in individual opportunity and their desire to preserve the existing structure of social privilege. If a college education earmarked a student for future occupational achievement and social status, was higher education in a democracy a privilege or a right? How many and who should attend? What criteria should apply? Between the world wars, elite liberal arts colleges drawing from a national pool of applicants emerged, but they were selective institutions often rooted in class and ethnic prejudice. Most well-known schools limited the number of Jewish and Catholic students. More subtle class distinctions among students were often reflected in student life on campus, for example in fraternity and sorority organizations.

Admissions policies became a battleground between traditional institutional prerogatives and democratic social policy. Despite decades of rapid enrollment growth, the 1947 President's Commission on Higher Education concluded that American collegiate education still had not realized its democratic potential because of its high cost, restrictive curriculum, and racial and religious discrimination in admissions. Free and universal access to at least two years of postsecondary work, the commission insisted, should be a public policy goal.

During the twentieth century, the federal government encouraged the growth of colleges and universities through financial support for individual students as well as through institutional support for faculty and research. In World War I, Washington created the Student Army Training Corps and the Reserve Officer Training Corps, but the number of participating students paled in comparison to the millions of veterans who flocked to college after *World War II thanks to the *Servicemen's Readjustment Act, or GI Bill of Rights (1944). The National Defense Student Loan Program of 1958, a response to the Soviet Union's launch of the *Sputnik* satellite, encouraged increased enrollment, particularly in science and *engineering programs. President Lyndon B. *Johnson's *Great Society reforms in the mid-1960s and subsequent domestic social policy initiatives included grant programs for disadvantaged students and general loan programs for a broader range of students. By the end of the twentieth century, the federal government was allocating well over ten billion dollars a year to college and university research and development activities, mostly from the Department of Health and Human Services and the *National Science Foundation, as well as the Department of Defense.

As enrollments grew and a college degree became highly valued, institutions found their niche in an increasingly differentiated structure. Name changes often signaled an institution's expanded offerings and its quest for prestige: the teacher-training "normal school" became, often around 1920, the "state teacher's college"; then the "state college"; and, finally, in the 1950s and 1960s, the "state university." Over one thousand public two-year junior and community colleges were established during the twentieth century to expand access to post-secondary education. At the same time, a select number of liberal arts colleges and research universities emerged at the apex of the higher education pyramid. In 1995, over 12.2 million undergraduates were enrolled in nearly 3,700 institutions, about 11 million of them in public institutions.

At the end of the twentieth century, colleges and universities constituted a significant industry in the United States, with annual expenditures in excess of $175 billion. Moreover, numerous high technology and biotechnology companies were affiliated with schools or their faculty. Intercollegiate athletics, especially football and basketball, supervised by the *National Collegiate Athletic Association (NCAA), figured prominently in the nation's *popular culture and media. From its beginnings in the 1630s, the American college had come a long way.

[*See also* African Americans; Anti-Semitism; Biological Sciences; Biotechnology Industry; Earth Sciences; Education: Education in Contemporary America; Education: The Rise of the University; Land Policy, Federal; Philanthropy and Philanthropic Foundations; Physical Sciences; Protestantism; Roman Catholicism; Social Class; Social Science; Sports: Amateur Sports and Recreation; Women's Rights Movements.]

• Frederick Rudolph, *The American College and University*, 1962. Laurence R. Veysey, *The Emergence of the American University*, 1965. Lawrence Cremin, *American Education*, 3 vols., 1970–1988. Frank Bowles and Frank A. DeCosta, *Between Two Worlds: A Profile of Negro Higher Education*, 1971. Frederick Rudolph, *Curriculum: A History of the American Undergraduate Course of Study since 1636*, 1977. Harold Wechsler, *The Qualified Student*, 1977. Barbara M. Solomon, *In the Company of Educated Women*, 1985. David O. Levine, *The American College and the Culture of Aspiration, 1915–1940*, 1986. Helen L. Horowitz, *Campus Life: Undergraduate Cultures from the End of the Eighteenth Century to the Present*, 1987.

—David O. Levine

EDUCATION: THE RISE OF THE UNIVERSITY

The original institution for advanced education in America was the liberal arts college. Soon after the *Revolutionary War, however, the term "university" arose, with several meanings implied. The University of the State of New York (1784–) and the short-lived University of Maryland (1784–1805) were overarching structures, designed to encompass individual colleges much like the universities of Oxford and Cambridge. The idea of a national university, first advocated by Benjamin *Rush in 1787, envisioned an institution providing advanced studies for college graduates. The most common usage of the term, however, implied a college possessing one or more professional schools, much like the universities of continental Europe.

The Pre-modern University. By the 1820s, Harvard and Yale, each with a full complement of professional schools, exemplified what might be called the premodern university. American realities were a far cry from European models, however. Schools of medicine and law were essentially proprietary undertakings that accepted students whether or not they had attended college. In the colleges, all students took the same course, and no modern subjects were taught in depth. The only postbaccalaureate course, theology, was intended to train ministers rather than scholars.

In the 1850s, critics lamented the inability of American institutions to cultivate and teach advanced knowledge. Henry Tappan in *University Education* (1851), praising the scientific achievements of German universities, advocated an American university that would teach beyond the collegiate level. As president of the University of Michigan (1853–1863), Tappan established an earned master's degree and encouraged faculty scholarship. More characteristic of the era, however, were the "scientific schools" established at Harvard and Yale. These new units accommodated both scientific studies and advanced learning without disturbing the separate operations of the college. Yale awarded the first American Ph.D.s in 1861 for work done in its scientific school.

The American University Takes Shape. Following the *Civil War, scientific schools, new institutes of technology, and colleges spawned by the 1862 *Morrill Land Grant Act offered practical science-based instruction. However, the issue of advanced learning reemerged most strongly at Harvard and the new Johns Hopkins University (1876). Charles William *Eliot assumed the presidency of Harvard in 1869 with a clear vision of reform. His elective system allowed students to choose their own studies and permitted the learned Harvard faculty to teach advanced subjects. Believing that professional studies should be pursued at the postgraduate level, Eliot restructured Harvard's professional schools accordingly. Daniel Coit Gilman, president of Johns Hopkins from 1876 to 1901, designed it largely as a graduate university committed first and foremost to the advancement of knowledge and the professional organization of scholarship. Clark University, which opened in 1889 in Worcester, Massachusetts, solely for graduate studies, carried this notion even further.

By 1890, a lively debate raged over the relation of the colleges to the emerging universities. Suggestions for shortening or subordinating the college course, however, were overcome by the college's resilience as a social and educational institution. Instead, the universities arose upon a collegiate base: a large faculty engaged in undergraduate teaching would also pursue scholarship and train future scholars. The new universities of Stanford (1891) and Chicago (1892), created through philanthropy, conformed in their own fashion to this pattern. This template also suited the stronger state universities, which included undergraduate professional schools as well as the arts and sciences core.

The new universities proved highly popular. Their mushroom growth outdistanced all other types of institutions for the next quarter-century, transforming American higher education. In 1900, the leaders in graduate education organized the Association of American Universities to define good practice in graduate education and also serve as an unofficial accrediting agency for colleges. The professional associations and learned journals of the various academic disciplines established a new canon of academic knowledge that ineluctably reshaped undergraduate colleges. Simultaneously, the new philanthropic foundations created by Andrew *Carnegie and John D. *Rockefeller employed their wealth to bolster standards in higher education—standards largely derived from universities.

The college at the heart of the American university became a source of considerable strength. Educators debated the nature of liberal education in an era of growing academic specialization, but the universities benefited from the high social value placed upon the collegiate experience. The collegiate dimension also ensured that American universities would differ markedly from one another.

After *World War I, these differences became more pronounced as public and private universities were shaped by different forces. The major state universities continued to grow by accommodating the burgeoning ranks of high-school graduates. The wealthy private universities looked for support largely from their alumni, who favored greater investment in educational quality, both in the classroom and collegiate life. Although private universities restricted enrollments, their relative affluence allowed them to hire and retain distinguished faculty. The role of advancing knowledge was nevertheless furthered most notably in the interwar years by philanthropic foundations.

Before World War I, universities could finance separate expenditures for research only through special gifts or endowments. The latter, for example, funded university *museums and *observatories, producing the characteristic American pattern of separately organized university research institutes. But such funds were rare. After the war, however, the Rockefeller and Carnegie foundations sought to advance the natural and social sciences, principally through academic research. Foundation support of academic research had a double-barreled effect. While it proved decisive in raising American *science to world-class status in many fields, especially nuclear physics, it was also instrumental in inducing universities consciously to expand their internal research capacity as a way of attracting foundation grants. By the 1930s, however, it became apparent that private research support was inadequate for the growing scientific needs of universities.

World War II and Beyond. The services of university scientists during *World War II demonstrated the value of academic research as a public investment. However, the blueprint for broad government support of pure science envisioned by Vannevar *Bush in *Science—The Endless Frontier* (1945) was not followed and research funding remained, with slight alternations, in military channels. University research underwent unprecedented expansion in the early postwar period, but largely in defense-related fields. University leaders continue to argue for greater support for disinterested basic research, and after the Soviet Union launched the *Sputnik* satellites in 1957, they got their wish.

Sputnik touched off a surge in civilian federal support for basic academic research. The *National Science Foundation, created in 1950, now received significant appropriations to support research. The *National Institutes of Health, aided by the spirit of the times and a powerful lobby, enormously increased its external grants. All told, federal support for academic research increased by 200 percent from 1959 to 1964, stimulating the most frenetic pace of academic development since the 1890s. In a veritable "academic revolution," the values and specialized approach of the university graduate schools spread throughout American higher education. Numerous institutions now transformed themselves into "research universities" and their doctoral graduates filled the faculties of other institutions. Pundits such as the sociologist Daniel Bell (*The Coming of Post-Industrial Society,* 1973) identified the university as a central institution of the postindustrial, knowledge-based societies.

At this moment of apparent triumph, American universities were sorely tested. Beginning in 1965, disaffected students protested against the complicity of universities in the *Vietnam War and *Cold War militarism, and the alleged irrelevance of theoretical, disciplinary scholarship. The federal government, meanwhile, demanded more applied knowledge from its huge investment in university research. Universities themselves advocated a new national agenda of egalitarianism and social meliorism, but those concerns ill fit their natural propensities toward pursuing excellence in science and scholarship and training society's elite.

American universities finally overcame the malaise of the 1970s by embracing a new role of economic relevance in the 1980s. Swept along by the revolution in the *biotechnology industry, universities forged partnerships with American industry. Although this new role enlarged and complicated the university's mission, it was largely accommodated, as in the past, by adding ancillary units to the academic core.

The twentieth-century American university succeeded most emphatically in the mission that had been most problematic in the previous century: the advancement of knowledge. At century's end, universities conducted approximately half of the nation's basic research. To maintain this role, they had to adapt continually to rapidly changing frontiers of knowledge. The close link between research and graduate education has made American universities the world's chief magnet for advanced students and scholars—the position occupied by Germany a century before. Having become huge, complex organizations, serving American society in numerous and contested ways, American universities retained a resilience and strength stemming from the core mission they fashioned at the end of the nineteenth century: advancing knowledge through free, systematic, rational inquiry.

[*See also* Agricultural Education and Extension; Education: Collegiate Education; Engineering; Gilded Age; Philanthropy and Philanthropic Foundations; Physical Sciences; Sixties, The; Social Sciences; Servicemen's Readjustment Act; Sports: Amateur Sports and Recreation.]

• Edwin E. Slosson, *Great American Universities,* 1910. Richard Storr, *The Beginnings of Graduate Education,* 1953. Laurence Veysey, *The Emergence of the American University,* 1965. Alexandra Oleson and John Voss, eds., *The Organization of Knowledge in Modern America,* 1979. Roger Geiger, *To Advance Knowledge: The Growth of American Research Universities, 1900–1914,* 1986. Richard M. Freeland, *Academia's Golden Age: Universities in Massachusetts, 1945–1970,* 1992. Roger Geiger, *Research and Relevant Knowledge: American Research Universities since World War II,* 1993. Burton R. Clark, *Places of Inquiry: Research and Advanced Education in the Modern Universities,* 1995.

—Roger L. Geiger

EDUCATION: EDUCATION IN CONTEMPORARY AMERICA

Few subjects generated more partisan rhetoric and less consensus in the 1990s than the fate of the public schools. The nation's schools have always had strident critics and impassioned defenders, but the demand for educational reforms echoed throughout the land as the twentieth century ended. Presidential hopefuls routinely aspired to become the "education president," even though public schools were largely funded and controlled by state and local officials. Governors' task forces, big-city mayors, and local worthies all favored school reforms and improvements, from charter schools to high-stakes testing, from voucher plans to more funding for Head Start. In his final State of the Union message in January 2000, President Bill *Clinton, proclaiming education central to the good life, called for a "twenty-first-century revolution in education, guided by our faith that every child can learn. Because education is more than ever the key to our children's future, we must make sure all our children have that key. That means quality preschool and after school, the best-trained teachers in every classroom, and college opportunities for all our children." What was at stake, he concluded, was the American dream.

The centrality of education in everyday life in 1990s America was nothing short of astounding. The nation made impressive emotional and financial investments in its schools. By 1997, more than 46 million pupils were enrolled in the public schools. In 1995, roughly 65 percent of public-school pupils were white, 35 percent minority (including 17 percent *African American and 14 percent *Hispanic American), reflecting America's ethnic and racial diversity. The teaching force (86 percent white) numbered well over 2 million, and the country spent many billions of dollars on salaries, school construction and repair, and innumerable school-related services and programs, from school transportation to hot lunches to educating children with special needs. All this occurred in the Western world's most decentralized school system. Compared to European ministries of education, the U.S. Department of Education (created only in 1976) was relatively weak, poorly funded, and vastly less important in educational matters than state and local governments. Formal control over the nation's tens of thousands of schools resided in the hands of lay people elected or appointed to the school boards of more than fifteen thousand independent districts. The enormous reach and diversity of this vast educational enterprise, ranging from inner cities to suburbs and rural America, gave ample scope to critics and friends alike.

The schools most often attracted criticisms as numerous campaigns for educational reform gained popularity. As in the past, many stakeholders in the schools—parents, politicians, educators, teachers, and pundits—joined the debate. Characterizing the countless reformers of the 1990s is complicated by the willingness of so many people to voice their complaints and offer proposals for improvement. One large strand of reform reflected the broad influence of a seminal report, *A Nation at Risk* (1983), published by a national commission under the auspices of the U.S. Department of Education during the early years of Ronald *Reagan's presidency. Despite the occasional insults they hurled at the department, Republicans effectively used this report as a catalyst for larger national debates on the public schools. Indeed, they set the terms of most subsequent educational debates.

Written at a time of national preoccupation with Japan's seemingly invincible economy and presumably superior educational system, *A Nation at Risk* blamed America's schools for the nation's economic woes and low industrial productivity. The sustained economic growth of the United States in the 1990s, in contrast, did not cause politicians to see public schools more favorably. Instead, Republicans and increasingly Democrats, too, chanted a familiar mantra: that the public schools were failing and test scores were unimpressive, reflecting permissive, liberal school policies and practices, leading to incivility and even violence in the classroom. Only more testing, accountability, and school choice could possibly save the beleaguered schools. Other interest groups agreed, while adding their own spin to school improvement. Evangelical Christians, among the strongest advocates of independent church schools and home schooling, lobbied conservative legislators to guarantee equal time for the teaching of "creation science" in biology classes and for voluntary prayer in the public schools. Back-to-basics zealots scrutinized textbooks for hints of anti-Americanism, whole-language teaching, and "secular humanism." Admirers of free markets and liberty, energized by the collapse of communism abroad, pressed for public aid to private schools, whether through tuition tax credits or vouchers, whose constitutionality in pilot programs in Milwaukee, Wisconsin; Cleveland, Ohio; and other places remained unclear. Conservatives differed on the means but not the ends: to restore competitiveness, discipline, high achievement, and character training to the schools. That might mean ending social promotion, tightening graduation standards, and expunging the permissiveness widely perceived as the offspring of 1960s-era social turmoil. Jeremiads on the state of youth and the schools proliferated.

As *Great Society liberalism became less influential within the *Democratic party and identity politics gained momentum, left-of-center activists lost political clout. Many eloquently defended the public schools, but Republican criticisms of education remained popular throughout the 1990s. To oppose higher standards, testing, discipline, and market solutions to school improvement seemed out of step with the times, while holding schools more accountable, weakening teachers' unions, and upgrading the curriculum and graduation requirements had considerable appeal. Like sporting events, the test scores of school districts were publicized by the local media, to applaud the high achievers and chastize the rest (usually the poorest, nonwhite districts). Schoolteachers had long been criticized for their failures, so much of this was familiar, but it was persistent. After all, the left had offered many of the same criticisms of the nation's schools in the 1960s, calling them racist, sexist, class biased, and unable to educate the poor and minorities well. By the 1980s and 1990s conservatives threw most of the stones and set the agenda for most policy debates.

More liberal or left-of-center educational activists remained on the defensive throughout the 1990s. Faculty who trained teachers on the nation's campuses had difficulty refuting attacks on teacher-certification programs. With few exceptions, schools of education were widely regarded as diploma mills. Teachers' unions faced considerable hostility in this age of accountability, even though Albert Shanker of the American Federation of Teachers and other union leaders endorsed more teacher and student testing and tougher standards. Civil-rights and feminist leaders in turn divided on the issue of single-sex education, despite the long tradition of coeducation in the public schools, and liberals and activists similarly split on the question of racial integration, with a resurgence of support for racial separatism. African American parents in inner cities, whose children often faced the greatest educational hurdles, increasingly embraced the idea of "school choice," even voucher plans, in defiance of traditional black leadership.

Culture wars, debates over standards, and occasionally struggles for economic justice preoccupied many activists. In a seemingly endless battle over religion in the classroom, groups such as Americans United for the Separation of Church and State and the *American Civil Liberties Union spent much time and money in court challenges to the teaching of "creation science" and the reestablishment of school prayer. Battle lines formed over attempts to frame national history standards; while white liberals and Afrocentrists debated academic content, Congress loudly rejected a more multicultural approach to social studies and history teaching. *California residents reflected the conservative mood by voting down state-sponsored bilingual education programs, further alienating liberal elites from the masses of voters. As liberal groups filed lawsuits on behalf of poor districts, some states declared existing school-funding formulas unconstitutional; legislatures proved less diligent in sharing the public purse with poorer districts.

Despite splits within both conservative and liberal ranks, Republicans largely shaped late twentieth-century educational debates. Democratic aspirants for office realized that conservative times required more moderate approaches to educational and social issues. Reacting to the wholesale rejection of liberalism in presidential elections in the 1980s, a new generation of politicians like Arkansas governor Bill Clinton shifted the Democratic party rightward. A leader in the moderate Democratic Leadership Council, Clinton joined with Republicans late in the decade to frame a series of national goals for America's schools for the year 2000. Less concerned with how to educate poor and minority children well, or with difficult issues related to multiculturalism, economic inequality, and racial injustice than with standards, discipline, competition, testing, and accountability, the goals reflected the broader public mood. While Democrats often resisted endorsing voucher or choice plans that included private and church-related schools, the two major parties had become nearly indistinguishable on most educational issues.

When President Clinton linked the fate of the public schools with the American dream in his 2000 State of the Union address, he tapped deep convictions about education's role in shaping the public good. To most students climbing the educational ladder, however, school seemed like a series of courses, tests, and quizzes on a wide variety of academic subjects. They often perceived the school as a social as much as an academic institution: a place offering sports teams, clubs, and peer groups. As a new century dawned, however, adults continued to argue mostly about how to toughen standards, enhance competition, and tighten discipline in institutions that seem forever in need of reform.

[*See also* Carnegie Foundation for the Advancement of Teaching; Cultural Pluralism; Evolution, Theory of; Federal Government, Executive Branch: Other Departments (Department of Education); Post–Cold War Era.]

• Diane Ravitch and Maris Vinovskis, eds., *Learning from the Past: Historical Perspectives on Current Educational Reforms*, 1994. Wayne J. Urban and Jennings L. Waggoner Jr., *American Education: A History*, 1996.

—William J. Reese

EDWARDS, JONATHAN (1703–1758), pastor, theologian, revivalist. Born in East Windsor, Connecticut, Jonathan Edwards enrolled at Yale College in 1716, where he encountered Newtonian science and the philosophy of John Locke and George Berkeley. Adapting Enlightenment thought to Reformed theology, Edwards set out to defend Protestant orthodoxy from "new schemes" of divinity, in the process formulating a version of Calvinist theology, eventually known as "Edwardseanism," that profoundly influenced American religious life and thought.

After completing his master's studies in 1723 and two years as a college tutor (1724–1726), Edwards joined his grandfather Solomon Stoddard in the ministry at Northampton, Massachusetts. He married Sarah Pierpont, notable for her piety, in 1727; they had eleven children. At Northampton, Edwards established himself as a practitioner and theorist of revival. Focusing his preaching on young people, he oversaw a revival in 1734–1735, which he described in *A Faithful Narrative of the Surprising Work of God* (1737).

Edwards's most famous sermon, *Sinners in the Hands of an Angry God* (1741), delivered during the Great Awakening of the 1740s, was a rhetorical masterpiece illustrating the uncertainty of earthly existence. *Millennialism and apocalypticism pervaded the new religious awakenings, and Edwards, too, saw them as harbingers of the end times. In this vein, he collaborated with Scottish evangelists in establishing a Concert of Prayer movement, which he described in a 1748 work.

In such sophisticated analyses of *revivalism and conversion as *Distinguishing Marks of a Work of the Spirit of God* (1741) and *Some Thoughts Concerning the Present Revival of Religion in New England* (1743), Edwards set forth the "signs" of true conversion. His masterful *Religious Affections* (1746) integrated religious experience in "holy affections," or a combination of intellect, emotion, and practice.

Meanwhile, however, Edwards's pastorate at Northampton was troubled. He criticized the town's business practices and its factional contention, or "party spirit." Following the awakening of 1734–1735, Edwards browbeat his congregants for backsliding so rapidly. Beginning in the early 1740s, a series of events alienated Edwards from his flock, including a controversy over covenant renewal, salary disputes, a mishandled disciplinary case, and paternity cases in which Edwards unsuccessfully tried to force marriages. Edwards's 1748 effort to change the requirements for church admission, which threatened community status and eligibility for baptism, prompted a bitter dispute that ended in his dismissal in 1750.

Long a supporter of missionary effort and an advocate of Christianizing and "civilizing" Indians, Edwards in 1751 became a missionary to Mahican and Mohawk Indians at Stockbridge, Massachusetts. He proved a tireless advocate for the Indians, defending them against English land speculators, presenting their grievances to the Massachusetts legislature, and raising funds for their care and education.

While at Stockbridge, Edwards wrote some of his most important treatises. *Freedom of the Will* (1754), an attempt to reconcile free human agency with God's foreknowledge and predetermination, long remained a central philosophical text. *Original Sin* (1758), a riposte against Enlightenment views of human nature, posited the fallen state of humankind and its utter dependence on divine grace. Two posthumously published works, *The Nature of True Virtue* and *The End for Which God Created the World*, comprised Edwards's ethical thought.

In 1757, Edwards was appointed president of the College of New Jersey at Princeton. However, he died a few months after his arrival from complications of a *smallpox inoculation.

[*See also* Colonial Era; Great Awakening, First and Second; Indian History and Culture: From 1500 to 1800; Missionary Movement, The; New England; Protestantism.]

• Perry Miller, *Jonathan Edwards*, 1949. Patricia J. Tracy, *Jonathan Edwards, Pastor: Religion and Society in Eighteenth-Century Northampton*, 1980. Norman Fiering, *Jonathan Edwards's Moral Thought and Its British Context*, 1981.

—Kenneth P. Minkema

EIGHTEENTH AMENDMENT. The Eighteenth Amendment to the U.S. *Constitution, instituting national prohibition, was born out of temperance reformers' efforts to remove the blight of alcoholic drinks from society, as they maneuvered within the intricacies of American federalism. In the 1880s and 1890s, prohibitionists in dry states struggled against the operations of a federal system that frustrated their efforts. Interstate commerce laws permitted liquor sellers from wet states to sell their products in dry territory. Also, the federal excise tax on liquor fostered a benign view of the liquor business as an economically vital industry. Drys (as prohibition advocates were called) responded by formulating a policy of concurrent state and federal action against liquor. In the twentieth century, the Anti-Saloon League (founded in 1895) carried this strategy to new heights. Through league pressure, prohibition spread to half the population of the United States by 1912, and Congress adopted laws, most notably the 1913 Webb-Kenyon Act, designed to aid prohibition states.

In 1913, the league called for a national constitutional amendment. Exploiting division in their opponents' ranks, drys drafted the bill and pressured Congress to pass it. Capitalizing on concerns associated with *World War I, including German-American dominance of the brewing industry and fears of diminished efficiency through alcohol consumption, the prohibitionists succeeded. Congress passed the amendment in December 1917 and sent it to the states for ratification, which occurred in January 1919. In January 1920 national prohibition went into effect. The amendment banned the manufacture, sale, transportation, and importation of intoxicating liquors within the United States. It granted Congress and the states "concurrent power" of enforcement. The Volstead Act of 1919 set up a specific federal enforcement apparatus.

The Eighteenth Amendment lasted only thirteen years before being repealed in 1933, the only time a constitutional amendment has ever been rescinded. Repeal was brought about by a number of factors, including the failure of enforcement. The concurrent-power provision let the states abdicate their enforcement responsibility to the federal government, which—though it expanded its efforts—could not fully curtail the illegal liquor trade. Although prohibition significantly reduced the amount of liquor being consumed and improved the health of Americans, it also stimulated the growth of *organized crime and corruption. A federal study, the Wickersham Report of 1930, documented the breakdown of enforcement, especially in the larger cities. Changes in cultural attitudes toward liquor consumption further eroded support for the policy. Antiprohibition editorial writers, newspaper cartoonists, and journalists like H. L. *Mencken heaped ridicule on the Eighteenth Amendment and its supporters. Moreover, the strongest organization behind the amendment, the Anti-Saloon League, lost much of its influence, just as lobbying organizations favoring repeal gained strength. Finally, the Great Depression, by destroying the claim that prohibition would assure national prosperity and by carrying predominantly "wet" Democrats into national office, assured the speedy demise of national prohibition.

The Eighteenth Amendment produced long-lasting consequences for American law and constitutionalism. National prohibition stimulated growth in the federal law-enforcement establishment, a process that did not disappear after repeal. The Eighteenth Amendment directly shaped the constitutional system by specifying a seven-year time limit for ratification. Such limits subsequently became customary, allowing amendment opponents to translate delay into defeat.

[*See also* Alcohol and Alcohol Abuse; Brewing and Distilling; Depressions, Economic; Progressive Era; Temperance and Prohibition; Woman's Christian Temperance Union.]

• Charles Merz, *Dry Decade*, 1931. Norman H. Clark, *Deliver Us from Evil*, 1976. Richard F. Hamm, *Shaping the Eighteenth Amendment*, 1995.

—Richard F. Hamm

EINSTEIN, ALBERT (1879–1955), physicist and Nobel Prize laureate. Born in Ulm, Germany, Albert Einstein graduated from the Swiss Federal Polytechnic in 1900 and two years later became a patent examiner in the Swiss Federal Patent Office in Bern. While there he wrote three path-breaking scientific papers in which he developed the theory of special relativity, conclusively demonstrated the existence of atoms, and presented the law of the photoelectric effect, the last of which brought him the Nobel Prize in Physics for 1921. He received his first academic appointment in 1909 in Zurich. Just before the outbreak of *World War I he moved to Berlin, where he assumed a research professorship without teaching obligations in the Prussian Academy of Sciences. In 1919, confirmation of his most lasting achievement—the theory of general relativity—granted him wide popular recognition and made him a media celebrity. This attention also gave him an international platform for his social concerns and established him as a moral arbiter of his age. Increasingly interested in political affairs after the war, he made his first trip to the United States in 1921 with Chaim Weizmann to raise money for the creation of the Hebrew University in Palestine.

In the fall of 1933, as Adolf Hitler gained power in Germany, Einstein took a position at the Institute for Advanced Study in Princeton, New Jersey, remaining in the United States for the rest of his life. Einstein's August 1939 letter to President Franklin Delano *Roosevelt, drafted by the Hungarian-born émigré physicist Leo Szilard, describing the military implications of recent developments in physics, eventually led to the establishment of the *Manhattan Project and U.S. development of the atomic bomb.

Becoming a U.S. citizen in 1940 (while also retaining Swiss citizenship), Einstein devoted himself to the search for a unified field theory, but also increasingly spoke out on public issues. Einstein retained an abiding commitment to establishing and maintaining a homeland for Jews, with an emphasis on equality of rights between Jews and Arabs. Like many fellow scientists, he feared a nuclear arms race after *World War II. He initially advocated a world government, and thereafter repeatedly supported the cause of disarmament and world peace. He invariably allied himself with those who sought legal protections for the well-being and civil rights of all.

[*See also* Internationalism; Nuclear Weapons; Peace Movements; Physical Sciences; Science: From 1914 to 1945; Science: Since 1945.]

• Alan J. Friedman and Carol C. Donley, *Einstein as Myth and Muse, 1985.* Otto Nathan and Heinz Norden, eds., *Einstein on Peace, 1960.* Jamie Sayen, *Einstein in America: The Scientist's Conscience in the Age of Hitler and Hiroshima*, 1985. Don Howard and John Stachel, eds., *Einstein and the History of General Relativity*, 1989.

—Robert J. Schulmann

EISENHOWER, DWIGHT D. (1890–1969), U.S. army general, Supreme Commander of Allied Forces in Europe during *World War II, and thirty-fourth president of the United States. Dwight David Eisenhower was born in Denison, Texas, but spent his youth in Abilene, Kansas. After high school he spent two years working before entering West Point, from which he was commissioned in 1915. The following year he married Mamie Doud; they had one son, John.

Eisenhower remained in the United States during *World War I. In the 1920s he served in Panama and attended both the General Staff School at Fort Leavenworth, Kansas, and the Army War College in Carlisle, Pennsylvania. From 1930 to 1935, he was assistant secretary of war and then chief of staff to General Douglas *MacArthur in Washington, D.C. In 1936 he accompanied MacArthur to the *Philippines, but returned to America when war broke out in Europe in 1939.

Eisenhower rose meteorically during World War II. His performance in the 1941 Louisiana Maneuvers earned him a summons to Washington to assist Army Chief of Staff George *Marshall. In 1942 he was given command of American and Allied forces in North Africa; his rout of General Erwin Rommel's forces led President Franklin Delano *Roosevelt to select him to lead the Allied invasion of Normandy (Operation Overlord). Eisenhower's key decision—to invade on 6 June 1944 (*D-Day) despite bad weather—proved critical to the operation's success. Although he was criticized by second-guessers, most notably for allowing Russian troops to liberate Berlin, his strategic decisions have withstood retrospective scrutiny.

After brief service as army chief of staff, Eisenhower returned to civilian life in 1948 as president of Columbia University. In 1951, President Harry S. *Truman appointed him as commander of the *North Atlantic Treaty Organization (NATO) forces in Europe. A year later, moderate Republicans successfully pressed Eisenhower to run in the New Hampshire Republican presidential primary; he did well there and in other primaries. At the *Republican party convention in July, his forces outmaneuvered those of Senator Robert *Taft to secure the nomination, thus launching the "nonpolitical" general's political career. With Senator Richard M. *Nixon as his vice presidential running-mate, he easily defeated Democrat Adlai *Stevenson in the general election.

As president, Eisenhower was less conservative than liberals feared, but more so than moderates hoped. A committed internationalist, he supported the *United Nations and engaged in a series of historic summit meetings with Soviet leaders. His differences with extreme conservatives included opposition to the communist-baiting Wisconsin senator Joseph *McCarthy. Although criticized at the time for his seemingly passive role, Eisenhower worked subtly to undermine McCarthy even while remaining publicly neutral. In foreign policy, he successfully brokered an armistice ending the *Korean War, and presided over a military build-up (mostly airpower and nuclear weaponry) while holding the federal budget virtually constant. He refused to send American troops to aid the 1956 Hungarian uprising against Soviet military rule, but acted decisively in invading Lebanon in 1958 to stabilize its prowestern government. His appeal across the political spectrum was reflected in his sweeping reelection in 1956, again defeating Stevenson.

Eisenhower sought to moderate American tendencies to over-militarize the *Cold War, defying public pressures to build up U.S. defenses after the Soviets launched the world's first space satellite, *Sputnik*, in October 1957. In domestic policy, he steered a moderately conservative course, opposing public power and direct support for farmers and labor, while compromising with a Democratic Congress. Although cool to the *civil rights movement, he did send federal troops to Arkansas in 1957 when Governor Orval Faubus defined a court order to integrate a Little Rock high school. A dramatic confrontation with the Soviets over the downing of an American surveillance (U–2) plane in 1960 only increased Eisenhower's popularity. His January 1961 farewell address, warning against the "military-industrial complex," proved to be one of his more enduring political contributions.

After leaving the White House, Eisenhower avoided partisan

activities. In 1964 he disappointed Republican moderates by refusing until the last minute to support their efforts to stave off Barry *Goldwater's presidential nomination.

A major figure of the twentieth century, Eisenhower was one of those rare American presidents whose reputation rests more on his prepresidential achievements than on his activities as president or afterward. His strategic decisions and political acumen are widely viewed as crucial to Allied victory in World War II. Still, his accomplishments as president were significant. As the first Republican to occupy the White House after the New Deal, he helped to legitimize the liberal political revolution it represented. He also introduced a staff system to the White House that became the model for succeeding presidents. Finally, the peace (after Korea), prosperity, and balanced federal budgets that characterized his White House years underscore the success of his moderate leadership.

[*See also* Conservatism; Federal Government, Executive Branch: The Presidency; Fifties, The; Foreign Relations; Liberalism; Military Service Academies; Military, The; New Deal Era, The; Nuclear Strategy; Nuclear Weapons; Space Program.]

• Piers Brendon, *Ike: The Life and Times of Dwight D. Eisenhower*, 1987. Stephen E. Ambrose, *Eisenhower: Soldier and President*, 1990.

—Gary W. Reichard

EISENHOWER DOCTRINE (1957). The Eisenhower Doctrine pledged that the United States would distribute economic and military aid and, if necessary, use military force to contain communism in the Middle East. President Dwight D. *Eisenhower proposed the doctrine in January 1957. Congress approved it in March despite misgivings about the administration's perspective on the Middle East, the preservation of Israeli interests under the doctrine, and the surrender of congressional prerogatives to the executive branch.

The doctrine resulted directly from the Suez War of late 1956. The Anglo-French-Israeli military assault on Egypt discredited Britain and France, traditional protectors of western interests in the Middle East; elevated the prestige of Egyptian Premier Gamal Abdel Nasser; and raised the specter in U.S. minds of Soviet intrusion into the region. The remaining pro-western rulers of the Middle East seemed vulnerable to Nasserist uprisings and Soviet influence. U.S. officials resolved to fill the power vacuum in the Middle East before the Soviets did.

Although never formally invoked, the Eisenhower Doctrine guided U.S. policy in three controversies. In spring 1957, Eisenhower provided economic aid to Jordan and dispatched the U.S. Sixth Fleet to the eastern Mediterranean to help Jordan's King Hussein survive a rebellion by army officers oriented toward Nasser. To counter growing Soviet influence in Syria, the United States sent arms to neighboring regimes and encouraged Turkey to concentrate forces on the Syrian border, prompting Syria to join Egypt in forming the United Arab Republic in January 1958. When a coup d'état in Baghdad in July 1958 threatened to spark revolution in Lebanon and Jordan, Eisenhower ordered U.S. soldiers to occupy Beirut and transport British paratroopers to Amman, the Jordanian capital.

By late 1958, officials in Washington realized that their resistance to Arab nationalism had failed to guarantee western interests in the region. The Eisenhower Doctrine faded as the administration adopted a policy that was more accommodating to nationalism.

[*See also* Cold War; Containment; Foreign Relations: U.S. Relations with the Middle East.]

• David W. Lesch, *Syria and the United States: Eisenhower's Cold War in the Middle East*, 1992. Irene L. Gendzier, *Notes from the Minefield: United States Intervention in Lebanon and the Middle East, 1945–1958*, 1997.

—Peter L. Hahn

ELECTORAL COLLEGE. The framers of the *Constitution, after rejecting proposals to have the president elected by Congress or by popular vote, contrived a novel and intricate alternative. Each state would appoint electors equal in number to its representation in Congress. On a specified day, the electors would meet in their respective states (not in a national "electoral college") and each would vote for two individuals for president. The compiled vote would be counted by the president of the Senate in the presence of the two houses of Congress. The candidate with the greatest number of votes (provided this constituted a majority) would become president. The person with the second highest vote would be vice president. If no individual obtained a majority, the Constitution provided for a contingent election by the House of Representatives, with each state delegation casting a single vote. Such elections occurred in 1801 and 1825.

The framers believed that they had designed a procedure that would be immune to politicization, but the rise of *political parties by the late 1790s destroyed that illusion. The electors, rather than acting independently, now voted on the basis of their party affiliations. It then became apparent that if all the electors of the majority party voted for the same two persons, the result would be a tie and the election would be thrown into the House of Representatives. To address this problem, the Twelfth Amendment was adopted in 1804. It required that the electors designate one of their two votes for president and the other for vice president. This amendment proved crucial to the maintenance of the two-party system.

Until 1824, electors were chosen in most states either by the legislature or by popular vote within districts. Least common, initially, was the general-ticket mode, in which party-nominated slates of electors were presented to the voters, thus enabling the majority party to win all of a state's electoral vote. This "winner-take-all" plan gained in favor and was adopted by 1836 in all states except South Carolina, which did not fall into line until 1868.

The late twentieth century saw support for abolishing the Electoral College, but opponents of such change warned that it would violate the "federative principle" in the Constitution. Criticism of the Electoral College increased, however, after the 2000 election, in which Democrat Al Gore won the popular vote, but Republican George W. Bush, after a fierce legal battle of the Florida outcome, carried the Electoral College.

[*See also* Constitutional Convention of 1787; Early Republic, Era of the; Federal Government, Executive Branch: Overview; Federal Government, Executive Branch: The Presidency; Federal Government, Legislative Branch.]

• Neil R. Pierce and Lawrence D. Longley, *The People's President: The Electoral College in American History and the Direct Vote Alternative*, rev. ed., 1981.

—Richard P. McCormick

ELECTRICAL INDUSTRY. By producing cheap power, the electrical industry contributed to America's emergence as an industrial leader and helped reshape American culture, powering the tools and appliances used in daily life. Building on Allessandro Volta's development of the battery in 1800 and Joseph *Henry's work on electromagnets, Samuel F. B. *Morse devised the first commercial application of electricity, the *telegraph. During the 1850s, as telegraph lines spread widely, entrepreneurs in *Philadelphia and *Boston produced telegraph equipment. Exploiting Michael Faraday's 1830 invention of the generator, Americans also pioneered in electrical lighting. Charles Brush's direct-current (DC) generator (1876) powered arc lights that illuminated streets, factories, and stores. In 1879 the California Electric Light Company in *San Francisco set up the first central utility station. Thomas *Edison, recognizing customers' desire for electric lighting similar to existing gas lights, invented in 1879 an incandescent lamp that produced light when current passed through a high-resistance filament in a vacuum. Edison's first DC central station opened in Manhattan in 1882. Inventors also used electricity to power streetcars. Charles J. Van De Poele introduced the overhead trolley, while Frank J. Sprague installed the first successful streetcar line involving an electrified third rail in Richmond, Virginia, in 1886.

As *Gilded-Age *industrialization and *urbanization increased demand for electric lighting and streetcars, electrical-equipment firms boomed, employing thousands of managers, engineers, and workers. Thanks to an AC motor invented in 1887 by Nikola Tesla (1856–1943), electricity soon replaced steam engines and waterwheels in factories. By 1890, Edison General Electric, the Westinghouse Electric and Manufacturing Company founded by George *Westinghouse, and the Thomson-Houston Electric Company were the key players. Westinghouse aggressively promoted the use of alternating-current (AC), while Thomson-Houston assisted fledgling utilities to fund power stations. AC, which could serve more customers over a wider area, soon became the industry standard. After Edison GE and Thomson-Houston merged in 1892 to form the General Electric Company, the new firm dominated in finance, incandescent lamp manufacture, and the manufacture of steam turbines to power generators. In 1896, the first *hydroelectric power station, at *Niagara Falls delivered abundant electricity to industries in Buffalo, twenty-five miles away, demonstrating AC's full potential.

By 1900 the basic pattern of the twentieth-century electrical industry was established, with two major firms manufacturing equipment used by investor-owned utilities to generate and distribute power. Seeking economies of scale, electrical utilities built ever-larger networks. Samuel *Insull of Chicago's Commonwealth Edison demonstrated how a utility could increase profitability by regional expansion and diversification. Soon Commonwealth Edison was the *Middle West's sole supplier of electricity. To protect his monopoly, Insull persuaded the Illinois legislature to create a utilities regulatory commission. As other states followed suit, utilities secured their monopolies by ceding rate-setting authority to the state.

After greatly expanding generating capacity during *World War I, the electrical industry in the 1920s campaigned to increase domestic consumption. Many households in this decade acquired electric stoves, washing machines, irons, *radios, and vacuum cleaners. The New Deal, in turn, heavily promoted electrification through the *Tennessee Valley Authority, the Rural Electrification Administration, and large-scale hydroelectric dam projects in the *West. Generating capacity further increased during *World War II, and the 1950s saw renewed efforts by the electrical industry and the government to stimulate domestic consumption. Flourescent lighting and the disappearance of electric streetcars reduced demand, but air conditioning added to summertime consumption. Seeking lower costs, electrical utilities adopted nuclear reactor technology; Westinghouse opened the first *nuclear power plant at Shippingport, Pennsylvania, in 1959. Predictions that electricity would soon be "too cheap to meter" went unfulfilled, however. Nuclear-power plants proved not only expensive to build but difficult to manage and prone to dangerous accidents. The Arab oil embargo of 1973–1974 further increased utilities' fuel costs, driving up consumer rates.

Yet consumer demand for electricity increased as Americans grew more dependent on reliable electric power to heat and cool buildings, control machinery, operate appliances and *computers, and supply indoor and outdoor *illumination. When parts of the East Coast suffered a major blackout in 1964, daily life briefly came to a near-halt. In response to rising demand, utilities encouraged conservation, and the federal and state governments established programs to promote wind, water, and solar power.

Deregulation of the electrical industry in the 1990s freed many utilities to buy and sell power on the open market. Where single utilities once held a monopoly, some states permitted companies to compete and customers to choose their electricity supplier. While some observers predicted that this would lower energy prices, others warned that deregulation threatened reliability. Whether the United States in an era of deregulation would continue to enjoy the cheap, reliable power essential to modern life remained to be seen as the twentieth century ended.

[*See also* Electricity and Electrification; Energy Crisis of the 1970s; Engineering; New Deal Era, The; Rural Life; Steam Power; Technology; Twenties, The.]

• Malcolm MacLaren, *The Rise of the Electrical Industry During the 19th Century,* 1943. Thomas Parke Hughes, *Networks of Power: The Electrification of Society, 1880–1920,* 1983. Richard F. Hirsh, *Technology and Transformation in the American Electric Utility Industry,* 1989. David E. Nye, *Electrifying America: Social Meaning of a New Technology,* 1990. James E. Brittain, *Alexanderson: Pioneer in American Electrical Engineering,* 1992. Mark H. Rose, *Cities of Light and Heat: Domesticating Gas and Electricity in American Homes,* 1995.

—W. Bernard Carlson

ELECTRICITY AND ELECTRIFICATION. Electricity—so named by the Englishman William Gilbert around 1600—was known since ancient times in the form of static electricity, which can be induced by rubbing amber, for example. From the seventeenth century onward, such scientists as Robert Boyle, Henry Cavendish, Alessandro Volta, G. S. Ohm, and the American Benjamin *Franklin added to electrical knowledge. Franklin, whose *Experiments and Observations on Electricity* (1751–1753) won international attention, is best remembered for his 1752 experiment with a kite and a key in a thunderstorm, which demonstrated that lightning is an electrical discharge. By the early nineteenth century, Michael Faraday and other scientists were developing techniques of generating electricity. Working independently of Faraday, the American Joseph *Henry began research on electromagnetism in 1827. Henry constructed an electromagnetic motor in 1829 and later discovered electrical induction, crucial to generating power, and demonstrated the oscillatory nature of electrical discharges.

Practical applications came slowly and piecemeal, long before anyone conceived of electrification as a universalizing process.

Most early electrical technologies, including fire-alarm systems, railway signaling, burglar alarms, doorbells, servant-calling systems, and the *telephone, were modifications of the *telegraph (1838). These devices relied on batteries to supply a modest direct current. A much more powerful current was needed for practical lighting, *heating, electroplating, and electric motors. Such applications developed only after about 1875, when improved generators and dynamos became available. After 1878 arc lighting, a powerful but crude form of *illumination, drew crowds to demonstrations in city centers and expositions. Large cities quickly adopted lights for streets and public places such as theaters and *department stores. Once Thomas *Edison's firm installed incandescent lighting systems across the country, beginning in *New York City in 1881, however, most indoor sites and street-lighting companies chose his technology. Edison and his assistants developed not only a practical incandescent lightbulb (1879), but the now familiar system of wiring, wall switches, sockets, meters, insulated transmission lines, and central power plants. Edison designed this distribution system to compete with gaslight on price, while offering brighter and safer *illumination. Rapidly adopted by the wealthy for fashionable indoor venues, including theaters, clubs, expensive homes, and the *New York Stock Exchange electric lighting became a prestigious and sought-after form of illumination.

Initially electrical technology had a separate energy source, as well as different financial backers. Lighting utilities, factories, and streetcar lines maintained their own power plants and delivery systems, with no uniform standards for wiring or current. The private systems installed by hotels, *skyscrapers, and large private homes in the 1880s were incompatible with one another, but they did have the advantage of not requiring overhead wires, which would soon become so numerous in the major cities as to constitute a public nuisance) or costly underground conduits. This pattern of development merely continued the earlier piecemeal commercialization of electricity.

The *electrical industry was the most dynamic sector of the economy between 1875 and 1900, growing into a $200-million-a-year industry with the backing of farsighted investors like J. P. *Morgan, who financed Edison's work. Once commercial development began, a flurry of mergers reduced the field from fifteen competitors in 1885 to only General Electric and Westinghouse in 1892. *Railroads, once America's largest corporations, were now a mature industry, in contrast to the rapidly expanding electric traction companies, local utilities, and equipment manufacturers that collectively exemplified the spread of managerial capitalism (as opposed to partnerships and family firms). From its inception, the electrical industry also relied heavily on scientific research and development, a fact formalized when General Electric founded the first corporate *research laboratory in 1900.

Electric trolleys, eagerly sought by burgeoning cities to replace dirty, slow horsecars, became practical after 1887, when Frank Sprague's new motor proved itself in hilly Richmond, Virginia. By 1890, two hundred cities had ordered similar systems. By 1902, two billion dollars had been invested in electric railways, and a typical urban family of four spent about fifty dollars a year on fares.

Electricity spread into factories with equal speed, starting with lighting in textile and flour mills. From a worker's point of view, incandescent lighting improved visibility and reduced pollution and the danger of fire, but it also made possible round-the-clock shifts. Furthermore, as electric motors and cranes provided more horsepower for production, they brought radical changes in the construction and layout of factories, most strikingly in Henry *Ford's assembly line (1912), an innovation partly anticipated by Edison's experiments with automating iron mining in the 1890s. The assembly line was literally impossible in any complex industry before electricity freed machines from fixed, steam-driven overhead drive shafts.

As electrical systems spread throughout the industrial, commercial, and residential worlds, utilities improved generating technologies and achieved economies of scale. They began to sell current and service so cheaply that the myriad small plants could no longer compete. Samuel *Insull of *Chicago early grasped the importance of consolidating power production and maximizing consumption. Insull convinced traction companies and factories to abandon their power plants and to purchase electricity from him. Through astute marketing he created one of the world's largest electrical utilities. As others copied his methods, holding companies created regional power companies and linked the many local systems into a national power grid. Private companies proved more agile in the consolidation process, for they possessed readier access to capital and had fewer jurisdictional problems than government-run utilities, and by the 1920s they owned all but a fraction of national generating capacity.

The spread of electrification, between the 1880s and the 1940s, first in cities and towns and then in rural areas, provided a major economic stimulus and transformed everyday life in the 1920s and beyond. As an array of electric appliances, from fans and mixers to vacuum cleaners, refrigerators, and washing machines, eased domestic labor for middle-class housewives, a different form of electric power, the storage battery, was crucial to automotive technology. Electricity made possible not only the *automotive and *aviation industries, but also the new mass media—*radio, *films, and recordings—as well as night *baseball, introduced in Cincinnati, Ohio, in 1935.

During the Depression of the 1930s, the federal government promoted public utilities, in part to create a yardstick to measure the price and performance of private power companies. It built a system of dams on the Tennessee River, administered by the *Tennessee Valley Authority (TVA), which sold power to rural cooperatives, as well as systems of dams on the Colorado and Columbia Rivers. Because private power had generally ignored farmers, only 10 percent of whom had electricity as late as 1935, President Franklin Delano *Roosevelt in 1935 established the Rural Electrification Administration (REA) to bring power to this neglected sector of the nation. Rural electrification spread comparatively slowly in the *South and *Middle West, where customers were widely dispersed, but more rapidly in the arid *West, where farmers wanted electric pumps for irrigation, and in areas served by interurban trolleys. The REA and TVA organized cooperatives and made available loans and technical expertise. By 1945, thanks to the New Deal, most of America was electrified. Electricity had important military applications as well, playing a crucial role in *World War II and the *Cold War era, for example, in the development of radar, rocketry, and the mainframe *computers essential to ballistic missiles and space technology.

Electric lighting dominated public spaces and changed the culture in ways that went far beyond the functional. American cities became the most intensively lighted in the world, not least because of the spread of electric *advertising. Spurred by the marketing campaigns of Westinghouse, General Electric, and the utilities, the illuminated skyline became a source of civic pride. Even small cities aspired to emulate New York City's "Great White Way," where millions of flashing bulbs in Times Square and the theater district created a scintillating artificial environment. Nightlife expanded as hundreds of brightly lit *amusement parks emerged as early as the 1890s, followed by stadiums and other outdoor venues.

As early as 1903, American cities were far more brightly lit than their European counterparts; Chicago, New York, and *Boston had three to five times as many electric lights per inhabitant as Paris, London, and Berlin. This reflected more than prosperity and wealth. Levels and methods of lighting varied from culture to culture, and what was considered dramatic and necessary in the United States often seemed a violation of tradition elsewhere. Many European communities continued throughout the twentieth century to resist electric signs and spectacular advertising displays. At the 1994 Winter Olympics in Lillehammer, Norway, for example, the city council refused corporate sponsors the right to erect illuminated signs.

Once American families acquired electrical lighting, they had less reason to cluster at night around the hearth, giving rise to a pattern of dispersed privacy. With power available at the flick of a switch, consumers ceased to associate lighting with physical *work such as hauling wood and ashes or cleaning lamps. Electricity also extended the range of usable space. Domestic activity after sunset was no longer confined to the hearth and the range of the kerosene lamp. In commerce, immense department stores, office buildings, and eventually malls could be built with adequate illumination far from any natural-light source.

In industry, while the flexibility of electrical power permitted the rearrangement of the work flow, the expansion of the electrical grid made it possible to locate a factory virtually anywhere, without regard for proximity to coal supplies or water power. Further, because not only factories, but also shops, homes, and businesses could spring up wherever the grid reached, electrification facilitated urban deconcentration. By the 1930s this trend was being assisted by the development of air-conditioning and climate control, and later by computers and the electrical transmission of information.

But if electrification homogenized space, delivering light, power, climate control, and information to any site, it also facilitated the concentration of people in cities. Indeed, night satellite photographs of the United States reveal the location of thousands of cities as intense blobs of light. Electricity, a scientific curiosity in 1800 and still a novelty for the rich in 1880, had become indispensable by the mid–twentieth century and beyond.

[*See also* Agriculture: The "Golden Age" (1890s–1920); Agriculture: Since 1920; Business Cycle; Consumer Culture; Dams and Hydraulic Engineering; Factory System; Gilded Age; Industrialization; Leisure; Mass Production; New Deal Era, The; Progressive Era; Shopping Centers and Malls; Twenties, The; Urbanization.]

• Thomas P. Hughes. *Networks of Power: Electrification in Western Society, 1880–1930,* 1983. Richard Rudolph and Scott Ridley, *Power Struggle,* 1986. David E. Nye, *Electrifying America: Social Meanings of a New Technology, 1880–1940,* 1990. Harold L. Platt, *The Electric City: Energy and the Growth of the Chicago Area, 1880–1930,* 1991. Mark H. Rose, *Cities of Light and Heat: Domesticating Gas and Electricity in Urban America,* 1995. Ronald C. Tobey, *Technology as Freedom: The New Deal and the Electrical Modernization of the Home,* 1996.

—David E. Nye

ELECTRIC LIGHT. *See* Edison, Thomas; Electrical Industry; Electricity and Electrifiction; Illumination.

ELIOT, CHARLES WILLIAM (1834–1926), president of Harvard University (1869–1909). Charles William Eliot sprang from *Boston Brahmin and Unitarian family roots. Graduating from Harvard in 1853, he taught chemistry there from 1854 to 1863, and then at the Massachusetts Institute of Technology from 1865 until elected Harvard's president four years later. His inaugural promise to innovate, while controversial, soon launched Harvard on the trajectory that would make it the nation's leading private university. Eliot's reforms aimed at turning the undergraduate college into a vital core surrounded by a growing cluster of professional graduate schools whose quality was ensured by his insistence on the A.B. degree as a credential for admission. For undergraduates he introduced his once notorious elective system, which gradually eliminated required courses in mathematics, *science, and classical languages until only English and a modern language requirement remained. This freed students to pursue personal academic interests and led, in turn, to a proliferation of advanced courses taught by professors in their special zones of expertise. To lure gifted scholars to the faculty, Eliot promoted research sabbaticals and ample salaries, but insisted that faculty in the arts and sciences teach undergraduates as well as graduate students. The scrapping of required chapel to secularize college life and widening women's access to Harvard, through the "Annex" that became Radcliffe College in 1894, were other changes under Eliot. His overarching goal was the preparation of the liberally educated expert, to guide contemporary American society and its government toward a more progressive future.

[*See also* Education: Collegiate Education; Education: Rise of the University; Professionalization; Secularization; Unitarianism and Universalism.]

• Hugh Hawkins, *Between Harvard and America: The Educational Leadership of Charles W. Eliot,* 1972.

—Geoffrey Blodgett

ELKINS ACT. *See* Antitrust Legislation.

ELLINGTON, EDWARD ("DUKE") (1899–1974), composer, bandleader, pianist. Born in *Washington, D.C., Duke Ellington learned to play *jazz in that city's saloons and clubs. In 1923 he moved to *New York City, where in 1927 his band became the house band at Harlem's Cotton Club. Some of Ellington's best-known songs, such as "East St. Louis Toodle-Oo," came from Cotton Club shows. Ellington and his band toured internationally in the 1930s, but periodically returned to the Cotton Club.

Beginning in the 1930s, Ellington traced the history of African-American life in a series of longer compositions, culminating in a 1943 suite entitled "Black, Brown, and Beige." Presented as a jazz concert in New York's Carnegie Hall, it showed Ellington's growing interest in classical music. Unlike Benny *Goodman, who played jazz and classical music separately, Ellington created an oeuvre combining classical and jazz influences.

Ellington wrote music to fit his players' talents and they in turn improvised on his compositions. Billy Strayhorn became his best-known collaborator and Ellington's son Mercer cowrote several numbers. Strayhorn's "Take the 'A' Train" (1941) became the band's theme. The post–World War II era that nearly wiped out big bands also affected Ellington. Like Ella *Fitzgerald, Ellington sold records in the 1960s by rerecording his earlier hits and covering other musicians' songs. He also wrote new long-form compositions, again toured internationally, and composed religious music. Ellington won his greatest recognition as a composer during the last decade of his life and posthumously, as his work contributed to the growing acceptance of jazz as a serious musical idiom.

[*See also* Harlem Renaissance; Music: Classical Music; Music: Popular Music.]

• John Edward Hasse, *Beyond Category: The Life and Genius of Duke Ellington,* 1993. Mark Tucker, ed., *The Duke Ellington Reader,* 1993.

—Jonathan Z. S. Pollack

ELLIS ISLAND served as the entry point for millions of immigrants to the United States. Situated in upper New York Bay, the island has had various names, including Gibbet Island, recalling its history as an execution site where pirates were hanged as late as the 1850s. The present name comes from Samuel Ellis, a butcher who owned it in the 1780s. *New York City ceded ownership to the state in 1794, which transferred it to the federal government in 1800. The city, however, retained jurisdiction for legal and tax purposes.

Enlarged to some twenty-seven acres, Ellis Island opened as an *immigration facility on 1 January 1892. Some 446,000 immigrants arrived that year. With the twelve million who followed came overcrowding, deterioration, and *public-health problems. Ellis Island also housed a hospital for immigrants detained for medical reasons. For those denied entry, Ellis became an "Island of Tears." During *World War II it was an enemy-alien detention facility. The immigration center briefly reopened after the war, but closed permanently in 1954 and was declared surplus property in 1955. It reopened in 1965 as a museum of immigration history administered by the National Park Service as part of the *Statue of Liberty National Monument.

Ellis Island lies between New York and New Jersey, and the two states long quarreled over it. In 1834, Congress approved a compact that granted New York jurisdiction over Ellis Island but gave New Jersey the submerged land west of the island. New Jersey revived its claim in the 1960s, arguing that its underwater land had subsequently been drained and made part of the island proper. Upholding this claim in 1998, the U.S. *Supreme Court divided Ellis Island between the two states.

[*See also* National Park System.]

• Thomas Monroe Pitkin, *Keepers of the State: A History of Ellis Island,* 1975. Barbara Benton, *Ellis Island, A Pictorial History,* 1985.

—Leo Hershkowitz

ELLISON, RALPH (1914–1994), novelist and essayist. Born in Oklahoma City, the grandson of slaves, Ralph Waldo Ellison played trumpet as a youth and later studied composition at Tuskegee Institution. In 1936, after his junior year there, he moved to *New York City to study sculpture. A friendship with Richard *Wright turned him to writing. From 1938 to *World War II he worked on the *Works Progress Administration's Federal Writers' Project and contributed reviews, essays, and short fiction to *New Masses, The Negro Quarterly* (which he edited for a time), and other periodicals. After service in the Merchant Marine (1942–1945), he held various jobs, including work as a freelance photographer. After a brief first marriage, he married Fanny McConnell in 1946; for more than forty years, they lived in Harlem.

Ellison's novel *Invisible Man* (1952) won the National Book Award and has since grown in critical esteem and popularity. Displaying a mastery of language, symbolism, and allegory, and a humane sensibility, it brilliantly probes the *African-American experience and American racial dynamics. After a fellowship at the American Academy in Rome (1955–1957), Ellison taught and lectured at several institutions, including Bard College, Yale, and Harvard. Excerpts from his unfinished second novel appeared in various literary magazines in the 1960s, and a version was published posthumously in 1999 as *Juneteenth*. Ellison's essays and interviews appeared in *Shadow and Act* (1964), *Going to the Territory* (1986), and the posthumous *Collected Essays* (1995) and his short fiction in *Flying Home and Other Stories* (1996).

Stubbornly committed to a vision of American life and culture rooted in complexity, diversity, and possibility, Ellison criticized some African Americans' tendencies to view their "relationship to American literature in a negative way." As a novelist, he said, he felt the same "personal responsibility for democracy" that he found in "our classic 19th-century novels." He received the Presidential Medal of Freedom in 1969.

• Kimberly W. Benston, ed., *Speaking for You: The Vision of Ralph Ellison*, 1987. Mark Busby, *Ralph Ellison*, 1992. Ralph Ellison, *The Collected Essays of Ralph Ellison*, ed. John F. Callahan, 1995. Ralph Ellison, *Conversations with Ralph Ellison*, eds. Maryemma Graham and Amritjit Singh, 1995.

—John F. Callahan

EMANCIPATION PROCLAMATION (1863). Issued by President Abraham *Lincoln on 1 January 1863, the Emancipation Proclamation declared that all slaves, in states or portions of states in rebellion against the United States, "are and henceforward shall be free." The president thus freed slaves in Arkansas, Texas, Mississippi, Alabama, Florida, Georgia, South Carolina, North Carolina, and parts of Virginia and Louisiana. Lincoln exempted those states remaining loyal to the Union, such as Maryland, and portions of Confederate states occupied by U.S. troops. Lincoln justified the proclamation by citing military necessity.

The proclamation was the culmination of a gradual process. Although Lincoln had initially declared the preservation of the Union, and not the abolition of *slavery, as his principal purpose in fighting the *Civil War, the two goals had become intertwined as the conflict progressed. Northerners were divided over the issue of slavery, and many were hostile to fighting a war on behalf of slaves. Lincoln also knew that any hope of compromise with the Confederacy ruled out the abolition of slavery as a war aim. He also feared that slave-holding states still loyal to the Union would secede if slavery were threatened. But the course of war determined Lincoln's actions and ensured that the abolition of slavery would become a central focus of the conflict.

Slaves, free blacks, and white abolitionists had, of course, immediately recognized the war's potential to end slavery. As the Union army and navy moved into portions of the *South, such as the Sea Islands of South Carolina, slaves sought freedom behind Union lines. In May 1861, General Benjamin F. Butler declared slaves who fled to the Union army headquartered at Fortress Monroe, Virginia, to be contraband of war—that is, enemy property open to confiscation by Union troops. Lincoln signed this policy into law as the First Confiscation Act on 6 August 1861. Other moves toward ending slavery followed. In April 1862, Republicans in Congress abolished slavery in the District of Columbia and in the territories. The Second Confiscation Act, passed 17 July 1862, freed all rebel-owned slaves who came behind Union lines, while the Militia Act of the same date freed slaves employed by the military. Lincoln and his military commanders recognized that undermining slavery would ultimately weaken the Confederacy and strengthen the Union. Military losses and the knowledge that reconciliation was unlikely also encouraged Lincoln to move toward emancipation. But his advisers encouraged him to refrain from issuing any proclamation until after a Union victory. On 22 September 1862, five days after Robert E. *Lee's army withdrew following the Battle of *Antietam, Lincoln released a preliminary proclamation announcing his intentions to free slaves in rebellious states on 1 January.

A crucial difference between the preliminary and the final proclamation was the latter's silence on the question of colonization—the repatriation of freed slaves to Africa. In the preliminary proclamation, Lincoln asserted his commitment to colonization, a measure that would appease loyal Southerners and Northerners who feared competition from free black labor. Lincoln's decision not to include a plan of colonization in the final proclamation bolstered its radical potential. In addition to freeing slaves in rebel states and recommending that able-bodied freedmen be "received into the armed service," Lincoln advised former slaves to immediately become free laborers, by working "faithfully for reasonable wages."

The Emancipation Proclamation had several important consequences. While freeing only slaves in areas outside the control of the federal government, it tied the abolition of slavery to the defeat of the Confederacy and ensured that northern victory would mean a reconstruction of southern society and economy. Before the Emancipation Proclamation, African American men and women had been employed by the Union army as servants, teamsters, laborers, scouts, cooks, and laundry workers. Although the Proclamations did not directly state that African American soldiers would serve in combat, former slaves and their allies quickly interpreted it this way. Approximately 190,000 black men would serve in the army and navy during the Civil War. The enlistment of *African Americans facilitated the abolition of slavery in border states and throughout the South. As black soldiers demonstrated their courage at Port Hudson, Louisiana; Milliken's Bend, Louisiana; and Fort Wagner, South Carolina, they gained northern respect and support for emancipation increased. In joining the Union army or seeking its protection, former slaves denied the Confederacy their labor, thereby hastening the destruction of slavery.

Providing a precedent for the *Reconstruction Era amendments to the *Constitution, especially the Thirteenth Amendment abolishing slavery, the Emancipation Proclamation revealed what slaves had known from the beginning: Slavery was the central issue of the Civil War.

[*See also* Antislavery; Colonization Movement, African; Confederate States of America.]

• Leon F. Litwack, *Been in the Storm So Long: The Aftermath of Slavery*, 1980. Eric Foner, *Reconstruction: America's Unfinished Revolution, 1863–1877*, 1988. James M. McPherson, *Battle Cry of Freedom: The Civil War Era*, 1988. Benjamin Quarles, *Lincoln and the Negro*, 1991. Ira Berlin, Barbara J. Fields, Steven F. Miller, Joseph P. Reidy, and Leslie Rowland, *Slaves No More: Three Essays on Emancipation and the Civil War*, 1992. John Hope Franklin, *The Emancipation Proclamation*, 1995.

—Carol Faulkner

EMBARGO ACTS. By 1807 the protracted war between Britain and Napoleonic France had reached a stalemate. The British navy had destroyed the Spanish and French fleets in October 1805, giving Britain control of the sea. But France dominated the European continent following Napoleon's victories over Austria, Prussia, and Russia. Without a military option, each side sought to starve the other into submission by depriving it of neutral trade. In this new war of Napoleonic Decrees and British Orders-in-Council, both sides preyed on American shipping.

President Thomas *Jefferson and Secretary of State James *Madison strongly believed in using commercial coercion to force England and France to rescind their offensive policies and to respect America's rights as a neutral nation. European economies, they reasoned, depended on American agricultural supplies, while the United States could easily survive without luxuries imported from the Old World. On 22 December 1807 Congress passed the Embargo Act, prohibiting all American exports.

The Embargo Act, amended several times in 1808 to tighten its enforcement, had disastrous effects for America. Neither France nor Britain altered its policy toward neutral trade. Instead, Napoleon seized American ships in European ports, claiming to believe that any ship trading under the American flag must be a British vessel in disguise. The U.S. economy plunged into a severe depression. Resentment against the embargo spread from merchants to farmers to urban workers and erupted into near rebellion in parts of *New England and New York. Jefferson, however, ignored the act's diplomatic failure and the widespread suffering it caused at home, praising it as late as 1815 as "a wise and powerful measure." Grievances arising from neutral rights issues ultimately helped bring on the *War of 1812.

[*See also* Depressions, Economic; Early Republic, Era of the; Foreign Relations: U.S. Relations with Europe.]

• Burton Spivac, *Jefferson's English Crisis: Commerce, Embargo, and the Republican Revolution*, 1979. Doron S. Ben-Atar, *The Origins of Jeffersonian Commercial Policy and Diplomacy*, 1993.

—Doron Ben-Atar

EMERSON, RALPH WALDO (1803–1882), essayist, poet, lecturer. Ralph Waldo Emerson, born in *Boston as the third son of William Emerson and Ruth Haskins Emerson, came from a long line of ministers. His father, minister at Boston's First Church, was a luminary of the Federalist cultural establishment. Emerson's youth, after his father's death in 1811, was marked by genteel poverty and frequent moves.

Emerson graduated from Harvard College in 1821, where he displayed an early interest in *poetry. After serving a brief teaching apprenticeship, he studied for the ministry at Harvard Divinity School. Approbated to preach in 1826, he was ordained colleague pastor of Boston's Second Church in 1829. This post provided him with sufficient social and financial stability to marry Ellen Tucker, from a New Hampshire merchant family, in September 1829. She died of tuberculosis in February 1831. Through this marriage Emerson eventually received a considerable monetary legacy.

Increasingly chafing under the restrictions of the Unitarian ministry and never blessed with easy sociability, Emerson proved ineffectual in the pastoral duties of his office. In his preaching, where he excelled, he interpreted Christianity symbolically, construing the teachings of scripture and revelation in ethical and humanitarian terms. When he insisted in 1832 that he could no longer in good conscience celebrate the Lord's Supper because it had become a source of division among persons of good conscience, his congregation decided to release him as minister. In an apparently amicable parting, he resigned in October 1832.

For most of 1833, Emerson traveled in Europe to broaden his horizons and consider his future. In November 1834 he moved to Concord, Massachusetts, his ancestral home, where he occasionally supplied pulpits while building the foundation for a career as an independent lecturer and essayist. A principal venue for the dissemination of his ideas became the lyceum, an institution for the spread of "useful knowledge" begun by Josiah Holbrook in 1826. The lyceum lecture circuit, of which Emerson was a leading light, eventually spread throughout much of the nation.

Freed from the necessity of defending a particular denominational position, Emerson entered upon a freelance career as spiritual sage, essayist, and public speaker that transformed him into an emblem of wisdom in a culture where attitudes toward the sacred were becoming increasingly individualized and privatized. His first published book, a slim volume entitled *Nature* (1836), imported into the United States some of the tenets of German transcendental philosophy that would become a significant source of inspiration for a small but visible segment of the *New England elite looking for an alternative to evangelical religion or secular entrepreneurialism. At Harvard, a Phi Beta Kappa Society oration later known as "The American Scholar" (1837) and a sermon before the graduating class of the divinity school (1838), earned for Emerson a local reputation as an advocate for American letters and harbinger of a radical new brand of spirituality.

Although Emerson gained an early reputation as an intellectual renegade, his popularity as a regional, then national, lecturer soared between 1840 and 1860. Two volumes, *Essays, First Series* (1841) and *Essays, Second Series* (1844) provided the public printed texts of his major lectures. Later publications largely based on lectures included *Representative Men* (1850), *English Traits* (1856), *The Conduct of Life* (1860), and *Society and Solitude* (1870). Two volumes of poems appeared as well.

Although Emerson at first eschewed organized reform as antithetical to the individual's need to carve out his or her own niche in the world, the 1840s and 1850s impelled him toward reforms of various sorts. Although never an organized program, the movement that became known as *transcendentalism coalesced around Emerson and the neighborhood of Concord during the 1840s. No firm core of beliefs marked adherents, but they shared a tendency to see the divine represented symbolically throughout nature, and nature as the emblem of a divinity in which humankind shared. Along with Margaret *Fuller, Emerson published and edited *The Dial* (1840–1844), a literary magazine inspired by transcendental philosophy. Emerson's Concord neighbor Henry David *Thoreau was profoundly influenced by transcendentalist ideas.

The *antislavery cause also drew Emerson's attention during these decades. At first repulsed by the rigidity of abolitionist thinking, Emerson increasingly spoke out against slavery and northern complicity with that institution, especially after passage of the *Fugitive Slave Act in 1850. Major addresses in Concord (1844 and 1851) and New York (1854) marked his escalating involvement in this major reform movement of his day.

By the mid-1860s, the most creative phase of Emerson's career was over. With age he grew forgetful and unable to lecture. He died in Concord in 1882, his reputation as a uniquely American seeker of wisdom already gargantuan.

[*See also* Antebellum Era; Federalist Party; Literature: Early National and Antebellum Eras; Romantic Movement; Unitarianism and Universalism.]

• Ralph Leslie Rusk, *The Life of Ralph Waldo Emerson*, 1949. Gay Wilson Allen, *Waldo Emerson: A Biography*, 1981. John McAleer, *Ralph Waldo Emerson: Days of Encounter*, 1984. Mary Kupiec Cayton, *Emerson's Emergence: Self and Society in the Transformation of New England, 1800–1845*, 1989. Len Gougeon, *Virtue's Hero: Emerson, Antislavery, and Reform*, 1990. Robert D. Richardson, *Emerson: The Mind on Fire*, 1995.

—Mary Kupiec Cayton

EMPIRE STATE BUILDING. Thanks to its familiar silhouette and status as the world's tallest building from 1931 until 1973, the Empire State Building, on *New York City's Fifth Avenue between Thirty-third and Thirty-fourth streets, ranks as the twentieth century's most famous *skyscraper. Designed by the architectural firm Shreve, Lamb, and Harmon, and erected on the site of the Waldorf-Astoria Hotel, it stands 102 stories (1,250 feet) high, with 85 floors of office space. A tourist promenade on the 86th floor offers a 360-degree view. The 200-foot tower, originally planned as a dirigible mooring mast, provides a grand crown. The idea for the building originated with John J. Raskob, chairman of the Democratic National Committee in 1928, when Alfred E. *Smith was the party's presidential nominee. After Smith's loss to Herbert *Hoover, Raskob decided to erect the world's tallest building, with Smith as president. He chose the name to emphasize the relationship between the building and Smith, the former governor of the Empire State. It was the first twentieth-century building to hold the "world's tallest" title that did not bear a corporate name such as Metropolitan Life, Woolworth, or Chrysler. Planned in the booming 1920s but completed during the Great Depression, the building attracted few tenants and for a time was dubbed the "Empty State Building." Further bad luck came in 1945 when a B–25 bomber crashed into the seventy-eighth floor, killing fourteen. Although the building is said to be Art Deco in design, the phrase did not exist at the time; the architects themselves simply described it as "modern." Seeking a practical, utilitarian structure, they little dreamed that it would become a tourist mecca, the symbol of New York, a national icon, and the setting for many movies, from *King Kong* (1933) to *Sleepless in Seattle* (1993).

[*See also* Architecture: Public Architecture.]

• John Tauranac, *The Empire State Building: The Making of a Landmark*, 1995.

—John Tauranac

EMPLOYMENT ACT OF 1946. This act created the Council of Economic Advisers as part of the White House staff, whose duty was to "formulate and recommend national economic policy" that would further the national goal of "maximum employment, production, and purchasing power." It reflected the conviction of many liberal policymakers that the greatest economic danger facing the United States after the war was a return to mass *unemployment, and that the surest way to avoid such a catastrophe was through economic growth. But the law provided no effective tools for achieving its goals, and its supporters soon became disillusioned.

The idea for the bill emerged from the National Resources Planning Board, the New Deal's official planning agency, which in the early 1940s promoted the idea of "full employment." It also reflected President Franklin Delano *Roosevelt's call in 1944 for an "economic bill of rights," which included "the right to a useful and remunerative job." Progressive labor and farm groups were also actively lobbying for legislation to promote government-guaranteed full employment, as were leading Keynesian economists. When the bill was introduced in Congress in January 1945, it was titled the Full Employment Bill; it called for the president to adopt economic policies that would create jobs for all who wanted them. The government would spend money on job-creation programs if the private sector appeared unlikely to generate enough employment. President Harry S. *Truman supported it after Roosevelt's death, as did most congressional New Dealers.

But by 1946, not enough New Dealers remained in Congress to enact the original bill. After strenuous opposition from employers, who feared that a full employment economy would drive up their labor costs, conservatives in Congress so diluted the legislation that many of its early supporters dismissed it as meaningless rhetoric. The phrase "full employment," which had resonated so strongly among liberals in the 1940s, disappeared from both the title and the body of the bill, as did all the specific policy requirements that were to have given the phrase meaning. But the Council of Economic Advisers created by the act did at times influence presidents to choose policies that promoted economic growth. While the Employment Act did not guarantee full employment, it did help make fiscal policy an important lever of economic planning in the postwar era.

[*See also* Federal Government, Executive Branch: The Presidency; Keynesianism; New Deal Era, The.]

• Stephen K. Bailey, *Congress Makes a Law: The Story behind the Employment Act of 1946*, 1950.

—Alan Brinkley

ENERGY CRISIS OF THE 1970s. The energy crisis of the 1970s damaged the American economy and decisively affected presidential politics. Retaliating for Western support of Israel in the October 1973 Mideast War, Arab members of the Organization of Petroleum Exporting Countries (OPEC) temporarily barred oil sales to the United States and dramatically raised prices for all customers. In six months the price of a barrel of crude oil soared from three to eighteen dollars. President Richard M. *Nixon advocated conservation and development of domestic energy sources, and also signed legislation controlling the prices charged by domestic oil producers. In 1975 Congress rejected President Gerald *Ford's proposal to decontrol domestic oil and natural gas to increase supply. Rising energy prices contributed to the economic "stagflation" that cost Ford the 1976 election.

Although President Jimmy *Carter called the energy crisis the "moral equivalent of war," Americans remained divided on the causes and cure of the problem. In 1978 Carter secured legislation that fostered conservation and decontrolled the price of some domestic natural gas. The Iranian revolution allowed OPEC again to raise prices rapidly in 1979. As stagflation worsened and lines of angry motorists formed at gas stations, Carter diagnosed a "crisis of confidence" and urged citizens to build their character by coping with austerity. Ridiculed as a prophet of "malaise" and blamed for the sagging economy, Carter lost to Ronald *Reagan in 1980. During the early 1980s, conservation, an international recession, and development of new fuel sources brought down energy prices. As memories of the crisis faded, the United States steadily increased its dependence on imported petroleum.

[*See also* Automotive Industry; Business; Environmentalism; Foreign Relations: U.S. Relations with the Middle East; Hydroelectric Power; Nuclear Power; Petroleum Industry.]

• Crauford D. Goodwin, ed., *Energy Policy in Perspective*, 1981. Franklin Tugwell, *The Energy Crisis and the American Political Economy*, 1988.

—Leo P. Ribuffo

ENGEL* v. *VITALE (1962), a U.S. *Supreme Court decision addressing the issue of school prayer. In the early 1960s some New York public school districts asked children to recite a state-composed prayer each day: "Almighty God, we acknowledge our dependence upon Thee, and we beg Thy blessings upon us, our parents, our teachers and our Country." Some non-Christian parents objected that the prayer, though supposedly not compulsory, was nonetheless required and that tax-supported facilities were used for a religious observance. While the *American Civil Liberties Union and the American Jewish Committee came to the aid of the parents, the New York Board of Regents, twenty state attorneys general, and Porter R. Chandler, a lawyer with close ties to the Roman Catholic Archdiocese of New York, joined in defense of the prayer requirement.

The case produced one of the Supreme Court's most controversial decisions under the chief justiceship of Earl *Warren. Justice Hugo *Black's majority opinion assuming a high wall of separation between church and state, declared the prayer an unconstitutional violation of the First Amendment's Establishment Clause. Using public schools to encourage prayer, Black argued, was "a practice wholly inconsistent with the Establishment Clause." Justice Potter Stewart's lone dissent reasoned that the Establishment Clause only forbade government from establishing an official church and coercing religious beliefs.

President John F. *Kennedy supported the Court by noting that Americans were still free to pray at home with their children. Yet fundamentalist religious groups charged that the Court in *Engel* had erected too high a barrier between church and state and had promoted atheism, agnosticism, and *secularization.

[*See also* Bill of Rights; Christian Coalition; Church and State, Separation of; Civil Liberties; Fundamentalist Movement; Moral Majority; Religion.]

• Kermit L. Hall, *The Magic Mirror: Law in American History*, 1989.

—Kermit L. Hall

ENGINEERING. Engineering as a profession has been linked historically to large-scale organizations such as the *military, or to the design, construction, and management of large-scale projects.

European Background and American Beginnings. Political and economic conditions sufficient to support an engineering profession, as opposed to isolated individuals, emerged in early modern Europe. By 1700 the expansion of French military power and the changing technological demands produced by the introduction of gunpowder had led to the creation of a corps of engineers in the French army. In the eighteenth century the French government created a special corps of road and bridge engineers and of mining engineers, with separate schools to systematize their training. In Britain, by contrast, state intervention and the military were less important to the emergence of professional engineering. There, a rapidly expanding industrial economy had provided sufficient large-scale projects (roads, harbors, canals) by the 1770s to support a significant number of full-time technical experts. These engineers, unlike their French counterparts, were neither formally trained nor dependent on the the state for employment; accordingly, they had much less faith in the value of scientific theory and mathematics for their work.

Because of engineering's dependence on large-scale organizations and large-scale projects, the profession hardly existed in colonial America where neither of these prerequisites was present. When the *Revolutionary War broke out in 1775, American armies had neither trained military engineers nor a reservoir of civilian engineers, forcing their dependence on French-trained ones.

Recognizing the need for military engineers, Congress created a Corps of Artillerists and Engineers in 1794 and a military academy at West Point in 1802 to train them. Modeled after French precedents (especially the École polytechnique), West Point served as a conduit for the transmission to America of the dominant French engineering tradition involving the use of an elite, disciplined corps of scientifically trained engineers employed by the state. Early America, however, was profoundly antimilitary and antielitist. The *Army Corps of Engineers and West Point survived only by adapting to American values. West Point's admissions policy was not as elitist and its engineering training not as mathematically rigorous as France's École polytechnique, and West Point early emphasized civilian engineering as much as military. Moreover, West Point for several decades produced more engineers than the country's miniscule military required, enabling the academy to contribute toward alleviating civilian engineering shortages.

The Antebellum Era: A Profession Takes Shape. Even in modified form, the French engineering tradition did not gain complete dominance in the early national period. American suspicion of elites, the frontier environment in which much early engineering was carried out, and a rapidly expanding economic environment provided fertile ground for the emergence of a profession modeled more along British lines, that is, based on practical, on-the-job training; suspicious of theory; and more dependent on the civilian economy than on government patronage. Large-scale transportation projects between 1815 and 1850 provided the foundations for the emergence of an engineering profession in America. The most influential was the *Erie Canal, begun in 1817. Drawing from British precedents, the state of New York appointed as chief engineers three men (Canvass White, Benjamin Wright, and James Geddes) without formal engineering education but with some technical skills, assuming that intelligent men could teach themselves what was necessary on the job. They, in turn, trained their survey crew chiefs as assistant engineers. By the completion of the canal in 1825, nearly seventy Americans had gained on-the-job training in engineering. Many left the Erie for similar projects elsewhere, taking the British-influenced system of engineering training with them.

Engineers trained in ways analogous to those used on the Erie Canal dominated American civil engineering until well after the *Civil War. Mid-nineteenth-century American machine and locomotive shops developed similar methods for training mechanical engineers, and the American *mining industry did the same for mining captains, the forerunners of mining engineers. Like job-trained civil engineers, job-trained American mechanical and mining engineers profoundly distrusted their academically trained counterparts and were skeptical of heavy reliance on theory and mathematics. They preferred, instead, using empirical methods based on established practices.

By the 1840s, American engineers had developed a distinct engineering style, adapted to American conditions and different from its European antecedents. Whereas British and French engineering were characterized by expensive, durable, and aesthetically appealing special-order products, American engineering was recognized for its ability to produce large quantities of routine, standardized designs cheaply and quickly. This American engineering tradition was further reinforced in the early twentieth century, when American mechanical engineers introduced *mass production techniques into the emerging *automotive industry and later into other industries as well.

Although most nineteenth-century American engineers were trained on the job, by the mid–nineteenth century engineering had begun to find a place in American colleges. In the 1830s and 1840s several dozen American schools introduced engineering coursework, and some, such as Rensselaer Polytechnic Institute, offered multiyear engineering curricula. The *Morrill Land Grant Act of 1862 further institutionalized engineering training by supporting collegiate-level education in the "mechanic arts" (usually interpreted as engineering) in each state.

Engineering in Twentieth Century America. By the early twentieth century, the attitudes, values, and working methods of engineering permeated American *business management and American thought more generally. The broader influence was especially evident in the *scientific management movement initiated by Frederick W. Taylor, and in the later writings of the economist Thorstein *Veblen, who saw the disinterested, production-oriented ethic of engineers as a model for the larger society.

By this period, too, the growing scale and complexity of *technology had begun to require American engineers to lean more heavily and regularly on mathematics and theory to supplement the empirical methods pioneered by early, job-trained engineers. This contributed to a steady expansion in the use of college-educated engineers between 1880 and 1920, by which time they had clearly displaced job-trained engineers in importance. Despite the growing use of mathematics and scientific methods in engineering, however, the engineering and scientific communities in America initially remained wholly distinct. Unlike its counterparts in many European countries, American engineering, having developed independently, did not look to the scientific community for recognition or approval. American engineering evolved its own institutions and reward system, which placed a high value on project-specific accomplishments and downplayed broad-based theoretical achievements.

Only around 1900 did American engineering and *science begin to converge. Faced with increasingly complex technical problems, especially in the newly emerging *electrical and *chemical industries, American engineering began to move away from its British antecedents and draw more heavily on mathematics and theory—though often in ways sharply different from those of scientists. This convergence was further encouraged by the growth of large corporations, which, through industrial *research laboratories employing both engineers and scientists, sought to institutionalize and control the pace of technological change. The convergence became especially noticeable after *World War II. Jealous of the leadership role given physicists and chemists in cutting-edge research projects during the war and lured by increased government support for basic scientific research after the war, American engineering schools and colleges began to place increased emphasis on scientific approaches to engineering work.

The scientization of American engineering in the twentieth

century was accompanied by other, equally significant changes, especially in work autonomy. Through much of the nineteenth century, American engineers functioned as independent professionals; heroic engineer-entrepreneurs like the bridge-builders James Eads and John Roebling dominated the profession. They and their peers worked as independent, outside experts brought in to solve particular technical problems or construct specific projects. By the late nineteenth century the independent engineering consultant's dominant role in the profession was in decline. American economic expansion and the growing scale and capabilities of technology had combined to create large corporations with large capital investments. To protect their investments, these corporations increasingly relied on staff engineers, rather than on outside consultants.

The emergence of large corporate organizations in America in the late nineteenth century and of large governmental agencies after World War II changed the nature of engineering in other ways. As engineers grew more dependent for employment on large organizations, engineering work was increasingly subjected to bureaucratic controls, and individual engineers became increasingly anonymous. By the mid–twentieth century, the typical engineer played only a small, specialized role in a project's development. The design of an automobile or aircraft and of the facilities necessary to manufacture it, for example, required hundreds, if not thousands, of engineers, each working on specific tasks.

The growing specialization of engineering work and the engineer's loss of independence in the workplace, however, were offset by engineers' increasingly central role in American life in the twentieth century. To secure needed technical expertise, corporations and government agencies employed engineers in larger numbers than ever before, making engineering the second largest profession (after public school teachers) in America. In addition, the engineer's role in management grew significantly. Technically oriented corporations came to regard engineers as a primary pool from which to draw their management personnel. As early as the 1920s, around 70 percent of all engineering graduates moved into managerial positions within fifteen years of graduation, and by midcentury a substantial proportion of the largest American corporations were headed by trained engineers. To supply a growing professional demand, engineering schools with many specialized subdivisions, including electrical engineering, chemical engineering, and computer engineering, had become increasingly important components of U.S. research universities as the twentieth century progressed.

[*See also* Canals and Waterways; Dams and Hydraulic Engineering; Education: Collegiate Education, Education: The Rise of the University; Mathematics and Statistics; Military Service Academies; Professionalization.]

• Forest G. Hill, *Roads, Rails and Waterways: The Army Engineers and Early Transportation*, 1957. Daniel Hovey Calhoun, *The American Civil Engineer: Origins and Conflict*, 1960. Monte A. Calvert, *The Mechanical Engineer in America, 1830–1910*, 1967. Raymond H. Merritt, *Engineering in American Society 1850–1875*, 1969. Edwin T. Layton Jr., *The Revolt of the Engineers: Social Responsibility and the American Engineering Profession*, 1971. A. Michael McMahon, *The Making of a Profession: A Century of Electrical Engineering in America*, 1984. Terry S. Reynolds, ed., *The Engineer in America: A Historical Anthology from* Technology and Culture, 1991. John Rae and Rudi Volti, *The Engineer in History*, 1993. Eda Kranakis, *Constructing a Bridge: An Exploration of Engineering Culture, Design, and Research in Nineteenth-Century France and America*, 1997.

—Terry S. Reynolds

ENVIRONMENTALISM. Although its roots go back much earlier, the social movement known as environmentalism first appeared in the 1960s. It soon became one of the most successful movements in modern history, with a national and global impact on politics, economics, *technology, design, and personal values. As the twentieth century ended, that impact seemed likely to endure, yet how truly profound it would be remained unclear. As it grew the movement came to mean different things to different groups, though at its core it remained an effort to improve human relationships with the other-than-human world.

In the early twentieth century, the word "environmentalism" referred mainly to the effects of external social influences (as opposed to genetic endowment) on the individual. But increasingly after *World War II, "environment" came to mean the natural world surrounding people, including flora, fauna, climate, water, and soil—the entire biosphere. At the same time, that natural world began to seem highly vulnerable to human activity; it was no longer an all-powerful Mother Earth providing boundless nourishment for her children but an endangered source of life. That sense of vulnerability inspired a social and political reform movement. Environmentalists called for a more responsible relationship between human beings and nature. Human survival was at stake, as was the stability and integrity of the whole fabric of life on the planet.

More and more citizens sensed that the human-nature umbilical link was itself under attack, and that defending it required a radically new way of thinking. The environment had to be seen holistically, they insisted. For them, nature was not a realm set above and apart from human beings, like another country one visits from time to time, but instead is a vast, intricate community interacting all around us, a system of connections and interchanges to which all belong. Human beings cannot move away from that condition, nor ignore it with impunity, they concluded, even in the midst of the largest metropolis.

A defining work in the emergence of environmentalism was Rachel *Carson's *Silent Spring* (1962), which warned of the wholesale contamination of the environment by chemical pesticides such as dichlorodiphenyltrichloroethane (DDT). Like many others of her generation, Carson was shaken by the fear of all-out nuclear war and worried about radioactive fallout from weapons-testing polluting food chains even in the most remote parts of the planet. In 1967, a group of scientists and lawyers founded the Environmental Defense Fund, which sought to get dangerous pesticides banned by the courts as a threat to the health of both human beings and natural ecosystems. The National Environmental Policy Act (1969) set up a federal regulatory agency, the *Environmental Protection Agency, and required an "environmental impact statement" for any federally funded project that might cause damage to the earth. The 1963 *Limited Nuclear Test Ban Treaty, a ban on DDT use in the United States, and the passage of many new laws (including the 1960 Clean Water Act and the 1963 Clean Air Act) all sprang from growing conviction that the human-nature relationship was more essential than Americans had generally realized, and that what happened to one side of the relationship inevitably affected the other. Capping a decade of ferment, environmentalists in 1970 declared the first Earth Day, an event to celebrate human-nature interdependence. An estimated twenty million people, most of them North Americans and most under the age of thirty, participated, far outnumbering student demonstrations for the *civil rights movement or for an end to the *Vietnam War. The event became an annual, and eventually a truly international, ritual—an unprecedented global "holiday." More substantially, almost all nations passed laws similar to those enacted in the United States, and several nations surpassed the United States in cleaning up their rivers and atmosphere, recycling their wastes, reducing toxic emissions, improving energy efficiency, and preserving a critical habitat for biodiversity.

Within the United States, environmentalism was an amalgamation of several older strands of intellectual and political consciousness. Among them were nineteenth-century *transcendentalism and the *Romantic movement. Rachel Carson acknowledged her indebtedness to such figures as Henry David *Thoreau and John *Muir, both of whom had celebrated American nature in its wilder state and sought to recover a direct personal relationship with the nonhuman. Both looked for ways of getting outside the confine of civilization now and then and into primeval woods or mountains. Painters and poets had encouraged people to seek the sublime in nature, alone or in small groups, in such awe-inspiring landscapes as Yellowstone, Yosemite, and the *Grand Canyon. Carson herself, a marine biologist with the U.S. Fish and Wildlife Service, was passionate about the sea; she found her wilderness in tidal pools along the Maine coast. But by the 1960s, in a highly urbanized nation of over 200 million people, with a far denser web of artifice obscuring the natural order, this kind of romantic quest had become increasingly difficult to satisfy by solitary, private excursions. Environmentalism, though inspired by romantic yearnings for contact with nature, could not be simply an individual act of reverence for or withdrawal from modernity; it must be a public project pursued collectively in the courtroom, the legislative chamber, and the corporate headquarters. Organization and lobbying were required to win passage of the 1964 Wilderness Act, which over the next three decades would protect 100 million acres and stand as one of the great successes of the American environmental movement.

A second strand was the *Progressive Era *conservation movement, which gained momentum in the early twentieth century under the leadership of Gifford Pinchot, chief forester during Theodore *Roosevelt's presidency, and of Roosevelt himself. That movement supported the preservation of national parks and wildlife refuges, but even more importantly it set up a national forest system based on sustained-yield management principles and called for protecting the nation's soils and minerals from overrapid development. The core ideal was "wise use." For Pinchot and his allies, that ideal required the federal government to be permanently in charge of managing land and overseeing national development. American society could not endure, they felt, without a secure, continuing permanent supply of natural resources. Unregulated private exploitation, they feared, threatened the nation's long-term security. The post-1960 environmental movement shared that same concern about stopping waste and inefficiency and safeguarding resources for the future, but it went further, calling for an overhaul of the entire modern economic system to fit consumption patterns to the limits of the land.

A third source of modern environmentalism was a *public-health movement working for cleaner, safer factories and urban neighborhoods. By the mid-nineteenth century, physicians and other professionals in Europe and North America were agitating for better sanitation to prevent devastating outbreaks of *cholera and *typhoid fever. The early targets had been water supplies contaminated by human waste, slaughterhouse offal, and garbage. As coal replaced wood as the nation's chief energy source after 1870, public-health concerns broadened to include air pollution, though clear medical evidence of the effects of such combustion on lungs and other body tissues was slow in coming. The urban environmentalist Alice Hamilton—a medical doctor, social worker at Jane *Addams's Hull House in *Chicago, and a sometime professor of industrial hygiene at Harvard University—pioneered in investigating the poisons that infected workplaces and tenement dwellings. Reformers found life in the modern city particularly degraded and unwholesome, but they soon extended their efforts into rural areas, including Indian reservations and sharecroppers' cabins, wherever poor people disproportionately bore the costs of progress. Not until Rachel Carson, however, did public-health reformers generally begin to realize that the human body is a part of nature too, and that its pollution by dangerous substances is one with the pollution of the earth.

Finally, the emergence of environmentalism owed something to a relatively obscure group of natural scientists and academics in such fields as ecology and geography who first perceived the environment as an interactive physical system connecting human beings and the rest of nature. Visualizing that system on a global scale, many of them dramatically transcended the nationalistic perspective of the Progressive conservationists or the localized concerns of urban health reformers. Their basic theories often came from abroad as well: from the Russian geologist V. I. Vernadskii, originator of the concept of the biosphere; from French and German geographers, who had long debated the question of nature as a limiting factor on human activity; and from a succession of English naturalists, including Charles Darwin, Charles Elton, and Arthur Tansley (who suggested the idea of the ecosystem). A key American figure in this emerging body of scientific thought was Aldo *Leopold, a University of Wisconsin wildlife expert, who introduced many readers to the science of ecology through his *Sand County Almanac* (1948).

By the 1950s, these scientific ideas had come together in a new integrative and interdisciplinary point of view that united the natural and *social sciences, a perspective that might be called human ecology. Avoiding the extremes of environmental determinism, which had tried to reduce cultures to their physical conditions, and of a technological optimism that was blind to all environmental limits, the new view insisted that human life must be lived within natural constraints, both physical and moral.

The concept of human ecology emerged on many fronts in the late 1940s and 1950s. Anthropologists Betty Meggers and Julian Steward—one working in Amazonia, the other in the American *Southwest—laid the foundations for "cultural ecology." Historian James Malin argued for an ecological approach and applied it in his own studies of the relations of plants, animals, soils, climate, and human populations on the Great Plains. Among geographers, Carl Sauer produced influential essays and books exploring the effects of European colonialism on New World peoples and landscapes. Several of those scholars and others from diverse disciplines gathered in Princeton, New Jersey, in 1956 for a symposium on the deteriorating state of the human-nature relationship. The resulting publication, *Man's Role in Changing the Face of the Earth* (1956), dedicated to the nineteenth-century American conservationist George Perkins Marsh, played a major role in preparing the deeper intellectual ground for the environmental movement.

Among the symposium participants was Paul B. Sears, a botanist who chaired the conservation program at Yale University. In his short but prophetic paper, "The Processes of Environmental Change by Man," Sears reviewed the global impact of human population growth, the intensification of agricultural land use, and water and air pollution in industrial areas, noting that the United States, with less than a tenth of the world's population, was consuming more than half of its mineral production. Neither Sears nor the other conference-goers called themselves environmentalists, but their concern over the growing effect of human beings on global ecology helped give environmentalism a set of defining ideas and theories. In 1972, when environmentalists from many countries assembled in Stockholm to resurvey the global situation, they drew on the perspective worked out by those pioneering human ecologists. By the later 1990s, that same perspective had become widely popularized in the United States, and ecology (however shallow or profound) was part of the daily language of masses of people worldwide.

What the environmentalist movement added to these fertile new ideas of human ecology was a growing sense of urgency, bordering at times on apocalyptic fear. By the *Sixties, activists warned of an environmental "crisis." Rachel Carson's nightmare of a future springtime when no birds would sing, all dead from manmade poisons, introduced a tone of anxiety missing from the writings of Thoreau, Pinchot, Hamilton, Leopold, or Sears. Following Carson, another anxious biologist, Paul Ehrlich, warned in *The Population Bomb* (1968) of a demographic hazard that "keeps ticking," ready to explode. In *The Closing Circle* (1971), the Washington University biologist Barry Commoner alerted the country to the death of Lake Erie from pollutants and the death of people from radioactivity, smog, and ground-water contamination. Commoner explained that he had first been alerted to the environmental crisis by the activities of the *Atomic Energy Commission (predecessor of the *Nuclear Regulatory Commission), which during the 1950s had exposed Americans and others to deadly Strontium 90 through nuclear-weapons testing and then failed to let the public know the full consequences of that exposure. The urgent need, in his view, was for an awakened public, led by informed scientists, to force the government and corporate America to develop less life-threatening technologies. The specter haunting each of these environmentalists was nothing less than death—the death of birds, of ecosystems, of nature itself, and, because of our dependence on nature, the death of human beings as well.

Only slightly less apocalyptic were those environmentalists who by the 1970s called for a reevaluation of the purposes and consequences of *economic development. In their view, an economy expanding geometrically using ever more energy, land, minerals, and water, must eventually encounter the limits of the earth's resources. The environment, they insisted, must be seen as more than a storehouse of commodities to be ransacked and consumed. Here the environmentalists confronted attitudes deeply engrained among economists, business leaders, politicians, and the public about the virtues of economic growth, attitudes underlying the modern economic system and indeed the whole materialistic ethos of contemporary culture. Although the popular response to this challenge was difficult to gauge, polls did show a growing tilt toward environmentalist views in all the industrial countries and a greater public willingness, at least in affluent societies, to make economic sacrifices to reduce pollution, preserve species, and consume less energy.

During the 1980s, as American politics turned conservative, a rising chorus of antienvironmentalists, led by President Ronald *Reagan and Secretary of the Interior James Watt, insisted that the environment was neither fragile nor a real constraint on human ambition. Environmentalists responded by renewing their sense of mission and increasing their numbers. They countered opposition by seeking alliances with other groups demanding cultural change: among feminists, some of whom insisted that women were more attuned to ecological interdependencies than men; among ethical radicals, who wanted to extend rights to animals, trees, and the rest of nature; and among social-justice advocates at home and abroad, who demanded protection for the poor from the environmental damage and toxic dumping by the rich. Above all, environmentalists tried to temper their gloomier tendencies with a more hopeful, and more politically acceptable, emphasis on creating a new "green future" in which environmentally sensitive cities, economies, and technologies would all be reembedded in the tangled web of life.

[*See also* Conservatism; Consumer Culture; Feminism; Forests and Forestry; Industrial Diseases and Hazards; Laissez-faire; Mass Production; National Park System; Nuclear Arms Control Treaties; Nuclear Weapons; Painting: To 1945; Three Mile Island; Yellowstone National Park; Yosemite National Park.]

• Stephen Fox, *The American Conservation Movement,* 1981. Samuel P. Hays, *Beauty, Health, and Permanence,* 1987. Robert C. Paehlke, *Environmentalism and the Future of Progressive Politics,* 1989. Riley E. Dunlap and Angela G. Mertig, eds., *American Environmentalism,* 1992. Bob Pepperman Taylor, *Our Limits Transgressed,* 1992. Robert Gottlieb, *Forcing the Spring,* 1993. Kirkpatrick Sale, *The Green Revolution,* 1993. Donald Worster, *Nature's Economy,* 2d. ed., 1994. Willett Kempton, James S. Boster, and Jennifer A. Hartley, *Environmental Values in American Culture,* 1995.

—Donald Worster

ENVIRONMENTAL PROTECTION AGENCY. Established by the Richard M. *Nixon administration in October 1970, in the wake of the first Earth Day that April, the Environmental Protection Agency (EPA) became the agent and symbol of a vast expansion of the federal government's role in addressing a widely perceived environmental crisis. Initially proposed by a Nixon advisory committee seeking ways to streamline the federal bureaucracy, the EPA brought together under one institutional umbrella several long-standing federal programs aimed mostly at pollution control. Through existing and new legislation that it implemented and defended in court, including Clean Water and Clean Air Acts, the Toxic Substances Control Act, and laws regulating pesticides and hazardous wastes, the EPA spearheaded the most far-reaching federal intervention into the American economy since the New Deal.

During its first three decades, the EPA grew steadily in its size, responsibilities, and regulatory strategies, even as its fortunes fluctuated with the political climate. Though its founding laws and early administrators envisioned an "ecological" protection encompassing nonhuman as well as human life, the agency found its scientific footing by stressing environmental threats to *public health. Initially quite decentralized, the EPA under President Jimmy *Carter centralized and coordinated its programs, largely through quantitative risk assessments (starting with carcinogenic risks) and cost-benefit analyses. Early appointees in the Ronald *Reagan administration assaulted the EPA's programs and damaged morale, but in the wake of the Love Canal exposé—a scandal involving long-term toxic pollution by the Hooker Chemical Company in Niagara Falls, New York—Congress mandated a new and ambitious EPA initiative to control industrial wastes. Friendlier Republican administrations of the later 1980s and early 1990s restored money and muscle to the EPA's older programs while expanding its regulatory tools. Experiments with dispute mediation and market-based incentives carried over into the Bill *Clinton administrations. During the 1990s, the EPA tightened pollution standards and began monitoring and regulating the effects of pollution on nonhuman species. In response to the environmental-justice movement, the agency also moved to shed its white, middle-class image by attending more closely to the disproportionate share of environmental risk borne by minorities and the poor.

[*See also* Carson, Rachel; Economic Regulation; Environmentalism; Industrial Diseases and Hazards; New Deal Era, The.]

• U.S. Environmental Protection Agency, *The Guardian: Origins of the Environmental Protection Agency,* 1992. Edmund Russell, "Lost among the Parts per Billion: Ecological Protection at the United States Environmental Protection Agency, 1970–1993," *Environmental History* 2 (1997): 29–51.

—Christopher Sellers

EQUALITY. "We hold these truths to be self-evident, that all men are created equal . . ." Although these words from the *Declaration of Independence are among the most familiar in the American canon, much of American history challenges the principle they proclaim. From the nation's beginnings onward, certain groups of Americans were judged unequal, not according to their virtue, intelligence, or talent, but rather on the basis of race, *religion, *gender, or wealth. Non-whites, women, some immigrants, and the propertyless were denied the privileges and obligations of citizenship, despite the nation's ostensible commitment to the principles of legal and political equality.

Yet Thomas *Jefferson's ringing declaration, even if not fully observed in practice, nevertheless echoed long and loud. Successive generations of reformers—Jeffersonians and Jacksonians challenging economic privilege; abolitionists challenging *slavery; women's-rights and woman-suffrage advocates challenging the subjugation of women; civil libertarians challenging the suppression of dissent; farmers and workers challenging the unchecked prerogatives of capital; and critics of intolerance challenging religious, ethnic, and racial injustice—invoked the principle of equality as one of their primary weapons. Protracted and sometimes bloody as their battles were, these crusaders prevailed: by the late twentieth century, legally imposed discrimination on the basis of religion, *race, ethnicity, gender, income, or sexual preference had been outlawed in the United States. Given the nation's long record of exclusion and oppression, this achievement testifies not only to the activists' heroic efforts, but also to the protean power of the principle of equality.

In the economic and social spheres, the record has been more equivocal. While most Americans' commitment in these areas was to equality of opportunity, not equality of outcome, even that more limited goal proved difficult to achieve. From 1913, when the quintessential progressive reform measure, the graduated income tax, was authorized, through the *New Deal of the 1930s and the *Great Society legislation of the 1960s, economic inequality diminished in the United States. Taxing the wealthy and regulating the economy to expand social and economic opportunities for the poor made a difference—albeit a less dramatic difference than that of the post–*World War II rights revolution.

The trend reversed in the two decades after 1980, however, as the gap between the richest and poorest Americans widened steadily. The *civil-rights and women's movements did not automatically assure equality of opportunity in the economic and social spheres. Many women, members of minority groups, and recent immigrants still in the late twentieth century faced barriers, and de facto racial *segregation persisted in urban America. The quality of public schools and other governmental services varied widely among neighborhoods of different ethnic make up and income level, as did the employment opportunities available to different groups. The late twentieth-century prosperity of highly educated, technologically sophisticated computer specialists and information-service providers, and of entrepreneurs in these fields, was accompanied by the decline of industries that had lifted earlier generations from *poverty, the eroding buying power of the minimum wage, and a proliferation of entry-level service-sector jobs leading nowhere. As a new century dawned, the goal of equality first promulgated in 1776 remained elusive.

[*See also* African Americans; Asian Americans; Antislavery; Capitalism; Civil Liberties; Economic Regulation; Equal Rights Amendment; Feminism; Hispanic Americans; Immigration; Immigration Law; Industrialization; Laissez-faire; Racism; Social Class; Social Darwinisn; Socialism; Suffrage; Taxation; Utopian and Communitarian Movements; Woman Suffrage Movement; Women's Rights Movements.]

• J. R. Pole, *The Pursuit of Equality in American History,* 2d ed., 1993. Rogers M. Smith, *Civil Ideals: Conflicting Visions of Citizenship in U.S. History,* 1997.

—James T. Kloppenberg

EQUAL RIGHTS AMENDMENT. The Equal Rights Amendment (ERA), written by Alice Paul and sponsored by the *National Woman's Party, was first proposed in 1923, on the seventy-fifth anniversary of the 1848 Seneca Falls women's rights convention. Inspired by the *Nineteenth Amendment, which had just secured equal suffrage for women, it was intended to push the feminist cause beyond political equality. The original wording declared that "men and women shall have equal rights throughout the United States and in every place subject to its jurisdiction." The ERA, which if ratified would have called into question the entire body of special protective labor legislation for women workers, created acrimonious divisions among former suffragists for four decades. Nonetheless, Paul and her small band of followers pushed the ERA year after year, in 1940 securing *Republican party endorsement. Serious prospects for the amendment developed in 1966, when a new feminist generation took up the cause. Now the wording demanded that "equal rights under the law shall not be abridged or denied . . . on account of sex," thus assuming that the purpose of the law was not to advance equality but to look without distinction at men and women. Carried forward by the energies of a new feminist wave, the ERA won quick congressional approval in 1972, but in the process stimulated an aggressive opposition, led by right-wing activist Phyllis Schlafly, who claimed that ratification would mean unisex toilets, gay marriages, and women in combat. Despite a congressionally authorized extension of the process to 1982, only thirty states ratified the amendment and it died. Nonetheless, the ERA campaign had important results: It helped to build both the feminist and antifeminist movements; and in its wake, judicial decisions regarding sex discrimination were significantly liberalized, in large part based on an expansive new reading of the *Fourteenth Amendment.

[*See also* Conservatism; Feminism; *Muller* v. *Oregon*; Seneca Falls Convention; Women in the Labor Force; Women's Rights Movements.]

• Joan Hoff-Wilson, *Rights of Passage: The Past and the Future of the ERA*, 1986.

—Ellen C. DuBois

ERA OF GOOD FEELINGS. *See* Early Republic, Era of the; Monroe, James; Political Parties.

ERIE CANAL. Begun in 1817 and completed in 1825, the Erie Canal stretched 363 miles across New York from Albany to Buffalo, linking the Hudson River and Lake Erie through the Mohawk River gap in the Appalachian Mountains. The state of New York built and financed the project, thanks in part to the promotional efforts of DeWitt *Clinton, the former mayor of *New York City.

This pioneering *engineering achievement was forty feet wide and four feet deep, with eighty-three locks and eighteen aqueducts. (It was later enlarged to seventy feet wide and seven feet deep; after 1905 it was rebuilt and renamed the Erie Barge Canal.) The self-taught engineers who designed the canal, such as Benjamin Wright, Canvass White, Nathan S. Thomas, and John B. Jervis, drew largely from English technology.

Celebrated in American folklore, the Erie Canal had a transforming influence. It increased settlement in western New York and the Great Lakes region, carried immigrants and merchandise west, and brought western grain to the Hudson. It created cites such as Buffalo, Rochester, and Syracuse; increased wheat production in western New York; and stimulated lateral canals to the Finger Lakes, Lake Champlain, and Lake Ontario. Spreading ideas as well as goods, the canal promoted such diverse social reforms as religious *revivalism, the *women's rights movements, and temperance. Into the 1880s the Erie Canal surpassed the competing New York Central Railroad in its freight traffic, but by the late twentieth century it served mainly as a corridor for recreational and commercial development.

[*See also* Antebellum Era; Canals and Waterways; Early Republic, Era of the; Railroads; Temperance and Prohibition.]

• Ronald E. Shaw, *Erie Water West: A History of the Erie Canal 1792–1854*, 1966. Carol Sheriff, *The Artificial River: The Erie Canal and the Paradox of Progress 1817–1862*, 1996.

—Ronald E. Shaw

ESPIONAGE. *See* Intelligence Gathering and Espionage.

ETHNICITY. *See* Race and Ethnicity.

ETIQUETTE AND MANNERS. Although they might seem trivial, manners have played an important role in American history. As anthropologists and sociologists have recognized, the rule-governed behaviors that people perform before each other communicate essential information. Whether through rules of precedence, customs of salutation, or norms for body carriage and facial expression, they enact power relations in face-to-face encounters, help people play their social roles, and communicate status. Americans have always been concerned with proper behavior, in part because these rituals maintain a social order often at odds with professed ideals. But the nature of this need for manners has changed over time. Indeed, changes in manners record the swings of America's waltz with *equality.

The array of symbolic behaviors that constitutes manners changes slowly. Traditional gestures of salutation such as the bow and the curtsey only gradually gave way to the handshake. It took some time for the custom of seating dinner guests by order of precedence to die out. What changed more quickly was the way these behaviors were learned and deployed, for what purposes, and by whom. In the *Colonial Era, for example, the Anglo-American males who ruled from council and church attempted to proclaim their superiority through their deportment, shoring up a hierarchy challenged by socioeconomic changes and their own less-than-exalted origins. But the reliance on manners to enforce social hierarchies actually enabled some of the socially inferior to masquerade as their betters. Indians and *African Americans could mimic the Europeans for their own ends, while also preserving their own rituals. The latter are hard to uncover, however, since they were not codified in Euroamerican discussions of proper behavior.

The colonial elite's near-monopoly on genteel behavior faced challenges after the mid–eighteenth century as social and economic changes undermined traditional hierarchies. This led to the co-option of formerly aristocratic behavior by those who openly embraced bourgeois modes of *work and *mobility. By the 1830s, manners had emerged as a key means of expression of a newly dominant urban middle class. Etiquette writers such as Catherine Sedgwick and Nathaniel Willis proclaimed a new "republican" code of etiquette, but the continuance of unspoken rules of *social class belied its democratic promise. Antebellum codes of manners excluded the poor, immigrants, the nonwhite, and children from the supposed level playing field of the bourgeois parlor.

By the late nineteenth century, the national myths of equality and universal upward mobility rang increasingly hollow amid the reality of *poverty, massive *immigration, and widening class divisions. The wealthy began to embrace an avowedly aristocratic and European code of manners, and etiquette writers such as Mary Sherwood made explicit class distinctions as they guided the social endeavors of the newly rich. As rules for entertaining grew ever more elaborate, the fancy table setting enjoyed its heyday.

In manners as in other areas, the trauma of *World War I brought a reaction against the practices of the late Victorian era. The rise of youth culture, the suburbs, the automobile, and continued *urbanization further challenged established social conventions. The *Progressive Era had partially discredited ostentatious displays of wealth, while the changing role of women also spelled trouble for the more restrictive rules. More relaxed behavior became the goal. As at other times, this did not put etiquette writers out of business, but merely set them to offering revised fare. Sophisticated behavior remained desirable, even if expressed more subtly than before. The first edition of Emily Post's perennially popular *Etiquette* appeared in 1922, followed by a radio program and a widely syndicated newspaper column.

After *World War II, the notion of "society" fell into eclipse. The wealthy no longer quite so ostentatiously set themselves off as a class distinguished by behavior and social activities. At the same time, America's increasingly multicultural identity confounded notions of one proper way of doing things. The women's movement and the accelerating divorce rate further undermined the old codes of manners. But manners did not disappear; Americans still needed symbolic gestures to act out the social order and keep face-to-face encounters from becoming chaotic. Elizabeth L. Post updated Emily Post's durable work in 1969, and the end of the century saw a new generation of behavior arbiters, including Letitia Baldridge and the newspaper columnist and author Judith Martin, who wrote under the name "Miss Manners." All evidence suggested that in the twenty-first century, manners advisers would continue to systematize current practices and reassure the uncertain.

[*See also* Antebellum Era; Courtship and Dating; Cultural Pluralism; Gilded Age; Leisure; Marriage and Divorce; Social Class; *Theory of the Leisure Class, The*; Twenties, The; Veblen, Thorstein; Working-Class Life and Culture.]

• Arthur M. Schlesinger Sr., *Learning How to Behave: A Historical Study of American Etiquette Books*, 1946. Karen Halttunen, *Confidence Men and Painted Women: A Study of Middle-Class Culture in America*, 1982. John Kasson, *Rudeness and Civility: Manners in Nineteenth-Century Urban America*, 1990. Richard Bushman, *The Refinement of America: Persons, Houses, Cities*, 1993. Mark Caldwell, *A Short History of Rudeness: Manners, Morals, and Misbehavior in Modern America*, 1999. C. Dallett Hemphill, *Bowing to Necessities: A History of Manners in America, 1620–1860*, 1999.

—C. Dallett Hemphill

EUGENICS. Eugenics had its modern roots in *Social Darwinism. Its proponents held that the quality of the human population could be improved by manipulating its biological heredity. The eugenics movement flourished in the Americas as well as in Europe and Asia during the early twentieth century. Its backbone in the United States consisted of biologists, physicians, psychologists, and middle-class, white Protestants of northern European origins. The zoologist Charles B. Davenport, director of a genetics research center at Cold Spring Harbor, Long Island, was an important proponent.

Eugenicists, exploiting Gregor Mendel's theory of heredity, which had been rediscovered in 1900, concluded that genes controlled a number of physical diseases and various mental deficiencies that were commonly termed "feeblemindedness." They further argued that mental deficiency underlay many adverse behavioral tendencies, including criminality, *poverty, alcoholism, and prostitution, and they contended that a biological propensity for such deleterious traits was disproportionately present among lower-income people, especially the "races" of immigrants arriving from eastern and southern Europe.

To the end of "improving" the American population, eugenicists joined other *immigration restrictionists in urging that fewer people from eastern and southern Europe be permitted entry to the United States. Many came to advocate contraception, arguing that if it were made available to lower-income groups, it would reduce the spread of bad genes. A number of eugenicists, contending that mentally deficient people were reproducing at a rate high enough to constitute a menace, called for the enactment of state programs of eugenic sterilization that would apply to the residents of state homes for the feebleminded.

Eugenicists helped obtain passage of the Immigration Restriction Act of 1924, providing biological reasons for the severe reductions it imposed on the immigration of people from eastern and southern Europe. By the late 1920s, some two dozen American states had enacted eugenic sterilization laws. The U.S. *Supreme Court upheld the constitutionality of such measures in the case of *Buck* v. *Bell* (1927). Justice Oliver Wendell *Holmes Jr., writing for the majority, declared "three generations of imbeciles are enough." By the mid-1930s, eugenic sterilizations had been performed on about twenty thousand people in the United States.

Few states actually enforced their eugenic laws, the leading exceptions being California and Virginia. The laws were widely regarded as an offense to *civil liberties, and during the second quarter of the century the eugenic science that undergirded them steadily lost credibility. Geneticists learned that few physical traits result from single genes and that human behavior is the product of a complex interplay of biology and environment. Social scientists showed that peoples from eastern and southern Europe were not races but ethnic and national groups who differed in culture but not biology. Eugenicists paid far too little attention to cultural, economic, and similar influences in their accounts of mental characteristics and social pathologies. Eugenic doctrine also came to be seen as pervaded by class and race prejudice. Although some eugenicists tried to remove such prejudice from their doctrines and goals, the revelations after *World War II of the extreme to which the Nazis had carried biological *racism made eugenics anathema. The specter of eugenics has continued to hang over all efforts to manipulate human heredity and formed a touchstone of late-twentieth-century debates over the acquisition and use of human genetic information.

[*See also* Anthropology; Birth Control and Family Planning; Boas, Franz; Crime; Cultural Pluralism; Genetics and Genetic Engineering; Human Genome Project; Immigration Law; Intelligence, Concepts of; Progressive Era; Prostitution and Antiprostitution; Race, Concept of; Sexual Morality and Sex Reform; Social Class.]

• Daniel J. Kevles, *In the Name of Eugenics: Genetics and the Uses of Human Heredity*, 1995. Edward J. Larson, *Sex, Race, and Science: Eugenics in the Deep South*, 1995.

—Daniel J. Kevles

EUROPEAN RECOVERY PROGRAM. *See* Marshall Plan.

EUROPE, U.S. RELATIONS WITH. *See* Foreign Relations: U.S. Relations with Europe.

EVANGELICALISM. *See* Fundamentalist Movement; Missionary Movement; Protestantism; Revivalism.

EVOLUTION, THEORY OF. Until the late 1850s, when the British philosopher Herbert Spencer introduced the term "evolution" to describe the history of the universe as a progression from the simple to the complex, writers discussing what came to be called evolution typically labeled it the "development" theory or, when referring to the organic world, the "transmutation" hypothesis. Few Americans paid any attention to such speculations until after 1844, when Robert Chambers, a Scot, anonymously published *Vestiges of the Natural History of Creation*, a synthesis of organic and inorganic development theories that elicited more ridicule than respect in the United States. Intense discussion of organic evolution did not begin until the appearance of the British naturalist Charles Darwin's *Origin of Species* in 1859. Although Darwin himself rarely used the term "evolution" to describe his views, they came to typify what others meant by evolution. Indeed, by the 1870s American commentators were commonly using "evolution" and "Darwinism" interchangeably.

Darwin's primary goal in writing the *Origin of Species* was to overthrow "the dogma of separate creations," which he regarded as "utterly useless" as a *scientific* explanation. By the mid-1870s the overwhelming majority of Darwin's fellow naturalists in America—botanists, zoologists, geologists, and anthropologists—had come to agree with him. Some were already calling evolution an "ascertained fact," though virtually none assigned as much importance as Darwin did to natural selection as the primary agent of organic change. Even Darwin's leading American champion, the Harvard botanist Asa *Gray, broke with his English friend in attributing the appearance of human beings and complex organs (such as the eye) to special divine intervention. Until the second third of the twentieth century, few American biologists identified natural selection as *the* mechanism of evolution.

During the early scientific debates over evolutionary theory and the efficacy of natural selection, religious leaders typically sat on the sidelines, many of them doubting that evolution would ever be accepted as serious science. By the mid-1870s, however, American naturalists were becoming evolutionists in such large numbers that the clergy could scarcely continue to ignore the issue. Some liberals simply baptized evolution as God's method of creation. But most religious leaders—whether Protestant, Catholic, or Jewish—rejected evolution, especially as it applied to human beings, or remained silent on the subject. Darwinism seemed not only to deny design in nature but, more important, to undermine the historical and ethical teachings of the *Bible. Americans who believed that God had created human beings in his image took umbrage at Darwin's assertion in *The Descent of Man* (1871) that "Man is descended from a hairy quadruped, furnished with a tail and pointed ears."

Despite widespread criticism of evolution in the late nineteenth and early twentieth centuries, no group mounted an organized crusade against it until after *World War I. Concerned by the increasing exposure of the nation's youth to evolution in high schools and emboldened by erroneous rumors that Darwinism (that is, evolution) lay on its "death-bed," Protestant fundamentalists in the 1920s sought to outlaw the teaching of human evolution in the public schools of America, which they accomplished in Tennessee, Mississippi, and Arkansas. In a celebrated 1925 trial, a court in Dayton, Tennessee, found John Thomas Scopes, a high-school science teacher, guilty of violating the state's antievolution law. Although the state supreme court later overturned Scopes's conviction, the groundswell of public opposition to evolution convinced many science teachers and most textbook publishers to soft-pedal discussions of evolution.

After seven decades of debating possible mechanisms of evolution—the inheritance of characters acquired by use and disuse, the influence of climatic changes and environmental catastrophes, the role of dramatic mutations and elusive internal forces—American biologists in the 1930s and 1940s finally reached a consensus about the central role played by natural selection operating on minute variations. Together various geneticists, systematists, paleontologists, embryologists, and botanists forged what came to be called the modern or evolutionary synthesis. Above all, as William B. Provine has pointed out, the so-called synthesis squeezed out mechanisms that allowed for purpose and design in evolution.

In the 1960s evolution reappeared in American classrooms with a vengeance, as school districts across the land adopted the federally funded Biological Sciences Curriculum Study textbooks, which featured evolution as "the warp and woof of modern biology." Outraged conservative Christians launched a counterattack that continued for the rest of the century. For a hundred years following the publication of the *Origin of Species*, antievolutionists had been united by their antipathy to human evolution, not by agreement on the mode of creation. They typically experienced little difficulty accommodating the evidence of ancient life forms with their reading of Genesis, either by interpreting the "days" of the first chapter of Genesis as geological ages or by assuming a huge chronological gap between the creation "in the beginning" and the much later Edenic creation. Beginning in the 1960s, however, large numbers of them turned their backs on such accommodating schemes in favor of young-earth, or scientific, creationism, which collapsed virtually the entire geological column into the year of Noah's flood and shrank Earth history to a mere 6,000–10,000 years. In the early 1980s two states, Arkansas and Louisiana, passed legislation mandating the teaching of this "creation science" whenever "evolution science" was taught, but the U. S. *Supreme Court in 1987 ruled that such laws violated the First Amendment to the *Constitution, requiring the separation of *church and state. This ruling prompted antievolutionists in the 1990s to push instead for the teaching of "intelligent design," based on the complexity of organic structures, and for treating evolution as a mere "theory."

By 2000 virtually all Americans, creationist and evolutionist alike, accepted the reality of "microevolution" (which for conservative Christians meant change within the originally created "kinds" of plants and animals), but the country remained bitterly divided over "macroevolution." Public-opinion polls in the 1990s revealed that 47 percent of Americans, including a quarter of college graduates, believed that "God created man pretty much in his present form at one time within the last 10,000 years." Another 40 percent thought that "Man has developed over millions of years from less advanced forms of life, but God guided this process, including man's creation." Only 9 percent supposed that "Man has developed over millions of years from less advanced forms of life" with God having no part in the process.

[*See also* Bill of Rights; Biological Sciences; Bryan, William Jennings; Education: Education in Contemporary America; Fundamentalist Movement; Religion; Science: Revolutionary Era to World War I; Science: From 1914 to 1945; Science: Since 1945; Scopes Trial.]

• James R. Moore, *The Post-Darwinian Controversies: A Study of the Protestant Struggle to Come to Terms with Darwin in Great Britain and America, 1870–1900,* 1979. Peter J. Bowler, *Evolution: The History of an Idea,* 1984. Jon H. Roberts, *Darwinism and the Divine in America: Protestant Intellectuals and Organic Evolution, 1859–1900,* 1988. Ronald L. Numbers, *The Creationists,* 1992. William B. Provine, "Progress in Evolution and Meaning in Life," in *Julian Huxley: Biologist and Statesman of Science,* ed. C. Kenneth Waters and Albert Van Helden, 1992, pp. 165–80. Gregg A. Mitman and Ronald L. Numbers, "Evolutionary Theory," in *Encyclopedia of the United States in the Twentieth Century,* ed. Stanley I. Kutler, 4 vols., 1996, 4:859–76. 1979. Ronald L. Numbers, *Darwinism Comes to America,* 1998. Ronald L. Numbers and John Stenhouse, eds., *Disseminating Darwinism: The Role of Place, Race, Religion, and Gender,* 1999.

—Ronald L. Numbers

EXECUTIVE BRANCH. *See* Federal Government, Executive Branch.

EXECUTIVE PRIVILEGE. Executive privilege has long been part of Anglo-Saxon jurisprudence and American constitutional history. In 1792, President George *Washington, citing the constitutional separation of powers, denied a congressional request for access to papers relevant to General Arthur St. Clair's defeat by Indian forces in Ohio. Three years later, Washington withheld documents pertaining to the negotiations that resulted in *Jay's Treaty. The nation's third president, Thomas *Jefferson, used similar grounds to defy a subpoena issued by U.S. *Supreme Court Justice John *Marshall during the treason trial of Aaron *Burr. More recently, Presidents Harry S. *Truman and Dwight D. *Eisenhower cited executive privilege—Truman in resisting a 1948 House resolution to turn over executive papers, and Eisenhower in rejecting a Senate demand for access to Defense Department files.

Subsequent Supreme Courts, however, sharply limited the executive-privilege claim. In *U.S.* v. *Nixon* (1974), the Court rejected Richard Nixon's assertion of executive privilege, ruling that his refusal to turn over the *Watergate tapes to Federal Judge John Sirica would "gravely impair" the judiciary's role under Article III of the *Constitution. More recently, when President Bill *Clinton claimed executive privilege in refusing to provide Congress with documents relating to activities of the White House Travel Office, the Supreme Court upheld a subpoena demanding the notes of relevant conversations between First Lady Hillary Clinton and White House attorneys. Moreover, in *Clinton* v. *Jones* (1998), a sexual-harassment case against the president, the Court unanimously required Clinton, while still in office, to answer civil lawsuits brought against him. As Justice John Paul Stevens noted, the president, like all other citizens, "is subject to judicial process in appropriate circumstances."

[*See also* Federal Government, Executive Branch: Overview; Federal Government Executive Branch: The Presidency; Federal Government, Judicial Branch.]

• Raoul Berger, *Executive Privilege: A Constitutional Myth,* 1974. Stanley I. Kutler, *The Wars of Watergate,* 1990.

—Herbert S. Parmet

EXERCISE. *See* Health and Fitness.

EXPANSIONISM. Expansionism—the desire of nations and empires to annex lands, peoples, or resources belonging to others—is a peculiar characteristic of a world order where boundaries are subject to the ambitions of those with the power and will to challenge them. War, as the instrument of coercion in the transfer of territory, dominated the history of the ancient world as successive conquering armies changed imperial configurations in accordance with their power and political designs. In Europe, the centuries of mass migrations and the slow emergence of the modern state system established myriad political boundaries without satisfying the needs and interests of the peoples affected. Conflicting expansionist interests and the resulting instability in international life were shaped by the interactions of three great historical realities: the economic universe of agriculture and trade, with its focus on rivers, harbors, and waterways; the cultural universe of ethnicity, language, and religion, which seldom conformed to national boundaries; and the political world of nations, more artificial and malleable than the others, with boundaries arising from natural lines of demarcation or war.

America's expansionism in the nineteenth century conformed to the European pattern of territorial change. It focused on bordering regions whose acquisition would enhance the nation's security and add valuable lands, resources, or waterways. Expansionism was usually justified by precepts of *Manifest Destiny, and throughout its expansionist career, the U.S. government never faced an invincible coalition committed to maintaining the status quo. Moreover, on every territorial issue the United States possessed the overwhelming strategic advantage. In its conflicts with such dominant European powers as Spain, England, and France, it always benefited from European rivalries and the weakening effects of distance. In conflicts with Indian nations, it benefited from tribal divisions, better armaments, and the sweep of European *diseases that had decimated Native peoples over the preceding two centuries. The United States achieved its continental empire in North America through the combination of diplomacy with Europe and wars against Indian nations and Mexico.

Continental Expansion. After the *Revolutionary War, U.S. continental expansion began with the *Louisiana Purchase of 1803, which at one stroke and with a cost of $15 million added 828,000 square miles to the national domain, from the *Mississippi River to the *Rocky Mountains.

Thomas *Jefferson's acquisition of Louisiana raised the issue of Florida's future. In 1764, Britain, then in possession of all Florida, divided the region at the Apalachicola River east of the Perdido, the historic line between French Louisiana and Spanish Florida. This created East and West Floridas. All Florida reverted to Spain in the Treaty of *Paris of 1783. Spain resisted U.S. efforts to acquire both Floridas, but in 1810, Spaniards in West Florida revolted against Spanish rule, took possession of Baton Rouge, declared their independence, and requested U.S. recognition. President James *Madison denied them recognition as American forces entered West Florida with orders to advance to the Perdido River. With Spanish garrisons defending Mobile and Pensacola, the Americans halted at the Pearl. When Britain protested the American occupation, Congress on 15 January 1811 passed a resolution declaring that the United States could not, "without serious inquietude, see any part of the said territory pass into the hands of a foreign power." While the United States continued to strengthen its position in West Florida, Congress early in 1812 annexed West Florida west of the Pearl River to Louisiana and added West Florida east of the Pearl to Mississippi Territory.

East Florida's disposition awaited the continuing decline of Spanish power in North America and the shrewd diplomacy of John Quincy *Adams. By 1817 Spain was too plagued with political and military disorders to maintain its authority in Florida. President James *Monroe in 1818 dispatched General Andrew *Jackson to fight against the Florida Indians. When

Jackson captured and executed two British agents as well as two Indian chiefs, all members of the cabinet except Secretary of State Adams argued that Jackson had exceeded his instructions and committed an act of war against Spain, which required an official disavowal. Adams retorted that Jackson had discretionary powers to terminate the Indian depredations; to disavow his actions was unthinkable. Adams carried the argument. On 23 July 1818, Adams reminded the Spanish minister, Don Luis de Onís, that Spain had an obligation to maintain order in Florida. Spain, recognizing its weakness, agreed to cede East Florida to the United States if the United States would assume the claims of U.S. citizens against Spain, estimated at five million dollars. Onís then raised the issue of the still-undefined southern boundary of the Louisiana Purchase. Convinced of his diplomatic advantage, Adams determined to push the boundary as far to the south and west as possible. Finally, on 20 February 1819, Onís capitulated. Spain ceded Florida and accepted a boundary from Louisiana to the Pacific coast highly favorable to the United States. Two days later, the two negotiators signed the *Adams-Onís Treaty.

Meanwhile, the boundary between the United States and Canada remained unsettled. In the Convention of 1818, Adams negotiated a boundary line from the Lake of the Woods westward along the 49th parallel to the Rocky Mountains. West of the Rockies, British fur trading interests centered largely in the Columbia River valley. Britain, therefore, demanded the Columbia River as the boundary between the mountains and the Pacific. Adams, however, seeking control of the Strait of Juan de Fuca and Puget Sound, one of the world's finest internal waterways, demanded the extension of the 49th parallel to the Pacific. When British negotiators proved intractable, Adams accepted a ten-year joint occupancy of the Oregon country.

Adams had delayed the final Oregon settlement until the United States could gain the diplomatic advantage. That came in the 1840s when American settlers began to occupy Oregon south of the Columbia. By late 1844, London was prepared to settle the Oregon question at the 49th parallel. This provided, in its estimation, an equitable distribution of waterways, with the United States acquiring Puget Sound and the British the magnificent harbor of Vancouver. This concession was a triumph for the congressional moderates, who favored a peaceful settlement at the 49th parallel, in contrast to the Democratic expansionists who demanded a line at 54°40'. The Oregon Treaty of 1846 established the boundary line of the 49th parallel between the Rockies and the continental shore. The line then continued to the Pacific through the Strait of Juan de Fuca. Meanwhile, in 1842, the United States and Britain reached a settlement of the disputed Maine boundary. The *Alaska Purchase of 1867, encompassing a region no longer desired by Russia, was, like Louisiana, largely a windfall.

Mexico's reluctance to part with its possessions in the American *Southwest meant that their acquisition by the United States would require threatened or actual force. The Republic of Texas, having established its independence in 1836 with the aid of American frontiersmen, entered the Union in December 1845, its boundary with an embittered Mexico still undefined. Following Texas's annexation, the James Knox *Polk administration pursued Texas's border claims to the Rio Grande. Early in 1846 Polk sent General Zachary *Taylor's army into the disputed region between the Nueces River and the Rio Grande to underscore those claims. In May, the predictable clash of arms led to the U.S. declaration of war against Mexico. From the outset, Polk and Secretary of the Navy George *Bancroft were determined to secure Mexico's *California territory as well, from San Francisco and Monterey in the north to the magnificent bay of San Diego in the south.

American victories in Mexico and California during 1847, ending with the occupation of Mexico City in September, provided the U.S. negotiator, Nicholas P. Trist, sufficient leverage to achieve the desired territorial settlement. In the Treaty of Guadalupe Hidalgo (1848), the United States acquired a boundary from the Gulf of Mexico to the Pacific that terminated just south of San Diego Bay. The *Gadsden Purchase of 1853, which added a strip of land in Arizona and New Mexico south of the original Gila River boundary, permanently fixed the borders of the United States on the North American continent.

Expansion in the Pacific and Caribbean. In the late nineteenth century, American expansionist impulses turned to the vast Pacific region, with its seemingly limitless opportunities for profit and adventure. Rendering the Pacific region especially inviting was the presumption that the civilizations of this area could not resist the power, *technology, and organizational skills of the West, especially the United States.

America's advance into the Pacific came in incremental stages. Prodded by Anson Burlingame, the first U.S. minister to China (1861–1867), the United States developed a paternalistic attitude toward that amorphous empire, eventually making its defense the keystone of U.S. policy in the Pacific. At the same time, the United States contributed much to Japan's nineteenth-century modernization and entertained some feelings of paternalism toward that country as well. Meanwhile, in 1867, the United States claimed the Midway Islands in the north-central Pacific. In subsequent years, Washington demonstrated a growing interest in *Hawai'i, Korea, and Samoa, where it faced powerful German and Japanese competition. Despite the potential dangers, two forces accelerated America's Pacific encroachments. One was the missionary zeal to bring Christianity, order, and progress to the world's "backward" regions. To expansionist Josiah Strong, a Congregationalist minister, Christianity and civil liberty, as keys to western civilization, had contributed most to the elevation of the human race. "The Anglo-Saxon, as the great representative of these two ideas," Strong wrote in *Our Country* (1885), "is divinely commissioned to be, in a peculiar sense, his brother's keeper. Add to this the fact of his rapidly increasing strength in modern times, and we have well nigh a demonstration of his destiny." The more tangible incentive to American expansion in the Pacific lay in the quest for markets that accompanied the rapid post–*Civil War growth of American industrial and agricultural production. Alfred Thayer *Mahan's influential book, *The Influence of Sea Power upon History* (1890), advocated the acquisition of island outposts to protect and service the country's shipping.

Except for Midway, the foundations of America's empire in the Pacific were laid during the administration of President Benjamin *Harrison (1889–1893). In August 1891, Secretary of State James G. *Blaine wrote to Harrison: "There are only three places that are of value enough to be taken that are not continental. One is Hawaii and the others Cuba and Porto Rico. . . . Hawaii may come up for decision at any unexpected hour." In February 1893, the Harrison administration negotiated an annexation treaty with Hawaiian commissioners, only to have the incoming Grover *Cleveland administration reject it and condemn the Harrison administration's involvement in a tripartite protectorate over Samoa (1889) as well. Anti-imperialists warned the nation against assuming commitments outside the Western Hemisphere. Colonial acquisitions, declared Yale sociologist William Graham Sumner, would be burdens, not assets. The anti-imperialists demonstrated their strength by defeating a second Hawaiian annexation treaty in 1897.

It required the *Spanish-American War of 1898, the result of journalistic jingoism and Americans' concern over conditions in Cuba, to stay the power of anti-imperialism and project the United States onto the world stage. Shortly after the outbreak of war, fought ostensibly to free Cuba from Spanish control, Commodore George Dewey's Pacific Squadron destroyed the Spanish fleet in Manila Bay. This display of naval power in the *Philippines, and the possibilities it opened for empire building, was welcomed by well-placed expansionists in Washington. In June 1898, against little opposition, Congress annexed Hawai'i by joint resolution. Meanwhile, President William *McKinley dispatched an army to occupy Manila, which Spanish officials surrendered to American forces on 13 August 1898. Having liberated the Philippines, the United States had either to restore them to Spain, free them, transfer them to another power, or retain them. As expansionists clamored for their retention, McKinley on 16 September instructed his peace commissioners to demand cession of the Philippines on the grounds that U.S. forces, with no thought of acquisition, had imposed upon the United States unavoidable obligations to the Filipino people. In the peace treaty signed that December in Paris, Spain conveyed the Philippines, Guam, and Puerto Rico to the United States in exchange for twenty million dollars. Critics warned the administration that it was assuming territorial commitments that the country could not defend. After a long and sometimes prophetic debate, the Senate, in February 1899, approved the treaty by a vote of fifty-seven to twenty-seven, one more than the necessary two-thirds. Philippine annexation triggered a costly war with Emilio Aguinaldo's Filipino insurgents for possession of the islands. The U.S. antiguerrilla campaign soon degenerated into a no-quarter struggle of burned villages, the torture of prisoners, and the deaths of many innocent men, women, and children. A special senate committee in 1902 heard harrowing testimony about this war, which cost the lives of some four thousand Americans and as many as twenty thousand Filipino independence fighters.

In the aftermath of the acquisition of the Philippines, anti-imperialist opposition grew so strong that the United States embarked on no more territorial acquisition. In 1903 Cuba and Panama became protectorates, and the United States came to exert administrative control over the Dominican Republic, Haiti, Liberia, and Nicaragua during the second and third decades of the twentieth century. But, generally, twentieth-century American expansion emphasized economic and cultural connections rather than territorial acquisition.

Thus, at the turn of the century, the United States made efforts to prevent China's dismemberment by Russia, Britain, France, Germany, Italy, and Japan, having Secretary of State John *Hay send his Open Door notes of 1899 and 1900. These countries, in principle, accepted China's economic, political, and administrative integrity and agreed to support equal access to China's trade. With U.S. policy objectives, in China and elsewhere, now anchored to the territorial status quo and supporting an "open door" trading system, the United States was prepared to oppose, at least in principle, any territorial expansion based on coercion or any spheres of special interest. In doing so during the 1930s, it confronted new expansionist powers—Japan and Germany—and a future threatened by global war.

[*See also* Agriculture: 1770s to 1890; Agriculture: The "Golden Age" (1890s–1920); Anti-Imperialist League; Business; Capitalism; Economic Development; Foreign Relations; Indian History and Culture: From 1800 to 1900; Indian Wars; Industrialization; Insular Cases; Mexican War; Missionary Movement; Multinational Enterprises; "Open Door" Policy; Protectorates and Dependencies; Spanish Settlements in North America; Texas Republic and Annexation.]

• E. W. Lyon, *Louisiana in French Diplomacy, 1759–1804*, 1934. Arthur P. Whitaker, *The Mississippi Question, 1795–1803*, 1934. Albert K. Weinberg, *Manifest Destiny: A Study of Nationalist Expansionism in American History*, 1935. Ernest R. May, *Imperial Democracy: The Emergence of America as a Great Power*, 1961. Frederick Merk, *Manifest Destiny and Mission in American History: A Reinterpretation*, 1963. H. Wayne Morgan, *America's Road to Empire: The War with Spain and Overseas Expansion*, 1965. Norman A. Graebner, *Manifest Destiny*, 1968. Richard E. Welch, *Imperialists and Anti-Imperialists: The Debate over Expansionism in the 1890s*, 1972. Goran Rystad, *Ambiguous Imperialism: American Foreign Policy and Domestic Politics at the Turn of the Century*, 1975. David L. Anderson, *Imperialism and Idealism: American Diplomats in China, 1861–1898*, 1985. Norman A. Graebner, *Foundations of American Foreign Policy: A Realist Appraisal From Franklin to McKinley*, 1985. Thomas R. Hietela, *Manifest Design*, 1985.

—Norman A. Graebner

EXPLORATION, CONQUEST, AND SETTLEMENT, ERA OF EUROPEAN. From 1487 to 1497, explorers sailing for the Portuguese, Castilian (Spanish), and English crowns opened three routes to "the Indies," soon learning that two led not to Asia, but to the Americas.

Early Voyages, Conflicts, and Colonizing Ventures. In 1487, Portuguese Bartholomeo Díaz explored the entire west coast of Africa. Nine years later, Vasco da Gama rounded Africa and established a dangerous but lucrative Indian Ocean trade link with Asia. In 1492, Christopher *Columbus, a Genoese working for the Spanish crown, sailed westward from Iberia and reached islands in the Caribbean, which he believed to be the eastern fringe of Asia. John Cabot, a fellow Genoese sailing for Henry VII of England, in 1497 crossed the North Atlantic and sighted land in Newfoundland or Cape Breton.

Europe's expansion arose from a restless striving for wealth and territory and the renewal of learning during the Renaissance and Reformation. The mastery of transoceanic travel culminated centuries of attempts by Christians to gain ascendancy over their Muslim rivals, who controlled trade routes into Africa and Asia. Western Europeans achieved these feats of exploration by borrowing from their adversaries' mathematical and navigational technology, such as the astrolabe, magnetic compass, and lateen (triangular) sails, which allowed tacking into the wind.

European fishermen seeking to feed a protein-hungry Europe may have reached Newfoundland before Cabot's voyage of 1497, although the documentary record is unclear. A cargo of Newfoundland fish reached England in 1502, and by 1506 the Portuguese were taxing cod caught off the Grand Banks. Soon upwards of three hundred ships and ten thousand men from Portugal, the Basque country, the Azores, France, and Spain were visiting the fishing banks every summer.

For most of the sixteenth century, the Iberians dominated European expansion, as dynastic controversies and religious upheavals preoccupied European powers. By mid-century, the Portuguese had established sugar plantations on islands off Africa's west coast, worked by black slaves purchased or captured in west Africa. In 1532, the Portuguese extended sugar plantation slavery into Brazil, their only colony in the Western Hemisphere.

The Spanish, meanwhile, established a colony on the islands claimed by Columbus in 1492. Fanning out from Hispaniola (modern-day Haiti/Dominican Republic), Spaniards enslaved Arawakan- and Taino-speaking "Indians" for *mining and agricultural enterprises. Abusive labor regimes, together with European *diseases such as *smallpox, *influenza, measles, chicken pox, and mumps, to which indigenous populations had no immunities, soon decimated entire tribes. Spanish conquistadors seeking gold, silver, pearls, and gems explored coastlines and portions of the North American mainland. Expeditions led by Juan Ponce de León to Florida (1512–1513; 1521), Lucas Vásquez de Ayllón to the Carolina coast (1526), Hernando de *Soto to Florida and the interior Southeast (1539–1542), Francisco Vásquez de *Coronado to the *Southwest (1540–1542), and Juan Rodriguez Cabrillo along the *California coast (1542–1543) left no permanent colonies.

Spain conquered the Aztec capital, Tenochtitlán (Mexico City) by 1521 and the Inca capital, Cuzco, by 1535. Both empires had amassed exquisite gold and silver objects, which the conquistadors under Hernando Cortés in Mexico and Francisco Pizarro in Peru plundered. Spain quickly established the viceroyalties of New Spain and Peru, claimed all native gold and silver mines, and forced Indians to work them. By mid-century, Spanish galleons loaded with treasure sailed annually

MAP 6: 1590 ENGLISH MAP OF ROANOKE ISLAND AND ALBEMARLE SOUND, IN PRESENT-DAY NORTH CAROLINA

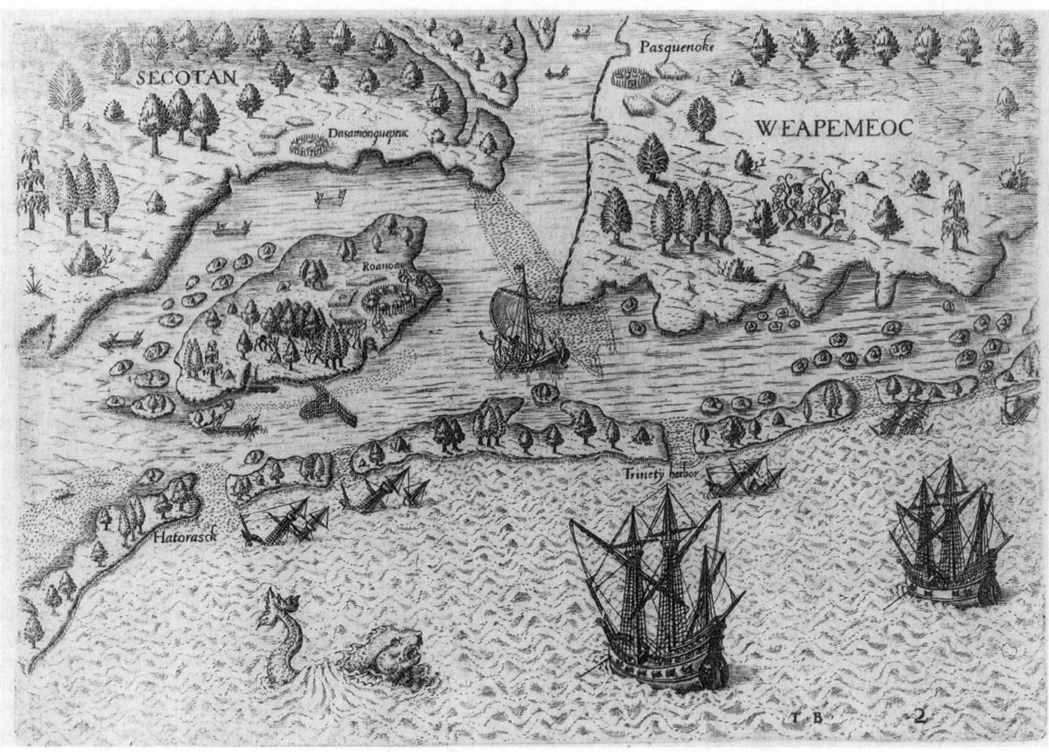

Theodor de Bry's engraving, based on drawings by John White, appeared in *A Briefe and True Report of the New Found Land of Virginia* (London, 1590) by Thomas Harriot, a tutor in the household of Sir Walter Raleigh. In addition to recording Indian place names and details of Indian life, the map also portrays English sailing vessels of the period—including several that have foundered on the treacherous shoals. While Indians on shore wield bows and arrows, a man on shipboard brandishes a cross.

[*See* Colonial Era; Exploration, Conquest, and Settlement, Era of European; Indian History and Culture: From 1500 to 1800; Jamestown; Smith, John.]

for Europe, becoming prey to pirates, many of them English, based in the Bahamas. Spain established Florida (1565) in response to the French colony at Fort Caroline (1562) and to reduce privateering by Elizabethan "seadogs" like Francis Drake. In 1598, a wealthy Spaniard sent five hundred colonists to present-day New Mexico, hoping to reap a fortune from silver mining. The resultant colony remained a permanent Spanish borderland, but did not produce the hoped-for wealth.

England and France had only a few royally sponsored voyages of discovery in the sixteenth century, mostly searching for the elusive Northwest Passage: Sebastian Cabot in 1507, and the French-sponsored Giovanni de Verrazano (1524) and Jacques Cartier (1535). Cartier's exploration and attempted colonization established France's claim to "Canada," an Iroquois term. The French and English made scattered attempts at colonization, but not until Samuel de Champlain established Port Royal in Acadia (1605) and Quebec City on the St. Lawrence (1608) did the French gain a permanent presence in North America.

European fishermen on the Grand Banks and in the Gulf of St. Lawrence had long bartered with local Indians, and the establishment of a permanent French presence profoundly affected Native political and economic alliances. Quebec (1608) and later Montreal (1642) were strategically located on an east-west trade axis linking Algonquian-speaking tribes of the Great Lakes and the St. Lawrence. French missionaries and merchants grafted themselves onto the system organized by the Hurons and their allies. (Similarly the Dutch, beginning in 1624, established *fur trade posts on the Hudson River and supplied the Iroquois and their allies with guns and other manufactured items.) To rebuild trade and alliances disrupted by epidemics and intertribal wars, French traders and missionaries moved into the western Great Lakes and southward into the *Mississippi River system. In 1663, Louis XIV took over the colony of Canada, and in 1698 established the province of Louisiana, controlling the entire Mississippi River with the founding of *Detroit (1701) and *New Orleans (1718).

The seventeenth century brought a wave of English colonization. The English woolen trade had flourished in the previous century, enriching the commercial elite. Farming improvements coupled with the enclosure of monastic estates displaced thousands of yeomen and day laborers, many of whom became indentured servants in the Americas. Religious strife in England between Protestants and Catholics and within the Church of England made colonization in North America an attractive alternative to many townspeople with capital.

English Colonization I: 1607–1640. English colonization falls into two distinct chronological phases: 1607–1640 and 1660–1681. Seven English efforts to establish colonies in Newfoundland all failed owing to the harsh winters and scarcity of food. Cecil Calvert, Lord Baltimore, attempted a Newfoundland colony before relocating to Maryland's more temperate clime in 1634. By the time the Calvinistic separatists known as the *Pilgrims landed at *Plymouth in 1620, English fishermen lived at year-round fishing stations from present-day Maine to Massachusetts Bay. English Puritans (nonseparatists seeking to purify the Church of England) secured a charter from Charles I for a Massachusetts Bay Colony in 1629. An advance party settled at Salem in 1628, followed in 1630 by a large fleet under John *Winthrop. Religious and political controversies soon led some Massachusetts Puritans to found nearby colonies in Connecticut and Rhode Island. Others, seeking economic gain, founded townships in the interior. A healthy climate, good diets, and high fertility rates along with steady *immigration led to a dramatic rise in population throughout southern *New England. By 1700, Massachusetts Bay Colony, now with a royal charter, had expanded to include adjacent Plymouth Colony.

The nascent Virginia Colony (*Jamestown, 1607) did poorly until John Rolfe introduced a hybrid variety of tobacco in 1611. Abuse of indentured servants, Indian warfare, and poor management prompted the Crown to revoke Virginia's commercial charter in 1624 and appoint a royal governor. Lord Baltimore's Maryland (founded 1634) paralleled Virginia economically, but its large Catholic population and its origins in a proprietary royal grant to a single family distinguished it from its larger neighbor. By 1700 both colonies had become more highly stratified in race and class as black slaves replaced white servants, especially after 1660.

For Englishmen seeking riches in the Americas, the Caribbean was the most attractive location, but also the least healthy. Taking small islands on the fringe of Spain's Caribbean holdings, the English soon held Barbados, Antigua, Nevis, St. Kitts, and the Bahamas, as well as Bermuda in the Atlantic. Barbados, founded in 1625, prospered through sugar and rum production. The transition to *slavery and sugar monoculture in the Caribbean drove out many English planters in the 1660s, some of whom relocated to mainland colonies, particularly the Carolinas. The Barbadians who founded Charleston in 1670 replicated Caribbean ways, replacing sugar with rice.

English Colonization II: 1660–1681. The English Civil War interrupted colonization, but the restoration of the monarchy in 1660 spawned expansionist projects by aristocrats jockeying for power. In 1663, Charles II chartered the Carolina Company, which planted a colony south of Virginia and north of Spanish Florida, and the Royal African Company, which challenged Dutch control of the slave trade. Early Carolinians suffered from *malaria and *yellow fever, but the colony succeeded through the labor of slaves, who by 1750 formed the largest black majority of any mainland colony.

To the north, Charles II sent a naval force in 1664 to take New Netherlands from the Dutch and made his brother, the Duke of York, the proprietor. England's chartering of the Hudson's Bay Company in 1670 put them in direct competition with the French in Canada for control of the fur trade. The last English colony established in the seventeenth century, Pennsylvania (1681), under the proprietorship of William *Penn, also incorporated Swedish settlements that had been on the Delaware River since 1655. Delaware gained its own legislative assembly in 1704, but it remained under the governor of Pennsylvania until 1776.

The Stages of Expansion and the Patterns of Interaction. The era of European exploration, conquest, and settlement illustrates the stages of expansion that historical geographer Donald P. Meinig has suggested as a model for trans-Atlantic interaction: seafaring, conquering, and planting of colonies. Recurrent general patterns within these three sequences include *exploration*, whereby information is acquired; *gathering* of staple commodities such as fish, timber, and salt, along with new cartographic information; *barter* with Native peoples who trade goods such as furs for goods brought by Europeans; *plunder*, where Europeans ignore the protocol of Native diplomacy and seize goods and peoples, alienating local populations; *establishment of outposts* as fixed points of commercial exchange, *imperial imposition*, whereby Europeans claim lands and introduce political, religious, and social hierarchies in the form of governors, missionaries, and soldiers; *implantation*, the establishment of permanent colonies; and finally, *imperial colonization*, where the full complex of European institutions and cultural preferences are transferred and nurtured to promote national goals and further expansion.

By 1700, many colonial regions of North America had reached the last stage of imperial colonization. European societies had been transplanted, along with their values, biases, and worldviews. Beginning with King William's War (1689), Spanish, French, and English colonists and their Native allies found themselves parties in repeated wars as European nations contested for dominance in North America.

Despite their vast claims, European nations in reality occupied only a small portion of the Americas by 1700. Most territory remained in control of Native peoples, on whom Europeans depended for trade, geographic expertise, and military support. While disease, warfare, and expanding settlements continued to decimate many Indian nations, most also found ways to adapt to the presence of Europeans and maintain control over their lives. Some resisted. The Pueblos of New Mexico drove Spaniards out of the region for twelve years in the Great Pueblo Revolt (1680–1692). The Comanche and Apache also rejected missionization and Hispanicization well into the nineteenth century. Others, such as Indian peoples in French-influenced areas, established ties through trade alliances and intermarriage that produced a creole population of mixed-bloods or Métis, who played a major role in North American development after 1700.

[*See also* Colonial Era; Columbian Exchange; Fisheries; French Settlements in North America; Indentured Servants; Indian History and Culture: Migration and Pre-Columbian Era; Indian History and Culture: Distribution of Major Groups; Indian History and Culture: Circa 1500; Indian History and Culture: From 1500 to 1800; Puritanism; Slavery: Development and Expansion of Slavery; Spanish Settlements in North America; Tobacco Industry.]

• Carl O. Sauer, *Sixteenth Century North America: The Land and the People as Seen by the Europeans*, 1971. W. J. Eccles, *The Canadian Frontier, 1534–1760*, rev. ed., 1974. David B. Quinn, *North America from Earliest Discovery to First Settlements: The Norse Voyages to 1612*, 1977. Kenneth R. Andrews, *Trade, Plunder and Settlement: Maritime Enterprise and the Genesis of the British Empire, 1480–1630*, 1984. D. W. Meinig, *The Shaping of America: A Geographical Perspective on 500 Years of History*, vol. 1, *Atlantic America, 1492–1800*, 1986. R. Cole Harris, ed., *Historical Atlas of Canada*, vol. 1, *From the Beginning to 1800*, 1987. Jack P. Greene, *Pursuits of Happiness: The Social Development of Early Modern British Colonies and the Formation of American Culture*, 1988. David J. Weber, *The Spanish Frontier in North America*, 1992. Bruce G. Trigger and William R. Swagerty, "Entertaining Strangers: North America in the Sixteenth Century," in *The Cambridge History of the Native Peoples of the Americas*, vol. 1, *North America*, part 1, Bruce G. Trigger and Wilcomb E. Washburn, eds., 1996, pp. 325–98.

—William R. Swagerty and Elizabeth Mancke

F

FACTORY SYSTEM. The shift of manufacturing from hand to machine processes was a central element of the Industrial Revolution that transformed the early modern economy and contributed to the emergence of modern industrial *capitalism. The coming of the modern factory led to a tremendous increase in labor *productivity, which contributed, in turn, to a rising standard of living, an increasingly complex division of labor, growing agricultural production, and a massive rural-to-urban population shift. It is no exaggeration to characterize the factory system as the major contributor to this interrelated complex of changes that distinguish modern society.

The factory system in the United States emerged with the growth of the cotton *textile industry in *New England after the *Revolutionary War. Customarily historians identify the cotton spinning mill of Almy, Brown, and Slater established in Pawtucket, Rhode Island, in 1790 as the first permanent factory in the new nation. Samuel Slater, a former apprentice in the Derbyshire, England, mill of Jedidiah Strutt, emigrated to the United States in 1789 with an extensive knowledge of English carding and spinning machinery. In Pawtucket, with the financial backing of two Providence merchants, William Almy and Smith Brown, he constructed the requisite machinery and set a small spinning mill in operation in December 1790. Rhode Island, eastern Connecticut, and southern Massachusetts dominated early cotton textile manufacturing in the United States. The reconstruction of a power loom at the Boston Manufacturing Company in Waltham, Massachusetts, in 1813 by a group of investors subsequently called by historians the Boston Associates, set the stage for further expansion of the industry, with the emergence of a vertically integrated system that combined all stages of the production process at a single site.

Before 1850, textiles were the single major consumer commodity successfully produced within a factory setting. The Waltham-Lowell–type mills of northern New England realized the full potential of factory production. In Lowell, for instance, by 1850 ten large mill complexes, with assets valued at twelve million dollars, employed more than ten thousand operatives producing a million yards of cloth weekly. With a population of some 33,000, Lowell was Massachusetts's second largest city and the leading factory town in the country. By 1850 textiles manufactured in New England and the *Philadelphia region clothed virtually the entire nation. Only on isolated frontiers might homespun fabrics still be found; only among urban elites did imported textiles have a substantial market.

Factory production soon spread to other sectors of the economy. By the mid–nineteenth century, shoemaking and garment manufacture were increasingly concentrated in urban factories. After the *Civil War, the *iron and steel industry emerged as the leader of a second industrial revolution, which shifted production from light consumer goods to heavy industry. Whereas textile, shoe, and garment manufacturing were localized operations, steel production created new national corporate enterprises by the turn of the twentieth century. Buying up coal and iron ore deposits, purchasing *railroads and steamship lines, and merging with potential competitors, steel magnates like Henry Clay Frick (1849–1919) and Andrew *Carnegie built and administered fortunes that dwarfed those of the antebellum New England cotton mill owners.

Given the economies of factory production, corporate managers sought to systematize factory operations to maximize their returns. The *scientific-management principles espoused by Frederick W. Taylor in the *Progressive Era captured the new imperatives. In the meatpacking, *automotive, rubber, and *electrical industries, new ways of organizing production emerged to take advantage of mechanization and increase the productivity of labor. As workers lost control of the *work process in the modern factory, their unions bargained for increased wages, offering American workers by the mid–twentieth century the highest standard of living in the world. Referring to feelings of powerlessness and purposelessness among factory workers in the post–*World War II decades, some sociologists discerned a growing sense of alienation. Radical social critics questioned whether labor's new contract was a pact with the devil.

At the end of the twentieth century the continuing growth of factory productivity transformed the American economy in still other ways, resulting in a sharp decline in manufacturing jobs and the growth of a newly dominant service sector. Financial and information services increasingly constituted the growth sectors of the nation's economy. Unions, traditionally strongest in the manufacturing sector, experienced dramatic declines in membership and economic and political power, as yet another consequence of the ongoing global transformation of factory production. What role the factory will continue to play in a postindustrial world economy remains an open question.

[*See also* Agriculture; "American System" of Manufactures; Antebellum Era; Automation and Computerization; Business; Cotton Industry; Economic Development; Gilded Age; Labor Markets; Labor Movements; Mass Production; Meatpacking and Meat Processing Industry; Multinational Enterprises; Post–Cold War Era; Technology; Urbanization.]

• Harry Braverman, *Labor and Monopoly Capitalism: The Degradation of Work in the Twentieth Century*, 1974. Alan Dawley, *Class and Community: The Industrial Revolution in Lynn*, 1976. Thomas Dublin, *Women at Work: The Transformation of Work and Community in Lowell, Massachusetts, 1826–1860*, 1979. Barry Bluestone and Bennett Harrison, *The Deindustrialization of America: Plant Closings, Community Abandonment and the Dismantling of American Industry*, 1982. Gary B. Kulik, "Industrialization," in *Encyclopedia of American Social History*, eds. Mary Kupiec Cayton, Elliot J. Gorn, and Peter W. Williams, 1993, pp. 593–604. Walter Licht, *Industrializing America: The Nineteenth Century*, 1995.

—Thomas Dublin

FAIR DEAL. *See* Truman, Harry S.

FAIR EMPLOYMENT PRACTICE COMMITTEE. In June 1941, President Franklin Delano *Roosevelt reluctantly created the Fair Employment Practice Committee (FEPC) to forestall a mass demonstration planned by the black labor leader A. Philip *Randolph to protest discrimination and segregation in defense industries. Executive Order 8802 authorized the FEPC to investigate job discrimination in war industries and federal agencies. Led by Lawrence Cramer and black *Chicago alderman Earl B. Dickerson, the committee and its interracial, interethnic staff, including appointees from business and labor, examined complaints of discrimination and held hearings. Howls of protest, particularly from southern politicians and editors, soon led Roosevelt to abolish the original committee.

The FEPC enjoyed strong support among blacks, liberals, religious groups, and labor unions, however, and in May 1943 Roosevelt created a new FEPC. The staff at the Washington headquarters, headed by the black law school dean George M. Johnson, oversaw thirteen regional offices. Significantly, the agency became the first in U.S. history to appoint blacks to policy-making positions. Dealing with other agencies often cool and even hostile toward its goals, the FEPC exposed the subterfuges used by private and federal employers to deny war-related jobs and upgrading to minorities. But the FEPC had little real power. By summer 1946 relentless congressional opposition led to its dismantling.

Many historians credit wartime labor shortages for decreasing job discrimination, not the parsimoniously funded FEPC. Others, however, cite the FEPC for establishing the principle that job bias constituted a denial of *civil rights. Blacks indeed used the FEPC in tight *labor markets to open up work opportunities, and in some regions the agency placed qualified minorities in skilled trades and professions ordinarily closed to them. In some ways a precursor of the postwar *civil rights movement, the FEPC's symbolic and long-term significance seems unquestioned.

[*See also* African Americans; Racism; Segregation, Racial; World War II: Domestic Effects.]

• James A. Neuchterlein, "The Politics of Civil Rights: The FEPC, 1941–1946," *Prologue* X (1978): 171–91. Merl E. Reed, *Seedtime for the Modern Civil Rights Movement: The President's Committee on Fair Employment Practice, 1941–1946*, 1991.

—Merl E. Reed

FAIRS, COUNTY AND STATE. The first agricultural fairs in the United States were the annual sheep-shearings held by George Washington Parke Custis, step-grandson of the first president. Begun in 1803, Custis's shearings expressed an American desire to achieve independence from Europe in the manufacture of textiles. Elkanah Watson, the so-called father of American agricultural fairs, had already dined with Custis at *Mount Vernon when, in 1811, he organized the Berkshire County Livestock Fair in western Massachusetts. This first fair consisted of fourteen farmers parading their animals to a designated fairground, socializing, and hearing speeches on the future of *agriculture.

The Berkshire Fair contained the key elements of fairs to come: exhibits, competitive judging, the award of prizes or premiums, and social events, including dances, oratory, and dinners. Women's work—sewing and preserving—was rewarded and honored. The object throughout was the improvement of agriculture, craft, and industry. The 1812 Berkshire Fair offered seventy dollars in premiums: Farmers willing to experiment with new breeds and methods were publicly rewarded for their efforts, thus encouraging others to do likewise. The fair idea stirred great enthusiasm. By the end of the *Civil War, the U.S. Department of Agriculture counted 1,367 agricultural societies in operation nationwide.

Agricultural societies, often made up of businesspeople and politicians rather than farmers, organized and ran most fairs. Implement manufacturers, grocers, lawyers, and railroad executives all had a stake in the health of the rural economy and worked tirelessly to promote fairs. Such societies held title to state and county fairgrounds. Nineteenth-century fairgrounds shared certain canonical architectural features: a peripheral fence to control entry, a grandstand and a racing oval (for "trials of speed," which were really horse races with illicit wagering), a Women's Building (or Floral Hall), and an exhibition hall. Around these permanent landmarks clustered other temporary structures, including cook-tents, lemonade stands, and the ubiquitous midway, with its freak shows and games of chance. Phil Stong's 1932 novel *State Fair*, while based on the Iowa State Fair at Des Moines, accurately describes most American fairs between 1870 and *World War II.

Fairs were important venues for the dissemination of knowledge about animal and plant genetics, new techniques and *farm machinery, and marketing strategies. Farmers first saw steel plows, gas-driven tractors, cream separators, and electric lights at fairs. Their wives bought sewing machines there. Their sons and daughters, after 1903, joined corn and calf and canning clubs—the forerunners of the *4-H club movement—to compete at fairs. In this way, club organizers spread word of the latest advances from children to parents. Midway and grandstand shows helped overcome rural isolation. On their annual pilgrimages to fairgrounds in Des Moines or St. Paul or Pomona, farm families saw the same kinds of entertainment that city dwellers enjoyed.

In the 1990s, 125 million Americans annually attended agricultural fairs. Some were farmers, following in Elkanah Watson's footsteps and bent on self-improvement, but most were city folk or suburbanites who came to the fair to stay in touch with the culture and values of a rural past, real or imagined.

[*See also* Antebellum Era; Circuses; Early Republic, Era of the; Federal Government, Executive Branch: Department of Agriculture; Homework; Horse Racing; Popular Culture; Regionalism.]

• Donald B. Mart, *Historical Directory of American Agricultural Fairs*, 1986. Karal Ann Marling, *Blue Ribbon: A Social and Pictorial History of the Minnesota State Fair*, 1990.

—Karal Ann Marling

FAMILY. As a complex social institution, the family is affected by both the processes of social and historical change and by natural variables such as biological and psychological processes. Society affects the family through cultural values, market conditions, demographic changes, industrial institutions, churches, government, and *welfare agencies. The relationships of individual family members with each other and with the collective family unit are defined differently under various cultural and historical contexts, the meaning of "family" can even differ among various members of the same family. A historical understanding of the family involves consideration of *courtship, *marriage, *life stages, *gender roles, sexuality, emotions, and human development.

Throughout American history, the family has been seen as the linchpin of the social order and the basis for stable governance. Though the family has changed more gradually than other institutions in response to external forces, educators, social planners, and the media have long expressed fear of family breakdown under the pressures of social change. Since the founding of the nation, every generation has voiced anxiety over what were perceived as threats to the "traditional" family.

This essay discusses historical changes in the American family, drawing upon research on the history of the family since this field emerged in the 1970s.

Households and Kin. A *nuclear family* is a unit consisting of parents and their children, a childless couple, or one parent and his or her children. In a nuclear *household*, the domestic group may include non-relatives as well, including apprentices, "life cycle servants" (typically teenagers placed by their own parents), or dependent members of the community.

In considering continuity and change in family behavior, social scientists and laypersons alike long assumed that "modern" family structures and demographic behavior such as nuclear households, family limitation, and the spacing of children were by-products of *industrialization, and that in preindustrial society the extended household form predominated, often with three generations co-residing. According to this view, industrialization destroyed the three-generation family structure and replaced it with an "isolated" nuclear family more compatible with the demands of the industrial system. Industrialization was thus considered a major watershed in family structure and demographic behavior. Historical research has revised these myths.

Contrary to such assumptions, households in the *Colonial Era were nuclear in structure. They were, however, enmeshed in close ties with extended kin, who usually resided nearby. Aging parents rarely shared the same household with their adult children, but lived in the vicinity, often on the same land. Thus industrialization did not break down a preindustrial extended family or produce an isolated nuclear family type. Indeed, owing to migration and housing shortages, industrialization and *urbanization may actually have *increased* the proportion of households containing extended kin.

Nuclear families of the past did, however, differ from contemporary ones in their age configurations and economic function. Because of higher fertility, children were spread over a larger age spectrum. Older children often took charge of their younger siblings; older sisters served as surrogate mothers. The preindustrial household also served as the basic site of production, vocational training, and welfare. Households collectively formed the fiber of neighborhoods and communities. Before the twentieth century, solitary residence was rare. Men and women expected to live out their lives in familial or surrogate familial settings. Through their control of housing space, family members engaged in economic exchange relations with both kin and non-relatives. Households could expand and contract over the life course of their members in accordance with the family's needs.

The distinguishing historical feature in the organization of households was not its extension through the presence of other kin, but its augmentation by non-relatives, such as boarders and lodgers, including young men and women in the transitional period between departure from their parents' households and marriage. For migrants and immigrants, boarding could provide both access to jobs and surrogate family arrangements. For older couples or widows whose children had left home, accommodating young boarders served as a social equivalent of the family while providing young migrants to the city a form of family life. Taking in boarders also provided middle-aged or older couples with supplemental income, and families with young children alternative sources of child care. By enabling homeowners to pay mortgages or wives to stay out of the labor force, the additional income from boarders made it easier for families to adhere to their traditional arrangements without slipping into *poverty.

Families occasionally took in kin as well, usually for a limited time during periods of need or at specific stages in the life course. Increased urban migration over the nineteenth century brought a corresponding increase in co-residence with extended kin. Newly arrived migrants or immigrants usually stayed with relatives for a limited time until they found jobs and housing. In turn, after having established themselves, they took other kin into households on a temporary basis. In the years around 1900, about 12 to 18 percent of all urban households contained relatives other than nuclear-family members. By 1950, however, the proportion of such households had declined to 7 percent.

During the era of industrialization, such kinship arrangements played an integral role in mediating between family and societal institutions. Kin organized migration, facilitated newcomers' settlement, helped them find employment, and cushioned the shock of the new industrial world. In the absence of a public welfare system, kin served as the major safety net for migrants. Stretching over several communities, kinship networks of migrants and immigrants assisted local communities in crisis.

The overall pattern of historical change, however, has been from family collectivity to individual goals and aspirations, reducing the integration of individuals into extended kinship networks. The pace and nature of these changes have varied considerably among various classes and ethnic groups.

Changes in the Timing of Life Transitions. From the nineteenth century to the late twentieth century, despite greater societal complexity, the timing of life-course transitions in American society became more uniform and more closely articulated to age grading and age norms. In the nineteenth century, young people often followed "erratic" patterns, unconnected to specific age norms, shuttling between school and work and in and out of the parental home. Even after marriage, young couples returned home temporarily if their parents needed assistance, or during housing shortages. The timing of early life transitions was shaped by a continuum of practical considerations and familial obligations.

Later life transitions were even more "erratic." When older men could no longer work at their physically demanding occupations, they alternated between periods of employment and joblessness. Women's work patterns fluctuated over their entire life course because of marriage, childbearing, *child rearing, and widowhood. The continuing presence of adult children or others in the household meant that widowhood did not necessarily result in an empty nest.

Over the twentieth century, by contrast, age norms and individual needs emerged as more important determinants of life-course transitions than familial obligations. As the century ended, however, the more flexible patterns of timing of life course transitions re-emerged, reflecting changes in family arrangements and values and new policies governing the work life. As the age of first marriage rose, young adult children once again moved in and out of the parental home. This pattern differed from the former one, however, in a fundamental way: In the late nineteenth century, children remained at home, or returned home, in response to the needs of their family. In late-twentieth-century society, young adult children (including divorced or unmarried daughters with their own young children) returned home in order to meet their own needs. The return of the "erratic" style of family life also coincided with changing patterns of retirement, as the once rigid end to a work career again became more flexible.

The Family and Industrialization. As we have seen, industrialization and urbanization were long viewed as major threats to traditional family life and as causes of family breakdown. Industrialization, sociologists argued, caused familial breakdown as rural-to-urban migration uprooted people from their kinship networks, eroded traditional culture, and precipitated disintegration of the family unit.

Recent research on the history of the family has challenged these simplistic models of social and economic change and demonstrated that industrial *capitalism did not cause family breakdown. In negotiating such larger processes as migration, urbanization, and industrialization, the family was not passive and inert, but a proactive agent in planning, initiating, or resisting change.

While following their own priorities, families facilitated the early phases of industrialization in several ways: Rural families released members to work in urban factories, or acquired machinery that transformed their own households into cottage industries. Families provided *housing, employment, and training for newly arriving relatives entering the industrial workforce.

The success of the industrial system depended on a continuous flow of labor from abroad and from rural areas. Much of the recruitment and migration of workers was carried out under the auspices of kinship networks. Kinship ties with communities of origin facilitated back-and-forth migration of individuals and the transmission of resources. The family type that best "fit" industrialization, therefore, was not the isolated nuclear type, but a nuclear family embedded in an extended kinship network.

Domesticity and Women's Work. Despite the large families typical of preindustrial society, women invested relatively less time in motherhood than did mothers in the industrial era. Childcare was part of the process of household production rather than women's exclusive preoccupation. Children were viewed not merely as objects of nurture but as productive members of the family. The integration of family and work allowed for the sharing of labor between husbands and wives as well as between parents and children.

Industrialization reordered the division of labor in the family along gender lines, especially in middle-class households, which were transformed from places of production to places of consumption and child rearing. The most crucial change was the transfer of functions from the family to other social institutions. The preindustrial family and household served as "workshop," "church," "reformatory," "school," and "asylum." With industrialization and urbanization, these functions became, in large part, the responsibility of other institutions. As the middle-class family ceased to be a work unit, unpaid housework, no longer involving the production of visible goods, lost its economic and productive role and was devalued by a modern society that measured achievement by systematic time-and-production schedules.

The separation between home and workplace enshrined the former as a domestic retreat from the outside world and made the family child-centered. The ideology of domesticity and the new view of childhood combined to revise expectations of parenthood. A clear division of labor between husbands and wives replaced the old economic cooperation, with wives concentrating on homemaking and child rearing while husbands worked outside the home. Arising in the early nineteenth century, these patterns marked the emergence of the domestic middle-class family, as it has been known over the past century.

The ideology of domesticity, originating in urban middle-class families, gradually became the dominant model for family life in the entire society. Second- and third-generation immigrant families who had originally viewed the family as a productive unit and accepted the wife's work outside the home now embraced the ideology of domesticity and viewed women's participation in the labor force as demeaning to the husband and harmful to the children. Consequently, married women entered the labor force only when driven by economic necessity. The post-*World War II re-entry of married women into the labor force in pursuit of a career thus represents a major historical transformation. Older attitudes toward working women and mothers' labor-force participation and stereotypes persisted, however.

As the values of *individualism and privacy triumphed, the nuclear family grew increasingly distant from extended kin network and non-relatives disappeared from the household. This trend toward privatization of the family exacerbated the isolation of the family from the community at the very time when families could have benefited from community interaction in areas such as child care, support for aged relatives, and other critical life situations.

Family-history research is currently examining family interaction with societal processes and institutions within specific community contexts. Although such work has already contributed to a revision of earlier generalizations, historians still face the challenge of developing a more comprehensive model of family behavior that covers a longer historical period and does justice to the full complexities of social change.

[*See also* Abortion; Architecture: Domestic Architecture; Birth Control and Family Planning; Childbirth; Child Labor; Consumer Culture; Demography; Domestic Labor; Domestic Violence; Education: The Public School Movement; Factory System; Homework; Immigrant Labor; Immigration; Mobility; Sexual Morality and Sexual Reform; Slavery: Slave Families, Communities, and Culture; Social Class; Suburbanization; Women in the Labor Force; Working-Class Life and Culture.]

• John Demos, "Notes on Family Life in Plymouth Colony," *William and Mary Quarterly* (1965) 22: 264–286. Glen H. Elder Jr., *Children of the Great Depression,* 1974. Herbert Gutman, *The Black Family in Slavery and Freedom, 1750–1925,* 1976. Joseph F. Kett, *Rites of Passage: Adolescence in America—1790 to the Present,* 1977. Carl N. Degler, *At Odds: Women and the Family in America from Revolution to the Present,* 1980. Tamara K. Hareven, *Family Time and Industrial Time: The Relationship between the Family and Work in a New England Industrial Community,* 1982. Frances K. and Calvin Goldscheider, *The Changing Transition to Adulthood—Leaving and Returning Home,* 1999. Tamara K. Hareven, *Families, History and Social Change: Life-Course and Cross-Cultural Perspectives,* 2000.

—Tamara K. Hareven

FAMILY PLANNING. *See* Birth Control and Family Planning.

FARMERS' ALLIANCE MOVEMENT. The Farmers' Alliance, the largest agricultural movement in American history, was triggered by worsening agricultural conditions in commercial crop producing areas of the southern and Great Plains states, particularly the fall in agricultural prices after the *Civil War and consequent loss of land by small farmers. To counter these conditions, the Texas Alliance appeared in the late 1870s, and by 1884 was promoting cooperative ideas and antimonopoly politics.

A democratic organization centered around local suballiances and a system of lecturers, the Texas Alliance in 1886 began its spread into the Southeast and north into Kansas. Women were encouraged to join but *African-American farmers could not, although the Southern Alliance did cooperate with the Colored Farmers' Alliance, organized in 1886. By 1889 Alliance cooperative enterprises, including statewide cooperative purchasing and marketing exchanges, had spread across the *South. The state exchanges failed or did not live up to expectations, but local cooperative efforts often succeeded temporarily.

In the latter half of the 1880s the Farmers' Alliance movement, still incorporating the message of cooperation and antimonopoly politics, appeared in the tier of states from the Dakotas to Nebraska and in parts of the *Middle West. Efforts in 1889 at St. Louis to combine all the organizations in the movement failed, but most joined the new National Farmers' Alliance and Industrial Union on an antimonopoly platform calling for an end to large landholding; government ownership of the *railroads and *telegraph systems; the free and unlimited coinage of silver; the replacement of national bank notes with legal tender notes issued by the federal government; and the subtreasury plan, a sophisticated proposal developed by Charles Macune for using nonperishable crops as collateral for federal loans to farmers and as a way to increase seasonal currency flexibility.

Between 1889 and early 1892 much of the Farmers' Alliance movement entered independent politics. Until then, support for the Farmers' Alliance movement had been strong, even among nonfarmers. Its entry into third party politics in 1892 with Populism—the *Populist party adopted the Farmers' Alliance St. Louis platform—produced opposition as well as many defections from the Alliance. Indeed, the Farmers' Alliance movement fell apart that year, a victim of internal dissension. By 1893 only a few local Alliances and Alliance cooperatives survived. While the movement did pass the cooperative ideal to another generation of farm organizations, it proved less successful in transmitting its conviction that a democratic government should play an active role in the political and economic life of its citizens.

[*See also* Agriculture: 1770s to 1890; Agriculture: The "Golden Age" (1890s–1920); Free Silver Movement; Gilded Age; Granger Laws; Granger Movement; Monetary Policy, Federal; Populist Era.]

• Lawrence Goodwyn, *Democratic Promise: The Populist Moment in America,* 1976. Robert C. McMath Jr., *American Populism: A Social History, 1877–1898,* 1993.

—Bruce Palmer

FARM MACHINERY. American farmers first used mechanized equipment during the *Revolutionary War, when some farmers adopted grain drills (seed-planting devices) based on English designs. A successful American innovation did not occur until 1841, however, when Moses and Samuel Pennock of Pennsylvania significantly improved the design of this implement to facilitate more uniform planting of seed. American farmers continued to plant corn with a hoe until 1853 when George Brown of Illinois marketed a two-row, horse-drawn corn planter.

In 1833, Obed Hussey patented the first successful reaper for small grains. This device consisted of an oscillating sickle bar and a platform to catch the cut stalks. The next year, Cyrus *McCormick of Virginia patented a reaper that included a reel to help catch and hold the stalks against an improved cutter bar. In 1854, the Brockport, New York, firm of Seymour and Morgan marketed the first commercially successful self-raking reaper, which automatically removed the stalks from the platform. By 1860 the reaper had spread across the *Middle West, and the McCormick factory in *Chicago had become one of the nation's great manufacturers of farm machinery. Although a machine designed to cut grain and bind sheaves with wire was patented in 1856, farmers disliked wire, in part because they could not easily dispose of it at threshing time. In 1880, twine binders began to replace wire binders after John Appleby of Wisconsin developed a mechanism for tying a knot in twine wrapped around a sheaf of grain. Reapers and binders enabled farmers to harvest from ten to twenty acres of grain per day, depending on field conditions, with far less labor than that required to cut the grain with a scythe and rake and bind the sheaves by hand. The next significant increase in daily harvested acreage and decrease in the labor needed at harvest and threshing time came with the adoption of the tractor-powered combine harvester threshers, called combines, during the 1920s.

During the twentieth century, tractors powered by internal combustion engines became the most important and widely adopted agricultural implement in American history. In 1918, Henry *Ford marketed the first affordable farm tractor, known as the "Fordson." Six years later, the International Harvester Company (successor to the McCormick Harvesting Machine Company) introduced the "Farmall," a tricycle-designed tractor that met the needs of small-scale, row-crop farmers.

The cotton picker, developed in the early 1940s, became the most important twentieth-century farm machine for a specific, regional crop. Before the International Harvester Company manufactured the first commercially successful cotton picker in 1942, however, scientists had to modify the cotton plant to eliminate foliage and ensure uniform ripening. The cotton picker initially proved most suitable for large-scale operations in *California, but in time it supplanted handpickers in the *South as well.

These and other forms of agricultural machinery enabled farmers to reduce labor costs and increase production, which contributed to lower agricultural and food prices. Farm machinery also eased the drudgery of farm work, but it necessitated an increase in farm size and capital investment and caused a corresponding decrease in the number of farms, farm workers, and agricultural families.

[*See also* Agricultural Education and Extension; Agriculture; Cotton Industry; Fairs, County and State; Industrialization.]

• Robert C. Williams, *Fordson, Farmall, and Poppin' Johnny: A History of the Farm Tractor and Its Impact on America*, 1987. R. Douglas Hurt, *American Agriculture: A Brief History*, 1994.

—R. Douglas Hurt

FARRAGUT, DAVID (1801–1870), admiral, U.S. Navy. David Glasgow Farragut is identified with his famous order, "Damn the torpedoes!" at the *Civil War battle of Mobile Bay in 1864. His service since 1810, however, had already assured his fame. Farragut's career paralleled the development of U.S. sea power. Born near Knoxville, Tennessee, he moved to *New Orleans in 1807 with his family. He went to sea in 1810 at age nine, the ward of Admiral David Dixon Porter, who appointed him first prize master of a captured ship in 1812. A lieutenant by 1825, he fought pirates in the Caribbean as the U.S. navy enforced the *Monroe Doctrine. Rising in the ranks, Farragut was promoted to commander in 1841; developed the Mare Island, California, Navy Yard after the *Mexican War; and became a captain in 1855.

When the Civil War broke out in 1861, Farragut, though a southerner by birth, moved his wife and son from Norfolk, Virginia, to New York. Commanding the Union's West Gulf Blockade Squadron, he posted ships from West Florida to the Rio Grande and captured the vital southern port of New Orleans in 1862. In 1863 Farragut led the great riverine victories that secured the *Mississippi River and its tributaries for the Union: Vicksburg, Port Hudson, and Island Number Ten. In the public mind he became "the American Nelson," after the British naval hero Lord Nelson, and Congress created the ranks of rear admiral, vice admiral, and admiral to reward his service.

After the war Farragut's poor health confined him to administrative duties. After making a triumphal tour as European Squadron commander, he died during a visit to the Portsmouth, New Hampshire, Navy Yard.

[*See also* Military, The; Vicksburg, Siege of.]

• Loyall Farragut, *The Life and Letters of Admiral Farragut, First Admiral of the United States Navy*, 1879. James C. Bradford, ed., *Captains of the Old Steam Navy*, 1976.

—Maxine Turner

FASHION. *See* Clothing and Fashion.

FAULKNER, WILLIAM (1897–1962), novelist and short story writer. Born in New Albany, Mississippi, and raised in nearby Oxford, William Faulkner dropped out of high school to pursue a writing career, first as a poet and later as a fiction writer. Influenced by the novelist Sherwood Anderson, whom he met while living in *New Orleans, Faulkner published his first two novels, *Soldier's Pay* (1926) and *Mosquitoes* (1927), to limited critical success.

In the late 1920s, Faulkner returned to Oxford and devoted his literary efforts to works exploring life in north Mississippi. His best novels and stories, including *The Sound and the Fury* (1929), *As I Lay Dying* (1930), *Sanctuary* (1931), *Light in August* (1932), *Absalom! Absalom!* (1936), and *Go Down, Moses* (1942), portrayed with often dizzying complexity the life and history of his fictional Mississippi county, Yoknapatawpha. Something close to tragic doom cloaks almost all of Faulkner's work, particularly his portrayal of the *South's massive cultural transformations wrought by forces of intolerance, modernization, and greed.

Faulkner's critical reputation—and financial solvency—floundered precariously in the 1930s and 1940s. Drinking heavily, he subsisted primarily by writing Hollywood screenplays. Malcolm Cowley's *The Portable Faulkner* (1946) initiated a resurgence of critical interest. Capping this stunning critical reappraisal, Faulkner received the Nobel Prize for Literature in 1950. Although he continued to write, little of his later fiction, including *A Requiem for a Nun* (1951), *A Fable* (1954), *The Town* (1957), and *The Mansion* (1959), matched the power and complexity of his earlier work.

Faulkner has come to be regarded as one of America's—and the world's—greatest writers. His dense writing style embodies his belief that every moment of existence is pressured almost to suffocation by all that has come before—the past is never past. His experiments with narrative form and structure were profoundly influential. As his fellow southern writer Flannery O'Connor once wrote, "The presence alone of Faulkner in our midst makes a great difference in what the writer can and cannot permit himself to do. Nobody wants his mule and wagon stalled on the same track the Dixie Limited is roaring down."

[*See also* Literature: Since World War I; Twenties, The.]

• Joseph Blotner, *Faulkner: A Biography*, 2 vols., 1974. Richard Gray, *The Life of William Faulkner*, 1994.

—Robert H. Brinkmeyer Jr.

FEDERAL BUREAU OF INVESTIGATION. The Federal Bureau of Investigation (FBI) is the principal investigative arm of the Department of Justice, with jurisdiction over more than two hundred categories of federal *crimes. Its major late twentieth-century priorities were counterterrorism, illicit *drugs and drug-related crime, foreign counterintelligence, violent crimes, and financial malfeasance. The Bureau provides local *police with training, fingerprint identification, and crime-laboratory services. Its National Crime Information Center compiles crime statistics. In 1997, with a budget of some $2.5 billion, the FBI employed 10,529 special agents and 15,398 support personnel in a network of field offices, special installations, and foreign liaison posts. The director, nominated by the president and approved by the Senate, is limited to a single ten-year term.

Founded in 1908, the FBI received its current name in 1935. Its earliest responsibilities included bankruptcy fraud, antitrust crimes, violation of neutrality regulations, and enforcement of interstate prostitution laws. Its jurisdiction expanded during *World War I to include espionage, sabotage, *sedition, and draft-law violation. The Bureau won the lasting enmity of radicals and civil libertarians during the 1919–1920 Red Scare when hundreds of aliens were arrested and deported. The Warren *Harding–era *Teapot Dome scandal further tarnished its reputation. To reform the Bureau, J. Edgar *Hoover, with whom the FBI's history is inextricably entwined, was appointed director in 1924; he served until his death in 1972.

Committed to professionalizing law enforcement, Hoover during the later 1920s sought to make the Bureau an indispensable resource for local police. The activist New Deal administration unleashed the Bureau on John Dillinger, Pretty Boy Floyd, and other celebrity gangsters of the era. During *World War II, the Bureau targeted homefront sabotage and espionage. Movies, radio programs, magazine features, and tours of the FBI's Washington headquarters enhanced the Bureau's reputation.

With the *Cold War, the Bureau entered its most controversial phase as it allied with the *House Committee on Un-American Activities to purge alleged communist sympathizers from unions, schools, and the entertainment industry. Despite notable successes in investigating Soviet espionage, especially in the Alger *Hiss and *Rosenberg cases, the Bureau became embroiled in partisan politics with Hoover feeding information to Red-hunting politicians like Richard M. *Nixon and Joseph *McCarthy.

During the 1950s and 1960s, the Bureau conducted surveillance of Martin Luther *King Jr.; assembled dossiers on thousands of citizens; and used infiltration and counterespionage techniques to disrupt the Communist party, then the *Ku Klux Klan, the *Black Panthers, *civil rights organizations, and *Vietnam War protesters. The Bureau's deep-dyed *conservatism and hostility to social protest widely discredited it. Revelations of illegalities and excesses that emerged during House and Senate investigations of the intelligence agencies in 1975–1976 led to the creation of formal congressional oversight committees and other reforms.

During the 1980s the Bureau used the Racketeer Influence and Corrupt Organizations Act (RICO, 1970) and wiretapping authority granted it in 1968 to build devastating cases against *organized crime figures. Under director Louis Freeh (appointed in 1993) it played a key role in international law enforcement, training foreign law officials at its Quantico, Virginia, academy and establishing FBI academies overseas. But the Bureau's disastrous handling of armed stand-offs with militant antigovernment groups at Ruby Ridge, Idaho (1992), and Waco, Texas (1993), coupled with revelations of slipshod laboratory procedures, complicated its efforts to restore its reputation as America's most professional, as well as most celebrated, law enforcement agency.

[*See also* Anticommunism; Civil Liberties; Civil Rights Movement; Communist Party—USA; Federal Government, Executive Branch: Other Departments (Department of Justice); Intelligence Gathering and Espionage; Prostitution and Antiprostitution; Twenties, The.]

• Richard Gid Powers, *Secrecy and Power: The Life of J. Edgar Hoover*, 1987. Ronald Kessler, *The FBI*, 1993.

—Richard Gid Powers

FEDERAL COMMUNICATIONS COMMISSION. The Federal Communications Commission (FCC), created by the Federal Communications Act of 1934, assumed all federal oversight of broadcasting, *telephone, and *telegraph services. Under the initial terms of the act, the president appointed seven commissioners to seven-year terms; in 1982, Congress reduced the number of commissioners to five, serving five-year terms.

Congress gave the FCC limited powers and scant funding; the first commissioners were obscure *radio engineers and attorneys with no incentive to alter the status quo. Like the Federal Radio Commission, which regulated broadcasting from 1927 to 1934, the FCC awarded radio licenses in ways that favored commercial over noncommercial broadcasters and punished only the most irresponsible behavior. The lethargy ended with the chairmanship of James Lawrence Fly (1939–1944). Under Fly, the commission forced the National Broadcasting Company to sell one of its two networks. Fly's successor, Paul O. Porter, fought to make stations honor their obligations to provide public-service programming.

The Fly-Porter years proved exceptional. In the 1950s, the agency bungled its greatest postwar challenge: *television. The FCC awarded TV licenses without consistent criteria except to reaffirm the dominance of two networks, NBC and CBS, at the expense of commercial and noncommercial rivals. In the 1960s, the commission adopted rules inhibiting the diffusion of cable TV systems, fearing they would undermine individual stations in smaller markets. For decades, FCC regulations similarly reinforced American Telephone and Telegraph's (AT&T) monopolistic control over the telephone industry, inhibiting competition and innovation. A 1982 district court ruling broke up AT&T.

Several key court decisions in the 1970s freed the cable industry. By then, the FCC itself had started to deregulate broadcasting. Yet the agency remained vigilant about what it considered indecent speech; individual commissioners, led by Chairman Reed Hundt (1993–1997), admonished the networks to air more educational children's programming.

[*See also* New Deal Era, The; Public Broadcasting.]

• Erwin G. Krasnow, Lawrence D. Longley, and Herbert A. Terry, *The Politics of Broadcast Regulation*, 3d. ed., 1983.

—James L. Baughman

FEDERAL GOVERNMENT, EXECUTIVE BRANCH

Overview
The Presidency
Department of State
Department of Defense
Department of the Treasury
Department of Agriculture
Other Departments

FEDERAL GOVERNMENT, EXECUTIVE BRANCH: OVERVIEW

The fear that drove the delegates to the *Constitutional Convention of 1787 was not the specter of monarchy but rather the anxiety created by a national Congress that was incapable of governing. For much of the convention, executive independence was threatened by a provision calling for election of the president by the legislature, but eventually the *electoral college compromise took the selection out of the hands of the legislature and laid the basis for the president's claim to popular support. In addition, the decision to give the president the power to appoint executive officers provided a foundation for the cabinet system that would be developed by George *Washington and used by all subsequent presidents.

Still, the potential for a popularly chosen and independent executive was not immediately realized. In the 1790s, supporters of executive independence became increasingly suspicious of popular opinion, and defenders of popular government were hostile to executive power. It was the Federalists who initially encouraged the growth of the executive branch, but Thomas *Jefferson helped solidify its power. Although Jefferson saw a powerful executive as a threat to democracy, in founding the Democratic Republican party he established the role of president as a popular leader. Moreover, despite his distrust of executive power, he allowed for the continued expansion of the executive branch to handle the exigencies of government.

It was, however, Andrew *Jackson who first embraced the idea of permanent political parties. Arguing that the president rather than Congress could best claim to represent the people, Jackson relied on that claim to defend extensive executive discretion. Jackson used the spoils system—giving federal jobs to one's political supporters—to tie the national government to the people through the party machinery and also to establish political control of the executive branch.

The *Civil War proved a catalyst for further expansion of the executive branch. President Abraham *Lincoln's exercise of emergency powers demonstrated the tremendous potential of an independent executive in time of war, a potential that would be exploited by presidents during the two world wars and the *Cold War. Presidents from Lincoln to Woodrow *Wilson saw the spoils system become a major threat to executive independence and energy. While *civil service reform in part arose from reformers' desire to clean up the corruption of the spoils system, presidential support for the reform was also motivated by the same goal that had moved Jackson to adopt the spoils system in the first place: increased control over the executive branch.

Since President Franklin Delano *Roosevelt in the 1930s, presidents have sought greater control of an executive branch that grew from 239,476 civilian employees in 1901 to 2,482,666 in 1951. Twentieth-century presidents also relied on popular leadership skills to enhance their power. Theodore *Roosevelt's concept of a "bully pulpit" and FDR's "fireside chats" because the models for other great communicators such as John F. *Kennedy and Ronald *Reagan, who used the new medium of *television very effectively. The increased reliance on popular leadership, however, weakened the president's ties to political parties and to Congress. Personal popularity proved an unreliable foundation for presidents from Lyndon B. *Johnson through Jimmy *Carter. Whether the 1998–1999 *impeachment of Bill *Clinton represented another blow to the popular presidency of the twentieth century or whether Clinton's ability to withstand the impeachment marked the beginning of a period of renewed strength for the office remained uncertain as the twentieth century ended.

[*See also* Constitution; Democratic Party; Federalist Party; Republican Party; Republicanism; Veto Power; Whig Party.]

• Sidney M. Milkis and Michael Nelson, *The American Presidency: Origins and Development*, 2d ed., 1994. Stephen Skowronek, *The Politics Presidents Make*, 2d ed., 1997.

—David K. Nicholas

FEDERAL GOVERNMENT, EXECUTIVE BRANCH: THE PRESIDENCY

The American presidency, the world's oldest continuous republican chief executive office, is the choicest prize in the nation's political system. It stands at the apex of national and international attention and power. When the framers of the *Constitution introduced Article II with the words, "The executive power shall be vested in a President of the United States of America," the word "president" was readily acceptable to the public, having been the title of the presiding officer of the *Continental Congress.

The office combines the political and symbolic functions that are ordinarily divided in other countries, so that the president is both chief of state and head of government. The executive function of the office, namely to see that the nation's laws are faithfully carried out, has expanded over the course of two centuries to include vast legislative, judicial, administrative, economic, and diplomatic responsibilities. The president serves also as the commander-in-chief of the armed forces. Since the early twentieth century, presidents have also functioned as the head of their parties, dispensing patronage and shaping party programs. In 1940 Franklin Delano *Roosevelt created the Executive Office of the President to bring executive-branch activities under tighter control. Its many subunits, staffed by about five hundred people by the 1990s, schedule the president's (and the first lady's) activities, deal with the media, and generally manage the far-flung activities of the office, including everything from advising on economics, scientific, and technological developments and maintaining cabinet records to drug control and safeguarding the codes for deploying *nuclear weapons.

Shaping the Presidency in the Early Republic and Beyond. The shaping of the presidency was a troubling issue at the *Constitutional Convention of 1787. Some of the delegates favored a plural executive, but James Wilson (1742–1798), a Scottish-born Pennsylvania lawyer and political theorist who deserves to be regarded as the father of the presidency, adamantly argued that only a single executive could give the necessary "energy, dispatch and responsibility to the office." Wilson also insisted that the office be independent of the legislature, have a *veto power, and control *foreign relations. He also pressed for the direct popular election of the chief executive—a novel idea at the time that continues to win advocates. Late in the Convention, a committee appointed to find an appropriate alternate solution invented a system of electors. Each state would have as many electors as the total number of its representatives and senators, to be chosen by any method on which the state legislature decided. Collectively known as the *electoral college, the arrangement plainly gave an advantage to the large states. Still, it was assumed that in many elections no aspirant would win the required electoral-college majority, and that the election would be thrown into the House of Representatives, which would choose the president from the top five (later changed to three) names, with each state having one vote. In fact, only in 1800, 1824, and 1876 were presidential elections decided by the House. Despite the complexity of the electoral-college arrangement, the selection of the president almost from the beginning has been regarded as the equivalent of a popular election. Nevertheless, in the elections of 1876 and 1888, the candidates who polled the most popular votes failed to win the presidency in the electoral college.

The presidential term was fixed at four years almost as an afterthought, with no limit on reelection. George *Washington, Thomas *Jefferson, and James *Madison retired after two terms, establishing a precedent that stood until Franklin D. Roosevelt won a third term in 1940 and a fourth in 1944, although Ulysses S. *Grant in 1880 and Theodore *Roosevelt in 1912 had sought third terms. The Twenty-second Amendment (1951), in a kind of posthumous rebuke to FDR, limited presidents constitutionally to two terms. Other amendments have also modified the original presidency: The Twelfth (1804) required the electoral college to vote separately for president and vice president to avoid the confusion that marred the election of 1800; the Nineteenth (1919) altered the voter base by granting the ballot to women and the Twenty-sixth (1971) altered it further by enfranchising eighteen-year olds; the Twentieth (1933) moved inauguration day from 4 March to 20 January; the Twenty-third (1961) gave electoral votes to the District of Columbia; the Twenty-fourth (1964) forbade the imposition of a poll tax on voters in presidential elections; and the Twenty-fifth (1967), in the aftermath of President Dwight D. *Eisenhower's major illnesses while in office, set forth procedures to be followed in case of presidential disability. The recurring idea of a single fixed presidential term is of long standing. Andrew *Jackson in his State of the Union messages repeatedly called for a single, six-year term.

The strong presidency provided for in the Constitution owed much to the expectation that George Washington would inaugurate the office. One delegate wrote, "I do [not] believe the [executive powers] would be so great had not many of the members cast their eyes toward General Washington as President; and shaped their Ideas of the Powers to be given a President, by their opinions of his Virtues." Washington, keenly aware that he was the first national president in history, knew that he would be setting precedents by almost everything he did, including choosing the heads of the executive departments—then state, treasury, war, and attorney general—and making of them a cabinet, an extraconstitutional institution. On formal occasions he received guests while standing on a raised platform and wearing a sword, and did not shake hands during his time in office. Still, neither he nor the American people desired a monarchy. After considerable discussion in Congress and elsewhere as to how to address him, including one suggestion that he be called "His Highness the President of the United States of America and Protector of their Liberties," the simple phrase "President of the United States" was deemed sufficient. When Washington left office in 1797, he created the matchless tradition that an elected executive departs on schedule, and all of his successors have followed suit, so that the fact seems ordinary when in fact it is extraordinary. As his successor, John *Adams, wrote to his wife on his inauguration day, "The sight of the sun setting . . . and another rising (though less splendid) was a novelty."

The third president, Thomas Jefferson, although a slaveholder, brought to the office a democratic manner that seemed better befitting to a republic. He walked to his inauguration, shook hands freely, and forbade presidential birthday celebrations. In greeting people at the newly completed "President's House" (later called the *White House), he took no account of differences in rank or prestige. His style, with many additions and variations, in time became the norm of presidential behavior. Democratization and responsiveness to public opinion constantly brought the chief executive closer to the public: Andrew Jackson was the first "man of the people," winning a national constituency with supporters in every section of the country; Abraham *Lincoln was metamorphosed in affectionate parlance from "Honest Abe," when he was the Republican candidate, to "Father Abraham," when he became the embattled Union's war leader; and Theodore Roosevelt came to be "Teddy"—a nickname immortalized in the Teddy Bear. Franklin D. Roosevelt entered America's homes via *radio "fireside chats." Dwight D. Eisenhower in the same spirit allowed his news conferences to be televised; James Earl Carter made himself officially Jimmy *Carter; William Jefferson Clinton, known everywhere as Bill *Clinton, opened the White House e-mail address to the public. In the later twentieth century, however, the tight security imposed by the U.S. Secret Service (a division of the Treasury Department), the trappings of what some called "the imperial presidency," symbolized by the giant presidential jet, Air Force One, and the vast entourage accompanying the president on every trip, tended to make these populist gestures more a matter of public relations than of participatory democracy.

The Presidency and Party Politics. Until 1824, presidential and vice presidential nominees were selected by congressional leaders meeting in secret—later public—sessions called caucuses. Attacked as undemocratic, "King Caucus" was replaced by national nominating conventions, introduced by the *Anti-Masonic party in 1831 and adopted by the two major parties in 1836. Now meeting quadrennially in the summertime, the conventions of the *Democratic and *Republican parties, consisting of 1,100 to 1,800 delegates chosen at the state level by primary elections, convention, or committees, nominate their candidates by majority vote. Until 1936, however, the Democratic party required a two-thirds majority. Thus it took the Democrats 46 ballots to nominate Woodrow *Wilson in 1912 and 103 ballots to agree upon John W. Davis in 1924. Not since 1952, however, has a major party proceeded past the first ballot to select a candidate, and the *television networks no longer offer gavel-to-gavel coverage of the extravaganzas.

The parties have ranged widely in their selection of presidential nominees: from governors and former governors (the Democrats' Adlai *Stevenson in 1952 and 1956, and the Republicans' Ronald *Reagan in 1980 and George W. Bush in 2000) to war heroes (the *Whig party's William Henry *Harrison in 1840 and Zachary *Taylor in 1848, and the Republicans' Ulysses S. Grant in 1868 and Dwight D. Eisenhower in 1952) and the Senate (the Republicans' Warren G. *Harding in 1920 and the Democrats' John F. *Kennedy in 1960).

As presidential election campaigns moved to the center of national political attention, they became filled with hoopla that included catchy songs and slogans, parades with marching bands, election eve bonfires, and cruising sound trucks. Some rallying cries are embedded in the national memory: "Tippecanoe and Tyler Too" (1840), "The Full Dinner Pail" (1900), "He Kept Us Out of War" (1916), "Keep Cool with Coolidge" (1924), "No Third Term" (1940), "I Like Ike" (1952), and "Nixon's the One" (1972). When the twenty-first century dawned, there was growing public concern over the astronomical cost of presidential campaigns, the methods used to raise the required money, and the role of attack ads and superficial sound bites in television-dominated campaigns.

Presidential Succession; Impeachment; First Ladies. Eight vice presidents have succeeded to the presidency upon the death or assassination of the president: John *Tyler (1841), Millard *Fillmore (1850), Andrew *Johnson (1865), Chester A. *Arthur (1881), Theodore Roosevelt (1901), Calvin *Coolidge (1923), Harry S. *Truman (1945), and Lyndon B. *Johnson (1963). When Richard M. *Nixon resigned in the wake of the *Watergate scandal—the first resignation in the history of the office—he was succeeded by Gerald *Ford (1974). Ford in 1973 in accordance with the Twenty-fifth Amendment had been named by President Nixon—and confirmed by Congress— to succeed Vice-president Spiro T. Agnew who had been forced to resign amidst bribery and tax-evasion charges. Ford, as president, selected Nelson A. Rockefeller to be vice president, giving the nation for the first time not only a president but also a vice president who were not elected. The line of succession to the presidency after the vice president was established by law in 1947: the Speaker of the House, the president pro tem of the Senate, and the members of the cabinet in order of the creation of their department, beginning with the secretary of state. Under the constitutional provision for the removal of presidents, vice presidents, and other ranking federal officers by *impeachment and trial, Andrew Johnson (1868) and Bill Clinton (1999) were impeached by the House of Representative for "high crimes and misdemeanors" but found not guilty by the Senate.

The role of the president's wife—the designation "First Lady" was not used until the *Civil War era—has sometimes made the presidency seem like a two-person position. Among the best-known spouses have been Martha Dandridge Custis Washington, an involved helpmate of the General; Dolley Payne Madison, who served as Jefferson's hostess in the White House and subsequently her husband's as well; Sarah Childress Polk, whose political savvy was legendary; Edith Galt Wilson, the president's second wife, who jealously guarded his privacy and even took over some of his duties after he was incapacitated by a stroke in October 1919, so that she is sometimes regarded as the "first woman president;" Eleanor *Roosevelt, whose constant travels made her FDR's "eyes and ears"; Jacqueline Bouvier Kennedy, whose grace and charm made her a national icon; Rosalynn Smith Carter, who sat in cabinet meetings and conducted diplomacy unofficially for the president; Nancy Davis Reagan, who was a dominant political force in the Reagan White House; and Hillary Rodham Clinton, whose powerful place in her husband's administration appeared to fulfill Clinton's campaign assertion that his election would give the nation "two-for-one" and in 2000 won election to the U.S. Senate from New York.

[*See also* Federal Government, Legislative Branch: House of Representatives; Federal Government, Legislative Branch: Senate; Political Parties; Washington, D.C.; *and entries on individual presidents.*]

• William Seale, *The President's House,* 2 vols., 1986. Stephen Hess, *Organizing the Presidency,* 2d ed., 1988. Richard E. Neustadt, *Presidential Power and the Modern Presidents: The Politics of Leadership from Roosevelt to Reagan,* 4th ed., 1990. William DeGregorio, *The Complete Book of U.S. Presidents: From George Washington to Bill Clinton,* rev. ed. 1993. Leonard W. Levy and Louis Fisher, eds., *Encyclopedia of the American Presidency,* 4 vols, 1994. Arthur M. Schlesinger Jr., et al., eds. *Running for President: The Candidates and Their Images,* 2 vols., 1994. Henry F. Graff, ed., *The Presidents: A Reference History,* 2d ed., 1996. Richard Pious, *The Presidency,* 1996. Philip B. Kunhardt Jr., Philip B. Kunhardt III, and Peter W. Kunhardt, eds, *The American President,* 1999.

—Henry F. Graff

FEDERAL GOVERNMENT, EXECUTIVE BRANCH: DEPARTMENT OF STATE

The State Department began as something of an institutional anomaly. It was patterned on the British government's secretary of state for foreign affairs, but had no counterpart comparable to the British secretary for domestic affairs. The department's early history reflected the revolutionary generation's ambivalent attitude toward formal diplomacy. Only with great reluctance had the *Continental Congress created a professional diplomatic corps. This meager political backing translated into a weak support structure for the conduct of early American foreign policy. Poor communication between Secretary of State James *Monroe and U.S. diplomats in London helped bring on the *War of 1812. Monroe's successor at the State Department, John Quincy *Adams, lacking a clerical staff, had to transcribe three copies of the *Adams-Onís Treaty himself. Later, Adams's uncertainty over whether to recognize Brazil was complicated by the fact that no one in his employ could translate Portuguese.

If ill-equipped to handle *foreign relations, the State Department from the first became enmeshed in partisan politics, with the wars of the French Revolutionary Era providing an early flashpoint. While the first secretary of state, Thomas *Jefferson, favored the French, Treasury Secretary Alexander *Hamilton advocated a pro-British neutrality. Hamilton's triumph in this dispute helped give rise to the first party system while also anticipating the department's later struggles to control foreign policy. As revolutionary passions faded, the department evolved into something of an incubator for presidents. Three successive secretaries of states—James *Madison, James Monroe, and John Quincy Adams—rose to the presidency.

While Adams's appointment of the westerner Henry *Clay as secretary of state in 1825 marked the end of the first cycle of American diplomacy, the election of Andrew *Jackson in 1828 began an interval in which the State Department was weaker than at perhaps any other time in U.S. history. It also suffered appalling organizational deficiencies. During a diplomatic crisis with Peru in the early 1850s, for example, departmental staff took several months to find a crucial memorandum documenting an agreement Secretary of State Daniel *Webster had reached with the Peruvians over offshore island guano rights.

Abraham *Lincoln's appointment of William *Seward as secretary of state in 1861 helped resolve these related problems of inefficiency and low prestige. Seward initiated an efficient indexing system, regional responsibilities for staff members, and the publication of diplomatic documents in the *Foreign Relations of the United States* series. Appointing a talented diplomatic corps, Seward pursued a risky but successful strategy of preventing European intervention in the *Civil War. Seward's tenure, however, also saw the emergence of a pattern of congressional thwarting of State Department initiatives. Congress stymied Seward's attempts to purchase the Danish West Indies and the efforts of his successor, Hamilton Fish (1869–1877), to annex the Dominican Republic.

The State Department, meanwhile, had developed a two-tier culture in which the consular service endured low pay and poor working conditions while top diplomats were appointed for patronage reasons or their social connections. With 80 percent of secretaries of state having served in Europe and most still coming from privileged backgrounds, the department became an inviting target for congressional critics who denounced its "elitism" and demanded less exclusionary recruitment policies. Their crusade culminated in the Rogers Act of 1924, which established a professional foreign service with improved pay, retirement benefits, and tenure provisions, while combining the diplomatic and consular services.

On substantive foreign-policy issues, secretaries of state James G. *Blaine (1881, 1889–1892), John *Hay (1898–1905), and Elihu Root (1905–1909) skillfully promoted the nation's turn-of-the-century emergence as a world power. President Woodrow *Wilson pleased the *Democratic party's agrarian wing by appointing William Jennings *Bryan as secretary of state in 1913, but the pacifist Bryan, unhappy over the belligerence of Wilson's protests of German U-boat attacks, resigned in 1915. His successor Robert Lansing proved ineffectual as Wilson, advised by Colonel Edward M. House, essentially acted as his own secretary of state, an approach taken by other strong presidents as well.

Despite congressional criticism, the State Department regained prestige in the 1920s under Charles Evans *Hughes, Frank Kellogg, and Henry *Stimson, one of the nation's most prescient diplomats. But the freewheeling presidential style of Franklin Delano *Roosevelt again lessened the department's influence, even as Cordell *Hull became the longest serving secretary of state in American history (1933–1944) and the number of State Department personnel swelled from under two thousand in 1940 to more than sixteen thousand by 1950.

The lawyer and career diplomat Dean *Acheson, secretary of state from 1949 to 1953, played a major role in shaping America's *Cold War policy—a policy built upon the *containment doctrine proposed in 1946 by George *Kennan, a U.S. diplomat in Moscow who later headed the State Department's policy planning staff. President Dwight D. *Eisenhower's first secretary of state, John Foster *Dulles (1953–1959), also played a strong role in building anti-Soviet Cold War alliances. But the department faced problems as well. Accusations of disloyalty against State Department officials, including Acheson and the respected George *Marshall (secretary of state from 1947 to 1949), leveled by Wisconsin senator Joseph *McCarthy and others, demoralized departmental personnel. Meanwhile, the department's policy-making role was challenged by such newly created entities as the Department of Defense, *Joint Chiefs of Staff, *Central Intelligence Agency, *National Security Council, and the National Security Advisor. Indeed, during the presidencies of John F. *Kennedy and Lyndon B. *Johnson, each of these agencies exerted more influence than did the State Department under Dean Rusk (1961–1969). The department's foreign-policy primacy was also threatened by such new bodies as the *Agency for International Development and the Arms Control and Disarmament Agency. Henry *Kissinger exerted great influence as President Richard M. *Nixon's national security advisor before himself becoming secretary of state in 1973.

In the post–Cold War era, the State Department again became a target of congressional criticism, this time from nationalists who saw it as a hotbed of Wilsonian interventionism. This period also brought a significant historical breakthrough with President Bill *Clinton's appointment of the first woman secretary of state, Madeleine K. Albright, in 1997.

[*See also* Anticommunism; Clayton-Bulwer Treaty; Collective Security; Dollar Diplomacy; Eisenhower Doctrine; Expansionism; Federal Government, Legislative Branch: Senate; Foreign Aid; Fourteen Points; Good Neighbor Policy; Internationalism; Jay's Treaty; Kellogg-Briand Pact; Marshall Plan; Monroe Doctrine; "Open Door" Policy; Pan American Union; Pinckney's Treaty; Truman Doctrine; Webster-Ashburton Treaty; Yalta Conference.]

• Samuel Flagg Bemis, ed., *American Secretaries of State and Their Diplomacy,* 10 vols., 1963. Waldo Henrichs, *American Ambassador: Joseph Grew and the Development of the United States Diplomatic Tradition,* 1966. Smith Simpson, *Anatomy of the State Department,* 1967. Hugh De Santis, *Diplomacy of Silence: The American Foreign Service, the Soviet Union, and the Cold War, 1933–1947,* 1980.

—Robert David Johnson

FEDERAL GOVERNMENT, EXECUTIVE BRANCH: DEPARTMENT OF DEFENSE

The Department of Defense, established in 1949, evolved from the National Military Establishment (NME), a hybrid organization created by Congress in 1947 to unify the previously separate War and Navy departments, dating from 1781 and 1798 respectively. Unification had its immediate origins in the experiences of *World War II, which demonstrated the need for new organizational mechanisms to achieve more effective military coordination. As the war ended, attention turned to enacting permanent reforms. One plan, sponsored by the War Department and endorsed by President Harry S. *Truman, called for a highly centralized defense organization, including a separate air force, under a single secretary of defense. A competing plan, advocated by the navy, urged closer coordination rather than outright unification.

The resulting legislative compromise under the *National Security Act of 1947 borrowed from both plans. Desiring the savings and increased efficiency promised by unification but fearing that an overly centralized system would produce a "Prussian-style general staff," Congress therefore incorporated aspects of the navy concept by loosely unifying the services under the NME and granting the secretary of defense only qualified authority. Additionally, the 1947 act gave statutory standing to the *Joint Chiefs of Staff (JCS), a body that had existed without a formal charter since 1942, and established two new organizations: the *National Security Council to oversee high-level policy coordination and the *Central Intelligence Agency to collect and analyze intelligence.

The first secretary of defense, James V. Forrestal (1947–1949), took office on 17 September 1947. As secretary of the navy during the unification debate, Forrestal had opposed service unification. Once installed in his new job he adopted a go-slow approach—"evolution, not revolution"—toward integrating service activities. Even so, he did not receive what he considered sufficient cooperation from the military services. Especially intense was interservice competition over roles and missions. Meanwhile, worsening relations with the Soviet Union intensified pressures to step up military preparedness, despite rigid budget ceilings imposed by President Truman for economic reasons.

Doing an about-face, Forrestal recommended that the secretary's powers and staff support be strengthened. In 1949 Congress removed the limitations on the secretary's authority and converted the NME into the Department of Defense, a full-scale executive department. With unencumbered powers and a larger staff, the secretary of defense became the focal point of an increasingly centralized administrative system. During the summer and fall of 1949, opponents of unification fought back, as senior navy officers, reeling from recent budget cuts, openly attacked service unification for causing a shift away from sea power toward growing reliance on strategic nuclear bombing as the country's first line of defense. But following the across-the-board rearmament precipitated by the *Korean War, money for defense became more plentiful and the stresses and strains of interservice relations eased.

The Korean War produced renewed complaints from Congress that the services continued to squander resources while unnecessarily duplicating activities. In 1953 and 1958, President Dwight D. *Eisenhower addressed these problems through organizational reforms that took the unification process nearly as far as it could go without abandoning the concept of individual military services. In the Defense Reorganization Act of 1958, Congress authorized the secretary to reassign service functions and approved a new chain of command that bypassed the service secretaries. Instead of being separately administered, as in the past, the military departments were merely to be "separately organized," a gesture toward preserving service autonomy but a distinct departure from the preunification days when the departments had operated as sovereign entities.

The first secretary of defense to make full use of these increased powers was Robert S. McNamara (1961–1968). His initial task was to fulfill President John F. *Kennedy's campaign promise to replace Eisenhower's "New Look" defense strategy, which had emphasized *nuclear weapons, with a "flexible response" posture giving greater weight to general purpose forces. To control rising defense costs, McNamara introduced a variety of reforms, including mission-oriented budgeting with five-year expenditure projections, "systems analysis" techniques that used computer models to evaluate the cost-effectiveness of weapons and programs, and consolidation of service activities under defensewide agencies. The net effect was an unprecedented degree of centralized civilian control.

McNamara's management successes contrasted sharply with the military debacle that developed in Southeast Asia during his tenure. Secretaries of defense had customarily stayed out of the operational side of military affairs, leaving them to the professionals, but McNamara inserted himself directly into the details of running the *Vietnam War. Initially a strong proponent of American involvement in Vietnam, he gradually became disillusioned and left office counseling stepped-up negotiations and disengagement.

After McNamara came a reaction to centralized authority. While the managerial and budgeting techniques he had pioneered generally survived, his use of civilians in roles traditionally reserved for military professionals aroused much resentment among the services and skepticism in Congress. By the mid-1980s, the question at issue was how to revitalize the Joint Chiefs of Staff, whose stature and effectiveness had diminished steadily since Vietnam. The Goldwater-Nichols Act of 1986 attempted to reverse this trend by giving the JCS chairman broader advisory powers and increased administrative authority over the Joint Staff (the JCS bureaucracy), and by mandating more "jointness" among the services. Although the performance of U.S. forces in the 1991 *Persian Gulf War seemed to bear out the soundness of the new emphasis on joint doctrine, subsequent misadventures in Somalia and command-and-control problems in the Middle East suggested a need for further refinements.

During the 1990s the Department of Defense faced the challenge of an international environment that, while no longer dominated by the threat of a global thermonuclear war, continued to exhibit unstable tendencies. At the same time, a revolution in military affairs, driven largely by new technologies, augured major changes in the role and composition of future military forces. In the circumstances, the demands on the secretary of defense and the JCS chairman to work together in providing unified policy and programmatic guidance appeared unlikely to diminish. Unification, born of necessity after World War II, had become a fact of life throughout the defense establishment.

[*See also* Cold War; Military, The; Nuclear Strategy; Post–Cold War Era.]

• Steven L. Rearden, *History of the Office of the Secretary of Defense: The Formative Years, 1947–1950*, 1984. Robert J. Art, Vincent Davis, and Samuel P. Huntington, eds., *Reorganizing America's Defense*, 1985. Doris M. Condit, *History of the Office of the Secretary of Defense: The Test of War, 1950–1953*, 1988. James A. Blackwell Jr. and Barry M. Blechman, eds., *Making Defense Reform Work*, 1990. Roger Trask and Alfred Goldberg, *The Department of Defense, 1947–1997*, 1997. Robert J. Watson, *History of the Office of the Secretary of Defense: Into the Missile Age, 1956–1961*, 1997.

—Steven L. Rearden

FEDERAL GOVERNMENT, EXECUTIVE BRANCH: DEPARTMENT OF THE TREASURY

Alexander *Hamilton, the first secretary of the treasury, said that most of the important measures of the government are connected with the Treasury Department. That remained as true at the end of the twentieth century as it was in Hamilton's time. From its *Revolutionary War beginnings to the present, the Department of the Treasury has played a key role in the nation's development. The secretary of the treasury is the president's senior economic adviser and supervises the operation of a vast executive department that has served the nation with distinction since 1789.

The demands of effective financial administration forced the *Continental Congress and then the U.S. Congress to overcome their misgivings about delegating the power of the purse. Accordingly, on 2 September 1789, Congress created the Treasury Department under the direction of a secretary, to be aided by a Comptroller (the superintendent of accounts), an Auditor (the certifier of accounts), a Register (the keeper of accounts), a Treasurer (in charge of receiving and disbursing funds), and a general assistant.

On 11 September 1789, Alexander Hamilton began his tenure as secretary and instituted an economic program that included proposals for funding the nation's debt, establishing a central bank, augmenting internal revenues, and promoting domestic industry. Hamilton's program, which envisioned an urban-based, manufacturing economy, proved controversial, as did his penchant for wielding his power over the budgets of other government departments to influence their policies.

Hamilton's successor, Albert *Gallatin—the longest serving secretary (1801–1813) in Treasury history—was an active crusader for government economy, which brought him into constant conflict with other department heads. (Treasury's control over government estimates and expenditures under Hamilton and Gallatin anticipated the function of today's Office of Management and Budget.) Thanks largely to Gallatin's economies, Treasury employed fewer people in 1826 than in 1801. Customs duties and land sales generated sufficient revenue to retire the national debt by 1834 and, in most years before the *Civil War, to generate a surplus that was refunded to the states. A growing national economy and a budget-minded government combined to make possible the elimination of excise taxes on products like whiskey and jewelry, as well as the Treasury machinery to collect those taxes.

From the beginning, the Treasury Department spawned myriad subsidiary agencies and functions. The Post Office Department, originally under Treasury supervision, gained autonomy in 1829; the General Land Office left Treasury to become part of the new Interior Department in 1849. At one time or another, the Public Health Service, the Bureau of Narcotics, and the Supervisory Architect of the United States operated under Treasury's umbrella.

Treasury has always functioned as the collector of customs duties. From the fleet of ten small ships authorized by Hamilton to enforce the customs laws evolved the U.S. Coast Guard, the oldest seagoing branch of the *military, whose functions were transferred to the Department of Transportation in 1967.

The National Currency Act of 1863, designed to end the chaos associated with the distribution of private bank notes and to help finance the Civil War, created an Office of the Comptroller of the Currency within the Department of the Treasury to administer a system of national banks authorized to distribute a uniform national currency, nicknamed greenbacks. (Treasury relinquished most of its monetary responsibilities to the newly created *Federal Reserve System in 1913.) The U.S. Secret Service, protector of the president and vice president and their families, is a division of the Department of the Treasury. It was initially established in 1865 to prevent counterfeiting of greenbacks. Until the creation of the *Federal Bureau of Investigation in 1935, the Secret Service was the government's principal general law enforcement agency.

The financial pressures of the Civil War led to a sweeping *taxation program, including the first federal *income tax, administered by a Commissioner of Internal Revenue under the secretary of the treasury. Many these taxes lapsed after the war, including the income tax, but the Sixteenth Amendment to the *Constitution (1913) authorizing a federal income tax brought the Internal Revenue Service back to life. Enforcement of the 1919 Volstead Act, prohibiting the sale of alcoholic beverages, also fell to Treasury. The unit created to combat liquor trafficking eventually evolved into the Bureau of Alcohol, Tobacco and Firearms.

The Great Depression caused hundreds of banks to fail and in 1933 led newly inaugurated President Franklin Delano *Roosevelt to declare a bank holiday to stop the panic. Treasury then supervised the reopening of the solvent banks and the orderly liquidation or reorganization of the others.

U.S. involvement in both *World War I and *World War II was partly financed by the sale of government bonds under Treasury supervision. The Defense Bond campaigns of World War II, modeled on the Liberty Bond drives of World War I, raised $211 billion, or about two-thirds of the war's cost. (U.S. savings bonds, administered by the Treasury Department's Bureau of Public Debt, are a direct offshoot of the wartime bond program.) A little known but influential function of Treasury during both wars was the implementation of freeze orders on enemy assets under the 1917 Trading With the Enemy Act.

After the 1944 *Bretton Woods Conference established a new international monetary system, Treasury Secretary Henry Morgenthau Jr. (1891–1967) was named chairman of the Board of Governors of both the International Bank for Reconstruction and Development (the *World Bank) and the *International Monetary Fund. In 1959, Treasury spearheaded the creation of the Inter-American Development Bank to promote economic development in Latin America.

In the later twentieth century, Treasury assisted a succession of presidential administrations in fighting inflation, *unemployment, negative trade balances, and a rising federal deficit. The department responded to the savings and loan crisis of the mid-1980s by overseeing the creation of the Office of Thrift Supervision to monitor the savings and loan industry more closely. In the early 1990s, Treasury played an important role in the negotiations that led to the *North American Free Trade Agreement (NAFTA). The economic expansion of the later 1990s and the decline in the budget deficit resulted in part from the Department's policies.

[*See also* Bank of the United States, First and Second; Banking and Finance; Business Cycle; Depressions, Economic; Early Republic, Era of the; Eighteenth Amendment; Foreign Trade;

Monetary Policy, Federal; New Deal Era, The; Savings and Loan Debacle; Tariffs; Temperance and Prohibition.]

• Esther Rogoff Taus, *Central Banking Functions of the United States Treasury,* 1943. Leonard D. White, *The Federalists: A Study in Administrative History,* 1965. Office of Information, Department of the Treasury, *The Department of the Treasury,* 1969. Bernard S. Katz and C. Daniel Vencill, eds., *Biographical Dictionary of United States Secretaries of the Treasury,* 1996.

—Jesse Stiller

FEDERAL GOVERNMENT EXECUTIVE BRANCH: DEPARTMENT OF AGRICULTURE

The United States Department of Agriculture (USDA) was established in 1862. The first commissioner of agriculture, Isaac Newton, organized the department by scientific fields such as entomology and botany, each represented initially by one person and later by a division. Early contact with farmers was limited to the distribution of seeds for trial and the publication of advisory pamphlets. The USDA began with a small budget and an uncertain relationship to the land-grant universities in the development of agricultural science. In 1887 the Hatch Act established state *agricultural experimental stations as institutions for basic research in agriculture-related fields.

In the late nineteenth century the USDA began reorganizing its research activities to focus on specific problems, such as livestock diseases. The first new unit was the Bureau of Animal Industry, created in 1884. With permanent status and funding, an approving interest group (cattle ranchers in this case), and regulatory power, this new bureau made rapid progress against livestock diseases and became the model for other problem-oriented bureaus. Harvey W. Wiley, head of the Bureau of Chemistry from 1883 to 1912, led a long campaign against food adulteration, culminating in the 1906 *Pure Food and Drug Act. The high-visibility activist Gifford Pinchot ran the Bureau of Forestry (later Forest Service) from 1898 to 1910, pursuing a policy of sustained use that has remained largely unchanged.

Working in the Bureau of Plant Industry during the early twentieth-century period when the boll-weevil infestation began to devastate the southern *cotton industry, Seaman A. Knapp started "demonstration farms" to persuade farmers to try new methods developed by agricultural scientists, particularly those in the Bureau of Entomology. Knapp's success led to the Smith-Lever Act of 1914, which formed the Extension Service as a cooperative program of the USDA and land-grant colleges.

The USDA became a cabinet-level department in 1889. Secretary James Wilson (1897–1913) oversaw the expansion of scientific work in the bureaus, the establishment of federal experiment stations in new territories such as *Hawai'i and *Puerto Rico, and the introduction of new crops and varieties by the "plant explorer" David Fairchild. Henry C. Wallace (1921–1923) increased the department's work in agricultural economics, recognizing that merely improving production did not guarantee prosperity for farmers. His son, Henry A. Wallace (1933–1940), implemented such New Deal programs as the *Agricultural Adjustment Acts, which introduced crop reduction and agricultural *subsidies to boost prices, policies that in some form would long remain in place.

Direct contact between department scientists and farmers declined over time. In 1954 the bureaus were abolished and their scientific work reorganized into the Agricultural Research Service. The Food and Drug Administration was removed from the department in 1940. By *World War II, the department was emphasizing pesticides to the near exclusion of other methods of insect control, opening it to a storm of criticism by environmentalists after the publication of Rachel *Carson's *Silent Spring* in 1962. The controversy reflected a long-standing ideological divide between advocates of maximum resource utilization in the USDA and preservationists in the Department of the Interior. During the late twentieth century the USDA came under criticism for favoring large agribusinesses and big, rich, white farmers in its scientific research, economic policies, and regulatory actions.

[*See also* Agricultural Education and Extension; Agriculture: 1770s to 1890; Agriculture: The "Golden Age" (1890–1920); Agriculture: Since 1920; Food and Diet; Forests and Forestry; Homestead Act; Livestock Industry; New Deal Era, The.]

• A. Hunter Dupree, *Science in the Federal Government,* 1957. Alan I Marcus and Richard Lowitt, eds., "The United States Department of Agriculture in Historical Perspective," *Agricultural History* 642, special issue, (1990).

—Richard C. Sawyer

FEDERAL GOVERNMENT, EXECUTIVE BRANCH: OTHER DEPARTMENTS

As the authority and sheer size of the federal government expanded over the course of American history, so did the number of cabinet-level departments within the executive branch. Since the creation in 1789 of three great executive departments (Treasury, State, and War), lawmakers have added eleven cabinet-level departments to address new problems, interest-group pressures, and functions that could not be met easily by the original three. Eight of the current fourteen departments in the executive branch were created in the twentieth century, and six alone after 1960. Charged with broad responsibilities, cabinet-level departments are the largest units of the contemporary executive branch.

Department of the Interior (1849). Although a "home affairs" or "interior" department was proposed in the earliest days of the republic, Congress resisted until the administration of James Knox *Polk. Polk's treasury secretary, Robert J. Walker, strongly supported an interior department, arguing that managing the public lands of an expanding nation was overly burdensome for his department. Walker was especially daunted by U.S. acquisitions of vast new territories following the *Mexican War and the 1848 treaty with Britain ceding much of the Oregon Territory to the United States. After heated debate, Congress in 1849 approved an administration plan establishing the Department of the Interior. The measure shifted to the Interior Department the General Land Office from Treasury, the Patent Office from State, and the *Bureau of Indian Affairs and Pension Office from War.

For most of its history, Interior's policies reflected the notion that the public lands and natural resources under its management were practically limitless and should be fully developed to promote national growth and prosperity. The environmental movement altered the politics and policies of the department, however. Stewart L. Udall, President John F. *Kennedy's interior secretary in the early 1960s, forged closer ties with the environmental movement. Udall, a supporter of national parks and environmental preservation during his years as a congressman, fostered department initiatives for improving the *national park system, resource planning, and outdoor recreation. After Udall's tenure, the Interior Department found itself drawn into heated political conflicts pitting environmental groups against *mining, logging, and other development interests. Secretary Cecil D. Andrus (1977–1981) drew fire from corporate interests for championing new controls on strip mining, stronger protection of the *Alaska wilderness, and new efforts to redress chemical contamination. His successor, Ronald *Reagan appointee James G. Watt, faced withering criticism from environmental groups who protested his plans for private use of resources in the public domain, stronger state control over public lands, and the appointment of prodevelopment personnel.

Former Arizona governor Bruce Babbitt, secretary of the interior in the Bill *Clinton administration, found himself at the center of tense struggles over grazing, mining, logging, and controlled-burn policies. As the twentieth century ended, Interior was responsible for managing the nation's natural resources, including its wildlife and nearly 600 million acres of public lands. Among its thirty major bureaus and agencies were the Bureau of Land Management, the U.S. Fish and Wildlife Service, the U.S. Geological Survey, the Bureau of Indian Affairs, and the National Park Service.

Department of Justice (1870). The Judiciary Act of 1789 established the U.S. attorney general's office as one of the earliest and most prominent within the executive branch. As the nation's chief legal officer, the attorney general joined the secretaries of Treasury, State, and War as a member of the cabinet. Yet President George *Washington's attorney general, Edmund Randolph, was assisted by only one clerk. Not until 1870 did Congress establish a Department of Justice headed by the attorney general. The new department was given responsibility for representing the U.S. government in all federal courts, providing legal advice to the White House and other executive agencies, prosecuting violations of federal law, and protecting the country from subversion.

During its early history, Justice primarily enforced *antitrust legislation, prosecuted tax evasion cases, and monitored so-called "subversives" and "public enemies." The *Federal Bureau of Investigation (FBI) was established in 1908 as the department's chief investigative arm. The department gained notoriety during the post–*World War I Red Scare when Attorney General A. Mitchell Palmer mobilized a vast campaign against radicals allegedly planning "to rise up and destroy the Government at one fell swoop." Working with local law enforcement officials, Palmer coordinated massive dragnet raids in 1919 and 1920 that targeted members of socialist or communist organizations, especially alien members. Not surprisingly, Congress placed the Immigration and Naturalization Service within Justice in 1940.

Sweeping *civil rights reforms in the 1960s and after expanded the department's mission and functions dramatically. In particular, the Justice Department's Civil Rights Division was given responsibility for prosecuting violations of the Civil Rights Act of 1964, the Voting Rights Act of 1965, the Fair Housing Act of 1968, the Equal Educational Opportunities Act of 1974, and the *Americans with Disabilities Act of 1990.

The post-1960 Justice Department also played a major role in presidential efforts to launch a "war on crime." Whereas President Lyndon B. *Johnson's attorney general, Ramsey Clark, championed *civil rights and due process, his successor John N. Mitchell embraced the Richard M. *Nixon administration's call for "law and order." As Mitchell insisted, Justice "was an institution for law enforcement, not social improvement." Ironically, Mitchell himself was convicted in 1975 of conspiracy and obstruction of justice in the *Watergate scandal. In the Clinton administration, Attorney General Janet Reno made Justice a key participant in debates over the 1994 crime bill and oversaw such varied departmental responsibilities as investigating violations of federal law, regulating immigration, policing narcotics trafficking, guarding domestic security from subversive attacks, assisting local law enforcement, providing legal advice to executive officials, and trying all government litigation before federal courts.

The Justice Department has long been authorized to name special prosecutors to investigate wrongdoing by executive branch officials. During the Nixon administration, for example, Archibald Cox was appointed to spearhead the Watergate investigation. Yet Cox's summary discharge for pursuing incriminating White House tapes highlighted dramatic limitations in how executive officials were policed. The Ethics in Government Act of 1978 established the office of independent counsel as well as formal procedures by which the Attorney General is required to initiate independent investigations of high-level executive officials for malfeasance. Since then, various White House challenges to the independent counsel's broad discretion over witness selection, investigatory strategies, and indictment decisions have routinely failed in the federal courts. The independent-counsel process thus has generated fierce debate and considerable fine-tuning whenever the law has required congressional reauthorization. This was especially true of the 1999 reauthorization which followed the controversial investigation of President Clinton by Independent Counsel Kenneth Starr.

Department of Commerce (1903). Amid rapid *industrialization and *economic development, a modest commerce agency was formed within the executive branch in 1888. After the Panic of 1893, *business interests such as the *National Association of Manufacturers lobbied strenuously for a cabinet-level department of commerce. In 1903, courting both business and labor support, President Theodore *Roosevelt won congressional approval for a Department of Commerce and Labor. With over ten thousand employees, the department's functions included regulating foreign and domestic commerce; the mining, manufacturing, shipping, and fishing industries; labor interests; and transportation. The 1913 creation of a Labor Department resulted in an independent Department of Commerce.

Departmental authority and resources expanded sharply under the ambitious leadership of commerce secretary and presidential aspirant Herbert *Hoover (1921–1928). Under Hoover, Commerce's budget soared from $860,000 in 1920 to $38 million in 1928. When Hoover became president in 1929, Commerce remained a powerful department. But in the antibusiness climate of the 1930s, President Franklin Delano *Roosevelt and the New Dealers did not look kindly at Commerce. Significantly reducing its budget and authority, they even considered dissolving the department altogether.

Although Commerce weathered *New Deal Era assaults, many of its traditional functions were subsequently taken over or shared by other executive agencies. Regulation of transportation was shifted to a new Department of Transportation in 1967. By the 1990s, responsibilities for commerce, trade, and economic analysis were shared with a host of other agencies, such as the Office of the U.S. Trade Representative, the Council of Economic Advisers, and Treasury. Nevertheless, Commerce continued to play an important collaborative part in these areas and to manage various programs to aid American businesses, encourage technological innovation, and enhance U.S. fortunes in international trade. Commerce Secretary Ron Brown died in a plane crash in 1996 while leading a group of U.S. businesspeople on a trade mission to the former Yugoslavia. The Commerce Department also is responsible for conducting the federal *census.

Department of Labor (1913). Labor activists lobbied vigorously in the 1880s for a cabinet-level department dedicated to the needs of organized labor. A small Bureau of Labor was created in 1884 within the Interior Department, followed in 1888 by an independent Department of Labor without cabinet rank. When a Department of Commerce and Labor was established in 1903, labor activists protested that it would be captured by business interests. In 1913, a Democratic Congress created a separate cabinet-level Department of Labor. During the New Deal Era under Secretary Frances *Perkins (1933–1945) the Department of Labor gained new prominence. The 1960s brought further expansion as Secretary W. Willard Wirtz forged close alliances with organized labor.

During the Reagan administration, the Labor Department faced budget cuts and charges of lax enforcement of worker-protection laws. President George *Bush's first Labor secretary, Elizabeth H. Dole, revitalized the department, winning budget increases, making worker safety a key objective, negotiating an increase in the minimum wage, and pressing companies receiving government contracts to move more women and minorities into managerial positions. Labor Secretary Robert B. Reich (1993–1997) further restored departmental prominence, emphasizing education and training for unskilled workers in a global economy while overseeing Labor's responsibility for occupational health and safety, antidiscrimination in employment, worker's compensation, *unemployment insurance, minimum wages and overtime pay, pension rights, and free collective bargaining. The department also maintains job training and manpower programs (such as Job Corps) and collects labor statistics.

Department of Health and Human Services (1953). The roots of the Department of Health and Human Services date to the Federal Security Administration (FSA), formed in 1939 to coordinate various agencies responsible for health, education, and *Social Security programs. The Federal Children's Bureau (1912) was transferred from Labor to the FSA a few years later. In 1953, President Dwight D. *Eisenhower won legislative approval for making the FSA a cabinet-level department, the Department of Health, Education, and Welfare (HEW), which soon grew into one of the largest departments in the federal government. Social Security expanded steadily, providing disability insurance in 1956 and gradually increasing retirement benefits while easing eligibility standards. HEW responsibilities grew again in 1965 with new Medicare hospital insurance for the elderly and a Medicaid program to fund medical expenses of the poor.

With the creation of the Department of Education in 1979, HEW became the Department of Health and Human Services (HHS). HHS functions were reduced again when the Social Security Administration became an independent agency in 1995, thereby distancing the program from political pressures. Despite this streamlining, HHS retained a broad mandate, administering *Medicare and Medicaid and overseeing the work of the surgeon general, the *Centers for Disease Control and Prevention (CDC), the *National Institutes of Health (NIH), and the Food and Drug Administration (FDA). Despite reforms in the Clinton years shifting responsibility for welfare to the states, HHS continued to oversee numerous programs designed to promote the welfare of children, families, and the elderly.

Department of Housing and Urban Development (1965). Endorsed by the Kennedy and Johnson administrations, the Department of Housing and Urban Development (HUD) was created in 1965 to address a host of urban problems: *housing shortages, pollution, poor mass transit and roadways, and a general decline of the urban infrastructure. Controversial from the start, HUD was called on to promote fair housing practices, provide rent supplements and public housing for the urban poor, and help poor families buy their own homes. During the 1980s, however, the Reagan administration sharply reduced federal housing programs and slashed HUD resources. President Bush's HUD secretary, Jack Kemp, tried to position the department at the vanguard of domestic policy innovation. In a 1990 housing-reform law, Kemp won approval for a plan to help public housing tenants and other poor persons purchase homes. After the 1991 riots in *Los Angeles, he successfully pressed Congress to create enterprise zones offering tax breaks to businesses locating in inner-city areas.

Department of Transportion (1966). Established to coordinate the government's labyrinthine transportation policy, the Department of Transportation (DOT) in fact never received broad authority to manage the national transportation system. Various key agencies, such as the National Transportation Safety Board, were made independent of the department's secretary. Despite its narrow authority, DOT played an important role in deregulating the airline, railroad, and trucking industries in the late 1970s, and in promulgating new rules for making public facilities handicapped-accessible. DOT oversees the Coast Guard, the Federal Aviation Administration, the Federal Railroad Administration, public mass transit systems, and the nation's *highway system.

Department of Energy (1977). The immediate impetus for an energy department was the 1973 Arab oil embargo, which led to the creation in 1974 of two federal agencies, the Energy Research and Development Administration and the Federal Energy Administration, to design and implement a national energy policy. These agencies were consolidated into a Department of Energy in 1977. President Jimmy *Carter gave the new department prominence, arguing that it should have broad discretion to address national energy problems. During the late 1970s, Energy promoted conservation by embracing solar power and other alternative technologies as well as new ways to burn fossil fuels. Federal regulation of energy markets was rolled back during the Reagan years, while Energy secretaries James B. Edwards and Donald P. Hodel promoted *nuclear power. The Nuclear Waste Policy Act of 1982 placed the Energy Department at the center of political controversy by giving it responsibility for locating, constructing, and operating sites for the disposal of civilian and military nuclear waste. The department also monitors U.S. energy consumption and promotes new energy technologies.

Department of Education (1979). Given the decentralized structure of the U.S. educational system, the creation of a federal education department was relatively late in coming and highly controversial. When the Department of Education was formed in 1979 with strong backing from the powerful *National Education Association, a teachers' union, Congress stipulated that the new department "shall not diminish the responsibility for *education which is reserved to the states and local school systems." Lacking a broad mandate to shape education policy, departmental efforts to overhaul American education were routinely frustrated by Congress, and Republican leaders periodically called for dismantling the department altogether. The department administers federal funds to enhance preschool, elementary, and secondary schooling; to educate handicapped children and rehabilitate disabled adults; and to help young adults pay for postsecondary education. In the 1990s, the department became embroiled in debate over "school choice" plans, a proposed national examination for students, and merit standards for teachers.

Department of Veterans' Affairs (1989). Since the *Revolutionary War, various government programs were established to assist veterans and their dependents. These programs were scattered among different federal agencies until Congress in 1930 placed them under the control of the *Veterans Administration (VA). The VA's resources and functions expanded significantly after *World War II, as the number of American veterans soared to nineteen million. By the 1980s, more than twenty-seven million Americans were veterans and roughly one-third of the population were dependents and survivors of veterans. Veterans groups lobbied vigorously for the VA's elevation to cabinet status, and the Reagan administration strongly agreed. Although a congressionally mandated report by the National Academy of Public Administration found "no compelling reason" to make the VA a cabinet-level department, lawmakers bowed to political pressure and established a Department of Veterans' Affairs in 1989. In the 1990s, the department won special benefits for *Vietnam War and *Persian Gulf War veterans suffering illnesses related to exposure to harmful chemicals. Its major responsibilities include oversight of an extensive veterans health care system, various benefits programs for veterans and their families, and maintenance of 147 national military cemeteries.

[*See also* Civil Rights Legislation; Forests and Forestry; Immigration Law; Land Policy, Federal; Energy Crisis of the 1970s; Patent and Copyright Law.]

• Mary L. Hinsdale, *A History of the President's Cabinet*, 1911. Henry Barrett Learned, *The President's Cabinet: Studies in the Origin, Formation, and Structure of an American Institution*, 1912. Richard Fenno, *The President's Cabinet*, 1959. Bradley H. Patterson Jr., *The President's Cabinet: Issues and Questions*, 1976. John P. Burke, *The Institutional Presidency*, 1992. W. Craig Bledsoe and Leslie Rigby, "The Cabinet and Executive Departments," in *Cabinets and Counselors: The President and the Executive Branch*, 1997, pp. 73–140. Ronald C. Moe, "The President's Cab-

inet," in *Understanding the Presidency*, eds. James P. Pfiffner and Roger H. Davidson, 1997, pp. 136–55.
—Daniel J. Tichenor

FEDERAL GOVERNMENT, JUDICIAL BRANCH. The framework of the federal judicial system was established by the Judiciary Act of 1789. Its principal author, Senator Oliver Ellsworth of Connecticut, a delegate to the *Constitutional Convention of 1787, would in 1796 become the second chief justice of the United States. Because Article III of the *Constitution merely provided for "one Supreme Court and such inferior Courts as the Congress may from time to time ordain and establish," it fell to the fledgling legislative branch to organize the judicial branch. It did so in the seminal 1789 Judiciary Act, which incorporated into the national judicial system the fundamental principle of federal supremacy.

The statute provided for a *Supreme Court composed of a chief justice and five associate justices, thirteen federal district courts of one judge each, and three circuit courts, each consisting of two justices of the Supreme Court sitting jointly with one district court judge. The legislation outlined the several courts' jurisdiction in considerable detail and spelled out their general organizational and procedural parameters. A key section of the act brought the state courts directly under federal appellate jurisdiction by providing for appeals from state courts to federal courts. This crucial power of federal judicial review over decisions by the state judiciary was challenged by the states in the U.S. Supreme Court, then headed by Chief Justice John *Marshall, in four seminal cases—all of which the states lost: *United States* v. *Peters* (1809), **Fletcher* v. *Peck* (1810), *Martin* v. *Hunter's Lessee* (1816), and *Cohens* v. *Virginia* (1821). The opinions, two written by Marshall and two by Joseph *Story, confirmed in perpetuity federal judicial supremacy and authority.

Another major issue of judicial power—perhaps *the* major issue—soon came to the fore: namely, the power of *judicial review, not only of actions by the states but also by the legislative and executive branches of the federal government. "Judicial review" in the United States is the power of a court (after painstaking reflection and due regard for legal precedent and the principle of judicial restraint) to hold unconstitutional and hence unenforceable any law, official action based on a law, or other action by a public official that it deems to be in conflict with the Constitution. (The judicial review process also may result, of course, in the finding that the law or official action in question *is* constitutional.)

The Supreme Court confronted the issue of judicial review in **Marbury* v. *Madison* (1803). The case turned on the fact that Congress, in the Judiciary Act of 1789, had extended to the Supreme Court the power to issue writs of mandamus (Latin for "we command"), an ancient Anglo-Saxon writ ordering a public official to perform his official duty. Petitioner Marbury, whose appointment as a justice of the peace by President John *Adams was deliberately not delivered by newly elected president Thomas *Jefferson's secretary of state, James *Madison, asked the Supreme Court to issue a writ of mandamus to compel the delivery of his commission. Although expressing sympathy for Marbury's plight, Marshall, speaking for a unanimous Court, rejected his petition. By granting the Supreme Court the power to issue writs of mandamus, Marshall held, Congress had unconstitutionally added to the Court's original jurisdiction spelled out in Article III of the Constitution. These powers could only be changed by an amendment to the Constitution, the chief justice went on, not by a mere law. "An act repugnant to the Constitution is void," Marshall concluded, and "it is emphatically the province and duty of the judicial department to say what the law is." Thus was offically born the Court's ultimate power, that of judicial review.

Readdressing the organization of the judicial branch, Congress in the Judiciary Act of 1801, created six new circuit courts to be staffed with their own judges rather than by circuit-riding Supreme Court justices (who loathed that collateral duty). In addition, the act established a number of new district courts. For jurisdictional as well as political and economic reasons, the Judiciary Act of 1801 was repealed once the Jefferson administration took office and replaced by the Circuit Court Act of 1802. This measure, the last to change the federal judicial structure until after the *Civil War, divided the country into six rather than three circuits, assigning a Supreme Court justice to each.

*Reconstruction Era politics resulted in various changes to both the number of circuit courts, and to the increasing or decreasing size of the Supreme Court. In 1869, however, responding to insistent pleas from the justices, Congress stabilized the Court at its present membership of nine and added nine circuit judges to relieve the Supreme Court justices of some of the burden of circuit riding. That duty ended entirely in the 1880s, although each of the nine justices continues to be responsibile for at least one of the now thirteen circuits.

Along with the federal courts mandated by Article III of the Constitution, known as the "constitutional" courts, Congress as the need arose created additional specialized courts under its constitutional power (art. 1, sec. 8, clause 9) to "constitute Tribunals inferior to the Supreme Court." Known as "legislative" rather than "constitutional" courts, these include the U.S. Court of Claims, the Tax Court, the U.S. Court of Military Appeals, and the U.S. Veterans Court. However, the center of gravity of federal judicial power remains in the three-tiered constitutional court structure. The number of Supreme Court justices remains nine, despite President Franklin Delano *Roosevelt's ill-fated 1937 attempt to persuade Congress to increase the membership to as many as fifteen. This bill, a product of Roosevelt's frustration with the Court's hostility toward New Deal legislation, elicited a fierce public reaction. What did change as the nation grew was the size of the high tribunal's docket, which by the end of the twentieth century had reached some seven thousand petitions for review annually. Most of these were disposed of by memorandum orders, but one hundred or so typically resulted in formal opinions.

The two lower constitutional court structures, the federal circuit and district courts, also remained in place as the twentieth century ended, but the number of courts, judges, and cases had all increased markedly. The thirteen U.S. circuit courts of appeals in 1998 (including the U.S. Circuit Court of Appeals for the District of Columbia, often called the second most important court in the land, and the U.S. Court of Appeals for the Federal Circuit) comprised a statutorily authorized total of 179 judges who handled some 50,000 cases annually. At the lowest level of the federal constitutional judiciary stand the 94 workhorse U.S. district courts, where federal trials commence and whose 649 judges field some 100,000 civil and criminal cases annually.

In general, the judicial branch of the federal government has enjoyed the people's trust, ranking above both the legislative and executive branches in poll after poll. It is endowed with awesome power, but, headed by the Supreme Court, it remains the nation's natural forum for individuals and groups as well as the fundamental guardian of law and order. On the whole, the system has done well in maintaining the balance between continuity and change that constitutes the sine qua non for stability in the governmental process of a democracy.

[*See also* other "Federal Government" essays; New Deal Era, The]

• Charles Warren, *The Supreme Court in United States History*, 1922–1935. Lawrence M. Friedman, *A History of American Law*, 2d ed., 1986. Henry M. Hart and Herbert Wechsler, *The Federal Courts and the Federal System*, 1988. Sheldon Goldman and Charles M. Lamb, *Judicial Conflict and Consensus: Behavioral Studies of American Appellate Courts*, 1989. Daniel J. Meador, *American Courts*, 1991. Charles M. Coffin, *Appellate Courts, Lawyering and Judging*, 1994. Daniel J. Meador and J. S.

Bernstein, *Appellate Courts in the United States,* 1994. Henry J. Abraham, *The Judiciary,* 10th ed., 1997. Henry J. Abraham, *The Judicial Process,* 7th ed., 1998. Henry J. Abraham, *Justices, Presidents, and Senators, 1999.*

—Henry J. Abraham

FEDERAL GOVERNMENT, LEGISLATIVE BRANCH

Overview
Senate
House of Representatives

FEDERAL GOVERNMENT, LEGISLATIVE BRANCH: OVERVIEW

The legislative branch of the U.S. government—the Congress—is a bicameral legislature composed of the House of Representatives, whose membership is based on proportional representation, and the Senate, made up of two members from each state. This arrangement resulted from a compromise at the *Constitutional Convention of 1787 between the representatives of states with large populations and those from small states, who feared being automatically outvoted under a wholly proportional system.

The House of Representatives was modeled on the British House of Commons: Elected directly by the citizens, representatives serve two-year terms. The Senate, in contrast, was a new creation, designed not only as a body where each state would have an equal number of votes, but also as a check on the popular emotions that might sway House members. To this end, senators were to be older—at least thirty years of age as opposed to twenty-five for representatives—and thus presumably more mature. To insulate them from popular pressures, senators would serve staggered six-year terms and be elected by the legislatures of their states instead of directly by the citizens.

Together, the House and Senate are responsible for making all laws, with tax bills originating in the House. Congress also possesses the power to declare war, oversee and investigate the administration of programs initiated by the executive branch, and override presidential vetoes by two-thirds votes of both houses. In addition, the Senate has sole responsibility for reviewing and approving treaties and confirming presidential nominations. The House has the power to impeach government officials who abuse their office, while the Senate acts as a court to try *impeachment cases brought by the House. Conviction by the Senate brings removal from office. Each house also has the power to discipline its own members and to expel a member by a two-thirds vote.

Until 1794 the Senate met in closed session, while meetings of the House were always open to the public. Although the House had two standing committees as early as 1795, both bodies generally operated with ad hoc committees chosen for each piece of legislation or for a single term until the early 1800s, when both the House and Senate established more permanent standing committees.

The basic structure of the legislative branch has generally remained stable, with only a few changes over time. As new states entered the Union, the membership of both bodies multiplied, from 26 senators in the first Congress to 100 after 1959, and from 65 representatives to 435 since 1911, when the total number of representatives was capped by statute. By the mid–1850s, the House and Senate had outgrown their chambers in the Capitol Building, leading to the addition of large north and south wings to provide spacious new chambers. Down to the first decade of the twentieth century, representatives and senators had little or no office space or staff, but as staff members were hired and more working space was needed, both bodies erected office buildings.

As the twentieth century progressed, the role of the federal government expanded and became more complex, a trend accelerated by the New Deal and *World War II. Legislative branch activities kept pace, leading to the hiring of additional staff, until by the 1990s the House had more than ten thousand staff members and the Senate more than six thousand, housed in seven congressional office buildings.

One structural change occurred with ratification in 1913 of the Seventeenth Amendment, which mandated that senators, like members of the House, be elected by direct popular vote. Also important, though less dramatic, was the Legislative Reorganization Act of 1947, which made such "housekeeping" changes as reducing the number of House and Senate committees, consolidating jurisdictions, and authorizing professional staff members for both members and committees.

Although most federal government agencies are part of the executive branch, the legislative branch has created several agencies to serve its particular needs. The *Library of Congress, established in 1800, serves as a repository and disseminator of knowledge for the entire nation; the Government Printing Office, set up in 1860, publishes official congressional and other governmental documents; and the General Accounting Office, established by the Budget and Accounting Act of 1921, audits and reviews the actions of federal agencies. In 1974, Congress established its own Congressional Budget Office as an independent source of fiscal information. A congressional Office of Technology Assessment existed from 1972 until it was abolished in 1995.

[*See also* Constitution; New Deal Era, The; Taxation; Veto Power.]

• George B. Galloway, *History of the House of Representatives,* 1961. Alvin M. Josephy Jr., *On the Hill: A History of the American Congress,* 1979. U.S. Congress, Senate, *Biographical Directory of the United States Congress, 1774–1989,* 1988. Robert C. Byrd, *The Senate, 1789–1989: Addresses on the History of the United States Senate,* 4 vols., 1989–1994. Joel H. Silbey, ed., *Encyclopedia of the American Legislative System,* 3 vols., 1994. Donald C. Bacon, Roger H. Davidson, and Morton Keller, eds., *The Encyclopedia of the United States Congress,* 4 vols., 1995.

—Wendy Wolff

FEDERAL GOVERNMENT, LEGISLATIVE BRANCH: SENATE

The Senate forms the upper house of the bicameral Congress established by the U.S. *Constitution. The earlier government under the *Articles of Confederation had consisted of a Congress of one house, in which each state had a single vote. With no executive branch, all officials were responsible to Congress. The *Constitutional Convention of 1787 was called because that government, a confederation of sovereign states rather than a union, did not meet the needs of the new nation.

After extensive discussions, the framers arrived at the so-called Great Compromise. They devised a House of Representatives in which a state's representation was proportional to its population and a Senate in which each state would be equally represented with two members, thus providing protection to the smaller states. The two senators representing each state would serve staggered, six-year terms, with only one-third of the Senate running in any election year. The Senate is thus a continuing body, unlike the House of Representatives whose entire membership is elected every two years. The Convention's members hoped the Senate would carefully review measures passed by the House, which, with frequent elections, would more likely be swayed by popular passions. With this goal in mind, they set the Senate's age requirement at thirty (in contrast to the House's twenty-five), and they provided for the election of senators by state legislatures rather than by popular vote.

To start the staggered terms, senators of the first Congress drew lots to determine who would have two-, four-, or six-year terms. The Senate continues to be divided into three "classes," depending on which year a member faces reelection. When a new state enters the Union, its senators are assigned to classes so that the number in each class remains nearly equal, with no class having more than one senator from any state.

Powers. The Senate shares with the House responsibility for making laws, declaring war, and appropriating funds to operate the federal government, as well as for instituting new programs and overseeing old ones. With the House, the Senate has the power to override presidential vetoes by a two-thirds vote. In addition, the Constitution assigned three powers exclusively to the Senate: reviewing and approving treaties, confirming nominations of judges and executive branch officials, and serving as the court for *impeachment trials.

Under the Articles of Confederation, congressional agents negotiated treaties, which required approval by nine of the thirteen states. The U.S. Constitution, by contrast, gives the treaty-making power to the executive, with the requirement of Senate approval. Having the Senate review treaties, the framers thought, would provide counsel to the president, as well as place checks and balances on the executive power. Since all states have equal representation in the Senate, the arrangement would also protect the interests of the states.

In practice, the president submits the text of each treaty to the Senate, which reviews it first in committee. If the committee approves, it sends the treaty to the full Senate for a vote. Presidents have frequently found it useful to consult the Senate while negotiating a treaty or to include senators in the delegation conducting the negotiations. On only twenty-one occasions has the Senate formally rejected a treaty, the most famous being the Treaty of *Versailles ending *World War I. After President Woodrow *Wilson failed either to consult the Senate or to accept reservations it had adopted, the body refused to approve the treaty in two votes in 1919 and 1920.

The requirement for Senate approval of presidential nominations to executive and judicial offices is another of the checks and balances written into the Constitution. Every year the Senate reviews thousands of military and civilian nominations, generally submitted to it in long lists, as well as the individual nominations of cabinet officers, federal judges, and ambassadors. Most of these nominees are confirmed, but occasionally the Senate objects. As of 1997, the Senate had failed to confirm a total of twenty-seven *Supreme Court nominees. While it has formally rejected only nine cabinet appointees, the nominations of eight others have been withdrawn in the face of Senate opposition.

Fearing that the president might abuse his position, the Constitutional Convention included an impeachment provision similar to those many of the new states had included in their constitutions. After considering whether the Supreme Court should try impeachment cases, the framers foresaw a possible conflict of interest, since the Court's members were presidential appointees. They settled instead on having the Senate try impeachments. Through 1999, the Senate had conducted impeachment trials of two presidents (Andrew *Johnson and Bill *Clinton, both acquitted); one senator (William Blount, 1797, already expelled, so impeachment failed); one cabinet officer (William Belknap, 1876, already resigned); one Supreme Court justice (Samuel Chase, 1804, acquitted); and twelve federal judges (seven found guilty and removed from office).

Structure. Under the Constitution, the vice president of the United States is the president and presiding officer of the Senate. The Constitution also gives the Senate the power to choose a president pro tempore to preside in his absence, as well as authority over its own membership, including the power to expel a member by a two-thirds vote and to serve as judge in contested election cases. Empowered to select its officers, the Senate elects a chaplain, a secretary, and a sergeant at arms. For more than two hundred years, these latter two officers have supervised the Senate's basic administrative structure. The secretary of the Senate, the body's chief administrative and financial officer, also oversees the official journals and records and the clerks who serve in the Senate chamber. The sergeant at arms is the chief law enforcement and protocol officer of the Senate and also manages most of the support services.

Many of the Senate's rules were originally based on English precedent, as well as on the rules of the Continental and Confederation congresses. The Senate has recodified its rules on seven occasions, most recently in 1979. Unlike the House, which strictly regulates the length of debate, the Senate prides itself on its right of extended debate, as a protection for the rights of the minority. Through the delaying tactic known as the filibuster, a minority of senators can block action on a measure. Not until 1917 did the Senate adopt its first "cloture" rule permitting a vote by two-thirds of the senators to shut off debate and bring a measure to a vote. Subsequent refinements to the rule now allow a vote by sixty senators (three-fifths of the Senate) to close debate.

Since the first Congress, the Senate has assigned proposed legislation (bills) to committees for review. Initially, temporary committees handled specific legislation and then disbanded. Not until 1816, except for three housekeeping panels, did the Senate create permanent standing legislative committees. The number of standing committees grew steadily thereafter, reaching more than seventy by 1913. The Legislative Reorganization Act of 1946 reduced the number of committees to seventeen, while providing for professional staff members. A further restructuring in 1977 produced the approximately sixteen standing committees that existed in 1997.

In designing the Senate, the framers did not envision political parties, but party divisions began almost immediately, and continued through the early nineteenth century. By 1860 the present *Democratic and *Republican parties were in place. Although Senate Democrats and Republicans elected chairs and secretaries in the late 1800s, not until the early twentieth century did the body adopt the modern system of party leadership. In the 1920s the party caucuses began electing floor leaders. These majority and minority leaders, assisted by party whips, manage legislation on the Senate floor.

Unlike the House of Representatives, which was open to the public from the beginning, the Senate initially met behind closed doors, not opening public galleries until 1795. Thus, in the early 1790s, newspapers reported the House debates but citizens knew little of what transpired in the Senate. Starting in 1802, the Senate admitted notetakers to record its debates, which were published initially by the newspaper the *National Intelligencer*, and later in other private publications such as the *Register of Debates* and the *Congressional Globe*. The official *Congressional Record*, a government publication, began reporting in 1873, at which time the Senate also hired its own official reporters.

The Senate considers treaties and nominations in executive session. Until 1929, these executive sessions were generally closed to the public, although detailed information about the debates regularly leaked to the press. Recognizing that the sources of the leaks must be the members themselves, the Senate in 1929 opened all executive sessions except those involving national security.

Development and Growth. The Senate's relative importance within the federal government has fluctuated over its history. In the early years, because the House met in open session, its debates had more public visibility than the Senate's. By the 1830s, the Senate had entered what became known as its Golden Age, as intense debates raged over *slavery and the very nature of the Union among such leaders as Henry *Clay of Kentucky, Daniel *Webster of Massachusetts, and John C. *Calhoun of South Carolina. When Alexis de Tocqueville visited Washington in 1832, he deplored the rowdiness of the House of Representatives, while praising the Senate for its articulate statesmen (apparently unaware that many senators had previously served in the House).

Memorable Senate debates and bargaining produced the *Missouri Compromise of 1820 and the *Compromise of 1850, both dealing with slavery and the admission of new states to the Union, but only temporarily defusing deepening sectional conflicts. When the *Civil War broke out in 1861, the Senate shrank temporarily from sixty-eight members to fewer than fifty, as senators from the seceding states withdrew or were expelled.

The dominance of Radical Republicans in Congress during the Civil War and after set up a confrontation with President Andrew Johnson that culminated in the impeachment of Johnson, whom the Senate failed to convict by a single vote in 1868. For the rest of the nineteenth century, the Senate, still led principally by Republicans, dominated the federal government until its position was challenged in the early 1900s by the powerful presidencies of Theodore *Roosevelt and Woodrow Wilson.

The turn of the twentieth century also saw growing public dissatisfaction with the method of electing U.S. senators. Political battles in state legislatures could lead to long vacancies in some Senate seats. This problem, combined with charges of corruption and purchased votes, led to adoption and ratification of the Seventeenth Amendment in 1913, directing that senators be elected by popular vote.

Influential during the 1920s, the Senate played a more subordinate role during the early *New Deal Era as President Franklin Delano *Roosevelt, enjoying overwhelming popularity and strong congressional majorities, proposed measure after measure that received prompt legislative approval. The Legislative Reorganization Act of 1946 streamlined the operations of both the Senate and House to deal with the flood of postwar legislation. Senator Joseph *McCarthy's anticommunist crusade of the early 1950s brought moments of high drama. The so-called *Army-McCarthy hearings of early 1954 attracted a vast television audience. That December, resorting to a rarely used expedient just short of expulsion, the Senate voted to censure the Wisconsin Republican.

In the 1950s and 1960s, the Senate struggled with *civil rights legislation before breaking a southern filibuster to pass the landmark Civil Rights Act of 1964, followed by President Lyndon B. *Johnson's *Great Society programs. As the *Vietnam War absorbed the nation's treasure and manpower during the later 1960s and early 1970s, the Senate and House eventually balked and cut off funding for the war. They also adopted the War Powers Resolution of 1973, requiring the president to notify Congress and seek congressional approval when sending U.S. troops into combat. Again asserting its authority in early 1991, the Senate held an intense debate before approving the use of military force to repel Iraq's invasion of Kuwait.

Since the 1920s, the Senate has energetically exerted its right to investigate executive branch activities, supported by a Supreme Court decision (*McGrain* v. *Daugherty*, 1927) that established the power of Senate committees to compel testimony from witnesses. The Senate's high-profile investigations have included the Teapot Dome inquiry of 1923–1924, probing the leasing of government oil reserves in Wyoming; the "Truman Committee's" investigation of defense contracts during and after *World War II; Tennessee Senator Estes Kefauver's investigation of *organized crime in the early 1950s; and the *Watergate Committee's inquiry into wrongdoing by the Richard M. *Nixon administration.

For more than two centuries, the Senate has fulfilled its unique constitutional role as the deliberative arm of the legislative branch, using its power to review treaties and nominations and its right of extended debate to slow executive branch or House pressures for more precipitous action.

[*See also* Continental Congress; Persian Gulf War; Teapot Dome Scandal.]

• Richard A. Baker, *The Senate of the United States: A Bicentennial History,* 1988. U.S. Congress, Senate, *Biographical Directory of the United States Congress, 1774–1989,* 1988. Robert C. Byrd, *The Senate, 1789–1989: Addresses on the History of the United States Senate,* 4 vols., 1989–1994. Bob Dole, *Historical Almanac of the United States Senate,* 1989. U.S. Congress, Senate, *Guide to the Records of the United States Senate at the National Archives, 1789–1989: Bicentennial Edition,* prepared by the National Archives' Center for Legislative Archives, 1989. Joel H. Silbey, *Encyclopedia of the American Legislative System,* 3 vols., 1994. Donald Bacon, Roger Davidson, and Morton Keller, eds., *The Encyclopedia of the United States Congress,* 4 vols., 1995. U.S. Congress, Senate, *Guide to Research Collections of Former United States Senators, 1789–1995,* 1995. U.S. Congress, Senate, *Senators of the United States: A Historical Bibliography,* 1995.

—Wendy Wolff

FEDERAL GOVERNMENT, LEGISLATIVE BRANCH: HOUSE OF REPRESENTATIVES

Of all the components of the federal government, the House of Representatives derives most directly from Great Britain, being closely patterned on the House of Commons and retaining many of that body's features, including a Speaker as presiding officer.

Creating the House of Representatives. The decision to create a House of Representatives elected directly by the people was made by the *Constitutional Convention of 1787 following earlier decisions establishing a three-part national government and a bicameral national legislature. The convention assigned eighteen specific powers to the legislative branch, including the power to levy and collect taxes, declare war, and regulate interstate and foreign commerce. The most divisive issue, and the one on which the convention might have foundered, was the manner in which seats in the House would be assigned to the thirteen states. Would the states be equally represented, or would they be given seats according to their populations? After lengthy debate, the convention decided that states should receive seats in proportion to their population of free citizens plus three-fifths of all others. (The latter provision, a concession to the southern states, with their vast populations of slaves, would continue until nullified after the *Civil War by the Thirteenth, *Fourteenth, and *Fifteenth Amendments to the *Constitution.) The delegates next settled on a two-year term for members of the House; decided that revenue bills should originate in the House but be subject to modification by the other branch of the national legislature, the Senate; and set the qualifications for membership in the House: to be elected, a person must have been a U.S. citizen for at least seven years, must be a resident of the state, and must be at least twenty-five years of age.

The Nineteenth Century. The first House, which convened on 1 April 1789, elected Frederick A. C. Muhlenberg of Pennsylvania as Speaker. As presiding officer of the House, the Speaker is the only official of the chamber specifically mentioned in the Constitution. The need for strong leadership was paramount in a chamber destined to grow larger as the nation's population expanded. Beginning with only 65 members, the size of the house nearly tripled by 1830 to 186 members, and it increased to 435 by 1910, at which point the number was fixed by statute. Speakers have played a central role throughout the House's history, although the influence of individual Speakers has varied widely.

In the early years of the republic, the House of Representatives, possessing the democratic legitimacy that came from its members' direct election by the people, was the dominant legislative chamber. (Senators were not directly elected until the ratification of the Seventeenth Amendment in 1913.) But equally important was the emergence of a forceful Speaker in Henry *Clay of Kentucky, who was elected Speaker on his first day in the House, 19 January 1811, and served almost continuously until 1825.

Because of the rough balance between slave and free states in the Senate, that chamber beginning around 1820 became the principal forum for debating the divisive issues of *slavery and *tariffs; the House proved less able to conciliate these differences. After the Civil War, however, the House again became dominant because one party or the other usually had a clear majority, and a number of unusually strong Speakers emerged, including Republicans James G. *Blaine and Thomas Brackett Reed of Maine, and Democrats John Carlisle of Kentucky and Charles F. Crisp of Georgia.

With the growth of the House came two important adaptations: legislative committees and an elaborate structure of rules that govern debate and the lawmaking process. Initially, House committees were "select" or "special committees," set up either for a brief period—such as a single two-year Congress—or to deal with a single bill. In the earliest period there were only two standing (that is, permanent) committees: a Committee of Elections and, to fulfill the House's constitutional role as the point of origin for revenue bills, the Committee on Ways and Means. The latter body established in 1795, is the only early committee that survives under its original name.

Originally, the House was governed by a simple set of rules, one of which allowed the members to resolve themselves into "The Committee of the Whole House" to expedite action. By the legal fiction of reconvening under a different name, quorum requirements could be relaxed. At first, debate was unlimited. Filibusters, or interminable speech-making to purposely block consideration of a bill, were common. Only in 1811, as war with Britain loomed, did the House adopt a motion that allowed members to cut off debate by calling for the previous question, a parliamentary procedure requiring an immediate vote on whatever motion is on the floor. Denounced as a "gag rule," this initial effort to limit debate proved ineffective, and not until 1841 was a rule adopted limiting each member to one hour of debate on each question. Filibustering was further restricted in 1847 with the adoption of a rule that gave members only five minutes to introduce, explain, and advocate amendments to bills. Resourceful representatives, however, continued a form of filibustering by offering many amendments—a tactic that was restricted in 1860.

One of the most radical steps ever taken by a Speaker came in response to members' practice of deliberately failing to respond to a roll call, so as to make it impossible to achieve a quorum. In January 1890, when minority Democrats refused to answer the roll call that would register them as present and prepared to vote, Speaker Reed ordered the clerk of the House to record as present all members who were actually in the chamber. By thwarting the "disappearing quorum" and other techniques used by the minority to obstruct the legislative process, Reed earned the enmity of Democrats, who denounced him as "Czar Reed," but he enabled the majority to work its will more easily and thereby moved the House closer to the majoritarian institution it would become.

Reforms and Changes in the Twentieth Century. Reed's six years as Speaker (1889–1891 and 1895–1899) marked the beginning of a period of extreme dominance by House Speakers. Joseph G. Cannon, an Illinois Republican who served as Speaker from 1903 until 1911, ruled the House with an iron hand and greatly reduced the influence of individual members. Cannon inherited Reed's powers to appoint the standing committees and name their chairs. He also appointed all five members of the Rules Committee, the most important procedural committee in the House, which was responsible for forwarding bills to the entire chamber for action. As presiding officer of the House, Cannon would refuse to recognize those who had incurred his disfavor. His dictatorial reign ended in 1910 when a group of Progressive Republicans joined with the Democrats to strip the Speaker of his membership on the Rules Committee (a position of vast influence that Speakers had enjoyed since 1858), denied him the power to appoint standing committees and their chairs, and restricted his discretion in recognizing or refusing to recognize members. While the revolt against Cannon divested the speakership of certain autocratic features, the Speaker retained an important core of powers that included the ability to influence—if not control—committee assignments and to interpret House rules.

One outgrowth of the limitations placed on Cannon was the principle that seniority would determine who would chair House committees. Ultimately, the seniority system meant that committee leadership was usually vested in those members—often conservative southern Democrats—from the safest districts. Reformers, strengthened by a large influx of younger Democrats in the election of 1974, succeeded in reducing the force of the seniority system in the 1970s when they required chairpersons of standing committees and of the powerful appropriations subcommittees to be approved by a vote of all the party's members (the Caucus). In 1975 the Caucus ousted three senior Democratic chairmen. Despite the reforms, however, there remained a presumption that seniority on a committee gave one a strong claim to the chairmanship. But even this presumption was eroded in the 104th Congress (1995–1997) when Republican Speaker Newt Gingrich of Georgia elevated some relatively junior members to committee chairmanships, most notably Bob Livingston of Louisiana as chair of Appropriations and John Kasich of Ohio as chair of Budget. As another by-product of dramatic Republican gains in the 1994 midterm elections, the Republican Conference (the counterpart of the Democratic Caucus) restricted chairs of standing committees to three two-year terms, altered the jurisdiction of committees, and changed the names of most of them.

While changes in many House rules reflected action by the party in power, other reforms resulted from nonpartisan statutory action. These include the legislative reorganization acts of 1946 and 1970, which reorganized committees and improved their staffing, and the 1974 Budget Control and Impoundment Act, which established budget committees for both chambers.

Throughout its history, certain persistent tensions have existed within the House: between the need for strong leadership to process legislation efficiently and the desire of individual members to have a role in shaping bills, and between the desire by party leaders to fashion comprehensive policies and the needs of the individual members to retain the support of their constituents or of special-interest groups.

Another source of tension that arose in the late twentieth century was that between the power of incumbency, which reinforced the overwhelming preponderance of white male representatives, and pressures to make the House more truly representative of the population as a whole. Because of the manner in which House districts are drawn by state legislatures, one party or the other often has disproportionate strength, making reelection all but certain for most members. Indeed, it is unusual for more than 25 percent of all House seats to be seriously contested. The resources available to incumbents further enhance their reelection chances. These factors contributed to the dominance of the Democrats between 1955 and 1995.

Efforts to promote racial diversity by redrawing district lines proved contentious. A succession of *Supreme Court cases, beginning in 1964 with *Wesberry* v. *Sanders*, coupled with the Voting Rights Act of 1965 and its subsequent amendments required state legislatures to maximize the chances that candidates who belonged to racial minority groups could win seats in the House. A generation later, however, Supreme Court decisions in the cases of *Shaw* v. *Reno* (1993) and *Miller* v. *Johnson* (1995) narrowed the role that race could play in redistricting. In 1996, thirty-eight *African Americans served as voting members of the House, all but one a Democrat. While African Americans, comprising 12 percent of the population, were slightly underrepresented in the House in the later 1990s, with about 7 percent of the membership, women, who make up more than 50 percent of the population, constituted only about 13 percent of the House. Latinos, with 9 percent of the population nationally, claimed only 4 percent of House seats in

1997. As a new century dawned, the House of Representatives continued to evolve, responding to the changing realities of American life while also reflecting the traditions and precedents deeply embedded in its more than two-hundred-year history.

[*See also* Federal Government.]

• George Rothwell Brown, *The Leadership of Congress,* 1922. George B. Galloway, *History of the House of Representatives,* 1961. Neil MacNeil, *Forge of Democracy,* 1963. Alvin M. Josephy Jr., *On the Hill,* 1979. Roger H. Davidson, *The Postreform Congress,* 1992. Barbara Sinclair, *Majority Leadership in the U.S. House,* 1983. Ronald M. Peters Jr., "The History and Character of the Speakership," in Ronald M. Peters Jr., ed., *The Speaker,* 1995.

—Ross K. Baker

FEDERALISM. Federalism is the division of governing power between the national and state governments. Advocates of federalism assert that it allows states to experiment with new programs that other states can adopt or modify, protects against tyranny by imposing checks on the national government, and provides the citizens of a diverse nation with a way of governing locally to achieve their distinctive interests while creating a national government to serve truly national purposes. Federalism's critics believe that local diversity is much less important in the modern world than it was in the past, and that a centralized government can encourage experimentation.

Conflicts over federalism have been a recurrent feature of U.S. history. Dividing power appropriately between the states and the nation was one of the central concerns of the *Constitutional Convention of 1787. Antifederalists feared that a powerful national government might tyrannize the people and displace the important power of self-government they associated with state government. A key compromise resolved the controversy by giving the national government a list of enumerated powers in the *Constitution and state legislatures the power to select senators.

Controversies over federalism in the *Antebellum Era frequently arose from the conflict over *slavery. Slavery's defenders were concerned that interpreting the Constitution expansively would ultimately authorize Congress to regulate slavery. They therefore opposed nationalist interpretations of Congress's power to regulate interstate commerce, as well as efforts by nationalist politicians to appropriate federal funds for the construction of roads and other elements of the national economic infrastructure.

The national government's reach grew during the *Civil War, as it developed the machinery to conduct a large-scale military conflict. Constitutional theory, however, remained focused on ensuring a federalism that protected state government power. The constitutional amendments adopted after the Civil War authorized Congress to protect the newly freed slaves and individual rights more generally, but in the **Slaughterhouse Cases* (1873) the *Supreme Court refused to give these new enumerated powers an interpretation that, in the Court's view, would allow Congress to exercise general governmental power.

As corporations operating in many states and internationally gained substantial influence, reformers took the position that the growth of private power made it impossible for any single state to regulate economic activity. From the late 1880s to the *Progressive Era, Congress enacted statutes that occupied terrain previously left to state governments. The Supreme Court gradually endorsed this expansion of national power, though often with reluctance.

The New Deal's response to the Great Depression produced a dramatic growth in national power and a displacement of state authority, as most Americans concluded that only the national government could alleviate the national economic disaster. President Franklin Delano *Roosevelt's administration developed programs of economic relief and reconstruction on far larger scale than any earlier national efforts. The Supreme Court initially held that these programs invaded areas the Constitution reserved for the states, but in 1937 the Court changed course and held that the national government could, in effect, exercise general governing authority: Congress could enact any program that it believed to be in the public interest, despite the apparent limitations implied by the Constitution's enumeration of powers.

Even after the New Deal, states remained important arenas for the development of innovative policies, but the focus of governing authority had clearly shifted from state capitals to *Washington, D.C. Although President Richard M. *Nixon articulated a program he called the "New Federalism," the first real assault on the New Deal–Great Society centralization of power occurred during the Ronald *Reagan administration, which sought to reduce the scope of government generally, not simply the reach of national government.

In the mid-1990s the Supreme Court imposed some modest limits on congressional power. It struck down a federal statute making it a crime to possess guns near schools, saying that the connection between crime and interstate commerce was so tenuous that upholding the statute would imply that Congress could constitutionally pass any statute whatsoever (*United States* v. *Lopez,* 1995). The Court also invalidated the 1993 Religious Freedom Restoration Act as beyond Congress's power to protect individual rights under the *Fourteenth Amendment (*City of Boerne* v. *Flores,* 1997). It protected the institutions of state government in two decisions denying Congress the power to "commandeer" either state legislatures or state executive officials to carry out national policy (*New York* v. *United States,* 1992; *Printz* v. *United States,* 1997). In 1999 the Court invoked the concept of a state's sovereign immunity from lawsuits seeking damages for copyright infringements and violations of national minimum wage law to expand the constitutional protection afforded state governments. As a group the decisions of the 1990s suggested that the Supreme Court might impose substantial limits on national power, but the decisions could be interpreted to make only modest revisions in the constitutional law developed through the twentieth century.

Even with these new limits on national power, the national government clearly remained vastly more powerful than state governments as the twentieth century ended, and almost certainly more powerful than the Constitution's framers had envisioned.

[*See also* New Deal Era, The; Roads and Turnpikes, Early; States' Rights.]

• Samuel H. Beer, *To Make a Nation: The Rediscovery of American Federalism,* 1993. Stanley Elkins and Eric McKitrick, *The Age of Federalism,* 1993. Edward Rubin and Malcolm Feeley, "Federalism: Some Notes on a National Neurosis," *UCLA Law Review* 41 (1994): 903–52. David L. Shapiro, *Federalism: A Dialogue,* 1995.

—Mark Tushnet

FEDERALIST ERA. *See* Early Republic, Era of the; Federalist Party.

FEDERALIST PAPERS (1787–1788). The Federalist Papers are the most important American contribution to political theory. Conceived by Alexander *Hamilton and John *Jay, this series of essays, written under the pseudonym "Publius," countered the political campaign mounted by opponents of the *Constitution during the months after the adjournment of the *Constitutional Convention of 1787. Planned as a modest series of essays to appear in *New York City newspapers, the Federalist Papers grew to eighty-five numbers. Newspapers in others states reprinted the first numbers, but with the announcement in January 1788 that the essays would appear as a book, the out-of-state reprintings dwindled. Eventually the series filled two volumes published in March and May 1788. Hamilton wrote about fifty of the essays. Illness restricted Jay to only five, and James *Madison (joining the consortium later) contributed the balance. Disagreement persists over whether Hamilton or Madison was the author of a handful of the essays. It was widely believed at the time that Hamilton and Madison were the primary contributors.

Written in a nonpartisan style, the Federalist Papers extolled the benefits of the union, demonstrated the inefficacy of the *Articles of Confederation, explained and clarified the principles and provisions of the Constitution, and justified the exclusion of various provisions such as a *Bill of Rights and a religious test for office-holding. Hamilton introduced the series on 27 October 1787 with an essay suggesting that Americans must "decide the important question, whether societies of men are really capable or not, of establishing good government from reflection and choice, or whether they are forever destined to depend, for their political constitutions, on accident and force." Conceding that the love of liberty could lead to an "illiberal distrust" of government, he nevertheless insisted that "the vigour of government is essential to the security of liberty."

While Hamilton's essays emphasized the importance of an energetic federal government, Madison, especially in Federalist No. 39 and 51, stressed the restraints placed on that government by free and frequent elections, the checks and balances built into the government through the separation of powers, and the healthy tension created by the division of power between the states and the federal government. Federalist No. 10, also by Madison, is particulary celebrated for its argument that in a large republic like the United States under the proposed Constitution, conflicting interest groups—notably economic interests—would be sufficiently numerous and dispersed to counterbalance each other, and thereby promote rather than endanger political stability, with no one interest group gaining complete dominance.

The original objective of the Federalist Papers was to convince New Yorkers to elect to their state ratifying convention delegates who would support the Constitution. In this the authors failed, as two-thirds of New York's convention delegates initially opposed ratification unless the Constitution was first altered by amendments. But the series succeeded beyond the authors' expectations in other ways. Arguments espoused by "Publius" became the standard explanations used by other Federalists in the public debate waged in newspapers and pamphlets as well as in speeches in the state ratifying conventions. Thomas *Jefferson, writing to Madison, praised the Federalist Papers as "the best commentary on the principles of government which ever was written." To his son-in-law Jefferson observed, "descending from theory to practice there is no better book than the Federalist." Since the adoption of the Constitution, scholars, judges, and lawyers have elevated the Federalist Papers to a unique status as the most authoritative source for discerning the framers' original intent.

[*See also* Federalism; Revolution and Constitution, Era of.]

• Jacob E. Cooke, ed., *The Federalist*, 1961. Thomas S. Engeman, Edward J. Erler, and Thomas B. Hofeller, eds., *The Federalist Concordance*, 1980.

—John P. Kaminski

FEDERALIST PARTY. By 1783 critics of the *Articles of Confederation—those who thought the *Continental Congress too weak and its powers insufficient—were using the word "federal" when discussing the powers and stature of Congress. In June 1783 George *Washington, as commander in chief of the army, sent a circular letter to state governors discussing the need to add "tone to our federal government." The term "federal" was thus both a description of the central government and a shorthand method of describing the program for enhancing its authority. By 1786 Washington, James *Madison, and their political friends were referring to those who opposed strengthening the Articles of Confederation as "antifederal."

At the *Constitutional Convention of 1787, the Federalists drafted a *Constitution that greatly increased the powers of Congress and the executive, and the debate over ratification sharpened the lines of division. Washington, elected president in 1789, solidified the organization of the embryonic Federalist party through the use of patronage. Although Washington's public criteria for federal offices were honesty and intelligence, in practice he found those qualities only in persons who agreed with him politically. Treasury Secretary Alexander *Hamilton took the next step in party development when he gave the new party a political creed. Hamilton's fiscal policy, which involved funding the national debt through the issue of bonds and the founding of a Bank of the United States to provide a national currency, advanced a Federalist political program that won the support of wealthy merchants and landowners. The outbreak of war in Europe in 1783 further polarized American opinion, and the political parties became associated with the contestants in Europe: the Federalists were regarded as pro-British, their "Republican" opponents, led by Thomas *Jefferson, as pro-French. By means of the *Alien and Sedition Acts, passed in 1798 as war with France loomed, the Federalist majority in Congress sought to silence their Republican critics.

By the middle of Washington's second term he was an avowed partisan, and his successor John *Adams was a staunch Federalist from Massachusetts. The election of Jefferson as president in 1800 ended Federalist rule, and the party never recovered control of the national government. The party's chief contribution was to convert the Constitution into a stable, relatively affluent government that they peacefully turned over to their electoral successors.

After 1800 the party's dwindling popular support was mainly confined to rural *New England and pockets of voters of German or Scots ancestry in the mountain valleys of the *South. The Federalists ran Charles Cotesworth Pinckney of South Carolina for president in 1804 and 1808, and DeWitt *Clinton of New York in 1812. The party's opposition to the *War of 1812 and flirtation with disunion in the *Hartford Convention of 1814 completed its ruin. In the presidential election of 1816, Rufus King of New York, the last Federalist presidential candidate, lost to Republican James *Monroe. Most Federalists, such as Daniel *Webster, who began his congressional career in 1814, became National Republicans in the 1820s and joined the *Whig party in the 1830s.

[*See also* Bank of the United States, First and Second; Conservatism; Early Republic, Era of the; Federal Government, Executive Branch: The Presidency; Federal Government, Legislative Branch: House of Representatives; Federal Government, Legislative Branch: Senate; Federalism; Political Parties; Quasi-War with France.]

• James M. Banner Jr., *To the Hartford Convention: The Federalists and the Origins of Party Politics in Massachusetts, 1789–1815*, 1970. Stanley Elkins and Eric McKitrick, *The Age of Federalism*, 1993.

—Norman Risjord

FEDERAL REGULATORY AGENCIES. The first federal regulatory agency was the Interstate Commerce Commission (ICC). Created in 1887 after decades of controversy over "the railroad problem," the ICC in many ways served as a model for future agencies. Like the ICC, they were established by Congress in response to crises in particular industries (or, occasionally, across industries). Staffed with persons thought to be experts and bipartisan or nonpartisan by law, most were nevertheless plagued by continual controversy.

The ICC found its power limited by the federal courts. In a pattern repeated later with other regulatory commissions, Congress then proceeded to strengthen the original *Interstate Commerce Act through a series of laws passed between 1903 and 1940 that, in effect, gave the commission de facto rate-making authority for *railroads, pipelines, trucks, and barges. The ICC's staff evolved complicated standards to set rates for passengers and freight carried by diverse modes of transportation over different routes. Its primary principle sought to assure transportation companies a "fair rate of return" on the "fair value of property used and useful" in performing their services. This seemingly simple idea involved the ICC in arbitrary estimates, dubious valuation schemes to determine the "rate base," and unworkable attempts to allocate traffic "fairly" among various modes of transportation.

In reality, American *capitalism proved too fluid and complex to lend itself to minute regulatory control as developed by the ICC, and industries under ICC supervision tended to stagnate because entrepreneurial opportunity was too constricted. Not until the deregulation movement of the 1980s and 1990s did some ICC-regulated industries again become vibrant parts of the national economy, by which time the ICC itself had been abolished by Congress.

Economic Regulation. Meanwhile Congress had created nine other federal regulatory agencies to address different areas of the economy. Five agencies were given primarily economic functions and four were assigned social or environmental regulatory duties. The five economic agencies are

1. The *Federal Trade Commission (FTC), created in 1914 and assigned the ambiguous task of maximizing competition in business. The FTC's biggest successes came in presenting to Congress detailed industry studies that prompted important legislation such as the Public Utility Holding Company Act of 1935 and several laws restricting the fixing of retail prices.

2. The Federal Power Commission (FPC), created in 1920, strengthened in 1930 and 1935, and in the 1980s renamed the Federal Energy Regulatory Commission. The dynamism of the energy sector overwhelmed this agency, and by the 1950s it could not manage its huge caseload effectively. Beginning in the 1960s and culminating with congressional deregulation of natural gas during the 1980s, a series of reforms alleviated the impossible pressures under which the FPC worked.

3. The *Federal Communications Commission (FCC), created in 1934 with jurisdiction over *radio, interstate *telephone communication, and later *television. The FCC was plagued by a fundamental lack of clarity about its proper functions. In the broadcasting industry, should it promote growth? Should it censor content? Should it take the draconian step of rescinding the licenses of wayward stations? As for the telephone industry, how could the FCC effectively regulate the monopolistic American Telephone and Telegraph Company, which, until the divestiture of regional operating companies in 1984, under pressure from antitrust authorities, was America's largest single business firm? The FCC never successfully resolved these questions.

4. The *Securities and Exchange Commission (SEC), created in 1934 and assigned the task of reviving and policing the nation's Depression-battered capital markets. Compared to other agencies, the SEC achieved remarkable success. It did so by working through allies in the private sector (especially lawyers, accountants, and officials of organized exchanges), whose interests were aligned by statutes and rulings with the goals the SEC defined as best for the industry and the public.

5. The Civil Aeronautics Board (CAB), created in 1938 and abolished during the 1980s. The CAB restricted entry into the airline industry, allocated the routes companies flew, standardized prices along these routes, and in general supervised a cartel. Although efforts to determine a fair rate of return made some sense for such "natural monopoly" industries as railroads and electric utilities, it did not for airlines, where entry was easy, competition keen, and business flexibility high.

Social and Environmental Regulation. The four social and environmental regulatory agencies reflected the heightened attention to civil rights, environmental, and consumer issues in the 1960s and 1970s. These agencies are:

1. The Equal Employment Opportunity Commission (EEOC), created in 1964 and charged with administering Title VII of the Civil Rights Act of that year. The EEOC coordinates federal efforts at affirmative action for the employment of women and minorities. It investigates charges of violation, promotes awareness of the law, and publishes statistical reports on employment patterns.

2. The *Environmental Protection Agency (EPA), created in 1970 and granted a broad range of responsibilities for the control of air and water pollution and the cleanup of hazardous waste sites. As the largest of all federal regulatory agencies measured by both size of budget and number of employees (over 10,000 by 1980), the EPA has formidable powers.

3. The Occupational Safety and Health Administration (OSHA), created in 1970, headed by an assistant secretary of labor, and charged with developing regulations for workplace safety. OSHA's effectiveness suffered from the difficulty of conducting a sufficient number of inspections at the nation's millions of worksites.

4. The Consumer Product Safety Commission, created in 1972 to enforce safety standards on potentially dangerous items such as hand tools, lawnmowers, flammable clothing, and children's toys. Its rules are often cited in product liability suits brought by private parties.

In addition to these major regulatory agencies, many other governmental bodies, including the National Highway Traffic Safety Administration, the Federal Aviation Administration, the Food and Drug Administration, the National Labor Relations Board, the *Nuclear Regulatory Commission, and the Federal Reserve Board, also have important regulatory responsibilities.

[*See also* Airplanes and Air Transport; Aviation Industry; Business; Civil Rights Legislation; Civil Rights Movement; Consumer Movement; Environmentalism; Federal Reserve System; Industrial Diseases and Hazards; Industrialization; New Deal Era, The; Progressive Era; Pure Food and Drug Act; Sixties, The; Stock Market.]

• Marver H. Bernstein, *Regulating Business by Independent Commission*, 1955. Ari and Olive Hoogenboom, *A History of the ICC*, 1976. James Q. Wilson, ed., *The Politics of Regulation*, 1980. David Vogel, "The New 'Social' Regulation in Historical and Comparative Perspective," in *Regulation in Perspective: Historical Essays*, ed. Thomas K. McCraw, 1981, pp. 155–85. Thomas K. McCraw, *Prophets of Regulation: Charles Francis Adams, Louis D. Brandeis, James M. Landis, Alfred E. Kahn*, 1984. Walter Rosenbaum, *Environmental Politics and Policy*, 1994. Walter Rosenbaum, *Environmental Politics and Policy*, 1994.

—Thomas K. McCraw

FEDERAL RESERVE ACT (1913). The Federal Reserve Act had its origins in the Panic of 1907, when the collapse of several loosely managed trust companies sparked a general financial crisis. Depositors frightened by the collapse of trust companies withdrew money from banks, which then called in loans and dumped securities on the market, contributing to a serious recession. Financier J. P. *Morgan saved the day, using a fund created by bankers and the federal government to prop up threatened but basically sound financial institutions.

The crisis illuminated severe weaknesses in the American banking system. National banks around the country issued currency backed with U.S. government bonds. They kept their reserves either in cash or on deposit in several designated money-center banks. The system produced an inelastic currency—since it was tied to the availability of Treasury bonds, it could not expand with the economy. The problem became particularly acute at harvest time, when the demand for money rose as farmers sold their crops. Moreover, because reserves were dispersed throughout the system, mobilizing them during a crisis proved extremely difficult.

The panic inspired Congress in 1908 to create the National Monetary Commission, chaired by Senator Nelson Aldrich of Rhode Island, to study banking reform. A Republican stalwart with personal ties to the John D. *Rockefeller family, Aldrich was in no sense a Progressive, yet in this case he was open to change. His commission toured Europe studying continental financial arrangements, but Aldrich made his most important contact in New York. There he met Paul Warburg, a member of the noted German-Jewish banking family and a partner at Kuhn, Loeb, who combined strong civic responsibility with wide financial experience.

In late 1910, Aldrich, Warburg, and several other leading bankers met secretly to hammer out a plan to create a central bank along European lines, but more decentralized. The group recommended the creation of fifteen regional banks, controlled by local bankers, to handle the issuance of currency. These institutions would issue money in exchange for either gold or "real bills"—short-term commercial paper backed by goods (inventories, for example). Such a currency would be "elastic," that is, able to expand with the economy. The regional banks would also hold the reserves of financial institutions in their region, permitting a concerted response to any crisis. Over the regional banks would stand a central board composed largely of representatives of business and finance but also including a few government appointees. Aldrich formally submitted the plan to Congress in January 1911.

Although Aldrich's proposals remained stalled in Congress for almost two years, the election of Woodrow *Wilson in 1912 opened the way for financial reform. In December 1912, even before Wilson's inauguration, Senator Carter Glass of Virginia, chairman of the Senate Banking Committee, put forward his own plan. It closely resembled Aldrich's, except that Glass, a *states' rights Democrat, sharply restricted the authority of the central board.

Glass quickly secured Wilson's support, but his plan horrified most congressional Progressives. Deeply suspicious of bankers, who they believed manipulated the financial system for their own ends, Progressives feared that Glass's measure would increase bankers' power. Fortunately Wilson, who knew little about finance and had few convictions on the subject, made enough concessions to win over Progressive critics. In a key concession, Wilson agreed to strengthen the authority of the central board and to make all of its members presidential appointees, giving Washington a predominant voice in the new system.

The financial community opposed the final version of the bill, which it feared gave the federal government too much authority over the nation's banking system. As a result Progressives rallied around the measure and gave the proposal a radical aura that it did not entirely merit. The bill, authorizing the creation of twelve regional banks and the Federal Reserve Board in Washington, became law in 1913. The Federal Reserve Act had one serious weakness, not rectified until the 1930s: It did not define precisely the relationship between the regional banks and the central board. Nevertheless, the Federal Reserve Act gave the United States a central bank able to pursue consistent monetary policies.

[*See also* Banking and Finance; Business Cycle; Depressions, Economic; Economic Regulation; Federal Reserve System; Monetary Policy, Federal; Progressive Era.]

• Arthur S. Link, *Woodrow Wilson and the Progressive Era*, 1954. Robert C. West, *Banking Reform and the Federal Reserve*, 1977. Ron Chernow, *The House of Morgan*, 1990. Ron Chernow, *The Warburgs*, 1993.

—Wyatt C. Wells

FEDERAL RESERVE SYSTEM. Congress created the Federal Reserve System, the central bank of the United States, in 1913. It consisted of twelve regional banks and the Federal Reserve Board in Washington, which had ill-defined powers of oversight. Lawmakers expected the system to regulate the supply of money and credit (*monetary policy), mitigating the effects of the *business cycle; to oversee, in concert with other federal and state agencies, the operations of commercial banks; and to carry out the government's international financial transactions. Ideally, the system's decentralized structure would reduce the influence of *New York City banks over the nation's credit system.

During *World War I, the Federal Reserve financed government deficits by expanding the money supply, and it broke the postwar inflation by raising interest rates and sharply restricting credit. In the 1930s, however, the shortcomings of the Federal Reserve's decentralized structure became apparent. During the Great Depression, infighting between the regional banks and the central board prevented a coordinated response to the crisis. Incoherent monetary policy permitted the money supply to contract by a third, contributing mightily to the catastrophe.

Accordingly, President Franklin Delano *Roosevelt and Marriner Eccles, his appointee as chair of the Federal Reserve Board, initiated reforms. Eccles persuaded Congress to enact new legislation confirming the board's authority over the regional banks, solidifying the position of its chair, and vesting in the Open Market Committee (a group consisting of members of the Federal Reserve Board and the presidents of the regional banks) control over monetary policy.

Despite its new organization, the Federal Reserve soon fell under the influence of the Treasury Department. Throughout *World War II and for many years after, the central bank at the behest of the Treasury "pegged" long-term interest rates at a low level, permitting Washington to finance its debt cheaply. This policy became controversial after 1945 because, by accommodating every demand for credit, it threatened to fuel inflation. Surging prices during the *Korean War forced the Treasury to relent and grant the Federal Reserve the authority to set interest rates as it saw fit. The subsequent increase in the cost of money, engineered by the central bank, helped stabilize prices.

Over the next twenty years, the Federal Reserve exercised its newfound autonomy carefully, following policies described as "leaning against the wind." Put simply, during recessions it cut interest rates to stimulate production, and when inflation threatened it increased rates to cool demand. But the stagflation of the 1970s—simultaneous inflation and recession—stymied the central bank. After years of vacillating between expansion and contraction, the Federal Reserve in 1979 under Chairperson Paul Volcker embraced a policy of fierce monetary stringency, driving interest rates to near 20 percent and triggering the worst recession since the 1930s. Hard times inspired calls for reforms to make the Federal Reserve more responsive to elected officials. Economic recovery after 1983, however, coupled with stable, low inflation, bore out the wisdom of Volcker's policy and garnered the Federal Reserve immense prestige. Subsequently, the central bank followed policies designed primarily to keep prices stable. Under the leadership of Alan Greenspan, the Federal Reserve continued this policy through the long boom of the 1990s.

[*See also* Banking and Finance; Depressions, Economic; Economic Regulation; Federal Government, Executive Branch: Department of the Treasury; Federal Reserve Act; New Deal Era, The; Progressive Era.]

• John T. Wooley, *Monetary Politics: The Federal Reserve and the Politics of Monetary Policy*, 1984. Donald F. Kettl, *Leadership at the Fed*, 1986.

—Wyatt C. Wells

FEDERAL TRADE COMMISSION (FTC), an independent federal regulatory agency. Created in 1914, the FTC was part of an antitrust settlement that included the Clayton Antitrust Act and congressional acceptance of a judicial "rule of reason," which tolerated aspects of business concentration. Consisting of five appointed commissioners, the agency inherited the investigatory powers of an earlier Bureau of Corporations and became the administrator of regulatory legislation outlawing "unfair methods of competition." Subsequently, it also became the administrator of laws under which it supervised export associations and enforced restraints on price discrimination, deceptive *advertising, proposed mergers, and certain labelling, lending, packaging, and warranty practices.

The FTC's creation was supported both by antimonopolists seeking to halt the "unfair competition" involved in trust-building and by businessmen seeking "fairness" as a basis for greater order and stability. Differing definitions of "fairness" could serve differing ends, however, and in practice the FTC pursued contradictory policies. At times it fought industrial concentration, most notably in its investigations of the electrical power, iron and steel, and cement industries in the 1930s and in its actions against "shared monopoly" in the 1970s. But at other times, especially under chairs William E. Humphrey (1925–1933), Edward F. Howry (1953–1955), and James C. Miller (1981–1985), it sponsored corporate collaboration and business stabilization schemes. In addition, its rulings tended to be more concerned with protecting complaining competitors than with encouraging competitive markets, especially in its enforcement of the Robinson-Patman Anti-Price Discrimination Act, which from 1945 to 1965 generated nearly 70 percent of the FTC's regulatory orders.

Historians generally regard the FTC as one of the least successful of America's regulatory commissions. It showed political staying power and conducted investigations of lasting importance for industrial policy. But it was more often characterized by contradictory impulses, unstable policies and standards, persisting organizational problems, and the squandering of its resources on relatively inconsequential matters.

[*See also* Antitrust Legislation; Electrical Industry; Federal Regulatory Agencies; Iron and Steel Industry; Progressive Era.]

• Alan Stone, *Economic Regulation and the Public Interest: The Federal Trade Commission in Theory and Practice*, 1977. Robert A. Katzmann, *Regulatory Bureaucracy: The Federal Trade Commission and Antitrust Policy*, 1980.

—Ellis W. Hawley

FEMININE MYSTIQUE, THE (1963). The feminist manifesto *The Feminine Mystique*, authored by Betty Friedan (1921–), a professional journalist, argued that American women suffered from deep discontent. Friedan blamed what she called "the feminine mystique," a repressive ideal promoted by journalists, magazine editors, advertisers, educators, and social scientists. This domestic ideal held that women could find fulfillment only as wives and mothers. It stunted women's aspirations and trapped them in the home. With conscious hyperbole, Friedan labeled the home a "comfortable concentration camp" in which housewives lost their freedom and sense of identity.

The Feminine Mystique reworked themes—individual freedom, suburban conformity, and domestic discontent—that pervaded postwar *popular culture. In framing her arguments, however, Friedan did not use a typical liberal language of rights and equality. Influenced by Abraham Maslow's human potential psychology, she focused instead on growth and fulfillment. Full-time domesticity, she argued, denied women's "basic human need to grow." In *The Feminine Mystique*, she did not push for a *women's rights movement; rather, she advocated individual fulfillment through achievement, especially through *education and careers. Critics have noted that Friedan's discussion of American women dwelled on affluent, white housewives and implicitly excluded the many women who were not middle or upper class, married, white, and domestic. They have also shown how Friedan, in presenting herself as a housewife, obscured her own activist history as a left-leaning labor journalist.

Nonetheless, *The Feminine Mystique* was a bestseller. It struck a chord among middle-class women, hundreds of whom wrote to Friedan to testify that the book resonated with their own sense of dissatisfaction. As a key inspiration to liberal feminists, the book helped launch the rebirth of the women's movement in the 1960s. Friedan emerged as a major figure in the reinvigorated movement, especially as a founder and first president of the *National Organization for Women.

[*See also* Feminism; Fifties, The; Homework; Sixties, The.]

• Joanne Meyerowitz, "Beyond *The Feminine Mystique*: A Reassessment of Postwar Mass Culture, 1946–1958," *Journal of American History* 79 (March 1993): 1455–82. Daniel Horowitz, *Betty Friedan and the Making of The Feminine Mystique: The American Left, the Cold War, & Modern Feminism*, 1998.

—Joanne Meyerowitz

FEMINISM. Throughout recorded history, some women have protested their exclusion from full participation in their society's educational, economic, social, cultural, sexual and/or political life. But most have not described themselves as feminists or professed a belief in feminism. The historian Gerda Lerner has addressed this problem by defining feminist consciousness rather than feminism.

From "Feminist Consciousness" to Feminism. "Feminist consciousness" is especially useful for embracing all those women who, over the centuries, have struggled against patriarchal constraints, but have not acted or written as participants in a larger women's movement. In *The Creation of Feminist Consciousness* (1993), Lerner defined feminist consciousness as women's awareness "that they belong to a subordinate group; that they have suffered wrongs as a group; that their condition of subordination is not natural, but societally determined; that they must join with other women to remedy these wrongs; and finally, that they must and can provide an alternate vision of societal organization in which women as well as men will enjoy autonomy and self-determination." Even with this broad definition, most women—including those who have protested women's condition—have not identified themselves as feminists.

The actual word "feminism," or *feminisme,* was coined by the French reformer Charles Fourier (1772–1837) in his *Théorie des quatres mouvements et des destinées généralises,* written sometime between 1808 and 1837. According to historian Karen Offen, Alexandre Dumas the Younger first used the word *feministe,* pejoratively, in 1872. In 1882, Hubertine Auclert, a French advocate of woman suffrage, began to employ the term and even used it in a letter to the American suffragists Elizabeth Cady *Stanton and Susan B. *Anthony. By the early 1890s, the words had entered common political discourse in Europe; in the *London Daily News* (1894); and appeared in Latin America, most notably in Argentina. About 1910, it appeared in the United States.

Most nineteenth-century American suffragists did not refer to themselves as "feminists" or espouse an ideology called "feminism." Rather, they saw themselves as advocates of women's rights or as suffragists. In 1910, a group of young women in *New York City formed a club they called Heterodoxy. In *The Grounding of Modern Feminism* (1987), historian Nancy Cott describes their commitment to personal emancipation, unconventional behavior, and self-fulfillment. Although they supported suffrage and other formal rights, they emphasized the individual psychological and social emancipation of women and prefigured the many young women of the 1920s, who similarly sought emancipation in personal realization rather than in any ideology or movement.

Shifting Views of Feminism, 1920–1970. After the *Nineteenth Amendment was ratified in 1920, some women in Alice Paul's *National Woman's Party called themselves feminists. Many of these women were independently wealthy and/or hostile to other progressive reforms. Some were stridently anti-Semitic or racist as well. By contrast, Progressive women of the Old Left, *civil rights movement, and labor unions, who joined the fight against fascism or organized unskilled workers during the Depression of the 1930s, subsumed feminist issues under the Marxist phrase "The Woman Question." To them, the word "feminist" conjured up an image of a conservative, wealthy woman who voted Republican, rather than supporting the New Deal, the *Communist or *Socialist parties, or radical labor unions. During *World War II, these same women continued to debate many issues subsumed under "The Woman Question" rubric, but without identifying themselves as feminists or espousing an ideology called feminism.

After the war, the very word "feminist" came to denote an unpatriotic woman who dared challenge the *Cold War effort to contain communism. Since women were expected to stay home and fight the Cold War as consumers for their families, feminists, like working women, emerged as major villains at the height of the anticommunist hysteria. During the 1960s, women's rights activists did not commonly use the word "feminism." Many of the women who founded the *National Organization for Women (1966) and who fought legal discrimination against women had deep roots in the progressive politics of the 1930s, 1940s, and 1950s. Furthermore, "feminism" still brought to mind images of bourgeois women unconcerned with issues of race, *social class, or *poverty.

To the younger women who created the highly publicized women's liberation movement in the late 1960s, the word feminism also seemed too tame. Having emerged from the civil rights or *New Left movements, they viewed themselves as radicals who were unconcerned with bourgeois feminist issues. The press dubbed all these young activists "Women's Libbers," a term of disparagement that trivialized the movement and which activists consciously avoided.

Feminism since 1970. By the 1970s, as the various branches of the women's movement began to fragment and merge, and new populations of American women embraced the women's movement and activists began to refer themselves as "feminists"—sometimes qualified as liberal, radical, socialist, or lesbian. To these activists, the term now expressed their determination to seek emancipation by challenging economic, political, sexual, cultural, and social traditions. In *The Politics of Women's Liberation* (1975), the political scientist Jo Freeman compared the difference between a "traditional" and "feminist" view of society. Feminists, she argued, recognize the changing, artificial, and highly arbitrary ways that men and women are permitted or denied access to the educational, political, and economic institutions of their society. Traditionalists, by comparison, view the organization of *gender in society as normal and natural.

Some feminists emphasized women's rights and demanded equality with men. Others argued that society needed to change to accommodate women and their capacity to bear children, rather than trying to squeeze women's experiences into a male life cycle. From this perspective came the feminist creation of "family-friendly" work policies that could embrace women both as workers and as mothers.

As women of various minority groups analyzed their own subordinate position within their communities, some resisted the word "feminism," viewing it as a "family quarrel" among white, middle-class women. In 1983, the African-American writer Alice Walker coined the term "womanism" to express the needs and aspirations of women of color. The word "womanist," she explained, grew out of a black folk expression that mothers often used with their daughters. "You acting womanish," a mother would say, meaning that the youngster was engaging in outrageous, audacious, or willful behavior. Minority women, many of whom had never been schooled in learned helplessness, Walker felt, could better express their desire for equality and freedom with this term. Not all minority women agreed, but the phrase did gain some currency.

With the conservative backlash of the 1970s and beyond, the phrase "I'm not a feminist, but . . ." became almost mandatory for women political candidates and other women entering the public arena, distancing them from media-generated stereotypes of man-hating superwomen, even as they worked for feminist goals.

By the 1980s and 1990s, many different populations of women—old, young, trade unionists, displaced homemakers—had reinvented feminism to address the specific realities of their lives. Four *United Nations' World Women's Conferences convened in 1975 (Mexico City), 1980 (Copenhagen), 1985 (Nairobi), and 1995 (Beijing), further broadened the term, so that "feminism" no longer belonged to American women or indeed to any particular society. The *Platform for Action* adopted by the Beijing conference urged all nations to view all social, political, economic, cultural, and military policies "through the eyes of women." This meant thinking about development, population control, *human rights, and other global issues *as if women mattered*. In Africa, for example, fuel and water and the ritual mutilation of the body became feminist issues. In other areas, feminist concerns included dowry deaths, *domestic violence, *child labor, and the traffic in sexual slaves.

With the spread of feminist perspectives to many nations, often referred to as "global feminism," these transnational feminist networks promoted the improvement of women's lives in countless ways. Though activists debated many issues, they all tended to emphasize that equality for women required an end to violence and poverty, and access to education. That, in the end, constituted the broadest and most inclusive description of feminism as the twenty-first century began.

[*See also* Antebellum Era; Anticommunism; Conservatism; Consumer Culture; Domestic Labor; *Feminine Mystique, The;* Fuller, Margaret; Gillman, Charlotte Perkins; Labor Movements; National American Woman Suffrage Association; New Deal Era, The; Prostitution and Antiprostitution; Radicalism; Socialism; Stone, Lucy; Twenties, The; Woman Suffrage Movement; Women in the Labor Force; Women's Rights Movement; Women's Trade Union League.]

• bell hooks, *Ain't I A Woman: Black Women and Feminism,* 1983. Alice Walker, *In Search of Our Mothers' Garden,* 1983. Nancy Cott, *The Grounding Of Modern Feminism,* 1987. Karen Offen, "Defining Feminism: A Comparative Historical Approach," *Signs* 14 (autumn 1988): 119–57. Karen Offen, "On the French Origin of the Word *Feminism* and Feminist," *Feminist Studies* 8.2 (Fall 1988): 45–61. Linda Kauffman, *American Feminist Thought at Century's End,* 1993. Gerda Lerner, *The Creation of Feminist Consciousness,* 1993. Joan Scott, *Feminism and History,* 1996. Robyn R. Warhol and Diane Price Herndl, eds., *Feminisms: An Anthology of Literary Theory and Crticism,* 2d ed., 1997. Ruth Rosen, *The World Split Open: How The Modern Women's Movement Changed America,* 2000.

—Ruth Rosen

FERMI, ENRICO (1901–1954), nuclear physicist, Nobel laureate, and inventor of *nuclear power. Born in Rome, Fermi obtained his doctorate at the Reale Scuole Normale Superiore in Pisa in 1922. After studies with Max Born in Göttingen, Germany, he returned to Italy, where in Florence he discovered Fermi-Dirac statistics, a system for mathematically analyzing the behavior of subatomic particles. Appointed a full professor at Rome shortly thereafter, he formulated the theory of nuclear beta-decay. In a series of experiments, he also found that slow neutrons were efficient agents of nuclear transformations and won the Nobel Prize in Physics in 1938. With his Jewish wife, he used the prize money to escape Fascist Italy and its anti-Semitic legislation. Coming to America, he joined the faculty of Columbia University (1939–1945).

Fermi learned of the discovery of fission from Niels Bohr early in 1939, shortly after his arrival at Columbia. With another emigré physicist, the Hungarian-born Leo Szilard, he devised and built a series of prototype fission reactors. He continued this work at the University of Chicago as a member of the *Manhattan Project, after the United States entered *World War II. On 2 December 1942, in a laboratory under the university football stadium, Fermi achieved the first self-sustaining nuclear chain reaction. His "pile," scaled up by the DuPont Corporation at Hanford, Washington, converted uranium into plutonium, the nuclear explosive used in the first successful nuclear device tested at Alamogordo, New Mexico in July 1945. Fat Man, the plutonium bomb dropped on Nagasaki, Japan on 9 August 1945, precipitated the Japanese surrender.

After the war, Fermi launched the Institute for Nuclear Studies at Chicago, where he was appointed professor in 1946, and pioneered scientific computation at Los Alamos. A member of the *Atomic Energy Commission's General Advisory Committee, he opposed the development of the hydrogen bomb, which he had conceived in 1942. Revered and much-beloved in the scientific community, he died in 1954 of stomach cancer.

[*See also* Einstein, Albert; Hiroshima and Nagasaki, Atomic Bombing of; Nuclear Strategy; Nuclear Weapons; Oppenheimer, J. Robert; Physical Sciences; Science: From 1914 to 1945; Science: Since 1945.]

• Emilio Segre, *Enrico Fermi, Physicist*, 1972. Laura Fermi, *Atoms in the Family*, reprint ed., 1995.

—Robert W. Seidel

FERTILITY. *See* Childbirth; Child Rearing.

FIELD, DAVID DUDLEY (1805–1894), law reformer. David Dudley Field's reputation rested on his advocacy of codification of the law, a process by which scattered court decisions and legislation were assembled into accessible codes. In 1846 Field was appointed to the New York state codification commission over which he exerted enormous influence. Two years later, the commission produced the so-called Field Code and over the next two decades Field helped to frame additional political, civil, and penal codes. Several other states adopted his civil procedure and penal codes. In 1873 Field extended his scope to include *international law, founding the Association for the Reform and Codification of the Law of Nations.

Field's legal career mixed high-profile constitutional cases and important business clients in ways that typified the most successful *Gilded Age practitioners. Field, for example, persuaded the U.S. *Supreme Court to reject the wartime practice of using military rather than civilian courts when the latter were still open. In 1869 he served as counsel to Jay Gould and James Fisk in the controversial Erie Railroad litigation. The New York City bar association accused him of unprofessional conduct, but its recommendations of censure were never adopted officially. Field's reputation also suffered because of his connections with William Magear *Tweed, a codirector of the Erie Railroad and the archetypical late nineteenth-century political boss.

[*See also* Jurisprudence; Legal Profession; Railroads.]

—Kermit L. Hall

FIFTEENTH AMENDMENT (1870). This amendment to the U.S. *Constitution declares that the right to vote shall not be denied or restricted by the federal or state governments on account of race. The amendment reflected both the egalitarian ideals of *Reconstruction and the self-interest of the *Republican party.

Two developments led to the framing of the amendment: the northern state elections of 1867, in which voters rejected black *suffrage, and the presidential election of 1868, which signaled future electoral trouble for the Republicans. Having enfranchised southern freedmen in 1867, Republican leaders proposed the enfranchisement of *African Americans—most of whom could be counted on to vote Republican—in those northern and border states that still prohibited black voting.

The Republican-controlled Congress approved the Fifteenth Amendment on 26 February 1869. In the brief but intense ratification struggle in the state legislatures, Democrats opposed and Republicans supported ratification. With the outcome uncertain, a combination of pressure and incentives brought about final ratification on 30 March 1870.

Upon ratification, adult black males in seventeen northern and border states became voters. With racist repression in the *South, growing political indifference in the North, and federal inaction, however, most southern and border state blacks lost the franchise.

During the long retreat from egalitarian principles after 1867, federal courts often interpreted the amendment narrowly to deny federal authority to prosecute violations of federal voting rights. From 1941 onward, however, courts began to reverse this trend. The landmark Voting Rights Act of 1965 owed its constitutional underpinning to the Fifteenth Amendment.

[*See also Civil Rights Cases;* Civil Rights Legislation; Fourteenth Amendment; Racism.]

• William Gillette, *The Right to Vote: Politics and the Passage of the Fifteenth Amendment*, 1969. Ward E. Y. Elliott, *The Rise of Guardian Democracy: The Supreme Court's Role in Voting Rights Disputes, 1845–1969*, 1974.

—William Gillette

FIFTH AMENDMENT. *See* Bill of Rights.

FIFTIES, THE. The *Cold War between the United States and the Soviet Union dominated American life in the 1950s. The *Korean War (1950–1953), a conflict formally fought under the flag of the *United Nations, represented America's resolve to contain Soviet expansion, but it also revealed the tensions dividing American society.

Anticommunism and Religion in Cold War America. While the Korean conflict was arguably America's last "good war," in which citizens rallied to support agreed-upon military and political objectives, the war coincided with a campaign to rid the country of domestic subversives. This wrenching process has been labeled "McCarthyism" in reference to its single most visible proponent Senator Joseph *McCarthy of Wisconsin, but it was not limited to the senator and his supporters. The search for subversives in the early 1950s, and its attendant anticommunist loyalty oaths, affected a large segment of society, ranging from labor unionists and government bureaucrats to university professors and Hollywood writers. And while post–Cold War archival research uncovered evidence that some of these targets did indeed spy for the Soviets, the entire movement represented a form of national insecurity. Many saw the Soviet Union's success in building an atomic bomb and testing it in 1949 as proof of leaks in American security. Two highly publicized spy cases at the start of the decade confirmed this fear for many Americans. The *Rosenberg and Alger *Hiss cases, in which American citizens were accused of conducting espionage for the Soviets, only increased the nation's worries about the enemy within.

The Cold War ideological climate, perhaps abetted by *suburbanization and nuclear anxieties, also contributed to an upsurge of religious activity in the 1950s. Church-attendance rates increased and in 1955 Congress added "In God We Trust" to the nation's currency and coins. Evangelist Billy *Graham conducted revivals that attracted millions worldwide. Catholic bishop Fulton J. Sheen became a television celebrity, and the Rev. Norman Vincent *Peale attracted a vast following with such therapeutic books as *The Power of Positive Thinking* (1952).

An Era of Prosperity and Domesticity. One of the many ironies of the 1950s is that this national self-doubt came at a time of great economic prosperity for many Americans, as economist John Kenneth Galbraith documented in *The *Affluent Society* (1958). With jobs plentiful and salaries rising, many families could afford an increasing array of consumer goods. The spread of suburban *shopping centers and malls facilitated the *mass marketing of this array of new products.

The economic growth of the 1950s arose partially from the increased ability of American corporations to export their wares, an ability aided by America's postwar political dominance as well as the reduced industrial capacity of other nations owing to war damage. Another important cause of the economic growth was heavy government defense spending, a further by-product of the Cold War. Even the prosperity enjoyed by individuals was filtered through the lens of the Cold War. The success of women during *World War II in entering the workforce partly dissolved in the face of renewed emphasis on the traditional family, with the devoted mother expected to use her many appliances to keep the home running efficiently.

Much of the *popular culture of the period linked the defense of American values at home with the struggle against communism abroad. The nuclear family would repel any insidious foreign influences or doctrines. The ideal of conformity was both espoused and criticized in many of the books and films of the period, ranging from intellectual concern with the "organization man" (the title of a 1956 book by William H. Whyte) to movies about the menace of alien influences, such as the paranoid thriller *Invasion of the Body Snatchers* (1956).

Increased Civil Rights Activism. Not everyone shared in the decade's prosperity. Many older Americans, rural people in *Appalachia, and Hispanic migrant farm workers or urban manual laborers remained mired in *poverty. Perhaps no group was as cut off from the mainstream of American life in the 1950s as *African Americans. At the start of the decade, southern racial *segregation laws and less formal—but no less powerful—forms of discrimination in the North excluded most African Americans from the economic opportunities and prosperity enjoyed by most white citizens. But in the middle part of the decade this situation began to change. The most visible event was the *Supreme Court's decision in **Brown* v. *Board of Education* (1954) declaring racially segregated school systems unconstitutional. The *Brown* ruling initiated a series of struggles over racial integration that pitted the federal government and civil rights workers against southern segregationists and state governments. To focus exclusively on the legal strategies that succeeded in the *Brown* case would be a mistake, however, as African Americans also had been working on more political strategies well before 1954. Efforts by African American labor and religious leaders in the 1930s and 1940s to press for political rights, for example, led to the desegregation of the armed forces in 1948. This facet of the African American movement for *civil rights gripped the popular consciousness in the 1956 Montgomery, Alabama, bus boycott led by a youthful Martin Luther *King Jr. In both legal and political realms, the 1950s saw an important phase of the movement by African Americans to gain equality, a movement that would culminate in the *civil rights legislation of the mid-1960s.

The gains made by African Americans in the 1950s triggered a reaction by some whites in both the North and the *South. In the South, this reaction produced a climate of violence that would set the stage for civil rights battles in the 1960s. It also contributed to a major change in the political culture of the region, where the lily-white electorate (most blacks were disenfranchised until the 1960s) had voted solidly Democratic since the end of *Reconstruction. As southern whites began to see the *Democratic party as a supporter of integration, they started a slow, decades-long exodus to the *Republican party. In the North and West, some urban whites followed the same path and identified the Democratic party's *liberalism and commitment to an activist federal government with attempts to integrate local schools and neighborhoods that were segregated in fact if not by law. Although the urban North did not see the massive shift to the Republican from the Democratic party that occurred in the South, the more progressive wing of the Democratic party in the North lost out to a more moderate and restrained version of liberalism. In the *West and especially the *Southwest, voters did turn to the Republican party in large numbers. Throughout the nation, the 1950s battles over civil rights set the stage for the political transformation of the 1970s and 1980s: the end of the "New Deal Order" and the ascendancy of *conservatism.

Consensus Politics and Underlying Tensions. On the surface, however, the politics of the 1950s seemed characterized by consensus rather than conflict. The Democratic and Republican parties were united in both their responses to the Cold War and their approaches to the New Deal welfare state. The Democratic party purged many of its more radical supporters in its anticommunist fervor while supporting military expansion. At the same time, many Democrats moved from an emphasis on economic issues in the 1930s and 1940s to a tentative focus on race relations, leading to a defense of the New Deal rather than any extension of its programs. Among Republicans, Dwight D. *Eisenhower's defeat of the party's isolationist wing eliminated any dissent on the issue of the Cold War. Under Secretary of State John Foster *Dulles, the Eisenhower administration initiated a series of regional military pacts aimed at the Soviet Union; financed and planned coups that overthrew left-leaning regimes in Iran, Chile, and elsewhere; and became more deeply involved in resisting a communist-led nationalist movement in Vietnam. At the same time the success of Eisenhower's "modern republicanism" against more strident forms of small-government conservatism represented an acceptance by the GOP of the New Deal state.

The deceptive sense of placid homogeneity was reinforced by *television, which spread like wildfire in this decade to become the dominant new mass medium. TV advertising spread the message of consumer abundance, while television programming especially domestic comedies such as *Father Knows Best, Leave It to Beaver*, and *The Nelson Family* focused mainly on the nation's white, affluent, middle-class suburbs where traditional gender roles prevailed.

The surface calm of the 1950s, however, obscured more fundamental disagreements over the nation's future direction. Although the Cold War and its economic prosperity provided an adhesive that seemed to bind the country together, America in the 1950s was a nation divided between incommensurable positions on race, women's roles, labor unions, nuclear testing, and foreign policy. As the decade wore on, the quickening tempo of black activism and a grassroots campaign to halt nuclear testing (a campaign rooted in well-founded fears of radioactive fallout and endorsed in 1956 by the 1952 and 1956 Democratic presidential candidate Adlai *Stevenson), coupled in the cultural realm with the rise of rock and roll; Elvis *Presley's erotic gyrations and songs of sexual longing; the Beat movement in literature led by Allen Ginsberg and Jack Kerouac; and movies like *Blackboard Jungle* (1955), *The Wild One* (1953) with Marlon Brando, and James Dean in *Rebel Without a Cause* (1955), all signaled that the fragile conformity of the decade was about to dissolve.

[*See also* Amusement Parks and Theme Parks; Anticommunism; Business Cycle; Civil Rights Movement; Consumer Culture; Containment; Family; Film; Foreign Relations; Foreign Trade, U.S.; Literature: Since World War I; Music: Popular Music; Nuclear Weapons; Segregation, Racial.]

• Harvard Sitkoff, *The Struggle for Black Equality, 1954–1980*, 1981. William Chafe, *The Unfinished Journey*, 1986. Elaine Tyler May, *Homeward Bound: American Families in the Cold War*, 1988. John Diggins, *The Proud Decades, 1941–1960*, 1989. Numan Bartley, *The New South, 1945–1980*, 1995.

—Charles Romney

FILLMORE, MILLARD (1800–1874), thirteenth president of the United States. The son of a tenant farmer in western New York, Millard Fillmore gained a minimal education before he was apprenticed as a clothier. After reading law with a local judge, he moved to Buffalo and gained admittance to the bar at the age of twenty-three. Capitalizing on the Anti-Masonic frenzy in New York, Fillmore won election to the state legislature in 1828. He joined the *Whig party in 1834 and served four terms in the U.S. Congress. A supporter of Henry *Clay's American System, Fillmore helped craft the Tariff of 1842. After retiring from Congress in 1844, Fillmore lost a campaign for governor of New York, but his continued service to the party won him the vice presidency in 1848. Fillmore initially deferred to President Zachary *Taylor, playing a small role in the new administration. As president of the Senate, he broke with Taylor to support the *Compromise of 1850. When Taylor died unexpectedly that July, Fillmore became president. He signed the compromise measures into law, confident that the sectional crisis had finally been resolved.

Capitalizing on his presidential patronage power, Fillmore removed his intraparty opponents from office. The ensuing battle led to the Whigs' decision in 1852 to bypass Fillmore and give the presidential nomination to the *Mexican War hero Winfield Scott, who subsequently lost to Democrat Franklin *Pierce. Out of office and skeptical about the prospects of the Whigs, Fillmore in 1855 joined the new nativist *Know-Nothing party, which nominated him for president in 1856. Fillmore used the campaign to promote his own nationalist vision, largely ignoring the nativism that brought the party together. After his defeat, Fillmore opposed the *Republican party and Abraham *Lincoln's administration, which were both controlled by his political foes. Although he continued to engage in politics in his later years, he exerted little influence, in part because of his personal vindictiveness.

[*See also* Antebellum Era; Anti-Masonic Party; Antislavery; Federal Government, Executive Branch: The Presidency; Nativist Movement; Slavery; Tariffs.]

• Robert J. Rayback, *Millard Fillmore,* 1959. Elbert B. Smith, *The Presidencies of Zachary Taylor and Millard Fillmore,* 1988.

—Eric D. Daniels

FILM. Film is a term for the visual medium also known as motion pictures, cinema, or the movies. The medium's history involves its various aspects as a *technology, an industry, an art form, and a means of delivering entertainment and information to spectators in theaters and at home. From its emergence in the 1890s, the film industry became in the twentieth century a major component of U.S. cultural life and a dominant force in global entertainment production.

A New Technology—A New Entertainment Medium. Film as a technology developed out of several nineteenth-century scientific pursuits. One was an interest in a visual phenomenon then known as "persistence of vision," which described the eye's retention of visual images. A sequence of individual still pictures, when set in motion, was found to give an illusion of movement. A further endeavor, building on the technology of still *photography, sought to record movement as a means of description and analysis.

A major advance occurred in the 1870s in *California when the British photographer Eadweard Muybridge, hired by railroad tycoon Leland Stanford to settle a bet whether racehorses ever had all four feet off the ground, took a sequence of photographs that demonstrated that a galloping horse did at times have all four feet off the ground. In the 1880s such sequence photography became more practical when the inventor George Eastman introduced roll "film" made of a synthetic plastic material, celluloid, to replace individual glass plates.

Among inventors working simultaneously in several countries, Thomas *Edison employed William K. L. Dickson to construct machines for recording and viewing moving images. By 1891 these machines, called the Kinetograph and the Kinetoscope, respectively, were in operation. In 1893 the first public exhibition of motion pictures took place, although only one viewer at a time could watch through Edison's "peephole" device. Projection machines for larger audiences were soon introduced in Europe (1895) and the United States (1896).

Early motion picture exhibitions took place as part of *vaudeville programs, at carnivals and fairgrounds, and in lecture halls and churches. Most films ran ten minutes or less, reflecting the amount of film that could be wound on a standard reel. The visual presentation lacked both recorded color and sound, although these were often provided through color tinting of prints and musical accompaniment. Film subjects included travel scenes, newsworthy events, comedies, trick films (using the medium's technology, for example, to make trains appear to run backward), and short narratives. *The Great Train Robbery* (1903), directed by Edwin S. Porter for Edison's company, was a popular success and demonstrated the medium's commercial entertainment potential.

The scale of film exhibition changed around 1905 when entrepreneurs began opening storefront theaters in urban immigrant and working-class districts. These nickelodeons, so called because they charged five cents for admission, fostered film production but also called forth public debate about film content and allegedly unsafe exhibition conditions. In 1908 Edison, among others, organized the Motion Picture Patents Company to pool patents and assert control over production, distribution, and exhibition, with a goal of eliminating cheap theaters and raising admission prices. Excluded companies, however, called independents, continued to thrive and innovated in longer feature-film production. In 1915 a federal district court ruled in a lawsuit that the Patents Company had attempted illegally to restrain trade in violation of *antitrust legislation. Its appeals failing, the company dissolved in 1918.

After 1910, film production, which had been centered in *New York City, began to shift to southern California, which offered more sunlight, more varied terrain, and lower wage scales. Hollywood, a *Los Angeles suburb, became synonymous with the film industry and American movie culture. During *World War I, with European film production disrupted, U.S. films dominated world markets. D. W. *Griffith directed *The Birth of a Nation* (1915), a three-hour historical epic on the *Civil War and *Reconstruction that set new standards for cinematic spectacle but also aroused lasting controversy over its racist themes. Charlie *Chaplin became world famous as the Tramp in silent comedies.

The 1920s and 1930s: Heyday of the Studio System. During the 1920s Hollywood perfected a so-called studio system with a few major, vertically integrated companies controlling the bulk of production, distribution, and exhibition. Producing around six hundred films per year, the industry organized its output around stars and genres. Films were sold and promoted on the basis of their star performers and genre category, such as western, mystery, horror, romance, or comedy. Stars like Greta Garbo and Rudolph *Valentino became public icons who embodied Hollywood glamour and screen romance. The comedies of Harold Lloyd, Buster Keaton, and Laurel and Hardy remain classics.

On the technological front, the mid-1920s saw the introduction of synchronized recorded sound, eventually standardized in a system that recorded sound directly onto the celluloid film strip. The shift to sound was almost complete by 1930. Although recorded color was less prevalent, the Technicolor process came into use in the 1930s and the number of color films gradually increased.

The advent of sound coincided with the Great Depression, and the technological and cultural transformations of the early 1930s created new controversies over movie content and the medium's social role. Agitation by religious groups and social reformers led to industry self-regulation in the form of a Production Code, introduced in 1930 and strengthened by establishment of a Production Code Administration in 1934. Although the Depression sent several major companies into receivership, the film industry remained remarkably stable during the 1930s. The major companies—Paramount, Warner Bros., Metro-Goldwyn-Mayer, and RKO (Radio-Keith-Orpheum), along with Universal, Columbia, and United Artists—all survived, while Fox grew stronger when it was taken over by a smaller company and became Twentieth Century–Fox. Walt *Disney emerged as a leader in film animation.

The 1930s are often viewed as Hollywood's "Golden Age." Sound fostered verbal comedy—at which the Marx Brothers excelled—musicals, and urban crime films as new genres, while filmmakers such as Frank Capra and John Ford shaped cultural and historical myths amid growing recognition of popular entertainment's social significance. Two movies of 1939—*Gone with the Wind* and *The Wizard of Oz*—now rank as much-loved icons of American popular film. Already a magnet for foreign film talent, Hollywood took on greater international character as a haven for refugees from European fascism.

As awareness of film's role in propaganda and persuasion increased, the U.S. government began producing documentary films, starting with two on agricultural and environmental issues, *The Plow That Broke the Plains* (1936) and *The River* (1937). Additionally, in 1938 the Justice Department, in *United States* v. *Paramount Pictures, Inc., et al.,* known as the *Paramount* case, charged the vertically integrated major film companies with violating antitrust laws. In 1948 the *Supreme Court ruled in the government's favor, ordering the movie firms to divest their theater ownership.

From World War II through the 1970s. During *World War II the film industry, considered vital to national morale, functioned as usual, with some supervision over movie content by the Office of War Information. Leading directors, including Capra, Ford, John Huston, and William Wyler, served in the armed forces and made military documentaries. Capra produced the *Why We Fight* series of seven films that explained U.S. war aims to service personnel and the public. Movie attendance soared during the war and reached its all-time peak in 1946.

But the postwar years brought multiple difficulties for the industry. Besides the *Paramount* case decision, which forced fundamental changes in business practices, the film world was divided beginning in 1947 by Congressional investigations into alleged communist infiltration, which led to an industrywide blacklist. Social and demographic transformations produced a decline in movie attendance, which accelerated as *television gained ground during the 1950s.

In the early 1950s film companies sought to combat audience loss by introducing technological innovations, including three dimensionality, or 3–D, and widescreen processes, such as CinemaScope, that accentuated the difference from television's then small, black-and-white image. 3–D proved a short-lived fad, but wider screen images (although not CinemaScope) became standard. Nevertheless, by 1957 attendance figures were half the 1946 total, and by 1964 they had fallen by 75 percent from the peak year.

Still, even if displaced as the leading mass medium, movies retained their aura of glamour and celebrity, and 1950s movie stars such as James Dean and Marilyn *Monroe became cultural icons comparable to Valentino and Garbo in the silent era. As social mores changed, the industry abandoned its Motion Picture Production Code in the mid-1960s and replaced it with a ratings system that evaluated sexual subject matter. The late 1960s were a major watershed as a generation of filmmakers and producers active since the silent years passed from the scene. In 1969–1970 many film companies sustained some of the greatest financial losses in their histories and several were taken over by nonentertainment conglomerates.

Amid business turmoil came signs of a revival. The studio system's demise gave film directors greater leeway to pursue artistic visions. The postwar generation took new interest in the medium and gave it new prominence through scholarly studies and cultural criticism. Open to fresh talent, the industry introduced promising young filmmakers such as Robert Altman, Francis Ford Coppola, and Martin Scorsese. The early 1970s became to some observers a second "golden age" of stylistic innovation and social engagement.

The film industry also modernized its distribution strategies, utilizing television advertising and releasing major films in hundreds of theaters simultaneously. This tactic, highlighted by the success of *Jaws* (1975), countered the artistic trends of the early 1970s by emphasizing "blockbuster" elements such as action-adventure stories and special-effects spectacle. Filmmakers George Lucas with *Star Wars* (1977) and Steven Spielberg with *E.T.—The Extra-Terrestrial* (1982) became leading practitioners of the new blockbuster film and collaborated as producer and director, respectively, on the Indiana Jones series, three films modeled on children's matinee serials featuring an intrepid archaeologist.

Since 1980: New Markets, New Technologies. Movies further prospered in the 1980s as the advent of cable television networks and video cassette recorders (VCRs) as home entertainment devices provided new outlets for film viewing. The number of theater screens increased with the construction of new multiscreen, or multiplex, cinemas, and release patterns led to major films appearing simultaneously on several thousand screens nationwide. Movies became a linchpin of new media empires encompassing film, television, publishing and music products, distribution systems, retail outlets, theaters (the *Paramount* case rulings had been vacated in the 1980s), and even sports teams.

As the major companies concentrated on so-called high-concept works with the potential for multiple revenue streams—including games, toys, and theme-park rides—an independent film movement sprang up in the late 1970s and 1980s, with assistance from organizations such as the Independent Film Project, based in New York, and actor Robert Redford's Sundance Institute in Utah. A niche market developed for these low-budget works that, by the 1990s, had become to some extent a subsidiary enterprise for the major firms. Meanwhile, mainstream films relied on advances in computer-generated imagery and ever-higher production budgets, exceeding $200 million with *Titanic* (1997), to expand their commitment to special-effects spectacles.

Critics and social analysts have been assessing the impact of movies on American society almost since their beginnings. While recent scholarly opinion has viewed the medium as a champion of dominant ideologies and the status quo, historically film has more often been feared as an agent of change and a threat to social stability. Both perspectives have validity. As a visual, story-telling medium, film brought spectators glimpses of unfamiliar behaviors, products, and places and fostered knowledge of other lives and unaccustomed possibilities. But if the movie experience destabilized static social structures, it also bound its audiences to visions of felicity that stimulated the desire not to overthrow, but to be included. Linked to cultures of modernity, celebrity, and consumption, movies have functioned simultaneously as transgressors and conservators in American social life.

[*See also* Anticommunism; Censorship; Consumer Culture; Foreign Relations: The Cultural Dimension; Modernist Culture; Multinational Enterprises; Popular Culture.]

• Larry Ceplair and Steven Englund, *The Inquisition in Hollywood: Politics in the Film Community, 1930–1960,* 1980. David Bordwell, Janet Staiger, and Kristin Thompson, *The Classical Hollywood Cinema: Film Style and Mode of Production to 1960,* 1985. Thomas Schatz, *The Genius of the System: Hollywood Filmmaking in the Studio Era,* 1988. Charles Musser, *The Emergence of Cinema: The American Screen to 1907,* 1990. Miriam Hansen, *Babel and Babylon: Spectatorship in American Silent Film,* 1991. Jeanine Basinger, *A Woman's View: How Hollywood Spoke to Women, 1930–1960,* 1993. Ed Guerrero, *Framing Blackness: The African American Image in Film,* 1993. Robert Sklar, *Movie-Made America: A Cultural History of American Movies,* 1975, rev. ed., 1994. Francis G. Couvares, ed., *Movie Censorship and American Culture,* 1996.

—Robert Sklar

FINNEY, CHARLES G. (1792–1875), revivalist, reformer, educator. Born in Connecticut and reared in western New York, Charles G. Finney became a schoolteacher and apprentice lawyer. In 1821, while practicing law in Adams, New York, Finney experienced a religious conversion. He received Presbyterian ordination in 1824 and became a missionary in the Lake Ontario region. In 1825 he began a seven-year series of revivals in Oneida County, New York, that brought him national fame and enabled him to develop new evangelistic techniques. With the exception of George Whitefield, earlier evangelists had usually worked within individual churches. Finney pioneered city-wide campaigns supported by numerous committees for publicity, prayer, and so forth. After conducting revivals in *Philadelphia, *New York City, *Boston, and elsewhere, he preached in Rochester, New York, for six months in 1830–1831, ushering in the great revival of 1831–1832. Eschewing emotionalism, Finney ministered especially to the professional classes, which responded in great numbers to his dignified meetings. Many of the techniques he pioneered would become standard in mass evangelism. Theologically he was a New School Calvinist, and placed particular emphasis on sanctification, or perfectionism.

In 1832 Finney became pastor of the Second Presbyterian Church in New York City, moving in 1835 to the Broadway Tabernacle, where he remained until 1837. His series of lectures on revivals, published in 1835, enjoyed a wide influence. In 1835 he also became professor of theology at Oberlin College in Ohio, dividing his time for many years thereafter between Oberlin and evangelistic campaigns across the North. He was president of Oberlin from 1851 to 1866. Active in numerous reform movements of the day, especially *antislavery, he inspired many to embrace these causes.

[*See also* Antebellum Era; Education: Collegiate Education; Great Awakening, First and Second; Missionary Movement; Revivalism.]

• Keith J. Hardman, *Charles G. Finney, Revivalist and Reformer, 1792–1875*, 1987. G. A. Rosell and R. A. G. Dupuis, eds., *Memoirs of C. G. Finney*, 1989. Charles E. Hambrick-Stowe, *Charles G. Finney and the Spirit of American Evangelicalism*, 1996.

—Keith J. Hardman

FIRESTONE, HARVEY (1868–1938), industrialist, corporate executive. Harvey Firestone was born near Columbiana, Ohio, to a well-to-do farm family. After graduating from high school in 1887, he held several clerical jobs, most notably with his uncle's Columbus Buggy Company. Firestone became interested in rubber carriage tires and developed a profitable tire dealership. In 1900 he moved to Akron, Ohio, the emerging center of the tire industry, to manufacture tires. Firestone quickly established his firm as an important producer of carriage, bicycle, and, increasingly, automobile tires. In 1905, Firestone Tire and Rubber Company obtained a large order from the Ford Motor Company for its new Model T. From that time it grew rapidly. By 1920 Firestone had become one of the best-known American industrialists.

In the 1920s and 1930s Firestone transformed his company into a vertically integrated corporation that participated in all aspects of tire production and distribution. He developed rubber plantations overseas, textile plants, specialized factories, a full line of tire-oriented products, retail stores, and a world-wide marketing organization. Firestone scorned growth through mergers with competing companies; instead, he emphasized his own brand-name products, which he promoted relentlessly through *advertising and public-relations activities, such as camping trips with Thomas *Edison, Henry *Ford, and other notables. Despite his company's growing size, Firestone insisted on personal control and family management and opposed labor unions. His five sons all became Firestone executives and played important roles in the firm until the 1970s.

[*See also* Automotive Industry; Foreign Relations: The Economic Dimension; Industrialization; Mass Marketing; Mass Production.]

• Alfred Lief, *The Firestone Story: A History of the Firestone Tire and Rubber Company*, 1951. Alfred Lief, *Harvey Firestone, Free Man of Enterprise*, 1951.

—Daniel Nelson

FIRST AMENDMENT. *See* Bill of Rights.

FISHERIES. From Indian subsistence to global markets, fisheries loom large in American history. Ancient weir sites under Boston Bay and along the Northwest coast and huge bone deposits at The Dalles in Oregon offer evidence that North Americans have fished intensively for more than nine thousand years. European cod fishermen venturing into the northwestern Atlantic in the 1480s soon came ashore in Newfoundland, Acadia, and *New England, establishing some of the earliest permanent settlements. By the 1700s, fishers caught Atlantic salmon, lobsters, and cod; indeed, control of the cod fisheries figured in the era's diplomacy and imperials wars.

Evolving technologies have included aboriginal spears, nets, and weirs and European purse seines. The salmon fisheries' adoption of pound nets and fish wheels in the 1870s and the introduction of the otter trawl net in 1905 increased catches. Early Europeans cured cod by salting the wet fish on shipboard, but by the later 1500s they were drying and salting fish on shore. Canning emerged in the mid-1800s, freezing late in the century. In the 1940s, giant factory trawlers combined these operations.

The history of fisheries varies by region. In New England, freshwater species began to disappear after 1800 as *agriculture, *urbanization, and manufacturing altered their habitats, but offshore fishing and whaling remained economic mainstays. In the twentieth century, cod, striped bass, tuna, and marlin were the principal commercial fish, while anglers prized eastern trout and Atlantic salmon. Along the middle and south Atlantic coast, Chesapeake Bay, and the Gulf Coast, crabs, oysters, striped bass, and shrimp were important, with Indians, African slaves, and poor whites the primary laborers. Anglers coveted warm-water fish such as bass and bonefish.

Fisheries also arose on inland rivers and lakes, including the *Mississippi, Illinois, and Nipigon Rivers; the Great Lakes; and Lake Winnipeg, sustaining major industries and communities until habitat destruction undermined them in the late nineteenth and twentieth centuries. Market species included catfish, whitefish, pike, and sturgeon; anglers favored trout and bass. Late twentieth-century fish culturists created Pacific salmon fisheries, but pollution prevented these stocks from becoming important food sources.

On the West Coast, aboriginal societies caught salmon, eulachon, shellfish, and pinnipeds, while nineteenth-century Euroamericans pursued Pacific salmon, fur seals, and whales. Commercial fishers in *Alaska formed communities that often preceded formal government. Indians, although important laborers initially, had by 1900 been displaced by southern Europeans, Scandinavians, and Asians. In the twentieth century, offshore fleets depleted salmon, halibut, whale, sardine, crab, pollack, and groundfish stocks. Anglers, meanwhile, fished for trout, stocked exotic species, and fought to control salmon and steelhead streams.

Fishery management and regulation were initially local perogatives. In the *Colonial Era, towns such as Concord, Massachusetts, set rules and sanctioned monopolies to conserve shad. State fish commissions did not appear until the 1860s. When the first federal fish commissioner tried in 1871 to resolve a conflict in New England over declining scup stocks, the states were ill-equipped to deal with the issue and the commissioner gave up. Only in Alaska, or when negotiating fishing treaties with Indians and other nations, did federal officials play a primary role, and even here states often contested their power. To avoid regulations, Americans relied on technical solutions such as hatcheries and fishways. When regulations proved unavoidable, they typically fell most heavily on the more marginal members of society.

[*See also* Exploration, Conquest, and Settlement, Era of European; Indian History and Culture; Work.]

• Harold A. Innis, *The Cod Fisheries: The History of an International Economy*, rev. ed., 1954. Joseph E. Taylor III, *Making Salmon: An Environmental History of the Northwest Fisheries Crisis*, 1999.

—Joseph E. Taylor III

FITZGERALD, ELLA (1917–1996), *jazz and popular music singer. Born in Newport News, Virginia, Ella Fitzgerald grew up in Yonkers, New York. Escaping an abusive household, she ran away to Harlem at the age of fifteen. Originally a dancer, she debuted as a singer at Harlem's Apollo Theater in 1934, winning over a tough Amateur Night crowd. In 1935 she joined the Chick Webb band, known for its up-tempo solos and the danceability of its music. To the dismay of jazz critics, who felt that she was wasting her talent, she first won fame with a series of novelty hits in the late 1930s and early 1940s. The first of these, "A-Tisket, A-Tasket," recorded in 1938, diverted audiences from the Great Depression. She became the Webb band's leader from his death in 1939 until 1942.

In the early 1940s, Fitzgerald began performing modern jazz. By singing syllables and isolated words in a stream-of-consciousness fashion, or "scatting," Fitzgerald offered a vocal analogue to modern jazz's rapid tempos and abrupt key changes, in the process becoming an important modern jazz artist. Later, she broadened her appeal by recording "songbook" albums featuring the music of Ira and George *Gershwin, Harold Arlen, and Irving *Berlin. By 1960, in a time when the record industry was targeting the youth market, she had sold millions of records to the audience that remembered her from the Swing Era. Worsening eyesight brought on by diabetes hampered Fitzgerald's career, though she continued to perform into her seventies.

[*See also* Music: Popular Music.]

• Stuart Nicholson, *Ella Fitzgerald*, 1993.

—Jonathan Z. S. Pollack

FITZGERALD, F. SCOTT (1896–1940), novelist and short story writer identified with the 1920s, which he named the "Jazz Age." Born in St. Paul, Minnesota, and educated at Princeton University, F. Scott Fitzgerald served briefly in the army and achieved early success with *This Side of Paradise* (1920), a coming-of-age novel mainly set at Princeton. *The Beautiful and Damned* (1922), his second novel, traces the deterioration of a wealthy young couple.

Fitzgerald's most famous novel, *The Great Gatsby* (1925), was neither a financial success nor a recognized masterpiece in its own time. This fictional assessment of the American Dream has become the most widely read and taught twentieth-century American novel, and Jay Gatsby is an American icon. The theme—as in all of Fitzgerald's best work—is aspiration and disillusionment: His questing heroes are invariably defeated. The emotional quality of Fitzgerald's fiction is intensified by its stylistic richness, combining wit, sensory appeal, accurate observation, and a keen sense of time and place.

The insanity of Fitzgerald's wife, Zelda—herself a 1920s celebrity—delayed his most profound novel, *Tender Is the Night* (1934). Set on the Riviera during the 1920s, it examines the failure of a brilliant young American psychiatrist during his marriage to a wealthy mental patient. This novel's disappointing reception, combined with financial worries and illness, contributed to Fitzgerald's breakdown, about which he wrote in a series of essays posthumously collected in *The Crack-Up* (1945). Fitzgerald went to Hollywood in 1937 to write for the movies. At the time of his death from a heart attack at age forty-four, he was writing a Hollywood novel; the work-in-progress appeared posthumously as *The Last Tycoon* (1941).

During his lifetime, Fitzgerald's reputation for extravagance and dissipation affected assessments of his writings. A reappraisal began in 1945, and by the 1960s and beyond, his work was read and studied in English and in translation throughout the world, both as literature and as documents of American social history. His 160 short stories for mass-circulation *magazines, dismissed as hack-work, included such masterpieces as "May Day," "The Diamond as Big as the Ritz," "The Rich Boy," "The Last of the Belles," and "Babylon Revisited."

[*See also* Literature: Since World War I; Twenties, The.]

• Matthew J. Bruccoli, Scottie Fitzgerald Smith, and Joan P. Kerr, eds., *The Romantic Egoists: A Pictorial Autobiography from the Scrapbooks and Albums of Scott and Zelda Fitzgerald*, 1974. Matthew J. Bruccoli, *Some Sort of Epic Grandeur: The Life of F. Scott Fitzgerald*, rev. ed., 1993. Matthew J. Bruccoli, ed., *F. Scott Fitzgerald: A Life in Letters*, 1994.

—Matthew J. Bruccoli

FLETCHER* v. *PECK (1810). In an opinion delivered by Chief Justice John *Marshall, the U.S. *Supreme Court in *Fletcher* v. *Peck* used the contract clause of the U.S. *Constitution (art. I, sec. 10) to protect individual property rights from state legislative action. The case arose from conflicting land claims to Georgia's Yazoo territory (modern Alabama and Mississippi). During the 1780s and early 1790s, Georgia sold much of this land to speculators. The largest sale, in 1795, involved the bribery of the state legislature. When Jeffersonian Republicans subsequently gained power in Georgia, the state assembly repealed the 1795 sale.

Later, John Peck of Massachusetts bought land that Georgia had sold under the 1795 act; Peck then sold it to Robert Fletcher of New Hampshire, who in 1803 sued Peck in federal court, claiming that Peck had not had clear title to the land. (This was a friendly suit; both parties wished to establish the legitimacy of land titles under the 1795 act.) In 1807, the federal Circuit Court upheld Peck's position, and Fletcher appealed to the Supreme Court.

Ruling in favor of Peck, Marshall held first that the Supreme Court was powerless to investigate the motives of the Georgia legislature in making the 1795 sale. In so doing, the Chief Justice further clarified the distinction between political questions, left to other branches of government, and judicial questions that the Court might properly decide. Marshall then voided the Georgia repeal act on two grounds, natural law and the contract clause. Even in the absence of specific constitutional protection, Marshall contended, the very nature of government and society constrained a legislature from seizing property without compensation. But in impairing a contract obligation between the state and the original purchasers, Marshall went on, Georgia's repeal act violated the contract clause of the Constitution. If fraud between two parties in the transfer of property could adversely affect the rights of subsequent buyers and sellers of that property, he argued, then "all titles would be insecure, and the intercourse between man and man would be seriously obstructed."

Marshall's ruling served to protect and stimulate private economic initiative. More generally, his opinion gave the federal courts a role, under the contract clause, in reviewing state regulation of private contract and property rights. The contract clause continued to be used by the Supreme Court throughout the nineteenth century to limit state regulatory power. In the *Gilded Age and beyond, the Court often invoked the contract clause, and cited *Fletcher* v. *Peck*, to shield corporations from state regulation and to block state reform efforts.

[*See also Charles River Bridge* v. *Warren Bridge; Dartmouth College Case*; Early Republic, Era of the; Economic Regulation; Judicial Review; Laissez-faire.]

• C. Peter Magrath, *Yazoo: Law and Politics in the New Republic: The Case of* Fletcher v. Peck, 1966.

—Paul G. E. Clemens

FLEXNER REPORT (1910). The Flexner Report, an evaluation of American *medical education, has become the exemplar of critical investigations of higher education. Abraham Flexner (1866–1959), a nonphysician with little knowledge of medicine or medical training, was employed by the *Carnegie Foundation for the Advancement of Teaching, established in 1905 by Andrew *Carnegie. The foundation shared the widespread concern that many medical schools were poorly equipped to teach the new discoveries in the medical sciences and clinical medicine. In 1909, under an agreement between the foundation and the *American Medical Association (AMA), Flexner participated in the AMA's second inspection of medical schools. Flexner's independently written report won wide publicity because of its descriptions of each medical school in the United States and Canada and its harsh denunciations of the education provided by many of them. The report gained a reputation as having been responsible for the closing of many medical schools, but mergers and closings had been under way for a decade. (Between 1904 and 1910 the number of medical students decreased by one-fourth.) Flexner also failed to observe that the weakest schools produced few graduates. Using as a model the renowned Johns Hopkins University medical school, which opened in Baltimore in 1893, Flexner advocated laboratory instruction as the principal form of preclinical education and hospital training as the core of clinical training. The former proved to be prohibitively expensive for most medical schools and the latter, which was widely adopted after midcentury, has been criticized for neglecting ambulatory patients and their social environment.

[*See also* Education: The Rise of the University; Medicine: From the 1870s to 1945.]

• Abraham Flexner, *Medical Education in the United States and Canada*, 1910. William G. Rothstein, *American Medical Schools and the Practice of Medicine: A History*, 1987.

—William G. Rothstein

FOLK ART AND CRAFTS. References to "folk art and crafts" arose in the early twentieth century to describe traditional handwork that stood in contrast to modern industrial systems of *mass production. Divergent meanings of the term reflected alternative visions of American society. As used in the urban art world, the term referred to an American tradition rooted in the white Protestant foundations of the *Colonial Era and the era of the *Early Republic. In the 1920s, art-world curators and writers began describing folk art as preindustrial painting and sculpture, often executed by anonymous artisans. *New York City galleries frequently celebrated folk crafts associated with early *New England. This "Americana," as it was sometimes called, suggested continuity from the founding of the nation to urban, industrial America of the twentieth century. In the freedom of expression and vernacular spirit of this work, art-world critics found both the source of a vernacular American culture and a precedent, indeed inspiration, for the abstraction of modernist art. Art-world curators and writers such as Holger Cahill, Jean Lipman, and Edith Halpert, influenced by the wealthy patronage of Abby Aldrich Rockefeller and Electra Havemeyer Webb, organized and publicized influential folk art exhibitions at the Museum of Modern Art in New York City and the Newark Museum during the 1930s. After *World War II, private collections of such folk-art patrons developed into major centers for the permanent exhibition of early American folk art and crafts at Williamsburg, Virginia (Rockefeller); Cooperstown, New York (Lipman); and Shelburne, Vermont (Webb). Around the time of the U.S. bicentennial in 1976, many exhibitions used preindustrial folk art and crafts to celebrate the "common man" and national vernacular aesthetic in American history. The largest of these exhibitions, entitled "The Flowering of American Folk Art," opened at the Whitney Museum of American Art in 1974.

Even when twentieth-century materials began to be called folk art by art-world critics after World War II, the examples often conveyed a nostalgia for a preindustrial past. Perhaps most notable was the fame of Anna Mary "Grandma" Moses during the 1950s for her memory paintings of rural New York life. The art world's use of folk art to emphasize a vernacular individuality continued with a movement in the 1980s to extend the definition of folk art to "outsider" art, the unusual creations of individuals working without deference to community or artistic conventions. The exhibition of Herbert Hemphill's major collection of twentieth-century folk art at the *Smithsonian Institution in 1990 legitimized the association of such works with American tradition.

Meanwhile, an alternative concept of folk art and crafts had unfolded as sociologists and folklorists viewed such works as evidence of America's ethnic and regional diversity and of the persistence of varied folk cultures in an era of modernization. Growing out of an anthropological concern for the communal arts and crafts of aboriginal and peasant groups, this interpretation emphasized persistent forms of social folklife within industrialized societies that did not necessarily blend into a dominant national culture. Distinctive traditions of groups within the United States that formed regional-ethnic cultures, such as the *Mennonites and Amish in Pennsylvania and elsewhere, Scots-Irish in *Appalachia, *African Americans in the Mississippi Delta, and French Acadians in Louisiana, offered examples of cultural persistence. Such long-standing subcultures could still be observed in contemporary life, helping to solidify community, rather than national, identity. Those who hold this view of folk art and crafts emphasize their function of preserving communal tradition and transmitting skills in everyday life, rather than the aesthetic and stylistic emphasis characteristic of the art-world view.

The opposing visions of folk art and crafts especially came into conflict during the 1920s debate over *immigration restriction. The Metropolitan Museum of Art, bemoaning the decline of an American aesthetic because of the diverse ethnic groups that had recently emigrated from eastern and southern Europe, in 1924, established an American Wing to show the virtue of American decorative arts produced mostly by colonial New England artisans.

Jane *Addams at Hull House and Allen Eaton at the Russell Sage Foundation meanwhile established exhibitions of living immigrant folk art and crafts, many combining Old World peasant traditions with American themes and materials. Their purpose, as the title of Eaton's 1932 book made clear, was to celebrate "Immigrant Gifts to American Life." Folk art and craft production, in this view, reflected a continuing, living tradition in an America of plural communities. The exhibition that Eaton organized, "Arts and Crafts of the Homelands," attracted unprecedented numbers of visitors at various sites in the Northeast from 1919 through the early 1930s. Rather than insisting upon a single dominant American colonial aesthetic, Eaton arranged his exhibition by social groups, each with its distinctive and enduring traditions. Eaton followed these exhibitions with folk art and craft displays that featured the living crafts of contemporary rural life (many from Appalachia) and art produced in World War II Japanese internment camps. Other social categories whose living folk art would later receive attention included women, children, old people, and members of diverse occupational and religious groups. In contrast, many in the art world continued to view folk art as a relic tradition associated with the preindustrial era out of which a unique and homogeneous American culture had emerged.

Exhibitions such as those organized by Allen Eaton often sought to encourage the revival and marketing of folk art and crafts, to enable residents of folk-culture regions threatened with displacement to remain in their ancestral homes and occupations. Festivals and programs in Appalachia and Pennsylvania during the 1950s stimulated interest in traditional handmade goods. In addition to providing opportunities for traditional artists and craftspeople to continue their work, such events offered authentic skills and experiences that provided emotional and spiritual renewal within an increasingly dominant mass culture. After World War II, the cultural conservationist enterprise became incorporated into state and federal programs including state folk-art offices. The first one was established in 1948 in Pennsylvania and spread to over forty states by the 1980s. Programs included apprenticeships, grants to artists and craftsworkers, exhibitions, publications, folk artists in the schools, and archives. At the federal level, the National Endowment for the Arts (NEA) included a folk-art program, and an American Folklife Center in the *Library of Congress was established as part of the Folklife Preservation Act of 1976. Beginning in 1967, the Smithsonian Institution featured folk art and crafts of American ethnic-regional groups on the Mall in *Washington, D.C., at its annual Festival of

American Folklife held around Independence Day. The NEA awarded national "Heritage" fellowships to recognize traditional folk artists representing American cultural diversity, including African-American blacksmith Philip Simmons and Mexican-American Santos carver George Lopez.

As a new wave of immigration from Asia, South America, and the Caribbean reached the United States in the 1980s, programs reminiscent of Allen Eaton's efforts to recognize the contributions of various ethnic cultures during the 1920s became evident. While folk art and crafts had previously been associated with transplanted European skills, community life in ethnic-regional cultures, or Native American crafts, new forms appeared as part of the American scene, especially in changing cities populated by mixtures of black, Hispanic, and Asian groups with their different legacies and complex interrelationships. Among the Hmong (from Laos), new forms of "story cloths" emerged based on an old textile tradition but now containing images of their *Vietnam War experiences. Among Puerto Ricans in New York City, home-built *casitas* (small houses) in abandoned urban lots sprang up to recreate the garden life of a community amid decaying apartment projects. As such productions came to be seen as a part of American folk art and crafts, students of folk culture recognized the value of ethnic and communal difference in a "multicultural" society. In this view, folk art and crafts appear not so much as relics of the Colonial Era, but as the material manifestations of an ongoing process of popular cultural expression that has been interpreted differently in various periods of American history.

[*See also* Asian Americans; Cultural Pluralism; Folklore; Hispanic Americans; Immigration Law; Indian History and Culture; Industrialization; Modernist Culture; Museums: Museums of Art; Music: Traditional Music; National Endowments for the Arts and the Humanities; Painting: To 1945; Puerto Rico; Race and Ethnicity; Regionalism; Settlement Houses.]

• Jean Lipman and Alice Winchester, *Flowering of American Folk Art, 1776–1876,* 1974. Kenneth L. Ames, *Beyond Necessity: Art in the Folk Tradition,* 1977. Ian M. G. Quimby and Scott T. Swank, eds., *Perspectives on American Folk Art,* 1980. Charles Camp, ed., *Traditional Craftsmanship in America,* 1983. Simon J. Bronner, *Grasping Things: Folk Material Culture and Mass Society in America,* 1986. John Michael Vlach and Simon J. Bronner, eds., *Folk Art and Art Worlds,* 1986. Michael Owen Jones, *Exploring Folk Art,* 1987. John Michael Vlach, *Plain Painters: Making Sense of American Folk Art,* 1988. Steve Siporin, *American Folk Masters: The National Heritage Fellows,* 1992.

—Simon J. Bronner

FOLKLORE. Folklore consists of cultural expressions learned through oral tradition and custom, typically enacted in social settings. Types of folklore prevalent in America include legends, beliefs, rituals, crafts, food, and architecture. As a lasting record of social expressions, folklore has been an important source of historical evidence for analyzing perceptions and attitudes of groups identified by region, *race and ethnicity, *religion, occupation, age, and *gender, among other categories. Folklore often provides essential information about groups lacking a documentary record. Even when such a record exists, folklore can provide valuable supplementary evidence. Folklore studies have helped scholars reconstruct the everyday life of the past and to comprehend the principal images and symbols that have developed in America. The cultural evidence of folklore has been central to debates over interpretations of a national culture and the role of diverse social traditions within it.

One approach to the study of folklore involves tracing the movement of ethnic folk cultures and their formation of *regional groups.* Because a group's traditions are usually relatively stable over time and variable over space, when changes occur, they are often a sign of major social structural shifts. One interpretive approach to this process sees cultural diffusion as emanating from four main "cultural hearths" on the eastern seaboard that influenced the formation of American regions. The *New England hearth, with its strong British stamp, spread north and west across the upper *Middle West. The Chesapeake-Tidewater hearth influenced the movement across Maryland and Virginia into the Upland *South. The Lowland South hearth, featuring both English and African influences, worked its way through South Carolina and Georgia into the Deep South. In Pennsylvania, the last hearth to form, Palatine Germans, Swiss Anabaptists, English Quakers, French Huguenots, and Scots-Irish people formed a plural society and strong inland Pennsylvania-German cultural subregion that spread into the Middle West. Further west, arguments have been made for a Mormon culture region (Utah and parts of Idaho, Nevada, and Arizona); the *Southwest (New Mexico, Arizona, and parts of Texas, Nevada, and Colorado); the Ozarks (Arkansas, Missouri, and part of Illinois); and Cajun country (Louisiana and part of Texas). Beyond the regional ties of ethnic groups, the long-standing cultural distinctiveness of such groups as *African Americans, Chinese Americans, and Pennsylvania-Germans suggests a pattern of multiculturalism in America dating back to the nineteenth century.

Another perspective, the *ethnographic,* concentrates less on broad historical-geographical patterns and more on contemporary observations of localized behavior and communication in a variety of social settings. When such observations can be recovered historically, an ethnographic view of the functioning of folklore in everyday life can be discerned through time. Using this approach, some authorities have characterized American folklore as heterogeneous and dynamic, subject to a variety of social variables, especially gender, age, and *social class, in addition to region and ethnicity. From this perspective, folklore is not a historic artifact, but a living process found in such diverse social settings as suburban developments, college campuses, and city neighborhoods. This approach, emphasizing changing settings and individual interactions in everyday life, suggests that cultural identities within America have been more variable, complex, and fluid than static models suggest.

A lingering historical question regarding folklore in America concerns its role in the development of a national culture. To be sure, some critics have questioned whether the culture of a nation-state as ethnically mixed and young as the United States may be equated with the older and more homogeneous national traditions of Europe and Asia. Others, however, drawing on the example of early American historical experience, posit a new American cultural hybrid forming from the cross-fertilization of European, Native American, and African traditions. The historian and folklorist Richard Dorson (1916–1981) drew attention to a unique set of historical forces—exploration and colonization, revolution and the establishment of a democratic republic, the westward movement, *immigration, *slavery and the *Civil War, and *industrialization and *technology—that shaped new folklore or adaptations of older folklore themes unique to American society. Among the favorite subjects for the emergence of such a national cultural consciousness was the American frontier, which bred national folk heroes like Davy *Crockett, the legendary lumberjack Paul Bunyan, and the mythic riverboat captain Mike Fink.

Dorson offered a periodization of American cultural history based on the development of folklore. The "religious impulse" represented by lore of witchcraft, divine providences, and supernatural judgments in the form of earthquakes or Indian attacks characterized the *Colonial Era. The "democratic impulse," Dorson suggested, flourished in the *Antebellum Era giving rise to legends of larger-than-life frontier adventurers and folk heroes. In the later nineteenth century, a changing economy fostered songs and stories of *cowboys, lumberjacks, miners, oil drillers, and railroaders. The later twentieth century, some contend, gave rise to "urban legends" and the folklore of a youth culture with its distinctive patterns of speech, fashion, and popular music.

Folklore also figures in the effort to describe, and sometimes create, a unique American historical mythology. According to influential American Studies scholars such as Henry Nash Smith and Russell Nye, American "myths" were not narrative texts in the usual sense. They were driving concepts or "collective representations" that unified Americans. Smith's "myth of the garden," for example, referred to Americans' belief in their ability to transform wilderness and desert into an Edenlike garden, while Nye's "myth of superabundance" alluded to the belief in the boundlessness of the nation's natural resources. Comparative studies of proverbs and games suggest that a national "worldview" or set of broadly held "folk ideas" exists, built on such themes as *individualism and an optimistic orientation toward the future. Folklore, in short, as a representation in everyday life of deep-seated values and long-standing beliefs, can provide a highly useful basis for historical studies examining both national traditions and multicultural movements.

[*See also* Cultural Pluralism; Folk Art and Crafts; Regionalism.]

• Henry Glassie, *Pattern in the Folk Material Culture of the Eastern United Studies,* 1968. Richard Dorson, *America in Legend,* 1973. Barre Toelken, *The Dynamics of Folklore,* 1979. Alan Dundes, *Interpreting Folklore,* 1981. Simon J. Bronner, *Grasping Things: Folk Material Culture and Mass Society in America,* 1986. Jan Harold Brunvand, ed., *American Folklore: An Encyclopedia,* 1996.

—Simon J. Bronner

FOLK MUSIC. *See* Music: Traditional Music.

FOOD AND DIET. If one had to sum up the history of Americans and their food in a word, it would likely be "abundance." Although the first English settlers suffered difficult times, most were soon much better fed than their counterparts across the Atlantic. Thanks mainly to better diets, George *Washington's *Revolutionary War troops were, on average, much taller than the British soldiers facing them. Citizens of the new republic prided themselves on what a Philadelphia physician called their "superabundance" of food. For most of the free population, this meant lots of meat, accompanied by breads made from corn, rye, and, increasingly, wheat. Fruits and vegetables were abundant in season, while wild animals inland and plentiful fish and seafood along the coasts provided additional sources of protein. The winter and early spring diet comprised preserved pork, bread, beans, and root vegetables—filling, if monotonous.

By the 1830s new roads, canals, and steamboats brought vast new areas of farmland into the market economy, making a wider variety of foodstuffs available for longer durations. Food reformers now cautioned against excessive indulgence. The minister and temperance advocate Sylvester Graham, warning that meat, alcohol, and spicy foods sapped the body's vital force, condemned such foods as processed white flour that had been altered from its God-given natural state.

America's slave population, totaling nearly four million by 1860, experienced a very different dietary environment. Slave families typically received a scant weekly ration of cornmeal and fatty pork. Some supplemented this unbalanced fare with fish, small game, eggs, and vegetables they provided for themselves.

After mid-century, the expanding *railroads transported affordable supplies of wheat, pork, and beef to the growing cities; market gardening and dairy farms proliferated around them; and steamships brought exotic foods from abroad. By 1900, skilled chefs were turning out elaborate multicourse meals in the style of French haute cuisine for the wealthy. The growing middle and upper-middle classes could readily purchase the abundant foods but could not afford the servants to prepare and serve them in this fashion and were thus amenable to calls by a new generation of food reformers for dietary restraint.

The scientific basis for the reformers' crusade was the so-called New Nutrition: the discovery by chemists of proteins, carbohydrates, and fats, each with its unique physiological function. Proper nutrition now meant consuming as much of these as necessary—any less was unhealthful; any more, wasteful. Urging immigrant workers to economize, the reformers insisted that the proteins in beans were fully as nutritious as those in beefsteak. The middle classes, heeding the call to choose foods on the basis of their "physiological economy" rather than taste, made culture-heroes out of dietary faddists like John Harvey Kellogg, who amplified Graham's theories with purgative nostrums based on recent scientific discoveries that the colon harbored large amounts of bacteria. The "scientific cooking" advocate Fannie Farmer offered simple menus and exact recipes in her *Boston Cooking School Cook Book* (1896). Women in the new profession of home economics, teaching about food and health in the schools, similarly insisted that science rather than taste should guide one's food choices.

For the urban immigrant poor, meanwhile, providing even subsistence nutrition for their families proved difficult. In hard times, such as the Depression of the 1890s, it was more difficult still. Impure water, tainted milk, and spoiled meat contributed to illness, infant mortality, and periodic epidemics in the slums. Tougher public-health measures such as the 1906 *Pure Food and Drug Act and milk pasteurization gradually ameliorated the worst of these dietary hazards, but their health ultimately improved mainly because of more ample and varied diets.

During *World War I, the federal Food Administration used the New Nutrition to persuade Americans to substitute beans, whole grains, and fresh vegetables for the meat and wheat being shipped to Europe. Meanwhile, the discovery of vitamins in the early twentieth century gave rise to a new nutritional paradigm. Its dissemination was encouraged by the transformation of food production by *mass-production industries characterized by large capital investments, mechanization, complex distribution networks, and large promotion and *advertising budgets. Servants having practically disappeared from middle-class homes, housewives were encouraged to buy labor-saving processed foods such as canned goods, as well as vitamin-rich citrus fruits and milk, which were said to be essential for children's health. Though still little understood, vitamins proved to be a food promoter's dream. Citrus growers, dairymen, the grain-milling industry, pickle producers—almost anyone could and did make extravagant claims. When synthesized vitamin pills became available in the late 1930s, food producers insisted that such supplements were unnecessary: A "balanced diet" would provide more than enough nutrients.

Neither the Depression of the 1930s nor *World War II undermined confidence in America's abundant food supply. Indeed, the Depression-era agricultural crisis was defined as one of overproduction of food and maldistribution of income. And despite wartime rationing, many doubted that the shortages were real. Recurring rumors insisted food supplies were more than adequate, but that government incompetence or crooked middlemen were keeping them off the market.

In the postwar "Baby Boom" years, 1946 to 1963, the long-term tendency of food preparation to move outside the home intensified as the food industries sold harried young mothers and homemakers on the "convenience" of their products. Frozen foods and other new kinds of processed, precooked, and packaged foods became popular. From 1949 to 1959, chemists developed more than four hundred additives to help food survive these new processes. Restaurants, especially the proliferating fast-food chains, welcomed this development: With food preparation reduced to defrosting, frying, or adding hot water, unskilled labor could replace expensive, often temperamental cooks.

Gastronomical considerations took a backseat in all of this, but few seemed to notice, since haute cuisine had long since fallen out of favor. In the 1920s, Prohibition had deprived expensive restaurants of the income from alcohol that had padded their profit margins. During World War II, a preoccupation with fine food had seemed unpatriotic. By the 1950s, food tastes were no longer an important mark of social distinction. Most Americas seemed satisfied by beefsteak, pizzas, fried chicken, canned-food casseroles, Jell-O molds, and frozen TV dinners. Regional differences, already undermined in the 1920s and 1930s, practically disappeared under the onslaught of mass-produced foods aimed at supposedly homogeneous Middle American tastes. Government officials, educators, journalists, and the food industries insisted that Americans were "The Best Fed People on Earth."

The self-satisfaction eroded in the 1960s with the realization that, amid massive agricultural surpluses, millions of poor citizens could not afford an adequate diet. Programs were instituted to distribute surplus commodities and food stamps to the poor. As middle-class concerns over the healthfulness of their own diet increased, a new dietary paradigm, which one might call Negative Nutrition, arose. Whereas earlier nutritional systems had emphasized consuming healthful foods, Negative Nutrition warned *against* eating certain foods, particularly those treated with potentially harmful pesticides and chemical fertilizers and those robbed of nutrients by overprocessing. Veterans of the *New Left, meanwhile, redirected their critique of *capitalism toward its effects on food and the environment. The giant corporations, they charged, used their immense advertising resources to brainwash Americans into eating overprocessed, denutrified, unhealthful, and environmentally hazardous products. They pointed out, for example, that the spread of cattle ranching in South America to meet U.S. demands for beef was contributing directly to the destruction of the rain forests. Both health and morality, they insisted, dictated a preference for "organic" and "natural" foods, preferably grown by small producers.

The food industry responded nimbly, reformulating and repackaging their products with labels such as "Natural" and "Nature's Own." However, new findings in nutritional science reinforced another aspect of Negative Nutrition, as specific foods came to identified as dangerous. Rising rates of *heart disease were now blamed on high levels of cholesterol in many of America's favorite foods. Sugar, long linked to diabetes and now thought by some to be a factor in other *diseases and psychological disorders, was called an addictive substance manipulated by food processors to "hook" children on nutritionally deficient products. Themes from the Graham and Kellogg eras resurfaced, as vegetarianism, once the domain of cranks, became a serious option for many. Issues relating to obesity added a new twist to the nutrition debate. In the later nineteenth century a full figure had been a mark of beauty for woman and a sign of health, wealth, and substance for men. Since the 1920s, however, evidence had accumulated of a relationship between excessive weight and higher mortality rates.

As in previous eras, food reformers mustered impressive scientific support. By the mid-1970s, the federal government was supporting research on diet and health and urging Americans to lose weight and reduce the animal fat, sugar, and sodium in their diets. Organizations such as the American Heart Association underscored the need for dietary change. "Low-fat," "lite," "no-cal," "cholesterol-free," and "sodium-free" products now lined supermarket shelves.

The result reflected the paradoxes of American abundance. Many took to frenetic diet-and-exercise regimens, yet the average weight of Americans continued to rise. Although consumption of full-fat dairy products and red meat fell, that of other fats soared, as did that of sugar and sodium. Dietary self-denial was undermined by the foreign travel boom, which encouraged indulgence and helped once again to make food tastes a sign of social distinction. Consumers now had an unprecedented choice of foods and ways to consume them. As more women entered the workplace, the trend for food production to move outside the home accelerated. "Take-home" foods boomed, as did eating out, particularly at fast-food and other chain restaurants.

Persisting moralism, in the form of guilty consciences, impeded indulging in the abundance of food choices, but the targets of the guilt constantly shifted, as experts regularly warned of new food dangers and absolved old ones. With the Negative Nutrition now superimposed on older nutritional ideas, many Americans simultaneously tried to eat more of foods that were supposed to prevent or cure illness and promote general good health, and less of those foods deemed unhealthy or likely to cause weight gain. Americans seemed doomed by their past to both celebrate their food abundance and avoid enjoying it too much.

[*See also* Agriculture; Alcohol and Alcohol Abuse; Canals and Waterways; Carson, Rachel; Dairy Industry; Depressions, Economic; Environmentalism; Health and Fitness; Immigration; Livestock Industry; Mass Marketing; Meatpacking and Meat Processing Industry; Roads and Turnpikes, Early; Slavery: Slave Families, Communities, and Culture; Temperance and and Prohibition; Urbanization.]

• Richard Cummings, *The American and His Food,* 1940. Waverly Root and Richard de Rochemont, *Eating in America: A History,* 1976. Stephen Nissenbaum, *Sex, Diet and Disability in Jacksonian America,* 1980. Richard Hooker, *Food and Drink in America: A History,* 1981. James Wharton, *Crusades for Fitness: The History of American Health Reformers,* 1982. Harvey Levenstein, *Revolution at the Table: The Transformation of the American Diet,* 1988. Warren Belasco, *Appetite for Change,* 1989. Harvey Levenstein, *Paradox of Plenty: The Social History of Eating in Modern America,* 1992. Peter Stearns, *Fat History: Bodies and Beauty in the Modern West,* 1997.

—Harvey Levenstein

FOOD AND DRUG ADMINISTRATION. *See* Economic Regulation; Pure Food and Drug Act.

FOOD AND DRUGS ACT. *See* Pure Food and Drug Act.

FOOTBALL. Versions of football were played in late seventeenth-century Massachusetts. In the early 1800s, college students representing their classes played the "football rush." Rutgers beat Princeton, six goals to four, in the first intercollegiate game in 1869, using rules similar to soccer. Players could bat the ball, but not carry or throw it. A crucial innovation occurred in 1874 following two Harvard-McGill football games, one contested under soccer-style rules, the second under rugby rules. The Harvard players enjoyed rugby's physical contact and ball carrying, and adopted the new game. In 1876, the Intercollegiate Football Association (IFA) was established using rules that emphasized kicking (one kicked goal equaled four touchdowns).

Yale's Walter Camp, a key figure, played for six years (1876–1882), and then became the unpaid coach. From 1883 to 1891, Yale lost just three games. Camp, an innovator, stressed rational management (organized practices, strategy, and precision) and commercialization. He arranged for off-campus championships, usually in *New York City on Thanksgiving Day, that drew over thirty thousand fans by the early 1890s. Camp was responsible for most major rules innovations as a leader of the Rules Committee (1878–1925), including the number of players and field dimensions. He introduced the "down system," requiring the offense to advance the ball at least five yards in three plays, and established a means to restart play after each down. At a time when elites worried about their sons' masculinity, the violent mass plays of the 1890s helped observers identify football as a moral equivalent of war, certifying players' manliness.

Midwestern and western universities adopted the sport in the 1890s to gain recognition. Pressures to win gave rise to the professional coach, such as Amos Alonzo Stagg of the University of Chicago, who won 323 games, a number that remained unsurpassed for many years. Success depended on recruiting top players through athletic scholarships and on using graduate students, "special students" who did not meet normal admission standards, and even nonstudents. Coaches enrolled their athletes in easy classes, hired tutors, and arranged special examinations.

Problems of eligibility, brutality, commercialism, and poor sportsmanship convinced some schools to drop the sport. In 1905 President Theodore *Roosevelt, the preeminent advocate of "the strenuous life," invited college football leaders to the White House to discuss reform. A national conference followed, leading to the establishment of the Intercollegiate Athletic Association (IAA), renamed the *National Collegiate Athletic Association (NCAA) in 1910. The IAA banned freshman participation, required transfers to sit out one year, and limited eligibility to three years. New rules were introduced to open up play, including ten yards for a first down, no tackling below the knees, and legalization of the forward pass. Other changes intended to promote safety and spectator interest included requiring seven men on the line of scrimmage, four tries for a first down, revaluing touchdowns from five to six points, and streamlining the ball to make it easier to throw. In 1913 Notre Dame used the forward pass to upset Army, 35–13, popularizing the tactic and opening up play.

As football's popularity grew, Harvard in 1903 built the 38,000-seat Soldier's Field, then the largest seating capacity of any American sports field. The Yale Bowl (1913) held 67,000, and similar edifices arose at Syracuse, Princeton, and Chicago. In 1928 the University of Michigan build a football stadium seating 87,000. During Knute Rockne's thirteen years as head coach at Notre Dame (1918–1931), his teams won 105 games, lost 12, and tied 15. To generate tourism, urban boosters instituted postseason bowl games on the model of Pasadena's Rose Bowl (1901) in Miami (Orange), New Orleans (Sugar), El Paso (Sun), Dallas (Cotton), and elsewhere.

Army, Notre Dame, Fordham, Pittsburgh, and the University of Southern California dominated the game in the 1940s, while in the 1950s Oklahoma won forty-seven straight games. In the 1960s attendance rose by 50 percent while *television fees soared from $3 million in 1964 to $29 million in 1981. In 1984 the U.S. *Supreme Court ended the NCAA's cartel operations, allowing groups or individual schools to sell their own games.

Professional football, meanwhile, originated in western Pennsylvania, where industrialists hired mill hands or former collegians to entertain workers and alleviate labor tensions. The first pro, Pudge Heffelfinger, was paid five hundred dollars in 1892 to play a game for the Allegheny Athletic Association. By 1903 the center of pro football shifted to Canton, Massillon, and other industrial towns in Ohio. By 1915, some eighty-six professional and semiprofessional teams were competing, sponsored by social clubs, ethnic fraternities, and especially industrial labor relations departments. In 1920 the American Professional Football Association (renamed the National Football League [NFL] in 1922) was organized. It was primarily a midwestern organization of company-sponsored squads, including the Decatur Staleys (the future Chicago Bears), the brainchild of labor-relations director George Halas. The APFA's first star was Jim Thorpe, the all-around athlete who had excelled at the 1912 Olympic games. Thorpe played for the APFA's Canton Bulldogs, and was also the organization's figurehead president.

Initially, the NFL had a hard time competing with college football for fan support. Public acceptance was bolstered when Red *Grange, a celebrated football hero at the University of Illinois, signed with the Chicago Bears in 1925. Nonetheless, the NFL still struggled, paying most players about one hundred dollars a game. By 1934, all smaller NFL cities except Green Bay, Wisconsin, had dropped out. Important innovations included divisional play (1933); the College All-Star game (1934); and a player draft (1936) to increase competition. After *World War II, the new All-American Football Conference (1946–1949), with franchises across the country, competed with the NFL.

Television in the 1950s boosted the pro game, which continued to grow in popularity thereafter. The establishment of the rival American Football League in 1960 encouraged the NFL to expand. The bidding war for players led to a merger in 1966, and the first "superbowl" one year later. The sport was dominated in the 1960s by Vince Lombardi's Green Bay Packers, who won five championships. By the end of the twentieth century, pro football teams were among the most profitable sports franchises, profiting from capacity crowds, concessions, product endorsements by players, and pooled TV revenues involving many millions of dollars.

[*See also* Baseball; Basketball; Education: Collegiate Education; Education: The Rise of the University; Popular Culture; Sports.]

• Tom Bennett et al., *The NFL's Official Encyclopedic History of Professional Football*, 1977. Ronald Smith, *Sports and Freedom: The Rise of Big-Time College Athletics*, 1988. David S. Neft and Richard M. Cohen, *The Football Encyclopedia: The Complete History of Professional Football from 1892 to the Present*, 1991. Murray Sperber, *Shake Down the Thunder: The Creation of Notre Dame Football*, 1993. Robin Lester, *Stagg's University: The Rise, Decline and Fall of Big-Time Football*, 1995. Robert W. Peterson, *Pigskin: The Early Years of Pro Football*, 1997.

—Steven A. Riess

FORD, GERALD (1913–), thirty-eighth president of the United States. Born Leslie L. King Jr. in Omaha, Nebraska, Ford moved with his mother, Dorothy, to her hometown, Grand Rapids, Michigan, following the breakup of her marriage in 1915. There Dorothy married Gerald R. Ford, a local merchant, who adopted her son and gave him his name. Young Ford excelled at sports and in the classroom. Graduating in 1935 from the University of Michigan, where he starred as a lineman on the football team, Ford attended Yale Law School before serving as a naval officer in the Pacific during *World War II. He entered politics as a Republican in 1948, winning a seat in the U.S. House of Representatives. That year he married Betty Warren, a Grand Rapids native.

Known as a conservative in fiscal matters, a moderate on social issues, and an internationalist in foreign policy, Ford initiated no major legislation during his long tenure in the House. Though he rose through Republican ranks to become minority leader in 1965, his true ambition—to be Speaker of the House—remained elusive, despite Republican presidential victories in 1968 and 1972. With Democrats firmly in control of Congress, Ford considered retirement from politics; but a series of Republican scandals altered his plans. In October 1973, Vice President Spiro Agnew resigned from office amid charges of bribery and tax fraud. President Richard M. *Nixon, facing investigation himself in the unfolding *Watergate drama, nominated the popular and easily confirmable Ford to succeed Agnew under the Twenty-fifth Amendment. When Nixon resigned in August 1974 to stave off *impeachment, Gerald Ford became president.

Americans appeared ready for an honest leader with decent values and an ordinary touch. As the new president joked, "I'm a Ford, not a Lincoln." Yet he, too, became enmeshed in the Watergate morass by granting Nixon a "full, free, and absolute pardon" in the hope of ending this "national nightmare." Within days, his public approval rating dropped from 72 to 49 percent.

He also faced a bleak economic picture. As energy costs spiraled, *unemployment and inflation reached the highest levels in years. Believing a balanced federal budget essential to recovery, Ford proposed sizeable cuts in government programs. But the Democratic Congress called for increased federal spending to spur the economy and create new jobs. As a result, Ford vetoed more than sixty major bills during his short tenure in office.

In foreign affairs, he sought unsuccessfully to extend emergency aid to the government of South Vietnam, which fell to the Communists in 1975. In May 1975, demonstrating American willpower after the Vietnam debacle, Ford ordered the Marines to free the crew of the *Mayagüez*, a U.S. merchant vessel siezed by Cambodia. The mission succeeded, but at a cost of forty-one Marines' lives. More broadly, he worked to maintain the policy of détente begun by Nixon and Henry *Kissinger, who remained as secretary of state. Aspiring to win the White House on his own, Ford, at the 1976 Republican National Convention, narrowly beat back a challenge from conservative Ronald *Reagan. In the general election he faced Democrat Jimmy *Carter, who portrayed himself as an "outsider" with no ties to the Washington "establishment." The media, meanwhile, caught Ford in a series of bumbling accidents and misstatements, such as his insistence that "there is no Soviet domination of Eastern Europe." On election day, Carter narrowly won.

Gerald Ford restored confidence and integrity to a badly damaged presidential office. In addition, his domestic policies laid the groundwork for the conservative Republican presidential administrations of the 1980s.

[*See also* Cold War; Energy Crisis of the 1970s; Federal Government, Executive Branch: The Presidency; Federal Government, Legislative Branch: House of Representatives; Republican Party; Vietnam War.]

• Gerald R. Ford, *A Time to Heal: The Autobiography of Gerald R. Ford*, 1979. A. James Reichley, *Conservatives in an Age of Change: The Nixon and Ford Administrations*, 1981.

—David M. Oshinsky

FORD, HENRY (1863–1947), automobile manufacturer. Born on a farm near Dearborn, Michigan, Henry Ford as a young man held various jobs in *Detroit, including machine-shop apprentice, traction car operator, and engineer for the Edison Illuminating Company. Tinkering with internal combustion engines in his spare time, he produced his first prototype automobile in 1896. His racing cars gained national attention, and in 1903 he formed the Ford Motor Company and began commercial production. In the turbulent world of early automobile manufacturing, Ford initially stood out primarily for his race cars and his 1911 legal defeat of George B. Selden, who had tried to gain a monopoly over automobile manufacturing by taking out a series of patents in 1895.

Three contributions coalesced to assure Ford's worldwide reputation and his iconic status in the pantheon of U.S. heroes: the Model T, the moving assembly line, and the five-dollar day. The 1908 Model T was a remarkable match of technical design and social context. Well-built and inexpensive in contrast to its competitors, the Model T succeeded despite terrible roads and primitive repair facilities thanks to an exceptionally strong frame, high wheel clearance, and a fix-it-yourself simplicity. Growing demand led to production breakthroughs between 1908 and 1915 that came to be known collectively as the "Assembly Line" or simply "Fordism." But Ford's integrated handling of materials and machine-tool specialization also involved an authoritarian management style that led to high worker turnover. In response, Ford in January 1914 not only announced completion of the moving assembly line, but also approximately doubled daily wages, to five dollars a day, and shortened the workday from nine to eight hours. This combination of technical achievement and beneficence dramatically enhanced Ford's image and brought him international fame.

In 1916, at a price of $316 each, Ford sold 730,000 Model Ts. Sales faltered by the mid-1920s, however, as rival General Motors offered a range of attractively designed models in color. (The boxy Model T came only in black.) After a period of retooling, Ford introduced the smart Model A in 1928. The innovative V–8 engine came in 1932, but the company never regained the market dominance it had once enjoyed.

For Ford himself, fame took its toll, as his eccentricities and prejudices became increasingly evident. In an abortive effort to end *World War I through arbitration, he chartered a "peace ship" in December 1915 to sail to Europe. Ford's newspaper *The Dearborn Independent*, distributed in the 1920s through Ford dealers, disseminated a virulent *anti-Semitism. Confronted with a libel suit by a Jewish attorney, Ford issued a retraction and halted publication in 1927. Adolf Hitler quoted Ford with approval in his 1924 manifesto *Mein Kampf*.

Increasingly autocratic, Ford drove away creative lieutenants; bought out stockholders; and enforced employee conformity, on the job and off, with spies and sometimes brutal company police. His bitter anti-unionism led to outbreaks of bloody labor violence at Ford plants during the Great Depression. Only in 1941 did Ford sign a contract with the United Automobile Workers union.

In later life Ford increasingly withdrew from the day-to-day operations at his company's massive River Rouge plant, and lived reclusely on his two-thousand-acre Dearborn estate, Fairlane, where he pursued various pet projects and philanthropies, including Detroit's Henry Ford Hospital (which initially excluded Jewish physicians). Ford's agents scoured Great Britain and the United States for artifacts relating to the history of *technology, which after 1929 he housed in a museum near his estate, called the Edison Institute. The museum was also a fully accredited school, where students from kindergarten through twelfth grade could study amid physical reminders of technological progress. Nearby stood Greenfield Village, Ford's replica of a bucolic preindustrial community. An elusive figure, Ford shunned visitors but roamed the grounds alone at night. He also restored the Old Wayside Inn in Sudbury, Massachusetts, immortalized by the poet Henry Wadsworth Longfellow.

Ford's obsession with these projects and his growing aversion to work-a-day management reveal a man caught in the classic ambivalence of the modernist technological aesthetic. He exulted in the march of inventive progress on display in his museum, while in Greenfield Village he nostalgically invoked a world untroubled by change. The paradox of Ford's attachment to his premodern fantasy world coupled with his heroic stature as a technological innovator helps explain his enduring grip on the American imagination.

The *Ford Foundation, established by Henry Ford and his son Edsel in 1936, ultimately received many millions in nonvoting Ford Motor Company stock, making it one of America's wealthiest foundations.

[*See also* Automobile Racing; Automotive Industry; Congress of Industrial Organizations; Industrialization; Mass Production; Motor Vehicles; Peace Movements; Reuther, Walter.]

• Allan Nevins with Frank E. Hill, *Ford*, 3 vol., 1954–1963. Anne Jardim, *The First Henry Ford: A Study in Personality and Business Leadership*, 1970. David L. Lewis, *The Public Image of Henry Ford: An American Folk Hero and His Company*, 1976. Stephen Meyer III, *The Five Dollar Day: Labor, Management and Social Control in the Ford Motor Company, 1908–1921*, 1981. Robert Lacey, *Ford: The Men and the Machine*, 1986. Donald Finlay Davis, *Conspicuous Production: Automobiles and Elites in Detroit, 1899–1933*, 1988.

—John M. Staudenmaier

FORD FOUNDATION. Through most of its modern history beginning in 1950, the Ford Foundation was the nation's largest philanthropic foundation. In 1999, its assets, $11.4 billion, were surpassed by the Bill and Melinda Gates Foundation ($17.1 billion) and the David and Lucille Packard Foundation ($13.0 billion). In 1998 the Ford Foundation made grants totaling $453.4 million, aimed at strengthening democratic values, reducing *poverty and injustice, promoting international cooperation, and advancing human achievement.

The foundation was established in 1936, in part to save the Ford family from having to sell the Ford Motor Company to pay taxes on the estates of Henry *Ford and his son Edsel. It was transformed from a small Michigan philanthropy in 1950 when it inherited 88 percent of the company's stock from their estates. Paul G. Hoffman, former head of the *Marshall Plan, was president from 1951 to 1953. By 1976 the foundation no longer held Ford company stock and no family members remained on the Board of Trustees. The greatly enlarged foundation spun off the Fund for the Advancement of Education, the Fund for Adult Education (a pioneer in educational *television), and the controversial Fund for the Republic. It was a leader in promoting public interest law, *civil rights, ballet and repertory theater, Third World agricultural development, and environmental protection.

The foundation's New York headquarters, a twelve-story structure near the *United Nations completed in 1967, has been designated a historical landmark by the New York City Landmarks Preservation Commission. The foundation also has fourteen offices in Asia, Africa, the Middle East, Latin America and the Caribbean, and Russia. Susan V. Berresford, who joined the foundation in 1970 as a program assistant, became its seventh president in 1996, succeeding Franklin A. Thomas, who had held the post for seventeen years.

[*See also* Philanthropy and Philanthropic Foundations.]

• Richard Magat, *The Ford Foundation at Work: Philanthropic Choices, Methods, and Styles*, Plenum Publishing 1979. Francis X. Sutton, "The Ford Foundation: The Early Years," *Daedalus* 116, no. 1 (Winter 1987): 41–91.

—Richard Magat

FORDISM. *See* Ford, Henry; Mass Production; Scientific Management.

FORD MOTOR COMPANY. *See* Automotive Industry.

FOREIGN AID. Foreign aid includes private or public bilateral or multilateral assistance to nations suffering the ravages of war, natural calamity, or long-standing poverty. Foreign aid may also be given for reasons relating to U.S. economic, diplomatic, or national-security interests. The concept derived from humanitarian concerns and, in a larger sense, from the processes of colonialism, world war, and economic depression. The Depression of the 1930s, *World War II, and the *Cold War, for example, demonstrated the necessity of resource transfers from rich to poor nations in order to correct the inherent capitalist tendency toward unequal income distribution and concomitant socioeconomic and political upheavals. Once poor nations received capital and technology, the conventional wisdom held, they would "take off" into self-sustained economic growth.

By the 1940s, U.S. public and private policy-makers had embraced an economic development theory that identified the causes of poverty and underdevelopment as internal to particular societies. Their solutions centered on external private capital transfers and technical assistance, as well as on the natural operation of free trade and comparative advantage. During the second half of the twentieth century, foreign aid meant giving capital (grants or loans), *technology, equipment, and food to the less developed world. It also entailed state efforts to enhance the proper functioning of the private market.

For the United States, giving foreign aid served overlapping economic, military, political, and humanitarian purposes. It could help expand export markets to alleviate domestic industrial and agricultural surpluses, guarantee the availability of strategic natural resources, or bolster the political fortunes of foreign allies. Whether operating through bilateral programs or international institutions (e.g., the *World Bank or *International Monetary Fund), foreign aid helped the United States to incorporate new states into an expanding capitalist world-economy.

Government foreign-aid programs originated with wartime relief and private philanthropic agencies. After *World War I, for example, the privately sponsored American Federated Russian Famine Relief Committee worked closely with the U.S. government to help alleviate large-scale famine in the Soviet Union, subsidize the sale of American agricultural surpluses, and aid anti-Bolshevik factions. During World War II, the government took control of voluntary relief agencies through licensing procedures and created new bureaucracies that directly dispensed foreign aid (e.g., the Office of Inter-American Affairs and the U.S.–dominated United Nations Relief and Rehabilitation Administration).

Foreign aid became a major government institution during the Cold War. The European Recovery Program or *Marshall Plan (1948–1952) sought to reconstruct European economies and reintegrate them into the capitalist world economy while creating a unified economic bloc against the Soviet Union's influence. The Point Four Program, created by the Act for International Development (1950), proposed that American technical experts help agrarian nations to stimulate their domestic economies—especially the export of selected crops and raw materials—enhance their ability to purchase American exports, attract private foreign capital, and become integrated into the global economy. Such economic growth supposedly would build Third World political stability and allegiance to the West. The Foreign Assistance Act of 1961, which created the *Agency for International Development (AID), also identified development aid as a mechanism for improving the lives of poor people in developing nations and undermining the appeal of non- or anticapitalist models of economic development.

During the Cold War, American aid funded large-scale infrastructure projects such as highways and hydroelectric dams. Recipient nations spent the bulk of their foreign aid in the United States to purchase needed technology, machinery, and other capital goods. While acknowledging that much of U.S. foreign assistance went to elites in the recipient nations, aid officials predicted that this process eventually would lead to expanded national output and higher living standards for all. Widespread disillusionment with this trickle-down strategy led to the Foreign Assistance Act of 1973 and the International Development and Food Assistance Act of 1975. Emphasizing "basic human needs" and "appropriate technology," this legislation targeted Third World poverty by providing assistance for health, nutrition, population planning, and rural development. But the "new direction" in foreign aid failed, in large part because it continued to ignore power and class conflicts between rich and poor at the local, national, and international levels.

The presidential administration of Ronald *Reagan refocused on general economic growth and direct aid to private businesses. Foreign-aid agencies during the 1980s and 1990s insisted that developing nations adopt austerity programs (especially in the sphere of social welfare and price controls); liberal trade policies; and market-oriented, open-door economies geared to export promotion. The demise of the Soviet Union in 1989 eliminated some of the strategic rationale for foreign aid, and levels of various forms of assistance reached new lows as Americans focused their attentions domestically. As the twentieth century ended, the concept of foreign aid found itself increasingly enervated by a fundamentalist belief in private markets and the global economy as engines of growth.

[*See also* Agriculture: Since 1920; Birth Control and Family Planning; Depressions, Economic; Economic Development; Foreign Relations; Foreign Trade, U.S.; United Nations.]

• Merle Curti and Kendal Birr, *Prelude to Point Four: American Technical Missions Overseas, 1838–1938*, 1954. Teresa Hayter, *Aid as Imperialism*, 1971. Emily S. Rosenberg, *Spreading the American Dream: American Economic and Cultural Expansion, 1890–1945*, 1982. Nathan Godfried, *Bridging the Gap between Rich and Poor: American Economic Development Policy toward the Arab East, 1942–1949*, 1987. Frances Moore Lappe, Rachel Schurman, and Kevin Danaher, *Betraying the National Interest*, 1987. Vernon W. Ruttan, *United States Development Assistance Policy: The Domestic Politics of Foreign Economic Aid*, 1996.

—Nathan Godfried

FOREIGN RELATIONS

FOREIGN RELATIONS: OVERVIEW

Although America's relations with other nations have varied according to specific regions and eras, certain themes often recur. These themes—including free trade, democracy, continental expansion, and *internationalism—have not always been intellectually consistent or gone uncontested. Still, their recurrent invocation suggests ongoing patterns in American foreign policy.

American leaders of the Revolutionary and early national periods sought to free their international trade from mercantile regulations. As colonials heavily dependent upon foreign commerce, Americans had resented British trade laws passed in a Parliament that accorded them no representation. After independence, American policy-makers continued to assert the right to trade freely with other nations, a policy that helped bring on the *Quasi-War with France and the *War of 1812 with Britain. In the 1820s and 1830s the United States officially recognized the new nations in Latin America, where independence movements similarly embraced free trade and sought to escape Spain's imperial restrictions.

American leaders viewed *republicanism and democracy as the political forms that logically accompanied free trade. Both free government and free trade arose from a liberal philosophy that opposed special privileges for entrenched or hereditary elites. Thomas *Jefferson expressed the popular view of America as a beacon of liberty for the world, although he, like most white Americans of his day, discussed liberty in the context of racial and gender ideologies that effectively excluded nonwhites and women from citizenship.

Twentieth-century American leaders continued to advocate free-trading policies and the spread of democracy. Secretary of State John *Hay championed the "*Open Door" policy in China and elsewhere. Woodrow *Wilson's insistence on the trading rights of neutral nations helped bring the United States into *World War I against Germany in 1917, and Wilson then pledged that the war would "save the world for democracy." His *Fourteen Points enshrined both the principles of "freedom of the seas" and political "self-determination." In 1941, President Franklin Delano *Roosevelt took the country into a second great conflict, *World War II, this time opposing Japanese and German fascism and the threat that these nations might build exclusive trading spheres. Roosevelt even pressured Britain, America's wartime ally, to end its system of imperial preference and embrace free trade, an expectation that ultimately shaped the *General Agreement on Tariffs and Trade in 1948.

During the *Cold War Era, free trade, once an ideology of the underdog in a mercantilist world, became a powerful tool for the global spread of U.S. *capitalism. Supporting open markets and opposing state ownership of economic enterprises, the United States created trade and investment opportunities for its business enterprises. The collapse of the communist bloc after 1989 signaled the triumph of American policy, and the first post–Cold War president, Bill *Clinton, worked strenuously for global trade, especially through the *North American Free Trade Agreement and the World Trade Organization.

The goal of spreading democracy played a prominent rhetorical role in Cold War policy-making. American leaders could support pro-U.S. dictators, especially in the Third World, on the claim that noncommunist regimes, whatever their character, strengthened the "Free World" and thus bolstered "democracy." The *Korean and *Vietnam Wars, and indeed Cold War rivalries throughout the world, were all justified within the "democracy-versus-communism" framework. President Ronald *Reagan and his successors even more explicitly promoted "democratization," particularly through the use of elections to transfer political power. Like free trade, this agenda received a boost with the collapse of Soviet power.

Continental *expansionism represents another powerful theme in early American foreign policy. Many colonists had supported the independence movement to avoid Britain's *Proclamation of 1763, restricting settlement west of the Appalachians. Once independent, Americans zealously pushed westward. Where European nations blocked their way, Washington successfully negotiated, concluding the *Louisiana Purchase in 1803, gaining East Florida from Spain in 1819, annexing Texas in 1845, and settling northern boundary controversies with England (the largest over Oregon in 1846). Victory in the *Mexican War (1848) brought a huge cession of land, including *California, and fulfilled the dreams of empire-builders who had proclaimed America's "*Manifest Destiny" to reach the Pacific. Through wars and treaties, and invoking an ideology of racial superiority, white Americans also took lands occupied by Indian nations. In the 1890s the last of the Indian resistance was quelled, and the continental empire secured.

In the twentieth century, the ideology of continental expansion evolved into the imperial acquisitions associated with the *Spanish-American War of 1898 and Theodore *Roosevelt's 1904 corollary to the *Monroe Doctrine, asserting U.S. police power over the Western Hemisphere. Entrenched beliefs about continental security also emerged, however, particularly after World War I, in the form of *isolationism—that is, the desire to avoid entanglements in foreign conflicts and to concentrate instead on domestic development.

In the twentieth century, the theme of internationalism modified or eclipsed the nineteenth century's emphasis on continental destiny. Woodrow Wilson provided the most powerful articulation of American internationalism: the view that peace for all nations could be achieved through "collective security." Although the United States never joined Wilson's *League of Nations, his internationalist vision underlay the later creation of the *United Nations and other international bodies. Regional collective-security pacts, especially the *North Atlantic Treaty Organization (1949), also expressed this internationalist policy.

Although differences over how to define and promote free trade, democracy, continental expansion, and internationalism engendered ongoing debates, these broad themes nonetheless shaped much of U.S. foreign policy.

[*See also* Federal Government, Executive Branch: Department of State; Texas Republic and Annexation.]

• Robert Dallek, *The American Style of Foreign Policy: Cultural Politics and Foreign Affairs,* 1983. Michael H. Hunt, *Ideology and U.S. Foreign Policy,* 1987. Walter LaFeber, *The American Age: United States Foreign Policy at Home and Abroad, 1750–the Present,* 1996. Walter A. McDougall, *Promised Land, Crusader State: The American Encounter with the World since 1776,* 1997.

—Emily S. Rosenberg

FOREIGN RELATIONS: THE ECONOMIC DIMENSION

From the time of Thomas *Jefferson to the present, U.S. policy-makers and private interest groups have viewed economic ties with the rest of the world as vital to the nation's well-being. The definition of U.S. economic objectives and their impact on foreign relations, however, have been hotly debated. U.S. foreign economic relations may be organized into three periods: the preindustrial era, roughly 1790–1850; the era of the industrial revolution, 1850–1920; and the era of U.S. economic pre-eminence, 1920 to the present.

Preindustrial America was not extensively involved in world

affairs. Preoccupied with continental expansion and the issue of *slavery, the nation focused inward. Yet the founders recognized the connections between internal development and overseas commerce. America's first foreign treaty, signed with France in 1778, included a section promising trade reciprocity. From George *Washington to James *Madison, U.S. presidents defended American commercial shipping and "neutral rights" from the Barbary pirates, Napoleonic conquest, and Great Britain's confiscation of ships and impressment of sailors. Presidents Jefferson and Madison tried to use trade as a diplomatic weapon, only to be disappointed when U.S. *embargo acts led to domestic unrest and the *War of 1812.

America's early economic diplomacy did not serve defensive ends alone. The effort to secure rights to warehouse agricultural products in New Orleans for transshipment elsewhere led Jefferson to conclude the 1803 *Louisiana Purchase with France, which ushered in a new era of territorial expansion. Indeed, land, rather than overseas markets, constituted the most alluring economic prize during the agrarian, preindustrial period.

The controversy over slavery expansion and the *Civil War temporarily interrupted U.S. expansion, but *Gilded Age *industrialization reinvigorated and reshaped the expansionist urge. Marxist analysts trace the late nineteenth-century imperialism of western powers and Japan to the rise of monopoly *capitalism and the need to find investment opportunities for surplus capital. "Revisionist" U.S. scholars, following the lead of historian William Appleman Williams, advanced an alternative thesis: that America's extremely competitive industrial economy necessitated the export of surplus goods rather than capital. Therefore, the United States sought an informal overseas empire based on the principle of liberal trade. The depression-plagued 1890s, these scholars point out, ended with the *Spanish-American War (leading to U.S. acquisition of Guam, *Puerto Rico, and the *Philippines), the enunciation of the "*Open Door" policy toward China, the construction of the *Panama Canal, and military interventions in the Caribbean. All these developments enhanced America's foreign-trade and investment prospects. The safeguarding of U.S. trade and loans to Britain and its allies also influenced the U.S. decision in 1917 to enter *World War I. Both these schools, the Marxist and the revisionist, saw economics as paramount in driving foreign policy.

Other historians, however, have contested the centrality of economics to U.S. foreign policy, and have emphasized instead the nation's security needs, journalistic jingoism, the influence of an imperialist-minded elite, and ideological ethnocentrism. These historians stress that the export of U.S. products was accompanied by the equally important export of U.S. culture. Popular entertainers, Christian missionaries, and philanthropic organizations, often acting independently of Washington, spearheaded the drive to spread American tastes, ideas, and values.

By 1920, when the United States had replaced Great Britain as the world's leading creditor nation and industrial power, America entered a new era of economic preeminence. Washington's failure to adjust to these new realities by lowering protective *tariffs and easing Europe's postwar debt, however, helped spark the global depression of the 1930s and *World War II. Last-minute economic sanctions against Japan, including revocation of petroleum-export licenses, only heightened Japan's long-festering grievances about global inequalities, and its surprise attack on *Pearl Harbor soon followed.

Eager to avoid a repetition of the mistakes of the interwar years, the United States in 1944 took the lead in establishing the Bretton Woods system, which stabilized global finances through the *International Monetary Fund and the *World Bank, and liberalized trade through the *General Agreement on Tariffs and Trade (GATT). The *Marshall Plan, the reconstruction of Japan, assistance to industrializing East Asia, and development aid to recently decolonized areas—coinciding with the *Cold War and Washington's anticommunist security policies—deepened America's embrace of economic *internationalism and global *Keynesianism. International trade, the growth of U.S.–based *multinational enterprises, and the activities of nongovernmental organizations such as the Ford and Rockefeller foundations further enhanced America's worldwide presence.

Revisionist historians, informed by "world systems" theory, see in America's recent economic expansion an effort by government and *business to achieve global hegemony for a capitalist elite. According to this view, U.S. economic power relegated less industrialized states to an inferior, "dependent" status within the world capitalist system as producers of raw materials and food stuffs. Others, invoking corporatist theory, stress that a variety of organized elements in the United States and abroad—business, labor, farmers, and government—forged a transnational postwar consensus in support of liberal internationalism. Still other "modernization" theorists conclude that America's economic dominance has confirmed capitalism's modernizing impact throughout the world.

The end of the Cold War highlighted the economic dimension of American foreign policy. Presidents George *Bush and Bill *Clinton emphasized the global liberalization of trade and investment and tried to address new problems: How could the United States assist the conversion of former communist societies to capitalism? How would regional trading blocs such as the European Union and the *North American Free Trade Agreement (NAFTA) affect the world economy? How did America's global commercial activity relate to the nation's desire to protect the environment, improve exploitive labor conditions, and advance human rights?

In summary, the economic dimension of American foreign relations has historically been multidimensional and subject to varied interpretations by historians. But all agree that as the twenty-first century unfolds, the U.S. economy is increasingly interconnected with the world economy, and the economic dimension of foreign relations overlaps an array of global issues.

[*See also* Bretton Woods Conference; Corporatism; Depressions, Economic; Economic Development; Expansionism; Ford Foundation; Foreign Trade, U.S; Missionary Movement; Post–Cold War Era.]

• William Appleman Williams, *The Tragedy of American Diplomacy*, 1959. Gabriel Kolko, *The Roots of American Foreign Policy: An Analysis of Power and Purpose*, 1969. Emily Rosenberg, *Spreading the American Dream: American Economic and Cultural Expansion, 1890–1945*, 1982. Robert L. Beisner, *From the Old Diplomacy to the New, 1865–1900*, 1986. Michael J. Hogan, *The Marshall Plan: America, Britain, and the Reconstruction of Western Europe, 1947–1952*, 1987. Thomas J. McCormick, *America's Half Century: United States Foreign Policy in the Cold War*, 1989. Michael J. Hogan and Thomas G. Paterson, *Explaining the History of American Foreign Relations*, 1991. Diane B. Kunz, *Guns and Butter: America's Cold War Economic Diplomacy*, 1997.

—Dennis Merrill

FOREIGN RELATIONS: THE CULTURAL DIMENSION

The nineteenth-century Protestant *missionary movement constituted the first significant attempt to spread American culture internationally. Inspired by Evangelical impulses and notions of racial destiny, American missionaries promoted their religious and cultural values in "heathen" countries. Although conversion rates proved disappointing and religious enthusiasm gradually waned, many foreign missionaries continued to play important roles as social reformers abroad, shifting their emphasis from saving souls to improving education, agriculture, and living standards.

In the early twentieth century, American mass entertainment also began to spread globally. Buffalo Bill *Cody's Wild West Show and Hollywood's silent *films played on all continents, erasing boundaries of language and culture. During *World War I, the Committee on Public Information (CPI), charged with selling America's ideals, vigorously promoted American films. Taking advantage of government support and the popularity of such films as D. W. *Griffith's *Civilization* and *Birth of a Nation*, Hollywood captured foreign film markets. In the 1920s, when some foreign governments enacted quotas to protect their film industries from U.S. competitors, pressure from Washington and evasive action by the American film industry overcame the barriers. Before 1930, American films constituted 95 percent of those shown in Britain and Canada, 70 percent in France, 80 percent in South America.

America's *radio industry also received a jump-start during World War I, when the U.S. government nationalized it and expanded its capacity. The Radio Corporation of America was founded by Owen D. Young in 1919 at President Woodrow *Wilson's urging, and the products of American broadcasters and radio manufacturers soon enjoyed a global reach.

During the 1920s, social reform movements also spread American values. Rotary clubs, the *YMCA and YWCA, the American Boy Scouts, the *American Federation of Labor, and the Women's International League for Peace and Freedom, among many others, internationalized their organizations. John *Dewey tried to bring educational change to China; the economist Edwin Kemmerer promoted American-style reserve banks and currency systems worldwide; and Elizabeth Washburn Wright crusaded internationally against narcotics. Political reformers even spread the American game of *baseball as a bulwark against instability. The Rockefeller Foundation launched global health programs and established colleges throughout Asia. Though these varied efforts projected no single cultural message or set of values, they did represent a quintessentially American faith in *voluntarism.

The outpouring of U.S.-made cars and appliances during the 1920s further extended American cultural influence. Woolworth, A&P, Safeway, and Montgomery Ward opened stores worldwide; Coca-Cola expanded its bottling; American *jazz won fans abroad; and mass *tourism brought throngs of Americans to Europe and to such resort destinations as Cuba. Meanwhile, American Studies became a respected academic field in major foreign universities.

These trends stirred a backlash among some groups of cultural nationalists, who assailed the "threat" of American culture. The Depression of the 1930s accentuated this cultural nationalism. In Germany, Adolf Hitler's National Socialists, charging that American *popular culture was dominated by Jews, banned U.S. films and jazz. Japan similarly restricted American film and news services. Left-leaning Mexico, embroiled in an oil controversy with the United States, embargoed films considered offensive and built its own highly successful film industry.

*World War II, however, brought new opportunities for American cultural expansion. The Office of Inter-American Affairs and the Office of War Information distributed American magazines and films. U.S. troops spread a taste for American chewing gum, blue jeans, T-shirts, jazz, Coke, and cigarettes worldwide. In postwar Germany, Austria, and Japan, U.S. agencies developed programs to introduce American values into education, journalism, and films.

After the war, *anticommunism became the central rationale for an assertive "cultural policy." Congress funded educational exchanges under the the Smith-Mundt Act of 1948, which created the Fulbright program. In 1950 the Harry S. *Truman administration increased funding for the *Voice of America and established information offices, libraries, and mass-media products in many countries. The American film industry's Motion Picture Export Association worked with Washington to extend Hollywood's dominance in foreign markets. The *United States Information Agency (1953) institutionalized and enlarged these cultural initiatives.

Consumer products continued to promote the American way of life. U.S.-style supermarkets, hotel and retail chains, and installment buying expanded globally in the postwar period. In western Europe, the *Marshall Plan's promise of consumer abundance and high wages constituted a powerful *Cold War cultural weapon. American-based nongovernmental organizations also flourished internationally.

American cultural power remained controversial, however. In the 1960s and 1970s, the United Nation's Economic and Social Council promoted a "New World Information Order" to help developing nations break the American media's dominance. But in the late 1980s, U.S. cultural expansion benefited from the decline of state-owned broadcasting systems and the collapse of communist governments in eastern Europe and the Soviet Union (with their controlled media). The proliferation of privately owned media outlets especially affected *television. As new networks sought to fill airtime, they turned to low-cost American producers, and U.S. entainment programs such as *Dallas* and *Baywatch* became global hits.

While most Americans assumed that their cultural influence was benevolent, critics spoke of "cultural imperialism," charging that Americanization "colonized" the minds of other peoples. Other observers argued that people in cultural "contact zones" quickly learn to borrow selectively and adapt cultural meanings to suit themselves. However interpreted, twentieth-century American-style culture clearly became a significant world force.

[*See also* Foreign Trade, U.S.; Philanthropy and Philanthropic Foundations.]

• Merle Curti, *American Philanthropy Abroad: A History*, 1963. Emily S. Rosenberg, *Spreading the American Dream: American Cultural and Economic Expansion, 1890–1945*, 1982. Frank Costigliola, *Awkward Dominion: American Political, Economic, and Cultural Relations with Europe, 1919–1933*, 1984. Akira Iriye, *The Globalizing of America, 1913–1945*, 1993. Gilbert M. Joseph, Catherine C. LeGrand, and Ricardo D. Salvatore, eds., *Close Encounters of Empire: Writing the Cultural History of U.S.–Latin American Relations*, 1998.

—Emily S. Rosenberg

FOREIGN RELATIONS: U.S. RELATIONS WITH EUROPE

John *Winthrop's image of a "city upon a hill," the biblical motif identifying America as a divinely inspired corrective of the ills of the Old World, had been secularized by the time of the *Revolutionary War. But its essence was expressed in Thomas *Paine's **Common Sense* (1776), which represented the colonies as victims of an alien and exploitive British imperialism that endangered the freedoms and prosperity of Americans.

Independence and the Early Republic: No "Entangling Alliances." This sense of independence from the ways of the Old World, which some scholars call "American exceptionalism," manifested itself in the first American effort to win support of Britain's European rivals in the struggle for independence. After the *Declaration of Independence, the colonies were convinced that France would be the instrument to secure their freedom without any entangling obligations on their part. Such was the reasoning behind John *Adams's Plan of 1776, which was based on an assumption that Europe would promote America's break with Britain both to open markets formerly monopolized by the mother country and to weaken Britain's economic power. France was a vital cog in the plan that would serve the war effort without reciprocal American commitments. Adams's language could not have been plainer: "I am not for soliciting any political connection, or military assistance . . . from France. I wish for nothing but commerce, a mere marine treaty with them."

American military setbacks on the field and France's hesitations about abetting rebellion against a monarchy, however, forced the new nation to settle for the Treaty of Paris in 1778. This treaty brought France into the war as an ally but at the price of assuming the entanglements that Paine and Adams had felt would be unnecessary as well as undesirable. The subsequent twenty-two years of experience with the French alliance confirmed for Americans the wisdom of abstaining from alliances with any nation of the Old World. It was not that France was more dangerous than the other two powers the United States had to confront: Britain and Spain. Rather, Americans under the weak Confederation and the somewhat stronger Federal Union recognized that their independence was not secure and that they needed maximum flexibility in negotiating the various threats posed by European rivalries. Thomas *Jefferson offered the definitive statement of this view in his first inaugural address in 1801, when he expressed America's goal: "Peace, Commerce, and honest friendship with all nations—entangling alliances with none."

Britain was the major problem for the United States in its first generation. British acceptance of American independence was accompanied by efforts to substitute economic for political dominance. The former mother country also nourished the idea that the United States would not long endure, and used America's unwillingness or inability to fulfill certain articles of the peace treaty as a pretext for retaining bases in the Northwest, promoting unrest among Indian nations, and encouraging an Anglophile American mercantile class to support British interests.

The replacement of the weak Confederation with a potentially stronger Federal Union in 1789 did not end the nation's problems with the Old World. Spain intrigued to separate western territories from the Union. Britain identified itself with a *Federalist party dependent on the British economy for the prosperity of mercantile interests. France, enmeshed in revolution, sought to exploit its alliance with the United States to promote its aggressive foreign policy. In brief, the administrations of George *Washington and John Adams in the 1790s were embroiled in foreign relations that threatened the stability, if not the survival, of the new nation. In this decade the United States managed to keep Spain at bay, win limited access to the British economy, and conclude a naval war with France by terminating the Treaty of Paris in the Convention of Mortefontaine (1800).

Disengagement from Europe did not follow immediately, however. The United States under presidents Thomas Jefferson and James *Madison could not escape the long reach of the Napoleonic wars. The wars led to disputes with both Britain and France over neutral rights, and ultimately to war with Britain in 1812. Not until the Treaty of *Ghent in 1814 did the United States feel free from the political power of Europe. The trauma attending Britain's impressment of American sailors and France's seizure of American ships had underscored the principle of freedom of the seas, which lingered on in attenuated forms into the twentieth century. Even more significant was the legacy of political nonentanglement with Europe that lasted well into the twentieth century. Not until 1949 when the *North Atlantic Treaty Organization (NATO) was created did the United States formally reenter "entangling alliances" with nations of the Old World.

The Monroe Doctrine and Beyond. America's pride in surmounting challenges from the three European powers found expression in the *Monroe Doctrine in 1823, the most notable symbol of American *isolationism in the nineteenth century. It had been presaged by American success in forcing Britain to accept a joint occupation of the Oregon territory in 1818 and Spain to cede Florida in the *Adams-Onís Treaty the following year. Additionally, Spain was forced to accept an American interpretation of the boundary between Mexico and Louisiana. Secretary of State John Quincy *Adams, perhaps the greatest statesman in American history, was the prime mover in these diplomatic victories, and even he might have achieved more in Texas had he pressed his advantage. In a sense the Monroe Doctrine was an anticlimax, an American challenge to France and Spain to abandon ideas of reconquering Latin America and to Russia to desist from its push down the west coast of North America. Adams knew that it was in Britain's interest to support these challenges, even as its leaders resented America's triumphalism.

But the Monroe Doctrine's significance lay less in its specific warnings against European interference in the Americas than in its insistence on America's intention to refrain from involvement with Europe. This abstention from European affairs was visible when the United States gave only sympathy to Greeks seeking the freedoms Americans enjoyed, and, a generation later, when Hungary won only America's good wishes in its revolution against Austria in 1848. Despite the emotional appeal of many of its causes, the Old World remained out of bounds for American intervention.

Having made its case for aloofness, the Monroe Doctrine essentially disappeared from American consciousness until the end of the nineteenth century. The nation turned inward to develop what Jefferson called "the empire of liberty" that would extend from coast to coast. Such was the concept of "*Manifest Destiny," a term coined in 1845 but expressive of America's aggressive westward expansion throughout its history. There was hostility to Manifest Destiny from the familiar adversary, Great Britain; from Canada to the north; and from the new nation of Mexico to the south. Britain no longer threatened U.S. security, but it was able to restrain American ambitions along the Maine–New Brunswick border and limit America's more expansive claims in the Oregon country, summed up in the rallying cry "54°40' or fight." Mexico proved less able to contain American expansionists, as the annexation of Texas and the *Mexican War in the 1840s demonstrated. But the measure of American power was less its acquisition of Mexican territory than in the deference Great Britain paid to the growing strength of the United States. Britain's willingness to accept compromise in the Pacific Northwest and to back off from support of Mexico resulted partly from the increasing contrast between a thinly populated Canada and a rapidly growing American population, and partly from an awareness of a need to keep the American market open to British manufacturers.

America at midcentury was not wholly absorbed in its own backyard. Isolation from the larger world was rarely equivalent to complete nonentanglement. While Latin America was neglected—aside from southern interest in Central America and the Caribbean—and Europe still held in suspicion, Americans looked to East Asia for economic opportunities and competed with Europeans in this arena. Nor did Europe, particularly Britain, hesitate to intervene again in America when opportunities arose. The *slavery controversy and a destructive *Civil War offered chances for Britain to consider recognizing the Confederacy and for France to establish a satellite empire in Mexico. The Confederacy's military setbacks aborted Britain's hopes in 1863, and the Union victory in 1865 extinguished Emperor Maximilian's pro-French reign in Mexico.

The Gilded Age through World War I: Deepening Engagement. Although an increasingly industrialized post–Civil War America found itself in closer proximity to Europe than ever before, the negative image of the Old World endured. Europe was still considered a continent of monarchs and tyrants, dangerous to American values. But on at least two levels close ties bound the two worlds. One was the continuing flow of European *immigration that swelled the population of the United States and kept transatlantic links alive. This did not signify pressure for intimate relations, however; indeed, refugees fleeing poverty or repression in Ireland or Germany in the mid–nineteenth century, and Russia and Italy at the end of the century, probably reinforced isolationist prejudices. The other factor linking the two worlds was rising U.S. competition with Europe, particularly Britain, for new territories and new markets for agricultural and industrial products. As Manifest Destiny evolved into imperialist dreams, the United States built a navy to serve an overseas empire in the Pacific and the Caribbean, European imperialism having preempted Africa and Asia.

Spain once again was the primary victim of American expansion, in the *Spanish-American War of 1898, but Germany displaced Britain as potentially the more serious adversary.

British challenges to America's conception of the Monroe Doctrine faded by the end of the century, as reflected in British support of the United States at Manila Bay during the Spanish-American War and in Britain's concern over the challenge of imperial Germany to its supremacy on the high seas. Theodore *Roosevelt's foreign policy involved an informal collaboration with Britain. The common ground of Anglo-Saxon kinship became more visible both to Britons witnessing the decline of their imperial power and to American leaders who identified their newfound sense of world power with their British cousins.

Anglophilia was clearly an element driving Woodrow *Wilson's outlook on Europe in 1914. Britain and France represented a democratic culture far closer to America's than that of Germany and Austria. Long before the United States entered *World War I in 1917, the nation under Wilson's leadership had tilted toward the Allies. But this sentiment did not mean an abandonment of the tradition of nonentanglement. From the onset of war in 1914, the president and nation looked upon it as a typical expression of Old World behavior. Sympathy for Britain did not preclude objections to its maritime practices, similar to those of the Napoleonic period. Pressure for neutrality was increased by *Irish Americans and *German Americans, who countered the eastern establishment's pro-Allied sentiments.

Whether Allied propaganda, America's economic ties, or revulsion against German submarine warfare were individually or collectively responsible for the decision for war in 1917, America's entry into the conflict was not as an ally but as an "associated power," with the avowed aim of ending for all time the nationalistic conflicts that created war. The United States may have fought alongside Britain and France, but not for the same objectives, any more than the United States in 1812 shared the objectives of its cobelligerent, Napoleonic France. The cynical Old World remained as dangerous to idealistic Americans as it had been in the eighteenth century. The difference was that in the twentieth century, Wilson believed, the New World had the power to change Europe's habits through a *League of Nations to end all wars.

Since 1920: Isolationism; Military Alliances; Post–Cold War Uncertainty. Disillusionment over the failure of Wilson's vision to transform world politics plunged the nation more deeply into isolationism than it had been in the nineteenth century. Revulsion took the form of high *tariffs, restrictive *immigration laws, and debt-management policies that increased tensions between Europe and America, helped to bring on the Great Depression of the 1930s, and accounted for America's initial passivity as fascism and Nazism gained strength in Europe. Congress in the 1930s passed a series of *neutrality acts designed to avoid a repeat of the experience of World War I. Consequently, the outbreak of *World War II in 1939 found the United States officially in the same neutral stance that it had held at the beginning of World War I in 1914.

Neutrality was of shorter duration in World War II, however. While it took a Japanese attack on *Pearl Harbor in December 1941 to elicit a U.S. declaration of war, the Franklin Delano *Roosevelt administration, supported by public opinion, had a greater awareness of the stakes than in the past. The administration's judgment that a Nazi victory in Europe would imperil America's security carried greater weight than had Wilson's idealistic vision of a world without war. Despite the efforts of an isolationist *America First Committee, the United States abandoned its neutrality laws before Pearl Harbor. It became a de facto cobelligerent against Hitler's Germany through a lend-lease program—extended to the Soviet Union in 1941—and through antisubmarine patrols serving Great Britain in the Atlantic. Unlike the situation in World War I, the United States was now the dominant Western partner, leading a successful invasion of Europe in 1944 and providing supplies to help Russia defeat Germany in the East.

As the war drew to a close, the United States intended to use its role as a superpower to correct the mistakes of 1919. America would not only join the new league of nations, the *United Nations (UN), but would take the lead in maintaining a new world order. Any assumption that Soviet communism would easily coexist with democratic capitalism was quickly dispelled. Less than two years after the war's end, Europe still despaired of its future, fearing that it might fall under communist control through subversion or the electoral process. Recognizing the errors of the interwar period, a bipartisan foreign policy resolved to rebuild Europe through economic aid via the *Marshall Plan, and ultimately through the creation of NATO, linking America's fate with Europe's in an alliance with eleven European nations, including Britain and France. The intention was to contain communist expansion and in the process strengthen America's own economy, while fashioning a United States of Europe in the American image.

Fifty years later, the linkage remained in place. The Soviet Union and its communist system collapsed in the late 1980s and early 1990s, and a united Europe appeared to be emerging. But with the end of the communist menace, centrifugal forces inevitably arose. Isolationist voices called for the withdrawal of U.S. troops from Europe; Europeans chafed over American domination of the alliance; questions about the wisdom of enlarging the membership of NATO as well as about its role in dealing with civil wars on its periphery gave rise to larger questions about the future of European-American relations. Without the centripetal pressures that the Soviet challenge had presented, the fifty-year alliance could collapse. A unified Europe in the future could be less reliant upon the American connection, and an America looking to the Pacific might become more aloof from Europe. But as the twentieth century ended, there was as yet no substitute for an intimate American presence in Europe as a guarantor of security for both continents.

[*See also* Cold War; Expansionism; Foreign Trade; U.S.; Neutrality Acts; Post–Cold War Era; Quasi-War with France; Texas Republic and Annexation.]

• Samuel Flagg Bemis, *John Quincy Adams and the Foundations of American Foreign Policy*, 1949. Jean-Baptiste Duroselle, *From Wilson to Roosevelt: Foreign Policy of the United States, 1913–1945*, 1963. Philip Van Doren Stern, *When the Guns Roared: World Aspects of the American Civil War*, 1965. Max Savelle, *The International History of Angloamerica, 1492–1763*, 1967. Robert L. Beisner, *From the Old Diplomacy to the New, 1865–1900*, 1975. Melvyn L. Leffler, *A Preponderance of Power: National Security, the Truman Administration, and the Cold War*, 1992. Bradford Perkins, *The Creation of a Republican Empire, 1776–1865*, vol. 1, *The Cambridge History of American Foreign Relations*, 1993. Lawrence S. Kaplan, *NATO and the United States: The Enduring Alliance*, rev. ed., 1994. Walter McDougall, *Promised Land, Crusader State: America's Encounter with the World since 1776*, 1997.

—Lawrence S. Kaplan

FOREIGN RELATIONS: U.S. RELATIONS WITH ASIA

Since 1784, when the *Empress of China* set sail from *Boston for the Middle Kingdom, U.S. relations with Asia have revolved around four principal themes: economic factors, *immigration, strategic interests, and war. The particular shape, texture, and importance of these themes have depended on the specific circumstances of different time periods, but all four have always been present to some degree.

From the Early Republic through 1945: Trade; Expansionism; War. From 1784 to 1898, American interests focused on developing trade opportunities, initially with China, but later with Japan and other Asian nations. Of enormous assistance to American designs was Great Britain's use of military force during the first Opium War (1839–1842), resulting in greater British access to Chinese ports. By the Treaty of Wangxia in 1844, the U.S. negotiated the same concession. Trade with Japan grew steadily after Commodore Matthew Perry opened some commercial ties with Japan in 1854.

Immigration developed alongside trade relations as a major issue in the nineteenth century. Chinese laborers traveled to the United States, settled on the West Coast, and played a critical role in the completion of the transcontinental railroad in

1869. Their growing presence—over 110,000 by the 1870s—raised concerns with organized labor and politicians, leading to the first of several exclusion acts in 1882. From then until 1943, U.S. immigration policy focused on barring Asians. Chinese were targeted first, but Filipinos and Japanese were also later restricted.

Economic and strategic interests converged in 1898 when the United States defeated Spain and, amid a chorus of imperialist arguments, took possession of the *Philippines rather than grant the islands independence. Under the leadership of Emilio Aguinaldo, the Filipinos fought back, dragging America into the first of four major wars in Asia over the next seventy-five years. Not until 1946 did the United States grant the Philippines full independence and for decades after the U.S. military maintained a major presence on the island.

Concern over European and Japanese efforts to carve out exclusive spheres of influence in China led Secretary of State John *Hay to issue the "Open Door" notes at the turn of the twentieth century. Eager to expand outlets for America's agricultural and manufacturing surpluses, Hay sought access to China, which meant, endorsing its territorial integrity and opposing exclusive spheres of influence in China by other powers. Antiforeign violence broke out in China in 1901 as a group called the Boxers rose up. European, Japanese, and American troops intervened to protect their citizens and restore order, but "Open Door" principles generally prevailed. From then until 1931, American interests in Asia were expressed largely through government-encouraged, but privately sponsored, loans, business initiatives, and Christian missionary efforts.

Japan, meanwhile, demonstrated its growing economic, military, and political vitality, first by defeating Chinese forces in 1894–1895 and more importantly by defeating Russia, especially its navy, in 1904–1905. Japan's development as a regional power raised fears in Europe and the United States. The outbreak of *World War I in 1914 temporarily diverted attention from Asia, but the *Washington Naval Arms Conference of 1921–1922 sought not only to prevent a naval arms race but also to curb Japan's power. This effort collapsed, however, along with the world economy in 1929. Economic depression reinforced Japanese militarism and fueled Japan's desire to create an exclusive sphere of influence in Asia. Japan embarked on the military occupation of China, starting with Manchuria in 1931 and expanding in 1937 into the central provinces. The U.S. reaction was rhetorical at first, but as the fascist danger grew, the Franklin Delano *Roosevelt administration came to see the problems of Asia and Europe as interrelated.

The Japanese attack on *Pearl Harbor in December 1941 officially brought the United States into *World War II. Despite the Europe-first strategy, the United States committed large forces to the Pacific. In a strategic move designed to prepare for the postwar world, President Roosevelt elevated the Chinese nationalist leader Chiang Kai-shek (Jiang Jieshi) to a position of equality with himself, British prime minister Winston Churchill, and the Soviet leader Joseph Stalin. The Pacific war ended abruptly and decisively in August 1945 with the atomic bombing of *Hiroshima and Nagasaki.

The Cold War and Vietnam. After 1945 the United States sought to build a nonmilitaristic Japan and to revive Japanese industry as the focal point for Asian economic growth. The new alliance with Japan became critical after the Chinese Communists led by Mao Tsetung (Mao Zedong) seized power on the mainland in 1949, forcing Chiang and his government to flee to the island of Formosa (Taiwan), where they proclaimed the Republic of China.

When Kim Il Sung's North Korean troops invaded South Korea in June 1950, communist aggression appeared to be spreading by military force. Under the aegis of the United Nations, the Harry S. *Truman administration committed U.S. troops to South Korea's defense. The dramatic success of General Douglas *MacArthur's Inchon landing in September and drive into North Korea was followed two months later by an equally dramatic retreat as Chinese communist troops crossed the border and joined the war. For the next two and half years, both sides fought bitterly back and forth over the thirty-eighth parallel, which became the dividing line when a ceasefire was agreed to in July 1953.

During the *Korean War, the United States began a military commitment to Southeast Asia as well, helping to finance and supply the French effort to restore its colonial presence in Vietnam and to defeat Ho Chi Minh, leader of the Vietnamese communists, who proclaimed the Democratic Republic of Vietnam in 1945. He appealed to the United States for assistance, but from Washington's perspective, his allegiance to *communism meant that he was part of an effort to undermine American interests around the world; that he was also a nationalist appeared irrelevant. When French troops were defeated at Dien Bien Phu in 1954, the Dwight D. *Eisenhower administration intervened, providing military and economic assistance to Ngo Dinh Diem's government in Saigon, as part of a general strategy to divide Vietnam and create a viable anticommunist government in the south. Although the United States was reluctant to commit itself to yet another land war in Asia, its engagement in Vietnam gradually deepened as Southeast Asia became important both as a symbol of America's anticommunist commitment to the region and as part of a regional economic structure with Japan serving as the hub.

The centrality of anticommunism in America's post–1945 Asian policy found further expression in the Southeast Asia Treaty Organization (SEATO), created in 1954 at the initiative of Secretary of State John Foster *Dulles. It brought together Australia, New Zealand, Pakistan, the Philippines, Thailand, Great Britain, France, and the United States in an association pledged to resist "communist aggression"; a separate protocol extended SEATO protection to South Vietnam, Cambodia, and Laos.

The revitalization of Japan, *anticommunism, the isolation of communist China, and military engagement in Korea and Vietnam shaped American policy in Asia from 1949 to 1972. What finally modified this strategy was a combination of economic considerations and the failure of the U.S. military effort in Vietnam. Beginning with President Truman, and continuing with presidents Eisenhower, John F. *Kennedy, Lyndon B. *Johnson, and Richard M. *Nixon, the United States committed itself, first indirectly and gradually, then directly and rapidly, to supporting South Vietnam. In 1965, Johnson significantly escalated a bombing campaign and sent U.S. combat troops. At its peak, the United States had more than 540,000 soldiers fighting in Vietnam, all in the hope of convincing the North Vietnam leadership that the United States was serious about its commitment to stopping communism. But stalemate was the best that could be achieved.

Beyond the Cold War: New Opportunities, New Issues. President Nixon's trip to China in 1972 signaled a change in American Asian strategy. Marking an end of the goal of isolating China in the hope of undermining Beijing's communist government, this visit signaled America's desire for access to new markets to help a sagging U.S. economy. Nixon also sought Mao's help in negotiating an end to the *Vietnam War. The United States reached an agreement with the North Vietnamese in January 1973 on the withdrawal of all American combat personnel, but the fighting did not end until Vietnam's unification under communist control in April 1975.

As the twentieth century ended, U.S. relations with Asia increasingly involved economic issues, including engaging and expanding the China market (while simultaneously pushing for democratic change), increasing U.S. exports and curbing Asian nations' trading practices considered unfair by the United States, and building free-market capitalism in Southeast Asia. Immigration returned as a major issue after the Immigration Act of 1965 and with it a new wave of refugees from Southeast

Asia. Strategic concerns included forestalling the development of weapons of mass destruction by North Korea, normalizing relations between the two Koreas, preventing a regional nuclear arms race between India and Pakistan, and avoiding a military conflict with China over the status of Taiwan.

[*See also* Asian Americans; Business; Capitalism; Cold War; Expansionism; Federal Government, Executive Branch: Department of State; Foreign Trade, U.S.; General Agreement on Tariffs and Trade; Immigration Law; Missionary Movement; Nuclear Weapons; "Open Door" Policy; Perry, Matthew and Oliver Hazard; Post–Cold War Era; Spanish-American War; Tet Offensive.]

• Akira Iriye, *Across the Pacific: An Inner History of American-East Asian Relations,* 1967. Emily Rosenberg, *Spreading the American Dream: American Economic and Cultural Expansion, 1890–1945,* 1982. Michael Hunt, *The Making of a Special Relationship: The United States and China to 1914,* 1983. George C. Herring, *America's Longest War: The United States and Vietnam, 1950–1975,* 2nd ed., 1986. Arthur Power Dudden, *The American Pacific: From the Old China Trade to the Present,* 1992. Nancy Bernkopf Tucker, *Taiwan, Hong Kong, and the United States, 1945–1992,* 1994. Walter LaFeber, *The Clash: U.S.-Japanese Relations Throughout History,* 1997. Don Oberdorfer, *The Two Koreas: A Contemporary History,* 1997. Michael Schaller, *Altered States: The United States and Japan Since the Occupation,* 1997.

—T. Christopher Jespersen

FOREIGN RELATIONS: U.S. RELATIONS WITH AFRICA

America's ties with Africa are rooted in the violent hemorrhaging of the slave trade. Beginning in 1618 and continuing for almost two centuries, an estimated two million slaves were wrenched from the West African coast and shipped to the Caribbean and North America. Discomfort with these reluctant immigrants led to the American Colonization Society's failed efforts in the 1820s to "repatriate" freed slaves to Liberia, which became a virtual U.S. protectorate. For the next century, only explorers' tales, missionary reports, and Theodore *Roosevelt's hunting safaris piqued Americans' interest in the "Dark Continent."

Severed from their ethnic roots, eager to prove their patriotism, and embarrassed by the prevailing stereotypes of Africa, *African Americans shunned identification with the continent. By the early twentieth century, however, pushed by virulent *racism at home and pulled by Ethiopia's defeat of Italy in 1896, some U.S. blacks reconsidered. Identification with Africa, they argued, would deepen black Americans' pride and political power. W. E. B. *Du Bois led a Pan-African delegation to the 1919 Versailles peace conference, and Marcus *Garvey promoted a back-to-Africa movement in the early 1920s. Black churches, especially the African Methodist Episcopal (AME) church, sponsored missionaries in Africa, and in the 1940s Paul *Robeson chaired the militant Council on African Affairs.

*World War II highlighted North Africa's strategic and South Africa's economic importance, but the United States, confident that Europeans would maintain control of the continent, remained on the sidelines, and African Americans, bowing to the superpatriotism of the early *Cold War, again distanced themselves from Africa. In the late 1950s and early 1960s, however, Washington, caught off guard as decolonization swept through the continent, finally turned its attention to Africa. Its policy, while influenced by the domestic politics of race, was determined by the exigencies of the Cold War. President John F. *Kennedy offered rhetorical support for the newly independent nations, more than doubled U.S. aid (to $460 million in 1961), and dispatched *Peace Corps volunteers.

The traffic was, for the first time, two-way: African students and diplomats came to the United States, where they encountered racism and *segregation. "African diplomats . . . consider the United States the most difficult post," the Malian embassy commented in 1961. Two years later, the Organization of African Unity formally expressed "deep concern over racial discrimination in the United States." Fear that African outrage at U.S. racism would give the Soviets a powerful propaganda weapon spurred Kennedy to support the *civil rights movement at home, while Cold War fears led him and President Lyndon B. *Johnson to quash revolts they considered procommunist in Africa. In the Congo, Johnson relied on the *Central Intelligence Agency (CIA) and white mercenary troops to maintain the pro-American regime—a policy that generated virtually no debate in the United States.

Washington's interest was short-lived. By 1968, the fall of leading African leftists, such as Ghana's Kwame Nkrumah, Algeria's Ben Bella, and Mali's Modibo Keita, and the frailty of anticolonialist guerrilla movements in Angola, Mozambique, and Rhodesia, lulled Washington back to complacency. The Richard M. *Nixon administration considered Africa's minority white regimes to be America's most reliable allies on the continent.

Blindsided in 1974 when a coup in Lisbon led to the decolonization of Portugal's African colonies, Washington colluded with South Africa's white government to prevent a leftist victory in Angola—a policy that was foiled by the intervention of thirty thousand Cuban troops in 1975–1976. As the Cubans moved on to Ethiopia in 1977 to repel an invasion from Somalia and Nigeria gained economic clout as a major oil exporter, Washington's concern increased. Heightened Cold War fears led the Ronald *Reagan administration to assist anticommunist insurgents in Angola. Meanwhile, TransAfrica, an activist organization founded in 1976 by African Americans, successfully challenged the administration's accommodationist policy toward South Africa's apartheid regime. In 1986, over Reagan's veto, Congress imposed economic sanctions on South Africa.

After the collapse of the Soviet Union and of white African regimes, U.S. interest in Africa subsided. President George *Bush sent U.S. troops to Somalia to assist in famine relief, but he withdrew them as factional fighting flared in the capital. Numbed by television images of famine, war, and the epidemic of *acquired immunodeficiency syndrome (AIDS); confused about humanitarian intevention; loath to join multilateral efforts; and convinced that Africa's problems were both intractable and marginal to U.S. interests, the United States at the end of the twentieth century lapsed back toward the indifference that had long characterized its stance toward Africa.

[*See also* African American Religion; Colonization Movement, African; Missionary Movement; Slavery: The Slave Trade.]

• Richard D. Mahoney, *JFK: Ordeal in Africa,* 1983. Gerald J. Bender, James S. Coleman, Richard L. Sklar, eds., *African Crisis Areas and U.S. Foreign Policy,* 1985. Zaki Laïdi, *The Superpowers and Africa: The Constraints of a Rivalry, 1960–1990,* trans. Patricia Baudoin, 1990. Thomas Borstelmann, *Apartheid's Reluctant Uncle: The United States and Southern Africa in the Early Cold War,* 1993. Peter J. Schraeder, *United States Foreign Policy toward Africa: Incrementalism, Crisis, and Change,* 1996. Brenda Gayle Plummer, *Rising Wind: Black Americans and U.S. Foreign Affairs, 1935–1960,* 1996.

—Nancy Mitchell

FOREIGN RELATIONS: U.S. RELATIONS WITH THE MIDDLE EAST

From the early nineteenth century, rivalry between the Russian and British empires unfolded in an arena extending from the Balkans to India. America's minor interests in the region up to *World War I involved mainly commerce and missionary work. After the United States entered the war in 1917, the Ottoman Empire broke relations, but the two powers did not engage in hostilities. As U.S. commercial interests expanded in the oil-rich Middle East, the "buffer" states that had emerged between the British and Soviet empires tried to balance great-power ambitions and allied among themselves against external threats.

Waging the Cold War in the Middle East. After 1945, America's dominant concerns in the Middle East were containing Soviet influence and resolving the Arab-Israeli conflict. As British power in the region waned, the potential Soviet threat preoccupied Washington planners. The *Cold War brought a series of presidential pronouncements, or "doctrines," asserting America's determination to resist Soviet threats to influence the region. While most Arab states welcomed Britain's departure, Turkey and Iran, bordering the Soviet Union, sought U.S. assistance. The *Truman Doctrine, enunciated in March 1947 by President Harry S. *Truman in response to Britain's withdrawal from Greece, marked a growing U.S. commitment to maintaining the balance of power in the region. Washington increasingly linked America's vital concerns in Europe and the Middle East, which supplied 75 percent of Europe's oil requirements. The *Joint Chiefs of Staff stressed Turkey's crucial role in both regions, and the Truman administration supported the admission of Turkey (and Greece) into the *North Atlantic Treaty Organization (NATO).

The gradual departure of the British (and the French from the eastern Mediterranean and North Africa) encouraged nationalist movements in the Middle East. In Arab eyes, the United States, initially free of colonialist taint, became identified with imperialism. Two factors reinforced this link: U.S. support for a Jewish state in Palestine and America's continued collaboration with the British. To U.S. strategists, *containment of the Soviet threat, even at the cost of association with the vestiges of colonialism, outranked better relations with the region's emerging nationalist forces.

The implications of these choices emerged starkly in Iran. The Dwight D. *Eisenhower administration, worried about Iran's drift toward neutrality, carried out in 1953 a British-sponsored plan to overthrow the nationalist Mohammed Mossadeq and reinstall the pro-Western Shah Reza Pahlavi. In supporting this policy, Washington violated the principle of sovereignty, with long-lasting consequences.

As the Soviet Union gained influence with Egypt, Iraq, and Syria (in part because of U.S. support for Israel), U.S. administrations redoubled their containment efforts. The 1956 Suez Crisis (see below) gave rise to the *Eisenhower Doctrine, which pledged the United States to defend the Middle East against a perceived Soviet threat. After a nationalist revolution in Iraq in 1958, Washington negotiated executive agreements with Turkey, Iran, and Pakistan (in the Central Treaty Organization) institutionalizing U.S. military support to these countries.

In 1968, Britain announced plans to withdraw entirely from the area east of Suez by 1971. The Richard M. *Nixon administration, fearing a power vacuum in the Persian Gulf at a time when the United States was preoccupied in Vietnam, proclaimed the Nixon Doctrine (1969) pledging support and military aid to key regional powers who assumed responsibility for their own defense. Under Nixon's "twin-pillar" policy, the United States relied primarily on Iran and Saudi Arabia. But the Shah's ability to protect U.S. interests in the Gulf proved short-lived. Enriched by oil price hikes organized by the Organization of Petroleum Exporting Countries (OPEC) following the 1973 Arab-Israeli war, the Shah purchased nine billion dollars of western arms and developed a ruthless secret police. The 1979 Iranian revolution that brought to power a fundamentalist Islamic regime under the Ayatollah Khomeini, scholars believe, derived less from what Khomeini stood for than from what he opposed: the Shah's regime and U.S. control and cultural domination.

The Iranian revolution and the Soviet invasion of Afghanistan later in the year underminded the security framework premised on the Nixon Doctrine. President Jimmy *Carter's response, the Carter Doctrine (1980), emphasized the U.S. stake in the Persian Gulf, asserted America's ultimate responsibility for regional defense, and developed a Rapid Deployment Force to deal with crises in the region. The Ronald *Reagan administration consolidated this security framework but also revived the policy of supporting "regional influentials," bolstering assistance to Turkey and Pakistan and strengthening relations with Saudi Arabia.

Revolutionary Ferment and the Palestinian–Israeli Conflict. After the Shah's fall, the foremost challenge to U.S. interests in the Persian Gulf came not from the Soviet Union but from revolutionary Iran and especially Iraq, whose leader, Saddam Hussein, invaded Iran in 1980, launching a war that cost a million lives. When Saddam invaded Kuwait in 1990, launching the *Persian Gulf War, the George *Bush administration coordinated a multination military operation to expel his army and deter him from intimidating Saudi Arabia. Saddam's subsequent defiance of the ceasefire conditions, persecution of Iraq's Shiite and Kurdish minorities, and secret chemical and biological weapons programs resulted in a continuing embargo on Iraqi oil, restrictions on Saddam's military activities within Iraq, and *United Nations inspections of weapons sites.

While pursuing the policy of containment (first of the Soviet Union, then of Iran and Iraq), Washington also confronted the Palestinian question. From the early Cold War on, regional specialists at the State Department worried that U.S. support for the partition of Palestine and the Zionist goal of a Jewish state would violate the principle of self-determination, alienate the Arabs, make them more receptive to the Soviets, and undermine the policy of containment. Truman, however, for political and humanitarian reasons, supported the desire of many Jews to build a new life after the Holocaust, and he did not believe that this position jeopardized U.S. interests. Truman recognized the new state of Israel in 1948. The conflict between Israel's search for security and the Palestinian quest for self-determination and a homeland was at the root of all subsequent Arab-Israeli wars. The State Department's fears, meanwhile, were borne out in February 1955, when an Israeli attack on the Gaza Strip triggered events that led Egyptian president Gamal Abdel Nasser to seek Soviet assistance. The Eisenhower administration, in turn, cancelled a proposed loan to Egypt to build a dam at Aswan on the Nile. In 1956, after Nasser nationalized the Suez Canal to pay for the dam, British, French, and Israeli forces colluded in an attack on Egypt. U.S. pressure and Soviet threats to intervene led to a ceasefire, but the episode increased Nasser's regional influence. The 1956 war, followed by U.S. intervention in Lebanon in 1958 and France's colonial war in Algeria, helps explain why Arab states, with firsthand knowledge of Western intervention but little direct experience with Soviet expansionism, embraced Soviet assistance. Following the 1967 war, in which Israel occupied the West Bank, Gaza, and the Golan Heights, the U.S.–Israeli relationship developed into a virtual alliance, while Palestinians who had looked to Nasser now took the nationalist movement into their own hands.

After yet another war in 1973, prodded by rising Palestinian nationalism and an Arab oil embargo, the United States adopted a more constructive response to Palestinian concerns and grievances, including an attempt to rectify some (but not all) historical injustices. This aim was not easily implemented, however, as shown in Henry *Kissinger's shuttle diplomacy and in Carter's search for a comprehensive peace, which fell short when the 1979 Camp David Accords ended in a separate peace between Israel and Egypt. A 1982 Israeli incursion into Lebanon, made possible by the Israeli-Egyptian peace and motivated by Israel's desire to crush Palestinian strongholds from which attacks were mounted on Israel, again illustrated the centrality of the Palestinian question. An Intifada, or Palestinian uprising, began in the West Bank and Gaza in 1987 after twenty years of Israeli occupation.

Israeli negotiations with Palestinian leader Yasir Arafat, promoted by the Bush administration and facilitated by the Norwegian government, reached fruition in the 1993 Oslo Accords. This agreement (as well as subsequent interim agreements) was grounded in the concept, framed by 1967 United Nations Security Council Resolution 242, of exchanging territory for peace. It provided the basis for a phased Israeli withdrawal from the occupied territories, and increasing Palestinian self-rule, but left in limbo the borders and final status of the Palestinian entity and the future of Jerusalem. The opposition of extremist elements in both Israel and the Palestinian territories resulted in the 1995 assassination of Israeli Prime Minister Yitzhak Rabin by a pro-settlement activist and in terrorist attacks that reinforced hardline opposition on both sides. The Bill *Clinton administration, like its predecessors, searched for a framework for further progress, and in 1999, with the election of new Israeli government under Ehud Barak, the peace process that had been suspended during the last year of the administration of Benjamin Netanyahu was once again a high priority. In July 2000, as his term wound down, President Clinton brought Arafat and Barak to Camp David for a final round of talks. Despite substantial progress, however, the two sides reached an impass over Jerusalem, and the negotiations, like so many in the past, ended inconclusively.

[*See also* Energy Crisis of the 1970s; Missionary Movement; Petroleum Industry.]

• Bruce Kuniholm, *The Persian Gulf and United States Policy*, 1984. William Quandt, *Camp David: Peacemaking and Politics*, 1986. William B. Quandt, *Peace Process: American Diplomacy and the Arab-Israeli Conflict since 1967*, 1993. Hanan Ashrawi, *This Side of Peace*, 1995. David Makovsky, *Making Peace with the PLO: The Rabin Government's Road to the Oslo Accords*, 1996. Charles Smith, *Palestine and the Arab-Israeli Conflict*, 3d ed., 1996. Rashid Khalidi, *Palestinian Identity: The Construction of Modern National Consciousness*, 1997. Benny Morris, *Righteous Victims: A History of the Zionist-Arab Conflict, 1881–1999, 1999.*

—Bruce Kuniholm

FOREIGN RELATIONS: U.S. RELATIONS WITH CANADA

American relations with Canada began in hostility. In the *Colonial Era, American colonists and their Indian allies warred regularly with French settlers on the St. Lawrence. In the *Revolutionary War, American troops invaded Canada, hoping to provoke an uprising against the British, who had conquered Canada in 1759. Although Montreal fell in 1775, Quebec withstood, and Canada did not revolt. After 1783, Loyalists fleeing patriot vengeance found refuge in British North America.

The Loyalists accentuated Canada's anti-Americanism. British North America was to be a different America, one still responsive to London, and many in the new United States viewed their northern neighbor suspiciously. The *War of 1812, again pitting the United States against the British, reinforced Canada's anti-Americanism. The Rush-Bagot Convention of 1817, the first gesture of reconciliation, demilitarized the Great Lakes. An 1818 convention resolved most outstanding border disputes, although the Oregon boundary remained uncertain and controversies over fishing rights dragged into the twentieth century. Canadian rebellions in 1837–1838, encouraged by American expansionists, created tensions in the Northeast, and a brief border skirmish, known as the Aroostook War, flared in 1839. The *Webster-Ashburton Treaty (1842) resolved several boundary controversies, and by the 1850s relations had eased.

Tensions flared again during the American *Civil War, however, fed by U.S. anger at British support for the Confederacy. The Union victory fed fears in British North America that the United States might try to restore internal harmony by an invasion northward. Such fears contributed to the unification movement that resulted in the confederation of four British colonies into the Dominion of Canada on 1 July 1867. The Canadian constitution adopted an American federal model while giving more power to the central government.

The new nation remained a colony, London nominally controlling foreign relations until 1931. Relations between Washington and Ottawa fluctuated, with periods of hostility and coolness interrupting two-way emigration and ever-increasing trade. When arbitration settled the turn-of-the-century Alaska boundary dispute in America's favor, Ottawa pressed for creation of an International Joint Commission, the first of a web of agencies for the resolution of disputes.

In 1911, over many Canadians' opposition, the two nations signed a free-trade reciprocity agreement. A viciously anti-American election in 1911 produced a new government and quickly killed reciprocity. But the outbreak of *World War I and the necessity to coordinate scarce commodity supplies led Canada to establish a quasi-diplomatic presence in Washington and to accept limited military cooperation. By 1927, when the two countries exchanged diplomatic missions, American investment in Canada far outstripped British. Increasingly, Canada was part of a continental economy, and the Depression of the 1930s, though it fostered protectionism, did not reverse the trend.

*World War II confirmed Canada's southward drift, as British military and economic weakness strengthened U.S.–Canadian ties. The Permanent Joint Board on Defense (1940) marked Canada's open reliance on the U.S. military; the Hyde Park Declaration (April 1941) signalled her economic dependency. By 1945, the United States had constructed the Alaska Highway, air bases, and weather stations in northern Canada. A still-wary Ottawa paid in full for all these installations at war's end and ushered the GIs home.

The *Cold War forced renewed cooperation. Canada provided troops for the *Korean War, built radar lines with the United States, and in 1957–1958 integrated its air defenses with the U.S. Air Force. While Canadians favored such measures, underlying tensions erupted in 1962–1963 over *nuclear weapons deployment, and the Liberal party, which had accepted the weapons, barely survived another anti-American election. During the *Vietnam War, Canada protested U.S. bombing and admitted an estimated 100,000 draft resisters.

Increasingly, however, U.S.–Canadian relations centered on economics. American dollars amounted to more than 75 percent of the total foreign investment in Canada in the 1960s, stirring fears for Canadian independence. Canadian corporations dependent on Wall Street defeated the Liberal party's effort to curb U.S. investment. Other proposals to increase Canada's economic autonomy provoked confrontations with Washington. In 1985, Prime Minister Brian Mulroney, who wanted "super" relations with the United States, changed course and pressed for free trade. The resulting agreement swept away tariff barriers while supposedly protecting Canada's still-fragile culture; Ottawa signed the *North American Free Trade Agreement (NAFTA), and Canada accepted its North Americanness at last.

Still, Canadian anti-Americanism remained powerful. American legislation against foreign companies doing business in Cuba irritated Canadians, as did U.S. objections to protective cultural measures. Increasingly, however, such disputes were resolved in bilateral or multilateral trade panels, and relations remained close as the twentieth century ended. The two governments consulted regularly, Washington fully supported Ottawa in its dealings with Quebec separatists, citizens crossed the borders freely, and the two nations were each other's biggest trading partners. The superpower inevitably overshadows the smaller country, but Canadians' national survival rests in their own hands.

[*See also* Expansionism; Foreign Trade, U.S.; French Settlements in North America; Multinational Enterprises.]

• Seymour Martin Lipset, *Continental Divide: The Values and Institutions of the United States and Canada*, 1990. Robert Bothwell, *Canada and the United States: The Politics of Partnership*, 1992. J. L. Granatstein and Norman Hillmer, *For Better or for Worse: Canada and the United States to the 1990s*, 1992. Gordon T. Stewart, *The American Response to Canada since 1776*, 1992. John H. Thompson and Stephen J. Randall, *Canada and the United States: Ambivalent Allies,* 1994. J. L. Granatstein, *Yankee Go Home? Canadians and Anti-Americanism,* 1996.

—J. L. Granatstein

FOREIGN RELATIONS: U.S. RELATIONS WITH LATIN AMERICA

The first independent republics arose in the Americas during "the age of democratic revolution" between 1775 and 1825. Conceived in the course of complicated revolts against European empires, the new nations professed devotion to free trade and representative government, but their actual practices varied widely. The United States, the first of these republics, presumed that they all would share common identities and purposes. In 1823, the *Monroe Doctrine supported Latin American independence by warning the Europeans against reconquest. It also established a myth of hemispheric unity, according to which common experiences and beliefs supposedly linked North and South Americans in a shared commitment to "the Western Hemisphere idea." Affirming the interconnectedness of commerce, republicanism, and political disengagement from Europe, this claim served useful rhetorical purposes. In actual practice, national interests based on disparities of wealth, power, and culture functioned as the primary determinants of international behavior.

Following formal recognition of their independence in the 1820s and 1830s, Latin American governments typically cultivated European connections. The United States, in contrast, engaged in westward expansion, conquering territory to the Pacific Ocean. In 1848, Mexico lost half of its territory to the United States in the Treaty of Guadalupe Hidalgo, which ended a war between the two countries. The United States then suffered the effects of the *Civil War, the outcome of which focused attention more on the pursuit of commercial than territorial gain. During the latter third of the nineteenth century, U.S. elites developed compelling interests in overseas markets to serve burgeoning industry and *agriculture.

The *Spanish-American War in 1898 marked an important transition. As a consequence of this three-month struggle, the United States obtained hegemonic status in the New World and something very much like an empire. Since the Teller Amendment (introduced by Colorado senator Henry M. Teller) blocked outright annexation of Cuba, Washington devised other means of control. Cuba became a protectorate under the terms of the Platt Amendment, an administration measure sponsored by Senator Orville H. Platt of Connecticut. The United States then expanded its protectorate system, which enabled U.S. officials to sustain order by working with indigenous elites when possible and to intervene administratively and militarily when necessary, to Panama, Haiti, the Dominican Republic, and Nicaragua. As justified by President Theodore *Roosevelt's "Corollary" to the Monroe Doctrine in 1904, "the exercise of an international police power" by the United States served the nation's basic interests in preventing "chronic wrongdoing" in the Caribbean regions, keeping away European nations, and safeguarding the *Panama Canal.

U.S. hegemony came under challenge in Mexico after the revolution of 1910. Threatened by violence and revolution, U.S. corporations operating in Mexico demanded strong measures. President Woodrow *Wilson intervened twice with military forces. Nevertheless, the Mexican Constitution of 1917 presented long-term dangers to U.S. propertyholders under authority of Article 27, which endorsed the principles of nationalization and expropriation. In Mexico, henceforth, foreign ownership of property would be a privilege, not a right. Meanwhile, the consequences of *World War I strengthened the U.S. economic position by cutting off Latin Americans from European consumers and investors and increasing dependence on the United States. Before the war, U.S. trading and strategic interests focused mainly on the Central American–Caribbean region; after the war, ties rapidly increased with South American nations.

Following Germany's defeat in 1918, the absence of European threats in the Western Hemisphere deprived U.S. interventionist policies of urgency and justification. Under Republican administrations in the 1920s, a shift away from these practices produced a new orientation, culminating in the 1930s with the *Good Neighbor Policy. Under President Franklin Delano *Roosevelt, this approach accomplished a turnabout. The United States stopped intervening in Latin America and dismantled most of the remnants of the protectorate system. The incentives emanated from the Great Depression. Seeking markets and resources, Washington gave up obsolete forms of military activity in hopes of cultivating Latin American cooperation. The change paid off. During *World War II, most of Latin America lined up in support of the United States, assuring a high degree of "hemispheric solidarity" against Germany, Italy, and Japan.

World War II further strengthened Latin America's economic dependence on the United States. Needing a market for their products, Latin American countries courted favor with Washington by declaring war on the Axis powers or severing relations with them. The exceptions, Argentina and Chile, preferred neutrality for their own reasons. The United States, meanwhile, rewarded its Latin American allies with promises of economic aid and assistance in future *industrialization and modernization.

During the *Cold War, U.S. priorities shifted away from Latin America, regarded as peripheral to the main contest with the Soviet Union. International relations in the Western Hemisphere featured military and political collaboration through the Rio Pact (1947) and the *Organization of American States (1948) but demonstrated no equivalent governmental focus on economic affairs. Contrary to wartime assurances, the Harry S. *Truman and Dwight D. *Eisenhower administrations did not pursue a "*Marshall Plan" for Latin America, encouraging instead time-honored techniques for promoting growth through free trade and private investment. Latin Americans, in contrast, wanted large-scale aid and assistance and also favored programs of state intervention in the economy. Such differences over basic strategies for economic development gave rise to Latin American charges of U.S. indifference and neglect.

The Cold War also produced reversions to intervention. Such acts usually came about when U.S. leaders linked revolutionary nationalism in Latin America with the Soviet threat. Radical regimes in Guatemala (1954), Cuba (1959), and Chile (1973) occasioned specific instances. U.S. leaders saw these regimes as Soviet vanguards, threatening U.S. security interests. To counter them, Washington employed clandestine means, more often than not attaining their immediate goals. Among the primary offenders, only Fidel Castro in Cuba survived the efforts to overthrow him, notably during the abortive *Bay of Pigs invasion in 1961. But the elected governments of Jacobo Arbenz Guzmán in Guatemala and Salvador Allende in Chile both fell when confronted with U.S. opposition. Critics of U.S. policy, meanwhile, pointed out that right-wing, anticommunist dictators—no matter how brutal—elicited much less impatience. As examples, they cited U.S. support for Fulgencio Batista in Cuba, Rafael Trujillo in the Dominican Republic, and Anastasio Somoza in Nicaragua.

Legacies of authoritarianism, repression, and poverty colored U.S.–Latin American relations in the 1980s. To combat Marxist enthusiasms within the revolutionary Sandinista regime in Nicaragua, President Ronald *Reagan's administration pursued counterrevolutionary policies by backing right-wing opposition forces, the so-called Contras. Reagan officials also warned of Soviet incursions. For them, revolutionary activity in Central America constituted an East-West encounter, that is, a Cold War confrontation by proxy. This position differed from the Jimmy *Carter administration's earlier view, which depicted such ferment as a North-South issue between the "developed" and "developing" worlds. Meanwhile, "the quiet invasion"—

the movement of people out of Mexico, Central America, and the Caribbean into the United States, often without sanction from U.S. immigration authorities—caused concern.

The end of the Cold War again altered the international context of U.S.–Latin American relations. The Soviet Union no longer served as a pretext for U.S. interventions, Marxist movements in Latin America moderated, and the *United Nations became more active as a peacemaker within the hemisphere. At the same time, significant issues and sources of tension defied resolution, in part because governments lacked the capability of stopping human migrations and the flow of illicit *drugs. At the same time, profound demographic and cultural changes held significant implications for the future. Census Bureau forecasts suggested that by 2050, Hispanics would constitute one-quarter of the U.S. population, and already at the end of the twentieth century, persons of Latin American antecedents constituted an emerging majority in the southeastern and southwestern United States.

[*See also* Depressions, Economic; Foreign Trade, U.S.; Hispanic Americans; Immigration; Immigration Law; Mexican War; Puerto Rico.]

• Arthur P. Whitaker, *The Western Hemisphere Idea*, 1954. Mark T. Gilderhus, *Pan American Visions: Woodrow Wilson in the Western Hemisphere*, 1986. Stephen G. Rabe, *Eisenhower and Latin America*, 1988. John J. Johnson, *A Hemisphere Apart: The Foundations of United States Policy toward Latin America*, 1990. Frederick B. Pike, *The United States and Latin America: Myths and Stereotypes of Civilization and Nature*, 1992. Walter LaFeber, *The American Search for Opportunity, 1865–1913*, vol. 2, *The Cambridge History of American Foreign Relations*, 1993. John H. Coatsworth, *Central America and the United States*, 1994. Fredrick B. Pike, *FDR's Good Neighbor Policy*, 1995. Peter H. Smith, *Talons of the Eagle: Dynamics of U.S.–Latin American Relations*, 1996.

—Mark T. Gilderhus

FOREIGN TRADE, U.S. Trade and commerce have had a formative influence on America from the *Colonial Era onward. The British colonial system embraced the doctrines of mercantilism, with its closely regulated trade, restricted economic development, and unfavorable balance of payments for the American colonists. After independence, Americans melded the free-trade doctrines of Adam Smith's *Wealth of Nations* (1776) with their revolutionary cause.

From the Early Republic to World War I. The federal *Constitution eliminated interstate trade barriers while providing for the consolidation of trade policy. Incorporating commercial values with national interest, Americans assumed that the territorial and commercial wars of the past would yield to a peaceful era of free economic exchange among nations. Foreign trade's relative importance declined in the nineteenth century, however, as internal development intensified. Exports fell to about 6 percent of gross domestic product (GDP), while exports and imports combined constituted an average 12 percent. The *South's cotton economy remained export-led; economic growth overall was not.

Following the Napoleonic wars (1803–1815), Great Britain adopted free-trade policies, stimulating phenomenal growth in world trade per capita between 1800 and 1910. After 1850, international economic relationships strengthened so that the national economies of the Atlantic region showed common features of specialization, *urbanization, trade cycles, and movements of capital and labor. In this same period, the United States moved steadily from the periphery of this system to the center, the core of the international economy.

Through the nineteenth century, American exports were largely raw materials. Primary products, including raw and processed foodstuffs, forest products, and minerals, constituted 80 percent of American exports. Manufactured and semimanufactured goods comprised about two-thirds of imports. As the trans-Mississippi *West came into production after the *Civil War, half of the increase in wheat production was exported. But the expansion of manufacturing counted most in the accelerating *rate* of economic *productivity. In 1860, manufactured goods accounted for 20 percent of U.S. exports; by *World War I, the figure had climbed to 50 percent. Overall, until 1895, Americans bought more abroad than they sold, setting the deficit account by borrowing from abroad, or paying in the internationally recognized exchange of gold.

Since tariff receipts were the largest source of federal revenue until 1913, when they were overtaken by tax revenues, tariff duties could only selectively restrict, not wholly prohibit, imports. American competitive advantage took the form of innovations in *mass production and *mass marketing of foodstuffs and retail goods, made possible by the large and comparatively affluent domestic market. The efficiency of these techniques, rather than the protective effects of the *tariffs, enabled U.S. manufactures to compete effectively and generate a surplus trade account for most of the twentieth century.

From World War I through the 1960s. The combined strength of agricultural and manufactured exports after World War I led to an anomalous situation in which the United States captured 27 percent of world trade while its exports constituted only 6 percent of the total U.S. GDP. Since tariff disputes in Congress originated mostly among specific business interests, economic groups, and regions, the U.S. government did not sufficiently recognize the profound implications of the lopsided trade and credit balance. Corrective action required that the United States reduce its tariffs and encourage private lending abroad. Instead, a business-labor alliance embraced more highly protective tariffs, to offset alleged differences between foreign and domestic production costs occasioned by higher wages in the United States. This outlook produced the high Fordney-McCumber tariff (1922) and the even higher Smoot-Hawley tariff (1930).

Tight credit policies further contributed to a world credit collapse in 1929, from which industrial nations sought relief in regional trade blocs. These encouraged import substitution, i.e., domestic production of what could be more cheaply produced and purchased abroad. The value of U.S. exports fell by half from 1929 to 1933, while the trade balance fell into a deficit position that lasted until 1940.

The economic and political crises precipitated by *World War II produced a trade agreement among the industrial nations, at the 1944 *Bretton Woods Conference in New Hampshire, to end trading blocs and import substitution. New international bodies, notably the *General Agreement on Tariffs and Trade (GATT) and the *International Monetary Fund (IMF), were established to negotiate tariff reduction and address precipitate currency fluctuations that jeopardized the free exchange of goods. Ostensibly multilateral (i.e., among all nations), tariff reduction as originated by U.S. Secretary of State Cordell *Hull actually proceeded through bilateral, or reciprocal, negotiations. At GATT's Geneva Conference in 1947, such negotiations reduced tariff barriers by an average of 50 percent. Most of the industrial economies, however, war-torn and plagued by competitive disadvantages, used nontariff barriers (e.g., quotas and subsidies) to protect recovering industry, *agriculture, and inadequate foreign currency reserves.

Overall, the GATT arrangement did reconstruct a multinational trading system. By 1953, Japan and a European Common Market, enjoying U.S. economic assistance and protected home markets, experienced economic growth at rates double that of the United States. From 1948 to 1957, world trade increased 77 percent, playing a crucial role in the recovery of the industrialized nations and the emergence of the export-led industrial economies of Southeast Asia. Fearing the exclusion of American products, particularly agricultural ones, from the emerging European Common Market, Congress in 1964 passed the Trade Expansion Act granting the president sweeping (multilateral) authority to place entire categories of products on the bargaining table.

1970 to 2000. In 1972, owing in part to the rising imports of high-priced foreign oil, the United States recorded its first postwar trade deficit on the merchandise account. Blue-collar jobs, especially those in steel, automobiles, and other heavy metallurgical industries, suffered from foreign competition. By 1985, Japan held 30 percent of the U.S. automobile market. American agricultural exports, which had doubled in the 1970s, fell as world agricultural trade declined in response to rising production and protectionism. China, meanwhile, began its meteoric rise to third place among suppliers to the U.S. consumer nondurables market.

The exports of American multinational corporations (which had proliferated as U.S. corporations invested abroad in the 1960s and 1970s), especially in chemicals, machinery, and transportation equipment, helped ease the U.S. trade deficit. Moreover, 40 percent of U.S. imports originated from the foreign affiliates of American multinationals. Although America's merchandise trade balance shifted decisively into the red (i.e., by the importation of far more goods than it exported), the often-criticized investment abroad partially countered the deficit by generating $100 billion more in exports to foreign affiliates than foreign firms gained from their investments in the United States.

Downward pressure on U.S. wage rates, popularly associated with the trade deficit, stimulated proposals to improve American "competitiveness" by retaliating against "unfair" trade barriers. These trading partners decried such actions pointing to excessive consumption indicated by historically low U.S. savings rates. When increased net borrowing in the 1990s erased the positive balance of foreign earnings (i.e., income on U.S. investment abroad), increasing the deficit, congressional trade restrictionists attacked U.S. capital exports, which had reached 25 percent of the world's total. These attacks proved ineffectual, but the restrictionists did have some success in extending trade controls.

Aware of the protectionist drift in Congress, Canada consolidated its premier position as the United States's largest trading partner by concluding a free-trade agreement (1988) that progressively eliminated tariffs over a ten-year period while making Canadian oil and gas more accessible to the U.S. market. The Mexican government, meanwhile, in pursuit of market-oriented reforms, sought closer economic ties with the United States. The resulting *North American Free Trade Agreement (NAFTA) passed Congress over bitter restrictionist opposition in January 1994. As Canadian and Mexican exports to the United States shot upward, most analysts anticipated greater efficiencies, lower prices, and an increase in high-tech jobs in the United States to compensate for the expected loss of blue-collar jobs to Mexico.

In 1999, the U.S. trade deficit reached about $200 billion, an increase to 2.5 percent of GDP (1998) from 1.7 percent in 1989. Some argued that the corresponding trade surpluses of foreign economies, much of which was reinvested in the United States, constituted an undependable component of U.S. financial markets (i.e., if withdrawn). Others emphasized that substantial rates of increase in government and business savings (represented by an apparent end to federal budget deficits and the phenomenally increased value of common stocks, respectively) showed that the nation had done well despite the trade deficit. While the trade deficit reduced the GDP by 1.5 percent in 1998, they noted, the U.S. economy still grew at a rate of nearly 4 percent.

[*See also* Agriculture: 1770s to 1890; Agriculture: The "Golden Age" (1890s–1920s); Automotive Industry; Business; Economic Development; Energy Crisis of the 1970s; Expansionism; Foreign Relations: The Economic Dimension; Global Economy, America and the; Iron and Steel Industry; Multinational Enterprises.]

• W. Elliot Brownlee, *Dynamics of Ascent,* 1988. Martin Feldstein, ed., *The United States in the World Economy,* 1988. Albert Fishlow and Stephen Haggard, *The United States and the Regionalization of the World Economy,* 1992. Anne Y. Kester, ed., *Behind the Numbers: U.S. Trade in the World Economy,* 1992. Henry C. Dethloff, *The United States and the Global Economy since 1945,* 1997.

—Paul P. Abrahams

FORESTS AND FORESTRY. In 1873, as the clearing of forests for agriculture, lumber, and fuelwood threatened the nation's future timber supply, the American Association for the Advancement of Science petitioned Congress and state legislatures to recognize the importance of timber cultivation and forest preservation. The resulting *Report on Forestry,* funded by Congress and compiled by Frederick B. Hough and Nathaniel Egleston, became the foundational document of American forestry. The establishment of the American Forestry Association in 1878 and a Forestry Division in the Department of Agriculture further signaled forestry's growing role. Bernard Fernow, a German forester, became the first chief of the division. He was succeeded in 1898 by Gifford Pinchot of Pennsylvania in a revamped Bureau of Forestry (renamed the U.S. Forest Service in 1905). Pinchot (1865–1946), a confidant of Theodore *Roosevelt, transferred federal forests held by the Interior Department to his own bureau, established the system of National Forests, and promoted conservation measures. He also helped to form the American Society of Foresters and establish at Yale the first graduate forestry program in 1900.

The period 1900–1960 saw frequent clashes between the Forest Service and private *lumbering interests over access to timber stands, and disputes with the National Park Service and the Fish and Wildlife Service, which sought to appropriate forest lands for their own purposes. After *World War II, however, forestry's earlier exclusive emphasis on lumber production gradually expanded to incorporate recreation and environmental protection. The Multiple Use–Sustained Yield Act of 1960 decreed that timber, wildlife, range land, water, and recreation were all legitimate National Forest concerns. From 1970 on, environmentalists' attention to clear-cutting practices and endangered-species protection steadily grew. As the century ended, the Forest Service and foresters, while still the guardians of the nation's arboreal heritage, increasingly shared that role with an informed and articulate public.

[*See also* Ballinger-Pinchot Controversy; Conservation Movement; Environmentalism; Leopold, Aldo; Muir, John; National Park System; Progressive Era.]

• Richard C. Davis, ed., *Encyclopedia of American Forest and Conservation History,* 2 vols., 1983. Michael Williams, *Americans and Their Forests,* 1989.

—Michael Williams

FORTY-NINERS. *See* Gold Rushes.

FOSTER, STEPHEN (1826–1864), musical arranger and the best-known nineteenth-century composer of American popular song. Born in Pittsburgh to a middle-class family, Stephen Foster received training in music from Henry Kleber, a musician and music publisher. Through Kleber, Foster came to know the music of Vincenzo Bellini and the *Irish Melodies* of Thomas Moore. The theater life of Pittsburgh acquainted him with blackface minstrels like Thomas Dartmouth ("Jim Crow") Rice. Drawing on diverse musical influences, Foster summarized the disparate vocal styles of the *Antebellum Era. His arrangements for *The Social Orchestra* (1854) included selections from Italian opera, Irish tunes, and the more spirited minstrel repertory. He incorporated these styles into his own songs, combining them with simple yet artful piano accompaniments. "Wilt Thou Be Gone Love" (1851) and "Beautiful Dreamer" (1864) represent the Italianate style, while "Jeanie with the Light Brown Hair" (1854) and "Gentle Annie" (1856) hint at Moore's *Irish Melodies.* His best-known songs, shaped by the minstrel tradition, include comic numbers like "Oh!

Susanna" (1848) and "Gwine to Run All Night or De Camptown Races" (1850), and blackface ballads like "Old Folks at Home" ("Way down upon de Swanee ribber," 1851) and "My Old Kentucky Home" (1853), which figured prominently in stage productions of *Uncle Tom's Cabin*. Foster's reputation enabled him to negotiate a lucrative royalty arrangement with Firth, Pond and Co. of New York, and he was the first American composer to live solely off his royalties. He died in New York in 1864.

[*See also* Minstrelsy Music: Popular Music; Popular Culture.]

• John Tasker Howard, *Stephen Foster, America's Troubadour*, 1953. William W. Austin, *"Susanna," "Jeanie," and "The Old Folks at Home": The Songs of Stephen Foster from His Time to Ours*, 2d. ed., 1987. Ken Emerson, *Doo-Dah! Stephen Foster and The Rise of American Popular Culture*, 1997.

—Jon W. Finson

4–H CLUB MOVEMENT. In 1914, the Cooperative Extension Service of the Department of Agriculture established a Rural Youth Division by bringing together a number of independent clubs for farm boys and girls under the direction of country agricultural agents. The term "4–H" (Head, Heart, Hands, and Health), popularized by Extension Agent Gertrude Warren, became the clubs' official name in 1919. The 4–H clubs, which proved highly popular, served as a useful vehicle for training young people in advanced farming and home economics techniques often resisted by their parents.

In the 1920s a *Chicago-based private organization, the National 4–H Service Committee, solicited contributions from corporate donors to underwrite 4–H prizes and established rules for participation in 4–H projects and county-fair competitions emphasizing animal husbandry, crop production, and home economics. In 1948 the Cooperative Extension Service established a second private organization, the National 4–H Foundation, in *Washington, D.C., primarily to underwrite international farm youth exchanges, an activity the 4–H Service Committee proved reluctant to sponsor. The two organizations sustained an uneasy working relationship until 1976 when they merged into a single National 4–H Council.

In the 1960s, as the farm population continued its long decline, 4–H added to its list of sponsored projects a number of hobby activities designed to appeal to small-town and urban youth. Although 4–H continued to promote traditional farm-related programs, it placed considerable emphasis on leadership training and community-development projects. As the twentieth century ended, 4–H continued to rank among the nation's largest youth organizations, and the only one federally sponsored.

[*See also* Agriculture: The "Golden Age" (1890s–1920); Agriculture: Since 1920; Federal Government, Executive Branch: Department of Agriculture.]

• Thomas Wessel and Marilyn Wessel, *4–H, An American Idea*, 1982.

—Thomas Wessel and Marilyn Wessel

FOURIER MOVEMENT. *See* Utopian and Communitarian Movements.

FOURTEEN POINTS (1918). President Woodrow *Wilson's pronouncement of 8 January 1918 was the most important statement of war aims during *World War I. Wilson made his address primarily in response to the revolutionary upheaval in Russia. By the end of 1917, Vladimir Lenin and Leon Trotsky had pulled their ravaged homeland out of the war, thus permitting Germany to transfer great numbers of troops to the Western Front, and called for a peace based on self-determination. Publishing the Allies' secret treaties (signed by the Tsarist regime) for carving up territory after victory, the Bolsheviks appealed to the soldiers of the Allied and Central Powers alike to lay down their arms and demand that their governments repudiate plans for conquest. Because many liberal and socialist groups among the Allies were already questioning the seemingly endless carnage, it fell to Wilson to remove the suspicions hanging over the Allied cause and explain why the conflict was still worth fighting.

The president argued that German militarism must be crushed in order to create a new and better world. Drawing upon his anti-imperialist "Peace without Victory" formula of 1917, he then outlined the American peace program. Seven of the points dealt with territorial readjustments, including the "unembarrassed opportunity" for Russia to shape her own destiny. The others were characteristically Wilsonian—open covenants openly arrived at free trade; national self-determination, reductions in armaments; impartial adjustment of colonial claims; freedom of the seas; and, the capstone, a *League of Nations.

Hailed by liberals and socialists throughout Europe and America, Wilson's progressive internationalist response to the Bolshevik challenge provided the ideological cement that held the Allied coalition together for the remainder of the war. Although not endorsed by the other Allies, the Fourteen Points set the public agenda for the Paris peace conference. They became a source of controversy, however, when the Treaty of *Versailles only partially fulfilled Wilson's program for a new world order.

[*See also* Foreign Relations: Overview; Foreign Relations: U.S. Relations with Europe; Internationalism.]

• Arno J. Mayer, *Political Origins of the New Diplomacy, 1917–1918*, 1959. Thomas J. Knock, *To End All Wars: Woodrow Wilson and the Quest for a New World Order*, 1992.

—Thomas J. Knock

FOURTEENTH AMENDMENT (1868), Congress's first attempt to settle the issues of the *Civil War and restore the former Confederate states to the Union. The first of the amendment's five sections defined state and national citizenship, reversing the ruling in **Scott* v. *Sandford* that *African Americans were not citizens of the United States. It also forbade states to deprive anyone of the rights of citizenship, infringe fundamental rights without due process of law, or deny equal protection of the laws. Other sections reduced the congressional representation of any state that denied voting rights to any class of men, disqualified many former government officials who had supported the Confederacy from holding public office, and guaranteed payment of debts incurred in suppressing the rebellion while barring payment of those incurred in support of it. Since the amendment appeared to sanction voting discrimination against women, some women's rights advocates opposed it. The fifth section authorized Congress to enforce the prior four.

Nearly all the states that had remained loyal to the Union quickly ratified the proposed amendment after Congress submitted it to the states for ratification in June 1866, but all the ex-Confederate states except Tennessee refused. Congress then passed the Reconstruction Act, which pronounced existing governments in the South provisional until they adopted new constitutions and ratified the amendment. With this prodding, the amendment was ratified on 9 July 1868.

In the decades following, the *Supreme Court defined the amendment narrowly in order to maintain a clear distinction between the powers of the federal and state governments. In the **Slaughterhouse Cases* (1873), the Court distinguished the rights Americans held as state citizens from their rights as U.S. citizens. The Fourteenth Amendment, the Court held, guaranteed only the latter. In the **Civil Rights Cases* (1883), the Court held that Congress could enforce the amendment only against state actions and could not punish private citizens for violating *civil rights. In **Plessy* v. *Ferguson* (1896), the Court ruled that racial *segregation did not deprive African Americans of equal protection of the law. Other decisions held that the amendment did not require the states to adhere to the protections written into the *Bill of Rights.

While the Court narrowed the Fourteenth Amendment's guarantee of civil rights and *civil liberties, it took an expansive view of the amendment's protection of property rights. From the 1880s to the later 1930s, in such cases as **Lochner* v. *New York* (1905), for example, the court held that the Fourteenth Amendment's due-process clause protected corporations from governmental regulation of such matters as workers' wages and working conditions and prices charged for goods and services. In the *New Deal Era, when this *laissez-faire interpretation of the Fourteenth Amendment hobbled governmental efforts to deal with the Great Depression, the Court reversed itself and ceased to overthrow economic regulation on constitutional grounds.

After *World War II the Supreme Court began to use the equal-protection clause of the Fourteenth Amendment to strike down state infringements of nonproperty civil rights and to sustain federal laws protecting such rights. Ruling that the Fourteenth Amendment "selectively incorporated" the most important provisions of the Bill of Rights, the court established a national body of rights that states cannot infringe. In **Brown* v. *Board of Education* (1954), the Court rejected the *Plessy* decision, ruling that the equal-protection clause forbade racial segregation. By expanding the scope of the Fourteenth Amendment, the Supreme Court after the 1930s became a major influence on public-policy issues relating to civil liberties and civil rights.

[*See also* Constitution; Depressions, Economic; Federalism; Reconstruction; States' Rights; Woman Suffrage Movement.]

• Richard C. Cortner, *The Supreme Court and the Second Bill of Rights*, 1981. William E. Nelson, *The Fourteenth Amendment: From Political Principle to Judicial Doctrine*, 1988.

—Michael Les Benedict

FRANKFURTER, FELIX (1882–1965), justice of the U.S. *Supreme Court. Arriving from Vienna as a boy in 1894, Felix Frankfurter could hardly have imagined the remarkable career he would have in his adopted country. He graduated from Harvard Law School in 1906, and was a professor there from 1913 to 1939. Frankfurter also held a number of public positions, including assistant to the secretary of war, assistant to the secretary of labor, and chair of the War Labor Policies Board in *World War I. A founder of the *American Civil Liberties Union, he strongly supported the cause of Nicola Sacco and Bartolomeo Vanzetti in the 1920s. In the 1930s Frankfurter informally advised President Franklin Delano *Roosevelt, recommending a number of his Harvard Law students for posts in the New Deal. Roosevelt made Frankfurter his third nominee to the Supreme Court in 1939, succeeding Benjamin Cardozo.

His judicial career, however, did not mirror the activism of his past. On the Court, Frankfurter argued that, with rare exceptions, judges should not invalidate the actions of other public officials. His philosophy was deeply grounded in *Progressivism, the early twentieth-century political movement that emphasized the fairness of the American political system, as well as the dangers associated with judicial decision-making. Only in rare instances, such as **Brown* v. *Board of Education* (1954), the unanimous public school desegregation ruling, did Frankfurter abandon his powerful commitment to judicial self-restraint.

[*See also* New Deal Era, The; Sacco and Vanzetti Case.]

• Bruce Allen Murphy, *The Brandeis/Frankfurter Connection*, 1982. Jeffrey D. Hockett, *New Deal Justice: The Constitutional Jurisprudence of Hugo L. Black, Felix Frankfurter, and Robert H. Jackson*, 1996.

—Jeffrey D. Hockett

FRANKLIN, BENJAMIN (1706–1790), writer, scientist, statesman, and philanthropist. Born in *Boston, Benjamin Franklin was apprenticed as a youth to his half-brother James, a printer. Largely self-taught and an avid reader, Benjamin at the age of sixteen published in James's *New England Courant* his "Silence Dogood" essays, the first essay-series in American literature. At seventeen, he ran away to *Philadelphia. Employed in Samuel Keimer's print shop, Franklin was befriended by Governor William Keith, who offered to lend him money to travel to London to buy a press, type, and printing supplies. After reaching England, Franklin learned that he had been deceived. Forced to make his own way, he worked briefly for two printing establishments in London.

Back in Philadelphia by 1726, Franklin soon became the city's premier printer. Shortly after he and Hugh Meredith purchased the failing *Pennsylvania Gazette* in 1729, they were chosen as the official printers for the province. In 1732 Franklin brought out the first issue of *Poor Richard's Almanac*, which quickly became the staple of his business. He also profitably printed the sermons and journals of the touring English revivalist George Whitefield. In 1730 Franklin and Deborah Read, whom he had courted before going to England, contracted a common-law marriage and raised in their home his illegitimate son, William. The couple also had two children of their own.

During his working years in Philadelphia, from 1726 through 1748, Franklin led the life of an involved urban citizen. He founded the Junto (1727), a self-improvement society for artisans, and joined the *Masonic Order. He established America's first subscription library, the Library Company of Philadelphia (1731), and drafted the founding document of what became the *American Philosophical Society, the nation's first learned society. He organized Philadelphia's first fire-fighting company and the nation's first mutual *insurance company, the Philadelphia Contributionship (1752). He also contributed to the opening of an academy that would evolve into the University of Pennsylvania and to the creation of the Pennsylvania Hospital, the first permanent hospital in what became the United States.

Franklin earned lasting fame as one of the eighteenth century's most original scientists, or "natural philosophers." He conducted experiments demonstrating that *electricity is a single fluid identical to lightning, publishing his findings in *Experiments and Observations on Electricity* (1751–1753). He also undertook important work on the Gulf Stream; conceived experiments on the conductivity of metals; and is remembered for several practical inventions, from the fuel-efficient Franklin stove and the lightning rod to the flexible catheter and bifocals.

Retiring from active management of his printing business in 1748, Franklin turned to politics. He sat in the Pennsylvania Assembly from 1751 to 1764. As Pennsylvania's delegate to the *Albany Congress of 1754, called in response to the outbreak of the French and Indian War, he drafted a Plan of Union that anticipated the later *Constitution of the United States. He undertook two missions to England (1757–1762 and 1764–1775) to represent Pennsylvania in its struggles with its proprietors, the Penn family. During his residence there he published numerous newspaper articles defending the American cause to the British government and people.

Between his missions to England, Franklin again immersed himself in Pennsylvania politics. The massacre of friendly Christian Indians by frontiersmen (the "Paxton Boys") and the movement for a petition to substitute royal government for the Penns' proprietorship prompted two of his most important polemical writings, *A Narrative of the Late Massacres* and *Cool Thoughts* (both 1764). His failure to win reelection to the Pennsylvania Assembly in 1764 was a bitter blow, but the new Assembly appointed him agent to England to petition the Crown for royal government in Pennsylvania.

The most pressing problem confronting Franklin upon his arrival in London in December 1764 was the *Stamp Act, recently proposed by George Grenville. Franklin initially opposed it, but after its passage by Parliament in February 1765 he urged acceptance, underestimating the depth of American resistance to the measure. After helping secure repeal of the Stamp Act in 1766, Franklin stayed on in England, serving in effect as the ambassador from the American colonies as the imperial crisis deepened.

Once Franklin sailed for America in March 1775, he abandoned all efforts at reconciliation and vociferously championed the patriot cause. He was unanimously chosen a delegate to the Second *Continental Congress, served on the committee that chose George *Washington to command the revolutionary army, and was one of four commissioners on a failed mission to urge Canada to join the independence movement. He also sat on the committee that drafted the *Declaration of Independence.

Named one of a three-person commission to seek diplomatic recognition and financial assistance from France, Franklin departed in October 1776 for an extended stay in France that brought him both diplomatic success and great personal satisfaction. He not only negotiated treaties of alliance, amity, and commerce with France (1778), but, as minister plenipotentiary, he raised substantial loans and gifts for the American cause from the French government, issued letters of marque for American privateers, and provided relief for American seamen held in English jails while he worked for prisoner exchanges. Lionized by Parisian society, he shrewdly played the role of the simple American democrat. With his colleagues John *Jay and John *Adams, Franklin negotiated the 1783 Treaty of *Paris with Great Britain that ended the *Revolutionary War and secured American independence.

Returning to Philadelphia in September 1785, Franklin, now nearing eighty, served as president of the Supreme Executive Council of Pennsylvania, represented his state in the *Constitutional Convention of 1787, and presided over the Pennsylvania Abolition Society. Among his last writings was an attack on *slavery and the slave trade published in the *Federal Gazette* in March 1790. His posthumously published *Autobiography* became the prototype of a classic American genre, the story of the self-made man. Although his historical reputation has fluctuated, Benjamin Franklin's status in the American pantheon seems secure.

[*See also* Antislavery; Colonial Era; Hospitals; Indian History and Culture: From 1500 to 1800; Penn, William; Revolution and Constitution, Era of; Science: Colonial Era; Seven Years' War.]

• Carl Van Doren, *Benjamin Franklin*, 1938. Leonard W. Labaree, William B. Willcox, and Barbara B. Oberg, eds., *The Papers of Benjamin Franklin*, 3 vols. to date, 1959– . Claude-Anne Lopez and Eugenia W. Herbert, *The Private Franklin*, 1975. J. A. Leo Lemay, ed., *Benjamin Franklin's Autobiography*, 1981. Jonathan R. Dull, *Franklin the Diplomat*, 1982.

—Barbara B. Oberg

FRATERNAL ORGANIZATIONS. Voluntary associations organized around secret rituals and seeking to create close, familial ties among their members enjoyed enormous popularity in nineteenth-century America. Freemasonry, the earliest and largest of these societies, provided the model for many of these groups. Imported from England about 1730, the *Masonic Order grew rapidly after the *Revolutionary War, but faced a massive AntiMasonic movement in the 1820s and 1830s. Masonry's temporary decline allowed other fraternal organizations to take root. Odd Fellowship, another English import, grew dramatically after the 1830s. Following the Masonic model of using regalia, initiation rituals, and symbolism to encourage fraternal bonding, mutual aid, and universal brotherhood, the Odd Fellows by the end of the century rivaled the earlier society in popularity. Many other national orders, including the Knights of Pythias, the Improved Order of Red Men, and the Benevolent and Protective Order of Elks, also developed in the mid–nineteenth century.

Typically claiming mythic origins and sponsoring convivial eating and drinking, moral training, mutual aid (sometimes including but almost always going beyond formal *insurance), and networking (both business and political), the fraternal order became a primary form of social organization in the late nineteenth and early twentieth centuries. The form was increasingly used for specific purposes—labor organization (the *Knights of Labor and the *Granger Movement), politics (the *Grand Army of the Republic and the *Ku Klux Klan), mutual insurance (the Modern Woodmen of the World), college life (Greek letter fraternities), and ethnic solidarity (B'nai Brith, the Ancient Order of Hibernians, and many other organizations). The Knights of Columbus, founded in 1882, provided fraternal fellowship for Roman Catholic men. *African Americans, excluded by almost universal racial discrimination, formed their own groups, including Prince Hall Freemasonry. The Fraternal Order of Elks removed their formal white-only restrictions only after a series of court battles in the 1970s. Women more often belonged to the ladies auxiliaries of national orders (the Odd Fellows formed one of the first such orders, the Daughters of Rebekah, in 1851). By 1900, probably more than 20 percent of all adult males (though many fewer women) belonged to a fraternal group.

These orders declined later in the century, undermined by the welfare state, the decline of single-sex sociability, and the broadened horizons offered by the automobile, *radio, and (later) *television. In the 1920s, a number of popular service organizations like the Rotary appropriated fraternalism's ability to encourage business contacts and public benevolence but stripped away its elaborate symbolism and rituals. The economic and social upheavals of the Great Depression dealt a more direct blow. Nearly all the orders lost substantial membership during the 1930s—and most never recovered. The size of the Odd Fellowship, for example, dropped by some three million members, nearly 90 percent of its total, in the sixty years after 1915. Although Freemasonry gained ground in the 1940s and 1950s, it and other fraternal orders subsequently declined markedly.

[See also Anti-Masonic Party; Voluntarism.]

• Mark C. Carnes, *Secret Ritual and Manhood in Victorian America*, 1989. Mary Ann Clawson, *Constructing Brotherhood: Class, Gender, and Fraternalism*, 1989.

—Steven C. Bullock

FREEDMEN'S BUREAU. To assist the adjustment of newly freed slaves in the post–*Civil War *South, Congress in March 1865 established the Bureau of Refugees, Freedmen, and Abandoned Lands under the leadership of General Oliver Otis Howard and the auspices of the War Department. Given an initial life of one year, the agency provided food, clothing, fuel, and medical treatment to destitute and dislocated freedpeople and white refugees. It was also supposed to parcel out abandoned and confiscated lands in forty-acre plots to freedmen, but President Andrew *Johnson, a staunch critic of the agency, undercut this effort by restoring most of the available land to its former white owners. Local Bureau agents thus spent much time mediating labor contracts and disputes between the freedmen and intransigent white employers and attempting to secure economic and civil justice for the freedmen—even as they slipped into a debilitating sharecropping system.

More positive was the Bureau's work with northern philanthropic groups to establish some three thousand freedpeople's schools by 1869. Congress renewed the Bureau for two years over Johnson's veto in July 1866 and personnel reached a high of nine hundred, but as the ex-Confederate states rejoined the Union, Congress limited the agency's work to education and bounty payments to African American soldiers. Sharply reduced in personnel by 1869, the Freedmen's Bureau ceased operations in June 1872. Overall the Bureau provided invaluable relief and educational aid for the 3.9 million former

slaves, but its initial promise was limited by inadequate funding and manpower, excessively paternalistic leadership, and deeply embedded racial antagonisms.
[See also African Americans; Reconstruction; Sharecropping and Tenantry.]

• George R. Bentley, *A History of the Freedmen's Bureau*, 1955. William S. McFeely, *Yankee Stepfather: General O. O. Howard and the Freedmen*, 1968.

—Terry L. Seip

FREEDOM OF INFORMATION ACT (1966). The Freedom of Information Act (FOIA) provides any person—individual or corporate, regardless of nationality—with presumptive access to identifiable unpublished federal agency records. Certain categories of information may permissibly be exempted from the rule of disclosure. Disputes over requested records may be settled in federal court. The FOIA overturned a "need-to-know" policy, initially asserted by federal bureaucrats after *World War II and based on the discretionary authority of agency heads to regulate the public availability of the records under their jurisdiction.

The product of years of deliberation in both houses of Congress, the FOIA was reluctantly signed into law by President Lyndon B. *Johnson. It became operative in July 1967, one year after its enactment. Among those prominent in the development and passage of the statute were representatives John E. Moss and Donald Rumsfeld and Senator Edward V. Long. In subsequent amendments between 1974 and 1996, Congress modified the FOIA to clarify its provisions or otherwise improve its functioning. The 1996 amendments brought electronically maintained information within the scope of the statute.

The Freedom of Information Act was not supported as legislation or welcomed as law by the executive branch. In spite of its less than vigorous implementation, however, the statute has proven to be a useful tool for journalists, historians, writers, and ordinary citizens to gain access to millions of pages of records that otherwise might never have been disclosed.

• Harold C. Relyea, "The Administration and Operation of the Freedom of Information Act: A Retrospective," *Government Information Quarterly* 11 (1994): 285–99. U.S. Congress, House of Representatives, Committee on Government Reform and Oversight, *A Citizen's Guide on Using the Freedom of Information Act and the Privacy Act of 1974 to Request Government Records* (House Report 105–37), 1997.

—Harold C. Relyea

FREEDOM OF THE PRESS. *See* Bill of Rights; Censorship; Civil Liberties.

FREEDOM OF RELIGION. *See* Bill of Rights; Church and State, Separation of; Civil Liberties.

FREEDOM OF SPEECH. *See* Bill of Rights; Civil Liberties.

FREE SILVER MOVEMENT. Traditionally the United States had a bimetallic monetary system in which sixteen ounces of silver equaled one ounce of gold. As the world supply of silver became scarce by the 1850s, the value of silver rose and it was rarely used to coin money. In the 1860s, western miners discovered new supplies of silver, which decreased the commodity's value. By then more nations were adopting the *gold standard. To maintain a stable currency, Congress passed a Coinage Act in 1873 that demonetized silver. At first there was little reaction, but as the price of silver fell, demands for the free and unlimited coinage of silver increased. To pacify the silver forces, Congress passed the Bland-Allison Act (1878) authorizing the Treasury to coin $2–$4 million in silver each month, and the Sherman Silver Purchase Act (1890), providing for the monthly coinage of 4.5 million ounces of silver.

To this point, the silver issue had not been deeply divisive. In 1893, however, in response to the Depression of 1893–1896, President Grover *Cleveland persuaded Congress to repeal the Sherman Silver Purchase Act, thereby again demonetizing silver. Many people then exchanged silver money for gold and the Treasury's gold reserve became seriously depleted. To bolster the reserve, the Cleveland administration sold bonds to New York bankers in return for gold bullion.

These developments revitalized the free silver movement. Within the *Democratic party, William Jennings *Bryan assumed leadership of the silver forces, and in 1896 the Democrats nominated Bryan for president on a free-silver platform, as did the *Populist party. The *Republican party, rallying behind William *McKinley, endorsed the gold standard. In the ensuing campaign, the two sides offered competing visions. Silverites argued that instead of rigidly adhering to the gold standard, the government should devise a more flexible monetary system; Republicans insisted that gold be the sole basis for money. Silverites desired price inflation to combat depression; Republicans feared that inflation would worsen the economy. Silverites charged that eastern bankers used the gold standard to exploit farmers and the working class; Republicans responded that only the gold standard could ensure prosperity for all.

McKinley won the election, and the silver issue soon faded. Free silver appealed mostly to indebted farmers and mine owners and the movement failed to bridge the division separating agriculturists and wage laborers. After 1897, however, new discoveries of gold enabled the nation to enjoy economic expansion and moderate inflation while maintaining the gold standard.

[*See also* Agriculture: 1770s to 1890; Agriculture: The "Golden Age" (1890s–1920); Depressions, Economic; Farmers' Alliance Movement; Gilded Age; Gold Rushes; Mining; Monetary Policy, Federal; Morgan, J. P.; Populist Era.]

• Walter T. K. Nugent, *The Money Question during Reconstruction*, 1967. Gretchen Ritter, *Goldbugs and Greenbacks: The Antimonopoly Tradition and the Politics of Finance in America*, 1997.

—William F. Holmes

FREE SOIL PARTY. As sectional tensions over *slavery increased following the *Mexican War, both the *Whig and *Democratic parties experienced internal disputes. *Antislavery members of both parties expressed disappointment in 1848 when their respective conventions nominated Zachary *Taylor and Lewis Cass for the presidency. So-called "Conscience Whigs" in Massachusetts, led by Charles Francis Adams, the son of ex-president John Quincy *Adams, joined with former *Liberty party supporters in calling for a new organization to oppose the growth of slavery. Their call attracted a faction of New York Democrats loyal to former president Martin *Van Buren, called Barnburners, who had bolted the party the previous year. At a meeting at Buffalo in August, the Free Soil party was born. The convention nominated Van Buren for president and Adams for vice president.

The party drew its strongest support from antislavery Whigs in the Northeast and *Middle West, northern antislavery Democrats, and former Liberty party backers. The party's 1848 platform, written by Benjamin F. Butler of Massachusetts and Salmon P. Chase of Ohio, called for an end to slavery in the District of Columbia and a halt to its extension in the territories. The rest of the party's planks, like its constituency, reflected a wide array of interests, including a high *tariff, support for internal improvements, and a free homestead land policy. Although the party won no electoral votes in the subsequent election, its nearly three hundred thousand popular votes more than quadrupled the Liberty party's support in 1844.

After a strong showing in state-level contests, many Free Soil politicians turned to coalition politics in the following years, joining whichever side would embrace their issues. With some success, coalition Free Soilers gained congressional seats and state offices. When Congress passed the series of measures known as the *Compromise of 1850, the Free Soil coalition broke down. Calling itself the Free Soil Democratic Convention, the party at its national meeting in 1852 nominated Senator John P. Hale of New Hampshire as its presidential candidate. The party polled poorly in the election, but hoped in vain that the faltering Whig party would offer a fresh influx of members. Outside of Ohio and Wisconsin, the party collapsed.

The passage of the *Kansas-Nebraska Act in 1854 again thrust sectional tensions to the forefront of national politics. In the next two years, the Whig and Democratic parties fragmented, resulting in political realignments along sectional lines. In 1856, former Free Soilers Salmon P. Chase and Charles Sumner joined discouraged Whigs, antislavery Know-Nothings, and former Liberty party men to form the *Republican party.

[*See also* Antebellum Era; Civil War: Causes; Know-Nothing Party; Political Parties.]

• Joseph G. Rayback, *Free Soil: The Election of 1848*, 1970. John R. Mayfield, *Rehearsal for Republicanism: Free Soil and the Politics of Antislavery*, 1979.

—Eric D. Daniels

FRÉMONT, JOHN CHARLES (1813–1890), explorer and Republican presidential candidate. Born in Savannah and reared in Charleston, Frémont in 1838 joined a team surveying a planned Charleston-to-Cincinnati *railroad. Next he assisted the French explorer Jean Nicollet in mapping the upper *Mississippi and Missouri River Valleys. In 1841, Frémont organized his own expedition to survey the Des Moines River. That October, in *Washington, D.C., he married Jessie Benton, daughter of the powerful Missouri senator Thomas Hart Benton, like Frémont, a champion of western expansion. Expeditions to Wyoming's Wind River Range and to the Pacific Northwest followed in 1842–1844.

In *California during the *Mexican War, Frémont became embroiled in a command dispute and was court-martialed. Leaving the army in 1848, he settled with his wife in California, grew temporarily wealthy during the California Gold Rush, and was elected a senator in 1850. His expeditions in 1848–1849 and 1853–1854 to find a railroad route across the Sierra proved unsuccessful. By then Frémont's fame as an explorer was secure, enhanced by popular accounts of his expeditions which he composed with his wife's skilled assistance.

Nominated for president by the new *Republican party in 1856, Frémont lost the election to James *Buchanan. When the *Civil War broke out, President Abraham *Lincoln appointed him one of four ranking generals of the Union Army. In his later years, Frémont lost heavily in railroad and mining speculations, but served as governor of Arizona Territory in 1878–1881. The Pathfinder, as he had come to be called, died in obscurity in *New York City, a forgotten hero.

[*See also* Expansionism; Gold Rushes.]

Allan Nevins, *Frémont, Pathmarker of the West*, 1939. Andrew Rolle, *John Charles Frémont: Character as Destiny*, 1991.

—Andrew Rolle

FRENCH AND INDIAN WAR. *See* Seven Years' War.

FRENCH SETTLEMENTS IN NORTH AMERICA. Because official French interest in North America began with the desire to find the fabled Northwest Passage to the riches of Asia, the crown lost interest in North America for almost fifty years following the unsuccessful attempts by Giovanni da Verranzano and Jacques *Cartier in 1524 and 1534 to find a transcontinental waterway. French fishermen, however, who had been plying the North Atlantic since the first decade of the sixteenth century, along with their Portuguese and Spanish counterparts, established a French presence along the North American coast. First landing along the coast to process fish for market, they quickly developed a parallel trading economy with the region's Algonquian and Montaignais Indians, exchanging European manufactured goods for furs.

While fishermen built temporary camps, sixteenth-century attempts to establish permanent French settlements along the St. Lawrence River and at both ends of North America's Atlantic coast failed. Cartier's short-lived Charlesbourg Royal, established in 1541 on the St. Lawrence near the Iroquois village of Stadacona, succumbed to harsh winters, scurvy, and attacks by nearby Iroquois, whom he had alienated by, among other things, kidnapping several Iroquois boys. In northern Florida in the 1560s, French Huguenots were repeatedly driven off by native Floridians and Spaniards, while a 1598 settlement on Sable Island (east of Nova Scotia) collapsed from internal dissent after four years.

Finally, in 1608, Samuel de Champlain, operating on behalf of sieur de Monts, who had received a monopoly on fur trade in exchange for funding colonization efforts, reoccupied the now-abandoned village of Stadacona, renamed it Quebec, and established the first permanent French settlement in North America. From Quebec, French settlement would eventually spread along the continent's waterways—up the St. Lawrence, along the Great Lakes, and down the *Mississippi River to the Gulf of Mexico—as well as along the Atlantic coast. By 1700, France would claim three-quarters of the North American continent, forming an arc from the mouth of the St. Lawrence to the mouth of the Mississippi, surrounding Great Britain's Atlantic colonies. The French population of this vast region was sparse, however, reaching only 85,000 in the 1760s. Despite the limited number of *habitants* (colonists), the sheer extent of French settlements (along with geography, especially the Appalachian Mountains) served to contain Anglo-American colonists' expansionist desires. French containment of the English colonies was also bolstered by those Native American nations, living between the lands claimed by the English and by the French, who parlayed their geographic location into positions of substantial power in their dealings with both until 1763 when, as a result of the so-called French and Indian War (*Seven Years' War), France lost its North American empire, leaving these Native Americans without a European ally in their opposition to English expansion and leaving the English colonists without a European enemy in the northern half of the continent.

French settlements in North America can be separated into five regions, each shaped by its particular political economy and population. Acadian settlements along the Atlantic coast continued to be dominated by fishermen, joined by immigrant soldiers, *engagés* (hired men), and some families who supplemented their subsistence with farming. The towns along the St. Lawrence River, from Quebec to Montreal (established upon another abandoned Iroquois village in 1642), served as administrative centers for secular and religious governance and for trade. Between these towns, farmers who had been recruited by seigneurial landowners filled the fertile river valley lands. Although primarily of French ancestry, colonists in Acadia and along the St. Lawrence also hailed from Portugal, the Basque Provinces, and Germany and included missionized Indians and *New England captives. Farther inland, in the *pays d'en haut*, outposts housed explorers, traders, missionaries, and soldiers but few *habitants*. The extent of French-claimed territories outstripped actual French control, and New France's dependence upon economic and political alliances with a variety of Native American groups required limiting the extent of French settlements. Antoine de la Mothe Cadillac established a civilian settlement at *Detroit in 1701, but even there the *habitants* were more interested in trade than in farming. Moving down the Mississippi River into what was known as the Illinois Country, French and Canadian fur traders became farmers, growing wheat, primarily for colonists in Louisiana, and developing multiethnic communities with their Native American wives around Jesuit missions and fur-trading posts, including Cahokia (1699), Kaskaskia (1703), and Sainte-Geneviève (1735). Finally, in the lower Mississippi valley, forts at Mobile (1702),

*New Orleans (1718), and Natchez (1716, originally Fort Rosalie) became centers of a staple-crop plantation colony that emerged gradually during the eighteenth century, inhabited by Canadian transplants, voluntary and involuntary immigrants from France, German peasants, French and Swiss soldiers, and Indian and African slaves.

The lives of many French North American *habitants* were disrupted by eighteenth-century geopolitical changes, but none more than the Acadians. As British-French tensions increased prior to the Seven Years' War, officials in the part of Acadia that had become British Nova Scotia decided to exile all French-speaking Acadians who refused to swear allegiance to the British Crown. Beginning in 1755, several thousand Acadians were forced to disperse, spreading out from New England south to the Caribbean and east to England and France. By the mid-1760s, unhappy with their original destinations, many Acadians began relocating to Louisiana, where they were welcomed by the colony's new Spanish government, which was seeking to increase the colony's population and was happy to do so with Catholic farmers. Settling among the isolated bayous of southern Louisiana, Acadians would become Cajuns.

Besides the Cajuns' significant contributions to the development of Louisiana and its culture (especially its music and cuisine), French habitants left reminders of their presence on the peoples, landscapes, and cultures throughout North America, including the future United States, from the Métis peoples of the Great Lakes through midwestern place names (such as Prairie du Chien, Wisconsin, and Des Moines, Iowa) to the cultural heritages of Sainte-Geneviève and New Orleans.

[*See also* Colonial Era; Exploration, Conquest, and Settlement, Era of European; Fisheries; Fur Trade; Indian History and Culture: From 1500 to 1800; Iroquois Confederacy; La Salle, René-Robert Cavelier, Sieur de; Roman Catholicism; Spanish Settlements in North America.]

• Carl A. Brasseaux, *The Founding of New Acadia: The Beginnings of Acadian Life in Louisiana, 1765–1803,* 1987. W. J. Eccles, *France in America,* rev. ed, 1990. Daniel H. Usner Jr., *Indians, Settlers, and Slaves in a Frontier Exchange Economy,* 1992. Carl J. Ekberg, *French Roots in the Illinois Country: The Mississippi Frontier in Colonial Times,* 1998.

—Jennifer M. Spear

FREUDIANISM. *See* Psychology; Psychotherapy.

FRIEDAN, BETTY. *See Feminine Mystique, The.*

FRIEDMAN, MILTON. *See* Economics; Monetarism.

FUGITIVE SLAVE ACT (1850). Drafted by Senator James Y. Mason of Virginia and the product of months of contentious debate in the Senate, the Fugitive Slave Act of 1850 was signed into law by President Millard *Fillmore as part of the *Compromise of 1850. Senator Charles Sumner of Massachusetts, an ardent critic, denounced the law as unconstitutional, but Daniel *Webster, in a famous speech on 7 March, supported it as part of a larger political effort to preserve the Union. The southern senators John C. *Calhoun and Jefferson *Davis doubted that the law would achieve its purpose, but they did not oppose it. Organized opposition to the law in the North faded after the summer of 1851. The *Supreme Court in *Ableman* v. *Booth* (1859) affirmed the law's constitutionality.

The Fugitive Slave Act authorized newly appointed fugitive slave commissioners to issue warrants for the arrest of runaway slaves. In a federal proceeding, before fugitive slave tribunals established by the act, the commissioner summarily ruled whether the person described in the warrant was indeed the person claimed by the slaveowner or the owner's agent. (A court record taken in the state from which the slave had escaped was deemed sufficient proof of ownership.) This summary decision could not be appealed, nor could state courts issue writs of habeas corpus.

The law's historical significance lay in the white South's belief that it was not vigorously enforced, that northerners had acted in bad faith in passing it, and that the southern states were therefore justified in seceding from the Union. Out of a total of 332 cases, federal tribunals remanded 157 slaves, 68 at government expense; 141 fugitive slaves were captured and returned without due process of law. The law was also of significance in inspiring Harriet Beecher Stowe's abolitionist novel **Uncle Tom's Cabin* (1852). Fugitive slaves were returned from *Washington, D.C., to owners in the free states as late as June 1863, but Congress repealed the Fugitive Slave Act in 1864.

[*See also* Antebellum Era; Antislavery; Civil War: Causes; Slavery: Development and Expansion of Slavery; Slave Uprisings and Resistance.]

• Stanley W. Campbell, *The Slave Catchers: Enforcement of the Fugitive Slave Law, 1850–1860,* 1970.

—Stanley W. Campbell

FULLER, MARGARET (1810–1850), critic, journalist, and transcendentalist leader. Born in Cambridge, Massachusetts, to Margarett Crane and Timothy Fuller, a four-term Republican congressman, Margaret Fuller received through her father's tutoring and private schooling the same advanced classical education available to boys of Boston-Cambridge's intellectually ambitious Unitarian elite, which she supplemented by self-education in the entire canon of European literature. Lacking a commensurate professional outlet, she soon carved out one for herself in the emerging transcendentalist movement. After teaching in its schools in *Boston and Providence, in 1839 she started a five-year series of "Conversations" for Boston's liberal and reform-minded women. In 1840–1842 she edited the transcendentalists' newly founded magazine, the *Dial.* In *Summer on the Lakes* (1844), she offered a self-reflexive critique of the American *West based on her previous summer's journey through the Great Lakes region. *Woman in the Nineteenth Century* (1845) was a pioneering philosophical study of womanhood and a prophetic plea for women's emancipation from social and psychological constraints.

In 1844 Fuller moved to New York to become the literary editor of Horace Greeley's *New-York Tribune*, regularly reviewing current books and the city's cultural events and benevolent institutions. In *Papers on Literature and Art* (1846), a collection of her criticism from the *Dial*, the *Tribune*, and other periodicals, she applied her Romantic cultural theories to both classic European works and to America's emerging *popular culture. In 1846 she sailed to Europe as the *Tribune*'s correspondent. Here she formed friendships with Giuseppe Mazzini and other prominent social Romantic exiles and ardently supported Italy's struggle for republican unification and independence. During the Roman Revolution of 1848–1849, she chronicled political developments in Italy and Europe from an increasingly socialist point of view. During the French siege of Rome she directed the city's principal hospital. After Rome's fall she fled to Florence, from which the following year she embarked for New York. She drowned with her husband, Giovanni Angelo Ossoli, a former officer in the Roman Republican Guard, and their out-of-wedlock, two-year-old son in a shipwreck off Fire Island.

Fuller was America's first public intellectual woman of letters. Her transcendentalist writings, along with those of Ralph Waldo *Emerson and Henry David *Thoreau, constitute the circle's most sustained effort to combine social reform and the Romantic claims of psychological self-development. As the first theoretical considerations of *gender in America, her feminist writings would remain influential through the twentieth century. Her criticism prefigured the two central themes of modern American critical discourse: finding a place for imaginative art and *literature in a market-driven, democratic culture and making American culture identity an integral part of the modern western conversation. America's quintessential questing Romantic, Fuller eventually became its first avant-garde, cosmopolitan intellectual.

[*See also* Feminism; Journalism; Romantic Movement; Transcendentalism; Unitarianism and Universalism; Women's Rights Movements.]

• Charles Capper, *Margaret Fuller: An American Romantic Life*, vol. 1, *The Private Years*, 1992. Bell Gale Chevigny, *The Woman and the Myth: Margaret Fuller's Life and Writings*, 1976, reprinted 1994.

—Charles Capper

FULTON, ROBERT. *See* Steam Power.

FUNDAMENTALIST MOVEMENT. American fundamentalism emerged within evangelical *Protestantism in the early twentieth century in opposition to "modernism," a term that encompassed liberal theology, the Darwinian theory of *evolution, and secular culture. Fundamentalists shared with other American evangelicals an emphasis on the classical Protestant doctrines of salvation, the authority of the *Bible, the importance of a personal conversion experience, and a missionary zeal to spread the gospel. What distinguished them from other evangelicals was their strident antimodernism.

The chief pillars of fundamentalist theology, such as biblical inerrancy, reflected this sentiment. The doctrine of inerrancy developed most fully by Presbyterian conservatives at Princeton Theological Seminary in the late nineteenth century in response to "higher criticism," a sociohistorical approach to the Bible advocated by theological liberals. Believers in inerrancy view the Bible as the infallible product of the Holy Spirit's guidance; as the Word of God it contains no errors of any sort and must be read "literally."

Strongly tied to biblical inerrancy was dispensational premillennialism, which predicted the imminent return of Jesus Christ to earth. Brought to America in the 1860s and 1870s by John Nelson Darby of Great Britain, this interpretation of endtime events was theologically antimodernist both in its hyperliteral approach to the Bible and in its view of the role of supernatural forces in controlling all of human history. Dispensationalism also prompted fundamentalists to view the institutional church as apostate and modern civilization as corrupt.

In the late nineteenth century, many evangelicals embraced inerrancy and dispensationalism. But the spread of theological liberalism in the major Protestant denominations, coupled with the growing sense of cultural peril engendered by *World War I, propelled some of these Protestant conservatives into becoming militant fundamentalists. Having organized the World's Christian Fundamentals Association in 1919, fundamentalist leaders mounted national crusades to rid Protestant denominations of modernist theology and the public schools of evolutionist teaching. Despite enthusiastic and well-publicized campaigns, led by such combatants as William Bell Riley of Minneapolis (1861–1947) and J. Gresham Machen of Princeton (1881–1937), the fundamentalists failed to capture control of the Northern Baptist and Northern Presbyterian denominations, where the struggle for control had been fiercest. Moreover, the anti-evolutionist movement, while experiencing some successes, sputtered and stalled in the years after the *Scopes trial of 1925. The end of the 1920s found the fundamentalist movement in retreat.

But these national defeats did not bring about the demise of American fundamentalism. Instead, fundamentalists created a rapidly expanding network of nondenominational organizations, including publishing houses, mission boards, and *radio stations. At the center of this fundamentalist network were approximately seventy Bible institutes across the country. These schools, such as Moody Bible Institute in Chicago and Riley's Northwestern Bible Training School in Minneapolis, provided nearby fundamentalist churches with ministers, teaching materials, Bible conferences, church secretaries, and a host of other services.

After flourishing for years at the grassroots level, fundamentalism reemerged in the 1940s on the national scene, using radio, evangelistic campaigns, and youth organizations (such as Youth for Christ, from whose ranks the evangelist Billy *Graham *arose) to bring the gospel to the masses. This emphasis on national revival, however, exacerbated tensions within the movement. Many fundamentalists had responded to the failures of the 1920s by adamantly refusing to cooperate with those who did not wholeheartedly share their views. In the 1940s and 1950s, a group of somewhat less rigid (and often younger) fundamentalists rejected both this extreme separatism and dispensationalism. By the latter half of the 1950s the fundamentalist movement had divided into two camps: those who called themselves "new evangelicals," or simply "evangelicals," and formed associations with evangelicals outside the fundamentalist tradition; and militant separatists who defiantly retained the fundamentalist label.

For the next two decades, fundamentalists concentrated on church-building and evangelizing. But in the late 1970s and 1980s the fundamentalist movement made a dramatic reappearance on the national scene. Fundamentalism had always been associated with patriotism, militarism, and free-market economics; in post–*Vietnam War, post-*Watergate America, when such sentiments came back into vogue, politically energized fundamentalists, who had long yearned to recreate a "Christian America," played an important and visible role in the resurgence of the Right.

Framing their involvement in religious and moral terms, fundamentalists rallied to the Reverend Jerry Falwell's *Moral Majority. Created in 1979 with the goal of electing to public office "pro-life, pro-family, and pro-America" candidates, the Moral Majority contributed to the election and reelection of Ronald *Reagan. Its demise in 1986, followed in 1988 by television evangelist Pat Robertson's failed candidacy for the Republican presidential nomination, did not mean the end of fundamentalist politics. From the ashes of Robertson's campaign arose the *Christian Coaltion. Under Ralph Reed's leadership this organization, which had attracted upwards of a million members by the early 1990s, became a formidable force in American politics, particularly within the *Republican party. Besides electoral politics, the fundamentalist movement addressed an array of related issues, aggressively opposing gay rights, the *Equal Rights Amendment, and, most important, *abortion rights.

Aroused by the spread of secularism in the public schools, fundamentalists campaigned for mandatory school prayer and equal time for "scientific creationism." More in keeping with the separatist side of their heritage, fundamentalists also created thousands of alternative schools for their children and energized the "home schooling" movement. In the 1980s, Southern Baptist fundamentalists successfully captured the levers of power in America's largest Protestant denomination and removed moderates from positions of authority.

Despite periodic predictions of its demise, the fundamentalist movement continued to flourish in cities and rural areas, particularly (but not exclusively) among lower-middle- and working-class whites. Although fundamentalists often displayed intolerance toward those who did not share their religious and political commitments, they offered believers certainty and community in a culture where both were often in short supply.

[*See also* Baptists; Conservatism; Millennialism and Apocalypticism; Missionary Movement, The, Modernist Culture; Religion; Revivalism; Secularization.]

• Ernest Sandeen, *The Roots of Fundamentalism: British and American Millenarianism, 1800–1930*, 1970. George M. Marsden, *Fundamentalism and American Culture: The Shaping of Twentieth-Century Evangelicalism, 1870–1925*, 1980. Kathleen C. Boone, *The Bible Tells Them So: The Discourse of Protestant Fundamentalism*, 1989. William Vance Trollinger Jr.,

God's Empire: William Bell Riley and Midwestern Fundamentalism, 1990. William Martin, *With God on Our Side: The Rise of the Religious Right in America*, 1996. Joel A. Carpenter, *Revive Us Again: The Reawakening of American Fundamentalism*, 1997.

—William Vance Trollinger Jr.

FUR TRADE. Animal pelts have probably been exchanged in North America since the beginning of human habitation, but large-scale fur trade began only after the arrival of Europeans. As the Eastern Hemisphere's fur stocks dwindled, Europeans regarded North America as a fur reservoir and created flourishing trade systems in New York, the lower *Mississippi River valley, and the Pacific Northwest. The principal fur-trading arena stretched from the Great Lakes and the Ohio Valley to the northern Great Plains and *Rocky Mountains. In the eighteenth and early nineteenth centuries, this region saw fierce rivalries among several American and Canadian enterprises that maintained hundreds of trading posts where Native trappers and processors bartered their deerskins and beaver, raccoon, and muskrat pelts for alcohol, firearms, metal tools, and other manufactured goods. The most powerful of these enterprises, John Jacob *Astor's New York–based American Fur Company (1808–1865), featured several regional divisions and field offices and an elaborate international marketing system. Small, high-value fur-bearers dominated the American fur trade until the 1830s when declining beaver populations, replacement of beaver hats by silk ones, and the introduction of steamboat transportation shifted the emphasis to bison robe production. The robe trade thrived until the 1870s when the destruction of bison herds on the Great Plains ended the traditional fur trade. By the late twentieth century, the fur trade involved extensive importation as well as limited domestic production of mink, fox, and muskrat coats and accessories, which employed numerous individual trappers, hunters, fur breeders, and furriers.

Even during its peak, the fur industry amounted to only about one percent of the United States's gross national product, and in many areas it formed only a transient phase that soon yielded to *mining, *lumbering, and *agriculture. Yet the fur trade integrated peripheral areas into the national economy by stimulating exploration and investment, and by boosting into prominence such distribution depots as St. Louis. The industry also wrought massive ecological changes. American "mountain men" virtually stripped the beaver from the central and northern Rocky Mountains in the 1820s and 1830s, and a three-way battle among Russian, British, and American traders on the Pacific coast threatened the sea otter with extinction by the 1850s. For the Indians, who formed the bulk of the industry's workforce, the fur trade proved a decidedly mixed blessing. While it gave them new technologies, it also spread European *diseases and tied the Native societies to a global economy over which they had little control.

[*See also* French Settlements in North America; Indian History and Culture: From 1500 to 1800; Indian History and Culture: From 1800 to 1900.]

• Paul C. Phillips, *The Fur Trade*, 2 vols., 1961. David J. Wishart, *The Fur Trade of the American West, 1807–1840*, 1979.

—Pekka Hämäläinen

G

GADSDEN PURCHASE (1854). The Gadsden Purchase was a wedge of land acquired by the United States from Mexico in 1854. Named after James Gadsden (1788–1858), an American diplomat and railroad entrepreneur, the territory comprised a narrow strip of today's New Mexico and nearly a quarter of southern Arizona. The purchase resulted from disagreements between the United States and Mexico over the 1848 Treaty of Guadalupe Hidalgo, which ended the *Mexican War. Besides defining the U.S.-Mexican border with an inaccurate map, the treaty obliged the United States to restrain marauding Indians along the border. U.S. failure to enforce this provision led Mexico to claim millions of dollars in damages.

When Franklin *Pierce entered the White House in 1853, he supported the building of a transcontinental railroad through territory claimed by Mexico. To this end, Pierce instructed Gadsden, the U.S. minister to Mexico, to attempt purchase of the Mexican state of Sonora. The Mexican president Antonio López de Santa Anna initially rebuffed Gadsden's offer. But his administration was in desperate financial straits, and Gadsden in December 1853 managed to negotiate a treaty under which the United States acquired a smaller piece of land for fifteen million dollars.

Despite Mexico's willingness to withdraw its damage claims and to abrogate the article pertaining to Indians, the treaty provoked bitter debate in the U.S. Senate. *Antislavery senators opposed the treaty as an effort by slave holders to expand the slave system. Although the opposition succeeded in reducing the size of the purchase and the price to ten million dollars, railroad and land speculators prevailed, and the Senate ratified the treaty in June 1854. The Gadsden Purchase represents a point of intersection between mid-nineteenth-century commercial expansionism and the debate over *slavery. While it did facilitate construction of a southern railroad route to the Pacific and the exploitation of mineral wealth in the region, it also helped to fuel the sectional conflict leading to the *Civil War.

[*See also* Economic Development; Expansionism; Foreign Relations: U.S. Relations with Latin America; Indian Wars; Railroads; Southwest.]

• Rodolfo Acuña, *Occupied America: A History of Chicanos,* 3d ed., 1988. Richard Griswold del Castillo, *The Treaty of Guadalupe Hidalgo: A Legacy of Conflict,* 1990.

—Norman Caulfield

GALBRAITH, JOHN KENNETH. *See Affluent Society, The.*

GALLATIN, ALBERT (1761–1849), secretary of the treasury and leading Republican financier. Born in Geneva, Switzerland, Gallatin came to America in 1780 and settled in western Pennsylvania, where his political career began. Elected to the state legislature in 1790, he ran successfully for the U.S. Senate as a Jeffersonian Republican three years later, only to be unseated in February 1794 by *Federalist party opponents on the grounds that he had not been a citizen for nine years, the Constitutional requirement for election to the Senate. Later that year, in 1794, Gallatin won election to the U.S. House of Representatives, where he served as minority leader. When Thomas *Jefferson assumed the presidency in 1801, he appointed Gallatin secretary of the treasury.

In this post, Gallatin stressed the Jeffersonian ideals of agricultural development and grassroots democracy. Believing that government is best when it governs least, he helped reduce the public debt from $80 million in 1801 to $45 million by 1804. But a series of foreign and domestic crises, including the *War of 1812, drove the debt up to $123 million, requiring the introduction of internal taxes.

After leaving the Treasury Department, Gallatin served as a diplomat for Presidents James *Madison and James *Monroe. He headed the commission that concluded the Treaty of *Ghent in 1814, and he spent the next decade as U.S. ambassador first to France and then to England. Ending his public career in 1827, Gallatin settled in *New York City, where he worked as a banker and founded the New York Historical Society. Symbolically, a statue of Gallatin faces the U.S. Treasury Building in Washington, D.C.

[*See also* Early Republic, Era of the; Federal Government, Legislative Branch: House of Representatives; Federal Government, Executive Branch: Department of the Treasury; Foreign Relations: U.S. Relations with Europe; Taxation.]

• Henry Adams, *The Life of Albert Gallatin,* 1879, reissued 1943. Raymond Walters, *Albert Gallatin: Jeffersonian Financier and Diplomat,* 1957. Alexander Balinky, *Albert Gallatin: Fiscal Theories and Policies,* 1958.

—Alexander Balinky

GALVESTON HURRICANE AND FLOOD (1900). The Galveston hurricane and flood was by far the deadliest natural disaster in United States history. On Saturday 8 September 1900, a powerful hurricane battered Galveston, Texas, and the surrounding countryside with 120-mile-per-hour winds and a storm surge (a wall of water, similar to a tidal wave) that briefly submerged the entire city. This inundation caused most of the estimated 6,000 deaths in Galveston, a city of 37,000 on Galveston Island, a barrier island in the Gulf of Mexico. The hurricane took another 4,000 to 6,000 lives in the surrounding rural areas of the island and on the Texas mainland.

After the storm, Galveston's business and professional elites coalesced to undertake three major projects to restore confidence in the city's safety and viability. First, capitalizing on general postdisaster civic-mindedness and emergency-induced cooperation from the city's strong maritime labor unions, they created a new city charter that gave Galveston the nation's first commission system of municipal government. The commission system, along with the city-manager system, spread to hundreds of medium-sized cities in subsequent years, becoming a major part of *Progressive Era urban reform. To mitigate the city's vulnerability to future hurricanes, the new city government undertook two ambitious engineering projects, building a massive, seventeen-foot-high seawall to protect Galveston's southern gulf front from storm surges, and raising by several feet many of the city's low-lying sections, using sand and silt dredged from Galveston Bay. Galveston was rebuilt but never again approached the prominence it had enjoyed in the Texas economy of the nineteenth century. Nevertheless, all three projects won national praise and soon became symbols of the country's Progressive Era romance with efficiency, bureaucracy, *technology, and *engineering.

[*See also* Johnstown Flood; Municipal and County Governments.]

• Bradley R. Rice, *Progressive Cities: The Commission Government Movement in America, 1901–1920,* 1977. Kai T. Erikson, *A New Species of Trouble: Explorations in Disaster, Trauma, and Community,* 1994.

—Stephen Kretzmann

GAMBLING AND LOTTERIES. Since the founding of *Jamestown in 1607, gambling has been a source of both pleasure and moral disapproval for Americans. The *New England Puritans classified it with idleness and waste. Colonial elites feared its effect on the poor. Nevertheless, until about 1830, many Americans gambled in taverns and at cockfights, while gentlemen bet on horse races. Gambling typically occurred among acquaintances, seldom involving persons who earned a living by promoting it, and thus did not generally concern the criminal-justice system. Indeed, colonial and later state governments sometimes chartered lottery companies to raise money for local improvements.

By the 1840s, under pressure from reformers, states began to ban lotteries and to criminalize gambling. The same period saw the emergence of a gambling culture and of illegal gambling entrepreneurs. Ever since, America has witnessed a shifting struggle between antigambling forces and an assertive gambling culture.

In the first stage of this struggle, until about 1900, state gambling laws became more specific, urban *police were expected to fight gambling, and moral reformers mounted antigambling movements. Yet at the same time, gambling continued to flourish. On riverboats and trains, professional gamblers offered travelers card games and other games of chance. Gambling houses sprang up in cities and frontier settlements. Resorts like Saratoga Springs, New York, established elegant, illegal casinos. Gambling accompanied the rise of professional *sports. *Horse racing, *boxing, and *baseball were all, to varying degrees, occasions for betting, with gambling becoming a part of a male culture of sports, drinking, and socializing.

By the 1890s, city gambling had become increasingly coordinated. The growing popularity of horse racing led to on-track bookmaking (determining odds and paying bets) and to off-track bookmaking syndicates. Policy gambling (an illegal form of betting on daily numbers) similarly involved local syndicates. Bookmaking and policy syndicates were often backed by *Irish Americans in saloons, barbershops, and other neighborhood outlets, so that syndicate backers became important local political figures.

In a second stage, the open and defiant gambling culture provoked a national antigambling crusade in the *Progressive Era. Reformers, by creating a threat that bookmaking at racetracks might be raided, caused the closing of most racetracks in America. Urban reformers battled gambling houses and policy syndicates. Racetrack gambling gradually reemerged in the 1920s and 1930s, however, as many states, following the example of the Kentucky Derby, legalized pari-mutuel betting, a system that pools the money from bettors and distributes it to the winners, minus a percentage kept by the track. Off-track bookmaking, meanwhile, was transformed by technology as bets were increasingly placed by *telephone. Numbers gambling, a new way to bet on a daily number, introduced into Harlem around 1920, soon surpassed policy gambling in popularity. As urban black ghettos grew in the 1920s, black entrepreneurs—later challenged by Jews and Italians—often replaced the Irish as heads of policy and numbers syndicates. Despite their illegality, small gambling houses and large casinos continued to flourish. Local governments often overlooked the bingo games in churches and the slot machines sponsored by the *American Legion.

The third stage, beginning in the 1950s, saw a renewed war on gambling and, ironically, a movement for state-operated lotteries and licensed casinos. The war on gambling grew chiefly from the widespread belief that a well-organized "mafia" controlled illegal gambling and used the profits for loan-sharking and drug trafficking. For the first time, the federal government entered the fight against gambling, using stringent federal laws that climaxed with the 1970 RICO statute (Racketeer Influenced and Corrupt Organizations Act). Federal enforcement virtually eliminated large illegal casinos, but a campaign against bookmakers proved unsuccessful. Although the declining popularity of horse racing gradually reduced illegal betting on the horses, after the introduction of the "spread" in the 1930s to equalize betting on each game, bookmakers increasingly took bets on college and professional *football and *basketball.

Concurrently, licensed casino gambling and state-operated lotteries gained popularity, chiefly to raise state revenue but sometimes to undercut illegal gambling. In Nevada, where licensed casino gambling had existed since the early 1930s, Las Vegas blossomed as a gambling and entertainment center after 1945, often backed by ex-bootleggers who ran illegal casinos in the 1930s and 1940s. In 1978, New Jersey launched casino gambling in Atlantic City. By 1994, twenty-four states and some seventy Indian tribes had or were planning licensed casinos. New York launched a state lottery in 1967, and by the mid-1990s more than thirty states had followed suit. In 1995, Utah and *Hawai'i were the only states that had no legal gambling. The result was an upsurge both in betting by Americans, including compulsive gambling, and in the gaming industry's political power. Although legal gambling often failed to generate the income projected by its backers, state economies increasingly became dependent upon the revenues and jobs it created. Would this lead to another cycle of antigambling activism? The odds remained uncertain.

[*See also* Indian History and Culture: Since 1950; Leisure; Organized Crime; Popular Culture; Puritanism; Stock Market.]

• John Samuel Ezell, *Fortune's Merry Wheel: The Lottery in America,* 1960. National Institute of Law Enforcement and Criminal Justice, *The Development of the Law of Gambling: 1776–1976,* 1977. Mark H. Haller, "The Changing Structure of American Gambling in the Twentieth Century," *Journal of Social Issues* 35 (1979): 87–114. Mark H. Haller, "Bootleggers as Businessmen: From City Slums to City Builders," in *Law, Alcohol, and Order: Perspectives on National Prohibition,* ed. David E. Kyvig, 1985, pp. 139–157. John M. Findlay, *People of Chance: Gambling in American Society from Jamestown to Las Vegas,* 1986. Elliott J. Gorn, *The Manly Art: Bare-Knuckle Prize Fighting in America,* 1986.

—Mark H. Haller

GARFIELD, JAMES (1831–1881), twentieth president of the United States. Born in poverty in a log cabin near Cleveland, Ohio, Garfield graduated from Williams College, taught at the Eclectic Institute in Hiram, Ohio (later Hiram College), in 1857–1861, and was a lay preacher in the Disciples of Christ church. Rising from colonel to major general in the *Civil War, he helped create the Forty-second Ohio Volunteer Infantry and saw action at Shiloh and Chickamauga. As a Republican Congressman (1863–1880), Garfield like his contemporary James G. *Blaine identified with the younger element of the party, oriented toward economic issues rather than residual matters from the Civil War. Although implicated in the 1873 Crédit Mobilier scandal, involving bribery of politicians by railroad interests, he survived politically. In 1880, he supported Ohio's favorite son, John Sherman, for the Republican presidential nomination, opposing a third term for Ulysses S. *Grant. A deadlocked convention chose Garfield himself, however, with Chester A.*Arthur as his running mate, in order to represent both factions in a bitterly divided party. Narrowly defeating the Democrat Winfield Scott Hancock in the popular vote, Garfield won overwhelmingly in the *electoral college.

The major issue confronting the new administration was the divisive matter of *civil service reform, which Garfield generally favored, even though he was preoccupied with distributing jobs to party loyalists. On 2 July 1881, at the Washington, D.C., railroad station, a delusional office-seeker, Charles J. Guiteau, shot Garfield. Lingering in pain through the summer, the president died on 19 September. Guiteau's plea of not guilty by reason of insanity sparked much discussion of the nature of mental disorder. He was convicted and hanged on 30 June 1882. Though himself immersed in the politics of patronage, Garfield after his death was widely viewed as a martyr to a corrupt political system, and his assassination helped spur passage of the Pendleton Civil Service Act of 1883.

[*See also* Gilded Age; Railroads; Republican Party.]

• Allan Peskin, *Garfield: A Biography*, 1978. Justus Doenecke, *The Presidencies of James A. Garfield and Chester A. Arthur*, 1981.

—H. Wayne Morgan

GARRISON, WILLIAM LLOYD (1805–1879), abolitionist. Born in poverty in Newburyport, Massachusetts, William Lloyd Garrison rose to international prominence by demanding the immediate abolition of American *slavery and insisting that all persons enjoy equal rights. Reflecting his mother's piety and willpower, Garrison first embraced the religious imperative of "immediate emancipation" in 1830. He launched his *antislavery newspaper *The Liberator* in Boston a year later, and in 1833 was a principal founder of the *American Anti-Slavery Society (AASS). For the next three decades, Garrison remained the nation's most visible and radical abolitionist. He urged churches, political parties, and the government itself to sever all ties with the *South and its unchristian labor system. His fiery language, in speeches and in *The Liberator*, stirred both passionate support and fierce opposition not only in the South but across the North. Even in abolitionist circles, his endorsement of women's rights, religious perfectionism, *pacifism, and political disunion proved divisive, and his opponents left the AASS after 1840 to found competing organizations. Yet his opposition to *racism won him strong support among northern free blacks, particularly in *New England, and in this respect his activities prefigured the *civil rights movement of the 1960s. Garrison opposed armed resistance to slavery, favoring "moral suasion" instead, yet his agitation sharply heightened the estrangement between North and South.

Once the *Civil War began, Garrison supported the government he had long condemned, pushed abolition as a central war aim, and urged the enlistment of black soldiers. With passage in 1865 of the Thirteenth Amendment outlawing slavery, Garrison terminated *The Liberator* and turned to woman suffrage, temperance, Indian rights, and other reforms, leading to criticism that he had abandoned the freedmen just as their struggle for full *civil rights had begun. Yet his unrelenting agitation and moral vision gives Garrison a preeminent position among those who challenged slavery and racism in the *Antebellum Era.

[*See also* African Americans; Brown, John; Temperance and Prohibition; *Uncle Tom's Cabin*; Woman Suffrage Movement; Women's Rights Movements.]

• James Brewer Stewart, *William Lloyd Garrison and the Challenge of Emancipation*, 1992. Henry Mayer, *All on Fire: William Lloyd Garrison and the Emancipation of Slavery*, 1998.

—James Brewer Stewart

GARVEY, MARCUS (1887–1940), black nationalist leader. Garvey founded the Universal Negro Improvement Association (UNIA) in his native Jamaica in 1914, and moved it to Harlem in 1916. The organization encouraged self-help and ethnic pride, sponsored black-owned business enterprises, and promoted Pan-African unity. Thanks to Garvey's flamboyant leadership, his popular *Negro World* newspaper, and colorful parades and mass rallies, the UNIA's membership soared to perhaps a million worldwide in the early 1920s. While Garvey's dream of a mass return of American blacks to Africa remained unfulfilled, he did establish, in 1920, the Negro Factories Corporation, which sponsored black businesses, and organized the ocean-going Black Star Line in 1919 to transport passengers and facilitate trade among black businesses in Africa and the Americas. Amid accusations by critics of corruption and mismanagement in these enterprises—the Black Star Line folded in 1922—Garvey was indicted on federal charges of mail fraud and, in 1925, sentenced to five years in prison. President Calvin *Coolidge commuted Garvey's sentence in 1927 and deported him to Jamaica. Historians disagree over whether Garvey's undoing resulted from his own failings or from attacks by other civil rights leaders and the U.S. government. In either case, Garvey's urban mass movement, the first among *African Americans, marked a significant chapter in the history of *black nationalism. He attracted many working-class blacks who were lukewarm to middle-class civil rights leaders and organizations like W. E. B. *Du Bois and the *National Association for the Advancement of Colored People. He combined the militancy of Du Bois with the capitalistic practicality of Booker T. *Washington, one of Garvey's sources of inspiration. Though some scholars place Garvey outside the main current of African-American nationalism, some later black nationalists—notably *Malcolm X—traced their roots to the Garvey movement.

[*See also* Civil Rights Movement; Harlem Renaissance; New York City; Twenties, The.]

• Judith Stein, *The World of Marcus Garvey: Race and Class in Modern Society*, 1986.

—William Jordan

GATES, WILLIAM H., III (1955–), computer software developer, businessman. Born in Seattle, Washington, Bill Gates attended one of the few secondary schools in America that had access to computers at the time. He later attended Harvard College but left before graduating. Gates and his friend Paul Allen learned of the invention of the Altair Personal Computer (PC) in 1975. Recognizing the potential market for PC software, they developed the BASIC program for the Altair. Moving to Albuquerque, New Mexico, where the Altair was produced, they incorporated their firm, Microsoft. In 1979, they moved the company to Seattle. Gates married Melinda French in 1994.

Challenging the amateur tradition of software development, Gates argued that unless software authors could recover their costs, they would have no incentive to provide high-quality software. In 1980, Microsoft won the contract to develop the operating system for the new International Business Machines (IBM) PC. Because IBM, unlike other PC manufacturers, used an open architecture in its machine, and because a number of other firms copied the IBM machine and used its operating system, this arrangement gave Microsoft a vast and elastic market. By 1990, as the dominant firm in the PC operating-systems market, Microsoft was expanding its product line by developing or acquiring applications software. Because of its market dominance, it also influenced the design of applications packages developed by other vendors. By the end of the decade, Gates, a billionaire many times over, had become the richest person in the world. The Bill & Melinda Gates Foundation, established in 1999 with assets of around $5.4 billion, initially focused on promoting computer and Internet access, global health, children's issues, and projects concerning the Pacific Northwest.

In 1998, the Justice Department brought an antitrust suit against Microsoft for allegedly using its control of the operating-systems market to promote its own Internet Web browser and to prevent other companies from entering the market. In June 2000, federal district judge Penfield Jackson ruled that Microsoft had violated the antitrust laws and should be divided into two companies. Microsoft appealed, and the case continued.

[*See also* Antitrust Legislation; Automation and Computerization; Computers; Internet and Worldwide Web; Philanthropy and Philanthropic Foundations.]

• Stephen Manes and Paul Andrews, *Gates: How Microsoft's Mogul Reinvented an Industry—and Made Himself the Richest Man in America*, 1993. Bill Gates, *The Road Ahead*, 1995.

—Robert W. Seidel

GAY AND LESBIAN RIGHTS MOVEMENT. The movement to protect gay and lesbian *civil rights emerged in the wake of *World War II. Thousands of men and women who had thrived in the military's same-sex worlds began understanding their sexual activities as central to their identities. They settled in the nation's cities, constructing social lives for themselves that dramatically expanded the previously small homosexual subcultures. Although in the past those subcultures—of private parties; select bars; and, for men, certain parks and bathhouses—were occasionally glimpsed and even celebrated by the larger public, from the mid-1930s onward homosexuality and cross-dressing were increasingly penalized. Bars were raided and patrons arrested, the *military instituted an elaborate homosexual-exclusion process, and states vigorously enforced sex-crime laws. The gay and lesbian civil rights movement was born of that simultaneous expansion and repression.

Its first phase, the homophile movement, started in 1950 when several homosexual men, most former communist and progressive activists, founded the Mattachine Society in *Los Angeles. Drawing on leftist theory, they created a network of discussion groups where men and women shared their experiences and constructed a common identity as an oppressed minority. Mattachine's membership peaked in the thousands with groups meeting across southern *California, and as far east as *Chicago and *New York City; other homophile groups soon appeared, including the lesbian Daughters of Bilitis. Members were generally middle-class with integrationist goals: They encouraged homosexuals to conform to social standards and sought out experts to convince society that homosexuals were otherwise normal. While never numerous, these groups for two decades held annual conventions, circulated newsletters, and even successfully appealed to the U.S. *Supreme Court the right to mail their literature. During the 1960s, they became somewhat more visible, staging small pickets in front of the *White House and *Philadelphia's Independence Hall to protest dismissals of homosexual federal employees. In New York, they even successfully challenged antihomosexual liquor laws and police entrapment.

These more public actions foreshadowed the dramatic explosion of aggressive, visible activism that erupted in 1969, marking the beginning of gay liberation, the movement's second wave. Fifty homophile organizations that year had turned into eight hundred gay liberation groups by 1973, and thousands by 1979. Inspired by other rights movements and by the counterculture, gay liberationists demanded "gay power" and insisted that homosexuals "come out of the closet" by announcing their homosexuality to friends, families, and colleagues. Younger and often less socially established than their homophile predecessors, gay liberationists forcibly resisted sanctions against homosexuality. Most famously, on 27 June 1969, at New York's Stonewall Inn bar, patrons refused to disperse after a police raid and instead fought back; street rioting ensued. Joining groups like the Gay Activists Alliance and Gay Liberation Front, activists around the country interrupted city council meetings and psychiatric conferences, sat in at magazine offices and political campaign headquarters, and marched through the streets. Subsequently, the American Psychiatric Association removed homosexuality from its disease list, countless editorial policies were modified, and several cities and Congress deliberated antidiscrimination legislation. Within the movement, often in reaction to its own sexism, strong lesbian-centered organizations also developed.

These political achievements produced a sharp backlash. In 1977, singer and orange-juice publicist Anita Bryant led a successful campaign in Florida to overturn Dade County's new gay-rights legislation, and other cities followed. In 1978, Harvey Milk, a gay city supervisor in *San Francisco, was assassinated, and California voters debated whether to deny homosexuals employment as public school teachers. These reactions drew into the fold of gay activism a conservative constituency that fought the backlash, and in some cases, including California, defeated it with traditional political actions. Lobbying groups established a gay presence in government, working to elect openly gay politicians and forging formal relationships with various administrations.

Much of the energy that might have augmented those efforts in the 1980s was instead lost to fighting AIDS (*acquired immunodeficiency syndrome). Only late in the decade, after suffering from inadequate treatment and devastating governmental disregard, did gay men and women return to the streets. Often led by ACT UP, the AIDS Coalition to Unleash Power, they fought successfully for improved care. That fight galvanized them with an energy that translated into political influence and inspired a cohort of proudly "queer" activists. At century's end, as the movies and *television portrayed gay characters and hundreds of cities and eleven states had antidiscrimination statutes, activism dissipated. Nevertheless, in the 1990s, the federal government reaffirmed the ban on military service by homosexuals and defined marriage as exclusively heterosexual for benefits purposes; seventeen states continued to criminalize gay sex; and antigay violence increased, most visibly in the 1998 murder of college student Matthew Shepard in Laramie, Wyoming. Vital protections still required action.

[*See also* Civil Rights Movement; Sexual Harassment; Sexual Morality and Sex Reform; Sixties, The.]

—Daniel Hurewitz

GENDER. To paraphrase the historian Joan Scott, "gender" is most usefully understood as an analytical category of historical thought. Although usage in this way dates only from the mid-1980s, it has largely displaced the analytical category from which it developed: the social history of women. The concept of "gender" brings together the many ways in which the distinctions between male and female operate in history. Put simply, it focuses on the history of concepts of "masculinity" and "femininity" rather than on the history of men and women. Together with the categories "race" and "*social class," "gender" forms the modern conceptual triad for analyzing the structures and workings of power and inequality in American society.

"Gender" has two long-standing meanings: an element of grammar and a colloquial, polite equivalent for "sex." With the revival of feminist thinking in the 1970s, "gender" became a term for distinguishing biological sexual differences from the historically variable and socially imposed meanings attached to those differences. This distinction underscored the fact that the biological differences between the sexes did not have inherent, inescapable meanings for people's lives. The proliferation of this usage in subsequent decades was a measure of the spread of the feminist claim that sex roles are socially imposed and largely arbitrary, and that they can and should be changed.

By the mid-1980s, when the concept of "gender" became increasingly common among historians, the first wave of modern historical writings about women was almost two decades old. Inspired by the 1960s burgeoning of social history, this scholarship had focused on the lives of people long ignored by historians. The proliferation of scholarship on women's experience concentrated on those very activities with which women were identified and which therefore had long been considered historically insignificant: *family, domesticity, kinship, emotion, private life. The dominant framework for women's social history initially reflected the nineteenth-century ideology of "separate sexual spheres" and the monumental divide it created between men's and women's lives; the historian's job was to investigate the women's side of the divide.

By the mid-1980s, however, historians began to realize that the social-historical information they were gathering on women needed to be supplemented with answers to other kinds of questions: how and why distinctions between men and women developed, operated, and changed in history; how and where men (as well as women) were positioned on the sexual divide; how "experience" was shaped by the wide range of women's class and racial backgrounds; and how discoveries about women could be made to change understandings of the core of U.S. history, rather than remain in a scholarly ghetto. The neglect of the ideological sources and functions of the "separate spheres" model of women's history, historians concluded, had led to a superficial and too literal description of social life and sexual difference.

These concerns resulted in the replacement of the category of "women's history" with the history of gender. This new focus has been producing scholarship that addresses historical topics left relatively untouched by the women's social-historical scholarship. *Work, citizenship, even military service, all historical areas associated with men, are being examined for the ways they assumed and helped to shape the historic divide between the sexes. Historians are asking whether anything women workers did was ever really considered "skilled labor," or if the meaning of the term shifted depending on where women were located in the wage-labor force. Gender-conscious studies on citizenship in the era of *Revolution and Constitution examine how the exclusion of women shaped the self-understanding of American republicans and their faith in their own civic virtue.

Scholarship organized around the concept of "gender" rather than that of "women" has also proved better able to address the relations of racial power. For example, historians of the *South in the decades after *Reconstruction, adopting an analytic approach informed by the new emphasis on gender, traced how postbellum upheavals in power relations between the races, as well as the efforts of former slaves to realize their freedom and to re-create their communities, led to dramatic shifts in the relations between men and women and tremendous conflicts over sexuality, culminating in the *lynching epidemic late in the nineteenth century.

[*See also* Domestic Labor; Feminism; Historiography, American; Race, Concept of; Racism; Republicanism; Sexual Morality and Sex Reform; Social Science; Women in the Labor Force.]

• Gayle Rubin, "The Traffic in Women: Notes on the 'Political Economy' of Sex," in *Toward an Anthropology of Women,* ed. Rayna Reiter, 1975, pp. 157–210. John Scott, *Gender and the Politics of History,* 1988. Linda Kerber et al., "Beyond Roles: Beyond Spheres: Thinking about Gender in the Early Republic," *William and Mary Quarterly*, 3d series, 46 (July 1989): 565–85. Ava Baron, ed., *Work Engendered: Toward a New History of American Labor,* 1991. Gail Bederman, *Manliness and Civilization: A Cultural History of Gender and Race in the United States, 1880–1917,* 1995.

—Ellen C. DuBois

GENERAL AGREEMENT ON TARIFFS AND TRADE (GATT), a never-signed but generally observed agreement that governed international trade from 1948 until 1995, when it was incorporated into the structure of the World Trade Organization (WTO). The ideas behind GATT originated during the 1930s. The Great Depression and the coming to power of fascist leaders had led to a breakdown in multilateral trade relations. Believing that non-cooperative trade policies would aggravate the economic depression and possibly lead to war, American diplomats, notably Secretary of State Cordell *Hull, pushed for a resumption of international trade. Under Hull's leadership, the United States entered into a series of bilateral reciprocal-trade agreements with various countries.

*World War II gave American planners the impetus to push for an international trade organization that would, they hoped, ensure a prosperous and therefore peaceful postwar world. The blueprint for an international trade organization (ITO) was set forth in December 1945, but the U.S. Congress failed to ratify the ITO in 1948. Rather than try to create another trade organization, diplomats decided to make the ITO's charter the basis of GATT, which the United States then adhered to by executive agreement.

Seven rounds of GATT negotiations were held between 1947 and 1994, all aimed at lowering tariffs barriers and thereby increasing the volume of world trade. These goals were based on the principles of nondiscrimination in trade, the elimination of quantitative restrictions, and the settlement of trade disputes through consultation, not confrontation. Most influential was the so-called Kennedy Round of discussions (1964–1967), which resulted in the deepest (around 35 percent) and broadest tariff reductions in history. Out of the Uruguay Round (1986–1994) came the genesis of the WTO, the first international-trade organization to be formalized and (in 1996) ratified by Congress. Political controversy over American involvement in GATT, and then in the WTO, involved the issue of whether such trade agreements entailed some loss of sovereignty and to what extent freer trade might disadvantage labor by keeping wages low.

[*See also* Depressions, Economic; Foreign Relations: The Economic Dimension; Foreign Trade, U.S.; Labor Movements; New Deal Era, The; Post–Cold War Era; Tariffs.]

• Kenneth W. Dam, *The GATT,* 1970.

— Diane B. Kunz

GENERAL ELECTRIC COMPANY. *See* Edison, Thomas; Electrical Industry.

GENERAL FEDERATION OF WOMEN'S CLUBS. *See* Women's Club Movement.

GENERAL MOTORS. *See* Automotive Industry.

GENETICS AND GENETIC ENGINEERING. The second half of the twentieth century brought a cornucopia of genetic marvels. Cloned human genes like insulin became the basis of genetically engineered medicines. Genetically-based diagnostic tests predicted the probability of hereditary *diseases like colon *cancer (in adults) and Tay-Sachs (in developing fetuses). Futuristic medical interventions, like gene therapy, were in the testing stage. American scientists were at the forefront of many of these discoveries, and American society was consequently often the first to confront the ethical and social implications of the biological revolution.

Though these developments seemed of relatively recent stamp, genetic engineering of the old-fashioned, methodical sort had in fact been a feature of *agriculture for centuries, whether breeding beefier cattle or juicier peaches. At the turn of the twentieth century, upon the rediscovery of Gregor Mendel's laws of inheritance, American genetics research rose to prominence, especially at Columbia University, where Thomas Hunt *Morgan identified a Mendelian pattern of inheritance in fruit fly mutations and, in 1910, linked a particular mutant trait to maleness—arguably the first mapping of a gene to a particular chromosome. In 1913, A. H. Sturtevant, an undergraduate in Morgan's lab, discovered that genes are arranged in linear fashion along chromosomes, establishing the basic principle of all subsequent genetic mapping.

As counterpoint to this basic research, a number of biologists became tantalized by the possibility of improving human society through genetic manipulation. This movement, known as *eugenics, first arose in England but was embraced with great fervor by some American researchers, in part as a reaction against the great wave of *immigration from southern and eastern Europe. The eugenicists ascribed a genetic component to such human traits as loyalty; humor; a propensity for crime and violence; and even "thallasophilia," a genetically predetermined love of the sea said to be inherited by ship captains. The American eugenics movement, led by the biologist Charles B. Davenport of the Carnegie Institution of *Washington, D.C., was attacked both for poor research techniques and its taint of *racism. Nonetheless, the Eugenics Record Office at Davenport's Cold Spring Harbor Laboratory on Long Island remained in operation until 1942.

Two years later, in 1944, Oswald Avery, Colin MacLeod, and Maclyn McCarthy at Rockefeller University first established the molecular nature of heredity by implicating deoxyribonucleic acid (DNA) in the inheritance of bacterial traits. But the modern era of genetics began in 1953 with the discovery of the double-helix structure of DNA by James D. *Watson, an American doing research in England, and Francis H. C. Crick. From that seminal discovery flowed decades of fabulously productive basic research into the biology of heredity.

DNA, an unusually long and supple molecule garrisoned in the nucleus of cells, contains in its pattern of chemical components (or bases) a code of instructions telling a cell how to make all the proteins essential to life. Discrete segments of DNA, known as genes, contain the instructions for particular proteins; the estimated 50,000 to 100,000 human genes are transmitted to offspring during the process of reproduction. By 1966 the basic genetic code was understood, and by 1969, the Harvard University biologists Mark Ptashne and Walter Gilbert, working independently on two separate organisms, had demonstrated that genes are not constantly active but rather are "regulated"—that is, turned on and off in response to environmental cues and stimuli.

By the early 1970s, molecular biologists had learned enough about DNA and its properties to begin manipulating it—a skill loosely called "genetic engineering." In 1973, Stanley Cohen of Stanford University and Herbert Boyer of the University of California at San Francisco first achieved what is commonly known as "cloning," or recombinant DNA. They spliced a piece of frog DNA into the DNA of a common bacterium known as *E. coli.* When these modified bacteria divided and replicated (which they do on average every twenty minutes), the frog DNA was copied as well. Because of concerns that virulent pathogens might be created by such a technology, biologists voluntarily observed a two-year moratorium between 1975 and 1977 before resuming cloning experiments.

As a research tool, cloning allowed biologists to replicate DNA of interest—a human gene, for example—many times. Such replication was necessary to provide the raw material for the next step in the revolution: reading the genetic text. Independently, two teams of scientists—led, respectively, by Frederick Sanger in Cambridge, England, and Alan Maxam and Walter Gilbert at Harvard—in the mid-1970s developed the technology to read, or "sequence," the chemical instructions in any piece of DNA.

The *biotechnology industry, which grew out of these academic experiments, was essentially an American invention. It emerged in the mid-1970s with the seemingly premature ambition of developing drugs using the techniques of molecular biology. In 1977, collaborators at the City of Hope Medical Center in Duarte, California, and Genentech, Inc., a company based in south San Francisco, for the first time synthesized a piece of human protein-encoding DNA—the gene for a brain hormone known as somatostatin—and inserted it into bacteria, which read the instructions and produced a form of the protein. A year later, the same researchers cloned the gene for human insulin, inserted it into bacteria, and coaxed single-celled organisms to manufacture this essential hormone. This process, with many refinements, provided the basis of the world's first genetically engineered product, human insulin, which won approval from the federal Food and Drug Administration in 1983 for the treatment of diabetes. Inspired by the success of Genentech, an estimated thirteen hundred biotech companies sprang up in the United States alone by the close of the twentieth century.

The notion of mapping and sequencing every human gene first gained serious attention in May 1985, at an informal meeting of biologists at the University of California at Santa Cruz. The initiative grew into the three-billion-dollar, fifteen-year federal effort known as the *Human Genome Project, launched in 1990.

This vast sequencing project generated considerable ethical controversy. As more and more disease-related genes—such as those associated with such devastating illnesses as Huntington's disease (a progressive, incurable neurological disorder) and colon cancer—were discovered through the genome project, geneticists and physicians faced the dilemma of whether to inform persons at risk even though no treatment was available. Medical consumers sometimes indicated their ambivalence about such tests. When the Utah-based biotech diagnostics company Myriad Genetics marketed a genetic test for an inherited form of breast cancer in 1997, for example, most eligible women chose not to use it.

The ultimate stunt of genetic engineering—cloning a human being—was solely the province of science fiction until April 1997, when Ian Wilmut and his colleagues at the Roslin Institute in Scotland reported that they had cloned a sheep named Dolly. American bioethicists generally warned against human cloning, but subsequent press reports suggested that several U.S. laboratories were actively pursuing the cloning of human beings. As the explosion in genetic research continued, the temptation of eugenics grew ever more alluring. As James Watson remarked in 1997, "Common sense tells us that if scientists find ways to greatly improve human capabilities, there will be no stopping the public from happily seizing them."

[*See also* Bioethics; Biological Sciences; Medicine: Since 1945; Science: Since 1945.]

• James D. Watson, *The Double-Helix: A Personal Account of the Discovery of the Structure of DNA,* 1968. Horace Freeland Judson, *The Eighth Day of Creation: The Makers of the Revolution in Biology,* 1979. Daniel J. Kevles, *In the Name of Eugenics: Genetics and the Uses of Human Heredity,* 1985. Stephen S. Hall, *Invisible Frontiers: The Race to Synthesize a Human Gene,* 1987. Daniel J. Kevles and Leroy Hood, eds., *The Code of Codes: Scientific and Social Issues in the Human Genome Project,* 1992. Robert Cook-Deegan, *The Gene Wars: Science, Politics, and the Human Genome,* 1994. Susan Wright, *Molecular Politics: Developing American and British Regulatory Policy for Genetic Engineering, 1972–1982,* 1994.

—Stephen S. Hall

GEOGRAPHY, PHYSICAL. *See* Earth Sciences.

GEOLOGICAL SURVEY, U.S. *See* Geological Surveys.

GEOLOGICAL SURVEYS. Geological surveys are among the earliest examples of government-supported science in the United States, with state surveys pre-dating the federal geological survey by nearly half a century. The North Carolina Geological Survey, begun in 1823, generally ranks as the first, though North Carolina supported only one individual (Denison Olmsted) part-time, and did not fund an ongoing institution. In other respects, however, North Carolina's survey typified state surveys to come. First, it was temporary and ended, with a report, in 1825. Nearly all early state surveys worked in fits and starts, flourishing in good times and disappearing during hard times. The longest continuously operating one, New York's, was founded in 1836. Second, the North Carolina survey, while not formally a part of a university, was conducted by a university professor. The association between state surveys and universities became common and, in many cases, endured. Finally, the North Carolina survey sought practical results. Emerging from a program of internal improvements within the state, it was designed primarily to produce geologic informa-

MAP 7: GEOLOGICAL MAP OF MASSACHUSETTS (1832)

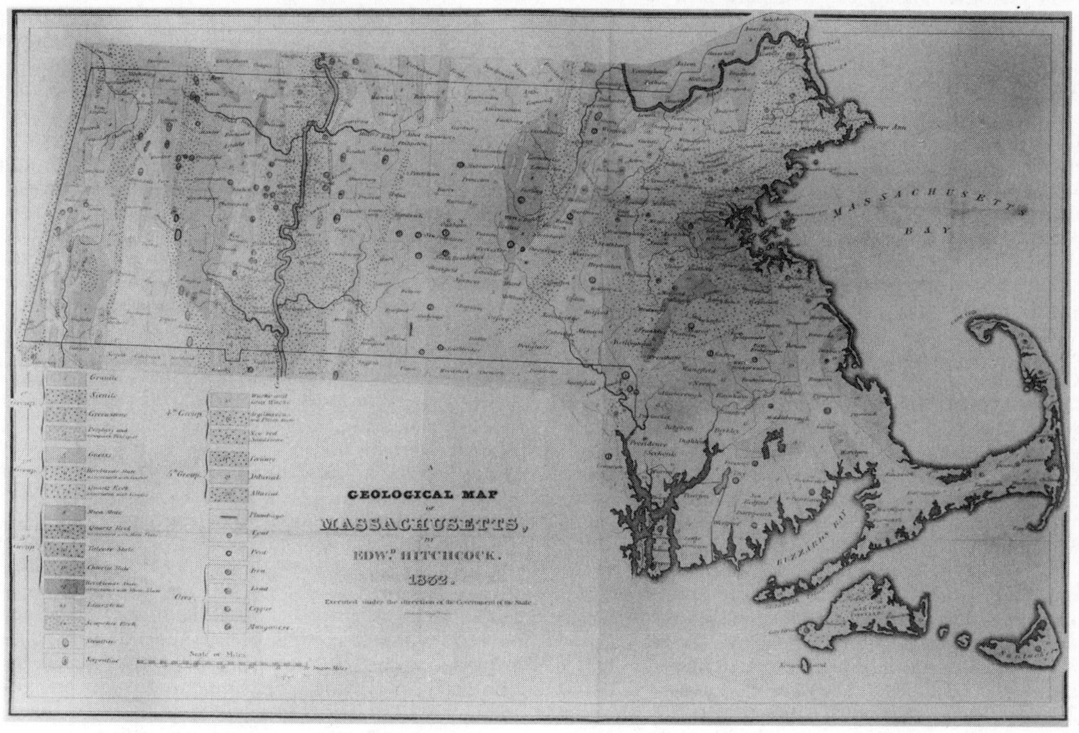

This is thought to be the earliest geological map of an entire state. It was prepared by the versatile Edward Hitchcock (1793–1864), Congregational minister, geologist, paleontologist, classicist, and president of Amherst College from 1845 to 1854. In this map, commissioned by the state government, Hitchcock concentrated on the underlying rock strata, organic substances, and minerals to be found within the state's borders.

[*See* Antebellum Era; Geological Surveys; Mining.]

tion for engineering applications, such as building *roads and bridges. Geological surveys in other states focused on minerals and *mining, or the relationship between soils and *agriculture.

By 1850 twenty states had established geological surveys. Others added surveys in the 1850s and 1860s, particularly in the burgeoning *West. Several western surveys, such as Nevada's and *California's, focused on mining and minerals. Between 1850 and 1900, thirteen western states created geological surveys, and three more territories—Arizona, New Mexico, and Oklahoma—started surveys soon after achieving statehood in the early twentieth century. Many of these surveys, in both the West and East, pursued two simultaneous, sometimes conflicting missions: generating practical results for utilitarian application while producing basic scientific knowledge, such as geologic maps or paleontologic reports.

Although the federal government did not establish a national survey until 1879, geologists were often associated with pre-*Civil War land and *railroad surveys of the Old Northwest and the trans-Mississippi West, frequently under the Army Corps of Topographical Engineers. In the postwar years Washington funded a number of western geological and geographical surveys: Clarence King's Army-sponsored Geological and Geographical Exploration of the Fortieth Parallel (begun in 1867); George M. Wheeler's Geographical Surveys West of the 100th Meridian (1869), also undertaken by the Army; John Wesley *Powell's Geographical and Topographical Survey of the Colorado River (1870), funded by the Department of the Interior; and Ferdinand V. Hayden's Geological and Geographical Survey of the Territories (1873). King, Powell, and Hayden were all experienced geologists, and Wheeler, an army lieutenant, recruited the geologist Grove Karl Gilbert to assist him. This proliferation of western surveys prompted Congress in 1879 to create a centralized United States Geological Survey (USGS), first under the direction of King, later under Powell, who made it the nation's premier scientific institution of the late nineteenth century.

By 1900 the state surveys were also becoming more permanent. The word "survey," at least as applied to state surveys, came to be used as a noun (referring to a "survey" as an organization), implying an enduring existence. Relations between the state surveys and the USGS, which generally concentrated on issues that cut across state lines, such as topographic mapping and water-resources studies, were not always smooth.

During the first half of the twentieth century, having completed the reconnaissance phase of their work and having gained a good idea of their state's general geology, many state surveys now undertook more detailed investigations of smaller areas. County studies were common, as were studies of minerals, especially petroleum in states such as Texas and metallic minerals in Nevada, Washington, and Wyoming.

After 1950, state geological surveys found their role changing. Some, such as Michigan's, were given increasing regulatory responsibility. Others, such as Utah's, were incorporated into state departments of natural resources, making them less research-oriented and more an arm of state government. Some surveys, such as Kentucky's and Illinois's, remained a university division. Even those surveys that were removed from the university environment usually maintained an academic connection.

During the 1960s and 1970s, concern about environmental issues—such as the relationship between subsurface geology and groundwater contamination, groundwater depletion, radioactive-waste disposal, and a host of other problems—gave geological surveys a renewed relevance. Individual surveys carved out scientific niches. The Kansas Geological Survey developed *computer software and pioneered the application of quantitative methods to geologic problems. State surveys in Utah and Colorado focused on geologic hazards. The Texas Bureau of Economic Geology did extensive petroleum research often funded by external grants and contracts. In the 1980s and 1990s, state surveys redoubled their efforts in geologic mapping, working with the USGS to develop funding for the National Mapping Act and collaborating on geographic information systems and other new cartographic methods. As the twenty-first century began, geological surveys were operating in every state, as well as at the federal level, a permanent but constantly changing feature of America's scientific landscape.

[*See also* Antebellum Era; Army Corps of Engineers; Education: The Rise of the University; Environmentalism; Land Policy, Federal; Petroleum Industry; Physical Science; Science.]

• George Merrill, *Contributions to a History of American State Geological and Natural History Surveys,* 1920. Thomas G. Manning, *Government in Science: The U.S. Geological Survey, 1867–1894,* 1967. William H. Goetzmann, *Exploration and Empire: The Explorer and the Scientist in the Winning of the American West,* 1971. Michele L. Aldrich, "American State Geological Surveys, 1820–1845," in *Two Hundred Years of Geology in America,* ed. Cecil J. Schneer, 1979. Anne Marie Millbrooke, "State Geological Surveys of the Nineteenth Century," Ph.D. diss., University of Pennsylvania, 1981. Arthur A. Socolow, ed., *The State Geological Surveys: A History,* 1988.

—Rex C. Buchanan

GEOLOGY. *See* Earth Sciences.

GEOPHYSICS. *See* Earth Sciences.

GEORGE, HENRY. *See* Single-Tax Movement.

GERMAN AMERICANS. Nearly six million Germans immigrated to America between 1830 and 1930, forming the country's largest ethnic group and by far the largest language minority. At the peak in 1900, German immigrants and their children comprised 10.5 percent of the U.S. population. Despite a substantial German presence in colonial America, especially in Pennsylvania, there was little institutional continuity into the nineteenth century. German immigration was second only to Irish in the 1830s and 1840s, then took the lead, making up over one-third of the total in the 1850s and 1860s and more than 27 percent in the 1870s and 1880s. Half or more of the migrants came as families, with women constituting a sizable 40 percent. Most Germans came motivated by economic hardship and—notwithstanding some religious and a few secular colonization groups—without formal organization. Refugees from the failed revolutions of 1830 and 1848 and from Prussian persecution of Catholics and socialists in the 1870s and 1880s emigrated as well.

Though predominantly of rural origins, German Americans were more heavily urbanized than the contemporaneous populations of either Germany or the United States. Prominent in Middle Atlantic cities, they dominated the ethnic population of the urban and rural Midwest. The 1980 census's ancestry data revealed a solid block of sixteen states stretching from Pennsylvania and Maryland to Colorado and Montana (along with Alaska) where Germans made up the largest ethnic element.

Widely distributed across the occupational spectrum, Germans were most heavily represented in skilled artisanal and industrial trades. Active as unionists and labor radicals, they formed a large contingent of the socialist movement. They dominated American brewing, were prominent in the entire food and drink sector, and often rose to prominence in more specialized branches of manufacturing. Their proportion in *agriculture, initially below the national average, increased across generations. Census figures suggest relatively low rates of labor-force participation for German women but overlook much work done on farms and in family businesses. Although occupational diversity suggests successful acculturation, it in fact allowed Germans to obtain everything they needed within their ethnic community.

Because of Germany's belated national unification (1871) and immigrants' religious, regional, and socioeconomic diversity, German Americans rarely united behind one political party, giving them a reputation for political impotence. Indeed, no other German immigrant approached the prominence of the diplomat, Republican senator, and cabinet member Carl Schurz (1829–1906). However, German Americans were nearly as successful as *Irish Americans in winning election as big-city mayors, and they used politics effectively to defend their culture. Resisting *nativist movements, Prohibition, and "blue laws," they promoted their language in the public and private arenas. Catholics and Lutherans—the two largest German confessional groups—built up substantial networks of parochial schools in the late nineteenth century, which operated largely in their native tongue. Public elementary schools in several dozen cities and towns also offered German instruction and in some instances truly bilingual education. An unofficial, incomplete survey taken around 1900 recorded 550,000 pupils studying German at the elementary level, 42 percent of them in public, 35 percent in Catholic, and 16 percent in Lutheran schools. The German-language press reinforced these efforts at cultural preservation. At its peak in 1894, with ninety-seven daily newspapers among eight hundred total publications, its combined circulation equaled half the German-born population.

The intolerance engendered by *World War I markedly accelerated the decline in German-American culture initiated by falling *immigration in the 1890s. The language was banned from schools and many areas of public life, and the number of German periodicals fell by half. Neither the 130,000 refugees from Nazi Germany nor some half million postwar immigrants effected an appreciable revival.

[*See also* Brewing and Distilling; Labor Movements; Lutheranism; Mennonites and Amish; Roman Catholicism; Socialism; Socialist Party of America; Temperance and Prohibition; Utopian and Communitarian Movements.]

• Frederick C. Luebke, *Bonds of Loyalty: German Americans and World War I*, 1974. Kathleen Neils Conzen, *Immigrant Milwaukee, 1836–1860*, 1976. La Vern J. Rippley, *The German-Americans*, 1976. Hartmut Keil and John B. Jentz, eds., *German Workers in Industrial Chicago: A Documentary History of Working-Class Culture from 1850 to World War I*, 1988. Walter D. Kamphoefner, Wolfgang Helbich, and Ulrike Sommer, eds., *News from the Land of Freedom: German Immigrants Write Home*, 1991. Linda Schelbitzki Pickle, *Contented among Strangers: Rural German-Speaking Women and Their Families in the Nineteenth-Century Midwest*, 1996.

—Walter D. Kamphoefner

GERONIMO (1823?–1909), Apache Indian leader. To Americans and Mexicans of the 1870s and 1880s, Geronimo personalized the horrors of Apache warfare. His surrender to U.S. officers in 1886 marked the end of four centuries of war between Indians and whites for possession of the North American continent.

Although the year of Geronimo's birth remains obscure, he was born a Bedonkohe Apache around the headwaters of the Gila River in the mountains of southwestern New Mexico. In later years, he became identified with the Chiricahua division of the Apaches. His Apache name was Goyahkla, or "One Who Yawns."

Never a chief, and despised by many of his people because of factionalism combined with an unappealing personality, Geronimo nonetheless attained leadership through mastery of the guerrilla fighting style that baffled United States and Mexican troops. With small followings, he alternated between reservation life in Arizona and raids from Mexico's Sierra Madre. In 1882, General George Crook, relying heavily on Apache scouts and pack mules, penetrated the Sierra Madre and secured Geronimo's surrender. In 1885, however, he again took refuge in Mexico. Crook and his scouts pursued, and again Geronimo surrendered but then fled to the mountains. Crook, under severe criticism from Washington, asked to be relieved and was replaced by General Nelson A. Miles. Geronimo surrendered to Miles at Skeleton Canyon, Arizona, on 4 September 1886. Confined in Florida, Alabama, and finally near Fort Sill in present-day Oklahoma, Geronimo in old age became a celebrity, appearing in parades and at expositions.

[*See also* Expansionism; Indian History and Culture: From 1800 to 1900; Indian Wars; Southwest, The.]

• Dan L. Thrapp, *The Conquest of Apacheria*, 1967. Angie Debo, *Geronimo: The Man, His Time, His Place*, 1976.

—Robert M. Utley

GERSHWIN, GEORGE (1898–1937), pianist, songwriter, composer. Born in *New York City, Gershwin quit school at age sixteen to take a job as a sheet music salesman. Influenced by *jazz and the popular songs of New York's Tin Pan Alley, he became a theater pianist and songwriter in 1917. *La La Lucille*, Gershwin's first complete score, opened on Broadway in 1919. Later that year, his reputation was established when Al Jolson interpolated "Swanee" into the show *Sinbad*. Between 1920 and 1924, Gershwin wrote songs for *George White's Scandals*, among them "Somebody Loves Me" and "I'll Build a Stairway to Paradise." His 1924 musical *Lady Be Good*, featuring Fred and Adele Astaire, achieved major success in New York and London. *Oh, Kay* (1926), *Strike Up the Band* (1927), *Funny Face* (1927), *Girl Crazy* (1930), and *Of Thee I Sing* (1931) followed, with lyrics by the composer's brother, Ira (1896–1983).

While Gershwin was preparing *Lady Be Good*, the orchestra leader Paul Whiteman asked him to compose a jazz piece for symphony orchestra. The resulting work, *Rhapsody in Blue* (1924), bridged the gap between serious and popular music and overnight made Gershwin a major figure in the music world. In 1925, he wrote *Concerto in F* at the request of Walter Damrosch (1862–1950), conductor of the New York Symphony, and three years later composed *An American in Paris*. His *Second Rhapsody* followed in 1931 and *Cuban Overture* in 1932. The musical *Porgy and Bess*, Gershwin's crowning achievement, opened on Broadway in 1935. This so-called folk opera, produced after the composer had studied orchestration with Joseph Schillinger, fused vernacular and cultivated traditions into an original masterpiece. Based on the successful novel and play by DuBose and Dorothy Heywood, it was set in Charleston, South Carolina, and featured an African-American cast. Although pleased to be taken seriously as a composer, Gershwin did not forsake popular songwriting; he spent his final months in Hollywood, writing such standards as "Love Walked In" and "Love Is Here to Stay" for motion pictures. His premature death resulted from a brain tumor.

[*See also* Music: Classical Music; Music: Popular Music; Musical Theater; Theater.]

• Deena Rosenberg, *Fascinating Rhythm*, 1991. Joan Peyser, *The Memory of All That: The Life of George Gershwin*, 1993.

—Ronald L. Davis

GETTYSBURG, BATTLE OF (1863). In early June 1863, General Robert E. *Lee marched his 75,000-man Army of Northern Virginia north across the Potomac River to take the war into Union territory. On 28 June, the 94,000-man Army of the Potomac under Major General George G. Meade marched into Pennsylvania to stop him.

On 30 June, Union cavalry deployed west and north of the crossroads town of Gettysburg. Uncertain about Meade's intentions, Lee sent his infantry toward Gettysburg early on 1 July with orders to avoid a fight. Nonetheless, the Confederates attacked the Union horsemen and their infantry reinforcements. The Union line north of Gettysburg collapsed in midafternoon. Shortly afterward, another Confederate assault broke stiffer Union resistance west of town. Northern survivors retreated to Cemetery Hill south of Gettysburg. Lee ordered General Richard Ewell to seize that hill immediately, if practicable, but Ewell, in a still-debated decision, took no action.

Meade's men, arriving at Gettysburg near midnight, estab-

MAP 8: THE BATTLE OF GETTYSBURG, JULY 1863

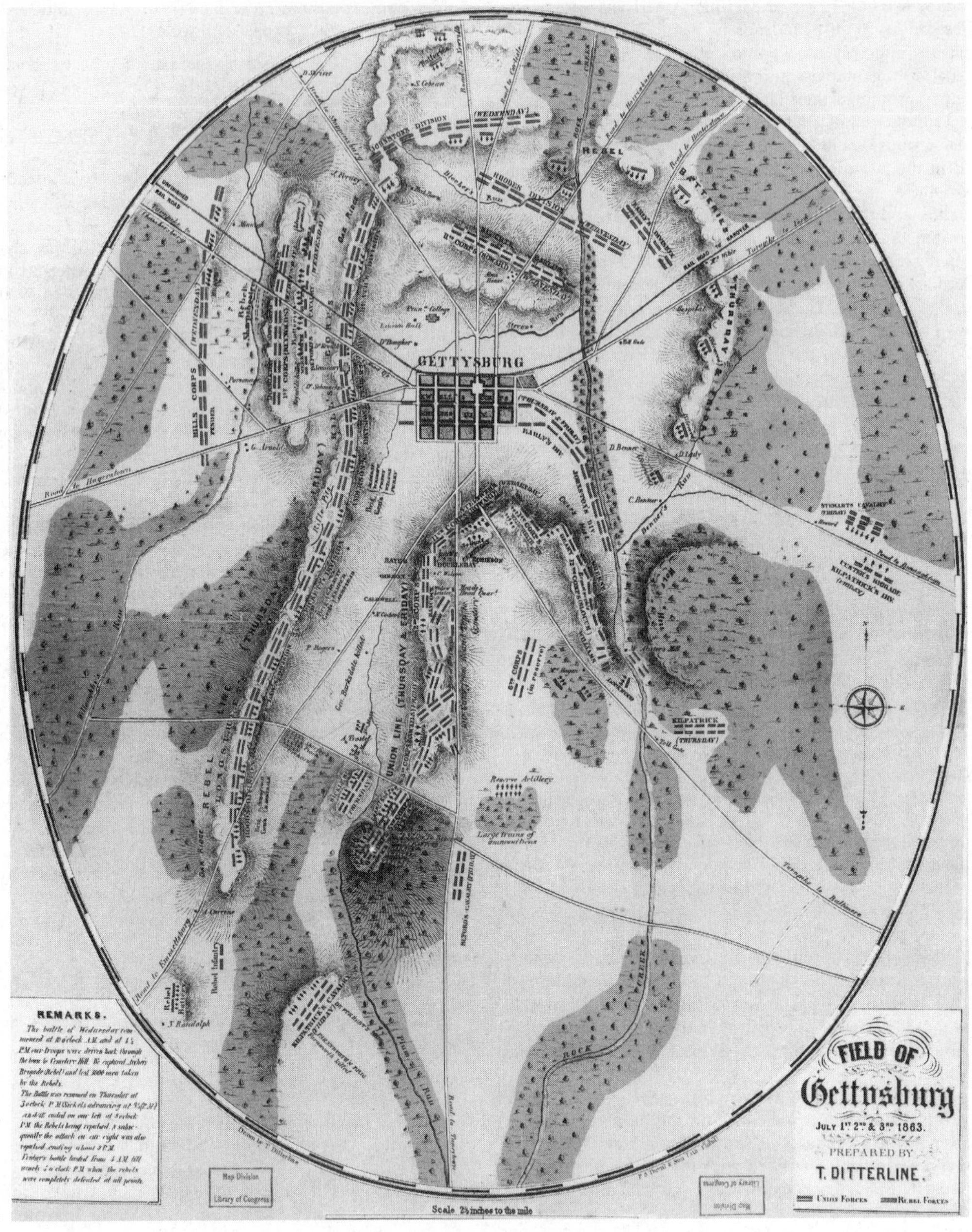

Drawn by Theodore Ditterline to illustrate his pamphlet *Sketch of the Battles of Gettysburg* (New York, 1863), this unusual oval map is valuable for its physical detail, chronology of the three-day battle, and information about Union and Confederate positions. Yet this curiously tranquil and static map hardly conveys the battle's terrible human toll, which would be commemorated by President Abraham Lincoln in a brief but eloquent address dedicating a military cemetery at Gettysburg on 19 November 1863.

[*See* Civil War: Military and Diplomatic Course; Gettysburg, Battle of; Gettysburg Address; Lincoln, Abraham.]

lished a fishhook-shaped defensive position anchored on Cemetery Hill, their right flank stretching southeastward to Culp's Hill, their left flank projecting south along Cemetery Ridge toward two hills, the Round Tops. On 2 July, Lee ordered Ewell to threaten the Union right while General James Longstreet, his second in command, assaulted the Union left. Although accused unfairly of slowness, Longstreet's attack ultimately smashed through the Union line at several points. But the key position—Little Round Top—remained in Northern hands when the fighting ended.

On 3 July, abandoning his earlier plan to renew the previous day's attacks on both Union flanks, Lee ordered an attack on the Union center at Cemetery Ridge. An artillery bombardment preceded an attack by perhaps 13,000 Confederate infantry known popularly as "Pickett's Charge," after General George E. Pickett. The southerners broke the Union line but in too few numbers to exploit the gap. Lee accepted blame for their failure. The southern army began its retreat to Virginia late on 4 July, its wagon train of wounded soldiers stretching for seventeen miles. Total casualties for both armies exceeded 51,000.

Although Gettysburg frequently is called the *Civil War's "high-water mark," the surrender of Vicksburg, Mississippi, on 4 July 1863 raised far greater interest at the time. President Abraham *Lincoln's *Gettysburg Address of November 1863, active postwar preservation efforts, and well-publicized reunions between Union and Confederate veterans gave this battle a larger place in American memory than its strategic or tactical importance warranted.

[*See also* Vicksburg, Siege of.]

• Frank A. Haskell, *The Battle of Gettysburg,* 1st ed., 1878. Edwin B. Coddington, *The Gettysburg Campaign: A Study in Command,* 1968.

—Carol Reardon

GETTYSBURG ADDRESS (1863). Union soldiers who died in the three fierce days of battle at *Gettysburg, Pennsylvania (1–3 July 1863), were buried in a cemetery specially created by a corporation of northern states. The leading orator of the day, Edward Everett of Massachusetts, was asked to deliver the funeral oration at the cemetery's formal opening on 19 November 1863. President Abraham *Lincoln, invited to make "remarks" on the same occasion, quickly accepted, since presidents had few occasions to deliver speeches at a time when the State of the Union address was sent to Congress in written form. Lincoln knew the power of his oratory and prepared very carefully all his formal statements as president. The myth that he scribbled his remarks on an envelope reflected a romantic ideal of "natural" inspiration, contrasting Lincoln's short (three-minute) speech with Everett's labored two-hour performance. In what became known as the Gettysburg Address, Lincoln distilled into 272 words a use of the *Declaration of Independence he had developed over the preceding six years—putting the clause "all men are created equal" at the center of American government. This prompted some protest in the North that Lincoln was enforcing a nonlegislative document, the Declaration, instead of the binding *Constitution. But Lincoln viewed the Constitution as a partial and developing document meant to put the ideals of the Declaration into practice.

The need for brevity made Lincoln pack a great deal into few words. His argument for union is contained in the triple invocation of "the people" in the last sentence—he and others had opposed secession on the grounds that "the people" as a whole had ratified the Constitution and only they, acting as a whole, could amend or dissolve the union formed by that document. He also drew on the idealistic, transcendental rhetoric associated with the rural-cemetery movement of the time.

Contrary to myth, both Everett's and Lincoln's speeches were successful with their original audience. Lincoln's was interrupted by applause five times and was widely reprinted. His assassination less than a year and a half following the address made it the most concentrated and memorable statement of his attitude toward the *Civil War. It has become his legacy, one of the great informal charters of the nation, competing with and eventually displacing *Washington's Farewell Address as a statement to rank with the Declaration and the Constitution as an expression of the spirit of American government.

[*See also* Equality; Republicanism.]

• David C. Mearns and Lloyd A. Dunlap, *Long Remembered: Facsimiles of the Five Versions of the Gettysburg Address in the Handwriting of Abraham Lincoln,* 1963. Garry Wills, *Lincoln at Gettysburg,* 1992.

—Garry Wills

GHENT, TREATY OF (1815). The Treaty of Ghent between the United States and Great Britain ended the *War of 1812. Signed by American and British negotiators on 24 December 1814, the pact was ratified by the Senate in February 1815.

Negotiations to end the "Second Anglo-American War" began soon after the war's start in June 1812. The United States proposed an armistice if the British would agree to stop boarding American merchant vessels on the high seas and seizing suspected deserters (a practice known as impressment) and stop capturing American merchant shipping destined for Napoleon's forces. Although the British had suspended their policy of ship seizures a week before the U.S. declaration of war, they refused to budge on impressment, and the talks failed. A Russian mediation effort collapsed in 1813.

In August 1814, talks between the two sides resumed in Ghent, Belgium, aided by the fact that Napoleon's defeat made one major point of contention moot. The final agreement essentially reestablished the prewar status quo, leaving unresolved the questions of impressment and neutral rights.

Insofar as the United States avoided concessions of territory or principle, the Treaty of Ghent represented an American diplomatic triumph. It cast a victorious glow over a conflict that had been for the most part a disaster on the battlefield. Thanks to the treaty (and the Battle of *New Orleans, fought two weeks after the treaty was signed), the bitterly divisive War of 1812 was popularly remembered as a victory.

[*See also* Early Republic, Era of the; Foreign Relations: U.S. Relations with Europe; Madison, James]

• J. C. A. Stagg. *Mr. Madison's War: Politics, Diplomacy, and Warfare in the Early American Republic, 1783–1830,* 1983. Donald R. Hickey, *The War of 1812: A Forgotten Conflict,* 1989.

—William Earl Weeks

GHOST DANCE. *See* Indian History and Culture: From 1800 to 1900; Wovoka.

GIBBONS, JAMES CARDINAL (1834–1921), Catholic prelate. Born in Baltimore, Maryland, and raised in Ireland, Gibbons studied at St. Mary's Seminary in Baltimore, where he was ordained a priest in 1861. Named vicar apostolic of North Carolina and consecrated a bishop in 1868, he attended the First Vatican Council in 1869–1870. In 1872, while retaining jurisdiction over North Carolina, he became bishop of Richmond, Virginia. Five years later, he was named coadjutor archbishop of Baltimore and immediately became archbishop at the death of his predecessor, James Roosevelt Bailey. In 1884, he presided over the Third Plenary Council, some of whose legislation continues to govern the U.S. Roman Catholic church. In 1886, he was named the nation's second cardinal—the first being John McCloskey (1810–1885), Archbishop of New York.

In Rome in 1887, he defended the *Knights of Labor, a position that began the close identification between the Catholic church and organized labor, and gave an address praising American religious liberty. As the nation's only cardinal until 1911, he became the most prominent American bishop. In the 1890s, when the bishops divided over such issues as the Americanization of immigrants, the question of parochial schools, and the general attempt to accommodate the church to American society led by Archbishop John Ireland (1838–1918) of St. Paul, Minnesota, Gibbons supported Ireland's progressive proposals that culminated in the "Americanism" movement condemned by Pope Leo XIII in 1899. Since his archdiocese included Washington, D.C., Gibbons was also chancellor of the Catholic University of America, founded in 1889, and acted as the principal Catholic spokesman to U.S. presidents, with some of whom, notably Theodore *Roosevelt, he was on close terms. Near the end of his life, in 1919, he presided over the formation of the National Catholic Welfare Council.

[*See also* Americanization Movement; Irish Americans; Roman Catholicisim.]

• John Tracy Ellis, *The Life of James Cardinal Gibbons: Archbishop of Baltimore, 1834–1921*, 2 vols., 1952. —Gerald P. Fogarty, S. J.

GIBBONS* v. *OGDEN (1824). In 1798, New York state gave Robert Livingston an exclusive fourteen-year franchise to operate a steamboat "within the state." In 1808, the legislature extended this monopoly, now shared with Robert Fulton, until 1838. Chief Justice James Kent, speaking for New York's highest court in 1812, approved the monopoly. In 1815, Livingston and Fulton sold part of their franchise rights to Aaron Ogden of New Jersey, who began operating a steamboat between New Jersey and *New York City. In 1819, Ogden's former partner Thomas Gibbons began operating his own boat between New Jersey and New York. Ogden sued Gibbons, and in 1820 the New York court again upheld the steamboat monopoly. Gibbons appealed to the U.S. *Supreme Court, which decided the case in 1824. Daniel *Webster, representing Gibbons, argued that his client had the right under federal law to "navigate freely" in all of the waters of the United States.

In one of his most important opinions, Chief Justice John *Marshall struck down the monopoly as it applied to interstate commerce. The authority the *Constitution granted the federal government to regulate interstate commerce, Marshall asserted, was a linchpin of the national government's power. Commerce, he declared, "is traffic, but it is something more; it is . . . the commercial intercourse between nations and parts of nations, in all its branches." The Constitution, Marshall ruled, vested in Congress alone the complete power to regulate all commerce "among the states." The states could regulate "completely internal commerce," Marshall conceded, but all commerce that began in one state and entered into a second state fell exclusively within the federal government's regulatory power. In striking down an unpopular monopoly, Marshall also skillfully interpreted the Constitution's commerce clause to expand the power of the federal government. His decision was widely applauded by nationalists and *states'-rights advocates alike.

[*See also* Capitalism; Early Republic, Era of the; Economic Regulation; Federalism.]

• M. G. Baxter, *The Steamboat Monopoly:* Gibbons *v.* Ogden, 1972. G. Edward White, *The Marshall Court and Cultural Change, 1815–35*, 1988. —Paul Finkelman

GIBBS, JOSIAH WILLARD (1839–1903), foremost mathematical physicist in nineteenth-century America. Born in New Haven, Connecticut, the son and namesake of a professor of philology at Yale College, Gibbs was the first of a new breed of physicists in America who were also highly trained in advanced mathematics. He received the first engineering Ph.D. awarded by an American institution, the Sheffield Scientific School at Yale, in 1863. After three years spent studying physics and mathematics abroad in Paris, Berlin, and Heidelberg, Gibbs returned to his beloved New Haven, where he served as professor of mathematical physics at Yale from 1871 until his death.

Equally at home parsing Latin and doing mathematics, Gibbs published his main contribution to physics in the obscure pages of the *Transactions of the Connecticut Academy of Arts and Sciences*: "On the Equilibrium of Heterogeneous Substances" (1876–1878), a two-part work that became the cornerstone of the field of physical chemistry. Although James Clerk Maxwell, the great Scottish physicist, early recognized Gibbs's brilliance, a full appreciation of his achievement came only posthumously. It took a new generation of industrial and pharmaceutical chemists wielding the "Gibbs Phase Rule"—specifying the number of solids, liquids, and gases present in complex chemical processes at equilibrium—to rediscover and champion his contributions. Because he made no assumptions about the ultimate nature of matter and based his system on a strictly phenomenological treatment of substances, his work avoided later controversies about the interpretation of thermodynamic functions and the statistical nature of quantum theory.

[*See also* Mathematics and Statistics; Physical Sciences; Science: Revolutionary War to World War I.]

• Lynde Phelps Wheeler, *Josiah Willard Gibbs: The History of a Great Mind*, 1952. Raymond J. Seeger, *J. Willard Gibbs: American Mathematical Physicist Par Excellence*, 1974. —David A. Tomlin

G.I. BILL. *See* Servicemen's Readjustment Act.

G.I. BILL OF RIGHTS. *See* Servicemen's Readjustment Act.

GILDED AGE. The quarter century between the end of *Reconstruction and Theodore *Roosevelt's accession to the presidency in 1901 obtained its name from an 1873 novel by Charles Dudley Warner and Mark Twain, *The Gilded Age*. The book's satirical, critical tone shaped the way historians viewed the period until the late twentieth century. The only distinct era in American history to have a pejorative title, the Gilded Age came to be remembered as a time of corrupt and issueless politics, corporate domination, and oppressive treatment of the less fortunate. Because public officials in the late nineteenth century failed to anticipate the expansion of government power and social programs of the century that followed it, historians deemed the era one when the United States failed to achieve minimal social advances for its population.

In the last quarter of the twentieth century, historical research revised the inherited stereotypical picture of the Gilded Age. Judging the period more on its own terms than from the perspective of the *New Deal Era and the *Great Society, historians reappraised the record of the post–*Civil War political and industrial system to produce a more nuanced assessment. They described the era's constructive accomplishments as well as its inequities and excesses. The decades from Rutherford *Hayes to William *McKinley appear not just as a flawed forerunner of the *Progressive Era but an equally important time with its own unique problems and achievements.

Corporate Expansion, Social Inequities, and Urban Growth. The growth of big *business represented the dominant economic fact of the era. An expanding railroad network brought the nation together and created a national market. In the process, the *railroads emerged as the nation's first big business. They employed thousands of people, created bureaucratic structures to carry on their operations, and posed large policy issues for the political system. The *iron and steel, *petroleum, and *electrical industries all loomed large in the economy. Consumers used processed foods in tin cans, ready-made clothing, and *telephones. *Farm machinery spurred *productivity in the agrarian sector. The skill and labor of workers and farmers helped drive down costs. Consolidation of industry and new forms of *mass production and mass distribution lowered price levels. Deflation and falling prices defined economic life between the Panic of 1873 and its counterpart two decades later in 1893, a worldwide reality that gave birth to the terms "economic depression" and "unemployment."

With economic growth came social inequities. Many workers toiled sixty-hour work weeks without pensions, compensation for on-the-job injuries, or *insurance against periodic layoffs.

Businesses competed ruthlessly, sometimes unethically, and corrupted the political system through bribes, kickbacks, and illegal rebates. Despite the growth of the *American Federation of Labor, unions represented only a minority of workers. The mass of the industrial workforce remained unorganized. Major strikes at Andrew *Carnegie's Homestead steel mill in 1892 and at George Pullman's railroad works in 1894 brought swift repression by employers and a government that sympathized with management. Economic downturns left poorer Americans at the mercy of the *business cycle.

Yet society sought to regulate industrialism in ways that seemed acceptable to a generation suspicious of governmental power. Congress through the *Interstate Commerce Act (1887) created a regulatory agency to oversee corporate behavior without eliminating private enterprise. The Sherman Antitrust Act, passed by Congress in 1890 in response to popular fear of big business, sought to restrain the spread of monopoly. By the end of the 1890s, citizens' demands for more state and federal regulation anticipated what would become a major domestic issue of the next century.

*Urbanization represented another important aspect of the Gilded Age. Large cities such as *New York City, *Chicago, and *Boston spread outward along the lines of the electric railway systems. Suburbs developed as rapid transit offered affluent city dwellers the benefits of country living with proximity to their jobs. The remaining urban inhabitants, often poor and of immigrant backgrounds, lived in dense neighborhoods, often called ethnic ghettos. Within the central city, vibrant communities emerged that mirrored the nation's growing cultural diversity. Urban political machines courted the votes of immigrants and their families through the provision of rudimentary social services. Middle-class residents, however, launched reform movements to curb the power of the machine bosses and shift political influence away from the urban masses.

Social and Cultural Developments. Gilded Age America exhibited the prejudices and biases of a society in which racial, religious, and ethnic bigotry commanded support from some quarters of the dominant white Protestant culture. In the *South, *African Americans saw the political and economic gains of Reconstruction slip away. White southerners imposed a system of institutionalized racial *segregation and disfranchised African Americans through literacy tests, poll taxes, and other means. *Lynching and political violence provided more direct means of coercing and subjugating blacks. Native Americans found armed resistance futile after 1876, as the 1890 *Wounded Knee Tragedy of the Sioux demonstrated. Public policy restricted the pacified tribes to reservations in the West where corruption and discrimination left the Indians impoverished and marginalized. Mexican Americans in the *Southwest experienced hostility and segregation as well. Religious tensions also pervaded society. The *anti-Catholic movement flared in the 1890s in the shape of the American Protective Association. *Anti-Semitism emerged among some protesting farmers in the *West and South and especially within the upper-class bastions of the Northeast.

For white, middle-class American women, the Gilded Age brought economic and political gains, though women still lacked the vote except in a few smaller western states. Women organized such voluntary associations as the General Federation of Women's Clubs (1890) and the Daughters of the American Revolution (1890). Other women, most notably Jane *Addams, set up *settlement houses in the slums of Chicago, New York, and other cities that sought to bridge the widening divisions of the immigrant city. In small towns and medium-sized cities, women in garden clubs and nature groups provided indispensable volunteers for the emerging *conservation movement.

Culturally, the Gilded Age was a period of notable literary and artistic achievement. While the novels of Horatio *Alger gained a wide readership for their depiction of energetic young capitalists pursuing middle-class respectability, the novels and poetry of Emily *Dickinson, Mark Twain (Samuel L. *Clemens), William Dean *Howells, and Henry *James proved more important and enduring. Twain's *Huckleberry Finn* (1884), the most significant novel of the period, depicted life on the *Mississippi River. Huck's rejection of social convention and his moral dilemma over *slavery influenced generations of writers.

*Religion dominated the lives of many citizens. Revivals led by such evangelical preachers as Dwight L. *Moody and J. Wilbur Chapman (1859–1918) tapped into deep convictions about the need for Christian faith while also addressing the challenges of the so-called higher criticism of the *Bible and Charles Darwin's theory of *evolution. To meet the ethical and human challenges of industrialism, liberal clergymen such as Walter *Rauschenbusch and Washington Gladden proclaimed a "*Social Gospel" that took *Protestantism into society to achieve economic and social justice. *Roman Catholicism and *Judaism experienced similar impulses to improve society.

Gilded Age *popular culture offered many attractions. Americans attended professional *baseball games and watched as college *football, first played in the late 1860s, grew in popularity. Dime novels recounted the western exploits of William ("Buffalo Bill") *Cody and the outlaw Billy the Kid (William Bonney). In the growing cities, music halls and the *vaudeville stage offered a dazzling variety of comedy, songs, and novelty acts. *Museums flourished in the major cities, and symphony orchestras became the hallmark of culturally ambitious population centers. In many respects, the Gilded Age produced the conditions for mass entertainment that would reach maturity in the twentieth century.

Party Politics and Protest Movements. Political life in the Gilded Age remained largely a white male preserve in voting and officeholding, but the rate of participation among these men reached heights unmatched in the twentieth century. A highly partisan and well-mobilized electorate voted in presidential and congressional contests at rates that often exceeded 70 percent in the North. Ethnocultural and religious issues shaped the outcome of elections as much as economic questions. Newspapers covered politics in lavish detail that often reflected the owner's ideological allegiance. Voters and their families, women included, attended campaign rallies in great numbers and listened to speeches on such issues as the protective tariff or the *free silver movement that could last several hours. The Gilded Age was the last great period of American oratory.

The two major parties contended for supremacy using such issues as the protective tariff, the civil service, and free silver. The more nationalistic *Republican party championed protection for American industry; the use of governmental power to stimulate the economy; and, with diminishing intensity, the rights of African Americans in the South. The *Democratic party embraced limited government, *states' rights, and white rule in the South.

Elections were closely contested, and neither major party established a clear claim to the allegiance of a majority of the electorate. Republicans controlled the White House except for Grover *Cleveland's eight years; Democrats held the upper hand in the House of Representatives, while the Senate, to which men were chosen by state legislatures, usually went Republican. Given the absence of a ruling party, legislators often deadlocked over significant issues.

By the end of the 1880s, however, gridlock gave way. The Republicans won control of both houses of Congress and the presidency in 1888. Their resulting legislative activism produced a reaction in favor of the Democrats in 1890 and 1892 that brought Grover Cleveland back to the White House with Democratic control of Congress. The Panic of 1893 and the hard times that followed created a voter backlash against the Democrats in the 1894 congressional elections.

Meanwhile, low prices and rising debt in the rural South

and West led to the emergence of the People's or *Populist party during the early 1890s. The Populists' call for government aid to agriculture evoked more opposition than support from the major parties. The Populists did well in the election of 1890 and ran a presidential campaign two years later that alarmed the political establishment. For a time, the agrarians and their allies seemed poised to become a major alternative to the existing parties.

Ultimately, however, the political revolution of the mid-1890s benefited the Republicans, who made substantial gains in the 1894 midterm election, positioning them as the majority party for a generation. The victory of William McKinley over William Jennings *Bryan two years later confirmed the political shift. The return of economic prosperity during McKinley's presidency solidified the Republican hold on voters outside the South for another decade at the presidential level.

As the 1890s ended, foreign-policy issues loomed large. The *Spanish-American War and its aftermath, including U.S. acquisition of the *Philippines, testified to the emergence of the United States as a world power.

Assessing the Era. The late nineteenth century was not a golden time in which Americans resolved all of the issues that confronted them. The answers that Gilded Age citizens devised for racial tensions, social inequities, and corporate power would seem inadequate to later generations. Yet their achievements were substantial. They industrialized the economy, created a national market, built the great modern cities, and established a durable two-party system that would govern the nation for the century that followed. The inventions of the Gilded Age, including the automobile, the telephone, and motion pictures, would profoundly influence American life in the century that followed.

A twentieth century of war, genocide, and suffering would make the optimism and confidence of the Gilded Age seem remote and quaint. Yet these qualities enabled post–Civil War Americans to create a solid foundation for the world leadership and economic growth of the century that followed. Indeed, the Gilded Age involved far more than gilt, tawdriness, and corruption. On balance, the era's material, political, and cultural accomplishments far overshadow its deficiencies and faults.

[*See also* Agriculture: 1770s to 1890; Agriculture: The "Golden Age" (1890s–1920); Antitrust Legislation; Automotive Industry; Business Cycle; Depressions, Economic; Economic Regulation; Foreign Relations; Homestead Lockout; Indian History and Culture: From 1800 to 1900; Industrialization; Labor Movements; Literature: Civil War to World War I; Mass Marketing; Music: Classical Music; Music: Popular Music; Municipal and County Governments; Populist Era; Pullman Strike and Boycott; Racism; Tariffs; Women's Club Movement.]

• H. Wayne Morgan, *From Hayes to McKinley: National Party Politics, 1877–1896,* 1969. H. Wayne Morgan, ed., *The Gilded Age: Revised and Enlarged Edition,* 1970. R. Hal Williams, *Years of Decision: American Politics in the 1890s,* 1978. Robert L. Beisner, *From the Old Diplomacy to the New, 1865–1900,* 1986. O. Gene Clanton, *Populism: The Humane Preference in America,* 1991. Edward Ayers, *The Promise of the New South,* 1992. Glenn Porter, *The Rise of Big Business, 1860–1920,* 1992. Charles W. Calhoun, ed., *The Gilded Age: Essays on the Origins of Modern America,* 1996.

—Lewis L. Gould

GILMAN, CHARLOTTE PERKINS (1860–1935), author, lecturer, feminist intellectual. Born in Hartford, Connecticut, to parents descended from William Bradford of the *Plymouth Colony and the evangelical revivalist Lyman Beecher, Charlotte Perkins Gilman grew up in poverty after her father left the family and withheld economic support. So began Gilman's lifelong attention to women's dependence on men, a concern intensified by her first marriage, in 1884, to Charles Stetson, which quickly led to depression, rest-cure treatment from the *Philadelphia neurologist S. Weir Mitchell, and her partially autobiographical short story "The Yellow Wall-Paper" (1892).

Having moved to *California in 1888, and after scandalously sending her daughter to live with her husband (whom she divorced in 1894), Gilman began her public life as a socialist and feminist reformer, taking up a tireless regimen of speaking and writing that culminated in her most important work, *Women and Economics* (1898). Marrying her cousin George Houghton Gilman in 1900 and relocating to *New York City, Gilman played a leading role in one of the most active periods of American *feminism. Always independent in thought, Gilman single-handedly produced the *Forerunner* (1909–1916), a monthly journal of literary and cultural criticism, *social science, fiction, and *poetry. In 1922, Gilman and her husband moved to Connecticut, where she wrote her autobiography. Suffering from breast cancer, Gilman took her own life in 1935, explaining that she "preferred chloroform to cancer."

Gilman made two major intellectual contributions to American feminism. First, influenced by the sociologist Lester *Ward and Edward Bellamy's utopian novel **Looking Backward*, Gilman used Darwinian evolutionary theory to expose how overemphasis on sexuality and motherhood had retarded woman's development. Matching social remedy with historical analysis, Gilman envisioned the collectivization and professionalization of child care, laundry service, and cooking, thereby freeing women to achieve coequal status with men through more meaningful work. Second, Gilman introduced the concept of "androcentricism": the broad-based set of social practices, relationships, and institutions that systematically subjugated women to men. Her delineation of a "man-made world" became a key building block in late twentieth-century understandings of *gender. Gilman implored women to "shake ourselves free" from constricted feminine identities by pursuing (in one of her favorite words) the quality of "humanness." This idea underlies her utopian novel *Herland* (1915), which tells of a communitarian society of women that has erased gender difference. Gilman's legacy is conflicted, as even sympathetic biographers find it difficult to explain her *racism and her ethnocentrism. Gilman's limitations are perhaps outweighed, however, by the boldness and originality of her contribution not only to feminist thought but to American intellectual history generally.

[*See also* Evolution, Theory of; Gilded Age; Progressive Era; Women's Rights Movements.]

• Mary Armfield Hill, *Charlotte Perkins Gilman: The Making of a Radical Feminist,* 1980. Ann J. Lane, *To "Herland" and Beyond: The Life and Work of Charlotte Perkins Gilman,* 1990.

—John Pettegrew

GIRL SCOUTS OF AMERICA. *See* Scouting.

GLOBAL ECONOMY, AMERICA AND THE. The terms "global economy" and "international economy" refer to the growth of integrated free markets worldwide. The *Bretton Woods Conference of 1944 created a multilateral postwar trading system with strong nationalistic characteristics, including bank regulation, use of the U.S. dollar as the global monetary standard, and reliance on Keynesian national planning. But the Bretton Woods agreements also included features that facilitated the emergence of a global economy, including an international reserve bank (the *International Monetary Fund), cooperation among the central banks of member nations, and an array of international agencies such as the *General Agreement on Tariffs and Trade (GATT) and the International Trade Organization. Between 1953 and 1973, world trade increased 15 percent a year, promoting prosperity in many national economies and facilitating the development of others.

As economic rivalries resumed and international competition sharpened following *World War II, the United States developed a negative trade balance, exacerbated in the early 1970s by a tripling of oil import prices. The resulting dollar glut on world currency markets terminated the Bretton Woods system in 1973. Stagflation (a combination of business stagnation and inflation) characterized domestic economies in which Keynesian stabilization policies no longer worked. The post-1973 decline in national economic power and the proliferation of *multinational enterprises gave rise to the idea that a "global" economy was emerging. Central to the evolution of this global economy was the communications revolution based on microchip *computers and fiber-optics networks that facilitated instantaneous economic transactions worldwide. Capital, labor, information, and *technology reorganized themselves on a cost-efficiency basis without regard to national boundaries.

The first and most thoroughly integrated movement toward a global economy occurred in *banking and finance. The floating exchange rate that followed the collapse of the Bretton Woods agreements together with the deregulation of the U.S. banking system facilitated the growth of offshore financial institutions (for example, London's Euromarket) not subject to U.S. government regulation. Coincidentally, as financial instruments and national stock markets proliferated, capital roamed the world in search of both long-term investment opportunities and fractional profits on interest or exchange-rate differences. Currency values fluctuated despite governmental stabilization efforts, and nations competed for favorable treatment from capital. Global pressure forced the United States to attack the large budget deficits of the 1980s, leading successive administrations to levy higher taxes, curb spending increases, and, in the 1990s, move credibly toward a balanced budget.

The United States also led in restructuring the debt of developing economies and strengthening international bank reserves. After the 1982 recession, world exports of goods rose 50 percent faster than output. In the later 1980s and 1990s, 40 percent of the U.S. gross national product (GNP) was estimated to have come from exports. Both trends suggested the increasing integration of the United States into the global economy.

The second area of globalization was in corporate organization. Deregulation and access to foreign capital helped American entrepreneurs bypass Wall Street as they engaged in raids and hostile corporate takeovers. Once again, the new fiber-optics technology intensified global economic competition, enabling multinational corporations to replace middle-management workers with computers and to decentralize and disperse production and trading units. While the new technologies transformed the organization of all economic activity, some 40 percent of "international" trade involved the exchange of goods and services among units of multinational corporations and was thus "global" without being truly international.

Responding to new opportunities for economies of scale, Japanese, European, and American corporations followed a three-continent strategy to secure markets through direct investment or partnerships in Asia, Europe, and North America. Such global integration among regions weakened American hegemony and fostered multipolarity. For example, Japanese and European direct investment poured into the United States, in areas including real estate, publishing, the mass media, Hollywood, and even the *automotive industry, once a fortress of American industrial supremacy.

The third area of globalization was in the generation of marketable knowledge, or information. The most profitable firms exploited advanced technologies. As readily communicable information comprised a growing proportion of the value added to products, integration of the factors of production for these goods proceeded on a global basis. Nations adept in these value-added techniques increasingly benefitted from the prosperity of the global economy, while those that were not fell behind.

In the new global information age, the main economic mission of the U.S. government and other national governments became one of organizing domestic resources for world competition. In this process, the United States enjoyed some advantages over many nations, including relative political stability, a well-developed infrastructure, and access to vast amounts of capital. Human resources, essential to economic flexibility, were promoted in the United States by a superior health-care system and an accessible public-education system from grade school through university. Since adaptation to the global economy requires high-income workers skilled in symbolic manipulation (converting information into useful knowledge), workers' concerns about the quality of life assumed political significance. Economists and public policy-makers began to explore how sustainable "quality of life" standards could be introduced into traditional measures of economic growth and well-being.

As the twentieth century ended, the public debate over the role of the United States in the global economy focused, first, on the devolution of power from Washington to state and local governments, whose flexibility might prove advantageous in addressing quality-of-life issues, and, second, on global trade policies. Organized labor and its allies called for trade controls to protect American workers and reverse the large foreign-trade deficit. These groups also advocated a government-guided industrial policy for capital investment in order to increase the world market share of American products. In contrast, "free" marketeers argued for further reduction of trade controls to stimulate the international integration necessary to realize the full potential of the new technologies. Hence they favored the regional integration promoted by such measures as the 1994 *North American Free Trade Association (NAFTA) agreement, by which Mexico, the United States, and Canada created an integrated trading region. The passage of the NAFTA agreement signaled the continuing support of U.S. policy-makers for the worldwide march toward free markets and further economic globalization.

[*See also* Business; Education; Federal Government, Executive Branch: Other Departments (Department of Commerce); Foreign Relations: The Cultural Dimension; Foreign Relations: The Economic Dimension; Foreign Trade, U.S.; Keynesianism; Labor Markets; Labor Movements; Monetary Policy, Federal; Energy Crisis of the 1970s; Productivity; Stock Market; Tariffs.]

• U.S. Senate, *Hearings before the Committee on Foreign Relations: The United States in a Global Economy*, 99th Cong., 1st sess., 1985. Martin Feldstein, ed., *The United States in the World Economy*, 1988. Bill Orr, *The Global Economy in the 1990s*, 1992. Martin Carnoy et al., eds., *The New Global Economy in the Information Age*, 1993. Marjorie Deane and Robert Pringle, *The Central Banks*, 1995.

—Paul P. Abrahams

GLORIOUS REVOLUTION IN AMERICA. Political principle and self-interest are the keys to understanding the American colonial rebellions of 1689. British imperial policy stiffened after the restoration of the monarchy in 1660. The *Navigation Acts established a monopoly of the empire's commerce in England's favor. Admiralty courts and the Royal Navy with enlarged powers bore down on offenders. The rules of empire narrowed political freedom. *New England, including New York and New Jersey, were consolidated into the Dominion of New England under a single governor, Sir Edmund Andros, vacating charters and eliminating representative assemblies. Marylanders struggled under a Catholic proprietary government that discriminated against the Protestant majority. The bishop of London, Henry Compton, encouraged Anglican churches even in dissenting colonies such as Massachusetts. The accession of James II in 1685 increased the threat of Catholicism, real and imagined. Between 1660 and 1689, the colonists' economy, governments, and religion all experienced more stringent control from London.

When news of the accession of William III and Queen Mary to the British throne in 1689—the so-called Glorious Revolution—reached America, it was welcomed as a release from James's arbitrary power, not just in England, but in the empire as well. The people of Massachusetts, hoping to reinstate their original charter, imprisoned Governor Andros and his close supporters. Rhode Island and Connecticut followed suit. In

New York, Jacob Leisler, a merchant of German origin, led a rebellious group that brought down James's local government. Leisler's rebels carried on precariously under strong protest, hoping the new king would accept their rebellion. Led by John Coode, Maryland Protestants toppled the Catholic proprietary and begged King William to absorb Maryland as a royal colony. Throughout, these rebellions were both a struggle for equal rights and violent attempts to exploit England's constitutional and religious crisis for colonial purposes.

The success of the rebellions hung on skillful negotiation with the Crown. The agent, Increase Mather, Massachusetts's foremost Puritan, extracted a new charter guaranteeing many, but not all, of the colony's earlier privileges. Massachusetts became a royal colony but lacked protection against further royal or imperial regulation as well as the religious underpinnings of its original charter. Jacob Leisler's regime in New York was thwarted by a strong royalist faction that bested the colony's weak negotiators in London. When Leisler hesitated to recognize a new royal governor appointed by William III, he and his deputy were tried and hanged as traitors. Maryland's effort to shed the Catholic proprietor succeeded, although without the guarantees of Englishmen's rights the colony sought. As in New York, London repeatedly vetoed the attempts of Maryland's new assembly to attain such rights by legislation.

The Glorious Revolution in America laid bare two distinct interpretations of empire that had emerged after the Restoration. Despite differences among the colonies, they had all assumed the rights of Englishmen overseas were equal to the rights of those in England. The Glorious Revolution taught them differently: From London's perspective, colonies in America existed for the benefit of the realm; they were the king's dominions and would be dealt with accordingly. Despite the lesson of 1689, however, the American colonists in the early eighteenth century generally continued to assume equality of rights. When these assumptions were again challenged by the Crown and Parliament in the 1760s and 1770s, independence resulted.

[*See also* Colonial Era; Mather, Increase and Cotton; Revolution and Constitution, Era of.]

• M. G. Hall, L. H. Leder, and M. G. Kammen, eds., *The Glorious Revolution in America: Documents on the Colonial Crisis of 1689*, 1964. David S. Lovejoy, *The Glorious Revolution in America*, 1972; 2d ed., 1987. Jack M. Sosin, *English America and the Revolution of 1688*, 1982.

—David S. Lovejoy

GODDARD, ROBERT. *See* Missiles and Rockets.

GOLDMAN, EMMA (1869–1940), anarchist, social activist, free-speech advocate, spokesperson for women's freedom. Born in a Jewish ghetto in present-day Lithuania, Goldman moved with her family to Prussia and in 1881 to St. Petersburg, Russia. Fleeing provincialism and *anti-Semitism, she migrated to the United States in 1885 with a half-sister, and settled in Rochester, New York, where she worked in a clothing factory. Her marriage to Jacob Kersner in 1887 ended in divorce. The *Haymarket affair, coupled with harsh industrial conditions and violence against striking workers by government and business propelled her toward *anarchism and support of the eight-hour-day movement. Moving to *New York City in 1889, she encountered such émigré radicals as Johann Most and Alexander Berkman. Goldman's involvement with Berkman's attempted assassination of the industrialist Henry Clay Frick and her alleged link to the 1901 assassination of President William *McKinley (by an anarchist who claimed to have been inspired by her speeches) resulted in her public demonization by the press.

She reclaimed her voice in 1906 by founding a literary and political magazine, *Mother Earth,* and through her lively cross-country tours lecturing on anarchism, *feminism, sexual radicalism, birth control, and new literary trends, especially modern *drama. Liberals and radicals formed free-speech clubs to protest the suppression of Goldman's talks and Roger Baldwin attributed his founding of the *American Civil Liberties Union to Goldman. Goldman had been a mentor to Margaret *Sanger and in 1916 was arrested for advocating birth control. Along with Berkman, she was tried, convicted, and imprisoned in 1917 for protesting wartime *conscription, and in 1919, amid the post–*World War I Red Scare, she and Berkman were deported with several hundred other alien radicals to Russia. In *My Disillusionment in Russia* (1923, full text 1925), she exposed the hypocrisy of Russia's Bolshevik regime and protested its suppression of dissent. Criticized and isolated by the Left and the Right, Goldman found refuge in southern France while frequently visiting England and Canada. Her compelling biography, *My Life* (1931), precipitated a final visit to the United States in 1934. Bereaved by the suicide of Berkman, her longtime comrade, in 1936, Goldman plunged into propaganda work for the Spanish anarchists during the Spanish Civil War, basing herself in London and Barcelona (1936–1938). She died in Canada, championing the cause of Spanish refugees and maintaining her lifelong commitment to free expression.

[*See also* Birth Control and Family Planning; Gilded Age; Homestead Lockout; Labor Movements; Progressive Era; Radicalism; Twenties, The.]

• Alice Wexler, *Emma Goldman in America,* 1984. Candace Falk et al., eds., *The Emma Goldman Papers: A Microfilm Edition,* 69 reels, 1991. Candace Falk et al., eds., *Emma Goldman: A Guide to Her Life and Documentary Sources,* 1995.

—Candace Falk

GOLD RUSHES. The nineteenth century was the great era of North American gold rushes. Beginning in North Carolina in 1799, gold rushes were initially a southern phenomenon, centered along the eastern piedmont of the Appalachians. A rush in the Cherokee Nation contributed to the forced removal of Cherokees in the 1830s.

The western rushes began in 1848 with a gold discovery in the foothills of the Sierra Nevada, just as the United States acquired *California from Mexico, and they shared characteristics with those in the *South. They dispossessed native peoples, focused on placers (surface gold deposits), and attracted disproportionately male and stunningly diverse populations. California's was the most male of the rushes, though native women were present in the diggings, and Miwok women, for example, took up mining in order to supplement older subsistence strategies. The rush drew gold seekers from around the world, especially from Mexico, Chile, the United States, China, and several European nations. California also set a pattern for future rushes whereby Anglo Americans, sometimes aided by the state, fought to control the placers. As Anglo women began to arrive, they, too, inaugurated a pattern common in later rushes by campaigning against such public amusements as dance halls and brothels, which often employed Mexican, Chilean, French, and Chinese women.

These patterns were repeated during gold rushes in Nevada and Colorado in the late 1850s; Montana, Idaho, and Arizona in the 1860s; and Dakota Territory in the 1870s. By the 1880s, the emphasis in western mining was shifting to the underground, hard-rock *mining of gold, silver, and copper, which required heavy capital investment, industrial processes, and large numbers of wage workers. Not until the 1890s, however, did hard-rock miners outnumber placer miners in the *West. And the 1890s saw new placer rushes following a series of discoveries in Alaska Territory and Canada's Yukon Territory.

The western rushes coincided with *industrialization and class formation in the United States and with an era of North Atlantic global economic dominance. For many in industrializing nations and in countries ruled by colonial powers, the rushes seemed to provide opportunities outside of the economic and geopolitical bounds that circumscribed their lives. That so many people from so many different places descended on the placers and contended with one another over access to gold, and that Anglo-American men often succeeded in limiting access for so many others, demonstrates that gold rushes were no sideshow; they were part of the main event of nineteenth-century history. Even Anglo men, however, try as they might to impose themselves as the rightful claimants of North American gold, could not extract from the hills the promise they sought—at most, a fortune; at least, an escape from a lifetime of wage labor. For most participants, gold rushes never lived up to the hopes they inspired.

[*See also* Capitalism; *Cherokee Cases*; Gilded Age; Indian History and Culture: From 1800 to 1900; Mexican War.]

• Rodman Wilson Paul and Elliott West, *Mining Frontiers of the Far West, 1848–1880,* 1974; rev. ed., forthcoming. David Williams, *The Georgia Gold Rush: Twenty-niners, Cherokees, and Gold Fever,* 1993.

—Susan Lee Johnson

GOLD STANDARD. A gold standard is adopted when a country establishes convertibility, at a fixed official price, between its currency and gold, thereby implicitly limiting its circulating money to the amount of gold it holds. Applied internationally, a gold standard establishes fixed exchange rates among different national currencies. Balance-of-payment settlements are made by transfers of gold.

An international financial system based on the gold standard emerged during the nineteenth century. Britain, already on a de facto gold basis, formally adopted the standard in 1821. From the 1870s through *World War I, most European and Latin American nations as well as Japan and the United States abandoned bimetallic standards, which based currencies on both gold and silver, and embraced the gold standard. Not only was it economically advantageous to join the currency standard used by the world's major industrial and financial power, Great Britain, but a huge rise in world silver production made it impossible to maintain a stable price between gold and silver, further undercutting bimetallism.

In the United States, the Coinage Act of 1873 officially demonetized silver, legally confirming a gold-based currency that—because of silver's relatively high price—was already the de facto standard. As gold entered a prolonged period of deflation, however, farmers (eager to expand the money supply and thus the availability of credit) joined U.S. silver-mining interests in denouncing this "Crime of '73." Advocating "free coinage of silver," they vocally embraced the new agriculturally based *Populist party. In 1896 the "free silver" forces captured the *Democratic party, as presidential candidate William Jennings *Bryan excoriated bankers and other monied elites for sacrificing the interests of common people on a "cross of gold." The Republican candidate, William *McKinley, argued that the gold standard would enhance trade and financial ties with the "civilized" world and stabilize banking and credit. McKinley's victory led to passage of the Gold Standard Act of 1900, fixing gold as the basis of the U.S. currency.

The international gold standard worked fairly well between 1870 to 1913, and economists came to accept the idea (or myth) that it was essential to global prosperity and peace. After World War I forced many nations to abandon the gold standard, most policy-makers and theoreticians urged its restoration. Throughout the 1920s, international conferences, economic advisers, and central banks all worked for this goal. By 1926 the gold standard was functioning in nearly forty countries (China and the Soviet Union were the principal exceptions). But the system proved too inflexible to counteract the banking crises of the late 1920s, which touched off the Great Depression of the 1930s. Indeed, the economic historian Barry Eichengreen argues that the the gold-standard's rigidity actually accelerated the economic and political crisis. Great Britain abandoned the gold standard in 1931, and most nations, including the United States, followed.

After *World War II, international leaders again tried to reconstruct a functioning gold standard, modifying its rules to provide greater oversight and flexibility. The 1944 *Bretton Woods Conference established the *International Monetary Fund to monitor economic policies, adjust the gold-based exchange rates of member nations, and provide credits for structural readjustments. This modified gold standard, which spread through much of the noncommunist world during the 1950s, also proved short-lived. For a variety of reasons, especially the mounting pressure against the U.S. dollar in the early 1970s, country after country abandoned the Bretton Woods system. After 1973, floating exchange rates, none pegged to gold, replaced the venerable gold standard.

[*See also* Banking and Finance; Depressions, Economic; Foreign Trade, U.S.; Free Silver Movement; Gilded Age; Monetary Policy, U.S.; Populist Era.]

• Barry Eichengreen, *Globalizing Capital: A History of the International Monetary System,* 1996.

—Emily S. Rosenberg

GOLDWATER, BARRY (1909–1998), U.S. Senator, Republican presidential candidate. Born in Phoenix, Arizona, Goldwater attended Staunton Military Academy in Virginia and the University of Arizona before entering the family's lucrative department store business. Of Jewish ancestry, Goldwater himself was an Episcopalian. During *World War II, he served in the Pacific as an officer in the U.S. Army Air Corp; he later became a major general in the U.S. Air Force Reserve.

A conservative Republican, Goldwater served on the Phoenix City Council before being elected to the U.S. Senate in 1952. In the Senate, he attacked the welfare state, supported the Red-hunting crusade of Senator Joseph *McCarthy, and denounced as appeasement any effort at diplomatic accommodation with the Soviet Union. His manifesto *The Conscience of a Conservative* appeared in 1960.

Winning the Republican presidential nomination in 1964, Goldwater gained a reputation for political extremism based partly on his staunch conservatism, which included his Senate vote against the Civil Rights Act of 1964, and partly on a shrewd campaign by the national *Democratic party, which portrayed Goldwater as a wild-eyed zealot who could not be trusted with his finger on the nuclear button. President Lyndon B. *Johnson defeated Goldwater in one of the great landslides in American electoral history. Nevertheless, in mobilizing a new army of "Goldwater conservatives" from the *South and the *Southwest, the 1964 campaign offered a portent of things to come.

Returning to the Senate, Goldwater somewhat softened his extremist image. Colorful as always, he described the *Vietnam War as "the biggest damn fool mistake we ever made." In 1974, he helped persuade Richard M. *Nixon, a friend and former political ally, to resign the presidency rather than face *impeachment in the *Watergate scandals. In retirement, he defended the rights of gays and lesbians. By the time of his death in 1998, Barry Goldwater had become a popular public figure, admired for his independence, plain speaking, and integrity.

[*See also* Anticommunism; Conservatism; Republican Party.]

• Robert Alan Goldberg, *Barry Goldwater,* 1995.

—David Burner

GOLF. Although "golf balls and sticks" from Scotland arrived in Charleston, South Carolina, in the mid–eighteenth century, not until the late 1880s did upper-class easterners and midwesterners found the nation's first permanent courses and country clubs. Representatives of the five most exclusive clubs met in New York in 1894 to organize the U.S. Golf Association. The USGA staged the first national amateur and open championships in 1895 and soon emerged as the game's governing body in America.

Between 1900 and 1920, sporting-goods companies supported construction of public courses and introduced improved equipment that made golf cheaper and easier to play. Although transplanted English and Scottish professionals initially dominated the game, a "homebred" pro first won the U.S. Open in 1911. When the young Boston amateur Francis Ouimet defeated Britain's two best professionals to win the 1913 Open, the game's popularity soared.

During the prosperous 1920s, the dominance of Americans both in tournaments and in the new Walker and Ryder Cup competitions against Great Britain assured golf's prominence. The 350,000 American golfers of 1913 increased to more than 2 million ten years later. Golf fans cheered the game's greatest amateur, Robert Tyre ("Bobby") Jones Jr., and professionals like Walter Hagen and Gene Sarazen; Jones's sweep of the amateur and open championships of Great Britain and America (the "Grand Slam") in 1930 was front-page news. An unrivaled generation of architects led by Donald Ross, Alister Mackenzie, and A. W. Tillinghast designed private and public courses, many linked to resorts and real-estate developments. Golf became more democratized, spreading beyond the bounds of the USGA's elite clubs, while gentlemen amateurs lost ground to professionals from poor and/or previously unrepresented ethnic groups.

The Great Depression and *World War II took a heavy toll, as many courses disappeared, but the fledgling Professional Golf Association tour survived, with such leading professionals as Byron Nelson, Ben Hogan, and Sam Snead displacing amateurs as the game's best players.

The 1950s ushered in another boom. President Dwight D. *Eisenhower was an avid golfer, and television made the charismatic Arnold Palmer a national hero whose unique status survived even Jack Nicklaus's preeminence. *Suburbanization, Sun Belt migration, and growing numbers of well-off retirees meant more courses and players.

By the 1990s, baby boomers helped make golf a major spectator and participant sport and a big business. Despite its continued reputation as an elite white male sport, golf made its greatest percentage gains among women and minorities, a trend furthered by the celebrity of the mixed-race superstar prodigy Eldrick "Tiger" Woods in the late 1990s. Woods won the 2000 British Open at historic St. Andrews golf course in Scotland, joining Sarazen, Hogan, Nicklaus, and Gary Player as the only golfers to have won all four major golf titles: the British Open, the U.S. Open, the Masters, and the PGA championship.

By the end of the twentieth century, the United States boasted more than fifteen thousand golf courses and an estimated 25 million golfers. Ironically, the game's soaring popularity represented its greatest challenge, as skyrocketing greens fees and new environmental restrictions posed daunting problems, particularly in metropolitan areas.

[*See also* Sports.]

• Herbert Warren Wind, *The Story of American Golf,* 3d rev. ed., 1975. George Pepper, ed., *Golf in America: The First One Hundred Years,* 1988.

—Howard N. Rabinowitz

GOMPERS, SAMUEL (1850–1924), labor leader, president of the *American Federation of Labor (AFL). Born into a poor family of Dutch Jewish cigarmakers in London's East End, Gompers emigrated to *New York City in 1863. The oldest of six children, he learned his father's trade and became a union member in his early teens. Working in the cigar shops of New York City, Gompers absorbed the culture of reform and self-improvement in the German-dominated cigar trade. By the early 1880s, he had reshaped the conservative Cigarmakers International Union into a dynamic workers' organization modeled after both British craft unions and German political labor organizations. As the representative of the cigarmakers, he was a founding member of the Federation of Trade and Labor Unions in 1881, and it was largely his energetic pursuit of a unified labor movement that led to the founding of the American Federation of Labor in 1886, with Gompers the first president. By then he had become well known not only as a union leader and organizer of the eight-hour-day movement in 1886, but also as a proponent of "pure and simple" trade unionism, which concentrated on higher wages and better working conditions and denigrated ethnic or party politics.

Gompers's hostility to the Marxist-led Socialist Labor party cost him the AFL presidency for one year in 1895. Once reinstated in the office, which he held until his death, he presided over a growing AFL, continuing his aggressive defense of workers' rights to organize, strike, and boycott. Working skillfully within the federal structure of the organization, Gompers at first tried to broaden the membership of its affiliated unions beyond skilled white workers but later largely abandoned this quest in favor of a dominant craft unionism. In 1901, he joined the *National Civic Federation, a group of employers, union representatives, and public figures who sought to mediate industrial disputes. Gompers refrained from supporting political parties and party programs but did selectively endorse candidates and legislative initiatives in the name of the labor movement. A supporter of President Woodrow *Wilson, Gompers served on the Advisory Committee of the Council on National Defense in *World War I, traveled to the European battlefronts, and participated in the Versailles peace negotiations. After the war, however, he could do little to prevent the erosion of organized labor. At his death, Gompers had come to symbolize the tremendous potential power of American labor, which seemed forever thwarted by its own internal divisions, the hostility of employers, and a mostly unsympathetic state.

[*See also* Communism; Gilded Age; Industrialization; Industrial Workers of the World; Knights of Labor; Labor Movements; Socialism; Socialist Party of America; Strikes and Industrial Conflict; Twenties, The.]

• Stuart B. Kaufman, *Samuel Gompers and the Origins of the American Federation of Labor,* 1973. J. H. M. Laslett, "Samuel Gompers," in *Labor Leaders in America,* ed. Melvyn Dubofsky and Warren van Tine, 1987, pp. 62–88.

—Dorothee Schneider

GOODMAN, BENNY (1909–1986), jazz clarinetist and bandleader. Born into a poor Russian-Jewish family in *Chicago, Benny Goodman studied clarinet at Jane *Addams's Hull House. A musical prodigy, he performed professionally at age twelve and in a traveling band at sixteen. As a teenager, Goodman became famous for playing "hot" clarinet solos, improvising like the *New Orleans musicians who had invented *jazz. Success in studio and *radio work led Goodman to form his own touring band in 1935, which received mixed reviews until it played the Palomar Ballroom in *Los Angeles on 21 August 1935. Teenagers who had heard Goodman's broadcasts packed the club, and "swing" music was born. While no one agreed exactly what "swing" was, promoters quickly dubbed Goodman the "King of Swing." On 16 January 1938 he became the first jazz bandleader to play Carnegie Hall, the country's premier high-culture musical venue.

Goodman was one of the first big-name bandleaders to feature African American musicians in his ensemble. The vibraphonist Lionel Hampton and the guitarist Charlie Christian received national exposure through his band. Black bandleaders like Edward ("Duke") *Ellington resented Goodman's raids on their bands, as Goodman offered salaries they could not match. Goodman's musicians were subject to his discipline and temper, however, and few stayed with him for more than one year.

High turnover coupled with physical exhaustion and the disruptions of *World War II ended Goodman's reign as "King of Swing." By the war's end, demand for small combos rendered Goodman's big bands obsolete. Playing concerts into his seventies, Goodman experimented with modern jazz and classical music; his later career, however, mostly celebrated his past.

[*See also* Music: Popular Music.]

• James Lincoln Collier, *Benny Goodman and the Swing Era,* 1989. Ross Firestone, *Swing, Swing, Swing,* 1993.

—Jonathan Z. S. Pollack

GOOD NEIGHBOR POLICY. The term "Good Neighbor," a diplomatic cliché, gained substance in U.S. relations with Latin America during the 1930s. Fundamentally a tactical shift motivated by a desire for access to trade and resources, the new policy abandoned older conceptions of America's international police power—specifically, military intervention in the Caribbean region—in favor of more subtle methods to win over Latin Americans.

Lacking a European threat (the traditional U.S. justification), Republican administrations in the 1920s initiated the move away from intervention. President Franklin Delano *Roosevelt's explicit "Good Neighbor policy," proclaimed at Pan American conferences in Montevideo, Uruguay, in 1933 and Buenos Aires, Argentina, in 1936, complied with Latin American demands by adopting noninterventionist principles. American protectorates in Cuba, Panama, Haiti, Nicaragua, and the Dominican Republic were modified or dismantled. The policy yielded significant dividends as the United States responded to the Great Depression and *World War II. These included fifteen reciprocal trade agreements with Latin American countries; the encouragement of "hemispheric solidarity" in opposition to Germany, Italy, and Japan; and the formulation of new "cultural initiatives" to bring U.S. perspectives to Latin American audiences.

When faced with the Axis threat, the Western Hemisphere nations tried to insulate their region against aggressive acts and later to coordinate wartime strategies. When the United States entered the conflict after the Japanese attack on *Pearl Harbor, eighteen of the Latin American republics followed its lead either by declaring war or breaking diplomatic relations with enemy states. Only Chile and Argentina remained neutral. Such unanimity avoided regional divisiveness and assured U.S. access to Latin American resources. Viewed in the context of World War II, the Good Neighbor policy proved its worth.

[*See also* Expansionism; Foreign Relations: The Economic Dimension; Foreign Relations: The Cultural Dimension; Foreign Relations: U.S. Relations with Latin America; Foreign Trade, U.S.]

• Irwin F. Gellman, *Good Neighbor Diplomacy: United States Policies in Latin America, 1933–1945,* 1979. Frederick B. Pike, *FDR's Good Neighbor Policy,* 1995.

—Mark T. Gilderhus

GOSPEL MUSIC, AFRICAN AMERICAN. Since its initial flowering in the late 1920s and 1930s, black gospel music has played a prominent role within the religious, artistic, and political spheres of American culture. The genre developed in tandem with the large-scale rural-to-urban and southern-to-northern migration of the early twentieth century and the Great Depression of the 1930s.

*Chicago-based Thomas Andrew Dorsey (1899–1993), inspired by the improvisational blues-inflected singing of W. M. Nix, successfully championed the gospel style as an evangelistic tool, a career path for talented performers, and an avenue for African American advancement. Dorsey himself composed one of the best-loved gospel songs of all time, "Take My Hand, Precious Lord," upon the death of his wife and newborn son in 1932. That same year, with Sallie Martin, Theodore Frye, Willie Mae Ford Smith, and Magnolia Lewis Butts, Dorsey cofounded the National Convention of Gospel Choirs and Choruses (NCGCC). A model for the Gospel Music Workshop of America (GMWA), founded by James Cleveland in 1968, the NCGCC fostered an elaborate apprenticeship and networking system for performers that linked together practitioners from Chicago, *St. Louis, *Philadelphia, *Detroit, Memphis, *Los Angeles, and smaller urban gospel centers across the country. At first, the gospel music of the 1920s and 1930s conflicted with the genteel sensibilities of old-line northern urban African American churches whose musical programs were oriented around a politics of respectability that sought to command the esteem of the white mainstream. While these churches initially viewed gospel music as retrogressive, they were gradually won over. By the early 1940s gospel music was thoroughly entrenched in black churches.

In her career-establishing 1947 hit recording of W. H. Brewster's "Move on up a Little Higher," Mahalia Jackson (1911–1972) combined Pentecostal shouting style, the deep resonance of *blues singers like Bessie Smith, and Baptist moaning. That same year the Ward Singers recorded Brewster's "Surely God Is Able." Both songs helped to make standard the use of "wandering couplets," pithy lines distilled from Negro *spirituals, sermons, and biblical texts. An everyday part of African American vernacular English, couplets such as "Sometimes I'm up, sometimes I'm down. Sometimes I'm almost level to the ground" transport the salience of myriad cultural contexts into the performance event. Reverend Cleophus Robinson, a St. Louis pastor and gospel powerhouse who recorded the 1969 hit "Wrapped up, Tied up, Tangled up," reinforced the interconnectedness of black religion, culture, and politics by singing gospel songs to raise funds for the *civil rights movement.

Edwin Hawkins's 1969 rhythm-and-blues-arranged Baptist hymn "O Happy Day" ushered in a period of stylistic innovation and unprecedented commercial success, as musicians fused elements of traditional gospel with rhythm and blues, soul, pop, *jazz, funk, and hip-hop. A showcase for rising talent, "Bobby Jones Gospel" became the first nationally syndicated black gospel television show upon its debut on the Black Entertainment Network in 1980. Kirk Franklin, the first gospel artist to sell more than a million copies of a debut CD album, saw his 1997 single "Stomp," featuring the rap group Salt-N-Pepa and importing a bass line from Parliament-Funkadelic, rise to the number-one spot on *Billboard* magazines' rhythm-and-blues and gospel charts.

As the twentieth century ended, the African American gospel tradition remained vital, merging the sacred cosmos, musical dialects, and sociopolitical discourses of *African Americans in the United States. Traditional styles (Richard Smallwood, Shirley Caesar, The Canton Spirituals) continued alongside contemporary (CeCe Winans, Fred Hammond & Radical for Christ, Helen Baylor) and urban styles (Trin-i-tee 5:7, Gospel Gangstaz, Yolanda Adams) as performers sought to package and deliver the gospel message in stylistically cogent ways relevant to the lives and times of their audience.

[*See also* African American Religion; Baptists; Bible, The; Music: Traditional Music; Music: Popular Music; Pentecostalism; Religion; Revivalism.]

• Michael Harris, *The Rise of Gospel Blues: The Music of Thomas Andrew Dorsey in the Urban Church,* 1992. Horace Clarence Boyer, *How Sweet the Sound: The Golden Age of Gospel,* 1995.

—Georgiary Bledsoe McElveen

GRAHAM, BILLY (1918–), evangelist. Born on a farm outside Charlotte, North Carolina, William Franklin Graham Jr. became the most famous and successful evangelist of the twentieth century. Graham preached the Christian gospel in person to more than eighty million people and reached countless millions more by radio, television, films, books, and newspaper columns.

A 1943 graduate of Wheaton College in Illinois, Graham gained experience and exposure in Youth for Christ International during the mid-1940s. A 1949 tent revival in *Los Angeles first propelled him into public view. Hugely successful revivals, his "Hour of Decision" radio program, numerous books, and periodic telecasts brought worldwide popularity and influence during the 1950s. His revival "crusades" and international conferences fostered ecumenical cooperation, particularly among conservative Christians known as evangelicals. *Christianity Today* magazine, which he founded in 1956, remained the flagship publication of the evangelical movement in the early twenty-first century. His association with presidents from Dwight D. *Eisenhower to Bill *Clinton encouraged religious conservatives to enter the political arena, despite warnings he sounded in later years regarding the perils of such ventures. Graham's connections and unique stature enabled him to overcome many formidable barriers, seen most dramatically in a series of increasingly successful forays behind the Iron Curtain between 1978 and, after the breakup of the communist bloc, 1992. By such actions as refusing to preach to racially segregated audiences, hiring an African American as an Associate Evangelist, inviting Martin Luther *King Jr. to appear at a crusade service, and calling on his audiences to espouse racial equality, Graham helped break down resistance to integration in the American South and elsewhere.

Graham and his wife, Ruth, reared five children, all of whom entered some form of Christian work. In 1995, his son Franklin was named leader-designate of the Billy Graham Evangelistic Association. Among many accolades and prizes, Graham received the Presidential Medal of Freedom (1983) and the Congressional Gold Medal (1996).

[*See also* Protestantism; Revivalism.]

• William Martin, *A Prophet with Honor: The Billy Graham Story,* 1991. Billy Graham, *Just As I Am,* 1997.

—William Martin

GRAHAM, MARTHA (1894–1991), dancer, choreographer, founder of the Martha Graham Dance Company and the Marthe Graham School of Dance in *New York City. During an extraordinarily long career, Graham was one of America's most honored cultural figures, her name synonymous with modern *dance. A visionary, she developed a new and wholly unique dance technique and vocabulary of steps and movements. Her theory of movement derived from the primary human activity, breathing, and the body's visible contraction and release when breathing is exaggerated by strong emotions. Her choreography, which eschews the gravity-defying lightness of classical ballet, is filled with tension, power, and strength. Graham's nearly two hundred works included highly charged retellings of Greek myths such as *Cave of the Heart* (1946), *Errand into the Maze* (1947), and *Clytemnestra* (1958); theatrical interpretations of ceremonial rites (*Lamentation* [1930], *El Penitente* [1940]); episodes from America's cultural landscape (*Frontier* [1935], *Appalachian Spring* [1944]); and dances with a literary or biographical context (*Letter to the World* [1940], *Deaths and Entrances* [1943]). A self-described "storyteller," Graham in many of her works created a new kind of theater fusing words and music, decor and movement.

Graham collaborated with such composers as Samuel Barber, Gian Carlo Menotti, Paul Hindemith, and Aaron *Copland, but her most celebrated and long-lasting collaboration was with the sculptor Isamu Noguchi (1904–1988). For works such as *Appalachian Spring, Cave of the Heart,* and *Clytemnestra,* Noguchi designed innovative sets and props, including three-dimensional sculptural forms that the dancers might move around or through, carry, manipulate, and even wear. Graham was also a noted teacher, and many of her students and members of her company went on to form their own troupes, including Merce Cunningham, Paul Taylor, and Twyla Tharp.

• Agnes de Mille, *Martha: The Life and Works of Martha Graham,* 1991. Martha Graham, *Blood Memory,* 1991.

—Trudy Garfunkel

GRAIN PROCESSING INDUSTRY. An ancient industry, grain processing in America can be traced from the simple mortar and pestle used by Native Americans and colonists alike to complex modern processing centers and *multinational enterprises. The industry's rise paralleled the broader economic, agricultural, and technological developments that made the United States the world's leading food exporter.

Gristmills, such as the one at *Jamestown in 1621, ground corn and wheat for meal and flour, helping to feed the colonists while making the millers key local figures. The earliest mills, and the vast majority up to about 1800, operated as custom mills that ground the farmer's grain for a toll in flour paid to the miller. The essential role of milling in local agricultural markets is evident in that public authorities offered development incentives and regulated the mills closely. Distant and foreign markets soon became important as well. As more farmers grew surplus wheat, many millers were acting more like merchants, buying and processing wheat for sale as flour. By 1792, these mills near the major seaports exported 824,000 barrels of flour to the West Indies and southern Europe. From 1815 to 1827, Baltimore was the leading U.S. flour market, with Rochester and Buffalo growing in stature after completion of the *Erie Canal.

As late as the 1780s, the milling process—sieving, cleaning, winnowing, and grinding the grain by millstones—involved strenuous human labor. The industry's subsequent history is linked to improvements in power sources and technological innovations, from human and animal labor (horses, mules, oxen), to wind, water, *steam, and electrical power. In 1782, Oliver Evans, a Delaware-born inventor, developed an automated process that used a waterwheel to turn the millstone, reducing by half the labor force needed in larger mills, eliminating much of the hard physical labor, and increasing the amount of flour extracted from wheat.

Grain processing mirrored the increasing corporatizing of the economy. The rise of St. Louis as an important milling center by 1870, for example, reflected not only its proximity to the prime winter-wheat growing areas, but also its access to river navigation and its ability to negotiate favorable *railroad rates.

In 1871, Edmond LaCroix built a new type of grinding machine that overcame Minnesota's hardy spring wheat which was difficult to grind and produced a poorer quality of flour. This "new process" gave spring-wheat flour, and Minneapolis, market dominance. Compact and efficient metal roller grinders that increased production and lowered costs, introduced from Hungary in 1873, marked another key technological advance. After 1900, bleaching processes improved quality and ended the adulteration of flour with alum or chalk.

Minneapolis's preeminence also reflected new modes of business operation, *mass production, aggressive marketing strategies, trade associations, strong local financial institutions, railroad expansion into new wheat areas—and the business acumen of Charles A. Pillsbury (1842–1899), whose Pillsbury Company led all others by 1880. By the 1890s, facing competition from the expanding *Kansas City Turkey Red wheat market, and a shift in consumption patterns from home-baked to store-bought bread, Minneapolis milling companies sought new locations, such as Buffalo, closer to urban markets in the East. Mergers in the 1920s consolidated milling and baking companies into such conglomerates as the General Mills Corporation. From the local mills of early America, the U.S. grain-processing industry by the late twentieth century had evolved into vast corporate enterprises with a global reach.

[*See also* Agriculture; Business; Canals and Waterways; Food and Diet; Foreign Trade, U.S.; Global Economy, America and the; Industrialization; Technology; Urbanization.]

• Charles Bryon Kuhlmann, *The Development of the Flour-Milling Industry in the United States,* 1929. Herman Steen, *Flour Milling in America,* 1963. George Terry Sharrer, "Flour Milling and the Growth of Baltimore, 1783–1830," Univ. of Maryland diss., 1975.

—Ginette Aley

GRAND ARMY OF THE REPUBLIC (GAR), largest and most powerful post–*Civil War organization of Union Army and Navy veterans. Founded on 6 April 1866, at Decatur, Illinois, by the former army surgeon Benjamin Franklin Stephenson

(1823–1871), its proclaimed goals were "fraternity, charity and loyalty." Simultaneously a political club, pension lobby, fraternal lodge, charitable society, and patriotic group, the GAR was perhaps the most influential voluntary organization of the *Gilded Age. Except for Grover *Cleveland, every president elected between 1868 and 1900 was a member; the unprecedented Dependent Pension Act of 1890 (which cost $1 billion by 1907) was the product of GAR lobbying; and the nearly seven thousand local posts that ultimately dotted the northern landscape were important centers of sociability. Grand Army membership crossed class lines, and to some extent it was interracial, though black veterans usually were relegated to segregated posts.

Between 1866 and 1872, the GAR operated as a virtual wing of the *Republican party, boosting the careers of soldier-politicians such as Illinois senator John A. Logan (1826–1886), who served several terms as GAR president. After 1872, it entered a steep decline, reaching a low of fewer than 27,000 members in 1876. In the 1880s, the GAR was revived as a fraternal order, emphasizing its secret initiation ritual and the provision of charity to needy veterans. It also began focusing on pensions and, by the 1890s, on a conservative version of American nationalism that stressed the ideals of independent producerism and the citizen-volunteer. At its peak membership of 409,489 in 1890, the Grand Army enrolled about 40 percent of eligible Union veterans.

The GAR declined in influence after 1900, holding its last encampment in 1949 and officially expiring with the death of its last member in 1956. Its chief legacies to the twentieth century were a pension system that acted as the template for subsequent entitlement spending and a conservative political agenda that later veterans' groups (notably the *American Legion) emulated.

[*See also* Welfare, Federal.]

• Mary R. Dearing, *Veterans in Politics: The Story of the G.A.R.,* 1952. Stuart McConnell, *Glorious Contentment: The Grand Army of the Republic, 1865–1900,* 1992.

—Stuart McConnell

GRAND CANYON. Arguably the single best-known American place, the Grand Canyon of the Colorado River is about a mile deep, twelve miles wide on average, and winds for 279 miles across the desert plateaus of northern Arizona. The chasm begins fourteen miles downstream from Glen Canyon Dam (1966), which forms Lake Powell. The lower forty miles of the Grand Canyon contains the headwaters of Lake Mead, which results from Hoover Dam (1936).

Although long known to and used by American Indians, the Grand Canyon was first viewed by Europeans in 1540, when Francisco Vásquez de *Coronado sent a small detachment of explorers to the South Rim. But the complex region below the rim was still unknown wilderness in 1869 when the one-armed *Civil War veteran, John Wesley *Powell, led a small group down the Colorado River and through the canyon. Powell's three-month journey made him a legend of the American imagination. Thomas Moran's paintings of the 1870s and Ferde Grofé's *Grand Canyon Suite* (1931) confirmed the Grand Canyon's status as an icon of sublime, romantic scenery.

A spur line from the Santa Fe Railroad to the South Rim, completed in 1901, opened the era of modern *tourism. Parts of the canyon were designated a national park in 1919, but the act left a loophole for hydropower dams. In 1968, after a bitter political struggle, Congress prohibited the damming of the Grand Canyon. By the 1990s, the Canyon was most threatened by the five million people who visited its rims and the 25,000 who traveled the river every year.

[*See also* Environmentalism; National Park System.]

• Robert Wallace, *The Grand Canyon,* 1972. J. Donald Hughes, *In the House of Stone and Light: A Human History of the Grand Canyon,* 1978.

—Roderick Frazier Nash

GRANGE, RED (1903–1991), football player and broadcaster. As the "Galloping Ghost" and the "Wheaton Ice Man" at the University of Illinois from 1923 to 1925, Harold "Red" Grange was the most famous *football player of the 1920s. Grange's career starkly reveals the power of the new mass media, *radio and *film, and of a popular press fully exploiting sports' appeal, to create a new phenomenon, the sport celebrity. By chance or exquisite timing, Grange's most spectacular football achievements came on the most media-focused occasions: against the University of Michigan on 18 October 1924, before 67,000 fans and a large regional media corps assembled for the dedication of Illinois's Memorial Stadium; then against Penn on 31 October 1925, before newsreel cameras and most of New York's major sportswriters.

Represented by the big-time sports promoter C. C. Pyle, another new figure of the 1920s, Grange provoked an unprecedented outpouring of media attention and controversy when he turned professional immediately after his final college game in 1925. At a time when pro players typically were paid $100–$150 a game, Grange earned as much as $200,000 for football, product endorsements, and a movie contract in just a few months. Following the media circus of his ten games with the Chicago Bears in 1925 and a subsequent barnstorming tour through the *South and *West, Grange's subsequent football career proved largely anticlimactic. After retiring from the Bears in 1934, he became a football broadcaster on radio and then *television, widely admired as a remarkably modest football hero, one of the greatest of all time.

[*See also* Journalism; Sports: Professional Sports; Twenties, The.]

• Michael Oriard, "Home Teams," *South Atlantic Quarterly* 95 (Spring 1996): 471–500. John M. Carroll, *Red Grange and the Rise of Modern Football,* 1999.

—Michael Oriard

GRANGER LAWS. A major goal of the *Granger movement of the early 1870s was to bring about public regulation of *railroads. Western farmers, who had applauded the rapid expansion of the rail system, now believed that rates were unreasonably high and fluctuated suspiciously, especially at noncompetitive points. These activist farmers also claimed that rail carriers discriminated between places and persons, formed illegal business combinations, and gave free passes to politicians and others who could serve the railroads' interests.

As the political power of organized farmers grew in the 1870s, agrarian representatives in the state legislatures, aided by spokesmen for certain business interests, pushed through legislation in Illinois, Iowa, Wisconsin, and Minnesota that collectively were known as the Granger Laws. These laws varied from state to state, but generally they sought to outlaw the widespread abuses by railroads, establish maximum rates in some instances, and create regulatory agencies to administer and enforce the laws. Beyond their immediate importance, the Granger Laws mark an early attempt by a previously rural nation to adjust to the conditions and challenges of an increasingly urban and industrial society.

The railroad corporations either ignored the Granger Laws or fought them in the courts. In due course, a case arising in Illinois found its way to the U.S. *Supreme Court. In *Munn* v. *Illinois* (1877), the Court upheld the constitutionality of the Granger Laws. Rejecting the contention of a warehouse operator that the regulatory actions of the Illinois Railroad and Warehouse Commission (the agency established to administer the Granger Law in that state) deprived the company of property and thus violated the *Fourteenth Amendment of the U.S. *Constitution, the Court ruled instead that enterprises such as railroads and warehouses that substantially affected the public interest had to submit to some degree of public control. This, in turn, opened the way for state regulation of a variety of businesses.

In 1886, the issue of state regulation of railroads again came before the courts. The Wabash railroad, an interstate carrier in the *Middle West, appealed a decision of the Illinois courts to the Supreme Court. In *Wabash* v. *Illinois* (1886), the Court found for the railroad, ruling that a state could not regulate interstate commerce, since the Constitution granted that power solely to the federal government. This decision led Congress to enact the *Interstate Commerce Act in 1887. That measure assigned the task of regulating railroads to the newly created Interstate Commerce Commission, the nation's first independent regulatory agency.

[*See also* Agriculture: 1770s to 1890; Gilded Age; Industrialization; Populist Era; Populist Party.]

• Solon J. Buck, *The Granger Movement,* 1913. George H. Miller, *Railroads and the Granger Laws,* 1971.

—Roy V. Scott

GRANGER MOVEMENT. The Granger movement was the first stage of the agrarian crusade of the late nineteenth century in which farmers voiced their dissatisfaction with deteriorating economic conditions and agriculture's declining status in a rapidly industrializing nation. The Patrons of Husbandry, or the Grange, was founded in 1867 in *Washington, D.C., by Oliver Hudson Kelley (1826–1913). A Minnesota farmer turned government clerk, Kelley believed that a rural social organization modeled on the *Masonic order but admitting women to full membership could improve the intellectual life of farmers and overcome rural isolation. As secretary of the group, Kelley set out to form local granges. He enjoyed little success at first, but beginning in 1869 the Grange grew rapidly. At its peak in the mid-1870s, with a network of county and state organizations, the national Grange claimed 775,000 members in twenty thousand local groups.

Although Kelley initially viewed the Grange as primarily a social organization, the order discovered other interests as it grew in strength. Its social role remained, especially at the local level, but the Grange also became an educational agency. Granges devoted a portion of each meeting to debate and discussion, thereby encouraging the members to read and to think about contemporary issues. Granges interested themselves in the one-room country schools, seeking to make the instruction more relevant to pupils' lives, and in the land-grant colleges, which they considered to be their institutions. The Patrons of Husbandry embraced economic cooperation as one way to improve farmers' economic condition, especially by reducing the role of middlemen. Members formed farmer-owned stores, elevators, and creameries, launched mutual *insurance companies, and in a few instances established factories to manufacture *farm machinery. Most of these enterprises failed, owing to inadequate capital and management, but they presaged the successful farm cooperatives of the twentieth century.

While the Grange was officially nonpartisan, discontented farmers organized by the Grange often turned to political action. Railroad abuses especially concerned them, and in the four states of the upper Mississippi Valley, they successfully campaigned for the so-called *Granger Laws that sought to bring *railroads under public control. These laws, in turn, laid the groundwork for the *Interstate Commerce Act of 1887. By then, however, the Grange had lost most of its membership and influence, although the organization remained a voice of agriculture and a social institution for farmers in the northeastern states.

[*See also* Agriculture: 1770s to 1890; Education: The Public School Movement; Education: The Rise of the University; Gilded Age; Homestead Act; Industrialization; Populist Era; Populist Party.]

• Dennis S. Nordin, *Rich Harvest: A History of the Grange, 1867–1900,* 1974. Thomas A. Woods, *Oliver H. Kelley and the Origins of the Grange in Republican Ideology,* 1991.

—Roy V. Scott

GRANT, ULYSSES S. (1822–1885), *Civil War general and eighteenth president of the United States. Grant was born at Point Pleasant, Ohio, the son of a tanner, Jesse Root Grant, and Hannah Simpson Grant. In 1839, he received a congressional appointment to the U.S. Military Academy at West Point. Disliking military education, Grant was a mediocre student, but mathematical aptitude secured his graduation in 1843. Appointed brevet second lieutenant and assigned to Jefferson Barracks near St. Louis, Missouri, he met Julia Dent, whom he married in 1848. Military events interrupted Grant's planned return to West Point to teach mathematics. *Mexican War service under Zachary *Taylor and Winfield Scott brought him promotion to brevet captain. Assigned to the Pacific Coast in 1852, Grant served in 1854 at isolated and dreary Fort Humboldt, *California, under an oppressive commanding officer. Lacking funds to bring his wife and two sons to join him, he resigned from the army. Rumors that heavy drinking was involved dogged Grant thereafter.

Intent on farming, he settled on land in St. Louis County owned by his father-in-law. Grant's farm failed during the 1857 depression and, unable to find employment in St. Louis, he moved to Galena, Illinois, to work in his father's leather-goods store.

When the Civil War erupted in April 1861, Grant accompanied volunteers to Springfield, Illinois, and assisted Governor Richard Yates in mustering troops. In June, Yates appointed Grant to command an Illinois regiment. Colonel Grant marched to Missouri, then was appointed brigadier general.

Stationed at Cairo, Illinois, in September 1861, Grant countered Confederate violations of Kentucky neutrality by occupying vital Paducah. In his first battle, at Belmont, Missouri (7 November 1861), he displayed characteristic aggressiveness. The Confederates' unconditional surrender of Fort Donelson, Tennessee, in February 1862, the war's first major Union victory, cracked the Confederate western defense line and yielded some fifteen thousand prisoners. Surprised at Shiloh on the Tennessee River (6 April 1862), Grant responded to a disastrous battle with a counterattack the next day that redeemed Union fortunes. Surviving a winter of frustration, Grant launched lightning thrusts against Vicksburg, a Confederate stronghold on the Mississippi; this campaign was considered his military masterpiece. Under siege, Vicksburg surrendered on 4 July 1863, and Grant rose to supreme command in the West. Another major victory, at Chattanooga, Tennessee (23–25 November 1863), brought a summons from President Abraham *Lincoln in March 1864 to assume overall command. Grant's spring campaign of attrition against Robert E. *Lee cost horrendous casualties before Grant besieged the Confederates south of Richmond. On 9 April 1865, Lee surrendered to Grant at Appomattox, Virginia.

Grant continued to command the U.S. Army during *Reconstruction, eventually breaking with President Andrew *Johnson and becoming a reluctant *Republican party presidential nominee in 1868. He was elected with a narrow popular majority over Democrat Horatio Seymour, the governor of New York. A nonmilitary general, Grant intended to govern as a nonpolitical president. In his first term, he protected freedmen's *civil rights, stabilized the currency, reformed Indian policy, and negotiated with Great Britain to settle Civil War grievances. Congress refused to annex Santo Domingo, Grant's pet project. Embarrassment arose in 1869 when his relatives became entangled in gold speculation that led to a financial crisis known as Black Friday. A further scandal implicated Vice President Schuyler Colfax in a scheme to defraud investors in the Union Pacific Railroad.

Nonetheless, Grant won a second term in 1872 with a decisive victory over Horace Greeley (1811–1872), editor of the *New York Tribune* and the candidate of the Democrats united with reform-minded Liberal Republicans. The country then slid into depression, Republicans continued to retreat from Reconstruction, and more government scandals burgeoned, including a scheme involving Grant's private secretary. Although

Grant's personal reputation for integrity survived, his judgment was questioned.

Out of office, Grant embarked upon a lengthy world tour. The leaders of a Republican faction known as Stalwarts fought fruitlessly for his nomination in 1880. Settled in *New York City, Grant was enticed into a fraudulent investment firm dominated by the swindler Ferdinand Ward. Bankrupt, suffering from inoperable throat cancer, and determined to leave his family financially secure, Grant heroically completed his highly regarded *Personal Memoirs* before his death.

[*See also* Depressions, Economic; Gilded Age; Military Service Academies; Shiloh, Battle of; Vicksburg, Siege of.]

• Bruce Catton, *Grant Moves South,* 1960. John Y. Simon, ed., *The Papers of Ulysses S. Grant,* 22 vols., 1967–. Bruce Catton, *Grant Takes Command,* 1970. William S. McFeely, *Grant,* 1981. Geoffrey Perret, *Ulysses S. Grant,* 1997. Brooks D. Simpson, *Ulysses S. Grant: Triumph Over Adversity, 1822–1865,* 2000.

—John Y. Simon

GRAPES OF WRATH, THE. John Steinbeck's masterpiece *The Grapes of Wrath* (1939) focused attention on the plight of *Dust Bowl migrants and made its author an international celebrity. An immediate success and winner of the 1940 Pulitzer Prize, the book also became the target of *censorship campaigns, particularly in Oklahoma and *California, where political and business leaders denounced it as obscene and distorted. This furor soon subsided, however, especially with the success of John Ford's uplifting 1940 film, starring Henry Fonda, and the novel remains one of America's all-time best-sellers.

Drawn from Steinbeck's research for a 1936 newspaper series on the conditions of California migrants, the novel chronicles the epic story of the Joad family, driven off their foreclosed Oklahoma farm and forced to join the exodus of displaced farmers heading west on *Route 66 for the "promised land" of California. Their dreams quickly fade, however, as the family disintegrates in the face of harsh labor conditions and the animosity of Californians toward what they see as degenerate "Okies." Yet this bitter experience also forces the Joads to recognize their fundamental connection to their fellow migrants, and, by extension, all humanity. Although Steinbeck proffered no explicit solution to the social problems he described, he clearly hoped that his target audience of progressive middle-class readers would embrace this new consciousness.

The novel's reputation among scholars declined after *World War II, as critics questioned its literary merits and historians demonstrated that both the migrants and their experiences in California were much more diverse than Steinbeck's monotone portrait. Despite this academic critique, Steinbeck's tale of social tragedy and spiritual awakening continues to echo through *popular culture, and the story of the Joads remains one of Depression-era America's most familiar and enduring images.

[*See also* Depressions, Economic; Literature: Since World War I; Migratory Agricultural Workers; New Deal Era, The.]

• Harold Bloom, ed., *John Steinbeck's* The Grapes of Wrath, 1988. Charles Shindo, *Dust Bowl Migrants in the American Imagination,* 1997.

—Anthony Harkins

GRAY, ASA (1810–1888), botanist. A native of upstate New York, Gray earned an M.D. degree from the Fairfield (New York) Medical School in 1831, at a time when medical schools required little preliminary education and awarded degrees after only eight months of coursework. Gray briefly practiced *medicine but increasingly turned his attention to botany. In 1842, Gray accepted Harvard College's offer of a professorship of natural history with special responsibility for botany. Although Gray quit teaching in 1873, he remained on the Harvard faculty until his death in 1888. His various textbooks brought him national fame, while his scientific work won him international acclaim as America's leading taxonomic botanist.

Gray is best remembered for the prominent role he played in the American debates over Charles Darwin's *Origin of Species* (1859). Gray, who had met Darwin during a visit to England in 1851 and had subsequently corresponded with him, sought to ensure that his English friend received "fair-play" in North America. An orthodox, if not particularly pious, Congregationalist Christian, Gray also strove to present Darwin's theory in a theistic light. He proposed that the unexplained organic variations on which natural selection acted be attributed to divine providence, a suggestion that Darwin rejected. Gray urged not only a "special origination" in connection with the appearance of human beings, but expressed skepticism about the ability of natural selection "to account for the formation of organs, the making of eyes, &c." Although he described himself as "one who is scientifically, and in his own fashion, a Darwinian," he confessed to a friend that his theistic interpretation of evolution was "*very anti-Darwin.*" Gray presented his views in two influential books: *Darwiniana* (1876), a collection of previously anonymous essays and reviews; and *Natural Science and Religion* (1880), based on a series of lectures at Yale Divinity School.

[*See also* Agassiz, Louis; Biological Sciences; Evolution, Theory of; Religion; Science: Revolutionary War to World War I.]

• A. Hunter Dupree, *Asa Gray, 1810–1888,* 1959. Ronald L. Numbers, *Darwinism Comes to America,* 1998.

—Ronald L. Numbers

GREAT AWAKENING, FIRST AND SECOND, evangelical religious movements in British colonial North America and the early United States characterized by revival meetings and emotional conversion experiences.

The term "Great Awakening" usually refers to the revivals in *New England and the Middle Colonies associated with the first American preaching tour of George Whitefield, 1739–1742; at other times it refers to the more general evangelical movement within *Protestantism, from about 1720 until 1750, sometimes including the spread of evangelicalism into the *South from the 1750s through the 1770s.

Whitefield (1714–1770), an itinerant English Calvinist Methodist, preached soul-searching sermons on conversion. He adapted commercial techniques, such as newspaper advertising, inexpensive publications, and the deliberate provocation of controversy, to stimulate interest. A consummate actor who spoke with charismatic spontaneity, he found in America a receptive audience for his message and preachers ready to imitate his style.

Whitefield's tour through the Middle Colonies in 1739 exacerbated divisions within the Presbyterian and the Dutch Reformed churches. Conservatives maintained orthodox doctrine and the prescribed liturgy; evangelicals sought experiential piety and spontaneous preaching. Theodorus Freylinghuysen (1691–c. 1748) introduced conversionist ministry to the Dutch Reformed in America in the 1720s and influenced the ministry of the Scottish Presbyterian Gilbert Tennent (1703–1764). The Philadelphia synod, to which Tennent belonged, was already divided over itinerant preaching and ordination qualifications when Whitefield arrived. Allying with the evangelical party, Whitefield attracted vast crowds to his outdoor assemblies and set off a series of local revivals. Whitefield's first New England tour, September and October 1740, initiated a year of local revivals that built upon an indigenous revival tradition already developed under Jonathan *Edwards.

The Great Awakening agitated several divisive issues, including itinerant preaching, church membership qualifications, and the role of emotion. Revivalists preached the terrors of hell to awaken sinners to their need of conversion, and people turned from their own ministers if they found more awakening preaching elsewhere. Many converts separated from established churches to form churches with stricter membership requirements. The antirevivalist *Boston minister Charles Chauncy (1705–1787) exploited these innovations as well as the faintings and visions of converts to discredit the awakening, while Edwards defended the revivals by separating such disorders from their spiritual essence. Colonial governments passed laws to keep ecclesiastical order, fueling sentiment for separation of *church and state.

Three waves of evangelicalism swept the South in the late eighteenth century. The Presbyterian denomination expanded into Virginia, under the Reverend Samuel Davies (1723–1761), beginning in the 1740s. Starting in the 1750s, *Baptists such as Shubal Stearns won converts among the unchurched of Virginia and the Carolina backcountry. And in the 1770s, circuit riders such as the Reverend Devereux Jarrett organized thousands into Methodist societies, mostly in Maryland and Virginia.

The Second Great Awakening began in the 1790s in the Northeast as followers of Edwards, such as Timothy Dwight (1752–1817) and Lyman Beecher (1775–1863), led a counteroffensive against *Deism. In the West, Presbyterians, Methodists, and Baptists employed revival meetings to evangelize unchurched frontier families. Camp meetings organized by preachers like James McGready, culminating in a massive interdenominational meeting at Cane Ridge, Kentucky, in 1801, brought dispersed settlers together to confirm their commitment to Christianity. Itinerant preachers spread the movement through the South among both whites and blacks.

Many new denominations emerged from the Second Great Awakening, while at the same time theological differences between denominations blurred. Like the First Great Awakening, the movement promoted belief in the imminence of the millennium, but it differed from the earlier movement in its trust in universal salvation and the perfectibility of society. This optimism led to the founding of missionary, education, tract, and Bible societies as well as moral-reform groups promoting temperance and chastity and opposing gambling and other vices. Some evangelicals sought to Christianize the republic by ending the delivery of mail and the operation of stage lines on Sundays. Participation in moral-reform movements enhanced women's moral and social authority. American Protestantism became more populist as older denominations, such as the Congregational and Episcopal bodies, lost ground to the more actively evangelistic, particularly Baptist and Methodist, which did not require a college-educated ministry.

The Second Great Awakening faded by the 1830s, as revivals lost their spontaneity. As a set of standardized practices promoted by Charles G. *Finney proved their effectiveness in the so-called Burned-Over District of upstate New York, revivals became practically an institutionalized element of American evangelical Christianity.

Because of the two Great Awakenings, evangelicalism supplanted rationalism in post-Revolutionary America. While strengthening denominationalism, the awakenings furnished a common evangelical tradition of emotional *religion. They implanted evangelical Protestant Christianity at the heart of African-American culture and reinvigorated missionary work among Native Americans. Some rationalists repelled by evangelical emotionalism embraced Unitarianism.

[*See also* African American Religion; Colonial Era; Early Republic, Era of the; Methodism; Millennialism and Apocalypticism; Missionary Movement; Revivalism; Temperance and Prohibition; Unitarianism and Universalism.]

• Whitney Cross, *The Burned-Over District: The Social and Intellectual History of Enthusiastic Religion in Western New York, 1800–1850,* 1950. Richard L. Bushman, *From Puritan to Yankee: Character and the Social Order in Connecticut, 1690–1765,* 1967. Donald G. Mathews, *Religion in the Old South,* 1977. William G. McLoughlin, *Revivals, Awakenings, and Reform: An Essay on Religion and Social Change in America, 1607–1977,* 1978. Patricia U. Bonomi, *Under the Cope of Heaven: Religion, Society, and Politics in Colonial America,* 1986. Nathan O. Hatch, *The Democratization of American Christianity,* 1989.

—Michael J. Crawford

GREAT CRASH. *See* Stock Market Crash of 1929.

GREAT DEPRESSION. *See* Depressions, Economic.

GREAT SOCIETY. The Great Society, President Lyndon B. *Johnson's sweeping reform program in the turbulent 1960s, represented the high-water mark of activist government. In response to seismic social changes and pressures, Johnson proposed an unprecedented array of legislation designed to transform society and advance individual fulfillment through a broad range of federal interventions.

Background. With John F. *Kennedy's assassination in November 1963, Johnson inherited more than the presidency. Many of the intellectuals whom Kennedy had drawn to Washington stayed to pursue an unfulfilled liberal agenda. A spirit of altruism, intensified by the assassination, provided an ideal climate for *liberalism. But as the martyred president's image grew to mythical proportions, Johnson appeared all too human by comparison. A constant reminder of this contrast was President Kennedy's brother Robert, Johnson's principal rival.

Johnson himself was a veteran of three decades of activist federal policy. His years as a youthful apostle of the *New Deal defined his liberal outlook. As a congressman during *World War II, he participated in the government's mobilization of resources against the Axis powers. As Senate Democratic leader in the 1950s, he pragmatically advanced a moderate agenda. Once he became president, the populist Johnson reemerged; he resolved to use all of his executive powers to extend and even surpass the New Deal's progressive record.

In 1964, a prosperous economy and the presidential election set the stage for a flurry of legislative initiatives. Johnson's landslide victory over the Republican candidate, Senator Barry *Goldwater, gave the president both a powerful mandate and large Democratic majorities in Congress to carry it out. Johnson articulated his "Great Society" vision, a broad-ranging statement of national purpose, in a commencement address at the University of Michigan in May 1964. His ambitious goals included equality of opportunity, enhancement of urban life, restoration of natural beauty, improvement of education, ending poverty, and implementing racial justice. He also unveiled a new approach for enlisting the nation's best minds to define problems and propose solutions: White House conferences would address such critical issues as *civil rights, the environment, and health care, and task forces would set the course toward the Great Society by developing legislative initiatives.

Civil Rights. Some of the Great Society's most significant achievements were in furthering racial equality. As the *civil rights movement turned from the courts to the streets, *television gave protests against discrimination a nationwide audience. Capitalizing on a groundswell of public opinion, Johnson used the presidency as a pulpit to define the cause as an urgent moral and civic issue. He quietly promoted a bipartisan coalition that overcame a two-month Senate filibuster and passed the 1964 Civil Rights Act, barring racial discrimination in public accommodations, employment, and schools receiving federal funds.

The following year, televised scenes of racial violence fueled support for the Voting Rights Act of 1965. Although Johnson accurately predicted that the legislation would make elected officials more responsive to minorities, he also recognized that he was delivering the white South to the *Republican party. The third sweeping civil rights measure—to ban discrimination in housing and to strengthen federal protection in other areas—was passed in 1968, after the assassination of Martin Luther *King Jr.

The radicalization of the black movement challenged LBJ's efforts to promote change from within the political system. As militant new leaders confronted the establishment and appealed to a rising black consciousness, urban *riots manifested the rage and hopelessness that gripped the nation's inner cities. While the problem of racial discrimination would persist, the Great Society fundamentally altered race relations in America. The sweeping changes wrought by the three civil rights measures created a new social framework for subsequent generations of all races.

The War on Poverty. To promote equal opportunity, Johnson launched an "unconditional" war against *poverty. With the creation in 1964 of a new government agency, the Office of Economic Opportunity (OEO), antipoverty programs were begun to assist the poor in helping themselves. The Job Corps and the Neighborhood Youth Corps provided income, remedial education, and job training to impoverished youths. VISTA, a domestic counterpart to the *Peace Corps, sent volunteer organizers into economically depressed areas. The Community Action Program made grants to local antipoverty initiatives and spawned such national projects as Head Start, an enrichment program for preschool children; and the Legal Services Program, which provided lawyers to defend the rights of low-income citizens. Other Great Society measures in addition to the OEO programs included an expanded food-stamp program and the Child Nutrition Act of 1966, both of which directly benefited the poor.

While conservatives argued that the "War on Poverty" stifled individual initiative and increased the demand for *welfare, others charged that the modestly funded programs deflected pressure for more radical solutions. The controversial Community Action Program, a favorite target of conservatives, drew fire for underwriting opposition to local power structures. Although the War on Poverty failed to achieve its idealistic goal of ending poverty in America, the program did improve the lives of many while focusing attention on the problem of chronic, long-term, transgenerational poverty, allowing neither the press nor the public to continue to ignore the plight of the poor. While the OEO was abolished by President Richard M. *Nixon in 1974, most of the component programs survived.

Housing, Education, Health, and Other Programs. Another Great Society goal—enhancement of urban life—was advanced through the creation in 1966 of the new Cabinet-level Department of Housing and Urban Development (HUD). With HUD came such urban initiatives as the Model Cities Program, which funded partnerships with local communities for urban revitalization and aid to low-income areas. Mass-transit legislation helped cities update their transportation infrastructure.

Convinced that *education was the best antidote for poverty, Johnson, a former teacher, envisioned the Great Society as one in which all children could enrich their minds. As president, he orchestrated the passage of scores of measures to provide massive federal aid to education. The Elementary and Secondary Education Act of 1965 employed a new formula of federal aid to circumvent the traditional stalemate imposed by the separation of *church and state issue. The Higher Education Act, also 1965, funded scholarships and aid to colleges for equipment, buildings, and libraries. Other grants were directed to vocational education. In all, the passage of sixty education measures earned LBJ the title "the education president."

The Great Society's landmark health legislation, which tripled the federal health budget, overcame three decades of opposition to "socialized medicine." The enactment of Medicare in 1965 dramatically increased accessibility to health care for the nation's elderly, providing for hospitalization and optional medical insurance. A companion measure, Medicaid, administered by the states through the welfare system, provided hospitalization coverage for poor Americans. Other Great Society health initiatives aided medical research, the construction of medical facilities, and regional medical programs.

The Great Society produced landmark legislation in almost every area of American life. Truth-in-lending and truth-in-packaging laws provided new protections for consumers. Automobile safety legislation reduced accidents and fatalities, while the Highway Beautification Act, championed by the president's wife, Lady Bird Johnson, enhanced the scenic beauty of the nation's roadsides. A new environmental consciousness brought the first nationwide attack on air and water pollution. To enrich cultural life, Johnson presided over the creation of the *National Endowments for the Arts and the Humanities and signed the Public Broadcasting Act of 1967. The Immigration Act of 1965 abolished the discriminatory national-origins policy.

The Great Society and Vietnam. While Johnson's willingness to expend political capital on the Great Society's costly and sometimes controversial reforms increased his political vulnerability, it was the *Vietnam War that ultimately undermined his presidency. As the American commitment of human resources increased from sixteen thousand advisers in November 1963 to more than half a million G.I.s, the prolonged, inconclusive conflict in Southeast Asia fueled inflation, limited domestic spending, ruptured the *Democratic party, ignited a youth rebellion, and caused deep divisions in American society. Tormented by his inability either to achieve victory or to withdraw honorably, Johnson in March 1968 announced that he would not seek reelection.

Tarnished by Vietnam, Johnson's presidency received the same mixed reviews in hindsight that marked contemporary assessments. Liberals praised the Great Society as a noble if idealistic crusade, cut short by a bitter, unpopular war. Conservatives criticized the period as the epitome of big-government excesses. Yet the Great Society's legislative landmarks remained, profoundly affecting the nation's economic, social, and political life for decades afterward.

[*See also* Civil Rights Legislation; Conservatism; Consumer Movement; Environmentalism; Federal Goverment, Executive Branch: Other Departments (Housing and Urban Development); Housing; Immigration; Immigration Law; Kennedy, Robert; Medicare and Medicaid; Public Broadcasting; Sixties, The.]

• Doris Kearns, *Lyndon Johnson and the American Dream,* 1976. Robert A. Divine, ed., *Exploring the Johnson Years,* 2 vols., 1981–1987. Vaughn Davis Bornet, *The Presidency of Lyndon B. Johnson,* 1983. Allen J. Matusow, *The Unraveling of America: A History of Liberalism in the 1960s,* 1984. Irving Bernstein, *Guns or Butter: The Presidency of Lyndon Johnson,* 1996. James T. Patterson, *Grand Expectations: The United States, 1945–1970,* 1996. Robert Dallek, *Flawed Giant: Lyndon Johnson and his Times, 1961–1973,* 1998.

—Michael Gillette

GREELEY, HORACE. *See* Journalism.

GREENBACK LABOR PARTY. The Greenback Labor party represented a brief but potent *Gilded Age expression of working-class anti-monopoly sentiment. In the aftermath of the depression of 1873, the formation of the agrarian-based Greenback Party in 1874–1875, the *railroad strikes of 1877, and the electoral success of local workingmen's parties in industrial states in 1877, 150 delegates assembled in Toledo, Ohio, in February 1878 to organize the National (or Greenback Labor) party. Its labor-oriented platform called for shorter working hours, a ban on contract prison labor, immigration restriction, and government bureaus of labor statistics. The party attracted a million votes in the 1878 midterm election and elected fifteen congressmen across the East, *South, and *Middle West. In some localities, it took on a distinctly radical character; in the coal districts of Alabama, black Greenback-Laborites exercised leadership among both black and white miners.

The party's 1880 platform included farmer-labor planks that foreshadowed the *Populist party's 1892 Omaha Platform, calling for government control of transportation and communications, a graduated federal *income tax, opposition to a standing army, and the lifting of all restrictions on *suffrage. Despite the party's impressive start, however, its 1880 presidential candidate, the *Civil War general James Weaver of Iowa, attracted only 3 percent of the vote, mostly in agricultural districts. The end of the depression in 1878 and the government's resumption of specie payments (the *gold standard) in 1879 had sapped the party's fortunes. Nevertheless, hopes for an independent labor party revived with the rise to prominence of the

*Knights of Labor after another wave of national strikes in the 1880s.

[*See also* Depressions, Economic; Immigration Law; Industrialization; Labor Movements; Monetary Policy, Federal; Populist Era; Strikes and Industrial Conflict.]

• Gretchen Ritter, *Goldbugs and Greenbacks: The Antimonopoly Tradition and the Politics of Finance in America*, 1997. Elizabeth Sanders, *Roots of Reform: Farmers, Workers, and the American State, 1877–1917*, 1999.
—Shelton Stromquist

GREENE, NATHANAEL (1742–1786), *Revolutionary War general. In May 1775, Greene, a member of the Rhode Island legislature, was appointed to command the Rhode Island troops besieging *Boston, making him the youngest general in the Continental Army. Appointed a major general in 1776, he commanded troops in several important battles in 1776–1777, performing so well that he soon became George *Washington's key adviser. At Washington's behest, Greene served as quartermaster general from 1778 until 1780, when he resigned to protest congressionally mandated changes in the department's staffing and operations. Named in October 1780 commander of the Southern Department, which included states from Pennsylvania to Georgia, he held this command until war's end, the only one of Washington's generals to serve throughout the war.

Greene was perhaps the greatest military strategist of the American Revolution. When he arrived in the *South to command a Continental Army bordering on dissolution, the British virtually controlled South Carolina and Georgia and were poised to overrun North Carolina. Greene reversed this situation in less than a year. Using available militia and partisan fighters brilliantly, and understanding the role that mounted troops could play in eroding British control and support, Greene lured British General Charles Cornwallis into an exhausting chase and finally, without scoring a clear-cut tactical victory, was able to retake all but two southern seaports.

Greene settled in Georgia after the war on a plantation given to him in recognition of his service to that state. His early death resulted from heat stroke.

• Theodore Thayer, *Nathanael Greene: Strategist of the American Revolution*, 1960. Richard Showman et al., eds., *The Papers of General Nathanael Greene*, 10 vols, 1976–.
—Dennis M. Conrad

GREENWICH VILLAGE, a neighborhood on Manhattan's lower West Side, was a separate community until *New York City's northern outskirts reached and passed the district in the early national period. Through much of the late nineteenth century, Greenwich Village was a mixed-class neighborhood. Mansions of elite families were situated around Washington Square; middle- and working-class homes lined the irregular streets west and south of the square.

During the *Progressive Era, Greenwich Village achieved fame as America's Bohemia. By the early 1910s, a modernist mood was challenging all artistic and political orthodoxies. Greenwich Village, long home to well-known American intellectuals, attracted many of the era's leading cultural radicals: artists, writers, poets, feminists, and anarchists (often overlapping categories). Between 1912 and 1917, these counterculturalists sponsored the *Armory Show; organized a pageant in support of striking workers in Paterson, New Jersey; founded and participated in the avante-garde Provincetown Players, Mabel Dodge's radical salon, and Heterodoxy (a feminist club); published the socialist magazine *Masses;* and held bacchanalian costume balls in the tradition of Paris's Left Bank. By 1917, Greenwich Village's association with free thought and free love had made the district a prime tourist attraction.

Greenwich Village's iconic status as a center of cultural radicalism endured through the years in part because its residents repeatedly updated the "Village" style in response to the latest assault on orthodoxy. This ever-evolving rebellion is exemplified by the Beat Village of the 1950s, the Hippie Village of the 1960s, and the high visibility of gay and lesbian rights activists following the so-called Stonewall Rebellion of 1969, when police raided a Village club popular with homosexuals.

[*See also* Fifties, The; Gay and Lesbian Rights Movement; Modernist Culture; Socialism; Sixties, The; Socialist Party of America.]

• Adele Heller and Lois Rudnick, eds., *1915: The Cultural Moment*, 1991. Rick Beard and Leslie Cohen Berlowitz, eds., *Greenwich Village: Culture and Counterculture*, 1993.
—Gerald W. McFarland

GRIFFITH, D. W. (1875–1948), motion picture director and producer. Born in Kentucky, David W. Griffith was a stage actor and playwright before becoming a movie actor in 1907. He was hired as a director for American Mutoscope and Biograph Company in 1908. His scores of one- and two-reel films cranked out for the burgeoning nickelodeon market established him as the most original American filmmaker. From *The Lonely Villa* (1908) to *The Musketeers of Pig Alley* (1912) and *The Mothering Heart* (1913), Griffith used rapid crosscutting to wring almost unbearable suspense out of last-minute rescues. Working with Mary Pickford, Lillian Gish, and other young performers, he pioneered an untheatrical *film acting style of small gestures and slight expressions.

Griffith yearned to make cinema a vehicle for sweeping spectacle and moral edification. After leaving Biograph to establish his own company, he made *The Birth of a Nation* (1915), adapted from Thomas Dixon's novel *The Clansman* (1905). Griffith provided the screen's first national epic, a fresco of the American *Civil War and its aftermath that displayed his technique at its most overwhelming. It also presented a deeply prejudiced view of *African Americans and the effects of *Reconstruction and an idealized image of the *Ku Klux Klan. The stupendous success of *The Birth of a Nation* encouraged Griffith to mount the still more grandiose *Intolerance* (1916), which traced bigotry through the ages, daringly interweaving stories from four different epochs.

Thereafter, Griffith alternated historical spectacles like the *World War I drama *Hearts of the World* (1918) and the *Revolutionary War adventure *America* (1924) with more intimate and lyrical romances like *True Heart Susie* and *Broken Blossoms* (both 1919). His attitudes and techniques seemed antiquated in the 1920s, and his last two films, *Abraham Lincoln* (1930) and the anti-alcohol melodrama *The Struggle* (1931), were strained efforts to move into talking pictures. Griffith spent his final years in seedy obscurity, ignored by the industry he had helped found. Yet he was the most celebrated and controversial American filmmaker of the silent era.

• Richard Schickel, *D. W. Griffith: An American Life*, 1984. Tom Gunning, *D. W. Griffith and the Origins of American Narrative Film: The Early Years at Biograph*, 1991.
—David Bordwell

GRIMKÉ, SARAH (1792–1873) and **ANGELINA** (1805–1879), reformers. Born into the antebellum aristocracy of Charleston, South Carolina, both sisters had household slaves in their youth. After a spiritual and moral transformation as young adults, however, both became active in the *antislavery crusade and other reforms.

Sarah, visiting *Philadelphia in 1819, was drawn to the Quakers' moral-reform interests. Moving to Philadelphia, she joined the *Society of Friends; Angelina followed in 1829. Engaging in local benevolent activity, the sisters emerged as antislavery activists with two 1836 tracts: Sarah's *Epistle to the Clergy of the Southern States* and Angelina's *Appeal to the Christian Women of the South*. The latter was banned in the *South and led to threats of imprisonment in South Carolina. Angelina, recruited by William Lloyd *Garrison, lectured and wrote for the *American Anti-Slavery Society in 1836–1838. In *Reply to an Essay on Slavery and Abolition* (1838), she denounced gradualism and called for immediate abolition.

When Massachusetts Congregational ministers denounced

their public lectures in 1837, the Grimkés responded forcefully. In *Appeal to the Women of the Nominally Free States* (1837), Angelina argued that women shared with men the nation's moral guilt over *slavery. Sarah's *Letters on the Equality of the Sexes and the Condition of Women* appeared in 1838. Along with antislavery and *women's rights, they also embraced the temperance and *peace movements.

The sisters stopped lecturing after Angelina's marriage to the abolitionist leader Theodore Dwight Weld in 1838, but they continued to circulate antislavery petitions, and Angelina collaborated with Weld on an influential documentary collection, *American Slavery as It Is* (1839). Angelina's extensive correspondence with Weld comments insightfully on the economics of slavery and the political realities of abolition and offers shrewd observations on politicians and antislavery leaders. Sarah's correspondence, too, with family members, antislavery associates, and leaders in reform and religion, including the evangelist Charles G. *Finney, illuminates her moral and religious views.

After years in Belleville and Perth Amboy, New Jersey, where they operated a school, Angelina and Theodore Weld, with Sarah, moved to West Newton, Massachusetts, in 1863, where for several years they were associated with a school conducted by the physical-culture advocate Dioclesian Lewis.

[*See also* Antebellum Era; Feminism; Temperance and Prohibition.]

• Larry Ceplair, ed., *The Public Years of Sarah and Angelina Grimké: Selected Writings 1835–1839,* 1989. Gerda Lerner, *The Grimké Sisters from South Carolina: Pioneers for Women's Rights and Abolition,* 1998.

—William H. Brackney

GROUP HEALTH PLANS. *See* Health Maintenance Organizations.

GROUP OF SEVEN CONFERENCES. Beginning in November 1975 at Rambouillet, France, the annual Group of Seven (G7)—later Group of Eight (G8)—conferences brought together senior officials from the United States, Germany, France, Japan, Italy, Great Britain, and Canada to coordinate policies. The gatherings began after the collapse of the post–*World War II Bretton Woods monetary system, and the delinking of the U.S. dollar from gold, as U.S. policy-makers sought new ways to coordinate international economic policies with their counterparts elsewhere. Participants also focused on arms control and, later, on such global issues as the environment, illicit *drugs, money laundering, and the *Internet. Each nation's delegation typically included the head of state or government, the foreign minister, the finance minister, and his or her leading economic advisors. Among the most important conferences was that of September 1985, which set up the managed floating of exchange rates. In addition to the regular summits, special meetings in 1985 and 1996 inaugurated Russian participation.

While the G7/G8 system evolved significantly over its first twenty-five years, it nevertheless lagged behind global economic and political changes. For example, the conferences neglected globalization's effects on national culture and law. Such important nations as China, India, Mexico, and Brazil remained outside, and international organizations such as the *International Monetary Fund, the World Trade Organization, the *United Nations, and the *World Bank were not regular participants. Nevertheless, the G7/G8 system did illustrate the ability of the United States and other nations to create informal political structures to coordinate international policies.

[*See also* Bretton Woods Conference; Economic Development; Foreign Relations: The Economic Dimension; Foreign Trade, U.S.; General Agreement on Tariffs and Trade; Global Economy, America and the; Monetary Policy, Federal; Multinational Enterprises; Post–Cold War Era.]

• C. Fred Bergsten and C. Randall Henning, *Global Economic Leadership and the Group of Seven,* 1996. Peter I. Hajnal, *The G7/G8 System,* 1999.

—Susan Ariel Aaronson

GUADALUPE HIDALGO, TREATY OF. *See* Mexican War.

GUAM. *See* Protectorates and Dependencies.

GULF OF TONKIN RESOLUTION (7 August 1964), resolution that provided much of the legal authority for President Lyndon B. *Johnson's escalation of the *Vietnam War. On 2 August 1964, North Vietnamese gunboats attacked the USS *Maddox,* an American ship engaged in electronic espionage in the Gulf of Tonkin. Two days later, the *Maddox* and USS *Turner Joy* again reported being under attack. Doubts were subsequently raised—and still exist—as to whether the second attack took place, but the Johnson administration used it as pretext for retaliation. Denouncing this "deliberate aggression on the high seas," the president authorized the first U.S. air strikes against North Vietnam. Seeking to bolster his presidential campaign against the hawkish Republican Barry *Goldwater and to secure congressional backing for his Vietnam policies, Johnson asked congressional approval of a resolution authorizing him to take "all necessary measures to repel any armed attacks against the forces of the United States and to prevent further aggression." Two Democratic senators, Wayne Morse of Oregon and Ernest Gruening of Alaska, raised questions about the attacks and the blanket transfer of authority to the executive, but the Senate discussed the resolution less than ten hours and approved it 88 to 2. The House took less than forty minutes and voted unanimous approval.

Johnson often pointed to the resolution when congressional "doves" later questioned his authority to wage the war. Many congressman, on the other hand, concluded that they had been tricked, and in a symbolic act of defiance, the Senate voted in June 1970 to terminate the resolution. The 1973 *War Powers Act sought to curb the power of presidents to wage war without specific congressional approval.

[*See also* Federal Government, Executive Branch: The Presidency.]

• John Galloway, *The Gulf of Tonkin Resolution,* 1971. Edwin E. Moise, *Tonkin Gulf and the Escalation of the Vietnam War,* 1997.

—George C. Herring

GUN CONTROL. Gun-control laws first appeared in urban America during the early twentieth century. They typically specified where and how firearms could be used and restricted the carrying of concealed weapons. The most sweeping early effort to regulate firearms, New York State's Sullivan Law (1911), strictly limited the sale, possession, and carrying of guns. By the late 1990s, some authorities estimated, more than twenty thousand state and local statutes regulated firearms.

Federal gun-control laws were enacted in 1927, 1934, and 1938. These forbade mail-order pistol sales, regulated firearms dealers, and limited possession of "gangster" weapons. The Gun Control Act of 1968 tightened the earlier laws and prohibited some categories of persons from gun ownership. The so-called Brady Law of 1993 imposed a waiting period on handgun purchases and banned sales of some types of semiautomatic weapons. (This act was named for James Brady, a presidential press secretary who was shot and disabled in the 1981 attempted assassination of President Ronald *Reagan, and a prominent gun-control advocate.) In 1972, enforcement of federal gun laws was assigned to the Treasury Department's Bureau of Alcohol, Tobacco, and Firearms.

Late twentieth-century gun-control strategies emphasized either selective or comprehensive policies. Selective policies regulate gun *use* in that they seek to keep firearms away from dangerous situations and people but to avoid inconveniencing owners. Examples include restrictions on carrying guns, prohibitions on ownership by felons and mental patients, and laws mandating longer prison sentences for crimes involving gun use. Selective policies proved difficult to enforce, because guns easily pass from legal to illegal uses.

Comprehensive policies limit general firearm *possession.*

Such laws ban guns with high potential for misuse, such as military-style rifles, inexpensive handguns (also called "Saturday night specials"), or all handguns. Comprehensive policies raise problems of definition ("military-style" and "inexpensive" are imprecise terms), and they cannot stop persons bent on violence from substituting other types of firearms. Because they affected more owners, comprehensive policies also stirred greater opposition.

The effectiveness of gun-control laws remained an unresolved question as the century ended. Studies that examined a disparate set of laws in many areas usually concluded that the laws did not influence violence. However, studies focusing on the effects of a single law in one area often found that they did reduce violence. Gun control ultimately remained as much a political and cultural issue as a matter of public safety. Although polls regularly found strong support for stricter firearm laws, most proposals failed in referenda and legislatures. Commentators usually attributed this outcome to the efforts of the powerful *National Rifle Association (NRA), a progun lobbying organization that contributes heavily to the campaigns of sympathetic legislators. The NRA could not be successful, however, without support from millions of persons who view firearms access as a basic right under the Second Amendment to the *Constitution. A late 1990s wave of multiple murders involving guns, some committed by schoolchildren, further energized the campaign for stricter gun-control laws.

[*See also* Bill of Rights.]

• Lee Kennett and James LaVerne Anderson, *The Gun in America: The Origins of a National Dilemma*, 1975. Jervis Anderson, *Guns in American Life*, 1984. Albert J. Reiss Jr. and Jeffrey A. Roth, eds., *Understanding and Preventing Violence*, 1993. Marjolin Bijlefeld, ed., *The Gun Control Debate: A Documentary History*, 1997.

—Alan Lizotte and David McDowall

H

HALE, GEORGE ELLERY (1868–1938), astronomer and creator of scientific organizations and institutions. Born into a wealthy *Chicago family, George Ellery Hale became interested in science at an early age. He graduated from the Massachusetts Institute of Technology in 1890 and in 1892 he joined the faculty of the new University of Chicago, to which he contributed the observatory his father had built for him beside the family home. With the financial help of the Chicago financier Charles T. Yerkes, Hale built and directed the university's Yerkes Observatory in Williams Bay, Wisconsin, which opened in 1897. Using funds from the newly created Carnegie Institution of *Washington, D.C., Hale in 1904 constructed the institution's Mount Wilson Observatory near Pasadena, California, which he also directed. In 1928, now retired, Hale persuaded the Rockefeller Foundation to build the Palomar Observatory, on Mount Palomar north of San Diego, for the California Institute of Technology. In each of these last three observatories, Hale succeeded in installing the world's largest telescope. Hale also gained prominence as an astronomer with his invention of the spectroheliograph and the discovery of magnetic fields in sunspots.

A key figure in the development of scientific institutions and organizations, Hale in 1895 founded the *Astrophysical Journal*, in 1904 created the International Union for Cooperation in Solar Research (later the International Astronomical Union), and in 1907 began the process of turning a Pasadena technical high school into the California Institute of Technology. During *World War I he helped to create the National Research Council, which he subsequently headed until 1918.

[*See also* Physical Sciences; Science: Revolutionary War to World War I.]

• Helen Wright, *Explorer of the Universe: A Biography of George Ellery Hale*, 1966, reprint 1994. H. Wright, J. N. Warnow, and C. Weiner, eds., *The Legacy of George Ellery Hale: Evolution of Astronomy and Scientific Institutions in Pictures and Documents*, 1972.

—Ronald Brashear

HALF-WAY COVENANT. The Half-way Covenant, as it was called by its eighteenth-century detractors, attempted to resolve *New England Puritans' conflicting commitments to constituting the church exclusively with Visible Saints while still extending its discipline over the widest possible population. Congregationalist theory restricted full membership to those who could testify to a personal experience of conversion, but allowed for baptizing their unredeemed children. Left unsettled was whether the offspring of baptized unregenerates could undergo the same rite. The issue became acute during the 1650s when second-generation New Englanders, many baptized but unsaved, began bringing their babies to the baptismal font. Led by Jonathan Mitchel, the Synod of 1662, held in Massachusetts, determined that these progeny did enjoy a measure of church fellowship and could consequently receive the sacrament. Despite overwhelming clerical support, however, the innovation faced determined resistance from John Davenport, Increase Mather, and many laity, who complained that it debased membership standards and traduced the traditional order. Acceptance mounted after Mather switched sides in 1671 and a series of misfortunes, widely conceded as manifesting God's wrath at New England's sins, encouraged congregations to rethink their dissent. By century's end perhaps 80 percent had adopted the practice, allowing them to discipline half-way members while, coincidentally, the number of full communicants surged. In the eighteenth century, churches influenced by New Light *revivalism discarded the arrangement as too lax, and by about 1825 Congregationalists had abandoned it.

[*See also* Colonial Era; Great Awakening, First and Second; Mather, Increase and Cotton; Puritanism; Religion.]

• Robert Pope, *The Half-Way Covenant: Church Membership in Puritan New England*, 1969.

—Charles L. Cohen

HALL, G. STANLEY (1844–1924), psychologist and educator. Born and raised in rural western Massachusetts, Granville Stanley Hall in 1863 entered Williams College, where he developed an interest in the theory of *evolution and in *philosophy. After a brief stint at Union Theological Seminary, he studied philosophy and physics in Germany. In 1876 he began graduate work at Harvard where, under William *James's direction, he earned the first American doctorate in *psychology. Returning to Germany, he studied the new experimental, physiological psychology under Wilhelm Wundt at Leipzig. When Hall returned to America in 1880, he found the field of education the most receptive to the new psychology. His lectures on pedagogy interested Daniel Coit Gilman, president of the recently founded Johns Hopkins University in Baltimore, who in 1883 appointed him America's first full-time professor of psychology. There Hall established the first U.S. psychological laboratory, attracting students such as John *Dewey and James McKeen Cattell, who would make lasting contributions to the profession, and founded the *American Journal of Psychology* (1887). In 1888, Hall was named president of Clark University in Worcester, Massachusetts, a graduate research institution modeled on Johns Hopkins. While carrying out his administrative duties, he launched other psychological journals, helped organize the American Psychological Association (1892), and played a role in introducing psychoanalysis to the United States by bringing Sigmund Freud and Carl Jung to Clark in 1909. Hall's most influential work, the two-volume *Adolescence* (1904), a pioneering contribution to child study and educational psychology, reflected changing perceptions of human development in American culture.

[*See also* Life Stages.]

• Dorothy Ross, *G. Stanley Hall: The Psychologist as Prophet*, 1972.

—Kerry W. Buckley

HALSTED, WILLIAM (1852–1922), surgeon. After graduation from medical school at the College of Physicians and Surgeons in *New York City, William Stewart Halsted spent two years studying at the Germanic clinics of central Europe. Returning to New York in 1880, he practiced *surgery at several hospitals while conducting a series of research studies. Experiments with the recently discovered local anesthetic effects of cocaine resulted in Halsted's becoming addicted to that drug in 1885. Following a long period of recovery, he was invited in 1888 to do laboratory research at the Johns Hopkins Hospital in Baltimore under the sponsorship and oversight of William H. *Welch, the professor of pathology. Halsted's work so impressed leading members of the faculty that he was appointed surgeon-in-chief to the Johns Hopkins Hospital and professor of surgery at the medical school, which opened in 1893.

During Halsted's thirty-year tenure in these positions, he founded a distinctive school of surgery, characterized by emphasis on the physiological basis of disease and therapy, laboratory and clinic research, and meticulous operative technique, all of which were marked advances over previous practices. A number of the men who completed Halsted's rigorous training established departments of their own at other universities, thus spreading his teachings throughout the academic community. He also devised the residency framework upon which modern surgical training is based, and made important contributions to the operative treatment of breast *cancer, thyroid disease, and inguinal hernia. By the time of his death, the methodology that is still called Halstedian had become the predominant style in American surgical teaching and clinical work. It is for this reason that William Halsted has been called "The Father of American Surgery."

[*See also* Hospitals; Medical Education; Medicine: From the 1870s to 1945.]

• Samuel J. Crowe, *Halsted of Johns Hopkins*, 1957. Sherwin B. Nuland, "Medical Science Comes to America: William Stewart Halsted of Johns Hopkins," in *Doctors: The Biography of Medicine*, pp. 386–421, 1988.

—Sherwin B. Nuland

HAMILTON, ALEXANDER (1755–1804), first secretary of the treasury and *Federalist party leader. Alexander Hamilton was born out of wedlock on the island of Nevis to Rachael Paucett Lavien and James Hamilton, a Scottish merchant. In 1765 the family moved to St. Croix. Abandoned by James, Rachel apprenticed Alexander to a merchant firm, where he remained after her death in 1768. In 1772, his employer paid Hamilton's way to New York, where he attended King's College (now Columbia University). Opposing British imperial policy, he joined a local militia and in March 1776 was appointed an artillery captain by the New York legislature. With George *Washington's forces when the British attacked Long Island, he participated in the retreat across New Jersey late in 1776 and in the successful counterattacks at Trenton and Princeton. In March 1777 he became one of Washington's aides-de-camp, an experience that sharpened his criticism of the weak *Articles of Confederation government. In March 1780 he married Elizabeth Schuyler, daughter of General Philip Schuyler, a wealthy and prominent New Yorker. They had eight children. Resigning as Washington's aide in 1781 and given command of a battalion at Yorktown, Hamilton fought in the *Revolutionary War's final major battle.

Returning to New York, he entered the bar and embarked on a political career. After service in the *Continental Congress (1782–1783), he helped establish the Bank of New York (1784) and in 1786 was elected to the state legislature. At the *Constitutional Convention of 1787, Hamilton unsuccessfully argued for a government modeled on the English system. Writing under the name "Publius," Hamilton—in collaboration with John *Jay and James *Madison—published a series of essays urging ratification of the *Constitution. Collectively known as the *Federalist Papers, they rank as classics of political thought.

As secretary of the treasury in the Washington administration, Hamilton prepared a set of influential reports on the nation's government and economy and how they might be strengthened. In *Report for the Support of Public Credit* (1790) he proposed that, to secure the credit of the new United States, the federal government should pay all foreign, domestic, and state debts remaining from the Revolutionary War. He also advocated an excise tax to supplement tariff revenues, and the establishment of a mint and a national bank. His *Report on Manufactures* (1791), written with Tench Coxe, (1755–1824), his assistant secretary, called for the protection and encouragement of nascent industries. Hamilton envisioned a powerful republic in which the national interest would be synonymous with the interests of the most economically successful and energetic citizens.

Most of Hamilton's proposals became law, but they also engendered mounting opposition. Clashes with Thomas *Jefferson, Washington's secretary of state, over Hamilton's alleged meddling in foreign policy, and Jefferson's conviction that Hamilton was power-hungry and corrupt, splintered the administration. The violence of the French Revolution and the outbreak of war between Great Britain and France further polarized American politics. Washington, Hamilton, and their "Federalist" supporters backed neutrality and *Jay's Treaty, which resolved outstanding differences with Great Britain; Jefferson, Madison, and a growing "Republican" interest, fearing monarchical plots, supported a more pro-French policy.

Hamilton resigned as treasury secretary in early 1795. Resuming his New York law practice, he remained immersed in the struggles between Federalists and Republicans. He substantially rewrote Madison's draft of Washington's Farewell Address, worked to assure that the Federalists would retain the presidency, and during John *Adams's administration (1797–1801) offered advice to friends in the cabinet.

Personal setbacks and political blunders marked Hamilton's final years. A 1791 affair with Maria Reynolds became a public scandal in 1797. As inspector general of the army in 1798 he proved ineffective. In 1800 he attempted to prevent Adams's reelection by publishing a vitriolic personal attack on him. In 1801, his oldest son, Philip, died in a duel. In 1804, Hamilton attacked Aaron *Burr, an old political enemy, when Burr ran for governor of New York. After the election, Burr challenged Hamilton to a duel. The two met at Weehawken, New Jersey, on 11 July 1804. Burr fatally shot Hamilton, who died the next day.

Despite contemporary suspicions of his motives, Alexander Hamilton played a monumental role in establishing the new nation, including his service as Washington's advisor and confidant, his brilliant collaborative defense of the Constitution in *The Federalist*, his shaping of the first national financial system, and his leadership of the Federalist party. His political thought, often contrasted with that of Jefferson, continued to influence American political discourse well into the twentieth century.

[*See also* Bank of the United States, First and Second; Business; Conservatism; Croly, Herbert; Early Republic, Era of the; Economic Development; Factory System; Federal Government, Executive Branch: Department of the Treasury; Monetary Policy, Federal; Revolution and Constitution, Era of; Tariffs; Taxation.]

• Gerald Stourzh, *Alexander Hamilton and the Idea of Republican Government*, 1970. Forrest McDonald, *Alexander Hamilton: A Biography*, 1979.

—Paul G. E. Clemens

HANNA, MARK (1837–1904), central figure in the politics of the 1890s and early 1900s. Based in Cleveland, Ohio, Marcus Alonzo Hanna became rich as a shipper and broker serving the coal and iron industries, which developed as a result of Cleveland's strategic location. One of the few industrialists fascinated less by profits than by the machinations of politics, Hanna served as a key advisor for Ohio Republican governor William *McKinley, who established himself as the outstanding Republican spokesman for high *tariffs, high wages, and renewed prosperity in the face of the depression of the 1890s. Hanna helped to secure McKinley's presidential nomination in 1896 and to defeat William Jennings *Bryan's *free silver movement. Hanna nationalized the GOP campaign, raising $3.5 million, mostly from corporations fearful of Bryan's policies. Hanna's campaign reached millions of voters with a firm, insistent message of sound money, prosperity, and *cultural pluralism. The Democrats caricatured him as an archvillain who put corporate interests ahead of the national interest. Serving as a U.S. senator (1900–1904), he emerged as a Republican leader in his own right. Hanna also worked with the *National Civic Federation to conciliate labor strife. He sought to bring unions into the Republican fold and to avert major strikes that would be economically damaging as well as politically and socially divisive. Hanna's death at the peak of his power in 1904 ended a struggle with Theodore *Roosevelt for control of the *Republican party.

[*See also* Depressions, Economic; Gilded Age; Industrialization; Political Parties; Populist Era.]

• Herbert Croly, *Marcus Alonzo Hanna: His Life and Work,* 1912. Robert D. Marcus, *Grand Old Party,* 1971.

—Richard Jensen

HARDING, WARREN G. (1865–1923), twenty-ninth president of the United States. Although tainted by scandal, Warren Gamaliel Harding also presided over two years of peace and prosperity and an innovative arms-control initiative, and laid a foundation for the conservative *Republican party of the late twentieth century.

After a decade as publisher of the *Marion Star* in his Ohio hometown, Harding entered Republican politics in the mid-1890s, encouraged by his able and ambitious wife Florence. After mixed success in state politics, he won a U.S. Senate seat in 1914. A lackluster legislator, he nevertheless gained the 1920 Republican presidential nomination as an amiable compromise candidate whose conservative views placed him in the mainstream of postwar Republicanism. Calling for a return to "normalcy" after an era of reform, war, and struggles over the *League of Nations, Harding defeated his Democratic opponent, Ohio governor James M. Cox, by a landslide. Despite early flirtation with such progressive programs as farm relief and health care for mothers and infants, Harding's key domestic policies—immigration restriction, tax cuts, budgetary restraint, tariff protection, and opposition to *economic regulation—reflected a solidly conservative approach.

A lax administrator and indecisive leader, Harding relied heavily on his appointees, some of whom achieved notable success. Secretary of State Charles Evans *Hughes initiated the pathbreaking *Washington Naval Arms Conference and improved relations with Latin America. Treasury Secretary Andrew Mellon (1855–1937), with Charles Dawes (1865–1951), director of the newly created Budget Bureau, helped fuel prosperity after a downturn in 1921 by a program of tax- and spending-cuts and federal-debt reduction. Commerce Secretary Herbert *Hoover promoted business cooperation while Henry C. Wallace (1866–1924) introduced innovative programs as secretary of agriculture.

Other appointees, however, grossly abused their public trust for personal gain. Charles Forbes, director of the Veteran's Bureau, was convicted of stealing government funds. Influence-peddling charges swirled around Attorney General Harry Daugherty. The Harding scandals collectively became known as "Teapot Dome" after revelations in 1924 that oilmen had bribed Interior Secretary Albert Fall to secure leases of government oil reserves at Teapot Dome in Wyoming and Elk Hills in California. On the personal side, Harding, having carried on a long-term affair with a woman from Marion, Ohio, in 1917 launched a relationship with young Nan Britton, whom he occasionally smuggled into the White House. Britton told her story in a sensational 1927 book, *The President's Daughter.*

Dying of a heart attack before either the personal or public scandals became widely known, Harding was widely mourned. His legacy lived on in a Republican party that by the later twentieth century had largely embraced his conservative domestic policies.

[*See also* Conservatism; Coolidge, Calvin; Federal Government, Executive Branch: The Presidency; Immigration Law; Tariffs; Teapot Dome Scandal; Twenties, The.]

• Robert K. Murray, *The Harding Era,* 1969. Eugene P. Trani and David L. Wilson, *The Presidency of Warren G. Harding,* 1977.

—Alan Lichtman

HARLAN, JOHN MARSHALL (1833–1911), justice of the U.S. *Supreme Court, 1877–1911. A native of Boyle County, Kentucky, John Marshall Harlan, during his thirty-four-year tenure on the Supreme Court, supported a strong national economy based on free trade among the states and expansive readings of the due process and equal protection clauses of the *Fourteenth Amendment. Harlan's somewhat idiosyncratic perspective as a judge was most vividly articulated in his 361 dissenting opinions.

Harlan wrote famous *civil rights dissents in the **Civil Rights Cases* (1883), *Hurtado* v. *California* (1886), and **Plessy* v. *Ferguson* (1896). In the *Civil Rights Cases,* he defended the constitutionality of the Civil Rights Act of 1875, which guaranteed "full and equal enjoyment" of public accommodations to all citizens. In *Hurtado,* Harlan became the first to espouse the theory that all the protections enumerated in the *Bill of Rights should be considered part of the right of "due process" guaranteed by the Fourteenth Amendment, thereby making the Bill of Rights a protection against infringements by the states as well as by the federal government. He pressed this position with little success. In *Plessy,* Harlan dissented from the majority's support for the constitutionality of "separate but equal" transportation facilities for blacks and whites, insisting that state laws segregating the races on public transportation denied blacks equal protection of the laws.

Harlan's constitutional decisions on issues of political economy upheld what he considered important boundaries between the regulatory spheres of the federal government and the states. He believed in strong federal power to maintain the free flow of commerce, but he also upheld the police powers of the states in cases such as **Lochner* v. *New York* (1905), involving state regulation of the banking industry, so long as he did not find any commercial self-interest motivating the legislation.

Harlan's approach was opinionated, intractable, and impassioned. In the words of Chief Justice Edward Douglass White, "he could lead but he could not follow." Nevertheless, on issues involving racial discrimination and civil rights, his isolated views subsequently resonated with many late twentieth-century Americans.

[*See also* Economic Regulation; Segregation, Racial.]

• G. Edward White, "John Marshall Harlan—The Precursor," in *The American Judicial Tradition,* pp. 129–45, 2d. ed., 1988. Loren Beth, *John Marshall Harlan: The Last Whig Justice,* 1992.

—G. Edward White

HARLEM RENAISSSANCE. Known also as the Negro Renaissance or the New Negro movement, this artistic and sociocultural awakening among *African-Americans was a national phenomenon, reverberating through many urban centers. Viewed by some scholars as a distinctly African-American experiment in modernism and/or *cultural pluralism, it found many outlets, from *literature, *painting, and *sculpture to *jazz, dance, and Broadway shows.

Though it peaked in 1923–1929, the movement can be dated from the founding of the *National Association for the Advancement of Colored People (NAACP) in 1909, the outbreak of *World War I in 1914, or the publication of Claude McKay's poem "Harlem Dancer" in 1917 to as late as 1937, when Zora Neale *Hurston published *Their Eyes Were Watching God,* or 1940, when Richard *Wright's *Native Son* introduced a harsh new realism into black writing. Politically, it was part of a continuing response—which included the 1905 Niagara Movement and the NAACP—to the failure of Booker T. *Washington's accommodationism to reverse the black disfranchisement that began after *Reconstruction and extended through the *Supreme Court's 1896 **Plessy* v. *Ferguson* decision and beyond.

The issues the renaissance addressed had been confronted by earlier writers such as Frederick *Douglass, Frances Ellen Watkins Harper, Paul Laurence Dunbar, and Charles W. Chesnutt. But Jazz Age Harlem, the capital of black America and "the greatest Negro city in the world" (Alain Locke), came to epitomize the larger changes transforming African-American life and art. blacks from throughout the United States, the West Indies, and even Africa interacted to produce a race-conscious community of unprecedented sophistication in this northern Manhattan neighborhood. Harlem-based *civil rights organizations included the NAACP; the National *Urban League; A. Philip *Randolph's all-black Brotherhood of Sleeping Car Porters and Maids; and, perhaps most important, Marcus *Garvey's Universal Negro Improvement Association (UNIA).

While UNIA's celebration of blackness and of Africa stirred race pride and self-assertion among the demoralized urban black masses, the Harlem Renaissance represented the educated, middle-class blacks' response to the same realities that drew the poor to Garvey. Extending the racial, cultural, and political thinking of the New Negro movement to art, music, and literature, the renaissance found outlets in such periodicals as the NAACP's *Crisis*, the Urban League's *Opportunity*, and Randolph's *Messenger*, as well as such general-circulation magazines as the *Nation*, *New Republic*, and *Saturday Review*. It gained great visibility through the *New Negro* (1925), an anthology edited by the Howard University philosophy professor Alain Locke (1886–1954), who also helped young writers secure contracts and in general acted as "midwife" to the movement. W. E. B. *Du Bois, James Weldon *Johnson, Walter White of the NAACP, and the Marxist editor Victor F. Calverton provided mentoring and support. Jessie Redmon Fauset, literary editor of the *Crisis*, modulated and broadened Du Bois's genteel and propagandistic approach to the arts. The urban sociologist Charles S. Johnson, editor of *Opportunity*, stressed the importance of the great migration from rural South to urban North and encouraged black writing "which shakes itself free of deliberate propaganda and protest." A'Lelia Walker's elegant "Dark Towers"—satirized as "Niggerati Manor" in Wallace Thurman's *Infants of the Spring* (1935)—proved a popular meeting place. The white writer and photographer Carl Van Vechten (1880–1964) helped young black writers find publishers, but the success of his novel about Harlem, *Nigger Heaven* (1926), demonstrating the commercial possibilities of the primitivistic formula, arguably made it harder for some black writers to find their distinctive voice. Wealthy and well-meaning white patrons could prove stifling as well, as Langston *Hughes recalled in his memoir *The Big Sea* (1940).

But writers as diverse as McKay, Hughes, Hurston, Rudolph Fisher, Nella Larsen, Georgia Douglas Johnson, George Schuyler, Arna Bontemps, Gwendolyn Bennett, and Dorothy West did achieve a measure of artistic freedom. Inspired by little magazines such as *Fire!!* and by works like Jean Toomer's *Cane* (1923), Marita Bonner's "On Being Young—a Woman—and Colored" (1925), Hughes's *Weary Blues* and "The Negro Artist and the Racial Mountain" (both 1926), and McKay's *Home to Harlem* (1928), these and other writers helped define the Harlem Renaissance. So, too, did musicians, artists, and performers such as the actor Paul *Robeson, the sculptor Aaron Douglas, the tenor Roland Hayes, the jazz artist Duke *Ellington, the blues singer Bessie Smith (1894–1937), and scores of others.

The Harlem Renaissance stimulated fruitful controversy over basic aesthetic issues, the racial matrix of artistic expression, and such latter-day concepts as "Black Aesthetic" and cultural nationalism. Even if its participants felt ambivalent about their endeavors, and conflicted in their feelings about race and art, the movement they created remains a vitally important landmark in African American—and American—cultural history.

[*See also* Modernist Culture; New York City; Twenties, The.]

• Nathan Huggins, *Harlem Renaissance*, 1971. Amritjit Singh, *The Novels of the Harlem Renaissance*, 1976. David Levering Lewis, *When Harlem Was in Vogue*, 1987. Houston A. Baker, *Modernism and the Harlem Renaissance*, 987. Amritjit Singh et al., eds. *The Harlem Renaissance: Revaluations*, 1989. Cheryl A. Wall, *Women of the Harlem Renaissance*, 1995. George Hutchinson, *The Harlem Renaissance in Black and White*, 1995. Mark Helbling, *The Harlem Renaissance: The One and the Many*, 1999.

—Amritjit Singh

HARRIMAN, E. H. (1848–1909), railroad financier. Born in Hempstead, New York, Edward Henry Harriman began his business career as a Wall Street stockbroker, but soon became a railroad financier by acquiring the all-important Illinois Central Railroad. His biggest coup was gaining control of the Southern Pacific and Union Pacific railroads. Joining with J. P. *Morgan, James J. *Hill, and others, he created the Northern Securities Company, a holding company that integrated the ownership of the Union Pacific, Northern Pacific, Great Northern, and Burlington railroads. In the **Northern Securities Case* of 1904, the *Supreme Court found this company an illegal combination in restraint of interstate commerce and ordered it dissolved. Harriman also earned notoriety following accusations of stock manipulation. Having purchased the Chicago and Alton Railroad in 1899, he issued stock that increased his personal profit with no benefit to the line. A classic example of the practice of "watering" stock, this action was investigated by the Interstate Commerce Commission (ICC) in 1906–1907. Some have seen the investigation as politically motivated, arising from personal animosity between Harriman and President Theodore *Roosevelt, but the ICC did find Harriman's corporate empire and business practices "contrary to public policy."

Harriman also engaged in philanthropy, funding the Tompkins Square Boys Club in *New York City and a scientific expedition to *Alaska (Harriman Fjord in Prince William Sound is named for him), and donating forest land to New York State that became Harriman State Park. It is, however, as the quintessential *Gilded Age "robber baron" that he is remembered by history.

[*See also* Antitrust Legislation; Economic Regulation; Interstate Commerce Act; Progressive Era; Railroads.]

• William Z. Ripley, *Railroads, Finance and Organization*, 1920. Lloyd J. Mercer, *E. H. Harriman: Master Railroader*, 1985.

—Colin J. Davis

HARRISON, BENJAMIN (1833–1901), twenty-third president of the United States. Born in North Bend, Ohio, Harrison graduated from Miami University in Oxford, Ohio, in 1852 and studied law in Cincinnati. He married Caroline Scott in 1853, and they moved to Indianapolis, Indiana, the following year. Leaders of the new *Republican party recognized Harrison's political potential. His great-grandfather, also Benjamin Harrison, had signed the *Declaration of Independence. His grandfather, General William Henry *Harrison, had been elected president in 1840. After holding a succession of minor political positions between 1857 and 1862, Benjamin Harrison organized the Seventieth Indiana Regiment and commanded it as a colonel in the *Civil War, winning promotion to brigadier general in 1865.

Resuming his legal practice after the war, Harrison became leader of the Republican party in Indiana. Elected to the Senate in 1881, he quickly emerged as a possible presidential candidate. Harrison failed to win a second Senate term in 1887, but James G. *Blaine, the most prominent Republican of the era, endorsed him for president in 1888. Harrison won the nomination and then the election, garnering 233 electoral votes to 168 for the incumbent Democrat, Grover *Cleveland.

A contemporary said that Harrison "in his contempt for flattery . . . seldom indulged in praise." Harrison has been rated an average president at best, based on perceived failures in domestic policy. He chose not to intervene when Congress passed two controversial laws in 1890, the McKinley Tariff, with record high rates, and the Sherman Silver Purchase Act, which undermined confidence in the *gold standard. Exploiting the unpopular McKinley Tariff, the Democrats won control of the House of Representatives in a landslide in 1890.

Harrison, working closely with Blaine as secretary of state, pursued a more activist foreign policy. He agreed to participate in the nation's first protectorate, with Great Britain and Germany, over the Samoan Islands in the Pacific, and in 1889 he welcomed to Washington, D.C., the representatives of the nations of the Western hemisphere for the first Pan American Conference.

After losing to Cleveland in a rematch in 1892, having endured the death of his wife during the election campaign, Harrison returned to Indianapolis. He married the much younger Mary Lord Dimmick, the widowed niece of his first wife, in 1896. They had a daughter in 1897. He died in Indianapolis, a leader of the generation of Republican party founders who fought in the Civil War and led the nation through the often chaotic years of the *Gilded Age.

[*See also* Conservatism; Democratic Party; Federal Government, Executive Branch: The Presidency; Foreign Relations: U.S. Relations with Asia; Foreign Relations: U.S. Relations with Latin American; Free Silver Movement; Monetary Policy, Federal; Pan American Union; Protectorates and Dependencies; Tariffs.]

• Harry J. Sievers, *Benjamin Harrison,* 3 vols., 1952–1968. Homer Socolofsky and Allan Spetter, *The Presidency of Benjamin Harrison,* 1987.

—Allan Burton Spetter

HARRISON, WILLIAM HENRY (1773–1841), ninth president of the United States. Born into Virginia's Tidewater elite, William Henry Harrison attended Hampden-Sidney College and in 1795 married Anna Symmes. Their ten sons and daughters included John Scott Harrison, father of President Benjamin *Harrison. William Henry Harrison studied medicine briefly, then served in the Northwest Territory as a soldier, territorial secretary, congressional delegate, and territorial governor of Indiana (1800–1812). Despite his efforts to deal fairly with the Indians, friction over land cessions united area tribes under the Shawnee warrior *Tecumseh, who allied with the British during the *War of 1812. At the Battle of the Thames (5 October 1813), Harrison's Army of the Northwest killed Tecumseh, smashed his confederacy, and prompted the British to vacate the Northwest.

After retiring to his North Bend estate near Vincennes, Ohio, Harrison served briefly in local offices and in both houses of Congress. In 1836, as part of an ill-conceived strategy to deny Martin *Van Buren an electoral majority, he sought the presidency as the favorite son of the Whig and Anti-Masonic parties in the West, winning 73 electoral votes. Harrison shrewdly kept his organization intact and in 1840 bested Henry *Clay for the Whig nomination. That year the Whigs elevated the politics of popular amusement to unrivaled levels, eschewing a platform and avoiding positions on substantive issues to promote Harrison, the Virginia aristocrat, as a humble farmer partial to log cabins and hard cider. The "Tippecanoe and Tyler too" campaign (an allusion to Harrison's running mate, John *Tyler) featured massive parades, rallies two and three days long, and an extraordinary array of ephemera, including cologne, bitters, and whiskey in log-cabin bottles, and huge buckskin balls rolled hundreds of miles. Harrison defeated Van Buren, but succumbed to pneumonia a month after his inauguration.

[*See also* Antebellum Era; Anti-Masonic Party; Federal Government, Executive Branch: The Presidency; Indian History and Culture: From 1800 to 1900; Indian Wars; Northwest Ordinance; Political Parties; Whig Party.]

• Dorothy Burne Goebel, *William Henry Harrison, A Political Biography,* 1926. Robert Gray Gunderson, *The Log-Cabin Campaign,* 1957.

—Roger A. Fischer

HARTFORD CONVENTION (1814–1815). The Hartford Convention was a conference of twenty-six New England Federalists who met behind closed doors in the Connecticut state capital from December 1814 to January 1815 to channel opposition to the *War of 1812. Rejecting extremist Federalist demands for resistance, *nullification, and disunion, the convention pursued a moderate course.

The final report of the Hartford Convention echoed longstanding grievances of New England Federalists against ex-president Thomas *Jefferson, incumbent James *Madison, and the Republican congressional majority. Conceding their party's permanent minority status, the Hartford Federalists recommended constitutional amendments that would give a congressional minority a qualified veto over unwanted legislation and would check the Jeffersonian Republican party's rising ascendancy. Under the proposed changes, a two-thirds congressional majority would be required to approve all future embargoes, war declarations, and admission of new states; presidents would be limited to a single term; the three-fifths constitutional compromise that gave southern slave states additional congressman and electoral votes would be repealed; and commercial embargoes would be limited to sixty days. The convention also demanded that Congress allow the state governments to use federal taxes collected within their own boundaries for their own defense, and recommended that states "interpose" their authority if a militia conscription proposal took effect.

Within *New England, the Hartford Convention probably helped to quiet extremism. Elsewhere it had no direct effect other than to discredit the *Federalist party as obstructionist. Fortuitously, news of the Treaty of *Ghent, which officially ended the war, and of Andrew *Jackson's victory at *New Orleans, arrived simultaneously in Washington with the Hartford delegation, and the proposed amendments died.

Historian Henry *Adams once implied that the Hartford Convention's real purpose was to promote New England's secession. In reality, the principal leaders were moderate Federalists whose purposes were to protest the war, advance constitutional proposals, protect the New England coast, and preempt radical acts by extremist Federalists.

[*See also* Constitution; Early Republic, Era of the; Embargo Acts.]

• James M. Banner Jr., *To the Hartford Convention: The Federalists and the Origins of Party Politics in Massachusetts, 1789–1815,* 1970. Donald R. Hickey, *The War of 1812: A Forgotten Conflict,* 1989.

—Roger H. Brown

HATFIELD-McCOY FEUD. The most famous feud in American history occurred in the mountains of southern West Virginia and northeastern Kentucky between 1878 and 1890. Legend attributes the feud to lingering *Civil War hostilities and a dispute over the ownership of a hog, but the evidence suggests that rapid economic and cultural change shaped the conflict.

Anderson "Devil Anse" Hatfield (1839–1921) and Randolph "Old Ranel" McCoy (1825–1913) first became entangled in a court case over land and logging rights in 1872. However, most writers claim the feud actually began with a legal dispute over a hog in 1878. From there things became worse. On Election Day in 1882, three sons of McCoy killed a brother of Hatfield, who fought back by ritually executing the three McCoy youths. No further incidents or press coverage occurred, however, until nearly six years later. By that time, the discovery of coal had brought the Norfolk and Western Railroad through Hatfield land, increasing its value. Almost overnight, state politicians became obsessed with economic development in the mountains. In this volatile context, a relative of Randolph McCoy, a lawyer named Perry Cline, in 1887 persuaded Kentucky governor Simon Buckner to authorize a posse to cross into West Virginia and arrest the Hatfields. The Kentucky posse fought several battles with a Hatfield group calling themselves "regulators," during which several individuals on both sides were killed. Finally, on New Year's morning 1888, a small group of Hatfield supporters (but not Devil Anse himself) crossed the Tug River and trudged up the mountain to the McCoy cabin, which they set on fire, killing two of Randolph McCoy's children. The rest of the family fled to Pikeville, Kentucky, never to return to their mountain home.

Meanwhile, West Virginia governor E. Willis Wilson, claiming that Buckner had violated extradition procedures, took the case to the *Supreme Court, which upheld Kentucky's right to try the Hatfields. Of the eight Hatfields convicted, seven spent time in prison and one was hanged. Devil Anse, however, died peacefully of old age. In contrast to legends suggesting that hundreds were killed over a period of a hundred years, the death toll was actually a dozen within as many years. Press sensationalism obscured the fact that economic development and modernization, not primitive mountain culture, had exacerbated the violence.

[*See also* Appalachia; Railroads.]

• Virgil Carington Jones, *The Hatfields and the McCoys,* 1948. Otis Rice, *The Hatfields and the McCoys,* 1978. Altina Waller, *Feud: Hatfields, McCoys and Social Change in Appalachia 1860–1890,* 1988.

—Altina Waller

HAWAI'I. The Hawaiian islands are volcanic and rise directly from the Pacific Ocean floor as high as thirteen thousand feet above sea level. The capital and principal city is Honolulu, on the island of Oahu. Polynesian people first arrived by canoe in the fifth century A.D., and by the thirteenth century, competing chiefs formed a hereditary caste. Land was divided into slices running from the mountains to the sea, within which commoners hunted pigs in the forests; grew taro, a major food source, in irrigated terraces; and constructed coastal fish ponds. Hawaiians built large stone temples to their gods, preserved their history through oral traditions and the hula (a storytelling dance), developed fine crafts without metal tools, and numbered at least half a million by the time of European contact.

In 1778, the British naval captain and explorer James Cook arrived in Hawai'i on his third Pacific expedition. He returned later that year, after failing to find a northwest passage to the Atlantic, and died in a conflict with Hawaiians over a stolen boat. Despite this inauspicious beginning, British and other explorers continued to visit Hawai'i, whose strategic location on sailing routes between Asia and America made it a frequent port of call for fur and sandalwood traders, whalers, and sealers. With help from purchased European firearms, Kamehameha I united the islands in a series of wars by 1810. Foreign contact, however, introduced epidemic diseases, new tools and weapons, and new codes of behavior, so that when Kamehameha died in 1819, the traditional law system was abolished.

The next year, Protestant missionaries arrived from *New England and began to convert the population through the chiefs, who formed a constitutional monarchy. In 1848–1850, the legislature privatized land, to the great disadvantage of most commoners, and foreign-owned plantations began to grow sugarcane and to recruit indentured laborers from China, Japan, and other Asian countries. In 1893, foreigners, especially Americans, overthrew Queen Lili'uokalani with intimidating backing from U.S. Marines and warships. Despite Hawaiian petitions against annexation, the islands became a U.S. territory in 1898. Five local corporations, two founded by missionary families, controlled the economy, and the *Republican party dominated politics.

With the Japanese attack on *Pearl Harbor in 1941 and America's entry into *World War II, Hawai'i became an important base of operation. Despite official suspicion directed against local-born Japanese, thousands volunteered to serve in the U.S. armed forces, especially in Europe, where their unit won more medals than any other. After the war, they used veterans' benefits to earn college degrees, notably as lawyers. Asians also formed powerful labor unions. These changes enabled the *Democratic party to win the 1954 legislative election and to dominate Hawai'i thereafter.

In 1959, Hawai'i was admitted to the union as the fiftieth state. The coming of statehood coincided with jet air travel, and *tourism boomed; agriculture declined owing to foreign competition. In the 1970s, Hawaiians revived their traditional culture, and the state recognized Hawaiian as an official language. Hawaiians also organized sovereignty protests, which yielded an apology by the U.S. Congress in 1993 for abetting the overthrow of the monarchy a century earlier. By the end of the twentieth century, however, Hawaiians numbered only one-fifth of the million-plus population, and Asians outnumbered Americans from the mainland.

[*See also* Expansionism; Missionary Movement; Spanish-American War.]

• Gavan Daws, *Shoal of Time,* 1968. Lilikala Kame'eleihiwa, *Native Land and Foreign Desires,* 1992.

—David A. Chappell

HAWTHORNE, NATHANIEL (1804–1864), novelist and short story writer. The second child of sea captain Nathaniel Hathorne and Elizabeth Manning Hathorne, Nathaniel Hawthorne (who inserted the "w" in his surname) was born in Salem, Massachusetts, the site of the 1692 witchcraft trials over which one of his ancestors had presided as a judge. A thriving seaport in the eighteenth century, Salem was in decline during Hawthorne's youth. Hawthorne's paternal family had also declined from its seventeenth-century prominence, and Hawthorne (whose father perished at sea when his son was four) associated his Hawthorne ancestry with a heroic yet tragically flawed American past that might be buried but was far from dead in the complacent, commercial nineteenth century of his Manning relatives.

Out of his own divided familial loyalties and historical affinities, Hawthorne forged a self-consciously national tradition of romance fiction in such early stories as "My Kinsman, Major Molineux" (1832), "Young Goodman Brown" (1835), "Alice Doane's Appeal" (1835), "The May-Pole of Merry Mount" (1836), and "Endicott and the Red Cross" (1838). In the scope of his literary ambition, and in his devotion to the craft of writing (exemplified in his often lonely twelve-year literary apprenticeship after his 1825 graduation from Bowdoin College), Hawthorne established the prototype of the professional American writer.

The promotion of Hawthorne's fiction as representative American literature by northeastern critics and publishers helped *New England retain its cultural centrality, despite the southward and westward shift of economic and political power in the *Antebellum Era. The claim for Hawthorne's civic importance also enabled friends and admirers to procure government employment for him, including terms as a customhouse official in *Boston (1839–1840) and Salem (1846–1849), and, during the presidency of his college classmate Franklin *Pierce (1853–1857), as U.S. consul at Liverpool, England. This income helped Hawthorne support the family he and his wife Sophia Peabody had started after their 1842 marriage.

Hawthorne's novels, in their force of rhetoric, social insight, and ethical complexity, as well as in their engagement with central issues of his own day and of earlier and subsequent eras, undergird his literary reputation and cultural significance. His masterwork, *The Scarlet Letter* (1850), poses the competing claims of civil authority and individual freedom, and of religious and secular values, and explores the entanglements of spiritual and sexual passion, knowledge, and desire. *The House of the Seven Gables* (1851) explores social relations under entrepreneurial and speculative *capitalism, the comforts and limitations of domesticity, and the burden of a familial (or national) inheritance founded on theft and violence. *The Blithedale Romance* (1852) considers the prospects and implications of social engineering, as exemplified by utopian-socialist, feminist, and prison-reform movements. This novel also expresses his wary attitude toward the *transcendentalism of idealists like Ralph Waldo *Emerson and Margaret *Fuller and the utopian community at Brook Farm near Boston (1841–1847) where he was briefly a resident. Finally, the ethics of aesthetic production and consumption, the shifting relations between the United States and Europe, and the appeal and terror of the foreign (as embodied in religious, racial, sexual, and cultural "others") for provincial Protestant Americans are among the themes of Hawthorne's Italian romance, *The Marble Faun* (1860). Of his literary and intellectual contemporaries, his closest affinity was probably with his younger friend and admirer Herman *Melville.

[*See also* Literature: Early National and Antebellum Eras; Utopian and Communitarian Movements.]

• Sacvan Bercovitch, *The Office of the Scarlet Letter*, 1991. Evan Carton, *The Marble Faun: Hawthorne's Transformations*, 1992. T. Walter Herbert, *Dearest Beloved: The Hawthornes and the Making of the Middle-Class Family*, 1993.

—Evan Carton

HAY, JOHN (1838–1905), secretary of state, advisor to three presidents, and architect of a major U.S. foreign-policy doctrine. Born in Indiana and a graduate of Brown University, John Milton Hay served as one of President Abraham *Lincoln's wartime secretaries. Between 1865 and 1897 he held various diplomatic posts, wrote popular poetry, and remained close to the *Republican party leadership. The historian Henry *Adams was a close friend. Appointed ambassador to Great Britain in 1897, he became President William *McKinley's secretary of state in 1898. Hay addressed diplomatic issues arising from the *Spanish-American War and U.S. acquisition of the *Philippines, the negotiations over a Central American canal, and the boundary and fishery controversies that troubled Anglo (Canadian)-American relations. His most important achievement was the *Open Door policy toward China. In a series of diplomatic notes in 1899 and 1900, Hay asked the major powers to agree to the principles of equal trading and investment opportunities in China (the "open door") and respect for China's territorial integrity. The doctrine remained central to U.S. foreign policy through the mid–twentieth century.

After McKinley's assassination in 1901, Hay continued as secretary of state under President Theodore *Roosevelt. He was much involved in the diplomatic maneuverings of 1903–1904 that ultimately enabled the United States to build the *Panama Canal. He negotiated the Hay-Herrán Convention of 1903 (later repudiated by Colombia), by which the United States would have paid Colombia $10 million outright and $250,000 annually for a 90-year lease on the proposed canal site in Panama. Hay remains one of the United States's most important and influential secretaries of state.

[*See also* Federal Government, Executive Branch: Department of State; Foreign Relations.]

• Tyler Dennett, *John Hay: From Poetry to Politics*, 1933. Kenton Clymer, *John Hay: The Gentleman as Diplomat*, 1957.

—Lewis L. Gould

HAYES, HELEN (1900–1993), American stage and film actress. Born Helen Hayes Brown in *Washington, D.C., Hayes became known as the "First Lady of the American Stage" after a series of acclaimed performances in such parts as Cleopatra in George Bernard Shaw's *Caesar and Cleopatra* (1925), the saucy flapper in George Abbott's *Coquette* (1927), Mary Queen of Scots in Maxwell Anderson's *Mary of Scotland* (1933), and Queen Victoria in Laurence Housman's *Victoria Regina* (1935), her greatest stage triumph. Her career continued to flourish as she essayed parts in Shakespeare's *Twelfth Night* (1940), the London production of Tennessee Williams's *The Glass Menagerie* (1948), Eugene *O'Neill's *A Touch of the Poet* (1958), and George Kelly's *The Show-Off* (1967). She retired from the stage in 1970 but continued to act in *films and *television. Her film work was honored with two Academy Awards: for best actress in *The Sin of Madelon Claudet* (1931) and for best supporting actress in *Airport* (1970). Other celebrated film performances include *Arrowsmith* (1931), *A Farewell to Arms* (1932), *Anastasia* (1956), and *Candleshoe* (1977). In 1928 she married playwright Charles MacArthur (1895–1956) and at the end of her stage career appeared in a revival of *The Front Page*, a comedy about *journalism by MacArthur and Ben Hecht. She coauthored three autobiographies, plus memoirs on aging and a novel of Hollywood. Her slight frame and elfin appearance suggested a coy, pixieish quality but her work revealed wit and tough-minded resourcefulness.

[*See also* Drama; Theater.]

• Helen Hayes and Lewis Funke, *A Gift of Joy*, 1965. Helen Hayes and Katherine Hatch, *My Life in Three Acts*, 1990. Donn B. Murphy and Stephen Moore, *Helen Hayes, A Bio-Bibliography*, 1993.

—Steven Dedalus Burch

HAYES, RUTHERFORD (1822–1893), nineteenth president of the United States. Born in Delaware, Ohio, Hayes graduated from Kenyon College and Harvard Law School and became a successful attorney in Cincinnati, Ohio. Strongly *antislavery and pro-Union, he led a company of volunteers in the *Civil War, rising to the rank of major general. Severely wounded at the Battle of South Mountain in 1862, he recovered to fight in the 1864 Shenandoah campaign. After the war, he entered politics, serving a term in Congress (1865–1867) and three terms (1868–1872, 1876–1877) as governor of Ohio. Hayes won the 1876 Republican presidential nomination when the front-runner, Senator James G. *Blaine of Maine, became enmeshed in a financial scandal. In the general election, the Democratic candidate, Samuel Tilden of New York, received 250,000 more popular votes than Hayes and appeared to win the electoral tally as well, but the Republican managers contested the result, challenging the returns in three southern states and Oregon. The ensuing controversy threatened to revive sectional conflict until a special electoral commission appointed by Congress awarded the presidency to Hayes by a single electoral vote. The bargaining that produced this outcome, the so-called *Compromise of 1877, which involved Republican support for southern *railroads and the withdrawal of federal troops from the *South, marked the end of *Reconstruction, opening the door to the restoration of white rule in the region and the suppression of freedmen's rights.

As president, Hayes's unruffled, sometimes deceptively optimistic personality helped to calm national politics and to shift attention from the "southern question." While Hayes did what he could to support the *Republican party in the South, he also focused on new issues, especially *civil service reform, which he saw as essential to modernizing the federal government. He challenged Republican and Democratic leaders alike to implement his motto: "He serves his party best who serves his country best." Hayes asserted executive power through his appointments and in general upheld the authority of the presidency. Not personally popular even within his own party, he gained respect as his administration proceeded. His wife Lucy promoted the cause of temperance, while the Hayes family epitomized the Victorian ideal of piety and domesticity. Believing in a single presidential term, Hayes did not seek reelection in

1880. As an ex-president, he focused on higher education, philanthropy, and educational opportunities for *African Americans. While his presidency had few dramatic accomplishments, Hayes did maintain the dignity of the office and raise new political and social issues.

[*See also* Gilded Age; Temperance and Prohibition.]

• Ari Hoogenboom, *The Presidency of Rutherford B. Hayes,* 1988. Ari Hoogenboom, *Rutherford B. Hayes: Warrior and President,* 1995.

—H. Wayne Morgan

HAYMARKET AFFAIR (1886). On 1 May 1886, workers throughout the United States struck to win the eight-hour day. On 4 May in *Chicago, the strike's center, workers gathered in Haymarket Square to protest a police attack on strikers the previous day that had left at least two dead. The meeting was called by anarchists affiliated with the revolutionary International Working People's Association. The rally was ending when a police squad under Inspector John Bonfield commanded the crowd to disperse. Suddenly someone threw a dynamite bomb into the ranks of the police. One officer died instantly and seven later succumbed, most as a result of bullets fired by panicked policemen.

Many Americans, including preeminent ministers, journalists, and conservative politicians, saw the bombing as part of a conspiracy by anarchist-inspired immigrants designed to overthrow the republic. Responding to public hysteria, Chicago officials banned public meetings and processions. Eight anarchist leaders stood trial for conspiracy to commit murder. Although the identity of the bomb thrower remained unknown, a court convicted the anarchists of murder. On 11 November 1887, August Spies, Albert Parsons, George Engel, and Adolph Fischer were hanged; Louis Lingg had earlier committed suicide. Illinois governor John P. Altgeld (1847–1902) commuted the sentences of the other three in 1893. The novelist William Dean *Howells was one of the few prominent figures to protest the executions.

The Haymarket tragedy was part of a reaction by *business leaders and public officials to labor's "great upheaval" of the mid-1880s, including the rapid growth of the *Knights of Labor. Despite repression, skilled workers made significant progress in organizing unions and winning trade agreements after Haymarket. The *American Federation of Labor sponsored another nationwide eight-hour strike on 1 May 1890 and in Paris the Socialist Second International adopted 1 May as an international labor day. Revolutionary *anarchism, meanwhile, evolved into the syndicalism that flourished at the margins of the labor movement in the early twentieth century.

[*See also* Gilded Age; Labor Movements; Radicalism; Socialism; Strikes and Industrial Conflict.]

• Paul Avrich, *The Haymarket Tragedy*, 1984. Richard Schneirov, *Labor and Urban Politics: Class Conflict and the Origins of Modern Liberalism in Chicago, 1864–97,* 1998.

—Richard Schneirov

HEALTH AND FITNESS. The pursuit of health and fitness in America has long connoted more than a desire for the absence of illness or *disease; it implied a search for the strength, energy, and vitality that were believed to occur naturally in human beings in a right relationship with nature, or appear by way of divine intervention, and to result in a profound sense of well-being and spiritual harmony. Whereas medication and the ministrations of a physician suggested the need for some external and "unnatural" agent, advocates of health and fitness typically embraced self-reliance mediated through spiritual law in their search for an idealized state in which mind, body, and spirit united in perfect harmony. Health, therefore, became not only the prerequisite but the justification for an abundant life on earth or in some future realm.

Colonial Era and Nineteenth Century. The quest for health in early America unfolded within a worldview that intertwined the natural and supernatural worlds. This conjunction, described in such works as Cotton *Mather's *Angel of Bethesda* (1724) and *Primitive Physick* (1747) by the British Methodist leader John Wesley, manifested itself most obviously through a belief in a direct connection between sin and sickness, morality and health. Health came not only through a correct balance of the bodily fluid, or humor; and proper attention to hygiene, but also by maintaining a proper relationship to God and ascertaining the divine purposes for one's life.

The Second *Great Awakening, beginning in the late eighteenth century, witnessed waves of religious fervor that by the mid-nineteenth century found *revivalism and reform linked in a kaleidoscope of social movements struggling against not only *poverty, *slavery, and war but also against meat, *alcohol, and unhealthful dress. Fed by millennial enthusiasm, armed with "science for the common man," and appealing to a widespread desire for improvement through *education and self-control, reformers set about to perfect the United States by saving bodies as well as souls.

*Food and dietary reform loomed large in this effort. Antebellum Americans drank vast quantities of alcohol and consumed appallingly rich, fatty meals of meats and heavy desserts washed down with coffee. Fruits and green vegetables were a rarity. Corn and pork formed the staples of the rural diet, whereas urban populations relied more on bread and beef. Potatoes, turnips, cabbage, and later, tomatoes completed the basic American diet.

Dismayed by these food-and-drink habits, reformers launched a *temperance movement and sought to change eating patterns. In the 1830s the Presbyterian preacher and health reformer Sylvester Graham (1794–1851) attacked the American diet, warning that intoxicating drink, stimulating spices, coffee, tea, and meat should be avoided because they debilitated mind and body and overstimulated the gross and sensual side of human nature. Both as remedy for and prevention of the sickness and immorality of society, Graham advocated coarse whole-wheat bread, pure water, and a vegetarian diet. Three technological innovations—the ice cutter, refrigerated railroad cars, and canning—made such dietary reforms increasingly feasible by improving the distribution and year-round availability of perishable and seasonal foods.

Beginning in the 1840s Grahamite health reformers forged links with water-cure enthusiasts, who sought to cure bodily ills with various water treatments and who believed they were following nature's way of maintaining health. During the middle decades of the century, more than 200 water-cure establishments catered to a wide public, including many women in search of better health, social exchange, and cures for a wide range of "female complaints." Hydropaths believed that the sick body's self-curative powers could be vitalized by copious amounts of water, taken internally and externally, a non-stimulating diet, sunlight, exercise, and relaxation. In the words of the hydropathic reformer Russell T. Trall, who built a "hygienic system" on such principles, "All healing or remedial power is inherent in the living system" and "health is found only in obedience" to the divinely ordained laws of nature (*The Hygienic System*, 1872).

The spiritual impulse underlying the nineteenth-century crusade for health became explicit among the adherents of *Mormonism and *Seventh-day Adventism, who not only aspired to a purity of spirit that would enable good to triumph over evil, but also believed that much sickness could be prevented by righteous living and self-discipline. Advocating natural remedies and eschewing alcohol, coffee, tea, tobacco, and all stimulants, which polluted the body and corrupted the spirit, Adventists and Mormons spiritualized their rules of healthful living. Later studies demonstrated the health benefits of these practices, documenting a correlation between the Mormon and Adventist lifestyles and a lower incidence of *cancer, *heart disease, and other life-shortening *diseases.

Numerous nineteenth-century reformers popularized the many dimensions of health reform. Dioclesian Lewis (1823–1886) preached the power of physical exercise and gymnastics; Catharine *Beecher warned of the dangers of corsets and tight lacing; Horace Fletcher (1849–1919) attributed his prodigious physical strength to the thorough chewing of food; and the Adventist John Harvey Kellogg (1852–1943) invented flaked breakfast cereals, founded a medical school, and established numerous sanitariums devoted to the gospel of healthful living, most notably at Battle Creek, Michigan.

The Twentieth Century. The health and fitness impulses of nineteenth-century Americans reached a zenith with the turn-of-the-century progressive movement. Allying *scientific management, education, *public health, and *religion with their middle- and upper-class sensibilities, progressives worked to reform corrupt city governments, improve the infrastructure of urban social services, reduce *venereal disease by combating *prostitution, enact a constitutional amendment imposing nationwide prohibition, and save the immigrant masses from their sordid ways. Their often paternalistic efforts to instruct working-class Americans, especially recent immigrants, in matters of personal hygiene, the principles of scientific nutrition, and the dangers of intemperance demonstrated their commitment to matters of health. But other ideological currents of the *Gilded Age and beyond revealed a changing understanding of "fitness" as no longer simply evidence of divine favor and spiritual well-being, but as a marker of an individual's ability to survive the competitive Darwinian struggle for existence in urban-industrial America.

The post–*World War II years witnessed an epidemiological shift from infectious diseases to ailments related to lifestyle and old age. This shift resulted in part from the impact of antibiotics on infectious diseases, but the increasing number of Americans holding white-collar jobs and leading sedentary lives contributed to obesity and its associated debilities. Moreover, scientific investigators began to produce compelling evidence of the health benefits of exercise, a proper diet, and the avoidance of tobacco.

In response to these developments, President Dwight D. *Eisenhower in 1956 established the President's Council on Youth Fitness (after 1968, the President's Council on Physical Fitness and Sports) to combat the lack of physical fitness among children and young people. In the 1960s the federal government began to warn citizens of the health dangers of cigarettes. But these efforts lacked the religious overtones that had characterized many earlier health-reform movements. Science and secular morality had replaced religion and virtue as the primary motivators for health reform; and physical health, greater longevity, and economic productivity had replaced moral perfection as the primary purpose of healthful living.

Much of the explosive interest in health, diet, and fitness that characterized the late twentieth century was concentrated among aging members of the so-called baby-boom generation. However, the increase in physical-fitness activities and the decline in smoking were not uniform; white, affluent Americans with a post-secondary education embraced those behaviors more often than did the poor and blue-collar workers, the less well educated, and members of ethnic minority groups.

The continuing popularity of the vogue for jogging that began in the 1970s, the health and fitness clubs that proliferated in the 1980s, and the mountain biking enthusiasm of the 1990s all illustrated the faddish side of the late twentieth-century exercise and fitness movement, revealed the increasingly commercial and technological aspect of the quest for health and fitness, and highlighted the way these goals, so deeply rooted in America's religious and cultural history, had become as much badges of status as a means to a better life either here or in the hereafter.

[*See also* Americanization Movement; Industrial Diseases and Hazards; Medicine; Post–Cold War Era; Progressive Era; Sexual Morality and Sex Reform; Social Class; Social Darwinism; Sports: Amateur Sports and Recreation; Tobacco Industry; Tobacco Products.]

• James C. Whorton, *Crusaders for Fitness: The History of American Health Reformers,* 1982. Harvey Green, *Fit for America: Health, Fitness, Sport and American Society,* 1986. Ronald L. Numbers and Darrel W. Amundsen, eds., *Caring and Curing: Health and Medicine in the Western Religious Traditions,* 1986. Susan E. Cayleff, *Wash and Be Healed: The Water-Cure Movement and Women's Health,* 1987. Harvey A. Levenstein, *Revolution at the Table: The Transformation of the American Diet,* 1988. Martha H. Verbrugge, *Able-Bodied Womanhood,* 1988. Michael S. Goldstein, *The Health Movement: Promoting Fitness in America,* 1992. Richard Kluger, *Ashes to Ashes: America's Hundred-Year Cigarette War, the Public Health, and the Unabashed Triumph of Philip Morris,* 1996. Allan M. Brandt and Paul Rozin, eds., *Morality and Health,* 1997.

—Rennie B. Schoepflin

HEALTH FADS AND PANACEAS. *See* Health and Fitness; Medicine: Alternative Medicine.

HEALTH FOODS. *See* Health and Fitness.

HEALTH INSURANCE. The history of health insurance in America is largely a twentieth-century story. Well beyond 1900, paying for medical care, with few exceptions, remained a private activity between patients and their physicians and *hospitals. Widespread interest in sickness insurance—as it was originally called—did not develop in the United States until the 1910s, and then attention focused on compulsory, not voluntary, insurance. Inspired by the rapid spread of government-sponsored sickness-insurance plans in Europe, the progressive American Association for Labor Legislation in 1912 set up a committee to prepare a model bill for introduction in state legislatures (on the assumption that the U.S. *Constitution prohibited a federal plan). The model bill required the enrollment of most manual laborers earning a hundred dollars a month or less and provided for both income protection and medical care. Although many physicians greeted this plan enthusiastically, sentiment turned against the measure during *World War I, and by 1920, when the *American Medical Association (AMA) formally declared its opposition, the campaign for compulsory health insurance—or socialized medicine, as it was sometimes called—was dead.

The Great Depression, beginning in 1929, again brought health insurance to the fore. As hospital receipts and physician income plummeted, interest in voluntary health insurance grew. In December 1929, the Baylor University Hospital in Dallas, Texas, announced a plan to sell hospitalization policies to the city's school teachers for fifty cents a month. Other hospitals around the country adopted similar plans, and within a few years groups of hospitals were banding together to offer what came to be called Blue Cross insurance. The AMA, which urged Americans "to save for sickness" rather than purchase insurance, initially opposed this development "as being economically unsound, unethical and inimical to the public interests." In 1937, however, in the face of a renewed push for compulsory health insurance, the AMA finally approved group hospitalization plans—as long as they left the payment of physicians out of the scheme. By this time the AMA was working on a physician-controlled plan to provide medical (as opposed to hospital) insurance. The resulting medical-society plans, which started in the Pacific Northwest, took the name Blue Shield. By 1952 over half of all Americans owned some health insurance, and although insurance benefits paid only 15 percent of private expenditures for health care, prepayment plans were being hailed by a presidential commission as "the medical success story of the past fifteen years."

With voluntary plans failing to protect so many Americans, the perennial debate over compulsory health insurance flared again. Pro-insurance reformers had been bitterly disappointed when President Franklin Delano *Roosevelt failed to include health insurance in the 1935 *Social Security Act. To remedy this omission, the Social Security Board in 1943 drafted a bill to provide health insurance to all persons paying *Social Security taxes, as well as to their families. Despite the strong backing of President Harry S. *Truman, neither this nor subsequent versions were enacted by Congress. The election of a Republican administration in 1952 temporarily ended the debate over compulsory health insurance.

The 1960 election of John F. *Kennedy, a Democrat, revived discussion of the government's responsibility to provide adequate health care for its citizens. Despite strong opposition from organized medicine, Kennedy's successor, Lyndon B. *Johnson, persuaded Congress in 1965 to include health insurance as a Social Security benefit (Medicare) and to provide for the indigent through grants to the states (Medicaid). Ironically, after years of warning that government health insurance would ruin the medical profession financially, physicians found that *Medicare and Medicaid—by bringing in more patients, raising fees, and facilitating bill collecting—greatly increased their income.

The last third of the twentieth century witnessed numerous attempts to solve the twin problems of access to health care and its ever increasing cost. In the private sector the most notable development was the rapid growth of *health maintenance organizations (HMOs) after 1973, when Congress passed the bipartisan HMO Act. By 1990, the California-based Kaiser Permanente, which had pioneered in developing prepaid group-practice arrangements, had enrolled more than 6.5 million members. Proposals offered by different advocacy groups ranged from a national health service, on the left, in which medical workers would become salaried employees, to income-tax credits for the purchase of commercial health insurance, on the right. None of these efforts succeeded, including President Bill *Clinton's ill-fated health security plan in 1993–1994, which would have covered all Americans through large health-insurance purchasing cooperatives. Instead, the United States continued its piecemeal response to health-care coverage, with considerable experimentation occurring at the state level. By the end of the century, nearly 84 percent of Americans enjoyed health-insurance coverage, but an estimated 44 million remained uninsured, some by choice (over 8 percent of the uninsured earned more than $75,000 annually), most by necessity.

[*See also* Great Society; Insurance; Medicine: From the 1870s to 1945; Medicine: Since 1945; New Deal Era, The; Progressive Era.]

• Daniel S. Hirshfield, *The Lost Reform: The Campaign for Compulsory Health Insurance in the United States from 1932 to 1943,* 1970. Ronald L. Numbers, *Almost Persuaded: American Physicians and Compulsory Health Insurance, 1912–1920,* 1978. Monte M. Poen, *Harry S. Truman versus the Medical Lobby: The Genesis of Medicare,* 1979. Ronald L. Numbers, ed., *Compulsory Health Insurance: The Continuing American Debate,* 1982. Paul Starr, *The Social Transformation of American Medicine,* 1982. Robert Cunningham III and Robert M. Cunningham Jr., *The Blues: A History of the Blue Cross and Blue Shield System,* 1997.

—Ronald L. Numbers

HEALTH MAINTENANCE ORGANIZATIONS. Alone among western industrialized nations, the United States at the end of the twentieth century lacked a system of socialized medicine or universal *health insurance. National health plans proposed by presidents Franklin Delano *Roosevelt in 1939, Harry S. *Truman in 1948, and Bill *Clinton in 1993 failed to win congressional approval. Instead, the United States, beginning in the 1930s, evolved a network of health-maintenance organizations (HMOs) by which a group of health-care providers contracted to deliver specified, prepaid medical services to a defined group of enrollees.

The HMO concept originated among practitioners in the *public-health, industrial-medicine, and preventive-medicine fields, who often advocated prepaid group practice as an alternative to the individual fee-for-service arrangement favored by the mainstream medical profession. An early advocate of "health maintenance," the Yale bacteriologist and public-health expert Charles-Edward Amory Winslow coined the term in 1920 to describe an approach that emphasized preventive medicine and broad access to comprehensive care for workers and their families. Winslow's *Medical Care for the American People* (1932) advocated group-health plans.

The concept gained credibility thanks to the West Coast industrialist Henry J. Kaiser. A group-medical plan created for the workers on Kaiser's Grand Coulee dam project in the 1930s was extended to employees in Kaiser's shipyards during *World War II. In 1946, with the support of organized labor, Kaiser-Permanente incorporated as the nation's largest and most fully integrated prepaid group health plan, with its own physicians, *hospitals, and medical facilities. Other plans soon emerged, particularly in the West. In the East, the idea was pioneered by the Group Health Association of Washington, D.C. (1937), and by the Health Insurance Plan of Greater New York (1947). The *American Medical Association (AMA), defending the fee-for-service model, resisted HMOs, attacking them as "socialized medicine." The U.S. *Supreme Court, however, in a landmark 1943 ruling, struck down the AMA's effort to bar Group Health Association physicians from using local hospitals. The high court found this effort a violation of *antitrust legislation.

The controversies stirred by HMOs highlighted the difficulty of achieving the goal of providing broad access to quality health care in a democratic society; the differing interests of consumers, employers, organized physicians, and the federal government; and the tensions between the emerging structure of corporate medicine and individual physicians' traditional autonomy. But mounting health-care costs, coupled with increasing emphasis on preventive care, propelled the movement forward. The Health Maintenance Organization Act of 1973, passed with the backing of the Richard M. *Nixon administration, codified the basic tenets of prepaid health care and provided start-up funding for HMOs. By the mid-1990s, over five hundred HMOs existed nationwide, enrolling over fifty million people, including persons enrolled under the federal *Medicare and Medicaid programs. While the first HMOs were not-for-profit, those formed in the later twentieth century were mostly for-profit corporations. Kaiser-Permanente, with 9.1 million members by 1998, remained an industry leader. HMOs, in turn, were part of a larger trend toward managed care, driven by cost-containment pressures. The same pressures brought stricter regulation and oversight of HMOs after 1980. By the mid-1990s, at least half of U.S. physicians were associated with HMOs or other managed-care arrangements.

[*See also* Health and Fitness; Industrial Diseases and Hazards; Medicine: From the 1870s to 1945; Medicine: Since 1945.]

• Paul Starr, *The Social Transformation of American Medicine,* 1982. Rickey Hendricks, *A Model for National Health Care: The History of Kaiser Permanente,* 1993.

—Rickey Hendricks

HEARST, WILLIAM RANDOLPH (1863–1951), newspaper publisher and son of *mining millionaire and *California Democratic senator George Hearst. Privately educated, William Randolph Hearst attended Harvard for several years. Having worked briefly on Joseph *Pulitzer's *New York World,* he used it as a model to remake his father's *San Francisco Examiner.* He made the paper successful by means of sensationalism, crusades against the Southern Pacific Railroad, and luring the best talent.

When his father died, Hearst's mother, Phoebe Apperson Hearst, gave him $7.5 million to buy the *New York Journal* in 1894. Raiding Pulitzer's staff, he launched a circulation war with the *World,* using crude sensationalism and crusades against "the money power." Accuracy was slighted in this "yellow journalism" and in the *Journal*'s exploitation of the Cuban revolution and the *Spanish-American War.

An egomaniac burning with political ambition, Hearst served two terms in Congress (1903–07), received 263 Convention votes for the Democratic presidential nomination in 1904, lost a third-party race for mayor of New York in 1905, and lost again as the Democratic candidate for governor of New York in 1906. After this he exercised his influence indirectly through his newspapers. By the 1920s he controlled a publishing empire of over twenty newspapers, several magazines, the International News Service, and the King Features Syndicate. But he spent more than he earned, collecting art and antiques; promoting the film career of his mistress Marion Davies; and building a palatial mansion, San Simeon, in California.

Hearst helped Franklin Delano *Roosevelt secure the 1932 presidential nomination, but his early support of the New Deal ended in 1935 with attacks on business regulation, new taxes, and Roosevelt's foreign policy.

The Depression battered Hearst's fortune. By 1937 he was forced to sell some of his newspapers and art and antiques, and to relinquish financial control of his publications. His papers prospered during *World War II, and he recovered some of his control in 1945. At his death in 1951, his remaining properties passed to his five sons. His biographer W. A. Swanberg concludes that Hearst "was essentially a showman and propagandist, not a newsman." Orson Welles's classic 1941 film *Citizen Kane* was based on Hearst's career.

[*See also* Journalism; New Deal Era, The.]

• W. A. Swanberg, *Citizen Hearst*, 1961. David Nasaw, *The Chief: The Life of William Randolph Hearst*, 2000.

—James L. Crouthamel

HEART DISEASE. Heart disease entails any abnormality—anatomic or functional—that reduces the heart's life-sustaining action in providing essential nutrients to cells and removing the waste products of metabolism via the circulating blood. Although the importance of this circulation was recognized by European physicians as early as the seventeenth century, doctors in America and elsewhere as late as 1900 were unable to do much more for patients than listen to heartbeats with stethoscopes and prescribe rest and a few ordinary medications, such as digitalis for congestive heart failure. The electrocardiograph, developed in Holland in 1902 to record the heart's electrical activity, was first installed in the United States at New York's Mount Sinai Hospital in 1909. One year later, Arthur Hirschfelder of Johns Hopkins University published *Diseases of the Heart and Aorta*, the first American monograph on heart disease. In 1912, James B. Herrick of Chicago first described what he termed coronary artery thrombosis (occlusion by clot), which later came to be known as myocardial infarction.

An emerging cadre of heart specialists created a national organization, the American Heart Association (AHA), in 1924, and started a professional periodical, the *American Heart Journal*, in 1925. Robert E. Gross of Boston in 1938 ligated a patent ductus arteriosus (a condition that arises when the channel between the pulmonary artery and the aorta fails to close at birth), thereby performing the first successful *surgery for congenital heart disease. Two years later, board examinations were initiated to certify cardiologists. Alfred *Blalock and Helen Taussig at Johns Hopkins in 1944 performed the first "blue baby" operation, using diagnostic cardiac catheterization to correct a septal defect with severe pulmonary stenosis (a narrowing of the valve that regulates blood flow into the lungs). Their success aroused excitement throughout the medical profession. Federal legislation in 1948 funded the National Heart Institute (renamed in 1972 the National Heart, Lung, and Blood Institute—NHLBI). In 1948, too, the AHA transformed itself from a professional society to a citizens-based advocacy group dedicated to fund-raising, publicity, and support of better health care and expanded research, becoming the major popular voice of the "heart lobby." The American College of Cardiology, a select professional society, was formed in 1949.

The year 1948 also witnessed the launching of the Framingham (Massachusetts) Heart Study, which continued into the twenty-first century. This study, which periodically monitors over 5,200 men and women for coronary risk factors, established, among other findings, the role of high blood cholesterol in causing artery obstructions. John E. Gibbons of Philadelphia in 1953 developed an extracorporeal pump oxygenator (heart-lung bypass machine) to maintain continual blood flow during invasive surgery, thereby inaugurating the era of open-heart surgery. Successful recoveries from myocardial infarctions, such as those experienced in 1955 by President Dwight D. *Eisenhower and the future president Lyndon B. *Johnson, generated popular acclaim for advances in cardiovascular knowledge and techniques. Prosthetic heart valves were developed in 1960 by Dwight Harken of Boston and Albert Starr of Portland, Oregon.

The era of modern cardiovascular surgery, often called the "golden age" of cardiology, began in the mid-twentieth century. Open-heart surgery became routine in the 1950s; the first coronary bypass operation occurred in 1968; angioplasty (balloon dilation to open or repair obstructed vessels) was implemented in 1980; artificial pacemakers to compensate for diseased myocardial pathways were first implanted in 1959. Improved diagnostic techniques, such as echocardiology, permitted precise delineation of the location, nature, and degree of disease in the heart and arterial system. Pharmacological therapies included cyclosporine, an immunosuppressant introduced in 1981, to prevent rejection of donor organs, thereby allowing a resurgence of heart transplantation. Many *hospitals set up special coronary-care units. Most important, widened public awareness of lifestyle values such as low-fat diets, regular physical exercise, not smoking, and avoidance of obesity and high blood pressure created a "prevention culture" for Americans eager to minimize their susceptibility to heart disease.

By the end of the twentieth century, about seventeen thousand physicians practiced cardiology—more than any other non–primary care, nonsurgical specialty, and the death rate from heart attacks had fallen 58 percent from 1963 levels, while the rate for all cardiovascular diseases during the same interval had dropped 55 percent. Still, heart disease caused more deaths than all other illnesses combined. Annual costs to the nation in lost productivity and health expenses exceeded sixty billion dollars. *Hospitals attributed 20 percent of their total charges to care of cardiovascular patients. Fifty thousand Americans waited for heart transplants, but the number of available hearts, at most, allowed only 5 percent to receive them. Better control of health risk factors remained the key strategy for reducing heart disease as the new century began.

[*See also* Health and Fitness; Medical Education; Medicine: From the 1870s to 1945; Medicine: Since 1945; Pharmaceutical Industry; Tobacco Products.]

• Paul Dudley White, *My Life and Medicine: An Autobiographical Memoir*, 1971. Louis J. Acierno, *The History of Cardiology*, 1994. W. Bruce Fye, *American Cardiology: The History of a Specialty and Its College*, 1996. Stephen Westaby with Cecil Bosher, *Landmarks in Cardiac Surgery*, 1997. Richard J. Bing, *Cardiology: The Evolution of the Science and the Art*, 1999.

—Charles T. Morrissey

HEATING. Homes and public buildings in early America depended on a central hearth or open fireplace for heating. The hearth provided a gathering place for the family and served for cooking as well as heating. Many families heated only one room during the winter; even so, fireplace heat often proved inadequate. Cast-iron stoves did not come into general use until the second quarter of the nineteenth century. Even Benjamin *Franklin's famous "Franklin stove" of the 1740s, while efficient, had not been widely adopted. By the 1830s, however, cast-iron stoves became popular as the scarcity of firewood in urban areas converged with improvements in stoves themselves and the increasing accessibility of stoves and coal.

Centrally installed coal-fired furnaces appeared in the homes of wealthy Americans during the latter half of the nineteenth century. Built-in steam or forced-air heating systems did not become the norm until well into the twentieth century, however, when furnaces powered by other fuels, such as natural gas, electricity, and heating oil, became available. As urban areas and the middle class grew and utility companies expanded their distribution networks in the twentieth century, especially after *World War II, heat consumption in homes and public buildings kept pace.

The steady increase in heating consumption ended in the early 1970s. With the energy crisis and a slowing of improvements in heating technologies, consumers became increasingly concerned with fuel and energy efficiency. "Alternative" heating methods, such as passive solar heating, became popular, although they represented only a small percentage of heating sources. By the early 1990s, natural gas led the heating fuels, followed by electricity, fuel oil, and all other sources.

Throughout the history of heating, older technologies have overlapped with new ones. Consumers in abundantly wooded rural areas continued to use fireplaces even as urban dwellers adopted stoves. Coal furnaces coexisted with cast-iron stoves, and gas and electric furnaces overlapped with coal. As late as the 1950s, coal and wood were still widely used heating fuels. Moreover, in a nation as vast and diverse as the United States, wide regional differences have existed in the choice of heating devices and fuels. In warm climate zones, heating has been less of a concern than keeping the indoors cool.

Shaped by markets and institutions, heating technologies have in turn influenced cultural standards. For example, eighteenth-century Americans largely rejected stoves because of cost, perceived dangers, and the abundance of wood fuel for fireplaces. In the twentieth century, by keeping rates low and advertising to targeted groups, utility companies encouraged Americans to consume more heat. Whereas eighteenth- and even nineteenth-century Americans endured smoky and unevenly heated homes and public buildings, by the post–World War II era Americans had become accustomed to automatic heating (and, increasingly, cooling) systems, and were taking a well-regulated and comfortable indoor environment for granted.

[*See also* Electrical Industry; Electricity and Electrification; Environmentalism; Energy Crisis of the 1970s; Petroleum Industry; Refrigeration and Air Conditioning; Urbanization.]

• Susan Strasser, *Never Done: A History of American Housework*, 1982, pp. 50–67. Mark H. Rose, *Cities of Light and Heat: Domesticating Gas and Electricity in Urban America*, 1995.

—Libbie J. Freed

HEMINGWAY, ERNEST (1899–1961), writer, novelist, Nobel Prize recipient. Born in Oak Park, Illinois, Ernest Hemingway completed high school and then worked briefly as a reporter on the *Kansas City Star* before enlisting as a Red Cross ambulance driver in *World War I. On 8 July 1918, in northern Italy, he was seriously wounded by a mortar shell. After the war he recuperated in northern Michigan, and wrote freelance stories for the *Toronto Star*. In December 1921, he and Hadley Richardson (the first of his four wives) arrived in Paris where he continued to write for the *Toronto Star*. A charter member of what the expatriate American writer Gertrude Stein (1874–1946) dubbed the "Lost Generation," Hemingway connected with Stein, Ezra *Pound, and Sylvia Beach, owner of a Paris bookstore and publisher of avant-garde literature. Through them he became closely associated with such Modernist writers and artists as Ford Madox Ford, Juan Gris, Joan Miro, and James Joyce. By 1924, while working on the *Transatlantic Review*, Hemingway was writing now-classic short stories, including "Big Two-Hearted River," published in *In Our Time* (1925). With the help of F. Scott *Fitzgerald, Hemingway signed with Charles Scribner's Sons, who published all of his post-1925 work. Maxwell Perkins, until his death in 1947, was his editor.

Hemingway's first two novels, *The Sun Also Rises* (1926) and *A Farewell to Arms* (1929), expressing the disillusionment of the era, moved him to the forefront of postwar American writers. He reached a mass audience with *For Whom the Bell Tolls* (1940), a politically engaged novel about the Spanish Civil War. While experimenting with nonfiction and drama, he continued to write short stories like "The Short Happy Life of Francis Macomber" and "The Snows of Kilimanjaro." In 1952, he published *The Old Man and the Sea*, a lesser work that nevertheless brought him the Nobel Prize in 1954.

Marlin fisherman, big-game hunter, bull-fight aficionado, and war reporter, Hemingway's public persona seemed to mirror his macho fiction. Behind the scenes, however, increasingly severe depression and paranoia led to his suicide on 2 July 1961. Three novels, a memoir, and one nonfiction book appeared posthumously. The most influential American writer of his generation, Hemingway enlarged the subject matter of American fiction; developed a distinctive, pared-down prose style; and changed the voice and structure of the short story.

[*See also* Literature: Since World War I; Modernist Culture; Red Cross, American; Twenties, The.]

• Carlos Baker, *Ernest Hemingway: A Life Story*, 1969. Bernice Kert, *The Hemingway Women*, 1983. Michael Reynolds, *The Young Hemingway*, 1986. Michael Reynolds, *Hemingway: The Paris Years*, 1989. Michael Reynolds, *Hemingway: The 1930s*, 1997. Michael Reynolds, *Hemingway: The Final Years*, 1999.

—Michael Reynolds

HENRY, JOSEPH (1797–1878), physicist and first director of the *Smithsonian Institution. Born in Albany, New York, Joseph Henry attended the Albany Academy between 1818 and 1822. He taught physics and mathematics at the Albany Academy (1826–1832) and physics at the College of New Jersey, now Princeton University (1832–1846), before being elected secretary (director) of the Smithsonian in 1846.

Henry was the first American since Benjamin *Franklin to gain an international reputation in experimental physics, especially electromagnetic induction. His pioneering work on the nature of *electricity, magnetism, and the interaction between the two was valued both for its own sake and because it demonstrated how understanding nature could lead to technological advancement. His research proved essential for the development of the *telegraph. Among his other discoveries were the concept of the transformer and the oscillatory nature of the discharge of a capacitor. In recognition of his discoveries in electromagnetic induction, the unit of inductance, the "henry," was named after him.

As director of the Smithsonian, he set aside his personal research program to become an administrator and spokesperson for the importance of basic scientific research. At the Smithsonian, Henry established a program of direct support of research, scholarly publication, and international exchange. He supported research not only in the natural sciences, but also in *anthropology and ethnography.

Often compared to Franklin, Henry became a larger-than-life symbol of American accomplishment in science and the acclaimed father of modern electrical technology, including the electric motor and the *telephone. The premier American physicist of the mid–nineteenth century and an able institution builder, Henry, as a leader of American science, sought to establish rigorous standards for the scientific community and to increase the level of public support for research. His early accomplishments in the laboratory and his important discoveries accorded him the prestige and respect necessary for his success as a science administrator and spokesperson.

[*See also* American Association for the Advancement of Science; Coast and Geodetic Survey, U.S.; Electrical Industry; Mathematics and Statistics; Physical Sciences; Science: Revolutionary War to World War I.]

• Robert V. Bruce, *The Launching of Modern American Science 1846–1876*, 1987. Albert E. Moyer, *Joseph Henry: The Rise of an American Scientist*, 1997.

—Marc Rothenberg

HENRY, PATRICK (1736–1799), lawyer, orator, and Revolutionary leader. Born in Hanover County, Virginia, Patrick Henry began the study of law in 1760. Although weak in legal training, his ability to argue a case with logic and passion brought him a thriving practice. Elected to the Virginia House of Burgesses in 1765, he opposed the *Stamp Act with stirring oratory and a set of resolutions that circulated among the colonies and established his reputation as a defender of American rights. Henry served in the First *Continental Congress in 1774, delivered his famous "give me liberty or give me death" speech in support of his Virginia Assembly resolution to arm Virginia for defense against the British in 1775, and was a leader in Virginia's May 1776 call for independence.

Elected first governor of the independent state of Virginia in 1776, Henry dominated Virginia politics through 1787. Preoccupied with state business, he declined to serve in the *Constitutional Convention of 1787, a decision he may have regretted when he saw its final product. Henry emerged as the foremost Antifederalist opponent of the federal *Constitution, and his opposition speeches in the 1778 Virginia Ratifying Convention constituted one of the first fully articulated formulations of *states'-rights ideology. Defeated in the convention, Henry used his influence in the Virginia Assembly over the next few years in seeking to scale back the powers of the central government. In his final years he deserted many of his former Antifederalist colleagues to support Federalists such as John *Adams and John *Marshall, perhaps less from genuine commitment to their principles than from pique at the prominence of his rivals Thomas *Jefferson and James *Madison.

[*See also* Early Republic, Era of the; Federalist Party; Revolution and Constitution, Era of; Revolutionary War.]

• Richard R. Beeman, *Patrick Henry: A Biography,* 1974. Henry Mayer, *A Son of Thunder: Patrick Henry and the American Republic,* 1986.

—Richard R. Beeman

HEPBURN ACT. *See* Antitrust Legislation.

HIGH SCHOOLS. *See* Education: The Public School Movement; Education: Education in Contemporary America.

HIGHWAY SYSTEM. The American highway system is a creation of the twentieth century. Before 1916, roads remained a local responsibility. Bicyclists and railroad executives lobbied for better roads in the 1890s, and by 1910 the *automotive industry echoed those demands. Reflecting many elements of the *Progressive Era reform movement (especially central administration by technical experts), the Federal-Aid Highway Act of 1916 created the first national road system, funded by fifty million dollars over five years for construction of rural roads for mail deliveries. Consistent with *federalism, the bill mandated cooperation between state highway departments and the Bureau of Public Roads (BPR, later the Federal Highway Administration). Thus states designed, built, and maintained the roads, while federal engineers inspected and approved plans, specifications, and construction. Initially costs were shared equally, although BPR engineers always exercised greater influence than this fifty-fifty balance would suggest, owing to their superior technical expertise.

In 1921, as automobile traffic increased, the post-road program gave way to federal authorization of a national network of primary and secondary roads between cities. As first planned in 1923, this federal-aid road system totaled 169,000 miles—some 7 percent of the nation's highway mileage. Under a numbering scheme adopted in 1925, U.S. 1 followed the Atlantic coast while U.S. 2 paralleled the Canadian border. Federal appropriations averaged about $75 million annually during the 1920s, and the gasoline tax, introduced in Oregon in 1919 and dedicated to road construction by some state legislatures beginning in the 1930s, provided matching state funds. System additions began with extensions into urban areas (1938), followed by secondary roads (1940) partially built with federal aid. The final addition to the highway network, the Interstate system, was authorized in 1944. The states and BPR first designated routes in 1947, although special funding began only in 1954. Massive appropriations for the 42,500–miles National System of Interstate and Defense Highways came in 1956, with the federal government assuming 90 percent of the estimated cost of $25 billion.

This network altered many facets of American life, facilitating the development of a mobile culture and the rise of standardized national fast-food and motel franchises. Long-distance family summer vacations spent in campgrounds or motels became common, and long-haul trucking replaced *railroads as primary freight haulers. The decline of central-city business districts, the "malling" of America, rapid *suburbanization, and new patterns of land use all resulted in part from easy access to express highways after 1950.

While few government programs were as popular as road building, the scale of Interstate highway construction inside cities engendered significant resistance from neighborhood groups and early environmentalists after 1960. A "Freeway Revolt" made headlines and its partisans won numerous court cases, halting Interstate construction projects in such cities as *San Francisco, *Boston, *New Orleans, and *Philadelphia. Although several disputed freeways were eventually completed in the late 1980s, the momentum for road construction was lost. Even so, the federal-aid system in 1997 encompassed 957,544 miles out of the national total of some 3.9 million miles of roads and highways. Annual appropiations for this system alone increased from $5 million in 1916 to $75 million in 1925, $585 million in 1954, and $20.8 billion in 1997. Highway spending at all levels of goverment surpassed $60 billion that same year.

[*See also* Bicycles and Bicycling; Mass Marketing; Motor Vehicles; Roads and Turnpikes, Early; Route 66; Shopping Centers and Malls; Tourism.]

• Bruce E. Seely, *Building the American Highway System: Engineers as Policy Makers,* 1987. Mark H. Rose, *Interstate: Express Highway Politics, 1939–1989,* rev. ed., 1990.

—Bruce E. Seely

HILL, JAMES J. (1838–1916), businessman and railroad promoter. As the creator of the railroad network that dominated the late nineteenth-century economic expansion in the Northwest, from the prairies of western Minnesota to Seattle, Washington, James J. Hill embodied the canny foresight, organizational brilliance, and ruthless drive that characterized his generation of capitalist leaders.

Born in Ontario, Canada, Hill moved to Minneapolis, Minnesota, two decades later and worked as a shipping clerk for a steamship line. In 1867, using his extensive knowledge of freight rates, he formed his own shipping company and contracted to furnish the St. Paul and Pacific Railroad with fuel. When the railroad fell into receivership in the 1870s, Hill and Canadian financier friends bought it and extended it first to Manitoba, then westward through the Dakotas and Montana to Great Falls (1887), and finally over the Cascades to the Pacific in 1893. In 1890, he consolidated separate lines into the Great Northern Railroad Company.

Mastering every detail of the railroad's organization and operation while retaining a vision of long-term goals, Hill drove his workers hard, fired anyone he disliked, and fought off hostile acquisition attempts. His personal fortune swelled as he invested in iron and copper mines, and he built an imposing mansion in St. Paul. His 1901 attempt to control his empire through the Northern Securities holding company was struck down by the *Supreme Court in 1904, but until his death Hill retained a reputation as the empire builder of the Northwest.

[*See also* Gilded Age; *Northern Securities Case*; Railroads.]

• Albro Martin, *James J. Hill and the Opening of the Northwest,* 1976. Michael P. Malone, *James J. Hill: Empire Builder of the Northwest,* 1996.

—Clifford E. Clark Jr.

HILLMAN, SIDNEY (1887–1946), labor leader. Born in Zagare, Lithuania, and reared in an orthodox Jewish family, Sidney Hillman rebelled as a teenager by joining Jewish social-democratic trade unionists and revolutionaries fighting tsarist rule. Arrested twice in 1905, he joined the emigration of Lithuanian Jews to the United States. In 1909 in *Chicago he began his American career as a labor leader among fellow immigrants. In 1914, at age twenty-eight, he became the first president of the Amalgamated Clothing Workers of America (ACWA), a position he held until his death.

Hillman's idealism, influenced by the practices of American trade unionists and *Progressive Era reformers, led him to promote industrial unionism as a social democratic reform of American *capitalism. His union's collective bargaining agreements with employers in the men's clothing industry brought a forty-four-hour work week, workshop efficiency, discipline, social welfare benefits, and arbitration arrangements for stabilizing a conflict-ridden industry. Without severing his links to Jewish labor movements at home and abroad, he steered the multiethnic union—it had 177,000 members by 1920—through the turmoil of the post–*World War I decade: Red scares; trade union decline; and, in the needle trades, competing passions of *socialism and *nationalism. During the Great Depression and the *New Deal Era, Hillman became a leader in the campaign to organize industrial workers throughout the economy. As vice president of the Committee of Industrial Organizations (1935) and in 1936 in coalition with the Labor Nonpartisan League and American Labor Party, he allied with President Franklin Delano *Roosevelt and the New Deal. In 1940 Roosevelt appointed him codirector of the Office of Production Management. Hillman fought for Roosevelt's reelection in 1944 and played a key role in the political solidification of organized workers as a liberal force in the *Democratic party. After Roosevelt's death, Hillman worked for a World Federation of Labor, which he envisioned as part of a new world order under U.S.–Soviet leadership.

[*See also* Congress of Industrial Organizations; Immigration; Labor Movements.]

• Steven Fraser, *Labor Will Rule: Sidney Hillman and the Rise of American Labor*, 1991. Gerd Korman, "New Jewish Politics for an American Labor Leader, 1942–1946," *American Jewish History* 82 (1994): 195–213.

—Gerd Korman

HIROSHIMA AND NAGASAKI, ATOMIC BOMBING OF. In the only uses of nuclear weapons in war, and on the order of President Harry S. *Truman, the American bomber *Enola Gay* attacked Hiroshima, Japan, on 6 August 1945 and the *Bock's Car* struck Nagasaki on 9 August. Blast, heat, and radiation from these attacks took over 200,000 lives, mostly civilians. In concert with Soviet entry into the Pacific war, and compounding years of destruction to Japan, the bomb's use forced Japan's capitulation and ended *World War II.

The bomb's secret development had originated in fears of a Nazi atomic bomb; its eventual use against a defeated Japan derived from differing, even competing, considerations. The war's ferocity sanctioned atomic attack: By 1945 both Allied and Axis powers had abandoned most restraints on attacking civilians; atomic bombing seemed a small step beyond the ongoing fire-bombing of Japan. Racial hatreds between Japanese and Americans had stirred exterminationist fantasies, and Truman justified the attacks as acts of revenge as well as victory. Some leaders sought the attacks in order to threaten the Soviet Union; others hoped the bomb's awful power would compel Soviet-American cooperation. The reason later cited as paramount—the desire to avoid American casualties in an invasion of Japan—did not dominate official deliberations at the time. In retrospect, however, the widespread assumption that the bomb had shortened the war deepened the American public's gratitude for its use. Japan's leaders also bore responsibility by continuing a war they knew to be futile.

Just as differing forces shaped the bomb's use, Americans derived competing truths from it. Depending on who was telling the story, it came to signify America's martial triumph and moral righteousness, its *racism and technological fanaticism, its entry into an agonizing nuclear age, its fate if undefended, its threat to others if unrestrained. *Cold War politics encouraged uncritical acceptance of the bomb's use and censorship of the historical record about atomic decision-making, research, and experimentation. As late as 1994, after the Cold War's end, opposition by veterans' groups and others convinced that the bomb's use was necessary and wholly justified forced cancellation of the National Air and Space Museum's plans to incorporate competing stories in a display of the *Enola Gay.*

[*See also* Manhattan Project; Nuclear Strategy; Nuclear Weapons.]

• Paul Boyer, *By the Bomb's Early Light: American Thought and Culture at the Dawn of the Atomic Age*, 1985. Michael S. Sherry, *The Rise of American Air Power: The Creation of Armageddon*, 1987.

—Michael S. Sherry

HISPANIC AMERICANS. In 2000, Hispanic, or Latino, Americans—persons of Latin American, Spanish, or Portuguese ancestry—in the United States numbered over 25 million, or about 10 percent of the population. This highly diverse group included recent immigrants and families whose U.S. roots extended back many generations. With more than 50 percent under the age of twenty-five, Latinos were among the nation's youngest population groups, and, with high levels of natural increase, the most rapidly growing minority group. Relatively concentrated geographically, approximately 90 percent of Latinos lived in Arizona, *California, Colorado, Florida, Illinois, New Mexico, New York, and Texas. Cities with major Latino concentrations included *Los Angeles, Miami, *New York, *Chicago, and Houston. Most were Roman Catholic, but many belonged to fundamentalist or charismatic Protestant churches.

Colonial Era to World War II. Hispanic colonists settled Florida, Louisiana, and New Mexico, and two of the oldest communities within present-day United States—St. Augustine, Florida (1565) and Santa Fe, New Mexico (1610)—have had Latino inhabitants from the beginning. Cities that have had Latino residents for more than two hundred years include San Antonio, Texas; *New Orleans; and San Diego. Louisiana governor Bernardo de Galvez contributed money, arms, and supplies to the Continental Army during the *Revolutionary War, and Captain Jorge Farragut from the Spanish island of Minorca served with distinction in the U.S. Navy in the Revolutionary War and the *War of 1812 (and fathered the *Civil War naval hero David *Farragut). Commemorating New Spain's contributions to American independence, Mexicans contributed a thousand silver pesos to help construct the first Catholic church in New York City. Spanish-speaking residents of Florida, Louisiana, Mexico's northern territories, and *Puerto Rico became U.S. citizens as these regions were absorbed over the course of the nineteenth century. With citizenship came political participation. Joseph Marion Hernandez was elected to Congress from Florida in 1822. Miguel A. Otero served as governor of New Mexico from 1897 to 1906.

As Americans settled these Hispanic regions they adopted Hispanic words, folkways, legal practices, mining and grazing laws, and agricultural and livestock methods. California retained women's community-property rights, derived from Hispanic law, when it became a state. California *gold-rush miners utilized Mexican, Peruvian, and Chilean mining techniques and Mexican laborers experienced in silver- and coppermining. Arizona's Bisbee Copper Mines, linchpin of the Arizona-New Mexico *mining industry, recruited a Latino labor force. Early western songs and stories often derived from those of Latino *vaqueros* (literally, "cowmen"). Hispanic architecture, well adapted to the arid *Southwest, was highly influential.

One of the more interesting individual Hispanic Americans

of an earlier era was California's Doña Arcadia Bandini (1827–1912). Twice widowed and an astute investor, Bandini left an estate conservatively estimated at $8 million. The state's wealthiest woman, she contributed generously to schools, parks, and hospitals.

Latinos have fought in every American war. During the Civil War, New Mexico and Arizona volunteers, including Mexican-American cavalry under Manuel Antonio Chavez and Rafael Chacon, resisted Confederate efforts to separate the western states from the Union. At *Gettysburg, Lt. Colonel Federico Fernandez Cavada fought on the Union side, Colonel Santos Benavides for the Confederacy. Mexican Americans and other Latinos volunteered for service during the *Spanish-American War. During *World War I, many Puerto Ricans and Mexican Americans volunteered or were drafted.

In the twentieth century, many Mexicans migrated northward. The restrictive immigration legislation of the 1920s did not apply to Latin America, and many Latino immigrants arrived, becoming agricultural laborers in the Southwest and California, or unskilled urban workers, living in the *barrios* of Los Angeles and other cities. During the Depression of the 1930s these migrants, earlier welcomed as cheap labor, faced hostility and deportation. In the 1930s Latino migrant workers in California's agricultural fields went on strike for higher pay and better working conditions. Many joined the Confederación de Uniones de Campesinos y Obreros Mexicanos (Confederation of Unions of Mexican Workers and Farm Laborers).

World War II to 2000. As described in Raul Morin's *Among the Valiant* (1963), as many as 400,000 Latinos fought in *World War II, often with great distinction. Air Force hero José L. Holguin, a Los Angeles Mexican American, won the Distinguished Flying Cross, the Air Medal, and the Silver Star for his exploits. Despite this record, Latinos became a focus of wartime hostility, most notoriously in the Los Angeles "zoot-suit riots" targeting Mexican-American youths. More than 200,000 Latinos proudly served in the military from 1945 to 2000, including many in Korea, Vietnam, and some 25,000 in the *Persian Gulf War. Of some 100,000 Hispanics in the armed services in 2000, about 5,000 were women.

The post-World War II era brought continued growth of the Hispanic population through legal and illegal *immigration and natural increase. Under the *bracero* program (1942–1965), Congress permitted the regular annual importation of Mexican farm laborers for seasonal work in the agricultural fields of California, Arizona, and Texas. The 1965 Immigration and Nationality Act set an annual ceiling of 120,000 on immigration from the Western Hemisphere, on a first-come, first-serve basis, with special provisions for reuniting families. Later legislation permitted the immigration of Cubans fleeing Fidel Castro's communist regime in Cuba, thousands of whom settled in Miami.

In many respects, the story of these years is one of achievement—economically, organizationally, politically, educationally, and culturally. In 1992, 85 percent of Latino men and 53 percent of Latina women were employed. Some 1.5 million belonged to labor unions. Latino business ownership surged in the 1990s, particularly in the Southwest, New York, Florida, Illinois, and Puerto Rico. By 2000 these enterprises had some 100,000 employees, and the total sales of the 500 largest Latino-owned businesses reached $20 billion. Many Latino businesspeople belonged to the United Hispanic Chamber of Commerce or some 200 state and local Latino chambers of commerce.

Latinas (Hispanic women) populated all sectors of the labor force in the 1990s. Linda Chavez-Thompson, executive vice-president of the AFL-CIO, was one of many Latinas active in labor unions. Like their male counterparts, many Latina workers held unskilled or entry-level jobs. In 1996, Latinas working full-time had median earnings of $17,500. But their ranks also included many managers and professionals. The number of Latinas in managerial positions grew from 110,000 in 1980 to 300,000 in 2000, twice the growth rate for Latino males. The number of Latina professionals in fields ranging from urban planning, personnel relations, and health care to teaching, counseling, and library science consistently exceeded that of male Latinos. In 2000, 10 percent of Latina women over age twenty-five were college graduates. Changing career and educational patterns among Latinas were among the most significant developments in the Hispanic community in these years.

The growing Latino community in the twentieth century generated numerous civic organizations. The largest, the League of United Latin American Citizens (LULAC), founded in the 1920s, had some 100,000 members in 200 chapters nationwide by 2000. LULAC's program included anti-discrimination and equal-rights campaigns and promotion of education. The American G.I. Forum (1948) addresses Latino veterans' interests, encourages education and patriotism, and offers job-training services. The bipartisan National Association of Latino Elected Officials (1975) provides issue-analysis and promotes information exchange, training for public service, and advocacy on matters of importance to Latinos. The Southwest Voter Registration Project, founded in 1974 by Willie Velasquez of San Antonio, with a small staff and a network of volunteers, focuses on increasing the Latino vote and electing Latino candidates nationwide. Other advocacy organizations include the National Council of La Raza, the National Council of Hispanic Women, and the Hispanic Association on Corporate Responsibility.

Twentieth-century Latinos continued to participate in politics and governance. Mexican-born Octaviano A. Larrazolo, governor of New Mexico in 1919–1923, in 1928 became the first Latino in the U.S. Senate when he was elected to complete the term of a deceased incumbent. In 2000, some 5,000 Hispanic Americans, including 1500 women, held elective office nationwide. Five Latinos have served as cabinet members, five as governors, and over 25 as members of Congress. In the 1990s over 100 Hispanic Americans served in state legislatures.

On the *education front, Latinos comprised 12 percent of public-school students, and perhaps 4 percent of the teachers, in the 1990s. From 1982 to 1992, Latino college enrollment rose from 520,000 to 950,000. Some 40,000 Hispanic Americans graduated from college annually in the mid-1990s, and over 5,000 were college and university faculty members. The Spanish-born molecular biologist Severo Ochoa shared the 1959 Nobel Prize in Medicine and Physiology for his discovery of RNA. Dr. Alfredo Baños, a theoretical physicist at UCLA, did significant work in nuclear technology.

Latinos' late-twentieth-century cultural contributions were too extensive to treat adequately in a brief essay. By 2000 the United States had some 250 Spanish language *radio and *television stations and over 1,000 Spanish or Spanish-English periodicals. Latinos were major players in the recording industry and were increasingly visible in *films and on television. Indeed, Latino participation in films began with such silent-era performers as Myrtle Gonzales and Beatriz Michelena. In the later 1920s and 1930s came Dolores del Rio, Lupe Velez, and Ramon Novarro. Mid-century Hispanic stars included Rita Hayworth, Fernando Lamas, Desi Arnez, Rita Moreno, Anthony Quinn, and Ricardo Montalban. The late twentieth century brought stardom to Charlie Sheen, Emilio Estevez, Raul Julia, Rosie Perez, and many others.

Latinos' cultural visibility increased markedly after the 1960s, as many intellectual and creative activities intended for Latino audiences demonstrated broader appeal. Latino poets, playwrights, novelists, musicians, and dancers won a large following. A Latino ethnic theater movement provided experience for young performers. In music, the traditional Latin styles enjoyed continued popularity. Hispanic dance—folkloric, modern, and classical—attracted enthusiastic audiences. The long-established Hispanic mural tradition remained vital, including work not only in the classical Mexican tradition of public murals but also by iconoclastic individual artists adopting a full range of contemporary styles.

The national pastime for millions of Latinos was *baseball. The long roster of Hispanic stars in the major leagues, beginning with the Cuban third baseman Esteban Bellan in 1871, includes Roberto and Sandy Alomar, Jose Canseco, hitter Juan Gonzalez (Most Valuable Player in 1996), homerun champion Sammy Sosa, and pitcher Pedro Martinez, the 1999 Cy Young Award winner. The most beloved Latino player was the Pittsburg Pirates' great Puerto Rican right fielder Roberto Clemente, killed in a plane crash in 1972 at thirty-eight while on a humanitarian mission to aid Nicaraguan earthquake victims.

The late-twentieth-century Hispanic-American experience included not only noteworthy achievement and economic and cultural progress, impressive as these were, but also *poverty and social problems. While many Latinos continued to work as migrant laborers, great numbers also lived in the nation's inner cities plagued by *unemployment, social disorganization, illicit *drugs, gang activity, and out-of-wedlock pregnancy. In the mid-1990s some thirty percent of Hispanics lived below the poverty line and a third of Latino children lived with a single parent, typically the mother. Lack of education, prejudice and discrimination, and a changing economy that required technical training and offered little to unskilled workers all contributed to the problem. Latinos in the United States illegally, perhaps 12 million in the early 1990s, faced special difficulties, working long hours for low wages and lacking health coverage or job benefits. But even at the lower economic ranks, family, community, and church ties remained strong, and Latino organizations and leaders mobilized to alleviate the problems of the poor. Cesar *Chavez, founder of the United Farm Workers Union, led organizational campaigns and boycotts to improve the lot of migrant workers from the 1950s to his death in 1993.

A vibrant and diverse group that has been a significant part of American history, the Latino community was clearly poised to play an increasingly important role in the nation's social, economic, political, and cultural life as the twenty-first century unfolded.

[*See also* Adams-Onís Treaty; Agriculture: Since 1920; Immigration Law; Korean War; Labor Markets, Labor Movements; Louisiana Purchase; Mexican War; Migratory Agricultural Workers; Mexican War; Pueblo Revolt; Race and Ethnicity; Roman Catholicism; Spanish Settlements in North America; Strikes and Industrial Conflict; Vietnam War.]

• Frank D. Bean and Marta Tienda, *The Hispanic Population of the United States*, 1988. Earl Shorris, *Latinos, A Biography of the People*, 1992. Frank de Varona, ed., *Hispanic Presence in the United States: Historical Beginnings*, 1993. James D. Cockcroft, *The Hispanic Struggle for Social Justice: The Hispanic Experience in the Americas*, 1994. *The Hispanic Almanac: From Columbus to Corporate America*, 1994. Bureau of the Census, *Population Projections of the United States, by Age, Sex, Race, and Hispanic Origin: 1995 to 2050*, 1997. Nick Kanellos and Cristelia Perez, Chronology of Hispanic American History, 1995. Geoffrey Fox, *Hispanic Nation: Culture, Politics, and the Construction of Identity*, 1996. Mike Davis, *Magical Urbanism: Latinos Reinvent the U.S. City*, 2000.

—Juan Gomez-Quinones

HISS, ALGER (1904–1996), central figure in a celebrated case of the late 1940s and early 1950s that embodied many of the central anxieties of the McCarthy Era. Hiss, a Harvard-trained lawyer who served in Franklin Delano *Roosevelt's administration during the 1930s and later as a State Department official, member of the U.S. delegation to the *Yalta Conference, secretary-general of the inaugural meeting of the *United Nations, and president of the *Carnegie Endowment for International Peace, exemplified the liberal "establishment" targeted by Senator Joseph *McCarthy and his allies.

In 1948, in testimony before the *House Committee on Un-American Activities (HUAC), the *Time* magazine editor and former communist Whittaker Chambers (1901–1961) accused Hiss of having been a member of the Communist party. In a dramatic HUAC appearance, Hiss confronted Chambers and denied the charges. When Hiss sued Chambers for libel, Chambers further accused him of having passed secret documents to the Soviet Union during the 1930s. As a Soviet courier, Chambers claimed, he had transmitted to the Russian State Department documents given him by Hiss and his wife. In evidence, he offered microfilms that he had concealed in a pumpkin on his Maryland farm. Because of the three-year statute of limitation on espionage, Hiss was indicted by a grand jury in December 1948 not for spying but for perjury in his HUAC testimony. His first trial, in July 1949, resulted in a hung jury. A second trial, conducted in January 1950 with looser rules of evidence, resulted in conviction. His appeal failed, and he was imprisoned from 1950 to 1954.

Although Hiss continued to protest his innocence, evidence from the Soviet archives after the end of the *Cold War convinced many historians that he had indeed committed espionage. The case was even murkier at the time, particularly as it became embroiled in Cold War domestic politics. Much of the ambiguity arose from the contrasting careers of the two principals: Hiss's background was patrician; Chambers's mediocre at best. Hiss graduated from Johns Hopkins and Harvard and enjoyed a brilliant public career; Chambers, a Columbia University dropout, had lived the marginal existence of a freelance writer, joining the Communist party in 1925. Because of such contrasts, most HUAC members initially doubted Chambers's charges. Freshman congressman and HUAC member Richard M. *Nixon pursued them, however, leading to the dramatic retrieval of a Hiss family typewriter, given away years before, that experts linked to documents in Chambers's microfilms. Nixon's dogged pursuit of Hiss raised his own national profile, helping him secure the 1952 Republican vice presidential nomination.

Even after his conviction, Hiss retained the loyalty of high-profile defenders, including Secretary of State Dean *Acheson. Against a backdrop of anticommunist hysteria, however, the case also helped fuel government loyalty investigations and efforts by HUAC, Senator McCarthy, and others to root out communist influences in America. The case also seriously tarnished American *liberalism, which fell under a general cloud of suspicion; for years after, liberals faced charges of being "soft on communism." In this sense, the Hiss case influenced policy debates of the 1960s, including President Lyndon B. *Johnson's rationale for escalating U.S. involvement in Vietnam.

[*See also* Anticommunism; Communism; Communist Party—USA.]

• Allen Weinstein, *Perjury: The Hiss-Chambers Case*, 1978. Richard Fried, *Nightmare in Red: The McCarthy Era in Perspective*, 1990. Alexander Vassilier, *The Haunted Wood: Soviet Espionage in America: The Stalin Era*, 1999.

—Mark L. Kleinman

HISTORIC PRESERVATION. The 1824 visit of the Marquis de Lafayette to *Philadelphia's Independence Hall, recently threatened by demolition, stirred memories of the *Revolutionary War and helped spark a preservation movement. Americans have since been preserving historic sites to freshen fading memories, promote *tourism, and influence contemporary debate. In the charged political atmosphere of 1850, as sectional divisions widened, the Hasbrouck House in Newburgh, New York, which once served as George *Washington's wartime headquarters, was saved as the nation's first historic house museum. Shortly after, a women's group rescued Washington's Virginia plantation, *Mount Vernon. The first statewide preservation movement arose in Virginia in 1889 in a campaign to preserve the colonial sites at *Jamestown and Williamsburg.

As *industrialization and *immigration transformed America, filiopietism and nativism prompted further preservation efforts by native-born Anglo Americans. In 1904, the Fairbanks family acquired and soon opened to the public its ancestral home (built around 1636) in Dedham, Massachusetts. Genealogical and patriotic groups, such as the Daughters of the American Revolution (1890), restored innumerable sites nationwide. Sometimes historic restorations created identities for local communities, as in 1876 when the mission at San Luis Obispo, California, was rescued. Historic sites served to Americanize newcomers, teach—or invent—traditions, and anchor a fast-changing society.

In the early 1900s, museum curators, notably at *New York City's Metropolitan Museum of Art, began to highlight architectural aesthetics, while antiquarians such as Boston's William Sumner Appleton Jr. carefully restored buildings to reveal their original design and construction. Rejecting the movement's earlier romanticism, Appleton melded historical archaeology and preservation. Influenced by the *Progressive Era's business and scientific drives, Appleton, and later the American Institute of Architects and the National Park Service, professionalized historic restorations.

The focus on individual buildings soon broadened, beginning in 1926 with the restoration of colonial Williamsburg by John D. Rockefeller Jr. Henry *Ford simultaneously created his ersatz "Greenfield Village" in Dearborn, Michigan. There followed a wave of remaking communities, such as Connecticut's idealized Mystic Seaport, and of preserving existing townscapes, as at Charleston, South Carolina. In the 1930s, historic districts were zoned to emphasize *architecture, as in *New Orleans's *Vieux Carré*. "*Urban renewal" nonetheless destroyed the historic fabric of countless cities by the 1960s.

With the growth of the market economy, tourism increasingly shaped preservation. In 1894 Abraham *Lincoln's birthplace in Hodgenville, Kentucky, was "re-created" simply to draw tourists. In San Antonio, Texas, site of the Alamo, preservationists of the 1920s considered historic sites their economy's golden goose. By the 1980s, restored neighborhoods, main streets, and festival marketplaces, such as *San Francisco's Ghirardelli Square, fueled a booming heritage tourism. Such capital-driven preservation often conflicted with the rights of poorer communities and neighborhoods, however.

With the Historic Preservation Act (1966), the *civil rights movement, and the women's movement, the scope of historic preservation became more culturally representative. Whether at the restored home of Frederick *Douglass in *Washington, D.C., Harriet Beecher Stowe's house in Hartford, Connecticut; or the Shapiro family home at Strawbery Banke, in Portsmouth, New Hampshire, which exhibits Jewish immigrant life, historic preservation by the end of the twentieth century had begun to reflect the nation's ethnic and cultural diversity.

[*See also* Alamo, Battle of the; National Park System; Nativist Movement; Texas Republic and Annexation.]

• James M. Lindgren, *Preserving the Old Dominion*, 1993. James M. Lindgren, *Preserving Historic New England*, 1995. Mike Wallace, *Mickey Mouse History*, 1996.

—James M. Lindgren

HISTORIOGRAPHY, AMERICAN. Within the vast and fluid domain of collective memory, historical writing serves a special purpose. It refines, stabilizes, and extends the recorded experience of groups, societies, and undertakings. Its practitioners are an intellectual elite, applying their own standards and traditions to the task at hand. Yet they can never escape the authority of the documents available to them or the guidance of the milieu in which they work. Historical writing arises from the interplay of a codifying tradition, an access to sources, and a changing, contemporary culture.

Colonial and Antebellum Eras. During the first century of European colonization of the North American mainland, *New England produced the most memorable historical writing. This was the period of Puritan history, when clergymen and magistrates celebrated the divine guidance that had led them to the New World and preserved their settlements through famine, war, and religious dissension. From William Bradford's simple story of remembered experience (*Of Plymouth Plantation*, ed. Samuel Eliot Morison, 1952) to Cotton Mather's pompous scholarship (*Magnalia Christi Americana*, 2 vols., 1702), the Puritan histories interpreted the oddities of everyday life and the great events of the colony with a pervasive sense of God's sovereignty and man's responsibility.

Throughout the eighteenth and nineteenth centuries most of America's leading historians still bore the stamp of New England. Some were sons of clergymen (Francis *Parkman, George *Bancroft, Richard Hildreth). Others, in New England colleges, received an education steeped in the moral earnestness that survived a slow transition to a more secular culture. To upper-class New Englanders, the solid lessons of character and the down-to-earth verities that history imparted remained clearly preferable to the fabrications of fiction or the abstractions of political theory.

In the rationalistic atmosphere of the eighteenth century, however, historiography became relatively independent of religious sponsorship. A new basis appeared with the accumulation of wealth and leisure in the hands of cultivated individuals who could devote much of their time to historical research and writing. This was the era of patrician history, when scholars followed the great classical historians in holding up to posterity examples of errors, failings, and laudable deeds.

Nevertheless, patrician historians moved with the times. They responded on the one hand to modern styles of scholarship coming out of Europe and, on the other, to a changing political culture. The foremost of the eighteenth-century historians, Thomas Hutchinson, combined in his *History of the Colony and Province of Massachusetts-Bay* (3 vols., 1764–1828) a patrician respect for English political institutions with a judicious, critical management of documentary evidence. After the *Revolutionary War, although historians remained the custodians of an English heritage, their field of vision widened. In place of the earlier concentration on individual colonies, the best historians now encompassed an American nation, and their grand theme heralded the opening on the American continent of a new era in the progress of liberty. This was the burden of Parkman's gripping, seven-volume narrative, *France and England in North America* (1865–1892) and of Bancroft's *History of the United States of America from the Discovery of the Continent* (6 vols., 1834–1885). Although a shallower historian than Parkman, Bancroft struck a deeper chord in midcentury opinion by celebrating the American people as the standard-bearers of democracy.

Gilded Age and Early Twentieth Century. The romantic exuberance that suffused the pages of Parkman and Bancroft faded among a younger generation who came to the fore in the 1870s and after. For them history was not primarily a branch of literature; it was becoming a science. Historians could discover regularities in the past and, to some extent, project their consequences. But the desire for a richly evocative historical literature endured, and Henry *Adams's *History of the United States of America during the Administrations of Thomas Jefferson and James Madison* (9 vols., 1889–1891) provided an unforgettable example of art persisting within the forms of scientific inquiry. Nonetheless, practitioners of a science of history gained an unassailable preeminence in the new universities that were springing up on a German model. There, historians created academic departments that trained students to make a career of teaching other students while writing scientific monographs that would reflect credit on their respective universities and draw still more students. Gentlemen like Adams did not fit comfortably into this rule-bound world of specialization, division of labor, credentialing, and uniformity. The era of professional history, in which we still live, had begun.

Although the early professional historians adopted a more neutral tone, they worked within the national myth that the patricians had constructed: the myth of a new nation uniquely qualified to lead the world in the blessings of liberty and the fruits of progress. At first, scholars argued chiefly over the origins of this distinctive history. Some dwelled on an Anglo-Saxon heritage of law and institutions. Others, such as Frederick Jackson *Turner, turned westward to highlight the leveling influence of the American frontier. In the twentieth century, under the influence of the Progressive movement, an interest in the dynamics of change challenged the more conservative study of continuities. Following the lead of Charles A. *Beard, whose *Rise of American Civilization* (1927) was the most widely read synthesis since Bancroft's, many scholars interpreted American history as a recurring struggle between social-economic elites and a broad popular party that was widening the distribution of power and wealth. In this revision, the story of a rising nation endured, but the cast of characters expanded significantly.

Post–World War II Developments. After *World War II, the vigor of the American economy, together with a worldwide *Cold War conflict between totalitarian and democratic systems, stirred a new generation of historians to reassess the depth of class conflict within the United States. The internal divisions that progressive historians had emphasized now seemed less salient; instead, fresh questions about what has held together an apparently heterogeneous society came to the fore, especially in books by David Potter and Louis Hartz. The consensus historians, as they were first dubbed in 1959, stressed the uniqueness of the American experience. They took national myths seriously as a force in history, analyzed national character, and flocked to cultural history and the history of ideas.

The consensus paradigm crashed abruptly in the late 1960s with nearly all its associated projects. A few historians strove to preserve the breadth of the consensus approach while opening up its content to conflicts and contradictions, but most chose an intensified specialization, which flourished in the absence of any unifying paradigm. The consensus approach simply could not cope with the social discontent that burst forth in the sixties among academics, students, young women, and most especially racial and ethnic minorities. Instead of claiming a place in a larger national history that had never given them adequate recognition, most of the historians of these emergent groups preferred a history of their own tenacious resistance to the "mainstream." In one sense American history was finally democratized. In another sense, it fragmented into many separate histories of particular groups and small places. The reality of an overall American identity, either as an incentive to progress or as a reassurance of continuity, was less apparent than ever. Shrinking from the teaching of survey courses and facing a constriction of publishing outlets and academic jobs, professional historians by the 1990s had to wonder if a specifically American history was still viable.

[*See also* Cultural Pluralism; Education: The Rise of the University; Fifties, The; Mather, Increase and Cotton; Progressive Era; Puritanism; Sixties, The; Social Science.]

• George H. Callcott, *History in the United States, 1800–1860*, 1970. Alden T. Vaughan, "The Evolution of Virginia History: Early Historians of the First Colony," and Harry M. Ward, "The Search for American Identity: Early Historians of New England," in *Perspectives on Early American History*, eds. Alden T. Vaughan and George Athan Billias, 1973, pp. 9–62. Peter Novick, *That Noble Dream: The "Objectivity Question" and the American Historical Profession*, 1988. John Higham, *History: Professional Scholarship in America*, updated ed., 1989. Michael Kammen, *Mystic Chords of Memory: The Transformation of Tradition in American Culture*, 1991. John Higham, "The Future of American History," *Journal of American History* 80 (March 1994): 1289–1309.

—John Higham

HODGE, CHARLES (1797–1878), Protestant theologian. A graduate of the College of New Jersey (later Princeton University) and Princeton Seminary, Charles Hodge in 1821 was ordained by the Presbyterian Church. Apart from two years of travel and study in Europe, Hodge taught at Princeton Seminary throughout his career, first as professor of Oriental and biblical literature and, after 1840, as professor of theology.

During a career of over half a century, Hodge instructed several thousand students in theology and in biblical languages—more than any other seminary professor in the United States. Adding to his influence was his long editorship of the *Princeton Review*, a theological quarterly that he founded in 1825 as a forum for his theological views. Hodge's books included commentaries on the Pauline epistles; works on Presbyterian ecclesiastical issues; *The Way of Life* (1841), an introduction to Christianity for Sunday school use; a rigorous critique of Darwinism (*What Is Darwinism?*, 1874); and a three-volume *Systematic Theology* (1872–1873).

Hodge prided himself on the scriptural exposition of venerable doctrines rather than on original theological contributions. He was a preeminent apologist for "the Princeton Theology," a confessional Calvinist posture rooted in Scottish Common Sense philosophy that sought a balance between piety and learning and affirmed belief in the authority of the *Bible, the inseparability of faith and doctrine, and the value of personal religious experience ratified by scriptural testimony. From this position, Hodge criticized views espousing human autonomy, the priority of feeling over intellect, and the fallibility of biblical revelation. This brought him into conflict with more liberal nineteenth-century religious leaders such as Andrews Norton, Horace Bushnell, Edwards Amasa Park, and the German biblical critics, but in evangelical circles his work remains influential even today.

[*See also* Evolution, Theory of; Philosophy; Protestantism; Religion.]

• Archibald Alexander Hodge, *The Life of Charles Hodge*, 1880. Charles Hodge, *What Is Darwinism? And Other Writings on Science and Religion*, eds. Mark A. Noll and David N. Livingstone, 1994.

—Jon H. Roberts

HOLMES, OLIVER WENDELL, JR. (1841–1935), judge, legal scholar, and justice of the U.S. *Supreme Court, 1902–1932. Oliver Wendell Holmes consistently ranks as one of the "great" justices to sit on the Supreme Court. Born in *Boston, the son of the physician, poet, and man of letters Oliver Wendell Holmes Sr., Holmes graduated from Harvard College in 1861. He was wounded three times while serving in the Union Army during the *Civil War. Graduating from Harvard Law School in 1866, he practiced law in Boston, edited a legal journal, and wrote several scholarly essays in legal history and jurisprudence. His *The Common Law* (1881) ranks as one of the most important works of nineteenth-century legal scholarship. This work earned Holmes a professorship at Harvard Law School in 1882, but he left after six months to become an associate justice on the Supreme Judicial Court of Massachusetts; he became its chief justice in 1898. President Theodore *Roosevelt appointed him to the U.S. Supreme Court in 1901.

In 1905, Holmes wrote one of his best known opinions, his dissent in **Lochner* v. *New York*, which argued that judges should defer to the wishes of legislators in most cases involving regulations of the economy. By the time of *World War I, a group of "progressive" intellectuals had become attracted to the principle of judicial deference enunciated in Holmes's *Lochner* dissent, and to Holmes himself. By the 1930s, judicial deference to legislatures in the economic arena had become orthodoxy, with Holmes lionized as a "progressive" and "liberal" judge. At his ninetieth birthday in 1931, when he was still active on the Court, he was honored in a nationwide radio broadcast.

A second source of Holmes's attractiveness as a judge to early twentieth-century commentators was his increasingly protective attitude toward freedom of speech. In a series of decisions extending from the World War I era to his retirement in 1932, Holmes reversed his normal deferential stance toward regulatory legislation and insisted that even "freedom for the thought we hate" be given constitutional protection. Although his free-speech decisions resist being associated with any consistent doctrinal theory, in the main they affirmed the proposition that unfettered speech is indispensable to a democratic society.

Holmes's own views had little in common with the political radicals whose speech he protected or with the legislators who sought to alleviate market inequalities. He remained a nineteenth-century Brahmin, conservative in his social instincts and doubtful that economic tinkering did much good. But his eloquent pronouncements on behalf of free speech and judicial deference in the realm of political economy—propositions that remained jurisprudential orthodoxy from the 1930s through the 1970s—made him an attractive figure to commentators long after his death. So did his arresting prose style, his academic contributions, his philosophical insight, and the memorable length of his career.

[*See also* Bill of Rights; Civil Liberties; Conservatism; Economic Regulation; Jurisprudence; Liberalism.]

• G. Edward White, *Justice Oliver Wendell Holmes: Law and the Inner Self*, 1993.

—G. Edward White

HOME ECONOMICS MOVEMENT, a social movement, discipline, and profession, crystallized in the writings of Catharine *Beecher, a leading mid-nineteenth-century educator. Beecher stressed that women needed scientific knowledge to fulfill their socially sanctioned roles of wife, mother, and homemaker. In the late nineteenth and early twentieth centuries, universities and land-grant colleges, as well as elementary and secondary schools, institutionalized these principles as domestic science, domestic economy, or household science. The most significant force behind home economics in this period was Ellen Swallow Richards, a graduate of Vassar College and the Massachusetts Institute of Technology. At ten conferences Richards convened at Lake Placid, New York, between 1899 and 1908, educators and social reformers debated the role of the growing movement. The last conference established the movement's professional organization, the American Home Economics Association (later renamed the American Association of Family and Consumer Sciences).

Richards and her followers believed that the application of science to domestic problems could save society from the social disintegration they saw at the turn of the century. This program of science education for women had benefits and limitations. On the positive side, women could pursue science degrees in higher education. Moreover, the movement's social-reform impetus encouraged women to apply this knowledge in the wider arena of public life. For example, nutrition was not only the healthful feeding of one's family; it was also educating other women, constructing healthful dietaries for schools and institutions, generating the knowledge base underlying these efforts, and more. Thus, professional avenues such as dietician, nutritionist, and extension specialist opened for women. On the negative side, the existence of home economics departments enabled schools to direct women interested in *science into a sex-segregated educational track and sex-segregated occupations, with relatively low prestige and limited resources.

Through the twentieth century, home economics was closely associated with public school education and cooperative extension service. These affiliations and federal legislation, namely the Smith-Lever Act (1914), which created home economics extension, and the Smith-Hughes Act (1917), which funded home economics education in the elementary and secondary schools, had similarly contradictory effects on the path of home economics. While bringing in additional resources, they also deflected attention from scientific research, further separating home economics from more prestigious science departments.

Throughout the twentieth century, home economists were employed in academic, educational, governmental, and business settings. Greater occupational opportunities expanded the field, but also fragmented it. As the century ended, home economics, also labelled family and consumer sciences and human ecology, was struggling to construct a clear identity for itself.

[*See also* Domestic Labor; Education: The Public School Movement; Education: The Rise of the University; Feminism; Food and Diet; Women's Rights Movements.]

• Margaret Rossiter, *Women Scientists in America: Struggles and Strategies to 1940*, 1982. Sarah Stage and Virginia Vincenti, eds., *Rethinking Women and Home Economics in the 20th Century*, 1997.

—Rima D. Apple

HOMELESSNESS AND VAGRANCY. Homelessness first became a national issue in the latter half of the nineteenth century when western railroad construction, crop harvesting, and *mining and lumber camps created a huge market for casual, "moving" workers. Armies of transient laborers filled seasonal jobs throughout the country, creating the great era of tramps and hoboes, 1870 to 1920. The era faded as widespread mechanization radically changed the labor market. The Depression of the 1930s brought a brief resurgence of homelessness, which again increased in the early 1980s as high unemployment, deinstitutionalization of dysfunctional persons, and a decline in the dollar value of welfare programs all combined with the reduced number of single-room-occupancy (SRO) hotels to put more people on the street or in overnight shelters—perhaps 300,000 on a typical night in the mid-1980s, a quarter of them women.

In the *Colonial Era, the homeless were the "strolling poor," a mix of itinerant laborers, poor widows and their children, and the disabled. As transiency became tied more closely to the casual labor market in the nineteenth century, the homeless were typically unattached white males in their twenties and thirties, usually native-born or immigrants from the British Isles. The social world of tramping was a robust bachelor subculture anchored in urban areas of cheap lodging houses and saloons known in hobo argot as "main stems." The largest of these, in *New York City, *Chicago, and *San Francisco, might house forty thousand to fifty thousand transients on a given night. After 1920, homeless men were fewer, older, and less mobile. By the 1950s most Americans associated homelessness with the small groups of "derelicts" in squalid "skid row" districts of major cities.

Transients had simply been "warned out" of colonial era communities. By the mid-nineteenth century, concerns about the urban poor prompted a debate among charity groups and public officials about "worthy" and "unworthy" indigents, and this informed the largely antagonistic response of communities to the surge of transients after 1870. Homeless men were arrested as vagrants or simply chased out of town. After 1890 the growth of organized charity work, epitomized by the National Conference of Charities and Correction, fostered explanations of homelessness that incorporated both class-based prejudices and a recognition of the vicissitudes of economic development. Some charged that the free overnight lodgings offered in police stations or mission shelters—the latter an innovation of charitable and religious groups such as the Salvation Army—encouraged tramping. This led to a largely unsuccessful experiment with municipally run lodging houses until about 1930, mostly in the cities of the *Middle West and Northeast. As homelessness in the later twentieth century became, to a considerable extent, a by-product of extreme *poverty, disability, alcoholism and drug abuse, and the shrinking SRO housing market, efforts to address it focused on government social welfare programs and on providing permanent, affordable lodging through a combination of private enterprise, public funding, and nonprofit organizations.

[*See also* Charity Organization Movement; Immigrant Labor;

Labor Markets; Mental Illness; Migratory Agricultural Workers; Railroads; Welfare, Federal.]

• Eric H. Monkkonen, ed., *Walking to Work: Tramps in America, 1790–1935*, 1984. Jeffrey S. Adler, "A Historical Analysis of the Law of Vagrancy," *Criminology* 27 (1989): 209–29. Christopher Jencks, *The Homeless*, 1994.

—John C. Schneider

HOMER, WINSLOW (1836–1910), oil and watercolor painter and illustrator. Although Winslow Homer began his career by drawing scenes of rural *New England life for popular magazines, critics acclaimed his style for precisely its lack of sentimental, moralizing narrative. Born in *Boston, where he trained as a graphic artist, he moved to New York in 1859 and supported himself as a freelance illustrator. Hired by *Harper's Weekly* to cover the *Civil War, he avoided topicality or sentimentality. Instead, his illustrations humanized the war by depicting incidents of daily life at the front. His *Prisoners from the Front*, depicting the surrender of a range of southern character "types" to an honorable Union officer, exhibited in New York in 1866, secured his reputation as a serious painter whose understated realism connoted honesty. Both during and after the war, Homer painted *African Americans as central subjects, though his representation shifted from the self-reliant independence of *Weaning the Calf* (1875) to the unrelieved grimness of *The Gulf Stream* (1899). Two visits to Europe influenced his style and themes: an 1866 trip to the Universal Exposition in France, where he encountered Japanese woodblock prints and Barbizon-school landscapes, and an 1881 stay at an English fishing village near Tynemouth. Between these trips Homer worked in New York, painting sun-lit images of women at fashionable resorts such as the beach at *Long Branch, New Jersey* (1869), or, in the 1870s, rural boys at play, as in *Snap the Whip* (1872). After 1883, when Homer settled in Prout's Neck, Maine, his subjects changed to muscular, monumental fishermen and -women struggling with the sea for survival, as in *The Life Line* (1884). These paintings, like his less dramatic Adirondack hunting scenes, presented a masculine, vigorous outdoor world. Vacations in Quebec, Florida, Bermuda, and the Bahamas resulted in watercolors of men and the sea, influential for their fluid brushwork and saturated color. His final paintings depict the confrontation between elemental forces of nature, largely without human involvement, as in *Fox Hunt* (1893).

[*See also* Gilded Age; Magazines; Painting: To 1945.]

• Center for Advanced Study in the Visual Arts at the National Gallery of Art, *Winslow Homer: A Symposium*, Studies in the History of Art, vol. 26, 1990. Nicolai Cikovsky Jr., Franklin Kelly, et al., *Winslow Homer*, 1995.

—Wendy J. Katz

HOMESTEAD ACT (1862). The Homestead Act was an attempt to transform the settlement of the public domain in the *West. Passed by Congress in 1862 and put into operation on 1 January 1863, it offered actual settlers free title to 160 acres (a quarter section) after they had established residence and improved the land for five years. The act also sought to bind the West to the North during the *Civil War. It altered the historic policy of cash sale of the public domain since the first Land Survey Act of 1785. Potential settlers saw the Homestead Act as a great boon, but much of the available land was in regions of insufficient rainfall such as the midcontinent High Plains. In fact, farmers west of the ninety-eighth meridian (which passes through central Kansas, Nebraska, and the Dakotas) needed four to eight times the allotted acres for successful settlement. In the 1870s, of some 1.3 million new farms carved out of the public domain, only around 320,000 were actual homestead entries. In some areas, fewer than a quarter of the original entries actually completed the process and established homesteads. Farm families that did persevere described the initial five years as their "period of starvation." Homesteading was abused by fraudulent surveys and deceptive multiple claims by ranchers, *lumbering interests, and other speculators. A series of legislative efforts between 1873 and 1916 to correct some of the problems resolved neither the climate realities nor the fraud. Dryland farming techniques, however, stabilized some High Plains settlement. Between 1863 and 1904, some 720,000 farms, totaling nearly 100 million acres, had been established under the Homestead Act. Homesteading of at least three million acres a year continued until the 1930s Depression.

[*See also* Agriculture: 1770s to 1890; Agriculture: The "Golden Age" (1890s–1920); Land Policy, Federal; Livestock Industry; Northwest Ordinance; Republican Party.]

• Paul W. Gates, *History of Public Land Law Development*, 1968. John Opie, *The Law of the Land: 200 Years of American Farmland Policy*, 1994.

—John Opie

HOMESTEAD LOCKOUT (1892). Arguably the most infamous confrontation between workers and employers in the nineteenth century, this dispute began on 1 July 1892 when Henry Clay Frick, the coal magnate who managed Andrew *Carnegie's steelmaking company, closed down the immense Homestead Steel Works near Pittsburgh rather than bargain with the Amalgamated Association of Iron and Steel Workers. Frick announced that the Carnegie company would no longer recognize any union and that all 3,800 employees would have to sign individual contracts. Homestead's workers knew that Frick had constructed fortified barriers around the mill as a defense for strikebreakers who would also be protected by the Pinkerton Detective Agency, a private police force the company had used earlier to suppress trade unionism.

The workers responded by mobilizing virtually all twelve thousand residents of the town of Homestead, whose government was dominated by committed trade unionists. The workers also blocked all access to the mill. An uneasy calm prevailed until 6 July, when three hundred Pinkertons arrived by riverbarge at the mill and engaged the workers in a pitched battle. Three Pinkerton agents and seven workers were killed; after surrendering, the Pinkertons were forced to run a gauntlet of thousands of enraged men, women, and children.

The workers' victory proved short-lived. At Frick's request, Pennsylvania Governor Robert E. Pattison sent in eight thousand state militiamen. Homestead was placed under martial law, and the company reclaimed the mill. Soon strikebreakers were at work, union leaders had been arrested on charges ranging from murder to treason, and the workers defeated. The strikers were convinced that labor had a fundamental right to employment and that Frick and Carnegie, by abrogating this right, had violated the most basic tenets of justice. Frick and Carnegie, however, believed that they enjoyed the right to dispose of their property as they saw fit and therefore to hire whomever they chose. Thus, in fundamental ways, the dispute at Homestead arose from conflicting concepts of right and property.

The victory of Frick and Carnegie decimated the Amalgamated Association and signaled an industrywide collapse of unionism that would not be reversed until the 1930s. The lockout also proved to many Americans that in a showdown, private industry could summon the power of the state to defeat unions.

[*See also* Gilded Age; Immigrant Labor; Iron and Steel Industry; Labor Movements; Strikes and Industrial Conflict.]

• Arthur G. Burgoyne, *The Homestead Strike of 1892*, 1893, reprint 1979. Paul Krause, *The Battle for Homestead, 1880–1892: Politics, Culture, and Steel*, 1992.

—Paul Krause

HOMEWORK. Homework, or manufacturing in family residences, first became common in the shoe and *textile industries. It characterized garment production in the nineteenth and early twentieth centuries, and reemerged in the late twentieth to include telecommuting and business services as well as high-fashion and cheap-apparel production. Concentrated in urban tenements and immigrant neighborhoods, from *New York City's Lower East Side to *San Francisco's Chinatown, it reached into southern mill towns, Appalachian farms, Pennsylvania villages, and East Coast suburbs. Relying on a chain of contractors, manufacturers lessened expenses by paying a temporary workforce by the piece and requiring the worker to use his or her own tools and workplace. Employers took advantage of the gender division of labor within the household and between the household and the larger society to hire married women with small children whose husbands earned inadequate wages and whose cultural traditions or family responsibilities kept them homebound. The homework labor force also included the elderly, disabled, children, and older daughters in rural regions—those who lacked other employment options.

Homework undercut the labor standards of factory workers, weakening unionization and threatening higher wages. Reformers condemned it for spreading *disease and disorder, turning homes into factories, and perverting motherhood and childlife. Beginning in the 1890s, states regulated health and sanitary conditions for homeworkers because courts blocked outright bans as violations of the rights of privacy and contract. The federal government prohibited homework on army uniforms during *World War I, but only in the *New Deal Era, initially through *National Recovery Administration codes, did the government impose more general restrictions on homework. In the early 1940s, the administrator of the Fair Labor Standards Act (1938) banned homework in seven garment industries to protect the standards won by factory workers. The Ronald *Reagan administration removed all bans except ladies' garments in the 1980s, however. As the twentieth century ended, the notion that home-workers might combine earnings with family care threatened a return to sweatshop conditions.

[*See also* Domestic Labor; Immigrant Labor; Immigration; Labor Movements; Work.]

• Eileen Boris and Cynthia Rae Daniels, eds., *Homework: Historical and Contemporary Perspectives on Paid Labor at Home*, 1989. Eileen Boris, *Home to Work: Motherhood and the Politics of Industrial Homework in the United States*, 1994.

—Eileen Boris

HOMOSEXUALITY. *See* Gay and Lesbian Rights Movement; Sex and Sexuality.

HOMOSEXUAL RIGHTS MOVEMENT. *See* Gay and Lesbian Rights Movement.

HOOVER, HERBERT (1874–1964), thirty-first president of the United States. Born in West Branch, Iowa, of Quaker parents, Herbert Clark Hoover was orphaned at the age of nine and subsequently reared by relatives in Oregon, where he attended Friends Pacific Academy. After graduating from the newly founded Stanford University in 1895, he entered the employ of *mining engineer Louis Janin. Hoover next joined the British firm of Bewick, Moering, initially as a manager in Australia, later as a company representative in China, and after 1901 as a partner. In business for himself after 1908, he specialized in reorganizing and refinancing "sick" mining enterprises. He married Lou Henry, a fellow Stanford graduate in 1899; they had two sons.

During *World War I, Hoover achieved world stature as both an engineer and a humanitarian. His role in rescuing stranded Americans and feeding starving Belgians made him the "master of relief." As food administrator in the Woodrow *Wilson administration he engaged in "Hooverizing" U.S. consumption habits to conserve scarce commodities and became the best known of America's wartime domestic managers. He remained in the limelight after the war, first as director of American relief abroad, then as a progressive leader of the *engineering profession, and, after 1921, as an active and highly visible secretary of commerce in the Republican presidential administrations of Warren *Harding and Calvin *Coolidge. In 1928 a legion of admirers helped him secure the Republican presidential nomination, and in November he easily defeated Democratic opponent Alfred E. *Smith.

During his pre-presidential government career, Hoover had launched regulatory and welfare agencies heavily reliant on private-sector resources, and in the process had worked out a progressive social agenda to be realized through government-encouraged "associational action" rather than through public administration. In 1928 he spoke of a "New Day" to be ushered in by this "cooperative system." As president, Hoover made extensions of this ideology the basis of his reform agenda and his battle against the Great Depression, which set in after the *stock market crash of October 1929. Rejecting *laissez-faire prescriptions, including those of Treasury Secretary Andrew Mellon, he tried to raise spending levels through government-sponsored cooperative action by business leaders and through federalization of parts of the credit system, creating in 1932 the Reconstruction Finance Corporation, modeled on the federal lending agency of World War I, to extend credit to major economic institutions such as banks and insurance companies. But he rejected allegedly "dangerous" forms of federal investment, financing, relief, and market control. Perversely, his success in raising *tariffs in 1930 and other taxes in 1932 worked at cross purposes with his economic recovery aims. Moreover, the Depression's persistence undercut most of the reform agenda he kept trying to implement. The construction of Hoover Dam on the Colorado River, begun in 1931, and passage of the Federal Home Loan Bank System Act in 1932, designed to help hard-pressed homeowners avoid foreclosure, were lasting achievements. But most of Hoover's attempts to promote cooperative, private-sector recovery and relief efforts, including those involving agricultural marketing associations, oil and timber conservation, and social-welfare organizations, eventually failed.

Abroad, Hoover's administration made only limited responses to the Depression's corrosive effects on international order. Disarmament initiatives produced only the ineffectual London Naval Treaty of 1930. Concerns about international debts brought only the one-year Hoover Debt Moratorium of 1931 and a renunciation of forced debt collection in Latin America. Japan's aggression in China produced only a policy of not recognizing Japan's puppet state in Manchuria. Proposals for war-debt cancellation, economic sanctions against aggressors, and the United States's becoming the international lender of last resort were all ruled out. These options were not only politically difficult but beyond the limits of Hoover's *internationalism.

Meanwhile, the deepening Depression was also sparking political realignment and a growing anti-Hoover national mood. The one-time "great engineer" and "great humanitarian" now became a national scapegoat. The floating communities of jobless men in the nation's cities were dubbed "Hoovervilles." Making matters worse were such public relations fiascoes as Hoover's opposition to more generous drought relief, his continued support for prohibition, and his administration's 1932 military action against a "*bonus army" of veterans in the nation's capital. Hoover won renomination in 1932, but in the November election he carried only six states. In March 1933, after a four-month interregnum marked by governmental stalemate and collapse of the banking system, his presidency gave way to Franklin Delano *Roosevelt's New Deal.

After leaving the White House, Hoover remained active in *Republican party politics and in debates concerning the New Deal. As *World War II approached, he backed the noninterventionist cause and tried unsuccessfully to establish food relief programs in German-occupied countries. After the war, he gradually attained elder-statesman status, advising on postwar relief problems, heading commissions on governmental reorganization, and publishing his memoirs and other works. He is buried in West Branch, Iowa, near the Hoover presidential library.

A man of immense energy, a sincere commitment to public service, legendary organizational and administrative skills, and enduring Quaker sensibilities, Hoover served his nation well as a relief director, wartime food czar, commerce department secretary, and promoter of executive reorganization. But he lacked the political skills, charisma, and capacity for economic learning needed to lead a nation caught in the throes of the Great Depression. And while scholars now reject the older label of "do-nothingism" and see his presidency as activist, reformist, intellectually sophisticated, and in some ways anticipatory of the New Deal, most still judge it a failure overall.

[*See also* Corporatism; Depressions, Economic; Federal Government, Executive Branch: Other Departments (Department of Commerce); Federal Government, Executive Branch: The Presidency; Foreign Relations; New Deal Era, The; Society of Friends; Taxation; Temperance and Prohibition; Twenties, The.]

• Craig Lloyd, *Aggressive Introvert: A Study of Herbert Hoover and Public Relations Management, 1912–1932*, 1972. Joan Hoff Wilson, *Herbert Hoover: Forgotten Progressive*, 1975. David Burner, *Herbert Hoover: A Public Life*, 1979. George H. Nash, *The Life of Herbert Hoover*, 3 vols., 1983, 1988, 1996. William J. Barber, *From New Era to New Deal: Herbert Hoover, the Economists, and American Economic Policy, 1921–1933*, 1985. Martin L. Fausold, *The Presidency of Herbert C. Hoover*, 1985.

—Ellis W. Hawley

HOOVER, J. EDGAR (1895–1972), director, *Federal Bureau of Investigation (FBI). Born in *Washington, D.C., Hoover earned a law degree from George Washington University night school in 1917 and obtained employment in the Justice Department's alien enemy registration section. His administrative abilities, strategic mind, and diligence quickly won him promotion in 1918 to head the General Intelligence Division, in 1921 to assistant director of the Bureau of Investigation (formally renamed the FBI in 1935), and in 1924 to bureau director, a post he held until his death. A lifelong bachelor, he devoted himself to the FBI.

Inheriting a scandal-ridden operation, Hoover refurbished the bureau's image and turned it into a powerful and respected agency by instituting a series of administrative reforms and then by capitalizing on public concerns, first about *organized crime during the 1930s and then about spies during *World War II and the *Cold War. Indeed, Cold War *anticommunism became the catalyst of Hoover's unquestioned power and influence on national politics. Hoover also astutely cultivated presidents, members of Congress, and the media, and promoted a public-relations campaign that successfully identified criticism of himself or the FBI with disloyalty. With Hoover's collaboration, the entertainment industry burnished the FBI's image, as in the radio program "The FBI in Peace and War." The story of Herbert Philbrick, who infiltrated the *Communist party for the FBI, was recounted in a movie, *I Was a Communist for the FBI* (1951); Philbrick's own *I Led Three Lives* (1952); and a 1950s television series. The FBI's "Ten Most Wanted" lists, posted in post offices across the nation, further enhanced Hoover's reputation as a crime fighter.

After the 1930s, FBI investigations were not confined to law enforcement. FBI agents also collected (in some cases, as FBI officials themselves conceded, through "clearly illegal" means such as break-ins, mail opening, telephone wiretaps, and electronic bugs), and Hoover and senior FBI officials covertly disseminated derogatory personal and political information. Such material went to Senator Joseph *McCarthy and the *House Committee on Un-American Activities, for example, either to influence public opinion or to "harass, disrupt, and discredit" targeted individuals and organizations. The subjects of FBI investigations ranged from Communist party activists to Eleanor *Roosevelt, the actor Rock Hudson, the author Ernest *Hemingway, the baseball star Mickey Mantle, the poet Allen Ginsberg, and the rock star John Lennon. Furthermore, Hoover authorized a series of programs that targeted *civil rights and radical organizations for the explicit purpose of discrediting and neutralizing them. Hoover particularly sought to discredit Martin Luther *King Jr., by circulating information about King's private life obtained through clandestine surveillance devices.

The scope and nature of these abuses first became known in the mid-1970s when Hoover's wall of secrecy immunizing FBI activities was first breached. The resultant disclosures tarnished Hoover's posthumous reputation and led to tighter administrative rules governing FBI operations.

• Athan Theoharis and John Stuart Cox, *The Boss: J. Edgar Hoover and the Great American Inquisition*, 1988. Curt Gentry, *J. Edgar Hoover: The Man and the Secrets*, 1991.

—Athan G. Theoharis

HOPKINS, HARRY (1890–1946), social worker, New Deal relief administrator, and key advisor to President Franklin Delano *Roosevelt. Born in Sioux City, Iowa, Harry Hopkins had a distinguished early career with various *New York City *social-work agencies. In the Depression year 1931, Roosevelt, then governor of New York, named him deputy director of the state's Temporary Emergency Relief Administration. With Roosevelt's election as president, he brought Hopkins to *Washington, D.C., in 1933 to head the Federal Emergency Relief Administration, charged with providing assistance to the unemployed. Believing that most of the needy were not at fault, Hopkins pushed for government-created jobs rather than handouts. A dole keeps a person physically alive, but often destroys self-respect and undermines job skills, Hopkins argued, while work sustains spirit and mind, as well as body. This argument produced the short-lived Civil Works Administration (1933–1934) and the *Works Progress Administration, which Hopkins supervised from its start in 1935.

From 1936 until Roosevelt's death in 1945, Hopkins was the president's closest confidant. He hoped to succeed Roosevelt as president in 1940, but his poor health and opposition from key Democrats blocked this ambition. Roosevelt sent Hopkins on critical missions to British Prime Minister Winston Churchill and Soviet dictator Josef Stalin in 1941. During *World War II, Hopkins served as assistant to the president and became his alter ego.

A central figure during the nation's two largest twentieth-century crises, Hopkins brought to his varied assignments a combination of idealism and practicality summarized by his retort to the claim that a plan would work in the long run: "People don't eat in the long run—they eat every day."

[*See also* Depressions, Economic; New Deal Era, The; Welfare, Federal.]

• Robert E. Sherwood, *Roosevelt and Hopkins*, 1948. George McJimsey, *Harry Hopkins*, 1987.

—Robert S. McElvaine

HORSE RACING. With a history extending from ancient Egypt, the Grecian Olympic Games, and Roman chariot races through medieval and early-modern Europe, horse racing emerged in late seventeenth century America in the *South, the Middle Atlantic colonies, and New York. As the sport developed in the eighteenth century, certain features stood out. In the absence of a hereditary aristocracy to support it, horse racing was intertwined with commerce. Proximity to cities was essential; city dwellers paid admissions and their betting fuelled the sport.

Horse racing flourished in the *Antebellum Era. Rampant dishonesty provoked efforts to suppress or restrict it, followed by further expansion. Races were two or three miles long, with several heats. The pace was slow since horses ran on dirt tracks, not turf. Sectional tensions were mirrored in "North versus South" match races. One such event in 1823 at the Union Course on Long Island—New York had by now established its predominance—drew an estimated sixty thousand spectators.

When the *Civil War devastated racing in the South, the North and *West established preeminence. Kentucky, as a breeding center, was the major exception. U.S. horse racing's premier event, the Kentucky Derby, was first run in 1875 at the newly opened Churchill Downs in Louisville. By the 1890s, three hundred racetracks were operating. Wealthy plutocrats like Leonard Jerome, August Belmont, William Whitney, and others built larger racetracks and established stables. Stakes increased and attendance swelled. Jockeys such as "Snapper" Garrison, Isaac Murphy, and Tod Sloan became celebrities, as did the horses they rode, including Hanover, Salvador, and Sysonby. Led by Sloan, U.S. jockeys revolutionized the style of riding by adopting the forward seat, America's most important contribution to the sport. While bookmakers' fees provided a major source of revenue for racetracks, their presence added to the pervasive sense of underhanded dealing.

*Progressive Era reformers almost ended professional horse racing, but by reforming itself the sport survived and entered a golden age from 1920 to around 1970. Parimutuel machines replaced bookmakers, automatic starting gates and photo-finish cameras removed sources of contention, and stricter supervision reduced the doping of horses and illegal gambling. Women were more often present at the track, behavior became more orderly, and handsome new racetracks offered larger purses. Brilliant jockeys such as Earl Sande, Eddie Arcaro, and Willie Shoemaker and horses like Man o' War, Whirlaway, Citation, and Secretariat captured the nation's attention. Fans avidly followed horse racing's "Triple Crown" events: the Kentucky Derby, the Preakness at Baltimore's Pimlico track, and the Belmont Stakes in New York. Harness racing, with the rider in a sulky (a low, two-wheeled vehicle harnessed to the horse), dating to the 1830s in America, enjoyed a considerable vogue after *World War II.

Horse racing fell on hard times as a spectator event in the later twentieth century as lotteries, casinos, off-track betting, and other professional sports usurped the track's appeal. Nevertheless, the riders' skill, the appeal of the horses, and the beauty of the running continued to captivate.

[*See also* Gambling and Lotteries; Sports.]

• William H. P. Robertson, *The History of Thoroughbred Racing in America*, 2 vols., 1964. David Alexander, *A Sound of Horses: The World of Racing, from Eclipse to Kelso*, 1966.

—John Dizikes

HOSPITALS. The first hospitals in America were makeshift: military hospitals during the *Colonial Era, and the *Revolutionary War, and quarantine and inoculation hospitals during epidemics. By the early nineteenth century, the sick poor were often relegated to *alms houses, many of which ultimately became tax-supported municipal hospitals run by local governments. The first permanent institutions for the general care of the sick were organized in northeastern cities in the eighteenth and early nineteenth centuries and included Pennsylvania Hospital in 1751, New York Hospital in 1771, and Massachusetts General Hospital in 1821. These were not intended for the general public; popular opinion regarded medical treatment in an institution by strangers as a last resort, appropriate only for those who had no other choice.

The Nineteenth Century. The number of hospitals increased during the *Antebellum Era, partly in response to growing optimism about the recuperative powers of a regulated moral and physical environment. The new institutions included general-care hospitals as well as a host of specialty hospitals or asylums: mental hospitals, lying-in hospitals usually associated with foundling homes, and hospitals for the care and treatment of the blind. The link between *poverty and hospitalization remained strong; whether municipally or privately owned, hospitals were primarily charity institutions.

After the *Civil War, the number of hospitals increased dramatically, reaching approximately fourteen hundred by 1900. This rapid growth resulted as much from social upheaval as from medical advances. Amid surging *immigration and rapid *urbanization, local governments, benevolent groups, and churches organized hospitals for the growing ranks of the needy sick. Religious and ethnic groups founded hospitals for religious and cultural reasons. Mullanphy Hospital in St. Louis, the first Roman Catholic hospital in the United States, was founded by the Sisters of Charity in 1828; German Jews in *New York City organized Mount Sinai Hospital in 1852. Hospitals mainly cared for the chronically ill, for whom the cultural aspects of daily hospital life were central. Religious hospitals rarely administrated distinctive therapeutics, but they did provide a comfortable and familiar environment—and gave visible proof that a denomination was caring for its own. Hospitals were also organized to provide treatment and clinical training for groups excluded or discriminated against elsewhere. Female physicians founded the New York Infirmary for Women and Children (1860) and the New England Hospital for Women and Children (1862). *African Americans organized Provident Hospital in *Chicago (189) and Douglass Hospital in *Philadelphia (1895). In addition to bed care, many hospitals maintained outpatient facilities, or dispensaries. For the poor, these often represented the only professional medical care available.

By the late nineteenth century, three types of hospitals had evolved: municipal, proprietary, and voluntary. Municipal hospitals, typically larger than the others, were supported by public funds and managed by public authorities; many developed reputations for grim conditions and poor care. For-profit proprietary hospitals, often owned by physicians, relied on patient payments. Voluntary hospitals derived most of their financial support from private philanthropy, supplemented in some cases by public funding. As expanding hospital populations outpaced traditional sources of funding, patients increasingly paid for their hospital stays. Ultimately this helped remove the stigma of hospitalization as a last resort for paupers.

Early Twentieth Century. Hospital growth continued unabated in the early twentieth century with the number soaring to more than six thousand by the mid-1920s. As the hospitals' image as a charity institution faded, they advertised comfortable private rooms to attract patients. Unlike nineteenth-century institutions, which mostly provided chronic care and treatment, these new hospitals typically welcomed the acutely ill as well as surgical and obstetrical cases. The number of women delivering their babies in hospitals increased, especially after 1914, when the introduction of the sedative scopolamine to induce "twilight sleep" offered the promise of painless childbirth. The *professionalization of *nursing proved crucial to the emergence of the modern hospital. Hospital nursing schools, which provided a supply of unpaid student nurses to staff wards, became essential components of the hospital economy. Hospital training for medical students also became the rule in this period. Efficiency, professionalization, and standardization came to dominate hospital development. Institutional and professional groups such as the American Hospital Association and the American College of Surgeons worked to modernize all aspects of hospital life, from record-keeping to laundry practices. During *World War I, the military relied on hospitals to provide medical services in Europe, with American hospitals and medical schools sending teams of physicians and nurses to replicate facilities at home.

By the end of the 1920s, deliveries and *abortions, adenoidectomies, appendectomies, tonsillectomies, and the treatment of accident victims accounted for 60 percent of hospital admissions. By 1935, a third of Americans were born in and died in a hospital, but regional and class differences persisted. Rural areas and the *South had relatively few hospitals. In an ironic twist, high fees now increasingly excluded the hospitals' traditional patients, the poor. Proposals for compulsory national *health insurance stirred powerful opposition, but voluntary hospital-insurance plans, such as Blue Cross, flourished. Although hospital lobbyists were unsuccessful in efforts to include federal funding for privately managed hospitals among the New Deal's programs, the 1946 Hill-Burton Act sought to improve hospital care and availability through federal grants to states for hospital construction. The federal government had provided health care for veterans since shortly after the Civil War, when the first soldiers' homes were established for disabled veterans, but *World War II spawned a vast new system of veterans' hospitals.

Post–World War II Developments. In the postwar era, hospitals assumed an ever-greater medical and cultural role. The availability of antibiotics improved the safety and sophistication of hospital treatment and stirred optimism about the future promise of medical research. Technological developments expanded hospital services and altered hospitals' physical organization, creating, for example, intensive-care, coronary, and neurosurgery units. Hospital admissions in 1960 were double those of 1930. Hospitals even played a prominent role in twentieth-century *popular culture, as evidenced by a series of television programs extending over several decades, from *Dr. Kildare, Marcus Welby, M.D.,* and the long-running soap opera *General Hospital* to *St. Elsewhere* and the enormously popular *E.R.*

Hospitals employed huge numbers of workers, skilled and unskilled. Excluded from the gains made by other workers under New Deal labor laws, hospital workers, despite opposition from hospital administrations, began to organize in the 1950s. In 1974, federal prohibitions on striking by hospital workers were lifted.

Financial issues were central to further hospital development. Greater federal involvement in hospital finances resulted from the *Medicare and Medicaid programs established in 1965, which reimbursed hospitals for the care of the elderly and the poor. In the 1970s and 1980s, as hospital costs climbed, many voluntary hospitals merged in efforts to cut costs, creating regional and national chains. The number of for-profit hospitals rose from 414 in 1977 to 797 in 1997. The 1990s found America's hospitals in a state of flux and financial crisis. As they tried to economize, patient stays were shortened, *surgery was more frequently performed on an ambulatory basis, medical testing was contracted out, and recuperating patients shifted to less-expensive venues. Further, more medical care was delivered outside the hospital: in physicians' offices, patients' residences, nursing homes, and long-term care facilities. Increasingly, the institution that had developed in the late nineteenth and early twentieth centuries known as the modern hospital seemed the product of specific historical circumstances, and one that might well evolve in radically different ways. For all their problems, however, America's more than six thousand hospitals (as of 1998), with over a million beds and 4.4 million staff and employees, remained fundamental to the nation's health-care system and an integral feature of U.S. life.

[*See also* Cancer; Childbirth; Death and Dying; Disease; Heart Disease; Medical Education; Medicine; Mental Health Institutions; New Deal Era, The; Philanthropy and Philanthropic Foundations; Roman Catholicism; Strikes and Industrial Conflict; Veterans Administration.]

• Gerald N. Grob, *Mental Institutions in America: Social Policy to 1875,* 1973. Morris J. Vogel, *The Invention of the Modern Hospital: Boston, 1870–1930,* 1980. Harry F. Dowling, *City Hospitals: The Undercare of the Underprivileged,* 1982. David Rosner, *A Once Charitable Enterprise: Hospitals and Health Care in Brooklyn and New York, 1888–1915,* 1982. Charles E. Rosenberg, *The Care of Strangers: The Rise of America's Hospital System,* 1987. Diana Elizabeth Long and Janet Golden, eds., *The American General Hospital: Communities and Social Contexts,* 1989. Rosemary Stevens, *In Sickness and in Wealth: American Hospitals in the Twentieth Century,* 1989. Vanessa Northington Gamble, *Making a Place for Ourselves: The Black Hospital Movement, 1920–1945,* 1995. Joel D. Howell, *Technology in the Hospital: Transforming Patient Care in the Early Twentieth Century,* 1995. Christopher J. Kauffman, *Ministry and Meaning: A Religious History of Catholic Health Care in the United States,* 1995. Guenter B. Risse, *Mending Bodies, Saving Souls: A History of Hospitals,* 1999.

—Bernadette McCauley

HOUSE COMMITTEE ON UN-AMERICAN ACTIVITIES. The House Committee on Un-American Activities (HUAC) was created in 1938 by legislators concerned about fascist groups in America and by conservative opponents of President Franklin Delano *Roosevelt's New Deal. First chaired by Congressman Martin Dies of Texas, the committee created a sensation by charging that communists dominated numerous federal agencies, including the *Works Progress Administration. The raucous committee hearings drew attention to the prominent role of left-wing radicals in the political life of the 1930s and abetted the *Republican party's resurgence in the 1938 midterm elections.

HUAC enjoyed its most dramatic hours in 1947 and 1948: the Hollywood hearings that resulted in the jailing of ten screenwriters and directors for contempt and led to a show-business blacklist that would linger for years; and the confrontation between the excommunist Whittaker Chambers and the former State Department official Alger *Hiss that would send Hiss to jail for perjury and propel Representative Richard M. *Nixon, a committee member, to national attention.

Much criticized for its bruising treatment of witnesses, its use of hearings as a weapon of repression, and its lack of legislative accomplishments, the committee did contribute to the 1950 *Internal Security Act that called for the registration of Communist party members. Subsequent investigations—into atomic scientists, colleges, churches, and labor unions—did not stir much excitement as the loyalty-security issue began to ebb in the 1950s. Despite a foray against anti-*Vietnam War protestors in the 1960s and the enduring support of *Federal Bureau of Investigation director J. Edgar *Hoover, HUAC was abolished in 1975.

[*See also* Anticommunism; Communism; Communist Party—USA; Fifties, The; New Deal Era, The.]

• Walter Goodman, *The Committee,* 1968.

—Walter Goodman

HOUSEHOLD TECHNOLOGY. *Industrialization transformed American society, permanently altering the tools and work processes of preindustrial America. New technologies helped change how households fed, clothed, cleaned, and cared for their members, though these technologies affected men, women, and children differently. In addition, the rich and the urban tended to gain access to new technologies before the poor and the rural. Despite the unevenness and inequities of these changes, developments in household technology played an important role in elevating the American standard of living through the nineteenth and twentieth centuries.

In the *Colonial Era, most households used simple tools to maintain their living standards, which for all but the very rich consisted of simple diets, limited wardrobes, and low standards of cleanliness. Open, wood-burning hearths provided heat and a place to cook, while candles gave light. Women prepared and preserved food, made medicines, and used spinning wheels, looms, and needles to turn wool and flax into clothing. Men farmed, cut and hauled wood, whittled, and sewed leather items. Metalware such as kettles, pots, axes, and knives eased food preparation, wood gathering, and agricultural labor. Servants, slaves, and children, as well as male and female heads of house, provided household labor. Occasional reliance on people outside the household who produced and repaired metalware and sold staples such as salt and lime linked relatively self-sufficient households to the developing market economy.

Through the nineteenth century, the *mass production of goods by new industries removed many traditionally male tasks from homes and placed most household technology in the hands of women and servants. Beginning in the 1830s, versions of Benjamin *Franklin's 1740s cast-iron stove, modified to include ovens and stove-top hot plates, began replacing open hearths and altering cooking practices. By 1850, many households were purchasing coal and commercially ground flour, eliminating traditional male tasks like gathering wood, shelling corn, pounding grain, and, increasingly, farming itself. New technology diversified women's housework as well, removing some jobs and adding others. Kerosene eliminated the job of making candles. Purchasing textiles reduced long hours spent spinning and weaving, and after the *Civil War Isaac Singer's manufacture of a practical, treadle-operated sewing machine allowed women to sew family clothes without hiring seamstresses. The shift from leather and woolen clothing to cotton garments boosted standards of cleanliness, but added the arduous weekly task of hand-cleaning laundry. As culinary standards advanced, women invested more time preparing more varied meals.

Between 1880 and 1920, private industries began providing even more of the goods and services that households had traditionally produced. As increasing numbers of Americans moved from rural to urban areas, for example, many families began purchasing goods and services they had previously provided themselves: foodstuffs from grocery stores, health care from physicians and *hospitals, and ready-made clothing from *department stores. As municipalities developed water systems, many homes acquired running water, water heaters, sanitary fixtures, and indoor bathrooms. Following Thomas *Edison's invention of electric lights in 1879 and the first electric power station in 1882, many urban families gradually switched from kerosene lamps to electric light bulbs. By 1910, after the Westinghouse Corporation introduced alternating-current motors, industries mass-produced electric fans, sewing machines, washing machines, and vacuum cleaners for a national market. By 1920, when 35 percent of American homes had *electricity, devices using resistance-coil heaters like irons and toasters were widely available. A small but growing number of families also owned *telephones and automobiles.

The national standard of living rose through the 1920s, fell in the 1930s, and rose steadily again after *World War II as household technologies spread. General Electric began the assembly-line production of home refrigerators in 1926, enhancing the ability to preserve food and enabling the Birdseye Corporation to make frozen food widely available by the 1930s. Owners of electric dishwashers and other new kitchen appliances found cooking and cleaning easier, if still time-consuming. *Radio, the phonograph, and then *television brought free entertainment into homes around the nation. Businesses cut back on home delivery services in response to the spread of automobiles. The Great Depression of the 1930s reduced the number of households that could afford servants, but labor-saving technologies such as automatic washing machines made it easier and more acceptable for housewives—still the primary operators of household technologies—to perform domestic work without hired help. New products, such as microwave ovens, compact-disk (CD) players, and personal *computers, continued to appear at the end of the twentieth century, but even more remarkable than the range of new technologies was the speed and extent to which citizens of all regions and social levels gained access to them.

[*See also* Agriculture; Automotive Industry; Clothing and Fashion; Electrical Industry; Family; Food and Diet; Gender; Health and Fitness; Mass Marketing; Motor Vehicles; Technology; Textile Industry; Urbanization.]

• Susan Strasser, *Never Done: A History of American Housework*, 1982. Ruth Schwartz Cowan, *More Work for Mother: The Ironies of Household Technology from the Open Hearth to the Microwave*, 1983. Jack Larkin, *The Reshaping of Everyday Life, 1790–1840*, 1988. Richard L. Bushman, *The Refinement of America: Persons, Houses, Cities*, 1992. Judith McGaw, ed., *Early American Technology: Making and Doing Things from the Colonial Era to 1850*, 1994.

—Christopher W. Wells

HOUSE OF REPRESENTATIVES. *See* Federal Government, Legislative Branch: House of Representatives.

HOUSES OF REFUGE. *See* Prostitution and Antiprostitution.

HOUSEWORK. *See* Domestic Labor.

HOUSING. Housing in America, from the earliest Native American homes to the present, has been shaped by a wide range of factors, including building traditions, techniques of construction, cost considerations, material availability, the homebuilder's skill, and class and ethnic differences. Not until the twentieth century did the two features of contemporary housing—government intervention in the form of building regulations, zoning requirements, and financing support; and the effective use of *technology in terms of indoor plumbing, *electricity, and central *heating and cooling—become widespread.

Native American Housing Traditions. The approximately three hundred different Native American groups who were the earliest builders on the North American continent utilized a variety of materials and construction processes. Eastern woodlands and Great Lakes tribes created domed houses using lightweight stick frames covered by bark or woven mats. The Iroquois's version, called a longhouse, could contain as many as thirty families. Plains Indians, in contrast, erected tentlike tepees, constructed out of poles wrapped with buffalo skins. In the Southeast, Cherokees built log houses out of small logs chinked with dirt and sand. In the *Southwest, the Anasazi created dramatic cliff dwellings, honeycombed with room clusters and kivas (social-ceremonial chambers).

Colonial Housing. Colonists, immigrants, slaves, and other newcomers in the seventeenth and eighteenth centuries used traditional housing forms and adapted construction techniques to the American environment. Slaves followed African or Caribbean practices of constructing one- or two-room cabins, often using mud-covered woven branches for the walls and grass thatched roofs. Both the English and Dutch used heavy timbers to construct mortise and tenon frames, which gave their early houses low, massive profiles. In *New England, houses often had large center fireplaces, whereas in the *South, kitchens with fireplaces were often constructed as separate buildings.

In the Southwest, Spanish and Mexican settlers built flat-roofed adobe houses with one to three rooms and hard-packed dirt floors. Larger Mexican-styled haciendas often had small, open courts at the center. In contrast, northern European settlers from Belgium and the Scandinavian countries built log houses and log barns in the *Middle West. In all cases, local materials and traditional building techniques were combined to provide the best quality shelter possible.

Middle-class Housing. Most American single-family housing was designed not by architects but by local carpenters. In the nineteenth century, however, the publication of pattern books and popular magazines enabled architects such as Andrew Jackson Downing (1815–1852) and Calvert Vaux (1824–1895) to promote the new Gothic and Italianate revival homes. With these new styles, and the proliferation of homes built in the classical revival tradition, middle- and upper-class citizens in America built spacious, three -or four-bedroom houses with broad front porches and large entrance hallways. The expansion of rail and streetcar systems in the late nineteenth century and freeways in the twentieth enabled the prosperous classes to develop new residential suburbs adjacent to major cities.

Although the Pullman Palace Car Company in Illinois and the Hershey Chocolate Company in Pennsylvania created planned company towns (in 1881 and 1903 respectively), most small-town and suburban housing has been financed and built on a piecemeal basis. In 1975 a typical builder produced fewer than twenty units a year, and those who built one thousand or more accounted for less than 5 percent of total production.

Urban Housing. In cities, crowded conditions and higher land prices forced a continuous search for more efficient housing types. Small wooden houses, often crowded with two or three families, came first. In *New York City in 1855, for example, an average of three families, totaling fifteen people, lived in each house. Connected row houses were also built. Later in the nineteenth century, tenements and narrow four- or five-story, twenty-five-by-one-hundred–foot apartments, called railroad flats because each room could be entered only by going through another room, were erected.

Hotels represented another urban housing option. Whether palatial structures like the Waldorf Astoria in New York (1893), designed for wealthy visitors, or residential hotels and cheap boarding houses that rented single rooms to the middle and lower-middle classes, hotels often pioneered new plumbing, air-conditioning, and electrical technologies.

Federal Intervention. Despite the growth of middle-class suburban housing and the vast array of boarding houses, hotels, and apartments (sometimes called flats) in America's cities, finding affordable housing remained a problem. From 1900 to 1929, rising wages and prices for lumber and technology dramatically increased the costs of single family homes. Although the decision to make home mortgage interest payments deductible when the federal income tax was introduced in 1913, and the creation of a Housing Corporation during *World War I, were signs of a more activist state, it was the Great Depression of the 1930s that forced Congress to intervene in the housing market in a major way.

The Depression threw millions out of work and forced banks to foreclose on thousands of home mortgages. Although the New York City Housing Corporation had earlier built low-income housing and the Amalgamated Clothing Workers Union had sponsored cooperative apartments in the Bronx and Manhattan, it was the Housing Division of the Public Works Administration (PWA), created as a part of the National Industrial Recovery Act of 1933, that marked the entrance of the federal government into slum clearance and the low-cost housing market. In its four years of existence, the PWA financed or helped build 58 housing developments containing nearly 25,000 dwelling units around the country. In 1937, the Wagner Public Housing Act formally linked public housing to slum clearance. Underfunded and poorly administered, the PWA's housing division built cramped, barrackslike complexes such as the one in the Red Hook section of New York City that remained poor people's housing. Although the National Housing Act of 1949 also proposed to expand public housing, by the 1980s only 3 percent of all housing units in the country were owned by nonprofit or government agencies. The long tradition of private home ownership effectively undercut reformers' attempts to create more publicly owned, low-income housing.

Most federal aid during the Depression, not surprisingly, went to individual homeowners. The Home Owners Loan Corporation (1933) refinanced mortgages and helped save many owner-occupied nonfarm residences. The National Housing Act (1934) created the Federal Housing Administration (FHA), which provided federal insurance for home rehabilitation loans and mortgages for new homes. By 1950, FHA mortgage guarantees made it possible for most white, middle-class families to buy comfortable homes in suburban neighborhoods. *African Americans were generally excluded by a variety of discriminatory devices. For example, William Levitt, the developer of Levittown, used racially exclusive covenants to bar blacks from his new postwar subdivisions.

Planned Towns and Communities. The search for new forms of housing increased after *World War II. Self-contained mobile homes accounted for 25 percent of new housing in nonmetropolitan America in the 1970s. Manufactured homes, sometimes called trailer homes, were also popular. As the cost of house construction rose, new building materials, including vinyl and metal siding, were developed to recreate the look of wood at a lower price. Younger buyers often purchased condominiums, connected apartment units managed by a homeowners' association. More extensive developments, called planned communities, pioneered by Forest Hills Gardens, New York, in 1909, have included Reston, Virginia (1966), Kentlands (Gaithersburg, Maryland, 1988), and the Disney Corporation's town of Celebration, Florida (1996). These developments gained space for parks and public areas by reducing lot sizes and clustering homes more closely together. As the twentieth century came to a close, increasing emphasis was placed not only on the housing, but on the environment in which it was placed.

[*See also* Architecture: Domestic Architecture; New Deal Era, The; Slums; Suburbanization; Urbanization; Urban Renewal.]

• Gwendolyn Wright, *Building the Dream: A Social History of Housing in America*, 1981. Kenneth T. Jackson, *Crabgrass Frontier: The Suburbanization of the United States*, 1985. Dell Upton, ed., *America's Architectural Roots: Ethnic Groups That Built America*, 1986. Bernard L. Herman, *Architecture and Rural Life in Central Delaware, 1700–1900*, 1987. Lisa Taylor, ed., *Housing: Symbol, Structure, Site*, 1987. Jessica Foy and Thomas J. Schlereth, eds., *American Home Life, 1880–1930: A Social History of Spaces and Services*, 1992. Fred W. Peterson, *Homes in the Heartland: Balloon Frame Farmhouses of the Upper Midwest, 1850–1920*, 1992. Peter Katz, ed., *The New Urbanism: Toward an Architecture of Community*, 1994. Gail Radford, *Modern Housing for America: Policy Struggles in the New Deal Era*, 1996.

—Clifford E. Clark Jr.

HOUSTON, SAM (1793–1863), antebellum Texas leader. Born in Virginia, Sam Houston moved to Tennessee in 1807. A youthful runaway, he lived with the Cherokees from 1809 to 1812 and in 1813 enlisted in the U.S. Army. He left the army in 1818, moved to Middle Tennessee, became a lawyer, and launched a political career. A Jacksonian Democrat, Houston served in Congress from 1823 to 1827, when he was elected governor of Tennessee. He abruptly resigned the governorship in April 1829, following the breakup of his marriage, and went into exile with the Cherokees in present-day Oklahoma.

Three years later, Houston traveled to Texas as an agent of the United States to the Comanches. Although little involved in planning the 1835–1836 Texas revolution against Mexico, Houston became commander-in-chief of the Texan forces. After initial setbacks suffered by units not under his immediate command, including the fall of the Alamo in March 1836, Houston's army won Texas independence at the Battle of San Jacinto (21 April 1836), defeating the Mexican commander Santa Anna. Houston was president of the Texas Republic in 1836–1838 and again in 1841–1844. Following the U.S. annexation of Texas in 1845, which he actively supported, he served in the U.S. Senate from 1846 to 1859.

During the 1850s, Houston's staunch unionism reduced his popularity in Texas. He won the governorship in 1859 but was removed from office when the *Civil War began in 1861 owing to his opposition to Texas's secession and his refusal to swear loyalty to the Confederacy. He retired to Huntsville, where he died. Sam Houston, more than any other individual, had brought Texas into the Union that he loved.

[*See also* Alamo, Battle of the; Confederate States of America; Democratic Party; Jackson, Andrew; Mexican War; Texas Republic and Annexation.]

• Llerena B. Friend, *Sam Houston: The Great Designer*, 1954. Randolph B. Campbell, *Sam Houston and the American Southwest*, 1993.

—Randolph B. Campbell

HOWELLS, WILLIAM DEAN (1837–1920), novelist, editor, and proponent of literary realism. Born in Ohio, William Dean

Howells wrote a campaign biography of Abraham *Lincoln and was U.S. consul in Venice (1861–1865) before moving to *Boston, where in 1871 he became the first midwesterner to edit the prestigious *Atlantic Monthly*. He began his career in fiction with such studies of middle-class married life as *A Chance Acquaintance* (1873) and *A Foregone Conclusion* (1875). Leaving the *Atlantic Monthly* in 1881, he increasingly shifted his professional focus to *New York City, where he settled in 1891. Discovering in European realism an alternative to what he regarded as the prettified falsehoods of romanticism, he began a campaign to change American fiction. In his influential column in *Harper's Monthly*, "The Editor's Study," (1886–1892), he defended a realism of "the simple, the natural, and the honest" and promoted novelists whose work embodied those principles.

Although often regarded by succeeding generations as timid, his 1880s novels opened new ground for literary representation. In *A Modern Instance* (1882), *The Rise of Silas Lapham* (1885), *Annie Kilburn* (1888), and *A Hazard of New Fortunes* (1890), he gave middle-class readers portrayals of unscrupulous journalism and divorce, the travails of the nouveau riche in polite society, class divisions in a factory town, and social conflict in *Gilded Age New York. Nearly alone among literary figures in condemning the 1887 Haymarket executions, he became more explicitly radical with his 1894 utopian novel, *A Traveler from Altruria*. Through his challenge in criticism and fiction to prevailing conventions, Howells, along with his friends Henry *James and Samuel L. *Clemens, redefined American literary standards after the *Civil War.

[*See also* Haymarket Affair; Literature: Civil War to World War I; Magazines; Socialism.]

• Kenneth Lynn, *William Dean Howells, An American Life*, 1971. Daniel H. Borus, *Writing Realism: Howells, James, and Norris in the Mass Market*, 1989.

—Daniel H. Borus

HOW THE OTHER HALF LIVES (1890). Jacob A. Riis's *How the Other Half Lives: Studies among the Tenements of New York* was illustrated by seventeen halftones of photographs from Riis's extensive collection (now held by the Museum of the City of New York) and twenty-six drawings, some copied from photographs. The book aimed to awaken *Progressive Era, middle-class readers to the urgent need for tenement house reform and regulation. A Danish immigrant police reporter, Riis was frustrated that his accounts of New York slum life stirred little interest. As he commented in his 1901 autobiography, *The Making of an American*, "I wrote, but it seemed to make no impression." Accordingly, Riis in 1888 turned to *photography—his own and others'—to show scenes in the tenements, saloons, and sweatshops of lower Manhattan's "Mulberry Bend," "Jewtown," and "Chinatown."

The book originated in illustrated lectures in which Riis used slides to dramatize his stories of appalling conditions endured by the immigrant "hordes" flooding into *New York City. Against the contrast of "the other half," his text forcefully affirmed the worth of middle-class identity and values in new urban circumstances, proposing ultimately no more than that wealthy citizens invest in tenements as a form of philanthropy.

Generally favorably reviewed, the book sold well, remained in print until 1947, and was subsequently republished several times. Although poorly reproduced in early editions, Riis's innovative photographic work was a key to the book's success. It marked the inception of a distinctive American social documentary tradition that continued through the 1930s. In both word and image, *How the Other Half Lives* initiated ideological perspectives and representational strategies that remained current in social thought and public sentiment for much of the twentieth century.

[*See also* Gilded Age; Immigration; Philanthropy and Philanthropic Foundations; Slums; Urbanization.]

• Jacob A. Riis, *How the Other Half Lives: Studies among the Tenements of New York*, ed. David Leviatin, 1996.

—Maren Stange

HUDSON RIVER SCHOOL. *See* Painting: To 1945.

HUGHES, CHARLES EVANS (1862–1948), chief justice of the U.S. *Supreme Court. Born in Glens Falls, New York, the son of a Welsh immigrant and Baptist preacher, Charles Evans Hughes received a Christian education mostly at home, attended Madison (later renamed Colgate) University, and graduated from Brown University. In 1884, Columbia University awarded him a law degree. During the next twenty years, he mainly practiced corporate law.

As counsel to a New York state legislative committee investigating the utility industry, his hard-hitting attacks on corporate corruption won widespread acclaim. President Theodore *Roosevelt engineered his nomination as a Republican for governor of New York in 1906. Serving two terms, he promoted the progressive goals of administrative efficiency and public service reform. In 1910, President William Howard *Taft appointed him to the U.S. Supreme Court. He resigned in 1916 after receiving the *Republican party's nomination for president. He narrowly lost to incumbent Woodrow *Wilson.

Hughes's support until 1918 for Wilson's foreign policy established him as a leading Republican proponent of *internationalism. In 1921, he became President Warren *Harding's secretary of state. Committed to the principles of antimilitarism and the rule of law, he proposed a series of agreements at the *Washington Naval Arms Conference of 1921–1922, including the Five-Power Naval Treaty that mandated capital-ship ratios and reductions. The treaty may ironically have strengthened Japan in the Pacific, the opposite of what Hughes had intended. He also spearheaded U.S. efforts to stabilize the European economy by extending loans to Germany and scaling back Germany's *World War I reparations payments. He supported the Dawes Plan of 1924, formulated by a commission headed by banker Charles G. Dawes (1865–1951), as a step toward this goal. Although he avoided diplomatic commitments in Europe, Hughes did initiate some informal cooperation with the *League of Nations.

Returning to private law practice in 1925, Hughes soon accepted appointment to the Permanent Court of Arbitration and, in 1928, to the World Court. In 1930, President Herbert *Hoover named him chief justice of the U.S. Supreme Court. A moderate conservative, Hughes in his written opinions reflected an unimaginative but deep commitment to constitutional procedures. Serving until 1941, he often, but not always, questioned the expansion of federal *economic regulation. His religious principles, which contributed to his libertarian sentiments and his sympathy for racial *equality, distanced him from the narrow partisanship of many New Deal opponents.

[See also Federal Government, Executive Branch: Department of State; Foreign Relations; New Deal Era, The; Progressive Era.]

• Merlo J. Pusey, *Charles Evans Hughes*, 2 vols., 1951. Betty Glad, *Charles Evans Hughes and the Illusions of Innocence*, 1966. Robert F. Wesser, *Charles Evans Hughes: Politics and Reform in New York, 1905–1910*, 1967. David J. Danelski and Joseph S. Tulchin, eds., *The Autobiographical Notes of Charles Evans Hughes*, 1973.

—Gary B. Ostrower

HUGHES, JOHN (1797–1864), Catholic prelate. Born in Ireland, John Hughes immigrated to Emmitsburg, Maryland, where he first worked as a gardener at Mount St. Mary's Seminary. He then remained at Mt. St. Mary's to study for the priesthood. Ordained in *Philadelphia in 1826, he soon emerged as an able defender of Catholic rights against nativism. Appointed coadjutor bishop of New York in 1837, he was consecrated the following year. In 1842, he became bishop of New York and in 1850 the first archbishop. In New York, he came to symbolize the Irish immigrants' arrival on the American scene. In 1842, he gained the support of Governor William *Seward in his battle with the Public School Society, a private organization that distributed state funds for education and assured its Protestant character. Despite state legislation requiring funds to be distributed through locally elected school supervisors, Hughes, like other bishops, opened parochial schools to educate Catholic children. In 1844, he defended his churches with armed men against a threatened nativist attack. In 1858, he laid the cornerstone for St. Patrick's Cathedral in *New York City. A powerful orator, Hughes rallied *Irish Americans in particular to support the *Mexican War. In the *Civil War, he endorsed President Abraham *Lincoln's call to defend the Union, but rejected emancipation as one of the war's purposes. He also undertook a mission to Rome for Lincoln to prevent Pope Pius IX from recognizing the Confederacy. His last public appearance was to help quell the New York City draft riots in July 1863.

[*See also* Anti-Catholic Movement; Draft Riots, Civil War; Nativist Movement; Roman Catholicism.]

• Richard Shaw, *Dagger John: The Unquiet Life and Times of Archbishop John Hughes of New York*, 1977.

—Gerald P. Fogarty, S. J.

HUGHES, LANGSTON (1902–1967), African American writer. Born in Joplin, Missouri, and educated at Columbia and Lincoln universities, Langston Hughes established himself as a writer with *The Weary Blues* (1926), a collection of poems influenced by *jazz rhythms. Subsequent *poetry collections, notably *Shakespeare in Harlem* (1942), *Montage of a Dream Deferred* (1951), and *The Panther and the Lash* (1967), solidified his reputation as the "Negro Poet Laureate." A central figure in the *Harlem Renaissance, Hughes wrote prolifically, producing a novel, *Not without Laughter* (1930), as well as children's books, plays, musicals, radio scripts, and two autobiographies, *The Big Sea* (1940) and *I Wonder as I Wander* (1956). His humorous columns in *The Chicago Defender* newspaper, featuring Jess B. Semple, a fictional character who offered commonsense but cutting critiques of American culture, enjoyed a large following. In the 1930s and after, Hughes's writing increasingly reflected his social activism. He founded black theaters in *Chicago, Harlem, and *Los Angeles, and traveled extensively in the United States and abroad investigating race relations. In 1960, the *National Association for the Advancement of Colored People awarded him its Spingarn Medal.

A voice of social protest, Hughes blurred the line between high and low culture, addressing black audiences through the use of oral tradition, improvisation, and mass cultural forms, including the gospel musical play. His writing for children, in particular, reflected his belief that race consciousness and pride could be transmitted through literature and art. Renowned for the humor and compassion that suffused his vision of social renewal, Hughes ranks among the most influential American writers of the twentieth century.

[*See also* African Americans; Literature: Since World War I.]

• Arnold Rampersad, *The Life of Langston Hughes*, 2 vols., 1988, 1989. Henry Louis Gates Jr. and K. A. Appiah, eds., *Langston Hughes: Critical Perspectives Past and Present*, 1993.

—Tanya Agathocleous

HULL, CORDELL (1871–1955), secretary of state, 1933–1944. A Tennessee Democrat, Cordell Hull was best known during his quarter century as a congressman (1907–1921, 1923–1931) and senator (1931–1933), as the author of the income tax law of 1913 and as a party leader who appealed both to northern-urban-wet and southern-rural-dry Democrats. In 1933, those were sufficient credentials for President-elect Franklin Delano *Roosevelt to appoint him secretary of state.

Having little interest in diplomacy but convinced that world peace depended on free trade, Hull saw the office as a platform for promoting his reciprocal trade agreements program. Although initially stalled by Roosevelt advisers who favored an economic nationalist policy, Hull eventually triumphed, moving the nation permanently away from the protective tariff. Diplomatically, Secretary Hull implemented the *Good Neighbor Policy in Latin America and jealously guarded his control over American policy in East Asia, where he insisted upon a cautious response to Japanese expansion.

Hull's influence waned during *World War II as Roosevelt took greater control of foreign policy and Hull's health failed. Nevertheless, Roosevelt insisted that Hull, still immensely popular, remain in office through November 1944. He seized the opportunity to gain support for the *United Nations and foster his vision of a postwar liberal economic order. For his support of the United Nations, Hull received the 1946 Nobel Peace Prize. An even more fitting legacy is the liberal commercial world order the United States embraced at the end of World War II.

[*See also* Democratic Party; Federal Government, Executive Branch: Department of State; Foreign Relations; Foreign Trade, U.S.; General Agreement on Tariffs and Trade; Internationalism; New Deal Era, The; Tariffs.]

• Cordell Hull, *The Memoirs of Cordell Hull*, 2 vols., 1948. Julius W. Pratt, *Cordell Hull, 1933–1944*, 2 vols., 1964.

—Jonathan G. Utley

HUMAN GENOME PROJECT. Launched as a small "initiative" at the U.S. Department of Energy (DOE) in 1985, the Human Genome Project (HGP) was a political response to the needs of the American *biotechnology industry, an effort to find a post–*Cold War mission for the DOE's system of national laboratories, and a dramatic manifestation of molecular biology's rising scientific power. After early debates about the feasibility and desirability of a "crash program" to map the human genome—all genetic material in the twenty-four human chromosomes—Congress in 1986 approved public funding through both the DOE and the *National Institutes of Health. With a projected completion date of 2005, the database on this average human male, an amalgam of thousands of individual genomes, was expected to serve as a medical and scientific resource analogous to the nineteenth-century geological maps of the American West.

HGP proved extremely controversial. Its scientific strategies, funding, relationship to the biotechnology industry, impact on young scientists, patenting issues, and long-term social and ethical implications all generated significant public debate. Members of Congress worried about the possible misuse of genetic information produced by the project, and critics characterized the project as a new form of colonial exploitation of resources—that is, of Third World blood and DNA.

The potential ethical ramifications led to congressional support for a novel funding arrangement: beginning in 1989, HGP appropriations include a funding set aside of 5 percent for scholarly studies of the ethical and social implications of the scientific work itself. While memorable for its scientific impact, the project was thus also noteworthy as an experiment, however flawed, in socially responsible science. The Human Genome Project produced many new genetic discoveries and remarkable insights into the complexities and contrarieties of genomic structure. Despite the safeguards, however, it continued to provoke widespread fears of a "new *eugenics" facilitated by high-tech gene mapping and predictive diagnostics.

At a White House Conference in June 2000, officials of the National Human Genome Research Institute and of the Celera Genomics Corporation, a private firm also working on mapping the human genome, made a simultaneous announcement that a "working draft" of the DNA sequence of the human genome had been completed.

[*See also* Bioethics; Biological Sciences; Federal Government, Executive Branch: Other Departments (Department of Energy); Medicine: Since 1945; Science: Science and Popular Culture; Science: Since 1945.]

• Daniel J. Kevles and Leroy Hood, eds., *The Code of Codes: Scientific and Social Issues in the Human Genome Project*, 1992. Robert Mullan Cook-Deegan, *The Gene Wars: Science, Politics, and the Human Genome Project*, 1994.

—Susan Lindee

HUMAN RIGHTS, INTERNATIONAL. Political and philosophical discussions of human rights can be traced to antiquity, but the movement to define and protect human rights internationally emerged in the last half of the twentieth century. The movement arose from the impact of *World War II with its massive human rights abuses. The punishment of war criminals for crimes against humanity was one reaction to these abuses. A second and more sustained reaction was the internationalization and expansion of standards of behavior relating to human rights.

The move to ground the protection of human rights in international agreements found broad support among the delegates at the 1945 *San Francisco Conference that launched the *United Nations. Written into the UN charter was the pledge of member states to promote and encourage respect for "human rights and fundamental freedoms for all without distinction as to race, sex, language, or religion" (1.3). The rights that were the subject of this general goal were detailed in the Universal Declaration of Human Rights, the work of a UN committee chaired by U.S. delegate Eleanor *Roosevelt and adopted by the UN General Assembly in 1948. The declaration set the pattern for many subsequent human rights agreements. While often nonbinding, they nevertheless, in the words of the declaration's preamble, serve "as a common standard of achievement for all peoples and nations."

The human rights movement found regional expression in such undertakings as the American Declaration of the Rights and Duties of Man (1948), the European Convention on Human Rights (1950), the European Social Charter (1961), and the African Charter on Human and Peoples' Rights (1981). The movement has also generated controversy over the legitimacy of economic as opposed to political rights. Two U.N.–sponsored covenants, the International Covenant on Civil and Political Rights (1966) and the International Covenant on Economic, Social, and Cultural Rights (1966), reflect this controversy. The opposition of some nations, including the United States, to incorporating economic rights in a document intended to be legally binding, was met by separating the types of rights, thus allowing for separate agreements.

The Helsinki Accords (1975) enhanced the effectiveness of international standards by establishing regular review conferences to encourage compliance with the accord's human rights provisions. An emphasis on human rights in the foreign policy of President Jimmy *Carter's administration (1977–1981) further boosted the movement, which continued to expand and generate controversy. Toward the end of the twentieth century, some Asian and African states questioned the universality of civil and political rights, especially as applied to their own regimes. Still, the movement continued, as concerns about the environment, unequal development, racial discrimination, breaches of humanitarian norms, and the rights of marginalized groups such as women, children, and indigenous peoples were all brought under the umbrella of international human rights.

[*See also* Internationalism.]

• Dorothy V. Jones, *Code of Peace: Ethics and Security in the World of the Warlord States*, 1991. Rein Mullerson, *Human Rights Diplomacy*, 1997.

—Dorothy V. Jones.

HUMOR. Although rooted in Old World cultures, identifiably American forms and traditions of humor began to emerge in the late *Colonial Era, particularly in Benjamin *Franklin's *Poor Richard's Almanack* (1733–1758) and other writings. Here, as in his self-presentation as a "child of the wilderness" while serving as American ambassador to France during the *Revolutionary War, Franklin popularized one of the longest-lived comic types in American culture—the unschooled rustic whose natural simplicity masked an innate shrewdness and tenacity.

While Franklin's Poor Richard enjoyed universal appeal in the new nation, most antebellum humor had an explicitly sectional flavor. Washington Irving's "Legend of Sleepy Hollow" (1820) delineated the emerging regional type of the *New England Yankee. Stemming from earlier "Brother Jonathan" representations, the Yankee character solidified in the 1830s and 1840s through such deceptively simple yet morally didactic yokels in the big city as Seba Smith's Major Jack Downing and Thomas Chandler Haliburton's Sam Slick. By the *Civil War, the character had become the basis of a national icon, Uncle Sam. A second staple of antebellum humor was the backwoodsmen and poor whites of the old *Southwest states. Oral and published tall-tales, such as Thomas Thorpe's "The Big Bear of Arkansas" (1841), celebrated the boasting and fighting prowess of the frontiersman, epitomized by the "ring-tailed roarer" persona of Davy *Crockett, featured in many narratives and almanacs. Comic writers also presented deceitful and socially subversive characters of the southern frontier such as Johnson J. Hooper's oily Simon Suggs (1845) and the prankster hero of George Washington Harris's *Sut Lovingood's Yarns* (1867) who revels in vicious assaults on social hierarchies and social gatherings, from weddings to quilting parties to African American church services.

Late Nineteenth and Early Twentieth Centuries. Not until after the Civil War would a writer succeed in forging a unifying national humor. Enormously popular by the end of his life, Samuel L. *Clemens (Mark Twain) was the first writer to present authentic American vernacular voices without an intermediating "respectable" narrator. Unlike the comical writings and lectures of Artemus Ward (Charles Farrar Browne), Josh Billings (Henry Wheeler Shaw), and other "Phunny Phellows" of the 1870s and 1880s who relied upon malapropisms, deliberate misspellings, and soon-forgotten contemporary events and personages, Clemens revealed the deeper possibilities of American humor. He wrote humorously but movingly about timeless human foibles and deftly blended comic passages and characters with social criticism on the central issues of his day from *racism to imperialism to the destructiveness of modern warfare.

By 1900, the locus of American humor began to shift from the printed word to the new mass entertainments of the *vaudeville stage, newspaper comic strips, and silent *films. Heavily influenced by earlier popular entertainments such as minstrel shows and burlesque theater, these productions initially targeted a broad, at first, mostly working-class audience of first- or second-generation immigrants. Much of this humor was based on a combination of ethnic/racial comedic traditions and blatant stereotypes of Irish, German (dubbed "Dutch"), Jewish, and "Negro" (white and black men in blackface) characters. Simultaneously offensive and celebratory of cultural distinctiveness, ethnic humor faded by the late 1920s in the face of accelerating assimilation and protests by middle-class pressure groups. Even more universally appealing was the slapstick comedy of many early comic strips (for instance Rudolph Dirk's "The Katzenjammer Kids" and Frederick Opper's "Happy Hooligan") and such early motion picture stars as Charlie *Chaplin, Buster Keaton, and Harold Lloyd.

In the interwar years, American humor continued to mirror an evolving American society and psyche. The comic writers and cartoonists of *The New Yorker* magazine (founded 1925), including James Thurber, Charles Addams, and Dorothy Parker, perfectly reflected the jaded cosmopolitan spirit of the post–*World War I boom years. Humor in the Depression-wracked 1930s, by contrast, revealed a waning confidence in modernity. The anarchic zaniness of the Marx Brothers, immigrant Jewish ex-vaudevillians turned movie stars, portrayed a world without rules or reason, while lariat-twirling and plain-spoken Will *Rogers, in his stage shows, films, and newspaper columns, drolly expressed his skepticism about industrial *technology and corporate *capitalism and celebrated the wisdom of the common folk.

*Radio comedians of the 1930s such as Jack Benny, Jimmy Durante, and the husband-and-wife team of George Burns and Gracie Allen (many of them vaudeville veterans who would soon graduate to *television) hastened the rise of commercially sponsored humor geared to a mass audience. The popular comedy show *Amos 'n' Andy,* featuring white actors impersonating blacks, continued the tradition of humor based on racial stereotyping.

The Cold War Era and the Late Twentieth Century. In the early *Cold War Era, amid anti-Communist witch-hunts and nuclear threats, most American humorists followed the safe path of presenting apolitical consensus-oriented material. The increasing dominance of television reinforced this emphasis on social conformity. Even the comic geniuses of the era such as Lucille Ball (*I Love Lucy*) and Sid Caesar (*Your Show of Shows*) presented largely non-controversial, non-political routines. The tepid nature of mass-media humor began to break down by the mid-1950s, however, as daring "standup" comics like Mort Sahl and Lenny Bruce, William Gaines and the other contributors to *MAD* magazine, and irreverent comedy troupes such as Chicago's Second City (which would evolve into the 1970s television comedy revue *Saturday Night Live*) challenged the limits of political and sexual commentary in professional humor. This trend accelerated in the 1960s and 1970s as the *civil rights, *antiwar, and *women's rights movements, as well as the counterculture and sexual revolution, shaped a new wave of American humor including G. B. (Garry) Trudeau's groundbreaking comic strip "Doonesbury," the acerbic standup comedy of George Carlin and Lily Tomlin, and the suburban-housewife angst of columnist Erma Bombeck. These years also marked the entry into the media mainstream of a generation of *African American (Flip Wilson, Richard Pryor) and *Hispanic American (Freddie Prinze) comics who emphasized not cultural integration but their distinct ethno-racial communities.

As the twentieth century ended, American humor continued to evolve in ways that reflected changing social values and demographics. Bill Cosby, Roseanne (Barr), and Jerry Seinfeld reinvented the television situation comedy, featuring such once-invisible protagonists as affluent African Americans and working-class women and previously taboo sexual and social topics. Further, although the late-night television talk shows still starred white male comedians like David Letterman and Jay Leno, the humor of nightclubs, network and cable television, and film was increasingly culturally diverse, featuring more women, people of color, and homosexual comedians. Despite changes in personalities and content, however, humor continued to play the critical role it had since the Colonial Era, helping Americans come to terms with both a rapidly changing world and the persistence of societal inequality.

[*See also* Literature; Literature, Popular; Minstrelsy; Popular Culture; Race and Ethnicity; Racism; Regionalism; South, The; Working-Class Life and Culture.]

• Constance Rourke, *American Humor: A Study of the National Character,* 1931. Walter Blair and Hamlin Hill, *America's Humor: From Poor Richard to Doonesbury,* 1978. William Bedford Clark and W. Craig Turner, eds., *Critical Essays on American Humor,* 1984. Tony Hendra, *Going Too Far,* 1987. Lawrence Mintz, ed., *Humor in America: A Research Guide to Genres and Topics,* 1988. Joseph Boskin, ed., *The Humor Prism in 20th-Century America,* 1997.

—Anthony A. Harkins

HUMPHREY, HUBERT (1911–1978), senator, vice president, and Democratic presidential candidate. Perhaps the most eloquent and forceful proponent of New Deal *liberalism after *World War II, Hubert Humphrey rose from mayor of Minneapolis (1945–1949), to the U.S. Senate (1949–1965), to vice president (1965–1969). Four times he sought the presidency and four times he was rejected. In 1968, amid bitter domestic divisions over the *Vietnam War, he won the Democratic nomination but lost in a close election to Republican Richard M. *Nixon. In 1971 he returned to the Senate, where he served until his death in 1978.

Humphrey's rise to national prominence coincided with a critical period in the evolution of American liberalism and the *Democratic party. During World War II, liberals and communists had worked together for progressive causes, but growing U.S.–Soviet hostility after 1945 convinced Humphrey and many others that liberalism and communism were incompatible. In 1947 he joined with theologian Reinhold *Niebuhr, historian Arthur Schlesinger Jr., and others to organize the anticommunist *Americans for Democratic Action (ADA) and conducted a successful purge of communists from Minnesota's new Democratic-Farmer-Labor party. The following year he gained national attention at the Democratic national convention with a stirring speech in support of *civil rights that established his reputation as one of the leading orators in American politics. Minnesota voters rewarded Humphrey by electing him to the Senate in 1948. Over the next fifteen years, he emerged as the Senate's most outspoken liberal and most effective lawmaker. He shaped some of the most important social legislation of his time, including the Civil Rights Act of 1964, which helped to erode racial *segregation in the *South.

In 1964, President Lyndon B. *Johnson picked Humphrey as his vice presidential running mate and the ticket won a landslide victory. But the administration's 1965 decision to escalate the war in Vietnam splintered the Democratic party and destroyed Humphrey's 1968 presidential bid.

[*See also* Anticommunism; Civil Rights Legislation; Cold War; Communism; Communist Party—USA; Federal Government, Legislative Branch: Senate; New Deal Era, The; Sixties, The.]

• Carl Solberg, *Hubert Humphrey: A Biography,* 1984. Timothy Thurber, *The Politics of Equality: Hubert H. Humphrey and the African American Freedom Struggle, 1945–1978,* 1999.

—Steven M. Gillon

HUNTINGTON, COLLIS P. (1821–1900), railroad entrepreneur. Born in Connecticut, Collis P. Huntington, after an early business career in New York City, moved to Sacramento, California, during the 1849 Gold Rush and started a merchandise business with Mark Hopkins. In 1861 he joined with Hopkins, Leland Stanford, and Charles Crocker (the "Big Four" as they became known) to create the Central Pacific Railroad. Using Chinese labor and relying on government loans and subsidies, the Central Pacific built nearly seven hundred miles of the transcontinental railroad that in 1869 linked with the Union Pacific at Promontory Point, Utah. Huntington and his partners reaped huge profits from the venture.

In 1865, Huntington and his partners started the Southern Pacific Railroad. To maintain the railroad's dominance over competitors in *California and the *Southwest, and to avoid government regulation, Huntington lobbied in Washington, dominated the California legislature, and showered bribes on corrupt politicians. His candid private letters, some of which became public in 1883, revealed his cynical calculations about who could be bought to achieve his purposes. During the 1870s and 1880s, the period of his greatest economic and political power, Huntington was controversial and hated, personifying as he did the acquisitive business practices of the *Gilded Age. His excesses helped spark a movement within the California *Democratic party in the 1880s and 1890s to curb the power of the Southern Pacific. The estate of his nephew and business partner Henry E. Huntington in San Marino, California, became the site of the Huntington Library and Art Gallery, a major cultural center near Pasadena.

[*See also* Asian Americans; Gold Rushes; Railroads.]

• David Lavender, *The Great Persuader,* 1970. R. Hal Williams, *The Democratic Party in California Politics, 1880–1896,* 1973.

—Lewis L. Gould

HURSTON, ZORA NEALE (1903–1960), writer, anthropologist, folklorist. Born in Notasulga, Alabama, Zora Neale Hurston grew up in Eatonville, Florida, where her father was three-term mayor of that first all-black incorporated town. Her mother's death in 1904 ended her stable family life. While a student at Howard University in *Washington, D.C. (1918–

1924), she published her first stories. In *New York City by 1925, among the *Harlem Renaissance writers, she produced prize-winning stories and studied at Barnard College with the anthropologist Franz *Boas. One of the few Harlem writers of the period born in the *South, she genuinely loved and appreciated black rural people and culture, especially oral culture. In the late 1920s and 1930s she returned to the region and went to Haiti and Jamaica as well to study and collect black music, *folklore, poetry, and other facets of black culture. Best known for the skillful blending of *anthropology and literature in her four novels, two collections of folklore, and autobiography, she was also interested in black folk performance, which led her into theater and folk concerts. Flamboyant and fiercely independent, she was not a favorite among her peers and by the late 1940s she and her works had disappeared from public view. Dying in poverty and obscurity, she was rediscovered in the 1970s. One of Hurston's most significant legacies to American literary traditions was her unwavering belief in the artistic merits of black folk culture. Hurston was posthumously hailed as a foremother by Alice Walker and many other writers. Her best novel, *Their Eyes Were Watching God* (1937), was a pioneering black feminist text.

[*See also* African Americans; Feminism; Literature: Since World War I.]

• Alice Walker, "In Search of Zora Neale Hurston," *Ms* (March 1975): 74–82. Robert Hemenway, *Zora Neale Hurston: A Literary Biography,* 1977. Mary Helen Washington, *Invented Lives: Narratives of Black Women 1860–1960,* 1987. Henry Louis Gates Jr. and K. A. Appiah, eds., *Zora Neale Hurston: Critical Perspectives Past and Present,* 1993. Cheryl A. Wall, *Women of the Harlem Renaissance,* 1995, pp. 139–99.

—Nellie Y. McKay

HUTCHINSON, ANNE (1591–1643), religious dissenter. Born in Alford, England, the daughter of a dissenting Anglican clergyman, Anne married merchant William Hutchinson in 1612. Of their fifteen children, twelve survived infancy.

An admirer of the Puritan minister John Cotton, Hutchinson with her family followed Cotton to *Boston in 1634. Soon she began holding religious meetings in her home, expounding Cotton's sermons and adding her interpretations. Her intelligence and skill as a midwife and herbalist assured her an audience. Mirroring the views of Anabaptists and other dissenters, and anticipating Quaker beliefs, Hutchinson rejected the so-called Covenant of Works, by which a moral life offered evidence of salvation. Instead, she espoused an extreme form of the Covenant of Grace, teaching that God could act directly upon the worst sinner through immediate revelation, and that believers were freed from the moral law of the Old Testament. This doctrine, called Antinomianism, alarmed the colony's leadership, particularly when Hutchinson's meetings attracted merchants and the young governor, Henry Vane. Her teachings were seen as undermining ministerial authority, elevating a woman as the judge of men, and authorizing sinful behavior. A synod of Massachusetts churches condemned eighty-two of Hutchinson's "errors" in September 1637, and in November she was tried before the General Court, presided over by Governor John *Winthrop, who had replaced Vane. John Cotton aided her defense, but when she claimed by divine revelation that God would destroy her persecutors, the Court banished her. Confined that winter awaiting exile, her mental condition deteriorated, and she made extreme claims that further alarmed visiting ministers. In March 1638, after a heresy trial, the clergy excommunicated her.

She moved with her family to Portsmouth, Rhode Island, and then, after her husband's death in 1642, to Pelham Bay, Long Island. Here in 1643 she and all but one of her six younger children perished in an Indian attack. Viewed in successive eras as a "disturber of social order," a champion of religious freedom, and a model of female assertiveness, Hutchinson is perhaps best understood in terms of the specific theological issues of her day and the religious doctrines that she embraced and taught.

[*See also* Colonial Era; Midwifery; New England; Puritanism; Society of Friends.]

• Francis J. Bremer, ed., *Anne Hutchinson,* 1981. Selma R. Williams, *Divine Rebel,* 1981.

—Lyle Koehler

HUTTERITES. *See* Mennonites and Amish.

HYDROELECTRIC POWER. Electricity generated through the use of waterwheels or hydraulic turbines is known as hydroelectric power. In the early 1880s, small water-powered mills were utilized to produce direct current (DC) electricity. However, the full potential of hydroelectric power was not realized until the proliferation of alternating current (AC) power systems in the 1890s. In contrast to direct current (which was difficult to transmit more than ten miles), polyphase AC systems proved capable of transmitting power hundreds of miles. As a result, AC systems allowed the development of large waterpower sites in remote locations far removed from urban markets.

America's first polyphase AC hydroelectric power system came on-line in 1893 near San Bernardino, *California. California subsequently led the nation in long-distance hydroelectric power development; Fresno received power over a thirty-five-mile-long transmission line in 1896, and by 1901 *San Francisco was connected to generating plants in the Sierra Nevada mountains, more than 140 miles away. In the eastern United States, *Niagara Falls became the focus of hydroelectric power development; in 1896, AC power was first transmitted over a 22-mile-long line connecting Niagara Falls to Buffalo, New York.

In the early twentieth century, the conservationist Gifford Pinchot championed a movement advocating government regulation of hydroelectric power systems built by privately owned utilities. In the 1920s, the struggle between public and private interests over control of the electric power industry focused on the Muscle Shoals (or Wilson) Dam on the Tennessee River in northern Alabama. The government had started the Muscle Shoals project during *World War I to manufacture nitrates used in explosives. After the war, Henry *Ford proposed buying the dam for general industrial purposes. However, public-power supporters in Congress blocked the transfer of control into private hands. In 1933, President Franklin Delano *Roosevelt successfully incorporated Wilson Dam—and several other proposed dams—into the newly created and publicly administered *Tennessee Valley Authority (TVA).

In the *West, hydroelectric power constituted a key component of the Boulder Canyon Project. Authorized in 1928 by President Calvin *Coolidge, this project included federal financing of the Hoover Dam across the Colorado River near Las Vegas, Nevada. During Roosevelt's New Deal, many other large-scale hydroelectric power dams were built in the West by the federal government. These included Grand Coulee Dam in Washington state, Shasta Dam in California, and Marshall Ford Dam in Texas.

After *World War II, still more hydropower dams were built (including Glen Canyon Dam in northern Arizona), but the economic importance of hydroelectricity waned as fossil-fuel and nuclear generating plants grew in size and numbers. By the end of the twentieth century, hydroelectric power accounted for about 10 percent of electricity used in the United States; concurrently, public concern over environmental costs associated with reservoir construction prompted a movement to remove hydroelectric dams in order to restore river valleys to a more natural state.

[*See also* Dams and Hydraulic Engineering; Electricity and Electrification; Environmentalism; New Deal Era, The; Nuclear Power.]

• Preston J. Hubbard, *Origins of the TVA: The Muscle Shoals Controversy, 1920–1932,* 1961. Thomas P. Hughes, *Networks of Power: Electrification in Western Society, 1880–1930,* 1983.

—Donald C. Jackson

HYDROGEN BOMB. *See* Nuclear Weapons; Teller, Edward.

HYGIENE, PERSONAL. Early European visitors to the United States frequently commented on the absence of reliable supplies of soap and water and the prevalence of mud and manure, flies and insects, and disgusting tobacco stains (from both spitting and chewing). More than four out of five *Antebellum Era Americans lived in hygienically primitive situations on small farms or in country villages. Even in the few big cities, where *cholera and *typhoid fever epidemics signaled the need for water and sewer systems and stimulated massive public-works contruction, changes in personal and domestic cleanliness practices came slowly.

American housewives tried to keep their homes tidy and their families clean. But much of what would later be considered essential, such as bathing and frequent washing of clothes, was not thought important. Since indoor plumbing was rare, basic hygiene was extremely laborious. To wash a load of clothes, housewives and hired girls (slaves in the *South) had to carry full buckets of water some distance, cut wood to heat it, and then lift and hang heavy wet laundry to dry. Soap was typically homemade from ashes, lye, and rendered animal fat.

Improvements in hygiene habits were rooted in technological innovations and changed attitudes. From the early nineteenth through the mid–twentieth centuries, the gradual spread of municipal water and sewage systems and the growing availability of indoor plumbing, hot water heaters, washing machines, and commercially manufactured soaps—developments that extended outward from urban centers to small towns and rural regions, and down the social scale from the elite to the poor—marked a major transition in hygiene, making possible higher standards of personal cleanliness, less exhausting laundry procedures, and the sanitary disposal of human wastes. Americans also heeded the advice and warnings of early nineteenth-century reformers and sanitarians such as Catharine *Beecher and the New England educator William Alcott (1798–1859). The work of the United States Sanitary Commission and women volunteers during the *Civil War proved especially important in stimulating a national campaign for better personal hygiene. Since *disease killed more soldiers than guns or cannons, sanitarians effectively demonstrated that sanitation was the war's crucial weapon. By wrapping cleanliness in the mantle of victory and patriotism, they taught army doctors, soldiers, and loved ones on the homefront that poor personal hygiene, which led to rampant camp diseases, was a fearsome enemy.

Nevertheless, hygienic problems continued to threaten vast numbers of Americans and immigrants who flocked to industrializing cities after the war. In congested working-class neighborhoods, the health of these newcomers was clearly at risk as outbreaks of cholera, typhoid, and *yellow fever took a heavy toll. Through the combined efforts of *public-health reformers, city officials, *settlement houses, public-works engineers, teachers, and employers, immigrants and native-born migrants from the countryside learned the significance of personal hygiene—first to their health, then to their opportunities for upward *mobility.

By the 1920s, reformers concerned with immigrant *assimilation successfully made cleanliness a hallmark of being "American." But it was the producers of hygiene products and household cleaning appliances, for whom cleanliness meant profits, who persuaded American consumers to accept nothing less than perfection, to look for "the cleanest clean possible." Incessant *advertising appeals in magazines, on *radio, and later on *television created a culture of cleanliness that by the 1950s set Americans apart. With houses cleaner and bodies better groomed than ever before, cleanliness became an obsession. Dependence on daily showers, sensitivity to body odors, desire for immaculately clean houses, and preoccupation with teeth that gleamed distinguished Americans as a people.

During the mid-1960s, however, as more married women (traditionally the quintessential agents of cleanliness) entered the workforce, they spent less time at housecleaning, and most husbands chose not to pick up the slack. Environmentalists, feminists, and members of the counterculture for reasons of their own also turned their backs on what had become an obsession. Thus, by the mid-1990s, Americans were less likely to be swayed by the old rationales for chasing dirt, yet they still took delight in their daily showers, "natural" soaps, and luxurious bathrooms.

[*See also* Consumer Culture; Health and Fitness; Household Technology; Immigration; Mass Marketing; Slums; Technology; Urbanization.]

• Ruth Schwartz Cowan, *More Work for Mother,* 1983. Phyllis Palmer, *Domesticity and Dirt,* 1989. John Duffy, *The Sanitarians,* 1990. Marilyn Thornton Williams, *Washing "The Great Unwashed",* 1991. Vincent Vinikas, *Soft Soap, Hard Sell,* 1992. Suellen Hoy, *Chasing Dirt,* 1995.

—Suellen Hoy

I

ILLEGITIMACY. Historically, the term "illegitimacy" has referred to children born to unmarried females; "unwed motherhood" and "single pregnancy" have referred to unmarried, pregnant girls and women. In the United States, the social, cultural, and political significance of these terms has varied according to the race (and often the *social class) of the women and children involved.

In the seventeenth and eighteenth centuries, illegitimacy rates among white colonists varied over time and between colonies, but generally remained low, reflecting the strength of community and religious control over sexual and marital norms. Despite civil and religious punishment of fornicators, evidence from *New England colonies shows that unmarried women who became pregnant, and their children, stayed within their families of origin, and most of the women eventually married.

Down to the *Civil War, laws in slave-holding states forbade marriage for *African Americans, and slave owners regularly directed and coerced female slave procreation in order to increase the return on their investments. According to civil and church law, then, all slave children were "illegitimate." They were recognized and valued, however, within their own communities. After the Civil War, white illegitimacy rates began to rise, partly owing to *urbanization and *industrialization, both of which increased the ranks of women living outside the *family and community sphere. Among poor and working-class whites, the incidence of illegitimacy was similar to African-American rates. Contrary to a widespread misapprehension, definitive data indicate that northern migration between 1880 and 1920 did not shatter the black family: four out of five African-American children in northern urban communities lived in households where the father was present.

In the early decades of the twentieth century, "single pregnancy" emerged as a public-policy obsession: as the family, not the community, became the locus of social and sexual control, the newly atomized family was accused of policing its daughters poorly. Both black and white single pregnancy became a proxy for anxieties about urbanization, *immigration, and industrialization. Single pregnancy and illegitimacy were cast as environmental plagues.

Beginning in the late 1930s, black and white single pregnancies were treated as two distinct phenomena. As the children of some African-American women became eligible for Aid to Dependent Children grants, under the *Social Security Act of 1935, the attitude of the white tax-paying public toward these expenditures—and toward black "illegitimate" children and their mothers—turned increasingly hostile. In succeeding decades, with the emergence of the *civil rights movement, politicians mounted campaigns against unmarried, black, childbearing women and their children. These attacks drew on "suitable home" laws that targeted poor, African-American unmarried women as unfit to provide such an environment for their children. Attackers typically claimed that these women had babies simply to collect *welfare checks.

In these same years, experts redefined illegitimate pregnancy among white women as proof of neurosis. This perspective promised illegitimately pregnant whites that they could resume normative lives after the "cure": relinquishment of the child. By mid-century, it was more important for a white woman to appear sexually pure, whatever her real history, than to be so. The white illegitimate baby was redefined as well, cleared of the biologically based taint associated with the bastard child, and rendered a valuable commodity on the emergent adoption market.

With the *Supreme Court's legalization of *abortion in the 1973 **Roe* v. *Wade* decision, many women embraced another innovative idea: If a woman could decide whether or not to stay pregnant, surely she could also decide whether to be the mother of the child she gave birth to. This idea revolutionized the consequences of illegitimate pregnancy by dramatically diminishing the relinquishment of white babies for adoption. White unwed mothers from all socioeconomic classes began behaving more like unwed mothers-of-color; that is, they kept and raised their "illegitimate" children.

Soon after 1973, conservative policy-makers and others began to preach against single motherhood as a moral evil; agitate for the revival of the pejorative term "illegitimacy"; and claim that the country's social problems resulted from out-of-wedlock childbearing, chiefly by poor, minority teenagers. In the 1980s and 1990s, political debate centered on recrafting welfare policy as the most effective way to halt "illegitimacy." Critics of welfare reforms, however, argued that single childbearing had become a cross-class and cross-race phenomenon, largely unrelated to welfare or to income level. Sixty-five percent of the late-twentieth-century increase of single motherhood in the United States, they pointed out, was among women who were not poor. Observers did agree, however, that extreme *poverty, along with a lack of educational and employment opportunities, may push some young, unmarried women to have babies.

[*See also* Demography; Marriage and Divorce; Sexual Morality and Sex Reform; Slavery: Slave Families, Communities, and Culture.]

• Joyce Ladner, *Tomorrow's Tomorrow: The Black Women,* 1971. Herbert Gutman, *The Black Family in Slavery and Freedom, 1750–1925,* 1976. Constance A. Nathanson, *Dangerous Passage: The Social Control of Sexuality in Women's Adolescence,* 1991. Regina G. Kunzel, *Fallen Women, Problem Girls: Unmarried Mothers and the Professionalization of Social Work, 1890–1945,* 1993. Elaine Bell Kaplan, *Not Our Kind of Girl: Unraveling the Myths of Black Teenage Motherhood,* 1997. Rickie Solinger, *Wake Up Little Susie: Single Pregnancy and Race before* Roe *v.* Wade, rev. ed., 2000.

—Rickie Solinger

ILLUMINATION. Although lighting might appear a necessity, the perception of needs has changed radically since the *Colonial Era, when the expense of illumination restricted it to domestic use, and night and day were sharply demarcated. To light their homes, early Americans relied on tallow candles, floating tapers that burned assorted greases, and lamps that burned fuels such as lard and turpentine. Whale oil, cleaner but more expensive, was in such demand by the early nineteenth century that American whaling ships circled the globe.

Kerosene came into use after 1859, when oil production began in western Pennsylvania. Incandescent electric lighting based on Thomas *Edison's system became available in *New York City after 1882 but spread only gradually. In 1910, about 15 percent of all homes had electricity. By 1930 the level in cities topped 90 percent and reached 50 percent in the irrigated *West, but remained under 10 percent in other farm areas. New Deal programs completed rural electrification only after 1935.

In terms of outdoor illumination, colonials who ventured out at night carried torches or lanterns. Benjamin *Franklin organized the first public lighting in 1751, placing lanterns on *Philadelphia's streets. Gaslight was introduced in 1816, when Baltimore started making artificial gas from coal. By 1828, New York's Broadway was brilliantly illuminated with gas flares, giving rise to a new urban phenomenon, nightlife. During the 1840s, gasworks spread to medium-sized cities; by 1860, 183 urban gaslighting companies served both domestic and commercial customers.

Although natural gas was used to light several buildings in Fredonia, New York, as early as 1821, it was long ignored as a light source because of difficulties in delivering it to consumers. In the 1870s natural gas began to overtake manufactured gas in some areas, but electrification seized much of the market before pipelines could be developed. Charles Brush's powerful arc lights, in which an electric current flows between two carbon rods, were first displayed in 1878 in Cleveland, Ohio. Common in cities and at expositions for a generation, incandescent lighting was little used outdoors before about 1900. As electric lighting spread, Americans debated whether it should be a public or a private utility. *Boston, New York, and *Chicago opted for private power, but a minority of cities, notably Cleveland and *Los Angeles, did not.

Artificial illumination expanded the workday. Early factories closed at dusk, but as lighting improved and became less costly, investors realized that several shifts were possible. Gaslight, dangerous in cotton mills, was installed in newspaper offices and other venues. California gold mines adopted arc lighting in the 1870s, and after incandescent light proved safe for cotton and flour mills, it spread wherever visual acuity mattered. After about 1900, banks, offices, libraries, and schools installed artificial lighting. The age-old distinction between day and night eroded, especially during the 1940s, when wartime needs necessitated round-the-clock production.

Although incandescent lighting remained dominant, other forms of electric illumination appeared in the twentieth century. Neon lights, developed in France in 1911, found many commercial uses, adding color and variety to the urban scene. Fluorescent lights, another French invention (1867), became commercially available in the United States in 1938, enjoying great success since they used less electricity than incandescent bulbs while providing the same illumination. As the century ended, powerful mercury-vapor and sodium-vapor lights illuminated highways, city streets, and public venues, while small, high-intensity halogen bulbs proved popular for reading and other purposes requiring bright, concentrated illumination.

[*See also* Electrical Industry; Electricity and Electrification; Factory System; Leisure; New Deal Era, The; Petroleum Industry; Urbanization.]

• Wolfgang Schivelbusch, *Disenchanted Night: The Industrialization of Light in the Nineteenth Century,* 1988. David E. Nye, *Electrifying America: Social Meanings of a New Technology, 1880–1940,* 1990.

—David E. Nye

IMMIGRANT LABOR. At least since the 1840s, when *Irish-American workers replaced the native-born "factory girls" of Lowell, Massachusetts, immigrants have loomed large in the American working classes. This was especially true between 1880 and 1924, when 25 million immigrants arrived in the United States. Soon Europeans and their children outnumbered native-born Americans in factories, mines, steel mills, and automobile plants, while Mexicans, *Hispanic Americans, and *Asian Americans predominated in the agricultural fields of the *West. Foreign-born women staffed canneries, textile mills, and garment factories and worked as cooks and child-care providers for middle-class Americans. The history of American *labor movements during these years is a tale of both immigrant activism and ethnocultural struggle.

With emancipated slaves relegated to the declining agriculture of the *South, *immigration made possible the "Second Industrial Revolution" of the late nineteenth century. Irish, Chinese, Italian, Slavic, and Mexican migrants built the transportation network (first canals, then *railroads) essential to a national mass market. As immigrants became "machine-tenders" for the new *mass-production industries, native-born skilled workers sought to protect their standard of living against low-wage, unskilled competitors. Legislation restricting immigration—from the Chinese Exclusion Act of 1882 to the discriminatory Immigration Act of 1924—invariably won organized labor's support.

Ironically, first- and second-generation immigrants dominated the American labor movement of the *Gilded Age and *Progressive Era. Abandoning reformist strategies that tied the interests of wage earners to independent small producers, second-generation Irish Americans and *German Americans contributed to the rapid growth of the *American Federation of Labor (AFL). After 1900, immigrant women—mostly Irish, Italians, and eastern European Jews—joined with middle-class American feminists in the *Women's Trade Union League to launch a women's movement that created female strongholds in the International Ladies Garment Workers' Union, an industrial union founded (and dominated) by immigrant men.

Immigrants were even more visible as radical activists. Germans dominated the Socialist Labor party and remained prominent in the multiethnic *Socialist Party of America. The *Industrial Workers of the World, with its ideology of revolutionary syndicalism and "one big union," particularly attracted unskilled immigrant workers, many of them women, as it led huge strikes in the *textile and *mining industries just prior to *World War I. Into the 1930s, Finnish, Slavic, and eastern European Jewish immigrants figured prominently in the *Communist Party—USA.

Overall, however, World War I, with its demands for "100 percent Americanism," ended this era of immigrant labor activism. Deportations of radicals accompanied the postwar Red Scare, and nativist fears ended unrestrained immigration. By the 1930s, older immigrants in the AFL, along with second-generation immigrants in the steel and *automotive industries created the *Congress of Industrial Organizations (CIO). Although radicals remained active in some of its unions, the CIO promised Americanized children of immigrants incorporation into the American mainstream through the *New Deal Era welfare state and the *Democratic party.

The number of immigrants began to rise again in the mid-1960s, but even so, unskilled workers constituted a much lower proportion among immigrants than a century earlier. Cesar *Chavez's United Farm Workers publicized the plight of low-wage, seasonal, immigrant (and largely Mexican) workers in southwestern agriculture in the 1960s and 1970s. New garment-industry sweatshops employing Latina and Asian women in Miami, New York, and Los Angeles recalled the travails and organizing campaigns of past generations. However, with industry and agriculture dropping in importance as employers of labor, and with American labor unions only slowly emerging from a long period of decline in membership and political influence, immigrant workers seemed more marginalized than ever as the twentieth century ended.

[*See also* Agriculture: Since 1920; Anticommunism; Canals and Waterways; Domestic Labor; Homework; Immigration

Law; Industrialization; Iron and Steel Industry; Labor Markets; Migratory Agricultural Workers; Nativist Movement; Socialism; Twenties, The; Women in the Labor Force.]

• Dirk Hoerder, ed., *"Struggle a Hard Battle": Essays on Working-Class Immigrants*, 1986. Robert Asher and Charles Stephenson, eds., *Labor Divided: Race and Ethnicity in United States Labor Struggles, 1835–1960*, 1990.

—Donna R. Gabaccia

IMMIGRATION. International migration, as an aspect of the process of globalization, has been taking place on a large scale since 1500. For the European powers, North America, as well as Asia, Africa, Australasia, and South America, became a site of competing imperial ambition and capitalist enterprise. Imperialism required the voluntary and involuntary migrations of labor to exploit resources, build markets, transportation networks, and other infrastructures, and operate agricultural, commercial, and industrial establishments. Human migration, however, has never been solely an economic phenomenon; persecution, genocide, war, and famine have also stimulated it. Similarly, the familiar dichotomy of slave and free migrations is too simple. In the coerced category, one can distinguish among slaves, exiles, deported convicts, and refugees, while the voluntary category includes colonists, labor migrants, sojourners, adventurers, and entrepreneurs. America has received all of these.

While the earliest migrations, some 30,000 years ago across the land bridge from Asia, brought the ancestors of the indigenous inhabitants of the Americas (denoted "Indians" by Europeans), this essay focuses on the post-1500 migrants who crossed national borders from adjacent as well as from transoceanic countries. The Spanish planted St. Augustine, Florida in 1565 and established early settlements in the *Southwest several decades before the English arrived at *Jamestown in 1606. French, Dutch, Swedish/Finnish, and Russian colonists were eventually incorporated into the British colonies (and then the United States) by means of territorial conquest or purchase. Meanwhile, of the 12 million Africans brought in chains to the New World, some 450,000 landed in the British mainland colonies (and then the United States).

Because of differing policies of proprietors and joint stock companies, natural resources, and land-distribution systems, various British colonies attracted different mixes of immigrants. Organized migrations of co-religionists established the *New England colonies, homogeneous communities with a strong Puritan character. By contrast, the Middle Colonies attracted a polyglot, religiously diverse population, sometimes including even Roman Catholics and Jews. Land-hungry German Lutherans and pietists and Scots-Irish Presbyterians flocked to Pennsylvania, settling the back country as far south as Georgia. Although religious motives impelled a minority, most colonists aspired to improve their material conditions. The southern colonies, growing staple crops such as tobacco and indigo, initially recruited British indentured servants or imported convicts, but by the eighteenth century, African slaves, first introduced in Virginia in 1619, had become the major source of labor. Colonial immigration thus determined longlasting regional racial, ethnic, and social patterns within the original states and beyond.

Far from being a homogeneous Anglo-American population, colonial America was very diverse in culture, language, religion, and race. Of the 3.9 million persons enumerated in the first federal *census in 1790 (Indians were not counted), those of English stock comprised only 48 percent; 19 percent were of African ancestry; and another 12 percent were Scots and Scots-Irish. Germans accounted for 10 percent, with smaller numbers of French, Irish, Welsh, Dutch, and Swedes.

Reflecting this heterogeneity, The *Revolutionary War was in a sense, a civil war pitting certain groups against others, often along ethnic and religious lines. After the war, in the first of a number of *emigrations*, some eighty thousand Loyalists left for Canada and Britain. Having achieved independence, the leaders of the new republic faced the task of nation-building. Lacking deep roots in the soil and ancient ties of blood, they fashioned an American identity from Enlightenment doctrine of natural rights; one became an American by assent, not by descent. Such a conception of nationhood well suited a "nation of immigrants." The *Constitution alluded to immigration only indirectly: it provided that slave importation would not be prohibited prior to 1808, and it gave Congress the power to regulate foreign commerce. The latter underlay the judicial doctrine granting the federal government exclusive jurisdiction over immigration. Authorized by the Constitution to establish "an uniform rule of naturalization," Congress in 1790 defined the criteria for naturalization as two years' residence (subsequently changed to five years); good character; an oath to support the Constitution, and the renunciation of all foreign allegiances. These liberal requirements enabled millions of immigrants to become American citizens. Equally important, the United States adopted the principle that place of birth, not blood, determined nationality, native-born children of foreign parents were citizens by birthright. The 1790 law, however, also restricted naturalization to "free white person[s]" making the racial test of "whiteness" essential to American citizenship. In 1870, during *Reconstruction, Congress extended the privilege of naturalization to "aliens of African nativity and to persons of African descent," but in 1882 the Chinese Exclusion Act explicitly excluded Chinese immigrants from citizenship. Only the Immigration and Nationality Act of 1952 finally removed all racial bars to citizenship.

Between 1790 and 1820, as war interrupted transatlantic commerce, only 1 million immigrants arrived. Immigration grew slowly thereafter, surpassing a million in the decade of the 1840s as canal and railroad projects, *mining and *lumbering, urban construction, and western land settlement created an insatiable demand for labor. Meanwhile, a more than doubling of Europe's population in the nineteenth century and the disruption of traditional livelihoods by the industrial revolution displaced millions of peasants and artisans. Not a desire for change, but a need to escape radical social and economic transformations, impelled many immigrants. They hoped in America to conserve their customary ways of life. Meanwhile burgeoning transoceanic commerce, resulting in regular and improved shipping (steamships were introduced by the 1840s), facilitated the migration process. Immigration became an integral part of an Atlantic economy involving the exchange of capital, commodities, and labor.

From the 1840s on, recurring waves of immigration brought some sixty million persons to America. But the volume of immigration has varied, with peaks and valleys reflecting economic and political conditions in both the United States and the sending countries. *Business cycles, famines, persecutions, wars, and migration policies on both ends of the migration process affected the volume and direction of migrations. Mostly voluntary immigrants, the newcomers chose when to leave, how to travel, and where to go. Individual migrants were atypical; families and even communities usually made collective decisions and departed together. Once established, the immigrants called on relatives and friends to join them. Thus international networks linked specific villages in Europe with settlements in the United States. The lure of America was exerted not only by the advertising of shipping companies, land speculators, and state agencies, but even more by the "America letters" from those who had already come.

The history of American mass immigration falls into four periods. During the first (1840–1890) almost 15 million arrived (over 4 million Germans, 3 million Irish, another 3 million British, and a million Scandinavians). The second period (1891–1920) brought an additional 18-plus million (almost 4

MAP 9: MAP PREPARED FOR GERMAN EMIGRANTS TO NORTH AMERICA

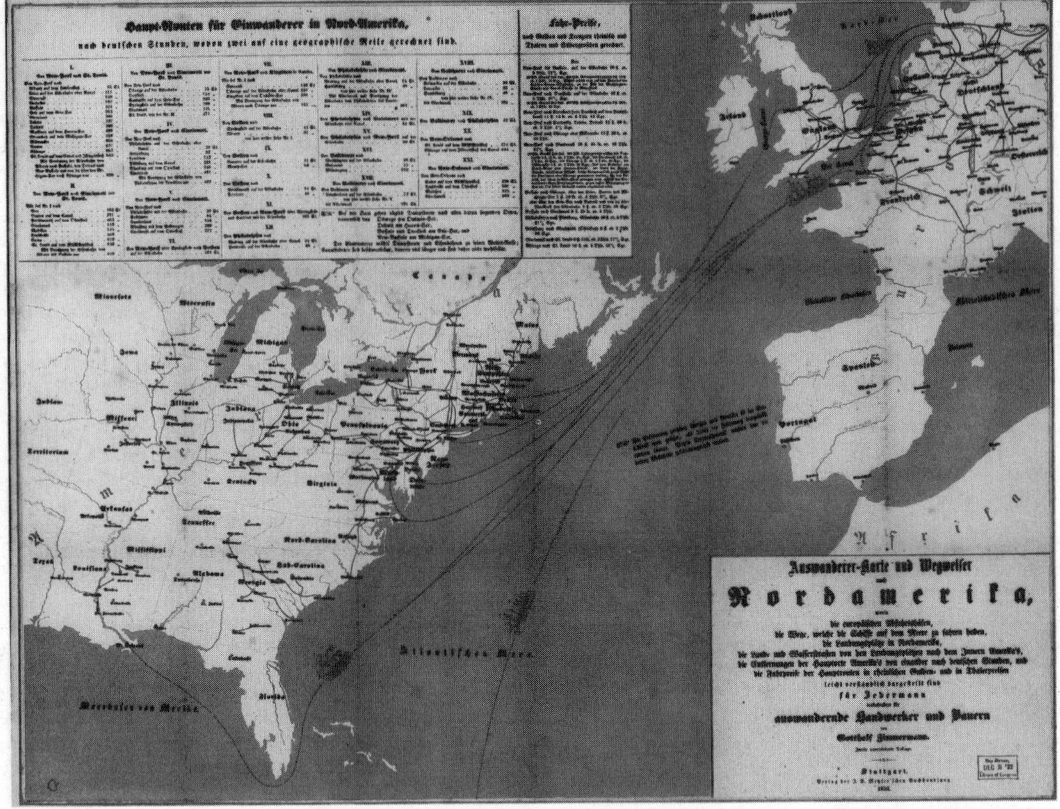

Germans contemplating emigration to the United States gained a wealth of information from this 1853 map, including major steamship routes and travel connections and railway ticket prices (converted into German thalers) from New York to such centers of German settlement as Cincinnati, Milwaukee, and St. Louis. From 1820 to 1900, more than 5 million German immigrants came to the United States.

[*See* German Americans; Immigrant Labor; Immigration; Immigration Law.]

million from Italy, 3.6 million from Austria-Hungary, and 3 million from Russia). In the third period (1920–1960), only 7.5 million immigrants (including many Mexicans) arrived—a decline reflecting restrictive U.S. immigration policies, economic *depressions, and wars hot and cold. The ongoing fourth period, which began in the 1960s accounted for approximately 20 million immigrants by 2000, of whom some 24 percent were from Mexico, another 24 percent from Central and South America and the Caribbean, and 35 percent from Asia. While almost 90 percent of immigrants of the first three periods originated in Europe, only 10 percent of the fourth period did.

1840–1890. During this expansive period, the United States admitted all comers with few restrictions. British immigrants, English-speaking and Protestant, were readily absorbed. While the Welsh, Scots, and Scots-Irish immigrants initially organized their own settlements, societies, and churches, they gradually merged into a British-American ethnicity, strengthening the emerging definition of the American as white, Anglo-Saxon, and Protestant. Although some established agricultural and utopian colonies, British tradesmen and industrial workers tended to settle in the urban centers of the East. The British often occupied managerial and skilled labor positions in such emerging industries as *mining, steel making, and textiles. Experienced in trade unionism, they provided leadership for the emerging American labor movement.

While Irish Catholic emigration began well before and continued long after the famine years of the 1840s, it was the more than 1 million fugitives from the "Great Hunger" who established the negative stereotype of the Irish immigrant as pauperized and disease-ridden. Few of the Irish chose to become farmers, preferring the cities and towns of the East and *Middle West. Some were craftsmen, but most held low-paid, dirty, and often dangerous jobs, as railroad and construction laborers, miners, and factory hands. From the 1860s, females, often single young women, predominated among the Irish immigrants. Many worked as domestic servants, textile hands, and seamstresses, sending money back to their families or to bring relatives to America.

Like the British, the Irish figured prominently in establishing trade unions. They also brought modes of resistance that had been used against landlords: sabotage and assassination. In the 1870s, the "Molly Maguires" conducted a campaign of violence against the mining companies in Pennsylvania's anthracite region. The Irish quickly demonstrated talent for American politics; the saloon keeper became an important agent for mobilizing Irish voters. By 1900, many mayors of northern cities and the majority of their policemen and firemen were of Irish origin.

Irish immigration made *Roman Catholicism a major force in America. Among the Irish themselves, the Church exerted political as well as spiritual leadership. The parish became synonymous with the community, and the priest the acknowledged authority. Irish immigrants had suffered religious as well as economic persecution at the hands of the British, and Catholicism became inextricably intertwined with Irish-American ethnicity.

Their Catholicism also subjected the Irish to fierce religious prejudice. The nativist movement that culminated in the *Know-Nothing party of the 1850s sought to exclude the Irish from political life and even from the country. The Irish suffered verbal abuse in Protestant churches and the U.S. Congress, and physical violence on city streets. *Anti-Catholicism remained a major theme of American nativism well into the twentieth century.

Objects of bigotry, *Irish Americans, ironically, became major antagonists of other racial groups. Competing with blacks for jobs, the Irish sought to achieve the privileges of "whiteness" by venting their hostility toward *African Americans. Irish workers also figured prominently in the anti-Chinese movement in *California and displayed hostility toward later immigrants from southern and eastern Europe. Nurturing memories of colonial oppression, Irish Americans reserved their deepest hatred for the British. Their support of Irish liberation movements extended from the 1850s to the 1990s. Irish-American ethnic nationalism, symbolized by the celebration of St. Patrick's Day, fused Catholicism, nostalgia for the "auld sod," and bitterness for injuries inflicted by Anglo-Americans.

Ethnic Germans (often espousing provincial identities as Bavarians, Pomeranians, and so forth) constituted the largest group of European immigrants, totaling over 6 million. Unlike the Irish, religion was not as unifying a force for German immigrants, who included Roman Catholics, Protestants (Lutheran and Reformed), Jews, and Free Thinkers. German-American ethnicity was thus largely "invented" in the United States, following the creation of the German empire in 1870. More than most immigrant groups, German immigrants came from various ranks of society, with merchants, professionals, artisans, skilled workers, and farmers well represented, along with a cultural elite of intellectuals and artists. Within "Little Germanies" in Cincinnati, St. Louis, Milwaukee, *Chicago, and other cities, Germans established clubs, churches, schools, and beer gardens, as well as newspapers, symphony orchestras, choral societies, and literary circles. Unlike other immigrant groups, German immigrants were not intimidated by American culture; indeed, many viewed their culture and language as superior to that of the uncouth Americans. Their attitude, plus beer drinking and boisterous singing, particularly on Sundays, antagonized Anglo-Americans. Conflicts over cultural issues such as Sabbatarianism, *temperance, and German-language schools long plagued German-Anglo relationships.

German immigrants were also denounced as dangerous radicals. Many "48ers" (veterans of the 1848 revolutions in Europe) and their Turnvereins (cultural and athletic clubs) did indeed profess radical republicanism and atheism. Some espoused Marxist *socialism and *anarchism. German immigrants established strong labor unions and socialist organizations modeled after those in Germany. The 1886 *Haymarket affair in Chicago resulted in the supression of the German-led anarchist movement and fixed in the minds of many Americans the image of the immigrant radical as a wild eyed bomb thrower. Recurring "Red Scares" based on such fears became yet another theme of American nativism.

Many German and Scandinavian immigrants shunned urban industrial areas for the rich and affordable farmlands of the Middle West. Arriving in family groups, often coming from the same localities, they settled large contiguous areas. Ethnic maps of rural America resembled patchwork quilts. While they adjusted to new crops, farming methods, agricultural markets, and environmental conditions, their relative isolation enabled them to maintain their cultures and languages over several generations. The church, whether Catholic or Lutheran, played a central role as community center as well as place of worship. But the lure of city lights attracted the youth, and urban migration gradually eroded the demographic base of these German and Scandinavian settlements.

Two other sources of immigration figured significantly in this first period: China and Canada. Although Chinese immigrants numbered only some 200,000, the reaction they elicited influenced U.S. immigration policy for a century. Initially drawn by the Gold Rush of 1849, Chinese workers in the *West provided an important labor supply for building the transcontinental railroad, mining, and *agriculture. Sojourners like many Europeans, these predominantly male immigrants came to make money and return home. The objects of vicious stereotypes depicting them as morally degenerate pagans, they were subjected to riots, *lynchings, and legal restrictions. Supported by many European immigrants and labor unions, the anti-Chinese movement gained national dimensions, culminating in the Chinese Exclusion Act of 1882. Erecting a racial barrier to immigration, this precedent-setting law was subsequently extended by law and judicial decisions to Asians generally.

Emigration from Canada, often slighted in accounts of U.S. immigration history, has been highly important, totaling over three million. Of these, some two-thirds were Anglo-Canadians who quickly blended into the larger American population. However, the other third, the French-Canadians, had a distinctive history and influence. In the province of Quebec, a peasantry with large families and few resources increasingly migrated to the mill towns of New England. Because the *textile industry employed women and children, this was a family migration. Strong kinship ties, proximity to places of origin, and the French language made the Quebecois resistant to assimilation. The Catholic Church's structure of parishes, parochial schools, and benefit societies represented another powerful cohesive force. For this colonized group subject to Anglo-Protestant domination, Catholicism became, as it did for Irish Catholics, a core element of Franco-American ethnicity.

1891–1930. These decades witnessed a level of immigration matched only by that of the late twentieth century. In several years, the annual total exceeded one million. In 1900, almost 14 percent of the U.S. population was foreign born; with their American-born children, immigrant families acccounted for over a third of the total population. In the succeeding decades, the "foreign" element grew ever larger and more diverse. Before the 1890s, most immigrants came from northern and western Europe, thereafter, eastern and southern Europeans predominated: Italians, eastern European Jews, and Slavs. This shift reflected the movement eastward of European industrial and agricultural *capitalism. Finns, Slovaks, and Greeks now migrated for reasons similar to those that had earlier uprooted Norwegians, Irish, and Germans: modernization was undermining time-honored forms of work and life. However, owing to improved transportation and differing aspirations, the post-1890s immigrants were much more likely than their predecessors to be temporary sojourners. Like the Chinese, they wanted to earn dollars and return home to buy land. For this reason, the southern and eastern European immigration was overwhelming male (the Finns were an exception). If they decided to remain, as many did, they sent for wives, brides, and children. The rate of return varied by nationality, but was often over 50 percent. Many immigrants made multiple trips back and forth across the Atlantic. The exceptions were Jews and Armenians fleeing religious and ethnic persecution.

This vast immigration also reflected the labor demands of an expansive, if volatile, American economy. *Industrialization and *urbanization required workers, skilled and unskilled. Few of the post-1890s immigrants became farmers; they sought out the cities, factory towns, and mining and lumber camps offering immediate wages. With few exceptions, these immigrants bypassed the still largely agrarian *South. Southern and eastern European immigrants for the most part entered the labor force as common laborers. Not only did employers consider them less desirable, but the Germans, Irish, and British who had preceded them (as well as old-stock Americans) resisted their entry into the skilled trades and trade unions. Though partly motivated by fear of labor competition, such discrimination also expressed prejudice against southern and eastern European "races" who were not truly "white men" but "black labor."

Although denounced as strikebreakers and wage cutters (which on occasion they were), the southern and eastern Europeans generally proved amenable to labor organization. Many in fact had been involved in socialist and anarchist movements, and participated in strikes and protests, in their home countries. When admitted into unions such as the United Mine Workers or the United Packinghouse Workers, Slavs, Lithuanians, and Hungarians demonstrated strong solidarity. Jews and Italians, excluded from craft unions, formed industrial unions in the clothing and textile industries. Eastern and southern European immigrants were in the forefront of early-twentieth-century labor struggles, and they and their children formed the backbone of what became the *Congress of Industrial Organizations (CIO) in the 1930s.

Some East European Jews and Italians dispersed throughout the country; the former often as peddlers and merchants; the latter as miners and in agriculture. Most, however, initially concentrated in Manhattan, Jews on the Lower East Side, the Italians in East Harlem. Migrants from the shtetls of Poland, Lithuania, and Russia, and the paesi of Sicily, Calabria, and Campania, they clustered in tenements with their townspeople. Orthodox Jews eager to observe their religion formed shuls and landsmanshaften and patronized kosher butchers and grocers. A large and important segment, however, was secular and socialist. Active in politics and labor activities, they sponsored bunds, theaters, newspapers, and discussions clubs. Many men and women were tailors and seamstresses, peddlers and small shopkeepers. Entreprenurial and thirsty for education, the second generation tended to move into business or the professions. These Yiddish-speaking Jews had a difficult relationship with the more established German Jews who feared a growth of *anti-Semitism because of the newcomers' exotic appearance and behavior. Religious, cultural, and political differences, including Zionism, divided Jewish immigrants, old and new, into numerous conflicting camps.

Internal divisions based on regional and local origins plagued the Italians even more. Membership in mutual benefit societies was often limited to those from the same paese. Among the Italians, family loyalties were so intense and exclusive that they created few other institutions. Although nominally Roman Catholics, even their religious piety focused upon the local patron saint whose annual festa was the year's high point. Their alleged religious "indifference" attracted Protestant proselitizers and the disdain of ardent Irish Catholics. Like the Jews, many Italians were radicals (particularly syndicalists and anarchists) and free thinkers. They were militant, active in the *Industrial Workers of the World, and some anarchists resorted to violence. Most Italian immigrants remained unmoved by Italian nationalism. However, patriotic passions aroused by *World War I evolved into a filio-fascism that, despite the opposition of an anti-fascist minority, dominated Italian-American communities into the 1930s.

Beginning as unskilled laborers on the *railroads and in mines and factories, few Italian Americans rose to the level of skilled workers. Exceptions were those with trades such as stone cutters, tailors, and barbers. Others engaged in petty commerce, providing goods and services in the Little Italies. The children normally left school at an early age. The second generation remained largely proletarian, although many moved into the ranks of skilled blue-collar workers. For Italian Americans, the breakthrough into the middle class was largely a post-World War II phenomenon.

Among the millions of Slavic immigrants from the German, Russian, and Austro-Hungarian empires, Poles were the most numerous. Largely unschooled peasants, they, too, entered the ranks of unskilled labor. Poles, however, valued by employers for their brawn and reliability, were largely employed in heavy industry: coal mining, meat packing, steel making, and automobile manufacturing. Unlike the Italian and Jewish women who worked in sweatshops and tenements, Polish women more often were employed as domestics and factory hands. Densely populated "Poletowns," dotting the industrial heartland from Cleveland to Chicago and south to Pittsburgh, provided an environment in which Polishness prevailed. Dominated by Germans or Russians since Poland's partition in the eighteenth century, Polish immigrants shared the Irish sense of being a colonial people and similarly found a source of identity and resistance in the Catholic Church. Community and parish were congruent, and within both the priest was the accepted leader.

The immigrants' Polish and Catholic identities sometimes

clashed, however, resulting, for example, in the formation of rival fraternal organizations, one nationalist, the other religious. Opposition to control by an Irish-American Catholic hierarchy gave rise to bitter conflicts and even a schismatic Polish National Catholic Church. World War I catalyzed Polish-American nationalism, and contributed greatly to Poland's reunification.

The tide of new immigrants evoked anxieties among Anglo-Americans and calls for greater immigration restriction. To the fears of Roman Catholicism and immigrant radicalism was now added the menace of biological pollution. In the late nineteenth century, "scientific" racialism based on *eugenics and an assumed hierarchy of races (Nordics being the superior race) became a major tenet of Anglo-American nationalism, justifying imperialism abroad and immigration restriction at home. The influx of southern and eastern Europeans of supposedly inferior racial stock triggered a nativist campaign against "undesirable and dangerous immigrants."

Already in 1882, along with entrance requirements (the Chinese Exclusion Act), a second law had established health and moral standards for admission. In 1890, New York's *Ellis Island became a federal immigrant-receiving station to screen immigrants arriving in steerage. The Immigration Restriction League, founded in Boston in 1894, and the *American Federation of Labor called for even stricter immigration laws.

World War I intensified the anti-immigrant climate, with demands for "One Hundred Percent Americanism" and attacks upon "hyphenated Americans." While this patriotic hysteria focused on *German-Americans, all foreigners became suspect. Linguistic and other aspects of ethnicity were suppressed or monitored by authorities and vigilante organizations. In this atmosphere, the nativist agenda prevailed. Wartime laws against "seditious" organizations, publications, and expressions were aimed particularly at immigrant radicals who opposed the war. Domestic labor strife and Bolshevism abroad further fueled the 1919–1920 "Red Scare" leading to the imprisonment of thousands of immigrants and the deportation of hundreds. The eugenic argument loomed especially large in public discussions and congressional debates. The immigration law of 1921 and the 1924 National Origins Acts allocated quotas according to the criteria of allegedly superior and inferior "races," favoring "Nordics" over "Alpines" and "Mediterraneans" and totally excluding Asians. These statutes sought to protect the genetic character of the American people from foreign contamination.

The debate over immigration involved no less than the issue of what America was to become. Americans differed on the issue. Countering the xenophobia of the restrictionists, proponents of a liberal immigration policy cited Christian and democratic ideals of universal brotherhood and quoted Emma Lazarus's 1883 sonnet "The New Colossus," enshrined on the *Statue of Liberty, portraying the United States as an asylum for the oppressed. During much of the nineteenth century, Americans had generally believed that by some alchemy immigrants would be melded into a common national identity. Israel Zangwill's play *The Melting Pot* (1909) provided the metaphor for this assimilationist ideology. However, the war and its aftermath caused many to question whether the world's "wretched refuse" could be transformed into worthy citizens. Others, including Horace Kallen and Randolph *Bourne, had an antithetical vision, espousing what was called *cultural pluralism. However, during the 1920s hardline Americanizers held the upper hand, and coercive Americanization programs demanded total Anglo conformity.

1930–1960. During these three decades, only 7.5 million immigrants arrived, most after 1945. World War I, by interrupting transatlantic migration and creating an urgent demand for labor, had stimulated two alternative intracontinental migrations: *African Americans from the rural south to the industrial north, and Mexicans from south of the border. (The National Origins Act did not apply to the Western Hemisphere.) Mexicans had long found employment in the agricultural fields and mines of the Southwest, but they now moved further afield, to work on the railroads and in the packing houses of the Midwest, establishing barrios in cities along the paths of migration. With the onset of the Depression of the 1930s, however, the government instituted a program of forced repatriation, sending hundreds of thousands, including native-born citizens, "home" to Mexico. Mexico continued to supply a "reserve army of labor" for American industry and agriculture, however. Federal agencies encouraged Mexican workers with the *World War II bracero program, and then reinstituted mass deportations in the 1950s.

The Depression ended a century of increasing, if fluctuating, immigration. In some years during the 1930s, thanks to both widespread unemployment and strict enforcement of the quota system, more persons left than entered the country. Even Jewish and other refugees desperately seeking asylum from fascist regimes were denied admission, partly due to a virulent anti-Semitism.

The thirties brought both heightened ethnic and racial conflict, as organized hate groups mimicked Europe's fascists, but also a blooming cultural democracy. In literature, the arts and popular culture, celebrated American diversity. In *The Native's Return* (1934) and other writings, the Austrian immigrant Louis Adamic popularized the idea that immigrants were as fully American as those whose ancestors had arrived at Plymouth Rock.

The outbreak of World War II further limited traditional sources of immigration and led to a campaign of national unity under the slogan "Americans All." Immigrants and their descendants with few exceptions supported the war effort through military service and work in defense industries. Compared to World War I, this war saw less persecution of suspected "enemy aliens" with one major exception: the confinement of some 112,000 Japanese Americans, including the American-born, in concentration camps, a policy clearly based on racial prejudice.

With the end of World War II came the *Cold War and an upsurge of *anti-communism that would influence American immigration policy for half a century. Some post-1945 efforts were made to resettle millions of European refugees, but Congress belatedly admitted only a modest number of these displaced persons. It became a principle of America's Cold War immigration policy to admit persons fleeing communist regimes, while excluding those escaping from sometimes brutal right wing dictatorships. Thus Hungarians, Czechs, Cubans after Fidel Castro's rise to power, and Jews from the Soviet Union received preferential treatment. Cold War immigration policy also concentrated on deporting, denying visas to, or seizing the passports of persons who allegedly had "subversive" ideas or associations. Paul *Robeson, W. E. B. *Du Bois, Charlie *Chaplin, Bertrand Russell, and many others fell afoul of these policies. The Immigration and Naturalization (McCarren-Walter) Act of 1952 embodied this anti-communist bias. While eliminating the racialist constraints on immigration and naturalization, the law perpetuated the national origins system. It also included special provisions for screening out "subversives" and deporting immigrants—even those who became U.S. citizens—who belonged to suspected communist organizations.

1960–2000. The 1960s brought many changes in American society, including rejection of the "melting pot" ideal and the affirmation of particularistic identities, initially by African Americans, then by other racial and ethnic groups. This process of ethnicization, a revolt against Anglo-American conformity and dominance, affirmed the survival, despite assimilationist pressures, of cultural memories, forms, and communities stemming from the great migrations of the past. Native Americans, Chicanos, *Asian Americans, and European descent groups (labeled "white ethnics"), celebrated their distinctive heritages and mobilized politically. Such manifestations of ethnicity among second and third generation European Americans, thought to have been thoroughly assimilated, surprised scholars and policy-makers.

After the 1970s, the ideology of "multiculturalism," celebrating racial and ethnic differences, proved profoundly influential, but also encountered vigorous opposition from political and religious champions of "traditional values." The resulting "culture wars" were exacerbated by an explosive growth in immigration in the wake of the Immigration Act of 1965, which radically altered the rules for entry. This law eliminated the national-origins quota system and instead established preferences favoring relatives of U.S. citizens or of resident aliens, persons with particular skills and talents, and refugees from communist countries or the Middle East. The law's annual caps on immigration were soon exceeded because of the principle of family reunification and special provisions for refugees. While legal immigration surged, exceeding 800,000 a year by the 1990s, an estimated several hundred thousand undocumented immigrants filtered through the country's porous borders annually. Not since early in the century had immigrants arrived in such numbers, totaling as many as twenty million from 1970 to 2000. Responding to growing concerns, Congress passed measures designed to curb illegal immigration, but did not alter the generous immigration policy established in 1965.

By opening America's gates to the world, the 1965 act reversed the historical pattern of a predominantly European immigration. The great majority of post-1965 immigrants—more than 80 per cent of the total—arrived from Asia and Latin America, with Mexicans, Chinese, Filipinos, and Koreans among the largest contingents. Increasing numbers also arrived from Central America, the Caribbean, the Middle East, and Africa.

The post-1965 immigration shook the American kaleidoscope, producing a dramatic reconfiguration of ethnicities. The range of skin hues expanded (some called it "browning of America"); the country's linguistic, musical, and culinary repertoire grew; and new forms of worship enriched the religious spectrum. The umbrella labels "Hispanic" and "Asian" marked an extraordinary diversity; Spanish-speaking immigrants included several million each of Puerto Ricans (who are U.S. citizens), Mexicans, and Caribbean islanders, while Chinese, Filipino, Korean, Asian Indian, and Southeast Asian (Vietnamese, Cambodians, Hmong, and Laotians) immigrant groups each totalled a million or more. A less noted influx brought several million Arabic, Persian and African speakers from Lebanon, Jordan, Syria, Iran, Nigeria, Somalia, and Ethiopia. With perhaps 3 million Muslims, and 500,000 each of Buddhists and Hindus, the familiar "Protestant-Catholic-Jewish" triad no longer adequately described the American religious scene.

While in certain respects these newest immigrants resembled those of past eras, they also displayed striking differences. Rather than being concentrated in the bottom economic strata, the foreign-born were now conspicuously present at all levels. Many, with education and technical, professional, or business skills, integrated smoothly into upper- and middle-class American life residing in ethnically diverse suburbs.

But immigrants of rural or working-class backgrounds experienced greater adjustment difficulties and sought security among their own kind. At the bottom of the ethnic-class hierarchy, they competed with disadvantaged native-born Americans for jobs, housing, and *welfare benefits. In fact, the availability of cheap Asian and Hispanic labor resulted in a revival of sweatshops in manufacturing. Since the economy no longer needed armies of workers to build railroads, mine coal, and tend machines, they often found traditional entry-level jobs unavailable. In many respects, their experience mirrored that of the Europeans who had preceded them. Families and clans settled in particular locations, creating new ethnic neighborhoods with specialty food shops, churches, temples, mosques, cultural centers, and publications. Constructing new ethnic identities, they created self-help and political organizations. And, as before, ethnic animosities and generational conflicts made the process of adjustment painful and tortuous.

While the cumulative impact of some 20 million post-1965 immigrants had profound implications for the nation's future, grim forebodings about an "unprecedented immigrant invasion" seemed exaggerated. The *rate* of immigration (the number of immigrants as a percentage of the total population) which was 10 per thousand in the 1900s, registered only 3.5 per thousand in the 1980s. While the number of foreign born reached an all-time high by 2000, they accounted for only 10 percent of the population, as compared with 14.7 percent in 1910. In short, the statistical impact of late-twentieth-century immigration was much smaller than that of the past.

Still, fears aroused by the newcomers—their color, languages, and cultures, as well as their numbers—spawned a neo-nativist reaction. While eschewing explicit racialism, advocates of immigration restriction expressed anxiety that the immigrants posed a threat to the homogeneity of the United States. Projecting immigration and birth rates forward, some demographers predicted that "minorities" (persons of American Indian, African, Asian, and Hispanic ancestry) would make up more than half of the American population by 2050 and that the United States would cease to be a predominantly white society.

The 1990 U.S. Census underscored the reality of ethnic diversity in America of the nineties. The 90 percent who responded to a question about ancestry or ethnic origin were classified into 215 ancestry groups. The largest was German, followed by Irish, English, and Afro-American; next came Italian, Mexican, French, Polish, American Indian, Dutch, and Scotch-Irish; another 21 groups accounted for over a million each, and even many smaller groups had sizeable representations: Maltese, Basque, Rom, Windish, Paraguayan, Belizian, Guyanese, Yemini, Khmer, and Micronesian, among others. Like glacial terminal moraines, these population groups represented deposits resulting from four centuries of immigration.

Bilingualism became a lightning rod for nativist anxieties in the 1990s. Some deplored school bilingual programs and the use of foreign languages in official documents as a threat to the nation's cultural and political integrity and lobbied for a constitutional amendment making English America's official language. Innocent of the country's linguistic history, proponents of this reform asserted that earlier immigrants had speedily and gladly Anglicized, and that new immigrants must do likewise. Proponents of bilingualism responded that coerced linguistic conformity violated the rights of non-English speakers and was in any case unnecessary, given the overwhelming dominance of English. The struggle over language, symptomatic of broader ideological and political conflict, seemed sure to continue.

Despite the neo-nativism, the newcomers generally received a more cordial welcome than had Japanese or Greeks at the turn of the century. In contrast to earlier eras' laissez-faire attitude, public programs and voluntary agencies provided assistance and social services to newcomers. Further, federal policies and *Supreme Court decisions regarding bilingualism, voting rights, and *affirmative action legitimized ethnic pluralism. Multiculturalism, a loosely defined movement to make American culture and institutions fully representative of the country's increasing diversity, influenced popular consciousness. While *racism and xenophobia persisted, Americans in 2000 appeared more accepting and even appreciative of racial and ethnic differences. What would happen if massive immigration continued (particularly, if the booming economy of the 1990s turned bad) or if fears of biological or ideological contamination revived, remained to be seen.

[*See also* Agriculture; Americanization Movement; Anti-Catholic Movement; Canals and Waterways; Erie Canal;

Exploration, Conquest, and Settlement, Era of European; Hispanic Americans; Immigrant Labor; Immigration Law; Indentured Servitude; Italian Americans; Judaism; Labor Markets; Labor Movements; Language, American; Lutheranism; Migrant Agricultural Workers; Polish Americans; Poverty; Protestantism; Puerto Rico; Scandinavian Americans; Slavery; Social Class; Race and Ethnicity; Race, Concept of; Urbanization.]

• John Higham, *Strangers in the Land: Patterns of American Nativism, 1860–1925,* 1963. David Reimers, *Still the Golden Door: The Third World Comes to America,* 1985. Gary R. Mormino and George Pozzetta, *The Immigrant World of Ybor City: Italians and Their Latin Neighbors in Tampa, 1885–1985,* 1987. Virginia Yans-McLaughlin, ed., *Immigration Reconsidered,* 1990. Roger Daniels, *Coming to America: A History of Immigration and Ethnicity in American Life,* 1991. Rudolph J. Vecoli and Suzanne M. Sinke, eds., *A Century of European Migrations, 1830–1930,* 1991. Kathleen Neils Conzen, David Gerber, Ewa Morawska, George E. Pozzetta, and Rudolph J. Vecoli, "The Invention of Ethnicity: A Perspective from the USA," and comments by Herbert J. Gans and Lawrence Fuchs, *Journal of American Ethnic History* 12 (Fall 1992): 3–63. Donna R. Gabaccia, ed., *Seeking Common Ground: Multidisciplinary Studies of Immigrant Women in the United States,* 1992. Philip Gleason, *Speaking of Diversity: Language and Ethnicity in Twentieth-Century America,* 1992. Jon Gjerde, *The Minds of the West: Ethnocultural Evolution in the Rural Middle West, 1830–1917,* 1997. Jan Lucassen and Leo Lucassen, eds., *Migration, Migration History, History: Old Paradigms and New Perspectives,* 1997. Matthew Frye Jacobson, *Whiteness of a Different Color: European Immigrants and the Alchemy of Race,* 1998.

—Rudolph J. Vecoli

IMMIGRATION LAW. As early as 1798, the *Alien and Sedition Acts provided for the deportation of enemy aliens and imposed a fourteen-year residency requirement for U.S. citizenship. In general, however, early Congressional oversight of *immigration was slight. The Steerage Act of 1819 directed ship captains to present lists of arriving passengers, and an 1855 law required that these rosters distinguish permanent immigrants from visitors. State laws relating to immigration were struck down by the U.S. *Supreme Court as infringements of Congress's power to regulate foreign commerce. In 1849, for example, the Court voided New York and Massachusetts laws that taxed arriving passengers to cover the costs of caring for indigent immigrants.

Congress's first direct control of immigration came in 1875, when it barred criminals and prostitutes. The Chinese Exclusion Act (1882), a response to native-born workers' complaints of job competition, suspended for ten years the immigration of Chinese laborers. The exclusion became permanent in 1904. The Immigration Act of 1882 established a system of immigration control under the secretary of the treasury. Congress subsequently barred numerous "undesirables," including lunatics, beggars, persons with contagious diseases, and advocates of political violence. To identify such persons, officials conducted interviews and medical examinations at New York's *Ellis Island and other entry points.

In 1907, as *San Francisco prepared to segregate Japanese and other Asian schoolchildren, President Theodore *Roosevelt averted an international incident by negotiating the so-called Gentlemen's Agreement by which Japan reaffirmed a 1900 pledge to bar Japanese laborers from emigrating to America. That same year, amid rising anti-immigrant sentiment, Congress created a Joint Commission on Immigration, popularly called the Dillingham Commission. Its 1911 report, reflecting contemporary assumptions about innate ethnic differences, found the recent wave of southern and eastern European immigrants generally inferior to the northern and western European immigrants of earlier eras. In 1915, culminating a long campaign, Congress passed over President Woodrow *Wilson's veto a *literacy requirement for immigrants.

As immigration resumed after *World War I, Congress imposed the first numerical limits. The Quota Law of 1921 restricted annual immigration to approximately 350,000 persons. To reduce immigration from southern and eastern Europe, this law limited annual immigration from any one nation to 3 percent of the number of foreign-born persons from that country living in America in 1910. The Immigration Act of 1924, while imposing even stricter and more discriminatory temporary restrictions, provided that, beginning in 1927, annual immigration by the end of the decade would be permanently limited to approximately 150,000, to be distributed proportionately to the ethnic composition of the U.S. population in 1920. The law also excluded Asians entirely.

Immigration from the Western Hemisphere, left largely unregulated by the 1924 law, was restricted by U.S. officials during the Great Depression of the 1930s under a provision barring persons "likely to become a public charge." In 1943, however, responding to wartime labor shortages, Congress permitted the recruitment of temporary agricultural workers from Mexico and other Latin American nations. This *bracero* (farmworker) program continued until 1964.

In the 1930s, U.S. immigration laws were intepreted strictly to exclude all but a handful of Jewish and other victims of Nazi persecution. *World War II and its aftermath brought some relaxation of immigration policies, however. In 1943, to counter Japanese propaganda about American *racism, the United States granted China an annual quota of 105 visas. The Displaced Persons Act of 1948, extending a policy inaugurated by President Harry S. *Truman in 1945, authorized the annual admission of 205,000 persons displaced by the war. In 1950, Congress raised the total to 415,744.

The Immigration and Nationality Act of 1952 (the McCarren-Walter Act), passed over Truman's veto, removed the ban on Asian immigration but retained the discriminatory national-quota system. (This *Cold War measure also barred "subversives" and authorized the deportation of immigrants who joined "Communist and Communist-front" organizations, even if they were U.S. citizens.) Amid mounting criticism, the McCarren-Walter Act was amended in 1965 to end, after more than forty years, the system that set different immigration quotas for people of different nations. After a further amendment in 1976, annual immigration from the Eastern and Western Hemispheres was set at 170,000 and 120,000 respectively, with a maximum total from any one nation of 20,000.

The issue of admitting refugees loomed large during the Cold War. Soviet dissidents, victims of Russia's suppression of the 1956 Hungarian uprising, anti-Castro Cubans, and Hmong and others allied with U.S. forces during the *Vietnam War were at various times admitted by presidential action. While Congress chafed at this broad presidential power, refugee advocates urged a more inclusive approach to the problem. The Refugee Act of 1980, sponsored by Senator Edward Kennedy, set at 50,000 the number of refugees who could be admitted annually and provided for consultation between the president and Congress regarding adjustments to that figure. This law also accepted the *United Nations' nonideological definition of a refugee as a person in flight from persecution on account of race, religion, nationality, politics, or social class.

Illegal or undocumented immigration captured congressional attention in the 1980s. The Immigration Reform and Control Act of 1986 made it illegal for employers knowingly to hire aliens not authorized for employment in the United States. As a concession to employers of alien workers, the law granted legal residence to certain aliens who had labored in U.S. agriculture during recent growing seasons and, in a one-time amnesty, to undocumented aliens who had arrived before 1982 and had lived in the United States continuously thereafter.

As the 1965 reform measures took effect, critics worried about a rising tide of immigration, and particularly about the proliferation of "family-reunification" visa requests—a loophole, they charged, that unfairly benefited recent arrivals from Latin America and Asia while disadvantaging European applicants. In response, the Immigration Act of 1990 set an annual limit of 675,000 immigrants but restricted in various ways the family-reunification provision. This law also increased the number of visas available for skilled workers and set aside 55,000 "diversity" visas for applicants from nations underrepresented in recent immigration. As the twenty-first century dawned, issues of immigration policy would clearly remain on the national agenda.

[*See also* Anticommunism; Asian Americans; Immigrant Labor; Industrialization; Labor Markets; Migratory Agricultural Workers; Nativist Movement; Progressive Era; Twenties, The.]

• Robert A. Divine, *American Immigration Policy, 1924–1952,* 1957. Edward Prince Hutchinson, *Legislative History of American Immigration Policy, 1798–1965,* 1981. Gil Loescher and John A. Scanlan, *Calculated Kindness: Refugees and America's Half-Open Door, 1945 to the Present,* 1986. John Higham, *Strangers in the Land: Patterns of American Nativeism, 1860–1925,* 2nd ed., 1988. Stephen Yale-Loehr, ed., *Understanding the Immigration Act of 1990,* 1991.

—Thomas J. Archdeacon

IMMIGRATION RESTRICTION LEAGUE. *See* Nativist Movement.

IMPEACHMENT, a procedure for removing government officials for malfeasance or criminal activity, is based on the English process in which the House of Commons brought charges against a powerful aristocrat or government official and the House of Lords conducted the trial and rendered the verdict. Although political motivations almost always underlay impeachments, the proceedings were judicial and significant evidence of wrongdoing was required for conviction. Since impeachment played an important role in the seventeenth-century struggle between Parliament and the Stuart monarchs, it became identified with liberty against overbearing executive power.

In the American colonies, impeachment was an important weapon in the colonial assemblies' struggles with governors appointed by proprietors or the king. As conflict grew between the colonies and Great Britain, the assemblies used impeachment against royal officials. The framers of the U.S. *Constitution made the president, vice president, and "all civil officers of the United States" liable to impeachment for "treason, bribery, or other high crimes and misdemeanors." Under the Constitution, impeachments are brought by the House of Representatives and tried by the Senate. Conviction requires a two-thirds vote, with punishment confined to removal from office.

Three presidents have been impeached, though none has been convicted by the Senate. In 1868, the House of Representatives impeached President Andrew *Johnson for dismissing Secretary of War Edwin M. Stanton, in violation of the 1867 Tenure of Office Acts and thereby seeking to obstruct Congress's program of *Reconstruction. The Senate failed by one vote to convict Johnson. In 1974, the House Judiciary Committee recommended the impeachment of President Richard M. *Nixon for obstructing the *Watergate investigation, but he resigned before the House voted impeachment articles. In 1998, the House voted articles of impeachment against President Bill *Clinton for perjury and other charges relating to his efforts to conceal a relationship with a White House intern, but in the Senate trial early in 1999, the vote fell far short of the two-thirds necessary for conviction.

Altogether, the House of Representatives has voted eighteen impeachments, nearly all of judges. (Members of Congress have not been subject to impeachment since the Senate in 1798–1799 dismissed articles of impeachment brought against Senator William Blount of Tennessee, declaring that a member of Congress was not a "civil officer" liable to impeachment under the Constitution.) The charges have usually involved corruption or serious misbehavior on the bench. One judge was removed for treason during the *Civil War. The most significant impeachment of a judge occurred in 1804, when Jeffersonian Republicans brought articles against *Supreme Court Justice Samuel Chase for abusive partisanship on the bench. Had the impeachment succeeded, the Jeffersonians in Congress and the state legislatures might have moved wholesale impeachments against federal and state judges, completely politicizing the process. However, Chase was acquitted in 1805, confirming the need to prove serious wrongdoing for an impeachment to succeed.

Federal impeachment has devolved largely into a process for maintaining the integrity of the judiciary, whose members serve during good behavior and can be removed in no other way. In the 1980s, the U.S. Judicial Conference, the top rule-making body for federal courts, established a procedure for referring recommendations for impeachment to Congress. The Senate streamlined impeachment by allowing proceedings before a committee rather than the whole Senate, which votes after the committee reports. State legislatures also continue to utilize impeachment to remove executive and judicial officials primarily for corruption and serious wrongdoing, but not primarily as a check on the abuse of executive power.

[*See also* Early Republic, Era of the; Federal Government, Executive Branch: The Presidency; Federal Government, Judicial Branch; Federal Government, Legislative Branch: Senate; Federal Government, Legislative Branch: House of Representatives; Jefferson, Thomas; State Governments.]

• Peter Hoffer and N. E. H. Hull, *Impeachment in America, 1635–1805,* 1984. Michael J. Gerhardt, *The Federal Impeachment Process: A Constitutional and Historical Analysis,* 1996.

—Michael Les Benedict

IMPERIALISM. *See* Expansionism.

IMPERIAL WARS. American warfare took on a new dimension near the end of the seventeenth century when conflicts between the principal imperial powers—France, Spain, and England—spread to their colonies in America.

The earliest English colonists had expected to be part of the rivalry between the European giants, and fighting occasionally occurred. On three occasions, English forces destroyed French settlements on Acadia (present-day Nova Scotia) and in Canada, and in the 1680s the French extirpated English trading posts on Hudson Bay. England also wrested control of New Netherlands from the Dutch in 1664.

The first European conflict to spread to the provinces was the War of the League of Augsburg, called King William's War by the English colonists, which erupted in 1689. However, in this struggle the American theater was deemed of secondary importance, and the French and the English colonists fought largely unaided by their parent states. Under the leadership of Count Louis de Frontenac, New France and its Indian allies struck first, launching surprise raids on frontier villages. The most devastating blow fell on Schenectady, New York, in February 1690; nearly ninety residents were killed or carried into captivity, and the settlement was razed. The English quickly retaliated. A Massachusetts army under the governor, Sir William Phips, seized Port Royal on Acadia. Phips's army, like those raised by other provinces in the course of the imperial wars, consisted of volunteers; as militiamen could not by law be sent beyond their provincial boundaries, recruits were garnered by cash and land bounties. Later in 1690, Massachusetts, Connecticut, Plymouth, and New York raised armies to strike at the heart of their adversary. Phips was to seize Quebec with an armada of 2,200 men, while another army of colonists and Iroquois was to drive up the Champlain Valley to Montreal. The plan miscarried. Phips's assault was repulsed, and the invasion army, disheartened by a dearth of Iroquois volunteers, disbanded without reaching Montreal.

The Treaty of Ryswick ended this inconclusive war in 1697. Despite the deaths of about one thousand English, three hundred Canadians, and countless Indians, nothing had been resolved. However, the English colonists had learned that their security hinged on the destruction of New France, an objective that was possible only with assistance from the mother country.

The peace was shattered in 1701 by the outbreak of the War of the Spanish Succession, known in the English provinces as Queen Anne's War. Because Spain was a belligerent, fighting erupted briefly in the southern colonies, but the North witnessed the heaviest action. French and Indian frontier raids commenced in 1703, although the best-remembered blow fell early the next year. Deerfield, Massachusetts, was attacked at night in February 1704. Killed immediately were 44 residents, including 25 children, and 109 others—40 percent of the town's population—were taken captive. As settlers elsewhere huddled in garrison houses, the English fought back, attacking Acadia and Abenaki Indian villages.

In 1710, responding to pleas from the colonies, imperial officials in London at last dispatched a fleet that cooperated with a Massachusetts-Connecticut army in taking Acadia. The following year, Great Britain sent Sir Hovenden Walker to America with 64 ships and 4,300 regulars to attack Quebec. *New England recruited 1,300 men to augment Walker's force, while several colonies contributed to another army of 2,300 men that was simultaneously to attack Montreal. Both ventures failed, the former when Walker's fleet ran aground in fog hundreds of miles from Quebec.

Great Britain was more successful elsewhere, however, and in the Treaty of Utrecht (1713) acquired Hudson Bay, Newfoundland, and Nova Scotia (as it renamed Acadia). But the colonists, especially in New England, had paid heavily for a war that failed to drive France from America. Many frontier inhabitants had perished, some cities had experienced food shortages, several colonies had been plunged into debt, and the citizenry groaned under heavy taxes.

The Treaty of Utrecht inaugurated a generation of international peace that endured until commercial clashes in the Caribbean led to hostilities between Britain and Spain in 1739, a conflict known as the War of Jenkins' Ear. Fighting quickly erupted between the English colonists in Georgia and the Spanish in Florida. However, the largest provincial undertaking in this war occurred in 1740, when the Americans raised a regiment of 3,600 men to assist in a British attack on the Spanish port of Cartagena. The unsuccessful campaign ended disastrously with the death of five-sixths of the colonial soldiery.

Soon thereafter, France allied with Spain, resulting in a larger conflict known as the War of the Austrian Succession, or King George's War. In 1745, London consented to a joint operation to seize Louisbourg, the French citadel that guarded the St. Lawrence River. An army of two thousand New England volunteers under William Pepperrell—united with a British naval force of ninety-four vessels commanded by Commodore Peter Warren—compelled the French to surrender after a brief siege. Although New France was now vulnerable, Britain's leaders soon agreed to peace. Moreover, in the Treaty of Aix-la-Chapelle, London returned Louisbourg to France in exchange for compensation in Europe. New England was furious, as more than a thousand of its sons had perished in securing the French installation.

Hostilities soon flared again. This time the first shot was fired in in America, when French and Virginian armies clashed in the Ohio Country in 1754. London immediately rushed an army of two thousand regulars to America and conducted Anglo-American operations on several frontiers in 1755, although most ended in failure. War was declared in 1756, beginning a conflict variously known as the *Seven Years' War, the French and Indian War, and the Great War for Empire.

The war went badly for Britain until 1758, when the policies of a new prime minister, William Pitt, bore fruit. Pitt sent more than twenty thousand regulars to America and revamped the Royal Navy, which trounced its adversary.

Britain ultimately gained victory as a result of several successful campaigns, especially an attack on Quebec in 1759. However, this worldwide conflict continued until 1763, when the Treaty of Paris brought peace. France abandoned its claims to the North American mainland, and Spain, which had entered the conflict in 1760, surrendered Florida.

Britain had scored a colossal victory, but the imperial wars had been costly. London was saddled with indebtedness, and many colonists had come to question their ties to a country so frequently at war, particularly now that New France no longer existed to threaten the provinces. Ironically, then, Great Britain's four costly wars to gain hegemony in North America sowed the seeds for the loss in 1776 of every mainland colony it had possessed when the first imperial war erupted in 1689.

[*See also* Colonial Era; Exploration, Conquest, and Settlement, Era of European; French Settlements in North America; Indian History and Culture: 1500 to 1800; Indian Wars; Iroquois Confederacy; Revolution and Constitution, Era of; Spanish Settlements in North America.]

• Francis Parkman, *France and England in North America,* 9 vols., 1865–1892. Gerald S. Graham, *Empire of the North Atlantic: The Maritime Struggle for North America,* 1950. Douglas Edward Leach, *Arms for Empire: A Military History of the American Colonies in North America, 1607–1762,* 1964. Howard H. Peckham, *The Colonial Wars, 1689–1762,* 1964. Ian K. Steele, *Guerrillas and Grenadiers: The Struggle for Canada, 1689–1760,* 1969. John Ferling, *A Wilderness of Miseries: War and Warriors in Early America,* 1981. John Ferling, *Struggle for a Continent: The Wars of Early America,* 1993.

—John Ferling

INCARCERATION OF JAPANESE AMERICANS. The forced removal from the West Coast in the Spring and Summer of 1942 of nearly 120,000 Japanese Americans, more than two-thirds of them native-born U.S. citizens, and their subsequent incarceration in ten desolate concentration camps has been called America's "worst wartime mistake." It is better understood as the culmination of a long history of discriminatory treatment of Asian immigrants and their descendants by the federal government, going back to such measures as the 1882 Chinese Exclusion Act. After 1870, Asian immigrants were defined as "aliens ineligible to citizenship," a category from which other forms of discrimination stemmed. By 1924, all Asian immigrants, except for Filipinos who were then "American nationals," were barred from immigrating to the United States.

When Japanese military forces attacked Pearl Harbor and other American bases on 7 and 8 December 1941, some 126,000 persons of Japanese ancestry or birth were living in the continental United States, all but a few thousand on the West Coast. According to plan, federal security authorities immediately interned some 11,000 enemy aliens, about 8,000 Japanese, 2,300 Germans, and a few hundred Italians. Although many if not most of those initially interned posed no threat to the United States, their confinement proceeded according to the statute and involved a rudimentary due process of law.

The mass incarceration of Japanese Americans, by contrast, was lawless. Pressured from both within and outside the federal government, President Franklin Delano *Roosevelt issued Executive Order 9066 on 19 February 1942, providing the initial authority for mass incarceration. It did not affect the few thousand Japanese Americans not living on the West Coast, and of the 150,000 Japanese Americans in *Hawai'i, only a few thousand were rounded up.

Although the removal was carried out by the U.S. Army, a separate wartime agency, the War Relocation Authority, operated the ten camps located in sparsely populated parts of *California, Arizona, Idaho, Wyoming, Colorado, and Arkansas. Without a dissenting vote, Congress passed ex post facto legislation to enforce the president's action; the mass incarceration was also hailed by the press and the general public. Many legal scholars anticipated that the U.S. *Supreme Court would strike down Roosevelt's order and the actions that stemmed from it, but the justices refused to do so in the so-called Japanese-

American cases of 1943–1944 (*Korematsu, Hirabayshi,* and *Endo*), although the *Endo* case (December 1944) did end the government's authority to incarcerate or otherwise limit the freedom of "loyal" American citizens. The last of these camps closed in March 1946.

In isolated incidents at three camps, soldiers shot and killed their fellow Americans. In general, however, the camps were run humanely; most inmates lived in family groups, and attempts were made to create communities behind barbed wire. As early as the Summer of 1942, some Japanese Americans were released to do farm work or attend college, and a few with language skills were recruited by military intelligence. In 1943, Japanese-American male citizens were encouraged to enlist in the U.S. Army, and in 1944 many were actually drafted for military service from behind barbed wire. Some 3,600 young men were inducted into the army from the camps, and more than 20,000 others served.

The vast majority of Japanese-American inmates did what officials told them to do, but a few challenged the government unsuccessfully in the courts. A significant minority participated in peaceful protests, including resisting the draft. For the latter offenses 263 young men were tried, convicted, and sent to federal prisons.

After a presidential commission in 1982 identified "race prejudice, war hysteria, and a failure of political leadership" as the underlying causes of the incarceration, Congress passed the Civil Liberties Act of 1988, which awarded 81,974 individuals $20 thousand each and apologized to them for the nation, as did President Ronald *Reagan and George *Bush. In 1999 a memorial to the ordeal of the Japanese Americans was approved for a small park near the Capitol in *Washington, D.C.

[*See also* Asian Americans; Immigration Law; *Korematsu* v. *United States*; Nativist Movement; Pearl Harbor, Attack on; Racism; World War II: Domestic Effects.]

• Commission on Wartime Relocation and Internment of Civilians, *Personal Justice Denied: Report of the Commission on Wartime Relocation and Internment of Civilians,* 1982, reprint 1997. Peter Irons, *Justice at War: The Story of the Japanese Internment Cases,* 1983. Roger Daniels, ed., *American Concentration Camps: A Documentary History of the Relocation and Incarceration of Japanese Americans, 1941–1945,* 9 vols., 1989. Arthur Hansen, ed., *Japanese American World War II Evacuation History Project,* 5 vols., 1990–1992. Roger Daniels, *Prisoners Without Trial: Japanese Americans in World War II,* 1993. Sandra C. Taylor, *Jewel of the Desert: Japanese American Internment at Topaz,* 1993.

—Roger Daniels

INCOME TAX, FEDERAL. The first U.S. income tax was introduced during the *Civil War and collected through a newly established Bureau of Internal Revenue in the Department of the Treasury. It was designed less as a money-raiser (though, at its height, it accounted for a fifth of Union revenues) than as a political diversion—conspicuously targeting the well-to-do in order to cloak the disproportionate burdens that higher *tariffs and new consumer excise taxes placed on typical Americans. Phased out by 1872, it was politically resurrected in succeeding decades in response to sectional (western and southern), partisan (Democrat and Populist), and economic resentments against the power and wealth of the Republican-dominated industrial East. Congress again enacted an income tax in 1894, only to have it declared unconstitutional by the *Supreme Court the following year. The income tax was revived permanently in 1913, with the ratification of the Sixteenth Amendment of the *Constitution and the passage by Congress of an income tax graduated up to a 7-percent rate but with exemption provisions that shielded all but the top two percent of households.

Substantial tax increases in *World War I (reaching a peak rate of 77 percent), reinforced by prosperous conditions that more than counterbalanced the Republican-sponsored income-tax cuts of the 1920s, transformed the individual income tax into a major federal revenue-raiser. The small minority of income-earners receiving over fifty thousand dollars annually shouldered most of this burden, however. *New Deal Era tax reforms heightened the class tilt of the income tax (including a new 79-percent top bracket applying only to John D. Rockefeller Jr.). Nevertheless, the erosion of incomes in the Great Depression, combined with new *Social Security and consumer taxes, meant that the personal income tax accounted for under a fifth of federal revenue collections in the 1930s.

Drastic rate increases and cuts in exemption to finance *World War II mobilization permanently converted the income tax into the federal government's primary revenue source. The income tax mutated from a class tax (only 5 percent of the public had filed taxable returns in the 1930s) to a mass tax, deducted directly from paychecks beginning in 1943 and applying to most American workers. In 1963–1965, embracing the "New Economics" of the Council of Economic Advisors, the John F. *Kennedy and Lyndon B. *Johnson administrations subordinated the income redistributional potential of the federal income tax to an apparently successful "Keynesian" countercyclical strategy of using broad income-tax cuts and temporary budget deficits to stimulate economic growth. Top rates (deceptively high due to gaping loopholes) fell from over 90 percent to 70 percent. In the 1980s, the Ronald *Reagan administration, adopting a "supply-side" logic of economic expansion that demonized tax burdens and privileged business investment, reduced income-tax rates further, and even subsequent increases left the top rate below 40 percent. Income-tax reform remained at the center of American debate in the 1990s, assuming a symbolic and political importance that often overshadowed its financial and redistributive significance.

[*See also* Depressions, Economic; Economic Development; Economic Regulation; Federal Government, Executive Branch: Department of the Treasury; Keynesianism; Monetary Policy, Federal; Taxation.]

• Sidney Ratner, *Taxation and Democracy in America,* 1967. W. Elliot Brownlee, *Federal Taxation in America: A Short History,* 1996

—Mark H. Leff

INDENTURED SERVITUDE. Indentured servitude, which had appeared in colonial America by 1620, was developed by the Virginia Company as a means to connect the English labor supply to colonial demand. Most hired labor in preindustrial England was performed by servants in husbandry—youths who lived and worked in the households of their masters on annual contracts. Since passage fares to America were high relative to the earnings of these servants, few could afford the voyage. The Virginia Company's solution was to pay the passage of prospective laborers who contracted to repay this debt from their earnings in America.

This arrangement was soon adopted by merchants in England's ports, as migrants signed indentures that the merchants sold to colonial planters upon the servants' arrival in America. Servitude became a central labor institution in early English America: Between one-half and two-thirds of all white immigrants to the British colonies arrived under indenture. Indentured servitude therefore enabled between 300,000 and 400,000 Europeans to migrate to the New World. Unmarried men predominated among the servants throughout the *Colonial Era. Most were in their late teens or early twenties—the same ages that were prevalent among servants in husbandry in England.

Indentured servants were most important in the early history of those regions that produced staple crops for export, particularly the sugar islands of the West Indies and the tobacco colonies on the Chesapeake Bay. Over time, as colonial conditions for servants deteriorated and economic conditions improved in England, attracting indentured workers to these colonies became more difficult. Planters increasingly found African slaves a less expensive source of labor and responded by substituting slaves for servants.

Some historians have characterized the indenture system as debased and the servants who participated in it as disreputable. Yet indentured workers were governed by the same basic legal conditions as English farm servants, and studies of emigration lists have shown that the servants were not drawn from England's poorest or least skilled workers, but rather from a broad cross section of English society. Historians have also argued that servants were exploited economically by English merchants. Yet the servants' long terms did not imply exploitation, for the large debt for passage meant that repayment would necessarily take longer than the standard single year worked by farm servants in England. Analysis of collections of contracts has furthermore revealed that more productive servants received shorter terms, evidently because they could repay their debts more quickly. Servants bound for less desirable colonial destinations also received shorter terms. Competition among merchants thus protected servants from economic exploitation.

[*See also* Agriculture: Colonial Era; Immigration; Labor Markets; Slavery; Tobacco Industry.]

• Abbot Emerson Smith, *Colonists in Bondage: White Servitude and Convict Labor in America, 1607–1776,* 1947. David W. Galenson, *White Servitude in Colonial America: An Economic Analysis,* 1981.

—David W. Galenson

INDIANAPOLIS 500. *See* Automobile Racing.

INDIAN CAPTIVITY NARRATIVES. *See* Captivity Narratives, Indian.

INDIAN HEALTH SERVICE. In 1873, amid growing national interest in social and public-health reforms, the Office of Indian Affairs in the Department of the Interior created a Medical and Educational Division, forerunner of today's extensive, multitasked Indian Health Service. At the time, only about half of the nation's seventy-four reservations employed physicians. Despite the subsequent construction of the first Indian *hospitals, more rigorous hiring standards for medical personnel, and a late-1880s policy shift toward *disease prevention, rampant epidemic disease and malnutrition persisted.

Throughout the nineteenth century, health care competed poorly with educational efforts for the Interior Department's meager resources. In the period 1900–1920, however, a number of bureaucratic changes and budgetary successes enhanced Indian health services. In 1908, the department created the position of chief medical supervisor to oversee the medical service. In 1911, the first congressional appropriation specifically for general health services to Indians resulted in the addition of dentists and public-health nurses.

A reorganization of the Indian Bureau in 1924 resulted in a separate Medical Division (in 1931 renamed the Health Division, later the Indian Health Service). In 1926, the medical division itself reorganized, expanded, and added supervisors detailed from the U.S. Public Health Service. The pre–*World War II period brought expansion for the medical department. Its staff successfully treated trachoma, conducted sanitation surveys, and built more hospitals. Service hospitals were now the site of 80 percent of Indian births, reflecting the degree of native trust.

Yet federal studies of reservations, such as the 1928 Meriam Report, consistently found abysmal health conditions. Controversies over salaries and limited resources persisted as well. Reformers and the National Tuberculosis Association called for transfer of medical services from the Interior Department to the Public Health Service, and in 1955 Public Law 568 did just that: The Indian Health Service became part of the new Department of Health, Education, and Welfare (now the Department of Health and Human Services). In subsequent years, personnel, budgets, facility construction, and the numbers of patients served increased dramatically. Troubling discrepancies persisted, however, between health statistics for the 1.5 million Native Americans and those of the general population.

[*See also* Bureau of Indian Affairs; Federal Government, Executive Branch: Other Departments (Department of Health and Human Services); Health and Fitness; Indian History and Culture: 1800 to 1900; Indian History and Culture: From 1900 to 1950; Since 1950; Indian History and Culture: Since Medicine: From the 1870s to 1945; Medicine: Since 1945; Public Health; Tuberculosis.]

• Todd Benson, "Race, Health, and Power: The Federal Government and American Indian Health, 1909–1955," Ph.D. diss., Stanford University, 1994. Robert A. Trannert, *White Man's Medicine: Government Doctors and the Navajo, 1863–1955,* 1998.

—Diane D. Edwards

INDIAN HISTORY AND CULTURE

Overview
Migration and Pre-Columbian Era
Distribution of Major Groups, circa 1500
From 1500 to 1800
From 1800 to 1900
From 1900 to 1950
Since 1950
The Indian in Popular Culture

INDIAN HISTORY AND CULTURE: OVERVIEW

People of Asiatic origins migrated into the Americas between forty thousand and twelve thousand years ago. Climatic change prompted the earliest foragers, who stone-chipped spear points throughout the hemisphere, to adapt to a wide variety of ecosystems. Southeastern peoples domesticated chenopod plants in step with other global centers of plant domestication. Peoples across North America adopted maize, beans, and squash from their Mexican neighbors. The largest population centers and state-level societies arose on the interior *Mississippi River drainage networks, leaving the coasts more vulnerable to invasion.

With Spain in the lead, Europeans colonized and brought new diseases to the Americas beginning in the late fifteenth century, causing the worst demographic disaster in human history. Epidemics took a toll in every sphere of Native American life. With remarkable adaptability, the survivors splintered, migrated, and ultimately amalgamated to form new groups and devise strategies for dealing with the invaders.

Exchange of pelts for European manufactured goods enhanced native economic and spiritual life for centuries before dependence eroded their autonomy. The continual drive of Euroamericans to expropriate native land by whatever means necessary, including genocide, reduced the native peoples to an indigenous minority engulfed in a sea of immigrants.

As the colonizer that ultimately retained the most native land, the United States inadvertently accorded native people limited sovereignty by employing treaties as the cheapest means for acquiring land. In the 1830s, the *Supreme Court defined Indians as wards of the U.S. government. Though nearly all treaties were broken, tribes in the twentieth century successfully used the courts to maintain their limited sovereignty. With the greatest rate of intermarriage of any U.S. minority group, the native population was on the rise as the twentieth century ended, though they remained the most impoverished.

[*See also* Columbian Exchange; Expansionism; Exploration, Conquest, and Settlement, Era of European; Indian Wars.]

• William C. Sturtevant, ed., *Handbook of North American Indians,* 10 vols. to date, 1978–. Francis Jennings, *The Founders of America,* 1993.

—Melissa L. Meyer

INDIAN HISTORY AND CULTURE: MIGRATION AND PRE-COLUMBIAN ERA

The Indians of the Americas, as well as the Aleuts and Inuit (Eskimos), originated in northeastern Asia and came to the

Americas in three or four major migratory episodes. Most American Indians descend from a migration that began about 15,000 years ago. Whether these people encountered a sparse population of people descended from a much earlier migration is a topic of much debate and research. A later migration that began about 9,500 years ago probably brought speakers of Na-déné languages to interior *Alaska and western Canada. However, genetic evidence is also consistent with the possibility that the Na-déné began as a branch of the previous migration, the split perhaps having occurred in northwestern North America rather than earlier in Siberia. Some of the Na-déné speakers later moved to the present-day southwestern United States, where their descendants are known as Apaches and Navajos. A final migration of ancestral Inuit (Eskimo) and Aleut people began around 4,500 years ago and led to their occupation of coastal Alaska as well as of forbidding and previously unoccupied regions above the Arctic Circle in Canada and Greenland.

At the end of the Ice Age around ten thousand years ago, all human beings lived as hunters, gatherers, and foragers. The highly mobile bands of American Indians living then in what is now the United States are generally referred to as Paleo-Indians. Changing environmental conditions and human predation drove many of the large Ice Age game animals to extinction as glaciers retreated and the environment shifted toward modern conditions. As conditions stabilized, Indian populations became less mobile, settled into territorial ranges, and developed specialized technologies and social organizations for the efficient exploitation of available food resources. This led to the development of habitations at key locations and the gradual regional diversification of what had earlier been a generally uniform culture.

Increasing familiarization with local resources eventually led to the partial domestication of wild plant foods. For example, in the Eastern Woodlands, native squash, sunflower, goosefoot, sumpweed, knotweed, maygrass, and little barley were all brought under domestication by the second millennium B.C. Along the Northwest Coast, Indian communities intensified the exploitation, storage, and redistribution of seasonal resources, most of them maritime. Populations remained thin in the western deserts and in the far north. Environmental variations were clearly major determinants of the specific directions taken by Indian cultures across the continent as they grew and evolved.

North American Indians were limited by the general lack of suitable animal domesticates. Native American horses had become extinct, and they might not have been suitable for domestication in any case, and there were no other animal candidates that might have served as domesticated sources of burden, wool, milk, meat, traction, or transportation in North America. This fact limited technological change and compelled a reliance on wild game for meat, hides, and animal fiber. The absence of any animal equivalent to the ox forestalled the development of plows and wheeled vehicles as well as grassy plant domesticates similar to Eurasian wheat and barley, which require plow technology.

Native domesticates supported the development of Adena culture in present-day southern Ohio and portions of four adjacent states by around 700 B.C. Adena is best known for large burial mounds containing high-quality grave offerings. Among these are tubular pipes and other evidence that tobacco, originally a South American domesticate, had spread to North America by this time. Some outlying Adena-style burials occur as far east as New Jersey and as far northeast as Vermont.

Adena lasted until around A.D. 1. The more elaborate Hopewell earthworks arose around 100 B.C. within Adena territory. These sometimes include very large geometric earthworks in the core area of southern Ohio. Hopewell lasted until around A.D. 350, spawning derivative mound-building cultures in the lower Great Lakes region, around Lake Michigan, and in the valleys of the *Mississippi River and its major tributaries from southern Minnesota to the Gulf of Mexico. Burial mounds eventually were built throughout the Eastern Woodlands and eastern prairies of the United States, except for *New England and the Middle-Atlantic coastal region. Some late examples in Wisconsin and parts of adjacent states were constructed as large animal effigies.

Plant domesticates that were first cultivated farther south eventually made up for some natural deficiencies. Maize was developed in Mexico as a plant domesticate that produced many large seeds from a comparatively small number of plants that could be tended using hand techniques. Beans, domesticated in South America, had the same characteristics and provided a partial substitute for meat protein. These were spread north by Indian farmers along with superior strains of squash, leading to major economic changes in eastern North America after A.D. 800.

Strains of these domesticates also reached the American Southwest by perhaps as early as 300 B.C. Here they made a desert and near desert marginally productive for farmers, and the Pueblo village cultures emerged. Three great cultural traditions, the Anasazi, Mogollon, and Hohokam, were centered in present-day Arizona and New Mexico, with extensions by the first two reaching into neighboring parts of the United States and Mexico. The Hohokam culture made use of intensive crop irrigation. The minor Patayan tradition developed to the west, partially in *California, and the Fremont culture developed in Utah.

The midcontinental prairies remained grasslands because, as we have seen, Indian farmers lacked the traction power necessary for plowing. Only the river valleys of the prairies supported farming before the coming of Europeans, for their alluvial soils could be cultivated with hand implements. The prairies and High Plains were the scene of cultural florescence only after domesticated horses introduced by the Spanish made pastoralism possible.

The rise of chiefdoms in the Eastern Woodlands occurred after A.D. 800 with the introduction of new strains of maize and other domesticates. Large towns appeared with flat-topped platform mounds clearly showing the architectural influence of developments in central Mexico. Four regional variants in the Southeast, all known as Mississippian, are designated as Middle, South Appalachian, Caddoan, and Plaquemine Mississippian, respectively. Northern variants are known as Oneota and Fort Ancient.

American Indians living north of the Great Lakes, in the High Plains, the Great Basin, California, and along the Northwest Coast remained hunters and gatherers throughout the pre-Columbian era. Populations there remained generally low, fewer than one person per hundred square kilometers on average. Those living along the West Coast and in some parts of interior California, however, enjoyed such natural abundance that they had higher population densities comparable to those of the Eastern Woodlands farmers. The elaborate societies of the Northwest Coast are especially noteworthy for their highly developed art and sophisticated sociopolitical systems.

Climatic changes in the last few centuries of the pre-Columbian era caused the abandonment of many farming villages in the Southwest, as well as village nucleation and increased competition that led to intensified warfare in many parts of the Eastern Woodlands. North America at the end of the pre-Columbian era was a cultural mosaic of hundreds of American Indian nations speaking distinct languages and following lifeways ranging from small hunting bands to large settled chiefdoms based on intensive farming. All aspects of American Indian culture displayed considerable regional and temporal variation. Reliable estimates of the aggregate size of North American Indian populations north of Mexico in A.D. 1492 approximate 2.2 million.

[*See also* Columbian Exchange; Exploration, Conquest, and Settlement, Era of European; Tobacco Products.]

• William Sturtevant, ed., *Handbook of North American Indians,* 10 vols. to date, 1978–. Michael Coe, Dean Snow, and Elizabeth Benson, *Atlas of Ancient America,* 1986. Alice B. Kehoe, *North American Indians: A Comprehensive Account,* 1992.

—Dean R. Snow

INDIAN HISTORY AND CULTURE: DISTRIBUTION OF MAJOR GROUPS, CIRCA 1500

Around A.D. 1500, approximately four hundred distinct and mutually unintelligible American Indian languages were spoken in the portion of North America lying north of Mexico. Generally, each language was spoken by members of a reasonably well-defined traditional society. These societies varied from small but widely scattered ones in areas of low natural productivity to large and dense ones in areas where farming was practiced. Descendants of many still survive, and references to the societies in the past tense in this essay do not necessarily imply that they are extinct.

The continent can be conveniently divided into eleven culture areas, each with a different set of typical subsistence practices, settlement types, house styles, social systems, and political organizations. North American Indian languages can be grouped into no fewer than twenty-one families, the final form of language diversification that took fifteen thousand years to develop. More than thirty languages are either unique isolates having no known relatives or extinct and so poorly known that they cannot be grouped with any others. Because unwritten languages preserve clues to their links with related languages for at most a few thousand years, it may never be possible to trace the ancient connections between even well-known languages and language families.

When Hernando de *Soto began his exploration of the Southeastern Woodlands in 1539, he encountered large towns with central plazas and earthen platform mounds surrounded by residences and fields of maize, beans, and squash. Cultivation tended to be carried out on rich, easily tilled, alluvial soils on broad river floodplains, often near oxbow lakes and other areas of high natural food productivity. Many societies were organized politically as chiefdoms, some having societies based on matrilineal principles, some based on patrilineal ones. Muskogean and Caddoan were the major language families of the region, although there were also representatives of the Siouan and Iroquoian families. The region was one of the first to experience depopulation owing to *smallpox and other diseases that spread from Europe in the sixteenth century.

The Northeastern Woodlands supported less intensive farming. Upland slash-and-burn farming was practiced in the lower Great Lakes and southern *New England areas, while wild-rice gathering predominated around the upper Great Lakes. Most societies spoke either Iroquoian or Algonquian languages in this culture area. Algonquian speakers, also widespread in eastern Canada, were in place earlier than the Iroquoian speakers. The latter intruded into the region from the central Appalachians, bringing with them plant domesticates and longhouse communities organized along matrilineal lines. Farming later spread to the Algonquian residents of southern New England. European diseases reached the Northeast later than the Southeast but with such devastating effects even prior to European exploration that we know little about the Indians of the upper Ohio Valley in this period.

Prior to the introduction of the domesticated horse, the upland Great Plains were occupied by bands of mobile hunter-gatherers, at least some of them speakers of Kiowa-Tanoan languages. Wooded valleys of the main western tributaries of the *Mississippi River, particularly the Missouri River, were occupied by sedentary farmers who had moved upstream from the Eastern Woodlands late in the pre-Columbian era. These were mainly speakers of Caddoan and Siouan languages. These farming peoples typically lived in villages of large multifamily earth lodges, and some were strongly matrilineal.

Algonquian-speaking hunters were thinly distributed across the eastern Canada culture area, which included northern New England and the Maritime Provinces. Small mobile bands were typically organized along patrilineal or bilateral lines. Those living near the seacoast had access to more abundant food resources and frequently lived in villages of bark wigwams for at least part of the year.

The western Canada culture area was occupied by speakers of various Na-déné languages, the largest fraction of which are called Athapaskan. Like the people of eastern Canada, they were hunter-gatherers who lived in small mobile bands. Some Athapaskans broke away and migrated to the *Southwest late in the pre-Columbian era, where they later became known as the Apache and Navajo peoples.

The settled Pueblo farmers of the Southwest, remnants of the great traditions of the region that flourished during the pre-Columbian era, comprised four language families: Uto-Aztecan, Hokan, Keresan, and Kiowa-Tanoan. One language, Zuni, defies classification. Pueblo villages were traditionally built of stone or adobe, and many housed strongly matrilineal societies built around clans and elaborate seasonal ceremonies. Prolonged drought forced all of them to contract their territories prior to A.D. 1500, a change that facilitated the immigration of Athapaskan speakers from the north. Southwestern Pueblo villages remain well known for their architecture and ceramics.

The Great Basin is an arid region that did not support much farming around A.D. 1500. Nearly all inhabitants of this culture area were Uto-Aztecan speakers that lived in small mobile bands.

Present-day *California, north of the portions of it that were part of the Great Basin or Southwest culture areas, was high in natural productivity. More than forty nations lived in small, densely populated tribal territories. None of them practiced farming, but all had elaborated special techniques for harvesting locally abundant resources that were virtual staples in their diets. The rich, wild resources varied from plant foods, such as acorns, to seafood. Long-term management of the food resources nearly turned some of them into domesticates. The tribes of California spoke languages belonging to at least seven families, including small representative enclaves of some language families spoken much more widely outside California.

The Northwest Coast, like California, was characterized by about forty independent tribes and chiefdoms showing considerable cultural and linguistic diversity. There were eight language families in the culture area and several languages that cannot now be classified. Rich maritime resources allowed the development of large sedentary towns. The chiefdoms of the central part of the coast are well known for their multifamily houses and elaborate cedar totem-pole art.

The interior Plateau culture area lies between the coastal mountains of the Northwest Coast and the interior Rocky Mountains. Most of the tribes of the Plateau lived along tributaries of the Columbia and Fraser Rivers and spoke Sahaptain, Salishan, and Na-déné languages that were related to languages of the same families along the Northwest Coast. They were largely hunter-gatherers who enjoyed resources rich enough to allow some of them to live in permanent earth lodges for at least part of the year.

Coastal *Alaska, northern Canada, and Greenland all lie within the Arctic culture area, whose inhabitants all spoke languages of the Eskimo-Aleut family. In 1500, all of the inhabited parts of the Arctic east of Alaska were occupied by Inuit people speaking dialects of a single language, the consequence of their rapid migratory expansion from northern Alaska only a few centuries earlier. Alaska itself, which had been occupied for much longer, was considerably more diverse, both culturally and linguistically. Arctic people lived in small mobile family bands that depended upon a light but highly elaborated *technology for survival in a harsh environment. The toggling harpoon, dogsled, compound bow, and kayak are only a few examples of their technological ingenuity.

North America on the eve of European exploration and colonization was, in short, a region of richly diverse Indian cultures that differed widely in all respects, including language, social organization, and means of subsistence. It was a diversity that matched the cultural diversity of the newcomers from across the Atlantic. Subsequent interactions produced the complex cultural mosaic that persists today.

[*See also* Architecture: Domestic Architecture; Columbian Exchange; Exploration, Conquest, and Settlement, Era of European.]

• William Sturtevant, ed., *Handbook of North American Indians,* 10 vols. to date, 1978–. Michael Coe, Dean Snow, and Elizabeth Benson, *Atlas of Ancient America,* 1986. Alice B. Kehoe, *North American Indians: A Comprehensive Account,* 1992.

—Dean R. Snow

INDIAN HISTORY AND CULTURE: FROM 1500 TO 1800

Aboriginal peoples entered the Eastern Woodlands (here defined broadly as the area bounded by the Atlantic Ocean, the St. Lawrence and *Mississippi Rivers, and the Gulf of Mexico) around ten thousand years ago. By the late fifteenth century, perhaps 500,000 Amerindians dwelled in the area, although estimates are at best highly conjectural. They divided into scores of bands, each of which considered itself a distinct people. Algonquian languages predominated (spoken by Abenakis, Delawares, and Ojibwas, among others), along with Iroquoian (the Five Nations, Hurons, Cherokees), Muskogean (Creeks, Choctaws, Appalachees), Siouan (Catawbas), and Timucuan (Potamos).

Amerindian Life and Social Institutions around 1500. With some exceptions, Woodlands Amerindians lived in villages of a few hundred residents. Most subsisted primarily on cultivated crops, especially corn, beans, and squash, supplementing their diets with meat and seafood; hunting prevailed north of the St. Lawrence and along the Ohio River, as did fishing in coastal Florida and southern *New England. Villages consisted of families grouped into two or more clans, which provided hospitality for visiting relatives and, in the absence of any statist legal system, functioned as a police, avenging injuries to kin. Woodlands peoples neither accumulated much material wealth nor developed stratified classes. Bands were headed by civil chiefs who took advice from elders, councils, or sometimes all adults. Lacking fiat power and thus unable to compel individual behavior, chiefs ruled instead by force of personality and example. Military chiefs, chosen for their feats of bravery, captained parties for hunting and combat. Wars, fought for honor or revenge rather than riches or territory, were endemic but not particularly lethal. Villages were joined in structures of various size and complexity, from tribes incorporating a few towns with headmen holding essentially equal authority to paramount chiefdoms integrating numerous band and kin groups governed by a ranked hierarchy of chiefs. Extensive polities were rare. Sometime in the sixteenth century, the Senecas, Cayugas, Onondagas, Oneidas, and Mohawks formed the League of the Iroquois to stop blood feuds among them; at the end of the century, *Powhatan created a paramount chiefdom among the James River Algonquians by force, intimidation, and negotiation; and in the eighteenth century, the Cherokees evolved a confederation to coordinate policies toward the British colonies. Amerindians undertook few tasks without engaging the spirits ("manitous," an Algonquian word), who were believed to inhabit the world and confer power on its denizens. Proper conduct entailed establishing relationships of mutual respect with every creature; such conduct would maximize a person's potency. Villages performed communal rituals to thank and propitiate spirits. Select individuals (shamans) acquired extraordinary magical and healing powers from the spirits, but no special clerical caste existed, and any person could communicate with manitous directly.

Early Contacts with Europeans. Repeated contacts between Woodlands Amerindians and Europeans first occurred during the sixteenth century. Along the North Atlantic littoral, they were sporadic. Algonquians in eastern Canada and New England exchanged goods with fishermen drying their catches. Iroquoians and Algonquians greeted Jacques *Cartier's three excursions up the St. Lawrence between 1534 and 1542, but the French did not return for more than half a century. Southeastern peoples experienced far greater intrusions; the incursions of Pánfilo de Narváez (1527–1528) and Hernando de *Soto (1539–1542) precipitated many clashes, and in their wake the region's paramount chiefdoms collapsed. The reasons for their demise are not entirely clear, but illness played the leading role, as it did in decimating aboriginal settlements throughout the hemisphere. Having existed in a static *disease environment for millennia, Amerindians had evolved no immunities to Old World pathogens and rapidly succumbed to *smallpox and respiratory ailments. "Virgin soil epidemics" struck the most productive age cohorts the hardest and left survivors unable to sustain themselves. Some scholars suggest that native populations may have declined by 90 percent within a century after contact; whatever the exact figure, pandemics loosened natives' grip on their land more than did any other factor.

During the seventeenth century, Amerindians had to contend with European incursions along the entire Atlantic seaboard. Around the St. Lawrence River and the Great Lakes, Algonquians and Hurons entered into an extensive trading network with the French. Thousands converted to *Roman Catholicism, some baptized by Jesuits as they lay dying, others because taking the cross afforded them greater access to guns. The *fur trade's profitability drew the attention of the Five Nations, the Hurons' inveterate enemies, who sought to take over the commerce and who in 1649 destroyed Huronia, some of whose survivors regrouped as Wyandots. The Five Nations, particularly the Mohawks, took their pelts to Fort Orange (later Albany), originally settled by the Dutch West India Company, which was far more interested in skins than souls. At first, the Algonquians of the lower Hudson Valley coexisted peacefully with New Netherland. As the number of farmers grew and their use of tribal lands increased the Dutch tried to control native movements more closely, and war broke out in 1643–1645, weakening both the river tribes and the colony, which fell to England in 1664.

In the English colonies, Amerindians confronted colonizers who constructed more extensive agricultural settlements than did any other Europeans and who thus posed the greatest threat to native lands. Algonquians were marginal to New England's commercial and spiritual economies; the quantity of fur-bearing animals could not support intensive trapping for long, nor did Puritan visions of constructing a godly society make converting the heathen a cardinal priority. The Wampanoags kept peace with the English for more than fifty years until, fearful about being dispossessed, they recruited the Narragansetts and other Algonquians into a pan-tribal alliance that devastated New England in Metacom's War (1675–1676), called *King Philip's War by the colonists. The conflict retarded English settlement for decades but also wrecked the tribes' capacity for further resistance. Around Chesapeake Bay, the Powhatans soon determined that the Virginians' desire for tobacco soils endangered their domain, and they launched major strikes in 1622 and 1644 to expel the invaders. The Virginians persevered, despite suffering significant casualties, and by the late seventeenth century had subdued the coastal tribes.

Spanish Franciscans gathered Guales of the Georgia coast, along with Timucuans and Appalachees in northern Florida, around *doctrinas,* church compounds circumscribed by native villages that contributed crops and labor. Disease and the Timucuan Rebellion of 1656 stunted the interior missions, and the English and Creeks destroyed the Guale outposts in 1702–1704.

Amerindians, the Atlantic Economy, and Imperial Conflicts. By the eighteenth century, the Eastern Woodlands peoples were inextricably tangled in two profound dynamics. First, exchanging furs for European textiles, metal goods, alcohol, and weapons had integrated them into the transatlantic market economy. Dependent on European commodities that they could neither reproduce nor replace because they had lost ancient skills, natives had to secure continuing access to colonial merchants. Second, rivalry between Great Britain, France, and Spain forced them to choose sides during the wars fought between 1689 and 1763 to control North America. Amerindians who lived near the colonies of two or more European nations could tease concessions from one side by threatening to do business with another, but none could disengage from imperial affairs. The tensions of dealing with aggressive states that were also sources of vital goods split many peoples between accommodationists, who believed that bands could best preserve their autonomy by coexisting with Europeans, and nativists willing to risk war. Stirred by "prophets" who decried Amerindians' departure from the old ways and their consequent loss of spiritual power, nativists urged armed struggle against encroachment and the complete rejection of European culture. Pontiac's Rebellion (1763–1765), a pan-tribal nativist movement instigated by the Delaware prophet Neolin (although named for an Ottawa chief), pressured the British to resume giving native allies gifts, declare their lands off-limits to future settlement, and issue a schedule of fair trade prices.

Soon, however, the situation of Woodlands peoples deteriorated. Britain's triumph in the *Seven Years' War (also known as the French and Indian War) gave it hegemony over the Eastern Woodlands and undermined tribes' ability to play foes against each other. The *Revolutionary War created a single national state that asserted sovereignty over virtually the entire area and upheld its citizens' rights to acreage within its borders. The United States regarded native peoples—most of whom had fought with Great Britain to curtail further American expansion—as either individuals to assimilate or as obstacles to overcome, but in any case as parties whose claims to autonomy and territory should not be largely credited. Tribal coalitions continued to resist, but the evacuation of British and Spanish troops from American soil during the 1790s made foreign aid more difficult for Woodlands peoples to obtain, and the last great uprising east of the Mississippi—led by the Shawnee chief *Tecumseh and his half brother, the prophet Tenskwatawa—was defeated in 1811, after which Amerindians had little remaining means to oppose land cessions and westward removal. Marginalized within the United States, the surviving natives nevertheless maintained their cultural integrity. The incipient sense of belonging to a larger racial or cultural group articulated during nativist movements would crystallize in the late twentieth century around the terms "Native Americans" and "First Nations."

[*See also* Colonial Era; Columbian Exchange; Dutch Settlements in North America; Exploration, Conquest, and Settlement, Era of European; French Settlements in North America; Indian Wars; Iroquois Confederacy; Pontiac; Revolution and Constitution, Era of; Spanish Settlements in North America; Tobacco Industry.]

• Neal Salisbury, *Manitou and Providence: Indians, Europeans, and the Making of New England, 1500–1643,* 1982. Ian Steele, *Warpaths: Invasions of North America* 1994. James Merrell, *The Indians' New World: Catawbas and Their Neighbors from European Contact through the Era of Removal,* 1989. Gregory Dowd, *A Spirited Resistance: The North American Indian Struggle for Unity, 1745–1815,* 1991. Richard White, *The Middle Ground: Indians, Empires, and Republics in the Great Lakes Region, 1650–1815,* 1991. James Axtell, *Beyond 1492: Encounters in Colonial North America,* 1992. Daniel Richter, *The Ordeal of the Longhouse: The Peoples of the Iroquois League in the Era of European Colonization,* 1992. Colin Calloway, *The American Revolution in Indian Country,* 1995. Colin Calloway, *New Worlds for All: Indians, Europeans, and the Remaking of Early America,* 1997.

—Charles L. Cohen

INDIAN HISTORY AND CULTURE: FROM 1800 TO 1900

Nineteenth-century American history might read like an unrelieved tragedy for native peoples if their actions and adaptations were not spotlighted. However, they were not simply victims. They actively participated in this history and affected its course and outcome.

Post-Revolutionary Euroamerican Expansion and Indian Migration. The *Revolutionary War and the subsequent defeat of the British in the *War of 1812 created an unprecedented situation for North America's native peoples. Never again could they play one European power against another. No longer would any nation regard their sovereignty in the North American interior as crucial for preserving peace and enhancing trade. Expansion underlay the U.S. agenda; any protection of native rights was a temporary deviation from that greater goal. While land acquisition and explosive population growth brought opportunity and prosperity to white Americans, it dispossessed and impoverished the native people. The close of the nineteenth century coincided with the nadir of the indigenous population.

Most native groups had allied with the British during the Revolutionary War, but they were too powerful to be treated as conquered enemies. The U.S. government, small, weak, and bankrupt, was in no position to dictate terms to native people. To avoid costly wars, Congress passed between 1790 and 1834 a series of Trade and Intercourse Acts regulating interaction with Indians. Native people would have sovereignty in "Indian Country;" intruders would be expelled. Only the federal government could buy Indian land. Traders were to be licensed and alcohol prohibited. The United States even established a nonprofit, credit-free, alcohol-free trading enterprise to wean native allies from British traders still in Canada.

The inherent contradiction between the dual goals of acquiring land and keeping the peace doomed the formula to failure. A series of Pre-emption Acts promised land titles to squatters who made "improvements." The overriding objective of expansion could not have been more clear.

Accustomed to collective land stewardship and consensus politics, native groups learned through hard experience the many strategems Euroamericans would use to acquire their land. Speculators preyed upon unauthorized individuals ready to "sell" land. Bolstered by Pre-emption Acts, squatters intruded illegally. U.S. negotiators sought land cessions at every turn: to liquidate trade debts; in return for money, goods, and services to be distributed annually (annuities); and as retribution against groups that resorted to military defiance. The United States claimed jurisdiction over huge parcels like the *Louisiana Purchase and the *Gadsden Purchase through deals with various European nations. It claimed the *Southwest, Northwest, and *California through wars with European nations. Despite the clear overall policy of expansion, government representatives dealt with the thousands of native inhabitants largely on an ad hoc basis. Treaties avoided costly wars, but military conquest and even genocide awaited recalcitrant tribes. Whatever appeared in print, U.S. policy toward native people was in reality one of expediency.

Many native groups migrated west to avoid direct conflict. The Ohio Valley and Great Lakes areas teemed with refugees, prompting others to move onto the Great Plains and hunt bison astride horses reintroduced into the Americas by Europeans centuries before. In the early nineteenth century, portions of southeastern groups chose to transplant themselves west of the *Mississippi River, to present-day Oklahoma and Kansas, at least temporarily escaping settler incursions.

Economic and Cultural Interactions. But migration alone could not extricate native peoples from interaction with Euroamericans. For centuries they had traded peltry and environmental produce for European manufactured goods like copper pots, knives, hatchets, guns and ammunition, cloth, and beads. Although this trade enriched native economic, artistic, and spiritual lives, it complicated their political lives, as commerce and diplomacy with Euroamericans and other natives drew men farther away from home and increased the potential for conflict and military confrontations.

Along with material exchange came intermarriage and cultural borrowing, especially in areas where amicable trade persisted the longest, such as the western Great Lakes, central Canada, and the interior Southeast. Traders relied on relationships with native women to cement trade alliances and to acquaint themselves with the cultural and environmental conditions. Growing numbers of people of mixed descent fostered biculturalism and served as cultural brokers.

Traders had to accept a nexus of reciprocal rituals embedded in kinship networks. They learned to give presents and demonstrate concern for group welfare. They adopted native items like canoes and snowshoes and relied on native food supplies.

European-manufactured goods often had native counterparts. Knives, hatchets, and cloth were improvements, not innovations. Trade goods could even be used for entirely different purposes; copper pots, for example, might be cut up for ornamentation. Beads, following upon quill work, brought a florescence of artistic expression. Firearms, however, intensified deadly violence in intertribal conflicts. Alcohol, the perfect trade good because it was totally consumed, also exacerbated social conflict, especially among uprooted and dislocated groups. Increasingly in the nineteenth century, treaty-annuity cash fueled a booming liquor trade in every frontier community west of the Mississippi River, despite federal prohibitions against selling alcohol in "Indian Country."

Over generations, native people came to understand credit and debt and learned to equate goods with a standard based on pelts. Those of mixed descent from fur-trade families learned market ways especially well and became petty merchants after the collapse of the regional *fur trade. In the Southeast, they kept step with the local economy by opening inns, mills, taverns, ferries, and toll roads, and even by establishing large plantations with African slaves. They extended their mediating skills into the reservation era, becoming outspoken politicians, though their interests often deviated from those of more conservative members of the group.

However, the encroaching agricultural frontier degraded the environment. As game was depleted, native people functioned as intermediaries, supplying manufactured goods to groups farther in the interior in exchange for pelts. Native middlemen faced a crisis when bypassed by Euroamerican traders. Having lost native craft skills, they found themselves dependent on Euroamericans with little to offer in return other than their land.

Innovations in Governance, Religious Movements, and Pantribal Initiatives. Escalating land loss prompted many native groups to centralize their governance and ally across tribal lines. The Cherokees, subordinating village autonomy to the common goal of retaining their homeland, created a state modeled after the tripartite U.S. government. Selling land without national approval was treason, punishable by death. Other groups, too, modified governance by consensus in the interest of political centralization. Land pressures, combined with the onslaught of formal treaty negotiations with the United States, crystallized social units that had formerly been more fluid.

Native people often sought spiritual solutions for the wrenching problems they faced. Prophets, often reformed alcoholics, experienced visions and conveyed instructions for reclaiming their society from degradation and despair. The more pragmatic the message, the greater was the likelihood of success. In 1799, as the Seneca of upstate New York were reeling from military defeat, land loss, and alcoholism, Handsome Lake began preaching a social and religious message that condemned alcohol, encouraged displaced men instead of women to farm, and subordinated the Senecas' matrilineal social structure to one favoring nuclear families. He also urged revival of religious rituals and farming for subsistence instead of the market.

Tenskwatawa, the Shawnee Prophet, however, at about the same time preached abstinence from all things Euroamerican. He encouraged all native people to assemble at Prophetstown, in northern Indiana. Unable to feed them, he secretly begged for supplies from the British. He claimed the ability to work miracles, but his followers nearly killed him when he failed to deliver.

Equally unrealistic and unsuccessful was the Ghost Dance movement of the 1890s. Large population losses drew native groups across the Plains to the message of *Wovoka, a Paiute. If the devout performed the Ghost Dance at intervals for four consecutive days and nights, Wovoka prophesied, a cataclysm would eliminate whites, return the former Plains ecosystem (especially buffalo), and resurrect the dead. The prophecy failed to materialize, and, tragically, more than 150 members of Big Foot's Lakota band were massacred by the United States cavalry at Wounded Knee, South Dakota, in 1890.

While Tenskwatawa held out spiritual solace through a return to Shawnee ways, diplomats representing his brother *Tecumseh were recruiting allies from the Great Lakes to the Gulf of Mexico. For a brief historical moment, in the most famous pan-tribal initiative, were natives from Canada to the Southeast united to halt the American advance into what had been officially recognized as "Indian Country," where tribes were sovereign nations. Disheartened when General William Henry *Harrison defeated the native people gathered at Prophetstown, in 1811 Tecumseh abandoned his dream of a pan-Indian union.

Forced Expulsion, Forced Assimilation. Neither political nor spiritual strategy could deliver native people from the power of the United States, which began to dictate terms that contradicted its own established policies. For example, despite the Cherokees' success in establishing an elective, democratic government, achieving literacy in both English and Cherokee, establishing plantations, and winning favorable *Supreme Court rulings, they were forcibly removed from their Georgia homeland in the later 1830s. On the trek west, between four thousand and eight thousand perished on what is remembered as the Trail of Tears. By 1850, most native people east of the Mississippi River had been relocated to "Indian Territory," which resembled an ethnic crazy quilt of displaced groups.

The discovery of gold in California in 1848 proved a momentous watershed for native people in the *West. Hordes of single men stampeded to find fortune. Unrestrained by family, community, or church, they decimated the native population near the goldfields. California natives suffered the most complete genocide in U.S. history.

The quest to link California and its gold to East Coast markets by an overland route placed intense pressures upon the native peoples of the Great Plains. The *Oregon Trail split the immense buffalo herd in two. Westering emigrants denuded the countryside adjacent to the trails. As native inhabitants retaliated, the United States erected forts and violence escalated, with many innocent people caught in the cross fire. Most white Americans viewed Great Plains natives as obstacles. Attacks multiplied even against groups under the protection of the U.S. Army. The 1864 massacre of Dull Knife's band of friendly Cheyenne at Sand Creek, Colorado, symbolized the genocide of the bloody Plains Wars between 1850 and 1880. To subdue the Plains people, the U.S. cavalry destroyed their possessions and exterminated the buffalo upon which they depended.

Policy-makers viewed reservations as temporary halfway houses on the road to assimilation. By the late nineteenth century, they were dismayed that many native people persisted in their customs and beliefs. Easterners hoping to assimilate Indians and westerners hoping to acquire reservation lands coalesced in 1887 to pass the *Dawes Severalty Act. Each individual Indian would receive between 40 and 160 acres of land, to be held in trust by the government for twenty-five years while native owners learned how to manage real estate. Homesteaders could buy any land left over. Policy-makers believed that private property would transform Indians' collective values; their cultural traditions would soon follow. The Dawes Act disregarded treaty terms nationwide, except in the arid Southwest. Although some enterprising Indians favored allotment, the vast majority opposed it, but to no avail. In *Worcester* v. *Georgia* (1832), the *Supreme Court had confirmed the absolute plenary power of the United States over native tribes, and Congress now fully exercised this right.

At the same time, the government imposed a massive forced assimilation program on native people. Agents withheld goods and services unless individuals complied with every federal directive. They had to move onto their allotments, cut their hair, assume surnames, attend Christian services, wear "citizens'" clothing, speak English, and, worst of all, send their children to distant boarding schools like Richard H. Pratt's Carlisle Indian Industrial School in Pennsylvania. Boarding schools offered vocational training. Half the day focused on rudimentary reading, writing, and math; the other half involved cleaning, farming, chopping wood, and sewing. Children were steeped in military discipline and forced to wear uniforms and accept English names. Speaking native languages brought punishment. Some homesick students found peer-group support, but others ran away or committed suicide. Overcrowding spread diseases. Graveyards were a regular feature of school grounds. The formula for forced assimilation amounted to cultural genocide.

But native adaptations did not simply mirror policy-makers' demands. Some converted to Christianity; others blended elements from both cultures. At the White Earth Reservation in Minnesota, Ojibwa Episcopal ministers preached and sang hymns in their own language. Mountain Wolf Woman, a Wisconsin Winnebago, practiced her traditional Medicine Lodge religion, attended Christian services, and was a devout Peyotist (a popular new syncretic religion emphasizing sobriety and using peyote as a sacrament). Son of a Star, a North Dakota Hidatsa, built a log cabin instead of an earth lodge but arranged furniture along the walls around the center wood stove. Men and women segregated themselves in customary fashion in relation to the door, on which a buffalo skull rested facing the rising sun. Others resisted change and secretly practiced religions like the Sun Dance away from the prying eyes of agents and missionaries.

As for the 1887 Dawes Act, most native people did not have a chance to learn to manage their allotments as real estate. The 1906 Burke Act permitted "competent" individuals to sell their land, and many did. By 1917, the Commissioner of Indian Affairs was forcing unrestricted land titles on individuals without their consent. They were then subject to property taxes and lost the land through tax forfeiture. Local corporate interests and their political allies connived to defraud native people. By 1920, most native people had lost their land, further pauperizing the most impoverished American minority.

The Situation in 1900. The year 1900 marked the nadir of the Indian population. Colonized, dispossessed, and infantilized by outsiders' iron-clad political and economic control, ultimate extinction seemed inevitable to many observers. Even so, individual responses ranged along a spectrum, with most falling somewhere between the extremes. On one hand, assimilationists championed the Dakota Charles Eastman (1858–1939), a physician who graduated from Boston University Medical School. Daklugie (1872–1955), an Apache leader, represents the other extreme. Daklugie survived the genocidal wars against the Chiricahua Apache, imprisonment at an old fort in Florida, and incarceration at Carlisle Indian School. Once freed, he helped his people turn to cattle raising. Yet he shared the vision of his father, Juh, and despondently reported that the Apache had become *Indeh*—the dead. They had suffered military conquest and could no longer recognize themselves. History, for them, had stopped. That the native population began to increase after 1900 is testimony to their human resiliency and perseverance.

[*See also* Agriculture: 1770s to 1890; Alcohol and Alcohol Abuse; Antebellum Era; *Cherokee Cases*; Early Republic, Era of the; Expansionism; Gilded Age; Gold Rushes; Indian Wars; Land Policy, Federal; Native American Church; Wounded Knee Tragedy.]

• Angie Debo, *And Still the Waters Run: The Betrayal of the Five Civilized Tribes,* 1940. Francis Paul Prucha, *The Great Father: The United States Government and the American Indians,* 2 vols., 1983. R. David Edmunds, *Tecumseh and the Quest for Indian Leadership,* 1984. Robert M. Utley, *The Indian Frontier of the American West, 1846–1890,* 1984. Albert L. Hurtado, *Indian Survival on the California Frontier,* 1988. Richard White, *"It's Your Misfortune and None of My Own": A New History of the American West,* 1991. Anthony F. C. Wallace, *The Long, Bitter Trail: Andrew Jackson and the Indians,* 1993. K. Tsianina Lomawaima, *They Called It Prairie Light: The Story of Chilocco Indian School,* 1994. Melissa L. Meyer, *The White Earth Tragedy: Ethnicity and Dispossession at a Minnesota Anishinaabe Reservation, 1889–1920,* 1994.

—Melissa L. Meyer

INDIAN HISTORY AND CULTURE: FROM 1900 TO 1950

Broad demographic, social, and cultural developments profoundly affected both American Indian tribes and individuals in the first half of the twentieth century, as they struggled to define a place for themselves in a changing America. Two different visions shaped that effort. While some sought to establish themselves and their families as full members of American society, others endeavored to retain distinctive tribal cultures, living within American society but not wholly a part of it.

The most fundamental change during these five decades was demographic. After some four hundred years of decline from an aboriginal population of more than five million, the American Indian population in the United States sank to a nadir of only about 250,000 around 1900. By 1950, according to the U.S. census, the figure had increased to 357,000, as mortality declined significantly and births outnumbered deaths. Accompanying the numerical increases were declining percentages of "full blood" individuals within the American Indian population; for example, 57 percent of American Indians enumerated in the 1910 census were "full bloods," as compared with only 46 percent in 1930. Census data also reveal small but steady increases in the proportion of the Indian population residing in urban areas: In 1900, less than one-half of one percent of American Indians lived in urban areas; by 1950, more than 13 percent did. This redistribution was in part a by-product of *World War II, as returning Indian servicemen and -women settled in cities and towns rather than on reservations or in rural areas where they had lived formerly. A *Bureau of Indian Affairs (BIA) relocation program that encouraged and assisted Indian people to relocate to urban areas, launched at midcentury, accelerated the *urbanization process.

Political developments in these decades affected American Indians as well. The Citizenship Act of 1934 made all American Indians in the United States citizens for the first time, and with citizenship came full voting privileges. The allotment of tribal lands to private owners, although primarily a phenomenon of the late nineteenth century, continued into the twentieth century, particularly in Oklahoma where the allotment of Cherokee lands went on until 1907. That same year the former Oklahoma Territory and Indian Territory merged to become the state of Oklahoma, thereby ending "Oklahoma" as a relocation area for Indian peoples from throughout the United States.

Driving the allotment process were political and corporate desires for Indian lands. In some instances, such as in Oklahoma, acreage allotted to tribal members amounted to mere portions of former tribal land, with the rest allocated for "settlement" by non-Indians. Even allotted lands were not secure under individual Indian ownership. As a result of rampant fraud, individual allotments often fell into the hands of future land barons, speculators, and corporations.

Allotment also undermined tribal life. American Indian groups that managed to retain tribal lands as reservations fared better as tribes. This included particularly Indians on the Plains and in the *Southwest and *West. The 1934 *Indian Reorganization Act, acknowledging Indian tribes' "rights to organize for [their] common welfare," legitimated and codified tribal self-government under the watchful eyes if not the actual dictates of the BIA. This act, in turn, provided the basis for formal tribal constitutions governing the operations of the more than three hundred federally recognized tribes and more than two hundred federally recognized Alaskan Native villages.

The early twentieth century also marked an era of social and cultural change for American Indians. The Chiricahua Apache *Geronimo, the last of the true Indian "warriors" fighting for their land, was captured in 1886 and lived on in Oklahoma until his death in 1909. In 1911, an Indian named Ishi, the last of the Yahis, wandered into Oroville, California, and was taken to the University of California at Berkeley under the supervision of anthropologist Alfred L. Kroeber and others. Apotheosized as the "last wild Indian," he died of tuberculosis in 1916. Symbolically, Ishi's death marked the extinction of truly distinctive American Indian ways of life that had developed over many thousands of years. The portrayal of Indians in the movies and other popular-culture media reinforced the tendency to relegate them to America's mythic past.

While Geronimo and Ishi symbolized the past, other American Indians attained prominence in the early twentieth century for different reasons. The athlete Jim Thorpe (1888–1953) of Oklahoma, a descendant of *Black Hawk, won fame at the 1912 Olympic Games and later played professional football. Other Indians constituted a cadre of intellectuals, operating on a newly established pan-Indian basis, who sought to define or redefine American Indians' identity and their place in twentieth-century America. This group, including such diverse individuals as Charles Eastman, Carlos Montezuma, Mary Baldwin, Arthur C. Parker, and Henry Standing Bear, sought primarily to assimilate Indians into wider society.

In large part, this intellectual cadre was a product of the system of Indian education that had gradually taken shape. Around 1900, more than two hundred government schools were operating on reservations, supplemented by state schools for Indian youth and some schools in the soon-to-be-ended Indian Territory, primarily under the auspices of the Cherokee, Chickasaw, Choctaw, Creek, and Seminole—the so-called Five Tribes. The Carlisle Indian School in Pennsylvania—where Jim Thorpe first won fame as a football player—dated to 1879. By 1925, however, doubts had arisen about the effectiveness of these schools in facilitating the movement of Indians into mainstream American life. The U.S. Senate established a commission to assess Indian education; it was headed by Lewis Meriam of the University of Chicago. Meriam's *The Problem of Indian Administration,* which became known as the *Meriam Report,* asserted in 1928 that the "Indian problem is essentially an educational one," and called for a redirection of Indian education. Beginning in the 1930s, schools for American Indians became more sympathetic to Indian cultures and slowly incorporated Indian history and culture into the curriculum. As boarding schools and day schools declined, the emphasis by midcentury had almost wholly shifted to public-school education for Indian youth.

While many intellectuals, educators, and government administrators sought to bring American Indians more fully into mainstream American society, other developments aimed at retaining a distinct Indian identity, even as the role of tribalism in Indian life declined. Although the Ghost Dance of the 1890s barely survived (in Oklahoma) into the early twentieth century, another new, pan-Indian religion, peyotism, also known as the *Native American Church, became a mainstay for American Indians seeking to maintain a distinct culture. Peyotism remained prominent through midcentury and continued to flourish thereafter in Oklahoma, the Southwest, and other areas, offering hope for American Indians' survival as a distinct people within the larger American society.

[*See also* Assimilation; Cultural Pluralism; Dawes Severalty Act.]

• Angie Debo, *And Still the Waters Run: The Betrayal of the Five Civilized Tribes,* 1940. Hazel W. Hertzberg, *The Search for an American Indian Identity: Modern Pan-Indian Movements,* 1971. Margaret Connell Szasz, *Education and the American Indian: The Road to Self-Determination since 1928,* 1979. Russell Thornton, *American Indian Holocaust and Survival: A Population History since 1942,* 1987. Melissa L. Meyer, *The White Earth Tragedy: Ethnicity and Dispossession at a Minnesota Anishinaabe Reservation,* 1994. Nancy Shoemaker, *American Indian Population Recovery in the Twentieth Century,* 1999.

—Russell Thornton

INDIAN HISTORY AND CULTURE: SINCE 1950

In the 1950s, the U.S. government attempted to assimilate Native Americans through treaty termination and relocation. In 1953, President Dwight D. *Eisenhower signed into law a bill designed to annul federal treaties with Indian nations and to subject Indians to the same laws, and entitle them to the same privileges, rights, and responsibilities, as other citizens. Initiating procedures for ending federal supervision of Indians in *California, Florida, New York, Texas, and specific tribes in other states, the legislation ordered the Secretary of the Interior to review existing treaties and statutes and recommend measures to end federal responsibility by 1 January 1954. A companion act in 1953 extended state laws over Indian reservations in Minnesota, Nebraska, Oregon, and Wisconsin.

In 1951, the Interior Department's *Bureau of Indian Affairs (BIA) launched an employment-assistance program that resettled Native peoples from high-*unemployment reservations to cities like *Chicago, Denver, *Los Angeles, and Oakland. After some job training on the reservation, people were taken to cities where BIA employees found them *housing and employment. After the training and adjustment period, specialized government services ceased. Over 100,000 Indians were resettled through the relocation program, but it was controversial from the start; some people relocated easily, while many others found the transition difficult and returned to their reservations.

In the early 1960s, the John F. *Kennedy administration largely ignored the termination policies and focused on Indian economic development, educational reform, vocational training, and housing. President Lyndon B. *Johnson's *Great Society legislation funneled more federal funds onto reservations than any previous programs. Head Start, the Job Corps, VISTA, and Upward Bound began operating on reservations. Pursuing a policy of self-determination, Johnson's Community Action Program authorized tribal governments to receive monies directly from the Office of Economic Opportunity (OEO) and to administer them without BIA supervision. A weakened BIA thus assumed an intermediary role between tribal governments and other federal agencies.

In 1966, Robert Bennett (Oneida) became the first American Indian to head the BIA since Ely S. Parker (Seneca) in the 1870s. A career BIA employee, Bennett was a skilled administrator who knew many Indian leaders and worked effectively behind the scenes in the federal bureaucracy. In a message to Congress on Indian problems in 1968, Johnson rejected the termination approach and asserted that self-determination would erase "old attitudes of paternalism." To coordinate the many agencies offering Indian services, Johnson appointed Vice President Hubert *Humphrey to head the National Council on Indian Opportunity (NCIO).

President Richard M. *Nixon retained NCIO; pledged to continue Johnson's self-determination policies; and appointed a Republican Indian, Louis R. Bruce (Sioux-Mohawk), as Commissioner of Indian Affairs. In a 1970 message to Congress, Nixon rejected the termination policy and endorsed programs to improve education, health, and economic development on reservations and to increase support for urban Indian centers. The Indian Self-Determination Law (1974) set up procedures whereby Indian tribes could manage federal programs on their lands.

The civil-rights era brought an upsurge in Indian militancy. In the mid-1960s, despite complaints from commercial and sport fishermen, Native fisherman in Washington State asserted their treaty rights to fish in the "usual and accustomed places" along the Nisqually River. In 1974, the federal courts upheld Native fishing rights in the Pacific Northwest. (Similar struggles for fishing rights would erupt in Minnesota and Wisconsin in the 1980s.) Occupying Alcatraz Island in San Francisco Bay in November 1969, American Indian militants sought to gain title to the island, build a Native American cultural center, and launch a Pan-Indian movement called the Confederation of American Indian Nations (CAIN). After a two-year occupation that spotlighted Indian demands, federal marshals removed the protesters.

For Taos Pueblo in New Mexico, the issue was nearby Blue Lake, an important water source and sacred site that the federal government had incorporated into Carson National Forest in 1904. In 1965, after extended protests, the Pueblo leaders rejected a proposed monetary settlement and demanded the lake's return. In 1970, the Nixon administration pushed through a bill restoring Blue Lake to Taos Pueblo.

The Alaska Native Land Claims Act (1971) granted some 40 million acres of federal land, and $962 million, to Indian villages and corporations in *Alaska. In 1972, Nixon by executive order restored to the Yakima Indians of Washington State some 21,000 acres that had been wrongfully incorporated into Mount Rainier forest reserve in 1908.

In 1968, meanwhile, the pan-Indian *American Indian Movement (AIM) had been founded in Minneapolis to deal with unemployment, alienation, and *poverty. Using audacious media tactics, AIM leaders occupied college buildings and staged protests at Mount Rushmore and the *Mayflower II*, a vessel commemorating the *Pilgrims' voyage of 1620. Organizing a "Trail of Broken Treaties," AIM activists occupied BIA headquarters in Washington on 2 November 1972. They demanded repeal of termination legislation, the replacement of the BIA with a three-person presidential commission, the restoration of tribal sovereignty through treaties, and an increase in the Indian land base. On the eve of the 1972 election, the Nixon administration negotiated a compromise agreement granting immunity to the occupiers and promising to review their demands. In February 1973, AIM leaders occupied the hamlet of Wounded Knee on the Pine Ridge Reservation in South Dakota, site of the 1890 massacre of over 300 Lakota people. The highly publicized occupation and armed confrontation with the *Federal Bureau of Investigation lasted for seventy-one days.

American Indian intellectuals and writers rose to prominence through a 1970s cultural renaissance. Vine Deloria Jr., Scott Momaday, and Leslie Silko published pathbreaking books portraying the lives, philosophies, and anger of Native peoples. By the 1980s, writers and activists like Joy Harjo, Louise Erdrich, and Wilma Mankiller became strong voices for Indian survival and well-being. American Indian intellectuals, politicians, activists, and medicine people sought new ways to survive in a spiritually desolate and materialistic Euroamerican world.

Despite many broken government promises to investigate grievances, AIM and the subsequent cultural renaissance increased Indian self-respect and cultural identity. The number of Americans identifying themselves as Indians in the federal *census more than doubled between 1970 and 1990. Media coverage also sensitized the public to Indian issues.

The chief beneficiaries of Indian militancy were moderate groups like the National Tribal Chairman's Association (NTCA) and the National Congress of American Indians (NCAI). As in the African-American *civil rights movement, the government cooperated with moderates to isolate the radicals. In 1973, NTCA and NCAI rejected AIM overtures for cooperation. During the 1970s, Indian moderates and Congress conducted numerous hearings that resulted in over a dozen major legislative acts and the appropriation of more than $100 million in aid for *education (including tribal colleges), health, and economic programs in Native American communities. The Joint Resolution on American Indian Religious Freedom (1978) extended religious freedom to Native Americans, but *Supreme Court decisions in the 1980s and 1990s undermined the practice of religious freedom for the *Native American Church and Indian burial grounds.

In 1980, Passamaquoddy, Penobscot, and other Indian tribes in Maine won land concessions and monetary awards of $81.5 million in settlement of their treaty claims. In the same year, the Supreme Court upheld a lower court's award of $107 million to the Sioux for the illegal seizure of their lands in the Black Hills in 1877.

Seeking economic self-sufficiency, Indian communities turned to manufacturing, *tourism, and other strategies. Following a 1987 Supreme Court ruling and 1988 congressional legislation permitting casino *gambling on reservations, seventy tribes in twenty states opened casinos. Total gambling revenue in 1993 was estimated at $6 billion, but the profits were distributed unevenly; some casinos near urban areas did well, while many others did not.

At the federal level, the Ronald *Reagan and George *Bush administrations saw little progress on such basic Indian issues as sovereignty, economic development, education, and unemployment. Although the Bill *Clinton administration produced few legislative or policy changes, it did restore to tribal governments some monies cut by the previous two administrations. In September 2000, as the Clinton administration ended, BIA head Kevin Gover (Pawnee) formally apologized for the BIA's past record of complicity in the removal of eastern Indians "by threats, deceit, and force"; the "ethnic cleansing" of western tribes; and "futile and destructive efforts to annihilate Indian cultures." In such a climate, and with 557 tribal entities officially recognized by the federal government, the path seemed open for the advancement of Indian self-determination as a new century dawned.

[*See also* Wounded Knee Tragedy; Sixties, The.]

• James S. Olsen and Raymond Wilson, *Native Americans in the Twentieth Century*, 1984. Sharon O'Brien, *American Indian Tribal Governments*, 1989. Marjane Ambler, *Breaking the Iron Bonds: Indian Control of Energy Development*, 1990. Oren Lyons, John Mohawk, et al., *Exiled in the Land of the Free: Democracy, Indian Nations, and the U.S. Constitution*, 1992. John R. Wunder, *"Retained by the People": A History of American Indians and the Bill of Rights*, 1994. Donald L. Parman, *Indians and the American West in the Twentieth Century*, 1994. Donald A. Grinde Jr. and Bruce E. Johansen, *Ecocide of Native America: Environmental Destruction of Indian Lands and Peoples*, 1995. Jeffrey B. Morris and Richard B. Morris, eds., *Encyclopedia of American History*, 7th ed., 1996, pp. 627–29. Bruce E. Johanasen and Donald A. Grinde Jr., *The Encyclopedia of Native American Biography*, 1997.

—Donald A. Grinde Jr.

INDIAN HISTORY AND CULTURE: THE INDIAN IN POPULAR CULTURE

From the first European contact, cultural representations of Native Americans were, for the most part, made by non-Indians and reflected non-Indian values and ideologies. Two stereotypes persisted: the noble Indian and the unredeemable savage. The noble Indian lives a simple life, is eloquent and independent, a child of nature, and helpful to whites. The savage Indian is lecherous, drunk, dirty, improvident, lazy, and hostile to whites. Both stereotypes imagined Indians as relics of the past, with no place in American society, always in the process of disappearing to make way for "civilization."

These imaginings reflected political and cultural conflicts. Idealizations of Indians as the "first Americans" proved useful in developing a national identity distinct from Europe, but actual Native Americans were obstacles to the conquest of the continent. In the end, Native Americans occupied a troubled place in American society: marginalized and oppressed in reality, idealized or demonized in the imagination.

To some seventeenth-century Protestant colonists, Indians were remnants of the Ten Lost Tribes of Israel. *Pocahontas, who allegedly saved the life of Captain John *Smith, became a mythic figure in the American imagination. But the prevailing view held that Indians were heathens who needed to be converted to Christianity or destroyed. Such unredeemable savages figured in the popular Puritan *captivity narratives. In *A Narrative of the Captivity and Restoration of Mrs. Mary Rowlandson* (1676), Indians are instruments of the devil sent to test Christians' faith. Variations of the captivity story long survived in paintings, gothic novels, dime novels, and movies.

During the Revolutionary Era and beyond, the noble savage appeared as a powerful symbol of independence, individual liberty, and an authentic American identity. Chief Logan's eloquent speech of 1774, published in Thomas *Jefferson's *Notes on the State of Virginia* (1785) and in *McGuffey *Readers* throughout the nineteenth century, seemed to represent an authentic American voice and served to naturalize the principles of democracy. The *Boston Tea Party was one of many instances of white men imitating the appearance and behavior of Indians to make a political point. "Playing Indian" persisted in nineteenth-century *fraternal organizations like the New York Tammany Society and the Improved Order of Red Men.

During the *Antebellum Era, the romantic view of the Indian as a pure primitive doomed to disappear as civilization advances prevailed in American literature and art. Vanishing, romanticized Indians appear in the 1830s canvases of George Catlin, Karl Bodmer, and Alfred Jacob Miller and in the novels of James Fenimore *Cooper, in Lydia Maria *Child's *Hobomok: A Tale of Early Times* (1824), and in Henry Wadsworth Longfellow's *The Song of Hiawatha* (1855).

The *Indian Removal Act (1830) forced Indians to the trans-Mississippi west. After the *Civil War, as the U.S. government forced Native Americans onto reservations and violent confrontations erupted between Indians and whites, Indians appeared in the popular culture as villains blocking the way of peaceful settlers. Plains Indians, the prevailing icon, were depicted as savage (though sometimes noble) warriors. Dime novels and *magazines featured adventure stories based on Indian-white conflict. In the Wild West shows that enjoyed popularity from the 1880s until well into the twentieth century, Indians were foils for white Western "heroes" such as William ("Buffalo Bill") *Cody. Helen Hunt Jackson's 1884 novel *Ramona* sought to do for the American Indian what **Uncle Tom's Cabin* had done for the slaves. Jackson's immensely popular tale of doomed lovers offered a variation on earlier sentimental literature about Indians.

Until the late nineteenth century, federal policy concentrated on exterminating Native Americans or isolating them on reservations. With the *Dawes Severalty Act of 1887, however, government policy moved toward assimilation; through land allotment, education, and missionization, Indians would become Americanized. At this point, the noble, vanishing Indian reemerged in nostalgic, elegiac icons such as James Earle Fraser's sculpture *End of the Trail* (1894); photographs by Edward S. Curtis; and paintings and sculptures by Frederic Remington, which evoked an America threatened by *industrialization and *urbanization.

In these decades, too, images of Indians proliferated on many products, such as tobacco, food, patent medicine, and cosmetics. *Railroads and, later, automobiles and motorcycles also used the iconography. This commercial use of Indians evoked qualities such as connection with the earth, purity, manliness, speed, strength, and a reputation for helping whites. *Tourism promoters, regionally and nationally, used images of local Indians (now safely vanished) to promote historical, scenic, or camping attractions. In addition, Native Americans were featured attractions at world's fairs and national parks.

The early twentieth century brought a renewed vogue of "playing Indian." In *scouting organizations such as the Boy Scouts of America, Woodcraft Indians, Girl Scouts, Camp Fire Girls, YMCA, and Boys' Clubs, young people learned Indian "lore," practiced Indian crafts, and performed Indian dances. In *New Orleans, African-American *Mardi Gras associations assumed "Indian" costumes and danced in Mardi Gras parades. These practices provided ways of imagining a national American identity and accessing a premodern, "authentic" state of being. Playing Indian continued in the *New Age movement's spiritual practices, and men's movements. Conservationist and environmental movements also evoked the idea of Native Americans as "close to nature."

In the twentieth century, movies, *radio, and *television shaped images of Indians. Some of the earliest movies, drawing on dime novels and Wild West shows, featured Indian-white conflict. In these films, Native Americans, stereotyped as violent, usually threatened some emblem of civilization such as the stagecoach, the train, the *telegraph, or a white settlement. If not savages, Indians were frequently noble figures who served as companions or wards of white heroes. The "Lone Ranger" and his faithful Indian companion Tonto of radio fame had many incarnations in movie serials, comic books, comic strips, and on television. Beginning in the 1980s, several films portrayed contemporary Indian life, including *Powwow Highway* (1988), *War Party* (1988), *Thunderheart* (1991), and *Smoke Signals* (1998). In addition, several post-1960s Native American filmmakers including George Burdeau, Phil Lucas, James Luna, and Victor Masayesva Jr. responded to stereotypical representations with their own films, as did Native American writers such as N. Scott Momaday, Leslie Marmon Silko, Louise Erdrich, and Sherman Alexie.

As the twentieth century ended, although most Native Americans remained politically and socially marginalized, Native American intellectuals, writers, artists, and filmmakers were taking matters into their own hands, exposing the politics behind popular representations of Indians and demanding recognition of their cultural forms.

[*See also* Indian Wars; Literature, Popular; Puritanism; Romantic Movement; World's Fairs and Expositions.]

• Rayna Green, "The Pocahontas Perplex: The Image of Indian Women in American Culture," *Massachusetts Review* 16 (autumn 1975): 698–714. Robert F. Berkhofer Jr., *The White Man's Indian: Images of the American Indian from Columbus to the Present,* 1978. Brian Dippie, *The Vanishing American: White Attitudes and U.S. Indian Policy,* 1982. Philip J. Deloria, *Playing Indian,* 1998. Wilcomb E. Washburn, ed., *History of Indian-White Relations,* vol. 4 of *Handbook of North American Indians,* ed. William C. Sturtevant, 1988.

—Leah Dilworth

INDIAN REMOVAL ACT. In the 1820s, land speculators called for the elimination of Native American communities that impeded white settlement. Particularly at issue were the Cherokee,

Choctaw, Creek, Chickasaw, and Seminole Indians of Mississippi, Alabama, Georgia, and Florida—the so-called Five Civilized Tribes. Thomas L. McKenney, head of the federal Indian Office from 1824 to 1830, viewing American Indians as children, proposed their removal west of the *Mississippi River. Some missionaries, eager to convert and "civilize" Indians in isolated western lands, welcomed his rhetoric. In 1829, newly elected president Andrew *Jackson endorsed the Indian-removal campaign.

Signed into law on 28 May 1830, the Indian Removal Act empowered the president to exchange Western lands for lands held by eastern tribes and appropriated $500,000 for that purpose. After negotiating divisive treaties with southern Indian nations for removal to Kansas and Oklahoma, Jackson launched prolonged wars of removal that decimated Seminole populations in Florida. In two important *Supreme Court cases, *Cherokee Nation* v. *Georgia* (1831) and *Worcester* v. *Georgia* (1832), Chief Justice John *Marshall, while denying Cherokee claims to be an independent nation, did partially uphold their claims on the basis of prolonged occupancy. But to no avail. The forced removal of the Cherokee, the so-called "Trail of Tears," reduced their population by over 30 percent. An eyewitness recalled: "Families at dinner were . . . driven by blows and oaths . . . to the stockade by soldiers to await removal." They had little choice, since the alternative to removal was often genocidal policies. After the forced expulsion to Indian territory (Oklahoma), many tribes suffered long-term trauma, discord, and violence between pro-removal and anti-removal factions. Although some whites opposed removal, the overwhelming majority supported Jackson's policies, contributing to his lopsided reelection victory in 1832.

[*See also* Antebellum Era; *Cherokee Cases*; Expansionism; Indian History and Culture: From 1800 to 1900; Indian Wars; Seminole Wars; Sequoyah.]

• Michael P. Rogan, *Fathers and Children: Andrew Jackson and the Subjugation of the American Indian,* 1975. Ronald N. Satz, *American Indian Policy in the Jacksonian Era,* 1975. Stephen Breyer, " 'For Their own Good': The Cherokees, the Supreme Court, and the Early History of American Conscience," *New Republic,* August 7, 2000, 32–39.

—Donald A. Grinde Jr.

INDIAN REORGANIZATION ACT (Wheeler-Howard Act). The Indian Reorganization Act of 1934 settled a bitter Indian-policy debate waged in the 1920s. The "protectors," led by Secretary of the Interior Albert B. Fall and his commissioner of Indian affairs, Charles H. Burke, wanted to continue government paternalism toward Indian people while denouncing Indian dances and traditional religious practices and advocating open access by non-Indians to reservation resources and land. The "reformers"—notably John Collier (1884–1968), founder of the American Indian Defense Association, and Gertrude Bonnin, a Yankton Dakota—sought to preserve Native American resources, crafts, culture, land, and spirituality. Collier agreed with the writer Hamlin Garland that government should prevent "missionaries from regulating the amusements and daily lives of the natives" and should protect native lands.

In 1934, Collier, who had become President Franklin Delano *Roosevelt's commissioner of Indian affairs, replaced the "protectors" and "missionaries" in the *Bureau of Indian Affairs with social scientists and reformers and worked actively for passage of the Indian Reorganization Act, sometimes called "the Indian New Deal." Although the act did not put native peoples in leadership positions in the Bureau of Indian Affairs, it sought to protect Native American religious rights, encourage self-determination, improve Indian education and health services, fund tribal enterprises, and end the allotment established by the *Dawes Severalty Act by which non-Indians could acquire title to reservation lands.

Although criticized by some Indians for its paternalism, the act did curb the erosion of the reservation land base. The tribal sovereignty and self-determination aspects of the act, however, were undermined after 1945. In spite of its shortcomings, the act remains the most significant Indian legislation passed in the twentieth century.

[*See also* Indian History and Culture: From 1900 to 1950; New Deal Era, The.]

• Kenneth R. Philp, *John Collier's Crusade for Indian Reform, 1920–1954,* 1977. Graham D. Taylor, *The New Deal and American Indian Tribalism: The Administration of the Indian Reorganization Act, 1934–1945,* 1980.

—Donald A. Grinde Jr.

INDIAN WARS. Warfare between whites and Indians began when the first colonists set foot in the New World. Whites posed a threat to Indian lands and way of life. For four centuries the struggle kept pace with the westward movement of whites. Often tribes met the invasion with aggressions against settlers and travelers. When hostilities escalated, both sides often resorted to full-scale war using organized military forces.

Colonial Era. Throughout the *Colonial Era, fighting periodically broke out along the Atlantic coast and the northern frontiers of New Spain. Some wars sprang from resistance to European intrusion, others from rivalries of colonial powers exploiting traditional tribal animosities. Among the more destructive wars were those between the English settlers of *Jamestown and the Algonquian tribes in 1622 and 1644; *King Philip's War in New England in 1675–1676; the *Pueblo Revolt of 1680, which expelled Spaniards from New Mexico for a decade; and the *Pontiac "conspiracy" of 1763–1766, which aimed at driving the English from the Great Lakes. All the wars took a frightful toll in life and property, and all ended in Indian defeat.

From 1790 to 1870. After the *Revolutionary War, hostilities continued from the Appalachian Mountains to the *Mississippi River. In 1790–1791, in Ohio, the Miami chief Little Turtle decisively defeated U.S. forces under Generals Josiah Harmer and Arthur St. Clair. These defeats led the infant American government to establish a regular army. In 1794, in the Battle of Fallen Timbers, General Anthony Wayne (1745–1796) crushed Little Turtle and opened the Ohio Country to settlers.

Early in the nineteenth century, the Shawnee chief *Tecumseh sought to unite all the tribes, north and south, against the white invader. General William Henry *Harrison destroyed this design in 1811 at the Battle of Tippecanoe, in Indiana. In 1814, a Creek faction, the Red Sticks, rose against settlers in the *South but was crushed by General Andrew *Jackson at the Battle of Horseshoe Bend, Alabama.

In the 1820s and 1830s, the United States backed diplomacy with force to move the eastern tribes to new homes west of the Mississippi River. Most went without major armed resistance. Under *Black Hawk, the Sacs and Foxes of Illinois briefly fought back in 1832 but were swiftly overpowered.

Federal authorities hoped to end Indian warfare by separating Indians and whites with a "Permanent Indian Frontier" extending from Minnesota to Louisiana. In 1845–1848, however, the settlement of the Oregon boundary dispute and the territorial acquisitions of the *Mexican War dashed this hope. Beginning with the California gold rush in 1848, Indian warfare attended the westward movement until the frontier closed in 1890.

In *California, most of the small native groups vanished as gold seekers overran the Sierra Nevada. In Oregon and Washington, stronger tribes fought back. The Yakima and Rogue River Wars of 1854–1856, followed by an uprising in the Columbia Basin, prompted a ruthless military offensive. In 1858, victories by Colonel George Wright ended Indian warfare in the Pacific Northwest.

The most intense fighting of the 1850s occurred in Texas, where settlers pushed westward and the army tried to protect them from raiding parties of Kiowas, Comanches, and Apaches from the north. A chain of military posts extending from the Red River to the Rio Grande failed to deter the raiders.

In New Mexico, American newcomers inherited old rivalries between Hispanic colonizers and Apaches and Navajos. The army established a system of forts, but they proved no more effective than in Texas.

On the Great Plains, transcontinental emigrant trails stirred Indian wrath. Near Fort Laramie, the Grattan Massacre of 1854, caused by the imprudent actions of a young officer, led to General William S. Harney's campaign of 1855. At the Battle of Bluewater, Harney destroyed a Sioux village and killed Chief Little Thunder. To the south, Kiowas, Comanches, and Cheyennes disrupted the trade with New Mexico and struck south into Texas.

The *Civil War years of 1861–1865, when volunteer units replaced regulars, intensified fighting. In Minnesota, years of injustice exploded in the Sioux uprising of 1862, which took the lives of four hundred settlers. General Henry H. Sibley quelled the rebellion. It spread west into Dakota territory, however, where other Sioux deplored gold seekers crossing their territory to mines in western Montana. In 1863–1865, both Sibley and General Alfred Sully fought successful battles against Indians on the upper Missouri River.

In New Mexico, as Apache and Navajo wars continued, General James H. Carleton ordered U.S. troops into the field. In 1863–1864, under Colonel Christopher "Kit" Carson (1809–1868), the troops rounded up Mescalero Apaches and Navajos and confined them on a bleak reservation far from their homelands.

In the Summer of 1864, Indian unrest on the roads connecting Colorado with the East formed the backdrop for the Sand Creek Massacre—a treacherous attack by Colonel John M. Chivington on Black Kettle's peaceful Cheyenne village. Sand Creek set off a general war that spread over all the Plains country in 1865.

The Late Nineteenth Century. At the close of the *Civil War, regular troops returned to frontier duty. In the desert Southwest and in Texas, hostilities persisted. On the northern Great Plains, Red Cloud's Sioux closed the Bozeman Trail to the Montana mines, besieged the three forts established to protect travelers, and in December 1866 destroyed a force of eighty soldiers under Captain William J. Fetterman.

The Fetterman disaster and other military setbacks led the government to devise a peace movement. Treaties established reservations that promised rations and other goods, attracting many Indians to surrender and accept government handouts. The Fort Laramie and Medicine Lodge Treaties of 1867–1868 bound Plains Indians to settle on reservations. Most of the remaining Indian wars were fought to force Indians onto reservations or to return to reservations from which they had fled.

In 1868–1869, military campaigns forced Cheyennes, Kiowas, and Comanches onto new reservations in the Indian Territory. During this operation, the Cheyenne chief Black Kettle, who had escaped Sand Creek, died when Lt. Col. George A. Custer (1839–1876) devastated his village in the Battle of the Washita. In 1874, these tribes, rebelling against reservation restraints, fled to the West. The Red River War lasted until the Spring of 1875 and, with the surrender of the Indians, ended fighting on the southern Plains and along the Texas frontier.

On the northern Plains, discovery of gold in the Black Hills stirred new tensions. The Sioux War of 1876 resulted, as the army tried to force *Sitting Bull, *Crazy Horse, and other chiefs to settle on the Great Sioux Reservation, created by the Fort Laramie Treaty of 1868. On 25 June 1876 along Montana's Little Bighorn River Indian warriors wiped out Custer and part of his command. Stunned by the disaster, federal authorities ordered large armies into the field. By Spring 1877, most of the Sioux and Cheyennes had surrendered. Sitting Bull sought refuge in Canada but gave up in 1881.

In 1872–1873, war broke out with the Modocs of northeastern California, after the government tried to force a band under Captain Jack and other leaders onto a reservation. Taking refuge in a lava flow, these Modocs held out for four months. During a peace conference, Jack and other Modocs killed General Edward R. S. Canby. The Indians were finally driven from their fortress, captured, and the leaders hanged.

In 1877, the government ordered all Nez Percés of Idaho and Oregon to go to their Idaho reservation. Under *Chief Joseph and other leaders, about eight hundred Nez Percés retreated across the mountains to Montana. They had almost reached sanctuary in Canada when a force under Colonel Nelson A. Miles (1839–1925) cut them off at Bear Paw Mountain and forced most to surrender.

Other mountain tribes also fought before surrendering. In 1878, the Bannocks and Paiutes of Idaho and eastern Oregon were defeated. In 1879 the Utes of Colorado met a like fate. The last holdouts were the Apaches of Arizona and New Mexico. Under Cochise (1812?–1874), Apache warriors terrorized the Southwest and Mexico from 1861 until General Oliver O. Howard made peace with him in 1872. General George Crook conducted a successful campaign against other Apaches in the Tonto Basin in 1872–1873. New fighting broke out when the government determined to collect all Apaches on the San Carlos Reservation. The Victorio War of 1879–1880 ravaged much of the Southwest until Mexican troops finally killed the chief and ended the rebellion.

The most famous Apache leader was *Geronimo. His little band of fighters scourged settlements on both sides of the Mexican boundary and stood off armies of two nations. General Crook enlisted other Apaches and penetrated the Apache refuges in Mexico. Twice he forced Geronimo to surrender, but it fell to General Nelson A. Miles to bring Geronimo to bay for the last time, in 1886, and end Apache warfare.

One final bloodletting, the *Wounded Knee Tragedy in South Dakota, occurred in 1890. Here the Ghost Dance, a revivalist movement, exploded with unintended and unexpected violence. Nearly two-thirds of Chief Big Foot's people were killed or wounded, while the military force also sustained heavy casualties. Wounded Knee was the last major military encounter between Indians and whites.

[*See also* Expansionism; Gold Rushes; Indian History and Culture: From 1500 to 1800; Indian History and Culture: From 1800 to 1900; Little Bighorn, Battle of the; Manifest Destiny; Seven Years' War; Spanish Settlements in North America; Yamassee War.]

• Douglas E. Leach, *The Northern Colonial Frontier, 1607–1763,* 1966. Robert M. Utley, *Frontiersmen in Blue: The United States Army and the Indian, 1846–1865,* 1967. Francis Paul Prucha, *The Sword of the Republic: The United States Army on the Frontier, 1783–1846,* 1969. Robert M. Utley, *Frontier Regulars: The United States Army and the Indian, 1866–1891,* 1973. Robert M. Utley and Wilcomb E. Washburn, *Indian Wars,* 1977. W. Stitt Robinson, *The Southern Colonial Frontier, 1607–1763,* 1979. Wilcomb E. Washburn, ed., *History of Indian-White Relations,* vol. 4 of *Handbook of North American Indians,* ed. William C. Sturtevant, 1988. Gregory Dowd, *A Spirited Resistance: The North American Indian Struggle for Unity, 1745–1815,* 1992.

—Robert M. Utley

INDIVIDUALISM. To speak of a person as an individual is to conceive of that man or woman as separate, autonomous, and self-interested, all qualities that distinguish the person from his or her group or family. Individualism refers to the nest of concepts that emphasize this independence of individuals in contrast to the earlier view of each human being as belonging to the overlapping social entities of church, family, craft, and locale.

The word "individualism" appeared for the first time in the 1835 English translation of Alexis de Tocqueville's **Democracy in America*, where he described individualism as a withdrawal from public life by Americans who felt deeply their own self-sufficiency. Tocqueville's contemporary, the English philosopher John Stuart Mill, viewed personal liberty in a far more positive light, and American transcendentalists like Ralph Waldo *Emerson and Henry David *Thoreau explored the dimensions of the individual conscience, giving greater weight to responsibilities than to rights.

Initially seen as a threat to a well-ordered society, individualism gained acceptance with the commercialization of traditional economies and the spread of participatory politics. Freedom underwent a redefinition as well. Where once people thought of freedom in terms of the group's power of self-government, during the eighteenth century freedom became linked with individual liberty, competitive opportunity, and free choice.

In the later twentieth century, individualism came to be contrasted with communitarianism, the former ideology stressing that people must stand on their own aided by institutions protecting their free choice, the latter promoting a society of mutually dependent members all willing to subordinate their personal desires to the good of the whole. These contrasting views rested on different conceptions of human nature as well as of human welfare.

[*See also* Conservativism; Laissez-faire; Social Darwinism; Transcendentalism.]

—Joyce Appleby

INDUSTRIAL DESIGN. As *industrialization accelerated and consumer goods proliferated after 1865, competition forced manufacturers to focus on product appearance. Ordinary citizens aspired to comfort, even luxury: patent furniture, lush domestic interiors, eclectic mail-order goods. New materials like celluloid simulated expensive ivory and tortoiseshell. Although an industrial-design profession did not exist in the late nineteenth century, the architect Frank Lloyd *Wright articulated its principles in 1901 by advising artists to abandon craft production and create prototypes for factory reproduction.

After 1900, manufacturers struggled to give form to electrical appliances, automobiles, and other new technologies. Consumers often demanded the future in the guise of the past. The "horseless carriage" was just one novelty whose acceptance depended in part on traditional associations. Engineers planning new products were uncertain how to proceed. Art schools trained applied artists to create commercial art and decorative furnishings but offered no training in new technologies. In the 1920s, some decorators adopted French "modernistic" styling to express the tempo of the Machine Age. Promoted by architects and museum curators, Art Deco reached industry in the later 1920s.

Industrial design emerged as a business response to the Great Depression, an application of the principles formulated by the efficiency expert Frederick W. Taylor. Commercial artists and stage designers turned to product design and employed streamlining as a comprehensive style for the Machine Age. Borrowed from aerodynamics, streamlining transformed automobiles, washing machines, and radios. For manufacturers it lubricated the flow of goods to consumers; for consumers it promised a future of material abundance. Consultant industrial designers such as Henry Dreyfuss, Norman Bel Geddes, Raymond Loewy, and Walter Dorwin Teague became celebrities. General Electric, Sears Roebuck, and other companies established in-house design departments. Some designers sought to transform society, as at the utopian New York World's Fair of 1939, but more commercial considerations inspired Egmont Arens to describe his profession as "consumer engineering." During *World War II, designers boosted morale by visualizing postwar products in magazine advertisements: prefabricated housing, bubble-domed automobiles, and push-button telephones. The profession became institutionalized in the American Designers Institute (1938) and the Society of Industrial Designers (1944); both later consolidated as the Industrial Designers Society of America (1965).

Beginning in the 1930s, art, business, and government contributed to a "high modernism" lasting into the 1960s. The Museum of Modern Art promoted a succession of noncommercial design statements: an abstract "machine art," a warmer "organic design," and a reformist "good design." Refugees from Nazism like László Moholy-Nagy brought to America the advanced ideas associated with the Bauhaus, the German school of design founded by Walter Gropius in 1919. Influenced by this climate of opinion, Walter Paepcke, president of the Container Corporation of America, supported Chicago's Institute of Design and established the Aspen Design Conference for business leaders and policy-makers. Eero Saarinen and Charles and Ray Eames designed organic furniture for institutional and corporate America. George Nelson publicized high modernism through the journal *Industrial Design* and such official consumerist celebrations as the U.S. pavilion at the Brussels World's Fair (1958) and the Moscow trade fair (1959).

"Good design" principles rarely inhibited profit-driven corporate marketers, however, whose approach was epitomized by the chrome-laden chariots produced by the postwar American *automotive industry. Abandoning 1930s idealism, J. Gordon Lippincott's *Design for Business* (1947) insisted that industrial design existed only to increase a client's profits. Although well-trained designers graduated from many educational programs in the 1950s, few became consultants. Most joined in-house departments that treated design as cosmetic styling that often became anonymous, dull, and repetitive. Harley Earl's styling division at General Motors, founded in the late 1920s to rationalize planned obsolescence, introduced flaring tailfins and two-tone paint jobs that influenced the appearance of gas pumps, coffee tables, sectional sofas, and even suburban carports. Amoeba and boomerang shapes of the "populuxe" era reflected faith in scientific progress and a cornucopia of essentially disposable products.

Reactions against postwar excess, mirroring countercultural disgust with American affluence, often targeted industrial design. Victor Papanek's *Design for the Real World* (1972) dismissed much design as worthless and admonished designers to address the needs of poorer nations, the disabled, and the aging. Beginning in 1968, Stewart Brand's series of *Whole Earth Catalogs* promoted decentralized living with limited reliance on technological systems. Such views contributed to subsequent environmentally sensitive "green design" and "eco design" movements. A series of expensive product-liability lawsuits forced corporations to adopt design awareness for safety as well as profits.

Just as the 1930s depression challenged designers to create a cohesive style for the Machine Age, global competition of the 1980s and 1990s compelled designers to give shape to the hardware and immaterial software of the information age. Prophets of quality urged executives to upgrade design from its status as a cosmetic afterthought and to expand the designer's responsibility to encompass corporate strategy. The result was a design revival reminiscent of the 1930s—with its utopianism based not on the machine but on flowing streams of electrons.

[*See also* Advertising; Consumer Culture; Consumer Movement; Depressions, Economic; Electrical Industry; Modernist Culture; Scientific Management; World's Fairs and Expositions.]

• Jeffrey L. Meikle, *Twentieth Century Limited: Industrial Design in America, 1925–1939,* 1979. James Sloan Allen, *The Romance of Commerce and Culture: Capitalism, Modernism, and the Chicago-Aspen Crusade for Cultural Reform,* 1983. Arthur J. Pulos, *American Design Ethic: A History of Industrial Design to 1940,* 1983. Thomas Hine, *Populuxe,* 1986. Richard Guy Wilson, Dianne H. Pilgrim, and Dickran Tashjian, *The Machine Age in America 1918–1941,* 1986. Arthur J. Pulos, *The American Design Adventure: 1940–1975,* 1988.

—Jeffrey L. Meikle

INDUSTRIAL DISEASES AND HAZARDS. America's rise to industrial supremacy came at great human cost. Throughout the technological revolution that unfolded between the 1820s and *World War I, mechanization and the harnessing of steam and then electric power, for all their benefits, also created new productive processes and new occupations that jeopardized the health of working men, women, and children. This revolution both generated novel acute and chronic diseases and increased the incidence of preexisting occupational disorders. In particular, the expansion of natural resource–based industries, like tanning and mining, fostered considerable morbidity.

Workplace hazards of all sorts sickened American employees during the era of *industrialization. Among toxic chemicals, naturally occurring substances posed the greatest risk. A host of dangerous elements, including arsenic, mercury, phosphorus, and especially lead, poisoned employees across the nation. Cotton, silica, coal, and other vegetable and mineral dusts threatened the respiratory functioning of millions of workers. Bacteria and other biological agents attacked not only health-care workers but also construction laborers and slaughterhouse employees. Among the common physical agents of disease, extremes of heat and cold and nonionizing radiation menaced outdoor workers, while noise deafened workers inside mills, foundries, and other manufacturing plants. Repetitive and strenuous movements strained workers' musculoskeletal systems. On the endless range of psychosocial stressors, the tensions of experimentation with the pace of new *technology and the uncertainties surrounding devalued skills, arbitrary employer power, and a highly volatile *business cycle all contributed to illness in the workforce.

Scientific recognition and public reporting of work-related diseases were very limited prior to 1920. Against this pattern of disregard, the pioneering early twentieth-century investigations by the Chicago physician Alice Hamilton (1869–1970), a resident of Jane *Addams's Hull House, stand out as exceptional. Within working-class culture, vernacular terms—"the jackhammer laugh," "hatter's shakes," "phossy jaw," "brain strain," "telegraphist's cramp"—reflected a widespread, if incomplete, understanding of industrial disease.

In the period commencing with World War I, a flood of synthetic chemicals transformed the working environment. Cracking petroleum, splitting coal-tar molecules, and other *chemical-industry processes yielded substances to which human beings had never before been exposed. At the same time, increased resistance to infectious *diseases meant that workers generally survived the long latent periods preceding the onset of *cancer and other insidious chronic conditions. By the 1970s, federal officials estimated that work-induced illness accounted for approximately 100,000 deaths per year and that approximately 2 million Americans were living with disabilies stemming from such maladies.

With countless new solvents, dyes, plastics, pesticides, and other synthetic chemicals producing toxicity, and with thousands of these substances exhibiting some carcinogenic potential, employees far beyond the chemical industry and, indeed, far beyond the manufacturing sector routinely encountered significant risks. Moreover, innovative materials and processes sometimes combined with older hazards, like asbestos and lead, to create dangerous new formulations. Mortality from asbestos-related cancers in the last quarter of the twentieth century has been estimated at more than 200,000. Though the threat of some biohazards receded for workers in health-care and other human services, the threat of others, such as hepatitis B virus, grew. Among the physical agents, radium, uranium, and other sources of ionizing radiation endangered diverse groups of employees. The rise of *computers fostered hazards of repetitive motion and related ergonomic problems. The spread of so-called *scientific management split many jobs into fragments, leaving workers with neither control over nor fulfillment in their work. Combined with job insecurity, such powerlessness and alienation became a scientific-managerial prescription for employee stress.

Clinical, toxicological, and epidemiological researchers clarified innumerable adverse effects of human-made chemicals, often despite industry obstruction. Hamilton's *Industrial Toxicology* (1934) and Wilhelm Hueper's *Occupational Tumors and Allied Diseases* (1942) represented significant early breakthroughs in extending awareness of the scope of this problem. With the passage of the landmark Occupational Safety and Health Act in 1970, attention by public and private institutions to the full spectrum of workplace hazards accelerated. Unions and their allies pressed initiatives to give workers a right to know about the probability of occupational disease.

The late twentieth century witnessed the resurrection of a holistic perspective and a retreat from the long-standing preoccupation with seeking a single, specific cause of work-related ailments. Instead, the multifactorial nature of workers' afflictions, commonly involving both occupational and nonoccupational causes, was increasingly acknowledged, as were the varied, often indistinct, syndromes resulting from complex combinations of risk factors. Phenomena such as ergonomic disorders, stress-induced disease, building-related illness, multiple chemical sensitivities, and workers' hypertension challenged the single cause–singular effect paradigm.

[*See also* Carson, Rachel; Consumer Movement; Factory System; Labor Movements.]

• David Rosner and Gerald Markowitz, eds., *Dying for Work,* 1987. Ronald Bayer, ed., *The Health and Safety of Workers,* 1988. David Rosner and Gerald Markowitz, *Deadly Dust,* 1991. Allard E. Dembe, *Occupation and Disease,* 1996. Christopher C. Sellers, *Hazards of the Job,* 1997. Alan Derickson, *Black Lung,* 1998.

—Alan Derickson

INDUSTRIALIZATION. Industrialization encompasses the growth of manufacturing, the increased adoption of mechanical means of production and natural-resource forms of energy, the spread of the wage-labor system, and the advent of factory enterprise. Although industrial development in the United States dates to the 1820s, the process unfolded unevenly in different trades and regions at different times and rates. In the late twentieth century, with plant closings and significant losses in manufacturing jobs, the United States experienced industrial decline.

Before 1800, many manufactured goods—for example, garments, shoes, furniture, and tools—were produced in the home for direct family consumption. European settlers in North America also relied on British imports. Urban artisans produced elite custom goods based on venerable craft traditions and practices. In theory, British mercantile policies and prohibitions on colonial manufacture may have constrained manufacturing—and sparked grievances among the colonialists—but, in practice, a limited market, natural transportation obstacles, and cheap imports effectively dampened colonial industrial progress.

Beginnings in the Early National Era. Despite their new nation's underdeveloped industry, Americans of the early national period vigorously debated the benefits and pitfalls of industrialization. Advocates such as Alexander *Hamilton and the Pennsylvania political economist Tench Coxe argued that it would ensure America's fiscal integrity and economic autonomy and eliminate idle labor. In the early 1790s, Coxe and Hamilton even promoted a failed experiment to build an industrial city in what later became Paterson, New Jersey. Thomas *Jefferson and his allies, on the contrary, feared that a large, permanent class of factory workers would threaten a democratic republic based on virtuous yeoman producers and citizens.

This debate shaped but did not thwart industrialization, especially in textile production. U.S. textile manufacturing, benefiting from a period of extraordinary invention of textile machinery in Great Britain, followed four distinct paths.

In 1789, Samuel Slater (1768–1835) immigrated to America from Great Britain fresh from an apprenticeship in a cotton textile mill. He was only the first of a cohort of immigrant British mechanics who brought new technologies. Financed by the Brown family of Providence, Rhode Island, Slater established the nation's first successful cotton mill in Pawtucket, Rhode Island, in 1793, and then built similar cotton-mill villages throughout southeastern *New England. They were characterized by water-powered spinning mills operated by women and children; hand-loom weaving by men in company-provided houses; and company-established schools, churches, and stores. Spreading across the Northeast and the *South, the company-owned mill village based on family labor became a basic component of American industrialization.

Francis Cabot Lowell (1775–1817) of Massachusetts had a grander vision. After observing the latest technological developments in Britain, Lowell secured financial support from other *Boston merchants and constructed a fully-integrated and mechanized textile factory in Waltham, Massachusetts, in 1814. When waterpower there limited expansion, Lowell and his associates planned a large industrial works at the falls of the Merrimack River, thirty-five miles north of Boston. Lowell died before the industrial city bearing his name was built.

Textile production at the *Lowell mills represented a revolution in business practices including: the corporate form of ownership and the amount of capital amassed; the concentration of all stages of production under a single roof, from the cleaning, carding, and spinning of raw fibers to the weaving and finishing of cloth; the application of *technology (including fully mechanized power looms); the scale of employment (by the 1850s, more than thirteen thousand workers labored in the city's fifty-two mills); and the encouragement of mass consumption as bolts of inexpensive broadcloth flowed from the mills. Lowell also entailed a remarkable human story, as young New England farm women came to work in the factories and reside in company boardinghouses. In the 1830s and 1840s, protesting deteriorating working conditions, they participated in the nation's earliest strikes by industrial workers.

Along with Lowell and Slater-like mill villages, a third kind of industrial system characterized by diversity and specialization emerged in the larger cities. Textile production in *Philadelphia, for example, involved the manufacture of fancy cloth in separate spinning, weaving, and finishing establishments. A vast array of products—from garments to jewelry, machine parts, fine surgical instruments, pottery, and paints—flowed from homes, sweatshops, craft shops, mills with hand-powered machinery and more mechanized factories in the nation's metropolitan centers. The typical nineteenth-century manufacturing firm in *New York City or Philadelphia was small-to-medium sized, was family owned and operated, produced small batches of quality or seasonal wares, and often relied on skilled labor. Insufficient waterpower, the presence of niche markets and skilled workers, and the technological know-how and entrepreneurialism of British and German immigrants all figured in the creation of an urban industrial base characterized by variety and small-scale modes of production.

The American South added a fourth strand to early American industrialization: industrial *slavery. Before the *Civil War, leased and directly owned *African-American slaves worked in southern textile factories, ironworks, tobacco-processing plants, and lumber and grain mills. However, profitability of cotton plantation agriculture, coupled with southern white fears of forming a concentrated urban work force of slaves as well as southerners' preference for northern and imported manufactured goods, limited industrialization in the antebellum South. Investment flowed more readily into the purchase of land, cottonseed, and slaves than into industrial facilities.

Factors Influencing Industrial Development. In North and South, population growth, abundant natural resources, prosperous agriculture, and an expanding market stimulated industrial development. Government played a minimal role. While the federal, state, and local governments subsidized canal and *railroad building, public moneys were not advanced toward manufacture. Protective *tariffs remained a politically contentious issue, and only in a few areas, such as the *iron and steel industry, did tariff protection significantly help domestic industries. The nation's political and legal system, however, did affect economic development. The U.S. *Constitution, for example, established patent procedures that encouraged invention and reserved to the states substantive powers that included authority to charter businesses. Thus, during the 1840s, states enacted general incorporation laws that promoted the corporate form of enterprise. Judicial decisions also fostered industrial expansion.

One seeming obstacle to industrial development, a relative scarcity of labor, especially skilled labor, actually proved an asset, motivating entrepreneurs to mechanize and to substitute capital for labor. In Lowell, for example, lacking a preexisting labor base, textile manufacture could only be conducted in fully mechanized ways. (Conversely, in places where skilled hands abounded, such as Philadelphia, handwork production persisted.) Similarly with few skilled assemblers of guns available, federal arsenals and private companies pioneered in *mass production of standardized interchangeable parts that could be assembled by relatively unskilled labor. British investigators, impressed by the progress achieved in U.S. mass-production techniques in gun manufacture, clock-making, sewing-machine production, and other trades, dubbed what they saw the "*American System" of Manufactures.

Yet, the so-called American System was slow in developing. In the late nineteenth century, U.S. factories still needed skilled assemblers to file and fit in place less than precision-tooled components. Only with the twentieth-century advent of conveyor-belt, mass assembly, first in the *automotive industry, did the system of interchangeable-parts production become fully realized.

Except in Lowell, U.S. industrial development encompassed older forms of production alongside new techniques. In Lynn, Massachusetts, the center of shoe manufacture, for example, shoes were first produced in homes through an outwork system; later, the attachment of the upper leathers to the soles moved into centralized handwork shops. Mechanized factories emerged by the mid-nineteenth century, but older work settings persisted.

Labor conflict also marked early American industrialization. Journeymen demonstrated against the dilution of craft practices in artisan shops and their subordination as wage laborers. In the new factories, industrial workers protested against the harsh conditions of work. Women especially led and participated in notable strikes in Lowell and Lynn.

From the Civil War to 1900. By the Civil War, industrialization had made great strides. While the war was affected by industrialization—accuracy of machine-tooled rifles increased casualties and altered military strategies—it did not modify the established path of economic growth. The post–Civil War Era, however, saw extraordinary manufacturing growth, with a five-fold increase in output between 1870 and 1900, by which time 35 percent of the world's production of manufactured goods was pouring from U.S. factories, more than the combined output of rivals Great Britain, Germany, and France.

This industrial growth was based primarily on more workers in more factories producing more goods rather than on technological innovation or gains in *productivity. The geographical expansion of industry in the late nineteenth century abetted the nation's rise to industrial supremacy. During this period, a wide manufacturing belt stretched from the Northeast to *Chicago, extending southward to Ohio and Pittsburgh, Pennsylvania, the world's center for iron and steel production. Chicago, with its mechanized *meatpacking and meat-processing plants, steel mills, and farm-machinery works, attracted the greatest attention, yet diversified industry flourished throughout the new industrial heartland. Philadelphia and New

York City, with their shops, mills, and factories, remained major manufacturing centers, and textile production spread across New England. Wilmington, Delaware, became famous for gunpowder, leather tanning, and—somewhat later—chemicals; Trenton, New Jersey, for ceramic wares and wire cable; Paterson for silk cloth; Providence for machinery and jewelry; Troy, New York, for iron stoves; Rochester, New York, for photographic materials and equipment; Buffalo, New York, and Cleveland, Ohio, for steel; Cincinnati, Ohio, for soap; and Grand Rapids, Michigan, for furniture.

Small-to-medium-sized firms dominated this Northeast and Midwest industrial belt, but a new kind of manufacturing concern emerged in the late nineteenth century, eventually to dominate the economic landscape: the large-scale, corporately owned, bureaucratically managed industrial enterprise. Several factors contributed to the rise of big *business. A transcontinental railroad system created a national marketplace that heightened competition and encouraged manufacturing concerns to grow vertically, from accessing raw materials to distributing final products. Intense competition also led to a wave of corporate mergers and consolidations, including J. P. *Morgan's amalgamation of key steel producers into the giant U.S. Steel Corporation in 1901. Finance capitalists encouraged mergers, as they profited by underwriting, issuing, and exchanging corporate securities. Those consolidated firms that created profitable economies of scale and scope through professional managerial structures justified the emergence of mammoth enterprises.

Labor Conflict in the Industrial Age. Intense labor conflict accompanied the geographical and corporate manufacturing expansions of the late nineteenth century. Between 1880 and 1900, an average of more than 1,000 strikes involving 200,000 workers, and ranging from crippling nationwide walkouts to local job actions, occurred. Workers struck for more than higher wages and shorter hours. The economic and political threat that giant corporations posed to belief in equality and yeoman producership fueled grievances and produced community support for workers' demands. The capricious rule of foremen in large enterprises generated strike activity and calls for union recognition as well as union-determined work rules to ensure fairness and security.

The power of skilled workers over production processes proved another source of labor tension. Business executives attempted to assert greater managerial control over their skilled employees through technology, embedding the production process in machines and measuring devices; through the *scientific management principles of Frederick Winslow Taylor and others; and through concerted antiunion efforts. Two dramatic late nineteenth-century labor battles involved skilled workers. In Chicago in May 1886, conflict between managers and craft unionists at the McCormick Reaper Company coincided with a nationwide labor protest for an eight-hour workday; the McCormick strike presaged the Haymarket Square bombing and police riot. In July 1892, a decision by the steel magnate Andrew *Carnegie and his chief associate, Henry Clay Frick, to eliminate craft unionism in Carnegie's Homestead, Pennsylvania steelworks led to a pitched battle between strikers and Pinkerton agents.

Not every firm dealt with labor tension through repressive tactics. Some tried to win their employees' loyalty through positive means. George Pullman, manufacturer of the famed Pullman railroad sleeping and dining cars, introduced a notable experiment in corporate benevolence by building a corporate town outside Chicago with housing and other amenities for his employees. Pullman's altruism, however, did not prevent his employees from striking in 1894. The *Pullman strike and railroad boycott dampened such paternalistic initiatives but did not deter other corporate efforts to gain worker allegiances through an elaboration of fringe benefits. Many large industrial firms introduced profit-sharing plans; social and sports activities; and medical, life and retirement insurance plans in the early twentieth century.

The rise of new corporate bureaucracies and of heavy industries such as steel and machine manufacture led scholars to characterize developments in the late nineteenth century as a "second industrial revolution." Yet important continuities link the ante- and postbellum periods. Product diversity; uneven technological progress; varied work environments; the persistence of specialized, small-batch production; and control by skilled workers and foremen of work processes, even in large-scale enterprises, remained hallmarks of American industrialization into the early twentieth century. Manufacturing growth could still be characterized as more extensive than intensive.

The Twentieth Century. A definite growth in productivity, however, occurred in the twentieth century. The most dramatic breakthrough came in automobile manufacturing with the introduction of the moving assembly line. Cars initially were produced by teams of skilled assemblers who fit together crudely made components. Henry *Ford, determined to produce an inexpensive car for the mass market, conceived of a different system. Ford first had to improve standardized-parts production. Rather than relying on suppliers, Ford assumed direct control of components manufacture, overseeing innovations with new precision measuring devices and machinery. Having standardized parts fabrication, Ford in 1910 opened a revolutionary car assembly plant in Highland Park, Michigan. Thousands of workers were stationed along a conveyor-belt-driven assembly line, each repetitiously adding parts to Ford's Model T car.

Ford's system did not work flawlessly. Until Ford introduced his innovative Five-Dollars-a-Day wage plan, the company experienced high labor turnover. By the late 1920s, Ford's standardized-production methods also proved an impediment. General Motors (GM), a new conglomerate of firms, quickly surpassed Ford with a sales strategy that offered a different car for every income level and implemented a more flexible production system involving multipurpose machinery and relying more on skilled labor. Ford adjusted to the challenge only slowly.

Despite its difficulties, assembly-line production spread rapidly in the 1920s, from food processing to electric appliances. Indeed, the 1920s saw a flowering of American manufacture. Automobile production stimulated additional growth in the steel and rubber industries. Such new industries as petrochemicals, electronics, and aviation appeared. Following the lead of the DuPont chemical company and GM, large-scale firms diversified their product lines, decentralized production and management, and widened their productive capacities in order to tap new mass consumer markets. Industrial workers shared somewhat in the prosperity of the 1920s as the recipients of broader corporate fringe benefits.

Below the surface, however, lay harbingers of economic crises to come—not just the collapse of the economy during the depression of the 1930s, but long-term declines in industrial production and employment. Indeed, deindustrialization had its origins in the 1920s. New England textile mills closed in the face of low-wage competition, particularly from the South. Boarded-up factories appeared in America's earliest industrial sites. To reduce competition, national corporations bought out firms in older industrial centers such as Trenton, New Jersey, and rather than modernize antiquated facilities, simply liquidated operations. In Philadelphia, older firms producing specialized goods failed as American consumers preferred cheaper mass-produced goods.

The depression-wracked 1930s witnessed a more general contraction in manufacture, industrial production falling by 35 percent. This was the worst of a series of depressions, including contractions in the 1830s, 1870s, and 1890s that severely tested America's economic development.

Industrial firms during the 1930s also faced a newly militant labor force. Unskilled and semiskilled workers in mass-production industries—largely first- and second-generation eastern and southern Europeans who remained outside the craft unions affiliated with the *American Federation of Labor—successfully organized and gained union recognition and contracts through the *Congress of Industrial Organizations. By the early 1940s, the U.S. mass-production industries were heavily unionized.

The Depression of the 1930s did not end until *World War II, when military production regenerated the economy. As in *World War I, war production provided employment opportunities for women as well as for African Americans and other minorities who had been discriminated against in hiring for better manufacturing jobs.

High military production continued during America's *Cold War Era arms race with the Soviet Union. For the first time, military manufacture constituted a critical element in the nation's industrial system. Military production also led to a geographic shift away from the older industrial heartland. Defense-related industries (including aerospace manufacture) clustered in southern *California and the Pacific Northwest near Seattle, Washington, and in an arc stretching across the South from Columbia, South Carolina, through Huntsville, Alabama, to Houston, Texas.

The end of the Cold War reduced defense spending and eliminated employment in areas that had prospered through military-goods production. These regions joined older industrial areas in experiencing industrial decline. Through factory closings and corporate downsizing, more than 1.4 million manufacturing jobs disappeared between 1970 and 1995, a 7-percent loss during a period when total employment grew by 66 percent. (Service-sector employment accounted for the vast growth in jobs.) While manufacturing jobs represented a quarter of the total in 1970, they constituted 15 percent by 1995; the contribution of service-sector employment grew, conversely, from 15 to 25 percent. The vanishing industrial jobs often had offered higher pay, union protection, and better fringe benefits.

Foreign competition, new communications and transportation technologies enabling firms to shift manufacturing overseas, poor managerial strategies, failure to modernize facilities, and high wages and inflexible union rules all contributed to the absolute and relative decline of American industry. But the process was uneven. While steel-industry employment fell by more than 60 percent between 1970 and 1995, the automotive work force grew by 6 percent, and with robotics and other automated technologies, their productivity increased by 33 percent. While employment in the metal and machine trades nearly halved, industrial-machinery and metal-products production expanded rapidly. With the spread of *computers, employment in computer manufacture grew by 50 percent. Abandoned and vandalized factory buildings and vacant lots in the nation's once proud industrial centers, however, overshadowed the bright spots as decline largely characterized American industrialization at the end of the twentieth century.

[*See also* Automation and Computerization; Aviation Industry; Business Cycle; Canals and Waterways; Capitalism; Chemical Industry; Consumer Culture; Cotton Industry; Dams and Hydraulic Engineering; Depressions, Economic; Economic Development; Electricity and Electrification; Expansionism; Factory System; Global Economy, America and the; Haymarket Affair; Homestead Lockout; Hydroelectric Power; Immigrant Labor; Industrial Relations; Labor Markets; Labor Movements; Mass Marketing; Stock Market; Strikes and Industrial Conflict; Textile Industry; Urbanization; Women in the Labor Force.]

• David Nelson, *Managers and Workers: Origins of the New Factory System in the United States, 1880–1900*, 1975. Alfred D. Chandler Jr., *The Visible Hand: The Managerial Revolution in American Business*, 1977. David Jeremy, *Transatlantic Industrial Revolution: The Diffusion of Textile Technologies between Britain and America, 1790–1830s*, 1981. Barry Bluestone and Bennett Harrison, *The Deindustrialization of America: Plant Closings, Community Abandonment, and the Dismantling of Basic Industry*, 1982. James C. Cobb, *Industrialization and Southern Society, 1877–1985*, 1984. David Hounshell, *From the American System to Mass Production, 1800–1932: The Development of Manufacturing Technology in the United States*, 1984. Michael Piore and Charles Sabel, *The Second Industrial Divide: Possibilities for Prosperity*, 1984. Sanford Jacoby, *Employing Bureaucracy: Managers, Unions and the Transformation of Work in American Industry, 1900–1945*, 1985. John Cumbler, *A Social History of Economic Decline: Business, Politics, and Workers in Trenton*, 1989. Ann Markusen, ed., *Rise of the Gunbelt: The Military Remapping of Industrial America*, 1991. Walter Licht, *Industrializing America: The Nineteenth Century*, 1995. Philip Scranton, *Endless Novelty: Specialty Production and American Industrialization, 1865–1925*, 1997.

—Walter Licht

INDUSTRIAL RELATIONS is a term signifying both an academic field of study and a functional area of business practice. The focus of industrial relations (IR) in both the academic and business arenas is on the employer-employee relationship. In particular, IR specialists examine the causes of various kinds of employment problems and maladjustments and seek to discover and implement new ideas, institutions, policies, and practices that can resolve or ameliorate these problems. IR is thus a field of both study and practice, involving economic, political, legal, social, and psychological aspects of employment. Historically, IR specialists have emphasized applied problem-solving and concern for employee rights and interests.

Origins. IR emerged at the beginning of the twentieth century with the widespread growth and development of a modern industry and a wage-earning labor force. First and foremost as a source of public concern was labor-management conflict, epitomized by violent strikes, riots, bombings, and destruction of property. Other labor problems also gained increasing attention. Several of these particularly affected employers, including high employee turnover, sporadic work effort, and wasteful production. Workers, meanwhile, suffered from poverty-level wages, long hours, and unsafe working conditions. Many of these problems also imposed large costs on society, as when children's health and education were stunted by long work hours in mills and mines. Public and business concern about labor-management problems coalesced during the *World War I period, giving rise to IR as a field of study and practice.

Development through World War II. In the 1920s, a consensus emerged concerning three distinct approaches to solving labor problems and, thus, improving IR. The first, sometimes called the "workers' solution," relied on trade unionism and collective bargaining. The second, known as the "community's solution," advocated protective labor legislation (for example, laws on minimum wages and *child labor) and social insurance programs (e.g., *unemployment compensation and old-age *insurance). The third, designated the "employers' solution," involved the practice of personnel management and human-relations in the workplace.

The post–1920 history of IR is a chronicle of the changing nature of labor problems in the workplace and of the attempts to redress them using one or more of the three approaches described above.

During the prosperous and politically conservative 1920s, employers held the upper hand and dealt with labor problems through new practices of personnel management. Progressive companies trained foremen in human relations, provided *health insurance and paid vacations, codified employment policies, and promoted from within on the basis of internal job ladders. Companies also introduced employee-representation plans, which they characterized as a form of industrial democracy or citizenship. Labor unions and government labor legislation, by contrast, lacked broad-based public, governmental, or business support between 1919 and 1929.

The Great Depression of the 1930s brought radical changes in IR. The depression forced most firms to resort to repeated rounds of employee layoffs, wage cuts, and work speedups. By 1932–1933, mass unemployment and the collapse of welfare capitalism had created a growing sense of disillusionment, demoralization and injustice among masses of workers. The New Deal labor policies of the Franklin Delano *Roosevelt administration, most particularly the *National Labor Relations Act (NLRA) of 1935, stimulated the growth of unions across the economy, especially in the *mass-production industries. The NLRA, a wave of militant strikes, the rejuvenation of the *American Federation of Labor (AFL), and the birth of a new labor federation, the *Congress of Industrial Organizations (CIO), all stimulated unionization.

Although less than 10 percent of the nonagricultural workforce was unionized in 1932, by 1940 the proportion had risen to 27 percent. During *World War II, union membership and coverage spread further, buoyed by a full-employment economy and government pressure on employers to avoid strikes and labor unrest. When the war ended in 1945, union membership had quadrupled over the 1932 level and encompassed more than one-third of all nonagricultural employees.

Post–World War II. The Great Depression and World War II fundamentally changed the IR landscape, as unions organized most employees in the mass-production industries. Whereas employers had pioneered innovative employment practices in the 1920s, now unions more often performed this role. Through collective bargaining, unions negotiated for cost-of-living adjustment clauses in their contracts, formal grievance systems, and extensive health and retirement benefit programs.

In the academic world, the rise of organized labor and the newfound importance of labor-management relations led to the establishment of several dozen IR centers and programs in major public and private universities. Although these programs recruited faculty and offered courses covering each of the three solutions to labor problems described above, most stressed trade unionism and collective bargaining as the preferred means to improve IR.

In the twentieth century's concluding decades, IR again underwent fundamental changes. As organized labor suffered a substantial long-term decline in membership and power, both human-resource management, the new name for personnel management, and government legislation assumed more influence. Although most unions proved unable or unwilling to combat racial, gender, and other forms of discrimination in the workplace, for example, the federal government addressed these issues through legislation and regulations. Also, because unions now represented a much smaller proportion of the workforce, many workers lacked protection against such abuses as pension fraud and unsafe working conditions. Again the government stepped in to enact legislation to protect workers against these abuses. A third area of new legislation treated such social issues in the workplace as family and medical leave for employees.

Beginning in the late 1960s, employers also regained power and prestige in IR. The renaming of personnel management to "human-resource management" (HRM) carried with it a stronger rhetorical emphasis on employees as valuable assets rather than as an expense to be minimized. Companies developed new HRM practices aimed at increasing organizational efficiency, enhancing workers' satisfaction, and reducing employees' desire for union representation. Managements instituted self-managed work teams, alternative methods of dispute resolution (for example, peer-review panels), profit-sharing plans, and employee involvement programs.

By the mid-1990s, the union share of the workforce had fallen to 16 percent. Unions had substantially increased their representation among public-sector employees since the 1960s, but in the private sector union membership fell to only 10 percent—a level not seen since the early 1930s. A number of factors underlay this trend, especially increased domestic and global competition, sophisticated union-avoidance practices by employers, overaggressive bargaining demands by some unions, and improved working conditions and management practices.

A similar decline affected IR as an academic field. After 1960, the field of personnel/human-resource management gradually broke away from IR and established itself as a separate and competing area of study located in university business schools. IR programs in academia thus became increasingly associated with the two remaining approaches to solving labor problems, government legislation and collective bargaining. But as labor unions' size and power declined, so did interest in IR, while the HRM side of the field grew commensurately.

Summary. Industrial relations as a topic of study and area of business practice began as a *Progressive Era reform-oriented movement to improve workplace efficiency, equity, and human well-being through some combination of improved management practices, collective bargaining, and legislation. The emphasis given to each solution changed markedly over the years in response to new events and ideas. Between 1933 and 1973, industrial relations became increasingly associated with trade unionism and collective bargaining. After 1973, the human-resource management approach became more popular. But whatever the name given to the field, or however it is subdivided, the study of the employment relationship, the problems that grow out of it, and the resolution of these problems remained high on the academic and social agenda as the twenty-first century began.

[*See also* Business; Civil Rights; Depressions, Economic; Global Economy, America and the; Haymarket Affair; Homestead Lockout; Industrialization; Industrial Disease and Hazards; Labor Markets; Labor Movements; New Deal Era, The; Post–Cold War Era; Pullman Strike and Boycott; Scientific Management; Strikes and Industrial Conflict; Twenties, The.]

• Thomas Kochan, Harry Katz, and Robert McKerzie, *The Transformation of American Industrial Relations,* 1984. Sanford Jacoby, *Employing Bureaucracy: Managers, Unions and the Transformation of Work in American Industry, 1900–1945,* 1985. Lizabeth Cohen, *Making a New Deal: Industrial Workers in Chicago, 1919–1939,* 1990. Bruce Kaufman, *The Origins and Evolution of the Field of Industrial Relations in the United States,* 1993. J. Dulebon, Gerald Ferris, and J. Stodd, "The History and Evolution of Human Resource Management," in *Handbook of Human Resource Management,* ed. G. Ferris, S. Rosen, and D. Barnum, 1995. Bruce Kaufman, ed., *Government Regulation of the Employment Relationship,* 1997. David Lewin, Daniel Mitchell, and Mamood Zaidi, eds., *Handbook of Human Resource Management,* 1997. Daniel Nelson, *Shifting Fortunes: The Rise and Decline of American Labor, from the 1820s to the Present,* 1997.

—Bruce E. Kaufman

INDUSTRIAL WORKERS OF THE WORLD. Founded in *Chicago in 1905, the Industrial Workers of the World (IWW) counted its membership only in the tens of thousands even at its peak. However, from 1906 until the early 1930s, its combination of revolutionary unionism, tactical experimentation, racial inclusiveness, and cultural creativity enabled the IWW to influence organized labor out of proportion to its numbers.

Inspired by European theorists of anarcho-syndicalism and by the growth of low-wage, unskilled, and insecure jobs within American industry, the IWW differed from the more conservative *American Federation of Labor by seeking to organize all workers into "One Big Union" across lines of skill, nationality, and gender. Disdaining gradual gains and collective bargaining, the IWW sought the "Abolition of the Wage System."

The IWW enjoyed its greatest success in the extractive and textile industries. Affiliated briefly with the Western Federation of Miners, the Wobblies (as IWW members were called) led mass strikes among miners at Goldfield, Nevada (1906–1907), and on the Mesabi Iron Range (1916). Its activities in the forests of Louisiana and Texas resulted in fiercely contested strikes in 1912–1913. More successful organizing marked IWW campaigns among timber workers in the Pacific Northwest. Although it also recruited agricultural workers, domestic servants, longshoremen, and cigarmakers, the IWW's most stirring and publicized moments came in the Lawrence, Massachusetts (1912), and Paterson, New Jersey (1913) textile strikes. The Wobblies' ability to maintain unity among highly diverse immigrant workers, to emphasize dignity as well as wages as strike goals, and to dramatize the issues of *child labor and industrial safety made these struggles significant.

The early IWW suffered severe repression. Between 1907 and 1917, the union waged many "free speech fights" to exercise First Amendment rights. During and after *World War I, IWW members were prosecuted under state "criminal syndicalism" laws and federal espionage statutes. Mob attacks on union halls and on individual Wobblies such as Frank Little and Wesley Everest, later revered as martyrs, further damaged the IWW. Internal conflicts and legal repression drained the IWW during the 1920s. By the 1930s, the organization was a shadow of its former self.

The IWW's lasting contributions to the U.S. labor movement were indirect and largely cultural. The founders included such well-known radical leaders as Mary "Mother" *Jones, Eugene V. *Debs, and William "Big Bill" Haywood (1869–1928), a Utah-born miner who had joined the Western Federation of Miners in 1896. Its leading figures included the labor songwriter Joe Hill, the poet Covington Hall, and the humorist T-Bone Slim. The anthem of organized labor, "Solidarity Forever," was written by the Wobbly Ralph Chaplin. The IWW also pioneered mass civil disobedience to secure free speech, the use of sit-down strikes, and integration with African-American–led labor organizations.

[*See also* Labor Movements; Mining; Progressive Era; Radicalism; Strikes and Industrial Conflict; Textile Industry.]

• Melvyn Dubofsky, *We Shall Be All,* 1969. Salvatore Salerno, *Red November, Black November,* 1989.

—David R. Roediger

INFANTILE PARALYSIS. *See* Poliomyelitis.

INFLUENZA, a highly contagious viral *disease marked by fever, muscular aches, respiratory inflammation, and, in severe cases, bronchitis and pneumonia. Although the evidence is sketchy, influenza may have arrived in America in 1493 with the New World's first pigs, a species with whom human beings share the disease. Influenza pandemics, spreading from Europe, swept Anglo-America in 1732 and 1781–1782. The nineteenth century brought more outbreaks, the worst in 1889–1890. Millions of Americans fell ill, but as in all known influenza outbreaks except for one, few died, and those who did were mostly the young and the old. During the next pandemic, in 1918–1919, however, the death rate was several times higher than that of any influenza outbreak before or since, and half the victims were young adults. This "flu" epidemic killed about 30 million worldwide, including 550,000 Americans—more than ten times the number of U.S. soldiers who died in *World War I.

In the early 1930s, the Americans Richard E. Shope and Paul A. Lewis and the Britishers Wilson Smith, C. H. Andrewes, and P. P. Laidlaw isolated the influenza virus and transmitted it to and recovered it from laboratory animals. In the 1940s, other researchers produced influenza vaccines, which unfortunately proved only ephemerally effective. By the 1990s, a network of stations existed around the globe to report new strains of influenza to the *World Health Organization in hope of giving humanity enough warning to defend itself. In 1976, a strain of influenza virus resembling that of 1918 appeared in New Jersey, prompting the U.S. government to spend millions of dollars to produce and distribute a vaccine. The feared pandemic never happened. As the twentieth century ended, there was no known cure for influenza and no certainty that an outbreak comparable to the 1918 pandemic, whose severity still remained a mystery, could not happen again.

[*See also* Medicine; Public Health.]

• K. David Patterson, *Pandemic Influenza, 1700–1900,* 1986. Alfred W. Crosby, *America's Forgotten Pandemic,* 1989.

—Alfred W. Crosby

INFORMATION TECHNOLOGY. *See* Computers; Internet and World Wide Web.

INSANE ASYLUMS. *See* Mental Health Institutions.

INSANITY. *See* Mental Illness.

INSTITUTE FOR PACIFIC RELATIONS. Founded in 1925 by Stanford University president Ray Lyman Wilbur, the businessman Frank Atherton, and Merle Davis, who, like many others, was formerly linked to the Young Men's Christian Association (YMCA), the Institute for Pacific Relations (IPR) sought to advance understanding of Asia through conferences with Asian leaders, annual meetings, research, and publications. By 1939, eleven national IPR councils had been established in the United States, Canada, Australia, New Zealand, China, Japan, the *Philippines, the Soviet Union, the Netherlands, Great Britain, and France. From the start, the American council exerted the greatest influence because of its size (nearly fourteen hundred members by 1939) and fund-raising abilities. In the 1930s, under Edward C. Carter, secretary of the American council and later secretary-general of IPR itself, IPR became the premier organization for the study of Asia. It published *Pacific Affairs* and *Eastern Survey;* gave scholarly research grants; and provided reliable information to scholars, the government, and the public at a time when such information was scarce. The respected Asian scholar Owen Lattimore, who edited *Pacific Affairs* from 1933 to 1941, brought to the post a wealth of experience; insatiable curiosity; and impressive language proficiency in Chinese, Mongolian, and Russian.

Despite its nonpartisan beginnings, IPR became embroiled in controversy in the 1940s, when some members resigned over what they considered its left-leaning slant. Principal among the disgruntled was the textile importer Alfred Kohlberg, who charged Lattimore and others with turning the organization into a front for communist propaganda. Senator Joseph *McCarthy picked up these charges in the early 1950s, particularly targeting Lattimore, who had moved to Johns Hopkins University. IPR never recovered; its membership declined, and it ended in 1960. In its heyday, however, IPR stood high among international nongovernmental organizations seeking to expand knowledge of Asia and to bring scholarly expertise to bear on the shaping of international relations.

[*See also* Anticommunism; Cold War; Foreign Relations: U.S. Relations with Asia; YMCA and YWCA.]

• John N. Thomas, *The Institute of Pacific Relations: Asian Scholars and American Politics,* 1974. Robert P. Newman, *Owen Lattimore and the "Loss" of China,* 1992.

—T. Christopher Jespersen

INSULAR CASES. In twenty-four cases decided between 1901 and 1922, the U.S. *Supreme Court held that the *Constitution does not apply automatically to territories acquired by the nation. Badly divided initially, the Court later unanimously held that the Constitution applied only after Congress had "incorporated" a territory into the United States.

Following the *Spanish-American War, the United States acquired the islands of *Puerto Rico and the *Philippines (thus the name "Insular" cases). Almost immediately, a dispute arose over whether the national government could tax goods imported from its newly acquired territory. The dispute involved two sources. First, the Constitution required that duties be uniform throughout "the United States"; second, tariff laws imposed *tariffs on goods imported from "foreign" countries. If the island territories were part of the United States, goods imported from them could not be taxed. From that mundane problem emerged constitutional issues of great significance, in particular whether the *Bill of Rights applied to the newly acquired territories. Behind the language lay issues of race and cultural hegemony: Were people in the territories "fit" for constitutional protections? Should the United States impose its constitutional values on other cultures?

In the most important of the early cases, *Downes* v. *Bidwell* (1901), the Court failed to agree on a rationale for its conclusion that a duty could be imposed on goods imported from Puerto Rico because it was not part of "the United States." In announcing the Court's conclusion, Justice Henry Billings Brown explained that a territory could not become a "state" until Congress said it was. Chief Justice Melville W. Fuller dissented, reasoning that the Constitution applied to every action taken by Congress. Between those two positions fell the concurring opinion of Justice Edward D. White, who proposed that the Constitution applied only to territories that had been "incorporated" into the United States and that incorporation could come only from an act of Congress. The entire Court eventually adopted White's interpretation, first in a majority opinion, *Dorr* v. *United States* (1904), and later in a unanimous decision, *Balzac* v. *Puerto Rico* (1922).

The Insular case decisions placed the Supreme Court's imprimatur on overseas expansion, allowing the president and Congress great flexibility in international affairs. Never having been overruled, the doctrine of the Insular cases has continuing vitality, especially in the efforts to enforce U.S. laws outside its borders and in the U.S. involvement in international organizations.

[*See also* Expansionism.]

• James E. Kerr, *The Insular Cases: The Role of the Judiciary in American Expansionism*, 1982.

—Walter F. Pratt Jr.

INSULL, SAMUEL (1859–1938), businessman, utilities-industry spokesman. Born near London, England, Insull learned stenography, emigrated to America, and landed a job in 1880 as the personal secretary of Thomas *Edison. Learning the electric-lighting business from the ground up, Insull helped establish the manufacturing arm of what would become the General Electric Company in Schenectady, New York. In 1892, he became president of the Chicago Edison Company, one of several electric companies in the city.

Over the following decade, he mastered the unique economics of the electric-utility business and emerged as a national leader of the industry. Proclaiming that "low rates may mean good business," Insull developed a business strategy that encouraged the use of electricity by all types of energy consumers. This approach made him an innovator in the use of novel technologies, financial instruments, rate structures, and promotional campaigns to create a mass market for electric light and power. Moreover, he mounted a successful effort to establish a monopoly of central station service in *Chicago for the renamed Commonwealth Edison Company. He also became a pioneer in building larger, regional networks of power and related holding-company devices to maintain control of his sprawling utilities empire.

During *World War I, Insull was appointed chairman of the Illinois Council of Defense. In the 1920s, he was regarded as one of the nation's leading businessmen. The Great Depression and the collapse of his utilities empire turned Insull into a target of popular anger. Arrested and tried for securities fraud, he was acquitted in 1934 but remained a broken man until his death.

[*See also* Depressions, Economic; Electrical Industry; Electricity and Electrification; Mass Marketing; New Deal Era, The.]

• Forrest McDonald, *Insull*, 1962. Harold L. Platt, *The Electric City: Energy and the Growth of the Chicago Area, 1880–1930*, 1991.

—Harold L. Platt

INSURANCE. The history of insurance in the United States involves two major themes: risk protection and capital accumulation. Early American insurance companies adopted British insurance firms' practices in covering marine and fire hazards. Organized underwriters, usually merchants and real-estate men who could assess risk and estimate profitable premium rates, insured policyholders for lost cargoes and the destruction of buildings by fire. (Risk is now calculated by professional actuaries using complex statistical techniques.)

The most significant ninteenth-century outgrowth of fire and marine insurance was life insurance. The nation's first life-insurance company was founded in *Philadelphia in 1812. Most major life-insurance companies, founded in the 1830–1870 period, were mutually owned by policyholders, as were many fire-insurance companies. After the *Civil War, these companies became fiduciary agents of middle-class (and eventually working-class) savings as well as key investors in transportation, financial, and industrial corporations. By 1900, life-insurance companies rivaled banks in terms of financial power. In *Paul* v. *Virginia* (1868), the *Supreme Court ruled that insurance was not "commerce" and therefore was not subject to federal regulation. Insurance remained subject to state regulation, however, and in 1871 state regulators formed the National Association of Insurance Commissioners to coordinate legislation and other matters.

Social and economic changes of the twentieth century coupled with the increasing sophistication of actuarial methods helped insurance spread to broader aspects of property and society, including such diverse areas as automobile insurance, crop insurance, comprehensive homeowners' policies, product-liability coverage, and malpractice insurance for physicians. The *New Deal Era saw the growth of various forms of social insurance, including bank-deposit insurance, workers' injury compensation, *unemployment coverage, and *Social Security. *Health insurance expanded rapidly with the founding of Blue Cross in New York in 1934 and its spread to other states. The *Medicare and Medicaid programs of the 1960s, coupled with many private employee systems, extended health insurance still further.

The insurance industry grew enormously, in both size and investment power, in the later twentieth century. The Financial Services Modernization Act (1999) gave insurance companies and banks greater freedom to compete and collaborate in various financial services. In the mid-1990s, the nation's leading life-insurance carrier, Prudential of America, had annual revenues of more than $40 billion. In 1997 the nation's insurance carriers employed more than 1.5 million people, and there were 724,000 insurance agents and brokers. With assets of some $3.4 trillion invested in banks, mortgages, and corporate and government securities, the insurance industry loomed as a major player in the American economy as the twentieth century ended.

[*See also* Banking and Finance; Business; Stock Market.]

• Kailin Tuan, ed., *Modern Insurance Theory and Education: A Social History of Insurance Evolution in the United States during the Twentieth Century*, 3 vols., 1972.

—Tom Mertes

INTELLIGENCE, CONCEPTS OF. In 1923, the American psychologist Edwin G. Boring (1886–1968), faced with the problem of defining intelligence, famously explained that intelligence is what intelligence tests test. This seemingly circular characterization was not an off-the-cuff remark, but a serious attempt to deal with one of the more vexing issues confronting early twentieth-century psychologists. From the development of the modern intelligence test by the French psychologist Alfred Binet in 1905, the practice of measuring intelligence had grown rapidly, especially in the Anglo-American world. However, little consensus had emerged concerning the actual capability that the tests sought to measure. Some argued that intelligence referred to an individual's potential for learning or adapting to new situations, others that it denoted ability to solve problems or generate abstract ideas. And all questioned whether it was one thing or many, produced by heredity or environment, and shared with animals or uniquely human.

Interest in some mental attribute characterizing overall ability to think or reason can be traced, in the West at least, to Aristotle's definition of human beings as creatures who reason. Intelligence became a sustained topic of scientific inquiry during the late eighteenth century, when various European naturalists began to compare human beings systematically with other animals as part of their grand taxonomic projects. Such comparisons often focused on differences in intelligence and were linked by many to the notion of a "great chain of being" stretching from the simplest organisms through human beings and up to God. During the late eighteenth and early nineteenth centuries, various physical features were used to rank intelligence, with cranial capacity and brain weight predominating, especially through the labors of the American Samuel G. Morton (1799–1851). By measures such as these, a number of nineteenth-century scientists—including the so-called American school of *anthropology, led by Morton—sought to demonstrate the inferiority of Africans by suggesting that their intelligence was closest of all human groups to that of the apes. By the century's end, however, this research program had largely been abandoned, as variations within groups proved to be much more significant than differences among them.

Apart from comparisons of races or groups, and medical assessments of profound mental deficiency, intelligence as a personal and differential characteristic elicited little concern until the later nineteenth century. Before then, American mental philosophers spoke of the intellect largely in terms of the universal attributes of human reason and conceived of the mind as possessing a wide variety of faculties or powers, a certain subset of which could be grouped under the general term "intelligence." The advent of evolutionism, however, heightened the importance of an organism's overall mental power, as it was considered a central factor influencing progressive adaptation to the environment. At the same time, the expansion of primary education rendered differences in individual intellect more visible, and the development of the new so-called "scientific" *psychology in the late nineteenth century placed a premium on analyzing the mind in terms of quantitative methods and laboratory techniques.

The first successful psychological technique for quantifying differences in individual mental ability came early in the twentieth century. Asked in 1904 to participate in a French commission on children falling behind in the classroom, Binet and his colleague Théodore Simon created a scale of tests to identify those lagging in intellectual development. Focused on the higher mental processes and implicitly viewing intelligence itself as singular and quantifiable, the 1905 Binet-Simon Intelligence Scale was constructed as a sequence of age-related tasks that quantified the test-taker's intellectual level vis-à-vis his or her chronological peers. Using the Binet-Simon scale as a model, the American psychologists Henry H. Goddard and Lewis M. Terman began in the 1910s to refine the test further and link it more closely to arguments for the biological and inheritable nature of intelligence. Terman's 1916 Stanford-Binet test, which rapidly became the dominant instrument for assessing mental ability, reported scores in terms of a chronologically invariant measure, the intelligence quotient (IQ), a ratio of mental age to chronological age developed by the German psychologist Wilhelm Stern. Frequently revised, the Stanford-Binet test remained a leading instrument for the individual measurement of intelligence at the end of the twentieth century, although after the 1930s it was somewhat eclipsed by two scales created by David Wechsler, the Wechsler Intelligence Scale for Children (WISC) and the Wechsler Adult Intelligence Scale (WAIS).

The outbreak of *World War I gave American psychologists the opportunity to promote their services and products to a broader public. Using assembly-line-like methods, which included the multiple-choice question and group testing, psychologists administered mental tests to approximately 1.75 million army recruits and cited this experience in the postwar period to convince schools and industry that intelligence testing offered an efficient means of assessing students and staff. Although critics such as Walter *Lippmann and William C. Bagley challenged the tests as flawed and inimical to democracy, and many business leaders shifted to measures of personality, by the end of the 1920s the concepts of "intelligence" and "intelligence assessment" were well entrenched. New instruments continued to be developed, and by the 1940s one test, the Scholastic Aptitude Test (S.A.T.), had become a gatekeeper for admission to many colleges and universities. In addition, organizations such as the Educational Testing Service (ETS) of Princeton, New Jersey, which administers the S.A.T., flourished. Founded in 1947 under the leadership of Henry Chauncey, ETS quickly became the nation's leading testing agency. In 1998, with 2,300 employees and revenues of nearly $500 million, the nonprofit ETS administered the S.A.T. and other tests to some nine million persons, signifying the continued power of the concept of intelligence.

Discussions of intelligence have historically focused on two main issues. First, is intelligence one thing or many? Beginning in 1904, the British psychologist Charles Spearman used factor analysis to argue that intelligence consists of a single mental trait he called "general intelligence" (g). Edward L. Thorndike of Columbia University, by contrast, contended that intelligence is thoroughly heterogeneous, while L. L. Thurstone of the University of Chicago argued that intelligence consists of a small number of relatively independent abilities. Later, Philip E. Vernon offered a hierarchical conception of intelligence in an attempt to achieve consensus on this issue. Nonetheless, alternative theories have abounded: in the 1960s and beyond, Joy P. Guilford argued that intelligence is composed of 150 independent factors; Howard Gardner discerned seven discrete types of intelligence; and Robert J. Sternberg contended that intelligence is triarchically organized. All the while, Spearman's (g) has continued to attract many proponents.

The second continuing issue focuses on the problem of nature versus nurture. The nineteenth-century interest in craniometry and the ranking of species and races had assumed that intelligence was both biological and inheritable. In the early twentieth century, advocates of *eugenics fortified this conviction and enlisted it to justify a variety of social programs, from ability-tracking in high schools to sterilization of "the unfit." Studies by the anthropologist Franz *Boas in the 1910s, however, suggested that the environment plays a significant role in shaping intelligence, a position strengthened by subsequent work in the 1930s and 1940s, especially at the Iowa Child Welfare Research Station. In the post–World War II era, both heredity and environment have received much attention. Identical-twin research was interpreted by some psychologists as indicating a close connection between intelligence and heredity. At the same time, data on the worldwide increase in IQ scores (the Flynn effect) and the demonstrated influence of nutrition and home conditions on intelligence suggested the equally strong role of environmental factors. While some interpreted the positive correlation of IQ scores with socioeconomic status as evidence of the meritocratic nature of Western societies, others argued that it underscored the culture-bound character of all intelligence-measurement instruments, especially when applied to the issue of IQ and race. Whether critical or supportive of intelligence testing, however, few have challenged the notion that intelligence itself is a characteristic of relevance to negotiating the contemporary world.

[*See also* Education: The Public School Movement; Evolution, Theory of; Race, Concept of; Racism.]

• N. J. Block and Gerald Dworkin, eds., *The IQ Controversy,* 1976. Stephen Jay Gould, *The Mismeasure of Man,* 1981. Raymond E. Fancher, *The Intelligence Men: Makers of the IQ Controversy,* 1985. Michael M. Sokal, ed., *Psychological Testing and American Society, 1890–1930,* 1987. Carl N. Degler, *In Search of Human Nature: The Decline and Revival of Darwinism in American Social Thought,* 1991. William H. Tucker, *The Science and Politics of Racial Research,* 1994. Russell Jacoby and Naomi Glauberman, eds., *The Bell Curve: History, Documents, Opinions,* 1995. Kurt Danziger, *Naming the Mind: How Psychology Found Its Language,* 1997. Leila Zenderland, *Measuring Minds: Henry Herbert Goddard and the Origins of American Intelligence Testing,* 1998.

—John Carson

INTELLIGENCE GATHERING AND ESPIONAGE. "Intelligence" is information gathered by a government or other institution to guide decisions and actions; "espionage" is the collection of intelligence through clandestine means. Deeply rooted in world history, both intelligence and espionage have figured in U.S. history from the earliest days of the republic. George *Washington wrote: "There is nothing more necessary than good Intelligence to frustrate a designing enemy, & nothing that requires greater pains to obtain." Benedict *Arnold, an American general in the *Revolutionary War, doomed himself to perpetual disgrace by secretly passing coded military intelligence to the British in 1779–1780.

Slow and uncertain modes of communication reduced the value of intelligence and its reputation in the early nineteenth century. Between 1815 and 1914, however, with improved means of communication and administration, information was collected more rapidly and thoroughly and used to greater effect. When the *Civil War ended in 1865, the Union Army's Bureau of Military Information was the world's leader in military intelligence, although it was quickly dismantled in the postwar period.

Intelligence gathering, once the province of diplomats and the military, gradually came to be handled by specialized bureaucracies that not only assessed information but increasingly conducted espionage. By 1914, most European states possessed small espionage and assessment bureaus, with American intelligence efforts lagging somewhat behind those of Great Britain. Intelligence proved more central in *World War I than in any previous conflict. It now included technical sources like aircraft photography and signals intelligence (the interception and deciphering of another nation's communications by *telegraph, *radio, or other means). In one well-known incident, British naval intelligence on 1 March 1917 intercepted a coded telegram from the German foreign secretary, Arthur Zimmermann, to Germany's ambassador in Mexico. The telegram suggested that if Mexico joined Germany in war against the United States, it could regain its "lost territories" of New Mexico, Texas, and Arizona. Transmitted to Washington by the British, the Zimmermann telegram helped buttress President Woodrow *Wilson's decision to call for a declaration of war against Germany.

Espionage had even greater value in *World War II, with successes in code-breaking hastening Allied victories in both Europe and the Pacific. U.S. Army intelligence broke the Japanese diplomatic code in 1940, providing invaluable information throughout the war. Despite the rise of new forms of espionage, a key to intelligence operations remained the secret agent who gained access to documents or other information of interest to his or her masters, such as the Soviet atomic spies of the 1940s who penetrated the *Manhattan Project and supplied information to Moscow.

Building on the wartime *Office of Strategic Services and the signals-intelligence operations of the military services, the *Cold War Era saw a vast expansion of U.S. intelligence gathering and analysis. Signals intelligence was conducted by the National Security Agency (NSA), created in 1952 from a combination of army and navy signals-intelligence programs; human intelligence by the *Central Intelligence Agency (CIA); and satellite imagery by the National Reconnaissance Office (NRO). Some of the more celebrated moments of the Cold War involved the unmasking, defection, or exchange of intelligence agents by the superpowers. Supplementing the traditional use of agents were increasingly sophisticated forms of signals intelligence and imagery, including satellite photography, which proved vital for such tasks as estimating Soviet nuclear capacity. As President Lyndon B. *Johnson said in 1967: "Before we had the [satellite] photography our guesses were way off. We were doing things we didn't need to do. Because of the satellites I know how many missiles the enemy has." The goal, in the words of Ray S. Cline, the CIA's deputy director for intelligence from 1962 to 1966, was to formulate "an evidence-based description of the real world around us, with as much objectivity and accuracy as possible."

The goal was not always realized, however. The process of gathering and analyzing intelligence was sometimes distorted by preconceptions and politicization. Since fragmentary and ambiguous data could be made to fit many explanations, analysts and politicians sometimes interpreted them to fit their preconceptions. While signals intelligence sometimes penetrated the deepest of foreign secrets, it could also be trivial in significance. One celebrated American code-breaking operation of the Cold War, "Gamma Guppy," essentially provided U.S. analysts with gossip by top Soviet leaders about their colleagues' sex lives. Aerial and satellite photography generated facts in such quantity as to overwhelm understanding. American intelligence agencies in the 1960s, clogged by millions of satellite images, most of which analysts could not examine for a year or more, missed evidence of such impending events as the Soviet invasion of Czechoslovakia in 1968.

Both the successes and failures of American intelligence decisively shaped U.S. history in the twentieth century, from the failure of U.S. intelligence to anticipate Japan's surprise attack on *Pearl Harbor on 7 December 1941 to the CIA's detection of Soviet missiles and delivery systems in Cuba in 1962, which gave rise to the U.S.-Soviet showdown known as the *Cuban Missile Crisis. Intelligence remained important at the end of the twentieth century, although several decades of controversy surrounding the CIA had diminished its standing and tarnished its reputation. With the end of the Cold War, as economic rivalries and trade competition came to shape relations among nations more and more, commercial and economic intelligence gathering and espionage became increasingly important.

• Walter Laqueur, *A World of Secrets,* 1985. Michael Handel, *War, Strategy, and Intelligence,* 1989. Michael Handel, ed., *Intelligence and Military Operations,* 1990. Keith Neilson and B. J. C. McKersher, *Go Spy the Land: Military Intelligence in History,* 1992. Michael Herman, *Intelligence and Power in Peace and War,* 1996.

—John Ferris

INTERCONTINENTAL BALLISTIC MISSILES. *See* Missiles and Rockets; Nuclear Weapons.

INTERNAL IMPROVEMENTS. *See* Economic Development.

INTERNAL SECURITY ACT (McCARRAN ACT). Enacted during the early *Cold War, shortly after the Soviet Union's detonation of an atomic bomb and North Korea's invasion of South Korea, the Internal Security Act of 1950 expressed the nation's growing fear of *communism, both at home and abroad, in the so-called McCarthy Era. Its main intention was to control the spread of domestic subversion. Title I—"The Subversive Activity Control Act"—required "communist-action" organizations and "communist front" organizations to register with the Justice Department. The original sponsors of this measure were Senator Karl E. Mundt (Rep.-S.D.) and Representative Richard M. *Nixon, (Rep.-Calif.). The act also contained provisions for the exclusion and deportation of, and the denial of passports to, communists and other "subversives."

Title II—"The Emergency Detention Act"—provided for the detention of potential espionage agents and subversives whenever the president proclaimed an "internal security emergency." Sponsored by seven Democratic senators as a substitute for Title I, it was added to the Internal Security Act through the efforts of Nixon, Mundt, and Senator Patrick McCarran (Dem.-Nev.), the bill's chief sponsor.

The measure became law on 23 September 1950, after Congress overrode a veto by President Harry S. *Truman. The registration and other measures of Title I were challenged in the courts until declared unconstitutional by the U.S. *Supreme Court in *Aptheker* v. *Secretary of State* (1964) and *Albertson* v. *Subversive Activities Control Board* (1965). The "Emergency Detention Act" was repealed by Congress in 1972 during Nixon's presidency and the controversial *Vietnam War protests.

[*See also* Anticommunism; Fifties, The; Korean War; McCarthy, Joseph.]

• Earl Latham, *The Communist Controversy in Washington,* 1966. William R. Tanner and Robert Griffith, "Legislative Politics and 'McCarthyism': The Internal Security Act of 1950," in *The Spectator,* ed. Robert Griffith and Athan Theoharis, 1974.

—William R. Tanner

INTERNATIONAL BANK FOR RECONSTRUCTION AND DEVELOPMENT. *See* World Bank.

INTERNATIONALISM. Although the term "international" was coined by Jeremy Bentham in 1770, historians usually locate the genesis of American internationalism in President Woodrow *Wilson's promotion of the *League of Nations during *World War I. Wilson, a progressive internationalist, believed that the League could lessen the chances of another catastrophic war by providing a framework for arbitration or conciliation, for the limitation of armaments, and *collective security against aggression—that is, the mutual guarantee of member nations' political independence and territorial integrity, enforced by economic and military sanctions.

Conservative internationalists—such as Massachusetts senator Henry Cabot Lodge and former president William Howard *Taft—looked upon these provisions as a diminution of national sovereignty. Whereas they advocated a world parliament to make appropriate changes to *international law and favored arbitration and conciliation to settle certain kinds of disputes, most conservative internationalists also believed that the United States should build up its *military and reserve the right to undertake independent coercive action whenever the "national interest" was threatened. They balked at the League's provisions for collective sanctions and feared that membership might restrict independent, unilateral military action. The Republican-controlled Senate prevented the United States from joining the League in 1919–1920.

*World War II caused Americans to reconsider Wilson's vision. In 1943, the Arkansas congressman (and future senator) J. William Fulbright (1905–1995) secured President Franklin Delano *Roosevelt's support for a resolution calling for a new peacekeeping organization; when Roosevelt assured doubters that its authority would not impinge on national sovereignty, most Republicans endorsed the Fulbright Resolution. In August 1945, the United Nations Organization was established, and President Harry S. *Truman declared Wilson vindicated.

Yet, in the postwar years, Democratic and Republican administrations alike mirrored the views of Wilson's conservative internationalist critics and came to regard the *United Nations (UN) as an unreliable instrument of foreign policy. In the bipolar *Cold War world, American internationalism metamorphosed into "globalism," characterized by unilateral interventionism (often in direct violation of the UN Charter) and the impulse to hegemonic power. In the 1980s, the U.S. grew hostile toward the UN and even hinted at withdrawal in part because the General Assembly, numerically dominated by Third World countries, frequently asserted itself against American economic and strategic interests. By the 1990s, as the Cold War ended, relations with the UN improved, aided by a growing recognition that many critical problems (especially those concerning the global environment) required concerted action. Still, the United States remained ambivalent about the UN's peace-keeping missions and highly selective about the use of international military force, invoking the UN's authority when Iraq invaded oil-rich Kuwait in 1990–1991 and virtually ignoring it when ethnic violence erupted in Kosovo in 1998–1999. Some politicians wanted to reduce America's financial contributions to the UN while others argued that American military units should never serve under any but American commanders in any circumstances. If, as Senator Fulbright once remarked, internationalism was "the one great new idea" of the twentieth century in the field of U.S. international relations, its basic Wilsonian tenets remained controversial and unfulfilled as the twentieth century ended.

[*See also* Foreign Relations; Isolationism; Post–Cold War Era.]

• Warren F. Kuehl, *Seeking World Order: The United States and International Organization to 1920,* 1969. Daniel Patrick Moynihan, *On the Law Of Nations,* 1990. Thomas J. Knock, *To End All Wars: Woodrow Wilson and the Quest for a New World Order,* 1992. Gary B. Ostrower, *The United Nations and the United States,* 1998.

—Thomas J. Knock

INTERNATIONAL LAW. International law is sometimes viewed as a by-product of the rise of the nation state in the seventeenth century. Others trace it to the *Jus Gentium* (Law of the Nations) of the Holy Roman Empire. In any event, by the time the United States was founded, international law was acknowledged to comprise rules binding nations in their relations with one another. While earlier concepts of international law focused only on the relationships between and among sovereign states, the twentieth century has gradually brought the individual to the foreground.

International and regional tribunals such as the International Court of Justice, the Court of European Communities, the Inter-American Court, and the European Court of Human Rights try cases alleging violations of international law. National courts are also competent to try cases alleging violations of international law, as long as their rules and procedures meet a minimum international standard.

The International Court (which succeeded the Permanent Court of International Justice established by the *League of Nations) can issue advisory opinions as well as resolve disputes. The United States, as a party to the agreement establishing the court, accepts as the source of international law the enumeration it sets forth. These include "international conventions" (which include bilateral and multilateral agreements between and among nations); "international custom" ("as evidence of a general practice accepted as law"); "the general principles of law recognized by civilized nations"; and, as a subsidiary means of finding the law, "judicial decisions and the teachings of the most highly qualified publicists of the various nations."

The rules for interpreting international conventions and determining under what circumstances they are binding are collectively known as "treaty law." A Convention on the Law of Treaties, an international equivalent of the codification of national rules of contract, sets forth these rules. Increasingly, nations have attempted to create bodies of law through agreements drafted at international conferences. In the late nineteenth and early twentieth centuries, the Law of War was the subject of such conferences. The Law of the Sea agreements and commercial agreements such as the *General Agreement on Tariffs and Trade (GATT) resulted from post–*World War II conferences. Recently *environmentalism has been the subject of international agreements: the Convention on International Trade in Endangered Species (1973); the Montreal Protocol on Ozone (1985–1987); and the conventions adopted at a 1992 *United Nations-sponsored Earth Summit conference in Rio de Janeiro to combat climate change, protect the world's wildlife and plants, resist the spread of deserts, and reduce "greenhouse gas" emissions.

Such international agreements often establish an organization with ongoing responsibilities for a given subject matter and provide a mechanism for resolving disputes. The United Nations (UN), itself established by international agreement in 1945 as a successor to the League of Nations, has spawned a multitude of specialized agencies responsible for specific subject areas. Many regional organizations have also been created by international agreement.

Customs accepted as binding by nations are also a developing source of international law. Controversy exists over when such a law can be imposed on a nation that does not itself accept such a custom, particularly on issues of great importance. For example, to apply international customary law relating to a nuclear issue would be difficult if a nuclear power objected, since the objection itself would belie the existence of uniform custom. On the other hand, alleged customary international law relating to the oceans could not as readily be challenged by a landlocked country, since that nation could not easily participate in activities creating the custom.

International law is dynamic. The second half of the twentieth century witnessed a new focus on the individual and the gradual erosion of nation-state sovereignty. Now individuals increasingly are viewed as having both rights and responsibilities under international, as well as national, law. At the 1945–1946 Nuremberg Trials of alleged Nazi War criminals, an international tribunal, acting under an agreement of the four World War II Allies occupying Germany, for the first time held individuals liable for certain crimes under international law. And a few post–World War II human-rights agreements granted to individuals whose rights had been infringed by their own governments the right to petition an international body. In the later 1990s, for the first time since Nuremberg, International Crime Tribunals were again convened as a result of conflicts in the former Yugoslavia and Rwanda. After years of discussion concerning the need for a permanent international criminal court, the Rome Statute of the International Criminal Court was adopted in July 1998. In a nonrecorded vote, 120 states favored it, 7 states (including the United States) opposed it, and there were 21 abstentions. As of September 2000, 19 states had ratified the statute. Sixty states must ratify it for the statute to enter into force. Developing international law relating to the environment also seemed likely in the future to bring an increasing focus on individual rights.

[*See also* Collective Security; Environmentalism; Human Rights, International; Internationalism; San Francisco Conference; War Crimes Trials, Nuremberg and Tokyo.]

• Fernando R. Tesón, *Humantarian Intevention: An Inquiry into Law and Morality,* 2d ed., 1997. Hofstra Law and Policy Symposium, *War Crimes and War Crimes Tribunals: Past, Present, and Future,* vol. 3, 1999. Mark W. Janis, *An Introduction to International Law,* 3d ed., 1999. Paul W. Kahn, "Nuclear Weapons and the Rule of Law," vol. 93, *American Journal of International Law* (January 1999): 349–415. Frances Nicholson and Patrick Twomey, eds., *Refugee Rights and Realities: Evolving International Concepts and Regimes,* 1999. Henry J. Steiner and Philip Alston, *International Human Rights in Context: Law, Politics, Morals,* 2d ed., 2000.

—Jane M. Picker

INTERNATIONAL MONETARY FUND. The International Monetary Fund (IMF) was the most important international organization to emerge from the *Bretton Woods Conference of 1944. Following the competitive monetary devaluations during the depression years of the 1930s, diplomats became convinced of the central importance of currency stability to the international economic system. Anglo-American discussions during *World War II focused on the creation of an institution that would promote international monetary cooperation and aid countries in maintaining the value of their currencies, particularly in times of crisis. While British diplomats, notably John Maynard Keynes, sought an activist institution, American planners, wary of giving a blank check to debtor nations, sought and won an IMF with circumscribed lending authority and stringent rules.

The IMF started operations in 1946 with around eight billion dollars in funds from its member nations. A weighted voting system allocated votes according to the size of each country's contribution. While this system gave the United States the largest voting share, the managing director of the IMF has never been an American. Yet the United States has made full use of the IMF as an instrument of its policy. During the period 1946–1971, the IMF helped nations to remain within a fixed-rate, dollar- and gold-based international economic order. After August 1971, when the administration of Richard M. *Nixon decoupled the link between the dollar and gold and moved currencies from fixed to floating valuations, the IMF began to play a more important role in international economic relations, especially during the *energy crisis of the 1970s and the Third World debt crisis of the 1980s. IMF loans were available to nations in financial distress, provided they agreed to various conditions designed to nurse the economy back to fiscal health.

The Soviet Union refused to join the IMF, but after its collapse, the IMF played a major role in distributing Western aid to Russia. The IMF was also instrumental in the *post–Cold War era financial rescue of Mexico in 1994–1955 and in handling the Asian economic crisis of 1998.

[*See also* Depressions, Economic; Gold Standard; Internationalism; Monetary Policy, Federal.]

• Margaret De Vries, *The IMF in a Changing World, 1945–1985,* 1986. Harold James, *International Monetary Cooperation since Bretton Woods,* 1996.

—Diane B. Kunz

INTERNET AND WORLD WIDE WEB. As early as 1962, John Licklider, computer scientist at the Massachusetts Institute of Technology, proposed an Internet-like system called the "Galactic Network" that would link *computers around the world and be accessible to everyone. It was not Licklider's vision, however, but the desire of government officials and the *military for a communications network that could survive a nuclear attack that prompted the first practical steps toward what would become the Internet. In December 1969, with funding from the Defense Department's Advanced Research Projects Agency (ARPA), scientists in California and Utah linked computers in four cities with dedicated, high-speed transmission lines to create the ARPANET. Information passed from site to site in such a way that if some of the sites or the connections between them stopped functioning, the rest of the network would be unaffected.

More and more sites, mainly universities and government laboratories, joined the ARPANET throughout the 1970s, attracted in large part by the ability it gave individuals to exchange electronic messages, or e-mail. By 1980, a number of networks were in operation, but because they relied on different information-passing rules, or protocols, they could not communicate with one another. That problem was solved by Robert Kahn of Bolt Beranek and Newman Inc., a Cambridge, Massachusetts, consulting company, and Vinton Cerf at Stanford University, who invented TCP/IP (Transmission Control Protocol/Internet Protocol), a method of exchanging information among networks; by 1983 the various networks had linked up. The Internet was born.

For most of the 1980s, the Internet remained accessible only to computer professionals and those willing to learn the complex commands necessary to traverse it. But in 1989 the British scientist Tim Berners-Lee at CERN, the European Center for Particle Physics, devised a new protocol for passing information around the Internet. The resulting virtual-information space, dubbed the World Wide Web by Berners-Lee, allowed users to move from site to site on the Internet and view whatever information they wished without paying attention to the physical location of the computers holding that information.

The Internet was opened to commercial use in the early 1990s, and companies began selling access to it and creating software programs tailored to nonscientists. By the end of the decade, the Internet and the World Wide Web had become ubiquitous in the developed world and were spreading into developing countries.

As the twenty-first century dawned, the Internet promised to reshape society in many ways. A rapidly increasing volume of commerce was being conducted over it, from retail sales and auctions to business-contract negotiations. For many people, e-mail had replaced letters and the *telephone for much of their communication with friends and colleagues. Discussion groups that met in electronic "chat rooms" had created new communities of people who might never meet but who shared common interests and bonds. Most significant, the Internet had broadened and quickened the dissemination of information more than anything since the development of the printing press in the fifteenth century, leading to predictions that it could be the most important technological advance in five hundred years.

• Katie Hafner and Matthew Lyons, *Where Wizards Stay Up Late: The Origins of the Internet*, 1996.

—Robert Pool

INTERNMENT OF JAPANESE AMERICANS. *See* Incarceration of Japanese Americans.

INTERSTATE COMMERCE ACT, 1887 regulatory law. *Railroads were the earliest major corporations whose interests transcended state boundaries. In some places, railroads competed for traffic, but over long stretches of their tracks they were monopolies. As common carriers, they were forbidden by their charters to discriminate among customers. Nevertheless, to lure traffic between competitive points, railroads offered larger shippers rebates—and charged less for a competitive long haul than for a monopolistic short haul. With their prosperity threatened by railroad pricing practices, farmers, merchants, communities, and even entire regions turned to politics for redress. Abandoning their free-market *laissez-faire notions, protestors convinced several states to regulate railroads.

The U.S. *Supreme Court upheld state regulation of railroads in *Munn* v. *Illinois* (1876), then reversed itself in *Wabash* v. *Illinois* (1886), triggering demands in the *West and the *South for federal action. In 1887, Congress passed the Interstate Commerce Act (ICA), designed to prevent railroad rate discrimination. The only significant opposition came from the Northeast and *California. Since divergent bills had passed the House and Senate, the ICA was a compromise measure that incorporated some provisions that railroads opposed and other features that reformers disliked. The ICA tried to eliminate price discrimination between long and short hauls, required railroads to charge their published rates and established the Interstate Commerce Commission (ICC) to administer the law.

The ICC worked effectively until 1897, when the Supreme Court outlawed its power to set rates and to prevent the long-haul/short-haul abuse. During the *Progressive Era, Congress amended the ICA through the Hepburn Act (1906), giving the ICC the power to set maximum freight rates and extending its jurisdiction to express companies and oil pipelines. In 1910, the Mann-Elkins Act again empowered the ICC to enforce the long-haul/short-haul clause. Following *World War I, the Esch-Cummins Transportation Act of 1920 amended the ICA by granting the ICC enormous power to consolidate railroads into about twenty competing systems and to regulate minimum rates as well as maximum ones. The Motor Carrier Act of 1935 subjected the trucking industry to ICC regulation, and the Transportation Act of 1940 gave the ICC jurisdiction over water carriers, while ordering it to protect equally all modes of transportation.

Railroads declined after *World War II, partly because minimum-rate regulation prevented them from competing successfully with motor and water carriers. In the Transportation Act of 1958, Congress attempted but failed to clarify minimum-rate-policy by giving the ICC two contradictory tasks: preserving rail, motor, and water carriers while also promoting competition among them. That act also facilitated railroads' abandonment of passenger service, which had become unprofitable because of airline competition. By the 1970s and 1980s, critics declared the much amended ICA a failure.

Presidents and Congress agreed. The Motor Carrier Act of 1980 deregulated the trucking business, and the Staggers Rail Act (1980) allowed railroads to compete with trucks. In 1982, Congress reduced the ICC from eleven to five members, and in 1985 the Office of Management and Budget proposed that the ICC by abolished. With budget-cutting mania sweeping Washington, that proposal was carried out, and the Interstate Commerce Act became a dead letter on 31 December 1995.

[*See also* Economic Regulation; Gilded Age; Granger Laws; Granger Movement.]

• Ari and Olive Hoogenboom, *A History of the ICC: From Panacea to Palliative*, 1976.

—Ari Hoogenboom

INTERSTATE COMMERCE COMMISSION. *See* Economic Regulation; Interstate Commerce Act.

INTERSTATE HIGHWAY SYSTEM. *See* Highway System.

INVENTIONS. *See* Technology.

IRAN-CONTRA AFFAIR. The Iran-Contra affair surfaced in 1986–1987 when evidence became public that President Ronald *Reagan's *National Security Council (NSC) staff had secretly sold arms to Iran, used the profits to provide aid to the Contra forces opposing Nicaragua's leftist government—aid expressly prohibited by Congress in 1984—and had then concealed the truth by lying to Congress and destroying evidence.

The affair began in 1985 when, at Israel's urging, Reagan secretly approved selling TOW antitank (and later anti-aircraft) missiles to Iran for use in its war against Iraq, which was viewed by Israel as its most dangerous enemy. Although Reagan had publicly vowed never to negotiate with hostage-takers, he hoped that the aid would encourage Tehran to facilitate the release of nine American hostages held in Beirut, including agents of the *Central Intelligence Agency (CIA). Some hostages were indeed released, but others were taken. As Reagan continued to approve arms shipments to Iran in 1986, Secretary of State George Schultz and Defense Secretary Caspar Weinberger objected, arguing that the shipments contradicted administration policy and violated a U.S. embargo imposed on Iran in 1979 because of its anti-American policies.

In November 1986, a Lebanese journal embarrassed the administration by revealing the arms shipments. At the same time, Attorney General Edwin Meese informed Reagan that NSC staff, led by Lieutenant Colonel Oliver North, had illegally diverted the arms-sale profits to buy military supplies for the Contras. North, an embittered *Vietnam War veteran, hated *communism and was determined to defeat Nicaragua's revolutionary government at any price. The diversion, however, was probably initiated by CIA Director William Casey, who died of a brain tumor just as the illegalities surfaced. Reagan appointed a review board led by the former senator John Tower of Texas. Its March 1987 report chastised the president for not controlling his administration and sharply criticized White House Chief of Staff Donald Regan, who resigned.

Later that spring, a joint House-Senate investigative committee uncovered crimes, including lying to Congress and destroying evidence, by North and his superiors, National Security Advisers Robert McFarlane and John Poindexter. The committee's televised hearing, especially the riveting testimony by Oliver North in full-dress Marine uniform, captured the nation's attention. The committee's report concluded that the actions had been concealed not for security reasons, as the administration claimed, but to circumvent the law to the detriment of America's democratic institutions. President Reagan was again judged an incompetent administrator, but he was found to have been unaware of the diversion of the arms' profits to the Contras. Meanwhile, Independent Prosecutor Lawrence Walsh, appointed by Attorney General Meese, charged fourteen persons with crimes. Eleven pleaded guilty or were convicted. An appeals court overturned North's and Poindexter's convictions on technicalities. In 1992, President George *Bush pardoned six others.

The Iran-Contra affair, the nadir of the Reagan presidency, formed a chapter in the long struggle between Congress and the executive branch over control of foreign policy. It also exemplified how officials could come to justify criminal activity in fighting what they considered to be righteous battles, even if a majority in Congress and the American public disagreed.

[*See also* Anticommunism; Foreign Relations: U.S. Relations with Latin America; Foreign Relations: U.S. Relations with the Middle East.]

• Theodore Draper, *A Very Thin Line: The Iran-Contra Affair,* 1991. Lawrence Walsh, *Final Report of the Independent Counsel for Iran/Contra Matters,* 1993.

—Walter LaFeber

IRANIAN HOSTAGE CRISIS. *See* Carter, Jimmy; Foreign Relations: U.S. Relations with the Middle East.

IRISH AMERICANS. Irish immigrants and their descendants virtually defined the American conception of "ethnic group." The Irish were the first European people to substantially challenge English cultural dominance in colonial America, to spark significant Anglo-American hostility, to develop a rich array of community institutions, and to demonstrate that ethnicity could have long-lasting social and demographic consequences.

English military operations and land confiscations in Ireland propelled over 10,000 Irish to the West Indies between the 1640s and the 1660s, with overflow into English North America. Population pressure and English land seizures accelerated emigration in the eighteenth century, with many of the Irish taking advantage of contractual servitude to provide for the Atlantic passage. By 1790, roughly 400,000 persons of Irish birth or descent populated the United States, three-quarters of them Roman Catholic. Between 1820 and the mid-1920s, some 4.75 million Irish migrated to the United States, second only to Germans among non-English immigrants. Irish *immigration peaked between 1846 and 1851, when the United States received most of the 1.5 million who fled the devastating potato famine. The number of Irish-born immigrants and their children reached an all-time high around 1900 at almost 3.5 million.

Until well into the twentieth century, a strong social and cultural Irish Catholic community existed in America by both choice and necessity. This community, which arose in the United States before the *Civil War, owed much to the nature of Irish immigration itself, a calculated movement—even in the famine years—of men and women seeking opportunities superior to those at home. Moreover, this was a chain migration, with relatives, neighbors, and coworkers paving the way for subsequent arrivals, and with families, parishes, and villages reassembling in America.

For much of the nineteenth century, Irish Americans found social and economic *mobility hampered by lack of capital, insufficiency of marketable skills, and outright prejudice. Most avenues of upward mobility—whether politics, the church, or trade—remained focused upon the immigrant subculture and held in the most ambitious youths rather than propelling them outward. One consequence was a highly concentrated population. In 1850, 80 percent of the Irish-born lived in the urban Northeast. In 1860, nearly one-third of the Irish-born lived in just ten American cities, and 40 percent of that number resided in *New York City alone. As late as 1920, approximately 90 percent of first-generation Irish Americans resided in urban areas. Not until after *World War I did these close-knit Irish neighborhoods begin to erode and disperse.

Irish Americans formed aid societies, fraternal groups, small businesses, Catholic parishes, and political organizations. The last offered protection against (while also provoking) periodic assaults by native-born Anglo-American Protestants upon the Irish Catholics' alleged loyalty, on account of their religion, to a "foreign prince." Episodes of nativist hostility reinforced Irish Americans' tendency to identify themselves as a people dispossessed—first by the English and subsequently by Anglo-Americans. The Roman Catholic church provided a source of strength and a path of upward mobility. By 1900, half of the bishops who had served the American church were Irish-born or -descended. Politics, too, served the community. Thousands of Irish-Americans earned their wages as policemen, firemen, city laborers, and clerks, while the politicians who secured their places built impressive urban vote-getting "machines" headed by "bosses" like New York City's "Honest John" Kelly and mayors like *Boston's James M. Curley (1874–1958) and, after *World War II, *Chicago's Richard J. *Daley.

Associated with the *Democratic party from the 1840s, Irish-American voters wavered when President Woodrow *Wilson showed little enthusiasm for Irish independence but returned to vote for the Catholic presidential candidate Alfred E. *Smith in 1928. The *New Deal Era's social welfare programs, which undercut the social services provided by ethnic politicians, and the erosion of Irish-American neighborhoods weakened pressures for political conformity. A residual ethnic pride emerged, however, in Irish-American support for John F. *Kennedy in 1960.

As the twentieth century wore on, Irish America slipped into a pan-Catholic culture that was no longer purely ethnic. With the growing *secularization of American life, a superficial "Irishness" was embraced as part of the American culture. Saint Patrick's Day, shorn of religious significance, became a national festival, and to claim Ireland as one's ancestral home became both fashionable and, ironically, a badge of *assimilation.

[*See also* Antebellum Era; Anti-Catholic Movement; Colonial Era; Indentured Servitude; Nativist Movement; New England; Race and Ethnicity; Roman Catholicism; Urbanization.]

• William V. Shannon, *The American Irish: A Political and Social Portrait,* 1963. Andrew Greeley, *That Most Distressful Nation: The Taming of the American Irish,* 1972. Lawrence McCaffrey, *The Irish Diaspora in America,* 1976. Timothy J. Meagher, ed., *From Paddy to Studs: Irish-American Communities in the Turn of the Century Era,* 1880–1920, 1986. Denis Clark, *Erin's Heirs: Irish Bonds of Community,* 1991. Ronald H. Bayor and Timothy J. Meagher, eds., *The New York Irish,* 1996.

—Dale T. Knobel

IRON AND STEEL INDUSTRY. The history of iron- and steel-making in the United States reflects the rise, fall, and partial recovery of the productive capacity of the nation's industrial sector, from its origins in the *Colonial Era, to the enormous productivity of the 1880–1970 period, to the cutbacks and restructuring of the 1980s and 1990s. This history has been marked by dramatic events, triumphant technological innovations, and well-known entrepreneurs.

Through the early 1800s, the three essential stages in the production of finished metal, typically conducted in small rural

MAP 10: PROPERTIES OF THE UNITED STATES STEEL CORPORATION (1903)

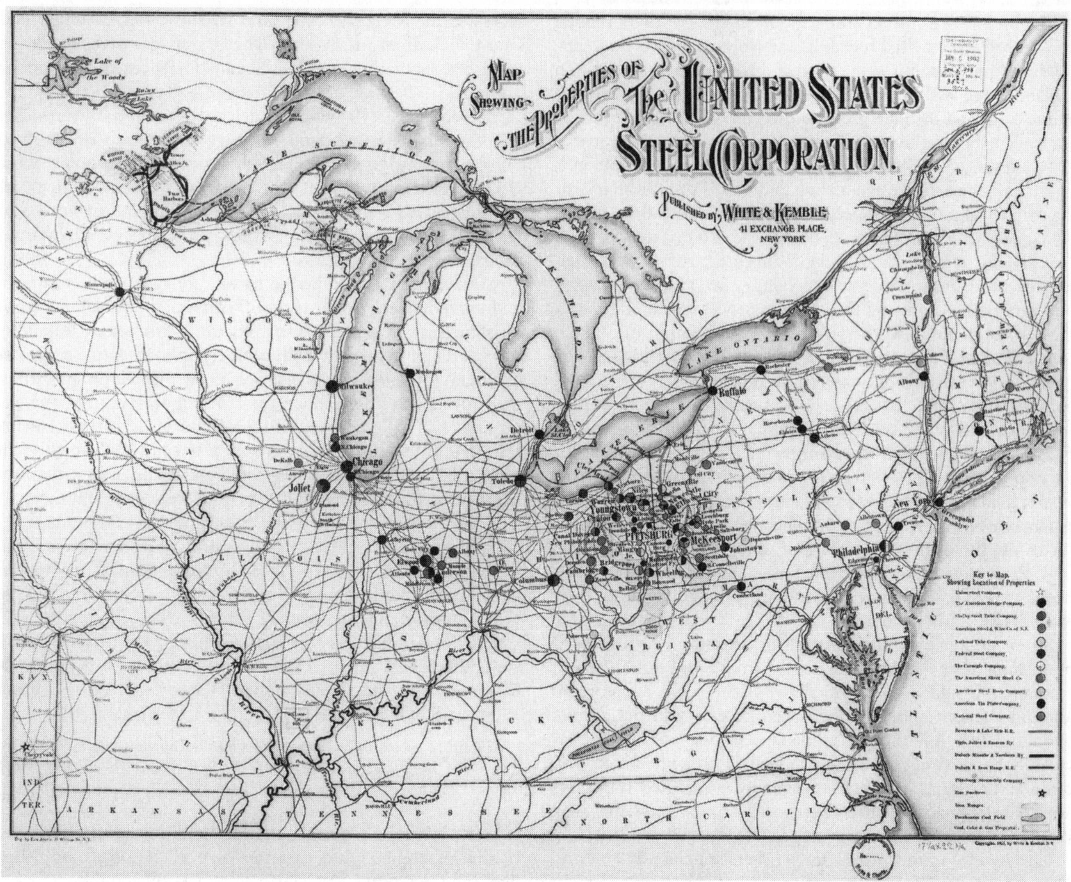

The U.S. Steel Company was formed in 1901 when J. P. Morgan bought out Andrew Carnegie and, with other financiers, combined Carnegie's mills with other steel companies to form a vast corporate conglomerate. This promotional map conveys the new company's far-flung holdings, including mills, mines, processing plants, steamship lines, railroads, corporate offices, and distribution facilities. U.S. Steel typified the concentrated corporate power that many Progressive-era reformers believed posed a serious threat to American democracy.

[*See* Capitalism; Carnegie, Andrew; Gilded Age; Industrialization; Iron and Steel Industry; Morgan, J. P.]

ironworks, consisted of smelting, which melted iron ore into a raw, intermediate material; refining, which imparted properties such as hardness or malleability; and shaping, which molded the metal into rails, beams, sheets, or tools and other objects. In the mid–nineteenth century, highly skilled workers refined and shaped the smelted metal. These workers, called puddlers, produced high-quality wrought iron through a demanding and expensive process. Before the iron could be used, however, it had to be rolled through grooved cylinders. Skilled rollers then controlled the production of small amounts of finished iron.

When the *Civil War began, U.S. mills output only one million tons per year through a slow and costly process that produced a wrought iron too weak to be made into rails, a much-demanded product. Fortunately for the ironmasters, a new *technology, named for its English inventor, Henry Bessemer, became available in the postwar years. This process bypassed puddlers by mechanizing the refining process. In a large, egg-shaped "converter," workers combined molten pig iron and a blast of air that produced an explosion so powerful that virtually all the impurities were removed. The result was a new, hard metal, Bessemer steel, ideal for rail-making. The new process sparked mechanical improvements throughout the industry, prompting steelmasters to integrate all stages of the production process. These integrated mills employed thousands of workers, many of them recent immigrants, and made three thousand tons of steel per day. The Bessemer process and its successor, the open-hearth method, underlay a second industrial revolution that transformed the United States into the world's premier industrial and military power.

Andrew *Carnegie was the first to see in the Bessemer process new possibilities for industrial organization. At his mammoth mills near Pittsburgh, Pennsylvania, he streamlined and automated production. Significantly, Carnegie's mills required less and cheaper labor than had been necessary in the days of puddling, and thousands of workers were displaced by the innovations that swept the metals industry in the late nineteenth century. Carnegie's initiatives essentially eliminated trade unionism in the steel industry until the 1930s, when the Steel Workers Organizing Committee succeeded in creating an industry-wide union open to workers of all skill levels. Throughout the twentieth century, *industrial relations in steelmaking were often marked by acrimony and, as in the nineteenth century, occasionally by violence.

The United States retained its premier position in metal-making until the 1970s, when international competition, higher production and labor costs, and questionable managerial decisions led to the collapse of the U.S. Steel Corporation, the direct heir of Carnegie's empire. In Pittsburgh and other locales in the Northeast, the effects were devastating. This region, which had profited so handsomely in the Age of Steel, was forced to look to service industries, education, and information technologies to rebuild its economic base. In other venues, however, the American steel industry staged a renaissance by the 1990s and succeeded in producing quality products in efficient and profitable mills, some large, others belonging to smaller competitors.

[*See also* Gilded Age; Global Economy, America and the; Homestead Lockout; Immigration; Industrialization; Labor Markets; Labor Movements; Railroads; Strikes and Industrial Conflict.]

• William T. Hogan, *Economic History of the Iron and Steel Industry in the United States*, 5 vols., 1971. John P. Hoerr, *And the Wolf Finally Came: The Decline of the American Steel Industry*, 1988.

—Paul Krause

IROQUOIS CONFEDERACY. The Iroquois Confederacy (League of the Iroquois) was a nonaggression pact formed during a period of warfare, probably between A.D. 1500 and 1600. Initially comprised of the Seneca, Cayuga, Onondaga, Oneida, and Mohawk nations of present-day New York state, its architectural metaphor was the multifamily longhouse they all used. Tradition has it that the Peacemaker, a Huron, and Ayonhwathah, an Onondaga, founded the confederacy, devising both a rationale and a ritual for ending internecine warfare. They first recruited the Mohawks. The Oneidas subsequently joined, and later the Cayugas and Senecas. The Onondagas were last, owing to an evil shaman named Thadodaho. Once cured, Thadodaho was made first among the confederacy's fifty equal chiefs.

The confederacy's structure derived from the Iroquois clan system, and its ritual from funerary ceremonies designed to prevent revenge warfare. The women of each nation's leading clan segments appointed league chiefs, each assuming the name of his deceased predecessor. The five nations had unequal representation, but this was not a voting problem since unanimous decisions were required.

Confederation facilitated joint warfare against other nations and confederacies in the region. With Dutch and later English assistance, the Iroquois destroyed the Hurons and others by the middle of the seventeenth century, often adopting survivors to counter population losses caused by *smallpox and other epidemics. The confederacy remained powerful until the expulsion of the French in the mid–eighteenth century. During this period, the Tuscaroras were admitted as a sixth constituent nation. However, dependence upon consensus and the requirement of unanimity proved a structural weakness, and the confederacy broke up during the *Revolutionary War. Separate confederacies re-formed in the United States and Canada in the nineteenth century, and these continue. While a few writers have viewed the Iroquois Confederacy as a model for the U.S. *Constitution, most scholars reject this idea.

[*See also* Indian History and Culture: Migration and Pre-Columbian Era; Indian History and Culture: Distribution of Major Groups, circa 1500; Indian History and Culture: From 1500 to 1800.]

• William N. Fenton, *The Great Law and the Longhouse: A Political History of the Iroquois Confederacy*, 1998. Dean R. Snow, *The Iroquois*, 1994.

—Dean R. Snow

ISLAM. Islam is a global religious tradition with about one billion adherents. Observing the "five pillars of Islam," Muslims pray five times a day, give alms, fast during the month of Ramadan, make the pilgrimage to Mecca, and testify to the oneness of God (Allah) and the messenger status of Muhammad, Islam's seventh-century founder. The religion is divided into two major groups, the Sunni and the smaller Shiite branch.

Islam first came to North America with the slave trade. Records from 1717 indicate that some African slaves spoke Arabic, refused to eat pork, and called God Allah. As many as 20 percent of the slaves in the North American colonies were Muslims, though most traces of their religious heritage vanished when they converted to Christianity. In the late nineteenth century, Muslims from the Middle East came to the United States, settling in eastern and midwestern cities. The South Asian agricultural workers who immigrated to *California at the turn of the twentieth century also included Muslims. The most rapid growth of the American Muslim population came after 1965, however, when legislation eased *immigration barriers.

By 2000, America had roughly one thousand mosques and many national Islamic organizations, including the Muslim Students Association (established in 1963) and the Islamic Society of North America (1981). Figures on America's total Muslim population at the end of the twentieth century varied widely, in part because the number was growing so rapidly. It seemed likely, however, that the United States was home to 3 to 6 million Muslims, or approximately 1–2 percent of the total population.

Many Americans associate Islam with the "Black Muslims" of the *Nation of Islam, a controversial African-American group founded in *Detroit in the early 1930s by Wallace Fard and later led by Elijah Muhammad. Most U.S. Muslims, however, are of either Middle Eastern or Asian origin. While some African-American Muslims continued in the late twentieth century to affiliate with the Nation of Islam, many more, including Elijah Muhammad's son, Wallace D. Muhammad, were orthodox members of American mosques.

American Muslims suffer from stereotypes that associate their *religion with terrorism, but because of its roots in *Judaism and Christianity, Islam is gradually coming to be seen as an important American faith. In 1991, a Muslim delivered the opening prayer at a session of the U.S. House of Representatives. Later in the 1990s, some American intellectuals spoke of one "Judeo-Christian-Islamic" faith common to the vast majority of U.S. citizens.

[*See also* African Americans; Immigration Law; Malcolm X; Post–Cold War Era, Protestantism; Roman Catholicism; Slavery: The Slave Trade.]

• C. Eric Lincoln, *The Black Muslims in America,* 3d ed., 1994. Jane I. Smith, *Islam in America,* 1999.

—Stephen Prothero

ISOLATIONISM. Isolationism is best defined as opposition to U.S. intervention in war outside the Western Hemisphere, particularly in Europe; to involvement in binding military alliances; and to participation in collective-security organizations. Historically, isolationists have sought above all to preserve the nation's freedom of action. In contrast to pacifists, isolationists can favor unilateral military action.

From the founding of the republic through the early twentieth century, the United States pursued an isolationist policy. In **Common Sense* (1776), Thomas *Paine warned that continued ties to Britain "tends directly to involve this continent in European wars and quarrels." John *Adams's Model Treaty of 1776 envisioned a purely commercial treaty with France, a proposal the French rejected. President George *Washington's Farewell Address of 1796 advised his countrymen "to steer clear of permanent Alliances." In his first inaugural address in 1801, Thomas *Jefferson sought "peace, commerce and honest friendship with all nations, entangling alliances with none." As part of what was later known as the *Monroe Doctrine, President James *Monroe proclaimed in his annual message of 1823: "In the wars of the European powers in matters relating to themselves we have never taken part, nor does it comport with our policy to do so."

Although the United States engaged in several major wars in the nineteenth century—the *War of 1812, the *Mexican War, and the *Spanish-American War—all these conflicts were fought unilaterally and therefore did not violate classic isolationist principles. Even when the United States entered *World War I in 1917, it did so as an "associated power," so as to avoid any obligations that might come from a binding military alliance. In 1919, President Woodrow *Wilson unsuccessfully sought American membership in the *League of Nations, whose covenant obligated member states to engage in collective security if one of its members faced "external aggression." The Republican senators Henry Cabot Lodge of Massachusetts, William E. Borah of Idaho, and Hiram Johnson of California invoked isolationist tenets to fight the proposal, as did the League for the Preservation of American Independence. Hence, throughout the 1920s and most of the 1930s, traditional isolationism remained intact.

The years 1934–1937 marked the peak of isolationist activism. As President Franklin Delano *Roosevelt sought discretionary power to aid nations facing fascist aggression, his foes rallied and strongly fought such entanglements. In 1934, Congress forbade private loans to nations in default of obligations; in 1935, it rejected American membership in the World Court; and from 1935 to 1937 it passed a battery of *neutrality acts that remained law until September 1939.

As more and more Americans endorsed collective action against rising dictatorships, however, isolationism became increasingly contested. As the word itself became more pejorative, isolationists preferred such terms as "noninterventionist," "hemispherist," "nationalist," and "continentalist"—the term favored by the historian Charles A. *Beard. After September 1939, when war again broke out in Europe, isolationists determinedly fought Roosevelt's interventionist proposals, though without success. Although a number of groups were involved, including the quasi-pacifist National Council for the Prevention of War and the short-lived No Foreign War Committee, the major isolationist organization was the *America First Committee, formed in September 1940.

Classic isolationism ended on 7 December 1941, with the Japanese attack on *Pearl Harbor. After both world wars, however, "revisionist" historians such as Beard, Charles Callan Tansill, and Harry Elmer Barnes wrote accounts claiming that in each case the isolationist position had been the correct one.

During the *Cold War, some citizens fought against America's major internationalist and interventionist moves: membership in the *United Nations (1945) and the *North Atlantic Treaty Organization (1949), entry into the *Korean War (1950), and early involvements in Indochina (1954). However, such former isolationists as Senator Robert A. *Taft (Rep.–Ohio) sacrificed consistency by supporting more militant action in Asia. Isolationists suffered a major defeat in 1953–1954 when the Senate defeated a constitutional amendment proposed by Senator John Bricker (Rep.–Ohio) limiting presidential treaty-making power.

Most opponents of the *Vietnam War could not be called isolationists in the traditional sense as they seldom, in principle, repudiated membership in international organizations, military aid overseas, economic sanctions, or the use of combat forces under certain circumstances. In the 1980s and 1990s, a few "neo-isolationist" political scientists and historians called for America's withdrawal from alliance systems, security arrangements, and international organizations and advocated a defense limited to the Western Hemisphere. Like their predecessors in the late 1930s, however, they shunned the discredited label "isolationism" and preferred such terms as "interest-based policies," "strategic disengagement," "strategic independence," or "national strategy."

[*See also* Foreign Relations: U.S. Relations with Europe; Internationalism; Pacifism; World War II: Military and Diplomatic Course.]

• Manfred Jonas, *Isolationism in America, 1935–1941,* 1966. John Milton Cooper Jr., *The Vanity of Power: American Isolationism and World War I, 1914–1917,* 1969. Justus D. Doenecke, *Not to the Swift: The Old Isolationists in the Cold War Era,* 1979. Wayne S. Cole, *Roosevelt and the Isolationists, 1932–45,* 1983. Justus D. Doenecke, *Anti-Intervention: A Bibliographical Introduction to Isolationism and Pacifism from World War I to the Early Cold War,* 1987. Justus D. Doenecke, *The Battle Against Intervention, 1939–1941,* 1997.

—Justus D. Doenecke

ITALIAN AMERICANS. The 1990 U.S. Census reported some 14.7 million persons of Italian ancestry, of whom the great majority were descended from 5 million Italians who immigrated to the United States after 1890. The high point of the immigration occurred in the first fifteen years of the twentieth century, when some 3.4 million Italians arrived. Predominantly males of working age, peasants, artisans, and laborers, about half remained and sent for wives and families.

This vast migration resulted from fundamental changes in Italian society, including population growth, capitalist innovations that disrupted traditional forms of agriculture and craft production, and burdensome taxes and military conscription imposed by the new Kingdom of Italy. Poverty and illiteracy characterized southern Italy, where two-thirds of the immigrants originated.

*World War I and American restrictive legislation reduced Italian *immigration to a trickle (the Immigration Act of 1924 established an annual quota for Italy of 3,845). Following

*World War II, the family-reunification provision of American immigration policy enabled a modest number of new immigrants to enter the United States. By the 1970s, however, Italy had become a country of immigration rather than emigration.

While the Italian immigrants included wine-makers and fishermen in California, stonecutters in Vermont, cigarmakers in Florida, sugarcane workers in Louisiana, and miners from Pennsylvania to Utah, over two-thirds were concentrated in cities along the East Coast from *Philadelphia to *Boston and west to *Chicago. Replacing the Irish, the Italians became the major source of unskilled labor in *railroads and construction. In time, increasing numbers, especially women, found jobs in factories and mills, particularly textiles and clothing manufacturing.

Immigrants who had been labor activists in Italy brought their radical ideologies to America. Italian-born anarchists, socialists, and syndicalists played an important role in such *Industrial Workers of the World-led strikes as those of Lawrence, Massachusetts, and Paterson, New Jersey. Italian immigrants figured in the leadership and rank-and-file of *American Federation of Labor unions and (with their children) of the *Congress of Industrial Organizations unions of the 1930s. Initially denounced as strikebreakers, Italians earned a reputation as radicals, a reputation reinforced by the *Sacco and Vanzetti case of the 1920s.

The immigrants formed clustered settlements, composed of persons from the same regions and even villages. Here they recreated their cultural patterns and social networks, including banks established by padrones (labor contractors), mutual-aid societies providing sickness and death benefits, and the *festa* of the town's patron saint. Nominally Roman Catholic, many immigrants were anticlerical, and Italian parishes were established with great difficulty. Parents preferred to send their children to free public schools rather than parochial schools. Yet, the second generation became acculturated to American Catholicism and more devout than the first.

Attached to the particular villages from which they came, the immigrants initially did not identify as "Italians." World War I and the rise of fascism engendered a nationalist spirit among many, however. Denounced as "dagoes," Italians faced prejudice and discrimination; thus, when Benito Mussolini encouraged pride in Italy, many embraced him as a savior. In the 1930s, fascist propaganda exploited this predisposition. Despite a militant antifascist minority, most Italian Americans initially sympathized with Mussolini's regime.

Slow to naturalize, Italians played a minor role in American politics until after World War II. Fiorello *La Guardia, first a congressman and then mayor of *New York City, and Vito Marcantonio, a radical congressman from East Harlem, were exceptions. Following the attack on *Pearl Harbor and Italy's declaration of war on the United States, the 600,000 Italian immigrants who were still not naturalized became "enemy aliens."

World War II marked a major turning point in Italian American history. Eager to prove their loyalty, Italian Americans served in the U.S. armed forces, purchased bonds, and otherwise supported the war effort. On 12 October 1942, Attorney General Francis Biddle removed the stigma of "enemy alien" from nonnaturalized Italians. In contrast to the mass internment of Japanese Americans, only a few hundred alleged Italian fascists were placed in concentration camps. The war also accelerated Americanization, as young people left their "Little Italy" neighborhoods for military service and jobs in war industries.

Following the war, the G.I. Bill (*Servicemen's Readjustment Act) and enlarged education and work opportunities accelerated the social *mobility of the second generation—a process reflected in increased migration to the suburbs. The Little Italies also suffered incursions by new migrants, *urban renewal, and highway construction. When the "black revolution" convulsed America's central cities in the 1960s, Italian Americans who sought to defend their turf were accused of a racist "backlash." Solidly Democratic since the *New Deal Era, they increasingly voted Republican in reaction to the cultural conflicts of those years and as an expression of their higher socioeconomic status.

Various indices show Italian Americans' assimilation to the norms of middle-class life. Indeed, by the 1980s, some had attained positions of power and prestige: New York governor Mario Cuomo; Lee Iacocca, head of Chrysler Corporation; Judge Antonin Scalia of the U.S. *Supreme Court; A. Bartlett Giamatti, president of Yale University; and the filmmaker Martin Scorsese.

Ethnic consciousness not only survived, however, but experienced a resurgence in late twentieth-century America. Italian Americans explored their experience through history and the arts, visited archives and cemeteries in Italy, and reestablished ties with long-lost cousins. Old organizations such as the Sons of Italy in America took on new life, while new organizations proliferated. Partially attributable to the general ascendance of the multicultural paradigm, this resurgence, for some, also offered compensation for the feeling that they were not yet fully accepted as Americans. (In the media, Italian Americans continued to be stereotyped as gangsters and stupid.) For others, it was a search for an identity to counter the impersonality of postmodern society. The Italian-American presence remained strong as the century ended and clearly would persist well into the future.

[*See also* Anarchism; Assimilation; Cultural Pluralism; Democratic Party; Immigration Law; Labor Markets; Nativist Movement; Roman Catholicism; Socialism; Suburbanization; Textile Industry; Urbanization; Women in the Labor Force; Working-Class Life and Culture.]

• Alexander De Conde, *Half Bitter, Half Sweet: An Excursion into Italian-American History,* 1971. Richard D. Alba, *Italian Americans: Into the Twilight of Ethnicity,* 1985. Rudolph J. Vecoli, "The Search for an Italian American Identity: Continuity and Change," in *Italian Americans,* ed. Lydio Tomasi, 1985, pp. 88–112. Jerre Mangione and Ben Morreale, *La Storia: Five Centuries of the Italian American Experience,* 1992. Michael J. Eula, *Between Peasant and Urban Villager: Italian-Americans of New Jersey and New York, 1880–1980,* 1993. Rudolph J. Vecoli, "The Italian Diaspora, 1876–1976," *Cambridge Survey of World Migrations,* ed. Robin Cohen, 1995, pp. 114–22.

—Rudolph J. Vecoli

IVES, CHARLES (1874–1954), composer. Born in Danbury, Connecticut, to George E. Ives, a former *Civil War bandleader and music teacher, and Mary Elizabeth Parmelee, Ives grew up in a rich musical environment. He excelled as a pianist, became a church organist at age fourteen, and later attended Yale (1894–1898), studying composition with Horatio Parker. From age twelve, Ives composed works that reflected his father's iconoclastic views about dissonant harmony and his own love of musical borrowing from patriotic and popular songs and hymns. Parker discouraged his experimentation, and Ives kept his innovations to himself while composing in the evenings and on weekends.

Following the wishes of his father, who had died unexpectedly in 1894, Ives chose a career in insurance over music. In 1908, he married Harmony Twichell, the daughter of the Reverend Joseph Twichell of Hartford, a close friend of Samuel L. *Clemens. In his *Memos* (1932), Ives identified Harmony as the greatest influence on his musical development other than his father. The couple settled in West Redding, Connecticut.

After a heart attack in 1918 left him unable to work, Ives revised and self-published his Second Piano Sonata, the *Concord Sonata,* his aesthetic statement *Essays before a Sonata* (both 1920), and later his *114 Songs* (1922). He wrote for solo piano, chamber ensembles, chorus, band, and orchestra, including multimovement symphonies and more than 140 solo songs. By 1925, he ceased composing new works and instead revised his existing oeuvre. Although working in seclusion, he won a following among young composers through occasional public performance of his music.

Ives's rugged musical language, with its unexpected harmonies, quotations of popular American music, and conscious ties to *transcendentalism, grew in influence after his death. By the end of the twentieth century, he was widely regarded as America's most important composer of concert music. His Third Symphony won the 1947 *Pulitzer Prize.

[*See also* Music: Classical Music; Music: Popular Music; New England.]

• Stuart Feder, *Charles Ives, "My Father's Song": A Psychoanalytic Biography,* 1992. J. Peter Burkholder, ed., *Charles Ives and His World,* 1996.

—Susan C. Cook

IWO JIMA, BATTLE OF (1945). Located 670 miles southeast of Tokyo and vital to Japan's defense, Iwo Jima became strategically important in the latter stages of the Pacific phase of *World War II. Dominated by Mount Suribachi, Iwo was defended by Lieutenant General Tadamichi Kuribayashi's 21,000 men and a thousand heavy guns. Foresaking Japan's usual tactics of defending at the water's edge, Kuribayashi decided instead to defend from an elaborate system of tunnels and caves dug into Iwo itself.

Assigned to capture Iwo was Marine Major General Harry Schmidt's Fifth Amphibious Corps (Third, Fourth, and Fifth Marine Divisions), comprising more than 80,000 men. At 9:30 A.M. on 19 February 1945, after ten weeks of continuous bombing, the first wave of armored amphibian tractors touched down on the island's black volcanic sand beaches. The capture of Suribachi on 23 February was immortalized by the Associated Press photographer Joe Rosenthal's photograph of the flag-raising on its heights.

Fierce and bloody fighting continued until 26 March, during which 5,931 Marines and navy hospital corpsmen were killed in action, and 17,372 wounded. For their heroism, twenty-two Marines, four navy corpsman, and one navy landing-craft commander were awarded the Medal of Honor, half of them posthumously. Japanese losses have never been determined exactly, but only 216 prisoners were taken, most of them Korean conscript laborers. The terrible cost to Americans was somewhat balanced by another statistic: By the war's end, 2,251 B-29 superfortresses, with crews totaling 24,761 airmen, had made emergency landings on Iwo. The horrific death toll on both sides led Americans to conclude that a land invasion of Japan itself, to end the war, would be long and very costly. Re-created in John Wayne's *The Sands of Iwo Jima* (1949), this battle looms large in the lore of World War II.

• Joseph H. Alexander, *Closing In: Marines in the Seizure of Iwo Jima,* 1995. George C. Garand and Truman R. Strobridge, *Western Pacific Operations,* vol. 4 of *History of U.S. Marine Corps Operations in World War II,* 1971.

—Benis M. Frank

IWW. *See* Industrial Workers of the World.

J

JACKSON, ANDREW (1767–1845), seventh president of the United States, founder of the *Democratic party. Born in Waxhaw, South Carolina to Scotch-Irish immigrants, Jackson fought as a boy in the *Revolutionary War, studied law, and in 1788 moved west to Nashville. In 1791, he married Rachel Robards, believing that her divorce had been finalized. When this proved incorrect, they were remarried in 1794. Malicious rumors relating to the contretemps followed Jackson throughout his career. After serving as a Tennessee prosecutor, judge, congressman, senator, and militia general, he won fame in the *War of 1812 with smashing victories against the Creek Indians in 1814 and against the British at the Battle of *New Orleans in January 1815.

His triumph at New Orleans, which eventually acquired an almost mythical coloring, gave Jackson a heroic stature unrivaled since George *Washington's. In 1818, he pursued Seminole Indians into Spanish Florida, creating an international incident. Appointed military governor of Florida (1821), he again served in the Senate in 1823–1825. In a confused, four-candidate presidential race in 1824, Jackson led the popular and electoral vote but lost in the House of Representatives to John Quincy *Adams through the machinations of Henry *Clay. Jackson challenged Adams again in 1828 and defeated him. The campaign introduced new vote-getting techniques but also exhibited a sectional pattern, with Jackson sweeping the *South and *West. In 1832, Jackson easily defeated Henry Clay.

Elected president more for his patriotic persona than his largely unformed political views, Jackson carved out a policy while in office and in doing so shaped his diffuse electoral coalition into an organized political party. He replaced many government officials on partisan grounds, inaugurating the so-called spoils system. Serving his core southwestern constituency, he condemned abolitionism, advocated cheaper public lands, and strong-armed Indian tribes into removing west of the Mississippi. In a confrontation between Georgia and the Cherokee Nation, Jackson backed state authority against tribal sovereignty and refused to protect Indians' treaty rights despite a ruling by U.S. *Supreme Court Chief Justice John *Marshall.

Jackson's presidency defined itself in two central episodes: the nullification crisis and the "Bank War." Jackson took office amid mounting sectional acrimony over the "*American System," a program of fostering *economic development through protective *tariffs and transportation improvements, policies that many southerners condemned as promoting northern growth at their expense. Jackson curbed the American System by vetoing congressional transportation subsidies (most famously the Maysville Road in 1830) on constitutional grounds and urging a lower tariff. When South Carolina, led by John *Calhoun, declared the 1828 tariff null and void in 1832, and prepared to resist its collection, Jackson acted quickly to uphold federal supremacy, by force if necessary. In a ringing proclamation he declared the country indivisible, and *nullification tantamount to treason. With Jackson's blessing, Congress lowered the tariff in 1833, and South Carolina backed down.

Another element in the American System was the Bank of the United States, a privately managed institution chartered by Congress to provide a stable currency and handle the government's finances. Following Thomas *Jefferson, Jackson deemed a national bank dangerous and unconstitutional. In 1832, he vetoed a bill engineered by bank president Nicholas Biddle (1786–1844) to renew its charter, scheduled to expire in 1836. His veto message counterposed the virtuous plain people against the bank's privileged stockholders. The following year, he transferred the federal government's deposits to selected state-chartered banks, triggering a brief financial panic and prompting the Senate to censure him in 1834. Undeterred, Jackson launched a broader assault against all forms of government-granted special privileges, including corporate charters. His Farewell Address in 1837 warned of the insidious "money power." After his presidency, Jackson retired to the Hermitage, his cotton plantation near Nashville, where he died.

Jackson's Bank War and its populistic, egalitarian rhetoric provided the platform and vocabulary for the emerging Democratic party. (His policies also arguably helped trigger the Panic of 1837, which deepened into a severe depression.) By casting himself as the people's tribune against the moneyed elite and their tools in government, he introduced an enduring theme in American politics. Jackson exercised executive powers vigorously, defying Congress, vetoing more bills than all his predecessors, and frequently reshuffling his cabinet.

Jackson's political philosophy adapted Jeffersonian precepts to a developing democratizing society. Combining energetic nationalism and attacks on privilege with *laissez-faire and limited government policies, Jackson appealed simultaneously to the longing of many Americans for a purer republic and to their ambition for a more open future. Strong-willed and sharp-tempered, a fierce patriot and rabid partisan, Jackson himself was always controversial. For him, politics was personal, whether the opponent was Henry Clay, John Marshall, John Calhoun, or Nicholas Biddle. A cabinet crisis erupted in 1829 when the wife of Vice President Calhoun ostracized Peggy Eaton, the daughter of a Washington innkeeper and wife of Jackson's secretary of war. Jackson defended Peggy, and the resulting controversy helped push Calhoun into opposition and open the way for Martin *Van Buren, Jackson's 1832 running mate to win the presidency in 1836.

Andrew Jackson was both a champion and symbol of democracy, the first westerner and self-made man to achieve the presidency, yet also a wealthy slaveholder. The preeminent public figure between Jefferson and Abraham *Lincoln, he dominated and gave his name to an era.

[*See also* Antebellum Era; Bank of the United States, First and Second; Depressions, Economic; Federal Government, Executive Branch: The Presidency; Indian History and Culture: From 1800 to 1900; Indian Wars; Monetary Policy, Federal; Roads and Turnpikes; Seminole Wars; Veto Power.]

• Arthur M. Schlesinger Jr., *The Age of Jackson,* 1945. John William Ward, *Andrew Jackson: Symbol for an Age,* 1955. Edward Pessen, *Jacksonian America,* rev. ed., 1978. Robert V. Remini, *Andrew Jackson,* 3 vols., 1977–1984. Harry L. Watson, *Liberty and Power: The Politics of Jacksonian America,* 1990. Charles Sellers, *The Market Revolution: Jacksonian America,* 1991. Daniel Feller, *The Jacksonian Promise: America, 1815–1840,* 1995.

—Daniel Feller

JACKSON, THOMAS J. ("STONEWALL") (1824–1863), Confederate military hero. A Virginian who graduated from the U.S. Military Academy at West Point in 1846, Jackson distinguished himself in the *Mexican War, winning brevets to major. In 1852, he resigned his commission to become a professor at the Virginia Military Institute. When Virginia seceded from the Union in April 1861, Jackson joined the Confederate Army. Soon promoted to brigadier general, he distinguished himself in a series of *Civil War battles. At the First Battle of *Bull Run (31 July 1861), he earned the sobriquet of "Stonewall" for his defense of a ridge, which helped turn a threatened Confederate defeat into a rout of the Union forces.

In the Spring of 1862, Jackson fought his Shenandoah Valley campaign, proving himself a brilliant strategist and driving the Union Army out of Virginia. He fought in the Seven Days' Battles, but his judgment was blunted by fatigue and sleep deprivation.

In August 1862, he destroyed General John Pope's principal supply depot at Manassas, Virginia. He fought in the Second Battle of Bull Run and defeated the Union forces at Chantilly. He commanded a corps that captured twelve thousand Union troops at Harpers Ferry and fought at Antietam and Fredericksburg. At Chancellorsville, his 2 May 1863 attack on the Union's right flank resulted in one of the most remarkable victories by an inferior force in the annals of warfare. That night, on a personal reconnaissance, he was mistakenly shot by Confederate soldiers. His shattered arm was amputated, but he died eight days later of pneumonia.

Jackson was a deeply religious Presbyterian and a secretive man, an aggressive soldier and stern disciplinarian. He died at the pinnacle of his reputation and entered American mythology as the symbol of a stubborn, persistent fighter.

[*See also* Antietam, Battle of.]

• Byron Farwell, *Stonewall: A Biography of General Thomas J. Jackson,* 1992. James I. Robertson Jr., *Stonewall Jackson: The Man, the Soldier, the Legend,* 1997.

—Byron Farwell

JACKSONIAN ERA. *See* Antebellum Era; Jackson, Andrew.

JACKSON STATE. *See* Kent State and Jackson State.

JACOBI, MARY PUTNAM (1842–1906), physician, feminist. Eldest of the eleven children of the publisher George Palmer Putnam and Victorine (Haven) Putnam, Mary grew up in the environs of *New York City. At age seventeen, she published an essay in the *Atlantic Monthly.* Graduating from the New York College of Pharmacy (1863), she received her M.D. from the Female Medical College of Pennsylvania in 1864, amid volunteer medical work in *Civil War military hospitals. After studying at the École de Médicine in Paris (the first woman to do so), she returned in 1871 to New York, where she built a successful practice and taught at the Woman's Medical College of the New York Infirmary for Women and Children. Incensed by male physicians' refusal to allow women doctors to care for hospital patients, she in 1872 founded the Association for the Advancement of Medical Education of Women. In 1873, she married the German immigrant Abraham Jacobi, a pediatrician, medical reformer, and social activist. The devastating death of their seven-year-old son Ernst from *diphtheria in 1883 impelled her to train students more rigorously in the developing field of bacteriology.

Highly regarded for her uncompromising professional standards, she published more than one hundred papers in medical journals on pathology, neurology, and other topics. Challenging anti-vivisectionists, she practiced and advocated animal experimentation in the search for new vaccines. Emphasizing women's and children's health issues, Jacobi also supported the *woman suffrage movement and campaigned to improve the lot of working women. Insisting on women's right to be scientists and physicians, she challenged all barriers to their professional advancement in these fields.

[*See also* Blackwell, Elizabeth; Hospitals; Medical Education; Medicine: From the 1870s to 1945; Women in the Labor Force.]

• Regina Markell Morantz, "Feminism, Professionalism and Germs: The Thought of Mary Putnam Jacobi and Elizabeth Blackwell," *American Quarterly* 34: 5 (Winter 1982): 459–78. Joy Harvey, " 'Clanging Eagles': The Marriage and Collaboration between Two Nineteenth-Century Physicians, Mary Putnam Jacobi and Abraham Jacobi," in *Creative Couples in the Sciences,* ed. Helena M. Pycior, Nancy G. Slack, and Pnina G. Abir-Am, 1995, pp. 185–95, 325–6.

—Jo Gladstone

JAMES, HENRY (1843–1916), novelist, writer of short stories, plays, critical essays, and travel accounts; prose stylist and theorist of fiction. Born in *New York City the son of Henry James Sr. and Mary Robertson Walsh, and the brother of William *James, Henry James was educated abroad in Geneva, Paris, and Bonn and attended Harvard University briefly to study law but read Balzac instead. After a series of transatlantic residences, James in 1876 lived for a time in Paris where he met Turgenev, Flaubert, Maupassant, Daudet, and Zola. Later in the year, he settled permanently in England: first in London and, in 1898, in Rye. He knew the principal literary men and women of the day, including Robert Browning and George Eliot, whose poetry and fiction he admired and emulated.

James found the American scene bereft of the cultural institutions that gave breadth and depth to a novelist's imagination: "no aristocracy, no church, no clergy, no army, no diplomatic service, no country gentlemen, no palaces. . . . no literature, no novels, no museums, no pictures, no political society, no sporting class—no Epsom nor Ascot!" Consequently, he made the subject of his fiction the complex fate of being an American testing the value of Europe. He brought the genre of the international novel to perfection in plots that examined American naiveté amidst European sophistication, New World morality in the arena of Old World manners. *The American* (1877), *Daisy Miller* (1879), and, especially, *The Portrait of a Lady* (1881) won for James artistic acclaim and fame as a psychological realist. His later international novels *The Wings of the Dove* (1902), *The Ambassadors* (1903), and *The Golden Bowl* (1904), written in his more demanding later style, achieved subtlety and sophistication, though little recognition in his own time. Later generations, raised on Joyce and Proust, praised them as James's "major phase." James also wrote novels and tales with exclusively American settings (like *Washington Square,* 1881; *The Bostonians,* 1886) and exclusively English settings (like *The Spoils of Poynton,* 1897; *The Awkward Age,* 1899), equally incisive psychologically and socially with his international fiction. He tried but failed to become a successful London playwright in the early 1890s.

James, who often wrote about artists and writers, said of himself in 1878 that he had an "imagination of disaster" and saw life as a battle in which "evil is insolent and strong; beauty enchanting but rare; goodness very apt to be weak; folly very apt to be defiant; wickedness to carry the day; imbeciles to be in great places, people of sense in small, and mankind generally unhappy." In this situation, life "bids us learn to will and seek to understand." A Jamesian novel presents this sense of life by constantly nourishing a character's consciousness and having him or her make choices based on an ever more informed sensibility. The novel *What Maisie Knew* (1897) is paradigmatic of this form, ending with a girl on the verge of adolescence who has learned enough as a child to acquire a moral sense and choose the way she will live.

In 1915, when the United States delayed entering *World War I to help England in its fight against Germany, James became a British subject; he was awarded the Order of Merit shortly before his death in 1916.

[*See also* Literature: Civil War to World War I.]

• Leon Edel, *Henry James,* 5 vols., 1953–72. *The Henry James Review,* (1979–), published three times a year. —Joseph Wiesenfarth

JAMES, JESSE (1847–1882), legendary midwestern bandit. Born near Kearney, Missouri, Jesse James and his brother Frank were "bushwhackers" (irregular Confederate guerrillas who attacked Union facilities) during the *Civil War. After the war, the James brothers' gang took up robbery and murder in Missouri and neighboring states. As newspaper articles and dime novels romanticized and justified his crimes, Jesse became famous. To defeated southerners, tales of former Confederate soldiers robbing Yankee banks and trains meant striking back at the enemy. Later, antirailroad sentiment enhanced his image. For the next fifteen years, as the James gang robbed banks and trains, an American Robin Hood legend was born. In a failed bank holdup in Northfield, Minnesota, in 1876, all the gang members except the James brothers were killed. In 1882, living as "Thomas Howard" in St. Joseph, Missouri, with his wife and two children, James was in his home planning the next bank robbery when Bob Ford, a new gang member who was secretly working for the Missouri governor, shot him in the back. According to the later folk song, Ford was "that dirty little coward that shot Mr. Howard, and laid poor Jesse in his grave."

Little evidence suggests that Jesse James robbed from the rich and gave to the poor, or that he espoused lofty social ideals, but his *folklore image as an unvanquished hero of the defeated *South endured. Others, perhaps bored with their own humdrum existence, envied the exciting life he led and the fame he attained.

• Paul I. Wellman, *A Dynasty of Western Outlaws,* 1961. William A. Settle Jr., *Jesse James Was His Name,* 1977. —David E. Conrad

JAMES, WILLIAM (1842–1910), psychologist, philosopher, religious thinker. William James was born in *New York City, the first of five children. His paternal grandfather, also named William James, had emigrated from Ireland and settled in Albany, New York, where he amassed a fortune in business, real estate, and *railroads. As the son of a romantic and spiritually minded father, Henry James Sr., and Mary James, and a close observer of science in the Darwinian Era, James came of age imbibing two major forces of nineteenth-century intellectual life: the urge to make *religion personally vital and the expanding role of science.

Though deeply influenced by his father's belief that the natural world harbored hints of deeper levels of reality, James could not accept the particulars of his father's faith, which included convictions shaped by the Swedish mystic Emanuel Swedenborg and the French utopian thinker Charles Fourier. He developed flexibility of mind during his early education with an idiosyncratic range of tutors, schools, and European trips. His intelligent and energetic siblings, including the diarist Alice James (1848–1892) and the novelist Henry *James, were his schoolmates and traveling companions.

In this intellectually stimulating setting, which included fluency in French and German and vigorous philosophical debate, the father discouraged specialization. William, however, decided to become a painter, and in 1860 the family moved to Newport, Rhode Island, so he could study with William Morris Hunt. After one year, however, prompted by his father's quest for spiritual meaning in science, he enrolled at Harvard's Lawrence Scientific School. He was briefly attracted to the ideas of young scientific enthusiasts who treated the evolutionary theory propounded by Charles Darwin in *The Origin of Species* (1859) as the symbolic centerpiece of their rejection of traditional religion and assertion of the professional authority of science.

Drawn to scientific naturalism, James rejected the anti-Darwinian idealism of the Harvard zoologist Louis *Agassiz, while at the same time accompanying Agassiz on a natural-history expedition to Brazil in 1865–1866. James studied physiological *psychology in Germany in 1867–1868 and in 1869 received his M.D. from Harvard Medical School.

Anticipating a dilemma of the early twentieth-century middle class, James with his excellent education had no clear vocation. He was also deeply troubled by the antireligious and amoral implications of materialistic and deterministic science. His inability to decide on a career or to choose among competing scientific and religious certainties led to a severe personal crisis in 1869–1871. His resolution of this crisis occurred gradually through the 1870s. In 1872, he was appointed an instructor in physiology and psychology at Harvard, where, in 1876, he established America's first psychological laboratory. Philosophically, he decided to accept the vitality of free will as formulated by the French neo-Kantian Charles Renouvier and the British psychologist Alexander Bain. His personal life gained stability in 1878 when he married Alice Howe Gibbens; they had five children, of whom four survived infancy.

James's discussions with the intensely logical and scientifically well-versed Charles *Peirce, in an informal Cambridge group known as the Metaphysical Club, contributed to his new outlook. Under Peirce's influence, James grasped the hypothetical and probabilistic elements underlying many claims for scientific authority—including Darwinism. The example of Darwin and the philosophy of Peirce reinforced James's impulses to adhere to the freedom of the will and to doubt dogma and determinism in his mediation of religion and science.

James's mature theories reflect his hard-won embrace of uncertainty and his integration of the religious and scientific elements in his education. His long-popular textbook *The Principles of Psychology* (1890) reflected an empirical and scientific viewpoint, collecting recent developments in the new science of psychology, but his emphasis on the active mind and on moral behavior, as well as his introspective methods and tentative conclusions, distanced the text from deterministic science.

True to his impatient and energetic mind, James's books were mostly collections of smaller pieces, often delivered as lectures, for which he became increasingly popular. The essays gathered in *The Will to Believe* (1897) recognize the role of science but assert the need for voluntary beliefs in situations empirically ambiguous or elusive. His Gifford Lectures at the University of Edinburgh, published in 1902 as *The Varieties of Religious Experience,* treat the subliminal realms of human consciousness as windows to religious experiences. The essays in *Radical Empiricism* (1912), seminally influential on modern process philosophy and philosophical psychology, grew from James's desire to evaluate empirically a wide range of human experience—including religious and psychic experiences—beyond the artificially simplified empiricism of professional scientific investigation. The Hibbert Lectures that became *A Pluralistic Universe* (1909) argue for looking at the multiplicity of the world's empirical parts without losing the sense of purpose derived from religious worldviews.

James is perhaps most famous for his theory of *pragmatism, developed in discussions with Peirce, first expressed in the 1898 lecture "Philosophical Conceptions and Practical Results" and given wide currency in his *Pragmatism* (1907) and *The Meaning of Truth* (1909). While often challenging conventional philosophical wisdom, he moved furthest outside the mainstream in his scientific curiosity for and experimentation in paranormal experiences. During and after the *Spanish-American War, he provided forceful leadership of the anti-imperialist movement.

Through his life and work, William James bridged religion and science as well as nineteenth- and twentieth-century culture.

[*See also* Dewey, John; Evolution, Theory of; Philosophy; Science: Revolutionary War to World War I.]

• Ralph Barton Perry, *The Thought and Character of William James,* 2 vols., 1935. Howard Feinstein, *Becoming William James,* 1984. Gerald Myers, *William James: His Life and Thought,* 1986. George Cotkin, *William James, Public Philosopher,* 1990. Paul Jerome Croce, *Science and Religion in the Era of William James,* vol. 1, *Eclipse of Certainty,* 1995. Eugene Taylor, *William James on Exceptional Mental States,* 1996.

—Paul Jerome Croce

JAMESTOWN. The first permanent English settlement on the North American continent, established in 1607 along the James River in southeastern Virginia, Jamestown was founded by the Virginia Company of London, a joint stock company chartered by King James I in 1606. The original 104 Jamestown colonists sailed from London on three ships, reaching Virginia on 26 April 1607 and founding Jamestown on 13 May. Initially, Jamestown was contained within James Fort, a defensive structure consisting of a substantial wooden palisade of triangular shape. As the town expanded, the original fort fell into ruin. From 1607 until 1699, Jamestown was the capital of the Virginia colony, and Virginia's first representative assembly met there in 1619.

Despite efforts to develop Jamestown as an important urban center, it remained small, sustained only by its governmental functions and by its role as the colony's principal port of entry. Burned during *Bacon's Rebellion in 1676, it never fully recovered. In 1699, the capital moved to Middle Plantation, now called Williamsburg. Soon thereafter, Jamestown ceased to exist as a town.

Today the site is owned by the U.S. National Park Service and the Association for the Preservation of Virginia Antiquities (APVA). Archaeological excavations by these organizations have uncovered much of the seventeenth-century town. In 1994, APVA archaeologists discovered the site of the original James Fort, long thought to have been destroyed by shoreline erosion.

[*See also* Colonial Era; Exploration, Conquest, and Discovery, Era of European; Smith, John.]

• Philip L. Barbour, ed., *The Complete Works of Captain John Smith (1580–1631),* 3 vols., 1986. James Horn, *Adapting to a New World: English Society in the Seventeenth Century Chesapeake,* 1994.

—Thomas E. Davidson

JAPANESE AMERICANS. *See* Asian Americans; Incarceration of Japanese Americans.

JAY, JOHN (1745–1829), statesman, diplomat, first chief justice of the *Supreme Court. Born to wealth in *New York City, John Jay was a rather a political lawyer until the eve of the *Revolutionary War. In 1775, he became a member of the Second *Continental Congress and a leader of the conservative faction that favored resistance to Britain but opposed independence. After independence, he drafted the constitution of the State of New York, served as president of Congress in 1779, became U.S. representative to Spain in 1780, and joined Benjamin *Franklin and John *Adams to negotiate peace with Great Britain.

Returning from Europe in 1783, Jay served Congress as secretary for foreign affairs for the next six years. Although not a member of the *Constitutional Convention of 1787, he supported its efforts by helping Alexander *Hamilton and James *Madison write the *Federalist Papers to defend the new *Constitution. President George *Washington rewarded Jay's efforts by appointing him the first chief justice of the U.S. Supreme Court. In 1794, Washington sent Jay to London to settle issues that threatened to drag the United States into war against Britain on the side of revolutionary France. The controversial concessions he made in the resultant *Jay's Treaty produced a major party battle between Jay's Federalists and the Republican opposition. After two terms as governor of New York, Jay retired from politics. Overshadowed by more illustrious contemporaries, John Jay was a steady conservative contributor to the creation and survival of the new nation.

[*See also* Early Republic, Era of the; Federalist Party; Revolution and Constitution, Era of.]

• Frank Monaghan, *John Jay: Defender of Liberty,* 1935. Richard B. Morris, *John Jay, the Nation, and the Court,* 1965.

—Jerald A. Combs

JAY'S TREATY (1795). After the end of the *Revolutionary War in 1783, the British refused to turn over the Great Lakes forts on the American side of the new border with Canada. This was only fair, they argued, because the Americans were refusing to honor their promises to compensate the Loyalists for their wartime losses and to enforce payment of prewar debts American citizens owed to British subjects. The British also refused to reopen their West Indian colonies to American ships and to compensate Americans for escaped slaves they had carried off at the end of the war.

The resulting tensions escalated dramatically when, after revolutionary France declared war on Great Britain in 1793, the British began to seize neutral American ships carrying goods to France. As Britain and the United States approached the brink of war in 1794, the embryonic Jeffersonian *Republican party in Congress wanted to force the British to settle on American terms by cutting off Anglo-American trade. Instead, President George *Washington commissioned the Federalist John *Jay to negotiate a settlement.

The terms of the resulting treaty became known in March 1795. In return for giving up America's right to retaliate commercially against Britain for ten years, the British relinquished the Great Lakes posts and agreed to turn over to neutral arbitration the issues of Loyalist compensation, prewar debts, Canadian border disputes, and the most egregious of British ship seizures. The British also agreed to open the West Indies to certain American ships, but the concession was so meager and contingent that the Senate rejected this part of the treaty. To the dismay of both northern shippers and southern slaveholders, Jay secured neither a guarantee of American neutral rights nor compensation for escaped slaves.

The Senate ratified the treaty in June 1795, and the House of Representatives voted the funds to implement it in 1796. But the acrimonious congressional and public debates over whether peace with the powerful British was worth the cost of the treaty helped to convert the Federalists and Republicans from limited congressional factions into full-scale party organizations among the public at large. The treaty also alienated France and helped bring on the 1798 Quasi-War with that country.

[*See also* Early Republic, Era of the; Federalist Party; Jefferson, Thomas; Political Parties; Quasi-War with France.]

• Samuel Flagg Bemis, *Jay's Treaty,* rev. ed., 1962. Jerald A. Combs, *The Jay Treaty,* 1970. Daniel G. Lang, *Foreign Policy in the Early Republic,* 1985.

—Jerald A. Combs

JAZZ. The most influential American music of the twentieth century, jazz was shaped by 1800s *minstrelsy, *vaudeville, *ragtime, and brass-band music. African-American *blues singing of the lower Mississippi Valley, however, was the decisive new influence in local river towns. By 1910, bands were flavoring ragtime marches and dances with indeterminate "blue" notes, rough vocal-style timbres, and imaginative improvisations on tunes. *New Orleans's extensive musical culture and diverse racial and ethnic identities nurtured the most distinctive new style. Beginning in 1906, black New Orleanians such as the pianist Jelly Roll Morton traveled the nation, popularizing their "hot" blues-oriented ragtime. In 1917, when a white New Orleans group, the Original Dixieland Jazz Band (ODJB), made its best-selling first recordings, the local term "jazz" (originally a reference to sexual activity, perhaps of distant African origin) became the world's name for the new music.

After 1920, commercial *New York City bands and songwriters further popularized the ODJB's comic cacophony. Southern musicians in search of commercial advancement joined the great black migration to northern cities. In *Chicago, Joe "King" Oliver's group popularized "hot" jazz, and the band member Louis *Armstrong, a brilliantly extroverted trumpeter, soon launched an independent career. In New York, pianists such as Eubie Blake blended ragtime dexterity with "swinging" jazz rhythms. Fletcher Henderson and Edward ("Duke") *Ellington independently built the first large black jazz orchestras, but white groups such as Paul Whiteman's—playing in comic, symphonic, or "sweet" styles—continued to shape the public's perception of jazz. The music came to symbolize a decade that witnessed the rebellion of white adolescents, northern blacks, and speakeasy customers against restrictive codes of behavior, and F. Scott *Fitzgerald labeled the 1920s the "Jazz Age."

The Great Depression eliminated many musicians' jobs, but the rise of *radio, recordings, and sound *films continued to aid jazz. Ellington's complex and sophisticated work and the blues-oriented, aggressively improvisational "Kansas City" style of the William ("Count") *Basie Orchestra refined the "hot" band traditions pioneered by Oliver and Morton. Ellington, Armstrong, and Cab Calloway, aided by effective management, became commercial successes. Hot jazz gained mass popularity, however, only after the white clarinetist Benny *Goodman made a successful 1935 tour. "Swing" bands suddenly became the vogue. Leaders such as Goodman, Tommy Dorsey, Artie Shaw, Glenn Miller, and Woody Herman carefully tailored "hot" jazz to more sedate white tastes. Jazz became a topic of serious inquiry in the 1930s, as writers researched its history and young white critics proclaimed aesthetic standards. Carnegie Hall concerts conferred respectability on "swing," and Manhattan's Fifty-second Street became a stylish mecca for curious listeners. While highly publicized racial integration occurred in some bands, and new black stars such as the vocalists Ella *Fitzgerald and Billie Holiday, the pianist Art Tatum, and the saxophonists Coleman Hawkins and Lester Young appeared, discrimination and segregation continued to hinder jazz.

During *World War II, the draft, labor disputes, and rationing limited recording and touring, but armed-services swing bands such as Glenn Miller's proved highly popular. This turbulent era saw both the nostalgic revival of "Dixieland" music and the rise of a group of assertive young black innovators. The saxophonist Charlie *Parker, a Kansas City native, along with the New Yorkers John ("Dizzy") Gillespie (trumpet), Kenny Clarke (drums), and Thelonious Monk (piano), pioneered a fleet, technically demanding blues style that scorned swing clichés and intimidated older, less gifted improvisers. This new style, soon labeled "bebop," created intense critical controversy. After 1945, the players' dress, unusual slang, and drug use made them notorious, but critics acknowledged their skill. Postwar inflation and changing public tastes forced most swing orchestras to disband, and jazz became the province of smaller audiences and more experimental musicians. Pedagogues introduced conservatory-style training in jazz. The composers John Lewis, George Russell, Pete Rugolo, and Boyd Raeburn introduced avant-garde classical dissonances and experimentation, and the bandleader Stan Kenton championed a strident "progressive" jazz style. The trumpeter Miles *Davis (a bebop pioneer) created a more subdued new sound in his 1949 *Birth of the Cool* recordings.

In the 1950s, the federal government enlisted jazz in *Cold War diplomacy. The Gillespie, Armstrong, and Goodman bands made goodwill tours. "Cool" jazz proved highly popular in the staid Eisenhower era. The white pianist Dave Brubeck advocated a "West Coast" style, while Davis, the arranger Gil Evans, and the saxophonist John *Coltrane explored the static pastels of modal improvisation. Younger musicians such as Charles Mingus, Horace Silver, Max Roach, and Abbey Lincoln, however, considered jazz the voice of a new African American militance, in favor of *civil rights and against ghetto despair. Their emphatic "hard bop" was abetted by the folklike improvisations of the Texas saxophonist Ornette Coleman. After 1960, Coleman and Coltrane's embrace of atonal "free" improvisation initiated a decade of dramatic jazz innovations. Atonality, distorted timbres, and chance improvisations characterized the music of Coltrane, Eric Dolphy, Cecil Taylor, and Albert Ayler. Black musicians forged closer ties with the avant-garde but also contributed to artistic projects in riot-torn inner cities. Their innovations won small audiences, though, as rock, soul, and the mass-market–oriented sound promoted by Motown Records dominated popular music. Miles Davis, the saxophonist Wayne Shorter, the pianist Joe Zawinul, and others responded by blending soul dance rhythms and electronic instruments with jazz. The resulting 1970s rock-jazz "fusion" brought success to the group Weather Report, the pianist Chick Corea, and others, and somewhat revived jazz's popularity. In a time of increasing opportunities for women, musicians such as the trombonist Melba Liston and the pianists Carla Bley and Toshiko Akiyoshi also gained well-deserved recognition.

As the twentieth century ended, jazz remained a prestigious music, supported by academe, foundation grants, and worldwide networks of festival organizers, producers, and fans. Indeed, young advocates of bebop improvisation such as the trumpeter Wynton Marsalis and the pianist Marcus Roberts stimulated a revival in jazz's popularity. While avant-garde, big-band, fusion, and other jazz forms were underfunded and relatively neglected, jazz's heritage was widely celebrated, and the music continued to influence genres—such as rock, rhythm and blues, soul, rap, and New Age—that dominated the world's musical culture.

[*See also* African Americans; Music: Popular Music; Popular Culture; Twenties, The.]

• Gunther Schuller, *Early Jazz: Its Roots and Musical Development,* 1968. John Litweiler, *The Freedom Principle: Jazz after 1958,* 1984. Gunther Schuller, *The Swing Era: The Development of Jazz, 1930–1945,* 1989. Ted Gioia, *West Coast Jazz: Modern Jazz in California, 1945–1960,* 1992. Paul F. Berliner, *Thinking in Jazz: The Infinite Art of Improvisation,* 1994. Thomas J. Hennessey, *From Jazz to Swing: African-American Jazz Musicians and Their Music, 1890–1935,* 1994.

—Burton W. Peretti

JEFFERSON, THOMAS (1743–1826), third president of the United States. Born in Virginia on the western edges of settlement, Jefferson would always feel a closeness to the land and to an agrarian way of life, and he built his own home, *Monticello, in Albemarle County, not far from his birthplace. Although his public career repeatedly drew him away, he eagerly returned to Monticello whenever possible.

Entering the College of William and Mary in 1760, Jefferson absorbed the ideas of the Enlightenment and became a devoted disciple of the Age of Reason and he subscribed to its preferred religious position, *Deism. He followed his college studies by reading law with George Wythe in Williamsburg. Here, in Virginia's colonial capital, Jefferson encountered the political world that would enlist his lifelong participation. Visiting the House of Burgesses in 1765, he heard Patrick *Henry's memorable "Give me liberty or give me death" speech against the *Stamp Act.

Elected to the House of Burgesses in 1769, at age twenty-six, Jefferson began the political career that would continue until he retired from the presidency forty years later. The young Jefferson actively supported colonial rights in the developing conflict with the British. His *Summary View of the Rights of British America* (1774) protested British policies and actions, insisting that "the British Parliament has no right to exercise authority over us." This pamphlet circulated among delegates to the First *Continental Congress, making its author well known when he took his seat in the Second Continental Congress in June 1775. A year later, appointed to the committee to draft the *Declaration of Independence, Jefferson achieved enduring fame as its principal author.

As a delegate in the Virginia Assembly, Jefferson was active in revising the laws of his state. His draft statute for religious freedom was eventually adopted in 1786. Elected governor of Virginia in 1779, Jefferson served during a trying period of the *Revolutionary War, when the British invaded the state. In June 1781 he barely escaped capture when the British raided Monticello. After two years as governor, Jefferson decided to retire from politics.

In his private life, Jefferson married Martha Wayles Skelton in 1772, and they had three children who survived infancy. Martha's death in 1782, following the birth of their last child, left Jefferson severely depressed. Recovering from his grief, Jefferson was again willing to leave Monticello and return to politics.

Although he inherited slaves from his father and from his wife, Jefferson was opposed to *slavery. In the revision of the laws of Virginia, he proposed gradual emancipation; and in his *Notes on the State of Virginia* (1785), he vigorously condemned the institution. Yet he failed to win support in Virginia for ending slavery and remained a slaveholder for the rest of his life.

Reports that Jefferson fathered children by his slave Sally Hemings (1773–1835), based on oral traditions among Hemings's descendants, have long been controversial. DNA analysis conducted in 1998 of the blood of descendants of Jefferson's uncle and descendants of Sally Hemings led some historians to conclude that Jefferson was the father of at least one of Hemings's children. Other historians, however, argued that such DNA analysis was not conclusive because Jefferson had a brother, Randolph, who with his five sons lived within easy distance of Monticello and visited Jefferson.

Jefferson was U.S. minister to France from 1785 to 1789 and thus did not participate in drafting or ratifying the U.S. *Constitution. In Paris at the outbreak of the French Revolution, he welcomed the struggle as following in the path of the American Revolution and remained sympathetic to the French revolutionary cause after returning to the United States late in 1789.

Jefferson served as the first secretary of state under President George *Washington from 1790 through 1793. In this post he played a major role not only in the direction of foreign affairs but also in the emerging political divisions between the Federalists and their Republican opponents. Opposing the fiscal policies of Treasury Secretary Alexander *Hamilton, he was recognized as the Republican leader. While Hamilton's policies favored business development and urban commercial interests, Jefferson remained suspicious of cities and saw yeoman farmers as the backbone of American democracy.

After three years in retirement during which he extensively remodeled Monticello, Jefferson was elected vice president in 1796, having come in second to Federalist John *Adams at a time when there was no separate balloting for vice president. Presiding over the Senate, he increasingly opposed the policies of the Federalists, who controlled Congress. In 1800, he accepted the Republican nomination for president to oppose Adams's reelection bid. In the electoral vote, Jefferson tied with his vice presidential running mate, Aaron *Burr, throwing the election to the House of Representatives, which chose Jefferson as president and Burr as vice president. (The Twelfth Amendment, adopted in 1804, revised *electoral college procedures to prevent such an outcome in the future.)

Jefferson's first term proved remarkably successful. Reversing Federalist policies that had produced the repressive *Alien and Sedition Acts, Jefferson also reduced military expenditures and set a tone of simplicity and frugality. The capstone of his first term was the *Louisiana Purchase of 1803. A strong president who provided leadership for Congress, Jefferson closely supervised his administration, drafting his own messages to Congress, wrestling with appointments, and working closely with his cabinet whom he involved in the decision-making process. Secretary of State James *Madison, a longtime friend and political ally, provided advice and support.

Defeating the Federalist Charles Cotesworth Pinckney to win reelection in 1804, President Jefferson faced increasing difficulties in his second term, including the British attack on the USS *Chesapeake;* the conspiracy trial of his former vice president, Aaron Burr; and the Napoleonic wars in Europe, which left American commerce caught in the conflict between Great Britain and France. Jefferson's embargo policy, enacted in 1807, forbade U.S. trading vessels to leave port for any foreign destination. Deeply unpopular with merchants, traders, seamen, and farmers growing crops for export, the Embargo Act was repealed in 1809.

Jefferson's retirement years at Monticello were filled with activity. An intellectual with wide-ranging interests, from music, painting, and architecture to political philosophy and natural history, he served as president of the *American Philosophical Society from 1797 to 1815. His extensive correspondence included a long series of letters with John Adams in which the onetime political rivals explored their differing views of politics and human nature. His most important retirement project was the founding of the University of Virginia, in Charlottesville. He not only rallied legislative support for the enterprise but also assumed the role of planner, architect, and director of building, together with establishing the curriculum and hiring professors. Jefferson lived to see the opening of the university on 7 March 1825. He died a year later on 4 July 1826, the fiftieth anniversary of the Declaration of Independence. In keeping with his instructions, his epitaph identifies him only as the author of the Declaration of Independence and the Virginia Statute for Religious Freedom, and father of the University of Virginia.

[*See also* Early Republic, Era of the; Embargo Acts; Federal Government, Executive Branch: The Presidency; Republicanism.]

• Dumas Malone, *Jefferson and His Time,* 6 vols., 1948–1981. Merrill D. Peterson, *Thomas Jefferson and the New Nation: A Biography,* 1970. John C. Miller, *The Wolf by the Ears: Thomas Jefferson and Slavery,* 1977. Noble E. Cunningham Jr., *The Process of Government under Jefferson,* 1978. Noble E. Cunningham Jr., *In Pursuit of Reason: The Life of Thomas Jefferson,* 1987. William Howard Adams, *The Paris Years of Thomas Jefferson,* 1997. Joseph J. Ellis, *American Sphinx: The Character of Thomas Jefferson,* 1997. Thomas Jefferson Memorial Foundation, *Report of the Research Committee on Thomas Jefferson and Sally Hemings,* January 2000. Philip Ranslet, "Communication," William and Mary Quarterly, 3d ser., 57, no. 3 (July 2000): 728.

—Noble E. Cunningham Jr.

JEFFERSONIAN ERA. *See* Early Republic, Era of the; Jefferson, Thomas.

JEHOVAH'S WITNESSES. Jehovah's Witnesses (originally Bible Students) originated in the 1870s under Charles Taze Russell (1852–1916) of Pittsburgh, Pennsylvania. He established what is known today as the *Watchtower* magazine in 1879 and incorporated Zion's Watch Tower Tract Society in 1884. In his preaching and his book *Millennial Dawn* (1886), Russell taught that Jesus Christ had returned invisibly in 1874 and that the present world would be replaced by Christ's Kingdom on earth in 1914. When this prophecy failed, Russell's successor, Joseph Franklin Rutherford (1869–1942), gradually reworked his teachings and posited that Christ had again come, invisibly, in 1914.

Rutherford reorganized the Bible Students; renamed them Jehovah's Witnesses, developed an authoritarian "Theocracy" that directed all Witnesses to engage in evangelism; condemned "politics, commerce, and religion"; and voiced outspoken anti-Catholicism.

Jehovah's Witnesses' condemnation of other religions and the secular state, coupled with their *conscientious objection to military service, led to their severe persecution in many lands during the 1930s and *World War II. In the United States, they suffered widespread mob violence over their refusal to salute the flag. By carrying many cases to the U.S. *Supreme Court, they greatly broadened the legal basis of *civil liberties.

Under Nathan Homer Knorr (1905–1977) and his successors, Jehovah's Witnesses became a worldwide movement. Officially known as the Watchtower Bible and Tract Society, the organization is controlled by a twelve-member Governing Body based in Brooklyn, New York, also the location of the church's vast book and periodical publishing enterprise. Witnesses engage actively in door-to-door evangelism. There were 974,719 Jehovah's Witnesses in the United States in 1997 and millions more in some 57,000 congregations worldwide.

Non-Trinitarians, the Witnesses believe in conditional immortality and hold that most of righteous mankind will live forever in an earthly paradise whose advent they continue to view as imminent. They refuse blood transfusions as unscriptural.

[*See also* Anti-Catholic Movement; Bill of Rights; Church and State, Separation of; Millennialism and Apocalypticism; Protestantism; Religion.]

• Alan Rogerson, *Millions Now Living Will Never Die: A Study of Jehovah's Witnesses,* 1969. M. James Penton, *Apocalypse Delayed: The Story of Jehovah's Witnesses,* 1997.

—M. James Penton

JIM CROW LAWS. *See* Segregation, Racial.

JINGOISM. *See* Expansionism.

JOGGING. *See* Health and Fitness.

JOHN BIRCH SOCIETY. The John Birch Society was founded in Indianapolis in 1958 by the former Massachusetts candy manufacturer and anticommunist conspiracy theorist Robert W. Welch (1899–1985). Named for an American Baptist missionary killed by communists in China in 1945, Welch's organization attracted a significant following of ardent anticommunist conservatives. Critics, including many conservatives, labeled Welch an extremist, pointing to the extraordinary accusations of treason and subversion in his writings. In a lengthy letter originally written in 1951 and eventually published as *The Politician* (1963), Welch denounced President Dwight D. *Eisenhower as a conscious agent of the communist conspiracy. In *The Blue Book of the John Birch Society* (1959), he equated *liberalism with collectivism and treason, charging that communists controlled, among other institutions, the federal government, organized labor, much of the nation's education system, and many religious organizations—not to mention most of Western Europe.

While many dismissed such thinking as beyond the pale, the John Birch Society was actually more mainstream than its critics realized. Welch's accusations were far from unusual during the early *Cold War and in many ways reflected a long tradition of popular fears about foreign conspiracies and internal subversion. Welch insisted on opening membership to Catholics, Jews, and other groups that had been the focus of past nativist movements. He also claimed that *African Americans were welcome. But in mixing legitimate concerns (in this case, over foreign conflicts in a nuclear age) with a reckless cultural nationalism that saw danger lurking in every shadow, Welch's movement helped perpetuate America's long-standing xenophobic tendencies.

Welch's criticism of New Deal liberalism as "collectivist" was also neither new nor uncommon; indeed, the John Birch Society played a significant role in connecting the older *conservatism of the 1930s, 1940s, and 1950s to the new conservatism of Barry *Goldwater, George C. *Wallace, and Ronald *Reagan. Goldwater and Reagan both found it convenient to quote Welch's anticommunist, antigovernment rhetoric, and the organization itself built a powerful grassroots network of conservative activists (perhaps as many as 100,000 at its zenith) who operated bookstores and reading rooms; waged local political struggles against *gun control, high taxes, sex education in the schools, and other emerging conservative concerns; and worked tirelessly to elect like-minded political candidates. Welch himself became increasingly paranoid and isolated after issuing even more bizarre conspiracy theories in 1964. The politics his organization nurtured, however, were just beginning to flourish.

[*See also* Anticommunism; Fifties, The; House Committee on Un-American Activities; McCarthy, Joseph.]

• Robert A. Goldberg, "Bridging McCarthyism and Reaganism: The John Birch Society," in *Grassroots Resistance: Social Movements in Twentieth Century America,* 1991, pp. 116–40.

—Leonard J. Moore

JOHNSON, ANDREW (1808–1875), seventeenth president of the United States. Born in extreme poverty in Raleigh, North Carolina, Johnson in 1826 moved to Greenville Tennessee, where he operated a tailor shop. Lacking formal education, he was taught to read and write by his wife, Eliza McCardle, whom he married in 1827, when she was sixteen. Johnson held a series of public offices, culminating in his election as governor in 1853 and U.S. senator in 1857. Throughout his career he stressed his plebian origins and claimed a special identification with ordinary people. Although he vigorously defended the *South and *slavery in Congress, he supported the Union in 1861 and was the only southern senator to refuse to resign when his state seceded. After Union troops occupied central Tennessee in 1862, President Abraham *Lincoln named Johnson military governor. In 1864, he was elected Lincoln's vice president on the National Union (*Republican) party ticket.

Becoming president on 15 April 1865, following Lincoln's assassination, Johnson announced a program for reconstructing the postwar South. He built upon Lincoln's wartime policy of appointing provisional governors in the seceding states, offering amnesty to Confederates who professed future loyalty to the Union, and requiring constitutional conventions to reinstitute southern state governments. Johnson's plan required the new state governments to renounce slavery and secession, but by limiting the vote to adult white men, he assured the dominance of lawmakers unsympathetic to the rights of the freepeople. The reestablished governments passed legislation that denied black southerners' political rights and circumscribed their *civil rights by enacting "black codes" to replace the prewar slave codes.

The Republican-dominated Congress refused to recognize the southern state governments restored under Johnson's authority and in June 1866 responded to their racially discriminatory legislation by proposing the *Fourteenth Amendment, which defined citizenship and guaranteed fundamental rights and equal protection to all. When all the Johnson-created governments but that of Tennessee rejected this amendment, Congress passed the Reconstruction Act of 1867 and supplementary legislation. These laws placed the recalcitrant states under military rule until they established new governments recognizing equal civil and political rights for all adult men regardless of race.

Supported by the *Democratic party and a few renegade Republicans, Johnson bitterly assailed Congress' civil-rights and *Reconstruction legislation, denying the constitutionality of these measures and using his influence and authority as president to obstruct their enforcement. His course threatened a dangerous confrontation over whether to count southern votes in the 1868 election. An initial House of Representatives effort to impeach Johnson, motivated in part by a desire to forestall the potential crisis, failed in December 1867. However, a second attempt succeeded in February 1868 after Johnson removed Secretary of War Edwin M. Stanton (1814–1869) in apparent violation of the 1867 Tenure of Office Act, which permitted removal of government officials only upon Senate confirmation of their successors.

The *impeachment trial before the Senate revealed significant weaknesses in the House's case. Despite the overwhelming Republican majority in the Senate, the House managers of the impeachment narrowly failed in two key Senate votes (16 and 28 May 1868) to secure the two-thirds majority needed to convict. However, Johnson stopped obstructing the congressional Reconstruction program and served out the balance of his term without incident.

Despite opposition from former secessionists, in March 1875 a coalition of Tennessee Republicans and dissident Democrats again elected Johnson to the U.S. Senate, where he served until his death that July.

[*See also* Confederate States of America; Federal Government, Executive Branch: The Presidency; Federal Government, Legislative Branch: House of Representatives; Federal Government, Legislative Branch: Senate.]

• Michael Les Benedict, *The Impeachment and Trial of Andrew Johnson*, 1973. Hans L. Trefousse, *Andrew Johnson: A Biography*, 1989.

—Michael Les Benedict

JOHNSON, JACK (1878–1946), prizefighter, world heavyweight *boxing champion from 1908 to 1915. John Arthur Johnson was born to former slaves in Galveston, Texas, just as *Reconstruction ended and he came of age in the Jim Crow Era of rigid racial *segregation. In boxing, the color line was firmly drawn. Although Johnson had established himself as an accomplished boxer by 1902, white heavyweight champions Jim Jeffries, Robert Fitzsimmons, and Tommy Burns refused to fight him. But Johnson persisted, allegedly following Burns all over the world until Burns in 1908 agreed to fight in Sydney, Australia. In the fourteenth round, with Burns defenseless, police stopped the fight.

Johnson's championship sparked a wave of antiblack hostility. For the next several years, he flaunted his wealth and fame. Not only was Johnson the heavyweight champion—and defiantly so—but he violated the ultimate racial taboo by conducting relationships with white women, eventually marrying two. The search for the "great white hope" was on. After Johnson disposed of a handful of opponents, former champion Jim Jeffries came out of retirement in 1910, proposing to uphold the honor of "that portion of the white race that has been looking to me to defend its athletic superiority." Johnson easily defeated him, touching off race riots.

Meanwhile, federal authorities began to compile a dossier on Johnson. Under the Mann Act of 1910, he was convicted of transporting a woman across state lines for sexual purposes. In 1913, Johnson fled the country to escape imprisonment. He lost his title to Jess Willard in Cuba in 1915, remained abroad until 1920, then returned to serve eight months in federal prison in Leavenworth, Kansas. He continued to fight until age fifty, worked as an entertainer, and died in a car crash in 1946. Considered by many the greatest boxer of all time, Johnson also came to symbolize racial relations in a singularly racist era.

[*See also* African Americans; Prostitution and Antiprostitution; Racism; Sports: Professional Sports.]

• Randy Roberts, *Papa Jack: Jack Johnson and the Era of White Hopes*, 1983.

—Elliott J. Gorn

JOHNSON, JAMES WELDON (1871–1938), educator, *civil rights leader, writer. Born in Jacksonville, Florida, Johnson graduated from Atlanta University in 1894 and three years later became the first African American to be admitted to the Florida bar. In 1901, he moved to *New York City, where he worked with his brother John Rosamund Johnson on musicals and wrote, among other songs, "Lift Every Voice and Sing," later to become an anthem of the *civil rights movement. Johnson's involvement in *Republican party politics led to his appointment as U.S. consul to Venezuela (1906–1909) and Nicaragua (1909–1912). While abroad, he wrote *Autobiography of an Ex-Colored Man* (1912), a novel that established his literary reputation and ignited a heated debate about *racism.

Johnson wrote explicitly for an interracial audience, in accordance with his belief that racial equality should be asserted on an artistic level, as well as legally and politically. A prominent figure of the *Harlem Renaissance, he promoted art patronage and education for *African Americans, taught creative writing, and extended his own literary output, including an autobiography, *Along This Way* (1933), and *Black Manhattan* (1930), a study of African American influences on New York life. *God's Trombones* (1927), poetry based on the rhythms and texts of the black preaching tradition, and *The Book of American Negro Poetry* (1922), the first publication to document African American *poetry, rank among his most innovative and influential works. Johnson also did much to increase African American visibility in the political sphere. As field secretary and then executive secretary of the *National Association for the Advancement of Colored People (1916–1930), he expanded the organization's membership and influence, leaving a powerful political force as part of his legacy.

[*See also* African American Religion.]

• Eugene Levy, *James Weldon Johnson: Black Leader, Black Voice*, 1973. Kenneth M. Price and Lawrence J. Oliver, eds., *Critical Essays on James Weldon Johnson*, 1997.

—Tanya Agathocleous

JOHNSON, LYNDON B. (1908–1973), thirty-sixth president of the United States. Lyndon Baines Johnson came from a moderately well-to-do family in the impoverished hill country of central Texas. After graduating from Southwest Texas State Teachers College in 1930, he spent a year teaching school before beginning his career in *Democratic party politics as a legislative assistant to a Texas congressman. In 1934, he married Claudia Alta ("Lady Bird") Taylor. They had two daughters.

Johnson returned to Texas in 1935 to head the state National Youth Administration office, a New Deal agency. Two years later, he won a special election to Congress, defeating a field of eight candidates by staunchly supporting the controversial programs of Franklin Delano *Roosevelt, who became the first of Johnson's many powerful patrons. As a congressman, Johnson strongly supported rural electrification and won federal funding for a key dam in his district. In 1941, he lost a close race for the U.S. Senate. In a second Senate race in 1948, Johnson defeated former governor Coke Stevenson by eighty-seven votes in an election marred by suspected voter fraud that gave rise to the nickname "Landslide Lyndon."

An extremely effective senator, Johnson moderated his New Deal *liberalism without giving up his belief that the federal government should aid the less fortunate. He staunchly backed Presidents Harry S. *Truman and Dwight D. *Eisenhower in waging the *Cold War, making sure that Texas benefited from heavy defense spending. He continued to cultivate powerful leaders, notably House Speaker Sam Rayburn (1882–1961) and Senator Richard Russell (1897–1971) of Georgia, to advance his career. In 1955, he became Senate majority leader. Criticized by liberal Democrats for his flexibility, Johnson prided himself on his ability to bargain with the Republican Eisenhower administration to secure needed legislation. Famous for his brand of personal persuasion, known as the "Johnson treatment," he helped in 1957 secure passage of the nation's first civil rights bill since *Reconstruction.

LBJ, as he liked to be called, proved less successful in a 1960 presidential bid. Outmaneuvered and outspent by John F. *Kennedy, Johnson finally agreed to become Kennedy's running mate in order to carry the *South. When Kennedy won, LBJ virtually disappeared from sight as vice president. After Kennedy's assassination in November 1963, however, Johnson displayed both sensitivity and statesmanship by stressing the theme of continuity in carrying out the programs of the fallen leader. In 1964, he persuaded Congress to pass two of Kennedy's most controversial measures, a civil rights bill desegregating public accommodations and a major tax cut, as well as inaugurating his own War on Poverty. With the Minnesota liberal Hubert *Humphrey as his running mate, he easily won a landslide victory over Republican Barry *Goldwater, an outspoken conservative, in the 1964 presidential election.

President Johnson's greatest success in domestic policy came with the enactment of his *Great Society program. Building on FDR's New Deal and Truman's Fair Deal proposals, LBJ persuaded Congress to enact more than sixty separate reform measures in 1965. The three most important Great Society achievements were greatly increased federal aid to *education, the enactment of *Medicare and Medicaid to provide health care for the elderly and the indigent, and a voting-rights act that gave previously disenfranchised *African Americans in the South the political power to protect and advance their interests. Johnson moved quickly to implement his Great Society program, capitalizing on the trauma of Kennedy's death as well as on the heavy Democratic majorities in Congress created by Goldwater's crushing defeat. Critics would charge that many of the programs were overly ambitious, inadequately funded, or carelessly administered. The Great Society, however, suffered most from LBJ's growing obsession with the *Vietnam War.

Against Johnson's legislative success must be balanced his failure in foreign policy. Less sure of himself on diplomatic issues, LBJ relied on advisers he had inherited from Kennedy, who were committed to the defense of South Vietnam, a policy successively upheld by Truman, Eisenhower, and Kennedy. Instead of reassessing America's role in what was essentially a civil war, Johnson accepted the domino theory—the Cold War belief that a North Vietnamese victory would doom all of Southeast Asia to *communism. In 1964, after a presumed attack on American destroyers in the Gulf of Tonkin, he persuaded Congress to grant him unlimited power to use force to defend South Vietnam. In early 1965, U.S. warplanes began bombing North Vietnam; in July, Johnson authorized sending 50,000 American combat troops to Vietnam. Yet he refused to declare war, disguised the heavy cost of the fighting, and failed to justify the conflict to the American people. By 1968, despite the presence of more than 500,000 American troops in Vietnam, he had achieved only a costly stalemate. After the *Tet offensive, a bloody setback for the enemy but a devastating blow to American confidence, Johnson rejected Pentagon requests for an additional 200,000 troops. Instead, on 31 March amid mounting domestic protests and facing a challenge for the nomination from antiwar Democrats Eugene McCarthy and Robert *Kennedy, he announced that he would not run for reelection in 1968, and would instead devote himself to peace negotiations with Hanoi. Humphrey won the nomination at a deeply divided Democratic Convention in Chicago but lost the general election to Richard M. *Nixon.

Johnson spent his final years in retirement on his Texas ranch. He died of a massive heart attack on 22 January 1973, just a day before the Nixon administration signed the Paris Peace Accords ending America's direct combat role in the Vietnam War. Ever since, Johnson's reputation as president has been clouded by his failure in Vietnam. In many ways, he was a tragic figure. In Vietnam, he simply tried to carry out the policies of his predecessors. Yet his refusal to explain the war candidly to the American public, in part out of fear that it would reduce support for the Great Society, cost him dearly. At the same time, he received little acclaim for his more enduring domestic achievements. The voting-rights act did help African Americans gain political office and influence; Medicare and Medicaid would give millions of elderly and impoverished citizens access to health care. Despite later conservative counterattacks, the Great Society remained deeply imbedded in modern American life. An ambitious, hard-driving politician with an outsized ego masking deep insecurities, particularly in his dealings with the wealthy, socially confident Kennedy clan, he could be devious, bullying, and crude while also displaying high idealism and great generosity of spirit.

[*See also* Antiwar Movements; Civil Rights Legislation; Federal Government: Executive Branch: The Presidency; Federal Government, Legislative Branch: Senate; Gulf of Tonkin Resolution; New Deal Era, The; Sixties, The.]

• Lyndon B. Johnson, *The Vantage Point,* 1971. Doris Kearns, *Lyndon Johnson and the American Dream,* 1976. Robert A. Caro, *The Years of Lyndon Johnson,* 2 vols., 1982–1990. Paul Conkin, *Big Daddy from the Pedernales: Lyndon Baines Johnson,* 1986. Joseph A. Califano, *The Triumph and the Tragedy of Lyndon Johnson,* 1991. Robert Dallek, *Lone Star Rising: Lyndon Johnson and His Times, 1908–1960,* 1991. Robert Dallek, *Flawed Giant: Lyndon Johnson and His Times, 1961–1973,* 1998.

—Robert A. Divine

JOHNSON, PHILIP (1906–), architect, museum curator. Born in Cleveland, Ohio, Johnson received from his father Alcoa stock, which made him very wealthy by the time he graduated in 1930 from Harvard, a student of philosophy and classics. His *International Style: Architecture since 1922* (1932), coauthored with Henry-Russell Hitchcock Jr., introduced many Americans to modern European *architecture. This book complemented the 1932 "Modern Architecture: International Exhibition" that Johnson helped to organized at New York's Museum of Modern Art (MoMA), where he served as first director of the Department of Architecture (1932–1934). Resolving to become an architect, Johnson returned to Harvard; he received an architecture degree in 1943.

Johnson's early buildings were strongly influenced by the refined and austere modern architecture of Ludwig Mies van der Rohe, as particularly seen in Johnson's own country residence, the Glass House (1947–1949), at New Canaan, Connecticut. His subsequent career was one of eclectic variation as he absorbed and championed ever-changing stylistic fashions, including modern classicism (Sheldon Memorial Art Gallery, 1961–1963, University of Nebraska, Lincoln), sculptural late modernism (Pennzoil Place, 1972–1976, Houston, Texas), *postmodernism (AT&T Corporate Headquarters, 1979–1984, New York), deconstructivism (Johnson was guest curator of the MoMA's 1988 "Deconstructivist Architecture" exhibition), and a new expressionism (Gate House at New Canaan, 1995). Johnson's partnership (1967–1991) with John Burgee resulted in many prominent and diverse *skyscrapers and public buildings across the United States. A constant in Johnson's architectural career was his rich understanding of the broad sweep of architectural history and his assertion of architecture as an art.

[*See also* Modernist Culture; Museums: Museums of Art.]

• Philip Johnson, Hilary Lewis, and John O'Connor, *Philip Johnson: The Architect in His Own Words,* 1994. Franz Schulze, *Philip Johnson: Life and Work,* 1994.

—Craig Zabel

JOHNSTOWN FLOOD (1889). This natural disaster devastated much of Johnstown, a steelmaking center in the Conemaugh River Valley of southwestern Pennsylvania. In the hills above the city, the industrial elite of nearby Pittsburgh had built a private resort, including an artificial lake contained by a poorly designed and ill-maintained earthen dam.

On 31 May 1889, weakened by torrential rain, the dam collapsed, sending a wall of water crashing down the valley. When it struck an unsuspecting Johnstown, after overwhelming four smaller towns, the deluge had risen to a height of forty feet. Some 2,200 of Johnstown's 30,000 people died, and much of the city was leveled.

The nation responded with a spontaneous charitable outpouring. Within weeks some four million dollars were collected and turned over to a commission established by the governor. Thousands of volunteers cleared wreckage and built temporary housing. Clara Barton, president of the American *Red Cross, personally supervised the relief effort. In this *laissez-faire age, the federal government limited its role to supplying a few temporary bridges. By year's end, Johnstown was nearly rebuilt. The wealthy resort owners escaped legal liability for their neglect.

While the *Galveston hurricane and flood of 1900 took more lives (six thousand), the Johnstown flood remained for decades the paradigmatic American disaster. The episode illustrated the depth of national compassion and the ability of the emerging industrial order to organize a vast relief and reconstruction effort with little government involvement. But it also demonstrated the power of that order to evade the negative consequences of its acts.

[*See also* Gilded Age.]

• David McCullough, *The Johnstown Flood,* 1987.

—Alan Clive

JOINT CHIEFS OF STAFF. In January 1942, President Franklin Delano *Roosevelt and British Prime Minister Winston S. Churchill created the Combined Chiefs of Staff (CCS) to direct global military strategy in *World War II. The American contingent on the CCS, faced with the highly organized British Chiefs of Staff Committee as its counterpart, responded by forming the Joint Chiefs of Staff (JCS), which first met on 9 February 1942. In addition to the military heads of the army, navy, and army air forces, the JCS included the presidential chief of staff as chairman. Supporting the body was an extensive committee system. The Joint Chiefs advised the president, served on the CCS, and, for the first time in American history, attempted to coordinate the work of the different military services.

The key role of the JCS in the Allied victory contributed to its continuation after the war, but its limited success in achieving interservice cooperation led to the creation of the Department of Defense by the *National Security Act of 1947. This act officially established the JCS as the military advisers to the president and the secretary of defense. Amendments specified that its chairman come from one of the services and work independently of the president's staff. In later legislation, civilian control over the JCS increased. The Marine Corps commandant, granted a partial vote in 1952, became a full member in 1978. A major reorganization in 1986 designated the chairman of the JCS, instead of the entire body, as the primary military adviser to the president, the secretary of defense, and the *National Security Council.

[*See also* Federal Government, Executive Branch: Department of Defense; Military, The.]

• Lawrence J. Korb, *The Joint Chiefs of Staff: The First Twenty-five Years,* 1976. Grace Person Hayes, *The History of the Joint Chiefs of Staff in World War II,* 1982.

—Anne Sharp Wells

JONES, JOHN PAUL (1747–1792), Continental Navy officer. Born in Scotland, Jones enlisted in the British merchant navy at the age of thirteen. He became a captain in 1768, following an apprenticeship in the West Indian trade. Discipline problems plagued his command. In 1770, Mungo Maxwell, a ship's carpenter, died after Jones ordered his whipping for insubordination. After narrowly avoiding a jail sentence for Maxwell's death, Jones killed another sailor during a mutiny. Afraid that a civil court might find him guilty of murder, Jones fled to Virginia in 1774.

The *Revolutionary War offered Jones a second chance. Appointed first lieutenant in the Continental Navy in 1775, Jones received the command of the *Ranger* in 1777. Based in France, Jones captured the British man-of-war *Drake* and attacked the port of Whitehaven during a cruise in 1778. The next year, he took over the command of the *Bonhomme Richard.* In April, he led the American assault on a British merchant squadron escorted by the *Serapis.* The *Bonhomme Richard* and the *Serapis* battled to a spectacular draw. In refusing to surrender his sinking ship, he is said to have uttered the famous phrase, "I have not yet begun to fight." The battle destroyed both ships, but it transformed the iron-willed Jones into the United States's first naval hero. Jones subsequently served a year in the Russian navy (1788–1789), an experience that left him physically and mentally disabled.

John Paul Jones died in Paris. In 1905 the burial site was rediscovered and his remains transferred to the U.S. Naval Academy at Annapolis, Maryland, where they now rest in a crypt.

• Samuel Eliot Morison, *John Paul Jones: A Sailor's Biography,* 1959.

—Jon T. Coleman

JONES, MARY ("MOTHER") (1830–1930), labor activist. Born in Ireland, Mary Harris Jones immigrated to the United States in 1835. She attended school in Toronto, Canada, and later worked as a teacher and a dressmaker in *Chicago and Memphis, Tennessee. In 1861, she married an iron molder and labor union member named Jones. Six years later, she lost her spouse and their four children to a *yellow fever epidemic. This tragedy forced her back into a life of wage-earning. By 1871, her resentment of social inequality found an outlet in the *Knights of Labor. In 1877, Jones helped to organize striking railroad workers in Pittsburgh, Pennsylvania, and by 1880 her career as an agitator was well under way.

A tiny woman dressed in black, with striking blue eyes, Mother Jones became known as "The Angel of the Miners" and was a beloved figure in the mine fields of West Virginia, Pennsylvania, Illinois, Arizona, and Colorado. Her incendiary speeches made her a legend. She was arrested four times in the years before *World War I, and in 1912, amid a bitter miners' strike, she was convicted in West Virginia of conspiracy to commit murder. Pardoned by the governor, Mother Jones continued her peripatetic activity among miners and other industrial workers.

Socialists embraced Mother Jones, but she remained politically unaffiliated. A founding member of the *Industrial Workers of the World in 1905, she also worked for the *American Federation of Labor, campaigned for the *Democratic party, and made her last public appearance in 1924 at the Farmer-Labor party convention. Although she became a late-twentieth feminist icon, Jones, like other radical labor activists of her day, viewed woman suffrage as trivial and the *women's rights movement as bourgeois. She reserved her compassion, her boundless energy, and her always tart tongue for the working man and his family. She died in Silver Spring, Maryland, soon after her hundredth birthday.

[*See also* Labor Movements; Mining; Radicalism; Socialism; Strikes and Industrial Conflict.]

• Mary Field Parton, ed., *The Autobiography of Mother Jones,* 1925. Dale Fetherling, *Mother Jones, the Miner's Angel,* 1974. Philip S. Foner, ed., *Mother Jones Speaks: Collected Writings and Speeches,* 1983.

—Ann Schofield

JORDAN, MICHAEL (1963–   ), athlete, celebrity. Jordan is widely considered a *basketball player without equal. To his trademark leaping ability that seemed to defy gravity, Jordan added an astonishing creativity around (and often above) the basket and a daunting competitive spirit. As he matured, Jordan developed outstanding skills as an outside shooter, passer, defensive player, and team leader, establishing a reputation for performing best at critical moments. His accomplishments included a national collegiate championship with the University of North Carolina (1982), two Olympic gold medals (1984, 1992), six professional championships with the Chicago Bulls (1991–1993, 1996–1998), ten individual scoring titles, and multiple Most Valuable Player awards.

Though his athletic feats were always at the core of his fame, Jordan became a major figure in the evolution of late twentieth-century popular commercial culture. His charisma heightened public interest in basketball and in sports generally and, as a result, helped generate unprecedented revenues for teams and players, including himself. Contributing to Jordan's immense following and very positive public image were his appearances in such mass-entertainment forms as *television, music videos, and *films and, far more extensively, in the *advertising of an array of consumer goods. Some manufacturers and marketers based entire product lines on his endorsements. This incessant public exposure made Jordan one of the most famous people in the world, in a class with Babe *Ruth as a great athlete and cultural icon.

[*See also* Popular Culture; Sports: Professional Sports.]

• Sam Smith, *The Jordan Rules*, 1992. David Halberstam, *Playing For Keeps: Michael Jordan and the World He Made*, 1999.

—Carl Smith

JOSEPH, CHIEF. *See* Chief Joseph.

JOURNALISM. The regular, periodic publication of information about contemporary affairs began in British North America in the early eighteenth century. At first, the notion that "news" should provide timely accounts of recent events was not self-evident. One early paper, *The Universal Instructor in All Arts and Sciences and Pennsylvania Gazette*, devoted most of its space to printing serially an encyclopedia, A through Z. In 1729, a new owner, Benjamin *Franklin, squashed the encyclopedia project and introduced a mode of journalism more literary and satirical, on the one hand, and more engaged in civic affairs on the other, something he learned from English literary models and from his brother's *New England Courant.*

*Colonial Era papers were typically four-page weeklies that provided an assortment of local advertising, short paragraphs of local hearsay, and large, unedited chunks of European political and economic news from the London press. Political news of other colonies rarely appeared. Local political news was scarce, too, until the 1760s. As conflict with England grew intense, colonial printers were compelled to choose sides. Print shops became hives of political activity. Pamphleteers reached new height of influence with Thomas *Paine's **Common Sense* in 1776. At a time when the largest newspapers sold no more than 2,000 copies of a weekly issue, *Common Sense* sold an estimated 150,000. Paine addressed the general populace, dropping esoteric classical references for familiar biblical ones, seeking a common language.

The first daily newspaper in North America appeared in *Philadelphia in 1783. By 1800, among more than two hundred newspapers, Philadelphia had six dailies, *New York City five, Baltimore, Maryland, three, and Charleston, South Carolina, two. The widespread habit of reading, and especially newspaper reading, astonished foreign visitors. By 1850, the United States had more than two thousand newspapers, including more than two hundred dailies. The press was aided by explicit protection of press freedom in many state constitutions and in the *Bill of Rights. Congress also supported the press with preferential postal rates. Nevertheless, *Federalist party leaders assaulted the Republican opposition with the Sedition Act (1798), which made it a crime to print "any false, scandalous and malicious writing . . . against the government of the United States."

In the first decades of the new nation, newspapers were frequently weapons for party or faction. Polemics overshadowed reports, but this began to change. In the 1820s, several New York papers began to send small boats out to incoming ships to get the news from London faster than their rivals. This turn toward reportage accelerated when, beginning with the *New York Sun* in 1833, a new breed of newspaper sought commercial success and a mass readership. Between 1833 and 1835, in New York, *Boston, Baltimore, and Philadelphia, "penny papers" began selling for a penny an issue rather than the six cents at which papers were commonly priced. Hawked on the streets by newsboys, instead of being available only by subscription, the penny papers aggressively sought out local news, assigning reporters to the courts and to the coverage of "society."

Low price, innovative distribution methods, and popular content brought large circulation gains that, in turn, encouraged an aggressive use of recently developed technologies. The *Sun* began with a traditional hand-run flatbed press but quickly switched to a cylinder press making a thousand, rather than two hundred, impressions an hour. In 1835, already selling twenty thousand copies a day, the *Sun* became the first newspaper in the country to purchase a steam-driven press. Penny papers also led the way in using the *telegraph. The *New York Herald* was the penny paper with the most sustained commercial success. Editor James Gordon Bennett (1841–1918), unlike most newspaper proprietors of the day, had never worked as a printer.

Another leader of the new journalism had a more conventional career. Horace Greeley, born in New Hampshire in 1811, entered journalism by printing a small weekly in Vermont. Moving to New York in 1831, he worked as a job printer, published a literary magazine and a *Whig party campaign paper, and in 1841 launched his own penny paper, the *New York Tribune.* Quickly reaching a circulation of 10,000, the *Tribune* was strongly *antislavery and, as a reform-minded journal of ideas, reported on *women's rights, socialist experiments, *temperance, and other reforms. Margaret *Fuller was among the talented writers Greeley recruited. By the 1850s, with the *Tribune* surpassing 250,000 in circulation and widely influential throughout the North and West, Greeley mounted thundering editorial attacks on the *Fugitive Slave Act, the *Kansas-Nebraska Act, and the Dred Scott decision (see **Scott* v. *Sandford*). A founder of the *Republican Party, he pushed President Abraham *Lincoln to make emancipation a central aim of the *Civil War, but his growing reputation for political instability was heightened by personal idiosyncracies and unsuccessful campaigns for political office. The *Tribune* continued to thrive, with 500 employees in 1871, but it was no longer under the day-to-day control of Greeley, who was increasingly immersed in politics as a Liberal Republican opposed to both the *Reconstruction policies of the Radical Republicans and the corruption of the Ulysses S. *Grant administration. Nominated for president in 1872 by both the Liberal Republican and *Democratic parties, he nevertheless lost to Grant by a lopsided margin and died a few weeks after the election.

The press reflected the pluralism of American society. Different churches and social movements had their own journals. A foreign-language press served immigrants; the German press was especially strong. In 1828, the *Cherokee Phoenix* became the first Native American newspaper, published bilingually in English and Cherokee. The African-American press began with *Freedom's Journal* (1827–1829) and the *Colored American* (1837–1841). Frederick *Douglass launched the *North Star* in Rochester in 1847.

News-gathering became the central function of the general-interest newspaper, but political reporting was not well institutionalized. As late as 1846, only Baltimore and *Washington, D.C., papers assigned special correspondents to cover Congress.

Country weeklies—the predominant form of American journalism in an agricultural society—were local town boosters providing some national but little or no state and local political coverage. As politics heated up in the 1850s, however, more than fifty papers hired Washington correspondents. Most wrote for half a dozen or more papers at once and earned further salary as clerks for congressional committees or speechwriters for politicians.

The frequently strong connection between paper and party began to weaken after the Civil War for two reasons. First, newspapers became highly profitable businesses. Circulation leaped forward while the cost of production plummeted with wood pulp as a new source of paper and mechanical typesetting, a new labor-saving device. *Advertising revenue surpassed subscription fees as the primary source of income as the papers courted new audiences (particularly women).

Second, liberal reformers began to criticize party loyalty. They promoted new forms of electoral campaigning, urging "educational" campaigns with more pamphlets and fewer parades. Newspapers at the same time became more willing to take an independent stance. By 1890, a quarter of daily newspapers in northern states, where the reform movement was most advanced, claimed independence of party.

A key figure in developing a big-business model of the newspaper was Joseph *Pulitzer, an Austrian Jewish immigrant who became a reporter and then publisher and editor in St. Louis. He bought the failing *New York World* (circulation 15,000) in 1883. By 1886, he brought its circulation to 250,000. By 1895, the *World,* with 1,200 employees, was the largest paper in the country. Pulitzer's crusading journalism, intensified attention to local news, lavish use of illustration, and relatively simple language appealed to New York's thousands of immigrants.

If Pulitzer inaugurated the new mass journalism, his rival William Randolph *Hearst made it notorious. Like Pulitzer, Hearst saw the press as both a political agency and a business. Taking over his father's *San Francisco Examiner* in 1887, he bought the *New York Journal* in 1895 and several *Chicago dailies soon thereafter. In New York, he brought to the *Journal* pages of comics, sensational news coverage, a self-promoting crusading spirit, and several hundred thousand readers. Battling for New York's mass readership, Hearst and Pulitzer pushed for a war with Spain over Cuba. Even so, the common view that yellow journalism "caused" the *Spanish-American War is dubious. Many other leading papers, including those with the greatest influence in elite circles, opposed American intervention.

While Pulitzer and Hearst competed for mass circulation, the Chattanooga publisher Adolph Ochs (1858–1935) in 1896 bought the languishing *New York Times,* with a circulation of 9,000 compared to the *World*'s 600,000 and the *Journal's* 430,000. In his inaugural declaration "to give the news impartially, without fear or favor," Ochs set out to distinguish his paper from the yellow journals, to capture a high-toned readership, and to set the standards of journalistic integrity.

Besides the general-circulation papers, newspapers continued to flourish as agents of various special communities. The United States had about 800 non-English-language newspapers in 1884, 1,300 by 1917. Black dailies attained large circulations: 300,000 for the *Pittsburgh Courier* by the 1940s; 230,000 for the *Chicago Defender* by 1920, two-thirds of it outside Chicago. The *Defender* was the first African-American publication with a broad, national circulation. Editor Robert S. Abbott helped stimulate black migration north by writing about the opportunities for blacks in northern cities. After *World War II, the black press declined as the mainstream press began to cover racial issues, the white-run media began to hire black journalists, advertising support weakened, and a growing black middle class left the inner city.

A small-town and rural press persisted and neighborhood and suburban newspapers sprang up, generally serving more as community cheerleaders than as community tribunes. Even establishment politics was of little account in the small-town press. But in the metropolitan press, hard-bitten reporters and hard-hitting reporting became the cultural ideals. In leading cities, reporting became a full-time occupation and reporters a self-conscious community, with their own organizations and informal watering holes.

New reporting practices gave reporters greater autonomy. Conducting and printing interviews, all but unknown before the Civil War, became a routine practice. Standard news stories shifted from a chronological ordering of events to the "summary lead" that placed important aspects of the news first, implicitly designating reporters as legitimate interpreters of a complex world.

The rise of mass-circulation monthly *magazines with an appreciative, national middle-class audience in the 1890s brought yet another sign of the reporter's authority: muckraking. *Progressive Era practitioners of this new investigative journalism revealed illegal and unsavory practices of capital, labor, and state and local government. It was Theodore *Roosevelt who, in a sizzling attack on their negativism, labeled them "*muckrakers."

Stimulated in part by muckraking attacks on business and in part by the general rationalization of corporate enterprise, public relations developed in the early twentieth century. Journalists grew self-conscious about the manipulability of information in an age of public relations and, as they learned in *World War I, an age of *propaganda. One response was the signed political column that openly acknowledged its subjective viewpoint. Columnists became popular features in leading newspapers, available nationwide through syndication.

Journalists typically had no formal training. After World War II, however, journalism schools multiplied, developing on a large scale in the state universities. By the late twentieth century, more than half of the nation's journalists held degrees in journalism or communication.

During and after World War I, the government suppressed radical newspapers and German-language newspapers. In 1925, in *Gitlow* v. *United States,* the *Supreme Court upheld a conviction of radical pamphleteers but acknowledged for the first time that First Amendment guarantees of press freedom applied to the states under the *Fourteenth Amendment. In **Near* v. *Minnesota* (1931), the High Court struck down a "gag law" that permitted the suppression of "malicious" and "scandalous" publications. The decision outlawed the prior restraint of publications and termed suppression a greater danger than journalistic irresponsibility.

Larger and larger corporate entities reaped the benefits of this enlarged press freedom. Chain or group newspaper ownership, begun around the turn of the century by E. W. Scripps, Hearst, and others, expanded. Hearst's empire, at its peak in 1935, included twenty-six daily newspapers with a seventh of the nation's total circulation. By 1980, two-thirds of one thousand seven hundred daily newspapers, commanding three-fourths of total daily circulation, were group-owned. City by city, newspaper competition dropped sharply; 181 cities had competing daily papers in 1940, 29 in 1986.

Broadcasting was a new influence in journalism. *Radio became a news medium in the 1920s and a significant source of breaking news during World War II. But it never challenged the dominance of newspapers as *television did. By 1963, polls found more Americans claiming to rely on television than on newspapers as their primary source of news. Watching the evening network news became in many homes a family ritual. Nothing established television's place more than John F. *Kennedy's assassination. Few people learned of the assassination first from television, but by the evening of 22 November 1963, millions of people were glued to their sets. They saw, on live television, Jack Ruby shoot Lee Harvey Oswald; they watched the funeral procession, listening to the solemn beat of the drum.

TV coverage of the *Vietnam War took on a symbolic centrality for both Washington elites and the public at large. Reporting in Vietnam, the media directly challenged the government. During the Lyndon B. *Johnson presidency, the press drew attention to the "credibility gap": official lies and half-truths about the war. With the presidency of Richard M. *Nixon, two events brought the press a new prominence. In 1971, the *New York Times* published the first installment of the "*Pentagon Papers," a classified Defense Department history of the Vietnam War secretly photocopied and released by a one-time Pentagon insider, Daniel Ellsberg. When the Nixon administration obtained a court injunction preventing the *Times* from further publication, the *Washington Post* and then the *Boston Globe, St. Louis Post-Dispatch,* and *Chicago Tribune* continued the series.

A second milestone for the press was *Watergate, the collective term for a tangle of illegal activities by Nixon-administration officials, and by the president himself. The uncovering of the scandal by Congress, the courts, and federal administrative agencies was initiated by the *Washington Post* reporters Bob Woodward and Carl Bernstein. Investigative reporting was already expanding, thanks to the growing distrust of government in the Vietnam War years, but Watergate served as the symbolic capstone to this newly aggressive journalism.

TV news expanded in the 1970s. *Sixty Minutes,* an hour-long program of investigative journalism that began in 1968, became the nation's most popular TV program. ABC began a late-night news program in 1979 as a daily update on the Iranian hostage crisis. In 1980, this became *Nightline,* another long-running and influential news program. In 1970, the television networks had no competition, but by 1990 more than half of American homes had cable systems, the networks' share of total television viewership had declined, and network investment in news shrank amid corporate buyouts and mergers. Cable's C-SPAN (1979) and the Atlanta businessman Ted Turner's twenty-four-hour Cable News Network (CNN, 1980) were important additions to the national news diet.

In print journalism, nationally oriented newspapers—notably the *New York Times, Wall Street Journal,* and *Washington Post,* joined in 1982 by *USA Today*—expanded their national reach. Metropolitan dailies lost readership, partly from TV's competition, partly from *suburbanization that meant increasing numbers of people who worked in cities did not live, vote, or pay taxes in them.

As the twentieth century ended, journalism became a target for criticism from insiders and outsiders. Women and minority groups mounted challenges to media stereotyping and media hiring practices. Before the 1960s, for instance, women journalists typically wrote exclusively about fashion and society; the National Press Club admitted women only in 1971. But changes were afoot. Whereas 80 percent of journalists were male in 1971, only 66 percent were by 1982 (the figure remained the same ten years later). Whereas about 4 percent of journalists were African American, Asian American, or Hispanic in 1982, the figure was 7 percent in 1992.

Conservative research institutes and think tanks, meanwhile, prominently criticized "liberal bias" in the press. Surveys confirmed that journalists for national news outlets (but not for "the press" at large) were more liberal than the general population. At the same time, many observers concluded that journalists' possible political bias was a lesser problem than their "professional" and commercial bias toward stories of conflict and sensation. News coverage of presidential candidates of both parties grew increasingly negative after 1980. In the 1990s, a "public journalism" or "civic journalism" movement emerged that called on the industry to reassess professional values and rededicate itself to the "public good." Meanwhile, technological change in the newsroom led to a new emphasis on computer-assisted reporting and a new blending of media forms, with one reporter preparing the same story in print, on-line, and on camera for a newspaper's cable station.

[*See also* Censorship; Political Parties; Printing and Publishing; Public Opinion; Sedition; Steam Power; Urbanization; Zenger Trial.]

• Frank Luther Mott, *American Journalism: A History, 1690–1960,* 3d ed., 1962. George Juergens, *Joseph Pulitzer and the New York World,* 1966. Michael Schudson, *Discovering the News,* 1978. Sally Miller, *The Ethnic Press in the United States,* 1987. Donald Ritchie, *The Press Gallery,* 1991. James Baughman, *The Republic of Mass Culture,* 1992. Charles E. Clark, *The Public Prints: The Newspaper in Anglo-American Culture, 1665–1740,* 1994. Michael Schudson, *The Power of News,* 1995. David H. Weaver and G. Cleveland Wilhoit, *The American Journalist in the 1990s,* 1996.

—Michael S. Schudson

JUDAISM. American Judaism began with the arrival in New Netherland of twenty-four Sephardic Jews from Recife, Brazil in 1654. To fulfill the requirements of Jewish law, a Jewish communal governing authority (kehillah) was formed. Among its early actions was to petition the authorities for a separate Jewish burial ground.

Fifteen years later, after New Amsterdam became *New York City, bringing a more tolerant English governance, cemetery land was purchased. A permanent synagogue, Shearith Israel, including a school and a mikveh (ritual bath), was completed in 1731. By 1815 it boasted 855 members and a spiritual leader, Gershon Seixas (1746–1816). Similar patterns prevailed in the four other large colonial towns where Jews had settled in numbers (*Philadelphia, Newport, *Boston, and Charleston). Philadelphia's Jewish community, for example, purchased cemetery land in 1740 and built its first synagogue, Mikveh Israel, in 1747. Architecturally, the most noteworthy was Newport's Touro synagogue (1759).

Early Adaptations to American Culture. From the outset, American Judaism endured communal strife rooted partly in divisions between comparatively well-established Jews of Sephardic (Iberian) origin, usually called "Portuguese," and Ashkenazim from central and eastern Europe. Although equally committed to their religion's monotheistic tenets, the congregations differed in social status and disagreed over variations in rituals. In addition, exilic Judaism is inherently congregational. Unlike many Christian denominations, it has no official priesthood or single head. Any ten adult Jewish males can establish a congregation; the rabbi is merely recognized as the most learned in Jewish texts. Until the late nineteenth century, with few rabbis to offer spiritual leadership, the rabbinate in England resolved questions of Jewish law.

Historic Judaism was a command religion with laws covering every detail of life. Community leaders exercised sanctions ranging from fines to the denial of Jewish burial and even, in drastic cases, excommunication. But in colonial America's comparatively free atmosphere, enforcing religious regulations, especially those pertaining to Sabbath observance, proved difficult.

Eventually, America's secularism, free atmosphere, separation of *church and state, and comparatively open economy profoundly altered the traditional cohesiveness of Jewish communities. Communal adherence became voluntary. As congregations became more democratic, the desires of the laity took precedence over Jewish law. The quest for economic well-being both released new energies and undermined traditional piety. Jews experienced growing prosperity, especially in merchandising, in relatively open areas of the economy such as the *tobacco industry and *fur trade, and in traditional crafts like wig and soap making, leather tanning, and cutting precious stones. After 1820, the arrival of many German-speaking Jews from central Europe further diminished prospects for establishing a single religious authority. Usually young, widely dispersed, poorly grounded in Judaism, and virtually bereft of spiritual leaders, these peddlers and merchants were poor prospects for strict religious observance. Unbound by communal fiat, the free Jews of America could no longer be commanded; they had to be persuaded.

Reform Judaism. The two principal religious leaders in this era were Isaac Leeser (1806–1868) and Isaac Mayer *Wise. Although not ordained, Leeser became the spiritual leader of Philadelphia's congregation Mikveh Israel and worked indefatigably to protect American Judaism from both external threats and what he saw as an internal one: a reform movement whose accommodationist approach he considered incompatible with traditional Judaism. His views found expression in *The Occident,* a monthly publication he founded in 1843.

Despite Leeser's efforts, Reform Judaism became dominant among the German-Jewish immigrants. Rooted in the spirit of science and enlightenment influential among German-Jewish scholars who sought to replace Judaism's obsession with rabbinic law with the social-justice vision of the Hebrew prophets, American Reform Judaism was also influenced by developments in Charleston's Beth Elohim congregation in the 1820s. The Charleston reformers, embracing a new aesthetic decorum for their services, introduced choral reading of prayer and family pews rather than separate seating for men and women, and ended the sale of privileges such as reading from the Torah. Their model naturally reflected the aesthetics of the surrounding Protestant churches.

The establishment of Hebrew Union College (HUC) in 1875 and the codification of Reformist principles and practices in the so-called Pittsburgh Platform ten years later, followed by the organization of the CCAR (Central Conference of American Rabbis) in 1889, was welcomed by CCAR's president Isaac Mayer Wise as evidence that an institutional structure for American Judaism was taking shape under Reform auspices. But Wise's vision proved premature. Rather than being one unified faith, American Judaism ultimately spawned four branches, developing a denominationalism not unlike that of Protestantism. The serving of unkosher clams at HUC's first graduation ceremony in 1883 aroused a storm of controversy that contributed to the founding of the Jewish Theological Seminary of America (JTS) five years later as an Orthodox response to the Reform movement. JTS languished for more than a decade until two Reform leaders, Jacob Schiff and Louis Marshall, and Cyrus Adler, a native-born Orthodox Jew linked to the leadership group of Philadelphia, set out to reenergize it.

Conservative Judaism. Convinced that some intermediary position between Reform and Orthodoxy could help stem the alarming religious indifference of Jewish immigrants, Schiff and Marshall in 1902 recruited Solomon Schechter, a Romanian-born scholar and reader in Rabbinics at Cambridge University, to head JTS. Schechter shaped what came to be known as Conservatism, a half-way house between Reform and Orthodox Judaism. He advocated cultural Zionism, an ideology of Jewish "peoplehood" that would permit newly secularized Jews, especially the children of immigrants, to preserve their cultural Jewishness without necessarily adhering to religious law.

In 1913, the United Synagogue, an umbrella organization for Conservative congregations, was founded. A professional organization for its Conservative rabbis, the Rabbinic Assembly, established in 1919, coopted the powerful Committee on Jewish Law ten years later. The Conservative movement, fully in place by 1930, valued tradition and religious law while also accommodating the social environment of modern America. As Conservative spokesmen seeking to balance tradition and change sometimes put it, the past should have "a voice, but not a veto."

Orthodox Judaism. Predictably, the Union of Orthodox Rabbis (Agudat Harabonim), established in 1902, opposed the Conservative accommodation. It gave high priority to establishing yeshivas, religious academies devoted to the study of Judaic texts and law. The Orthodox organizational structure, which began with the establishment of the Rabbi Isaac Elchanan Yeshiva in New York City in 1897 and the Union of Orthodox Congregations a year later, was completed in 1927 when the two existing yehivas, Isaac Elchanan and Etz Chaim, merged to form the nucleus of Yeshiva University. It contained Yeshiva College (1928), the first liberal arts college established under Orthodox auspices. By 1930, the three-way religious division of American Judaism was complete.

Of the three branches, the Orthodox proved the least cohesive and the least willing to adopt "American" patterns of governance. Assuming that its decisions were fiat for the committed Jewish laity, the Union named Jacob Josef chief rabbi in 1901. Steeped in the ways of Polish Orthodoxy and unable to master English, Josef failed to gain acceptance, highlighting the powerlessness of those who claimed spiritual leadership without first winning a mandate from the laity. The overextended power claims of a group of Orthodox rabbis in New York City, who imposed a tax on the sale of kosher meat and poultry, coupled with the unclear lines of Orthodox authority, set the stage for several bitter "kosher meat wars" in the early years of the twentieth century. Ultimately the civil courts arbitrated the conflict.

The Reconstruction Movement. The Orthodox branch experienced further attrition after *World War I, as part of a larger postwar "crisis of faith." Among the earliest to recognize the impact of the crisis was Rabbi Mordecai Kaplan (1881–1993), who became head of the Jewish Theological Seminary's Teacher's Institute in 1909. Kaplan understood the appeal for Jewish immigrants and their children of secularism's claims of individual autonomy and freedom. Yet he also realized that *secularization posed a grave challenge to Judaism's corporate character. If its influence was not neutralized and reshaped, Kaplan believed, American Judaism faced an uncertain future. This fear led to the founding of the Reconstruction movement, which he envisioned as a fourth branch of Judaism, situated between the Conservative and Reform movements.

Judaism, Kaplan believed, was not merely a religion but an "evolving religious civilization," the sum of what Jews actually did culturally and religiously. The umbrella institution for such combined cultural and religious activities would be the Jewish Center. Like Solomon Schechter, Kaplan emphasized the strong sense of Jewish peoplehood inherent in Zionism. To put his strategy into effect, Kaplan organized the Society for the Advancement of Judaism in 1922, but his strategy remained largely in the realm of ideas. A 1926 religious census found only one Reconstructionist congregation among America's 3,118 Jewish congregations. Only after 1968, when the Reconstructionist Rabbinic College was established in Philadelphia, did the movement make significant advances.

American Judaism, 1950–2000. By 1950, the three major branches of American Judaism broke down approximately as follows: 2 million Conservatives Jews, 1.3 million Reform Jews, and 1 million Orthodox Jews. Orthodoxy burgeoned after *World War II—a resurgence hardly presaged by its condition in the early part of the century, when it had been confined mostly to eastern European immigrants gathered in small congregations with few and poorly paid rabbis, and when Orthodoxy had failed to develop a way to allow its followers to combine piety with social mobility. Yet Orthodoxy's deep commitment to religious law and tradition, combined with the infusion of new leadership and energy from the remnants of European Orthodoxy that survived the Holocaust, belied the once widespread assumption that American Orthodoxy would not survive the immigrant generation. Included in the Holocaust remnant was Agudath Israel of America, part of the worldwide Agudath movement, which established its American headquarters in 1939 in New York City. Among the refugees from Nazism to reach America were Rabbi Moses Feinstein, a renowned authority on Jewish law; Menachem Mendel Schneersohn, the Lubavitcher Rebbe; and Rabbi Aaron Kutler, a well-known Talmudic scholar.

Wracked by such issues as ordination of women, patrilineal descent, and other facets of the perennial "who is a Jew" question, late twentieth-century American Judaism was more divided than ever. The intensity of the struggle between its several branches was deepened by the Orthodox rabbinate's control of the religious establishment in Israel. By recognizing only marriages, divorces, and conversions conducted under its auspices, Orthodoxy could delegitimize the Reform and Conservative movements to which most affiliated American Jews belonged. Simultaneously, the perennial "crisis of faith" continued to weaken all branches of Judaism. Late twentieth-century Jews were America's most avid secularists. Less than 40 percent belonged to a congregation, and many members attended only on the high holy days. None of the branches had yet discovered a way to rejoin the normative Jewishness—the cuisine, the humor, the emphasis on education, the cultural interests, the middle-class lifestyle—that shaped Jews' daily lives, with the historic Judaism of faith and piety. Finding a way to reunite Judaism, the faith, and Jewishness, the ethnic culture, loomed large on the Jewish agenda in the twenty-first century.

[*See also* Anti-Semitism; Immigration; Protestantism; Religion; Roman Catholicism; Wise, Stephen S.]

• Jack Wertheimer, ed., *The American Synagogue: A Sanctuary Transformed,* 1987. Henry L. Feingold, ed., *The Jewish People in America,* 5 vols., 1992. Sefton D. Temkin, *Isaac Mayer Wise: Shaping American Judaism,* 1992. Samuel G. Freedman, *Jew vs. Jew: The Struggle for the Soul of American Jewry,* 2000.

—Henry L. Feingold

JUDICIAL BRANCH. *See* Federal Government, Judicial Branch.

JUDICIAL REVIEW. Judicial review, the power of courts to determine the legality of governmental acts, usually refers to the authority of judges to decide a law's constitutionality. Although state courts exercised judicial review prior to the ratification of the *Constitution, the doctrine is most often traced to the landmark U.S. *Supreme Court decision **Marbury* v. *Madison* (1803), which struck down an act of Congress as unconstitutional. In a now classic opinion, Chief Justice John *Marshall found the power of judicial review implied in the Constitution's status as "the supreme Law of the Land" prevailing over ordinary laws.

Both federal and state courts have exercised judicial review. Federal courts review federal and state acts to ensure their conformity to the Constitution and the supremacy of federal over state law; state courts review laws to ensure their conformity to the U.S. Constitution and their own state constitutions. The power of judicial review can be exercised by any court in which a constitutional issue arises.

Judicial review gained added importance in the late nineteenth and early twentieth centuries, as courts passed judgment on laws regulating corporate behavior and working conditions. In these years, the Supreme Court repeatedly struck down laws regulating wages, hours of labor, and safety standards. This is often called the *Lochner* Era, after **Lochner* v. *New York,* a 1905 decision ruling a New York maximum-hours law unconstitutional on the grounds that it violated the due-process clause of the *Fourteenth Amendment. During this period, the Supreme Court invalidated no fewer than 228 state laws.

Justice Oliver Wendell *Holmes Jr., dissenting from many of these decisions, urged judges to defer to legislatures. In the later 1930s, the Supreme Court adopted the Holmes approach—partly in response to the threat of President Franklin Delano *Roosevelt's "court packing" plan of 1937. Deferring to legislative judgment, the Supreme Court thereafter upheld virtually all laws regulating business and property rights, including laws similar to those invalidated during the *Lochner* Era.

Under the chief justiceship of Earl *Warren (1953–1969) and beyond, however, the Court moved toward striking down laws restricting the personal rights and liberties guaranteed by the *Bill of Rights, particularly measures limiting freedom of expression, freedom of religion, the rights of criminal defendants, equal treatment of the sexes, and the rights of minorities to equal protection of the law. In another extension of judicial review, the Court read new rights into the Constitution, notably the right of privacy (including *abortion rights), and invalidated laws restricting those rights. Many other countries, including Germany, Italy, France, and Japan, adopted the principle of judicial review after *World War II, making constitutional law one of the more important recent American exports.

[*See also* Federal Government: Judicial Branch; Federalism; State Governments.]

• Bernard Schwartz, *A History of the Supreme Court,* 1993.

—Bernard Schwartz

JUDICIAL SYSTEM. *See* Federal Government, Judicial System; Municipal Judicial Systems.

JUNGLE, THE (1906). Published in 1906, Upton *Sinclair's *The Jungle* remains one of the most influential novels in American political and social history. Sinclair was a socialist writer who had just published a book on chattel slavery and an article on the meatpackers' failed 1904 strike for the socialist periodical *Appeal to Reason.* Invited by the journal's editor, Fred Warren, to do another exposé, this time of wage slavery, Sinclair in the autumn of 1904 lived for seven weeks in *Chicago's meatpacking district, investigating both the plants and the adjoining workers' residences.

Based on this research, Sinclair wrote a graphic description of conditions encountered by a fictional family of Lithuanian immigrants. Jurgis Rudkus, the protagonist, is optimistic that he will succeed in America because of his physical strength and his work ethic. Instead, the industrial order grinds down not only Jurgis but every member of his family, several of whom die or suffer other terrible fates.

While Sinclair's goal was to expose the evils of industrial *capitalism and demonstrate the need for *socialism, the public's reaction was very different. At a time when middle-class consumers were being taught to trust national name brands as symbols of purity and quality, Sinclair offered a very different message. *The Jungle* portrayed an industry in which monopolistic corporations sold diseased and damaged meat and invested in *advertising rather than in pure and safe products. In the resulting uproar, Congress passed the *Pure Food and Drug Act and the Meat Inspection Act in 1906. Commented a disappointed Sinclair: "I aimed at the public's heart and by accident I hit it in the stomach." Later critics attacked the pessimism of the book, especially Sinclair's failure to recognize the resourcefulness of immigrant workers.

[*See also* Immigration; Industrialization; Meatpacking and Meat Processing Industry; Progressive Era.]

• James Barrett, introduction to *The Jungle,* by Upton Sinclair, 1988, pp. xi–xxxii.

—Robert A. Slayton

JURISPRUDENCE. The term "jurisprudence" technically means skill in the science of the law. That definition rests on the premise that law is a science, a premise deeply rooted in Anglo-American legal education since at least the eighteenth century, but one that came under severe assault in the twentieth century. The conception of law as a science presupposes its methodological and even substantive universality as a set of fundamental principles that can be analyzed and discerned in an unchanging fashion, akin to the traditional view of "the scientific method." Many conventional treatments of jurisprudence have been organized around these premises. However, jurisprudence can also be thought of as the cumulative history of ideas about the nature and cultural significance of law and legal institutions in a given nation. This essay takes the latter approach, emphasizing ideas about the law in successive periods of American history.

Fundamental to an examination of the stages in American jurisprudence is the assumption that a sea change in conceptions of the nature of law occurred over the course of the nineteenth century. Once thought of as a repository of essentialist, unchanging principles, akin to other fundamental causative forces in the universe, law came to be thought of as equivalent to the ideologies and policies of officials empowered to make legal decisions. While this change in the meaning of law as a causative agent in society took place gradually, the view of law as essentialist and external to human will, dominant at the time of the framing of the *Constitution, had by the 1930s been replaced by one that defined law as largely indistinguishable from the legal decisions of authoritative officials.

Nineteenth-century Jurisprudence. This sea change in attitudes involved two fundamental stages, the "classical" (nineteenth-century) and the "modern" stage, each associated with certain jurisprudential movements. The jurisprudential issues contested in the classical period revolved around whether judges had correctly "discerned the course prescribed by law"—in other words, whether they had accurately adapted fundamental legal principles to emerging social issues. Thus, the struggles that produced the leading constitutional decisions of the nineteenth century—over the federal government's authority to supplant the authority of the states, the constitutional status of *slavery, federal enforcement of the *civil rights of former slaves, income tax, *antitrust legislation, or states' efforts to regulate contractual relationships among employers and their employees—were not thought of as raising fundamental questions about the the legitimacy of judges making law or entering into the domain of policy. They were thought of, instead, as raising questions of whether the judges deciding those cases had accurately discerned the course prescribed by law.

During the *Gilded Age, some American legal commentators, influenced by the growing prestige of *science and its secularized explanations for the flow of events in the universe, began to question the essentialist nature of law. This group of "modernist" commentators concluded that the distinction between the will of officials, including judges, and the "will of the law" was simply a fiction. Legal decision-makers, including judges, were now characterized as "making" law. This characterization naturally raised issues that centered on the problem of separating politics from law, and of checking the potentially tyrannical or arbitrary tendency of legal decisions by human actors, in a society premised on the supremacy of a written Constitution and on democratic theory.

Early Twentieth-century Developments. In response to these problems, three successive twentieth-century jurisprudential movements sought to erect constraints on legal decision-makers, especially judges. "Sociological jurisprudence," an early twentieth-century movement, insisted that judicial decisions must be grounded in an empirical understanding of current social conditions. Legal realism, the next movement, abandoned the idea of essentialist legal principles altogether and proposed that judging be seen as the equivalent of policy-making and that legal rules be frankly recast in a functional form. Some legal realists pressed the idea of judging as human will so insistently that, in the context of totalitarian threats to American democracy, it appeared frightening.

The next influential twentieth-century jurisprudential movement, "process jurisprudence," attempted to constrain the unsettling implications of the realist movement. Because process jurisprudence beliefs continued to be widely held by lawyers and judges of the late twentieth century, it merits a more extended treatment. Process jurisprudence attempted to justify a selective approach to *judicial review, in which a degree of activism in common law-judging and in certain constitutional realms—notably free speech—was combined with judicial deference to legislatures and to the federal administrative agencies that had proliferated from the 1930s on. Process jurisprudence correlated selective judicial review with a set of institutional spheres in "the legal process," each with its own set of competence requirements.

For its adherents, process jurisprudence "solved" the jurisprudence dilemma of activist judging in a constitutional democracy by providing criteria for determining whether a particular judicial decision had been been grounded in institutional competence theory and was thus rational. Aggressive judicial review in the free speech area was seen as competent because the justifications for that review articulated the vital role of freedom of expression in a modern democracy. Deferential judicial review in the realm of political economy was equally viewed as competent because the collapse of orthodox capitalism had demonstrated that American democracy was not committed to an essentialist economic policy, but rather to experimentation, embodied in legislative solutions.

In an influential series of decisions highlighted by **Brown v. Board of Education* (1954), the *Supreme Court expanded aggressive judicial review into areas beyond free speech, such as race relations, reapportionment, and criminal procedure. Process theorists insisted that these decisions be justified by a grounding in "neutral principles of law" that would demonstrate their rationality and competence. Eventually, after finding the Court's justifications inadequate, process theorists supplied their own justifications by formulating two additional essentialist policies to which the judiciary could subscribe: the policy of antidiscrimination on the basis of race or skin color, which justified the Court's desegregation decisions; and the policy of reinforcing the democratic principle of representation by ensuring that if a minority group was unrepresented or underrepresented in a legislature, the judiciary could invoke aggressive constitutional review on its behalf.

The Late Twentieth Century. In the late twentieth century, the governing assumptions that linked sociological jurisprudence, legal realism, and process jurisprudence were called into question. Specifically, a series of theoretical perspectives appeared in legal scholarship that collectively denied that modern scientific methodology actually amounts to a constraint on its practitioners, whether in law or in any other human "science." Critical legal studies, feminist theory, critical race theory, *republicanism, and communtiarianism all were openly normative perspectives that made no pretense of being a positive, objective "science." Their implicit jurisprudential theory appeared to be that no legal actors, including judges, are constrained in any meaningful fashion in their decision-making. From this perspective, the effort of modern jurisprudence to substitute empirically derived and rationally justified essentialist policies for the essentialist principles of classical jurisprudence is simply incoherent.

Some commentators suggested that with the collective surfacing of these diverse perspectives, process jurisprudence had disintegrated, resulting in the dawn of a "postmodern" stage of American jurisprudence. This conclusion was perhaps premature. The problem of distinguishing the "will" of the law from the will of those who make legal decisions seems to transcend history, given that law, unlike economics or physics or literature, is assumed to be a regime that provides authoritative rules for governing human conduct. Unless "postmodern" jurisprudential perspectives devoted themselves to fashioning some techniques—whether derived from modern science or elsewhere—they were not likely to gain the lasting influence of their predecessors. The purported emergence of "*postmodernism" in jurisprudence may have signalled not so much the collapse of modernist epistemology as the collapse of the idea, from which conventional treatments of jurisprudence had started, of law as a science. That is to say, law resists being analogized to a field with predictive universalistic rules; it is too grounded in human complexity. But at the same time, law's authoritative force, at least in democratic societies, derives from its ascribed ability to function as an alternative to tyranny and arbitrariness. Thus, at least in the United States, the subject of jurisprudence appears integrally bound to the recurrent dilemmas posed by law as both a facilitator of, and a constraint upon, human willfulness.

[*See also* Federal Government, Judicial Branch; Legal Profession.]

• G. Edward White, *Patterns of American Legal Thought,* 1978. Daniel Rodgers, *Contested Truths,* 1987. G. Edward White, *The American Judicial Tradition,* 1988. Dorothy Ross, *The Origins of American Social Science,* 1993. Dorothy Ross, ed., *Modernist Impulses in the Human Sciences,* 1994. G. Edward White, *Intervention and Detachment: Essays in Legal History and Jurisprudence,* 1994. Neil Duxbury, *Patterns of American Jurisprudence,* 1995. Laura Kalman, *The Strange Career of Legal Liberalism,* 1996. Gary Minda, *Postmodern Legal Movements: Law and Jurisprudence at Century's End,* 1995.

—G. Edward White

JUVENILE DELINQUENCY. Although children and youth have always misbehaved, the concept of juvenile delinquency as a distinct social phenomenon arose in the United States only in the early nineteenth century, when it was associated with the breakdown of traditional familial controls in a period of emerging *industrialization, *urbanization, and *immigration. Delinquency included both criminal acts (such as theft) and noncriminal activities (such as "incorrigibility" and "stubbornness"). Reflecting a new faith in the power of the environment to curb delinquent tendencies, philanthropists in the 1820s founded the first "houses of refuge" in northern cities. By the late nineteenth century, most states had established juvenile reformatories, most of which quickly degenerated into repressive, overcrowded institutions.

After 1900, a new generation of Progressive reformers, lauded as "child savers," sought innovative means to save children from a life of *crime. In Illinois, they established the first juvenile court in 1899. Other states followed suit. Juvenile-court procedures, designed to be informal, lacked the legal rights accorded to adult defendants, including the right to a lawyer; social workers, psychologists, and psychiatrists were to guide the judge. Juvenile courts never lived up to their founders' ideals however. Few had specialized treatment services, and most defined delinquency in highly gendered ways, routinely sentencing girls to reformatories for sexual behavior for which boys were rarely punished.

Scholars have offered many competing theories of juvenile delinquency. *Progressive Era sociologists stressed environmental causes such as *poverty. Biological determinists regarded juvenile delinquents as physically and mentally degenerate. From the 1920s to the 1950s, social and psychological explanations of delinquency predominated, as sociologists focused on family breakdown, social strains, deviant subcultures, and class and racial discrimination.

Treatment of juvenile delinquents changed radically after the 1967 *Supreme Court decision *In re Gault,* which gave juveniles unprecedented legal rights. Congress's landmark 1974 Juvenile Justice and Delinquency Prevention Act encouraged states to define delinquency far more narrowly, removing truants and runaways from court jurisdiction. As a result, juvenile courts became more formal and legalistic institutions. In the 1980s and 1990s, fueled by perceptions of spreading gang warfare and drug-related inner-city violence, states became much more punitive, "criminalizing" or "adultifying" their juvenile-justice systems, imposing longer sentences, transferring juveniles to adult court, and holding them in adult prisons and jails. Widespread anxiety over juvenile delinquency characterized nearly every twentieth-century decade. During *World War II, with many fathers at war and many mothers working, fears of escalating delinquency mounted. The 1950s witnessed a juvenile-delinquency "panic" (captured by Hollywood in such films as *The Wild One* [1954], *Rebel without a Cause* [1955], and *Blackboard Jungle* [1955]), while the protests, riots, and counterculture of the 1960s sparked new concerns. Whether delinquency changed significantly over the twentieth century remains unclear. Crime statistics, affected by changes in *police practice and reporting, must be treated with caution; increasing arrests do not necessarily indicate an increase in delinquency rates. In the 1990s, police were more likely to arrest juveniles than they had been in earlier decades. Nevertheless, only 6 percent of juvenile arrests in the 1990s involved serious, violent offenses. While public attitudes toward juvenile delinquents became more punitive after the 1960s, most "juvenile delinquency" continued to consist of petty larceny, disorderly conduct, underage drinking, truancy, and running away from home.

[*See also* Family; Fifties, The; Gender; Life Stages; Prisons and Penitentiaries; Sixties, The; Social Class.]

• John R. Sutton, *Stubborn Children: Controlling Delinquency in the United States, 1640–1981,* 1988. Thomas J. Bernard, *The Cycle of Juvenile Justice,* 1992.

—L. Mara Dodge

K

KAISER PERMANENTE. *See* Health Maintenance Organizations.

KANSAS CITY. The Missouri settlement that by the 1850s would be called Kansas City arose in the 1820s as a fur trading center at the junction of the Kansas and Missouri Rivers. By the 1830s hemp farming and the outfitting of settlers migrating west on the *Santa Fe Trail had replaced the *fur trade as the region's major cash sources.

Kansas Territory opened to settlement in 1854, and Kansas City grew from a few hundred residents to over 4,000 in 1860. The *Civil War in the region was largely a guerrilla conflict, resulting in rural depopulation and economic stagnation. After the war, *railroads became the major concern. Local promoters persuaded the Hannibal & St. Joseph railroad to build a bridge across the Missouri River at Kansas City. Together with the Missouri Pacific connection to St. Louis (1865) and the Kansas Pacific connection to Abilene (1867), this made Kansas City a major transfer point and railroad hub for the *Middle West. Stockyards, *meatpacking, and related businesses located across the State line in Kansas processed livestock from western Missouri, Kansas, and the *Southwest. Wholesaling companies made Kansas City the economic center for the Southwest in the later nineteenth century.

Kansas City, Missouri, reached a population of 132,000 by 1890 and 400,000 by 1930. Kansas City, Kansas meanwhile, grew from several small towns into a city of 50,000 by 1900 and over 100,000 by 1920. Trade, transportation, and related services such as conventions and hotels were the central businesses into the 1920s. The Kansas City metropolitan region was only secondarily a manufacturing center. Though sometimes portrayed as a "cow town," Kansas City contained no stockyards or meatpacking facilities after 1990.

From the mid-1920s to 1939 (when he went to prison for income-tax evasion), Kansas City politics was controlled by Democratic boss Thomas Pendergast (1872–1945), whose best-known protégé was the future president Harry S. *Truman. Under Pendergast the city gained a reputation for lax law enforcement and prostitution.

By 1950 approximately 1 million persons lived in the Kansas City metropolitan area. Downtown Kansas City, Missouri, retained its position as the financial center, but suburban Johnson County, Kansas, contained over 400,000 residents and many business offices by 2000.

Metropolitan Kansas City hosts an American League *baseball team, The Royals, and the National Football League's Chiefs. As the twentieth century ended, its economy was quite diversified with low unemployment. The 1.8 million residents were proud of the city's *jazz heritage, including pianist and bandleader William ("Count") *Basie, and of the strong role of *African Americans—15 percent of the metropolitan population—in developing the region's image. It was also a regional center for the federal government, the largest single employer.

[*See also* Livestock Industry.]

• Shirl Kasper and Rick Montgomery, *Kansas City: An American Story*, 1999.

—William S. Worley

KANSAS-NEBRASKA ACT (1854). The 1840s brought a rising tide of foreign immigrants and internal migrants to the trans-Mississippi West, generating interest in promoting orderly settlement of the Great Plains. However, the Mexican Cession of 1848 became the focus of fierce sectional debates over the spread of *slavery. Senator Stephen A. *Douglas of Illinois played a crucial role in congressional adoption of the *Compromise of 1850, which implicitly opened new southwestern territories to slavery on the principle of "congressional nonintervention" and "popular sovereignty," whereby the people of a territory, like those of a state, would decide the issue for themselves. To Douglas and his *Democratic party, this principle was superior to the 1820 *Missouri Compromise's federal dictate that slavery could not exist in the *Louisiana Purchase territory north of the 36°30' line of latitude. Extending "popular sovereignty" to the still unorganized northern portion of the Louisiana Purchase, they believed, would represent a victory for local self-government; further, it would promote national political unity and economic development by securing the Democratic party against the threat of sectional fracture and by expediting settlement and *railroad construction on the Great Plains.

Hence, in January 1854, Senator Douglas's Committee on Territories reported a "Nebraska Bill" that, with subsequent amendments, became the Kansas-Nebraska Act. Bowing to pressure from his party's powerful southern wing, but fully expecting that climate would exclude slavery from the Great Plains, Douglas agreed that the act should explicitly repeal the Missouri Compromise line and provide for the organization of two territories, Kansas and Nebraska. The bill passed the Senate by a vote of 37–14 and the House of Representatives by a much closer vote of 113–100, with northern Democrats evenly split. President Franklin *Pierce signed it into law on 30 May. Douglas hoped that the Kansas-Nebraska Act would settle the slavery issue in the territories, coalesce national Democratic support for "popular sovereignty," and further his presidential aspirations. In reality, the law triggered a violent struggle in Kansas between pro- and *antislavery forces; deepened antislavery sentiment in the North; and set the stage for a new *Republican party opposed to the expansion of slavery, whose 1860 presidential nominee, Abraham *Lincoln, frustrated Douglas's bid for the White House.

[*See also* Antebellum Era; Brown, John; Civil War: Causes.]

• Michael A. Morrison, *Slavery and the American West: The Eclipse of Manifest Destiny and the Coming of the Civil War*, 1997.

—Shearer Davis Bowman

KELLEY, FLORENCE (1859–1932), social reformer. Kelley was born into a patrician *Philadelphia Quaker and Unitarian family, the daughter of William Darrah Kelley, a leading *Republican party politician, and Caroline Bonsall Kelley. Graduating from Cornell University in 1882, Kelley studied at the University of Zurich where in 1884 she married Lazare Wischnewetzky, a Russian Jewish socialist medical student, and forged a lifelong identity as a socialist. Between 1885 and 1888, she gave birth to three children. Returning to *New York City in 1886, she found it impossible to continue the political commitments begun in Zurich. In 1891, after Lazare began beating her, she fled with their children to *Chicago, residing at Jane *Addams's Hull House until 1899. In 1895, she completed a law degree at Northwestern University.

Kelley established her national reputation during a three-year tenure as Illinois's Chief Factory Inspector (1893–1896), enforcing the state's pathbreaking eight-hour law for working women and children. In 1899, she assumed the position she occupied until her death, secretary-general of the newly-formed *National Consumers' League (NCL). Returning to New York City, she lived at the Henry Street Settlement on Manhattan's Lower East Side.

Building sixty-four local leagues by 1906, Kelley, in cooperation with other women's organizations, worked to make American government more responsive to the needs of working people, especially wage-earning women and children. Using gender-specific legislation as a surrogate for class legislation, Kelley defended the constitutionality of legislation limiting the hours of working women, then successfully extended those protections to men. Similarly, the NCL pioneered the passage of state minimum-wage laws for women that in 1938 led to a federal minimum-wage law for women and men.

[*See also* Child Labor; Consumer Movement; Progressive Era; Socialism; Women in the Labor Force.]

• Kathryn Kish Sklar, ed., *Notes of Sixty Years: The Autobiography of Florence Kelley*, 1986. Kathryn Kish Sklar, *Florence Kelley and the Nation's Work: The Rise of Women's Political Culture, 1830–1900*, 1995.

—Kathryn Kish Sklar

KELLOGG-BRIAND PACT (1928). A treaty purporting to outlaw war in *international law, the Kellogg-Briand Pact, or Pact of Paris, was initially signed by fifteen nations and shortly gained the adherence of sixty-two nations, including the United States, which ratified it in 1929.

The pact reflected a French search for security in the wake of *World War I. Hoping for at least a moral sanction against possible German aggression, the French foreign minister, Aristide Briand, in 1928 proposed a U.S.-French treaty to renounce war between them. U.S. Secretary of State Frank B. Kellogg (1856–1937), seeking to preserve unilateral policymaking, finessed the French initiative by universalizing it. Kellogg proposed a treaty that would pledge all signatories to "condemn recourse to war for the solution of international controversies, and renounce it as an instrument of national policy. . . ." Implicitly at least, the pact reaffirmed the 1899 Hague Convention for the Pacific Settlement of International Disputes by pledging to settle conflicts solely "by pacific means." It carried no mechanism for enforcement.

The acceptance of the pact in the United States reflected a widespread disillusionment with warfare and the emergence of antiwar pressure groups. With political leadership from the Republican senator William E. Borah of Idaho, the pact aligned advocates of outlawing war with proponents of international law. It forged the basis of a broad coalition of peace societies while deflecting stronger commitments to *internationalism and more specific challenges to military defense.

The pact was widely understood to preclude only aggressive war, though that was not specified, leaving in place the option of defensive warfare. It was violated by aggressor states during the 1930s, leading up to *World War II. Although widely disparaged by foreign policy realists for its idealistic framework, the Kellogg-Briand Pact was invoked as the main precedent in international law prohibiting the "crimes against peace" that supplemented traditional war crimes in the trials at Nuremberg and, especially, Tokyo following World War II.

[*See also* Peace Movements; War Crimes Trials, Nuremberg and Tokyo.]

• Robert H. Ferrell, *Peace in Their Time: The Origins of the Kellogg-Briand Pact*, 1952. Charles DeBenedetti, *Origins of the Modern American Peace Movement, 1915–1929*, 1978.

—E. Charles Chatfield

KENNAN, GEORGE (1904–), diplomat, historian, foreign policy critic. Born in Milwaukee, Wisconsin, Kennan attended Princeton University and joined the United States Foreign Service in 1926. He served as a diplomat at various European postings over the next two decades and earned some reputation for expertise on the Soviet Union, but he had minimal influence on policy. His obscurity ended with the dispatch from Moscow of his "Long Telegram" in February 1946 and especially with the publication of his 1947 article "The Sources of Soviet Conduct," written under the pseudonym "X" and espousing the *containment doctrine, in *Foreign Affairs*. The latter secured his standing as a principal architect of America's *Cold War strategy

As director of the State Department Policy Planning Staff from 1947 to 1950, Kennan advocated political and economic measures, such as the *Marshall Plan, to implement containment. He unsuccessfully objected to what he considered containment's overmilitarization as evidenced by the *North Atlantic Treaty Organization, the hydrogen bomb, and *National Security Council Document #68. Dissenting from the expansive national security strategy favored by Dean *Acheson, Kennan left the State Department in 1950. His direct role in U.S. foreign policy formulation ended then, although he later served as ambassador to the Soviet Union (1952) and to Yugoslavia (1961–1963).

After leaving government, Kennan pursued a distinguished career as a historian at the Institute for Advanced Studies at Princeton. He also emerged as an important realist critic of American foreign policy. In the 1950s he proposed the reunification of Germany and the withdrawal of American troops from Europe. Later, he opposed U.S. involvement in the *Vietnam War, offered constructively critical support to the Richard M. *Nixon–Henry *Kissinger policy of détente, and passionately advocated nuclear arms–control measures. With the end of the Cold War, Kennan continued to emphasize the limits of American power and the need for restraint in its exercise.

[*See also* Federal Government, Executive Branch: Department of State; Foreign Relations; Nuclear Arms Control Treaties; Nuclear Weapons.]

• David Mayers, *George Kennan and the Dilemmas of U.S. Foreign Policy*, 1988. Wilson D. Miscamble, *George F. Kennan and the Making of American Foreign Policy, 1947–1950*, 1992.

—Wilson D. Miscamble

KENNEDY, JOHN F. (1917–1963), thirty-fifth president of the United States. Kennedy's standing in American political history far supersedes the actual achievements of his tragically foreshortened administration. Born in Brookline, Massachusetts, the son of Joseph P. Kennedy, a wealthy and ambitious *Irish-American businessman, and his wife, Rose Fitzgerald, the daughter of a popular mayor of *Boston, Kennedy early absorbed his father's expectations that he would go far in politics. Although plagued with lifelong serious health problems, he became a naval hero in *World War II and won election to the House of Representatives in 1946 and to the Senate in 1952 and 1958, aided by his rugged good looks and youthful, energetic campaign style. He won the *Democratic party's 1960 presidential nomination after a hotly contested series of primaries and went on to defeat the Republican Richard M. *Nixon by the narrowest of margins. He thus became the youngest person (and the first Roman Catholic) ever elected to the White House. With his attractive and glamorous wife Jacqueline Bouvier (whom he married in 1953) as First Lady, Kennedy infused the presidency with an aura of excitement and sophistication.

Foreign policy was Kennedy's principal concern. The *Cold War, he argued, required a more active use of American power than the inflexible policies of the Dwight D. *Eisenhower administration had permitted. While enlarging the nation's nuclear arsenal, he also backed the military's commitment to new forms of warfare suitable for fighting insurgences in what was becoming known as the "Third World." He escalated the American drive to unseat Fidel Castro's communist regime in Cuba, first through the disastrous 1961 *Bay of Pigs invasion (whose plans he had inherited from his predecessor) and then through a series of covert assassination schemes hatched by the *Central Intelligence Agency. A tense 1961 confrontation with the Soviet premier Nikita Khrushchev over Berlin was defused only by the Soviets' construction of the Berlin Wall. The *Peace Corps, launched in 1961, stands as one of his most admired initiatives.

In the defining international event of his presidency, the 1962 *Cuban Missile Crisis, Kennedy went to the brink of war to pressure the Soviets to remove nuclear missiles from Cuba. Perhaps ironically, the successful resolution of that crisis seemed to ease Soviet-American relations. In 1963, Kennedy negotiated a ban on atmospheric nuclear tests and called for a new and more cooperative relationship with Moscow. At the same time, however, he increased Washington's commitment to the survival of a noncommunist government in South Vietnam, and in the Fall of 1963 he authorized a coup to topple South Vietnam's unpopular president, Ngo Dinh Diem, who was subsequently murdered by the coup leaders.

Domestically, the administration developed ambitious plans for a war on *poverty, national health insurance for the elderly, and other initiatives, but none was implemented, stalled by an essentially conservative Congress. Kennedy's principal domestic achievement was one that Attorney General Robert *Kennedy (his brother) at first sought to avoid: allying the federal government with the African American drive for *civil rights. In June 1963, after the savage attacks of southern authorities against civil rights demonstrators had galvanized public opinion, Kennedy in a notable television speech expressed his and the nation's commitment to equal rights and proposed a bill that, after his death, would become the Civil Rights Act of 1964.

Kennedy was assassinated while riding in a motorcade in Dallas, Texas, on 22 November 1963. In death, he came to symbolize a youthful idealism and optimism that many Americans ultimately concluded had died with him. For decades after, despite revelations of character blemishes largely unacknowledged during his lifetime, he loomed large in the American political imagination—his dynamism and radiant charm a reminder to millions of citizens of what seemed a better time and a loftier politics than what they had come to know in the difficult years that followed.

[*See also* Civil Rights Legislation; Civil Rights Movement; Federal Government, Executive Branch: The Presidency; Limited Nuclear Test Ban Treaty; Nuclear Strategy; Roman Catholicism; Sixties, The; Vietnam War.]

• Arthur M. Schlesinger Jr., *A Thousand Days,* 1965. Garry Wills, *The Kennedy Imprisonment,* 1982. Herbert Parmet, *J. F. K: The Presidency of John F. Kennedy,* 1983. Richard Reeves, *President Kennedy,* 1993.

—Alan Brinkley

KENNEDY, ROBERT (1925–1968), attorney general of the United States, senator from New York. Born in Brookline, Massachusetts, third son of Rose Fitzgerald Kennedy and Joseph P. Kennedy, a wealthy businessman and former ambassador to Great Britain, Robert Francis Kennedy served in the navy during *World War II, graduated from Harvard in 1948, and received a law degree from the University of Virginia in 1951. He first came to public notice in the 1950s as a staff member of Senator Joseph *McCarthy's Red-hunting Subcommittee on Investigations and later as the twenty-nine-year-old chief counsel to the so-called Rackets Committee headed by Senator John McClellan, which publicized criminal activity in organized labor.

In 1960, he successfully managed his brother John F. *Kennedy's campaign for the presidency. To the surprise and disapproval of many, President Kennedy appointed Robert attorney general, joking that he wanted his brother, who had never tried a case, to get some experience before he practiced law. In fact, Robert won high marks as attorney general, orchestrating a campaign against *organized crime that resulted in the conviction of the teamster president James R. Hoffa, among others, and definitively entering the *civil rights struggle on behalf of racial integration. The Kennedy Justice Department was widely criticized, however, for illegal wiretapping, supporting segregationist judges for federal judicial appointments, and tolerating the *Federal Bureau of Investigation excesses of J. Edgar *Hoover.

After President Kennedy's assassination in November 1963, Robert emerged from a season of despair and in 1964 won election to the U.S. Senate from New York. As a senator, he investigated the underside of American life, including hunger in the Mississippi Delta, joblessness in northern ghettos, and squalid conditions in the migrant labor camps of *California. In 1968, he campaigned for president as a law-and-order candidate, a champion of the disadvantaged, and an opponent of the *Vietnam War. The Kennedy charisma won enthusiastic support from the young, the poor, the alienated, members of minority groups, and others. Yet he was resented by some on the left as an opportunist and by others on the right as an integrationist.

On 5 June 1968, Robert Kennedy was shot to death in *Los Angeles, having just won the California primary. The assassin was Sirhan Sirhan, a supporter of the Palestinian cause. His murder shocked a nation already reeling from the assassinations of President Kennedy, *Malcolm X, and Martin Luther *King Jr. Robert Kennedy never got the chance to fulfill the possibilities he so eloquently described.

[*See also* Civil Rights Movement; Federal Government, Executive Branch: Other Departments (Department of Justice); Sixties, The.]

• Victor S. Navasky, *Kennedy Justice,* 1971. Arthur M. Schlesinger Jr., *Robert Kennedy and His Times,* 1978.

—Victor S. Navasky

KENT STATE AND JACKSON STATE. In May 1970, amid escalating protests against the *Vietnam War, six students died in violent incidents at Kent State University in Ohio and Jackson State College in Mississippi. On Thursday, 30 April, protests had erupted as President Richard M. *Nixon revealed that American troops had entered neutral Cambodia to attack Vietcong sanctuaries. The next day at Kent State, a peaceful campus protest was followed in the evening by a disruptive disturbance in downtown Kent that prompted Ohio's Republican governor, James Rhodes, to declare a civil emergency and call out the National Guard. On Saturday, arsonists burned the ROTC building on campus. After clashes between students and guardsmen on Sunday, authorities banned a noon rally planned for Monday, 4 May. When two thousand students gathered on campus anyway, the guardsmen first used tear gas to disperse the crowd and then, a few seconds later, for reasons never fully explained, twenty-eight guardsmen fired more than sixty shots that killed four students—Jeffrey Glenn Miller, Allison B. Krause, William K. Schroeder, and Sandra Lee Scheuer—and wounded nine others.

Meanwhile, tensions were running high at all-black Jackson State, where students often clashed on spring evenings with local youths, passersby, and police along Lynch Street, which cut through the campus. On 13 May, when students hurled rocks at white motorists driving along Lynch Street, the National Guard was placed on alert as police and state patrolmen used an armored car and tear gas to disperse several hundred students. When the rock-throwing resumed the next night, the police, highway patrol, and National Guard returned. Around midnight, shooting suddenly began. In twenty-eight seconds, law-enforcement officers fired more than 150 rounds into a dormitory, killing two students, Phillip Lafayette Gibbs and James Earl Green, and injuring a dozen others.

The killings at Kent State, compounded by the Jackson State shootings, triggered a wave of outraged protest that marked the high point of the antiwar movement. An investigative commission appointed by President Nixon found the Kent State shootings "unnecessary, unwarranted, and inexcusable" and attributed the Jackson State deaths to "the historic pattern of *racism that substantially affects daily life in Mississippi." Nevertheless, a significant portion of the public supported the forcible suppression of campus protests. In 1979, in a suit arising from the Kent State case, twenty-eight defendants, including national guardsmen and Governor Rhodes, paid the victims or their families $675,000, accepted responsibility for the shootings, and expressed regret over the deaths and injuries. A decade-long lawsuit against city and state authorities in the Jackson State case failed.

[*See also* Antiwar Movements; Sixties, The.]

• *The Report of the President's Commission on Campus Unrest,* 1970. Scott L. Bills, ed., *Kent State/May 4: Echoes through a Decade,* 1982. Tim Spofford, *Lynch Street: The May 1970 Slayings at Jackson State College,* 1988.

—Charles W. Eagles

KEYNESIANISM, an economic theory originally derived from the British economist John Maynard Keynes. In his *General Theory of Employment, Interest and Money* (1936), written during the Great Depression of the 1930s, Keynes challenged the orthodox view that market forces would necessarily bring about recovery. Rather, Keynes postulated that the historical evolution of capitalist economics limited the ability of private investment to stimulate renewed economic growth. Hence, public investment would be required to lift Western economies from an indefinite state of stagnation. American economists initially understood Keynes's analysis in this light.

In the climate of post–*World War II prosperity, however, Keynesianism came primarily to be understood as a series of fiscal-policy strategies: the use of government spending or tax reduction to boost a sagging economy; the introduction of government retrenchment or tax increases to cool an overheated one. Widely supported among U.S. economists, this contracyclical version of Keynesianism largely displaced the original formulation. Keynesianism thus evolved from a general theory repudiating *laissez-faire economic orthodoxy into a kit of policy tools. This revision of orthodox economic theory was dubbed the "neoclassical synthesis."

During the 1970s, this post–World War II view of Keynesianism fell into disrepute. The simultaneous appearance of recession and inflation—labeled "stagflation"—rendered Keynesian fiscal tools ineffectual. Accordingly, the form of Keynesianism widely accepted after 1945 stood indicted as simpleminded, and younger economists by and large abandoned it. Other economists, however, worked to retrieve or develop a form of Keynesianism more in keeping with Keynes's original theoretical and policy intent: to save *capitalism from a historical tendency toward long-term stagnation and mass *unemployment.

[*See also* Business Cycle; Depressions, Economic; Economics; Monetarism; Monetary Policy, Federal; New Deal Era, The; Taxation.]

• Walter S. Salant, "The Spread of Keynesian Doctrines and Practices in the United States," in *The Political Power of Economic Ideas: Keynesianism across Nations,* ed. Peter A. Hall, 1989, pp. 27–51.

—Theodore Rosenof

KING, BILLIE JEAN (1943–), tennis champion and advocate of women's equality in sport. Born in Long Beach, California, Billie Jean King learned tennis on public courts under the tutelage of Clyde Walker and later honed her skills with the help of former champion Alice Marble and Australian Mervyn Rose. One of the most successful women's tennis players of all time, King captured many championships during a playing career that spanned more than two decades. Included among these were six singles, four mixed doubles, and ten doubles titles at Wimbledon; four singles, four mixed doubles, and four doubles titles at the U.S. Open; one Australian Open singles title; and one singles and one doubles title in the French Open. She also competed for several years on both the U.S. Federation and Wightman Cup teams, defeated Bobby Riggs in a much ballyhooed "Battle of the Sexes" in 1973, and served in 1974 as the player-coach for the Philadelphia Freedoms in World Team Tennis. Besides her exploits on the court, King founded *Women Sports* magazine, coauthored five books on tennis technique, and wrote two autobiographies. Her many awards include the Associated Press Athlete of the Year, *Sports Illustrated* Sports Woman of the Year, the United States Lawn Tennis Association Service Bowl, and the Marlboro award (along with husband Larry King) for promoting tennis through public clinics. She was also honored by election into the Women's Sports Foundation Hall of Fame in 1980 and the International Tennis Hall of Fame in 1987.

[*See also* Feminism; Sports: Professional Sports.]

• Marshall Buchard, *Sports Hero, Billie Jean King,* 1975. James Hahn and Linda Hahn, *King! The Sports Career of Billie Jean King,* 1981.

—David K. Wiggins

KING, ERNEST J. (1877–1956), *World War II strategist and commander. Born in Lorain, Ohio, King entered the U.S. Naval Academy in 1897, served on the cruiser *San Francisco* off Cuba during the *Spanish-American War, and graduated in 1901. Before *World War I, he served as an aide to Rear Admiral Hugo Osterhaus. While on the staff of Henry T. Mayo during the war, King became suspicious of British political motives and developed a low opinion of the Royal Navy that would last a lifetime. After World War I, King became both a submariner and an aviator. His experience in surface, submarine, and aviation forces gave him a unique understanding of their capabilities, something he drew upon as World War II commander-in-chief of the U.S. fleet and Chief of Naval Operations.

During World War II, King devoted his attention to the work of the *Joint Chiefs of Staff while still directing the greatest naval buildup in U.S. history, overseeing conduct of the Battle of the Atlantic, and formulating U.S. strategy for the war against Japan. A shrewd judge of character, King appointed capable assistants and delegated power to them, retaining for himself broad oversight of policy, strategy, and personnel. He accepted the "Europe first" strategy but fought for resources for the Pacific. Inflexible and difficult to get along with, King was nevertheless supportive and considerate of men he respected, and thoroughly dedicated to the interests of the navy and the United States. He retired as a five-star fleet admiral in December 1945.

[*See also* Military, The; Military Service Academies; Submarines.]

• Ernest J. King, *Fleet Admiral King,* 1952. Thomas Buell, *Master of Sea Power,* 1980.

—James C. Bradford

KING, MARTIN LUTHER, JR. (1929–1968), *civil rights leader, preeminent voice of the post–*World War II African American freedom movement. Born in Atlanta, Georgia, the son and namesake of a prominent Baptist minister, King entered Atlanta's Morehouse College at age fifteen. After graduation he enrolled at Crozer Theological Seminary in Pennsylvania, where he encountered Walter *Rauschenbusch's *Social Gospel theology, Reinhold *Niebuhr's justifications for the use of coercion to combat evil, and Gandhi's philosophy of nonviolent direct action. Enrolling at Boston University, he earned a Ph.D. in systematic theology (1955). He married Coretta Scott in 1953; they had four children.

In 1954, King was appointed pastor of Dexter Avenue Baptist Church in Montgomery, Alabama. On 1 December 1955, the arrest of Rosa Parks for violating the city's racial-segregation ordinances sparked a bus boycott, and local organizers selected the twenty-six-year-old King to lead it. "It happened so fast," King remembered, "that I did not even have time to think it through." At the boycott's first mass meeting, King delivered a speech that revealed not only his oratorical gifts and his expansive vision of African American liberation, but also a political strategy. Declaring "the only weapon we have . . . is the weapon of nonviolence," King situated the movement within U.S. civic traditions and *Cold War politics. "If we were incarcerated behind the iron curtains of a communistic nation we couldn't do this," he said, "but the great glory of American democracy is the right to protest for right." Underlining the threat that black protest could pose to U.S. foreign policy, King envisioned God proclaiming to the United States: "Be still and know that I am God—and if you don't obey Me I'm going to break the backbone of your power—and cast you out of the arms of your international and national relationships." He concluded with a prophetic call for African-American self-affirmation: "Right here in Montgomery, when the history books are written in the future, somebody will have to say, 'There lived a race of people, black people, fleecy locks and black complexion, who had the moral courage to stand up for their rights.' " Nonviolent direct action, Cold War realism, and appeals to what he later called "a sense of somebodiness" among *African Americans summed up King's ensuing strategy. After a 381-day bus boycott, a federal district court declared Alabama's bus-segregation statutes unconstitutional, and the U.S. *Supreme Court concurred. King told the Montgomery bus boycott story in *Stride toward Freedom* (1958).

Following up this victory, King in 1957 founded the *Southern Christian Leadership Conference (SCLC). Based in the black churches, SCLC led a series of campaigns in southern cities to expose the reality of *racism for all to see, with the goal of securing federal *civil rights legislation. A self-described reformer, King invoked the *Bible, the U.S. *Constitution, and the "American dream"—even though he declared in 1957 that he "could never accommodate [him]self" to *capitalism "because it denies necessities to the many to provide luxuries to the few." Moving to Atlanta in 1960, he became co-pastor, with his father, of Ebenezer Baptist Church. That fall he was imprisoned following a sit-in at an Atlanta snack bar. John F. *Kennedy's intervention to secure his release helped Kennedy solidify the black vote in the November presidential election.

King's strategy failed in Albany, Georgia, in 1962, when shrewd local authorities responded mildly to the demonstrations, but succeeded spectacularly in Birmingham, Alabama, in 1963. As the *television cameras rolled, Police Commissioner Eugene "Bull" Connor battled peaceful demonstrators with firehoses and snarling dogs, and imprisoned King, whose "Letter from Birmingham Jail" eloquently summarized his goals and strategy. That August, thousands flocked to Washington, D.C., for an interracial civil rights rally at the *Lincoln Memorial, where King delivered his memorable "I Have a Dream" speech. The landmark Civil Rights Act of 1964 resulted directly from these events. Further demonstrations led by King and SCLC, including one in Selma, Alabama, in 1965, led to the Voting Rights Act of 1965. The Selma demonstrations, which also triggered police violence, culminated in a major demonstration at the capital in Montgomery, where 25,000 protesters heard King's powerful oratory and sang the movement's anthem, "We Shall Overcome."

King's protests were predicated on Cold War realpolitik. America was "battling for the hearts of men in Asia and Africa," he declared, "and they aren't going to respect the United States . . . if she deprives men and women of the basic rights of life because of the color of their skins." Images of violence against protestors, broadcast worldwide, forced the federal government to intervene. The movement that King symbolized brought about the 1964–1965 civil rights legislation, which, along with the Supreme Court's earlier **Brown* v. *Board of Education* ruling, stands as enduring achievements of a freedom movement that toppled the formal racial caste system in the United States and created a new black sense of self.

By 1965, as King took up the issues of *poverty and structural *racism in northern cities, and began to criticize the *Vietnam War, his popularity waned. Young black activists in the *Student Non-Violent Coordinating Committee and the *Congress of Racial Equality, together with the *Nation of Islam leader *Malcolm X, urged a more militant approach. The *Federal Bureau of Investigation, seizing upon King's sexual indiscretions, sought to destroy him by a campaign of spying, blackmail, and humiliation. On 4 April 1968, as he lent support to striking garbage workers in Memphis, Tennessee, King was assassinated by James Earl Ray, a white racist who was convicted of the crime, though aspects of the killing remain unclear.

The brief career of Martin Luther King Jr. took him to the heights of world leadership, capped by the Nobel Peace Prize (1964), and led him to die fighting for garbage workers, urging a nonviolent revolution of the poor, and denouncing America's military role in Southeast Asia. His legacy as a symbol of nonviolent direct action and progressive social change continues to resonate throughout the world. Martin Luther King Jr. Day is observed as a national holiday on the third Monday in January.

[*See also* African American Religion; Baptists; Black Nationalism; Civil Rights Movement; Segregation, Racial; Sixties, The.]

• David Levering Lewis, *King: A Critical Biography*, 1970. David Garrow, *Bearing the Cross: Martin Luther King, Jr., and the Southern Christian Leadership Conference*, 1986. Adam Fairclough, *To Redeem the Soul of America: The Southern Christian Leadership Conference and Martin Luther King, Jr.*, 1987. Taylor Branch, *Parting the Waters: America in the King Years, 1954–63*, 1988. Adam Fairclough, *Martin Luther King, Jr.*, 1995.

—Timothy B. Tyson

KING PHILIP'S WAR (1675–1676), also called Metacom's War and Metacom's Rebellion. The war resulted from a transformation of Anglo-Indian relations in southern *New England. Except during the *Pequot War, Indians and the English settlers had avoided war since colonization began. But in the 1660s, the region's *fur trade ended as overhunting depleted the beaver population and English demographic and economic growth created pressures on Indians to cede additional lands. Natives' abilities to resist these pressures were limited by their continued population decline owing to European diseases and by the colonies' growing assertions of authority over them. These issues came to a head in March 1675 when a Christian Indian informed authorities of the *Plymouth Colony that the Wampanoag sachem, Metacom ("King Philip" to the English), was plotting all-out war. Metacom was the son of Massasoit, who had earlier befriended the Plymouth colonists. After the informer was murdered, three associates of Metacom were found guilty and hanged. In late June, bands of Wampanoags warriors began attacking Plymouth towns.

With the advent of war, Plymouth gained support from New England's other colonies and from Mohegans, Pequots, and many Christian Indians. Metacom's cause was aided by Nipmuc, Pocumtuc, and other Indians in central and western Massachusetts, who raided English towns during the Summer and Fall of 1675. Massachusetts's ability to respond was limited by many colonists' distrust of Christian Indians. Although "praying Indians" had proven themselves as warriors and scouts, the colony interned them on Deer Island in Boston harbor. In December 1675, the colonists launched a surprise attack on the Narragansetts in their Great Swamp Fort in Rhode Island, hoping to weaken them before they could join Metacom's cause. Despite killing several hundred warriors and noncombatants, they could not prevent the Narragansetts and Wampanoags from escaping southeastern New England and joining their western sympathizers. Metacom attempted to expand the war in January 1676 by meeting with French-allied Indians at Hoosic, New York, but a Mohawk attack broke up the gathering. Returning eastward, Metacom's forces launched attacks on outlying Massachusetts towns in hopes of pushing the line of settlement eastward, but disease and starvation weakened their ranks. In March, the western Indians began negotiating for peace while the Wampanoags and Narragansetts returned to their homelands in search of food. By July, English troops and their Indian allies had quashed the last pockets of resistance. Metacom himself was slain by a Christian Indian. Plymouth troops carried his head to the colony's capital, also called Plymouth, and put it on public display.

With the deaths of about 5,000 Indians of New England and 2,500 colonists (40 and 5 percent of their respective populations), King Philip's War is one of the bloodiest in American history relative to population size. The English precluded future resistance by executing and enslaving those most actively hostile and by replacing the alliances and trade networks, which formerly characterized their ties to Indians, with reservations and legislation that rendered all natives—whether supporting or opposing them during the war—as outcast subjects.

[*See also* Colonial Era; Indian History and Culture: From 1500 to 1800; Indian Wars.]

• Douglas Edward Leach, *Flintlock and Tomahawk: New England in King Philip's War,* 1958. Neal Salisbury, "Introduction," *The Sovereignty and Goodness of God,* ed. Neal Salisbury, 1997, pp. 1–60.

—Neal Salisbury

KINSEY, ALFRED (1894–1956), zoologist, sex researcher, reformer. Born in Hoboken, New Jersey, Kinsey was a sickly child. At his parents' insistence he spent much time attending the Methodist church, thoroughly absorbing the tenets of evangelical *Protestantism. Following two fruitless years at Stevens Institute of Technology, he broke with his domineering father and transferred to Bowdoin College in Maine. Majoring in biology, he graduated magna cum laude in 1916. Three years later he received a doctorate in zoology from Harvard. In 1920 he joined the faculty of Indiana University. Here he abandoned religion, raised a family, and won a reputation as a respected teacher and preeminent authority on gall wasps.

Privately, Kinsey experienced sadomasochistic and homoerotic urges deeply at odds with conventional morality. Like many closeted homosexuals of his day, he lived a double life, pursuing same-sex liaisons at every opportunity. Rejecting society's judgment that homosexuality was abnormal, he in 1938 began to study human sexuality, using essentially the same taxonomic methodology he had developed in his gall-wasp research. Attracting grants from the National Research Council and the Rockefeller Foundation, he founded the Institute for Sex Reserch at Indiana University in 1947. Defended against critics by the university president, Kinsey and his staff interviewed thousands of subjects nationwide. The value of the massive data they compiled remains contested, however, because of methodological and sampling flaws. In the studies that made him famous, *Sexual Behavior in the Human Male* (1948) and *Sexual Behavior in the Human Female* (1953), Kinsey and his coworkers shattered the conspiracy of silence surrounding sexuality. Showing that millions of American men and women routinely violated middle-class morality, these books sparked sustained debates about sexual mores and practices.

Along with the library and archive of his institute, Kinsey left three important legacies, summed up in his beliefs that human sexuality can be studied scientifically, that social and legal policies relating to sex should be informed by scientific knowledge, and that society should cultivate tolerance in the face of such diversity in sexual behavior.

[*See also* Gay and Lesbian Rights Movement; Methodism; Sexual Morality and Sex Reform; Social Science.]

• James H. Jones, *Alfred C. Kinsey: A Public/Private Life,* 1997. Jonathan Gathome-Hardy, *Sex the Measure of All Things: A Life of Alfred C. Kinsey,* 2000.

—James H. Jones

KISSINGER, HENRY (1923–), statesman. Born in Germany, Kissinger immigrated to the United States with his family in 1938 to escape anti-Jewish persecution. He received his B.A. and Ph.D. from Harvard University and became professor of government there in 1962, gaining attention for his scholarly work on *nuclear strategy. A consultant to the Kennedy-Johnson administrations, he was appointed by President Richard M. *Nixon in 1969 as assistant for national security affairs, a position he retained under Nixon and Gerald *Ford until 1975. From 1973 to 1977, he was secretary of state.

Deeply conservative, Kissinger believed that effective diplomacy must be backed by force and guided by toughmindedness rather than abstract ideals. At the same time, he championed a romantic notion of statesmanship and the role of such strong historical figures as Metternich and Bismarck. Like Nixon, he was manipulative and fearful of bureaucratic inertia, and was a perfect ally in Nixon's efforts to centralize policy-making in the White House.

As Nixon's envoy, Kissinger met secretly with the North Vietnamese starting in 1969, seeking an agreement that would preserve America's "credibility" yet allow U.S. disengagement from the *Vietnam War. When efforts to link improved relations with Moscow to a mutual withdrawal from South Vietnam proved unsuccessful, Nixon and Kissinger were reduced to offering Hanoi more favorable terms, finally negotiating a cease-fire-in-place in January 1973. In the interim, to counter increasing homefront opposition to the war, they exploited Sino-Soviet hostility to accomplish a dramatic "opening" to China and generated arms-control incentives and trade inducements to achieve a surprising détente with Russia, including the 1972 Strategic Arms Limitation Treaty (Salt I).

After the 1973 Arab-Israeli War provoked new *Cold War tensions, Kissinger devoted himself to a "shuttle diplomacy" that achieved revised truce lines on Israel's borders. Meanwhile, détente came under increasing criticism at home despite the Ford-Brezhnev Vladivostok accords (1974), establishing a SALT II framework, and the multination Helsinki Agreements (1975), formalizing Europe's post–World War II territorial boundaries and pledging support for *human rights. In the short run, Moscow's arms buildup, Soviet-Cuban intervention in Africa, and the collapse of South Vietnam (1975) led to widespread skepticism regarding Kissinger's professed hope that the USSR could be prodded and rewarded into becoming a nonrevolutionary power. Later, although Kissinger was one of the few high Nixon-administration officials to emerge unscathed from the *Watergate scandals, his secretive administrative style and power-oriented approach to foreign policy would elicit harsh criticism from journalists, historians, and biographers. His role in Nixon's secret bombing of Cambodia in 1969 and in the CIA-backed coup that resulted in the death of Chile's left-leaning president Salvador Allende in 1973 came in for special censure.

[*See also* Antiwar Movements; Central Intelligence Agency; Conservatism; Federal Government, Executive Branch: Department of State; Foreign Relations; National Security Council; Nuclear Arms Control Treaties; Nuclear Weapons.]

• Henry Kissinger, *White House Years,* 1979; *Years of Upheaval,* 1982; *Years of Renewal,* 1999. Raymond Garthoff, *Détente and Confrontation: American-Soviet Relations from Nixon to Reagan,* 2d ed., 1994. William Bundy, *A Tangled Web: The Making of Foreign Policy in the Nixon Presidency,* 1998.

—Keith L. Nelson

KLONDIKE. *See* Gold Rushes.

KNIGHTS OF LABOR. Founded in 1869 as a secret society of *Philadelphia garment cutters, the Noble and Holy Order of the Knights of Labor by the early 1880s emerged at the center of a powerful movement among working people determined to challenge the terms of American industrialism. Under the leadership first of the Philadelphia tailor Uriah S. Stephens (1821–1882) and then the former machinist Terence *Powderly, the Knights and their missionary message—"An Injury to One Is an Injury to All"—gained national prominence with a successful strike against Jay Gould's Wabash railway system in 1885. For the next year, the order experienced explosive growth, recruiting 700,000-plus members distributed in every state and territory. Knights of Labor cooperatives planned large-scale manufacturing and even *mining operations. Boycotts, strikes, or the threat of a strike by the Knights won negotiated settlements from hundreds of employers. Knights-based political tickets, operating both inside and outside the two-party system, competed in municipal elections nationwide. Perhaps most significant was the Knights' encompassing appeal to "producers" across the divisions of crafts, race, and gender.

The Knights' decline, however, was equally precipitous. Following unsuccessful strikes against the railroad and meatpacking industries, and suffering from the repression that followed Chicago's *Haymarket affair of 4 May 1886, the order collapsed into feuding disarray. The trade-union base of the labor movement moved into the new *American Federation of Labor. By the time the Knights linked up with the *Populist party in 1895, their ranks had dwindled to fewer than fifty thousand members, and the order had lost all real influence.

[*See also* Gilded Age; Industrialization; Labor Movements; Meatpacking and Meat Processing Industry; Populist Era; Railroads; Strikes and Industrial Conflict; Working-Class Life and Culture.]

• Gerald N. Grob, *Workers and Utopia: A Study of Ideological Conflict in the American Labor Movement, 1865–1900,* 1961. Leon Fink, *Workingmen's Democracy: The Knights of Labor and American Politics,* 1985.

—Leon Fink

KNOW-NOTHING PARTY. The group that would come to be known by this name arose in the 1840s amid nativist sentiment roused by the influx of Irish Catholics to East Coast cities. The American Republican party (later simply the American party) was founded in *New York City in 1843; in coalition with the Whigs, it elected a nativist mayor of New York in 1844. Advocating a ban on Catholic and foreign-born officeholders and a twenty-year time limit for naturalization, the party made headway in *Philadelphia also, sparking anti-Catholic riots. It gained momentum in 1849 when Charles B. Allen founded the secret Order of the Star Spangled Banner in New York. Lodges soon spread to other cities. When questioned, members were instructed to answer "I know nothing," leading the *New York Tribune* to deride them in 1853 as "Know Nothings."

In the early 1850s, as the *Whig party split over *slavery in the territories, a Whig faction that supported the *Compromise of 1850, called the Union Whigs, aligned with the American party. In 1854, the Whig James W. Barker replaced Allen as leader. The party now added to its platform a new theme, pro-Unionism, first enunciated by Thomas Whitney, editor of a nativist periodical called the *Republic.* The nation faced two major threats, Whitney warned: abolitionism and politicized Catholicism. Members now swore to do everything possible to preserve the Union. At a party convention in 1855, when the leadership added a platform plank proclaiming: "Congress ought not to legislate upon the subject of slavery within the Territories" northern delegates opposed to slavery extension bolted, dividing the party. In 1856, the southern Know Nothings nominated Millard *Fillmore for president. The election proved a disaster for the party, however. Amid deep sectional divisions evident in the vote for Democrat James *Buchanan and Republican John C. *Frémont, Fillmore carried only the slave state of Maryland. The party subsequently disbanded, and organized nativism subsided for a time.

[*See also* Antebellum Era; Anti-Catholic Movement; Antislavery; Civil War: Causes; Democratic Party; Immigration; Irish Americans; Nativist Movement; Political Parties; Republican Party; Roman Catholicism.]

• Ray A. Billington, *The Protestant Crusade, 1800–1860: A Study of the Origins of American Nativism,* 1938. Jean H. Baker, *Ambivalent Americans: The Know Nothing Party in Maryland,* 1977. Tyler Abinder, *Nativism and Slavery: The Northern Know Nothings and the Politics of the 1850s,* 1992.

—Thomas J. Curran

KOREAN WAR (1950–1953). This conflict grew out of the August 1945 division of Korea into U.S. and Soviet occupation zones. During *World War II, U.S. leaders believed that the Korean peninsula should eventually receive independence from Japan but that it would need a period of tutelage before enjoying full self-government. The United States made only vague agreements on Korea's future at wartime conferences with Soviet, Chinese, and British allies.

Background of the Conflict. As the Pacific war moved toward conclusion, American officials worried that the impending entry of the Soviet Union into the fight against Japan would result in Soviet occupation and domination of the entire peninsula. Some Soviet troops entered Korea after the Soviet Union declared war on Japan on 8 August 1945, but they did not advance rapidly. A week later, Washington proposed that the Soviets occupy the country as far south as the thirty-eighth parallel and that the United States occupy the rest. Soviet Premier Joseph Stalin agreed.

Stalin wanted the peninsula unified under a friendly regime. The Americans primarily wanted to contain Soviet influence. Despite a qualified agreement in December 1945 for a provisional national government and a multipower trusteeship, subsequent negotiations failed to produce either. In November 1947, beset by unrest within its zone and burgeoning commitments elsewhere, the United States pushed through the General Assembly of the *United Nations a resolution calling for elections throughout Korea aimed at creating an independent government. When the Soviets refused to permit a UN commission into its zone, the United States, with UN approval, went ahead on 10 May 1948 with elections in the south. In August, the Republic of Korea (ROK) was inaugurated at Seoul with the conservative Syngman Rhee as its president. In December, the UN General Assembly recognized the ROK as Korea's only legitimate government, with authority below the thirty-eighth parallel. In the north, meanwhile, the Soviets had set up the leftist Democratic People's Republic of Korea (DPRK) under Premier Kim Il Sung.

Soviet troops withdrew from the north at the end of 1948; American troops left the south the following June. Yet worries continued about armed clashes along the thirty-eighth parallel between units of the ROK and DPRK armies and ongoing guerrilla activities. In the fall of 1949, guerrillas launched an offensive against the ROK army and police that lasted for several months.

Meanwhile, Kim Il Sung pressed Stalin to support a full-scale North Korean military offensive to overthrow the ROK. Stalin hesitated, fearing the U.S. response. At the end of January 1950, perhaps encouraged by U.S. Secretary of State Dean *Acheson's omission of South Korea from a speech describing the American defense perimeter in the Pacific, Stalin agreed to plans for such a venture. In April, he began funneling heavy weapons to the DPRK army. In May, Kim received the go-ahead from Mao Tsetung (Mao Zedong), the leader of the People's Republic of China. Already the Chinese had returned to the north tens of thousands of Koreans who had fought on the communist side in the Chinese civil war and would now comprise the lead units of the DPRK army.

The Fighting Begins. The DPRK surprise attack began on 25 June 1950. The North Koreans advanced rapidly, but the United States responded vigorously, fearing a loss of international credibility if its client fell. Washington took the issue to the UN Security Council, which the Soviet Union was boycotting, and secured resolutions, calling for a cease-fire and the withdrawal of North Korean forces behind the thirty-eighth parallel and urging members to provide assistance to help the ROK repulse the attack. U.S. President Harry S. *Truman approved the use of American air forces from Japan in support of ROK resistance. On 30 June, with the North Koreans still advancing, he committed U.S. ground forces to Korea with the objective of restoring the thirty-eighth parallel. On 7 July, after passage of a Security Council resolution calling on the United States to designate a commander of UN forces in Korea, Truman appointed General Douglas *MacArthur. Rhee immediately placed ROK forces under him.

Retreating U.S. troops and remnants of the ROK army fought desperately just to maintain a foothold around the southeastern port of Pusan. Then, on 15 September, the U.N. command launched a counteroffensive at Inch'ŏn on the west coast, sending the North Koreans into a headlong retreat. By the end of the month, U.N. units approached the thirty-eighth parallel. Only some 25,000 DPRK troops managed to escape across that line, and on the thirtieth ROK units crossed in pursuit. Three days earlier, Washington had authorized MacArthur to move his ground forces into North Korea to destroy enemy forces. On 7 October, a UN General Assembly resolution called for action "to ensure conditions of stability in Korea" and to establish "a unified, independent and democratic government" there. Non-Korean units in the UN command crossed the thirty-eighth parallel the next day.

The Chinese Intervene. The Chinese communists already had warned the United States that they would enter the fray if non-Korean forces moved into North Korea. Irate over a U.S. decision of 27 June 1950 to protect the Nationalist Chinese on Taiwan, suspecting Washington of aggressive designs on the mainland, and anxious to reestablish China to its historic place in East Asia, the government of China began considering intervention in Korea in July. Still, concerned about American firepower, including *nuclear weapons, uncertain of Soviet air support, and anxious to concentrate on domestic reconstruction, Mao did not decide conclusively to intervene until 13 October. The "Chinese People's Volunteers" (CPV) entered Korea six days later, concentrating their first offensive on ROK units.

Although the Chinese intervention caused an urgent reevaluation of policy in Washington, MacArthur pleaded successfully that his instructions not be altered. On 24 November, he launched what he hoped would be an "end-the-war offensive." The CPV countered with their own offensive, however, producing what MacArthur conceded was "an entirely new war."

The Chinese offensive of late November, combined with another early in 1951, sent UN ground forces reeling southward for nearly two months. During that time, U.S. allies, especially Great Britain, and *Cold War neutrals, led by India, worked in the UN to contain the war. They delayed the imposition of sanctions against China until May 1951 and limited them to relatively mild economic and political measures.

Two facts eased their task: First, top officials in Washington, adhering to a Europe-first strategy, preferred to limit the war in Korea; second, by late January, UN forces had ended their retreat below Seoul and were again moving northward. MacArthur pressed for authority to extend his operations into China with the objective of clearing the peninsula of enemy forces and persisted in making public his disagreements with official policy. On 11 April 1951, Truman relieved him of all commands. Clearly Washington was willing to settle for its initial objective of restoring the status quo prior to the beginning of the war. With the failure of Chinese spring offensives and the establishment of a relatively stable battle line mostly north of the thirty-eighth parallel, that objective appeared within reach.

Armistice. Truce talks commenced on 10 July 1951. On 27 November, after long debate, the communist side accepted the UN command's position that the armistice line be the battle line rather than the indefensible thirty-eighth parallel. The issue of the fate of prisoners of war remained unresolved, however. The Americans insisted on the principle of no forced repatriation, whereas the communists clung to the more conventional position of automatic repatriation.

While UN ground forces had advanced slightly northward during the fall of 1951, by the spring of 1952 the communists were well dug in, and UN operations thereafter were mostly limited to air strikes on North Korea. Kim appears from the spring of 1952 to have desired an end to the fighting. Mao and Stalin resisted a concession on Chinese prisoners, however, and not until 4 June 1953, with a new Republican administration headed by President Dwight D. *Eisenhower in power in Washington, did the communists concede the point. Stalin's death on 5 March 1953, coupled with the U.S. bombing of dikes in North Korea in May and the threat of a termination of armistice talks and of further military escalation, paved the way for key concessions on the communist side. After delays resulting from Rhee's attempt to sabotage any settlement that did not achieve Korea's unification, the armistice was signed by the UN command, the North Koreans, and the Chinese on 27 July.

Aftereffects. The war left Korea divided, but the destruction caused by the conflict discouraged a repeat performance. Koreans suffered at least 2 million civilian and probably more than 1 million combat casualties. Chinese casualties were anywhere from 382,000 (Chinese estimate) to 1 to 1.5 million (U.S. estimate). American forces endured more than 33,000 deaths as a result of battlefield injuries, over 20,000 more from other causes, and a total of more than 142,000 casualties. The United States and the ROK provided over 90 percent of the manpower to the UN command, but the fifteen other contributor-countries suffered more than 17,000 casualties.

To discourage a disappointed Syngman Rhee from resuming hostilities, the United States made clear that it would not support such a move and attempted to mollify Rhee with a defensive military alliance and large-scale economic aid. To deter the other side, the United States and other contributors to the UN cause declared that any renewed hostilities would in all likelihood not be confined to Korea. The war already had sparked massive rearmament programs in the United States and western Europe, which narrowed the Soviet bloc's advantage in conventional forces and widened the U.S. superiority in nuclear weapons.

In the United States, the war imposed limited sacrifices; indeed, it helped to produce an economic boom. Yet it also added fuel to a domestic Red Scare; in 1952, widespread frustration with the continuing stalemate helped propel the Republicans to victory over the incumbent Democrats in both the presidential and congressional elections. On the eve of the 1952 election, Eisenhower dramatically pledged to go to Korea in his quest to end the unpopular war. Finally, the war provoked a high state of military readiness that would last for the remainder of the Cold War.

[*See also* Anticommunism; Fifties, The; Foreign Relations: U.S. Relations with Asia; McCarthy, Joseph; National Security Council Document #68; Nuclear Strategy.]

• Bruce Cumings, *The Origins of the Korean War,* 2 vols., 1981–1990. James I. Matray, ed., *Historical Dictionary of the Korean War,* 1991. Cold War International History Project, Woodrow Wilson Center for Scholars, *Bulletin* nos. 3, 6–7 (Fall 1993 and Winter 1995–1996). Sergei Goncharvo, John W. Lewis, and Xue Litai, *Uncertain Partners: Stalin, Mao, and the Korean War,* 1993. Jian Chen, *China's Road to the Korean War,* 1994. William Stueck, *The Korean War,* 1995. Shu Guang Zhang, *Mao's Military Romanticism,* 1995. Burton Kaufman, *The Korean War,* 2d ed., 1997.

—William Stueck

KOREMATSU* v. *UNITED STATES (1944), *Supreme Court decision arising from the 1942 military order forcing West Coast Japanese Americans into "assembly centers" from which they were interned in "relocation camps." Fred Korematsu of *San Francisco, an American-born citizen of Japanese ancestry, attempted to enlist when *World War II began but was rejected for medical reasons. Working in a defense job when the internment began, he moved, changed his name, and claimed to be Mexican American. He was arrested, sentenced to five years in prison, immediately paroled, and interned in the camp at Topaz, Utah. By a 6–3 vote, the Supreme Court rejected his appeal. Writing for the majority, Justice Hugo *Black conceded that "all legal restrictions which curtail the *civil rights of a single racial group are immediately suspect" and required "the most rigid scrutiny." Further, Black questioned the army's contention that the impossibility of distinguishing between loyal and disloyal Japanese Americans justified "the temporary exclusion of the entire group." Nevertheless, he argued that the internment policy reflected legitimate military considerations, not "antagonism to those of Japanese ancestry." To blame the case on "racial prejudice, without reference to the real military dangers . . . ," Black went on, "merely confuses the issue." Since Korematsu was charged only with remaining in a restricted area and failing to report to the assembly center, the Court did not explicitly address the constitutionality of forced relocation.

Justices Owen Roberts, Frank Murphy, and Robert Jackson dissented. The internment program that had ensnared Korematsu did not really rest on military grounds, argued Murphy, but "mainly upon questionable racial and sociological grounds not ordinarily within the realm of expert military judgment." Japanese Americans should have been treated "on an individual basis," Murphy argued, through "investigations and hearings to separate the loyal from the disloyal."

[*See also* Asian Americans; Incarceration of Japanese Americans; Racism; World War II: Domestic Effects.]

• Roger Daniels, *The Decision to Relocate the Japanese Americans,* 1985. Peter Trans, *Justice at War,* 1993.

—Paul Finkelman

KORESH, DAVID. *See* Millennialism and Apocalypticism; Religion.

KU KLUX KLAN, the most notorious of terrorist groups that arose in the *Reconstruction Era to uphold white supremacy and *Democratic party rule in the *South. Founded as a social club (*kuklos,* the Greek word for circle, inspired the name) by six Confederate veterans in Pulaski, Tennessee, in 1866, the Klan soon became a powerful and frightening vehicle of vigilante violence and lawlessness. Racial terrorists from all walks of life adopted the Klan's white hoods and secret rituals to protect their identities and lend an aura of legitimacy to their activities. Their aim was to punish anyone perceived as threatening white supremacy, including assertive black workers, black or white teachers in black schools, and those who violated interracial sexual taboos. The overwhelming focus of Klan violence and intimidation, however, was *Republican party politicians, black and white, and black voters. During the election year of 1868, in Louisiana alone, the Klan and other terrorist groups murdered between eight hundred and one thousand people, the vast majority of whom were Republican leaders, political candidates, and others challenging white, Democratic rule. Similar murderous waves across the South kept countless black voters away from the polls. A congressional investigation and anti-Klan state and federal legislation diminished the Klan's influence after 1871, but the movement left a powerful legacy.

Later, historians, novelists, and filmmakers offered racist apologies for the Reconstruction Klan. The most notorious of these, D. W. *Griffith's film *Birth of a Nation* (1915), based on Thomas Dixon's 1905 novel *The Clansman,* inspired a second Klan movement. This revived Klan, founded at Stone Mountain, Georgia, by William J. Simmons and later taken over by the Texan Hiram W. Evans, differed markedly from the first. It attracted millions of male and female members from throughout the nation, especially in the Midwest and *West, enriching paid recruiters (called Kleagles) as well as Simmons, Evans, and other leaders at the national headquarters in Atlanta. It was racist, but in an era when the institutions of white supremacy faced no serious challenge, race was not the exclusive focus. The second Klan's central message was that white Protestant hegemony was threatened by Roman Catholics, Jews, *African Americans, immigrants, Prohibition violation, *gambling and other crimes, political corruption, sexual immorality, materialism, and the erosion of *religion and traditional family values. This Klan sometimes used intimidation and violence, but most frequently targeted fellow white Protestants who violated traditional morality. Political mobilization, parades, and social events were the Klan chapters' primary activities. By the mid-1920s, the Klan elected its candidates to local office in many communities, dominated politics in Indiana, Colorado, Oregon, Oklahoma, Alabama, and other states, and exerted a strong national influence within both major parties. A motion to condemn the Klan bitterly divided the 1924 Democratic party convention. The second Klan declined dramatically after 1925 as a result of bitter divisions among Klan leaders, the imprisonment of Indiana "Grand Dragon" D. C. Stephenson on rape and manslaughter charges, and declining faith that the Klan could accomplish its goals.

In the following decades, pockets of support lingered, and racial vigilantes continued to invoke the Klan's name and regalia. During the era of the *civil rights movement, a variety of Klan organizations surfaced with newfound support and, like their predecessors of the Reconstruction Era, attacked and terrorized African Americans and racial reformers. As the twentieth century ended, isolated Klan groups, while generally discredited, continued to perpetuate an occasionally violent right-wing subculture.

[*See also* Anti-Catholic Movement; Anti-Semitism; Eighteenth Amendment; Immigration; Immigration Law; Nativist Movement; Progressive Era; Protestantism; Racism; Roman Catholicism; Temperance and Prohibition; Twenties, The.]

• Allen W. Trelease, *White Terror: The Ku Klux Klan Conspiracy and Southern Reconstruction,* 1971. David M. Chalmers, *Hooded Americanism: The History of the Ku Klux Klan,* 3d ed., 1981. Nancy MacLean, *Behind the Mask of Chivalry: The Making of the Second Ku Klux Klan,* 1994.

—Leonard J. Moore

L

LABOR MARKETS. The term "labor market" does not refer to a particular location or set of institutions. Instead it describes the processes of labor allocation in an economy, that is, the methods by which employers fill vacancies and workers find jobs, as well as the internal allocation of labor within businesses, households, and other economic organizations. The interaction of supply and demand in the market determines wages and employment.

The historical study of labor markets has two major objectives. The first is to describe how labor is allocated over time and how markets have evolved. The second is to document the consequences for wages, employment, the distribution of income and jobs, and the overall efficiency of the market. Although American labor markets have rarely if ever achieved perfect efficiency, the American economy's sustained growth and American workers' high standard of living could not have been achieved without the development of effective labor-market institutions.

The Colonial Period. From the beginning of European settlement in North America, American labor markets have been characterized by the scarcity of labor in relationship to land and natural resources. Natural abundance raised the productivity of labor, enabling ordinary Americans to enjoy a higher standard of living than comparable Europeans. Realizing these economic opportunities required labor-market mechanisms capable of overcoming the obstacles of high passage costs and imperfect communication.

In the colonial period, labor moved in three ways: free migration, *indentured servitude, and the forced migration of African slaves. Because of the high cost of transatlantic passage, only a small fraction of potential migrants could afford transport to the Americas. The cost barrier was especially problematic for the young, landless laborers who stood to gain the most from such migration.

Under the indenture system, migrants signed contracts with merchants in England committing themselves to work for a specified period of years in exchange for passage to the New World. Once in America, the merchants sold these contracts to planters needing labor. Because land abundance made it hard for planters to hire free labor, the use of unfree workers—either indentured servants or slaves—was the only way they could expand cultivation beyond the limits set by their family's labor. Demand for servants varied geographically, depending on crops and climates. Consistent with the existence of a well-functioning market, terms of service appear to have varied with individual productivity and employment conditions in the specific locality.

In the mainland British colonies, African slaves began to replace indentured servants as the principal source of unfree labor in the late seventeenth century. From 1700 to 1770, the proportion of blacks in the Chesapeake region grew from 13 percent to around 40 percent. In South Carolina and Georgia, the black proportion of the population climbed from 18 percent to about 45 percent in the same time period. The transition from indentured European to enslaved African labor reflected the effects of shifting supply-and-demand conditions. Improved economic conditions in Europe after 1650 reduced the supply of servants and raised their cost. Meanwhile, increasing competition in the slave trade caused slave prices to fall.

Because export opportunities were more limited in northern colonies, they imported few slaves. Yet abundant land created opportunities for small-scale agriculture in Pennsylvania, New York, and New Jersey that enabled employers to attract indentured servants throughout the eighteenth century. In *New England, where farming was less profitable and little demand existed for hired labor, immigrants, either free or slave, were infrequent.

By 1776, market forces had created a sharp regional division in labor-market regimes. Across the *South, large-scale plantation agriculture utilizing slave labor was well established. In the North, family farms predominated. Hired labor might be used on occasion, but limited markets did not justify expansion. What had emerged by accident was soon codified into law. After the Revolution, all the northern states adopted some form of gradual emancipation, and in 1787 the *Northwest Ordinance prohibited the introduction of *slavery into territories north of the Ohio River.

From Independence to World War I. Three related developments dominated the history of labor markets between the *Revolutionary War and *World War I: westward expansion, the growth of manufacturing, and mass *immigration. From 1800 to 1910, the labor force grew from 2.3 million to 37.5 million. In these same years, the agricultural labor force's share of total employment dropped from 74 percent to 31 percent. Manufacturing, which had employed 3 percent of the labor force in 1800, employed 22 percent of all workers in 1910.

American independence eliminated British restrictions on expansion and initiated a century-long process of western settlement. Fertile land and abundant natural resources drew population toward less densely settled regions in the *West. This movement was accelerated by improvements in transportation, which lowered shipping costs while increasing the speed, comfort, and reliability of travel.

Northern and southern responses to frontier expansion differed, with profound effects on settlement patterns and regional development. The large size of southern slave plantations made it relatively easy for planters to recover the fixed costs of obtaining information and relocating production onto new lands. Plantations were also largely self-sufficient, requiring little urban or commercial infrastructure to make them economically viable. Well-established slave markets facilitated migration by enabling western planters to acquire additional labor in the East. In the North, the small scale of family farms made it more difficult to recover the costs of migration. Consequently, the task of mobilizing labor fell on promoters who bought up large tracts of land at low prices and then subdivided them. Promoters offered generous loans, invested heavily in recruiting settlers, and actively encouraged the development of such urban services as blacksmith shops, grain merchants, wagon builders, and general stores. Population density, *urbanization, and *industrialization thus were all much higher in the North than in the South in 1860.

As improved transportation lowered the cost of midwestern

agricultural products, the value of agricultural land and labor declined in New England. The result was a pool of underemployed agricultural labor—especially young women—who were available to work in the manufacturing establishments that developed in the Northeast during the *War of 1812 and after the imposition of protective *tariffs in 1816.

Throughout the nineteenth century, migration costs remained a significant though declining obstacle to transatlantic labor movements. Immigration accelerated in the late 1840s following the Irish potato famine of 1845–1847 and the failed German revolution of 1848. While northeastern industries drew arrivals who had few resources (mostly Irish), agriculture and commerce in the *Middle West attracted wealthier immigrants (mostly German). Few immigrants, however, settled in the South.

More than 25 million immigrants arrived in the United States between 1870 and 1915. By 1900, about 20 percent of the population was foreign born, but because working-age males immigrated in disproportionate numbers, they constituted about 25 percent of the labor force. Immigrants were even more concentrated in manufacturing, where they often comprised a majority of the labor force. In 1907–1908, for example, foreign-born workers represented 72 percent of the factory labor force in textiles, 58 percent in iron and steel, 61 percent in slaughtering and meatpacking, and 34 percent in boots and shoes.

The close correlation between immigration levels and the American *business cycle, on the one hand, and the narrowing of transatlantic wage differentials, on the other, indicates a growing integration of American and European labor markets. The mechanisms linking European villages to American factories relied on informal networks of friends and family as well as the recruitment efforts of steamship agents, employment agencies, and employers. The increased supply of labor that resulted appears to have depressed wages among less-skilled workers who competed directly with the new arrivals. Workers with more skills, however, may actually have benefited from the influx of unskilled labor. Rising immigration and its adverse effects on less-skilled workers produced increasing anti-immigrant sentiments. But efforts to limit immigration proved unsuccessful, except on the West Coast, where the Chinese Exclusion Act (1882) effectively constrained labor supplies.

Mass immigration and the post–Civil War expansion of manufacturing brought substantial changes in the nature of employment relationships. In the *Antebellum Era, most people worked on family farms or in small artisanal workshops. After the *Civil War, however, urbanization, improved transportation and communication, and the introduction of high-volume, capital-intensive production processes created enormous factories. Workers became more isolated from managers and more dependent on wage labor.

One symptom of these changes was growing public concern about industrial *unemployment and other labor issues. The late nineteenth century also saw a considerable increase in labor conflict. Early labor organizations had functioned primarily as benevolent associations—providing mutual insurance for illness, death, or unemployment. But after the Civil War effective labor unions began to emerge for the first time.

During the 1880s, the *Knights of Labor enjoyed a brief surge of popularity, but membership collapsed after a series of failures in 1886. In the 1890s, the *American Federation of Labor (AFL) consolidated the union movement, with membership reaching 2 million (5.9 percent of the labor force) by 1910.

The First World War to the Late Twentieth Century. Declining rates of natural increase and immigration restrictions imposed in the 1920s slowed the growth of population and labor force in the twentieth century. Nonetheless, by 1995 the labor force had increased to 132 million. Agricultural employment continued to decline, now falling in both absolute and relative terms. By 1990, just 3.4 million workers (2.6 percent of the labor force) were employed in agriculture. Meanwhile, manufacturing's share of the labor force had dropped to only 17 percent. The service-producing and government sectors grew most rapidly, employing close to two-thirds of all workers by 1990. Accompanying these sectoral shifts were pronounced changes in labor-force composition, as more women entered the workplace and children and older men exited. By the 1990s, nearly 45 percent of the labor force was female, up from about 18 percent in 1900. Westward expansion had ceased, but shifting regional fortunes continued to produce substantial population redistribution. Finally, the twentieth century was characterized by the growth of long-term employment relationships and increasing government regulation of labor markets.

World War I ended mass immigration, and following the war Congress imposed a stringent quota system. Immigration rates remained low until 1965, when Congress liberalized immigration policies. Arrivals increased from 3.3 million in the 1960s to 4.5 million in the 1970s, and continued to grow into the 1990s, raising concern about the labor-market impacts of uncontrolled immigration.

The interruption of immigration caused by World War I initiated new patterns of internal population movements. Although the South's defeat in the Civil War ended slavery, postbellum southern labor markets had remained largely isolated from the rest of the country. The shock of the war, emancipation, and the slow growth of demand for the region's principal crop—cotton—caused southern wages to fall well below northern levels by the 1880s. Yet migration to the North was limited. Northern employers could meet their labor needs with immigrant labor, and potential southern migrants lacked contacts to help them find work in northern cities. Only during World War I did northern employers begin actively to recruit southern workers. Northward migration, once begun, continued into the 1970s, interrupted only by the Great Depression.

The effects of this population redistribution on regional wages became apparent in the 1960s with a significant narrowing of interregional differences in wages and earnings. By 1980, per capita incomes in much of the South had reached approximately 90 percent of the national average, up from about 60 percent in 1940.

In the 1970s and 1980s, the industrial heartland of the Northeast and Midwest experienced a series of shocks caused by rising energy prices and increasing international competition. Declining manufacturing employment coupled with the shift of service-sector jobs to the South and West initiated a new pattern of population movements in the 1980s.

World War I also contributed to changes in employment relationships. Prompted partly by the high costs of labor turnover, employers had adopted policies to encourage longer-term employment relationships. Tight wartime labor markets accelerated this process and led companies to establish centralized personnel departments that shifted responsibility for hiring, promotion, wage setting, and discipline away from shop foremen. These developments heralded the emergence of modern "internal" labor markets.

The twentieth century also brought expanded government intervention in labor markets. Protective legislation limiting hours and regulating working conditions was initially restricted mainly to women and children. The turning point came in the 1930s with New Deal legislation, which regulated *industrial relations and other aspects of the labor market. In 1938, the Fair Labor Standards Act for the first time established national minimum wage and maximum hours standards.

New Deal laws contributed to a rapid expansion of union membership. Between 1934 and 1938, membership nearly doubled, reaching close to 30 percent of nonagricultural workers. It continued to climb in the 1940s, reaching an all-time high of close to 40 percent of nonagricultural workers in 1953. Unionization rates declined consistently thereafter, however, despite a rise in public-sector unions after the 1960s.

The introduction of federal *unemployment insurance and passage of the *Employment Act of 1946, which committed the government to pursue macroeconomic policies intended to insure full employment, represent other important instances of government intervention in the labor market. While scholars disagree over the effect of macroeconomic policies on employment, workers at the end of the twentieth century were much less likely than workers in 1900 to become unemployed, although those who did were likely to spend considerably more time between jobs.

The pattern of women's participation in the labor force has changed markedly. In 1900, less than 6 percent of married women worked outside the home; by 1990, more than 50 percent held paying jobs. This dramatic shift is attributable to changes in both supply—falling fertility rates, increased education, and the women's movement—and demand—the rise of white-collar and clerical jobs, evolving social attitudes, and technological changes reducing the physical demands of most kinds of work. With rising female participation came an increase in relative wages. Median female earnings were about 70 percent of median male earnings in the late 1990s, up from around 55 percent in 1900. Women continued to be disproportionately concentrated in some occupations and substantially underrepresented in others, however.

As women entered the labor force, other groups of workers left. Rising education and legal prohibitions substantially reduced *child labor. Participation among elderly workers declined with a shift toward earlier retirement. More years of education and earlier retirement contributed to a reduction in total work over the average worker's lifetime, as did the decline in the length of the average workweek from sixty hours at the turn of the century to around forty hours by 1940.

The economic progress of *African Americans was painfully slow from emancipation until the mid–twentieth century, but between 1940 and 1980 black male wages rose from 43 percent of white male wages to just over 84 percent. While considerable evidence indicated that increases in the quality and quantity of education and training were important in improving economic conditions among blacks, equally compelling evidence suggested that federal antidiscrimination programs adopted in the 1960s were instrumental in promoting progress as well.

Labor Markets and U.S. History. Labor markets have played a prominent role in shaping the development of the United States. The early settlement of the colonies, slavery, westward migration, industrialization, immigration, the changing status of blacks and women, the rise of high school and college education, and the growth of retirement are among the many phenomena that cannot be understood without examining the influence of labor markets. Despite the impressive efficiency with which changing labor-market institutions have mobilized human resources in response to economic incentives, imperfections in market allocation have been at least as important in shaping the country's history.

[*See also* Agriculture; Automation and Computerization; Congress of Industrial Organizations; Cotton Industry; Expansionism; Factory System; Immigrant Labor; Immigration Law; Labor Movements; New Deal Era, The; Scientific Management; Technology; Tobacco Industry; Women in the Labor Force; Work; Working-Class Life and Culture.]

• Stanley Lebergott, *Manpower in Economic Growth: The American Record since 1800*, 1964. Daniel Nelson, *Managers and Workers: Origins of the New Factory System in the United States, 1880–1920*, 1975. Sanford M. Jacoby, *Employing Bureaucracy: Managers, Unions, and the Transformation of Work in American Industry, 1900–1945*, 1985. Alexander Keyssar, *Out of Work: The First Century of Unemployment in Massachusetts*, 1986. Gavin Wright, *Old South, New South: Revolutions in the Southern Economy since the Civil War*, 1986. John Bodnar, *The Transplanted: A History of Immigrants in Urban America*, 1987. Robert William Fogel, *Without Consent or Contract: The Rise and Fall of American Slavery*, 1989. Bruce Laurie, *Artisans into Workers: Labor in Nineteenth-Century America*, 1989. Claudia Goldin, *Understanding the Gender Gap: An Economic History of American Women*, 1990. Robert A. Margo, *Race and Schooling in the South, 1880–1950*, 1990. David W. Galenson, "The Settlement and Growth of the Colonies: Population, Labor, and Economic Development," in *The Cambridge Economic History of the United States*, ed. Stanley L. Engerman and Robert E. Gallman, vol. 1, 1996, pp. 135–208. Joshua L. Rosenbloom, "The Extent of the Labor Market in the United States," *Social Science History* 22.3 (Fall 1998): 287–318.

—Joshua L. Rosenbloom

LABOR MOVEMENTS. Protective organizations appeared among working people as early as the 1750s, well before the industrial revolution in the United States. By the first years of the nineteenth century, journeymen artisans organized independently of their masters to protect the prices for their work and their terms of employment and apprenticeship. For the first half of the century, however, prosecutions for conspiracy left such organizations on the legal margins. As the traditional master-journeymen relationship evolved into a more market-oriented association, journeymen ignited a period of intense labor organization and conflict.

The Antebellum Era. Most early trade unionists were skilled workers, but others joined the fray as well. Female textile operatives in Lowell, Massachusetts; women shoe binders throughout Massachusetts and northern *New England; and less-skilled common laborers caught the infectious spirit of revolt. The demand for shorter hours proved a common bond, and the movement for a ten-hour day won support in *Boston, *Philadelphia, and other cities. However, a depression between 1837 and 1843 led to the collapse of this first general trade-union movement.

The labor movement took on new life during the 1850s. Trade unions of skilled iron molders, puddlers, and textile workers joined forces with struggling societies of artisan craftsmen—printers, shoemakers, and tailors. The massive *immigration of Irish and German workers between 1845 and 1855 provided cheap labor for *railroad and canal construction as well as craftsmen to compete in the labor market. A "great shoemakers' strike" in 1860 reflected a last, massive stand by craft workers—but not the new factory operatives, who would come to dominate the industry.

The *Civil War profoundly changed the American labor movement. By the war's end, the trade-union movement included new and old trades such as the Brotherhood of the Footboard (locomotive engineers) and a revived Iron Molders' Union. In 1866 the first truly national organization, the National Labor Union (NLU), led by William Sylvis, appeared. The NLU, like the new unions of wage earners in shoemaking, the Knights and Daughters of St. Crispin, demanded the eight-hour day and the right to organize. It also challenged the basis of the wage system by calling for land reform and cooperative production. Freedmen organized under the auspices of the Colored National Labor Union in cities like Baltimore, Maryland, and Richmond, Virginia, giving added salience to labor's demand that "wage slavery" be ended.

The Gilded Age through World War I. The NLU collapsed during the early 1870s, soon to be replaced by a new fledgling national organization, the Noble and Holy Order of the *Knights of Labor (KOL). Founded in 1869 by Philadelphia garment cutters as a secret fraternal society, the KOL grew rapidly after the 1877 railroad strikes and under Terence *Powderly became the dynamic center of labor organizing. The Knights organized all sectors of workers, regardless of skill, and also attracted women and *African Americans. But white hostility to black workers, especially in the *South where the latter were concentrated, doomed the KOL's attempt to practice biracial unionism.

The labor movement reached its nineteenth-century peak in 1886 with more than 700,000 workers in the Knights and another 250,000 in trade unions. That growth quickly eroded however, as employers resisted union growth and broke strikes. By 1890, KOL membership had dwindled to 200,000, and it declined even more rapidly thereafter.

The 1890s represented a turning point for the labor movement. The *American Federation of Labor (AFL), led by the former socialist cigarmaker Samuel *Gompers, preached a philosophy of "pure and simple" trade unionism. Gompers urged skilled workers to "look to your union" and to distance themselves from utopian campaigns to overthrow *capitalism. While he stressed caution, some workers and AFL-affiliated unions during the 1890s proved more venturesome, particularly the United Mine Workers of America (UMWA), the Brewery Workers, the Western Federation of Miners, and the Boot and Shoe Workers, which included former Knights, Populists, and socialists. The American Railway Union (ARU), led by Eugene V. *Debs, embraced all categories of railroad workers but was destroyed by federal judicial and military power in the 1894 *Pullman strike and boycott.

Unions affiliated with the AFL benefited from the economic growth that followed the depression of 1893–1897. Trade unions expanded rapidly between 1897 and 1904. The UMWA secured a national agreement in 1898 for most bituminous coal production, and the International Association of Machinists in 1901 won a national contract covering major firms in the metal trades. In response, many employers mounted an open-shop (anti-union) drive that stymied labor's growth. Facing a period of crisis, the AFL turned to politics. In the congressional campaign of 1906 and later, the AFL supported the *Democratic party in the hopes of winning more union-friendly government policies.

Socialists and syndicalists contested Gompers's power before *World War I. In 1902 and 1912 socialists challenged his presidency. The syndicalist *Industrial Workers of the World (IWW), formed in 1905, confronted the AFL from another direction. Revolts by less-skilled immigrant workers in McKees Rocks, Pennsylvania; Lawrence, Massachusetts; Paterson, New Jersey; and other eastern manufacturing centers foreshadowed a new phase of labor mobilization, as did the IWW's organizing success among western miners, timber workers, and *migratory agricultural workers.

The outbreak of World War I created both opportunities and perils for the labor movement. As war orders drove unemployment levels to near zero and American workers struck to win gains, the Woodrow *Wilson administration designed new federal mechanisms to maintain labor peace. Following America's entry into the war in April 1917, Wilson created a War Labor Board (WLB) to investigate and resolve labor disputes. The WLB endorsed wage increases, the eight-hour day, collective bargaining for union members, and representation of nonunion workers through shop committees. By the war's end, 4.2 million American workers belonged to unions. The AFL now included quasi-industrial unions in steel and meatpacking. Large numbers of black workers for the first time entered the *mass-production industries of northern cities, where they maintained, at best, an uneasy relationship with white-dominated unions.

The 1920s and the New Deal Era. The immediate postwar years weakened the labor movement. *Unemployment rose and employers, freed from the WLB oversight, fought to roll back wartime union gains. A major strike wave in 1919 resulted in labor defeats. Left-wingers split into rival socialist and communist factions following the Bolshevik revolution in Russia, and a wave of antiradical hysteria shattered their influence within the labor movement. Employers promoted a new open-shop movement through the "American Plan," and they fought unions with company welfare programs and more worker-friendly forms of *scientific management. As a result, the proportion of organized workers fell by half.

The Depression of the 1930s and the consequent suffering of broad segments of the working class reenergized labor organizing across industrial America. The inauguration of Franklin Delano *Roosevelt as president in 1933 brightened the prospects for the labor movement's renewal, as labor's political influence within the New Deal coalition stimulated expectations of a more sympathetic government climate. Passage of the National Industrial Recovery Act (NIRA) ignited a wave of labor organizing in the mass-production industries. In the coal fields, automobile plants, textile and steel mills, and on the docks, workers heeded John L. *Lewis's hyperbolic assertion: "The president wants you to join a union." In 1934 major and at times violent strikes swept the nation. Despite some initial success, union organizing efforts failed against firm corporate opposition. Congressional friends of labor led by Senator Robert F. *Wagner of New York drafted legislation to ensure union recognition. The *National Labor Relations Act (Wagner Act) that Roosevelt signed in 1935 intensified the process of union organizing.

Emboldened by rising worker militancy and the Wagner Act, leaders of a number of AFL unions joined Lewis, president of the UMWA, to form a Committee for Industrial Organization (CIO). Charged by AFL leaders with splitting the labor movement, Lewis and his allies persisted in organizing mass-production workers. Dramatic success in February 1937—in a strike against General Motors, spearheaded by the sit-down strike at Flint, Michigan, and in steel through a secretly negotiated contract with U.S. Steel in March 1937—catapulted the CIO into national prominence and made it a real rival to the AFL. Although the CIO's organizing drive stalled in the summer and fall of 1937, as it lost several strikes, faced more bitter employer opposition, and confronted heavy unemployment in a new economic downturn, Lewis moved to turn it into a permanent, independent organization. In October 1938, the CIO held its first constitutional convention and emerged as the *Congress of Industrial Organizations.

When European war erupted in 1939, the CIO again began to grow, as did the AFL. By the time the United States entered *World War II in December 1941, American mass-production industries had signed union contracts. The war also brought new restraints on labor, however. In early 1942, Roosevelt created a National War Labor Board (NWLB), which regulated *industrial relations for the duration of the war. The NWLB controlled wages in order to limit inflation, guaranteed union security in return for labor peace, and pressured employers to bargain with unions. Wartime labor scarcity brought large numbers of women and African Americans in the mass production industries. Some CIO unions, like the United Packinghouse Workers of America, took aggressive action to attack racial intolerance in the unions' ranks. By war's end, the labor movement had made unprecedented gains, having unionized nearly 35 percent of the nonagricultural labor force.

The Post–World War II Years. A postwar strike wave—the largest in American history—swept through the nation's mass-production industries in 1946. Unlike the 1919 strikes, this time employers did not break the unions. Instead they established a pattern of postwar collective bargaining through which workers conceded much to management in return for higher wages and fringe benefits. A 1950 agreement between the Ford Motor Company and the UAW, the so-called Treaty of Detroit, exemplified the postwar union-management bargain.

Politically, the labor movement suffered a number of defeats in the immediate postwar years. Republicans regained control of Congress in 1946 and the following year passed the anti-union *Taft-Hartley Act. That law, combined with rising anti-communist and anti-Soviet hysteria, caused a split in the CIO. In 1949–1950, the CIO expelled eleven left-led unions, because their leaders refused to sign non-communist affidavits.

Despite the booming postwar economy, the labor movement, especially the CIO, showed signs of decline. New technologies associated with automation swept across unionized industries. Overseas competition and the shift from manufacturing to service-sector employment further reduced union membership. Despite the merger of the AFL and CIO in 1955, unions failed to advance. Organizing in the South faced added obstacles as whites mobilized against the *civil rights demands of African Americans.

The factors that curtailed postwar organizing intensified after 1960. Unions found themselves restrained by new government regulation such as the 1957 *Landrum-Griffin Act and rising corporate resistance. The *Vietnam War deeply divided the labor movement as Walter *Reuther of the UAW led a revolt against AFL-CIO support for the war. Insurgencies challenged many union leaders who had lost touch with younger rank-and-file workers. One of the more prominent opposition movements—Miners for Democracy—witnessed the 1969 assassination of its popular leader, Jock Yablonski, by hirelings of UMWA president Tony Boyle. In steel, rank-and-file insurgencies challenged leaders who promoted labor-management cooperation.

The Late Twentieth Century. Economic contraction and deindustrialization in mass-production industries in the 1970s and early 1980s accelerated the decline in union membership. *Republican party hegemony in national politics in the 1980s weakened labor and made the National Labor Relations Board less effective in protecting workers' right to unionize. Key strike losses by the air-traffic controllers (1981), Hormel packinghouse workers (1987), and corn-processing workers in Clinton, Iowa (1980), and in Decatur, Illinois (1994), further depleted union ranks and morale. Isolated victories occurred, but by the mid-1990s union membership had reached its lowest point since the early 1930s: less than 15 percent of the nonagricultural labor force (and under 10 percent in the private sector).

Two signs of revival appeared in the late 1990s. First, service-sector workers won significant gains, largely as a result of the entry of women and minority workers into unions, led by a new cadre of organizers dedicated to building a more diverse and militant labor movement. Second, the AFL-CIO chose a new leadership in 1995, with John Sweeney of the Service Employees' International Union as president. This leadership revitalized organizing campaigns, encouraged city and state federations to act politically, and sought to rebuild labor's alliances with other social movements. The U.S. labor movement, moreover, evinced new interest in building international alliances with workers overseas while simultaneously fighting international trade agreements, such as the *North American Free Trade Agreement (NAFTA), that free capital from national regulation.

[*See also* Anticommunism; Automation and Computerization; Automotive Industry; Canals and Waterways; Depressions, Economic; Foreign Trade, U.S.; Industrialization; Iron and Steel Industry; Labor Markets; Lowell Mills; Mining; Multinational Enterprises; National Association of Manufacturers; National Recovery Administration; New Deal Era, The; Populist Era; Racism; Sit-down Strike, Flint; Social Class; Socialism; Socialist Party of America; Strikes and Industrial Conflict; Work; Working-Class Life and Culture.]

• David Brody, *Steelworkers in America: The Nonunion Era,* 1960; reprint, 1998. Richard Oestricher, *Solidarity and Fragmentation: Working People and Class Consciousness in Detroit, 1875–1900,* 1986. Robert Zieger, *American Workers, American Unions, 1920–1985,* 1986. Melvyn Dubofsky, ed., *Labor Leaders in America,* 1987. David Montgomery, *The Fall of the House of Labor: The Workplace, the State, and American Labor Activism, 1865–1925,* 1987. Kim Moody, *An Injury to All: The Decline of American Unionism,* 1988. Bruce Laurie, *From Artisan to Worker: Labor in Nineteenth-Century America,* 1989. Lizabeth Cohen, *Making a New Deal: Industrial Workers in Chicago, 1919–1939,* 1990. Melvyn Dubofsky, *The State and Labor in Modern America,* 1994.

—Shelton Stromquist

LA FOLLETTE, ROBERT (1855–1925), *Progressive Era politician and reformer. Born and raised in Wisconsin, La Follette won election as district attorney of Dane County in 1880. As a Republican congressman between 1885 and 1891, he found himself increasingly at odds with the conservative state leaders of his party, led by Senator Philetus Sawyer. As governor of Wisconsin (1901–1905), he joined the ranks of Republican insurgents, presiding over a reform administration that received national attention and came to be called, in Theodore *Roosevelt's phrase, the "laboratory of democracy." Working closely with the economist John R. Commons (1862–1945) and other experts at the University of Wisconsin, La Follette successfully battled for social-reform laws, measures promoting majoritarian democracy such as the direct primary, tax-law changes designed to equalize the tax burden, and new regulatory commissions aimed at bringing *railroads and large corporations under control.

In the U.S. Senate from 1906 on, La Follette continued many of the same campaigns he had pursued at the state level, making the "Wisconsin Idea" a blueprint for federal reform. He promoted his ideas through *La Follette's Weekly Magazine* (founded 1909), later the *Progressive.* His hopes for the presidency in 1912 were dashed as William Howard *Taft won the Republican nomination and Theodore Roosevelt headed the insurgent *Progressive party ticket. La Follette vocally opposed U.S. participation in *World War I and in April 1917 was one of six senators to vote against President Woodrow *Wilson's call for a declaration of war, a position that cost him heavily in popularity. In 1924, he ran unsuccessfully for president as the candidate of a new Progressive party.

La Follette passionately advocated the causes he embraced. Like many Progressives, he believed in a rational, scientific approach to reform. Unlike such leaders as Theodore Roosevelt, who were willing to compromise, he believed, as he asserted in his autobiography, that "in legislation *no bread* is often better than *half a loaf.*"

[*See also* Economic Regulation; Republican Party; Taxation; Twenties, The.]

• Robert M. La Follette, *La Follette's Autobiography: A Personal Narrative of Political Experiences,* forward by Allan Nevins, 1960. David P. Thelen, *Robert M. La Follette and the Insurgent Spirit,* 1976.

—Allan M. Winkler

LA GUARDIA, FIORELLO (1882–1947), congressman, mayor of *New York City. Born in New York City, La Guardia grew up in the West and moved to Italy. Returning to New York at age twenty-four and earning a law degree from New York University in 1910, he plunged into *Republican party politics. In 1916, he became the first Italian American to be elected to Congress, serving in the House of Representatives until 1932, with interruptions for *World War I service in Italy and a brief tenure as president of the New York City Board of Alderman. In 1933, running on the Republican and City Fusion tickets, La Guardia was elected mayor of normally Democratic New York with less than 40 percent of the votes, as two candidates from the scandal-ridden *Democratic party split the rest. He won reelection in 1937 and 1941 with backing from the American Labor party. After leaving office in 1946 he served as director-general of the *United Nations Relief and Rehabilitation Administration.

During his long political career, La Guardia emerged as one of the nation's most prominent advocates of urban *liberalism. A one-man balanced ticket (the Episcopalian son of a Jewish mother, he married a Catholic and spoke Italian, Yiddish, German, and Hungarian), the "Little Flower" projected a cosmopolitan Americanism at odds with the rampant nativism and *racism of his day. In Congress, he opposed prohibition, defended labor and immigrants, and sought checks on corporate power, allying with a minority bloc of midwestern progressives. As mayor, he worked to rationalize the sprawling city government and root out corruption, using his close ties to the New Deal to fund a massive expansion of the city's infrastructure and social services. Though never as popular with voters as his Democratic predecessors and successors, La Guardia after his death came to be seen as the political embodiment of modern New York.

[*See also* Italian Americans; New Deal Era, The; Temperance and Prohibition.]

• Arthur Mann, *La Guardia: A Fighter against His Times, 1882–1933,* 1959. Thomas Kessner, *Fiorello H. La Guardia and the Making of Modern New York,* 1989.

—Joshua B. Freeman

LAISSEZ-FAIRE, a French term literally meaning "let [people] do [as they choose]," refers to the view that governments should not intervene in the economic and social realm. First proclaimed by the eighteenth-century French school of economists known as the physiocrats, and more fully developed by British classical economists such as Adam Smith, laissez-faire ideas soon found their way to the United States. In the *Antebellum Era, hostility to governmental action gained strength not only from the precepts of classical economics but also from the doctrine of natural rights, Americans' belief in individual self-sufficiency, and the conditions of U.S. life and experience. An influential pre–*Civil War expression of laissez-faire dogma, Francis Wayland's *Elements of Political Economy* (1837), had gone through eighteen editions by 1861.

After the Civil War, the case against state intervention was made by businessmen, clergymen, jurists, social Darwinists, economists, political scientists, and sociologists like William Graham Sumner (1840–1910) of Yale. Insofar as Americans had any theory of government, observed the English visitor James Bryce in 1888, that theory was laissez-faire.

Whatever the theory, state and federal governments did not, in practice, confine themselves to the limited, passive role recommended by laissez-faire advocates. Although the proponents of small government continued to criticize the interventionist state after 1900, they appeared to be in retreat in the first six decades of the twentieth century, when reform and war vastly expanded government's role.

But the small-government ideology survived. Frederick Hayek's influential *Road to Serfdom* (1944) championed economic freedom as the indispensable prerequisite to political freedom. Milton Friedman's theory of *monetarism, supply-side economics, and other economic doctrines of the 1960s and 1970s involved a preference for the free market as opposed to public action in the economic sphere. Although unwilling to surrender the benefits they derived from state action, Americans from the 1960s onward expressed a growing distrust of government. As the twentieth century ended, laissez-faire ideas remained alive and well.

[*See also* Conservatism; Economic Regulation; Economics; Individualism; New Deal Era, The; Social Darwinism; Socialism.]

• Sidney Fine, *Laissez Faire and the General-Welfare State: A Study of Conflict in American Thought, 1805–1901,* 1956. John Kenneth Galbraith, *Economics in Perspective: A Critical History,* 1987.

—Sidney Fine

LAND POLICY, FEDERAL. In a country where private property is a sacred ideal, the federal government has, ironically, always been the nation's largest landowner. Following the lead of European imperialism, the United States through purchase, negotiation, treaty, and war acquired a vast territory from France, Spain, England, Mexico, Russia, and Native Americans. The 1803 *Louisiana Purchase doubled the territory of the United States and opened a vast frontier for *agriculture. Most of the 2.3 billion acres comprising today's nation were at one point under federal ownership, and even now some one-third of the country—740 million acres—remains in federal possession.

A policy of disposal went hand in hand with acquisition. The *Northwest Ordinance of 1787 established a system for creating new states out of the public domain as the population moved westward. The largest group of federal-land recipients were the states, but *railroads, war veterans, and rich entrepreneurs also received large acreages. Beginning in the 1840s, as citizens without capital agitated for free land in the form of agricultural homesteads, the federal government disposed of 288 million acres, free or at low cost, to homesteaders. Both the program's scope and its purpose, to create a *West of small rural property owners, were unprecedented; even today it remains unique among developing countries. The *Homestead Act of 1862 authorized any citizen or intended citizen to select 160 acres of surveyed but unclaimed lands and, after five years' residence, to gain title. But homestead grants comprised only one-fourth of all the land disposed of by the federal government, and the government made little effort to ensure that homesteaders would be able to stay on their holdings.

Beginning with *Yellowstone National Park in 1872 and the Forest Reserve Act in 1891, the government set aside public lands in perpetuity. President Theodore *Roosevelt vastly accelerated that policy, creating a national forest system that by the end of the twentieth century covered nearly two hundred million acres. While all of these reservations were made in the name of conserving natural resources, the government continued its policy of disposal, giving away or selling land well beyond the "closing of the frontier" supposedly documented in the census of 1890. But withdrawals for conservation did mark a significant change in federal policy, whether saving spectacular natural scenery or safeguarding economic resources. The plunder of the Great Lakes forests by timber companies in the later nineteenth century convinced many that government must retain some of its lands in the interest of future generations. Livestock grazers on the western public domain posed another threat; they appropriated pasture without permission, paying no fees and putting up illegal fences, until checked in 1934 by the Taylor Grazing Act, again in the name of conservation. Grazers on federal land were now organized into districts, supervised by federal agents, and required to pay fees and follow rules. Homesteading officially ended. The General Land Office, long the chief agency for land disposal, disappeared in 1946, and a new Bureau of Land Management took its place alongside the Forest Service, the Park Service, and the Fish and Wildlife Service as managers of the federal estate.

As the twentieth century wore on, federal land policy became more contested. The nation turned increasingly to the public lands for minerals, fiber, and food, as well as recreation, solitude, and ecological understanding. As private timberlands reached their maximum output, timber companies turned to the national forests to supply the market demand. After decades of relative quiet, the national forests were opened up to logging trucks, chain saws, clear-cutting, and herbicide spraying. In the mid-1950s, land-management officials nearly quadrupled the "allowable cut" in several federal forests and, despite an official policy of "multiple-use," they retained that level until, by the 1980s, it could no longer be sustained. Similarly, the federal lands were expected to produce more beef, oil, coal, and uranium, as well as to pack more tourists into their parks and wildlife refuges, all enhancing local economies. Western states, meanwhile, where federal lands often amounted to over 50 percent of the territory, began to demand that these lands be turned over to them or sold to private developers. The "Sagebrush Rebellion" of the early 1980s, centered in Nevada and Utah, did not succeed in getting any such transfers, but the anger directed against federal agencies remained.

The environmental movement, gathering force after 1960, insisted on maintaining or even extending public ownership in some form, but it was often bitterly critical of federal stewardship. Stung by these criticisms, federal agencies proclaimed a new policy of "ecosystem management," though how they would balance ecology and economics remained unclear. The

MAP 11: TOWNSHIP MAP (1815)

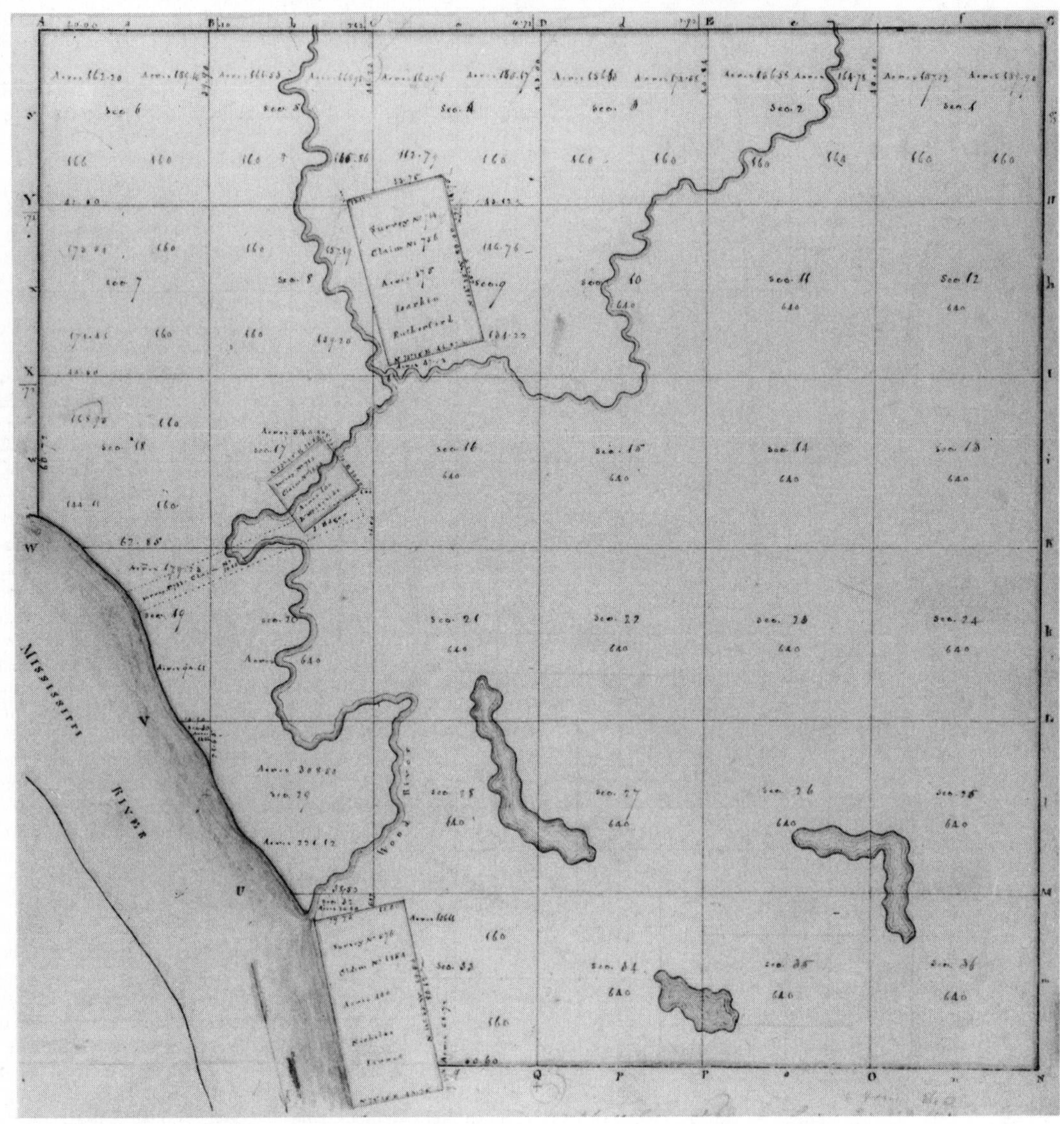

As millions of acres of public lands were subdivided and sold in the early nineteenth century, General Land Office surveyors prepared township maps like this one to assist the process. Each township was six miles square and divided into thirty-six sections of one square mile each. The maps also included identifying physical features and landmarks. Copies were held by the local land office, the territorial or state government, and the General Land Office in Washington, D.C.

[*See* Land Policy, Federal; Louisiana Purchase; Middle West, The; Northwest Ordinance.]

federal lands are probably here to stay, but how and by whom they are used remains an abiding national issue.

[*See also* Conservation Movement; Environmentalism; Expansionism; Federalism; Forests and Forestry; Livestock Industry; Lumbering; National Park System; States' Rights.]

• Paul W. Gates, *History of Public Land Law Development,* 1968. Malcolm J. Rohrbough, *The Land Office Business: The Settlement and Administration of American Public Lands, 1789–1837,* 1968. R. McGregor Cawley, *Federal Land, Western Anger: The Sagebrush Rebellion and Environmental Politics,* 1993. Paul Hirt, *A Conspiracy of Optimism: Management of the National Forests since World War Two,* 1994. Paul W. Gates, *The Jeffersonian Dream: Studies in the History of American Land Policy and Development,* eds. Allan G. Bogue and Margaret B. Bogue, 1996.

—Donald Worster

LANDRUM-GRIFFIN ACT (1959). By 1958, nearly a decade of well-publicized hearings by congressional committees had saturated the public with stories of corruption in labor unions, especially by the Teamsters' union presidents David Beck and the even more ruthless Jimmy Hoffa (1913–1975). In this climate, legislators formulated federal legislation to curb union power and make unions more democratic, a drive that peaked in the second Dwight D. *Eisenhower administration.

Two senators with presidential ambitions played a role as John F. *Kennedy developed legislation acceptable to the AFL-CIO while Lyndon B. *Johnson, the democratic majority leader, guided it through the Senate. The Eisenhower administration, however, supported legislation that business interests preferred. Through effective staff work, a public appeal by the popular president, and a canny use of a bipartisan pair of congressmen as sponsors—Phillip Landrum, a Democrat, and Robert Griffin, a Republican—the administration built sufficient support among antiunion congressmen to enact its bill.

The Labor-Management Reporting and Disclosure Act of 1959 (Landrum-Griffin) required the *National Labor Relations Board (NLRB) to referee internal union affairs. It circumscribed boycotts and forms of picketing that teamsters and other unions used to establish their power. It also empowered the NLRB to conduct and supervise union elections, to ensure democratic procedures, to require financial reporting and bonding of union officials, and to outlaw embezzlements and misuse of union funds. Landrum-Griffin, however, failed to meet its authors' expectations, contained ill-considered provisions, and ignored certain vital problems in *industrial relations. This law and the *Taft-Hartley Act did combine to dilute the original promise of the *National Labor Relations Act of 1935 to promote industrial democracy through independent unionism.

[*See also* Fifties, The; Labor Movements.]

• Alan K. Adams, *Power and Politics in Labor Legislation,* 1964. R. Alton Lee, *Eisenhower and Landrum-Griffin,* 1990.

—R. Alton Lee

LANDSCAPE DESIGN. Landscape design means shaping land forms, plants, and site features such as walls or water courses for utilitarian and aesthetic purposes. The term "landscape architecture" connotes the work of professionals. Landscape design began in America with the arrival of Europeans, who adapted landscape forms to the terrain, climates, and flora they encountered. Colonists created landscapes in the wilderness, ordering the arrangement of dwellings, gardens, fields, mills, and roads, in juxtaposition to the unknown world beyond the edges of settlements. These alterations to the land reflected economic practices and belief systems. Virginia planters organized their farms to earn a living and to demonstrate that they were masters of their realm. The few geometric gardens they made were decorative correlatives to well-drained fields and securely fenced yards. Thomas *Jefferson, who recorded his horticultural and aesthetic observations in his journals, introduced aspects of picturesque design to his plantation gardens at *Monticello, based on his reading of English and French treatises and his garden tours in England and France.

By the nineteenth century, gardening was a popular pastime, and a variety of public landscapes—cemeteries, campuses, suburbs, and urban *parks—were shaped by America's first generation of professional designers. The horticulturist and popular writer Andrew Jackson Downing (1815–1852) promoted the morally uplifting art of "rural improvement," adapting the English picturesque aesthetic to American villa and cottage grounds. Downing also advocated public parks, and his partner Calvert Vaux (1824–1895) later worked with Frederick Law *Olmsted to design Central Park in *New York City in 1858. Dozens of American cities followed suit, creating large "pleasure grounds" that provided healthy recreation and naturalistic scenery. Olmsted, sometimes called the father of American landscape architecture, combined a philosophy of social purpose with aesthetic and managerial expertise over the course of a long professional career. His two sons continued his practice through the 1940s.

Frederick Law Olmsted Jr. (1870–1957) led the professionalization of landscape architecture as a writer, as a founder and first president of the American Society of Landscape Architects (1899), as creator of Harvard University's first landscape-architecture course (1900), and through his public service and important commissions. His work, epitomizing the broadening of professional expertise in the early twentieth century, included *city planning studies, designs for suburbs and private estates, and the promotion of national and regional parks. Many landscape architects of this era, including Charles Platt (1861–1933) and Beatrix Jones Farrand (1872–1959), combined horticultural expertise with aesthetic sensibilities derived from formal Italian Renaissance gardens. Others, such as Jens Jensen (1860–1951), emulated patterns of indigenous natural landscapes. Modernist landscape design was propagated in the late 1930s by Christopher Tunnard (1910–1979), Garrett Eckbo (1910–), and Dan Kiley (1912–), who advocated designs based on human needs and on an aesthetic of geometric abstractions and continuous spatial patterns. In the 1960s, Ian McHarg (1920–) led the landscape-planning movement, which advocated shaping urban development to preserve landscape resources as determined by visual, cultural, and scientific criteria.

[*See also* Architecture, Public; Suburbanization.]

• John R. Stilgoe, *Common Landscape of America, 1580–1845,* 1982. William Tishler, ed., *American Landscape Architecture: Designers and Places,* 1989.

—Joan E. Draper

LANGUAGE, AMERICAN. The meaning and significance of the term "American Language" has changed considerably since Roger *Williams published *A Key into the Language of America* in 1643. For Williams, the term referred exclusively to Native American speech. While this usage persisted into the twentieth century, primarily among anthropologists, by the time H. L. *Mencken published his landmark study *The American Language* in 1919, he could with confidence and bravado use the term to refer to English.

In part, the shift reflects the substantive changes that characterize the linguistic history of the United States. With the conquest, settlement, and expansion that established first British and then federal sovereignty over a large part of North America, English became its dominant idiom, the de facto language. At the same time, the particularities of American experience, including the persistence and influx of other languages (native, African, European, and Asian), differentiated the English of the United States from that of Great Britain, transforming it into a distinctively American language.

But the change relates to intellectual and ideological shifts as much as linguistic developments. With the coming of independence, Americans became concerned about the character and quality of the language—or languages—they spoke. The American experiment in self-government, they believed, depended largely on the integrity of public discourse: Political speech had to be free and sincere, and, most fundamentally, the citizens of the new republic had to be able to understand one another. Moreover, British culture, once a source of pride to the colonists, now became a source of anxiety. How truly independent were they, some questioned, if Americans still read the same literature and spoke the same language as their former oppressors?

Spurred by the heady nationalism that followed the *Revolutionary War and sustained by philosophies of linguistic relativism that suggested an intimate, necessary relationship between a nation and its speech, linguistic patriots set out to identify and institute a properly American language. Proposals were even offered in the immediate postwar period (all of them abortive) to change the official language of the United States. Some suggested Greek, the ancient language of democracy; others felt that Hebrew, the language of the chosen people, would be suitable for the new promised land. Most, however, while ambivalent about their cultural heritage, remained content with English. Regardless of its origin, they argued, the quality of the language was the true source of its Americanness. Even before the Revolution ended, John *Adams offered a proposal—never implemented—that Congress establish a language academy to ensure a qualitative edge for American English. Others suggested a variety of orthographic and other reforms to purify, improve, and standardize English in America.

The most prominent champion of American English was Noah *Webster. While some British and Anglophile linguists denigrated American English as provincial and corrupt, Webster inverted the argument. Combining the Whig mythology of the Revolution with ideas from the relativistic philosophies of the Abbé de Condillac, Johann David Michaelis, and others, Webster argued in such works as *Dissertations on the English Language* (1789) that just as the government of Great Britain had become corrupt, so had its culture, and in particular its language, which had fallen victim to linguistic tyrants such as Samuel Johnson and Thomas Sheridan. And just as America was a political asylum for Englishmen escaping tyranny, so was it a haven for the unadulterated English of William Shakespeare and Joseph Addison. Moreover, just as the authority of the American government rested upon the consent of the governed, so language use (his primary concern was pronunciation) was not dictated by pedants but determined by common usage, that is, by the people themselves—or, at least, by those of pure Anglo-Saxon descent.

Throughout American history, intellectuals advanced theories of American English that reflected the philosophies and ideologies of their times. For instance, inspired on one hand by the work of historical and comparative philologists such as Wilhelm von Humboldt and Max Müller and on the other by the expansionism of Jacksonian democracy, Walt *Whitman developed an intricate mythology of the *Manifest Destiny of American English. For Whitman, the Americanness of English lay in its composite nature (Anglo-Saxon, Celtic, Romance, Greek, and Latin) and its seemingly unlimited ability, especially in the United States, to appropriate words and phrases from the languages with which it came into contact. In the 1855 preface to *Leaves of Grass* and the posthumously published *An American Primer* (1904),Whitman depicted English as the ultimate, eternal, cosmopolitan language, with its roots in the obscure Indo-European past and its future as limitless as that of America itself.

Of all accounts of the subject, Mencken's *The American Language,* which saw several editions and was enlarged by two supplements between 1919 and 1948, is the most ambitious and well known. Both a study in philology and a history of ideas, *The American Language* continued in the tradition of Webster and Whitman to defend American English against its detractors. Conceived in a period that witnessed both America's emergence as a world power and Mencken's ongoing battle against genteel philosophy, Victorian moralism, and bourgeois mediocrity, it portrayed the history of English in America as a manifestation of the nation's true character, its inventiveness, ingenuity, exuberance, and audacity.

As the twentieth century ended, against the background of popular calls for English-only legislation, some academics, in the spirit of multiculturalism, challenged the notion of English as the exclusive American language, arguing that the United States is and has always been a polyglot nation. Studies of black English (sometimes called Ebonics), the movement for bilingual education, and the project sponsored by Marc Shell and Werner Sollors at Harvard University to study American literary works written in languages other than English all offered evidence of a shift in thinking about American language.

[*See also* Antebellum Era; Cultural Pluralism; Early Republic, Era of the; Literacy; Literature.]

• George Philip Krapp, *The English Language in America,* 1925. Charlton Laird, *Language in America,* 1970. Dennis E. Baron, *Grammar and Good Taste: Reforming the American Language,* 1982. David Simpson, *The Politics of American English, 1776–1850,* 1986. Thomas Gustafson, *Representative Words: Politics, Literature, and the American Language, 1776–1865,* 1992. Michael P. Kramer, *Imagining Language in America from the Revolution to the Civil War,* 1992.

—Michael P. Kramer

LA SALLE, RENÉ-ROBERT CAVELIER, SIEUR DE (1643–1687), French explorer. In 1666, La Salle left France for New France to seek his fortune. He quickly established himself as a landowner and fur trader at Lachine on the St. Lawrence River, near Montreal. With the patronage of Governor Frontenac, La Salle began exploring the western reaches of the colony, endeavoring to extend French control over the land, its peoples, and the *fur trade. Named commandant of Fort Frontenac (at present-day Kingston, Ontario) in 1673, he was granted noble rank by the crown on a return trip to France. After receiving permission to establish a trade monopoly along the *Mississippi River (reached in 1673 by the French trader Louis Jolliet and Jesuit priest Jacques Marquette), La Salle and his lieutenant Henri de Tonti set off in 1679 with a crew of French men and Indian men, women, and children. Three years later, having built several forts along the Illinois and Mississippi Rivers, La Salle reached the Gulf of Mexico and claimed all the lands drained by the river for France, naming them Louisiana.

Back in France, La Salle gained the crown's support to colonize the newly claimed region and set off again for the Mississippi River with several hundred colonists, but he failed to find the river's mouth from the Gulf, landing about five hundred miles west. On the last of several overland attempts to find the Mississippi, La Salle was murdered by some of his own dissatisfied colonists. In much the same way that the crosses La Salle planted along the Mississippi River symbolized French possession of the territory, La Salle himself stands as a symbol for French colonialism in North America, its grand expansionist schemes, and its eventual demise.

[*See also* Exploration, Conquest, and Settlement, Era of European; French Settlements in North America; Indian History and Culture: From 1500 to 1800.]

• John Upton Terrell, *La Salle: The Life and Times of an Explorer,* 1968. Anka Muhlstein, *La Salle: Explorer of the North American Frontier,* trans. Willard Wood, 1994.

—Jennifer M. Spear

LATIN AMERICA, U.S. RELATIONS WITH. *See* Foreign Relations: U.S. Relations with Latin America.

LATINOS/LATINAS. *See* Hispanic Americans.

LAW, INTERNATIONAL. *See* International Law.

LAWRENCE, ERNEST O. (1901–1958), physicist, Nobel laureate. E. O. Lawrence invented the cyclotron and created a new style of physics in his University of California Radiation Laboratory (UCRL), now the Ernest O. Lawrence Berkeley National Laboratory and the Ernest O. Lawrence Livermore National Laboratory. Later he helped develop the atomic bomb and promoted the hydrogen bomb.

Born in Canton, South Dakota, he attended the Universities of South Dakota, Minnesota, and Chicago before earning his Ph.D. (1925) at Yale University, where he became an instructor. In 1928, he moved to the University of California, Berkeley, where he planned and developed the cyclotron particle accelerator. Supported by the university, federal funds, and private philanthropy, he created the UCRL, which by the outbreak of *World War II had produced three cyclotrons of increasing size and power. In 1939, Lawrence won the Nobel Prize in physics for his invention of the cyclotron. During the war, Lawrence turned the laboratory's capability to the separation of uranium isotopes to provide the critical material for the first atomic bomb.

After World War II, Lawrence built a much larger laboratory, with new accelerators such as Louis Alvarez's proton linear accelerator and Edwin M. McMillan's synchrotron. Between 1949 and 1955, with McMillan and William Brobeck, he oversaw the construction of a six-billion–electron-volt accelerator, the Bevatron. This machine permitted the discovery of many subatomic particles in the 1950s and 1960s. At the same time, Lawrence built massive production accelerators for enriching depleted uranium and, later, a second *nuclear weapons laboratory at Livermore.

More than any other scientist, Lawrence created modern big physics, with its large laboratories, collaborative, interdisciplinary teams of scientists and engineers, and massive particle accelerators and detectors. His abilities and enthusiasm made him one of the most influential scientists in the United States during the World War II and *Cold War Eras. He died shortly after returning from the 1958 Geneva Conference on nuclear arms control.

[*See also* Manhattan Project; Nuclear Arms Control Treaties; Physical Sciences; Science: From 1914 to 1945; Science: Since 1945.]

• John L. Heilbron and Robert W. Seidel, *Lawrence and His Laboratory*, vol. 1 of *A History of the Lawrence Berkeley Laboratory*, 1989.

—Robert W. Seidel

LAWYERS. *See* Legal Profession.

LEAGUE OF NATIONS. This international organization came to life in 1919 when President Woodrow *Wilson secured the inclusion of its charter in the Treaty of *Versailles. The League "Covenant," the work of many internationalists on both sides of the Atlantic, contained provisions for the arbitration of international disputes, armaments reduction, and the imposition of collective military and economic sanctions against any nation that violated the political independence and territorial integrity of another. The last obligation (embodied in the controversial Article 10), in tandem with the arbitration requirement, also implied a restriction against unilateral coercive action by a league member.

The Covenant, like all constitutions, was subject to interpretation. Thus, upon Wilson's return from the Paris Peace Conference, one senator observed, "Internationalism has come, and we must choose what form the internationalism is to take." This apt remark referred to two divergent tendencies within the American internationalist movement that had arisen during the impassioned debate over American military preparedness that had raged in 1915–1916, when the United States was still officially neutral. "Progressive internationalists" considered peace essential to domestic reform. Like Wilson, they saw European imperialism, militarism, and balance-of-power politics as the root causes of the war; in place of these evils, they envisioned a "community of nations" sustained by disarmament, self-determination for subject peoples, and a multinational world organization.

"Conservative internationalists," led by the former president William Howard *Taft and the League to Enforce Peace, also advocated a world parliament. But while tentatively endorsing the principle of *collective security, most conservative internationalists believed as well that the United States should expand its army and navy and reserve the right to exercise force independently whenever the national interest so warranted. Disarmament and self-determination were not among their concerns. Progressive internationalists viewed their conservative rivals as enemies of reform and as advocates of militarism and imperialism. For their part, most conservative internationalists regarded as socialistic the social welfare legislation (progressive taxation, the eight-hour day, restrictions on *child labor, and so forth) that Wilson, aided by progressive internationalists, had shepherded through Congress in his first term. Thus, disagreements over domestic politics and foreign policy alike complicated the impending League debate.

Had a national referendum been held in July 1919, the United States almost certainly would have joined the league. Two main factors, however, compounded the larger problem of ratifying the treaty. First, the Republicans, having captured control of Congress in the 1918 midterm elections, launched a fierce, ultraconsevative attack on Wilson's overall program. Second, many progressive internationalists had begun to distance themselves from Wilson because the peace settlement had fallen short of the promise of the *Fourteen Points; Wilson's acquiescence in the wartime suppression of *civil liberties further eroded his support among progressives.

In the Senate, opposition was grounded in both partisanship and principle; only a few of the league's critics, however, were irreconcilable isolationists. Most Republicans were conservative internationalists; they believed Wilson had consigned too many vital national interests to the will of an international authority. In part to preserve America's freedom of action, the Republicans, led by Henry Cabot Lodge (1850–1924) of Massachusetts, drew up fourteen reservations as conditions for ratification. Some of these reservations were intended to curtail the league's ability to arbitrate disputes, to supervise a reduction of armaments, and to impose sanctions under Article 10, and to restrict independent unilateral military interventions, as those actions might affect U.S. sovereignty. Wilson was unable to persuade the Republicans to accept the treaty as it was written. In September 1919, Wilson embarked upon a strenuous 10,000-mile speaking tour across the nation to build public support for unqualified American membership. His exertions brought on a nearly fatal paralytic stroke that rendered him an invalid for the remainder of his term, resulting in political gridlock.

The Senate voted on the treaty three times, in November 1919 and March 1920, but failed to muster a two-thirds majority either on motions to ratify unconditionally or with the Lodge reservations. In November 1920, the Republican presidential nominee Warren G. *Harding won a landslide victory over Democrat James M. Cox. Alluding to Wilson's earlier wish that the election should become a "solemn referendum" on the issue, Lodge declared, "that League is dead."

In assessing the debacle, some historians have argued that Wilson's stroke prevented him from finding a middle ground on the Lodge reservations. Other scholars maintain that even a healthy Wilson would have refused to compromise, given his sometimes rigid personality. Still others have contended that the ideological gulf that separated the two forms of American *internationalism, along with the president's failure to rally his own progressive coalition as the congressional struggle began, sealed the fate of a *Wilsonian* league.

In part because of America's absence, the fledgling organization recorded few achievements in the interwar period. Republican administrations assiduously avoided all formal association with the league throughout the 1920s. In promulgating the 1924 Dawes Plan to alleviate Europe's reparations-war debt tangle, in the *Washington Naval Arms Conference of 1921–

1922, and even in the innocuous *Kellogg-Briand Pact of 1928, Washington conspicuously ignored the League. Perhaps the nadir came during the Manchurian incident of 1931–1932. While condemning Japanese aggression and Japan's puppet state, Manchukuo, the League undertook no meaningful sanctions. The League receded further into impotence as the 1930s wore on, and mounting crises heightened international tensions.

By 1944–1945, many Americans had come to believe that *World War II might have been averted had the nation followed Wilson's counsel and joined the League. President Franklin Delano *Roosevelt championed a new international organization, the *United Nations (UN), but he and his advisers incorporated in its Charter most of the reservations prescribed by the Republicans in 1919. With the creation of the UN in 1945, the League of Nations ceased to exist. Although the UN was largely their conception and design, American foreign-policy-makers within two years of its creation deemed it an inadequate instrument of international security. Instead, the United States adopted the Lodgian strategy of unilateralism in world affairs in pursuit of the doctrine of *containment throughout the *Cold War.

[*See also* Isolationism; International Law; Progressive Era; Twenties, The.]

• Thomas A. Bailey, *Woodrow Wilson and the Great Betrayal,* 1945. Alexander L. George and Juliette L. George, *Woodrow Wilson and Colonel House,* 1956. Arthur S. Link, *Woodrow Wilson, Revolution, War and Peace,* 1979. William C. Widenor, *Henry Cabot Lodge and the Search for an American Foreign Policy,* 1980. Lloyd E. Ambrosius, *Woodrow Wilson and the American Diplomatic Tradition: The Treaty Fight in Perspective,* 1987. Thomas J. Knock, *To End All Wars: Woodrow Wilson and the Quest for a New World Order,* 1992.

—Thomas J. Knock

LEAGUE OF WOMEN VOTERS. The League of Women Voters occupies a unique place in American political and women's history. Founded in 1920 as a direct offshoot of the *National American Woman Suffrage Association, its program of intensive study, citizenship training, and issue-oriented nonpartisanship exemplifies one direction that women's political activism took in the postsuffrage era.

Voter education—providing information about candidates and campaign platforms—remains the league's best-known activity. A Voters Education Fund was incorporated in 1957 to sustain this function. But from the first, the league had a broader agenda. Under the leadership of the former suffragists Maud Wood Park and Carrie Chapman *Catt, the organization lobbied for the 1921 Sheppard-Towner Act, which appropriated funds for rural prenatal and baby care, and the 1922 Cable Act, which guaranteed married women's citizenship rights. During the 1930s, it mobilized public support for *Social Security, the *Tennessee Valley Authority, and *civil service reform. As part of its long-standing commitment to *internationalism, it staunchly supported the *United Nations throughout the post–*World War II era. Its 1972 endorsement of the *Equal Rights Amendment aligned the league with the revival of *feminism.

Although men were admitted in 1974, the membership remained primarily white, female, and middle class. Never a mass organization, the league's real vitality lay in grassroots activism, strengthened by a major change in the 1940s when it shifted from a federation of state leagues to an association of individual members. Throughout its history, the League of Women Voters produced a corps of committed volunteers whose contributions to government, especially at the local level, were vital to the democratic process.

[*See also* Twenties, The; Women's Club Movement; Women's Rights Movements.]

• Louise M. Young, *In the Public Interest: The League of Women Voters, 1920–1970,* 1989.

—Susan Ware

LEAHY, WILLIAM D. (1875–1959), fleet admiral, chairman of the *Joint Chiefs of Staff (JCS), chief of staff to Presidents Franklin Delano *Roosevelt and Harry S. *Truman, 1942–1949. Born in Hampton, Iowa, Leahy graduated from the U.S. Naval Academy in 1897. After a distinguished naval career and a term as chief of naval operations (1937–1939), he was appointed by President Roosevelt, a longtime friend, as governor of *Puerto Rico and then in 1940 as ambassador to Vichy France. In April 1942, to protest the Vichy government's cooperation with Nazi Germany, Roosevelt ordered Leahy home.

As presidential chief of staff and chairman of the JCS through much of *World War II, Leahy functioned primarily as a liaison between the military-service chiefs and the president. Professionally and personally close to Roosevelt, Leahy advised the president daily, drafted much of his correspondence, and accompanied him to major allied conferences. He also alternated with his British counterpart as chairman of the Anglo-American Combined Chiefs of Staff. In December 1944, Leahy received the five-star rank of fleet admiral.

After Roosevelt's death in 1945, Leahy became an integral part of the Truman administration. An early and avid cold warrior, Leahy worked with Truman to counter Soviet influence worldwide. From 1942 to 1949, Leahy participated in the highest levels of decision-making, but he kept the presidents' confidences so well that his own role is difficult to measure. Unquestionably, however, he played a vital role in the development of U.S. strategic policy during World War II and the early *Cold War.

[*See also* Federal Government, Executive Branch: Department of Defense; Federal Government, Executive Branch: The Presidency.]

• William D. Leahy, *I Was There: The Personal Story of the Chief of Staff to Presidents Roosevelt and Truman Based on His Notes and Diaries Made at the Time,* 1950. Henry H. Adams, *Witness to Power: The Life of Fleet Admiral William D. Leahy,* 1985.

—Anne Sharp Wells

LEE, ANN. *See* Shakerism.

LEE, ROBERT E. (1807–1870), Confederate general. Born in Virginia, Lee was the son of Henry ("Lighthorse Harry") Lee of *Revolutionary War fame and a descendant of other prominent Virginia families. Graduating from West Point in 1829, he enjoyed a distinguished army career, including *Mexican War service, and was a protégé of General Winfield Scott, general in chief of the U.S. Army. Contrary to a popular myth he owned and trafficked in slaves and pursued the capture and punishment of his own fugitive slaves. He also accepted the prewar southern claims of northern oppression. When Virginia seceded from the Union in 1861, Lee rejected President Abraham *Lincoln's appeals and resigned from the U.S. Army. As the *Civil War began, he became first a leader of Virginia forces and then a general officer of the *Confederate States of America.

From 1862 to 1865, Lee commanded the Confederacy's premier Army of Northern Virginia. An accomplished tactician, he favored offensive strategies and achieved a number of stunning victories over larger Union armies, most notably at the battle of Chancellorsville (May 1863). In the course of these victories, however, he suffered disproportionate and irreplaceable losses. Defeated at the Battle of *Gettysburg (July 1863) and ultimately unsuccessful in the defense of Richmond, Virginia, he surrendered his army at Appomattox in April 1865. After the war, Lee served as president of Washington College in Virginia. Not conciliatory toward the North, he championed southern grievances and was antagonistic toward the freedmen. As sectional reconciliation took place, however, he posthumously came to be viewed as a heroic American in the North as well as the South.

• Thomas Connelly, *The Marble Man: R. E. Lee and His Image in American Society,* 1971. Alan T. Nolan, *Lee Considered: General Robert E. Lee and Civil War History,* 1991. Emory M. Thomas, *Robert E. Lee: A Biography,* 1995.

—Alan T. Nolan

LEGAL PROFESSION. Lawyers are disproportionately represented in the political branches of American government and hold a virtual monopoly over the judiciary. The extraordinary legal cast of the American Revolution first gave prominence to the idea that lawyers were the high priests of America's civic religion of law. Yet a populist ethic scorning them as money grubbers who mystified the law while profiting from the miseries of others has persisted.

The early bar responded to these concerns with a combination of formal legal education and self-policing. Tapping Reeve in 1784 founded the Litchfield Law School in Connecticut, which trained more than one thousand lawyers before it closed in 1833. Yet most nineteenth-century lawyers prepared for law practice by serving an apprenticeship with an established attorney or judge. Their reading included *Supreme Court Justice Joseph *Story's famous *Commentaries,* which first appeared in the 1830s.

Nevertheless, by 1870 the United States had thirty-five law schools. Business corporations seeking specialized legal talent provided the impetus for some of this growth. Paul D. Cravath of *New York City in the 1890s pioneered the factory system of law practice. Although lawyers in these large firms (five or more persons) were an infinitesimal percentage of all lawyers in the country, they garnered a disproportionate share of the financial rewards. During the twentieth century, the practice of law turned into a gigantic business, with more than 250 firms of one hundred or more lawyers commanding about 40 percent of the nation's total legal revenues.

The bar-association movement also grew rapidly at the end of the nineteenth century. The *American Bar Association (ABA), founded in 1878 by Judge Simeon E. Baldwin, advocated higher standards for practitioners. The ABA and local associations attempted to elevate quality by limiting access, especially of the foreign born, women, and racial minorities.

Despite opposition, however, all of these groups gradually joined the profession. Night law schools accommodated the rising tide of immigrants and other daytime workers seeking a career at the bar. Women's exclusion from the profession continued longer because the men who dominated it believed women's proper place was in the home, a cultural bias sustained by the Supreme Court in *Bradwell* v. *Illinois* (1873). By 1997, however, women constituted about 24 percent of all lawyers, up from 2.5 percent in 1950, and about half of all law school graduates. The number of African American lawyers also increased, though less dramatically. In 1997, when *African Americans constituted 12 percent of the population, they represented about 7 percent of law graduates but only 3 percent of the bar. Women and all minorities remained distinctly underrepresented as partners in large law firms at the end of the twentieth century.

Dean Christopher Columbus Langdell of Harvard Law School introduced in the 1870s the most enduring reforms in legal education. Langdell's "scientific" method involved formal entrance requirements, the case method of teaching, core subjects, large libraries filled with state and national reports, and law reviews edited by law students.

Langdell's method survived, but his assumptions came under attack, first from advocates of "sociological jurisprudence," including Oliver Wendell *Holmes Jr. and Louis *Brandeis, and then in the 1930s and 1940s from the Legal Realists, who insisted on measuring the law's success by its social consequences rather than its scientific logic. Some of the Realists, such as Jerome Frank, moved into the New Deal as lawyers, where they became the vanguard of a new segment of the profession—the government lawyers—and the regulators of consumer safety, occupational health, *civil rights, and environmental matters.

This commitment to law as an instrument of social policy produced a surge in the number of lawyers. In 1960 there were 286,000 lawyers in the United States; in 1997 the number was almost 1 million, or roughly one lawyer for every 250 people, a ratio unrivaled in American history and in the rest of the world. The nation's 175 law schools continued to turn out many thousands more each year. Moreover, the Supreme Court's decision in *Bates* v. *State Bar of Arizona* (1977)—that bar-association codes against lawyer advertising violated lawyers' First Amendment rights to commercial free speech—opened the legal market to more competition.

As the twentieth century ended, the American legal profession was more diverse, more influential, and more embedded in popular consciousness than ever before. As interest in the profession soared, however, these high priests of America's civic religion frequently exhibited feet of clay. The reputational ranking of lawyers sank along with President Richard M. *Nixon and his lawyer-laden staff during the *Watergate crisis and in the aftermath of celebrity cases such as the 1995 murder trial of the football star O. J. Simpson. Lawyers, it sometimes seemed, had become the profession that Americans loved to hate but could not live without.

[*See also* Federal Government, Judicial Branch; Jurisprudence; New Deal Era, The; Professionalization; Shaw, Lemuel.]

• Wayne K. Hobson, *The American Legal Profession and the Organizational Society, 1890–1930,* 1986. Peter Irons, *New Deal Lawyers,* 1982. Robert Stevens, *Law School: Legal Education in America from the 1850s to the 1980s,* 1983. Kermit L. Hall, *The Magic Mirror: Law in American History,* 1989. Jennifer L. Pierce, *Gender Trials: Emotional Lives in Contemporary Law Firms,* 1995. American Bar Association, *Miles to Go: Progress of Minorities in the Legal Profession,* 1998.

—Kermit L. Hall

LEGAL THOUGHT. *See* Jurisprudence.

LEGISLATIVE BRANCH. *See* Federal Government, Legislative Branch.

LEISURE. Recreation and leisure figure importantly in America's cultural, social, and economic history. In the Colonial and earlier national eras, leisure activities were shaped by the agrarian nature of the economy, as well as by regional, *gender, and class differences. In colonial *New England, leisure was subject to religious strictures and close community oversight, though the Puritans, contrary to popular stereotypes, enjoyed beer drinking, games, recreational hunting, and social occasions, and the region's court records recount many instances of colonists engaging in a wide range of diversions discountenanced by the authorities, even on the Sabbath. The more easygoing middle and southern colonies tolerated a variety of leisure activities, including tavern going, dancing, *gambling, and *horse racing. Among the southern landed gentry, horse racing and fox hunting provided occasions for social display. Slaves enjoyed scant leisure, though records of African-influenced singing and dancing in the slave quarters make clear that even this brutal labor system failed to extinguish the impulse for amusement and diversion.

In the cities of early America, opportunities for leisure pursuits gradually increased, including musical performances, theaters featuring visiting troupes from England, and even balls and dances. Charleston's St. Cecilia Society sponsored an annual subscription ball beginning in 1762. Most Americans through the mid-nineteenth century were farmers, however, and leisure activities were largely centered around *family, church, or other local institutions. Barn raisings, corn huskings, and harvest festivals; weddings and baptisms; and holidays such as Thanksgiving and Christmas provided breaks in the work routine, and occasions for family and community celebrations, as did elections, muster days (when local militias assembled and marched), and—after 1776—the Fourth of July. Women, while more closely tied to the home, organized quilting parties and sewing bees, and corresponded extensively with friends and relatives.

Profound social and economic changes in the mid- and later

nineteenth century affected leisure practices. *Urbanization encouraged commercialized leisure, stratified by *social class and varying among different immigrant groups. Canals, *railroads, the National Road, and steamboats allowed lecturers, performers, *circuses, and theatrical companies to reach interior cities. In the larger cities, a new commercial elite patronized the *opera, concert halls, theaters, and art *museums. Boston's Academy of Music and New York's Astor Place Opera House (1847) became shrines of upper-class leisure. The New York Yacht Club, established by wealthy sportsmen in 1844, sponsored the first America's Cup Race in 1851.

The rich sought out summer resorts such as Newport, Rhode Island; the Berkshires in western Massachusetts; Long Branch, New Jersey; and White Sulpher Springs, West Virginia. In the 1880s and 1890s, the railroad entrepreneur Henry M. Flagler built a string of luxurious vacation hotels, notably The Breakers at Palm Beach, along Florida's Atlantic coast. They also traveled more widely. Samuel L. *Clemens' *Innocents Abroad* (1869) describes a tour of Europe and the Middle East by well-to-do Americans.

Middle-class citizens seeking diversion flocked to lecture series, ranging from high-minded discourses by the likes of Ralph Waldo *Emerson to comic routines. A summer institute established for Sunday-school teachers at Lake Chautauqua, New York, in 1874 by John H. Vincent evolved into a popular summer resort combining leisure and cultural uplift; it eventually spawned hundreds of local "Chautauquas" nationwide.

The quest for leisure and recreation took many forms. Urban *parks, developed at mid-century, offered islands of tranquility in the city. The first professional *baseball team, the New York Knickerbockers, was founded in 1845, and baseball—both amateur and professional—surged in popularity after the *Civil War. New York's Bowery Theater (1825), P. T. *Barnum's American Museum (1842), and similar popular venues offered crowd-pleasing melodramas, freak shows, and other amusements to a leisure-seeking urban public. The 1850–1852 tour of singer Jenny Lind, the "Swedish nightingale," arranged by Barnum, proved a tremendous success.

The waves of immigrants arriving between 1870 and 1920 introduced their own forms of leisure: the Yiddish theater popular with Eastern European Jews, the saints' feast days beloved of *Italian Americans, the *German-American beer gardens and *Turnvereins* (athletic and singing clubs). While immigrant working-class males patronized saloons, prizefights, and social clubs, young working women found other diversions, from *department stores to ferry-boat rides and amusement parks.

Urban commercialized leisure expanded as the nineteenth century wore on. The antebellum ministrel show evolved into *vaudeville. Music halls such as Tony Pastor's in New York City (1865) offered popular songs, comedy routines, and variety sketches. Bandmaster John Philip Sousa (1854–1932), the "March King," toured with great success. As new technologies developed, movies and recorded music made their appearance. Amusement parks modeled on the Midway Plaisance at the 1893 Chicago World's Fair sprang up, including three built by entrepreneurs at New York's Coney Island between 1895 and 1903. *Progressive-era reformers worried about this explosion of urban commercialized leisure. While some urged dance-hall regulation and movie *censorship, others organized civic pageants to entertain and instruct the immigrant masses and established supervised playgrounds to provide recreation and moral guidance for their children.

By the 1920s, leisure was both more standardized and more democratized. Americans flocked to Hollywood *films, listened to network *radio programs and popular songs produced in New York's Tin Pan Alley, and devoured mass *magazines such as *Reader's Digest* and *The Saturday Evening Post.* The spread of automobiles, paved highways, and tourist cabins (which soon evolved into motels) stimulated family *tourism to national parks, beaches, and big cities.

In the generally affluent decades from 1950 through the close of the century, commercialized leisure, increasingly controlled by multinational media conglomerates, expanded its reach. *Television viewing exploded; the film and recording industries and professional *sports thrived; computer video games diverted the young; and the travel industry flourished. With the introduction of jet aircraft, foreign travel, once an elite activity, became accessible to a broader range of Americans. The nation's first theme park, Disneyland, opened in Anaheim, California, in 1955, followed by scores of others, including Hersheypark in Pennsylvania, Nashville's Opryland, Cedar Point in Ohio, and the Six Flags chain. Thousands flocked to Branson, Missouri, to see aging pop stars perform one last time. Walt *Disney World in Orlando, Florida (1971), became enormously popular. By the 1990s, leisure was very big business in America.

Not all leisure was commercialized, however. Late-twentieth-century Americans continued to find more small-scale diversions, from camping, hiking, and biking to such age-old pursuits as reading, gardening, and picnicking with family and friends. They joined in community- and church-based recreational events; visited local parks, public gardens, and zoos; and engaged in such recreational activities as bowling, skiing, and competing in amateur baseball or soccer leagues. Despite its mass-culture aspects and commercial trappings, leisure in America as the twentieth century ended remained highly diverse and resisted easy generalization.

[*See also* Amusement Parks and Theme Parks; Automobile Racing; Automotive Industry; Basketball; Bicycles and Bicycling; Boxing; Chautauqua Movement; Dance; Football; Immigration; Minstrelsy; Music; Musical Theater; Popular Culture; Puritanism; Quilts and Quilting; Shopping Centers and Malls; Theater; Worlds Fairs and Expositions.]

• Carl Bode, *The Anatomy of American Popular Culture, 1840–1861,* 1959. Foster R. Dulles, *A History of Recreation: America Learns to Play,* 1965. John F. Kasson, *Amusing the Million: Coney Island at the Turn of the Century,* 1978. Warren James Belasco, *Americans on the Road: From Autocamp to Motel, 1910–1945,* 1979. Judith A. Adams, *The American Amusement Park Industry,* 1991. Peter G. Buckley, "Popular Entertainment Before the Civil War"; Richard V. Smith, "Travel and Vacations"; and Don B. Wilmeth, "Amusement and Theme Parks," in Mary Kupiec Cayton, Elliott J. Gorn, and Peter W. Williams, eds., *Encyclopedia of American Social History,* III (1993), pp. 1611–25, 1677–88, 1705–11.

—Paul S. Boyer

LEOPOLD, ALDO (1887–1948), conservation scientist, writer, and philosopher. Following graduation from Yale University's Forest School in 1909, Leopold joined the U.S. Forest Service, where he became a leading innovator in soil conservation, range management, recreation planning, game management, and wilderness protection. Concerned by the accelerating loss of the nation's wild lands, he led efforts that in 1924 resulted in the designation of the nation's first wilderness area within the Gila National Forest in New Mexico. After 1928, Leopold devoted himself to the development of wildlife management as a distinct field, first as an independent researcher (1928–1933), then as professor at the University of Wisconsin (1933–1948). His fundamental contribution in these years was to apply concepts from the science of ecology to the management of wildlife populations and habitats. His text *Game Management* (1933) was the first in the field.

Through his many nontechnical writings, including policy statements, editorials, and nature essays, Leopold defined a new approach to conservation, one that sought to blend elements of older utilitarian and preservationist traditions within the broader context of contemporary ecological understanding. In the final years of his life, Leopold compiled many of his essays into a collection published posthumously as *A Sand County Almanac* (1949). *Sand County* became, along with Rachel *Carson's *Silent Spring* (1962), a basic text for the later environmental movement. Especially influential was its capstone essay, "The Land Ethic," in which Leopold argued for an expansion of the sphere of human ethical concern to include the natural world. Leopold's writings provided important foundations for such emerging interdisciplinary fields as environmental history, ecological economics, environmental ethics, restoration ecology, and conservation biology.

[*See also* Conservation Movement; Environmentalism; Forests and Forestry; Muir, John.]

• Susan Flader, *Thinking Like a Mountain: Aldo Leopold and the Evolution of an Ecological Attitude toward Deer, Wolves, and Forest,* 1974. Curt Meine, *Aldo Leopold: His Life and Work,* 1988.

—Curt Meine

LESBIANISM. *See* Gay and Lesbian Rights Movement.

LEWIS, JOHN L. (1880–1969), labor leader. Born in Lucas, Iowa, to Welsh immigrant parents. Lewis as a young man wandered the *West and attempted to establish several businesses. He became a coal miner and in 1908 moved to Panama, Illinois. A year later, Lewis became president of the United Mine Workers (UMW) local. Thereafter, he rose rapidly in the labor movement, becoming in 1917 a UMW vice president. Lewis's political ability and his adroit handling of the 1919 coal strike won him the union's presidency in 1920.

The union over which Lewis assumed command soon entered an era of decline. Ironically, as the power of the UMW eroded in the 1920s, Lewis's personal power in the union grew. With Franklin Delano *Roosevelt's election in 1932, Lewis rebuilt the UMW. In 1933, he launched a spectacular organizing drive that brought over 90 percent of the nation's coal miners into the UMW. Lewis emerged as the dominant labor leader of the 1930s and an effective advocate of aggressive organizing. In 1935, with the passage of the prolabor *National Labor Relations Act, he created the Committee for Industrial Organization (CIO) within the *American Federation of Labor (AFL) to unionize workers in the *mass production industries. As president of the CIO (which was expelled from the AFL in 1938 and changed its name to the *Congress of Industrial Organizations), Lewis helped unionize the *automotive industry, the *iron and steel industry, and others.

At first allied with Roosevelt and the New Deal, Lewis broke with the president during the 1940 election. Roosevelt's reelection caused Lewis to resign as president of the CIO and in 1942 to withdraw the UMW from the CIO.

During *World War II, Lewis played the militant loner. In 1943, he led a series of unpopular strikes. After the war, Lewis led more massive coal strikes that spurred the passage of the 1947 *Taft-Hartley Act. In the 1950s, he shifted from militancy to accommodation with mine owners. He transformed himself into an industrial statesman, urging trade policies that would increase coal exports, building a string of union hospitals, and seeking the passage of the first Federal Mine Safety Law. When he retired from his union presidency in 1960, Lewis left an ailing industry and a debilitated, corrupt union.

[*See also* Labor Movements; Mining; New Deal Era, The; Strikes and Industrial Conflict.]

• Melvyn Dubofsky and Warren Van Tine, *John L. Lewis: A Biography,* 1977.

—Warren Van Tine

LEWIS, SINCLAIR (1885–1951), novelist. Although he attended Yale, Harry Sinclair Lewis, a native of Sauk Centre, Minnesota, always remained something of a provincial midwesterner. Deeply insecure about his personal appearance, ill at ease among intellectuals, prone to alcoholic binges, and in and out of well-publicized marriages, he remains a perennial critical problem, an uncouth realist in an age of uncertain modernism. Perhaps the most gifted mimic in American letters, he was best at seeming to caricature small-town businessmen and religious hucksters.

Although cosmopolitan eastern critics such as H. L. *Mencken assumed that he shared their scorn at the cultural wasteland west of the Hudson River, Lewis in fact was deeply sympathetic to those he only appeared to satirize. *Main Street* (1920), loosely based on Sauk Centre, and *Babbitt* (1922), about a Republican real-estate broker in the fictional midwestern city of Zenith, entered the language as generic terms for the aridity of American culture and the emptiness of business values. Both novels became best-sellers, securing Lewis's reputation and epitomizing the post–*World War I mood of cynicism and condescension toward rural and provincial America. Almost as popular were *Arrowsmith* (1925), on the pressures that constricted a career devoted to medical research; *Elmer Gantry* (1927), featuring a flamboyantly hypocritical touring evangelist; and *Dodsworth* (1929), about the impact of European values and behavior patterns on a seemingly conventional business couple.

Awarded the Nobel Prize for literature in 1930, Lewis won a huge following abroad, as foreigners saw in his work some essence of capitalist democracy. His later works, dealing with social problems, included *Ann Vickers* (1933), on gender issues, *It Can't Happen Here* (1935), on fascism; and *Kingsblood Royal* (1947), on race and miscegenation. Sinclair Lewis remains a somewhat ambiguous observer of American mores, a critic of bourgeois life who was deeply implicated in its consumer values and *advertising techniques.

[*See also* Literature: Since World War I; Twenties, The; Urbanization.]

• Mark Schorer, *Sinclair Lewis,* 1961. Christopher P. Wilson, *White Collar Fictions: Class and Social Representation in American Literature, 1885–1925,* 1992.

—Robert M. Crunden

LEWIS AND CLARK EXPEDITION (1804–1806). In a January 1803 message to Congress, President Thomas *Jefferson called for an expedition up the Missouri River and west to the Pacific. With the *Louisiana Purchase later that year, the project took on even greater significance. Jefferson chose the army captain Meriwether Lewis (1774–1809) to lead the expedition. Lewis selected as his partner a fellow officer, William Clark (1770–1838). More than forty men, including York, Clark's slave, composed the Corps of Discovery as it started up the Missouri in a keelboat and three canoes on 14 May 1804. By late October the expedition had reached present-day central North Dakota, where the members established their winter quarters, Fort Mandan.

In April 1805, Lewis and Clark sent the keelboat downriver before resuming their journey west, accompanied by a young Shoshone woman, Sacagawea (1786–1812), and her French Canadian husband. They reached the source of the Missouri and advanced up a tributary, the Jefferson, before having to abandon their boats. Using horses obtained from Sacagawea's Shoshones, the expedition crossed the Continental Divide at Lemhi Pass and surmounted the Bitterroot Mountains via the Lolo Trail. At the Clearwater River they entrusted their horses to the Nez Percés, built canoes, and floated down the Clearwater, Snake, and Columbia Rivers to the Pacific, which they reached on 18 November 1805. They named their winter quarters Fort Clatsop.

In late March 1806, the corps started home. At the mouth of Lolo Creek the expedition split, Clark's contingent returning as they had come and Lewis's group advancing directly east to the Falls of the Missouri, where the units were reunited. On 23 September 1806, after an absence of twenty-eight months, the Corps of Discovery arrived at St. Louis.

The Lewis and Clark Expedition, which produced extensive published records and journals, was one of the most successful in the annals of world exploration. It destroyed the concept of an all-water route to the Pacific and helped fix in the public mind the vast extent of the Louisiana Purchase territory and the Pacific Northwest.

MAP 12: MAP OF THE LEWIS AND CLARK EXPEDITION

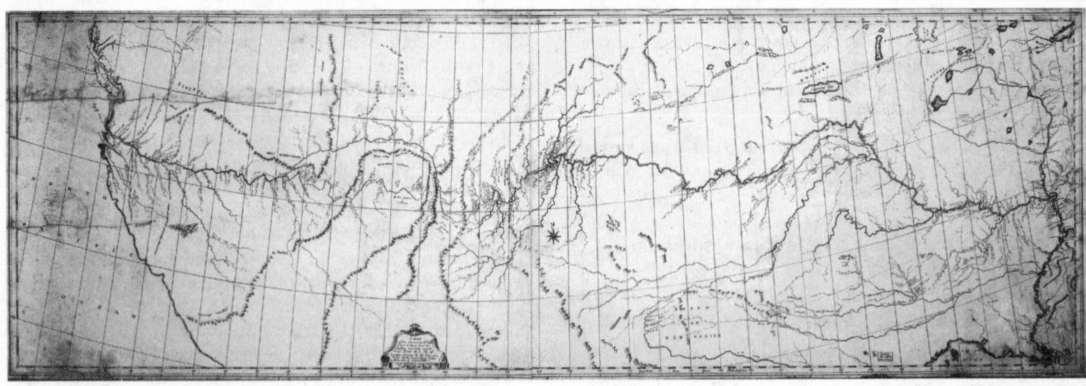

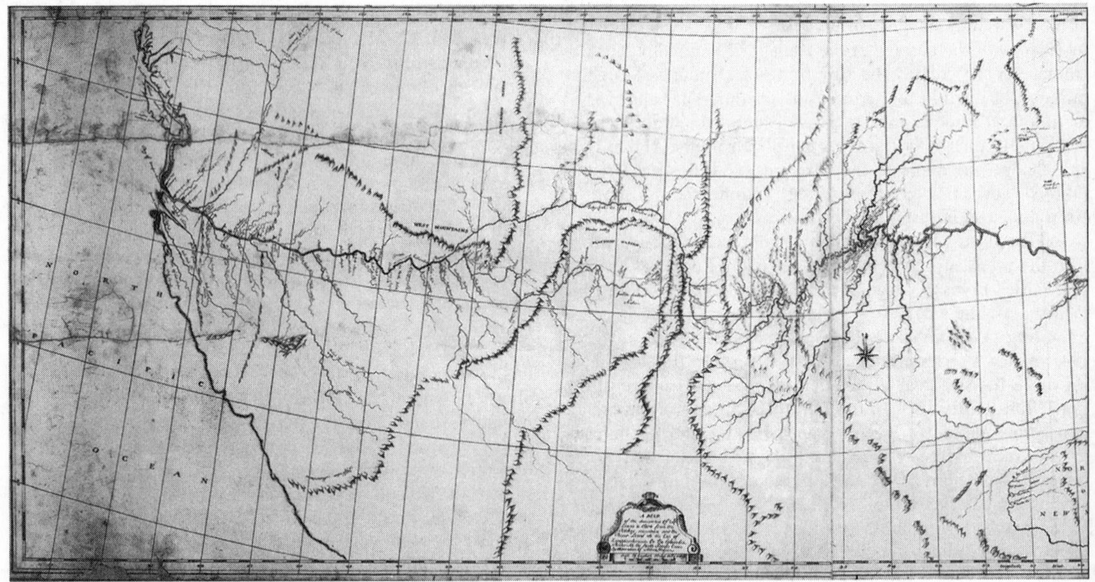

Top: This 1807 map was made by Robert Frazer, a U.S. Army private who accompanied the Lewis and Clark Expedition (1803–06) and made pen-and-ink sketches of each day's travels from the Rocky Mountains to the expedition's final terminus at the mouth of the Columbia River. The many rivers and streams the expedition encountered—each one of which was named by the expedition leaders—are shown in great detail. The mountain ranges, represented by darker, snaking lines, were based largely on guesswork and Indian reports. Bottom: Detail of the western portion of the expedition.

[*See* Expansionism; Lewis and Clark Expedition; Louisiana Purchase; Rocky Mountains; West, The.]

[*See also* Early Republic, Era of the; Expansionism; Indian History and Culture: From 1800 to 1900; Science: Revolutionary War to World War I.]

• Gary E. Moulton, ed., *The Journals of the Lewis and Clark Expedition,* 1986–. Stephen E. Ambrose, *Undaunted Courage: Meriwether Lewis, Thomas Jefferson, and the Opening of the American West,* 1996.

—Richard A. Bartlett

LEYTE GULF, BATTLE OF (23–25 October 1994). The largest and one of the most complex naval engagements in history, this *World War II battle represented an all-or-nothing gamble by the Imperial Japanese Navy to maintain control of the *Philippines in the face of American landings. The Japanese, gravely outnumbered in ships and planes, executed a complex, three-pronged plan to use their carriers—ships lacking effective striking power because of earlier losses—as decoys to draw off the American battle fleet under Admiral William Halsey, and then to strike with their battleships and cruisers the American transports in Leyte Gulf, located between the eastern Philippine islands of Samar and Leyte.

From the start, the Japanese offensive went awry. American submarines sounded the alarm and inflicted dispiriting losses on the vessels the Japanese had designated as their Center Force as it got to sea. Pummeled by Halsey's carriers, these gunships suffered severely, while those of the Southern Force were virtually annihilated by the aging U.S. battleships guarding Suriago Strait. Fortunes briefly turned when the impotent Japanese carriers to the north managed to lure Halsey away from his blocking position. Grasping this opportunity, the Center Force descended upon the American amphibious ships, protected to the east by a weak detachment of escort carriers and destroyers. Surprised and outgunned, these U.S. warships nevertheless put up such a resolute and skillful fight that the Japanese retreated. Halsey, chasing the carriers, doubled back too late, and some Japanese ships escaped.

Still, Leyte Gulf was a crushing American victory and Japan's fleet never recovered. The worst American casualties, inflicted by Japanese Kamikaze attacks (organized suicide missions) came late in the battle; overall U.S. losses totaled six warships sunk; for the Japanese, twenty-six.

[*See also* Nimitz, Chester.]

• Samuel E. Morison, *Leyte: June 1944–January 1945,* vol. 12 of *History of United States Naval Operations in World War II,* 1963. Thomas J. Cutler, *The Battle of Leyte Gulf, 23–26 October 1944,* 1994.

—Malcolm Muir Jr.

LIBERALISM. The term "liberalism" is best understood historically as a language of individual rights with widely variant, and sometimes contradictory, political applications. The origins of the American liberal tradition lie in seventeenth- and eighteenth-century English political philosophy. As science, *technology, and civil war challenged the organic social order of medieval society, Thomas Hobbes, John Locke, and Adam Smith envisioned new relationships among the individual, the church, and the state. While Hobbes deduced political rights from the harsh conditions of life in a state of nature—"nasty, brutish, and short"—Locke more optimistically redefined civil society as a voluntary social contract among rational individuals. In his view, legitimate authority derived not from monarchs, nobles, or clerics, but from the consent of the governed, insofar as they accurately interpreted God's unchanging natural law. If a regime abrogated the rights to life, liberty, and property, its subjects could overthrow it and choose a new one. Tempering his philosophy's revolutionary implications, Locke stressed fidelity to Christian virtue, but on an individual level only. The state, reduced to a neutral arbiter of economic disputes, would leave matters of faith to individual conscience.

The notion that the state exists primarily to preserve private property emerged as one of free-market liberalism's two core principles; Adam Smith provided the second, arguing in *Inquiry into the Nature and Causes of the Wealth of Nations* (1776) that markets, left alone, function with optimum allocative efficiency. Though Smith cautioned against the excesses of unbridled free enterprise, he insisted that society benefited when the state allowed acquisitive *individualism full scope.

In America, the potent union of Lockean and Smithian principles, generally called "classical" or "*laissez-faire" liberalism, pervaded Revolutionary Era political texts and formed a central tenet of early national political economy. It also undergirded Thomas *Jefferson's idealization of the independent yeoman farmer. Equating large-scale urban manufacturing with poverty and vice, Jefferson favored a rural economy based on agricultural exports and small-scale manufacturing. The frontier's seemingly limitless supply of natural resources, he suggested, guaranteed immunity from the Old World's class struggles and moral corruption. The frontier ethos helped sustain Americans' commitment to Locke's calculus of property and liberty—despite the emergence of evangelical Christianity, labor unionism, and government-sponsored internal improvements, all part of an urban industrial order at variance with Locke's idealized "state of nature."

During the *Progressive Era, John *Dewey, Herbert *Croly, and other reformers redefined liberalism by affixing the term to what was, in fact, a sharp departure from classical liberalism. Locke, considering labor a form of property, was untroubled by the dehumanizing effects of industrial work. In the new liberal discourse, however, government emerged as the benevolent guardian of individual liberties against laissez-faire *capitalism run amok. Thus, the states passed laws shielding children from labor exploitation and small businesses from unfair monopolies. For pragmatists like Dewey, a new science of administrative efficiency would replace the now closed frontier as a guarantor of perpetual progress.

During the Great Depression of the 1930s, Franklin Delano *Roosevelt's *New Deal accelerated the departure from classical liberalism by shifting emphasis from individual property rights to utilitarian governance on behalf of the public good. Through massive work programs, government sought to restore the economic independence once exclusively provided by property and wealth. *World War II hastened the emergence of a managerial ethos that stressed group psychology over individualism. Throughout his presidency, Roosevelt stressed liberalism's secondary dictionary definitions: generous support for those in need and a broad-minded tolerance for diversity, in stark contrast to the rise of totalitarianism elsewhere.

Cast into the realm of political rhetoric in postwar America, liberalism came to represent one side of a partisan debate. Post–New Deal liberals generally opposed *socialism but favored the state's heightened role as an active agent for promoting individual well-being and social equality. Conservatives, by contrast, raised the discarded banner of classical liberalism, which in the 1950s enjoyed a brief renaissance as a subject of scholarly debate. In 1955, Louis Hartz construed *The Liberal Tradition in America* as a broad historical consensus about freedom that bred a natural distrust of extremism. While acknowledging the dangers of conformity, Hartz found no room in a centrist, classless political system for radical ideologies like *communism or messianic leaders like Senator Joseph *McCarthy. Political scientists elaborated Hartz's vision of a nonpartisan liberal consensus, portraying municipal governance as an open, self-correcting system of group competition, absorbing the discontent manifested abroad as riot and revolution.

During the 1960s, Lyndon B. *Johnson completed liberalism's break from its roots in Lockean individualism. Johnson's *Great Society initiatives extended government's advocacy into relationships between parents and children (*welfare), patients and doctors (*Medicare and Medicaid), and consumers and manufacturers (consumer protection). In Johnson's liberal vision of the good society, the benefits of economic growth accrued to all citizens more fairly, a principle underlying legislation banning discrimination on the basis of race, sex, age, and national origin. But while Johnson's support for *civil rights alienated many southern Democrats, weakening liberalism's political base, the *Vietnam War discredited the notion of liberalism as a humane philosophy and fueled a younger generation's revolt against the *Democratic party's procorporate strategy. The *Watergate scandal further eroded trust in government as an agent of change. Faced with a soaring national debt and opposition from a revitalized conservative movement, New Deal–style liberalism lost favor in the 1980s and 1990s, and politicians avoided the term. Blamed for a variety of evils, including an alleged decline of moral consensus, liberals found themselves relying, ironically, on the federal court system—the most undemocratic of government institutions—to continue the pursuit of social justice.

In the late twentieth century, commentators debated whether the so-called crisis of liberalism resulted from its failures or its successes. Those who argued the former position cited such measures as *affirmative action (racial preferences to redress past discrimination) as examples of government's excessive infringement of individual rights. Others suggested that the successful civil rights struggle had made the goal of equality in public life part of a new consensus, and that liberalism remained salient as a continuing appeal to the public conscience for tolerance and understanding of all racial and ethnic groups in an increasingly diverse society.

The focus on diversity, however, entailed new problems. Should liberalism maintain official neutrality among competing claims for the good, or should it affirm a set of core principles? Building on John *Rawls's assertion, in *A Theory of Justice* (1971), that individuals naturally gravitate to a conception of justice, Ronald Dworkin argued that liberal activism derived from "a theory of equality that requires official neutrality amongst theories of what is valuable in life." This argument found favor among advocates of multiculturalism but dismayed communitarians, who argued that liberalism rested on a sense of fixed values shared by all members of a liberal community.

Despite the accrual of competing meanings over its long history, liberalism remains a focal point of Americans' efforts to balance the benefits of *capitalism with larger moral and ethical priorities.

[*See also* Conservatism; Pragmatism; Radicalism; Republicanism.]

• C. B. Macpherson, *The Political Theory of Possessive Individualism: Hobbes to Locke,* 1962. Ronald Dworkin, "Liberalism," in *Public and Private Morality,* ed. Stuart Hampshire, 1978, pp. 113–43. Drew R. McCoy, *The Elusive Republic: Political Economy in Jeffersonian America,* 1980. Michael J. Sandel, *Liberalism and the Limits of Justice,* 1982. Joyce Appleby, *Capitalism and a New Social Order,* 1984. Dorothy Ross, "Liberalism" in *Encyclopedia of American Political History,* ed. Jack P. Greene, 1984, pp. 750–763. William A. Galston, *Liberal Purposes: Goods, Virtues, and Diversity in the Liberal State,* 1991.

—Andrew Chamberlin Rieser

LIBERTARIAN PARTY. Founded in Colorado in 1971, the Libertarian party became a significant, if somewhat exotic, variation on late twentieth-century antigovernment politics. Dedicated to challenging "the cult of the omnipotent state," the party nominated its first presidential candidate in 1972 on a platform best described as antigovernment fundamentalism. Among other things, it demanded an immediate or eventual end to: mandatory *taxation; all social *welfare and economic subsidies; government funding for *education; and any government restrictions on *immigration, freedom of speech, drug use, and consensual sex. Later, the party proposed an end to all government regulation of food and drugs and any restrictions on discrimination in housing, employment, or other areas of "private trade." It also adopted a variety of isolationist foreign-policy positions.

The party nominated the television producer and children's author Roger MacBride for president in 1976. An articulate former *Republican party activist, he won more than 170,000 votes. In 1980, with growing support in the *West and among some intellectuals, the party turned to Ed Clark, who had recently helped lead the popular California property-tax revolt. Clark garnered nearly a million votes. The party lost support in the 1980s and 1990s, however, a time of ample opportunity to oppose government power without resorting to a marginal third party. MacBride himself returned to the Republican fold in 1983 and promoted Libertarian ideas in an increasingly receptive mainstream setting. The Libertarian party itself softened some of its positions but remained committed to private, free-market solutions to social and cultural as well as economic problems. In 1998, it claimed to have elected more than one hundred local officials throughout the nation but showed little promise of significant future growth.

[*See also* Conservatism; Isolationism; Laissez-faire; Political Parties.]

• Joseph M. Hazlett, *The Libertarian Party and Other Minor Parties in the United States,* 1992.

—Leonard J. Moore

LIBERTY. Rich and poor, the leaders and the led, from Carolina to *New England, almost any group of *Revolutionary War–era Americans, if asked what they were seeking, would almost certainly have used this word—liberty or death, as Patrick *Henry put it. A representative collection of late twentieth-century Americans might say "democracy" and have as many different things in mind. The revolutionaries drew on several interlinking patterns of ideas, less distinct for them than for modern analysts looking for roots in different intellectual traditions.

By liberty, the revolutionaries clearly meant, from the beginning of the crisis in imperial relations, the liberties or rights to which all Englishmen, including British Americans, were entitled by birth—that is, by virtue of the traditions, common-law decisions, colonial charters, and parliamentary statutes (such as the Magna Carta or the English Bill of Rights of 1689) that eighteenth-century Britons called their "constitution." Trial by jury, security against cruel punishments or warrantless searches, the writ of habeas corpus, freedom of the press, and toleration of dissenting religious faiths were generally agreed to be among these rights. When Americans could no longer claim them as Englishmen and had come to insist on written rather than unwritten constitutions, they wrote them into the states' first declarations of rights and ultimately into amendments to the new federal *Constitution.

Between 1765 and 1776, Britons on opposite sides of the Atlantic increasingly differed in their definitions of English rights. As this happened, Americans appealed to the rights of man, which they had long supposed to be closely related to English rights in any case. In doing so, they drew on a long succession of modern natural-law and law-of-nations writers—most famously, John Locke—who taught that it was "sacred," "undeniable," or evident to any inquiring mind that no man was born with a natural right to rule another or to take by force what others had by right: their lives, their property, and their capacity to make their own decisions about the things in which their happiness might seem to consist. Thomas *Jefferson captured much of what the revolutionary generation meant by liberty in the eloquent second paragraph of the *Declaration of Independence, including the conclusion that legitimate political authority can only rest on the consent of the governed and that the governed retain a right to withdraw their consent and make their government anew if it threatens the natural rights that governments are instituted to protect.

But liberty in this final sense, for Revolutionary War–era Americans, meant more than ultimate or tacit consent to whatever sort of government might rule. It meant the right, initially of Englishmen and then of citizens of the American republics, to a representative political system: the right of a people to govern themselves continuously and actively through elections, petitions, and free assemblies. Valuing this participation for its own sake, not merely as a means of protecting their individual rights, they drew on a republican tradition extending back to ancient Greece and Rome. James *Madison was plainly using the word in this sense when he wrote in *Federalist Paper number 51 that "justice" or security for fundamental rights was "the end of civil society" and would "ever be pursued until it be obtained, or until liberty be lost in the pursuit." Self-governance, inalienable rights, and ancient, common-law protections and procedures were all encapsulated in this potent word.

[*See also* Conservatism; Laissez-faire; Liberalism; Republicanism; Revolution and Constitution, Era of.]

• Jack P. Greene, ed., *Colonies to Nation: A Documentary History of the American Revolution, 1763–1789,* 1975.

—Lance Banning

LIBERTY PARTY. The Liberty party was organized in Warsaw, New York, in 1839 by abolitionists convinced that they must take their decade-long *antislavery propaganda campaign into the polling booth to accomplish their purpose. The party campaigned in two presidential elections, in 1840 and 1844, nominating in both years James G. Birney (1792–1857), a former slaveholder from Kentucky and long-time abolitionist. The party contested a number of local and state races as well. Rooted in *New England, upstate New York, and the Western Reserve area of northern Ohio, the Liberty party drew support largely from Protestant groups opposed to slavery on moral and religious grounds. Party leaders tried to broaden their appeal by stressing in their platform an economic argument against *slavery, claiming that wasteful expenditures by slaveholders drained resources from workers and the middle class in the North.

The party fared poorly at a time when deep loyalties to the two major parties, the Democrats and Whigs, and a lack of widespread antislavery sentiment dominated American political culture. Liberty party activists also encountered difficulties with other abolitionists who feared that electoral politics would compromise their beliefs. The party drew less than 1 percent of the national vote in the 1840 presidential election, and just over 2 percent in 1844. Some historians suggest that its New York State vote in the latter year denied the state to the Whig candidate, Henry *Clay, and insured the election of the slaveholder James Knox *Polk, but this involves the unlikely assumption that in the Liberty party's absence, its voters would have cast their ballots for Clay. It is more useful to see the Liberty party as an early manifestation a gathering movement that would culminate in the crusades of the *Free Soil and *Republican parties against slavery's expansion.

[*See also* Antebellum Era; Democratic Party; Political Parties; Whig Party.]

• Richard H. Sewell, *Ballots for Freedom: Antislavery Politics in the United States, 1837–1860,* 1976.

—Joel H. Silbey

LIBRARIES. "Libraries have improved the general conversation of the Americans," Benjamin *Franklin observed in his autobiography, "and perhaps . . . contributed in some degree to the stand so generally made throughout the colonies in defense of their privileges." Franklin was in a good position to know. In 1731 he had organized the Library Company of *Philadelphia, a joint-stock venture in which stockholders pooled their money to acquire a collection of books that all could borrow. It differed from institutional predecessors like the Harvard College Library, which originated in 1636 with a gift of three hundred mostly theological books, and the seventy religious libraries set up by the Anglican clergyman Thomas Bray between 1695 and 1704 to combat heresy and induce English clergy to emigrate to the colonies. Franklin's library avoided religious subjects, favoring travel, philosophy, and biography.

For the next century the Library Company became the model for other types of social libraries, including athenaeums (which added newspapers and periodicals), "subscription" libraries (where patrons paid a fee to draw from collections others owned), "mercantile" libraries (created by young urban clerks for self-improvement), and "mechanics" libraries (often funded by capitalists to improve employee efficiency).

As *literacy increased, as *education became compulsory, and as improved technologies reduced the cost of printed materials, the model shifted. In 1854, Boston opened a "public library" funded by local tax dollars. Democracy required an informed citizenry, founders argued, and making "good books" accessible to the public was a civic responsibility.

To encourage uniform library practices, Melvil Dewey in 1876 helped organize the American Library Association (ALA), published his decimal classification system for library collections, began editing a new periodical entitled *Library Journal,* and started a library supplies company. In 1887, Dewey opened the world's first library school at New York's Columbia College (where, on the otherwise all-male campus, seventeen of the first twenty students were women). By 1900, Dewey had cemented into library practice his own brand of library science, which emphasized efficient service and management and delegated to other professionals the authority to identify the "good books" libraries would collect.

By that time, the steel magnate Andrew *Carnegie had articulated a philosophy that challenged all wealthy Americans to support self-improvement institutions like libraries. Between 1890 and 1919, Carnegie himself contributed $45,000,000 to construct 108 academic and 1,679 public library buildings. To qualify, communities had to provide a suitable site and promise annual support of 10 percent of the construction grant.

During *World War I, an ALA Library War Service Committee supervised two fund-raising and three book-collecting campaigns that eventually netted five million dollars and ten million books and magazines, most of which went to thirty-six training camps in the United States and thousands of mobile library stations in Europe.

By the time the war ended, the public library had matured into a civic reading institution staffed mostly by women, who found in librarianship one of the few professions that welcomed them. But except for children's literature—an area of collection development for which their gender "naturally" qualified them—librarians continued to look to experts in the academy and literary establishment for guidance in identifying "good books." Despite librarians' best efforts, however, public library users were much more interested in popular reading.

Academic libraries experienced a different history. In antebellum America they consisted mostly of donated and carefully guarded books; the classical curriculum did not require library use. After 1876, however, academic libraries responded to the growing emphasis on research and graduate work by increasing collections, extending hours, and improving access and bibliographic control. A second burst of growth occurred after *World War II as higher education expanded dramatically.

About midcentury the federal government greatly increased its presence in American library development. The Library Services Act of 1956 funded extension services to rural people through state library agencies. The 1964 Library Services and Construction Act helped thousands of public and academic libraries increase collections and construct new buildings. The Elementary and Secondary Education Act (1965) put libraries in thousands of American public schools.

At century's end, the fourteen thousand public, eighty thousand school, five thousand academic, and ten thousand special libraries maintained by private and public-sector institutions combined to make the library a ubiquitous site for the nation's diverse reading communities. By that time, most libraries were following institutions like the *Library of Congress and the New York Public Library and adopting newer electronic technologies. Many libraries automated routine work like circulation, replaced card catalogs with computerized access to their holdings, and tapped into huge databases that vastly expanded the information and bibliographic resources available to their patrons.

[*See also* Philanthropy and Philanthropic Foundations.]

• Jesse H. Shera, *Foundations of the Public Library: The Origins of the Public Library Movement in New England, 1629–1855,* 1949. Jane Aikin Rosenberg, *The Nation's Great Library: Herbert Putnam and the Library of Congress, 1899–1939,* 1993. Joanne E. Passet, *Cultural Crusaders: Women Librarians in the American West, 1900–1917,* 1994. Abigail A. Van Slyck, *Free to All: Carnegie Libraries and American Culture, 1890–1920,* 1995. Louise S. Robbins, *Censorship and the American Library: The American Library Association's Response to Threats to Intellectual Freedom, 1939–1969,* 1996. Wayne A. Wiegand, *Irrepressible Reformer: A Biography of Melvil Dewey,* 1996.

—Wayne A. Wiegand

LIBRARY OF CONGRESS. Established in 1800, the Library of Congress is the world's largest and most comprehensive research institution. Although never the official national library of the United States, it has been run continuously by the federal government's legislative branch and serves all the functions of a national library, including copyright repository (since 1870) and reference service to Congress and other branches of government. A fire destroyed the library's core collections in 1814, but it recovered by acquiring the great library of Thomas *Jefferson the following year. The institution grew slowly through the nineteenth century, obtaining collections of books, pamphlets, maps, manuscripts, newspapers, pictorial materials, and broadsides through purchase, exchange, and donation. In addition, the nation's earliest documents and the papers of the founders (George *Washington, Jefferson, James *Madison, and others) were transferred to the library from the State Department.

With the appointment of the library's first professional administrator, Herbert Putnam, in 1899, the collections grew dramatically, numbering over 100 million items in three buildings a century later. The library became a leader in cataloging, description, and technology, first by distributing its catalog cards to libraries worldwide, and then with the development of the machine-readable cataloging (MARC) format that became the international standard. Its American Memory page on the Worldwide Web contains images of thousands of items from the collections, giving researchers instant off-site access to them. The library's paper preservation accomplishments, cultural programs, and services to the blind and persons with disabilities are notable as well.

[*See also* Internet and Worldwide Web; Libraries.]

• Jane Aikin Rosenberg, *The Nation's Great Library: Herbert Putnam and the Library of Congress, 1899–1939,* 1993. John Y. Cole, *Jefferson's Legacy: A Brief History of the Library of Congress,* 1997.

—Ronald Becker

LIFE EXPECTANCY. One of modern America's greatest achievements has been the reduction of death rates and the prolongation of human life. One way to summarize this development is by the concept of life expectancy, which expresses the average number of years of life remaining to a person at some age, often at birth. This measure is derived from life tables and can be calculated from data at a point in time for persons of different ages (period life expectancy) or by following the same groups of people over time as they age (cohort life expectancy). The data used usually come from federal *census counts by age and sex as well as vital statistics of deaths, also by age and sex. Other data, such as genealogies and family reconstitutions, are useable, however, and other methods may be employed.

Life expectancy in the United States has evolved through several stages. During the early *Colonial Era, life expectancy was relatively short, death rates were high and variable, and epidemics of infectious *disease were common. Life expectancy at birth generally ranged from twenty to thirty years. By the late seventeenth century mortality conditions had begun to improve, and by the late eighteenth century, were quite favorable by world standards. In his *Essay on the Principle of Population* (1798), the Englishman Thomas R. Malthus commented that mortality conditions had for some time been quite benign in America. Mortality was lowest in *New England (with life expectancy at birth ranging from 35 to 60 years), more severe in the Middle Colonies (30–45), and highest in the *South (25–35). Gradually epidemic diseases such as measles and *smallpox became endemic and joined *malaria, dysentery, pneumonia, bronchitis, and *tuberculosis as major causes of endemic, baseline mortality. Infectious and parasitic diseases accounted for most deaths until the twentieth century, when degenerative conditions (e.g., *cancer and *heart disease) became dominant.

Life expectancy likely reached a high point in the late eighteenth century and then declined until the later nineteenth century. For example, genealogical data yield an expectation of life at age ten of almost fifty-seven years for white males in 1790–1794, but by 1855–1859 the figure had declined to forty-eight years. Data on human stature, another indicator of physical well-being, support these results. Heights of *Civil War military recruits, West Point cadets, college students, and others (mostly males) declined from those born in the 1830s to those born in the 1870s, consistent with a deteriorating disease environment. Information on specific cities with adequate vital statistics (*New York City, *Boston, *Philadelphia, Baltimore, and *New Orleans) reveals constant or rising mortality prior to the Civil War with substantial mortality peaks resulting from *cholera (which first appeared in the United States in 1832), *typhoid fever, and *yellow fever.

During the nineteenth century, the sources of data improved. The census, a federal mandate, was taken decennially from 1790. Questions about mortality in the year prior to the census were asked from 1850 through 1900. But vital-statistics collection, left to state and local governments, was uneven. Massachusetts in 1842 became the first state to commence comprehensive registration of births, deaths, and marriages. Quality was good by about 1855. Several states followed suit, but the Death Registration Area formed in 1900 by the U.S. Bureau of the Census initially included only ten states and the District of Columbia. Not until 1933 did it cover the entire United States.

From the middle of the nineteenth century on, sufficient information exists to support reasonable national estimates of life expectancy. Table 1 reports life expectancy and infant mortality rates (deaths in the first year of life per one thousand live births) for the white and African American populations from 1850 to 1990. It is apparent that the sustained mortality transition did not begin until about 1880. Life expectancy at birth for whites overall changed little between 1850 and 1880—but then rose from about forty years in 1880 to fifty-two years in 1900, sixty-nine years in 1950, and seventy-six years in 1990. The black population suffered a substantial mortality disadvantage, although protected somewhat by their concentration in rural areas earlier in the twentieth century. (About 80 percent of *African Americans lived in rural areas in 1900 in contrast to 58 percent of whites.) Life expectancy at birth for blacks was about 20 percent lower than for whites in 1900, and their infant mortality rate about 54 percent higher. The situation had been even worse around 1850, when African Americans (mostly slaves) had an estimated life expectancy at birth of 23 years (40 percent lower than for whites) and an estimated infant mortality rate of about 340 (61 percent higher than for whites). While infant mortality rates for both groups had declined sharply by 1990, the black rate still remained more than double that of whites.

In terms of other mortality differentials, women have tended to live longer than men. In 1850, girls at birth had a life ex-

Table 1. Mortality in the United States, 1850–1990

Approx. Date	Expectation of Life[a]						Infant Mortality Rate	
	At Birth		At Age 10		At Age 20			
	White	Black[b]	White	Black[b]	White	Black[b]	White	Black[b]
1850	38.4	23.0	47.3		39.5		216.8	340.0
1860	43.6		49.4		41.3		181.3	
1870	45.2		50.6		42.5		175.5	
1880	40.5		48.3		40.4		214.8	
1890	46.8		50.4		42.2		150.7	
1900	51.8	41.8	52.5	47.2	44.1	39.5	110.8	170.3
1910	52.7	43.1	53.0	47.9	44.5	40.1	106.1	161.9
1920	57.4	47.0	54.6	45.3	46.0	37.8	82.1	131.7
1930	60.8	48.5	56.3	44.8	47.2	36.6	60.1	99.9
1940	64.9	53.9	58.8	49.5	49.5	40.7	43.2	73.8
1950	69.0	60.7	61.5	54.5	51.9	45.2	26.8	44.5
1960	70.7	63.9	62.8	57.4	53.2	47.9	22.9	43.2
1970	71.6	65.2	63.3	56.8	53.7	47.3	17.8	30.9
1980	74.5	68.1	65.6	60.4	56.0	50.8	11.0	21.4
1990	76.1	69.1	66.9	60.7	57.2	51.1	7.6	18.0

(a) The numbers listed in the columns refer to the statistically probable *average years of life remaining* to whites and blacks at birth, at age ten, and at age twenty. (b) For 1950 and 1960, black and other population.

Source: For sources, see Haines, 2000.

pectancy 6 percent higher than boys, a gap that narrowed to only about 2 percent by 1900. By 1990 women were living almost 10 percent longer than men (seven years). Rural-urban differences have also been significant. In the nineteenth century, cities were distinctly less healthful places to live. Around 1830, life expectancy at birth was 51 years in 44 New England towns, 42 percent higher than the average for Boston, New York City, and Philadelphia (35.9 years). By 1900, the probability of a child surviving to age five was 22 percent worse in urban than rural areas. This urban penalty had disappeared by 1920, when improved *public-health programs and other reforms in urban America diminished the problems of overcrowding, impure water, food contamination, and poor rubbish removal and sewage disposal. Among the foreign born, life expectancy has usually been lower than that of native-born whites, partly because of initially lower socioeconomic status and partly from their concentration in urban areas. Regional variations in mortality were substantial since at least 1900, the first point for which they can be observed for the nation as a whole. The lowest mortality areas were in the *Middle West; the highest, in the South and New England. These differences diminished over the twentieth century, however, with the spread of public-health programs and better medical care.

[*See also* Death and Dying; Demography; Immigration; Medicine; Slavery; Urbanization.]

• Stephen J. Kunitz, "Mortality Change in America, 1620–1920," *Human Biology* 56, no. 3 (1984): 559–82. Samuel H. Preston and Michael R. Haines, *Fatal Years: Child Mortality in Late Nineteenth-Century America*, 1991. Clayne L. Pope, "Adult Mortality in America before 1900: A View from Family Histories," in *Strategic Factors in Nineteenth Century American Economic History: A Volume to Honor Robert W. Fogel*, eds. Claudia Goldin and Hugh Rockoff, 1992, pp. 267–96. U.S. Department of Health and Human Services, Social Security Administration, *Life Tables for the United States Social Security Area, 1900–2080*, Actuarial Study No. 107, 1992. Richard A. Easterlin, "The Nature and Causes of the Mortality Revolution," in *Growth Triumphant: The Twenty-first Century in Historical Perspective*, 1996, pp. 69–82. Michael R. Haines, "The American Population, 1790–1920," in *The Cambridge Economic History of the United States*, vol. 2, eds. Stanley Engerman and Robert Gallman, 2000.

—Michael Haines

LIFE STAGES. Research on the historical meaning and importance of different life stages is relatively recent, A growing interest in family history from the early 1960s on resulted in studies of the evolution of childhood, the progression to adolescence and young adulthood, and the transition from adulthood to old age. The development of specialized subfields devoted to the status and roles of the youngest and oldest members of society produced a greater understanding of the aging process.

An important landmark in the study of specific life stages was the 1962 English translation of Philippe Ariés's *Centuries of Childhood.* In western Europe prior to the sixteenth century, Ariés argued, children were quickly socialized into the adult world; childhood, he contended, was a concept that evolved only in recent centuries. Although few historians shared Ariés's nostalgia for a time when children enjoyed greater freedom but few institutionalized protections, his view of childhood as in many ways a social construction proved very influential.

Childhood and Adolescence. Historians of colonial America generally portrayed childhood as a period lasting no later than the age of eight. At this relatively young age, most children began a sort of apprenticeship that encompassed their integration into the religious, social, and economic world of adults. Early research on colonial *New England also indicated that the strong affective bonds that typically characterized parent-child relations in the late twentieth century were conspicuously absent. However, this depiction of childhood in early America has undergone some revision. Research on the Chesapeake region indicated that parents outside Puritan New England were more likely to have stronger emotional attachments to their children. Other scholars argue that even in New England, relations between parents and children were probably closer than once thought.

Nonetheless, childhood has clearly changed in profound ways over the past three centuries. The nineteenth century, for example, witnessed the increasing acceptance of childhood vulnerability and the need to protect children from undesirable moral influences. This recognition contributed to the expansion of compulsory public-school *education, *Progressive Era *child labor legislation, and social welfare services designed to deal with delinquency, *poverty, and child abuse.

The reasons' for these changes remain under discussion. Some research, for example, has focused on demographic effects, linking the apparent lack of affection for children in early America to high child mortality. According to this view, the relatively high death rate among children resulted in a psychological reaction whereby parents avoided deep emotional attachments to offspring who quite possibly would not survive to adulthood. Large *family sizes, a consequence of women continuing to give birth past the age of forty, meant that many families ultimately contained children ranging from infants to young adults. This tended to blur the distinction between the various stages of early life that eventually became sharply distinguished.

Other scholars link the emergence of childhood as a distinct life stage to the Industrial Revolution. While the necessity of training a skilled industrial workforce contributed to the expansion of formal schooling as an important part of childhood, the demise of family-based economies made the early socialization of children the exclusive domain of mothers. This transition, some argue, increased awareness of the emotional value of children.

Demographic and economic change also played a more indirect role in the development of modern childhood. The reform movements of late nineteenth- and early twentieth-century America were in many ways a response to increased levels of *immigration, *urbanization, and *industrialization. A key component of the Progressive Era was the emergence of specialists—medical and health professionals, educators, social scientists, and social welfare advocates—who increasingly used specific age groupings as an organizing framework. In addition, many of these professionals focused on the problems and developmental needs of children.

The recognition of adolescence as a specific developmental stage shows how specialists played a role in the evolution of modern childhood. Early in the twentieth century, psychologists popularized the notion that the onset of puberty marked the beginning of a stressful time in terms of identity formation. The discovery of adolescence—often dated from the publication of a book of that title by the psychologist G. Stanley *Hall in 1904—played a major role in reorganizing the lives of American teenagers. Compulsory high-school attendance and the growth of youth organizations added adult-sanctioned structures not present before. This fundamental change helped lay the groundwork for the development of a pervasive youth culture in the twentieth century.

Although these changes in American childhood were profound, their timing varied. The need to contribute to the family economy is often credited with lower school-attendance rates for many ethnic groups and working-class youths during the nineteenth and early twentieth centuries. The lack of facilities and racial *segregation resulted in lower school attendance among *African American children, especially in the *South. *Gender differences in education were also evident. Young women's education was seen as preparation for their anticipated role as homemakers and mothers. Although gendered socialization (as well as the influence of race and *social class) remains influential, by the post–*World War II period, these distinctions generally diminished.

Ironically, even as the experience of childhood became more homogenized, childhood as a protected stage of life eroded over the last decades of the twentieth century, as children were exposed to mass-media depictions of sex and violence and the rise in divorce forced many children to confront adult realities at relatively young ages. In addition, two distinct child-rearing models based largely on social class emerged. Middle- and upper-class parents strove to provide a nurturing environment including access to better educational facilities. This achievement-oriented style contrasted with that of parents who lacked the means, time, or energy to improve their children's probability of success later in life.

Much of the impetus for achievement-oriented parenting came from research done by developmental psychologists and social scientists, and from the central assumption that a child's environment and experiences have profound effects on later life. Glen Elder's *Children of the Great Depression* (1974), an important historical study using this approach, examined the impact of the Depression of the 1930s on the lives of successive cohorts of California children. Elder's research model, often referred to as the life-course approach, influenced historians studying life stages. According to this model, the timing of significant life-defining transitional events—leaving home, leaving school, marriage, and entry into the labor force—varies from individual to individual, and also according to gender, class, and culture, and the timing of a specific event in turn affects the timing of subsequent events.

Marriage and Adulthood. The transition to adulthood, most historians believe, proceeded more gradually in the past. In 1900, men and women typically left home, married, and established independent households later in life. Gradually, young adults accomplished these transitions at younger ages, with this trend accelerating after World War II. By the end of the twentieth century, most young adults accomplished the transition to adulthood in a far shorter period of time than they had a century earlier.

Why did the transition to adulthood become a more rigidly age-defined process? One theory is that in the past the timing of these transitions was articulated more by the family's collective needs. Children remained at home because they had an obligation to contribute to the family income. In addition, marriage and the establishment of an independent household were often contingent on attaining a minimum resource level, which for the urban working class could be a lengthy process. Over the twentieth century, as the economic well-being of most families became less dependent on the contributions of children, young adults increasingly accomplished these transitions not because of collective family needs, but rather according to specific age norms. However, the post-1970 era saw a slight reversal of this trend. As postsecondary education became a more protracted process, young men and women tended to leave home at later ages, and the marriage age increased. Nonetheless, the experience of young adulthood (like that of childhood and adolescence) was acutely affected by an increasing age consciousness.

Old Age. The development of a more age-regimented society also affected older Americans. In the preindustrial past, according to a widely held view, the elderly enjoyed an exalted status. In agrarian-based, traditional economies, they maintained control of land and were repositories of knowledge acquired over a lifetime of productive work. In colonial America, historians have found, the elderly enjoyed a respected place in society but were often a focus of generational conflicts over family and community authority and the transfer of economic assets. By 1900, however, the elderly were no longer seen as merely older adults, but rather as a distinct group with special needs. Like children, they drew the attention of reformers and social scientists who claimed that many older Americans suffered from poverty and isolation from their kin.

Recent historical research suggests that the alarmist warnings concerning the state of the elderly at the end of the nineteenth century were exaggerated. Little evidence exists that their economic position was deteriorating. Older men maintained high labor-force participation rates, while home ownership (often the result of relatively high rates of savings) provided many widows with an important economic asset. In addition, most older Americans lived with kin—either a spouse or, in the case of widows and widowers, an adult child.

Nonetheless, the perception that the elderly needed public assistance instigated a variety of lobbying efforts on their behalf, which contributed to the passage of the *Social Security Act in 1935. The provisions for old-age assistance reduced poverty among the elderly, but it also set in motion two significant trends. Although earlier reformers had claimed that industrialization had increased unemployment among older men, labor-force participation rates among the elderly declined sharply after the 1930s. *Social Security benefits also significantly affected the living arrangements of the elderly. Whereas in 1900 most formerly married elderly men and women lived with an adult child or other relative, by the end of the twentieth century most lived independently in single-person households. Social Security began this trend, some researchers believe, by providing widows and widowers with the resources to maintain an independent residence after the death of a spouse.

Demographic trends have also profoundly affected the lives of older Americans. A lower age at marriage and declining fertility rates (specifically the ending of childbearing at earlier ages) combined with increased *life expectancy resulted in the so-called empty-nest syndrome: the increasing time span experienced by parents after their youngest child leaves home. Increased longevity also contributed to a fundamental population shift, with approximately 13 percent of the American population over the age of 65 in 1990, compared to 4 percent a century earlier. In their multiplying numbers, the elderly became a potent force in American politics through various lobbying organizations. Although the United States remained a youth-oriented society as the twenty-first century began, the needs and concerns of the elderly, including the provision of health and retirement services, had important economic implications and seemed likely to loom even larger in the future.

[*See also* American Association of Retired Persons; Birth Control and Family Planning; Child Rearing; Colonial Era; Death and Dying; Demography; Depressions, Economic; Disease; Health and Fitness; Housing; Marriage and Divorce; Medicare and Medicaid; Professionalization; Psychology; Puritanism; Romantic Movement; Social Science; Welfare, Federal; Women in the Labor Force; Work.]

• Glen H. Elder Jr., *Children of the Great Depression*, 1974. Joseph M. Hawes and N. Ray Hiner, eds., *American Childhood: A Research Guide and Historical Handbook*, 1985. John Demos, *Past, Present, and Personal: The Family and the Life Course in American History*, 1986. David Van Tassel and Peter N. Stearns, eds., *Old Age in a Bureaucratic Society: The Elderly, The Experts, and the State in American History*, 1986. Howard Chudacoff, *How Old Are You?: Age Consciousness in American Culture*, 1989. John Modell, *Into One's Own: From Youth to Adulthood in the United States, 1920–1975*, 1989. Carole Haber and Brian Gratton, *Old Age and the Search for Security: An American Social History*, 1994.

—Ron Goeken

LIL'UOKALANI (1838–1917), last queen of *Hawai'i. She was born Lydia Kamaka'eha to parents who were first cousins, following the Hawaiian custom requiring high-ranking personages to marry closely in their lineage to increase the family mana, or spiritual power. Lil'uokalani served as regent in 1880–1881 when her brother King Kalakaua made a world tour, and again in 1890 when he sought medical treatment in San Francisco. Well educated, well read, and fluent in Hawaiian and English, she accompanied her sister-in-law, Queen Kap'iolani, to London in 1887 for Queen Victoria's Golden Jubilee, where they were received as befit their royal status.

Lil'uokalani became queen in 1891, upon the death of King Kalakaua. Her reign was cut short in January 1893 by a coup d'état led by Lorrin Thurston and other descendants of American missionaries, in collusion with the U.S. minister to Hawai'i, John L. Stevens. Stevens ordered troops from the USS *Boston* ashore, ostensibly to support Thurston and what became known as the "Provisional Government." Thurston and his associates sought greater profits for their sugar plantations through U.S. annexation, so Hawaiian sugar could be marketed in America without payment of the duties imposed on foreign sugar.

To prevent bloodshed, Queen Lil'uokalani forbade her people to engage militarily with U.S. troops or American citizens, although armed Hawaiian volunteers outnumbered the American forces. Hawaiians, regarding their queen as a spiritual as well as political leader, unhesitatingly obeyed. The queen sent emissaries to Washington, D.C., to seek peaceful removal of American troops, but the American military chose the Pearl Harbor lagoon as headquarters for the Pacific fleet. The United States annexed Hawai'i in 1898, without allowing the Hawaiian people to vote on the matter. Because the queen ceded the country under military threat, the coup has been deemed illegal under *international law. In November 1993, President Bill *Clinton signed Public Law 103–150, acknowledging the illegality of the invasion and Hawaiians' inherent right of sovereignty over their lands.

A gifted composer and beloved humanitarian, Lil'uokalani died in Hawai'i in 1917, her dream of independence unfulfilled.

[*See also* Expansionism; Spanish-American War.]

• James Blount, *Report to the United States Congress: Hawaiian Islands*, 53d Cong., 2d sess., Doc. 47, 1893. Lili'uokalani, *Hawai'i's Story by Hawai'i's Queen*, 1898, reprint 1986.

—Lilikala Kame'eleihiwa

LIMITED NUCLEAR TEST BAN TREATY (1963). The advent of the hydrogen bomb in the mid-1950s led to a worldwide outcry over the deadly radioactive fallout from American and Soviet nuclear tests. As protests mounted, American leaders from Dwight D. *Eisenhower to John F. *Kennedy sought a test ban not only to stop this global fallout but also to limit the spread of nuclear weapons to other countries.

When negotiations between the United States and the Soviet Union over a comprehensive nuclear test ban failed in 1958, Eisenhower and the Soviet leader Nikita Khrushchev agreed to a voluntary moratorium on testing. In September 1961, the Soviet Union resumed atmospheric tests; President Kennedy immediately authorized American testing, at first only underground, and then in the atmosphere in April 1962.

After the *Cuban Missile Crisis, Kennedy and Khrushchev resumed the quest for a comprehensive test ban, but Soviet opposition to on-site inspection doomed this effort. In July 1963, special envoy W. Averell Harriman (1891–1986) secured Khrushchev's agreement to a treaty to outlaw nuclear tests in the atmosphere, outer space, and underwater. Kennedy succeeded in winning Senate approval for this limited nuclear test ban in September 1963 by pledging to continue U.S. underground testing indefinitely.

The limited test ban treaty succeeded in allaying public concern over global fallout, but it had little impact on the nuclear arms race. Countries such as China, which refused to sign, perfected their own nuclear weapons through extensive testing, and the superpowers continued to build ever larger and more deadly arsenals of destruction. The 1963 treaty was but a halting first step toward genuine nuclear disarmament.

[*See also* Cold War; Nuclear Arms Control Treaties; Nuclear Weapons.]

• Robert A. Divine, *Blowing on the Wind: The Nuclear Test Ban Debate,* 1978. Glenn T. Seaborg, *Kennedy, Khrushchev, and the Test Ban,* 1981.

—Robert A. Divine

LINCOLN, ABRAHAM (1809–1865), sixteenth president of the United States. Lincoln was born in a log cabin near Hodgenville, Kentucky. A paternal ancestor had arrived in Massachusetts from England in 1637. Abraham's father, Thomas, a respected farmer though semiliterate, shared the restlessness of the frontier, and in 1816 the family moved to Indiana. In 1818, when Lincoln was nine, his mother, Nancy Hanks, died. His father soon married Sarah Bush Johnston, who became a loving stepmother. Abraham attended school for scarcely a year, but he read such works as the *Bible, *Pilgrim's Progress,* and Aesop's *Fables* and displayed a remarkable capacity for self-education. Migrating with his family to Illinois in 1830, young Lincoln tried various occupations and served briefly in the Black Hawk War (1832). Passing the bar exam in 1836, he moved in 1837 to Springfield, the state capital, where law and politics absorbed his interests. Joining the *Whig party, he served in the Illinois legislature (1834–1841) and a term in Congress (1847–1849), during which he opposed the *Mexican War and proposed a bill providing for the gradual, compensated emancipation of slaves with local consent. Returning to Springfield, Lincoln virtually abandoned politics while developing a thriving law practice with his partner, William Herndon, and rearing a family. In 1842 he had married Mary Todd, who was from a prominent Kentucky family. Of their four sons, only the eldest, Robert, lived to maturity.

The *Kansas-Nebraska Act of 1854, opening the territories to *slavery, aroused Lincoln and thrust him back into politics. At the 1856 convention of the new *Republican party, he was a favorite-son candidate for the vice presidential nomination. Lincoln's skill as a stump speaker, enhanced by his six-foot-four-inch height, contributed to his political rise. In 1858, Illinois Republicans nominated him for the U.S. Senate; in accepting, Lincoln asserted: "'A house divided against itself cannot stand.' I believe the government cannot endure permanently half slave and half free." In seven well-publicized debates with his Democratic opponent, Stephen A. *Douglas, Lincoln attacked slavery expansion. He lost the election but gained national recognition.

In 1860, the Republicans nominated Lincoln for president. A four-way contest in a divided nation gave him the presidency, but only 39 percent of the popular vote and no electoral votes in any of the eleven southern states that would soon secede. By 1 February 1861—more than a month before Lincoln's inauguration—seven states of the Lower *South had seceded to form the Confederacy. Confronting a gathering crisis, Lincoln in his inaugural address pledged not to interfere with slavery where it already existed, but he insisted that the Union must be preserved, and affirmed the duty of any president "to administer the present Government... and to transmit it, unimpaired by him, to his successors." With the surrender of Fort Sumter in Charleston harbor on 13 April, the *Civil War began.

Further inflamed by Lincoln's call to arms, four more states seceded. Four border states remained loyal, however, and keeping them in the Union became one of Lincoln's prime concerns. By the time Lincoln summoned the fractured Congress to Washington on 4 July 1861, he had already adopted war measures that stretched the *Constitution, declaring martial law and suspending habeas corpus in areas of the Union where antiwar sentiment ran high.

Inevitably, the war dominated Lincoln's presidency. The rout of Union forces at the Battle of *Bull Run near Washington in July 1861 spurred Congress to make abundant authorizations of money and men, but Lincoln had trouble finding generals who could use these resources effectively. George B. McClellan (1826–1885), while skillful in organizing troops, proved reluctant to confide in Lincoln or to conduct an aggressive war. Not until March 1862 did McClellan's huge Army of the Potomac advance, approaching Richmond, Virginia, the Confederate capital, by the peninsula formed by the York and James Rivers, contrary to Lincoln's preference for an overland march shielding Washington.

Frustrated by McClellan's caution, his overestimation of enemy strength, and his complaints of lack of support, Lincoln relieved him in August 1862 but reappointed him after a second Union reverse at Bull Run. At the Battle of *Antietam, 17 September 1862, McClellan repelled General Robert E. *Lee's invading forces but failed to pursue the enemy. The partial victory at Antietam did, however, enable Lincoln to issue the *Emancipation Proclamation, on 1 January 1863, freeing the slaves in rebel areas, welcoming freedmen into military service, and laying the groundwork for the Thirteenth Amendment of 1865, officially ending slavery.

Lincoln's troubles continued with defeats at Fredericksburg and Chancellorsville, Virginia. The tide turned in July 1863, however, as Union forces repulsed the Confederates' northern advance at the Battle of *Gettysburg, and Ulysses S. *Grant took Vicksburg, Mississippi, dividing the Confederacy in the *West. On 9 March 1864, Lincoln appointed Grant to command all Union armies. Leaving the western campaign to General William T. *Sherman, Grant laid plans to defeat Lee's army in Virginia and invade the Lower South. By late 1864, Sherman's march through the South had brought him to Savannah, Georgia, while Grant, although failing to defeat Lee in the field, had enveloped Lee's forces at Petersburg, Virginia.

Throughout 1864, Lincoln's reelection remained doubtful. His generals' inability to end the war conclusively was accompanied by a growing peace movement and a congressional struggle over postwar *Reconstruction. The Democrats nominated McClellan and adopted a peace platform (which McClellan repudiated). Lincoln himself despaired of reelection, but Union successes in Georgia and Mobile Bay brought him victory with 55 percent of the popular vote. His Second Inaugural Address of March 1865, meditating on the war's meaning and looking forward to peace ("With malice toward none, with charity for all..."), ranks with his brief but eloquent *Gettysburg Address of 19 November 1863 as a masterpiece of American public oratory.

Looking to the postwar period, Lincoln in December 1863 had proclaimed a *Reconstruction plan that Congress believed too lenient and an infringement on its authority. Proceeding with plans for dealing with the collapsing Confederacy, Lincoln pocket-vetoed the Wade-Davis Bill of July 1864, which required a harsher approach. By early 1865, Lincoln was moving in the direction of enfranchising and educating some freedmen while displaying flexibility in restoring seceding states to the Union. His cabinet failed to support his suggestion for compensating slaveholders, however.

On 9 April 1865, Lee surrendered at Appomattox, Virginia. Lincoln, however, had little time to savor victory. On the night of 15 April, as he sat with his wife at Ford's Theatre in Washington, he was shot by John Wilkes Booth, an actor and rabid Confederate supporter. He died the following morning. Grief enveloped the North as his body was borne back to Springfield for burial.

Historians have long probed Lincoln's life and character,

seeking the key to his almost saintlike standing in the American pantheon. His earthy humor, his ability to joke when things seemed darkest, and his endless supply of homespun stories certainly helped him cope with the crises of war. Beneath the humor, however, lay a profound melancholy. His relations with the temperamental and unstable Mary Todd Lincoln were often strained, and the death of his beloved son Willie in 1862 brought further grief. His frontier origins, his plainspoken eloquence, his magnanimity toward the defeated South, and the circumstances of his death all contributed to his enduring reputation as perhaps the greatest of presidents. Walt *Whitman's elegiac "When Lilacs Last in the Dooryard Bloom'd" and "Oh Captain, My Captain," beloved of school orators, launched a tide of commemorative poems, biographies, and works of art. The *Lincoln Memorial in *Washington, D.C. (1914–1917), housing Daniel Chester French's heroic seated statue, remains one of the capital's best-known icons. Carl Sandburg's multivolume biography (1926–1939) presented Lincoln as a son of the West who supremely embodied the straightforward frontier virtues that underlay his grandeur of character and nobility of thought. Although debunking historians have presented Lincoln as a calculating politician, vacillating and temporizing in his approach to *racism and slavery, and psychohistorians have dissected his enigmatic and sometimes tortured personality, Abraham Lincoln's standing in the hearts of the American people seems unassailable.

[*See also* Antebellum Era; Antislavery; Confederate States of America; Federal Government, Executive Branch: The Presidency; Lincoln-Douglas Debates.]

• Albert J. Beveridge, *Abraham Lincoln, 1809–1858,* 2 vol., 1928. J. G. Randall, *Lincoln the President,* 4 vols., the 4th completed by R. N. Current, 1946–1955. T. Harry Williams, *Lincoln and His Generals,* 1952. Merrill D. Peterson, *Lincoln in American Memory,* 1994. David Herbert Donald, *Lincoln,* 1995. James A. Rawley, *Abraham Lincoln and a Nation Worth Fighting For,* 1996.

—James A. Rawley

LINCOLN-DOUGLAS DEBATES (1858). A fabled series of political duels, the Lincoln-Douglas debates comprised seven joint appearances during the 1858 U.S. Senate contest in Illinois between the Democratic incumbent, Stephen A. *Douglas, and his Republican challenger, Abraham *Lincoln. The debates began at Ottawa on 21 August and concluded at Alton on 15 October. They aroused intense state and national interest because they involved the political future of Douglas, probably the nation's most influential Democrat, and because they concentrated on the intensifying sectional conflict over *slavery. They are remembered in history for elevating Abraham Lincoln to national prominence.

Both candidates elaborated long-held positions on the issues of slavery in the *South, the extension of the institution westward, and race. Lincoln insisted that slavery was a moral wrong that should be placed on a course toward extinction. Although the *Constitution obliged Americans to give each state plenary control over slavery within its jurisdiction, he said, citizens were equally obliged by moral principle to prevent slavery from extending its geographical reach. Douglas, refusing to take a position on the morality of slavery, declared that the Union and slavery were compatible institutions; whether a territory adopted slavery was a matter for its settlers to decide—the doctrine known as "popular sovereignty." Lincoln retorted that Douglas's hidden object was to inculcate popular indifference to the injustice of slavery as part of a conspiracy to spread bondage not only throughout the territories but ultimately into the free states as well.

Douglas, in turn, asserted that his policy on slavery arose from his belief that the republic was a white man's government in which blacks were entitled only to those privileges that whites chose to extend to them. Lincoln, he alleged, was not only an abolitionist and a reckless inciter of sectional warfare, but also a proponent of racial *equality. The power of this last charge was registered in Lincoln's tortured response that the equality he claimed for blacks was compatible with white supremacy and did not extend to the rights to vote, serve on juries, or marry whites.

In the election, the Democrats narrowly prevailed where it mattered: they held control of the Illinois legislature, which proceeded to return Douglas to the Senate. Although Lincoln lost the contest, his respectable showing against Douglas in the debates proved a major step toward a grander prize, the *Republican party nomination for president in the fateful election of 1860.

[*See also* Antislavery; Civil War: Causes; Kansas-Nebraska Act.]

• Harry V. Jaffa, *Crisis of the House Divided: An Interpretation of the Lincoln-Douglas Debates,* 1959. Don E. Fehrenbacher, *Prelude to Greatness: Lincoln in the 1850's,* 1962.

—George B. Forgie

LINCOLN MEMORIAL. Located on the west end of the Mall in *Washington, D.C., the Lincoln Memorial features Daniel Chester French's statue of a seated Abraham *Lincoln in a building designed by Henry Bacon and modeled after a classical Greek temple. Authorized by Congress in 1911 and built by the Lincoln Memorial Commission, it stresses Lincoln's role as savior of the Union and the importance of sectional reconciliation between North and *South. The speakers who dedicated the memorial on 30 May 1922, including President Warren G. *Harding, made scant mention of Lincoln's role as the "Great Emancipator" of African American slaves.

In 1939, however, the *National Association for the Advancement of Colored People (NAACP) helped to reshape Lincoln's memory by turning the memorial into a locus for *civil rights activity. That year, Secretary of the Interior Harold Ickes gave the NAACP permission to sponsor an Easter concert by Marian *Anderson, an African American singer, after the Daughters of the American Revolution had denied her the use of Washington's Constitution Hall on account of her race. Widely attended and publicized, Anderson's appearance made the memorial a popular site for future civil rights rallies and protests. In August 1963, the memorial became the focal point of the March on Washington, attended by hundreds of thousands of people demanding passage of what became the landmark Civil Rights Act of 1964. It served as the backdrop that afternoon for Dr. Martin Luther *King's memorable "I Have a Dream" speech.

• Scott A. Sandage, "A Marble House Divided: The Lincoln Memorial, the Civil Rights Movement, and the Politics of Memory, 1939–1963," *Journal of American History* 80 (June 1993): 135–67. Merrill D. Peterson, *Lincoln in American Memory,* 1994.

—G. Kurt Piehler

LINDBERGH, CHARLES (1902–1974), aviator. Lindbergh burst upon the world stage on 20–21 May 1927 when he piloted his single-engine Ryan monoplane, *The Spirit of St. Louis,* solo across the Atlantic. Although this was the signature achievement of his life, Lindbergh's impact went well beyond his epic flight. Reared on a farm in Little Falls, Minnesota, the son of a farm-bloc congressman, Lindbergh in 1920 enrolled as an engineering student at the University of Wisconsin. He dropped out after two years, learned to fly, and spent the summer of 1923 barnstorming through the West. Seeking more experience and training, Lindbergh enlisted as a U.S. Army flying cadet; trained in San Antonio, Texas; and graduated first in his class in 1925. After the military, he found employment as an airmail pilot, the most demanding and dangerous type of flying in this period.

Learning of a $25,000 prize to fly from New York to Paris, Lindbergh saw an unmatched aviator's challenge. But he also sought to further the cause of aviation and to demonstrate the capabilities and reliability of the airplane. His successful 33½ hour, nonstop flight from Roosevelt Field on Long Island, New

York, to Le Bourget Field just outside Paris not only vaulted Lindbergh to instant fame but also contributed to renewed enthusiasm and investment in the nascent U.S. *aviation industry and commercial air transport. Other crucial building blocks in the 1920s contributed to later American preeminence in aerospace, such as the Air Commerce Act of 1926 and the Guggenheim Fund for the Promotion of Aeronautics, but Lindbergh's achievement provided an important catalyst.

Lindbergh's impact on aeronautics continued in the 1930s as he made several pioneering transoceanic flights with his wife, Anne Morrow Lindbergh, for Pan American Airways and other emerging airlines. He was an early and ardent supporter of the research of the rocket pioneer Robert H. Goddard. During *World War II, Lindbergh served as a consultant to several aircraft manufacturers and as a civilian adviser to the U.S. military. In 1944, as a civilian, he flew fifty combat missions in the Pacific theater and shot down one Japanese fighter. After the war he served as a special consultant for research and development to the U.S. Air Force.

The 1932 kidnapping and murder of the Lindberghs' infant son, and the ensuing trial and execution of Bruno Hauptmann in 1935, stirred nearly as much public and media attention as Lindbergh's Atlantic crossing. On the eve of World War II, as a leading spokesman for the noninterventionist pressure group the *America First Committee, Lindbergh drew widespread criticism for highly publicized statements regarding the superiority of German airpower, for his consistent failure to denounce German atrocities, and for anti–Semitic utterances made in a speech delivered in Des Moines, Iowa, on 11 September 1941. Lindbergh later restored his reputation somewhat as an activist in the environmentalist movement. A talented and prolific writer, he wrote seven books and numerous articles.

[*See also* Airplanes and Air Transport; Anti-Semitism; Environmentalism; Popular Culture; Twenties, The.]

• Kenneth S. Davis, *The Hero: Charles A. Lindbergh and the American Dream,* 1959. Charles A. Lindbergh, *Autobiography of Values,* 1976. Tom D. Crouch, ed., *Charles A. Lindbergh: An American Life,* 1977.

—Peter L. Jakab

LIPPMANN, WALTER (1889–1974), author, columnist, public-affairs commentator. Born into a wealthy German-Jewish family in *New York City, Lippmann graduated from Harvard in 1910. A college socialist who grew more conservative over time, Lippmann epitomized the stresses of twentieth-century American *liberalism. Active over more than six decades, he advised Theodore *Roosevelt, helped craft Woodrow *Wilson's *Fourteen Points, aided in drafting John F. *Kennedy's inaugural address, and assailed Lyndon B. *Johnson's *Vietnam War policies.

A founding editor of the *New Republic* magazine in 1914, Lippmann emerged as one of the *Progressive Era's leading social theorists with two influential early books. *A Preface to Politics* (1913), reflecting his encounter with Sigmund Freud's work, examined the irrational aspects of politics. *Drift and Mastery* (1914) explored the transition from premodern to modern society, delineated the interest groups emerging in the new industrial order, and proposed loyalty to scientific method as a unifying force.

*World War I soured Lippmann on progressive idealism. His *Public Opinion* (1922) and *The Phantom Public* (1925) criticized the media and advocated intervention by experts to help the masses deal with complex issues. *A Preface to Morals* (1929), his most enduring book, examined the alienation and aimlessness of the postwar "lost generation." Turning once again to *journalism, Lippmann wrote a daily column for the *New York Herald Tribune* from 1931 to 1967, and later for the *Washington Post.* Syndicated in more than two hundred newspapers and read by some fifty million people, his columns influenced both the political elite and the educated public. Critical of the New Deal in the 1930s, he forsook his neo-Hamiltonianism, with its emphasis on governmental activism, to defend a market-oriented liberalism that some critics mistook for warmed-over *laissez-faire ideology. With the rise of totalitarianism abroad, Lippmann abandoned his youthful *pragmatism and its attendant relativism. During and after *World War II he criticized U.S. *Cold War ideology for oversimplifying complex international realities, becoming an articulate exponent of a tough–minded foreign policy "realism." Because he wrote so much, for so long, about so many issues, Lippmann occasionally seemed a man for every season. But a fundamental skepticism and elitism consistently characterized his views of public affairs and foreign policy.

[*See also* Croly, Herbert; New Deal Era, The; Sixties, The; Twenties, The.]

• Ronald Steel, *Walter Lippmann and the American Century,* 1980. Barry D. Riccio, *Walter Lippmann—Odyssey of a Liberal,* 1994.

—Barry D. Riccio

LITERACY. Historically, literacy has meant the ability to read and/or write at a certain level of competence. But conceptions of literacy and its uses have been closely tied to specific historical contexts. In medieval and Renaissance Europe, before European settlers reached North America, the term *litteratus,* or "lettered," meant competence in Latin and was associated with the clergy or the aristocracy. By the eighteenth and nineteenth centuries, the focus had shifted from Latin to vernacular languages, and the equation of literacy with aristocratic or clerical rank had been broken, despite the continuing complaints of cultural elites about the spread of literacy to the lower order.

Definitions and measures of literacy, especially for comparative purposes, are notoriously difficult. Until the mid–nineteenth century, signatures or marks on wills, petitions, or other documents offered the most direct and widest evidence of literacy or the lack thereof. In more recent times, censuses, school records, and various educational and "literacy" tests have been used. All measures, however, remain problematic and controversial.

Many researchers have treated literacy as a gauge of social, political, or cultural development. For some, it is a sign of modernity. In other interpretations, literacy has symbolic, ideological, and even mythic value. Interpretations of its meaning often conflict. In American history, literacy has been linked to the advancement of individuals and groups, but it has also been used to maintain inequalities associated with *social class, race, *gender, and other factors. Researchers, therefore, must consider literacy not as a neutral and abstract skill, but in relation to the value accorded to reading and writing by society at large or by particular subgroups in successive time periods. These values, in turn, have influenced the institutional resources that have been allocated to the spread or restriction of literacy. Legislatures in the antebellum *South, for example, often made it illegal to teach a slave to read or write.

These distinctions divide American historians as they have divided Americans historically. For example, historians long assumed, with scant evidence, that the mainland North American British colonies, and then the United States, were more literate than Europe. Recent research has both confirmed and qualified this received wisdom. *Colonial Era literacy levels, ranging from perhaps 50–60 to more than 90 percent for European immigrants and their descendents, were, indeed, high by European standards, but not unprecedentedly so. Literacy levels tended to reflect the levels of the regions from which the emigrants came and to reproduce existing social differences. Excepting enslaved Africans, literate individuals were more likely to emigrate, giving America a long-standing social and developmental advantage. Yet, as literacy became more common and valued, it intertwined with the oral in American culture.

*Religion—first a *Protestantism rooted in individual access to the *Bible—was long a spur to literacy, along with the desire for economic and social progress and concerns for social control and national status. Residents of *New England and the Old Northwest particularly endorsed and diffused literacy. For many reasons, literacy was more restricted in the South and among racial and some ethnic minorities. Women's rates of literacy increased rapidly in the nineteenth century. *African Americans and members of other minority groups waged impressive struggles for literacy. Over time, public schools increasingly took on responsibility for literacy training, replacing less formal ways of learning to read and write. As the literacy levels of virtually all groups rose in the nineteenth and twentieth centuries, literacy's symbolic role as a marker of class distinctions declined.

Concerns about literacy have also masked a nativist desire to restrict the *immigration of ethnic groups considered undesirable. In the late nineteenth and early twentieth centuries, the Immigration Restriction League repeatedly urged Congress to impose a literacy test for immigrants, as a means of controlling and reducing the influx of newcomers from southern and eastern Europe.

In the late twentieth century, issues related to literacy continued to stir intense controversy. Many observations and tests suggested that levels of "functional" literacy were dangerously low. Debate raged over whether *Asian American and *Hispanic American immigrant children should be taught in English or in their own languages, and over the establishment of English as the official national language. The rise of the new electronic media and the recognition of diverse modes of understanding and communicating suggested that the concept of literacy itself needed to be reexamined. Conservatives trumpeted their fears of an endangered "cultural literacy."

But such controversies were hardly new. Throughout U.S. history, literacy has been a source of controversy and contention. What seemed clear, as the century ended, was that there are many forms of "literacy," and that the whole issue would likely remain a volatile arena of ideological contestation.

[*See also* Education: The Public School Movement; Immigration Law; Mobility; Nativist Movement; Slavery: Development and Expansion of Slavery.]

• Lawrence A. Cremin, *American Education,* 3 vols., 1970–1988. Daniel H. Calhoun, *The Intelligence of a People,* 1973. Harvey J. Graff, *The Literacy Myth: Literacy and Social Structure in the Nineteenth-Century City,* 1979, reprint 1991. Lee Soltow and Edward Stevens, *The Rise of Literacy and the Common School in the United States: A Socioeconomic Analysis to 1870,* 1981. Harvey J. Graff, *The Legacies of Literacy: Continuities and Contradictions in Western Society and Culture,* 1987. Mike Rose, *Lives on the Boundary: The Struggles and Achievements of America's Underprepared,* 1989. Carl Kaestle et al., *Literacy in the United States: Readers and Reading since 1880,* 1991.

—Harvey J. Graff

LITERARY CRITICISM, the formal discussion of literary works, first flowered in America in early nineteenth-century debates over the quality and characteristics of American writing—debates intensified by the notorious 1821 jibe of the British critic Sydney Smith, "Who reads an American book?" Critics such as William Tudor, James Kirke Paulding, and Cornelius Mathews debated whether American authors should write in "American" or English, and whether they should celebrate the nation's democratic principles or its landscapes, waterways, and indigenous peoples. Cultural critics such as Ralph Waldo *Emerson and Theodore *Parker, meanwhile, reflected more broadly on the role of writers, poets, and scholars in democratic America. Some writers themselves, including Edgar Allan *Poe, Margaret *Fuller, and James Russell Lowell produced illuminating critical studies. Otherwise, criticism was largely left to partisan journalists who reviewed books according to their readers' political expectations.

Post–*Civil War literary criticism—indeed, the whole culture industry—was dominated by defenders of the genteel tradition. A vast informal network of editors, publishers, and ministers insisted on literature's central duty to uphold Christian morality. Tastemakers like Edmund Clarence Stedman and Thomas Bailey Aldrich valued harmony, coherence, and beauty above all. The new professors of American literature, which became an academic subject in the 1870s, fully concurred. Late nineteenth-century literary histories by Moses Coit Tyler, Barrett Wendell, and others celebrated the *New England tradition.

Against this regime of pallid good taste, William Dean *Howells, Henry *James, and Samuel L. *Clemens called for serious adult realism. Early modern authors like Edgar Lee Masters, Theodore *Dreiser, and Sherwood Anderson, encouraged by the journalist-critic H. L. *Mencken, along with new generation of self-conscious intellectuals writing in such magazines as the *New Republic,* the *Dial,* the *Smart Set,* the *Nation,* and ultimately Mencken's *American Mercury* criticized bourgeois America's commercialism, philistinism, and xenophobia. The international modernist movement, including such Americans as the poet T. S. Eliot, further undermined the genteel tradition.

A reaction soon set in, however, as the poet-critic John Crowe Ransom and his circle in Nashville initiated the so-called Agrarian movement. Calling themselves Fugitives, they were in flight from a modernity they identified with the urban industrial North. Influenced by European formalists like Benedetto Croce and T. E. Hulme, as well as the linguists William Empson and I. A. Richards, their literary criticism focused almost exclusively on the text. Christened the "New Criticism" by Ransom in the late 1930s, this formalist approach dominated academic textual analysis for a generation.

Mid–twentieth-century cultural critics, meanwhile, writing in journals of opinion, explored literature's social and ethical responsibilities. Freelance critics like Philip Rahv and Alfred Kazin functioned largely outside academia. Even if they were professors, like Lionel Trilling or Leslie Fiedler, they addressed a broader public. Rejecting their Depression-Era radical pasts, these critics embraced the vision of democratic humanism that became the *Cold War's hegemonic consensus and shaped the literary canon.

By the early 1970s, such nonacademic literary criticism had faded. Burgeoning instead was an academic movement that rejected formalist orthodoxies and explicitly embraced radical political agendas. At the same time, formalism itself was in upheaval, as archetypal or psychoanalytic criticism gave way to phenomenology, structuralism, and, later, deconstruction and reader-response criticism. These new ways of examining texts and their social context spurred demands to rediscover writers excluded from the canon, especially women and *African Americans. Linked to the era's liberationist movements, these trends contributed to a new consciousness of literary criticism as cultural argument. The younger scholars' self-conscious political motivation itself soon became a point of cultural contention.

In the 1980s and 1990s, cultural criticism dominated American writing about literature. The "culture wars"—as that term applied to literary criticism—focused on whether literary works are written in a special language, requiring arbiters of taste to determine their merit, or whether they are essentially like other kinds of writing and thus subject to a broad range of social, political, and philosophical inquiry. Proponents of the former position were cast as conservative upholders of Enlightenment verities clinging to modernism as the last bastion of a Eurocentric culture. Their opponents saw themselves as postmodernists, willing to live and argue in a world without clear national or epistemological boundaries. They looked to European theorists who specialized in the formation of power relations, like Michel Foucault, or in counterintuitive concepts of language, like Jacques Derrida.

In this climate, new critical voices emerged at the century's end. Feminist critics and scholars like Sandra Gilbert and Nina Baym, noting how previous critics and literary historians had marginalized women's writing, questioned how canons are made and literature is valued. Other younger critics espoused gay, Chicano, *Asian-American, and Third World literature, while writers and scholars like Toni Morrison and Henry Louis Gates Jr. approached criticism of African American literature as both an academic subject and a form of literary expression.

[*See also* Feminism; Gay and Lesbian Rights Movement; Language, American; Literature; Literature, Popular; Modernist Culture; Poetry; Postmodernism.]

• Richard Ruland, *Rediscovery of American Literature: Premises of Critical Taste,* 1967. Evan Carbon and Gerald Graff, "Criticism Since 1940," in *Cambridge History of American Literature,* vol. 8, ed. Sacvan Bercovitch, 1996, pp. 261–472.

—Gordon Hutner

LITERATURE, POPULAR. Although Native American and African-American cultures of the seventeenth and eighteenth centuries had rich and varied traditions of oral narrative, the first popular printed literature in what is now the United States came from colonial *New England. As David D. Hall argues in *Worlds of Wonder, Days of Judgment* (1989), learning to read and absorbing one's religious faith were indistinguishable for the New England Puritans. Thus, this period's popular literature was religious, its literary formulas borrowed from the era's best-seller, the *Bible. The Puritans read published sermons; spiritual biographies and autobiographies that dramatized the struggles of ordinary men and women with doubt and sin; and Indian *captivity narratives like those of Mary Rowlandson and John Williams that detailed how their sufferings had tested and strengthened their religious faith. All of these literatures were designed to show the hand of God at work in the world. This "respectable" popular literature existed alongside less reputable works—chapbooks featuring romances, plays, ballads, crime stories, and other fictional materials whose lack of "truth" made them anathema to the clerical elite.

The novel became important in the early republic, although as "fiction" it remained a morally suspect genre. As Cathy Davidson argues in *Revolution and the Word* (1986), the novel during this period was a profoundly democratic form. Novels were written in simple language, they did not require a minister or other cultural authority to guide one's interpretation, and they featured poor or poorly educated protagonists whose pursuit of *literacy and *education could serve as a model for the reader's own. Novels of the early republic implicitly welcomed women, the poor, and others excluded from political life by the framers of the *Constitution to become citizens of a more democratic republic of letters. Moreover, these novels took the concerns of young women seriously. Both Susanna Rowson's *Charlotte Temple* (1791) and Hannah Foster's *The Coquette* (1797) addressed decisions regarding marriage—decisions of great importance in an era when a married woman's property and political rights were subsumed under her husband's.

By the 1850s, rising levels of literacy and education, combined with improved transportation networks, created a national market for popular books and magazines. The first best-seller, Susanna Warner's *Wide, Wide World* (1850), was followed by Harriet Beecher Stowe's **Uncle Tom's Cabin* (1852), Maria Susanna Cummins's *The Lamplighter* (1854), Fanny Fern's *Ruth Hall* (1855), and Mrs. E. D. E. N. Southworth's *The Hidden Hand* (1859), most of which were first serialized in *magazines. Later called "sentimental fiction," these texts were written by women, for women, and largely dealt with the domestic issues that made up women's "separate sphere" in the nineteenth century. Espousing Christian values, these books were intended to supplement the widely circulated religious tracts and Sunday school literature. This literature had what Jane Tompkins in *Sensational Designs* (1985) has called "designs" on the world: a desire to address pressing issues, to educate readers, and to change their hearts and minds so they would, in turn, act to change the social order. Although scholars disagree over the ideologies embraced by this fiction, at least some of it, Tompkins has suggested, involved a radical reimagining of the world, the replacement of patriarchal, capitalist values with matriarchal, Christian ones.

Slave narratives by authors like Frederick *Douglass, Harriet Jacobs, Olaudah Equiano, and Mary Prince circulated widely in the antebellum North from the late eighteenth century onward. Linking literacy and freedom, testifying to the evils of *slavery, and serving as a kind of collective autobiography, these narratives linked *antislavery speeches and other oral traditions with the world of print. Because these narratives often targeted white, middle-class women who made up the largest class of readers in the nineteenth century, they drew upon the conventions of popular sentimental fiction to find common ground between black and white women as mothers.

Between 1840 and 1890, publishers like Street and Smith, Beadle and Adams, Frank Tousey, and others began printing and distributing inexpensive fiction variously called dime novels, story papers, or cheap libraries. In *Mechanic Accents* (1987), Michael Denning identified the targeted readers of this fiction as workers, often of Irish or German descent, who labored in cities and mill towns of the North and West. Although Horatio *Alger's rags-to-respectability tales are the best known of these narratives, these sensational stories also explored the mysteries of the city, the drama of the great strike, and romance between honest workmen and virtuous mill girls. The popularity of these texts incited controversies about the relationship between "legitimate" literature sanctioned by cultural authorities and the fiction read by a largely immigrant working class. Ought dime novels be allowed to pollute the public *libraries? Did sensation fiction corrupt the morals of youth? Was this fiction even worth the (cheap) paper it was printed on?

The controversies continued in the twentieth century as changes in postal rates forced most of the dime-novel publishers to repackage their cheap fiction as pulp magazines, named for the inexpensive pulp paper on which they were printed. Distinguished from respectable "slick-paper" periodicals like the *Saturday Evening Post* and the *Ladies' Home Journal,* pulp magazines flooded the newsstands between 1896 and 1953, offering readers Westerns, romances, detective fiction, sports stories, war stories, and tales of the supernatural. In 1939, Pocket Books originated yet another form for popular literature, the paperback book. Selling for twenty-five cents rather than the two dollars or more that "trade" hardcover books cost, this innovation enabled people who could not afford trade books to build personal libraries of popular texts.

Throughout the history of popular literature, the same critical debates have been enacted. While some critics viewed these mass-produced texts as simply a means by which those in control of cultural production manipulated the masses, others saw these narratives as expressions of the authentic dreams and desires of ordinary readers. The critical consensus at the end of the twentieth century viewed these narratives as contested terrain—multivocal texts alternately claimed, rejected, and appropriated in a struggle over social meanings between the class that produces cultural texts and the classes of people who consume them.

Increasingly, scholars have redefined "popular" to refer not to a distinct body of texts but to a way of using texts, of creatively interpreting them in light of one's own concerns. Michel de Certeau in *The Practice of Everyday Life* (1984) calls such reading "poaching" and argues that it makes readers into active producers of meaning rather than passive consumers of mass-produced texts. This focus on popular appropriations of cultural texts raises questions about the social construction of the category of "popular" across time. As Lawrence Levine argues in *Highbrow, Lowbrow* (1988), Shakespeare in nineteenth-century America was *popular culture—widely performed, widely known, and widely parodied in a variety of venues—although in the twentieth century Shakespeare came to be sacralized as "high art." The study of popular literature, then, has moved beyond a literary analysis of widely read texts to include studies of the publishing and educational institutions that shaped their production and reception studies of the way individual readers and communities of readers have taken them up.

[*See also* Capitalism; Censorship; Feminism; Folklore; Journalism; Literary Criticism; Literature; Printing and Publishing; Puritanism; Religion; Social Class; Working-Class Life and Culture.]

• John G. Cawelti, *Adventure, Mystery, and Romance,* 1976. Nina Baym, *Woman's Fiction,* 1978, 2nd. ed., 1993. Mary Kelley, *Private Woman, Public Stage,* 1984. Janice Radway, *Reading the Romance,* 1984, 2d ed., 1991. David Reynolds, *Beneath the American Renaissance,* 1988. Susan Coultrap-McQuin, *Doing Literary Business,* 1990. Glenwood Irons, ed., *Gender, Language, and Myth,* 1992. Jane Tompkins, *West of Everything,* 1992. Marcus Klein, *Easterns, Westerns, and Private Eyes,* 1994.

—Erin A. Smith

LITERATURE

Colonial Era
Early National and Antebellum Eras
Civil War to World War I
Since World War I

LITERATURE: COLONIAL ERA

Previously somewhat neglected, the literature of the *Colonial Era was recognized in the later twentieth century as a rich and fascinating part of American literature. In the 1940s and 1950s, scholarship on colonial literature—now usually seen as part of the field of early American literature—was heavily influenced by the work of the Harvard English professor Perry Miller and other intellectual historians. As a result, much attention focused on *Puritanism and on continuities between colonial American literature and the later literature of the United States. Both Miller and the Puritans later came to loom less large, and the study of literature became more independent of historical scholarship, though literary continuities remained important to many specialists.

Scholars and critics of the late twentieth century asked large and serious questions about colonial literature. Is early American literature confined to writings in English by sometime residents of those colonies that later became the United States? Should writings in languages other than English be included in the canon? Are there distinctive qualities that a work of literature must possess to be designated American? Though no definitive answers to these questions emerged, the canon of colonial literature was expanded to include previously unrecognized writers and marginalized groups: women, Native Americans, and *African Americans. Increasingly, colonial writers were viewed in the context of the development of a distinctive American culture, with some writings valued as belles lettres.

The writers of colonial America generally identified as most important to literature are William Bradford (1590–1657), Anne *Bradstreet, Edward Taylor (c. 1644–1729), William *Byrd II, Jonathan *Edwards, Benjamin *Franklin, and J. Hector St. John *Crèvecoeur, with others placed at a somewhat lower level: Cotton *Mather, the African American poet Phillis *Wheatley, and Captain John *Smith, who is now recognized as a credible writer.

Bradford's well-crafted history of the *Plymouth colony (written c. 1630–1650) enjoys a preeminent place because of its early date and because of the author's efforts to understand what was happening in his tiny settlement; it continues to be read as adumbrating later critiques of the American dream. Bradford addressed the young men of Plymouth Plantation and stressed the virtues of the founders. Anne Bradstreet of Boston, who began a feminist tradition in American *poetry, learned her craft by composing conventional, public verse but later turned to personal themes of family, love, faith, nature, and loss. Fully aware that her society did not expect women to express themselves as she did, she nevertheless, like Bradford, struggled to interpret her experience in the framework of her religious beliefs. In such poems as "Contemplations," "Before the Birth of One of Her Children," and "A Letter to Her Husband," she left an enduring legacy.

Edward Taylor, whose poetry was unknown until the 1930s, has been the beneficiary of excellent editors; his work—prose and verse—fills thirteen published volumes. The founder of a frontier church in Westfield, Massachusetts, and deeply engaged in the liturgical arguments of his day, he struggled with wit and imagination to apply biblical texts to his personal situation in his major work, *Preparatory Meditations before My Approach to the Lords Supper.* Once seen as an aberration in *New England Puritanism, Taylor is now acknowledged as an orthodox Calvinist, and his passionate work has led to a new understanding of the role of emotion in New England Puritanism.

Jonathan Edwards, despite his theological preoccupations, also has an important place in colonial literature. His "Personal Narrative" is both a work of real literary merit and, with its focus on the subjective—"the sense of the heart"—a precursor of Ralph Waldo *Emerson's early writings. Also notable are his *Treatise Concerning Religious Affections, The Nature of True Virtue,* and his sermons, especially the classic "Sinners in the Hands of an Angry God." The customary contrast between Edwards and Benjamin Franklin focuses on their autobiographical writings, but some of Franklin's other writings, such as his satires and bagatelles, are now recognized as comprising a large, impressive body of literature. As a writer, he has been judged the peer of his British contemporary Dr. Samuel Johnson.

Turning from New England southward, perhaps the greatest legacy of the Chesapeake Bay area is William Byrd's *History of the Dividing Line betwixt Virginia and North Carolina,* which deals with a quintessential early American concern, bringing order to the wilderness, as recounted by a witty gentleman whose prose features antithesis, analogy, puns, and epigrams, and contrasts industry and idleness as well as the gentlemen of Tidewater, Virginia, and the inhabitants of "Lubberland," Byrd's term for North Carolina. Byrd obviously wrote to be read, though he had no interest in print publication. Other Chesapeake area writers now admired are the poets Richard Lewis (1700–1734) and Ebenezer Cooke (c. 1667–c. 1732), and Dr. Alexander Hamilton (1712–1756), author of the three-volume *History of the . . . Tuesday Club* of Annapolis as well as his *Itinerarium,* an account of his journey to Maine.

St. John de Crèvecoeur, who emigrated from France at age twenty, developed a broader knowledge of the American scene than any other colonial writer. His powers of observation and keen insight provide, in *Letters from an American Farmer,* the classic statement of the American dream. He originated the melting-pot metaphor of America as a place where "individuals of all nations are melted into a new one." In America an oppressed European could become a new man "from the new life he has embraced, the new government he obeys, and the new rank he holds."

The riches of colonial literature are still being explored. The slave narrative, an important American genre, is well represented in the colonial period by Olaudah Equiano's prototypic *Interesting Narrative* (1789). The spiritual autobiography of the Pennsylvania Quaker Elizabeth Ashbridge (1713–1755) complements the many autobiographical accounts by men. Mary White Rowlandson's 1682 account of her three-month captivity by Indians during *King Philip's War enjoyed immediate success and remains in print. A 1997 anthology introduced attractive new finds: the 1665 account by Pierre-Esprit Radisson (c. 1636–1710) of his adoption and acculturation by the Iroquois; the loyalist portrait of Benjamin Franklin by Peter Oliver (1731–1791), first published in 1961; and a 1772 sermon by the Mohegan Samson Occom (1723–1792), in which he addresses "the Indians, my brethren and kindred according to the flesh."

[*See also* Bible, The; Feminism; Indian History and Culture: From 1500 to 1800; Literary Criticism; Protestantism; Religion.]

• *Early American Literature* (journal), University of North Carolina at Chapel Hill, 1966–. Everett Emerson, ed., *Major Writers of Early American Literature,* 1972. J. A. Leo Lemay, *Men of Letters in Colonial Maryland,* 1972. Emory Elliott, ed., *Columbia Literary History of the United States,* 1988, pp. 5–135. Philip F. Gura, "The Study of Colonial American Literature, 1966–1987: A Vade Mecum," *William and Mary Quarterly* 45 (Apr. 1988): 305–41. William C. Spengemann, *A New World of Words: Redefining Early American Literature,* 1994. Myra Jehlen and Michael Warner, eds., *The English Literatures of America,* 1997.

—Everett Emerson

LITERATURE: EARLY NATIONAL AND ANTEBELLUM ERAS

Literature in the early republic was a means to an end, helping to instigate the revolution and to contain it, instructing and disputing as well as entertaining. Copyright law and other economic factors made authorship less a profession than a vocation or occasional practice.

Political Texts, Science and Nature Writing, Biography and Autobiography. No strict boundaries separated art from moral or political writing. Indeed, political texts and public documents constitute the early national period's most famous literature, from the wartime pamphlets of Thomas *Paine to the *Declaration of Independence, the *Federalist Papers, and the *Constitution. In creating a new nation and outlining the principles of constitutional *republicanism, these texts and others undertook imaginative burdens as great as any fiction or poetry, giving life to theories of natural law and abstractions like "We the People." The same could be said of the antifederalists, women, *African Americans, and others who highlighted the hypocrisies and exclusions of republican principles. Since, as Michael Warner has observed (*The Letters of the Republic,* 1990), the print medium carried with it implicit assumptions about authors' whiteness and masculinity, many of these interventions questioned the very foundations of the early national culture of letters.

Scientific, nature, and travel writing also addressed these political questions, helping shape national debates about *race and ethnicity, *slavery, and expansion. Thomas *Jefferson's *Notes on the State of Virginia* (1784), while matter-of-factly cataloging the state's natural resources, also contains lengthy discourses on African Americans and Native Americans, setting the terms for scientific *racism in the United States. Territorial expansion underlay two of the period's most important travel narratives, William Bartram's *Travels* (1792) and the journals of Lewis and Clark (1814).

Biography and autobiography valorized exemplary lives, as in the overt mythmaking of John Filson's life of Daniel *Boone (1784), celebrating the frontiersman as hero, or Mason Weems's moralizing life of George *Washington (1800). Benjamin *Franklin's equally moralizing *Autobiography* (written 1771–1790, published 1818) mirrors contemporary novels in its concern with fictions of the self. Olaudah Equiano's autobiography (1789), another exercise in capitalist self-fashioning, is the best-known early example of the slave narrative in English. J. Hector St. John *Crèvecoeur's fictional *Letters from an American Farmer* (1782) creates an exemplary American in the title figure; yet as the pastoral bliss of the early letters gives way to descriptions of slavery and frontier paranoia, social and political disruptions shatter neoclassical order.

Novels, Poetry, and Literature of Transcendentalism. A conservative society suspicious of the power of fiction insisted that novels advertise both their foundation in fact and their morally improving nature. Sentimental and often epistolary, many early American novels utilized seduction plots, warning of the dangers awaiting young women outside the bounds of conventional morality and institutions. Although American novels of this era were not usually commercially successful, some achieved wide popularity, including Hannah Foster's *The Coquette* (1797), based on an actual scandal, and Susanna Rowson's *Charlotte Temple* (1791), a seduction narrative that functioned as an allegory of national identity and retained a devoted readership for more than a century.

The gothic novels of Charles Brockden Brown (1771–1810) captured the paranoid 1790s of *yellow fever outbreaks, the Reign of Terror, and the *Alien and Sedition Acts, especially *Wieland* (1798), *Arthur Mervyn* (1799–1800), and *Edgar Huntly* (1799). Tabitha Tenney's *Female Quixotism* (1801) and Hugh Henry Brackenridge's picaresque *Modern Chivalry* (1792–1815) satirized changing mores and social practices (including novel-reading itself), as did the first American play, Royall Tyler's *The Contrast* (1787).

*Poetry, the most conservative of early national genres, adapted European neoclassical modes to "native" uses, as in Timothy Dwight's pastoral *Greenfield Hill* (1794), Joel Barlow's epic, *The Vision of Columbus* (1787), and Sarah Wentworth Morton's long poems on Native American and revolutionary subjects. Americans also explored the limits of eighteenth-century poetic conventions. Philip Freneau's personal, symbolic nature lyrics introduced romanticism to American poetry. The Massachusetts slave Phillis *Wheatley both embraces and subverts conventional religious and Augustan poetry, commenting subtly on slavery, race, and the revolution in *Poems on Various Subjects* (1773).

The 1820s saw the emergence of a literary marketplace, authorship as a viable profession, and calls for a "native" literature. Literary careers became possible, not only for such men as Washington Irving (1783–1859) and James Fenimore *Cooper, but also for women like Lydia Maria *Child and Fanny Fern (Sara Parton). Irving's *Sketch-Book of Geoffrey Crayon* (1819–1820) exemplified this transition, packaging genteel nostalgia in an elegant prose style for a middle-class audience.

Ralph Waldo *Emerson's essay *Nature* (1836) ushered in the age of *transcendentalism, as the Concord circle—including Henry David *Thoreau, Margaret *Fuller, Theodore *Parker, and Bronson Alcott—produced such classics as Fuller's *Woman in the Nineteenth Century* (1844) and Thoreau's *Walden* (1849). Transcendentalism, rooted in the primacy of the individual's unmediated encounter with nature, insisted on the power of the individual to remake the world in his (or her) own image. Despite the transcendentalists' generally oppositional politics, their idealism and antimaterialism ironically provided the basis for an informal national philosophy not incompatible with a violent, expanding materialistic society.

The Literature of Westward Expansion and Frontier Adventure. Much antebellum literature addressed westward expansion and relations with Native Americans—issues that came to a head in the 1820s and 1830s. Long narrative poems like James Eastburn's and Robert Sands's *Yamoyden* (1820) and Henry Wadsworth Longfellow's *Hiawatha* (1855), as well as John Augustus Stone's popular *Metamora* (1829), memorialized Indians, often condemning conquest morally while simultaneously treating it as inevitable. The histories of William Prescott and Francis *Parkman and the ethnographic writings of Henry Rowe Schoolcraft and others justified European imperialism in the Americas and attempted to delineate a distinctive white American identity out of confrontation with, and appropriation of, Indian culture. Drawing on this newer material as well as the long-standing conventions of captivity and Indian-fighting narratives, Cooper's Leatherstocking Tales were only the best-known of the "frontier romances," which also included Child's *Hobomok* (1824), Catherine Sedgwick's *Hope Leslie* (1827), and Robert Montgomery Bird's *Nick of the Woods* (1837).

The new popular press thrived on frontier adventure, from

the Davy *Crockett almanacs and story papers of the thirties and forties to the first dime novel, Ann S. Stephens's *Malaeska* (1860). Eastern urban settings proved popular also, as in the best-sellers of the radical novelist George Lippard, whose *The Quaker City* (1843–1844) exposes the corruption of *Philadelphia's elite. Equally sensationalist was Maria Monk's notorious anti-Catholic captivity narrative, *Awful Disclosures of the Hôtel Dieu Nunnery* (1836).

Sentimental Novels and Social Protest Literature. Sentimental novels such as Susan Warner's *The Wide, Wide World* (1850), Harriet Beecher Stowe's **Uncle Tom's Cabin* (1851), and Maria Cummins's *The Lamplighter* (1854) won popularity in the 1850s. As Jane Tompkins has argued (*Sensational Designs: The Cultural Work of American Fiction 1790–1860,* 1985), sentimental and domestic fiction used the central values of *family and *religion to encourage radical reforms, including *antislavery and women's rights. Of these novels, *Uncle Tom's Cabin* enjoyed the greatest impact, selling an unprecedented million copies and, some argue, helping to precipitate the *Civil War.

Social protest also inspired African-American literature, especially the slave-narrative genre, which helped animate the abolitionist movement. *The Narrative of the Life of Frederick *Douglass* (1845) perfected the form and galvanized both white and black antislavery activity. Harriet Jacobs's *Incidents in the Life of a Slave Girl* (1861) addresses a specifically female audience, using novelistic techniques to dramatize the sexual exploitation of slave women. The 1850s also witnessed a brief flowering of African-American fiction, such as Harriet Wilson's autobiographical *Our Nig* (1859), about northern racism. Similarly, Native American writing began to appear in print, notably the "as-told-to" *Life of *Black Hawk,* the Sauk chief (1833), and the radical writings of William Apess, a Pequot preacher, activist, and autobiographer.

The Canonical Writers and Poets. Social issues figure more obliquely (though still vitally) in the works of three white men who were subsequently canonized as the preeminent antebellum American writers. Edgar Allan *Poe, Nathaniel *Hawthorne, and Herman *Melville produced ambivalent, at times tortured examinations of social and moral issues, including race and gender. Poe invented the detective genre with his Auguste Dupin stories, while his tales of madness and psychological terror epitomized the American gothic. Hawthorne's romances offered a subtler strain of the gothic, a genre he described and exemplified in *The Scarlet Letter* (1850) and *The House of the Seven Gables* (1851). His fiction, often set in colonial *New England, also engages with historical memory. Melville, in his speculative, philosophical novels, as in shorter fiction like "Bartleby the Scrivener" (1853) and "Benito Cereno" (1855), confronts problems of identity, nation, and *capitalism. After his masterpiece *Moby-Dick* (1851), Melville's style grew increasingly experimental, notably in *The Confidence-Man* (1857). All three writers enjoyed moments of market success, but each also contributed to the myth of romantic authorship, the image of the tormented artist pursuing aesthetic and moral concerns rather than pandering to the marketplace.

The so-called "schoolroom poets"—Longfellow (1794–1878), William Cullen Bryant (1807–1892), and John Greenleaf Whittier—developed romantic styles that made them popular during their lives and after. From a twentieth-century perspective, however, the era's most significant poets were Walt *Whitman and Emily *Dickinson. Whitman's sexual frankness and willingness to experiment with form and content achieved notoriety, while the intensely private Dickinson's meditations on sex, death, and nature remained almost completely unknown. Although sometimes reduced to stereotype, the contrast between Dickinson's elliptical but tightly wound lyrics and Whitman's expansive, epic experiments in free verse helped define the range of possibilities for later poets. Much of twentieth-century poetry is implicit in their work.

[*See also* Antebellum Era; Anti-Catholic Movement; Bartram, John and William; Early Republic, Era of the; Expansionism; Historiography, American; Indian History and Culture: From 1800 to 1900; Indian History and Culture: The Indian in Popular Culture; Lewis and Clark Expedition; Literature, Popular; Printing and Publishing; Romantic Movement.]

• F. O. Matthiessen, *American Renaissance,* 1941. Richard Slotkin, *The Fatal Environment: The Myth of the Frontier in the Age of Industrialization, 1800–1890,* 1985. William L. Andrews, *To Tell a Free Story: The First Century of Afro-American Autobiography, 1760–1865,* 1986. Cathy N. Davidson, *Revolution and the Word,* 1986. David S. Reynolds, *Beneath the American Renaissance,* 1988. Emory Elliott, ed., *Columbia Literary History of The United States, Part II (1810–1865),* ed. Terence Martin, 1988. Dana D. Nelson, *The Word in Black and White: Reading "Race" in American Literature 1638–1867,* 1993. Eric Sundquist, *To Wake the Nations: Race in the Making of American Literature,* 1993. Michael Moon and Cathy Davidson, eds., *Subjects and Citizens: Nation, Race, and Gender from Oroonoko to Anita Hill,* 1995. Christopher Newfield, *The Emerson Effect,* 1996.

—Gary Ashwill

LITERATURE: CIVIL WAR TO WORLD WAR I

American literature in the half-century from 1865 to 1914 matched the radical changes that transformed U.S. society in these years.

Overview. This era witnessed the progression from romantic to realist conventions and then the advent of modernism. Throughout the period, poets, dramatists, and, most of all, fiction writers increasingly saw themselves as social critics. Although the *Civil War left a legacy of disillusionment, a forceful sentimental tradition arose in response to the felt loss of national innocence. These five decades produced a powerful progressive literature responding to the social upheavals associated with *urbanization and *industrialization. The era also saw the rise of ethnic and African-American writing, along with an increasingly critical feminist tradition.

Perhaps the period's principal contribution to world literature was the emergence of the American novel and short story. A few masters stand out, notably Henry *James, Samuel L. *Clemens, and William Dean *Howells. The expatriate James was acknowledged as the consummate artist; Clemens the popular favorite; and Howells the craftsman, astute social observer, and highly influential critic who introduced many new writers.

The period's intermingling of romance, realism, and modernism reveals how rich and varied were its energies. Herman *Melville completed his last work, *Billy Budd,* just before his death in 1891. The fireside poets William Cullen Bryant, Henry Wadsworth Longfellow, James Russell Lowell, and John Greenleaf Whittier wrote into the 1870s and 1880s, while Walt *Whitman revised and reissued *Leaves of Grass* (first published in 1855) for more than thirty years. Three volumes of Emily *Dickinson's poems were published in this period. Other significant poets of the time include John Hay, Sidney Lanier, Edwin Arlington Robinson, Trumbull Stickney, and Paul Laurence Dunbar. The era also produced such once-popular poetic voices as Eugene Field, Emma Lazarus, Edwin Markham, and James Whitcomb Riley. Yet by 1914 the *modernist movement was well under way. T. S. Eliot, Ezra *Pound, Robinson Jeffers, and Robert Frost had all published their first poems; Willa *Cather, Gertrude Stein, Ellen Glasgow, and Mary Austin had begun their careers; and Sherwood Anderson, Sinclair *Lewis, and Eugene *O'Neill would soon emerge.

Regional, "Local Color," and Ethnic Literature. Like the transcontinental railroad, postbellum American literature was engaged in the general project of national unification. Western writers like Clemens and Bret Hart reached a national audience through prestigious eastern magazines like the *Atlantic Monthly.* Sarah Orne Jewett in *The Country of the Pointed Firs* (1896) evoked small-town life in coastal Maine, and Kate Chopin described Cajun culture in *Bayou Folk* (1894). Such "local-color" writing gratified readers' appetite for information about the nation's varied regions. Sometimes satirical in tone and cast in dialect, local-color writing refreshingly supplemented the earnest, pious portrayals of character and morality in conventional literature, such as Thomas Bailey Aldrich's popular *Story of a Bad Boy* (1870). Local colorists like George Washington Cable, Edward Eggleston, Mary Wilkins Freeman, and Charles Chesnutt introduced regional folkways and vernacular expression. Joel Chandler Harris drew upon African American folk culture in a series of popular works extending from *Uncle Remus, His Songs and His Sayings* (1880) to *Uncle Remus and Brer Rabbit* (1906). (Pauline Hopkins gave a different idea of racial politics in a series of fictions that included *Contending Forces* [1900].) Others, like Chopin in *The Awakening* (1899) and Abraham Cahan in *Yekl: A Tale of the New York Ghetto* (1896), went further, skeptically probing prevailing moral codes and customs.

Social Criticism. Even at its most critical, however, local color did not achieve the ethical intensity of European critical realists who found an audience in America through Howells's support. Ibsen, Turgenev, Dostoyevsky, Tolstoy, and Zola exemplified how writers could exert a social and philosophical claim on educated readers' imagination. The need for such a critique seemed pressing in the *Gilded Age (the title of an 1873 novel by Clemens and Charles Dudley Warner attacking postwar materialism and vulgarity). An incipient protest literature addressing the social effects of industrialism had already emerged, as in Rebecca Harding Davis's "Life in the Iron Mills" (1861) and *John Andross* (1874), but the most lasting indictments were Howells's *The Rise of Silas Lapham* (1885) and *A Hazard of New Fortunes* (1890) and Frank Norris's *The Octopus* (1901), probing such by-products of industrial capitalism as widening class divisions, the erosion of ethics, and the ravaging of natural resources. Henry Blake Fuller's *The Cliff-Dwellers* (1893) addressed another of industrialization's consequences, the rise of a new class of urban office workers. While the nature writers John Burroughs and John *Muir evoked a preindustrial America and promoted wilderness preservation, the Philadelphian Owen Wister in *The Virginian* (1902) implicitly contrasted the physical challenges and moral clarity of ranch life in Wyoming with the urbanizing East, creating in the process an enduring American icon, the strong, silent cowboy hero.

Gilded Age and *Progressive Era writers took their obligations as political and social critics with increasing seriousness. Fictions like John William De Forest's *Honest John Vane* (1875) and Henry *Adams's *Democracy* (1880) examined the debased level of public life, as did some of the later novels of the American writer Winston Churchill. Howells publicly protested the injustices of the *Haymarket affair prosecutions, while Clemens was among those who denounced U.S. imperialist expansion in the 1890s and later. Helen Hunt Jackson documented the mistreatment of Native Americans in *A Century of Dishonor* (1881), while Cable and Albion Tourgée, among whites, and Chesnutt, Simon Griggs, and James Weldon *Johnson, among blacks, dramatized the racial oppression of *African Americans. The feminist Charlotte Perkins *Gilman in her short story "The Yellow Wall-Paper" (1892) and her utopian novel *Herland* (1915) portrayed the psychologically crippling effects of gender stereotypes and envisioned a world of equality between the sexes. Hamlin Garland's short-story collection *Main-Travelled Roads* (1891) evoked the loneliness and cultural barrenness of midwestern rural life, while Harold Frederic's *The Damnation of Theron Ware* (1891) portrayed the struggles of a small-town upstate New York minister confronting social changes and new intellectual currents that threaten his provincial worldview.

Following the example of Jacob Riis's investigative report **How the Other Half Lives* (1890), American authors also turned their attention to the underside of urban life, as in Stephen Crane's *Maggie: A Girl of the Streets* (1893); Cahan's stories from the Jewish ghetto; and David Graham Phillips's *Susan Lenox: Her Fall and Rise* (published posthumously in 1917), exposing urban political corruption and the sexual exploitation of young working women. Robert Herrick's *The Common Lot* (1904) and *Memoirs of an American Citizen* (1905) probed the unscrupulous behavior of industrialists and urban professionals in an age of cutthroat capitalist competition, the theme also of Theodore *Dreiser's *The Financier* (1912) and *The Titan* (1914). The most influential reform novels of the era included Edward Bellamy's **Looking Backward* (1888), a utopian fantasy of a harmonious and equitable social order; Charles M. Sheldon's Social Gospel novel *In His Steps* (1896), about a minister who tries to follow Jesus's example in addressing contemporary urban conditions; and Upton *Sinclair's *The *Jungle* (1906), an exposé of the *Chicago stockyards that inspired the *Pure Food and Drug Act of 1906.

The Naturalist Movement. Following the critical ascendancy of realism (a vogue to which the book-buying public remained cool) came its most important permutation, naturalism. If realist novels posited a choice between two worldviews, naturalist fiction presented a world governed by forces outside the self: Blind chance or determinism rules the individual, the social order, and the cosmos. E. W. Howe's *The Story of a Country Town* (1883), an early popular version of determinism, was followed by such works as Crane's naturalistic Civil War novel *The Red Badge of Courage* (1895); Norris' *McTeague* (1899) and *The Octopus*; Dreiser's *Sister Carrie* (1900), recounting an amoral young woman's career in Chicago and *New York City; and Edith *Wharton's *The House of Mirth* (1905), *Ethan Frome* (1911), and *The Custom of the Country* (1913), in all of which individuals struggle with events and social forces beyond their control.

American naturalist writers were influenced by such authors as Flaubert and Zola; Charles Darwin's theory of *evolution; and the *laissez-faire ideology of Herbert Spencer and William Graham Sumner. In an era of rapid cultural change, some of these novels, including Crane's *Maggie* and Dreiser's *Sister Carrie,* received a fiercely negative critical reception and even faced *censorship pressures. The novelist and short-story writer Jack London also presented a naturalistic philosophy and a deterministic world of struggle and conflict in such books as *The Call of the Wild* (1903), *The People of the Abyss* (1903), *The Sea-Wolf* (1904), the semiautobiographical *Martin Eden* (1909), and *The Iron Heel* (1907). A gifted and prolific storyteller, London won a worldwide following.

Popular Fiction. Along with the ubiquitous dime novels, the era's popular literature included sentimental romances and historical fiction, especially books about the *Revolutionary War. Louisa May *Alcott's *Little Women* (1868–1869) became a beloved favorite, while Horatio *Alger's popular boys' stories of city street life, starting with *Ragged Dick* (1867), offered a formula for rising from poverty to middle-class respectability. Detective novels were also popular, especially those of Anne Katharine Green. Other formula fiction included Edgar Rice Burroughs' first Tarzan novel (1914) and Gilbert Patten's Frank Merriwell tales about a Yale football hero.

Best-sellers—the term was coined in the 1890s—frequently sold hundreds of thousands of copies. The foremost example is Lew Wallace's *Ben Hur* (1880), but other commercial successes included Edward Noyes Westcott's *David Harum* (1898), Charles Major's *When Knighthood Was in Flower* (1898), Elbert Hubbard's inspirational "A Message to Garcia" (1899), Paul Leicester Ford's *Janice Meredith* (1899), and Churchill's *Richard Carvel* (1899). Mary Johnston's novels idealizing the Confederacy, *The Long Roll* (1911) and *Cease Firing* (1912), enjoyed a great vogue, especially in the *South. Thomas Dixon's *The Clansman* (1912), celebrating the *Ku Klux Klan, led to a revival of the Klan and inspired D. W. *Griffith's notoriously racist 1915 movie *Birth of a Nation.* Other best-selling authors included Irving Bacheller, F. Marion Crawford, Robert W. Chambers, Richard Harding Davis, George Barr McCutcheon, and Mrs. Humphrey Ward. The early 1900s also brought to the fore novelists whose popularity would extend well into the century, including Emerson Hough, Harold Bell Wright, Henry Van Dyke, Kathleen Norris, the mystery writer Mary Roberts Rinehart, and Zane Grey, who launched his long career as a Western writer with *Spirit of the Border* (1905) and *Riders of the Purple Sage* (1912).

Drama and Autobiography. Despite the continuing popularity of melodramas like *Uncle Tom's Cabin* and Augustin Daly's *Under the Gaslight* (1867), dramatic literature generally moved toward greater realism and more attention to current social issues in these years. Bronson Howard's *Saratoga* (1870) and *Young Mrs. Winthrop* (1882) focused on contemporary society, and by 1900 David Belasco's productions were synonymous with new levels of realism. Other playwrights included James Herne, who was supported by leading realists like Howells and Garland; the versatile Clyde Fitch, whose dramas ranged from farces to problem plays to psychological studies; and Edward Sheldon, a prolific dramatist and product of George P. Baker's famous playwriting class at Harvard, who wrote nine plays between 1908 and 1914. Rachel Crothers examined gender relations in several noteworthy pre-1914 plays.

These years also brought renewed interest in autobiography, a literary form pioneered in America by such varied antebellum figures as Benjamin *Franklin, Davy *Crockett, and Henry David *Thoreau. Ulysses S. *Grant's straightforward *Personal Memoirs* (2 vols., 1885–1886) later won praise from Gertrude Stein as a masterpiece of American literature. Not only public figures but also less well-known individuals now offered their life stories. In part, the impetus came from Frederick *Douglass's 1845 autobiography and other antebellum slave narratives. Gertrude Bonnin (Zitkala-Sa) published her memoirs of an Indian girlhood in the *Atlantic Monthly* (1900–1902); Henry Adams's classic *The Education of Henry Adams* circulated among friends for several years before its publication in 1918; and Mary Antin's *The Promised Land* (1912) helped launch a genre of immigrant writing describing the transformation "from alien to citizen."

Huckleberry Finn. The most widely studied novel of this remarkably productive era in American literature, Clemens's *Adventures of Huckleberry Finn* (1884), set forty years earlier, envisions a dream of freedom and autonomy that, paradoxically, was already anachronistic in Gilded Age America. The wilderness for which Huck sets out in 1845 was fast becoming "sivilized" by 1884. Although the Civil War and the *Emancipation Proclamation cast a different light on Clemens's story of a white boy's friendship with an adult black man, so compelling was the novel's ethical expression of love and *pragmatism, and so deeply did it speak to the possibilities of an American literary language, that the novel stands not only as the major literary achievement of these years but as the font of much modern literature.

[*See also* Drama; Feminism; Folklore; Journalism; Literary Criticism; Literature, Popular; Magazines; Poetry; Regionalism; Romantic Movement; Social Darwinism.]

• Henry F. May, *The End of American Innocence: A Study of the First Years of Our Time, 1912–1917,* 1959. Warner Berthoff, *The Ferment of Realism,* 1965. Larzer Ziff, *The American 1890s,* 1966. Jay Martin, *Harvest of Change,* 1967. Eric J. Sundquist, ed., *American Realism: New Essays,* 1982. June Howard, *Form and History in American Literary Naturalism,* 1985. Emory Elliott, ed., *Columbia Literary History of the United States,* part 3 (1865–1910), ed. Martha Banta, 1988, pp. 463–689. Amy Kaplan, *The Social Construction of American Realism,* 1988. Dickson D. Bruce, *Black American Writing from the Nadir: The Evolution of a Literary Tradition, 1877–1915,* rpt. ed. 1992.

—Gordon Hutner

LITERATURE: SINCE WORLD WAR I

In the twentieth century, American literature came into its own. Still mindful at century's beginning of their cultural roots in British traditions and literature, American writers by mid-century had rediscovered Ralph Waldo *Emerson, Herman *Melville, Emily *Dickinson, and Walt *Whitman, and produced a literature distinctly and powerfully their own.

Overview. Even before *World War I, Gertrude Stein, Robert Frost, Carl Sandburg, Ezra *Pound, Hilda Doolittle (H. D.), and Harriet Monroe had created a new *poetry based in American vernacular and speech rhythms. H. L. *Mencken underlined this fact with his scholarly project *The American Language* (1919), while the authentically American voices of Whitman and Mark Twain (Samuel L. *Clemens) were taken up and stylized in the fiction of Stein, Willa *Cather, Sherwood Anderson, Ring Lardner, F. Scott *Fitzgerald, Ernest *Hemingway, and William *Faulkner.

Twentieth-century American literature not only came of age, but also became many-voiced, as women and ethnic writers gained public stature. As the examples of Stein, H. D., Cather, Monroe, Mina Loy, and Marianne Moore testify, women writers took a greater role in literary culture, as did *African Americans. By the century's close, writers from all of America's ethnic cultures were published in the nation's literatures.

The new directions in the arts of the early twentieth century were urban and international developments. Local and rural experience gave way to life in the city. Cather wrote of immigrants on the Great Plains—but from New York. Hemingway in Paris described fishing in northern Michigan; Frost published his first poems about *New England farm life while in London. Crowded with immigrants, New York and *Chicago were the places where identity was the most plastic and the self could be remade, the story told in Theodore *Dreiser's *Sister Carrie* (1900).

Modernism and Social Criticism. American modernism began in a pre–World War I rebellion against the older generation's culture and politics, evident in Randolph *Bourne's *Youth and Life* (1913), Van Wyck Brooks's *America's Coming of Age* (1915), and "little magazines" like Harriet Monroe's *Poetry* (1912) and Margaret Anderson's *The Little Review* (1914). Ford Madox Ford's *Transatlantic Review* and Robert McAlmon's *Contact* would soon follow. Ezra Pound, writing his own path-breaking *poetry, found publishers and patrons for modernist writers.

American poets created the modernist style. Experimenting in free verse and breaking with British verse forms and iambic rhythms, they sought to make a reality rather than merely describe or reflect it. This took the form of experiments in capturing moments of complex illumination, which Pound first called "images" and then "vortices" to connote a confluence of energies and recognitions. Such experiments were antinarrative, seeking the spatial gestalt of sudden recognition. Originally expressed in short poems, the same techniques underlay such modern epics as T. S. Eliot's *The Wasteland* (1922), Pound's *Cantos* (1915–1970), William Carlos Williams's *Spring and All* (1922) and *Paterson* (1946–1958), and H. D.'s *Trilogy* (1944–1946) and *Helen in Egypt* (1961).

In the novel and short story, Stein, Hemingway, Fitzgerald, Faulkner, Jean Toomer, and John Dos Passos produced collages featuring multiple points of view from which narrative omniscience is withdrawn or limited. With narrative itself associated with prewar sentimentality, a new effort to present facts shorn of sentiment underlay the best of American writing in the 1920s. Partly the result of war experiences, Dos Passos's *Three Soldiers* (1920), e. e. cummings's *The Enormous Room* (1920), Pound's poem sequence *Hugh Selwyn Mauberly* (1920), and Hemingway's *In Our Time* (1925) and *A Farewell to Arms* (1929) offered bitter antiheroic views of military life and international politics. Responses ranged from Nick Carraway's moral retreat in Fitzgerald's *The Great Gatsby* (1925) to Jake Barnes's stoic resignation in Hemingway's *The Sun Also Rises* (1926).

Apart from Cather, writers of the 1920s typically attacked small-town life as narrow and mean-spirited. Sinclair *Lewis, the first American to win the Nobel Prize for Literature (1930), satirized small-town life and America's crass boosterism in the best-selling *Main Street* (1920), *Babbitt* (1922), *Arrowsmith* (1925), and *Elmer Gantry* (1927). Influenced by Freud, writers portrayed the family as a source of repression and emotional turmoil, as in Faulkner's *The Sound and the Fury* (1929). The playwright Eugene *O'Neill's first successes—*The Emperor Jones* (1921), *The Hairy Ape* (1922), and *Desire under the Elms* (1924)—addressed taboo subjects of race and sexuality. O'Neill's major tragedies, *Mourning Becomes Electra* (1931) and the autobiographical *Long Day's Journey into Night* (1941), treat the family as the source of personal trauma. In much of this literature, freedom and growth come from leaving the family and the small town for the challenge of the city, as Tom Willard does at the end of Sherwood Anderson's *Winesburg, Ohio* (1919).

African-American Literature. As African Americans migrated to northern cities seeking jobs and greater social freedom, *New York City's Harlem emerged as a vibrant community of intellectuals, writers, artists, and musicians. W. E. B. *Du Bois's *Crisis* magazine, published by the *National Association for the Advancement of Colored People, and Charles Johnson's *Opportunity,* founded by the National *Urban League, provided outlets for creative work by African Americans. James Weldon *Johnson, himself best known for *Autobiography of an Ex-Colored Man* (1912), showcased black writers in his 1922 anthology *The Book of American Negro Poetry.*

The decade of creativity that emerged from this matrix of talent, prosperity, and patronage, represents a landmark in twentieth-century American literature. Along with Jean Toomer, author of the memorable and idiosyncratic *Cane* (1923), notable *Harlem Renaissance writers included the poets Countee Cullen, Claude McKay, and Langston *Hughes, whose *Weary Blues* appeared in 1926, and the novelists Rudolph Fisher and Nella Larsen, author of *Quicksand* (1928) and *Passing* (1929). Hughes and Zora Neale *Hurston may be taken as representative in their insistence upon the value of black experience and culture, a view Hughes articulated in "The Negro Artist and the Racial Mountain" (1926). While Hurston published short fiction in the 1920s, her major novels and folk-culture studies appeared in the 1930s, including her most polished novel *Their Eyes Were Watching God* (1937). Alain Locke's *The New Negro* (1925), a collection of poetry, prose, art, and essays representing the strength and accomplishments of black culture, remains a significant point of access to this fertile moment in U.S. literary history.

The 1930s. With the *stock market crash of 1929 followed by a decade of economic hardship, literary culture moved left. Concern with *social class and disparities of wealth and power, never far from the surface of American literature, became overt in this decade. Many writers joined or supported the *Communist party and many more attended the leftist American writers congresses in New York City in 1935 and 1937. Because of these developments and the proliferation of proletarian writing, the 1930s are often labeled the "red decade."

Amid widespread *unemployment, the tradition of American naturalism developed by Dreiser, Frank Norris, and Jack London reappeared in novels portraying capitalism's victims, such as Anna Yerzierska's *The Breadgivers* (1925), Michael Gold's *Jews without Money* (1930), James T. Farrell's Studs Lonigan trilogy (1932–1935), and Henry Roth's *Call It Sleep* (1934). In drama, Clifford Odets's *Waiting for Lefty* and *Awake and Sing* (both 1935) explored the plight of workers, while Maxwell Anderson's *Winterset* (1935) dealt with the *Sacco and Vanzetti case. Using devices of modernist collage, John Dos Passos's *U.S.A.* trilogy (1930–1936) provides a historical panorama of twentieth-century social history, and in the third volume, *The Big Money* (1936), indicts the wealthy and powerful for creating "two nations." John Steinbeck's Dust Bowl epic, *The *Grapes of Wrath,* and Lillian Hellman's searing *The Little Foxes* appeared in 1939. With Richard *Wright's *Native Son* (1940), African-American literature entered the mainstream. Selected by the *Book of the Month Club, this violent novel sold over 200,000 copies in three weeks.

Southern writers, viewing history as more organic and impervious to change than did northern activists, produced poetry, fiction, and essays in the thirties that would dominate midcentury literary culture. Their conservative manifesto *I'll Take My Stand* (1930) included essays by Allen Tate, John Crowe Ransom, and Robert Penn Warren. Admirers of modernist poetry, especially Eliot's, these three established "the Fugitives" at Vanderbilt University; in 1939, Ransom founded the influential *Kenyon Review.* Along with Cleanth Brooks, these writers helped theorize the idea of the "well wrought" poem that underlay the "new criticism." Warren continued to write novels and poetry into the 1990s, including the great political novel *All the King's Men* (1946), based on the life of Huey *Long. The South's legacy of slaveholding is Faulkner's great theme, especially in his epic novels *Light in August* (1932), *Absalom! Absalom!* (1936), and *Go Down Moses* (1942).

The Post–World War II Decades. The *Cold War profoundly influenced American literature in the second half of the twentieth century. Domestically, the United States enjoyed renewed prosperity, but the *civil rights movement, campus unrest, environmental activism, and anti–*Vietnam War protests affected American culture dramatically in the fifties and sixties. Paul Goodman's *Growing up Absurd* (1960), Rachel *Carson's *Silent Spring* (1962), Michael Harrington's *The *Other America* (1962), and Betty Friedan's *The *Feminine Mystique* (1963) helped initiate the new radicalism. From the 1970s to the century's end, American literature became more ethnically diverse and less susceptible to easy characterization.

*Postmodernism offers an umbrella term for the breakup of old distinctions and hierarchies between elite and popular literatures and between once dominant white male writers and a rich blooming of writers from diverse backgrounds. The term also signifies a far-reaching and radically democratic decentering of authority, of aesthetic standards, and of the notion of fixed truth existing outside language.

These developments originated in the postwar culture of *anticommunism, conformity, and middle-class malaise, in which literature depicted the moral quandaries of alienated loners. American theater witnessed such productions as Tennessee Williams's *A Streetcar Named Desire* (1947), Arthur Miller's *Death of a Salesman* (1949), Lorraine Hansberry's *A Raisin in the Sun* (1959), and Edward Albee's *A Zoo Story* (1959) and *Who's Afraid of Virginia Woolf?* (1962). These years saw the publication of J. D. Salinger's *Catcher in the Rye* (1951) and Vladimir Nabokov's transgressive novel, *Lolita* (1958). Work by "the Beats" included Allen Ginsberg's *Howl and Other Poems* (1957), Jack Kerouac's *On the Road* (1957), and William Burroughs's *Naked Lunch* (1959) as well as the poetry of Diane DiPrima, LeRoi Jones, Gregory Corso, Philip Whalen, and Lawrence Ferlinghetti. John *Updike published the first of his Rabbit tetrology, *Rabbit, Run* (1960), while southerners Truman Capote, William Styron, Carson McCullers, Flannery O'Connor, Eudora Welty, and Walker Percy extended the heritage of Faulkner. Jewish writers emerged at the forefront of American writing at this time, as Norman Mailer, Bernard Malamud, Philip Roth, and Saul *Bellow began their careers. Ralph *Ellison and James *Baldwin were characteristic of the era in presenting portraits of alienated individuals while offering a more psychologically complex portrait of black life than did Wright in *Native Son.* Ellison's *Invisible Man* (1952), winner of the National Book Award, is often ranked as the most important novel of the post–World War II era.

A new generation of poets that included Elizabeth Bishop, Theodore Roethke, John Berryman, Robert Lowell, James

Dickey, Denise Levertov, Richard Wilbur, and Adrienne Rich emerged in the 1940s and 1950s, producing well-made formal poems indebted to Eliot and the New Criticism. But learned formalism soon gave way to looser, more "confessional" poetry in the work of Ginsberg, Anne Sexton, and Sylvia Plath. Acknowledging Bishop's influence in *North and South* (1946) and *Poems* (1956), Lowell himself developed a more personal style in *Life Studies* (1959). New directions could also be found in the poetry of the Black Mountain poets Charles Olson, Robert Duncan, and Robert Creeley; the San Francisco and Beat poets; and the experiments of the New York poets John Ashbery and Frank O'Hara, all represented in Donald Allen's watershed anthology *The New American Poetry* (1960). Subsequently, the Language poets Charles Bernstein, Susan Howe, Ron Silliman, and Lyn Hejinian built on the traditions of Pound and Ashbery while James Merrill displayed brilliant formal artistry in his epic *The Changing Light at Sandover* (1982). The influences of Whitman and William Carlos Williams could be seen in the visionary poetry of James Wright and Philip Levine, while the southern poet Charles Wright paid homage to Emily *Dickinson.

The Late Twentieth Century. The twentieth-century's concluding decades also saw a remarkable flourishing of fiction—a fiction marked by a paranoid sensibility rooted in the perception that social structures, public policy, and perhaps even history itself are conspiracies against the self. Indebted to *Invisible Man,* this line of satire and dissent included Joseph Heller's *Catch-22* (1960); Kurt Vonnegut's *Cat's Cradle* (1963) and *Slaughterhouse-Five* (1969); Ken Kesey's *One Flew over the Cuckoo's Nest* (1962); Thomas Pynchon's *The Crying of Lot 49* (1966); Diane Johnson's *The Shadow Knows* (1974); and Don DeLillo's *White Noise* (1985), *The Names* (1989), and *Libra* (1991). The satiric and revisionary impulse extended to the literary medium itself in the novels of Donald Barthelme, John Barth, William Gass, and Robert Coover; and to historical fiction in Pynchon's *V.* (1963) and *Gravity's Rainbow* (1973), Styron's *Confessions of Nat Turner* (1967), E. L. Doctorow's *Book of Daniel* (1971), and Robert Coover's *The Public Burning* (1977); and the New Journalism of Mailer's *Armies of the Night* (1968) and Joan Didion's *Slouching toward Bethlehem* (1968) and *The White Album* (1979). The compelling novels of Joyce Carol Oates showed the emotional impact on the defenseless of modern culture's violence and lack of center. Ishmael Reed's novels *Mumbo Jumbo* (1972) and *Flight to Canada* (1976) treat history as an instrument of white oppression. Indeed, in these years history writing became a battleground for identity formation, not only of individuals, but of groups and the nation itself. In stories like *The Autobiography of *Malcolm X* (1964), Ernest Gaines's *The Autobiography of Miss Jane Pittman* (1971), and Alice Walker's *Meridian* (1976), African Americans wrote their history into literature. Drawing energy from the civil rights and black-power movements, writers and artists formed the Black Arts movement of the 1960s. Under the leadership of Amiri Baraka (formerly LeRoi Jones), this movement promoted works of political engagement accessible to the black masses. Its influence continued in the poetry of Gwendolyn Brooks, Audre Lorde, Michelle Cliff, Lucille Clifton, Yusef Komunyakaa, and Rita Dove; the plays of Ntozake Shange and August Wilson; and the novels of Charles Johnson, David Bradley, Gloria Naylor, Jamaica Kincaid, Octavia Butler, and Toni *Morrison, who won the Nobel Prize for Literature after publication of her fifth novel, *Beloved* (1987).

Influenced by the antiwar and civil rights movements, fiction and poetry by women—already central to American literary history—addressed issues of *gender in society. Adrienne Rich's *Diving into the Wreck* (1973), a landmark in feminist poetry, marked a turn from her earlier formalism and paved the way for Jorie Graham, Carolyn Forché, and others. In such novels as Joanna Russ's *The Female Man* (1986), Marge Piercy's *Woman on the Edge of Time* (1977), and Ursula K. Le Guin's *Left Hand of Darkness* (1971), women writers employed science fiction to imagine alternate worlds, while Anne Tyler, Anne Beattie, and Marilynne Robinson created haunting pictures of domestic space. Maxine Hong Kingston's *The Woman Warrior* (1976) and *China Men* (1980), Fae Myenne Ng's *Bone* (1993), and David Hwang's *M. Butterfly* (1988), meanwhile, explored *Asian Americans' experiences.

Carson's *Silent Spring* revived environmental writing, as in the work of Gary Snyder, Ernest Callenbach, Edward Abbey, Annie Dillard, and Barry Lopez. The consciousness of the natural world at the center of Native American culture found expression in N. Scott Momaday's *House Made of Dawn* (1968) and *The Way to Rainy Mountain* (1969), Leslie Marmion Silko's *Ceremony* (1977), and Louise Erdrich's novel *Love Medicine* (1984) and *Jacklight* (1984), a book of poems. James Welch's extraordinary *Fool's Crow* (1986), narrated from the point of view of Montana's Blackfeet tribe, conveys the coherence of the natural and tribal world.

Attempts to sum up the nation's history as the twentieth century ended included Updike's *In the Beauty of the Lilies* (1996) and *Rabbit at Rest* (1994), Steven Milhauser's *Martin Dressler* (1996), Paul Auster's *Mr. Vertigo* (1994), Roth's *American Pastoral* (1997), DeLillo's *Underworld* (1997), Pynchon's *Mason and Dixon* (1997), and Robert Stone's *Damascus Gate* (1998). In the era of the world wide web, writers of hypertext used the new technology to create an interactive literature. Indeed, like the little magazines of Modernism, the *Internet could become the medium of literary culture in the twenty-first century.

[*See also* Environmentalism; Immigration; Indian History and Culture: From 1900 to 1950; Indian History and Culture: Since 1950; Literature, Popular; Modernist Culture; New Deal Era, The; Post–Cold War Era; Twenties, The; Urbanization; World War II.]

• Hugh Kenner, *The Pound Era,* 1971. Tony Tanner, *City of Words: American Fiction 1950–70,* 1971. Malcolm Bradbury and Ames McFarlane, eds., *Modernism,* 1976. James B. Breslin, *From Modern to Contemporary: American Poetry 1945–65,* 1984. Linda Hutcheon, *A Poetics of Postmodernism,* 1988. Thomas H. Schaub, *American Fiction in The Cold War,* 1991. Barbara Foley, *Radical Representations,* 1993. Jay Parini, ed., *The Columbia History of American Poetry,* 1993. Henry Louis Gates Jr. and Nellie Y. McKay, eds., *The Norton Anthology of African American Literature,* 1997. Paula Geyh, Fred G. Leebron, and Andrew Levy, eds., *Postmodern American Fiction,* 1998. Paul Lauter, ed., *The Heath Anthology of American Literature,* vol. 2, 3d ed., 1998.

—Thomas H. Schaub

LITTLE BIGHORN, BATTLE OF THE (25–26 June 1876), clash between U.S. cavalry and Sioux and Cheyenne Indians, renowned in history and legend. Although a triumph for the Indians, the disaster celebrated as "Custer's Last Stand" so outraged whites that the army launched a determined counteroffensive to end Indian resistance on the northern Plains.

The Sioux War of 1876 originated in the Treaty of 1868, which established the Great Sioux Reservation in Dakota Territory. Part of the seven tribes of Lakota Sioux and their Cheyenne allies settled on the reservation, while the rest gathered with *Sitting Bull, *Crazy Horse, and other "nontreaty Indians" in the "unceded" Powder River country to the west. After the discovery of gold in the Black Hills in 1874, the government sought to buy the hills from the reservation chiefs. The attempt failed largely because of the opposition of the nontreaty chiefs. To destroy their independence, the government ordered all Indians to go to their agencies by 31 January 1876 or face military action. The nontreaty chiefs did not comply.

Lieutenant Colonel George A. Custer (1839–1876) commanded the Seventh Cavalry, which marched with one of three columns that converged on the unceded territory. Battlefield reverses turned back General George Crook, but General Alfred H. Terry and Colonel John Gibbon united on the Yellowstone

River at the mouth of the Rosebud Creek and formed plans to strike the Indians, thought to be in the Little Bighorn Valley. Custer would march up the Rosebud and hit from the south, while Terry and Gibbon would ascend the Yellowstone and Bighorn to head off any Indians flushed by Custer.

On 25 June, before Terry and Gibbon were in position, Custer attacked the Indian village on the Little Bighorn, which contained about 7,000 people, including 2,000 fighting men. Custer's regiment numbered about 600, which he divided into three battalions. While Captain Frederick W. Benteen departed on a mission to ensure that no Indians camped in the valley above the main village, Custer and Major Marcus A. Reno approached the village from two directions. When Custer and five companies rode downstream behind masking bluffs, Reno and three companies charged the upper end of the village. Although surprised, the warriors rallied and threw Reno's small command back across the river with heavy casualties. Reno's retreat freed the Indians to concentrate on Custer. Within an hour, all five of Custer's companies, 210 men, had been wiped out. No man survived. Joined by Benteen, Reno held hilltop positions four miles to the south through the next day, when the Indians, discovering Terry's approach from the north, pulled off to the south.

The disaster promptly set off a controversy that still rages. Whether a reckless glory-hunter or a capable field commander victimized by bad luck, Custer in defeat gained an immortality that no victory could have conferred. Controversy still rages, and the Little Bighorn battlesite remains contested terrain, a monument to the tortured and tragic history of Indian-white encounters.

[*See also* Expansionism; Gold Rushes; Indian History and Culture: From 1800 to 1900; Indian Wars.]

• John S. Gray, *Centennial Campaign: The Sioux War of 1876,* 1976. John S. Gray, *Mitch Boyer and the Little Bighorn Reconstructed,* 1991. Paul Andrew Hutton, ed., *The Custer Reader,* 1992.

—Robert M. Utley

LIVESTOCK INDUSTRY. Various means of marketing livestock developed in colonial America. *Boston became a market town in the seventeenth century, as did nearby Brighton a century later, as holding pens surrounded slaughterhouses where citizens purchased fresh meat. Similar arrangements existed at Lancaster, Pennsylvania and on Manhattan Island in the Middle Colonies and farther south in Carolina "cowpens." As settlers migrated westward to Kentucky and Ohio, Louisville and Cincinnati emerged as leaders in the livestock industry. Processing techniques introduced by German hog butchers influenced the mid-nineteenth-century meat industries while turnpikes and canals facilitated marketing.

The industry boomed after the *Civil War with three new developments: cattle raised on the West Texas frontier were driven northward to reach more lucrative markets; the transcontinental *railroad expanded westward through Kansas; and insulated (later refrigerated) railroad cars were built to carry processed meat to burgeoning eastern cities. Businessmen like Gustavus *Swift and Philip Armour of *Chicago, investing in modern meat slaughtering facilities near railroad-terminal locations and becoming part-owners of large stockyards adjacent to the meat packing plants, made the livestock industry the nation's largest business in the 1880s and 1890s.

Early market centers, with the incorporation dates of their stockyards, included Chicago in 1865 and Milwaukee, Wisconsin, in 1869. *Kansas City, St. Louis, and St. Joseph, Missouri; Peoria, Illinois; and Indianapolis, Indiana, followed in the 1870s. The 1880s brought very rapid growth, with stockyards incorporated in Omaha, Nebraska; Sioux City, Iowa; Denver, Colorado; St. Paul, Minnesota; Fort Worth and San Antonio, Texas; and Wichita, Kansas. Between 1889 and 1916, a new group of livestock centers combining with packing plants emerged, including Sioux Falls, South Dakota; *San Francisco; Portland, Oregon; Oklahoma City; and Ogden, Utah. Facilitated by this network of large market centers, packing facilities, stockyards, and booming railroads, the nation's livestock moved rapidly, expanded to a world market, and supplied the nation's allies in *World War I. Fears of excessive profits and monopoly brought calls for regulation resulting in the creation of the federal Packers and Stockyards Administration in 1921. This agency in the U.S. Department of Agriculture began court proceedings and forced meatpackers to divest themselves of stockyards, railroads, cattle-loan companies, and similar businesses. The agency remains a watchdog for the industry.

Following *World War II, the livestock industry accelerated an earlier decentralization into country auctions or direct sales to packers that avoided federal regulation. In addition, railroads declined in importance as large trucks increasingly carried animals to market. As consumers demanded grain-fed beef, feedlots developed near grain-producing areas and modern meatpacking facilities relocated near the feedlots. The large stockyards' century of dominance faded as more and more of them closed.

By the end of the twentieth century a new group of packers with a new process called "boxed beef" marketed a large percentage of the nation's meat supply. The twenty-first-century livestock industry involves *computer technology in management and marketing, stricter environmental and pollution laws, and increased trading opportunities in animal futures. Country auctions for small operators, video sales, new breeds, specialty breed shows, and the use of private airplanes to locate animals all had a place in this enduring and ever-evolving industry.

[*See also* Agriculture; Canals and Waterways; Cowboys; Economic Regulation; Mass Production; Meatpacking and Meat Processing Industry; Roads and Turnpikes, Early; Urbanization; West, The.]

• J'Nell L. Pate, *Livestock Legacy: The Fort Worth Stockyards 1887–1987,* 1988. Charles Ball, *The Finishing Touch: A History of the Cattle Feeders Association and Cattle Feeding in the Southwest,* 1992.

—J'Nell L. Pate

LOCHNER* v. *NEW YORK (1905). In 1895, New York State passed a law limiting the hours of work for employees in bakeries to ten hours per day and sixty hours per week. Spearheaded by the bakers' union and tenement-house reformers, this statute reflected the labor movement's long struggle to achieve shorter work hours. In 1902, the Utica bakeshop owner Joseph Lochner was fined for violating the new law. Appealing to the U.S. *Supreme Court, Lochner claimed that the statute violated the *Fourteenth Amendment guarantee that no person shall be denied life, liberty, or property without due process of law. Voting 5–4, the Court in 1905 voided Lochner's conviction and ruled the bakeshop law unconstitutional. Justice Rufus Peckham's majority opinion reasoned that among the liberties protected by the Fourteenth Amendment was "liberty of contract," including the right of the employee and employer voluntarily to contract about the hours of work. A state might interfere with that liberty, Peckham admitted, but only if its regulation fell under the legitimate police powers of the states. Peckham defined the police power narrowly, saying that the bakeshop law was not a reasonable use of the state's power to protect the bakers' health.

Justice Oliver Wendell *Holmes Jr. dissented vigorously. Attacking the majority's underlying premise, he argued that the majority had based its decision on *laissez-faire economic theory rather than on the *Constitution, substituting its own judgment for that of the state legislature.

Lochner became the symbol of laissez-faire constitutionalism and judicial activism. For more than thirty years, critics complained that the Court had erected an insurmountable barrier to economic reform. The "*Lochner* Era" came to an end in 1937, when **West Coast Hotel Company* v. *Parrish* rejected the liberty-of-contract doctrine.

[*See also* Conservatism; Economic Regulation; Gilded Age; Industrialization; Progressive Era; New Deal Era, The.]

• Paul Kens, *Judicial Power and Reform Politics: The Anatomy of* Lochner v. New York, 1990. Howard Gillman, *The Constitution Besieged: The Rise and Demise of* Lochner *Era Police Power Jurisprudence,* 1993.

—Paul Kens

LOGGING. *See* Lumbering.

LONDON ECONOMIC CONFERENCE (1933). The World Monetary and Economic Conference, commonly called the London Economic Conference, took place in the depths of the Great Depression, with fascism and *communism on the rise and the capitalist system in crisis. Most countries had abandoned the *gold standard as their currencies faced collapse; tariff wars raged; *World War I debts were in default; and Germany refused to pay its reparations. Hoping to cure these ills by stabilizing currencies, settling debt issues, and reducing trade barriers, the *League of Nations called an economic conference to convene in London. The conference opened in June 1933 with sixty-six nations represented. The U.S. delegate was Secretary of State Cordell *Hull. Despite initial optimism, squabbling soon erupted between three divergent groups: a bloc of European nations that favored returning to the gold standard as a way of stablizing world currencies; a sterling bloc made up of British Commonwealth nations and Scandinavia that backed a silver standard; and an independent bloc, including the United States and South America, determined to follow its own monetary policies.

Domestic political considerations dictated the U.S. position. The Franklin Delano *Roosevelt administration was in the process of abandoning the gold standard at the very time the London conference was taking place, and President Roosevelt was unwilling to support any international currency-stabilization measures that would tie his hands in dealing with the domestic currency crisis. Moreover, Roosevelt did not want national attention diverted from what he saw as the more fundamental problem—U.S. economic recovery. The administration did support tariff reduction, but the gold-bloc nations saw this as secondary to currency stabilization.

The conference ended in late July with no significant accomplishments. Many blamed the United States for its failure, and even, in retrospect, for hastening the onset of *World War II. In reality, the war's fundamental causes were already in place, and adjusting world currencies and *tariffs would probably have done little to change the course of events.

[*See also* Capitalism; Depressions, Economic; Monetary Policy, Federal; New Deal Era, The.]

• Raymond Moley, *After Seven Years,* 1939. Lloyd C. Gardner, *Economic Aspects of New Deal Diplomacy,* 1964.

—David E. Conrad

LONELY CROWD, THE (1950). This influential study by the Harvard sociologist David Riesman, with Nathan Glazer and Reuel Denney, rests upon the premise that socioeconomic structure influences personality. Applying this concept to post–*World War II American society, the authors investigated the personality type, or "national character," produced by advanced industrial *capitalism. In a time of economic scarcity (nineteenth-century America), they argued, survival depended upon an individual's ability to respond innovatively to unfamiliar situations. This they termed "inner-direction." Conversely, during an age of abundance (postwar America), economic success came as one learned to cooperate and adapt to the values of others. The authors labeled this an "other-directed" personality type. Although the authors discussed ways for twentieth-century white-collar workers (the focus of their analysis) to maintain autonomy in an increasingly collectivized culture, *Lonely Crowd* readers interpreted the dichotomy between inner and outer-direction as an indicator that American society was becoming more conformist and less individualistic.

Despite the alarm it engendered, *The Lonely Crowd* was enthusiastically received. Riesman, the principal author, was featured in a 1954 *Time* magazine cover story as a defender of *individualism in an age of mass culture. This popularity had two sources. A clear articulation of how one could maintain autonomy in a mass society struck a responsive chord with intellectuals traumatized by the horrors of twentieth-century totalitarian movements where individual will had succumbed to the will of the collective. Further, its analysis of an expanding managerial class made *The Lonely Crowd* a popular and influential book for self-reflective middle-income Americans. Indeed, contemporaries argued that it perfectly captured and contributed to the 1950s mood of national soul-searching. It continues to influence understanding of postwar society.

[*See also Affluent Society, The;* Fifties, The; Social Class; Social Science; Sociology; Urbanization.]

• Wilfred M. McClay, *Masterless Self and Society in Modern America,* 1994.

—Jennifer L. Kalish

LONG, HUEY (1893–1935), Louisiana political leader and would-be presidential candidate. A populistic and politically ambitious lawyer from the northern Louisiana town of Winnfield, Long won election to the state railroad commission in 1918. His relentless opposition to corporate privilege, especially the unbridled power of the Standard Oil Company, led to an unsuccessful run for governor in 1924. Fours years later he won the governorship thanks to a folksy style and shrewd maneuvering that disrupted traditional alliances. As governor, Long did what other reformist politicians only talked about: He built roads, schools, and hospitals, and he shifted the tax burden to the corporations and the wealthy. He also organized a statewide machine that all but destroyed the conservative "Bourbon" oligarchy that had controlled Louisiana politics since the end of *Reconstruction. Long offered the downtrodden a long-awaited taste of power, but his increasingly ruthless and graft-driven methods polarized the state. Followers regarded him as a populist champion and a political messiah; critics labeled him a demagogue and political gangster. After surviving a 1929 impeachment trial, he won election to the U.S. Senate in 1930.

Long strongly supported Franklin Delano *Roosevelt during the 1932 presidential race, but he later became a sharp critic of the New Deal's measured response to the Great Depression. In 1934, after publishing a manifesto entitled *Every Man a King,* Long launched a nationwide "Share Our Wealth" campaign. He used *radio broadcasts and high-profile personal appearances to promote his radically progressive tax proposals that he claimed would alleviate *unemployment and the maldistribution of wealth. In 1935 he planned a run for the presidency and even wrote a book entitled *My First Days in the White House.* But his insurgent candidacy ended abruptly on 9 September, when he was fatally shot by Dr. Carl Weiss (the son-in-law of Judge Benjamin Pavy, an anti-Long leader), in the Louisiana statehouse in Baton Rouge.

During his brief but remarkable career, Huey Long ruled Louisiana with an iron hand, dispensing economic panaceas and political retribution with a ferocity seldom seen in American politics. The most powerful southern politician of his day, the "Kingfish," as he liked to be called, spawned a political dynasty that influenced state and national politics decades after his death. Immortalized in Robert Penn Warren's novel *All the King's Men* (1946), a semifictional meditation on the temptations of power, this talented but tragically flawed leader left an ambiguous and troubling legacy.

[*See also* Depressions, Economic; New Deal Era, The; Political Parties.]

• T. Harry Williams, *Huey Long,* 1969. William Ivy Hair, *The Kingfish and His Realm: The Life and Times of Huey Long,* 1991.

—Raymond O. Arsenault

LOOKING BACKWARD 2000–1887 (1888), a utopian novel by Edward Bellamy (1850–1898). *Looking Backward* is the story of a privileged but troubled nineteenth-century Bostonian who awakens from a hypnotic sleep in the year 2000 to find a commonwealth of abundance and solidarity instead of the competition, egotism, and waste of industrial *capitalism. Influenced by Protestant millennialism and Fourierism, an antebellum utopian movement, Bellamy intended his tale to demonstrate how "Nationalism" (the term he used to distinguish his version of the cooperative society from materialistic *socialism) would peacefully evolve by accelerating industrial capitalism's tendencies toward consolidation. In Bellamy's vision of the future, every able person owes society a reasonable service and in turn receives an equal share of a productive output that belongs to the whole nation, not to select individuals. The society depicted in the novel is one in which equitable distribution of goods, rational planning, and industrial progress render *poverty, class conflict, and *gender discrimination relics of the past.

Attracted by the book's moral vision of social harmony, its forecast of the peaceful transition to the new society, and its celebration of the middle-class virtues of work, character, and expertise, 500,000 Americans bought the work in its first year alone, and many joined Nationalist clubs to bring Bellamy's vision to fruition. Among those who acknowledged their debt to *Looking Backward* were the socialist Eugene V. *Debs, the philosopher John *Dewey, the feminist Charlotte Perkins *Gilman, the social analyst Thorstein *Veblen, and numerous Populists, whose cause Bellamy endorsed. In subsequent years, it inspired Arthur Morgan, first director of the *Tennessee Valley Authority, and Al Haber, a founder of *Students for a Democratic Society.

Although criticized for its unrealistic view of human nature, its misunderstanding of markets, its constricted view of human possibilities, and its undemocratic reliance on experts, *Looking Backward* remains one of the most striking American visions of an alternative to capitalism.

[*See also* Gilded Age; Haymarket Affair; Populist Era; Populist Party; Protestantism; Social Gospel; Utopian and Communitarian Movements.]

• John Thomas, *Alternative America: Henry George, Edward Bellamy, Henry Demarest Lloyd, and the Adversary Tradition,* 1983.

—Daniel H. Borus

LOS ANGELES. El Pueblo de la Reina de Los Angeles was founded in 1781 at Yanga, a Tongva Indian village along the Pacific coast in present-day *California. Decades of Mexican rule gave way after the *Mexican War (1848) to U.S. conquest and settlement. After a relatively tranquil interval in the 1870s and 1880s came a period of frenzied real-estate boosterism, accellerated by the rise of Hollywood. By the 1920s, Los Angeles' population surpassed one million—90 percent of European origin, two-thirds transplanted Midwesterners. The Depression of the 1930s roused social tensions that included the forced repatriation of Mexican aliens.

During *World War II more newcomers arrived to work in the city's defense industries. The war stirred further ethnic tensions, including a 1942 outbreak of violence against Mexican youths. The postwar years brought a vast urban sprawl and a tangle of freeways, along with increasing ethnic and class divisions. Wealthy areas coexisted with black ghettos and Hispanic barrios. Indeed, from 1848 through the 1960s, most non-Anglos, including Native Americans, Mexicans, *Asian Americans, and *African Americans, were marginalized as a subordinate labor force. By the 1990s, with more than three million inhabitants, Los Angeles was a global city with immigrants from 100 nations. Hispanics comprised 40 percent of the population, African Americans 14 percent, and Asian/Pacific islanders 10 percent.

"Los Angeles" has always been in part a media creation. Health-seekers and journalists celebrated it in the 1870s and 1880s as the Garden City; the Chamber of Commerce and real-estate promoters of the 1920s called it the All-American Pacific Metropolis. It was "Hollywoodland" in the 1930s and "America's first Global City" in the 1980s and 1990s—an image reenforced when it hosted the 1984 Olympic Games. From Aimee Semple *McPherson's Angelus Temple in the 1920s to Forest Lawn Cemetery and Disneyland more recently, Los Angeles has long been a tourist mecca.

Countless filmmakers and *television producers also appropriated the city. The celebrated final scene of *Casablanca* (1942) was filmed at Los Angeles airport. The 1950s TV series *Dragnet* made the Los Angeles City Hall an icon as well-known as London's Big Ben. In literature, the mystery writer Raymond Chandler exploited Los Angeles locales to a high camp perfection, Nathaniel West offered a nightmarish vision of rootless, rioting masses in *The Day of the Locust* (1939), and Evelyn Waugh concocted a hilarious send-up of Forest Lawn cemetery in *The Loved One* (1965). World War II expatriates such as Thomas Mann and Igor Stravinsky, by contrast, generally ignored the city except as a source of Hollywood largess. Columnist Herb Caen articulated a San Francisco/New York view of Los Angeles as one big parking lot. Stung, Angelenos pointed to their art museums and institutions of higher learning, including UCLA and the University of Southern California.

Rioting in the black district of Watts in 1965 burned through the media hype to reveal a divided city undergoing wrenching sociolcultural change. The election of Tom Bradley as the city's first black mayor in 1973 underscored the changes. The 1992 rioting that followed the brutal beating of a black motorist, Rodney King, and the acquittal of the white policemen responsible, made clear that the social tensions remained potent. But Los Angeles in the 1990s overcame a severe economic recession (related to the collapse of an inflated real estate market and to post-*Cold War cuts in the defense industry). With the economy booming and the city growing ever more diverse, Los Angeles seemed poised to reinvent itself once again.

[See also, Disney, Walt; Film; Hispanic Americans; Riots, Urban; Suburbanization; Urbanization; World War II: Domestic Effects.]

• Robert M. Fogelson, *The Fragmented Metropolis: Los Angeles, 1850–1930,* 2d ed., 1990. Leonard Pitt and Dale Pitt, *Los Angeles A to Z: An Encyclopedia of the City and County,* 1997.

—Antonio Rios-Bustamante

LOUIS, JOE (1914–1983), boxer and heavyweight champion. Born near LaFayette, Alabama, Joe Louis moved to Detroit with his mother at the age of ten. He became an amateur boxer in 1932 and two years later turned professional. Under the guidance of his trainer and confidant Jack "Chappie" Blackburn and managers John Roxborough and Julian Black, Louis quickly established a reputation as a devastating puncher and skilled fighter. He captured the heavyweight championship from James Braddock in 1937 and went on to defend his title a record twenty-five times. Among his many legendary fights was a first-round knockout of the German fighter Max Schmeling in a return match in 1938, a final-round knockout of Billy Conn in 1941, and a highly controversial defeat of Jersey Joe Walcott in 1947. His defeat of Schmeling took on symbolic importance, as many Americans viewed it as a triumph of American democracy over Nazi racism and totalitarianism. Louis retired as heavyweight champion in 1949, only to be thwarted in comeback attempts against Ezzard Charles and Rocky Marciano over the next two years. As with many former boxers, Louis's postretirement years were troubled. He married four times (twice to Marva Trotter), failed in the fast-food business, at one time owed over a million dollars in federal taxes, and spent five months in a mental hospital. Louis spent his last years as a greeter at Caesar's Palace Casino in Las Vegas. In 1990, he was posthumously honored by election to the International Boxing Hall of Fame. An American hero, Joe Louis was especially revered in the *African-American community.

[*See also* Boxing; Sports: Professional Sports.]

• Anthony O. Edmonds, *Joe Louis,* 1973. Chris Mead, *Joe Louis: Black Hero in White America,* 1985.

—David K. Wiggins

LOUISIANA PURCHASE (1803), an agreement by which the United States bought from France that part of France's North American empire roughly defined by the Missouri and *Mississippi River watersheds. The deal doubled the size of the nation, creating what Thomas *Jefferson termed an "empire for liberty."

French control of the region dated from 1682, when the explorer René-Robert Cavelier, Sieur de *La Salle, claimed on behalf of King Louis IX a vaguely defined area he named "Louisiana." Rather than lose the colony to Britain as a result of its defeat in the *Seven Years' War, France ceded Louisiana to Spain in 1763. Rising tensions between the United States and Spain led to *Pinckney's Treaty (1795), which guaranteed American navigation rights on the Mississippi River and the right to deposit goods for export at *New Orleans, through which most of the trade of the western states passed.

In 1801, rumors that Spain had transferred Louisiana back to France alarmed many Americans. Fearing that access to the Gulf of Mexico might be interrupted, some Americans, mostly from the West, called for the territory to be taken by force. To head off this sentiment, President Thomas Jefferson dispatched Robert Livingston of New York and, later, James *Monroe to Paris to negotiate the purchase from France of New Orleans and the province of Florida west of the Perdido River.

Meanwhile, Emperor Napoleon Bonaparte, faced with defeat in the French sugar colony of Santo Domingo, decided to sell all of Louisiana in order to consolidate his forces in Europe. Although their instructions empowered them only to acquire New Orleans and West Florida, Livingston and Monroe jumped at the French offer. Understanding the territorial ambitions of many Americans, they recognized this acquisition as a unique opportunity. On 30 April 1803, American and French negotiators initialed agreements transferring the Louisiana territory to the United States in exchange for $11,250,000. In addition, the United States assumed $3,750,000 in claims of its citizens against France.

The *Lewis and Clark expedition of 1804–1806 brought back the first scientific and economic knowledge of a land purchased sight unseen by the United States. The expedition also helped undergird a U.S. claim extending the limits of the Louisiana territory as far west as the Columbia River region and as far south as West Florida and Texas. Spanish objections, first to the legality of France's sale of the territory, and then over its boundaries, resulted in a diplomatic dispute with the United States that lasted until the signing of the *Adams-Onís Treaty in 1819.

In the long run the United States paid a steep price in blood and treasure for the Louisiana territory. The region saw a series of bitter conflicts with Indians, and the controversial question of *slavery in the new lands exacerbated sectional tensions between northern and southern states, leading to both the *Missouri Compromise of 1820 and its eventual repeal in the *Kansas-Nebraska Act of 1854. In this respect the Louisiana Purchase can be understood as one of the long-term causes of the *Civil War.

[*See also* Early Republic, Era of the; Expansionism; Indian History and Culture: From 1800 to 1900; Indian Wars.]

• Henry Adams, *History of the United States of America during the Administrations of Jefferson and Madison,* vols. 2 and 3, 1889–1891. Alexander DeConde, *This Affair of Louisiana,* 1976. Dolores Egger Labbé, *The Louisiana Purchase and Its Aftermath,* 1998.

—William Earl Weeks

LOWELL MILLS. The cotton textile mills of Lowell, Massachusetts, were the most famous factories in the United States in the first half of the nineteenth century. From them emanated innovations in *technology, the organization of work, and *business practices that made signal contributions to industrial *capitalism in the United States.

In the early 1820s, *Boston capitalists, organized as the Boston Manufacturing Company of Waltham, sought a site for expansion. They purchased land, a transportation canal, and water-power rights at the Pawucket Falls of the Merrimack River in East Chelmsford. There they began manufacturing printed cotton cloth in 1823.

Implementing their grand vision, the mill owners incorporated the town of Lowell in 1826, naming it for the late Francis Cabot Lowell, a founder of the Waltham venture. High profits led to rapid expansion, and by 1850 the Lowell mills, employing more than 10,000 workers, were the nation's leading textile-manufacturing center. With a population of 33,000, Lowell was the second largest city in Massachusetts.

Mill towns patterned after Lowell arose across *New England and collectively came to constitute the Waltham-Lowell system. Large, redbrick, water-powered mills housed all the machinery needed to manufacture cotton cloth from raw cotton. Employing a work force consisting of native-born single daughters of Yankee farmers, the mills erected boardinghouses for their workers. Combining corporate paternalism with monthly cash wages, the owners of the Lowell mills sought to industrialize without replicating the social ills associated with English factory towns in this era. Later, immigrant workers replaced native-born young women.

The Lowell mills offered the first major source of wage work for women in the nation. After the *Civil War, Lowell occupied a less important place in the *textile industry and the industrial economy. Employment and production in Lowell grew until *World War I but declined thereafter, as textile production shifted to the *South. By 1980 only scattered, minor textile production continued in Lowell, the dominant center of the early American industrial revolution. In 1978, Congress created the Lowell National Historical Park on the site of a restored mill and associated buildings.

[*See also* Antebellum Era; Cotton Industry; Factory System; Immigrant Labor; Industrialization; Labor Movements; Strikes and Industrial Conflicts; Women in the Labor Force.]

• Thomas Dublin, *Women at Work: The Transformation of Work and Community in Lowell, Massachusetts, 1826–1860,* 1979, rev. ed. 1994. Robert F. Dalzell Jr., *Enterprising Elite: The Boston Associates and the World They Made,* 1987.

—Thomas Dublin

LUCE, CLARE BOOTHE (1903–1987), editor, playwright, war correspondent, two-term Republican congresswoman from Connecticut (1943–1947), ambassador to Italy (1953–1956). Born in *New York City, she became a writer and editor for *Vogue* and *Vanity Fair* magazines, after divorcing her first husband, the wealthy George Tuttle Brokaw (with whom she had a daughter, Ann). In 1935, she married Henry R. *Luce, founder of *Time, Fortune,* and *Life* magazines. By 1939 she had written three successful and acerbic Broadway plays, *The Women, Kiss the Boys Goodbye,* and the anti-Nazi *Margin for Error.*

Luce was a vociferous *World War II interventionist and champion of Lend-Lease and China Relief. In Congress, she was something of a maverick, making provocative speeches, supporting liberal immigration laws, and opposing a 1942 tax cut as being a windfall for the rich. As a member of the House Military Affairs Committee, she visited hard-pressed Allied forces at the Italian front and publicized their plight in articles and broadcasts. Luce flamboyantly converted to *Roman Catholicism in 1946, lectured nationwide, wrote theological pamphlets, and edited a book of essays, *Saints for Now.* While ambassador to Italy, she protested communist influence in industry and government and supervised the distribution of American aid. Awed by her brilliance, charm, and beauty, Italians dubbed her *La Luce*—the luminescent one. Luce's lifelong interest in espionage led Richard M. *Nixon and Ronald *Reagan to appoint her to their President's Foreign Intelligence Advisory Board.

[*See also* Anticommunism; Drama; Feminism; Immigration Law; Journalism.]

• Stephen Shadegg, *Clare Boothe Luce,* 1970. Wilfrid Sheed, *Clare Boothe Luce,* 1982. Sylvia Jukes Morris, *Rage for Fame: The Ascent of Clare Boothe Luce,* 1997.

—Sylvia Jukes Morris

LUCE, HENRY R. (1898–1967), magazine publisher and editor. Born in China, the son of Presbyterian missionaries, he graduated from Yale in 1920. With his college classmate Briton Hadden, Luce in 1923 founded *Time* magazine, the first and most successful news *magazine. Possessing a knowing point of view, *Time* offered a weekly synthesis of news and culture in a distinctive style of compounded and invented words and inverted sentences. It appealed to middle-class readers in smaller cities and towns whose local newspapers provided little national news or analysis.

Hadden's death in 1929 left Luce in control of Time Inc. He oversaw the creation of a lavish business monthly, *Fortune,* in 1930, and a spectacularly popular picture magazine, *Life,* six years later. Also in the 1930s, Time Inc., launched "The March of Time" radio news program and movie newsreel. In 1954, Luce started *Sports Illustrated.*

The expansion of his magazine empire coincided with changes in Luce's personal life. In 1936 he divorced his first wife, Lila, to marry the playwright Clare Boothe. Soon thereafter, he became more involved in public affairs. Although no reactionary, he opposed what he regarded as the Franklin Delano *Roosevelt administration's antibusiness policies. Together with other East Coast publishers and editors, he lobbied for American involvement on behalf of the Allies in *World War II. In a famous 1941 *Life* essay, he contended that Americans had no choice. The twentieth century was, Luce wrote, "the American Century."

To his frustration, Luce's magazines, up to the mid-1940s, often expressed views at variance with his own. He replaced more independent-minded editors, however, and by the 1950s, writers for *Life* and *Time* generally conformed to the publishers's opinions, notably his support for an aggressive stance against communist regimes worldwide. Only after Luce's death did his magazines begin to moderate their politics.

[*See also* Anticommunism; Conservatism; Journalism; Luce, Clare Boothe.]

• James L. Baughman, *Henry R. Luce and the Rise of the American News Media,* 1987. Robert E. Herzstein, *Henry R. Luce,* 1994.

—James L. Baughman

LUMBERING. From the early *Colonial Era, European settlers tapped North America's forests. Initially, lumbering was more an adjunct of farming than an industrial activity. In the early eighteenth century, however, a primitive lumber industry arose land in northern *New England. By 1830, Bangor, Maine, was the world's largest lumber-producing center, supplying markets along the Atlantic seaboard and in Europe.

In the mid-nineteenth century, lumbering flourished in Pennsylvania and New York. Williamsport, Pennsylvania, became the new leader in production. There in 1872 the industry's first great strike occurred, its failure hastening the collapse of the National Labor Union. The *Erie Canal opened new opportunities. Vast quantities of lumber went eastward over it, especially from Saginaw and Bay City, Michigan, which by the 1880s had come to primacy as producers. Albany, New York, the canal's eastern terminus, became the nation's major wholesale lumber mart.

As settlement pushed westward, the industry followed. *Chicago became a distribution center, production expanded into Wisconsin, and large mills arose that served markets down the *Mississippi River and on the Great Plains. In the upper Midwest, Frederick Weyerhaeuser and his associates created the industry's largest enterprise.

Lumbering lagged in the antebellum *South owing to natural barriers. However, a few centers emerged that catered to markets in *New Orleans and in the Caribbean sugar islands. With extensive *railroad construction following the *Civil War, the southern pine industry burgeoned. Much of its expansion derived from northern capital and leadership. At Bogalusa, Louisiana, for example, Pennsylvania's Goodyear brothers in 1904 built the world's largest sawmill.

In the early twentieth century, many companies transferred to the Far West, competing with older mills that had arisen following California's Gold Rush, while continuing to serve midwestern markets by rail.

In the late nineteenth century, operators in the South and Far West had turned increasingly to timberland acquisition to ensure stable supplies of logs and to justify investments in logging railroads, ever more necessary as stands near floatable streams disappeared. Earlier lumbermen had put nearly all their investment capital into production facilities (and, in the West, into ships to carry their output), but this no longer sufficed. The need to acquire timberland, combined with expensive technological advances, fostered bigger enterprises, yet the industry remained highly fragmented. Bulky, abundant raw material, still relatively simple *technology, and ease of entry discouraged centralization. Repeated efforts at cooperation or consolidation failed.

By the end of *World War II, private timber holdings in the *West had been heavily cut. With no new forested frontiers available, lumbermen turned to the national forests for logs. This led to changes in the National Forest Service, previously largely a custodial agency, and to clashes with environmentalists, who extolled the noncommodity values of forests. Partly in response, some producers shifted back to the South, where new forests had grown and most timber was on private land more insulated from environmentalist pressure. Declining per capita lumber consumption and rising demand for more sophisticated wood products accompanied these shifts and encouraged consolidation anew, but as the twentieth century ended the industry remained decentralized and fragmented.

[*See also* Conservation Movement; Environmentalism; Forest and Forestry; Labor Movements; Land Policy, Federal.]

• Thomas R. Cox et al., *This Well-Wooded Land,* 1985. Michael Williams, *Americans and Their Forests,* 1989.

—Thomas R. Cox

LUTHERANISM. Lutheranism, the oldest and largest branch of Protestant Christianity worldwide, has over eight million members in the United States, nearly all in two denominations, the Evangelical Lutheran Church in America (ELCA) and the Lutheran Church Missouri Synod (LCMS). Lutheranism, emerging from the early sixteenth-century reformation of Martin Luther, was formalized in the Augsburg Confession (1530) and spread to northern and central Europe. Dutch and Swedish Lutherans first came to America in the 1620s, with larger groups of German Lutherans arriving after 1680. Lutheran settlements stretched from New York to South Carolina but were heaviest in Pennsylvania, where Henry Melchior Mühlenberg organized scattered congregations into the Pennsylvania Ministerium in 1748. Other regional groupings of congregations, called synods, were organized, and in 1820 many formed a national organization, the General Synod, under the leadership of Samuel Simon Schmucker. By the early nineteenth century many colonial Lutherans had acculturated to the United States and, led by Schmucker, this "American Lutheranism" moved closer to Reformed and Evangelical Christianity.

From the 1840s until *World War I, another, larger wave of Lutheran immigrants from Germany and Scandinavia organized independent denominations along linguistic and theological lines. These immigrant Lutherans settled primarily in a broad band of territory from Ohio to the Dakotas, which remains the center of Lutheran strength. These immigrants were often more conservative in doctrine and practice than the "American Lutherans." One group of Germans formed the LCMS in 1847, under the direction of C. F. W. Walther. A similar conservative movement within the General Synod led by Charles Porterfield Krauth resulted in the formation of the General Council in 1867. The later immigrants assimilated into American society early in the twentieth century, pushed by nativist feelings during World War I. From 1917 to 1962 a wave of denominational realignments resulted in three major Lutheran denominations. After *World War II, American Lutherans began to play an important leadership role in American Christianity and world Lutheranism through various ecumenical organizations. In the early 1970s, the LCMS underwent a struggle between moderates and conservatives; the moderates left and eventually merged with two other Lutheran groups in 1988 to form the ELCA. The 5.2-million-member ELCA is generally identified with mainline American *Protestantism, while the 2.6-million-member LCMS is much more conservative. Of a number of other, much smaller conservative Lutheran denominations, the largest is the Wisconsin Evangelical Lutheran Synod, with 400,000 members.

[*See also* German Americans; Immigration; Religion; Scandinavian Americans.]

• E. Clifford Nelson, ed., *The Lutherans in North America,* 1975.

—Mark A. Granquist

LYNCHING, a form of illegal execution, usually of a person accused of a crime or some type of deviant behavior. Historically, most lynching victims in the United States have been African-American males. However, women, native-born white males, and members of other minority groups (including European immigrants, Chinese, and Hispanics), were also lynched, though in much smaller numbers. Although lynchings are often equated with hanging, other methods that have been used include shooting, burning, and drowning, sometimes followed by the mutilation and/or public display of the corpse. Some lynchings were carried out by large mobs, while others involved groups of only three or four members. White supremacist or nativist groups like the *Ku Klux Klan perpetrated some lynchings, but the informal and spontaneous organization of citizens into lynch mobs was more common. Most lynch victims had been accused, but not convicted, of such serious crimes as murder, assault, or rape. Other victims were killed because of transgressions of racial codes such as insulting a white person or using inflammatory language.

Lynchings have occurred throughout U.S. history but have been concentrated more heavily in specific time periods. The number of *African Americans lynched in the *South increased sharply during *Reconstruction as southern whites reacted to the federal occupation of the former Confederacy and to the increasing political and economic power of blacks. Lynchings peaked during the 1890s, when the annual total of victims regularly exceeded eighty. The rate declined during the next four decades, with temporary upswings between 1905 and 1910, and again immediately following *World War I. After 1930 lynchings became relatively rare, though some of the most highly publicized incidents occurred in the 1940s, 1950s, and even as late as the 1960s (for example, the 1955 lynching of the fourteen-year-old Emmett Till near Greenwood, Mississippi, and lynchings of Claude Neal, Charles Mack Parker, and *civil rights activists James Chaney, Andrew Goodman, and Michael Schwerner). The number of lynchings of whites followed a different trend, declining through the late 1800s and virtually disappearing by the twentieth century.

Lynching was primarily a southern phenomenon. Mississippi and Georgia claimed significantly more victims than any other state. However, the rate of lynching in relation to the size of the black population was highest in Florida. Outside the Southeast, lynchings were most likely to occur in the *Southwest and *West, though in considerably smaller numbers. Lynchings in the Southwest differed in important respects from those in the Southeast. For example, victims were more likely to be white or Latino and were more often accused of being horse thieves, bandits, or outlaws. Lynchings in the North Central and Northeast states were rare.

Because most lynching victims had been accused of serious crimes, lynching has sometimes been viewed, particularly by southern newspapers and commentators, as a form of "popular justice," substituting for, or reinforcing the formal criminal justice system. More recently, explanations for lynching have drawn from *social science theory. One theory describes lynchings as a form of aggression resulting from southern whites' economic frustrations. And, indeed, larger numbers of lynchings did occur during years when the southern economy faltered. Another theoretical perspective views lynching as a form of social control practiced by southern whites when they felt threatened by African Americans. According to this "racial threat" perspective, whites felt threatened when blacks competed with them for political power, economic security, or social status.

The sharp decline in lynchings after the mid-1920s is attributed by some to improved law enforcement, especially the increased use of patrol cars and radios. Another explanation emphasizes the increasingly critical treatment of lynch-mob behavior by southern newspapers. Some claim that antilynching organizations played a critical role. The *National Association for the Advancement of Colored People (NAACP) fought vigorously against lynching, as did the Association of Southern Women for the Prevention of Lynching and the Committee on Interracial Cooperation. Activists such as the NAACP's Walter White, Jessie Daniel Ames, and Ida B. *Wells-Barnett were especially visible opponents of lynching. Still others suggested that increasingly fierce resistance, sometimes armed, by African Americans discouraged mob behavior in whites. Finally, the decline of lynching has also been linked to major social and economic transformations in the South that fundamentally altered the relation between whites and African Americans.

At their peak, lynching and the fear of lynching had a profound effect on the African American population. It posed a deadly danger to those who challenged the privileged position of whites in southern society. It also motivated many blacks to leave the South. While some southern whites persisted in defending lynching as a "necessary evil," increasing numbers of whites in all regions came to view the phenomenon as a barbaric national embarrassment and moral disgrace. The ample representation of lynching in American fiction, such as in Lillian Smith's *Strange Fruit* (1944), and frequent allusion to lynching—real and metaphorical—in discussions of contemporary race relations attest to its lasting influence.

[See also Civil Rights Movement; Racism; Segregation, Racial.]

• Arthur Raper, *The Tragedy of Lynching,* 1933. Robert L. Zangrando, *The NAACP Crusade against Lynching, 1909–1950,* 1980. James R. McGovern, *Anatomy of a Lynching: The Killing of Claude Neal,* 1982. George C. Wright, *Racial Violence in Kentucky, 1865–1940: Lynchings, Mob Rule, and "Legal Lynchings,"* 1990. W. Fitzhugh Brundage, *Lynchings in the New South: Georgia and Virginia, 1880–1930,* 1993. Stewart E. Tolnay and E. M. Beck, *A Festival of Violence: An Analysis of Southern Lynchings, 1882–1930,* 1995.

—Stewart E. Tolnay and E. M. Beck

LYON, MARY (1797–1849), educator, founder of Mount Holyoke College. Born in Buckland, Massachusetts, the descendant of *Baptists who had helped establish religious liberty in the 1770s, Lyon began teaching in 1814 and enrolled in Sanderson Academy in 1817, commencing a period that alternated school-teaching with study. She experienced religious conversion in 1821 while a student at Rev. Joseph Emerson's Byfield Female Seminary. In 1824, Lyon founded Buckland Female Seminary, a successful girls' school whose graduates were eagerly sought as teachers by western Masschusetts school boards.

Seeking ways to carry her Buckland innovations to a larger constituency, and shunning the elite female seminaries that emphasized "refined" accomplishments like dancing and painting, Lyon in 1834 began to raise money for a seminary for "the adult female youth in the common walks of life." Her efforts bore fruit in 1837 with the opening of Mount Holyoke Female Seminary in South Hadley, Massachusetts.

Mount Holyoke set a new standard for women's education. Keeping costs low, the seminary offered the daughters of artisans and farmers the same high quality of education available at male colleges like Amherst and Harvard. Responding to a national demand, the seminary supplied a steady stream of female teachers to the new nation, helping to feminize that profession and providing many young women with an interlude of autonomy before marriage. Many Mount Holyoke graduates also want abroad as missionaries. Lyon served as principal and teacher until her death.

[*See also* Education: Collegiate Education; Missionary Movement; Women's Rights Movements.]

• Elizabeth Alden Green, *Mary Lyon and Mount Holyoke: Opening the Gates,* 1979. Amanda Porterfield, *Mary Lyon and the Mount Holyoke Missionaries,* 1997.

—Kathryn Kish Sklar

M

MacARTHUR, DOUGLAS (1880–1964), commander of Allied forces in the Pacific in *World War II and *United Nations commander in the *Korean War. Born to a military family, Douglas MacArthur was a flamboyant, vain, and brilliant field commander, arguably the best general in World War II. Graduating from West Point in 1903, MacArthur established a distinguished military record in *World War I. Commander in the *Philippines when the Japanese attacked Pearl Harbor in December 1941, MacArthur led the resistance to Japan's invasion of the islands. When the Philippines fell, MacArthur established new headquarters in Australia, pledging, "I shall return."

When Allied forces halted the Japanese advance in the South Pacific, MacArthur took up the attack with a successful "island hopping" strategy of bypassing strongly held Japanese islands. He was preparing for the final assault on Japan when the United States dropped the atomic bombs on Japan in August 1945 and the war abruptly ended.

Given complete control of the occupation of Japan, MacArthur reformed and modernized the Japanese government and economy. When North Korea attacked South Korea in 1950, the United Nations called on its members to "repel" the invasion. MacArthur was appointed commander of the newly formed UN command. When UN troops halted the North Korean advance into South Korea, MacArthur ordered a counterattack, including an amphibious landing at Inchon. The strategy succeeded, and the North Korean invaders were partially trapped. UN forces drove deep into North Korea, but when they approached the Chinese border, large elements of the Chinese army crossed the border and drove the UN forces back to South Korea.

Outraged, MacArthur called for all-out war with communist China, using *nuclear weapons if necessary. President Harry S. *Truman refused, fearing World War III. In April 1951, accusing MacArthur of defying presidential authority, Truman removed MacArthur from command. He came home to a hero's welcome, delivered an emotional address to Congress, but failed in his goal of winning the Republican presidential nomination in 1952.

[*See also* Cold War; Pearl Harbor, Attack on.]

• Douglas MacArthur, *Reminiscences: General of the Army*, 1964. William Manchester, *American Caesar*, 1979.

—David E. Conrad

MADISON, JAMES (1751–1836), "Father of the *Constitution" and fourth president of the United States. Born in King George County, Virginia, James Madison spent his childhood at Montpelier in Orange County, Virginia. After attending local schools, he entered the College of New Jersey at Princeton in 1769 and graduated in 1771.

Poor health and small stature prevented Madison from participating in the *Revolutionary War, but in the Summer of 1776, as a delegate to the Virginia Convention, he played a decisive role in altering George Mason's draft of the *Virginia Declaration of Rights. Mason had proposed to grant religious dissenters toleration under the law, but Madison persuaded the Convention to make religious freedom a matter of right rather than a mere concession.

Between 1777 and 1779, while advising the governors of Virginia as a member of the Council of State, Madison commenced his friendship with Thomas *Jefferson. During the 1780s Madison served in the *Continental Congress (1780–1783 and 1786–1788) and the Virginia House of Delegates (1783–1786). In the latter body, he further advanced the goal of religious liberty by ensuring the passage in 1786 of Jefferson's Statute for Establishing Religious Freedom. In the Continental Congress, Madison joined the effort to replace the *Articles of Confederation with a new constitutional structure. Madison drafted the "Virginia Plan," which defined the agenda for the *Constitutional Convention of 1787 and ultimately became, with modifications, the blueprint for the federal Constitution. Playing an equally prominent role in the ratification process, Madison collaborated with Alexander *Hamilton and John *Jay on the *Federalist Papers, writing twenty-nine of the eighty-five essays; led the Federalist forces in the Virginia ratifying convention; and in 1789 headed the campaign to add the first amendments to the Constitution in the form of the *Bill of Rights.

Madison served four terms in the U.S. House of Representatives (1789–1797). At first, he cooperated with George *Washington's administration, but differences over economic policy and foreign affairs drove Madison into leading the political opposition that coalesced into the Jeffersonian Republican party. In 1797 Madison and his wife Dolley Payne Todd (whom he had married in 1794) retired to Montpelier. He continued to act as an opposition leader, however, by drafting the 1798 Virginia Resolutions protesting the violations of *civil liberties and *states' rights embodied in the 1798 *Alien and Sedition Acts.

In 1801 Madison became President Thomas Jefferson's secretary of state. In this capacity he served as Jefferson's closest advisor and contributed to both the successes of his administration (such as the 1803 *Louisiana Purchase) and its failures (such as the *Embargo Acts of 1807–1809). His tenure in the State Department after 1803 was dominated by efforts to protect American neutral trade during the Napoleonic wars (1803–1815). Madison tried, without success, to implement policies of commercial restriction against France and Great Britain as an alternative to armed force and war, an approach he also pursued during his own presidency.

Madison's two terms as president (1809–1817) were troubled ones. He was beset by trade quarrels with France and Great Britain and by a territorial dispute with Spain. By 1810, France had repealed its anti–neutral trade policies, and in the same year Madison seized West Florida from Spain, thereby consolidating U.S. control of the Gulf Coast. With Great Britain, however, his efforts proved unavailing. Madison became the first president to act as commander-in-chief when Congress declared war on Great Britain on 18 June 1812. Madison's purpose in the *War of 1812 was to conquer Canada, thereby compelling Great Britain to sign a treaty that guaranteed the neutral rights of U.S. vessels, but the war effort—hobbled by inadequate preparation, bad generalship, untrained troops, and logistical difficulties—was largely ineffective. For Madison the nadir of the conflict came in August 1814 when British forces captured and burned *Washington, D.C., forcing Madison and his wife into ignominious flight. Peace with Great Britain was restored under the December 1814 Treaty of *Ghent, after which Madison enjoyed the final years of his second administration in tranquility and prosperity. Vivacious and outgoing Dolley Madison, seventeen years her husband's junior, presided as White House hostess during Madison's presidency.

In retirement at Montpelier, Madison assumed the role of elder statesman. He prepared his records of the 1787 Federal Convention for publication, worked to establish the University of Virginia, and made an appearance at the 1829 Virginia Constitutional Convention. Of all the Founding Fathers, none was more important than Madison in conceiving of the possibilities of a national republic. In his protests against the excesses of Federalism in the 1790s, however, Madison also contributed ideas that were instrumental in dissolving the Union after his death. Had Madison himself lived until 1861, he probably would not have been altogether surprised at this development.

[*See also* Church and State, Separation of; Early Republic, Era of the; Federal Government, Executive Branch: Department of State; Federal Government, Executive Branch: The Presidency; Federal Government, Legislative Branch: House of Representatives; Federalist Party; Political Parties; Revolution and Constitution, Era of.]

• Ralph Ketcham, *James Madison: A Biography,* 1971. J. C. A. Stagg, *Mr. Madison's War: Politics, Diplomacy and Warfare in the Early American Republic, 1783–1830,* 1983. Drew McCoy, *The Last of the Fathers: James Madison and the Republican Legacy,* 1989. Jack N. Rakove, *James Madison and the Creation of the American Republic,* 1990. Lance Banning, *The Sacred Fire of Liberty: James Madison and the Founding of the Federal Republic,* 1995. Richard Matthews, *If Men Were Angels: James Madison and the Heartless Empire of Reason,* 1995.

—J. C. A. Stagg

MAFIA. *See* Organized Crime.

MAGAZINES. The first American magazines, Andrew Bradford's *American Magazine* and Benjamin *Franklin's *General Magazine,* appeared in 1741, but neither lasted the year. Magazines remained shaky ventures for the next century and a half, low in income, circulation, *advertising, and life span. Conditions improved with the Postal Mailing Act of 1879, which lowered mailing rates for periodicals. Between 1865 and 1885 the number of U.S. periodicals increased fourfold, from 700 to 3,300.

This boom in magazine founding was also fostered by the invention of the rotary press, which allowed for halftone (instead of hand-engraved) illustrations; faster delivery through railroads and rural free delivery postal routes; businesses seeking national markets; and the shift from bulk to packaged merchandise, leading in turn to brand names and advertising campaigns.

Cyrus and Louisa Knapp Curtis of *Philadelphia, two of the many *Gilded Age businesspeople to take advantage of these conditions, in 1883 launched the *Ladies Home Journal.* The Curtises' son-in-law Edward Bok (1863–1930) edited it from 1889 to 1919. The *Journal* was the prototype of the modern national magazine, with its combination of low subscription price, heavy advertising content (30 percent of the first issue), audience segmented by *gender, and direct and indirect understandings of gender throughout. Building the *Journal*'s circulation to over a million by the turn of the century, the Curtises in 1897 first published a magazine for men. The *Saturday Evening Post* was masterfully edited by George Horace Lorimer (1868–1937), but not until the formula was broadened to include the family did it hit its stride. In the *Progressive Era, *McClure's* and other muckraking magazines helped build sentiment for reform.

In 1922, Henry R. *Luce and Briton Hadden created *Time* magazine, targeting men primarily, but intending to condense and simplify for all educated Americans the proliferation of news in print. Hadden died in 1929, but the Luce/Hadden company, Time Inc., had already created *Fortune* magazine and would go on to create highly successful periodicals like *Life, Sports Illustrated,* and *Architectural Digest.* These magazines eventually gave rise to a host of imitators, including *Newsweek, U.S. News, Look,* and *Jet.*

Gender and race combined to shape the magazine market after Luce as demonstrated by the vicissitudes of periodicals intended for *African-American readers. Some founders of magazines for blacks, like W. E. B. *Du Bois, eschewed advertising and tried to foster serious political debate. His magazine, *The Call,* did not thrive, however, often teetering on the brink of financial disaster. In contrast, publisher John H. Johnson won black readers with magazine formulae already popular with whites. His *Negro Digest* (1942) did so well that he created several other magazines, including *Ebony* (1945). Like the *Saturday Evening Post, Ebony* originally targeted men but broadened its formula to include women as well, to attract more advertising.

Popular magazines of the nineteenth and twentieth centuries reflected and reinforced a culture divided by gender, *race and ethnicity, and *social class—stubbornly persistent divisions thoroughly entwined with *capitalism and consumption. Magazines helped set the stage for future forms of *popular culture in the United States, such as *radio, movies, and *television.

With the rise of television in the 1950s, many mass-market, general-interest magazines ceased publication. Special-interest and niche magazines continued to proliferate, however. The 1990s brought experiments with publishing magazines on the *Internet, including a political magazine called *Slate,* owned by the Microsoft Corporation.

[*See also* Journalism; Muckrakers; Printing and Publishing.]

• Frank Luther Mott, *A History of American Magazines,* 5 vols., 1958–1968. A. J. van Zuilen, *The Life Cycle of Magazines: A Historical Study of the Decline and Fall of the General Interest Mass Audience Magazine in the United States During the Period 1946–1972,* 1977. Jan Cohn, *Creating America: George Horace Lorimer and the* Saturday Evening Post, 1989. Alan Nourie and Barbara Nourie, eds., *American Mass-Market Magazines,* 1990. Helen Damon-Moore, *Magazines for the Millions: Gender and Commerce in the* Ladies' Home Journal *and the* Saturday Evening Post, 1994.

—Helen Damon-Moore

MAHAN, ALFRED THAYER (1840–1914), naval historian and strategist. Alfred Thayer Mahan, the son of Dennis Hart Mahan, a professor of engineering at West Point, graduated second in his class at the Naval Academy in 1859. During the *Civil War he taught at the Naval Academy and participated in the naval blockade of the Confederacy. Routine duty followed as he rose by seniority to captain in 1885. An essay on naval reform and a short monograph on Civil War naval operations led to his assignment to the new Naval War College at Newport, Rhode Island, in 1885. Mahan's lectures there formed the basis of *The Influence of Sea Power upon History, 1660–1783* (1892) and *The Influence of Sea Power upon the French Revolution and Empire, 1793–1812* (1897), in which he analyzed the characteristics of a sea power and the advantages such nations enjoy over land powers.

Applying his ideas to U.S. foreign and naval policies, Mahan in a series of essays advocated constructing a Central American canal and a battle fleet and expanding commerce and the merchant marine. He also urged a naval strategy based on fleet engagements aimed at gaining command of the sea, in place of the traditional U.S. strategy of coastal defense and commerce raiding. Mahan's thought rested on *Social Darwinism, economic determinism, and tactical principles first developed by others. Deftly synthesized and cogently stated in numerous publications, Mahan's ideas laid the philosophical basis for an era of global navalism, influenced leaders such as Germany's Kaiser Wilhelm II and Theodore *Roosevelt, and popularized American *expansionism. Mahan served as president of the Naval War College from 1886 to 1889 and in 1892–1893; on the Board of Naval Strategy during the *Spanish-American War; as a delegate to the Hague Peace Conference in 1899; and as president of the American Historical Association in 1902. He was promoted to rear admiral on the retired list in 1906.

[*See also* Military, The; Military Service Academies.]

• Alfred Thayer Mahan, *From Sail to Steam: Recollections of a Naval Life*, 1907. Robert Seager II, *Alfred Thayer Mahan: The Man and His Letters*, 1977. William E. Livesey, *Mahan on Sea Power*, 1981.

—James C. Bradford

MAJOR LEAGUE BASEBALL. *See* Baseball.

MALARIA. A mosquito-borne *disease once attributed to foul air emanating from swamps, malaria came to America in the bodies of both African and European colonists during the seventeenth century. While at times it appeared in states as far north as New Hampshire and Minnesota, it was a particular scourge of the *South. The ravages of the most severe type of malaria (falciparum) influenced the choice of African slave labor for plantations in Carolina and Virginia, because African workers tolerated the disease and remained at work after European field hands had become incapacitated. Malaria also played an important role on the early frontier, since the principal form of transportation, river travel, dictated prolonged exposure to wetland areas.

By the twentieth century malaria, for a variety of environmental reasons, had retreated largely to the southern states. British physician Ronald Ross's discovery in 1897 that the anopheles mosquito transmitted malaria prompted southern towns in the early twentieth century to the destruction of mosquito larvae. A similar strategy of eradication eliminated the scourge of malaria from the *Panama Canal Zone. Still, rural malaria persisted in the South because the cost per capita for malaria control in the sparsely populated countryside was so high. The federal government supported antimosquito work in the South, including drainage programs in the 1930s and extensive spraying of the pesticide DDT after 1945. These measures, along with the migration of susceptible sharecroppers from the rural South into disease-free cities and towns, contributed to the disappearance of indigenous malaria from the United States by 1950.

[*See also* Public Health; Sickle-Cell Anemia; Slavery: Development and Expansion of Slavery.]

• Erwin H. Ackerknecht, *Malaria in the Upper Mississippi Valley, 1760–1900*, 1945. Margaret Humphreys, "Kicking a Dying Dog: DDT and the Demise of Malaria in the American South, 1942–1952," *Isis* 87 (1996): 1–17.

—Margaret Humphreys

MALCOLM X, born Malcolm Little; later adopted the name El-Hajj Malik El-Shabazz (1925–1965), *African American leader. As a thinker, activist, and especially an icon, Malcolm X was perhaps the most important black nationalist figure in post-*World War II America. Born in Omaha, the son of Louisa and Earl Little—a *Baptist preacher active in the Garvey movement—Malcolm and his siblings experienced poverty and racial injustice in childhood. Hooded Klansmen burned their home in Lansing, Michigan; Earl Little was killed under mysterious circumstances; welfare agencies split up the children and eventually committed Louisa Little to a state mental institution. By the eighth grade he left school, moved to *Boston to live with his half-sister Ella, and turned to petty crime to earn money. In 1946 he was arrested for burglary and began a ten-year prison sentence.

In prison, he began studying the teachings of the Lost-Found *Nation of Islam (NOI), the Muslim group founded by Wallace Fard and led by Elijah Muhammad (Elijah Poole). Submitting to NOI discipline and guidance, he became a voracious reader of the Koran, the *Bible, and works of literature and history. Upon his release in 1952, he was renamed Malcolm "X," symbolically repudiating the "white man's name." As a devoted follower of Elijah Muhammad, Malcolm X rose quickly within the NOI ranks, serving as minister of Harlem's Temple No. 7 in 1954. Through national speaking engagements, television appearances, and by establishing *Muhammad Speaks*, Malcolm X put the NOI on the map. His criticisms of *civil rights leaders for advocating integration into white society instead of building black institutions and defending themselves from racist violence generated opposition from both conservatives and liberals. To those who claimed that the NOI undermined their efforts toward integration by preaching racial separatism, Malcolm responded: "It is not integration that Negroes in America want, it is human dignity."

Early on, however, Malcolm showed signs of independence from NOI. During the mid-1950s, for example, he privately scoffed at Muhammad's interpretation of the genesis of the "white race" and clearly disagreed with the NOI's policy of not participating in politics. He not only believed that political mobilization was indispensable but occasionally defied the rule by supporting boycotts and other forms of protest. And as early as 1954, Malcolm gave a speech comparing the situation in Vietnam with the Mau Mau rebellion in colonial Kenya, framing both movements as uprisings of the "Darker races" creating a "Tidal Wave" against U.S. and European imperialism. Indeed, Africa remained his primary political interest outside of black America. He toured Egypt, Sudan, Nigeria, and Ghana in 1959.

Although Malcolm X tried to conceal his differences with Elijah Muhammad, tensions between them erupted. These were exacerbated by the threat that Malcolm's popularity posed to Muhammad's leadership, and by Malcolm's disillusionment with Elijah upon learning that the NOI's moral and spiritual leader had fathered children by two former secretaries. On 8 March 1964, he announced his resignation and formed the Muslim Mosque, Inc., an Islamic movement devoted to working in the political sphere and cooperating with civil rights leaders. That same year he made his first pilgrimage to Mecca and took a second tour of several African and Arab nations. Upon his return he re-named himself El-Hajj Malik El-Shabazz, adopted Sunni *Islam, and announced that he had found the "true brotherhood" of man. He publicly acknowledged that whites were no longer devils, though he still remained a black nationalist and staunch believer in black self-determination and self-organization.

During the Summer of 1964 he formed the Organization of Afro-American Unity (OAAU). Inspired by the Organization of African Unity made up of independent African states, the OAAU's program combined advocacy for independent black institutions (e.g., schools and cultural centers) with support for black participation in mainstream politics, including electoral campaigns. Following the example of Paul *Robeson and W. E. B. *Du Bois, Malcolm planned in 1965 to submit to the *United Nations a petition documenting human-rights violations and acts of genocide against African Americans. His assassination in *New York City on 21 February 1965 by gunmen affiliated with the NOI intervened, however, and the OAAU died soon after Malcolm was laid to rest.

[*See also* Black Nationalism; Civil Rights Movement; Garvey, Marcus; King, Martin Luther, Jr.; Ku Klux Klan; Racism; Segregation, Racial; Sixties, The; Race, Concept of; Vienam War.]

• Malcolm X with Alex Haley, *The Autobiography of Malcolm X*, 1964. James Cone, *Martin and Malcolm and America: A Dream or Nightmare?*, 1991. Joe Wood, ed., *Malcolm X: In Our Own Image*, 1992. William

Sales, Jr., *From Civil Rights to Black Liberation: Malcolm X and the Organization of Afro-American Unity,* 1994. Louis DeCaro, *On the Side of My People: A Religious Life of Malcolm X,* 1996.

—Robin D. G. Kelley

MALLS. *See* Shopping Centers and Malls.

MANHATTAN PROJECT. The Manhattan Project refers to the *Army Corps of Engineers' "Manhattan Engineer District," the code name of the military project established in June 1942 for atomic-bomb research and development. In the years leading up to *World War II, many scientists pondered building *nuclear weapons, particularly after Lise Meitner's and Otto Frisch's startling interpretation in 1938 of earlier uranium and neutron bombardment experiments (by Enrico *Fermi and others) as nuclear fission.

Albert *Einstein's August 1939 letter to President Franklin Delano *Roosevelt (actually written by the Hungarian-born emigré physicist Leo Szilard [1898–1964]) was one means by which the U.S. government became aware of the atomic potential. In late 1940, the British and American governments joined forces to establish an atomic-bomb project in the industrially stronger and more protected country. Vannevar *Bush, director of the government's new Office of Scientific Research and Development, drafted plans for the Manhattan Project, whose urgency was underscored by Japan's attack on *Pearl Harbor on 7 December 1941. On 2 December 1942, less than three months after the appointment of Colonel (later Brigadier General) Leslie Groves as director of the Manhattan Project, Fermi demonstrated the first chain reaction at the University of Chicago. The Manhattan Project eventually grew into a three-billion-dollar conglomeration, which included the Chicago Metallurgical Laboratory; the Berkeley Radiation Laboratory; the Oak Ridge, Tennessee, and Hanford, Washington, materials-production facilities; and the Los Alamos, New Mexico, laboratory, where the first atomic bombs were built.

Centralizing the many separate research efforts devoted to atomic-bomb research was essential, both for efficiency and to maintain secrecy. J. Robert *Oppenheimer, whom Groves appointed in 1942 to head the project, selected a site on a high mesa in New Mexico, the Los Alamos Ranch School. Here a large community of scientists, engineers, and military personnel worked behind a security fence in a town identified only by its post-office box number (1663). Everyone at Los Alamos—even scientific luminaries, such as Fermi, Hans Bethe, Edward *Teller, Richard Feynman, John *von Neumann, George Kistiakowsky, Stanislav Ulam, and Niels Bohr—was assigned and reassigned as needed and required to work collaboratively in the mode later known as "big science."

The technical program, geared initially toward "gun-type" uranium and plutonium bombs (in which the fissionable material would be shot together), was abruptly realigned after the April 1944 discovery of a high level of spontaneous fission in reactor-made plutonium. Attention then turned to the more rapid, and technically complex, assembly known as implosion. Despite enormous hurdles, an implosion bomb was successfully detonated at the "Trinity" test at Alamogordo, New Mexico, on 16 July 1945.

Told of the successful test while at the *Potsdam Conference, President Harry S. *Truman authorized dropping the uranium bomb that fell on Hiroshima on 6 August and the plutonium bomb dropped on Nagasaki on 9 August. These weapons, which killed more than 120,000 Japanese, are widely believed to have led directly to the Japanese surrender on 14 August. They marked the start of the nuclear age and touched off an arms race that persisted throughout the *Cold War Era.

[*See also* Hiroshima and Nagasaki, Atomic Bombing of; Nuclear Power; Nuclear Strategy; Physical Sciences; Science: From 1914 to 1945; Science: Since 1945.]

• Richard Rhodes, *The Making of the Atomic Bomb,* 1986. Lillian Hoddeson, Paul W. Henriksen, Roger A. Meade, and Catherine Westfall, *Critical Assembly: A Technical History of Los Alamos during the Oppenheimer Years, 1943–1945,* 1993.

—Lillian Hoddeson

MANIFEST DESTINY, a term first used in the 1840s to justify U.S. expansion into Texas, Oregon, and Mexico. The Jacksonian journalist John O'Sullivan originated the phrase. The "manifest destiny" of the United States, he wrote in 1845, was "to overspread the continent allotted by Providence for the free development of our yearly multiplying millions." With roots in both evangelical *Protestantism and the ideology of *republicanism, the logic of the phrase was straightforward: History had a purpose and this design or "destiny" manifested (revealed) itself in specific situations. Providence had clearly designated North America as a stage for demonstrating history's larger trajectory. Armed with this divine mandate, politicians and publicists justified the territorial expansion of the United States into contiguous areas. In the *Antebellum Era, the "manifest destiny" impulse culminated most spectacularly in the appropriation of half of Mexico by means of war (1846–1848). Critics tended to turn "manifest destiny" into a contested slogan. Although most agreed that the United States was, in fact, invested with some sanctified mission, they argued, for various reasons, that expansion would pervert, not promote, that mission.

Notions of manifest destiny returned when territorial *expansionism again beckoned in the late 1890s, but the discourse now took the form of an imperialist Western duty to conquer and/or uplift alien territories that would never become part of the Union. Destinarian thinking remained integral to twentieth-century American politics. Typically, however, it took diametrically opposite forms. While some argued that the United States, as the carrier of world-historical purposes, had an innate duty to act or intervene in the world to save or regenerate it, others claimed that any such intervention would stain the purity of America's distinctive identity.

[*See also* Gilded Age; Mexican War; Spanish-American War.]

• Albert Weinberg, *Manifest Destiny,* 1935. Frederick Merk, *Manifest Destiny and Mission in American History,* 1963. Anders Stephanson, *Manifest Destiny,* 1995.

—Anders Stephanson

MANN, HORACE (1796–1859), lawyer, *Whig party politician, leader of the common-school reform movement. Born in Franklin, Massachusetts, Horace Mann was the son of a struggling farmer. After chores, he and his sisters braided straw hats to supplement the family's income. "Industry," wrote Mann, "became my second nature." The family's religion was also austere. When Horace's brother drowned on a Sunday, their Congregational minister, Nathaniel Emmons, seized on the tragedy as an occasion to preach against Sabbath breaking. Reacting against both of these harsh realities, Mann eventually became an ambitious lawyer and a Unitarian. To his district school education, Mann added private lessons in Latin and mathematics, and, at age twenty, took his small inheritance and enrolled at Brown University.

Emerging from Brown in 1819 as a skilled debater and class valedictorian, Mann proceeded during the next decade from practicing law in Dedham, Massachusetts, to serving as president of the Massachusetts Senate. An enthusiastic Whig, he promoted *railroads, helped establish the state insane asylum, and generally supported an active government role in the economic and social realm. Thus, he was open to a surprising career change when the Whig philanthropist and manufacturer Edmund Dwight persuaded him in 1837 to become secretary to the newly created Massachusetts Board of Education. With *industrialization and *immigration accelerating, the time was ripe for the creation of tax-supported, state school systems throughout the Northeast and the Midwest. Perfectly consistent with the Protestant, Whig ideology that informed Mann's career, the common-school reform movement made him a national figure. The state's Democrats, with some dissident Whigs, attempted to abolish the Board of Education in 1840, but Mann survived in a close vote. Subsequently, in a series of annual reports that circulated nationally, he laid out the rationale and desired policies for common public schools, with moral education and stability at the center, but promising economic growth, more equal opportunity, and lessened *social-class tensions as well. Mann helped articulate and launch two enduring trends in American educational history: the centralization of public-school oversight, from the local to the state level; and the strategy of making public schools inclusive by attempting to make them politically uncontroversial and religiously neutral. After resigning from the Board of Education, Mann served two terms in the U.S. House of Representatives (1848–1852) and seven years as president of Antioch College in Ohio.

[*See also* Antebellum Era; Education: The Public School Movement; Protestantism; Unitarianism and Universalism.]

• Jonathan Messerli, *Horace Mann,* 1971. —Carl F. Kaestle

MANN ACT. *See* Prostitution and Antiprostitution.

MARBURY* v. *MADISON (1803). In this decision, the U.S. *Supreme Court, speaking through Chief Justice John *Marshall, for the first time declared an act of Congress unconstitutional and thus established the precedent for *judicial review of legislative acts. The case arose from the appointment of the so-called "midnight judges"—judicial appointments made by President John *Adams during the last days of his administration. Adams appointed William Marbury a justice of the peace in the District of Columbia, and his commission was signed by the outgoing secretary of state, John Marshall, but not delivered. When Thomas *Jefferson's Republican administration took power, the new secretary of state, James *Madison, refused to deliver the commission. Marbury filed suit against Madison in the Supreme Court under section 13 of the Judiciary Act of 1789, which had established the particulars of the new federal court system. That section, Marbury contended, gave the Supreme Court the right to hear the case and issue a writ of mandamus directing the secretary of state to deliver his commission.

Marshall well knew that an order to Madison to deliver the commission might be ignored, irreparably damaging the authority of the Supreme Court and effectively neutralizing the *Federalist party's strength in the federal judiciary. Marshall began his opinion by stating unequivocally that Marbury deserved the commission and that the Republican administration was wrong in not delivering it. That said, however, Marshall held that the Supreme Court did not have the power to aid Marbury because section 13 of the Judiciary Act had improperly enlarged the Supreme Court's original jurisdiction (the right to hear a case in the first instance). That jurisdiction had been established by the *Constitution itself, Marshall stated, and a federal law in contravention of the Constitution was void.

The notion that courts could strike down acts of a legislature did not originate with Marshall. In both seventeenth-century England and late eighteenth-century America, courts had suggested that legislation that violated "natural law" or the fundamental principles of government might be void. Alexander *Hamilton, defending the proposed Constitution in *Federalist Paper No. 78, had sketched out the logic of judicial review that Marshall would follow in *Marbury* v. *Madison.* Marshall, however, established this specific judicial power in the American constitutional system, and while no other federal law was declared unconstitutional until 1857, the Marshall court subsequently reaffirmed in a number of cases its power to consider the constitutionality of federal laws. Marshall's opinion also first articulated the distinction between political questions (in this case, the powers of a coordinate branch of the government), which the court would not resolve, and judicial ones, which were properly its responsibility.

[*See also* Early Republic, Era of the; Federal Government, Judicial Branch; Jurisprudence.]

• Robert L. Clinton, *Marbury v. Madison and Judicial Review,* 1968. Charles F. Hobson, *The Great Chief Justice: John Marshall and the Rule of Law,* 1996. —Paul G. E. Clemens

MARCH ON WASHINGTON (1963). *See* Civil Rights Movement.

MARDI GRAS. *New Orleans's annual pre-Lenten celebration of Mardi Gras ("Fat Tuesday"), or Carnival, long a ritual of both civic self-definition and cultural conflict, owes its origins to the region's French, Spanish, and Afro-Caribbean population. The celebration begins on January 6 and culminates on Mardi Gras day, Shrove Tuesday. Although informal parades and festive masquerades date to the early nineteenth century, the modern Mardi Gras—with its themed parades, costumed maskers, and elaborate balls—began in 1857 with the establishment of the city's first exclusive Carnival organization, the "Mystick Krewe of Comus." Other all-white "krewes" like Rex, Momus, and Proteus soon arose and quickly became social networks for the city's Anglo and Creole (French or Spanish) elites.

In 1909 members of New Orleans's black middle class created the Zulu Social Aid and Pleasure Club as a sly critique of white stereotypes of *African Americans as "savages," and as a protest against the city's harsh Jim Crow culture. The "Zulu" parade mocked the ruling white social order as paraders donned blackface and grass skirts and threw rubber spears and highly prized decorated coconuts; eventually this parade became one of the city's most important. Black working-class people also asserted group pride by subverting white hegemony: Beginning in the 1880s, away from the center city, the black "Mardi Gras Indians" masqueraded in highly stylized Plains Indians costumes that played upon white stereotypes of both Indians and African Americans.

By the late 1990s more than seventy krewes paraded in the two weeks leading up to and including Mardi Gras day. Some used central city routes while many more preferred suburban neighborhoods. In the wake of a proposed 1991 ordinance to desegregate the exclusive Carnival organizations, several of the elite old-line krewes chose to stop parading. Their disappearance, combined with New Orleans's growing *tourism-based economy focused more attention on newer, nonexclusive superkrewes, like Bacchus and Orpheus, whose parades featured flamboyant floats and abundant Carnival beads.

[*See also* Segregation, Racial.]

• Samuel Kinser, *Carnival, American Style: Mardi Gras at New Orleans and Mobile,* 1990. Reid Mitchell, *All on a Mardi Gras Day: Episodes in the History of New Orleans Carnival,* 1995. —Steven Hoelscher

MARINE CORPS. *See* Military, The.

MARITIME TRANSPORT. Water-borne transportation has been central to the American economy since Europeans first crossed the Atlantic. Oceans, bays, and rivers offer surfaces across which heavy vessels can be moved with comparatively little effort, and the earliest European settlers knew how to build boats and use the wind to propel them. Maritime transport remained the only practical way to move freight long distances until canals and *railroads began to be built in the 1820s and 1830s. In the nineteenth and twentieth centuries, new modes of transportation created new markets and greatly diversified the ways people and goods travel.

Three basic distinctions help explain the rise and decline of maritime transport in the United States. First, commercial ships normally operate in two quite distinct geopolitical settings. Coastal voyages between U.S. seaports and inland navigation along its rivers and canals are governed by state and federal laws. Foreign trade, on the other hand, is governed by agreements among the nations involved. From its beginnings, the United States, like the nations of Europe, restricted its coastal and internal trade to vessels built, owned, and crewed by its citizens. In international trade, however, the lowest-cost carrier who provides acceptable service normally prevails.

A second broad distinction concerns what is being carried. Ships, trains, automobiles, and airplanes can all move people, but in maritime transport the movement of commodities and goods is of greater significance. The development of railroads, automobiles, and airplanes reduced the importance of passengers in maritime transport, yet ships are still needed to carry commodities such as petroleum and the huge volume of manufactured goods and agricultural commodities that moves among continents.

A third distinction focuses on the evolving technologies employed in maritime transport. The nineteenth-century displacement of wooden-hulled, wind-driven ships by steam-driven iron- and then steel-hulled ships was profoundly important. Many other new technologies have been introduced during the long history of maritime transport, yet none has been nearly as consequential as the shift from wood and wind to metal and *steam power.

These distinctions help illuminate the history of maritime transport in the United States. The period from the *Revolutionary War to the *Civil War was a flourishing age of sail. In this early industrial era, Americans drew upon the shipbuilding skills of their ancestors, the timber resources of the continent, and their own talents as seafarers and merchants to create a vibrant commercial society centered on such seaport cities as *Boston, *Philadelphia, and Savannah. They applied the lessons they had learned as colonists operating within the British Empire to the global opportunities available to them after they had been excluded from imperial trade. In this period, American ships ranked as the best and the least expensive in international trade and U.S. ships consistently carried a high percentage of the nation's foreign trade. The development of steam propulsion on inland waterways, especially on the Ohio and *Mississippi River systems, enabled the United States to expand rapidly into its trans-Appalachian hinterland.

A second phase in U.S. maritime transport began in the second half of the nineteenth century as British-built iron steamships increasingly dominated the international carrying trade, gradually squeezing out the United States. The loss was hardly noticed, however, as the nation turned westward and focused on the continental drama of railroad building. Although the coastal and inland trades remained protected from foreign competition, the railroads soon captured most of their markets. By 1900, U.S. ships were carrying only a small percentage of the nation's trade.

A third phase encompassed the world wars of the twentieth century, including the *Cold War. Even before the United States entered *World War I, President Woodrow *Wilson and Congress had committed the nation to building and operating a world-class merchant marine, a service capable of providing auxiliary support for the armed forces fighting abroad and insuring that the nation's international trade would not again be disrupted by the withdrawal of foreign carriers. The massive shipbuilding programs of World War I and *World War II provided the hulls while government operating programs, subsidies, and cargo-protection laws sustained the maritime industry through the Cold War. The rapid expansion of global markets that followed the end of the Cold War, together with increasing deregulation of U.S. industry, created conditions that worked against the survival of the U.S. merchant marine. The increasing globalization of markets, services, and manufacture may render this decline a matter of limited significance. Although infrequently provided by U.S.–owned companies, maritime transport services continued to play a vital role in America's participation in the *global economy as the twentieth century ended.

[*See also* Automotive Industry; Aviation Industry; Canals and Waterways; Expansionism; Foreign Trade, U.S.; Industrialization; Multinational Enterprises; Petroleum Industry.]

• John G. B. Hutchins, *The American Maritime Industries and Public Policy, 1789–1914,* 1941. George Rogers Taylor, *The Transportation Revolution, 1815–1860,* 1951. K. Jack Bauer, *A Maritime History of the United States,* 1988. Benjamin W. Labaree et. al. *America and the Sea: A Maritime History,* 1998. Andrew Gibson and Arthur Donovan, *The Abandoned Ocean: A History of U.S. Maritime Policy,* 1999.

—Arthur Donovan

MARRIAGE AND DIVORCE. Historically the preferred form of legal cohabitation, marriage is widely thought to promote social stability and individual well-being, and to be the most desirable means to procreate and raise children. When, who, and how one marries and what constraints affect those choices have varied over time by social, legal, cultural, and economic circumstances. Anglo-American attitudes traditionally embraced the inviolability of marriage and *family, fostering social attitudes and laws that made divorce difficult.

During the *Colonial Era and into the early nineteenth century, marriage functioned primarily as a pragmatic, economic, and procreative alliance, binding a couple and extended families together. Choosing a partner wisely was important, especially for a woman, in a period when divorce was difficult, for one's future happiness depended on that choice. *New England Puritans saw marriage as a civil contract based on mutual consent, and to this end, they closely monitored courting procedures to insure sound decisions. Puritans believed that well-ordered families fostered a well-ordered society.

The length of marriage has varied significantly. In the past, death usually was the limiting factor; today divorce often plays this role. In the seventeenth-century Chesapeake, marriages averaged only seven years owing to the high mortality rate. Serial marriages were common as successive spouses died, resulting in complex step-family relationships. In the healthier New England climate, colonial couples experienced long marriages, creating more stable family situations.

Divorce was rare in the colonial period, because it was considered disgraceful, and was difficult to achieve, especially for women. Yet Puritans permitted marital dissolution under certain circumstances because they believed marriage and family life should be happy. Adultery, bigamy, and desertion were acceptable legal grounds. Acquiring an absolute divorce that permitted remarriage was complicated and expensive. Many unhappy spouses simply ran away or sought a legal separation. Before 1800, most divorce petitioners were male, but after the *Revolutionary War, more women succeeded in obtaining divorces.

Southern colonies and states adopted more conservative policies concerning divorce; in the *Antebellum Era, South Carolina prohibited it entirely. Elsewhere, equity and chancery courts handled the proceedings, as did colonial and state legislative bodies. The unhappy partner had to petition the legislature or court to plead his or her case. The marriage and divorce laws of each colony and state determined property rights, residency requirements, the minimum age for marriage, and other rules relating to marriage and divorce. By the mid-nineteenth century, states began to turn over divorce proceedings to courts and to codify laws rather than operate on an ad hoc basis.

When women wed, they forfeited the property rights that they enjoyed as single women. This situation did not begin to change until 1839, when Mississippi became the first state to protect married women's property rights. By the early twentieth century, many states had granted wives the right to control their own property and earnings.

Slaves faced a different situation. Although not allowed to marry legally, since this would have interfered with masters' rights to sell slaves and separate couples, they did wed. Finding a partner could be difficult; many slave couples lived apart on separate plantations. When nearby, a man and woman might move in together, with or without a formal ceremony. Slave breeding that forced couples to marry and procreate existed, but was rare. Dissolving a slave marriage occurred when a couple simply decided to terminate their relationship.

The marriage ritual has varied from an informal exchange of vows before a judge or preacher to a full-scale church wedding. In some cases, pre-nuptial contracts were drawn up to protect personal property. Slaves ritually jumped over a broomstick or heard words read by their master or preacher. Common-law marriages allowed couples who had lived together for several years to claim legal marital status.

A number of variables influenced the age at which men and women married. In colonial New England, most women married in their early twenties, men in their late twenties. Seventeenth-century indentured servants in the *South, required to remain single while fulfilling their indentures, wedded late. By the second and third generation after settlement, southern men were marrying in their mid- to late twenties and women in their late teens. Economic factors affected marriage age. Struggling immigrants in the nineteenth century tended to marry later than did the native-born because *poverty made it difficult to establish households. Without an inheritance or assured income, many young men could not afford to marry. Age at marriage remained relatively stable until the late 1940s and 1950s when it declined. It rose again in the 1960s, as more women pursued higher education and paid jobs, and by the 1980s, the average age when women first married reached a new high.

Gauging marital happiness is virtually impossible. That few marriages in the past ended in divorce does not mean that couples were happier, since laws, traditions, and religious beliefs made divorce difficult and few women had the means to live independently. Despite what is often assumed, the past was not a golden era of marital bliss, as numerous separations, public notices for runaway spouses, separations, and private lamentations in letters and diaries attest.

Parental involvement in children's marital choices has varied over time. In the colonial period, property influenced who and when one married. Daughters who needed a dowry and sons who required land to establish an independent household depended on parents, who could therefore exert some control, if not actually dictate the choice. Strict rules governed young women's courtship behavior because of the possibility of pregnancy and the importance of a prudent choice. Parental involvement declined by the mid-eighteenth century, evidenced in part by siblings marrying out of birth order. By the nineteenth century, more women remained single owing to a shortage of men and more opportunities for females to survive on their own. By the late twentieth century parents usually played a minor role in their children's choice, though this varied among different cultural and ethnic groups.

Another change was the growing importance of romance in marriage and of love and a desire for personal happiness in selecting a spouse. Women, in particular, began by the early nineteenth century to favor suitors likely to fulfill their ideal of a companionate marriage. As romantic ideals of marriage spread, especially among middle-class women, disappointment invariably increased as well, and the divorce rate climbed steadily from 1840 on. By the late nineteenth century, as women became better educated and gained some financial independence, divorce became a likelier option. The legal grounds for divorce were expanded as well, contributing to the rising rate. This phenomenon cut across all social classes, and many working-class couples sought divorce. A 1909 Census Bureau study on marriage and divorce showed a significant increase in the divorce rate. In 1870, there were 81 divorces per 100,000 of the nation's married population; by 1900 this number rose to 200 divorces.

During the twentieth century, the divorce rate rose noticeably after each major war and dropped during the Depression of the 1930s, when many couples stayed together to survive tough times. The divorce rate rose sharply after 1965, peaking around 1980 and stabilizing thereafter. In the 1990s, about half of all marriages ended in divorce, giving the United States the highest divorce rate of any Western nation. Frequent divorces and remarriages created complex extended family relationships involving stepparents and stepchildren, half brothers and sisters, that in some respects resembled colonial households.

Some observers blamed the decline of the traditional family and high divorce rates on easy divorce laws, especially the initiation of so-called no-fault divorce in the 1970s. Others, however, viewed this phenomenon as less a result of changing laws and more a reflection of higher expectations about marriage and a safety valve for the more emotionally charged nuclear family setting. The high divorce rate may also reflect women's greater autonomy, with a corresponding lessening of tolerance for unrewarding relationships or a spouse's bad behavior.

In a legal sense, most twentieth century marriages involved monogamous, heterosexual relationships. In the past, some Native American tribes and Mormons practiced polygamy, but legislation largely ended this practice by the late nineteenth century. The 1990s brought a movement for legalizing same-sex marriages, but it initially enjoyed little success. A modern and widespread alternative or precursor to marriage is cohabitation. From the 1960s on, increasing numbers of young people chose to live together without a legally binding ceremony, especially before they had children. Nevertheless, the majority of Americans eventually married, as they always had.

[*See also* Courtship and Dating; Domestic Violence; Gay and Lesbian Rights Movement; Indian History and Culture; Life Stages; Mormonism; Puritanism; Slavery: Slave Families, Communities, and Culture; Social Class; Women's Rights Movements.]

• William O'Neill, *Divorce in the Progressive Era,* 1967. Carl N. Degler, *At Odds: Women and the Family in America from the Revolution to the Present,* 1980. Elaine Tyler May, *Great Expectations: Marriage and Divorce in Post-Victorian America,* 1980. Marilyn Salmon, *Women and the Law of Property in Early America,* 1986. Elizabeth Pleck, *Domestic Tyranny: The Making of American Social Policy against Family Violence from Colonial Times to the Present,* 1987. Stephen Mintz and Susan Kellogg, *Domestic Revolutions: A Social History of American Family Life,* 1988. Karen Lystra, *Searching the Heart: Women, Men, and Romantic Love in Nineteenth Century America,* 1989. Andrew Cherlin, *Marriage, Divorce, Remarriage,* 1992. Brenda Stevenson, *Life in Black and White: Family and Community in the Slave South,* 1996.

—Sally G. McMillen

MARSHALL, GEORGE (1880–1959), soldier, *World War II army chief of staff, secretary of state (1947–1949), and secretary of defense (1950–1951). George Catlett Marshall Jr. was born in Uniontown, Pennsylvania; graduated from the Virginia Military Institute in 1901; and was commissioned in 1902. A protégé of General John J. *Pershing during *World War I, Marshall played a key role in planning the 1918 U.S. offensives. His most important assignment during the interwar years was as head of the Fort Benning Infantry School in Georgia (1927–1932), where he trained what would become the *World War II army high command. In 1939 he became chief of staff, a position he held throughout the war. He created the largest army in U.S. history, became the leading figure on the Joint and Combined Chiefs of Staff as well as President Franklin

Delano *Roosevelt's chief military adviser, and developed an extraordinary reputation with Congress and the public. After the war he served as special emissary to China in an unsuccessful effort to avert civil war. As secretary of state he played a major role in defining, implementing, and winning bipartisan support for an activist U.S. *Cold War policy of containing Soviet expansion, most notably with the European Recovery Program. He proposed this program, subsequently called the *Marshall Plan, at a Harvard University commencement address on 5 June 1947. As secretary of defense during the *Korean War he rebuilt U.S. military forces and played a key role in the controversial removal of General Douglas *MacArthur. He retired in 1951.

Marshall is considered the organizer of Allied victory in World War II, the architect of key U.S. Cold War policies, one of the foremost defenders of the principle of civilian control of the military, a key definer of the military's proper role in a democratic society, and a model of personal integrity and selfless public service. He was twice named *Time* magazine's "Man of the Year" and in 1953 he received the Nobel Peace Prize—the only professional U.S. soldier ever so honored.

[*See also* Containment; Federal Government, Executive Branch: Department of Defense; Federal Government, Executive Branch: Department of State; Joint Chiefs of Staff; Military, The.]

• Forrest C. Pogue, *George C. Marshall,* 4 vols., 1963–1987. Larry I. Bland, ed., *The Papers of George Catlett Marshall,* 6 vols., 1981–.

—Mark A. Stoler

MARSHALL, JOHN (1755–1835), fourth chief justice of the United States. Born into the Virginia gentry, John Marshall had little formal schooling. During the *Revolutionary War, he saw combat with the Culpepper Minutemen and the Continental army, spent the Winter of 1778 at *Valley Forge, and came to revere George *Washington. He resigned his commission in 1781. This military service reinforced his *nationalism.

In 1780, Marshall studied law briefly at the College of William and Mary under George Wythe, one of Virginia's most respected lawyers; passed the bar; and received a license to practice from Governor Thomas *Jefferson. In 1782, he was elected to the Virginia House of Delegates. He married Mary Willis Ambler, called Polly, in 1783; they had ten children. Moving to Richmond, Virginia's new capital, Marshall enjoyed an extensive practice and was recognized as the leader of the local bar. As a delegate to the Virginia Convention of 1788, he helped win approval of the new federal *Constitution, delivering a noteworthy speech defending the judiciary.

Through the 1790s, Marshall stalwartly supported the Washington and John *Adams administrations. In 1797, Adams sent him as an envoy to settle grievances during the *Quasi-War with France. There with Charles Pinckney and Elbridge Gerry he became part of the so-called *XYZ Affair. Welcomed as a hero upon returning to America in 1798, he was the subject of the famous toast, "Millions for Defense but not a cent for Tribute," and won a seat in Congress in 1799. President Adams appointed him secretary of state in 1800, in which capacity he supervised the federal government's move to *Washington, D.C., the new capital. In 1801, Adams appointed him chief justice of the United States, a post he held until his death in 1835.

Marshall is known as the "Great Chief Justice" because he established the institutional integrity of the U.S. *Supreme Court. The Court decided over 1,100 cases in his tenure; he wrote the decisions in over 500—including 36 of 62 constitutional decisions. Among these were some of the most important precedents in American constitutional law: **Marbury* v. *Madison* (1803); **Fletcher* v. *Peck* (1810); **McCulloch* v. *Maryland* (1819); *Dartmouth College* v. *Woodward* (1819); *Cohens* v. *Virginia* (1821); and **Gibbons* v. *Ogden* (1824).

Marshall's greatness traces to the timing of his appointment, his sociable temperament and engaging personality, and his remarkable ability to get to the heart of issues and express himself with compelling logic. An unwavering nationalist, Marshall believed in a living Constitution, a strong national government, and a vigorous and independent judiciary within the federal system. Defining the role of chief justice through his long tenure, he initiated the practice of the court's speaking with one majority opinion and regularly suppressed his own views to help his colleagues reach a majority opinion. He dissented only once in a constitutional case, *Ogden* v. *Sanders* (1827). Although sometimes prone to stating general principles and then making the facts and statutes in a case conform to them, John Marshall was a brilliant jurist who always remained keenly sensitive to the political and economic consequences of the Court's decisions.

[*See also Dartmouth College Case*; Early Republic, Era of the; Federal Government, Judicial Branch; Federalism; Federalist Party; Judicial Review; Jurisprudence; States' Rights.]

• Albert J. Beveridge, *The Life of John Marshall,* 4 vols., 1916–1919. Charles F. Hobson, *The Great Chief Justice: John Marshall and the Rule of Law,* 1996.

—Francis N. Stites

MARSHALL, THURGOOD (1908–1993), *civil rights lawyer, first African American *Supreme Court justice, architect of the attack on legally mandated racial *segregation that culminated in **Brown* v. *Board of Education* (1954). Raised in Baltimore, Thurgood Marshall graduated from Howard University Law School where he was one of a group of talented students who adopted the vision of their mentor, Dean Charles Hamilton Houston, of law as a form of social engineering. After working with Houston on the legal staff of the *National Association for the Advancement of Colored People (NAACP) from 1936 to 1939, Marshall succeeded him as the NAACP's chief lawyer.

After *World War II, Marshall coordinated legal challenges to segregated university education, which led to Supreme Court decisions in 1950 requiring the desegregation of graduate education in Oklahoma and Texas. Marshall himself acted as the chief trial lawyer in the South Carolina school desegregation case that was decided along with *Brown.* Among the other Supreme Court cases Marshall argued and won was a 1948 challenge to legal restrictions on the ability of *African Americans to purchase homes in white neighborhoods.

In 1961 President John F. *Kennedy gave Marshall a recess appointment to the Court of Appeals for the Second Circuit in New York, where he served until 1965. President Lyndon B. *Johnson then named Marshall solicitor general, and in 1967 appointed him to the Supreme Court, commenting that it was "the right thing to do, the right time to do it, the right man, and the right place."

As a justice, Marshall's major contribution to constitutional law was his formulation of a test for determining whether a state law violated the *Constitution's requirement of "equal protection of the laws." According to Marshall, courts should balance the public purposes promoted by a statute and the burden it imposed on particular group against the characteristics of the group affected, including its ability to achieve its goals through legislation, and the nature of the rights affected, including whether society deemed these rights to be important, even if not constitutionally protected (*San Antonio Independent School District* v. *Rodriguez,* 1973).

During his years on the Court, Marshall insisted that the poor and dispossessed were as fully protected by the Constitution as any other group. As the Court turned more conservative, Marshall found himself increasingly in dissent. By the time he retired in 1991, his achievements as a civil rights lawyer and a Supreme Court justice had earned him a distinguished place in American *jurisprudence.

[*See also* Civil Rights Legislation; Civil Rights Movement; Segregation, Racial.]

• Mark Tushnet, *Making Civil Rights Law: Thurgood Marshall and the Supreme Court, 1936–1961,* 1994. Mark Tushnet, *Making Constitutional Law: Thurgood Marshall and the Supreme Court, 1961–1991,* 1997.

—Mark Tushnet

MARSHALL PLAN. The European Recovery Program (ERP), popularly known as the Marshall Plan, America's most successful *foreign-aid program, was a landmark in the struggle to contain *communism abroad and *isolationism at home. The plan was fueled by a humanitarian impulse to rebuild war-ravaged Europe and by fears that Depression conditions might return in the United States.

The Marshall Plan addressed three post–*World War II crises: the collapse of Britain's imperial role in the world balance of power; the instability of France and Italy; and West Germany's economic and moral deterioration. Interim aid programs by the *United Nations and the U.S. Army in Germany and Austria failed to bring economic recovery, and by early 1946 U.S. elite circles were discussing a long-term European recovery program, including occupied Germany. The severe Winter of 1946–1947 brought Western Europe's economy to a standstill. The announcement of President Harry S. *Truman's *containment doctrine and the East-West deadlock over German reparations at the Moscow foreign-ministers' meeting in early 1947 deepened the sense of crisis. In this setting, the principal advisors of Secretary of State George *Marshall developed an aid program that Marshall announced at Harvard University on 5 June 1947. Promising aid to all European nations willing to help themselves, Marshall encouraged the Europeans to take the initiative.

Led by Ernest Bevin and Georges Bidault, the British and French foreign ministers, the Europeans responded enthusiastically and met in Paris late in June. A Soviet delegation initially participated but stormed out of the meeting. Moscow forbade its satellites to participate and attacked the United States for building an anti-Soviet bloc and dividing Europe. While sixteen European nations asked for $28 billion in U.S. aid, Truman set up three committees led by prominent citizens to sell the Marshall Plan to the American public. After the communist coup in Prague in 1948, Congress passed a four-year aid package.

Between 1948 and 1952, some thirteen billion dollars in economic assistance poured into Western Europe. The aid was designed to bring in food, machinery, raw materials, and capital investments to stimulate production and trade. European exports, it was hoped, would pay for future imports. The sale of American products in Europe generated "counterpart funds" that participating countries used in different ways. France and Italy used their counterpart funds to combat inflation and enforce budgetary restraint. The British and Norwegians retired state debts; the Austrians invested in state-owned steel and electrical industries. The Belgians imported machinery and steel products; the Germans, Austrians, and Italians bought food. Initially fueling economic recovery, the Marshall Plan subsequently funded military rearmament and fostered Western European integration by financing intra-European trade through the European Payments Union. By 1950, prewar production levels had been exceeded by 25 percent, dollar deficits had sunk, inflation and unemployment had decreased, and intergovernmental cooperation had grown, especially between France and West Germany.

Traditional *Cold War historians depict the Marshall Plan as a humanitarian effort to revive Western Europe and alleviate suffering. Revisionists interpret it as Washington's attempt to rescue liberal *capitalism and defeat *socialism. Corporatists stress its role in exporting American-style *scientific management and *mass-production techniques. Economic historians argue that Western Europe was already recovering by 1947 without ERP funds. Others portray the plan as solving a severe "marketing crisis" by restoring financial stability and liberalizing production and prices.

[*See also* Acheson, Dean; Anticommunism; Foreign Relations: U.S. Relations with Europe; Foreign Trade, U.S.]

• Harry B. Price, *The Marshall Plan and Its Meaning,* 1955. Alan S. Milward, *The Reconstruction of Western Europe 1945–51,* 1984. Charles S. Maier, *In Search of Stability,* 1987. Michael J. Hogan, *The Marshall Plan,* 1987. Barry Eichengreen, ed., *Europe's Postwar Recovery,* 1995.

—Günter Bischof

MASON-DIXON LINE. The Mason-Dixon Line initially established the boundary between Pennsylvania and Maryland, resolving a lengthy dispute between the Penn and Calvert families, proprietors of the respective colonies. Both families claimed land that included *Philadelphia, while Pennsylvania claimed the so-called lower counties that make up present-day Delaware. The dispute produced armed conflicts over tax collection and occasional uprisings against one proprietary regime or the other. Under a 1760 agreement, the two families accepted a proposal for a survey to be conducted by a pair of English astronomers and surveyors, Charles Mason and Jeremiah Dixon. The agreement required the use of a complex series of calculations incorporating the most advanced surveying methods of the day. Mason and Dixon conducted their survey between 1763 and 1767, encountering rugged terrain, political intrigues, and hostile Native Americans in the western country. Their final demarcation determined the Maryland-Pennsylvania boundary at parallel 39°43'17.6" N. In 1769 the British crown ratified the line ; in 1784 it was extended to settle the Pennsylvania and Virginia (now West Virginia) boundary. The novelist Thomas Pynchon offered a fictionalized account of the project in *Mason and Dixon* (1997).

In the *Antebellum Era the Mason-Dixon Line marked the division between the northern free-soil and southern slave states. With the 1820 *Missouri Compromise, Congress applied the term to a line extending from the Pennsylvania border, down the Ohio River to its *Mississippi River outlet. Since the Ohio River flowed in a southwesterly direction, Congress established the line at 36°30' west of the Mississippi. The Mason-Dixon Line, thereby, divided the nation geographically over the slave issue. It later became embedded in popular usage as a convenient shorthand for demarcating the northern boundary of the *South.

[*See also* Colonial Era; Penn, William; Regionalism; Slavery: Development and Expansion of Slavery.]

• Judith St. George, *Mason and Dixon's Line of Fire,* 1991.

—Nicholas Casner

MASONIC ORDER. The Ancient and Accepted Order of Freemasons originated in London in the early 1700s and spread to colonial America. The all-male secret organization flourished among colonial leaders who were attracted to its deistic religion and its ideology of equality and fraternity. George *Washington, Benjamin *Franklin, John Hancock, and Paul *Revere were among the prominent American Masons of the Revolutionary Era. An Anti-Masonic furor in the 1820s nearly destroyed the order, however. Opponents accused the Masons of subverting democracy and orthodox *Protestantism. When William Morgan, who threatened to expose Masonic secrets, disappeared in Batavia, New York, in 1825, suspicions of the fraternity's conspiratorial nature seemed confirmed. Anti-Masonry became embroiled in partisan politics and decimated the fraternity's ranks.

Shortly before the *Civil War, the fraternity regrouped and became the model for dozens of other *fraternal organizations that enjoyed tremendous popularity in the late nineteenth and early twentieth centuries. With the leadership carefully assuaging fears about its secrecy, religious ideas, and effects on politics, the Masonic order flourished. The organization claimed to stand for morality, piety, and charity. And, although it consisted primarily of white skilled workers and middle-class Protestants, it boasted that in the lodge room, all men were equal. The order's most egregious lapse from its egalitarian ideal was its steadfast refusal to acknowledge the Prince Hall Masons, a black version of the fraternity founded in 1787. White and black Masonry continued as separate organizations throughout the twentieth century.

Roman Catholics were absent from Masonic lodges primarily because of a Papal interdiction against Masonic membership. Masons, however, also were influenced by the anti-Catholicism that pervaded much of Protestant America.

With over three million members, Freemasonry reached a high point in the 1920s but it never completely recovered from the devastation of the Great Depression. While many men continued to enjoy membership in the fraternity as the twentieth century ended, the organization proved too static and old-fashioned to sustain its popularity.

[*See also* Antebellum Era; Anti-Catholic Movement; Anti-Masonic Party; Deism; Fraternal Organizations; Roman Catholicism; Twenties, The.]

• Dorothy Ann Lipson, *Freemasonry in Federalist Connecticut,* 1977. Lynn Dumenil, *Freemasonry and American Culture, 1880–1930,* 1984.

—Lynn Dumenil

MASS CULTURE. *See* Popular Culture.

MASS MARKETING, targeting a large percentage of the relevant population as purchasers of a particular product or service. The size of the market depends on the nature of the product sold and the goals of the company. Typically, mass marketers want to sell in a range between half the relevant population and everyone.

The history of *photography offers a good example of the mass-marketing process. In 1877, when George Eastman purchased his first picture-taking equipment at a cost of some fifty-five dollars, photography was a mysterious art demanding chemical knowledge, mechanical ability, and a considerable sum of money. Photographers were either professional portraitists or serious amateurs. Few Americans had ever taken a picture or mastered the technical processes of developing and printing. Eastman set out to eliminate these financial and technical hurdles by devising photographic methods that were simple and cheap. As he did so, however, he discovered that barriers related to consumer behavior remained. Finding a less than enthusiastic response to his innovations, he concluded that "in order to make a large business we would have to reach the general public and create a new class of patrons." Eastman consciously "created" a mass market for his camera and film. He intensively distributed his product, simplified it so that a child could use it, advertised it widely, and—most importantly—slashed the price. The Kodak Brownie camera sold in 1900 for one dollar and film for fifteen cents. By the time of Eastman's death in 1932, cameras and photography had become ubiquitous features of American mass culture.

Eastman's story contains within it many of the elements that defined mass marketing from the late nineteenth century through the 1960s. These elements include the vision of the mass market; the willingness to sacrifice profit margin for volume; and the preconditions, in terms of income, logistics, and psychology, for the creation of a receptive market.

Vision. Without the belief that a product will have a broad appeal, there would be no mass marketing. When mass marketing began in earnest in the United States, that belief did not grow from systematic market research. Instead it came from entrepreneurs' sense of what people wanted. Thus, Eastman intuitively grasped that people would like to take pictures. When they did not respond at first, he coaxed them with persuasive *advertising. Such visionary mass marketers have played a vital role in American *business history. Henry J. Heinz (1844–1916) knew people really wanted his pickles, relishes, and beans in cans or jars. He went bankrupt in the 1870s seeking to mass market his products but tried again in the 1880s with happier results. Henry *Ford felt the same way about the automobile. The American people wanted and deserved the benefits of automotive transport, he was convinced. Therefore the fact that the first two companies with which he was associated failed was merely an historical accident. Only after such failures and at a relatively advanced age did Ford produce his first Model T in 1908. Through this product, Ford became the most important mass marketer in the twentieth century. He put a high-quality automobile within the reach of a theretofore-unimaginably large market.

Visionary mass marketers enabled millions of Americans to purchase products and services undreamed of when mass marketing began in the 1880s. These include all the apparatuses of kitchen and bathroom, of home entertainment, and, in recent years, personal *computers. They also include air travel, *telephones, and financial investment services.

Margin and Volume. The willingness and, indeed, the insistence on selling many units of a product and making money on volume, rather than selling fewer units and making money on the margin between cost and selling price, is an exceptionally difficult decision to make and sustain. Mass marketers sometimes have made decisions that seem contrary to the logic of the profit system. Henry Ford, for example, continuously cut the price of the Model T. As he did, demand skyrocketed. Even when demand exceeded supply, Ford permitted shortages to occur rather than raise prices. This seemed economically irrational but illustrates the commitment to low prices that is a crucial element in mass marketing.

Preconditions. America would have had no mass marketing without mass consumption. Mass consumption required a population with enough wealth to purchase the products being marketed, the means to deliver these products to their purchasers, and the desire to buy. All these existed in the United States by the 1880s. After a devastating *Civil War and a deep depression in the 1870s, America's economic and political life by the 1880s had achieved a level of stability allowing for increased consumption. The producers of expensive consumer durables developed time-payment programs, placing their products within reach of ever-widening circles of consumers. But economic well being was not constant. The overall trend toward greater mass purchasing power was punctuated by periodic collapses. When those occurred, as in the 1930s, the mass market, especially for expensive consumer durables, quickly shrunk in size.

A second essential precondition is logistics. The United States is a continental nation of over three million square miles. For a mass market to arise, goods had to be transported and business information transmitted at affordable prices. The *railroads and the *telegraph initially made this possible.

A third precondition for the mass-marketing revolution was that Americans had to harbor "wants" that exceeded their "needs" for survival such as food, clothing, and shelter. People had to feel that they *deserved* consumer products, that they would be happier owning them, and that they could afford them. A socialist once deplored "the damned wantlessness of the poor." Thanks to a deep-rooted national ideology of personal fulfillment summed up in the resonant phrase "the pursuit of happiness," and powerfully reinforced by advertising, "wantlessness" has not been a problem in the United States.

Marketing Segmentation. Perhaps the most important trend in marketing in the later twentieth century was the rise of market segmentation and the relative decline of mass marketing. Market segmentation sought to divide a market in a multitude of ways—the most common being demographic (age, income, and education) and psychographic (lifestyle). Market segmentation permitted price customization. For example, an airline that charged the same fare for every seat of a jumbo jet might be thought of as following a "mass market" approach to travel. The same airplane with three classes (first class, business, and tourist) has segmented its service in accord with customers' willingness to pay and has thus made possible higher revenues.

With the spread of personal computers, the Internet, and other new information technologies at the end of the twentieth century, most observers envisioned a data-rich environment, in which products could be customized to individual taste, giving currency to the phrase "mass customization." Simultaneously, however, this era saw the rise of such giant firms as Wal-Mart that used information *technology to build a mass market through low prices. Thus, predictions of mass customization must be viewed with caution. Mass marketing remained a vital part of the American economy as the century ended.

[*See also* Automotive Industry; Consumer Culture; Department Stores; Gilded Age; Internet and World Wide Web; Mass Production; McDonald's; Shopping Centers and Malls.]

• Alfred D. Chandler Jr., *The Visible Hand: The Managerial Revolution in American Business,* 1977. David A. Hounshell, *From the American System to Mass Production, 1800–1932: The Development of Manufacturing Technology in the United States,* 1984. Alfred D. Chandler Jr., Thomas K. McCraw, and Richard S. Tedlow, *Management, Past and Present: A Casebook on the History of American Business,* 1996. Robert J. Dolan and Hermann Simon, *Power Pricing: How Managing Price Transforms the Bottom Line,* 1996. Richard S. Tedlow, *New and Improved: The Story of Mass Marketing,* 1996.

—Richard Tedlow

MASS PRODUCTION. Mass production transformed the way Americans lived and worked at the beginning of the twentieth century. Understandable only as part of the larger socioeconomic system in which it operates, mass production encompasses far more than a set of manufacturing principles and technologies. Thanks to its role in creating mass *consumer culture, it constitutes a vital part of contemporary life. It was responsible for the dehumanizing assembly-line work of the twentieth century as well as the physical comfort enjoyed by most people in industrialized countries. The 1926 edition of the *Encyclopaedia Britannica* formally introduced the term in an article titled "Mass production." Ghostwritten by the Ford Motor Company's publicity secretary, the article appeared over Henry *Ford's name. The actual authorship matters little, for Henry Ford is indeed recognized as the man who popularized the term and, more important, made mass production work.

Mass production is characterized by the high-volume manufacture of standardized goods resulting in lower prices. Dependent on economies of scale and efficiency in production, it relies heavily on a mechanized workplace, the division of labor, and a far larger proportion of machine operators than of skilled workers. It also requires absolute uniformity in production: each piece or component must be made exactly the same each time. This feature of mass production—the manufacture of interchangeable parts—proved so difficult and expensive that it took almost a century to achieve.

The idea that work could be made routine and more productive through mechanization, standardization, and the division of labor long antedated Henry Ford; it can be found in eighteenth-century England, France, and America. In *From the American System to Mass Production* (1984), David Hounshell traced the technical development of mass production in the United States, beginning with the arms industry and proceeding through the sewing machine and woodworking industries; agricultural equipment and bicycles; and, finally, the *automotive industry. Like that of any invention, mass production's history is one of genius and frustration. With the support of the U.S. government, early nineteenth-century armories successfully experimented with the mechanized production of guns with interchangeable parts, the essential components of mass production. One after another, American industries mechanized production, but the manufacture of interchangeable parts proved too expensive for many, and without perfect interchangeability, true mass production remains impossible. Lacking this, some manufacturers, such as the Singer Sewing Machine Company, settled for the older system of "fitting" the parts together machine by machine. This resulted not in mass-produced machines whose parts could be assembled randomly, but in unique machines whose components had to be filed by trained machinists to make the parts fit properly.

The response to mass production is as interesting as the story of its invention. Perfected and most widespread in the United States, mass production and its products have been introduced around the world, rejected nowhere. The inspiration for art, *architecture, *poetry, and *music, it was also criticized as the root cause of the modern ecological crisis and twentieth-century alienation. Mass production was one of the icons, both beloved and reviled, of the so-called American century—the twentieth—when the United States became the world's premier military and industrial power.

As the new system of manufacturing developed, workers complained about the growing restrictions in the workplace. Some expressed their discontent by quitting, others by joining unions. No factory had more trouble keeping workers than the Ford Motor Company's Highland Park plant near *Detroit, where the assembly line in its fully realized form was introduced in 1914. Workers quit in such large numbers that in 1913 turnover was 380 percent, even before the assembly line became fully operational. Henry Ford addressed the turnover and made himself famous with a single act: to keep his employees on the job in the face of work that many deemed unacceptable, Ford offered them an unheard-of wage rate of five dollars per day.

The European response to Ford's style of mass production, known as "Fordism," is surprising compared to the labor response in the United States. During the interwar years, Fordism, along with Frederick W. Taylor's *scientific management, was praised, especially in Germany and the Soviet Union, by both conservative engineers and socialist reformers as the way to economic security. Fordism and Taylorism were seen as the keys to the success of modern America and the obvious path for any country seeking modernity.

A widespread and diverse artistic response to mass production can be found in film, painting, photography, literature, and music. The central inspiration for this response, sometimes called "machine-age modernism," was the mass-production factory. Film provides the clearest and most unambiguous initial reaction to mass production. Movies like Charlie *Chaplin's *Modern Times* (1936), which used Ford's factory as a model; René Clair's *A nous la liberté* (1931); and Fritz Lang's *Metropolis* (1926) unabashedly criticized mass production and the socioeconomic system that supported it. Other artists, however, found the modern factory a positive inspiration. The painters Charles Sheeler and Diego Rivera both portrayed Ford's Detroit factories and praised them (in very different ways) in their art. Modern architecture, beginning with the Bauhaus designs of Walter Gropius, derived much of its inspiration from American factories. As practitioners of a wide range of art forms embraced the symbols of mass production and the machine age in general, these technological developments became increasingly accepted as part of *modernist culture, no longer questioned but taken for granted as integral components of the social and economic landscape.

[*See also* Advertising; "American System" of Manufactures; Bicycles and Bicycling; Business; Business Cycle; Capitalism; Factory System; Industrialization; Labor Markets; Labor Movements; Mass Marketing; Strikes and Industrial Conflict; Technology; Whitney, Eli.]

• Alfred D. Chandler, *The Visible Hand: The Managerial Revelation in American Business,* 1977. Stephen Meyer, *The Five Dollar Day,* 1981. Cecilia Tichi, *Shifting Gears,* 1987. Thomas P. Hughes, *American Genesis,* 1989. Lindy Biggs, *The Rational Factory,* 1996. Robert Kanigel, *The One Best Way,* 1997.

—Lindy Biggs

MATHEMATICS AND STATISTICS. Mathematics has been part of American higher education since the founding of Harvard College in 1636. In the seventeenth century, however, the level of instruction was low—arithmetic and the rudiments of Euclidean geometry—reflecting the primitive state of elementary education and the underlying aim of preparing young men for the ministry.

By 1800, new colleges had been founded that focused more on liberal education. The mathematics curriculum grew accordingly to include algebra, trigonometry, and sometimes even Newton's fluxional calculus. Colonial professors of mathematics drew, however, from Great Britain, a country that had fallen behind the Continent—especially France—in pedagogical innovations and original research.

This situation began to change by the 1820s. Beginning in 1817, the U.S. Military Academy at West Point followed the example of France's state-of-the-art École Polytechnique and incorporated into its curriculum not only Leibnizian calculus but also the descriptive geometry that had been developed by Gaspard Monge. At midcentury at Harvard, Benjamin Peirce (1809–1880) crafted a curriculum in the mathematical sciences for the new Lawrence Scientific School (1847) that included some of the latest foreign research. Nevertheless, prior to 1876, America's colleges were almost exclusively undergraduate institutions. Research was not part of the faculty's mission, although some, like Peirce with his abstract theory of algebras (1870), pursued research anyway.

Colleges were not the sole locus of mathematical activity in nineteenth-century America. In a few instances, mathematicians worked individually: Robert Adrain discovered the law of least squares in 1809 independently of Carl Friedrich Gauss, while Nathaniel *Bowditch translated and wrote penetrating mathematical commentary on Pierre Simon de Laplace's challenging *Mécanique céleste* (1828–1839). The federal government supported mathematical activity in its U.S. Coast Survey and Nautical Almanac Office, where George William Hill did ground-breaking work on the three-body problem (1877).

After 1870, new research-oriented universities were founded and many colleges began to emphasize research. The first mathematics program to offer research-level training opened in 1876 at Johns Hopkins University under a British algebraist, James Joseph Sylvester. Following Sylvester's departure in 1883, mathematically inclined Americans turned to Germany, particularly the University of Göttingen and Felix Klein. There they absorbed the latest mathematics and the notion that academic mathematics encompassed both teaching and research. Returning to American institutions newly receptive to this ideal, they set up graduate programs and pursued their research agendas. By 1900, a professional community of mathematical researchers supported programs, notably at the University of Chicago under Eliakim Hastings Moore and at Harvard under William Fogg Osgood and Maxime Bôcher, and sustained at least four research journals as well as the American Mathematical Society (1888).

While American mathematicians embraced all of pure mathematics, certain areas of strength emerged. At Chicago, Leonard Eugene Dickson and his student A. Adrian Albert established a center for algebra. Princeton, with Oswald Veblen, Luther Pfahler Eisenhart, James Alexander, and Solomon Lefschetz, excelled in geometry and topology. Robert L. Moore created a school of point set topology at the University of Texas at Austin. Harvard built on its strength in analysis with George David Birkhoff, Joseph Walsh, and Marshall Stone.

Newer mathematical areas strengthened in the 1920s and 1930s owing both to the influx of European refugees and to the establishment of new research venues. Statistics as a tool for social analysis had grown during the *Progressive Era with its practitioners conveying their findings through the American Statistical Association (1839). Activists such as Harry Carver at the University of Michigan, however, worked to establish statistics as a more mathematical field. Their efforts, including the formation of the Institute for Mathematical Statistics in 1935, received a considerable boost after the rise of Nazism brought refugees such as Jerzy Neyman to Berkeley and Mark Kac to Cornell. Others also fled to American shores, among them Hermann Weyl to Princeton's Institute for Advanced Study; Richard von Mises to Harvard; and Emil Artin, Richard Brauer, and Emmy Noether. Applied mathematics likewise profited from the European influx, as well as from the formation of industrial-research facilities like Bell Telephone Laboratories (1925). During *World War II, the Applied Mathematics Panel within the federal Office of Research and Development coordinated mathematical work on war-related questions.

Thanks partly to wartime successes, the postwar period witnessed a dramatic increase in federal support of mathematics, as the *National Science Foundation led an institutionalization of academic grants that contributed to an explosive growth of American mathematical research. Late twentieth-century American mathematicians solved such noted problems as the Bieberbach conjecture, the classification of finite simple groups, the four-color problem, and Fermat's Last Theorem. The immigration of mathematicians from China, the former Soviet bloc, and elsewhere also contributed to the country's mathematical strength as the century ended.

[*See also* Coast and Geodetic Survey, U.S.; Education: Collegiate Education; Education: The Rise of the University; Research Laboratories, Industrial; Service Academies, Military.]

• Florian Cajori, *The Teaching and History of Mathematics in the United States,* 1890. Peter L. Duren, Richard A. Askey, Harold M. Edwards, and Uta C. Merzbach, eds., *A Century of Mathematics in America: Parts I–III,* 1988–1989. Larry Owens, "Mathematics at War: Warren Weaver and the Applied Mathematics Panel, 1942–1945," in *The History of Modern Mathematics,* eds. David E. Rowe and John McCleary, 2 vols., 1989, II: 287–305. Karen Hunger Parshall and David E. Rowe, *The Emergence of the American Mathematical Research Community, 1876–1900: J. J. Sylvester, Felix Klein, and E. H. Moore,* 1994. Patti Wilger Hunter, "Drawing the Boundaries: Mathematical Statistics in 20th-Century America," *Historia Mathematica* 23 (February 1996): 7–30.

—Karen Hunger Parshall

MATHER, INCREASE (1639–1723), and his son **COTTON** (1663–1728), Congregational ministers, writers, and leaders in church and society. Increase, the son of Richard Mather (1596–1669), felt himself be the heir of the founders of *New England, colonies settled to demonstrate to the world the New England way in church and state. He conveyed this sense of mission to his son, who strove to live up to the ideals of his father and his grandfathers, Richard Mather and John Cotton (1584–1652), after whom he was named.

Though filled with conflict and struggle, the lives of both Increase and Cotton showed moral and intellectual growth. Increase, never satisfied with his achievements, strove throughout his life to manage his complicated psyche. A conservative in theology, he proved an innovator in politics; a devoted husband and father, he left his family for years to travel to England in defense of New England's interests; a lover of New England, he still yearned for old England. By any standard of his time his was a successful ministry: he preached for fifty years at *Boston's North Church (or Second Church) and figured prominently in the political life of Massachusetts, sometimes virtually choosing its governors and magistrates. In 1688 he went to England to persuade the Crown to replace the Massachusetts charter it had revoked in 1684. A Royal charter was granted in 1697 and Increase's choice as governor, William Phips, was appointed.

When Increase and Phips reached Boston in 1692, the *Salem witchcraft crisis was raging. Increase, like his son Cotton, believed in witches, as did almost everyone in the seventeenth century. Nevertheless, he acted to end the upheaval, working behind the scenes and in the open, convinced that the court trying the witches had acted improperly. His critique of the court's procedures, *Cases of Conscience Concerning Evil Spirits,* was published in London in 1693.

Increase Mather's influence slowly declined in the following years. He originally opposed both the *Half-Way Covenant (an ecclesiastical contrivance of 1662 that eased the terms of church membership) and the open communion instituted in Northampton by Solomon Stoddard (1643–1728/29), a long-time opponent. In his eyes, such measures eroded the foundations of the churches. Nor was he pleased by the introduction early in the eighteenth century of ministerial associations and standing councils, an additional blow to the independence of every Puritan church and to New England's mission.

Cotton Mather's character and personality were even more complicated than his father's. His antagonist in the Salem witch hunt, the Boston merchant Robert Calef, accused him of having an "ambidexter" quality, a word intended to suggest that his attitudes were never quite what they seemed. In the Salem trials, for example, he praised the judges while criticizing their procedures.

Born in Boston, he graduated from Harvard in 1678, took an M.A. in 1681, was ordained at Boston's North Church in 1685, and in 1686 married Abigail Phillips—the first of three wives, with whom he had fifteen children.

This complicated man was a minister who shared the pulpit with his father, preaching to the poor as well as the mighty, and published 388 sermons, tracts, and books and left many others in manuscript, including the "Biblia Americana," his immense *Bible commentary. Unlike his father, Cotton never left New England, yet he led an active life: He played a significant role in the Glorious Revolution in Boston, which saw Governor Edmund Andros overthrown, and in the years immediately following he defended the new charter. He also defended the witchcraft trials in *Wonders of the Invisible World* (1693) and sought influence in the political world. But like his father, he saw his public influence decline. This was an immense disappointment, for he shared the vision of New England as an example to the world. Other disappointments included his failure to secure the presidency of Harvard after his father gave it up in 1701.

His preaching became more enthusiastical after 1700 as he attempted to convert the unregenerate and draw Presbyterians, Congregationalists, and others into a great Christian union. He studied nature—the stars in the heavens and New England's flora and fauna—and when *smallpox broke out in Boston in 1721, he attempted to persuade local physicians to adopt inoculation, an early form of vaccination. Many of his efforts miscarried, but there were rewards too: His great historical work, *The Magnalia Christi Americana*, appeared in 1702; his submissions of scientific reports brought election to the Royal Society in 1713; and in 1726 *Ratio Disciplinae*, a formidable account of Congregational polity, appeared.

Both Mathers achieved much, and their lives tell much about the early history of America and *Puritanism in England and America.

[*See also* Colonial Era; Glorious Revolution in America; Protestantism; Religion.]

• Kenneth Ballard Murdock, *Increase Mather,* 1926. Perry Miller, *The New England Mind: From Colony to Province,* 1953. Robert Middlekauff, *The Mathers,* 1971. David Levin, *Cotton Mather,* 1978. Kenneth Silverman, *The Life and Times of Cotton Mather,* 1984. Michael G. Hall, *The Last American Puritan: The Life of Increase Mather,* 1988.

—Robert L. Middlekauff

MAYFLOWER COMPACT (21 November 1620). The first written framework of government in English America, the Mayflower Compact was an agreement made among the forty-one adult male passengers aboard the *Mayflower* on arrival at Cape Cod. It bound the signers to form a civil government and to obey its laws for their "better Ordering and Preservation," while pledging them to enact "just and equal Laws . . . for the General Good of the Colony."

The compact aimed to legitimize the new government and to prevent disorder, especially among those recruits who were not *Pilgrims and who, according to Governor William Bradford, wanted to "use their own libertie." The issue of legitimacy was important, since the settlers lacked a valid charter, having landed several hundred miles north of their intended destination in Virginia. The only recorded copy of the document is in an anonymous account of the voyage called *Mourt's Relation* (1622). Modeled on Puritan church covenants, it contained few specifics about the structure of government and had questionable legal status other than common consent. Nevertheless, it established a government in which people were bound to obey laws voted by the majority of adult males and served as a precedent for more elaborate covenants like the "Fundamental Orders" of Connecticut (1639).

Although the Mayflower Compact is commonly regarded as having embodied the democratic principles of self-government and consent, it was far from establishing an actual democracy of universal adult *suffrage. Voting rights, initially limited to adult males, became gradually more exclusive until *Plymouth was absorbed by the short-lived Dominion of New England in 1686 and then annexed by the Massachusetts Bay Colony in 1691.

[*See also* Colonial Era; Exploration, Conquest, and Settlement, Era of European; Puritanism]

• William Bradford, *Of Plymouth Plantation, 1620–47,* ed. Samuel Eliot Morison, 1952. Jack P. Greene, ed., *Settlements to Society 1607–1763: A Documentary History of Colonial America,* 1975. Mark L. Sargent, "The Conservative Covenant: The Rise of the Mayflower Compact in American Myth," *New England Quarterly* 61 (1988): 233–51.

—Andrew J. O'Shaughnessy

MAYO, WILLIAM AND CHARLES. *See* Mayo Clinic.

MAYO CLINIC, innovative medical center in Rochester, Minnesota. In 1863, an English-born, nomadic country doctor, William Worrall Mayo, moved his wife, three daughters, and infant son, William James Mayo, to the frontier town of Rochester (pop. 3,000), where a second son, Charles Horace Mayo, was born in 1865. The unwillingness of W. W. Mayo's wife to move again compelled the restless doctor to remain in Rochester. When a tornado devastated the town in 1883, the local sisters of the Order of St. Francis offered to build a hospital there if Dr. Mayo and his two physician sons, affectionately known as Drs. Will and Charlie, would staff it. Saint Mary's, the first general hospital in southeastern Minnesota, opened in 1889. Drs. Will and Charlie tirelessly traveled throughout Europe and the United States to learn the newest surgical techniques, and soon their reputation for expert diagnoses and safe *surgery lured physicians from around the world to Rochester to watch the brothers perform. In 1892, the Mayos began inviting other doctors to join their practice. Among the first was Dr. Henry Plummer, whose vision of a private, coordinated, multispecialty group practice of medicine dedicated to patient care became the core of the Mayo Clinic philosophy. The Mayo Graduate School of Medicine, the world's first formal program to train medical specialists, opened in 1915 with an endowment from the Mayo brothers. In 1919, the Mayos turned over their personal assets to form what is now the Mayo Foundation; the partnerships were dissolved and the entire staff became salaried. The Mayo Medical School was started in 1972. The Mayo Foundation opened its first "satellite" Mayo Clinic in Jacksonville, Florida, in 1986 and its second in Scottsdale, Arizona, in 1987.

Mayo milestones include sharing the Nobel Prize for the discovery of cortisone, creation of a system to grade different types of *cancer, development of the first effective *tuberculosis treatment, performing the first hip replacement, pioneering open-heart surgery, and pivotal work in the development of successful organ transplantation.

[*See also* Health and Fitness; Health Maintenance Organizations; Heart Disease; Hospitals; Medical Education; Medicine: From the 1870s to 1945; Medicine: Since 1945.]

• Helen Clapesattle, *The Doctors Mayo,* 1990. C. D. B. Bryan, *The Mayo Clinic,* 1999.

—C. D. B. Bryan

McCARTHY, JOSEPH (1908–1957), Republican senator from Wisconsin, notorious "Red-hunter" during the early *Cold War years. Born on a dairy farm near Appleton, Wisconsin, McCarthy quit school at age fourteen to raise chickens. He subsequently went bankrupt, returned to high school, crammed four years of work into two terms, and entered Marquette, a Jesuit college in Milwaukee. Earning a law degree in 1935, McCarthy established a small practice before winning a circuit judgeship by frantic campaigning and smearing the incumbent's good name.

At twenty-nine, the youngest judge in Wisconsin, McCarthy raised eyebrows by providing "quickie divorces" to political supporters. The state supreme court also censured him for destroying crucial evidence in a price-fixing case. Although judges were exempt from the draft, McCarthy joined the Marines in 1942 and spent *World War II as an intelligence officer in the Pacific. He later claimed to have suffered wounds as a "tail-gunner" when his plane crash-landed under Japanese fire. In fact, his only war injury occurred during a troopship hazing incident, when he fell down a flight of stairs and broke his foot.

In 1946, McCarthy defeated three-term incumbent Robert M. La Follette Jr., a member of Wisconsin's leading political family, in the Republican senatorial primary. The overconfident La Follette barely bothered to campaign; McCarthy never stopped. A few months later, McCarthy buried his Democratic opponent, Howard McMurray, under a mountain of baseless allegations.

As a senator, McCarthy became known for his raucous, erratic behavior. Then, in February 1950, his political career in trouble and his reelection chances looking grim, he told a Republican gathering in Wheeling, West Virginia, that he held in his hand a list of 205 communists presently "working in the State Department." The claim was preposterous; McCarthy knew nothing about communists in government or anywhere else. But his aim was publicity, and his timing was right. Americans were alarmed by Soviet aggression in Europe, China's recent fall to communist rule, Alger *Hiss's conviction for perjury, and Russia's successful atomic-bomb test. McCarthy provided a simple explanation for these disturbing events. The communists were "winning" the Cold War, he insisted, thanks to traitors within the U.S. government. The real enemy wasn't in Moscow; it was in Washington, D.C.

When communist North Korea invaded anticommunist South Korea in June 1950, McCarthy's message took on special force. In the November elections, Republicans gained five seats in the Senate and twenty-eight in the House. As the 1952 presidential campaign approached, McCarthy grew bolder. He called Secretary of Defense George *Marshall a traitor, mocked Secretary of State Dean *Acheson as the "red Dean of Fashion," and described President Harry S. *Truman as a drunkard, adding, "The son-of-a-bitch should be impeached." During the campaign, McCarthy claimed, falsely, that the communist *Daily Worker* had endorsed the Democrat Adlai *Stevenson for president. And he made the intentional slip "Alger . . . I mean Adlai" in a nationally televised address. So long as his targets were Democrats, leading Republicans were generally supportive. Senator Robert *Taft advised: "Keep talking and if one case doesn't work out, proceed with another."

Not only did McCarthy easily win reelection in the Republican landslide of 1952, but four of the Democratic senators he campaigned against lost, including Millard Tydings of Maryland, chair of a Senate committee that in 1950 had labeled McCarthy's charges "a fraud and a hoax." At his peak of influence, McCarthy became chairman of the Committee on Government Operations and its powerful Subcommittee on Investigations. Filling key staff positions with former agents of the *Federal Bureau of Investigation and former prosecutors like Roy M. Cohn from New York, McCarthy set out to uncover "communist influence" in the federal government. His targets included the Voice of America, the Government Printing Office, and the Foreign Service. He even questioned the anticommunist credentials of President Dwight D. *Eisenhower, a member of his own party. McCarthy's hearings did not uncover any communists. They did, however, ruin numerous careers, undermine government morale, and make America look ridiculous in the eyes of the world.

McCarthy's downfall began with his investigation of "subversive activities" in the U.S. Army. The public got to see him for thirty-six days in the televised Army-McCarthy hearings during the Spring of 1954, and the cumulative impression was devastating, as the senator insulted witnesses, attacked fellow senators, and launched crude personal attacks against his critics. A 1954 TV documentary on McCarthy by the respected and influential CBS newsman Edward R. *Murrow further eroded his influence. In November, the Senate censured McCarthy for bringing that body into "into dishonor and disrepute." Many linked his censure to an easing of Cold War tensions. The *Korean War was over, the Soviet dictator Joseph Stalin dead, and the radical right in disarray. His demagoguery no longer effective, McCarthy grew increasingly depressed. He died of alcoholism in 1957, utterly discredited, but the word "McCarthyism" lived on, a reminder of the worst times of the early Cold War.

[*See also* Anticommunism; Hoover, J. Edgar; House Committee on Un-American Activities; Republican Party; Rosenberg Case.]

• Edwin R. Bayley, *Joe McCarthy and the Press,* 1981. David M. Oshinsky, *A Conspiracy So Immense: The World of Joe McCarthy,* 1983. Richard M. Fried, *Nightmare in Red: The McCarthy Era in Perspective,* 1990.

—David M. Oshinsky

McCARTHYISM. *See* McCarthy, Joseph.

McCLINTOCK, BARBARA (1902–1992), biologist and Nobel laureate. Born in Hartford, Barbara McClintock was educated at Cornell, from which she received a Ph.D. in botany in 1927. She taught at Cornell and the University of Missouri before joining the Department of Genetics at the Carnegie-funded research center at Cold Spring Harbor, Long Island, in 1941, where she remained for the rest of her career.

McClintock's place in the history of biology is guaranteed by a lifelong career of pathbreaking research in genetics and cytology. The year of her birth coincided with the rediscovery of Gregor Mendel's work, and her coming of age with that of genetics. Her early work on maize at Cornell University in the 1920s and 1930s, combining microscopic studies of chromosome structure with the new science of genetics, provided crucial evidence for the chromosomal basis of genetic crossover. But it was her pioneering work on the transposition of genes in the 1940s and 1950s for which she is best known. This work, performed after she moved to Cold Spring Harbor, demonstrated that chromosomes are dynamic structures, but it went against the prevailing view of the time that the position of genes on the chromosome was fixed. As a result, her findings seemed incomprehensible to many scientists and went largely unheeded for years. In the 1970s, however, with the identification of "jumping genes" in the bacteria *E. coli,* McClintock's much earlier work with maize was recalled and granted new recognition. In 1983, she was awarded the Nobel Prize, thirty-two years after her first definitive paper on the subject.

McClintock particularly interests historians of biology for

her success in breaking with tradition on a number of fronts: as a geneticist whose understanding of genes was shaped by her interests in development, as a woman who refused to be constrained by conventional notions of *gender, and as a scientist who dared to affirm the necessity of a "feeling for the organism" in the rational construction of knowledge.

[*See also* Genetics and Genetic Engineering; Science: From 1914 to 1945; Science: Since 1945.]

• E. F. Keller, *A Feeling for the Organism,* 1983. N. Federoff and D. Botstein, *The Dynamic Genome,* 1992.

—Evelyn Fox Keller

McCORMICK, CYRUS HALL (1809–1884), inventor and manufacturer. Cyrus Hall McCormick was born on a farm in Rockbridge County, Virginia. In 1831, he took up the project his father had pursued unsuccessfully for twenty years: building a reaper to speed the harvesting of small grains. In July 1831, he gave a public demonstration of his new design, which embodied key innovations common to every subsequent reaper. McCormick started a business to manufacture his reaper, locating in *Chicago in 1847, closer to the agricultural heartland. His company quickly became the industry leader, maintaining that position until the *Civil War.

During the war, while McCormick lived in London, his company lost its leadership as a manufacturer of farm machinery, though it remained important. After the war, he left the company management to his brother Leander. When the devastating *Chicago fire destroyed his factory in 1871, McCormick considered abandoning the business, but his wife Nettie Fowler (whom he married in 1858) intervened, urging reconstruction of the factory. Thereafter she played a central role in the management of the McCormick Company and its successor, the International Harvester Corporation.

From 1857 until his death, McCormick was deeply involved in *Democratic party politics. He was also a committed Presbyterian layman. In 1859, he endowed four professorships at the Presbyterian Theological Seminary of the Northwest (renamed McCormick Theological Seminary in 1886). McCormick's inventive genius transformed grain harvesting and agricultural practices, yet the success of his company (and, perhaps, his reputation) resulted primarily from the business acumen of his wife and, subsequently, his eldest son, Cyrus Jr.

[*See also* Agriculture: 1770s to 1890; Gilded Age; Industrialization; Technology.]

• William T. Hutchinson, *Cyrus Hall McCormick,* 2 vols., 1930, 1935. R. Douglas Hurt, *American Farm Tools: From Hand-Power to Steam-Power,* 1982. J. Sanford Rikoon, *Threshing in the Middle West, 1820–1948: A Study of Traditional Culture and Technological Change,* 1989.

—Fred V. Carstensen

McCORMICK REAPER. *See* Farm Machinery; Technology.

McCULLOCH* v. *MARYLAND (1819). Chief Justice John *Marshall's memorable phrases and magisterial reasoning make his opinion in this case the classic formulation of the implied powers of the national government and of the relation between the national government and the states. Congress had incorporated the Second Bank of the United States (BUS) in 1816 and given it the power to establish branches in the states without their consent. Maryland imposed a tax on banks issuing notes without state consent, and James McCulloch, treasurer of the Baltimore branch of the BUS, refused to pay. Maryland then sued McCulloch, who, after losing twice in state court, appealed to the U.S. *Supreme Court.

The case attracted intense public interest. Many held the BUS, the "Monster," responsible for the Panic of 1819. Further, agricultural depression and debates over *slavery in Missouri were reviving interest in old *states'-rights arguments. Beginning on 22 February 1819, some of the nations' best lawyers argued the case for nine days. On 17 March, Marshall spoke for a unanimous Court in upholding Congress's power to incorporate the bank and in ruling Maryland's tax unconstitutional.

Maryland's state's-rights, strict-construction argument, Marshall said, would retard national growth and turn the *Constitution into a "splendid bauble." The people of the United States, not the states, had created the Constitution as their instrument of government and had given the government limited, enumerated powers. It was unimportant that the power to incorporate a bank or anything else was not among those enumerated powers, Marshall argued, because the "necessary and proper" clause of Article I, section 8 of the Constitution granted the government broad discretion in devising ways to execute its powers. If the end was legitimate and within the scope of the Constitution, he concluded, then "all means which are appropriate, which are plainly adapted to that end, which are not prohibited, but consist with the letter and spirit of the constitution, are constitutional."

The supremacy clause (Article VI) established that the national government was supreme within its sphere. Lawful congressional acts took precedence over state law. States could not threaten or impede the national government in exercising its constitutional power. So, because the power to tax "involved" the power to destroy, Maryland's tax was unconstitutional. The Constitution, Marshall proclaimed, was intended for "ages to come" and must be adaptable to circumstances its framers could not have imagined.

[*See also* Antebellum Era; Bank of the United States, First and Second; Early Republic, Era of the; Jurisprudence; Nationalism.]

• Gerald Gunther, ed., *John Marshall's Defense of* McCulloch v. Maryland, 1969. G. Edward White, *The Marshall Court and Cultural Change, 1815–1835,* vols. III–IV, in *The Oliver Wendell Holmes Devise History of the Supreme Court of the United States,* 1988.

—Francis N. Stites

McDONALD'S, fast-food restaurant franchiser. Richard and Maurice McDonald introduced assembly-line techniques at the hamburger drive-in they opened in San Bernardino, *California, in the 1940s. Their "Speedy Service System," combined with economies of scale made possible by serving many customers quickly, proved far more profitable that the traditional labor-intensive approach. Their success attracted potential franchisees, including Ray Kroc (1902–1984), who supplied the Multimixers used to prepare McDonald's milk shakes. Overcoming the McDonalds' reluctance to invest time or money in franchising, Kroc offered to take all responsibility as the sole franchise agent. The brothers accepted Kroc's offer, and in 1955 McDonald's restaurants began to appear nationwide. Kroc bought out his contract with the McDonald brothers in 1962. Kroc's vision of clean, quick, family restaurants with an instantly recognizable logo—the golden arches—fit beautifully with postwar trends of *suburbanization, highway expansion, working mothers, and consumer preference for standardized, mass-marketed products.

Fast-food franchising had a mixed record before Kroc. Earlier franchisers had tended to sell off large territories to raise capital quickly, or to operate as the supplier for the franchisees (as the Howard Johnson's restaurants did in the 1930s), creating potential conflicts of interest and temptations to overcharge franchisees. Kroc emphasized efficient restaurant operations and guaranteed franchisees' profits before McDonald's Corporation took its cut. A key to McDonald's success was chief financial officer Harry Sonneborn, who structured franchise deals that insured profitability not by food sales alone, but through the real estate the restaurants occupied.

By the mid-1990s, McDonald's was the world's largest private real-estate enterprise, as well as its largest food service provider, serving nearly forty million meals daily in more than one hundred countries, with annual sales in excess of thirty billion dollars. A host of competitors such as Kentucky Fried Chicken, Taco Bell, Wendy's, and Burger King testified to the success of the McDonald's formula.

[*See also* Consumer Culture; Fifties, The; Food and Diet; Highway System; Mass Marketing.]

• Ray Kroc with Robert Anderson, *Grinding It Out: The Making of McDonald's,* 1977. John F. Love, *McDonald's: Behind the Arches,* 1986.

—Christopher Berkeley

McGILLIVRAY, ALEXANDER (1751–1793), *Isti acagagi thlucco* (Great Beloved Man) of the Creek Indians and opponent of Georgia's expansion. Alexander McGillivray's father, Lachlan McGillivray, was a trader, planter, and colonial Georgia assemblyman. His mother, Sehoy Marchand of the Creek Wind Clan, was the daughter of a French officer and a Creek woman. Until age five or seven he lived at Little Tallassee in the Creek Nation. Later he lived in Augusta, Savannah, and Charleston, where he was formally educated. He apprenticed to a slave-trading firm in Savannah. During the *Revolutionary War he served the British Indian service in dealings with the Creeks, among whom he remained after 1783. His maternal connection to the Wind Clan provided his tribal status.

McGillivray led Creek efforts both to strengthen the Creek National Council and to coordinate Creek resistance to U.S. expansion. When town leaders Hoboithle Mico (Tame King) of Tallassee and Eneah Mico (Fat King) of Cusseta sold land to Georgia without the consent of the National Council, McGillivray had them disciplined. He secured aid from Spanish Florida and helped the British firm of Panton, Leslie, and Company operate in Spanish territory. Through these measures he sought to keep the Creeks independent of the United States and prepared to oppose Georgia with force. He gained federal promises of protection against Georgia in the Treaty of New York (1790), but the treaty both alienated the Spanish and, through secret clauses granting him a large American salary, damaged his later reputation. McGillivray died in Pensacola in 1793.

[*See also* Colonial Era; Expansionism; Indian History and Culture: From 1500 to 1800.]

• John W. Caughey, *McGillivray of the Creeks,* 1938. Edward J. Cashin, *Lachlan McGillivray, Indian Trader: The Shaping of the Southern Colonial Frontier,* 1992.

—Gregory Evans Dowd

McGUFFEY *READERS.* In 1835 Winthrop Smith, a Cincinnati publisher, invited William Holmes McGuffey (1800–1873), a popular teacher of ancient languages at Miami University in Oxford, Ohio, to produce a set of school reading books, characterized by Smith as "a western reader for western children." The first two *Readers* appeared in 1836, featuring moral and biblical tales, excerpts from the classics, and historical snippets. They quickly became the best-selling school texts nationwide. With help from his brother Alexander, McGuffey eventually produced six *Readers,* frequently revised and updated (notably in 1857 and 1879) to answer criticisms or outdo the innovations of competing texts. The *Readers* made Smith a millionaire; they made McGuffey famous. The politics of the books were conservative, even by nineteenth-century standards, but this was not unusual for school texts. McGuffey's *Readers* leaned toward the Federalist position in their constitutional views; they tip-toed past *slavery and the *Civil War; and they promoted a morality of individual industry, not collective responsibility. They had an enduring appeal, based on some combination of their staunchly moral views, their support of American institutions, their praise of American goodness, and the literary quality of their selected passages. The American Book Company, long the copyright holder, estimated that 122 million copies were sold from 1836 to 1920. They were still selling over 200,000 copies a year in the 1990s, a decade that witnessed a revival of interest in McGuffey's *Readers* based on a resurgence of conservative values and a reaction against the "basal" readers of public schools as bland, noncommittal, and "dumbed down."

[*See also* Antebellum Era; Conservatism; Education: The Public School Movement; Individualism; Literacy; Literature, Popular; Printing and Publishing.]

• Richard D. Mosier, *Making the American Mind: Social and Moral Ideas in the McGuffey Readers,* 1947. Dolores P. Sullivan, *William Holmes McGuffey: Schoolmaster to the Nation,* 1994.

—Carl F. Kaestle

McKINLEY, WILLIAM (1843–1901), twenty-fifth president of the United States. Born in Niles, Ohio, William McKinley attended Allegheny College briefly before volunteering for the *Civil War. He rose to the rank of major in the Union Army, a title that he carried into national politics. Practicing as an attorney in Canton, Ohio, he married Ida Sexton in 1871 and became an active Republican. Elected to Congress in 1876, he served until defeated in 1890. He chaired the House Ways and Means Committee, hence the McKinley Tariff of 1890 bears his name. He was elected governor of Ohio in 1891 and reelected in 1893. The frontrunner for the Republican presidential nomination in 1896, he won on the first ballot, went on to defeat his Democratic opponent, William Jennings *Bryan, the candidate of western agrarians and the *free silver movement.

Although his close friendship with Cleveland industrialist Mark *Hanna aided McKinley's political rise as governor and president, he was the dominant figure in their relationship. In the White House from 1897 to 1901, McKinley is sometimes considered the first modern president: He cultivated the press, traveled frequently to push his programs, and exercised significant influence on Congress.

McKinley's reputation rests on his handling of the crisis in Cuba that led to the *Spanish-American War. Unlike his predecessor Grover *Cleveland, McKinley insisted that the Cuban rebels have a role in any negotiated settlement. He also specified that Spain must end the rebellion quickly. This policy intensified the pressure on Madrid, which refused to relinquish Cuba peacefully. Popular sentiment for war increased sharply in February 1898 after an explosion of unknown origin destroyed the USS *Maine* in Havana harbor, killing many sailors. By late March it was clear that Spain would not concede, and McKinley asked Congress for authority to intervene in Cuba. Within weeks, the two nations were at war.

A strong and effective war president, McKinley also dominated the negotiations that produced an armistice in August 1898. He made the decision that the United States should acquire the *Philippines in the Treaty of Paris. McKinley's leadership assured Senate approval of the pact in February 1899. For the two years that followed, McKinley used his war powers to subdue an insurrection in the Philippines and establish a civilian government. His forceful approach to foreign affairs, reinforced by Secretary of State John *Hay, also produced the *"Open Door" policy in China (1899), the dispatching of American troops to China to help subdue the Boxer Rebellion (1900), and the talks with Great Britain that facilitated construction of the *Panama Canal. In domestic affairs, McKinley championed the *gold standard and the protective tariff, but also advocated reciprocal trade treaties to open up markets overseas to American exporters.

McKinley won reelection in 1900, again defeating Bryan, but he was assassinated in September 1901 in Buffalo, New York, by anarchist Leon Czolgosz. McKinley was an important architect of the twentieth-century presidency and a decisive force in the nation's rise to world power.

[*See also* Democratic Party; Expansionism; Federal Government, Executive Branch: The Presidency; Foreign Relations: U.S. Relations with Asia; Foreign Relations: U.S. Relations with Latin America; Foreign Trade, U.S.; Populist Era; Populist Party; Republican Party; Tariffs.]

• Lewis L. Gould, *The Presidency of William McKinley,* 1980. Lewis L. Gould and Craig H. Roell, *William McKinley: A Bibliography,* 1988.

—Lewis L. Gould

McKINLEY TARIFF. *See* Tariffs.

McNARY-HAUGEN BILL (1924). In the years following *World War I, farmers received prices for their products that represented a purchasing power far below prewar levels. This resulted in an effort by the farm bloc in Congress to secure a larger share for these producers, in part by making the protective tariff as effective for agricultural products as it was for manufactured goods. In 1924, Senator Charles McNary of Oregon and Representative Gilbert Haugen of Iowa introduced a bill designed to assist farmers by requiring the federal government to sell surplus crops abroad at whatever price the commodities could command, thereby allowing domestic prices to rise. The cost of the program would be met by an equalization fee levied on farmers. Congress passed two versions of McNary-Haugen only to have President Calvin *Coolidge veto both because, in his view, they fixed prices and abused the power to tax. Although unable to override the president's vetoes, congressional supporters did succeed in bringing the plight of agriculture to national attention. Both political parties included planks in their 1928 platforms calling for legislation to give equality to agriculture.

The goal of the McNary-Haugen bills was to achieve parity, a fair exchange value between agricultural prices and the general price index. It is doubtful if the law could have succeeded during the 1920s owing to the huge agricultural surpluses that kept prices low. During the Coolidge presidency, moreover, the government lacked the administrative ability and facilities to manage complex agricultural production and storage programs. But the campaign for the McNary-Haugen bills laid the foundation for some of the agricultural reforms of the *New Deal Era and for the federal agricultural programs in place from the 1940s into the 1990s.

[*See also* Agriculture: Since 1920; Economic Development; Laissez-faire; Republican Party; Tariffs; Taxation; Twenties, The.]

• Theodore Saloutos and John D. Hicks, *Twentieth Century Populism: Agricultural Dissent in the Middle West 1900–1939,* 1951. Gilbert Fite, *George N. Peek and the Fight for Farm Parity,* 1954.

—Richard Lowitt

McPHERSON, AIMEE SEMPLE (1890–1944), evangelist and founder of the International Church of the Foursquare Gospel. Aimee Kennedy was born in Canada near the southern Ontario village of Salford, where her early religious impressions were shaped by her father's *Methodism and her mother's enthusiasm for the Salvation Army. In 1908, Aimee embraced *Pentecostalism and married Robert Semple, the evangelist who converted her. They sailed as missionaries to Hong Kong in 1910. Six weeks later, Robert died of malaria and other complications. Married again in 1912 to Harold McPherson, a bookkeeper, Aimee could not settle into a housewife's routine. In 1915, Living in Providence, Rhode Island, she left Harold and dedicated her life to Robert Semple's work of evangelism. The couple divorced in 1921.

Aimee enjoyed instant success as an evangelist. In 1917, she began publishing *The Bridal Call,* a monthly magazine that helped her build an international network. Late in 1918, she moved to *Los Angeles where she opened the 5,300–seat Angelus Temple and a Bible school in 1923 and her own *radio station in 1924. Her charismatic sermons, often illustrated with visual props, attracted thousands. Fame turned to notoriety in 1926 when McPherson disappeared for six weeks. The district attorney's office sought to disprove her widely doubted claim that she had been kidnapped, but eventually dropped all charges. Rumors persisted that she had spent the time with a male staff member of Angelus Temple. Her third marriage, in 1931, ended in divorce two years later. Ill health curtailed McPherson's activities thereafter, but her son Rolf McPherson carried on her ministry with considerable success.

[*See also* Protestantism; Religion; Revivalism; Sunday, Billy; Twenties, The.]

• Edith L. Blumhofer, *Aimee Semple McPherson: Everybody's Sister,* 1993. Daniel Epstein, *Sister Aimee: The Life of Aimee Semple McPherson,* 1993.

—Edith L. Blumhofer

MEAD, MARGARET (1901–1978), anthropologist and social reformer. Margaret Mead was born in *Philadelphia to Emily Fogg, a sociologist, and Edward Sherwood Mead, an economist. She graduated from Barnard College and in 1929 received a Ph.D. in *anthropology from Columbia University, where she was trained by Franz *Boas, a pioneer in cultural anthropology. Initially specializing in children and women, Mead later extended her interests to psychological and applied anthropology, *gender and cultural change, human settlements, and diet and nutrition. Her *Coming of Age in Samoa: A Psychological Study of Primitive Youth for Western Civilization* (1928) established her reputation as a field researcher and writer. With hindsight, later critics would note that in this and later works, such as *Sex and Temperament in Three Primitive Societies* (1935), she neglected the biological determinants of human behavior. In *Margaret Mead and Samoa: The Making and Unmaking of an Anthropological Myth* (1983), anthropologist Derek Freeman criticized her research methodology and suggested that her idyllic picture of polymorphous, guilt-free sexual activity among adolescent Samoans was intended primarily as a critique of Western sexual repressiveness. Still, these and other works by Mead remain acknowledged classics. As a fieldworker, she encouraged the use of photography, film, and tape recorders.

Mead believed that science could and should promote human betterment. Appalled by America's atomic bombing of *Hiroshima and Nagasaki in 1945, she sought to ameliorate social problems through anthropological understanding. During the 1950s and 1960s she became a media celebrity, projecting the image of a wise, advice-giving grandmother commenting on a wide range of issues. She testified at congressional hearings and spoke in public forums on U.S. foreign policy, family and child-rearing issues, drug laws, and *nuclear-power regulation; participated in international and *United Nations conferences concerning population control, food supply, and health; and served as president of the Scientists' Institute for Public Information (1972), the World Federation of Mental Health (1956–1957), and the American Association for the Advancement of Science (1975). A prolific writer, Mead published some thirty-five books and hundreds of articles, both scholarly and popular.

[*See also* Courtship and Dating; Family; Life Stages; Marriage and Divorce; Sex Education; Sexual Morality and Sex Reform; Social Science.]

• Margaret Mead, *Blackberry Winter: My Earlier Years,* 1972. Mary Catherine Bateson, *With a Daughter's Eye: A Memoir of Margaret Mead and Gregory Bateson,* 1982.

—Virginia Yans

MEANY, GEORGE (1894–1980), labor leader. Born in *New York City, George Meany in 1915 joined the United Association of Plumbers and Steam Fitters, his father's union. In 1922 he attained his first union office, winning election as business agent of New York City Local 463. He served as president of the New York State Federation of Labor from 1934 to 1939, and in 1939 was elected secretary-treasurer of the *American Federation of Labor (AFL). Upon the death of William Green in 1952, the Executive Council elected Meany president of the AFL. In 1955, successful in his efforts to effect a merger with the once-rival *Congress of Industrial Organizations (CIO), Meany was elected president of the AFL-CIO, a post he held for twenty-four years.

Meany acted forcefully as an advocate of labor's views from within the political system. He supported *civil rights legislation but rarely challenged the racially discriminatory practices of craft unions. Meany was an ardent cold warrior who fought procommunist unionism at home and abroad, and also supported the *Vietnam War. During his AFL presidency, union membership declined as a proportion of the nonagricultural labor force, a circumstance that Meany viewed with equanimity so long as the AFL-CIO remained influential in government and *Democratic party circles. Meany clashed frequently with United Automobile Workers president Walter *Reuther, who urged revitalization of labor's activist traditions and a less strident approach to foreign-policy questions.

As a labor leader, Meany championed workers' economic interests and allied with the mainstream *civil rights movement. He did little, however, to accommodate the concerns of women, minority or marginal workers, or more militant trade unionists.

[*See also* Anticommunism; Cold War; Immigrant Labor; Labor Movements; Women in the Labor Force.]

• Joseph C. Meany, *Meany,* 1972. Robert H. Zieger, "George Meany: Labor's Organization Man," in *Labor Leaders in America,* eds. Melvyn Dubofsky and Warren Van Tine, 1987, pp. 324–49.

—Robert H. Zieger

MEATPACKING AND MEAT PROCESSING INDUSTRY. Commercial meatpacking in North America dates from 1660, when entrepreneur William Pynchon began selling preserved pork from an abandoned warehouse in Springfield, Massachusetts. In the *Antebellum Era, meatpacking and processing concentrated in Cincinnati, where the Ohio River provided low-cost transport of pork to distant markets. By the late 1840s, Cincinnati boasted more than forty pork-packing plants using an advanced division of labor that integrated packing with slaughtering and dressing. By the end of the *Civil War, however, Cincinnati had been displaced as the meatpacking capital by *Chicago, strategically located along rail lines linking western livestock supplies to eastern urban markets.

Between 1865 and *World War I, meatpacking changed from a mostly local, seasonal, and small-scale business into a giant, nationally integrated, and year-round industry dominated by five massive corporations led by Swift's and Armour's. At the heart of this transformation lay Chicago-based firms' use of refrigerated railroad cars to ship dressed beef from Chicago and other western packing centers to eastern, urban markets. These firms also developed networks of refrigerated branch distribution outlets, deployed armies of salespeople, developed and marketed broad ranges of animal by-products, and subdivided a mostly unskilled labor force in massive, multispecies packing establishments. Collectively keeping labor costs low and pricing their goods on the basis of average costs rather than supply and demand, they dominated the industry through the 1940s.

After *World War II, the advantage shifted to three upstart firms (Con-Agra, Excell, and especially Iowa Beef Processors) that challenged the older rail- and river-connected packing centers and slaughtered 70 percent of the nation's cattle by 1989. These companies deployed new technologies to eliminate skilled labor, advance the industry's legendary specialization of tasks, and increase *productivity. They built single-species plants closer to livestock supplies and revolutionized the meat trade by trimming red meats to retail specifications within their slaughterhouses and selling the resulting "boxed beef" directly to grocery stores and supermarkets. They undertook an effective campaign against established wage standards, reduced plant safety, sped up production, and recruited nonunion workers from rural areas in the United States, Latin America, and Asia. As the twentieth century ended, the meatpacking and meat-processing industry remained one of the nation's leading employers, important to the economies of Midwestern and Mid-Atlantic states as well as Texas and *California.

Upton *Sinclair's *The *Jungle* (1906), an exposé of labor exploitation and unsanitary conditions in the meatpacking industry, had led to stricter federal regulation. The industry continued, however, to be plagued by charges of labor exploitation, noxious conditions, workplace danger, nutritional risk, and environmental damage.

[*See also* Agriculture; Immigrant Labor; Labor Markets; Livestock Industry; Mass Marketing; Pure Food and Drug Act; Refrigeration and Air Conditioning; Swift, Gustavus.]

• Jimmy Skaggs, *Prime Cut: Livestock Raising and Meatpacking in the United States,* 1986. Roger Horowitz, *"Negro and White, Unite and Fight": A Social History of Industrial Unionism in Meatpacking, 1930–1960,* 1997.

—Paul Street

MEDICAL EDUCATION. Medical education in colonial and antebellum America typically involved individual apprentices laboring under older doctors. These apprenticeships varied widely in length and quality, while always emphasizing practical experience. Those with the desire and the resources could pursue more formal training in a European medical school, but most American doctors remained content with domestic education.

The advantages of some form of institutional medical training, particularly as a means of imparting formal scientific knowledge, encouraged the growth of medical schools along the proprietary (physician-owned) model. These schools, which were self-governing even when associated with universities, functioned as a supplement to apprenticeship. Although most taught so-called regular medicine, homeopathic, eclectic, and other sectarian physicians also established medical schools. A few medical schools offered training to blacks and women. The number of medical schools burgeoned in the late nineteenth century, leading to a rapid increase in physician supply.

The establishment of the Johns Hopkins Medical School in Baltimore in 1893 provided a new model. This institution was from the beginning integrated into the Johns Hopkins University. It emphasized research and established high standards for admission and graduation. Concern about the quality of medical education in America had been growing during the late 1800s. Issues of clinical quality, social position, financial gain, licensing, and research opportunities led medical reformers to call for fewer and more rigorous schools. This movement, well established by the early 1900s, received validation in the *Flexner Report of 1910. Abraham Flexner, an educator from Louisville, Kentucky, had been hired by the *Carnegie Foundation for the Advancement of Teaching to survey medical education in the United States and Canada. He used his report to praise the Hopkins model, and later, as an official at the Rockefeller Foundation philanthropies, funneled resources to institutions adhering to that model.

The number of medical schools in America fell rapidly as the Hopkins model became dominant. Standards rose across the board, but the number of women and *African Americans entering medical school declined sharply. The Hopkins model remains the dominant paradigm of medical education in America. By the 1930s, medical schools were becoming heavily involved in postgraduate education, with the establishment of hospital internships and residency programs. Initially utilized by only a few practitioners, these programs soon became a required extension of medical training.

The rapid expansion in federal funding for scientific research after *World War II proved a bonanza for medical faculties, as did the growth of federal spending for health care associated with the *Medicare and Medicaid legislation of 1965 and the introduction of many new modes of treatment. The cost of medical education and health care, however, soared to prohibitive levels as the twentieth century wore on. As state and federal governments adopted ever more stringent cost-containment measures, medical schools found themselves tightly strapped. At the same time, more women and minorities began to enter medicine, and concern grew over the grueling and sometimes dehumanizing nature of medical training.

In 1997, the nation's 125 medical schools awarded 16,000 M.D. degrees. Medical education in the 1990s enjoyed access to advanced technologies, but faced ever greater challenges. Money continued to be tight, while crises such as the *acquired immunodeficiency syndrome (AIDS) epidemic and the debate over genetic technologies embroiled medical schools in troubling and complicated issues. Pressures to compete with private-sector health providers caused many schools to place their *hospitals and clinics at least partially under commercial control, and criticism of the exhausting demands placed on medical students and residents continued. American medical education left the twentieth century as it had entered it—worried and apprehensive on the one hand, but excited and hopeful on the other.

[*See also* Biological Sciences; Biotechnology Industry; Education: The Rise of the University; Medicine; Philanthropy and Philanthropic Foundations.]

• Abraham Flexner, *Medical Education in the United States and Canada: A Report to the Carnegie Foundation for the Advancement of Teaching,* 1910. E. Richard Brown, *Rockefeller Medicine Men: Medicine and Capitalism in America,* 1979. Ronald L. Numbers, ed., *The Education of American Physicians: Historical Essays,* 1979. Kenneth M. Ludmerer, *Learning to Heal: The Development of American Medical Education,* 1985. Thomas N. Bonner, *Becoming a Physician: Medical Education in Britain, Germany, France, and the United States, 1750–1945,* 1995. Kenneth M. Ludmerer, *Time to Heal: American Medical Education in the 20th Century,* 1999.

—Robert Oliver

MEDICARE AND MEDICAID. On 31 July 1965, at the Truman Library in Independence, Missouri, President Lyndon B. *Johnson signed the Medicare and Medicaid Bill into law. The site was chosen to honor former president Harry S. *Truman, who had supported national *health insurance during his presidency. The date of the signing anticipated by only two weeks the thirtieth anniversary of the 1935 *Social Security Act, to which Medicare was attached.

The new law contained three parts that had been put together a year earlier by the House Ways and Means Committee chairman, Wilbur Mills, an Arkansas Democrat. The first part, Medicare, expanded the Social Security Act's old-age pension program. Through wage deductions, employees would contribute to a Medicare trust fund. At retirement, those eligible for *Social Security benefits would also receive coverage for *hospital care, some surgical care, and nursing-home reimbursements. The original law specified 120 days of hospital benefits and 120 days of nursing-home follow-up benefits. The Medicare program also included general revenue funds for hospital construction, diagnostic equipment purchase, and grants to teaching hospitals for *medical education.

A second part of the 1965 law, called Part B, covered visits to physicians. This option had to be selected by eligible individuals on retirement. If this option were chosen, deductions were made from the recipient's monthly Social Security checks. Part B originated as the *American Medical Association's (AMA) alternative to Medicare, called Eldercare, which Mills had streamlined and turned into an optional addition to Medicare.

The third part of the bill, Medicaid, funded from general tax revenue, provided health care for the needy poor and others. Administered by the individual states, Medicaid covered a broad range of people, including welfare recipients, persons who were blind or disabled, and low-income elderly citizens who did not qualify for Social Security or whose Medicare benefits had run out. The Medicaid idea had originated in the early 1960s as a Republican alternative to the Johnson administration's push for a compulsory health-insurance plan.

The enactment of Medicare and Medicaid in 1965 culminated three decades of political controversy. Agitation for federal (as opposed to state) health-care coverage arose with the passage of the 1935 Social Security Act, which left out any provision for health insurance. Repeated failures over the next two decades to establish a comprehensive national health-insurance plan, in large part because of fierce opposition by the AMA, led reformers to try for more limited plans covering the neediest groups. In 1957, advocates of health insurance for the elderly enlisted the support of Representative Aime Forand (Dem.-R.I.), but the resulting Forand Bill, the direct ancestor of Medicare, failed to win passage. In 1960, President John F. *Kennedy made Medicare part of his national agenda. Representative Cecil King (Dem.-Calif.) and Senator Clinton Anderson (Dem.-N. Mex.) sponsored the bill in Congress. After a number of hearings in the House and Senate—and the Democratic landslide in the 1964 elections—Medicare became President Johnson's top priority.

In the years after 1965, Medicare and Medicaid were modified periodically by Congress in an effort to control escalating costs. Changes in 1971 and 1974 instituted a review of standards and costs and tried to eliminate duplication of equipment and hospitals. Revisions in 1983 standardized charges for medical procedures. Both state and federal agencies waged a continual battle to control fraud and abuse in the system. In the 1980s health-care discussion turned to the long-term needs of the elderly, coverage for medical catastrophes, and ways to preserve the Medicare system when the large baby-boomer cohort of the population reached retirement age. *Health maintenance organizations (HMOs), introduced by the private sector after being enabled by legislation passed by Congress in 1973 as a way to control rising costs, were subsequently included as an option for Medicare and Medicaid recipients. At the end of the century, debate focused on ways to cover the approximately forty-four million uninsured Americans and to provide reimbursement to Medicare recipients for expensive pharmaceuticals.

[*See also* Great Society; Medicine: From the 1870s to 1945; Medicine: Since 1945; New Deal Era, The; Welfare, Federal.]

• Richard Harris, *A Sacred Trust,* 1966. Theodore Marmor, *The Politics of Medicare,* 1970. Robert J. Myers, *Medicare,* 1970. Robert Stevens and Rosemary Stevens, *Welfare Medicine in America: A Case Study of Medicaid,* 1974. Sheri I. David, *With Dignity: The Search for Medicare and Medicaid,* 1985. Edward Berkowitz, *America's Welfare State: From Roosevelt to Reagan,* 1991.

—Sheri I. David

MEDICINE

MEDICINE: OVERVIEW

For centuries, sick and injured Americans typically received their medical care at home, either from family members or informally trained healers. The first permanent hospital did not open until 1751; the first medical school in 1765. The medical profession remained weak and divided; even the creation of the *American Medical Association in 1847 did little to help. The half-century spanning the years 1875 to 1925 brought revolutionary changes to American medicine. The germ theory of *disease led to the availability of new diagnostic and therapeutic procedures, such as *diphtheria antitoxin (1894). The locus of practice shifted from home to hospital as the number of general *hospitals mushroomed from no more than 150 in 1875 to nearly 7,000 50 years later. Medical practice, heretofore virtually unregulated, became subject to licensing laws. With the new Johns Hopkins Medical School (1893) leading the way, *medical education improved dramatically.

In one of the most significant developments in all of American history, *life expectancy at birth increased from under thirty years at the time of the *Revolutionary War to about seventy-seven years in 2000. Surprisingly, before the mid-twentieth century, when antibiotics became available, therapeutic medicine contributed little to this improvement. The great killers of nineteenth-century Americans—infectious diseases such as *tuberculosis, *influenza, and pneumonia—were declining for decades before physicians discovered effective ways to treat or prevent them. Of greater importance were *public-health measures such as improved sanitation, purified water, and compulsory *smallpox vaccinations for children. Better *food, *housing, and personal hygiene also helped reduce mortality rates.

—Ronald L. Numbers

MEDICINE: COLONIAL ERA

For all the grievances against Great Britain enumerated in the *Declaration of Independence, the American revolutionaries offered no evidence that imperial regulations had inhibited colonial medical practice. This simple fact of noninterference is important for a general understanding of health care in colonial America. Indeed, during the *Colonial Era, perhaps fewer than 20 percent of all identified medical practitioners were immigrants. Of these, most came from provincial England, where the regulatory powers of London's medical guilds, such as the Royal College of Physicians, were relatively weak. Few were college or medical-school graduates, although many had gained experience by serving apprenticeships or working as surgeons in the military or on passenger and cargo vessels. Of the vast majority of colonial medical practitioners who were native-born, most had no formal training; those who did typically served an apprenticeship, averaging little more than a year, with an established doctor. The first American medical school did not open its doors until 1765 in *Philadelphia.

A diversity of Old World medical practices and healing traditions, including self-medication, formed an important part of the cultural baggage colonists brought to America. The absence of effective regulation assured the continuation of such diversity. As in provincial England, the American landscape abounded in general practitioners, herbalists, minister-physicians, and innumerable self-taught itinerants who offered their services as dentists, bone-setters, and fever doctors. Given the high colonial birthrate, female midwives modestly prospered until the eighteenth century, when male physicians became competitors in larger communities. Medical services were usually delivered at the patient's residence rather than in an office or *hospital. Although poorhouses and workhouses occasionally cared for the sick, the first permanent hospital did not open until 1751, again in Philadelphia. The evidence suggests that these colonial healers exercised considerable independent judgment and avoided dogmatic adherence to such practices as vigorous bloodletting, purging, or the administration of highly active drugs. Healers included some Native American herbal remedies among their generally imported armamentarium.

With the notable exceptions of African-American slaves and the very poor, colonial Americans generally enjoyed better health and greater longevity than their English counterparts. Their most common complaints included injuries, dysentery, common colds, and ague or *malaria. Periodic epidemics of measles, *diphtheria, and *smallpox afflicted European and Native Americans alike.

The most important *public-health development of the Colonial Era occurred in connection with a smallpox epidemic that struck *New England in 1721. To combat the epidemic in *Boston, the Reverend Cotton *Mather enlisted Dr. Zabdiel Boylston in a pioneering effort to inoculate volunteers with the live smallpox virum. Despite considerable medical opposition, led by the town's only school-trained physician, William Douglass, the risky experiment saved many lives. Douglass himself became a convert and in 1730 helped to organize the first colonial medical guild, the Boston Medical Society, which collectively endorsed smallpox inoculation. During the *Revolutionary War this practice was employed successfully by the medical corps of the Continental Army.

Efforts by colonial legislatures to regulate medical practice began as early as the 1640s in Massachusetts. In the later Colonial Era, one finds in the larger colonial cities a growing professionalism, manifested especially in the formation of medical societies. Perhaps the epitome of the colonial surgeon was Dr. Silvester Gardiner (1708–1786) of Boston. A colonial-trained apprentice, Gardiner studied with surgical luminaries in Paris and London, and in Boston compiled an impressive record in lithotomy (removal of stones, or urinary calculi, in the bladder), and in general *surgery. In 1741, before the Boston Medical Society, Gardiner successfully removed a large stone from a six-year-old boy. To combat the improper dispensing of drugs, Gardiner also established apothecary shops in Boston as well as in Meriden and Hartford, Connecticut.

In general, however, licensing laws and the move toward professionalization had little effect on the practice of medicine throughout the colonial period. Local medical societies, though more numerous than in provincial England, proved ineffective as regulatory agencies. The experience of medical practitioners in the Revolutionary War would inspire the creation of various state medical societies, but on the eve of independence, the estimated 3,500 medical practitioners in the American colonies were little regulated and enjoyed few legal protections against the encroachment of ill-trained interlopers or quacks. More than a century would pass before these problems were solved. Nevertheless, Dr. Benjamin *Rush of Philadelphia, a signer of the Declaration of Independence, saw the Revolution as a foundational event in the exuberant, patriotic process of creating an American medical profession.

[*See also* Demography; Dentistry; Disease; Health and Fitness; Indian History and Culture: From 1500 to 1800; Midwifery; Slavery: Slave Families, Community, and Culture.]

• John Duffy, *Epidemics in Colonial America*, 1953. Philip Cash, *Medical Men at the Siege of Boston, April 1775–April 1776*, 1973. Whitfield J. Bell Jr., *The Colonial Physician and Other Essays*, 1975. Jane B. Donegan, *Women and Men Midwives: Medicine, Morality and Misogyny*, 1978. J. Worth Estes, "Therapeutic Practice in Colonial New England," in *Medicine in Colonial Massachusetts, 1620–1820*, eds. Philip Cash, Eric H. Christianson, and J. Worth Estes, 1980, pp. 289–383. Eric H. Christianson, "Medicine in New England," in *Medicine in the New World: New Spain, New France, and New England*, ed. Ronald L. Numbers, 1987, pp. 102–53. Laurel Thatcher Ulrich, *A Midwife's Tale: The Life of Martha Ballard, Based on Her Diary, 1785–1812*, 1990.

—Eric Howard Christianson

MEDICINE: FROM 1776 TO THE 1870s

Of about 3,500 physicians in America at the time of the *Revolutionary War, only one in ten held an M.D. degree. The establishment during the 1760s of the first medical schools, societies, and licensing laws had encouraged a growing sense of corporate identity. Yet male physicians played a modest role in the medical care of sick Americans, who more frequently turned to midwives and other women healers and to herbalists, bone-setters, nostrum vendors, and domestic medical guidebooks.

During the early decades of the republic, expanding medical institutions sustained a new, confident professionalism. The organization of local and state medical societies—which adopted ethical codes and fixed fee scales—helped regularly trained physicians distinguish themselves from other healers, a move state legislatures reinforced by placing licensing power in the hands of the societies. Apprenticeship, sometimes supplemented by lectures, remained the core of *medical education. Harvard (1783) and Dartmouth (1798) joined existing medical schools in *Philadelphia and *New York City, while an elite continued to study in London and Edinburgh. Starting in the 1810s, medical schools proliferated rapidly—twenty-six were founded between 1810 and 1840, and another forty-seven by 1877. Most were proprietary ventures, run by the professors for profit. Typically the student attended lectures for four months, duplicating in the second year the courses attended during the first. Keen competition for paying pupils kept requirements low.

Although Americans insisted that European precepts were often unsuited to New World practice, their understanding of *disease was strongly informed by the theoretically elaborate, rationalistic systems of eighteenth-century British medicine. University of Pennsylvania professor Benjamin *Rush, who received his M.D. in Edinburgh, was in the late eighteenth century the most influential medical teacher in America, and his theories promoted the so-called "heroic" therapeutics that dominated American practice through the 1830s. Disease in Rush's scheme was essentially an overexcited condition remedied by aggressively depleting the body by bloodletting and mineral purgatives such as calomel (mercurous chloride). If depletion was sometimes practiced by rote, physicians nonetheless argued that treatment should be individuated to patients and environments, an attitude that promoted investigations of the relationships among topography, climate, and disease.

From the 1820s through the 1860s, Americans who traveled to Europe for medical study favored the *hospitals of Paris, which offered unrivaled access to the body, living and dead. These physicians returned committed to grounding medicine on empirical observation and *symptom-lesion* correlation—that is, tracing the symptoms of disease viewed in the living patient to their underlying pathological lesions in the body's tissues revealed at autopsy. They denounced rationalistic systems, like that of Rush, and challenged heroic drugging while calling for greater trust in nature's healing powers. By midcentury, supportive and stimulative treatment was supplanting depletion.

The ideas, practices, and social pretensions of the regular profession also came under assaults from antiorthodox healers. Samuel Thomson's botanic system of domestic practice, consolidated by his *New Guide to Health* (1822), gained a large following. Thomsonians attacked heroic medicine and tapped into the Jacksonian Era's egalitarian distrust of claims to privilege based on special learning. Eclecticism (a parallel botanical healing system in which professional practitioners supplanted self-help), hydropathy (water cure), and a wider health-reform movement flourished in the 1840s and 1850s. During the same decades homeopathy, introduced to America in 1825, became the most powerful challenge to the regular profession, boasting institutions such as the Homoeopathic Medical College of Pennsylvania (1848) and the first national medical association, the American Institute of Homoeopathy (1844). During this period the states revoked virtually all medical licensing laws, leaving American medicine the freest from regulation in the western world.

It was in this *laissez-faire context that a movement toward orthodoxy arose. In 1847 the *American Medical Association (AMA) was founded, partly to promote educational reforms but chiefly to establish a unified front and demarcate the orthodox faithful. The association initially exerted little political influence, but its code of ethics was a culturally powerful device to enforce orthodoxy by forbidding members to associate professionally with practitioners the AMA derisively called "sectarians."

The absence of state regulation facilitated women's access to M.D. degrees earlier than in any other nation. When in 1849 Elizabeth *Blackwell received an M.D. from Geneva College in upstate New York, she became the first woman anywhere to win that degree. Male opposition kept most schools closed to women. In 1850, however, the Female Medical College of Pennsylvania opened as the world's first M.D.-granting medical school entirely for women. Over the next several decades a number of other women's medical colleges (orthodox and homeopathic) opened, as did women's dispensaries and hospitals.

Hospitals in antebellum America remained chiefly charitable asylums for the sick poor. Elite physicians sought hospital appointments for access to clinical teaching, experience, and investigation; thus, at the Pennsylvania Hospital in Philadelphia, William Gerhard used his Parisian experiences as the model for the clinical instruction he offered starting in the 1830s and for research that differentiated *typhoid fever from typhus (1843). While some institutions for the mentally ill dated from the *Colonial Era, the emergence of moral treatment and the campaign that Dorothea *Dix launched in 1841 to reform the care of the insane poor fostered a host of state insane asylums created before the *Civil War.

American innovations, chiefly in *surgery, won international attention. Ephraim McDowell's 1809 operation in Kentucky for an ovarian cyst and J. Marion Sim's operation for vesicovaginal fistula, developed on slave women during the 1840s, were celebrated as exemplifying native mechanical ingenuity. William *Beaumont's experiments on the physiology of digestion—performed during the 1820s and 1830s on a patient with a gastric fistula that provided a direct opening to the stomach—also drew European notice. The most celebrated American achievement, although clouded by priority disputes, was the first public operation on a patient anesthetized with ether, an 1846 performance at the Massachusetts General Hospital in Boston during which William T. G. Morton administered the anesthetic and John Collins Warren performed the surgery.

The state, little involved in regulating the medical profession, also had meager involvement in *public health. *Cholera and *yellow fever epidemics prompted the creation of municipal boards of health to orchestrate sanitation (based on the belief that miasms or emanations from filth produced disease) and quarantine. But through the mid–nineteenth century, such activities were temporary. The Civil War did not transform medicine, but the organizational skills and commitments on display in the U.S. Sanitary Commission (1861) raised expectations of state responsibility for public health. In 1869 Massachusetts established the first state board of health; by 1880, twenty such boards existed. In 1879 Congress created the National Board of Health, a short-lived but important precedent for federal involvement in public medicine.

After the war in 1868, Howard University in *Washington, D.C., established the first medical school for *African Americans. In 1871, Harvard adopted a three-year graded medical curriculum, but with diploma mills still flourishing, few other schools followed this lead. In 1873 New York's Bellevue Hospital established a *nursing school modeled after Florence Nightingale's plan, and over a dozen such institutions appeared before the end of the decade. Reflecting the elevated status of expert knowledge in *Gilded Age American culture, by the 1870s some states reinstituted medical licensing laws, usually broad enough to encompass homeopathic, eclectic, and orthodox physicians.

Although few important new therapies had arisen by the 1870s, some doctors were looking to the experimental laboratory as the wellspring of therapeutic progress. Americans studying abroad shifted to German laboratories and clinics, and in 1871 Henry Pickering Bowditch returned from Leipzig to set up at Harvard the nation's first laboratory for experimental physiology and to occupy the first full-time post in physiology. The most dramatic early post–Civil War change in American medical practice was the rise of specialization, patterned after German models. Ophthalmologists formed their own society in 1864; otologists (who specialized in diseases of the ear) in 1868. During the 1870s such specialty societies proliferated, testimony both to social reality and to the public's esteem for specialization as a hallmark of the emerging medical order.

[*See also* Mental Illness; Professionalization.]

• William G. Rothstein, *American Physicians in the Nineteenth Century,* 1972, reprint 1992. Paul Starr, *The Social Transformation of American Medicine,* 1982. Regina Markell Morantz-Sanchez, *Sympathy and Science: Women Physicians in American Medicine,* 1985. John Harley Warner, *The Therapeutic Perspective: Medical Practice, Knowledge, and Identity in America, 1820–1885,* 1986; reprint 1997. Charles E. Rosenberg, *The Care of Strangers: The Rise of America's Hospital System,* 1987, reprint 1995. John Duffy, *The Sanitarians: A History of American Public Health,* 1990. Gerald N. Grob, *The Mad among Us: A History of the Care of America's Mentally Ill,* 1994. Judith Walzer Leavitt and Ronald L. Numbers, eds., *Sickness and Health in America: Readings in the History of Medicine and Public Health,* 3d ed., 1997. John Harley Warner, *Against the Spirit of Systems: The French Impulse in Nineteenth-Century American Medicine,* 1998.

—John Harley Warner

MEDICINE: FROM THE 1870s TO 1945

In 1876, American physicians gathered in *Philadelphia to survey the nation's first hundred years of medical progress. A parade of speakers celebrated the introduction of anesthesia and antisepsis in *surgery, the use of new chemical discoveries to treat fever, and the profession's growing knowledge of *disease, grounded in the pathological and microscopical research of the previous fifty years. America's special genius, they suggested, lay in applying these European accomplishments. Laboratory studies shed new light on the workings of blood and bodily chemistry, while American sanitary institutions contained the once dreaded *cholera when it had last arrived in 1866 and 1873. At the same time, speakers warned, American *medical education remained in a parlous state, while sanitary reform lacked the public support it deserved. Nor, they might have added, did physicians get the material rewards and respect they sought.

The next seventy years witnessed unprecedented improvements in the social and economic status of U.S. physicians, in medical knowledge about the causes of specific diseases, and in *life expectancy. *Hospitals were transformed from refuges for the urban poor to surgeons' workshops patronized by the middle and working classes. Bacteriologists identified the causes of the major infectious diseases, though control over viral diseases eluded them. But if physicians gained new frameworks for understanding disease from the laboratory, they clung to their caste's prejudices in making sense of their society: categories of race and *gender figured prominently in medical thought and action. Meanwhile, both professional and social progress were unevenly distributed. Specialists and urban practitioners earned far more than their rural counterparts, while sanitary improvements only slowly reached working-class, rural, immigrant, and *African-American citizens. Nonetheless, medicine's scientific and institutional accomplishments engendered a belief in progress that neither social inequality nor injustice could refute.

Science, Disease, and Public Health. In 1882, the German physician Robert Koch (1843–1910) demonstrated that *tuberculosis, probably the leading cause of death in western Europe and the United States, was caused by a living microorganism, the tubercle bacillus. More important, he laid down a set of procedures (Koch's postulates) for researchers to follow in determining the bacterial causes of specific diseases. By 1906, European researchers had identified the microorganisms responsible for *typhoid fever (1880–1884), *diphtheria (1883), cholera (1884), gonorrhea (1885), pneumonia (1886), tetanus (1889), plague (1894), dysentery (1898), and syphilis (1905). Americans doctors like William H. *Welch and Frederick Novy (1864–1957) traveled to Europe to train in the new bacteriological techniques. American companies, quick to realize the commercial potential of the new "germ" theories, marketed disinfectants like Listerine and Radam's Microbe Killer. Bacteriological concepts held less appeal for medical practitioners, who continued to view disease as a complex interaction among the "constitution" of individual patients, the susceptibility of particular "racial" groups, and exposure to specific bacteria.

Although physicians who were trained after 1890 increasingly viewed infectious diseases as caused by specific microorganisms, the new science failed to fulfill its early therapeutic promise. Although diphtheria antitoxin (1894) rescued thousands from a disease that had routinely killed a quarter of those infected, subsequent vaccines and antisera proved far less effective, as did chemical anti-infectives prior to the introduction of sulfa drugs in the 1930s. Many practitioners avoided innovative treatments with dangerous side effects, such as pneumonia serum or Paul Ehrlich's salvarsan, a celebrated antisyphilis drug. Nowhere was medicine's therapeutic impotence more vividly demonstrated than in the viral epidemics of *poliomyelitis, which in 1916 killed 2,400 children in *New York City alone, and *influenza, which killed more than 315,000 Americans in 1918–1919, many of them young adults.

In contrast to medical practitioners, *public-health departments readily embraced the new bacteriological science. New York City's public-health laboratory, opened in 1892, was but the first to adopt routine bacteriological testing. By 1906, health officer Charles V. Chapin of Providence, Rhode Island, could write disparagingly of the "fetich [*sic*] of disinfection" that had led earlier sanitarians to emphasize the removal of offensive but innocuous urban nuisances. Stop worrying about rotting vegetables and "sewer gas," Chapin advocated, and instead block the specific infection path of each disease-causing organism: for *yellow fever, kill the mosquito; for typhoid, purify water, milk, and food.

Chapin's advice fit well with the *Progressive Era's "social-engineering" ethos, which sought to put all social reforms on a "scientific" basis. By *World War I, Chapin and others increasingly emphasized the importance of personal habits in stopping infectious disease. Scientific policing of water and food supplies could do little, they argued, if housewives did not wash their hands and refrigerate their milk. Sanitary fairs, public-health "propaganda," and school-hygiene campaigns joined other contemporary efforts aimed at the "Americanization" of immigrants and the "modernization" of the poor. Forced testing of prostitutes for *venereal disease marked another area where new science sanctioned existing middle-class mores.

Long before the germ theory's triumph, urban reformers had championed purified water systems and underground sewers for waste disposal. In the closing decades of the nineteenth century, death rates for waterborne diseases like typhoid fever plummeted in cities adopting these reforms. Not everyone benefited: Residents of Pittsburgh's low-lying, working-class districts experienced five to six times the typhoid mortality of middle-class districts. African Americans living in Kansas City, Cincinnati, and Indianapolis between 1910 and 1920 had typhoid mortality rates two to four times those of whites in the same cities. Regional variations compounded those of race and class. Despite northern-led campaigns against hookworm and pellagra, most rural counties in the *South remained without full-time health officers until Franklin Delano *Roosevelt's New Deal. As late as 1940, the heavily rural and African-American states of South Carolina, Georgia, and Alabama reported some of the nation's highest rates of typhoid and enteritis mortality. Local initiatives sometimes countered the effects of regional *poverty and prejudice. African-American women in Atlanta, Georgia, and Salisbury, North Carolina, for example, launched antituberculosis campaigns that reached across racial lines, as did North Carolina's dynamic public-health department, led by Watson S. Rankin (1879–1970).

Between 1900 and 1930, American life expectancy at birth climbed from 47.3 to 59.7 years. Many observers concluded that infectious diseases were "conquered," despite continued deaths from tuberculosis, pneumonia, and syphilis. By 1920, medical researchers were turning their attention to the detailed workings of the body's "chemical machinery," the chemical reactions that regulate nutrition and excretion, growth and reproduction, activity and rest. Biochemists like the University of

Wisconsin's Conrad A. Elvehjem (1901–1962) and Johns Hopkins University's Elmer V. McCollum (1879–1967) discovered numerous vitamins, while other researchers studied "metabolic pathways," the chemical reactions that govern the body's use of carbohydrates, proteins, and electrolytes. Apart from the discovery of insulin in 1922, however, this added knowledge had little impact on everyday medical practice. Vitamins nonetheless became the best-selling drug products of the 1930s, while numerous urban practitioners measured the "basic metabolic rate" of middle-class women, to identify the causes of their irritability, anxiety, and fatigue. Here again, new science underwrote existing social beliefs.

Political Economy of Medical Practice. In 1870, some 64,000 physicians were practicing in the United States. For the majority, economic security was uncertain at best. Much illness was self-treated; for the rest, physicians faced competition from midwives, lay healers, and patent-medicine vendors. In rural Wisconsin, for example, three-quarters of all physicians had to supplement their medical earnings by farming, teaching, or operating small businesses. In metropolitan centers such as New York or Philadelphia, a handful of physicians succeeded by offering postgraduate hospital training that gave them opportunities both to teach and to cultivate the socially prominent benefactors of the city's charitable hospitals. Yet even well-connected young physicians could fail. John Sedgwick Billings, son of one of the country's most prominent physicians, ended his career where it began, as an employee of New York City's health department, after several unsuccessful efforts to build a private practice.

Most physicians in 1870 had been trained through an apprenticeship, supplemented by up to two years of study at a medical college. Virtually any group of physicians could start a medical college. From midcentury, medical leaders sought to raise standards of medical training, and with it practitioners' social and economic status. Success came in the early twentieth century, when Abraham Flexner's *Medical Education in the United States and Canada: A Report to the Carnegie Foundation for the Advancement of Teaching* (1910) capped educational reforms begun by the *American Medical Association. Flexner (1866–1959), a lay educator, called for the closure of 124 of the country's 155 medical schools as either redundant, inadequately staffed and equipped, or lax in their entrance requirements. By 1920 only eighty-five schools remained. (Of these, only two were dedicated to training African-American physicians and one to training women.)

After 1900, new physicians increasingly opted to practice in larger cities, especially in the newly emerging downtown business districts. Doctors' preferences for urban, wealthy communities paid off. By 1928, physicians' mean annual income ($9,000) put them above all but 1 percent of the population. Doctors were overwhelmingly white, native-born males at a time when 11 percent of the population were immigrants, nearly 10 percent were African Americans, and 49 percent were women.

Sharing the prejudices of their class and gender, physicians endorsed public-health policies that held immigrants and African Americans responsible for spreading infectious disease, and attempted to regulate sexual and reproductive behavior through educational campaigns and, at times, the active sterilization of poor women.

Most physicians worked in solo "private" practice. Like other small business owners, they fared badly in the Great Depression of the 1930s, with average net annual incomes declining nearly two thousand dollars. Specialty practice was one means to make good: From 1930 on, a majority of medical-school graduates eventually became specialists.

*Surgery was among the first of the full-time specialties. The advent of antiseptic and then aseptic surgery in the late nineteenth century enabled surgeons safely to perform intra-abdominal surgery on a routine basis. Operations like appendectomies flourished, as hospitals became the preferred surgical sites for surgeons and middle-class patients alike. By 1928, 74 percent of admissions to Philadelphia's hospitals were surgical or obstetrical.

Social as well as technical innovations engendered the modern hospital. Religious groups—Protestant, Catholic, and Jewish—founded hospitals, as did small-town doctors who saw the advantages in hospitalizing patients. Hospitals not only provided surgeons with operating rooms, x-ray equipment, and diagnostic laboratories, but with nurses to care for patients. By 1939, more than half of the nation's babies were being delivered in hospitals, as obstetricians (and their patients) followed surgeons into the hospital.

As with sanitary reforms, use of the new hospitals varied by class, race, and place. Only one-quarter of African-American women gave birth in-hospital in 1939; a decade earlier, families earning over $5,000 had more than twice the number of tonsillectomies per capita as families with incomes under $1,200, while rural families of all incomes had surgery at rates well below those of city dwellers.

Much health care remained outside the orbit of the new, "scientific" medicine. In the 1930s, roughly 20 percent of "medical care" expenditures went for patent medicines and medical supplies, while another 8 to 10 percent went to midwives, chiropractors, and other practitioners condemned by orthodox physicians. In most years, Americans spent at least as much on funeral expenses as on hospitals.

From many perspectives, American medicine in 1945 had little in common with that of 1870. Discoveries in bacteriology, the reform of medical education, the rise of medical specialization, advances in surgery and public health, and the emergence of the modern hospital all contributed to the transformation. Yet the rewards of modernity were distributed along well-established lines of place, race, class, and gender.

[*See also* Biological Sciences; Childbirth; Death and Dying; Depressions, Economic; Eugenics; Flexner Report; Health and Fitness; Medicine: Alternative Medicine; Nursing; Professionalization; Prostitution and Antiprostitution; Social Class.]

• Barbara Gutman Rosenkrantz, *Public Health and the State: Changing Views in Massachusetts, 1842–1936,* 1972. George Rosen, *Preventive Medicine in the U.S., 1900–1975: Trends and Interpretations,* 1975. Harry F. Dowling, *Fighting Infection: Conquests of the Twentieth Century,* 1977. Paul Starr, *The Social Transformation of American Medicine,* 1982. Regina Markell Morantz-Sanchez, *Sympathy and Science: Women Physicians in American Medicine,* 1985. John Harley Warner, *The Therapeutic Perspective: Medical Practice, Knowledge, and Identity in America, 1820–1885,* 1986. Edward H. Beardsley, *A History of Neglect: Health Care for Blacks and Mill Workers in the Twentieth-Century South,* 1987. Allan M. Brandt, *No Magic Bullet: A Social History of Venereal Disease in the United States since 1880,* expanded ed., 1987. William G. Rothstein, *American Medical Schools and the Practice of Medicine: A History,* 1987. Rosemary Stevens, *In Sickness and in Wealth: American Hospitals in the Twentieth Century,* 1989.

—Harry M. Marks

MEDICINE: SINCE 1945

In the second half of the twentieth century, American medicine was characterized by unprecedented technological progress and profound social disagreements over how medical care should be organized, financed, and regulated. In the years from *World War II through the mid-1960s, widely publicized technological developments encouraged expansive optimism about what *science and *technology could ultimately do for the health of Americans. After the later 1960s, skepticism about the fruits of medical science and technology dominated public discussions, just as researchers finally began to realize their ambitions of re-engineering the human machine.

A similar chronological divide marks contrasting approaches to financing medical services. Between 1945 and 1965, middle- and working-class Americans looked to employment-based, private *health insurance to secure access to medical care, while the federal government's role was largely restricted to infrastructural investments in hospital facilities and medical research. After 1965, Washington's role in financing health-care markets expanded elevenfold, from three cents of every dollar spent in 1965 to thirty-three cents in 1995. The ensuing ideological debates over the government's regulatory and budgetary role in health care largely eclipsed the more basic question of whether any one party could or should control the nation's highly decentralized $879 billion health economy.

The Early Postwar Era. In the immediate aftermath of World War II, American physicians attempted to assimilate the legacy of war medicine. For some, the war experience offered new models of medical care and research. In July 1945, more than one in four American physicians was serving in the military. War medicine encouraged specialization, the delegation of tasks to nurses and technicians, and a hierarchical model of medical organization, with academic consultants and *hospitals at the pinnacle. Such a system, postwar planners argued, had delivered wartime medical innovations in an efficient, organized way. Rather than returning to the isolated conditions of individual general practice, planners insisted, physicians should work in groups, supported by modern, well-equipped hospitals.

Although prewar trends toward specialization continued (three-fourths of 1945 medical graduates entered specialty practices), the lucrative private-practice model remained strong. In 1965, only 10 percent of U.S. physicians worked in group practices.

Development of the regional medical centers envisioned by postwar planners proved similarly slow. Although the number of cottage hospitals (under twenty-five beds) declined after the war, the supply of small community hospitals of between twenty-five and one hundred beds increased, abetted by federal subsidies designed to distribute hospitals more widely. Overall per capita use of hospitals doubled between 1945 and 1975. By 1960, nearly all (white) women delivered their babies in hospitals.

Patients financed their increased use of hospital and medical services through private health insurance, medical opposition having defeated successive initiatives for publicly financed insurance. Court rulings in 1949 making health insurance benefits a legitimate subject for collective bargaining accelerated the growth of private, employment-linked health insurance. Middle-class and unionized workers especially benefited from this development. By 1956, more than 116 million Americans had some health insurance, but the private, job-based system meant that rural, poor, and black citizens were less likely to be insured, and thus they saw doctors and stayed in hospitals less often.

A series of innovations making *surgery easier and safer fueled increased hospital use. Intravenously administered fluids that mimicked the blood's chemical makeup and volume minimized postsurgical shock. Penicillin, the product of a publicly financed World War II crash program, was the first of many new antibiotics for controlling postsurgical infection. Intensive-care units, the symbol of high-technology medicine, were standard features of U.S. hospitals by 1970. Publicists promoting magazine sales, drugs, and medical charities spread awareness of these life-saving innovations, ushering in what historian John Burnham has termed the "golden age" of American medicine.

Penicillin aside, the best-known medical triumph of this era was Jonas *Salk's *poliomyelitis vaccine, publicized in a 1954 field test involving nearly two million school children. Although the media hailed Salk, his scientific colleagues, while acknowledging his technical skill and dedication, deemed his contribution less significant than that of John Enders, Thomas Weller, and Frederick Robbins, who received the 1954 Nobel Prize in medicine for developing the underlying technique of cultivating poliovirus in tissue culture.

The Salk episode points to a divide between medical scientists and the lay public regarding the means, if not the aims, of medical research. The most significant research in the *biological sciences in the 1950s and 1960s, which studied the structure and operations of the cell, was remote from "practical" results and everyday medical concerns. Those who sought immediate relief from suffering emphasized organized research programs targeting specific diseases. In their quest for new antibiotic and anticancer therapies, researchers built on the wartime model of screening for antimalarial drugs. Laboratory researchers following standardized protocols systematically tested thousands of substances to see what microorganisms they killed, or which tumors they might inhibit.

Methodic and resource-intensive, such research helped produce the antibiotics streptomycin (1944), chloramphenicol (1947), aureomycin (1948), neomycin (1949), and terramycin (1950). The National Cancer Institute's (NCI) search for anticancer drugs adopted a similar screening model but produced fewer tangible results. University scientists argued that such narrowly targeted research lacked imagination and could not produce the deeper understanding of *disease essential to its eventual control. American Cancer Society publicists drew a different lesson: The NCI program was not practical enough. New drugs needed to be tested in human beings, not test tubes.

Until the late 1960s, Congress generally sided with basic science, allowing university scientists to determine where federal funds should be spent, while rejecting proposals that medical research dollars be distributed broadly, like agricultural research support or highway construction funds. Between 1945 and 1960, as annual congressional funding for the *National Institutes of Health (NIH) increased from $2.8 million to $300 million, NIH's administrators convinced Congress that long-term investment in basic research would ultimately bring better health.

To demographers, who measure improvements in health by increases in *life expectancy, progress after midcentury seemed almost imperceptible. But most citizens, and many physicians, measured postwar medical progress by its more tangible technological accomplishments: the penicillin shot that saved an elderly person from death by pneumonia or painlessly cured syphilis; the polio vaccine that allowed children to swim in the community pool without fear of paralysis or death. In the 1950s, only a few medical specialists gave much attention to the fact that the widespread use of antibiotics gave rise to antibiotic-resistant pathogens, that the sexual behaviors that transmitted syphilis remained unaltered by penicillin, or that the risks of death from polio were small compared to other childhood hazards. Even the rising mortality rates from *heart disease and *cancer seemed a problem that more science and improved medical-care delivery arrangements would resolve.

Government and Markets: Health Care, 1965–1995. Following the defeat of national health-insurance proposals in the 1940s, congressional Democratic leaders adopted a new strategy, seeking government subsidies for groups excluded from the private insurance system. Building on *New Deal-Era and wartime programs, such legislation extended federal support to state governments that would provide health insurance to welfare clients and other medically needy groups. This supplementation strategy culminated with the 1965 passage of Medicare, which provided health insurance for all Americans over sixty-five, and Medicaid, a cost-sharing program with the states to pay for the medical care of the poor. These two laws extended medical-care coverage to millions of underserved Americans.

To ensure the participation of doctors, hospitals, and state governments in the new programs, federal officials promised to pay for any medical care provided. They even offered special inducements, such as a 2 percent premium to participating hospitals beyond their direct operating costs. Participation mushroomed, but so did program costs. By 1975, the two programs served 47 million people at a cost of $28 billion, nearly a quarter of the nation's total health-care expenditures.

Health care remained a national problem for the rest of the century. Federal programs created new political interests in health policy. No longer solely a concern of physicians and labor unions, health-care policies affected hospitals, nursing homes, the *pharmaceutical industry, home health-care vendors, and state governments. New fault lines appeared in the political landscape: medical specialists versus primary-care physicians, teaching versus community hospitals, home care versus nursing homes, Medicare versus Medicaid recipients. The proliferation of interest groups led to a new kind of health politics, in which conventional partisan differences over such issues as "competition versus regulation" or "market versus government" were replaced by a managerial politics that emphasized administrative innovations and technocratic expertise.

By the early 1970s, policy debates focused on the explosive growth in health-care costs, from 10 to 13 percent annually. President Jimmy *Carter promoted regional health planning under which community groups would assess medical needs and limit new hospital construction. President Richard M. *Nixon first imposed wage and price controls and then supported legislation providing federal subsidies for *health maintenance organizations (HMOs) to compete with traditional fee-for-service medicine. President Ronald *Reagan attempted to limit the federal share of Medicaid expenses by administrative changes in cost-sharing formulas and eligibility rules. Following the advice of Harvard economists, President George *Bush's administration redesigned Medicare fee schedules to favor primary-care physicians over more costly specialists.

But the federal government refrained from imposing direct limits on health expenditures. Although Washington's share of total health-care costs rose to 28 percent by 1990, only the Medicare program was fully controlled by the federal government. Most federal initiatives in the 1970s and 1980s were indirect efforts to steer the health-care system away from hospital-based, specialty-oriented care (health planning and fee-schedule reform) and toward more cost-conscious organizations (such as HMOs), with the overall aim of lowering costs without compromising access to medical care. These government efforts to influence decentralized, largely private health-care markets had limited, even perverse effects. The shift from hospital and nursing-home care, for example, fueled explosive growth in the harder-to-regulate home health-care industry.

In the 1980s, public debates over soaring health-care costs became private contests over who should pay for these costs. Businesses saddled with expensive employee-benefit programs sought to shift a greater share of the premiums to employees while reducing coverage for retirees and dependents. The growing ranks of part-time workers and employees of small firms often found themselves without insurance entirely. After the defeat of President Bill *Clinton's proposal for national health insurance in 1993, cutbacks in coverage reached previously protected employees in large manufacturing firms. The greatest gaps in coverage, however, remained among the poor, *African Americans, *Hispanic Americans, and citizens of rural states such as Arkansas, Mississippi, and Texas where one in four adults lacked health insurance at the end of the twentieth century.

The postwar social contract, which had offered employers labor peace in exchange for generous benefits, eroded in the 1980s. Simultaneously, the working conditions of America's physicians changed radically. As the pattern of independent practice faded at the end of the twentieth century, roughly two in five physicians engaged in patient care were employed by a hospital or other health-care organization, and the remainder received about 40 percent of their income from managed-care organizations that oversaw the amount and kind of treatment provided. While medicine remained among the highest paid occupations, these changes caused great anxiety among physicians.

Medical Progress and Medical Care, 1960–1995. The details of health-care policy concerned most Americans less than what happened when they got sick. In this realm, the changing treatment of heart disease offers a window on medical progress. In 1960, doctors could offer relatively little for the heart-attack patient who survived long enough to reach the hospital: anticoagulants to thin blood clots and diuretics to reduce the work of the damaged heart. Coronary-artery bypass surgery became widely available by the late 1960s, accompanied by specialized wards for monitoring the recovering patient. New therapies emerged at the end of the 1970s to dissolve or remove clots in the coronary arteries, allowing many patients to avoid open-heart surgery. By the late 1980s, a broad array of drugs was available for treating the underlying conditions that bring on heart attacks, including drugs to lower cholesterol and regulate the heartbeat.

While the gains in treating heart disease were exceptional, there are few cases where medical researchers cannot point to substantial differences between the "dark ages" of the 1960s and the ever-emerging present. The return of infectious diseases in the 1980s, including new infections such as *acquired immunodeficiency syndrome (AIDS) and older infections in newer, drug-resistant forms, such as *tuberculosis and pneumonia, suggested the limits of technological progress. Although the emergence of new infections was rooted in social behaviors, including sexual practices, drug use, and the medical and commercial abuse of antibiotics, the preferred solution for medical researchers and the general public alike remained technological.

Beginning in the late 1960s, a disparate group of economists, philosophers, and *public-health advocates vocally challenged contemporary medicine's technological orientation as intrusive, financially ruinous, and ultimately counterproductive. The trajectory of the women's health movement was instructive. In the 1970s, feminist activists, defending women's autonomy against medical domination, challenged existing obstetrical practices and explored alternatives to technologically oriented hospital births; popularized surgical alternatives to radical mastectomy for breast cancer; and identified the risks of technologically defined birth control, such as oral contraceptive hormones. Yet the autonomy of the 1970s became the consumer activism of the 1990s, as activists lobbied to assure that women's diseases would be researched and treated as aggressively as those of men. AIDS activists similarly demanded quicker access to experimental drugs. Autonomy was redefined as the right to pursue nontraditional treatments alongside the latest NIH innovations in cancer therapy. As with the politics of health care, the nation's social arrangements for assuring medical progress as the twentieth century ended were embroiled in struggles among groups of consumers over who would win the most favorable position at the medical table, and who would be left waiting.

[*See also* Bioethics; Biological Sciences; Birth Control and Family Planning; Childbirth; Feminism; Health and Fitness; Medical Education; Medicare and Medicaid; Medicine: Alternative Medicine; Nursing; Science: Since 1945; Welfare, Federal.]

• Stephen Strickland, *Politics, Science and Dread Disease: A Short History of United States Medical Research Policy*, 1972. John C. Burnham, "American Medicine's Golden Age: What Happened to It?" *Science* 215 (19 March 1982): 1472–9. Paul Starr, *The Social Transformation of American Medicine*, 1982. Daniel M. Fox, *Health Policies, Health Politics: The British and American Experience, 1911–1965*, 1986. Rosemary Stevens, *In Sickness and in Wealth: American Hospitals in the Twentieth Century*, 1989. Alan Derickson, "Health Security for All? Social Unionism and Universal Health Insurance, 1935–1958," *Journal of American History* 80 (1994): 1333–56. Harry M. Marks, *The Progress of Experiment: Science and Therapeutic Reform in the United States, 1900–1990*, 1997. David J. Rothman, *Beginnings Count: The Technological Imperative in American*

Health Care, 1997. Rosemary Stevens, *American Medicine and the Public Interest: A History of Specialization,* 1998.

—Harry M. Marks

MEDICINE: ALTERNATIVE MEDICINE

Although the cast of healers has changed dramatically, the medical marketplace in America has always been diverse and competitive. In the *Colonial Era, patients sought out bonesetters, midwives, preacher-healers, and root-and-herb doctors, as well as a broad range of school-trained and apprentice-trained physicians, known as regular, orthodox, or, in the nineteenth century, allopathic practitioners. At a time when many regular physicians bled, blistered, puked, and purged their patients—and when the population was largely rural and scattered—Americans often treated themselves and their families, relying on domestic recipes, almanacs, or, by the later eighteenth century, medical manuals.

Thomsonianism, Physiomedicalism, Eclecticism, Homeopathy, Hydropathy. Some medical entrepreneurs offered patients distinctive forms of treatment. In the 1790s, for example, the Connecticut physician Elisha Perkins began treating pain and *disease with metal rods, or "tractors." The state medical society expelled him, but he obtained a patent for his device and built up a considerable practice. In 1806, the New Hampshire farmer turned healer Samuel Thomson (1769–1843) began selling "family rights" to his system of botanical medicine, which relied heavily on the emetic *lobelia,* steam baths, and hot pepper. Proclaiming "Every Man His Own Physician," he attacked not only physicians but priests and lawyers as well. In the 1830s, Thomson's supporters pressured state legislatures to repeal licensing laws, which in any event had had little effect on medical practice. At the height of his popularity Thomson (generously) estimated that three million Americans were using his system, but by the late 1830s his movement was in sharp decline.

With the demise of Thomsonianism, two other botanic groups arose to fill the vacuum. The first, physiomedicalism, was formed by restless Thomsonians who wanted trained botanical physicians. The second, eclecticism, was started in the 1830s by a regularly trained physician, Wooster Beach. Like their physiomedical competitors, the eclectics established medical schools and societies. Their largest institution, the Eclectic Medical Institute in Cincinnati, Ohio, ranked among America's largest medical schools at midcentury. Eclecticism flourished well into the twentieth century.

Even more successful were the homeopaths, followers of a system developed by the German physician Samuel Hahnemann in the early nineteenth century and brought to the United States around 1825 by German-speaking immigrants. Rejecting orthodox drugs and doses, homeopathic practitioners relied on the law of similars (like cures like) and the law of infinitesimals (the smaller the dose the more potent). During the second half of the nineteenth century, homeopathy became the most significant professional and economic rival to orthodox medicine. By the 1880s homeopathic medical colleges and hospitals existed in most major cities, including women's homeopathic schools in Cleveland, Ohio, and *New York City.

A much smaller medical movement, hydropathy or the water cure, appeared in the mid-1840s. Relying on various water therapies developed by a Silesian peasant, Vincent Priessnitz, American hydropaths set up coeducational schools to train hydropathic physicians, established scores of water-cure institutions, and published the popular *Water-Cure Journal,* which claimed 100,000 subscribers. Many water-cure enthusiasts also embraced the health-reform movement launched in the 1830s by the Massachusetts temperance lecturer and sex reformer Sylvester Graham (1794–1851), who preached the virtues of a twice-a-day diet devoid of meat, rich foods, tea, coffee, spices, and commercially made bread.

The growing popularity of alternative-healing movements spurred the founding in 1847 of the *American Medical Association (AMA). Its code of ethics, made compulsory for member societies in 1855, barred consultation with anyone "whose practice is based on exclusive dogma," an obvious reference to eclectics, homeopaths, hydropaths, and other sectarians. Enforcement of the code frequently created awkward moments, as when in 1878 a county medical society in Connecticut expelled Moses Pardee, a regular physician, for consulting with his wife, Emily, a homeopathic practitioner. In 1884 the New York State Medical Society split, with rural general practitioners upholding the AMA code while urban specialists, often German-trained, claimed that truly scientific physicians could recognize legitimate expertise regardless of creed. A revision of the code in 1903 recognized this latter view. Henceforth, homeopaths and eclectics who embraced "scientific medicine" and abandoned their sectarian identities were welcomed as members.

Christian Science, Osteopathy, and Chiropractic. In the late nineteenth century, as the practices of allopaths, homeopaths, and eclectics increasingly converged under the banner of science, three new alternative-healing movements, all offshoots of mesmerism or animal magnetism, rose to prominence: *Christian Science, osteopathy, and chiropractic. Christian Science, a religion founded by Mary Baker Eddy in the 1860s, taught that disease and death do not exist physically but only mentally; thus treatment consists of helping the sick alter their state of mind. Osteopathy, originated by a magnetic healer and bonesetter, Andrew Taylor Still, focused on removing obstructions to the flow of body fluids by manipulating out-of-place bones, particularly vertebrae. In 1892, Still opened the American School of Osteopathy in Kirksville, Missouri. Daniel David Palmer, a magnetic healer from Davenport, Iowa, started the chiropractic movement in 1895, initially as a spiritual healing sect employing spinal adjustments to relieve pinched nerves that impeded the flow of "Innate Intelligence." Despite the return of medical licensing laws in the later nineteenth century, by the early 1930s roughly 20 percent of all healers in the United States were unorthodox. Some forty-six states legally recognized osteopathy, and thirty-nine permitted chiropractic practice. After many legal battles, Christian Science practitioners, too, had won the right to pursue their activities.

When Abraham Flexner issued his muckraking survey *Medical Education in the United States and Canada* (1910), he excoriated the homeopathic, eclectic, and osteopathic schools he had visited and dismissed chiropractors as "unconscionable quacks" unworthy of "serious notice in an education discussion." The *Flexner Report and Flexner's unwillingness to "compromise between science and revelation" profoundly shaped elite attitudes toward alternative medicine in America. But the public's increasing reliance on *hospitals and medical specialists did not necessarily undermine support for medical alternatives. And the often racist and anti-Semitic admissions policies of many orthodox medical schools led many *African Americans and Jews to study osteopathy and chiropractic (as well as *dentistry and *optometry) instead of medicine. Throughout the twentieth century, ethnic and racially segregated communities commonly used herbalists, midwives, medical advisers, and spiritual healers—often for complementary rather than alternative care.

Alternative Medicine in the Later Twentieth Century. By the 1960s and 1970s, American physicians faced increasing criticism as elitist, overly interventionist, and too Eurocentric. Critics compared Western scientific medicine to the allegedly gentler, more humane, and more natural *health practices of other cultures, such as those of Native Americans, Asians, and Hispanics. Communes and some college campuses welcomed alternative medicine. In 1969, Michigan State University established the first university-affiliated osteopathic school, followed in the 1970s by state universities in Texas, West Virginia, Oklahoma, Ohio, New Jersey, New York, and Maine. In 1966 the U.S. Department of Defense accepted osteopaths as military physicians and surgeons, and soon thereafter osteopaths gained admission to hospital residency and fellowship programs. In 1972, Congress mandated Medicare coverage of chiropractic, but, facing continuing discrimination, American chiropractors in 1976 sued the AMA for violating antitrust laws. Although the AMA revised its code of ethics to allow physicians the freedom "to choose whom to serve, with whom to associate, and the environment in which to provide medical services," it eventually lost the suit.

During the 1980s and 1990s, growing public fascination with so-called *New Age healing (a mixture of naturopathy, homeopathy, Ayurvedic healing, and other Eastern vitalist systems) gave rise to various alternative schools and numerous health-food stores and magazines. The growing incidence of chronic diseases for which orthodox medicine offered no cure—especially *cancer, rheumatoid arthritis, persistent fatigue, and *acquired immunodeficiency syndrome (AIDS)—spurred interest in unorthodox treatments. Recognizing the public's growing interest in alternative healing, Congress in 1991 created an Office of Alternative Medicine in the *National Institutes of Health.

Meanwhile, the practice of alternative healing flourished. In 1993 the prestigious *New England Journal of Medicine* published news of a recent survey in which over a third of the respondents "reported using at least one unconventional therapy in the past year, and a third of these saw providers for unconventional therapy." This report also revealed that Americans annually paid more visits (425 million) to alternative practitioners than to "all U.S. primary care physicians" combined, and spent more money on alternative healers ($13.7 billion) than on out-of-pocket expenditures for hospitalization. A follow-up survey seven years later reported a 47.3 percent increase in visits to alternative healers. Among the fastest-growing unconventional therapies were "herbal medicine, massage, megavitamins, self-help groups, folk remedies, energy healing, and homeopathy." So popular had alternative medicine become that by 2000 well over half of American medical schools were offering courses on the subject.

[*See also* Childbirth; Food and Diet; Medical Education; Medicare and Medicaid.]

• Guenter Risse, Ronald L. Numbers, and Judith W. Leavitt, eds., *Medicine without Doctors: Home Health Care in American History,* 1977. Norman Gevitz, ed., *Other Healers: Unorthodox Medicine in America,* 1988. Barbara Barzansky and Norman Gevitz, eds., *Beyond Flexner: Medical Education in the Twentieth Century,* 1992. John S. Haller Jr., *Medical Protestants: The Eclectics in American Medicine, 1825–1939,* 1994. Ronald L. Numbers and Darrel Amundson, eds., *Caring and Curing: Health and Medicine in the Western Religious Traditions,* 1998. Naomi Rogers, *The Making and Remaking of Hahnemann Medical College and Hospital of Philadelphia,* 1998. Robert B. Baker, et al., eds., *The American Medical Ethics Revolution: How the AMA's Code of Ethics Has Transformed Physicians' Relationships to Patients, Professionals, and Society,* 1999.

—Naomi Rogers

MELVILLE, HERMAN (1819–1891), author. Born in *New York City, Herman Melville was descended from *Revolutionary War heroes on both sides of his family. His family plunged from affluence into genteel poverty in 1832 when his father died shortly after the failure of his import business. Melville shipped out to Liverpool in 1839 and in 1841 went on a whaling voyage to the South Seas. He returned in 1844 after serving in the U.S. Navy. In 1847 he married Elizabeth Shaw, daughter of the chief justice of the Massachusetts Supreme Court, Lemuel *Shaw, a friend of his father; they had four children. Melville began working as a customs inspector for the Port of New York in 1866. In 1867 his eldest son Malcolm died at eighteen, probably a suicide. In that same year Melville's wife, suspecting his sanity, seriously considered leaving him to escape his emotional abuse.

Melville's popular early novels *Typee* (1846) and *Omoo* (1847), while published as travel narratives, actually fictionalized his adventures as a sailor in the South Seas. *Typee* embellished his sojourn with a cannibal tribe in the Marquesas Islands. With *Mardi* (1849), Melville's wide-ranging reading in literature and *philosophy led him to imagine an archipelago of islands, each symbolizing specific ethical, social, and political problems. Its risk-taking allegorical approach damaged his literary reputation. Melville's deepening power as a social critic became evident in his next two novels. *Redburn* (1849), based on his first voyage, vividly portrayed Liverpool's poverty. *White-Jacket* (1850), drawn from Melville's experiences in the navy, compellingly condemned the practice of flogging, and may have influenced its outlawing.

These early novels give hints of the rich symbolism, stylistic range, and depth of human insight that make *Moby Dick* (1851) a masterpiece of world literature. A first serious reading of Shakespeare and the impact of a new friendship with Nathaniel *Hawthorne caused Melville to transform his novel about whaling into a richly comic, darkly tragic tour de force. After *Moby Dick*'s critical and commercial failure, Melville's literary vision darkened.

Pierre (1852) parodied the sentimental fiction of the period, poking fun at Melville's literary friends, and, according to some controversial biographical evidence, may explore the possibility that Melville's father sired an illegitimate daughter. After *Pierre*'s disastrous reception by readers and critics, Melville claimed he was "prevented" from publishing his next novel, "The Isle of the Cross" (1853), about a Nantucket widow. The manuscript has not survived.

Turning to the short story genre, Melville produced such masterpieces as "Bartleby, the Scrivener" and "Benito Cereno," collected in *The Piazza Tales* (1856). The historical novel *Israel Potter* (1855) is set in the Revolutionary period and includes Ethan Allen, John Paul *Jones, and Benjamin *Franklin among the characters. Melville's last novel, *The Confidence Man* (1857), is a dark, allegorical work that grimly critiques the lack of trust pervading American culture.

Under family pressure and showing signs of psychological stress, Melville turned to *poetry. His *Civil War verse, collected in *Battle-Pieces* (1866), was his last commercial publication. *Clarel* (1876), portraying a religious pilgrimage to the Holy Land, dramatizes Melville's unresolved spiritual yearnings. *John Marr and Other Sailors* (1888) and *Timoleon* (1891) were printed in twenty-five-copy editions. The great novella *Billy Budd, Sailor,* discovered in unfinished form after Melville's death, was first published in 1924. Melville's literary reputation began to revive in 1919, the centennial of his birth, and grew steadily in the decades that followed.

[*See also* Antebellum Era; Literature, Popular; Literature: Early National and Antebellum Eras.]

• Herschel Parker, *Herman Melville: A Biography, volume 1, 1819–1851,* 1996. Laurie Robertson-Lorant, *Herman Melville: A Biography,* 1996.

—Neal Tolchin

MENCKEN, H. L. (1880–1956), writer, editor, newspaperman. Throughout his life Henry Louis Mencken relished his role as a working newspaperman. Starting with the *Baltimore Sun* in 1906, he was associated with that paper for most of his life. He rose to literary prominence as coeditor (with George Jean Nathan) of *The Smart Set* (1914–1923) and *The American Mercury* (1924–1933). As editor and literary reviewer for these magazines, he championed numerous European and young American writers, including Sherwood Anderson, Theodore *Dreiser, and Sinclair *Lewis, frequently becoming involved in volcanic literary battles with the literary establishment and partisans of the older genteel tradition.

In 1925 Mencken covered the *Scopes Trial challenging a Tennessee law banning the teaching of evolution, and wrote a savagely satirical attack on William Jennings *Bryan, who died shortly after testifying in the trial. An outspoken opponent of *censorship, he successfully challenged a 1926 effort in *Boston to suppress an issue of the *American Mercury* that included an article about a small-town prostitute.

In a great many essays, gathered in a series of seven books entitled *Prejudices,* Mencken excoriated, with brilliant, savage humor, the low estate of American politics, the dreariness of *popular culture, religious fundamentalism, Prohibition, and the smug, self-satisfied life of what he called the booboisie. One of the best-known figures of the 1920s, Mencken was a social and cultural critic of mordant wit and powerful literary skill.

In his years of greatest fame he wrote other successful books, including *A Book of Burlesques* (1916), *In Defense of Women* (1918), and *Notes on Democracy* (1926). An early work, *The Philosophy of Friedrich Nietzsche* (1908), helped introduce that German philosopher to American readers. Over several decades Mencken produced a scholarly three-volume study of *The American Language* (1919–1936), written in a lucid nonacademic style. After the Depression of the 1930s his role as a literary and cultural firebrand faded, but he wrote, in a more mellow and charming manner, three volumes of autobiography: *Happy Days, Newspaper Days,* and *Heathen Days.*

[*See also* Eighteenth Amendment; Fundamentalist Movement; Journalism; Literature: Since World War I; Literary Criticism; Magazines; Temperance and Prohibition; Twenties, The.]

• Fred Hobson, *Mencken; A Life,* 1955. Charles A. Fecher, *Mencken: A Study of His Thought,* 1978.

—George H. Douglas

MENNINGER, KARL (1893–1990), and **WILLIAM** (1899–1966), psychiatrists, founders of the Menninger Foundation. Karl Menninger, together with his father, Charles Frederick Menninger, founded the Menninger Clinic in Topeka, Kansas, in 1919. The clinic began as a small psychiatric facility in a renovated farmhouse. William Menninger, Karl's brother, joined the clinic in 1925, and a few years later it grew into a full-scale psychiatric hospital named the Menninger Sanitarium. In 1941, the hospital became part of the newly incorporated Menninger Foundation. Five years later, Karl Menninger founded the Menninger School of Psychiatry, which soon emerged as one of the nation's largest and most respected training facilities for psychiatrists, clinical psychologists, and psychiatric social workers.

In addition to his work for the Menninger Foundation, Karl Menninger helped popularize Sigmund Freud's psychoanalytic theories among American psychiatrists as well as the general public. He discussed Freud's ideas in several influential books, including *The Human Mind* (1930), *Man against Himself* (1938), *Love against Hate* (1942), and *The Vital Balance* (1963). He became especially well known for his espousal of Freud's dual-drive theory, which postulates that there are basic types of instincts—those that serve life (Eros) and those that serve death (Thanatos). In 1942, he organized the Topeka Institute for Psychoanalysis, which helped train new psychoanalysts along Freudian lines.

William Menninger, too, also had a career outside the Menninger Foundation as a leader in the psychiatric treatment of American soldiers. Beginning his *World War II military career as a neuropsychiatric consultant, by 1944 he was head of the Army's psychiatric programs and held the rank of brigadier general.

[*See also* Mental Health Institutions; Mental Illness; Psychotheraphy.]

• Lawrence J. Friedman, *Menninger: The Family and the Clinic,* 1990.

—Mark I. West

MENNONITES AND AMISH, religious bodies that originated in the Anabaptist wing of the sixteenth-century Protestant Reformation and were forced by persecution into sectarian isolation. The name "Mennonite" derives from Menno Simons, an early Dutch leader. In 1683, upon William *Penn's invitation, Mennonites from Krefeld, Germany, settled near *Philadelphia. Others followed, coming from Germany, Switzerland, and Holland. Among the migrants were Amish, followers of Jacob Amman who had split from the main body of Mennonites over issues of religious practice in the 1690s.

Gradually Mennonites and Amish spread to Ontario, Virginia, Ohio, Indiana, Kansas, and the West Coast. The 1870s brought a wave of ethnic German Mennonite immigrants from Russia and Eastern Europe to the Great Plains, where they constituted a branch known as the Mennonite Brethren. The 1870s migration included Hutterites, an Anabaptist group that had originated in Moravia and later migrated to Russia to escape persecution. Settling in South Dakota and later Montana, the Hutterites lived in rural communities and held all property in common. When a community grew to about 150 members, it divided to start a new colony. To avoid military conscription during *World War I, some Hutterites moved to Canada.

The central tenets of all Anabaptist groups included adult baptism on confession of faith, the authority of the *Bible, rejection of military service, and a church of mutual accountability. During America's wars, their peace doctrine led to conflicts with federal authorities and local communities. Prominent Mennonite leaders of the nineteenth and twentieth centuries have included Christian Burkholder, John F. Funk, Edmund G. Kaufman, and Harold S. Bender.

While sharing core values, the various Mennonite and Amish groups made different choices in accommodating to American society. Traditionalist groups such as the Old Order Amish and Old Order Mennonites resisted new technologies, an educated ministry, and denominational institutions. Typically they avoided jewelry, "worldly" fashions, and—in the case of the Amish—electrification and the automobile. Conservative evangelical Mennonites in all groups, especially the Mennonite Brethren, stressed evangelism, personal conversion, prescriptive creeds, and the literal authority of scripture. The progressives, by contrast, promoted a socially relevant gospel, educated leadership, ecumenical association, and openness to new ideas. In the late nineteenth and twentieth centuries, the progressives, especially in the (Old) Mennonite church and the General Conference Mennonite church, the two largest groups, created an array of denominational institutions for education, publication, mutual aid, health care, and missions. A strong sense of history, as well as the continuing growth of the Old Order groups, kept all Mennonite groups generally conservative.

In the 1990s, the various Mennonite, Amish, and Hutterite groups of the United States included about 266,000 baptized members. The strongest Mennonite population and institutional centers were in Pennsylvania, Iowa, Indiana, and Kansas. Mennonites have exerted an influence beyond their numbers on American society, however, especially in their refusal of military service (together with the *Society of Friends and Church of the Brethren). Their quest for alternatives to war and violence has led to creative programs of benevolent service, including the Mennonite Central Committee (1920), Mennonite Disaster Service, and the Victim-Offender Reconciliation program. In the late twentieth century, Mennonite theology enjoyed a belated flowering, with theologians John Howard Yoder and Gordon Kaufman representing different strands of Mennonite thought.

[*See also* Conscientious Objection; German Americans; Immigration; Pacifism; Peace Movements; Protestantism; Religion.]

• Cornelius J. Dyck, *An Introduction to Mennonite History,* 3d ed., 1993. Richard K. MacMaster, Theron Schlabach, James C. Juhnke, and Paul Toews, eds., *The Mennonite Experience in America,* 4 vols., 1985-1996.

—James C. Juhnke

MENTAL HEALTH INSTITUTIONS. Before the *Revolutionary War, most mentally ill persons in the colonies lived either with their families or in local *alms houses. With *urbanization, specialized institutions emerged to care for the dependent and ill. In 1752, the Pennsylvania Hospital in *Philadelphia, the colonies' first general hospital, accepted insane patients. In 1773, the Virginia House of Burgesses established a freestanding "madhouse" in Williamsburg, modeled on London's Bethlem Royal Hospital (from whence the word "bedlam" derives). When the New York Hospital opened in 1791, it too made provision for "maniacs," along with medical and surgical cases. Charity hospitals' decision to include lunatics manifested the Enlightenment view of insanity as a treatable affliction. Among the best-known advocates of more active therapeutics was Benjamin *Rush, a physician who developed a "tranquilizing chair" to soothe the agitated. Nonetheless, care generally remained harsh; *hospitals relied on bleedings, purgings, and emetics to calm the disturbed and often locked in basement cells those considered dangerous.

In the 1820s, a very different regimen, known as "moral therapy," appeared, first at private nonprofit institutions like the Friends' Asylum at Frankford, Pennsylvania (1817), and the McLean Asylum outside *Boston (1818), and then at state-funded institutions, like Massachusetts's Worcester State Hospital (1833). Inspired by the work of Philippe Pinel in France and William Tuke in England, advocates of moral therapy supported treatment of the insane by psychological methods, in particular a carefully constructed round of activities designed to stimulate patients' latent reason and capacity for self-control. Specialized lunatic asylums in peaceful, rural areas became the preferred therapeutic setting. By the second half of the nineteenth century, most states and many major cities had at least one public psychiatric institution, while corporate and proprietary hospitals continued to serve the wealthy. As the number and size of state hospitals increased, however, overcrowded wards housed chronic cases: long-term schizophrenics, the senile, paralytics, and epileptics. As a result, both the internal environment and the external image of the state asylums began to deteriorate. By 1900, hospital superintendents found themselves under bitter attack from other medical professionals (especially neurologists), ex-patients, and state legislators.

By the early twentieth century, the most innovative psychiatric research was taking place in research institutes, laboratories, and private practice. Psychopathic hospitals, intended to provide acute care, opened in a number of major cities. A mental-hygiene movement, aimed at promoting general mental health, emerged. Yet, in part because many psychiatrists were uninterested in the severely and chronically mentally ill, state hospital populations continued to grow. Underfunded and desperate for treatments that would control if not cure their patients, hospitals experimented with somatic therapies, including insulin shock, malarial fever, and lobotomies (surgical removal of part of the brain).

Staffing shortages during *World War II further exacerbated this situation. During the 1940s and 1950s, however, new drug therapies and the increasing involvement of the federal government began to reshape mental health institutions. Two federal laws of 1946—the Mental Health Act and the Hill-Burton Act—helped to fund the rebuilding of the public hospital system, the expansion of general hospitals (including psychiatric units), and the development of community services. The hope that antipsychotic drugs, like chlorpromazine, and antidepressants, like reserpine, would enable the long-term mentally ill to return to their communities prompted state legislatures and mental-health advocates to press for the downsizing of large psychiatric facilities. Mary Jane Ward's 1946 novel *The Snake Pit*, exposing the dreadful conditions in state mental institutions (made into a successful movie in 1948), intensified the pressures for reform.

During the 1950s and 1960s, as enthusiasm for community mental-health centers swept the nation, new groups of mental health care consumers began to use them. Public institutions, however, continued to provide most of the inpatient care, especially for the severely impaired, although the average length of stay decreased. Some patients seemed caught in a "revolving door" syndrome, moving in and out of psychiatric facilities to little long-term effect. Others, particularly those with a dual diagnosis of mental illness and substance abuse, lived marginal but highly visible lives in shelters and on city streets. During the 1970s and 1980s, a loose coalition of politicians, advocacy groups like the National Alliance for the Mentally Ill, and health-care professionals pressured community mental-health centers to refocus on the severely ill. The managed care movement of the 1990s increased the proliferation of halfway houses, supported-care facilities, and other quasi-independent residential facilities. As a result, the institutional landscape was highly diverse as the century ended, although the challenge of chronic mental illness remained.

[*See also* Dix, Dorothea; Drugs, Illicit; Medicine; Menninger, Karl and William; Mental Retardation; Prisons and Penitentiaries; Psychology; Psychotherapy.]

• David Rothman, *The Discovery of the Asylum,* 1971. Gerald Grob, *The Mad among Us,* 1974. Nancy Tomes, *A Generous Confidence: Thomas Story Kirkbride and the Art of Asylum Keeping, 1840–1883,* 1984. Ellen Dwyer, *Homes for the Mad,* 1987. George Dowdall, *The Eclipse of the State Mental Hospital,* 1996. Joel Braslow, *Mental Ills and Bodily Cures,* 1997.

—Ellen Dwyer

MENTAL ILLNESS. During the early *Colonial Era, Americans attributed mental illness to both natural and supernatural forces. Folk belief also linked it to the lunar cycles; hence, the term "lunacy." While ministers talked of "demonic possession," doctors attributed mental illnesses to an imbalance of the four bodily "humors": blood, phlegm, choler, and black bile. During the eighteenth-century Enlightenment, insanity came to be seen as involving defects of reason. In 1812, the Philadelphia physician Benjamin *Rush published *Medical Inquiries and Observations upon Diseases of the Mind,* the first major American treatise on mental illness.

Nineteenth-century notions of mental illness were shaped by the first generation of physicians to work in large psychiatric institutions. Asylum doctors divided mental illness into four categories: mania (with an important subcategory, monomania), melancholia, dementia, and idiocy. They sometimes added "moral insanity," later called psychopathy. In 1869, the New York neurologist and prolific writer on medical subjects George M. Beard (1839–1883) coined the term "neurasthenia" to describe a range of less serious but still debilitating nervous conditions, including headaches, insomnia, depression, and anxiety. Finally, in 1899, the German doctor Emil Kraepelin, in *The Compendium of Psychiatry,* offered a synthesis of the major diagnostic categories of the day, which was rapidly adopted in the United States. Among the illnesses he described were manic-depression and dementia praecox, a disorder renamed schizophrenia (split mind) by the Swiss psychiatrist Eugene Bleuler in 1911.

By the late nineteenth century, despite much neurological research into the structure and function of the brain and nervous system, the causes of insanity remained unknown. Frustrated by the growing numbers of chronic patients in psychiatric hospitals and influenced by evolutionary theory, many psychiatrists turned to hereditarian explanations. Particularly influential, if extreme, was degeneration theory, which held that degenerates (a category that included criminals, the long-term mentally ill, and the mentally handicapped) could be recognized by physical and mental characteristics indicative of regressive breeding. Once detected, such persons were to be sterilized or institutionalized for life.

This brief excursion into biological psychiatry was soon overshadowed by psychoanalysis (brought to the United States by Sigmund Freud in 1909) and other psychosocial perspectives on mental illness. Psychiatrists and neurologists paid increasing attention to private patients with neuroses and maladjustments, to the relative neglect of those with serious mental illnesses such as senile dementia and neurosyphilis who filled the large state psychiatric institutions. In 1948, the American Psychiatric Association published the first edition of its *Diagnostic and Statistical Manual [of] Mental Disorders,* which described both minor problems such as psychosomatic disorders and combat fatigue and major mental illnesses such as depression and schizophrenia.

The later twentieth century brought many changes in popular and medical conceptions of mental illness. Leaders of the antipsychiatry movement of the 1960s, including Thomas Szasz and R. D. Laing, attacked what they called the "myth of mental illness." Mental illness, they argued, was primarily a social, not a medical, label attached to anomalous or nonconforming behavior. By the 1990s, however, in both professional and popular discourse, this perspective had been swamped by a resurgent biological psychiatry that emphasized the somatic bases of serious mental illnesses and responded to psychic symptoms with powerful drug therapies.

[*See also* Eugenics; Hospitals; Medicine; Mental Health Institutions; Mental Retardation; Psychology; Psychotherapy; Sixties, The.]

• Lynn Gamwell and Nancy Tomes, *Madness in America: Cultural and Medical Perceptions of Mental Illness before 1914,* 1995. Edward Shorter, *A History of Psychiatry, From the Era of the Asylum to the Age of Prozac,* 1997.

—Ellen Dwyer

MENTAL RETARDATION, a term adopted by educators and physicians to explain intellectual disabilities. From the *Colonial Era to the *Civil War, Americans distinguished between two types of mental limitations: "idiocy" and "imbecility." Idiocy identified people who appeared to function with very low intellectual ability. Imbecility labeled individuals who seemed to have higher abilities than idiots, but still appeared disabled.

Beginning in the 1840s, American physicians Samuel Gridley Howe, Hervey Wilbur, and others read reports of the techniques of the French educator Edouard Séguin in training idiots. Encouraged by Séguin's success, these reformers founded private schools and public asylums for people with intellectual disability. Established for education, these facilities by the 1850s were housing graduates who had failed to find employment in their communities. By the 1870s, many states were transforming such schools into custodial institutions for the "feebleminded." Although they continued to provide classroom instruction, by 1900 most institutions had become fully custodial.

The new century marked the beginning of special education and the *eugenics movement. Special education provided schooling to "mentally defectives." Henry H. Goddard's 1905 adaptation of the Binet intelligence tests launched a movement to identify intellectual disability among American grade schoolers and other groups such as *World War I draftees. Paralleling the introduction of testing, the *eugenics movement linked intellectual limitations with heredity and "bad breeding." In 1914, the Committee on Provision for the Feebleminded launched a nationwide campaign against the "menace of the feebleminded." Invoking the authority of eugenics, the committee promoted involuntary sterilization, institutional segregation, and laws to restrict marriage.

The Great Depression of the 1930s and *World War II marked a period of underfunding and overcrowding of public institutions. Exposés that appeared during and after the war focused attention on the inhuman conditions of institutions housing the "mentally deficient." Nevertheless, these facilities continued to grow until the mid-1960s, when their populations reached over 190,000 residents. Beginning in the later 1960s, the efforts of two groups led to the rapid depopulation of the state institutions. These groups comprised civil libertarians critical of overcrowded institutions and state governments interested in transferring the costs of care to the federal Medicaid system. Both the civil libertarians and the funding provisions of the Medicaid program encouraged states to reduce the populations of their facilities. Policy-makers called the strategy deinstitutionalization. The populations of state institutions steadily declined from the 1970s on, and by the end of the century most people labeled intellectually disabled lived independently, in group homes, or in community facilities.

[*See also* Civil Liberties; Intelligence, Concepts of; Medicare and Medicaid; Mental Health Institutions.]

• Philip M. Ferguson, *Abandoned to Their Fate: Social Policy and Practice toward Severely Retarded People in America, 1820–1920,* 1994. James W. Trent Jr., *Inventing the Feeble Mind: A History of Mental Retardation in the United States,* 1994.

—James W. Trent Jr.

METHODISM, one of the most successful forms of popular *Protestantism in American history, matched only by the *Baptists. With lay beginnings in the 1760s and official missionaries commissioned in the 1770s by its English founder John Wesley, Methodism grew from a marginal sect into the nation's largest Christian denomination by the early 1840s.

In 1844 Methodists experienced a major split between North and South over the issue of *slavery. Throughout the nineteenth century, other denominations emerged from Methodism over matters of polity and theology and social issues. Race also divided the Methodists with the formation of the African Methodist Episcopal church (1816) and the African Methodist Episcopal Zion church (1821). The twentieth century saw merger rather than division. In 1939 the northern and southern branches and a smaller group reunited to form the Methodist church. In 1968 another merger produced the United Methodist church.

During its period of greatest growth, between the Revolutionary and Civil wars, Methodism flourished because of its ability to combine methodical organization and personal self-discipline with emotional spontaneity and a warm, familylike religious community. Its theology stressed free grace and human agency in the quest not only to be "born again," but also to attain "Christian Perfection," a distinctive Methodist doctrine that claims grace to overcome all desire to sin. Its class meetings, love feasts, and camp meetings were major engines of *revivalism. Its circuit-riding clergy emerged from the laity and kept close to them even while a paternalistic episcopal organization, headed first by Bishop Francis Asbury (1745–1816), insured that Methodism kept pace with a mobile and growing population.

Between the *Civil War and *World War I, Methodism was an established institution, almost an unofficial national church. Bishop Matthew Simpson, whose sermons celebrated American nationhood, advised President Abraham *Lincoln and preached his funeral sermon. As Methodism became an escalator into the middle class, the revivalistic ethos was replaced by an interest in benevolent enterprises such as missions, education, and *temperance. Frances *Willard, leader of the *Woman's Christian Temperance Union; Lucy Webb Hayes, wife of President Rutherford *Hayes and president of the Methodist Woman's Home Missionary Society; and Bishop John Heyl Vincent, founder of the *Chautauqua movement, were prominent Methodists who embodied these changes. A "holiness" movement, advocating a renewed experience of Christian Perfection, dissented from such changes, but by the turn of the century many in this movement had withdrawn into new holiness sects.

Methodism's late nineteenth-century identification with American nationhood and culture anticipated the evolution of mainstream Protestantism during the twentieth century. Methodism played major roles in the promotion of the Protestant *ecumenical movement and the *Social Gospel even as it coped with *secularization and the end of Protestant cultural hegemony in America in the 1930s and after. As the twentieth century ended, Methodism struggled to find its own distinctive voice among the many religious and secular options competing in America's spiritual marketplace.

[*See also* African American Religion; Antebellum Era; Cultural Pluralism; Education: Collegiate Education; Great Awakening, First and Second; Missionary Movement; Mobility; National Council of Churches; Religion; Social Class.]

• Russell E. Richey, Kenneth E. Rowe, and Jean Miller Schmidt, eds. *Perspectives on American Methodism: Interpretive Essays,* 1993. Nathan Hatch, "The Puzzle of American Methodism," *Church History* 63 (June 1994): 175–89.

—A. Gregory Schneider

MEXICAN AMERICANS. *See* Hispanic Americans.

MEXICAN WAR (1846–1848), the first photographed war, the first U.S. war covered by newspaper correspondents, and the first fought mostly on foreign soil. One of America's most successful conflicts militarily, the Mexican War added vast territories to the national domain. It also, however, provoked anti-Americanism in Mexico and contributed to the sectional tension that culminated in the *Civil War.

Although some historians trace the Mexican War's underlying causes to political instability in Mexico and the bellicosity of Mexico's leaders, most interpret the conflict as an outgrowth of U.S. *expansionism (expressed in the popular slogan "*Manifest Destiny," coined in 1845). According to this view, President James Knox *Polk was so bent upon acquiring *California ports and other Mexican territory, in part to preempt rumored British designs on California, that he provoked war as a pretext for conquest. Other scholars, however, contend that Polk sought a peaceful resolution of outstanding issues and conducted his prewar diplomacy with Mexico in good faith.

In an immediate sense, warfare erupted because of a dispute over the boundary separating Mexico and Texas, exacerbated by Mexico's defaulting in 1844 on payments to satisfy American citizens' claims for losses sustained in Mexico. The U.S. government, after annexing the Republic of Texas in 1845, upheld Texas's claim to the Rio Grande River as its border with Mexico. Mexican authorities neither recognized Texas's independence from Mexico (achieved in 1836) nor its annexation by the United States; they also claimed that Texas extended only to the Nueces River. On 13 January 1846, the Polk administration ordered General Zachary *Taylor's "Army of Occupation" to advance through the disputed region to the Rio Grande. On 23 April, Mexican cavalry crossed the Rio Grande and two days later ambushed a scouting party of Taylor's dragoons, killing eleven soldiers, wounding others, and taking sixty-three prisoners. Polk asked Congress for war on 11 May, asserting that Mexico had "shed American blood upon American soil." That same day the House of Representatives passed a war bill by a vote of 173–14. The Senate followed suit on 12 May, by a 40–2 margin.

Although the United States entered the war with an army of fewer than seven thousand officers and men (less than one-third the size of Mexico's establishment), American troops invaded Mexico and repeatedly defeated numerically superior Mexican forces while U.S. naval vessels blockaded Mexican ports. After routing Mexican troops at Palo Alto (8 May) and Resaca de la Palma (9 May), Taylor's army crossed the Rio Grande on 18 May and subsequently conquered much of northern Mexico, including Monterrey, the capital of the state of Nuevo León, which Taylor occupied under an armistice accord with Mexican officials following heavy fighting on 21 and 23 September. Taylor's campaigns culminated in his defeat of Mexican general Antonio López de Santa Anna's army at Buena Vista, on 22–23 February 1847. By then, General Stephen W. Kearny's Army of the West had occupied New Mexico and U.S. naval and ground forces had conquered California. The American military effort climaxed with Winfield Scott's Mexico City campaign. Scott (1786–1866), the U.S. Army's commanding general, captured Veracruz on the Gulf of Mexico in March 1847 after extensive siege operations, and then invaded Mexico's interior, routing Santa Anna's army at Cerro Gordo (17–18 April). Following victories near Mexico City on 20 August and a costly, avoidable action at Molino del Rey (8 September), Scott's forces routed Mexican defenders from Chapultepec Castle on 13 September and the next day occupied Mexico City, evacuated by Santa Anna the previous night.

The Treaty of Guadalupe-Hidalgo, signed by U.S. negotiator Nicholas P. Trist with Mexican officials on 2 February 1848 and ratified by the U.S. Senate on 10 March, ended the war. It ceded to the United States some 500,000 square miles—including the disputed boundary area and what would become today's states of California, New Mexico, Arizona, Utah, Nevada, and parts of Colorado and Wyoming—in return for $15 million and the U.S. government's assumption of up to $3.25 million in American claims against Mexico. The United States agreed to honor the property rights of current inhabitants of the ceded territories, though the process was unevenly applied, and most residents lost their land over time. The last U.S. forces evacuated Mexico in August 1848.

Firm presidential leadership, competent generalship, contributions by junior officers trained at West Point, and superior field artillery contributed to the American victory, as did Mexican disorganization and strategic errors. Scott's advance on Mexico City ranks as a brilliantly executed campaign: he did not lose a single man in his amphibious landing near Veracruz; he daringly cut his lines to the coast in order to consolidate his army; he conciliated the Mexican people by keeping his troops under tight discipline; and, finally, he conserved manpower by circumventing several Mexican strongpoints.

The support of the American people, however, may have been the most decisive factor in the U.S. victory. Some did oppose the war, including pacifists, *New England abolitionists (who wrongly saw the war as a southern plot to extend *slavery), and antiexpansionists in the *Whig party such as Congressman Abraham *Lincoln of Illinois. But prowar enthusiasm predominated, allowing the U.S. government to raise more than 75,000 volunteer troops. During the war, Congress authorized a substantial expansion of the regular army, but American success depended upon volunteers.

The U.S. war record, however, was by no means unblemished. Although only 1,721 American soldiers were killed in combat, nearly 11,000 died of *disease. Over 8 percent of U.S. enlisted men deserted, a higher percentage than in any other American foreign conflict. President Polk, a partisan Democrat, allowed politics to influence his military appointments. The campaign was marred by disputes between army and navy officers, friction between volunteers and regulars, and confusion about volunteers' enlistment terms. Bitter infighting among U.S. officers over rank and postbattle reports led to courts-martial and even the removal of Scott from command. U.S. troops, most notoriously Texas Rangers serving with Taylor, committed crimes against the property and persons of Mexican civilians. The war also aroused racist passions in the United States. Starting in the Summer of 1847, some U.S. expansionists began calling for the United States to take over all of Mexico, but Polk's administration settled for a considerably smaller conquest—in part because of a popular outcry against absorbing multitudes of mixed-race Mexicans into the American body politic. Most importantly, the never-passed Wilmot Proviso, introduced by Pennsylvania congressman David Wilmot in August 1846 as an amendment to an appropriations bill, helped set the stage for the Civil War. By proposing to prohibit slavery in any territory acquired from Mexico, the measure renewed debate about slavery expansion—the issue often viewed as the most important cause of the Civil War.

[*See also* Antebellum Era; Antislavery; Civil War: Causes;

Compromise of 1850; Democratic Party; Racism; Slavery: Development and Expansion of Slavery; Texas Republic and Annexation.]

• Otis A. Singletary, *The Mexican War,* 1960. Frederick Merk, *Manifest Destiny and Mission in American History,* 1963. K. Jack Bauer, *The Mexican War,* 1974. Robert W. Johannsen, *To the Halls of the Montezumas: The Mexican War in the American Imagination,* 1985. John S. D. Eisenhower, *So Far from God: The War with Mexico 1846–1848,* 1989. James M. McCaffrey, *Army of Manifest Destiny: The American Soldier in the Mexican War, 1846–1848,* 1992.

—Robert E. May

MIDDLE EAST, U.S. RELATIONS WITH. *See* Foreign Relations: U.S Relations with the Middle East.

MIDDLETOWN, influential 1920s sociological study. When Robert S. Lynd and his wife Helen Merrell Lynd arrived in Muncie, Indiana, early in 1924, the 38,000 residents of this Midwestern industrial community little realized the consequences of the "field investigation" mounted by these earnest "social anthropologists" that would appear in *Middletown: A Study in Modern American Culture* (1929), which has never been out of print since its publication.

Intended as an analysis of a typical American community incorporating the newest sociological methods, *Middletown* was in fact an anomaly in many ways: the "Small City Study" the Lynds headed was funded by John D. Rockefeller Jr. whose *industrial-relations policies Robert Lynd had earlier attacked; educated in theology and philosophy, neither of the Lynds was a trained sociologist; and Muncie was hardly typical since it was selected for the homogeneity of its population (92 percent native-born white). Notwithstanding these quirks, the importance of *Middletown* and its sequel, *Middletown in Transition: A Study in Cultural Conflicts* (1937), is widely recognized. *Middletown,* in particular, is noteworthy for the richness of its oral material; its careful attention to *work, homemaking, education, *leisure time, and religious and community activities; and its comparisons of community life in 1890 and 1924.

After the Lynds' books, "Middletown" studies continued as a kind of cottage-industry. The photographer Margaret *Bourke-White featured Muncie in a 1937 *Life* magazine photo-essay. In 1975 a team of researchers for the "Middletown III" project arrived to start work on a series of new studies. In 1976 the National Endowment for the Humanities funded a five-part public television documentary broadcast in 1982. The impact of the Lynds' enterprise spread far beyond Muncie, as other "field investigators" sought out other communities in an attempt to analyze what it means to "live American."

[*See also* Middle West, The; Social Science; Sociology; Twenties, The; Urbanization.]

• Theodore Caplow, Howard M. Bahr, Bruce A. Chadwick, Reuben Hill, and Margaret Holmes Williamson, *Middletown Families: Fifty Years of Change and Continuity,* 1982. Dwight W. Hoover, "Middletown Again," *Prospects: An Annual of American Cultural Studies* 15 (1990): 445–86.

—Martha Banta

MIDDLE WEST, THE. Among the great subnational regions of the United States, the Middle West is the vaguest in location and identity. Although some situate the area entirely west of the *Mississippi River and others entirely to the east, consensus opinion places twelve states within the region: Illinois, Indiana, Iowa, Kansas, Michigan, Minnesota, Missouri, Ohio, Nebraska, North and South Dakota, and Wisconsin. People in the plains sections of Colorado, Montana, Oklahoma, and Wyoming also have some attachment to the label.

The confusion over the "Middle West's" precise location has its roots in identity. Unlike many other places, the region lacks an obvious defining trait or moment. It was settled in distinct east-west bands by peoples from the Northeast, the Mid-Atlantic states, and the *South; its *agriculture is split among the corn, dairy, and wheat belts; and its economy features both large industrial cities and extensive farming lands. Physiographically, the region is more united. It is largely a subdued landscape of sedimentary rock, one that has been leveled further by relatively recent glaciation. Exceptions are found along the northern and southern fringes, where the ancient rocks and infertile soils of the Canadian Shield extend into parts of Minnesota, Wisconsin, and Michigan, and eroded hill lands characterize sections near the Ohio River and in southern Missouri. From a climatological perspective, the Middle West is a region of extremes. Precipitation becomes scarce and highly unreliable in the western borderlands and the growing season north of Milwaukee and Detroit is too short for corn.

When Euro-Americans first moved into the Ohio country shortly after the *Revolutionary War, eastern politicians feared anarchy and secession. They therefore enacted the *Northwest Ordinance of 1787, which provided for public education, orderly government, and free labor. These regulations applied only temporarily, but residents later came to see them as defining elements. *Capitalism was the real glue that unified the emerging region, however, especially after the *Erie Canal linked the Midwest to eastern markets in 1825. With an abundance of good soil, coal, iron ore, lumber, and other resources at hand, a *business mentality came to dominate the culture. Investors financed factories and *railroads, and a pervading sense of material progress rapidly overcame local and ethnic idiosyncrasies. By the 1850s, Cincinnati and St. Louis were major import-export cities on the Mississippi River system, *Chicago was becoming a focus for regional railroads, and middle westerners saw themselves as fulfilling the promise of America.

Capitalist enthusiasm gripped farmers and urban speculators alike, and opinions varied only over the degree to which such progress should be regulated. Democrats favored minimal regulation, whereas Whigs thought bank credit and government aid essential to the development process. This latter view characterized Abraham *Lincoln's new *Republican party. Gaining tremendous stature during the *Civil War, the Republican party emerged from the war dominant in the region. Both the place and the party stood for middle-class, Protestant values and a hard-working, moralistic bourgeois society. Roman Catholic immigrants and those from the rural South, premodern intrusions into the new capitalist world, were sometimes marginalized at first as lazy, unproductive folk.

Regional zeal for *economic development continued unabated through the twentieth century. The urban face of the region was transformed in the first half of the century by millions of immigrants drawn to steel mills and automobile plants. But cultural losses accompanied the gains. As the scale of manufacturing increased, control passed from local entrepreneurs to outside investors. A few cities grew rapidly, but many smaller places stagnated or declined. With such change came nostalgia for the rural and small-town life of the past, and through an outpouring of gauzy novels, songs, and movies such as *State Fair* (1945), the Middle West was at least partially reinvented as a pastoral Eden. This process was geographical as well as historical, as the core of the perceived region shifted toward the relatively rural plains states, while residents of Michigan and Ohio began to label themselves as easterners. Meanwhile, novelists such as Hamlin Garland, Theodore *Dreiser, Sherwood Anderson, and Sinclair *Lewis offered a more jaundiced view of life in the Middle West.

The Middle West at the end of the twentieth century remained an agricultural area without peer, a highly efficient producer of corn, soybeans, hogs, and cattle. Marginal lands on the northern and southern borders had given way to resorts and national forests. Although heavy manufacturing had declined, Chicago, *Detroit, Minneapolis-St. Paul, and Cleveland remained among the nation's top ten industrial centers. Chicago, with a metropolitan population of nearly eight million people, is by far the region's largest urban place.

[*See also* Automotive Industry; Democratic Party; Factory

System; Indian History and Culture: From 1800 to 1900; Industrialization; Lumbering; Mining; Protestantism; Regionalism; Whig Party.]

• John Mack Faragher, *Sugar Creek: Life on the Illinois Prairie,* 1986. James H. Madison, ed., *Heartland: Comparative Histories of the Midwestern States,* 1988. James R. Shortridge, *The Middle West: Its Meaning in American Culture,* 1989. Andrew R. L. Cayton and Peter S. Onuf, eds., *The Midwest and the Nation: Rethinking the History of an American Region,* 1990. William Cronon, *Nature's Metropolis: Chicago and the Great West,* 1991. John C. Hudson, *Making the Corn Belt: A Geographical History of Middle-Western Agriculture,* 1994.

—James R. Shortridge

MIDWAY, BATTLE OF (1942), a decisive naval battle of *World War II. Disappointed with the results of his attack on the U.S. Pacific fleet at *Pearl Harbor in December 1941, Admiral Isoroku Yamamoto, commander of Japan's combined fleet, planned to capture Midway, a defended American atoll 1,100 miles northwest of Pearl Harbor. He hoped to lure the U.S. Pacific fleet into battle and destroy it. Such a success could have opened the prospect of invading *Hawai'i and perhaps, he hoped, ending the war. The preliminary air attack on Midway was scheduled for 4 June 1942 and the invasion on 6 June. Warned of the forthcoming attack by U.S. cryptanalysts who had penetrated the Japanese Navy's communications, Admiral Chester *Nimitz, commander of the U.S. Pacific fleet, strengthened Midway and quietly stationed three aircraft carriers nearby.

The Japanese air attack on Midway's air base on 4 June devastated most of the base's aircraft. But U.S. planes, attacking from nearby carriers, destroyed all four of the Japanese aircraft carriers, with all their airplanes and many of their pilots. Japan's losses in carriers and pilots proved irreplaceable; the American losses did not. Having saved Midway, and perhaps Hawai'i, from invasion, the United States took advantage of the Japanese losses to go on the offensive in the South Pacific—an offensive that ended with Japan's surrender in August 1945. The Battle of Midway was a crucial turning point in the Pacific war.

• John B. Lundstrom, *The First South Pacific Campaign: Pacific Fleet Strategy December 1941–June 1942,* 1976. Gordon W. Prange, Donald M. Goldstein, and Katherine V. Dillon, *Miracle at Midway,* 1982.

—Frank Uhlig Jr.

MIDWIFERY. Until the twentieth century, midwives delivered most of America's babies. Self-trained neighbor women, who assisted family members or nearby friends, were the most common, but increasingly aspiring midwives served apprenticeships with older, more experienced practitioners. A few, especially in urban areas, built up large practices, but the average midwife probably delivered no more than a dozen babies a year. Martha Ballard, who began practicing midwifery in the late eighteenth century in the village of Augusta, Maine, delivered at least 998 babies in 35 years of practice. Like other midwives of her time, she not only delivered babies but performed a wide range of medical services for her patients and their families. In rural areas especially, busy physicians often relied on midwives to attend time-consuming births, preferring to be called only in cases of emergency.

The typical midwife was a middle-aged, married, immigrant woman from the working class. Delivering babies, like taking in boarders and lodgers, allowed her to contribute to the domestic economy and still take care of her family's needs. By the late nineteenth century a few schools for midwives had appeared, most of them controlled by physicians. Indeed, an Illinois law, passed in 1896, required that only "legally qualified" physicians could teach in state-recognized midwifery schools. Although some midwifery schools were little more than diploma mills, others tried to provide an education comparable to that offered in Europe. The municipally controlled Bellevue Hospital School for Midwives in *New York City, founded in 1911, was reputed to be exemplary. Unlike nurses and teachers, midwives seldom aspired to professional status. They claimed neither a distinct body of knowledge nor control over the training and licensing of practitioners. Although some states regulated the practice of midwifery, Massachusetts banned midwifery in the 1890s and many southern states left midwifery free of control.

As late as 1900, about half of all the children born in the United States were delivered by midwives; by 1930 midwife-attended births had dropped to less than 15 percent of all births in the United States, and most of these were among *African Americans in the *South. Although obstetrics was the worst taught clinical specialty in American medical schools in the early twentieth century, and the safety record of midwives generally equaled that of physicians, parturient women increasingly opted for hospital-based, physician-assisted, pain-free birthing experiences. General practitioners and, increasingly after 1950, obstetricians attended most parturient women. Because midwives traditionally served their own ethnic communities, the decline in the number of immigrant families sharply reduced the practice of midwifery. By 1950, with the federal government picking up much of the cost of building new *hospitals, 93 percent of births to white mothers were taking place in hospitals; ten years later the figure had risen to virtually 100 percent. Midwives, however, still attended 28 percent of all minority women and 50 percent of rural nonwhite Americans in 1950.

By this time, however, some women were beginning to question the desirability of a fully drugged, physician-controlled delivery, and to protest what they regarded as inhumane and insensitive hospital care. Women in the feminist and countercultural movements helped to kindle a reexamination of physician-dominated obstetrics and to launch an alternative birthing movement. The movement did not survive the 1980s, but it did encourage the revival of midwifery in two forms: nurse-midwives, who worked primarily in hospitals under the aegis of physicians, and lay midwives, who worked independently and often extralegally. At the end of the century, midwives were attending under 5 percent of the nation's births.

[*See also* American Medical Association; Childbirth; Feminism; Medicine; Nursing.]

• Jane Donegan, *Women and Men Midwives: Medicine, Mortality, and Misogyny in Early America,* 1978. Judy Barrett Litoff, *American Midwives: 1860 to the Present,* 1978. Laurel Thatcher Ulrich, *A Midwife's Tale: The Life of Martha Ballard, Based on Her Diary, 1785–1812,* 1990. Charlotte G. Borst, *Catching Babies: The Professionalization of Childbirth, 1870–1920,* 1995. Gertrude Jacinta Fraser, *African American Midwifery in the South: Dialogues of Birth, Race, and Memory,* 1998.

—Charlotte G. Borst

MIGRATORY AGRICULTURAL WORKERS. Following the *Civil War, a migratory labor system of mobile, low-paid workers emerged in the United States to meet the seasonal demands of expanding capitalist *agriculture. Growers recruited an international pool of workers whose *poverty, racial stigmatization, and political disfranchisement made them willing to migrate. Dispossessed tenant farmers, sharecroppers, and small farmers, both native-born and immigrants, also joined the migrant pool. The 1924 immigration law created a vulnerable group of "illegal" immigrant workers, excluded from protective labor legislation. Government-sponsored contract-labor programs during both world wars and after 1945, developed in collaboration with agricultural interests, enlarged and diminished the migrant labor force as needed.

Resisting exploitation, migrant workers organized spontaneous strikes, ad hoc collective bargaining, temporary labor organizations, and eventually more permanent unions. Ignored by the *American Federation of Labor, they turned to left-wing and ethnic associations for collective bargaining. By 1910 the radical *Industrial Workers of the World, allied with the Partido Liberal Mexicano, organized migrants on both sides of the border. Ethnic labor organizations arose in *California in the 1920s, including the Mexican-based Confederación de Uniónes de Campesinos y Obreros Mexicanos (CUCOM). In 1928 the *Communist Party–USA's Trade Union Unity League, followed in 1931 by the Cannery and Agricultural Workers Industrial Union (CAWIU), organized migrant workers. In the 1930s, 140 strikes erupted in California, including one by 18,000 cotton workers. The CAWIU was broken by 1935, but in 1937 organizers formed the United Cannery, Agricultural, Packing and Allied Workers of America (UCAPAWA–CIO). The federal, state, and local governments usually backed the interests of the large farmers, however, while workers' exclusion from *New Deal–Era labor legislation weakened their position. The federally sponsored contract labor program undermined unionization efforts from 1942 until the program's demise in 1964. In 1965 Filipino and Mexican workers, led by farm worker and organizer Cesar *Chavez, formed the United Farm Workers, which led a protracted fight to improve conditions. Other unions followed, such as the Ohio-based Farmworker Labor Organizing Committee.

As the twentieth century ended, U.S. agriculture still depended heavily on migratory labor. Mixtec and Zapotec Indians from Mexico were the newest migrants, augmented by Jamaicans, Yemenites, and others. In response to economic globalization, binational organizations worked with domestic unions to organize these migrants.

[*See also* Agriculture: The "Golden Age" (1890s–1920); Agriculture: Since 1920; Hispanic Americans; Immigrant Labor; Immigration Law; Labor Movements; Sharecropping and Tenantry; Strikes and Industrial Conflict.]

• Dennis Nodin Valdes, *Al Norte: Agricultural Workers in the Great Lakes Region, 1917 to 1970,* 1991. Devra Weber, *Dark Sweat, White Gold: California Farm Workers, Cotton and the New Deal,* 1994.

—Devra Weber

MILITARY, THE. The military exists principally to counter external threats to the nation, although on occasion it may react to domestic unrest such as civil disorder. The American military has often mirrored other nations' armed forces, but unique circumstances have led to significant differences as well. Two influences account for these variations. European rulers often used their armies to exploit the citizenry. Many immigrants abhorred such treatment and harbored antimilitarist sentiments, which tended to limit the military and denied it an influential societal function. Moreover, the American colonies did not require a large military. To provide local defense and maintain order, voluntary (although sometimes conscripted) militia performed temporary, part-time service.

Colonial Era to 1900. Colonial militiamen often served under British commanders during the colonial wars. The inadequacy of colonial militia as a defense against French and Spanish incursions, however, led to the stationing of British regular army units in the colonies, especially during the *Seven Years' War. The militia tradition, together with the growing dislike for British professional troops, reinforced the antimilitary bent in the colonies and encouraged a tradition that demanded the subservience of military to civil authority. The *Revolutionary War confirmed the main lines of defense policy. The nation relied on volunteers to augment the regulars in the Continental Army, which demobilized rapidly after the war. The *War of 1812 did not significantly alter this policy, and for more than a century after the 1814 Treaty of *Ghent ending the Napoleonic wars, the United States maintained a small regular army and navy, augmented with volunteers when necessary. In addition to the army and the navy, the post–revolutionary U.S. military also included the Marine Corps, established by Congress in 1798 under the command of the secretary of the navy, with responsibilities for carrying out all land operations essential to naval campaigns. Under their motto "Semper Fidelis," the Marines have seen service in every American war.

Nineteenth-century America enjoyed a high level of security stemming from the restored European balance of power after Napoleon's defeat. Secure behind oceanic moats, the United States, while maintaining economic and cultural ties to the Old World, concentrated on domestic issues and continental projects. The army policed the *West as the frontier moved to the Pacific. The navy provided coastal defense and "showed the flag" in areas such as the Mediterranean Sea and the Pacific, notably in Admiral Matthew Perry's visit to Japan in 1853. The minuscule military, assuming continued peace, neglected preparation for warfare and failed to reach full professional competence.

In addition to the frontier Indian wars, the nation fought only two foreign wars between 1815 and 1914: the *Mexican War (1846–1848) and the *Spanish-American War (1898). In both these conflicts, the volunteer system produced sufficient manpower to defeat weak opponents at small cost, so no fundamental changes in the military seemed necessary. The creation of the U.S. Military Academy at West Point (1802) and a U.S. "Naval School" at Annapolis in 1845 (renamed the U.S. Naval Academy in 1850), however, helped professionalize officer training.

The one departure from this lengthy calm was the *Civil War. Neither the Union nor the Confederacy gained an early victory, forcing both to mobilize huge war-fighting military establishments. These forces, consisting mostly of state militiamen, volunteers, and conscripts, endured heavy casualties. Battle deaths were about 140,000 for the Union army and about 65,000 for the Confederates. But while the Civil War had a profound impact on those who fought in it, and on American society and politics, it had little long-term effect on the military. Confederate units melted away immediately after Appomattox, and the Union's forces quickly shrank to prewar size and influence. Some Civil War veterans were detailed westward to fight the Indian wars, but no foreign nation posed a vital threat. Statistics suggest why the old military paradigm emphasizing a small, quasiprofessional army endured for so long. Casualties for the major wars between 1775 and 1916 averaged but 2,200 per conflict. Expecting peace and eager to avoid expenditures, the nation continued to embrace the ideal of the citizen-soldier.

The U.S. military protected the insular possessions that the nation acquired in the aftermath of the Spanish-American War, but this function, analogous to that of frontier police, did not necessitate forces in any way comparable to the powerful military establishments of Europe. Although the foundation of the U.S. Naval War College at Newport, Rhode Island, in 1884 hastened the development of a modern navy, the army's turn-of-the-century efforts to modernize, including the establishment of an Army War College at Carlisle, Pennsylvania, in 1901 and the creation of a General Staff Corps in 1903, to reduce conflicts between the secretary of war and army generals, proved only moderately effective.

1900 through World War I. All this changed in the twentieth century as the United States emerged as a great power with global interests and responsibilities. The turning point was the outbreak of *World War I in August 1914, as vast historical processes such as *industrialization, nationalism, and imperialism undermined the balance of power that had underlain America's "free security" since 1815 and launched a violent century in which warfare became almost the norm. The coming of the war did not at first dictate extensive military changes for the United States. President Woodrow *Wilson, recognizing that the United States had vital interests at stake, attempted to mediate the conflict. When diplomacy failed and "peace without victory" proved anathema to the warring parties, Wilson realized that he could not influence the belligerents until he possessed a strong military, and he supported the Preparedness movement promoted by bankers, industrialists, and others with an interest in the Allied cause.

Wilson became the first U.S. president to attempt a significant, long-term upgrading of American military might, which he expected to continue until disarmament and collective security under a new world organization rendered it unnecessary. The Naval Act of 1916 reflected Wilson's determination to build "a navy second to none." Rejecting the principle of military volunteerism, Wilson in May 1917 pushed through Congress a Selective Service Act, establishing a national draft. *Conscription helped amass some 2.8 million men for military service. This rapid expansion foreshadowed a new military paradigm—active defense based on huge and highly professionalized armed forces, with war-fighting as a primary objective. Although the inexperienced American Expeditionary Forces did not perform well as an independent army in France, its sheer numbers gave the Allies the manpower superiority essential to victory, and the U.S. Navy made an undramatic but indispensable contribution to the antisubmarine campaign against German U-boats.

In the long run, Wilson envisioned a new world order based on self-determination and the peaceful resolution of conflict. Rejecting the traditional, European-based balance-of-power system as unstable and inequitable, he called for a new approach, *collective security, under a *League of Nations. The League, he believed, would preserve the peace by arbitrating disputes and eliminating the underlying causes of war. These ideas lay at the heart of Wilson's promise of a "just and lasting peace" and his hope for eventual general disarmament. The utter exhaustion of the European powers allowed Wilson to dominate the peace settlement and secure the inclusion of a covenant establishing the League of Nations in the Treaty of *Versailles.

The subsequent failure of the United States to lead the way toward Wilson's new system of international-security arrangements came not from the actions of other countries, but at the hands of the American people themselves. The brevity of the American intervention in World War I, and the shock of the conflict's appalling destructiveness, led Americans of the 1920s to revert to the old military paradigm. While Wilson's dream included eventual general disarmament, he insisted that in the interim the United States must maintain a military capable of assuming an appropriate role in peacekeeping. The postwar American public thought differently, however. Wilson's interventionism appeared unnecessary, the Allied victory having seemingly restored European stability and guaranteed a return to peaceful conditions. America's characteristically rapid postwar demobilization paralleled its refusal to accept international political responsibilities, even on issues that affected U.S. vital interests.

1920 through World War II. During the post–World War I period, a small military establishment, especially U.S. marines and naval vessels, engaged sporadically in constabulary tasks in U.S. dependencies—notably Cuba, the Dominican Republic, Haiti, and Nicaragua—but public opinion opposed more extensive engagement in world politics. In the 1930s, unpreparedness, appeasement, and a preoccupation with the domestic economic crisis helped open the door to the rise of dictators abroad, as Germany under Adolf Hitler renewed its aggression, the Japanese invaded China and pursued an expansionist policy throughout Southeast Asia, and Italy under the fascist regime of Benito Mussolini staked out imperial claims in Africa. Efforts to curb these threatening developments failed because the antihegemonic nations, including the United States, lacked the will to coordinate their efforts.

German and Japanese conquests finally brought on *World War II and U.S. intervention became inevitable after Japan's December 1941 attack on *Pearl Harbor. A huge economic and military mobilization eventually ensured the victory of the Grand Alliance, led by the United States, Britain, and the Soviet Union. Massive U.S. ground and naval forces, augmented by the Army Air Force and led by a professional command structure headed by Chief of Staff George *Marshall, provided the margin of victory in Europe and then defeated Japan. By war's end, some twelve million Americans had served in the armed forces. A powerful symbol of the military's enhanced wartime status was the Pentagon, a massive, five-sided structure covering thirty-four acres across the Potomac from Washington, D.C., completed in 1943 as the nerve center of the nation's military establishment.

The Cold-War and Vietnam-War Eras. President Franklin Delano *Roosevelt's vision for the postwar world order resembled Woodrow Wilson's grand design. The U.S. decision to join the *United Nations, another effort at collective security, came as America stood at the summit of world power, underlined by its early postwar monopoly of atomic weaponry. The Soviet Union soon emerged as a rival claimant for superpower status, however, consolidating its position by testing an atomic bomb in 1949. As the *Cold War began, hopes for a new international-security system faded. The veto granted to the great powers in the UN Security Council hamstrung that organization's peacekeeping capacity, and the United States instead relied on its own military strength and on regional alliances, especially the *North Atlantic Treaty Organization (NATO), founded in 1949 to preserve security. In building up a powerful military in order to wage the Cold War, however, the United States embraced Wilson's vision of America's military and foreign-policy role in preserving peace and maintaining a world balance of power in the interim, before new international organizations could assume responsibility for collective security.

Another effect of the Cold War on the U.S. military was the major administrative restructuring brought about by the *National Security Act of 1947. Under this law, the War Department became the cabinet-level Department of Defense; the Army Air Corps became an independent service, the U.S. Air Force; and the heads of the various military services were brought into a single body, the *Joint Chiefs of Staff, under the overall authority of the civilian secretary of defense. The aim of this law (which also created the *National Security Council and the *Central Intelligence Agency) was to bring greater coherence and rationality into U.S. military and strategic planning, and to reduce interservice rivalries as the nation geared up for a long-term struggle with the Soviet empire.

The shadow of *nuclear weapons hung over the Cold War. Both the United States and the Soviet Union recognized that to deter nuclear war, each side's nuclear forces must be credible—that is, capable of inflicting unacceptable damage on the other. A rough balance of threat, summed up in the phrase "mutual assured destruction," was attained by the 1960s. President John F. *Kennedy, while accepting the basic principle of nuclear deterrence, also championed "flexible response," a strategic posture stressing the nation's capacity to fight not only a major war, but also small-scale insurgencies. After the 1962 *Cuban Missile Crisis, Kennedy also pursued nuclear arms control and welcomed the *Limited Nuclear Test Ban Treaty of 1963. Presidents Richard M. *Nixon and Jimmy *Carter continued this trend, negotiating important treaties with the Russian leader Leonid Brezhnev. Arms control lost steam during the later 1970s, however, when various crises, notably the Soviet intervention in Afghanistan and the overthrow of the pro-U.S. Shah of Iran, derailed détente. President Ronald *Reagan sponsored an arms build-up during the early 1980s, but eventually resumed arms control and disarmament negotiations with Russian leader Mikhail Gorbachev.

The mutual deterrence that prevented all-out war between the superpowers did not extend to regional conflicts. In the *Korean War (1950–1953) and the *Vietnam War (1965–1972), the United States intervened to prevent communist conquests of divided countries. Washington gained its objectives in the first of these proxy wars, but not in the second. Successive administrations from the 1950s on endorsed the "domino theory," which held that communist success in one locale would inevitably lead to a series of further conquests, but this notion proved unreliable as a guide to military policy in Southeast Asia.

U.S. war-planning in Vietnam, as well as the development of U.S. *nuclear strategy, reflected the increasing use of game theory, mathematically based planning and assessment, and computer-assisted statistical analyses. Robert S. McNamara, U.S. secretary of defense from 1961 to 1968, a business statistician who had served as president of Ford Motor Company before entering government, strongly encouraged these approaches, an aspect of his desire to preserve civilian control of the military.

Despite the debacle of Vietnam, the American military reached its zenith of prestige during the Cold War. The necessity of maintaining a credible military deterrent, involving both nuclear and conventional forces, created a permanent military class, including several million personnel. Military leaders and their civilian counterparts in the defense industry gained extensive influence in national decision-making, sometimes opposing domestic programs they deemed threatening to the defense budget. This unprecedented development in a nation with a strong antimilitarist tradition raised fears of military dominance in collusion with defense contractors. President Dwight D. *Eisenhower, the most revered U.S. military commander of the twentieth century, warned in his 1961 Farewell Address to the American people that a "military-industrial complex" might gain such power as to compromise the democratic process. Scholars who traced the growth and influence of the military and the defense industry in Cold War America lent plausibility to Eisenhower's thesis, as did antiwar activists in the Vietnam War Era, who used it to explain President Lyndon B. *Johnson's dogged pursuit of an increasingly unpopular war.

Fears of an all-powerful military-industrial complex proved exaggerated, however, largely because of strong countervailing pressures. Various interests resisted excessive military influence in politics, some reflecting traditional antimilitarism, others concerned about soaring budget deficits, and still others competing for scarce resources to fund nonmilitary programs. Further, the military itself proved faithful to the professional credo of civilian control. Military counsel inevitably played an influential Cold War role, but civilian control remained firm, surviving even President Harry S. *Truman's unpopular dismissal of the World War II hero General Douglas *MacArthur in 1951, for insubordination in his role as commander of UN forces in Korea. Civilian defense intellectuals in foundations such as California's RAND Corporation, although fully committed to the new military paradigm, also reinforced the principle of civilian control.

The Post–Cold-War Era. With the end of the Cold War, regional conflicts and crises again came to the fore, initially in the Persian Gulf, where Iraq's 1990 invasion of Kuwait threatened oil shipments to the West. South Korea, where U.S. troops remained to deter possible aggression from North Korea, constituted a potential flashpoint as well. In some areas, the post–Cold War United Nations played a larger role in dealing with regional conflicts. Woodrow Wilson's vision of collective security became feasible whenever unanimity could be mustered within the Security Council. During the 1990s the United States supported UN missions in several areas, including Somalia and Bosnia. The defeat of Iraq in the *Persian Gulf War involved the mobilization of a multinational force totaling nearly 500,000 troops, with the U.S. military in overall command. When the UN could not take the lead, the United States still tried to act in some other multilateral framework, as in the 1999 NATO bombing of Serbia, in response to Serbian attacks on ethnic Albanians in the province of Kosovo.

Such operations seemed comparable in some respects to the earlier peacetime work of the army on the western frontier and in the management of the American empire at the beginning of the twentieth century. As Pentagon planning centered on "low intensity" or "middle intensity" conflicts, the post–Cold War changes in mission portended alterations—and reductions—in force structures. Budget planners of the late 1990s assumed significantly lower annual defense outlays than during the Cold War. President Bill *Clinton sought to redress the balance between military and nonmilitary expenditures in favor of the latter. In his second inaugural address, in 1997, Clinton dealt only briefly with national-security matters—a clear indication of the lower priority accorded to the military in the aftermath of the Cold War. The operations in the Persian Gulf and Serbia also showed a desire to minimize casualities on the ground by the massive application of America's overwhelming superiority in air power and sophisticated military technology.

As a new century dawned, some observers saw in these trends the potential for a turn toward *isolationism and a resurgence of the nation's long antimilitarist tradition, but this seemed unlikely. America stood alone as a superpower with extensive international interests and deeply immersed in the world's affairs. Global economic interdependence alone precluded retreat. Despite scaled-back budgets and objectives, the U.S. military headed into the twenty-first century with continued high prestige and, after the end of the draft in 1973, an all-volunteer service. It was also an institution with a very different demographic profile from that of earlier generations. A 1948 executive order by President Truman requiring racial integration was implemented during the Korean War, and opportunities for minorities and women increased substantially as the services worked to recruit volunteers.

Despite the antimilitarist tradition, Americans have always held their military leaders in high regard, as evidenced by the election of a succession of war heroes as president, from George *Washington to Dwight Eisenhower, and including Andrew *Jackson, William Henry *Harrison, Zachary *Taylor, and Ulysses S. *Grant. The military exploits of other presidents, including Rutherford *Hayes, Theodore *Roosevelt, John F. *Kennedy, and George *Bush, proved decided political assets. But Americans have also treasured the principle of civilian control, recognizing its indispensability to the preservation of government of, by, and for the people.

[*See also* American Legion; Antiwar Movements; Army Corps of Engineers; Conscientious Objection; Draft Riots, Civil War; Federal Government, Executive Branch: Department of Defense; Foreign Relations; Grand Army of the Republic; Indian History and Culture: From 1800 to 1900; Indian Wars; Military Service Academies; Pershing, John J.; Preparedness Controversy; Veterans Administration.]

• Arthur A. Ekirch Jr., *The Civilian and the Military: A History of the American Antimilitarist Tradition,* 1956. Samuel P. Huntington, *The Soldier and the State: The Theory and Politics of Civil-Military Relations,* 1957. Russell F. Weigley, *Towards an American Army: Military Thought from Washington to Marshall,* 1962. Russell F. Weigley, *The American Way of War: A History of United States Military Strategy and Policy,* 1973. Allan R. Millett, *Semper Fidelis: The History of the United States Marine Corps,* 1980. Kenneth J. Hagan, ed., *In Peace and War: Interpretations of American Naval History, 1775–1984,* 2d. ed., 1984. Allan R. Millett and Peter Maslowski, *For the Common Defense,* 1984. Kenneth J. Hagan and William R. Roberts, eds., *Against All Enemies: Interpretations of American Military History from Colonial Times to the Present,* 1986. Kenneth J. Hagan, *This People's Navy: The Making of American Sea Power,* 1991. John E. Jessup and Louise B. Ketz, eds., *Encyclopedia of the American Military,* 3 vols., 1994. John Whiteclay Chambers II, ed., *The Oxford Companion to American Military History,* 1999.

—David F. Trask

MILITARY-INDUSTRIAL COMPLEX. *See* Weaponry, Nonnuclear; Eisenhower, Dwight D.

MILITARY SERVICE ACADEMIES. Americans have long had an ambivalent relationship with their military service academies. In general, they appreciate traditions that emphasize patriotism, hard work, and discipline, but are skeptical of institutions that smack of military elitism or appear to perpetuate a distinct military caste with values and agendas different from those of society.

The nation's founders viewed willingness for military service as a key indicator of the health of the nation's republican ideals. Civic virtue meant bearing one's share of the nation's defense. A corollary of this citizen-soldier ideal was fear of professional soldiers who did not owe allegiance to society but to the institutions that employed them. The *Revolutionary War, however, raised doubts about the skills of the citizen-soldier, especially in a severe national emergency. Ex–Continental Army officers and *Federalist party members like George *Washington and Alexander *Hamilton advocated a regular officer corps. Ironically, it was the Federalists' archrival, Thomas *Jefferson, who authorized the establishment of the U.S. Military Academy at West Point, New York, in 1802. West Point's founders, understanding the fears about a professional officer corps, emphasized the school's *engineering reputation rather than its military functions. The army's combat record in the *War of 1812 convinced national leaders of the need for better-trained officers. Sylvanus Thayer's appointment as superintendent in 1817 led to many reforms, including more courses directly related to leading troops in battle.

The U.S. Navy initially patterned itself after Great Britain's Royal Navy in educating its officers. Midshipmen were trained at sea and their education varied, depending on the particular captain under whom they served. Concerns about this irregular system escalated following the 1842 *Somers* incident in which a midshipman, whose father happened to be the secretary of war, led a shipboard mutiny. In 1845, Secretary of the Navy George *Bancroft, temporarily serving as secretary of war, established the Naval Academy at Fort Severn in Annapolis, Maryland. It almost closed during the *Civil War after its relocation to Rhode Island and with many students assigned to the naval blockade of the Confederacy. Naval reformers like David Porter and Stephen Luce, however, revitalized the school in the postwar years.

As the nation's military expanded in the twentieth century, the academies became central to a highly stratified system of officer education. Academy graduates dominated the leadership of both services during the two world wars and solidified public faith in the service academy system. The *Cold War Era, however, saw the end of the service academies' monopoly as the sole providers of regular officers. New programs like Reserve Officers Training Corps (ROTC) and Officer Candidate School (OCS), based in civilian colleges and universities, eventually provided the bulk of regular officers to both services. The academies began emphasizing instead their role in maintaining service traditions and values and in providing officers who remained for an entire career. The U.S. Air Force Academy was established at Colorado Springs, Colorado, in 1954, confirming the importance of airpower to strategic planning. During the 1970s and 1980s, each of the academies made greater efforts to incorporate minorities and eventually women into their ranks because of pressure to make the officer corps more representative of society.

[*See also* Military, The.]

• Stephen Ambrose, *Duty, Honor, Country: A History of West Point,* 1966. Joseph Ellis and Robert Moore, *School for Soldiers: West Point and the Profession of Arms,* 1974. Allan R. Millett and Peter Maslowski, *For the Common Defense,* 1984. Jack Sweetman and Thomas Cutler, *The U.S. Naval Academy: An Illustrated History,* 1995.

—Todd Forney

MILLENNIALISM AND APOCALYPTICISM. The *Bible contains prophecies about a future golden age and the cataclysmic end of the world. Some of these texts are apocalyptic (from the Greek "to reveal" or "uncover") visions of impending disaster and divine rescue (Daniel, Ezekiel, Revelation). In the New Testament, such texts include the Second Coming of Christ (Matthew 24 and Mark 13, for example) and Christ's millennial (from the Latin *mille,* "thousand") reign (Revelation 20). Over time, many Christians have developed elaborate scenarios of the "end times" (including a coming Antichrist; persecution, famines, and plagues; and the battle of Armageddon) and have speculated about "signs of the times" that point to such prophetic fulfillments.

During the *Colonial Era, the Puritans John Cotton and Increase and Cotton *Mather identified the Roman papacy as the Antichrist and found prophetic significance in their own "errand into the wilderness." Others like Jonathan *Edwards foresaw Christ's return *after* the world's gradual "christianization" ("postmillennialism"). Christian patriots during the *Revolutionary War viewed George III as the Antichrist and America as the persecuted "Woman in the Wilderness" (Revelation 12). Later, Timothy Dwight and others interpreted the excesses of the French Revolution in apocalyptic terms and feared their spread to the New World.

In the *Antebellum Era, most Evangelical Protestants were optimistic postmillennialists. Lyman Beecher and Charles G. *Finney saw revivals and social reform as signs that the millennium was imminent. Many communal or utopian experiments espoused millennialist views including Mother Ann Lee's United Society of Believers in Christ's Second Coming (Shakers). Shakers saw Lee as the female incarnation of the Second Coming and started communities to prepare for the approaching millennium. John Humphrey *Noyes taught that Christ had returned in A.D. 70 but did not establish the earthly millennium because his followers lacked Christian love. To correct this deficit, Noyes founded a community near Putney, Vermont, in 1838, but opposition to his views of "complex marriage" forced a move to Oneida, New York, in 1848. There, commercial success eventually overshadowed millennialist concerns.

A more successful communal group was Joseph Smith's Church of Jesus Christ of Latter-Day Saints. Citing a series of divine revelations, including the Book of Mormon, Smith proclaimed Christ's imminent return and even produced a city plan for the new Zion in Jackson County, Missouri, to which site he instructed all Mormons to move. However, the Mormons were driven out of Missouri, and, after a short stay in Nauvoo, Illinois, and Smith's murder, relocated in Utah, where they still await Christ's return.

Also in the 1830s, William Miller (1782–1849), a Baptist preacher from New England, adopting an interpretive approach popular in Great Britain, used "millennial arithmetic" drawn primarily from the Book of Daniel to calculate Christ's return in 1843–1844. The Millerites rejected notions of gradual "christianization," taught that Christ will come *before* the millennium ("premillennialism"), and used sophisticated publicity to promote their beliefs. After the "great disappointment" on 22 October 1844 (the date Miller eventually settled on), some Millerites regrouped as Seventh-day Adventists, who continued to take prophecy seriously, though avoiding date-setting.

After the *Civil War, a new kind of premillennialism, "dispensationalism," gained popularity. Based on the Englishman John Nelson Darby's interpretations of various prophetic texts, dispensationalists fashioned a detailed end-time scenario, including worsening world conditions (which made sense in an era of often turbulent social change); the rebirth of Israel; Antichrist's rise and the "pretribulation rapture," whereby the faithful are snatched from the earth to escape the horrors of Antichrist's reign. Spread through prophecy conferences, Bible institutes, and the popular *Scofield Reference Bible* (1909), dispensationalism became almost synonymous with *Pentecostalism and fundamentalism in the twentieth century. Hal Lindsey's best-selling *The Late Great Planet Earth* (1970), the Left Behind novels of Tim LaHaye and Jerry B. Jenkins in the 1990s, and countless other paperbacks, television programs, video tapes, and films spread the dispensationalist doctrine. The strong support for Israel among fundamentalists like Jerry Falwell, Pat Robertson, and James Hagee was rooted in dispensationalism.

During the 1990s, apocalyptic views were tied to two well-publicized and ill-fated groups: David Koresh's Branch Davidians, a defection from the Seventh-day Adventists, who died in a confrontation with federal agents in Waco, Texas (1993); and Marshall Applewhite's Heaven's Gate followers, who combined New Age and millennialist teachings to justify group suicide in Southern California (1997). A revival of postmillennialism was also apparent in the New Christian Right's efforts to create a "Christian America."

[*See also* Christian Coalition; Fundamentalist Movement; Moral Majority; Mormonism; New Age Movement; Protestantism; Religion; Revivalism; Roman Catholicism; Seventh-day Adventism; Shakerism; Utopian and Communitarian Movements.]

• Michael Barkun, *Disaster and the Millennium,* 1974. Ronald Numbers and Jonathan Butler, eds., *The Disappointed,* 1987. Timothy Weber, *Living in the Shadow of the Second Coming,* 1987. Paul Boyer, *When Time Shall Be No More,* 1992. Thomas Robbins and Susan Palmer, eds., *Millennium, Messiahs, and Mayhem,* 1997.

—Timothy P. Weber

MILLIKAN, ROBERT A. (1868–1953), physicist and Nobel laureate. Robert A. Millikan was born in Morrison, Illinois, the son of a Congregational minister. In 1875, the family moved to Maquoketa, Iowa. He entered Oberlin College in 1886, intending to study Greek and Latin, but found physics more interesting. After receiving his A.B. (1891) and M.A. (1893) from Oberlin, Millikan enrolled as a graduate student at Columbia University, earning his Ph.D. in physics in 1895. In 1896, after a year at the universities of Berlin and Göttingen, he joined the University of Chicago physics department. Millikan married Greta Blanchard in 1902; they had three sons.

Millikan's scientific reputation rests on his measurement of the charge on the electron (1907–1917), his verification of Albert *Einstein's quantum equation for the photoelectric effect (1916), and his numerical determination of Max Planck's constant. The success of these experiments made him one of America's best known and most distinguished physicists well before he won the Nobel Prize for Physics in 1923. Actively involved in the organization of American science, Millikan during *World War I headed the science and research division of the Army Signal Corps. He also organized the physics work of the new National Research Council.

Moving to the California Institute of Technology in 1921, Millikan, as director of the Norman Bridge physics laboratory, began research on cosmic rays, a term he coined. As chair of the Institute's executive council he functioned as its de facto president and played a major role in its early development until his retirement in 1945.

[*See also* Physical Sciences; Science: From 1914 to 1945.]

• Robert A. Kargon, *The Rise of Robert Millikan: Portrait of a Life in American Science,* 1982. Judith R. Goodstein, *Millikan's School: A History of the California Institute of Technology,* 1991.

—Judith R. Goodstein

MINING has played a central role in American *economic development. Coal, petroleum, natural gas, and uranium helped fuel *industrialization. Iron, cement, copper, and other mine products were transformed into manufactured goods and buildings. Gold and silver have at times served as monetary metals. Mining and drilling contributed to the accumulation of numerous family fortunes, including those of the Guggenheims, Rockefellers, Hearsts, and Mellons. Historically, the growth of mining and the growth of the economy were strongly intertwined. Between 1880 and 1970, mining output was cyclical and the trend rate of growth for mining and real gross domestic product were similar. After 1970, however, mining output remained flat.

Iron, copper, and coal were originally mined from outcroppings at or near the earth's surface, and gold was panned in streams. As the demand for mine products increased, miners searched farther afield, dug deeper, and drilled in the ocean. The increased difficulty of tapping these resources led to increased capital investment and dramatic changes in mine technologies. Through the early 1920s, many mines depended on workers using hand tools and rule-of-thumb techniques, while mules and steam-run hoists or pumps moved the materials to the surface. Increases in mine output required more mine workers, although technological improvements in blasting and machinery based on steam, compressed air, and then electricity contributed to steady growth in output per miner. After the 1920s the pace of technological change increased dramatically. New machinery dug, drilled, pumped, and clawed underground, and many mines began using large-scale earth movers to strip the hillsides above the mine seams. Consequently, mine output rose nearly eight-fold from the mid-1920s to the 1970s despite a 40 percent reduction in the number of miners. The improvements in mining *technology also cut accident rates in half. Mining remained dangerous, however, as evidenced by a series of mining disasters, including those in Mather, Pennsylvania (1928, 195 dead); Centralia, Illinois (1947, 111 dead); and West Frankfort, Illinois (1951, 119 dead).

Mining was often the leading edge of development in isolated areas. *Gold rushes and silver rushes opened up *California, Nevada, Arizona, and the Black Hills. When coal and copper mines opened in unpopulated and undeveloped areas, employers attracted workers from outside the region by establishing company towns with housing, stores, and schools. As the number of mines increased or other industries developed, company towns gave way to independent towns and cities. In some isolated regions, however, the population dwindled when the resource was depleted, leaving ghost towns behind.

During the employment booms in the early 1900s, mine owners competed fiercely for labor. Consequently, miners were often highly mobile; they earned high hourly wages to compensate for the dangers of mining, and employers hired an ethnically diverse workforce. Competition among numerous mines in combination with the miners' use of collective action limited the employers' abilities to exploit their monopoly power in company towns. Miners went on strike more frequently than other workers, and several violent episodes erupted in the mine fields. Mine workers often were leaders in the major union movements. The hardrock miner William D. ("Big Bill") Haywood led the radical *Industrial Workers of the World. The United Mine Workers of America, led by John L. *Lewis, played a leading role in the *American Federation of Labor and the *Congress of Industrial Organizations.

[*See also* Carnegie, Andrew; Hearst, William Randolph; Iron and Steel Industry; Labor Markets; Petroleum Industry; Rockefeller, John D.; Strikes and Industrial Conflict.]

• John Laslett, ed., *The United Mine Workers of America: A Model of Industrial Solidarity?,* 1996. David Pearson, *This Was Mining in the West,* 1996.

—Price Fishback

MINSTRELSY, a popular form of nineteenth-century urban entertainment. Between 1843 and the *Civil War, dozens of troupes of white men in blackface performed minstrelsy in cities across America. Presented as a loosely structured series of songs, jokes, dances, variety acts, and skits, minstrelsy depicted foolish, sensual, and sentimental images of *African Americans for native-born workers, Irish immigrants, rural newcomers, and other white working-class males who constituted its primary audience. By presenting images of a degraded Other, minstrelsy helped to bridge ethnic and cultural differences among white workers, who consequently came to define their class allegiances in racial terms. After the Civil War, the production and reception of minstrelsy changed, as women and African Americans performed on the minstrel stage and audiences included more middle-class, white spectators and some

MAP 13: NEVADA SILVER MINES IN THE 1870S

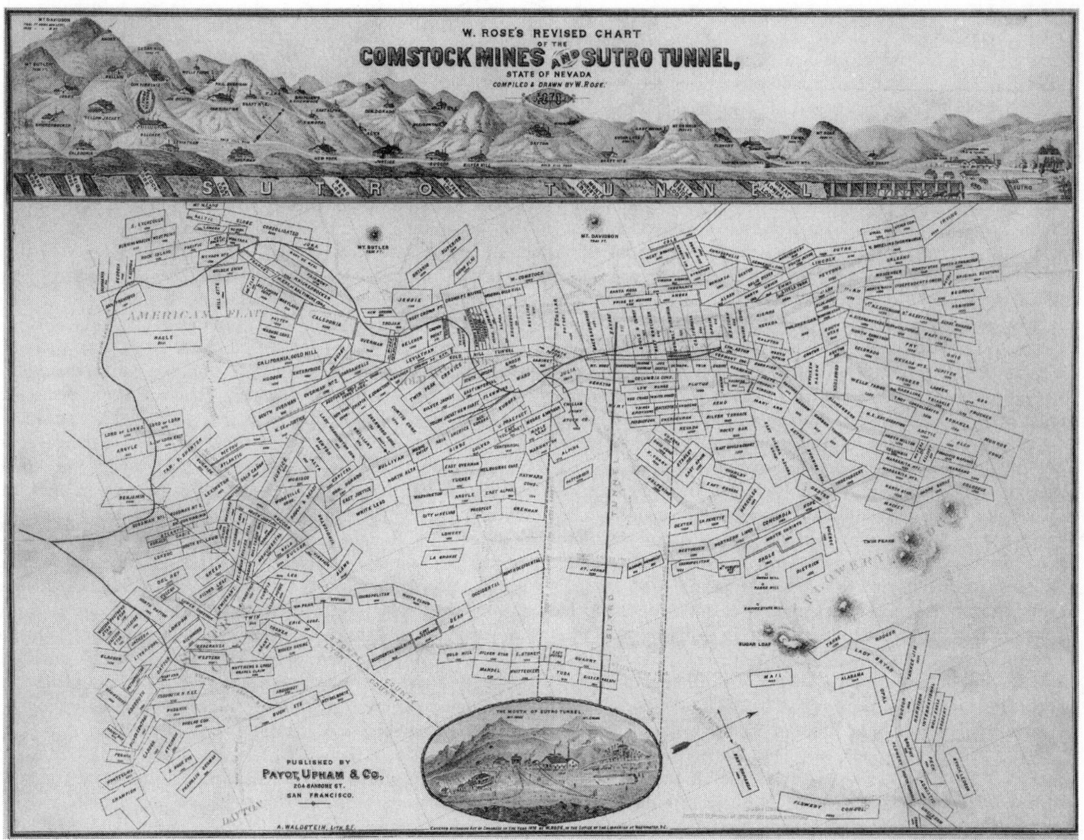

This 1878 map shows scores of small mining claims staked out by prospectors who had rushed to western Nevada to exploit a rich vein of silver, the Comstock Lode, which was named after a local sheepherder and prospector. The sketch at the top shows mining settlements with such names as Justice, Succor, Europa, Silver Hill, and Yellow Jacket. By 1898 most of these settlements had been abandoned. The Comstock Lode's fabulous output of silver, a monetary metal, affected the economy and politics of the late nineteenth century.

[*See* Bryan, William Jennings; Free Silver Movement; Gilded Age; Gold Standard; Mining; Monetary Policy, Federal; Populist Party.]

African Americans. Blackface acts remained generally racist, however, even as individual performers joined *vaudeville, burlesque, and other forms of *popular culture in the 1890s.

The conventions of white performers "blacking up" derived from European traditions. The black face had long signified a trickster figure in folk rituals of inversion, including charivari shaming rites and many Anglo-American festivals. Thomas D. Rice, George Washington Dixon, and other blackface performers popular in the 1830s combined these musical and theatrical traditions with African-American costuming, dancing, and instrumental practices. After the formation of the first minstrel troupe in 1843, blackface musicians appropriated other performance elements from the intercultural life of the plantation *South. These included the corn-shucking ritual, which influenced the beginning of the show and the banter among minstrel comics.

Both Jacksonian *republicanism and northern conceptions of the slave South shaped this working-class entertainment. Idealized images of happy slaves and generous masters (especially evident in the minstrel music of Stephen *Foster) pervaded minstrelsy in the 1850s, encouraging audiences to denigrate free as well as enslaved African Americans. At the same time, minstrelsy lampooned professional pretensions by parodying lawyers and politicians, and undercut elite power by satirizing the rich. In addition to sentimentalizing light-skinned female slaves, minstrelsy attacked assertive women through its ridicule of the "wench" character; men played both of these female roles in ways that encouraged homosocial enjoyment.

Although African Americans had appeared on minstrel stages before 1861, their numbers increased after the Civil War. Successful in part because of their claim to delineate authentic Negro life, black troupes nonetheless continued the stereotypes of the carefree Jim Crow, loyal Uncle Tom, and dandified Zip Coon. The interracial popularity of African-American performer Billy Kersands induced some southern theater owners to suspend racially segregated seating practices when his troupe came to town. The success of burlesque in the late 1860s spawned several all-female white troupes performing standard minstrel routines in whiteface. Bourgeois interest in *gender difference and sexual desire also led to the popularity of female impersonators. The large companies and sumptuous productions of Jack H. Haverly revived minstrely in the 1880s, but the rise of vaudeville soon splintered the troupes and dispersed their performers.

Minstrelsy traditions continued to shape the careers of such performers as Bert Williams and Al Jolson; popular entertainment, including the "Amos 'n' Andy" *radio show; and the larger contours of race relations in the United States. Minstrelsy also proved immensely popular in England and the British Empire; indeed, it influenced the social construction of "whiteness" throughout the world.

[*See also* Antebellum Era; Gilded Age; Music: Popular Music; Race and Ethnicity; Racism; Slavery; Social Class; Working-Class Life and Culture.]

• Robert C. Toll, *Blacking-Up: The Minstrel Show in Nineteenth-Century America,* 1974.

—Bruce McConachie

MIRANDA* v. *ARIZONA (1966), landmark *Supreme Court case involving the rights of arrested persons. Prior to *Miranda,* the "voluntariness" test governed the admissibility of confessions. But determining whether a confession was "voluntary" involved so many variables that the test became extremely subjective. Moreover, trial judges almost always resolved in the government's favor the inevitable disagreements over what tactics police interrogators had utilized. Addressing the shortcomings of the "voluntariness" test, the Supreme Court in *Miranda* offered a clearer, more manageable alternative.

On the basis of his confession, Ernesto Miranda, an indigent, poorly educated twenty-three-year-old, had been convicted in Arizona of kidnapping and rape. On appeal, the case reached the Supreme Court. Although his two hours of questioning had been comparatively mild, Miranda had not been advised of his right to consult with an attorney, or to have a lawyer present, before answering any questions. Because the confession was obtained under circumstances the High Court found constitutionally unacceptable, Miranda's conviction was reversed.

The Fifth Amendment provides that no person "shall be compelled in any criminal case to be a witness against himself." The pre-*Miranda* view was that this provision applied only to judicial or other formal proceedings. But in *Miranda,* a 5–4 majority led by Chief Justice Earl *Warren held that the self-incrimination clause also applied to the informal compulsion exerted by the *police during their interrogations after a suspect has been arrested.

In the "interrogation environment," the *Miranda* majority concluded, a suspect typically assumed (erroneously) or was misled by the police into believing that he or she had to answer their questions. Thus, unless "adequate protective devices" were utilized to dispel the anxiety and coercion inherent in police interrogation, no statement obtained from a suspect could truly be the product of a free choice. The "adequate protective devices" set down by the Court (unless the government adopted other equally effective means) were the now-familiar *Miranda* warnings against self-incrimination and notification of the right to counsel.

In reality, *Miranda* is a much more limited ruling than was at first realized. Its principal weakness (or, depending upon one's viewpoint, its saving grace) is that it permits someone subjected to the inherent pressures of arrest and detention to waive his or her rights without obtaining the advice of counsel. Moreover, *Miranda* permits the police to obtain the waiver of a suspect's rights without the presence of a judicial officer or any disinterested observer and without making any formal record of the "waiver" transaction.

When President Richard M. *Nixon, after sharply criticizing *Miranda* during his successful 1968 presidential campaign, appointed four new Supreme Court justices, many thought *Miranda* would be overruled. But this did not happen, and by the 1990s the Supreme Court understood *Miranda*'s limited scope. Further, most empirical studies indicated that it had no significant adverse effect on law enforcement. The police, despite their initial anger, had similarly learned to live with the rule.

To some, *Miranda* remains the "red flag" of the Warren Court's activism in the criminal law area. To others it symbolizes the willingness of the American legal system to treat even the lowliest criminal suspect as worthy of respect and consideration.

[*See also* Civil Rights; Crime.]

• Yale Kamisar, *Police Interrogation and Confessions,* 1980. Liva Baker, *Miranda: Crime, Law and Politics,* 1983. Yale Kamisar, "Miranda, the Case, the Man, and the Players," *Michigan Law Review* 82 (February 1984): 1074–92. Stephen J. Schulhofer, "Reconsidering *Miranda,*" *University of Chicago Law Review* 54 (Spring 1987): 435–61. Richard A. Leo, "The Impact of *Miranda* Revisited," *Journal of Criminal Law and Criminology* 86 (Spring 1996): 621–92.

—Yale Kamisar

MISSILES AND ROCKETS. In 1814, as the British besieged Fort McHenry at Baltimore, Francis Scott Key observed their rocket barrages; his poem describing the scene eventually became America's national anthem, making his descriptive phrase, "rockets' red glare," part of the nation's heritage. Later, Americans used similar solid-powder rockets during the *Mexican War and to carry life lines to stricken ships.

Advances in metallurgy and chemistry led to more powerful liquid-propellant rockets in the twentieth century. In 1926, on his aunt's farm in Massachusetts, Robert Goddard (1882–1945), a professor of physics at Clark University, launched the first successful rocket of this type. The American Interplanetary Society (AIS, 1933) and the California Institute of Technology figured prominently in subsequent developments. AIS members formed a company, Reaction Motors, that developed many *World War II production techniques and engines, which powered experimental rocket planes such as the postwar X–1 and the X–15. Caltech researchers organized the famed Jet Propulsion Laboratory and established companies like Aerojet General that manufactured wartime propulsion and guidance systems. Such activities created an infrastructure that quickly absorbed the advanced wartime rocket technology developed by Germany, especially the V–2 ballistic missile. In 1945, Wernher von Braun (1912–1977) and other German experts were brought to America to continue development of military missiles and high-altitude research rockets.

*Cold War tensions led to massive expenditures for land and submarine-based ballistic missiles. After the Soviets orbited the first artificial satellite (Sputnik) in 1957, America overhauled its civilian *space program, creating the *National Aeronautics and Space Administration (NASA), which developed rockets to lift astronauts on a trajectory for the first lunar landing in 1969. Subsequent research enhanced military rocket boosters for warheads as well as surveillance satellites; modified versions lifted civilian weather and communications satellites. By the end of the twentieth century, the NASA space shuttle and booster rockets from the former Soviet Union were being configured to launch components of an international space station.

[*See also* Nuclear Strategy; Nuclear Weapons; Technology.]

• Walter McDougal, *The Heavens and the Earth: A Political History of the Space Age*, 1985. Frank Winter. *Rockets into Space*, 1990.

—Roger E. Bilstein

MISSIONARY MOVEMENT. Christian missionaries from several nations participated in the earliest European settlement of the Americas. Roman Catholic priests accompanied Spanish and Portuguese conquistadors in Latin America in their assaults on Indian populations, and evangelizing Jesuits and Franciscans in the eighteenth century established an Hispanic presence in present-day *California. In eastern North America, French Jesuits preceded French settlers into Indian territory. In the late seventeenth century, the Church of England sent Protestant missionaries to the Maryland Tidewater.

The English dissenters who settled Massachusetts, however, were not primarily missionaries. They focused less on evangelizing pagans than on establishing a godly community among themselves. Even during the First Great Awakening, which crested in the 1740s, revivalists stressed the conversion of sinners in their midst rather than the evangelizing of Indians or foreign heathen. The Second Great Awakening of the early nineteenth century, however, stimulated a missionary movement focused on converting heathen at home and abroad. A group of seminarians gained the support of both Presbyterian and Congregational parishes in organizing the long-lived American Board of Commissioners for Foreign Missions (ABCFM) in 1810. In 1812, the ABCFM sent its first missionaries to India, among them Adoniram Judson. Becoming a *Baptist, Judson played a key role in organizing a Baptist foreign missionary society. With denominationalism on the rise, the Presbyterians established their own Board of Foreign Missions in 1837, and many other denominations followed suit.

Although important to home congregations, the foreign missionary movement sent relatively few missionaries to such fields as India, Africa, and China prior to the *Civil War. With the war's end, however, as missionary organizations increasingly targeted the American *West and the foreign field, the numbers of missionaries increased to the thousands, their ranks augmented by women. For years wives had accompanied their missionary husbands as "assistant missionaries." Confined largely to the domestic sphere, they had provided only limited ministry to indigenous women, who were frequently barred by social taboos from contact with foreign men. After the Civil War, however, churchwomen began to address the needs of "heathen" women by organizing separate boards to send single women to the field. "Woman's Work for Woman," a Presbyterian periodical proclaimed. Soon single and married women missionaries outnumbered men by a ratio as high as two to one.

The appointment of women missionaries coincided with an expanding emphasis on lay work and the introduction of the *Social Gospel to missions. Early missionaries had been ordained ministers eager to save souls. In the late nineteenth century, conditions in crowded urban slums persuaded home churches to supplement gospel preaching with needed social services. In *Our Country* (1885), home-missionary Josiah Strong argued for a broadened mission, advocating the "Anglo-Saxonizing" of the world. ABCFM missionaries had played a critical role in Christianizing and colonizing *Hawai'i following their arrival in 1820, thereby contributing to the annexation of that territory in 1894. By 1900, both proponents and opponents of such American imperialism saw missionaries as vital to the dissemination of American cultural influence abroad.

Equally important to the reenergizing of late nineteenth-century missions was the influence of a collegiate student movement that emerged from the revivalism of Dwight L. *Moody. In 1886, Moody encouraged some one hundred students to volunteer as foreign missionaries, and they became the first recruits for an ecumenical revivalistic movement, the Student Volunteer Movement (SVM, 1888), which attracted many campus leaders. Under the direction of Methodist John R. Mott and Presbyterian Robert E. Speer, the SVM linked a revivalistic call for "the evangelization of the world in this generation" with a patriotic and worldly zeal. This group of so-called missionary statesmen exercised considerable influence in American and world affairs during the early twentieth century.

Even as missionary activity in the established Protestant denominations peaked in the 1920s, however, the movement was in crisis, racked by the fundamentalist controversy at home and challenges by indigenous nationalists abroad. One result was an extended self-examination of the missionary movement funded by the wealthy Baptist layman John D. Rockefeller Jr. and supported by the major denominations. The resulting multivolume report, summarized as *Re-thinking Missions* (1932), caused a furor within the missionary movement because it welcomed the contributions of the other world religions and searched for common spiritual ground. Thereafter, the liberal denominations officially encouraged indigenous leadership and strove to avoid charges of cultural imperialism.

The United States remained a Catholic mission field during much of the nineteenth century, with European societies contributing substantially to building the Catholic Church among Indians, western settlers, and nominally Catholic immigrant populations. Heroic, short-lived efforts had earlier supported individual American Catholic missionaries in India, Hawai'i, and Africa, but sustained missionary outreach overseas awaited the founding of the Catholic Foreign Mission Society of America, known as the Maryknoll Order, in 1911. The Maryknolls were especially active in China until expelled at the time of the Chinese Revolution. Beginning in the 1960s American Catholic orders, diocesan clergy, and lay workers turned more of their attention to Latin America, addressing the need for social and economic development. Catholic missionaries suffered persecution for their "liberation theology" and social activism, with occasional imprisonment and death at the hands of local political regimes.

In the later twentieth century, evangelical and conservative Protestant denominations, too, conducted fervent missionary activity abroad. During the 1990s, after decades of missionary activity, the Seventh-day Adventist Church claimed seven million members worldwide, compared with 780,000 within the continental United States. The Church of Jesus Christ of Latter-Day Saints (Mormons) sent many of its youth on missions abroad and by the late 1990s, nearly half its eight million members lived overseas. American Holiness and Pentecostal churches, too, won converts around the world, making especially significant inroads in traditionally Catholic Latin America.

At the close of the century, Christian missionaries played a critical and continuing role both in representing the United States abroad and in speaking for other nations and cultures back home.

[*See also* Ecumenical Movement; Expansionism; Exploration, Conquest, and Settlement, Era of European; Foreign Relations: The Cultural Dimension; French Settlements in North America; Fundamentalist Movement; Great Awakening, First and Second; Immigration; Methodism; Mormonism; Pentecostalism; Protestantism; Religion; Revivalism; Roman Catholicism; Serra, Junipero; Seventh-day Adventism; Spanish Settlements in North America; Urbanization.]

• Clifton Phillips, *Protestant America and the Pagan World: The First Half Century of the American Board of Commissioners for Foreign Missions, 1810–1860*, 1969. Patricia R. Hill, *The World Their Household: The American Woman's Foreign Missions Movement and Cultural Transformation, 1870–1920*, 1984. William Hutchison, *Errand to the World: American Protestant Thought and Foreign Missions*, 1987. Joel A. Carpenter, *Earthern Vessels: American Evangelicals and Foreign Missions, 1880–1980*, 1990. Timothy Yates, *Christian Mission in the Twentieth Century*, 1994. William J. Collinge, ed., *Historical Dictionary of Catholicism*, 1997.

—Jane Hunter

MISSISSIPPI RIVER. Samuel L. *Clemens, quoting *Harper's* magazine, pronounced the Mississippi River the "Body of the Nation." The metaphor is appropriate, for the story of the Mississippi mirrors many central themes in American history and culture.

Draining the North American continent from its headwaters in Minnesota's Lake Itasca to the Gulf of Mexico, the Mississippi is home to diverse species of flora and fauna. Between A.D. 500 and 1500, mound-building Mississippian peoples built an agrarian civilization along its banks. Beginning in 1541, Spanish and French explorers including Hernando de *Soto, Jacques Marquette, and Louis Joliet, traversed the Mississippi valley. British and American explorers, traders, and adventurers eventually followed.

Events along the Mississippi form a microcosm of American history. *Revolutionary War soldier George Rogers *Clark fought at Kaskaskias; the *Lewis and Clark expedition wintered in 1803–1804 at Wood River; Andrew *Jackson defeated the British at the Battle of *New Orleans in 1815; Chief *Black Hawk's 1832 defeat, followed by the Cherokee's forced march across the frozen Lower Mississippi, marked the extirpation of America's woodland Indians; Ulysses S. *Grant turned the tide of the *Civil War at the Siege of *Vicksburg in 1863; the "Steamboat Age" on the Mississippi hugely affected the nineteenth-century economy; the twentieth century was influenced by the diesel towboat and the evolution of the *Army Corps of Engineers; and American life was forever marked by the eras of Mississippi valley *slavery, racial *segregation, and *civil-rights activism.

Artists and writers like George Caleb Bingham, Samuel Clemens (Mark Twain), Hamlin Garland, William *Faulkner, and Thomas Hart Benton mined the Mississippi's stories, most memorably in Clemens's autobiographical *Life on the Mississippi* (1883). Many forms of indigenous American music—gospel, *blues, country, *jazz, and rock-and-roll—were born or flourished along its banks. From geography to history to *folk arts and crafts, the Mississippi and its people reflect the core of the American experience.

[*See also* Canals and Waterways; Exploration, Conquest and Settlement, Era of European; Gospel Music, African American; Indian History and Culture: Migration and Pre-Columbian Era; Indian History and Culture: From 1800 to 1900; Music: Popular Music; Music: Traditional Music.]

• Mark Twain, *Life on the Mississippi*, 1883, reprint 1990. Louis C. Hunter, *Steamboats on the Western Rivers: An Economic and Technological History*, 1949, reprint 1993. Michael Allen, *Western Rivermen, 1763–1861: Ohio and Mississippi and the Myth of the Alligator Horse*, 1990.

—Michael Allen

MISSOURI COMPROMISE (1820). In 1817, Missouri became the first territory within the boundaries of the *Louisiana Purchase, apart from Louisiana itself, to apply for statehood. Subsequent congressional consideration of the issue led to the first major national debate between free and slave interests. Although the resulting compromise lasted for several decades, the dispute served as an omen of future sectional tensions, one that an aging Thomas *Jefferson described with remarkable prescience as "a fireball in the night" and "a [death] knell for the Union."

In February 1819, Congressman James Tallmadge of New York introduced an amendment to the Missouri statehood bill requiring that no further slaves be allowed into Missouri and that children of slaves already in the state (over ten thousand in 1820) be freed at age twenty-five.

Tallmadge's amendment, coupled with a similar one banning *slavery in the adjacent Arkansas Territory, sparked impassioned debate. The House of Representatives, on votes falling almost entirely along sectional lines, narrowly approved both amendments. The Senate, by a wider margin, rejected them and imposed no restrictions on slavery, present or future, in Missouri. When the next Congress convened in early December, Senator Jesse B. Thomas of Illinois proposed a compromise that, despite initial rejection in the House, passed in March 1820 when each provision was voted on separately. Under its terms, Maine, whose bid for statehood had been blocked by southern senators, was admitted as a free state; Missouri came in as a slave state; and, most significantly, Missouri's southern border, the 36°30' parallel, was extended westward as the boundary north of which slavery would not be permitted within the Louisiana Purchase.

The significance of the Missouri controversy became fully apparent only in hindsight. It provided the impetus for the first full-scale debate on what would emerge by midcentury as the central issue of the gathering sectional crisis: the territorial expansion of slavery. It also revealed the power of sectional interests to overwhelm partisan loyalties when this issue arose, and set a precedent for congressional authority in determining the limits and conditions of slavery's expansion. The Missouri Compromise defined the terms and the dynamics of a sectional crisis that would reemerge with even greater intensity in the later 1840s in the wake of the territorial gains resulting from the *Mexican War.

[*See also* Antebellum Era; Antislavery; Civil War: Causes; Compromise of 1850; Kansas-Nebraska Act; *Scott* v. *Sandford*.]

• Glover Moore, *The Missouri Controversy, 1819–1821*, 1937. William W. Freehling, *The Road to Disunion: Secessionists at Bay, 1776–1854*, 1990, chapter 8.

—John C. Inscoe

MITCHELL, BILLY (1879–1936), Army brigadier general, advocate of air power. The son of U.S. Senator John Mitchell of Oregon, William ("Billy") Mitchell served in the *Spanish-American War and entered the regular army in 1901. Abandoning a conventional army career, Mitchell in 1916 began to focus on aviation and quickly gained a position of authority. Capitalizing on his family's influence and displaying a flair for the dramatic, he vocally championed the potential of military air power. Influenced by discussions with French, British, and Italian aviation pioneers, he became convinced that air power could be decisive in future warfare and advanced a revolutionary argument for strategic bombing: Long-range aircraft, operating independently, could strike enemy industrial targets and nerve centers, resulting in a less expensive and arguably less bloody form of warfare. Campaigning for an independent air force, Mitchell organized a series of highly publicized, if somewhat contrived, tests in which bombers sank the decommissioned U.S.S. *Alabama* and the German dreadnought *Ostfriesland.* If the results failed to confirm Mitchell's more extreme claims, they did spur the navy to improve and expand carrier-based aviation.

Increasingly strident, Mitchell in 1925 was banished from Washington and admonished to keep silent. He nonetheless goaded the War Department into confrontation and in 1926 was court martialed for insubordination and prejudicial conduct. Despite the predictable guilty verdict, he successfully turned his trial into a forum for his views. Nevertheless, much of the impetus for change had already been provided by 1926 legislation establishing the nation's broad aeronautical policy. Although Mitchell never regained the prominence he had enjoyed in the early 1920s, he was later hailed as a prophet.

[*See also* Aviation Industry; Federal Government, Executive Branch: Department of Defense; Military, The.]

• William Mitchell, *Winged Defense,* 1925. Alfred F. Hurley, *Billy Mitchell: Crusader for Air Power,* 1975.

—Mark K. Wells

MITCHELL, MARIA (1818–1889), astronomer. Born on Massachusetts' Nantucket Island, Mitchell was the daughter of a Quaker schoolmaster who also checked the accuracy of the chronometers of Nantucket's whaling fleet, a task in which Maria assisted. As librarian of the Nantucket Atheneum from 1836 to 1857, she had ample leisure to pursue her astronomical studies. The precision of her observations attracted the notice of leading scientists, including William C. Bond, director of the Harvard Observatory, and Alexander Dallas Bach, head of the U.S. Coast Survey. Her discovery of a new comet in October 1847 added to her reputation. The comet was named for her, and she was elected to the American Academy of Arts and Sciences (1848) and admitted to the *American Association for the Advancement of Science (1850). In 1865, though lacking a college degree herself, she joined the faculty of the newly opened Vassar Female College in Poughkeepsie, New York, where the founder, brewer Matthew Vassar, built her an observatory with a twelve-inch telescope, the third largest in America at the time. Although refusing to give grades or take attendance, she won recognition as an inspiring teacher. Several of her students pursued careers in science or other disciplines. Continuing her astronomical research, she photographed solar phenomena and published on solar eclipses and surface changes of the planets. A founder of the Association for the Advancement of Women in 1873, Mitchell was particularly interested in furthering the cause of women in science. "Nature made woman an observer," she observed; ". . . the natural sciences are well fitted for woman's power of minute observation."

[*See also* Coast and Geodetic Survey, U.S.; Education: Collegiate Education; Observatories; Physical Sciences; Science: Revolutionary War to World War I.]

• Phebe Mitchell Kendall, *Maria Mitchell: Life, Letters, and Journals,* 1896. Helen L. Morgan, *Maria Mitchell: First Lady of American Astronomy,* 1977.

—Paul S. Boyer

MOBILITY. The concept of mobility includes both geographic and social components. Geographical mobility refers to any change of residence, including migration, defined in the United States as movement across county lines. Social mobility entails changes in social position, usually focusing on upward (or, less frequently, downward) movement in *social class. Much work on geographical mobility posits a relationship between these two processes. The labor-mobility model, dominant in migration research, suggests that people flow from areas of few economic opportunities to areas with surplus opportunities. Thus, the model suggests, geographical movement typically produces social mobility, as people move to new locations with better jobs.

American society has historically valued both types of mobility. The nation's founders had moved, or had ancestors who had moved, from the "Old World," setting the tone for a restless, highly mobile society. Americans continued moving, searching for better conditions. Some estimates suggest that as much as half the population moved during each decade of the nineteenth century. While these estimates may be high, census data show that about one-fourth of the mid-nineteenth-century population lived outside its state of birth. Alexis de Tocqueville in **Democracy in America* wrote eloquently of Americans' love for pulling up stakes and moving on.

The Era of Western Migration. First settling along the Atlantic coast, the European newcomers quickly looked westward. Even before the *Revolutionary War, Massachusetts, Connecticut, Pennsylvania, Maryland, and Virginia experienced net out-migration of native-born men of militia service age. The British *Proclamation of 1763 restricted settlements to the east of the Appalachian Mountains; hence, colonists from the Middle Atlantic states moved down the mountains' eastern side as far as Georgia. Northern colonists moved into upper *New England and upstate New York. Following independence, Americans, including those from southern states, spread westward. The 1790 census reported about half a million people living west of the original thirteen states. By 1860, after a decade during which the population center moved a greater distance west than during any other decade between 1790 and 1930, over half the population, about sixteen million people, lived west of the Appalachians.

Considering it their "*Manifest Destiny" to settle the continent, Americans followed Horace Greeley's advice, "Go west, young man," and sought opportunities in the vast interior, which Frederick Jackson *Turner described in *The Frontier in American History* (1920). As explorers, trappers, and traders blazed trails, more permanent settlers followed. Daniel *Boone forged a trail through the Cumberland Gap in 1775, and settlers followed him to Kentucky, Tennessee, and beyond. The *Lewis and Clark Expedition mapped a route for fur traders and, by the 1840s, settlers bound for Oregon and *California. Discovery of gold and silver stimulated further mobility, most notably the 1849 California gold rush. Although prospectors moved first, support and service personnel followed rapidly. While some boom towns became ghost towns when the ore was exhausted, others evolved into stable communities, attracting even more settlers. About the same time (1847), Mormons seeking freedom from religious persecution arrived in Utah, ending a trek that originated in New York with brief stays in Ohio, Missouri, and Illinois.

Farther south, by 1824, more than two thousand settlers had moved into Texas despite the Mexican government's restrictions on immigration. The Mexican authorities did allow movement along what would become the *Santa Fe Trail, demonstrating that heavy wagons could make the journey across the plains and the mountains, and helping refute the view of the *West as an inhospitable Great American Desert. Back East, the *Erie Canal, which opened in 1825, provided a northern route for movement of goods and people into the *Middle West.

Land availability figured prominently in attracting settlers. The 1862 *Homestead Act provided a land parcel to any citizen who paid a small fee and agreed to cultivate the land for five years. In 1866, another Homestead Act provided land in the Southwest for freed slaves. While some *African Americans took advantage of this opportunity, neither act stimulated a land rush comparable to the 1899 opening of the Oklahoma territory. Not all agreed on opening these lands. Industrialists opposed the idea because they felt it would decrease their factories' labor supply. Additionally, *railroads gained control of substantial land in an attempt to control western development.

Westward settlers faced many hardships from the social and physical environment. Whites fought frequent wars and skirmishes through the later nineteenth century as they pushed into Native Americans' lands. Treaties forced Indians to move westward into small reservations with poor environments and few opportunities, reversing the typical pattern of migration producing upward mobility. Mastery of the physical environment also proved problematic. In the 1880s, settlers on the Great Plains faced devastating drought. As recently as the 1930s, drought conditions (worsened by destructive agricultural practices) drove many *Dust Bowl farmers from their lands. For women, as diaries and letters reveal, the quest for economic mobility through westward migration often meant hardship on the trail, unremitting labor on the new farm, and a gnawing sense of isolation.

Toward the end of the nineteenth century, settlers, including lower-class laborers, moved to fill the Great Plains. The agricultural communities had high mobility rates as settlers continually sought better conditions on other farms or in the towns developing along the railroads and other transportation routes. Millions of farmers moved to Kansas, Nebraska, the Dakotas, Wyoming, and Montana between 1870 and 1890, leading the director of the census at the century's end to note the closing of the frontier.

Mobility in Industrial and Post–Industrial America. The western frontier's closing coincided with accelerated manufacturing growth and increased rural-to-urban migration. The appeal of industrial and, later, service jobs replaced land as migration's driving force. The *textile industry, first in New England and later in the *South, created opportunities for social mobility in early industrial cities. Textile factories attracted women as well as men, although women typically quit their jobs when they married. Agricultural mechanization, improved transportation systems, and the lure of bright lights and urban culture all contributed to the flow of Americans cityward. In 1790, about 5 percent of the population lived in urban places. By the *Civil War, the total had risen to about 20 percent. By 1920, a majority was urbanized, including many African Americans who moved to cities in the North and South during *World War I. (The 1920 census reported an increase of 695,000 southern-born blacks in the North.) Black migration to cities continued through the 1920s and surged again during *World War II. By the late 1990s, about three-fourths of all Americans lived in urban areas.

As cities filled, often with immigrants, minorities, and the poor, many who could afford it moved to the surrounding suburbs. While *suburbanization began earlier, it accelerated during the 1950s, accounting for approximately 80 percent of metropolitan growth during this decade. By 1970, more people lived in suburbs than in cities or rural areas. Suburbs offered affordable family housing during the post–World War II baby boom, yet with access to cities' jobs and cultural opportunities. The thriving economy, expanding interstate *highway system, lower tax rate, and home-building standardization promoted suburban movement. Initially suburbanization was a mainly white phenomenon, with African Americans, *Hispanic Americans, and other minorities excluded by either economic considerations or overt discrimination. As the twentieth century wore on, suburbs attracted many blacks and other minorities, but many suburban neighborhoods continued to be highly stratified along lines of race, ethnicity, and social class.

During the 1970s, countering the earlier rural-to-urban pattern, nonmetropolitan areas grew faster than metropolitan areas. Movement to nonmetropolitan areas occurred for many of the same reasons as the suburban migration. Improved transportation and communication made it possible to move farther away from the city and still take advantage of opportunities there. Additionally, many businesses and services relocated to nonmetropolitan areas. After dipping in the 1980s, the movement to nonmetropolitan areas resumed in the 1990s.

Following Peter Rossi's *Why Families Move* (1955, 1980), much research on mobility has suggested that families move as units after careful balancings of demographic, economic, and psychological calculations. Upon marriage, Rossi found, the wife was expected to give up her job and move with her husband. Recent research suggests changes in this view, however, particularly as more women have careers, limiting their desire to follow their husbands to new locations.

Mobility among regions has played an important role in U.S. development. The later twentieth century saw substantial population shifts to the so-called Sunbelt. Older, industrial areas of the Northeast and Midwest lost population as the South attracted migrants, especially those of the educated middle class, because of its expanding economy, natural resources, favorable climate, lower taxes, and more *leisure opportunities. Businesses were attracted by the lower cost of (nonunionized) labor. From the 1970s on, African Americans returned to the South in increasing numbers because of both economic opportunities and a perceived decline in racial discrimination. This migration southward also included retirees seeking a moderate climate, not necessarily social mobility. These recent trends exemplify the degree to which not simply a desire for better economic opportunity, but a combination of economic, cultural, and social factors, along with personal "lifestyle" choices, shaped patterns of geographic mobility at the close of the twentieth century.

[*See also* Agriculture; Alger, Horatio; Census, Federal; Expansionism; Franklin, Benjamin; Gold Rushes; Immigrant Labor; Immigration; Indian History and Culture: From 1500 to 1800; Indian History and Culture: From 1800 to 1900; Indian Wars; Labor Markets; Mormonism; Race and Ethnicity; Racism; Urbanization; Women in the Labor Force.]

• Simon S. Kuznets and Dorothy Swaine Thomas, eds., *Population Redistribution and Economic Growth: United States, 1870–1950,* 3 vols. 1957–1964. Stephen Thernstrom, *Progress and Poverty: Social Mobility in a Nineteenth-Century City,* 1964. Peter M. Blau and Otis Dudley Duncan, *The American Occupational Structure,* 1967. Jeanne C. Biggar, "The Sunning of America: Migration to the Sunbelt," *Population Bulletin* 34, no. 1 (1979). Daniel M. Johnson and Rex R. Campbell, *Black Migration in America: A Social Demographic History,* 1981. Larry Long, *Migration and Residential Mobility in the United States,* 1988. David R. Gerhan and Robert V. Wells, compilers, *A Retrospective Bibliography of American Demographic History from Colonial Times to 1983,* 1989. William H. Frey, "Metropolitan America: Beyond the Transition," *Population Bulletin* 45, no. 2 (1990). Patricia Gober, "Americans on the Move," *Population Bulletin* 48, no. 3 (1993).

—Robert H. Freymeyer

MODERNIST CULTURE. Only recently have historians come to appreciate the significance of modernist culture in the United States. Modernism was long considered a movement of the European avant-garde that could be found in the United States primarily in bohemian enclaves such as New York's *Greenwich Village or *San Francisco's North Beach. In reality modernist culture played a major role in determining how twentieth-century Americans understood and shaped their world. Far from being monopolized by a tiny intellectual and artistic elite, modernism exerted its influence everywhere, in areas ranging from *architecture to *literature to the visual arts to the social and natural sciences, as well as in *popular culture. Indeed, some scholars view it as the dominant—though assuredly not the only—cultural sensibility of twentieth-century America.

Although the constellation of beliefs and values now known as modernism first appeared in Paris in the final decades of the nineteenth century among the symbolist poets and impressionist painters, the movement soon reached the United States. A band of cultural radicals who had gathered in *New York City shortly after 1900 supplied the main point of entry. The group included fledgling journalists such as John Reed (1887–1920), Max Eastman (1883–1969), Randolph *Bourne, and Walter *Lippmann, as well as the playwright Eugene *O'Neill, the dancer Isadora Duncan (1878–1927), and the controversial birth-control advocate, Margaret *Sanger. Another key member of this circle, the photographer Alfred *Stieglitz, began exhibiting the works of Cezanne, Picasso, and Matisse at his Little Gallery of the Photo-Secession, leading to the New York *Armory Show of 1913—a display of 1,200 works by foreign and native-born modernist artists that heralded the arrival of the new culture on American shores.

Not all of the action took place in New York. During the first decade of the century, early modernist writers from the *Middle West, such as Theodore *Dreiser, Vachel Lindsay, and Sherwood Anderson, assembled in *Chicago, where publications vital to the movement like *Poetry* and *The Little Review* were headquartered. By then Gertrude Stein had settled in Paris as the *grande doyenne* of American modernist expatriates, while the London-based American poets Ezra *Pound and Thomas Stearns Eliot (1888–1965) were turning out daring aesthetic manifestos and masterpieces of contemporary verse. Equally influential were two pioneering academics, the psychologist William *James and the philosopher John *Dewey, whose writings on *pragmatism and radical empiricism helped to supply the conceptual framework for modernist thought in both the United States and Europe.

At its core, modernism arose by way of rebellion against the major historical culture that preceded it. During the nineteenth century the emerging bourgeoisie in those societies caught up in the Industrial Revolution embraced Victorianism, a belief system that, as they saw it, ordained a glorious future of progress and prosperity based on technological advancement and the continuous spread of civilization. To ensure that progress, Victorians struggled to maintain a firm moral dividing line between the secure, tranquil world of the middle class, in which emotions were kept under strict control, and the "savage," violence-ridden world of the lower classes and noncivilized nations where the "animal" passions were allowed to run riot. To a proper Victorian, nothing could be worse than permitting savagery to contaminate the purified precincts of "high" civilization.

Modernist culture, by contrast, was premised on recovering the very animal component of human nature that the Victorians had sought to suppress and, at the social level, on bringing together all that the nineteenth century had struggled to keep apart. Viewing Victorian life as fatally severed from reality, modernists sought to reorient human existence toward the cultivation of direct experience, no matter how discomforting that might be. Following the dictates of Sigmund Freud, they insisted on reconnecting the faculties of the mind governing rationality and logic with those subconscious forces governing the senses and emotions in order to produce a more "authentic" self. At the cosmic level, modernists banished the Victorian conception of a stable, predictable universe presided over by a benevolent deity, putting in its place what James called an "unfinished" universe characterized by constant and unforeseeable change. As a consequence, knowledge of the empirical world would always be imperfect at best, and the moral values constructed on the basis of that knowledge would need to stay provisional, evolving to keep pace with the incessant evolution of historical circumstances. The one thing of which we can be sure, Dewey declared in *The Quest for Certainty* (1929), is that we can never obtain certainty about anything.

The reality discovered by modernism may have been filled with flux and fragmentation, but the foremost impulse within the culture nonetheless consisted of a deep yearning for integration in all aspects of human life. Over the course of the twentieth century, modernists attempted to heal the many divisions that the Victorians had bequeathed, from those separating mind from body and thought from emotion to those involving race, *social class, and *gender. This powerful desire to eradicate boundaries helped fuel the movements to gain equal rights and status for *African Americans and women, as well as a more general campaign against elitism within American society, all of which had gained sufficient momentum to transform national mores and politics by the 1960s and 1970s. In this way, what began as an "adversary" culture (to borrow the critic Lionel Trilling's term) matured into one of abiding achievement.

As the twentieth century ended, modernism appeared to have reached its final phase, with *postmodernism replacing it among the intellectual avant-garde. Whether or not postmodernism truly represented a new cultural entity or was in fact better understood as an extension and exaggeration of basic modernist precepts remained a matter for debate. What did seem clear was that anyone seeking to understand twentieth-century American historians must give modernism, in all its manifestations, very close attention.

[*See also* Feminism; Gilded Age; Literature: Civil War to World War I; Literature: Since World War I; Painting: To 1945; Photography; Poetry; Progressive Era; Secularization; Social Science; Women's Rights Movements.]

• Malcolm Bradbury and James McFarlane, eds., *Modernism, 1890–1930,* 1976. Sanford Schwartz, *The Matrix of Modernism: Pound, Eliot and Early Twentieth-Century Thought,* 1985. Daniel J. Singal, ed., *Modernist Culture in America,* 1991. Dorothy Ross, ed., *Modernist Impulses in the Human Sciences, 1870–1930,* 1994. Steven Watts, *The Magic Kingdom: Walt Disney and Modern American Culture,* 1996. Daniel J. Singal, *William Faulkner: The Making of a Modernist,* 1997.

—Daniel J. Singal

MOLECULAR BIOLOGY. *See* Biological Sciences.

MONETARISM. The economic theory known as monetarism holds that the money stock exerts an important influence on economic activity and prices. Economists who embrace monetarism hold that changes in the quantity of money are crucial in increasing aggregate income and productivity in the short run, and the inflation rate in the long run. The University of Chicago economist Milton Friedman (1912–) was the most prominent twentieth-century proponent of monetarism, but the theory's intellectual origins extend back more than two centuries to the quantity theory of money of classical *economics. According to such theories, changes in the money stock or the velocity of the circulation of money (the ratio of total spending to the money stock) determine nominal spending. Because velocity changes less over the longer run than the total money stock, the effects of the latter dominate.

Friedman and Anna Schwartz offered important empirical support for monetarism in *A Monetary History of the United States, 1867–1960* (1963). They showed that since the *Civil War, fluctuations in the rate of monetary growth led the peaks and troughs of all U.S. *business cycles. Moreover, they associated especially severe economic downturns, such as 1929–1933, with large monetary contractions. While money powerfully affected the economy in the short run, its long-term effect was less predictable. This fact underlies another precept of monetarism: Rather than actively using monetary policy to smooth business cycles, as Keynesians advocate, the monetary authority (in the United States, the *Federal Reserve System) should adhere to a fixed rule such as maintaining a constant rate of growth of the money supply.

While changes in the money supply may affect the physical volume of output in the short run, over the long run nonmonetary factors determine economic growth. Monetary changes primarily affect the price level. Hence, monetarists argue, inflation or deflation are directly related to the rate of growth of the money supply.

[*See also* Banking and Finance; Depressions, Economic; Economic Development; Keynesianism; Monetary Policy, Federal.]

• Milton Friedman, *A Program for Monetary Stability,* 1960. Neil DeMarachi and Abraham Hirsch, *Milton Friedman: Economics in Theory and Practice,* 1990.

—John A. James

MONETARY POLICY, FEDERAL. Encompassing two major components, the coining of currency and the creation of a banking system, U.S. monetary policy is as old as the national government itself.

Currency. Following Alexander *Hamilton's recommendations, the Coinage Act of 1792 established the dollar as the official unit of account and established a bimetallic standard that defined the dollar in relation to gold and silver. The silver dollar contained fifteen times as much silver as the gold in the gold dollar. Originally the fifteen-to-one ratio was close to the prevailing market value, but as market values changed over time, one of the metals became overvalued at the mint price. In the early nineteenth century, silver became overvalued, and its possessors presented silver to the mint for coinage. Gold coins began to disappear from circulation. In 1834 the Treasury adjusted the mint ratio to around sixteen to one, now overvaluing gold. Hence, gold began to replace silver in circulation, causing the latter to be hoarded or exported.

This system whereby the value of the dollar and foreign currencies was defined by their specie (gold or silver) content in turn fixed the value of currencies relative to each other. In other words, a system of fixed exchange rates enabled specie, dollars, and foreign exchange all to be freely convertible. *Civil War economic exigencies, however, led Congress to pass the Legal Tender Act of 1862, which provided for the issue of fiat money, commonly know as greenbacks, not convertible into specie at a fixed rate. Market forces determined the value of the greenback (paper) dollar relative to gold and foreign currencies in a system of floating or flexible exchange rates. At one point, greenbacks in New York fell to a gold price as low as thirty-five cents on the dollar.

To restore the prewar parity between the U.S. dollar and the British pound sterling (the standard for global exchange rates), the post–Civil War American government adopted fiscal policies to deflate prices and bring greenbacks onto a par with gold. The ensuing sharp deflation, which hurt debtors and aided creditors, caused fierce opposition. The *Greenback Labor party (founded in 1874) appealed to debtors and entrepreneurs who wanted to expand the issue of greenbacks, increase the money supply, and raise the price level. Later, the *free silver movement advocated the free and unlimited coinage of silver at the old ratio (16 to 1) to accomplish the same ends. Only after a decade of deflation did Congress pass the Resumption Act of 1875 and commit the Treasury to exchange gold dollars and paper dollars at par. On 1 January 1879 greenbacks became freely convertible to gold with fixed exchange rates restored at the prewar parity.

The victims of deflation, however, continued to condemn the *gold standard as the congressional "Crime of '73." (In 1873, ancillary to its deflationary policy, Congress had "demonitized" silver by ordering the U.S. Mint to stop making silver coins.) The 1880s and early 1890s remained a period of intense controversy as to the appropriate monetary standard. The election of William *McKinley over William Jennings *Bryan in 1896 and, subsequently, rising prices stilled the protests of debtors and free-silver advocates. In 1900 the U.S. formally committed itself to the gold standard.

After the financial crises and disruptions of the 1930s and *World War II, the United States and its major allies agreed to restore fixed exchange rates at the 1944 *Bretton Woods Conference. The dollar, set at a price of thirty-five dollars per ounce of gold, replaced the pound sterling as the international currency of record. The Bretton Woods system lasted into the early 1970s when domestic inflation prompted President Richard M. *Nixon to end fixed exchange rates. Afterward the dollar floated against other currencies, its value determined by the demand and supply of foreign exchange.

Banking. Congress chartered the first Bank of the United States in 1791 as proposed by Alexander Hamilton, who modeled it after the Bank of England. The bank was a combined public and private enterprise with branches in major cities, the authority to issue notes, and a role as a commercial bank as well as the fiscal agent of the government. When the bank's charter came up for renewal in 1811, the recharter bill failed in the Senate after a hotly contested debate about its constitutionality.

Shortly thereafter, however, in 1816, Congress established a second Bank of the United States with charter provisions similar to those of the first. After a rather undistinguished early history, the Second Bank came into its own in 1823 with the appointment of Nicholas Biddle of Philadelphia as director. Biddle actively pursued a policy of pressing state banks to redeem their outstanding banknotes at promised par or face value in specie. Such a policy restrained the temptation of such banks to "overissue" notes, dampened inflation, and increased public confidence in circulating banknotes. During the 1820s Biddle's policy narrowed the range of discounts among state banknotes. This policy promoted soundness and confidence in the banking system but produced discontent in western regions and among individuals desirous of easier credit.

President Andrew *Jackson, who vetoed a bank recharter bill in 1832, represented the enemies of Biddle. In his veto message, Jackson criticized the bank's monopoly status, its domination by financiers and foreigners, and its regulation of economic growth in the *West. He even questioned its constitutionality. Jackson resolved to cripple the bank's power by removing government deposits and redepositing them in selected state banks known as "pet banks." Jackson's war against the Second Bank was followed by a speculative boom (with the highest peacetime inflation rate before the 1970s) and an ensuing financial panic and deep depression (1837–1843). After 1836 the federal government withdrew from the banking system altogether, later establishing an independent treasury to administer revenues and their disbursement. This system lasted nearly three-quarters of a century until the establishment in 1913 of the *Federal Reserve System.

To replace the circulation of heterogeneous state banknotes with a uniform currency and simultaneously increase the demand for government bonds, the National Banking Act of 1863–1864 established a national banking system. Banks with national charters were allowed to issue banknotes backed by U.S. government bonds. The dominance of national banks proved short-lived. Increasing use of checks and demand deposits made banks' inability to issue notes less of a disadvantage, so that by 1890 the non-national banks surpassed national banks both in number and assets. This system of small, independent local banks (as opposed to branch banks) proved particularly vulnerable to financial crises. In the late nineteenth century, financial panics and subsequent suspensions of cash payments by banks became common. A panic in 1907 was the last straw, leading Congress to establish the congressional National Monetary Commission to consider banking reform. The result was the *Federal Reserve Act of 1913.

The Federal Reserve System created a central bank to alleviate the problem of recurrent panics. The new institution was to furnish "an elastic currency," smooth seasonal money-market stringencies, and act as the lender of last resort during crises. The law established a decentralized structure that dispersed power and reflected popular and congressional suspicion of the concentration of economic power in Washington or among Wall Street bankers. Twelve regional Federal Reserve Banks operated under a coordinating board in Washington.

In its initial years the new system appeared successful in adjusting seasonal credit flows and smoothing seasonal interest rates. The Federal Reserve, however, failed to avert the Great Depression of the 1930s. Indeed, many economists cite its inaction as the principal factor underlying the severity of the depression. The failure of the Federal Reserve System between 1929 and 1933 led the Franklin Delano *Roosevelt administration to propose further reforms. The Banking Act of 1933, known as the Glass-Steagall Act, created the Federal Deposit Insurance Corporation (FDIC) to protect depositors' accounts. Glass-Steagall also divorced investment and commercial banking operations. The Banking Act of 1935 further centralized and extended the power of the Federal Reserve Board, now called the Board of Governors. Thereafter, the Federal Reserve Board had greater power to regulate the money supply and set interest rates.

The high inflation and interest rates of the 1970s created great problems for regulated banks, which were limited as to the loans they could make and the rate of interest they could pay. Depositors thus withdrew funds from banks and redeposited them in unregulated money market mutual funds that offered higher interest rates. The Depository and Monetary Control Act of 1980 partly deregulated commercial banks and savings-and-loan associations, allowing them to offer higher interest rates by making more diverse investments. The ensuing pattern of highly speculative investment led to the *savings-and-loan scandal of the 1980s. As the twentieth century ended, however, further deregulation of banking seemed likely.

[*See also* Banking and Finance; Bank of the United States, First and Second; Depressions, Economic; Federal Government, Executive Branch: Department of the Treasury; Taxation.]

• Bray Hammond, *Banks and Politics in America from the Revolution to the Civil War,* 1957. Milton Friedman and Anna Schwartz, *A Monetary History of the United States, 1867–1960,* 1963. Paul Studenski and Herman Krooss, *Financial History of the United States,* 1963. Peter Temin, *The Jacksonian Economy,* 1969. Richard Timberlake, *The Origins of Central Banking in the United States,* 1978. Eugene N. White, *The Regulation and Reform of the American Banking System, 1900–1929,* 1983.

—John A. James

MONROE, JAMES (1758–1831), fifth president of the United States. Born in Westmoreland County, Virginia, James Monroe entered the College of William and Mary in 1774, but left two years later to fight in the *Revolutionary War. Rising to the rank of lieutenant colonel, Monroe saw active service at Long Island, Manhattan, Trenton, Brandywine, *Valley Forge, and Monmouth Courthouse.

Elected to the Virginia House of Delegates in 1782, Monroe soon went to Philadelphia for a term in the *Continental Congress (1783–1786). He opposed ratification of the federal *Constitution, but was nevertheless elected to the U.S. Senate in 1790. He represented the United States in Paris from 1793 to 1796, but was recalled after disagreeing with the George *Washington administration over foreign policy. He served three terms as Virginia governor (1799–1802) before President Thomas *Jefferson sent him back to Paris for the final stage of the negotiations for the *Louisiana Purchase (1803). Thereafter, until 1807, Monroe was, alternately, U.S. minister in London and Madrid, but he achieved little success. Jefferson rejected a commercial treaty he negotiated with Great Britain in 1806, and in Spain Monroe failed to obtain the Floridas for the United States.

In 1808 Monroe ran unsuccessfully for the presidency. He began another term as governor of Virginia in 1811, but resigned the same year when President James *Madison appointed him secretary of state. During the *War of 1812 Monroe contemplated resuming a military career but he remained in the State Department while simultaneously serving as secretary of war in the Winter of 1812–1813 and again in 1814–1815.

In 1816 Monroe was elected to the first of two terms as president. Winning on each occasion without significant opposition, he presided over the "Era of Good Feelings" following the collapse of the Federalist and Jeffersonian Republican parties. On the domestic front, the Monroe administration undertook few initiatives. The president played no active role in the debates occasioned by the Missouri Crisis, though he did ultimately support the measures that resolved the dispute by linking the admission of Maine and Missouri to the Union to the restriction on *slavery throughout the remainder of the Louisiana Purchase. In foreign affairs, Monroe's accomplishments were more substantial. He worked closely with his secretary of state, John Quincy *Adams, on the negotiations with Spain that produced the 1819 *Adams-Onís Treaty granting the United States clear title to the Floridas, establishing the final boundaries of the Louisiana Purchase, and extending U.S. territory to the Pacific. A section of his 1823 annual message, drafted by Adams, warning European powers against intervening in the Americas and opposing the incorporation of South American territory into European colonial empires, was subsequently enshrined as the "*Monroe Doctrine," which helped lay the foundation for U.S. diplomatic hegemony in the Americas.

[*See also* Early Republic, Era of the; Federal Government, Executive Branch: The Presidency; Expansionism; Federalist Party; Foreign Relations: U.S. Relations with Europe; Missouri Compromise; Political Parties.]

• Harry Ammon, *James Monroe: The Quest for National Identity,* 1971. Noble E. Cunningham Jr., *The Presidency of James Monroe,* 1996.

—J. C. A. Stagg

MONROE, MARILYN (1926–1962), film actress. Marilyn Monroe was born Norma Jean Mortenson in *Los Angeles. She did not complete high school, marrying James Dougherty in 1942 and divorcing him in 1946. An army photographer discovered her working in an airplane factory during *World War II, and she parlayed her photogenic face and figure into modeling assignments. Signing her first movie contract in 1946, she appeared in small but provocative roles before receiving star treatment in *Niagara* and *Gentlemen Prefer Blondes* (both 1953). She married retired baseball hero Joe *DiMaggio in January 1954. When their stormy marriage ended nine months later, she embarked on the films that would consolidate her place in the history of American *popular culture: *The Seven Year Itch* (1955), *Bus Stop* (1956), *Some Like It Hot* (1959), and *The Misfits* (1960). She married playwright Arthur Miller in 1956 and divorced him in 1961. Monroe died, a suicide, amid rumors of involvements with President John F. *Kennedy and his brother Attorney General Robert *Kennedy.

In the years after her death, Monroe became a national—indeed, a world—icon, symbolizing American innocence and ambition, the desire to remain a genuine person and yet invent a new self. Her last interviews, her attraction to men of power and celebrity, and her determination to protect her image from misguided Hollywood decisions demonstrate her awareness of her mythic status. Her major films reveal a talent transcending limited, repetitive roles and finding ways to make stereotypes yield a complex humanity.

• Norman Mailer, *Marilyn,* 1973. Carl Rollyson, *Marilyn Monroe: A Life of the Actress,* 1986.

—Carl Rollyson

MONROE DOCTRINE (1823). The Monroe Doctrine proclaimed the United States as guardian of the Americas while pledging no U.S. political intervention in Europe. President James *Monroe's annual message to Congress, delivered on 2 December 1823, declared the American republics free from further colonization by European powers and, in exchange, promised no U.S. interference with existing European possessions.

The origins of the Monroe Doctrine date to the end of the Napoleonic wars. The victorious European powers, leery of liberal ideas that had culminated in the French Revolution followed by war, seemed determined to revive monarchical government. By early 1823, Americans feared that France had agreed to restore the Spanish monarchy in exchange for Cuba. In August, British Foreign Secretary George Canning recommended a joint Anglo-American statement opposing intervention in Spanish America. But Secretary of State John Quincy

*Adams, warning Monroe that such a joint declaration would constitute an American renunciation of all hemispheric expansion as well, persuaded the president to announce a unilateral American policy in his annual message to Congress. The United States should act alone, Adams declared, rather than "come in as a cockboat in the wake of the British man-of-war."

The Monroe Doctrine drew mixed reactions. The European powers were too preoccupied with other matters to pay much attention. Latin American spokesmen sought formal alliances with the United States, but Adams refused. Canning was incensed at U.S. pretensions and boasted that he had already secured a noninterventionist pledge from France. As American power grew, however, American presidents increasingly asserted the doctrine to justify U.S. commercial and territorial expansion. In the 1840s, President James Knox *Polk articulated what later became known as the Polk Corollary to the Monroe Doctrine in opposing British claims in the Pacific Northwest. The following decade, Americans for the first time referred to the doctrine by name in arguing against British claims in Central America. During the *Civil War, Secretary of State William *Seward referred to Monroe's principles in denouncing French intervention in Mexico. Almost thirty years later, in 1895, President Grover *Cleveland again identified U.S. security with restraining European intervention in Latin America. In 1904 President Theodore *Roosevelt broadened the doctrine with a corollary that proclaimed the right of the United States to police the Western Hemisphere in cases of "chronic wrongdoing" or "impotence." Under the Roosevelt Corollary, the doctrine served as a justification for U.S. intervention in the Caribbean area through the 1920s and became hotly contested within Latin America.

During the *Cold War, American presidents occasionally invoked the Monroe Doctrine in security matters. In the *Cuban missile crisis, James Monroe made the cover of *Time* magazine as President John F. *Kennedy resisted Soviet intrusions in Cuba. The doctrine was also invoked by Lyndon B. *Johnson in the 1965 invasion of the Dominican Republic. With the end of the Cold War and the demise of the Soviet Union, the Monroe Doctrine became somewhat irrelevant, and American presidents seldom referred to it.

[*See also* Early Republic, Era of the; Expansionism; Foreign Relations: U.S. Relations with Europe; Foreign Relations: U.S. Relations with Latin America.]

• Dexter Perkins, *A History of the Monroe Doctrine,* 1955. Ernest R. May, *The Making of the Monroe Doctrine,* 1975. Gaddis Smith, *The Last Years of the Monroe Doctrine, 1945–1994,* 1994.

—Howard Jones

MONTGOMERY BUS BOYCOTT. *See* Civil Rights Movement.

MONTICELLO. This eighteenth-century Virginia mansion manifests the evolving ideals of its designer and original owner, Thomas *Jefferson, who began constructing Monticello in 1770 and continued to work on it for the rest of his life. Selecting an elevated site in Charlottesville, Jefferson gained impressive angles of approach and splendid views. Monticello, or "Little Mountain," originally comprised a two-story central section with two flanking, one-story wings. Jefferson distinguished Monticello with rigorous classical porticoes on the east and west elevations and replaced the usual scattering of outbuildings with two L-shaped service wings connected to the north and south ends of the house at its cellar level.

The appearance of the house was altered considerably in 1796 by major changes that reflected Jefferson's experiences as a revolutionary, nation-builder, and diplomat. The revised Monticello was less diagrammatically classical than the original. Jefferson replaced the second-story library with America's first dome. He also addressed the pressing issues of civic obligation and private autonomy in the new republic by doubling Monticello's plan and differentiating public and private zones of activity.

Monticello was Jefferson's quintessential essay in *architecture. The opposing porticoes of the first Monticello inspired his design for the Virginia state capitol, the first temple-form public building in America. Monticello's rigorous geometry anticipated Jefferson's octagonal plan for Poplar Forest, the Bedford County retreat he built for himself in 1806. The dome, the hierarchical arrangement of spaces, and the U-shaped configuration of house and service wings adumbrated his scheme for the University of Virginia. All of Jefferson's architecture reflects his belief in the inherent legibility of correct architecture and his conviction that fine buildings inspire to higher goals all who see and use them.

[*See also* Early Republic, Era of the; Mount Vernon; Revolution and Constitution, Era of.]

• Jack McLaughlin, *Jefferson and Monticello: The Biography of a Builder,* 1988. William L. Beiswanger, ed., *Monticello in Measured Drawings,* 1998.

—Camille Wells

MOODY, DWIGHT L. (1837–1899), revivalist. Born in rural western Massachusetts, Dwight L. Moody moved to *Boston at age seventeen, then quickly to *Chicago where he became a shoe salesman. An evangelical Protestant, he joined the Young Men's Christian Association (YMCA) in Boston, continued those connections in Chicago, and in off hours scoured poor neighborhoods on the near North Side for urchins to join his fast-growing Sunday School. His religious enthusiasms soon supplanted his purely commercial interests, especially after 1871 when he experienced a deep spiritual conversion. This set the stage for his decision to go to England, where he launched his career as a revivalist. In 1873–1875 Moody preached throughout the British Isles, perfecting his revival techniques. Upon his return to the United States he launched a series of urban-based mass revivals that attracted thousands. His hearers responded to this "father-figure" who spoke softly, not of fire and brimstone but of Christ's love, who looked and in some ways acted like the business and political leaders of the age, and who mastered the large-scale organizational techniques that adapted the revival tradition to urban, industrialized America. By 1880 he had become America's premier popular religious leader.

Although never giving up his revivalistic work, Moody after 1880 turned increasingly to education and other means of evangelism. He founded two private secondary academies in his hometown of Northfield, Massachusetts, which today constitute the Northfield Schools, and a school in Chicago, now the Moody Bible Institute, devoted to training missionaries and religious workers. Suffering a heart attack while conducting a revival in Kansas City in 1899, Moody died at his home in Northfield.

[*See also* Gilded Age; Missionary Movement; Protestantism; Religion; Revivalism; Urbanization; YMCA and YWCA.]

• William G. McLoughlin, *Modern Revivalism,* 1959. James Findlay, *Dwight L. Moody, American Evangelist, 1837–1899,* 1969.

—James Findlay

MORAL MAJORITY. The televangelist Jerry Falwell (1933–) established the Moral Majority, the first prominent manifestation of a resurgent Religious Right, in 1979. A "pro-life, pro-family, pro-moral, and pro-America" political organization, the Moral Majority mobilized grassroots Americans to oppose pornography, *abortion, the *gay and lesbian rights movement, and the welfare state; to support increased defense spending, the death penalty, and the free-enterprise system; and to elect candidates who shared these goals. Targeting Protestant fundamentalists, who traditionally had been politically inactive, Falwell's organization used direct mailings to fundamentalist churches and an estimated four million individuals to spread the word on candidates and issues.

While interested in electing conservatives at all levels of government, Falwell and the Moral Majority especially focused on electing Ronald *Reagan as president. The organization played a visibly active role in the 1980 campaign, and Reagan's stunning victory ensured that it would enjoy a high public profile in the early 1980s.

Despite the publicity, the Moral Majority was in reality an amateurish organization. Lacking both long-term plans and a grassroots organizational base, it had little success at putting substantive political pressure on the Reagan administration. By the mid-1980s the Moral Majority was in serious decline, and it officially disbanded in 1989. Numerous pundits saw the collapse of the Moral Majority as an indication of the Religious Right's imminent demise, but in reality it opened the way for much more sophisticated forms of fundamentalist politics.

[*See also* Christian Coalition; Conservatism; Fundamentalist Movement; Protestantism; Religion; Televangelism.]

• Frances Fitzgerald, *Cities on a Hill,* 1981. William Martin, *With God on Our Side: The Rise of the Religious Right in America,* 1996.

—William Vance Trollinger Jr.

MORGAN, J. P. (1837–1913), banker, financier, and art patron. The son of the international banker Junius Spencer Morgan and his wife Juliet Pierpont, of Hartford, John Pierpont Morgan became America's dominant financier of steel and *railroad enterprises. Schooled in Boston, Switzerland, and Germany, he returned to New York in 1857, a year of economic panic. Joining a banking firm representing the London-based George Peabody and Company, he acted as his father's eyes and ears. In 1861, he married Amelia Sturges, of a Manhattan cotton-trading family. Soon after her death in 1862 he married Frances Louise Tracy; they had four children.

During the *Civil War, Morgan arranged Union loans on the London market, but also resold guns originally bought from the Army, the often-defective Hall carbines, making a substantial and perhaps unethical profit. Avoiding military service by paying for a substitute (as did many other well-to-do young men), Morgan instead sold government bonds and supported charities for war widows and the wounded. He also became a partner in the new banking house of J. S. Morgan and Company, which became Drexel, Morgan in 1871, and J. P. Morgan and Company in 1895.

Coming of age in the era of ruthless capitalist entrepreneurs such as Cornelius *Vanderbilt, Daniel Drew, Andrew *Carnegie, and Jay Gould, Morgan invested heavily in and eventually gained control of Gould's Erie Railroad. He also combined the New York Central and Wabash railroads, and acquired or reorganized the Lehigh Valley and Northern Pacific railroads. In 1895, at a considerable profit, he successfully halted a run on the gold reserves of the U.S. Treasury. Purchasing Carnegie Steel in 1901, he combined it with other holdings to form the United States Steel Corporation, which dominated the industry. During a financial panic in 1907, Morgan led a consortium of New York bankers who ended the crisis by guaranteeing the stability of weaker banks—a demonstration of his dominance over the economy that intensified pressures for reform of the nation's banking system. His vast economic power prompted congressional investigators to call him to testify in 1912 before the Pujo Committee, which investigated the small circle of New York financiers who controlled the nation's banks, corporations, railroads, and stock exchange. Morgan emerged with his prestige intact, his position unchallenged.

A collector even as a boy, Morgan during his many trips to Europe acquired a horde of valuable works. Among the first patrons of the Metropolitan Museum of Art, he also supported the American Museum of Natural History. His acquisitions included Chinese porcelains, medieval and Renaissance paintings, and rare books, especially on religion. His treasures became the nucleus of the Morgan Library, housed in his Madison Avenue mansion.

Some of Morgan's contemporaries saw him as ruthless, secretive, and acquisitive to an extreme, taking more from society than he gave. Others viewed him as a major contributor to corporate growth, *philanthropy, and American culture. Larger than life, he was simply J. P. Morgan.

[*See also* Banking and Finance; Capitalism; Depressions, Economic; Economic Development; Federal Reserve Act; Gilded Age; Iron and Steel Industry; Museums: Museums of Art; Progressive Era.]

• Ron Chernow, *The House of Morgan,* 1990. Jean Strouse, *Morgan: American Financier,* 1999.

—Leo Hershkowitz

MORGAN, LEWIS HENRY (1818–1881), anthropologist. A Rochester, New York, lawyer, Lewis Henry Morgan played a leading role in establishing *anthropology in the United States and through his writings gained worldwide influence. Interested in the Indians of his area, he became an honorary Seneca in 1847. Morgan chiefly studied kinship, one of the two central topics around which anthropology arose (the other being "primitive" religion). Indeed, he largely invented kinship as an anthropological subject, making it the focus of his three major books. *The League of the Iroquois* (1851) documented the matrilineal family relationships underlying the Iroquois's political structure. His masterwork, the massive *Systems of Consanguinity and Affinity of the Human Family* (1871), published by the *Smithsonian Institution, compared kinship systems worldwide, arguing that American Indian systems were similar among themselves and to those of Asia, so proving the Indians' Asian origins. In this work, Morgan created most of the basic analytic tools still used in kinship analysis. *Ancient Society* (1877) integrated his kinship studies into an evolutionary framework, drawing all societies into a unitary story of progress. Writing at a time when the great antiquity of human history had suddenly become evident, Morgan theorized a progressive series of kinship stages, from "primitive promiscuity" through matriarchy and patriarchy to monogamy, thus thoroughly historicizing contemporary marriage norms. This work appealed to a diverse range of groups and individuals, including feminists; the evolutionary theorist Charles Darwin; the conservative English legal historian Sir Henry Maine; and Karl Marx and Friedrich Engels, who believed that Morgan's evolutionary kinship model strengthened their materialist view of history.

[*See also* Indian History and Culture: From 1500 to 1800; Indian History and Culture: From 1800 to 1900; Iroquois Confederacy.]

• Elisabeth Tooker, "The Structure of the Iroquois League: Lewis H. Morgan's Research and Observations," *Ethnohistory* 30 (1983): 141–54. Thomas R. Trautmann, *Lewis Henry Morgan and the Invention of Kinship,* 1987.

—Thomas Trautmann

MORGAN, THOMAS HUNT (1866–1945), embryologist, geneticist, Nobel Laureate in medicine in 1933. The son of Charlton Hunt Morgan and Ellen Key Howard, Thomas Hunt Morgan grew up in Lexington, Kentucky. After receiving a B.S. in zoology at the State College of Kentucky (1886) and a Ph.D. at Johns Hopkins University (1890), he spent his academic career at Bryn Mawr College (1891–1904), Columbia (1904–1928), and the California Institute of Technology (1928–1945). During the summers he conducted research at the Marine Biological Laboratory at Woods Hole, Massachusetts. In 1904 Morgan married Lilian Vaughan Sampson, with whom he had four children.

Trained as a morphologist, Morgan soon grew disenchanted by the descriptive methods of this field and became a champion of the experimental approach to biological research. He published important studies on regeneration, embryology, sex-determination, and evolution, but is best known for his work on variation and inheritance in the fruit fly (*Drosophila melan-*

ogaster). Discovering that certain characteristics were present in one sex only, he explained this by postulating the existence of genes in chromosomes behaving in Mendelian fashion. With the collaboration of a small group of students he published *The Mechanism of Mendelian Heredity* (1915), a landmark in early genetics. A central figure in the establishment of experimental zoology and genetics in the early twentieth century, Morgan published 24 books and about 370 papers, was the president of many professional organizations, and received numerous honors in addition to the Nobel Prize.

[*See also* Biological Sciences; Evolution, Theory of; Genetics and Genetic Engineering; Science: From 1914 to 1945.]

• Garland E. Allen, *Thomas Hunt Morgan: The Man and His Science,* 1978.

—Marga Vicedo

MORMONISM. A worldwide faith by the late twentieth century, Mormonism arose in western New York in the 1820s as seekers gathered around Joseph Smith (1805–1844), a young farmer reputed to be translating a text engraved in hieroglyphics on golden plates. This translation, which Smith said he managed with spiritual help, was published in 1830 as the Book of Mormon. A scripturelike history of ancient Hebrew peoples who settled in North America, it included an account of Jesus bringing the Christian message to the New World.

Assuming prophetic powers, Smith warned of the world's end and told his followers that neither the authentic priesthood nor the true Christian church was presently on the earth. In 1829, Smith claimed that the priesthood had been restored to him, and a year later he presided over the organization of an ecclesiastical institution that Smith, claiming divine revelation, identified as the restored New Testament church. Although its members are generally called Mormons, the church's official name is the Church of Jesus Christ of Latter-Day Saints (LDS).

Initially the Book of Mormon and the doctrine of continuing revelation principally distinguished the LDS church from other forms of American Christianity. But further revelations promulgated by Smith quickly established the church's theological distinctiveness by adding the claim that the movement was also engaged in a literal re-gathering of Israel in the New World. Some practical consequences of this were that Mormonism had patriarchs as well as pastors, temples in addition to meeting houses, and an ideological basis for Mormon ethnicity. Revelation also declared that with the formation of Mormonism, ancient temple rituals had been restored that conferred spiritual power on worthy Saints and created eternal families through celestial marriage and sealing ordinances. Down to 1890, Mormon men could contract celestial marriages with multiple wives.

During a tempestuous first decade, the initial LDS converts, both prosperous and clannish, were driven from their enclave in Kirtland, Ohio, and from several Missouri settlements. In 1839 they fled back to Illinois, settling in a hamlet they named Nauvoo. What they wrought there—at one time Nauvoo was Illinois's largest city—seemed miraculous to the Saints, but so dangerous to their neighbors that Joseph Smith and his brother were murdered in 1844. The Saints were forced to evacuate Nauvoo in 1847.

The murder of the prophet (as Smith was called among Mormons) disclosed a rift within the LDS community. The majority, desiring to preserve the entire theology of restoration and the enclave settlement pattern with its ecclesiastical oversight of all dimensions of existence, followed Brigham Young (1801–1877) to Utah. But a substantial minority remained behind. Committed to Mormonism in its original form, many of these Saints in 1860 "reorganized" the church under Joseph Smith III's leadership. Headquartered in Independence, Missouri, the Reorganized Church of Jesus Christ of Latter-Day Saints (RLDS) had 250,000 members in 1996.

Meanwhile, the main body of Mormons in Utah, centered in Salt Lake City and other settlements, grew to forty thousand by 1860. The church's involvement in politics and business, as well as its acceptance of plural marriage, brought it into conflict with the federal government, and in 1857 President James *Buchanan sent an army occupation force that remained until 1861. In 1896, with LDS leaders having agreed to modify the church's political and economic activities and to give up plural marriage, Utah entered the Union.

The LDS church grew steadily in the twentieth century, sustained by the missionary efforts of young volunteers. Governed by a prophet–president and a Council of Twelve Apostles, the church stressed strong family ties, a work ethic, and education, sponsoring Brigham Young University. The Mormon Tabernacle Choir became widely known. By 1996 worldwide LDS membership approached ten million. Important because it tested the nation's tolerance for religious freedom, this indigenous American religion obliged the United States to clarify the implications of the First Amendment's guarantee of the free exercise of religion.

[*See also* Antebellum Era; Church and State, Separation of; Missionary Movement; Protestantism; Race and Ethnicity; Religion; West, The.]

• Leonard J. Arrington and Davis Bitton, *The Mormon Experience: A History of the Latter-day Saints,* 1979, reprint 1992. Jan Shipps, *Mormonism: The Story of a New Religious Tradition,* 1985. Grant Underwood, *The Millenarian World of Early Mormonism,* 1993. John L. Brooke, *The Refiner's Fire: The Making of Mormon Cosmology, 1644–1844,* 1994.

—Jan Shipps

MORRILL LAND GRANT ACT (1862). This law, which provided land grants to the states for the founding of colleges to teach "agriculture and the mechanic arts," was first introduced in Congress in 1857 by Representative Justin Morrill, a Vermont Whig (later Republican). Morrill was convinced that existing colleges were failing to provide practical education for the nation's farmers and workers, whose productivity might be greatly improved through the diffusion of "useful knowledge." Although Morrill's first bill encountered strong southern opposition and was ultimately vetoed by President James *Buchanan, a similar bill was passed in 1862 after southern secession and was signed into law by President Abraham *Lincoln.

The Morrill Act entitled each state to a grant of thirty thousand acres of federal land for each member of Congress. Funds from the sale of these lands were to be used as a permanent endowment for "at least one college where the leading object shall be, without excluding other scientific and classical studies . . . , to teach such branches of learning as are related to agriculture and the mechanic arts." The states themselves had authority to choose their parcels of federal land, arrange for their sales, and designate the recipients of the income. States either chose existing universities (as in Wisconsin), founded new flagship universities (California), or named special agricultural and mechanical colleges (Indiana). Some southern states (which received grants after the *Civil War) split the funds among separate agricultural and mechanical (A&M) colleges for whites and blacks.

Most land-grant colleges struggled at first, lacking both students and a body of useful scientific knowledge to teach. Rising demand for *engineering education and a surge in high-school graduates, however, eventually caused these institutions to prosper. They were assisted materially by two subsequent acts passed in part because of lobbying efforts by the colleges themselves. The Hatch Act (1887) provided federal funds for *agricultural experiment stations, which considerably furthered agricultural science, and the Second Morrill Act (1890) legislated annual federal appropriations.

The Morrill Act shaped American higher education in important respects. It promoted the equal standing of practical and liberal studies; encouraged publicly supported higher education by inducing states to found universities and materially assist their development; and fostered a system of agricultural education, research, and dissemination that ultimately brought useful knowledge to the farmers Justin Morrill had originally sought to help.

[*See also* Agricultural Education and Extension; Agriculture: 1770s to 1890; Agriculture: The "Golden Age" (1890s–1920); Education: Collegiate Education; Education: The Rise of the University; Land Policy, Federal.]

• Edward D. Eddy Jr., *Colleges for Our Land and Time: The Land-Grant Idea in American Education,* 1957. Roger L. Williams, *The Origins of Federal Support for Higher Education: George W. Atherton and the Land-Grant College Movement,* 1991. "The Land–Grant Act and American Higher Education," *History of Higher Education Annual,* 1998.

—Roger L. Geiger

MORRISON, TONI (1931–), author. Toni Morrison's many achievements include a Nobel Prize for literature in 1993, a Pulitzer Prize (1987), and the National Book Critics Circle and American Academy and Institute of Arts and Letters Awards (1977). Born and raised in Lorain, Ohio, Morrison was christened Chloe Anthony Wofford, a name she later changed. She studied English at Howard University (B.A., 1953) and Cornell University (M.A., 1955). She taught briefly at Texas Southern and Howard Universities, edited textbooks, and in 1968, with two sons from a short-lived, late-1950s marriage, moved to *New York City as a senior editor at Random House, where she promoted the careers of several now well-known black writers. From 1971 to 1988 Morrison taught at the State University of New York at Albany, then became Robert F. Goheen Professor of the Humanities at Princeton University. By the late 1990s she had written a play, *Dreaming Emmett* (1992); a collection of essays, *Playing in the Dark: Whiteness and the Literary Imagination* (1992); and seven novels: *The Bluest Eye* (1970), *Sula* (1973), *Song of Solomon* (1977), *Tar Baby* (1981), *Beloved* (1987), *Jazz* (1992), and *Paradise* (1998); as well as two edited or coedited works. A versatile and gifted writer, Morrison was especially acclaimed for her novels. In beautiful but often disturbing language she created literary masterpieces out of the effects of the most debilitating problems in American life. Morrison's genius earned her praise as the most internationally celebrated African American writer in history, and indeed as one of western culture's premier twentieth-century authors.

[*See also* African Americans; Literature: Since World War I.]

• Nellie Y. McKay, ed., *Critical Essays on Toni Morrison,* 1988. Henry Louis Gates Jr. and K. A. Appiah, eds., *Toni Morrison: Critical Perspectives Past and Present,* 1993. Nancy J. Peterson, ed., special issue of *Modern Fiction Studies* 39, nos. 3–4 (1993): 461–859. Danille Taylor-Guthrie, ed., *Conversations with Toni Morrison,* 1994.

—Nellie Y. McKay

MORSE, SAMUEL F. B. (1791–1872), artist and inventor. Born in Charlestown, Massachusetts, and educated at Yale University, Samuel F. B. Morse began his career as an artist, studying *painting at London's Royal Academy (1811–1815), but is best known for his work in telegraphy. After settling in *New York City in 1823, Morse helped to found the National Academy of Design, serving as its first president. In 1832, the same year he became professor of painting and *sculpture at the University of the City of New York, he drafted his first ideas for an electric *telegraph. He worked alone on his system for several years before congressional interest in establishing a semaphore telegraphy system led him to propose his electrical system as a superior alternative. Morse then acquired the assistance of a former student, Alfred Vail (1807–1859), whose father, Stephen, supported their work at his Speedwell Iron Works in Morristown, New Jersey. Alfred Vail, who converted Morse's crude instrument designs into commercially practical devices, deserves credit as a coinventor of the American telegraph. He may also have revised the telegraph code, named for Morse, into its common form. With additional help from chemist Leonard Gale and physicist Joseph *Henry—and thirty thousand dollars from Congress—Morse and Vail built the first telegraph line, between *Washington, D.C., and Baltimore. After its completion in 1844, Congress refused to purchase Morse's patents or pay for additional lines. Morse and his associates, who included former Postmaster General Amos Kendall, subsequently sold the patent rights to private companies. Morse played only a small role in the subsequent development of the telegraph business, although he continued to defend his patents against legal challenge.

• Carleton Mabee, *The American Leonardo: A Life of Samuel F. B. Morse,* 1943. Paul J. Staiti, *Samuel F. B. Morse,* 1989.

—Paul Israel

MORTALITY. *See* Death and Dying; Life Expectancy.

MOTION PICTURES. *See* Film.

MOTOR VEHICLES. The pioneer mechanical engineer Oliver Evans built a steam-powered amphibious dredge in 1805, but the first significant American experiments with mechanized vehicles came in the 1820s. These heavy, smoky, and unreliable steam-driven vehicles ran on rails, which were smoother than any pavement and guided the vehicles through turns, but sharply limited their utility.

Other inventors, notably J. K. Fisher and Richard Dudgeon, built smaller, more reliable vehicles around 1860, potential replacements for horses for at least some transportation functions, especially in cities where paved streets provided good surfaces. Urban residents, however, feared these "steamers," worrying about accidents, smoke, and boiler explosions. Popular resistance, marked by occasional riots, led to municipal prohibitions on steamers.

In the 1880s European inventors such as Karl Benz, Gottlieb Daimler, and Jean-Joseph Lenoir built the first internal combustion cars, which a few wealthy Americans imported. The *Chicago Times-Herald* organized a race in 1895 that generated enormous publicity for the new internal combustion technology. It inspired Charles and Frank Duryea, Elwood Haynes, Ransom E. Olds, and others to become the first American car producers. The public proved more willing to accept internal combustion than steam. Early carmakers merely strapped engines on carriages, a less-threatening sight with lower speeds (rarely exceeding ten miles per hour [mph]) than the old steamers. Traffic congestion did not seem a problem since the high cost of prototype cars suggested that they would only be playthings for the wealthy. In any case, courts had overturned bans on other new mechanical vehicles, notably bicycles and trolleys, so cities could no longer contemplate outright prohibition.

Henry *Ford forever changed the luxury status of cars by designing the Model T, a durable car reliable enough for poor rural roads. He then mass produced (a Ford-coined word) them, setting up his first assembly-line factory in Highland Park, Michigan, in 1913. By 1922, despite a high rate of inflation, he had cut Model T prices from $850 to $265 (under $2,000 in 1990 dollars). Ford sold over fifteen million Model Ts before 1927, putting America on wheels. By 1925 a majority of American families possessed cars.

The Ford Corporation fell from dominance in the mid-1920s. Its nemesis was the General Motors Corporation (G.M.), founded in 1908 through the consolidation of several independent auto companies. Alfred P. *Sloan, who became G.M.'s president in 1923, turned to aggressive marketing after he realized that G.M. could not compete in price. He extended customer credit through the General Motors Acceptance Corporation (1919), and offered a variety of brands marketed for different audiences, from the plebeian Chevrolet to the patrician Cadillac. Brand marketing and annual model changes—another Sloan innovation—relied on the styling genius of onetime Hollywood car customizer Harley Earl, G.M.'s head designer. (Earl would later introduce the garish tailfins that characterized 1950s cars.) The stodgy Model T could not compete with such marketing, and its successor, the Model A, fared little better. Eventually Ford and the other major car company, Chrysler (founded in 1924 by Walter P. Chrysler [1875–1940]), adopted G.M.-style marketing.

The automobile contributed to massive social changes between the two world wars. The 1920s saw a boom in suburban and resort housing, as cars made outlying areas near big cities more accessible. They helped end the isolation of rural Americans, allowing farmers access to markets and facilitating rural-urban migration, including the well-known movement of *Dust Bowl farmers to *California during the Great Depression. They allowed poor blacks and whites from impoverished rural areas to move to booming northern industrial cities. Providing private space, cars encouraged personal freedom. Blacks could escape the stigma of racial *segregation enforced on southern *railroads and buses. Courting adolescents could evade the social oversight of family and neighbors. Workers in milltowns could choose from workplaces spread over wider areas.

The auto increased access to consumer goods at, for example, the first self-service grocery store, Piggly-Wiggly (Memphis, 1916) and the first mall, Country Club Plaza (Kansas City, 1923). The drive-in culture extended to movies (Camden, New Jersey, 1933), restaurants (Dallas, 1921), and banks (Ventura, California, 1931). The first "motel" (motor hotel) opened in San Luis Obispo, California, in 1926. The Rev. Robert Schuller even opened a drive-in church in Garden Grove, California, in 1954, which he described as "a shopping center for Jesus Christ." The first restaurant chains (White Tower and A&W Root Beer, 1924) catered to a motoring public looking for predictability in food and speed in service. The new roadside businesses borrowed a plastic architecture from *amusement parks and ignored regional vernaculars. Shell-shaped gas stations, milk bottle-shaped ice cream stands, and duck-shaped restaurants proliferated in the 1920s and 1930s.

The automobile also introduced hazards. By 1926 cars had become the fifth leading cause of fatalities, with most victims pedestrians or children. By the end of the twentieth century, cars had killed more than two million Americans. The big-city traffic jam emerged by 1914. Cities lost one third of their street space to parked cars and by the 1930s were razing downtown buildings for parking lots. In 1914 Cleveland introduced the first traffic light and *Detroit police sergeant Harry Jackson built the first octagonal stop sign. Using stop signs to create high-speed boulevards and adding progressively timed lights briefly improved urban traffic flow. When traffic jams worsened in the 1920s, cities turned to highway building. Rural interests initially dominated road policy, however. At both the federal and state levels, governments funded farm-to-market roads that rarely served cities or suburbs. The 1920s federal *highway system choked immediately with traffic generated by uncontrolled roadside businesses.

The limited access highway, rooted in traditional urban planning, provided a better long-term solution to traffic-flow problems. Well before the advent of the automobile, Frederick Law *Olmsted had pioneered the grade separation of cross traffic in New York's Central Park (1857) and limited access to high-speed carriage arteries such as Brooklyn's Eastern Parkway (1868). At the end of the nineteenth century, *Boston's Charles River Speedway built slowdown exit lanes for speedy carriage drivers. The Bronx River Parkway (1922), a toll route, adapted these high-speed design elements to automobile travel. New York highway builder Robert Moses (1888–1981) created a massive commuting road system on Long Island in the 1920s. *New York City's West Side Highway, built in 1927, was the first elevated urban road. New Jersey added another element, constructing the first cloverleaf interchange (Woodbridge, 1929). Massachusetts engineer Franklin Pillsbury designed the first beltway (Route 128 outside Boston, planned in 1930, finished in 1949). Using *Works Progress Administration funds, Connecticut built the first intercity parkway in 1937. Pennsylvania borrowed parkway techniques for its 1940 turnpike, the prototype for the state toll roads of the 1950s and for the interstate highway system begun in 1956.

As the automobile transformed American life, other motorized vehicles had profound effects as well. By 1940 growing fleets of buses were carrying passengers within cities and on longer trips, 4.1 million trucks were vying with the railroads for transporting freight, and the nation's 1.5 million tractors were revolutionizing U.S. *agriculture. Motorcycles, while never a major form of motorized transport, proved popular with police and open-air enthusiasts.

While *World War II halted the production of automobiles for civilian use, the production of motor vehicles for the *military surged. Major Detroit firms produced 49,000 tanks, 126,000 armored cars, and 2,600,000 trucks (as well as 27,000 airplanes and nearly 6 million guns) during the war. Moreover, confiscated Ford and G.M. overseas factories produced more than 70 percent of Germany's trucks. Ford faltered badly at wartime production, however, leading the U.S. government to force Henry Ford out in favor of his grandson, Henry Ford II.

By war's end the big three auto firms, G.M., Ford, and Chrysler, had become an oligopoly, since most smaller firms had failed in the Depression of the 1930s. Henry Kaiser, Preston Tucker, and other independent producers tried but failed to introduce new automobile brands after the war. The oligopoly concentrated on marketing and increasing engine power in the postwar decades, choking off European innovations like front-wheel drive, radial tires, and disk brakes. Consumers could buy cars with 42-inch tailfins, 58 pounds of chrome, and more than 500 horsepower. Germany began to export Volkswagens to the United States in 1958, controlling 8 percent of the American market with a compact car of the kind that Detroit refused to make. New (but short-lived) compacts, like the Ford Falcon, blunted the Volkswagen threat.

The anti-authority movements that characterized the 1960s affected the nation's car culture. Urban activists blocked the completion of many inner-city interstate highways, just as the economic center of American metropolises was shifting from downtown to the beltway. Muckraking attorney Ralph *Nader, noting how fatalities to automobile occupants had soared in the postwar decades, attacked the auto industry on safety grounds. Detroit was slow to install brakes adequate for high horsepower and resisted seat belts and air bags for nearly forty years. Quality control faltered and hazardous design became all too common. As Americans car guzzled more gasoline, smog became an urban health problem. Los Angeles biochemist Aarlie Hagen-Smit demonstrated the relationship between auto emissions and smog in 1950. After much lobbying by environmentalists, Congress passed the Clean Air Act (1970), which banned leaded gasoline and required catalytic converters, significantly reducing some pollutants.

In the 1970s, the Detroit oligopoly faced the challenge of Japanese car makers, which began to export highly reliable, fuel-efficient models to the United States in large numbers, capturing up to a third of the American market. In a decade of oil shortages, Detroit could not match the Japanese in cost, quality, or fuel efficiency. Chrysler escaped bankruptcy only by a government bailout and President Lee Iacocca's success at marketing.

Import taxes and quotas somewhat protected the battered domestic auto industry, and the 1980s brought a revival. Ford responded first, marketing the German-designed, Japanese-engined Escort and Taurus (also German engineered) in the mid-1980s. Chrysler also rebounded in the 1980s, adopting Japanese design and production techniques. General Motors continued to falter through the 1980s, however, losing 25 percent of its domestic market and laying off 74,000 workers. Even when successful, the domestic industry's response to the Japanese import boom took its toll. Imported cars, Japanese style "lean production" techniques, and the outsourcing of work, especially to Mexico, turned much of the *Middle West into a "rust belt."

As the twentieth century ended, the United States remained the most auto-(and petroleum-)dependent nation. The economy was increasingly centered in auto dependent "edge cities." By 1990 the two-car family was the norm and annual mileage per car was up, increasing gasoline imports. The 1950s love of heavy cars returned, with four-wheel-drive cars, pickup trucks, and vans becoming popular. Traffic jams and air pollution worsened in major cities. In 1994, Seattle planners reported a 120 percent increase in traffic and *Los Angeles commuters reported a doubling of travel time over the previous ten years. The statistics did reveal one bright spot, however: As auto safety standards grew more rigorous, seat belt use and airbags became more common, drunken drivers faced increasing social stigma, and the grim annual toll of traffic fatalities decreased.

[*See also* Automobile Racing; Automotive Industry; Bicycles and Bicycling; Courtship and Dating; Energy Crisis of the 1970s; Environmentalism; Foreign Trade, U.S.; Global Economy, America and the; Labor Markets; Mass Marketing; Mass Production; Mobility; Petroleum Industry; Popular Culture; Roads and Turnpikes, Early; Shopping Centers and Malls; Steam Power; Suburbanization; Twenties, The; Urbanization.]

• National Automobile Chamber of Commerce, *Automobile Facts and Figures*, 1921–present. Michael Berger, *The Devil Wagon in God's Country*, 1971. Robert A. Caro, *The Power Broker: Robert Moses and the Fall of New York*, 1975. Pierre Bardou, Jean-Jacques Chinaron, Patrick M. Fridenson, and James M. Laux, *The Automobile Revolution: The Impact of an Industry*, 1982. David Halberstam, *The Reckoning*, 1986. U.S. Department of Transportation, *Personal Travel in the U.S.*, 1986. Jan Jennings, ed., *Roadside America: The Car in Design and Culture*, 1990. Virginia Scharff, *Taking the Wheel: Women and the Coming of the Motor Age*, 1991. Clay McShane, *Down the Asphalt Path: American Cities and the Automobile*, 1995.

—Clay McShane

MOTT, LUCRETIA (1793–1880), Quaker (*Society of Friends) minister, peace activist, abolitionist, and women's rights pioneer. Born in Nantucket, Massachusetts, the daughter of sea captain Thomas Coffin and his wife Anna, Lucretia in 1808 became an assistant teacher at Nine Partners Quaker boarding school in Dutchess County, New York. There she met James Mott, a teacher/businessman. They married in 1811 and settled in *Philadelphia. Five children survived infancy. In 1821 Lucretia was officially recognized as a Quaker minister. Devoted to social justice, she challenged Quaker rules and doctrine, violent means of protest, and the oppression of women and *African Americans. The Motts were ardent "Non-Resistants" (pacifists), believing that "moral force" alone could end *slavery. Lucretia helped organize the Anti-Slavery Convention of American Women in 1837.

At the 1840 World's Anti-Slavery Convention in London, where she and other women delegates were refused recognition, Mott conversed with Elizabeth Cady *Stanton about women's unequal status. This led them, with Mott's sister Martha Coffin Wright, to call the first American women's rights convention at Seneca Falls, New York, in 1848.

Remembered today for her advocacy of women's rights and abolitionism, Mott was equally known in her time as a pacifist and as one of the most effective and recognized American reformers. Her speeches and sermons frequently appeared as pamphlets. She harbored runaway slaves; presided over the 1852 women's rights convention in Syracuse, New York, and the first annual convention of the American Equal Rights Association (1866); spoke regularly on women's and African-American rights, including addresses to state legislatures; and raised funds for her causes, including Swarthmore College, a Quaker school.

[*See also* Antebellum Era; Antislavery; Pacifism; Peace Movements; Seneca Falls Convention; Women's Rights Movements.]

• Margaret Hope Bacon, *Valiant Friend: The Life of Lucretia Mott*, 1980. Margaret Hope Bacon, "Lucretia Mott: Pioneer for Peace," *Quaker History* 82 (Fall 1993); 63–78.

—Susan Gonda

MOUNT RUSHMORE. Located in the Black Hills of South Dakota, this mountain contains the massive carved sculptural heads of Presidents George *Washington, Thomas *Jefferson, Abraham *Lincoln, and Theodore *Roosevelt, each sixty feet in height. In 1923, Doane Robinson, a South Dakota historian, proposed a monument in this region to commemorate the settling of the West. With the aid of U.S. Senator Peter Norbeck, Robinson enlisted the sculptor Gutzon Borglum, who instead proposed a national memorial on Mount Rushmore that would feature the four presidents. In 1925, the South Dakota Legislature and the U.S. Congress authorized the use of state and federal lands for the memorial. Borglum began work on the figure of Washington in 1927. Two years later, Congress established the first of two commissions to oversee completion of the memorial and to provide financial assistance.

The Mount Rushmore project was a massive artistic and engineering feat requiring a staff of assistants who used dynamite and power drills to carve the heads under Borglum's supervision. When Borglum died in 1941, his son Lincoln Borglum supervised the final work, which ended that October. A part of the *National Park System, Mount Rushmore National Memorial is one of the most frequently visited sites in the United States.

• Gilbert C. Fite, *Mount Rushmore*, 1952.

—G. Kurt Piehler

MOUNT VERNON. Situated on the Potomac River in Fairfax County, Virginia, Mount Vernon originated in a 1674 land grant to English emigrant John Washington, the great-grandfather of George *Washington. Inheriting the estate, then an unexceptional tobacco plantation, from his half-brother Lawrence in 1761, George Washington gradually enlarged it to eight thousand acres and diversified its economy with grain cultivation, a grist mill, a fishery, and a ferry.

The *Revolutionary War imparted a civic purpose to such activities. After returning home from the war in 1783, Washington, dedicated to agricultural improvement, attempted to transform Mount Vernon into the new nation's most advanced farming operation, hoping to offer all Americans a model of efficiency, productivity, and industrious labor. Although this grand design never reached fruition (not least because Washington's slaves and free white laborers did not share his vision), innovations undertaken at the estate long influenced agricultural reform.

Following the deaths of George and Martha Washington and their burial on the grounds, even as heirs owned and lived at Mount Vernon, thousands visited "the American Mecca" annually, commemorating the Revolution and honoring the man credited above all others with securing independence and creating the nation. Beginning in the 1820s, politicians and public-spirited citizens periodically urged the federal government or the state of Virginia to buy and preserve the site. This proved unattainable, however, because of sectional animosities and the lack of any precedent for historic preservation in the United States. An apolitical solution to the impasse was achieved when the Mount Vernon Ladies' Association of the Union (1853) conducted a national fund-raising campaign and bought the site in 1858. So great was public reverence that Mount Vernon was by common consent of both sides preserved as neutral ground during the *Civil War.

[*See also* Agriculture: Colonial Era; Agriculture: 1770s to

1890; Architecture: Domestic Architecture; Slavery; Tobacco Industry.]

• Robert F. Dalzell Jr., *George Washington's Mount Vernon: At Home in Revolutionary America,* 1998. Jean B. Lee, *Mount Vernon and the Nation, from the Revolution to the Civil War,* forthcoming.

—Jean B. Lee

MOVIES. *See* Film.

MUCKRAKERS. Theodore *Roosevelt first applied the term "muckrakers" to a group of journalists and writers who exposed corruption in business and government in the early twentieth century. Roosevelt intended the term, borrowed from John Bunyan's *Pilgrim's Progress,* to be somewhat pejorative, but the muckrakers were very influential for a time and provided strong impetus to the ongoing *Progressive Era reform movement.

Around 1902, a number of prominent *magazines, including *McClure's, Collier's, Cosmopolitan, Everybody's,* and the *Arena,* began featuring crusading exposés or "muckraking" articles. Some of these pieces were later expanded into full-length books. Among the best-known were Ida Tarbell's *History of the Standard Oil Company* (1902); Lincoln *Steffens's *The Shame of the Cities* (1904), documenting corruption in municipal government; Samuel Hopkins Adams's *The Great American Fraud* (1906), lambasting the patent-medicine industry; and Ray Stannard Baker's *Following the Color Line* (1908), a pioneering exposé of American *racism.

A few muckrakers made their case in works of fiction. Upton *Sinclair's *The *Jungle* (1906), a fictionalized account of the *Chicago meatpacking industry, was the best known of the genre, but David Graham Phillips was perhaps the most prolific of the muckraking novelists. Among his numerous works were *Lightfingered Gentry* (1907), on the insurance industry; *Susan Lenox: Her Fall and Rise* (1908, published in 1917), on prostitution; and many others.

The muckracking spirit also influenced some of the major novelists of the time, although usually in less tractarian form. Frank Norris's *The Octopus* (1901) and *The Pit* (1903); Theodore *Dreiser's *The Financier* (1912) and *The Titan* (1914); and Jack London's *Iron Heel* (1908) all address the social consequences of unregulated capitalist expansion.

After about 1912, the muckraking movement abated. The public tired of the exposés, some of which seemed sensationalized and overly sordid. But muckraking already had exerted a major impact on the reform movement and would influence the policies of President Woodrow *Wilson. Indeed, Ray Stannard Baker became an aide to Wilson and later edited a six-volume collection of Wilson's public papers (1926–1927). Assuming many different forms, the muckraking impulse continued to influence American *journalism as the twentieth century wore on.

[*See also* Capitalism; Industrialization; Literature: Civil War to World War I; Meatpacking and Meat Processing Industry; Prostitution and Antiprostitution; Urbanization.]

• J. M. Harrison and H. H. Stein, eds., *Muckraking,* 1974. Walter M. Brasch, *Forerunners of Revolution,* 1990.

—George H. Douglas

MUGWUMPS, late nineteenth-century reformers who blamed partisanship for the rampant corruption of *Gilded Age politics. By voting independently of party lines, Mugwumps attempted to pressure regular Republicans and Democrats to support *civil service reform, lower *tariffs, and a hard-money policy based on the *gold standard.

In 1884, members of the *Republican party's independent wing rejected their party's presidential candidate, James G. *Blaine, to support the *Democratic party nominee, Grover *Cleveland. Republican loyalists called the insurgents "Mugwumps," an Algonquian word for "great man," used in this context to deride the bolters' claim to moral superiority.

Most Mugwumps were college-educated business and professional men from New York or *New England. Their spokesmen in 1884 were veteran Republicans such as Carl Schurz (1829–1906), a former U.S. senator and cabinet official, and George William Curtis (1824–1892) and E. L. Godkin (1831–1902), editors respectively of *Harper's Weekly* and *The Nation.* But younger men such as R. R. Bowker, a New York publisher, and George Fred Williams, a Boston lawyer, did the day-to-day organizational work.

Cleveland's slim victory margin in 1884 seemed to underscore the importance of the Mugwump vote, and Cleveland courted their support by backing civil service reform and lower tariffs. After 1884, some bolters became Democrats and helped revive Democratic strength in New England in the early 1890s. But Mugwump-Democratic cooperation was never wholehearted. Irish-American Democrats and the Mugwumps distrusted each other from the start, and the Democrats' 1896 presidential candidate, William Jennings *Bryan, advocated populist programs that the Mugwumps abhored. The last national campaign in which the Mugwumps figured prominently was the anti-imperialist opposition to U.S. annexation of the *Philippines following the *Spanish-American War.

[*See also* Political Parties; Populist Era.]

• John G. Sproat, *"The Best Men": Liberal Reformers in the Gilded Age,* 1968. Gerald W. McFarland, *Mugwumps, Morals and Politics, 1884–1920,* 1975.

—Gerald W. McFarland

MUIR, JOHN (1838–1914), naturalist and a founder of the environmental movement. John Muir was born near Edinburgh, Scotland. His family emigrated to America in 1849, settling on a farm in southeastern Wisconsin. After a grim childhood and adolescence, Muir in 1861 escaped to the state university at Madison, where he studied botany and geology. Years of travel through Canada and the United States followed. On a long hike in 1867 he intuited the central insight of his life: the need for human forbearance toward nature.

His initial encounter with *California's Yosemite Valley, in 1869, moved him profoundly; he was thereafter identified with Yosemite and the Sierra Nevada Mountains. Independent geological work on the valley's glacial origins led to his first published articles in the 1870s. After a hiatus for family and farming, he resumed writing and conservation work in 1889. Muir cofounded the *Sierra Club in 1892 and served as its president until his death.

In the intramural battles of the nascent *conservation movement, Muir led the amateur, preservationist wing, which fought both with and against the professional, utilitarian faction under Gifford Pinchot. Possessed of sparkling if verbose charm, Muir formed friendships with powerful men (such as Theodore *Roosevelt and the financier E. H. *Harriman), which proved useful to his causes. His passionate nature writings—in the tradition of Henry David *Thoreau and implicitly pantheistic—gained him wide attention and support. Muir's protracted final battle, to forestall the Hetch Hetchy reservoir within *Yosemite National Park, ended in a loss for the preservationists.

[*See also* Environmentalism; Forests and Forestry; Progressive Era; West, The.]

• Stephen Fox, *John Muir and His Legacy,* 1981. Michael P. Cohen, *The Pathless Way,* 1984.

—Stephen Fox

MULLER* v. *OREGON (1908), a U.S. *Supreme Court decision granting states the right to regulate the hours of women workers. The case began when laundry-owner Curt Muller, convicted of violating Oregon's ten-hour law for women, carried his appeal to the Supreme Court, arguing that the statute infringed his right to contract freely with his workers. At issue, then, was whether states had the power to intervene on behalf of employees in employment relationships. In **Lochner* v. *New York* (1905), the Supreme Court had overthrown a New York law regulating the hours of bakers. The opportunity to prepare evidence in defense of the Oregon law fell to Florence *Kelley and her research chief at the *National Consumers' League (NCL), Josephine Goldmark. The case exemplified Kelley's strategy of using gender-specific means to achieve classwide goals. Goldmark collected extensive evidence to prove that long hours jeopardized women's health and morals, and her brother-in-law Louis *Brandeis argued the case before the Court. His famous "Brandeis Brief," a compilation of sociological and medical evidence, persuaded the high court to uphold Oregon's law. Writing for the majority, Justice David Brewer accepted the argument that overwork was injurious to women, and that the state bore a responsibility for protecting women "to preserve the strength . . . of the race."

The ruling led many more states to regulate working conditions. It also popularized the practice of introducing sociological and medical data to establish legal claims. This approach, central to the concept that came to be known as "legal realism," helped lay the groundwork for such later landmark decisions as **Brown* v. *Board of Education.* While women's organizations supported the *Muller* decision at the time, changes in working conditions and in ideology brought about a reversal of attitude, and in the 1960s and 1970s the *National Organization for Women and other feminist organizations successfully campaigned for the removal of gender-specific laws.

[*See also* Progressive Era; Women in the Labor Force.]

• Josephine Goldmark, *Impatient Crusader: Florence Kelley's Life Story,* 1953. Nancy Woloch, Muller v. Oregon: *A Brief History with Documents,* 1996.

—Kathryn Kish Sklar

MULTICULTURALISM. *See* Cultural Pluralism.

MULTINATIONAL CORPORATIONS. *See* Global Economy, America and the; Multinational Enterprises.

MULTINATIONAL ENTERPRISES. Multinational enterprises are firms that control facilities—other than those exclusively devoted to sales—in two or more countries. This control of foreign subsidiaries can be exercised through either total or partial ownership, joint ventures, or less binding agreements. Success abroad depends upon some firm-specific skills, such as expertise in marketing, management, *technology, or finance. Foreign direct investment (FDI) also relies upon the extraordinary transformations in transportation, communication, and corporate organization that began in the late nineteenth century. Political considerations, especially in the host countries, vitally shape the size and direction of multinational investment.

The first wave of American direct investment abroad occurred between the 1880s and 1920s, in a response to the great organizational and technological changes of that era. The Singer Sewing Machine Company, seeking markets for its innovative machines, led the way. As sales mounted abroad, Singer built factories to assemble and eventually build sewing machines in Scotland. Other *mass-production manufacturers followed, initially seeking markets in developed countries such as Canada, Great Britain, France, and Germany. After 1900, the focus of most American investment shifted to less developed countries, as American corporations vied to exploit these nations' natural resources. U.S. funds flowed into the Western Hemisphere, especially into agriculture—for tobacco, coffee, sugar, and bananas—and into *mining and drilling, to extract oil, silver, gold, lead, zinc, and copper. These capital-intensive ventures yielded raw materials that were shipped to the United States for refining (if necessary) and then consumption domestically and abroad.

The second great wave of American multinational investment dates from 1955. As Europe rapidly recovered from the devastation of *World War II, the United States had the needed capital, management, and especially technology. By 1966, American FDI exceeded that of the rest of the noncommunist world combined. This burst of FDI aroused alarm in Europe about the "American invasion" and Europe's "technology gap." In contrast to the previous era, when most investment went into raw-material ventures in developing countries, early post–World War II FDI tended to be concentrated in manufacturing in Europe and Canada. After an initial flurry of investment in petroleum, money flowed into industries such as automobiles, chemicals, machinery, foods, and fabricated metals. This multinational spread was typically accomplished through the acquisition of foreign firms rather than the construction of new facilities by an American company.

The post-1970 period brought a bewildering array of developments, as the complexity of multinational activity increased. As other nations closed the technological and organizational gap, they began to invest abroad as well. The United States, with its huge open market, became the largest target of FDI by British, Dutch, German, and increasingly Japanese firms. U.S. investments, meanwhile, sought ever wider outlets geographically, particularly as production became more specialized. Increasingly, American firms relied upon foreign subsidiaries not to produce for their own national markets, but to build products for shipment to the United States or elsewhere for final assembly. By the end of the twentieth century, perhaps half of the United States' foreign trade consisted of imports and exports within multinational companies. While American service firms such as banking always had some multinational spread, others such as management consulting, consumer finance, automobile rental, hotels, and legal services grew rapidly after 1980.

American multinational enterprises have historically been the nation's largest, most technologically and managerially sophisticated, and, on the whole, most profitable companies. While their beneficial impact upon the economic well-being of Americans seemed clear, their political clout, sheer size, and geographical flexibility, posed problems domestically and abroad. As multinationals formed strategic alliances and grew ever more powerful, the ability of governments even in developed economies to regulate their activities remained in doubt.

[*See also* Banking and Finance; Business; Capitalism; Economic Development; Economic Regulation; Foreign Relations: The Economic Dimension; Industrialization; Post–Cold War Era.]

• Mira Wilkins, *The Emergence of Multinational Enterprise: American Business Abroad from the Colonial Era to 1914,* 1970. Mira Wilkins, *The Maturing of Multinational Enterprise: American Business Abroad from 1914 to 1970,* 1974.

—Diane Lindstrom

MUMFORD, LEWIS (1895–1990), social philosopher, architectural critic, and moral reformer. Mumford was born in *New York City and educated in its public schools. In a succession of bold and brilliant books, beginning with *The Story of Utopias* (1922), and in his "Sky Line" column for the *New Yorker* Magazine, he did more than any other American writer to heighten awareness of the role of *architecture, cities, and *technology in history and everyday life.

His two landmark works on urban civilization, *The Culture of Cities* (1938) and *The City in History* (1961), helped establish the city as a subject of scholarly concern. An activist as well as an intellectual, Mumford played a central role in some of the leading public-policy debates of the later twentieth century, including those on highways and *urban renewal, *nuclear weapons, and the problems and promise of technology. As a founder of the Regional Planning Association of America in 1924, he fashioned a program of regional development that resulted in the building of two model communities: Radburn, New Jersey, and Sunnyside Gardens, Queens. One of the outstanding public intellectuals of his era, Mumford produced a body of writing unmatched in modern American letters for its range and richness.

[*See also* Highway System; Regionalism; Urbanization.]

• Donald L. Miller, *Lewis Mumford, A Life,* 1992. Donald L. Miller, ed., *The Lewis Mumford Reader,* 1995.

—Donald L. Miller

MUNICIPAL AND COUNTY GOVERNMENTS. Americans inherited both the institution of the municipal corporation and the county form of government from seventeenth-century England, but over the course of four centuries these units of local rule have changed markedly.

Colonial Era. During the *Colonial Era, the county was the principal unit of local government in the *South with county courts, composed of local gentry, acting both as judicial and administrative bodies. These courts settled legal disputes and supervised the construction and maintenance of roads. In the middle colonies, counties and townships shared authority, whereas in *New England the town was the most significant local unit, though county justices were authorized to preside over civil and criminal cases, license taverns, and order the construction of roads and bridges.

Operating under royal charters, municipal corporations ruled the emerging commercial centers of the middle and southern colonies. During the seventeenth and early eighteenth centuries, these corporations dedicated themselves primarily to promoting and regulating commerce and managing the municipal corporations' property. They fixed bread prices, licensed carters, guaranteed standard weights and measures, and oversaw corporation-owned ferries, wharves, and markets. By the mid–eighteenth century, however, the municipal corporations were devoting increased attention to such services as fire protection and street lighting. Some of these colonial municipalities, such as *Philadelphia, Williamsburg, and Norfolk, were closed corporations with incumbent aldermen filling all vacancies on the governing boards and the general populace having no voice in the selection of their municipal rulers. In *New York City and Albany, as well as other less prominent municipal corporations in the middle colonies, the municipal charters provided for popular elections of city councils. Devoted to their town governments, colonial New Englanders eschewed the municipal corporation, and none of the commercial centers of New England operated under a municipal charter.

Revolutionary Era to Late Nineteenth Century. The half century following the *Revolutionary War brought notable changes in local government. The closed corporation disappeared, and in all municipalities the electorate chose the members of the governing council. New Englanders finally accepted the municipal corporation, with six communities in Connecticut and Rhode Island securing municipal charters in the 1780s and *Boston becoming a chartered city in 1822. Whereas during the Colonial Era a municipal charter was a privilege granted by the royal governors to a selected group of communities, by the 1820s and 1830s the state legislatures rubber-stamped charters for every village or town aspiring to corporate status. During the course of the nineteenth century, thousands of communities, including many with only a few hundred residents, became municipal corporations and enjoyed the right of local self-government.

Meanwhile, the new states west of the Appalachians were creating county governments modeled on those in the East. Those north of the *Mason-Dixon line opted for a county and township governance structure similar to that in Pennsylvania or New York. In some northern states the legislature vested responsibility for county government in boards of supervisors, composed of at least one supervisor from each township, but other states adopted the commission form of rule, with a small panel of officials elected at large overseeing each county's business. New southern states, however, followed the examples of Virginia and North Carolina, assigning responsibility for rural government to county courts and rejecting the township unit.

During the second half of the nineteenth century, county governments generally underwent little change, but in the fast-growing cities, municipal governments expanded their role. The larger municipalities invested in expansive parks, state-of-the-art water and sewer systems, and professional fire and police departments. New York City boasted of such magnificent municipal enterprises as Central Park, the Croton Aqueduct, and the *Brooklyn Bridge, whereas Boston's public library and intercepting sewer system won plaudits from domestic and foreign observers.

Yet many criticized American city government. The *police forces were too often corrupt, ignoring prostitution and the illegal sale of liquor in exchange for bribes. Some urban political leaders grew rich by exploiting their influence and winning lucrative contracts from the city. Streetcar and public-utility companies paid off aldermen to secure valuable franchises. Wardheelers of questionable competence obtained jobs in city hall simply through loyal service to the political party in power. During the early 1870s, New York City's Democratic party leader William M. ("Boss") *Tweed won nationwide notoriety for his peculations and those of his cronies, and many late nineteenth-century Americans claimed that minor-league Tweeds were operating in municipalities throughout the nation. To a growing number of Protestant, upper middle-class moralists, municipal governments were compromising their honor by welcoming Irish-Catholic ward bosses and tolerating the infractions of saloonkeepers, prostitutes, dishonest aldermen, and venal police officers.

Progressive Era Municipal Reforms. To clean up city government, municipal reformers of the late nineteenth and early twentieth centuries suggested a long list of remedies. Seeking to keep party hacks off the public payrolls, they urged the adoption of civil service rules that provided for the selection of municipal workers by competitive examinations. Municipal legislatures appeared especially prone to corruption, and consequently reformers proposed a shift in authority from the board of aldermen or city council to the mayor. Moreover, they sought to weaken the clout of party ward bosses through the creation of nonpartisan city councils elected at large. This reform would supposedly shift control of city government from neighborhood party potentates to upright citizens of citywide repute. Yet another highly touted remedy was home rule, which enabled municipalities to draft and adopt their own charters. No longer would cities have to seek state legislative approval for their structures of government or bargain with party bosses and special interests at the state capital. Instead, a municipality could tailor its charter to its needs and the local electorate would have the final say whether to accept a proposed charter. Not every state or locality adopted all these reforms, but by the early twentieth century the tendency nationwide was toward enhanced mayoral authority, smaller at-large councils, nonpartisan administration, and home rule.

Some reformers sought even more radical changes. Advocates of the commission plan of municipal government jettisoned the traditional mayor-council structure and placed all executive and legislative authority in the hands of a small body of commissioners. Each commissioner was elected at large and responsible for a certain branch of administration. Thus the commissioner of public works met with the commissioners of finance, public safety, parks, and sanitation, and together they governed the city just as a board of directors governed a business corporation. First adopted in Galveston, Texas, in 1901, after a devastating hurricane and flood, the commission plan swept the nation; by 1922 over five hundred cities had converted to this scheme of government.

Meanwhile, another reform plan was also attracting adherents. In 1908 Staunton, Virginia, introduced city-manager government; Dayton, Ohio, followed suit after a terrible flood in 1913, and by 1920 164 American cities had embraced this plan. Under the city-manager scheme, the city council retained legislative authority but an appointed, professional manager was put in charge of municipal administration. Thus elected officials determined basic policy questions, yet the implementation of policy and the overall operation of the city was the responsibility of an expert administrator. The administration of a city was supposedly too complex to assign a mere politician fortunate enough to be elected mayor.

As the twentieth century wore on, the commission plan waned in popularity, and by 1987 only 364 American municipalities still adhered to it, whereas nearly 2,500 cities employed managers, and over 13,000 municipalities retained traditional mayor-council government. Large, heterogeneous cities that needed political leadership as well as technical expertise were most often in the mayor-council column, but many homogeneous suburban municipalities and smaller cities favored the manager plan.

Reforms in County Government. As municipalities shifted to manager rule, good-government reformers and public-administration experts also found county governments wanting. In 1917 H. S. Gilbertson exposed the previously unexplored shortcomings of county rule in *The County: The "Dark Continent" of American Politics.* Characterizing the irrational county structure as a jungle, Gilbertson called for reform. Others were suggesting changes as well. Some proposed a county-manager scheme to ensure professional, expert administration. The county-manager idea only slowly gained momentum, however, with Iredell County, North Carolina, appointing the first in 1927. As of 1950, only sixteen of the more than three thousand American counties had hired such professional chieftains. In 1911 *California contributed to the county-reform movement when it authorized county home rule. The following year, *Los Angeles County became the first in the United States to adopt a locally drafted charter and eschew the general scheme for county government authorized by the state legislature. The county home-rule idea did not initially spread rapidly, and prior to 1930, only California and Maryland had incorporated this reform in their constitutions.

Gradually, however, the traditional structure of county rule came under assault, especially in fast-growing suburban areas where county authorities needed to assume new responsibilities that the myriad miniature suburban municipalities could not adequately perform. From 1920 to 1940, the number of municipalities in Long Island's Nassau County soared from twenty to sixty-five. Believing that an overarching county government could impose needed order and unity on Nassau's fragmented governmental structure, Long Islanders voted in 1936 to adopt a county charter that enhanced the county's planning powers and transferred responsibility for welfare, *public health, and tax assessment from the townships and municipalities to the county. Moreover, the charter provided for the nation's first elected county executive, comparable to a big-city mayor, to preside over the new governance structure. This represented a marked deviation from the traditional reliance on county boards to exercise both legislative and executive authority. Other counties followed Nassau's example, but as late as 1960 only eight could boast of elected executives. During the following quarter century, the number of converts to this reform scheme rose markedly, and by 1987, nearly four hundred counties had elected executives comparable to mayors, while another four hundred had adopted the county-manager plan, hiring administrators comparable to city managers. These reforms became possible in part because of a growing willingness to grant home rule to counties. By 1987, eighty-five counties had framed and approved their own blueprints for government.

Post–1950 Developments. As the number of municipal governments in metropolitan areas soared during the mid–twentieth century, pressure for more centralized governance mounted. Political scientists and good-government leagues proposed plans to shift governing power from cities and villages to metropolitanwide authorities. As older central cities lost population, businesses, and tax revenues to outlying municipalities, proponents of metropolitan reform argued that new schemes of regional cooperation or consolidation would correct the growing inequities between cities and their suburbs. For example, in the late 1950s and early 1960s, two proposals to promote metropolitan unity among ninety-eight suburban municipalities and the city of Saint Louis appeared on the ballot. Voters resoundingly rejected both proposals, however, and residents of small municipalities elsewhere proved equally wedded to local self-government. Nevertheless, county governments gradually succeeded in imposing some coordination upon smaller local units, and many municipalities agreed to join special-function metropolitan districts providing such services as water or sewerage. But wholesale consolidation remained elusive. As the twentieth century ended, the United States had almost twenty thousand municipalities, and there seemed little likelihood that the number would decline.

[*See also* City Planning; Civil Service Reform; Galveston Hurricane and Flood; Muckrakers; Municipal Judicial Systems; Prostitution and Antiprostitution; Suburbanization; Urbanization.]

• Alexander B. Callow Jr., *The Tweed Ring,* 1966. Robert M. Ireland, *The County Courts in Antebellum Kentucky,* 1972. Jon C. Teaford, *The Municipal Revolution: Origins of Modern Urban Government, 1650–1825,* 1975. Bradley R. Rice, *Progressive Cities: The Commission Government Movement in America, 1901–1920,* 1977. Jon C. Teaford, *The Unheralded Triumph: City Government in America, 1870–1900,* 1984. David R. Berman, ed., *County Governments in an Era of Change,* 1993. Jon C. Teaford, *Post-Suburbia: Government and Politics in the Edge Cities,* 1997.

—Jon C. Teaford

MUNICIPAL JUDICIAL SYSTEMS encompass a variety of courts of limited or special jurisdiction that form the base of the American justice system. They are termed "municipal" courts not because they are in cities, although they often are, but because they oversee the exercise of municipal or, as they are more frequently called, police powers. These are the powers of government—historically left to the cities and states—to regulate the health, safety, morals, and welfare of the population. In contrast to state courts of general jurisdiction, which also exercise police powers, these lower-level courts typically hear and decide cases that result in a fine of less than $1,000 or a jail term of less than 12 months; misdemeanor violations involving traffic, petty larceny, prostitution, and similar criminal acts; and matters covered under municipal ordinances. The initial hearing of some felony charges also occurs in municipal courts. Together they account for 90 percent of all courts in the nation and 80 percent of all litigation.

Modern courts of limited jurisdiction have their roots in the American colonies and more distantly in the judicial institutions and common-law experience of England. The first local colonial courts were rough approximations of their seventeenth- and eighteenth-century English counterparts. Most colonies had local judges, usually called justices of the peace or magistrates, who possessed limited legal training, served by appointment of the governor, and handled matters ranging from immoral behavior to economic regulation. These local courts, the forerunners of the modern municipal courts, were also important in reminding the colonists that they were entirely capable of delivering their own brand of justice, independent of their English governors.

This powerful heritage of local legal control carried beyond the ratification of the *Constitution and reminds us that the most immediate impact of American law is at the local level. The nineteenth-century justice-of-the-peace courts, for example, operated on a neighborhood basis. The justice was a quasi-paternal figure, often untrained formally in the law, but a local notable who knew the people who appeared before him. Justices of the peace and magistrates, who depended in most cases on the fines and fees assessed on defendants, viewed themselves as semi-autonomous figures who managed their own case flows and finances, and more often than not held a presumption of guilt about the defendants who appeared before them.

This scheme of local justice, like the rest of the American judicial system, came under growing pressure during the *Progressive Era. Since relatively few records of the actions of these courts survive, it is hard to establish their real level of business. It was surely vast, however. By 1900, for example, over 500 separate courts existed in the *Chicago metropolitan area alone, more than double the number in 1880. The courts of *Kansas City had 5,100 cases on the dockets in December 1903, twice the total a decade earlier.

As the number of courts and cases grew, so, too, did the work of those courts. European *immigration and *industrialization, for example, prompted cities and states to criminalize an increasingly broad range of human conduct. Thus, municipal courts typically became the place where judges unfamiliar with immigrant culture and language meted out justice to drunks, petty thieves, and status offenders, such as prostitutes.

The judges were invariably political rather than legal figures. Municipal judgeships were filled in various ways, but whatever the method, the office, especially in light of the court's role as an agent of local social control, had powerful and often pernicious political overtones. These conditions drew the wrath of increasingly organized and professionally oriented municipal bar associations that by 1900 made municipal-court reform a priority.

The leaders of these bar associations preached that justice would only flow from a politically disinterested court system presided over by legal professionals. Businessmen joined the chorus to protest the waste, corruption, and political influence associated with these municipal courts. Chicago in 1900, for example, had fifty-two justices of the peace, whose salaries were paid by the fees of litigants, and whose courts suffered from endless delays. The poor who could not afford an appeal were forced to accept the justices' ruling. At the same time, police magistrates, who heard petty criminal cases, were appointed by the mayor, who wielded extensive political influence over the courts.

Faced with these challenges, Chicago's bar and business leaders adopted reform measures that produced the nation's first modern municipal court system. The Illinois legislature in 1904 authorized an amendment to the Illinois Constitution that granted extensive home-rule powers to Chicago, including the authority to establish a unified municipal court. This new court, created in 1905, won broad popular support at the polls after a vigorous campaign. It involved a network of branch courts under a single chief justice. The court had jurisdiction to hear civil complaints, ordinance violations, and misdemeanors, and even had preliminary jurisdiction over felonies. The act empowered the chief justice, Harry Olson, to bring a corporate style of management to the courts, including setting a trial calendar, developing civil procedures for the courts, assigning the twenty-seven associate justices to either the civil or criminal branch, and requiring a monthly reporting of activity. The judges were popularly elected on non-partisan ballots to six-year terms.

Under Olson's leadership, the Chicago Municipal Court became a national model. Within a decade, Cleveland, Milwaukee, Pittsburgh, Buffalo, *New York City, *Atlanta, *Philadelphia, Birmingham, St. Louis, and Kansas City had adopted the Chicago model. The reformers who fashioned these new courts also embraced a different approach to the relationship of law and society. They expected municipal judges to approach each offender as a social worker might, using knowledge of the person's mental abnormalities, family history, and social experiences to shape appropriate punishments. As a result, a host of new, special-jurisdiction courts developed, including those dealing with juvenile justice, domestic relations, small claims, and public morals.

The promise of Progressive reform, however, was never fully realized. While the corporate administrative model offered a more effective way to manage case loads, city and state governments often failed to provide funding sufficient to keep pace with rapid population growth. The municipal courts became the subject of increasing complaint because they often provided only assembly-line justice. While the general ethic of American law presumes innocence, by the 1960s the day-to-day practice at the lowest level was a working presumption of guilt, a simple fact of judicial life in heavily overworked local court systems. The Progressive attempt to enlist the voters as a way of eliminating political and partisan influence in the selection of municipal judges fared just as poorly. Turnout in local judicial elections was invariably low; candidates for judgeships were frequently unknown to the electorate. Moreover, outside major metropolitan centers, the tradition of local justice remained strong, especially in the *South, where it was so intimately tied to racial control.

Beginning in the 1970s a new reform effort took hold. The National League of Cities pioneered efforts to bring *technology to the courtroom, making it possible for judges to administer growing case loads, to settle matters outside the courtroom through mediation and arbitration, and to share information about defendants that would prevent known criminals charged in one court from walking free in another court. Some of the most significant changes took place in *California. At the end of the twentieth century, for example, *Los Angeles County had the largest municipal justice system in America. It included 50 law enforcement agencies and 24 municipal court districts with 300 judges presiding over half a million arrests a year and more than 2 million traffic citations. California in 1995 gave local judges the opportunities to eliminate justice courts altogether and fold them into municipal courts. Moreover, voters in 1998 passed Proposition 220 that authorized the municipal courts to unify with the general-jurisdiction superior courts, if the judges of the two court systems could agree to do so. This unification process transferred many of the tasks formerly performed by the municipal courts to the superior courts and streamlined judicial business overall.

Despite these continuing efforts at consolidation and centralization, the American scheme of municipal justice retains strong local ties, extraordinary diversity, and a compelling role as an agency of social control. That tradition means that these courts are often shaped to fit local circumstances, but it also means that local justice does not mean exactly the same thing everywhere in America.

[*See also* Crime; Gambling and Lotteries; Jurisprudence; Legal Profession; Police; Prostitution and Antiprostitution; Sexual Mortality and Sex Reform; Social Work; Urbanization; Working-Class Life and Culture.]

• Hiram T. Gilbert, *The Municipal Court of Chicago*, 1928. Herbert Jacob, *Urban Justice: Law and Order in American Cities*, 1976. Kermit L. Hall, *The Magic Mirror: Law in American History*, 1989. Jon'a Meyer, *"Doing Justice" in the People's Court: Sentencing by Municipal Court Judges*, 1997. Eric Monkkonen, *Police in Urban America, 1860–1920*, 1981. Samuel Walker, *Popular Justice*, 2d ed., 1998. Michael Willrich, "The Two Percent Solution: Eugenic Jurisprudence and the Socialization of American Law, 1900–1930," *Law & History Review* 16 (Spring 1998): 63–111.

—Kermit L. Hall

MURROW, EDWARD R. (1908–1965), *radio and *television journalist. Born in North Carolina and raised in Washington State, Edward R. Murrow gravitated toward broadcasting without prior newspaper or magazine experience. Employed by the Columbia Broadcasting System (CBS), he reported from Europe on the advance of Nazism in the 1930s; his resonant and harrowing accounts of the Battle of Britain and other aspects of *World War II made him famous. Returning to the United

States after the war, Murrow became a vice-president of CBS and its director of public affairs. His shift from radio to television coincided with the intensification of the *Cold War, which haunted *See It Now,* the public-affairs program he produced in partnership with Fred W. Friendly beginning in 1951. When they directly attacked Senator Joseph *McCarthy in a *See It Now* episode broadcast on 9 March 1954, television journalism conveyed liberal revulsion at the Wisconsin Senator's unscrupulous demagoguery, but the ideal of objectivity was weakened. Murrow's delayed but emphatic anti-McCarthyism (and disappointing ratings) may have led CBS to drop television's most-honored weekly public-affairs program four years later, despite his effort to downplay controversy by interviewing celebrities on an entertainment program, *Person to Person* (1953–1959). Disillusioned with television, Murrow directed the *United States Information Agency from 1961 to 1964, when lung cancer forced his retirement. An exemplary professional reputation enabled Murrow to push a temperate *liberalism about as far as the mass medium of television would permit; his frustration and disaffection suggested the power of the new medium's commercial and regulatory constraints.

[*See also* Journalism.]

• Alexander Kendrick, *Prime Time: The Life of Edward R. Murrow,* 1969. A. M. Sperber, *Murrow: His Life and Times,* 1986.

—Stephen J. Whitfield

MUSEUMS

Museums of Art
Museums of Science and Technology

MUSEUMS: MUSEUMS OF ART

Nationalism and concern for cultural development impelled nineteenth-century Americans to create art museums. With industrial growth, wealthy individuals formed collections that became the basis for such institutions. Assisted by voluntary groups of literary figures, philanthropists, civic leaders, and artists, they founded academies and museums designed to mount regular exhibitions and provide art education programs to the public.

The first important art museum in the United States was established by the artist Charles Willson Peale (1741–1827) in *Philadelphia. Founded as a museum of natural history in 1784, by 1791 it included a portrait gallery of American revolutionary heroes. Before Peale, short-lived enterprises, such as du-Simitière's in Philadelphia or the Tammany Society's in New York occasionally exhibited works of art, as did early art academies such as *New York City's American Academy of Fine Arts (1802–1808) and Philadelphia's Pennsylvania Academy of the Fine Arts (1805). The academies gradually accumulated permanent collections as did the Boston Athenaeum's Gallery (1822), the National Academy of Design in New York (1825), Yale College's Trumbull Gallery (1832), and the Hartford or Wadsworth Athenaeum in Connecticut (1841–1844), becoming in effect museums of art. Throughout the first half of the nineteenth century, cities such as Albany and Troy in New York, Cincinnati, Pittsburgh, Louisville, and *New Orleans encouraged artistic interests through exhibitions; however, limited funds and the absence of artists' communities undercut such enterprises.

The movement to found art museums accelerated after the *Civil War. The popularity of art exhibitions at the Sanitary Fairs held in northern cities to aid Union soldiers convinced many civic leaders that permanent art institutions were desirable. In 1867, the New York Historical Society, enriched by the Luman Reed collection in 1858 and the Bryan Gallery of Christian Art (1867), unsuccessfully sought a site for a museum. Its efforts stirred enough interest for a group of eminent New Yorkers, members of the Union League Club, to launch the Metropolitan Museum of Art "free alike from bungling government officials and from the control of a single individual" (1869). At the same time, Bostonians voted to establish a Museum of Fine Arts, under the auspices of the Athenaeum, which since 1827 had held annual loan exhibitions. Incorporated in 1870, the museum opened its first section in Copley Square on 3 July 1876.

With New York and *Boston having taken the lead, prominent citizens and women's clubs in Philadelphia, Cleveland, *Detroit, Milwaukee, *Chicago, Minneapolis, and other cities raised funds for art museums. The *Progressive Era reform movement, with its emphasis on education and city beautification, encouraged private citizens and public institutions to mount exhibitions that became the nucleus of local museums. At the turn of the century, universities introduced art-history courses and, in turn, were given buildings and collections designed to educate students in art history. College and university museums at such institutions as Mount Holyoke, Smith, Bowdoin, Princeton, Harvard, Rochester, and Stanford strengthened the movement for public art institutions.

Individual entrepreneurs shared the enthusiasm for museums. Through institutions that either bore their names or fostered their aesthetic beliefs, they hoped to influence the American public. The Isabella Stewart Gardner Museum in Boston and the Henry C. Frick Collection in New York were personal creations, reflecting the collector's taste for Europe's masters; the Freer Gallery, accepted by the U.S. government in 1906, proclaimed Charles Lang Freer's love of Oriental art, while the Whitney Museum of American Art (1930) expressed the determination of sculptor Gertrude Vanderbilt Whitney to support American artists. The industrialist Solomon R. Guggenheim brought modern expressionist art to New York in 1937 in a museum that bore his name, as a counterpoint to the conservative policies of the Metropolitan Museum adopted during the presidency of the financier J. P. *Morgan. Frank Lloyd *Wright's circular Guggenheim Museum (1959) became a New York landmark.

French and American impressionist art constituted the Washington collection of Duncan Phillips, heir to a steel fortune. Financier Andrew Mellon's decision to found a National Gallery of Art (1937–1941) influenced the Wideners, Kresses, Chester Dale, and Lessing Rosenwald to donate their collections to that institution. The *Smithsonian Institution benefited from the gift of the Hirshhorn Collection in 1971; its art museums in Washington and New York made it a national cultural force. In the mid-twentieth century, a new generation of business benefactors endowed such *California art institutions as the Norton Simon Museum in Pasadena and the J. Paul Getty Museum in *Los Angeles.

By 1977, the United States boasted at least 150 important art museums, with collections ranging from antiquity through contemporary art. Subsequently, numerous private collections became public institutions, providing both general and special art education and experience in cities throughout the country.

[*See also* Education: Collegiate Education; Education: The Rise of the University; Gilded Age; Painting; Philanthropy and Philanthropic Foundations; Sculpture; Women's Club Movement.]

• Lillian B. Miller, *Patrons and Patriotism: The Encouragement of the Fine Arts in the United States, 1790–1860,* 1966. Calvin Tomkins, *Merchants and Masterpieces: The Story of the Metropolitan Museum of Art,* 1970. Walter M. Whitehill, *Museum of Fine Arts Boston: A Centennial History,* 1970. Nathaniel Burt, *Palaces for the People: A Social History of the American Art Museum,* 1977. E. P. Richardson, Brooke Hindle, and Lillian B. Miller, *Charles Willson Peale and His World,* 1983. Joel Orosz, *Curators and Culture: The Museum Movement in America, 1740–1870,* 1990.

—Lillian B. Miller

MUSEUMS: MUSEUMS OF SCIENCE AND TECHNOLOGY

Museums originated as a way to manage collections of objects that had special meaning to owners and, usually, a larger community as well. By the eighteenth century, museums had become well-established agencies for housing and displaying unusual natural specimens that exploring expeditions brought to European collectors. In North America, *Philadelphia's *American Philosophical Society (APS), founded in 1769, collected animal, vegetable, and fossil specimens, as well as models of machines and other instruments.

The Peabody Museum of Salem, Massachusetts, established by the shipmasters of the East India Marine Society (1799), displayed a rich array of items from the Pacific islands and Japan; maritime instruments and ship models; and botanical, zoological, and geological samples from surrounding Essex County. In Philadelphia, artist Charles Willson Peale started a display in his home that soon moved to the APS and then to Independence Hall, creating a commercial museum that was imitated by his sons in Baltimore and New York as well as by ambitious savants and entrepreneurs from Cincinnati to St. Louis.

Simultaneously, a number of natural-history societies established shared collections to be used primarily for serious research, artistic representations, and educational purposes. Thus the Philadelphia Academy of Natural Sciences, the *Boston Society of Natural History, and the New York Lyceum all built collections that attracted visiting European scholars. Members acted as voluntary curators, but the collections grew faster than reliable staff, and all these voluntary societies experienced periods of financial hardship. More successful was the well-endowed, federally subsidized *Smithsonian Institution, opened in *Washington, D.C., in 1846, whose holdings came to include materials from the Wilkes expedition (1838–1842) and various western exploring trips. With its excellent library, publication facilities, and natural-history collections, the Smithsonian became a scientific clearinghouse. Under George Brown Goode, the leading museum theorist of the late nineteenth century, the Smithsonian's displays focused on educational exhibits featuring instructive labels.

Post–*Civil War *urbanization and industrial growth led to an expansive period of museum building. Symbolizing the new public-museum movement was the American Museum of Natural History in *New York City, where wealthy patrons created the nation's largest museum. Drawing children as well as adults, it relied in part on connections with Columbia University to facilitate research activities. The appearance of the great Field Museum of Natural History in *Chicago, endowed by the merchant Marshall Field and using collections first displayed at the World's Columbian Exposition of 1893, marked the end of the "golden age of museums."

During the nineteenth century, as colleges included more natural sciences in their curricula, they relied on museums to provide specimens for student reference and research. Louis *Agassiz's Museum of Comparative Zoology at Harvard was the best known, but other significant collegiate museums dotted the country, from Princeton to Berkeley. The natural-history museums reflected changing research agendas as well as different audiences. While zoology had dominated early nineteenth-century collections, *anthropology loomed large in the early twentieth century. Curators, who sought to maintain a scientific outlook while serving a diverse public, debated whether to arrange materials by type or to demonstrate some theory of development.

The impulse to display machinery and other technological objects, which dated back to the APS's early museum, increased during the era of "world fairs" that followed England's Crystal Palace Exhibition in 1851. The Smithsonian and other museums held such materials, but only began systematically developing them in the 1880s. Inspired by Munich's Deutsches Museum, which developed active displays with working machinery, Julius Rosenwald, head of Sears, Roebuck, and Company, endowed the Museum of Science and Industry in Chicago, which opened in 1933. Economic circumstances forced it to rely heavily on industrial sponsorship for its major exhibits, however. After *World War II, increasing interest in the *physical sciences and *technology led to the establishment of a range of museums, from the adult-oriented Corning Museum in New York and Hagley Museum in Delaware to the child-friendly Boston Museum of Science (1939), the Lawrence Hall of Science at the University of California, Berkeley (1968), and San Francisco's Exploratorium (1969). Moving beyond merely celebrating science and technology, public museums of the late twentieth century increasingly tried to explore their social and cultural contexts and implications in a balanced way.

[*See also* Industrialization; Philanthropy and Philanthropic Foundations; Science; World's Fairs and Expositions.]

• Edward P. Alexander, *Museums in Motion: An Introduction to the History and Functions of Museums,* 1979. Charles Coleman Sellers, *Mr. Peale's Museum: Charles Willson Peale and the First Popular Museum of Natural Science and Art,* 1979. Sally Gregory Kohlstedt, "Museums on Campus: A Tradition of Inquiry and Teaching," in *The American Development of Biology,* eds. Ronald Rainger, Keth Benson, and Jane Maienschein, 1988. Joel Orosz, *Curators and Culture: The Museum Movement in America, 1740–1870,* 1990. Karen Wonders, *Habitat Dioramas: Illusions of Wilderness in Museums of Natural History,* 1993.

—Sally Gregory Kohlstedt

MUSIC

MUSIC: TRADITIONAL MUSIC

American popular entertainers, such as the blackface minstrels of the early nineteenth century, have always utilized ballads, songs, and dances of no known origins. No conscious concept of "traditional music" emerged, however, until the late nineteenth century. The first published collection of slave *spirituals (1867) by William Francis Allen and others, Francis James Child's compendium of English and Scottish popular ballads (1882–1898), and the founding of the American Folklore Society (1887) signaled a growing impulse among academicians to preserve traditional ballads and folk songs. Convinced that such music was becoming a casualty of modernization, scholars and collectors undertook a search for remnants of the British tradition in America. The most significant product of this quest was *English Folk Songs from the Southern Appalachians* (1917), compiled by Olive Dame Campbell and Cecil Sharp. After that time, the study, preservation, and popularization of traditional music assumed many, and often conflicting, forms. Scholars and other collectors preserved versions of old music in books and articles; "interpreters" (that is, performers from outside the tradition) presented adaptations in concerts, recitals, and recordings; and "the folk" themselves (singers from traditional communities) continued to make music in ways only peripherally related to the expectations of scholars and interpreters.

Interpreters of folk music first appeared in the 1870s after the Fisk Jubilee Singers of Nashville popularized "Negro Spirituals" among northern audiences, and again during *World War I when such musicians and composers as Elaine Wyman, Howard Brockway, and Edna Thomas gave concerts, often in period costumes, of Appalachian ballads, Creole songs, and African-American spirituals. Musicians like John Jacob Niles, Richard Dyer-Bennett, and Burl Ives continued such performances through the 1930s and 1940s, and this approach survived thereafter in the music of Harry Belafonte, Pete Seeger, Joan Baez, Odetta, Bob *Dylan, and other popular singers. Under the impact of the Great Depression of the 1930s and later of the *civil rights movement, authentic folk singers like Woody Guthrie (1912–1967), "Aunt Molly" Jackson, and Huddie "Leadbelly" Ledbetter (1885–1949), linked traditional music with working-class aspirations. Pete Seeger (1919–) and other socially conscious interpreters went further and lent to the music a strong left-wing cast, encouraging the equation of folk music with protest.

Genuine folk musicians began to appear on *radio broadcasts and commercial recordings in the 1920s when the entertainment industry first exploited such genres as hillbilly, cowboy, mountain, blues, Cajun, and gospel. In the later 1920s and early 1930s, other traditional musicians having styles more conservative or archaic than the "commercial" entertainers began to appear on *Library of Congress recordings, or at the newly emergent folk festivals in Asheville, North Carolina, and White Top Mountain, Virginia. Eventually, many of these musicians, such as Texas Gladden, Hobart Smith, and Horton Barker, appeared on commercial recording labels aimed at an urban, largely nonfolk audience.

The urban folk-music revival of the late fifties and early sixties triggered an explosion of interest in folk or folklike music. Although interpreters dominated the revival, authentic folk musicians such as Jean Ritchie, Elizabeth Cotton, and Almeda Riddle contributed as well. Gradually, many participants in the revival recognized the affinity between commercial country, blues, Cajun, gospel, and older traditional forms. The term "folk" itself, however, was appropriated by a contingent of musicians and fans who believed that they constituted a "folk community," not because they performed traditional material, but because they liked or performed newly created songs that had a "folk" feeling or ambience.

[*See also* Appalachia; Folklore; Gospel Music, African American; Minstrelsy; Sixties, The; Working-Class Life and Culture.]

• Bill C. Malone, *Southern Music/American Music,* 1979. Neil V. Rosenberg, ed., *Transforming Tradition: Folk Music Revivals Examined,* 1993. Robert Cantwell, *When We Were Good: The Urban Folk Music Revival,* 1996.

—Bill C. Malone

MUSIC: CLASSICAL MUSIC

When the Czech composer Antonín Dvořák arrived in the United States in 1892 to become director of *New York City's National Conservatory of Music, his dual mandate was to create a world-class educational institution for American musicians and to help foster an indigenous American musical high culture. Previously, leading American composers and performers had studied in Europe; such gifted German-trained composers as John Knowles Paine (1839–1906) and George Whitefield Chadwick (1854–1931) wrote German-sounding symphonies. Antonín Dvořák's search for an American folk music led him to *African Americans and Native Americans, and to the composition of his symphony "From the New World" (1893). Simultaneously (and unknown to Dvořák), Charles *Ives, who spurned European training, was creating a body of concert music saturated with the sounds of his *New England boyhood.

Notwithstanding the efforts of Dvořák and Ives, turn-of-the-century American classical music essentially remained what it had been: borrowed European goods. The "New World" Symphony—a Central European symphony with an American accent—spawned countless "Indianist" works by Americans, many based on actual Native American melodies, and nearly all more or less forgettable. Ives's achievement remained obscure until after *World War I. Of America's symphonic composers, the most celebrated was Edward MacDowell (1860–1908), who had made his name in Germany. In *opera, American composers, including many Indianists, produced nothing of enduring interest.

If, in fact, the emerging history of classical music in America was primarily a history of music in performance, however, this history was impressive. Three strains are traceable from the mid–nineteenth century: ballyhoo, symphony, and opera.

Ballyhoo. The American passion for pageantry and display, *circuses and parades, produced a native species of musical celebrity tour: New World entrepreneurs promoted Old World singers and instrumentalists in a manner common to sideshow freaks and blackface minstrels. The acme was P. T. *Barnum's presentation of the "Swedish Nightingale," Jenny Lind, in 1850–1851—accurately described in Barnum's autobiography as "an enterprise never before or since equalled in managerial annals." Leopold de Meyer, known as the "Lion Pianist," was the first celebrity pianist to tour America, arriving in 1845; his programs featured his own sleight-of-hand concoctions, larded with such Americana as "Yankee Doodle." *New Orleans's Louis Moreau Gottschalk (1829–1869) was the first important American-born pianist and a significant composer whose Creole sources were homegrown.

Symphony. Massive German immigration, peaking in the 1880s, spread trained musicians throughout many parts of the United States. The resulting symphonic culture—propagating Germanic masterworks, rejecting ballyhoo—was devotional; it resonated with New England church music reform. In this regard, the educator/composer Lowell Mason (1792–1872) was a major force. His hymn tunes, based on European sources including Mozart and Haydn, dominated nineteenth-century American hymnals. Mason campaigned to promote higher standards in church music and to democratize music education. Another New Englander, the critic John Sullivan Dwight (1813–1893), influentially espoused the moral purity of instrumental music; Beethoven was his godhead. Meanwhile, in New York, the Philharmonic was founded by *German Americans in 1842, the same year as the Vienna Philharmonic. The German-born Theodore *Thomas, who joined the New York Philharmonic's violinists in 1854, later created his own orchestra and began touring with it in 1869. Preaching that a symphony orchestra "shows the culture of a community," Thomas took over the New York Philharmonic (1877), then the new *Chicago Orchestra (1891). By 1903, orchestras had also been started in *Boston, Cincinnati, Pittsburgh, *Philadelphia, Minneapolis, and St. Louis. The Boston Symphony, founded in 1881, outstripped all others in frequency and caliber of performance. Its early conductors included Arthur Nikisch and Karl Muck, both towering figures abroad. Its supporters proclaimed, "A symphony orchestra pure and simple does not exist in all of Europe.... In no city in Germany, Italy, France or Russia is there an orchestra which is made up of players whose only business it is to perform such music as is to be found on programmes of symphony concerts." In fact, the American penchant for concert orchestras, versus the opera orchestras of Europe, was a singular phenomenon. The term "symphony orchestra" is itself an American coinage, dating from 1878.

Opera. America's operatic culture was vigorous and diverse by 1850. Opera was variously elevated and elegant, popular and cheap. In New York, where the world's great vocalists clustered, the Academy of Music, opened in 1854, was the leading opera house for nearly three decades. Its paucity of boxes dictated a larger, more opulent venue for a new elite: the 3,615-seat Metropolitan Opera House, opened in 1883. In certain respects, the Met's pre–World War I achievements were not later equaled. As in subsequent decades, illustrious vocal talent was regularly showcased. At the same time, the house was ruled (as never after) by master conductors: Anton Seidl (1885–1898), Gustav Mahler (1908–1909), and Arturo *Toscanini (1908–1915). In these years, as well, the repertoire incorporated a higher percentage of important new and recent works than subsequently. Between 1889 and 1891, with Wagnerism at its height, the entire repertoire was given in German. Thereafter, a tradition was established of presenting operas in the language in which they were written—usually German, Italian, or French. In Europe, by contrast, opera in translation—in the language of the audience—was more the custom. American resistance to opera in the vernacular discouraged the emergence of a body of important American operas; it also served to deemphasize the theatrical dimension of opera. Compared to its nineteenth-century diversity, opera in America more preponderantly became a glamorous vocal medium.

With the outbreak of the Russian Revolution in 1917 and the rise of European fascism in the 1920s and 1930s, a plethora of great performing artists became residents of the United States. During and after *World War I, Germanophobia diminished the predominance of Germanic performers. One infamous episode was the 1918 internment of Boston's Karl Muck as an enemy alien; upon leaving for Europe (permanently) following the Armistice, he called the United States a country "controlled by a sentiment which closely borders on mob rule." Of the non-Germans who now took over, Arturo Toscanini, with his New York Philharmonic (1926–1936) and NBC Symphony (1937–1954), symbolized classical music for Americans. Called "priest of music" and "vicar of the immortals," he personified the continued moral rectitude of the European symphonic canon (its uses in Hitler's Germany notwithstanding). Leopold Stokowski in Philadelphia (1912–1936) and Serge Koussevitzky in Boston (1924–1949) were also famous non-Germanic leaders of remarkable American orchestras. Such phenomenal immigrant Russians as the pianist Vladimir Horowitz and the violinist Jascha Heifetz were fervently embraced and celebrated. Such inspired proponents of the Germanic tradition as the pianists Artur Schnabel and Rudolf Serkin, if less famous, were notably influential, not least on colleagues and students. After *World War II, important American-born and -trained performers emerged, the most notable being Leonard *Bernstein, a Koussevitzky protégé. No previous American classical musician had exercised such influence at home, or achieved such renown abroad, as an interpreter of both American and European works.

Compared to the impact of a Toscanini, Horowitz, or Heifetz, twentieth-century American composers occupied a back seat. Dvořák's "New World" Symphony remains the most popular composed on American soil; Ives's achievement, cresting before World War I, proved less a starting point than a solitary summit. As in performance, the Germanic influence on composing waned with World War I; an important new generation of Americans, whose most prominent representative was Aaron *Copland, was schooled in France. Koussevitzky proclaimed, "The next Beethoven vill [sic] from Colorado come." Although a significant school of interwar symphonists emerged, the great American symphony was not composed, and America's core creative contributions in music during these decades came in popular music and *jazz. A bridge between popular and classical traditions was attempted, most auspiciously by George *Gershwin, whose early death in 1937 aborted a major legacy. An antipopulist influence was exerted by Igor Stravinsky, Arnold Schoenberg, and Paul Hindemith, all Europeans who emigrated to the United States.

After World War II, the multitalented Bernstein, among others, anticipated fresh American achievements outside the European genres. Bernstein's own *West Side Story* (1957) notably melded opera and Broadway. Other late twentieth-century American composers of world reputation included Elliott Carter, a formidable modernist. Younger composers such as Philip Glass, Steve Reich, and John Adams, all born after 1936, challenged traditional distinctions between popular and classical, Eastern and Western cultures. For them, "classical music" became a defunct category of artistic experience.

[*See also* Gilded Age; Museums: Museums of Art; Musical Theater.]

• Gilbert Chase, *America's Music,* 1955, reprint 1987. Wilfrid Mellers, *Music in a New Found Land,* 1964. H. Wiley Hitchcock, *Music in the United States: An Historical Introduction,* 1969, reprint 1988. Charles Hamm, *Music in the New World,* 1983. Joseph Horowitz, *Understanding Toscanini: A Social History of American Concert Life,* 1987. John Dizikes, *Opera in America,* 1993. Joseph Horowitz, *Wagner Nights: An American History,* 1994.

—Joseph Horowitz

MUSIC: POPULAR MUSIC

The first popular music in the American colonies consisted of hymns, psalms, ballads, and patriotic airs imported from Europe. From the *Colonial Era to the present, popular music has remained a vital and constantly evolving feature of American culture.

Early National and Antebellum Eras. After the *Revolutionary War, political and patriotic themes dominated the new nation's popular songs, although sacred music persisted and melodies from English ballad *operas remained in vogue among the urban classes. Battles, heroes, frontier life, social crusades, current events, disasters, fads, and follies were all favorite subjects for singing in young America. Sentimentality and melodramatic expression pervaded these lyrics, and many told of human suffering with melancholy emphasis. Songs that spoke of piety, morbidity, and grief were deemed suitable for the family parlor, whereas humorous songs, common in taverns and other such venues, were viewed skeptically inside genteel circles.

Music publishing increased during the *Antebellum Era, and in the 1840s Stephen *Foster emerged as the country's most celebrated songwriter. Foster's first published song, "Open Thy Lattice, Love," was written in 1843, but he quickly won fame with minstrel tunes such as "Camptown Races," "Old Folks at Home," "My Old Kentucky Home," and "Old Black Joe." At his best, Foster was a master of melody and nostalgic narration. Although his songs for blackface performers enjoyed greater popularity, the composer considered his love songs, among them "Jeanie with the Light Brown Hair" and "Beautiful Dreamer," better efforts since they conformed to genteel standards of decorum.

The minstrel stage served as a major vehicle for spreading the popularity of songs. Dan Emmett (1815–1904), one of the Virginia Minstrels, wrote "Dixie" (1859) and "Old Dan Tucker" for blackface performers, and the tradition continued after the *Civil War with such songwriters as James A. Bland, composer of "Carry Me Back to Old Virginny" and "Oh Dem Golden Slippers."

Gilded Age to World War I. The commercial music business grew during the late nineteenth century with *New York City becoming its headquarters. The popular music business, known as Tin Pan Alley, centered first around Fourteenth Street, then moved to Twenty-eighth Street, and eventually beyond Times Square, as publishers followed the theaters up Broadway. Charles K. Harris, whose "After the Ball" (1892) became the first popular song to sell more than a million copies, is often regarded as the father of Tin Pan Alley. Later, Harris's "Hello Central, Give Me Heaven" combined three prevalent themes in contemporary songwriting: children, the death of a parent, and new *technology. Another turn-of-the-century tunesmith, Paul Dresser, brother of novelist Theodore *Dreiser, won fame with sentimental ballads such as "The Pardon Came Too Late," "My Gal Sal," and "On the Banks of the Wabash," adopted as the Indiana state song.

During the late nineteenth century, *vaudeville, burlesque, musical comedy, and operetta supplied much of the nation's popular music. Vaudeville performers were courted by music publishers like T. B. Harms and M. Witmark and Sons, since they could introduce songs and stimulate the sale of sheet music. Turn-of-the-century headliners such as Eva Tanguay, George M. Cohan, and Nora Bayes attracted loyal followings on national tours and were in constant need of fresh material. Bayes wrote "Shine on Harvest Moon" with her husband, Jack Norworth; Cohan composed such favorites as "Give My Regards to Broadway" and "You're a Grand Old Flag" after he graduated to writing story-line musicals as opposed to plotless revues.

Operettas supplied a loftier variety of popular music, patterned after central European models. Franz Lehar's *The Merry Widow* proved a sensation when it opened in New York in 1907, inspiring dozens of imitations. Irish-born Victor Herbert arrived in the United States in 1886 and within two decades had established himself as Broadway's foremost composer of light operas. Herbert filled his scores for *The Fortune Teller, Mlle. Modeste, The Red Mill,* and *Naughty Marietta* with such numbers as "Gypsy Love Song," "Kiss Me Again," and "Ah! Sweet Mystery of Life," many of which were later revived by Hollywood.

Rudolf Friml and Sigmund Romberg, both central European immigrants, extended the vogue for operetta into the 1920s. Friml's scores for *Rose Marie, The Vagabond King,* and *The Three Musketeers* contain such popular hits as "Indian Love Call," "Only a Rose," and "Love Me Tonight." Romberg established himself with *Maytime* in 1917 but achieved even greater popularity in the 1920s with *The Student Prince, The Desert Song,* and *New Moon.* Such songs as "Lover Come Back to Me," "One Kiss," "Deep in My Heart, Dear" and "Serenade" illustrate Romberg's lasting appeal.

Popular music became big business in America in the early twentieth century, aided by recordings, *radio, and *film. A copyright law passed in 1909 provided for a payment of two cents to the copyright holder for each phonograph record or piano roll sold containing a copyrighted song. The American Society of Composers, Authors, and Publishers (ASCAP) was founded in 1914 to collect royalties more effectively.

Although an increased sense of professionalism infused Tin Pan Alley, old formulas persisted. Harry von Tilzer carried the sentimental tradition into the new century with numbers like "A Bird in a Gilded Cage" and "Wait till the Sun Shines Nellie." Gus Edwards, closely linked to vaudeville, proved equally sentimental; his songs "School Days" and "By the Light of the Silvery Moon" became perennials.

During the 1890s a more rambunctious commercial music resulted from the black exodus to the north. These songs were syncopated and employed more natural wording than the stilted phrasing of the sentimental ballads. Many were initially sung by black vaudeville performers, but the impact of such songs soon reached white entertainers. Some of these songs were humorous; others, such as "The Warmest Colored Gal in Town," contained sexual innuendoes. Still others spoke of the economic rise and growing sophistication of urban blacks.

*Ragtime, another product of the black community in the 1890s, profoundly influenced popular songs and dance styles. The first ragtime piano number was probably William Krell's "Mississippi Rag," published in 1897, but Scott Joplin (1868–1917) became the most famous of the ragtime composers with such numbers as "Maple Leaf Rag" and "The Entertainer."

By 1910 classic ragtime was coming to an end, replaced by such Tin Pan Alley imitations as "Put Your Arms around Me Honey" and "Ragtime Cowboy Joe." Irving *Berlin's "Alexander's Ragtime Band," published in 1911, brought the ragtime craze to a peak, although the song was a corruption of the black idiom. The ragtime vogue revolutionized social *dance. Syncopated rhythm made dancing simpler; anyone who could march could dance. The two-step and the cakewalk soon spawned dances like the Grizzly Bear, the Bunny Hug, the Turkey Trot, and the Kangaroo Dip. As the rage continued, night clubs opened, and restaurants and hotels introduced dancing during meal hours. Vernon and Irene Castle emerged as the nation's dancing idols and in 1914 starred in the ragtime revue *Watch Your Step,* Irving Berlin's first complete Broadway score.

Berlin did much to liberate American popular music from the clichés of the previous century. Polished and versatile in style, Berlin's melodies were simple, yet his tunes possessed a haunting beauty and craftsmanship that lifted them beyond the ordinary. Romantic ballads like "All Alone," "Remember," and "What'll I Do?" proved Berlin's forte, yet he rose to fame during the ragtime era with such numbers as "That Mysterious Rag," "Everybody's Doin' It," and "The International Rag."

Meanwhile *jazz, having arisen in the *South, began expanding north prior to *World War I. After the success of the Original Dixieland Jazz Band in New York in 1917, jazz musicians found themselves in demand both in the urban North and Europe. Black jazzmen, among them trumpeters King Oliver and Louis *Armstrong, moved from *New Orleans to *Chicago and later to New York, while jazz staples like "Tiger Rag," "Livery Stable Blues," and "High Society" entered the popular music of the American middle class.

The 1920s to World War II. Prohibition brought speakeasies during the 1920s, many of which hired jazz musicians to attract customers. Dances such as the Charleston and the Black Bottom became popular, although moralists condemned such gyrations. Indeed, conservatives viewed jazz itself as a threat to traditional values, since the music was improvised and often played by performers of dubious reputation. "Moral disaster is coming to hundreds of young American girls through the pathological, nerve-irritating sex-exciting music of jazz orchestras," thundered the New York *American* in 1922.

By 1925, as jazz became more commercialized, New York drew the most successful artists, since Manhattan was the center of music publishing, the recording industry, and network radio stations. Harlem clubs, most notably the Cotton Club, which opened in 1927, became venues for such popular jazzmen as Edward ("Duke") *Ellington and Cab Calloway. Ellington, while maintaining ties with Tin Pan Alley, composed such classics as "Sophisticated Lady," "Mood Indigo," and "Solitude."

Radio revolutionized the popular music business by cutting the length of time a song could remain popular. But radio also brought music to more consumers and stimulated the sale of sheet music and phonograph records—another electronic innovation. The 1920s was a golden age for American popular music with such great songwriters as Berlin, Vincent Youmans, George *Gershwin, Jerome Kern, Cole Porter, and Richard Rodgers reaching maturity, along with adroit lyricists like Lorenz Hart, Oscar Hammerstein II, and Ira Gershwin.

Each of these celebrated composers wrote for the musical stage. Youmans's *No, No, Nanette* captured the flavor of the 1920s and reflects the buoyancy of the decade's middle-class youth. Two of the show's best songs, "I Want to Be Happy" and "Tea for Two," became international hits. For *Hit the Deck* (1927), Youmans wrote "Hallelujah" and "Sometimes I'm Happy," both lasting favorites.

George Gershwin capitalized on the growing popularity of jazz in such Broadway shows as *Lady Be Good, Oh, Kay,* and *Funny Face,* which included such perennials as "Fascinating Rhythm," "Someone to Watch over Me," and " 'S Wonderful." Gershwin's musical idol, Jerome Kern, helped modernize the musical theater with his scores for Princess Theatre productions between 1915 and 1918. In 1927 Kern altered the course of the big Broadway musical with *Show Boat,* which contained "Make Believe," "Can't Help Lovin' Dat Man," and "Ol' Man River." Gershwin died young, but Kern's career lasted for another two decades. His score for *Roberta* in 1932 included "Smoke Gets in Your Eyes," "The Touch of Your Hand," "Yesterdays," "I Won't Dance," and "I'll Be Hard to Handle," all popular standards.

Irving Berlin and Cole Porter wrote their own lyrics for the songs they composed, and both had strings of Broadway successes during careers that flourished until after *World War II. Berlin reached his pinnacle with *Annie Get Your Gun* in 1946, and few scores have offered such a concentration of hits, among them "The Girl That I Marry," "Doin' What Comes Naturally," "They Say It's Wonderful," "I Got the Sun in the Morning and the Moon at Night," and "There's No Business Like Show Business." Cole Porter's masterwork came in 1948 with *Kiss Me, Kate,* for which he wrote "So in Love," "Were

Thine That Special Face," "Wunderbar," and "Always True to You in My Fashion." Porter specialized in sophisticated, sometimes risqué lyrics, whereas Berlin was content to lift sentimentality to refined levels.

Richard Rodgers worked successfully with two lyricists, Lorenz Hart and Oscar Hammerstein II. The songs he wrote with Hart were imaginative, melodic, and literate. Hart was a master of intricate rhymes and tart figures of speech, while Rodgers colored his music with the unexpected. Their collaboration resulted in such shows as *The Girl Friend, A Connecticut Yankee,* and *Spring Is Here,* which contained such songs as "The Blue Room," "Thou Swell," "My Heart Stood Still," and "With a Song in My Heart." Their partnership ended in 1942 with *By Jupiter,* but Rodgers's talent continued to develop after Hammerstein became his lyricist. *Oklahoma!* (1943), their first effort, proved the sensation of the World War II years and offered a score that included "Oh, What a Beautiful Mornin'," "People Will Say We're in Love," and a title number that became the state song of Oklahoma. *Carousel, South Pacific, The King and I,* and *The Sound of Music* were equally rich in songs that won international renown.

Broadway musicals remained a major source of popular music until the 1960s. Various singers recorded numbers from Frank Loesser's *Guys and Dolls* (1950), Richard Adler and Jerry Ross's *The Pajama Game* (1954), Allan Jay Lerner and Frederick Loewe's *My Fair Lady* (1956), Meredith Willson's *The Music Man* (1957), and Jerry Herman's *Hello, Dolly!* (1964). The trend ended when young performers preferred to write their own music, thereby eliminating the need to pay outside royalties.

Swing, which dominated the American jazz scene from 1935 through World War II, brought respectability but increased commercialization to what had originally been an inventive, popular art form. Benny *Goodman's orchestra is credited with launching the swing craze and thrusting American popular music into the big-band era. Swing depended upon technically brilliant arrangers and virtuoso performers who could improvise solo passages and work from notation during ensembles. The big bands relied heavily on Tin Pan Alley songwriters and extensive publicity, but their music was heard on jukeboxes, over the radio, from the stage, and in movies around the globe. Glenn Miller, Artie Shaw, Harry James, Gene Krupa, Tommy and Jimmy Dorsey, and Ray Anthony became leaders in the big-band movement, which eventually turned into something of a personality cult. By the late 1930s hundreds of dance bands were playing in hotels, ballrooms, nightclubs, and gymnasia across the country.

As the swing era progressed, the band vocalist became increasingly important. Billie Holiday and Ella *Fitzgerald were two of the most celebrated black band singers, but such white vocalists as Peggy Lee, Frank Sinatra, Doris Day, and Rosemary Clooney gained early recognition performing with swing bands. By the end of World War II many of these singers had become stars in their own right. Some developed an individual technique, and vocalizing moved from the soft stylings of Rudy Vallee and Bing Crosby, both of whom gained fame in early radio, toward more dynamic approaches. Sinatra particularly showed an understanding of lyrics, which enabled him to outlive the "Bobby Soxer" mania of World War II and establish lasting fame in *popular culture.

Although the finest and most innovative popular songs before 1960 had come from the theater, motion pictures—even before the advent of sound—contributed an impressive number of standards. "Charmaine," interpolated into the film *What Price Glory* in 1926, was the first movie theme song to become an immediate hit. "Diane" for *Seventh Heaven* and "Angela Mia" for *Street Angel* followed. With the coming of sound, screen musicals were in demand, and such composers as Richard Whiting, Harry Warren, Nacio Herb Brown, and Johnny Mercer devoted much of their careers to motion pictures.

By 1930, radio had taken over the role once filled by vaudeville in plugging popular songs. *Your Hit Parade,* a Saturday night program that presented the "top ten" tunes of the week, began in 1935 and, having successfully made the transition to *television, stayed on the air for twenty-five years.

The 1950s to the Present. By the end of the World War II the pivotal figure in promoting songs was the radio disc jockey, who spun records between news and weather reports on thousands of local stations. With the expansion of record production in the 1950s, a radio station might receive three hundred new releases a week. Major disc jockeys became powerful figures in keeping records before the public. During 1959 and 1960 "payola" (bribery) scandals shook the popular music field, and eventually 255 disc jockeys were convicted of accepting cash or expensive gifts from record companies and music publishers for promoting their material.

In the early 1950s rhythm and blues began to invade popular music, expressing some of the realities of the black ghetto. In 1954 "Gee," recorded by the Crows, became the first rhythm-and-blues number to appear on the charts of bestselling songs. Soon white groups began to cover the more popular rhythm-and-blues hits, adapting them to mass audiences.

Such rock-and-roll performers as Ray Charles, Chuck Berry, and "Little Richard" (Richard Penniman) served as a connecting link between black and white audiences. But the single most important event in bringing rock-and-roll into the mainstream of American popular music was the appearance of Bill Haley's recording of "Rock around the Clock" in 1955. The next year Elvis *Presley erupted onto the scene with his recording of "Heartbreak Hotel." The younger generation was in a mood for its own music, and Presley became their musical idol despite parental protests about his tight pants, swaying hips, and long sideburns. A rash of Presley imitators soon appeared.

By 1962 Bob *Dylan emerged as an important force in reviving folk music, and such groups as the Kingston Trio, The Brothers Four, and Peter, Paul, and Mary rose to prominence. In 1964, rock experienced a British invasion when the Beatles first toured the United States. Their recording of "I Want to Hold Your Hand" sold over a million copies in ten days. After 1965 the counterculture movement ushered in a harder form of rock, accompanied by the use of drugs and psychedelic light shows. The Grateful Dead, the Doors, and Grand Funk Railroad became leaders in what was termed acid rock, while groups like Jefferson Airplane showed musical sophistication.

The Motown sound, out of *Detroit, spearheaded by Diana Ross and the Supremes, won acceptance within the American middle class, since the music was polished and mild mannered, yet furnished a firm, danceable beat. As the counterculture rebellion faded, disco became the fad of the late 1970s. Amid a farrago of strobe lights and deafening music, young dancers moved to recordings by Donna Summer, K. C. and the Sunshine Band, and the Bee Gees.

In the 1980s American popular music showed the continuing impact of rock, but also a strong influence from country music. New Wave groups from Britain like Duran Duran hit the American market stressing pure electronics, although rhythm and sound became dominant over melody and lyrics in other trends. African-American rap music in the 1990s reflected the anger of the inner city, while college students listened to contemporary jazz and alternative rock but danced to techno and rave.

Popular music, a lively feature of American life for two hundred years or more, has in each era mirrored the social, cultural, and technological realities of the age. As the twenty-first century dawned, this ever-evolving form of popular expression seemed certain to continue to underscore the nation's cultural moods, as each new generation adopts its own music.

[*See also* Blues; Gospel Music, African American; Harlem Renaissance; Mass Marketing; Minstrelsy; Musical Theater; Urbanization.]

• Sigmund Spaeth, *A History of Popular Music in America,* 1948. David Ewen, *Panorama of American Popular Music,* 1957. Isaac Goldberg, *Tin Pan Alley,* 1961. Neil Leonard, *Jazz and the White Americans,* 1962. Lester S. Levy, *Grace Notes in American History,* 1967. John Rublowsky, *Popular Music,* 1967. Alec Wilder, *American Popular Song,* 1972. Lester S. Levy, *Give Me Yesterday,* 1975. Ronald L. Davis, *A History of Music in American Life,* 3 vols., 1980–1982. Russell Sanjek, *American Popular Music and Its Business,* 1988. Gunther Schuller, *The Swing Era,* 1989. Kenneth J. Bindas, ed., *America's Musical Pulse,* 1992.

—Ronald L. Davis

MUSICAL THEATER. Although imported ballad operas and romantic light operas alongside native musical burlesques and occasional spectacles lit American stages from the early eighteenth century onward, *The Black Crook* (1866), which ran for over a year in New York, with its darkly romantic plot and line of beautiful chorus girls in flesh-colored tights, is often cited as the beginning of modern American musical theater. Other contenders are Jacques Offenbach's better plotted and musically more sophisticated *La Grande Duchesse de Gérolstein* (1867) and the even wittier and equally well scored *H.M.S. Pinafore* (1879), by W. S. Gilbert and Arthur Sullivan. This comic opera, with its wholesome lyrics, opened many American stages, hitherto regularly denied to often risqué lyric entertainments, to song-and-dance mountings. Soon playgoers were applauding native operettas by composers such as Reginald De Koven and Victor Herbert (1859–1924), and librettist Harry B. Smith.

In the same season that *Pinafore* appeared, Ned Harrigan's and Tony Hart's raucous, song-filled plays of *New York City life launched a loosely structured genre known as farce-comedy, which allowed performers to do their stuff within the confines of a flimsy book. Charles Hoyt and George M. Cohan (1878–1942) were early masters in this field. A third major, if short-lived, genre, the revue, first delighted audiences in *The Passing Show* (1894). Florenz Ziegfeld (1869–1932) and his annual *Follies,* beginning in 1907, represented the apogee of this sort of frolic.

The *World War I Era saw the emergence of a brilliant group of creative artists—composers Jerome Kern, Irving *Berlin, Sigmund Romberg, Rudolf Friml, George *Gershwin, Vincent Youmans, Cole Porter, and Richard Rodgers, and lyricists and librettists P. G. Wodehouse, Guy Bolton, Oscar Hammerstein II, Lorenz Hart, and Dorothy Fields. These and others helped make the 1920s the heyday of the musical as pure, melodic fun.

The Depression of the 1930s and sound *films ended that heyday, and following the path of the pioneering *Show Boat* (1927), musicals during and after *World War II became more serious, proclaiming their "integration" of song, story, and *dance, ignoring how well these elements had been integrated as far back as Offenbach and Gilbert and Sullivan. Richard Rodgers and Oscar Hammerstein II led the way with *Oklahoma!* (1943). Their subsequent masterpieces, along with such works as Leonard *Bernstein's and Stephen Sondheim's *West Side Story* (1957) and Alan Jay Lerner's and Frederick Loewe's *My Fair Lady* (1956), marked a second glorious era of American musicals that lasted until the mid-1960s. Thereafter, amid a wave of hugely successful importations from Great Britain, the lone major, uniquely American voice was that of Sondheim (1930–), whose musicals, marked by complex wordplay and unconventional, sometimes distasteful subject matter, carried the venerable tradition of musical theater into new territory.

[*See also* Drama; Music: Popular Music; Popular Culture; Theater.]

• Gerald Bordman, *American Musical Theatre: A Chronicle,* 3d ed., 2000. Kurt Gänzl, *Encyclopedia of the Musical Theatre,* 2d ed., 2000.

—Gerald Bordman

MY LAI. The My Lai massacre was an atrocity committed by American troops during the *Vietnam War. Charlie Company, Americal Division, was assigned to the My Lai area, where the National Liberation Front (known as the Viet Cong) fought with land mines, booby traps, and hit-and-run attacks. In the weeks before the massacre, Charlie Company suffered heavy casualties but never engaged the enemy. On 16 March 1968, one hundred soldiers were airlifted to My Lai. Although they received no fire and observed no enemy combatants, the unit advanced and began to shoot women, children, and old men who inhabited the village. Over the next four hours more than five hundred Vietnamese were murdered. A few G.I.s refused to obey orders. Pilot Hugh Thompson witnessed the slaughter from his helicopter, rescued a number of children, and had an armed confrontation with Lieutenant William Calley of Charlie Company, commander of the operation.

The My Lai massacre became public news in 1970 when an investigative report by Seymour Hersch appeared in the *New York Times.* The army charged twenty-five soldiers in the incident, but only one, Lieutenant Calley, was found guilty. A bitter national debate ensued in which Calley was widely portrayed as a scapegoat. Some Americans insisted that My Lai was an aberration, while others, including antiwar Vietnam veterans, claimed that attacks on civilians in Vietnam were depressingly routine. Although President Richard M. *Nixon commuted Calley's prison sentence in 1974, the My Lai massacre would generate controversy for years to come.

[*See also* Sixties, The.]

• Seymour Hersch, *My Lai-4: A Report of the Massacre and Its Aftermath,* 1970. David L. Anderson, *Facing My Lai,* 1997.

—Richard Moser

N

NADER, RALPH (1934–), consumer advocate. Ralph Nader dominated the U.S. *consumer movement during the last third of the twentieth century. Born in Winsted, Connecticut, to Lebanese immigrant parents, Nader graduated from Princeton College and Harvard Law School and began his law practice in Hartford. He first came to public attention in 1965 with *Unsafe at Any Speed,* an indictment of the design of the General Motors Corvair automobile and of the *automotive industry's more general failure to attend to the "second collision," the impact of occupants with the inside of the vehicle in an accident. This book and Nader's congressional testimony played a key role in passage of legislation in 1966 allowing the federal government to set vehicle-safety standards.

Nader branched out quickly from his initial interest in auto safety, and his efforts resulted in a proliferation of federal consumer-protection legislation during the 1960s and early 1970s, including the 1972 act creating the Federal Consumer Product Safety Commission. Nader also established numerous consumer organizations, including the Center of Auto Safety, Health Research Group, and Public Citizen, Inc., staffed by young activists nicknamed "Nader's Raiders." His legislative influence faded after 1977, following a failed, acrimonious effort to create a federal consumer protection agency.

Nader's determination and idealism elicited both admiration and condemnation. While his achievements won praise, he was criticized as unwilling to compromise, insensitive to the costs of his consumer-protection initiatives, and excessively beholden to trial lawyers (the latter connection allegedly explaining his antipathy to no-fault auto insurance).

His activist energies undiminished, Nader in the early 1990s campaigned against trade agreements that he believed jeopardized hard-won consumer, environmental, and labor protections. In 1996, he ran as the Green party's candidate for president, refusing contributions and urging campaign finance reform. He received 685,128 votes. Again the Green party presidential nominee in 2000, he received 2.7 million votes.

[*See also* Environmentalism; Foreign Trade, U.S.; Legal Profession; North American Free Trade Agreement.]

• Hays Gorey, *Nader and the Power of Everyman,* 1975. David Bollier, *Citizen Action and Other Big Ideas: A History of Ralph Nader and the Modern Consumer Movement,* 1989.

—Robert N. Mayer

NATIONAL ACADEMY OF SCIENCES. The National Academy of Sciences (NAS) was the brainchild of three nineteenth-century figures prominent in the American scientific community: Joseph *Henry; Alexander Dallas Bache, superintendent of the U.S. Coast Survey; and Charles Henry Davis, a naval officer and scientist. These men hoped to create a body analogous to Great Britain's Royal Society and the French Academy. In 1863 they obtained a government charter for this organization, which they hoped would centralize control over American science, recognize the achievements of the scientific community, and serve as an agency for advising the federal government on scientific matters. Passage of legislation creating the academy in March 1863 depended on skillful use of legislative procedure by Republican Senator Henry Wilson of Massachusetts.

During the NAS's first half-century, the federal government rarely sought its advice. Its impact on federal policy, however, increased markedly when it established the National Research Council (NRC)—a collaboration of academic and industrial scientific elites—at the onset of *World War I. On behalf of the government, the NRC helped achieve large-scale production of optical glass, nitrates, and poison gas, among other materials. The NAS did not play a prominent role in organizing science during *World War II. During the *Cold War, however, it received many contracts to provide advice to the government, and thereafter it continued to produce reports on a wide range of subjects.

Election to the NAS is considered a high honor among American scientists. Like the American scientific community generally, the NAS has been dominated by white males throughout its history. The first woman was elected to academy membership in 1925. At the close of the twentieth century, the academy comprised about 1,800 members and 300 foreign associates.

[*See also* Coast and Geodetic Survey, U.S.; Science: Revolutionary War to World War I; Science: From 1914 to 1945; Science: Since 1945.]

• A. Hunter Dupree, *Science in the Federal Government: A History of Policies and Activities,* 1957, reprint 1986. Daniel J. Kevles, *The Physicists: The History of a Scientific Community in Modern America,* 1987.

—Daniel Lee Kleinman

NATIONAL AERONAUTICS AND SPACE ADMINISTRATION (NASA). NASA emerged in 1958 at the height of the *Cold War rivalry between the United States and the Soviet Union. In the field of space exploration, the Soviets scored a dramatic coup on 4 October 1957, when they launched *Sputnik 1,* the first artificial satellite to orbit the Earth, as part of a larger scientific effort associated with the International Geophysical Year. Concerned about the perception that the United States had fallen behind the Soviet Union in *technology, Congress established NASA to explore and use space for the benefit "of all mankind."

The new agency's space missions began with Project Mercury to study the possibilities of human space flight. The efforts expanded significantly in 1961 when President John F. *Kennedy, responding to perceived challenges to U.S. leadership in *science and technology, announced Project Apollo, whose goal was to place an American on the moon by 1970. For the next eleven years this project consumed NASA's energies. Between 1969 and 1972 NASA landed six teams of astronauts on the moon. The first landing mission, *Apollo II,* achieved success on 20 July 1969, when astronaut Neil Armstrong (1930–)first set foot on the lunar surface, proclaiming to millions of listeners: "That's one small step for [a] man—one giant leap for mankind." Subsequent landings, coming at approximately six-month intervals thereafter, spent more time on the moon and conducted more sophisticated experiments.

NASA went into a holding pattern after Project Apollo. The reusable space shuttle, its major program of the 1970s, first flew in 1981 and by the end of 1985 had made twenty-four flights. During the launch of *Challenger* on 28 January 1986, however, a leak in the joints of a solid rocket booster detonated the main fuel tank. Six astronauts and high-school social studies teacher Christa McAuliffe died in this accident, the worst in NASA's history. Following the **Challenger* disaster, the shuttle program experienced a two-year hiatus, while NASA redesigned the system and revamped its management structure. Space shuttle flights resumed on 29 September 1988. Through 1999, NASA launched more than seventy accident-free shuttle missions. In November 1998, seventy-seven-year-old John H. Glenn Jr. returned to space for a ten-day mission in the shuttle *Discovery,* thirty-six years after he flew a mission in Project Mercury in 1962.

In addition to the human space-flight programs, scientific probes were sent to the moon and planets, particularly Mars. The space vehicle Viking landed on Mars in 1976; the Mars Pathfinder in 1997. The Voyager mission to the outer solar system in the 1970s and early 1980s provided stunning images and data about distant planets and their moons. In the 1990s the Hubble space telescope, initially impaired, began returning exceptional scientific data about the origins and development of the universe; the Magellan mission radar-imaged Venus; and the Galileo probe to Jupiter generated important scientific data.

The effort to develop an international space station, inaugurated in the 1980s with the launch of the first components in 1998, promised a future presence in space and the possibility of renewed exploration of the moon and nearby planets. At the same time, the high cost of space exploration dampened the enthusiasm of some members of Congress, which provided the funding. From the beginning, some critics had argued that NASA's budget might be better spent on social needs at home, but this remained a minority view, as the romance of space continued to exert its allure.

[*See also* Science: Since 1945; Space Program.]

• Walter A. McDougall, *The Heavens and the Earth: A Political History of the Space Age,* 1985. Roger D. Launius, *NASA: A History of the U.S. Civil Space Program,* 1994.

—Roger D. Launius

NATIONAL AMERICAN WOMAN SUFFRAGE ASSOCIATION. The National American Woman Suffrage Association (NAWSA) was founded in 1890, healing the split among the suffrage forces that had occurred in 1869 and joining together the National Woman Suffrage Association (headed by Elizabeth Cady *Stanton and Susan B. *Anthony), and Lucy *Stone's American Woman Suffrage Association. Initially, the new organization failed to make many gains, either at the state or the national level. This was a conservative era, but the problems were internal as well. The NAWSA's key early leader, Anna Howard Shaw, first as vice president (1892–1900) under Anthony and then as president (1904–1915), was a gifted orator but a poor administrator and strategist and essentially conservative in many of her social views. Thus, in this early period, the NAWSA was sometimes identified with conservative political positions, anti-immigrant pronouncements, and even, among its southern members, racist views. Around 1910, however, a new group of younger, more progressive leaders emerged, mostly in state branches and sometimes influenced by the British militant suffrage leaders. Including Harriot Stanton Blatch of New York, the daughter of Elizabeth Cady Stanton, they introduced such dynamic tactics as parades, rallies, aggressive lobbying, and alliances with working-class groups, and they won notable successes. Before 1910, women could vote in only four states: Wyoming, Utah, Colorado, and Idaho; between 1910 and 1914, six states were added: Illinois, Washington, California, Arizona, Kansas, and Oregon.

While the NAWSA focused on state referenda, the Quaker Alice Paul (1885–1977), closely following the English example, split with the NAWSA in 1913 to found the Congressional Union. Her organization focused on congressional passage of the long-dormant woman-suffrage amendment to the *Constitution. In 1916 the Congressional Union regrouped into the Woman's party and began a campaign to unseat antisuffrage legislators in state elections.

Relations between the much larger NAWSA and the Woman's party were generally cordial until the war year 1917, when the NAWSA, led by the dynamic and tireless Carrie Chapman *Catt, disavowed the militancy of the Woman's party as members of the latter group picketed the White House; were arrested and jailed; and, embarking on hunger strikes, were force-fed.

The NAWSA strongly supported the war effort during *World War I, maintaining a hospital in France and supporting the work of Shaw and Catt on the Women's Committee of the Council for National Defense and of Blatch as an official of the Food Administration. Meanwhile, however, the organization also continued its steady work for woman suffrage, following Catt's "Winning Plan" announced in 1916. This plan involved tight national discipline combined with forceful grassroots agitation to increase the number of states with women's suffrage and to pressure congressmen, senators, and state legislators to support the suffrage amendment in Congress and, later, during the state ratification process. The plan succeeded. The *Nineteenth Amendment was passed by Congress in 1919 and ratified in 1920, whereupon, the NAWSA became the *League of Women Voters.

[*See also* Feminism; Progressive Era; Woman Suffrage Movement; Women's Rights Movements.]

• Eleanor Flexner, *Century of Struggle: The Woman's Rights Movement in the United States,* 1959, revised ed., 1975. Ellen C. DuBois, *Harriot Stanton Blatch and the Winning of Woman Suffrage,* 1997.

—Lois W. Banner

NATIONAL ASSOCIATION FOR THE ADVANCEMENT OF COLORED PEOPLE. Founded in 1909, the National Association for the Advancement of Colored People (NAACP) arose from two American reform traditions, one rooted in white *philanthropy and the *antislavery movement, the other in various black self-help organizations created in the antebellum free states to promote group solidarity and racial power. In the decades following emancipation, *African Americans formed a number of organizations committed to the struggle for equal rights. Among these were T. Thomas Fortune's Afro-American League and Josephine St. Pierre Ruffin's National Federation of Afro-American Women. Other groups, such as Alexander Crummell's American Negro Academy, utilized research and publications to combat theories of black inferiority. These organizations maintained ties with white progressives and encouraged interracial cooperation toward the goal of a more egalitarian society in which African Americans might fully enjoy the benefits of American citizenship—both as individuals and as members of an ethnic community.

In the early twentieth century, Booker T. *Washington worked with white progressives and northern capitalists behind the scenes to encourage a form of industrial democracy for the benefit of black workers and white capital alike. Washington's so-called "Tuskegee machine" was challenged by the elitist but racially conscious W. E. B. *Du Bois, who in 1905 founded the so-called Niagara movement, which advocated militant propaganda and political activism to achieve black advancement.

The NAACP originated as a philanthropic movement among white progressives, including Oswald Garrison Villard, Joel Spingarn, William English Walling, and Mary White Ovington. Black "founders" immediately entered its ranks from across the political spectrum, including Du Bois; Mary Church Terrell, a Tuskegee sympathizer; and Ida B. *Wells-Barnett, a radical anti-

Bookerite. The immediate impetus was the *lynching of two African Americans in Springfield, Illinois, in 1908, and the antilynching crusade became a major early focus. Du Bois effectively functioned as the NAACP's voice through his editorship of its monthly magazine, the *Crisis*, until his ouster in 1934 for advocating a degree of voluntary segregation embodying modified *socialism within the black community.

From 1934 to the 1960s, the NAACP emphasized the legal struggle against *de jure* racial *segregation. After Du Bois's departure, leadership passed to field secretary Walter White (1893–1955) and chief legal counsel Thurgood *Marshall, whose arguments before the U.S. *Supreme Court led to the 1954 **Brown* v. *Board of Education* decision, which outlawed *de jure* public school segregation in the *South. Under Roy Wilkins (1910–1981), executive director from 1955 to 1977, the NAACP, through its national office and local branches throughout the country, was active in the struggle for passage of the Civil Rights Act of 1964 and the Voting Rights Act of 1965. It also fought against public acts of defamation and the negative stereotyping of African Americans and other people of color. (As early as 1915, the NAACP had organized a boycott of D. W. *Griffith's racist movie *The Birth of a Nation*.)

By the early 1970s, *de jure* segregation had been at least temporarily eradicated through a combination of court decisions, acts of Congress, and executive orders. Legal barriers to black participation in the electoral processes of the southern states had also been effectively overcome. With these objectives largely achieved, the NAACP under president Kweisi Mfume (1948–) and board chairman Julian Bond (1940–) searched for new ways to define its mission and reinforce its identity as a black-controlled self-help organization as the twentieth century ended. With more than 500,000 members in over 2,200 branches, it remains the nation's oldest, largest, and most influential African-American organization.

[*See also* Civil Rights; Civil Rights Legislation; Civil Rights Movement; Progressive Era; Racism; Urban League, National.]

• Charles Flint Kellogg, *NAACP: A History of the National Association for the Advancement of Colored People*, 1967. John H. Bracey and August Meier, eds., *Papers of the NAACP*, 1992. Christopher Robert Reed, *The Chicago NAACP and the Rise of Black Professional Leadership, 1910–1966*, 1997.

—Wilson J. Moses

NATIONAL ASSOCIATION OF MANUFACTURERS. The National Association of Manufacturers (NAM) was founded in 1895 to facilitate manufacturers' influence in promoting U.S. *foreign trade and setting protective *tariffs. Its leaders soon turned their attention to fighting trade unions. In the aftermath of *World War I, the NAM's *Industrial Relations Department assumed leadership of the "open shop" drive against organized labor. Anti-union southern firms and protectionist northern firms, especially in the metal trades, the *textile industry, and *shipbuilding, dominated the NAM throughout the 1920s. Its anti-union policies hardened in the *New Deal Era, as leading steel, automobile, chemical, domestic oil, food, and tobacco firms focused the NAM's attention on the threat that big government and big labor allegedly posed to employers' "right to manage."

While many enterprises gradually accommodated the New Deal system of contractual labor relations, a limited welfare state, and increased federal spending, the NAM served as the voice of anti-union and anti-statist business interests. It proved especially active in postwar struggles over full employment, business *taxation, and labor law reform, and played a central role in the passage of the *Taft-Hartley Act in 1947 that weakened trade unions. Like other national multi-industry business groups, the NAM operated primarily as a public-relations service. Its activities in the 1930s and beyond anticipated the institutionalized interest-group lobbying of modern politics.

Especially after 1945, the NAM prepared congressional testimony, supplied *radio stations and newspapers with probusiness stories, and launched a series of educational campaigns on behalf of "free enterprise." While NAM was less prominent and influential than such moderate business organizations as the *Business Roundtable or the *Chamber of Commerce, its "cold war" against labor and *liberalism after 1945 undermined the political legitimacy of the labor movement and paved the way for the more widespread managerial and political attacks on organized labor that began in the 1970s.

[*See also* Business; Capitalism; Industrialization; Labor Movements; National Industrial Conference Board.]

• Albert Steigerwalt, *The National Association of Manufacturers, 1895–1914: A Study in Business Leadership*, 1964. Elizabeth Fones-Wolf, *Selling Free Enterprise: The Business Assault on Labor and Liberalism, 1945–1960*, 1994.

—Colin Gordon

NATIONAL BASKETBALL ASSOCIATION. *See* Basketball.

NATIONAL CIVIC FEDERATION. The National Civic Federation (NCF), founded in 1900, sought to improve labor-capital relations by finding middle ground between the "socialism" of radical labor unions and the "anarchism" of short-sighted *business interests. The founders were Ralph Easley, a midwestern journalist and economist earlier associated with the Chicago Civic Federation, and his wife, Gertrude Beeks Easley, a former director of employee-welfare programs at Chicago's International Harvester company. The NCF was most active from 1900 to 1920. Primarily an organization of prominent business leaders (its first president was the Cleveland, Ohio, business tycoon and *Republican party leader Mark Hanna), the NCF gained credibility and prominence through its alliance with Samuel *Gompers and other moderate labor leaders. In promoting harmony between capital and labor, it sought, by extension, to strengthen and legitimate American *capitalism. To this end, the federation urged businesses to bargain with trade unions; to offer voluntary benefits to workers (sometimes called "welfare capitalism") as an alternative to radical unionism or state intervention; and to tolerate a limited range of prolabor legislation, such as a ban on *child labor and laws requiring compensation of workers injured on the job.

Easley became obsessed with the threat of *communism after the 1917 Bolshevik Revolution and increasingly channeled NCF attention and resources into a campaign against U.S. recognition of the Soviet Union. Neither progressive employers nor moderate unions showed much interest, and business and labor support for NCF evaporated after 1920. Easley's view of labor-capital relations proved increasingly irrelevant amid the bitter anti-union "open shop" campaign waged by many corporations in the 1920s, and in the Great Depression and New Deal decade of the 1930s. Gertrude Beeks Easley took over after her husband's death in 1939, but by then the NCF, a relic of the *Progressive Era, had drifted into obscurity.

[*See also* Anticommunism; Corporatism; Industrialization; Labor Movements; National Association of Manufacturers; New Deal Era, The; Strikes and Industrial Conflict; Twenties, The.]

• Marguerite Green, *The National Civic Federation and the American Labor Movement, 1900–1925*, 1956. James Weinstein, *The Corporate Ideal in the Liberal State, 1900–1918*, 1968.

—Colin Gordon

NATIONAL CIVIL SERVICE REFORM LEAGUE. *See* Civil Service Reform.

NATIONAL COLLEGIATE ATHLETIC ASSOCIATION (NCAA). The NCAA, the major organization controlling college sports for men and women, was created after the turbulent and brutal 1905 college *football season. The death of a Union

College player in a game with New York University (NYU) aroused Henry MacCracken, chancellor of NYU, to call for a national conference to reform football rules. With the backing of President Theodore *Roosevelt, a series of meetings was held and new football rules written, including the introduction of the forward pass. Palmer Pierce of the United States Military Academy was elected the NCAA's first president. Except for writing game rules, the NCAA initially was a debating society; it had the power of moral suasion but lacked legislative and enforcement powers. These were left to individual institutions and conferences. The association did, however, sponsor national tournaments, first in track and field in 1921.

Shortly after *World War II, the NCAA hired its first executive director, Walter Byers, and began enacting enforceable legislation. The NCAA passed a major piece of legislation in 1951 to control football telecasts to prevent the loss of gate receipts. By the 1970s, nearly all NCAA income came from a percentage of football telecast fees and from its sponsorship of an annual college *basketball tournament, which began in 1939. With revenue from *television, the NCAA effectively battled the Amateur Athletic Union for power over amateur athletics, including women's athletics. When the NCAA offered to fund college championships in women's sports in the early 1980s, the Association for Intercollegiate Athletics for Women (founded in 1971) went out of existence.

[*See also* Education: Collegiate Education; Education: The Rise of the University; Sports: Amateur Sports and Recreation.]

• Jack Falla, *NCAA: The Voice of College Sports,* 1981. Ronald A. Smith, *Sports and Freedom: The Rise of Big-time College Athletics,* 1988.

—Ronald A. Smith

NATIONAL CONSUMERS' LEAGUE. Formed in 1898 from several local leagues that united to fight urban sweatshops, the National Consumers' League (NCL) is one of the oldest organizations in the United States devoted to improving the conditions under which goods are made. The league's impact was especially great during the *Progressive Era, when it championed the passage of state labor laws protecting women wage earners and restricting *child labor. Based largely on a constituency of middle-class women, the NCL also worked closely with labor unions.

The NCL's first executive director, Florence *Kelley, was also its most historically significant. Serving from 1898 until her death in 1932, Kelley motivated the organization to challenge business practices that exploited wage-earning women, children, and men. In **Muller* v. *Oregon* (1908), the NCL prepared a brief that persuaded the U.S. *Supreme Court to uphold the constitutionality of state laws limiting the hours of women workers. Between 1910 and 1920, the league pioneered in the passage of state minimum wage laws for women, which established precedents for the minimum wage provisions of the federal Fair Labor Standards Act of 1938, which included men. In the 1920s and 1930s, the NCL investigated and publicized the exploitation of agricultural workers.

After *World War II, reflecting the growth of *consumer culture, the NCL expanded its goals to include the defense of consumers' as well as workers' interests. Today the league monitors the effectiveness of legislation and regulations affecting consumers and reports on the conditions under which goods are made.

[*See also* Consumer Movement; Economic Regulation; Nader, Ralph; Women in the Labor Force.]

• Josephine Goldmark, *Impatient Crusader: Florence Kelley's Life Story,* 1953. David J. Rothman and Sheila M. Rothman, eds., *The Consumers' League of New York: Behind the Scenes of Women's Work,* 1987. Kathryn Kish Sklar, *Florence Kelley and the Nation's Work,* 1995.

—Kathryn Kish Sklar

NATIONAL COUNCIL OF CHURCHES. The National Council of Churches of Christ in America (commonly known as the National Council of Churches [NCC]), an association of major Protestant denominations, was founded in Cleveland, Ohio, in 1950. It was rooted in earlier Protestant interdenominational efforts, including the Evangelical Alliance, 1837; the *Civil War Christian Commission; the revivals of Dwight L. *Moody; and the late nineteenth century Student Volunteer Movement. The Federal Council of Churches, founded in 1908, served as the principal institutional expression of Protestant ecumenism in the United States until the NCC superseded it in 1950. The NCC, initially representing twenty-nine denominations, also assumed the foreign and domestic missionary responsibilities of earlier interdenominational groups. The NCC reflected the ecumenical drive within mainstream American *Protestantism during and after *World War II and perhaps also, in a more secular context, the "consensus" attitudes of the 1950s as well as the expansion of large-scale administrative and managerial practices throughout American institutions.

Led initially by holdovers from the Federal Council of Churches, the NCC also gave programmatic priority to the social activism of the Federal Council. Throughout much of the 1950s, as the NCC struggled to establish its own identity, it muted somewhat its liberal public voice, but the early 1960s brought a return to activism reminiscent of the early twentieth century *Social Gospel era. Younger white leaders as well as pressure from *African Americans like Martin Luther *King Jr. pushed the ecumenical agency, and mainstream Protestantism generally, to the left, especially concerning racial issues. Nudged by the NCC, church people played important roles in the 1963 March on Washington, in lobbying for the Civil Rights Act of 1964, in supporting civil rights activists in Mississippi, and in assisting King in Selma, Alabama, in 1965 as a prelude to the passage of the Voting Rights Act of 1965.

In the late 1960s, the NCC's influence began to wane. The council adopted stances often at variance with former allies, especially with the Lyndon B. *Johnson administration over the *Vietnam War, Black Power with African Americans, and with the burgeoning women's movement; such conflict created deep fissures within the liberal churches and thus in the council, as in the larger liberal society. Declining membership in the member churches affected revenues and forced cutbacks. The post–1970 conservative shift nationally was reflected in the religious world in the growth of evangelical churches and the decline of mainline Protestantism, including the National Council of Churches.

[*See also* Baptists; Civil Rights Legislation; Civil Rights Movement; Methodism; Missionary Movement; Religion; Sixties, The.]

• Dean M. Kelley, *The National Council of Churches and the Social Outlook of the Nation,* 1971. James Findlay, *Church People in the Struggle: The National Council of Churches and the Black Freedom Movement, 1950–1970,* 1993.

—James F. Findlay Jr.

NATIONAL EDUCATION ASSOCIATION. The National Teachers Association, founded in 1857, became the National Education Association (NEA) in 1871. Its members met annually to discuss educational issues. By the late nineteenth century, the NEA leadership was dominated by college presidents like Nicholas Murray Butler of Columbia University. Beyond its annual meetings and proceedings, its chief influence came from committees. The Committee of Ten (1893), led by President Charles Eliot of Harvard, recommended four equivalent and thoroughly academic high-school curricula, putting modern subjects on a par with the classics. After 1900, three developments shaped the NEA: The activism of college presidents waned while school administrators came to dominate; women successfully challenged male dominance and occupied offices (including the presidency, with the election of Ella Flagg Young in 1910); and the organization's committees (especially its Commission on the Reorganization of Secondary Education in 1918) endorsed school curricula that emphasized a variety of nonacademic purposes. The organization grew from 2,300 members in 1900 to 53,000 in 1920 and 454,000 by 1950.

By the 1950s, a majority of NEA members were classroom teachers, and the organization faced a challenge from the American Federation of Teachers (AFT). Unlike the NEA, the AFT accepted collective bargaining, and it began to sanction strikes by teachers in the 1960s. The NEA accepted collective bargaining (but not strikes) in 1962, thus becoming more like a union. In the 1960s and 1970s, the NEA achieved two major lobbying goals: federal assistance to elementary and secondary education and the creation of a federal Department of Education. By blending its long-standing emphasis on teacher professionalism and a somewhat reluctant endorsement of collective bargaining, the NEA retained the loyalty of most organized teachers, with 2.2 million members in 1996, compared to 830,000 in the AFT. While the NEA moved toward collective bargaining, the AFT began emphasizing teacher professionalism. This convergence bred serious talk of merger throughout the 1990s.

[*See also* Education: The Public School Movement; Labor Movements.]

• Edgar B. Wesley, *NEA: The First Hundred Years. The Building of the Teaching Profession,* 1957. Marjorie Murphy, *Blackboard Unions: The AFT and the NEA, 1900–1980,* 1990.

—Carl F. Kaestle

NATIONAL ENDOWMENTS FOR THE ARTS AND THE HUMANITIES. The federal government handsomely supported the arts and humanities from at least 1917, when the income-tax law permitted exemption for contributions to nonprofit organizations. In the *New Deal Era, the *Works Progress Administration included visual and performing arts in its programs. In the early 1960s, fears that the communists were winning the cultural *Cold War bolstered President John F. *Kennedy's modest plans for federal arts funding. Following Kennedy's assassination, President Lyndon B *Johnson in 1965 persuaded Congress to establish "endowments" for both arts and humanities with initial funding of ten million dollars, a token gesture toward balancing the government's massive subsidies for *science. The endowments, initially envisioned as two arms of the same agency, quickly became separate entities. The National Endowment for the Humanities (NEH), under its first chair, Barnaby Keeney, funded mostly university research. The National Endowment for the Arts (NEA), under Roger Stevens, funded individuals and institutions in performing and visual arts. Both organizations used peer panels to select grantees, approved by national councils of prominent individuals in the humanities and the arts. By law, both endowments distributed 20 percent of their appropriation among state humanities and arts councils.

During President Richard M. *Nixon's administration, appropriations for both endowments expanded to more than $100 million each, with consequent growth of their constituencies. NEH chairman Ronald Berman expanded NEH support to public television programs and blockbuster museum exhibitions. NEA chair Nancy Hanks added *jazz, crafts, and *folk arts and crafts.

As funding crept toward $200 million for each endowment in the late 1970s, conservative critics disparaged what they dismissed as frivolous or arcane grants, such as the NEH's support of obscure linguistic research. But both endowments maintained strong congressional support, forcing President Ronald *Reagan to retreat from his vow to abolish them. The NEH quietly continued to dole out its funds mostly to universities and museums, but the NEA, despite its substantial support of *opera, *music, and *dance, became increasingly controversial for smaller grants to such projects as an artist's dropping of crepe paper streamers from an airplane over Wyoming. Besieged by insistent constituencies, the NEA never developed coherent goals. The problem exploded in 1988, when chairman Frank Hodsoll unwittingly approved expansion of an exhibition to include sexually explicit photographs by Robert Mapplethorpe.

Both endowments suffered in the 1980s and 1990s from a combination of congressional budget-cutting pressures and conservative criticism of a few grants that opponents attacked as trivial, bizarre, or repulsive. Appropriations dwindled toward $100 million, and the NEA was damaged when President George *Bush appointed a weak chairman who vacillated over several controversial grants. Under his successor, the actress Jane Alexander, the NEA lost almost half its staff and was required to give the states 35 percent of its appropriation. The folklorist William Ferris, President Bill *Clinton's choice to head the NEH, worked with considerable success to build a congressional and public constituency for his agency, focusing on public-private partnerships in funding regional humanities centers and other projects. As the twentieth century ended, both agencies continued their efforts to clarify their goals, fend off conservative attacks, and build public support for the arts and the humanities.

[*See also* Education: The Rise of the University; Great Society; Public Broadcasting.]

• Livingston Biddle, *Our Government and the Arts,* 1988. Joseph Wesley Zeigler, *Arts in Crisis: The National Endowment for the Arts versus America,* 1994. Alice Goldfarb Marquis, *Art Lessons: Learning from the Rise and Fall of Public Arts Funding,* 1995.

—Alice Goldfarb Marquis

NATIONAL FOOTBALL LEAGUE. *See* Football.

NATIONAL GUARD. *See* Military, The.

NATIONAL INDUSTRIAL CONFERENCE BOARD (since 1970, the Conference Board), founded in 1916, an association of business firms that sponsors research on a variety of business topics, notably labor and personnel issues. Until the 1930s, the National Industrial Conference Board (NICB) was largely an extension of the personality and interests of its principal founder and executive secretary, Magnus W. Alexander (1870–1932). Alexander sought to enhance the image of American manufacturing firms by encouraging them to embrace voluntary labor reforms and modest state regulation. Yet he was also instrumental in shifting the focus of the NICB from advocacy to research.

Alexander's interests derived from his experiences at the General Electric Corporation, where he was an engineer and, after 1905, employment manager. Recognizing the desirability of improving working conditions, he helped organize the National Safety Council and the National Association of Corporation Schools. He gathered personnel experts from different firms in "conference boards" devoted to such issues as safety and sanitation, medical services in industry, and apprenticeship systems. Convinced that business was the victim of unfair trade union and media criticism, he mobilized employers to defend themselves. He coordinated a series of informal conferences in the Catskills that led to the formation of the NICB.

During *World War I, the NICB played an important role in the formation of wartime labor-policy boards, including the National War Labor Board. Wartime prosperity and labor turmoil also enabled Alexander to create individual corporate memberships, expand the staff, and redefine the NICB as a nonpartisan business research organization.

After *World War II, the NICB became more international and expansive, emphasizing economic and financial issues as well as personnel topics. As the Conference Board, it remained an important source of information on business activity at the end of the twentieth century.

[*See also* Business; Business Roundtable; Industrial Diseases and Hazards; Industrial Relations; Labor Movements; National Association of Manufacturers; National Civic Federation.]

• H. M. Gitelman, "Management's Crisis of Confidence and the Origin of the National Industrial Conference Board, 1914–1916," *Business History Review* 58 (1984): 153–157. Joseph L. Naar, *The Conference Board: An Historical Celebration of the Conference Board's Seventy-fifth Anniversary,* 1991.

—Daniel Nelson

NATIONAL INSTITUTES OF HEALTH. The National Institutes of Health (NIH)—a component of the Public Health Service, a division of the Department of Health and Human Services—is the United States's principal federal agency for medical research. The NIH funds basic and clinical research across the United States and in some foreign countries. By the end of the twentieth century its annual budget exceeded $17 billion, 80 percent of which was distributed as research grants to investigators at universities and other institutions. The NIH also maintained laboratories staffed by government scientists at its main campus in Bethesda, Maryland, and other locations.

What is now known as the NIH began in 1887 as a one-room Hygienic Laboratory at the Marine Hospital on Staten Island, New York. Under Assistant Surgeon Joseph J. Kinyoun, the founder and at first the only permanent staff member, the laboratory focused on applying the new science of bacteriology to federal quarantine work. In 1891 the facility moved to *Washington, D.C. In 1902 the laboratory established a formal research program on infectious *diseases and assumed regulatory responsibility for licensing vaccines and antitoxins. In 1912, the research scope was broadened to include noninfectious diseases. Congress in 1930 changed the laboratory's name to the National Institute of Health, and in 1937 created a National Cancer Institute, the first of more than twenty NIH institutes focusing on specific disease categories. The 1944 Public Health Service Act authorized the NIH to award grants and fellowships. In 1948, as more specialized institutes were created, the name of the umbrella agency became plural: the National Institutes of Health.

The NIH budget and staff expanded rapidly from 1955 through 1968, and more slowly thereafter. Among the thousands of discoveries made by NIH investigators are the cause and cure of pellagra; a vaccine against Rocky Mountain spotted fever; a typhus vaccine and confirmation of plasma's lifesaving value during *World War II; and, in the 1990s, breaking the genetic code and developing therapies for *acquired immunodeficiency syndrome (AIDS).

[*See also* Biological Sciences; Cancer; Federal Government, Executive Branch: Other Departments (Department of Health and Human Services); Genetics and Genetic Engineering; Medicine: From the 1870s to 1945; Medicine: Since 1945; Public Health.]

• Stephen P. Strickland, *Politics, Science, and Dread Disease: A Short History of Medical Research Policy,* 1972. Victoria A. Harden, *Inventing the NIH: Federal Biomedical Research Policy, 1887–1937,* 1986. For an annually updated bibliography on NIH history, see http://www.nih.gov/od/museum/nihbib.htm.

—Victoria A. Harden

NATIONALISM. Nationalism is a political ideology based on the assertion by some bounded social group—usually, though not always, a culturally or linguistically homogenous one—of its right to its own state or a sphere of autonomy. Nationalists demand that citizens subordinate other loyalties (to class, party, church, geographic region, or ethnic group, for example) to national loyalty. In the United States, nationalism has often taken the form of unstinting support for the federal government and suspicion of groups perceived as threats to it. In many periods, nationalism has carried racial, cultural, and linguistic overtones, with nativists trying to limit the term "American" to English-speaking Protestant whites. Yet countertraditions of American nationalism also exist among *African Americans, immigrants, and workers.

In antebellum America, nationalist arguments were most frequently deployed against Southern disunionists or foreign states. The 1850s saw the first national political parties explicitly dedicated to cultural or linguistic nationalism. Variously calling themselves "Americans" or "Know Nothings," these parties reacted to a massive Irish influx by demanding immigration restriction and curbs on *Roman Catholicism. Nativist Americanism reappeared in the 1890s as a second great wave of *immigration began. In that decade, veterans' organizations such as the *Grand Army of the Republic joined hereditary societies such as the Sons and Daughters of the American Revolution in a patriotic onslaught. Public campaigns sought textbook revision, military drill in schools, and protection of the national flag from "desecration." The Pledge of Allegiance to the flag was written and Francis Scott Key's "The Star Spangled Banner" proposed as the national anthem. This nervous upsurge of nationalism among native-born whites was a reaction not only to immigration, but also to industrial unrest and to the *Spanish-American War.

During *World War I, the federal government attempted to manufacture nationalist sentiment through *propaganda agencies such as the Committee on Public Information (CPI). Wartime demands for "100-percent-Americanism" led to a postwar Red Scare that targeted socialists and radicals as "un-American" and resulted in the arrests of more than 6,000 alleged subversives. Meanwhile, however, writers such as Randolph *Bourne, Louis *Brandeis, and Horace Kallen urged a more inclusive Americanism that recognized ethnic and political pluralism as a source of national strength. In the interwar period, immigrants and industrial workers, too, emphasized alternative nationalisms rooted in the ideals of democracy and equal rights rather than in ethnicity or middle-class respectability. Still, powerful ethnic nationalisms persisted through the 1920s among nativist whites in a revived *Ku Klux Klan, and among separatist blacks led by Marcus *Garvey.

The administrations of Franklin Delano *Roosevelt promoted inclusive nationalism, first through the *New Deal cultural agencies' rediscovery of American folk cultures, then through *World War II propaganda contrasting American diversity and tolerance to Nazi *racism. In the *Cold War, this vision was joined to a celebration of American material abundance, with communists portrayed as not only anti-democratic but also anti-consumption. In the 1960s, this version of American nationalism came under attack from the political left as a mystification obscuring racial and class oppression. Post–1990 nationalist arguments were deployed mostly by the Right, and more frequently against internationalist targets (such as the *United Nations or the World Trade Organization) than against internal enemies. In its many permutations, nationalism has remained a powerful ideological force throughout U.S. history, paradoxically both uniting and dividing the American people.

[*See also* Antebellum Era; Anticommunism; Immigration Law; Internationalism; Irish Americans; Know-Nothing Party; Race and Ethnicity; Social Class.]

• Merle Curti, *The Roots of American Loyalty,* 1946. Stuart McConnell, "Nationalism," in *Encyclopedia of the United States in the Twentieth Century,* Stanley I. Kutler, ed., vol. 1, pp. 251–271, 1995.

——Stuart McConnell

NATIONAL LABOR RELATIONS ACT (WAGNER ACT). Signed by President Franklin Delano *Roosevelt on 5 July 1935, and upheld by the U.S. *Supreme Court in 1937, the act was a major part of FDR's New Deal revolution. Senator Robert F. *Wagner of New York, who supervised the drafting of the act, asserted that its provisions embodied two principles: first, that there must be democracy in industry as in government; second, that workers can participate in the decisions that affect their workplace lives only if allowed to organize and bargain collectively through representatives of their own choosing.

The Wagner Act constituted a fundamental change in labor policy, particularly in regard to the government's role in labor relations. As a matter of policy, the act committed the U.S.

government to encourage collective bargaining and to protect "the exercise by workers of full freedom of association, self-organization, and designation of representatives of their choosing, for the purpose of negotiating the terms and conditions of their employment or other mutual aid or protection." After the Wagner Act, union recognition was a right, no longer something to be decided by economic warfare.

The act outlawed employer interference with or coercion of employees' statutory rights to organize, to bargain collectively, and to engage in strikes and picketing. In addition, it required employers to bargain collectively with their employees' chosen representatives. The Wagner Act established a *National Labor Relations Board to implement and enforce its provisions.

The Wagner Act also sought to create labor peace as well as to promote economic recovery by increasing workers' earnings and purchasing power. Yet the law was vigorously opposed by employers, most of the press, and the legal community, all of whom claimed that it was either impractical or unconstitutional. The *Communist party opposed it as well, warning of government control of unions and a consequent loss of the right to strike.

In part because of the Wagner Act, the giant steel, automobile, rubber, and *electrical industries were unionized and obliged to bargain with their employees' representatives. Most significantly, the Wagner Act established the most democratic procedure in U.S. labor history for the participation of workers in the determination of their wages, hours, and working conditions.

[*See also* Automotive Industry; Industrial Relations; Iron and Steel Industries; Labor Movements; New Deal Era, The; Strikes and Industrial Conflict.]

• Irving Bernstein, *The New Deal Collective Bargaining Policy,* 1950. Milton Derber, *The American Ideal of Industrial Democracy, 1865–1965,* 1970. Peter H. Irons, *The New Deal Lawyers,* 1982.

—James A. Gross

NATIONAL LABOR RELATIONS BOARD. The *National Labor Relations Act of 1935 (Wagner Act) established a three-member National Labor Relations Board (NLRB) to interpret and apply the act. As an independent quasi-judicial administrative agency with the power to enforce its rulings, the NLRB decided cases through a formal adversary process and developed a body of binding case law.

After the U.S. *Supreme Court ruled the act constitutional in 1937, the NLRB, under chairman J. Warren Madden, initially enforced it vigorously and literally. An unlikely coalition of critics, including business interests, congressional conservatives, old-style union leaders, and even President Franklin Delano *Roosevelt, sought to weaken the board, however, and consequently it began to act more cautiously and less decisively on behalf of labor.

The 1947 *Taft-Hartley Act further limited the NLRB, restricting it to adjudicative responsibilities and creating the office of general counsel to investigate charges, prosecute complaints, and represent the agency in court proceedings. By the 1990s, the NLRB, headquartered in *Washington, D.C., had more than thirty regional offices across the United States.

The NLRB implements statutory language that, while broad, can also be unclear or ambiguous. In carrying out its statutory mandate, the board chooses among alternatives that affect opposed constituencies and that reflect conflicting views of what national labor policy should be. After 1954, when the NLRB had its first Republican-appointed majority and general counsel, case doctrine underwent periodic modification depending on which political party held power. Democrats interpreted Taft-Hartley in ways that encouraged collective bargaining and facilitated union organizing, while Republicans focused on provisions in Taft-Harley protecting individual choice and the right to reject collective bargaining.

[*See also* Industrial Relations; Labor Movements; New Deal Era, The; Strikes and Industrial Conflict.]

• James A. Gross, *The Making of the National Labor Relations Board: A Study in Economics, Politics, and the Law,* 1974. James A. Gross, *The Reshaping of the NLRB: National Labor Policy in Transition, 1937–1947,* 1981. James A. Gross, *Broken Promise: The Subversion of U.S. Labor Relations Policy, 1947–1994,* 1995.

—James A. Gross

NATIONAL LEAGUE. *See* Baseball.

NATIONAL MEDICAL ASSOCIATION. After several unsuccessful attempts to desegregate the *American Medical Association, the National Medical Association (NMA) was founded by a group of African-American physicians meeting in *Atlanta's First Congregational Church on 18 November 1895. Committed from the first to promoting the science and art of medicine, to improving *public health, and to representing the men and women of African descent legally engaged in the practice of medicine in the United States, the NMA at the end of its first century remained predominantly African American, enrolling more than two-thirds of the nation's sixteen thousand black physicians, who in turn comprised 2.8 percent of all U.S. physicians.

NMA's founding president, Robert F. Boyd (1858–1912) of Nashville, and vice-president, Daniel Hale *Williams of *Chicago, worked to make the association a major force for improving the quality of life of *African Americans. In 1909, C. V. Roman (1864–1934) launched the *Journal of the National Medical Association,* the oldest continuous black publication in America. Led by physicians such as John A. Kenney (1874–1950) and W. Montague Cobb (1904–1990), the NMA became an advocate for civil rights; for the desegregation of medical institutions; and, at times, for national health insurance. Over the years it actively supported quality health care for all Americans, regardless of race, ethnicity, *gender, creed, or socioeconomic status.

[See also Civil Rights Movement; Medical Education; Medicine: From 1870s to 1945; Medicine: Since 1945; Segregation, Racial.]

• Herbert M. Morais, The History of the Negro in Medicine, 1967. "Health Care and Health Care Porviders," Health Legislation," "Medical Associations," in Jack Salzman, David Lionel Smith, and Cornel West, eds., *Encyclopedia of African-American Culture and History,* 5 vols., 1996, pp. 1247–55, 1255–57, 1257–58, 1747–49. W. Michael Byrd and Linda A. Clayton, *An American Health Dilemma, vol. 1: A Medical History of African Americans and the Problem of Race,* 2000, and *An American Health Dilemma, vol. 2: Race, Medicine and Health Care in the United States,* forthcoming.

—W. Michael Byrd and Linda A. Clayton

NATIONAL ORGANIZATION FOR WOMEN. The first formal organization of the late twentieth-century feminist movement, the National Organization for Women (NOW) was founded in 1966 by reformers frustrated by the government's failure to enforce Title VII of the 1964 Civil Rights Act, which prohibited sex discrimination in employment. Most founders were professional women, union activists, or members of state commissions on the status of women. Under the leadership of president Betty Friedan and board chair Kathryn Clarenbach, and with support from the United Automobile Workers union, NOW set out "to bring women into full participation in the mainstream of American society . . . in truly equal partnership with men." Seven initial task forces focused action on employment, education, religion, family, mass media, politics, and poverty.

A national membership organization with state and local chapters, NOW grew from 1,000 members in 1967 to 220,000 in 1982. Internal conflicts arose over the *Equal Rights Amendment (ERA), *abortion, lesbian rights, and the organization's bureaucratic structure. By the late 1970s, facing growing national opposition to feminist gains, NOW concentrated on working for ratification of the ERA, defending abortion rights, and increasing its involvement in electoral politics. Subsequently, NOW targeted violence against women, *racism, homophobia, and economic inequity as priority issues. "To eliminate sexism and end all oppression" became NOW's expanded purpose. By 1998, with 250,000 members in 550 chapters, NOW was the nation's largest feminist membership organization, a key partner in a women's policy lobby, and an important forum for the ongoing development of feminist ideas.

[*See also* Civil Rights Legislation; Domestic Violence; *Feminine Mystique, The;* Feminism; Gay and Lesbian Rights Movement; Women in the Labor Force; Women's Rights Movements.]

• Winifred D. Wandersee, *On the Move: American Women in the 1970s*, 1988. Myra Marx Ferree and Beth B. Hess, *Controversy and Coalition: The New Feminist Movement across Three Decades of Change*, rev. ed., 1994.

—Joyce C. Follet

NATIONAL PARK SERVICE. *See* National Park System.

NATIONAL PARK SYSTEM. In 1872, President Ulysses S. *Grant designated 4.2 million acres of public land in Wyoming as *Yellowstone National Park. Thus began a vast park system eventually administered by the National Park Service, established in 1916 within the Department of the Interior. By the 1990s, the NPS oversaw 54 national parks and 112 national historic sites and historical parks, along with an array of national memorials, monuments, battlefields, seashores, parkways, scenic trails, and recreation areas.

The origins of the national-park idea go back to the earlier growth of urban parks. Starting with *New York City's Central Park in 1857, many cities created parks to provide healthful recreation for their residents. This goal, in turn, influenced the wilderness-preservation movement. The first legislation aimed at preserving a wilderness area, *California's Yosemite Grant of 1864, setting aside the Yosemite Valley, was explicitly intended to provide healthful *leisure for Californians. The valley was protected on the condition that it be kept open to the public. This goal of promoting public relaxation and enjoyment was reflected in the subsequent management of the valley and of *Yosemite National Park (1890). The commissioners thinned trees and dredged lakes, for example, to make the valley more "park-like."

From the first, changes in *technology profoundly affected the National Park System. Transcontinental *railroads allowed easier access to parks, and the dry-printing process made possible the mass production of photographs that enhanced park publicity. As the parks became democratized, urban, middle-class tourists arrived in growing numbers. The rise of the automobile and a national *highway system brought still more visitors. Managers at Yellowstone, Yosemite, and other parks responded by building more roads, hotels, and tourist facilities.

With more tourists came congestion and many of the problems associated with *urbanization. By the 1950s, visitors were voicing unhappiness with park management because of overcrowding. By the 1990s, the parks and sites administered by the NPS were attracting upward of 250 million visitors annually, creating profound tensions between the dual goals of public access and wilderness preservation. However, the founders of the National Park System had from the first encouraged citizens to enjoy recreation in a newly "civilized" wilderness. The problems confronting America's National Park System at the end of the twentieth century were thus rooted, ironically, in the overwhelming success of the system's original goal: to provide outdoor recreation on a large scale to the American people.

[*See also* Conservation Movement; Motor Vehicles; Muir, John; Parks, Urban.]

• Samuel P. Hays, *Conservation and the Gospel of Efficiency: The Progressive Conservation Movement, 1890–1920,* 1959. Alfred Runte, *National Parks: The American Experience,* 1979.

—Michelle Lee Park

NATIONAL PRISON ASSOCIATION. The National Prison Association, founded in 1870, is today the American Correctional Association (ACA), the main professional organization of U.S. prison administrators. The ACA traces its origins to the National Congress on Penitentiary and Reformatory Discipline, an 1870 convention of prison reformers held in Cincinnati, Ohio. Many of these reformers were veterans of the *antislavery movement; now they found a new cause in the improvement of prison conditions and prisoners themselves. The congress's chief organizer, Enoch C. Wines of the New York Prison Association, joined forces with Franklin B. Sanborn of the Massachusetts Board of State Charities and Zebulon Brockway, superintendent of the Detroit House of Correction, to write a *Declaration of Principles,* which the congress endorsed. This document articulated the rehabilitative approach that dominated prison administration (in theory, if not always in practice) for the next century.

Incorporated in 1871, the National Prison Association met sporadically through the 1870s and 1880s as it defined its membership, goals, and structure. It became the American Prison Association in 1907 and the ACA in 1954, at which time it also broadened its base to include noninstitutional members. By the late twentieth century the ACA was a multipurpose organization with numerous affiliates. It compiled guidelines for accrediting the nation's prisons and jails; formulated policy; and published a journal, *Corrections Today,* and an annual directory of all U.S. institutions and agencies dealing with adult and juvenile offenders.

[*See also* Prisons and Penitentiaries.]

• E. C. Wines, ed., *Transactions of the National Congress on Penitentiary and Reformatory Discipline,* 1870, reprint 1970. Anthony P. Travisono and Mary Q. Hawkes, *Building a Voice: The American Correctional Association—125 Years of History,* 1995.

—Nicole Hahn Rafter

NATIONAL RECOVERY ADMINISTRATION (NRA), a federal agency created under the National Industrial Recovery Act of 1933 and abolished after the *Supreme Court held this act unconstitutional in 1935. The agency was modeled on the *War Industries Board (WIB), the *World War I agency that sought to promote industrial self-government. A similar system, advocates claimed, could end the "destructive competition" allegedly perpetuating the Great Depression. In 1933, as part of his *New Deal, President Franklin Delano *Roosevelt secured an emergency two-year measure suspending the antitrust laws and authorizing government-recognized industrial organizations to formulate a new regulatory system consisting of codes of fair competition and fair labor practices. Presidential approval made such codes federal law, and where no approvable codes were adopted by industrial sectors, federal authorities were authorized to impose them.

To administer the law, Roosevelt created the NRA under General Hugh Johnson, a former WIB member. A massive propaganda campaign followed, depicting support for the NRA's codes of fair competition as patriotic, and urging citizens to boycott businesses operating without the NRA's official Blue Eagle emblems. Eventually 541 codes were approved, each combining regulation of *business practice with a required guarantee of workers' rights to organize and bargain collectively. Despite widespread noncompliance, codification did reduce competition, foster labor and business organization, and largely end *child labor. Yet such results failed to bring recovery, and owing to this failure a code structure disproportionately fashioned by big businessmen came under severe criticism from smaller businesses, labor, consumers, and political dissidents, many demanding extensive code revision. In 1934 a new administrative board replaced Johnson, but policy conflicts and deadlocks only worsened. By May 1935, when the Supreme Court ruled that the system involved both an unconstitutional delegation of legislative power to the executive branch and an unconstitutional expansion of the government's power to regulate commerce, it had few supporters left. The NRA that lingered on under a six-months extension busied itself mostly with writing official histories of the codification experience.

Historians have generally regarded the NRA as a huge mistake, an unfortunate flirtation with *corporatism that, in effect, turned policy-making over to big business with disastrous results. Recently, however, scholars have complicated the picture by using the history of the NRA to illuminate patterns of business organization and disorganization, federal administrative structures and incapacities, and liberal ideas concerning planning. Some have also shown that parts of the code structure reflected the demands of small and medium-sized rather than big business. In addition, the historical significance of the NRA has become clearer, both as an example of failed corporatism in America and as an unsuccessful experiment that opened the way to more innovative reforms and the new regulatory agencies of the later New Deal.

[*See also* Depressions, Economic; Economic Regulation.]

• Bernard Bellush, *The Failure of the NRA,* 1975. Donald R. Brand, *Corporatism and the Rule of Law: A Study of the National Recovery Administration,* 1988.

—Ellis W. Hawley

NATIONAL RESEARCH COUNCIL. *See* National Academy of Sciences.

NATIONAL RIFLE ASSOCIATION. The National Rifle Association of America (NRA) was incorporated in 1871 by William C. Church and other *Civil War veterans. Military doctrine of the time emphasized massed rifle fire, downplaying marksmanship. The NRA stressed accurate shooting and promoted competitions at its rifle range. The early NRA focused its efforts on state militia units, and its fortunes varied with their support. In 1880, New York state stopped funding NRA activities, leaving it effectively moribund. The organization revived after the U.S. Congress established the National Board for the Promotion of Rifle Practice in 1903 and in Public Law 149 (1905) allowed members of NRA-approved clubs to purchase guns and ammunition at low cost.

Through the twentieth century, the NRA steadily expanded its scope and membership and broadened its interests to include safety instruction, firearm collecting, hunting, and police training. From the 1960s on, the NRA also devoted increasing attention to firearm-control legislation. It supported laws that punished armed criminals but fought most limits on general gun ownership and use. A lobbying arm, the Institute for Legislative Action, was formed in 1975. At the 1977 annual meeting, a group led by the activist Harlon Carter gained control of the organization. Carter's group increased the membership's role in governance and launched an unyielding campaign against *gun control. By 1995, membership exceeded 3 million.

• James B. Trefethen, comp., *Americans and Their Guns: The National Rifle Association Story through Nearly a Century of Service to the Nation,* 1967. Osha Gray Davidson, *Under Fire: The NRA and the Battle for Gun Control,* 1993.

—David McDowall and Alan Lizotte

NATIONAL SCIENCE FOUNDATION (NSF), an independent agency within the executive branch of the federal government. Created in 1950, the NSF awards grants and fellowships to institutions and individuals to support scientific research and science education. Its 2000 budget exceeded $3.9 billion. Policy is set by a twenty-five–member board named by the president and approved by Congress. While the NSF does not itself conduct research, it does maintain several research centers, such as the Kitt Peak National Observatory in Arizona.

The foundation's origins are rooted in two contrasting visions, one articulated by the Democratic senator Harley Kilgore of West Virginia, the other by the scientist Vannevar *Bush. Kilgore's proposals, dating from the early 1940s and reflecting his populist belief in broad-based democratic participation in, and government coordination of, science for public purposes, envisioned a central science agency to set research priorities and to support research that would promote economic growth. Bush, head of the *World War II Office of Scientific Research and Development, proposed in *Science—the Endless Frontier* (1945) an agency controlled by scientists and dedicated to the support of "basic" science.

By the time President Harry S. *Truman signed legislation creating the NSF in 1950, many of the functions envisioned by Kilgore had been assumed by other agencies, such as the *Atomic Energy Commission and the *National Institutes of Health. In its early years, therefore, the NSF largely confined its grants to basic research. From the first, however, it had to justify its funding policies to a utilitarian-oriented public and Congress.

The Soviets' launch of the *Sputnik* satellite in 1957 led to a substantial boost in the NSF's budget and made it a serious player in research funding, responsible for some 13 percent of all federally supported academic research. But the upheavals of the 1960s prompted President Lyndon B. *Johnson in 1968 to sign legislation proposed by Congressman Emilio Daddario, (Dem.-Conn.) that fundamentally altered the agency's mission in the direction of "applied" research. This set a pattern by which the NSF's funding priorities reflected current congressional and public concerns. During the oil crises of the 1970s, high priority went to developing alternative energy technologies. In the 1980s, worried that the United States was losing economic competitiveness, Congress pushed the NSF to support economically relevant research. In the 1980s, too, *engineering, which had remained precarious within the NSF's priorities because of its image as a vocational field rather than a basic research field, gained greater representation and status within the foundation.

[*See also* Cold War; Energy Crisis of the 1970s; National Aeronautics and Space Administration; Science: Since 1945; Sixties, The; Space Program.]

• Daniel J. Kevles, *The Physicists: The History of a Scientific Community in Modern America,* 1987. Daniel Lee Kleinman, *Politics on the Endless Frontier: Postwar Research Policy in the United States,* 1995.

—Daniel Lee Kleinman

NATIONAL SECURITY ACT OF 1947. This measure, signed into law by President Harry S. *Truman on 26 July 1947, created four new coordinating agencies: the National Military Establishment, directed by a secretary of defense; a National Security Resources Board to ensure preparedness for a future war; a *National Security Council to advise the president on national security policy; and a director of central intelligence to coordinate the military and civilian intelligence services.

The 1947 act reflected the experience of *World War II and the subsequent recognition that the institutions shaping American strategic and foreign policy were inadequate for a global power. It originated in President Truman's determination to unify the armed forces before the outbreak of another war. Truman was strongly supported in this effort by General George *Marshall and vehemently opposed by Secretary of the Navy James Forrestal (1892–1949), whose objections were fueled by the suspicions that, given the Soviet Union's massive land army, a unified U.S. armed services would be dominated by the army to the detriment of the navy.

But Forrestal also viewed the Soviet Union as a dangerous antagonist and was therefore determined to add a military and intelligence component to American foreign policy, to coordinate means and ends. Seeking a more comprehensive alternative to the army plan, Forrestal commissioned a study to recommend a new national security process. As a result, Forrestal became a major architect of the act.

Debate over the proposed National Security Act continued for two years because of intense opposition within the navy, and among its congressional supporters, to unification of the military services. Disagreements also arose over the position of the director of central intelligence and the agency that would support that position: Military intelligence agencies maneuvered to maintain their own autonomy, and the State Department sought to control the proposed new intelligence agency. In addition, President Truman and his advisers opposed the creation of a statutory National Security Council and worked to weaken what they saw as a threat to the independence of the presidency.

The act that emerged was, consequently, the result of a series of compromises. With the help of congressional supporters, for example, Forrestal weakened the authority of the secretary of defense, thereby undercutting the attempts at unity and enhancing, he hoped, the position of the navy.

In 1949 amendments to the act finally created a Department of Defense that diminished the power of the civilian service secretaries and strengthened the position of the secretary of defense. The amendments also removed the service secretaries from the National Security Council, thus augmenting the State Department's influence within the council.

In the following decade, both the National Security Council and the *Central Intelligence Agency grew into formidable agencies; the National Security Resources Board expired; and the Department of Defense, seeking an elusive unity, periodically reorganized itself. The National Security Act created the basic structure of U.S. strategic and foreign policy decision-making in the *Cold War. It was one of the most significant pieces of legislation passed in the second half of the twentieth century.

[*See also* Federal Government, Executive Branch: Department of Defense; Federal Government, Executive Branch: Department of State; Federal Government, Executive Branch: The Presidency; Joint Chiefs of Staff; Military, The.]

• Demetrios Caraley, *The Politics of Military Unification: A Study of Conflict and the Policy Process,* 1966. Charles E. Neu, "The Rise of the National Security Bureaucracy," in *The New American State,* ed. Louis Galambos, 1987, pp. 85–108.

—Anna Kasten Nelson

NATIONAL SECURITY COUNCIL. Established by the *National Security Act of 1947, the National Security Council was created largely by Secretary of the Navy James Forrestal, who wanted to ensure that civilian secretaries of the military services as well as the secretary of defense would have close contact with the president. After amendments to the National Security Act in 1949 eliminated the service secretaries, the National Security Council consisted of the president (as chair), the vice president, and the secretaries of state and defense, although other participants were added by succeeding presidents. The council's duty is to "advise the President with respect to the integration of domestic, foreign, and military policies relating to the national security," and also to "assess and appraise the [nation's] objectives, commitments, and risks . . . in relation to our actual and potential military power."

Although the National Security Council was originally housed in the Defense Department, Admiral Sidney W. Souers, its first executive secretary, moved it into the Office of the President. President Harry S. *Truman actively participated in the council until the *Korean War. President Dwight D. *Eisenhower added a Planning Board and Operations Coordinating Board to the structure and relied upon it for information and coordination, often leaving the impression that the council actually made national security policy.

Beginning with the administration of President John F. *Kennedy, the functions of the National Security Council were for all practical purposes assumed by the national security adviser to the president and a White House staff. Presidents after 1961 had few all-inclusive council meetings. Instead, they relied on strong national security advisers, such as McGeorge Bundy, Walt Rostow, Henry *Kissinger, and Zbigniew Brzezinski, who coordinated policy by chairing interdepartmental groups. President Ronald *Reagan briefly turned the National Security Council into an operational agency, which figured in the *Iran-Contra Affair, but the disastrous result seemed likely to assure its future as only an advisory body.

[*See also* Cold War; Federal Government, Executive Branch: Department of Defense; Federal Government, Executive Branch: Department of State; Federal Government, Executive Branch: The Presidency; Joint Chiefs of Staff; National Security Council Document #68.]

• Anna Kasten Nelson, "National Security I: Inventing a Process (1945–1960)," in *The Illusion of Presidential Government,* ed. Hugh Heclo and Lester M. Salamon, 1981, 229–262. John Prados, *Keepers of the Keys: A History of the National Security Council from Truman to Bush,* 1991.

—Anna Kasten Nelson

NATIONAL SECURITY COUNCIL DOCUMENT #68 (1950), officially titled "U.S. Objectives and Programs for National Security," the quintessential policy document of the *Cold War. The final victory of the Chinese communists, the detonation of an atomic bomb by the Soviet Union in the Fall of 1949, and the prospect of developing a hydrogen bomb convinced President Harry S. *Truman and Secretary of State Dean *Acheson of the need for a reevaluation of U.S. national security objectives. In January 1950, Paul Nitze, director of the State Department's Policy Planning Staff, assembled a small group from the State and Defense Departments to formulate a policy paper for this evaluation. By the following April, a draft was handed to the president and other members of the *National Security Council (NSC).

National Security Council Document #68 (NSC 68) constituted a clarion call for a concerted long-term effort by the entire national security apparatus to fight the threat of Soviet communism. Along with the necessity of a total military, political, and economic commitment, the document proclaimed, the nation must also develop a balance between conventional and atomic capability and a program of psychological warfare.

Financing this total commitment to protect national security, NSC 68 warned, would require substantially higher budgets. Whether President Truman and his advisers would accept such a large national security budget remained uncertain until the *Korean War began on 25 June 1950. This seemed to substantiate NSC 68's pessimistic prognosis and its call for a total Cold War commitment.

Together, the Korean War and NSC 68 marked a crucial turning point in the Cold War and in U.S. military spending. When the national security budget soared from \$13.5 billion in 1950 to \$50 billion in 1952, the modern defense budget was born.

[*See also* Containment; Federal Government, Executive Branch: Department of Defense; Federal Government, Executive Branch: Department of State; Joint Chiefs of Staff; Military, The; Nuclear Strategy; Nuclear Weapons.]

• Ernest May, ed., *American Cold War Strategy: Interpreting NSC 68,* 1993.

—Anna Kasten Nelson

NATIONAL WOMAN'S PARTY. The National Woman's party (NWP), formed in 1917, had its roots in two earlier organizations. In 1913, two American students, Alice Paul (1885–1977) and Lucy Burns, fresh from "suffragette" actions in London, returned to the United States to revive the nearly defunct campaign for a constitutional amendment to enfranchise women. (American suffragists at the time were focused on winning suffrage through individual state constitutional amendment campaigns.) Paul and Burns formed the Congressional Union (CU), initially a wing of the *National American Woman Suffrage Association (NAWSA), but soon a separate and rival organization. The CU's first action was a controversial suffrage parade held in *Washington, D.C., on the eve of Woodrow *Wilson's first inaugural. It then embarked on a campaign to convince women already enfranchised by state action to vote against Democratic candidates in the 1914 congressional elections; the goal was to force the *Democratic party, which controlled Congress and the White House, to support the suffrage amendment. A similar campaign was mounted for the 1916 elections, at which time a second organization, made up entirely of women voters and named the Woman's party, was formed. Members tended to be younger, more militant suffragists. Important figures included Mary *Beard; Florence *Kelley; Harriot Stanton Blatch, the daughter of Elizabeth Cady *Stanton; and Alva Belmont, a wealthy New York socialite.

Despite the militants' campaign, Woodrow Wilson, who promised to keep the United States out of the European war, was reelected in 1916. The militants now formed a single organization, the NWP, which abandoned electoral techniques in favor of propaganda and demonstrations. In January 1917, picketing of the White House began. After America entered the war in April, the picketers were arrested; though tried on minor charges, some, including Paul herself, received sentences of up to six months. The resulting publicity so embarrassed the Wilson administration that all charges were dismissed and arrests ceased.

In January 1918, the House of Representatives passed the *Nineteenth Amendment to the *Constitution, followed sixteen months later by the Senate. By August 1920 the ratification process was complete. The NWP and the NAWSA each claimed that its approach—militant civil disobedience versus law-abiding lobbying—produced the victorious result, but more likely the combination, against the background of wartime politics, was responsible.

After enfranchisement, Paul was determined to keep the NWP an active feminist force. Claiming to have learned from the suffrage struggle the importance of concentrating on a "single issue," she in 1923 committed the NWP to a campaign for another constitutional amendment that would ensure "equal rights before the law" for women and men. However, most postsuffragists objected to this platform, and within a few years the NWP's membership had dramatically shrunk. It survived, however, fighting for equal rights nationally and internationally. Paul stayed at the organization's helm until her death in 1977, at which time the campaign for the *Equal Rights Amendment was taken up by a younger organization, the *National Organization for Women. Formally the NWP still existed at the end of the twentieth century, sustained by its ownership of a headquarters building, the Alva Belmont House, in Washington, D.C., within sight of the White House.

[*See also* Catt, Carrie Chapman; Feminism; Woman Suffrage Movement; Women's Rights Movements.]

• Christine A. Lunardini, *From Equal Suffrage to Equal Rights: Alice Paul and the National Woman's Party, 1910–1928,* 1986. Ellen Carol DuBois, *Harriot Stanton Blatch and the Winning of Woman Suffrage,* 1997.

—Ellen C. Dubois

NATION OF ISLAM. The religious organization that became the Nation of Islam (NOI) originated in *Detroit in 1930 with the teaching of W. D. Fard, also known as Fard Muhammad. Born of obscure parentage in 1891 in either Oregon or New Zealand, Fard had been imprisoned in *California in 1926 for selling drugs. His theology, combining *Islam and *Black Nationalism, captured the imagination of Elijah Poole. Born in Sandersville, Georgia, in 1897, Poole's formal education ended with elementary school. At age ten he witnessed the *lynching of a black man—an event that profoundly impressed him. At fourteen he joined the Baptist church. In 1923 Poole, migrated to *Detroit with his wife and two children, where he became a factory worker. In 1931 he encountered Fard Muhammad, who preached that "the Original Man," a "Black Man," evolved 76 trillion years ago, adopted the name "Allah" or God, and created others in his image. *African Americans were therefore inherently Islamic. But an evil scientist, Yacub, created a white race of innately wicked "devils." The reign of the "white devils" would soon end, however, and the "Black Man's" rule would resume.

By 1934, Fard Muhammad had disappeared and Poole, now Elijah Muhammad, assumed leadership of the organization, whose small membership was concentrated in Detroit and *Chicago. During *World War II he was imprisoned for pro-Japanese pronouncements. After the war, more African Americans embraced the NOI's message of economic self-reliance, black nationalism, and virtuous living. The NOI's growth was furthered by *Malcolm X, the former Malcolm Little, a charismatic recruit who led a successful Harlem mosque and helped launch NOI's widely sold weekly newspaper, *Muhammad Speaks.* Prisons supplied many recruits. Membership estimates vary, but at its peak, the NOI had perhaps 100,000 adherents. Malcolm X broke with Elijah Muhammad in the early 1960s, and his 1965 assassination by NOI gunmen caused significant defections. After Elijah Muhammad's death in 1975, his son, W. D. Muhammad, changed the organization's name to the World Community of Islam in the West and sought to turn believers toward orthodox Islam. This led to more defections. The minister Louis Farrakhan (1933–), moving into Elijah Muhammad's former residence in Chicago, revived both the NOI name and the discarded theology. The NOI's "Million Man March" of October 1995, which brought thousands of (mostly) African American males to *Washington, D.C., confirmed the disillusionment of many African Americans with the failed promise of racial equality and integration and the continued attraction of the NOI's blend of racial chauvinism, *capitalism, and strict standards of personal morality.

[*See also* African American Religion.]

• C. Eric Lincoln, *The Black Muslims in America,* 1997. Richard Brent Turner, *Islam in the African-American Experience,* 1997.

—Gerald Horne

NATIVE AMERICAN CHURCH, is a loosely confederated religious organization with some 250,000 American Indian adherents in the United States, Canada, and Mexico. Its distinctive characteristic is the sacramental use of peyote (*Lophophora williamsii*), a cactus found in the Chihuahuan Desert that contains the psychedelic mescaline. An important part of the twentieth-century Pan-Indian movement, the Native American Church has been further influential by expanding the scope of religious practice protected under the First Amendment.

Suppression of peyote use began during the Spanish colonial period; starting in the 1880s, U.S. government Indian agents issued new prohibitions. At that time, the peyote ceremony was spreading into Oklahoma from the Rio Grande region as two Lipan Apaches, Billy Chiwat and Pinero, introduced it to Quanah Parker (Comanche), who along with John Wilson (Caddo) became the ceremony's principal systematizers. The ceremony proved popular among tribes throughout the Great Plains and *Southwest in the late nineteenth and early twentieth centuries as a way to revitalize Native American culture, which was under stress from dispossession, forced acculturation, alcoholism, and family breakdown. The Native American Church's formal history commenced in 1918, when practitioners of the ancient peyote ceremony, seeking legal protection, incorporated the church in Oklahoma.

In light of its crisis origins, the Native American Church's tenets emphasize social unity, hard work, sobriety, and monogamy. The ritual use of peyote is believed to advance these goals through the plant's powers to heal and to elevate consciousness. The two main ritual forms, the Half Moon Way and the Big Moon or Cross Fire Way, both of which last all night and take their names from the shape of the altar used, were developed by Parker and Wilson, respectively. A recurring issue for the Native American Church has been the extent of syncretism between Christianity and traditional Native American religion.

After a series of conflicts in which peyote use fell afoul of antidrug laws, the Native American Church committed itself to expanding the First Amendment's guarantees of religious freedom. Led by Reuben Snake, the church built a coalition that lobbied Congress in the early 1990s. In response, Congress enacted the American Indian Religious Freedom Act Amendments of 1994 guaranteeing that the religious use of peyote by Native Americans would not be prohibited or subject to discrimination by either federal or state authorities.

[*See also* Church and State, Separation of; Drugs, Illicit; Indian History and Culture; Religion.]

• Omer C. Stewart, *Peyote Religion: A History,* 1987. Huston Smith and Reuben Snake, comps. and eds., *One Nation under God: The Triumph of the Native American Church,* 1996.

—Jonathan D. Sassi

NATIVE AMERICANS. *See* Indian History and Culture.

NATIVIST MOVEMENT. Nativism, the fear and hatred of aliens, particularly religious or ethnic minorities or political radicals, emerged with the earliest settlements from Europe. The first victims were Catholics. Anti-Catholicism, rampant in England before the era of American colonization, was rooted in imperial rivalries with Catholic Spain and France. It gained new life in America, particularly among the New England Puritans determined to build a church "purged of Romish corruptions." *Colonial Era school primers instructed children to "abhor that arrant Whore of Rome and all her Blasphemies."

By the 1830s, as *immigration from Ireland and Germany swelled the Catholic population, anti-Catholicism increased. In 1834 a mob of "ordinary Americans"—teamsters, bricklayers, volunteer firemen—sacked and burned an Ursuline convent near *Boston. Nativists feared, as expressed in the title of a work by Samuel F. B. *Morse, *Foreign Conspiracy against the Liberties of the United States.* They stigmatized Irish Catholic immigrants as an unassimilable horde of criminals, slum dwellers, lunatics, and drunkards. Anti-Catholic publications proliferated, including the best-seller *Maria Monk's Awful Disclosures* (1836), recounting the alleged immoral goings-on in a Montreal, Canada, convent. Street battles between Catholics and Protestants in *Philadelphia in 1845 over the issue of Catholicism in the schools left thirty dead and hundreds wounded.

With the Irish potato famine beginning in 1846, immigration to America mushroomed, and the Catholic population reached almost three million in the 1850s. Nativist secret societies such as the Order of the Star Spangled Banner spawned a political movement, the American party, nicknamed the *Know-Nothing party because members were instructed to respond "I know nothing" when asked about it. Swollen by recruits from mainstream parties fractured by the abolitionist and free-soil issues in the 1850s, the American party briefly became the nation's second largest political organization. But it, too, like the *Democratic and *Whig parties, split over the issue of *slavery.

After the *Civil War, as "new immigration" from southern and eastern Europe brought millions of Italian Catholics, Jews, Russians, and Slavs, nativism gained strength, particularly during the depression of the 1890s. The American Protective Association (APA), the largest of many nativist organizations, had 500,000 members nationwide. Nativism declined in the *Progressive Era, but *World War I and the postwar Red Scare revived it. In 1917–1918, APA members tracked and exposed opponents of the war. With the 1919 Palmer raids, organized by Attorney General A. Mitchell Palmer, the federal government itself became the instrument for protecting America from aliens, communists, and "un-American" ideas. "Where Do the Reds Come From: Chiefly Imported and So Are Their Red Theories," explained one magazine.

In the 1920s, a new organization with an old name, the *Ku Klux Klan, recruited at least 2.5 million members to an anti-Catholic, anti-Semitic, anti-alien, anti-black crusade. Although nativism was the common bond, the Klan also stressed the defense of traditional values imperiled by the social changes of the 1920s. The farmers, blue-collar workers, and day laborers who supported the Klan were in some places joined by lawyers, physicians, ministers, and prosperous businessmen. The Immigration Act of 1924, restricting immigration and establishing national quotas directed against southern and eastern Europe, culminated a long nativist campaign led by the Immigration Restriction League (founded in 1894).

Nativism faded after the 1920s. With Franklin Delano *Roosevelt's New Deal encompassing Catholics, Jews, and a variety of former immigrant subcultures, and with G.I.s of all ethnic groups fighting and dying in *World War II, it became harder to assail any group of citizens as "un-American." (The wartime *incarceration of Japanese Americans represented a final nativist assault, however.) In these years, too, leading social scientists repudiated the racist theories embraced by earlier generations of political and social elites. Postwar prosperity removed some of the economic anxieties on which nativism had fed. As discriminatory educational barriers fell and an ideology of pluralism and openness underlay the success ethic in America, nativism became increasingly unacceptable in academia, commerce, and the professions. Though a climate of repression pervaded the early *Cold War Era, it targeted not religious or ethnic groups but political radicals. Indeed, it was an Irish-American Catholic senator, Joseph *McCarthy, who became the chief communist hunter of the 1950s, and his targets were often members of the native-born elite.

Despite broadly supported efforts in the 1980s and 1990s to limit immigration and bar illegal aliens, old-style nativism did not return. As ethnic and religious conflicts raged elsewhere in the post–Cold War world, the decline of nativism in the United States was striking. Indeed, by the 1990s, America was the world's preeminent example of a continent-wide multiethnic, multireligious, multiracial democracy. Only fragmentary and extremist cells in the racist underground—the Aryan Nation, the tiny Klan chapters, and skinhead gangs—perpetuated the nativist rhetoric of the past.

[*See also* Antebellum Era; Anti-Catholic Movement; Anticommunism; Anti-Semitism; Antislavery; Asian Americans; Depressions, Economic; German Americans; Immigration Law; Irish Americans; Political Parties; Protestantism; Puritanism; Race, Concept of; Racism.]

• John Higham, *Strangers in the Land: Patterns of American Nativism, 1860–1925,* 2d ed., 1963. Ray Allen Billington, *The Protestant Crusade, 1800–1860,* 1964. Michael Barkun, *Religion and the Racist Right,* 1994. David H. Bennett, *The Party of Fear: The American Far Right from Nativism to the Militia Movement,* 2d ed., 1995.

—David Harry Bennett

NAT TURNER'S UPRISING (1831). The bloodiest slave rebellion in American history, organized and led by Nat Turner, broke out on 22 August 1831 in Southampton County, Virginia. In this remote tidewater county where *African Americans outnumbered whites, Turner and a group of slaves killed more than fifty whites over a two-day period. Turner's revolt panicked southern slaveholders and crystallized the tensions between proslavery forces and abolitionists.

Born in 1800, Nat Turner took the name of his original owner, Benjamin Turner. During his years on the plantation, Turner's literacy and his carpentry skills gained him the respect and admiration of his fellow slaves. In sermons to other slaves, he told of seeing visions and hearing voices. Turner's father is said to have escaped from the Virginia plantation to seek refuge in the North, and Nat himself fled in 1821 but returned a month later. Turner's owner went bankrupt in 1822 and sold him to a neighboring planter. Six years later, Turner had a religious vision that instructed him to liberate his fellow slaves by killing every white person residing between his master's plantation and the nearest town of Jerusalem. Three years later, he interpreted a solar eclipse as the sign that he should carry out his plan. Recruiting up to sixty slaves from nearby plantations, Turner and five co-conspirators murdered fifty-nine whites before local authorities quelled the uprising. In the days following, local whites detained and executed a number of African Americans, many of whom had no involvement in the rebellion. Turner evaded capture for two months by hiding in the woods. Following his arrest, Turner was tried and found guilty on 5 November. Six days later, he was hanged.

Nat Turner's rebellion radicalized opponents of *slavery and provided a preview of the impending sectional crisis. In the North, the nascent *antislavery movement intensified. Only emancipation, abolitionists argued, could prevent future outbreaks of violence. The revolt also alarmed southern slaveholders in general and Virginia masters in particular. In the immediate aftermath, Virginia legislators considered abolishing slavery. A number of politicians, including Governor John Floyd, proposed plans of gradual abolition to prevent any future uprisings. Floyd's proposal was defeated in January 1832, however, and proslavery forces passed legislation tightening controls on both slaves and free blacks. Other southern states followed suit. These new restrictions silenced African-American slave preachers; limited the independence of free black churches and schools; and, in some cases, called for the removal of free people of color. Despite the ferocity of the reaction, however, African Americans seized hope and strength from Nat Turner's uprising as a fierce assault on the institution of slavery.

[*See also* African American Religion; Antebellum Era; Slavery: Slave Uprisings and Resistance; South, The.]

• Henry Irving Tragle, *The Southampton Slave Revolt of 1831: A Compilation of Source Material,* 1971. John B. Duff and Peter M. Mitchell, eds., *The Nat Turner Rebellion: The Historical Event and the Modern Controversy,* 1971. Stephen B. Oates, *The Fires of Jubilee: Nat Turner's Fierce Rebellion,* 1975. James Baker Thomas, *Nat Turner: Cry Freedom in America,* 1998.

—Jane E. Dabel

NAVAL ACADEMY. *See* Military, The; Military Service Academies.

NAVIGATION ACTS (1651–1696). The outbreak of the English Civil War in 1642 temporarily cut the American colonies' supply lines to the mother country, leading the colonists to establish commercial relations with the Dutch and French. At the end of the war, England sought to reassert control over the American trade by passing a series of laws that came to be known as the "Navigation Acts."

The first statute, passed by Parliament in 1651 and reenacted in 1660 upon the restoration of the monarchy under Charles II, stipulated that all goods brought into England be imported only in English ships, and that "enumerated commodities," such as tobacco and sugar grown in the Americas, be exported only to England or English colonies. The second Navigation Act, passed in 1663 and known as the Staple Act, required that European commodities be exported to the English American colonies only via approved ports in England. A third Navigation Act (1673) set customs duties for the colonies and established a cadre of officers in the colonies to collect them, in the hope of better controlling the flow of "enumerated commodities" to England and its possessions. A fourth Navigation Act, the 1696 Act of Trade and Plantations, strengthened the machinery of metropolitan control by setting up admiralty courts in the colonies. Together, these statutes summed up seventeenth-century English mercantilist thought by creating an exclusionary imperial commercial system restricted to English and colonial traders and designed to benefit the mother country. Subsequent statutes passed with similar intent, such as the Molasses Act of 1733, exhibited the same mercantilist spirit.

In considering the Navigation Acts and the empire's mercantile regime, British and American historians have divided over two issues. The first is the extent of smuggling to contravene the acts. The surviving evidence seems to confirm the effectiveness of the parliamentary laws, coupled as they were with the threat of prosecution. On the other hand, the evidence is incomplete, since successful smuggling leaves few traces, and the presence of French, Dutch, and Spanish imports in American markets seems too great to be accounted for in any other way.

Whether the Navigation Acts contributed to the ferment that led to the *Revolutionary War has engendered more heated debate. Historians long viewed the laws as exploitative and debt-inducing, at least after 1763 when the ministry decided to make the colonists pay for the *Seven Years' War. However, Robert P. Thomas in 1965 estimated the burden of the acts in the 1760s and 1770s to be less than 0.5 percent of average annual American income. So slight a burden, Thomas suggested, could not have caused revolt. Thomas's conclusion, hotly debated at first, eventually became historical orthodoxy. Subsequent scholarship, however, showed that the burden of the acts was not evenly distributed, and that they did impose significant costs on certain groups—in particular, tobacco and rice planters, colonial merchants and manufacturers, and artisans and mechanics—actors central to pre-Revolutionary agitation. These groups may have thought the burden intolerable enough to warrant rebellion.

[*See also* Colonial Era; Tobacco Industry.]

• Lawrence A. Harper, *The English Navigation Laws: A Seventeenth-Century Experiment in Social Engineering,* 1939. Robert P. Thomas, "A Quantitative Approach to the Study of the Effects of British Imperial Policy on Colonial Warfare: Some Preliminary Findings," *Journal of Economic History* 25 (1965): 336–355. Larry Sawers, "The Navigation Acts Revisited," *Economic History Review* 45 (1992): 262–284.

—David Hancock

NAVY. *See* Military, The.

NEAR* v. *MINNESOTA (1931). In *Near* v. *Minnesota,* the U.S. *Supreme Court by a 5–4 vote declared state gag laws an unconstitutional prior restraint on speech. These laws, enacted in response to the proliferation of yellow *journalism in the 1920s, allowed judges to halt the publication of newspapers seen as engaging in malicious, scandalous, or defamatory criticism of public officials.

Near involved a newspaper that had been shut down under Minnesota's gag law for accusing a mayor and police chief of being under the control of a gangster. Instead of addressing the unsettled question of whether defamatory criticism of public officials was protected speech under the First Amendment, the Court concentrated on the means of suppression. Comparing prior restraints and subsequent sanctions, it reasoned that the former posed a far greater danger because it prevented the speech from entering the public realm. Regardless of the content of the speech, the majority ruled, the state must rely on subsequent sanction rather than prior restraint in its efforts at suppression.

The legacy of *Near* is threefold. First, the decision firmly established the freedom of the press against *censorship and prior restraint. Second, it applied the First Amendment to the states, thereby curtailing the use of state police power to silence unpopular speech. Third, the Court adopted the marketplace-of-ideas rationale for protecting free speech. This rationale views speech in terms of its social value in a democratic community: enhancing the deliberative process by injecting controversial ideas that might otherwise have been excluded.

[*See also Abrams* v. *United States;* Bill of Rights; *Schenck* v. *United States..*]

• Paul L. Murphy, *The Meaning of Freedom of Speech,* 1972.

—Patrick M. Garry

NEUTRALITY. The concept of neutrality as a legal status applies to a nation that seeks to avoid military involvement in an armed conflict between belligerent states. Under *international law, a neutral power is permitted to engage in all legal international trade and transactions.

The early American republic grappled with issues of neutral rights in a world roiled by European conflicts that disrupted trade. As a commercial nation, the United States embraced the concept of "free ships, free goods" as the cornerstone of its definition of neutral rights. This formulation held that the nationality of a ship determined the status of its cargo and that only contraband (forbidden goods) on neutral ships could be subject to capture. The widely unpopular *Jay's Treaty of 1794 violated the "free ships, free goods" doctrine, however, conceding to Britain the right to seize goods on American ships bound for an enemy port. France's 1797 declaration that neutral vessels even partly laden with enemy property were legitimate prizes led to the so-called *Quasi-War with France. During the Napoleonic wars, France and Britain both illegally seized American ships, and Congress in 1808–1809 passed several *Embargo Acts to force them to alter their policies. In 1810, France informed the United States that it would stop such practices if the British ended their blockade of the French-dominated European continent. Though France continued its illegal captures, the United States ignored such behavior while continuing to hold Britain accountable for seizures of cargo and impressment of seamen. The British on 23 June 1812 revoked the orders-in-council that had initiated such practices, but the United States—unaware of this action—had declared war on Britain five days earlier. Issues of neutral rights thus led to the *War of 1812, but, at the war's end, the United States still obtained no British guarantee of "free ships, free goods." Only in 1856 did the European powers agree to apply the American tenet of "free ships, free goods" to neutral powers in wartime.

When *World War I began in 1914, Britain vastly expanded its contraband list and sought to enforce a "continuous voyage" doctrine under which a ship en route from one neutral port to another could be seized by a belligerent if its cargo were ultimately destined to an enemy. President Woodrow *Wilson protested these and other British actions as violations of neutral rights. Germany also violated American notions of neutrality by declaring the waters around Britain a war zone in which even neutral merchant ships could be sunk without warning. Wilson threatened war if Germany sank American merchant ships without warning or without provision for the safety of passengers and crew. Germany initiated unrestricted *submarine warfare in February 1917, and the United States declared war in April. Wilson identified violations of U.S. neutral rights as his major reason for entering the war.

To avoid such entanglements arising from neutral-rights grievances, Congress in the 1930s legislated a series of so-called *Neutrality Acts that in effect abandoned traditional definitions of neutrality and neutral rights. These acts sought simply to preserve American impartiality by restricting loans and trade to belligerents. After *World War II, issues of neutral rights largely faded as a theme of U.S. foreign policy.

[*See also* Early Republic, Era of the; Foreign Relations: U.S. Relations with Europe; Isolationism; World War II: Causes.]

• Philip C. Jessup, et al., *Neutrality: Its History, Economics, and Law,* 4 vols., 1936. Ruhl J. Bartlett, "Neutrality," in *Encyclopedia of American Foreign Policy,* 3 vols., ed. Alexander DeConde, 1978, pp. 679–87.

—Justus D. Doenecke

NEUTRALITY ACTS. Neutrality Acts have been considered by Congress at various times to keep the United States aloof from actual or imminent European wars. When in 1793 France declared war on Britain, the newly appointed French minister to the United States, "Citizen" Edmond Genêt, began to recruit American volunteers and sought to stimulate the revolt of British and Spanish colonists in Canada and Louisiana. In response, Congress in June 1794 passed its first neutrality law, confirming President George *Washington's "Rules Governing Belligerents," which prohibited the arming of belligerent vessels within American ports and military recruitment by belligerent powers within U.S. borders.

A different kind of legislation became an issue when *World War I broke out. On 11 February 1916, in an effort to crack the British blockade, Germany announced that it would attack enemy merchant ships, endangering citizens of neutral states who might be traveling on such vessels. President Woodrow *Wilson believed that travel by neutrals was a neutral right, but some in Congress wanted to ensure America's continued neutrality in the war by eliminating the possibility of provocation. In mid-February 1916, Representative Jeff McLemore (Dem.-Tex.) introduced a resolution requesting the president to warn Americans not to travel on armed belligerent vessels, and Senator Thomas P. Gore (Dem.-Okla.) introduced a resolution denying passports—and protection—to Americans seeking passage on such ships. Under pressure from President Wilson, Congress early in March tabled both resolutions.

In the aftermath of World War I, when many Americans became convinced that the United States had entered the conflict because of the Wilson administration's pro-Allied partisanship, Congress enacted various neutrality bills. The Johnson Act of 1934, not technically a neutrality act, prohibited private loans to any government in default of obligations to the U.S. government. In August 1935, in its first general neutrality act, Congress legislated that an arms embargo would become mandatory once the president declared that a war existed between two or more foreign powers. The bill also authorized the president to proclaim that Americans traveling on belligerents' ships did so at their own risk.

In a second neutrality bill enacted in February 1936, Congress extended the existing law by fourteen months while adding a prohibition on loans to belligerents. In 1937, Congress, by overwhelming majorities in both houses, reacted to the Spanish Civil War by enacting a nondiscriminatory embargo designed to minimize U.S. involvement on either side.

In May 1937, Congress passed a third neutrality bill. It retained bans on arms sales, loans, credit, and travel on belligerent ships whenever the president found a foreign or civil war endangering the United States. In addition, the 1937 act banned the arming of all merchant ships trading with belligerents. It gave the president discretionary authority to put the sale of nonembargoed goods on a "cash-and-carry" basis, requiring belligerents to pay at the time of purchase and to transport the goods on their own ships. The act also gave the president discretionary authority to prohibit armed belligerent ships from using American ports.

The neutrality laws of the 1930s proved short-lived. In November 1939, two months after *World War II began, Congress repealed the arms embargo. By December 1941, when the United States entered the war, it was already convoying munitions to Britain, making most neutrality legislation a dead letter.

[*See also* Early Republic, Era of the; Foreign Relations: U.S. Relations with Europe; Isolationism; Neutrality; Peace Movements.]

• Robert A. Divine, *The Illusion of Neutrality,* 1962. Arthur S. Link, *Wilson,* vol. 4, *Confusion and Crises, 1915–1916,* 1964.

—Justus D. Doenecke

NEW AGE MOVEMENT. The name popularly given to a constellation of ideas originating in the late 1960s and related to paradigmatic cultural changes in the last third of the twentieth century. Broadly, such changes may be characterized as the move from a modern to a postmodern worldview; from Newtonian to Einsteinian physics; and from mechanistic to organic understandings of reality. These shifts emphasized the resacralization of the cosmos; the interconnectedness of all things; change or process, rather than stasis, as the nature of reality; the emergence of a planetary culture; and the reintegration of such dualisms as spirit and matter, emotion and reason, and *science and *religion.

The origin of the New Age movement has been traced variously to the "occult explosion" of the 1960s; metaphysical movements and interest in alternative and Eastern religions in the nineteenth century; and even to ancient Gnosticism, alchemy, Renaissance magic, and the search for the "perennial philosophy." Evaluations of the New Age movement are polarized, ranging from accusations of self-serving foolishness, crass marketing of products, satanism, and idolatry to the conviction that the New Age will bring with it spiritual transformation and hitherto unknown global harmony and ecological responsibility.

With its fluid boundaries; eclectic sources, concerns, and practices; and multiple levels of sophistication and depth, the New Age movement helped give shape to a wide-ranging cultural conversation related to the search for an adequate worldview for American culture as the twentieth century ended. This worldview, New Age representatives insisted, must recognize the realities of religious pluralism; discoveries in the physical and biological sciences; the efficacy of alternative healing methods; and the place of humankind within, rather than outside, nature. The New Age can also be seen as a reblossoming of America's persistent metaphysical tradition and as offering an arena outside established religions for spiritual speculation and experimentation.

[*See also* Environmental Movement; Post–Cold War Era; Postmodernism; Sixties, The.]

• David Spangler, *Emergence: The Rebirth of the Sacred,* 1984. James R. Lewis and J. Gordon Melton, eds., *Perspectives on the New Age,* 1992. Duncan S. Ferguson, ed., *New Age Spirituality: An Assessment,* 1993.

—Mary Farrell Bednarowski

NEWCOMB, SIMON (1835–1909), mathematical astronomer, political economist, science commentator. Born in Wallace, Nova Scotia, Simon Newcomb showed exceptional intellectual promise under the tutelage of his school-teacher father. Displaying a particular aptitude for mathematics and astronomy, Newcomb in 1856 became a computational assistant at the U.S. Navy's Nautical Almanac Office in Cambridge, Massachusetts. He received a bachelor of science degree from Harvard in 1858. In 1861, he advanced to professor of mathematics at the Naval Observatory in *Washington, D.C., becoming a naturalized U.S. citizen three years later. Gaining an international reputation among astronomers not only for his observational but also for his calculative skills, he served as superintendent of the Nautical Almanac Office, now located in Washington, from 1877 to 1897.

Newcomb excelled in mathematical analyses of the orbital motions of the moon and planets in relation to one another and to the sun. He helped bring international uniformity to classical, positional astronomy by overseeing an ambitious program of recasting computational methods, reevaluating astronomical constants, rectifying old observational data, recalculating commonly accepted orbits, and refining the positional tables for the planets and the moon. By the time of his death, he ranked among the era's most acclaimed American scientists.

Newcomb's work as a political economist further enhanced his reputation. Building on John Stuart Mill's classical *liberalism, Newcomb published in 1885 a mathematically rigorous textbook on labor, currency, *taxation, trade, and finance. Sensitive to other social and cultural issues, he criticized Christian natural theology, psychical research, and the nation's meager support for science. He underpinned his commentaries with appeals to a positivistic conception of the scientific method, aligning himself with the budding American movement later labeled *pragmatism. Also adept at writing scientific popularizations and textbooks, and even science fiction, he published all told over five hundred technical, popular, and pedagogic books and articles.

[*See also* Mathematics and Statistics; Observatories; Physical Sciences; Science: Revolutionary War to World War I.]

• Albert E. Moyer, *A Scientist's Voice in American Culture: Simon Newcomb and the Rhetoric of Scientific Method,* 1992.

—Albert E. Moyer

NEW DEAL ERA, THE. A period of political, economic, cultural, and social ferment that spanned President Franklin Delano *Roosevelt's first two terms in office, the New Deal Era (1932–ca. 1940) takes its name from the slogan that Roosevelt first used in his acceptance speech at the 1932 Democratic National Convention and later adopted to describe his administration. This era saw an unprecedented level of federal intervention to regulate economic life and provide basic welfare to citizens in response to the Great Depression. This redefinition of government in turn facilitated the realignment of both major *political parties, the rise of unionism among *mass-production workers, demands for progress by women and minorities, and the growth of populist influences in culture and the arts.

Above all, the New Deal Era changed American government. President Herbert *Hoover's administration, though more active than any previous government in combating economic depression, remained hostage to the belief that privately coordinated economic action was preferable to government regulation. Hoover's policies proved incapable of halting economic decline or reviving public confidence amid *unemployment rates that exceeded 25 percent of nonagricultural workers. In his first hundred days in office, President Roosevelt broke decisively from Hoover's example in favor of experimentation with new government programs. In those early months, Roosevelt pushed fifteen major bills through a compliant Democratic Congress.

The First New Deal. Among the acts of 1933 were such reforms as the Emergency Banking Act, the passage of which was accompanied by a "bank holiday" (the temporary closing of the nation's banks), and the Glass-Steagall Act, which separated commercial and investment banking. Other acts focused on relief: The Federal Emergency Relief Administration dispensed $500 million in aid to the poor; the *Civilian Conservation Corps put two million men to work on environmental projects; the Civil Works Administration provided work-relief; and the Home Owners Loan Corporation refinanced mortgages. A massive construction program, the *Tennessee Valley Authority (TVA), built some thirty flood-controlling dams and thirteen power plants that provided cheap electricity to regional consumers. Through the TVA in the *South and large public works projects in the *West, the New Deal stimulated *economic development and *urbanization in those regions.

But the most significant programs aimed to restart a floundering economy. The *Agricultural Adjustment Administration (AAA) boosted farm prices by reducing production. It paid farmers to take acreage out of cultivation and to reduce livestock herds. The *National Recovery Administration (NRA) reinvigorated industry by restraining competitive forces and raising prices. It created industry boards composed of business and government officials who jointly wrote codes that set minimum wages, maximum hours, and price guidelines. The National Industrial Recovery Act (NIRA), the law that created the NRA, also launched a $3.3 billion Public Works Administration which initiated projects from airport construction to school building and protected workers' right to join a union (through Section 7a of the act).

In 1934, the "First New Deal," as it is often called, came to an end with a flurry of legislation that included the Securities and Exchange Act, which prohibited such abuses as insider trading—a contributor to the *stock market crash of 1929. Already it was clear that government would never again be quite the same. The proliferation of "alphabet soup" agencies attracted to Washington a new governing class of lawyers and economists. With "Brains Trust" advisers such as Ben Cohen (a Jew) and Tommy Corcoran (an Irish Catholic), the New Deal reached beyond the conventional Protestant elite for talent. This new governing class experimented with economic planning. The NRA took a step in this direction, as government attempted to boost prices by having consumers patronize companies that complied with NRA codes and displayed "Blue Eagle" logos. In truth, however, no single approach animated Roosevelt's advisers, nor did any one philosophy characterize the president's early initiatives.

Yet by 1935 a host of developments sent the New Deal in a new direction. First, Roosevelt found it increasingly difficult to placate *business. Small businesses denounced NRA policies that favored larger competitors. Even big business leaders, who initially supported the NRA, soon chafed under its codes. A powerful business lobby, the American Liberty League, emerged in 1934 to promote anti-Roosevelt candidates.

Meanwhile, the New Deal's effort to make government an instrument of social justice inspired a wide range of activist demands during 1934–1935. In *California, the novelist Upton *Sinclair nearly won election as governor in 1934 on a left-wing platform. Militant strikes broke out in textiles, trucking, and longshoring, as workers sought to realize the right to organize promised by Section 7a. Democrats unexpectedly augmented their majorities in both houses in the 1934 congressional elections. A mass movement demanding regular government payments to retirees emerged under the leadership of Dr. Francis Townsend. And two skillful demagogues—Father Charles Coughlin and Senator Huey *Long—castigated the New Deal's inadequacies. Coughlin, a Catholic priest who hosted a radio program with a fervent national following, called for currency reform. Long, the corrupt boss of Louisiana politics, demanded that the nation "Share Our Wealth" by expropriating vast fortunes and distributing them to all.

Losing business support and facing demands for action from other quarters, Roosevelt's First New Deal was finally undermined by the U.S. *Supreme Court's decision in **Schechter Poultry Corp.* v. *United States,* which declared the NRA unconstitutional. Searching for an alternative program, Roosevelt embraced the ideas of advisers who believed that the fundamental problem of the Great Depression was underconsumption. This thinking corresponded to the new theories of the British economist John Maynard Keynes (although New Dealers had little knowledge of *Keynesianism). Legislation launched in 1935, often termed the "Second New Deal," attempted to build purchasing power among the unemployed, industrial workers, the elderly, and others. This demand-side approach represented a departure in fiscal policy, inaugurating what became the Keynesian revolution in the U.S. political economy.

The Second New Deal. Among the programs launched in 1935 were the *Works Progress Administration (WPA), a relief program that dwarfed previous New Deal efforts by employing nearly one-third of the nation's jobless. The Emergency Relief Appropriation disbursed some five billion dollars in aid to the distressed. The Public Utilities Holding Company Act, which broke up the thirteen companies that controlled most of the nation's utilities, drove down electricity prices. The Rural Electrification Act provided federal funds to electrify hamlets and farmsteads. And the Wealth Tax Act increased taxes on corporations and the rich. Together these laws tapped corporate wealth while boosting the incomes of the poorest Americans.

The two most significant pieces of legislation to emerge from the Second New Deal were the *Social Security Act (SSA) and the *National Labor Relations Act (NLRA). The SSA enrolled a majority of Americans in a federal pension program that guaranteed them retirement income. It also provided funds to the states for unemployment and disability *insurance and aid to single mothers of dependent children. The act set the foundation on which the American welfare state was built. The NLRA (or "Wagner Act," after its sponsor, Senator Robert F. *Wagner of New York) guaranteed workers' right to organize, prohibited company unions from representing them, and established a *National Labor Relations Board to oversee collective bargaining. It opened the door to mass-production unionism.

The legislation of the Second New Deal defined the government's role in American life for the remainder of the century: the New Deal state regulated and stimulated the economy, promoted workers' rights, and offered welfare to the poor. The Second New Deal did not go as far as some supporters hoped (no national health plan was adopted, for example), but its direction was clear. For decades to come, political debate would no longer focus on *whether* government should intervene to steer the economy and foster social justice, but rather on *how* and to what extent such intervention should take place.

The New Deal Era also witnessed a shift in U.S. foreign policy away from unilateralism and toward *internationalism. In December 1933, announcing a *"Good Neighbor Policy" toward Latin America, Roosevelt renounced unilateral military intervention as a tool of American policy in the Western Hemisphere. Although Roosevelt continued to defend perceived U.S. interests in South America, he did so with more restraint than his recent predecessors. Reversing the policy adopted by previous administrations since 1917, the administration also granted diplomatic recognition to the Soviet Union. And, as a depression-fighting tactic, Roosevelt pursued reciprocal trade agreements between the United States and its trading partners that lowered *tariffs and facilitated *foreign trade.

The New Deal's Domestic Impact. But the impact of the New Deal Era was visible above all in domestic developments, and nowhere more so than in politics. Since the *Civil War, the *Republican party had dominated presidential politics. Only two Democrats went to the White House between 1856 and 1932—and neither gained a majority of popular votes in their elections. The New Deal, however, built a powerful Democratic coalition, appealing to urban voters and some previously Republican blocs, including midwestern farmers and *African Americans. The *Democratic party emerged from Roosevelt's 1936 reelection as the nation's majority party, a status it would hold for decades.

In his 1936 campaign against Alfred M. ("Alf") Landon (1887–1987), the Republican governor of Kansas, Roosevelt attacked Republicans as "economic royalists" and reactionaries and enthusiastically defended the New Deal's achievements. Voters gave him 61 percent of the popular vote and all but eight electoral votes—the largest electoral landslide in American history. More important, Roosevelt not only swept Democratic strongholds in the "Solid South" and urban America, he won new constituencies to his party. Never before had a president received more unified or enthusiastic support from organized labor. Roosevelt also gained votes from more than 80 percent of the poorest Americans and won a similar majority among first-time voters, most from immigrant stock. Significantly, he also won large majorities among African Americans, breaking black ties to the party of Abraham *Lincoln and creating thereafter the Democrats' most loyal voting bloc.

The 1936 New Deal coalition also swept Democrats to large majorities in both houses of Congress and to power in many traditionally Republican statehouses. For more than a generation, the Democratic party would be seen as the party of reform, government action, and the "common man" (a phrase invoked by Roosevelt in 1932). So well did Roosevelt align the Democrats with such ideas that even long-time third-party protest voters flocked to the Democratic banner.

Ultimately, though, the New Deal Era proved how deeply rooted were America's conservative tendencies. The New Deal's political realignment went only so far. Roosevelt's party also enjoyed the support of powerful business forces, especially those with an interest in promoting consumption-oriented economic policies. Mass retailers, the investment banking houses connected to them, some powerful legal firms, influential building contractors, real-estate developers, and consumer-oriented banks all benefited from the New Deal's political *capitalism. Their voices checked the influence of unions and liberals within the party. Similarly, the power of southern Democrats, especially in Congress, blocked the party from moving very far leftward. Entrenched segregationists with years of seniority on powerful committees enacted provisions that weakened key New Deal reforms—for example, exempting agricultural and domestic workers from protection by the SSA or NLRA. When Roosevelt challenged some of these southern conservatives by endorsing their liberal opponents in the 1938 Democratic primaries, the strategy failed. As a result, the Democratic party emerged from this era divided between hopeful black masses, labor unionists, and liberals on the one hand and die-hard southern segregationists on the other.

Nonetheless, the political shifts of the New Deal Era awakened the hopes of previously subordinated groups in American society. Workers, radicals, blacks, and women alike enjoyed rising expectations.

To no group did the New Deal promise more than to industrial workers. The protection of the right to organize embodied in Section 7a of the NIRA sparked a wave of unionizing efforts in basic industry. That ferment in turn stirred reform within the *American Federation of Labor (AFL). Unable to meet the needs of mass-production workers owing to its anachronistic craft structure, the AFL floundered in response to Section 7a. By 1935, a group of union reformers led by John L. *Lewis of the United Mine Workers of America demanded that the AFL issue charters to industrial unions to reach mass-production workers. When AFL president William Green balked, Lewis and others formed the Committee for Industrial Organization (CIO).

The CIO sponsored mass organizing drives in the *iron and steel, *automotive, rubber, and *electrical industries that came to fruition in a series of dramatic breakthroughs in 1937. The most important, a *sit-down strike in a Flint, Michigan, auto plant, forced General Motors to recognize the CIO's United Automobile Workers union. Shortly thereafter the U.S. Steel Corporation recognized the CIO. When the Supreme Court unexpectedly upheld the constitutionality of the NLRA in April 1937, the CIO's position was further strengthened. Before the end of the year, Lewis led industrial unionists out of the AFL to institutionalize the CIO as the *Congress of Industrial Organizations. Breaking with AFL policies that excluded blacks, women, and most radicals, the CIO forged a new path for American labor. By the end of *World War II, the CIO had unionized much of mass-production industry and established itself as a power in Democratic politics.

The rise of the CIO was in part aided by an alliance that developed among unionists, liberals, and radicals. During the Depression, the. U.S *Communist party grew into the dominant left-wing presence, despite its policy of spurning alliances with the democratic left. In 1935, however, the Communist International, mindful of the threat of fascism, abandoned its previous sectarianism and inaugurated the Popular Front, urging communists everywhere to ally with liberal, antifascist forces. In America, communist workers abandoned efforts to build their own unions and instead streamed into the CIO, becoming in many cases its best organizers and rising to positions of leadership in several CIO unions. Although especially important for labor, the Popular Front strategy was broadly influential. Communists entered New Deal agencies (without disclosing their party connections) and joined with liberals in *civil rights, peace, and *civil liberties efforts. Never before had radicals exerted more influence in government or mainstream political causes—a fact that would haunt liberals during the *Cold War when Republicans attacked them as one-time "fellow travelers" of the communists.

Among the causes that communists helped advance during this period were African-American civil rights. Communists played an active role in publicizing the *Scottsboro case, which involved nine black youths dubiously charged with raping two white women in Alabama in 1931. Communists also organized southern black sharecroppers into the Share Croppers Union. (Socialists, meanwhile, founded their own Southern Tenant Farmers Union.) And they helped launch civil rights groups such as the National Negro Congress and the Southern Negro Youth Congress.

The New Deal's own record on civil rights was less luminous. Roosevelt refused to support antilynching legislation for fear of angering powerful southern Democrats, the CCC ran segregated camps, relief programs frequently discriminated against blacks, and nearly all TVA employees were white. Still, the administration did evince solicitude for black concerns. Roosevelt regularly consulted with an informal "Black Cabinet"; he appointed such black leaders as Mary McLeod *Bethune to secondary-level administration posts; and Eleanor *Roosevelt, the president's wife, championed black demands for equality. In 1939 the First Lady and Secretary of the Interior Harold Ickes (1874–1952) intervened when the Daughters of the American Revolution barred the black opera singer Marian *Anderson from performing at their Washington, D.C., concert hall. Mrs. Roosevelt and Ickes arranged for Anderson to sing instead on the steps of the *Lincoln Memorial, staging a stirring *radio broadcast of the event.

Likewise, although the New Deal did little to advance feminist goals in programmatic terms, women gained increasing influence in government during this period. Molly Dewson, a feminist activist, headed the newly established Women's Division of the Democratic National Committee. Working with Eleanor Roosevelt and other allies, Dewson helped secure appointment of the first women to hold the positions of cabinet secretary (Frances *Perkins of the Department of Labor), ambassador, U.S. Court of Appeals judge, and a score of lesser posts. Meanwhile, Eleanor Roosevelt's travels, speeches, syndicated newspaper column, and frequent interventions in policy debates within the administration transformed the role of First Lady.

The New Deal also brought improvements for Native Americans. The long-time reformer John Collier (1884–1968), appointed head of the *Bureau of Indian Affairs by Roosevelt, pushed through Congress a series of laws that aided beleaguered Native American communities. These culminated in the *Indian Reorganization Act of 1934, which granted Indians rights of self-government and cultural freedom on reservations.

While such social changes should not be exaggerated, they did encourage an emerging ideal of *cultural pluralism among liberals who celebrated America's cultural diversity. This tendency was greatly strengthened by simultaneous developments in music and the arts. Here, too, government played a role. Under the aegis of the WPA in 1935, the Federal Arts Project, the Federal Music Project, the Federal Writers Project, and the Federal Theatre Project were born. These programs employed jobless artists and writers to compose and perform music and plays, to write local histories, to paint murals in public buildings, and more. Such projects encouraged artists to draw upon folk culture and everyday life for themes, making the arts more accessible to the masses.

By the end of the 1930s, American arts and letters had been permeated by a concern for everyday people's struggles. The paintings of John Steuart Curry, the proletarian fiction of John Dos Passos and John Steinbeck—whose novel *The *Grapes of Wrath* (1939) celebrated the endurance of *Dust Bowl migrants—and the composer Aaron *Copland's "Fanfare for the Common Man" all revealed an effort to give voice to the voiceless.

Developments in *popular culture reinforced this trend. The New Deal Era saw *film and *radio gain a vast following. The movies offered the fantasy world of *The Wizard of Oz* and escape into the past with *Gone with the Wind* (both 1939). Radio diverted listeners with the comedy shows of Jack Benny, George Burns and Gracie Allen, and the mildly racist stereotypes of "Amos 'n' Andy." Radio also made mass opinion a force as never before, as Roosevelt's "Fireside Chats" showed. Moviegoers watched newsreels touting the New Deal's efforts, cheered the populist heroes of the director Frank Capra's films, and admired strong women such as Bette Davis and Joan Crawford. Just as the federal government supplanted local, ethnic, or religious institutions unable to care for the Depression's victims, the new mass media partially supplanted their audiences' distinctive subcultures with a national mass culture at once democratic and consumerist.

The New Deal's Demise and Its Legacy. Yet the New Deal that had initiated such vast changes began to fade by 1937, in part because of difficulties created by Roosevelt himself. Frustrated by the Supreme Court's conservative rulings, Roosevelt in early 1937 led a vain effort to expand the number of justices on the court. This transparent attempt to "pack" the court and thereby influence its decisions alienated many of the president's allies and reinvigorated his foes. Later in 1937, worried about deficit spending and assuming that the economy was rebounding, Roosevelt decided to cut back relief programs. The *stock market promptly crashed and jobless rates again soared.

Other calamities ensued. Smaller steel companies refused to follow the lead of U.S. Steel, successfully avoiding recognition of the CIO in a bitter 1937 strike that weakened Roosevelt's labor allies. Then, in 1938, conservatives on the *House Committee on Un-American Activities mounted a damaging investigation into communist influence in New Deal agencies. These same conservatives ensured that the last great piece of New Deal legislation—the Fair Labor Standards Act of 1938—exempted agricultural workers and set minimum wages at a level that would not hurt low-waged southern industry. Increasingly under attack after 1938, administration liberals retreated from ambitious efforts to restructure the economy and contented themselves with pursuing economic growth policies.

By the time Adolf Hitler's storm troopers invaded Poland on 1 September 1939, unleashing *World War II, the New Deal Era was waning. Conservative and liberal political forces became locked in a stalemate that blocked significant reforms until the United States went to war in December 1941. Only in wartime was Roosevelt able to place the New Deal's central legacy—a powerful regulatory government—on a durable footing. By then, however, those interests that had most resisted the New Deal's changes had regrouped to ensure that their power would not be undermined by the postwar political dispensation.

What is the legacy of the New Deal Era? Historians differ, and their views have shifted over time. During the early *Cold War years, most saw the New Deal as the triumph of democracy and liberal *capitalism at a time when the future of both looked bleak. By the 1960s, however, revisionists began focusing on the missed opportunities and the conservative achievements of this era, the spread of an entrenched government bureaucracy, and the co-opting of militant unionism. The New Deal's failure to address the grievances of minorities and women also received increasing scrutiny. In the last years of the century, however, as the era of "big government" faded, scholars seemed willing to grant that the New Deal Era witnessed a profound broadening of American democracy against great odds. Workers, consumers, and minorities benefited from the developments of this period, even if they gained little direct influence over public policy. Their advances may be the era's most enduring legacy.

[*See also* Agriculture: Since 1920; Banking and Finance; Conservatism; Consumer Culture; Depressions, Economic; Folk Art and Crafts; Foreign Relations; Indian History and Culture: From 1900 to 1950; Labor Movements; Liberalism; Lynching; Peace Movements; Securities and Exchange Commission; Segregation, Racial; Sharecropping and Tenantry; Socialism; Socialist Party of America; Strikes and Industrial Conflict; Welfare, Federal.]

• William E. Leuchtenberg, *Franklin D. Roosevelt and the New Deal, 1932–1940,* 1963. Ellis Hawley, *The New Deal and the Problem of Monopoly,* 1966. Richard Pells, *Radical Visions, American Dreams: Culture and Social Thought in the Depression Years,* 1973. Harvard Sitkoff, *A New Deal for Blacks,* 1978. Susan Ware, *Holding Their Own: American Women in the 1930s,* 1982. Robert McElvaine, *The Great Depression,* 1984. Steve Fraser and Gary Gerstle, eds., *The Rise and Fall of the New Deal Order, 1930–1980,* 1989. Lizabeth Cohen, *Making a New Deal: Industrial Workers in Chicago, 1919–1939,* 1990. Melvyn Dubofsky, ed., *The New Deal: Conflicting Interpretations and Shifting Perspectives,* 1992. Alan Brinkley, *The End of Reform: New Deal Liberalism in Recession and War,* 1995. Robert H. Zieger, *The CIO, 1935–1955,* 1995. David Plotke, *Building a Democratic Political Order: Reshaping Liberalism in the 1930s and 1940s,* 1996.

—Joseph A. McCartin

NEW ENGLAND. Consisting of six states (five of them among the nation's smallest), New England, named by Captain John *Smith in 1614, is the only U.S. region with clearly defined political boundaries. The region's first substantial European settlement was organized by Puritans in the late 1620s. Despite rapid diversification—Rhode Island and Connecticut emerged as rival colonies to Massachusetts-Bay within the first decade—and the presence of non-Puritans from the very beginning, a form of Puritan hegemony was imposed, especially in Massachusetts, by restricting the franchise to a religious elite. This hegemony was successfully challenged by England, which in 1686 imposed a central government, the "Dominion of New England," on the entire region (plus New York). Although the dominion was dissolved in 1689, only Rhode Island and Connecticut retained political autonomy.

During the eighteenth century, New England came increasingly to resemble England itself. Society polarized economically, and its elite (like that of other regions) aspired to the cultural style of the English gentry, a development sometimes termed "anglicization." Still, far more than other regions, New England maintained its ethnic homogeneity, in large measure by using the *family itself as its primary labor supply—in contrast not only to the *South's slave-labor system but also to the wage labor of the Middle Colonies. Largely for that reason, regional population growth stemmed from natural increase rather than *immigration: as late as 1773–1776, less than 1 percent of Britons who immigrated to America landed in New England—a mere 77 out of 9,364 individuals.

One element now deeply associated with New England—the nucleated village gathered around a central common—did not develop until about 1800. Far from being the product of early Puritan settlement, the nucleated village emerged only with the advent of strong regional markets and a protocapitalist rural economy. Nevertheless, the "New England village" and the stable cultural practices it was believed to engender became a model for the social order that many prominent *antebellum New Englanders wished to export to the rest of the United States especially to the contested western regions. But in the decades after 1815, New England underwent a radical transformation as the region's mercantile elite (brought low economically by the *War of 1812 and politically by their opposition to that war) came to invest in industrial production. The industrial revolution carried New England to a position of national strength and in the process transformed its social structure. By 1860 the region was more highly industrialized and urbanized, and contained more immigrants (mostly Roman Catholics, including many from Ireland), than any other part of the nation—a rapid and dramatic reversal of its ethnic composition and labor system. This same transformation helped generate the various reform movements that swept over New England after 1830: *temperance and prohibition, body reform, and *antislavery, all linked by a shared commitment to individual self-discipline and self-fulfillment.

The *Civil War strengthened New England's industrial might. But many native-born New Englanders found the side effects of *industrialization—vast cotton mills and floods of non-English-speaking immigrants—deeply disturbing. Some of New England's most prominent reformers disengaged themselves from urban problems. For a new generation of authors, artists, and tourists, the declining villages of northern and coastal New England began to seem quaint and old-fashioned, the repository of everything industrial society was leaving behind.

By 1920, more than two-thirds of the Massachusetts population were first- or second-generation immigrants. Old-stock Yankees began to lose control over the economy. Even the *Republican party's long-standing regional hegemony was crumbling; the Democrat Alfred E. *Smith won a majority of Massachusetts votes for president in 1928. The depression of the 1930s continued this development, though slowly. In 1936, when Connecticut, New Hampshire, and Rhode Island joined the New Deal, casting their electoral votes for Franklin Delano *Roosevelt, Maine and Vermont became the only two states in the United States to hold out against the Roosevelt landslide.

In the first half of the twentieth century, New England underwent prolonged economic depression, resulting in massive deindustrialization as textile mills were dismantled, textile production moved south, and industrial cities became slums. But *World War II fueled the growth of new industries and prosperity. Government contracts led to the rapid expansion of research and development in weapons, electronics systems, and what would later become *computer technology. Cambridge, Massachusetts—home of the laboratories of Harvard and the Massachusetts Institute of Technology—was at the center of the new expansion. *The Cold War fueled this military technology boom. The ripples of economic transformation were felt even in the marginal parts of New England, as those regions were transformed into highly developed tourist destinations catering to the vacation demand of newly leisured workers.

[*See also* Agriculture: Colonial Era; Boston; Factory System; Federalist Party; Hartford Convention; Immigration; Indian History and Culture: From 1500 to 1800; Industrialization; Irish Americans; Italian Americans; King Philip's War; Literature: Colonial Era; Lowell Mills; Pequot War; Pilgrims; Poetry; Puritanism; Roman Catholicism; Salem Witchcraft; Textile Industry; Transcendentalism; Unitarianism and Universalism; Utopian and Communitarian Movements.]

• Hal Barron, *Those Who Stayed Behind: Rural Society in Nineteenth Century New England*, 1984. Stephen Nissenbaum, "New England as Region and Nation," in Edward L. Ayers, et al., eds., *All Over the Map: Rethinking American Regions*, 1989. Theodore Steinberg, *Nature Incorporated: Industrialization and the Waters of New England*, 1991. David A. Zonderman, *Aspirations and Anxieties: New England Workers and the Mechanized Factory System, 1815–1850*, 1992. Dona Brown, *Inventing New England: Regional Tourism in the Nineteenth Century*, 1995. Joseph A. Conforti, *Imagining New England: Explorations of Regional Identity from the Pilgrims to the Mid-Twentieth Century*, 2001.

—Stephen Nissenbaum

NEW LEFT. An uprising of students against the dominant policies and cultural mores of American society, the New Left emerged in the early 1960s, peaked at mid-decade, and dissipated in the early 1970s. Arising from the *civil rights movement, fears of nuclear war, and socialist movements of the 1930s (the so-called Old Left), the New Left became closely identified with protests against the *Vietnam War and related campus uprisings as the 1960s progressed. The spread of left-leaning periodicals, most notably *Liberation, Ramparts,* and *Studies on the Left;* the specter of student protests, black and white; and the formation of leftist organizations, particularly *Students for a Democratic Society (SDS), the *Student Nonviolent Coordinating Committee (SNCC), and the *Congress of Racial Equality (CORE), signaled the emergence of the New Left.

The movement's espousal of "participatory democracy" emphasized widespread popular engagement in political decision-making. The slow pace of change, meanwhile, reinforced the New Left's disdain for political *liberalism. While SDS supported the idea of a war on *poverty, it found President Lyndon B. *Johnson's policies lacking and established its own Economic Research and Action Project, aimed at forging an interracial movement of the poor. Furthermore, while applauding the Civil Rights Act of 1964, SNCC and other New Left voices condemned Johnson's forces for refusing to seat the Mississippi Freedom Democratic party at the Democratic National Convention that same year.

The New Left gained a devoted following, particularly among college students, through its leadership of the antiwar movement and association with black power advocates and the counterculture. Together, these forces broke down the liberal consensus represented by President Johnson's landslide victory in 1964 and fueled a host of other movements on issues such as *feminism and *environmentalism. Whether the New Left actually shortened the Vietnam War remains a problematic question, since radical student protests created a backlash among mainstream Americans.

While most prominent on the East and West coasts, on campuses like Columbia and Berkeley, the New Left attracted supporters nationwide, at such institutions as the University of Texas, the University of Wisconsin, and Kent State in Ohio. Moreover, the youth-led rebellions in France, Czechoslovakia, and elsewhere during the 1960s demonstrated that New Left–type protests were not confined to the United States. Convinced that a worldwide revolution was at hand, some New Left students abandoned their initial goals and methods in favor of more traditional Marxist-Leninist tactics. Most prominently, the Weathermen, a violent offshoot of SDS, cast itself as the vanguard of a global struggle against racist imperialism.

Several factors produced the New Left's demise. Increased militancy alienated some movement supporters, while prompting a government crackdown on radical insurgencies. The end of the Vietnam War also took its toll, turning leftist attention and energy to other social and political movements. Paradoxically, some New Right groups adopted the tactics and vocabulary of the New Left in their own crusades of the 1970s and beyond.

While some scholars present the New Left in a favorable light, as an idealistic movement dedicated to increasing minority rights and ending a disastrous war, others focus more on its excesses, including the defense of terrorism by some and its divisive impact on the *Democratic party and its liberal agenda. Nearly all scholars, however, agree that the New Left played a key role during the 1960s, leaving a powerful legacy of youthful protest and political change.

[*See also* Antiwar Movements; Black Nationalism; Black Panthers; Civil Rights Legislation; Great Society; Kent State and Jackson State; Nixon, Richard M.; Radicalism; Sixties, The; Socialism.]

• Kirkpatrick Sale, *SDS*, 1973. Irwin Unger, *The Movement: A History of the New Left, 1959–1972*, 1974. James Miller, *Democracy Is in the Streets: From Port Huron to the Siege of Chicago*, 1984. Todd Gitlin, *The Sixties: Years of Hope and Days of Rage*, 1987. Peter B. Levy, *The New Left and Labor in the 1960s*, 1994. Terry Anderson, *The Movement and the Sixties*, 1995.

—Peter B. Levy

NEW ORLEANS. Situated on the first high ground rising from the Gulf of Mexico near the mouth of the *Mississippi River, New Orleans is a culturally diverse, historically Roman Catholic city. Founded as the capital of France's Louisiana colony in

1718, the swampy, mosquito-infested site remained a largely undeveloped economic liability when the French ceded it to Spain in 1762–1763. The "Crescent City" (named for its location on a bend in the Mississippi River) began to prosper as it attracted large numbers of American settlers. Spain retroceded the colony to France just prior to Napoleon's sale of the Louisiana territory to the United States in 1803. Notable *Colonial Era developments included the genesis of New Orleans's large community of free people of color.

A regional economic boom in cotton, land, and slaves fueled rapid antebellum growth in a city fragmented into largely American "uptown" and Creole "downtown" sectors. The arrival of thousands of Irish and German immigrants contributed to the city's unique cultural tapestry and the inviting blend of music, food, and festival that was represented by the appearance in 1857 of the first modern *Mardi Gras "krewes" (companies of costumed paraders).

By 1860, with a population of 168,675, New Orleans was the largest city in the *South and fifth largest in the United States. The *Civil War and *Reconstruction accelerated New Orleans's "Americanization," as evidenced by the imposition of an uncompromising system of racial *segregation that divided white from black. Remnants of the city's unusual origins could be found, however, in a Creole protest tradition that surfaced in Homer Plessy's unsuccessful legal assault on Jim Crow in the landmark **Plessy* v. *Ferguson* case of 1896.

Late nineteenth- and early twentieth-century New Orleans stagnated economically even as its African-American musicians took the lead in demonstrating the city's cultural vitality by developing *jazz. The new music, Storyville (the fabled red-light district), the corrupt Louisiana lottery, and *gambling combined to enhance the city's exotic and sensual reputation. "Reformers" battled "Ring" politicians until 1904, when Martin Behrman consolidated one of the urban South's rare political machines.

After *World War II, *suburbanization, changing racial demographics, and the *civil rights movement dramatically reshaped the city. New bridges, highways, and swamp-draining pumps permitted geographic expansion, with whites concentrated in a suburban collar around an increasingly black urban core. Ernest Nathan "Dutch" Morial, a prominent civil rights leader, became the city's first black mayor in 1978. The city's population dropped to 496,938 in 1990 and, despite its flirtation with gambling as a solution to long-standing economic problems, New Orleans increasingly resembled other racially segmented, economically troubled American cities as the twentieth century ended.

[*See also* African Americans; Cotton Industry; German Americans; Irish Americans; Louisiana Purchase; Roman Catholicism; Slavery: Development and Expansion of Slavery.]

• Arnold R. Hirsch and Joseph Logsdon, eds., *Creole New Orleans: Race and Americanization,* 1992. Reid Mitchell, *All on a Mardi Gras Day: Episodes in the History of New Orleans Carnival,* 1995.

—Arnold R. Hirsch

NEW ORLEANS, BATTLE OF (1815). In the Battle of New Orleans at the end of the *War of 1812, General Andrew *Jackson and an assortment of forces that included Tennessee volunteers, Jean Laffite and his band of pirates, and a corps of free black soldiers from Santo Domingo defeated a British invasion of the Gulf Coast.

British success appeared likely until Jackson took command of New Orleans's defense on 1 December 1814 and imposed conscription and martial law on the city's inhabitants, some of whom still remained unreconciled to American rule. Jackson began the battle on 23 December with a surprise attack on the British positions outside the city. A British counterattack on 27–28 December silenced American gunboats but failed to penetrate Jackson's defensive line. On 8 January 1815, after waiting for reinforcements, five thousand British regulars commanded by General Edward Pakenham launched a frontal assault on the American defenses surrounding the city. A withering cannon, rifle, and musket fire devastated the brightly clad redcoats who suffered more than two thousand casualties. The American casualties numbered only twenty-one. The British forces withdrew from the region in late January.

The Battle of New Orleans made Jackson a national hero and a presidential prospect, even though the decisive clash occurred two weeks after the signing in Ghent, Belgium, of a peace treaty ending the war. The victory, though strategically meaningless, was one of the few bright spots in a war otherwise marked by stalemate or defeat; it became an enduring symbol of American nationalism.

[*See also* Antebellum Era; Early Republic, Era of the; Ghent, Treaty of; New Orleans.]

• Robert Remini, *Andrew Jackson and the Course of American Empire, 1767–1821,* 1977. Donald R. Hickey, *The War of 1812: A Forgotten Conflict,* 1989.

—William Earl Weeks

NEW RIGHT. *See* Conservatism.

NEWSPAPERS. *See* Journalism.

NEW YORK CITY. Geography favored the future city of New York, providing a huge protected harbor, river access to the interior, a temperate climate, and stable bedrock. Various Algonkin people, including Carnarsies and Manhattans, first inhabited the site. The first European explorer to visit the area was probably Giovanni da Verrazano, in 1524. In 1609, Englishman Henry Hudson, employed by the Dutch, sailed by Manhattan Island in a futile search for the Northwest Passage.

Others followed, lured by commercial possibilities, especially the *fur trade. In 1621, the Dutch government granted a trade monopoly to the Dutch West India Company. By 1624, some thirty families, Protestant Walloons, established the first European settlement, New Amsterdam. Two years later, Peter Minuit, the first director general, purchased Manhattan Island (fifteen thousand acres) from local Indians, probably Carnarsies, for sixty guilders in trade goods. In 1653, during the administration of Peter Stuyvesant (1610?–1672), a city council was established. England seized the land in 1664, changing its name to New York and introducing jury trials and a permanent court system. The settlement, which had grown to 1,500 people, contained a city hall, a church, a canal (later Broad Street), a wall (Wall Street), a main street (Broadway), and about 300 houses.

In 1665, Governor Richard Nichols extended the city limits to include the entire island. By 1680, the population stood at three thousand, and trade in furs and flour was thriving. Six years later, Governor Thomas Dongan, an Irish Catholic, granted the "Dongan Charter," dividing the city into six wards. A common council was given the power to make laws not contrary to those of England or the province. The overthrow of James II in 1689 led to a political crisis, however, as followers of Jacob Leisler (1640–1691), a German immigrant, seized control of the city and governed it for two years. Leisler was arrested and executed, but the affair left deep political scars as New Yorkers struggled for power. Other notable events in the *Colonial Era included the trial of John Peter Zenger in 1735, slave insurrections in 1712 and 1741, and the launching of William Bradford's *New York Gazette* in 1725. The New York Society Library was created in 1754, John Street Theater in 1764, and New York Hospital in 1771.

Although it hosted the *Stamp Act Congress in 1765, New York entered the *Revolutionary War reluctantly. The city's 25,000 inhabitants, flourishing under English rule, valued their trade with the empire. After the disastrous Battle of Long Island on 27 August 1776, British forces seized unresisting New York and held it throughout the war.

New York recovered quickly. George *Washington was in-

MAP 14: MAP OF NEW YORK CITY'S ELEVATED RAILROADS (1881)

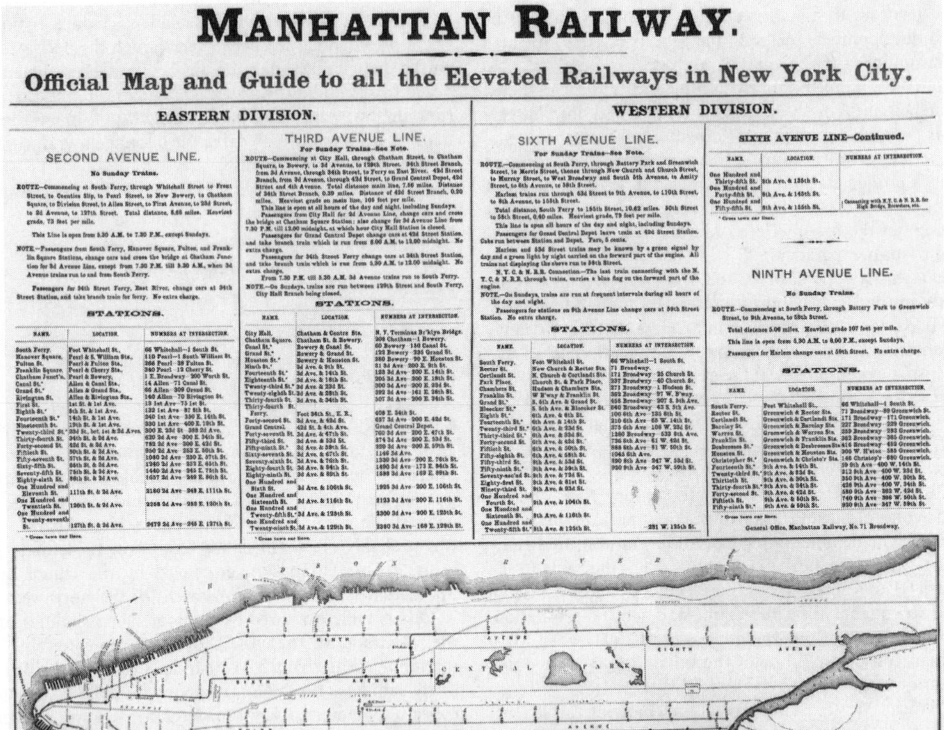
MANHATTAN RAILWAY.
Official Map and Guide to all the Elevated Railways in New York City.
EASTERN DIVISION.
WESTERN DIVISION.
SECOND AVENUE LINE.
THIRD AVENUE LINE.
SIXTH AVENUE LINE.
SIXTH AVENUE LINE—Continued.
NINTH AVENUE LINE.
STATIONS.
NINTH
AVENUE
EIGHTH
SIXTH
CENTRAL PARK
THIRD
SECOND
AVENUE
BLACKWELL'S ISLAND
WARD'S ISLAND
Points of Interest and How to Reach them.
F. K. HAIN, General Manager.
CHAS. P. McFADDIN, General Ticket Agent.

Not only routes and fare information, but also directions to many public institutions were included in this early map of Manhattan's elevated railway system. New York City's population grew from 1 million to 3.4 million between 1860 and 1900, and this map's "Points of Interest"—including hotels, clubs, theaters, opera houses, railroad stations, ferry-boat and steamship lines, German Hospital, Orphan Asylum, Foundling Asylum, Lunatic Asylum, Children's Aid Society, "Base Ball Grounds," St. Patrick's Cathedral, Tammany Hall, and the new Brooklyn Bridge (the world's first steel-wire suspension bridge)—suggests its burgeoning growth, teeming vitality, ethnic diversity, and extremes of wealth and poverty.

[*See* Business; Gilded Age; Immigration; Industrialization; New York City; Railroads; Urbanization.]

augurated president on 30 April 1789 on the balcony of City Hall, renamed Federal Hall, as New York City became the nation's first capital. Adding to the city's growing importance was the founding of the New York Stock Exchange in 1792 and Bellevue Hospital in 1794; the voyage of Robert Fulton's steamboat, the *Clermont,* to Albany in 1807; the adoption of the grid or Commissioners Plan in 1811; and the opening of Central Park in 1857. The population grew from sixty thousand in 1800 to nearly one million, almost half foreign-born, by 1860. Most immigrants in the 1840s were from Ireland, with German immigration rising sharply in the 1850s. But with growth came problems. Rising *crime and city-state competition led to the creation of a centralized state-controlled *police force in 1857. Outbreaks of *yellow fever and *cholera increased the role of city government in public-health matters. In 1834, after years of pressure to expand the elective process, New York held its first post-colonial popular mayoral election, won by Democrat Cornelius Lawrence.

During the *Civil War, most New Yorkers rallied to the Union cause. More than 400,000 city and state residents served, and 50,000 died. The bloody 1863 Civil War *draft riots were an aberration, not indicative of the city's patriotism. Following the war, the city continued its economic expansion and tradition of rough-and-tumble politics. In 1871, *The New York Times* allied with cartoonist Thomas Nast (1840–1902) and *Harper's Weekly,* all Republican supporters, to pillory William M. "Boss" *Tweed, a Democrat whose name quickly became synonymous with municipal corruption. Despite such attacks, greater New York was created in 1898 as the five boroughs—Manhattan, Brooklyn, Queens, the Bronx, and Staten Island—were incorporated into a single municipality.

By 1900, the city's population exceeded three million. Two-thirds were foreign born, with 300,000 immigrants from Germany, followed by Ireland with 275,000, Russia (180,000), and Italy (145,000). Jewish immigrants fleeing persecution in eastern Europe arrived in great numbers as well. *African Americans comprised 10 percent of the population. The *Statue of Liberty (1886) in New York harbor symbolized the city's role as a mecca for immigrants. Bridges linked Manhattan and the boroughs, including the *Brooklyn Bridge (1883), Manhattan Bridge (1909), and Queensborough Bridge (1909). Subway construction began in 1900. Steel enabled the growth of skyscrapers, including the Flatiron Building (1902), Woolworth Building (1913), and *Empire State Building (1931).

Harlem. The 1920s brought the *Harlem Renaissance, a cultural flowering centered in a district of New York City sometimes called "the capital of Black America." Bounded on the north by the Harlem River and on the south by Central Park, it was named Nieuw Haarlem by the seventeenth-century Dutch farmers who first settled here. Home to prominent colonial-era families, it later drew Irish squatters, middle-class German Jews who lived in spacious brownstones, and poor Eastern European Jews escaping the crowded Lower East Side. By 1917, Harlem's Jewish population stood at 80,000. African Americans from the South as well as Caribbean newcomers arrived as well, and by 1930, with more than 200,000 blacks, Harlem had become largely African American. In the 1920s, Harlem boasted not only a vibrant literary scene, but also *jazz and variety shows at venues like the Cotton Club, the Apollo Theater, and the Savoy Ballroom; the headquarters of the National *Urban League and the *National Association for the Advancement of Colored People; and a rich religious life ranging from storefront places of worship to the thriving Abyssinian Baptist Church (1923). Social problems associated with overcrowding, poor schools, racial discrimination, and lack of jobs worsened in the 1930s, and rioting erupted in 1935. As protests against racism and Harlem's economic plight increased, riots again broke out in 1943, 1964, and 1968.

The 1980s brought signs of community renewal—a growing middle- and professional class; new construction; political leaders, including New York's first black mayor, David Dinkins; and such highly regarded cultural institutions as the Dance Theatre of Harlem—but also continuing problems of joblessness and high school-dropout rates, compounded by drugs—especially crack cocaine—gangs; high out-of-wedlock birth rates; and single-parent households. Harlem also grew more ethnically diverse as the twentieth century progressed, including a growing African community and a large Hispanic population in "Spanish Harlem."

In the larger history of the city, meanwhile, the 1920s also brought Prohibition-era speakeasies and the rise of the city's favorite son, Alfred E. *Smith, to national prominence. The 1929 *stock market crash, reverberating from Wall Street, coupled with the resignation of Mayor James "Gentleman Jimmy" Walker amid charges of corruption, marked the end of an era. Fiorello *La Guardia, the "Little Flower," was elected mayor on a reform ticket in 1933. A new charter in 1936 increased the mayor's power and created a city planning commission.

The post–*World War II decades accelerated New York's rise to global economic and cultural dominance. In 1945 the newly formed *United Nations made the city its permanent home. Parks commissioner Robert Moses (1889–1981) razed entire neighborhoods to build parks, parkways, playgrounds, and public beaches, and inaugurated other monumental undertakings, including the 1964–1965 New York World's Fair. The completion of the World Trade Center in 1972 bore witness to New York's vitality as an international center not only of commerce and finance, but also publishing, theater, fashion, the arts, intellectual life, and *popular culture. But urban unrest and teachers' strikes in 1962 and 1967 exemplified both the city's financial problems and racial divisions. The public schools were decentralized, but the educational system remained troubled. The growing need for social services by the city's vast underclass, mostly African Americans and *Hispanic Americans, strained economic resources. As in the late nineteenth century, vast concentrations of wealth coexisted with grinding *poverty. Along with imposing and glittering districts, parts of the city resembled war zones, marked by abandoned buildings, joblessness, and drug-related crime and violence. Adding to the aura of decline, some large corporations moved their headquarters out of Manhattan.

The economic upsurge of the late 1980s and 1990s brought revitalization, however, marked by growing *tourism, rising office occupancy rates, a real-estate boom, and declining crime statistics. As newcomers continued to arrive, including aspiring young people from across America and immigrants from around the world, New York City remained a symbol of hope, glamour, and opportunity.

[*See also* Architecture: Public Architecture; Armory Show; Dutch Settlements in North America; German Americans; Glorious Revolution in America; Harlem Renaissance; Immigration; Irish Americans; Italian Americans; Judaism; Parks, Urban; Roman Catholicism; Stock Market; Urbanization; World's Fairs and Expositions; Zenger Trial.]

• Isaac N. P. Stokes, *Iconography of Manhattan Island,* 6 vols., 1915–1928. Ira Rosenwaike, *Population History of New York City,* 1972. Susan Lyman, *The Story of New York,* 1975. Edwin G. Burrows and Mike Wallace, *Gotham: A History of New York City to 1898,* 1998.

—Leo Hershkowitz

NEW YORK STOCK EXCHANGE. The largest of the country's organized securities exchanges. Tracing its origins to the 1792 Buttonwood Agreement among street brokers, the exchange developed from an outdoor market on Wall Street in lower Manhattan into the New York Stock and Exchange Board in 1817. The current name was adopted in 1863.

The exchange trades stocks that it lists, or registers. Trading takes place on the exchange at various official posts where markets are maintained by traders known as specialists. They buy and sell their assigned stocks from other floor brokers who represent themselves and the public. Specialists and other brokers purchase their seats on the exchange and are required to meet certain capital requirements in order to trade. From just a handful of stocks in its first decade, the exchange by the end of the twentieth century listed more than 2,900 different companies, both foreign and domestic. In terms of value represented, this made it the world's largest stock exchange.

After many smaller disasters, the exchange suffered its most serious decline in the *stock market crash of 1929. As a result of congressional investigations that followed, the exchange was subjected to federal regulation by the Securities Exchange Act of 1934. This act put all stock exchanges under the jurisdiction of the *Securities and Exchange Commission. Two 1975 developments affecting the New York Stock Exchange were the consolidation of the ticker tape reporting transactions into a national integrated system with other exchanges and the abolition of fixed commission rates in favor of negotiated rates.

[*See also* Banking and Finance; New York City; Stock Market.]

• Robert Sobel, *The Big Board: A History of the New York Stock Exchange,* 1975. Charles Geisst, *Wall Street: A History,* 1997.

—Charles Geisst

NIAGARA FALLS, 160-foot waterfall on the border of the United States and Canada, over which the Niagara River waters of Lake Erie flow into Lake Ontario. Niagara Falls was first seen by Europeans in the late seventeenth century. With the opening of the *Erie Canal in 1825, Niagara became America's most popular tourist destination. For the romantic "pilgrims" who visited Niagara before the *Civil War, it evoked the emotions of the sublime and symbolized the nation's grand destiny. Niagara's image as a national shrine was enhanced by the many artists who painted it, notably Frederick Church and his panoramic *Niagara* of 1857. Though often depicted in a pristine state, Niagara Falls became increasingly desecrated by shops, sideshows, and factories. In response, Church, Frederick Law *Olmsted, and other prominent citizens succeeded in 1883 in securing legislation to establish the New York State Niagara Falls Reservation, one of the first parks to protect scenery. Although the park only pushed back the surrounding commercial and industrial activity, it did restore naturalness and free access to the falls.

From the Civil War to the 1930s, Niagara Falls enjoyed a great vogue as a honeymoon destination. Niagara also attracted performers, such as the celebrated jumper Sam Patch, and daredevils who went over the falls in barrels. In 1895, Niagara became a major source of cheap *hydroelectric power, and at the end of the twentieth century about one-half of Niagara's water was diverted to drive turbines. Although no longer as important culturally as in the nineteenth century, Niagara continued to play a role in popular culture—as in the 1953 Marilyn *Monroe movie *Niagara* and the 1980 film *Superman II,* for example—and to epitomize America for many foreign tourists.

[*See also* Painting: To 1945; Romantic Movement; Tourism.]

• Elizabeth R. McKinsey, *Niagara Falls: Icon of the American Sublime,* 1985. John F. Sears, *Sacred Places: American Tourist Attractions in the Nineteenth Century,* 1989.

—John F. Sears

NIEBUHR, REINHOLD (1892–1971), theologian. The most influential American theologian of the twentieth century, Niebuhr spoke authoritatively about politics and culture as well as the Christian Gospel. Like Ralph Waldo *Emerson and William *James, he believed that religious vitality was ebbing in the churches and could be revived only by an energetic encounter with the wider world. Like Emerson and James, too, he developed his thinking in tension with secular currents of thought, but unlike them he was also a man of action. He was a gifted political journalist and a tireless political activist from the 1920s to the 1960s.

Born in Missouri to a German immigrant preacher and his second-generation German immigrant wife, Niebuhr was ordained at the age of twenty-one into his father's German Evangelical Synod of North America. But he sought a larger sphere, and soon departed for Yale Divinity School, where he received a master's degree in 1915. Yale deepened the liberal Protestant convictions he had inherited from his father: the critical study of the *Bible, the *Social Gospel, God as forgiving companion rather than irascible judge. As minister of a small middle-class German Evangelical Synod church in *Detroit (1915–1928), he turned it into a thriving liberal institution. By 1928, when he became a professor of ethics at Union Theological Seminary in *New York City, he had become, thanks to his masterful oratory and biting essays in the *Christian Century* magazine, a leading voice of liberal *Protestantism.

At Union, Niebuhr moved to the center of the national political and intellectual debate. His *Moral Man and Immoral Society* (1932) argued that Christians must engage the world of power politics, and resist evil with force, and even violence, rather than merely preach love and goodwill as the all-purpose solution to social conflict. His "realism" profoundly influenced Protestant opinion, which moved during the 1930s and 1940s toward support for organized labor at home and for military intervention against fascism abroad. A *Socialist party member in the 1930s (and twice a candidate for office), Niebuhr moved in the 1940s toward the political center, from which he lambasted both the communists and the business-dominated Republicans. His masterpiece, *The Nature and Destiny of Man* (1941–1943), laid a theological groundwork for the chastened *liberalism of the *Cold War Era: Human progress was still open-ended, since men and women were creative beings made in God's image, but they were also sinners who undermined their own achievements through pride and self-aggrandizement. Democratic, interest-group politics offered the right combination of freedom and restraint for beings so demonstrably divided against themselves. In this spirit, in 1947, he helped launch *Americans for Democratic Action to mobilize the noncommunist left. In the 1960s, however, he sharply criticized the Lyndon B. *Johnson administration's escalation of the *Vietnam War.

[*See also* Anticommunism; New Deal Era, The; Pacifism; Twenties, The.]

• Charles W. Kegley, ed., *Reinhold Niebuhr: His Religious, Social, and Political Thought,* rev. ed., 1984. Richard Wightman Fox, *Reinhold Niebuhr: A Biography,* 1985; reprint, 1996.

—Richard Wightman Fox

NIMITZ, CHESTER (1885–1966), officer in the U.S. Navy. Born in Fredericksburg, Texas, and a graduate of the U.S. Naval Academy, Nimitz commanded successively a gunboat, a destroyer, and a submarine division and made himself an authority on diesel engines. In *World War I, as engineering aide to the commander of the U.S. Atlantic Fleet Submarine Force, he served his last duty with machinery. Thereafter he was concerned mainly with people: selecting, instructing, commanding.

In a series of land and sea commands, Nimitz's achievements earned him such a favorable reputation that when the United States entered *World War II in 1941, President Franklin Delano *Roosevelt selected him to command the U.S. Pacific Fleet. After six months of ineffectual carrier air raids on Japanese bases and on Japan itself, Nimitz, commanding from his headquarters at Pearl Harbor, *Hawai'i, sent his three-carrier fleet out to a calculated location, and in the Battle of *Midway it defeated a more numerous Japanese fleet.

Nimitz next sent land-sea-air forces to oust the Japanese from their island strongholds on Guadalcanal and in the Aleutians. In late 1943 he launched a greatly enlarged Central Pacific

Fleet in a westward drive, which landed and supported troops in the Gilbert, Marshall, Mariana, and *Philippine Islands and reduced the Japanese fleet to impotence in the Battle of the Philippine Sea and the Battle of *Leyte Gulf. Nimitz's forces then headed north via the Ryukyu Islands.

After Japan's surrender in 1945, Nimitz was appointed chief of naval operations, a popular choice even though never in his long career had he been onboard a ship or plane in combat.

• Elmer Belmont Potter, *Nimitz*, 1976.

—E. B. Potter

NINETEENTH AMENDMENT. Ratified in 1920, the Nineteenth Amendment inscribed women's right to vote into the U.S. *Constitution. No other constitutional amendment required such a long, hard-fought struggle. The *woman suffrage movement, launched by Elizabeth Cady *Stanton at the 1848 women's rights convention in Seneca Falls, New York, was initially understood to involve a state-by-state process. After the *Civil War, in response to the constitutional amendments that granted citizenship to former slaves and established suffrage rights "regardless of race, color or previous condition of servitude," woman suffragists shifted their sights to the federal Constitution. A woman-suffrage amendment was introduced in 1878 by Senator Aaron Sargent of California, but for the next thirty-five years suffrage efforts focused on the state level.

In 1913, however, a new, more concerted drive for a federal amendment was initiated by Alice Paul, a charismatic young woman from Pennsylvania. Paul's followers, first known as the Congressional Union and then as the *National Woman's party, forthrightly challenged Congress and the president to support the amendment; they were soon joined by the *National American Woman Suffrage Association, a larger and more moderate group, under the leadership of Carrie Chapman *Catt. In 1918 (with President Woodrow *Wilson, praising women's contributions to the war effort, finally endorsing the cause), these combined forces won House passage of the amendment; eighteen months later the Senate, less amenable to public pressure, passed the measure. Ratification proved difficult because Democrats from the *South, where most blacks were excluded from the franchise, opposed an assertion of federal control over *suffrage. After sixteen months, however, the border state of Tennessee ratified the Nineteenth Amendment, bringing the seventy-two-year effort for woman suffrage to a successful conclusion.

[*See also* Anthony, Susan B.; Feminism; League of Women Voters; Progressive Era; Women's Rights Movements; World War I.]

• Christine A. Lunardi, *From Equal Suffrage to Equal Rights: Alice Paul and the National Woman's Party, 1910–1928*, 1986. Eleanor Flexner with Ellen Fitzpatrick, *Century of Struggle: The Woman's Rights Movement in the United States*, enlarged ed., 1996.

—Ellen C. DuBois

NIXON, RICHARD M. (1913–1994), thirty-seventh president of the United States. Born in Yorba Linda, *California, to Quaker (*Society of Friends) parents who had moved from the *Middle West, Richard Milhous Nixon excelled at Whittier College, a Quaker school. A scholarship student at Duke Law School, he graduated third in his class in 1937. Returning to Whittier, he married Catherine (Pat) Ryan in 1940; they had two daughters. After working in the wartime Office of Price Administration, Nixon obtained a naval commission in 1942 and served in the South Pacific during *World War II, rising to the rank of lieutenant commander.

Running for Congress as a Republican in 1946, he defeated five-term liberal Democrat Jerry Vorhees. In 1950 he won a U.S. Senate seat from California, defeating the equally liberal Helen Gahagan Douglas. From the first, Nixon generated controversy, as he accused his opponents of communist leanings. Such tactics earned him a reputation as a ruthless political polarizer who would do anything to win. In 1948 he proposed the Mundt-Nixon bill requiring communist organizations and individuals to register with the government. On the *House Committee on Un-American Activities, he effectively ended the career of Alger *Hiss by accusing him of communist connections and espionage in the 1930s. Although many scholars now believe Hiss guilty of the perjury charge for which he was convicted, some liberals never forgave Nixon for bringing down Hiss and using the case to promote his own career. He did not make *anticommunism a major theme after the Hiss case, however, and kept his distance from Senator Joseph *McCarthy.

Tapped as Dwight D. *Eisenhower's running mate in 1952, Nixon faced charges that wealthy friends had created a secret fund to further his career. In a nationwide *television broadcast, Nixon successfully defended himself and salvaged his place on the ticket. The speech is best remembered for Nixon's maudlin declaration that his daughters would keep their cocker spaniel "Checkers," a gift from a supporter.

During eight years as vice president, Nixon campaigned widely for Republican candidates. His reputation as the party's hatchet man related especially to his attacks on Adlai *Stevenson, the Democrats' presidential candidate in 1952 and 1956. He also, however, supported educational reform and *civil rights; honed his foreign-policy skills; and campaigned for moderate as well as conservative Republicans, broadening his base of party support. His popularity rose after his car was stoned during a 1958 visit to Venezuela and his 1959 "kitchen debate" with Soviet premier Nikita Khrushchev at a U.S. exhibition in Moscow. Although Eisenhower excluded Nixon from his inner circle, gave him few responsibilities, and occasionally humiliated him in public, Nixon upgraded the vice presidency to a more meaningful office than it had been before. Through Eisenhower's various medical crises in 1955–1957, Nixon displayed tact and restraint, presiding over numerous cabinet and *National Security Council meetings.

Nixon's party services and "centrist" image assured his presidential nomination in 1960, but his loss to John F. *Kennedy created bitternesses—and taught him lessons—he never forgot. While the press described Kennedy as a "youthful" candidate representing a new generation, Nixon was in reality only four years older. Nixon's more liberal record on social and foreign-policy issues was generally ignored in the media blitz surrounding the charismatic Kennedy, as were Kennedy's womanizing and medical problems. Finally, the one-on-one TV debates with Kennedy taught Nixon that the television tactics he had honed in the 1950s were outmoded. Nixon lost by 112,000 votes—the closest presidential election since 1884. To his credit, he did not challenge the results despite evidence of election fraud in Illinois and Texas.

Returning to private life, Nixon practiced law in New York and wrote a political memoir, *Six Crises* (1961). His defeat in the 1962 California gubernatorial race prompted his much-quoted remark to reporters that they would not "have Nixon to kick around anymore." He tirelessly campaigned for Republican candidates and played a centrist role, especially after the arch-conservative Barry *Goldwater's 1964 loss to Lyndon B. *Johnson.

Winning the 1968 Republican presidential nomination, Nixon faced a *Democratic party divided over the *Vietnam War, shaken by demonstrations at its *Chicago convention, and haplessly led by Hubert *Humphrey after Johnson's withdrawal. Appealing to a "silent majority" of northern blue-collar workers and southern whites, Nixon campaigned as a "law and order" candidate who would quell domestic protests and end the war. He won by 500,000 popular votes, garnering 301 electoral votes to Humphrey's 191 and George *Wallace's 46. He did well in the *South, Wallace's home turf.

Publically committing himself to "government reform such as this nation has not witnessed in half a century," Nixon focused on five areas of domestic policy: *welfare, the environment, some aspects of *civil rights, and executive-branch reorganization. He supported increased *Social Security benefits, expansion of the Job Corps, quotas to increase minority access to skilled employment, an innovative plan to replace welfare with a guaranteed annual income for the poor, and creation of the *Environmental Protection Agency (1970). On the economic front, he adopted various strategies—including, for a time, Keynesian deficit spending—to combat the inflation and budget deficits inherited from Johnson's efforts to wage the Vietnam War and fund his *Great Society programs without raising taxes. Underrated at the time, Nixon's domestic record appears more impressive in retrospect. Pursuing his "southern strategy," Nixon opposed court-ordered school busing and extension of the 1965 Voting Rights Act, urged a slowdown of southern school integration, and unsuccessfully nominated two southern conservatives to the *Supreme Court. (He also made four successful Supreme Court appointments: Warren Burger as chief justice, Harry Blackmun, Lewis Powell, and future chief justice William Rehnquist.)

In the global arena, Nixon and his national security adviser (and later secretary of state) Henry *Kissinger pursued better relations with America's *Cold War adversaries, the People's Republic of China and the Soviet Union. Nixon triumphantly visited China in February 1972, laying the groundwork for later diplomatic recognition, and that May in Moscow signed agreements with the Soviets to reduce the risk of military confrontations and to promote cooperation in *science, *technology, health, environmental matters, and space exploration. The two powers also signed the Anti-Ballistic Missile Treaty, an interim Strategic Arms Limitation Treaty (SALT I), and a document entitled "Basic Principles of U.S.-Soviet Relations." This brief détente anticipated the Cold War's eventual end, but in the short run it foundered in the later 1970s and early 1980s.

A central goal of these initiatives was to improve chances for a favorable Vietnam settlement, but this effort failed. Despite Nixon's strategy of "Vietnamization" and protracted U.S.-North Vietnamese negotiations, the conflict dragged on until 1975, finally ending in a North Vietnamese victory. Elsewhere, the Nixon-Kissinger foreign policy involved geopolitical considerations largely unrelated to economic realities or the interests of the peoples involved. Among other instances, these priorities emerged in the United States' tilt toward Pakistan in its 1971 war with India and in the clandestine use of U.S. power to overthrow the democratically elected leftist government of Salvadore Allende in Chile. In the Middle East, Kissinger's shuttle diplomacy produced more show than substance. Overall, Nixon's foreign-policy record was mixed at best, despite his unquestioned expertise in this area.

Though hardly photogenic, Nixon employed television in innovative and widely imitated ways, including effective use of prime-time broadcasts, interviews on morning talk shows, speaking live with orbiting astronauts, and assuring satellite coverage of his foreign policy triumphs. These public-relations tactics, coupled with his domestic record and foreign-policy achievements, all but assured Nixon's reelection in 1972. By nominating the antiwar candidate George McGovern, the badly divided Democrats turned the election into a rout. Nixon amassed a plurality of almost 18 million popular votes, and won 520 electoral votes to McGovern's 17.

Nixon's second term proved disastrous. In 1973 came Vice President Spiro Agnew's resignation amid charges of tax evasion and accepting bribes, to be replaced by Congressman Gerald *Ford. Far more serious was the *Watergate crisis, involving a foiled break-in at the Democratic National Committee headquarters on 17 June 1972 by burglars linked to the White House, and the administration's subsequent cover-up of its involvement, including payoffs to the arrested burglars. The break-in was conducted by a secret White House unit, dubbed "the Plumbers," created in 1971 to plug leaks and to harrass persons on Nixon's "enemies list." As the media, federal judge John Sirica, Special Prosecutor Leon Jaworski, a special Senate committee, and eventually the House Judiciary Committee conducted investigations, the pressure on Nixon built steadily in 1973–1974, especially after the release of White House tapes with incriminating Oval Office conversations. On 9 August 1974, with impeachment looming, Nixon resigned—the only president ever to do so. The Watergate scandal ultimately resulted in the conviction of twenty men, including not only those directly involved in the burglary, but also such top administration figures as Nixon advisers John Ehrlichman and H. R. (Bob) Haldeman, presidential counsel John Dean, special assistant Charles Colson, and Attorney General John Mitchell. Nixon himself received a full pardon in September 1974 from President Ford. Phoenix-like, ex-president Nixon worked to rehabilitate his reputation, by publishing books on foreign policy, for example. As a younger generation arose that did not remember Watergate, the scandal's centrality somewhat faded. (It had never loomed as large abroad as it did domestically.)

Richard Nixon remains one of the most enigmatic and controversial politicians of the post–World War II era. Highly intelligent and a master of politics, he was also consumed by gnawing grievances and a preoccupation with shadowy "enemies." Nevertheless, he ranks without question as one of the most important presidents of the twentieth century.

[*See also* Federal Government, Executive Branch: The Presidency; Foreign Relations; Keynesianism; Nuclear Arms Control Treaties; Republican Party; Sixties, The.]

• Garry Wills, *Nixon Agonistes: The Crisis of a Self-Made Man*, 1970. Daniel Patrick Moynihan, *The Politics of a Guaranteed Income: The Nixon Administration and the Family Assistance Plan*, 1973. Richard Nixon, *RN: The Memoirs of Richard Nixon*, 1978. James Reichley, *Conservatives in an Age of Change: The Nixon and Ford Administrations*, 1981. Robert S. Litwack, *Détente and the Nixon Doctrine*, 1984. Stephen E. Ambrose, *Nixon: The Triumph of a Politician*, 1987. Herbert Parmet, *Richard Nixon and His America*, 1990. Joan Hoff, *Nixon Reconsidered*, 1994. Stanley Kutler, *Abuse of Power*, 1997.

—Joan Hoff

NORMANDY INVASION. *See* D-Day.

NORTH AMERICAN FREE TRADE AGREEMENT (NAFTA). In June 1991, the administration of President George *Bush opened talks designed to achieve a trilateral trade agreement among the United States, Canada, and Mexico. The largely secret negotiations came to fruition in December 1992 with the signing of a two-thousand-page agreement by President Bush, Prime Minister Brian Mulroney of Canada, and President Carlos Salinas of Mexico. President Bill *Clinton in 1993, after initiating and signing side agreements addressing concerns raised by labor and environmental groups, lobbied vigorously for ratification of NAFTA. Congress approved the agreement in 1993, and it went into effect in 1994.

Under the terms of NAFTA, *tariffs among the three countries were to be gradually phased out. The detailed agreements also reduced nontariff barriers to trade and investment by outlawing preferential treatment of government monopolies and by exempting businesses from many forms of local, state, and national regulation. Disputes arising under NAFTA are referred to a supranational panel of trade officials and lawyers whose hearings are secret.

Some of the largest corporations in Canada, Mexico, and the United States lobbied intensively on behalf of NAFTA, arguing that the treaty would bring widespread prosperity by creating the world's largest free trade bloc. Opposition surfaced in all three countries, however, among those who feared that the agreement would cost jobs and undermine labor organizations, environmental protections, small-scale agriculture, and public-sector service and transportation programs.

[*See also* Agriculture: Since 1920; Environmentalism; Foreign Relations: U.S. Relations with Canada; Foreign Relations: U.S. Relations with Latin America; Foreign Trade, U.S.; Global Economy, America and the.]

• Noam Chomsky, *World Orders Old and New*, 1994. Esmail Hossein-Zadeh, "NAFTA and Sovereignty," *Science and Society* 61 (Summer 1997): 243–254. United States International Trade Commission, *The Impact of the North American Free Trade Agreement on the U.S. Economy and Industries: A Three-Year Review*, 1997.

—Elizabeth McKillen

NORTH ATLANTIC TREATY ORGANIZATION. On 4 April 1949, the United States signed a treaty of alliance with eleven Western European nations, thereby creating the North Atlantic Treaty Organization (NATO) and ending a long tradition of nonentanglement in Europe's political and military affairs. Under Article 5 of the treaty, the United States promised to help defend western Europe in the event of an invasion. Underlying this momentous reversal was U.S. recognition that its disengagement from Europe had helped bring on two world wars in the twentieth century. Even more central to America's change of policy were the new threat posed to the West by the expansion of Soviet communism and the opportunity to promote western Europe's political and economic integration.

The outbreak of the *Korean War in 1950 spurred NATO's transformation from an abstract U.S. commitment to western Europe's defense into an actual military organization. A divided Germany, like a divided Korea, Western leaders feared, might invite Soviet aggression. To forestall an attack from the Soviet Union or its satellites, NATO was expanded to include Greece and Turkey in 1952 and West Germany in 1955. (In response, the Soviet Union in 1955 set up its own military alliance, the Warsaw Pact.) NATO's military character, under U.S. leadership, dominated the alliance's early years. Beginning with General Dwight D. *Eisenhower in 1950, Americans served as the military commanders of NATO, while European statesmen held the lesser post of secretary-general of the alliance's bureaucracy. Europe's dependence on U.S. military power inhibited, but did not conceal, its resentment of this U.S. dominance.

As a revived and confident Europe moved toward integration, America's leadership of NATO faced growing challenges. Such challenges increased after the launching of the Soviet space satellite *Sputnik* in 1957, making America vulnerable to an intercontinental missile attack; coupled with America's preoccupation with Cuba and Vietnam in the 1960s, the developments raised doubts about the reliability of the U.S. nuclear umbrella and about America's commitment to Europe. The result was France's departure from the NATO organization in 1966 (although not from the military alliance) and the smaller allies' calls for détente with, as well as defense against, the Soviet Union. Despite rising tensions, however, the allies' recognition of NATO's military importance held the alliance intact.

As fear of the Soviets receded in the 1970s, the United States and its NATO allies achieved a détente of their own. A dual-track initiative in 1979, envisioning both defense and détente, led to negotiations in the 1980s that de-escalated the military contest with the Warsaw Pact. NATO's solidarity, coupled with Soviet economic difficulties, most scholars agree, brought about the unexpected implosion of the Soviet Union in 1991, the collapse of the Warsaw Pact, and the end of the *Cold War. The 1990s found the alliance focusing on crisis management on its periphery—particularly in Bosnia—and on expansion eastward through the admission of Poland, Hungary, and the Czech Republic, as NATO redefined its role in the *post–Cold War Era.

[*See also* Anticommunism; Containment; Foreign Relations: U.S. Relations with Europe; Internationalism; Isolationism; Marshall Plan; Nuclear Strategy; Vietnam War.]

• Lawrence S. Kaplan, *NATO and the United States: The Enduring Alliance*, 1994. Sean Kay, *NATO and the Future of European Security*, 1998.

—Lawrence S. Kaplan

***NORTHERN SECURITIES* CASE** (1904), landmark antitrust case. In 1901 three powerful business leaders, J. Pierpont *Morgan, James. J. *Hill, and E. H. *Harriman, decided to cooperate rather than compete, forming the Northern Securities holding company, which held the stock of their rival railroad interests in the Northwest. Their action was part of a great wave of corporate mergers that began in 1895 after the *Supreme Court ruled that the E. C. Knight Company, a holding company that monopolized U.S. sugar production, did not violate the Sherman Antitrust Act of 1890.

By 1900 state and federal courts had found a variety of monopolistic practices illegal under the Sherman Act and state laws. Yet no holding company was successfully prosecuted until the Theodore *Roosevelt administration brought an antitrust action against the Northern Securities Company in 1903. The trial court upheld the government's contention that the creation of the Northern Securities Company violated the Sherman Act. Upon appeal the following year, the Supreme Court upheld this ruling by a 5–4 vote. The majority, led by John Marshall *Harlan, ruled that the holding company's intent to eliminate competition was illegal. The four dissenters, led by Oliver Wendell *Holmes Jr. and Edward D. White, argued that a more flexible standard of reasonableness should have been applied to sustain the combination.

The decision ended the great wave of mergers. Federal officials, some business leaders, their lawyers, and members of the Supreme Court nonetheless concluded that in the future a "rule of reason" should govern merger cases. The Court adopted this doctrine in its *Standard Oil* and *American Tobacco* opinions of 1911. That same year, however, the Court reaffirmed that many monopolistic practices by companies working in collusion were illegal. These remained the prevailing doctrines of American antitrust law thereafter, encouraging an economic order in which both big and small business could prosper.

[*See also* Antitrust Legislation; Business; Capitalism; Economic Regulation; Progressive Era; Railroads.]

• Naomi R. Lamoreaux, *The Great Merger Movement in American Business, 1895–1904*, 1985. Martin J. Sklar, *The Corporate Reconstruction of American Capitalism, 1890–1916: The Market, The Law, and Politics*, 1988.

—Tony A. Freyer

NORTHWEST ORDINANCE (1787), a measure adopted by the *Continental Congress, acting under the *Articles of Confederation, to provide an orderly system of government leading to statehood for the territory north and west of the Ohio River. In 1789, after ratification of the *Constitution, Congress reenacted the ordinance with minor modifications.

When the *Revolutionary War began, seven states claimed lands in the Transappalachian west on the basis of their colonial charters or treaties with Native Americans. As the war grew more protracted and costly, these states faced growing pressure to cede the lands to Congress to provide funds (through land sales) to pay war debts and soldiers' pensions. By 1786, Congress controlled most of the Ohio territory.

Congress faced three problems: governing the region, selling the land, and dealing with the numerous Native American inhabitants of the region. Congress was committed to establishing republican governments in the territory and to the formation of states that would join the union on an equal basis with the existing states. Some in Congress also feared that unruly westerners might try to form states independent of the nascent United States. Addressing these concerns, a committee chaired by Thomas *Jefferson produced a general statement of principles (often called the "Ordinance of 1784") that recommended moving the western territory toward statehood in stages of increasing self-government.

Congress addressed the land-sale issue in the Ordinance of 1785. It directed that land be surveyed in six-mile-square townships, each containing thirty-six one-mile-square (640 acre) "sections" to be auctioned off for a dollar an acre. One section in each township would be set aside to support education. Most settlers, unable to afford the $640 minimum price, bought farms from land companies and speculators. With land now for sale, Manasseh Cutler, an agent for the Ohio Company (a group of speculators), and others pressured Congress to provide a more specific plan of governance.

The 1787 Ordinance set forth this plan. It called for the eventual establishment of three to five states in the region. Congress would initially appoint a governor and other officials for each future state. When the free adult male population reached five thousand, an elected assembly and an appointed legislative council would jointly elect a nonvoting delegate to Congress. When the territory's population reached sixty thousand free inhabitants, the residents could frame a constitution and apply for statehood. The ordinance also included a bill of rights, a pledge that Indian lands would not be taken without Indian consent, encouragement for the development of schools, and a prohibition on *slavery. (In fact, slavery persisted in the region, becoming a political issue in Indiana and Illinois territories.)

Early settlement clustered along the Ohio River. Native American groups resisted further incursions, encouraged by the British, who retained troops and fur-trading posts in the region. By 1789, white settlement on lands of the Shawnee, Miami, and other Indian groups led to war. In 1795, an army led by Anthony Wayne (1745–1796) defeated the Algonquian-speaking peoples of the region at the Battle of Fallen Timbers, forcing them in the Treaty of Greenville to surrender their land claims north of the Ohio. Meanwhile the British agreed, in *Jay's Treaty, to remove their troops. As settlers poured in, Ohio became a state in 1803, Indiana in 1816, Illinois in 1818, Michigan in 1837, and Wisconsin in 1848.

The Northwest Ordinance left an ambiguous legacy. It established the principle that with territorial expansion would come republican government, while simultaneously reflecting an assumption that Native Americans would make way for new settlers. Though the ordinance prohibited slavery, its persistence in the region underscored Abraham *Lincoln's claim, in the *Lincoln-Douglas debates, that "not only law, but the enforcement of law" was necessary to prevent slavery's expansion.

[*See also* Education: The Public School Movement; Fur Trade; Indian History and Culture: From 1500 to 1800; Indian Wars; Land Policy, Federal; Revolution and Constitution, Era of.]

• Peter S. Onuf, *Statehood and Union: A History of the Northwest Ordinance,* 1987. Frederick D. Williams, ed., *The Northwest Ordinance: Essays on Its Formation, Provisions, and Legacy,* 1989.

—Paul G. E. Clemens

NOYES, JOHN HUMPHREY (1811–1886), religious reformer, founder of the Oneida Community. Born to a prominent family in Brattleboro, Vermont, Noyes attended theological seminaries at Andover and Yale. In his early twenties he developed heretical "perfectionist" religious beliefs that eventually led him to advocate a form of tightly regulated "free love." From 1834 to 1879, he propagated his ideas through self-published newspapers. After returning home to Putney, Vermont, in 1836, he began to form a small community, which in 1845 embraced the communal ownership of property. The community's attempt to institute a form of group marriage in 1846 led to its expulsion from Putney in 1847 and its reestablishment at Oneida, New York, in 1848.

At Oneida, community members, numbering some two hundred adults, gradually established a system of "complex marriage." Considering themselves married to each other in an enlarged family, men and women exchanged sexual partners frequently. Exclusive romantic attachments were broken up as threats to group stability. Members lived, ate, and worked together, practiced communal child rearing, and held most property in common. Although less sex-role stereotyping occurred at Oneida than in comparable groups, tight control was maintained by group-criticism sessions, *birth control by *coitus reservatus,* and an informal status hierarchy dominated by Noyes and his closest male and female associates. Beset by internal dissent and external opposition, the community discontinued complex marriage in 1879 and formally dissolved in 1881. Noyes spent his final years in exile in Canada.

John Humphrey Noyes was a serious religious reformer and an incisive social critic, but scholars and popular writers have been most fascinated by his unorthodox sexual ideas and practices, which have impressed some as prototypes for a more liberated future.

[*See also* Antebellum Era; Protestantism; Religion; Sexual Morality and Sex Reform; Shakerism; Utopian and Communitarian Movements.]

• Robert Allerton Parker, *A Yankee Saint: John Humphrey Noyes and the Oneida Community,* 1935. Maren Lockwood Carden, *Oneida: Utopian Community to Modern Corporation,* 1969, reprint 1998. Spencer Klaw, *Without Sin: The Life and Death of the Oneida Community,* 1993.

—Lawrence Foster

NUCLEAR ARMS CONTROL TREATIES. Efforts to control *nuclear weapons began in the first session of the *United Nations General Assembly in 1946, when U.S. delegate Bernard *Baruch and Soviet delegate Andrei Gromyko put forward high-profile plans. The Baruch Plan sought international verification prior to international control, while the Gromyko Plan called for nuclear disarmament before agreement on verification procedures. The *Cold War's onset produced an impasse, and in 1949 the Soviet Union tested its atomic bomb.

The first nuclear-weapons control agreement, the Partial Test Ban Treaty (PTBT), signed by the United States, the Soviet Union, and Great Britain in 1963, reflected pervasive public fears of radioactive fallout from nuclear testing. It prohibited nuclear testing in the atmosphere, the oceans, and outer space, but permitted continued underground testing.

The Nuclear Non-Proliferation Treaty (NPT), put forward in 1968 by the United States, Great Britain, and the Soviet Union, went into effect in 1970. Nonnuclear states that signed this treaty pledged not to acquire or develop nuclear weapons. The nuclear-weapons states, for their part, promised not to assist other nations with nuclear-weapons development and, under Article VI, to "pursue negotiations in good faith" on timely measures to end the nuclear arms race and achieve nuclear disarmament. The treaty supported nuclear-energy projects for peaceful purposes and promised developing nations assistance with such projects. It also called for an extension conference in twenty-five years. Other treaties prohibited nuclear weapons in specific geographic areas: the Antarctic Treaty (1959), the Outer Space Treaty (1967), the Latin American Nuclear-Free Zone Treaty (1968), the Seabed Arms Control Treaty (1972), the South Pacific Nuclear-Free Zone Treaty (1986), the Southeast Asia Nuclear-Free Zone Treaty (1996), and the African Nuclear-Free Zone Treaty (1996).

The 1972 Anti-Ballistic Missile (ABM) Treaty limited U.S. and Soviet antimissile defenses to two sites: each nation's capital and one other site (the level was reduced in 1974 to one site in each nation). Based on deterrence theory, this treaty sought to prevent a defensive arms race that would in turn spur a further offensive build up. President Ronald *Reagan's 1983 *Strategic Defense Initiative was criticized for undermining the ABM Treaty. In 1997, reflecting post–Cold War fears of nuclear threats from nations such as North Korea and Iraq, the ABM Treaty was clarified in a joint U.S.–Russian statement to allow development of shorter-range defensive systems.

The 1972 Strategic Arms Limitation Treaty (SALT I) limited for five years the superpowers' testing and deployment of nuclear-weapons delivery systems. The next stage, SALT II, further limiting offensive nuclear weapons, was signed by the United States and the Soviet Union in 1979, but withdrawn from Senate ratification proceedings by President Jimmy *Carter after the Soviets invaded Afghanistan.

As the Cold War wound down, treaty negotiations continued. The 1988 Intermediate Nuclear Forces (INF) Treaty eliminated an entire class of intermediate and short-range nuclear weapons from Europe. The 1991 Strategic Arms Reduction Treaty (START I) called for phased reductions of some 30 percent in each sides' offensive nuclear arsenal. The break up of the Soviet Union, leaving nuclear weapons in newly independent Ukraine, Kazakhstan, and Belarus, delayed implementation of START I until 1994. Under START II (1993, revised 1997), the United States and Russia agreed to cut their long-range nuclear-weapons levels by two-thirds and to disable and dismantle specified launching systems by 2007. The Southeast Asia Nuclear-Free Zone Treaty (1995) and the African Nuclear-Free Zone Treaty (1996), combined with earlier regional treaties, made the Southern Hemisphere a de facto nuclear weapons-free zone.

At the 1995 NPT Review and Extension Conference, the nuclear-weapons states argued for the treaty's indefinite extension. Some non nuclear-weapons nations, however, opposed this, since, in their view, the nuclear-weapons states had not fulfilled their Article VI pledge of good-faith negotiations on nuclear disarmament. The nuclear-weapons states prevailed, and the treaty was extended indefinitely. The nonnuclear-weapons states did, however, succeed in adding a nonbinding pledge by all signatories to work for a comprehensive nuclear test ban and a treaty banning production of fissile material for nuclear weapons and calling for "a determined pursuit by the nuclear-weapons States" of the reduction and ultimate elimination of all nuclear weapons. The NPT's continued effectiveness clearly depended upon the willingness of the nuclear-weapons states to fulfill their treaty commitments to work seriously for the total elimination of nuclear weapons. If the non nuclear-weapons states concluded that these promises were not being kept, and exercised their right to withdraw from the NPT, nuclear arms control would suffer a major setback.

In 1996, a Comprehensive Test Ban Treaty was opened for signatures, with the requirement that its implementation required ratification by all forty-four states with a nuclear capacity. As of Spring 2000, 155 nations had ratified it, including more than half of the states with nuclear capacity. Among the nuclear-weapons states, Great Britain, France, and Russia had ratified, while the United States, China, India, Pakistan, and Israel had not.

[*See also* Acheson, Dean; Antinuclear Protest Movements; Hiroshima and Nagasaki, Atomic Bombing of; Limited Nuclear Test Ban Treaty; Manhattan Project; Nuclear Power; Nuclear Strategy; Post–Cold War Era; Teller, Edward.]

• *Arms Control and Disarmament Agreements*, 1982. Richard Dean Burns, ed., *Encyclopedia of Arms Control and Disarmament*, 3 vols., 1993. Ved Nanda and David Krieger, *Nuclear Weapons and the World Court*, 1998. Robert D. Green, *Fast Track to Zero Nuclear Weapons*, rev. ed., 1999.

—David Krieger

NUCLEAR POWER. In the aftermath of *World War II and the beginning of the widely hailed "Atomic Age," a plethora of books and articles suggested that the dangers of atomic weapons would be offset, at least partially, by the potential peaceful benefits of nuclear technology. Most of the projected applications, such as atomic automobiles and small reactors to heat and cool individual homes, were hopelessly fanciful. Proposals for building reactors to generate electricity in central power stations were more realistic, but progress was slow, especially with the Harry S. *Truman administration's focus on the military uses of atomic energy.

In 1954, Congress passed a law intended to speed nuclear-power development. The 1954 Atomic Energy Act made possible for the first time the wide commercial use of atomic energy by ending the government's monopoly of the *technology. It assigned the *Atomic Energy Commission (AEC) responsibility for both promoting nuclear power and regulating its safety. To the frustration of the AEC and the congressional Joint Committee on Atomic Energy, many utilities refrained from making a major commitment to nuclear power because of the abundance of conventional fuels and because of economic uncertainties and unresolved safety questions about the technology.

Beginning in the mid-1960s, however, nuclear-power development experienced a sudden and unanticipated boom. This came about for several reasons, including indications that large nuclear plants could compete economically with coal, the rise of interconnected electrical grids that encouraged the construction of large plants, and intensifying concern about air pollution from fossil-fuel units. The nuclear boom not only produced a rapid growth in the number of nuclear plants but also in the size of individual plants, which in less than a decade grew from small demonstration facilities to behemoths.

The expansion of the nuclear industry took place at virtually the same time as the development of *environmentalism as a potent political force. By the early 1970s, nuclear power had become a leading target of environmental activism and the subject of a highly visible and increasingly strident debate. Critics claimed that the technology was neither safe nor necessary; supporters argued that it was both safe and essential for the nation's energy future. At the center of the controversy were the unresolved issues of the likelihood and consequences of a major reactor accident and the effects of exposure to low levels of radiation. As the debate continued, public uneasiness about the risks of nuclear power increased substantially, and by the end of the 1970s orders for new plants has slowed dramatically. The slump in the industry resulted more from inflation and reduced demand for electricity than antinuclear activism, but the complaints of nuclear opponents strongly influenced public attitudes.

The debate over nuclear power intensified after the most serious accident in a U.S. nuclear power plant occurred at the *Three Mile Island station near Harrisburg, Pennsylvania, in March 1979. The accident's severity was caused by mechanical failures and human error, and although only small amounts of radiation were released, the political fallout was heavy. The accident undermined the credibility of the *Nuclear Regulatory Commission (NRC) and the nuclear industry while enhancing that of antinuclear critics.

After the shock of Three Mile Island, the NRC and the nuclear industry focused on a series of issues that had commanded only limited interest before the accident. These were intended to reduce the likelihood of another major accident, and, if one did occur, to enhance the ability of the NRC, the utility, and the public to cope with it. At the direction of the NRC, power companies improved plants that were operating or under construction. After a moratorium of more than one year, the NRC resumed issuing operating licenses for completed nuclear units in August 1980. By 1989, it had granted full-power licenses to more than forty reactors, most of which had been under construction since the mid-1970s. No new nuclear-power reactors were ordered after 1978, and many earlier orders were canceled.

In 2000, 103 nuclear-power plants were operating in the United States, providing about 20 percent of the nation's generating capacity. By that time, the debate over nuclear power had faded as a national issue, though it continued to trigger heated arguments in many local areas where plants were located.

[*See also* Antinuclear Protest Movements; Electrical Industry; Electricity and Electrification; Hydroelectric Power; Nuclear Weapons.]

• George T. Mazuzan and J. Samuel Walker, *Controlling the Atom: The Beginnings of Nuclear Regulation, 1946–1962,* 1984. Joseph G. Morone and Edward J. Woodhouse, *The Demise of Nuclear Energy?,* 1989. Brian Balogh, *Chain Reaction: Expert Debate and Public Participation in American Commercial Nuclear Power, 1945–1975,* 1991. J. Samuel Walker, *Containing the Atom: Nuclear Regulation in a Changing Environment, 1963–1971,* 1992. Joseph V. Rees, *Hostages of Each Other: The Transformation of Nuclear Safety since Three Mile Island,* 1994.

—J. Samuel Walker

NUCLEAR REGULATORY COMMISSION. The Nuclear Regulatory Commission (NRC) was created by the Energy Reorganization Act of 1974 to assume the regulatory duties of the *Atomic Energy Commission (AEC), which the law abolished. The AEC had become the target of sharp criticism in the public debate over the safety of commercial *nuclear power, partly because it had a statutory mandate both to regulate and to promote the nuclear industry. The NRC's responsibilities were limited to regulating the safety of nuclear power and other civilian applications of nuclear energy.

The NRC, headed by five commissioners appointed by the president of United States, began operations in January 1975. Most of its staff members were holdovers from the AEC, but the new agency hoped to dispel the widespread public suspicion of the AEC by demonstrating its toughness as a regulator. This proved difficult, if not impossible. As the public debate over nuclear-power safety raged on, former critics of the AEC were not inclined to regard the NRC more charitably. The NRC's efforts to overcome these suspicions were hampered by a serious fire at an Alabama nuclear-power plant in 1975, highly publicized allegations that the NRC's radiation-protection regulations and reactor-safety requirements were too lax, and growing concern about *nuclear weapons proliferation.

In March 1979, the worst accident in the history of commercial nuclear power in the United States occurred at Unit 2 of the *Three Mile Island plant near Harrisburg, Pennsylvania. A series of mechanical failures and human errors uncovered the core of the reactor and melted about half of it. The plant suffered irreparable damage, and the credibility of the nuclear industry and the NRC fared almost as badly. Although very little radiation escaped into the environment, the accident intensified doubts about nuclear-power safety and seriously undermined public support for the technology.

In the aftermath of Three Mile Island, the NRC devoted increased attention to a number of issues that the accident highlighted. These included ways in which a series of minor failures could lead to a major accident, the need for improved operator training, better means to assess the probability of reactor accidents, and upgraded emergency preparedness and planning. In the absence of orders for new plants, the agency allocated more of its resources to regulating the safety of existing plants, setting standards for the decommissioning of closed plants, and evaluating the complex and politically sensitive issue of the disposal of radioactive waste materials.

[*See also* Antinuclear Protest Movements; Environmentalism; Federal Government, Executive Branch: Other Departments (Department of Energy).]

• David Okrent, *Nuclear Reactor Safety: On the History of the Regulatory Process,* 1981. J. Samuel Walker, *A Short History of Nuclear Regulation, 1946–1990,* 1993.

—J. Samuel Walker

NUCLEAR STRATEGY. Until 1945, Americans could assume that any wars they fought would not be fundamentally ruinous to their society. The nuclear era challenged that assumption not only because of the destructiveness of *nuclear weapons, but also because of the dangers associated with the *Cold War. For many years, U.S. military planners, policy-oriented savants, and political leaders would ponder how nuclear war could or should be fought, how it could be prevented, and whether such outcomes as victory, survival, or defense were even conceivable. Nuclear strategy became an academic discipline as well as a preoccupation of civil servants, think-tank intellectuals, and military officers, most of whom worked in strict secrecy. The last were nuclear strategy's most significant practitioners and were strongly resistant to civilian pressures. Military secrecy, however, could not prevent ethical and political critiques by scholars and political activists.

During the Cold War and after, nuclear strategy's guiding concept was deterrence. U.S. presidents from Harry S. *Truman to George *Bush believed that only the threat of nuclear attack would dissuade an expansionist Soviet leadership from escalating political conflicts into military ones. If deterrence failed and war broke out, they further believed, nuclear war plans and capabilities were essential. To prepare for the worst case and to make deterrence credible as the Soviets developed their own nuclear capabilities, U.S. presidents approved massive investments in a nuclear weapons complex that between 1940 and 1997 totaled $5.4 trillion (in 1996 dollars).

The Truman and Eisenhower Years. Organizationally, the U.S. Air Force's Strategic Air Command (SAC), created in 1946, underpinned U.S. nuclear planning and operations. At first possessing only a handful of weapons and nuclear-capable bombers, SAC by 1950 had more than 250 nuclear-capable aircraft, and nearly 300 atomic weapons were in the U.S. stockpile.

Although President Truman had come to see atomic weapons as instruments of "terror" with no legitimate military purpose, in the Fall of 1948, with tensions over Berlin mounting, he authorized the military to incorporate atomic weapons into their planning. (The Air Force had unilaterally done so in 1947.) So that bombers could reach targets in the Soviet Union without refueling, Truman also approved deployments of nuclear bombers in the United Kingdom. U.S. capability to produce fissile material (highly enriched uranium and plutonium) expanded rapidly in 1949–1950, facilitating development of tremendously destructive thermonuclear weapons (H-bombs) and permitting the "overkill" nuclear posture that soon emerged. By 1966, the *Atomic Energy Commission (AEC) had produced 32,200 nuclear weapons, many in the multimegaton class.

Even before Dwight D. *Eisenhower's presidency, U.S. nuclear strategy was premised upon "massive retaliation." In the late 1940s, SAC and the *Joint Chiefs of Staff formulated atomic war plans involving a single massive bomber strike against Soviet targets. Viewing defense against strategic bombing attacks as hopeless, SAC commander in chief General Curtis LeMay (1906–1990) insisted that whoever took the offensive first would prevail and that a preemptive attack would be justified if a Soviet attack seemed likely. Although SAC's early plans focused on Soviet industrial and energy targets, after the Soviets tested an atomic bomb in 1949 military planners stressed "counterforce" targeting of Soviet nuclear installations and weapons delivery capabilities.

President Eisenhower and his advisers publicly embraced this concept of a massive nuclear strike, or "massive retaliation." Despite Eisenhower's private misgivings that thermonuclear weapons endangered civilization, he presided over multibillion-dollar investments in long-range delivery systems, both bombers and intercontinental ballistic missiles (ICBMs) as well as submarine-launched ballistic missiles (SLBMs). By the late 1950s, SAC had developed an "Air Power Battle Target System" comprising more than fourteen hundred Soviet targets, with most requiring "immediate attack" in the event of war: air bases, nuclear stockpiles and production facilities, and command and control systems. After a LeMay briefing on SAC's war plans, a naval officer commented that it would leave Russia "a smoking radiating ruin at the end of two hours."

The 1950s brought an outpouring of academic writing on nuclear strategy. Henry *Kissinger's *Nuclear Weapons and Foreign Policy* (1957), a study of "limited nuclear war," was best known, but other strategists, including Bernard Brodie, Herman Kahn, William W. Kaufmann, Thomas Schelling, and Albert Wohlstetter, at the air force-supported RAND Corporation, shared Kissinger's assumption that threatening massive use of nuclear weapons lacked credibility. Chief of Naval Operations Arleigh Burke argued for "finite deterrence" rather than massive retaliation. The nearly invulnerable Polaris submarine-launched missile, Burke asserted, in contrast to vulnerable ground-based missiles, which had to be used quickly, would allow presidents to respond in a measured way in a crisis.

At the close of his administration, Eisenhower presided over the formulation of a new war plan, the Single Integrated Operational Plan (SIOP). Produced by a SAC-directed Joint Strategic Target Planning Staff, the first SIOP—for fiscal year 1962—envisioned launching 3,200 nuclear weapons against 2,600 installations in the Soviet Union, China, and the satellite nations, with up to 425 million casualties. These details "frightened the devil" out of Eisenhower; nevertheless, he approved SIOP-62 in late 1960 as the basis of force deployments, warhead production, and alert postures.

From the late 1940s on, antinuclear protest movements in the United States and abroad stressed the threat to humane values and to civilization itself that nuclear weapons posed. Public opinion may have helped incline successive administrations toward a "late use" posture, with nuclear weapons justified only in the most extreme circumstances.

The Kennedy-Johnson and Nixon Years. The John F. *Kennedy administration took a key step toward facilitating "late use" by supporting "flexible response" strategies to provide nonnuclear deterrence options. Determined to make nuclear war more "controllable," Secretary of Defense Robert McNamara (1961–1968) expressed interest in William W. Kaufmann's counterforce "no cities" strategy designed to give civilian leaders supposedly more credible choices than mass slaughter of civilians. Although SAC planners considered "controlled response" impractical, they agreed that the SIOP should include a range of attack options as well as "withholds," such as taking China or satellite countries off the target list if they were not at war. Nevertheless, SIOP-63 still envisioned huge attacks reflecting a "massive retaliation" approach.

Although McNamara's public rhetoric initially emphasized "damage limiting" strategies that could reduce Soviet capabilities to strike American targets without devastating cities and killing millions, that approach proved controversial because of its first-strike implications. McNamara soon changed his deterrent focus to "assured destruction"—a capability to destroy Soviet industry and war-making capability even if the Soviets struck first. Nevertheless, operational planning continued to emphasize targeting of Soviet strategic sites, suggesting that nuclear planners anticipated making the first blow in any military confrontation before absorbing a Soviet attack. Satellite photography, improvements in missile accuracy, and the development of multiple independently targetable reentry vehicles (MIRVs) underscored America's growing capability to strike specific military targets such as missile bases.

New satellite warning systems enabled Richard M. *Nixon to insist more successfully than his predecessors that the military develop credible alternatives to the SIOP's all-out attacks. By 1974, studies ordered by Nixon and Kissinger, the national security adviser, led to a secret directive requiring distinct nuclear attack options—limited, selected, major, and regional—to enhance control over escalation and encourage early termination of a war. Recognizing that deterrence could fail (and tacitly confirming Soviet arguments that nuclear conflict could not be contained), Nixon in 1974 also requested plans to enhance the U.S. postwar position by destroying targets critical to Soviet recovery, which meant the indirect targeting of the civilian population. Moreover, military planners were instructed to set aside a strategic reserve of survivable forces, such as SLBMs, for "protection and coercion during and after major nuclear conflict." Within two years the SIOP provided the White House with a greater variety of nuclear options.

In part because of domestic political pressures to control a spiraling arms race, arms control loomed large in Nixon administration nuclear strategy. Pursuing détente with Moscow, Nixon and Kissinger sought limits on strategic forces while preserving strategic options in the event of conflict.

The Carter and Reagan Years. As détente collapsed in the late 1970s, President Jimmy *Carter approved significant changes in nuclear strategy in Presidential Directive 59 authorizing planning for a protracted nuclear war if deterrence failed. Carter also directed targeting of underground Soviet command posts on the grounds that a threat to the Soviet political and military leadership would strengthen deterrence. In 1981, President Ronald *Reagan reaffirmed Carter's concept of a prolonged nuclear war, adding that in such a conflict the United States "must prevail" and "force the Soviet Union to seek earliest termination of hostilities." In his 1983 *Strategic Defense Initiative, Reagan also proposed a protective shield against incoming missiles. The goal of "prevailing" remained national strategy until President Bill *Clinton rescinded it in 1997.

The Post–Cold War Era. The end of the Cold War produced significant changes in nuclear-force deployments and war plans, if not in strategy. Defense officials removed thousands of former Soviet-bloc targets from the SIOP and deactivated thousands of nuclear weapons. Budgetary trends suggested the impact of global political developments; in 1990, the nuclear-weapons budget stood at about $56 billion (in 1996 dollars); 1998, it was $35 billion. Nevertheless, President Clinton did not challenge the military's commitment to deterrence. Secrecy cloaked his administration's nuclear-policy deliberations, but nuclear-strategy and targeting guidelines approved by Clinton in 1997 apparently embodied long-standing concerns with Russian and Chinese strategic forces while also reflecting new worries about countries capable of developing weapons of mass destruction—nuclear, biological, or chemical—outside the constraints of international agreements. While Washington officials doubtless continued to hold "late-use" assumptions, veiled threats during confrontations with China in 1996 and Iraq in 1998 suggested continued reliance on nuclear weapons as instruments of policy.

That the Cold War had ended without a nuclear cataclysm led analysts and historians to explore the relationship between deterrence and the resolution of great power conflict. Some argued that U.S. nuclear strategy and forces had deterred superpower war and would remain indispensable for preventing future confrontations with other adversaries. Others looked at the massive expenditure on nuclear weapons and questioned whether deterrence needed to be so expensive. Moreover, some former military leaders, arguing that deterrence involved unacceptable risks, proposed renewed efforts to abolish nuclear weapons altogether.

[*See also* Civil Defense; Dulles, John Foster; Hiroshima and Nagasaki, Atomic Bombing of; Nuclear Arms Control Treaties; Post–Cold War Era.]

• David A. Rosenberg, "The Origins of Overkill: Nuclear Weapons and American Strategy, 1945–1960," *International Security* 7 (Spring 1983): 3–71. Desmond Ball and Jeffrey Richelson, eds., *Strategic Nuclear Targeting,* 1986. Scott Sagan, *Moving Targets: Nuclear Strategy and National*

Security, 1989. Desmond Ball and Robert C. Toth, "Revising the SIOP: Taking War-Fighting to Dangerous Extremes," *International Security* 14 (Spring 1990): 65–92. Fred Kaplan, *The Wizards of Armageddon,* 1991. Peter Feaver, *Guarding the Guardians: Civilian Control of Nuclear Weapons in the United States,* 1992. Bruce Blair, *The Logic of Accidental Nuclear War,* 1993. Lawrence Wittner, *The Struggle against the Bomb,* 2 vols., 1993–1997. Steven Schwartz, ed., *Atomic Audit: The Costs and Consequences of U.S. Nuclear Weapons since 1940,* 1998.

—William Burr

NUCLEAR TEST BAN TREATY. *See* Limited Nuclear Test Ban Treaty.

NUCLEAR WEAPONS. The history of nuclear weapons began well before the United States entered *World War II. Spurred by the German discovery of nuclear fission announced early in 1939, scientists at several universities had confirmed the feasibility of an unimaginably powerful chain-reacting bomb and suggested how to build one. In August 1939, the émigré physicist Albert *Einstein wrote a letter to President Franklin Delano *Roosevelt (drafted by another émigré physicist, Leo Szilard) reporting these developments; in response, Roosevelt authorized a modest research program. In the Summer of 1941, the federal Office of Scientific Research and Development transferred this small, scattered research program to the *Army Corps of Engineers. Taking charge of what became known as the *Manhattan Project, General Leslie R. Groves organized a crash program of expanded research, industrial production of fissionable materials, and bomb development.

Research was consolidated at the University of Chicago's new Metallurgical Laboratory, where Enrico *Fermi and his team achieved the first controlled nuclear reaction in December 1942. Chicago also developed the health and safety measures adopted throughout the project. Construction of production facilities for enriched uranium at Oak Ridge, Tennessee, and for plutonium at Hanford, Washington, proceeded in parallel. Groves picked J. Robert *Oppenheimer to direct bomb development in a new laboratory at Los Alamos, New Mexico, managed by the University of California. Buildings were still going up when scientists began work in April 1943.

By 1945, Oppenheimer's team had designed and built two fission bombs. One used enriched uranium in a gun-type assembly, a design deemed so reliable as to need no proof-testing before deployment. The other depended on the newly discovered fissionable element plutonium assembled by implosion, a much less certain technique that did demand testing. A secret test, code-named Trinity, took place at Alamogordo, New Mexico, on 16 July 1945, producing energy equivalent to 21,000 tons (21 kilotons) of high explosives.

On 6–9 August 1945, the United States launched its nuclear attack on Japan, dropping the uranium bomb on Hiroshima, the plutonium bomb on Nagasaki. At Bikini Atoll in July 1946, two more plutonium bombs furnished the firepower for a test series called Operation Crossroads. Part public spectacle intended to demonstrate America's nuclear might, part attempt to assess the effect of nuclear weapons on ships, Operation Crossroads became the Manhattan Project's last hurrah.

After heated congressional debate, the Atomic Energy Act of 1946 settled responsibility for developing future nuclear weapons on a civilian agency, the *Atomic Energy Commission (AEC). Civilian control of nuclear weapons remained intact when the AEC gave way in 1974 to the Energy Research and Development Administration, itself succeeded in 1977 by the Department of Energy. The Manhattan Project officially transferred its facilities to the AEC on 1 January 1947. Its remaining, specifically military components merged under the new Department of Defense as the Armed Forces Special Weapons Project (after two subsequent name changes, it eventually became the Defense Special Weapons Agency).

Of the major transferred facilities, only Los Alamos remained concerned primarily with nuclear-weapons research and development. Its former engineering division, however, had grown rapidly after moving to Albuquerque, New Mexico, in 1945. In 1949, it became the independent Sandia Laboratories, its management transferred from the University of California to Bell Laboratories. Its primary function was providing the engineering support to turn Los Alamos designs into working weapons.

With the *Cold War now well under way, nuclear-weapons development became a high national priority. The AEC inaugurated its nuclear-weapons testing program in the Spring of 1948 with Operation Sandstone. Supported by a joint army-navy task force, Los Alamos scientists tested three new fission-bomb designs at Enewetak Atoll. Part of the United Nations Trust Territory of the Marshall Islands administered by the United States, Enewetak officially became the Pacific Proving Ground, which expanded in 1951 to include Bikini. When the outbreak of the *Korean War threatened to disrupt schedules for Operation Greenhouse, the next Pacific test series, the AEC selected a continental test site in Nevada, first used for Operation Ranger in January 1951.

During the 1950s, annual testing alternated between Nevada, where operations were cheaper but restrictions greater, and the Marshall Islands, which served as the site for testing very-large-yield thermonuclear weapons. A Soviet atomic-bomb test in August 1949, decidedly sooner than many expected, had severely jolted American complacency. To meet the perceived challenge, Edward *Teller (among others) vigorously advocated accelerated development of the hydrogen bomb, the so-called Super, based on thermonuclear fusion, the main subject of Teller's research at wartime Los Alamos. Although no one yet knew how to design such a weapon, President Harry S. *Truman in January 1950 authorized a crash program.

The conceptual breakthrough came a year later, in February and March 1951, from a suggestion by the Los Alamos mathematician Stanislaw Ulam, which Teller improved and extended. A fission first stage (primary) would provide the energy to ignite the thermonuclear fuel (deuterium and tritium, the heavy isotopes of hydrogen) in a second stage (secondary). In essence, the Ulam-Teller idea was to couple the primary's energy to the secondary via X-rays. Hydrogen bombs (H-bombs) promised yields measured in megatons rather than the kilotons of fission bombs.

Although not based on the Ulam-Teller principle, the Greenhouse George test in May 1951 showed that a fission detonation could indeed ignite small amounts of thermonuclear fuel. Teller still deemed H-bomb progress too slow, however, and with air force support and backing from the cyclotron inventor and Nobelist Ernest O. *Lawrence, he successfully lobbied the AEC for a second nuclear-weapons laboratory. It opened in September 1952 as the Livermore branch of Lawrence's Berkeley Radiation Laboratory. Two decades later it became the independent Lawrence Livermore Laboratory, still under University of California management.

The new Livermore laboratory contributed little to early thermonuclear development, which remained largely a Los Alamos enterprise. The "Mike" test in Operation Ivy at Enewetak on 1 November 1952 demonstrated a full-scale thermonuclear detonation. Sixteen months later at Bikini, on 1 March 1954, the Bravo test of Operation Castle proved the design of an aircraft-deliverable H-bomb. Twice as powerful as predicted, Bravo caused heavy fallout that injured Marshall Islanders and Japanese fishermen a hundred miles and more from ground zero. Public outcry led to the test moratorium of 1958–1961, then to the Partial Nuclear Test Ban Treaty of 1963 that ended above-ground testing. Testing moved underground.

The peak of innovation in nuclear-weapons design, with Livermore now playing a major role, came in the period 1955–1965. Despite the three-year moratorium, at least two and as many as five new types of warheads entered the stockpile each year. Gravity bombs continued to improve; the introduction in 1955 of the long-range jet-powered B-52 gave the air force a bomber that could plausibly deliver them on strategic targets. Intercontinental ballistic missiles (ICBMs) benefited even more from the trend toward efficient, lighter warheads. The first air force squadron of Atlas ICBMs became operational in 1958, followed in 1960 by the navy's nuclear-powered, missile-equipped Polaris *submarine. Nuclear warheads for a variety of tactical missiles, artillery shells, torpedoes, and other munitions also proliferated.

By the mid-1960s, with nuclear-weapons development no longer posing major scientific challenges, the focus of innovation shifted from warheads to delivery systems. In 1967, the air force completed replacing its first-generation ICBMs, which used cryogenic propellants, with technically safer and more reliable missiles using solid (Minuteman) or hypergolic (Titan II) propellants. Protected in underground silos, the new missiles were ready for immediate launch. When the last Polaris submarine went to sea, also in 1967, the strategic triad of manned bombers, land-based missiles, and missile-armed submarines was in place.

The next missile generation, fitted with MIRVs (multiple independently targetable reentry vehicles), followed quickly. The air force deployed the first Minuteman IIIs in 1970, the navy its first Poseidon fleet ballistic missile systems in 1971. With land-based and sea-launched MIRV missiles, the United States acquired a reliable and essentially invulnerable means of responding to, and so deterring, nuclear attack.

Delivery systems and guidance, like warheads, continued to improve, but not radically. Although the air force's Peacekeeper missile (first deployed in 1986) and the navy's Trident system (1979) marked advances in accuracy over their predecessors, their basic character remained unchanged. Efforts to develop an antiballistic missile (ABM) system in the late 1960s and early 1970s produced only a modest deployment and were limited by the ABM Treaty of 1972. The much more ambitious *Strategic Defense Initiative (Star Wars), pursued in the 1980s, cost more and produced less.

The end of the Cold War brought reductions in nuclear stockpiles and, in 1992, a halt to U.S. nuclear-weapons testing. The United States retained its nuclear arsenal at reduced levels, however, and the Department of Energy instituted a laboratory science–based "stockpile stewardship" program to insure that aging weapons would remain both safe in storage and reliable if ever required.

[*See also* Antinuclear Protest Movement; Civil Defense; Federal Government, Executive Branch: Department of Defense; Federal Government, Executive Branch: Other Departments (Department of Energy); Hiroshima and Nagasaki, Atomic Bombings of; Nuclear Arms Control Treaties; Nuclear Strategy.]

• Richard Hewlett et al., *A History of the United States Atomic Energy Commission*, 3 vols., 1962–1989. Herbert F. York, *The Advisers: Oppenheimer, Teller, and the Superbomb*, 1976. Samuel Glasstone and Philip J. Dolan, eds., *The Effects of Atomic Weapons*, 3d ed., 1977. Richard Rhodes, *The Making of the Atomic Bomb*, 1986. Barton C. Hacker, *The Dragon's Tail: Radiation Safety in the Manhattan Project, 1942–1946*, 1988. Chuck Hansen, *U.S. Nuclear Weapons: the Secret History*, 1988. Donald Mackenzie, *Inventing Accuracy: A Historical Sociology of Nuclear Missile Guidance*, 1990. Norman Polmar and Timothy M. Laur, eds., *Strategic Air Command: People, Aircraft, Missiles*, 2d ed., 1990. Barton C. Hacker, *Elements of Controversy: The Atomic Energy Commission and Radiation Safety in Nuclear Weapons Testing, 1947–1974*, 1994.

—Barton C. Hacker

NULLIFICATION. The origins of the doctrine of nullification lie in the 1790s, when strict construction of the *Constitution, *states' rights, and hostility to national "consolidation" became the principles of the new Jeffersonian Republican party. When a Congress dominated by the *Federalist party passed the *Alien and Sedition Acts in 1798 to stifle domestic dissent in anticipation of war with France, Republican leader Thomas *Jefferson, in his draft of the Kentucky Resolutions, declared "nullification" the "natural right" of a state in response to a federal act deemed unconstitutional. James *Madison's complementary Virginia Resolutions asserted that states "have the right and are in duty bound to interpose for arresting the evil" of unconstitutional federal legislation. Exactly how a state could exercise the right of nullification remained unclear.

In response to high import duties adopted by Congress in 1828 and 1832, many citizens of South Carolina ardently embraced ideas of nullification and interposition. A high protective tariff, as distinct from low import duties levied to raise revenue, they had come to believe, represented an unconstitutional tax designed to enrich the industrializing Northeast at the expense of the agricultural *South. Moreover, South Carolina's leaders, governing the only state with a population more than half slave, feared that the enhanced federal authority encouraged by the protective tariff could eventually be turned against the institution of *slavery. John C. *Calhoun, the foremost exponent of nullification theory, repeatedly invoked the language and principles of 1798. As his "Fort Hill Address" of 1831 insisted, "This right of interposition, thus solemnly asserted by the State of Virginia, be called what it may—State-right, veto, nullification, or by any other name—I conceive to be the fundamental principle of our system." A state's right to declare null and void within its borders a federal branch of the solemn constitutional compact among sovereign and independent states, Calhoun concluded, would serve to prevent the creation of a "consolidated" government dictating the agenda of a numerical majority. Once a state convention had vetoed a federal law, the contested legislation could be legitimated only through a constitutional amendment ratified by conventions in the requisite three-quarters of the states. When a South Carolina convention voted in 1832 to nullify the contested tariffs, and no other state followed suit, the possibility that President Andrew *Jackson, an ardent nationalist, might use military means to enforce federal authority was averted only by a congressional compromise in 1833 that promised lower import duties. Calhoun always portrayed nullification as a process designed to preserve the union, but he himself acknowledged that secession could follow interposition if repeated abuses of the Constitution went uncorrected.

Although the outcome of the *Civil War seemed to negate the principle of state sovereignty that underpinned both secession and nullification, in 1956 and 1957 eight southern states, led by Virginia, exhumed the doctrine of interposition against court-ordered school desegregation. The *Supreme Court had the final say, upholding a lower court ruling in *United States* v. *Louisiana* (1960) "that interposition is not a constitutional doctrine. If taken seriously, it is illegal defiance of constitutional authority."

[*See also* Antebellum Era; Early Republic, Era of the; Segregation, Racial; States' Rights Party; Tariffs.]

• William W. Freehling, *Prelude to Civil War: The Nullification Controversy in South Carolina, 1816–1836*, 1966. Numan V. Bartley, *The New South, 1945–1980: The Story of the South's Modernization*, 1995.

—Shearer Davis Bowman

NUREMBERG TRIALS. *See* War Crimes Trials, Nuremberg and Tokyo.

NURSING. Nursing of the sick, injured, and wounded has been performed by a variety of individuals, from the Roman tent companions and recuperating patients to Catholic nuns and Protestant deaconesses. Modern American nursing, however, developed in the post–*Civil War period as part of the women's movement. Its impetus lay in the British example of Florence Nightingale, as well as the many women who gained recognition in the American Civil War for nursing soldiers. It quickly became one of the breakthrough "new" occupations—along with librarian, social worker, elementary school teacher, and secretary—pioneered by women.

Professional nursing accompanied the rise of general *hospitals in America. The first three "Nightingale" schools opened in 1876: at the Massachusetts General Hospital in *Boston, Bellevue Hospital in *New York City, and the Connecticut Training School in New Haven. Others quickly followed. By 1900, over four hundred were in existence. Nursing schools not only saved hospital administrators money but offered patients better care. Student nurses furnished almost all the nursing needs in hospitals until after *World War II. Graduate nurses primarily engaged in private-duty nursing, became teachers or administrators in nursing schools, or, after the 1920s, worked as *public-health nurses. The first major hospital to employ graduate nurses for staff was the newly opened University of Chicago Hospital, in 1929.

In 1894 professionalizing nurses organized the Society of Superintendents of Nursing Schools of the United States and Canada (later called the National League for Nursing Education) and the Associated Alumnae, shortly thereafter renamed the American Nurses Association (ANA), comprising graduates of various training schools. These two nursing groups were among the early national ones organized by and for women. (Male nurses were not admitted to the ANA until the 1930s.) The first priority of the fledgling ANA was to distinguish between training-school graduates and other "nurses," primarily through state registration. Thus early nursing leaders concentrated on securing the right to the title "R.N." (registered nurse). They also sought to upgrade the credentials of nursing school faculty, an effort that began in 1899 with an extension program at Teachers College, Columbia University.

Nurses were both more protected and more emancipated than most other women. Hospitals, for example, often required nurses in their employ to live in a nurses' residence so they would be available for emergencies or because of split shifts. This meant that for the most part the married women in nursing engaged in home nursing or part-time work, although by the end of World War II the demand for nurses was such that hospitals generally abandoned the residence requirement. At the same time, nurses could go where few other American women could: working in urban slums, isolated rural communities, and foreign mission fields; crisscrossing the country as airline stewardesses (who originally had to be nurses); or serving in the military.

To meet the need for more nurses during *World War II, the U.S. government enacted the Nurse Training Act of 1943, establishing the Cadet Nurse Corps, which gave nurses free training, a uniform, and a small stipend for thirty months. The program played a major role in raising nursing-education standards, because schools had to meet certain fixed criteria to be accepted. By the time the program ended, some 170,000 women had become cadet nurses at 1,125 different nursing schools. The program marked the massive entrance of government into nursing education, which increased substantially in the 1960s as the U.S. government became more and more involved in health planning.

The military's official policy of refusing to use male nurses during World War II led to a rapid drop in the number of male students, even in the all-male nursing schools. The low point was reached in 1945, when only 169 men were enrolled nationwide. An upward swing began after 1954 when the military commissioned the first male nurses.

From the beginning, nurses played a subordinate role to (usually male) physicians, but inspired by the feminist movement of the 1960s, nurses began demanding more independence and recognition. Despite considerable physician opposition, nurses succeeded in expanding their roles and power, sometimes through legislative action. As health care became more complex and nursing grew more sophisticated, the number of baccalaureate programs increased. Hospital-based nursing schools found that they could no longer depend on nursing students for their free labor and had to provide a costly education as well. Beginning in 1952 the hospital-based schools moved to community colleges, where students earned associate degrees. Increasingly community-health nursing required a baccalaureate degree, while most of the nursing specialties—nurse anesthetist, nurse midwife, nurse practitioner, the clinical nurse specialist, and nursing administration—demanded a master's degree.

As the profession redefined itself, a number of functions once performed by nurses fell into the hands of nursing aides, licensed practical nurses, and other health-care specialists, such as physical therapists.

[*See also* Death and Dying; Disease; Education: Education in Contemporary America; Health Maintenance Organizations; Medicine: From the 1870s to 1945; Medicine: Since 1945; Missionary Movement; Professionalization.]

• Vern L. Bullough and Bonnie Bullough, *The Care of the Sick: The Emergence of Modern Nursing,* 1978. Vern L. Bullough, Bonnie Bullough, and Barret Elcano, *Nursing: A Historical Bibliography,* 1981. Barbara Melosh, *"The Physician's Hand": Work Culture and Conflict in American Nursing,* 1982. Susan M. Reverby, *Ordered to Care: The Dilemma of American Nursing, 1850–1945,* 1987. Julie Fairman and Joan Lynaugh, *Critical Care Nursing: A History,* 1998.

—Vern L. Bullough

O

OBSERVATORIES. Observatories are astronomical institutions equipped with telescopes. In the United States, the 1830s and 1840s marked a landmark for observatory development, with the formation of a national network of astronomers and the founding of the Harvard College Observatory (1839), the Cincinnati Observatory (1843), and the U.S. Naval Observatory in *Washington, D.C. (1844). The next sixty years saw a rapid expansion of observatories. By 1904, when George Ellery *Hale established the Mount Wilson Observatory near Pasadena, *California, with its hundred-inch reflecting telescope, the United States had the greatest number of observatories, and the largest telescopes, in the world. Several factors contributed to this growth. Religious believers hoped that study of the heavens would reinforce biblical accounts of creation; for patriots, astronomy supported science, which promised utilitarian benefits to the nation. Big telescopes embodied the prestige of science, so civic boosters and university administrators competed for ownership of the largest telescopes. For example, when the former Wisconsin governor Cadwallader C. Washburn donated an observatory to the University of Wisconsin in 1877, he specified that its refractor telescope must be larger than Harvard's—as it was, by one-half inch. The rise of business fortunes in the *Gilded Age enabled single donors to fund observatories. In 1892, for example, the *Chicago financier and street-railway tycoon Charles Yerkes (1837–1905) gave the Yerkes Observatory, at Lake Geneva, Wisconsin, to the University of Chicago. The development of astrophysics spurred observatory growth as well, as the spectroscopic analysis of starlight enabled astronomers to study not just the position of celestial bodies, but their composition as well.

In the absence of federal support, the advocates of observatories initially based their funding strategies on business models. The Cincinnati and Harvard observatory projects started as joint-stock enterprises, to which many patrons donated relatively small sums. By the early twentieth century, observatory builders turned to new philanthropies such as the Carnegie Foundation. The *Cold War Era brought increased federal, university, and foundation funding. The 1948 Mount Palomar Observatory near San Diego, California, with its two-hundred-inch telescope, was jointly administered by the Carnegie Institution and the California Institute of Technology. The 1958 Kitt Peak National Observatory in Arizona, administered by a consortium of universities, was initially funded by the *National Science Foundation. The late twentieth century saw the advent of radio astronomy, which measured radio waves emitted by celestial objects, and space-based observatories, such as the Hubble Space Telescope, launched in 1990.

[*See also* Education: The Rise of the University; Mitchell, Maria; Philanthropy and Philanthropic Foundations; Physical Sciences; Science: Revolutionary War to World War I; Science: From 1914 to 1945; Science: Since 1945.]

• Owen Gingerich, ed., *Astrophysics and Twentieth-Century Astronomy to 1950,* vol. 4A of *The General History of Astronomy,* ed. M. A. Hoskin, 1984. John Lankford, *American Astronomy: Community, Career, and Power, 1859–1940,* 1997.

—Philip Shoemaker

O'CONNOR, SANDRA DAY (1930–), first woman justice of the U.S. *Supreme Court. A native of El Paso, Texas, O'Connor graduated third in her class at Stanford Law School in 1952, but encountered difficulty in finding employment in the legal profession, which was still largely closed to women. Eventually, after a career in the public sector, including a term as an Arizona state senator and a judgeship on the Arizona Court of Appeals, O'Connor was appointed to the Supreme Court by President Ronald *Reagan in 1981.

O'Connor's principal contributions to the Court's constitutional *jurisprudence came in the areas of religion and *federalism. In *Lynch* v. *Donnelly* (1984), she outlined an approach to cases involving the First Amendment's establishment clause that focused on when the government could be said to have "endorsed" religion. A decade later, that approach appeared to command a majority of the Court.

In federalism cases, O'Connor ardently defended state sovereignty. Her dissent in *Garcia* v. *San Antonio Metropolitan Transit Authority* (1985) described the "essence" of federalism as a recognition "that the States have legitimate interests which the National Government is bound to respect." In *New York* v. *United States* (1992), she led the first Court effort in decades to put teeth in the Tenth Amendment as a substantive limitation on federal power. After initially appearing to endorse a constitutional jurisprudence favored by conservatives during the chief justiceship of Warren Burger, O'Connor moved to a more centrist position during William Rehnquist's tenure as chief justice, often joining majorities in closely divided cases. Despite her status as the first woman justice, she did not play a conspicuous role in gender discrimination cases.

[*See also* Church and State, Separation of; States' Rights.]

• M. David Gelfand and Keith Werthan, "Federalism and the Separation of Powers on a 'Conservative' Court," *Tulane Law Review* 64 (1990): 1443–1476. Peter Huber, *Sandra Day O'Connor: Supreme Court Justice,* 1990.

—G. Edward White

OFFICE OF STRATEGIC SERVICES (OSS), one of several American intelligence agencies during *World War II, is inextricably linked with William "Wild Bill" Donovan, a Republican but also an associate of Franklin Delano *Roosevelt. In 1940, as one of Roosevelt's contacts with Winston Churchill, Donovan established close ties with British intelligence. He wished to become coordinator of American intelligence as a whole, but instead, in 1942, FDR appointed him director of the newly established OSS, which was placed under the *Joint Chiefs of Staff and ordered to analyze strategic intelligence, conduct covert action, and run agents in Asia and Europe. The OSS's three-year history was marked by political controversy, a search for missions and successes to justify its existence, and some real achievement. The OSS's exploits have been romanticized. Some of its undertakings were extravagant failures, and it often functioned as a junior partner to British intelligence. Still, it proved a competent espionage service, with particular successes in running agents in Germany, and in providing tactical intelligence to U.S. field commanders in Europe. American academics figured prominently in the OSS's analytical branches, where they pioneered new techniques of strategic analysis. Nonetheless, the OSS was less significant to the war effort than the signals intelligence services of the army and the navy, and in September 1945, President Harry S. *Truman disbanded it. Contrary to OSS mythology, Truman did so not out of a naïve opposition to intelligence—he preserved the code-breaking agencies of the army and the navy, and retained some other intelligence organizations—but because he distrusted Donovan and regarded the OSS as being penetrated by the British. Many leading figures of the early *Central Intelligence Agency were OSS veterans. The OSS tradition, with its focus on action, bureaucratic and operational buccaneering, covert operations, and links with the academic community, influenced the CIA, and the two agencies' functions in the American intelligence community were similar.

• Thomas F. Troy, *Donovan and the CIA,* 1981. Bradley Smith, *The Shadow Warriors: OSS and the Origins of the CIA,* 1983. Thomas F. Troy, *Wild Bill and Intrepid: Donovan, Stephenson, and the Origin of the CIA,* 1996.

—John Ferris

OFFICE TECHNOLOGY. U.S. inventors built mechanical prototypes of typewriters and computing machines as early as the mid-nineteenth century, but little demand for them arose until the economy became more sophisticated after the *Civil War. Christopher Latham Sholes and James Demsmore convinced E. Remington and Sons, a Hartford, Connecticut, arms manufacturer, to advertise the first mass-produced typewriting machine in the 1870s. In the 1890s both Underwood and Royal marketed more efficient versions of the typewriter, which by 1900 was ubiquitous in North American offices. After William Patterson devised cash registers (adding machines with drawers) for use in his Dayton, Ohio, coal business in 1882, he founded the National Cash Register Company. Joseph Burroughs, Frank Baldwin, and Jay Monroe were among the entrepreneurs and inventors who established adding-machine companies at the turn of the twentieth century. The Felt and Tarrant Company of *Chicago produced a popular lightweight "comptometer," which could execute all the basic arithmetic functions.

Herman Hollerith adapted Jacquard loom technology in the 1880s to develop sorting machines using punched cards, allowing for more efficient production and analysis of cost-accounting records, census data, and actuarial tables. First used in the federal *census of 1890, the Hollerith machines were soon installed at large offices such as the Baltimore Department of Health, the New York Central Railroad, and the Marshall Field department store in Chicago. Hollerith's Computing Tabulating and Recording Company merged with the smaller International Business Machine (IBM) Corporation in 1924 and took its name. By leasing machines and selling keypunch cards to large business establishments, IBM became one of America's most powerful and profitable corporations, eventually dominating the office-machine industry.

Other office machines complemented this basic computing, typewriting, and tabulating technology. Mimeograph machines used typewritten stencils to reproduce office documents. "Addressograph" machines (featuring detachable metal name-and-address plates on a mimeographing device) and bookkeeping and billing machines (combinations of adding and typewriting machines) made billing, tax collecting, and advertising more efficient. With the dictaphone, a combination of the sewing machine, the phonograph, and the *telephone that reproduced the human voice on a wax cylinder, business correspondence could be dictated for later transcription by someone using a typewriter. Along with the telephone and switchboard, these machines completed the modern office and allowed *scientific management experts to rationalize most office functions, making the organization of office workers and their use of machines akin to light factory work.

U.S. employers created 3 million new clerical jobs between 1900 and 1920. Functions that could be mechanized and routinized were often "feminized" as well, and by 1930, 82 percent of all bookkeepers, cashiers, stenographers, and typists were female. These mostly young women were paid far less than men and subjected to discrimination based on marital status (the so-called marriage bar). Business colleges and high-school business-education courses prepared tens of thousands of them for office machine jobs, and young women flocked to major cities to take up clerical work. These urban pioneers helped create new standards of female dress, sexual behavior, and independence from family supervision, and they soon appeared as standard characters in movies and novels. During the Great Depression of the 1930s, some of them overcame the resistance of employers and male-dominated unions and organized office-worker unions, protesting low wages, uncompensated overtime, and the increased pace of mechanized work. By 1950 more than 4.5 million women were employed in office work, far outnumbering those in factories.

Beginning in the 1920s, electrification amplified the efficiency of some office machines, and after *World War II, early prototypes of the digital *computer, financed largely by the federal government, allowed for still more elaborate compilations of data. The widespread introduction of personal-computer stations after 1980 integrated multiple office-work functions into the same machine. Some workers used the new technology for creative and varied work, but many found their computerized jobs more routinized than ever. By the end of the century, some clerical functions were being assigned to home offices or back-office electronic sweatshops in inexpensive *labor markets, some of them outside the United States. Clerical workers (mostly female) and better-paid middle managers (mostly male) were particularly hard hit in the 1990s by the disappearance or downgrading of their jobs.

Office technology facilitated the growth of the modern corporation and the sophisticated nation-state after 1900. North America's development and dominance of that technology made the United States a major exporter of office machinery and office-management methods. By the end of the twentieth century, thanks to ever-more-sophisticated office technology, white-collar workers dominated the U.S. job market, and the continued refinement of microchip and telecommunications technology had made office functions fundamental to an increasingly integrated global economy.

[*See also* Business; Department Stores; Electricity and Electrification; Global Economy, America and the; Industrialization; Railroads; Urbanization; Women in the Labor Force.]

• Geoffrey D. Austrian, *Herman Hollerith,* 1982. Heidi I. Hartmann, Robert E. Kraut, and Louise A. Tilly, eds., *Computer Chips and Paper Clips,* 1986. Barbara A. Garson, *The Electronic Sweatshop,* 1988. Lisa M. Fine, *The Souls of the Skyscraper: Female Clerical Workers in Chicago, 1870–1930,* 1990. Shoshana Zuboff, *In the Age of the Smart Machine,* 1990. Sharon Hartman Strom, *Beyond the Typewriter,* 1992. James W. Cortada, *Before the Computer: IBM, NCR, Burroughs, and Remington Rand and the Industry They Created, 1865–1956,* 1993.

—Sharon Hartman Strom

OIL INDUSTRY. *See* Petroleum Industry.

O'KEEFFE, GEORGIA (1887–1986), painter. Born in Sun Prairie, Wisconsin, O'Keeffe attended high school in nearby Madison until her family moved to Williamsburg, Virginia. After graduating from Chatham Episcopal Institute she attended the Chicago Art Institute, the Art Students League in New York, the University of Virginia, and Teachers College, Columbia University, where she studied with the well-known art educator Arthur Wesley Dow. During the 1910s she held a variety of teaching jobs, including supervisor of the art program for the public schools in Amarillo, Texas.

In 1916 she met Alfred *Stieglitz, who exhibited her latest

work—primarily watercolor abstractions—in his gallery at 291 Fifth Avenue. By 1924, when they married, her nonfigurative oil paintings of the climate, light, and space of West Texas influenced his *photography, as he abandoned urban-realist subjects for cropped sky studies called "Equivalents." During the mid-1920s, O'Keeffe created her best-known works, the magnified flower blossoms. Beneath their decorative abstractness these are commonly viewed as expressing a provocative sexuality. In 1929 she spent her first summer in Taos, New Mexico, as a guest of Mabel Dodge Luhan. By 1940 she had settled in the area; in 1945 she bought an isolated house in nearby Abiquiu, where she lived the rest of her life.

Avoiding the influence of Picasso's cubism in any form, O'Keeffe epitomized the independence of the American avant-garde. Whether referring to *New York City *skyscrapers, Lake George barns, parched pelvic bones, skulls, distant mountains, adobe buildings, or clouds, her paintings project precisely contoured configurations of sharply contrasting color. Extracting a given object from its immediate setting, she suspended it in space, or in what she termed "a wonderful emptiness." Thereby, she advanced an expansive tendency in American art, as opposed to a European tradition of containment.

[*See also* Painting.]

• Georgia O'Keeffe, *Georgia O'Keeffe,* 1976. Laurie Lisle, *Portrait of an Artist: A Biography of Georgia O'Keeffe,* 1986. Peter H. Hassrick, ed., *The Georgia O'Keeffe Museum*; introduction by Mark Stevens; essays by Lisa Mintz Messinger, Barbara Novak, and Barbara Rose, 1997. Jeffrey Hogrefe, *O'Keeffe: The Life of an American Legend,* 1999.

—James M. Dennis

OKLAHOMA CITY BOMBING. On the morning of 19 April 1995, a huge explosion ripped through the Alfred P. Murrah Federal Building in downtown Oklahoma City. Caused by a lethal mixture of diesel fuel and ammonium nitrate packed into a rental truck parked nearby, the blast spread death and destruction throughout a forty-eight-square-block area, overturning automobiles and damaging three hundred buildings. At the time of the explosion, nearly a thousand people were in the Murrah Building, which housed sixteen federal agencies and a day-care center. The entire north face of the structure collapsed and each of the nine floors received extensive damage. Emergency personnel frantically searched the Murrah Building for survivors. The final human toll numbered 168 killed, including many children, and at least 700 injured.

A short time later, two men were arrested and charged with the bombing. Both had ties to ultra–right-wing paramilitary groups that viewed the federal government as an evil force to be confronted and destroyed. Timothy McVeigh, a U.S. Army veteran who planted the bomb, was convicted and sentenced to death. Terry Nichols, his accomplice, was sentenced to life in prison. Evidence suggested that the bombing was timed to coincide with the second anniversary of a raid by the Bureau of Alcohol, Tobacco, and Firearms on the compound of the Branch Davidians, a heavily armed apocalyptic sect in Waco, Texas, led by David Koresh. The raid, in which some eighty Branch Davidians perished when fire of undetermined origin destroyed the compound, had infuriated McVeigh as an example of overweening federal power.

The Oklahoma City bombing stands as the worst act of domestic terrorism in American history. An active survivors' association soon took shape, and the Murrah Building site became a major focus of mourning rituals, including thousands of poems, memorabilia, and teddy bears left at the chain-link fence surrounding the ruin. In October 1998, architectural plans for a permanent memorial on the site were unveiled at a ceremony attended by Vice President Al Gore and other officials. It was completed and opened to the public on 19 April 2000, the fifth anniversary of the bombing.

[*See also* Post–Cold War Era.]

• Oklahoma Department of Civil Emergency Management, *After Action Report: Alfred R. Murrah Federal Building Bombing, 10 April 1995, Oklahoma City, Oklahoma.* Jon Hansen, *Oklahoma Rescue,* 1995. Mark Hamm, *Apocalypse in Oklahoma,* 1997. Richard Serrano, *One of Ours: Timothy McVeigh and the Oklahoma City Bombing,* 1998.

—Richard Lowitt

OLD AGE. *See* Life Stages.

OLMSTED, FREDERICK LAW (1822–1903), landscape architect. Born in Hartford, Connecticut, Olmsted farmed from 1847 to 1852 and then toured the *South for the *New York Times.* Three books of description and analysis resulted: *A Journey in the Seaboard Slave States* (1856), *A Journey through Texas* (1857), and *A Journey through the Backcountry* (1860). Stressing *slavery's adverse social effects, these works helped shape the ideology of the early *Republican party. As editor of *Putnam's Monthly Magazine* (1855–1857), he opposed slavery and promoted American authors. In 1858, Olmsted and the architect Calvert Vaux won the design competition for *New York City's Central Park, and Olmsted directed its construction. In 1861–1863, during the *Civil War, he headed the U.S. Sanitary Commission, organizing camp inspections and relief distribution for the Union Army.

After the war, Olmsted with various partners carried out five hundred landscape design commissions. With Vaux he designed Brooklyn's Prospect Park, Washington and Jackson parks in *Chicago, and a park system for Buffalo, New York. He subsequently designed Mount Royal Park in Montreal, Canada, and comprehensive park systems for *Boston, Rochester, New York, and Louisville, Kentucky. Olmsted planned his urban parks so that they would have a restorative psychological effect, serving as an antidote to the artificiality of city life. His parks also promoted community by giving city dwellers a common meeting-ground.

Beginning with Riverside, Illinois, in 1868, Olmsted planned suburban communities where extensive public open space preserved areas of natural scenery, while curvilinear streets and sidewalks provided special amenity. He and Vaux also developed the concept of the "parkway," a wide, well-paved and tree-lined boulevard for non-commercial traffic—the forerunner of the landscaped automobile parkway. A leader in scenic preservation, particularly at Yosemite valley and *Niagara Falls, Olmsted also planned the site of Chicago's 1893 World's Columbian Exposition; the grounds and West Front terrace of the U.S. Capitol; the Stanford University campus; and Biltmore, the Vanderbilt estate in North Carolina.

[*See also* Landscape Design; Leisure; Parks, Urban; Urbanization; World's Fairs and Expositions; Yosemite National Park.]

• Laura Wood Roper, *FLO: A Biography,* 1973. Charles E. Beveridge and Paul Rocheleau, *Frederick Law Olmsted: Designing the American Landscape,* 1995.

—Charles E. Beveridge

ONEIDA COMMUNITY. *See* Utopian and Communitarian Movements.

O'NEILL, EUGENE (1888–1953), playwright. In his most famous play, *Long Day's Journey into Night* (1956), O'Neill drew upon the most formative aspects of his own family life: Irish, Roman Catholic, alcoholic, contentious. His actor father, famous for his role in *The Count of Monte Cristo,* was lower class and sexually profligate; his mother, middle class and ineffectual, escaped her miseries through morphine. O'Neill educated himself chiefly at the Unique Book Shop of the New York anarchist Benjamin Tucker and by attendance at plays by such avant-garde dramatists as Henrik Ibsen and George Bernard Shaw. The thinkers who most influenced him included the philosopher Max Stirner, the radical Emma *Goldman, the philosopher Friedrich Nietzsche, and the playwright August

Strindberg. A lover of the sea, O'Neill also absorbed the novels of Joseph Conrad and distilled their contents in numerous short plays.

Carrying to America the Scandinavian revolt against conventional middle-class drama, O'Neill made his first permanent mark with *The Emperor Jones* (1920), incidentally creating a major role for such black actors as Charles Gilpin and Paul *Robeson. *The Hairy Ape* (1922), exploring the lower depths of the working class in an age of *technology, confirmed his place as the leading American expressionist in any art. Fascinated by ideas of atavism and free association that he discovered in the work of the Swiss Freudian Carl Jung, he enjoyed great popular success with *Strange Interlude* (1928), a work whose sexually liberated heroine, based in part on the journalist Louise Bryant, became for many emblematic of *Greenwich Village bohemianism. *Strange Interlude* won a Pulitzer Prize; the Nobel Prize followed in 1936. Most contemporary critics rank *The Iceman Cometh,* a bleak drama of 1946, or *Long Day's Journey into Night* (1956) as O'Neill's best play. O'Neill's obsessions still dominated serious theater in America a half century after his death, and foreigners continued to rank him as the only American playwright worthy of a place beside Ibsen and Strindberg.

[*See also* Drama; Theater; Twenties, The.]

• Louis Sheaffer, *O'Neill,* 2 vols., 1968–1973. Travis Bogard, *Contour in Time: The Plays of Eugene O'Neill,* 1972. Michael Manheim, ed., *The Cambridge Companion to Eugene O'Neill,* 1998.

—Robert M. Crunden

OPEC OIL EMBARGO. *See* Ford, Gerald; Foreign Relations: U.S. Relations with the Middle East.

"OPEN DOOR" POLICY. The "Open Door" notes, issued by Secretary of State John *Hay in 1899–1901, represented the U.S. hope and expectation of maintaining access to the China market at a time when European colonial powers and Japan, taking advantage of China's weakness after the Sino-Japanese War of 1894–1895, threatened to exclude U.S. business by carving out exclusive spheres of influence for themselves. Seeking to prevent this without resort to force, and drawing upon ideas already developed by British observers, Hay articulated a series of principles for the interested nations—Great Britain, France, Italy, Germany, Japan, Russia, and the United States—to adopt. Hay's first note, issued as a circular letter on 6 September 1899, asked the other powers to follow most-favored-nation practices in China, permitting equal access to commercial activity within their spheres of influence. Despite evasive and ambiguous answers, Hay announced in March 1900 that his principles had been accepted. That the other powers did not object demonstrated America's growing power, the largely unobjectionable content of the notes themselves, the tactful manner of their presentation, and the unwillingness of the Europeans and Japanese to appear manifestly rapacious in their Chinese dealings.

The second note, dispatched on 3 July 1900, came during the Boxer Uprising, when groups of antiforeign Chinese calling themselves Boxers (after a martial-arts style) attacked foreigners, especially Christian missionaries and their Chinese converts. In response, the outside powers, including the United States, sent military forces to suppress the Boxers, protect the lives and property of their citizens, and restore order. In this context, Hay's second note pushed for guarantees of China's territorial and administrative integrity, which he feared was endangered by the foreign intervention.

Down to the communist victory in China in 1949, the "Open Door" policy stood for safeguarding U.S. access to the China market. In a larger sense, it also reinforced self-serving notions of American exceptionalism and disinterestedness. Indeed, the views set forth in the "Open Door" notes rested on two divergent, yet symbiotic, sets of ideas about American foreign policy. One was the belief that the "Open Door" policy embodied the principles of fairness, equal opportunity, and reasonableness in U.S. treatment of China. (In the late twentieth century, similar ideas would reappear in the argument by U.S. policy-makers that China's repressive political system would change if the Chinese opened their markets to free trade by entering the World Trade Organization.) Also embedded in the "Open Door" policy, however, were underlying imperialist pretensions and commercial assumptions. In seeking to shape the China policy of the major world powers, Hay never consulted Chinese officials themselves about how they defined their nation's best interests. Moreover, Hay was persuaded that the "Open Door" policy would not only prevent the Japanese and Europeans from carving up China, but would ultimately lead to American commercial dominance in China. The "Open Door" policy thus illuminates not only certain illusions about America's world role, but also the U.S. government's growing activism in shaping an international environment conducive to the expansion of American trade and investment.

[*See also* Business; Capitalism; Federal Government, Executive Branch: Department of State; Foreign Relations: The Economic Dimension; Foreign Relations: U.S. Relations with Asia; Foreign Trade, U.S.; Multinational Enterprises.]

• Marilyn B. Young, *The Rhetoric of Empire: American China Policy, 1895–1901,* 1969. Michael H. Hunt, *The Making of a Special Relationship: The United States and China to 1914,* 1983.

—T. Christopher Jespersen

OPERA. Opera came to America in 1735, in the form of English ballad opera featuring spoken dialogue, new lyrics set to familiar tunes, and subjects taken from ordinary life. In the 1790s, French opera reached *New Orleans. Italian opera made its debut in 1825 with the appearance of the Manuel Garcia Company in *New York City. Lacking both court and aristocratic patronage and state subsidy, opera in America confronted the vagaries of a market economy. With no music schools to train native-born performers and composers, American operagoers until well into the twentieth century depended on touring companies, unknown itinerants, and the occasional celebrated star. William Henry Fry's *Leonora,* the first known performance of an opera by an American composer, premiered in *Philadelphia in 1845.

So emerged nineteenth-century America's dual operatic culture. Small companies with modest resources and without famous singers continued the English-language tradition, crisscrossing the country, bringing to small-town opera houses the operas of the Irish composer Michael William Balfe, and the English team of W. S. Gilbert and Arthur Sullivan. This was long dwarfed, however, by the high-culture "European" tradition, featuring large orchestras and star singers performing in a foreign language, centered in the major cities, and dominated by an elite seeking social prestige. Large opera houses—Philadelphia's Academy of Music (1857), the first Metropolitan Opera House in New York City (1883), the Auditorium Building in *Chicago (1889)—flaunted the plutocrats' wealth in a style appropriate to "grand opera," as the operas of Rossini, Bellini, and Donizetti gave way to those of Meyerbeer, Verdi, Gounod, and Wagner.

In the twentieth century, this European tradition, vastly broadened by *radio, recordings, and English supertitles, spread throughout the nation and attracted a more diverse audience and a more musically mature one, as demonstrated by the fact that Mozart's operas, represented primarily by *Don Giovanni* in the nineteenth century, now all entered the repertory. Regional opera companies proved particularly receptive to the works of American composers. Meanwhile, the English-language opera tradition evolved to incorporate operettas and *musical theater. The tradition of spoken dialogue, modest scale, melodious music, and subjects drawn from contemporary life was transformed by Sigmund Romberg, George *Gershwin, Jerome Kern, Richard Rodgers, Oscar Hammerstein, Leonard *Bernstein, and Stephen Sondheim (among others) into a distinctively American form, reaching a vast international audience, multiplied by *film and *television.

The outlook for opera appeared mixed as the twentieth century ended. Governmental subsidies for the arts, originating in a modest way with the *New Deal Era of the 1930s and institutionalized in the 1960s, remained precarious, leaving opera dependent, as always, on wealthy patrons, supplemented now by corporate and foundation support. But there were also reasons for optimism about the future of this four-hundred-year-old artform as the new century dawned. Two generations of American singers and conductors, trained in music schools and university departments, and—with racial barriers diminishing—broadly representative of American society as a whole, now played a major role in the U.S. operatic world. Innovative productions drew upon modern technology, and the cross-fertilization of opera and *popular culture offered exciting possibilities. Late twentieth-century operas by American composers utilizing American themes included Aaron *Copland's *The Tender Land* (1954); Douglas Moore's *The Ballad of Baby Doe* (1956); Jack Beeson's *Lizzie Borden* (1965); Scott Joplin's *Treemonisha* (composed 1907–1911, first performed in 1972); John Adams's *Nixon in China* (1987); Daron Hagen's *Shining Brow* (1992), about Frank Lloyd *Wright; William Bolcom's *McTeague* (1992), based on a novel by Frank Norris; and John Harbison's *The Great Gatsby* (1999).

[*See also* Music: Classical Music; National Endowments for the Arts and the Humanities.]

• John Dizikes, *Opera in America: A Cultural History,* 1993. Karly Lynn Zietz, *National Trust Guide to Great Opera Houses in America,* 1996.

—John Dizikes

OPPENHEIMER, J. ROBERT (1904–1967), physicist. Born in *New York City, J. Robert Oppenheimer attended Harvard University and in 1927 received a Ph.D. in theoretical physics from Germany's Göttingen University where he studied with Max Born. In 1929, after lecturing at Europe's leading centers of physics, he accepted an unusual joint appointment at the University of California, Berkeley, and the California Institute of Technology. While teaching half-time at Cal Tech (and seriously studying the arts, languages, and literature), he nevertheless transformed Berkeley into the top U.S. center for quantum physics. He also became friendly with members of the Communist party in northern California, married the widow of a party official, and supported causes championed by the party.

In 1942, despite opposition by security officers, General Leslie Groves, military head of the *Manhattan Project, appointed Oppenheimer director of the Los Alamos laboratory responsible for designing and constructing atomic bombs. He proved an effective leader, and on 16 July 1945, the first atomic device was tested at Alamagordo, New Mexico. On 6–9 August, atomic bombs obliterated the Japanese cities of Hiroshima and Nagasaki. Transformed into a national hero, "the father of the atomic bomb," Oppenheimer used his new-found fame to promote the Acheson-Lilienthal plan for the international control of atomic energy.

In 1947–1953, while directing the Institute for Advanced Study in Princeton, New Jersey, he served on numerous government advisory committees and chaired the General Advisory Committee of the *Atomic Energy Commission (AEC). His former communist associations and his opposition to the hydrogen-bomb project led in 1953 to the suspension of his security clearance—an action coordinated by Lewis L. Strauss, appointed by President Dwight D. *Eisenhower as AEC chairman. In 1954 a biased and inquisitorial AEC hearing board, while affirming Oppenheimer's loyalty, nevertheless declared him a security risk. The decision ended his career as a government adviser but made him a martyr in the eyes of many. In 1963, in a gesture of reconciliation, President Lyndon B. *Johnson awarded Oppenheimer the prestigious Enrico *Fermi Prize.

[*See also* Acheson, Dean; Cold War; Communist Party—USA; Hiroshima and Nagasaki, Atomic Bombing of; Nuclear Strategy; Nuclear Weapons; Physical Sciences; Science: From 1914 to 1945; Science: Since 1945.]

• Philip Stern, *The Oppenheimer Case: Security on Trial,* 1969. Peter Goodchild, *J. Robert Oppenheimer: Shatterer of Worlds,* 1980.

—Martin J. Sherwin

OPTOMETRY. The word "optometry," from the Greek *optos* and *metron* meaning "visible" and "measure," was apparently first used in the 1890s to describe a profession that today encompasses doctors trained and licensed to diagnose and treat diseases and disorders of the visual system. Colonial merchants selling European-made spectacles and lenses launched what would become professional optometry in the United States. Two developments by Americans, bifocal lenses and better spectacle frames, helped move optometry from a vendor trade toward a recognized profession by making fitting and selecting eyeglasses more complicated. In 1760, Benjamin *Franklin instructed a London firm to make him spectacles with two types of lenses fitted together, thus inventing bifocals. Late in the eighteenth century, American inventors, like those overseas, began patenting lighter-weight rims and springs and pads for comfort, as well as improved construction techniques.

Nineteenth-century American optometry made further advances with the growth of optical companies, the development of new diagnostic equipment, and cooperative efforts by prescriber-purveyors of spectacles to gain professional status as optometrists. Many of the diagnostic advances, such as Bausch and Lomb's 1902 retinoscope and the improved opthalmoscopes made in 1905 by the New Jersey-based DeZeng Standard Company, extended *technology developed earlier in Europe. More grounded in American soil were the optical companies, which also influenced an emergent profession of opticians. Denied traditional supplies from Europe during the *Revolutionary War, American manufacturers and merchants built a domestic industry. John McAllister, a *Philadelphia cane and whip manufacturer who began selling spectacles in 1783, became the first U.S. optician and his firm, the first American optical company. Several frame-making factories followed, often begun by jewelers or by European-trained immigrants. When the *Civil War again disrupted glass imports from Europe, the American Optical Company and other firms began production of their own lenses. In consultation with those who sold spectacles, American Optical and Bausch and Lomb, among others, developed improved sets of trial lenses to determine patient prescriptions. By 1904 the United States was exporting lenses to Europe.

With improved tools and clinical expertise, practitioners who once labeled themselves refracting or applied opticians now identified themselves as more highly trained optometrists; took steps to establish optometry's professional identity and prestige; and launched specialized periodicals such as *Johnson's Eye Echo* (1886), *The Optician* (1891), *Optical Journal* (1895), and *Optical Review* (1907).

With *professionalization came controversies over licensing laws and government regulations. Until the late nineteenth century, the field had no official standards of practice, education, or competency. In 1896, seeking stricter controls over who could prescribe eyeglasses, Charles F. Prentice and Andrew Jay Cross formed the Optical Society of New York. As other state societies arose, practitioners lobbied legislatures for regulatory statutes. Minnesota imposed the first regulations, in 1901, and by 1925 all the states and the District of Columbia had passed such legislation.

Inspired by the early lobbying efforts, periodical editors, officials of state organizations, and practitioners founded the American Association of Opticians in *New York City in 1898.

Initially, anyone interested in optics could join, but the retail merchants soon dropped out and over the next decade stricter education and professional standards resulted in a more exclusive membership. In 1910 the organization was renamed the American Optical Association, and in 1919, the American Optometric Association. In 1929 it launched its own *AOA Organizer,* renamed the *Journal of the American Optometric Association* in 1930.

In 1915 the National Board of State Examiners in Optometry (established by the national association in 1919) set two twenty-six-week school terms as a minimum education standard for certification. This reflected a continuing emphasis on education as one guarantee of quality care. Around 1900, America had an estimated sixty optometry schools of varying quality; by 2000, fewer than twenty were accredited by the Council on Optometric Education. Four-year programs included anatomy, pharmacology, pathology, vision screening, optics, and applied lens technology. Graduates needed to pass a state board examination to practice, and nearly all states required continuing-education courses for license renewal.

The scope of optometric practice expanded in the 1970s as some states authorized optometrists to treat certain eye diseases with pharmaceuticals. By 1989 all states had authorized specifically trained optometrists to use drugs for diagnostic purposes. By 2000, changing Medicare regulations, the growth of managed-care systems, and cooperative networks with ophthalmologists and other specialists were altering optometric practices. But America's thirty thousand optometrists, 25 percent of whom were women, still performed over 60 percent of the nation's primary eye examinations.

[*See also* Health Maintenance Organizations; Medicare and Medicaid.]

• James R. Gregg, *The Story of Optometry,* 1965. James R. Gregg, *American Optometric Association,* 1972. Robert Koetting, *The American Optometric Association's First Century,* 1997.

—Diane D. Edwards

OREGON TRAIL. The Oregon Trail, important in American westward expansion, began at Independence, Missouri. Following the Platte River to Fort Laramie, it crossed the *Rocky Mountains at South Pass, continued westward through Wyoming to James Bridger's fort and Fort Hall on the Snake River, and on to Oregon's Willamette valley.

The trail's role in American history dates to the early 1840s. Although the United States and Great Britain jointly administered Oregon, and Hudson's Bay Trading Company operated a major fur-trading post there, expansion-minded U.S. politicians and American settlers were determined to win the territory for the United States. Migration and settlement, they concluded, would best assure this goal. The glowing accounts of U.S. Protestant missionaries in Oregon aided the cause.

As "Oregon fever" swept the Mississippi valley, several small wagon trains made the six-month trek over the Oregon Trail in 1841–1842; mass migration began in 1843. Injuries, thirst, poor diet, exhaustion, *disease, and Indian attacks took a terrible toll. (Indians often assisted the migrants as well.) By 1844, with more than five thousand Americans in the Willamette valley, the "Oregon question" dominated U.S. politics. In that year's presidential election, voters in effect risked war with Great Britain by selecting the Democrat James Knox *Polk on a platform committed to acquiring Oregon and the slogan "Fifty-four forty or Fight." The slogan referred to a willingness to fight Great Britain to secure all of the jointly administered Oregon territory. Fifty-four degrees and forty minutes of north latitude was the northern boundary of the territory. By an 1846 treaty with Great Britain, the United States gained sole possession of Oregon, with the forty ninth parallel as its northern boundary; statehood followed in 1859. The Oregon Trail remained in heavy use until the *railroads superseded it. Francis Parkman's classic *The Oregon Trail* (1849) helped secure its place in American memory.

[*See also* Expansionism; Fur Trade; Indian History and Culture: From 1800 to 1900; Missionary Movement.]

• Francis Parkman, *The Oregon Trail,* 1849. Jean Van Leeuwen, *Bound for Oregon,* 1994.

—David E. Conrad

ORGANIZATION OF AMERICAN STATES. The Organization of American States (OAS) emerged from the Ninth International Conference of American States held in Bogotá, Colombia, in 1948. As a regional entry sanctioned by Article 51 of the *United Nations Charter, the OAS provided the political means for implementing the Rio Pact of 1947, a *collective security alliance among Western Hemisphere nations.

The OAS charter set forth the following aims: advancing peace and security; resolving disputes among members by amicable means; enforcing collective security provisions against aggressors; and promoting economic, social, and cultural development. The governing principles also affirmed respect for international law, national sovereignty and independence, and the goal of unity among American states through the exercise of representative government.

From the Latin American viewpoint, Article 15 of the Charter embodied a most important provision: a statement of the nonintervention principle affirming that "No State or group of States has the right to intervene, directly or indirectly, for any reason whatever, in the internal or external affairs of any other State." This prohibition applied to the use of "armed force" and also to "any other form of interference or attempted threat against the personality of the State or against its political, economic and cultural elements."

Divergent expectations impeded OAS activities from the beginning. For the United States, the organization served primarily anticommunist purposes—that is, to orchestrate political and military responses in the *Cold War with the Soviet Union. For Latin Americans, in contrast, the OAS represented a shield against U.S. intervention and a structure for administering anticipated programs of economic aid and assistance. These divergent understandings caused special controversy during the U.S. intervention in the Dominican Republic in 1965 and other Cold War Era interventions.

[*See also* Anticommunism; Foreign Relations: U.S. Relations with Latin America; Pan American Union.]

• O. Carlos Stoetzer, *The Organization of American States,* 2d ed., 1993. David Sheinin, *The Organization of American States,* 1995.

—Mark T. Gilderhus

ORGANIZED CRIME, a term that has been used selectively in the twentieth century to identify particular criminal coalitions that were often ethnically based and which others wished to define as especially dangerous illegal conspiracies. Generally speaking, the criminal groups identified as "organized crime" have possessed neither the hierarchical structure nor the power ascribed to them. But the label has, nevertheless, strongly influenced both popular attitudes toward the groups involved and the policies of law enforcement. The history of "organized crime," therefore, must include both a history of criminal structure itself and of the use of the term.

From the 1860s until well into the twentieth century, certain types of *gambling became increasingly coordinated in some urban neighborhoods. During and after the *Civil War, policy gambling—a kind of illegal lottery—enjoyed wide popularity. Fans could bet on the numbers in bars, barber shops, newspaper kiosks, and other neighborhood outlets. At the same time, policy entrepreneurs backed the local retailers, so that the retailer retained a fixed percent of each bet while the backer(s) assumed the risk when betters won. By the 1880s, as *horse racing became a national, professional sport, fans wished for an opportunity to bet off-track as well as at the track. Off-track bookmaking was coordinated much like policy, with bets taken in local retail outlets while bookmakers backed the local sellers.

MAP 15: THE OREGON TRAIL (1846)

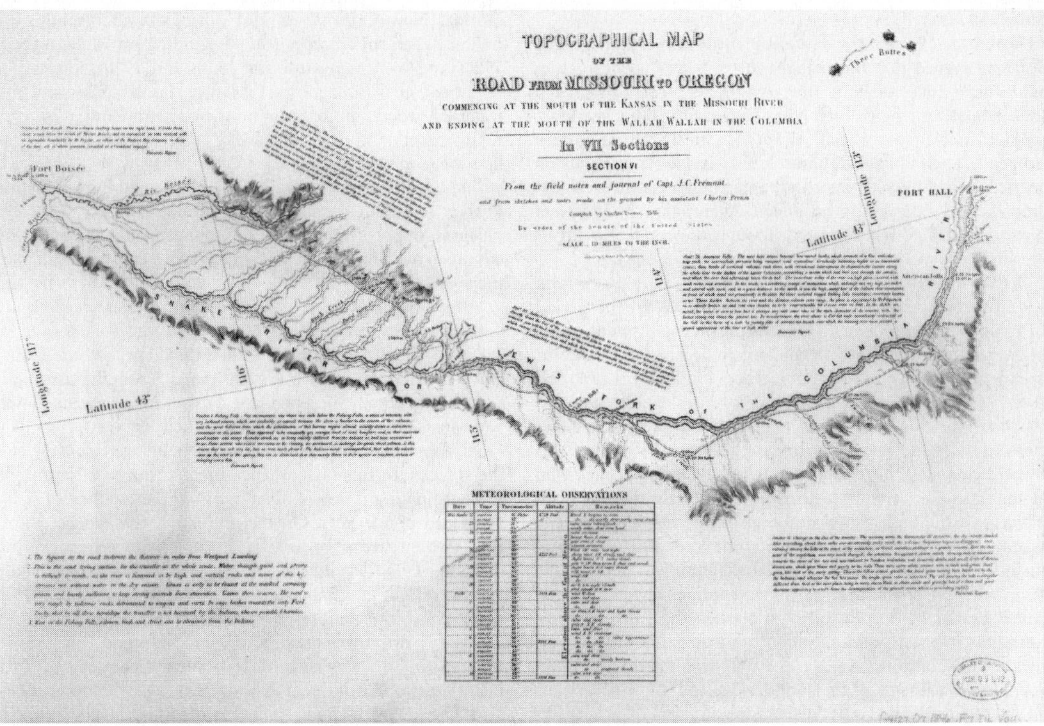

A portion of the Oregon Trail passing through the Snake River region of present-day Idaho appears in this 1846 map. Featuring extensive information about topography, natural landmarks, and the weather, the seven-part map was prepared by order of the Senate in 1846, as the "Oregon Question"—the issue of the northwestern boundary between the United States and Canada—gripped the nation. The map was based on the 1842–43 field notes and journal of the explorer John C. Frémont.

[*See* Expansionism; Foreign Relations: U.S. Relations with Canada; Frémont, John C.; Mexican War; Oregon Trail; Polk, James K.]

As a result, especially by the 1890s, policy and off-track bookmaking syndicates had the support of betters as well as local businesses and politicians. The activities of these important criminal entrepreneurs were not yet labelled "organized crime," however.

During the *Progressive-Era antiprostitution crusade, many reformers argued that the redlight districts in American cities could not exist without the systematic recruitment of thousands of young girls each year. They claimed that shadowy, organized networks of "white slavers"—often with an Eastern European Jewish background—lured innocent girls from American small towns, port cities, and foreign countries to become slaves in the cities' bordellos. Again, the specific term "organized crime" was not used, though the concept, with its exaggerations, was clearly present.

The term itself was first used in the 1920s, perhaps in John Landesco's *Organized Crime in Chicago* (1929). In the period of Prohibition, the press and movies, in their treatment of the bootleggers, often ascribed to the largely decentralized and independent bootleggers a mythical centralized control and power. *Chicago, where the violence of bootlegging wars was capped by the famous 1929 St. Valentine's Day massacre and where Al *Capone revelled in media attention, was the focus of worldwide attention. Capone was one of four partners who entered into partnerships with others to establish numerous relatively small bootlegging, gambling, and vice enterprises. Because he lived chiefly at his Miami home after 1927 and spent much of 1929 in a *Philadelphia jail, Capone was perhaps the least important of the four partners. The media, nevertheless, defined him as the lord of Chicago bootlegging and a controlling figure in local politics. Such *films as *Little Caesar* with Edward G. Robinson (1932) and Paul Muni's *Scarface* (1932) provided vivid images of the gangsters' power and ruthlessness and made Capone a symbol of "organized crime."

The most important twentieth century development involving the split between the reality of criminal structure and the mythical uses of the term "organized crime" was the creation of the idea that "the mafia" coordinated crime in the United States. An important early step came in 1950 to 1951 when the U.S. Senate's Special Committee to Investigate Organized Crime (popularly known as the Kefauver Committee after its chair, Senator Estes Kefauver of Tennessee) held widely-watched televised hearings in a number of cities and concluded officially that a secret society called "the mafia," operated across the United States to oversee crime. In 1963–1964, Joseph Valachi, a long-time member of a New York City Italian-American crime family, testified before Congress and for the first time provided a public description of the structure of such groups. He was motivated to do so because, while in prison for drug dealing, he had killed a fellow prisoner and then sought leniency by agreeing to talk. More important, perhaps, the President's Commission on Law Enforcement and the Administration of Justice published a report on *Organized Crime* (1967), based chiefly upon information gained from telephone wiretaps. The report claimed that 24 "Cosa Nostra" cartels in some 20 cities, with membership restricted to *Italian Americans, controlled criminal activities in their own cities and cooperated across city boundaries in gambling, loansharking, and *drugs. Building on such developments, Hollywood contributed vivid and exaggerated images of "the mafia" in movies like *The Godfather* (1972) and *Prizzi's Honor* (1985).

In the process of identifying a "mafia" menace, newspaper reporters and criminologists created a history of the American "mafia" that mixed myth with fact. During Prohibition, successful bootleggers, although often young men from poor neighborhoods, learned to think in terms of national and even international markets as the importers and manufacturers made deals with processors and wholesalers so that booze could be moved from its multiple sources to its millions of consumers. During and after Prohibition many bootleggers and their business associates invested in gambling casinos and other gambling enterprises; with a broadened understanding of markets, they sometimes jointly invested in tourist centers like Florida, New Orleans, or Hot Springs. Concurrently, some Italian-American entrepreneurs, beginning probably in the late 1920s and continuing into the 1930s and 1940s, formed local membership organizations. Like the Masons, Elks, and other fraternal orders, the organizations had formal initiation rituals for members and often acted like secret societies; like Chambers of Commerce or Rotary Clubs, they were a framework within which members, while generally remaining independent in their economic pursuits, could develop contacts, learn about business opportunities, and sometimes settle disputes under circumstances in which the legal system was not available to them.

After *World War II, then, investigators discovered both the joint partnerships of independent entrepreneurs and the Italian-American "families" (which they labelled "the mafia"). They then constructed a history based upon the assumption that the generally independent businessmen in the families were instead controlled by and worked for the profit of the "mafia" and that non-Italian entrepreneurs were subservient to the Italians. In this history, the "mafia" rose to a central place in coordinating crime nationally through the power of Italian-American bootleggers. On the one hand, this ignores the fact that entrepreneurs of Eastern-European Jewish background dominated bootlegging. (Some 50 percent of leading bootleggers were Jewish, 25 percent were Italian-American.) On the other hand, this ignores that many leading bootleggers (like Capone) were not members of "families" and that many of those who formed the families were not bootleggers. In the history, Lucky Luciano, after a series of assassinations in *New York City, consolidated "mafia" control nationally. While Luciano certainly emerged, briefly, as a highly respected "don" in New York, it is an exaggeration to ascribe national power to him. After World War II, according to the dominant history, the "mafia" moved into and controlled the casinos in Nevada. No doubt many entrepreneurs who had operated illegal casinos in the 1930s and 1940s were leaders in the expansion of legal gambling in Las Vegas. But this history overlooks the predominance of Jewish entrepreneurs in the rise of Las Vegas as a national entertainment center; equally important, it overlooks that they were largely independent, acting in their own interests and not seeking profit for a "mafia."

As the fight against the "mafia" menace became a central focus of law enforcement, the Federal government established Organized Crime Task Forces in many cities where Italian-Americans were active in criminal activities. States and cities followed suit. Naturally, the focus of federal, state, and local prosecutions almost solely on Italian-Americans, combined with the media attention, necessarily publicized the exaggerated notions of the power of "the mafia" while obscuring the complexity and diverse roots of criminal activities and generally ignoring similar activities by persons not of Italian-American background.

In the 1970s, with the launching of the "war on drugs," drug trafficking gradually supplanted "the mafia" as the focus of law enforcement and media attention. It became clear that Italian-Americans could not bear the blame for the multiple drug trafficking activities that provided LSD, marijuana, cocaine, and heroin to a diversity of users. As a result, the term "organized crime" was now transferred to drug "cartels," often centered in other countries like Mexico, Jamaica, or Colombia. This had the effect of again oversimplifying a complex problem while also externalizing America's drug problem by blaming it on powerful foreign organizations. At the end of the twentieth century, with the expansion of international banking and trade and the management of the international economy by computers, the term "organized crime" was expanded to encompass a variety of criminal activities embedded in the new economy, such as money laundering and investment fraud.

The term "organized crime," introduced in the 1920s, has been applied to a diversity of criminal markets and ethnic groups. While criminal entrepreneurs often enter into joint ventures or use violence as part of market competition, the effect of the term has been to oversimplify the structure of complex and loosely coordinated activities, to suggest that a danger originates abroad, and generally to exaggerate the centralized power and control of those engaged in illegal pursuits.

[*See also* Federal Bureau of Investigation; Hoover, J. Edgar; Police; Prostitution and Antiprostitution; Temperance and Prohibition.]

• Mark H. Haller, "The Changing Structure of American Gambling in the Twentieth Century," *Journal of Social Issues* 35, no. 3 (1979), 87–114. Stephen Fox, *Blood and Power: Organized Crime in Twentieth-Century America,* 1989. Mark H. Haller, "Policy Gambling, Entertainment, and the Emergence of Black Politics: Chicago from 1900 to 1940," *Journal of Social History* 24 (Summer 1991), 719–39. David E. Ruth, *Inventing the Public Enemy: The Gangster in American Culture, 1918–1934,* 1996. Terry M. Parssinen and Kathryn Meyer, *Web of Smoke,* 1999.

—Mark H. Haller

ORPHANAGES, public or private institutions for the care of children without parents, date to ancient times. Charity for parentless children is mentioned in the New Testament and is included in Jewish and Islamic religious law. Christian monasteries and convents assumed this role in the Middle Ages to discourage the abandonment of children and unwanted infants. Protestant churches continued this work of mercy, inspiring governments to provide for orphans. By 1550, orphanages were combined with educational reform in England, Germany, Switzerland, and Holland.

The orphanage appeared early in America when an English philanthropist, James Oglethorpe, established Georgia as a proprietary colony in 1732 and as a refugee for English orphans and paupers. But orphan asylums were rare because all British colonies enforced the English Poor Law of 1601, which gave orphans and other worthy poor persons a legal right to assistance from the state. Transplanted to the New World, the Elizabethan social welfare system relied on the *family and the local government to care for orphans.

*Colonial Era orphans were typically apprenticed by the town selectmen (the overseers of the poor) to craftsmen or farmers to learn a trade in a well-ordered Christian family. However, by 1780 growing seaports like *Boston, *New York City, *Philadelphia, and Baltimore, Maryland, had larger, more heterogeneous populations, and not every homeless child could be apprenticed or farmed out. When Boston opened its first *alms house in 1660, following the examples of New York (1657) and Plymouth, Massachusetts (1658), children were among the first inmates. By the 1760s, more than one-quarter of Massachusetts poorhouse residents were minors. Matrons cared for children until they could be apprenticed, sent to live with relatives, or placed as domestic servants. Many citizens, however, criticized the mixing of young children with adult inmates—including the indigent, insane, senile, crippled, diseased, drunken and criminal—as deplorable and unwise.

After the *Revolutionary War a new solution appeared when philanthropic ladies and gentlemen established private institutions for orphans. The Boston Female Asylum opened in 1799 to care for young girls, and this example spread to New York, Philadelphia, *Chicago, and most large cities. Public officials cooperated with private charities to reduce the taxpayers' burden. This pattern of genteel private charity continued through the nineteenth century, and each community or denomination demonstrated its humanitarianism by operating a wide variety of orphanages and charities.

The *Civil War disrupted family life in every community, placing a heavy burden on both private and public charities. Many Northern states established orphanages to care for the children of soldiers, including half-orphans, a child with only one surviving parent. In 1864 a group of Boston Methodists founded the New England Home for Little Wanderers as a response to *poverty and social disorder on the Civil War homefront. This regional orphanage cared for hundreds of boys and girls each year and developed into a large congregate asylum and (by 1900) a modern, professional child-welfare institution. Like most orphanages, it was racially segregated.

Religious rivalry prompted each denomination to sponsor its own orphanage, often to counter proselytizing or "child stealing" from one sect to another. The Home for Destitute Catholic Children opened in Boston in 1865 in response to the threat that Irish Catholics saw in the Evangelicalism of the New England Home for Little Wanderers. New York City Catholics were similarly motivated by the alleged "child-snatching" of the nonsectarian New York Children's Aid Society, founded in 1853 by the Reverend Charles Loring Brace (1826–1890), a Congregationalist. Similar competition to rescue orphans arose in most major cities throughout the nineteenth century.

In the *Progressive Era, the public and private orphanage was criticized by the new professional social workers as obsolete, expensive, and inhumane. Adoption, foster care, and smaller cottage-style child-welfare institutions replaced the large congregate orphanage in many states. Economy-minded state and federal officials doubted the efficacy of orphanages, and by the time of the New Deal with its social welfare programs, the era of the traditional orphanage was ending, although established institutions remained active in many states into the 1950s. Perhaps America's most famous orphanage was Boys Town, founded in Omaha, Nebraska in 1917 by a Catholic priest. Father Edward J. Flanagan's shelter for homeless and delinquent boys became a self-governing nonsectarian farm community. The 1938 film, *Boys Town,* made Flanagan's institution the most beloved (although controversial) orphanage in the United States. This was one reason cited for interest in reviving orphanages in the 1990s, but the opposition of child-welfare specialists prevailed against the idea.

[*See also* New Deal Era, The; Philanthropy and Philanthropic Foundations; Social Work; Urbanization.]

• Joan Gittens, *Poor Relations: The Children of the State in Illinois, 1818–1990,* 1994. Peter C. Holloran, *Boston's Wayward Children: Social Services for Homeless Children, 1830–1930,* 1994. Kenneth Cmiel, *A Home of Another Kind: One Chicago Orphanage and the Tangle of Child Welfare,* 1995.

—Peter C. Holloran

OSLER, WILLIAM (1849–1919), physician and medical educator. Osler was born at Bond Head, Canada, the son of the Reverend Featherstone Lake Osler and Ellen Free Picton Osler. He graduated in medicine from McGill University in Montreal, Canada, in 1872 and after studies abroad returned to McGill as professor of the institutes of medicine in 1874. In 1884 he moved to the University of Pennsylvania, and in 1889 he was appointed professor of medicine at Johns Hopkins University and physician in chief at Johns Hopkins Hospital.

Drawing on European models, Osler introduced to the Johns Hopkins Medical School, which opened in 1893, a system of clinical clerkships that put a premium on bedside instruction. A charismatic teacher, he became a role model for a generation of U.S. medical students. His influence was further extended through his best-selling textbook, *The Principles and Practice of Medicine* (1892), and numerous essays on the medical life. In 1905 he became Regius Professor at Oxford and in 1911 was made a baronet. In England, Osler and his wife made their home a haven for a generation of Rhodes scholars and other visiting Americans. He died at Oxford in 1919.

A clergyman's son, Osler became a high priest of modern medicine and contributed greatly to America's rise to international medical prominence. His patient-centered teaching and his genteel, bibliophilic scholarship inspired later medical humanists. His legacy is perpetuated through various clubs, lectureships, and the American Osler Society.

[*See also* Medical Education; Medicine: From the 1870s to 1945; Welch, William H.]

• Harvey Cushing, *The Life of Sir William Osler*, 2 vols. 1925. Michael Bliss, *William Osler: A Life in Medicine*, 1999.

—Michael Bliss

OTHER AMERICA, THE. *The Other America: Poverty in the United States* (1962) was written by Michael Harrington (1928–1989), a young socialist whose first encounter with *poverty had come during the two years he lived on *New York City's Lower East Side as part of the Catholic Worker movement, a ministry to the poor founded by Dorothy Day (1897–1980). Harrington became known as "the man who discovered poverty" when his book caught the eye of President John F. *Kennedy. Influenced by the book, Kennedy proposed to his advisers shortly before his assassination that the federal government undertake a "War on Poverty."

Harrington's book made two main points. First, poverty was rampant in the United States, with 40 to 50 million victims, despite the prevailing national belief in the "affluent society." "That the poor are invisible is one of the most important things about them," Harrington wrote. "They are not simply neglected and forgotten as in the old rhetoric of reform; what is much worse, they are not seen."

Second, Harrington argued that a "culture of poverty" existed in the United States. Suffering the effects of generations of inadequate education, nutrition, *housing, and medical care, the poor lacked both the ability and the aspiration to improve their lot in life. Thus, poverty could not be eliminated either by an expanding economy or by exhortations to the poor to lift themselves up by their own bootstraps. "Society," Harrington concluded, "must help [the poor] before they can help themselves."

[*See also Affluent Society, The*; Great Society; Sixties, The; Socialism; Socialist Party; Welfare, Federal.]

• James T. Patterson, *America's Struggle against Poverty*, 1900–1985, rev. ed. 1986. Michael Katz, *The Undeserving Poor: From the War on Poverty to the War on Welfare*, 1989.

—Maurice Isserman

OWENS, JESSE (1913–1980), track-and-field star, winner of four gold medals in the 1936 Berlin Olympics. Born in Oakville, Alabama, Owens first gained notice as a track-and-field performer at East Technical High School in Cleveland, Ohio. Under the tutelage of coach Charles Riley, Owens captured three titles at the National Interscholastic Track and Field Meet in 1933 in *Chicago. Continuing his athletic career at Ohio State University, he further enhanced his reputation as one of the nation's greatest track-and-field stars. At the Western Conference Championships in Ann Arbor, Michigan, in 1935, Owens put on one of the most memorable single-day performances in the history of the sport. Within a span of 45 minutes, he tied the world record in the 100-meter dash and broke world records in the broad jump, 200-yard dash, and 220-yard low hurdles. Remarkable as these performances were, it was Owens's triumphs in the politically charged 1936 Berlin Olympics that brought him lasting fame. His four gold medals helped discredit Adolf Hitler's assertions of Aryan racial superiority and laid the groundwork for an unprecedented record of performance by *African Americans in Olympic track and field.

Following the Berlin games, Owens was reduced to running races against horses for money and pursued several failed business ventures. Later in life he worked for several public agencies; toured on behalf of the U.S. Department of State; and spoke to business, religious, civic, and sports groups. In 1974, he was elected as a charter member of the National Track and Field Hall of Fame.

[*See also* Sports: Amateur Sports and Recreation.]

• Marc Bloom, "Jesse Owens: The Legacy of an American Hero," *Runner*, June 1980, 30–31. William J. Baker, *Jesse Owens: An American Life*, 1986.

—David K. Wiggins

P

PACIFISM. Pacifism is the principled rejection of war. European peace advocates coined the word in 1901 to describe the goal of replacing national wars with *international law and organization. During *World War I the term was narrowed to mean an individual's total renunciation of war and social violence. This essay refers primarily to the latter, more restrictive use of the term.

Pacifism has roots in Buddhism and the Janist tradition of Hinduism, but its modern and Western forms have Christian origins, notably the Anabaptist sects of the Protestant Reformation such as the Mennonites, *Society of Friends (Quakers), and Brethren. For some Anabaptists, a corollary of pacifism was withdrawal from the political life of the state, which was based on military force. Pacifism in that sense may be called nonresistance. Pacifism also has led individuals to active social involvement through pacifist groups like the Fellowship of Reconciliation (FOR, 1915), *American Friends Service Committee (1917), and Mennonite Central Committee (1920).

One expression of pacifism has been *conscientious objection to military service, the principle of the War Resisters League (1923). U.S. and British law during World War I exempted conscientious objectors (COs) whose pacifism was religious and applied to all wars. It did not exempt COs who were not sectarian or who objected (like many socialists) only to that particular war or (like anarchists) to conscription itself. In *World War II the U.S. government liberalized its administration of *conscription without essentially changing the law. Subsequently, however, judicial decisions eroded the religious requirement for CO status, and the *Vietnam War brought considerable public support for the right of selective objection. By that time the Roman Catholic church sanctioned conscientious objection and western European countries typically offered their enlistees alternative service.

Another expression of pacifism has been peacemaking. The carnage of World War I deeply moved a number of men and women who came to pacifism from a Progressive, often a *Social Gospel, orientation. Pacifists like Jane *Addams, Emily Green Balch, Dorothy Detzer, Frederick Libby, A. J. Muste, Kirby Page, and Nevin Sayre played leading roles in peace movements working for *internationalism, challenging U.S. intervention in World War II, and protesting the Vietnam War and the nuclear arms race. Nonresistant sects, notably Mennonites and Brethren, also developed active forms of pacifism such as humanitarian service for war victims.

A third expression of pacifism has been nonviolent direct action for justice. Struck by the conjunction of injustice and war during World War I, Progressive pacifists came to see working for justice as a corollary of peace-seeking. Inspired by Mohandas Gandhi, some American pacifists experimented with nonviolent direct action. In race relations, for example, the FOR and *Congress of Racial Equality (1943) counseled Martin Luther *King Jr. and other civil rights leaders. Nonviolent direct action also shaped the Vietnam War protests and the campaign against *nuclear weapons.

Still an essentially individual witness to principle, pacifism has become secular as well as religious, inspiring a range of collective action from humanitarian service and political activism to nonviolent direct action.

[*See also* Anarchism; Antinuclear Protest Movements; Antiwar Movements; Civil Rights Movement; Mennonites and Amish; Peace Movements; Socialism.]

• Peter Brock, *Pacifism in the United States from the Colonial Era to the First World War,* 1968. Peter Brock, *Twentieth-Century Pacifism,* 1979. Harvey Dyck, ed., *The Pacifist Impulse in Historical Perspective,* 1996. Anne Klejment and Nancy L. Roberts, *American Catholic Pacifism: The Influence of Dorothy Day and the Catholic Worker Movement,* 1996.

—E. Charles Chatfield

PAINE, THOMAS (1737–1809), political philosopher and pamphleteer. Born in England, Paine grew up in the small-town artisan milieu of Thetford, Norfolk, where his Quaker father taught him corset-making. He failed in this trade and as a minor excise officer. In 1774, jobless, debt-ridden, and separated from his second wife, he sailed for *Philadelphia bearing letters of recommendation from Benjamin *Franklin. Pursuing a new career as a political pamphleteer, he made history by advocating American independence in the best-selling pamphlet **Common Sense,* published in January 1776. He supported the *Revolutionary War through rousing articles and a pamphlet series called *The Crisis* (1776–1783). Service as a military aide-de-camp, secretary of the *Continental Congress's Committee for Foreign Affairs (1777–1778), and clerk to Pennsylvania's legislature (1779–1780) did not hold his attention for long.

In 1787, Paine returned to Europe, moving between London and Paris to promote a single-arch iron bridge he had invented and patented. He supported the moderate wing of the French revolutionaries, sat in the French National Assembly for Calais, and narrowly escaped the guillotine. His two-part treatise, *The Rights of Man: Being an Answer to Mr. Burke's Attack on the French Revolution* (1791–1792), defended republican government and its natural-rights foundation. His *Age of Reason* (1795–1796), a major statement of Enlightenment criticism of traditional Christian theology, tarnished him as an "infidel." Returning to the United States in 1802, Paine died, impoverished, in New Rochelle, New York. A brilliant polemicist with an independent critical mind that personified the Enlightenment's international aspect, Paine during his first American stay played a crucial role in arguing the case for revolution and in sustaining support for the war once it began.

• Jack Fruchtman Jr., *Thomas Paine: Apostle of Freedom,* 1994. John Keane, *Tom Paine: A Political Life,* 1995.

—Willi Paul Adams

PAINTING

To 1945
Since 1945

PAINTING: TO 1945

The Protestant cultural heritage of Anglo settlers in the eastern colonies brought with it a long-lived suspicion of visual experience. Dissenting Protestants associated visual display with

*Roman Catholicism and with absolutist forms of government. From its origins in the 1660s, therefore, visual expression in the English colonies was expected to serve moral and spiritual lessons. In contrast to the iconophobic Anglo cultures of the east were the devotional images of saints *(retablos)* produced by the Spanish Catholic colonies of the *Southwest, annexed to the United States following the *Mexican War.

Colonial and Antebellum Eras. Seventeenth-century Anglo-American painting, indebted to Elizabethan courtly styles as adapted by provincial English "limners" and devoted to portraits of prosperous mercantile families such as the Freakes, focused on the external attributes of godliness in the forms of material prosperity. A nonillusionistic emphasis on pattern over volume or depth governed visual representation until the early eighteenth century, when a growing market in mezzotints after baroque masters introduced Renaissance principles of perspective and chiaroscuro. Along with the increasingly worldly *New England mercantile elite, the land-based colonial aristocracy of the New York Dutch patroons and the tidewater plantations produced a form of colonial baroque and later rococo portraiture relying on English print sources. With the *Boston-born John Singleton *Copley, colonial elites found a self-trained artist fully able to realize their self-projections as independent artisans (*Paul Revere,* 1768–1770) or fashionable men of wealth (*Nicholas Boylston,* 1767). In the absence of inherited titles, portraiture emphasized self-fashioning through clothing and consumer goods.

Frustrated by limited cultural opportunities, promising colonials like Copley and Benjamin West (1738–1820) pursued careers in England. Following his appointment as painter to King George III, West in *Death of General Wolfe* (1771) redefined British history painting with figures dressed in contemporary clothing and a Christ-like martyred hero. The *Revolutionary War furthered heroic modern history painting, as in a series of battle scenes by John Trumbull (1786–1832) that anticipated his large-scale works in the U.S. Capitol rotunda.

London remained the artistic metropolis for Americans in the early nineteenth century; history painters such as Washington Allston (1779–1843) and Samuel F. B. *Morse occupied an international arena. When Morse returned to the fledgling republic, however, his career floundered as interest in history painting waned. Allston, however, sustained by Boston's affluent Unitarians, forged a richly associative art combining figures and landscapes and shaped by European romanticism, Venetian colorism, and "Grand Manner" history painting. Celebrated during his lifetime, Allston created in America the cultural type of the artist-visionary at odds with the materialism of society.

After the opening of the *Erie Canal in 1825, *New York City emerged as the center of cultural production. The 1826 establishment of the artist-run National Academy of Design (NAD) in New York gave institutional focus to the growing *nationalism of American art production. Thomas *Cole, an English émigré, established a youthful reputation for native and Biblical landscapes by the late 1820s; his subsequent work, notably the cautionary allegory *The Course of Empire* (1833–1836), offered lessons in the prophetic and instructive content of landscape art. Cole's conservative message and his distrust of national hubris went largely ignored by the landscape painters of the midcentury. His pupil Frederick Church (1862–1900), along with Asher B. Durand (1796–1886), later president of the NAD, celebrated America's cultural mission with images of a providentially blessed nature even as the eastern wilderness succumbed to industrialization. John James *Audubon's monumental project *The Birds of America* included his meticulous, vivid painting of some five hundred different species.

Concurrently, genre painting—scenes of everyday life such as W. S. Mount's *The Painter's Triumph* (1836)—took its cue from theater and popular culture in revealing subtle social distinctions while also expressing a truculent sense of national pride. The Düsseldorf Academy in Germany, with its emphasis on theatrical narrative and staged effects, replaced London as the preferred destination for antebellum American artists seeking European training.

1865 to 1920. After the *Civil War, the growing cosmopolitanism of American culture was furthered by the availability of transcontinental rail travel, the increasing presence of European dealers in New York City, the emergence of a capitalist elite dedicated to acquiring European art, and the opening of major art museums in Boston, New York, *Philadelphia, *Detroit, and elsewhere. While landscape and genre painting remained dominant into the late nineteenth century, American art gradually assumed a more retrospective and academic character. The Colonial Revival introduced antiquarian themes, along with a preference for muted interiors and preurban folkways. Landscape artists preferred intimist views of rural eastern scenery painted at dawn and twilight or through a softening atmospheric veil. Tonalist artists, following the lead of the American expatriate James McNeill *Whistler, preferred subtle modulations of color within a limited chromatic range.

After the 1870s, Paris and Munich emerged as major destinations for younger American artists who, repudiating the meticulous and nonpainterly realism of the so-called Hudson River school, favored a self-conscious artistry cultivated as a unique form of expertise. No longer serving nationalist cultural ideals, they joined a cosmopolitan and often expatriate international brotherhood "in pursuit of beauty," beholden only to aesthetic principles of art for art's sake. Stylistically, much American painting in these decades was indistinguishable from that of Europe, as American artists reaped awards at the Parisian Académie des Beaux-Arts and vied with French artists for the patronage of wealthy American collectors. Mary *Cassatt of Pennsylvania lived after 1874 in Paris, where her luminous paintings of domestic and maternal scenes showed the influence of Edgar Degas and the impressionists.

Around 1900, critical attention swung toward the so-called native realists. Thomas *Eakins, although trained in Paris, focused his analytic gaze on his native Philadelphia in ambitious portraits of professional men such as his 1875 *Clinic of Doctor Samuel Gross*; psychologically probing portraits of women; and outdoor genre scenes combining a scientific interest in motion and light refraction with a commitment to modern life and an escape from Victorian euphemism, called for by his friend Walt *Whitman. Though national fame awaited a New York retrospective following his death, Eakins furnished inspiration for the "ashcan" artists around Robert Henri (1865–1929), who rejected the "genteel" overrefinement of American painting at the end of the century.

Winslow *Homer, largely self-taught, enjoyed a growing national reputation in the late nineteenth century as a "purely American" painter. Despite his denial of external influences, his painting, with its elegant formal reductions and attention to surface forms, reveals a debt to Japanese art *(Japonisme)* as well as French *plein-aire* and English and French academic art. Homer's late seascapes of the 1890s and early 1900s, however, gave substance to the critical repudiation of cosmopolitan art and a resurgent nationalism.

The year 1908 marked the waning institutional grip of the National Academy in the independent exhibition of the "Eight," bringing together social realists around Henri with the postimpressionist Charles Prendergast and others. Concurrently, Alfred *Stieglitz, a photographer dedicated to establishing his medium as a fine art, introduced New Yorkers to European postimpressionism, cubism, and African art at his Fifth Avenue gallery "291" (1905–1917). Viewing modern art as an agent of cultural change, Stieglitz promoted such early American modernists as Georgia *O'Keeffe, Marsden Hartley, John Marin, and Arthur Dove (1880–1946). Dove's early abstractions (ca. 1910) were exactly contemporaneous with those of the first "pure" European abstractionist, Wassily Kandinsky. The 1913 *Armory Show in New York City, offering audiences their first major exposure to European modernism, polarized the American art world into traditionalist academic and progressive camps. Among the latter were Stuart Davis (1893–1964), whose youthful work registered a dramatic shift in style after 1913. Other Americans like Max Weber and Dove had already gained exposure to European modernism in Paris. The migration of French artists to New York during *World War I, notably Marcel Duchamp, engendered native awareness of the ironic artistic possibilities of *technology and urban mass culture, producing a brief New York "proto-Dada" movement that left its mark on American art long after its immediate influence.

1920 to 1945. After a decade of apprenticeship to European modernism and the wartime disruption of New York cultural life, American artists in the 1920s turned to the cultural landscapes of the regions. While artists such as Stuart Davis continued to exploit *advertising and urban culture, creatively interpreting the syncopated rhythms of *jazz, others, from Charles Demuth to O'Keeffe, used modernist lessons of irony, geometric abstraction, scale distortion, and decontextualization to engage regional subjects from rural Pennsylvania to Hispanic New Mexico. By the 1930s, this "rediscovery of America" had broadened into "American Scene" painting, ranging from the rural, small town, and urban images of Edward Hopper (1882–1967) and Charles Burchfield to the embrace of metropolitan culture in the work of Reginald Marsh and others of New York's "Fourteenth Street School." Leading the "regionalists" (so dubbed by *Time* magazine in a 1934 cover story) were Grant Wood, John Steuart Curry, and Thomas Hart Benton (1889–1975), whose repudiation of his modernist roots and virulent isolationism point to a resurgent populism. The social hardship of the 1930s Depression produced a growing affiliation of artists with workers; themes of labor, urban *unemployment, and working-class martyrdom abound in the social realism of Philip Evergood, the Soyer brothers, Ben Shahn (1898–1969), and others. *New Deal Era work relief programs for artists produced many public murals—influenced by the presence in the United States of the Mexican muralists Diego Rivera, Clemente Orozco, and David Siqueiros from the late 1920s into the early 1930s—as well as easel paintings.

The cultural impact of *World War II, along with a second wave of European artistic migration to New York, brought a turn from social themes and politically engaged art toward new techniques of automatism that drew on the uncensored energies of the unconscious. Blending surrealist influences, an interest in cross-cultural myth, and the art of tribal cultures, Jackson *Pollock, Mark Rothko (1903–1970), and other figurative artists of the 1930s turned during World War II to subject-based abstraction dedicated to universal themes that explored the tragic dimensions of human experience. Such developments prepared the way for the innovations of *abstract expressionism that combined the muralism of the 1930s with a commitment to the role of American art in articulating mythic truths.

[*See also* Architecture; Folk Art and Crafts; Modernist Culture; Romantic Movement.]

• Milton Brown, *American Painting, from the Armory Show to the Depression,* 1955. Neil Harris, *The Artist in American Society: The Formative Years, 1790–1860,* 1966. Joshua C. Taylor, *America as Art,* 1979. H. Wayne Morgan, *New Muses: Art in American Culture, 1865–1920,* 1978. Theodore E. Stebbins et al., *A New World: Masterpieces of American Painting, 1760–1910* (exhibit catalog, Museum of Fine Arts, Boston), 1983. Wayne Craven, *Colonial American Portraiture,* 1986. Elizabeth Johns, *American Genre Painting: The Politics of Everyday Life,* 1991. Michael Leja, *Reframing Abstract Expressionism: Subjectivity and Painting in the 1940s,* 1993. Terry Smith, *Making the Modern: Industry, Art, and Design in America,* 1993. Sarah Burns, *Inventing the Modern Artist: Art and Culture in the Gilded Age America,* 1996.

—Angela Miller

PAINTING: SINCE 1945

Eclecticism ruled nineteenth-century American painting as artists looked to Europe for traditional styles and subject matter. By *World War I, the Picasso-led revolution of cubism and its offshoots had licensed independent self-assertion. Thus, the earliest American abstractionists, including John Marin and Stuart Davis, created a wide range of individualistic expression with significant content as well as modernist form. Following *World War II, as *New York City replaced Paris as the capital of art in the West, American painters declared their ultimate independence from European influences. The shift was signaled by Peggy Guggenheim in her gallery, Art of This Century. After showing works by leading exiled Europeans in 1942, including Max Ernst (1903–1970), Guggenheim held one-artist exhibitions of recent works by Jackson *Pollock, Mark Rothko, Clyfford Still, Robert Motherwell, and William Baziotes. Each revealed the influence of surrealist psychic automatism, which in its purest doodle-like process resulted in biomorphic imagery, a highly ambiguous metamorphosis of plant and animal appearances. Representing the avant-garde of modernism, the Americans had moved beyond the social realism, regionalism, and stylized cubism of the 1930s.

By 1950, Pollock, Rothko, and Willem *de Kooning, varying greatly in style and subject matter, led the movement hailed as "*abstract expression" by the formalist critic Clement Greenberg or "action art" by the content-oriented critic Harold Rosenberg. Both labels suggested disturbance, whether from painterly turmoil or a sociopsychological origin. Though Pollock did not necessarily invent his signature technique of dripping, splattering, and pouring compositions of enamel over large areas of unprimed canvas, he vastly extended its scale and free associations of meaning. Jungian analysis underlay his free-flowing compositions and stream-of-consciousness imagery as he struggled to harmonize the conflicting forces of his psyche. Rothko's paintings, comprised of luminous layers of what appear to be chromatic vapor, invite meditation, especially when presented in a chapel-like setting. Sadly, the shades of his consistently formatted canvases gradually descended into melancholy, depression, and suicide, ending whatever relationship their early, heightened color schemes may have had to an American tradition of decorative optimism. De Kooning, more outwardly expressive than either Pollock or Rothko, culminated a series of single female figures with the provocative *Woman I* in 1952. Its painterly configuration of seemingly spontaneous gestures of primary hues, scumbled whites, and black contours distorts the body into a large-breasted, primeval goddess image and the face into a rodent-toothed, bug-eyed mask. De Kooning alluded to both an Oedipus complex and the ubiquitous commercialized glamour-girl as motivating factors in his best-known work. He followed it up with a Marilyn *Monroe painting and a progression of large, nonfigurative, urbanscapes. Moving to the end of Long Island, he luxuriated in thickly painted pink, white, and yellow sun-bathed nudes through the 1960s. For twenty more years, beautifully painted abstractions grew increasingly linear in their decorative patterning by the time of his death in 1997.

Meanwhile, modern American painting evolved from early reactions in the 1950s against painterly expressionism; through the movements of pop art, geometric minimalism, and photo realism in the 1960s; to a revival of expressionist painting in the 1970s that ended in a near chaos of postmodernist diversity as the century ended. Barnett Newman and Ellsworth Kelly introduced a minimalist subversion of abstract expressionism as Pollock came into public view. Beginning in 1948 with *One-ment,* a humorous "zip" of heavy orange pigment bisecting a modulated brown "field," Newman expanded his color-fields onto enormous, vertically divided canvases. His compositions were strictly intuitive, he maintained, defying the search for momentary self-identity of existentialist action art. Kelly, returning to America in 1954 from a six-year stay in Paris, offered geometric abstraction comprised of gestureless, solid-color shapes that he said "shifted the visual reality of painting to include the space around it." He thereby, to a greater extent than Newman, liberated the medium from both the picture frame and the picture plane. As instructed by *ArtForum* critics influenced by Greenberg, minimalist painters of the 1960s were well aware of the precedents set by the Dutch modernist Piet Mondrian and the Russian revolutionary artist Kasimir Malevich, both highly reductive in designing geometric paintings. Kenneth Noland, Gene Davis, Robert Mangold, and Brice Marden maintained their predecessors' level of precisely ruled abstraction. Though this was not particularly true of Frank Stella (1936–), his work was often categorized as "hard-edge" minimalism in spite of his penchant for decorative designs.

Cool detachment in American painting emerged by the mid-1950s when Jasper Johns (1930–) exhibited his flag and target paintings, and his loft-mate, Robert Rauschenberg (1925–), introduced his "combine" paintings, including *Bed.* From that point forward, through many varieties of object matter and media, including encaustic on newsprint and silkscreen collages of magazine clippings, they insisted that their purpose was simply a chance, inconsequential display of random actuality. Free from subjective attachment, their increasingly complicated compositions were supposed to be viewed "the same way you look at a radiator," according to Johns. In Rauschenberg's case, his visual noise, from black-and-white to color, might well correspond to the information explosion of *television, especially experienced with a quick-action remote control. This detachment persisted as the central concept of 1960s painting, no matter how hot the decade became politically and culturally.

Drawing upon mass-media imagery and a booming *consumer culture, pop art stole the show by the early 1960s. The British artists Eduardo Paolozzi and Richard Hamilton anticipated the process in the 1950s, but the most authentic instigator was Andy *Warhol, a New York advertising artist who aspired to fame as a fine artist. In 1960, Warhol produced a casein-and-crayon head of the comic-strip character Dick Tracy on canvas and a synthetic polymer painting of an ad for a storm door. In 1961 he began his series of repetitive silkscreen paintings, including Campbell's soup cans, Coca-Cola bottles, and promotional shots of Marilyn Monroe. Promoted through Leo Castelli Gallery, Warhol was joined in the burgeoning pop art market by Roy Lichtenstein with his oil-on-canvas blowups of comic-strip frames. The former billboard painter James Rosenquist outdid Rauschenberg by painting enormous montages of consumer goods intermingled with glamorous female faces and other human-figure fragments. This mixture climaxed in his *F-111* (1965), an eighty-six-foot, fifty-one-panel mural featuring the new U.S. fighter-bomber identified with the *Vietnam War. Social commentary not to be denied, Romare Bearden (1911–1988) during the peak of the *civil rights movement, applied a similar cut-and-paste composition of masklike faces to rhythmic depictions of black ghetto life.

Stylized sexuality became the hallmark of Tom Wesselmann, who garnished his Great American Nude paintings with an assortment of supermarket items, including, of course, Coca-Cola. The *San Francisco-born Peter Saul heated up his pop iconography with Day-glo compositions of elastic, bubble-gum figures reenacting the inhuman horrors of Vietnam. His idiosyncratic style influenced the figural fantasies of *Chicago artists Gladys Nilsson, Jim Nutt, and Karl Wirsum. The Chicagoan Ed Paschke's TV wrestlers, sideshow freaks, streetwalkers, and transvestites, as well as Roger Brown's cartoon fantasies of Chicago and its suburbs, with silhouetted figures at yellow-lit windows, are inventions of their own. Because of pop art's diversity, debate continues about how coolly objective it could have been, when its characteristic "take offs" may readily be interpreted as satirical cultural commentary.

Urban appeal and abstract objectivity fused in another strain of painting by the end of the 1960s, photo realism, a manual, photocopy technique guaranteed to attract a following in a materialistic society. All kinds of consumer goods, from kosher meats to shoes and silverware, fill the colorful show-window paintings of Richard Estes and Don Eddy. An arrangement of details and reflections, rendered with small-scale brushes and airbrushes, extracts factual renderings from photographs. Audrey Flack accomplished the same in her autobiographic still-life paintings, while Chuck Close tediously enlarged black-and-white face-shots of himself and friends to enormous sizes and then simulated the dot-by-dot process of three-color reproduction. Whatever the object matter—Robert Cottingham's neon signs, Robert Bechtle's Buicks and Chevys, Ralph Goings's Airstream trailers, or John Salt's rusted-out junkers—the transcribed data of these paintings add up to impersonal inventories, as aesthetically significant as uniform abstractions. In this sense they, too, were a product of the "cool" 1960s, despite their reactionary distance from mainstream minimalism.

In keeping with the stylistic dialect characteristic of the history of painting since the Renaissance, a counterresponse to the "cool" reactions against abstract expressionism came in the form of a painterly synthesis that critics labeled neoexpressionism. This, in turn, spawned what was commonly termed *postmodernism. In the neoexpressionist work of Philip Guston (1912–1980) in the 1970s, paintings of alternating interior and exterior spaces were occupied by *Ku Klux Klan hoods, comic hands holding cigars, knobby legs bent at right angles, shoe bottoms, clocks, and backs of stretched canvases. These heavily painted oddities lack overt relevance to each other and refuse to coalesce as an overall configuration. This defiance of order, whether expressive of sociopsychological disturbance or a visual counterpart to the poststructuralism that prevailed in literary theory and criticism after 1980, invaded fashionable painting on both sides of the Atlantic. Modernist principles of harmonious balance, traceable to Cezanne and cubism, virtually vanished in the decentered, deconstructive paintings of young postmodernist celebrities. Susan Rothenberg "deenergized" crudely drawn images of horses in a surface of dense pigment, while Julian Schnabel overloaded enormous canvases with broken dinnerware and undisciplined drawing. Jean-Michel Basquiat ceased defacing subway station walls for a seven-year career of eye-catching, drug-addicted, figural scrawls accompanied by essentially undecipherable graffiti texts. Elizabeth Murray abandoned the rectangular format entirely, fragmenting such domestic objects as tables, beds, and coffee mugs into bulky pictorial pieces that project like sculpture from the wall. All in all, an engaging eccentricity, free from the dictates of institutionalized patronage or traditional stylistic prescriptions, characterized advanced American painting as the twentieth century ended. No longer restricted to a New York avant-garde, the postmodern license of creative self-indulgence infiltrated the entire art world as American culture spread over the globe.

[*See also* Fifties, The; Foreign Relations: The Cultural Dimension; Literature: Since World War I; Modernist Culture; Photography; Sixties, The.]

• Irving Sandler, *The Triumph of American Painting: A History of Abstract Expressionism,* 1976. Louis K. Meisel. *Photo-Realism,* 1989. David Anfam, *Abstract Expressionism,* 1990. Christin J. Mamiya, *Pop Art and Consumer Culture, American Super Market,* 1992. Norma Broude and Mary D. Gerrard, *The Power of Feminist Art: The American Movement of the 1970s, History and Impact,* 1994. Brandon Taylor, *Avant-Garde and After, Rethinking Art Now,* 1995. Thomas Crow, *The Rise of the Sixties: American and European Art in the Era of Dissent,* 1996. Irving Sandler, *Art of the Postmodern Era, from the Late 1960s to the Early 1990s,* 1996. Kenneth Baker, *Minimalism: Art of Circumstance,* 1998.

—James M. Dennis

PALEY, WILLIAM (1901–1990), chairman of the Columbia Broadcasting System (CBS). Born in *Chicago to Russian immigrants, Paley first became aware of *radio's power by *advertising cigars over the air and seeing sales soar. In 1928 he spearheaded his now wealthy family's purchase of a controlling interest in the struggling CBS radio network connecting sixteen stations. Intending to remain active in radio only briefly, Paley stayed on to develop a managerial team and attract the entertainment stars (and later the journalists) who propelled CBS to a leading position in audience ratings and revenue. Columbia Records, purchased by CBS in the 1930s, became an industry leader and introduced the long-playing record in 1948. Naming Frank Stanton his successor as CBS president in 1946, Paley became chairman of the board. Staying on long after the retirement age of sixty-five, mandatory for all CBS employees, and after the often-forced departure of several potential successors, Paley retired in 1982, only to be brought back as a figurehead in the late 1980s. He thus remained a key figure as CBS emerged as a dominant *television network in the 1950s and after.

Paley combined an interest in the fine arts (he was a longtime supporter of New York's Museum of Modern Art) and enjoyment of high society with an almost uncanny feel for programming that the general public would appreciate. Confident in his financial independence and social and managerial abilities, Paley dominated CBS, participating in programming decisions, wooing stars, basking in the reflected glory of *CBS News,* and seeking acquisitions that fed CBS's image as the "Tiffany Network." Through its news and entertainment programming during Paley's tenure, CBS both reflected and helped shape American *popular culture.

• William S. Paley, *As It Happened: A Memoir,* 1979. Sally Bedell Smith, *In All His Glory: The Life of William S. Paley—The Legendary Tycoon and His Brilliant Circle,* 1990.

—Christopher H. Sterling

PANAMA. *See* Panama Canal; Protectorates and Dependencies.

PANAMA CANAL, a fifty-one-mile ship canal through the Isthmus of Panama that connects the Caribbean Sea with the Pacific Ocean. The Spanish recognized the importance of such a canal as early as the sixteenth century. From 1879 to 1881, the French engineer Ferdinand de Lesseps attempted to build a canal at Panama, but the project failed because of disease, poor planning, and lack of funding. Late nineteenth-century commercial and military interests prompted the U.S. government to undertake the project. After actively promoting Panama's independence, the Theodore *Roosevelt administration completed the Hay-Bunau-Varilla Treaty in 1903, negotiated by Secretary of State John *Hay, by which Panama granted the United States the right to construct, maintain, operate, and defend the canal.

Between 1907 and 1914, after a major *public-health program to eradicate the mosquitos that transmitted *yellow fever, the U.S. army colonel George W. Goethals (1858–1928) directed nearly 35,000 workers who completed the greatest construction project the world had seen to that time. Seven sets of locks raise and lower approximately fifty ships every twenty-four hours en route between the Caribbean Sea and Pacific Ocean. To pass through the canal takes approximately eight hours. For ships traveling between the East and West coasts of the United States, the canal route is some 8,000 nautical miles shorter than the route around the tip of South America. On voyages between the East coast of North America and the West coast of South America and Asia, the savings is some 3,500 miles.

Almost immediately after the signing of the Hay-Bunau-Varilla Treaty, the Panamanian government protested its provisions that granted the United States titular sovereignty and economic control over the ten-mile-wide Canal Zone. As a result of the Hull-Alfaro Treaty (1936) and the Eisenhower-Remón Treaty (1955), the Republic of Panama's share of administrative responsibilities in the Canal Zone was increased, and Panamanians gained greater economic opportunities in the Canal Zone.

A rising wave of Panamanian nationalism after *World War II demanded more. After violent demonstrations in Panama in 1958 and 1964, new treaty negotiations began. Finally, the 1977 New Panama Canal Treaties provided for a joint U.S.-Panamanian Commission that administered the canal's operations until the year 2000, when the canal was turned over to the Panamanian government. The treaties included safeguards for U.S. security interests. While Panamanians readily approved the treaties in a plebiscite, the U.S. Senate ratified them only after a bitter debate over the "abandonment" of a prized U.S. possession.

[*See also* Expansionism; Foreign Relations: U.S. Relations with Latin America; Maritime Transport.]

• Thomas M. Leonard, *Panama, the Canal and the United States: A Guide to Issues and References,* 1993. John L. Major, *Prize Possession: The United States and the Panama Canal, 1903–1977,* 1993.

—Thomas M. Leonard

PANAMA INCURSION OF 1989. *See* Panama Canal.

PAN AMERICAN UNION. The First International Conference of American States, held in *Washington, D.C., in 1889–1890, established the foundations of the Pan American Union. Initially called the Commercial Bureau of the American Republics, this apparatus served common interests in trade by collecting economic information concerned with production, commerce, and customs law. Secretary of State James G. *Blaine (1889–1892) championed these ideas to promote hemispheric economic ties. The designation "Pan American Union" (PAU) emerged from a conference at Buenos Aires in 1910, and a building to house the organization was built in Washington, D.C.

The organization functioned informally and irregularly during the early years, sponsoring meetings at Mexico City, Mexico, in 1902 and Rio de Janeiro, Brazil, in 1906. After 1910 an executive director took charge of the governing board and exercised administrative authority. Meanwhile, specialized agencies such as the Pan American Sanitary Bureau (1902), the International Law Commission (1915), and the Inter-American High Commission (1915) coordinated other endeavors.

The PAU also assumed political functions. At conferences in Santiago, Chile, in 1923, and Havana, Cuba, in 1928, Latin Americans pressed for a statement supporting the principle of nonintervention. At Montevideo, Uruguay, in 1933, and Buenos Aires, Argentina, in 1936, the Franklin Delano *Roosevelt administration, in the spirit of the *Good Neighbor policy, accepted the idea. Nonintervention provided a basis for "hemispheric solidarity" during *World War II, including various forms of cooperation against the Axis powers.

Near unanimity in wartime entailed advantages for the United States, specifically Latin American political support and access to the region's raw materials. In 1948, the PAU merged with the *Organization of American States.

[*See also* Cold War; Foreign Aid; Foreign Relations: U.S. Relations with Latin America.]

• Alonso Aguilar, *Pan-Americanism from Monroe to the Present,* 1965. Samuel G. Inman, *Inter-American Conference, 1826–1954,* 1965.

—Mark T. Gilderhus

PARIS, TREATY OF (1783). One of the greatest triumphs of American diplomatic history, the Peace of Paris between the United States and Great Britain ended the *Revolutionary War and achieved American independence. After the victory of George *Washington and his French allies at Yorktown in 1782, the *Continental Congress named five commissioners to conduct peace talks with the British in Paris. Only three were able to attend—John *Adams, Benjamin *Franklin, and John *Jay—but their combined talents proved indispensable to the final outcome.

Although the French expected a coordinated diplomatic strategy because of the Franco-American alliance of 1778, the U.S. envoys distrusted European diplomats and pursued their

MAP 16: TREATY MAP (1775–1782)

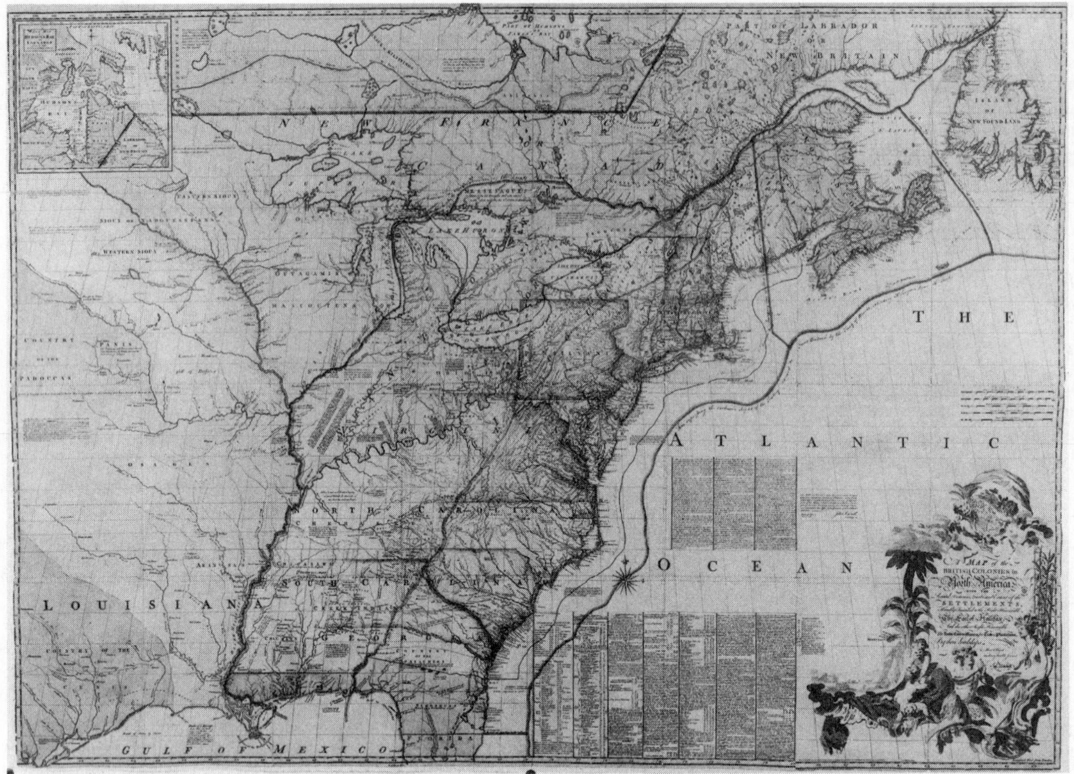

This 1775 map of Great Britain's North American colonies, annotated in 1782, was used by the British and American negotiators who drafted the Treaty of Paris, which ended the Revolutionary War and set the initial boundaries of the United States.

[*See* Adams-Onís Treaty; Early Republic, Era of the; Expansionism; Paris, Treaty of; Revolution and Constitution, Era of; Revolutionary War.]

own goals. The results justified their decision. They won from the British recognition of American independence, fishing rights for Americans in Canadian waters, and control of the vast area from the Allegheny Mountains to the *Mississippi River. The British negotiators insisted only on language safeguarding Loyalists to the British cause against persecution by state and local governments in the United States. The treaty was officially signed on 3 September 1783, and the Continental Congress gave its approval a few months later. Adams, Franklin, and Jay had achieved the maximum success from the victories that American troops, aided by French strength, had won on the battlefield.

[*See also* Foreign Relations: U.S. Relations with Europe; Revolution and Constitution, Era of.]

• Richard B. Morris, *The Peacemakers: The Great Powers and American Independence,* 1965. Jonathan R. Dull, *A Diplomatic History of the American Revolution,* 1985.

—Lewis L. Gould

PARK, ROBERT (1864–1944), sociologist. Born in Pennsylvania and reared in Red Wing, Minnesota, where his father ran a wholesale grocery firm, Park studied *philosophy at the University of Michigan, Harvard University, and at Strasbourg and Heidelberg in Europe. At Michigan and Harvard, his teachers included John *Dewey, William *James, and the idealist philosopher Josiah Royce. In Germany, he attended lectures by the social theorist Georg Simmel and wrote a dissertation under the neo-Kantian philosopher Wilhelm Windelband on the problem of the crowd and the public. Back in America, he put scholarship aside to work with the Congo Reform Association, and this led to his employment as an assistant to Booker T. *Washington at Tuskegee Institute.

In 1913, he took his first academic post, in the sociology department at the University of Chicago. Joining an already distinguished group of sociologists, he emerged as leader of the Chicago school of urban sociology. In an important 1915 essay, "The City," and in his textbook *Introduction to the Science of Sociology* (1921), coauthored with Ernest W. Burgess, Park conceptualized the American urban experience within a holistic ecological framework that combined economic, demographic, and cultural factors. The tension between the civilizing process of *urbanization and the persistence of discrete cultural enclaves remained a consistent theme through his work, which drew upon what he and his students observed in the dynamic "laboratory" of early twentieth-century industrial *Chicago. Park's integrative vision continued long after his death to appeal to students of ethnicity, race, and the social geography of the city.

[*See also* Cultural Pluralism; Demography; Race and Ethnicity; Social Science; Sociology.]

• Fred H. Matthews, *Quest for an American Sociology: Robert E. Park and the Chicago School,* 1977. Edward Shils, "Robert E. Park, 1864–1944," *American Scholar* 60 (Winter 1991): 120–127.

—J. Nicholas Entrikin

PARKER, CHARLIE (1920–1955), *jazz saxophonist and leader in the "bop" revolution of the 1940s. Born in *Kansas City, Kansas, Parker grew up across the river in Missouri. At age nineteen he joined the Jay McShann Orchestra and became the band's principal soloist, acquiring the name "Yardbird," shortened to "Bird." In 1941, when the McShann Orchestra played at the Savoy Ballroom and the Apollo Theater in *New York City, Parker discovered the Harlem clubs that were centers of jazz experimentation. When he left McShann in 1942, he had already acquired the narcotics problem that would ultimately take his life. He played for most of 1943 with the Earl Hines Orchestra, working with the trumpeter Dizzy Gillespie, another formulator of the "bop" style. When the singer Billy Eckstine left Hines to form his own band, both Parker and Gillespie went with him. Tired of big bands and preferring the freedom of a small combo, Parker quit Eckstine in 1944.

His eccentric style, subtle and complex, won followers among young urban blacks and jazz enthusiasts, and his improvised sounds combined with his unorthodox lifestyle to make "Bird" a cultural icon. In 1947, Parker formed his own quintet and often played in after-hours jam sessions at Minton's Playhouse in Harlem and the clubs along Fifty-second Street in midtown New York. He played his last engagement at Birdland, a Broadway club named for him, shortly before his death. Always controversial, Parker deepened the emotional intensity of jazz and became a hero within the emerging *Black Nationalism of postwar America.

• Ross Russell, *Bird Lives!,* 1973. Brian Priestley, *Charlie Parker,* 1984.

—Ronald L. Davis

PARKER, THEODORE (1810–1860), Unitarian clergyman, theologian, and abolitionist. A Unitarian minister associated with the intuitive rationalism of *transcendentalism, Theodore Parker was one of New England's most zealous social and religious reformers. The grandson of Captain John Parker, one of the Lexington minutemen of *Revolutionary War fame, Theodore grew up in modest circumstances. A precocious child, he read voraciously and soon revealed an extraordinary aptitude for languages. Supported by the tutelage of Watertown's scholarly minister Convers Francis, Parker entered Harvard Divinity School in 1834, where he encountered German higher criticism. Ordained and settled over the Spring Street Church in West Roxbury in 1837, he was soon regarded by his fellow Unitarian clergy as a more radical figure than Ralph Waldo *Emerson. In an ordination sermon on *The Transient and Permanent in Christianity* (1841), Parker denied the personal authority of Jesus but celebrated Jesus's apprehension of the absolute, pure religion that reposes in the hearts of all people. As Parker focused on the immanence of God and downplayed the centrality of Jesus, he became a virtual pariah among the Boston Association of Ministers.

In 1845, through the intervention of some Unitarian laymen, Parker left West Roxbury and took his ministry to Melodeon Hall in *Boston, forming the Twenty-eighth Congregational Society. From this pulpit Parker vigorously addressed the social issues of the day—temperance, penal reform, *education, and *slavery. Aroused by the *Fugitive Slave Act (1850), he became active in efforts to resist the arrest of escaped slaves and became a staunch supporter of abolitionist John *Brown. His health began to decline in 1857 and he died three years later in Florence, Italy.

[*See also* Antislavery; Channing, William Ellery; Religion; Temperance and Prohibition; Unitarianism and Universalism.]

• Henry S. Commager, *Theodore Parker,* 1936. Charles Capper and Conrad Wright, eds., *Transient and Permanent: The Transcendentalist Movement and Its Contexts,* 1999.

—Robert J. Wilson III

PARKMAN, FRANCIS (1823–1893), historian. The son of a prominent Unitarian minister of *Boston, he read widely in his father's library. At Boston's Chauncy Place School he drilled in Greek, Latin, and mathematics. Parkman became a skilled linguist, and at Harvard, from which he graduated in 1844, he completed requirements for a law degree. In his last year of college he toured Europe, gaining firsthand contact with French culture and the Catholic church. In 1846, he embarked on an expedition to the *West, following the *Oregon Trail as far as Fort Laramie, Wyoming, to study Plains Indian culture and thereby better understand the seventeenth-century Iroquois. His *Oregon Trail: Sketches of Prairie and Rocky-Mountain Life* appeared in 1849.

Parkman's *History of the Conspiracy of Pontiac* (1851) combined comparative ethnological and ethnohistorical research with documentary evidence to analyze and describe the history of Anglo-French rivalry in North America and Indian affairs. This launched his life's project, a vast eight-volume history of France and England in North America until 1763, published between 1850 and 1892. Expanding on *Pontiac*'s main themes, the series included histories of the pioneers; the Jesuits; *La Salle; Frontenac, the energetic seventeenth-century governor of New France; and the *Seven Years' War.

In a novelistic style, Parkman portrayed the struggle between France and England as a heroic contest between rival civilizations with wilderness as a modifying force. Plagued by partial blindness, arthritis, and mental disorders, Parkman was a heroic figure himself, overcoming what he called his "enemy-illness" to complete a masterly narrative. Some part of his own struggle was undoubtedly projected into his writings.

[*See also* French Settlements in North America; Historiography, American; Indian History and Culture: From 1500 to 1800; Indian History and Culture: From 1800 to 1900; Indian History and Culture: The Indian in Popular Culture; Pontiac; Roman Catholicism; Unitarianism and Universalism.]

• Wilbur R. Jacobs, ed., *The Letters of Francis Parkman,* 2 vols., 1960. Edward C. Atwater, "The Lifelong Sickness of Francis Parkman," *Bulletin of the History of Medicine* 41 (1967): 413–439. Wilbur R. Jacobs, *Francis Parkman, Historian as Hero: The Formative Years,* 1991.

—Wilbur R. Jacobs

PARKS, NATIONAL. *See* National Park System.

PARKS, URBAN. American urban parks developed from a blending of two traditions—rural landscape parks and urban public space. Many early cities, including *New Orleans, *Philadelphia, *San Francisco, and Savannah, Georgia, contained small squares or plazas, while more than three hundred *New England towns and cities, most notably *Boston, preserved a grassy central area as a common. Landscape parks originated in England from hunting grounds and gardens. Aesthetically complex, landscape-park principles were first applied to rural American cemeteries in the 1830s and two decades later to the urban park.

The history of urban parks falls into three periods: the romantic (1850s–1890s); the rationalistic (1890s–1950s); and the regenerative (1950s–). In each, advocates promoted urban parks as social-reform vehicles that would foster healthy, wealthy, democratic, and orderly societies. In each period, too, the arguments advanced by park advocates reflected changing perceptions of society's major problems so that park landscapes became cultural palimpsests as new features were added. By design and accretion, urban parks and park systems became functionally more complex and spatially segmented.

Romantic parks tended to be large (three hundred or more acres) and so arranged that a strolling or horseback-riding visitor would encounter a series of natural vistas. To bring the beneficent influence of the countryside into the city, parks provided "uplifting" rural scenery. The first romantic park, New York City's Central Park, followed an initial proposal in 1851 by Andrew Jackson Downing (1815–1852), America's premier landscape gardener, but considerable wrangling preceded the selection of the park's final location in 1854. Much of the land was developed and legally occupied by residents who fought their removal by eminent domain. Calvert Vaux (1824–1895) and Frederick Law *Olmsted developed the initial landscape plan for the 778-acre park in 1858. (It was soon expanded to 843 acres.) Their design of open meadows and lawns backed by thick plantings of border vegetation reflected the ideas of Downing and an English designer, Joseph Paxton (1803–1865). Largely complete by 1860, Central Park became the model and inspiration for numerous other parks during the romantic era. Baltimore, Maryland; Boston; Brooklyn and Buffalo, New York; *Detroit; Hartford, Connecticut; Philadelphia; St. Louis, Missouri; San Francisco, and many other cities started similar projects by 1876.

Rationalistic parks, which varied in size from several to several thousand acres, were developed by advocates who saw urban life as chaotic because it failed to recapitulate human social history. Parks, they claimed, would be the settings for surrogate activities. Small rationalistic parks tended to be functionally specialized as, for example, neighborhood flower gardens, playgrounds, athletic fields, or swimming pools. Large parks were spatially segmented to include the same functions as small ones plus other, more didactic features like *museums and music pavilions. To promote "efficiency," municipal authorities organized their parks into integrated systems. These urban-park systems provided a model for urban planning as well as for the National Park Service, begun in 1916. Recreation facilities and museums dominated urban parks until the 1950s.

Advocates of the regenerative park movement see parks as parts of a larger, unbounded natural ecology that helps reconnect society both to the past and to the physical environment. Parks, these advocates declare, regenerate identity by recalling local and regional traditions even as they provide links in the damaged ecosystem's web. Reflecting this outlook, the National Park Service in 1965 declared Central Park and Brooklyn's Prospect Park National Historic Landmarks. Rather than being remodeled, these and other parks were restored and preserved. Like great paintings by the Old Masters, parks such as San Francisco's Golden Gate underwent restoration to preserve society's roots and act as cultural guideposts. At the same time, urban parks were seen as ecological reserves, acting as floodplains, wildlife corridors, or natural habitats. Clearly, the urban park is a malleable idea, continuing to change form as American society itself evolves.

[*See also* Environmentalism; Landscape Design; National Park System; Progressive Era; Romantic Movement; Urbanization.]

• Galen Cranz, *The Politics of Park Design: A History of Urban Parks in America,* 1982. Stephen Hardy, *How Boston Played,* 1982. David Schuyler, *The New Urban Landscape,* 1986. Roy Rosenzweig and Elizabeth Blackmar, *The Park and the People: A History of Central Park,* 1992. Ethan Carr, "The Twentieth-Century Landscape Park" *George Wright Forum* 13 (Jan. 1996): 11–26. Mona Domosh, "Preserving Boston's Common and Planning Its Park System," in *Invented Cities,* 1996, pp. 127–154. Mike Eberts, *Griffith Park: A Centennial History,* 1996.

—Terence Young

PARSONS, TALCOTT (1902–1979), sociologist. Born in Colorado Springs, Colorado, the son of a Congregational minister, Parsons studied at Amherst College (1920–1924), the London School of Economics, and Heidelberg (1924–1926). Although his education included little formal training in *sociology, it introduced him to the institutional economics of Thorstein *Veblen, the functionalism of the anthropologist Alfred Radcliffe-Brown, and the sociology of Max Weber. He joined Harvard University's sociology department in 1927.

Parsons' sociological theory developed in several phases. During his first two decades at Harvard, and particularly in *The Structure of Social Action* (1937), he elaborated a voluntaristic "action" theory that he traced to Weber, Alfred Marshall, Emile Durkheim, and Vifredo Pareto. In the two decades following Harvard's establishment of a new Department of Social Relations in 1946, notably in *The Social System* (1951), he treated social structures in terms of the functions they served, now describing his work as "structural-functionalism" and "systems theory." From the late 1950s on, returning to interests evident in his earlier work on the professions, he refined his "systems theory" to deal with the interaction of social subsystems and to develop a cybernetic model of the ways the culture controls social change.

From 1945 to the early 1960s, Parsons was *the* major figure in American sociology, serving as president of the American

Sociological Association in 1949. During the 1960s, criticism of his system mounted on the left, from the sociologists C. Wright Mills and Alvin Gouldner and from feminists, as in Betty Friedan's *The *Feminine Mystique* (1963). A revival of interest in the 1980s, however, reestablished his preeminence among American sociologists.

[*See also* Social Science.]

• Peter Hamilton, *Talcott Parsons*, 1983. William Buxton, *Talcott Parsons and the Capitalist Nation-State: Political Sociology as a Strategic Vocation*, 1985.

—Robert C. Bannister

PARTIAL NUCLEAR TEST BAN TREATY. *See* Limited Nuclear Test Ban Treaty.

PATENT AND COPYRIGHT LAW. U.S. patent and copyright law is based on Article 1, Section 8 of the *Constitution, which gives Congress the power "to promote the progress of science and useful arts, by securing for limited times to authors and inventors the exclusive right to their respective writings and discoveries." This clause, when drafted in 1787, represented a culmination of legal and economic theory and practice regarding intellectual property going back at least as far as Renaissance Europe, where similar grants of exclusive rights were first recorded. In colonial America, though few patents and no copyrights in the modern sense were granted, practice generally followed English precedents. But whereas in England the Crown granted patents and copyrights as a royal prerogative, in America they were granted at first by colonial legislatures as private acts and later under general statutes enacted by the states.

In 1790, exercising its constitutional authority, Congress enacted the nation's first general patent and copyright statutes, effectively supplanting those of the states. The new statutes spelled out preconditions for the grants, general penalties to be imposed on infringers, and other details. Responsibility for issuing both patents and copyrights was assigned to the executive branch of the new government. The task of interpreting the statutes in disputed cases was left to the courts, whose decisions over the years constitute an enormous body of *jurisprudence, much of which has found its way into statutory law. Periodic revisions in this body of law have sought to fine-tune the balance of interests of inventors and authors, patent and copyright owners, and the general public. Most far-reaching, perhaps, have been changes to what the statutes specify as patentable and copyrightable subject matter, changes made necessary by the ever unforeseen evolution of *technology in new directions.

Through much of the nineteenth century, books or other materials published abroad enjoyed little copyright protection in the United States, and U.S. publishers freely pirated foreign works. The Berne Convention of 1887, updated most recently in 1971 by the Universal Copyright Convention at Paris (accepted by the United States in 1974), helped close this loophole. At the end of the twentieth century, the genetic manipulation of plants and even animal species, as well as the rise of the *Internet and on-line publishing, raised complicated new patent and copyright issues.

[*See also* Printing and Publishing.]

• Bruce W. Bugbee, *The Genesis of American Patent and Copyright Law*, 1967.

—Kendall J. Dood

PATRIOTISM. *See* Nationalism.

PATRONS OF HUSBANDRY. *See* Granger Movement.

PATTON, GEORGE S., JR. (1885–1945), U.S. Army general. Born in San Gabriel, California, Patton graduated from the U.S. Military Academy in 1909 and entered the cavalry. He accompanied General John J. *Pershing into Mexico in 1916–1917, and then to France. In November 1917, as the first U.S. officer assigned to tanks, Patton commanded his brigade of light tanks and fought at Saint-Mihiel and in the Argonne until wounded. A colonel, he received the Distinguished Service Cross.

During *World War II, Patton headed the Desert Training Center around Indio in southern California in early 1942 and then commanded the I Armored Corps, landing in French Morocco in November 1942. After General Erwin Rommel's February 1943 breakthrough at Kasserine Pass in Tunisia, Patton took command of the II Corps, quickly rehabilitated the American troops, and led them to capture El Guettar.

At the head of the Seventh U.S. Army, Patton invaded Sicily in July 1943, taking Palermo and Messina. His Third U.S. Army, which became operational on 1 August 1944, liberated France from Brest to the Meuse River. In December, he turned north; relieved the U.S. forces surrounded in Bastogne, Belgium; and helped drive German forces back in the Battle of the *Bulge. Crossing the Rhine in March 1945, Patton took Pilsen, Czechoslovakia, in early May.

Patton was controversial, particularly after he slapped and berated two shell-shocked U.S. soldiers in a military hospital on Sicily in August 1943. Nevertheless, his professional skill, audacity, and personal inspiration shortened the war. Of all the Allied commanders in Europe, Patton was the most feared by the Germans.

Heading the occupation of eastern Bavaria, but insisting that the United States should be more aggressively anticommunist, Patton was reassigned in October 1945 to write historical studies. He suffered fatal injuries in an automobile accident on 9 December near Mannheim, Germany, and is interred in the American Military Cemetery in Hamm, Luxembourg. A legendary cultural figure (played by George C. Scott in a celebrated 1970 film), Patton symbolizes American military genius.

[*See also* Military, The.]

• Martin Blumenson, *Patton: The Man behind the Legend*, 1985. Carlo D'Este, *Patton: A Genius for War*, 1995.

—Martin Blumenson

PAULING, LINUS (1901–1994), chemist, peace activist. Born to an Oregon family of modest means, Pauling found a scientific home at the California Institute of Technology, where he earned his doctorate in 1925 and taught for nearly forty years.

While traveling in Europe on a fellowship, Pauling learned quantum mechanics as it was being discovered. Upon returning to Caltech in 1927, he helped revolutionize chemistry by aligning it with the new physics, popularizing his ideas through an intuitive mix of bold theory and empirical research, memorable lectures, persuasive papers, and best-selling textbooks. His *Nature of the Chemical Bond* (1939) proved particularly influential.

Convinced that the structure of molecules explained their activity, Pauling made his point brilliantly in a series of groundbreaking discoveries about biomolecules, explaining the workings of hemoglobin and antibodies, the cause of *sickle-cell anemia, and the secondary structure of proteins. He won the Nobel Prize in Chemistry in 1954.

After *World War II, at the urging of his wife, he focused his attention on political causes, especially efforts to end nuclear-bomb testing. He persevered despite government harassment, becoming a world leader in the *peace movement. His efforts brought him the 1962 Nobel Peace Prize, making him the only person to win two unshared Nobels. Pauling spent his last years at a California research institute he cofounded in 1973, studying the health effects of vitamin C and other nutrients.

[*See also* Antinuclear Protest Movements; Biological Sciences; Health and Fitness; Limited Nuclear Test Ban Treaty; Medicine: Alternative Medicine; Nuclear Arms Control Treaties; Nuclear Weapons; Physical Sciences.]

• Thomas Hager, *Force of Nature: The Life of Linus Pauling*, 1995. Barbara Marinacci, ed., *Linus Pauling in His Own Words*, 1995.

—Thomas Hager

PEACE CORPS. Created by President John F. *Kennedy on 1 March 1961 and headed by R. Sargent Shriver, the Peace Corps became a popular symbol of Kennedy's "New Frontier." Its purpose was to send American volunteers abroad for two years to work in developing countries in order to cement U.S. relations with the Third World, contribute to economic development, and promote peace. The Peace Corps gave citizens an opportunity to respond to the spirit of civic activism stimulated by the young president's stirring exhortation, "Ask not what your country can do for you—but what you can do for your country."

The Peace Corps Act, passed by Congress in September 1961, established three goals: "1) To help people of interested countries and areas in meeting their needs for trained manpower; 2) To help promote a better understanding of Americans on the part of the peoples served; and 3) To help promote a better understanding of other peoples on the part of Americans."

The first volunteers went to Ghana in August 1961 and were immediately followed by volunteers to twelve other countries in Africa, Asia, and Latin America. Participants numbered 545 in 1961, increasing to 15,556 men and women by 1966. The average age was twenty-four. Volunteers brought a wide range of professional skills, from *medicine to agronomy, but most were college graduates with liberal arts degrees. The largest program, elementary and secondary *education, was strongest in Africa, where the corps responded to requests for teachers from newly independent nations. The Peace Corps also focused on rural and urban community development, primarily in Latin America. This activity, Kennedy believed, would supplement the efforts of the *Alliance for Progress to direct revolutionary ferment into channels consistent with American strategic interests.

The Peace Corps declined in the late 1960s as U.S. policies in Latin America and Southeast Asia alienated many young people. By the end of the *Vietnam War, the agency had shrunk more than 50 percent. The gender ratio of volunteers, roughly equal in the mid-1960s, also became skewed toward males, as young men sought to avoid the draft by joining the Peace Corps.

The Peace Corps survived, however, and continued sending some 6,000 volunteers abroad annually. By the year 2000, over 150,000 Americans had served in 132 counties.

[*See also* Foreign Relations: U.S. Relations with Africa; Foreign Relations: U.S. Relations with Asia; Foreign Relations: U.S. Relations with Latin America; Sixties, The; Voluntarism.]

• Gerard T. Rice, *The Bold Experiment*, 1985. Elizabeth Cobbs Hoffman, *All You Need Is Love*, 1998.

—Elizabeth Cobbs Hoffman

PEACE MOVEMENTS. From the early nineteenth century to the end of the twentieth, a series of disparate peace movements arose from temporary political coalitions that coalesced around a core group of peace organizations in response to specific national issues. The mobilizing issues have varied—from arbitration and *international law to the nuclear-arms race—but all have had in common the goal of replacing warfare with the peaceful resolution of conflict.

The American peace movement started with small, religiously based peace societies in New York and Massachusetts (1815). The pacifist New York group totally renounced war; the Massachusetts organization pursued all forms of peace advocacy. The latter, broader approach also characterized the American Peace Society (1828), whose leaders Alan Ladd and Elihu Burritt advocated international law, a congress of nations, and the arbitration of international disputes. Arbitration and international law attracted some U.S. and English political leaders and by the turn of the century had become the fulcrum for the first large peace coalition. These were the issues of choice for prestigious peace societies founded by businessmen like Andrew *Carnegie and directed by intellectuals like Elihu Root, John Bates Clark, and Hamilton Holt.

The outbreak of *World War I in 1914 gave currency to the idea of an international security organization. Combined with arbitration, this goal was promoted by the League to Enforce Peace (1915) and became the centerpiece for President Woodrow *Wilson's peace policy. But acceptance of Wilson's *League of Nations foundered on U.S. political divisions. The established peace movement split on the question of U.S. league membership, a remnant emerging in 1923 as the League of Nations Nonpartisan Association (in 1929 renamed the League of Nations Association, or LNA).

Meanwhile, as U.S. neutrality had become a salient issue in 1914–1917, progressive reformers, *Social Gospel ministers, women suffragists, and social workers had created a second peace-movement coalition. Such groups as the Women's Peace Society (1915, subsequently the American Branch of the Women's International League for Peace and Freedom, or WILPF); the pacifist Fellowship of Reconciliation (FOR); the American Union Against Militarism; and the *American Friends Service Committee (AFSC, 1917) promoted U.S. leadership in peacemaking but opposed intervention in the European war.

With the U.S. declaration of war in 1917, this new constituency shrank to a few uncompromising pacifists like Jane *Addams, Emily Green Balch, Dorothy Detzer, Frederick Libby, Kirby Page, Nevin Sayre, and A. J. Muste. After the war they spearheaded a broad, politically active peace movement that, however, promoted contending programs, including arms limitation, outlawry of war, and international organization.

In the 1930s, the threat of renewed European war generated a third coalition, the Emergency Peace Campaign, that mobilized public and legislative support for neutrality. James T. Shotwell and Clark Eichelberger of the LNA broke with the movement's pacifist wing, however, to campaign for aiding the European democracies and, during *World War II, to mobilize a fourth peace coalition that rallied support for the *United Nations.

The next peace coalition coalesced around the 1950s campaign to ban atmospheric nuclear tests. Leaders from the FOR and AFSC created the 1957 Committee for a Sane Nuclear Policy (SANE) and the Committee for Non-Violent Action (CNVA), which organized protests such as sailing into Pacific test zones. SANE, with Women Strike for Peace (WSP, 1961), mobilized public opinion and lobbied in Washington, contributing to the 1963 *Limited Nuclear Test Ban Treaty.

The largest and most tumultuous of all peace coalitions was the Vietnam-era antiwar movement. Core peace groups initially included the FOR, AFSC, WILPF, SANE, and WSP. New constituencies were quickly added, including *Students for a Democratic Society, Clergy and Laymen Concerned, and business, professional and *civil rights groups. Within this shifting coalition arose tension between the liberals' goal of ending the war and the radical objective of exploiting the war and cultural conflict to promote broader economic and social change. The movement's radical phase peaked in 1968–1970, after which a liberal antiwar constituency became dominant.

When the nuclear-weapons issue again arose in the 1980s, peace groups helped mobilize still another large political coalition: the Nuclear Weapons Freeze Campaign to halt the U.S.-Soviet arms race. Although Congress compromised the freeze proposal, and its popular support dissolved after President Ronald *Reagan proposed his *Strategic Defense Initiative in March 1983, the campaign revived arms-control pressures and strengthened support for détente.

The historian Charles DeBenedetti has aptly described the peace movement as a social-reform movement in the area of foreign policy. Indeed, American peace advocates have been integral to a transnational social movement that has interacted with international agencies and national governments to create institutions and procedures that offer alternatives to war.

[*See also* Antinuclear Protest Movements; Antiwar Movements; Collective Security; Internationalism; Nuclear Arms Control Treaties; Nuclear Weapons; Sixties, The; Vietnam War.]

• Warren F. Kuehl, *Seeking World Order: The United States and International Organization to 1920,* 1969. Charles DeBenedetti, *The Peace Reform in American History,* 1980. Charles Howlett, *The American Peace Movement: References and Resources,* 1991. Charles Chatfield, *The American Peace Movement: Ideals and Activism,* 1992. Harriet Hyman Alonso, *Peace as a Women's Issue: A History of the U.S. Movement for World Peace and Women's Right,* 1993. Lawrence Wittner, *One World or None: A History of the World Nuclear Disarmament Movement through 1953,* vol. 1 of *The Struggle against the Bomb* (3 vols.), 1993. Warren F. Kuehl and Lynne K. Dunn, *Keeping the Covenant: American Internationalists and the League of Nations, 1920–1939,* 1997.

—E. Charles Chatfield

PEALE, NORMAN VINCENT (1898–1993), minister, author, public speaker. Born in central Ohio to a Methodist minister and his wife, Peale received divinity training from Boston University and was ordained by the United Methodist Church in 1922. He left *Methodism in 1932, however, to become a minister of the Reformed church in America's Marble Collegiate Church in *New York City, serving there for more than fifty years. While in this post, Peale expanded his ministry to nonchurchgoers through books, *journalism, *radio programs, speaking engagements, and television.

Peale preached a distinctive brand of popular Christianity, using a straightforward, anecdotal style and emphasizing the practical qualities of *religion and the power of affirmative prayer. In his sermons, lectures, and numerous published works, including most notably the best-seller *The Power of Positive Thinking* (1952) and *Guideposts* magazine (founded 1944), Peale stressed that a positive attitude along with a strong commitment to Christian morality and love of God would lead to an improved life.

This philosophy generated attacks from some Protestant ministers and theologians, who believed that Peale's simplified theology and utilitarian focus on religion as merely a means to materialistic ends, namely a vaguely defined "success," inappropriately promoted individual agency over God's saving grace. Despite these critiques, Peale remained extremely popular throughout his life, reaching millions annually via his lectures and writings and playing a leading role in the religious revival of the 1950s. Although indeed simplistic, Peale's ideas clearly resonated with many Americans, who discovered through them a new commitment to and appreciation for personal religion.

[*See also* Fifties, The; Protestantism.]

• Carol V. R. George, *God's Salesman: Norman Vincent Peale and the Power of Positive Thinking,* 1993.

—Margaret A. Hogan

PEARL HARBOR, ATTACK ON (7 December 1941). U.S.-Japanese relations, often tense after 1900, worsened as the United States extended assistance to China following Japan's 1937 invasion of that nation and imposed economic sanctions, including a ban on U.S. aviation fuel, steel, and scrap metal exports to Japan. Hoping to deter further Japanese expansion, President Franklin Delano *Roosevelt ordered the Pacific Fleet to remain forwardly deployed at Pearl Harbor in Oahu, *Hawai'i, after its 1940 maneuvers. Viewing war as inevitable, Admiral Isoroku Yamamoto, commander in chief of the Japanese navy, on 7 January 1941 began plans for an attack on Pearl Harbor. In October, a new, more militaristic government under war minister Hideki Tojo took power in Tokyo. On 26 November, a thirty-two-ship fleet under Yamamoto's command left the Kuril Islands. Thanks to intercepted codes, the United States knew that war was imminent, and warnings went out to all Pacific commanders on 27 November, but without specific mention of Hawai'i. Indeed U.S. officials expected that the first assault would come against the *Philippines or British or Dutch possessions in the Pacific.

On Sunday, 7 December, from a position 275 miles north of Oahu, Yamamoto launched two waves of planes against the U.S. fleet anchored at Pearl Harbor. Achieving complete tactical surprise, the first wave of 183 planes from 6 Japanese carriers struck U.S. airfields and U.S. battleships moored along Ford Island at 7:55 a.m. The planes reached their targets shortly before Japanese diplomats delivered a message to U.S. officials in Washington, breaking diplomatic relations. The 167 planes of the second wave, arriving at 8:40 a.m., continued the onslaught. U.S. losses included 2,403 killed and 1,178 wounded as well as 187 aircraft, 8 battleships, 3 cruisers, 3 destroyers, 2 auxiliary craft, a minelayer, and a target ship. Japan lost only 29 planes, 6 submarines, and 64 men. Only the absence of U.S. aircraft carriers, which were delivering planes to Midway, and Japan's failure to destroy repair facilities, submarine pens, and fuel-storage tanks prevented total disaster. Addressing Congress, President Roosevelt called 7 December a day that would "live in infamy." "Remember Pearl Harbor" became America's *World War II rallying cry.

On 22 December, a commission chaired by Supreme Court Justice Owen J. Roberts launched the first of eight investigations conducted over the next five years, none of which clearly fixed specific blame for the catastrophe. However, Rear Admiral Husband Kimmel and Major General Walter C. Short, the navy and army commanders at Pearl Harbor, were held negligent and relieved of duty. Debate continued for more than fifty years, some writers blaming Roosevelt and other officials in Washington, and others defending them. Still others lay a preponderance of blame on Short and Kimmel, or on British and Russian officials who, some have alleged, knew the Japanese fleet was sailing eastward but failed to inform the United States. No credible evidence supports the conspiracy theory that Roosevelt knew of the attack in advance but allowed it to occur to create a pretext for war.

Pearl Harbor is today a national historic landmark. The partially-submerged battleship *Arizona,* with the bodies of 1,103 U.S. sailors still entombed within, remains as a memorial of the attack. The battleship *Missouri,* on whose deck Japanese officials signed surrender papers ending the war, is anchored nearby as a war memorial.

[*See also* Foreign Relations: U.S. Relations with Asia.]

• Martin V. Melosi, *The Shadow of Pearl Harbor: Political Controversy over the Surprise Attack, 1941–1946,* 1977. Gordon W. Prange et al., *At Dawn We Slept,* 1991. Gordon W. Prange et al., *Pearl Harbor: The Verdict of History,* 1991. John Costello, *In Days of Infamy,* 1994.

—James C. Bradford

PEI, I. M. (1917–), architect. Ieoh Ming Pei was born in Canton, China, the son of a banker. In 1935, Pei left China to study architecture in the United States. He graduated in 1940 from the Massachusetts Institute of Technology and received a master's degree in 1946 from the Harvard University Graduate School of Design. The rise of communism ended Pei's plans to return to China and he eventually became a U.S. citizen. From 1948 to 1960, Pei worked for the real estate developer William Zeckendorf and his firm Webb and Knapp, primarily on urban redevelopment projects. Pei established the New York–based I. M. Pei and Associates in 1955, later renamed I. M. Pei and Partners in 1966, and Pei Cobb Freed and Partners in 1989.

One of Pei's most accomplished designs is the East Building of the National Gallery of Art (1968–1978) in *Washington, D.C. This structure reflects his modernist faith in pure geometry, precise detailing, and creative engineering, while asserting an appropriate institutional monumentality and a sensitivity for the site. Some of Pei's prestigious commissions generated controversy before their successful completion, including the John F. Kennedy Library (1964–1979, originally intended for Cambridge, Massachusetts, and eventually built in *Boston), and his much-discussed glass pyramid (1983–1989) providing a new entrance to an expanded Louvre in Paris. Pei's boldly sculptural and publicly pleasing modern buildings often became iconic symbols for their respective cities, as exemplified by the Rock and Roll Hall of Fame and Museum (1987–1995) in Cleveland.

[*See also* Architecture: Public Architecture.]

• Carter Wiseman, *I. M. Pei: A Profile in American Architecture,* 1990. Michael Cannell, *I. M. Pei: Mandarin of Modernism,* 1995.

—Craig Zabel

PEIRCE, CHARLES SANDERS (1839–1914), philosopher, scientist, mathematician, logician, semiotician, founder of *pragmatism, America's greatest contribution to *philosophy. With Augustus de Morgan, Peirce is one of the founders of the logic of relatives. His pioneering work in semiotics, the study of signs, provides in the judgment of such figures as the philosopher Hilary Putnam and the novelist Walker Percy, a fruitful means of inquiry for the humanities and sciences alike. A polymath, Peirce also made significant contributions to geodesy, geology, metrology, computing, photometrics, spectroscopy, astronomy, cartography, psychology, metaphysics, phenomenology, and the history, philosophy, and logic of science. Peirce's father, Benjamin Peirce (1809–1880), a distinguished mathematician, was professor of mathematics and astronomy at Harvard. There Charles Peirce, despite his brilliance, graduated seventy-ninth of ninety in 1859, in part because his father had rigorously educated him in mathematics, science, and philosophy, but with little regard for academic requirements. At college, Peirce earned a reputation for arrogance, brilliance, iconoclasm, dangerous mood swings, and dissipation, behaviors owing in part to neurological pathologies. This reputation followed him into old age, undermining both his personal and professional life and resulting in two disastrous marriages and two dismissals, from the faculty of Johns Hopkins University in 1884 and from the U.S. Coast Survey, his employer for thirty years, in 1891.

Peirce's lifelong pursuit of the methods of inquiry into truth derived from his work as an experimental scientist. At age twenty-five, he began conducting experiments on star brightness at the Harvard Observatory. These resulted in his *Photometric Researches* (1879), the first modern compilation of star magnitudes and among the first works to suggest a disk shape for the Milky Way galaxy. In 1872, his father, then superintendent of the Coast Survey, placed Peirce in charge of the measurement of gravity. At the 1877 meeting of the International Geodetic Association, his work in gravimetry was recognized as an important advance. In the early 1880s, he used a wavelength of light to determine the length of the meter, a major refinement in metrology.

Peirce integrated this grounding in exact science with a knowledge of *philosophy and its history. He was indebted to Aristotle, Plato, medieval realism, Leibnitz, Berkeley, Boole, de Morgan, Scottish commonsense philosophy, Schelling, Hegel, and especially Kant, whose concept of "pragmatic belief" he extended to mean that truth is the ultimate opinion that would survive all possible logical scrutiny and experiential evidence. Peirce is best known for his "Illustrations of the Logic of Science," six essays (1877–1878), the first two of which—"The Fixation of Belief" and "How to Make Our Ideas Clear"—William *James, in 1898, called "the birth certificates of pragmatism." His only volume of philosophy, *Studies in Logic,* appeared in 1883. Peirce spent his last twenty-five years in Milford, Pennsylvania, in increasing isolation and poverty. He left more than eighty thousand pages of unpublished philosophical manuscripts, from which the Peirce Edition Project is publishing a projected thirty-volume selection.

Peirce's influence on William James, John *Dewey, and the idealist philosopher Josiah Royce was fundamental. He greatly influenced such subsequent thinkers as C. I. Lewis, Ilya Prigogine, Jacques Derrida, Umberto Eco, Jurgen Habermas, Jacques Lacan, Richard *Rorty, and Karl Popper.

After 1970, Peirce's thought became an important source for philosophers and scientists internationally. For these thinkers, he offered a point of departure for new approaches to issues in metaphysics, philosophy of science, logic, language, computer design, artificial intelligence, cultural studies, and many other fields.

[*See also* Coast and Geodetic Surveys, U.S.; Science: Revolutionary War to World War I.]

• Murray G. Murphey, *The Development of Peirce's Philosophy,* 1961. R. Jackson Wilson, *In Quest of Community: Social Philosopny in the United States, 1860–1920,* 1968, pp. 32–59. Christopher Hookway, *Peirce,* 1992. Charles Sanders Peirce, *The Essential Peirce: Selected Philosophical Writings Volume I (1867–1893),* ed. Nathan Houser and Christian Kloesel and with an introduction by N. Houser, 1992, and *Volume II (1893–1913),* ed. The Pierce Edition Project, 1998. Charles Sanders Peirce, *Reasoning and the Logic of Things,* ed. Kenneth Laine Ketner and with an introduction by K. L. Ketner and Hilary Putnam, 1992. Joseph Brent, *Charles Sanders Peirce,* 1993.

—Joseph Brent

PENDLETON ACT. *See* Civil Service Reform.

PENITENTIARIES. *See* Prisons and Penitentiaries.

PENN, WILLIAM (1644–1718), Quaker leader, colonial proprietor. Penn was born in London, the son of Admiral William Penn. The family moved briefly to Ireland, where the boy first encountered Quakerism. He entered Oxford when his father was knighted in 1660, but he was dismissed in 1662 for defying its Anglican regulations. He read law at Lincoln's Inn, London, then returned to the family estates in Ireland, where he embraced Quakerism, a reviled and officially persecuted radical sect. Imprisoned four times for publicly affirming his beliefs, Penn won a leadership position in the *Society of Friends as the movement turned from martyrdom to political pragmatism. He led the way from zeal to moderation, publishing tracts on religious toleration that aligned him with the emerging Whig party despite his personal acquaintance with Charles II and Charles's brother, the future James II.

These political connections served him well when he turned to America as a place to conduct a "holy experiment" based on his religious and political principles. The charter for Pennsylvania, granted to Penn by Charles in 1681 in payment of a debt owed to Penn's father, named Penn supreme governor. True to his ideals, Penn drafted a Frame of Government guaranteeing liberty of conscience and granting the freemen the right to alter the government. The city of *Philadelphia was laid out according to Penn's plan. Penn divided his proprietary energies between the demands of the turbulent provincial legislature for augmented power and the efforts of English officials to expand Crown control. In 1682, Penn negotiated with Delaware chiefs a treaty that assured good relations between settlers and local Indian tribes. A boundary dispute with Maryland drove him back to England in 1684, where he became caught up in the ill-fated reign of James II. Amid continuing attacks on his executive power, Penn returned to Pennsylvania in 1699. Yielding to the provincial assembly's demands, he granted it preeminence through the Charter of Privileges (1701). Returning to England in discouragement in 1701, he opened negotiations to sell his proprietorship, an action halted by his crippling stroke in 1712. Pennsylvania remained a Penn family possession until the *Revolutionary War.

[*See also* Colonial Era; Indian History and Culture: From 1500 to 1800.]

• Richard S. Dunn and Mary Maples Dunn, eds., *The Papers of William Penn*, 5 vols., 1981–1986. Melvin B. Endy, *William Penn and Early Quakerism*, 1973. Jean R. Soderlund, ed., *William Penn and the Founding of Pennsylvania, 1680–1684*, 1983.

—Joseph E. Illick

PENSIONS, CIVIL WAR. Often considered a welfare laggard, the United States pioneered generous disability and old-age benefits for Union veterans of the *Civil War. This was a break with precedent, because paltry benefits were opened to surviving veterans of the *Revolutionary War only in the 1830s. When the South seceded in 1861, however, the federal government needed to recruit an army without the capabilities of a central bureaucracy. To help recruit citizen-soldiers, Congress in February 1862 promised pensions to those disabled "from causes which can be directly traced to injuries received or disease contracted while in military service." Benefits were graded by rank; yet privates as well as officers were eligible, and family dependents of the dead could also apply for aid.

Although the Civil War left millions dead and disabled, pension expenditures initially peaked in the mid-1870s, with less than 10 percent of veterans enrolled. Then Congress passed the 1879 Arrears of Pension Act, which promised cumulative pensions from the date of discharge if veterans could prove that later disabilities were service-related. Tempted by lump sums often sufficient to finance new homes, tens of thousands discovered latent injuries. A growing backlog enabled U.S. commissioners of pensions to influence close elections by speeding up the processing of applications from swing states.

Responding to southern voters after 1876, Democrats (including the two-time president Grover *Cleveland) sought to limit expenditures and trim the rolls. Hard-pressed former Confederate states had to help pay for Union pensions, yet they could afford only hardship aid for Confederate veterans and survivors. Meanwhile, Republicans competed to fund ever more help for the "saviors of the Union" from "surplus" federal revenues generated by protective *tariffs.

After capturing both houses of Congress and the presidency in 1888, Republicans in 1890 passed the Dependent Pension Act. Henceforth anyone who had honorably served the Union for ninety days or more could be pensioned when unable to do manual labor. Pension administrators soon decided that veterans met this criterion at age sixty-two. By 1910, some 90 percent of surviving Union veterans—more than a third of elderly men in the North—received benefits that were very generous by the international standards of the day. Expenditures dwindled as the old soldiers died, but as late as the mid-1970s, pensions were still being paid to a few widows who, in their youth, had married aging Union veterans.

[*See also* Confederate States of America; Grand Army of the Republic; Republican Party; Welfare, Federal.]

• William H. Glasson, *Federal Military Pensions in the United States*, 1918. Theda Skocpol, *Protecting Soldiers and Mothers*, 1992, Ch. 2, pp. 102–151.

—Theda Skocpol

PENTAGON PAPERS. Commissioned by Secretary of Defense Robert McNamara in June 1967 to determine what had gone wrong in Vietnam, the research project that came to be called the Pentagon Papers played a critical role in the *Vietnam War saga. Completed in 1969, the study comprised forty-seven volumes and more than seven thousand pages of text and government documents analyzing U.S. involvement in Vietnam from *World War II forward, especially during the presidential administrations of John F. *Kennedy and Lyndon B. *Johnson. It raised fundamental policy questions and confirmed antiwar critics' charges of high-level deception and duplicity.

The former Defense Department official Daniel Ellsberg leaked the papers to the *New York Times*, which began to publish them in June 1971, provoking a political and constitutional crisis. Revelations from the Pentagon Papers fueled popular disillusionment with an already discredited war. Obsessed with government secrecy, President Richard M. *Nixon sought a court injunction to prevent further publication. In *New York Times Co.* v. *United States* (1971), the *Supreme Court ruled that the government had not met constitutional tests for prior restraint. Large portions of the papers subsequently appeared in the *Times* and other newspapers, as well as in various paperback editions.

The Pentagon Papers had a profound impact in a tumultuous period. Strengthening public and congressional opposition to U.S. involvement in Vietnam, they also initiated an era of aggressive investigative *journalism. Their leak provoked a vengeful Nixon to take steps that would culminate in the *Watergate scandal and his resignation. The papers remained for many years the basis for much of the scholarship on the Vietnam War.

• David Rudenstine, *The Day the Presses Stopped: A History of the Pentagon Papers Case*, 1996.

—George C. Herring

PENTECOSTALISM, an early twentieth-century religious movement among American evangelicals that connected the baptism of the Holy Spirit with speaking in tongues (the Pentecost experience described in the New Testament). Pentecostals believe that all Christians may receive spiritual gifts and that those anointed by the Holy Spirit can work mighty signs and miracles. Though the rise of Pentecostalism cannot be traced to a single event, important dates in the movement's early history include an outbreak of speaking in tongues (glossolalia), considered evidence of the baptism of the Holy Spirit, on New Year's Day 1901 in a Topeka, Kansas, Bible school operated by the itinerant evangelist Charles F. Parham (1873–1929), and a three-year-long revival at the Azusa Street Mission in *Los Angeles (1906–1909) that precipitated worldwide interest.

In the succeeding years, scores of small Pentecostal sects sprang up; the most successful were the Assemblies of God church and the Church of God. Growing slowly at first, the Pentecostal churches expanded rapidly after 1950, both in the United States and abroad. Early Pentecostal churches flourished among the poor; they often challenged accepted practices by ordaining women and forming racially integrated churches. Segregation appeared by the 1920s, however, and one of the largest late twentieth-century Pentecostal denominations was the predominantly African American Church of God in Christ.

After *World War II a pan-Pentecostal revival erupted, spawning a generation of independent evangelists, including Oral Roberts (1918–) and Jimmy Swaggart (1935–). These preachers, along with ecumenically minded Pentecostal leaders such as David Du Plessis (1905–1987), encouraged the spread of the charismatic movement to mainstream Protestant churches and the Roman Catholic church.

In all of its modern variations—Pentecostal denominations, independent ministries and churches, and charismatic movements within *Protestantism and *Roman Catholicism—Pentecostal religion strongly influenced twentieth-century American Christianity and transformed the religious demography of much of the developing world.

[*See also* African American Religion; McPherson, Aimee Semple; Religion; Televangelism.]

• David Edwin Harrell Jr., *All Things Are Possible*, 1975. Robert Mapes Anderson, *Vision of the Disinherited*, 1979. Edith L. Blumhofer, Russell P. Spittler, and Grant A. Wacker, eds., *Pentecostal Currents in American Protestantism*, 1999.

—David Edwin Harrell Jr.

PEQUOT WAR (1636–1637). The Pequot War originated in conflicts over trade and colonization in south-central *New England. From the early 1620s, coastal Indians supplied wampum (sacred shell beads, polished and strung in strands, belts, or sashes) to Dutch traders who exchanged it with inland natives for beaver pelts. The Pequots attempted in the early 1630s to control this trade but were resisted by the Narragansetts, Mohegans, and Dutch. Politically isolated, the Pequots allied in 1634 with the English colonists of Massachusetts Bay, only to find that the alliance encouraged English settlement in the Connecticut Valley and the formation, in 1636, of a new colony, Connecticut. Pequot alarm at this incursion was compounded after Massachusetts demanded restitution for the murder of English traders. When the Pequots denied the accusation, the colonies determined to punish them.

Fighting began in September 1636 when an English expedition burned Pequot homes and crops, after which the Pequots besieged Connecticut's Fort Saybrook. In April 1637 the Pequots raided Wethersfield, Connecticut, killing nine colonists and capturing two. With Mohegan and Narragansett support, the English attacked the Pequot town of Mystic on 26 May 1637. With most combatants away, Mystic's three hundred to seven hundred inhabitants were largely old men, women, and children, most of whom perished when the English burned the town. English and Indians routed the remaining Pequots by July. In the Treaty of Hartford (1638), surviving Pequots were divided as slaves or tributaries among the English and their Indian allies. The war secured Connecticut for the English and forestalled further Indian resistance in southern New England until *King Philip's War in the 1670s.

[*See also* Colonial Era; Indian History and Culture: 1500 to 1800; Indian Wars.]

• Neal Salisbury, *Manitou and Providence: Indians, Europeans, and the Making of New England, 1500–1643,* 1982. Alfred A. Cave, *The Pequot War,* 1996.

—Neal Salisbury

PERKINS, FRANCES (1880–1965), secretary of labor under President Franklin Delano *Roosevelt, first woman cabinet member. Graduating from Mount Holyoke College in 1902, Frances Perkins received her M.S. in political science from Columbia University in 1910. She married the economist Paul Wilson in 1913 and had one child, a daughter.

Perkins began her career investigating factory conditions and later held labor posts under New York governors Alfred E. *Smith and Roosevelt. Upon his election as president in 1932, Roosevelt asked Perkins to be secretary of labor. She accepted on the condition that he support a host of reforms including *unemployment, old age, and health *insurance; a federal employment service; and the end of *child labor. She served as secretary of labor until 1945, throughout Roosevelt's entire administration. Thereafter, following six years as a member of the Civil Service Commission, Perkins turned to teaching, first briefly at the University of Illinois and then at Cornell University's School of Industrial and Labor Relations.

Perkins's accomplishments place her in the first rank of secretaries of labor. She founded the Division of Labor Standards, a precursor to the Occupational Safety and Health Administration, and she successfully fought for legislation to regulate wages and hours and to guarantee employees' right to organize. Most important, as chair of the 1935 Committee on Economic Security, Perkins was an engineer of the New Deal's social welfare legislation including *Social Security and unemployment insurance, which built the system of worker protection still in place.

[*See also* Federal Government, Executive Branch: Other Departments (Department of Labor); New Deal Era, The.]

• Don Lawson, *Frances Perkins: First Lady of the Cabinet,* 1966. Penny Coleman, *A Woman Unafraid: The Achievements of Frances Perkins,* 1993.

—Deborah J. Anderson and Francine D. Blau

PERMANENT COURT OF INTERNATIONAL JUSTICE. The creation of the Permanent Court of International Justice (World Court) after *World War I stemmed from earlier efforts of lawyers, peace advocates, and reform-minded citizens to promote peaceful alternatives to international violence by widening the practice of international arbitration. While welcoming the creation of a Permanent Court of Arbitration by the First Hague Peace Conference (1899), these individuals had also pointed out that because the Hague Court allowed the litigating states to select their own arbiters, it was hardly "permanent" or a "court." To limit political influence in arbitrations, they advocated the creation of a new world court composed of renowned jurists. The Second Hague Peace Conference (1907) adopted a convention establishing a new court of arbitral justice but could not agree on a procedure for appointing the judges.

The cataclysm of World War I convinced many internationalists that more imaginative approaches to world order were needed. A new movement for broader and more authoritative international institutions resulted in the creation of the *League of Nations. Interest in a world court to handle legal issues nonetheless persisted. Article 14 of the Covenant of the League of Nations authorized the League Council to formulate plans for a Permanent Court of International Justice, and Article 13 defined the "justiciable" questions that could be brought before it. The U.S. Senate rejected membership in the league, but Elihu Root (1845–1937), the most prominent American promoter of a world court, served on the Advisory Committee of Jurists (1920) that designed the details for the new court at The Hague and devised an acceptable formula for the selection of the fifteen jurists.

In seeking U.S. adherence to the World Court, the administration of President Warren G. *Harding supported five reservations, which minimized the court's connections to the League of Nations; stated that the United States would not be bound without its consent by the court's advisory opinions; and, to satisfy the Senate's concern over its prerogatives, required that body's consent to a separate treaty specifying the issues in each dispute before cases could come before it. In January 1926 the Senate approved, 76–17, U.S. adherence to the World Court with these reservations. After lengthy talks, the league reluctantly acquiesced in the U.S. position, but by that time Senate support had eroded. The Senate vote on the proposal in January 1935 fell seven votes short of the necessary two-thirds majority. President Franklin Delano *Roosevelt endorsed U.S. adherence but was unwilling to champion it vigorously. The defeat of this modest internationalist proposal underscored the virulent *isolationism that permeated the nation in the interwar years.

Despite these setbacks, many citizens' groups and the two major political parties endorsed U.S. adherence to a world judiciary. Support for American membership, the proponents argued, would have allowed the United States to participate more actively in international affairs without potentially entangling political commitments.

[*See also* Internationalism; International Law; Peace Movements.]

• Denna Frank Fleming, *The United States and the World Court, 1920–1966,* rev. ed. 1968. Michla Pomerance, *The United States and the World Court as a "Supreme Court of the Nations,"* 1996.

—David S. Patterson

PERRY, OLIVER HAZARD (1785–1819) and **MATTHEW** (1794–1858), naval officers. Born in Rhode Island, the sons of Captain Christopher R. Perry, both enjoyed distinguished careers. Oliver Hazard Perry in 1798 became a midshipman on board his father's ship, the *General Greene,* which attacked French commerce and supported Haitian revolutionaries during the *Quasi-War with France. After service in the Mediterranean he directed construction of gunboats in 1807–1809 before taking command of the schooner *Revenge.* Commanding a Great Lakes fleet during the *War of 1812, he defeated the British at the Battle of Put-in-Bay (Battle of Lake Erie), near present-day Sandusky, Ohio. This victory assured U.S. control of Lake Erie, forced the British from *Detroit, and made possible a U.S. invasion of Canada. Perry's terse report, "We have met the enemy and they are ours," entered American military lore. In 1816–1817, he commanded the *Java* on a Mediterranean expedition against Barbary Corsairs. He contracted *yellow fever when traveling on the Orinoco River to meet with Venezuelan officials about piracy in the Caribbean, and died off Trinidad a week later.

Matthew Perry, after serving as a midshipman aboard the *Revenge* under his brother's command in 1809–1810, spent the War of 1812 on board the warship *President.* Over the next twenty years he won recognition as a reformer in naval education, training, and steam engineering. During the *Mexican War, Perry led attacks on Frontera and Carman. Given command of naval forces, he directed Winfield Scott's landing at Veracruz, the capture of Tuxpan and Tabasco, and the blockade of Mexico. His command of the U.S. fleet that opened Japan to trade with the United States in 1852–1854 culminated his career. In retirement he wrote a history of the mission to Japan.

[*See also* Foreign Relations: U.S. Relations with Asia; Military, The.]

• Samuel E. Morison, *Old Bruin: Commodore Matthew C. Perry, 1794–1858,* 1967. Richard Dillon, *We Have Met the Enemy: Oliver Hazard Perry,* 1978.

—James C. Bradford

PERSHING, JOHN J. (1860–1948), leader of the American Expeditionary Forces (AEF) in Europe during *World War I. Missouri-born, Pershing was a U.S. Military Academy graduate, Indian fighter, commander of the *African-American Tenth Cavalry (hence his nickname, "Black Jack"), founder of the Bureau of Insular Affairs during the *Spanish-American War, and a military campaigner against the Moros of the *Philippines in the aftermath of that war. He married Frances Warren in 1905. A fire at their army quarters took her life and the lives of three of their four children. Promoted by President Theodore *Roosevelt from captain to brigadier general, Pershing led the punitive expedition into Mexico against Pancho Villa in 1916. Pershing's fighting and command experience led President Woodrow *Wilson to name him in 1917 to lead the American forces sent to join the Allies in France after the United States entered the war against Germany. (Ironically, Pershing himself was of *German-American stock; the name was originally Pfoershing.)

Quickly grasping the desperate Allied situation, Pershing realized that Britain and France wanted to use American troops in their war-torn ranks. Resisting this pressure, Pershing preserved the integrity of the AEF and launched his First Army in a successful attack against German-held Saint-Mihiel Salient in September 1917. After a swift shift northward, his army attacked strong German positions in the Meuse-Argonne sector in late September. Bitter fighting enabled the Americans to drive toward Sedan, a key rail center. Pershing's leadership made the AEF a vital factor in Allied victory.

Awarded the unique rank of General of the Armies, Pershing was army chief of staff from 1921 to 1924, chaired the American Battle Monuments Commission, and sometimes consulted with his protégé, General George *Marshall, during *World War II.

[*See also* Foreign Relations: U.S. Relations with Latin America; Indian Wars; Military, The.]

• John J. Pershing, *My Experiences in the World War,* 2 vols., 1931; reprint 1995. Donald Smythe, *Guerrilla Warrior: The Early Life of John J. Pershing,* 1973. Frank E. Vandiver, *Black Jack: The Life and Times of John J. Pershing,* 2 vols., 1977. Donald Smythe, *Pershing: General of the Armies,* 1986.

—Frank E. Vandiver

PERSIAN GULF WAR (1991). On 1 August 1990, Iraq's leader, Saddam Hussein, invaded Kuwait and proclaimed it a province of Iraq. This action led to the Persian Gulf War, which had two major phases. The first, "Desert Shield," was a largely defensive operation aimed at protecting Saudi Arabia and the rest of the Gulf, and employing *United Nations (UN) economic sanctions to force Iraq out of Kuwait. In the second phase, known as "Desert Storm," a UN coalition commanded by General H. Norman Schwarzkopf of the U.S. Army expelled the Iraqi forces from Kuwait. General Colin *Powell, chairman of the *Joint Chiefs of Staff, played a key role in planning the war's strategy.

Saddam Hussein almost certainly saw the annexation of oil-rich Kuwait as a means of solving Iraq's economic problems and counted on the world's unwillingness to mount any effective opposition. Saudi Arabia and the other Gulf States supported Kuwait's government in exile, however, and President George *Bush ordered U.S. military forces to the Gulf on 7 August. Japan, Britain, France, most other European nations, and the Soviet Union condemned the invasion, as did key Arab states like Algeria, Egypt, and Syria. Jordan, Libya, Mauritania, and the Palestinian Liberation Organization (PLO), however, supported Iraq. On 29 November, the United States obtained a UN Security Council resolution authorizing the use of "all necessary means" if Iraq did not withdraw by 15 January 1991.

In "Desert Shield," the United States deployed some 527,000 personnel, 100 naval vessels, 2,000 tanks, 1,800 fixed-wing aircraft, and 1,700 helicopters. Britain deployed 43,000 troops, and France, 16,000, each with supporting tanks, combat aircraft, and other military hardware. Of the Arab states, Saudi Arabia deployed 50,000 troops; Egypt, 30,200; and Syria, 14,000. Oman, Qatar, and the United Arab Emirates (UAE) each deployed a significant portion of their small forces.

Iraq responded by building up its military forces in Kuwait to 336,000 men and some 9,000 battle tanks, other armored vehicles, and major artillery weapons. Despite UN economic sanctions and diplomatic efforts, Iraq further expanded its military capabilities in Kuwait and along its border with Saudi Arabia.

The air-war phase of "Desert Storm" began on 17 January 1991 when the United States and its coalition allies launched devastating attacks on Iraqi command-and-control facilities, communications systems, air bases, and land-based air defenses. U.S. sea-launched cruise missiles and F-117 stealth aircraft quickly demonstrated that they could attack even heavily defended targets like Baghdad, Iraq's capital. Within three days, U.S., British, and Saudi fighters had established near air superiority. Over the next month, UN coalition aircraft went after Iraqi armor and artillery in Kuwait and attacked Iraq's forward defenses; elite Republican Guard units; air bases and sheltered aircraft; hardened command-and-control facilities; military supply depots; and biological, chemical, and nuclear warfare installations.

Iraq retaliated by launching modified Scud missiles against targets in Saudi Arabia and Israel, but these strikes did not alter the course of the war. Iraqi ground forces were struck by more than 40,000 air sorties, causing 84,000 Iraqis to desert and destroying 1,385 tanks, 930 other armored vehicles, and 1,155 artillery pieces. The air attacks also severely reduced the flow of supplies to Iraqi ground forces in Kuwait and heavily damaged Iraq's military command and communications centers, ammunition storage sites, naval vessels, and electric-power-generating capability.

The land offensive to liberate Kuwait began on 24 February. UN land forces attacked along a broad front from the Persian Gulf to the Iraqi-Saudi border. This attack had two principal thrusts: a highly mobile "left hook" around and through Iraqi positions in western Kuwait and a move straight through Iraq's defenses along the Kuwaiti border. While some Republican Guard units fought well, many Iraqi troops, poorly trained conscripts with low morale and little motivation, fled after putting up brief resistance; others surrendered. As a result, UN forces reached their objectives in Kuwait in half the time originally planned.

By 26 February, coalition land forces were in Kuwait City, and U.S. forces had advanced to positions in southern Iraq. These nighttime advances had taken place despite heavy rain, mud, and weather problems that hampered air support. Baghdad announced on 26 February that all Iraqi forces would withdraw from Kuwait in compliance with UN Resolution 660. Military operations ended on 28 February.

The Persian Gulf War achieved all of the United Nations' original objectives, principally the restoration of Kuwait. Iraqi casualties totaled 25,000 to 65,000. In contrast, UN forces lost fewer than 200 personnel, excluding losses to friendly fire, plus four tanks and nine other armored vehicles. The conflict demonstrated the importance of joint operations, high-tempo air and armored operations, precision-strike systems, night and all-weather warfare capabilities, and sophisticated electronic warfare and command-and-control capabilities.

President Bush's mobilization of a broad anti-Iraq coalition and his rallying of public opinion behind the war represented the high point of his presidency, producing a spike of popularity. Gulf War veterans returned to heroes' welcomes. The Pentagon, having learned in the *Vietnam War the power of the media to shape home-front perceptions, strictly controlled journalistic coverage of the Gulf War. Most Americans experienced the conflict through fleeting *television images of bombing raids and streaking missiles.

The Gulf War did not, however, bring stability to the region or drive Saddam Hussein from power. These failures led many observers to argue that the United Nations should have expanded its objectives and invaded Iraq to destroy Saddam Hussein's regime. Others point out, however, that this might have caused an Iraqi civil war, led to bloody urban combat, or forced a long UN occupation of a sovereign state.

[*See also* Foreign Relations: U.S. Relations with the Middle East; Military, The; Post–Cold War Era.]

• H. Norman Schwarzkopf, *It Doesn't Take a Hero,* 1992. U.S. Department of Defense, *Conduct of the Persian Gulf War: Final Report to Congress,* 1992. Anthony H. Cordesman, *After the Storm: The Changing Military Balance in the Middle East,* 1993. U.S. Air Force, *Gulf War Power Survey,* ed. Eliot Cohen, 1993. U.S. Army, *Certain Victory: The U.S. Army in the Gulf War,* directed by Robert H. Scales, 1993.

—Anthony H. Cordesman

PETROLEUM INDUSTRY. The petroleum age began in 1859 when Edwin L. Drake's construction of the first oil well in northwestern Pennsylvania launched several oil rushes in the Appalachian fields and a refinery boom. For the rest of the nineteenth century the United States was the world's leading oil producer, refiner, consumer, and exporter. While demand for American illuminating oil expanded, continual improvements in processing petroleum, such as larger stills, pipeline gathering systems, and railroad tank cars, reduced costs.

Aggressively applying economies of processing and distribution, John D. *Rockefeller's Standard Oil Trust captured about 90 percent of oil refining in the 1880s. Friendly and unfriendly takeovers, rebates and drawbacks on *railroad rates, and control of pipelines paved the way for Rockefeller's monopoly. But antitrust complaints from oil-well owners, politicians, and journalists culminated in a 1911 *Supreme Court decision dissolving his empire into thirty-four companies.

Even before the divestiture, rivals had arisen to challenge Standard Oil. In Europe and Asia, Royal Dutch Shell marketed oil from Russia and the East Indies. Around 1900, oil discoveries in the Texas Gulf Coast region, the midcontinent states, and *California provided opportunities for smaller oil companies to develop into integrated corporations such as Gulf Oil, the Texas Company (Texaco), Sun, and Sinclair. While the Standard Oil subsidiaries focused on their traditional sales territories, the new "majors" competed aggressively for markets. By the 1920s, as a result of the new majors as well as the hundreds of small nonintegrated, independent refiners, oil producers, marketers, and jobbers who had entered the market, the Standard Oil companies controlled only about 40 percent of the oil industry.

A second great change occurred in the early twentieth century. With the rapid expansion of the truck, tractor, and *automotive industries, gasoline replaced kerosene as the oil industry's leading product. In order to extract more gasoline from crude oil, oil companies in the 1920s developed methods of thermal cracking or refining with higher temperatures and pressure. Simultaneously, Charles F. Kettering of Dayton, Ohio, discovered that adding tetraethyl lead to gasoline improved automobile performance. By the end of the 1930s refiners employed the Houdry process of catalytic cracking to increase their yields of gasoline with higher octane.

During the Depression of the 1930s, oil companies, like other businesses, turned to government regulation to restore profits. The industry's problems had been exacerbated by overproduction following the discovery of an enormous oil field in East Texas in 1930. During the *New Deal Era, state and federal regulations curtailed output from American wells, especially in new oil fields. In 1959, President Dwight D. *Eisenhower bolstered these regulations by limiting oil imports. However, this system of production control broke down in the early 1970s. By then the American demand for petroleum far exceeded domestic production capacity. Despite sharp price increases by foreign oil producers in the 1970s, oil imports rose steadily, reaching 50 percent of total U.S. consumption in 1994 and leaving the country vulnerable to oil crises precipitated by developments that affected overseas producers.

[*See also* Antitrust Legislation; Carter, Jimmy; Energy Crisis of the 1970s; Ford, Gerald.]

• Harold F. Williamson et al., *The American Petroleum Industry,* 2 vols., 1963. Daniel Yergin, *The Prize,* 1991.

—Norman Norhauser

PHARMACEUTICAL INDUSTRY. The American pharmaceutical industry, like its older counterpart in Europe, grew out of the ancient practice of pharmacy, as commercial production gradually superseded the traditional compounding of medications by individuals. The need for medicine chests during the *Revolutionary War necessitated some large-scale pharmaceutical compounding in the 1770s, but significant manufacturing activity did not appear until about the 1820s, in *Philadelphia. This growth accelerated after the *Civil War with the emergence of many pharmaceutical firms in the mid-Atlantic and Great Lakes regions, such as Squibb, Parke-Davis, Lilly, Abbott, Upjohn, and Searle, that would soon dominate the industry. Though these and many other old firms remain in existence, mergers have obscured their origins. From the 1960s on, economic considerations shifted much pharmaceutical manufacturing to *Puerto Rico.

Several factors account for the pharmaceutical industry's evolution and rapid growth. Wars and their concomitant demands on the therapeutic armamentarium stimulated the development of drug manufacturing. Advances in medical sciences and technology, especially from the late nineteenth century forward, had a major impact. Such disparate factors as *urbanization, population growth, and the broader corporate model of the *mass production, *advertising, and *mass marketing of consumer goods all played a role.

Like other comparatively young enterprises in the late nineteenth century, such as the *petroleum and *electrical industries, pharmaceutical manufacturers embraced scientific research to enhance both their product line and their marketing strategies. As pharmacology, bacteriology, organic and analytical chemistry, and other relevant sciences became established in the United States, some pharmaceutical companies drew upon them to improve quality control and develop new products. Not until the 1920–1940 era, however, and the industry's emergence as a global competitor, did all pharmaceutical companies rely on scientific research as a matter of course.

Beginning as early as 1902, when the government first required firms to secure licenses to produce therapeutic agents of biological origin, federal regulation played an important role in the way the industry conducted its affairs. The *Pure Food and Drug Act of 1906, which required truth in labeling, applied to established pharmaceutical firms as well as to manufacturers of patent medicines and cure-all panaceas. The 1938 Food, Drug, and Cosmetic Act, which required that a drug be certified as safe by the federal Food and Drug Administration before it could be marketed, had a much greater impact. An amendment in 1962 demanded proof of efficacy as well. The post–*World War II surge of chemical treatments for mental and emotional disorders, from schizophrenia to depression, proved a boon for the pharmaceutical industry. By the mid-twentieth century, drug companies achieved a major and profitable role in the chemotherapeutic revolution, from the laboratory to the home medicine cabinet.

[*See also* Drugs, Illicit; Medicine; Mental Illness; Psychotherapy; Research Laboratories, Industrial.]

• Tom Mahoney, *The Merchants of Life: An Account of the Pharmaceutical Industry,* 1959. John P. Swann, *Academic Scientists and the Pharmaceutical Industry: Cooperative Research in Twentieth-Century America,* 1988.

—John P. Swann

PHILADELPHIA. Founded by William *Penn in 1682, Philadelphia was the last of the major Atlantic coastal cities to be established. Penn envisioned a Quaker city, but his policy of religious freedom and his promotion of Pennsylvania's potential wealth attracted a multinational *immigration that eventually became the prototype of American heterogeneity. Although Quakers early became a minority of Philadelphia's population, their ideas continued to exert a strong influence on the city's culture. The career of Benjamin *Franklin, who arrived as a youth from *Boston in 1723, is inextricably linked to Philadelphia.

By 1750, Philadelphia was not only the largest city in British North America but the most modern as well, providing public amenities such as street lighting and an architecturally advanced cityscape featuring up-to-date buildings like Independence Hall (1735). For the next fifty years, Philadelphia also enjoyed something of a golden age in its politics, economy, and culture. Many key events in the formation of the new nation were centered there: the *Declaration of Independence, the *Articles of Confederation, and the *Constitution were all born in Philadelphia; and the national government was located there from 1790 to 1799. Its commerce, both overseas and coastwise, surpassed all other American ports, and a broad industrial base led by shipbuilding encouraged new systems of technology and labor practices, as well as a sophisticated banking system. European-style *libraries, *museums, learned societies, and a rapidly developing publishing industry assured the city's cultural preeminence.

In the two centuries following removal of the national government to *Washington, D.C., Philadelphia's preeminence gradually declined. Overtaken in population by *New York City in the early 1800s and by *Chicago in 1890, it nevertheless remained significant in industry and commerce until after *World War II. Philadelphia expressed its civic pride through an international Centennial Exposition in 1876, but by 1900 a "corrupt but contented" city increasingly became the butt of comedians' jokes. By 1950, although its suburbs continued to grow, the city's population had begun a long decline, dropping 25 percent over the next half century, with matching losses in industry and jobs.

As the fifth largest city in the United States, Philadelphia in the 1990s built on decades of government reform and an improved economic outlook to stimulate new vitality, positioning itself to exploit its historical and cultural advantages. Some of the character of late twentieth-century Philadelphia reflected its history as an older eastern city with an outdated infrastructure; social problems arising from centuries of unplanned growth; and tensions as well as cooperation among religious, ethnic, and racial groups. On the other hand, the city was also marked by a unique dynamic between the strong grip of tradition and local innovations of national significance. This dynamic is well exemplified in Independence National Historical Park, where the Liberty Bell, Independence Hall, and other eighteenth-century icons represent both what was innovative and forward-looking in the creation of the United States and what remains most traditional and lasting.

[*See also* Anti-Catholic Movement; Bartram, John and William; Colonial Era; Constitutional Convention of 1787; Early Republic, Era of the; Mott, Lucretia; Nativism; Revolution and Constitution, Era of; Society of Friends; Wanamaker, John; World's Fairs and Expositions.]

• Russell F. Weigley, Nicholas B. Wainwright, and Edwin Wolf 2d, eds., *Philadelphia: A 300-Year History,* 1982.

—Stephanie Grauman Wolf

PHILANTHROPY AND PHILANTHROPIC FOUNDATIONS. John *Winthrop, governor of the Massachusetts Bay Colony, dreamed of a "City on a Hill": an ideal society of Puritan saints imbued with a religious obligation to do good. This vision soon faded with the rise of cities, commerce, and trade, but the idea of the New World as a place where people not only pursued their own interests but also helped others took deep root. In common with the practice of a minority of the rich for centuries, colonial American philanthropy included efforts by the wealthy to create worthy memorials to themselves. When, in 1638, John Harvard bequeathed £780 and a collection of four hundred books to a new college recently established in Cambridge, Massachusetts, which was promptly named Harvard College in his honor, he was only one of hundreds of prosperous colonists who endowed libraries, reading societies, schools, and other institutions that benefited their communities while perpetuating their benefactors' names.

By the eighteenth century, charitable activities in the colonies also included something more uniquely American that Europeans noted with curiosity: institutions to which large numbers of individuals of relatively modest means contributed. By the end of his life Benjamin *Franklin was one of the country's most famous and wealthy men, but long before, while still a little-known printer of modest means, Franklin had enthusiastically subscribed to voluntary associations like the Philadelphia Free Library created to encourage self-improvement among "middling" people like himself without inherited money or important social contacts. In doing so, he typified an idea more enthusiastically promoted in America than anywhere else at the time: that not only rich people should do good works, but that entire communities should organize philanthropically. By the time of the *Revolutionary War, scores of charitable societies had been established. Especially in *New England, philanthropic giving had become a cooperative and highly organized activity. The shipbuilders who attended *Boston's Old South Church gathered monthly to supervise the delivery of firewood to the indigent. Other prominent congregations in the city declared regular fasts, decreeing that all money ordinarily spent for food on that day be distributed to the poor instead.

Many communities found such giving insufficient, however. *Alms houses provided shelter and food, though often minimal, to the needy. After independence, as Americans created new economic, political, and social institutions, they also continued others, including the tradition that alms houses, as well as schools, be supported cooperatively through public taxation and private contributions. Repudiating the state-sanctioned and state-funded churches, centralized educational systems, and government-owned museums of Europe, the Founding Fathers adopted the First Amendment to the *Constitution formally separating church and state and guaranteeing citizens' right to meet when they wished, say what they wanted, and form associations as they pleased.

Nineteenth-century Americans exercised these rights with a vengeance. Indeed, the French aristocrat Alexis de Tocqueville, who toured the United States in 1830–1832 to prepare a report on American penitentiaries for his government, was astonished by the country's zeal for private associations. Thousands of non-profit organizations, from burial societies to *orphanages, flourished. Although women did not receive the right to vote until 1920, they powerfully influenced American politics and culture throughout the nineteenth century as prime movers behind a host of these philanthropic institutions. Some, like the Philadelphia Ladies' Depository, emphasized female self-help by establishing "exchanges" where impoverished women could sell handmade goods on consignment. Others embraced a wide variety of reforms. Dorothea *Dix of Massachusetts demanded better treatment for the mentally ill, often chained like animals in the back rooms of alms houses. Others championed first freedom, and then education, for *African Americans.

By the end of the century, in a rapidly growing nation transformed by *industrialization and *urbanization, Jane *Addams of *Chicago's Hull House and Lillian Wald of *New York City's Henry Street Settlement, promoted the establishment of *settlement houses in the crowded immigrant wards of the burgeoning cities. These institutions sought to improve living conditions, promote social interaction, and help acclimate the new arrivals to American life.

The years from 1870 to 1900 saw an unprecedented burst of economic growth in the United States that generated vast wealth for the new captains of industry and, in turn, opened a fresh chapter in the history of American philanthropy. The generation that won the *Civil War went on to create the modern business corporation and then its offshoot, the charitable foundation, a vehicle for philanthropy that proved more popular in America than anywhere else in the world. Just as the post–Civil War business fortunes were mostly concentrated in the victorious North, so, too, were the new foundations. Even those that promoted charitable causes in the *South, such as the improvement of education in the region, were rarely located there.

Only a fraction of the wealthy capitalists of the late nineteenth century became philanthropists. William Rockefeller, for example, a partner with his brother John D. *Rockefeller in the Standard Oil Company, gave almost nothing to charity. But of those who did, some did so on a massive scale. Best known were the foundations established by John D. Rockefeller, the Scottish-born steel baron Andrew *Carnegie, and the *Detroit automaker Henry *Ford.

The vast benefactions of Carnegie, who preached that "the man who dies rich dies disgraced," included New York's Carnegie Hall (1892), the Carnegie Institute of Technology (1900), the *Carnegie Foundation for the Advancement of Teaching (1905), the *Carnegie Endowment for International Peace (1911), and some 2,800 Carnegie libraries. The Carnegie Corporation of New York (1911) was established to administer his remaining fortune for philanthropic purposes.

Rockefeller was the major benefactor of the University of Chicago (1892) and in 1901 endowed the *Rockefeller Institute for Medical Research (later Rockefeller University) in New York City. It conducted important research on such endemic parasitical diseases as hookworm, *malaria, and *yellow fever. He established the Rockefeller Foundation in 1913 to promote "the well-being of mankind throughout the world." The Laura Spelman Rockefeller Memorial Foundation, named for his wife, followed in 1918. In total, Rockefeller gave some $245 million to these foundations.

The *Ford Foundation, established by Henry Ford and his son Edsel in 1936, initially concentrated its philanthropy in the Detroit area, but eventually emerged as the nation's largest philanthropic foundation and funded a wide range of projects worldwide. From 1950 to 1975, the Ford Foundation granted some $3.8 billion in programs to aid higher education, developing nations, public television, the arts, and other causes. The foundation's endowment in 2000 was about $13 billion.

The modern business corporation was an invention of the nineteenth century, and the philanthropic foundation, a creature of the twentieth century, was modeled on it. The Rockefeller Institute for Medical Research set the pattern. Like all subsequent philanthropic foundations, it followed a corporate model, with a board of trustees, a written statement of purpose, and a government-issued charter.

By 2000, the number of charitable foundations in America, which had totaled about 150 in 1930, stood at more than 42,000. A few extremely large ones bore famous business names like Rockefeller, Carnegie, or Ford—or, more recently, Pew, Danforth, Lilley, Packard, Kellogg, or Gates—and conducted large-scale programs on a national or international scale. Most, however, were smaller and more insular, the creations of wealthy individuals or families seeking the kind of indirect, institutionalized giving that buffered them from direct pleas for help. The beneficiaries of their philanthropy were mostly close at hand: local schools, *hospitals, *parks, symphonies, *museums, dance and theater companies, and so forth.

The trustees of these foundations were insiders. Legally, the board of a foundation, as with any corporation, conducted all its business. Appointed by founders who wanted people on whom they could rely, foundation trustees were typically wealthy white men in their sixties—a long-time family lawyer, a business partner, a trusted relative. Most were Protestant, Republican, and graduates of Ivy League colleges. Although foundation trustees with rare exceptions served without pay, most boards nonetheless had highly conflicted relationships with the sources of their money. Foundations linked with the *automotive industry did not fund research on exhaust pollution. Those funded by fortunes tied to the *tobacco industry did not investigate connections between smoking and *cancer. Foundation philanthropy, moreover, could never be entirely separated from corporate self-promotion. To patronize improvements in society, however defined, was good public relations.

This insulated world began to change in the 1970s, prodded by Texas Congressman Wright Patman's eight-year crusade, which culminated in the Tax Reform Act of 1969, to require nonprofit foundations to disclose their assets and other information, and to tax their investment income. Since Republicans interested in endowing local hospitals or similarly noncontroversial projects ran the vast majority of foundations, Patman's accusation that foundation philanthropy supported unpatriotic "left wing" causes was wildly exaggerated. But so, too, were the charges of leftist critics convinced that philanthropies practiced a shadowy kind of social control through their charitable donations.

The truth has always been more complicated. Of course, since the seventeenth century, patrons rarely consulted the wishes of the recipients of their largesse. The eighteenth- and nineteenth-century merchants who endowed reading rooms chose books they deemed morally improving. The "friendly visitors" in late nineteenth-century *Charity Organization societies sought to impose middle-class values as they dispensed aid to the urban poor. Nonetheless, in a pluralistic society, philanthropy was only one of many sources of power. When philanthropic projects ran counter to prevailing cultural norms, they usually foundered. Between 1917 and 1930, for example, philanthropist Julius Rosenwald of the Sears-Roebuck Company built schools for over half a million black children in the South. His hope, however, to "shame" white southern politicians and education officials into spending more money on African-American education failed miserably. The few philanthropists who ventured beyond traditional charitable donations in their own communities succeeded most strikingly when they supported a venture that had broad public support: medical research. At the beginning of the twentieth century researchers at the Rockefeller Institute created a vaccine against yellow fever, generating enormous favorable comment. At century's end, the William and Melissa Gates Foundation, established by Microsoft founder Bill *Gates, donated hundreds of millions of dollars to promote research on HIV/AIDS.

Despite the visibility of a few high-profile, multi-billion-dollar foundations, American philanthropy has always been fundamentally a democratic phenomenon. Throughout the twentieth century, and especially after 1940, the very rich gave far less, per capita, than did ordinary Americans. In the 1990s, almost 85 percent of the more than $170 billion that Americans contributed annually to charity came from middle-class families, who usually directed their giving to local religious and cultural institutions, social agencies, or self-help organizations. In so doing, they were Benjamin Franklin's true heirs.

[*See also* Capitalism; *Democracy in America*; Peace Corps; Religion; Social Class; Social Gospel; Voluntarism.]

• Kathleen McCarthy, *Noblesse Oblige: Charity and Cultural Philanthropy in Chicago, 1849–1929*, 1982. Dwight Burlingame and Dennis Young, eds., *Corporate Philanthropy at the Crossroads*, 1996. Judith Sealander, *Private Wealth and Public Life: Foundation Philanthropy and the Re-Shaping of American Social Policy from the Progressive Era through the New Deal*, 1997. David Hammack, ed., *Making the Nonprofit Sector in the United States: A Reader*, 1998. Charles Clotfelter and Thomas Erlich, eds., *Philanthropy and the Nonprofit Sector in a Changing America*, 1999. Ellen Lagemann, ed., *Philanthropic Foundations: New Scholarship, New Possibilities*, 1999.

—Judith Sealander

PHILIPPINES. The Philippine Islands, located in the western Pacific and named for King Philip of Spain, became a Spanish colony in 1571 and so remained for 325 years. American contact commenced in 1790, and regular trade began in 1796 with the voyage to Manila of the Salem ship *Astrea* with Nathaniel *Bowditch as its supercargo. Between the 1820s and the 1880s, *New England traders imported hemp, sugar, and other commodities from the Philippines.

The Filipinos' war for independence from Spain began in 1896. America intervened on 1 May 1898 when, as part of the *Spanish-American War, Commodore George Dewey's fleet defeated the Spanish navy in the Battle of Manila Bay. A Philippine movement under Emilio Aguinaldo (1869–1964) proclaimed independence on 12 June 1898 and subsequently established a constitutional government. This initiative failed, however, after Spain transferred the archipelago to the United States by the Treaty of Paris, signed in December 1898 and ratified by the U.S. Senate in February 1899. From 1899 to 1903 the United States waged a war against forces of the First Philippine Republic that cost the lives, from injury and disease, of hundreds of thousands of Filipinos and some 4,200 Americans. Involving both open battles and guerrilla campaigns, the war, especially the latter phase, was marked by atrocities later investigated by a U.S. Senate committee.

From the appointment of William Howard *Taft to head the first civil commission in 1900, America's expressed intention was to limit its control over the colony. Filipino officials ran local government from the outset, and by 1907 the first Philippine legislature met and shared lawmaking responsibility with the Philippine Commission, appointed by the U.S. president. The 1916 Jones Act provided for an elected senate, completing the turnover of legislative responsibility to the Filipinos. The executive remained under U.S. control until 1935 when the Tydings-McDuffie Act (1934) created the Philippine Commonwealth. Manuel Luis Quezon became the first elected Filipino president.

During *World War II, Filipino guerrilla forces provided critical help in resisting the Japanese occupation, and the Philippines became independent on 4 July 1946. Subsequently, American economic and military assistance kept the Philippines and the United States closely allied. America exerted considerable control over the Philippine economy through tariff arrangements and leased military bases in the archipelago as part of the its *Cold War strategy in Asia, particularly Clark Air Force Base and Subic Naval Base. The United States provided military aid to help the Philippine government suppress the communist Hukbalahap movement from 1946 to 1956. Philippine nationalists and others have dubbed these postwar relations neocolonialism.

U.S. support of Ferdinand Marcos's repressive martial law regime (1972–1986) elicited growing Filipino resentment of American influence, and in September 1991 the Philippine Senate voted to terminate the leases on the military bases. Despite the Philippines' growing affiliation with other Pacific Rim nations, American business investment in the Philippines and ties with a large Philippine-American community kept the bonds between the two countries strong as the twentieth century ended.

[*See also* Expansionism; Foreign Relations: The Economic Dimension; Foreign Relations: U.S. Relations with Asia; Foreign Trade; Insular Cases; Protectorates and Dependencies.]

• H. W. Brands, *Bound to Empire: The United States and the Philippines*, 1992. John A. Larkin, *Sugar and the Origins of Modern Philippine Society*, 1993.

—John A. Larkin

PHILOSOPHY. Philosophy in America has a long history, traceable at least to Jonathan *Edwards in the mid–eighteenth century. For the most part, the discipline has been centered in colleges and universities where philosophy has taken on many roles: handmaiden to theology, instructor in morals for young men, mediator of the conflicting claims of science and religion, foundational ground for human thought and action, and participant in a wider cultural conversation. From Edwards in his study, the discipline has grown to encompass several thousand men and women teaching and writing philosophy. Like the other academic disciplines, philosophy in the twentieth century developed characteristic institutions: Ph.D.-granting graduate departments, refereed journals, professional organizations, and academic meetings. The development of American philosophy has thus been marked by both the achievements of individual philosophers and the rise of an academic discipline.

Colonial and Antebellum Eras. The first significant American philosopher was the evangelical minister and theologian Jonathan Edwards. As a young student at Yale College, Edwards encountered the works of John Locke and Isaac Newton. His earliest writings reflect his preoccupation with philosophical and metaphysical problems posed by these writers. Following his own conversion experience; pastorate at Northampton, Massachusetts; and leading role in the *Great Awakening, Edwards increasingly employed his metaphysical rationalism in the service of Calvinist theology. In his *Treatise Concerning Religious Affections* (1746), Edwards wrestled with the problem of knowledge, which would preoccupy American philosophers for the next 250 years. An idealist, he argued that both sensation and reflection produced direct knowledge of mind and nature. In *Freedom of the Will* (1754), Edwards argued that belief in freedom was possible even for a determinist. He defended freedom by dividing the universe into two spheres—God's world ruled by determinism and the finite world in which real freedom of choice was possible. Edwards's writing on knowledge, religious belief, and free will influenced theological and philosophic thought well into the nineteenth century.

Early nineteenth-century philosophy retained close ties to theology, but philosophers increasingly congregated in the colleges and universities of the eastern states. After Edwards, philosophy developed in several directions. Philosophers in *New England, especially, worked in an Edwardsian tradition that focused on problems of the relations of God and man, nature and spirit, and the freedom of the will. Another strain derived from the philosophy of Scottish realism. James McCosh (1811–1894) at Princeton and Noah Porter (1811–1892) at Yale developed subtle versions of the Scottish position that the task of philosophy is to examine and make explicit the implicit assumptions of commonsense belief. Sensation and perception provided reliable knowledge of the external world and made scientific knowledge possible. The third strain of academic philosophy was moral philosophy. Often taught by the college president as a culminating class for seniors, moral philosophy was designed to inculcate the moral values of the culture in each generation of future leaders. Usually taught from texts, such as Francis Wayland's *Elements of Moral Science* (1835) or Mark Hopkins's *Lectures on Moral Science* (1862), moral philosophy rooted individual and national morality firmly within the Christian tradition. These philosophers broke little new ground, and the challenge to these orthodoxies came from outside the academy.

Ralph Waldo *Emerson represents the late stage of New England Calvinism and a bridge to the more secular philosophers of the late nineteenth century. Emerson's *transcendentalism was rooted in the liberal Unitarianism to which was added an element of German idealism ultimately derived from Immanuel Kant. As much a literary movement as a philosophical one, transcendentalism's key text was Emerson's short book *Nature* (1836). Nature was the vehicle by which human beings gained insight into the ideal world that transcended the mundane reality. Through nature, the individual consciousness could have direct contact with, and understanding of, this higher reality. The transcendentalists' reliance on the authority of individual consciousness and the primacy of action and creativity over contemplation and theory helped lay the groundwork for the development of *pragmatism, the most significant distinctively American philosophy.

Pragmatism and Instrumentalism. Pragmatism originated in the meetings of the Metaphysical Club, a group of young men who gathered in Cambridge, Massachusetts, in the 1870s to discuss philosophical issues. The participants included Chauncey Wright (1830–1875), Charles Sanders *Peirce, and William *James. As it developed in the work of Peirce, James, and later John *Dewey, pragmatism focused on the problems of knowledge, truth, and meaning. Drawing on the emerging sciences, including Charles Darwin's theory of *evolution, pragmatism emphasized the primacy of action over theory and the value of contingency, novelty, and progress that for James was centered on the individual and for Peirce and Dewey on the community.

Peirce articulated the basic premises of pragmatism in articles published in the 1870s, especially "The Fixation of Belief" (1877) and "How to Make Our Ideas Clear" (1878). Our conception of an object, Peirce argued, lies in its practical consequences. For him, pragmatism was a method for clarifying the meaning and truth of objects and theories by determining their future practical consequences. Invoking the scientific method, he saw truth as contingent and evolving and determined by a consensus of those competent to judge in a particular situation. Peirce's pragmatism depended upon his influential semiotics, or theory of signs. All thinking, meaning, and truth, he believed, relies upon socially standardized signs contingently established by a community of interpreters.

James was an innovative psychologist as well as a philosopher. His *Principles of Psychology* (1890) helped establish experimental *psychology in the United States and defined the field for many years to come. Upon the completion of this work, James turned more fully to the pragmatic philosophy being elaborated by his friend Peirce. James's more individualistic version of pragmatism was rooted in his psychology and in his own personal need to establish a means of finding truth in the fluid contingency of the modern world. James tended to conflate meaning and truth, and to describe as true any idea that leads to a satisfactory and beneficial experience. For James, Peirce's reliance on scientific experimentalism was too narrow to deal adequately with the manifold pluralities confronting individuals. By focusing on what worked for the individual in a particular cultural context, James sought a reliable means to establish truth and knowledge without resting on the bedrock of some absolute. More accessible and popular than Peirce, James outlined pragmatism for a wide audience in *Pragmatism* (1907) and *The Meaning of Truth* (1909).

Dewey, whose long academic career took him from the University of Michigan to the University of Chicago and ultimately Columbia University, developed the third major version of pragmatism. Dewey's pragmatism, like Peirce's, was more communitarian in that it emphasized the adaptation of the individual and the community to changed circumstances. Dewey situated the individual in the social context and developed pragmatism as a process of social reconstruction based on communal inquiry and experimentation. Dewey's instrumentalism was both a theory and a method of inquiry for solving problems and for generating truth, or what he called warranted assertion. Pragmatism was thus an activist philosophy operating within a democratic community to direct beneficial adaptive change to altered social circumstances. Dewey exemplified his call to action through his own extensive commitment to education reform and a variety of social and political reforms.

Idealism and Realism. James's friend and Harvard colleague Josiah Royce (1855–1916), the strongest American proponent of absolute idealism at the turn of the century, provided a powerful counter to the generally realistic philosophy of the pragmatists. In his early writings, Royce postulated the Absolute as the solution to the problem of error. Under James's influence, Royce modified his views, moving toward what he called absolute pragmatism. In later work influenced by Peirce's semiotics, Royce developed the idea of the community of interpretation as providing a social basis for reality. The Universal Community, which possessed truth in its totality, became for Royce a viable alternative to the Absolute.

Epistemological realism also found new adherents in the early twentieth century. The new realists, which included Edwin B. Holt (1873–1946) and Ralph Barton Perry (1876–1957), argued for realism in which we can directly apprehend the qualities of an object. The critical realists, which included George Santayana (1863–1952) of Harvard and Arthur O. Lovejoy (1873–1962) of Johns Hopkins University, countered by arguing for a dualistic realism in which objects are only indirectly perceived through the mediation of ideas. Santayana was noted not only for his realism, but also for his skepticism and naturalism and his highly literary style of philosophizing. Lovejoy went on to develop the influential method of tracing fundamental ideas through history, as in *The Great Chain of Being* (1936).

Professionalization and European Influences. With the exception of Peirce, all of the philosophers following Emerson had successful careers in colleges and universities. By the late nineteenth century, philosophy was loosening its ties to theology on the one hand and to psychology on the other. Although many turn-of-the-twentieth-century philosophers had a traditional Christian upbringing and may have even considered the ministry, their philosophical training took place in the secularizing graduate schools patterned on that of Johns Hopkins, established in 1876. In this milieu, the path to a career in philosophy was increasingly well defined: graduate training, especially at universities such as Harvard, Johns Hopkins, Cornell, and Columbia; appointment to a collegiate or university faculty; publication in one of the new journals such as *Philosophical Review* (1892) or *The Journal of Philosophy, Psychology, and Scientific Methods* (1904); and membership in the new

American Philosophical Association (1901). By the early twentieth century, American philosophy had become thoroughly secularized and was seeking to emulate the sciences in its methods, rigor, and explanatory power.

During the interwar years, American philosophy was substantially influenced by European ideas and philosophers. The first significant immigrant was the English philosopher and logician Alfred North Whitehead (1861–1947), appointed at Harvard in 1924. His early work in logic and mathematics with his student Bertrand Russell contributed to the development of an analytic tradition in the United States. Much of his work at Harvard focused on metaphysics, especially his emphasis on organicism and process. His stress on the organism's selective responses to the changing environment in which it operates proved particularly significant for American social thought. During the 1930s, other philosophers immigrated to the United States, especially from central Europe following the rise of fascism. Rudolf Carnap (1891–1970), a German logical positivist, and Hans Reichenbach (1891–1953), a German philosopher of *science, both accepted positions at American universities in the late 1930s.

The writings of these and other European analytic philosophers and logical positivists had already crossed the Atlantic to a favorable reception. The pragmatists, with their emphasis on the problems of truth and knowledge, and reliance on scientific methods, had created an intellectual climate congenial to the seemingly more rigorous methods of the Europeans. Philosophy, in this context, means the careful definition of terms, the analysis and reduction of linguistic complexities to simple terms, and the study of logical syntax. The logical positivists stressed several related ideas including a verifiable theory of meaning, rejection of metaphysics, the unity of the sciences, and the logical analysis of *mathematics and science. Because they promised a more rigorous and scientific approach to the problems of truth and knowledge so prevalent in American philosophy, these ideas, once they took hold, dominated philosophical thinking until well into the 1970s.

Post–World War II Developments. Following *World War II, American philosophers largely focused on the problems raised by analytic philosophy and logical positivism. The most important philosopher in this tradition was Harvard's W. V. O. Quine (1908–2000), the foremost logician of the twentieth century. Quine's work in logic was especially important in the development of set theory. He drew both on the pragmatic tradition and the analytic and positivistic traditions to elucidate how we use language to describe and understand the workings of the world. Other important postwar philosophers included John *Rawls, whose *A Theory of Justice* (1971) helped revive the close study of moral theory, and Thomas Kuhn (1922–1996), whose *The Structure of Scientific Revolutions* (1962) reconfigured both the history and the philosophy of science. As a counter to the prevailing analytic and logical traditions, American philosophy was also invigorated by new European imports, including existentialism immediately following World War II and later the work of such contemporary French philosophers as Jacques Derrida and Michel Foucault and the German Martin Heidegger.

In the last quarter of the twentieth century, American philosophy became increasingly diverse in both its subject matter and its methodology. This period was marked by Richard *Rorty's notable rejection of the hegemony of the analytic tradition. Rorty in the 1970s returned to an earlier pragmatic tradition in giving up the search for absolute foundations for knowledge in either science or logic. In his influential *Philosophy and the Mirror of Nature* (1979), Rorty abandoned a representational theory of reality, in which the mind more or less accurately mirrors the absolute reality, in favor of the argument that knowledge is always constructed by the individual in a particular context for a particular need. If philosophers were no longer to serve as the final arbiters of truth and knowledge, they could and should, Rorty argued, still participate in the conversations that create and critique the cultures in which we live.

At the end of the century, postanalytic and neopragmatic philosophers predominated. Philosophical approaches had become much more diverse, as had the profession itself, which now encompassed such fields of inquiry as feminist philosophy and environmental ethics. For example, Sandra Harding (1935–) developed an influential feminist approach to knowing and to the philosophy of science, and Tom Regan (1938–) did significant work in environmental ethics, with a particular focus on animal rights. Pragmatic thought experienced a revival, both in renewed study of Peirce, James, and Dewey, and in works by Rorty, Hilary Putnam, Richard Bernstein, John Smith, Cornel West, and others. All these philosophers tried to articulate a neopragmatism that was broadly conceived as problem-solving adaptability, rather than narrowly focused on establishing the bases of truth, meaning, and the possibility of knowledge. Philosophy in the United States was well established within higher education as the twenty-first century began, but with rare exceptions, contemporary philosophers lacked the broad cultural appeal and influence exercised by James and Dewey at the beginning of the twentieth century.

[*See also* Education: The Rise of the University; Professionalization; Religion; Secularization; Unitarianism and Universalism.]

• Herbert W. Schneider, *A History of American Philosophy,* 1946. Morton White, *Science and Sentiment in America: Philosophical Thought from Jonathan Edwards to John Dewey,* 1972. Bruce Kuklick, *The Rise of American Philosophy: Cambridge, Massachusetts, 1860–1930,* 1977. Elizabeth Flower and Murray G. Murphey, *A History of Philosophy in America,* 2 vols., 1977. Bruce Kuklick, *Churchmen and Philosophers: From Jonathan Edwards to John Dewey,* 1985. Cornel West, *The American Evasion of Philosophy: A Genealogy of Pragmatism,* 1989. Daniel J. Wilson, *Science, Community, and the Transformation of American Philosophy, 1860–1930,* 1990. John Patrick Diggins, *The Promise of Pragmatism: Modernism and the Crisis of Knowledge and Authority,* 1995. Robert Hollinger and David Depew, eds., *Pragamatism: From Progressivism to Postmodernism,* 1995.

—Daniel J. Wilson

PHOTOGRAPHY. From its arrival in 1839 to its 1990s immersion in the digital world of *computers and on-line information, photography both reflected and influenced American culture. The first widespread form of photography in America was the daguerreotype process, which produced images on a small silver plate. This "mirror with a memory" attracted entrepreneurs who bought inexpensive kits that included a camera, materials, and such studio accessories as pastoral backdrops and a neck brace for the long exposures. Daguerreotype businesses ranged from ornate palaces in major cities to itinerant flatboat studios on inland rivers.

In the 1850s the daguerreotype gave way to a cheap hybrid, the tintype, and to a new form of negative-to-positive photography known as wet-plate or wet-collodion. While the tintype served the mass-portraiture market, wet-plate lent itself to landscapes, cityscapes, and mass-reproduced celebrity portraits. West Coast photographers like Carleton Watkins and Isaiah Taber exploited the mass-reproduction capacity of the new process to take landscape photographs that advertised the *West's scenic wonders, especially those of Yosemite. Eastern studios produced images of presidents and ministers, writers and orators. Mathew Brady's studios in *New York City and *Washington, D.C., disseminated canonical portraits of public figures; Abraham *Lincoln's public image was effectively invented and refined by the Brady Studios. The *Civil War sent the studio photographers into the field to record the conflict and produce narrative books that combined memorial texts with resonant images of battlefields, sometimes with the dead still awaiting burial.

Postwar photographers turned to the next great cultural adventure: westward expansion. While Andrew Joseph Russell and Alexander Gardner tracked the transcontinental railroad's construction, others like Eadweard Muybridge and William Henry Jackson, working as private entrepreneurs or government surveyors, recorded and celebrated the West. This golden era of landscape photography produced a subgenre of images of American Indians that memorialized the vanishing races while justifying Euro-American expansion. Urban America, meanwhile, inspired tourist photographs and then, in the 1890s, documentary reform photography. The journalist-reformer Jacob Riis's pictures of New York City slum life in *How the Other Half Lives* (1890), and Lewis Hine's photographs of street urchins and child laborers, helped inspire the *Progressive Era reform effort.

By the turn of the century, photography had become ubiquitous in *journalism, illustrated books, cheap postcards, and family "snap-shot" albums. The advent of flexible film, miniature cameras, the popular "Kodak" box camera, introduced in 1888 by George Eastman (1854–1932), and cheap film-development services democratized photography. Meanwhile, art galleries began to display the delicate, painterly work of Alfred *Stieglitz, Gertrude Kasebier, and others. The circle around Stieglitz brought photography into the world of high modernism and largely created elite art photography in America, nurturing such luminaries as Edward Weston and Imogen Cunningham.

The rise of picture *magazines like *Life* and *Look* in the 1930s provided a mass-market alternative to high modernist photography. Exploiting the new medium, the Franklin Delano *Roosevelt administration instituted numerous photography projects. The most legendary was that of the Farm Security Administration (FSA) run by Roy Emerson Stryker, who hired such important photographers as Walker Evans, Dorothea Lange, Marion Post Wolcott, and Russell Lee. While displaying nostalgia for a vanishing rural and small-town America, their work also adeptly propagandized for the New Deal. Ansel Adams, meanwhile, carried on the tradition of western landscape photography. *World War II produced many memorable photographs, including the raising of the American flag over Iwo Jima, the mushroom cloud over Hiroshima, and haunting images of the Nazi death camps.

The twentieth century's three dominant photographic communities—snapshot amateurs, elite artists, and photojournalists—often came together, especially during the 1950s, when the profitable photography market drew amateurs and artists alike into the professional realm. This combination was embodied in the Museum of Modern Art's 1955 exhibit *The Family of Man,* curated by the Stieglitz-acolyte Edward Jean *Steichen. The exhibit presented photography as an ideal medium to editorialize, to inspire, and to unite the disparate cultures of America and the globe into a commodified universal human culture.

This theme dominated *advertising, editorial, and much art photography throughout the *Cold War, but it also engendered a reaction as in the caustic photographs of Robert Frank, whose *The Americans* (1959) brought a Beat sensibility to the medium, shocking critics and inspiring a generation of ironic documentarians. Photographers like Garry Winogrand and Diane Arbus abandoned lucrative commercial careers to haunt the social landscape, creating a genre known as the "new documentary." That their work garnered influential exhibitions, gallery shows, book contracts, and high sale prices caught the attention of a new generation of photographers trained not in journalism or advertising but in university art departments. Schooled in *literature and *painting, these practitioners moved the medium into the center of postmodernist artistic discourse. Photography's omnipresence, its blurring of the constructed and the "real," and its immersion in *consumer culture all made it a central icon of *postmodernism, though individual photographs often disappeared into larger collaged works in which painting, *sculpture, literature, and the mass media uneasily coexisted. The insertion of photography into postmodernism signaled a significant change. Once a medium of Truth, photography had lost its authority, becoming, instead, simply one among a host of image-making processes.

[*See also* Indian History and Culture: The Indian in Popular Culture; New Deal Era, The; Tourism; Yosemite National Park.]

• Beaumont Newhall, *The Daguerreotype in America,* 1961. Weston Naef, *Era of Exploration: The Rise of Landscape Photography in the American West, 1860–1885,* 1975. Jonathan Greene, *American Photography: A Critical History, 1945 to the Present,* 1984. Naomi Rosenblum, *A World History of Photography,* 1984. Martha A. Sandweiss, ed., *Photography in Nineteenth-Century America,* 1991. Peter Galassi, *American Photography, 1890–1965,* 1995.

—Peter Bacon Hales

PHYSICAL FITNESS MOVEMENT. *See* Health and Fitness.

PHYSICAL SCIENCES. Sharing a common subject of study—the inanimate universe of matter and energy—the sciences of astronomy, physics, and chemistry also share aspects of a common history. In many instances, these three basic physical sciences even overlap, giving rise to joint disciplines such as astrophysics and chemical physics. Moreover, when viewed in the context of U.S. history, the three sciences' patterns of development tend to synchronize with national social and cultural trends. Despite the shared patterns, however, the three sciences throughout their histories have retained their individuality and nuance as distinct realms of scientific inquiry. In particular, during the early decades of the American republic, practitioners of all three sciences were few in number, isolated from one another, and reliant on European colleagues for direction. By the mid–nineteenth century the physical scientists enjoyed broader public support, clearer professional identities, and more reliable institutional bases, particularly within burgeoning colleges and universities. By the early twentieth century, they had established themselves as full participants—if not leaders—in the international scientific arena, and by midcentury, had added strong links to American government and industry as they expanded their research initiatives and capabilities.

Scientific Colonialism. During the late *Colonial Era and early national period, citizens interested in astronomy, physics, and chemistry found camaraderie and support in a few regional learned societies and colleges. *Philadelphia's *American Philosophical Society (1743) and *Boston's American Academy of Arts and Sciences (1780) fostered scientific study and inquiry, as did early colleges such as Harvard and William and Mary. Working within European frameworks and reflecting an Enlightenment fascination with science's practical and philosophical aspects, a few Americans generated results of an international caliber. In astronomy, Philadelphia's David Rittenhouse (1732–1796) built his own telescopes in 1769 and after for precise celestial observations, while Nathaniel *Bowditch contributed to mathematical astronomy and its ties to nautical navigation. In physics—or, as it was then known, natural philosophy—the legacy of Benjamin *Franklin and his electrical investigations boosted the young nation's overseas image. Whereas physician Benjamin *Rush taught European-style chemistry at the University of Pennsylvania, the English scientist and religious radical Joseph Priestley (1733–1804) brought his trailblazing knowledge of experimental chemistry to America after his emigration to Pennsylvania in 1794.

Although presidents Thomas *Jefferson and John Quincy *Adams championed government support of scientific projects, parsimonious and constitutionally sensitive members of Congress objected. Furthermore, while colleges proliferated during the *Antebellum Era, they tended to teach astronomy, physics, and chemistry as merely accoutrements of a liberal education. Original scientific research, whether directed toward practical applications or arcane theories, still originated with self-motivated individual investigators who faced substantial constraints, including burdensome teaching loads, a scarcity of apparatus and materials, and insufficient access to the primary international practitioners, societies, and journals. To be sure, astronomers enjoyed an advantage because of a national flurry of observatory building—including the U.S. Naval Observatory in *Washington, D.C., completed in 1844. But physicist Joseph *Henry and chemist-naturalist Benjamin *Silliman were more typical of the American self-initiating, self-reliant investigator. With minimal technical resources, Henry still matched wits with his European counterparts in the new field of electromagnetism, while Silliman bolstered scientifically minded compatriots by publishing the only consequential national outlet for research, the interdisciplinary *American Journal of Science.*

Professionalism. As the nineteenth century proceeded, physical scientists moved into an era of heightened professionalism and increased specialization. The *American Association for the Advancement of Science (1848) and *National Academy of Sciences (1863) provided institutional support and a sense of community. The *Smithsonian Institution (1846), under Joseph Henry's direction, served as a clearinghouse for the nation's scattered scientists. Near the end of the century, the physical scientists carved out separate disciplinary organizations and specialized journals: the American Astronomical Society and the *Astronomical Journal*; the American Physical Society and the *Physical Review*; and, with the largest outreach, the American Chemical Society and its *Journal.*

Through two midcentury institutions—Harvard's Lawrence Scientific School and Yale's Sheffield Scientific School—astronomers, physicists, and chemists trained a new generation of experts in these three often overlapping disciplines. Jobs opened for these scientists at technically oriented land-grant colleges and universities, mandated by Congress in the 1862 *Morrill Land Grant Act. By the 1880s, American educational institutions such as the new Johns Hopkins University (1876) were awarding doctoral degrees in the sciences, thus lessening the need for aspiring researchers to study abroad, as had been the pattern. Although a few physical scientists had found employment in early federal agencies such as the U.S. *Coast and Geodetic Survey and the Nautical Almanac Office, the government expanded job opportunities by creating new science-oriented divisions such as the National Bureau of Standards and the Department of Agriculture. Physical scientists also gained support from private foundations such as the Carnegie Institution of Washington. Physicists and particularly chemists (along with chemical engineers) also found positions in *medicine and industry, especially the *electrical industry. Increasingly these scientists provided not merely technical assistance but also worked in industrial *research laboratories underwritten by corporations such as American Telephone and Telegraph, General Electric, DuPont, and Eastman Kodak. The physical scientists who enjoyed these expanding professional opportunities were overwhelmingly male and white. Except for a scattering of female astronomers, women and minorities had little representation in the physical sciences throughout the nineteenth century.

Enjoying increased support and expanded resources in the later nineteenth century, a still small but growing number of American physical scientists gained international prominence. Simon Newcomb of Johns Hopkins led the way in astronomy with mathematical studies of lunar and planetary orbits. In physics, Henry Rowland of Johns Hopkins and Albert A. Michelson of the University of Chicago broke new ground with experiments on diffraction gratings and interferometer studies of light waves—the latter helping earn Michelson the first Nobel Prize awarded to an American scientist (1907). Although the chemists greatly outnumbered the astronomers and physicists, their ranks included fewer luminaries. The chemists, however, gained recognition not only in basic research but also in practical applications: Charles M. Hall, for example, produced cheap aluminum through electrolysis. Josiah Willard *Gibbs bridged physics and chemistry with innovations in thermodynamics and statistical mechanics—and, in the process, by concentrating on abstract theory, complemented his colleagues' propensity for experiment and measurement.

International Parity. In the early twentieth century, American physical scientists achieved strength in numbers, funding, and performance comparable to that of their European counterparts. They now occupied positions in universities, industries, private foundations, and state and federal governments. The tie to the federal government strengthened during *World War I through both the Chemical Warfare Service and the National Research Council (NRC). The council, organized by astrophysicist George Ellery *Hale and later directed by physicist Robert A. *Millikan, coordinated a successful series of *military research projects. Earlier, Hale had shown the advantages of centralized, large-scale, cooperative research by building successively bigger and more costly telescopes at the Yerkes and Mount Wilson *observatories and later the even more ambitious Mount Palomar Observatory. Indeed, through the *observatories and the NRC, Hale blazed the trail for the "big science" of the 1930s and 1940s. The University of California physicist Ernest O. *Lawrence, winner of the Nobel Prize in 1939, reinforced the trend by building progressively more powerful and expensive cyclotrons. Collaborating with chemists such as his Berkeley colleague Glenn T. Seaborg (1912–1999), Lawrence used these particle accelerators to generate radioisotopes (often with medical applications) and, eventually, transuranium elements (including plutonium).

In the period between 1920 and 1940, American physical scientists assimilated such radical new theories as special and general relativity, quantum mechanics, and nuclear science. Applying these new perspectives to cosmological issues (such as stellar evolution, galactic structure, and expansion of the universe) were astronomers Henry N. Russell, Harlow Shapley, and Edwin P. Hubble. Physicists who tackled quantum complexities included Arthur Compton and the team of Clinton Davisson and Lester Germer. Chemist Linus *Pauling clarified the significance of quantum theory for chemical bonds. The arrival in the 1930s of immigrants escaping persecution in Europe reinforced these various investigations. George Gamow and Peter J. W. Debye, for example, drew on the new theories to explore the interfaces of astronomy, physics, and chemistry. Albert *Einstein's emigration to America in 1933 further bolstered the already high international standing not merely of physics in the United States but of all the physical sciences.

Ties to Government and Industry. During *World War II, physicists and chemists worked with engineers on a wide range of war-related projects. Often through contracts with industries or universities, the military funded a series of crash programs to develop devices such as radar and the proximity fuse, to refine armaments such as incendiary weapons and solid-propellant rockets, and to produce synthetic versions of scarce materials such as rubber and fuel. Although all of these front-line technologies helped assure the Allies' victory, the atomic bomb (utilizing the recent discovery of nuclear fission) was the scientists' most dramatic and ultimately crucial undertaking. The *Manhattan Project, the war's most ambitious and expensive scientific and *engineering enterprise, brought together the leading native-born and immigrant physical scientists, who not only overcame the problems of producing fissionable uranium and plutonium, but also assumed the lead in designing the actual bombs. The success of the Manhattan Project, so dramatically demonstrated by the atomic bombing of *Hiroshima and Nagasaki, helped rally the nation's political, military, industrial, and scientific leaders to the idea of federally funded big science. This idea informed the postwar creation of such scientific giants as the *Atomic Energy Commission (1946) and the *National Science Foundation (1950), both initially dominated by Manhattan Project veterans.

During the second half of the twentieth century, big science flourished at major facilities structured around *nuclear weapons (as hydrogen or fusion bombs superseded the original atomic or fission bombs), nuclear reactors, magnetic fusion reactors, particle accelerators, and radio telescopes. These facilities included Argonne National Laboratory, Brookhaven National Laboratory, Fermi National Accelerator Laboratory, Lawrence Berkeley Laboratory, Los Alamos National Laboratory, Oak Ridge National Laboratory, and the Stanford Linear Accelerator Center. The *National Aeronautics and Space Administration (NASA) similarly fostered astronomical research into pulsars, quasars, black holes, and other celestial oddities through various lunar and planetary probes, satellites to detect x-rays and other emissions, and the Hubble Space Telescope. Smaller, less expensive research initiatives also flourished, particularly in academic and industrial settings, and especially for chemists. Narrower networks of researchers, for example, pioneered the transistor and the laser and helped detect residual cosmic effects from the Big Bang, the primal event astrophysicists hypothesize as the origin of the knowable universe. In the sprawling and diverse community of chemical scientists, local researchers continued to use versatile instruments such as mass spectrometers to make breakthroughs in fields ranging from medicine to *agriculture.

End of the Twentieth Century and Beyond. The generation of physical scientists who led the Manhattan Project and kindred wartime endeavors dominated American scientific policy—in all fields—through at least the 1960s. In the aftermath of the *Vietnam War, however, the influence of this aging generation eroded as Americans reevaluated the nation's scientific priorities. The erosion quickened with the end of the *Cold War and the growing prominence of such life-science fields as molecular biology, *genetics and genetic engineering, and medical research. "Accountability" and "relevance" became the new bywords of American science. Physicists were particularly affected by the resultant national reallocation of resources, facing diminished or no funding for an ambitious space-weapons project (the *Strategic Defense Initiative) and a gargantuan particle accelerator. Physics was also more affected by an ongoing problem: the underrepresentation of women and, to an even greater degree, *African Americans and *Hispanic Americans. Despite recurrent corrective campaigns, physicists in particular—but also astronomers and chemists—achieved only modest improvements in establishing gender and racial balance.

Even as they adjusted to changing national priorities, however, the physical scientists maintained commanding positions in international research arenas as the century ended. Their achievements ranged, as they had throughout the nation's history, from the highly esoteric to the immediately practical—from probing the cosmological theory of an expanding universe to developing the medical tool of magnetic-resonance imaging (MRI). Whether working in academic, industrial, or governmental settings—and whether allied with one another, with life scientists, or with engineers—American astronomers, physicists, and chemists continued to extend the bounds of scientific inquiry.

[*See also* Agricultural Experiment Stations; Biological Sciences; Chemical Industry; Earth Sciences; Education: Collegiate Education; Education: The Rise of the University; Education: Education in Contemporary America; Federal Government, Executive Branch: Department of Agriculture; Mathematics and Statistics; Nuclear Power; Oppenheimer, J. Robert; Professionalization; Rabi, Isidor I.; Science; Space Program; Technology; Teller, Edward.]

• Daniel J. Kevles, *The Physicists: The History of a Scientific Community in Modern America,* 1977. Daniel J. Kevles, "The Physics, Mathematics, and Chemistry Communities: A Comparative Analysis," in *The Organization of Knowledge in Modern America, 1860–1920,* eds., Alexandra Oleson and John Voss, 1979, pp. 139–72. Albert E. Moyer, *American Physics in Transition: A History of Conceptual Change in the Late Nineteenth Century,* 1983. Sally Gregory Kohlstedt and Margaret W. Rossiter, eds., *Historical Writing on American Science: Perspectives and Prospects,* 1985. Arnold Thackray et al., *Chemistry in America, 1876–1976,* 1985. John W. Servos, "Mathematics and the Physical Sciences in America, 1880–1930," *Isis* 77 (1986): 611–629. John W. Servos, *Physical Chemistry from Ostwald to Pauling: The Making of a Science in America,* 1990. Ronald E. Doel, *Solar System Astronomy in America: Communities, Patronage, and Interdisciplinary Research, 1920–1960,* 1996. John Lankford, *American Astronomy: Community, Careers, and Power, 1859–1940,* 1997.

—Albert E. Moyer

PHYSICS. *See* Physical Sciences.

PIERCE, FRANKLIN (1804–1869), fourteenth president (1853–1857) of the United States. Pierce was born and reared in Hillsboro, New Hampshire. His father, Benjamin, a *Revolutionary War general and later governor of New Hampshire, influenced his son toward a career in *Democratic party politics. After graduating from Bowdoin College, Pierce read law with several jurists and joined the bar in 1827. He first entered politics as a representative in the state legislature, then in 1833 became one of the youngest members of the U.S. House of Representatives. A fervent supporter of Andrew *Jackson, Pierce fully embraced the Democratic creed of small government and *states' rights. In 1837 he won election to the U.S. Senate. His unexpected nomination as the presidential candidate of a divided Democratic party in 1852, coming on the forty-ninth ballot, made him the first "dark-horse candidate" in American history. He defeated the *Whig party candidate, General Winfield Scott (1786–1866).

Pierce's presidential significance lies primarily in his failure to achieve the sectional harmony he hoped for. He supported the 1854 *Kansas-Nebraska Act, believing that southerners should be allowed to take their slaves wherever they wished, and hoping that leaving the *slavery issue to local decision-making would end sectional friction. In fact, most of his presidency was preoccupied with the fierce and sometimes violent conflict between proslavery and antislavery settlers in Kansas. Criticizing the newly formed *Republican party as disruptive and sectionalist, Pierce struck most northerners as a "doughface": a northerner who favored southern interests. An expansionist, he tried without success to buy Cuba from Spain, but by means of the *Gadsden Purchase (1853) he did acquire a sliver of land from Mexico for a southern railroad line. Overall, Franklin Pierce represents that group of northern Democrats sympathetic to southern positions but whose efforts at sectional compromise proved unsuccessful. As president, he exemplified passive, mid-nineteenth-century chief executives during a time of congressional domination.

[*See also* Antebellum Era; Buchanan, James; Civil War: Causes; Douglas, Stephen A.; Expansionism; Federal Government, Executive Branch: The Presidency; Railroads.]

• Roy Nichols, *Franklin Pierce: Young Hickory of the Granite Hills,* 1931. Larry Gara, *The Presidency of Franklin Pierce.* 1991.

—Jean Harvey Baker

PILGRIMS. The term "Pilgrims" (used in Hebrews 11:13) was first bestowed by William Bradford (1590–1657), governor and historian of *Plymouth Colony, on the band of Separatist Puritans that originated in Scrooby, England, but it has been variously applied to all passengers on the *Mayflower,* to everyone who settled in Plymouth before 1631, and to any early inhabitant of the colony. Separatists differed from most Puritans in maintaining that the Church of England could not be reformed and that true churches were constituted only by members' voluntary covenants. Since Separatists challenged the Church of England's exclusive claim to ecclesiastical legitimacy, and thus traduced its royal head, they suffered persecution; in the years around 1600, hundreds fled to the Netherlands, a haven for religious dissenters from throughout Europe. In 1608 the Scrooby meeting escaped to Amsterdam, relocating to Leiden under pastor John Robinson the next year. Economic hardship, fears that their children were becoming too Dutch, and concern about their neighbors' religious laxity encouraged some congregants to contemplate a further move; in 1620 roughly one-third of them sailed to America. Having signed the *Mayflower Compact aboard ship on 11 November, the Pilgrims went ashore on Cape Cod and, after several exploratory expeditions, established their permanent colony at Plymouth. Although contemporary accounts do not mention landing at a specific site, traditions about the colonists' first footfall on "Plymouth Rock" were locally extant by the mid–eighteenth century and became part of *New England's founding legend during the 1770s, when patriots used the Pilgrims' earlier flight from persecution to excoriate contemporary British tyranny. As notions of national identity cohered in the nineteenth century, the Pilgrims were (and continue to be) widely apotheosized for exemplifying such core American virtues as industry, piety, fortitude, self-government, and tolerance.

[*See also* Colonial Era; Exploration, Conquest, and Settlement, Era of European; Puritanism; Religion.]

• William Bradford, *Of Plymouth Plantation 1620–1647,* ed. Samuel Eliot Morison, 1952.

—Charles L. Cohen

PINCKNEY'S TREATY (1795). During the *Revolutionary War, Spain reconquered Florida from Great Britain. Contrary to the border agreed to by the British and Americans (31° north latitude), Spain claimed that Florida extended into the Ohio valley. By this border claim, Spain sought to keep the expansive United States away from the *Mississippi River and Spain's other major colony in the area, Louisiana. With Louisiana occupying the west bank of the Mississippi and Florida controlling the east bank from at least 31° southward, Spain in 1784 closed the mouth of the river to U.S. navigation. This made the river useless as a means of getting goods from U.S. territory west of the Appalachian Mountains to markets in the East. To further discourage settlement beyond the Appalachians, the Spanish also supported the hostile southwestern Indian tribes.

By 1794, however, the Spanish feared that the Americans might use the opportunity of the ongoing European war to attack Spanish territory. Consequently, they negotiated a treaty with the U.S. minister Thomas Pinckney (1750–1828) that guaranteed Americans free navigation of the entire Mississippi and a three-year renewable right to unload riverboat goods at *New Orleans for reshipment on oceangoing vessels. The treaty (signed in Madrid on 27 October 1795) also set the Florida boundary at 31° and promised noninterference with the Indians along the border between Spanish territory and the United States.

President George *Washington and the Senate welcomed Pinckney's Treaty, and it was ratified in 1796. But it only temporarily settled Spanish-U.S. border disputes because expansionists in the United States were determined to acquire Florida and New Orleans and gain sole control of the navigation of the Mississippi. Within twenty-five years, both goals were accomplished.

[*See also* Adams-Onís Treaty; Early Republic, Era of the; Expansionism; Foreign Relations: U.S. Relations with Europe; Indian History and Culture: From 1500 to 1800; Louisiana Purchase; Spanish Settlements in North America.]

• Arthur P. Whitaker, *The Spanish-American Frontier, 1783–1795,* 1927. Samuel Flagg Bemis, *Pinckney's Treaty,* rev. ed. 1960.

—Jerald A. Combs

PLANETARIUMS. *See* Museums: Museums of Science and Technology.

PLASTICS. Plastics are resinous substances molded, cast, or extruded into desired shapes. Until 1869, when John Wesley Hyatt invented celluloid by combining cellulose and camphor, the only plastics were such natural materials as shellac, hard rubber, and gutta percha, used for daguerreotype cases, buttons, and other small artifacts. Celluloid, a sheet material shaped with heat, replaced ivory or tortoiseshell in combs and accessories. Celluloid addressed such issues as the uncertain supply of raw materials, the need for precisely dimensioned manufacturing materials, and the demand for democratization of goods. From the first, its imitative qualities signified both technological ingenuity and second-rate cheapness.

After finding a shellac substitute for electrical insulation in 1907, Leo Baekeland realized that his durable phenolic resin had many applications—from pipe stems to skillet handles—and commercialized it as "the material of a thousand uses." While Bakelite became a household word during the 1920s and 1930s, other plastics appeared: colorful cast phenolic, pastel-colored urea formaldehyde, cellulose acetate, vinyl, and transparent acrylic—all promoted as utopian materials derived from such abundant sources as coal, water, and air. Independent custom molders, who made marketable parts and products, experimented in the 1930s with injection molding of thermoplastics, which eventually almost replaced compression molding of thermoset resins. A journal (*Modern Plastics,* 1925) and a trade association (The Society of the Plastics Industry, 1937) served the fledgling industry.

The DuPont corporation's introduction of nylon in 1938 marked a major transition. Rather than trying to commercialize a random laboratory gunk, Wallace Carothers and Julian Hill set out to synthesize a precise substitute for silk. Nylon's success as a fiber for stockings and as a molding resin signaled the dominance of large chemical companies. The industry came to maturity during *World War II, providing cockpit enclosures, mortar fuses, even bugles. Its wartime advertising promised a plastic miracle world, but homefront substitutes reinforced an image of cheapness. Many new plastics—among them polyethylene, polypropylene, and polyester—were commercialized after the war. Mirroring an expanding economy, a host of new products—Tupperware, hula hoops, fiberglass chairs, Formica laminate, bubble packaging, dry-cleaning bags, Teflon-coated pans—moved so quickly into everyday life that moviegoers laughed nervously in 1968 when a booster in *The Graduate* told Dustin Hoffman, "Just one word. . . . Plastics. . . . There's a great future in plastics."

Although vinyl go-go boots and inflatable domes expressed the youth culture of the 1960s and 1970s, distrust of plastic developed into hostility. Journalists and writers expressed fears of toxicity, flammability, and overflowing landfills (themes used to great effect by the novelist Norman Mailer). "Plastic," once a symbol of humanity's power to transcend natural limits, became instead a metaphor of *technology out of control and a pejorative adjective meaning fake or phony. Eventually, as engineering resins and composites revolutionized sports equipment and other consumer goods in the 1980s and 1990s, plastic regained its good name. At the same time, as cultural attention shifted from intractable natural materials to more malleable plastics, and finally to virtual environments electronically synthesized by computer, the concept of plasticity embodied a traditional American faith in an ability to remold the world.

[*See also* Chemical Industry; Consumer Culture; Mass Production.]

• J. Harry DuBois, *Plastics History U.S.A.,* 1972. Jeffrey L. Meikle, *American Plastic: A Cultural History,* 1995.

—Jeffrey L. Meikle

PLESSY* v. *FERGUSON (1896). *Supreme Court decision upholding racial *segregation. The state of Louisiana in 1890 required *railroads to provide "equal but separate accommodations for the white and colored races." The railroads objected to the legislation because of the additional cost it imposed in providing separate cars. The Louisiana law, however, had little to do with economic efficiency; instead, it represented an attempt by white legislators to restrict racial mixing. In response, a group of Creoles and *African Americans in *New Orleans organized the Citizens' Committee to Test the Constitutionality of the Separate Car Law. In 1892, Homer Plessy, a person who was one-eighth black and therefore appeared to be white, agreed to test the law. Plessy purchased a ticket on a train traveling solely within the state of Louisiana and made sure that the train's conductor understood that he was a "colored" person. When the conductor ordered Plessy from an all-white car, he refused to leave and was arrested. At his trial before Judge John H. Ferguson, Plessy argued that the Louisiana law violated the Thirteenth and *Fourteenth Amendments to the federal *Constitution. The trial judge disagreed, as did the Louisiana Supreme Court, giving Plessy and his supporters the opportunity they wanted to test the meaning of the Thirteenth Amendment's prohibition against *slavery and the Fourteenth Amendment's guaranteeing to all citizens "equal protection" of the laws.

Speaking for an 8–1 Supreme Court majority, Justice Henry Billings Brown, an admiralty lawyer from Detroit, disposed of Plessy's case in a precedent-setting fashion. Brown found that the Thirteenth Amendment applied only to actions intended to reintroduce slavery and that distinctions resting on color and race, by themselves, did not constitute slavery. Brown also proclaimed that the Louisiana law's requirement that passengers be separated on the basis of race did not violate the equal protection clause of the Fourteenth Amendment, since both races enjoyed equal facilities.

Brown rested his opinion on two important nonconstitutional assumptions: first, that segregation by race was not a mark of inferiority, and, second, that race-mixing enjoyed little public support. To prove his point that separate but equal facilities were acceptable, he cited an 1849 Massachusetts decision, *Roberts* v. *City of Boston,* that upheld segregation by race in the Boston public schools. According to Brown, as long as the facilities provided were equal, even if separate, the state had satisfied the constitutional burden imposed by the equal protection clause.

Justice John Marshall *Harlan, a former slaveholder from Kentucky, issued the lone dissent. Harlan insisted that the Thirteenth Amendment did apply, since segregation was a "badge of servitude" and that, in any case, the "Constitution is colorblind, and neither knows nor tolerates classes among citizens." Harlan's dissent proved prophetic. In 1954, the Supreme Court in **Brown* v. *Board of Education* overturned the "separate but equal" doctrine written into the Constitution by *Plessy* v. *Ferguson* and began the process of dismantling legally imposed racial segregation in the United States.

[*See also Civil Rights Cases*; Gilded Age; Racism.]

• Charles A. Lofgren, *The Plessy Case,* 1987.

—Kermit L. Hall

PLYMOUTH, town in Massachusetts, site of a 1620 settlement of English religious dissenters. Unlike the Puritans who founded *Boston in 1630, these were separatists, believing in total separation from the corrupt Church of England. They became known as *Pilgrims, as many had left England in 1608 for the more tolerant Netherlands. In 1619, however, concerned about the corrupting influence of Dutch prosperity, they secured from the Virginia Company a land patent in America. The *Mayflower* sailed from Southampton, England, in September 1620 with some one hundred colonists aboard, about sixty-five of them Pilgrims. Their intended landfall was somewhere north of *Jamestown, but by November storms had carried them far north, beyond the area where their patent was valid, to Massachusetts Bay. Concluding that the isolated location would discourage interference in their religious affairs, they settled on a protected harbor they called Plymouth. The *Mayflower* stayed through the winter; while still on board, the adult males signed the *Mayflower Compact, the colony's basic governing framework.

More than half the population perished the first winter, but by the following autumn the survivors celebrated a day of thanksgiving with the local Indians, an event remembered in the present-day Thanksgiving holiday. For the first generation, Plymouth provided what the founders sought: a place to practice their religion freely. Plymouth lost its independence in 1688 with the formation of the short-lived Dominion of New England and was absorbed by the Massachusett Bay Colony in 1691. The often moving and quietly eloquent journal of the colony's first governor, William Bradford (1590–1657), published as *Historie of Plimouth Plantation,* ranks as a classic of early American literature.

[*See also* Colonial Era; Literature: Colonial Era; New England; Puritanism.]

• John Demos, *A Little Commonwealth: Family Life in Plymouth Colony,* 1970. John D. Seelye, *Memory's Nation: The Place of Plymouth Rock,* 1998.

—Christopher Berkeley

POCAHONTAS (c. 1595/1596–1617), favorite daughter of *Powhatan—his people's paramount chieftain—and friend to the *Jamestown colonists. Her clan name was Matoaka; Pocahontas, her public name, means "playful." The Virginia colonist and adventurer John *Smith claimed that she saved his life when Powhatan was about to execute him; her performance was more likely part of a ritual adopting Smith into the tribe. Some scholars question whether this incident actually occurred, although the most exhaustive study, J. A. Leo Lemay's *Did Pocahontas Save Captain John Smith?* (1992), affirms its historicity. Pocahontas held Smith in special esteem, on one occasion warning that Powhatan planned to ambush him, but there are no grounds for thinking their relationship amorous.

In 1613, during the first Anglo-Powhatan War, Captain Samuel Argall abducted her to leverage the return of captives and materiél held by the Powhatans. The next year she entered the Church of England, taking the baptismal name Rebecca, and married John Rolfe, one of her tutors. The marriage stabilized relations between the English and Powhatans until after her death. The Virginia Company brought her to England in 1616 to publicize the plantation; she charmed London society but soon died of natural causes. As an individual Pocahontas performed numerous kindnesses for the English settlers in Virginia, but she had little influence on the diplomatic policies conducted by the *weroances* (chieftains). Virtually forgotten for two centuries, she became a favorite subject for nineteenth-century authors romanticizing "noble savages" and glorifying "founders" of the United States, attaining a mythic status that survives to the present.

[*See also* Colonial Era; Indian History and Culture: From 1500 to 1800; Indian History and Culture: The Indian in Popular Culture; Indian Wars.]

• Philip L. Barbour, *Pocahontas and Her World,* 1970. Frances Mossiker, *Pocahontas: The Life and Legend,* 1976. Gregory Evans Dowd, *A Spirited Resistance: The North American Indian Struggle for Unity, 1745–1815,* 1992.

—Charles L. Cohen

POE, EDGAR ALLAN (1809–1849), poet, short-story writer, critic, essayist. Born in *Boston to itinerant actors and orphaned in 1811, Poe was reared by his godfather, the Richmond, Virginia, merchant John Allan. After a stay in England with the Allans (1815–1820), Poe quarrelled with John Allan and returned to America. He briefly attended the University of Virginia and the U.S. Military Academy. His first book, *Tamarlane and Other Poems,* appeared in 1827. From 1835 on, Poe worked in Richmond, *New York City, and *Philadelphia as a journalist and magazine editor. His incisive literary reviews were highly regarded.

Influenced by romantic and Gothic writers, Poe was drawn to the fantastic, grotesque, paranormal, and necrophilic. Poems such as "The Raven" and "The Bells" are marked by a wistful musicality and innovative techniques. His best-known tales include "MS. Found in a Bottle," "The Fall of the House of Usher," "The Masque of the Red Death," "The Pit and the

Pendulum," and "The Tell-tale Heart." A pioneer of science fiction, he also invented the detective story with "Murders in the Rue Morgue" and "The Purloined Letter." The deductive reasoning of his fictional detective C. A. Dupin influenced Sir Arthur Conan Doyle's character Sherlock Holmes.

In 1836, Poe married his thirteen-year-old cousin, Virginia Clemm, for whom he wrote the poem "Annabel Lee." She died in 1847. Poe himself died in Baltimore, Maryland, two years later after a bout of drinking. A giant of American letters and indeed of world literature, Poe particularly influenced the French symbolist poets.

[*See also* Literature: Early National and Antebellum Eras; Poetry; Romantic Movement.]

• Bettina L. Knapp, *Edgar Allan Poe,* 1984. Scott Peoples, *Edgar Allan Poe Revisited,* 1998.

—Bettina L. Knapp

POETRY. American poetry, the history of which spans more than 350 years, is notable for its variety, energy, contrarian tendencies, and feistiness. True, the earliest verse was imitative and derivative, displaying a heavy reliance on British prosody, diction, and verse forms (particularly pastorals, odes, elegies, epistles, and satires). By the nineteenth century, however, poets were expressing an emergent national identity and making significant strides toward liberating themselves from foreign models. By the twentieth century, American poetry commanded international attention and respect, for it had attained a high level of quality—indeed, had achieved parity among the world's poetries, including European poetry.

*Colonial Era poetry was primarily metaphysical and devotional. Among the *New England Puritans, the three most important poets were Anne *Bradstreet, Edward Taylor (1645–1729), and Michael Wigglesworth (1631–1705). Though her work was conventional and often didactic, Bradstreet nevertheless wrote with honesty and sensitivity, especially concerning familial matters. Moreover, she ranks as the author of the first book of American poetry: *The Tenth Muse, Lately Sprung up in America* (published in England in 1650). Taylor's poetry, which resembles that of such English metaphysicals as George Herbert and John Donne, was written for private purposes between 1682 and 1725 and did not appear in print until 1937. Calling his poems "preparatory meditations," Taylor viewed them chiefly as exercises leading to the sermons he delivered as a clergyman. Wigglesworth's *The Day of Doom* (1662), a long, fulminating epic on the Last Judgment, became, in its day, the most popular of all Puritan poems.

Like their seventeenth-century predecessors, eighteenth-century American poets continued to adhere to English poetic modes and methods. From 1725 to 1820, in the sometimes turbulent years preceding and following the *Revolutionary War, no major figures materialized. Nevertheless, there were some noteworthy developments, and often these had a political rather than religious focus. At Yale, for instance, a "school" of poets arose who became known as the Connecticut Wits. This group's principal members included Joel Barlow, John Trumbull, and Timothy Dwight, all of whom patterned themselves, with mixed success, after such British satirists as Alexander Pope, Jonathan Swift, and John Gay. In *Boston, Phillis *Wheatley, brought from Africa as a slave, wrote methodically but well enough to win recognition as America's first significant black poet. Her *Poems on Various Subjects, Religious and Moral* appeared in England in 1773. At Princeton, New Jersey, Philip Freneau (1752–1832) launched a poetic career in the 1770s that would freely combine nationalistic and romantic subjects and would ultimately make him not a great figure but still the most notable American poet of the eighteenth century.

In the early and mid–nineteenth century, poetry began to move in fresh directions. Among the most popular poets of the American *Romantic movement was Edgar Allan *Poe, some of whose spellbinding verse appeared in *The Raven and Other Poems* (1845). Also immensely popular in their day were the authors known as the Fireside Poets: William Cullen Bryant, Henry Wadsworth Longfellow, John Greenleaf Whittier, Oliver Wendell Holmes Sr., and James Russell Lowell. Once-beloved poems such as Bryant's "Thanatopsis" (1821), Lowell's *The Vision of Sir Launfal* (1848), Longfellow's *The Song of Hiawatha* (1855), Holmes's "The Chambered Nautilus" (1858), and Whittier's *Snow-Bound* (1866) are generally viewed by modern critics as sentimental, diffuse, moralistic, and excessively hortatory.

Sometimes grouped with the Fireside Poets is Ralph Waldo *Emerson, best known as a lecturer, essayist, and the doyen of New England *transcendentalism, but also the author of such once-revered poems as "Concord Hymn" (1837) and "The Snow-Storm" (1841). Indeed, because of his various commentaries on poetics, particularly his 1844 essay "The Poet," Emerson is often regarded as a watershed figure in American poetic history. Urging poets to be visionary rather than literary, to use organic rather than predetermined forms, and to exploit hitherto unsung native materials, Emerson contributed profoundly to the nineteenth-century American effort to formulate an indigenous theory of poetry and to achieve literary independence from British and European culture.

Influenced by Emerson's pronouncements were both Walt *Whitman and Emily *Dickinson, the two greatest American poets of the nineteenth century. Avowedly inspired by Emerson, Whitman's *Leaves of Grass* (1855) is regarded by some critics as the most revolutionary volume in American poetry. Whitman would spend the remaining thirty-six years of his life revising and augmenting this book, publishing expanded editions in 1856, 1860, 1867, 1871–1872, and 1881–1882. In sprawling, highly rhythmical free verse lines expressing his passionate commitment to the democratic ideals of America, Whitman in *Leaves of Grass* explored two central themes: first, the freedom and dignity of the individual and the equality of all people; and, second, the beauty and innocence of the human body and the naturalness and healthiness of sex. Dickinson wrote 1,775 poems during her lifetime but published only eleven of them. Indeed, her entire body of work did not appear in print exactly as she wrote it until 1955. Modeling her brief, intense, often elliptical poems on the metric pattern of hymns, Dickinson explored the interior life. Freely employing oblique rhymes, unorthodox punctuation, and eccentric capitalization, she plumbed such subjects as pain, death, immortality, nature, imagination, and love.

Other nineteenth-century poets deserve at least minimal acknowledgment: Jones Very and Frederick Goddard Tuckerman, two reclusive New Englanders, were among the century's best sonneteers; Herman *Melville's *Battle-Pieces and Aspects of the War* (1866) ranks as one of the two best books of poems on the *Civil War (the other being Whitman's *Drum-Taps,* 1865); in both theory and practice, Georgia-born Sidney Lanier tried in novel ways to fuse poetry and music; in *The Black Riders* (1895) and *War Is Kind* (1899), the fiction writer Stephen Crane published terse, ironic, aphoristic poems that anticipate the modern era; and in fine lyrics such as "Frederick Douglass" (1896) and "We Wear the Mask" (1896), Paul Laurence Dunbar explored themes that spoke to the condition of *African Americans.

Considering the level of achievement of its poets, the modernist period, extending roughly from 1900 to 1945, is perhaps the richest in American poetic history. The period began auspiciously in 1912 when, in *Chicago, Harriet Monroe founded *Poetry: A Magazine of Verse* that would become the most distinguished journal of its kind. Among the poets published in the early issues of *Poetry* were Carl Sandburg, Vachel Lindsay, Edna St. Vincent Millay, Edgar Lee Masters, Sara Teasdale, and Elinor Wylie—all minor figures, to be sure, but notable for their contributions, either in theme or technique, to the flowering of modernism. Their work appeared in such collections as *Chicago Poems* (Sandburg, 1916), *Spoon River Anthology*

(Masters, 1915), and *Renascence and Other Poems* (Millay, 1917).

The two most important early modernists or, more accurately, premodernists, were Edwin Arlington Robinson (1869–1935) and Robert Frost (1874–1963). Robinson, revitalizing traditional forms, examined the alienation and social failure of individuals unable to adapt to a materialistic and mechanistic age. In poems such as "Richard Cory," "Mr. Flood's Party," and "Eros Turannos," published in *Children of the Night* (1897), *The Town Down the River* (1910), and other works, he reveals a thorough understanding of frustration, ostracism, defeat, and loneliness. Frost insisted on the necessity of traditional metrics; favored speech idioms and conversational tones; and exhibited a fascination with metaphor, symbol, and synecdoche. In poems collected in *A Boy's Will* (1913), *North of Boston* (1914), and later works, Frost, like Robinson, wrote of the lives and landscapes of New England, sometimes expressing affirmative themes, more often negative ones, including isolation, fear, and despair. Among his best-known poems are "Mending Wall," "Birches," "Home Burial," and "The Road Not Taken."

Two highly significant aesthetic developments of the early twentieth century had important implications for poetry: the Imagist movement and the *Harlem Renaissance. From about 1909 to 1917, and primarily in reaction to the sentimentality, didacticism, and abstract language of much nineteenth-century verse, poets in both England and America articulated a theory known as Imagism. This theory advocated the use of concrete particulars, common speech, free verse, and mundane subject matter. Imagists also called for observation without generalization or explanation, and precise and concentrated language. The American poets most conspicuously involved in Imagism included Ezra *Pound, Amy Lowell, and H. D. (Hilda Doolittle). Though short-lived, the Imagist movement exerted an enormous influence on subsequent American poetry.

Poets associated with the Harlem Renaissance of the 1920s, the first large-scale movement in the arts created by African Americans, included Countee Cullen, Claude McKay, James Weldon *Johnson, and, most notably, Langston *Hughes. *The Weary Blues* (1926), by Hughes; *Harlem Shadows* (1922), by McKay; and *The Book of American Negro Poetry* (1922, enlarged 1931), edited by Johnson, would appear on any list of significant works in the history of American poetry.

Ezra Pound and T. S. Eliot (1888–1965) were the American poets most responsible for defining the ideology and practice of modernism. In the twentieth century's early decades, Pound seemed ubiquitous as he advocated "the new" in dozens of critical essays; championed the Imagist and Vorticist movements; compiled anthologies; edited or coedited influential little magazines such as *Blast* and *Poetry*; assisted and advised many other poets, including H. D., Frost, Eliot, Williams, and Marianne Moore (1887–1972); and published his own poems, notably *Hugh Selwyn Mauberly* (1920) and the initial sections of his lifelong epic, *The Cantos*. Eliot, strongly influenced by the French symbolists, particularly Laforgue and Baudelaire, would eventually be as widely acclaimed as any modern poet. His best poetry appeared early in his career: *Prufrock and Other Observations* (1917), *Poems* (1919), and *The Waste Land* (1922). The latter, because it so effectively expressed post–*World War I disillusionment and contained so many radical technical innovations, became one of the most celebrated poems in American literature. Eliot also had a towering reputation as a critic. In oft-quoted essays he argued that poetry should be impersonal and that it necessarily existed in a self-referential world—ideas that had a profound impact on the so-called New Critics and, hence, on the way poetry was taught for many years in American universities.

Among the modernists, Wallace Stevens (1879–1955), William Carlos Williams (1883–1963), and Marianne Moore rank as major figures. In poems whose language is often described as elegant, colorful, and epigrammatic, the symbolist Stevens (an insurance-company executive in Hartford) explored metaphysical and aesthetic questions, like the relationship between the perceiver and the perceived, or between reality and the imagination, for example. He also promoted poetry, an art that shapes reality and gives order, as "the supreme fiction," believing that the "fiction" of traditional religion had lost its vitality in the modern world. Like Whitman's "Song of Myself" and Eliot's *The Waste Land*, Stevens's "Sunday Morning," published in his first collection, *Harmonium* (1923), ranks among America's truly great poems. Williams, vociferously opposing the expatriates Pound and Eliot and the allusive, recondite, academic poetry that they and their followers produced, dedicated himself to using American speech cadences and to writing about American materials, particularly the details of everyday urban life. "No ideas but in things," the imagist Williams insisted, and this credo resulted in fine poems as short as "The Red Wheelbarrow" and as long as his five-part epic *Paterson* (1946–1958). Like Williams, Moore tried to break with tradition. Her poems in *The Dial*, an influential literary magazine of the 1920s, and other periodicals, displayed her experiments with stanzaic patterns; her employment of syllabic verse; her obsession with precise observations; and her innovative use of quotations drawn from such unlikely and far-flung sources as science journals, sports magazines, travel brochures, and advertising flyers. Moore's definitive *Complete Poems* appeared in 1967.

Other noteworthy poets of the modernist era include Hart Crane, who, inspired by Whitman, composed *The Bridge* (1930), a long, visionary poem on spiritual possibilities in an industrialized America; e. e. cummings, who used visual pyrotechnics in poems satirizing advertising, politics, and mass culture and celebrating individuals, lovers, and nonconformists; Muriel Rukeyser, whose poems reflected her passionate commitment to political freedom and social justice; and Robinson Jeffers, who, in long narratives, denounced mankind as self-centered and perverse in its unmitigated destruction of the world's natural beauty.

Within the larger modernist movement, two interesting subgroups arose: the Objectivists and the Fugitives. The Objectivists—including Louis Zukofsky, Charles Reznikoff, George Oppen, and Lorine Niedecker—viewed a poem as an autonomous object, a physiological entity, rather than a conveyor of symbolic value. The Fugitives—notably John Crowe Ransom, Allen Tate, and Robert Penn Warren, were southern poets who in the 1920s embraced classical modes of literature and valued poetry that is structured, impersonal, ironic, and complex. The critical principles of the Fugitives, in turn, laid the foundation for the New Criticism, a formalist and internalist approach to literary analysis identified with I. A. Richards, R. P. Blackmur, Cleanth Brooks, Kenneth Burke, and others.

The early post–*World War II period was dominated by what was called (often disparagingly) "academic poetry." If the early-twentieth century poets had been aggressive and experimental, their post-1945 successors were cautious and conservative, writing in the manner of the English Metaphysicals or the American Fugitives, publishing intellectual, well-wrought, impersonal, technically sophisticated poems in closed or traditional forms. But if these midcentury formalists were not daring, they nevertheless wrote impressively, and their ranks included such gifted figures as Elizabeth Bishop, Robert Lowell, Richard Wilbur, Theodore Roethke, Howard Nemerov, and Randall Jarrell.

Eventually a strong reaction to the dominance of the formalists set in, giving rise to poetry so varied in voice, theme, and style as to defy easy categorization. As early as 1950, Charles Olson published a seminal essay, "Projective Verse." A few years later, Olson and other poets associated with Black Mountain College in North Carolina, including Robert Creeley, Robert Duncan, and Denise Levertov, put projective verse theory into practice, writing open-form poems with lines determined by breath rather than by metrical feet. Led by Allen Ginsberg, author of the landmark volume *Howl and Other Poems* (1956), Beat generation writers such as Jack Kerouac, Gregory Corso, Lawrence Ferlinghetti, Gary Snyder, Michael McClure, and Brother Antoninus (William Everson) rejected the classicism of the academic poets, opting instead for revitalized romanticism, vatic pronouncement, and countercultural protest. In the late 1950s, inspired by Lowell's *Life Studies* (1959), the so-called confessional poets—Sylvia Plath, Anne Sexton, W. D. Snodgrass, and John Berryman—wrote lyrics about highly personal matters, for example, *mental illness, sexual inhibitions, marital discord, menstrual problems, and bouts with alcoholism, and in so doing jettisoned the doctrine of impersonality espoused by Eliot and his disciples.

The antiformalist reaction manifested itself in other ways as well. Believing that academic verse privileged only the external and rationalistic life, poets such as James Wright, Robert Bly, Galway Kinnell, and W. S. Merwin explored the possibilities of a "deep" or subjective imagism, attempting thereby to gain access to the reader's unconscious and thus deepen awareness of the inward and affective life. In the late 1960s and early 1970s, a Black Arts movement developed, as poets such as Imamu Amiri Baraka, (LeRoi Jones), Gwendolyn Brooks, and Sonia Sanchez, finding most contemporary poetry only marginally relevant to their concerns, set about fully utilizing African-American cultural experience and language, as in Baraka's *Reggae or Not!* (1982) and Sanchez's *homegirls and handgrenades* (1984). Last, but by no means least, the New York school, which included Kenneth Koch, Frank O'Hara, and, most notably, John Ashbery, produced painterly, surrealistic poems that perhaps owed more to the techniques of abstract expressionist painting than to the practices of poetic predecessors.

Many outstanding poets whose work does not fall conveniently into a specific "school" or category flourished in the second half of the twentieth century. Simply to cite some representatives figures—Adrienne Rich, Stanley Kunitz, William Stafford, Mary Oliver, Lucille Clifton, James Dickey, Robert Hayden, Mark Strand, A. R. Ammons, Audre Lord, Charles Simic, Philip Dacey, Billy Collins, Carolyn Forché, Sharon Olds—is to suggest the vitality of American poetry in these years. Of the various movements that were influential in the 1980s and 1990s, the three most prominent were women's poetry, Language poetry, and neoformalism. At the century's end, the most significant development by far was the emergence of multicultural poetry. The vibrant and impressive contributions coming from African Americans, Latinos, Native Americans, *Asian Americans, and other ethnic minorities seemed finally to confirm Walt Whitman's description of America as a "teeming nation of nations."

[*See also* Cultural Pluralism; Literature; Modernist Culture.]

• Roy Harvey Pearce, *The Continuity of American Poetry,* 1961; rev. ed., 1965. Hyatt H. Waggoner, *American Poets from the Puritans to the Present,* 1968; rev. ed., 1984. Donald B. Gibson, *Modern Black Poets: A Collection of Critical Essays,* 1973. Alicia Suskin Ostriker, *Stealing the Language: The Emergence of Women's Poetry in America,* 1986. Alan Shucard, *American Poetry: The Puritans through Walt Whitman,* 1988. Alan Shucard, Fred Moramarco, and William Sullivan, *Modern American Poetry, 1865–1950,* 1989. Jay Parini, ed., *The Columbia History of American Poetry,* 1993. Sacvan Bercovitch, ed., *The Cambridge History of American Literature,* vol. 8, *Poetry and Criticism, 1940–1995,* 1996. Fred Moramarco and William Sullivan, *Containing Multitudes: Poetry in the United States since 1950,* 1998.

—Donald D. Kummings

POLICE. In colonial America, policing relied on community consensus and citizens' service as constables and in sheriffs' posses. Public punishments were the most important means of encouraging conformity and order. Modern American police forces, patrols to prevent and detect crime and maintain order, arose in the nineteenth century. Like their *Colonial Era predecessors, they were adaptations of English institutions.

After the *Revolutionary War, northern cities employed constables, who served warrants and acted as detectives, and night watchmen, who patrolled the streets calling out the hour. In contrast, southern cities (Charleston, South Carolina, first, in 1783) developed uniformed, heavily armed, military-style forces primarily to control slaves.

Reflecting the democratic spirit of the 1830s associated with Andrew *Jackson, New Orleans abandoned the military style for a civilian, plainclothes day and night patrol. It lacked central direction, however, so *New York City's police force (1845) is considered the first modern one in America, modeled on London's Metropolitan Police (1829). Adopted after years of debate, the New York police system emulated London's centralization of day and night police. The policemen walked beats, and they had power to arrest without a warrant. They also performed services such as rescuing lost children or animals or lodging the homeless temporarily in station houses. Other cities, and later small towns, followed this model. The new forces were distinctly American: Originally appointed for limited terms by local politicians, they did not wear uniforms, but in New York by the end of the 1850s they were carrying revolvers as well as clubs. These developments in policing reflected the fears of vice and *crime that accompanied rapid *urbanization and the increasing cultural heterogeneity resulting from *immigration.

The big-city police forces themselves became a source of conflict, however. Reformers fought to eliminate political patronage and corruption through bipartisan commissions, *civil service reform, and state control (in New York from 1857 to 1870, and in *Boston from 1885 to 1962). Administration improved, but political interference proved difficult to eliminate. Reformers also sought to outlaw gambling and prostitution and to regulate or prohibit liquor. Such unenforceable laws only opened new opportunities for corruption. By the early twentieth century, reformers emphasized *professionalization, a more military-style organization, higher educational standards, better training, concentration on crime-fighting over general service, and freedom from politics. However, professionalization sometimes widened the distance between the police and local communities.

Police technology steadily advanced. Mobility evolved from walking the beat to horse-drawn patrol wagons (first introduced in *Chicago in 1881) to motorcycles, automobiles, and helicopters. Communications progressed from rapping a club on the street to radios and computers. Uniforms (first adopted in New York City in 1853) identified the policeman to citizens and to fellow officers. Investigative methods progressed from mug shots to up-to-date crime labs (1930s), computerization, and DNA analysis.

American police operated within a larger urban culture often characterized by fears of racial minorities, immigrants, and the poor. Arbitrary treatment or brutality toward such groups sometimes resulted. In strikes and labor disputes, the police usually sided with employers (notable exceptions were small towns with prolabor mayors or police chiefs). In the twentieth century, courts increasingly regulated police conduct through standards of evidence-gathering and suspects' rights, as in the landmark 1966 case **Miranda* v. *Arizona.*

The American police tradition also includes private policing. Vigilante movements of the nineteenth and early twentieth centuries, such as the vigilantes of early *San Francisco or the *Ku Klux Klan, expressed fear of outsiders or minority groups. Formal private police forces, like the Pennsylvania Coal and Iron Police and the strikebreaking Pinkerton Detective Agency, founded in 1852 by Allan Pinkerton, served industrialists' interests in labor disputes.

State and federal governments did little policing until the early twentieth century. Pennsylvania formed a state police in

1905 for more efficient control of strikes. New York (1917) and some other states followed. The federal government always had a police system, made up of U.S. marshals. Marshals kept the peace in many western territories until statehood brought eastern-style urban police forces. During the *Reconstruction Era, U.S. marshals in the *South struggled to enforce *civil rights laws. Several federal departments of the late nineteenth century maintained small police agencies. In the Treasury Department, the revenue bureau tracked down excise-tax evaders, while the secret service investigated counterfeiting. Post Office inspectors kept an eye out for obscene mail. The Immigration and Naturalization Service also has police functions. The army or National Guard acted as police, briefly upholding Reconstruction in the post–Civil War South, and later controlling strikes or riots and maintaining law and order following natural disasters. The premier federal police agency is the *Federal Bureau of Investigation (1908), which rose to prominence under the directorship of J. Edgar *Hoover.

With improved training, entry of minorities and women, and community-relations programs, American police forces became more efficient and responsive to diverse communities. Yet an old problem remained: How are the police to mediate social conflict without contributing to it?

[*See also* Censorship; Federal Government, Executive Branch: Department of the Treasury; Gambling and Lotteries; Prisons and Penitentiaries; Prostitution and Antiprostitution; Racism; Strikes and Industrial Conflict.]

• David R. Johnson, *American Law Enforcement: A History,* 1981. Eric Monkkonen, *Police in Urban America, 1860–1920,* 1981. Edward L. Ayers, *Vengeance and Justice: Crime and Punishment in the Nineteenth-Century American South,* 1984. Peter C. Hoffer, *Law and People in Colonial America,* 1992. Lawrence M. Friedman, *Crime and Punishment in American History,* 1993.

—Wilbur R. Miller

POLIOMYELITIS. Until 1894 when Vermont reported 132 cases, poliomyelitis, also known as infantile paralysis, remained rare. Between 1905 and 1909, however, when the United States reported two-thirds of the world's eight thousand cases, it became a peculiarly American epidemic. Although never a major factor in overall morbidity or mortality rates, polio by the 1930s had become one of America's most feared *diseases because it tended to strike children and had no known prevention or cure. In 1909 pathologist Simon Flexner at New York's *Rockefeller Institute of Medical Research, building on pathologist Karl Landsteiner's work, had demonstrated that polio was caused by a virus, but full understanding eluded investigators.

In 1921, polio left thirty-nine-year-old Franklin Delano *Roosevelt partially paralyzed. Although Roosevelt hid the extent of his disability, he made Warm Springs, Georgia, a polio rehabilitation center and inspired the founding in 1937 of the National Foundation for Infantile Paralysis. The National Foundation, directed by Roosevelt's former law partner Basil O'Connor, became America's largest, most successful disease *philanthropy. By 1945 its "March of Dimes" campaign had raised more than twenty million dollars.

During the 1930s and 1940s American scientists, funded by the National Foundation, made crucial contributions to polio research. The 1948 Foundation-supported tissue-culture experiments of John Enders, Frederick Robbins, and Thomas Weller at the Boston Children's Hospital, which won them a Nobel Prize in 1954, demonstrated that the virus could be grown in non-neurological tissue—and gave University of Pittsburgh virologist Jonas *Salk the means to develop the first safe and effective polio vaccine.

In 1954 the National Foundation organized the world's largest clinical trial, in which 1.8 million U.S. school children were injected with Salk's killed-virus vaccine or a placebo. The Salk vaccine was widely administered thereafter, bringing a dramatic decline in the incidence of polio. In the late 1950s, Dr. Albert Sabin (1906–1993) at the University of Cincinnati developed an attenuated live-virus vaccine that the Soviet Union tested in 1958. Between 1961 and 1998, Sabin's oral vaccine, which was riskier but more effective than Salk's, remained the officially recommended U.S. polio vaccine. As part of the worldwide effort to eliminate polio, the U.S. Public Health Service then began to reintroduce the Salk vaccine. After decades as a symbol of America's victory over infectious disease, polio won renewed scientific and public interest in the 1980s with the identification of postpolio syndrome, in which polio survivors experienced muscle weakness and fatigue thirty or forty years after the initial attack. Still largely unexplained, this condition spurred many "polios" to become active in the disability-rights movement of the 1980s and 1990s.

[*See also* Biological Sciences: Medicine: From the 1870s to 1945; Medicine: Since 1945; Public Health.]

• John R. Paul, *A History of Poliomyelitis,* 1971. Jane S. Smith, *Patenting the Sun: Polio and the Salk Vaccine,* 1990. Naomi Rogers, *Dirt and Disease: Polio before FDR,* 1992. Nina Gilden Seavly, et al., *A Paralyzing Fear: The Triumph over Polio in America,* 1996.

—Naomi Rogers

POLISH AMERICANS. A few Poles settled in *Jamestown and other colonies, and the *Revolutionary War enlisted democratically inclined Polish nobles like the generals Kazimierz Pulaski and Tadeuz Kościuszko, a military engineer whose fortifications helped win the Battle of Saratoga. Polish *immigration grew after the 1830s, when veterans of several failed Polish insurrections against foreign rule (by Prussia, Austria, and Russia) fled to America. Numbering only a thousand or so, these early immigrants of the "Great Emigration" organized the first Polish-American periodicals, literary societies, and nationalist political groups and, by their presence, helped establish later Polish immigrants' claims to authenticity as Americans. Only after the 1850s, however, with economic upheavals in Poland, did Polish immigration to America reach major proportions. The mass migration "for bread" of economically motivated immigrants (1850–1920) brought about 2.5 million ethnic Poles, including a variety of regional subgroups like the Kashubes and Górali, or Tatra highlanders. Though Polish immigrants came from all classes, most had rural backgrounds and tended to be young, male, and unmarried. Immigrant Poles entered many occupations, including farming, shopkeeping, the professions, skilled labor, and the arts, but 80 percent took unskilled jobs in heavy industry.

Rural Panna Maria, Texas, is recognized as this era's first Polish settlement (1854), but most Poles settled in northeastern and midwestern towns and cities (*Chicago became the second largest "Polish" city, after Warsaw). Their social dislocations were documented in William I. Thomas and Florian Znaniecki's sociological classic, *The Polish Peasant in Europe and America* (1918–1920), but Polish communities (known individually and collectively as Polonia) sustained a vital immigrant life. Polish Roman Catholic parishes (over eight hundred at their 1930s peak), with their parochial schools and teaching nuns, provided cradle-to-grave social services and encapsulated immigrant spiritual and aesthetic life. The largest, in Chicago, with over forty thousand parishioners, also gave rise to the first notable Polish-American leaders, such as the Resurrectionist priest, Reverend Wincenty Barzyński.

Two rival fraternal organizations, the Polish Roman Catholic Union (1873) and the secular Polish National Alliance (1880) argued about, then compromised on Polish American ethnic identity: Polish *and* Roman Catholic. Within the Catholic church, other Poles, led by Reverend Wenceslaus Kruszka, fought for Polish equality within the heavily Irish hierarchy. This campaign succeeded modestly in 1908 when the Reverend Paul Rhode became the first Polish-American Roman Catholic bishop. Polish nationalism and lay-trusteeism produced the largest schism ever to rock American Roman Catholicism, the

1904 founding of the Polish National Catholic church by the Scranton cleric, the Reverend Francis Hodur. The Polish nationalist movement won a major victory after *World War I, when the pianist Ignacy Jan Paderewski and others persuaded the Woodrow *Wilson administration to support a united, independent Poland.

Involved in the *Progressive Era's labor and radical movements (a Polish anarchist assassinated President William *McKinley in 1901), Polish workers later played a key role in the rise of the United Automobile Workers and other industrial unions. Polish Americans overwhelmingly supported Franklin Delano *Roosevelt and the *Democratic party in the 1930s, a loyalty shaken by the 1945 *Yalta Conference, which left Poland a Soviet satellite and sparked fifty years of anitcommunist activism by the Polish American Congress, Polonia's political umbrella organization.

From the 1940s through 1965, about 250,000 Polish "displaced persons" came to America. The 1965 reform of the U.S. *immigration law combined with Poland's 1968 political crackdowns brought 67,000 more. Émigrés from Poland's anticommunist labor movement, Solidarity, with others seeking economic opportunity, added another 64,000 after 1980. Another 668,000 Poles visited between 1965 and 1989, many illegally extending tourist visas. Meanwhile, with high rates of home ownership, older urban Polish-American communities endured. But suburban out-migration, intermarriage, language loss, *assimilation, and upward *mobility undercut the ethnic group identification of Polish Americans—estimated at 10 million in 1998.

Despite their economic and cultural achievements, Polish Americans tended to score low in "social status" rankings owing to persistent ethnic stereotyping. Late twentieth-century Polish-American politics focused on antidefamation, cultural survival, Poland's membership in the *North Atlantic Treaty Organization, accurate census enumeration, and improvement in Polish-Jewish relations, historically a difficult issue. In Democratic party politics, Polish-American visibility peaked with Senator Edmund Muskie's 1968 vice-presidential nomination. Thereafter, however, Polish Americans, like other white ethnics, voted increasingly Republican.

[*See also* Anarchism; Anticommunism; Immigrant Labor; Industrialization; Labor Movements; Race and Ethnicity; Roman Catholicism; Working-Class Life and Culture.]

• Victor Greene, "Poles," in *Harvard Encyclopedia of American Ethnic Groups*, ed. Stephan Thernstrom, 1980, pp. 787–803. Norman Davies, *God's Playground: A History of Poland*, 2 vols., 1984. John J. Bukowczyk, *And My Children Did Not Know Me: A History of Polish-Americans*, 1987. Thomas S. Gladsky, *Princes, Peasants, and Other Polish Selves: Ethnicity in American Literature*, 1992. James S. Pula, *Polish Americans: An Ethnic Community*, 1995. John J. Bukowczyk, ed., *Polish Americans and Their History: Community, Culture, and Politics*, 1996.

—John J. Bukowczyk

POLITICAL PARTIES. Influenced by the eighteenth century's classical republican intellectual tradition, America's founding fathers were hostile to political parties, believing them to be corrupt advocates of narrow factional interests. Political parties emerged, nevertheless, when Hamiltonians and Jeffersonians, soon Federalists and Republicans, squared off to define the authority of the new federal government in the 1790s. Much was at stake as a multitude of social, economic, and regional interests bred unremitting conflict. As political leaders addressed these issues, they mobilized support across a large landscape in order to contest regular elections on behalf of different policy initiatives. The Federalists, their strength centered among the social and economic elite of the *New England and Middle Atlantic states, advocated a vigorous national government that would guarantee the nation's security and develop its commercial and manufacturing resources. The Republicans, in contrast, were more socially pluralist, wary of federal power, and supportive of economic policies that sustained the nation's dominant agricultural economy.

Political Parties in Antebellum America. With much at stake, the contests between the *Federalist party and the Jeffersonian Republican party were intense. But party activities remained limited, intermittent, and ephemeral. Turnout at the polls was low. Few voters were deeply committed to either party, policy disagreements were largely confined to small groups of political leaders, and the antiparty tendencies of the political culture remained influential. Neither party developed extensive organizations to promote its interests, and whatever furor the parties provoked in Congress or state legislatures did not survive for long. As a result, the history of the first parties was brief. The Federalists faded after 1815, while Republicans splintered into factions. What conflict remained in this "era of good feelings" was fragmented and shallowly rooted.

Party politics reappeared in the 1820s with more intensity and staying power. The nation's rapid development reinvigorated battles over the authority of the central government, while the expansion of the electorate, which by 1840 encompassed most white males, increased the need to organize voters and draw them into the electoral process. Democrats and Whigs, the respective successors to the Republicans and Federalists, were, like their predecessors, coalitions of social and economic interests united by their commitments to distinct policy perspectives. The Democrats, having elected Andrew *Jackson as president in 1828, pushed an agenda favoring limited government. The *Whig party, arising in opposition to Jackson, tended to be more commercially oriented, favoring the use of national power to develop an integrated market economy. Socially, the parties differed on ethnic and religious lines. Historic tensions between Catholics and Protestants, different Protestant denominations, and people of different national background continued to shape political outlooks in the New World and to influence party choice. Party leaders articulated alternative policy agendas so starkly, and made the differences between them seem so wide, that party loyalists felt they had to participate in partisan warfare for fear of losing their birthright should the other side win. Election campaigns became raucous nationwide extravaganzas drawing thousands to rallies spiced by debates among candidates and rousing speeches by party heroes. Each party maintained a newspaper network to spread the partisan word. Each energetically brought out the faithful on Election Day. Politics was about parties. Voters loyally followed their party's direction and turned out at the polls in record numbers. Once in office, party representatives worked assiduously to implement their declared policies.

With these developments came a significant ideological shift. Parties were now accepted as necessary. Their authority was great. Still, aspects of the constitutional system, such as the need to amass an absolute majority in the *Electoral College in order to win the presidency, limited the number of parties at the national level. Locally, the major parties used their power to restrict the number of candidates on the ballot. Minor parties never attracted a large vote, their hopes thwarted by most voters' strong partisan commitments. Nevertheless, given the close competition between the two major parties, minor parties were sometimes important in determining electoral outcomes and—in the case of the *Liberty and *Free Soil parties—in signaling the rise of sectional tensions.

Electoral realignments, sharp political shocks that jolted voters from their partisan moorings and affected the subsequent course of party warfare, occurred at regular intervals after the 1830s. The first of these came in the 1850s. Neither Whigs nor Democrats had spent time discussing sectional matters, but as new territories were acquired, as a campaign against the further spread of *slavery took root, and as a bipartisan nativist backlash against Irish Catholic *immigration beset the major parties, a new organization, the *Republican party, arose. It brought together *antislavery sectionalists and other northern dissenters from the old party system. The Republicans' victory as a sectional party in 1860 led to the *South's secession and the *Civil War, during which party conflict remained as vigorous as ever in the North. The Republicans won support as the pro-Union party, while the *Democratic party suffered because of its adherents' alleged treasonous sympathy for the South. In the Confederacy, party warfare subsided during the war but reappeared with renewed vigor thereafter.

From the Gilded Age through the New Deal Era. Partisan warfare was unusually intense in the postwar decades. The two parties fought to a standstill in some of the closest, best organized, and most partisan elections in American history. Nevertheless, much was changing. With rapid *industrialization, a new economic elite of investment bankers and manufacturers sought federal policy support for their efforts, and the Republican party best embodied the pro-business position. The Democrats, in contrast, were strong in the agrarian South and among urban immigrant laborers put off by the Republicans' traditional hostility to ethnic outsiders. The latter supported the new urban political machines that pushed policy initiatives stressing government's responsibility to protect recent arrivals, the unemployed, and others in need.

Despite the Republicans' industrial tilt, the Democrats did not entirely win over the agricultural and labor sectors. Old party loyalties, Civil War memories, and ethnic antagonisms held thousands to their Republican loyalties. In the *Gilded Age and *Populist Era, economically marginalized workers and especially Western farmers challenged the existing order through third parties, notably the *Greenback Labor and *Populist parties. The Democrats behind William Jennings *Bryan successfully attracted many of these have-nots in the mid-1890s but were soundly beaten by William *McKinley and the Republicans in 1896 in another transforming electoral realignment that solidified Republican control of national politics for a generation.

In the *Progressive Era, modernizing economic elites joined forces with the political reformers in a coalition that reinvigorated residual antiparty sentiment and presaged a massive change in American political culture. In the name of unselfish and uncorrupt politics, these antipartisans pushed legislation that weakened party control of the nominating and electoral process, significantly cut off the parties' major source of funds necessary to fight elections (the spoils system), and, in general, made the parties' operations more difficult. This attack had significant long-range consequences. Parties remained influential, but a process of destabilization and decline was underway.

The first third of the twentieth century also brought a major ideological reshuffling of party positions. Within the Democratic party the rise of urban political groups seeking federal *welfare legislation affected its traditional commitment to limited government. The Great Depression of the 1930s provoked a new electoral realignment that, this time, badly hurt the Republicans. Rallying behind Franklin Delano *Roosevelt's New Deal, liberal Democrats vastly expanded the federal government's role to make it the guarantor of citizens' social and economic well-being. They were constrained, however, by resistance from the party's southern wing. Southern Democratic opposition also prevented action on *civil rights, even as *African Americans shed their traditional Republican loyalties in gratitude for Democratic economic policies.

So popular were Democratic policy initiatives from the 1930s onward that some Republicans embraced them in the name of political survival. Although still verbally confrontational, the parties lost some of their polarizing edge as a result. Under President Dwight D. *Eisenhower in the 1950s, the Republicans briefly regained national power but with an agenda that accepted many of their rivals' initiatives. Back in power after 1960, the Democrats extended their social legislation, this time including civil rights, with the support of liberal Republicans.

The Declining Influence of Political Parties. The conditions for a partisan realignment again seemed present in the 1960s. Some liberal Republicans did join the Democrats, and many southern whites became Republicans. But the effect of the Progressive Era assault on parties was now increasingly evident, aided by the decline of party-reinforcing mechanisms, such as the fervent campaign rally, as well as by the rise of alternative means of political communication, especially *television, which shaped election campaigns in nonpartisan, often antipartisan ways. Party identification weakened as voters grew more unsettled in their behavior, primarily reacting to dramatic crises and to the appeal of charismatic candidates, rather than expressing long-standing party loyalty. Electoral stability declined. The elements necessary for a realignment no longer existed.

Accompanying this voter defection from the party system was a strong popular reaction against the excesses and abuse of federal power identified with the *Vietnam War and the *Watergate scandals. The antigovernment mood benefited the Republicans in the 1980s behind the conservative Ronald *Reagan. The Democrats, charged with policy excesses that produced inflation and violent confrontations over civil rights, fell apart at the polls. The Reagan revolution undid or weakened much of the Democratic policy agenda of the previous era and reinvigorated sharp ideological polarities between the parties. In 1994, the backlash against the Democrats brought in the first Republican-controlled Congress in forty years. But Republican gains were limited, with Democrats winning successive presidential elections in the 1990s. These divided outcomes suggested that a stable, partisan electoral order no longer existed. Without effective partisan anchoring, unpredictable voter swings became the rule. Whatever role parties still played, their influence was increasingly problematic in what was turning into a postpartisan political environment as the twentieth century ended.

[*See also* Civil Service Reform; Depressions, Economic; Federal Government; Municipal and County Governments; National Woman's Party; Nativist Movement; New Deal Era, The; Progressive Party of 1912–1924; Progressive Party of 1948; Race and Ethnicity; Socialist Party of America; State Governments; States' Rights Party; Suffrage.]

• Roy Nichols, *The Invention of the American Political Parties,* 1967. William Nisbet Chambers and Walter Dean Burnham, eds., *The American Party Systems,* 1975. Paul Kleppner et al., *The Evolution of the American Electoral Systems,* 1981. Michael McGerr, *The Decline of Popular Politics, the American North, 1865–1928,* 1986. Joel H. Silbey, *The American Political Nation, 1838–1893,* 1991. Sidney Milkis, *The President and the Parties: The Transformation of the American Party System since the New Deal,* 1993. L. Sandy Maisel and William Shade, eds., *Parties and Politics in American History,* 1994. Martin Wattenberg, *The Decline of American Political Parties, 1952–1992,* 1994.

—Joel H. Silbey

POLITICAL SCIENCE. Like other social scientists, American political scientists have long questioned whether their field of study constitutes, or ought to constitute, a coherent discipline. The result has been a vibrant field, but one whose whole is less than the sum of its parts. Though lively and productive, it lacks even a wavering consensus about its proper methodology, theory, or subject matter. What is called "political science" in America is, in fact, an amalgam of philosophy, history, *sociology, *economics, law, *psychology, systems theory, institutional analysis, quantitative analysis, and a dozen other perspectives, all with competing presuppositions and clashing *raisons d'être.*

The problem with defining political science begins with the term itself. In what sense can the study of politics be called a science? The discipline's lineage extends back to Aristotle's *Pol-*

itics which embedded a rich account of political life in a more general "scientific" perspective on the natural and human worlds. Yet Aristotle did not mean "science" in the modern sense, nor did he envision the study of politics as something independent of what one might call "moral philosophy." Rejecting Aristotle's approach, the founders of modern political science sought to make the field more "scientific" precisely by distancing it from moral philosophy, focusing instead on the value-neutral, quantitative study of human behavior. David Easton's 1953 definition of politics—"the behaviors or set of interactions through which authoritative allocations (or binding decisions) are made and implemented for a society"—sums up this view. Such behaviorist, realist, or structuralist-fuctionalist approaches largely dominated much of twentieth century American political science—though outlines emerged as early as the 1780s, in James *Madison's *Federalist* number 10.

Challenging this approach, conservative traditionalists and admirers of the German refugee scholars Leo Strauss, Eric Voegelin, and Hannah Arendt continued to insist that the study of politics is a fundamentally philosophical and moral undertaking. Marxist, feminist, socialist, and other "engaged" scholars meanwhile rejected the goal of scholarly detachment and value-neutrality, espousing a political science openly committed to political goals. Both approaches were amply represented in the discipline at the end of the twentieth century. Indeed, the tension between engagement and detachment lies at the very heart of political science and is unlikely ever to be finally resolved.

Views of political science's proper subject matter have shifted as well. American founders of the discipline, such as Columbia University's John W. Burgess (1844–1931), following their German mentors, focused on the state and other governmental institutions—a natural enough preoccupation for academics who had experienced the breakdown of the American nation-state in the *Civil War. But subsequent generations changed and expanded this focus. Scholars such as Charles A. *Beard, Arthur Bentley, E. Pendleton Herring, V. O. Key Jr., and David Truman cast aside the legalism and formalism of Burgess's generation, substituting more pragmatic and experimental approaches to American politics, emphasizing extraconstitutional, extralegal, and extragovernmental groups. Writers such as Walter *Lippmann, Harold Lasswell, and Charles Merriam explored the influence of psychology, particularly mass psychology, upon modern politics.

Post–*World War II social scientists, epitomized by Talcott *Parsons, exuded confidence in the application of science to human affairs, yet they were leery of the notion that politics ought to involve public arguments over fundamental values, believing that fanaticism bred by political ideology had in part caused the war. Therefore they sought to manage social conflict through value-neutral doctrines of functionalism and pluralism, pitting faction against faction in the neo-Madisonian fashion to produce a social equilibrium. Their mantle continued to be carried in the late twentieth century by the advocates of "rational choice" theory. *New Left scholars of the 1960s vehemently rejected this value-neutrality as both an apology and a prop for the status quo; they sought instead to reinfuse political science with moral purpose. After the 1960s, the study of elections and political institutions had to compete with sympathetic interest in social movements, particularly those of minorities or "subaltern" groups, and in the nongovernmental institutions of "civil society."

Noteworthy in this pattern was the steady retreat from the consideration of the "political" per se. Instead, twentieth-century American political science, particularly after the postwar "behavioral revolution," increasingly reduced politics to the social, the economic, the psychological, or the cultural. Arendt warned against this process, particularly the tendency to conflate the "social" and the "political." Arendt's observations were perhaps borne out by the perceived erosion of the public realm in late twentieth-century America. That problem could not be addressed without reviving an older tradition of reflection on politics, as a distinctive form of human activity involving public deliberation by citizens in public spaces. Try as it may, political science appears unable to escape its normative dimension, for that dimension is implicit in the very concept of politics.

[*See also* Federalist Papers; Political Parties; Sixties, The; Social Science.]

• John W. Burgess, *The Foundations of Political Science,* 1933. Leo Strauss, *Natural Right and History,* 1950. Bernard Crick, *The American Science of Politics: Its Origins and Conditions,* 1953. Albert Somit and Joseph Tanenhaus, *The Development of American Politic Science: From Burgess to Behavioralism,* 1982. James Ceaser, *Liberal Democracy and Political Science,* 1990. Dorothy Ross, *The Origins of American Social Science,* 1992.

—Wilfred M. McClay

POLK, JAMES KNOX (1795–1849), eleventh president of the United States. A Jacksonian Democrat and devotee of Thomas *Jefferson's agrarian political ideology, Polk was born in Mecklenburg County, North Carolina, and reared in Maury County, Tennessee. Graduating with honors from the University of North Carolina in 1818, he first practiced law and in 1823 won election to the Tennessee legislature. He married Sarah Childress in 1824. Elected to Congress in 1825, he opposed President John Quincy *Adams's domestic program of economic development and political consolidation. As chair of the House Ways and Means Committee in Andrew *Jackson's first term, he led the *Democratic party's opposition to federally funded internal improvements and renewal of the national bank's charter. He served two terms (1835–1839) as speaker of the House.

Polk backed the Democrat Martin *Van Buren for president in 1836, but Tennessee voted Whig. Determined to regain political control of his state, he won the governorship in 1839. Tennessee again voted Whig in 1840, however, and Polk himself lost gubernatorial bids in 1841 and 1843. In 1844, seeing near-certain Democratic defeat if Van Buren again headed the ticket, the aged Andrew Jackson persuaded the party to nominate Polk, a westerner who, he hoped, would annex Texas while bridging the deepening sectional divide. The first "dark horse" presidential candidate, Polk defeated both the Whig Henry *Clay and James G. Birney of the tiny *antislavery *Liberty party by a razor-thin plurality. Clay hurt his candidacy by issuing ambiguous statements on Texas annexation, while Polk limited his public utterances to a single statement on the *tariff. The election revealed a nation almost evenly divided over *expansionism, the tariff, *immigration policy, and agrarianism versus the market revolution.

As president, Polk pursued five major goals: Texas annexation (already approved by Congress), settlement of the Oregon boundary dispute with Britain, tariff reduction, establishment of an independent treasury, and the purchase of *California. In pursuing Texas annexation, Polk first tried diplomacy. He offered to purchase Mexico's northern provinces, not from a belief in so-called *Manifest Destiny but from a desire to preserve the agrarian republic. Each new generation of independent farmers, he believed, must find its own rich soil or sink into wage dependency. Mexico, rejecting America's right to annex lands west of the Sabine River, broke diplomatic relations shortly after Polk's inauguration. Polk sought to restore amicable ties, but Mexico's military rulers feared that the loss of Texas would precipitate other provincial uprisings and a further erosion of centralized control. For his part, Polk saw annexation as preferable to a drawn-out defensive border war upholding Texas's sovereignty and its claims to the Rio Grande as its southern boundary. Convinced that Mexico intended to invade Texas and frustrated when Mexico snubbed John Slidell, his diplomatic emissary, Polk ordered Zachary *Taylor and his troops to the Rio Grande. On 24 April 1846, a large Mexican force crossed the river and captured an American patrol. Reacting forcefully, Polk on 11 May informed Congress that "war exists by the act of Mexico itself." The resulting war led to U.S. acquisition of Texas, California, and Mexico's other territories north of the Rio Grande.

The British cabinet, meanwhile, had decided to settle the Oregon dispute by accepting a boundary line at the forty-ninth parallel. Contrary to the view of his secretary of state, James *Buchanan, Polk had calculated correctly that the British would not go to war over its commercial interests in North America. Polk's diplomatic and military successes failed to bring political consensus at home, however, as the *Whig party blamed him for giving up half of Oregon and denounced the *Mexican War as immoral. Polk's expansionist policies postponed the demise of the agrarian republic, but left unresolved the profound economic, religious, and racial issues dividing the nation. Having accomplished his goals, he honored his pledge not to seek a second term. Polk succumbed to *cholera at his Nashville, Tennessee, home just three months after leaving office.

[*See also* Antebellum Era; Bank of the United States, First and Second; Texas Republic and Annexation.]

• Milo Milton Quaife, ed., *The Diary of James K. Polk,* 4 vols., 1910. Charles Grier Sellers Jr., *James K. Polk, Jacksonian,* 1957. Herbert Weaver and Wayne Cutler, eds., *Correspondence of James K. Polk,* 9 vols., 1969–1996.

—Wayne Cutler

POLLOCK, JACKSON (1912–1956), artist, member of the abstract expressionist movement. Born in Cody, Wyoming, Pollock moved to *New York City in 1930 to study with Thomas Hart Benton at the Art Students League. Pollock eventually rejected Benton's emphasis on representational subject matter, but he retained Benton's proclivity to articulate compositions based on pictorial dynamics. In New York, Pollock's work was informed by the Mexican muralists' use of large scale, synthetic paints, and experimental techniques, as well as by the work of the European surrealists, whose ideas about myth and the relevance of the unconscious to artistic creativity dovetailed with his own appreciation for non-Western art. He married Lee Krasner, also an artist, in 1945.

Moving to Long Island, Pollock created his characteristic large-scale abstractions between 1947 and 1950. In a bigger studio, Pollock began placing the canvas on the floor, approaching it from all directions, pouring pigment directly on the canvas, a technique he compared to that of Indian sand painters. Interested in issues of meaning and interpretation, Pollock described his abstractions as an attempt to evoke the rhythmic and dynamic energy of nature, a point he reinforced by applying paint with a physicality unprecedented in Western art and by achieving an "allover" effect (a term coined by critics to describe paintings without a visual center of attention). In the early *Cold War era, *Life* magazine promoted Pollock as evidence of Western artistic freedom and America's cultural coming-of-age. Pollock's work proved remarkably influential on later artists, including Morris Louis, Robert Morris, Allan Kaprow, and Robert Smithson.

[*See also* Abstract Expressionism; Painting: Since 1945.]

• B. H. Friedman, *Jackson Pollock: Energy Made Visible,* 1972. Claude Cernuschi, *Jackson Pollock: Meaning and Significance,* 1992.

—Claude Cernuschi

POLYGAMY. *See* Mormonism; Sex and Sexuality.

PONTIAC (d. 1769), Ottawa *ogema* (respected man), leader of what became known as Pontiac's Rebellion or Pontiac's Conspiracy, an unsuccessful campaign of resistance to Anglo-American expansion. In May 1763, at the close of the *Seven Years' War, Pontiac led an assault on the British at Fort *Detroit. His call for war represented a fusion of the teachings of Neolin, a Delaware spiritual leader, and an effort to win French support. The attack on Detroit inspired warriors from at least eight other Indian peoples to attack British garrisons, communications networks, and traders in the Great Lakes region above Niagara and in Ohio, eliminating nine outposts. Indians also struck garrisons and farmsteads in Pennsylvania, Maryland, and Virginia. Some 450 British soldiers perished; Indian and Anglo-American civilian casualties are unknown.

Pontiac's seige of Detroit lasted until October 1763, when he withdrew to the Maumee River in Ohio. Having corresponded with French officers in Illinois, Pontiac visited them in April 1764. He won over the region's Indians, who obstructed British efforts to occupy the territory. The French supplied ammunition but refused to fight alongside Pontiac, and he left Illinois in July.

The British successfully defended their forts at Detroit, Pittsburgh, and Niagara, and Pontiac's allies found themselves negotiating with, rather than fighting, the British. Back in Illinois by spring 1765, Pontiac made formal peace with the British at Detroit in 1766. When he killed an Illinois, his authority deteriorated. In April 1769 he was killed by a Peoria in Cahokia, Illinois. Apart from the events of 1763–1766, and a visit to the French Fort Dusquesne (Pittsburgh) in 1757, uncertainty surrounds most details of Pontiac's life.

[*See also* French Settlements in North America; Indian History and Culture: From 1500 to 1800; Indian Wars; Proclamation of 1763.]

• Francis Parkman, *History of the Conspiracy of Pontiac,* 1851. Howard H. Peckham, *Pontiac and the Indian Uprising,* 1947.

—Gregory Evans Dowd

PONTIAC'S REBELLION. *See* Pontiac.

PONY EXPRESS. The Pony Express was a mail service that carried mail by horse relay from St. Joseph, Missouri, to Sacramento, *California—nearly two thousand miles—in an average time of ten days. Despite its legendary status, the Pony Express operated for only eighteen months, from April 1860 to October 1861. The freighting firm of Russell, Majors, and Waddell ran the operation.

The federal government first subsidized overland mail to California in the 1850s, when a southern postmaster general awarded the contract to a company that carried the mail along a southern route from Missouri through Texas into southern California. California Senator William Gwinn convinced businessman William Russell to develop a central route, from St. Joseph (where *telegraph lines from the East ended) to Sacramento. A horse relay, Gwinn believed, would halve the time required to deliver mail and convince Congress that the central route deserved the federal contract.

Russell built 190 stations every 10 to 12 miles over the route, and purchased 500 horses. Each rider rode thirty-five to seventy miles before passing the mail to the next rider. Pony Express riders set their fastest time at seven days, seventeen hours, carrying the text of Abraham *Lincoln's 1861 inaugural address. Despite his efforts, Russell was at first unable to secure the federal contract necessary to make the Pony Express profitable. But in March 1861, when the *Civil War interrupted the southern mail route, the government transferred its contract to the central route. Only six months later, however, completion of the transcontinental telegraph made the Pony Express obsolete and drove Russell, Majors, and Waddell into bankruptcy.

[*See also* Postal Service, U.S.; West, The.]

• Raymond W. Settle and Mary L. Settle, *Saddle and Spurs: The Pony Express Saga,* 1955. Roy S. Bloss, *Pony Express: The Great Gamble,* 1959.

—James W. Feldman

POOR HOUSES. *See* Alms Houses.

POPULAR CULTURE. "Popular culture" is a problematic term. To use it as an antonym of "high culture" is both illogical and ahistorical: illogical because the antonyms of "popular" and "high" are, respectively, "elite" and "low"; ahistorical because many civilizations have produced art that is both high *and* popular. Examples from western Europe include the plays of Shakespeare, Beethoven's symphonies, and the paintings of the impressionists. In the United States the novels of Samuel L. *Clemens, the silent films of Charlie *Chaplin, and the *jazz of Louis *Armstrong are generally understood to possess both high artistic merit and broad appeal.

Matters of commerce and *technology further complicate the task of definition. Concerns about commercialism in culture date to eighteenth-century England, where increasing *literacy among the middle classes created a market for the inexpensive novels and periodicals pouring out of the "penny presses" on London's Grub Street. To the educated aristocracy, this flood of cheap reading matter threatened to engulf serious literature—and for a century the novel itself was considered an inferior art form.

Elite and Popular Taste in Colonial and Nineteenth-Century America. In the American *Colonial Era, such aristocratic attitudes were associated with British rule and had little to do with vital developments such as the emergence of a vernacular style of mechanical design now admired for its economy, simplicity, and ease of reproduction. After the *Revolutionary War, European disdain for American culture was countered by a new pride in republican ideals and a rejection of Old World models. For example, in early nineteenth-century sheet music, English and French tunes were spurned in favor of homegrown fare: *New England shape-note hymns, patriotic ballads, and drinking songs such as Thomas *Paine's "Adams and Liberty."

But the dream of a new "new Arcadia" did not last. By the late *Antebellum Era, the battle lines were redrawn between the educated elite who, despising popular taste and commercialism, urged Americans to emulate their cultural betters in Europe; and the common people who, embracing the frontier egalitarianism of Andrew *Jackson, displayed a more aggressive cultural populism. These tensions were evident in the public theaters, where the rich in their "boxes" applauded anything they considered refined and European, while the poor in the "pit" (ground floor) and "gallery" (balcony) hurled missiles at anything they considered pretentious and foreign. Sometimes open conflict ensued. The 1849 Astor Place Riot in *New York City, which claimed twenty-two lives, began in a brawl between rival supporters of the American actor Edwin Forrest and the "aristocratic" British actor William Macready.

Nonetheless, the nineteenth century brought distinctively American styles of comedy, *drama, music, and *dance within such popular entertainments as traveling *circuses, built into a national enterprise by the promotional hype of P. T. *Barnum; variety theater, which originated in the all-male frontier saloon but was dominated for several years by female impresarios; and blackface *minstrelsy, which traded in demeaning racial stereotypes but introduced white audiences to at least a semblance of African-American culture. After the *Civil War, minstrelsy was opened to black performers and became a unique training ground for their talents. Similarly, the well-organized and well-financed form of entertainment known as *vaudeville, which replaced minstrelsy in the 1880s and thrived until 1930, provided opportunities for countless first- and second-generation immigrants. In their day, none of these entertainments was regarded as high art, usually with good reason. Yet out of this rough-and-tumble milieu exploded the phenomenon of twentieth-century popular culture.

The Popular Culture Debate in the Twentieth Century. With the advent of the electronic media (*film, *radio, recorded music, and *television), these popular forms gained new outlets and, in the case of jazz and film, began a rapid ascent to the level of genuine art. Soon, old aristocratic concerns about the vulgarizing effects of commerce were joined with new worries about the homogenizing effects of *technology. Alarmed by Adolf Hitler's use of the radio and influenced by the work of Karl Marx and Sigmund Freud, the European émigré intellectuals who presided over the "mass culture debate" of the 1940s and 1950s, notably Theodor Adorno and Max Horkheimer, warned of an American future in which the ruling elite would dominate the populace through a "consciousness industry" based in the mass media.

Were they right? It sometimes appeared so in the twentieth century's closing decades, as huge conglomerates such as the Disney corporation sought to control and profit from every stage of cultural production and distribution; educators deplored the power of movies, television, and popular music to supplant books and the traditional fine arts; and children's advocacy groups warned of the potential social and psychological harm of youthful exposure to increasingly explicit portrayals of sex and violence. And a few survivors from the older generation of cultural theorists continued to dissect the ways in which "commodified" cultural products reinforce the social, economic, and political status quo.

Yet a countervailing trend arose among cultural theorists who came of age during the 1960s. For these analysts, popular culture was not simply a top-down phenomenon but also a bottom-up one. While acknowledging the power of the media to disseminate "hegemonic" beliefs and values, they also paid attention to the ways popular culture had become an arena for symbolic self-assertion on the part of oppressed minorities and socially marginal groups.

Fragmentation and Consolidation. An important development not predicted by the postwar "mass culture" theorists was the fragmentation of the "mass audience" into several different markets—some overlapping and others quite distinct. The process was initiated by the entertainment industry itself, when it began to divide the audience by categories such as race (in the 1940s, when local radio stations began to program specifically for blacks), age (in the 1950s, when the recording industry discovered teenagers), and gender (in the 1970s, when network television began to "target" young adult women). Soon this splintering of the audience acquired its own momentum, spinning out of the industry's control and unfolding in tandem with technological changes from cable and the videocassette recorder to satellite broadcasting and the *Internet.

At the same time, huge audiences continued to coalesce around phenomena such as blockbuster films, hit television shows, major sports events, notorious murder trials, celebrity funerals, terrorist catastrophes, and political scandals. The dangers once thought to inhere in such upwellings of "mass consciousness" came to be mitigated by some observers' perception that certain media events may serve to unite an increasingly diverse population. Another mitigating factor was the mass audience's skepticism, even hostility, toward the media—even as that same audience demonstrated an insatiable appetite for saturation coverage of topics that a few years earlier would have been considered off-limits to public scrutiny.

The Intertwining and Cross-Fertilization of Popular and Elite Culture. Also unforeseen by the "mass culture" theorists was the complex intertwining of popular with elite culture that accompanied the maturing of the electronic media. Curiously, a majority of both the critics and the champions of popular culture defined this process as a leveling one. The critics, lamenting the "contamination" of high culture by popular culture, sounded the death-knell of taste and excellence. The more vociferous champions of popular culture, celebrating what they saw as a much-needed blow to elitist standards, called for the total elimination of standards in the name of democracy.

Meanwhile, a minority of observers insisted on placing the process in a more positive light—as part of a healthy, ongoing, inevitable cross-fertilization between the culture of the many and the culture of the few. This view was reinforced by history. Many major American artists have been inspired by popular genres: Herman *Melville by the explorer's journal, Ralph *Ellison by African-American *folklore, the architect Robert Venturi (1925–) by the casinos of Las Vegas. At other times, modes of expression considered mere entertainment have gained acceptance as genuine art: the jazz compositions of Duke *Ellington, the Hollywood films of John Ford, the "Pogo" comic strips of Walt Kelly, the detective novels of Dashiell Hammett, the songs of Cole Porter. And on occasion a figure labeled "serious" and a figure labeled "popular" have engaged in fruitful interaction: the American cubist painter Stuart Davis and the jazz pianist Earl Hines, for example.

Yet this straightforward approach to popular culture remains a minority one. Why? The complicating factor here has been the long-standing tendency of those who study "folk" or "vernacular" culture to dismiss anything that bears the taint of commerce. Thus, purist folklorists have endorsed the painstaking collection of orally-transmitted materials (such as tales and songs) while roundly denouncing anyone who adapts those materials for sale in the marketplace. In the purist view, such "commodification" instantly renders its object inauthentic.

Even when all of the above obstacles to definition have been sorted out, a daunting task remains: to evaluate the good or ill wrought by popular culture. If traditional artistic standards do not apply, what shall replace them? Rare indeed is the observer who refrains from making some sort of "value judgment," whether on aesthetic or ideological grounds. Popular culture is simply not a phenomenon that one contemplates with passionless neutrality. But after all, isn't that a tribute to its amazing vitality?

[*See also* African Americans; Amusement Parks and Theme Parks; Capitalism; Disney, Walt; Folk Art and Crafts; Foreign Relations: The Cultural Dimension; Leisure; Literature, Popular; Mass Marketing; Multinational Enterprises; Music: Popular Music; Musical Theater; Painting; Social Class; Sports; Theater; Urbanization.]

• Bernard Rosenberg and David Manning White, eds., *Mass Culture,* 1957. John A. Kouwenhoven, *The Arts in Modern American Civilization,* 1967 (originally *Made in America,* 1948). Henry Pleasants, *The Great American Popular Singers,* 1974. Ian M. G. Quimby and Scott T. Swank, eds., *Perspectives on American Folk Art,* 1980. Richard Schickel, *Intimate Strangers: The Culture of Celebrity,* 1985. Neal Gabler, *An Empire of Their Own: How the Jews Invented Hollywood,* 1988. Lawrence W. Levine, *Highbrow/Lowbrow: The Emergence of Cultural Hierarchy in America,* 1988. Chandra Mukerji and Michael Schudsen, eds., *Rethinking Popular Culture,* 1991. Ralph Ellison, *The Collected Essays of Ralph Ellison,* 1995.

—Martha Bayles

POPULATION. *See* Census, Federal; Demography.

POPULIST ERA. No historical period conforms precisely to a specific span of years, and the Populist Era is no exception. The events of the 1890s—the time period known as the Populist Era—reflected social and economic pressures, and reactions to those pressures, that had been building for decades. Similarly, the Populist movement itself, a response to long-term political, economic, and social changes, was rooted in earlier agrarian protest movements—the *Farmers' Alliance movement of the 1880s, the *Granger movement of the 1870s—and even in rural folkways antedating the *Civil War.

Populist Politics. The politics of the Populist Era were issue-oriented. Following several decades of weak presidents, corrupt politicians serving corporate interests, and dominance by two parties that often seemed indistinguishable, the *Populist party and Populists generally took a sharply different approach. Whereas both the *Republican party and the *Democratic party usually nominated candidates allied with corporate interests, Populists championed America's workers, small farmers, tenants, and sharecroppers. While the dominant parties espoused *Social Darwinism, *laissez-faire (at least in theory), and governmental passivity, Populists advocated active government intervention in the economy and regulation of trusts and corporations in the public interest. Whereas Presidents Benjamin *Harrison, Grover *Cleveland, and William *McKinley all advocated a sound-money policy to protect creditors, and used force to break strikes and unions, Populists favored the unlimited coinage of silver and other measures to increase the money supply and help debtors, and opposed the use of troops against striking workers.

The Economy. The 1890s was a decade of depression, *unemployment, widespread *poverty, and crisis in rural America. In the period after 1870, the rapid settlement of western lands, improved agricultural *technology, and the spread of *railroads and steamship lines resulted in agricultural overproduction and increased competition in world markets, driving prices down and putting farmers in a harsh credit squeeze. The Panic of 1893, triggered by the failure of a London banking firm, caused many British investors to unload their American stocks, precipitating a stock market crash. The sell-off came just as the high McKinley Tariff of 1890 depressed the agricultural export market. The resulting three-year depression, the worst in American history up to the 1930s, saw soup kitchens, desperate strikes, farm foreclosures, and ragged armies of the unemployed.

Evidence of unrest abounded. In July 1892, strikers at Andrew *Carnegie's Homestead Steel Works near Pittsburgh, Pennsylvania, fired on two barges loaded with Pinkerton detectives, killing seven and wounding many more. State militia broke the strike, and a steelworkers' union did not emerge until the 1930s. An 1894 strike at George Pullman's sleeping-car works near *Chicago, protesting wage cuts combined with rent increases in Pullman's company town, precipitated a confrontation between the American Railway Union and the General Managers Association, the latter representing twenty-four railroads operating through Chicago. The Cleveland administration, securing a court injunction against the strike, sent in federal troops when escalating violence threatened delivery of the mail. Meanwhile, in the spring of 1894, "Coxey's Army," three hundred unemployed workers led by the Ohio Populist Jacob S. Coxey (1854–1951), staged one of the earliest marches on Washington, demanding jobs and relief.

The *South and the Great Plains, both Populist strongholds, suffered severe economic deprivation exacerbated by drought in the 1890s. Indeed, the rural South experienced a prolonged economic downturn that extended from the end of the Civil War through the 1930s. Along with agrarian protest, factory workers' discontent in industrialized areas of the South, such as northern Alabama, contributed to the climate of unrest.

Desperate economic conditions were widespread. Some 40 percent of Americans lived in poverty in 1900, a higher percentage than in the Great Depression of the 1930s. No organized social service network, no minimum wage laws, no unemployment insurance, and no federal welfare programs protected the poor. Poverty fell especially hard on the unemployed, marginal farmers, urban immigrants, and other particularly vulnerable groups. *African Americans experienced not only high rates of poverty but the added burden of *racism. Jim Crow laws spread across the South in these years, imposing a rigid system of racial *segregation. In **Plessy* v. *Ferguson* (1898), the U.S. *Supreme Court upheld racially segregated public facilities, from schools to transit systems. A record of 226 *lynchings occurred in 1892, mostly in the South and *Southwest. The total number of lynchings from 1889 to 1918 exceeded 2,500, and most victims were African American. Even in the North, de facto segregation and discrimination prevailed. Speaking in *Atlanta in 1895, the era's most prominent black leader, Booker T. *Washington, urged African Americans to acquire useful vocational skills and to avoid agitation for racial equality.

Society and Culture. Battered by economic crisis and political upheaval, American society and culture also underwent major transformations. The nation's ethnic composition was changing dramatically. Nineteenth-century *immigration peaked at 790,000 in 1882, and even during the depression of the later 1890s, between 250,000 and 350,000 newcomers arrived annually. The massive immigrant influx contributed both to desperate overcrowding and appalling conditions in city *slums and to a vibrant urban culture of immigrant festivals, and social organizations; churches, saloons, dance halls, and beer gardens; and music halls offering *vaudeville shows featuring broad ethnic *humor and the latest songs from Tin Pan Alley, such as "After the Ball" (1892) and "Only a Bird in a Gilded Cage" (1900).

The "new immigration" from southern and eastern Europe unsettled many native-born Americans of northern and western European ancestry. The increasing numbers of Jews, Catholics, and Orthodox Christians alarmed many American Protestants and gave rise to urgent strategies to convert and assimilate the newcomers. The waves of immigrants placed tremendous pressure on local governments and city services, providing convenient scapegoats for those seeking explanations for municipal corruption, labor unrest, and political *radicalism. Blacks moving to cities—although only a trickle compared to the Great Migration ahead—experienced disruption as well. Between 1880 and 1915, 25 to 30 percent of urban black households had a mother but no father present, twice the percentage for rural black families. The economic crisis affected the family life of immigrants and native-born, white and black alike. Across America, unemployed men left home to seek jobs in other cities and even other regions, sometimes abandoning their families in the process. On foot and in freight trains, tramps scoured the country seeking employment or, if not a job, a handout.

Reform Movements. Populism was only one manifestation of a larger reform current in the 1890s that launched the *Progressive Era. Through the leadership of Jane *Addams and others, *settlement houses arose in the immigrant districts of most big cities. The *Woman's Christian Temperance Union, under its energetic president Frances *Willard, pursued a broad reform agenda, while the Anti-Saloon League, founded in 1895, launched a coordinated campaign for national prohibition. *Social Gospel advocates like W. D. P. Bliss and Washington Gladden exhorted middle-class churchgoers to apply their Christian principles to the social problems of the new industrial order. Charles M. Sheldon's best-selling Social Gospel novel *In His Steps* (1896) told of an urban congregation that commits itself to reform by posing the question "What would Jesus do?" The British journalist William T. Stead made a similar plea in *If Christ Came to Chicago* (1893). The photojournalist Jacob Riis offered middle-class readers a harrowing picture of slum life in **How the Other Half Lives* (1890), as did the novelist Stephen Crane in *Maggie: A Girl of the Streets* (1893). William Dean *Howells addressed urban labor unrest and the economic roots of crime in such novels as *A Hazard of New Fortunes* (1890) and *The Quality of Mercy* (1892), while Theodore *Dreiser's *Sister Carrie* (1900) portrayed the corrupting effects of city life on an ambitious young woman from the country.

The 1890s saw activist stirrings among middle-class American women, signaling the revival of the *woman-suffrage movement and women's broad-scale reform involvement in the Progressive Era. Kate Chopin in *The Awakening* (1899) portrayed the stultifying life of a vivacious young wife in the tradition-bound and patriarchal culture of *New Orleans, while Charlotte Perkins *Gilman explored the effects of women's economic subordination in *Women and Economics* (1898). A vogue for *bicycles and bicycling, a prelude to the automobile era just ahead, put many young women as well as young men on wheels in the 1890s.

America and the World. Expansionist fever pervaded the Populist Era, fueled by missionary zeal, a quest for overseas markets, desires for an empire to match those of the European powers, and the jingoism of tabloid newspapers. In *Our Country* (1885), the Reverend Josiah Strong offered a potent array of nationalistic, racial, and religious arguments to awaken Americans to their global destiny. In *The Influence of Sea Power upon History* (1890), Alfred Thayer *Mahan urged an expansion of U.S. naval power, including acquisition of the refueling stations that a two-ocean navy demanded. After a series of diplomatic interventions in South America, the decade ended with a major expansion beyond the nation's continental borders: The United States annexed *Hawai'i in 1898 and, in the same year, in the aftermath of the *Spanish-American War, acquired Cuba, *Puerto Rico, Guam, and the *Philippines from Spain. An anti-imperialist movement recruited such varied supporters as William Graham Sumner, William *James, and Andrew Carnegie, but most Americans approved of the nation's imperial aspirations. In foreign affairs, as in the domestic arena, the last decade of the nineteenth century stands as a kind of curtain-raiser to the twentieth.

The Culture of Populism. The Populist movement unfolded in a rapidly changing society. Many Populists lived in a traditional world that preserved rhythms of life dating to the pre–Civil War era and earlier. In the small towns of rural America, churches and the village store nourished community life. Cooperative patterns of work, common rites and rituals such as hunting and fishing, land-inheritance customs, and grazing on common lands in the West all encouraged premodern and anti-commercial values and patterns of life. But this traditional life was under siege. The spread of railroads brought "drummers" (traveling salesmen), mail-order catalogs, and national *magazines whose advertisements offered an array of mass-produced goods. And farm life itself was evolving under the economic pressures posed by expensive new equipment; rising land prices; a global market; and new systems of transporting, processing, and marketing agricultural products.

Threats to traditional folkways from *industrialization, business consolidation, commercial agriculture, and the rise of urban-immigrant America spurred the agrarian protest spirit known as Populism. Some historians have seen Populism as a reactionary phenomenon, a last stand for agrarian values before the juggernaut of modernization. Richard Hofstadter, in his influential *Age of Reform* (1955), viewed the Populists as deluded reactionaries who scapegoated Jewish bankers and big-city immigrants, oversimplified complicated economic issues, and romanticized an idealized past of self-sufficient yeomanry.

Certainly Populism had a darker side. One leader, Thomas E. Watson (1856–1922) of Georgia, soured by his foray into biracial agrarian protest, became a virulent nativist and racist. Yet recent historians generally adopt a more positive approach, viewing Populists as realistic in their analysis of their problems and the remedies they espoused, and tolerant by the standards of their time, providing a place for women in their movement—the first American political movement to do so—and even, in the South, for a time making common cause with blacks in a class-based political campaign. The historian Lawrence Goodwyn, in *The Populist Moment* (1978), emphasized the creation of a "movement culture" based on a shared commitment to democratic forms and institutions. From this perspective, Populism appears at heart a cooperative movement, not only in the narrow sense of establishing purchasing-and-marketing cooperatives, but also in the broader sense of seeking to promote cooperation among agrarian communities with similar values, a shared culture, and a remembered past. From the perspective of a century later, Populists can be seen as precariously suspended between two worlds: one of agrarian values and cooperative, grassroots, democratic institutions and the other a modernizing, corporate, impersonal world. The Populists' attempt to adapt to that emerging modern world while preserving as much as possible of their traditional values, folkways, and institutions gave their movement—and the decade that bears its name—its unique character as an epoch in American history.

[*See also* Advertising; Agriculture: The "Golden Age" (1890–1920); Americanization Movement; Anti-Semitism; Bryan, William Jennings; Depressions, Economic; Expansionism; Feminism; Foreign Relations: U.S. Relations with Latin America; Free Silver Movement; Homestead Lockout; Labor Movements; Literature: Civil War to World War I; Missionary Movement; Popular Culture; Populist Party; Pullman Strike and Boycott; Race and Ethnicity; Strikes and Industrial Conflict; Tariffs; Temperance and Prohibition.]

• John D. Hicks, *The Populist Revolt: A History of the Farmers' Alliance and the People's Party,* 1931. Norman Pollack, *The Populist Response to Industrial America,* 1962. Gilbert C. Fite, *The Farmers' Frontier, 1865–1900,* 1966. Lawrence Goodwyn, *The Populist Moment: A Short History of the Agrarian Revolt in America,* 1978. Bruce Palmer, *"Man Over Money": The Southern Populist Critique of American Capitalism,* 1980. Steven Hahn, *The Roots of Southern Populism: Yeoman Farmers and the Transformation of the Georgia Upcountry, 1850–1890,* 1983. Barton C. Shaw, *The Wool Hat Boys: Georgia's Populist Party,* 1984. Robert C. McMath Jr., *American Populism: A Social History, 1877–1898,* 1993. William F. Holmes, ed., *American Populism,* 1994.

—Wayne Flynt

POPULIST PARTY, popular name for a third party of the 1890s, the People's Party of America. Organized nationally in May 1891 in Cincinnati, Ohio, the Populist party's first national nominating convention met in Omaha, Nebraska, the following year. There, the party nominated a presidential ticket headed by James B. Weaver of Iowa and James G. Field of Virginia, and fashioned what came to be called the Omaha platform, ratified and promulgated on 4 July 1892. To its adherents, this document symbolized a "second declaration of independence," designed to restore the nation to a course they believed had been abandoned in *Gilded Age America's headlong rush into a new urban-industrial age in a political environment that placed corporate and financial interests above the general welfare. Thus, Populism came to stand for a politics designed to put the people first.

The Omaha platform emerged from political protests and organizational efforts that had been building since the 1870s among the nation's farmers. Southern and western farm organizations, together with earlier third parties, were especially active in formulating a program aimed at helping America's rural majority. This program, encompassed in the Omaha platform and its accompanying resolutions, called for the national government to exert a new and positive role on behalf of the general welfare and democratic reform. It urged government ownership of all transportation and communication systems; a graduated income tax; immigration restriction; the direct election of U.S. senators and other electoral reforms; and, in a bid for labor support, a shorter work week in industry. Although not without precedents, the call was historically significant in an era when most political leaders envisioned only a limited role for government, apart from government aid to *business interests. In the 1892 election (in which Democrat Grover Cleveland defeated Republican Benjamin *Harrison), Weaver received just over 1 million votes, or about 9 percent of the total. The party failed, however, to win much support in the *South or in urban-industrial districts.

In 1896, the *Democratic party coopted an aspect of the Populists' financial program, the free and unlimited coinage of silver, on behalf of the candidacy of William Jennings *Bryan. The Populist party thus faced a dilemma: either nominate Bryan and support his fight against the *gold standard or divide the reform vote and insure the election of Republican William *McKinley. In the end McKinley won despite Populist support for Bryan, and the party gradually faded, leaving Populists with only the consoling thought that they had contributed to the conversion of the Democratic party to the cause of reform.

Throughout, the Populist party was strongest in Kansas, Nebraska, Colorado, Texas, and North Carolina, although its influence was also felt in other southern and western states. Out of its ranks emerged many talented and colorful figures, among them Ignatius Donnelly of Minnesota; Jeremiah Simpson, William A. Peffer, Mary E. Lease, and Annie Diggs of Kansas; and William V. Allen and William Neville of Nebraska. Among the prominent southern leaders were Thomas E. Watson of Georgia, Marion Butler of North Carolina, and James Harvey Davis of Texas.

From 1891 to 1903, fifty Populist party candidates, representing sixteen states and one territory, were elected to Congress, where they waged an educational campaign on behalf of the Populist program and spoke out on a wide range of issues, from the economic depression of 1893–96 to the nation's imperialist expansion. For many, the Populist movement remains a source of inspiration. As one historian has written: "The Populists' message remains as relevant today as . . . in the nineteenth century, and their vision of community still serves as a powerful critique of American society."

[*See also* Agriculture: Revolutionary War to 1890; Agriculture: The "Golden Age" (1890s–1920); Farmers' Alliance Movement; Free Silver Movement; Greenback Labor Party; Immigration Law; Industrialization; Political Parties; Populist Era; Republican Party.]

• Lawrence Goodwyn, *The Populist Moment,* 1978. Steven Hahn, *The Roots of Southern Populism,* 1983. Gene Clanton, *Populism: The Humane Preference in America, 1890–1900,* 1991. Robert C. McMath, *American Populism: A Social History,* 1993. Peter H. Argersinger, *The Limits of Agrarian Radicalism,* 1995. Gene Clanton, *Congressional Populism and the Crisis of the Nineties,* 1998.

—Gene Clanton

PORT HURON STATEMENT. *See* New Left; Students for a Democratic Society.

POSTAL SERVICE, U.S. For most of its history, the postal service was the nation's largest civilian institution and the federal government's most visible manifestation in Americans' everyday lives. Empowered by the *Constitution to "establish Post Offices and post Roads," Congress created a communication network to unite the fragile young nation. Some of the first postal connections, for instance, linked county seats to state capitals and ultimately to *Washington, D.C. The Post Office Department itself did not build many *roads or operate many long-distance transports. But contracts with private carriers—stagecoach and steamship lines, *railroads, trucking firms, and airlines—helped create a nationwide transportation system.

Politics pervaded the Post Office through most of its history. From Andrew *Jackson's administration until 1971, the postmaster general customarily served as the president's chief political lieutenant, some having previously headed the party's national committee. Postmasters general dispensed patronage—tens of thousands of local postmasterships and thousands of contracts—throughout the nation. Congress itself set postage rates, often arguing for years over a fraction of a cent for one category or another. Residents of rural areas, and their representatives in Congress, lobbied assiduously for special postal services to reduce their isolation. Rural free delivery (1896) was the most direct response, but postal savings banks (1911–1966) and parcel post (1913) also helped.

Although the postal service facilitated personal correspondence, most material sent by mail related to the press, business, or commerce. The volume of mail grew from 7 billion pieces in 1900 to 85 billion in 1970. The number of post offices peaked at 76,688 in 1900, dropping to 32,002 in 1970. Between 1926 and 1970, by contrast, the number of postal employees more than doubled to 741,000.

The postal service long maintained a dual relationship with the press. Newspapers and *magazines enjoyed free or below-cost postage rates from the 1790s to the 1970s, and vestiges of the subsidies continued even longer. But the very centrality of the postal service also made it the federal government's principal censor of printed material. From the passage of a federal postal censorship act in 1873 through the mid–twentieth century, the Post Office Department, often in tandem with the U.S. Customs Service, barred from circulation printed matter or other materials considered indecent and obscene. The Post Office also suppressed material deemed treasonable or subversive, notably during the abolitionist controversy, the *Civil War, *World War I, and the *Cold War.

The Postal Reorganization Act of 1970 transformed the Post Office Department into the U.S. Postal Service, a quasi-corporate agency. Seeking to rectify the shortcomings of legislative rate-making by elevating economic considerations over politics, the act removed rate-making control from Congress and vested it in an independent regulatory body, the Postal Rate Commission.

While a late-twentieth-century surge in direct-mail marketing increased the volume of parcels and catalogs in the mail stream, new private carriers such as Federal Express and United Parcel Service (UPS), promising faster, more efficient service, aggressively competed with the U.S. Postal Service for this business. At the same time, e-mail messages via the *Internet increasingly supplanted the U.S. mails as a favored mode of communication. The future of the postal service in the new era of privatization and electronic information-exchange remained unclear as the twenty-first century dawned.

[*See also* Censorship; Journalism.]

• Wayne E. Fuller, *The American Mail: Enlarger of the Common Life*, 1972. Richard R. John Jr., *Spreading the News: The American Postal System from Franklin to Morse*, 1995.

— Richard B. Kielbowicz

POST–COLD WAR ERA. The end of the *Cold War in the late 1980s and early 1990s, one of the most momentous developments in modern world history, brought a reorientation in a number of areas of American life. The impact was greatest on foreign policy, as the United States sought a new role in international affairs. But the disappearance of a unifying external threat also led to serious disagreements about domestic policy and contributed to a fragmentation in social and cultural life.

The collapse of communism in Eastern Europe and in the Soviet Union led to the overthrow of authoritarian regimes and the creation of often precarious democratic governments. President George *Bush spoke hopefully of the dawn of a more stable and peaceful "New World Order," but he and his successor, Bill *Clinton, found themselves confronting an international arena torn by racial, cultural, and religious tensions that sometimes seemed even less stable than before.

Problems surfaced worldwide. Russia moved toward democracy but found the process painful. In Russia and neighboring countries such as Poland, the transition to a free-market economy caused serious shortages and dislocations that threatened political and social stability. Soviet leader Mikhail Gorbachev proved unable to contain the forces of change he had helped set in motion, and his successor, an increasingly frail Boris Yeltsin, struggled constantly with his opponents for political control. Former spy Vladimir Putin replaced Yeltsin in 1999, restoring a degree of stability, but deepening doubts about the future of democracy in the former Soviet state. In what was formerly Yugoslavia, long-submerged ethnic hostility burst forth with the collapse of central authority and violence escalated.

The Middle East was similarly turbulent. Here, too, the United States hoped to preserve stability as the Cold War ended. President Bush mobilized a military coalition against Iraq when its ruler Saddam Hussein invaded Kuwait in the summer of 1990. With the conclusion of the *Persian Gulf War, American leaders sought to promote peace between Israel and the Palestine Liberation Organization (PLO) and in a dramatic White House ceremony managed to get PLO leader Yasir Arafat and Israeli prime minister Yitzhak Rabin to shake hands, only to watch the tenuous agreement later unravel. A further round of talks between Israeli leaders and the Palestinians initiated by President Clinton in 2000 proved equally inconclusive.

In Africa, the end of the Cold War created a vacuum. In South Africa, the Western-aided struggle against apartheid succeeded and Nelson Mandela created a multiracial state. But elsewhere, dictators long propped up by the United States for their value in the struggle against communism now found themselves vulnerable. Without Western support, such countries as Somalia and Zaire descended into chaos and intertribal conflict, often with horrendous loss of life. Here, as elsewhere, the United States found it difficult to maintain the stability it sought.

This unsettled world situation posed difficult questions for the United States. What kind of leadership would America exert as the world's one remaining superpower? How actively would it support the *United Nations and participate in international peacekeeping missions? And what kind of assistance would it extend to developing nations absent the Cold War competition that had fueled foreign aid? Increasingly in the post–Cold War Era, Washington concentrated on promoting America's global trading interests, including trade with former adversaries such as China.

Domestically, the conservative transformation that had taken place in the Ronald *Reagan and Bush years increasingly influenced public policy. The coalition of religious fundamentalists, free-market advocates, and politicians who decried pornography as well as preferential treatment for minorities proved increasingly successful at the polls. Though Bill Clinton won the presidency in 1992, Republicans captured both houses of Congress in the 1994 midterm elections for the first time in more than forty years. Newt Gingrich, an aggressive Georgia congressman who became the new Speaker of the House, championed a Republican "Contract with America" to scale back the role of the federal government, eliminate burdensome regulations, balance the budget, and reduce taxes. Though the House passed some of the measures proposed in the "Contract with America," few became law. The Senate resisted some; the president vetoed others. Clinton also stole the Republican's thunder by moving skillfully to the political right, thereby securing his own reelection in 1996. Clinton was aided as well by the booming prosperity, low inflation, and surging *stock market that characterized the American economy throughout most of the 1990s.

With these changes, the president and Congress weakened the commitment to the welfare state dating back to the *New Deal Era. In a welfare-reform law agreed upon by Clinton and the Republican Congress in 1996, Washington scaled back or eliminated federal assistance programs and turned much of the responsibility for welfare policy over to the states, operating with sharply reduced federal block grants. While welfare reform proved popular, it left many Americans without needed help.

The attack on the welfare state paralleled a diminished commitment to social reform. Enough had been done already for the disadvantaged groups in American society, conservatives argued; middle-class Americans were suffering from such efforts and deserved an end to intrusive federal policies that they believed hampered them from getting ahead.

The federal commitment to *civil rights diminished as conservative judicial appointees reinterpreted the law. In 1992, the *Supreme Court's *Freeman* v. *Pitts* decision granted a suburban Atlanta school board relief from a desegregation order by arguing that it was not possible to counteract major demographic shifts. Three years later, in 1995, the Court let stand a lower court ruling prohibiting colleges and universities from awarding special scholarships to *African Americans and other minorities.

These years saw an even stronger backlash against *affirmative action programs. Conservatives, energized by their political victories in 1994, launched a powerful attack on the policy of giving preference in hiring or promotion to groups that had suffered discrimination in the past. Arguing that government officials had never intended for these policies to become permanent, conservatives called for their elimination. In *California, voters voiced their opposition to affirmative action in 1996 by approving Proposition 209, prohibiting preferential treatment based on *gender or race.

Other groups faced a similar backlash. *Hispanic Americans and Native Americans, unemployed in far greater numbers than whites, suffered from the erosion of affirmative action. Though President Clinton appointed Ruth Bader Ginsburg as the second woman on the Supreme Court, women still faced a "glass ceiling" in their efforts to rise to the top of American corporations and watched as state and federal courts continued to chip away at women's right to *abortion affirmed by the Supreme Court in **Roe* v. *Wade* (1973).

Post–Cold War America also saw an upsurge of the anti-immigrant feeling that had reverberated so loudly in the past, expressed in strenuous efforts to halt illegal *immigration and to lower annual quotas for new arrivals. In 1994, California voters passed Proposition 187, which required teachers and clinic doctors to deny assistance to illegal aliens and report them to government authorities. Other states moved to follow suit. In 1996, a new federal immigration law expanded the list of crimes for which legal resident aliens could be deported, regardless of when the crime was committed. It also provided for a policy of "expedited removal," whereby aliens could be deported immediately, and banned from reentry for five years, on instructions from a single immigration agent, without a hearing or judicial review by a judge.

The post–Cold War Era also brought "culture wars": bitter disagreements over basic values, from abortion and homosexuality to Creationism, *gun control, *censorship of the mass media, and prayer in the schools. An exhibition planned by the Smithsonian Institution to commemorate the fiftieth anniversary of the dropping of the first atomic bombs (1945) set off a fierce debate that finally reached the halls of Congress. Veterans convinced that the atomic bomb had saved their lives by preventing an invasion of Japan fought furiously with historians who had studied the reasons the bombs were used. In the end, the Smithsonian canceled the larger exhibition and simply put the fuselage of the *Enola Gay*, the plane that had carried the Hiroshima bomb, on display. At the same time, the public became polarized over the question of national history standards that could guide public-school teachers. In both of these conflicts, the underlying issue was whose version of the past would prevail. Some observers linked these debates directly to the end of the Cold War. The demise of the Soviet Union and the end of the struggle that for fifty years had consumed America's economic and emotional resources had eliminated the external focus of hostility, they argued; now some of that tension and hostility turned inward, as the nation attempted in so many different areas to define a new role.

The U.S. economy and the stock market enjoyed a sustained boom in the 1990s, but an undercurrent of uneasiness could also be detected. As America became increasingly multicultural and multiethnic, urgent public-policy issues clamored for attention, including long term environmental concerns, genetic engineering, and health-care costs associated with an aging population. An emerging global economy of multinational corporations and mass-entertainment conglomerates, as well as an array of new electronic technologies—from cellular phones to the burgeoning *Internet, heralded social and cultural changes whose contours could barely be discerned as the twenty-first century dawned.

In the quadrennial election year 2000, the Democrats nominated President Clinton's vice-president, Albert (Al) Gore Jr. (1948–), a former senator from Tennessee and the son of a Tennessee senator. As his running mate, Gore broke precedent by selecting Joseph Lieberman of Connecticut, the first person of the Jewish faith to be nominated on a national party ticket. The Republicans, too, turned to an established political family, nominating Texas governor George W. Bush (1946–), the son of former president George Bush. As his running mate, Bush chose Dick Cheney, a conservative former congressman who had served his father as secretary of defense.

The election was one of the closest in U.S. history. Gore won the popular vote by a margin of some 263,000, but the Electoral College outcome depended on the extremely close Florida vote. When Gore's legal battle to secure a hand recount in some counties failed, Bush won Florida and the presidency.

[*See also* Business Cycle; Computers; Conservatism; Cultural Pluralism; Evolution, Theory of; Foreign Relations; Foreign Trade, U.S.; Global Economy, America and the; Hiroshima and Nagasaki, Atomic Bombing of; Indian History and Culture: Since 1950; Multinational Enterprises; North American Free Trade Agreement; Postmodernism; Welfare, Federal.]

• Colin Campbell and Bert A. Rickman, eds., *The Bush Presidency: First Appraisals*, 1991. Christopher Jencks, *Rethinking Social Policy: Race, Poverty, and the Underclass*, 1992. Walter LaFeber, *America, Russia, and the Cold War, 1945–1992*, 7th ed., 1993. Ronald Takaki, *A Different Mirror: A History of Multicultural America*, 1993. John Hope Franklin and Alfred A. Moss, Jr., *From Slavery to Freedom: A History of African Americans*, 7th ed., 1994. Geir Lundestad, ed., *The Fall of Great Powers: Peace, Stability, and Legitimacy*, 1994. David G. Gutiérrez, *Walls and Mirrors: Mexican Americans, Mexican Immigrants, and the Politics of Identity*, 1995. David Moraniss, *First in His Class: The Biography of Bill Clinton*, 1995. Ronald Steel, *Temptations of a Superpower*, 1995.

—Allan M. Winkler

POSTMODERNISM, a concept frequently employed by artists, intellectuals, and academics internationally, refers to what they identified as the dominant cultural tendencies in the last quarter of the twentieth century. In contemporary usage, the prefix "post" indicates not only "after" but also "contrary to," or even "anti."

The three art movements most relevant to the concept of postmodernism are *architecture, *dance, and fine art (*painting, *sculpture, and *photography). Postmodern architecture emerged in the late 1950s in opposition to the austerity of modern architecture, as in the work of Le Corbusier. It heralded a return to ornamentation, expression, and allusion to previous architectural styles, as evident in the work of Michael Graves. Postmodern dance, which arose in *New York City in the early 1960s under the leadership of figures like Yvonne Rainer, attempted to dissolve the distinction between dance and ordinary movement; its nemesis was modern dance, as practiced by choreographers like Martha *Graham. Postmodernist fine art had become a consolidated movement by the late 1970s. It was expressly opposed to the aestheticism of high modernist art, as explicated by the critic Clement Greenburg, and to minimalism. Like postmodern dance, postmodernist fine art sought to dissolve rigid distinctions between art and everyday life, while, like postmodern architecture, it employed techniques of allusion, juxtaposition, and ironic distance, as exemplified by the work of Cindy Sherman. Often politicized, postmodernist fine art was frequently said to be in the service of interrogating or deconstructing the symbolic and representational practices of capitalist society.

The emphasis on the topic of representation provides a major link between postmodern artistic practice and *philosophy. Poststructuralist theorists, like Jean Baudrillard and Jean-François Lyotard, became important touchstones for discussion of postmodernism because of their emphasis on representation. According to Baurillard, the postmodern epoch is marked by a tendency for simulation (symbols without reference) to predominate. Lyotard, on the other hand, focusing on narrative as a mode of representation, argued that the late twentieth century can be characterized by its suspicion of meta-narratives (world-historical narratives after the fashion of Hegel and Marx). In this, Lyotard recalled the nineteenth-century philosopher Friedrich Nietzsche. In fact, in many ways philosophical postmodernism, inclining to often extreme forms of relativism, owed its major intellectual debt to Nietzsche.

The concept of postmodernism was broadly influential in the 1980s and early 1990s. Though this influence was most pronounced among literary critics and art critics, it extended to the social sciences, cultural studies, and philosophy. Because postmodernism is associated with a suspicion of metanarratives, intellectual tendencies such as post-structuralism, relativism and *pragmatism have been labeled postmodernist. For this reason, some consider the American thinker Richard *Rorty to belong to the postmodern camp.

[*See also* Abstract Expressionism; Capitalism; Modernist Culture; Post–Cold War Era.]

• Fredric Jameson, *Postmodernism; or, The Cultural Logic of Late Capitalism,* 1991. Hans Bertans, *The Idea of Postmodernism: A History,* 1995. Noël Carroll, "The Concept of Postmodernism from a Philosophical Point of View," in *International Postmodernism,* ed. Hans Bertans and Douwe Fokkema, 1997, 89–102.

—Noël Carroll

POTSDAM CONFERENCE. The *World War II Allies met in Potsdam, near Berlin, Germany, from 17 July to 2 August, 1945, following their victory in Europe. Representatives at the conference included President Harry S. *Truman, in office only since April; Soviet premier Joseph Stalin, and British prime ministers Winston Churchill and his successor Clement Attlee.

The conference's closing agreement confirmed an earlier plan to divide the administration of Germany and of Berlin into four zones of military occupation by the United States, Britain, France, and the Soviet Union; established a four-power Allied Control Council to resolve overall issues of occupation policy; and suggested a territorial settlement that would place German-held lands east of the Oder and Neisse rivers under Polish jurisdiction. Austria was also divided into zones. In addition, the Allies agreed to permit each occupying power to seize reparations from their zone and promised the Soviet Union greater compensation owing to the extraordinary war damage it had suffered. The conference established a process to draft peace treaties, to plan for demilitarizing and eliminating Nazi influence from Germany, and to try Axis officials as war criminals.

The United States, Britain, and China also issued on 26 July the Potsdam Declaration, calling for the unconditional surrender of Japan. Some historians believe that the nature of Japanese militarism and Allied public opinion demanded this ultimatum. Others argue that, by making it harder for Japanese moderates to press for a negotiated end to the war, the policy led inexorably to the use of the atomic bomb.

During the conference, receiving word of the *Manhattan Project's successful test at Alamogordo, Truman with studied casualness told Stalin that the United States now had a weapon of vast destructive force. Stalin (who already knew of the atomic-bomb project through espionage) calmly replied that he hoped it would be used against Japan. Recent research reveals that Stalin then urgently accelerated his program to develop a Soviet bomb, fearing that his ally's new weapon would threaten Soviet security. Historians still debate the extent to which America's unilateral possession of this fearsome bomb hastened the cooling of relations between Truman and Stalin. Certainly, the growing hostility between these two leaders and their countries, aggravated by America's atomic monopoly and Stalin's determination to force Soviet-led communism on Eastern European countries, did not bode well for harmonious execution of the Potsdam agreements. The United States subsequently refused to support additional reparations for the Soviet Union. Acrimony developed within the Allied Control Council over zonal governance and the nature of future German reunification. Although considered successful at the time, the Potsdam Conference would come to be seen by many historians as marking the emergence of the *Cold War.

[*See also* Hiroshima and Nagasaki, Atomic Bombing of; Nuclear Weapons; Yalta Conference.]

• Charles L. Mee Jr., *Meeting at Potsdam,* 1975. James L. Gormly, *From Potsdam to Cold War: Big Three Diplomacy, 1945–1947,* 1990.

—Emily S. Rosenberg

POUND, EZRA (1885–1972), poet, critic. Born in Idaho, Pound grew up near *Philadelphia. A precocious Latinist, he entered the University of Pennsylvania at age fifteen but transferred to Hamilton College, graduating in 1905. He returned to Penn to earn an M.A. in Romance languages in 1906. After teaching briefly at Wabash College in Indiana, he settled in London in 1908. Pound revolutionized *poetry in the early twentieth century, befriending William Butler Yeats and Ford Maddox Ford; helping to found the Imagist and Vorticist movements; and sponsoring the work of then unknowns such as H.D. (Hilda Doolittle), T. S. Eliot, James Joyce, and William Carlos Williams. His own early poems appeared in a series of small books (1909–1912). During *World War I, Pound began *The Cantos,* an epic on which he continued to work until 1960. He married Dorothy Shakespear in 1914; moved to Paris in 1921; and to Rapallo, Italy, in 1925.

A vocal supporter of the Italian dictator Benito Mussolini, Pound broadcast over Rome Radio in support of the fascist regime. Indicted for treason in 1943, he was declared mentally incompetent in 1946 and confined in St. Elizabeths Hospital in *Washington, D.C. His *Pisan Cantos* (1948) won the 1949 Bolligen Award, reigniting controversy over his wartime activities. The indictment was quashed in 1958, and Pound returned to Italy with his wife. He lapsed into silence in 1962 and was cared for during his remaining years by his companion, Olga Rudge. He died in Venice, where he is buried. Ezra Pound was the most influential poet of the twentieth century, but his support of fascism and his wartime *anti-Semitism have marred his reputation.

[*See also* Literature: Since World War I; Modernist Culture.]

• Hugh Kenner, *The Pound Era,* 1971. Ira Nadel, ed., *The Cambridge Companion to Pound,* 1998.

—Tim Redman

POVERTY. Poverty has always been a serious problem in America. Throughout its history, large numbers of Americans have been unable to purchase food, shelter, and clothing, or to achieve a reasonable standard of living according to the standards of their time. Their poverty has reflected a variety of factors, from sickness, disability, and natural disaster to *labor market conditions, structural problems of economics or *demography, the absence of a social safety net, racial and *gender discrimination, and other failures of public policy. Yet public authorities and private charities often have adopted moral definitions of poverty, blaming poor people for their inability to support themselves.

A Chronological and Demographic Overview of America. Expenses for poor relief started to rise in the late eighteenth century. Destitute immigrants crowded nineteenth- and early twentieth-century cities, and homeless children wandered the streets. By any objective measure, half the population of large cities at the end of the nineteenth century—including many who worked full-time—must be counted as poor. The number of poor people, which remained very high in the early decades of the twentieth century, soared during the Great Depression of the 1930s. Although *World War II and the postwar prosperity reduced poverty, the ranks of the poor remained far higher in the 1950s than popular images of the period suggested.

Estimates of poverty remain crude for the years before the

federal government instituted an official poverty line in the 1960s. However, poverty rates clearly declined from the 1960s until 1973, when they again began to rise. From the mid-1970s to the late 1990s, the national poverty rate fluctuated around 14 percent.

Women, too, have figured disproportionately in the ranks of the poor. Excluded from jobs that paid living wages throughout most of American history, many women depended on men for material support. Indeed, virtually all self-supporting women struggled constantly against poverty. Young women on their own in nineteenth- and twentieth-century cities earned so little that many turned to forms of prostitution to survive. With no public social safety net in place, job opportunities restricted, and wages low, widows, usually left without payments from life insurance, often found themselves destitute. Even in the late twentieth century, a number of factors—including limited work opportunities and low wages, public benefit programs that discriminated by gender, and an increase in female-headed families—kept poverty rates higher among women. In 1960, single mothers headed about 8 percent of all families with children; by 1990, the proportion had increased to 25 percent. Nearly half of all families supported by women were poor.

*African Americans have, on average, always been poorer than whites. As slaves, most owned no assets whatsoever. From the post–*Civil War Era through *World War II, southern planters and state legislatures worked to keep blacks in the *South as a low-wage labor force picking cotton and working in domestic service. In 1935, under pressure from southern white politicians, *Social Security legislation excluded agricultural and domestic workers, which meant most blacks. In the North, before the Civil War, white immigrants often replaced blacks in occupations customarily open to them, such as barbering and catering, and well into the twentieth century, northern employers relegated blacks to the harshest and most poorly paid jobs.

As they migrated to northern cities in the twentieth century, African Americans increasingly concentrated in segregated, high-poverty neighborhoods drained of mortgage capital by banks practicing redlining—that is, using loan criteria, originally supported by federal government agencies, that defined black neighborhoods as poor credit risks. Unequal educational opportunities in both the North and South combined with racial *segregation and job discrimination to reinforce high levels of poverty among African Americans. However, between 1959 and 1974, as a result of the *civil rights movement, *affirmative action, and expanded education opportunities, the poverty rate for African Americans dropped from 55.1 percent to 30.3 percent. By 1990, *Hispanic Americans experienced poverty at about the same rate as blacks—about 30 percent, compared to less than 12 percent among whites. Both Hispanics and blacks suffered from discrimination and the lack of the educational credentials essential for well-paying work.

As for unskilled and semiskilled workers, their experience in nineteenth- and early twentieth-century cities was framed by a combination of low wages, irregular work, and periodic illness, rather than long-term *unemployment. In the best of times, they earned barely enough to feed and clothe a family, but seasonal labor demands as well as shifts in the *business cycle left them often with no work at all. In and out of work, they alternated between bare self-sufficiency and dependence. Work-related accidents and sickness struck ordinary workers and their families frequently and with devastating impact. With little or no *insurance, a serious illness could devastate the capacity of families to support themselves; well into the twentieth century sickness and accidents remained prime causes of poverty.

The working poor, ubiquitous in towns and cities before World War II, became less common as economic growth and trade unions fueled rising wages. By the 1980s, however, as real wages declined, their numbers had started to grow once again. Among families with children and an unemployed household head, the poverty rate rose by nearly half—7.7 percent to 11.4 percent—from 1977 to 1993. In the late twentieth century, chronic joblessness also became a new and widespread source of poverty. As manufacturing disappeared from cities, many people found themselves more or less permanently out of the regular labor force, a problem prevalent especially among young black men. Many had not worked in the regular labor market for a long time, if at all, and their prospects for steady, remunerative work remained dim. With neither jobs nor public assistance sufficient to lift them out of poverty, chronic joblessness defined a large, new component of urban poverty.

Throughout American history, poverty has displayed a rural as well as an urban face. In rural areas, low wages, soil exhaustion, the exploitation of sharecroppers and miners, declining prices of farm commodities, and natural disasters all promoted poverty. Rural poverty in southern *Appalachia initially inspired the War on Poverty in the early 1960s and the redesign and vast expansion of the food-stamp program a few years later. Although rural poverty persisted, by the 1970s public attention focused more on urban poverty, especially the concentration and persistence of poverty in inner cities. The number of city census tracts where the rate of poverty reached 20 to 40 percent increased alarmingly in northern and midwestern cities during the 1970s; in the 1980s it spread to cities in the South and *West as well. In the nation as a whole, the number of census tracts with a population at least 40 percent poor rose 50.1 percent in the 1970s and 54.3 percent in the 1980s.

From the early *Colonial Era, public authorities grappled with poverty. Colonial poor laws initially followed British precedents, which included outdoor relief—that is, aid to people outside institutions. Although widely condemned, outdoor relief remained a staple of public policy throughout American history. In the late twentieth century, state-level outdoor relief was called "general assistance" (or something similar); at the federal level, it became Aid to Families with Dependent Children, Food Stamps, Supplemental Social Insurance, or, simply, what most Americans called "welfare." Public authorities also built institutions for the poor, including *alms houses (which, by the early twentieth century, largely had become public old-age homes), *hospitals, dispensaries, and *orphanages. This combination of outdoor relief and institutional support kept public spending on poverty high and contentious.

Private Charity and Governmental Responses. A myriad of voluntary associations and private charities also responded to poverty with direct relief, institutions, and advice for the poor. Through the *charity organization movement, which flourished in the 1870s and 1880s, private *philanthropy unsuccessfully attempted to abolish outdoor relief and rationalize charitable giving across the country. Private charity and voluntary associations never proved capable of meeting the needs of America's poor. Economic *depressions—such as the depression of 1893–1896 and the Great Depression of the 1930s—only underlined the limits of the voluntarist approach. Nonetheless, private organizations played an indispensable role in the nation's response to destitution, less as an alternative to government than as a partner. Because all levels of government have always depended on the private sector to operate services or institutions with public money, America's response to poverty has rested on a mixed economy.

The major federal government response to poverty began with the *New Deal Era of the 1930s. For the first time in American history, the federal government provided direct relief—initially through short-term measures such as the Federal Emergency Relief Administration and the Civilian Works Administration. Of more lasting importance were the Economic Security Act of 1935 (often called the *Social Security Act), which instituted unemployment insurance, old-age insurance, and aid to dependent children; the Fair Labor Standards Act, which regulated working conditions; and the Wagner Act, which established labor's right to bargain collectively. In the 1960s, influenced by Michael Harrington's pathbreaking book *The *Other America* (1962), the federal government extended its antipoverty efforts through President Lyndon B. *Johnson's War on Poverty, whose programs, notably Operation Headstart and Legal Services, attempted to expand and equalize opportunities and to empower poor people through community action. The *Great Society programs of the same era expanded social security and other income-related programs, increased public housing, and with *Medicare and Medicaid created the first national *health insurance. These programs reduced poverty, hunger, and substandard housing and extended health care to millions.

Though poverty arises mainly from objective factors, as we have seen, public discussions often trace it to moral failure or flaws in individual character. Since the early nineteenth century, discussions of poverty have stressed a distinction between the deserving and undeserving, or the worthy and unworthy, poor. Although contradicted by empirical evidence, this moral definition has retained a powerful hold on the way issues of poverty have been addressed in America. In the 1870s, it legitimated attempts to abolish outdoor relief; in the 1980s and 1990s, it helped justify reductions in public benefits and the passage of a federal welfare bill that ended the poorest Americans' entitlement to public assistance.

The 1980s and 1990s proved years of paradox. Homelessness increased (sometimes related to problems of addiction or *mental illness); poverty was endemic in many inner-city districts; the share of children living in poverty increased; factory jobs declined, diminishing the prospects of unskilled or poorly educated youth, especially in the inner cities. Yet, public policy rested increasingly on market models that emphasized individual rather than social responsibility. Federal, state, and local governments redesigned programs by reducing funding, tightening eligibility standards for public assistance, and emphasizing sanctions intended to force the dependent poor into the workforce. At the century's end, were there enough jobs to substitute work for welfare? Would forcing individuals to accept responsibility for their fate motivate them to improve their lives? Answers to these questions promised to reconfigure poverty once again and profoundly affect American society in the twenty-first century.

[*See also* Alcohol and Alcohol Abuse; Cotton Industry; Drugs, Illicit; Homelessness and Vagrancy; *How the Other Half Lives;* Immigration; Individualism; Industrial Diseases and Hazards; Laissez-faire; Migratory Agricultural Workers; National Labor Relations Act; Prostitution and Antiprostitution; Racism; Sharecropping and Tenantry; Sixties, The; Slums; Social Class; Wagner, Robert F.; Welfare, Federal; Women in the Labor Force.]

• Charles Loring Brace, *The Dangerous Classes of New York, and Twenty Years Work among Them,* 1872. Jacob A. Riis, *How the Other Half Lives,* 1890. Robert Hunter, *Poverty,* 1904. Raymond A. Mohl, *Poverty in New York, 1783–1825,* 1971. Michael B. Katz, *The Undeserving Poor: From the War on Poverty to the War on Welfare,* 1989. Michael B. Katz, ed., *The "Underclass" Debate: Views from History,* 1993. James Patterson, *America's Struggle against Poverty 1900–1994,* 1994. William Julius Wilson, *When Work Disappears: The World of the New Urban Poor,* 1996.

—Michael B. Katz

POWDERLY, TERENCE (1849–1924), organizer and leader of the *Knights of Labor. Born in Carbondale, Pennsylvania, to Irish Catholic immigrants, Powderly apprenticed as a machinist before taking a job in a railroad shop. He joined the Knights of Labor in 1876 and rose quickly through this secret order's ranks, becoming secretary for a district assembly in 1877. In 1878, running on the *Greenback Labor party ticket, he was elected mayor of Scranton, Pennsylvania. A charismatic orator, Powderly replaced Uriah Stephens as the Knights' grand master workman in 1879.

Within three years, Powderly transformed a 10,000-member organization into a thriving movement that welcomed virtually all toilers. Under Powderly, the Knights abandoned secrecy in 1882, sparking further rapid growth. After victorious railroad strikes in 1884–1885, the Knights' membership rose as high as 750,000. Powderly's vision of labor organization and his articulate opposition to the wage system fostered this growth. His advocacy of producers' cooperatives and arbitration, disdain for strikes and craft unionism, and support for educational agitation and inclusive labor organization proved popular.

Yet Powderly was an erratic administrator. After 1886, the Knights descended into factionalism and chaos, hastened by his vanity and vague ideas. Driven from leadership in 1893, Powderly subsequently served as the U.S. commissioner of immigration in 1897 and held other federal posts before his retirement. Powderly's leadership of the Knights in their heyday left behind a vision of inclusive labor unionism that subsequent generations would seek to fulfill.

[*See also* Gilded Age; Labor Movements; Strikes and Industrial Conflict.]

• Norman J. Ware, *The Labor Movement in the United States, 1860–1895,* 1929. Harry J. Carman, Henry David, and Paul N. Guthrie, eds., *The Path I Trod: The Autobiography of Terence V. Powderly,* 1940, reprint 1967. David Montgomery, *The Fall of the House of Labor: The Workplace, the State, and American Labor Activism, 1865–1925,* 1987. Kim Voss, *The Making of American Exceptionalism: The Knights of Labor and Class Formation in the Nineteenth Century,* 1993.

—Joseph A. McCartin

POWELL, COLIN (1937–), chairman of the *Joint Chiefs of Staff. Born in Harlem, New York City, to immigrants from Jamaica, Powell joined the Reserve Officers' Training Corps while enrolled at the City College of New York. He received a U.S. Army commission as a second lieutenant upon graduating in 1958. He served in Vietnam in 1962–1963 and again in 1968–1969, when he was injured in a helicopter crash.

Receiving an M.B.A. from George Washington University in 1971, Powell possessed the necessary combat and educational background to profit by efforts to bring *African Americans into leading military positions. In 1972–1973, he was a White House fellow in the Office of Management and Budget, directed by Caspar Weinberger.

After commanding a battalion in South Korea, attending the National War College, and serving in the Department of Defense, Powell in 1983 became military assistant to Weinberger, President Ronald *Reagan's first secretary of defense. Powell's policy, management, and political skills led to his appointment as Reagan's national security adviser in 1987. Promoted to four-star general, he became head of the Army Forces Command in 1989. Shortly thereafter, President George *Bush nominated Powell to chair the Joint Chiefs of Staff, making him the first African American to hold the highest position in the U.S. military.

Powell helped shape U.S. defense strategy during the *Cold War's final years and developed plans to reshape and reduce post–Cold War U.S. military forces. He played a major role in the U.S. intervention in Panama in 1989 and in the *Persian Gulf War. He retired in 1993. In 1994, at the request of President Bill *Clinton, Powell joined former president Jimmy *Carter and Senator Sam Nunn in a mission to persuade Haiti's military dictators to relinquish power without a U.S. invasion. A moderate Republican, Powell received support for the party's presidential nomination in 1996 and again in 2000, but chose not to run.

[*See also* Federal Government, Executive Branch: Department of Defense; Military, The; Post–Cold War Era; Vietnam War.]

• Bob Woodward, *The Commanders,* 1991. Colin L. Powell, *My American Journey,* 1995.

—Anthony H. Cordesman

POWELL, JOHN WESLEY (1834–1902), geologist, anthropologist, director of the U.S. Geological Survey (USGS). Born in New York and raised on the Ohio and Illinois frontiers, Powell attended Oberlin College and was a teacher before joining the Union Army in the *Civil War. Losing an arm at the Battle of Shiloh in 1862, he left the military with the rank of major. Active in the Illinois State Natural History Society before the war, he returned in 1865 to become professor of geology at Illinois Wesleyan College. An 1869 expedition down the Colorado River brought Powell national notice and a federal appropriation. His U.S. Geographical and Geological Survey of the *Rocky Mountain region (1870–1879) won him recognition for explaining the role of structure, uplift, and stream erosion in shaping topography. Also a student of native Indian language and culture, Powell organized the *Smithsonian Institution's Bureau of Ethnology in 1879 and directed it until his death.

Concerned about the risks of American expansion into the arid *West, Powell in his 1878 *Report on the Lands of the Arid Region of the United States* warned policy-makers about settlement laws that ignored scarcity of water. His desire for a scientific bureau to replace Land Office surveys was partially realized in 1879, when he worked with Clarence King to establish the USGS. Powell became its second director in 1881. Buoyed by a Spencerian faith in science and progress, Powell worked to extend the survey beyond the mining regions and into general geology, topographic mapping, and natural-resource assessment.

The USGS under Powell won international acclaim. The most prominent federal scientific institution of the late nineteenth century, it laid a foundation for the growth of federal scientific agencies during the *Progressive Era. It also sparked controversy when it clashed with traditional congressional prerogatives. Powell's planning of irrigation development (1888–1890) angered some members of Congress and led to his retirement in 1894.

[*See also* Earth Sciences; Geological Surveys]

• William Culp Darrah, *Powell of the Colorado,* 1951. Mary C. Rabbitt, *Minerals, Lands, and Geology for the Common Defense and General Welfare,* 2 vols., 1979–1980.

—John J. Zernel

POWHATAN (Wahunsonacock) (d. 1618), paramount chief of the Chesapeake Bay Region when *Jamestown was founded in 1607. Historians have doubted the English colonists' attribution of imperial authority to Powhatan, but recent scholarship argues that he did exercise great power over his subject peoples. Captain John *Smith wrote that Powhatan had "such a grave and Majesticall countenance, as drave me into admiration to see such state in a naked Salvage."

Powhatan and his people were familiar with Europeans and knew their strengths and weaknesses. He and Smith settled into a pattern of wary sparring, each attempting to force the other to conform to his plan for the relationship. Powhatan's young daughter *Pocahontas was often the emissary between her father and the fort. Smith accorded Powhatan grudging respect for his subtlety and command. Many of Jamestown's problems, Smith argued, stemmed from its inept leaders' underestimating Powhatan's intelligence and determination, combined with the colony's dependence on Indian supplies of food.

Powhatan died in 1618, just as the Virginia Company was reorganizing the colony so as to attract large numbers of colonists. He had believed that his people could benefit from the presence of the English and their supplies of manufactured goods from Europe, but always keep the upper hand through control of the food supply and the threat of military action. In the four years after his death, the colony grew dramatically. When his brother Opechancanough tried to wipe out the entire settlement in 1622, the colony's resilience showed the scale of Powhatan's miscalculation.

[*See also* Colonial Era; Indian History and Culture: From 1500 to 1800; Indian Wars.]

• Helen C. Rountree, ed., *Powhatan Foreign Relations, 1500–1722,* 1993.

—Karen Ordahl Kupperman

PRAGMATISM. The most important and controversial philosophical tradition to originate in the United States since *transcendentalism, pragmatism remained central to American intellectual life at the twentieth century's end. A cluster of ideas first articulated by Charles Sanders *Peirce, William *James, John *Dewey, George Herbert Mead (1863–1931), and Oliver Wendell *Holmes Jr., pragmatism generates debate in fields as diverse as *philosophy, *feminism, and legal theory.

Peirce, James, and Holmes developed their ideas in the Metaphysical Club in Cambridge, Massachusetts, in the 1870s. Collisions between the world of chance and change disclosed by Darwinian science, on the one hand, and, on the other, traditional philosophical systems, whether premised on religious dogmas or on the Cartesian dualisms of spirits and matter and mind and body, persuaded these thinkers to reject claims to absolute certainty. They chose instead the experimental method and accepted the provisionality of all knowledge. But if their embrace of uncertainty accounted for the renewed interest in their ideas in the late twentieth century, the early pragmatists' devotion to democratic ideals and their moral earnestness distinguished them from cynics who celebrate the postmodern culture of irony.

Peirce argued that communities of inquiry—outside as well as within the natural sciences—should proceed toward a hypothetical Omega point at which unconstrained investigation would yield truth, which remained for him a regulative ideal. James doubted that such consensus could ever emerge. Much in human experience, he believed, flowing in the stream of consciousness that he explored in his masterpiece *The Principles of Psychology* (1890), defies scientific explanation or even adequate linguistic expression. Developing Peirce's ideas in ways Peirce himself found unpalatable, James insisted that dimensions of human life, including questions of metaphysics, faith, and morals, elude scientific explanation. In *Pragmatism* (1907), James argued that in certain circumstances—and *only* in such circumstances, which he clarified in *The Meaning of Truth* (1909)—individuals should ask what difference believing a hypothesis would make in their lives. When a question cannot be tested empirically (the existence of God, for example) and the question is alive, momentous, and inescapable for an individual, then the "will to believe" might well replace the normal scientific attitude of open-minded skepticism. Despite the jibes of critics who accused him of authorizing wishful thinking and valorizing material success, James neither doubted that reality always constrains belief nor adopted a crudely functionalist definition of what it means for a hypothesis to "work." Instead he sought to open individual lives and cultural debate to unpopular options, whether unfashionably traditional (such as religious belief) or radical (such as anti-imperialism), that might fruitfully be tested in individual or collective experience.

Dewey and Mead extended these insights into social analysis, Dewey through his wide-ranging and often misunderstood writings about progressive *education and democratic politics, Mead through theories of symbolic interaction and intersubjectivity that powerfully shaped twentieth-century *sociology from the Chicago School to the seminal German theorists Jürgen Habermas and Hans Joas.

The thought of the early pragmatists is incomprehensible outside the context of American Progressivism. Among reformist currents that inspired them and in which they participated were the social experiments of *settlement-house leaders such as Jane *Addams and Lillian Wald, the feminism of Jessie Taft and Charlotte Perkins *Gilman, the *Social Gospel of Walter *Rauschenbusch and W. D. P. Bliss, the socially engaged economics of Richard T. Ely and John Commons, the political ideas of Herbert *Croly and Walter *Lippmann, the cultural *radicalism of such founders of the *National Association for the Advancement of Colored People as W. E. B.*Du Bois and William English Walling, and the *jurisprudence of Holmes and Louis *Brandeis.

Pragmatism's alliance with progressivism did not survive *World War I, however. Stinging critiques by writers such as Randolph *Bourne, Van Wyck Brooks, Lewis *Mumford, Arthur Lovejoy, and Reinhold *Niebuhr, who from diverse perspectives accused pragmatists of abandoning their ethical and political ideals to become accomplices of power, corresponded with the broader interwar cultural transformations. To critics, early pragmatists' ideal of individuals in a democratically constituted community of inquiry deliberating and testing hypotheses seemed either too fragile in the face of power, too constraining of personal liberty, or too sunny-minded in the face of evil. In Dewey's writings and teaching, in the work of legal realists such as Felix Frankfurter and Jerome Frank, and in some of the more experimental corners of the *New Deal Era, however, pragmatism survived.

Pragmatism faced renewed opposition after *World War II as the natural sciences—and the certainty they promised—emerged as models for scholarship and politics. The *behaviorism that dominated *psychology, sociology, and politics preserved Dewey's enthusiasm for experimentation but lost his concern with the qualitative dimensions of experience and inquiry in human sciences. The rise of linguistic analysis displaced pragmatism in American philosophy. James and Dewey had worried that Bertrand Russell would guide philosophers toward a new scholasticism of propositional logic and, indeed Russell's and Rudolf Carnap's American disciples, leaders of a professionalizing discipline aspiring to scientific status and entranced by the intricacies of logical positivism, dismissed as meaningless all questions of metaphysics, ethics, and politics. Not surprisingly, they had no patience with the early pragmatists. Popularizers of pragmatism such as Will Durant simplified the ideas of the founders for mass consumption, but this merely reinforced the tendency of critics and vulgarizers alike to identify pragmatism with the can-do attitude and assumptions of self-satisfied middle-class Americans.

The years after the 1960s, however, saw a multifaceted and rapidly proliferating resurgence of pragmatism. Inspired by Thomas Kuhn's *The Structure of Scientific Revolutions* (1962) to see the natural sciences as human creations subject to paradigm shifts, and by the anthropologist Clifford Geertz to see the social sciences as inevitably value-laden, many analysts of American culture returned to the early pragmatists for ammunition. In the process they resurrected some ideas and transformed others. Philosophers such as Richard *Rorty and various cultural and literary critics invoke pragmatism as the American source for their own versions of antifoundationalism. By contrast, philosophers and legal theorists such as Hilary Putnam, Richard J. Bernstein, Cornel West, and Joan Williams, and historians such as Thomas Haskell, David Hollinger, and Robert Westbrook, tried to recover and extend the earlier pragmatists' ethical and political commitments. If, as James and Dewey argued, neither tradition nor *science can provide universal, unchanging truths, a democratic culture should seek provisional agreements—and negotiate inevitable differences—through open, uncoerced discussions among autonomous participants whose status is presumed equal rather than fixed by their race, *gender, or *social class. For insights into that project and how it should proceed, pragmatism remained a vital source.

[*See also* Evolution, Theory of; Gilded Age; Postmodernism; Progressive Era; Religion; Social Science.]

• John E. Smith, *Purpose and Thought: The Meaning of Pragmatism,* 1978. Horace Standish Thayer, *Meaning and Action: A Critical History of Pragmatism,* 1981. James T. Kloppenberg, *Uncertain Victory: Social Democracy and Progressivism in European and American Thought, 1870–1920,* 1986. Hans Joas, *Pragmatism and Feminism: Reweaving the Social Fabric,* 1996. James T. Kloppenberg, "Pragmatism: An Old Name for Some New Ways of Thinking?," in *The Revival of Pragmatism,* ed. Morris Dickstein, 1998, pp. 83–127.

—James T. Kloppenberg

PREPAREDNESS CONTROVERSY (1914–1917). The outbreak of war in Europe in August 1914 provoked significant disagreement in the United States over its implications for America. Conservatives, who had espoused patriotic service and national power since the 1890s, saw the war as clear proof of the need to enlarge the military establishment. Reformers and radicals, suspicious of the motives of conservative business interests, viewed the conflict as an impressive argument against abandoning America's traditional antimilitarism.

The earliest agitation for greater "preparedness" was led by a small group of northeastern Anglophiles including the former president Theodore *Roosevelt and Senator Henry Cabot Lodge. Their message, however, fell on largely deaf ears in the Woodrow *Wilson administration and in the country.

All this changed when Germany initiated submarine warfare and especially after German U-boats sank the *Lusitania* in May 1915. Newly formed and well-financed preparedness organizations like the National Security League were swamped with applications. Magazines, books, and even movies described a possible military invasion of the United States. By July, Wilson, frustrated by the *Lusitania* negotiations and fearful of leaving the preparedness issue to his Republican opponents, was rethinking his position. On 20 October, in a stunning reversal, Wilson approved a proposal for a five-year naval building program. On 4 November, he announced plans to expand the regular army and create a centralized new reserve, the "continental army."

The left reacted with extreme hostility, for Wilson seemed to be renouncing a widely held belief that war is necessarily destructive of efforts to achieve social justice. In the resultant split in reformist ranks, a number of Democratic and Republican progressives united to oppose the president. Facing a strong congressional antipreparedness coalition, Wilson in February 1916 abandoned the continental-army idea and accepted the federalization, in emergencies, of the National Guard—making a concession that led his secretary of war to resign. However, Wilson's new flexibility, together with the appointment of the antimilitarist Newton D. Baker as a secretary of war, rekindled confidence in the president among his former supporters. In March, the House voted to increase the army from 100,000 to 140,000 troops.

Subsequent events further weakened the antipreparedness forces. In May 1916, American intervention in Mexico and the German torpedoing of the *Sussex* prompted Congress to more than double the peacetime army and enlarge the National Guard. In June, the Senate, inspired by the sea battle of Jutland, voted to complete the administration's naval proposal in three, not five years; the House approved this in August.

During the 1916 presidential campaign, both parties posed as champions of preparedness, yet almost no one talked in terms of sending U.S. forces to Europe. Astonishingly, when Congress declared war in April 1917, the army still numbered only 5,791 officers and 121,797 enlisted men. Wilson had moved in the direction of preparedness but critics such as Theodore Roosevelt continued to argue that the nation remained ill-prepared to assume its role as a global power.

[*See also* Military, The; Peace Movements; World War I.]

• John Patrick Finnegan, *Against the Specter of a Dragon: The Campaign for American Military Preparedness, 1914–1917,* 1974. David M. Kennedy, *Over Here: The First World War and American Society,* 1980.

—Keith L. Nelson

PRESERVATIONISM. *See* Environmentalism.

PRESIDENCY. *See* Federal Government, Executive Branch: The Presidency.

PRESLEY, ELVIS (1935–1977), singer, actor. Elvis Aaron Presley was born in a two-room shack in Tupelo, Mississippi, in the depths of the Great Depression of the 1930s. When he was a toddler, his father was imprisoned for forgery, and the family sank further into poverty. The Presleys moved to Memphis in 1948. Here Elvis sang in the Assemblies of God choir, graduated from high school in 1953, and briefly was a truck driver.

Music—rock-and-roll—took Elvis to pop-culture immortality. His first recording, on Sam Phillips's Sun label in 1954, featured "That's All Right Mama" and "Blue Moon of Kentucky." Like Phillips, Elvis had color-blind musical tastes; in high school he even emulated the "look" of *African-American musicians and dyed his blond hair inky black. Likewise, his 1956 appearance on Ed Sullivan's *Talk of the Town* *television show, which made him a household name, was as much visual as musical. His on-stage gyrations stunned audiences, his pelvic thrusts outraging parents and delighting teenagers. In retrospect, Presley's wiggles seem perfectly suited to a medium that showed the movements and performance styles that *radio listeners could only imagine. This full-body style epitomized the freedom and spirit of sexual exploration implicit in the new postwar culture.

The year 1956 also brought his first million-record hit, "Heartbreak Hotel," and the first of his thirty-three movies, *Love Me Tender.* After military service (1958–1960), he resumed a phenomenal career of records, movies, and personal appearances. Until his premature death (from long-term abuse of prescription drugs), Elvis reigned as a pop-culture icon. Critics scoffed at the low-budget films; forgettable songs; and, in his later years, the extravagant costumes and operetta-like musical arrangements of his Las Vegas shows. But he remained a towering presence whose capacity to reinvent himself ultimately transcended questions of musicianship or movie quality. Elvis was a star, an American original. Graceland, his antebellum-style Memphis mansion, symbolizing his rise from poverty and obscurity to wealth and fame, seemed a concrete validation of the American dream. Two decades after his death, Graceland was, after the *White House, the most visited private home in America.

[*See also* Fifties, The; Music: Popular, Music; Popular Culture.]

• Peter Guralnick, *Last Train to Memphis: The Rise of Elvis Presley,* 1994. Karal Ann Marling, *Graceland: Going Home with Elvis,* 1996.

—Karal Ann Marling

PRICE SUPPORTS, AGRICULTURAL. *See* Subsidies, Agricultural.

PRINTING AND PUBLISHING. Since 1640, when a Cambridge, Massachusetts, printer produced a hymnal popularly called the **Bay Psalm Book,* printing and publishing have loomed large in American culture. The eighteenth-century *Philadelphia printer Benjamin *Franklin published numerous works, including popular almanacs. Revolutionary-era printers produced influential political pamphlets. Isaiah Thomas (1750–1831) of Worcester, Massachusetts, published high-quality books and *magazines that he sold through his bookshops in various cities.

Nineteenth-century technological developments transformed a craft into a major industry. New York's Richard Hoe invented the steam-powered rotary press with curved stereotype plates in 1846. The web press (1871), developed by Hoe and Stephen Tucker, printing on both sides of a continuous roll of paper, could produce 18,000 newspapers per hour. The linotype machine, patented in 1884 by Ottmar Mergenthaler (1854–1899), eliminated hand-set type, creating metal type slugs that could be melted down and reused. The *New York Tribune* adopted the linotype process in 1886. High-speed rotary presses made possible mass-circulation newspapers and magazines; low-cost books; and mass-produced Bibles, religious tracts, and Sunday-school literature.

Nineteenth-century book publishers—including New York's Charles Scribner's Sons (1846) and Putnam's (1848); J. B. Lippincott (1836) of Philadelphia; and *Boston's Little, Brown (1847) and Houghton Mifflin (1852)—produced religious works, histories, novels, dictionaries, gift books, and school textbooks. Books were sold through bookshops, by advance subscription, and door-to-door. Prior to the International Copyright Convention (1891), U.S. publishers regularly peddled pirated editions of popular British writers like Walter Scott and Charles Dickens without paying royalties. Dime novels and juveniles, published by Erastus Beadle (1821–1894) and others, proved highly profitable as well.

The early twentieth century brought a wave of new houses, including Alfred A. Knopf (1915), Boni & Liveright (1917), Harcourt Brace (1919), Simon & Schuster (1924), and Bennett Cerf's Random House (1925). Publishing contemporary European and American authors, they sometimes faced *censorship pressures from antivice societies such as Boston's Watch and Ward Society. These new publishers also introduced marketing innovations such as Boni & Liveright's Modern Library (acquired by Random House in 1925), an inexpensive series in a standardized format. The direct-mail *Book-of-the-Month Club and Literary Guild (1926) spawned a host of special-interest book clubs. The paperback revolution, launched by Pocket Books (1939) and Bantam Books (1946), burgeoned after *World War II. By the 1980s, paperbacks comprised one-third of U.S. book sales.

Like U.S. *business generally, the later twentieth century brought mergers and consolidation, such as Random House's 1960 acquisition of Knopf. Venerable houses became divisions of corporate conglomerates: RCA acquired Random House in 1966; CBS bought the textbook publisher Holt Rinehart & Winston (itself a product of earlier mergers) in 1967. Multinational media empires such as Germany's Bertelsmann and Rupert Murdoch's Australian-based News Company became major players in the acquisitions game. Printing technology evolved as well, with composition directly from computer disk to high-speed, continuously operating presses, and new techniques of high-quality color and fine-art reproduction.

By century's end, with independent bookstores hard-pressed by high-volume chains such as Borders and Barnes & Noble, the major publishers concentrated on blockbuster books by authors with name-brand recognition. As book publishing and marketing were transformed, the book itself seemed vulnerable in an age of electronic information processing. When the best-selling author Stephen King published several books on the *Internet in the late 1990s, some observers saw this as the wave of the future.

[*See also* Bible, The; Computers; Global Economy, America and the; Journalism; Literature; Literature, Popular; Mass Marketing; Mass Production; Multinational Enterprises; Technology.]

• Isaiah Thomas, *History of Printing in America,* 2 vols., 1810, reprint 1972. Charles A. Madison, *Book Publishing in America,* 1966. Thomas Whiteside, *The Blockbuster Complex: Conglomerates, Show Business, and Book Publishing,* 1981. John W. Tebbel, *Between Covers: The Rise and Transformation of Book Publishing in America,* 1987.

—Paul S. Boyer

PRISONS AND PENITENTIARIES. Perhaps the most critical fact about the origins of the penitentiary in the United States is a frank recognition that the institution does have a history. Prisons were not always the central feature of the American criminal justice system, an inevitable and logical method for punishing unlawful actions. Rather, beginning in the early nineteenth century, Americans, with some debt to the English, invented the prison, and it has been a fixture of American life ever since.

In the *Colonial Era, a wide range of punishments existed, none of which included extended periods of incarceration. The colonists levied penalties of fines, whippings, and public shaming (in the stocks). They relied even more heavily on banishment, assuming that those who committed a crime and were not legal residents of the town were best sent on their way, whatever the consequences for the next town down the road. The local jails were reserved for those who were either awaiting trial, or who had been convicted but not yet punished; the jails were ancillary to punishment, not its core. And of course, the colonists used the gallows, executing not only those guilty of capital crimes but repeat offenders as well. In effect, the system of punishment oscillated between the lenient and the harsh, with nothing in between.

In the decades following independence, Americans struggled to devise new modes of criminal sanctions. *Capital punishment seemed an unacceptable relic of monarchical governments, out of place in a republic. (As Benjamin *Rush remarked: "An execution in a republic is like a human sacrifice in religion.") Moreover, capital punishment seemed not only wrong but ineffective. The harsher the punishment, the more likely that American jurors would exonerate the guilty, and thereby reduce its deterrent effects. At the same time, banishment appeared altogether inappropriate. Now that citizens thought not only in terms of their locality but of their state and nation, it made no sense simply to pass the criminal along.

But what then to do? How should *crime be punished? In the 1790s and early 1800s, the idea emerged to have the offender serve time behind bars. The prison would serve the purpose of incapacitation; during the period of confinement, the offender would not be able to commit further offenses. But the system did not work as intended. Riots and break-outs occurred, and no one was satisfied that the prisons were meeting the challenge of crime. However, rather than being abandoned, the prison experiment took on new life. Beginning in the 1830s, incarceration acquired a grander function: to reform the criminal and return him to society as a law-abiding citizen.

The idea was a curious, if long-lasting, one. It is by no means apparent why a period of confinement should rehabilitate an offender. But the Jacksonians had a ready answer, and one that had enormous appeal not only in the United States, but abroad. The prison was to be structured as a kind of model society, with an internal organization marked by the discipline and order that was so lacking in the outside society. Would-be reformers were convinced that the roots of crime were to be found in the weakness of traditional institutions, including the *family, the church, the school, and the community itself. The prison would substitute for them, inculcating habits of obedience that the offenders had not learned before. Accordingly, the new prisons, as designed primarily in New York (the so-called Auburn, Sing-Sing, or congregate system) or in *Philadelphia and Pittsburgh (the so-called Pennsylvania or separate system), established very fixed and steady routines for inmates.

A surprisingly fierce debate broke out on the merits of the two systems, even though in retrospect they seem far more similar than different. In New York, inmates slept one to a cell but worked and ate together; in Pennsylvania, inmates slept, ate, and worked alone in continuous solitary confinement. To the New York systems' defenders, the solitary life of the Pennsylvania system seemed so excessive as to drive inmates mad; to Pennsylvania's defenders, the New York system allowed inmates to corrupt one another. But both systems relied upon a bell-ringing regularity to inculcate discipline and order. At the sound of a bell, the men woke; another bell signaled mealtime; still another, work time; still another, meals and bedtime. The only book allowed into the cells was the *Bible, and the only visitors, those who would promote religious beliefs.

Around this program, state after state built large, expensive, and isolated institutions, embracing the idea that prisons would reform inmates. Indeed, this promise gave the prisons or penitentiaries, as they were now often called, enormous legitimacy, making them the pride, not the shame, of the new republic. Europeans viewed the American prisons in this very light. Alexis de Tocqueville came to America, along with his collaborator Gustave de Beaumont, not to write **Democracy in America* but to study its prisons and make recommendations to the French government.

What happened to the dream of rehabilitation? It persisted long after it had become apparent that the prisons were not meeting the ideal. By the 1850s, and even more clearly by the 1880s and 1890s, the prisons were overcrowded, with several inmates to a cell; brutal, with guards inflicting harsh punishments upon inmates; and corrupt, with favors and special treatment bought and sold. But few objected to the decline of the prison system, or used it as the occasion to think about alternatives. Part of the reason is that institutions once legitimated are hard to topple. To this day, there are those who believe that incarceration can reform. Part of the reason, too, was the changing characteristics of the prisoners themselves. By the mid-nineteenth century, the inmates were predominantly *Irish Americans. In the opening decades of the twentieth century, they were predominantly Eastern European. In the late twentieth century, they were disproportionately *African American. In effect, prison populations became minority populations, and in the process the institutions seemed less in need of improvement than expansion. They might not be rehabilitative, the reasoning went, but that was the fault of the prisoner, not of the system. All the while, prisons and penitentiaries did confine a troublesome and dangerous class and thereby justified their centrality to punishment.

[*See also* Antebellum Era; Early Republic, Era of the; Immigration; Police; Poverty.]

• W. David Lewis, *From Newgate to Dannemora: The Rise of the Penitentiary in New York, 1796–1848*, 1965. David J. Rothman, *The Discovery of the Asylum: Social Order and Disorder in the New Republic*, 1971. Margaret Calahan, "Trends in Incarceration in the United States Since 1880," *Crime and Delinquency* 24, no. 1, 1979. Bradley Chapin, *Criminal Justice in Colonial America, 1606–1660*, 1983. Edward L. Ayers, *Vengeance and Justice: Crime and Punishment in the Nineteenth-Century American South*, 1984. Herbert A. Johnson, *A History of Criminal Justice*, 1988. Norvall Morris and David J. Rothman, eds., *The Oxford History of the Prison*, 1995. David Ray Papke, "Crime and Punishment," in Mary Kupiec Cayton, Elliott J. Gorn, and Peter W. Williams, eds., *Encyclopedia of American Social History*, III, pp. 2073–87, 1993.

—David J. Rothman

PRIZE FIGHTING. *See* Boxing.

PROCLAMATION OF 1763. The Royal Proclamation of 7 October 1763 is best known for establishing a boundary along the crest of the Appalachian Mountains, separating European and Indian settlement. (This decree also created governments for three colonies newly acquired by Great Britain in the aftermath of the *Seven Years' War: East Florida, West Florida, and Canada, which the British now called Quebec.)

The fear of native hostilities—underscored by the uprising known as Pontiac's Rebellion (1763–1765)—encouraged the British to draw this line. It was, however, hardly permanent. The English acknowledged certain Indian claims east of the mountains, while pressure from settlers and speculators forced Indians to concede large tracts to the west. Negotiations with the Iroquois, concluded at the Treaty of Fort Stanwix (1768), pushed the boundary of European settlement into present-day West Virginia and Kentucky, and dealings with the Cherokees, Creeks, Choctaws, and Chickasaws led to other modifications. Quarrels among native groups, and among colonists with conflicting claims, helped shape these treaties.

Although squatters ignored the proclamation and colonial leaders such as George *Washington believed it would never be enforced, the decree was nevertheless a grievance for the Americans. It led the British to keep a standing army in the colonies to make certain that this border was respected and it symbolized the clash between a British government determined to guide colonial development and the boisterous, expansion-minded colonists.

[*See also* Colonial Era; Imperial Wars; Indian History and Culture: From 1500 to 1800; Iroquois Confederacy; Pontiac; Revolutionary War.]

• Jack M. Sosin, *Whitehall and the Wilderness: The Middle West in British Colonial Policy, 1760–1775,* 1961.

—Marc Egnal

PRODUCTIVITY. For any economic system, including that of the United States, productivity is the key to economic performance. Determining whether nations prosper or languish, productivity measures the rate at which factor inputs—land, labor, and capital—are transformed into output. The term "productivity" actually encompasses two separate but related concepts. "Total-factor productivity" refers to the relationship between *all* inputs and output, while "partial-factor productivity" refers to the relationship between a *single* factor input and total output.

The relative importance of different input factors to productivity growth has varied over time. In early-nineteenth-century America, for example, when the economy was still primarily agricultural, labor accounted for around 60–65 percent of productivity, and land for about 15 percent. By the end of the twentieth century, labor's share stood at around 75 percent, while land's share was well under 5 percent.

Defining a "factor input" precisely is anything but straightforward. The measure of labor input, for example, must take account of the age distribution of the workforce, which in turn serves as a proxy for physical strength, vigor and endurance, and accumulated work experience. It must also take account of the intensity of work effort, which might vary widely from handicraft settings (such as preindustrial America) to a speeded-up production line. Calculating the labor factor in productivity also involves assessing such intangibles as the skills, education, and willingness and ability to learn and adapt that economists call "human capital."

In the study of productivity, the term "capital" does not mean money *per se.* Rather, it refers to the machines and buildings used directly and indirectly in production. Assessing this factor, too, involves consideration of innovations; organizational changes; and the vintages (that is, ages) of machines and buildings, which in turn provides information about wear-and-tear and the rate of technical progress.

American economic history—indeed all human economic history—is a product of these forces. For example, the transition from a two-field system of *agriculture (where half the land is kept fallow each year) to a three-field system (where only one-third is kept fallow each year) raised land productivity by at least 16 percent, quite apart from increases related to mechanization and crop diversification. The steam engines introduced into Cornish tin mines made possible better-drained and better-ventilated mines that could then be dug deeper in search of mineral wealth. Indeed, most productivity improvements had similar multiple spillover effects. For example, the use of water-actuated trip hammers (capital) in forging iron reduced workers' fatigue (labor), increasing output while simultaneously producing a superior product.

Not all productivity-enhancing changes have been desirable from the perspective of human well-being. For example, the division of labor such as that practiced in Adam Smith's pin factory in the late eighteenth century, and readily introduced into industrializing America, stimulated labor productivity and fostered mechanization by breaking down complex tasks into simple, repetitive operations. This, in turn, however, led to fatigue, production speed-ups, repetitive motion injuries, and labor deskilling. These unwelcome by-products of increased productivity became the focus of activism by *Progressive-era social reformers such as Florence *Kelley, Josephine Goldmark, and Louis *Brandeis.

Some sources of productivity growth, such as patented devices, have been private. Some have been public, involving innovative processes that cannot be kept private, such as "just in time" inventory control. Others have resulted from social factors, such as public education, and improved *public health and sanitation or from externalities such as the freer interchange of ideas in more densely settled areas.

A certain portion of productivity growth is unexplained by changes in factor inputs. This, in the words of economist Moses Abramovitz, is a measure of economists' ignorance. Unfortunately for our understanding of productivity, the increases not explainable by conventional factor-input analysis accounted for more and more of the economic growth of the late twentieth century.

[*See also* "American System" of Manufactures; Automation and Computerization; Automotive Industry; Business Cycle; Capitalism; Depressions, Economic; Economic Development; Economics; Electrical Industry; Electricity and Electrification; Factory System; Industrialization; Iron and Steel Industry; Labor Markets; Mass Production; Patent and Copyright Law; Steam Power; Technology.]

• Edward F. Denison, *The Sources of Economic Growth in the United States,* 1962. Joel Mokyr, *The Lever of Riches: Technological Creativity and Economic Progress,* 1990.

—Jeremy Atack

PROFESSIONALIZATION. Professionalization, the rise of particular occupations to positions of authority and honor, began in eighteenth-century America. The professions of that era, notably law, *medicine, and ministry, especially flourished in prosperous seaboard cities experiencing rapid social stratification. They became occupations that a gentleman could pursue without demeaning himself and, indeed, that could make a man a gentleman simply by the fact of his taking them up. *Social class and occupational characteristics merged. The professional exercised authority not only over his work, but over his clientele as well. The tradesman sold his customers what they wanted; the professional gave his clients, patients, or parishioners what they needed. The traits of professionalism—honor, authority, a secure income—carried over from these preindustrial professions to those of the late twentieth century.

The early nineteenth century brought an ambivalent egalitarianism that mixed a vague leveling impulse with an eagerness for upward *mobility—unsurprising in an expanding democratic society dominated by small farmers. As the traditional hierarchical society eroded, any well-behaved white male could aspire to the rank of "gentleman." The professional associations, with their restrictive membership requirements and their state licensing laws, came under attack. In 1800, three-quarters of the states had educational requirements for the practice of law; by 1860, only one-quarter did. In 1800, almost all states had medical licensing laws; by 1860, almost none did.

Despite the unfavorable social circumstances, the professions maintained gentlemanly authority and honor within their own ranks while surrendering both in society at large. The lowering of entry standards brought the professions within reach of ordinary folk. *Dentistry and pharmacy, previously considered merely trades, became "professionalized" in this era. Women and *African Americans found places at the margins of the professions. (They would be excluded again, however, as the professions regained power in the late nineteenth century.)

Post–Civil War *industrialization and capital accumulation produced new kinds of social stratification in the burgeoning cities, revitalizing the professions and providing new rationales for their existence. The period from 1880 to 1920 was a heyday of professionalism in the United States, with scores of professional societies arising in many realms of American life. Expanding rapidly, the professions raised requirements for admission to their associations and, through new state licensing laws, to the professions themselves. Even in this very different social milieu, the ideal of the gentleman professional survived. For example, the *American Medical Association's celebrated code of ethics, retained into the twentieth century, was mostly written by an eighteenth-century English physician.

The principal new profession of this era was *engineering. Though the engineering societies were dominated by consulting engineers, whose situation was closest to that of the traditional professions, most engineers were employees of large firms. For them, status and prestige within the corporate hierarchy replaced the broader social authority and honor once accorded to professionals.

As the twentieth century wore on, the percentage of Americans employed in *agriculture and in the production of goods declined sharply, while the percentage of those in the service sector rose. In these new circumstances, the professions—in a sense, the first service industries—stood out as models of a special kind of success. To be a "professional," or so it seemed, meant autonomy; status; a secure income; and escape from the indignities, depersonalization, and uncertainties of bureaucracies and markets. The professions brought into the modern world ideals that were premodern and predemocratic. This gave them great appeal and helped fuel a powerful drive for professionalization within the growing service industries that was a central fact of late twentieth-century American social history.

[*See also* American Bar Association; Capitalism; Legal Profession; Libraries; Women in the Labor Force.]

• Samuel Haber. *The Quest for Authority and Honor in the American Professions, 1750–1900,* 1990. Amitai Etzioni, ed., *The Semi-Professions and Their Organization,* 1969. Thomas M. Stanback, *Understanding the Service Economy,* 1979. Gerald Geison, ed., *Professions and Professional Ideologies in America,* 1983. Michael Burrage and Rolf Torstendahl, eds., *Professions in Theory and History: Rethinking the Study of the Professions,* 1990. Elliot A. Krause, *Death of the Guilds: Professions, States, and the Advance of Capitalism, 1930 to the Present,* 1996.

—Samuel Haber

PROGRESSIVE ERA. The Progressive Era takes its name from the *Progressive party of 1912–1924 and from the general feeling both at the time and in subsequent histories that the early years of the twentieth century were focused on a coherent body of democratic reforms that changed important aspects of the American political system. Interpretations of the Progressive Era have undergone many changes. Autobiographies and early histories stressed the return to popular control over political actions and the gradual shift from local to state to national authority. The next generation stressed points of continuity between Progressive reforms and those of the *New Deal Era in a presumptive march toward a moderate welfare state. In the 1950s, historians stressed the "status resentment" of middle-class reformers who, presumably fearing a loss of social power, had enacted laws to preserve an economic system in which they did well. Radical historians subsequently derided the extent of Progressivism's reform achievement and stressed its conservative nature; their successors focused on such matter as *professionalization and bureaucratization. The subject remains contentious, but few in the early twenty-first century regard the actual legislative achievements of the Progressive Era as more than tentative first steps toward substantive reform.

Viewed chronologically, the "Progressive Era" normally covers three discrete time periods. Toward the end of the 1880s, a significant number of women and their male allies came to the conclusion that *Social Darwinism, the reigning ideology that had justified economic expansion since the *Civil War, was inhumane in its effects and unchristian in its implications. Seeking more meaningful vocational choices than those the order of the day supplied, they pioneered such new professions as *social work, or reinvented such older ones as teaching and *journalism to make them more ethically meaningful. Following the precedents of Toynbee Hall in London, Jane *Addams and Ellen Gates Starr opened Hull House in *Chicago in 1889, in a quiet way beginning the era with a concrete achievement. The social settlement movement, with its efforts at adult education, *public health, political lobbying, and immigrant assimilation, gave women a respectable place in society. When John *Dewey, George Herbert Mead, and other academics joined various clergy and a few doctors in associating themselves with *settlement houses, Progressivism was essentially under way.

The growing body of reformers soon included such local politicians as Hazen Pingree in *Detroit; Samuel M. "Golden Rule" Jones in Toledo, Ohio, and Governor John P. Altgeld of Illinois. As these locations attest, the upper Midwest particularly nurtured the movement. The focus was on "gas and water socialism," that is, requiring de facto monopolies to charge fair prices in the absence of true competition. Municipal transit fares were often popular issues, but water, gas, *electricity, and eventually *telephone rates all drew attention. *Taxation of real estate, an issue that Henry George had made central to *California reform activity, was basic. Allied issues included low wage rates, dangerous working conditions, polluted water supplies, and conditions in the schools.

Attention shifted to the national level with the inauguration of Theodore *Roosevelt as president in 1901. A former member of the U.S. Civil Service Commission and of the *New York City Police Commission, Roosevelt not only knew *crime and corruption firsthand, he was friendly with reform journalists such as Lincoln *Steffens. A moderate reformer by temperament, Roosevelt was sympathetic to early efforts at "muckraking" journalism. Steffens, Ida Tarbell, Ray Stannard Baker, and Samuel Hopkins Adams focused public attention on the underworld of contemporary *capitalism, and Roosevelt supported efforts to break up large trusts, regulate railways, purify food and drugs, and protect public lands from private exploitation. He rebelled, however, against writers such as Upton *Sinclair and David Graham Phillips, whom he felt went overboard in denouncing corrupt business or political behavior.

An aroused public reelected Roosevelt in 1904, enabled William Howard *Taft to win in 1908, and carried Woodrow *Wilson to the White House in 1912. Taft proved inept, but Wilson managed to lower *tariffs; increase *economic regulation of business; assist education, agriculture, and labor; and above all to enact the *Federal Reserve Act, a long overdue measure that proved the most enduring of all Progressive reforms. During these years as well, local reformers adopted "initiative, referendum, and recall" measures enabling voters to initiate legislation, ratify legislative acts, and remove public officials who violated their trust. Certain states notably California, Oregon, and Wisconsin proved especially friendly to reform activity.

The outbreak of *World War I in 1914 began a slow but inexorable shift from domestic to international preoccupations. At first favoring neutrality, Wilson took America into the war in 1917, an act that, in Wilson's obsessively theological mind, seemed quintessentially Progressive: America could bring its reform mentality to the supreme task of assuring a permanent world peace. Through a series of "covenants" he would conduct a war to end all wars and instill democratic principles everywhere. Wilson's failure to win the kind of peace treaty he sought at Versailles, and the U.S. Senate's repudiation of American membership in the *League of Nations, marked the end of the Progressive impulse as a political force.

Early interpretations of the Progressive Era dwelled on political and diplomatic goals, but in reality the movement was a broad-based cultural and even religious phenomenon. Most Progressive leaders came from Protestant and often clerical families, they had learned Christian moral principles from an early age, and they tended to assume that sin was somehow at the core of social problems. Sin implied sinners; sinners needed to repent; and thus the period comes increasingly to look like a massive revival effort, with journalists, professors, lawyers, social workers, and clergy exhorting their audiences in sermons, secular or otherwise. Roosevelt was not simply using rhetoric opportunistically when he twice urged voters at national conventions to "stand at Armageddon" and "battle for the Lord."

The era was more a third "Great Awakening" than an "early New Deal."

In fact, the greatest achievements of the Progressive impulse were not legislative at all. "Progressive education," for example, remains a major legacy of the period. Drawing ideas from *psychology and pragmatic *philosophy, John Dewey supervised a Laboratory School during his years (1894–1904) at the University of Chicago, publishing a number of influential papers consolidating the results. Insisting that traditional methods that stressed sheer memorization and an outmoded morality merely stifled intelligence, he demanded a schooling experience that would be less oriented toward "reading, writing, and 'rithmetic" and more focused on re-creating the educational effect of a vanishing rural life. Students needed to work on projects; familiarize themselves with fabrics, carpentry, and crafts; learn about local governments and fire laws, take trips to observe biology and botany in their nature setting; and, in general, use their arms and legs more than their vocabularies. When he shifted to Columbia University in 1904, Dewey founded one of the more forceful institutions in modern life, the Progressive educational establishment, a bureaucracy that in time caused many parents to equate the word "Progressive" with "child-centered" and "undisciplined."

In intellectual life, Progressivism reshaped church and university. Led by George D. Herron and Walter *Rauschenbusch, most Protestant denominations developed versions of a *Social Gospel closely tied to British and continental *socialism. The true Christian had a moral duty to do good in this world rather than withdrawing from society to pursue his or her own salvation. In *social science, new graduate schools such as Johns Hopkins and the University of Chicago were soon turning out Ph.D.s intent on social investigation as a prelude to reform. Woodrow Wilson and John Dewey, both with Ph.D.s from Johns Hopkins, offered models of the socially engaged intellectual. At Chicago, *sociology was especially strong, as William I. Thomas pioneered in the study of *immigration and Robert Park in study of the city. Charles A. *Beard at Columbia and Carl Becker at Cornell were only two of the historians who recast American history in terms of present needs rather than some abstract "scientific knowledge."

In journalism, the *muckrakers generated an astonishing number of reform novels. Upton Sinclair took on the meatpacking industry in *The *Jungle* (1906) and Brand Whitlock the criminal mentality in *The Turn of the Balance* (1907), David Graham Philipps produced books on one industry in need of moral reform after another. In the arts, Vachel Lindsay was only the most eloquent of several poets who celebrated William Jennings *Bryan, three-time reform candidate for president, or William Booth, the Salvation Army general who devoted himself to helping society's outcasts. The painter John Sloan of the "ashcan school" worked for socialist candidates while picturing scenes of urban *poverty.

Like Progressives in other arenas, reformers in the arts yearned nostalgically for the moral, natural, God-centered world of their grandparents, creating comparable solutions for contemporary problems. Unlike the modernists of *Greenwich Village, who valued the new in and of itself, without reference to Protestant moral values, the Progressives always combined their innovations with nostalgia.

In this context of "innovative nostalgia," the composer Charles *Ives looked back to the *Revolutionary War, *antislavery, and the *Civil War to find materials for his radical innovations. He named movements of a *Concord Sonata* after Ralph Waldo *Emerson, Nathaniel *Hawthorne, the Alcotts, and Henry David *Thoreau; the String Quartet no. 1 bears the subtitle "A Revival Service"; and the most innovative piece of all, "Putnam's Camp," from *Three Places in New England*, fuses tales of the Revolutionary War and a stream-of-consciousness dream sequence with memories of a Fourth of July celebration when two uncoordinated brass bands marched into Danbury, Connecticut, each competing for sonic dominance.

Most famous of all, Frank Lloyd *Wright brought Progressive concerns into *architecture. From a background of Unitarianism, he adapted the educational ideals of Friedrich Froebel to the concerns of Hull-House and the University of Chicago, fitting easily into the world of Addams and Dewey. Developing a "prairie style" of single-unit construction, usually of houses or churches, he sought in the manner of the transcendentalists, to fit his works into nature. Form and function were one; generations of efforts to impose on the landscape, to ornament without regard to useful purpose, went out the window.

Defeated politically in 1920, Progressivism persisted in identifiable ways at least until *World War II. It helped shape both sides of the interior foreign policy debates, as Progressive internationalists fought isolationists. Some Progressive moralists resisted the secular and nationalizing tendencies of the New Deal, while others adapted with little trouble. In time, the Progressive image became increasingly tarnished. National prohibition, adopted by the Eighteenth Amendment in 1919, seemed a fiasco, the effort to remoralize drinking habits eventually leading to more drink and much more crime. Once devoted to moral reform, America turned toward secularism and social democracy in 1933, only to return to at least one strand of the Progressive ethos in the Ronald *Reagan years, when issues like the legality of *abortion and *religion in the public schools focused public debate in ways eerily reminiscent of the years before World War I.

[*See also* Antitrust Legislation; City Planning; Education: The Public School Movement; Great Awakening, First and Second; Lippmann, Walter; Modernist Culture; Painting: To 1945; Pragmatism; Pure Food and Drug Act; Revivalism; Secularization; Temperance and Prohibition; Transcendentalism; Unitarianism and Universalism.]

• Allen Davis, *Spearheads for Reform: The Social Settlements and the Progressive Movement, 1890–1914*, 1967. Paul Boyer, *Urban Masses and Moral Order in America, 1820–1920*, 1978. Robert M. Crunden, *Ministers of Reform: The Progressives' Achievement in American Civilization, 1889–1920*, 1982. Daniel Rodgers, "In Search of Progressivism," *Reviews in American History*, 10.4 (Dec. 1982): 113–32. Arthur S. Link and Richard L. McCormick, *Progressivism*, 1983. James T. Kloppenberg, *Uncertain Victory: Social Democracy and Progressivism in European and American Tought, 1870–1920*, 1986. Alan Dawley, *Struggles for Justice: Social Responsibility and the Liberal State*. 1991. Nora Lee Frankel and Nancy S. Dye, eds., *Gender, Class, Race, and Reform in the Progressive Era*, 1991. William A. Link, *The Paradox of Southern Progressivism*, 1992.

—Robert M. Crunden

PROGRESSIVE PARTY OF 1912–1924. Founded in *Chicago in August 1912 by *Republican party dissenters who favored the nomination of the former president Theodore *Roosevelt over the incumbent William Howard *Taft, the Progressive party was the culmination of an internecine battle between Regulars and western and midwestern Insurgents, led by the Wisconsin senator Robert M. *La Follette. The two factions had clashed bitterly over tariff reduction, income taxation, conservation, business regulation, the direct election of senators, and other reform measures. In 1911, Insurgents had formed the national Progressive Republican League and promoted La Follette's candidacy for the Republican presidential nomination. When Roosevelt, disillusioned with his handpicked successor, Taft, bested the incumbent in several primaries, he alienated not only Taft but La Follette as well.

Despite Roosevelt's popularity with the party rank and file, Taft's control of the Republican National Committee assured his nomination by the convention. Prepared in advance, the Roosevelt forces regrouped in another hall and nominated Roosevelt on what became the "Bull Moose" ticket. The party was a curious mixture of professional politicians, idealistic neophytes, social reformers, and businessmen who saw in Roosevelt's "New Nationalism" potential for a "corporate liberalism," in which the nation's largest corporations would work through federal government agencies to promote a stable, national, efficient socioeconomic order. The platform's "Social and Industrial Justice" section, drafted by social settlement residents, constituted a blueprint for the welfare state. A "top-down" creation, the party hastened to field a full ticket for the 1912 congressional and state elections, guaranteeing Democratic victories in numerous states. Roosevelt garnered nearly 28 percent of the popular vote and eighty-eight electoral votes, humiliating Taft and assuring the election of the Democrat Woodrow *Wilson with a substantial working majority in both congressional houses.

The Progressive party fared poorly in 1914, and party diehards pleaded unsuccessfully with Roosevelt to carry the banner in 1916. When Senator La Follette resurrected the party label for his final run at the presidency in 1924, he appropriated only the name and some of the 1912 platform. Marginalized by his opposition to *World War I and U.S. membership in the *League of Nations, he was endorsed by the *American Federation of Labor, the Nonpartisan League, the *Socialist party of America, and other antiestablishment organizations that had rallied to La Follette's Conference for Progressive Political Action. La Follette won almost 17 percent of the popular vote but carried only Wisconsin and North Dakota. His major support came from west of the Mississippi, a protest vote against Calvin *Coolidge's business-oriented Republicanism. He also ran well among working-class voters in several northeastern industrial cities and served as a "way station" for many who would later support Franklin Delano *Roosevelt's New Deal. Failing at grass roots organization, the Progressive party collapsed after La Follette's death in 1925. The *Progressive party of 1948 bore no relationship to the earlier party of the same name.

[*See also* New Deal Era, The; Political Parties; Progressive Era; Twenties, The.]

• Kenneth Campbell MacKay, *The Progressive Movement of 1924,* 1947. John Allen Gable, *The Bull Moose Years: Theodore Roosevelt and the Progressive Party,* 1978.

—John D. Buenker

PROGRESSIVE PARTY OF 1948. Only nominally related to the *Progressive Party of 1912–1924, this national political party was established in July 1948 to support the presidential candidacy of the New Deal liberal Henry A. Wallace (1888–1965), secretary of agriculture (1933–1941) and vice president (1941–1945) in the Franklin Delano *Roosevelt administration. Created from the membership of the Progressive Citizens of America (PCA), itself an amalgam of several left-liberal political-action organizations, the Progressive party was dominated by professionals of the middle and upper-middle classes, with many high-profile members drawn from the arts and sciences. Along with Wallace's candidacy, the party's formation marked the culmination of a crucial breach in American liberal ranks between anticommunist or *Cold War liberals, in organizations such as *Americans for Democratic Action, and the liberals of the Progressive party, who accepted communists in their ranks and leadership. The Progressives advocated a range of domestic policies somewhat to the left of New Deal *liberalism, including the socialization of several large components of the American economy and the expansion of *civil rights. After their nomination, Wallace and his running mate, the Idaho senator Glen Taylor, dramatically campaigned through the *South, holding integrated rallies in the face of often violent protests. It was the party's stand on *foreign relations, however, that aroused the most vehement attacks. Representing, by 1948, one of the few high-profile critiques of the Harry S. *Truman administration's hard-line policies toward the Soviet Union, the Progressives—and Wallace in particular—faced sustained and often innuendo-laden denunciations of their policies and their loyalty.

Never in serious contention, the Progressives garnered less than 3 percent of the popular vote as Truman narrowly defeated the Republican Thomas E. Dewey. Although the party persisted after the 1948 election, still espousing Progressive positions, it never regained even the modest stature it attained at its founding. In 1950, the Progressives lost the little credibility they still retained when Wallace broke with the party over its opposition to American involvement in the *Korean War.

[*See also* Anticommunism; Communist Party—USA; New Deal Era, The; Political Parties.]

• Norman D. Markowitz, *The Rise and Fall of the People's Century: Henry A. Wallace and American Liberalism, 1941–1948,* 1973. Mark L. Kleinman, *A World of Hope, a World of Fear: Henry A. Wallace, Reinhold Niebuhr, and American Liberalism,* 2000.

—Mark L. Kleinman

PROHIBITION. *See* Eighteenth Amendment; Temperance and Prohibition.

PROHIBITION PARTY. *See* Temperance and Prohibition.

PROMISE OF AMERICAN LIFE, THE. *See* Croly, Herbert.

PROPAGANDA. Defined as the deliberate attempt by the few to influence the beliefs and actions of the many through the manipulation of ideas, facts, and lies, propaganda has been widely practiced and frequently condemned throughout American history. In the *Colonial Era, religious writers and trading companies disseminated glowing tracts urging settlement in the Americas. Advocates of American independence and the adoption of the U.S. *Constitution promoted their causes through the *Declaration of Independence, pamphlets like Thomas *Paine's **Common Sense,* and the *Federalist Papers. Before the *Civil War, supporters and opponents of *slavery spread their ideas through literature and lobbying. In the late nineteenth and early twentieth centuries, propaganda techniques became more refined and effective with the growth of new communication technologies together with the development of the *advertising and public-relations professions.

During *World War I, the government became officially involved in the creation of propaganda. To encourage enlistment and war bond sales, the Woodrow *Wilson administration established the Committee on Public Information (CPI), which deployed posters, films, and speakers known as the Four Minute Men. CPI propaganda tried to convince a skeptical public to support the war by portraying the German enemy as the brutal "Hun" guilty of atrocities while selling America's effort as one that would save the world for democracy and lasting peace. In the interwar period, the term acquired a sinister connotation because of the exposure of the false atrocity stories the Allies had spread in 1914–1918 and because of its association with the fascist and communist regimes of Mussolini's Italy, Nazi Germany, and the Soviet Union. The U.S. government called its own propaganda effort during *World War II a "strategy of truth," using a news and information format as a persuasive method. Organized by the Office of War Information (OWI), U.S. propaganda portrayed the war as a contest between democracy and dictatorship, good and evil. With the cooperation of the news media, industry, and Hollywood, the OWI directed messages toward the home front, the Allies, and neutral countries. Propaganda directed against the enemy, known as psychological warfare, was conducted by the military and the *Office of Strategic Services.

During the *Cold War, propaganda became an institutionalized part of government. The presentation of the Cold War struggle as an ideological confrontation between democratic "freedom" and communist "slavery" was assisted by the *Voice of America, the *United States Information Agency, and the allegedly private Radio Free Europe, which was supported by the *Central Intelligence Agency. Secrecy and manipulation of information in the Cold War era led to a "credibility gap" most noticeable during the *Vietnam War, when much evidence contradicted the upbeat official line. During the *Persian Gulf War, the U.S. government depended on official briefings and controlling journalists' access as strategies for assuring supportive news coverage.

In the "information age" of the late twentieth century, both the private and public sectors targeted audiences with the sophisticated use of symbols. Much of the ensuing controversy surrounding propaganda centered on whether it creates consensus by informing or by manipulating *public opinion. Propaganda has been used to unite and mobilize the country in times of crisis by employing patriotic symbols and by demonizing the enemy. But social cohesion based on fear or hatred can promote intolerance and suppression of dissent, a lesson learned during all major wars. Scholars recognize the difficulties in analyzing propaganda's effectiveness, but many agree that it is most successful when it builds upon rather than challenges widely held attitudes and beliefs.

• Robert Cole, *Propaganda in Twentieth Century War and Politics: An Annotated Bibliography,* 1996. Richard Alan Nelson, *A Chronology and Glossary of Propaganda in the United States,* 1996.

—Susan A. Brewer

PROSTITUTION AND ANTIPROSTITUTION. Prostitutes—persons who provide sexual services for payment—may be of either sex and may serve clients of either sex but historically were women who promiscuously provided sexual services to men.

Colonial Era to 1890. In colonial America, prostitution was confined mainly to ports. In the 1820s and after, as the nation became urbanized, prostitution increased, fostered by the anonymity of city life. In 1831, the Reverend John R. McDowall, an antiprostitution crusader, claimed that *New York City, with a population of some 250,000, had 10,000 prostitutes. The New York Female Moral Reform Society (1834), led by the wife of revivalist Charles G. *Finney, spearheaded an early effort to combat prostitution.

By the mid–nineteenth century, authorities no longer prosecuted illicit sexual activities, as they had in the *Colonial Era, provided those activities occurred out of public view. Brothels were tolerated if they remained confined to informally designated "red light" districts. Open street prostitution was sporadically suppressed, but from the 1850s until around 1910, virtually every American city of even modest size had its bordello district. The more expensive bordellos in major cities were elaborate affairs and attracted an elite clientele. Brothel districts such as *Chicago's Levee, *San Francisco's Barbary Coast, *Washington, D.C.'s "Hooker's Division" (sometimes said to commemorate the *Civil War general Joseph Hooker), and *New Orleans's Storyville (named for the alderman who introduced the legislation setting its boundaries) were well-known and even clandestine tourist attractions. Some brothels, such as Chicago's Everleigh Club, run by Ada and Minna Everleigh of Omaha, were elegant and opulent establishments.

In the nineteenth century, prostitution in itself was not illegal. Prostitutes who solicited openly on the streets might be arrested as "vagrants," but those who worked inside were generally safe from arrest. Although brothels by common-law tradition were classed as "public nuisances," city officials rarely exercised their authority to close them. By the 1870s, many progressive municipal leaders favored the European approach of legalizing and regulating bordellos, an innovation adopted in St. Louis in 1870. This campaign, however, triggered a protest movement led by the *Woman's Christian Temperance Union and the so-called Social Purity movement, which sponsored annual conferences and published antiprostitution periodicals. Such groups opposed legalization and demanded instead that brothels be closed. Throughout the *Gilded Age, the suppressionists and the regulators debated prostitution policy.

1890 to 1960. The tide began to turn in favor of suppression in the 1890s. The English reformer William T. Stead, having documented the prevalence of prostitution in London in an 1885 magazine article, "The Maiden Tribute of Modern Babylon," brought his crusade to America in the muckraking exposé *If Christ Came to Chicago* (1894). American attitudes and laws regarding prostitution changed greatly during the *Progressive Era as the *public-health movement spread and the relationship of *venereal disease (VD) to sexual activity became more clearly understood, thanks to such works as *Social Diseases and Marriage* (1904) by the prominent New York physician Prince A. Morrow. Among the hazards was the risk that a man who contracted VD from a prostitute might infect his wife and, through her, their future children. The American Social Hygiene Association (1913), funded by John D. Rockefeller Jr., spurred the antiprostitution campaign through its periodical *Social Hygiene.*

A kind of moral panic known as the "white slave" hysteria gripped the United States in these years, as millions of Americans became convinced that vast numbers of innocent young women were being abducted and forced into brothels. While brothel owners or their agents did sometimes prey on naive young female immigrants, the panic in retrospect seems primarily an irrational response to *urbanization, *immigration, and the new phenomenon of unchaperoned working women. At the time, however, Americans took "white slavery" very seriously, as novelists, politicians, moviemakers, and muckraking journalists hammered away at its horrors. In response, Chicago and many other cities appointed vice commissions to investigate prostitution and make recommendations. These commissions found few "white slaves," but did document the prevalence of prostitution and bordellos. Prodded by public opinion and by such reports, municipal officials launched a wave of brothel closings that crested in 1909–1912.

At the federal level, the government had played little role in prostitution policy in the nineteenth century; indeed, only in 1875 did immigration officials begin to bar prostitutes seeking entry to the country. In response to the white-slave hysteria, however, Congress in 1910 passed the Mann Act, named for its sponsor, Illinois congressman James R. Mann. Designed to combat the white-slave trade by prohibiting the transport of prostitutes across state lines, it was sometimes used selectively to harrass private citizens, including the African-American boxer Jack *Johnson. During *World War I, the War Department closed red-light districts near military installations and warned doughboys against prostitutes through posters, lectures, and films.

The closing of traditional bordellos and red-light districts did not end prostitution, but only dispersed it. The more expensive prostitutes, now designated "call girls," made appointments by telephone and met their clients in hotel rooms. Other prostitutes worked out of bars or hotels, or on the streets. During the 1920s, many states criminalized prostitution, and over the following decades it became officially illegal almost everywhere. Enforcement of these laws varied widely, however, depending on the local climate. Prostitutes who too freely congregated on street corners might be driven into bars by a police campaign stimulated by a journalistic exposé or a wave of reform. Some jurisdictions periodically cracked down on bars that harbored prostitutes, usually by revoking their licenses.

Prostitution in Late-Twentiety-Century America. The sexual revolution of the 1960s, with its climate of permissiveness, undermined traditional forms of prostitution by easing taboos on sexual activity outside marriage, but also gave rise to a new phenomenon: "massage parlors," "health clubs," facilities offering "private lingerie modeling," or other euphemistically named establishments where, for a series of escalating fees, topless or nude women provided sexual services to male customers. By the 1970s, these small-scale, low-cost operations had become ubiquitous in American cities. In contrast to the old-style bordello, the women worked part-time; they were usually not professionals; and they set the terms of the encounter in the process of negotiating the client's "tip."

The differences in legal regulation were important as well. In principle, at least, the traditional brothel became illegal with the criminalization of prostitution. Massage parlors and their ilk, by contrast, were technically legal even though they were often covers for prostitution. Charges brought against such establishments were often dismissed because the plain-clothes police officer had first suggested explicit sexual activity, enabling the defendants to plead entrapment. By the end of the twentieth century, stricter zoning and licensing regulations, coupled with fears of AIDS and other sexually-transmitted diseases, had reduced the number of such establishments.

The post–1960s women's movement spurred both antiprostitution campaigns and efforts to improve the status and occupational conditions of "sex workers." Some feminists, citing the health risks, physical abuse, and economic exploitation endured by prostitutes, campaigned for more strenuous repressive efforts, including the arrest of male customers. Some municipalities placed provocatively dressed young women in areas known for prostitution and arrested the men who solicited them. These latter-day antiprostitution activists also criticized movies such as the Julia Roberts vehicle *Pretty Woman* (1990) for romanticizing a dangerous and often debasing way of life.

But calls continued to be heard for the legalization and regulation of prostitution. Organizations of prostitutes such as PONY (Prostitutes of New York); HIRE (Hooking Is Real Employment) in Atlanta; and COYOTE (Call off Your Tired Old Ethics), with branches in San Francisco, Los Angeles, and Seattle, campaigned for legalization and for better working conditions. Despite considerable publicity, these efforts enjoyed little success. As the twentieth century ended, the cultural context of prostitution had changed dramatically from a century earlier, but it remained an important if clandestine feature of American life.

[*See also* Acquired Immunodeficiency Syndrome; Feminism; Muckrakers; Temperance and Prohibition; Urbanization; Women in the Labor Force; Women's Rights Movements.]

• David J. Pivar, *Purity Crusade: Sexual Morality and Social Control, 1858–1900*, 1973. Mark Thomas Connelly, *The Response to Prostitution in the Progressive Era*, 1980. Allan M. Brandt, *No Magic Bullet: A Social History of Venereal Disease in the United States since 1880*, 1985. Barbara Meil Hobson, *Uneasy Virtue: The Politics of Prostitution and the American Reform Tradition*, 1987. David J. Langum, *Crossing over the Line: Legislating Morality and the Mann Act*, 1994. Timothy J. Gilfoyle, "Prostitutes in History: From Parables of Pornography to Metaphors of Modernity," *American Historical Review* 104 (February 1999): 117–41.

—David J. Langum

PROTECTORATES AND DEPENDENCIES. By 1898, when the *Spanish-American War was fought, American territorial claims already included the vast area of *Alaska as well as several guano-producing islands in the Pacific. It was the war with Spain, however, that marked the United States' emergence as a colonial power. As a war measure, the United States annexed the Hawaiian Islands, which were already dominated by American sugar interests and had been the focus of several annexation attempts during the 1890s. With the treaty of peace signed in Paris on 10 December 1898, Spain ceded to the United States control over *Puerto Rico, the *Philippines, and Guam. It also relinquished sovereignty over Cuba, which subsequently became a U.S. protectorate. Panama, too, became a protectorate with the signing of the Hay-Bunau-Varilla Treaty in 1903. In addition, an agreement among Britain, Germany, and the United States in 1899 resulted in the partition of the Samoan Islands between Germany and the United States.

To administer its territories and dependencies, the United States did not establish a centralized colonial bureaucracy like those of the European powers. Instead, responsibility for managing the affairs of different possessions devolved upon various existing government agencies. An office created within the War Department, called the Division of Customs and Insular Affairs (later the Bureau of Insular Affairs), took responsibility for Cuba, Puerto Rico, and the Philippines. Guam, American Samoa, and the U.S. Virgin Islands, first administered by the navy, were transferred to the Division of Territories and Island Possessions within the Department of the Interior.

The provisions for governing American possessions as well as their status vis-à-vis the United States have varied greatly over time. A series of *Supreme Court decisions in 1900 and 1901 known collectively as the **Insular Cases* distinguished between two groups of U.S. territories: incorporated and unincorporated. Incorporated territories such as *Hawai'i followed the path taken by other contiguous portions of the United States toward eventual statehood and citizenship for the inhabitants. Unincorporated territories, the Court held, were "appurtenant and belonging to the United States, but not a part of the United States. . . ." Residents of unincorporated territories were not granted U.S. citizenship.

Cuba. As war with Spain loomed in 1898, Congress passed the Teller Resolution, which renounced "any disposition or intention to exercise sovereignty" over Cuba. While never formally a territory of the United States, Cuba nevertheless became its dependency after Spain relinquished control the following year. After a brief period of direct U.S. military government (1899–1901), Cuba was forced to incorporate into its constitution the protectorate provisions known as the Platt Amendment. These provisions, confirmed by treaty in 1903, stipulated that Cuba could not enter into treaties or financial relationships with any other countries and gave the United States the right to intervene in Cuba and to maintain a naval base on the island. The Platt Amendment remained in force, providing the rationale for several interventions by the United States, until 1934, when it was abrogated by President Franklin Delano *Roosevelt as part of his *Good Neighbor policy toward Latin America. The American naval base at Guantánamo Bay remains as a legacy of Cuba's U.S. dependency.

Puerto Rico. U.S. military government in Puerto Rico ended on 1 May 1900, when the Foraker Act took effect. This law established a government for Puerto Rico in which both the island's governor and the upper house of the legislature were appointed by the United States. Representatives to the lower house were elected by Puerto Ricans. The Foraker Act also defined Puerto Ricans as "citizens of Puerto Rico," an ambiguous status that was not resolved until the Jones Act of 1917 extended U.S. citizenship to Puerto Ricans and gave them the right to elect members to both houses of the legislature. In 1952 the island became the Commonwealth of Puerto Rico by an act of Congress. Commonwealth status increased local autonomy and provided for a new constitution, but it did not increase Puerto Ricans' participation in the U.S. federal government or erase the unequal status that was the legacy of colonialism.

The Philippines. An easy early victory over Spain in the Philippines turned into a bloody three-year war of conquest, as Filipinos resisted American attempts to take possession of the archipelago. Estimates of Filipino casualties in the war ran into the hundreds of thousands; some four thousand American troops also died. As in Puerto Rico, an organic act passed for the Philippines in 1902 provided for an American-appointed governor and upper house and an elected lower house. In 1916 the Jones Act declared "the intention of the people of the United States to withdraw their sovereignty over the Philippine Islands and to recognize their sovereignty as soon as a stable government can be established." The Tydings-McDuffy Act, signed by President Roosevelt in 1934, made the Philippines a self-governing commonwealth of the United States for ten years, after which the act promised independence. Delayed slightly by *World War II, during which the Philippines were occupied by Japan, independence was proclaimed on 4 July 1946.

Hawai'i. As early as 1842, Secretary of State Daniel *Webster warned European nations that the United States was more interested "in the fate of the [Hawaiian] islands and of their government than any other nation can be." Hawai'i became an important supplier of sugar to the North during the *Civil War, and in 1875 a reciprocity treaty guaranteed Hawaiian sugar duty-free entry to the United States. Twelve years later, an amendment to the reciprocity treaty granted the United States exclusive right to establish a coaling station at Pearl Harbor. In 1893, pro-U.S. sugar planters overthrew the Hawaiian monarchy and called for annexation to the United States, but the U.S. Senate refused to act until the islands became an important staging ground for U.S. troops in the Philippines during the Spanish-American War. Hawai'i was annexed to the United States by joint resolution of Congress on 7 July 1898, and the Organic Act of 30 April 1900 made it an incorporated territory. After the Japanese bombing of *Pearl Harbor and American entry into World War II, Hawai'i was placed under martial law. It became a state in 1959.

Guam. One of the Mariana Islands, Guam lies 5,200 miles west of San Francisco. Seized to serve as a coaling station for American ships en route to the Philippines during the Spanish-American War, Guam acquired new significance for American military and commercial interests with the completion of the *Panama Canal in 1914. The island was administered by the U.S. Navy from 1899 until 1950, except for two and a half years of Japanese occupation during World War II. Civil government was initiated by its transfer to the Department of the Interior and the passage of the Guam Organic Act in 1950. Despite political initiatives aimed at redefining Guam's status as a U.S. commonwealth, it remained an unincorporated territory as the twentieth century ended. Several other islands in the Mariana chain were incorporated as U.S. territory in "political union" with the United States in 1975 as the Commonwealth of the Northern Mariana Islands. Inhabitants of the Northern Marianas became U.S. citizens in 1986.

Panama. The Panamanian isthmus—then a part of Colombia—became the focus of U.S. attentions after the Spanish-American War as the possible site of a canal that would facilitate interocean military and commercial shipping. After lending support to a Panamanian separatist movement, the United States, under the Hay-Bunau-Varilla Treaty of 1903, secured a permanent lease on a ten-mile-wide Canal Zone and also retained the right to intervene in the new, nominally independent nation. Panama remained a U.S. protectorate until 1936. In the Panama Canal Treaties of 1978, control over the Canal Zone reverted to Panama, and the United States passed jurisdiction over the canal itself to Panama in 2000.

The U.S. Virgin Islands. The United States purchased the Virgin Islands (formerly the Danish West Indies) from Denmark in 1917 as a strategic precaution to keep them out of German hands and to maintain control over the Caribbean passage to the Panama Canal during *World War I. The U.S. Navy administered the Virgins until 1936, when an organic act established municipal government under the jurisdiction of the Department of the Interior. A second organic act (1954) provided for a more centralized government and more local autonomy, although not until 1970 did Virgin Islanders begin to elect their own governor.

The Trust Territory of the Pacific Islands. After World War II, as part of a *United Nations (UN) program of administering territories formerly belonging to Germany, Turkey, and Japan, the United States became the "administering authority" for the Trust Territory of the Pacific Islands, comprising more than two thousand islands spread among three archipelagoes: the Marshalls, the Carolines, and the Marianas (excluding Guam). In 1986, the United States, with the approval of the UN Trusteeship Council, terminated the Trust Territory agreement. While the United States retained responsibility for their defense, the Federated States of Micronesia and the Republic of the Marshall Islands became independent states at that time.

[*See also* Expansionism; Foreign Relations: U.S. Relations with Asia; Foreign Relations: U.S. Relations with Latin America.]

• Noel Kent, *Hawaii: Islands under the Influence,* 1933. Julius W. Pratt, *America's Colonial Experiment: How the United States Gained, Governed, and in Part Gave Away a Colonial Empire,* 1950. Philip Foner, *The Spanish-Cuban-American War and the Birth of American Imperialism, 1895–1902,* 1972. Gordon K. Lewis, *The Virgin Islands: A Caribbean Lilliput,* 1972. Peter H. Stanley, ed., *Reappraising an Empire: New Perspectives on Philippine-American History,* 1984. George Black, *The Good Neighbor: How the U.S. Wrote the History of Central America and the Caribbean,* 1988. Louis Pérez, *Cuba under the Platt Amendment, 1902–1934,* 1991. Robert F. Rogers, *Destiny's Landfall: A History of Guam,* 1995. Walter La Feber, *The New Empire: An Interpretation of American Expansion, 1860–1898,* 1998.

—Katharine Bjork

PROTESTANTISM. Protestantism is a complex Western Christian movement that derives from the sixteenth-century Reformation in Europe. Rejecting the authority of the Pope and thus becoming separated from *Roman Catholicism, the movement stresses the authority of the *Bible, an accent on grace as the agent that brings God and human beings together, and "the priesthood of all believers," a way of acknowledging the positive role of lay people in the church.

Protestant Foundings. Though the first Europeans who came to the Americas were Catholic, the original thirteen colonies that would become the United States were, with the exception of Maryland, settled by Protestants. Most settlers came from England, which meant that they were either Anglicans, who established themselves in southern colonies such as Virginia and the Carolinas, or Puritans, who settled New England. The "Middle Colonies" such as New York, New Jersey, and Pennsylvania attracted Lutherans and the Reformed from northern Europe, English Quakers (members of the *Society of Friends who settled mainly in Pennsylvania), and Scottish Presbyterians to add to the Protestant mix.

By the end of the *Colonial Era, despite an estimated thirty thousand Catholics and three thousand Jews, the white settlers of British North America were overwhelmingly Protestant. So, too, were the founders of the nation who drafted the *Constitution, but of a special sort. Influenced by the Enlightenment and promoting human reason over divine revelation in Scripture, they saw to it that none of the Protestant churches was established—which included being tax-supported—or officially favored. By 1833 the last state establishment ended, in Massachusetts. Henceforth the Protestant churches were on their own, forming what is sometimes called "the voluntary church" and developing a form of Christian polity called "denominationalism."

The Spread of Protestantism. The voluntary denominational pattern forced the Protestants to compete with each other, even as most of them tried to keep Catholics from migrating to or feeling at home in the United States. Competition took the form of revivals and "awakenings," efforts to convert people and get them to join the churches. Already in the colonial period revivalists like George Whitefield (1715–1770), who commuted from England and regularly traversed the colonies, and Jonathan *Edwards of Connecticut set the pattern for conversion efforts in the First Great Awakening.

What historians call a Second Great Awakening was promoted early in the nineteenth century, with particular success in the new settlements in the *South and on the Transappalachian western frontiers. Revivalists like Charles G. *Finney in the 1820s and 1830s invented "new measures" to stimulate conversions, employing techniques that all but guaranteed a successful response. As Finney and his colleagues turned Protestant *revivalism into an instrument of reform, many of their followers became *antislavery abolitionists, advocates of temperance, and founders of denominational colleges, some of which would become highly prestigious. Though Protestants provided biblical justifications for *slavery in the South, where most of the clergy supported it, those in the North, where slavery was less economically rewarding, came to oppose it, also on biblical grounds. Spreading through the plantation system, Protestant Christianity was adopted and adapted by African-American slaves and freedmen and most of their descendants. Well over a century after the *Emancipation Proclamation in 1863, despite racial *segregation within the churches and church-supported prejudice by whites against blacks, the nation's *African Americans remained overwhelmingly Protestant, mainly Baptist, Methodist, and Pentecostal.

Social Policies and Divisions. The social movements to reform individuals in the nineteenth century became efforts to spread a *Social Gospel early in the twentieth. Now Protestants attacked what the leaders saw as structural and social evils: wage slavery, unregulated corporate life, *slums, prostitution, exploitative liquor interests. Through the Social Gospel among liberals and more individualized reform efforts by evangelical groups, Protestants continued to influence American social policy.

The nonsectarian Salvation Army, founded in England in 1865 by the Methodist minister William Booth and brought to America in 1880 by George Railton and seven army "lassies," represented a unique form of evangelical social action to combat *poverty and other social ills. With their military-like uniforms, street-corner rallies, soup kitchens, work programs for the poor, and proliferating social programs in the twentieth century, the Salvation Army became a distinctive and highly visible feature of American Protestantism. In another arena of social action, the *civil rights movement of the 1950s–1970s was led largely by ministers—for example, the Baptist Martin Luther *King Jr.—and backed by much white church leadership.

The Evangelical movement emerged in reaction to the liberalization in Progressive social policies and modernism in theology embraced by many Congregationalists, Presbyterians, Episcopalians, Methodists, and other Protestants of the old mainstream. The extreme element among Evangelicals formed the especially reactive *Fundamentalist movement, which lost battles for control of various denominations around 1925. Led by the National Association of Evangelicals (1942) and Evangelists like Billy *Graham, the Evangelicals won new church members through conversion to "Born-Again Christianity," and by the mid–twentieth century were outfacing the mainstream churches, which became statistically static or even declined.

The newly assertive conservatives also emerged from political passivity, and by the time Ronald *Reagan won the presidency in 1980, they had become the most aggressive religious group in politics. Favoring "family values" and constitutionally supported prayer in public schools, and opposing legalized *abortion, they gained control locally of many school, library, and town boards and influenced national politics through organizations such as the Reverend Jerry Falwell's *Moral Majority in the 1980s and the Reverend Pat Robertson's *Christian Coalition in the 1990s.

Theology. Theology, a word deriving from the Greek for "the word" about "god," is the systematic interpretation of the life of a people in the light of God. Although U.S. Protestantism is better known for activism and good works than for formal theology, the American circumstance did prompt Protestant leaders to develop certain themes integral to life in the colonies and the United States. First among these had to do with making sense of divine activity in the New World. Jonathan Edwards, the most notable colonial theologian, concentrated on "the religious affections," the meaning of the experience of God among the revived. He also contemplated the colonies' role in the plan of God. The Edwardsians came to be called "postmillennialists" because they believed that efforts at conversion and reform would spread righteousness and justice, after which (hence, "post") Jesus Christ would return to rule for a thousand years (hence, "millennial"), as foretold in the Book of Revelation. Later, a "premillennialist" view, impelled by the evangelist Dwight L. *Moody and others, came to prevail among conservatives. They turned to biblical prophesies that suggested the world will resist conversion and that wars and wickedness will increase until, in an apocalyptic end of history, Christ will return to rule for a thousand years.

The postmillennialists, prevailing between the mid–eighteenth century and the *Civil War, sponsored great movements of reform through religiously motivated voluntary associations. Along with antislavery and antiliquor agencies, these associations produced Sunday School unions, Bible societies, antipoverty endeavors, and an American version of the modern Protestant *missionary movements. Protestant missionaries labored on the frontier and in the cities, and, along with Catholics, set out to convert and educate Native Americans.

But frustrations on the domestic missionary front led many Protestants to seek to rebuild their "Kingdom," which was being progressively crowded by Catholic and other immigrant newcomers, through missionary efforts in *Hawai'i, Africa, India, China, Palestine, and elsewhere abroad. An American Board of Commissioners for Foreign Missions, founded in 1810, was the first sign of a thrust that consumed Protestant energies for a century and a half and lived on, especially in conservative Evangelicalism, through the twentieth century.

Meanwhile, theologians continued to work on both "religious affections" and the theological meaning of America. The most notable nineteenth-century Protestant was the Congregationalist pastor Horace Bushnell (1802–1876) of Hartford, Connecticut. In his book *Christian Nurture* (1847), Bushnell opposed the revivalists and the prorevivalist theologians. Instead of preaching human sinfulness and the need for a radical conversion experience, Bushnell and the modernists who followed him suggested that the potential good in people should be nurtured through education, example, and acts of love.

Late in the nineteenth century the liberal and modernist Protestants developed a theological justification for their social programs, notably the Social Gospel. While they treated the millennium symbolically as opposed to literally, they could still be classified as postmillennialists. In alliance with secular Progressives, they worked to make the world, beginning in America, a more righteous place. For the theologian Walter *Rauschenbusch of Rochester Theological Seminary, who wrote *A Theology for the Social Gospel* (1918), the key idea became "bringing in the Kingdom of God." By advancing public ownership of corporations, the organization of labor, and efforts to fight *crime, *unemployment, and exploitation of the poor in *slums, they saw themselves as following Christ.

A reaction to the Social Gospel modernism came after the 1920s under the leadership of the theological brothers H. Richard Niebuhr (1894–1962) of Yale and Reinhold *Niebuhr of New York's Union Theological Seminary. The former, through works like *The Kingdom of God in America* (1937) and *Christ and Culture* (1951), criticized optimistic and Progressive theology as shallow. Reinhold, through journal articles, lectures, and such influential books as *Moral Man and Immoral Society* (1932) and *The Nature and Destiny of Man* (1941–1943), was even more critical and searching. He resurrected terms like "original sin" to describe human nature and stressed divine activity more than progressive human creativity. Both Niebuhrs, especially Reinhold, continued to urge Protestant engagement with the social order, but now on what were often called "Christian realist" terms.

Pluralism as a Protestant Theme. While other theologians concentrated on the revelation of God, as H. Richard Niebuhr himself did in *The Meaning of Revelation* (1941), and on hermeneutics, the art and science of interpreting texts, still others dwelled on themes as old as Protestantism in America, themes that could be gathered under a code word seldom used before the 1950s: pluralism.

Pluralism acknowledged the reality that America harbored all sorts of Protestant and other religious groups and that theologians needed ways to interpret this reality. From the fourth to the eighteenth century throughout the West, in Europe into recent times, and in colonial America, one form of the church—such as Catholicism until the sixteenth century—was privileged and dominant. All others were "dissenters," to be hampered or persecuted. This form of religious establishment did not long survive in America.

After the First Amendment to the *Constitution in 1789 and progressively since, the United States became home to every kind of religious and nonreligious philosophy and cause. What sense should Protestants make of this diversity? Many informally followed what the University of California sociologist and religious thinker Robert Bellah in 1967 called "Civil Religion"—a blend of patriotism and generalized religious piety that transcended all sectarian and denominational divisions. Another sociologist, Peter Berger, called this a "sacred canopy" that allowed for the churches to prosper, but rendered their particular theologies irrelevant to the public purposes.

In the 1980s and 1990s, criticism by Bellah himself and others of banal civil religion and extreme individualism led to the articulation of what came to be called "public theology." The public theologians assumed that "private religion" was relatively prospering; that "church theology" remained important for its purposes; but that an interpretation of public life "under God" was also needed.

Public theology did not have the field to itself in Protestantism. Beginning in the 1960s, Protestant women began to make major feminist theological contributions. And African-American Protestants, inspired by books like James M. Cone's *A Black Theology of Liberation* (1970), developed a theology that interpreted their liberation from slavery, segregation, and oppression. Other groups and theologians, stressing ethnicity, *gender, sexual orientation, or environmental themes, further "particularized" American theology, the interpretation of life in a bewildering and creative national circumstance.

[*See also* African American Religion; Anti-Catholic Movement; Baptists; Bill of Rights; Church and State, Separation of; Ecumenical Movement; Education: Collegiate Education; Feminism; Great Awakening, First and Second; Judaism; Lutheranism; McPherson, Aimee Semple; Methodism; Millennialism and Apocalypticism; Peale, Norman Vincent; Pentecostalism; Progressive Era; Prostitution and Antiprostitution; Puritanism; Race and Ethnicity; Religion; Sunday, Billy; Temperance and Prohibition; Unitarianism and Universalism; Voluntarism.]

• Jerald C. Brauer, *Protestantism in America,* 1955. John Dillenberger and Claude Welch, *Protestant Christianity, Interpreted through its Development,* 1958. James H. Nichols, *The Meaning of Protestantism,* 1959. Winthrop S. Hudson, *American Protestantism,* 1961. Sidney E. Mead, *The Lively Experiment: The Shaping of Christianity in America,* 1963. Sydney E. Ahlstrom, *A Religious History of the American People,* 1972. Martin E. Marty, *Protestantism,* 1972. Edwin S. Gaustad, *A Documentary History of Religion in America,* 2 vols., 1982–1983. Robert T. Handy, *A Christian America: Protestant Hopes and Historical Realities,* 2d ed., 1984.

—Martin E. Marty

PSEUDOSCIENCE AND QUACKERY. Americans have long used these pejorative terms to designate scientific and medical theories and practices for which they have no respect. The meaning of the terms remains contested, however, because one person's "*science" and "*medicine" is often another's "pseudoscience" or "quackery." Further, the line between pseudoscience and bad science, between quackery and malpractice, has always been blurry. Thus many late-twentieth-century scholars dismissed demarcating between science and pseudoscience as "a pseudo-problem."

By the early eighteenth century, the term "quack" (from the Dutch word *quacksalver,* meaning one who boasts about his salves) was already gaining currency in the American colonies as a medical synonym for a charlatan. By the early nineteenth century, American physicians, who lacked the protection of strict licensing laws, were complaining that "quacks abound like locusts in Egypt." Typical of the person they had in mind was the untutored botanical healer Samuel Thomson, who sought wealth and fame by aggressively selling "family rights" to his system. Thomson, who saw himself as a life-saving reformer, acknowledged that critics called him a quack, but alleged that the real quacks were the regular physicians who gave their patients "poisonous medicines" such as calomel (mercurous chloride).

After 1847, when regular doctors organized the *American Medical Association (AMA), that body led the war on "quackery," especially targeting dissenting medical groups such as homeopaths, who prescribed infinitesimally small doses of medicine. Ironically, even as the AMA attacked all homeopathy as quackery, educated homeopathic physicians were expelling untrained "quacks" from their ranks.

Around the 1830s, as "science" took on its present-day meaning, scientific and other writers introduced a new term of opprobrium, "pseudoscience," to describe such novel ideas as phrenology (the science of "reading" a person's character by examining the skull) and the transmutation of species (later called *evolution). Leaders of American science often contrasted reputable "men of science," such as themselves, with ignorant and sometimes immoral "quacks" and "charlatans."

Early in the twentieth century, about the time Congress passed the first Food and Drugs Act regulating patent medicines (1906), the AMA created the first organized anti-quackery unit in the country. Often collaborating with government agencies, the AMA's Bureau of Investigation sought to suppress "quacks" and "charlatans" who advertised quick cures for *cancer, rheumatism, sexual weakness, or other conditions. By the 1930s the AMA was using "pseudomedicine" as a synonym for quackery.

No species of "quackery" stirred the wrath of organized medicine more than chiropractic, discovered in 1895 by D. D. Palmer, a magnetic healer from Iowa. Palmer believed that sickness resulted primarily from obstructions to the flow of "Innate Intelligence," which could be relieved by adjustments to the spinal column. Chiropractors described their practice as "the only truly scientific method of healing"; the AMA called it "quackery." After decades watching chiropractic prosper despite its opposition, the AMA in 1963 created a Committee on Quackery, whose "prime mission" was the containment and elimination of the "unscientific cult" of chiropractic. (The AMA had only recently stopped referring to *optometry as a cult.) The strategy backfired, however; chiropractors in 1976 filed an antitrust suit alleging illegal restraint of trade against a licensed profession, and a decade later won a stunning victory in federal court.

In the later twentieth century, many writers and organizations softened the language they used in discussing healing practices outside the medical mainstream. Inflammatory terms such as quackery and charlatanism gave way to the more neutral "complementary," "alternative," or "unconventional" medicine. In part this reflected the immense popularity of heterodox healing, employed by over 40 percent of Americans in the late 1990s. Responding to this widespread use, many medical schools began offering courses on complementary and alternative medicine, and in 1992 Congress created an Office of Alternative Medicine in the *National Institutes of Health.

No such euphemisms replaced "pseudoscience," which, if anything, increased in usage during the late twentieth century with the rise of watchdog groups such as the Committee for the Scientific Investigation of the Paranormal. Although employed most commonly to target ideas marginal to the scientific establishment, such as creation science, Afrocentric science, parapsychology, and "ufology," (the study of unidentified flying objects), the label pseudoscience also proved useful in besmirching scientific colleagues with whom one strongly disagreed: over racial differences in *intelligence, the links between social behavior and genetic makeup, or claims to have discovered cold nuclear fusion. To the public, the labeling often seemed arbitrary, as when scientists engaging in the Search for Extraterrestrial Intelligence (SETI) fell within the boundaries of "science," while those searching for evidence of Intelligence Design were dismissed as "pseudo-scientists."

[*See also* American Association for the Advancement of Science; Medical Education; Pure Food and Drug Act.]

• James Harvey Young, *The Toadstool Millionaires: A Social History of Patent Medicines in America before Federal Regulation,* 1961. James Harvey Young, *The Medical Messiahs: A Social History of Health Quackery in Twentieth-Century America,* 1967. Norman Gevitz, ed., *Other Healers: Unorthodox Medicine in America,* 1988. Ronald L. Numbers, *The Creationists,* 1992. Steven C. Martin, "'The Only Truly Scientific Method of Healing': Chiropractic and American Science, 1895–1990," *Isis* 85 (1994): 207–27. Ullica Segerstråle, *Defenders of the Truth: The Battle for Science in the Sociobiology Debate and Beyond,* 2000.

—Ronald L. Numbers

PSYCHOANALYSIS. *See* Psychology; Psychotherapy.

PSYCHOLOGY. The science of psychology was a late nineteenth-century invention whose origins lay in several German universities, particularly the University of Leipzig laboratory begun in 1879 by Wilhelm Wundt (1832–1920), usually acknowledged as the founder of scientific psychology. By the beginning of the twentieth century, the new experimental psychology had replaced nineteenth-century American mental philosophy, a form of Scottish faculty psychology that emphasized the empirical study of the intellect, emotions, and will.

The Beginnings of Experimental Psychology. The demise of the old psychology proceeded rapidly as the new psychologists, many of them trained in Germany, returned to America to pursue experimental work. In the late nineteenth century, America was undergoing a great transformation spurred by *industrialization, *urbanization, *immigration, and educational reform. The human problems caused by these changes created the need for an applied science of the mind. The stage was set for the rapid growth of psychology as a science and as a profession.

G. Stanley *Hall established the first American psychology laboratory at Johns Hopkins University in 1883. Four years later he founded the *American Journal of Psychology* to publish the new experimental work. America boasted seven psychology laboratories by the end of the 1880s, and nearly forty by 1900. A national organization, the American Psychological Association (APA), founded by Hall in 1892, brought psychologists together for annual meetings to share research findings and to promote their science.

Harvard University's William *James was the new discipline's most visible figure at the turn of the twentieth century, thanks to his *Principles of Psychology* (1890), arguably the most influential book in the history of American psychology. James's compendium of the latest experimental studies, his insightful analysis and integration of that research, his elegant prose and use of metaphor, and his optimistic predictions of psychology's importance as the science of the twentieth century assured his centrality in the new psychology in America.

Early psychologists sought to study the mind, or, more specifically, consciousness. They did so with experimental methods from Germany, the mental tests popularized by England's Francis Galton (1822–1911), questionnaires, and several varieties of introspection. At Cornell University, Edward Bradford Titchener (1867–1927) pursued a reductionistic analysis of consciousness that he would call structuralism. Relying almost exclusively on the method of introspection, Titchener sought to map the structure of consciousness by identifying its most basic elements, which he labeled sensations, emotions, and images.

The Functionalist Approach. Other American psychologists, influenced by the writings of William James and Charles Darwin (1809–1882), focused instead on understanding the functions of consciousness, particularly how consciousness enables the organism to adapt to changing environments. More eclectic in their methods, these psychologists used nonhuman animals in their research and promoted the application of psychology outside the university laboratories. Whereas the structuralists focused their research principally on sensation and perception—processes by which information is acquired—the functionalists were more interested in learning and motivation. If consciousness had adaptive significance, they reasoned, then learning must be the mechanism by which adaptation operated.

In addition to James, the functionalist group included G. Stanley Hall, who, beginning in the 1890s at Clark University, involved psychologists and schoolteachers in a nationwide effort to gather information about the psychological nature of children. The child-study movement, as it was known, used questionnaires in an attempt to learn everything there was to know about children: sensory capabilities, humor, play, religious ideas, memory, attention span, and so forth. In Hall's view, the field of education offered the most fertile possibilities for psychology's application. His child-study program—the earliest application in America of the new psychology—was aimed at curricular reform and teacher training.

Another early functionalist, Columbia University's James McKeen Cattell (1860–1944), pioneered mental testing in America. He developed a battery of sensory, cognitive, and motor tests that he used in a research program focused on individual differences. Some of these tests, touted as measures of intelligence, proved to have little validity in that regard and were replaced in the first decade of the twentieth century by the Binet and Simon tests imported from France. Intelligence testing, which reached its zenith in America, was part of a broader program of mental testing, an activity that defined much of the first fifty years of American psychology.

Behaviorism. While structuralists and functionalists debated the study of consciousness, other psychologists suggested shifting psychology's focus to behavior. Their champion was John B. Watson (1878–1958), who in 1913 published what has been called the "behaviorist manifesto." Psychologists who thought that their science could study consciousness were deluding themselves, Watson argued. Instead, he believed that psychology would take its rightful place as a science by restricting its study to what could be observed and scientifically measured, namely behavior. Convinced that psychology could be a wholly objective science, Watson called for reform in its content and its methods and for the rejection of mentalistic terms such as "mind" and "consciousness." Over the next twenty years American psychology was increasingly influenced by *behaviorism, an approach that dominated the discipline's thought and research into the 1970s.

Behaviorism continued the functionalist emphasis on learning, primarily using animal subjects (mostly the albino rat), and fostering a number of competing learning theories. The best known of these was the operant conditioning work of B. F. Skinner (1904–1990). Skinner developed a behavioral psychology based on the use of reinforcers and punishers as behavioral contingencies in changing behavioral rates. His work was widely applied in business, education, and the field of mental-health care.

The Rise of Subspecialities. As American psychology developed in the twentieth century, its divisions were marked not only by philosophical and methodological differences—structuralism, functionalism, behaviorism, and so forth—but also by the growth of specialty areas. Applied specialties, such as school and industrial psychology, began in the late 1890s, as psychologists used their science to help children overcome learning problems and businesses to evaluate *advertising effectiveness. Concern with personnel selection and the vocational guidance of youth gave rise to counseling psychology, whereas clinical psychology emerged initially in the mental testing used in clinical assessment and diagnosis. All of the applied fields grew rapidly after *World War II, especially clinical psychology, which was stimulated by a joint program among the APA, the *Veterans Administration, and university graduate programs interested in training psychologists to be psychotherapists and clinical researchers. As psychology's role evolved in the mental-health field from the late 1940s through the 1970s, psychologists worked with state legislatures to establish licensing laws to protect consumers and ensure quality in the growing fields of clinical and counseling psychology.

In addition to their various specialties defined by practical application, psychologists increasingly differentiated themselves by the subject matter of their studies, for example, social psychology, biopsychology, developmental psychology, and cognitive psychology. Cognitive psychology—which focused on many of the topics that behaviorism had expunged, such as thinking, memory, language, and consciousness—appeared in the 1960s with the use of *computers in psychology, the emergence of new methods for researching internal states, and a growing dissatisfaction in psychology with the narrowness of behaviorism. By the 1970s behaviorism shared center stage with cognitive approaches.

Psychoanalytic and Humanistic Psychology. Other influences on American psychology were psychoanalysis and humanistic psychology. Psychoanalytic theory spread in America in the decades following the 1909 U.S. visit of the Austrian Sigmund Freud (1856–1939), who came at the invitation of G. Stanley Hall. Freud's ideas, emphasizing the role of early childhood experiences and of the unconscious as the primary determinants of behavior, soon won an American following. America's first journal of Freudian psychology, the *Psychoanalytic Review,* was founded by William Alanson White and Smith Ely Jelliffe in 1913. The rise of fascism in the 1930s brought a number of Freudian psychoanalysts to the United States as refugees, including Erich Fromm (1900–1980) and Karen Horney (1885–1952). By the mid-twentieth century, the United States had became a major center of psychoanalytic practice. But American-based psychoanalysts and psychiatrists influenced by Freud, including Fromm, Horney, and Harry Stack Sullivan (1892–1949), first editor of the journal *Psychiatry,* were among the sharpest critics of Freudian orthodoxy. These American neo-Freudians stressed the role of sociocultural factors in psychological development; the power of the individual to address and overcome psychological problems; and, in the case of Horney, the psychosexual experience of women, downplayed by Freud. Fromm's *Escape from Freedom* (1941) and Horney's *Our Inner Conflicts* (1945) were particularly influential books. While Freud loomed large in the arts and the humanities, and in mid-twentieth-century *popular culture, his influence in psychology was largely limited to therapeutic practice. By the end of the twentieth century, Freudian theory had come under heavy challenge for a variety of reasons, and declined even as a therapeutic technique.

Humanistic psychology emerged in the 1960s, principally based on the ideas of Carl Rogers (1902–1987) and Abraham Maslow (1908–1970). It opposed the determinism implicit in behaviorism and psychoanalysis and proposed instead that individuals could choose how they behaved. Humanistic psychology led to some alternative psychotherapies but had little influence on the science of psychology.

By the beginning of the twenty-first century, the American Psychological Association had more than 159,000 members and affiliates who belonged to at least one of the APA's more than fifty divisions reflecting the diversity of interests in psychology (e.g., sports psychology, media psychology, psychology and law, and addictions). One of the newer divisions, health psychology, promised considerable growth in the twenty-first century because of the significant number of illnesses and deaths caused by behavioral variables such as smoking, overeating, stress, violence, and lack of exercise. Beginning as a laboratory science in the universities of the 1880s, psychology a century later was one of the larger professions in the United States. By the 1990s, more than half of the world's psychologists resided in the United States. Of that number, a majority were involved directly in the practice of psychology in diverse applied specialties.

[*See also* The Education: The Rise of the University; Intelligence, Concepts of; Mental Illness; Professionalization; Psychotherapy.]

• Donald S. Napoli, *Architects of Adjustment: The History of the Psychological Profession in the United States,* 1981. Josef Brozek, *Explorations in the History of Psychology in the United States,* 1984. John M. O'Donnell, *The Origins of Behaviorism: American Psychology, 1870–1920,* 1985. Ernest R. Hilgard, *Psychology in America: A Historical Survey,* 1987. Elizabeth Scarborough and Laurel Furumoto, *Untold Lives: The First Generation of American Women Psychologists,* 1987. Michael M. Sokal, *Psychological Testing and American Society, 1890–1930,* 1987. Jill G. Morawski, *The Rise of Experimentation in American Psychology,* 1988. Donald K. Freedheim, *History of Psychotherapy,* 1992. Ludy T. Benjamin Jr., *A History of Psychology: Original Sources and Contemporary Research,* 2d ed., 1997.

—Ludy T. Benjamin Jr.

PSYCHOTHERAPY. Psychotherapy is the term applied to a wide variety of efforts to foster personal growth and behavioral modification by treating mental and emotional maladies through the use of conversations between therapists and patients designed to disclose inner conflicts and yield psychological insights. Several elements that lent credence to such talking cures were deeply rooted within American culture. Not only did "folk psychology" promote the value of talking things over with a trusted confidant, but nineteenth-century theological and philosophical discussions of human nature emphasized the importance of the mind as a causal agent in self-fashioning. Still, the birth of psychotherapy as a set of determinate ideas and clinical procedures awaited the discovery of the "subconscious" by the French psychopathologist Pierre Janet and others in the 1880s and 1890s and the use of a variety of techniques—hypnosis, suggestion, and the like—based on persuasion and the "re-education" of those suffering psychological distress.

European-based psychotherapeutic ideas and strategies initially encountered fierce resistance from the American medical community. Notwithstanding their inability to discern a physical cause for numerous forms of mental distress and their disturbingly low rate of success in treating those disorders, American physicians continued to attribute *mental illness to organic rather than psychological causes. During the late nineteenth and early twentieth centuries, however, several developments converged to foster interest in psychotherapy. Within the larger culture, many Americans became enthralled with *Christian Science, New Thought, the Episcopalian-based Emmanuel movement, and other groups that dissented from "medical materialism." At the same time, a small but influential group of neurologists, psychiatrists, and psychologists centered in the *Boston area—including James Jackson Putnam, Morton Prince, Boris Sidis, Adolf Meyer, William *James, and G. Stanley *Hall—began to assign great significance to psychological factors in the cause and treatment of hysteria, anxiety, depression, and a variety of other maladies. During the first decade of the twentieth century the prestige of these individuals, coupled with the desire of many physicians to compete more effectively with what William James termed the "mind-cure" movement, helped to give psychotherapy a foothold within American society.

Freudianism in America. One beneficiary of Americans' increasing tendency to look favorably on psychotherapy was the Austrian physician Sigmund Freud. In Freud's exposition of "depth psychology," the powerful, amoral "drives" residing in the unconscious—most notably the sexual drive, which he termed the libido—played a central role in motivating human behavior. Freud also held that these drives prompted human beings, often in their early years, to generate ideas and wishes so radically at odds with the standards they embraced in their conscious minds that they "repressed" them. This psychic defense mechanism, however, was not always successful; and when repressed material did surface, it was capable of causing a wide variety of mental and behavioral disorders. The appropriate therapy for such disorders, Freud maintained, was analysis: a series of sustained discussions with a trained analyst, during which patients could bring repressed material fully to light and integrate it into the conscious mind. Eventually, some patients would even achieve insight into the motives that had led to the initial repression.

After 1909, the year that Freud delivered a series of lectures at Clark University in Worcester, Massachusetts, psychoanalysis not only took root in the United States, but also evolved considerably. This is partly because Freud himself continued to modify his views and partly because many professed Freudians altered his emphases. In the process of "Americanizing" Freud, proponents of psychoanalysis muted the conflict between the individual and society and downplayed the master's emphasis on sexuality, aggression, and the centrality of infancy and childhood in the psychological lives of human beings. They also tended to focus more on the role of the ego—the conscious self—and the external environment and less on the intractability of the unconscious. By the early 1940s these views had become institutionalized in a neo-Freudian movement. Karen Horney, Harry Stack Sullivan, Erich Fromm, and other neo-Freudians highlighted the importance of anxiety and the role of interpersonal relationships in personality development.

The Rise of Psychological Counseling. Freudianism often receives the lion's share of attention in historical treatments of psychotherapy, and indeed prior to 1945 most of the psychotherapists in private practice and many of the best-known treatment centers, such as the Menninger Clinic in Topeka, Kansas, were psychoanalytically oriented. Nevertheless, throughout the twentieth century psychoanalysis remained a relatively minor component of the broader psychotherapeutic enterprise. Many people found both the cost and the time involved in analysis prohibitive. In addition, for much of the twentieth century, analysts, like the institutes where they were trained, remained concentrated almost entirely in a relatively few large urban areas. Although the medical profession worked assiduously to secure a monopoly on psychoanalytic practice, this effort did not extend to psychotherapy as a whole. The realization quickly spread that psychotherapeutic skill did not require a medical degree, and during the 1920s and 1930s; practitioners in university counseling centers and community-based child-guidance clinics provided psychotherapy to their clients. The clergy, who were beginning to receive formal training in pastoral counseling, increasingly practiced psychotherapy as part of their vocational effort to cure souls. In fact, prior to *World War II, ministers may have provided more hours of therapy in America than all other professional groups combined.

Before 1941, however, few Americans were inclined to describe conversations with their clergy or the other varieties of counseling to which they were exposed as psychotherapy. Rather, most tended to stigmatize psychotherapy as a clinical treatment used exclusively with "crazy people." World War II, however, proved to be a watershed in both the availability and the popularity of therapy. The sheer number of war-related mental disorders made it necessary to bring a growing number of clinical psychologists, who had previously worked in institutional settings assisting educators, physicians, and business executives with aptitude and personality tests, into the counseling setting.

Post-World War II Trends. After the war, clinical psychologists continued to practice psychotherapy. Indeed, during the second half of the twentieth century the number of professionally trained psychotherapists—psychiatrists, clinical psychologists, marriage and school-guidance counselors, clinical social workers, and clergy who provided counseling—increased dramatically. By the 1990s, depending on one's criteria for training and licensure, between 100,000 and 250,000 psychotherapists were practicing in the United States.

World War II also helped to democratize psychotherapy. The vigorous campaign of psychiatrists to screen the population for military fitness, coupled with the numerous instances of psychological disturbance associated with the war, suggested that many "normal" people could profit from therapy. In turn, psychotherapy lost much of its stigma. At the same time, *health insurance increasingly included coverage for therapeutic practices. By 1990 approximately a third of all Americans had received psychotherapy at some point in their lives.

Post-World War II psychotherapeutic theories and practices varied enormously. Between 1945 and 1970 ego *psychology continued to dominate American psychoanalysis. Subsequently, however, many analysts in the United States, influenced especially by British "object relations" theory and the "self psychology" of Hans Kohut, tended to focus on issues relating to representations of self and object and the relationship between them. Within the larger realm of psychotherapy, eclecticism reigned. In the quarter century after 1945, humanistic psychology, most notably the non-directive, "client-centered" practice of Carl Rogers and the "self-actualization" theory associated most closely with Abraham Maslow, became increasingly influential. Humanistic psychologists, who regarded the self as the ultimate source of values, insisted on the ability of individuals to achieve self-determination. Personal growth, rather than mental stability, they maintained, constituted the appropriate goal of human life. Even after the mid-1970s, when mainstream psychological theory began to move away from humanistic psychology, the importance of choice and the desirability of growth continued to be emphasized within therapeutic circles.

Criticism of Psychotherapy and the Pharmacological Challenge. Criticism of psychotherapy intensified even as its popularity increased. In 1952, for example, the eminent British experimental psychologist Hans Eysenck denied that there was persuasive evidence of psychotherapy's value. Other psychologists and cultural critics echoed this charge. People of the left assailed psychotherapy for fostering adjustment to a corrupt and inhumane status quo, while critics on the right charged that it fostered a victim mentality. The assaults on psychoanalysis, and particularly on the legitimacy of Freudian theory and practice, became so intense as the twentieth century ended as to constitute almost a cottage industry.

Perhaps the most serious post-1970 challenge to psychotherapy came from pharmacology. A growing number of newly developed drugs treated not only major mental illnesses but also less serious conditions that in previous years would have prompted people to enter therapy. Mood-altering drugs such as Prozac enjoyed great popularity. Whether drugs served as an appropriate substitute for psychotherapy or simply alleviated symptoms while leaving the underlying causes of mental distress untreated remained a point of controversy.

Notwithstanding the hostility of critics and the presence of alternative approaches, many Americans continued to look to psychotherapy not only as a means of grappling with acute emotional and mental distress but also as a route to self-knowledge and personal growth. So popular and persuasive did psychotherapy's approach to the human condition become that a number of observers characterized late-twentieth-century America as a "therapeutic society."

[*See also* Health and Fitness; Intelligence, Concepts of; Medicine: From the 1870s to 1945; Medicine: Since 1945; Menninger, Karl and William; Mental Health Institutions; Pharmaceutical Industry; Religion; Sexual Morality and Sex Reform.]

• Nathan G. Hale Jr., *Freud and the Americans: The Beginnings of Psychoanalysis in the United States, 1876–1917,* 1971. Morris N. Eagle, *Recent Developments in Psychoanalysis: A Critical Evaluation,* 1987. John C. Burnham, *Paths into American Culture: Psychology, Medicine, and Morals,* 1988. John C. Burnham, "Psychology and Counseling: Convergence into a Profession," in *The Professions in American History,* ed. Nathan O. Hatch, 1988, pp. 181–197. Donald K. Freedheim, ed., *History of Psychotherapy: A Century of Change,* 1992. Nathan G. Hale Jr., *The Rise and Crisis of Psychoanalysis in the United States: Freud and the Americans, 1917–1985,* 1995. Ellen Herman, *The Romance of American Psychology: Political Culture in the Age of Experts,* 1995. Eric Caplan, *Mind Games: American Culture and the Birth of Psychotherapy,* 1998.

—Jon H. Roberts

PUBLIC BROADCASTING. Throughout their history, public *radio and *television have struggled to survive in a minimally regulated broadcasting system dominated by commercial interests. Although educational radio stations airing instructional programming were prevalent in the 1920s, their numbers plummeted in the 1930s in the face of economic hard times and powerful national commercial radio networks. The limited federal regulatory legislation of the interwar years, primarily the Communications Act of 1934 that established the *Federal Communications Commission (FCC), made no explicit provision for educational and nonprofit stations.

This situation remained largely unchanged for the next thirty years despite the FCC's reservation of a small number of radio bands and television channels for nonprofit stations. Then, in 1966, spurred by the FCC's failure to diversify commercial television and reflecting the spirit of President Lyndon B. *Johnson's *Great Society initiatives, a report by the Carnegie Commission on Educational Television on the state of public broadcasting led to the most significant event in the history of the medium: the passage of the Public Broadcasting Act of 1967. To address congressional concerns about the dangers of both political interference and the creation of a "fourth network," the legislation established a highly decentralized structure under which the newly formed Corporation for Public Broadcasting (CPB) would allocate federal grants to separate national associations of noncommercial television and radio stations—incorporated in 1969 as the Public Broadcasting Service (PBS) and National Public Radio (NPR). These associations would in turn coordinate interconnection among their member stations.

Over the following three decades, federal funding, the number of stations, and the audience for public programming all grew substantially, and the medium solidified its position in American culture. Many programs attracted a large and loyal audience including public radio's news feature *All Things Considered* and Garrison Keillor's variety show *A Prairie Home Companion*; PBS's educational and witty children's show *Sesame Street*; the British drama import *Masterpiece Theatre*; the science series *Cosmos* and *Nova*; and *Eyes on the Prize,* the 1987 series documenting the history of the *civil rights movement. Charged with the sometimes contradictory mandate of providing unique, high-quality, and diverse programming to the most varied audience possible while maintaining strict objectivity and balance, public broadcasting faced increasing criticism from both the political left and right. From the left came charges that women and minorities were underrepresented, that programming catered too much to an elite audience, and that the system had become overly reliant on corporate underwriters. Conservatives complained that the CPB and public-broadcasting networks were overly centralized bureaucracies that reflected a liberal, even left-wing bias and used federal funds to glorify aberrant social practices. The conservative critique came to a head in 1995 when the Republican-controlled Congress called for the phased-in elimination of all federal funding for public broadcasting. However, a widespread show of support (particularly for the beloved *Sesame Street*) defeated this effort.

In the heyday of the major networks' almost exclusive control of the airwaves, public broadcasting clearly provided innovative and influential children's, cultural, and public-affairs programming that was otherwise unavailable. Although public television and radio continued to provide moments of national cultural import, such as Ken Burns's 1990 documentary series *The Civil War,* in the far more diverse and expansive communication environment at the turn of the century, its future remained unclear.

[*See also* Journalism.]

• John Witherspoon and Roselle Kovitz, *The History of Public Broadcasting,* 1989. Marilyn Lashley, *Public Television—Panacea, Pork Barrel, or Public Trust?,* 1992.

—Anthony Harkins

PUBLIC HEALTH. For much of American history, protecting local business figured prominently in public-health efforts. During the *Colonial Era, *smallpox and *yellow fever ravaged seaports, paralyzing business activity. Townspeople fled; shops closed; visitors avoided the stricken cities. To revitalize trade, local authorities often published false reports minimizing the danger. They also quarantined ships, established pesthouses (isolation hospitals), introduced short-term sanitary reforms, and experimented with smallpox inoculation. A major vindication of inoculation came during a 1721 *Boston epidemic that claimed nine-hundred lives. Cotton Mather championed the procedure, while Boston's most prominent physicians opposed it. Smallpox vaccination, developed by the English physician Edward Jenner, became available by 1800.

During the nineteenth century, outbreaks of *cholera, especially in 1832–1833, 1849–1850, and 1866, and other epidemic *diseases shaped public-health practice. As yellow fever devastated southern cities, physicians disagreed about whether it was contagious and how to combat it. Those who supported the broad exercise of government authority sought to quarantine incoming ships, whereas those favoring free trade and individual liberty urged the removal of decaying organic wastes, whose noxious "miasmas," they believed, caused most epidemics. (In 1900 an army medical team led by Dr. Walter *Reed at last discovered yellow fever's mode of transmission: the *Aëdes egypti* mosquito.)

By midcentury, local governments increasingly addressed public-health issues. *New York City built a municipal water system in 1842. Dr. John H. Griscom's *The Sanitary Condition of the Laboring Class of New York with Suggestions for Its Improvement* (1845) proved highly influential. New York created a permanent Metropolitan Board of Health in 1866, in response to a threatened cholera epidemic, and reformers in other cities soon followed suit. As municipal water and sewer systems replaced backyard wells, cesspools, and privies, outbreaks of cholera, *typhoid fever, dysentery, *malaria, and typhus diminished. As in the past, local business groups often led these sanitary reforms.

At the federal level, Congress in 1798 had created the U.S. Marine Hospital Service, under a Surgeon General, to care for ailing seamen. The U.S. Sanitary Commission, a volunteer agency headed by Frederick Law *Olmsted, worked to improve health and sanitary conditions in *Civil War military camps. Meanwhile, the Marine Hospital Service steadily expanded its activities, including a bacteriological research laboratory founded in the 1890s. Renamed the U.S. Public Health and

Marine Hospital Service in 1902, it eventually became simply the U.S. Public Health Service (PHS). Early PHS campaigns combated hookworm and pellagra.

With the triumph of the germ theory of disease and the advent of bacteriology in the early twentieth century, the rationale for public-health efforts shifted from ridding the environment of "miasmas" to attacking disease-causing microbes. Public health became professionalized as lay reformers gave way to physicians and scientists. The laboratory became the principal battleground against disease, with impressive results. Vaccines, serums, and tests attacked rabies, *diphtheria, typhoid fever, tuberculosis, and later, yellow fever, *poliomyelitis, measles, and whooping cough. The *Progressive Era's reform ethos opened new public-health vistas, including school-vaccination programs, maternal and child care, rural health efforts, medical inspection of immigrants, regulation of nuisance industries, inspection of food processors and providers, and campaigns to reduce infant mortality and *tuberculosis. In many of these programs, the federal government played a central role. By *World War I, there existed a vast network of governmental public-health agencies, supported by the American *Red Cross, *settlement houses, and other volunteer groups. Although organized *medicine, led by the *American Medical Association, enthusiastically supported the public-health movement, it strenuously sought to limit activities to prevention, not treatment.

As the acute, communicable diseases were defeated, attention shifted to the chronic and degenerative afflictions, especially *cancer, diabetes, stroke, and *heart disease. Public-health workers alerted the public to risk factors they could control, such as obesity; poor nutrition; lack of exercise; and, in the case of *venereal disease, unprotected sex. In the 1930s, Surgeon General Thomas Parran lifted the veil of silence surrounding syphilis. Beginning in the *New Deal Era, the federal government increasingly funded municipal and state public-health programs.

By the late twentieth century, public-health efforts at all governmental levels had vastly expanded in size and complexity. In the 1990s the PHS, now a part of the Department of Health and Human Services, included the Surgeon General's Office, with a corps of over six thousand public-health professionals; specialized agencies such as the *Indian Health Service, the Food and Drug Administration, the data-gathering *Centers for Disease Control, and the research-oriented *National Institutes of Health; and offices addressing such issues as aging, *mental illness, minority health, women's health, physical fitness, and the AIDS epidemic. The landmark *Surgeon General's Report on Smoking and Health* (1964) alerted citizens to the hazards of smoking and led to health warnings on cigarette packages, advertising restrictions, congressional investigations, and major legal challenges to the *tobacco industry. Other federal bodies addressing public-health issues included the Bureau of Prisons, the *Environmental Protection Agency, the Consumer Product Safety Commission, the Immigration and Naturalization Service, and the Occupational Safety and Health Agency. Globally, the PHS cooperated with the *World Health Organization, a *United Nations agency. From small beginnings, public health had emerged as a major governmental responsibility as the twenty-first century dawned.

[*See also* Acquired Immunodeficiency Syndrome; Federal Government, Executive Branch: Other Departments (Department of Health and Human Services); Health and Fitness; Hospitals; Immigration; Immigration Law; Industrial Diseases and Hazards; Mather, Increase and Cotton; Professionalization; Pure Food and Drug Act; Tobacco Products; Tuskegee Experiment; Urbanization.]

• Charles E. Rosenberg, *The Cholera Years: The United States in 1832, 1849, and 1866,* 1962. Judith Walzer Leavitt, *The Healthiest City: Milwaukee and the Politics of Health Reform,* 1982. Allan M. Brandt, *No Magic Bullet: A Social History of Venereal Disease in the United States since 1880,* 1985. Stuart Galishoff, *Newark, the Nation's Unhealthiest City, 1832–1895,* 1988. John Duffy, *The Sanitarians: A History of American Public Health,* 1990. Margaret Humphreys, *Yellow Fever in the South,* 1992.

—Stuart Galishoff

PUBLIC LANDS. *See* Land Policy, Federal.

PUBLIC OPINION. Since democratic theory requires leaders to respect "the will of the people" in directing the affairs of the nation, public opinion holds an exhalted place in democracies like the United States. It was an essential concept in Enlightenment political thought, and social observers from Alexis de Tocqueville to Walter *Lippmann (*Public Opinion,* 1922; *The Phantom Public,* 1925) have noted its importance in America. Most philosophers and scholars writing about public opinion in the United States agree on its role: It embodies the consent of the governed and confers legitimacy on the government. Americans have expressed their opinions on policy issues and political actions, while leaders have sought to know the popular will. Scholars have had a harder time agreeing on a definition of public opinion. However, with both the terms "public" (or "the public") and "opinion" stirring debate. Contemporary scholars appear to be comfortable defining public opinion as "the aggregated views of large numbers of people in a society on issues central to how that society functions."

Methods for determining "public opinion" have varied throughout American history. The most basic of these has been an electoral one: popular referenda on public issues, proposed laws, and enactment of (or changes to) constitutions. Tens of thousands of these have been conducted from the eighteenth century to the present. In the late twentieth century, between two hundred and three hundred referenda were typically voted upon in each election year. In the eighteenth and nineteenth centuries, less formal means were also employed, including the use of informed observers (notables, public figures, ward heelers in urban political machines), "straw polls" dating from as early as the 1820s, through the first systematic opinion surveys beginning in the late nineteenth century. Though these forms of collecting information on public opinion were reported widely in the press and avidly consumed by an increasingly literate and engaged mass readership, historians generally agree that they were not very accurate and were subject to reporting bias.

In the 1930s and 1940s, scientific polling and the use of probability samples improved methods for collecting information on the public's opinion. Notable in this era were George Gallup's founding of the influential American Institute of Public Opinion (Gallup Poll) in 1935 and the establishment of such university-based survey organizations as the National Opinion Research Center (NORC) at the University of Chicago and the Survey Research Center at the University of Michigan. As regular polls and somewhat more scientific nationwide surveys proliferated, these investigations of the public's "opinion" more accurately reflected society as a whole. Topics expanded from electoral and policy-related issues to include social problems and individuals' consumer tastes, *radio and *television preferences, and economic behavior. By the end of the twentieth century, the mass media had joined commercial and university-based survey organizations in constantly monitoring (and reporting) public attitudes. Despite ever-present concerns over the ways of manipulating public opinion (including *advertising and *propaganda), the appetite of both decision-makers and the general citizenry for information on what the public "thinks" appeared undiminished.

[*See also Democracy in America.*]

• Jean M. Converse, *Survey Research in the United States: Roots and Emergence, 1890–1960,* 1987. Susan Herbst, *Numbered Voices: How Opinion Polling Has Shaped American Politics,* 1993.

—Erik W. Austin

PUBLIC SCHOOLS. *See* Education: The Public School Movement; Education: Education in Contemporary America.

PUBLISHING. *See* Printing and Publishing.

PUEBLO REVOLT (1680). This uprising against Spanish rule in New Mexico, resulting in a rare retreat by a European colonial power, involved a complex mix of ethnic, religious, administrative, and economic grievances rooted in the Pueblo Indians' and mixed-bloods' resentment of European rule. Spanish colonizers and Franciscan missionaries had established themselves in New Mexico by 1598. Initially most of the Pueblos adapted to Spanish rule and Catholicism, but drought in the 1660s led to anti-Spanish unrest and a revival of traditional religion. Tensions worsened when Spanish soldiers under Governor Juan Francisco Trevino sacked the Pueblos' sacred kivas, publicly whipped native religious leaders, hanged three, and arrested others. One arrestee, Popé, of San Juan Pueblo, escaped to Taos Pueblo, a center of anti-Spanish resistance. Taos's economy, dependent on trading corn to the Apache to the north, had been disrupted by Spanish demands for corn. Under Popé and others, Taos fostered anti-Spanish agitation from the 1670s on. Trevino, confronted with armed insurgents, released the prisoners but tensions continued. Beginning on 10 August 1680, the insurgents killed sixty-eight Spanish colonists, destroyed Catholic churches and killed missionaries, and besieged Santa Fe. The surviving Spanish fled to Mexico.

After the violence came negotiations over the precipitating grievances. Some Pueblos, fearing Apache raiders, reestablished their Spanish ties. In 1692, Spanish authorities under Governor Diego de Vargas returned to New Mexico, having negotiated reforms that curbed Spanish power and benefited some of the revolt's mixed-blood leaders. Even so, Pueblo resistance erupted again in 1696. Contemporary historians, emphasizing the complexity of the issues and groups involved, view the revolt as a microcosm of sociocultural differences and amalgamation in a colonial setting.

[*See also* Indian History and Culture: 1500 to 1800; Spanish Settlements in North America.]

• Charles W. Hackett and C. C. Shelby, *Revolt of the Pueblo Indians of New Mexico and Otermin's Attempted Reconquest, 1680–1682,* 2 vols., 1942. David J. Weber, ed., *What Caused the Pueblo Revolt of 1680?*, 1999.

—Juan Gomez-Quinones

PUERTO RICO. An island in the Greater Antilles called "Borinquén" by the Taino (Arawakan-speaking) people who were living there when Christopher *Columbus landed in 1493, "Puerto Rico" ("wealthy port") was the name given to the island by the first Spanish governor of the island. One of the most densely populated places in the world, Puerto Rico is today home to 3.8 million people. The island's principal economic activities include pharmaceuticals, electronics, *agriculture, and *tourism.

A Spanish colony for more than four hundred years, Puerto Rico was ceded to the United States by the Treaty of Paris (1898) that ended the *Spanish-American War. After a period of U.S. military government, Congress by the Foraker Act (1900) declared the inhabitants "citizens of Puerto Rico, and as such, entitled to the protection of the United States." This act also provided for a governor and executive council to be appointed by the president; a popularly elected legislative assembly; and an elected Puerto Rican resident commissioner who could introduce legislation and speak, but not vote, in the U.S. House of Representatives. Amid continuing Puerto Rican demands for greater autonomy and representation, the Jones Act (1917) replaced the legislative council with an elected upper house and extended U.S. citizenship to Puerto Ricans. However, Puerto Rico remained, in the words of the U.S. *Supreme Court in *Downes* v. *Bidwell* (1901), an "unincorporated territory." In essence, still a U.S. colony.

Despite efforts for greater autonomy and a concerted independence movement in the 1920s and 1930s, not until the 1940s were Puerto Rico's self-government aspirations partially realized. In 1947 Congress permitted Puerto Ricans to elect their governor. Luis Muñoz Marín, the first Puerto Rican elected to this office (1949–1965), spearheaded a program of industrial development called "Operation Bootstrap" ("Operación Manos a la Obra"). Transforming an agricultural economy based on sugar, coffee, fruit, livestock, and dairy products, this program used tax incentives to attract U.S. corporations. Operation Bootstrap did bring economic betterment, but the island's population density and class divisions left many Puerto Ricans in *poverty.

Emigration, which began shortly after U.S. acquisition, has been one of the major features of the island's twentieth century history. Early migration took thousands of Puerto Ricans to *Hawai'i, as well as to parts of the Caribbean. After *World War I, migration to the mainland United States increased, concentrating in Florida as well as in urban areas of the northeastern United States, especially New York and New Jersey. At the end of the century the number of Puerto Ricans living on the mainland (almost 3 million) rivaled that on the island itself.

In 1950 the island won the right to draft and enact its own constitution. The constitution, which became law in 1952, established the Commonwealth of Puerto Rico, an anomalous status the island still retained at the end of the twentieth century. As the Estado Libre Asociado de Puerto Rico (Free Associated State of Puerto Rico), it is self-governing territory but subject to the authority of the United States. Aside from the nonvoting resident commissioner, Puerto Ricans lack representation in Congress.

As the twentieth century ended, Puerto Rico's long-term status remained unresolved. A referendum approved by the U.S. Congress and held in December 1998 placed the question of political status before the Puerto Rican electorate for the second time that decade. Forty-seven percent voted for statehood; independence and two other variants on Commonwealth status received a total of 4 percent of the vote; while 50 percent voted for "none of the above," producing a result that amounted to an ambivalent endorsement of the status quo.

[*See also* Exploration, Conquest, and Settlement, Era of European; Immigration; *Insular Cases;* Protectorates and Dependencies.]

• Gordon K. Lewis, *Puerto Rico: Freedom and Power in the Caribbean,* 1975.

—Katherine Bjork

PULITZER, JOSEPH (1847–1911), journalist. Born in Hungary, Pulitzer immigrated to America in 1864 and joined the Union army. Rootless after the *Civil War, he went to St. Louis, Missouri, and became a reporter for a German newspaper. Following the failure in 1872 of the Liberal Republican movement he had actively supported, he became a Democrat. After buying and selling several bankrupt newspapers at a profit, Pulitzer in 1878 acquired the *St. Louis Dispatch,* merged it with the *Post,* and turned the *Post-Dispatch* into a profitable newspaper with a formula of sensationalism and attacks on municipal corruption. With its profits he bought the floundering *New York World* in 1883.

The *World* quickly became a morning leader, attacking political corruption and the aristocracy of wealth. Such coverage, supplemented with cartoons, pictures, headlines, and crime news, appealed to *New York City's growing immigrant population. In 1887, Pulitzer added a more sensational evening edition. He "retired" that year because of poor health and failing eyesight but continued to offer daily criticism and suggestions from his vacation retreats and yachts. The *World*'s sensationalism, especially its Cuban coverage, reached a peak in 1896–1898 during a circulation war with William Randolph *Hearst's *Journal.* Pulitzer's paper grew more responsible after the *Spanish-American War, opposing imperialism and supporting reforms favored by the *Democratic party. The *World* opposed Tammany Hall, New York City's corrupt Democratic organization, and Pulitzer bolted the party in 1896 in opposition to William Jennings *Bryan and the *free silver movement. In 1908, the *World* was sued for libel by the government for its exposés of corruption in Theodore *Roosevelt's acquisition of the *Panama Canal Zone, but in 1911, in an important First Amendment case, the *Supreme Court upheld a lower court's dismissal of the indictment.

Pulitzer's sons proved unable to keep the *World* profitable after his death, and in 1931 it was sold to the Scripps-Howard group. Before Pulitzer's death he gave two million dollars to Columbia University to establish a school of *journalism and the *Pulitzer Prizes.

[*See also* Gilded Age; Urbanization.]

• W. A. Swanberg, *Pulitzer*, 1967.

—James L. Crouthamel

PULITZER PRIZES. First awarded by Columbia University in 1917, the Pulitzer Prizes in *journalism and the arts were established by the newspaper publisher Joseph *Pulitzer. To the original categories of fiction, drama, history, biography, meritorious public service, editorial writing, and reporting were later added *poetry, *music, general nonfiction, commentary, criticism, *photography (spot news and feature), and editorial cartooning; reporting was separated into local (general and specialized investigative), national, and international. The initial terms of the arts awards, requiring wholesome manners and moral uplift, were soon liberalized. A sizable number of women have been honorees in letters—though fewer in journalism. By the late twentieth century, the awards honored authors who were racially and ethnically diverse, and dramatists treating gay themes. Biographies about presidents and literary figures have dominated the prize as have histories of westward expansion, the *Civil War, and, eventually, the *civil rights movement. Journalistic articles against the *Ku Klux Klan and political corruption; defenses of *civil liberties and freedom of the press; accounts of school desegregation, race riots, and environmental pollution; and coverage of human-rights violations, famine, and refugees abroad have all been recognized.

Beginning in 1975, after the *New York Times* had won a Pulitzer Prize for publishing the *Pentagon Papers about the United States' involvement in Southeast Asia as had the *Washington Post* for coverage of the *Watergate break-in, the trustees of Columbia University withdrew from ratifying the awards, leaving sole authority to the Pulitzer Prize Advisory Board. Two spot-news photographs from the early 1970s, of an antiwar protester killed by a National Guardsman at Kent State University and of a screaming South Vietnamese girl running naked after being napalmed by U.S. bombers captured the conscience of the nation.

[*See also* Bill of Rights; Kent State and Jackson State; Vietnam War.]

• John Hohenberg, *The Pulitzer Prizes: A History of the Awards in Books, Drama, Music, and Journalism, Based on the Private Files over Six Decades*, 1974. Sheryle Leekley and John Leekley, eds., *Moments: The Pulitzer Prize Photographs*, 1978. John Hohenberg, ed., *The Pulitzer Prize Story II: Award-Winning News Stories, Columns, Editorials, Cartoons, and News Pictures, 1959–1980*, 1980. Hall Buell, *Moments: The Pulitzer Prize-Winning Photographs, A Visual Chronicle of Our Time*, 1999.

—Thomas P. Adler

PULLMAN STRIKE AND BOYCOTT. On 11 May 1894, employees at the Pullman Car Works on *Chicago's far South Side walked off their jobs, launching one of the most notable labor actions of the late nineteenth century. Recently organized by the American Railway Union (ARU), the strikers protested the company's wage cuts in response to the depression of 1893 that left them, their families, and their communities impoverished.

The strike quickly attracted national attention. The company town of Pullman that the industrialist George Pullman (1831–1897) had built adjacent to his railroad car works had for a dozen years stood as a highly contested model of a managed urban environment where workers' families could theoretically enjoy *capitalism's opportunities in a carefully planned, closely supervised paternalistic environment. By striking, Pullman's employees, half of whom lived in Pullman, challenged the idea of shared labor-capital interests that underlay the town's design and corporate control.

The strike spread in late June when the ARU national convention voted to boycott all trains carrying Pullman sleeping cars. Beginning 26 June, the boycott disrupted rail traffic nationwide. When the railroads tried to resume operations, violence erupted in Chicago. The federal government under President Grover *Cleveland intervened, sending troops to restore order. Attorney General Richard Olney (himself on the board of several *railroads) secured an injunction against the boycott, on the grounds that the strike was disrupting the U.S. mail. ARU officers, including the president, Eugene V. *Debs, were prosecuted and imprisoned. The success of the injunction, upheld by the U.S. *Supreme Court in 1895, ensured that similar injunctions would be used against unions for years to come.

Although the railroad boycott collapsed in mid-July, the strike at Pullman continued for another month. By then, many political and business leaders sympathized with the strikers. Pullman's stubbornness, they felt, had possibly caused the strike and definitely prolonged it. The U.S. Strike Commission chaired by Carroll Wright, head of the Bureau of Labor in the Department of the Interior, concurred, acknowledging that unions and government regulation might be necessary safeguards against unbounded corporate power.

[*See also* Depressions, Economic; Gilded Age; Industrialization; Labor Movements; Strikes and Industrial Conflict.]

• Almont Lindsey, *The Pullman Strike*, 1942. Carl Smith, *Urban Disorder and the Shape of Belief*, 1995.

—Janice L. Reiff

PURE FOOD AND DRUG ACT. Signed into law on 30 June 1906 by President Theodore *Roosevelt, the Food and Drugs Act—popularly know as the Pure Food and Drug Act—with its companion piece the Meat Inspection Amendment, originated the regulatory apparatus that became the Food and Drug Administration. This landmark statute prohibited the "misbranding" of any foodstuff or pharmaceutical offered for sale or their "adulteration" by any ingredient not specified on the label. Congress authorized the Bureau of Chemistry of the Department of Agriculture to enforce the law by testing random specimens for misbranding or adulteration, notifying suspect manufacturers, and granting them a hearing. Only if a manufacturer refused to comply could the bureau turn the case over to a district attorney for prosecution. Convictions carried fines of up to three hundred dollars and imprisonment for up to one year, with confiscation of the offending product the ultimate punishment.

Dr. Harvey W. Wiley (1844–1930), chief chemist of the Department of Agriculture from 1883 to 1912, was the moving force behind the law. Wiley publicized the problem by feeding dubious preservatives to volunteers dubbed the "poison squad." For over two decades, Wiley functioned as the chief propagandist, organizer, and strategist for the law, and then as its principal enforcer. Public support for such a law grew steadily thanks to a series of reports on harmful and unsanitary meatpacking processes published in muckraking magazines and in Upton *Sinclair's 1906 exposé, *The *Jungle*. The measure won backing from a broad-based coalition including the National Association of State Dairy and Food Departments, the *National Consumers' League, the *American Medical Association, and the General Federation of Women's Clubs, joined by some well-established manufacturers seeking to eliminate marginal competitors. Its opponents included the National Food Manufacturers' Association; the National Liquor Wholesale Dealers' Association; and the Proprietary Association of America, the drug industry's lobbying arm. Sponsored by two Republican senators and by two GOP congressmen, and aided by an eleventh-hour endorsement by Roosevelt, the final bill passed both houses by overwhelming margins and stands as a major *Progressive Era legislative achievement.

[*See also* Consumer Movement; Economic Regulation; Federal Government, Executive Branch: Department of Agriculture; Food and Diet; Health and Fitness; Meatpacking and Meat Processing Industry; Muckrakers; Pharmaceutical Industry; Women's Club Movement.]

• Oscar E. Anderson Jr., *The Health of a Nation: Harvey W. Wiley and the Fight for Pure Food,* 1958. James Harvey Young, *Pure Food: Securing the Federal Food and Drugs Act of 1906,* 1989.

—John D. Buenker

PURITANISM. Puritanism has been defined variously in intellectual, political, or cultural terms, but it is best understood as a religious sensibility centered around conversion—the Holy Spirit's regeneration of the soul—and the concomitant determination to restore the purity of the apostolic church and reform society according to God's laws. Theologically, Puritanism represents an emphasis within the Reformed Protestant (Calvinist) tradition on intense personal devotion and extreme ethical probity. During the late sixteenth and early seventeenth centuries, English divines described how during conversion those whom God elects to save (the saints) undergo a protracted spiritual experience in which they regret their sins, despair of obtaining eternal life, discover that they are redeemed by their faith in Christ alone, and celebrate the assurance that through him their salvation is absolutely secure. This "new birth" instills in the elect feelings of spiritual power and a zeal to demonstrate their love to God and to fellow saints by carrying out the Lord's commands. Puritan piety was characterized by a veneration of the *Bible as the rule for living righteously and a pervasive sense that God providentially supervises all human affairs.

Puritanism emerged in Elizabethan England among a minority of ministers and laypeople upset that the Church of England had neither fully eliminated "papist" practices nor organized itself according to what Puritans considered the proper biblical pattern. The ecclesiastical hierarchy and the government resisted their efforts to, for example, eliminate ornate clerical vestments, and with the suppression in 1590 of the classical movement, which advocated using local ministerial boards instead of church courts to administer discipline, most Puritans gave up direct institutional challenges, instead concentrating their efforts on encouraging conversion and assembling "the godly" into parish groups for mutual edification and moral oversight. A few hundred Separatists left the Church of England completely, holding it to be false; one such band, the *Pilgrims, settled *Plymouth Colony in Massachusetts in 1620. William Laud's rise to power, culminating with his becoming archbishop of Canterbury in 1633, once again crystallized Puritan discontents; Laud championed a different theology, forbade Puritan liturgical practices, and harassed nonconforming ministers. Puritans interpreted his ascendance along with Charles I's dismissal of Parliament, economic depression, and social dislocation as signs of God's displeasure with England. The voyage to Massachusetts of Governor John *Winthrop and seven hundred colonists in 1630 inaugurated the decade-long "great migration" during which thousands traveled to *New England hoping to erect a properly constituted church and a morally ordered society.

Once in America, Puritans developed an ecclesiastical government along lines advised by the Puritan ministers John Cotton (1584–1652) and Thomas Hooker (1586–1647). Formally codified in the Cambridge Platform of 1648, it granted each Congregational church autonomy over its own business, expanded the laity's disciplinary power, revised the liturgy, and obliged the state to support the churches—by such means as punishing heresy, for example—without giving the magistrates authority over religious practice. Churches were gathered by laymen who covenanted together to worship with and watch over each other, and who then called a minister to lead them. Every person within a town was obliged to attend services, but only regenerates—individuals who had demonstrated that they had been born again—received the sacraments. The clergy and membership admitted new members after scrutinizing their behavior, conversion experience, and knowledge of doctrine, and excommunicated any found to be ungodly. Public worship focused on the sermon and also included singing from *The *Bay Psalm Book;* private devotion featured family prayers and individual meditation. Each church ruled itself, although clergymen did meet informally to discuss issues of mutual concern. The magistracy upheld church order by punishing immorality, convening ministerial synods to resolve doctrinal disputes, and suppressing unorthodoxy, banishing dissenters like Roger *Williams and Anne *Hutchinson.

Having set up their ecclesiastical and devotional order, Puritans struggled to sustain it in the face of their children's declining conversion rate, congregational contentions over such issues as clerical salaries, and the appearance of a competing folk culture manifested in gaming and immoderate drinking. In response, Puritans reasserted traditional values, stepped up campaigns against misbehavior, and devised novel means of recruiting churchgoers. Preachers warned audiences against breaking New England's special relationship with God and urged magistrates to intensify their vigilance against immorality. Spurred by Increase Mather, the leading Puritan minister of *Boston, the Reforming Synod of 1679–1680 cataloged the population's sins and demanded redress; in its wake, churches renewed their covenants to revitalize personal piety and families refurbished domestic spiritual exercises, abetted by the growing availability of imported devotional manuals. In 1702, Cotton Mather (the son of Increase) founded a male society to help suppress social disorder in Boston, the prototype of moral-reform associations. To ensure continuing church discipline, the *Half-Way Covenant (1662) allowed baptizing the children of regenerate grandparents even if the childrens' parents had not been born again. Solomon Stoddard (1643–1729) opened the Lord's Supper to unregenerates in hopes of converting them, and he led his Northampton, Massachusetts, congregation in five "refreshings," periods of intensified spirituality that heightened church membership. These devices obtained mixed results. The number of Congregational churches expanded, conversions increased, and Puritan moral values continued as New England's norms. Nevertheless, Saints remained a minority of the population, rival denominations gained adherents, secular cultural forms thrived, and England's growing imperial presence destroyed the magistrates' ability to support the Congregational churches exclusively.

Puritanism made a substantial impact on Anglo-America. Seventeenth-century New England possessed a far more powerful religious establishment than did other English colonies. The Puritan method of gathering churches through voluntary lay action, replicated in the formation of town meetings, helped stimulate popular participation in politics. Puritan moral values made New England a watchword for sobriety—it had a lower percentage of illegitimate births than other regions—and may have instilled habits of economic discipline that abetted commercial growth. More generally, Puritanism underlay the colonies' dominant religious style; from its doctrinal and experiential matrix issued not only New England Congregationalism, but also varieties of Presbyterian and Baptist practice. Updated by Jonathan *Edwards in the mid–eighteenth century, Reformed Protestantism became America's leading theological tradition. Finally, the awakenings generated by Stoddard, Edwards, and others evolved into one type of religious revival, the most potent evangelical mechanism in American religious history.

[*See also* Baptists; Colonial Era; Mather, Increase and Cotton; Protestantism; Religion; Revivalism; Salem Witchcraft; Society of Friends.]

• Charles E. Hambrick-Stowe, *The Practice of Piety,* 1982. Charles L. Cohen, *God's Caress,* 1986. Harry Stout, *The New England Soul,* 1986. David D. Hall, *Worlds of Wonder, Days of Judgment,* 1989. Stephen Foster, *The Long Argument,* 1991. Richard Gildrie, *The Profane, the Civil, and the Godly,* 1994.

—Charles L. Cohen

Q

QUAKERISM. *See* Society of Friends.

QUANTUM PHYSICS. *See* Physical Sciences.

QUASI-WAR WITH FRANCE. In 1797, during the Anglo-French war that had started four years earlier, France began capturing American ships and cargoes in retaliation for the failure of the United States to protect its neutral commerce with France against British searches and seizures. France was dependent on American shipping to supply its empire because the superior British navy had swept French merchant vessels from the seas. When *Jay's Treaty between the United States and Great Britain was ratified and implemented in 1796 with no guarantee of American neutral rights, France announced that it would henceforth seize neutral American shipping just as the British did.

President John *Adams sent a delegation to France to try to resolve the dispute. But the French foreign minister, Talleyrand, demanded a bribe and treated the delegation with contempt. This so-called *XYZ Affair led Adams and Congress to prepare for war by increasing military appropriations and permitting American ships to fire on marauding French vessels. Neither the United States nor France formally declared war, hence the term "Quasi-War." Hostilities were limited to a few ship-to-ship battles. But Talleyrand had not wished the conflict to go even that far. He informed American diplomats that France would accept another American mission. Against the wishes of many in his own *Federalist party, Adams authorized William Vans Murray, Oliver Ellsworth, and William R. Davie to negotiate a settlement. In the resulting Treaty of Mortefontaine (also known as the Convention of 1800), France agreed to stop illegal seizures.

France also agreed to suspend the Franco-American alliance that had been in effect since the *Revolutionary War. The United States would avoid all further "entangling alliances" (a phrase used by Thomas *Jefferson in his first inaugural address in 1801) until *World War II. Meanwhile, although most Americans supported Adams's peace, the president's peacemaking divided his party and Republican Thomas Jefferson defeated him for the presidency in 1800.

[*See also* Early Republic, Era of the; Foreign Relations: U.S. Relations with Europe.]

• Alexander DeConde, *The Quasi-War,* 1966. Daniel G. Lang, *Foreign Policy in the Early Republic,* 1985.

—Jerald A. Combs

QUILTS AND QUILTING, folk craft and art form. The distinctive patterns of quilts are created from sewn-together pieces of cloth, appliquéd cutout designs, or a solid piece of fabric called whole cloth. A middle insulating layer of batting and two layers of pieced, appliqued, or whole cloth form the completed quilt. While being made, the quilt is held and stretched by a frame or hoop. Quilted garments are depicted on ancient Egyptian sculpture and appear as medieval armor and eighteenth century petticoats. In colonial America, quilted coverlets were imported from Europe. By the mid-nineteenth century, patchwork quilts were created and appreciated throughout America at every socioeconomic level.

In addition to their original utilitarian function as bedding, quilts are made to mark national and community events, births, friendships, betrothals, marriages or death. The U.S. AIDS Memorial Quilt, begun in 1985, grew to contain over 32,000 panels. A lexicon of over four thousand patchwork patterns was compiled and recorded by quilt historian Barbara Brackman in the *Encyclopedia of Pieced Quilt Patterns* (1993). Distinct categories of quilt designs include African American, Native American, Amish, and Hawaiian.

By the late twentieth century, quilts had come to be recognized as important artifacts of North American women's history and testaments to otherwise suppressed artistic voices. The growing awareness of quilts as an art form was marked in 1971 by an exhibition at the Whitney Museum of Art in New York. The American Quilt Study Group (San Francisco) was formed in 1980. A 1987 study by the American Folklife Center at the *Library of Congress identified over 700 public, corporate, and private museums and quilt collections in the United States and Canada housing over 25,000 quilts, related diaries, letters, photographs, taped interviews, films, and publications. Many states, counties, and regions have initiated projects to document quilts. Today quilting may encompass traditional craft, folk art, or abstract art, and quilts are as likely to be found on a museum wall as on a bed.

[*See also* Domestic Labor; Folk Art and Crafts; Mennonites and Amish.]

• Roderick Kiracofe, *The American Quilt: A History of Cloth and Comfort 1750–1950,* 1993. Robert Shaw, *Quilts: A Living Tradition,* 1995.

—Lisa Turner Oshins

R

RABI, ISIDOR I. (1898–1988), physicist and Nobel laureate. Born in eastern Europe, Isidor Isaac Rabi was brought by his parents to the United States when he was two years old. After obtaining his Ph.D. in physics from Columbia University in 1926, he went to Europe to study with the physicists who created quantum mechanics. In Otto Stern's Hamburg laboratory, Rabi began his work in molecular beam physics. From 1929 to 1967, he was a professor of physics at Columbia University. His discovery of the magnetic resonance method in 1938 won him the Nobel Prize in physics in 1944. A major field of study after *World War II, the magnetic resonance method became the basis for the medical diagnostic method called magnetic resonance imaging (MRI).

During World War II, Rabi served as the associate director of the Radiation Laboratory at the Massachusetts Institute of Technology, where radar systems were developed. Rabi was also one of J. Robert *Oppenheimer's senior advisers on the *Manhattan Project in Los Alamos, New Mexico.

After the war, Rabi became active in public affairs. As a member and chair of the Science Advisory Committee during President Dwight D. *Eisenhower's administration, he reconstituted the group as the President's Science Advisory Committee, which reported directly to the president. With Dag Hammarskjöld, secretary general of the *United Nations, he organized the first International Conference on the Peaceful Uses of Atomic Energy, held in Geneva, in 1955.

[*See also* Medicine: Since 1945; Nuclear Weapons; Physical Sciences; Science: From 1914 to 1945; Science: Since 1945.]

• John S. Rigden, *Rabi: Scientist and Citizen*, 1987.

—John S. Rigden

RACE, CONCEPT OF. The term "race" with reference to human beings first appeared in English literature in the sixteenth century as a classifactory term with a meaning similar to "kind" or "type," as in "a race of bishops" or "a race of saints." In the eighteenth century the term was more frequently applied to the diverse populations in England's American colonies: the Native Americans, Africans, and Europeans. Here race evolved as a ranking system reflecting the dominant English attitudes toward these populations. Conquered Indians were kept separate and apart from Europeans, often exploited, or moved off their lands for new settlers. *Slavery for Africans and their descendants was gradually institutionalized over the late seventeenth and early eighteenth centuries, and most Africans were identified primarily as property and sources of wealth.

In that same century, European scientists were collecting and organizing materials on the newly discovered indigenous peoples of the New World, Asia, and Africa. Carolus Linnaeus, Johann Blumenbach, and other systematists perceived physically differing groups as representing variants within a single human species. They established categories based on skin color and other physical traits, but they often included customs and habits as reported by travelers, missionaries, sailors, and merchants. These data were often not objective, but the rudimentary classifications helped to make sense of increasingly complex world realities. As these descriptions and classifications spread to learned people in Europe and America, they were readily assimilated to existing folk ideas about human differences.

During the late eighteenth century, a growing *antislavery movement, promoting the Revolutionary Era ideology of liberty, justice, equality, and democracy, threatened the deeply entrenched system of American slavery. Defenders of the institution developed new, stronger rationalizations for slavery, focusing on the nature of the slaves themselves and exaggerating the differences between Africans and Europeans. Linking certain behaviors with "negro" biology, they concocted an image of Africans as innately wild and uncivilized and an inferior human type whose natural state was slavery.

The earliest sustained arguments on black inferiority thus emerged during this period. Scholarly publications on race differences by such men as Edward Long, a Jamaican jurist and plantation owner, and Charles White, an English physician, drew upon an ancient model, the hierarchical "Great Chain of Being," to argue for the natural inferiority of Africans. Thomas *Jefferson and other slaveowners speculated on, and most accepted, this rationalization. In his *Notes on the State of Virginia* (1784–1785), Jefferson advanced "as a suspicion only" the view that blacks were "inferior to the whites in the endowments both of body and mind."

As abolitionism strengthened during the early nineteenth century, folk images of blacks and Indians (and later Chinese) as inherently lesser forms of human beings were magnified and widely publicized. Scientific writings mirrored and legitimated evolving folk beliefs. By mid-century, *Philadelphia physician Samuel Morton, who collected and measured skulls; Harvard zoologist Louis *Agassiz; Alabama physician Josiah Nott; and others were identifying "the negro" as a separate human species. A major scientific debate at mid-century centered on "the negro's place in nature." On one side were polygenists who, using cranial measurements and archeological evidence, asserted that blacks had been created separately and were a distinct species; on the other were the monogenists who, for equally scientific reasons, supported the notion of a single creation, but claimed that "the negro" had degenerated. Both camps and the general public accepted an image of "the negro" that was tantamount to a species distinction. The assumption of the biological, intellectual, moral, and social inequality of races continued long after the *Civil War, shaping laws, customs, social policies, and popular beliefs.

Thus, race in the nineteenth century was institutionalized as a form of social stratification predicated on beliefs about the innate inequality of human groups. Visible physical differences once attributed to geography and climate (or to a divine curse visited upon Noah's son Ham in the biblical account of the flood) had become markers of social status. Popular pejorative beliefs about low-status races served to justify exploitation and discrimination. As the ideology evolved, race became the premier explanation for the morals, character, and cultural achievement of all peoples. More important, racial characteristics were perceived as inherited and relatively immutable.

Race was soon reified as a category with important sociopolitical implications. Francis Galton and Herbert Spencer in England buttressed the notion of hereditary inequality, and Charles Darwin's theory of *evolution provided a "natural" explanation for whatever human differences were assumed to exist. Europeans began to segment their own populations into superior (Nordic) and inferior (Alpine and Mediterranean) races—views reflected in the influential publications of French writer Arthur de Gobineau (1853–1855) and Englishman Houston S. Chamberlain (1899). In Germany, Jews and other ethnic minorities were consciously transformed into inferior "racial" populations. As the Nazi party won power in Germany in the 1930s, the racial worldview reached its zenith with sterilization policies and genocide as the end products.

In the United States, some twentieth-century psychologists promoted IQ tests to determine intellectual differences among races. Such tests, however, have been shown to reflect levels of education and cultural experience. Numerous popular writers, such as Madison Grant in *The Passing of the Great Race* (1916), reiterated the ideology of race differences and the need for segregation and differential treatment. This continued (absent the argument for segregation) with publications like Richard Herrnstein's and Charles Murray's *The Bell Curve* (1994).

Throughout this history, some scholars and others have opposed the idea of race and its stereotypes, especially the notion of inequality. Frederick *Douglass and John *Brown in the nineteenth century and anthropologists Franz *Boas and Ashley Montagu (and many others) in the twentieth strongly combated popular race beliefs. While most Americans of the late twentieth century disavowed *racism, belief in the objective reality of race as identity persisted, linked to observable physical differences. Because races are significant social constructs, race remained a category in the 2000 U.S. *Census and continued to constitute an important topic in public discourse.

With advances in the science of *genetics, scientists have found greater genetic differences *within* purported "racial" groups than *between* them. Some scientists deny that "races" are exclusive and distinct biogenetic groups and increasingly argue that race has no meaning in the biological world. It is a cultural invention about human differences.

[*See also* African Americans; Anthropology; Anti-Semitism; Cultural Pluralism; Eugenics; Indian History and Culture: The Indian in Popular Culture; Nativist Movement; Psychology; Race and Ethnicity.]

• Alexander Alland Jr., *Human Diversity*, 1971. George M. Fredrickson, *The Black Image in the White Mind*, 1971, reprint 1987. John S. Haller, *Outcasts from Evolution: Scientific Attitudes of Racial Inferiority, 1859–1900*, 1971. Edmund S. Morgan, *American Slavery, American Freedom*, 1975. Elazar Barkan, *The Retreat of Scientific Racism*, 1992. Audrey Smedley, *Race in North America: Origin and Evolution of a Worldview*, 2d ed., 1998.

—Audrey Smedley

RACE AND ETHNICITY. Race and ethnicity have always mattered in the American experience. But their meanings and actualizations have changed over time and space, suggesting that they are social, not scientific, categories. Neither fixed nor permanent, they are continually negotiated and renegotiated. Race and ethnicity, or supposed physical and cultural groupings, respectively, were not always so defined or distinguished. America's first peoples formed economic, political, and ethnic groupings by language, kinship, and religious belief. They created idealized hierarchies that favored their own group over others. These perceived commonalities and differences justified belief systems and practices, alliances and fractures, cooperation and exploitation that shifted as time passed and situations changed.

America's Indigenous Peoples and the Columbian Encounter. Hunters and gatherers organized bands that competed for land and resources with one another and also with herders and agriculturists. Language formed a basis for unions such as the *Iroquois Confederacy that arose during the mid–fifteenth century in present-day central New York involving the Seneca, Cayuga, Onondaga, Oneida, and Mohawk "nations." Ethnic relations sometimes were expressed in terms of *gender. During the mid–eighteenth century, for example, the Mohawks considered their dependents, the Delawares, to be "women," while classing themselves as "men." These diverse social organizations and ethnic relations among native peoples became blurred and racialized with the entry of Europeans into the Americas. The conquest of America's peoples by Europeans was represented by the victors in ethnic, racial, and sometimes sexual terms. Christopher *Columbus on his first voyage in 1492 abducted some ten to twenty-five Indians to exhibit in Spain as specimens from exotic lands. During subsequent visits, Columbus and his men exerted themselves as conquerors over the Indians, demanding their labor and property, capturing and exporting them as slaves, and raping women. Indian resistance—refusing to plant crops, running away, or rebelling—prompted Spanish retaliation and warfare that, together with introduced *diseases, decimated the Indian population. The Spaniards who first settled on the North American continent in 1519 petitioned King Charles V for permission to punish natives who opposed them because, the colonists claimed, they were infidels and practiced homosexuality.

Conquest involved both extermination and propagation. Sexual relations and intermarriage between Spanish men and Indian women, common during the colonial period, resulted in the formation of a new group called "mestizos" or mixed peoples. Mestizos, as a distinct group, occupied a third position that was neither Spanish nor Indian and revealed the porous boundaries of racial categories. Nevertheless, the borders that delimited the racialized categories of Europeans, mestizos, and Indians generally reflected their respective political class positions with Europeans on top, mestizos in the middle, Indians at the bottom. Wealth and social status, however, could blur categories and hierarchies of race, so that "Spanish"—which could be either a racial or national designation—came to indicate a member of the ruling *social class.

Plantation economies and horrific population declines among the Indians led to the traffic in enslaved peoples from West Africa that introduced another element in the American racial equation. Sugar, its cultivation and its products, was the initial reason for the eventual enslavement of an estimated ten million Africans and their transport across the Atlantic to the Americas that began in 1503 and ended in 1888 when the last slaves were emancipated in Brazil. Throughout the Caribbean, a small white elite governed large numbers of Indians, mestizos, and enslaved Africans, who provided much of the labor required for sugar production. Legal codes enforced the supremacy of masters over servants, and economic gain determined social relationships. Like the islands' indigenous peoples, Africans resisted their enslavement, ran away, and initiated rebellions, the most significant of which was the Haitian revolution of 1791–1804 that installed a free, African-led republic. The pattern established in the Caribbean of a plantation society and its system of labor and race relations became a template for kindred European settlements to the north.

English Colonization and Slavery. Like the Spaniards before them, the English were drawn to North America in large part by the allure of commerce, and they brought with them ideas about race and ethnicity that had guided them in Britain. During the second half of the sixteenth century, the English had embarked upon a colonizing mission in Ireland that involved its conquest and settlement. The Irish were wild, ignorant, beast-like savages, the English held; accordingly, both the land and its inhabitants had to be cleared and tamed before civilized "plantations" of settlers could take root and grow. Ideas derived from that venture—of the innately superior English and inferior natives, of wars of subjugation, and of separate enclaves of English settlers that reproduced English society and remained apart from indigenous societies—guided the English in their settlement of the Americas.

Among most English settlers, despite occasional sexual relationships and less frequent marriages between English men and Indian women, the perceived divide between themselves and the indigenous peoples was wide and unbridgeable. There arose no distinctive mestizo class, as among the Spanish, in English North America. Instead, mixed peoples belonged to the subject class. Some historians attribute that difference in race relations to a tolerant *Roman Catholicism in Spanish America and an intolerant *Protestantism, especially Calvinism, in English America. Others cite the allegedly more benign characteristics of Spanish American Indians in contrast to the threat to English settlement posed by the more warlike Indians of North America. Still other scholars point to the greater number of marriages between Spanish men and Indian women, and the consequent motivation to legitimate unions and their offspring. Whatever the causes, racial concepts and relationships evolved differently in the different parts of the Americas.

A third racialized group in English America was constituted when twenty enslaved Africans arrived in *Jamestown in 1619. Some historians maintain that Europeans believed in the innate inferiority of Africans and took those ideas with them to the New World, and thus this form of *racism preceded African enslavement. Other historians, however, argue that the notion of African inferiority arose as a consequence of and justification for their enslavement. *Slavery, according to this view, spawned a racism that included both physical and cultural distinctions and hierarchies to justify a system of labor. All agree that America's English settlers commonly viewed Africans as heathens whose enslavement was preparatory to their eventual conversion to Christianity. By the early eighteenth century, relations between Africans and Europeans became institutionalized in slave codes passed by colonial assemblies. Despite slavemasters' frequent sexual encounters with female slaves, sexual relations and marriage between Europeans and Africans were officially forbidden and punishable by law.

Race in Theory, Law, and Social Practice. Europeans developed a science of race in the eighteenth century as part of an attempt to classify and thereby order nature. Common to these theories were the association of culture or behavior with race or physical type and the ranking of these "races" as superior or inferior. A particular species of "scientific" racism arose in the American *South about the mid–nineteenth century in defense of African enslavement. These theorists rejected the environmental determinist explanation for racial differences and promoted the belief that blacks were innately and unalterably inferior to whites. The publication of Charles Darwin's *Origin of Species* in 1859 generally ended the debate over single or multiple descent, but it failed to eradicate the idea of race as a natural or scientific category. Indeed, Darwin's work spawned new evolutionary theories of race.

These efforts produced greater differentiation in racial classification. Europeans, for example, were subdivided into various "races" that included the Germanic or Teutonic "race" and its British branch, the Anglo-Saxons. Their alleged superior vigor, intellect, masculinity, love of liberty, and democratic institutions were celebrated by many English and American intellectuals as the racial inheritance of Anglo-Saxons and their American transplants. While the seventeenth-century view of Anglo-Saxons had stressed their Germanic origins and Protestantism, the nineteenth-century view equated it with Anglo-American whiteness or a blend of European races produced by the American melting pot. The racial career of the Irish exemplifies that trajectory of Anglo-Saxonism and whiteness. A Catholic, non–Anglo-Saxon people earlier racialized as bestial by the English, the Irish who migrated to America worked with and lived among free blacks in northern areas like *New York City. Before the *Civil War, the Irish were deemed, like blacks, to be lazy, sensual, and savage, but beginning in the 1850s the Irish assumed the mantle of whiteness when contrasted with the American Indian, African, or Asian.

Whiteness was acquired through the instrument of law and through everyday belief and common speech. One of the earliest and most basic expressions of whiteness in the new American republic was the 1790 Naturalization Act that limited naturalization to "free white persons." In 1868, the *Fourteenth Amendment granted citizenship to "all persons born or naturalized in the United States," and naturalization was extended to blacks in 1870 but the 1790 racial requirement for naturalization and its 1870 modification remained in forced until 1952. Like the Irish, groups racialized as nonwhite sought the protections and guarantees of citizenship and whiteness. The 1848 Treaty of Guadalupe Hidalgo that ended the *Mexican War granted U.S. citizenship to Mexican residents of the ceded territories. Mexicans thus were rendered "white" by treaty. In 1878, three Chinese migrants petitioned for naturalization under the claim that Asians were white. The judge, in his ruling, wrestled with the meaning of the term "white persons" as intended by Congress in 1790 and as used in contemporary common or scientific discourse, and concluded that the Chinese were not white. Immigrants from Armenia were originally classed as Asians and hence nonwhite, but through a 1909 court decision they were rendered white. Immigrants and would-be immigrants from Syria and India underwent even more complicated legal transformations from "nonwhite" to "white" and back again.

These court decisions relied upon what was considered scientific evidence as well as common knowledge or everyday speech. A 1923 U.S. *Supreme Court decision ruling that Asian Indians were nonwhites exemplified the shifting ground: "the blond Scandinavian" and "the brown Hindu" might have shared a common ancestor in the distant past, the Court noted, but "the average man" clearly knows the differences between them today.

Like whiteness, nonwhiteness was fraught with ambiguity. Persons were defined as "black," for instance, in Alabama, Arkansas, Tennessee, Texas, and Virginia if they had any ancestral trace of so-called "Negro blood." That category included those with one-sixteenth "Negro blood" in Kentucky; one-eighth in Florida, Indiana, Mississippi, Missouri, Nebraska, North Carolina, and North Dakota; and one-fourth in Oregon. By law, thus, a person might be black in one state but not in another. Chinese Americans were classified as whites in Louisiana in 1860; in 1870, they were enumerated as Chinese; in 1880, the children of Chinese men and non-Chinese women were classed as Chinese; but in 1890, those biracial children were reclassified as either blacks or whites and only those born in China or with two Chinese parents were deemed to be Chinese.

Race concepts have wielded extraordinary influence throughout American history. Race determined citizenship, immunities, and privileges. American Indian tribes were deemed sovereign entities by the Supreme Court during the 1800s, but were also considered "wards" of the federal government. Even as the Court devolved guardianship to the federal government, Congress, the states, and successive chief executives pursued policies of Indian removal. Similar racial preoccupations underlay the initiatives pursued during the 1840s and 1850s by Middlewestern states such as Indiana and Illinois to prohibit the entry of *African Americans. Other white supremacists in the North proposed the removal of all African Americans and peoples of color from the entire United States.

Yet people crossed racialized boundaries. American Indians and whites lived side-by-side in the South and *West during the nineteenth century and created communities that advanced the welfare of both groups. Blacks and *Irish Americans worked together, formed a waiters' union in New York City in 1853, lived in close proximity, and sometimes intermarried. Likewise, about 25 percent of New York City's Chinese men from the 1820s to the 1870s married Irish-American women. Despite conflicts between racialized groups, there were countervailing examples of cooperation, acculturation, and intimate relations. Racial ideologies sometimes had to be taught to and imposed upon America's people.

Racial *segregation was a crucial instrument of social control in the American South. Small farmers chafed under the paternalism of the planter elite, but benefited from their racialized identities as whites. Racialist ideologies, reinforced by gendered and sexualized images and sanctions that included white men's sexual access to black slave women and the myths that grew up around white southern womanhood, supported the male planters' power over the state and its peoples. Segregation reached new heights in the post-*Reconstruction South with laws and practices that policed the racial borders between black and white. The *Fifteenth Amendment guaranteed a citizen's right to vote irrespective of "race, color, or previous condition of servitude," yet African Americans were routinely denied the ballot by states that imposed property and literacy requirements from the end of Reconstruction down to the voting Rights Act of 1965.

Racial Ideas, Expansionism, and Immigration Policy. Expansionists invoked white nationalism in promoting America's push westward. Ordained by God and history, they contended, whites should implant the blessings of liberty and democracy across the continent. White settlers and U.S. soldiers—including African Americans—moved west through Indian country, initiating wars and policies that decimated and dispersed the Indians. The 1840s expansion in the *Southwest, culminating in Mexico's surrender of its northern territories, proved a precursor of the *Manifest Destiny dogmas of the 1890s that drove American civilization to the Pacific and beyond. War against Filipino nationalists was justified in part as a beneficent mission—the white man's burden—to uplift what President William *McKinley called our "little brown brothers."

*Immigration recast racial and ethnic relations in major cities of the late nineteenth century. Urban centers attracted whites and blacks from America's rural districts, as well as immigrants from southern and eastern Europe, Asia, Canada, and Mexico. By 1890, cities like *Chicago, *Detroit, Milwaukee, and New York had very high proportions of immigrants. Italian, Polish, Jewish, Chinese, Mexican, and other ethnic and racial neighborhoods took root because of immigrant choices and discrimination that forced residential segregation upon the new Americans. Ethnicity persisted, but it was also subject to change through pressures to assimilate, often called Americanization, effected through the public-school education of American-born generations. And while ethnicity stirred nativist agitation (itself a kind of ethnic identification), it also offered a means of political and economic mobilization. Ethnic politics and ethnic labor dominated the early twentieth-century urban landscape, fueling the engine of *mass production and consumption.

The law long functioned as an instrument of the racialized state by favoring the entry of British and northern Europeans, and restricting the immigration of racial and ethnic others. Congress excluded Chinese laborers in 1882; imposed restrictive quotas on southern and eastern Europeans in 1924; and successively excluded Japanese and Koreans, Asian Indians, and Filipinos before *World War II. Not until the Immigration Act of 1965 did Congress eliminate national (and hence racial and ethnic) quotas.

Challenging the Primacy of Race. The struggle against racial discrimination peaked with the African American *civil rights movement of the 1950s and 1960s. The legal basis for segregation in the public schools and with it the "separate but equal" doctrine fell in the Supreme Court's 1954 **Brown* v. *Board of Education* decision, and individuals and organizations challenged racial segregation in public facilities and transportation. Yet the gap between promise and practice remained.

Race and ethnicity are neither natural nor given: they have no basis in human biology. They are defined and actualized by people who impose, accept, and contest these terms' meanings and their workings. They are therefore historical insofar as they are made and remade in place and over time. Although they are culturally constructed abstractions, race and ethnicity are given substance in the institutions and cultures of America's peoples, providing justifications and means for division and union, inequality and equality.

[*See also* Americanization Movement; Anti-Semitism; Asian Americans; Evolution, Theory of; Expansionism; Exploration, Conquest, and Settlement, Era of European; German Americans; Hispanic Americans; Immigrant Labor; Immigration Law; Indian History and Culture; Italian Americans; Nativist Movement; Race, Concept of; Social Class; Spanish Settlements in North America.]

• George M. Fredrickson, *The Black Image in the White Mind: The Debate on Afro-American Character and Destiny, 1817–1914,* 1971. Stephen Jay Gould, *The Mismeasure of Man,* 1981. David R. Roediger, *The Wages of Whiteness: Race and the Making of the American Working Class,* 1991. Michael Omi and Howard Winant, *Racial Formation in the United States: From the 1960s to 1990s,* 1994. Gail Bederman, *Manliness and Civilization: A Cultural History of Gender and Race in the United States, 1880–1917,* 1995. Richard C. Trexler, *Sex and Conquest: Gendered Violence, Political Order, and the European Conquest of the Americas,* 1995. Ian F. Haney Lopez, *White by Law: The Legal Construction of Race,* 1996. Thomas F. Gossett, *Race: A History of an Idea in America,* 1997.

—Gary Y. Okihiro

RACISM, an ideology that views "race" as a fundamental human category rooted in nature and sees some races as inherently inferior. Racism in America has functioned as a means by which the white majority asserted its superiority and rationalized its dominance over Native Americans, *Asian Americans, and *African Americans. In the *Colonial Era, European settlers often expressed racist views toward the native population, reinforced by religious beliefs in the Indians' satanic nature and God's mandate to the colonists to conquer them. Racist assumptions continued thereafter to justify white appropriation of Indian lands and even campaigns of extermination.

Racist ideas have long been directed against African Americans. When Africans were first brought to America, some historians argue, their treatment was roughly equivalent to that of white indentured servants. The large-scale influx of Africans in the late seventeenth century, however, historian George Frederickson suggests, engendered fears that hardened prejudice into racism. As Virginia legalized *slavery in the 1670s, racist ideas took deep root. Racism underlay not only slavery but also the African *colonization movement, which arose in the *South after Gabriel Prosser's slave uprising in Virginia in 1800. Supporters of colonization—the return of blacks to Africa—included such notables as Thomas *Jefferson and James *Monroe. Discussing the peoples of North America in *Notes on the State of Virginia* (1785), Jefferson revealed racist notions, portraying African Americans as subhuman while idealizing Indians.

White racism so pervaded antebellum America that the free black leader Martin Delany (1812–1885) argued only that when blacks gained political power would it diminish. Southern religious leaders offered biblical defenses of racism and by the 1850s, an elaborate pseudo-scientific racism, based largely on measurements of cranial capacity, was devised by the so-called American School of Anthropology, which included the distinguished naturalist Louis *Agassiz and the Mobile, Alabama, physician and ethnologist Josiah Nott (1804–1873). The U.S. *Supreme Court's 1857 *Dred Scott* decision (**Scott* v. *Sandford*), declaring that blacks had no rights that whites were bound to respect, rested on a web of racist assumptions. Although abolitionist opposition to slavery threatened its racist foundations, many white abolitionists themselves held racist views and opposed social equality with blacks. Black abolitionists such as David Walker, Henry Highland Garnet, and Frederick *Douglass, by contrast, urged a struggle not only against slavery but also against the pervasive racism that underlay racial discrimination in the North.

Rooted in phobia and activated by the reflex of color, racism long survived its social construction in the slavery era. Post–*Civil War racism found expression in the *Ku Klux Klan's reign of terror, in the spread of segregation across the South, and in the 1896 Supreme Court ruling in *Plessy v. Ferguson* upholding racial *segregation in schools and public facilities. Racist assumptions underlay the biased intelligence and psychological tests introduced in *World War I, as well as historian Ulrich B. Phillips's *American Negro Slavery* (1918), long the reigning text on the subject. Racism also pervaded popular culture, including the blackface minstrel shows and D. W. *Griffith's film *The Birth of a Nation* (1915), celebrating the Ku Klux Klan and portraying blacks in hostile, stereotyped terms. Racism shaped the history of populism and American *labor movements, since poor white farmers and workers, while sometimes joining interracial movements, more often identified with white planters and capitalists than with their fellow black workers.

Opposition to racism continued, however, as the *National Association for the Advancement of Colored People (NAACP, 1910) conducted its long legal campaign against discriminatory laws and practices rooted in racist ideas. In addition, during the 1930s the U.S. Communist party mounted an impressive campaign to eliminate racism from its ranks. Its very success, however, militated against efforts to attract white workers, whose racist phobias are explored at length by David Roediger.

Meanwhile, immigrants who arrived in vast numbers from southern and eastern Europe in the late nineteenth and early twentieth centuries often embraced racist ideas as a way of identifying with the native-born white majority. At the same time, however, nativists used racist language to attack the new immigrants. In *The Passing of the Great Race* (1916), the New York lawyer and philanthropist Madison Grant, drawing upon the work of the Frenchman Joseph Gobineau and others, stridently insisted on the superiority of the "Nordic" race over all others. Grant proposed immigrant restriction, racial segregation, and sterilization of the "unfit." The term "race" was loosely applied in these years, and racism often blurred into *anti-Semitism and hatred of various ethnic and national groups. Racist ideology targeted Asian Americans as well, underlying restrictive immigration laws and the *incarceration of Japanese Americans in *World War II. Pervading anti-Japanese *propaganda, racism also surfaced in the *Vietnam War.

But, on balance, developments during and following World War II provided the context in which blatant expressions of racism were reduced. The horrors of the Nazi Holocaust, labor leader A. Philip *Randolph's call for a march of blacks on the nation's capital demanding fair employment in the war industries, and opposition to *lynching by such eminent figures as Paul *Robeson and Albert *Einstein helped to discredit racism. Moreover, America's *Cold War priority of recruiting allies in Asia and Africa, a diminished emphasis on race in the *social sciences, and especially the militancy of the *civil rights movement were changing the nation's attitude toward issues of race.

The civil rights movement gained inspiration from the school-desegregation decision **Brown* v. *Board of Education* (1954), in which the plaintiff's case, argued by Thurgood *Marshall of the NAACP, included sociological evidence demonstrating the psychological effects of racism on black children. The Montgomery bus boycott led by Martin Luther *King Jr., and the heavily publicized brutality of southern racists against civil rights demonstrators further discredited racism.

Racism did not disappear, however. The Mississippi novelist and Nobel Laureate William *Faulkner in 1956, speaking of "blood," "kin," and "home," declared that if necessary he would resort to arms to resist government efforts to end racial segregation. The Kerner Commission, appointed by President Lyndon B. *Johnson in 1967 to investigate racial disturbances in northern cities, identified white racism as a central cause and warned that America was in danger of becoming two societies, one white, one black. As the twentieth century ended, some observers saw a declining significance of race, emphasizing class differences instead, and social scientists increasingly stressed the social construction of the concept of "race" itself. Nevertheless, as the nation's weakening commitment to racial justice threatened the gains of the civil rights movement, a renewed emphasis on inherent racial difference was evident in such controversial works as *The Bell Curve* (1996) by Charles Murray and Richard J. Herrnstein, which claimed to find a genetic basis for racial variation in intelligence tests.

[*See also* Antislavery; Communist Party—USA; Eugenics; Garvey, Marcus; Immigration; Immigration Law; Indentured Servitude; Indian History and Culture; Intelligence, Concepts of; Malcolm X; Minstrelsy; Nation of Islam; Nativist Movement; Populist Era; Race, Concept of; Race and Ethnicity; Riots, Urban; Slave Uprisings and Resistance.]

• W. E. B. Du Bois, *Dusk of Dawn,* 1940, reprint ed., 1984. Winthrop Jordan, *White over Black,* 1968. George M. Frederickson, *The Black Image in the White Mind,* 1971. St. Clair Drake, *Black Folk Here and There: An Essay in History and Anthropology,* 1987. David Roediger, *Wages of Whiteness,* 1991. Alden T. Vaughn, *The Roots of American Racism,* 1995.

—Sterling Stuckey

RADICALISM. Radicalism in the United States owes its origins to the so-called Radical Reformation of the sixteenth century and to civil rebellions and millenarian movements reaching far back in human memory. Indian rebellions against European colonizers and transplanted pietist communes offer the clearest precursors of American political radicalism. Thomas *Paine's antimonarchical **Common Sense* (1776), the first widely read document with direct bearing upon the fate of the incipient nation, was characteristic in two ways. The revolution Paine helped inspire stopped well short of addressing *social class, race, and *gender inequities. Yet Paine's continuing attack on wrongful authority nevertheless gained him the enmity of ungrateful American conservatives, forcing him into postrevolutionary political exile. The burden of radicalism had already passed to the direct action of *Shays's Rebellion in Massachusetts in 1786, which sought to redress economic privilege. Fifteen citizens received death sentences (two actually were hanged), a small figure compared to the vengeance visited upon the organizers of and participants in a long series of Indian and slave uprisings, real and potential.

Radicalism found new outlets in the early *labor movements and the *utopian and communitarian movements of the *Antebellum Era. Urging shorter hours, free public schools, and free land in the *West, early workers' movements ultimately failed, but they did make their mark upon public life and Democratic machine politics. The great reform movements of the mid–nineteenth century—women's rights, *antislavery, and *spiritualism—began from a different standpoint. Social class as such concerned them less than the vision of universal citizenship and multifaceted social improvement. Meeting in Seneca Falls, New York, in 1848, the first women's rights convention declared a new revolutionary principle for half the human race. Abolitionists likewise demanded the expropriation of wrongfully held human "property." Spiritualism, an often misunderstood link between the various reform movements and a larger population of sympathizers, grew from a rejection of patriarchal Calvinism and a belief in the oneness of the human spirit with nature.

The outbreak of the *Civil War eclipsed every movement but war itself—and emancipation of the slaves. *African Americans abandoning the plantations helped speed the Union victory, but *Republican party "Radicals" finally abandoned* African Americans to what W. E. B. *Du Bois called "a new capitalism and a new enslavement of labor," establishing a model for global economic expansion. The first American followers of Karl Marx, mostly German immigrants, renewed efforts to create a radicalized labor movement. Swept away in the postwar conservative reaction, *socialism arose in different forms following the national *railroad strikes of 1877, and re-emerged in the labor and populist movements of the 1880s and 1890s.

Intermittently for the next half-century, African Americans, *Hispanic Americans, and *Asian Americans would find a thin section of socialists and labor radicals ready to address race issues with special urgency. The *Knights of Labor briefly mobilized a half-million working people during the mid–1880s. Populism (and its constituent movements known as the *Farmers' Alliance) revived multiracial radicalism in other forms, including cooperatives and third-party politics. Socialists struggled in vain to halt the *Spanish-American War and the American slaughter of Filipino nationalists. A large and influential Socialist party found a constituency of working people early in the twentieth century, only to be crushed by the repression of the Woodrow *Wilson administration after 1917.

Twentieth-century intellectuals like Du Bois, labor activists such as A. Philip *Randolph, and advanced figures within such labor movements as the *Industrial Workers of the World (IWW) proposed drastic changes in society's racial orientation as well its economic-political character. A thoroughgoing antiracism emerged in the 1920s when a defeated American Left, looked abroad to forces shaking the colonial world. American communists, altogether too closely tied to the Soviet Union but sometimes heroic in their own local circumstances, struggled to build an antiracist movement. In part, they achieved impressive success—at least until the *Cold War—in building egalitarian industrial unions and a radical interracial culture.

The Cold War and its concomitant domestic repression chilled radicalism severely. *Civil rights radicals, however, never quite as crushed as labor radicals had been, revived the direct-action approach, from the Montgomery bus boycott to the lunch-counter sit-ins to the Black Power movement of the 1960s. The anti–*Vietnam War movement; *environmentalism; *feminism; activism by Indian, Chicano, and Asian-American groups; and, still later the gay-rights movement, added new dimension to the American radical tradition. But by the 1980s, the hegemonic power of *capitalism had overwhelmed resistance in most quarters. Radicalism again consisted, as it had during earlier low periods, largely of support for revolutionary movements abroad and *antinuclear protest movements at home. The close of the twentieth century found American radicalism dispersed and institutionally weak. Nevertheless, the partial revival of a weakened and corrupted labor movement, and the appearance of new immigrant populations (most notably from the Dominican Republic and Haiti) with definite radical sentiments, showed signs of reawakening a radicalism damped down by defeat and disappointment.

[*See also* Black Nationalism; Civil Rights Movement; Communist Party—USA; Debs, Eugene V.; Gay and Lesbian Rights Movement; Goldman, Emma; Indian Wars; Populist Era; Populist Party; Sixties, The; Slave Uprisings and Resistance; Socialist Party of America; Students for a Democratic; Society; Women's Rights Movements.]

• Alden Whitman, ed., *American Reformers: An H. W. Wilson Biographical Dictionary,* 1985. Richard Flacks, *Making History: The American Left and the American Mind,* 1988. Mari Jo Buhle, Paul Buhle, and Harvey J. Kaye, eds., *The American Radical,* 1995. Jeremy Brecher, *Strike!,* 1988. Mari Jo Buhle, Paul Buhle, and Dan Georgakas, eds., *Encyclopedia of the American Left,* 1998. Paul Buhle and Edmund Sullivan, *Images of American Radicalism,* 1998.

—Paul Buhle

RADIO. Radio developed from wired and later wireless *telegraph and *telephone *technology, and adapted its broadcasting contents from *vaudeville, the phonograph, the popular press, and *film. In the early 1920s, these elements combined to create a new medium.

Before 1920. Radio developed first outside the United States. A few American experimenters sought improved point-to-point communication to compete with existing wired services and to transmit to ships at sea. Lee de Forest (1874–1961), the first important American wireless inventor, developed his Audion three-element vacuum tube in 1906. But it took years to realize its ability to amplify sound and thus its wireless applications. Perhaps the first broadcast took place on Christmas Eve 1906 when Reginald Fessenden transmitted signals of his voice and recorded music near *Boston. Early public attention focused on radio's lifesaving role in such disasters as the 1912 *Titanic* sinking. Edwin Howard Armstrong (1890–1954), another key American inventor, patented several circuits widely used in radio receivers and fought lengthy patent battles with de Forest and others. Thousands of soldiers learned to use radio during *World War I, but postwar development was slowed by the cancellation of government manufacturing contracts and by the fact that the patents needed to make radios were held by competing firms. Cooperation was imperative, and the Radio Corporation of America (RCA) was founded in 1919 to coordinate American radio manufacturing through a shared patent pool. But this hard-won legal agreement did not foresee broadcasting.

1920–1927. The inception of service by station KDKA in East Pittsburgh on 2 November 1920 is widely accepted as the birth of regular American broadcasting. Operated by the Westinghouse Corporation to encourage purchase of its radios, the station offered a regular weekly schedule of a few hours of talk and music designed for general listening. RCA built stations (also to sell radios), as did American Telephone and Telegraph (AT&T), which perceived radio as similar to toll telephony. As public interest soared, some five hundred stations went on the air by 1922, creating a cacophony of interference. Under a 1912 Radio Act that had not foreseen broadcasting's demand, the U.S. Department of Commerce had to license all applicants. Secretary of Commerce Herbert *Hoover called four radio conferences (1922–1926) to develop industry agreement on new legislation, then persuaded Congress to pass it. The resulting Radio Act of 1927 established a Federal Radio Commission (FRC) to license and regulate stations.

How to support these stations created further controversy. AT&T's New York station, WEAF, first sold time to advertisers in 1922, and eventually this became the accepted means of meeting operating costs. WEAF also first interconnected stations with telephone lines (1923) to allow program sharing, thereby creating the first experimental networks. The National Broadcasting Company (NBC) was the first company established (in 1926 by owner RCA) as a national radio network. The Columbia Broadcasting System (CBS) followed in 1927. There were then nearly seven hundred AM (amplitude modulation) stations on the air.

1928–1948. The years before *television competition marked radio's golden age. Despite the Depression of the 1930s, radio prospered as it provided free entertainment and news to anyone who owned a receiver. By the early 1930s, popular formats were well established, including half-hour situation comedies, variety and music programs, brief daily newscasts, fifteen-minute daytime serial dramas, and evening dramas of many kinds. Radio stars ranked in public appeal with those of film and stage. One indicator of radio's growing role came on Halloween in 1938, when a CBS adaptation of H. G. Wells's *War of the Worlds,* directed by and starring the young actor Orson Welles, frightened millions into believing that America was under attack by invading Martians.

Audience ratings based on telephone surveys conducted by the C. E. Hooper Company measured radio's growing appeal to advertisers. Radio's share of all *advertising soared—from less than 1 percent in 1928 to a high of 15 percent in 1945 when radio profited from wartime paper shortages that limited newspapers' advertisements. Despite the networks' dominance, radio's local appeal was evident as local advertising revenue grew from 20 percent of radio income in the late 1920s to twice that two decades later. This encouraged station growth—from just over 600 AM outlets in 1930 to 765 in 1940 and 1,612 in 1948.

Meanwhile, more regional and national networks appeared. Mutual Broadcasting System began operating in 1934 based on cooperative sharing of programs among its stations. The dominance of CBS and NBC (which operated two parallel national networks) over programs and advertising led the *Federal Communications Commission (FCC, created in 1934 to replace the FRC) to investigate in 1938–1941. The FCC ordered NBC to divest one network, a decision upheld by the *Supreme Court in 1943. NBC's Blue network was sold and became the American Broadcasting Company in 1945.

The search for interference-free operation eventually led to frequency modulation (FM) radio in the late 1930s. Based on a new transmission system perfected by Edwin Armstrong, the first experimental station aired in 1938. FM generally eliminated on-air static and provided much improved sound quality over AM stations. The FCC approved commercial FM operation in 1941. Few FM stations aired before America's entry into *World War II froze further expansion, but by 1948 some 460 FM stations were on the air.

1948–1980. Network radio declined after network television's first season in 1948–1949, and stations began a difficult transition back to the role of a local, music-based medium. Network programming disappeared by the early 1950s as audiences and advertisers moved to television. Whereas more than 90 percent of the 1,000 radio stations on the air in 1947 had been affiliated with a national network, a decade later fewer than half the 3,000 stations held network agreements, while only a quarter of 1967's 5,700 AM–FM stations were tied to any network's hourly newscasts, special events, and sports coverage.

The continued growth in the number of stations offered solid evidence of radio's successful transition to something quite different from television. A return to music-based programming (as in radio's earliest days) was paced by "Top-40" stations that attracted youth who learned a lifelong radio habit (as adults, many would tune to "golden oldies" outlets). Although the number of FM stations declined through 1957 because of few receivers, smaller audiences, and industry focus on television and AM, FM expanded in the 1960s aided by FCC approval of stereo FM in 1961. By 1979 FM stations collectively surpassed the more numerous AM outlets in total national listening.

The FCC reserved some FM frequencies for noncommercial or educational service. From 15 such stations in 1948, what later became known as public radio grew to 162 outlets in 1960, more than 400 in 1970, and over 1,000 by 1980. National Public Radio tied many of these outlets together beginning in the early 1970s and numerous states had networks of stations. Public radio offered drama, music, in-depth news reporting, and special programs. Audiences were small but intensely loyal.

Since 1980. As the twentieth century ended, radio was characterized by program specialization, use of satellites for distribution of programs, and continued expansion—to some twelve thousand AM and FM stations by 2000. Fully three-quarters of all radio listening was to FM stations. Deregulation in 1996 encouraged ownership of chains of hundreds of stations—and up to eight outlets in the largest cities. With little FCC program oversight, often strident right-wing talk shows, conservative religious station, and other controversial formats thrived. Early in 2000, the FCC established Low Power FM (LPFM), which could in time place hundreds of mini-stations on the air. Further change loomed with the inception of digital radio services projected early in the new century.

[*See also* Electricity and Electrification; Mass Marketing; New Deal Era, The; Popular Culture; Public Broadcasting; Twenties, The.]

• Erik Barnouw, *A Tower in Babel: A History of Broadcasting in the United States to 1933*, 1966. Erik Barnouw, *The Golden Web: A History of Broadcasting in the United States, 1933–1953*, 1968. Susan J. Douglas, *Inventing American Broadcasting, 1899–1922*, 1987. Christopher H. Sterling and John Michael Kittros, *Stay Tuned: A Concise History of American Broadcasting*, 2d ed., 1990. Susan Smulyan, *Selling Radio: The Commercialization of American Broadcasting, 1920–1934*, 1994. Ray Barfield, *Listening to Radio, 1920–1950*, 1996. Robert L. Hilliard and Michael C. Keith, *The Broadcast Century: A Biography of American Broadcasting*, 2d ed., 1997. Michele Hilmes, *Radio Voices: American Broadcasting, 1922–1952*, 1997. John Dunning, *On the Air: The Encyclopedia of Old-Time Radio*, 1998. Donald G. Godfrey and Frederic A. Leigh, *Historical Dictionary of American Radio*, 1998. Christopher H. Sterling, ed. *Encyclopedia of Radio*, 2001.

—Christopher H. Sterling

RAGTIME, the descriptive term for a uniquely American style of popular music and, more broadly, for the time period (ca. 1890–1920) when it emerged and gained popularity. A colloquial contraction of "ragged time," "ragtime" underscores the music's most identifying feature—its highly syncopated rhythms. The term also evokes the energy, optimism, and insecurity of the national culture during the transitional years between the Chicago World's Fair of 1893, where ragtime first reached the general public, and the end of *World War I, when *jazz replaced it.

The earliest appearance of ragtime is impossible to date or place precisely, but itinerant African-American piano players in such cities as St. Louis, *New Orleans, and Baltimore in the post-*Reconstruction Era created a synthesis that by the early 1890s came to define a distinct style. Drawing from the ubiquitous brass bands and minstrel shows, as well as from traditional dance music, these performers developed a two-handed, percussive approach that, once it became available through sheet music, piano rolls, and—eventually—recordings, offered a spirited change from the more sedate and sentimental styles of the period. At their most basic, ragtime rhythms consisted of a syncopated treble line (melody) juxtaposed against a regular bass and chord (harmony) pulse. By the mid-1890s, such rhythms were being applied to both the standard form of the march and to the song form. The emerging popular-music business, centralized in *New York City after 1900, quickly appropriated both ragtime rhythms and the expression (Irving *Berlin's "Alexander's Ragtime Band" of 1911 is a notable example). In addition, beginning with the Cakewalk fad of the 1890s, the association of ragtime with new forms of social dancing made it a focus of the larger debate over changing patterns of urban social behavior.

Instrumental ragtime, the style's more enduring strain, evolved from the application of ragtime rhythms to the form and beat of the march. The first instrumental rag to appear in print, William Krell's "Mississippi Rag" (1897), was soon followed by Tom Turpin's "Harlem Rag," the first by a black composer. In 1899, Scott Joplin (1868–1917) began publishing his ragtime compositions in Sedalia, Missouri, including "Maple Leaf Rag," which became the most celebrated rag of all time. A formally trained serious musician, Joplin dominated ragtime composition during his lifetime, writing dozens of rags as well as two "ragtime" operas—"The Guest of Honor" (1903) and "Treemonisha" (1911). His compositions, along with those of his pupils, collaborators, and followers, comprise a body of work, often described as "classic ragtime," intended to be performed as written—for piano, primarily, but also in orchestral arrangements.

By 1920 the term ragtime began to seem old fashioned, and both classic ragtime and the once-popular ragtime songs and dances lost their currency. The music continued to influence American popular music, however, and was crucial to the emergence and diffusion of jazz. The mid-1940s witnessed a modest revival of interest, and in the 1970s a more substantial and lasting reassessment was initiated by a series of best-selling recordings of classic ragtime, a new production of Joplin's "Treemonisha" by the Houston Grand Opera (a work never fully performed in his lifetime), and the adaptation of Joplin's music for the movie *The Sting*, which received an Academy Award for best film score in 1974.

[*See also* African Americans; Dance; Music: Popular Music; Popular Culture; Progressive Era.]

• Rudy Blesh and Harriet Janis, *They All Played Ragtime,* 1950. Edward A. Berlin, *King of Ragtime: Scott Joplin and His Era,* 1994.

—Reid Badger

RAILROADS. The railroad's basic principle—lessening the power needed to move objects over land by putting them on rails—had been used since the late eighteenth century, but the railroad took on its modern form in the late 1820s when steam locomotives came into use. English engineers established an early lead in this development, but Americans quickly caught up, often by visiting England to examine the latest innovations. By the 1830s, civil and military engineers such as Horatio Allen, Major William Gibbs McNeill, and Moncure Robinson had become railroad experts in their own right.

As in Europe, the earliest American railroads (e.g., the Granite Railroad in Quincy, Massachusetts, 1826) were powered by horses, and well into the 1830s, the superiority of steam-powered railroads remained an open question. Not only were steam railroads expensive to build and technologically complex, but the country had recently embarked on a canal-building boom, sparked by construction of the *Erie Canal. As coastal cities from *Boston to Charleston weighed transportation projects that would enable them to compete with *New York City for western markets, experts debated the relative utility of *canals and waterways versus steam-powered railroads. Pennsylvania pushed ahead with its Main Line canal system, linking *Philadelphia to Pittsburgh, but *steam power gradually prevailed. Construction of the first U.S. passenger railroad, the Baltimore and Ohio, began on 4 July 1828. Work proceeded slowly, however, and the first long-distance railroad actually brought into operation, in 1833, was the 136-mile South Carolina Canal and Railroad.

By 1840 a distinctive "American system" of railroad construction had emerged, characterized by economy of construction obtained by minimizing excavation and by substituting wood for iron wherever possible (including in the rails themselves). This resulted in railroads of light construction with sharp curves and steep grades as well as comparatively high operating costs and low speeds. While a wide diversity of construction styles marked U.S. railroad development, this American system of construction proved especially attractive when the terrain was rough, distances long, or capital scarce. The first locomotives were English imports, but a style more appropriate to the United States soon developed—powerful enough to haul heavy loads up steep grades and with swiveling front wheels to handle sharp curves.

From the 1830s, construction proceeded rapidly and absorbed increasing amounts of capital. By 1850, canal mileage had leveled off at about 3,700 miles, while the nation boasted 9,000 miles of railroads. Railroad investment, meanwhile, climbed from an estimated $96 million in 1839 to some $300 million in 1850. *New England claimed the greatest density of lines, but construction proceeded throughout the country. The largest firms soon commanded capital in the tens of millions, and by the mid–1850s four trunkline railroads stretched from northeastern coastal cities into the Old Northwest. By 1860, American railroads had more than tripled in length, to some thirty thousand miles, while investment soared to more than one billion dollars. Sectional conflict delayed transcontinental railroad construction until after the *Civil War, but four lines were chartered between 1862 and 1871. The first was completed on 10 May 1869 when the Central Pacific Railroad of Collis P. *Huntington and Leland Stanford (1824–1893), building from *California eastward, met the Union Pacific at Promontory, Utah. The rail system tripled in size again by 1880, reaching more than ninety thousand miles as railroad capital exceeded five billion dollars. Over the next two decades, net growth continued—turbulently and well beyond need. James J. *Hill's Great Northern Railroad, based in St. Paul, reached Seattle in 1893. In 1900 American railroads totaled more than 190,000 miles and claimed a net capitalization of nearly $10 billion. Rail expansion peaked in 1920 at more than a quarter million miles, while net capitalization rose for another decade before beginning to decline.

An array of supportive government policies underlay this phenomenal expansion. Beginning in 1838, the federal government transferred the mails from stagecoaches to railroads. Iron imported for railroad construction enjoyed lower *tariffs. The War Department lent early railroads its military engineers or permitted them to take leave while working on railroads. When such leaves were restricted in the 1830s, many engineers resigned to work for the railroads. In the 1850s, military engineers on active duty surveyed transcontinental routes.

State and local governments also energetically promoted railroads. Because the state legislatures that incorporated railroad companies saw transportation projects as a means of competing with other states, railroad charters—generally with liberal terms—were much easier to obtain in the United States than in Europe. Incorporation became even easier when "general incorporation" laws (Illinois, 1849; New York, 1850) made it a purely administrative process. Such easily obtained charters heightened investment risk, but the states offset this by contributing large amounts of capital themselves. In the 1830s, nearly half of the capital invested in American railroads came from state governments. When the depression of 1837–1843 curtailed state investment, local support increased. Overall, state and local governments accounted for an estimated 25 to 30 percent of *Antebellum–Era railroad investment. State and local courts also facilitated railroad construction, particularly in their interpretation of liability and eminent-domain law.

While the states, especially in the *South, continued to offer abundant aid after the Civil War, federal support now became more central. Western states gave railroads nearly 50 million acres in land grants, but the federal government gave much more. Before the Civil War, sectional conflict had held federal grants in check, but federal grants multiplied during and after the war, especially to the transcontinental railroads, which ran through sparsely settled territories. By 1871, when such grants ended, the federal government had given more than 130 million acres to the railroads. Washington also issued millions of dollars in bonds to promote transcontinental railroad construction, and by various indirect means funnelled even more capital into railroad securities.

The effects of railroad construction and operations rippled through the nineteenth-century economy. Railroads linked distant markets, enhanced communications, and drove down transportation rates—often spelling life or death for small towns. Their unprecedented demand for capital helped to centralize capital markets in New York and stimulated the creation of new financial instruments. Railway equipment suppliers such as Philadelphia's Baldwin Locomotive Works and George Pullman's sleeping-car factory in *Chicago sprang up to manufacture locomotives, passenger cars, switching equipment, and so on. In 1889, railroads consumed 29 percent of the nation's domestic iron and steel production.

The railroads also introduced two phenomena that would characterize American industrial *capitalism in the *Gilded Age: large geographic scale and capital intensity. As railroad construction intensified in the *Middle West in the 1850s, the trunk lines found themselves in direct competition. Grappling simultaneously with unprecedented competition and with the

MAP 17: ATCHISON, TOPEKA & SANTA FE RAILROAD

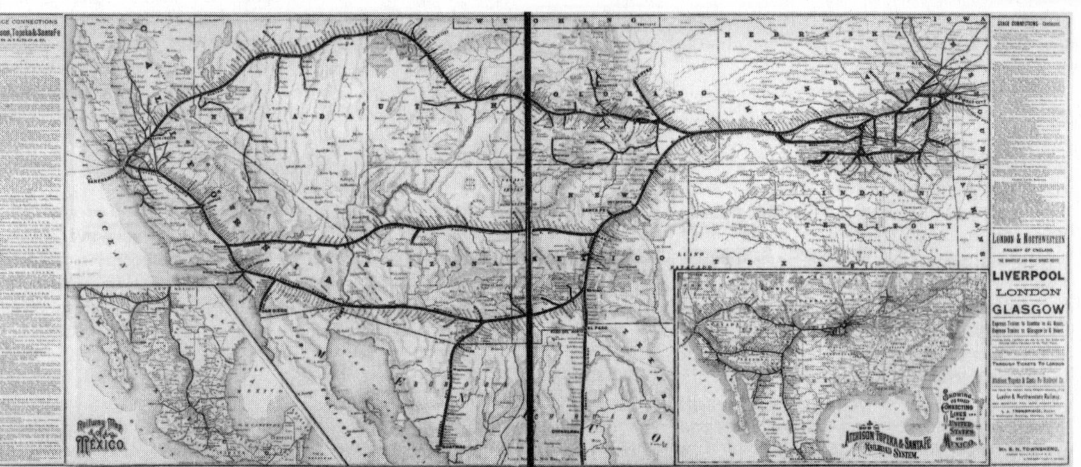

One part of the vast railroad grid that by the 1880s extended throughout the United States is shown in this 1884 promotional map. The Atchison, Topeka & Santa Fe with its connecting lines actually comprised an extensive railway system extending westward from Kansas City to San Francisco, Los Angeles, and San Diego, and, via a link with the Mexican Central Railroad, south to Mexico City. The railroad inspired a popular Johnny Mercer song of 1946, "On the Atchison, Topeka, and the Santa Fe."

[*See* Kansas City; Railroads; Southwest, The; West, The.]

novel challenges of long-distance operation, top executives such as Benjamin Latrobe of the Baltimore and Ohio, Daniel C. McCallum of the Erie, and J. Edgar Thomson of the Pennsylvania Railroad pioneered new management techniques—a decentralized divisional structure, innovative accounting methods, and a systematic flow of information—that were adopted and refined by other industries.

Employing labor on an unprecedented scale, railroads stimulated the rise of an industrial workforce and encouraged massive *immigration. The first transcontinental railroad was largely built by Chinese and Irish immigrant labor. The railway brotherhoods formed in the 1860s became the most powerful unions of their time. Major railroad strikes in 1877, 1886, and 1894, and the government's intervention with troops and court injunctions, intensified the labor unrest of these years. The railroad shaped American culture as well, as a favorite theme of painters, writers, photographers, filmmakers, and songwriters. Frank Norris's novel *The Octopus* (1901) evoked the vast economic and political power of California's railroads.

Railroad development had equally momentous political consequences. The chaotic expansion of competing lines profoundly shaped Gilded Age politics at all levels. Legislative bribery and corruption were common. In 1868, Jay Gould, James Fisk, and Daniel Drew, locked in a battle for control of the Erie Railroad, distributed more than one million dollars in bribes to New York politicians. The administration of President Ulysses S. *Grant was tainted by the Credit Mobilier scandal of 1872, involving a fraudulent company set up to siphon off money granted by the federal government to the Union Pacific to build a transcontinental railroad.

As the railroads expanded, they quickly outgrew the states that had created them. This challenged the state legislatures' long-standing right to regulate transportation rates on common carriers—a right predicated on traditional norms of competition, which the railroads (unlike canals) completely upset by monopolizing carriage on their own lines while competing with other lines. Because of their peculiar cost structure, moreover, the railroads engaged in rate discrimination, which became rampant as competition heated up. As the issue of railroad-rate regulation intensified, a decades-long battle erupted first in state legislatures and courts, then in federal courts, and finally in Congress. The U.S. *Supreme Court initially upheld state legislatures' right to regulate interstate rates in *Munn* v. *Illinois* (1877), but soon reversed itself in the *Wabash Case* (1886). In 1887, Congress established the Interstate Commerce Commission (ICC), the nation's first independent federal regulatory commission. Although weak in many ways, the ICC marked a shift in regulatory power from the states to the federal government that would continue in the twentieth century. Western farmers' fight for railroad regulation and their anger at the railroads' discriminatory rate-setting policies helped fuel late nineteenth-century agrarian protest and the rise of the *Populist party.

In the meantime, however, costly rate wars and regulatory threats galvanized the railroads to organize themselves to control competition. When self-regulation through "pooling" failed, the major lines built large "systems" in the 1870s and 1880s to establish regional monopolies. To head off regulation, they also worked collectively to standardize equipment and operations across state lines, formalizing their efforts in 1886 by founding the American Railway Association. (By-products of these initiatives were a uniform gauge and standard time zones.) But system-building proved expensive and encouraged overconstruction, which exacerbated competition; between 1873 and 1897, railroads controlling one-third of the nation's rail went bankrupt. Only concerted intervention by J. P. *Morgan and other investment bankers reorganized the industry on a firmer footing. But consolidation at the turn of the century produced giant holding companies that attracted federal scrutiny. The government's success in breaking up one such company in the **Northern Securities Case* (1904), under the Sherman Anti-Trust Act, ended industry efforts at self-regulation.

The twentieth century found the railroads in decline, as they faced increased federal regulation and intense competition—now from other modes of transportation. The Hepburn Act (1906) and the Mann-Elkins Act (1910) expanded the ICC's powers, while the Adamson Act of 1916 granted railroad workers an eight-hour day. The federal government operated the railroads during *World War I, then again increased the ICC's powers when it returned them to private hands in 1920. Increasingly, most scholars agree, federal regulation hampered the railroads' competitive ability.

As the federal government's regulatory power over railroads increased, it also put its formidable promotional powers behind new modes of transportation: aviation and *motor vehicles. The U.S. Postal Service shifted long-distance mail from railroads to airplanes in the 1920s, while the Air Commerce Act of 1926 aided civil aviation (e.g., through airport construction). An interlude of renewed prosperity for the railroad industry during *World War II continued after the war, thanks to operational and technical improvements such as dieselization. But the Highway Act of 1956, which authorized construction of a 41,000–mile interstate *highway system, signaled further decline. The government sought to address railroad problems by creating Amtrak (the National Railroad Passenger Corporation) in 1971 and Conrail (the Consolidated Rail Corporation) in 1976. The volume of freight transported by rail nearly doubled between 1970 and 1997, but except for the high-traffic Boston–to–*Washington, D.C., corridor, passenger traffic remained depressed. The century concluded with deregulation (the Staggers Act of 1980), massive rail mergers, and—most symbolic of all—abolition of the Interstate Commerce Commission in 1996. With the railroads' decline came a wave of nostalgia for the age of rail, marked by the opening of railway museums, efforts to save and preserve old equipment, and a proliferation of short-line railroad trips for tourists.

[*See also* Airplanes and Air Transport; Antitrust Legislation; Automotive Industry; Aviation Industry; Depressions, Economic; Economic Development; Economic Regulation; Granger Movement; Immigrant Labor; Industrialization; Interstate Commerce Act; Iron and Steel Industry; Labor Markets; Labor Movements; Pullman Strike and Boycott; Railroad Strikes of 1877; Strikes and Industrial Conflict.]

• Robert W. Fogel, *Railroads and American Economic Growth*, 1964. Alfred D. Chandler Jr., *The Railroads: The Nation's First Big Business*, 1965. Albro Martin, *Railroads Triumphant*, 1992. Gerald Berk, *Alternative Tracks*, 1994. Colleen A. Dunlavy, *Politics and Industrialization: Early Railroads in the United States and Prussia*, 1994. Maury Klein, *Unfinished Business: The Railroad in American Life*, 1994. John F. Stover, *American Railroads*, 2d ed., 1997. John H. White Jr., *American Locomotives*, rev. ed., 1997.

—Colleen A. Dunlavy

RAILROAD STRIKES OF 1877. The strikes that spread over the nation's *railroads and other workplaces in July 1877 were so massive that they sometimes have been called the "Great Labor Uprising." The strikes unfolded in the middle of the so-called Long Depression that began in 1873. Seeking to economize during the depression, the Pennsylvania Railroad and several of its competitors instituted 10 percent wage cuts in the summer of 1877. Almost immediately a secret society of the various railway crafts, the Trainmen's Union, organized in protest. On 16 July, 1,200 brakemen and firemen in West Virginia followed the example of Baltimore railway workers and struck against the wage cuts. Seizing the depot at Martinsburg, they stopped all freight traffic. Despite the dispatch of federal troops, the strike spread. When Pennsylvania Railroad strikers and their supporters in Pittsburgh confronted state militiamen, indiscriminate firing from the troops caused twenty deaths and sparked a pitched battle during which the city's roundhouse and Union Depot burned. Ultimately the strike stretched from coast to coast, halting movement of freight on the Erie Railroad, the New York Central, the Pennsylvania, the Baltimore and Ohio, and scores of lesser lines. In St. Louis, the socialist Workingmen's party (WPUSA) led a general strike shutting down production in all industries for nearly a week. In *Chicago, a similar WPUSA initiative led to a police attack on demonstrators and onlookers that killed at least eighteen people. In *San Francisco, demonstrations by strike supporters degenerated into violence against Chinese Americans. The railroad strikes ended, mostly in defeat, by the end of July, in large part because of state intervention. The enduring impact of the strike wave included a successful campaign for a more effective militia and an impetus toward stronger labor organization by railroad employees and other workers.

[*See also* Depressions, Economic; Gilded Age; Industrial Relations; Labor Movements; Pullman Strike and Boycott; Strikes and Industrial Conflict.]

• Robert V. Bruce, *1877: Year of Violence*, 1959. Philip S. Foner, *The Great Labor Uprising of 1877*, 1977.

—David R. Roediger

RANDOLPH, A. PHILIP (1889–1979), union head and *civil rights leader. A socialist, Asa Philip Randolph saw economic empowerment as the key to *African-American advancement, a philosophy he espoused in his *Messenger* magazine in the 1920s. In 1925 he organized the Brotherhood of Sleeping Car Porters, the nation's first predominantly black union, which he led until 1968. In 1937, Randolph won union recognition from the Pullman Company. Two years earlier, he had become president of the National Negro Congress (NCC), an African-American labor organization created in response to the Great Depression. His experience with communists in the NCC strengthened his *anticommunism.

In 1941 Randolph threatened a mass protest march in *Washington, D.C., that led President Franklin Delano *Roosevelt to create a *Fair Employment Practice Committee (FEPC). Randolph subsequently lobbied to make the FEPC permanent, and his advice to African-American men to refuse conscription into a segregated military prompted President Harry S. *Truman's 1948 executive order integrating the military.

With his younger associate Bayard Rustin (1912–1987), Randolph played a key role in devising the strategy of mass, nonviolent civil disobedience that fueled the midcentury *civil rights movement. He was the primary force behind the historic 1963 civil rights march in Washington, D.C. Although vice president of the merged *American Federation of Labor–*Congress of Industrial Organizations (AFL–CIO), he also created the Negro American Labor Council in 1959 to fight *racism within the union movement. The A. Philip Randolph Institute, which he founded in 1964, promoted his lifelong goals, especially the struggle against economic inequality that would bring together working people of all races.

[*See also* Labor Movements; Segregation, Racial; Socialism; Socialist Party of America.]

• Jervis Anderson, *A. Philip Randolph: A Biographical Portrait*, 1973. Paula F. Pfeffer, *A. Philip Randolph: Pioneer of the Civil Rights Movement*, 1996.

—Paula F. Pfeffer

RANKIN, JEANNETTE (1880–1973), suffragist, pacifist, first woman elected to the U.S. Congress. Born near Missoula, Montana Territory, the eldest of seven children of schoolteacher Olive Pickering and rancher John Rankin, Jeannette earned a B.S. in biology from the University of Montana in 1902 and studied *social work at the New York School of Philanthropy and the University of Washington. While working in Seattle in 1909, Rankin joined Washington's successful *woman suffrage movement. After campaigning for the cause in fifteen states in 1912–1914, she returned home to help win the vote for women in Montana. Elected to Montana's at-large seat in Congress in 1916, Rankin was only four days into her term when she voted (with fifty-six others) against a U.S. declaration of war on Germany. Failing in a reelection bid in 1918, she became a lobbyist and organizer for various peace groups. Throughout her life, Rankin championed two causes she believed were intertwined: women's rights and peace. Female voters, she contended, would counterbalance male militarism and eventually render war obsolete.

In 1940, Rankin returned to Congress and became the only member to vote against a declaration of war against Japan on 8 December 1941. This vote ended her political career; she resumed her efforts for peaceful alternatives to war. In 1968, at age eighty-eight, Rankin led five thousand women calling themselves the Jeannette Rankin Brigade in marching in *Washington, D.C. against the *Vietnam War. Rankin died of a heart attack in 1973 while considering a third congressional race to oppose what she saw as the growing risk of another world war.

[*See also* Feminism; Pacifism; Peace Movements; Women's Rights Movements; World War I.]

• Hannah Geffen Josephson, *First Lady in Congress*, 1974. Joan Hoff Wilson, " 'Peace Is a Woman's Job . . . ' Jeanette Rankin and American Foreign Policy: The Origins of Her Pacifism," *Montana: The Magazine of Western History* (Winter 1980): 28–41. Joan Hoff Wilson, " 'Peace Is a Woman's Job . . . ' Jeanette Rankin and American Foreign Policy: Her Life Work as a Pacifist," *Montana: The Magazine of Western History* (Spring 1980): 38–53.

—Janann Sherman

RAPE. All crimes must be viewed within their social and historical context, and this is certainly true of the crime of rape in America. Complicating the problem is the lack of a definitive historical study of the topic in the United States.

While both the legal history and the social and cultural understandings of rape have shifted dramatically from the *Colonial Era to the present, several themes clearly emerge. For much of the period, rape was understood as a kind of theft by one man of another man's property (that is, a daughter or a wife). Further, some property was deemed especially valuable. In colonial *New England, for example, rape was punishable by death, but of the tiny fraction of rape accusations that actually resulted in execution, all involved instances where the victim was married, engaged, or a young child; in other words, when she obviously and unambiguously "belonged" to a man. Another major theme in the history of rape has been a distinction based on the victim's race. Southern slave codes, for example, did not recognize the rape of a black female slave by her white owner as a crime.

Indeed, the racial politics of rape make the issue extremely complicated. Myths of the sexual voraciousness of African-American males and females enabled white men during and after *slavery to exert control over the bodies of blacks, male and female, as well as white women, to whom they stood as self-appointed protectors. The notion that black men were genetically predisposed to rape, and that their preferred victims were white women, flourished in the postemancipation era. In these years, as Jacquelyn Dowd Hall has put it, rape stories functioned as the "folk porn[ography] of the Bible belt." In this setting, *lynching became an ever more popular response to these imagined fears. While only about a quarter of the lynchings of black males were actually motivated by rape accusations, the fusion of racial and sexual politics meant that lynching was widely understood as the honorable act of white men protecting "their" women. Leaders of the antilynching campaign, including such women as Ida B. *Wells-Barnett and Jessie Daniel Ames, of course, rejected the attempt to justify lynching as an expression of chivalry. Wells-Barnett, an African American, further noted that black women were absent from the rhetorical defense of lynching as a means of protecting female virtue.

Studies of the history of rape in Canada, England, and other Western countries all suggest that it is and has been a crime that tends to take place within, not across, the boundaries of race, *social class, and ethnic group. The American obsession with black men as rapists (though not the response of lynching) has a historical parallel, in Canada and England, with the notion that working-class men are similarly incapable of controlling their animal instincts. But historical and contemporary studies suggest that the more similar in background and the better acquainted the alleged victim and the alleged rapist, the less likely that the alleged victim would be believed in court. This underscored the persistence, at least among judges and juries, of the popular misperception that rapists are most likely to come from outside their victim's social group.

The often humiliating treatment of rape complainants by the legal system, coupled with the emergence of a revived *women's rights movement, helped to politicize rape again in the 1960s and beyond. The redefinition of rape by feminists, especially Susan Brownmiller's highly influential book about rape, *Against Our Will* (1975), changed the politics of the issue. Many feminists now viewed rape as a crime of *gender power alone. As the foundation of a system of male dominance, some argued, rape united all women as victims, and all men—whatever their class or color—as potential rapists or beneficiaries of women's fears of rape. In this view, rape was seen as the key to patriarchal rule, the ultimate act of domination by which all men keep all women in a near-constant state of fear. Yet as black feminists have continually pointed out, the racial dynamics of rape, and the legacy of the myth of the menacing black man, had yet to be directly addressed.

By the 1990s a reaction had set in, as some women writers criticized some feminists' obsession with rape as a revival, in a new guise, of old notions of women's sexual innocence and helplessness in the face of sexually aggressive male behavior. Nevertheless, a belief in women's bodily inviolability remained at the forefront of the antirape campaigns, campus marches, and rape crisis centers that proliferated in the United States as the twentieth century ended.

[*See also* Crime; Feminism; Racism; Sexual Morality and Sex Reform.]

• Susan Brownmiller, *Against Our Will: Men, Women and Rape*, 1975. Jacquelyn Dowd Hall, *Revolt against Chivalry: Jessie Daniel Ames and the Women's Campaign against Lynching*, 1979. Angela Y. Davis, *Women, Race and Class*, 1981. Thelma Jennings, " 'Us Colored Women Had to Go through a Plenty': Sexual Exploitation of African American Slave Women," *Journal of Women's History* 1 (1990): 45–66. Karen Dubinsky, *Improper Advances: Rape and Heterosexual Conflict in Ontario, 1880–1929*, 1993. Mary Odem, *Delinquent Daughters: Protecting and Policing Adolescent Female Sexuality in the United States, 1885–1920*, 1995.

—Karen Dubinsky

RAUSCHENBUSCH, WALTER (1861–1918), theologian of the *Social Gospel. Born in Rochester, New York, the son of a prominent German-American Baptist minister, Walter Rauschenbusch graduated from the University of Rochester and Rochester Theological Seminary. From 1886 to 1897 he served the Second German Baptist Church in *New York City, where exposure to *poverty and *disease profoundly reoriented his thinking toward the social significance of the gospel. Returning to the Rochester seminary in 1897, he taught there until his death.

The central motif that emerged from Rauschenbusch's pastoral experience and theological, historical, and sociological studies, including a European sabbatical in 1891, was the coming Kingdom of God. For him, the kingdom idea encompassed all of Christianity, including its evangelical aspects and its social mission. With several associates, he formed the Brotherhood of the Kingdom (1893), a small but influential mutual-support network and forum for theological exploration.

Rauschenbusch's critique of *capitalism, especially in *Christianity and the Social Crisis* (1907), which brought him national prominence, and *Christianizing the Social Order* (1912), identified him as one of the Social Gospel's most radical thinkers. He believed that *socialism was spiritually and morally congruent with Christianity. Although he never joined the *Socialist party, he spoke and wrote under its auspices (and voted for its candidates). His writings, including also *The Social Principles of Jesus* (1916) and *A Theology for the Social Gospel* (1917), influenced an entire generation of ministers and lay people far beyond his own classroom.

[*See also* Niebuhr, Reinhold; Progressive Era; Protestantism; Religion.]

• Dores R. Sharpe, *Walter Rauschenbusch*, 1942. Paul M. Minus, *Walter Rauschenbusch: American Reformer*, 1988.

—Jacob H. Dorn

RAWLS, JOHN (1921–), moral and political philosopher. Born in Baltimore, John Bordley Rawls attended Princeton, served in the Pacific in *World War II, and received his Princeton Ph.D. in 1950 for a dissertation entitled "A Study in the Grounds of Ethical Knowledge." He taught briefly at Princeton, Cornell, and the Massachusetts Institute of Technology, and for thirty years at Harvard, training many leading philosophers in ethics and political *philosophy.

Rawls's major work, *A Theory of Justice* (1971), used a hypothetical social contract (the "Original Position") to argue for an alternative to the utilitarianism that dominated Anglo-American philosophy. Deliberating behind a "veil of ignorance" that blinds them to distinguishing and potentially biasing facts about themselves, contractors in Rawls's hypothetical scenario choose principles that protect certain basic liberties, guarantee fair equality of opportunity, and permit inequalities (measured by an index of primary social goods) only if the inequalities work to make those who are worst off as well off as possible. These principles, he argued, match our considered moral judgments in "reflective equilibrium" better than utilitarianism and produce a system that is more stable. Rawls revised his account of stability and political justification in *Political Liberalism* (1993) to address the pluralism of comprehensive moral views that arise in free nation states.

Rawls's work became the dominant influence in discussions of *liberalism and democratic theory in the last quarter of the century, influencing such fields as *jurisprudence, *economics, and *political science. Its focus on substantive issues rather than on questions about the "language" of moral discourse also contributed to a broad resurgence in applied ethics.

• Norman Daniels, ed., *Reading Rawls: Critical Studies of* A Theory of Justice, 1975. Symposium on Rawlsian Theory of Justice: Recent Developments, *Ethics* 99 (1989). Samuel Freeman, ed., *Companion to Rawls*, 2001.

—Norman Daniels

REAGAN, RONALD (1911–), fortieth president of the United States. A political liberal in his youth, Ronald Wilson Reagan helped create a conservative coalition in middle age and moved American politics rightward after winning the presidency at age sixty-nine. Born in Tampico, Illinois, he grew up in a family that was by the standards of the day socially as well as politically liberal. His Roman Catholic father Jack and his evangelical Protestant mother Nelle condemned *racism, and young Ron received help from a Jewish mentor. Jack's job with the *Works Progress Administration helped the family survive the Depression of the 1930s, but Jack's alcoholism left a mark on his son's personality. Outwardly amiable and optimistic, Reagan typically concealed his feelings, avoided confrontations, and cultivated many acquaintances but few close friends.

After graduating from Eureka College in 1932, Reagan became a *radio sportscaster in the *Middle West and then began a *film acting career in Hollywood. Generally avoiding the movie colony's often wild social life, he nevertheless became active in the Screen Actors Guild (SAG) and a master of Hollywood politics. In 1940 he helped to arrange production of his most famous film, *Knute Rockne: All American,* in which he starred as Notre Dame football legend George Gipp. That same year he married actress Jane Wyman. Involved in national politics as well, he voted for Franklin Delano *Roosevelt four times and bled for liberal causes so easily, he would later joke, that he was "hemophiliac." Barred from *World War II combat by weak vision, he acted in films and plays produced by the army.

A series of crises in the late 1940s permanently altered Reagan's life. He almost died of pneumonia, his marriage collapsed, and his movie career stalled. A *Cold War liberal Democrat during this period, he testified before the *House Committee on Un-American Activities as president of SAG and was a secret informant for the *Federal Bureau of Investigation. Nancy Davis, an actress whom he met in 1949 and married three years later, restored stability to his life and nudged him rightward. He became a public spokesman for General Electric during the 1950s, joined the *Republican party in the early 1960s, and won a national conservative following while campaigning for Republican presidential nominee Barry *Goldwater in 1964. As governor of *California from 1967 to 1975, Reagan sounded conservative but often acted moderately. He compromised with Democratic legislators, allowed state budget increases, and signed a bill liberalizing *abortion. Bids for the Republican presidential nomination in 1968 and 1976 proved unsuccessful.

Like the country as a whole, Reagan became more conservative during the late 1970s, yet he won the presidency in 1980, defeating President Jimmy *Carter, as the inspirational head of a broad coalition that included "Reagan Democrats" who blamed Carter for economic "stagflation" and a perceived decline of American power abroad. Moreover, except for his action to curb unions (most notably when he fired striking federal employees who belonged to the air-traffic controllers' union), Reagan had no intention of dismantling the New Deal. Cuts in federal expenditures centered on antipoverty programs created during President Lyndon B. *Johnson's administration rather than on middle-class entitlements. Overall, his economic program benefited the affluent. His administration lowered taxes, especially in the upper brackets; accepted a recession to stop runaway inflation; and promoted reduced governmental regulation of business. "Reaganomics" proved less popular than "the Gipper" himself, whose standing soared when he responded bravely to an assassination attempt in March 1981. He and his vice president, George *Bush, won a sweeping reelection victory in 1984, defeating Democrat Walter Mondale and his running mate Geraldine Ferraro.

After twenty-five years of Cold War détente in practice if not in name, Reagan resumed vigorous denunciation of the Soviet Union as an evil, totalitarian empire. He also sponsored the largest military buildup in U.S. history. In March 1983, confronted with a strong *antinuclear protest movement, he proposed a high-tech missile defense system known as the Strategic Defense Initiative. Heavy military spending, coupled with tax cuts, produced massive budget deficits, compounded by a severe trade imbalance. Elsewhere, Reagan's diplomacy mixed prudence with exaggerated fears of Third World radicalism. He retained diplomatic relations with communist China and, after a disastrous intervention in the Lebanese civil war cost more than three hundred American lives in guerrilla bombings, prudently withdrew. On the other hand, he ordered the bombing of Libya and the invasion of Grenada on the dubious grounds that their governments profoundly threatened U.S. interests, and he worked tirelessly to overthrow the Marxist Sandinista regime in Nicaragua. Although the full story may never be known, Reagan in the mid-1980s at least acquiesced in a clandestine and illegal plan to sell arms to Iran and divert the profits to anti-Sandinista rebels known as the Contras. A congressional investigation of the *Iran-Contra Affair in 1986 temporarily damaged Reagan's popularity, but this crisis was soon eclipsed by the end of the Cold War. The degree to which Reagan's military buildup contributed to the collapse of *communism remains conjectural, but Reagan unquestionably responded flexibly as the Soviet Union moved toward democracy under Mikhail Gorbachev. Nancy Reagan, an influential behind-the-scenes figure in the Reagan White House, encouraged this flexibility. Reagan left office in 1989 as the most popular president since Dwight D. *Eisenhower. Diagnosed with *Alzheimer's disease in 1994, he withdrew from public life.

[*See also* Anticommunism; Conservatism; Foreign Relations; New Deal Era, The.]

• Lou Cannon, *Reagan,* 1982. Larry Berman, ed., *Looking Back on the Reagan Presidency,* 1990. Lou Cannon, *President Reagan: The Role of a Lifetime,* 1991. William E. Pemberton, *Exit with Honor: The Life and Presidency of Ronald Reagan,* 1997. Edmund Morris, *Dutch: A Memoir of Ronald Reagan,* 1999.

—Leo P. Ribuffo

RECONSTRUCTION, the attempt to rebuild and reform the *South politically, economically, and socially after the *Civil War, and to refashion race relations throughout the nation. Historians of the era have focused on four questions: How much change occurred between the antebellum and postbellum eras? Was Reconstruction too radical or too conservative? When did it start and end? How and why did it fail?

Background to Reconstruction. Reconstruction proved as deeply political as the controversies over *slavery and secession, and all three followed the same pattern: *liberalism triumphed when reactionaries overreached. In 1861, southern secession freed Republicans from the pressure to compromise to preserve the Union. Over time, the Abraham *Lincoln administration and the Republican majority in Congress repealed racist laws, freed secessionists' slaves, enrolled African-American troops, and eventually passed the Thirteenth Amendment abolishing slavery throughout the country. Slaves effectively freed themselves by escaping to Union territory, and they fought valiantly against their former masters. The most deadly war in American history destroyed not only slavery but most of the South's physical and financial capital. Defeated, demoralized, and economically depressed, the South in 1865 seemingly lay helpless before the self-confident, prosperous North, whose activist government, bathed in the moral authority of a patriotic, reformist war, appeared poised to remake what many northerners considered the country's nether region.

The Reconstruction Era: 1865–1877. White southerners, however, behaved as though the war had settled nothing except the impracticality of secession and the nominal abolition of slavery. After Lincoln's assassination and accession of Tennessee Democrat Andrew *Johnson to the presidency, southern states passed "Black Codes" that denied *African Americans the right to vote, serve on juries, testify against whites in court, buy or lease real estate, or refuse to sign yearly labor contracts. Blacks were excluded from public schools, black orphans "apprenticed" to their former owners, and black "servants" required to labor from sunup to sundown for their "masters." White southerners also demanded that former Confederate officers and politicians be immediately seated in Congress.

But the Republicans who controlled Congress refused to admit the erstwhile rebels and they took decisive control of Reconstruction. When Johnson vetoed a bill extending the *Freedmen's Bureau, which provided food to destitute southerners of both races, supervised labor contracts, and started schools where ex-slaves could be educated and courts where their rights could be protected, Republicans in Congress overrode his action, as they did his veto of a Civil Rights Bill that outlawed the Black Codes and mandated basic legal *equality. Over unanimous Democratic opposition, Republicans passed the *Fourteenth Amendment, which constitutionalized *civil rights by guaranteeing due process and equality before the law for all.

In the critical 1866 election campaign, Johnson demagogically lambasted Congress, northern Democrats endlessly race-baited, and white southerners rioted in Memphis and *New Orleans, killing eighty-nine African Americans in full view of the national press. Northern voters reacted by giving the Republicans a landslide victory, which turned Reconstruction more radical. Ten southern states were placed under temporary military rule, forced to enfranchise African-American men, and granted congressional representation only after they had ratified the Fourteenth Amendment and rewritten their state constitutions to make them more liberal. Because Johnson persisted in trying to subvert the antiracist settlement, he was impeached, almost convicted, and practically rendered powerless.

Although buttressed by federal troops; by the *Fifteenth Amendment, which mandated racially impartial *suffrage nationally; and by federal jobs with which to reward supporters, the new Republican governments of the South faced three obstacles that ultimately proved insuperable. First, they had to rebuild the southern infrastructure and satisfy a greatly increased demand for government services, especially education, by raising taxes in a devastated region that after 1873 also faced a severe economic depression. Second, they had to overcome two centuries of ingrained *racism and convince one in four white men to vote for the party that had just defeated their section in a bloody war. Third, they had to compete at the polls against opponents willing to use any amount of fraud and violence to win elections and to employ election-law trickery and discriminatory practices to retain power once they gained it. After northern voters reacted to the economic depression and northern ethno-religious conflicts by electing a Democratic majority in the House in 1874, the survival of Reconstruction became increasingly problematic. Although Republicans rebounded to win the closest presidential election in U.S. history in 1876, part of the price for settling disputes over the election outcome was the implicit promise to stop using the army to protect southern Republicans. The *Compromise of 1877, as the settlement came to be called, marked what is usually treated as the end of Reconstruction.

Evaluating Reconstruction. Many historians believe that Reconstruction brought profound changes. As slaves, African Americans had worked very intensively, often in large groups or "gangs," under the constant threat of physical punishment. They could not legally marry or learn to read and write. They could be sold or moved against their wills and their families could be broken up. Masters constantly intervened in their lives. After emancipation, blacks first worked in "squads," usually headed by independent black contractors, and gradually convinced landowners to let them reside on small family plots, where they enjoyed a degree of privacy and independence. Through sharecropping arrangements, in which workers were paid a percentage of the value of crops after sale, landowners and workers shared the risk of crop failure and guarded against contract violations by either party. Ex-slaves used their new freedom of mobility to bargain with employers. By 1900, 20 percent of black farm operators owned the land they worked.

The United States was the only large slave society that quickly enfranchised ex-slaves, and the eagerness and skill with which the freedmen took to politics surprised and dismayed their former masters, who had expected docility and incompetence. Almost unanimously supporting the *Republican party—the party of abolition and enfranchisement—the freedmen participated in the constitutional conventions of 1867–1868 and elected governments that launched statewide education systems, encouraged *railroads, passed civil rights laws, protected the rights of laborers, established orphanages and other public institutions, and mandated universal manhood suffrage. African Americans sat in all southern legislatures and filled high state posts in Lousiana, Mississippi, and South Carolina. Several, mostly from South Carolina, were elected to the House of Representatives, and two went to the Senate: Hiram Revels and Blanche K. Bruce of Mississippi. Most black males retained the vote until around 1900 when suffrage restrictions adopted by Democratic legislatures and constitutional conventions disfranchised the vast majority of African Americans and many poor whites.

Reconstruction-era social changes were also striking. Blacks could now legally marry; worship as they wished; form private clubs; receive at least some education at public expense; and often patronize public accommodations such as restaurants, theaters, and railroads on a non-segregated basis, if they could afford to pay. Absolute racial *segregation of public places arrived only toward the turn of the century, and it was a matter of law, not custom.

Despite such transformations, however, historians who stress continuity between the antebellum and postbellum periods point to the persistent, often increased *poverty of southern African Americans; the continuation of the plantation system; the survival of many former plantation owners or their sons among the postwar economic and social elite; the eventual disfranchisement and segregation of blacks; and the frequent outbreaks of racist violence, particularly the surge of *lynching in the 1890s, which was horrifying enough, though far below the levels of the 1860s and 1870s The change-or-continuity question turns on which comparisons are made: One side emphasizes that post–Civil War blacks were far from being slaves; the other, that they were far from being fully equal citizens.

Historians who believe that Reconstruction was too radical contend that more gradual enfranchisement, a stronger Republican alliance with former southern Whigs, and less vigorous attacks on segregation and discrimination would have led to more lasting change. Critics of the conservative position respond that in the short interval when significant change was possible, Radical Republicans had to push for as much reform as they could get, and that the former Whigs, who were largely responsible for the 1865–1866 Black Codes, were hardly attractive allies for a party of blacks and poor whites. Those who criticize Reconstruction as too conservative hold that only widespread land redistribution from former masters to former slaves, and perhaps even the extermination of the planter class, would have achieved a true social revolution. Those who reject this position reply that a full-scale radical assault on the southern order might have frightened northern voters into ending Republican dominance earlier and hazarded a holocaust of revenge violence. In any event, they suggest that to have given the freed slaves small, undercapitalized farms, most on marginal land, might only have shackled them and the South to even deeper poverty.

If the end of Reconstruction is placed in 1877, then violence, ballot-box stuffing, and the repudiation of the Republicans for mostly economic reasons must figure prominently in explanations of its failure. If Reconstruction is thought to have collapsed a generation later, however, with the imposition of strict segregation and disfranchisement across the South, then a succession of incremental legal changes and their validation by the *Supreme Court account better for its demise. The upsurge of *civil rights legislation in the North in the 1870s and 1880s and the near-passage of the Lodge Elections Bill, a measure strongly attacking fraud in southern congressional elections, in 1890 support the view that Reconstruction extended beyond 1877, and suggest that diffuse northern racism did not account for its waning. Throughout the later nineteenth century, almost all congressional Republicans, but not a single Democrat, supported civil rights measures. Reconstruction, in short, was born, evolved, and died in political struggle.

[*See also* Agriculture: 1770s to 1890; *Civil Rights Cases;* Cotton Industry; Democratic Party; Depressions, Economic; Hayes, Rutherford; Impeachment; Sharecropping and Tenantry; Whig Party.]

• J. Morgan Kousser, *The Shaping of Southern Politics*, 1974. C. Vann Woodward, *The Strange Career of Jim Crow*, 1974. Thomas Holt, *Black over White*, 1977. William Gillette, *Retreat from Reconstruction*, 1979. Michael Wayne, *The Reshaping of Plantation Society*, 1983. Michael Per-man, *The Road to Redemption*, 1984. Dan T. Carter, *When the War Was Over*, 1985. Gerald David Jaynes, *Branches without Roots*, 1986. Eric Foner, *Reconstruction*, 1988.

—J. Morgan Kousser

RECREATION. *See* Leisure; Sports: Amateur Sports and Recreation.

RED CROSS, AMERICAN. Clara Barton (1821–1912) founded the American Red Cross in 1881, one year before Congress belatedly ratified the 1864 Geneva Convention concerning wartime help for sick and wounded soldiers. Although Barton played a modest role during the *Spanish-American War, full official recognition eluded her, and impromptu disaster relief became her first priority. After 1900 she was pushed aside by prominent New Yorkers who reorganized the Red Cross and redefined its status, role, and scope: Theodore *Roosevelt drafted a new charter that defined a closer relationship to the government and the army; Robert W. DeForest grounded its relief work on the principles of scientific philanthropy and the *charity organization movement; and Henry P. Davison gave it legitimacy on Wall Street, headed its endowment fund, and directed its extensive operations during *World War I. The Red Cross provided both planned assistance to the *military and an outlet for civilian patriotic enthusiasm; the wartime boom brought the organization 20 million members and a treasury surplus of $127 million by 1919. Salaried administrators proliferated despite its tradition of *voluntarism.

Ambitious plans for innovative peacetime *public-health and social-welfare programs at home and abroad soon foundered on war-weariness and *isolationism, opposition from established agencies and interest groups, hostility from the newspapers controlled by William Randolph *Hearst, and a grassroots suspicion among volunteers that the central office had been taken over by careerist professionals. Red Cross personnel and aspirations were quickly, if reluctantly, scaled back in response to diminished public expectations and a postwar drop in membership and contributions. Further criticism arose during the Depression of the 1930s, when the Red Cross refused a federal subsidy for assisting drought victims, soliciting private contributions instead, and then agreed to distribute government surplus wheat and cotton. Public controversy was fueled by claims that Red Cross leaders opposed the New Deal, disliked labor unions, and embodied typically white racial attitudes.

Beginning with *World War II, improvements in the U.S. military's medical and *nursing services changed the Red Cross's wartime role to one of providing generalized recreational services instead of auxiliary medical assistance. In the second half of the twentieth century, despite periodic pressure to assist the State Department's foreign-policy agenda or White House public-relations efforts, civilian disaster relief became its principal peacetime function. Over the years, the Red Cross's relationship with the American press and public has fluctuated from adulation to vilification and indifference. Unlike the great philanthropic foundations, its visibility and income varied with the public mood, increasing at times of natural disasters or other crises. An early 1990s survey found that it was the most highly regarded of major U.S. charities. During the *Persian Gulf War, for example, donations soared to $26 million.

By the mid-1990s, the American Red Cross was one of America's largest charitable organizations, with more than 1,300 local chapters, an annual budget of $1.8 billion (mostly raised by private and corporate contributions), a paid staff of around 30,000, and some 1.3 million volunteers annually. A fifty-member volunteer board of directors governed the organization. Its national programs included disaster relief, a blood-donor program that supplied about one-half of the nation's blood supply, and health and safety services including minor-injury treatment and blood-pressure and cholesterol-testing programs. A major initiative focused on increasing health services to minority groups and recruiting minority volunteers. The American Red Cross also worked with the International Red Cross and Red Crescent movement to meet human needs arising from natural disaster or conflicts in many countries, including, at the end of the 1990s, Kosovo and East Timor.

[*See also* Galveston Hurricane and Flood; New Deal Era, The; Philanthropy and Philanthropic Foundations.]

• Foster Rhea Dulles, *The American Red Cross: A History*, 1950. Patrick F. Gilbo, *The American Red Cross: The First Century*, 1981.

—John F. Hutchinson

REED, WALTER (1851–1902), physician and microbiologist, leader of the U.S. Army Yellow Fever Board that established the mosquito vector of *yellow fever. Born in Belroi, Virginia, Walter Reed received his first M.D. degree from the University of Virginia in 1869 and a second in 1870 from Bellevue Hospital Medical College in New York. From 1875 until his death he served in the Medical Corps of the U.S. Army. In 1898 he headed an army investigation of the spread of *typhoid fever in military camps during the *Spanish-American War. Two years later, Army Surgeon General George Sternberg appointed him head of the Yellow Fever Board, charged with investigating the yellow fever problem in Havana.

Reed, together with his fellow physicians Jesse Lazear, Aristides Agramonte, and James Carroll, conducted an extensive series of experiments to determine the mode of transmission of yellow fever. Lacking an animal model for studying the disease, Reed's colleagues used their own bodies for experimentation, as well as those of American soldier volunteers and Spanish immigrants. In 1900 Reed's board successfully demonstrated that the mosquito *Aedes aegypti* transmits yellow fever, a discovery that facilitated the eradication of the disease in Havana, the southern United States, and the *Panama Canal Zone. Initially lionized for the yellow fever discovery, Reed also came to be regarded as a model for ethical human experimentation, in recognition of his concern for the men who participated in the dangerous yellow fever studies and his introduction of written consent forms for medical volunteers.

[*See also* Disease; Medicine: From the 1870s to 1945; Public Health.]

• William B. Bean, *Walter Reed, a Biography*, 1982. Susan E. Lederer, *Subjected to Science: Human Experimentation in America before the Second World War*, 1995.

—Susan E. Lederer

REFRIGERATION AND AIR CONDITIONING. The development after 1850 of machines to control the temperature and moisture content of air profoundly affected the way Americans lived and worked. Although refrigeration and air conditioning are historically and technologically entwined, their purposes differ. Refrigeration preserves food and other perishables; air conditioning—a term coined in 1906 by textile engineer Stuart Cramer—controls temperature and humidity in spaces generally occupied by human beings.

Refrigeration arose from the early nineteenth century practice of "harvesting" *New England lake ice and shipping huge blocks, packed in sawdust, to cold-storage warehouses. By mid-century, ice processing and transport had improved enough to supply growing U.S. cities and an overseas market. By the 1880s, ice-making machinery was widely used in southern cities and spreading nationwide.

In 1902, pioneering air cooling systems were installed at the New York Stock Exchange by Alfred R. Wolff and at Brooklyn's Sackett-Wilhelms printing plant by Willis H. Carrier, the "Father of Air Conditioning."

Both refrigeration and air conditioning benefited from technical improvements in compressor and pump design. The DuPont Corporation's 1930 development of the refrigerant Freon proved a major breakthrough. Safer than commonly used ammonia, Freon made possible smaller, more efficient refrigerators and air conditioners.

Costly home refrigerators caught on slowly, but by 1920 the spread of commercial refrigeration had already affected food production and marketing, reshaping the American diet. As fresh and frozen foods edged out salted, dried, and canned goods, Americans developed new expectations of food safety and palatability.

The effects of air conditioning proved even more diverse. In factories and offices, controlled climate encouraged *productivity and facilitated heat-sensitive processes such as microchip manufacture. Introduced in movie palaces in the 1920s, comfort air conditioning became popular in residences only after 1950. By the end of the century it had become a standard appliance in many households. The environmental costs of both inventions, however, as demonstrated by summer power outages and a ban on atmosphere-degrading Freon, raised concerns about their basic safety.

[*See also* Environmentalism; Food and Diet; Technology.]

• Oscar E. Anderson Jr., *Refrigeration in America: A History of a New Technology and Its Impact,* 1953, reprint 1972. Gail Cooper, *Air-Conditioning America: Engineers and the Controlled Environment, 1900–1960,* 1998.

—Marsha E. Ackermann

REGIONALISM. Regionalism has persisted in the United States in spite of social and economic *mobility and telecommunications innovations that tend to homogenize culture and diminish geographic isolation. Studies of regionalism may be divided into two groups: those that emphasize material factors and those that emphasize ideas. The first considers the region as a form of classification that differentiates cultural traits geographically. These classifications identify culture areas, which become the basis for cultural-diffusion studies. Questions of regional identity may arise in such studies, but more often the analysis is limited to material culture and *folk art and crafts. The second type of study views regionalism as a form of collective solidarity and identity, often set against a national identity of the standardizing forces of modernization and globalization. Attempts to construct a theoretical understanding of regionalism have tended to conflate these two emphases, as was the case with early twentieth-century theories of environmental determinism and folk *sociology.

The story of regionalism in American history begins at different times, depending on which view of regionalism is given greater importance. For example, indigenous North American populations developed regionally distinct ways of life associated with different resource bases and forms of social organization. Clearly, distinct culture areas existed before the arrival of European settlers, but speculation about regionalist sentiment makes little sense in light of the strength of tribal identity and the absence of any compelling reason to conceptualize one's place in the world in terms of territorial parts in relation to a whole.

Similarly, in the early *Colonial Era, particular ecological settings and different national and religious identities of European settlers led to distinct culture areas and forms of life within the colonies. These differences were associated with regional identities, however, only after being cast in relation to a spatially more extensive protonational spirit. Differing colonial experiences and the settlement of the western frontier created strong and persistent regional political interests. The unique ways of life that divided the northern and southern colonies and the trans-Appalachian West, and that set individual colonies apart from one another, helped to shape American politics through the nineteenth century, despite the strong sense of continentalism that dictated the federal government's geopolitical strategies.

The *Civil War was the most violent and destructive expression of these competing sectional interests. The war's decisive military outcome did little to diminish the sense of separateness between the North and the *South, as reflected in the several regionalist movements associated with southern intellectuals in the nineteenth and twentieth centuries. The latter half of the nineteenth century also witnessed a growing sense of the particularity of western political interests. Here, regionalism provided a frame for the economic interests of an industrial, commercial, and urban Northeast; an agricultural and rural South; and a transitional *Middle West, astride a burgeoning industrial belt and rich agricultural lands; and an American *West rich in natural resources and characterized by extensive *agriculture. To the American eye, the nation was a federal union made up of distinct regional societies and cultures. To others, and especially to Europeans, what most characterized American culture was its homogeneity.

The importance of regionalism in twentieth-century American intellectual life varied widely. It also underwent a gradual semantic shift. Once an expression of subnational political interests, it gradually came to refer to antimodernist cultural themes. In this respect, regionalist movements were influential in *painting, *literature, and *architecture, usually as a counterpoint to modernist canons. Regionalist movements in planning, sociology, and human ecology emphasized decentralization and presented the region as an effective antidote to the perceived placelessness of an increasingly urban, corporate, and bureaucratic America. Such diverse American intellectuals as the philosophers Josiah Royce and John *Dewey, the historians Frederick Jackson *Turner and Walter Prescott Webb, and the sociologist Howard Odum and geographer Carl Sauer expressed concern about the loss of regional sentiment in twentieth-century America. The urbanist Lewis *Mumford championed a relatively unique regionalist vision that he though compatible with *urbanization, *technology, and professional planning.

Many of these writers shared a utopian communitarian vision of an America composed of decentralized democratic polities. Regionalism was thus one defense against the perceived coercion associate with centralization. In fact, however, it has more often been associated with isolation from the mainstream, which explains in part why regionalism as a concept has been more important to folklorists and American Studies specialists than to political scientists, sociologists, and economists. Regionalism has, however, played a role in subdisciplines that focus on social and economic ties between cities and their hinterlands, such as urban sociology or functionalism or regional economies.

The social scientific study of American life has tended to view regional studies, outside of urban regions, as nostalgic and conservative, especially in relation to divisions of social life along class and ethnic lines. This perception changed gradually at the end of the twentieth century, however, as regionalism gained some prominence in postmodernist studies and as attachment to places and regions figured in discussion of modern identities. Environmentalist thought also turned its attention to regionalist themes, as in the concept of bioregionalism and in other attempts to conceptualize the relation of human communities to the natural environment.

[*See also* Nationalism; New England; Social Class; Social Science; Utopian and Communitarian Movements.]

• Howard W. Odum and Harry Estill Moore, *American Regionalism: A Cultural-Historical Approach to National Integration,* 1938. Merrill Jensen, ed., *Regionalism in America,* 1965. Michael Steiner and Clarence Mondale, *Region and Regionalism in the United States,* 1988. Barbara Allen and Thomas J. Schlerth, eds., *Sense of Place: American Regional Cultures,* 1990. David M. Holman, *A Certain Slant of Light: Regionalism and the Form of Southern and Midwestern Fiction,* 1995. James M. Dennis, *Renegade Regionalists: The Modern Independence of Grant Wood, Thomas Hart Benton, and John Steuart Curry,* 1998. Bruce Katz, ed., *Reflections on Regionalism,* 2000.

—J. Nicholas Entrikin

REISMAN, D. *See Lonely Crowd, The.*

RELIGION. As the twentieth century ended, almost everything was up for grabs in American religious history. Social scientists argued whether the United States was nearly unique in its religiosity (e.g., with church attendance rates higher than anywhere else in the Western world except Poland, Ireland, and South Africa) or far gone in a process of *secularization (e.g., with no obvious religious influence on the great economic realities that define the United States' place in the world). Historians quarreled over how to incorporate the voices of women, ethnic minorities, and representatives of nonwestern religions in accounts that traditionally focused on men, British-stock communities, and the main Christian denominations. Theologians debated whether American ways of life undercut, supported, or supplanted authentic religion. The one exception to academic contention was the growing conviction that the religious practices, narratives, values, and habits of ordinary people deserve more attention than they have yet received in telling the story.

Beginnings. About the centrality of religion throughout American history—at the end of the twentieth century no less than in the supposedly less secular periods of the past—there can be no doubt. An idiosyncratic understanding of scripture figured prominently among the motives that drove Christopher *Columbus to the New World; a cosmology sensitive to the intrusion of outsiders functioned in a similar religious way for the Native Americans who witnessed his arrival. In the first period of European settlement, a variety of Roman Catholics and Protestants used religion to rationalize the destruction of Native populations. Others, like the Dominicans Bartolomé de Las Casas (1474–1566) and Francisco de Vitoria (1483–1546), defended with specific Christian reasoning the property, lives, and souls of the Indians. During the seventeenth century, English immigrants established several *New England colonies on a foundation of private family faith as well as on public church covenants and a general sense that God was a partner in their enterprise. Conditions of settlement in the Middle Colonies—with thriving bands of Presbyterians, Quakers, Mennonites, Dutch Reformed, Moravians, *Baptists, and more—soon made that region one of the most religiously pluralistic parts of the world. By the 1740s, subjective and evangelical forms of Christianity were exerting more influence in America than corresponding movements did in Britain or the Continent. During the *Seven Years' War, religious passions sustained Protestant British resistance to Roman Catholic France. And the *Revolutionary War was as much a religious civil war as it was an international conflict. While the Patriots' confidence that God favored the new nation received attention in later American *historiography, the Loyalists' conviction that God wanted the American colonies to remain a part of Britain was almost as strong, while a significant minority of religious pacifists rejected war as a means of settling international disputes.

The Religious Nineteenth Century. The reach of religion was most evident in the nineteenth century, which began with an unprecedented mobilization of Protestant energies. Led by grand visions of a Christian America among northern Congregationalists and Presbyterians, and fueled by the diligent labors of Methodist itinerants and Baptist farmer-preachers, Protestant leaders, local churches, denominations, and voluntary agencies transformed the religious landscape of the country. In the wake of the Revolution, the United States had been a substantially unchurched society. Slightly more than a generation later in 1835, the visiting Alexis de Tocqueville wrote in **Democracy in America*: "There is no country in the world where the Christian religion retains a greater influence over the souls of men than in America." By that date a great migration of European Roman Catholics had also begun; by the end of the century, it would make the Catholic church the country's largest, most diverse Christian denomination. And by *that* time, migrations from eastern and central Europe that would soon make the United States home to more Jews than anywhere else in the world were well under way.

The effects of active religious life were everywhere manifest throughout the century. Some form of Christian (usually Protestant) faith was integral in a long list of social movements: *antislavery and the defense of *slavery, anti-Catholic and *nativist movements, temperance and diet reform, attacks on the sexual double standard, efforts to improve treatment of the insane, and factory conditions for women and children. The nineteenth century also witnessed the remarkable combination of black chattel slavery and the rise of vigorous Christian movements among *African Americans, followed after the *Civil War by the explosive growth of African-American denominations.

The centrality of religion to the clash between North and *South that led to the Civil War is indicated by the religious revivals that became a major feature of camp life for both armies (in contrast to the more dissolute camps of the War for Independence). Abraham *Lincoln, who never joined a church, nonetheless evocatively used themes from the *Bible in his Second Inaugural Address of March 1865.

Religion played a major role in the emergence of women into public life. Whether as founder of a religious order like Mother Elizabeth Ann *Seton; novelist like Harriet Beecher Stowe, author of **Uncle Tom's Cabin*; abolitionist and promoter of women's rights like the freed slave *Sojourner Truth; or antislavery and women's-rights reformers like Sarah and Angelina *Grimké, the nineteenth century's expansion of women's roles rested on a religious foundation.

The century was also a golden age for religious thought in both *Protestantism and many other religious traditions. In New England, William Ellery *Channing, Lydia Maria *Child, and Theodore *Parker pioneered progressive forms of Christianity that pleased many and angered more. During the century's middle decades a phalanx of conservative Protestants—Congregationalist Nathaniel W. Taylor (1786–1858) at Yale, Presbyterians Charles *Hodge of Princeton and Henry Boynton Smith of New York, and the German Reformed John W. Nevin—offered competing varieties of Calvinism modified for American use. The antebellum revivalist Phoebe Palmer (1807–1874) became an effective advocate for Christian holiness, or sanctification. The African Methodist Episcopal bishop Daniel Alexander Payne (1811–1893) added themes from slave experience to a solidly conservative Protestantism. Samuel Schmucker (Lutheran), Philip Schaff (German Reformed), and John Ireland (Roman Catholic) were among those who gave immigrant communities fresh theological confidence. In Hartford, Horace Bushnell (1802–1876) combined his reading of the English poet Samuel Taylor Coleridge with his Congregational heritage to create America's most distinctive Romantic theology, most notably in *Christian Nurture* (1847). Out of *Boston, Mary Baker Eddy, healed spontaneously of a serious injury in 1866, founded *Christian Science as a way of overcoming the "false claims" of sickness and sin by appropriate deployment of mind and spirit. In Cincinnati, Rabbi Isaac Mayer *Wise became the architect of Reform *Judaism. And hymn writers like Lowell Mason, Fanny Crosby, and the anonymous authors of African-American *spirituals provided even more effective forms of religious language for everyday life. During the first half of the nineteenth century, in short, before the Civil War and the rise of industry dramatically shifted the nation's intellectual center of gravity, religious ideas played a central role in stabilizing American society.

The great exception to the obvious importance of religion during the nineteenth century was the economy. In its early decades, evangelical Protestant reformers like Lyman Beecher (1775–1863) tried to subject some aspects of economic life to systematic Christian critique. The same would be attempted by other evangelicals like Frances *Willard (of the *Woman's

Christian Temperance Union), the Catholic editor Orestes Brownson (1803–1876), and *Social Gospel advocates like Walter *Rauschenbusch. But such attempts were far less successful than religious efforts to shape family, personal, ecclesiastical, and cultural values.

Twentieth-Century Diffusion. In the twentieth century, religion figured somewhat less prominently in the national consciousness, but more for reasons concerning the kind of religion present than because of a decline in religious interest. As the century began, a major division in the historically dominant Protestant churches had the indirect effect of distancing cultural elites from religion. This division, known as the fundamentalist-modernist controversy, pitted aggressive defenders of contemporary intellectual fashion (the modernists who at their worst promoted little more than optimistic progressivism lightly coated with soothing God-talk) against militant fundamentalist defenders of nineteenth-century Christian *revivalism (who at their worst abandoned public life, higher education, and social reform for an anti-intellectual and reactionary biblical literalism). In consequence, religion became passé or an embarrassment in learned circles. As a result, prejudice against the academic study of religion was greater in the United States than in Europe, even though the rate of religious participation remained much higher in the United States.

An additional factor obscuring the visibility of religion in the twentieth-century America is the wide diffusion of religious practice beyond the standard categories of Protestant, Catholic, and Jew, including new religions and religions new to the United States. According to the 1996 edition of the *Encyclopedia of American Religion,* at least 2,150 organized religious groups existed in the United States in the 1990s, with many new variations of traditional European faiths joined by indigenous products as well as those related in some way to religions in other parts of the world. The very names of the groups suggest their bewildering multiplicity: Perfect Liberty Kyodon, New Enlightened Inspired Living, Nudist Christian Church of the Blessed Virgin Jesus, Kanzeonji Non-Sectarian Buddhist Temple, Original Hebrew Israelite Nation, Monastery of the Seven Rays.

By the end of the twentieth century two historic monotheistic faiths—Judaism and *Islam—also enjoyed a significant presence in North America. Judaism had come to flourish in many ways, especially as an object of vigorous study in yeshivot, Jewish universities, and many secular campuses. All the major expressions of Jewish ethnic and religious life (each with several subgroups) had assumed a heightened visibility: Reform, which now allowed for women rabbis; Conservative, which balanced modernity with Judaic tradition; and Orthodox, which maintained the study of the Talmud and the culture of the *shtetl.* American Jews also experienced mounting worry over intermarriage and cultural *assimilation along with internal division over the kinds and degree of support to offer the state of Israel, including the claim of Israel's Orthodox rabbinate to exercise sole authority to determine "who is a Jew." Islam, though newer to America, grew very rapidly after the 1960s with large-scale *immigration from Pakistan, Iran, Egypt, and Turkey joining the long-established smaller communities of Lebanese, Syrian, and various Arab groups. Most of the perhaps three million Muslims in the United States in the mid-1990s were of the more liberal Sunni branch. The African-American *Nation of Islam was a small but visible group that under Wallace D. Muhammad, son of Elijah Muhammad, found increasing acceptance in the worldwide Muslim community.

Alongside the rapid expansion of religions new to the United States, considerable power still attended the traditional faiths. The evangelist Billy *Graham, for instance, from the later 1940s through the 1990s, preached his evangelical Protestant message to more people, personally and by electronic means, than any other individual in the two millennia of Christian history. Chicago's Roman Catholic Joseph Cardinal Bernardin (1928–1996) was at his death one of America's most widely respected persons. The flourishing of *Pentecostalism and charismatic versions of Christian faith—with stress on healing, special empowerment by the Holy Spirit, and affective forms of worship—not only produced a host of new denominations, but also renewed traditional Protestant bodies as well as segments of the Catholic church.

Beginning in the early 1970s, religion reemerged as a force in American politics to a degree that had not been true since the time when such religiously charged issues as slavery, temperance, and the *World War I crusade to make the world safe for democracy had loomed large in public life. Now the resonant issues were *abortion, prayer in the public schools, and connections between private morality and public life.

End-Time Belief in American Religion. The perennial American fascination with eschatology (religiously infused theories about the end of the world) offered another indication of continuing religious ferment. In the mid-eighteenth century, Protestant evangelists had discerned the dawn of the millennium in the spread of revival. Revolutionary-Era patriots felt that American independence might inaugurate a divinely inspired Golden Age of freedom for all humanity. William Miller's Bible-based prediction of the world's end in 1843 (later postponed to 1844) was only the most widely publicized of many apocalyptic visions that enraptured millions of Americans during the nineteenth century. Miller's near contemporary Joseph Smith left a broader legacy in the Church of Jesus Christ of Latter-day Saints (or Mormons), another movement inspired in part by relevations concerning the fulfillment of ancient scripture and the end of time. In the twentieth century *Mormonism became a major missionary force, with about two-thirds of the denomination's fifteen million adherents in the 1990s located overseas. Mormons emerged as leaders in the politics of several western states, in education with Brigham Young University and a host of other institutions, and in some high-tech industries. Mormon concerns for family life, preference for the King James version of the Bible, and defense of traditional morality drew them closer to conservative Protestants, even as their loyalty to the distinctive teachings of Smith's Book of Mormon kept them separate.

Such currents again ran strong at the end of the twentieth century, now with a panoply of nontraditional sources like horoscopes augmenting more traditionally religious means of foretelling the future. Eschatological interest often percolated beyond the attention of the national media as with *The Late Great Planet Earth* (1970), a book by campus evangelist Hal Lindsey, who applied biblical prophecy to current events. With perhaps thirty million copies in circulation, it was *the* best-selling American nonfiction book of the 1970s. But eschatology could also leap boldly into public consciousness, as during the lengthy and tragic siege at Waco, Texas, in 1993. The struggle that pitted David Koresh (1959–1993) and his Branch Davidians against the U.S. government occurred in part because Koresh's end-time beliefs both nerved his followers and confused government agencies. An initial clash in February 1993 left four federal agents and six Davidians dead. Two months later, on 19 April, some eighty Davidians died when fire enveloped their compound as federal agents moved in. The mass suicide in San Diego, California, of thirty-nine members of the Heaven's Gate sect in 1997 also involved apocalyptic beliefs. With fatal consequences, the leader of the movement, Marshall Herff Applewhite amalgamated New Age, Christian, and astrological elements to convince his followers that the Hale-Bopp Comet was a sign that their destinies lay in another realm.

Comparisons, Regions, Practices. While a broad national survey reveals much about religion in American history, studies of individual regions, as well as comparisons with other nations, are illuminating as well. It is revealing, for example, to speculate on why church-going in Canada until about 1960 was more common than in the United States, but after 1970 became much less widely practiced. (While reported rates of church attendance in the United States remained about 40–45 percent per week from the 1950s through the 1990s, the rate in Canada declined from about 65 percent to 25 percent in the same period.) Whereas in Canada modern media, a rising standard of living, and the commodification of culture appeared to have displaced traditional religious practice, in the United States these same phenomena of modern life seemingly were incorporated into traditional religion.

Regional variation is an important part of the story as well. For most matters of religious belief and practice, geography has always been a factor. Thus, the American *West—without a history of church-state establishment but with a pluralism of denominations, ethnic groups, and economic patterns from the start of European settlement—is now more typical of religion in America generally than other regions, even though New England, the Mid-Atlantic, the South, and even the *Middle West enjoy fuller traditions of religious scholarship. Geography matters because history matters—whether in the South with its preponderant affiliation of conservative and evangelical forms of Protestantism; the regions with intensive concentrations of Roman Catholics (urban New England, the Upper Midwest, and the *Southwest); Mormon Utah and environs; or the concentration of Asian religions and nontraditional spirituality on the Pacific coast.

Whether defined as a structured response to divine revelation or as the rituals, values, and practices that embody a community's orientation to reality more generally, religion has always loomed large in American history. And religious stories, whether one is considering broad national characteristics or the particularities of specific places, enrich the American story. It is well to remember, however, that religion makes a difference in large-scale American narratives only because the practices of religion have been a part of ordinary daily life—prayer; ritual; sermons; sacred songs and hymns; a broad range of responses to divine revelation; a mighty river of religious publications, including the Bible and other sacred books; and a cornucopia of sanctified material objects from statues and garments to buildings and broadcasts.

Although religious connections with politics, commerce, and entertainment have sometimes been obscured, U.S. history can never be fathomed fully without understanding the rich substratum created by the presence and creative multiplication of religious practices and beliefs.

[*See also* African American Religion; Anti-Catholic Movement; Fundamentalist Movement; Gospel Music, African American; Indian History and Culture; Lutheranism; Methodism; Millennialism and Apocaplypticism; Missionary Movement; New Age Movements; Pacifism; Peace Movements; Puritanism; Seventh-day Adventism; Sexual Morality and Sex Reform; Slavery: Slave Families, Communities, and Culture; Temperance and Prohibition; Voluntarism; Woman Suffrage Movement; Women's Rights Movements.]

• Sydney A. Ahlstrom, *A Religious History of the American People,* 1972. George M. Marsden, *Fundamentalism and American Culture, 1870–1925,* 1980. Charles H. Lippy and Peter W. Williams, eds., *Encyclopedia of the American Religious Experience: Studies of Traditions and Movements,* 3 vols., 1988. Daniel G. Reid et al., eds., *Dictionary of Christianity in America,* 1990. Catherine L. Albanese, *America: Religions and Religion,* 2d ed., 1992. Mark A. Noll, *A History of Christianity in the United States and Canada,* 1992. Susan Hill Lindley, *"You Have Stept Out of Your Place": A History of Women and Religion in America,* 1996. Colleen McDannell, *Material Christianity: Religion and Popular Culture in America,* 1996. Timothy E. Fulop and Albert J. Raboteau, eds., *African-American Religion: Interpretive Essays in History and Culture,* 1997. Jonathan Sarna, ed., *The American Jewish Experience,* 2d ed., 1997. Thomas A. Tweed, ed., *Retelling U.S. Religious History,* 1997.

—Mark A. Noll

REPUBLICANISM. Imported from the civic humanism of Renaissance Italy via the English dissenting tradition, republicanism attracted eighteenth-century Americans who adopted the ideology as a rationale for establishing an independent republic. Americans of the revolutionary generation warmly embraced the republican ideal of civic virtue, historian Gordon Wood argued in *The Creation of the American Republic, 1776–1787* (1969), so that the eventual triumph of a politics of self-interest constituted a profound transformation of values.

While some historians have characterized quite different ideas as "republican" in order to distinguish a public-spirited "republicanism" from a selfish "liberalism," such characterizations are problematical. Eighteenth-century American republicans trusted the capacity of autonomous, public-spirited citizens to preserve civic virtue by participating in local politics, so republicanism does represent a clear alternative to the late twentieth century's emphasis on individual rights as the core value in American culture. But beyond the central commitment to civic virtue, historians have disagreed about the republican legacy. Because republicans scorned dependency, celebrated sacrifice for national glory, and feared that change meant decline, they excluded unpropertied workers, women, and slaves from citizenship, advocated military conquest, rejected interest groups of any kind, and prized austerity over economic growth—hardly a program for latter-day American egalitarians or communitarians. But viewed historically, both republicanism and *liberalism comprised multiple arguments deployed in changing contexts to solve diverse problems and articulate different ideals, and the discourses of both civic virtue and individual rights must be understood within the overarching context of America's persistent and pervasive religiosity. When the classical Aristotelian idea of man as a political animal and the Italian Renaissance conception of civic virtue are placed within the framework of Augustinian Christianity, republican ideas assume different meanings. When Samuel *Adams defined the future American republic as a "Christian Sparta," the qualifier carried enormous weight. Since the central theme of the classical republican tradition, autonomous citizens participating in public affairs, resonated with American ideals and experience and overlapped with the Lockean idea of responsible freedom and the Christian idea of the covenant formed by God's people, Americans could think of themselves simultaneously as republicans, liberals, and Christians, although the first two categories are ours rather than theirs. In the absence of entrenched traditions differentiating people by heredity, *social class, or creed, diverse interpretations of these ideas could coexist and loose coalitions could form and dissolve over time.

James *Madison in the *Federalist Papers offered a republican justification for institutions that might produce civic virtue despite the moral and political frailties of the body politic, but Madison's foes, the Antifederalists, also sought to defend local republican public life by opposing commerce, centralized authority, and the corruption they detected in the *Federalist party gentry. If Jeffersonians invoked civic virtue to legitimate their policies and accused Federalists of scheming to undermine the autonomy of independent craftsmen and farmers, Federalists understood their own call for a strong standing army, stable elites, and the suppression of selfish *individualism as a straightforward republican program. As for the Jacksonians of the 1820s and 1830s, whose ranks included slaveholders, craftsmen, and frontiersmen espousing diverse programs, characterizing them simply as "republican" distorts their complex amalgamation of values. Members of the *Whig party, too, considered themselves legitimate heirs of republicanism, thanks to their emphasis on duty, organic unity, and hierarchical order, but neither party succeeded in laying exclusive claim to the republican heritage.

While Republican terminology survived in the *Antebellum Era, meanings and contexts changed. Some Americans began identifying virtue not with citizens as a whole, but with women safely cordoned off from the now poisonous public sphere. Further, whereas John Locke and Adam Smith had conceived of political rights and economic activity within the contexts of religious duty and ethical life, some Americans began thinking of liberty as freedom from restraint. Nevertheless, as William J. Novak shows in *The People's Welfare: Law and Regulation in Nineteenth-Century America* (1996), the states' lower courts continued to enforce the republican doctrine "salus populi"—the people's welfare—by effectively regulating economic activity.

Abraham *Lincoln's *Republican party succeeded in part because it was able to revitalize older republican ideals of autonomy and ethical citizenship by linking them with appeals to the property rights of free men and to biblical injunctions against injustice. Champions of the Confederacy likewise stood firmly on the republican principle of autonomous and honorable service to the public good and homage to biblically justified forms of hierarchy. Republican echoes continued to reverberate, after the *Civil War, although more faintly, as champions of *laissez-faire endorsed a new ethos of greed and discarded civic virtue as quaint or counter-productive. Workingmen's parties likewise developed laborers' sense of themselves as a distinctive group with particular interests, thereby helping transform American public life into a contest to satisfy individual desires rather than a cultural project devoted to shaping and channeling those desires toward the common good.

Republican themes persisted in twentieth-century political rhetoric, but they fit poorly into the dominant discourse of rights. Some American progressives, such as John *Dewey, Jane *Addams, and Herbert *Croly, worked to resuscitate the ideal of a public interest emerging from the active participation of all citizens in democratically organized communities. But in the wake of *World War I, their pragmatist conception of knowledge as uncertain, and of politics as egalitarian and open-ended, seemed to most Americans shapeless and naive. New Dealers of the 1930s preferred a coalition of different groups attracted to an ill-defined agenda promising prosperity for all. In the late twentieth century, the *Democratic party sometimes tried to refashion the republican ideal by invoking themes of justice and *equality, if not civic virtue. But Democrats more often appealed in the language of rights to the interests of particular groups rather than trying to forge a united republican citizenry. Given the absence of resources in republicanism for oppressed groups like *African Americans, Indians, *Hispanic Americans, and women struggling for equality, such a shift from republican to liberal and religious discourse was hardly surprising.

The Republican party, by contrast, packaged itself for national consumption by incorporating classical republican themes of its own. Republican candidates denounced centralized power as a source of corruption, deprecated *welfare dependency and interest groups, defended hierarchy and patriarchy, honored valor in battle, interpreted cultural (although not economic) change as decline, and claimed to find virtue in austerity—at least for those without tax shelters. Although few American politicians in either party displayed much interest in (or evident familiarity with) civic virtue as the twenty-first century began, Republicans had as legitimate a claim to aspects of the republican tradition as did Democrats, whose vision, it often seemed, had narrowed to the demands of well-organized interest groups.

[*See also* Adams, John; Calhoun, John C.; Capitalism; Civil Rights; Clay, Henry; Conservatism; Constitution; Constitutional Convention of 1787; *Democracy in America*; Early Republic, Era of the; Gilded Age; Jackson, Andrew; Jefferson, Thomas; New Deal Era, The; Progressive Era; Religion; Revolution and Constitution, Era of; States' Rights; Suffrage; Webster, Daniel; Women's Rights Movements.]

• Drew R. McCoy, *The Elusive Republic: Political Economy in Jeffersonian America*, 1980. Joyce Appleby, *Liberalism and Republicanism in the Historical Imagination*, 1992. Daniel T. Rodgers, "Republicanism: The Career of a Concept," *The Journal of American History* 79 (1992): 11–38. Lance Banning, *James Madison and the Founding of the Federal Republic*, 1995. Michael Sandel, *Democracy's Discontent: America in Search of a Public Philosophy*, 1996. James T. Kloppenberg, *The Virtues of Liberalism*, 1998.

—James T. Kloppenberg

REPUBLICAN PARTY. The Republican party emerged in the 1850s from a party system torn by political pressures it could not contain. The organizers of the new party brought together formerly hostile groups, including Northern Whigs, *antislavery *Free Soil Party members, and dissident Democrats—all affected by worsening North-South tensions unleashed by the struggle for control of the Kansas territory—along with nativist Know-Nothings reacting against the flood of Irish Catholic immigrants. Republicans portrayed the *Democratic party as controlled by an expansionist Southern "slavocracy" abetted in the urban North by immigrant votes, and the new party grew rapidly as sectional conflict intensified in the late 1850s. Its opposition to the expansion of *slavery and its backing of free labor and federal support for *economic development—a reflection of its Whig ancestry—as well as its nativism all won support in the North.

The election in 1860 of Abraham *Lincoln, the first Republican president, and the *Civil War that followed solidified Republican dominance. The Lincoln administration, in the name of saving the Union, greatly expanded federal power. At first prepared only to restrict slavery, not to abolish it, Republican leaders gradually accepted emancipation both as a war measure and as an expression of the expanded understanding of liberty forged in the heat of conflict.

From the Gilded Age through the 1930s. In the postwar years, Republicans won support in the small-town and rural North by portraying the Democrats as the party of rebellion, a tactic known as "waving the bloody shirt." The *Grand Army of the Republic, an association of Union veterans, mobilized votes as a Republican pressure group. Union veterans headed party tickets for decades, starting with Ulysses S. *Grant in 1868. Republican orators also continued to appeal to nativists by picturing the Democrats as the party of immigrants. In this era, too, while retaining their support among northern farmers and shopkeepers, the Republicans championed the era's new industrial conglomerates and financial institutions. The party agenda focused on aiding capitalist development through high *tariffs, railroad subsidies, and generous support for the nation's economic infrastructure.

Like all political parties, the Republicans experienced factional tensions rooted in regional differences and policy conflicts. Early in the twentieth century, these tensions produced a wrenching split. Progressive Republicans, led by Robert *La Follette and Theodore *Roosevelt, argued that unbridled *industialization was harming farmers and laborers and promoted policies of social amelioration and corporate regulation. The party's corporate wing, predictably, opposed higher *taxation, business regulation, and legislation extending workers' rights. The party split allowed the election and reelection of a Democratic president, Woodrow *Wilson, in 1912 and 1916, respectively.

The most able Republican leader of the 1920s, Herbert *Hoover, first as secretary of commerce and then as president, succeeded for a time in reconciling the party's warring wings. Down to 1929, the Republicans, despite their factionalism, remained sufficiently united to dominate national politics. But the 1929 *stock market crash and the ensuing economic collapse ended the party's electoral dominance and threatened its survival. From 1932 to 1952, the Republicans found themselves for the first time a minority in a sea of Democrats, tainted by their association with the Great Depression, Hoover's failed presidency, and their opposition to the *New Deal.

Liberal Republicans in the urban Northeast, ignoring conservative charges of "me tooism," demanded action. The party would collapse, they warned, unless it accepted parts of the New Deal's regulative and social welfare program. Most congressional Republicans, however, were from small towns and rural areas, and they followed their leader, Senator Robert *Taft of Ohio, in rejecting the New Deal. The factional battle raged for thirty years. Liberal Republicans, led by Wendell Willkie (1892–1944) and New York governor Thomas Dewey (1902–1971), gained control of the party in the 1940s, at least at the presidential level, but failed to win the White House until the election of Dwight D. *Eisenhower in 1952. Eisenhower and Richard M. *Nixon, the first Republican presidents since Hoover, accepted New Deal programs and insisted that Republicans could be as caring as Democrats in the face of want and despair. In the Nixon years, particularly, support for the welfare state and an active government role in the economy became Republican orthodoxy.

To the party's conservative midwestern wing, all this remained unacceptable despite the anticommunist *Cold War pronouncements of Eisenhower and Nixon. To conservatives, the issues were big government, high taxes, and the strangling of free enterprise in governmental red tape. At first, conservatives made little headway against the liberal wing. Their strength was not in the voter-rich regions of the country. Senator Taft and other conservative Republicans initially welcomed the anticommunist crusade of Senator Joseph *McCarthy of Wisconsin, but when McCarthy attacked prominent Republicans and even the U.S. Army, many members of his own party joined in a 1954 Senate censure vote. When Senator Barry *Goldwater of Arizona defeated Governor Nelson Rockefeller of New York to win the 1964 Republican nomination, the result was an electoral disaster, the landslide victory of Democrat Lyndon B. *Johnson.

Amid the urban riots, campus unrest, economic strains, and *Vietnam War controversies of the late 1960s, however, Republican conservatism revived. As a Democrat-supported racial revolution turned from expanding *civil rights to promoting programs that seemed to favor ethnic minorities and women at the expense of white males, and as Democratic candidates became more liberal (or radical, in conservatives' eyes), traditional Democratic voters turned to Republican candidates espousing once-unfashionable conservative positions.

The 1980s and 1990s. Ronald *Reagan, a New Dealer turned conservative Republican, won the presidency in 1980 by excoriating the excesses and failures of the welfare state. Reagan also flexed America's Cold War military muscle, challenging alleged Democratic weaknesses on foreign policy. His success underscored the exhaustion of both Democratic *liberalism and me-too Republicanism. As Republicans made signficant inroads in the white South and in Democratic strongholds of the urban North, the conservative mood within the party hardened. Although conservative Republicans were themselves divided, they clearly controlled the party in the 1980s and 1990s. The emergence of an uncompromising conservatism among highly individualistic entrepreneurs, small shopkeepers, and middle managers typically living and working in the suburbs on the burgeoning Pacific Coast and in the Old South and *Southwest (rechristened the Sun Belt) sharpened the party's *laissez-faire, antigovernment outlook. The rise of Republican-oriented religious, moral-reform movements such as Jerry Falwell's *Moral Majority and Pat Robertson's *Christian Coalition and the revival of Republican nativism added new issues—tougher immigration controls, school prayer, pornography regulation, opposition to abortion and gay rights, and other matters of personal and group morality—to the Republican agenda.

Conservative Republicans triumphed electorally in the early 1990s, winning in 1994 control of both houses of Congress for the first time in almost fifty years. Espousing themes of individual responsibility and suspicion of government deeply rooted in the party's history, conservative Republicans—with Democratic support—pushed through a sweeping reform of a federal welfare system dating to the New Deal Era. But new economic and social issues sorely tested Republican unity and promoted internecine warfare, contributing to Democratic presidential victories in 1992 and 1996 and further gains in the 1998 midterm elections.

Republican Divisions over Foreign Policy. Republican divisions were important in the foreign policy arena as well, in long-term conflicts between internationalists and isolationists. President Theodore Roosevelt favored vigorous U.S. engagement in world affairs, but after *World War I, Republican isolationists rejected U.S. membership in the *League of Nations and generally withdrew from the international arena. Midwestern Republican senators like Taft, Idaho's William Borah (1865–1940), and Arthur Vandenberg (1884–1951) of Michigan opposed U.S. interventionism in the 1930s and, while supporting *World War II, reiterated their isolationism after the war. A turning point came in 1947, however, when Vandenberg supported President Harry S. *Truman's call for U.S. aid to Greece and Turkey, and a bipartisan approach to foreign policy generally prevailed during the Cold War. But the intraparty split reemerged the 1990s, as most Republican business leaders supported the global economy and lower trade barriers, while other Republicans, such as the TV commentator and sometime presidential candidate Pat Buchanan, espoused protectionism and a more nationalistic economic program.

As the twentieth century ended, many Americans viewed the Republican party's conservative wing as too extreme, suggesting the imminence of yet another realignment in the party's ever-shifting balance of power among competing factions.

[*See also* Blaine, James G.; Civil War: Causes; Conservatism; Depressions, Economic; Expansionism; Fifties, The; Gilded Age; Know-Nothing Party; Nativist Movement; Progressive Era; Political Parties; Progressive Party of 1912–1914; Twenties, The; Whig Party.]

• Donald B. Johnson, *The Republican Party and Wendell Willkie*, 1960. Robert Marcus, *Grand Old Party: Political Structure in the Gilded Age, 1880–1896*, 1971. James T. Patterson, *Mr. Republican: A Biography of Robert A. Taft*, 1972. Joan Hoff-Wilson, *Herbert Hoover: Forgotten Progressive*, 1975. David Thelen, *Robert M. La Follette and the Insurgent Spirit*, 1976. William Gienapp, *The Origins of the Republican Party, 1852–1856*, 1987. Herbert Parmet, *Richard Nixon and His America*, 1990. Joel H. Silbey, *The American Political Nation, 1838–1893*, 1991. Theodore J. Lowi, *The End of the Republican Era*, 1995. Robert Rutland, *The Republicans: From Lincoln to Bush, 1996.*

—Joel H. Silbey

RESEARCH LABORATORIES, INDUSTRIAL. Organized research on new products and processes began in large *business organizations in the last decades of the nineteenth century. The pioneers were companies in the new fields of electricity, chemistry, and telecommunications, which faced stiff international competition and rapidly changing *technology. Until Thomas *Edison established his famous Menlo Park laboratory in New Jersey in 1876, industrial laboratories concentrated on product-testing and improvement rather than exploring new technology. Edison's innovative idea was that organized research could develop new products in a wide range of fields and that the process could be managed like any other industrial endeavor. His Menlo Park and West Orange laboratories proved his point by producing a steady flow of innovations, including the incandescent electric light, phonograph, and motion-picture camera.

The scope and scale of Edison's laboratories provided an example for others to follow. By 1900 his West Orange laboratory employed over a hundred workers who experimented in areas as diverse as motion pictures and automobile storage batteries. Edison organized his laboratory to move into promising new areas. Companies such as General Electric and American Telephone and Telegraph (AT&T) also sponsored industrial research but never matched the scale or the ambitions of Edison; their goals were to improve existing products and seek out new technologies to serve established businesses. The commercial rewards of new types of light bulbs and long-distance telephony convinced these companies that industrial research was not only a vital part of their core business but also the key to new and more profitable endeavors. AT&T's Western Electric laboratories opened up the fields of wireless communication and sound *films for the parent company in addition to maintaining its dominance in telephony.

While industrial research laboratories in the big companies involved extensive facilities at several sites staffed by large numbers of workers, many smaller businesses maintained modest laboratories employing only one or two experimenters. The independent research laboratory pioneered by Edison virtually died out in the twentieth century as the corporation became the primary source of new technology. In 1885 only 12 percent of patents were issued to corporations, but by 1950 this figure had risen to 75 percent. Industrial research had become an activity carried out by large, integrated companies that could afford the high cost of research.

While Edison had hired both formally trained scientists and skilled craftsmen, industrial research laboratories tended to hire engineers and scientists with advanced degrees. The presence of well-known scientists such as Charles Steinmetz and William Coolidge at General Electric's laboratories gave that institution great prestige; Bell Laboratories could later claim several Nobel Prize laureates in its employ. Industrial research laboratories also helped business organizations increase their public visibility and sell products.

The union of business and academe in industrial research grew dramatically closer during times of war, when the U.S. government took over the laboratories and accelerated the pace of technological development. Government involvement in research began in *World War I and grew substantially during *World War II, when industrial research was carried out on an unprecedented scale. The *Manhattan Project to develop the atomic bomb used the same research principles established by Thomas Edison but employed an army of scientists and engineers at a cost of some three billion dollars. After the war, government-sponsored industrial research remained at high levels and contributed to numerous important technologies such as space exploration and *computers.

In the post–World War II economy, companies large and small carried out industrial research. As dramatic technological advances captured the American imagination, "new and improved" became something that every company wanted to claim for its products, even though it might not have employed industrial research. Industrial giants such as General Electric, Radio Corporation of America (RCA), and DuPont used well-known research laboratories to differentiate their products from those of their competitors and impress their customers. Slogans such as "Better Living through Chemistry" (DuPont) became the foundation for *advertising campaigns aimed at connecting industrial research with the benefits of new technology. The U.S. government used the same strategy to promote *nuclear power and to justify massive federal expenditures on research and development. By the end of the twentieth century, industrial research had become a vital part of modern life, viewed as essential to a healthy economy. It served as a barometer of economic well-being and helped set the standards of scientific education.

[*See also* Chemical Industry; Electrical Industry; Industrialization; Space Program; Telephone.]

• David Noble, *America by Design: Science, Technology, and the Rise of Corporate Capitalism,* 1977. Leonard Reich, *The Making of American Industrial Research: Science and Business at GE and Bell,* 1985. George Wise, *Willis R. Whitney, General Electric, and the Origins of U.S. Industrial Research,* 1985. Andre Millard, *Edison and the Business of Innovation,* 1990. Ronald R. Kline, *Steinmetz: Engineer and Socialist,* 1992.

—Andre Millard

RETIREMENT. *See* Life Stages; Work.

REUTHER, WALTER (1907–1970), labor leader. Walter Philip Reuther was born in Wheeling, West Virginia, the son of German immigrants. His father, a trade unionist and socialist, taught his sons that workers needed unions and capitalist society needed reform. A diemaker, Reuther worked for the Ford Motor Company (1927–1932) and then spent three years abroad, including a stint in a Soviet factory. Back in *Detroit, he organized for the infant United Automobile Workers (UAW), served on its executive board, and participated in its strikes, often in collaboration with his younger brothers Roy and Victor. In May 1937 Reuther and other UAW organizers were brutally beaten by Ford Motor Company security thugs in front of a Ford plant.

From the directorship of the UAW's General Motors Department (1939–1946), he became the union's vice president (1942–1946) and, in 1946, its president (until 1970). Concurrently he headed the *Congress of Industrial Organizations (1952–1955) and was vice president of the combined AFL-CIO (1955–1967). A *Cold War leader of the anticommunist left, he helped expell communist-dominated unions from the CIO in 1949.

An eloquent speaker, Reuther was also a bold strike strategist and nimble negotiator. During his presidency the UAW won numerous benefits for its members, including cost-of-living and *productivity wage increases, pensions, health coverage, and supplementary unemployment benefits during layoffs. The union brought auto workers a middle-class living standard and protection from some hazards of an industrial economy. As a social democrat, Reuther sought a more egalitarian society, enlisting himself and the UAW in efforts for social betterment, culminating in the *Great Society and *civil rights campaigns of the 1960s. Breaking with other labor leaders, he opposed the *Vietnam War. Despite his untimely death in a plane crash, Reuther's legacy lived on in the UAW's continuing commitment to social reform.

[*See also* Anticommunism; Automotive Industry; Labor Movements; New Deal Era, The; Sixties, The; Socialism; Strikes and Industrial Conflict.]

• John Barnard, *Walter Reuther and the Rise of the Auto Workers,* 1983. Nelson Lichtenstein, *The Most Dangerous Man in Detroit: Walter Reuther and the Fate of American Labor,* 1995.

—John Barnard

REVERE, PAUL (1735–1818), *Boston silversmith, engraver, legendary patriot hero. Although Revere's silver masterpieces place him among the finest craftsmen in colonial America, his wider fame has resulted from Henry Wadsworth Longfellow's "Paul Revere's Ride" (1861), the inaccurate but patriotic poem memorized by generations of schoolchildren.

Revere's famous ride came about through his involvement with Boston's Committee of Correspondence, which kept patriots informed of the movements of British soldiers occupying Boston. In April 1775, the British commander, General Thomas Gage, ordered his troops to capture a store of the colonists' gunpowder in Concord. When committee members learned of the plan (perhaps from Gage's wife), couriers were assigned to spread the news. Among those designated to warn Concord were Revere and William Dawes, who traveled by different routes.

On 18 April, the evening before the scheduled attack, Revere

MAP 18: TWO VERSIONS OF THE BOSTON MASSACRE BY PAUL REVERE

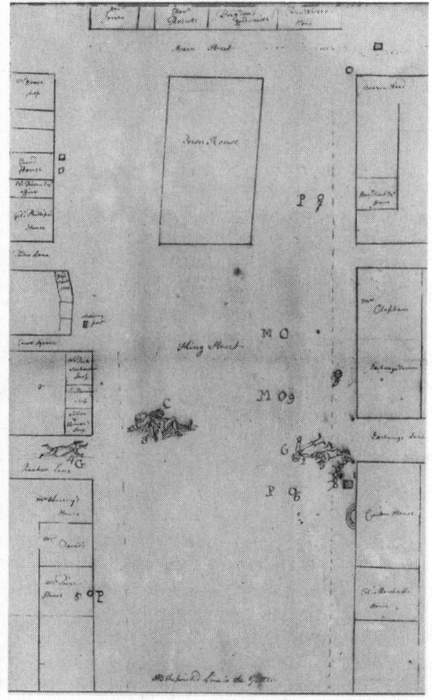

Revere's diagram of the fatal shots fired into a crowd of rock-throwing Bostonians by British troops guarding the customs house on 5 March 1770 (top) conveys the confusion and ambiguity of the encounter. This sketch was prepared in connection with the trial of the soldiers for murder. By contrast, Revere's engraving "The Bloody Massacre Perpetrated in King Street, Boston" (below), which circulated throughout the colonies, shows the soldiers in military formation, mowing down the unoffending colonists at point-blank range. The Redcoats, declared an accompanying poem,

> Like fierce Barbarians grinning o'er their Prey;
> Approve the Carnage, and enjoy the Day

[*See* Boston; Boston Massacre; Propaganda; Revere, Paul; Revolutionary War.]

rowed across Boston harbor to Charlestown, where he mounted a horse and rode into Medford and Menotomy (now Arlington). By chance, he met Dr. Samuel Prescott, who volunteered to help spread the alarm. Soon a British patrol overtook the two; Prescott escaped, but Revere was detained for several hours while Prescott, Dawes, and others got the news to Lexington and Concord.

While Longfellow's poem gave Revere greater celebrity than other Revolutionary-Era patriots who performed similar duties, he remains significant. Revere's occupation as an urban artisan connected with nearly every patriot and civic organization of his day, such as the Committee of Correspondence, Sons of Liberty, North End Caucus, and Freemasons, place him in the nexus of the Boston Revolutionary movement. In later years, his copper-rolling and brass foundry at Canton, Massachusetts, brought him great wealth. A portrait of Revere by John Singleton *Copley is highly regarded.

[*See also* Revolution and Constitution, Era of; Revolutionary War.]

• David H. Fischer, *Paul Revere's Ride*, 1994.

—Christopher Berkeley

REVIVALISM, the periodic movement of shared religious intensity in Protestant churches by which believers are spiritually renewed and outsiders are called to repentance and Christian faith. A feature of evangelical *Protestantism, revivals derive from several basic evangelical assumptions, including the conviction that all are sinners whose only hope for eternal salvation is in repentance and conversion, the emphasis on preaching, and the widespread influence of a pietist stress on religion of the heart.

In the *Colonial Era, revivals were often considered to come at God's discretion rather than as the result of human effort. Early American Puritans believed that hardships like natural calamities, plagues, or Indian raids represented God's judgments on a community that had broken faith with God's law. As in the Old Testament, repentance, fasting, and prayer with a renewed commitment to "walk in God's ways" were one prescribed response. "Seasons of awakening" followed in scattered parishes in seventeenth-century America. The first general religious revival came early in the eighteenth century, first appearing among the Dutch in the Middle Colonies in the 1720s, in *New England in the 1730s and 1740s, and intermittently in the southern colonies until the *Revolutionary War.

This revival was so widespread, intense, and remarkable that it came to be known as the Great Awakening. The travels and preaching of the British evangelist George Whitefield gave a degree of unity to widely scattered religious stirrings. At times, the Great Awakening was marked by intense emotional outbursts. Its ablest American defender, chronicler, and theologian was Jonathan *Edwards. The revival augmented the membership rolls of the churches, created and divided congregations, and fostered a new degree of intercolonial communication and cooperation. Detractors objected to the emotionalism and unrestrained "enthusiasm" that seemed to threaten standards of truth and decorum.

After the Revolutionary War, another religious revival emerged. Once again, although it began locally, it spread to many parts of the country and so became known as the Second Great Awakening. In parts of New England, it spread through local congregations from the 1790s, manifesting itself in concern for religion, responsiveness to preaching, increased church attendance, and greater attention to public morality. In these early manifestations, it was not often marked by the emotional excesses that had troubled the critics of the First Great Awakening.

In the first decade of the nineteenth century, revival gripped Yale University's student body, shaping the careers of some of the century's most prominent religious leaders. Again, this seemed a "surprising work of God," an unpredictable phenomenon in which God graciously chose to renew the church by converting sinners and renewing believers. By 1810, the revival had stimulated the formation of the first American foreign missionary association, the American Board of Commissioners for Foreign Missions, and the first foreign missionaries had sailed for India.

In the *West, the Second Great Awakening's defining moment came at a camp meeting near Cane Ridge, Kentucky, in 1801. Marked by spontaneous preaching that generated intensely emotional responses, camp meetings became a favored means for revival. An array of voluntary associations supporting home and foreign missions, Bible and tract societies, Sunday schools, and social reform movements owed much to the Second Great Awakening. Whereas leadership in the First Great Awakening had been Congregationalist, Presbyterian, and Baptist, the Second Great Awakening, especially in the West was strongly influenced by Baptists and Methodists.

In the 1820s, Charles G. *Finney helped routinize revivals. Revivals resulted from the right use of the right means, Finney believed; they would happen whenever right conditions prevailed. Acting on this assumption, Finney became the first of many nationally known revivalists. His *Lectures on Revivals of Religion* (1835) became standard reading for those who longed for personal and national spiritual renewal.

After the *Civil War, Dwight L. *Moody dominated revivalism. With his chorister Ira D. Sankey, who gave impetus to the use of gospel songs in revival services, Moody crisscrossed the United States and enjoyed enormous popularity in Britain. Successful revivalists among Moody's contemporaries included Daniel Whittle, Philip Paul Bliss, and Maria B. Woodworth-Etter, who traveled the country with a tent, praying for the sick and attracting large crowds. These national figures worked in conjunction with area churches so the converts of citywide revivals could join local congregations. At the same time, denominational and independent revivalists conducted local revival meetings. By 1900, revivalism had become a major tool of evangelical churches. Thousands of congregations held annual and semiannual revivals.

The proliferation of lesser known evangelists did not diminish the importance of national revivalists. In the twentieth century, Billy *Sunday, Aimee Semple *McPherson, and Billy *Graham spoke to ever larger crowds and used new media, including *television, to expand their efforts. By the end of the century, the terms "evangelist" and "revivalist" were almost interchangeable. Evangelism—converting the unsaved—perhaps more than renewal of the church, had come to be the heart of revivalism.

[*See also* Chautauqua Movement; Great Awakening, First and Second; Methodism; Missionary Movement; Pentecostalism; Protestantism; Puritanism; Religion; Televangelism.]

• Edwin S. Gaustad, *The Great Awakening in New England*, 1957. William G. McLoughlin, *Modern Revivalism*, 1959. William G. McLoughlin, *Revivals, Awakenings and Reform*, 1978. Keith J. Hardman, *Charles Grandison Finney, 1792–1875: Revivalist and Reformer*, 1987. Harry Stout, *The Divine Dramatist: George Whitefield and the Rise of Modern Evangelicalism*, 1991.

—Edith L. Blumhofer

REVOLUTION AND CONSTITUTION, ERA OF. The American Revolution, the first great democratic revolution, differed profoundly from those that followed. It did not originate in bitter discontent with the organization and governance of contemporary society, or in a desire to make the world anew. Rather, it began with a determination to *defeat* a fundamental change in the traditional order. For Americans, moreover, a sense of a separate national identity, of being a distinct people, was a *product* of an imperial crisis, not a cause.

Background to Revolution. In 1763, at the conclusion of the *Seven Years' War, the fourth and greatest of the eighteenth-century wars between the French and British, George III's loyal subjects from *New England to the Carolinas were a thriving and rapidly expanding preindustrial people. The region's white population probably enjoyed—and certainly believed that they enjoyed—the highest standard of living in the world. New Englanders, Virginians, Carolinians, and Pennsylvanians had many times displayed a powerful determination to defend their local interests, but always within the standing frame of government—in practice, if not in theory, a working federal system. Every province had a government in which a house of elected representatives enjoyed substantial autonomy over the province's internal affairs. The British empire was essentially cemented by a set of laws, called the *Navigation Acts, designed to keep the empire's trade in British (and British colonial) hands. Although this system rendered the colonies subservient in some respects, it offered many benefits as well. To be British in colonial America in 1763 was to enjoy a special relationship with the world's most advanced economy, to be a part of the nation whose ships dominated the Atlantic, whose armies had conquered its western shores, whose free political institutions were the envy of the enlightened world. Indeed, in the glow of the great victory over the French, the colonial pride in being British may never have been higher.

The crisis, then, originated not with a colonial initiative, but in Great Britain. There, some bureaucrats and politicians had long been troubled by London's dangerously loose supervision of its empire. The Seven Years' War, moreover, had left England with a larger empire to govern, entailing new administrative costs, and with a staggering debt. In these circumstances, the ministry of George Grenville considered it entirely reasonable for Parliament to require the thriving colonies, for the first time in their history, to pay a portion of the costs of their own administration and defense. This, together with stricter enforcement of the Navigation Acts, was the declared purpose, first of the American Revenue (or Sugar) Act of 1764, then of the *Stamp Act of 1765, against which the colonials rose with a ferocity that threatened civil war.

From the Stamp Act to the Articles of Confederation (1765–1781). When the colonials rallied to nullify the stamp tax, nobody meant to make a revolution, no identifiable leader espoused American independence. Proclaiming their loyalty to the Crown, they did not dispute Parliament's right to regulate the empire's trade. The British Americans simply demanded, as they conceived it, the rights of all Englishmen—especially the right to be taxed only by representatives elected by themselves, which the members of the House of Commons were not and could not be. If the authority of Parliament had no limits, the colonials asked themselves, how far might its exactions ultimately extend? If the people, through their provincial legislatures, could not preserve their traditional, exclusive control of taxation, how could they defend the other liberties that made colonials Englishmen and free? These were the principles of the British constitution, of natural rights, and of government based on an inviolable social contract proclaimed by English thinkers themselves—John Locke in the seventeenth century and more recently political journalists such as John Trenchard and Thomas Gordon. In the end, colonials would fight before conceding that Parliament's sovereignty was absolute, and Englishmen would fight before conceding that it was not. The empire shattered on its inability to solve—or even clearly define—the federal puzzle of a mutually acceptable division of authority between the provinces and the center, a riddle that would trouble the independent Americans for a further dozen years after independence before the *Constitution brought a fragile and temporary solution.

The American colonists' profound transformation of outlook did not occur quickly or casually. The nine years that elapsed between the Stamp Act crisis and the clashes at Lexington and Concord, and the fourteen months of warfare that passed before the Americans decided that their objective should be independence and a republican revolution, not a restoration of the eighteenth-century status quo, testify to the colonists' deep attachment to the empire and the difficulty of achieving concord among thirteen widely different colonies, even as England stubbornly insisted on the central principle of parliamentary rule.

In 1766, facing a colonial boycott of British imports and a threatened civil war, a new ministry headed by the marquis of Rockingham secured the repeal of the Stamp Act, accompanied, however, by a declaration of Parliament's authority to bind the colonies in all cases whatsoever. In 1767, its revenue needs still unmet, Parliament passed the Townshend Acts, taxing colonial imports of certain British goods (an "external" rather than an "internal" tax, but one soon perceived as aimed at raising revenue, not regulating trade). Another boycott followed, along with clashes culminating in 1770 in a "massacre" of *Boston townsmen rioting against the customs regulations and the troops who had been sent to quell their fractious spirit. Years of mounting crisis, with each British action triggering a more outraged response and every episode of colonial resistance bringing an angrier British reaction, underlay a general conclusion that the Tea Act of 1773 was a conspiracy to tempt the colonies to pay the single Townshend duty not repealed three years before. This vicious cycle prepared the way, too, for the *Boston Tea Party, at which the radicals dumped the tea ship *Dartmouth*'s cargo into Boston harbor.

Parliament responded with the Coercive Acts of 1774, closing Boston harbor and altering the charter of Massachusetts Bay. "Intolerable Acts," colonials called them, seeing in the punishment of Massachusetts (and in the new nonrepresentative government imposed by the Quebec Act of the same year) a fate that might await them all. With a unanimity reminiscent of the Stamp Act protests, several colonies called concurrently for a *Continental Congress to prepare a unified response. Meeting in the fall of 1774, Congress resolved to support Massachusetts's defiance of the Coercive Acts and to impose an escalating program of commercial resistance to Parliament's acts: the tested tool of nonimportation of British goods followed by nonexportation to Britain and nonconsumption of British products. A Second Continental Congress, assembled in the spring of 1775, confronted war, the people of Massachusetts having resisted at Lexington and Concord a ministerial order to seize the province's military supplies and arrest the resistance leaders. Only then did growing numbers of colonial leaders move toward the conclusion that their liberties could never be secure under the rule of a corrupt and corrupting Britain, that Americans were different from the British and could not sustain their special way of life without a revolutionary reorganization fully based on elections and popular consent. **Common Sense*, Thomas *Paine's explosive call for independence and a republican revolution, appeared in January 1776.

Six months later, on 7 June 1776, Virginia's Richard Henry Lee (1732–1794) proposed three resolutions in Congress: a declaration of independence, the forging of foreign alliances, and the creation of a permanent American confederation. It took two years to conclude an alliance with France, seven years to win the *Revolutionary War, and twelve to frame and ratify a Constitution that solved the federal problem that had wrecked the British empire. As Thomas *Jefferson drafted the *Declaration of Independence, Congress struggled to devise a plan of intercolonial union. Not until 15 November 1777 did Congress finally forward a plan to the states for their approval, and not until February 1781 were the *Articles of Confederation ratified by Maryland, the thirteenth state.

From the Confederation Era to the Constitutional Convention of 1787. By this point, many in Congress and its executive departments already considered the federal government created by the Articles seriously inadequate, dependent as it was on state actions to enforce its revenue requisitions and most of its other commands. In February 1781, as Maryland approved the Articles, Congress, seeking an independent source of federal funds, requested an amendment authorizing it to levy a 5 percent duty on foreign imports. Rhode Island rejected the proposal. In 1783, Robert Morris, the superintendent of finance, initiated an even more ambitious but equally unsuccessful campaign for a program of independent federal funding. In the end, every such effort to revise the Articles, including attempts to secure a federal authority to regulate the country's trade, fell victim to interstate jealousies or the fact that the Articles could only be amended by unanimous consent. As Congress limped along and a sharp postwar depression set in, thoughts turned increasingly toward extralegal action.

By September 1786, when delegates from six states met at Annapolis, Maryland, to consider better means of regulating interstate and international commerce, crisis loomed. Congress owed huge debts to foreign governments and bankers, to revolutionary soldiers, and to citizens who had lent their money or had had their goods conscripted to finance the war. Congress could not even pay the interest on its domestic debt and was financing its foreign debts only by contracting additional loans. Since Congress also lacked authority to deal with the depression, states were passing separate and conflicting commercial regulations, issuing paper money, and extending moratoria on taxes that dismayed property holders. Every lesser effort at reform having failed, and lacking a quorum even to make authoritative proposals concerning trade, the handful of reformers at Annapolis recommended another convention empowered to consider *all* the defects of the current constitution. Congress endorsed the recommendation. That autumn, *Shays's Rebellion, a tax revolt in Massachusetts, seemed to many a final warning that the union might be on the verge of collapse. This alarming uprising helped ensure a full attendance at the *Constitutional Convention that convened at *Philadelphia in May 1787—a convention that would draft the Constitution that still endures.

[*See also* Adams, John; Adams, Samuel; Albany Congress; Bill of Rights; Boston Massacre; Colonial Era; Committees of Correspondence; Early Republic, Era of the; Federalism; Franklin, Benjamin; Henry, Patrick; Imperial Wars; Republicanism; Sons of Liberty; Zenger Trial.]

• Edmund S. Morgan, *The Birth of the Republic, 1763–1789,* 1956. James Madison, *Notes of Debates in the Federal Convention of 1787,* ed. Adrienne Koch, 1966. Bernard Bailyn, *The Ideological Origins of the American Revolution,* 1967. Gordon S. Wood, *The Creation of the American Republic, 1776–1787,* 1969. Jack P. Greene, ed., *Colonies to Nation: A Documentary History of the American Revolution, 1763–1789,* 1975. Jack N. Rakove, *The Beginnings of National Politics: An Interpretive History of the Continental Congress,* 1979. Edward Countryman, *The American Revolution,* 1985.

—Lance Banning

REVOLUTIONARY WAR. The Revolutionary War (1775–1783) was simultaneously an ideological and a military struggle that pitted the rebellious British colonists in North America—and eventually their French, Dutch, and Spanish allies—against Great Britain, supported by German mercenaries. Although the imperial forces held significant advantages, the colonists won the war that established American independence. Victory was rooted in the Americans' belief in a revolutionary republican ideology, the willingness of an armed yeomanry to fight in defense of their locales, the advantages provided to the American forces by interior lines of supply, strong leadership in the person of George *Washington, and the assistance provided by European powers hostile to Great Britain.

Origins. The Revolution originated in constitutional, ideological, and demographic changes in the empire that converged in the aftermath of the *Seven Years' War. Seeking to retire an enormous war debt and pay for the garrisoning of troops in North America, the imperial government instituted a series of internal and external taxes in North America. These taxes, especially the Sugar and *Stamp Acts, were bitterly resented by the colonial population and led to a series of violent protests. At the core of the unrest was a constitutional claim by the colonists that they had to be actually represented in any legislative body that taxed them. In essence, they nullified the idea of the King-in-parliament as the empire's supreme authority, insisting on the supremacy of their local legislatures in matters of internal governance. This position was maintained and expanded throughout the 1760s and 1770s as Parliament passed first the Declaratory Act (1766), the Townshend Duties (1767), the Tea Acts (1773), and finally the Boston Port Bill (1774) in order to collect revenues and assert parliamentary authority. With each such effort, resistance expanded, leading to dramatic incidents like the *Boston Massacre of March 1770 in which five rioters were shot by British troops; the burning of the revenue cutter *Gaspée* in Narragansett Bay, Rhode Island, in 1772; and the *Boston Tea Party in December 1773. When Parliament passed the Boston Port Bill to punish the colonists for their actions in the Tea Party, aroused Americans began to announce their intentions to resist British tyranny—by force if necessary. In 1774, the first *Continental Congress met in one last-ditch effort to seek redress within the empire, and in early 1775, with a military confrontation brewing near *Boston, Parliament declared Massachusetts in rebellion.

While the unraveling of empire between 1764 and 1775 was extraordinarily complex, two underlying factors seem crucial to understanding the formation of an autonomous American identity, one that scarcely existed consciously before the imperial crisis. One was the infiltration of country, republican, and libertarian discourse into American political and social life in the fifty or so years before the Revolution. These languages ultimately provided alternative models of social, political, and economic behavior for provincial Americans. They were used to criticize the existing imperial order and ultimately to establish new behavioral norms in the infant republic. The second factor that helped unravel the empire was the American population's extraordinary physical mobility. Such mobility weakened traditional social bonds and encourage the acceptance of new forms of social organization at all levels and in all regions of the colonies. It was this new people, still only half-formed in 1775, that went to war against the eighteenth century's foremost military power.

Early Battles and the French Alliance. Fighting commenced in earnest in April 1775 when the British commander General Thomas Gage sought to seize munitions hidden in the countryside near Boston and arrest the patriot leaders Samuel *Adams and John Hancock. A light British force marching toward the Massachusetts village of Concord on this mission dispersed a small militia unit at Lexington before reaching Concord. There they encountered a larger colonial force and realized that militia from across the Commonwealth, warned by Paul *Revere and others, had anticipated their "surprise" march. In a running battle that took a heavy toll of British soldiers' lives, the *New England militia forced the redcoats back to Boston and besieged the port city. On 17 June, a British assault force initiated the Battle of *Bunker Hill to break the siege. Although the British emerged victorious, they received over a thousand casualties. The strength of opposition in New England led the British commanders to evacuate Boston in order to seek a decisive military victory in the Mid-Atlantic region in 1776.

This decision rested on a sound strategic assessment. Not only were the major Mid-Atlantic cities' ports easily held by the powerful British navy, but imperial authorities were convinced that a significant body of the King's Friends—as those Americans who were loyal to the Crown were called—were ready to rise when the royal army arrived. Moreover, victory in the Middle Colonies would cut land communication between the *South and New England, isolating the rebellious regions. Accordingly, an army of more than 30,000 British regulars and Hessian mercenaries commanded by William Howe descended on New York harbor in July 1776, just as the Second

Continental Congress, meeting in *Philadelphia, declared American independence. A British fleet commanded by Howe's brother Richard supported the invasion of New York.

In a near-disastrous failure of strategic thinking, George Washington and the American commanders deployed their forces on Long Island and Manhattan, in effect inviting Britain's amphibious armada to trap them. In late August, a British force decisively defeated the Continental Army at Brooklyn Heights. The American army escaped total annihilation by retreating by rowboat past the British navy to Manhattan. Realizing that their position in New York was untenable, the American forces withdrew from Manhattan after fighting Howe's troops at Harlem Heights, leaving behind a force of three thousand that was subsequently captured. *New York City, at that time comprising only the southern tip of Manhattan, was partially burned, probably by American sympathizers.

The subsequent months were the most desperate of the war. The rump of the Continental army fled across New Jersey, pursued by British forces under General Charles Cornwallis. Compounding Washington's problems was a serious split in the American general staff concerning tactics. Washington and the core of the officers wanted to create a European-style army that could engage the enemy in close combat. However, Charles Lee, a British-born military adventurer of considerable ability who received the rank of general in the American army through congressional patronage, recommended a guerrilla-style battle of attrition against the invaders. The disagreement became pronounced in the fall of 1776 when Lee, commanding American forces east of the Hudson River near White Plains, New York, refused to move to help the beleaguered Washington as the main army fled across New Jersey. Only when Lee was captured in early December did this clash temporarily abate.

With his army disintegrating and his officers in conflict, Washington needed a victory to revive the American cause. With this in mind he recrossed the Delaware River on 26 December and launched successful counterattacks at Trenton and later at Princeton. Although of limited military significance, these victories lifted American morale. However, the American cause suffered new defeats in 1777 as Washington lost Philadelphia after being defeated at Brandywine Creek and Germantown. But that October an American army led by Horatio Gates and Benedict *Arnold surrounded a British force under General John Burgoyne advancing southward through upstate New York and decisively defeated it near Saratoga. On 17 October, Burgoyne and his army of 5,700 surrendered. This disastrous defeat ended the British efforts to split New England from the rest of the colonies.

The American victories in 1776 and 1777 encouraged diplomatic initiatives in Europe that became vital to ultimate victory. From the outbreak of fighting in 1775, the Congress and the American military realized the importance of securing foreign aid. These efforts centered on France, but also involved diplomatic initiatives to the Dutch Republic and Spain. All three powers had reason to fear British influence, and were thus cautiously inclined to support the rebellious colonists. While none endorsed the radical *republicanism pervasive in the colonies, they were anxious to take the opportunity to weaken Britain. Led by Silas Deane and Benjamin *Franklin, American diplomats as early as 1776 gained nonofficial assistance in the form of guns and money from the three European powers. After the Battle of *Saratoga, the French recognized America as an independent country and signed a military alliance with the new nation. French military help proved to be critical to the American cause.

The addition of the powerful French fleet to balance the overwhelming British naval supremacy immediately improved America's strategic position. Although American privateers and commerce raiders had been able to significantly hinder British resupply of their forces in America, the French had a formal fleet of the line and provided bases from which American ships could operate in European waters. It was from such a base that John Paul *Jones, sailing the *Bonhomme Richard,* defeated the heavily armed British warship *Serapis* in September 1779. And it was the French fleet that made possible the victory at Yorktown in 1781 when they drove off a British naval force sent to aid Cornwallis.

American Society at War. Had the French monarchy known the true condition of Washington's army and American society in the winter of 1777, it might have hesitated before signing the treaty of assistance. After defeats at Brandywine Creek and Germantown in Pennsylvania, Washington's army went into the first of a series of brutally uncomfortable winter encampments in Pennsylvania and New Jersey. The following summer, as the armies again maneuvered against one another in the Mid-Atlantic colonies, widespread fighting among Americans broke out in New York, New Jersey, and Pennsylvania. While this fighting was diffuse, it was probably far more widespread in the region than historians have suspected. In New Jersey's Hackensack River Valley and Pine Barrens, in Pennsylvania's Wyoming Valley, and throughout upstate New York and on Long Island, Americans fell on one another in a series of struggles for local supremacy. Religious and ethnic divisions seem to have shaped loyalties in this civil strife. In the Wyoming Valley, for instance, German settlers and Native Americans assisted by British troops warred against New Englanders who had been trying to settle in the area since the 1750s, basing their claims on a Connecticut land grant. Their bloody conflict led to widespread assaults on civilians as well as combatants, and violence continued in the area well into the 1790s.

The war also encouraged fighting along ethnic, religious, and racial lines in the South. From the late 1770s until 1783, violence between contending groups of Americans—and between them and various Native American groups—turned large parts of the southern countryside into combat zones. These conflicts fell out along ethnic lines, with religion and locale playing secondary roles in deciding allegiance. In South Carolina, German and Scots-Irish settlers in the interior strongly tended towards loyalism. They were culturally alienated from the Charlestown elite and bitter at their treatment before the war during the upheaval known as the South Carolina Regulation.

The civil fighting in the South was as vicious, if not more so, than that in the North. Whigs and Tories routinely targeted civilians in parts of South Carolina and North Carolina, and in some areas refugee crises were intentionally created as a means of controlling the countryside. One Whig militia unit operating in Surry County, North Carolina, routinely used torture to extract information, even threatening prisoners with castration if they did not cooperate. In South Carolina, the term "Tarleton's Quarter"—that is, the refusal to take prisoners in battle—became commonplace after Tories serving under Banastre Tarleton massacred prisoners after the Battle of Waxhaw Creek in 1780. At one point, Nathanael *Greene begged Anthony Wayne to restrain the militia from attacking Tory civilians in retaliation, so vicious had the fighting become.

The war between the Whigs and Tories was not the only war fought. South Carolina had another civil war, between the powerful Cherokee Indian nation, which sided with the British, and the American militia. Cherokee resentments had been growing since the 1760s, when settlers from South Carolina and Georgia had pushed onto Cherokee lands. The Cherokee also had longstanding economic relationships with British traders. Like the war between the Whigs and Tories, this war was ferocious. Massacre followed massacre, atrocity followed atrocity, until all bounds of civil order collapsed.

The army's travails and the civil fighting were in part indicative of political and social problems in the new republic. A displaced and squabbling Congress struggled to supply the army. It was only nominally successful. The troops suffered widespread winter shortages of food and clothing, first at *Valley Forge and later at Morristown, New Jersey. To complicate matters, the *Articles of Confederation limited Congress's powers, and its relationship to the state governments was poorly defined. The states' economies began to experience hyperinflation as state governments printed paper money to meet war expenditures. The resulting currency devaluation and the erosion of the states' financial power posed a serious threat to the war effort because the state governments, the only bodies empowered to raise troops, used bounties as a key incentive for enlistment. All the states, moreover, lost considerable political, legal, and economic talent as loyalists fled into New York City and other British strongholds.

Despite these problems, several key factors sustained the American cause. The revolutionaries were fighting for independence and a republicanized society. These compelling goals gave them the will to continue the war. America was a society dominated by farmers, the majority of whom—around 80 percent—supported the Revolution's goals. These yeomen might not have rushed to join the Continental army, but they fought in the militia in defense of their towns and farms, making it difficult for the British army to operate in the countryside. Finally, Americans had in George Washington a leader in whom the soldiers, politicians, and people could believe. Washington's qualities as a general have been debated, but his leadership abilities are beyond doubt. A skilled politician, he adeptly handled the Congress, the French allies, and his own troops at numerous difficult moments.

The Shift South and the War's Final Phase. Military stalemate in the Mid-Atlantic region in 1778 encouraged British commanders to reconsider again their strategic policy. It was then that the war shifted to the South and entered its final (1779–1783) phase. The southern campaign started auspiciously for the British. In late 1778 and 1779, British forces reconquered Georgia, the only state completely subdued during the war. The British restored the royal governor and displaced the radical unicameral legislature that had assumed power in the state in 1776. Georgians who supported American independence were arrested by British authorities. Early in 1780, Georgia became a launching pad for a serious British offensive in the Carolinas that seemed likely to result in the complete reconquest of these states as well. In May 1780 General Henry Clinton captured Charleston, South Carolina, and over 3,000 American troops under the command of Benjamin Lincoln. Resistance to the British in South Carolina collapsed. Alarmed by these developments, General Washington and the Congress dispatched the hero of Saratoga, Horatio Gates, with reinforcements for the southern department. Gates, with ill-trained and ill-armed troops, rushed to engage Cornwallis without proper preparation and the subsequent battle at Camden, South Carolina, is generally regarded as the single worst defeat in American military history. A bayonet charge by the redcoats put Gates's army to flight, and Gates himself galloped off the battlefield on horseback. After this disaster, guerrilla war waged by Francis Marion, Thomas Sumner, and several other American commanders, with followers in the Carolina countryside, was the only visible sign of American resistance to the British in South Carolina.

It was in this darkest moment that American prospects began to brighten. New hope arrived in the American camp from two sources. Late in 1780, a group of hill country militia thoroughly defeated a loyalist force at the Battle of King's Mountain. This victory secured the southern interior for the American cause. The Congress dispatched one of Washington's ablest subordinates, Nathanael Greene, to take command of the southern department. Greene, a Rhode Island Quaker, had served with Washington since the beginning of the war and developed a reputation for courage and sound judgment. Arriving with few resources and men, Greene began to rebuild the American army in the Carolinas in the late fall of 1780. Harassed by Cornwallis's army, Greene took the audacious step of dividing his forces. Taking most of his inexperienced men into winter quarters for training, he sent a picked group out to battle under the command of Daniel Morgan.

Morgan maneuvered shrewdly in northern South Carolina, setting the stage for one of the war's critical battles. Pursued by Cornwallis's best subordinate, Banastre Tarleton, Morgan, with a mixed force of militia and Continental regulars numbering around 1,000 men, turned to fight on a low series of hills known locally as "Cowpens." Morgan understood how to use frontier militia to his advantage. He instructed them to fire twice and then run; when Tarleton's infantry surged forward in pursuit, Morgan's cavalry enveloped their wing and won a crushing victory. Although only several thousand combatants were involved in the Battle of Cowpens on 17 January 1780, it ranks along with Trenton and Saratoga as one of the war's crucial victories. Had Morgan been defeated, Greene's army would have likely been beaten in turn, resulting in at least a partial failure of the struggle for American independence.

Instead, 1781 saw a renewed American army in the field in the South. Greene's army engaged Cornwallis's at Guilford Court House in March, inflicting heavy losses on the British. After recovering in North Carolina, Cornwallis marched north to Virginia's Yorktown peninsula, where he was soon trapped by combined American and French land-sea forces. After a final assault on 17 October led by Washington's young aide Alexander *Hamilton, the British forces asked for terms, and on the 19th, 7,000 British soldiers surrendered as their musicians fittingly played the old tune "A World Turned Upside Down."

Aftermath. The official termination of hostilities took almost two years after the Yorktown surrender. The American negotiators in Paris, led by Benjamin Franklin, John *Adams, and John *Jay, secured important concessions from the British, including the recognition of the United States of America with the *Mississippi River as its western boundary.

American authorities faced many problems at home. The currency had been devalued, the army—units of which were owed years of pay—needed to be demobilized, British troops remained in many locales, and the American loyalists needed to be dealt with. Mutinies in the Pennsylvania and New Jersey Continental lines over lack of pay and insufferable conditions had broken out in January 1781, and discontent remained strong at the war's end. Rumors circulated of mutiny or even a coup by disgruntled officers who had been promised pensions for life and who realized that Congress would likely renege on all or part of these promises. But General Washington, always careful to yield to civil authority, calmed the army and controlled the unruly tempers within the officers' corps with a powerful address at his Newburgh, New York, headquarters in March 1783.

The problem of the American loyalists was less easily solved. Many had borne arms or given aid to George III's armies. The Treaty of *Paris that officially ended the war included language intended to encourage their reintegration into American society and the restoration of their seized property. But hatreds on both sides, reflecting political differences as well as the intense civil fighting of the war years, remained too deep. Tens of thousands of the King's Friends went into exile in Canada, Britain, and the British West Indies. Particularly difficult was the plight of former slaves who had served the king in order to gain their freedom. Some of them had been fighting since the outbreak of war in 1775 and 1776, when Lord Dunmore, Virginia's last royal governor, set up the Kings' Standard and offered freedom to African-American slaves who fled from their masters to serve the British army. But at the war's end, they were in grave danger of losing that freedom. Some were resold into slavery in the West Indies; British authorities settled a much larger population in Nova Scotia; and still others eventually made their way to Sierra Leone in West Africa, where they established several communities.

The Revolution unleashed a host of social changes. It disrupted old patterns of life and replaced them with new social relationships; led to the creation of new private and public institutions; changed the relationship of men to women; affected the lives of the Native American tribes east of the Mississippi (generally negatively); and partially ruptured the slaveholding system. Not only had over 20,000 slaves run away to the British army, but thousands more served in the American army, and *slavery would gradually disappear in the northern states after the war's end.

The Revolution's meaning cannot be grasped simply by recounting the military course of events. The military and political revolutions intersected with and were part of other changes—in population, economy, physical and social mobility, in *science, learning, and eventually *technology—that would remake American society in profound ways in the fifty years after the war's end. And yet to acknowledge these things is not to diminish the centrality of the Revolutionary War to the American nation and the American experience.

[*See also* Agriculture: 1770s to 1890; Albany Congress; Colonial Era; Early Republic, Era of the; Expansionism; German Americans; Immigration; Indian History and Culture: From 1500 to 1800; Indian Wars; Irish Americans; Jefferson, Thomas; Middle West, The; Military, The; Proclamation of 1763; Revolution and Constitution, Era of; Yorktown, Battle of.]

• John Shy, *Toward Lexington: The Role of the British Army in the Coming of the Revolution,* 1965. Bernard Bailyn, *The Ideological Origins of the American Revolution,* 1967, 1992. George A. Billias, ed., *George Washington's Opponents,* 1969. Gordon Wood, *The Creation of the American Republic,* 1969. Stephen G. Kurtz and James H. Hutson, eds., *Essays on the American Revolution,* 1973. Robert Gross, *The Minutemen and Their World,* 1976. Charles Royster, *A Revolutionary People at War: The Continental Army and American Character, 1775–1783,* 1979. Edward Countryman, *A People in Revolution,* 1984. Ronald Hoffman, et al., *Arms and Independence: The Military Character of the American Revolution,* 1984. John Shy, *A People Numerous and Armed,* 1990. Colin G. Calloway, *The American Revolution in Indian Country,* 1995. David Hackett Fischer, *Paul Revere's Ride,* 1994.

—Brendan McConville

RIOTS, URBAN. From the *Colonial Era to the late twentieth century, groups of people in American cities have expressed their grievances or enforced their collective will through the use or threat of violence. The nature and context of such rioting, however, has changed over time.

Colonial Era through the Civil War. Colonial riots usually centered on community regulation. In 1710, 1713, and 1729, for example, Bostonians rioted to protest the export of bread that would increase local prices. New Yorkers rioted in 1754 over an unfavorable exchange rate between colonial and British currency that added to the cost of bread and other daily necessities. These disturbances usually did not involve direct physical assaults, but rather street demonstrations and sometimes an attack on property such as a warehouse.

Opposition to British press gangs that forced men into the Royal Navy led to a number of colonial riots, most notably the 1747 Knowles riot in *Boston, in which a crowd held British officials hostage and burned a longboat. Elections sometimes triggered collective violence, as in *Philadelphia in 1741 when sailors attacked supporters of the Quaker-German alliance at the polls. Rowdy street celebrations could lead to riots that reflected neighborhood tensions or class antagonisms, as in Boston's Guy Fawkes Day celebrations starting in the 1740s.

The years preceding the *Revolutionary War saw hundreds of disturbances directed against imperial regulations. Anti–*Stamp Act riots in 1765 resulted in considerable property damage, including the destruction of Lieutenant-Governor Thomas Hutchinson's elegant house in Boston. The years 1767–1770 brought riots against customs collectors enforcing the hated Townshend Duties. A confrontation between British redcoats and local laborers over jobs, with the imperial crisis as a backdrop, led to what patriots called the *Boston Massacre of 5 March 1770. On 16 December 1773, the destruction of property and collective defiance of British authority known as the *Boston Tea Party helped transform resistance into revolution. Independence did not bring an end to rioting, however. Several bread riots broke out during the Revolutionary War, and two antiprostitution riots occurred in *New York City during the 1790s.

Urban riots changed character in the early nineteenth century, as cities became larger and more polyglot. No longer feeling part of a larger community, rioters engaged in acts of physical violence that led to a greater loss of life. By the 1830s and 1840s, ethnic, racial, and class conflict was becoming commonplace on the streets of American cities. Ethnic violence sometimes took political form. In 1834, New York City experienced massive rioting as nativist Whigs and *Irish-American Democrats squared off. Less overtly political were two riots in Philadelphia in 1844 between Protestant nativists and (mostly Irish) Catholics during debates over religion in the public schools. In the first riot, on 6 May, one nativist was killed. The second, on 5 July, erupted when nativists heard rumors that the Irish were arming to defend themselves. Twelve people died as Protestant crowds battled the militia. More politically inspired nativist rioting broke out in the 1850s as gangs linked to the *Know-Nothing party intimidated Catholic voters in Baltimore, Louisville, St. Louis, and other cities. Irish immigrants sometimes battled among themselves along religious lines. The most serious such clash, in New York City on 14 July 1871, left forty-one dead.

Class tensions also sparked rioting in the nineteenth century, as in the 1849 Astor Place riot in New York City. This conflict arose from a long-running feud between two actors, the genteel Briton William Macready, a favorite of elite theatergoers, and the flamboyant American Edwin Forrest, popular with the masses. Some thirty people were killed in the clash between partisans of the two performers.

Urban race riots appeared in the North as early as the Jacksonian Era, as whites physically assaulted *African Americans and destroyed their homes and institutions. In a Cincinnati riot in August 1841, determined African Americans beat off an invasion of their neighborhood, but fell back when whites armed with cannon cleared the streets of opposition. The next day, 250 to 300 blacks surrendered to officials for protection as a white mob ransacked African-American houses and destroyed the African-American church.

The worst outbreak of urban violence in nineteenth-century America, the New York City Civil War *draft riots of July 1863, combined ethnic, racial, and class tensions. The rioters, many of them Irish immigrants, objected to a draft law that favored the wealthy. In a murderous four-day rampage, rioters lynched African Americans, burned draft offices and a black orphanage, and attacked the houses of city officials. At least 120 people died before federal troops rushed to New York by President Abraham *Lincoln finally quelled the uprising.

Gilded Age to Late Twentiety Century. Rapid *industrialization after the *Civil War brought a wave of riots arising from *strikes and industrial conflict in which workers fought *police, troops, or strikebreakers protecting business interests. During the *railroad strikes of 1877, armed confrontations broke out from Baltimore to *San Francisco. In Pittsburgh, for example, workers battled militia imported from Philadelphia. Other confrontations rooted in labor unrest occurred at Haymarket in *Chicago in 1886; at the Carnegie steel mill in Homestead, Pennsylvania, in 1892; and in various cities during the *Pullman strike and boycott of 1894. Several cities experienced rioting during streetcar strikes around the turn of the century as urban workers rallied to support exploited streetcar employees.

Race riots continued as well. Collective violence directed against African Americans broke out sporadically in the North in the later nineteenth century, and the great migration of southern blacks to northern cities in the early twentieth century led to dozens of riots from 1917 to 1921. The worst of these erupted in East St. Louis in July 1917, leaving forty-eight dead; Chicago in July 1919 (at least thirty-eight killed); and Tulsa in 1921 (at least eighty-five killed).

Around the mid–twentieth century, the nature of rioting once again began to change. As labor unions gained legitimacy during the New Deal, strike-related rioting faded. Indeed, state and federal governments even tolerated sit-down strikes (the peaceful occupation of factories by workers), a form of rioting that minimized violence. As open ethnic hostilities became more muted, the older form of race riot involving collective white attacks on black communities ended. The last race riot of this type occurred in *Detroit in 1943. *Civil rights demonstrators in the *South, however, often faced attacks by white segregationists in the 1950s and early 1960s.

Politically motivated disturbances arose on college and university campuses and in some cities, including *Washington, D.C., in the later 1960s and early 1970s in opposition to the *Vietnam War. These actions usually consisted of the occupation of buildings, but destruction of property and mild attacks on police occurred as well. The attack by Chicago police on antiwar demonstrators at the 1968 Democratic National Convention was widely condemned as a "police riot."

A new form of urban rioting erupted in Harlem in 1943 as African Americans protesting job discrimination and other manifestations of *racism looted and destroyed white-owned businesses in Harlem. This form of rioting by poor blacks directed against property in their own neighborhoods, often through arson, spread in the 1960s as hundreds of disturbances erupted in black urban neighborhoods, most notably in the *Watts district of *Los Angeles in 1964, and in Newark and Detroit in 1967. The assassination of Martin Luther *King Jr. in 1968 led to riots and arson in Washington, D.C., and other cities. Similar outbreaks occasionally occurred after the 1960s, often triggered by police violence or rumors of police misconduct. The most extensive of these disturbances broke out in an African American district of Los Angeles in 1992, following a jury's acquittal of white policemen who had been videotaped beating Rodney King, a black motorist.

[*See also* Antebellum Era; Anti-Catholic Movement; Haymarket Affair; Homestead Lockout; Lynching; Nativist Movement; New Deal Era, The; Revolution and Constitution, Era of; Sit-Down Strike, Flint; Sixties, The; Whig Party.]

• Elliott Rudwick, *Race Riot at East St. Louis, July 2, 1917*, 1964. Joseph Boskin, *Urban Racial Violence in the Twentieth Century*, 1969. William M. Tuttle Jr., *Race Riot: Chicago in the Red Summer of 1919*, 1970. Michael Feldberg, *The Turbulent Era: Riot and Disorder in Jacksonian America*, 1980. Paul A. Gilje, *The Road to Mobocracy: Popular Disorder in New York City, 1763–1834*, 1987. Iver Bernstein, *The New York City Draft Riots: Their Significance for American Society and Politics in the Age of the Civil War*, 1990. Michael A. Gordon, *The Orange Riots: Irish Political Violence in New York City, 1870–1871*, 1993. Paul A. Gilje, *Rioting in America*, 1996. David Grimsted, *American Mobbing, 1828–1861: Toward Civil War*, 1998.

—Paul A. Gilje

ROADS AND TURNPIKES, EARLY. Turnpikes, an important organizational innovation that significantly improved roads in nineteenth-century America, were state-chartered corporations that built roads (sometimes on a preexisting roadbed) in return for the right to charge travelers a specified toll. The financial resources of the turnpike corporations gave them a significant advantage over local governments, which usually relied on the labor of uncooperative farmers and the dubious *engineering skills of unqualified commissioners to construct roads. Turnpikes put lengthy stretches of road under unified management, thereby dispensing with the need for coordination among a multiplicity of local governments to improve roads.

Although some historians have labeled the early nineteenth century the "turnpike age," it would be more accurate to view turnpike growth as coming in waves. Beginning with the opening of the *Philadelphia to Lancaster tollroad, the initial turnpike movement spread rapidly during the first quarter of the nineteenth century, especially in the Northeast. The *New England and Middle Atlantic states alone chartered more than nine hundred companies before 1830. By that time, turnpikes had begun to spread throughout the *Middle West and *South. Although these first waves subsided with the advent of canals and *railroads, individual turnpikes continued to operate as feeder lines to the canals and railroads for many decades. Moreover, new turnpikes remained an option for areas without access to water or rail transport. Turnpike chartering and construction, for example, continued in *California into the 1870s.

Although organized as corporations, most turnpikes were financial disasters. Higher-than-expected maintenance costs meant that many turnpikes had to channel toll revenue into maintaining roads. Travelers often managed to carve out "shunpike" trails around tollgates, thereby avoiding the necessity of paying tolls. State regulations granted numerous exemptions that compounded the problems of collecting tolls. In New York, for example, the legislature exempted from paying tolls travelers residing with one mile of a gate, performing militia duties, serving on juries, or going to a grist mill. Shunpiking and political pressure for toll exemptions reflected an undercurrent of popular distrust of turnpikes, as many common folk viewed the corporations as unjustified grants of state privilege to "aristocratic" proprietors.

Despite the well-known lack of profitability, Americans eagerly invested in turnpikes because they provided indirect benefits in the form of higher land values and increased commerce. Turnpikes were part of the town rivalries endemic to nineteenth-century America; residents of small towns and villages hoped that a turnpike would transform their locality into a great regional trade depot. Although such dreams usually proved elusive, contemporary observers nevertheless remained convinced that turnpikes significantly improved transportation, raised land values, and spurred local commerce. The combination of poor direct returns and high indirect benefits undermined charges that turnpikes were "aristocratic institutions"; consequently, they came to be viewed as mechanisms of community improvement. The strong relationship between community support and the turnpike corporations perhaps accounts for the popularity of turnpikes throughout the nineteenth century.

Roads and turnpikes figured in national politics as well. In 1816, Congress authorized federal support for a road into the interior. Construction of such a road had already begun at Cumberland, Maryland, in 1811. This so-called National Road reached Wheeling, West Virginia, on the Ohio River by 1818, and Vandalia, Illinois, where it ended, by 1838. The *Whig party's program of federally funded internal improvements included road construction. Democrats also supported the National Road, but Andrew *Jackson's 1830 veto of the Whig leader Henry *Clay's bill to fund a sixty-mile road in Kentucky—the so-called Maysville Road Veto—came to symbolize the party divisions of the day.

[*See also* Antebellum Era; Canals and Waterways; Early Republic, Era of the; Economic Development; Highway System.]

• Daniel B. Klein, "The Voluntary Provision of the Public Goods? The Turnpike Companies of Early America," *Economic Inquiry* 28 (1990): 788–812. Daniel B. Klein and John Majewski, "Economy, Community, and Law: The Turnpike Movement in New York, 1797–1845," *Law and Society Review* 26, no. 3 (1993): 469–512.

—John Majewski

ROBESON, PAUL (1898–1976), African-American singer, actor, and social activist. Born in Princeton, New Jersey, the son of a Presbyterian minister, Paul Robeson attended Rutgers University, distinguishing himself as a scholar, athlete, singer, and actor. He graduated from Columbia Law School in 1923 and briefly practiced law, but soon turned to the *theater. His roles in Eugene *O'Neill's *All God's Chillun Got Wings* (1924) and *The Emperor Jones* (1924 in New York, 1925 in London) catapulted him to international prominence as a serious actor at a time when stage opportunities for *African Americans were generally limited to racist stereotypes. Robeson's Shakespeare roles, particularly *Othello*, were popular and critical successes. He appeared in several *films and won fame at home and in Europe for his vocal recitals featuring Negro *spirituals and show tunes such as "Old Man River."

Robeson understood the fight against *racism within the context of antifascism. Supporting the Loyalist forces during the Spanish Civil War, he became increasingly interested in *communism and the American Communist party from the mid-1930s on, particularly as the party embraced antifascism and spoke to the plight of African Americans and on behalf of organized labor. Robeson's political leanings limited his opportunities to perform. During the *Cold War he became a target of Senator Joseph *McCarthy and the *House Committee on Un-American Activities. From 1950 to 1958, the U.S. government revoked his passport. Plagued by ill health and mental disorders, Robeson spent several years in Europe, but eventually returned to America. Increasingly withdrawn and reclusive, he died in Harlem.

[*See also* Anticommunism; Communist Party—USA; Drama; Harlem Renaissance; Music: Traditional Music.]

• Paul Robeson, *Here I Stand*, 1958. Martin Duberman, *Paul Robeson* 1988. Jeffrey C. Stewart, ed., *Paul Robeson: Artist and Citizen*, 1998.

—Theodore O. Mason Jr.

ROBINSON, JACKIE (1919–1972), *baseball player, *civil rights leader, businessman, first *African American in modern major league baseball. Born in Georgia and raised in Pasadena, California, Jackie Robinson attended the University of California at Los Angeles where he excelled as an All-American *football player, and in *basketball, broad jump, and baseball. Robinson later played for the Kansas City Monarchs of the Negro American League.

In 1945, Branch Rickey, owner of the Brooklyn Dodgers, selected Robinson to become the first African-American player in major league baseball since the 1890s. His promotion to the Dodgers in 1947 triggered opposition from other players. Nonetheless, he batted .297, won the Rookie-of-the-Year Award, and led the Dodgers to the pennant. Over the next decade, playing mostly second base, Robinson emerged as one of the most dominant players and foremost gate attractions in baseball history, winning the National League Most Valuable Player Award in 1949, compiling a .311 lifetime batting average and winning election to the Baseball Hall of Fame.

Robinson was a leading symbol of and spokesperson for the postwar *civil rights movement. Upon retirement he became a newspaper columnist and fundraiser for the *National Association for the Advancement of Colored People. A believer in "black capitalism," Robinson engaged in many business ventures in the black community, including Harlem's Freedom National Bank. Active in *Republican party politics, he was appointed special assistant for Community Affairs by New York Governor Nelson Rockefeller. By the late 1960s Robinson had become "bitterly disillusioned" with both baseball and American society. His 1972 autobiography, *I Never Had It Made*, criticized the nation's retreat on civil rights issues.

[*See also* Racism; Segregation, Racial; Sports: Amateur Sports and Recreation; Sports: Professional Sports.]

• Jackie Robinson with Alfred Duckett, *I Never Had It Made*, 1972. Jules Tygiel, *Baseball's Great Experiment: Jackie Robinson and His Legacy*, 1983.

—Jules Tygiel

ROCK-AND-ROLL. *See* Blues; Music: Popular Music; Presley, Elvis.

ROCKEFELLER, JOHN D. (1839–1937), oil-industry leader and philanthropist, dominated the U.S. *petroleum industry, developed management techniques that revolutionized American *business, and—perhaps his greatest legacy—contributed more than $550 million to philanthropic institutions.

Rockefeller was born in Richford, New York, the son of William Avery Rockefeller, a commodities dealer, and his wife Eliza (Davison) Rockefeller. In 1853 the family moved to a farm near Cleveland, Ohio. Combining his mother's pious humility and his father's brash ambition, Rockefeller early sought "something big." Becoming a partner in a produce business in 1859, Rockefeller began his business career in Cleveland as a bookkeeper. Viewing a contract as a covenant and trust as the basis of all business relationships, he won the respect of Cleveland's business community for his piety, seriousness, and perseverance. Coming of age at the dawn of the petroleum boom, Rockefeller, in partnership with his brother William, Henry M. Flagler, and others, opened an oil refinery in 1863; by 1865, it was Cleveland's largest. The Standard Oil Company of Ohio, incorporated by Rockefeller and his partners in 1867, soon dominated the industry and commanded markets worldwide. His innovative vertical integration, from oil wells and pipelines to retail-distribution outlets, secured his company a competitive edge in a cut-throat business. His ruthless horizontal integration, involving merging with or eliminating competitors, won for Standard Oil a near monopoly.

The Standard Oil trust, created in 1881 to run the far-flung Rockefeller empire, transformed the corporate world. It also became the target of *antitrust legislation and of exposés by journalistic *muckrakers, including Henry Demarest Lloyd's *Wealth against Commonwealth* (1894) and Ida Tarbell's devastating *History of the Standard Oil Company* (1904). The Ohio Supreme Court outlawed the Standard Oil trust in 1892. Its successor, the Standard Oil Company of New Jersey, a holding company, was dissolved by the U.S. *Supreme Court in 1911 in a landmark antitrust case.

Despite a fortune of more than $900 million, Rockefeller lived simply, riding the elevated train to work in *New York City, dining at home, attending the Baptist Church regularly, belonging to no clubs, and pursuing his avocation as a landscape gardener at estates in Ohio and New York.

In later years Rockefeller devoted himself to philanthropy. Among his more notable benefactions were the YMCA; the Anti-Saloon League; the Baptist Church; the University of Chicago (1892); the *Rockefeller Institute for Medical Research (1901); the General Education Board (1902), which made grants to educational institutions; the Rockefeller Foundation (1913); and the Laura Spelman Rockefeller Memorial Foundation (1918). In 1955, the *New York Times* estimated the total of Rockefeller family gifts at more than $2.5 billion.

Rockefeller married Laura Celestia Spelman in 1864. She provided wise counsel, and shared with him a warm and affectionate relationship. Their four children included John D. Rockefeller Jr. (1874–1960), who was active in managing the family's financial affairs and philanthropic interests, and who, in turn, fathered several children who became prominent in finance and politics, including New York governor Nelson A. Rockefeller (1908–1979) and the banker and philanthropist Laurence Rockefeller (1910–).

[*See also* Capitalism; Gilded Age; Industrialization; Philanthropy and Philanthropic Foundations; Temperance and Prohibition; YMCA and YWCA.]

• Allan Nevins, *Study in Power: John D. Rockefeller, Industrialist and Philanthropist*, 2 vols., 1953. Ron Chernow, *Titan: The Life of John D. Rockefeller, Sr.*, 1998.

—Joe Torre

ROCKEFELLER INSTITUTE. Founded in 1901 by John D. *Rockefeller Sr., the Rockefeller Institute for Medical Research initially provided grants to scientific investigators at various institutions. The institute moved to Manhattan's Upper East Side in 1906 with the construction of its first permanent laboratory. A research hospital was built in 1910, the first such American facility dedicated to experimental medicine.

Rockefeller's two main advisers, his son John D. Rockefeller Jr. and Frederick T. Gates, convinced that *philanthropy had a vital role in promoting the benefits of science and medicine, were determined to create a research institute of international caliber. Initially pledging $20,000 a year over a ten-year period, Rockefeller added an additional $2.6 million in 1907 and $3.8 million in 1910. Reflecting European research models, the Rockefeller Institute was organized under the directorship of Simon Flexner around senior investigators and their laboratories rather than by academic departments. This afforded researchers the freedom to cross disciplinary boundaries freely in the course of their investigations. Such diverse fields as cellular and molecular biology, infectious diseases, genetics, biochemistry, neurobiology, immunology, mathematics, physics, and behavioral sciences have all been studied at Rockefeller.

The institute became a graduate degree–granting institution in 1954 and in 1965 changed its name to Rockefeller University. The university and its hospital have been at the forefront of research in numerous medical areas including the identification of human blood groups, the production of antibiotics, and the study of aging, diabetes, *heart disease, *acquired immunodeficiency syndrome (AIDS), and genetic disorders. Twenty Nobel laureates have been associated with the institution.

[*See also* Biological Sciences; Disease; Genetics and Genetic Engineering; Hospitals; Mathematics and Statistics; Medical Education; Medicine: From the 1870s to 1945; Medicine: Since 1945; Physical Sciences; Science: From 1914 to 1945; Science: Since 1945.]

• George W. Corner, *A History of the Rockefeller Institute, 1901–1953: Origins and Growth,* 1964.

—Lee R. Hiltzik

ROCKY MOUNTAINS, a series of largely parallel ranges in western North America, including the Sangre de Cristo, Front, Wind, Absaroka, and Bitterroot ranges. They extend chiefly through New Mexico, Colorado, Wyoming, Idaho, and Montana, rising sharply from the Great Plains and contrasting with the intermontane plateaus and Great Basin farther west. Geologically young, the Rockies exhibit faulting, glaciation, and volcanism, resulting in rugged, spectacularly scenic terrain. Colorado's Mount Elbert, at 14,433 feet, is the highest point in the Rockies. National parks like Grand Teton, Rocky Mountain, Glacier, and Yellowstone preserve this stunning scenery.

The Rockies initially represented a barrier to settlement and travel. Their crest constitutes the Continental Divide, and many important rivers issue from these mountains, including the Arkansas, Colorado, Missouri, Snake, and Columbia. Explorers like Alexander MacKenzie (1793), Lewis and Clark (1804–1806), Zebulon Pike (1806–1807), John Colter (1807), Jedediah Smith (1826–1829), and Benjamin de Bonneville (1832–1834) eventually found gaps through the mountains. Chief among these was South Pass through which the Oregon, Mormon, and California trails passed after 1843. Later, *railroads and interstate highways utilized other passes.

The Rockies have influenced American art and literature. Samuel Seymour first sketched the Rockies in 1823, while Albert Bierstadt and Thomas Moran followed with many paintings after 1859. Washington Irving captured the early excitement of the Rockies in *The Adventures of Captain Bonneville* (1837), a theme revisited by more recent writers like James Michener in *Centennial* (1974). The region remains popular with tourists, as well as a source of timber, minerals, and grazing.

[*See also* Lewis and Clark Expedition; Literature: Early National and Antebellum Eras; Mining; Oregon Trail; Painting: To 1945; Tourism; West, The; Yellowstone National Park.]

• Patricia Trenton and Peter H. Hassrick, *The Rocky Mountains: A Vision for Artists in the Nineteenth Century,* 1983. Duane A. Smith, *Rocky Mountain West: Colorado, Wyoming, and Montana, 1859–1915,* 1992.

—Jon T. Kilpinen

ROE* v. *WADE (1973). In *Roe* v. *Wade,* the U.S *Supreme Court found unconstitutional state criminal *abortion laws dating back to the 1860s and 1870s. By a 7–2 vote, announced on 22 January 1973, the court ruled that prohibiting abortion violated a woman's right to privacy in determining whether or not to carry a pregnancy to term. The Court declared, however, that this right was not "absolute," but balanced against state interests. States were prohibited from interfering with abortion during the first trimester of pregnancy; they were allowed to regulate abortions in the second trimester to ensure the safety of the woman; and they could prohibit abortion in the third trimester to protect fetal life, unless the pregnancy jeopardized the woman's life or health. In a companion opinion, *Doe* v. *Bolton,* the Court found that policies designed to restrict abortions by reviewing (and often overturning) physicians' recommendations for abortion were unconstitutional because they violated doctors' rights to make medical decisions.

The principal author of both decisions was Justice Harry A. Blackmun (1908–1999). Blackmun's decision derived the right-to-privacy principle (not mentioned in the *Constitution) from the due process clause of the *Fourteenth Amendment. The two dissenters, Justice Byron White and future chief justice William Rehnquist, criticized the right-to-privacy argument as constitutionally dubious and the trimester approach as arbitrary.

Roe v. *Wade* grew out of a changing legal and political context. Several states (*Alaska, *Hawai'i, and New York) had already legalized abortion, and a dozen more had liberalized their laws to make it easier for women to obtain "therapeutic" abortions. (Therapeutic abortions to protect the life of the pregnant woman were always permitted.) The movement toward legalization began in the mid-1950s among physicians and lawyers, and by 1970 had won the support of numerous feminist, religious, professional, student, and labor organizations.

Underpinning this support was a heretofore quiet and private tradition of accepting abortion as well as the frightening history of the injury and death of women seeking illegal abortions. During the century of illegal abortion, American women of every class, ethnic, religious, and racial background obtained abortions. By the 1960s, however, low-income and nonwhite women were over-represented among those who died from illegal abortions. As legal abortions replaced illegal and self-induced abortions, maternal mortality fell and hospital septic abortion wards closed. In 1973, nearly 800,000 legal abortions were performed.

With the legalization of abortion nationwide, the pro-life movement, an anti-abortion campaign initially financed by the Catholic church and fundamentalist Protestants, grew in political power. This volatile issue was used to mobilize voters and swing elections at all levels. By the mid-1990s, 80 percent of all U.S. counties had no abortion providers. The reduced availability of legal abortion was achieved by various means: political pressure; laws, such as those requiring women under eighteen to obtain parental permission; the elimination of state funding for abortions for low-income women; and criminal anti-abortion activity, including the bombing of clinics and the murder of abortion providers. Nonetheless, opinion polls found that a growing proportion of the population supported legal abortion.

[*See also* Birth Control and Family Planning; Christian Coalition; Feminism; Fundamentalist Movement; Moral Majority; Roman Catholicism.]

• Carole Joffe, *Doctors of Conscience: The Struggle to Provide Abortion before and after* Roe v. Wade, 1995. Leslie J. Reagan, *When Abortion Was a Crime: Women, Medicine, and Law in the United States, 1867–1973,* 1997.

—Leslie J. Reagan

ROGERS, WILL (1879–1935), humorist and performer. Will Rogers, one-quarter Cherokee, mounted the *vaudeville stage in 1904, performing the rope tricks he had learned in his youth in the Indian Territory (later Oklahoma). Some offhand remarks elicited unexpected laughter and over time the talk in his act crowded out the roping; when he joined the Ziegfeld Follies in 1918, it was as a monologist. With the Follies, Rogers became known for his political commentary (usually preceded by his slogan, "All I know is just what I read in the papers"). In the 1920s, he was successively popular as a widely syndicated newspaper columnist, on the lecture circuit, as a *radio performer, and as the star of more than twenty films for Fox pictures. He died in a 1935 plane crash over Point Barrow, Alaska, that also killed the aviator Wiley Post.

Rogers enjoyed an unprecedented popularity in the 1920s and early 1930s. While another of his famous sayings—"I never met a man I didn't like"—was clear hyperbole, it was difficult to find anyone who didn't like *him*. Among national politicians—most of whom he knew and some of whom were his friends—to be kidded by Rogers was a badge of high status. He combined an inherent amiability and decency, a lightning-fast wit, and shrewd and opportunistic appreciation of the emerging media of his era, with a canny awareness of how far satire could go without giving offense.

[*See also* Cowboys; Film; Humor; New Deal Era, The; Twenties, The.]

• *The Writings of Will Rogers,* 21 vols., 1973–1983. Ben Yagoda, *Will Rogers: A Biography,* 1993.

—Ben Yagoda

ROMAN CATHOLICISM. Spanish and French explorers brought Roman Catholicism to America in the sixteenth and seventeenth centuries. St. Augustine, Florida, founded by Spanish explorers in 1565, became the site of the oldest Christian community in the United States. Missionary priests intent on Christianizing and "civilizing" the Native population established mission towns that stretched northward to Georgia. By the mid-seventeenth century, seventy missionaries were working in thirty-eight missions; these Spanish missions declined, however, and by the early eighteenth century St. Augustine was the only one left. The mission era ended when the British gained control of Florida in 1763.

The French, meanwhile, in 1608 established a permanent settlement at Quebec, from which Catholic missionary priests traveled down the St. Lawrence through the Great Lakes region evangelizing the Native population. This mission era ended in 1763 when the British took over all of Canada. Throughout the *Middle West, French missionaries and explorers left their mark in places like St. Ignace and Sault Ste. Marie, Michigan, and St. Louis, Missouri.

The Catholic presence in the *Southwest was widespread. Spanish explorers settled Santa Fe in 1610 and branched out to areas in what is now Arizona and Texas. In the eighteenth century, Spanish missionaries led by the friar Junipero *Serra traveled the Pacific coast founding twenty-one mission towns stretching from San Diego to *San Francisco. The Mexican government's takeover of the missions in 1833 marked the end of the Spanish mission era. The church survived, however, ministering to the needs of *Hispanic Americans and Catholic Indians. This territory became part of the United States in 1848 after the *Mexican War, opening a new chapter in the Catholic church's history.

Catholicism in British America. In 1634 Cecil Calvert, a convert to Catholicism, together with a small group of English colonists founded Maryland. This colony and its capital, St. Mary's City, became the center of the Catholic presence in the English colonies. Maryland farms established by Jesuit missionaries from England and Europe became centers of Catholic worship and home bases for traveling missionaries who ministered to rural Catholics of southern Maryland. Catholics were always a minority in Maryland, but while the Calvert family retained control, they enjoyed prestige and power. This changed in 1689 when William and Mary assumed the English throne and the Calverts lost ownership of the colony. As Maryland became a royal colony, English laws that discriminated against Catholics by proscribing such rights as voting and public worship also became law in Maryland. Nonetheless, thanks to *immigration from Ireland, Maryland's Catholic population continued to grow. By 1765, it stood at twenty thousand, with another six thousand in Pennsylvania.

The vast majority of Maryland Catholics supported the Revolution of 1776. One of them, Charles Carroll of Carrollton (1737–1832), became a delegate to the *Continental Congress, a signer of the *Declaration of Independence, and an author of the Maryland constitution.

In 1790 John Carroll (1735–1815), an American-born and European-educated priest, was ordained as the first bishop of Baltimore. Although only about 35,000 Catholics then lived in the United States, Carroll, together with other Catholics, articulated a vision of Catholicism that was unique at this time. He foresaw a national, American church that would be independent of foreign jurisdiction and would endorse religious pluralism and toleration, in which religion would be grounded in the Enlightenment principle of intelligibility, where a vernacular liturgy would be normative and in which the spirit of democracy would permeate parish government. By 1800 this republican model of Catholicism gave way to a more traditional European model, owing mainly to the influx of French clergy who brought with them a monarchical vision of the church.

The Immigrant Church. With large-scale immigration in the 1820s and 1830s, particularly from Ireland and Germany, the U.S. Catholic population increased dramatically. After the *Civil War, Catholic immigrants from southern and eastern Europe arrived in large numbers. By 1920 the Catholic population numbered about seventeen million and included some twenty-eight ethnic groups. Catholics mainly lived in the urbanized Northeast and Middle West, a region stretching from *Boston to *Chicago, Baltimore to St. Louis. The neighborhood parish organized by nationality became the hallmark of the urban immigrant church. Most parishes supported an elementary school staffed by nuns recruited from Europe and Ireland. Parish organizations strengthened the bond between church and people. Hospitals and orphanages, also staffed by nuns, extended the ministry of the urban church.

In the *Antebellum Era, a Protestant crusade against Catholics swept the nation. Anti-Catholic riots erupted, and in a few instances convents and churches were destroyed. The crusade peaked in the early 1850s when a new anti-immigrant, anti-Catholic political organization, the *Know-Nothing party, gained power in several states. Archbishop John *Hughes of New York became a forceful defender of Catholic rights. Encountering discrimination, Catholics developed their own subculture and an outsider mentality.

Some Catholics wanted the church to abandon this outsider mentality and become more American and less foreign. The Catholic convert Isaac Hecker (1819–1888), founder of the Paulist Fathers, forcefully advocated this vision in the antebellum period, while Archbishop John Ireland and James Cardinal *Gibbons promoted it in the 1880s and 1890s. These "Americanists" endorsed the separation of church and state, political democracy, religious toleration, and some type of merger of Catholic and public elementary education. In 1889, however, Pope Leo XIII issued an encyclical letter that condemned "Americanism." This papal intervention ended the campaign of Ireland and Gibbons and solidified the Romanization of American Catholicism.

1920–1960: Consolidation, Acculturation, and Growing Confidence. The 1920–1960 era was one of consolidation. New churches were built, colleges founded, and record numbers of American Catholics entered seminaries and convents. At the neighborhood parish level, Catholicism remained very ethnic and clannish into the 1940s. Educated middle-class Catholics, however, whose numbers were increasing, sought greater involvement in the public life of the nation. What contemporaries called a "Catholic renaissance" took place in these years as Catholics grew more confident of their place in the United

States. Catholics supported the New Deal and many held influential positions in President Franklin Delano *Roosevelt's administration and in the growing *labor movement. John Ryan (1869–1945), a priest and professor at the Catholic University of America, gained a national reputation as an advocate of social action and workers' rights. Dorothy Day (1897–1980) founded the Catholic Worker movement in 1933; her commitment to the poor inspired many young Catholics to work for social justice. By the 1950s Catholicism was riding a wave of popularity and confidence. New churches and schools opened their doors, the church drew record numbers of converts, and more than 70 percent of Catholics regularly attended Sunday Mass. The Catholic college population increased significantly. Bishop Fulton J. Sheen had his own award-winning television show that attracted millions of viewers. In 1958 a new pope, John XXIII, charmed the world and filled Catholics with pride. The 1960 election of an Irish American Catholic, John F. *Kennedy, to the presidency reinforced the optimism and confidence of Catholics.

1960–2000: Liturgical Reforms and Demographic Changes. In the 1960s, prodded by the Second Vatican Council (1962–1965), the Catholic church worldwide underwent a period of reform. Coupled with broader social changes under way in the United States, the reforms initiated by the council ushered in a new age for American Catholicism. The most dramatic change took place in the Catholic Mass; a new liturgy celebrated in English replaced an ancient Latin ritual. An ecumenical spirit inspired Catholics to break down the fences that separated them from people of other religious traditions. Emerging from a cultural ghetto, Catholics adopted a more public presence in society, joining the war against *poverty and *racism. While some members of the Catholic hierarchy such as Francis Cardinal *Spellman of New York supported the *Vietnam War, Catholics such as Daniel and Philip Berrigan were in the forefront of the peace movement. In the 1980s, the Catholic hierarchy issued pastoral letters addressing issues of war and peace in the nuclear age and economic justice. At the same time, an educated laity displayed a greater readiness to challenge the church's teaching on birth control, clerical celibacy, an exclusively male clergy, and the teaching authority of the Pope. Other Catholics opposed such dissent, however, and strongly defended the authority of the Pope and the hierarchy. Ideological diversity became a trademark of contemporary Catholicism.

Beginning in the 1960s, the number of priests and nuns declined. As a result, lay men and women assumed more responsibility for the church's many ministries. As new *immigration laws admitted more newcomers from Asia and South America, many of them Catholic, the church in the 1990s was more ethnically diverse than ever; in some cities, Sunday Mass was celebrated in as many as forty-five different languages. Spanish-speaking Catholics comprised the single largest group of these new immigrants.

As the twentieth century ended, Catholicism in the United States entered still another new period in its history. No longer religious outsiders, Catholics were better integrated into American life, more ethnically diverse than ever, and more heterogeneous intellectually and politically. While the hierarchy had become more theologically conservative, the laity had grown more independent. All these developments, coupled with the declining number of priests and nuns, presented the church, after more than four hundred years in America, with great challenges for the future.

[*See also* Abortion; Anti-Catholic Movement; Assimilation; Birth Control and Family Planning; Exploration, Conquest and Settlement, Era of European; French Settlements in North America; German Americans; Irish Americans; Italian Americans; New Deal Era, The; Polish Americans; Religion; Secularization; Seton, Elizabeth Ann ("Mother"); Sixties, The; Spanish Settlements in North America.]

• John Tracy Ellis, *The Life of James Cardinal Gibbons, Archbishop of Baltimore, 1834–1921*, 2 vols., 1952. Andrew M. Greeley, *The American Catholic: A Social Portrait*, 1977. James Hennessey, S.J., *American Catholics: A History of the Roman Catholic Community in the United States*, 1981. Jay P. Dolan, *The American Catholic Experience: A History from Colonial Times to the Present*, 1985. Robert A. Orsi, *The Madonna of 115th Street: Faith and Community in Italian Harlem, 1880–1950*, 1985. Patrick W. Carey, *People, Priests, and Prelates: Ecclesiastical Democracy and the Tensions of Trusteeism*, 1987. Philip Gleason, *Keeping the Faith: American Catholicism Past and Present*, 1987. James M. O'Toole, *Militant and Triumphant: William Henry O'Connell and the Catholic Church in Boston, 1859–1944*, 1992. Jay P. Dolan and Allan Figueroa Deck, S.J., eds., *Hispanic Catholic Culture in the U.S.*, 1994. John T. McGreevy, *Parish Boundaries: The Catholic Encounter with Race in the Twentieth Century Urban North*, 1996.

—Jay P. Dolan

ROMANTIC MOVEMENT. The initial phase of the American romantic movement is largely identical with *New England *transcendentalism. From that standpoint, its origin could be dated to the publication of Ralph Waldo *Emerson's *Nature* in 1836. Like transcendentalism itself, however, the antecedents of the American romantic movement are complex. It owes its inspiration to German biblical criticism and comparative mythology; to the rise of American Unitarianism; and, perhaps most of all, to the cultural revolution brought about by European romanticism (ca. 1770–1830). Among many European romantic authors, a few—Coleridge, Wordsworth, Shelley, Mme. de Staël, Balzac, and Goethe—stand out for their influence on the American scene. Prominent European scientists—Pierre Simon Laplace, Georges Cuvier, Etienne Geoffroy Saint-Hillaire, and Humphry Davy—played a role as well.

In the early phase of the American romantic movement, the significant presences were those of the transcendentalist circle: Emerson, Theodore *Parker, Margaret *Fuller, Amos Bronson Alcott, and Henry David *Thoreau. Their concerns included pantheism, the relation of subjectivity to objectivity (or, more broadly, of self or consciousness to the external world), symbolism in nature and literature, the *secularization of *religion, and, most importantly, self-development.

The later phase of the romantic movement in the United States is in some respects even more complex because of the additional complications created by the American assimilation of Victorian culture. As a result, social concerns such as *antislavery and women's rights acquired greater importance. But both of these clearly derived from the romantic notion of self-development. Its Victorian expression, the *Bildungsroman*, or novel of education, informs even slave narratives such as those of Frederick *Douglass, especially *My Bondage and My Freedom* (1855). Combined with self-development was the affirmation of a religion of the affections (traceable to later romantics like Keats and Shelley but also to Dickens and other Victorian novelists) and, simultaneously, a growing awareness of the problems of intersubjectivity, as in the work of Nathaniel *Hawthorne and the female slave narratives of Harriet Jacobs (1813–1897) and others. Much of the work produced in the 1850s reflects a tendency toward retrenchment. The sentimental fiction of Maria Cummins, Fanny Fern, Louisa May *Alcott, and others reveals a strong emphasis on emotional self-discipline. The works of Herman *Melville (especially *Pierre*, 1852) offer an even more radical questioning of many concepts and values professed by the American romantic movement in its initial phase. What one sees throughout the decade is a collective effort to respond to a perceived cultural/social crisis that would soon culminate in the *Civil War.

Echoes of the American romantic movement appear after the Civil War in Melville, Walt *Whitman, and Emily *Dickinson, who explore the immanent value of experiences, eternal recurrence, and new forms of spirituality. The enduring legacy of American romanticism may be seen as well in the *pragmatism of William *James, John *Dewey, and Josiah Royce.

[*See also* Antebellum Era; Cole, Thomas; Literature: Early

National and Antebellum Eras; Painting: To 1945; Philosophy; Poetry; Unitarianism and Universalism; Women's Rights Movements.]

• Michael T. Gilmore, *American Romanticism and the Marketplace*, 1985. Leon Chai, *The Romantic Foundations of the American Renaissance*, 1987. Barbara Novak, *Nature and Culture: American Landscape Painting, 1825–1875*, 1993.

—Leon Chai

ROOSEVELT, ELEANOR (1884–1962), First Lady, humanitarian, social activist. Eleanor Roosevelt (ER) was born in *New York City into an affluent, aristocratic, troubled family. Eleanor was eight when her mother Anna died, and ten when her beloved father Elliott died of alcoholism at thirty-four. She was nurtured and influenced by her maternal grandmother and her paternal uncle Theodore *Roosevelt.

Sent to Allenswood school in England at fifteen, Eleanor was inspired by headmistress Marie Souvestre. ER excelled, debated fiercely, made the first team at field hockey, and emerged a leader. But her grandmother insisted that she return to New York City to perform the debutante ritual of "coming out" when she was eighteen. In 1903, surrounded by friends who founded the Junior League as a smart-set rebellion, including Mary Harriman and Jean Reid, ER taught dancing and calisthenics to the immigrant girls of New York's Lower East Side at their new University Settlement. There she met her mentors and allies, social work pioneers Florence *Kelley and Lillian Wald (1867–1940).

Becoming engaged to her fifth cousin Franklin Delano *Roosevelt, she introduced him to issues of *poverty and struggle; encouraged his Harvard studies; and promoted his ambitions. Their love deepened despite the opposition of his mother, Sara Delano Roosevelt, and they married in 1905. Of their six children, five survived: Anna (1906), James (1907), Elliott (1909), Franklin, Jr. (1914), and John (1916). Sara Delano Roosevelt remained a dominant presence in their lives.

In 1910 FDR was elected to the New York State Assembly, and ER flourished in Albany's political climate. She established important alliances with reform politicians, notably Alfred E. *Smith, Robert F. *Wagner, and Frances *Perkins. In 1913 President Woodrow *Wilson named FDR assistant secretary of the navy, and their move to Washington was initially happy. But ER's life felt momentarily derailed when she discovered her husband's affair with her social secretary Lucy Mercer. She offered a divorce, but they agreed to carry on—to repair their hearts, and protect the children and his career. With FDR's nomination for the vice-presidency in 1920, and ER campaigned fully for the first time.

During that failed effort, she forged a new partnership with Louis Howe, FDR's primary adviser, who became the bridge between them. Together, they battled to keep FDR interested in public life, and promoted his political ambitions during the years of his convalescence from polio. In the 1920s, too, ER became the center of a powerful network of political women in the *Democratic party and the new *League of Women Voters. With Esther Lape and Elizabeth Read, ER campaigned for the U.S. membership in the World Court. With three partners, Marion Dickerman, Nancy Cook, and Caroline O'Day, she co-owned Val-Kill, a model furniture factory two miles from the Roosevelts' Hyde Park, New York, home. After her husband's death, she converted Val-Kill into her residence. She also taught history and literature and was co-principal at New York's Todhunter School, and edited the *Women's Democratic News*. By 1928, when FDR was elected New York State governor, ER was the women's political "boss" of the Democratic party, and a bipartisan leader for women's rights and equity.

In 1932 when FDR was elected president, ER's circle was in place to demand patronage, power, and New Deal justice for women. Her work with Mary (Molly) Dewson, secretary of labor Frances Perkins, Ellen Sullivan Woodward, Mary Anderson, Florence Kerr, and Hilda Worthington Smith, successfully enlarged the New Deal's scope. With Mary McLeod *Bethune, Walter White, and the *National Association for the Advancement of Colored People (NAACP), ER battled racial *segregation and discrimination. In 1938 she helped launch the Southern Conference on Human Welfare, a network of race radicals dedicated to end the poll tax and all discrimination. In 1939 she resigned from the Daughters of the American Revolution (DAR) when it refused to permit Marian *Anderson to perform in the DAR's Constitution Hall in *Washington, D.C. Associated Press reporter Lorena Hickok (Hick), ER's intimate friend during the White House years, influenced her career as a writer, encouraged her to hold press conferences for women journalists only, and write a daily column, "My Day."

Although ER generally supported her husband's policies, during the 1930s, they differed on such international issues as the World Court, *collective security, and the Spanish Civil War. Journalist, editor, and radio broadcaster, ER was the only First Lady to disagree publicly with her husband. In *This Troubled World* (1938), she offered a point by point alternative to FDR's isolationist policies. On domestic issues FDR encouraged his wife to speak out. If she could "warm up" an issue, he would run with it. Their unique partnership allowed each to do more than either could have achieved alone. In the area of *housing, for example, ER in 1934 with the support of her network created a model community, Arthurdale, in West Virginia, that became a prototype for other New Deal model communities.

ER lobbied less successfully for refugees fleeing Nazi persecution. In 1940, she became involved in a covert operation headed by Varian Fry that resulted in the rescue of over 2,000 refugees, including Hannah Arendt, Pablo Casals, Marc Chagall, Wanda Landowska, and Alma Mahler. But the State Department had Fry arrested and terminated the operation in 1941. During *World War II, ER citicized the *incarceration of Japanese Americans and campaigned for women's rights, *civil rights, and the survival of New Deal programs.

Distraught by FDR's death on 12 April 1945 in Warm Springs, Georgia (and dismayed to learn that Lucy Mercer had been with him at the end), ER announced her retirement from public life. But President Harry S. *Truman appointed her a delegate to the *United Nations and she used the opportunity to carry on her vision of the best of FDR's legacy: a New Deal for the world; dignity for all people. She helped create the UN Declaration of Human Rights, which passed the General Assembly on 10 December 1948, and spent the rest of her life lobbying for the UN, human rights, and nuclear disarmament. In 1961 President John F. *Kennedy appointed her chair of his new Commission on the Status of Women, which helped launch the second wave of the women's movement. Her final book *Tomorrow Is Now*, was published posthumously in 1963. She is buried beside her husband at Hyde Park.

[*See also* Antinuclear Protest Movements; Civil Rights Movement; Federal Government, Executive Branch: The Presidency; Feminism; International Law; Internationalism; New Deal Era, The; Progressive Era; Racism; Settlement Houses; Women's Rights Movements.]

• Joseph P. Lash, *Eleanor and Franklin*, 1971. Joseph P. Lash, *Eleanor: The Years Alone*, 1972. Susan Ware, *Partner and I: Molly Dewson, Feminism, and New Deal Politics*, 1987. Blanche Wiesen Cook, *Eleanor Roosevelt, 1884–1933*, 1992. Allida M. Black, *Casting Her Own Shadow*, 1997. Allida M. Black, ed., *Courage in a Dangerous World: The Political Writings of Eleanor Roosevelt*, 1999. Blanche Wiesen Cook, *Eleanor Roosevelt: The Defining Years, 1933–1938*, 1999.

—Blanche Wiesen Cook

ROOSEVELT, FRANKLIN DELANO (1882–1945), thirty-second president of the United States. Born in Hyde Park, New York, Franklin Delano Roosevelt enjoyed a privileged upbringing that gave him great self-confidence and a strong sense of noblesse oblige. He attended Groton School, Harvard College (Class of 1904), and Columbia Law School. Having as a young adult fantasized about following in the footsteps of his distant cousin, President Theodore *Roosevelt, he gained a closer relationship with his idol in 1905 when he married the president's niece (and his own fifth cousin, once removed), Eleanor *Roosevelt. They had five children.

A New York State senator (1911–1913) and assistant secretary of the navy (1913–1920), Roosevelt won the *Democratic party's vice presidential nomination in 1920, running unsuccessfully on a ticket headed by James M. Cox. His confidence was temporarily shaken in 1921 when *poliomyelitis cost him the use of his legs and thereafter confined him mostly to a wheelchair. But his paralysis enabled him to identify with people who suffered in other ways—and they with him. After he was elected governor of New York in 1928, his presidential aspirations were boosted by the *stock market crash of 1929 and the ensuing Great Depression, which discredited President Herbert *Hoover and allowed Roosevelt to win the Democratic nomination and sweep to victory in 1932.

As the economy hit bottom, Roosevelt launched an unprecedented legislative program—the New Deal—that addressed the immediate crisis and instituted lasting reform. The New Deal's first "Hundred Days" produced a flurry of Depression-fighting agencies, including the *National Recovery Administration, the *Agricultural Adjustment Administration, the *Tennessee Valley Authority, the Federal Emergency Relief Administration, and the *Civilian Conservation Corps, to list only a few. Roosevelt's informal *radio talks, billed as "Fireside Chats," reassured a fearful nation.

The Depression created a constituency for active government and bold new approaches, and Roosevelt, never a systematic thinker, oversaw an eclectic program. The *Social Security Act (1935); the *National Labor Relations Act (1935), assuring workers' right to join unions; and the Fair Labor Standards Act (1938), setting maximum working hours and a minimum wage, rank among the New Deal's lasting achievements. The 1936 election produced a Roosevelt landslide. His ill-advised 1937 effort to reorganize the U.S. *Supreme Court produced a significant backlash, however, and Republicans made steady gains in subsequent elections.

Roosevelt drew advisers and top administrators from outsider groups, including Jews, Catholics, *African Americans, and recent immigrants. He appointed the first woman Cabinet member (Frances *Perkins as secretary of labor); provided the first federal aid to the arts; redefined the Democratic party as the champion of the poor, the middle class, and organized labor; and moved toward an alliance with African Americans and other minority groups. For the rest of the twentieth century, the Democrats would be identified as the party of activist government, the disadvantaged, and a variously defined "*liberalism." For half a century after his death, Franklin Roosevelt would be the magnet around which politicians arranged themselves, like iron filings attracted to or repelled by the polarizing force of his record and policies.

An altered relationship between the American people and their government was another of Roosevelt's legacies. Before 1933, most Americans had contact with the federal government only through mail delivery or wartime drafts. When Roosevelt died in 1945, the government's increased involvement in the economy and society, in *World War II even more than during the Depression, had vastly expanded the variety and frequency of contacts between the people and Washington.

Eleanor Roosevelt loomed large in her husband's presidency, traveling widely, reporting her observations, and championing the underdog. Despite their political partnership, however, the Roosevelts grew apart personally, and each found intimacy outside marriage, FDR with Lucy Mercer Rutherfurd, with whom he had a long-term relationship.

The outbreak of war in 1939 presented Roosevelt with a new crisis and a new rationale to remain in office. Breaking with the two-term tradition established by George *Washington, Roosevelt handily won a third term in 1940. World War II dominated the rest of his presidency. Japan's 1941 surprise attack on *Pearl Harbor, combined with the clear evil of Nazism, united the American people to an extraordinary degree. This unity helped Roosevelt mobilize previously depressed industries to a remarkable level of military production. Working with British Prime Minister Winston Churchill, Roosevelt not only forged a wartime alliance, but laid the groundwork for a postwar order, including the *United Nations and international economic organizations, designed to lessen the chances of another depression or world war.

Roosevelt's presidency coincided with Adolf Hitler's years as dictator of Germany, and the contrast between them says much about FDR. He was supremely assured; Hitler pathologically insecure. Both were highly effective orators, but with markedly different techniques. While FDR rallied his friends (his radio talks customarily began, "My friends"), Hitler railed against his enemies. Roosevelt stirred compassion; Hitler incited hatred. Roosevelt's first inaugural address assured Americans that all they had to fear was "fear itself"; Hitler exacerbated his followers' irrational fears and prejudices. Roosevelt championed democracy; Hitler personified dictatorship. When the two men opposed each other in war, the world's fate rested on the outcome. Roosevelt's part in democracy's victory over fascism (albeit in alliance with the brutal regime of Soviet dictator Joseph Stalin), combined with his role in bringing the United States through the Depression, secures his place in history. Critics would later fault Roosevelt for yielding too much to Stalin at the 1945 *Yalta Conference, but most diplomatic historians contend that he played a weak hand as effectively as he could. As for one of Roosevelt's most momentous wartime decisions—to fund atomic-bomb research—its full significance emerged only after his death.

At a time when democracy and *capitalism were in crisis, Roosevelt revived confidence in both. Although the New Deal did not achieve full recovery (that came only with the war), the combination of Roosevelt's contagious optimism with the New Deal's palliative measures helped Americans surmount the worst economic crisis in their history without abandoning constitutional democracy. Similarly, the New Deal's relatively minor adjustments in the free-enterprise system helped ensure capitalism's long-term viability. Victory in the war against fascism, in which Roosevelt played a vital part, further strengthened both democracy and capitalism.

Franklin Roosevelt is generally acknowledged, even by those who disagree with some of his policies, as the most important U.S. president of the twentieth century, and among all presidents second only to Abraham *Lincoln. His death in Warm Springs, Georgia, on 12 April 1945, on the eve of victory in World War II, produced a national outpouring of grief. His memory is preserved in his birthplace and burial site at Hyde Park, and in the Franklin Roosevelt Memorial in Washington, D.C., opened in 1998.

[*See also* Atlantic Charter; Bretton Woods Conference; Depressions, Economic; Federal Government, Executive Branch: The Presidency; Foreign Relations; Labor Movements; Manhattan Project; New Deal Era, The; Political Parties.]

• James MacGregor Burns, *Roosevelt: The Lion and the Fox,* 1956. William E. Leuchtenburg, *Franklin D. Roosevelt and the New Deal,* 1964. James MacGregor Burns. *The Soldier of Freedom,* 1970. Kenneth S. Davis, *FDR,* 4 vols., 1985– . Frank Freidel, *Franklin D. Roosevelt: A Rendezvous with Destiny,* 1990. Patrick J. Maney. *The Roosevelt Presence,* 1992. Doris Kearns Goodwin, *No Ordinary Time,* 1995.

—Robert S. McElvaine

ROOSEVELT, THEODORE (1858–1919), twenty-sixth president of the United States. Born in *New York City, Theodore Roosevelt grew up in comfortable circumstances in the wealthy family of Theodore Roosevelt Sr. and Mittie Bulloch Roosevelt. He struggled with asthma and poor eyesight as a child but also showed the determination to excel, love of books, and fascination with the outdoors that marked his life. A graduate of Harvard, he married Alice Lee in 1880. Fascinated with politics, he won election to the New York Assembly in 1881. The sudden deaths of his mother and his wife on the same day in February 1884 left him with a baby daughter, Alice Lee Roosevelt, and a desire to escape New York. He ranched in the Dakotas for several years.

In 1886, Roosevelt married Edith Kermit Carow, a childhood friend, with whom he had five children. He ran for mayor of New York that year, but came in third. Appointed to the U.S. Civil Service Commission in 1889, he served until 1895. In 1897, after two years as the president of New York City's Board of Police Commissioners, he resigned to become assistant secretary of the navy in the administration of President William *McKinley. In that office he urged the expansion of the navy and lobbied for war with Spain.

When the *Spanish-American War began in April 1898, Roosevelt volunteered. The regiment that he led, known as the Rough Riders, attacked the Spanish in Cuba on 1 July 1898 in a battle that made him a national hero. That fall, running on the *Republican party ticket, he was elected governor of New York State in a close election. An activist governor, Roosevelt spoke out for worker protection, the conservation of natural resources, and the mild regulation of corporations, lending the state's Republican boss, Thomas C. Platt, to conclude that Roosevelt would be less troublesome as vice president. In the absence of credible alternatives, and since he also had the support of western Republicans and younger party members, Roosevelt joined the national Republican ticket in 1900 and campaigned vigorously for McKinley's reelection. He was inaugurated as vice president on 4 March 1901.

On 6 September 1901, McKinley was shot by an assassin; he died eight days later. At forty-two, Roosevelt became the nation's youngest president. He promised to continue McKinley's policies, but his energy, activism, and distinct leadership style soon led him in fresh directions. Taking on corporate America and revitalizing the 1890 Sherman Antitrust Act, he ordered the Justice Department to file what proved to be a successful suit to break up the Northern Securities Company, a railroad conglomerate, early in 1902. He also helped settle a bitter anthracite coal strike later that year on terms that established him as a champion of the "Square Deal" for labor. In foreign policy, he settled an Alaska boundary dispute with Canada, and in 1903 secured control of the Panama Canal Zone in a manner that outraged Colombia but pleased most Americans. He pushed construction of the *Panama Canal and became the first president to leave the continental United States when he visited the Canal Zone in 1906. Roosevelt's achievements and popularity secured his election to the presidency in his own right in 1904 when he decisively defeated the Democratic nominee, Alton B. Parker. On election night he announced that he would not be a candidate in 1908.

Roosevelt pursued a more activist course in his second term. In foreign affairs, he acted as peacemaker for the Russo-Japanese War in 1905, winning the Nobel Peace Prize for his efforts. His diplomacy facilitated the Algeciras Conference of 1906 that quieted differences between France and Germany over Morocco, and he sent a powerful naval force, the "Great White Fleet," around the world in 1907–1909 as a display of American strength. In Latin America, he proclaimed the Roosevelt Corollary to the *Monroe Doctrine, warning European nations against exploiting the troubles of Caribbean countries for military or political advantage.

In domestic affairs, Roosevelt championed railroad regulation through the Hepburn Act, sponsored the *Pure Food and Drug Act, and secured meat-inspection legislation, all in a single year, 1906. More reformist as his term progressed, he pushed for corporate regulation, toughened the antitrust laws, and promoted sweeping conservation policies. Although he invited Booker T. *Washington to the White House, his peremptory dishonorable discharge of African-American soldiers in 1906 because of their purported participation in a shooting incident in Brownsville, Texas, marred his record and reflected his ambiguity on the race issue.

Roosevelt hand-picked William Howard *Taft as his successor and helped Taft win the White House in 1908. Upon leaving office, he went on safari in Africa in 1909–1910. Progressive Republicans' increasing unhappiness with Taft's policies, culminating in the *Ballinger-Pinchot controversy, led Roosevelt to announce his candidacy for the Republican nomination in 1912. Losing the nomination to Taft after a bruising primary battle and a tumultuous national convention, Roosevelt bolted the Republican party and ran on the Progressive party ticket. He spoke out for social justice, but finished second to the Democratic nominee, Woodrow *Wilson.

The Progressive party did not prosper and Roosevelt returned to his Republican roots soon after *World War I broke out in 1914. Unhappy with Wilson's neutrality, he urged the country to prepare for war and, if necessary, intervene on the side of the Allies. Roosevelt lost to Charles Evans *Hughes in the race for the 1916 Republican nomination. Once the United States entered the war in April 1917, Roosevelt sought to raise a volunteer division to fight in France. Wilson and the army refused. Theodore Roosevelt was the likely candidate for the Republican presidential race in 1920, but he died on 6 January 1919.

A major figure in establishing the presidency in its modern form, TR (a nickname he favored) was both intensely controversial and a political celebrity of vast popularity. A forceful orator and an advocate of the strenuous life (he installed a *boxing ring in the White House), Roosevelt with his bushy mustache, pince-nez, and wide, toothy grin was a caricaturist's delight. Vigorous and outspoken, he basked in the limelight: "He wanted to be the bride at every wedding, the corpse at every funeral," a relative commented. A century after he came to the White House, his fame still endured.

[*See also* Antitrust Legislation; Brownsville Incident; Civil Service Reform; Conservation Movement; Economic Regulation; Expansionism; Federal Government, Executive Branch: The Presidency; Foreign Relations: U.S. Relations with Asia; Foreign Relations: U.S. Relations with Latin America; *Northern Securities Case;* Progressive Party of 1912–1924.]

• John Morton Blum, *The Republican Roosevelt,* 1954. Willard B. Gatewood, *Theodore Roosevelt and the Art of Controversy: Episodes of the White House Years,* 1970. William H. Harbaugh, *The Life and Times of Theodore Roosevelt,* 1975. David McCullough, *Mornings on Horseback,* 1981. John Milton Cooper Jr., *The Warrior and the Priest: Woodrow Wilson and Theodore Roosevelt,* 1983. Lewis L. Gould, *The Presidency of Theodore Roosevelt,* 1991.

—Lewis L. Gould

RORTY, RICHARD (1931–), philosopher and leading exponent of neopragmatism. Educated at Chicago and Yale, Richard Rorty taught *philosophy at Princeton before taking a chair as humanities professor at the University of Virginia in 1982. In 1998, he became Professor of Comparative Literature at Stanford. These institutional moves followed and partly expressed his philosophical conversion from conventional analytic philosophy to a *pragmatism that emphasized the poetic. *Philosophy and the Mirror of Nature* (1979) revealed the logic of his conversion by presenting a systematic, immanent critique of analytic philosophy of language, mind, and epistemology, showing that analytic philosophy's own developing arguments progressively dismantle its founding project and lead to the sort of pragmatism Rorty favors. Rorty's pragmatism was mainly inspired by John *Dewey, though it was strengthened by his continuing use of influential analytic ideas (e.g., those of Ludwig Wittgenstein and Donald Davidson). It is also enriched by integrating contemporary continental thought, particularly the work of Martin Heidegger, Hans-Georg Gadamer, Jacques Derrida, and Michel Foucault.

Rorty's main philosophical doctrines include the rejection of the correspondence theory of truth (i.e., that truth mirrors an altogether mind-independent reality) and the quest for indubitable foundations for knowledge. Such antifoundationalism is complemented by anti-essentialism about concepts, a recognition of the changing historicity of human thought and the inescapable hermeneutic and linguistic dimension of experience. Inspired, perhaps, by Dewey's example as a public intellectual, Rorty also turned his attention to politics. In defending progressive *liberalism against Marxist critiques from the cultural left, Rorty made two firm but controversial distinctions: the private versus the public spheres, and cultural versus real politics. His writings in the 1990s defended the value of American patriotism for achieving political reform toward greater democracy. In these views and others, he highlighted the power of poetic imagination over standard scientific thought.

• Richard Rorty, *Contingency, Irony, and Solidarity*, 1989. Richard Rorty, *Philosophical Papers*, 3 vols., 1991. John Pettegrew, ed., *A Pragmatist's Process?: Richard Rorty and American Intellectual Culture*, 2000.

—Richard M. Shusterman

ROSENBERG CASE. The early 1950s conviction and execution of Julius and Ethel Rosenberg for providing classified information to the Soviet Union about America's atomic bomb development remain among the most controversial events of the early *Cold War.

A graduate of the City College of New York, Julius Rosenberg joined the Communist party, along with his wife Ethel, in 1939. Working for Soviet intelligence during *World War II, he provided Russian contacts with the super-secret information he received from well-placed spies at the *Manhattan Project's Los Alamos, New Mexico, atomic research facility. Despite clues from Soviet defectors, American authorities did not learn about atomic espionage until 1948, when the Federal Bureau of Investigation, working with code breakers in the U.S. Army, decrypted and interpreted nearly three thousand messages, called the Venona Cables, between Soviet intelligence agencies in Moscow and spies in the United States. The cables quickly led to David Greenglass, Ethel's brother, who had worked as a machinist at Los Alamos during the war. Greenglass soon implicated Julius Rosenberg—code-named "Liberal" in the Venona cables—as the leader of an atomic spy ring. Arrested in 1950, against a Cold War backdrop that included the second Alger *Hiss trial, the fall of China to communism, the *Korean War, and the 1949 confession of the German-born British scientist Klaus Fuchs that he had spied for the Russians while assigned to Los Alamos, the Rosenbergs were tried and convicted the following year on the charge of conspiracy to commit espionage. Before issuing the death sentence, trial judge Irving R. Kaufman accused the couple of causing "the Communist aggression in Korea, with the resultant casualties exceeding 50,000, and who knows but that millions more innocent people may pay the price for your treason."

The government's case against Julius Rosenberg was far stronger than its case against Ethel. While she undoubtedly knew about—and may well have supported—her husband's spying, she was not, by any reasonable standard, an active co-conspirator. It appears she was arrested in order to pressure Julius into confessing. This was part of the government's "lever strategy"—a strategy that would lead an unyielding woman directly to her death. When Ethel was arrested one of the prosecutors said privately that "the case is not too strong against Mrs. Rosenberg," and it grew no stronger as time passed. A death-house questionnaire, prepared by prosecutors should Julius break down at the last moment, included this startling question: "Was your wife cognizant of your activities?"

Despite international protests, the Rosenbergs were electrocuted at New York's Sing Sing prison on 19 June 1953, proclaiming their innocence to the end. By the 1990s, however, the declassification of the Venona files and other documents led all but their most fervent supporters to acknowledge the guilt of Julius Rosenberg and, at least, the partial complicity of his wife. While the Rosenbergs' crimes were real indeed, millions still remember their executions as a vindictive act of Cold War justice.

[*See also* Anticommunism; Communist Party—USA.]

• Ronald Radosh and Joyce Milton, *The Rosenberg File*, 2d ed., 1997. Robert J. Lamphere and Tom Schachtman, *The FBI–KGB Wars: A Special Agent's Story*, 1986. John Earl Haynes and Harvey Klehr, *Venona: Decoding Soviet Intelligence in America*, 1999.

—Richard Gid Powers

ROTC. *See* Military, The.

ROUTE 66. Route 66 begins in *Chicago's Grant Park and arrives, 2,400 miles and 8 states later, in Santa Monica, *California. A reminder of the American love affair with cars and freedom, it was one of the first continuous spans of paved highway linking the East with the dream of the golden *West.

Route 66 incorporated sections of the Pontiac Trail, the Mormon Trail, and the Osage Indian Trail. Envisioned as an interstate highway spanning two-thirds of the nation, it was officially dedicated in 1926, a by-product of the "good roads movement" even though only about eight hundred miles were actually paved. The rest consisted of a series of dirt and gravel tracks linked by signs and promises. Thanks to balky local governments, the full length was not finally surfaced with concrete or macadam until 1937.

The physical character of Route 66 was probably always less important than its place in the imagination. Towns fought for the chance to become landmarks on this self-proclaimed "Main Street of America." Gas stations, diners, motels in the form of concrete wigwams—businesses of all sorts boomed along Route 66 in the 1920s. In the 1930s, when the Great Depression sent many Americans limping westward in search of jobs, Oklahomans bound for California dubbed it "the glory road." Novelist John Steinbeck, chronicling the plight of the Okies in *The *Grapes of Wrath*, called it "the mother road, the road of flight."

In the 1960s, a popular TV series, *Route 66*, followed the adventures of two young explorers in a sports car in search of America. In an age of a fast, anonymous interstate *highway system, the old Route 66 continued to evoke the lure of the open road.

[*See also* New Deal Era, The.]

• Phil Patton, *Open Road*, 1986. Michael Wallis, *Route 66: The Mother Road*, 1990.

—Karal Ann Marling

RULE OF REASON, a standard created by the judiciary for judging business behavior under the Sherman Act (1890). Because this act spread a very wide net by prohibiting "every contract, combination . . . , or conspiracy, in restraint of trade or commerce," the U.S. *Supreme Court quickly narrowed this prohibition to *unreasonable* restraints, to be defined through "a standard of reason" and an analysis of the particular facts in each case.

The result was the development over the twentieth century of a federal common law of fair business practices, one that changed as notions of "reasonableness" evolved. Some conduct was consistently condemned as unreasonable per se, such as most forms of price-fixing, output restrictions, and market divisions among competitors. The courts forbade other forms of "restraints" for many years, only to then reverse themselves and find that the outlawed practices instead promote "consumer welfare."

The rule of reason has had a controversial history. Many *Progressive Era reformers saw it as a loophole that weakened the fight against the giant trusts. Business leaders, by contrast, criticized the rule's ambiguous reach and its failure to offer clear guidelines. Beginning late in the *New Deal Era and continuing through the 1960s, a growing number of business practices were struck down as unreasonable, resulting in criticism of the courts as being antibusiness. The trend was reversed after 1970, leading to charges that the courts were too pro-business and too quick to protect economic efficiency over other values.

The rule of reason, like other vague statutory and constitutional standards, gave courts enormous authority in regulating American life. The rule has been used to police a variety of practices in virtually every field of business endeavor, and its ambiguity accommodated changes in economic theory, political power, and attitudes toward business throughout the twentieth century.

[*See also* Antitrust Legislation; Business; Corporatism.]

• Thomas K. McCraw, *Prophets of Regulation*, 1984. Philip E. Areeda, *Antitrust Law*, vols. 7 and 8, 1986.

—Charles G. Curtis Jr.

RURAL LIFE. No revolution has more profoundly changed America than the long transition from farm to city. This change was especially wrenching since the national mythology, dating to Thomas *Jefferson's day, had long held that rural life defined what was best and most distinctive about America, and that farmers were uniquely virtuous, individualistic, and independent.

In 1790, fewer than one in thirty Americans lived in urban centers, and the United States remained predominantly rural until 1920, when for the first time the balance shifted toward the city. Between 1929 and 1965, 30 million people moved off farms, 8.5 million in the 1940s alone. By 1970, fewer than 5 percent of Americans were farmers. Changing agricultural technology and rising efficiency accelerated this exodus. In 1820, one farmworker could feed four people. By 1945, the ratio was 1:15, and by 1969, 1:45. To produce a bale of cotton in 1841 required about 148 hours of labor; by 1969, only 25 hours. With growing agricultural efficiency, more rural people deserted the countryside.

Government policies also hastened this displacement. Despite their legendary independence, farmers often turned to the government for assistance. The 1862 *Homestead Act encouraged western settlement by offering free land. The land-grant universities authorized by the *Morrill Land Grant Act (1862) helped farmers develop applied skills. The Hatch Act (1887) and Smith-Lever Act (1914) established agricultural research and extension programs at land-grant universities that enhanced agricultural productivity, reducing both commodity prices and labor demands. The *Agricultural Adjustment Administration, established in 1933, paid owners to withdraw land from production, displacing millions of tenants and farm laborers.

Rural life evolved differently in different regions. The Northeast, ill-suited to agriculture, industrialized and diversified its economy early. The *South's rural economy persisted longer and was more diverse than most Americans realized. Although cotton monoculture dominated some sections, other subregions—*Appalachia, the Kentucky Bluegrass, the Nashville Basin, the Pineywoods, the Ozarks—produced diversified crops and livestock and different patterns of rural life. In 1890, most rural Arkansas Ozarkers lived near a country store, which supplied clothing, tools, dry goods, some food items, and a venue for socializing. As the twentieth century wore on, *railroads and mail-order catalogs supplanted the country stores.

In the Corn Belt and Great Lakes region, the rich, glaciated forests and prairies produced timber, plentiful livestock, and abundant crops. The Great Plains, with rich soil but low rainfall, required irrigation to produce crops. Livestock flourished, however, as did wheat when sufficiently watered. In the Mountain states, with low rainfall and poor soil, rural life generally involved *mining and raising livestock.

In the Far West, rural life centered on logging and forest products in Washington, Oregon, and northern *California, while central and southern California boasted the nation's most prosperous agriculture; by the 1970s, California ranked near the top in cotton production, livestock, and citrus. Irrigation made agriculture California's largest enterprise, even though only 1 percent of the state's population was engaged in farming. As elsewhere in rural America, giant agribusinesses, often worked by migrant laborers, gradually replaced California's family farms.

As late nineteenth-century farmers realized the gap between myth and reality, they protested their declining status and economic exploitation. Protests took political form: the *Granger movement, the *Greenback Labor party, the *Farmers' Alliance movement, the Populist movement. Caught in a cycle of declining commodity prices, eroding rural institutions, and the lure of the city, farmers fought valiantly but often ineffectively to preserve their way of life.

In the early twentieth century, concern about the eclipse of an idealized farm life stimulated renewal efforts. The Rural Life movement proposed revitalization strategies. President Theodore *Roosevelt convened a Country Life Commission, land-grant universities launched programs to improve farm life, and the *4-H Club movement (1914) targeted rural youth. Rural electrification, continued mechanization, and the spread of the *telephone, automobile, *radio, and *television all diminished the hardships and isolation of rural life. Still, problems continued.

In the 1960s, President Lyndon B. *Johnson appointed a National Advisory Commission on Rural Poverty. Its somber report, *The People Left Behind* (1967), revealed that only one in five rural dwellers actually worked on or owned a farm. Some 80 percent of rural people lived in small villages where they either worked or commuted to nearby cities. Some 14 million rural Americans lived in *poverty, concentrated in four zones: Appalachia, the old cotton belt from South Carolina to east Texas, the Rio Grande Valley, and the southwestern Indian reservations. The rural poor endured the nation's highest rates of *unemployment, malnutrition, *disease, premature death, and infant mortality. Their education also lagged. Consolidated churches and schools improved efficiency but reduced the sense of community. Cycles of drought and overproduction hobbled rural economies, while technological changes and government programs perpetuated the long process of displacement. Rural life continued to be celebrated in country music and elsewhere in the culture, but by the twentieth century's end, the gap between the rural America idealized in *folklore and the actual lives of hard-pressed rural Americans (apart from a prospering minority engaged in agribusinesses) made a mockery of Jefferson's dream of America as an agrarian utopia.

[*See also* Agricultural Education and Extension; Agricultural Experiment Stations; Agriculture; Automotive Industry; Cotton Industry; Federal Government, Executive Branch: Department of Agriculture; Indian History and Culture; Livestock Industry; Lumbering; Migratory Agricultural Workers; Motor Vehicles; Music: Traditional Music; Populist Era; Populist Party; Regionalism; Sharecropping and Tenantry; Urbanization.]

• Samuel R. Ogden, ed., *America the Vanishing: Rural Life and the Price of Progress*, 1969. John L. Shover, *First Majority—Last Minority: The Transforming of Rural Life in America*, 1976. Gilbert C. Fite, *Cotton Fields No More: Southern Agriculture, 1865–1980*, 1984. Stanford J. Layton, *To No Privileged Class: The Rationalization of Homesteading and Rural Life in the Early Twentieth Century American West*, 1988. Sarah Burns, *Pastoral Inventions: Rural Life in Nineteenth-Century American Art and Cul-*

ture, 1989. George E. Pozzetta, *Immigrants on the Land: Agriculture, Rural Life and Small Towns,* 1991.

—Wayne Flynt

RUSH, BENJAMIN (1746–1813), physician, medical educator, signer of the *Declaration of Independence. Born near *Philadelphia, Benjamin Rush earned his bachelor's degree from the College of New Jersey (Princeton) at age fourteen. He did a medical apprenticeship in Philadelphia and then continued his *medical education at the University of Edinburgh in Scotland, receiving his degree there in 1768. When Rush began his medical practice in Philadelphia in 1769, the College of Philadelphia appointed him the first native-born American professor of chemistry.

Outspokenly patriotic, Rush in 1776 took his seat with the Pennsylvania delegation in the Second *Continental Congress and signed the Declaration of Independence, later becoming surgeon-general of the Middle Department of the Continental Army. In 1786, Rush opened the first medical dispensary in the United States and in 1787 helped found the College of Physicians of Philadelphia. Rush assumed the chair of theory and practice of medicine at the University of Pennsylvania in 1796.

Rush theorized that all *disease arose from convulsive action in the blood vessels, which he treated by purging and bleeding his patients, and inducing vomiting. Rush's theory became famous after 1793 when a *yellow fever epidemic carried off about one-tenth of Philadelphia's population. While others fled, Rush stayed behind to administer his controversial treatments to hundreds. His devotion made him a popular hero. In 1813, ill with fever, Rush had himself bled twice before dying at home in Philadelphia.

Rush's prolific writings made him the first American physician to become widely known both at home and abroad. He established the reputation of Philadelphia, where he taught some three thousand medical students, as a center for medical training. He campaigned to make public schools free, broaden education for women, and humanize the treatment of mental patients. Rush also opposed *slavery and *capital punishment and in widely distributed tracts advocated temperance in the use of alcohol.

[*See also* Early Republic, Era of the; Medicine: From 1776 to the 1870s; Revolution and Constitution, Era of; Temperance and Prohibition.]

• Carl Alfred Lanning Binger, *Revolutionary Doctor: Benjamin Rush, 1746–1813,* 1966. Claire G. Fox, Gordon L. Miller, and Jacquelyn C. Miller, compilers, *Benjamin Rush, M.D.: A Bibliographic Guide,* 1996.

—Robert B. Sullivan

RUTH, GEORGE HERMAN ("Babe") (1895–1948), *baseball player. Born to a German saloon-owning family, George Herman Ruth Jr. played ball at a Baltimore industrial school before turning professional in 1914. He was soon the ace of the Boston Red Sox pitching staff, winning eighty-nine games over six seasons and setting a World Series record in 1918 for consecutive scoreless innings. Astoundingly, the next year he hit twenty-nine home runs, another record, prompting the Red Sox to sell him to the New York Yankees as a hitter for an unheard-of $125,000.

Babe Ruth (the nickname by which he was universally known) virtually made the Yankees. Before 1920 they had never won a pennant. In Ruth's fifteen years, they won seven, plus four World Series championships. Ruth led the league in homers twelve times, hitting 60 in 1927 alone and finishing with a total of 714. He also batted a career .342 and was a fine fielder. Yankee Stadium became "The House that Ruth Built." Millions saw him play. The all-powerful New York press loved him. He was the "Sultan of Swat," best paid and most acclaimed athlete of his day, a charter member of the Baseball Hall of Fame in Cooperstown, New York.

People idolized Ruth because of his hitting, which transformed baseball offense from singles-and-steals to raw power, and baseball itself into mass entertainment. But they also loved his undisciplined high spirits, his good humor, even his extravagant eating, drinking, and womanizing. He would sign autographs for hours, visit hospitals, then step into a convertible and carouse all night. He golfed, hunted, smoked huge cigars, made movies, and barnstormed around the world. Demonstrating how much fun life could be, Babe Ruth symbolized the hedonism and exuberance of the 1920s. While this image cost him a chance to manage, fans loved him for it. When he died of cancer, a hundred thousand mourners viewed his bier.

[*See also* Sports: Professional Sports; Twenties, The.]

• Ken Sobol, *Babe Ruth and the American Dream,* 1974. Marshall Smelser, *The Life that Ruth Built,* 1975.

—Ronald Story

S

SACCO AND VANZETTI CASE (1920). In May 1920, Nicola Sacco, a shoemaker, and Bartolomeo Vanzetti, a fish peddler, were arrested in Braintree, Massachusetts, for the robbery and murder of a shoe company's paymaster. In a trial marked by flimsy evidence and flawed procedures, they were convicted and sentenced to death. Critical observers recognized at the time that the police, jurors, prosecutors, and judge were responding less to the evidence than to the fact that Sacco and Vanzetti were immigrant Italian anarchists who had evaded the draft in *World War I. Their case was set against the backdrop of the Red Scare of 1919–1920, when Americans, fearful that the Bolshevik Revolution could spread to their country, and resentful of rising prices, a wave of labor strikes, and a growing immigrant presence, were catapulted into an antiradical, anti-immigrant furor. As Vanzetti himself put it, "The jury were hating us" because it was "a time when there was a hysteria of resentment and hate against the foreigner, against slackers."

The conviction sparked a wave of protest among reformers and radicals, as well as artists, such as Ben Shahn, and writers, including the novelist John Dos Passos and the poet Edna St. Vincent Millay. The future *Supreme Court justice Felix *Frankfurter wrote a lengthy exposé for the *Atlantic Monthly* in 1927, in which he concluded that Judge Webster Thayer's handling of the case was characterized by "misquotations, misrepresentations, suppressions, and mutilations." A special commission appointed by the governor of Massachusetts, however, upheld the conduct of the trial and dismissed the evidence suggesting the pair's innocence. Both men were electrocuted in August 1927. Historians still debate the guilt of Sacco and Vanzetti, but most concur that the two men did not receive a fair trial and the case stands as an example of the excesses of the post–World War I Red Scare.

[*See also* Anarchism; Anti-Communism; Nativist Movement; Radicalism; Twenties, The.]

• Francis Russell, *Sacco and Vanzetti: The Case Resolved,* 1985. William Young and David E. Kaiser, *Postmortem: New Evidence in the Case of Sacco and Vanzetti,* 1985.

—Lynn Dumenil

SALEM WITCHCRAFT. It began early in 1692 in Salem Village, an outlying region of the town of Salem, Massachusetts, and a community long beset by deep divisions, focused on the local church. The outbreak started in the household of the Village's beleaguered minister, Samuel Parris, where a group of girls engaged in fortune-telling rituals. (The most active of these girls was twelve-year-old Ann Putnam, daughter of Parris's chief supporter.) By February the girls were experiencing fits, and witchcraft was diagnosed. Pressed to say who was "hurting" them, the girls first named three marginal neighborhood women, including Parris's West Indian slave Tituba. The three were questioned and jailed. But the girls' "afflictions" continued, and through the spring their accusations escalated, targeting people (some 30 percent of them male) who were increasingly respectable, pious, and prosperous.

In May, with the prisons filling up, the newly appointed Massachusetts governor, Sir William Phips, established a special court of Oyer and Terminer to try the cases. In early June, after the court condemned to death its first defendant, Bridget Bishop, one of the judges resigned in protest. The key legal dispute concerned the validity of "spectral" evidence, when the afflicted girls testified that they were being hurt by a visual representation of their tormentor—presumably the Devil in the accused person's shape. Although the court sought other corroboratory evidence (voluntary confession at best, or at least such circumstantial evidence as preternatural "witch's tits" in the genital region, or testimony that threats by the accused had been mysteriously fulfilled), spectral evidence was accepted. A number of accused persons did confess (Tituba among them), and none of these was executed. Approximately 150 people were jailed, and between June and September, twenty were hanged. (In addition, Giles Cory was pressed to death, in an old English legal procedure designed to force recalcitrant prisoners to plead to the charges against them.)

From the start, the trials had been opposed from many quarters, and early in October, Increase Mather and other prominent clergymen interceded to stop them. ("It were better that ten suspected witches should escape, than that one innocent person be condemned," Mather wrote.) Phips immediately halted the executions, and by the spring of 1693 the remaining prisoners were released. While Increase Mather's son Cotton defended the trials, public opinion rapidly shifted the other way. In 1697 the Massachusetts General Court declared an official day of atonement, and in 1711 it granted financial compensation to some of the victims or their families. Never again would anyone be tried for witchcraft in *New England.

Although small in scale when compared to European witch trials, this was the largest such event in colonial America. In previous New England cases the clergy and the courts had generally acted to suppress witchcraft charges, distrusting them as folk superstition; but in 1692 these authorities, convinced of a satanic conspiracy to subvert the Puritan commonwealth, sided with the afflicted girls. Further, the trials took place at a time of political change in Massachusetts: in 1692 church members lost their monopoly over the franchise and the colony itself lost the right to choose its governor.

The trials are arguably the most infamous event in New England history, and the year 1692 remains etched in American consciousness. Fictionalized by writers from Henry Wadsworth Longfellow to Arthur Miller, Salem witchcraft has become an enduring if somewhat misplaced symbol of *Puritanism.

[*See also* Colonial Era; Mather, Increase and Cotton.]

• Paul Boyer and Stephen Nissenbaum, *Salem Possessed: The Social Origins of Witchcraft,* 1974. Richard Godbeer, *The Devil's Dominion: Magic and Religion in Early New England,* 1992.

—Stephen Nissenbaum

SALK, JONAS (1914–1995), virologist and developer of the first successful polio vaccine. Born in New York to immigrant parents, Jonas Salk received his B.A. from the City College of New York in 1934 and his M.D. from New York University's College of Medicine in 1939. He conducted virus research at the University of Michigan and the University of Pittsburgh. Salk became an international hero at forty when he and his associates developed a vaccine against *poliomyelitis, a viral disease that had paralyzed hundreds of thousands of victims, mostly children, in mysterious and terrifying epidemics that swept the industrialized world in the first half of the twentieth century. Traditional theory held that immunity to virus diseases came only from actual infection, but Salk showed that a vaccine made from killed-virus particles could spur immunity without danger. His vaccine was tested on 1.8 million school children in 1954 in a massive field trial sponsored by the National Foundation for Infantile Paralysis ("March of Dimes"), and received a federal license the following year. Although an early batch of faulty vaccine caused several cases of paralysis, polio incidences dropped by 80 percent after two years in areas where Salk's vaccine was used. Still, many scientists dismissed his work as "cook-book biology," and Salk was never honored in any way by his peers. After 1960, Salk's vaccine (but not his fame) was overshadowed by Albert Sabin's live-virus oral polio vaccine; since 1 January 2000, however, the *Centers for Disease Control and Prevention have recommended a return to the injected polio vaccine and the elimination of live-virus oral vaccine use. In 1963, Salk became founding director of the Salk Institute for Biological Studies at the University of California, San Diego. His later research sought vaccines to fight *cancer and to boost immune system activity after HIV infection. He married twice and had three sons.

[*See also* Acquired Immunodeficiency Syndrome; Disease; Medicine: Since 1945.]

• Richard Carter, *Breakthrough: The Saga of Jonas Salk,* 1966. Jane S. Smith, *Patenting the Sun: Polio and the Salk Vaccine,* 1990.

—Jane S. Smith

SALK VACCINE. *See* Poliomyelitis; Salk, Jonas.

SALVATION ARMY. *See* Protestantism.

SAMOA. *See* Protectorates and Dependencies.

SAN FRANCISCO. Archaeological evidence dates settlement in present-day San Francisco, *California, to 3100 B.C.; some 500 Native Americans lived on the site when a Spanish mission and presidio (military garrison) were established in 1776. American conquest took place in 1846, and the first American mayor changed the name of the village from Yerba Buena to San Francisco in 1847. An influx of newcomers following the discovery of gold near Sacramento in 1848 pushed the population from 1,000 to 25,000 and propelled San Francisco into the front rank of the nation's cities. It remained the Pacific coast's premier financial, commercial, and manufacturing city until *World War I. Subsequently, the city thrived on *tourism and the provision of financial, business, and personal services to Bay Area, regional, and transpacific customers. Despite the 1906 earthquake and fire, which killed more than 3,000 people, the population increased gradually until *World War II. That conflict and the subsequent *Cold War created a "second gold rush" that pushed the population to 775,400 by 1950. It stabilized thereafter and in 2000 stood at around 750,000, with 6.5 million in the larger metropolitan area.

San Francisco has always had large numbers of Asians as well as a diverse array of Euro-American residents; its Chinatown was long the nation's largest. Its Mediterranean climate, cosmopolitan ambience, and reputation for cultural bohemianism and political radicalism attracted a large and influential gay and lesbian population after World War II. San Francisco was a mecca of the Beat literary movement in the 1950s, and its Haight-Ashbury district flourished as a center of the 1960s counterculture.

Hyperbole abounds in the mythology of "the cool, grey city of love," as poet George Sterling called it, and its Golden Gate Bridge and cable cars are international tourist icons. San Francisco allusions abound in American *popular culture, including Alfred Hitchcock's classic 1958 film *Vertigo* and the 1968 ballad "I Left My Heart in San Francisco." Writers from Bret Harte and Samuel L. *Clemens to Armistead Maupin (*Tales of the City,* 1978) have drawn inspiration from the city.

At the same time, San Francisco has a deserved reputation for *philanthropy and social reform. San Francisco women played key roles in the national *woman suffrage and kindergarten movements in the late nineteenth century. The *Sierra Club was founded there in 1892, and *environmentalism remains a high priority. San Franciscans were the first to limit freeway construction in the 1950s and downtown high-rise construction in the 1980s. City residents also took the lead in the national response to the AIDS epidemic.

[*See also* Acquired Immunodeficiency Syndrome; Asian Americans; Gold Rushes; Indian History and Culture: Migration and Pre-Columbian Era; Literature: Since World War I; San Francisco Earthquake and Fire; Sixties, The; Spanish Settlements in North America.]

• William Issel and Robert W. Cherny, *San Francisco 1865–1932: Politics, Power, and Urban Development,* 1986. Richard Edward DeLeon, *Left Coast City: Progressive Politics in San Francisco, 1975–1991,* 1992.

—William Issel

SAN FRANCISCO CONFERENCE (25 April–26 June 1945). This conference drafted the *United Nations Charter. Its origins lay in a 1942 "Declaration by the United Nations" issued by twenty-six countries that had declared war against the Axis powers, and the 1943 Moscow Declaration by the United States, the Soviet Union, Great Britain, and China calling for a new international organization to replace the *League of Nations. Further planning occurred at the 1944 Dumbarton Oaks conference and a draft charter was prepared at the February 1945 Yalta conference. Fifty nations attended the San Francisco Conference. President Franklin Delano *Roosevelt having died two weeks earlier, President Harry S. *Truman addressed the opening ceremonies. To assure bipartisan U.S. support, Truman named two prominent Republicans, Senator Arthur Vandenberg of Michigan and lawyer John Foster *Dulles, to the American delegation. The conference quickly agreed on most of the Charter's 111 articles, but in early June a dispute arose over the veto power. The draft charter approved at Yalta had granted a veto to Security Council members, but at San Francisco the Soviet delegate, Andrei Gromyko, insisted that the veto power extend even to the discussion of issues—a demand that threatened to break up the conference. The crisis was resolved only when President Truman instructed presidential aide Harry Hopkins, then in Moscow, to take the issue directly to Soviet premier Josef Stalin. Stalin agreed to modify the Soviet position, and a compromise was reached. With this hurdle passed, the delegates unanimously approved the Charter on 25 June, and signed it the following day at San Francisco's War Memorial Opera House, with Truman again in attendance. The required number of nations ratified the Charter by 24 October (United Nations Day), and the United Nations came into existence. Despite the euphoria surrounding these events, however, the United Nations soon ran afoul of *Cold War conflicts, and the San Francisco Conference did not herald the new international order that many had hoped for.

[*See also* Yalta Conference.]

• R. B. Russell, *A History of the United Nations Charter: The Role of the United States, 1940–1945,* 1958. Leland M. Goodrich, *The United Nations,* 1959.

—Norman A. Graebner

SAN FRANCISCO EARTHQUAKE AND FIRE. At 5:12 A.M. on 18 April 1906, an earthquake estimated at 8.3 on today's Richter scale shook a great portion of northern *California for forty-five seconds, setting in motion the nation's largest natural disaster ever. Many San Franciscans found the jolt itself rather benign; some deep-sleepers in structures built on bedrock never even awoke. With few exceptions, such as collapsed buildings erected on landfill and the toppled City Hall, it was the ensuing fire that made 250,000 people homeless, destroyed 28,000 structures over four square miles, and caused $500 million in property damage. Within hours of the tremor, several isolated fires united in the city's southern districts, then progressed northward and westward. Only a shift in wind and the dynamiting of wood-framed houses along Van Ness Avenue finally halted the three-day inferno. *San Francisco's official list of deaths totaled 500, though the actual number of disaster-related fatalities likely reached 3,000.

Immediately following the calamity—as tramps and capitalists stood in the same bread lines—"social leveling" seemed to force intimate contact of San Francisco's heterogeneous population, stirring fears of urban disorder and crime. San Franciscans quickly set out to replicate the city's precrisis social order. To handle the predicted chaos, the San Francisco police, the U.S. Army, and local volunteers closed saloons and shot looters on sight. While distributing earthquake aid, relief workers restored San Francisco's established social hierarchy by offering loans only to those with a high pre-earthquake status. In their attempt to prove San Francisco's resilience, civic boosters quickly reproduced the city's prefire street configuration and district layout. Yet despite its quick repair, San Francisco declined in mercantile rank as *Los Angeles and nearby Oakland built new competitive seaports.

• William Bronson, *The Earth Shook, the Sky Burned,* 1959. Gladys Hansen and Emmet Condon, *Denial of Disaster,* ed. David Fowler, 1989.

—James L. Mallery

SANGER, MARGARET (1879–1966), birth control pioneer and sex reformer, founder of the international family planning movement. Born Margaret Louisa Higgins, the middle child of a large Irish-Catholic family, Sanger emerged on the American scene in the early years of the twentieth century, a follower of labor radicals, free-thinkers, and bohemians. Married to William Sanger, an itinerant architect, she help to support three young children by working as a visiting nurse. Following the death of a patient from an illegal abortion, she vowed to give all women ownership and control over their own bodies.

In 1914, she coined the term "birth control" as a simple way of talking about a still clandestine and delicate subject. Three years later she went to jail for opening a clinic to distribute diaphragms and spermicidal jellies. Appeal of her conviction led to licensed medical prescription of contraception in many states and led to the founding of what later became the Planned Parenthood Federation of America.

For more than half a century, Sanger battled religious and political opponents who identified birth control with moral and sexual license. At her death, contraception was publicly funded and constitutionally protected. The oral anovulant contraceptive pill had been developed privately with her assistance. And a world population movement had emerged from her pioneering efforts.

But controversy remains over the extent to which Sanger's pragmatic alliances with middle-class reformers and social and professional elites, many of whom espoused *eugenic arguments for limiting fertility, compromised her early idealism. Under the sanitized guise of family planning, has contraception primarily been a force for social reconstruction or a tool of social control?

[*See also* Birth Control and Family Planning; Censorship; Progressive Era; Sexual Morality and Sex Reform; Socialism.]

• Linda Gordon, *Woman's Body: Woman's Right: A Social History of Birth Control in America,* 1976. James Reed, *The Birth Control Movement and American Society: From Private Vice to Public Virtue,* 1984. Ellen Chesler, *Woman of Valor: Margaret Sanger and the Birth Control Movement in America,* 1992.

—Ellen Chesler

SAN JUAN HILL, BATTLE OF. *See* Spanish-American War; Roosevelt, Theodore.

SANTA FE TRAIL. The Santa Fe Trail stretched nine hundred miles from what is now central Missouri through Kansas, Oklahoma, and Colorado to Santa Fe, New Mexico. Native Americans first used sections of this route for trade, especially between peoples of the Great Plains and the Pueblo Indians of the *Southwest. Spanish conquistadores followed it as they explored the interior of North America. French and American fur trappers knew it as a route to the *Rocky Mountains.

In 1821 the Missourian William Becknell took a variety of frontier trade goods along the trail, thereby opening a commercial link to New Mexico, then part of the Republic of Mexico. This trade flourished, soon engaging thousands of men, wagons, and draft animals and drawing capital investment from both U.S. and Mexican citizens. In 1846 the U.S. Army of the West marched down the trail when it invaded and occupied the Southwest, subsequently annexed by the United States in the Treaty of Guadalupe Hidalgo, which ended the *Mexican War. For the next thirty years freighting on the trail, particularly to supply southwestern army posts, reached as much as a million dollars a year.

The westward progress of various *railroads shortened the trail in the 1860s. Its day ended in 1880 with the completion of the Atchison, Topeka, and Santa Fe railroad into New Mexico. Not an avenue of pioneer settlement, the Santa Fe Trail was a route to commerce and conquest and has been thus enshrined in the mythology of the American *West.

• Josiah Gregg, *Commerce of the Prairies,* 1844. Max L. Moorhead, *New Mexico's Royal Road: Trade and Travel on the Chihuahua Trail,* 1958.

—Michael L. Olsen

SARATOGA, BATTLE OF (1777). In 1777 the British strategy to quell the American Revolution involved plans to seize the Lake Champlain–Hudson River channel of communication, thereby isolating rebellious *New England. As formulated by the appointed commander, John Burgoyne, and authorized by the secretary of state for the colonies, George Germain, the main army would descend from Montreal, Canada, while an auxiliary force under Barry St. Leger would sweep westward through Lake Ontario, both to unite at Albany with William Howe's army ascending from *New York City. Germain, however, failed to send adequate instructions to Howe, who chose to sail south to capture *Philadelphia. Burgoyne, with 4,135 British regulars, 3,116 German mercenaries, 500 Indians, and 500 French Canadian militia, captured the inadequately defended Fort Ticonderoga on 6 July 1777. Believing his orders mandatory, and despite St. Leger's failure to capture Fort Stanwix, he then crossed the Hudson, cutting his Canadian supply line.

Horatio Gates (ca. 1728–1806) replaced the unpopular Philip Schuyler as commander of the American army, now camped at Stillwater, New York. On 19 September, at the Battle of Freeman's Farm, the 10,277 Americans, spearheaded by Daniel Morgan's riflemen and spurred by Benedict *Arnold, defeated Burgoyne's three-pronged offensive. The British suffered 566 casualties, the Americans 313. On 7 October, at the Battle of Bemis Heights, an unauthorized American attack led by Arnold repulsed Burgoyne's 1,723-man advance force. British losses were 631, American 130. Burgoyne waited futilely for reinforcements from New York and finally retreated to Saratoga, where on 17 October he surrendered his army of nearly 6,000 men. A major turning point of the war, the American victory in the Battle of Saratoga encouraged France to conclude the treaty of alliance, which assured American independence.

[*See also* Revolutionary War.]

• Hoffman Nickerson, *The Turning Point of the American Revolution,* 1928, reprint 1967. Max M. Mintz, *The Generals of Saratoga: John Burgoyne and Horatio Gates,* 1990.

—Max M. Mintz

SARNOFF, DAVID (1891–1971), president and chairman of the Radio Corporation of America. Born in Minsk, Russia, Sarnoff immigrated to the United States in 1900. He became an office boy in Gugilelmo Marconi's wireless *telegraph company in New York in 1906, rising to management roles by *World War I. On the formation of the Radio Corporation of America (RCA) in 1909, Sarnoff became RCA's commercial manager, then president (1930) and chairman of the board (1947). He retired from his executive positions in 1969. Unlike his chief competitor, William S. *Paley of CBS, Sarnoff directed research and manufacturing of *radio broadcasting equipment and receivers. Beginning in 1926, he also directed the National Broadcasting Company's radio and later *television services. Referred to as General Sarnoff after his brief European service in *World War II, he cultivated legends to enhance his own background. (He did not operate the world's key wireless link to rescue efforts when the *Titanic* sank in 1912, nor did he write a famously prescient "radio music box" memo when still in his twenties.) His real accomplishments included helping to establish network radio broadcasting in the 1920s, leading RCA's development of black-and-white television in the late 1930s, and likewise pushing compatible color television in the 1940s and 1950s. While never educated beyond grade school, Sarnoff could see the commercial possibilities of technical innovations, and he actively supported RCA's substantial research and development program. He was an industrial autocrat who passed RCA leadership on (though for only a few years) to his oldest son, Robert. Purchased by General Electric in 1985, RCA lasted barely fifteen years after its long-time leader's death.

• David Sarnoff, *Looking Ahead: The Papers of David Sarnoff,* 1968. Kenneth Bilby, *The General: David Sarnoff and the Rise of the Communications Industry,* 1986.

—Christopher H. Sterling

SATELLITE COMMUNICATIONS. Satellite communication was the only truly commercial space *technology to be developed in the first forty years or so after the beginning of the space age in 1957. Perhaps the first person to evaluate the technical and financial aspects of satellite communications was John R. Pierce of AT&T's Bell Telephone Laboratories, who in the mid-1950s outlined the utility of a communications "mirror" in space, estimating that such a satellite would be worth a billion dollars. Under Pierce's leadership, AT&T in 1960 petitioned the *Federal Communications Commission (FCC) for permission to launch an experimental communications satellite with a view toward implementing an operational system. Caught off guard, the government scrambled to develop a policy to regulate this new medium of communication. The John F. *Kennedy administration opposed allowing AT&T a monopoly of satellite communications, as it already enjoyed one on Earth. Accordingly, in 1961, to offset AT&T's lead in technological development, the *National Aeronautics and Space Administration awarded contracts to RCA and Hughes Aircraft to build communication satellites, *Relay* and *Syncom.* By 1964, two AT&T *Telstars,* two *Relays,* and two *Syncoms* had been successfully launched, and technological know-how had been transferred to companies other than AT&T. Live *television broadcasts from the 1964 Tokyo Olympics provided a glimpse of the dawning age of instantaneous global communications.

The Kennedy administration also sponsored legislation in 1962 that created the Communications Satellite Corporation (COMSTAT), with ownership divided evenly between the public and telecommunications corporations such as AT&T, ITT, RCA, and Western Union, to lead the U.S. effort in global satellite communications. Later, COMSTAT became the American component of an emerging global system known as the International Telecommunications Satellite Consortium (INTELSAT), formed in August 1964. On 6 April 1965, COMSTAT's first satellite, *Early Bird,* was launched from Cape Canaveral, Florida. Global satellite communications had begun.

Although COMSTAT and the initial launch vehicles and satellites were American, other countries had been involved from the beginning. By the time *Early Bird* was launched, the United Kingdom, France, Germany, Italy, Brazil, and Japan had established communications ground stations. From a few hundred *telephone circuits and a handful of members in 1965, the INTELSAT system grew to embrace more members than the *United Nations and to possess the technical capability to provide millions of telephone circuits. Cost to carriers per circuit, and to individual customers, declined dramatically as the system matured. By the end of the century, orbiting satellites were generating billions of dollars annually in sales of products and services and had transformed global communication by facilitating commercial broadcasting, business and scientific exchanges, and telephone and *Internet communication among individuals worldwide.

[*See also* Space Program.]

• Heather E. Hudson, *Communications Satellites: Their Development and Impact,* 1990. Donald H. Martin, *Communication Satellites, 1958–1992,* 1991. Andrew J. Butrica, ed., *Beyond the Ionosphere: Fifty Years of Satellite Communication,* 1997.

—Roger D. Launius

SAVINGS AND LOAN DEBACLE. The insolvencies of hundreds of savings and loan associations (S&Ls) in the 1980s, one of the major financial disasters of American history, cost American taxpayers about $150 billion. The debacle's origins lay in federal and state regulation of S&Ls, which restricted them to accepting savings deposits and making long-term fixed-interest residential mortgage loans ("borrowing short and lending long"). When interest rates rose sharply in the late 1970s, these institutions faced a financial squeeze.

In the early 1980s the government acted to help S&Ls by allowing them to engage in riskier ventures and to increase interest rates paid on deposits. Though reasonable, these reforms lacked the strengthening of safety-and-soundness regulation necessary to prevent S&Ls from undue risk-taking (at the expense of federal deposit insurance, which had been raised to $100,000 per account in 1980). Instead, the government weakened its prudential regulation. Armed with new opportunities and reduced restraints, hundreds of S&Ls grew rapidly between 1983 and 1985. They made risky loans and investments in commercial real estate, much of it dependent on the expectation of rising oil prices. A majority of S&Ls acted prudently but were nevertheless tarred by association with the more reckless institutions.

Though federal regulation had tightened considerably by 1986, too many S&Ls had already made imprudent loans and investments. When oil prices fell after 1981 and federal tax reform in 1986 made commercial real estate a poorer investment, the weaker S&Ls collapsed. Such failures were inevitable, though historical cost-based accounting methods delayed the recognition of losses and the legal insolvencies of many S&Ls until the late 1980s. One of the most spectacular collapses, that of California's Lincoln Savings and Loan, involved the notorious Charles H. Keating Jr., who spent five years in prison after his conviction on fraud charges. In 1989 and 1991 legislators appropriated the funds to honor federal deposit insurance guarantees and further tightened prudential regulation. A major episode in American financial history had ended.

[*See also* Banking and Finance; Economic Regulation; Reagan, Ronald.]

• Lawrence J. White, *The S&L Debacle: Public Policy Lessons for Bank and Thrift Regulation,* 1991.

—Lawrence J. White

SCANDINAVIAN AMERICANS. Immigrants from Denmark, Finland, Norway, Sweden, and the area that became Iceland, mainly arriving in the years 1840–1914, are broadly identified as Scandinavian Americans, despite significant differences among them. Sharing a pride in the Viking landfall in North America, a Nordic heritage, and a preference for settling in the Upper *Middle West, they formed common institutions and in urban areas were often perceived as one ethnic group. In rural areas, each national group typically formed its own enclave.

Often religiously motivated before 1850, emigration was mainly for economic reasons thereafter, as overpopulation, commercialized agriculture, improved transportation, and intra-Scandinavian migration combined with an expanding American economy to stimulate transatlantic migration. Scandinavian young women found work as domestic servants; males obtained farms under the 1862 *Homestead Act. From 1820 to 1990, some 2.8 million Scandinavian immigrants arrived. As Protestant northern Europeans, they were welcomed by the English-speaking majority as allies helping to preserve "Anglo-Saxon" hegemony. Some Finnish Americans were harassed, however, as socialists and unmeltable ethnics. In cities, a "Scandinavian melting pot" hastened assimilation—first, to an ersatz "Scandinavian" ethnicity, then to the American mainstream. Scandinavian Americans created a rich array of voluntary associations—cooperatives, churches, cultural societies, *fraternal organizations, and lending libraries. High *literacy rates and a tendency to form associations also led to political activism, often as progressive *Republican party members. As the agricultural frontier moved west, Scandinavian ethnic groups purchased large tracts of farmland to form virtual colonies. Here, assimilation was slow, even after the conformist pressures associated with *World War I nativism, and ethnic foods, festivals, and furnishings survived into the twenty-first century. In 1990, more than 10 million Americans claimed Scandinavian ancestry.

[*See also* Agriculture: 1770s to 1890; Agriculture: The "Golden Age" (1890s–1920); Immigration; Nativist Movement; Race and Ethnicity; Socialism; Voluntarism.]

• Hans Norman and Harald Runblom, *Transatlantic Connections: Nordic Migration to the New World after 1800,* 1988. Robert Clifford Ostergren, *A Community Transplanted: The Trans-Atlantic Experience of a Swedish Immigrant Settlement in the Upper Middle West, 1835–1915,* 1988.

—Steven J. Keillor

SCHECHTER POULTRY CORP.* v. *UNITED STATES (1935). The National Industrial Recovery Act (NIRA), passed in 1933, was President Franklin Delano *Roosevelt's major effort to combat the Great Depression. Among other things, the act authorized industry groups, operating through the *National Recovery Administration (NRA), to establish codes of fair competition. These codes, subject to presidential approval, affected such matters as wages, hours, working conditions, and methods of competition.

The Schechter brothers, owners of a small Brooklyn slaughterhouse, were convicted of violating the Live Poultry Code on several counts, including selling diseased chicken and filing false sales and price reports. They appealed, and in a unanimous 1935 ruling, the *Supreme Court declared the NIRA unconstitutional. Speaking for the Court, Chief Justice Charles Evans *Hughes said that the law failed to provide adequate guidance concerning what matters the codes would cover. As a result, the NIRA unconstitutionally delegated legislative power to the executive branch. Hughes further argued that the poultry code violated the commerce clause of the *Constitution (art. I, sec. 8). According to past cases, Congress could only regulate intrastate activity having a "direct" impact on interstate commerce. The Schechters' local commercial activity, Hughes noted, was clearly "indirect." While Roosevelt accused the Supreme Court of possessing an anachronistic view of the Constitution, he was not sorry to see the unwieldy and unworkable NRA dismantled. Indeed, the *Schechter* decision prompted more careful drafting of New Deal legislation in the future. While this decision has not been explicitly overruled, later justices abandoned the nondelegation doctrine and the distinction between direct and indirect effects enunciated therein. Some scholars regarded this development as a necessary jurisprudential response to an increasingly complicated world. Others argued, however, that the Court has merely encouraged Congress to renounce its legislative duties.

[*See also* Economic Regulation; New Deal Era, The.]

• Robert G. McCloskey, *The American Supreme Court,* 2d ed., 1994.

—Jeffrey D. Hockett

SCHENCK* v. *UNITED STATES, 1919 *Supreme Court case involving free-speech rights. During *World War I, free speech in the United States was sharply curtailed, especially under the 1917 Espionage Act, which made it a felony to use the U.S. mails to encourage disloyalty to the government or refusal of military service. When Charles Schenck, a *Socialist party official, was convicted under this law for mailing an antidraft and antiwar pamphlet, he appealed to the Supreme Court. Marking the first time in the Court's 130-year history that anyone had claimed First Amendment protection against government prosecution, the case gave the Court its first opportunity to interpret and apply the First Amendment.

In a unanimous opinion written by Justice Oliver Wendell *Holmes Jr., the Court upheld Schenck's conviction and found the Espionage Act constitutional. Formulating a "clear and present danger" test to distinguish between protected and unprotected speech, Holmes introduced a metaphor that would long influence free-speech debates: The First Amendment, he declared, would not protect a man who falsely shouted fire in a theater, thereby creating a panic. *Schenck* thus established an exception to the constitutional guarantee of free speech: Words that create a "clear and present" danger to the nation, particularly in wartime, do not enjoy First Amendment protection. Holmes's ruling thus focused on the possible consequences of the speech rather than on the content of the speech itself. In a subsequent case, **Abrams* v. *United States* (1919), Holmes in dissent (joined by Louis *Brandeis) narrowed the "clear and present danger" test to immediate hazards and specific actions, not remote or theoretical possibilities.

[*See also* Bill of Rights; Censorship; Civil Liberties.]

• Paul L. Murphy, *World War I and the Origin of Civil Liberties in the United States,* 1979. Patrick M. Garry, "Oliver Wendell Holmes and the Democratic Foundations of the First Amendment," in *Great Justices of the U.S. Supreme Court,* ed. William Pederson and Norman Provizer, 1993, pp. 125–47.

—Patrick M. Garry

SCHOOLS. *See* Education: The Public School Movement; Education: Education in Contemporary America.

SCIENCE

Overview
Colonial Era
Revolutionary War to World War I
From 1914 to 1945
Since 1945
Science and Religion
Science and Popular Culture

SCIENCE: OVERVIEW

Before the early nineteenth century, "science" referred to organized knowledge generally. The few Americans who systematically studied nature spoke of doing "philosophy"; thus they called the first permanent scientific society, established in *Philadelphia in 1769, the *American Philosophical Society. By the 1830s, however, "science" increasingly designated knowledge of the natural world. Between the *Revolutionary War and the *Civil War, the number of Americans earning a living by doing science swelled from fewer than 25 to an estimated 1,500, most of them working for government agencies or educational institutions. By *World War I, the United States had reached parity with the leading science-producing nations and was supporting over 14,000 scientists, perhaps 400 of whom did original research.

In the post–Civil War decades, as the popularity of science soared because of its association with medical and technological wonders, science increasingly came to represent "another name for truth." By the early twentieth century, philanthropists were underwriting such scientific centers as *New York City's *Rockefeller Institute for Medical Research and the Carnegie Institution of Washington, while corporations, led by General Electric, were opening the first industrial *research laboratories. Science's contributions to the two world wars elevated it to the status of a valuable national resource. During *World War II the federal government emerged as the nation's primary patron of basic science, and this lavish support continued during the *Cold War and beyond, swelling from roughly $1 billion in 1950 to about $70 billion as the century closed. By 2000 the United States was funding nearly half of the world's total expenditures on science and *technology.

—Ronald L. Numbers

SCIENCE: COLONIAL ERA

Early Spanish missionaries and explorers employed an Aristotelian cosmology; most early reports also used Pliny's *Natural History* as a guide to describing the fauna and flora of the Americas. Throughout the seventeenth century, Renaissance and Scholastic thought dominated American understandings of the natural world and even persisted into the eighteenth century. Throughout the *Colonial Era, astrology figured prominently in almanacs and herbals, especially in discussions of *medicine, *agriculture and meteorology. Alchemy was conspicuous in the science curriculum at colonial colleges; several Harvard theses on the philosophers' stone were accepted during the eighteenth century. Both astrology and alchemy were taught at Yale and the College of William and Mary but Renaissance science received its most comprehensive treatment at Harvard, where Charles Morton's *Compendium Physicae* was used until the 1720s.

The eventual triumph of Newtonian science and the acceptance of Enlightenment thought in the eighteenth century coincided with the appearance of small communities of savants throughout the colonies. For many Americans, the Royal Society of London provided inspiration, books, patronage, and scientific instruments; around fifty Americans in the colonial period were elected Fellows of the Royal Society and many more published scientific communications in the society's *Philosophical Transactions*. Bostonians organized a philosophical society as early as 1683 to converse on natural history, astronomy, and natural philosophy, but it survived only five years. New Englanders, whether Puritan ministers or college tutors, were disproportionately influential in colonial scientific circles until the 1730s. Among their most notable publications were Cotton Mather's *The Christian Philosopher: A Collection of the Best Discoveries in Nature* (1721) and Isaac Greenwood's *A Philosophical Discourse Concerning the Mutability and Changes of the Material World* (1731).

During the eighteenth century, science was promoted most comprehensively and effectively by the colonial colleges. In 1711 the College of William and Mary named a professor of natural philosophy and mathematics, the first such appointment at an American college. At Yale, a gift in 1714 of several hundred books, including Isaac Newton's 1687 work *Principia Mathematica*, from Jeremiah Dummer, Connecticut's colonial agent in London, transformed the teaching of science at the college, most notably through the introduction of advanced algebra. Harvard established the Hollis professorship of mathematics and natural philosophy in 1727, appointing Isaac Greenwood as the first incumbent. His successor, John Winthrop, who taught at Harvard from 1738 until his death in 1779, introduced modern textbooks; conducted research; established a large private scientific library; and re-built Harvard's collection of scientific instruments after fire destroyed Harvard Hall in 1764.

Mathematics and natural philosophy were introduced at Princeton (then the College of New-Jersey) during the 1760s and at Brown (Rhode-Island College) during the 1770s and 1780s, but science at both colleges depended more on the efforts of individual tutors than on initiatives of college administrators. At the end of the Colonial Era, science was especially prominent at the University of Pennsylvania (College of Philadelphia) and Columbia University (King's College). Both institutions established medical schools before the *Revolutionary War (in 1765 and 1767, respectively), thus inaugurating the systematic teaching of botany, chemistry, and anatomy in the American colonies. Both colleges, moreover, were led by men who emphasized the importance of science in the undergraduate curriculum. William Smith, appointed provost at Penn in 1756 by Benjamin *Franklin, not only introduced a full program of algebra, geometry, surveying, navigation, natural philosophy, and agricultural science but provided apparatus for experimental demonstrations. Science accounted for approximately 40 percent of classroom time. Although Samuel Johnson, president of Columbia from 1753 to 1763, promoted the teaching of mathematics, natural philosophy, and natural history, the scientific curriculum remained modest for many years. Nevertheless, Columbia, like Penn and William and Mary, offered science instruction in all four years of college.

The commercial and demographic growth of *Philadelphia and *New York City triggered the appearance of scientific, cultural, and educational institutions in each city. After moving to Philadelphia from *Boston in 1723, Benjamin Franklin helped organize, *inter alia*, the Library Company of Philadelphia, Pennsylvania Hospital, the *American Philosophical Society (APS), and the University of Pennsylvania. He won international acclaim for his research in *electricity, published in 1751 as *Experiments and Observations on Electricity*; the Royal Society awarded him the Copley Medal in 1753 and elected him a Fellow in 1756. Although Franklin's American Philosophical Society, founded in 1743, survived only two years, a second attempt in 1769 resulted in a permanent society. Society members observed the transit of Venus across the face of the sun in 1769 and published the first volume of *Transactions* in 1771. John *Adams, as American minister to France, was sufficiently impressed with the APS's reputation among the intellectuals of Paris to establish, in 1780, a similar organization in Boston: the American Academy of Arts and Sciences. With these institutions, science in America achieved a critical mass; in subsequent decades, American scientists would build on and extend the achievements of the Colonial Era.

[*See also* Bartram, John and William; Education: Collegiate Education; Mathematics and Statistics; Mather, Increase and Cotton; Medical Education.]

• Theodore Hornberger, *Scientific Thought in the American Colleges, 1638–1800*, 1946. Brooke Hindle, *The Pursuit of Science in Revolutionary America, 1735–1789*, 1956. Raymond Phineas Stearns, *Science in the British Colonies in America*, 1970. Herbert Leventhal, *In the Shadow of the Enlightenment: Occultism and Renaissance Science in Eighteenth Century America*, 1976. Henry F. May, *The Enlightenment in America*, 1976. I. Bernard Cohen, *Benjamin Franklin's Science*, 1990. William R. Newman, *Gehennical Fire: The Lives of George Starkey, an American Alchemist in the Scientific Revolution*, 1994.

—Simon Baatz

SCIENCE: REVOLUTIONARY WAR TO WORLD WAR I

When Henry *Adams wrote in his autobiography, "the American boy of 1854 stood nearer the year 1 than to the year 1900," he was invoking the enormous upheavals—intellectual, social, cultural, and national—of the second half of the nineteenth century. He was also alluding to his favorite thesis: that the pace of history was accelerating, in large part owing to developments in science and *technology. Indeed, the era between the *Revolutionary War and *World War I saw exponential growth in the organizations, journals, and amount of patronage devoted to science. As the U.S. population and economy expanded, so, too, did the industrial infrastructure and the capacity to produce precision instruments. Educational opportunities improved, and career paths, primarily for men, opened up in scientific research and engineering. Religious conservatives' resistance to such scientific theories as geological chronology and biological evolution had no lasting negative impact on science. Most notably, the federal government and a reformed university system became major players in the establishment of a national infrastructure supporting science in America.

Early National and Antebellum Eras. In 1782 the new nation could boast of one scientist of international repute (Benjamin *Franklin, whose 1751 *Experiments and Observations on Electricity* was widely translated and reprinted) and two scholarly societies (the *American Philosophical Society, based in *Philadelphia, and the American Academy of Arts and Sciences, in *Boston). While the Revolutionary War stimulated domestic manufactures, science itself played no role in the struggle for independence other than to enhance Franklin's reputation as a diplomat. Franklin's colleague, Thomas *Jefferson, however, both promoted American science and symbolized American respect for science. Indeed many of the Founding Fathers employed scientific metaphors in designing and justifying the American "experiment" in government.

Throughout the early republic and *Antebellum Eras, most scientists—or men of science, as they were commonly called—were either self-educated or trained at eastern liberal arts colleges such as Harvard and Yale. Many had earned a B.A. degree; some, an M.D. A few had spent a postgraduate year in Europe studying, touring, and purchasing books and apparatuses; still fewer had received Ph.D.s at European universities. Most scientists identified their special interests in either natural history (botany, zoology, and geology) or in *medicine and *agriculture. Research in Antebellum America was typically conducted by individual scientists with very limited resources. Much research was done "out of doors" by specimen collectors, weather observers, and explorers. The naturalist William *Bartram (whose father, John Bartram, had established America's first botanical garden in Philadelphia in 1728) explored the Southeast in the 1770s, recording plants, wildlife, and 215 species of native birds. Some government funding existed, particularly for geographical and geological exploration. The *Lewis and Clark Expedition (1803–1806) gathered geologic, mineralogical, and natural-history data. The U.S. Coast Survey mapped and improved the nation's harbors; the Army Medical Department conducted a continent-wide survey of medical geography. The *Wilkes Expedition (1838–1842), a six-ship U.S. naval mission led by Lieutenant Charles Wilkes, explored coastal South America, the South Pacific, *Hawai'i, and the Pacific Northwest and produced twenty volumes of scientific reports.

Individual scientists of note whose careers began in the Antebellum Era include the zoologist Louis *Agassiz and the botanist Asa *Gray, both of Harvard; the chemist Benjamin *Silliman, appointed professor at Yale in 1802, who did important work on carbon vaporization and also trained a notable group of geologists, including Edward Hitchcock (1793–1864) of Amherst College; the physicist Joseph *Henry, who published pathbreaking studies in electromagnetism while a professor at the College of New Jersey, later becoming the first secretary of the *Smithsonian Institution in 1846; and the chemist John William Draper (1811–1882) of the University of the City of New York, a pioneer in spectrum analysis and human physiology, and, in 1839, using the new daguerreotype process, the first to photograph the moon.

But with a few exceptions, such as the Harvard mathematician Benjamin Peirce (1809–1880), American scientists had little mathematical sophistication, and few possessed well-equipped laboratories. Those who conducted research generally did so in more than one field; for example Elias Loomis was both an astronomer and meteorologist. The theoretical foundations and boundaries of physics, chemistry, and biology remained ill-defined. Scientific papers on all subjects appeared in unspecialized journals such as Silliman's *American Journal of Science and Arts*, the *Journal of the Franklin Institute*, and the *Proceedings* of the American Philosophical Society.

The Gilded Age. The situation changed dramatically as the nineteenth century wore on. The *Civil War was the first major conflict affected by the industrial revolution. Although it drew on existing technology rather than generating much that was new, the Union's organizational and administrative accomplishments introduced new national networks—*railroads, banking, *telegraph lines—and infused new technologies into American society. The earth and agricultural sciences continued to receive the greatest share of federal patronage during and after the Civil War, as they had earlier. In 1862, President Abraham *Lincoln established the Department of Agriculture and signed the *Morrill Land Grant Act for the support of agricultural and mechanical colleges. A national weather service was established by the Army Signal Corps in 1870. The Hatch Act (1887) provided for basic research at state *agricultural experiment stations.

Despite the existence of a *National Academy of Sciences (1863), centralization of effort proved elusive. By 1886, the federal government had spent an estimated $68 million on various, often overlapping, surveys of the *West. The overarching concern motivating most of these government efforts was the central role of western settlement. Scientists who could connect their research to that nationalizing agenda, whether by extending telegraph wires into Indian Territory, mapping mineral deposits, or developing arid-land agricultural techniques were first in line for government support.

Liberal arts colleges and the new research universities such as Johns Hopkins (incorporated in 1869), Clark (1889), and Chicago (1892) became major patrons of science in the late nineteenth century. Some of the older colleges began offering degrees in science and *engineering. The new Massachusetts Institute of Technology (1861) and the post–1862 land-grant colleges supported applied sciences and engineering. Between 1870 and 1900, the number of bachelor's degrees granted by colleges and universities more than tripled, from about 10,000 to almost 30,000. During the same period the number of American Ph.D.s awarded soared from 1 in 1870 to 382 in 1900.

Specialization and *professionalization loomed large as advanced training became a prerequisite for a career in science. Institutional support structures—associations, specialized journals, laboratories, and professional standards—grew up around the new divisions of knowledge established by the universities. As early as 1874, the *American Association for the Advancement of Science reorganized itself into special-interest sections. The first scientific society based on a single discipline was the American Chemical Society, established in New York in 1876. A flurry of professional organization followed a decade or two later. The American Physiological Society (1887), the Association of American Anatomists (1888), the American Society of Zoologists (1890), the Botanical Society of America (1894), the American Mathematical Society (1894), the American Astronomical Society (1897), the American Society for Microbiology (1899), and the American Physical Society (1899) shared the common goals of raising disciplinary standards and insulating their community of discourse from nonspecialists.

The Early Twentieth Century. In the first decade of the twentieth century, after this era of dramatic disciplinary and professional growth, developments in the corporate board room, in the laboratory, and in scientific theory and practice all prefigured the coming of a new order in American science. In 1901, the General Electric Company opened an industrial research laboratory and the federal government established the

National Bureau of Standards; in 1902, the Carnegie Institution of *Washington, D.C., began funding scientific research with an initial bequest of $10 million; in 1903, Wilbur and Orville *Wright flew their airplane at Kitty Hawk, North Carolina; in 1904, George Ellery *Hale established the Mount Wilson Observatory; and before World War I, Americans won the nation's first two Nobel Prizes in science: A. A. Michelson for his spectroscopic studies and measurements of light (1907) and Theodore Richards for his study of atomic weights (1914). Intellectuals and the general public alike were coming to believe that the key to progress lay in the increased application of the knowledge and methods of science and technology to all spheres of human activity. Science, it was widely believed, was the mother of technology; technology, the worker of wonders. Throughout the *Progressive Era an optimistic nation remained convinced that the great engine of progress would operate ever more efficiently thanks to the forces of science and technology. Charles Sanders *Peirce (son of the Harvard mathematician Benjamin Peirce), John *Dewey, Walter *Lippman, and other pre–World War I social thinkers all saw the methods and values of science—or an idealized version of those methods and ideals—as a model for society as a whole.

America's brief involvement in World War I reinforced this trend. Although the contributions of scientists did little to affect the outcome directly, the National Research Council, founded in 1916 to coordinate research for national security and welfare, made clear to both scientists and the general public that a new era of cooperation between science and government had dawned.

[*See also* Airplanes and Air Transport; Banking and Finance; Biological Sciences; Coast and Geodetic Survey, U.S.; Early Republic, Era of the; Economic Development; Education: Collegiate Education; Education: The Rise of the University; Evolution, Theory of; Geological Surveys; Industrialization; Mathematics and Statistics; Photography; Physical Sciences; Professionalization; Research Laboratories, Industrial.]

• A. Hunter Dupree, *Science in the Federal Government: A History of Policies and Activities to 1940,* 1957. Nathan Reingold, ed., *Science in Nineteenth-Century America: A Documentary History,* 1964. Alexandra Oleson and John Voss, eds., *The Organization of Knowledge in Modern America, 1860–1920,* 1979. Margaret Rossiter, *Women Scientists in America: Struggles and Strategies to 1940,* 1982. Marc Rothenberg, *The History of Science and Technology in the United States: A Critical and Selective Bibliography,* 2 vols., 1982–1993. Sally Gregory Kohlstedt and Margaret W. Rossiter, eds., *Historical Writing on American Science, Osiris,* 2d ser., 1 (1985). Robert V. Bruce, *The Launching of Modern American Science, 1846–1876,* 1987. James Rodger Fleming, *Meteorology in America,* 1800–1870, 1990. Clark A Elliott, *History of Science in the United States: A Chronology and Research Guide,* 1996. Ronald L. Numbers and Charles E. Rosenberg, eds., *The Scientific Enterprise in America: Readings from* Isis, 1996.

—James Rodger Fleming

SCIENCE: FROM 1914 TO 1945

In 1916, two years after war erupted in Europe but before America's declaration of war, the astronomer George Ellery *Hale began to organize and recruit scientists in universities and industrial laboratories across the nation to work on military problems. His plans for an organization to support such work, operating under the auspices of the *National Academy of Sciences (NAS), culminated in the creation of the National Research Council (NRC). As a wartime science advisory board, the council dealt with problems ranging from the manufacture of nitrogen compounds for the production of explosives to the building and testing of submarine-detection devices and the physiology of battlefield shock. With the help of two coworkers, the chemist Arthur A. Noyes and the physicist Robert A. *Millikan, Hale, who saw *World War I as a great opportunity to promote the advancement of science in America, then orchestrated the transformation of the NRC into a permanent arm of the NAS. Reorganized on a peacetime basis in 1919, Hale's NRC now included a postdoctoral fellowship program for research in physics and chemistry, with the Rockefeller Foundation putting up the money and the council selecting the fellows and administering the program. The program, which later encompassed other disciplines, reinforced the role of universities as the traditional seats of American research. By the end of *World War II, universities had emerged as the strongest and largest centers of scientific research in the United States. The number of Ph.D. degrees in science and mathematics awarded by American universities rose from 525 in 1920 to more than 6,000 in 1950.

The period 1920–1940 saw the rapid development of many scientific fields and the expansion of the scientific research establishment in the United States. While some government agencies carried out research with the help of government funds, the American scientific community relied largely on private patronage and *philanthropy, especially from the Rockefeller, Carnegie, and Guggenheim foundations, to pay for research.

The research ranged from *Drosophila* (fruit fly) genetics and the biochemistry of *Neurospora crassa* (bread mold) in biology to the development of particle accelerators and cosmic rays in physics. Geographically, scientific research spanned the nation; indeed, three of the important early developments in nuclear physics—Carl Anderson's discovery of the positron, Harold C. *Urey's discovery of deuterium, and Ernest O. *Lawrence's invention of the cyclotron—took place in *California. In astronomy, Edwin Hubble's discovery of the expansion of the universe and the construction of the two-hundred-inch telescope, the world's largest optical telescope, paved the way for a revolution in cosmology. The theory of turbulence and airplane wing design in aeronautics opened new vistas in the applied sciences. Linus *Pauling's application of quantum mechanics to molecular structure provided a deeper understanding of the nature of chemical bonding. Glenn Seaborg's research on the chemistry of the transuranium elements, starting with the discovery of neptunium in 1941, played a crucial role in the *Manhattan Project's plutonium project and the development of the atomic bomb.

Pure mathematics was among the most successful scientific fields in the United States during the early twentieth century. The initial stimulus came from the contact of Eliakin Hastings Moore, Norbert *Wiener, Griffith Evans, and other aspiring mathematicians with particular German, English, and Italian mathematical schools. As a result, American mathematicians were able, within a short time, to play prominent roles in developing research groups in academic settings in the areas of analysis, number theory, and the new fields of topology and mathematical logic. The leading centers of mathematical research and graduate education included the University of Chicago, Harvard University, the University of California at Berkeley, Princeton University, and the nearby Institute for Advanced Study.

While American mathematicians tackled problems in pure mathematics, applied mathematics was at first largely ignored. The subject first emerged as an independent discipline in the United States during World War II. European-born scientists played an important role in closing this particular scientific gap in the United States. Theodore von Kármán, a Hungarian-born engineer and applied scientist and the first director of the Graduate School of Aeronautics at the California Institute of Technology (Caltech), was among those who campaigned vigorously before the war to make applied mathematics respectable to engineers and mathematicians. In 1941, Brown University's R. G. D. Richardson inaugurated the nation's first program in applied mathematics. Later, New York University's Richard Courant, who immigrated to the United States in 1934, established its program. The head of the Rockefeller Foundation's Natural Science Division, Warren Weaver, was also instrumental in advancing and expanding the academic base for applied mathematics in the United States in the 1930s. During World War II, Richard Courant served as a member of Weaver's Applied Mathematics Panel of the Office of Scientific Research and Development.

The arrival of émigré scientists from Europe, which coincided with the Great Depression of the 1930s, brought out the best and the worst in university deans, college presidents, and other representatives of American higher education. Relatively few institutions opened their doors to these displaced scientists, many of whom were Jewish. Latent *anti-Semitism, a resistance in many physics departments to theoretical physics (a specialty of many of these refugees), antipathy in some quarters to foreigners, and a concern for young unemployed American-born scientists all exacerbated the problem.

Nevertheless, several hundred central European refugee physicists, mathematicians, and physical chemists, dismissed from academic positions on racial grounds following the Nazi rise to power in Germany and other countries after 1933, eventually found new employment in American universities and colleges, industry, and research institutions. Albert *Einstein, fleeing Europe in 1933, accepted an appointment at Princeton's Institute for Advanced Study. Later on, many of the émigré theoretical physicists, including Hans Bethe, Enrico *Fermi, Emilio Segrè, Edward *Teller, and Victor Weisskopf, were recruited to work on the Mahattan Project. Despite their technical status as enemy aliens, these physicists proved essential to the atomic-bomb enterprise. Ironically, fascist dictators overseas helped level the playing field in science. In physics, especially, the émigré scientists contributed substantially to a marked shift of the centers of excellence from Europe to America.

Between the two world wars, the American geological community resisted the theory of continental drift and the notion of plate tectonics, subjects popular in Europe. Seismologists, however, at such universities as California at Berkeley, Caltech, and St. Louis, turned their research into a powerful tool for exploring the Earth's interior. Although interdisciplinary fields such as geochemistry and planetary science took off after World War II, war-related research, which brought together nuclear physicists and chemists, provided the intellectual spark.

The roots of molecular genetics, too, go back to two revolutionary World War II discoveries. By the early 1940s, Stanford University professors George Beadle and Edward Tatum had shown that the absence (or presence) of an enzyme was inherited as a single-gene trait. Their *Neurospora* genetics research cemented the idea that genes control enzymes (the one-gene, one-enzyme theory), the chemical stuff of life, and led to the rise of a discipline that cut across conventional boundaries—biochemical genetics. In 1944, Oswald T. Avery, Colin M. MacLeod, and Maclyn McCarty at the Rockefeller Institute produced the first experimental evidence that genes are made of deoxyribonucleic acid (DNA). Their discovery that DNA alone was the carrier of genetic information greatly influenced the later work of James D. *Watson and Francis Crick on the structure of DNA.

The growing strength of science in the United States in the interwar years was signaled by a substantial number of Nobel prizes awarded to Americans in the 1914–1945 era. These included, in physics, Robert A. Millikan, Arthur H. *Compton, Isidor Isaac *Rabi, Otto Stern, Ernest O. Lawrence, and Carl D. Anderson, and, in chemistry, Theodore W. Richards, Irving Langmuir, and Harold C. Urey.

In July 1945, Vannevar *Bush, the director of the wartime Office of Scientific Research and Development, sent President Harry S. *Truman an influential report, *Science: The Endless Frontier,* laying out a program for postwar scientific research. Insisting on the federal government's duty to support scientific research and scientific education, Bush argued eloquently that economic progress, the health and well-being of Americans, and national security depended on advances in science. He recommended the creation of a federal agency to carry out these activities. The *National Science Foundation, established in 1950 in fulfillment of Bush's vision, would play a crucial role in the further development of science in America.

[*See also* Biological Sciences; Education: The Rise of the University; Engineering; Genetics and Genetic Engineering; Mathematics and Statistics; Medicine: From the 1870s to 1945; New Deal Era, The; Physical Sciences; Professionalization; Research Laboratories, Industrial; Scopes Trial; Technology; Twenties, The; Wigner, Eugene.]

• Daniel J. Kevles, *The Physicists: The History of a Scientific Community in Modern America,* 1977. Nathan Reingold and Ida H. Reingold, *Science in America: A Documentary History, 1900–1939,* 1981. Paul S. Hoch, "The Reception of Central European Refugee Physicists of the 1930s: U.S.S.R., U.K., U.S.A.," *Annals of Science* 40 (1983): 217–46. Maclyn McCarty, *The Transforming Principle,* 1985. Richard Rhodes, *The Making of the Atomic Bomb,* 1986. John W. Servos, *Physical Chemistry from Ostwald to Pauling: The Making of a Science in America,* 1990. Judith R. Goodstein, *Millikan's School: A History of the California Institute of Technology,* 1991. Nathan Reingold, *Science, American Style,* 1991. John Lankford, *American Astronomy: Community, Careers, and Power, 1859–1940,* 1997.

—Judith R. Goodstein

SCIENCE: SINCE 1945

*World War II transformed American science. Before the war, the private foundations—Rockefeller, Carnegie, Macy, Guggenheim, and others—were the dominant patrons of university-based research in the natural and social sciences. Beginning with the mobilization of science for war in 1940, the federal government, especially the armed services, assumed this role, dwarfing prewar *philanthropy while transforming both the political economy of science and the content of technical knowledge. Understanding this profound transformation lies at the center of much recent scholarship in the history of American science and *technology.

Science and the Military in Cold War America. At war's end, the leaders of the wartime research and development effort—including Vannevar *Bush, James B. *Conant, and Karl T. Compton (1887–1954)—attempted to craft the postwar relationship of science and the federal government through Bush's landmark 1945 report, *Science—The Endless Frontier.* Bush sought to insulate federal patronage of the natural sciences from political interference while arguing that only basic research guided and performed by academic scientists would produce the knowledge necessary both to fuel the nation's economy and to protect national security. Bush proposed a National Research Foundation to support research in the physical and biomedical sciences, leaving out the social sciences. Although Congress established a *National Science Foundation in 1950, the foundation envisioned by Bush and his colleagues never materialized. Instead, between 1945 and 1950, the American *military became the patron of choice on American campuses. Bush tried to manage this dominance through his chairmanship of the national military establishment's Joint Research and Development Board, but this effort, like many to follow, failed to control the military's appetite for science and technology.

Military support of academic research rested on an assumption derived from wartime research: Given enough money, one could build any weapon. For example, the *Manhattan Project, with two billion dollars of federal funding, took a rare laboratory-bound phenomenon, nuclear fission, and transformed it into an awesome new bomb. For the military, this suggested that the scientist could deliver almost anything with enough funds. Believing this, the Air Force and Navy assumed that a massive research investment would produce the ballistic missile, a weapon (the V–2) that the Nazis had developed during the war. Although millions of dollars flowed into countless guided missile projects, the United States did not have a successful and operational ballistic weapon until the late 1950s.

Weapons research was not isolated or secluded. Instead, such work took place in academic and corporate laboratories under various labels. For example, researchers at a variety of institutions used captured German V–2 rockets to investigate the upper atmosphere. The knowledge gained was not only of academic interest but of value to missile design. Basic research in the *physical sciences was deemed essential to national security. Researchers might claim that they were using the military to fund "pure science," but such claims erroneously assumed that military patrons were easily duped. In fact, an important byproduct of the war was the development of a technological intelligentsia within the military. University laboratories became sites for the education of a new kind of military officer, as familiar with calculus as the carbine. Members of this new class, possessing master's and doctoral degrees, understood the complexity of the technologies under development as well as the science behind them.

The ballistic-missile and continental-defense programs dominated the physical sciences in *Cold War America. These massive projects had significant consequences at both the institutional and intellectual levels. New institutions, including the Defense Advanced Research Projects Agency (DARPA), now famous for its funding of the ARPANET, a forerunner of the Internet, were created. Others, such as the Lincoln Laboratories of the Massachusetts Institute of Technology or the MITRE Corporation, became important actors in national security research and development. The digital *computer and mass-produced semiconductor owe their existence to the military's ability to fund research that produced expensive and rare technologies. Military production experience allowed for semiconductor manufacturers, including Fairchild Semiconductor and Texas Instruments, to learn the art of growing silicon wafers and writing on them. Although the computer industry has been portrayed as an example of *laissez-faire *capitalism at work, in truth, the capital fueling research at *California's Silicon Valley and *Boston's Route 128 were as much a product of government contracts as they were of private investment. The massive government-funded projects often produced unexpected results. The ballistic-missile program yielded the Atlas booster that launched John Glenn into orbit and other feats of the early *space program. The IBM corporation repackaged software developed at government expense (SAGE) to produce the automated airline-reservation system (SABRE).

An emphasis on utilitarian projects turned American physical science into a large-scale development effort in which the crafting and manufacture of new technologies became more important than the work conducted with the apparatus. The industrial mindset directly affected laboratory life and practice, especially in so-called "big science." Before the war, successful laboratory instruments were often cannibalized for new investigations. In high-energy physics, for example, accelerators quickly became obsolete and new ones were constructed. The built-in obsolescence of *mass production entered the physical sciences. Old accelerators might lose their cutting-edge research function, but they were easily turned to other purposes, such as medical research or the production of radioactive isotopes, atomic physics' most commercial product. Skills once essential for research changed. Prewar scientists had been forced to build apparatus from scratch: their postwar successors simply modified preexisting hardware and software to perform research, and purchased lab equipment and instruments from catalogs.

Military patronage also affected the *social sciences. A key element of military social science, operations research (OR), illustrates the point. OR's origins lay in the application of mathematical techniques to strategic and logistical problems. Two campaigns secured OR's fame: the wartime antisubmarine effort in the North Atlantic, in which physicists, economists, mathematicians, and others developed new means of searching for submarines under various conditions and constraints; and the mining of the Sea of Japan. These successes generated support for continuing military investment in this new field, both at American universities and at new research institutions such as the RAND Corporation of Santa Monica, California, and the Johns Hopkins University Operations Research Office. OR became the leading edge of mathematical thinking in the social sciences, a trend that included the development of game theory, systems thinking, rational-choice theory, and econometrics. The spread of this quantitative approach to military strategy allowed for the rice paddies and villages of Vietnam to become laboratories for social science.

The Biomedical Disciplines. The other great federal patron of science after World War II, the *National Institutes of Health (NIH), concentrated on the biomedical disciplines. A multimillion dollar enterprise with ever increasing budgets, the NIH set the tone of U.S. biomedical research. Only with the arrival of the Howard Hughes Medical Institute's grants program in 1987 did a private institution rival NIH in support of biomedical research. At the same time, NIH research was increasingly directed by Congress toward particular diseases. Although President Richard M. *Nixon declared war on *cancer in 1970, members of Congress were always eager to support disease-directed research for constituents, partly to compensate for their failure to establish national health insurance.

Two landmarks greatly affected the biomedical disciplines in the postwar era. First, the HIV/AIDS epidemic provided NIH with a disease that required research at multiple levels, from etiology through treatment. In turn, government-funded research catalyzed work in the *pharmaceutical industry and other corporate settings. AIDS activists brought the military's assumption that "with enough money we can do anything" to the biomedical disciplines, as did those suffering from other diseases, such as breast cancer. Second, the *Human Genome Project (HGP), which mapped and sequenced the genetic blueprint for *Homo sapiens,* profoundly altered conceptions of illness and causality. Wielding computers and drawing on molecular biology and medical science, the HGP promised to alter the biomedical disciplines in ways previously unimagined. By the end of the century, big science, once the physicists' domain, had invaded the biomedical disciplines, with an important twist. For the physical sciences, big science was about location: a single accelerator or telescope served as the focus of research by individuals at an array of institutions. The HGP form of big science was decentralized, with multiple laboratories, public and private, sequencing genes and circulating this information on the Internet. Given the HGP's commercial potential, issues of intellectual property and government ownership arose in unprecedented ways, although the U.S. government preferred to see the genome remain in the public domain. At the same time, HGP threatened to become the biomedical equivalent of the Internet, that is, a foundational technology with standards set by the federal government that served as the base for a massive commercial enterprise. After 1945, science in America became a ward of the state; it remained so as the post–Cold War marketplace increasingly directed the aims and goals of federal funding.

[*See also* Acquired Immunodeficiency Syndrome; Bioethics; Biological Sciences; Biotechnology Industry; Education: Education in Contemporary America; Genetics and Genetic Engineering; Internet and World Wide Web; Mathematics and Statistics; Medicine: Since 1945; Missiles and Rockets; National Aeronautics and Space Administration; Nuclear Strategy; Technology; Vietnam War.]

• Stephen P. Strickland, *Politics, Science, and Dread Disease: A Short History of United States Medical Research Policy,* 1972. Paul Forman, "Behind Quantum Electronics: National Security as Basis for Physical Research in the United States, 1940–1960," *Historical Studies in the Physical Sciences* 18 (1987): 149–229. Stuart W. Leslie, *The Cold War and American Science: The Military-Industrial-Academic Complex at MIT and Stanford,* 1993. Daniel S. Greenberg, *The Politics of Pure Science,* rev. ed.,

1999. Jessica Wang, *American Science in an Age of Anxiety: Scientists, Anticommunism, and the Cold War,* 1999.

—Michael A. Dennis

SCIENCE: SCIENCE AND RELIGION

Beginning at least as early as the last third of the nineteenth century, the metaphor of war came to dominate discussions of science and *religion in America. The historian Andrew Dickson White sounded the keynote in 1869 with a public lecture on "The Battle-Fields of Science," which he eventually expanded into a two-volume best-seller, *History of the Warfare of Science with Theology in Christendom* (1896). White's characterization dominated scholarly opinion for nearly a century, but in the last quarter of the twentieth century historians of science and religion increasingly came to regard his view as inaccurate and simplistic. They found as much religious support for science as opposition, and they noted the slipperiness of the categories "science" and "religion." White, for example, sought to avoid being labeled anti-religious by equating "religion" (which he professed to value) with the Golden Rule, and "theology" (which he scorned) with dogmatic ignorance. Similarly, conservative Christians commonly praised "true science," based on observable facts, even as they railed against "science falsely so-called," based on theories that challenged their religious views.

Colonial Americans, who were carving a society out of a "howling wilderness" during the so-called scientific revolution in Europe, displayed more indifference than hostility to science. The *New England Puritans, who left the best records of their feelings toward what was then called natural philosophy, led the way in embracing the new physics and astronomy. Cotton *Mather, for example, wrote a book to "demonstrate, that *Philosophy* is no *Enemy,* but a mighty and wondrous *Incentive* to *Religion.*" In the early 1720s he proposed the novel measure of inoculating the citizens of Boston against *smallpox, widely regarded as a divinely sent punishment. The town's leading physician, William Douglass, denounced Mather for his impious attempt to thwart God's will. In this struggle for authority, a man of science wielded a theological weapon to attack a man of God for promoting what turned out to be a life-saving medical procedure.

The more that science explained about epidemics, earthquakes, and *electricity, the less colonial Americans invoked the direct agency of God. This troubled some religious leaders, such as the Anglican divine Samuel Johnson, who complained that "it is a fashionable sort of philosophy (a science falsely so-called) to conceive that God governs the world only by a general providence according to certain fixed laws of nature." Most Christian writers, however, seemed content with attributing the laws of nature to divine will.

The decades preceding the *Civil War presented a number of scientific challenges to devout Christians: astronomers traced the origin of the solar system to a primitive nebula, geologists discovered the antiquity of life on Earth and the absence of evidence of a worldwide flood, anthropologists speculated about the existence of human beings before Adam and Eve, and phrenologists correlated personality traits with the contours of the head. As God-fearing Christians themselves, most American men of science assured the faithful of their genuine desire to reveal God's wisdom, power, and goodness in nature, and repeatedly demonstrated the harmony of God's two books: the *Bible and nature. Some Christians disapproved of the tendency to make "science lead the way and the Bible follow," but perhaps the sharpest criticisms came from competing scholars. Biblical exegetes with hard-won expertise in ancient languages and history resented the presumption of scientists, who presumably didn't know one Hebrew letter from another, in instructing them on how to interpret ancient texts. The quarrel involved scientific and religious matters, but it centered on the protection of professional turf.

No topic in the history of science and religion in America attracted more attention than the debates over organic *evolution that erupted with the publication of Charles Darwin's *Origin of Species* (1859). Scientists and laypersons alike disputed the implications of evolution for natural and revealed religion, but there was little pattern to the sides. Although religious orthodoxy correlated with antievolution sentiment, conservative and liberal Christians, like traditionalist and reform Jews, could be found in both camps.

In the later nineteenth century, the meaning of "science" grew increasingly narrow and rigid. As the Princeton theologian Charles Hodge (1797–1878) observed in 1874, the very word science was "becoming more and more restricted to the knowledge of a particular class of facts, and of their relations, namely, the facts of nature or of the external world," which scientists insisted on explaining naturalistically. Long fond of science, Hodge sensed a growing "alienation" between scientists and theologians, which he attributed to the former's "assumption of superiority" and practice of stigmatizing their religious critics "as narrow-minded, bigots, old women, Bible worshippers, etc." The aging theologian may have overreacted, but he accurately observed the increasing compartmentalization of science and religion among American intellectuals.

The early-twentieth-century rise of the social and behavioral sciences, which made religion itself an object of scientific study, threatened to become the focal point of science-religion interactions, but evolution, particularly human evolution, continued to occupy center stage. During the 1920s Christian fundamentalists waged a holy war against evolution, symbolized most memorably by the *Scopes trial in 1925. But even the most outspoken critics of evolution typically lauded what they regarded as true science. "It is not 'science' that orthodox Christians oppose," a fundamentalist editor explained in *Bible Champion* in 1925. "No! no! a thousand times, No! They are opposed only to the theory of evolution, which has not yet been proved, and therefore is not to be called by the sacred name of *science.*"

The late-twentieth-century battles between creationists and evolutionists appeared to provide one more example of White's "warfare" thesis, but appearances were deceiving. In one celebrated contest between the two sides, in a federal courtroom in Little Rock, Arkansas, in 1981, the plaintiffs, who opposed "creation science," overwhelmingly represented religious organizations. In contrast, virtually all the experts testifying in support of creationism possessed graduate degrees in science. It was confusing enough to make a latter-day White long for the imaginary days when a predictable dichotomy between science and religion prevailed.

[*See also* Biological Sciences; Fundamentalist Movement; Physical Sciences; Puritanism; Social Sciences.]

• Theodore Dwight Bozeman, *Protestants in an Age of Science: The Baconian Ideal and Antebellum American Religious Thought,* 1977. Ronald L. Numbers. *Creation by Natural Law: Laplace's Nebular Hypothesis in American Thought,* 1977. Ronald L. Numbers, "Science and Religion," *Osiris,* 2d ser. 1 (1985): 59–80. Jon H. Roberts, *Darwinism and the Divine in America: Protestant Intellectuals and Organic Evolution, 1859–1900,* 1988. Ronald L. Numbers, *The Creationists,* 1992. David N. Livingstone, *The Preadamite Theory and the Marriage of Science and Religion,* vol. 82 of the *Transactions of the American Philosophical Society,* 1992. Ronald L. Numbers, *Darwinism Comes to America,* 1998. Jon H. Roberts and James Turner, *The Sacred and the Secular University,* 2000. David C. Lindberg and Ronald L. Numbers, eds., *Science and the Christian Tradition,* 2001.

—Ronald L. Numbers

SCIENCE: SCIENCE AND POPULAR CULTURE

From *Colonial Era newspapers to twentieth-century *television, American *popular culture has always incorporated science, presenting images and information adapted to changing media formats and evolving audience interests. Even when presented as entertainment, popularized science has been packaged as "useful knowledge," with implied utilitarian benefit.

In the early republic, ideals of democracy, progress, and egalitarian education determined the popular diffusion of scientific information. Interest in North American natural history and resources ran high. As the new nation defined itself in relation to European civilization, its periodicals offered descriptions of newly discovered flora, fauna, and fossils, alongside discussions of inventions, politics, and civic life.

The most democratic venue for popularization was the science museum. When the portrait painter Charles Willson Peale (1741–1827) in 1786 assembled a "cabinet of curiosities" and promoted his *Philadelphia museum as appropriate Sunday entertainment, visitors could admire "God's handiwork" by peering at entomologists' carefully arranged insects or models of marvelous inventions.

During the nineteenth century, popular lectures by European and American scientists and increased attention to science in general periodicals such as *Harper's Monthly* attested to Americans' continuing appetite for scientific information. Specialized *magazines such as *Scientific American* (1845), *Popular Science Monthly* (1872), and *National Geographic Magazine* (1886) disseminated the latest scientific findings and convinced readers of science's importance. The *Smithsonian Institution became another important venue for popular consumption of scientific knowledge. When the Smithsonian expanded to include inventions as well as natural history, and created a "living" collection in its National Zoo, it placed science at the heart of national culture.

Early twentieth-century newspapers and magazines treated scientists such as the physicist Robert A. *Millikan and the astronomer George Ellery *Hale as celebrities. Even the rarified ideas of theoretical scientists such as Albert *Einstein, were translated for the mass media. Readership of general science books grew; "dime novels," such as the Tom Swift series (1910–1941), entertained young readers with descriptions of fanciful inventions, while the new genre of "science fiction" infused fantasy with scientific credibility.

From the 1920s on, the burgeoning *film industry treated scientists primarily as colorful stock characters, although Hollywood also perpetuated the cultural image of the menacing "mad scientist" with various "Frankenstein" movies based loosely on Mary Shelley's 1818 novel. A few films such as *The Story of Louis Pasteur* (1936) and *Madame Curie* (1943) featured scientists as heroes, but science-fiction movies more typically portrayed them as well-meaning, politically naive, and manipulable. After 1945, the atomic bomb provided new images of terror for moviemakers.

Most mid-twentieth-century science popularizers saw themselves as explainers, not apologists, yet they were among science's biggest boosters. Some were themselves scientists. In the post–World War II decades, biologist Isaac Asimov (1920–1992) emerged as a prolific nonfiction communicator, while physician Michael Crichton successfully translated scientific fact into fiction in novels such as *The Andromeda Strain* (1971) and *Jurassic Park* (1993), which also became successful movies. Science-based periodicals such as *Omni* and *Discovery* attested to the public's strong interest in science, but also underscored the continuing appeal of sensationalized science. Although books by biologist James D. *Watson, paleontologist Stephen Jay Gould, and the British astrophysicist Stephen Hawking topped bestseller lists, serious attention to science never eclipsed the frivolous or fictionalized treatments.

Americans incorporated science into the popular culture on their terms, not necessarily those of the scientific community. Early television shows about science mimicked scientists' formal tone and manner of presentation, preserving a dignified distance between teacher and pupil, but this model eventually gave way to lively demonstrations such as *Watch Mr. Wizard,* first broadcast in 1951, and to narrated film footage of animals and natural phenomena in such shows as *Wild Kingdom,* launched in 1962; *Nova,* first shown in 1973, and astronomer Carl Sagan's *Cosmos'* series (1977). More often, television wove discussions of biomedical research into hospital dramas, as in *Ben Casey* and *Dr. Kildare,* or fantasized it within science fiction, as in the popular *Star Trek* series.

In the 1980s, science museums, zoos, and aquaria, responding to the ever-increasing importance of *technology, built interactive exhibits and invited visitors to participate in demonstration activities. The Exploratorium in *San Francisco pioneered this combination of *education and entertainment; its exhibits replaced static collections with light, sound, puppets, films, and *computer terminals. Extending this process, science content on videos, CD-ROMs, and computer networks in the 1990s, produced by many diverse institutions and organizations, allowed audiences of all ages and educational backgrounds to access and select from popularized science on their own terms and on demand. While some observers praised these imaginative efforts to popularize science, others found them too celebratory and insufficiently attentive to the social and ethical issues associated with science and technology.

[*See also* Hospitals; Literature, Popular; Medicine; Museums: Museums of Science and Technology; Nuclear Weapons.]

• Rae Goodell, *The Visible Scientists,* 1977. John C. Burnham, *How Superstition Won and Science Lost: Popularizing Science and Health in the United States,* 1987. Dorothy Nelkin, *Selling Science: How the Press Covers Science and Technology,* 1987. Marcel C. LaFollette, *Making Science Our Own: Public Images of Science, 1910–1955,* 1989. Christopher P. Toumey, *Conjuring Science: Scientific Symbols and Cultural Meanings in American Life,* 1996. Gregg Mitman, *Reel Nature: America's Romance with Wildlife on Film,* 1999.

—Marcel C. LaFollette

SCIENTIFIC MANAGEMENT, term coined in 1910 to describe the system of industrial management created and promoted by Frederick W. Taylor (1856–1915) and his followers. Though Taylor, a native of *Philadelphia, had used the term informally to describe his contributions to factory management, his associates, particularly Morris L. Cooke, deliberately chose the label "scientific management" to dramatize the novelty and significance of their work. This strategy worked brilliantly as the term came to be applied to managerial practices based on clear-cut responsibilities, rational organization, close attention to detail, and the centralized direction of work.

Scientific management arose from what historians have termed "systematic management," a wide-ranging late nineteenth-century effort to improve factory performance through cost accounting, inventory and production controls, incentive wage plans, and other modern management techniques. Working at Midvale Steel, Bethlehem Steel, and other plants in the 1880s and 1890s, Taylor refined these managerial practices, added innovations such as stopwatch time study, and combined the disparate features into a single comprehensive management package. After his retirement in 1901, he and a group of associates effectively promoted his managerial system to manufacturers. Only after the publication of Taylor's *The Principles of Scientific Management* (1911), mostly written by Cooke, however, did their work become well known outside *engineering circles, contributing to a *Progressive Era "efficiency" vogue. The impact of scientific management on industry is harder to assess. Taylor's full system was too rigorous for most manufacturers; they adopted bits and pieces according to their needs. By the 1930s most American and European and many Asian factories had introduced isolated features of scientific management, but apparently no plant had introduced and maintained every feature of Taylor's original, carefully prescribed system. The intellectual currents Taylor set in motion, however, proved more profound. By the 1920s, "Taylorism" had disciples in virtually every industrialized nation, and they succeeded in publicizing the value of the precise, systematic management of economic resources, from machinery to national economies.

In the 1930s, American social scientists rediscovered Taylor's writings and began to stigmatize "scientific management" or "Taylorism" as a shorthand designation for an oppressive industrial system. In particular, Taylor and scientific management became straw men for theorists and consultants who advocated more humanistic approaches to industrial organization. Both the criticism and the application of Taylor's principles continued as the twentieth century ended. Scientific management has thus proven to be a highly malleable and ambiguous term defined by diverse, conflicting constituencies.

[*See also* Automation and Computerization; Capitalism; Factory System; Industrial Relations; Industrialization; Labor Movements; Mass Production; Social Science; Twenties, The.]

• Daniel Nelson, ed., *A Mental Revolution: Scientific Management since Taylor,* 1992. Robert Kanigel, *The One Best Way,* 1997.

—Daniel Nelson

SCOPES TRIAL, celebrated 1925 case involving the teaching of evolution in public schools. By 1920, Protestant fundamentalism had coalesced from various conservative religious traditions into an organized movement fighting the spread of the religious modernism and cultural secularism. Fundamentalist leaders viewed evolutionary naturalism, propounded by Charles Darwin in *The Origin of Species* (1859), as a root cause of both developments. Joined by William Jennings *Bryan, they launched a national crusade against Darwinism. Their first major legal victory came in 1925, when Tennessee outlawed teaching about human evolution in public schools. The *American Civil Liberties Union invited local teachers to challenge the law. John Scopes, a young science teacher in Dayton, Tennessee, accepted the challenge at the urging of local school and civic leaders, who sought to promote their town.

The case resulted in a highly publicized clash of ideas rather than a serious prosecution of Scopes, who was never threatened with jail or loss of job. Bryan joined the prosecution, which vigorously asserted popular and parental control over public education. Clarence Darrow, a famed Chicago lawyer, led a team of prominent attorneys and scientists in defense of Scopes and the concept of *academic freedom. H. L. *Mencken and many other journalists covered the trial, which was also carried live on a Chicago *radio station.

Throughout the eight-day trial (10–21 July 1925), Bryan and Darrow sparred over the validity of evolutionary science and revealed *religion. The jury convicted Scopes, but not before Darrow exposed Bryan to ridicule as an "expert witness" on the *Bible. Bryan died a week later, and the crusade against Darwinism gradually lost momentum over the next few years. In 1927, the Tennessee Supreme Court reversed Scopes' conviction on a technicality but upheld the law. Several southern states adopted similar restrictions, though none was enforced in court.

Although the Scopes trial had little impact on popular religious or scientific beliefs, it passed into folklore as a object lesson in the danger of intolerance in a democratic society. The defense theory of individual freedom and strict separation of *church and state was later adopted by the U.S. *Supreme Court in a series of decisions, most notably *McCollum* v. *Board of Education* (1948), barring public-school religious instruction; *Abington Township School District* v. *Schempp* (1963), against officially sponsored prayer in public schools; and *Epperson* v. *Arkansas* (1968), overturning a state statute based on the Tennessee antievolution law.

[*See also* Evolution, Theory of; Fundamentalist Movement; Journalism; Modernist Culture; Science: Revolutionary War to World War I; Science: From 1914 to 1945; Science: Science and Religion; Secularization; South, The; Twenties, The.]

• Edward J. Larson, *Summer of the Gods,* 1997. Ronald L. Numbers, *Darwinism Comes to America,* 1998.

—Edward J. Larson

SCOTTSBORO CASE. The Scottsboro Case, a cause célèbre in modern American race relations, began in April of 1931 with a brawl between whites and blacks riding a freight train through northern Alabama. When Jackson County officials stopped the train near Scottsboro, two white women—Victoria Price and Ruby Bates—accused nine black teenagers of raping them.

A Scottsboro jury quickly convicted eight of the nine boys and sentenced them to death. The U.S. *Communist party took up the case, mobilizing mass protests across America and in Europe and mounting an appeal to the U.S. *Supreme Court. In *Powell* v. *Alabama* (1932), the Supreme Court ordered a new trial on the grounds that defendants in capital cases were entitled to more than a pro forma defense. (The two attorneys for the nine youths had been given less than thirty minutes to prepare their case; one was drunk, the other senile).

In a 1933 retrial, Ruby Bates recanted her accusation, and new evidence strongly contradicted Victoria Price. The jury nevertheless convicted. When the presiding judge James Edwin Horton ordered yet another trial, state officials removed him from the case, found a more amenable judge, and pushed through convictions and death sentences for two defendants, Haywood Patterson and Clarence Morris.

In *Norris* v. *Alabama* (1934), the Supreme Court ruled that the two defendants had been denied a fair trial because of Alabama's systematic exclusion of *African Americans from its jury rolls. In 1937, with the Communist party no longer in the case, the defense attorney Samuel Leibowitz brokered a deal whereby four of the defendants were released and state prosecutors tacitly promised that the others would be paroled once publicity had died down. Not for thirteen years, however, did Alabama release the last of the Scottsboro defendants.

[*See also* New Deal Era, The; Racism; Rape; Segregation, Racial; South, The.]

• Dan T. Carter, *Scottsboro: A Tragedy of the American South,* rev. ed., 1979. James Goodman, *Stories of Scottsboro,* 1994.

—Dan T. Carter

SCOTT* v. *SANDFORD (1857). In the 1830s, Dr. John Emerson took his slave, Dred Scott, to the free state of Illinois and then to Fort Snelling, in Wisconsin territory (now Minnesota), where the *Missouri Compromise had prohibited *slavery. In 1846, Scott sued Emerson's widow to gain his freedom. A Missouri court freed him in 1850, ruling that he had become free while living in Illinois and at Fort Snelling. This decision conformed to a long line of earlier cases in Missouri, other states, and England. In 1852 the Missouri Supreme Court reversed the lower court, and in 1854 Scott took his case to the federal courts, suing his new owner, John Sanford (the name is misspelled "Sandford" in the official report of the case), under the clause in Article 3, Section 2 of the U.S. *Constitution that allows a citizen of one state to sue a citizen of another state in federal court. As a "citizen of Missouri," Scott argued, he could sue Sanford, a New Yorker, in federal court. In opposing this suit, Sanford rejected Scott's claim to citizenship, "because he is a negro of African descent; his ancestors were of pure African blood, and were brought into this country and sold as negro slaves."

Federal district judge Robert W. Wells ruled that if Scott were free he could sue as a citizen of Missouri. However, on the merits of the case, Wells held that Scott was still a slave. Scott then appealed to the U.S. *Supreme Court, where, in an aggressively proslavery majority opinion, Chief Justice Roger B. *Taney held that the Missouri Compromise was unconstitutional because it deprived southerners of their property in slaves without due process of law or just compensation, in violation of the Fifth Amendment. Taney also denied that *African Americans could ever be U.S. citizens. Ignoring that free black men in a number of states could vote when the Constitution was ratified, Taney declared that blacks were not included under the word "citizens" in the Constitution. According to him, blacks were "so far inferior, that they had no rights which the white man was bound to respect."

This decision shocked many northerners, who had long seen the Missouri Compromise as a barrier against the expansion of slavery and a means of accommodating sectional differences. Abraham *Lincoln attacked it in his 1858 debates with Stephen A. *Douglas and again during the 1860 presidential campaign.

The Lincoln administration and the *Civil War Congress ignored the Dred Scott decision. During the war, Congress banned slavery in the western territories, and the *Fourteenth Amendment, ratified in 1868, declared all native-born persons citizens of the United States and of the state in which they lived.

[*See also* Antislavery; Bill of Rights; Civil Rights; Civil Rights Legislation; Civil War: Causes; Lincoln-Douglas Debates; Race, Concept of; Racism.]

• Don E. Fehrenbacher, *The Dred Scott Case: Its Significance in American Law and Politics*, 1978. Paul Finkelman, Scott *v.* Sandford: *A Brief History with Documents*, 1997.

—Paul Finkelman

SCOUTING. Scouting, the world's largest movement for boys and girls, exists in more than 180 countries, Scouting began in Great Britain, founded in 1908 by the military officer Robert Baden-Powell, the author of several books on methods of training army scouts. After gaining fame in the Boer War, Baden-Powell had become a popular speaker to various youth groups such as the YMCA. This experience led him to adapt one of his military manuals into *Scouting for Boys* (1908), a handbook for a new youth organization he called the Boy Scouts. The movement stressed military skills, leadership, respect for nature, and adherence to democratic values. Scouting quickly spread. The Boy Scouts of America (BSA) was founded in 1910 by a diverse group of reformers. Heavily influenced by the Progressive movement, the BSA placed greater emphasis on religious values than on military skills.

Juliette Gordon Low (1860–1927), a wealthy Georgia socialite and close friend of Baden-Powell, founded the Girl Scouts of America (GSA) in 1912. Girl scouting was initially quite controversial, as it encouraged girls to engage in military-style training, sports, and other activities some deemed inappropriate. For years, the BSA tried to prevent the GSA from using the name "scout," arguing that it undermined their movement by "feminizing" scouting.

During *World War I, scouts engaged in a wide variety of volunteer activities to aid the Allied war effort. After the war the movement shifted away from militarism to stress character development and unity among young people of different nations. This focus continues, encouraged by international scouting events and an emphasis on sisterhood and brotherhood across cultures. In the United States, more than 130 million people have been scouts.

[*See also* Child Rearing; Life Stages; Progressive Era; YMCA and YWCA.]

• Charles E. Strickland, "Juliette Low, the Girl Scouts, and the Role of American Women," in *Women's Being, Women's Place*, ed. Mary Kelley, 1979, pp. 252–64. Michael Rosenthal, *The Character Factory: Baden-Powell and the Origins of the Boy Scout Movement*, 1984.

—M. Langley Biegert

SCULPTURE. During the *Colonial Era, untrained artisans carved gravestones, ship figureheads, and furniture. William Rush (1756–1833) represents the culmination of the wood-carving tradition with his ship figureheads and outdoor public sculpture such as *Water Nymph and Bittern* (1809), once located in a *Philadelphia town square.

Sculpture emerged as a profession during the 1820s as Americans traveled to Florence or Rome to study ancient prototypes, hire stonecutters, and purchase marble. Horatio Greenough (1805–1852), Thomas Crawford (1813–1857), and Hiram Powers (1805–1873) carved idealized stone busts; allegorical, historical, and literary parlor statues; and full-length portraits of national heroes such as George *Washington, Benjamin *Franklin, and Thomas *Jefferson. Powers's *The Greek Slave* (1842–1847), the first female nude to be accepted by the American public, achieved renown at home and abroad. Receiving federal patronage, Greenough and Crawford created works for the U.S. Capitol that promoted the nation's *Manifest Destiny and the subjugation of the Native Americans.

Other U.S. artists lived and worked in Italy, rendering idealized, neoclassical marble works with clear contours and smooth, polished surfaces. Of a notable group of women sculptors, Edmonia Lewis (ca.1843–after 1909), half Chippewa and half *African American, drew upon her dual heritage, creating images of Hiawatha and the emancipation of slaves, while Harriet Hosmer (1830–1908) rendered heroic captive women. William Wetmore Story (1819–1895), Benjamin Paul Akers (1825–1861), and William Rinehart (1825–1874) also opened studios in Italy, where they sold their neoclassical marble statuary to American and European patrons. Some Americans, such as Erastus Dow Palmer (1817–1904), stayed home to create idealized marble statues of national themes such as *Indian Girl: or, The Dawn of Christianity* (1853–1856).

After the *Civil War, most American sculptors studied at the École des Beaux Arts and in independent ateliers in Paris where they learned to create more realistic bronze statues with individualized facial expressions, rich modeling, and lively surface textures. At the same time, sculpture became an organized and respected profession of fine artists who formed new organizations such as the National Sculpture Society. Augustus Saint-Gaudens (1848–1907), Daniel Chester French (1850–1931), and Frederick MacMonnies (1863–1937) combined portraiture and allegory as well as realism to create civic monuments as part of the *Progressive Era City Beautiful movement. They collaborated with architects to complete elaborate, harmonious buildings (such as the U.S. Customs House in *New York City, 1900–1907), expositions such as the 1893 World's Columbian Exposition in *Chicago, and public portrait monuments such as Saint-Gaudens's bas-relief memorial to the Civil War hero Robert Gould Shaw on the *Boston Common (1884–1896) and French's monumental seated Abraham *Lincoln for the *Lincoln Memorial in *Washington, D.C. (dedicated 1917). Supported by wealthy patrons seeking to promote patriotism, cosmopolitanism, and aesthetic taste, and to evoke Italian Renaissance culture, *Gilded Age sculptors and architects joined forces to create opulent, artistically unified public spaces.

Despite the emergence of modernism in Europe and its introduction to the United States through the 1913 *Armory Show and the photographer Alfred *Stieglitz's "291" gallery, American sculpture remained conservative during the first half of the twentieth century. Paul Manship (1885–1966), William Zorach (1887–1966), Elie Nadelman (1882–1946), and Hugo Robus (1885–1966) rendered figurative and narrative works in a stylized and simplified manner. Only a few artists, such as Alexander *Calder and Joseph Cornell (1903–1973), experimented with new types of sculptural forms.

After *World War II, formalist and conceptual considerations brought major changes to sculpture in the United States. David Smith (1906–1965), Theodore Roszak (1907–1981), Louise Nevelson (1899–1988), and Isamu Noguchi (1904–1988) challenged traditional notions of sculpture, sometimes creating abstract and nonfigurative works that often eliminated the base; the patriotic, narrative, and allegorical themes; and the expectation that the work should be viewed from all sides. From the 1960s to the end of the century, artists created even more non-traditional sculpture, experimenting with medium (from earth to the human figure), subject matter and content, form (abstract, realistic, hyper-realistic), setting, and scale. The range of styles was extensive (pop art, minimal art, light sculpture, assemblage, earthworks, performance, and new realism), as a host of artists created their own unique form of sculpture. These included Christo (1935–), Robert Smithson (1938–1973), Donald Judd (1928–1994), Claes Oldenburg (1929–), Sol LeWitt (1928–), Edward Keinholz (1927–1994), Duane Hanson (1925–), Robert Morris (1931–), and Vito Acconci (1940–). Artists also challenged the distinction between *painting and sculpture and between *architecture and sculpture, creating controversial works for public spaces such as Maya Lin's **Vietnam Veterans Memorial* (1981) in Washington, D.C., and Richard Serra's *Tilted Arc* in New York City (1981, removed 1989).

[*See also* Folk Art and Crafts; Modernist Culture; Museums: Art Museums; World's Fairs and Expositions.]

• Wayne Craven, *Sculpture in America,* 2d ed., 1984. Michele H. Bogart, *Public Sculpture and the Civic Ideal in New York City, 1890–1930,* 1989. Joy S. Kasson, *Marble Queens and Captives: Women in Nineteenth-Century American Sculpture,* 1990. Vivien Green Fryd, *Art and Empire: The Politics of Ethnicity in the U.S. Capitol 1815–1860,* 1992. Harriet F. Senie, *Contemporary Public Sculpture,* 1992. Kirk Savage, *Standing Soldiers, Kneeling Slaves: Race, War, and Monument in Nineteenth-Century America,* 1997.

—Vivien Green Fryd

SEC. *See* Economic Regulation.

SECOND AMENDMENT. *See* Bill of Rights; Gun Control.

SECRET SERVICE, U.S.. *See* Federal Government, Executive Branch: Department of the Treasury.

SECULARIZATION, the process by which church and state become separated and by which individuals gradually lose the sense of awe and mystery often associated with religious beliefs. Secularization generally occurs because forces such as *urbanization and natural *science undermine established community-based belief systems. In Europe, where royal authority and ecclesiastical power were often allied against emerging forces of rationalism and natural science, battles to secularize political power have been particularly hard fought and perennial. In America, despite the close connections between church and state in the *Colonial Era, later political battles over secularization were minor. But while political participation did not involve ecclesiastical requirements, a religious sensibility remained a lively and continuing presence in the minds of Americans.

The initial European settlers in America brought with them a God-centered vision of the world. In the *South, the *Jamestown colonists desired both financial profits and conversion of Native Americans to Christianity. In the North, John *Winthrop well captured the religious zeal of *Puritanism with his proclamation of a "city upon a Hill." The rhetoric of the *Revolutionary War retained much of a Calvinistic theology of sin and redemption. While the First Amendment to the *Constitution specifically separated church and state, the *Declaration of Independence had invoked a notion of Americans as "endowed by their Creator with certain unalienable rights."

In late eighteenth-century America, the strength of *religion seemed to be waning, as Enlightenment beliefs transformed God from a majestic, mysterious figure into a passive clockmaker who had set the universe into motion and then withdrawn. However, in the midst of secularizing forces, Americans remained intensely religious. The Second Great Awakening played a major role in *antislavery, *temperance and prohibition, and other reforms. Moreover, an impending sense of apocalypse contributed to the political stalemate that led to the *Civil War, a conflict that President Abraham *Lincoln comprehended in religious terms.

The years after the Civil War brought multiple pressures toward secularization, with massive *immigration, urbanization, *mobility, demographic changes, and *labor movements upsetting traditional beliefs. Many middle-class Americans found their belief in God compromised by Charles Darwin's theory of *evolution, advanced in *The Origin of Species* (1859), with its view of the natural order as an arena of unending chaos and struggle. Yet many Americans resisted the secularizing thrust of evolution and urbanization. Evolutionary theories that invoked the idea of God as a first cause gained popularity because they retained a sense of progress under the direction of divine power. Although the growth of cities had undermined traditional bonds of community, religious reformers attempted to reinvigorate religion in the immigrant cities through *revivalism, the *social gospel, and Progressive reform.

As immigrants from southern and eastern Europe flocked to America, the ideal of the United States as a religiously homogeneous Protestant nation became increasingly difficult to uphold. In response, many native-born Protestants reasserted traditional beliefs through politics and culture. Thus, some states banned the teaching of the theory of evolution. The rise of the *Ku Klux Klan in the 1920s was in part a reaction against the growing secularization of American society. Throughout the 1920s, however, with the power of consumerism and the mass media (*radio, *magazines, *film), Americans increasingly viewed worldly success as a matter of individual initiative, severely distanced from any religious imperatives.

For a time after *World War II, the further secularization of American society seemed assured. While large numbers of Americans professed religious belief, the depth of their conviction appeared weak. God could be referred to by an actress, in all seriousness, as "a living doll," while *cultural pluralism, in theory and practice, suggested that religion played an important social rather than spiritual role. Indeed, in *The Secular City* (1965), the theologian Harvey Cox took it for granted that America had become, once and for all, a secular culture. As he and others later realized, however, such a perception was premature. As the twentieth century ended, religion appeared to grow in strength, while secularization receded. Fundamentalist *Protestantism became central to many Americans' religious lives and political activities. The once neat division between church and state came under attack, as many religious Americans sought to return prayer to public schools. Prophetic Christianity defined the political understanding of both U.S. history and world politics for millions of Americans. A religious sensibility clearly remained vital in American culture, undermining the hypothesis that as a nation becomes more urbanized and mobile, more influenced by mass culture, and more open to the interpretive power of science, it must become more secular. But one component of secularization, the American tradition of a firm separation between church and state, while occasionally bending under pressure, did not appear to be in serious danger.

[*See also* Bill of Rights; Church and State, Separation of; Deism; Education: Rise of the University; Fundamentalist Movement; Great Awakening, First and Second; Modernist Culture; Science: Science and Religion.]

• James Turner, *Without God, without Creed: The Origins of Unbelief in America,* 1985. Paul Boyer, *When Time Shall Be No More: Prophecy Belief in Modern American Culture,* 1992. George Cotkin, *Reluctant Modernism: American Thought and Culture, 1880–1900,* 1992, pp. 1–26. Andrew Delbanco, *The Death of Satan: How Americans Lost the Sense of Evil,* 1995. Martin E. Marty, *Modern American Religion: Under God, Indivisible, 1941–1960,* vol. 3, 1996.

—George Cotkin

SECURITIES AND EXCHANGE COMMISSION. Established by the Securities Exchange Act of 1934, the Securities and Exchange Commission (SEC) was given broad authority to regulate stock exchanges, brokers, and dealers. The previous year, President Franklin Delano *Roosevelt had urged Congress to mandate "full and fair disclosure" of all new security issues, and to require sellers to provide accurate information. Meanwhile, the Senate Banking and Currency Committee, directed by chief counsel Ferdinand Pecora, uncovered evidence of fraud, corruption, and gross misrepresentation in the buying and selling of securities.

In response, Congress passed the Securities Act of 1933, requiring all companies issuing stock to file with the *Federal Trade Commission detailed information regarding their business and financial condition. Barraged with business complaints that the 1933 law was too intrusive, Congress in the 1934 measure limited the law's scope and transferred its administration to the newly created SEC. The SEC later gained additional regulatory authority through the Public Utilities Holding Company Act (1935), the Investment Companies Act (1940), the Investment Advisers Act (1940), and other measures. In 1977, the SEC mandated an end to fixed broker commissions and, in 1988, gained new authority over stock-index futures. Possessed of quasijudicial powers, the SEC's decisions can be appealed in federal court.

For many observers, the SEC epitomizes the reform spirit of the *New Deal Era and has set a standard of excellence for federal regulatory commissions. Some critics, however, insist that the agency's reliance on self-regulation has served the interests of the securities industry better than those of investors and the general public.

[*See also* Banking and Finance; Business; Business Cycle; Depressions, Economic; Economic Regulation; New York Stock Exchange; Stock Market; Stock Market Crash of 1929.]

• Michael E. Parrish, *Securities Regulation and the New Deal,* 1970. Joel Seligman, *The Transformation of Wall Street: A History of the Securities and Exchange Commission and Modern Corporate Finance,* 1982.

—John D. Buenker

SEDITION. Also known as seditious libel, this crime initially covered any "dangerous words" threatening the authority of the state, the sanctity of its laws, or the reputation of its officers. Under the interpretation of seditious libel that emerged during the seventeenth century, judges determined the "law of the case" (whether a statement or publication was seditious), permitted juries to determine only the "facts of the case" (whether the defendant has expressed the words), and disallowed evidence of truth as a defense.

During the eighteenth century, an alternative interpretation emerged. The guarantees of freedom of speech and press, critics insisted, required that juries determine the seditious nature of political statements, and that truth constitute a defense. The *Federalist party incorporated these ideas, which had emerged in the 1735 *Zenger trial, into the Sedition Act of 1798. Jeffersonians tried under this law, however, found it useless to argue either the nonseditious quality of their words or their truth to Federalist judges and juries. Although some Jeffersonian lawyers argued that the First Amendment barred any federal prosecution for sedition, the Sedition Act expired in 1801 without a *Supreme Court ruling on its validity.

Attempts to suppress dissent, especially during wartime, revived debates over the issue of sedition in the twentieth century. The 1918 Sedition Law restricted criticism of U.S. participation in *World War I. The *Smith Act (1940), passed on the eve of U.S. entry into *World War II, made it a crime to advocate or teach the desirability of violently overthrowing the government. The Supreme Court upheld these laws' constitutionality but divided over how they should be applied. The more libertarian justices, building on Justice Oliver Wendell *Holmes Jr.'s dissent in **Abrams* v. *United States* (1919), insisted that the government could criminalize political speech only if it posed a "clear and present danger" of "substantive" harm to the state. This position, suggesting that speech could not be criminalized solely on the basis of its allegedly dangerous content, remained contested, however, especially when the Court heard cases involving *Communist party members during the 1950s.

Important rulings during the next decade, however, translated the libertarian position into constitutional doctrine. In two 1964 political libel cases (*New York Times* v. *Sullivan* and *Garrison* v. *Louisiana*), the Court ruled that the Sedition Act of 1798 had violated the First Amendment's "core meaning"— "a profound national commitment to the principle that debate on public issues should be uninhibited, robust, and wide open." In *Brandenburg* v. *Ohio* (1969), the Court held that only words intended to incite or produce "imminent lawless action" could, in light of the First Amendment, be the object of criminal sanctions. These decisions effectively denied the legitimacy of prosecuting "dangerous" political discourse, the core notion in the old crime of sedition.

[*See also* Alien and Sedition Acts; Anticommunism; Bill of Rights; Censorship.]

• Harry Kalven Jr., *A Worthy Tradition: Free Speech in America,* 1988. Norman L. Rosenberg, *Protecting the Best Men: An Interpretive History of the Law of Libel,* 1990.

—Norman L. Rosenberg

SEGREGATION, RACIAL, the southern social, economic, and political system that enforced the separation of races from the post-*Reconstruction era to the mid-twentieth century. Racial segregation was also called "Jim Crow," an expression derived from the caricatured portrayal of blacks in antebellum minstrel shows. By the 1890s, however, "Jim Crow" had come to describe the segregation, social control, and political and economic subjugation of black people in the *South. Upheld by the *Supreme Court in **Plessy* v. *Ferguson* (1896) and other decisions, segregation persisted until challenged by the anticolonialist politics of *World War II and the postwar *civil rights movement.

While C. Vann Woodward's *The Strange Career of Jim Crow* (1955) launched a debate over the origins and nature of racial segregation in the South, comparative studies of segregation in South Africa and the American South by John W. Cell and George Fredericks0n linked the phenomenon to a broader white-supremacist ideology and demonstrated its variation over space and time. In America, restrictive customs and practices designed to separate the races were first devised by whites of the antebellum North in the 1840s. As historian Leon Litwack has noted, many abolitionist newspapers used the term "segregation" to describe separate facilities for blacks and whites in northern cities.

Segregation Imposed. After the *Civil War, southern whites unwilling to accept the social and political equality of freedmen adopted the practice. The earliest postwar southern legislatures passed restrictive laws to maintain the prewar racial hierarchy and secure a cheap labor force perpetually tied to the land. These so-called Black Codes were overturned as Radical Republicans took charge of Reconstruction, but in their place arose a system of *sharecropping, crop lien, disfranchisement, and violent repression. *African Americans struggled against the poverty and degradation born of tenancy and sharecropping, but as northern attitudes shifted, federal troops left, the southern *Democratic Party revived, and the *Ku Klux Klan and other racist organizations inaugurated a reign of terror, conditions very similar to *slavery took root.

Many historians hold that Jim Crow was already so firmly entrenched by custom that the rise of *de jure* segregation in the late nineteenth and early twentieth centuries merely ratified the prevailing situation. Historian Howard Rabinowitz, for example, has found that Baton Rouge, *Atlanta, Charlotte, Birmingham, and other southern cities excluded free blacks from militias, education, and welfare services in the antebellum and immediate post–Civil War eras. While radical legislators, Reconstruction officials, and black political leaders favored racially integrated facilities, fears of further antagonizing white southerners inhibited their efforts, and neither Republicans nor black legislatures proposed constitutional or legislative measures for achieving that goal. Indeed, as black churches, fraternal organizations, and mutual-aid societies proliferated, patterns of voluntary racial separation arose. Government, political, and judicial bodies were often the only integrated institutions in the Reconstruction South.

By the 1880s, however, *railroads and streetcars, involving close contact between black and white passengers, became the focus of challenges to segregation. Amid growing racial tensions, exacerbated by *urbanization and *industrialization, southern state legislatures enacted railroad separate-car laws that reshaped the region's social and political landscape. Blacks vigorously resisted. Prominent African-American business and professional leaders staged boycotts and sued railroads, insisting on equal access, but to little avail. After the U.S. Supreme Court in 1883 sharply restricted the 1875 Civil Rights Act (see **Civil Rights Cases*) and sanctioned the separate-but-equal doctrine in *Plessy* v. *Ferguson*, a torrent of segregation laws increasingly regulated all black-white contact throughout the South, banning or sharply restricting black access to public and private facilities including schools, theaters, hotels, parks, libraries, and the like. Simultaneously, employers and labor leaders blocked blacks' access to skilled jobs, limiting them to unskilled, semiskilled, or domestic occupations.

The spread of segregation and deteriorating race relations in the 1890s arose from southern white fears of racial mixing and miscegnation and from a desire to curb black aspirations for education and property. It coincided with an epidemic of *lynchings; antiblack riots in Atlanta, New Orleans, East St. Louis, Tulsa, and other cities; discrimination against black soldiers, as in the *Brownsville incident; and the propagation of racist ideas by politicians like Benjamin Tillman, James K. Vardaman, and Thomas Watson, and writers such as Thomas Nelson Page and Thomas Dixon, whose 1905 novel *The Clansman* inspired D. W. *Griffith's racist movie *The Birth of a Nation.* The legal imposition of strict racial segregation was also paralleled by a campaign of black disfranchisement through intimidation and terror; state constitutional amendments (in Mississippi, South Carolina, and Georgia); and poll taxes, literacy tests, property and residency requirements, and other devices intended to circumvent the *Fifteenth Amendment.

Segregation Challenged. Black southerners responded to these developments in a variety of ways. Some embraced Booker T. *Washington's strategy of conciliation, racial uplift, and group solidarity. Others, such as Ida B. *Wells-Barnett and W. E. B. *Du Bois, advocated militant challenges to the racist assumptions underpinning segregation. Still others, like Bishop Henry M. Turner (1834–1915) of the African Methodist Episcopal Church, West African chief Alfred Sam, and Marcus *Garvey, stressed racial solidarity, ethnic pride, and emigration to Africa. While novelists from Charles Chesnutt (1858–1932) to Langston *Hughes, Zora Neale *Hurston, and Richard *Wright, along with a host of African-American *ragtime, *blues, and *jazz musicians, implicitly challenged segregation by underscoring African Americans' cultural contribution to the nation as a whole, millions of southern blacks voted with their feet by moving north.

Amid black migration northward, the growing importance of the black vote, and the rising political awareness of African peoples worldwide in the 1920s and 1930s, African Americans fashioned a viable critique of the South's white-supremacist and segregationist ideology. The international and domestic politics developed from this transformed perspective underlay the Supreme Court's landmark 1954 **Brown* v. *Board of Education* decision outlawing racial segregation in public schools, and fueled the black freedom struggles of the 1950s and 1960s. By 1965 racial segregation had been all but dismantled throughout the South. The promise of economic, social, and political *equality in the region—and the nation—however, has yet to be fulfilled.

[*See also* African American Religion; Antislavery; Civil Rights; Civil Rights Movement; Gilded Age; King, Martin Luther Jr.; Minstrelsy; National Association for the Advancement of Colored People; New Deal Era, The; Progressive Era; Race and Ethnicity; Race, Concept of; Racism; Randolph, A. Phillip; Scottsboro Case; Southern Christian Leadership Conference; Student Nonviolent Coordinating Committee; Trotter, William Monroe; Twenties, The.]

• C. Vann Woodward, *The Strange Career of Jim Crow,* 3d ed., 1955; rep. 1974. Lawrence W. Levine, *Black Culture and Black Consciousness: Afro-American Folk Thought from Slavery to Freedom,* 1977. Howard N. Rabinowitz, *Race Relations in the Urban South, 1865–1980,* 1978. John W. Cell, *The Highest Stage of White Supremacy: The Origins of Segregation in South Africa and the American South,* 1982. William Fitzhugh Brundage, *Lynching in the New South: Georgia and Virginia, 1880–1930,* 1993. Leon F. Litwack, *Trouble in Mind: Black Southerners in the Age of Jim Crow,* 1998. Deborah Gray White, *Too Heavy a Load: Black Women in Defense of Themselves, 1894–1994,* 2000.

—Robert F. Jefferson

SELECTIVE SERVICE. *See* Conscription.

SEMINOLE WARS, three wars that extended from 1817 to 1858 and pitted U.S. forces against first the Spanish and then the Seminole Indians of Florida. The major causes were white lust for land and the gap between Indian and white cultures. The escape of African slaves into Florida was also a prime cause of the first and second wars.

The First Seminole War began in November 1817. Charging that Spain was unable to control the Indians, President James *Monroe ordered Major General Andrew *Jackson to invade Spanish Florida along the Apalachicola River; Monroe understood that given the opportunity, Jackson would seize Florida. After destroying the Indian settlements west of the Suwannee River, Jackson occupied Spain's two settlements in West Florida, St. Marks and Pensacola. When Pensacola surrendered on 24 May 1818, Jackson withdrew. In the *Adams-Onís Treaty (1821), Spain transferred Florida to the United States. Having assumed sovereignty over some five thousand Indians, called Seminoles, the U.S. government prepared to transfer them west of the *Mississippi River.

The Seminoles were a loose association of disparate bands, including Creek from Georgia, local Apalachee, and runaway black slaves. As white settlers crowded in, Osceola, part white and not a hereditary chief, assumed leadership and rallied the Seminoles against the government's resettlement plans. On 28 December 1835, Osceola shot the U.S. government's Indian agent at Fort King, while another party of Seminoles killed 108 U.S. soldiers marching to relieve the fort. Thus began the second Seminole War (1835–1842). For nine months, the Indians confined the whites of North Florida to three strong points. But then increasing U.S. military power, coupled with Osceola's illness, reversed the Seminoles' dominance.

The first three U.S. generals, especially Winfield Scott, employed conventional military strategy, but it failed in the swampy wilderness. Major General Thomas Jesup, however, initiated a strategy of seizing the war leaders. Most notorious was his capture of Osceola under a flag of truce on 27 October 1837. Indian leadership now passed to Wildcat, Alligator, Jumper, Halleck Tustenuggee, Billy Bowlegs, and Sam Jones.

On Christmas Day 1837, Colonel Zachary *Taylor positioned 800 U.S. soldiers on the north shore of Lake Okeechobee, held by three bands of Seminoles. At a cost of 26 U.S. soldiers killed and 112 wounded, Taylor's force drove the Indians away. Indian casualties were 11 killed and 14 wounded.

In March 1838, Jesup further diluted Seminole strength by promising freedom to all escaped slaves who would change sides. The last two U.S. generals in the Second Seminole War sent detachments of 20 to 40 soldiers, guided by blacks or captive Seminoles, to search and destroy hidden Seminole camps and fields. Deprived of essentials, ragged and hungry bands of

Indians surrendered. In all, 3,428 were shipped west. The 200 to 400 who remained withdrew south of the Caloosahatchee River and Lake Okeechobee. In August 1842, Brigadier General William J. Worth ended hostilities.

In the 1850s, U.S. soldiers and surveyors pushed south of the Caloosahatchee. On 20 December 1855, these incursions induced Billy Bowlegs to attack a U.S. military camp. Thus began the Third Seminole War. By 1858, facing the same search-and-destroy tactics that had ended the second war, Chief Bowlegs considered further struggle futile. After paying $44,000 to the departing Indians, U.S. officials on 8 May 1858 shipped Bowlegs and 165 followers to the West. Left behind were only 120 Seminoles.

[*See also* Expansionism; Indian History and Culture: From 1800 to 1900; Indian Wars; Slavery; Slave Uprisings and Resistance; Spanish Settlements in North America.]

• John K. Mahon, *History of the Second Seminole War,* 1967. Virginia Peters, *The Florida Wars,* 1979. James W. Covington, *The Seminoles of Florida,* 1993.

—John K. Mahon

SENATE. *See* Federal Government, Legislative Branch: Senate.

SENECA FALLS CONVENTION, 19–20 July 1848. The first meeting on behalf of *women's rights in U.S. history, the Seneca Falls Convention inaugurated a movement that led to the constitutional enfranchisement of women in 1920. The chief figure was Elizabeth Cady *Stanton, a mother of four living in this upstate New York industrial city. She was aided by Lucretia *Mott, the nation's foremost woman abolitionist. The two had met eight years before, at the World's Antislavery Convention in London, where Mott began to share with Stanton, an apt pupil, her Quaker-based convictions about the equality of the sexes. The public expression of their partnership waited eight years because of Stanton's domestic obligations, but 1848 was also a year of international political upheaval and revolutionary inspiration. One hundred people, two-thirds of them women, and almost all Quakers, attended the convention.

The convention's chief activity was discussion of a Declaration of Sentiments, Grievances and Resolutions. The preamble, written by Stanton, was modeled on that of the *Declaration of Independence: "We hold these truths to be self-evident: that all men and women are created equal." The Declaration went on to indict the long "history of repeated injuries and usurpations on the part of man toward women." Specific grievances began with man's denial to woman of "the inalienable right to the elective franchise"; went on to the disabilities that law and custom imposed on wives by regarding them as the property of their husbands; and further encompassed woman's exclusion from higher education, trades, and professions, church authority and moral responsibility, and indeed from all that would build "faith in her own powers." Of the thirteen resolutions, only the ninth, proclaiming "the duty of the women of this country to secure to themselves their sacred right of franchise," proved controversial at the meeting, both because politics was customarily seen as exclusively masculine and because many of the Quaker, abolitionist members of the convention considered moral suasion superior to the corruption of politics. But Stanton's defense of the franchise demand, supported by the African-American leader Frederick *Douglass, carried the day, and the resolution passed. Two weeks later, a second session of the convention, held in Douglass's hometown of Rochester, New York, focused on the grievances of working women. Newspaper coverage was widespread but uniformly satirical and disrespectful. Beginning in 1850, national women's rights conventions were held annually, and a generation of female reformers began the complex task of undoing the engrained legal bias against women's autonomy and establishing sexual equality.

[*See also* Antebellum Era; Anthony, Susan B.; Antislavery; Feminism; Gender; Woman Suffrage Movement.]

• Ellen Carol DuBois, *Feminism and Suffrage: The Emergence of an Independent Women's Movement in the U.S., 1848–1869,* 1978.

—Ellen C. DuBois

SEPARATION OF CHURCH AND STATE. *See* Church and State, Separation of.

SEQUOYAH (ca. 1770–1843), Cherokee leader, inventor of the Cherokee syllabary. Sequoyah, also known as George Guess (or Gist), was born in the Cherokee Nation in Tennessee to an English father and a Cherokee mother. He later lived in the Cherokee country in Georgia. A hunter, fur trader, warrior, and silversmith Sequoyah around 1809 began work on a Cherokee alphabet. He recognized that a written language enabled Euro-Americans to preserve and communicate information over great distances and believed that it would provide the Cherokees with the same capabilities and instill in them a renewed sense of power and self-expression. After considerable effort, Sequoyah concluded that a Cherokee alphabet would require over a thousand pictographs and be extremely difficult to learn. He then shifted his efforts to devising a syllabary, a system in which the syllables of a spoken language are represented by phonetic symbols. After over a decade of work, Sequoyah settled on a syllabary of eighty-six characters. In 1821, he demonstrated his invention before the Cherokee national council by exchanging written messages with his young daughter.

Within a few years, most Cherokees had become literate in their own language. The Cherokees recorded their laws and constitution and translated the *Bible and numerous other works into Cherokee. In 1828, the Cherokees began publishing a weekly newspaper, the *Cherokee Phoenix and Indian Advocate,* in both Cherokee and English. (Sequoyah himself never learned English.) Sequoyah later supplemented the syllabary with a Cherokee numerical system. Because of his invention, Sequoyah became an influential leader and diplomat for the Cherokee nation. He accompanied his people on their forced removal to the trans-Mississippi West in 1838.

[*See also* Cherokee Cases; Indian History and Culture: From 1800 to 1900; Indian Removal Act; Literacy.]

• Jack F. Kilpatrick and Anna Gritts Kilpatrick, eds., *New Echota Letters,* 1968. Grant Forman, *Sequoyah,* 1938; 7th printing, Civilization of the American Indian series, vol. 16, 1984.

—Tim Alan Garrison

SERRA, JUNIPERO (1713–1784), Franciscan missionary, founder of *California missions. Born in Majorca, he sailed for America in 1749 and arrived in Mexico City in 1750. Beginning in 1769, he established a system of nine missions between San Diego and *San Francisco. They were San Diego De Acala (1769), San Carlos Borromeo De Carmelo (1770), San Antonio De Padua (1771), San Gabriel Arcangel (1771), San Luis Obispo De Tolosa (1772), San Francisco De Asis (1776), San Juan Capistrano (1776), Santa Clara De Asis (1777), and San Buenaventura (1782). These missions played a pivotal role in the West Coast's formative history. Serra also assisted in founding four presidios (military garrisons) and two pueblos.

Indians from at least six linguistic stocks were gathered into the missions. More than 6,000 were baptized and 5,276 confirmed. Junipero Serra professed love for the Indians; understood their customs and manners; and defended their interests on such issues as the rightful payment for labor, proper punishment (if any), and the sharing of supplies. This involved him in conflicts with the Spanish military authorities, one of whom, Don Felipe de Neve, military commander of Alta California, found him "arrogant" and "obstinate."

All, however, acknowledged his tireless devotion to the

cause. "What good is a man's life," he once asked, "if he doesn't bring miracles to this earth for his brothers?" Junipero Serra was beatified for sainthood by Pope John Paul II in 1984, at his grave in the sanctuary of Mission San Carlos Borromeo in Carmel, California.

[*See also* Colonial Era; Indian History and Culture: From 1500 to 1800; Religion; Roman Catholicism; Spanish Settlements in North America.]

• Maynard Joseph Geiger, trans., *Palóu's Life of Fray Junipero Serra* [1787], 1955. Maynard Joseph Geiger, *The Life and Times of Fray Junipero Serra, O.F.M.*, vols. 1–2, 1959. Jacinto Fernandez, *Summarium, Patris Juniperi Serra,* 1984.

—Don De Nevi

SERVICEMEN'S READJUSTMENT ACT (1944). In 1944, during the height of *World War II, President Franklin Delano *Roosevelt signed the Servicemen's Readjustment Act, designed to enhance the future of the more than sixteen million men and women who served in the armed forces. The *American Legion had drafted the legislation and lobbied for its passage, calling it "a bill of rights for G.I. Joe and G.I. Jane." The "G.I. Bill of Rights," or "G.I. Bill," as it is commonly known, authorized payments for tuition, books, and living expenses for up to four years of college or vocational school, low-interest mortgages for homeowners, loans for veterans to buy farms and start businesses, and a "readjustment allowance" of twenty dollars per week while veterans sought employment.

In important ways, the G.I. Bill shaped the economic and social history of postwar America. Over one million veterans enrolled in colleges in 1946—half of that year's total enrollment. By 1956, almost ten million men and women had benefited from the law's educational and training provisions. Colleges often made places for male veterans by turning away qualified women, however. Furthermore, almost four million veterans received *Veterans Administration loans for houses, spurring the *suburbanization process, the postwar baby boom, and record demand for goods and services. The importance of the G.I. Bill lies not only in its immediate economic and social impact, but also in the fact that its provisions were later extended to millions of veterans of other conflicts, including the *Korean and *Vietnam Wars.

[See also Education: Collegiate Education; Education: The Rise of the University; Fifties, The; Housing; World War II: Domestic Effects.]

• Keith W. Olson, *The G.I. Bill, the Veterans, and the Colleges,* 1974. Michael J. Bennett, *When Dreams Came True: The GI Bill and the Making of Modern America,* 1996.

—William M. Tuttle Jr.

SETON, MOTHER ELIZABETH ANN (1774–1821), founder of the Sisters of Charity in the United States, educator, first American-born citizen to be canonized as a saint by the Roman Catholic church. Born in *New York City, Seton was the daughter of Richard Bayley, a physician, and his wife, Catherine Charlton, a daughter of the rector of Saint Andrew's Episcopal Church on Staten Island. Married at age twenty to the New York merchant William Magee Seton, she bore five children before being widowed in 1803. The death of her husband and her conversion to *Roman Catholicism in 1805 precipitated both her estrangement from her family and her dedication to charitable work among the immigrant poor. She opened her first school in her New York home as a means of supporting herself and her children and reestablished it in Emmitsburg, Maryland, in 1809 at the invitation of Archbishop John Carroll. Her holiness soon attracted women desirous of living and working with her. Accepting responsibility for leading the women, she adapted the European Daughters of Charity rule to suit their needs. The tuition-free day school, conducted in conjunction with a residential academy, set the pattern for the parochial school system that grew rapidly as other religious orders responded to the needs of a growing Catholic population. Within a few years of her death from *tuberculosis, her Sisters of Charity undertook the direction of Catholic hospitals, thereby forming the nucleus of the Catholic health-care system. She was canonized by Pope Paul VI in 1975.

[*See also* Immigration; Poverty; Religion.]

• Annabelle M. Melville, *Elizabeth Bayley Seton, 1774–1821,* 1951. Annabelle M. Melville and Ellin M. Kelly, eds., *Elizabeth Seton: Selected Writings,* 1984.

—Karen M. Kennelly

SETTLEMENT HOUSES. By the 1880s, rapid *urbanization, *immigration, and unregulated industrial *capitalism had produced deplorable living and working conditions in America's cities, but pro-business legislatures and a tradition of limited government retarded the regulation of conditions affecting workers' health and safety. Impelled partly by Christian *socialism's vision of class harmony and partly by a search for more authentic experience (which they romantically ascribed to the poor), a generation of young activists moved into the *slums to take reform into their own hands. Building on English precedents, they formed small colonies or "settlements" amid the people they sought to help. The best known of the settlement houses, which by 1900 numbered in the hundreds, were Hull House in *Chicago, founded by Jane *Addams in 1889; Henry Street in *New York City (Lillian Wald, 1893); and university settlements such as College Settlement in *Philadelphia (1893). The settlement movement remained loosely organized even after the National Federation of Settlements, headed by Jane Addams, was founded in 1911. Settlement-type institutions proliferated in all regions, some resembling religious missions (both Catholic and Protestant), others community centers. *African Americans, often excluded from white-dominated settlement houses, sometimes established separate houses.

Exemplifying the contradictions of early twentieth-century reform, the settlements combined empirical social-scientific research and moral uplift. Residents conducted research, producing social surveys such as *Hull House Maps and Papers* (1895) that formed the basis for campaigns against *prostitution, sweatshops, environmental hazards, and *child labor. Settlements were also social-service agencies whose residents ran well-baby clinics, day nurseries, pure milk stations, and playgrounds. They offered immigrants classes in English and citizenship as well as vocational subjects. The settlement served as a common ground for immigrants, and settlement workers lauded immigrants' contributions to American culture and defended them against nativist attacks. At the same time, they encouraged immigrants to adapt to American society and tended to regard ethnic and cultural differences as picturesque but archaic.

The settlement houses attracted middle-class female college graduates who preferred a period of useful volunteer work in the slums to the customary return to the parental household to await marriage. Intellectuals like Addams or Florence *Kelley who became long-term residents created what scholars see as a new kind of social space that connected the public associational life of policy-making with the private realms of love and family.

The settlements have fascinated historians for a variety of reasons. For some, the settlements facilitated the fashioning of modern selves by a new intellectual elite who believed that authentic experience could be found among the poor. Others have depicted settlements as "spearheads for reform" that initiated a range of Progressive legislation as settlement residents lobbied legislatures and drew on their close personal observation to publicize conditions in urban immigrant wards. As neighborhood associations, settlements may have been less important overall than community-based ethnic organizations, but as conduits to government and the media they helped shape American perceptions of the urban-immigrant poor for a generation. The *Progressive Era's enactment of mothers' pensions, protective labor legislation, and municipal reform was largely owing to their effort.

Feminist historians have recognized in the settlements the institutional basis for a distinctive women's culture. Residents explored new possibilities of working and living collectively as professionals and friends, demonstrated new roles for female social experts, and brought the influence of organized women into national politics as "social housekeepers." However, the feminist lives of settlement pioneers like Addams contradicted the settlement houses' teaching of "maternalist" family values and male breadwinner ideology. Viewed in a context of modernization broadly defined, settlements were the cutting edge of a Progressivism whose pursuit of efficiency and uplift could have unexpected consequences, including new uses of expertise.

Settlements lost their distinctiveness after *World War I, becoming part of a broader network of community agencies and social-work federations, and joining business Progressives in campaigns for *public health and the *Americanization of immigrants. Residency by a community of volunteers, the settlements' hallmark, gradually faded. By 1945, facing pressure to become more representative of their neighborhoods, settlements added community residents to their boards. Racially segregated settlements, created in the North at the time of heavy black migration to northern cities, were reintegrated. The National Federation of Settlements became the United Neighborhood Centers of America in 1979.

As the twentieth century ended, settlement houses continued to serve poor neighborhoods in America's major cities; in 1996, thirty-eight existed in New York City alone. Meanwhile, knowledge of the early settlements continued to grow as their papers became available to scholars.

[*See also* Cultural Pluralism; Feminism; Gilded Age; Nativist Movement; Poverty; Race and Ethnicity; Segregation, Racial; Social Class; Social Science; Social Work; Volunteerism.]

• Allen F. Davis, *Spearheads for Reform: The Social Settlements and the Progressive Movement,* 2d ed., 1984. John P. Rousmaniere, "Cultural Hybrid in the Slums: The College Woman and the Settlement House, 1889–1894," *American Quarterly* 22 (Spring 1970): 45–66. Judith Ann Trolander, *Professionalism and Social Change: From the Settlement Movement to Neighborhood Centers, 1886 to the Present,* 1987. Mina Carson, *Settlement Folk: Social Thought and the American Settlement Movement, 1885–1930,* 1990. Ruth Crocker, *Social Work and Social Order: The Settlement Movement in Two Industrial Cities, 1889–1930,* 1992. Elisabeth Lasch-Quinn, *Black Neighbors: Race and the Limits of Reform in the American Settlement House Movement, 1890–1945,* 1993.

—Ruth Crocker

SEVENTH-DAY ADVENTISM. Emerging from the prophetic interpretations of William Miller (1782–1849) about the second coming of Christ, Adventism coalesced around three beliefs during the late 1840s. First, the "sanctuary" doctrine of Hiram Edson held that on 22 October 1844, when Millerites had expected Christ's return to earth, Christ instead had entered the second apartment of the heavenly sanctuary (Hebrews 9) to begin determining the final fate of all human beings. Second, Joseph Bates promoted Saturday as the true Sabbath (Exodus 20: 8–10). Third, Ellen G. White (1827–1915) began experiencing "visions" regarded by her followers as resulting from the "spirit of prophecy" (Revelation 19:10). Sabbatarian Adventists also denied the immortality of the soul and practiced baptism by immersion. In 1850, Ellen White's husband, James, launched the *Advent Review and Sabbath Herald,* and in 1863, in Battle Creek, Michigan, the Whites led in organizing the General Conference of Seventh-day Adventists, with 3,500 members. In 1876 the church adopted tithing, which required members to contribute a tenth of their income, as its primary means of economic support.

After the *Civil War, Adventism expanded across the United States, flourishing especially in the *West. In 1874 the church sent John Nevins Andrews to Europe as its missionary. Meanwhile, Ellen White had begun advocating vegetarianism and drugless medicine. The Battle Creek Sanitarium established in 1866 as the first of many Adventist medical institutions, achieved prominence under the leadership of John Harvey Kellogg (1852–1943), promoter of flaked breakfast cereals. Beginning with Battle Creek College (established 1874), the Adventists created an extensive school system. Opposed to bearing arms in wartime, the church achieved noncombatant status for its draftees during *World War II. One of its most influential members, George McCready Price (1870–1963), laid the foundations of the modern creationist movement.

By the close of the twentieth century, over 900,000 Adventists were living in the United States, but most growth in America was occurring among ethnic minorities. The overwhelming majority of the more than 8 million Adventists in the world resided in Latin America, Africa, and Asia.

[*See also* Antebellum Era; Bible, The; Millennialism and Apocalypticism; Protestantism; Religion.]

• Gary Land, ed., *Adventism in America: A History,* 1986. Malcolm Bull and Keith Lockhart, *Seeking a Sanctuary: Seventh-day Adventism and the American Dream,* 1989.

—Gary Land

SEVEN YEARS' WAR (1756–1763). Whereas all previous *imperial wars had erupted in Europe, Anglo-French contention over the North American Ohio Country triggered the Seven Years' War. In 1754, Virginia dispatched an army under Lieutenant Colonel George *Washington to construct a fort at the head of the Ohio River (present-day Pittsburgh, Pennsylvania). Simultaneously, a larger French force marched south on a similar mission. Hostilities commenced when the Virginians encountered a small party of French troops about forty miles south of the river. Washington ordered an attack that resulted in the death of ten French soldiers.

Great Britain quickly committed two regiments to America. Its initial object was to compel France to withdraw from frontier territories that London claimed. Several southern colonies raised armies to assist the regulars west of the Appalachians, while some northern colonies recruited armies to strike at French installations in the Champlain Valley and along the boundary separating New France and Anglo-America.

In 1755 the British succeeded only in Nova Scotia, after which they loaded more than six thousand Acadian, or French, inhabitants onto ships, confiscated their property, and removed them to scattered locations elsewhere in the thirteen colonies. (Some later moved to French Louisiana, where their descendants were called Cajuns.) Otherwise, Governor William Shirley of Massachusetts failed to take Fort Niagara, the gateway to the St. Lawrence River, and Colonel William Johnson's army of colonists and Indians suffered heavy losses attempting to reach Fort St. Frédéric at Crown Point, New York. First ambushed south of Lake George, in an engagement known as Bloody Morning Scout, then attacked by the French at the partially constructed Fort William Henry, Johnson retreated after losing about 20 percent of his men.

Meanwhile, the regulars under General Edward Braddock, joined by nearly six hundred men from Virginia, Maryland, and North Carolina, lumbered west. The Anglo-American force had penetrated to within ten miles of the Ohio when, on 9 July 1755, it was attacked. Braddock perished and two-thirds of his soldiers—about nine hundred men—were killed or wounded.

Early in 1756, Britain and France finally declared war. The English colonists called the conflict the French War, but historians have known it as the Seven Years' War, the French and Indian War, and the Great War for the Empire. Involving hostilities in Europe as well as in America, the war took on religious overtones, with Protestant England and its allies pitted against Catholic France and its allies.

As never before, both France and Great Britain devoted considerable energy to the American theater. Each now understood that this was a war for supremacy, perhaps even survival, as an imperial power. London appointed the earl of Loudoun to command its armies; France dispatched the marquis de Montcalm to lead its forces.

Britain's military fortunes remained at low ebb for two years. The French and their Indian allies seized Forts Oswego and William Henry. Following the surrender of the latter installation, some 270 Anglo-American soldiers, 11 percent of the garrison, were killed or carried into captivity. Loudoun was recalled in 1757 after the failure of his principal offensive, an attempted siege of Louisbourg on Cape Breton Island.

The emergence of William Pitt as prime minister in 1756 changed the course of the war. He expanded the Royal Navy, which by 1759 had so decimated the French fleet that France was unable to supply its army across the Atlantic. Pitt's skillful diplomacy secured new European allies, enabling him to transfer approximately twenty thousand British regulars to America. He assigned quotas to each colony, and in both 1758 and 1759 the provinces raised twenty thousand volunteers. However, the colonies seldom coordinated their efforts. Indeed, every colony rejected Benjamin *Franklin's Albany Plan of Union, (1754), which had urged an intercolonial union for military purposes.

British successes came slowly. Pitt's strategy in 1758 called for General James Abercrombie to clear the Champlain Valley, while General Jeffrey Amherst took Louisbourg and an army under General John Forbes wrested the Ohio from France. Abercrombie failed egregiously. His assault on Fort Ticonderoga was repulsed with even heavier losses than Braddock had sustained. However, Louisbourg fell after a brief siege, and the French relinquished Fort Duquesne (Pittsburgh) as Forbes's regulars and colonials approached the forks of the Ohio.

The decisive engagement occurred in 1759 when an Anglo-American force of nine thousand men under General James Wolfe attacked Quebec, New France. Victory eluded the British for three months, until Wolfe successfully landed men on the Plains of Abraham above the citadel. Both Montcalm and Wolfe perished in the ensuing battle; French losses exceeded 15 percent. Six days later the garrison inside Quebec capitulated. Mopping-up operations concluded a year later when Montreal was taken.

Although American hostilities in the North had ended, the conflict raged against the Cherokees in the South until 1761 and continued elsewhere until the Treaty of Paris brought peace in 1763. France surrendered its claims to Canada and all territory east of the *Mississippi River. Spain, which entered the war after the fall of Montreal only to lose both Havana and Manila to British forces, ceded Florida to Great Britain. Western Indians rejected the treaty, denying that France had authority to cede their lands.

Although the Treaty of Paris was celebrated as a great victory for the British empire, in just twelve years the first shots for American independence would be fired. Tensions between Britain and its American colonies increased after 1763, partly because the war removed the French threat and also because its aftermath highlighted differences between London and its American colonies over policies relating to westward expansion, Indian relations, taxation, and defense.

[*See also* Albany Congress; Colonial Era; French Settlements in North America; Indian History and Culture: From 1500 to 1800: Indian Wars.]

• Francis Parkman, *Montcalm and Wolfe,* 2 vols., 1884. Lawrence H. Gipson, *The British Empire before the American Revolution,* 15 vols., 1935–1970. Charles P. Stacey, *Quebec, 1759: The Siege and the Battle,* 1959. Fred Anderson, *A People's Army: Massachusetts Soldiers and Society in the Seven Years' War,* 1984. James G. Lydon, ed., *Struggle for Empire: A Bibliography of the French and Indian War,* 1986. James Titus, *The Old Dominion at War: Society, Politics and Warfare in Late Colonial Virginia,* 1991.

—John Ferling

SEWALL, SAMUEL (1652–1730), merchant, judicial magistrate, diarist. One of *Boston's most influential men in his day, Judge Samuel Sewall provided a steadying influence as the Massachusetts Bay Colony became a royal province and as Puritan society was drawn into the English imperial orbit. Son of a prosperous yeoman from Newbury, Massachusetts, Sewall attended Harvard (M.A., 1674). He married Hannah Hull, the daughter of a well-to-do Boston merchant, in 1676, and entered upon a successful mercantile and public career. Elected to the General Court in 1683, he was appointed to the Council in 1691 and the Superior Court of Judicature in 1692, and was elevated to Chief Justice in 1718.

Although an active merchant, Sewall disliked worldly extravagance, worried about the growing secularization of Boston life, and applauded those merchants who resisted Anglicization by keeping their shops open on Christmas Day. As a commissioner of Oyer and Terminer he served on the panel of judges that heard the *Salem witchcraft cases in 1692, but in 1697, his Puritan conscience led him publicly to repent his role in these events. He became increasingly uncomfortable with the enslavement of Africans and, in 1700, composed "The Selling of Joseph," the first known published *antislavery tract. His *Phaenomena Quaedam Apocalyptica ad Aspectum Novi Orbis Configurata* (1697), a millennial treatise, argued that *New England might literally be the seat of the New Jerusalem.

For all his prominence among his contemporaries, Sewall's principal historic legacy is his diary (1674–1729), which richly documents life in the late Puritan period, affording revealing glimpses into Boston's changing political and social milieu.

[*See also* Colonial Era; Millennialism and Apocalypticism; Puritanism; Slavery.]

• Ola Elizabeth Winslow, *Samuel Sewall of Boston,* 1964. M. Halsey Thomas, ed., *The Diary of Samuel Sewall, 1674–1729,* 2 vols., 1973.

—Robert J. Wilson III

SEWARD, WILLIAM (1801–1872), statesman. A New York lawyer, Seward adhered to the *Anti-Masonic party and later the *Whig party. Elected governor (1839) and U.S. senator (1848), he championed internal improvements, educational reform, and *antislavery. A leading candidate for the *Republican party's presidential nomination in 1860, Seward served Abraham *Lincoln and Andrew *Johnson as secretary of state (1861–1869). During the *Civil War he worked with the U.S. minister to Great Britain, Charles Francis Adams, to prevent the Crown from recognizing and aiding the Confederacy and in resolving potential sources of conflict. He also pressured Emperor Napoleon III of France into remaining neutral and withdrawing French forces from Mexico (1866).

Seward vigorously promoted American commercial and territorial interests in the Pacific. Urging open markets and territorial integrity of China, he pledged, in the Burlingame Treaty of 1868, to respect the Chinese government's control of its domestic affairs. Conversely, he aggressively and willingly used naval force in *foreign-trade issues relating to China, Korea, and Japan. Seward's Pacific policy included the assertion of a U.S. claim to the Midway Islands (1867), support for the annexation of *Hawai'i, and the controversial purchase of *Alaska from Russia in 1867 for $7.2 million—a transaction some called "Seward's Folly."

Seward's expansionist goals in the Caribbean proved less successful. He failed to buy the Virgin Islands from Denmark (1867), secure naval bases in Santo Domingo and Central America, or obtain Senate ratification of a *Panama Canal treaty with Colombia. Seward's vision and accomplishments were those of a shrewd diplomat with an expansive view of America's destiny.

[*See also* Expansionism; Federal Government, Executive Branch: Department of State; Foreign Relations: U.S. Relations with Europe; Foreign Relations: U.S. Relations with Asia; Foreign Relations: U.S. Relations with Latin America; Manifest Destiny.]

• Glyndon Van Deusen, *William Henry Seward,* 1967. Ernest N. Paolino, *The Foundations of American Empire: William Henry Seward and U.S. Foreign Policy,* 1973.

—John M. Belohlavek

SEWING MACHINE. *See* Household Technology.

SEX EDUCATION. Before the twentieth century, sex education took the form primarily of personal observation and informal talks, but a handful of books such as *Aristotle's Masterpiece* (first published in English around 1684) and the Reverend John Todd's moralistic *Student's Manual* (1837) also conveyed rudimentary information about sexual functions. In the 1880s and 1890s, the *Woman's Christian Temperance Union called for students to take a vague pledge of premarital sexual abstinence as part of its White Cross Movement for personal purity. Countless religious writers and moralists issued veiled but dire warnings against prostitution, masturbation, and all forms of sexual activity outside the bonds of matrimony.

The modern movement to place sex education in the public schools grew out of a broader *Progressive Era crusade against prostitution and *venereal diseases that came to be known as the social-hygiene movement. *Social Diseases and Marriage* (1904) by Dr. Prince A. Morrow (1846–1913), a New York dermatologist, became the central document for the American Social Hygiene Association, a union of *public-health physicians, educators, and antiprostitution activists funded by John D. Rockefeller Jr. From its founding in 1914 to its decline and withdrawal from the field in the early 1960s, this organization led the fight for sex education. Prompted as much by fears of moral breakdown as by medical concern, Morrow and others insisted that almost all venereal diseases were transmitted through prostitution and that the social-hygiene movement must therefore attack both problems simultaneously. Despite what they perceived as a "conspiracy of silence" surrounding sexual matters, social hygienists argued that sex education was essential to dispel the ignorance about sex, *disease, and immorality that made prostitution and other misbehavior possible. After experimenting with public lectures to adult audiences, sex educators by 1914 turned decisively toward the public schools to teach young people a mixture of medical and moral lessons about anatomy; proper thoughts; and Protestant, middle-class morality.

Sex education in universities and public schools expanded significantly during *World War I with funding from the Chamberlain-Kahn Act (1918), so that by 1920 at least 25 percent of public high schools offered some form of sex education through biology and social-studies classes, poster exhibits, or lectures by physicians. Despite attempts by sex educators to ally with the progressive-education and mental-hygiene movements, sex education drew most of its funding and energy from public-health officials in individual cities and states. Although most sex educators took a generally sober and conservative approach, opponents in the late 1960s publicly attacked the allegedly radical programs favored by the U.S. Sex Information Education Council and its leader Mary Steichen Calderone. Sex education was subsequently marked by public acrimony, even as the AIDS crisis and concerns over teenage pregnancy prompted more schools to institute some form of instruction.

Central questions dating from the earliest days of the sex-education movement persisted nearly a century later: Is sex education's mission primarily moral or medical? Is sex education the school's or the parents' responsibility? Does knowledge of sexual facts lead young people to experiment sexually? Conversely, is sexual information by itself sufficient to alter sexual behavior at all?

[*See also* Acquired Immunodeficiency Syndrome; Prostitution and Antiprostitution; Sexual Morality and Sex Reform.]

• James T. Sears, ed., *Sexuality and the Curriculum: The Politics and Practices of Sexuality Education,* 1992. Jeffrey P. Moran, *Teaching Sex: The Shaping of Adolescence in the Twentieth Century,* 2000.

—Jeffrey P. Moran

SEXUAL HARASSMENT. The campaign to criminalize sexual harassment in the workplace began in the late 1970s. In cases brought to the federal courts, the lawyer Catharine MacKinnon sought to classify sexual harassment as a form of sex discrimination in violation of *civil rights legislation. In 1980 the Equal Employment Opportunity Commission (EEOC) adopted three tests for determining whether "unwelcome verbal or physical conduct" in the workplace violated Title VII of the Civil Rights Act of 1964, which bans sex discrimination in employment. Under EEOC guidelines, the unwelcome conduct had to be: (1) "quid pro quo" behavior that made submission to sex an explicit or implicit condition of advancement, (2) behavior that "unreasonably interferes with an individual's job performance," or (3) behavior that creates an "intimidating, hostile, or offensive working environment."

The *Supreme Court endorsed both the concept of sexual harassment as sex discrimination and the hostile-environment test in *Meritor Savings Bank* v. *Vinson* (1986), a case brought by a bank employee against a supervisor. Defining a hostile environment, however, proved difficult. In *Ellison* v. *Brady* (1991), the Ninth Circuit Court of Appeals held that issues of sexual harassment and the climate of the working environment should be evaluated from the perspective of a "reasonable woman." In *Harris* v. *Forklift Systems* (1993), the Supreme Court defined a hostile environment as one that a "reasonable person" would find hostile, abusive, or detrimental to job performance. A series of Supreme Court decisions in 1998 and 1999 extended employer liability for workplace harassment and further clarified the scope of sexual harassment law.

In *Sexual Harassment of Working Women* (1979), MacKinnon defined sexual harassment as "an unwanted imposition of sexual requirements in the context of a relationship of unequal power." Researchers in the 1980s agreed that sexual harassment was an abuse of power and a way to control or intimidate employees. Some studies found the greatest sexual harassment in occupations where women were new or in a minority, such as blue-collar jobs. Other studies held that women in white-collar work, such as office employees, were the most common targets. Surveys in the 1980s found that 42 percent of women employed in federal agencies had experienced harassment, as had 14 percent of the men. However, under 20 percent of workers who felt they had been harassed complained to their superiors, and even fewer left their jobs or pressed charges.

The issue gained national visibility in 1991, when the law-school professor Anita Hill, a former aide to the Supreme Court nominee Clarence Thomas, accused him of offensive conduct a decade earlier when he had been her superior at the Department of Education and as head of the EEOC. Hill's testimony before the all-male Senate Judiciary Committee during the Thomas hearings spurred an increase in harassment complaints and impelled several women to run for Congress in 1992. A few weeks after the Thomas hearings, Congress passed a civil rights law that for the first time awarded damages to victims of discrimination, including sexual harassment. The later 1990s brought an upsurge of highly publicized sexual-harassment charges, particularly in the *military, as well as an accusation against President Bill *Clinton by a former Arkansas state employee involving an alleged incident while he was governor of that state. The charge led indirectly to *impeachment of the president, though not to conviction.

[*See also* Civil Rights; Feminism; Gender; Women in the Labor Force; Women's Rights Movements.]

• Laura W. Stein, ed., *Sexual Harassment in America: A Documentary History*, 1999.

—Nancy Woloch

SEXUAL MORALITY AND SEX REFORM. The American colonies were settled by diverse ethnic, linguistic, and religious groups and had significant populations of indigenous peoples and slaves imported from Africa. The dominant influence on sexual attitudes, however, was *Protestantism, particularly from those Protestant groups emphasizing a conversion experience separating the believer from the mass of humanity and endowing him or her with the privileges and duties of the elect. Conversion brought with it not only assurance of salvation but also a dedication to opposing sin, including sexual sins. Protestants in general, and Calvinist groups in particular, however, viewed procreation as a fact of creation; sex within marriage could neither pollute nor corrupt, they held, and within the confines of the conjugal bed, the wife was equal to the husband and had the same rights. Fornication outside marriage was a scandal and a sin, and adultery was worse because it violated the sanctity of marriage, a covenant consecrated by God. Sodomy, or same-sex contacts, and bestiality were regarded as a particularly heinous. Colonial *New England apparently saw more prosecutions for bestiality than for same-sex activity, perhaps because the latter was easier to conceal. Intercourse during menstruation was a sin, masturbation and oral-genital contacts were immodest as well as wrong, and the former was widely condemned in sermons.

Given such attitudes, the laws in the early *Colonial Era dealt harshly with sexual deviance. A major difficulty, however, was the shortage of women, and many colonies adopted laws to punish female indentured servants who engaged in sex outside marriage. Native Americans held different views about sexuality, and many records tell of contacts between indigenous females and male European settlers, though few resulted in marriage. Indeed, many colonies forbade such marriages, as did Massachusetts in 1786.

The first conviction for a homosexual offense was recorded in Virginia in 1624 when an adult male was executed for allegedly forcing a young man into sexual relations. When some publicly cast doubt on the man's guilt, two such objectors were pilloried, lost their ears, and were indentured. Cross-dressing and cross-gender behavior were not so severely punished, particularly if the cross-dresser was female. During the *Revolutionary War, Deborah Sampson fought as a man in the Continental Army for more than a year under the name Robert Shirtliff.

The Eighteenth and Nineteenth Centuries. More tolerant sexual attitudes gained force in the eighteenth century from the *philosophes* and Enlightenment writers in general. Some of these ideas found expression in the bawdy writings of Benjamin *Franklin. Opponents of Thomas *Jefferson, however, used stories of his sexual adventures to discredit him. The reaction to the French Revolution diminished the *philosophes'* influence, but the romantic movement, with its emphasis on passion and emotion, carried on the challenge to traditional ideas about sex. The romantic sensibility challenged convention, welcomed physical passion, recognized sexual inconstancy, and cultivated sensation. The romantic challenge to sexual mores was less defined in the writings of the transcendentalists, but many antebellum utopian communities, such as New Harmony (Indiana), Brook Farm (Massachusetts), and John Humphrey *Noyes's Oneida Community (New York) challenged the conventional sexual attitudes of the day. The polygamist Mormons inspired particularly intense attacks, perhaps because of their political dominance in Utah.

The nineteenth century also saw the "medicalization" of many sexual activities. Reflecting the new medical theories, both treatment and prevention came to emphasize homeostasis, the need for balance between bodily intake and outgo. Especially influential in terms of sexual activity was the eighteenth-century Swiss physician Simon-André-D. Tissot, whose book *Onanism,* translated into English in 1766, went through many printings. Tissot taught that the human body experiences continual waste, and unless this is periodically restored, death results. Even with an adequate diet, the body could waste away through diarrhea, loss of blood, and especially (for men) seminal emission. While reproduction required seminal loss, nonprocreative sex, particularly masturbation, could lead to all kinds of illness, even insanity.

The most significant American popularizer of Tissot's ideas was the *Philadelphia physician Benjamin *Rush. The dangers of nonprocreative sexual activity loomed large in American sex writings throughout the nineteenth century, reaching its extreme in the career of John Harvey Kellogg (1852–1943), a Seventh-day Adventist leader; founder of a Battle Creek, Michigan, sanatorium (1876); and manufacturer of ready-to-eat grain cereals. Kellogg especially warned against masturbation, a term he used to describe various nonprocreative sexual activities, and taught that his grain-based breakfast foods would calm the sexual passions.

In this ideological climate, many physicians blamed an active sexual life for what were in fact the physical effects of sexually transmitted diseases such as gonorrhea and syphilis. Not until the end of the nineteenth century, following the work of William Koch and Louis Pasteur, were the bacterial causes of sexually transmitted diseases understood.

Fear of excessive sex activity persisted, however, largely owing to the writings of the American physician George M. Beard (1839–1882), who in 1869 advanced the idea of sexual neurasthenia, or nervous exhaustion. Urban-industrial civilization involved such stress, Beard theorized, that many people, particularly the well educated, succumbed to neurological disorders and nervous exhaustion. As humanity advanced, Beard argued, the conservation of nervous energy in order to keep the body in homeostasis became increasingly necessary. The main cause of nervous exhaustion and the resulting neurasthenia, he concluded, was the rash expenditure of sexual energy. The medical community in general agreed with Beard. Another influential writer who argued in the same vein was the English physician William Acton, who contended in *The Functions and Disorders of the Reproductive Organs* (1871) that seminal emission so drained the male nervous system that men must limit their sexual activity in order to survive.

Rapid *urbanization of cities in the late nineteenth century, coupled with heavy *immigration from southern and eastern Europe, led to renewed concerns about sexuality. Prostitution, which flourished in every major city, could no longer be ignored, while the greater visibility of same-sex relationships led authorities to seek advice from the medical community. As early as midcentury, concern about the influx of young men into the cities had led reformers to establish the Young Men's Christian Association and other organizations to counter the perceived dangers of urban life, including sexual temptation.

Widespread acceptance of the sexual double standard reinforced the urban commercialization of sex. Surviving diaries and letters make clear that antebellum women were recognized as sexual creatures who enjoyed sexual activity as much as men, but in the later nineteenth century this understanding was subordinated to an emphasis on women's responsibilities as moral guardians of the family. Motherhood became a special calling, demanding absolute moral purity and an almost childlike innocence. The ideal woman as envisioned by both science and religion was an ethereal, spiritualized creature—an image sharply at variance with reality, especially the reality of working-class and immigrant women. Fashion encouraged this image with corsets and trailing skirts suggesting the wearer's inability to venture into the world without protection. Since chastity and decorum were central to this idealized image, some medical writers asserted that women by nature were asexual beings who only reluctantly consented to sex in order to bear children. Some women used this exalted concept of womanhood for political leverage, justifying their demand for suffrage, for example, as a way of raising the moral level of society. But the idealized conception of womanhood inhibited the public discussion of sex except to emphasize its dangers. Contraception, too, fell under the ban. A principal aim of Anthony Comstock (1844–1915), longtime head of the New York Society for the Suppression of Vice, for example, was to prevent the dissemination of contraceptives and contraceptive information.

The Progressive Era through World War II. This nexus of ideas about sex was challenged by various demographic and scientific developments. Some immigrant groups lacked the sexual inhibitions mandated by the prevailing ideology. Further, the above-noted discovery of the bacterial causes of sexually transmitted diseases, and the realization that sexual activity itself did not cause the illnesses, encouraged a more open discussion of sex as a means of combating *venereal disease. Prostitution, once tolerated as a safety valve for male sexuality, was now attacked for *public-health reasons, since the prostitute was seen as the repository of diseases that could be transmitted to innocent women and children. The result was widespread discussion of sexual issues and an emphasis on *sex education for young people focusing on purity and abstinence. The Mann Act of 1910 prohibited the transportation of women across state borders for immoral (i.e., sexual) purposes, while local and state authorities investigated and legislated against prostitution. In short, the early twentieth century saw more open discussion about sex, but the emphasis was less on understanding it than on encouraging abstinence from it, publicizing its risks, and eliminating its illicit manifestations.

But as America changed from a rural to an urban nation, the comparative anonymity of urban life allowed for greater freedom of sexual activities that had in the past been either ignored or repressed. As traditional restraints on females eased, women's clothing became less restrictive and first the bicycle and then the automobile freed young couples to escape from the rigid chaperonage of previous generations. Symbolic of the new freedom were the pre–*World War I bohemians of New York's *Greenwich Village and the sexually precocious young women of the 1920s, the so-called flappers.

As confidence diminished in the dogmatic and simplistic answers to the moral issues raised by pornography, prostitution, homosexuality, and other sexual activities, interest in serious research on sexual topics increased. While the campaigns to abolish prostitution and other condemned sexual practices continued, sex research also advanced. John D. Rockefeller Jr. established the Bureau of Social Hygiene in 1911 to conduct research on prostitution. This, in turn, led to the establishment in 1921 of the Committee for Research into Problems of Sex (CRPS), funded by Rockefeller and sponsored by the National Research Council. Until the 1940s the CRPS subsidized most American sex studies. These included major endocrinology research that clarified the menstrual cycle and the role of hormones.

With the post–World War I vogue of Sigmund Freud and his emphasis on human sexuality, psychiatry became the authority on sexual matters, and ideas about homeostasis and the dangers of sex were replaced by discussion of repression, inhibition, and other such topics. World War I had also brought changes in official attitudes toward sex because of the disastrous consequences of the U.S. government's initial unwillingness to supply soldiers with condoms. Faced with an epidemic of gonorrhea and syphilis, American commanders overseas ignored domestic advice-givers and followed the French practice of providing their men with prophylactics.

The English writer Havelock Ellis, most of whose *Psychology of Sex* series of books (1896–1928) appeared first in the United States, also contributed to the changed thinking about sex. Redefining masturbation as "autoeroticism," Ellis included in the term a variety of psychosexual phenomena ranging from erotic dreams to daytime fantasies, in the process transforming a dangerous "vice" into a benign inevitability. Ellis did not dismiss the idea that excessive masturbation might result in slight physical disorders, but he removed it from the category of an illness. Gradually his view prevailed in American medical writing on the subject.

Equally important was the campaign to disseminate birth control information and contraceptives led by Margaret *Sanger and others, which both encouraged women to accept their own sexuality and helped men rethink the topic. Further fueling this trend were studies by two American researchers on female sexuality, Katherine Bement Davis (1860–1935) and Robert Latou Dickinson (1861–1950), both of whom dismissed the canard that women lacked sexual desire and disliked sexual activity.

The interwar period also brought marriage manuals that encouraged experimentation and the enjoyment of sex. Marie Stopes (1880–1958), in a series of books beginning with *Married Love* (1918) emphasized the importance of sex in marriage. Less didactic than Stopes but probably more influential was the Dutch writer Theodoor van de Velde whose *Ideal Marriage* (1926) enjoyed a long popularity.

Since World War II. The most famous recipient of CRPS grants was Alfred *Kinsey whose *Sexual Behavior in the Human Male* (1948) and *Sexual Behavior in the Human Female* (1953) revolutionized American thinking about sex and *gender issues. Although Kinsey's statistical data and sampling techniques would later be questioned, his work had a liberating effect in bringing sexuality fully into the arena of public discourse and in showing that American men and women not only enjoyed sex but engaged in a wide variety of sexual practices, some of which, such as homosexuality, remained illegal. Kinsey's attackers forced a congressional investigation into tax-exempt foundations that resulted in the closing of the CRPS and the termination of funding for most sex research. Kinsey's institute at Indiana University survived, however, by conducting more specialized sex-oriented studies such as those on *abortion, contraception, and the sex habits of prisoners.

Several developments of the 1960s further undermined longstanding sexual mores. The marketing of the oral contraceptive, approved by the U.S. Food and Drug Administration in 1960, allowed women greater control of their sexual choices in terms of reproductive consequences. The physiological studies of William Masters and Virginia Johnson, reported in *Human Sexual Response* (1963), further illuminated female sexuality and the female response cycle, including the capacity for multiple orgasms. Betty Friedan's *The *Feminine Mystique* (1963) expressed the rising discontent of many educated middle-class women with their traditional roles. The antiwar and counterculture movements of the 1960s with their slogan "Make love, not war" played a role as well, as flouting the sexual conventions of the older generation became a means of signaling one's broader rejection of the established political and corporate order. One result of these cumulative developments was an increasingly open discussion of sexuality and the weakening of many traditional inhibitors.

The more tolerant climate continued in the 1970s. First the psychologists (1973) and then the psychiatrists (1974) dropped their diagnosis of homosexuality as a mental illness. In **Roe* v. *Wade* (1973), the U.S. *Supreme Court upheld a woman's constitutional right to terminate her pregnancy. Nudity and explicit sex appeared more openly in the movies, and the courts relaxed the pornography laws (while still leaving obscenity—which remained ill defined—outside the pale of First Amendment protection). The influx of baby boomers into colleges and universities throughout these years undermined the traditional *in loco parentis* moral-oversight role of administrators. As young people experimented with a variety of living arrangements, it seemed to conservative critics that the entire younger generation was in full-scale sexual rebellion. Their parents, however, at the same time were reading Alex Comfort's *The Joy of Sex* (1974). The appearance of AIDS and an increasing incidence of sexually transmitted diseases in the 1980s led to a reassessment of the new sexual freedom, but with little attempt to deny human sexuality, only to emphasize safe sex.

Many of these changes reflected the shifting role and status of women in American society, including two-career families and single mothers (the majority of whom were not teenagers). Women in the 1990s enjoyed far more opportunities than in the past, including the ability to control when they would bear children. The emergence of women as a force in defining sexual mores significantly influenced male-female relationships, particularly with the enactment of laws against *sexual harassment and more inclusive definitions of *rape. By the end of the century, sexually explicit materials remained widely available, although with prohibitions on sexually provocative depictions of children. The nature of pornography had also changed, with more erotic writing now produced by and for women.

Viewed broadly, the twentieth century, particularly in the latter part, brought nothing less than a reformulation of social attitudes toward sexuality and a redefinition of the sexual roles of men and women. Although no unanimity was reached, a broad consensus by the end of the century viewed the private sexual activity of consenting adults as of concern to them only. This still left many issues open to sometimes heated debate, however, including *abortion, gay rights, sex education in the schools, sexual explicitness in the mass media, and the dangers of children venturing into the uncensored sexual world of the Internet. Clearly sex and sexuality would remain lively topics for Americans in the twenty-first century, as they had been since the beginning.

[*See also* Acquired Immunodeficiency Syndrome; Birth Control and Family Planning; Censorship; Courtship and Dating; Feminism; Gay and Lesbian Rights Movement; Marriage and Divorce; Mormonism; Prostitution and Antiprostitution; Psychology; Psychotherapy; Seventh-day Adventism; Sixties, The; Utopian and Communitarian Movements; Veneral Disease; Women's Rights Movements; YMCA and YWCA.]

• Allan M. Brandt, *No Magic Bullet: A Social History of Venereal Disease in the United States Since 1880*, 1985. John d'Emilio and Estelle B. Freedman, *Intimate Matters: A History of Sexuality in America*, 1988. Vern L. Bullough, *Science in the Bedroom: A History of Sex Research*, 1994. David J. Garrow, *Liberty and Sexuality*, 1994. Vern L. Bullough and Bonnie Bullough, *Sexual Attitudes: Myths and Misconceptions*, 1996. Ira Reiss, *Solving America's Sexual Crises*, 1997.

—Vern L. Bullough

SHAKERISM, the religious movement brought to America in 1774 by the English prophetess Ann Lee (ca. 1736–1784). In England, Lee, an illiterate factory worker and visionary, had joined a sectarian community—the "Shaking Quakers"—and emerged as a leader. Upon coming to America, Lee and a handful of followers eventually located at Watervliet near Albany, New York. The small community first attracted attention in 1780 because of its inhabitants' refusal to participate in the *Revolutionary War. The next year Lee and a group of disciples launched a missionary journey lasting twenty-six months. They traveled throughout *New England and eastern New York, gaining converts to their cause while also experiencing hostility. Proclaiming a new dispensation of regeneration, Lee taught her followers to flee sin, which she associated with sexual intercourse, and to strive for perfection. Shaker traditions describe her as a powerful charismatic who worked miracles.

Following Lee's death, leadership passed first to her English colleague James Whittaker, and then to her American disciples Joseph Meacham and Lucy Wright. They guided the young movement through critical organizational stages, consolidated the institutional side of Shakerism, and supervised its expansion into the Ohio Valley. By 1821 the Shakers had established a national society, formally entitled the United Society of Believers in Christ's Second Appearing, and gathered into settlements stretching from Maine to Indiana. They adopted a body of rules, the "Millennial Laws," and codified their theological views in major publications including the *Testimony of Christ's Second Appearing* (1808). They held several distinctive ideas, including the notion of God as Father and Mother. The Shakers demanded confession of sin, celibacy, communal ownership of property, and obedience to the ministry. Men and women shared leadership. The United Society attracted converts for different reasons: For some it offered a refuge; for others a challenge to a higher life. Shakerism reached its numerical height in the 1840s with nearly 4,500 members. Its organizational headquarters was at New Lebanon, New York. The Shakers were successful economically thanks to the pooling of resources, a vigorous work ethic, and abundant labor. They were noted for both agricultural products and hand-manufactured items. After the *Civil War, facing competition from new forms of manufacturing and unable to attract young persons or to retain male members, a numerical decline occurred. In 1875 villages began to close, and geographical retreat followed. The society changed in other ways, too. Some members, notably Frederick W. Evans and Antoinette Doolittle at Mount Lebanon, adopted increasingly liberal religious and social views, leaving behind the sectarian mentality. By 1900 the aging society included fewer than 600 members. At the end of the twentieth century only one village—Sabbathday Lake, Maine—remained.

The Shakers influenced American religion and culture to a degree beyond their numbers. A revival of interest in the Shakers' material culture occurred during the second half of the twentieth century. Village sites became historical museums; chairs and other objects commanded attention from collectors, designers, and entrepreneurs. Even Shaker religion enjoyed renewed respect as the twentieth century ended.

[*See also* Religion; Society of Friends; Utopian and Communitarian Movements.]

• Priscilla J. Brewer, *Shaker Communities, Shaker Lives*, 1986. Stephen J. Stein, *The Shaker Experience in America: A History of the United Society of Believers*, 1992.

—Stephen J. Stein

SHARECROPPING AND TENANTRY, once common forms of farming throughout the United States. The tenant paid the landowner rent; the landowner paid the sharecropper wages. After the *Civil War, landowners, former slaves, and yeomen in southern states often disputed rights of land tenure, ownership of crops, and the legal priority of their respective claims. The complex arrangements negotiated by landlord and tenant resulted in frequent litigation.

Sharecroppers brought only their labor to the bargaining table; landowners customarily supervised farming operations, marketed crops, and paid sharecroppers an agreed-upon sum. Legally, sharecroppers were wage laborers. A sharecropper's claim for wages might conflict with the economic interests of a landowner or a credit merchant. Some states gave the sharecropper's claim priority in such cases, but after *Reconstruction, the legislatures and courts generally favored landlords and credit merchants. The number of sharecroppers peaked at 776,000 in the early 1930s. During and after *World War II, the number declined, causing the Census Bureau to drop the category after 1959.

Tenant farmers, by contrast, usually brought such resources as implements, draft animals, and credit to the bargaining table. A tenant in effect rented the land and conducted farming operations and marketing independently. After he sold the crop, the tenant paid the landowner an agreed-upon percentage of the proceeds. A tenant, unlike a sharecropper, could use the growing crop to secure credit through what was termed a crop lien. A 1935 census listed 2.2 million tenant farms; half of the 1 million in the *South were farmed by *African Americans. Rapid mechanization and government policies reduced tenant farms to 539,000 by 1964.

Local customs often departed from written law, and power, cunning, and particular circumstances figured into tenure arrangements. To enhance landowners' power, many southern states by the end of the nineteenth century passed punitive laws that restricted farm laborers' mobility during the crop year. A complex legal history, as well as literary and historical sources, traces the varied tenure arrangements negotiated by farmers and the endless clashes between landowner and tenant. The labor needs and peculiarities of such cash crops as cotton, tobacco, wheat, and rice also shaped tenure contracts and customs.

Beginning in 1933, New Deal agricultural programs delegated enormous power to local agricultural committees composed primarily of wealthier farmers. Such county committees set acreage allotments and mediated landowner-tenant disputes. Farmers who could take advantage of federal programs and mechanize production prospered. But labor-intensive farm operations involving tenants and sharecroppers soon faded into insignificance. Millions of farmers left the land as *science, *technology, and government programs reconfigured U.S. *agriculture.

[*See also* Agricultural Adjustment Administration; Cotton Industry; New Deal Era, The; Populism; Southern Tenant Farmers' Union and National Farm Labor Union; Subsidies, Agricultural; Tobacco Industry.]

• Harold D. Woodman, *New South, New Law: The Legal Foundations of Credit and Labor Relations in the Postbellum Agricultural South,* 1995.

—Pete Daniel

SHAW, LEMUEL (1781–1861), jurist. A Harvard graduate who began legal practice after a three-year apprenticeship in a *Boston law office, Shaw first gained famed and fortune as the legal voice of Boston's leading mercantile families in the early nineteenth century. A Federalist, he vehemently opposed the *War of 1812 and drafted Boston's first city charter in 1822. He was appointed chief justice of the supreme judicial court of Massachusetts in 1830, at a time when whole areas of the law remained unsettled. For the next thirty years he dominated the court, writing some two thousand majority opinions. No other state judge before or since has exerted so great an impact. Oliver Wendell *Holmes Jr. labeled Shaw "the greatest magistrate which this country has produced."

Shaw has sometimes been portrayed as a "liberal" because of one well-known decision, *Commonwealth* v. *Hunt* (1842), in which he ruled that workers could strike whenever an employer hired nonunion labor. This opinion, freeing labor unions from the old doctrine of criminal conspiracy, has been hailed as labor's Magna Carta. But most of Shaw's decisions favored corporate interests, especially *railroads, and the burgeoning market economy. In 1849, upholding racial *segregation in Boston's public schools, he originated the "separate but equal" doctrine that later became the legal justification for segregation throughout much of the nation. Hostile to *slavery, Shaw freed slaves brought into Massachusetts by their master. In 1851, however, he refused to release the fugitive slave Thomas Sims and wrote the leading opinion justifying the constitutionality of the *Fugitive Slave Act of 1850.

[*See also* Antebellum Era; Jurisprudence; Labor Movements; Legal Profession; Strikes and Industrial Conflict.]

• Leonard W. Levy, *The Law of the Commonwealth and Chief Justice Shaw,* 1957.

—Leonard L. Richards

SHAYS'S REBELLION, political label attached to the rural protest movement of 1786–1787 against the government of Massachusetts. The protest was neither directed by Captain Daniel Shays, the Continental Army veteran from Pelham, Massachusetts, on whom it was blamed, nor was it unmistakably a rebellion. Dubbed "the Regulation" by participants, the movement was triggered by economic distress in the aftermath of independence. Determined to redeem its *Revolutionary War debts, Massachusetts imposed heavy taxes, payable in hard money, in the midst of a severe depression in transatlantic trade. With cash scarce, lawsuits for debts mounting, and taxes due, many farmers feared foreclosure and jail and pressed the state for relief. Their program called for paper money and tender laws to ease payment of debts, court reforms and lower salaries for officials to reduce public expenses, and changes in political institutions to bring government closer to the people. From 1784 to 1786, the state legislature, dominated by commercial interests and intent on upholding credit, rejected all these proposals.

The result was an angry protest movement in western Massachusetts that revived the methods and rhetoric that had been used a decade earlier to resist British rule. The movement started with petitions from town meetings, a traditional means of seeking redress; expanded into extralegal county conventions; and escalated into crowd actions, involving hundreds of armed men, that prevented courts from meeting in several counties during the fall and winter of 1786. When Governor James Bowdoin dispatched an army to defend the courts, events reached a climax. On 25 January 1787, Shays led some twelve hundred men in a march on the federal arsenal at Springfield. A burst of cannon fire from defending militia routed the insurgents, leaving four dead on the field; ten days later, General Benjamin Lincoln crushed the remnants of resistance at Petersham. Thus ended what the Massachusetts General Court proclaimed "a horrid and unnatural rebellion."

The Massachusetts uprising dramatized rural unrest throughout the new republic, and though only a minority of dissidents took up arms, it symbolized for conservatives a republic in peril. In their view, ambitious demagogues like Shays, exploiting an unruly people, jeopardized the liberty gained in the Revolution. Nationalists seized upon the specter of Shays to underscore the weakness of the *Articles of Confederation government and to urge support for the *Constitution produced by the Philadelphia Convention in 1787. Shays's Rebellion and the Constitution have been linked ever since. The crisis in the countryside illuminates the difficult passage of the new nation to a republican political order.

[*See also* Revolution and Constitution, Era of; Taxation.]

• David P. Szatmary, *Shays' Rebellion,* 1980. Robert A. Gross, ed., *In Debt to Shays,* 1993.

—Robert A. Gross

SHERMAN, WILLIAM T. (1820–1891), *Civil War leader, postwar commanding general. Born in Lancaster, Ohio, and the foster son of the *Whig party politician Thomas Ewing, Sherman graduated from the U.S. Military Academy at West Point in 1840 and served his earliest army tours of duty in the *South. In the 1850s, he resigned his commission to become a California banker and experienced a series of business failures there, in New York, and in Kansas. When the South seceded in 1861, Sherman was superintendent of the Louisiana Military Seminary, forerunner of the modern-day Louisiana State University.

Returning to the U.S. Army, he participated in many of the Civil War's major battles and campaigns, including *Bull Run, *Shiloh, *Vicksburg, Chattanooga, and Atlanta. He conducted marches of selective destruction through Mississippi, Georgia, and the Carolinas. He then negotiated the controversially mild surrender agreement with the Confederate general Joseph E. Johnston and, during *Reconstruction, was the South's leading northern supporter. In 1869, he became commanding general of the army, a post he held until he retired in 1884. He was the driving force in the *Indian wars of those years and the implementer of the concept of professional schools for army officers.

Sherman is most famous for his psychologically intimidating strategy of selective destruction against southern society. He saw this approach as helping to end the war in the shortest time possible with the fewest casualties; southern whites would long denounce his campaign as one of particular devastation and brutality. He is also remembered for two sayings: "War is hell" and (when mentioned as a possible presidential candidate) "I will not accept if nominated and will not serve if elected."

[*See also* Military, The.]

• William T. Sherman, *Memoirs of General W. T. Sherman,* Library of America ed., 1990. John F. Marszalek, *Sherman, a Soldier's Passion for Order,* 1993.

—John F. Marszalek

SHERMAN ANTI-TRUST ACT. *See* Antitrust Legislation.

SHILOH, BATTLE OF (1862), costly *Civil War engagement. In February 1862, a Union campaign along the Cumberland and Tennessee Rivers had forced the Confederates under General Albert Sidney Johnston to cede much of middle and western Tennessee. By spring forty thousand Federal troops under Major General Ulysses S. *Grant were massed near Pittsburg Landing on the Tennessee River, preparing to attack the vital rail junction of Corinth, Mississippi.

On 6 April after a dilatory march northward from Corinth, 44,000 Confederates under Johnston and General P. G. T. Beauregard attacked the Federal troops near a Methodist meetinghouse, Shiloh Church. Surprising their foes, the Southerners drove the Union right flank back nearly a mile in three hours of savage fighting. Yet the attack failed to turn Grant's left flank near the river, a prime tactical goal, and stubborn resistance in the Union center stalled the offensive. As Union defenders held out until late in the day, bloodied Confederates dubbed the area the "Hornet's Nest." By that time, Johnston was dead, struck by a stray minié ball that severed an artery in his leg. Beauregard assumed command and, although the Hornet's Nest was subdued, called off further attacks. Grant received reinforcements under Major General Don Carlos Buell, and at dawn on 7 April he seized the offensive. In a reversal of the previous day's action, the Federals forced the Confederates back, and Beauregard withdrew in midafternoon.

Shiloh failed to alter the strategic situation in the *West, although the Union followed with subsequent victories. The engagement was particularly significant, however, because its appalling casualty toll—over 23,000 men killed, wounded or missing—disabused both sides of the notion that the war would be short-lived.

• Wiley Sword, *Shiloh: Bloody April,* 1974. James Lee McDonough, *Shiloh—in Hell before Night,* 1977.

—Christopher Losson

SHIPBUILDING. Shipbuilding flourished in Colonial America. Colonial shipyards, numbering over 125 by 1750, constructed about one-third of the registered tonnage in the British Empire. England predominated shipbuilding because of its abundance of the variety of timber needed in building wooden ships; construction costs were 30 to 50 percent lower than in England; and London's mercantile laws gave British-built ships a near monopoly of the carrying trade with the empire.

During the golden age of the American merchant marine, 1785 to 1860, shipbuilding boomed. The rapid growth of U.S. commerce worldwide largely accounted for the upsurge. Moreover, the growing North Atlantic traffic and the demand for fast clipper ships for the *California trade stimulated the industry. In 1855, the peak year, more than two thousand vessels of all types were built by American shipyards.

The end of the *Civil War in 1865 largely halted construction until the "New Navy" was created in the 1880s. The primary reason U.S. shipbuilding suffered a precipitous decline during this period was its failure to convert to iron (and then steel) and steam construction. Foreign steam packets soon replaced American wooden sailing packets on the vital transatlantic trade routes. U.S. vessels carried only 8.7 percent of the nation's imports by 1910, a figure destined to drop lower despite government subsidies to the merchant-marine and shipbuilding industries. Only the coastal trade, in which American vessels were given a monopoly after 1817 in the cabotage laws by the federal government, remained firmly in U.S. hands.

*World War I benefited American shipbuilding as the nation sought to build a "bridge of ships" across the Atlantic to win the war; most of the ships were delivered only after the November 1918 armistice, however. A postwar oversupply of ships, coupled with the Washington Naval Arms Treaty of 1922, sent shipbuilding into a depression for the next decade. Congress's attempts to aid the industry through various laws passed between 1920 and 1936 proved ineffective. Only New Deal naval building contracts and the need for merchant and naval ships during *World War II ended the industry's depression. Shipbuilders produced almost 6,000 combatant vessels, cargo ships, tankers, and minor types of vessels during the conflict. This record of prodigious construction resulted from the federal government's expanding the number of shipways in the nation's nineteen private shipyards and building twenty-one new emergency shipyards, plus the adoption of new and faster shipbuilding methods including welding and modular construction. The shipyards of Henry J. Kaiser (1882–1967) were leaders in this regard.

In the last half of the twentieth century, commercial shipbuilding enjoyed a modest resurgence with the advent of giant tankers and container vessels, but a glut of ships, higher U.S. costs, and the growth of foreign-built and foreign-flagged vessels kept commercial shipbuilding in the doldrums. By the 1990s less than 5 percent of U.S. imports and exports were carried in American-flagged bottoms. Naval construction expanded greatly during the Ronald *Reagan administration, but after the collapse of the Soviet Union, U.S. military expenditures declined. Despite periodic bursts of activity, American shipbuilding has been a chronically irregular and unsettled industry since the Civil War.

[*See also* Foreign Trade, U.S.; Mahan, Alfred Thayer; Maritime Transport; Military, The; Navigation Acts; Washington Naval Arms Conference.]

• Robert A. Kilmarx, ed., *America's Maritime Legacy: A History of the U.S. Merchant Marine and Shipbuilding Industry since Colonial Times,* 1979. Clinton Whitehurst Jr., *The U.S. Shipbuilding Industry: Past, Present, and Future,* 1986.

—James M. Morris

SHOPPING CENTERS AND MALLS. Modern shopping centers are responses to automobility. As the old pedestrian downtown yielded in the 1920s to the demands of impatient drivers seeking quick access to merchandise, strips of shops began to open adjacent to curbside parking slots. By the mid-1920s this new relationship between car and store had made leisurely strolling a kind of luxury item in its own right. On the suburban fringes of *Kansas City, Missouri, in 1923, the developer J. C. Nichols offered motorists the chance to park and walk through an ersatz Spanish city embellished with imported mosaics and fountains. Nichols maintained the illusion that this was Old Seville with parking ramps concealed behind adobe walls. In this Country Club Plaza, shopping became an adventure straight out of a movie matinee.

World's fairs had offered exotic if temporary shopping venues since the nineteenth century, as had some of the larger *department stores, with periodic festivals of goods from faraway places in equally atmospheric settings. But the conjunction of pedestrianism, shopping, and theme began with Country Club Plaza. In the depression-ridden 1930s, hard-pressed retailers increasingly appealed to customers by enforcing the separation between driver and vehicle. *Los Angeles, a city soon to be transformed by the car, became the site of much experimentation with protomalls. The Farmers' Market (1934), designed to resemble a midwestern farm, and Crossroads of the World (1936), in which blocks of shops ranged from Elizabethan quaintness to the moderne style, presaged the postwar invention of the themed mall.

Southdale (1956), the first fully enclosed shopping mall, was built by the architect Victor Gruen in Edina, Minnesota. Roughly contemporary with Disneyland in Anaheim, California, Southdale took as its theme a modernist, minimalist elegance, with sculpture positioned about a decorous interior evoking a posh art museum.

As conceived by Gruen, Southdale represented a kind of surrogate civic center for American suburbia. Set like a jewel amid acres of free parking, Southdale offered the Minneapolis suburbs their closest approximation of a spiritual and physical core. Later in the 1950s, in Midtown Plaza, in Rochester, New York, Gruen tried to revitalize a cold-weather inner city decimated by white flight with a vertical mall built over an underground parking ramp topped by an office tower. By then the lessons of Disneyland were clear to anyone planning a pedestrian environment: Like the theme park, Midtown was brash, bright, colorful, and fun. Entertainment and atmosphere became the keys to retailing success.

Mall of America, which opened in 1992 in Bloomington, Minnesota, not far from Southdale, was America's largest and best publicized shopping mall. Despite provision for elderly mall-walkers and the occasional concert, arts fair, or church service, few malls served as true civic centers. They did, however, evoke the feeling of an old urban core: walking for pleasure, crowds, spectacle, and the sense of being part of an ephemeral public. But for most consumers, the mall with its themed stores, restaurants, and even tree-shaded (indoor) amusement parks made shopping a glamorous diversion. Transcending mundane commercial transactions, the modern megamall turned buying and selling into a kind of conceptual time travel.

[*See also* Amusement Parks and Theme Parks; Automotive Industry; Business; Capitalism; Consumer Culture; Fifties, The; Leisure; Mass Marketing; Suburbanization; Urbanization; World's Fairs and Expositions.]

• William Severini Kowinski, *The Malling of America,* 1985. Chester H. Liebs, *Main Street to Miracle Mile,* 1985.

—Karal Ann Marling

SICKLE CELL ANEMIA. A genetically transmitted blood disease most commonly found in persons of African-American ancestry. In late-twentieth-century America an estimated 72,000 persons had sickle cell disease and approximately 8 percent of the African-American population carried the sickle cell genetic trait.

In 1910 James B. Herrick published an article describing a twenty-year-old Grenadian dental student in *Chicago with "sickle-shaped and crescent-shaped" red blood cells. This was the first fully documented description of sickle cell anemia (SCA). The condition, which had existed for centuries in Africa and the southern Mediterranean, had been transported by black slaves to North and South America. Sickle cell genes were thus present among blacks in early America, where white planters and physicians noted that blacks often appeared immune to *malaria. Racial theories regarding medical differences between whites and blacks arose around such observations and became incorporated into the pro-slavery arguments of antebellum America. (Today it is known that people carrying at least one sickle cell gene are resistant to the most virulent form of malarial parasite.)

Other case reports followed Herrick's, and by the mid- to late 1920s medical investigators were identifying SCA as a genetic disease usually seen in blacks. In 1933 L. W. Diggs of Memphis demonstrated the existence of both the asymptomatic sickle-cell trait and the actual disease SCA. In 1949, when Linus *Pauling revealed that SCA was caused by an alteration in the usual structure of the hemoglobin molecule, a new era in SCA research and molecular biology began.

Until the *civil rights movement of the 1960s and 1970s, neither physicians nor community health leaders paid much attention to SCA, although SCA was occasionally used as a reason for segregating blood supplies or as a test for racial "whiteness." Government funding for testing and research remained low. When public-health officials attempted to institute genetic screening for sickle cell carriers, some *African-Americans suspected their motives.

By the end of the twentieth century, sickle cell anemia was the subject of extensive research. Treatment included pain control; regular blood transfusion; and, in rare instances, bone-marrow transplant. To facilitate early identification and treatment, a number of states required sickle cell screening of all newborns. Through government pamphlets, the *Internet, and other means, much information was available to persons with the disease or the genetic trait. The Georgia Comprehensive Sickle Cell Center at Grady Health Systems in Atlanta was a major research and information center.

[*See also* Disease; Medicine: From the 1870s to 1945; Medicine: Since 1945; Public Health; Race, Concept of.]

• Todd L. Savitt, "The Invisible Malady: Sickle Cell Anemia in America, 1910–1970," *Journal of the National Medical Association* 73 (1981), 739–746. Keith Wailoo, *Drawing Blood: Technology and Disease Identity in Twentieth-Century America,* 1997.

—Todd L. Savitt

SIERRA CLUB. The Sierra Club of *California was founded by *San Francisco Bay area businessmen and university professors in 1892, "To explore, enjoy, and render accessible the mountain regions of the Pacific Coast; to publish authentic information concerning them; [and] to enlist the support and cooperation of the people and the government in preserving the forests and other natural features of the Sierra Nevada Mountains." Under the founding president John *Muir, it acted as a protective association for *Yosemite National Park during the controversy over a reservoir proposed in Hetch Hetchy Valley.

Expanding its mission nationwide, the club grew meteorically after *World War II. Its first paid executive director, David Brower, enlisted a large membership, engaged in national campaigns against hydroelectric dams in Dinosaur National Monument and the *Grand Canyon, lobbied for the Wilderness Act (1964), and promoted national parks in the North Cascades (1968) and California's redwood groves (1968). Publishing, lobbying, and grassroots political activities made the Sierra Club the most powerful environmental organization in the United States in the years preceding the first Earth Day (22 April 1970).

By the end of the twentieth century, with some 580,000 members and an annual budget of $52 million, the San Francisco–based Sierra Club once again enlarged its mission, now launching a global effort to "protect the wild places of the earth; to practice and promote the responsible use of the earth's ecosystems, and resources; [and] to educate and enlist humanity to protect and restore the quality of the natural and human environment."

[*See also* Conservation Movement; Environmentalism; National Park System.]

• Michael P. Cohen, *The History of the Sierra Club: 1892–1970,* 1988.

—Michael P. Cohen

SILLIMAN, BENJAMIN (1779–1864), educator, editor, scientist. Silliman was born in Trumbull, Connecticut, to a family of modest means. His father was a general during the *Revolutionary War. Continuing a family tradition, Silliman studied law after his graduation from Yale College in 1796. The course of his life was radically altered in 1802, however, when Yale's president offered Silliman the new professorship of chemistry and natural history. Silliman accepted, but spent the next four years in various American and European cities learning the sciences he was to teach.

By the end of his active teaching career at Yale in 1853, Silliman was widely acknowledged as the patriarch of American science. He achieved this status not through his own largely descriptive work in chemistry, mineralogy, and geology, but through the achievements of his many students and through his *American Journal of Science* (1818). His students included Amos Eaton, Edward Hitchcock, James Dwight Dana, Benjamin Silliman Jr., Oliver P. Hubbard, and Charles Upham Shepard. The *American Journal of Science*, the nation's first general scientific periodical, offered a venue where Americans could read about the experiments and observations of their countrymen and publish their own work. Silliman also served as the hub of a wide system of correspondence that linked Americans interested in science to one another and to kindred spirits in Europe.

Originally chosen for the Yale faculty primarily on the strength of his Christian character, Silliman actively promoted the union of faith and science in his teaching and in the appendices he attached to his American editions of Robert Bakewell's *Introduction to Geology*. His characteristic blend of Genesis and geology made Silliman one of the most popular public lecturers of the *Antebellum Era.

[*See also* Henry, Joseph; Physical Sciences; Religion; Science: Revolutionary War to World War I; Science: Science and Religion.]

• John F. Fulton and Elizabeth H. Thomson, *Benjamin Silliman, 1779–1864: Pathfinder in American Science*, 1947. Chandos Michael Brown, *Benjamin Silliman: A Life in the Young Republic*, 1989.

—Julie R. Newell

SINCLAIR, UPTON (1878–1968), muckraking author, social activist. Born in Baltimore, Maryland, Sinclair graduated from the College of the City of New York in 1897, briefly attended graduate school at Columbia, and joined the *Socialist party in 1902. In 1905, with the novelist Jack London, he helped found the Intercollegiate Socialist Society. A brief trip to *Chicago led to the novel on which his reputation largely rests, *The *Jungle* (1906), an exposé of the meatpacking industry widely credited with having inspired passage of the *Pure Food and Drug Act. Unlike most other *muckrakers, Sinclair was a book writer, not a journalist; a tireless advocate of radical causes and self-promoter, he ultimately produced more than one hundred books. He wrote vegetarian and temperance tracts; investigative novels on the petroleum industry and the *Sacco and Vanzetti case; and nonfiction attacks on organized religion, the universities, and the press. He rarely received the critical respect he craved, but some of his books proved popular, and most caused a stir. At one time he was, in the estimation of H. L. *Mencken, the most widely translated American author.

Sinclair ran for office several times, most spectacularly in 1934 when his End Poverty in California (EPIC) movement won him that state's gubernatorial nomination. A well-financed hostile advertising campaign against him, including radio, billboards, and film, and involving techniques that would later become staples of political campaigning, contributed to his loss that November. Sinclair retired from politics thereafter but continued to write, producing a series of novels featuring the dashing globetrotter Lanny Budd, one of which won the *Pulitzer Prize in 1943.

[*See also* Meatpacking and Meat Processing Industry; New Deal Era, The; Progressive Era; Socialism; Temperance and Prohibition.]

• Leon Harris, *Upton Sinclair: American Rebel*, 1975. Greg Mitchell, *The Campaign of the Century: Upton Sinclair's Race for Governor of California and the Birth of Media Politics*, 1992.

—Greg Mitchell

SINGLE-TAX MOVEMENT. The Single-Tax movement was inspired by the plan of the *San Francisco journalist and political economist Henry George (1839–1897), first articulated in an 1871 pamphlet and then in *Progress and Poverty* (1879), to return the profits of growth to society by imposing a uniform land tax that would end land monopoly and real-estate speculation. Rising land values, George argued, were created by community development rather than by landlords and real estate speculators who unjustly reaped the benefits of economic growth by paying lower taxes on undeveloped land. The "Single Tax," so dubbed by Thomas Shearman in 1887, proposed that the government appropriate unearned real-estate profits by setting a uniform tax on all land whether developed or not. George envisioned the Single Tax as a great panacea. Speculators, faced with the prospect of paying high taxes on non-income-producing lands, would be forced to sell or develop their holdings. This would spur the construction of more homes and factories, thereby lowering rents, increasing profits and wages, and alleviating *unemployment and urban congestion. Moreover, the Single Tax would generate funds sufficient to eliminate all other taxes and yet leave a surplus that would be returned to citizens in the form of increased public services.

Progress and Poverty became a best-seller, and the Single-Tax movement attracted national and international attention during George's trips to England and Ireland in the 1880s and his unsuccessful campaigns for mayor of *New York City in 1886 and 1897. Despite George's death in 1897, the movement over the next several decades spread throughout the United States, Canada, Australia, Great Britain, Denmark, and Hungary. The Single Tax was opposed by economists, who thought it unworkable, and by wealthy landowners, churches, and farmers who feared losing their lands or profits. Although the movement declined after the 1920s, a number of Single-Tax advocates succeeded in shifting the burden of local property taxes from buildings and improvements to land. In 2000, Single Tax groups still operated in over twenty-two countries.

[*See also* Gilded Age; Populist Era; Radicalism; Taxation]

• Charles Albro Barker, *Henry George*, 1955. Robert V. Adelson, ed., *The Critics of Henry George: A Centenary Appraisal of Their Strictures on Progress and Poverty*, 1979.

—Steven J. Ross

SIT-DOWN STRIKE, FLINT. The sit-down strike of 1936–1937 pitted General Motors (GM), the world's largest manufacturing corporation, against the fledgling United Automobile Workers of America (UAW). After GM refused a UAW request for a conference to discuss outstanding grievances, a small group of workers, adopting a tactic the UAW had first used in November 1936, occupied the Cleveland, Ohio, Fisher Body plant on 28 December 1936. Two days later, strikers occupied the two Fisher Body plants in Flint, Michigan, heart of the GM empire. Eventually the strike spread to GM plants nationwide, idling 136,000 workers.

GM secured a court injunction on 2 January 1937 ordering the sit-downers to evacuate the two Flint plants. The union ignored the injunction, and Michigan's Governor Frank Murphy delayed its enforcement. Flint police made a futile effort on 11 January to dislodge the strikers in the No. 2 plant. Responding to the request of Flint officials, Murphy then sent the Michigan National Guard to Flint to preserve order but not to take sides. While the sit-down strikers carefully protected company property, wives and others on the outside supplied food and otherwise supported the cause. In a daring maneuver on 1 February, the UAW enlarged the strike by seizing the Chevrolet No. 4 plant, the sole producer of engines for Chevrolet cars.

Governor Murphy played the crucial role in resolving the dispute. The strike ended on 11 February, when GM agreed to recognize the UAW as the bargaining agency for its GM members. Arguably the twentieth century's most important labor conflict, the GM sit-down proved a boon not only to the UAW but to *mass-production unionism in general during the 1930s.

[*See also* Automotive Industry; Congress of Industrial Organizations; Labor Movements; National Labor Relations Act;

New Deal Era, The; Reuther, Walter; Strikes and Industrial Conflict.]

• Henry Kraus, *The Many and the Few: A Chronicle of the Dynamic Auto Workers,* 1947. Sidney Fine, *Sit-Down: The General Motors Strike of 1936–1937,* 1969.

—Sidney Fine

SITTING BULL (1831–1890), Hunkpapa Lakota Sioux chief. One of the most significant of all Indian leaders, Sitting Bull achieved distinction not only as a war leader but also as a political chief and holy man. His record in war with enemy tribes was exemplary even before he came to the notice of whites in the 1860s. He led the fighting against the armies of Generals Henry H. Sibley, Alfred Sully, and Patrick E. Connor, who headed strong columns into Sioux ranges of Dakota and Montana in 1863–1865.

The Fort Laramie Treaty of 1868 divided the Lakota tribes into factions, one accommodating to white authority, the other resisting. The former settled on the Great Sioux Reservation in western Dakota and accepted government rations. The latter remained in the "unceded" Indian territory to the west, the buffalo ranges of the Powder River country. Sitting Bull was the leading chief of the "nontreaty" Lakotas, whom government officials labeled "hostiles."

A staunch foe of all government programs, Sitting Bull disdained treaties, agents, rations, or any course that interfered with the Indians' traditional way of life. For eight years he held together an alliance of Lakota and Northern Cheyenne tribes that pursued their old free existence.

The construction of the Northern Pacific Railroad and the discovery of gold in the Black Hills destabilized this already precarious situation and brought on the Sioux War of 1876. As three armies converged on the Sioux country, Sitting Bull reached the zenith of his power and leadership. He was present at the Battle of the *Little Bighorn, 25–26 June 1876, when Sioux and Cheyenne warriors wiped out General George A. Custer and part of his command. As an "old-man" chief, however, Sitting Bull did not play a conspicuous part. His true significance lay in holding together and imbuing with his spirit of resistance the tribal alliance that defeated Custer.

After the Little Bighorn, the Indian coalition fell apart under military pressure. In 1877, Sitting Bull and a small following sought refuge in Canada. Dwindling buffalo forced his surrender in July 1881.

On the Standing Rock Reservation in Dakota, Sitting Bull feuded with the government agent and assumed a prominent role in the Ghost Dance movement, which swept the Sioux reservations in 1889–1891, promising a return of the old way of life. He was one of several perceived "troublemakers" whom authorities determined to remove. On 15 December 1890, while attempting his arrest, Indian policemen shot and killed him.

[*See also* Gold Rushes; Indian History and Culture: From 1800 to 1900; Indian Wars; Railroads; Wounded Knee Tragedy.]

• Stanley Vestal, *Sitting Bull, Champion of the Sioux,* 1957. Robert M. Utley, *The Lance and the Shield: The Life and Times of Sitting Bull,* 1993.

—Robert M. Utley

SIXTEENTH AMENDMENT. This 1913 amendment to the *Constitution empowers Congress to "lay and collect taxes on incomes, from whatever source derived, without apportionment among the several states . . . ," specifically exempting income taxes from the constitutional mandate governing "direct taxes." Even though an 1881 *Supreme Court decision had upheld the constitutionality of the *Civil War income taxes, a sharply divided Court in *Pollock* v. *Farmers' Loan and Trust Company* (1895) invalidated the income tax inserted into the 1894 Wilson-Gorman *tariff by the Democratic-controlled Congress.

In the years after *Pollock,* a variety of groups and concepts interacted to produce a broad-based consensus in favor of federal income taxation. Increases in government spending mandated a significant flow of revenue, especially if tariff reformers achieved their goal of major downward revision. The *West and the *South, regarding themselves as colonial regions exploited by the industrial Northeast, embraced the income tax as a weapon to redress the sectional balance. Believing that customs duties and excise taxes fell heaviest on the great mass of workers and consumers, largely missing the huge fortunes accumulated by the principal holders of financial and industrial assets, a growing number of Americans advocated income taxation as a matter of "tax equity." The conviction that taxation should be based on "the ability to pay" and that it should come "from whatever source derived" increasingly united southerners and westerners, economists and tax experts, social reformers, urban machine politicians, organized labor, agrarian groups, socialists, and mass-circulation newspapers and *magazines.

The *Democratic party platform of 1908 called for a constitutional amendment to overturn the *Pollock* decision, while the Republican presidential candidate William Howard *Taft proclaimed that a properly drafted tax bill would be sufficient. In 1909, however, when the Republican leaders in Congress sought Taft's aid to prevent a coalition of Democrats and insurgent Republicans from inserting an income tax into the Payne-Aldrich tariff, Taft proposed both a corporation excise tax and a constitutional amendment. Despite initial denunciations of the amendment as a ploy to defeat the income-tax clause of the tariff bill (a charge the Republican leadership freely admitted), the amendment process went forward. Congress proposed the Sixteenth Amendment to the states in September 1909, and by February 1913 the ratification process was complete. Every state except Virginia, Florida, Utah, Rhode Island, Connecticut, and Pennsylvania eventually concurred, as political upheavals in several urban, industrial states of the Northeast and *Middle West produced unexpected Democratic control of their legislatures. Ratification was staunchly opposed by conservative politicians, both Republicans and Democrats, and by prominent industrialists and financiers.

Urged on by President Woodrow *Wilson, majority Democrats swiftly added an income tax to the 1913 Underwood-Simmons tariff. It levied a tax of 1 percent on incomes over $3,000 for single persons and $4,000 for married couples, thereby exempting over 95 percent of Americans. An "additional tax," graduated to 6 percent on income over $500,000 reinforced the concept of taxation according to "ability to pay." Quickly emerging as the federal government's chief source of revenue, the income tax also become a major political battleground between those who viewed it as an instrument for the redistribution of wealth and those who favored lower rates to stimulate economic growth.

[*See also* Income Tax, Federal; Progressive Era.]

• John D. Buenker, *The Income Tax and the Progressive Era,* 1985. W. Elliott Brownlee, *Federal Taxation in America: A Short History,* 1996.

—John D. Buenker

SIXTIES, THE. Stirring restlessly in American memory, the 1960s can still rouse bitter contention. Even a brief overview makes clear why.

Political and Cultural Overview. Politically, the decade began with a presidential election in which Republican Richard M. *Nixon narrowly lost to a glamorous, young Democratic senator, John F. *Kennedy. The Kennedy administration saw several confrontations with the Soviet Union, including a showdown over Berlin and the 1962 *Cuban Missile Crisis. Kennedy also started the *Peace Corps, signed the *Limited Nuclear Test Ban Treaty, and proposed to put an astronaut on the moon—a goal fulfilled on 20 July 1969 when Neil Armstrong set foot on the lunar surface.

Kennedy's presidency—and his life—ended on 22 November 1963, when he was shot by Lee Harvey Oswald. Shocking at the time, the assassination would spawn myriad conspiracy theories by those convinced that Oswald did not act alone. Quickly assuming the reins of power, Vice President Lyndon B. *Johnson pressured Congress to enact an ambitious domestic program. Adding urgency to Johnson's efforts was a quickening pace of *civil rights protest in the *South and in northern cities. The 1963 March on Washington represented a moment of interracial unity, but the black freedom struggle increasingly turned to African American leaders and grew more militant under such groups as the *Student Non-Violent Coordinating Committee and the *Black Panthers. In 1965 and 1966, black neighborhoods in *Los Angeles, *Chicago, *Detroit, Newark, and other cities exploded in riots and arson. The landmark Civil Rights Act of 1965 and the Voting Rights Act of 1966, strongly pushed by Johnson, represented one response to the protests.

Emulating his hero Franklin Delano *Roosevelt, Johnson proposed a far-reaching reform program dubbed the *Great Society, addressing health, education, and environmental issues. The 1964 War on Poverty, launched with great fanfare, included jobs programs; the Head Start project for disadvantaged school children; and VISTA, a kind of domestic Peace Corps.

Challenged in 1964 by Arizona senator Barry *Goldwater, a deeply conservative Republican, Johnson won a landslide victory, in part by running as a peace candidate in contrast to Goldwater's saber rattling. Soon after the election, ironically, Johnson himself led the nation into a full-scale if undeclared war. America's military role in Vietnam had been increasing since the French withdrawal in 1954, and in 1965, citing the 1964 *Gulf of Tonkin Resolution, Johnson vastly escalated the U.S. commitment. As U.S. troops and hardware poured into Vietnam, the casualty figures mounted and domestic unease intensified. The January 1968 *Tet Offensive deepened the opposition. The *Vietnam War further unsettled a nation already torn by racial conflict. While some Americans strongly supported the war, protests mounted, particularly on college campuses, where the *New Left organization *Students for a Democratic Society played a leading role.

The divisions were cultural and generational as well as political. A youthful counterculture expressed its alienation in more open sexuality; long hair, and cast-off clothing; rock music, the Beatles, and Bob *Dylan; and marijuana and other consciousness-altering substances. At Woodstock, New York, in August 1969, 400,000 young people gathered for a three-day music festival laced with political and cultural protest.

Meanwhile, the political climate was changing. Ronald *Reagan, elected governor of California in 1966, denounced campus protests. Johnson, overwhelmed by protests and challenged within his own party, withdrew from the upcoming presidential race in March 1968. Vice President Hubert *Humphrey won the nomination at a chaotic Democratic convention in Chicago marked by violent street clashes between police and antiwar protesters. Richard Nixon, staging a political comeback, won the Republican nomination and went on to defeat Humphrey. Alabama governor George C. *Wallace, appealing to southern and working-class whites angered by racial protest and campus unrest, garnered 13.5 percent of the vote. The grim year 1968 also saw two shocking assassinations. On 4 April, an assassin's bullet killed Martin Luther *King Jr.; riots exploded in Chicago, *Washington, D.C., and elsewhere. In June, Robert *Kennedy, John Kennedy's brother and a presidential candidate in his own right, was shot and killed in Los Angeles.

While President Nixon curbed Johnson's domestic reforms, he and his national security adviser Henry *Kissinger reoriented U.S. foreign policy with overtures to the People's Republic of China and the Soviet Union. In Vietnam, Nixon pursued a policy of "Vietnamization," slowly withdrawing American forces while continuing heavy bombing, including secret raids in neutral Cambodia. Domestic protest continued, culminating in May 1970 with the killing of four Kent State University students by Ohio National Guardsmen. As antiwar protests waned, new social movements arose, including *environmentalism, consumer activism, anti–nuclear-power demonstrations, and a revived *women's rights movement. The conservative backlash continued as well, contributing to Nixon's reelection in 1972 and ultimately to Ronald Reagan's election as president in 1980.

Debating and Exploiting the Sixties. But a mere recital of dates, events, and organizations hardly conveys the complex role of "the Sixties" in subsequent American political and historical discourse. Although a commonly used historical marker, there is little agreement about what it signifies or even what time period it covers. Although the obvious answer is the years between 1960 and 1970, different formulations of a "long Sixties" usually prevail. "The Sixties" often evokes the Vietnam War, the disintegration of a liberal political coalition; and revolutionary changes in legally protected rights, social practices, and cultural forms. When associated with such political and cultural upheavals, the sixties is typically cast as emerging before 1960. One history is quite specific: The sixties arrived on 15 June 1955, when antinuclear activists protested a civil-defense drill. Similarly, Nixon's 1974 resignation or the final U.S. withdrawal from Vietnam in 1975 are often cited as end points for the era. In historical discourse, in short, "the Sixties" may not be the same as "the 1960s."

Mass-culture industries, particularly *advertising, have played an important role in creating images of the sixties. By the mid–1960s, the advertising industry was heralding a "youth revolution" to sell products to baby-boomers and those who hoped to remain in the words of a Dylan song, "forever young." The Chrysler Corporation proclaimed the "Dodge Rebellion"; the countercultural musical *Hair* was a hit on Broadway. Motion-picture directors such as Oliver Stone in *JFK* (1991) and other movies translated the sixties into a recognizable film genre. In mass culture, then, "the Sixties" has functioned as a kind of designer label for coffee-table photo books, hit-music packages, retro-clothing styles, history courses, and television programs—all of which, inevitably, helped shape perceptions of the era.

Attributing meanings to the sixties and to movements associated with it, such as the "counterculture" or the "new *conservatism," generally involves qualitative and normative judgments. Oftentimes, this process becomes intertwined with evaluations of "the *Fifties," the era against which the sixties are often measured. Explicit or implicit comparisons between these two periods, for example, often helps to draw the line between them. Trust in government and passivity among college students are commonly said to mark the fifties, while a growing credibility gap between the state and the citizenry and campus unrest are seen as characteristic of the sixties. Accounts that judge the sixties harshly generally view the fifties much more leniently—and vice versa.

There is nothing preordained about using "the Sixties" as a historical label. The "Gay Nineties" has all but disappeared as a marker for the close of the nineteenth century, and even the "Jazz Age" label for the 1920s has faded. The persistence of "the Sixties" as a historical label depends on the power and saliency of familiar background stories. At least four background frameworks have helped to organize the multitude of historical and popular accounts that have shaped public perceptions of the period.

Interpreting the Sixties: The Declension and Transformation Models. One common background narrative orders the sixties along a trajectory of bright promise followed by disillusionment and decline. Stories in this mold trace the downward course of political *liberalism as the "promise" of John F. Kennedy's Camelot (and/or Lyndon Johnson's Great Society) faded away during, or because of, the sixties. The disintegration of Johnson's presidency looms large in this narrative framework, with the year 1968 a powerful symbolic date. Stories in this "from-promise-to-decline" or "declension" mode often feature the evocative image of Richard Nixon entering the White House, trouncing George McGovern in 1972, or leaving the White House in post-*Watergate disgrace.

Toward the end of the twentieth century, after two decades of "postliberal" politics, accounts based on this paradigm proliferated. Many of these narratives recounted, with a mixture of approval and nostalgia, the liberal politics of the early sixties. The *civil rights movement and organized labor received credit as forces for reform; Kennedy for demonstrating deft leadership during the Cuban Missile Crisis; and Johnson for skillfully managing the presidential transition after Kennedy's assassination. But eventually, in this paradigm, the sixties ended with, or even helped to bring about, the "unraveling," "destruction," or "coming apart" of liberalism.

Another group of stories in this declension framework examine the "radical" challenges to liberalism such as the New Left. These accounts begin with youthful insurgents who see liberalism, even as practiced by Kennedy and Johnson, as failing to address adequately such problems as inequality, *racism, and militarism. Although often critical of the "excesses" of the radical activists, these histories portray them as helping to end racial *segregation, to halt U.S. involvement in Vietnam, and to articulate a new political and social agenda for the United States. But the initial promise of radicalism, like that of liberalism, declines in these stories, and appears defunct by the symbolic year 1968.

In these narratives, many interrelated forces share the blame for the decline of both liberalism and radical insurgency, including the emergence of "divisive" political agendas based on racial and *gender identities, a supposed infatuation with violence and Third World revolutionaries, and the media's ability to deflect attention from political issues to cultural spectacles featuring the antics of countercultural celebrities. The sixties end with squabbling interest groups that cannot compete effectively with a powerful conservative political movement.

The declension paradigm confronts its mirror opposite in a competing paradigm of "transformation." Histories in this vein see the countercultural values, the resurgent *feminism, and the various forms of identity politics that emerged during the late 1960s and early 1970s not as the spoilers of liberalism but as its legitimate heirs and as the seedbed for a renewal of public and private life. Adopting a "long Sixties" chronology, these stories extend into the late–1970s and even well beyond.

Accounts in this transformation framework refuse to concede the political impotency of insurgency and, by expanding the definition of "political," credit the sixties (or movements associated with this label) for promoting lasting and positive changes. Even before the sixties ended, histories that adopt this framework argue, America's social and cultural landscape had been altered: Controls over personal lifestyle choices were eroding; racial and gender hierarchies were being challenged; political and economic institutions were becoming accessible to once-excluded groups, especially women and nonwhite ethnics; new social institutions, such as neighborhood-development organizations and public-interest law firms were taking root; and cultural expression, while not as exuberant as in countercultural dreams, was far more vibrant and iconoclastic.

The Bifurcation Model. A third framework for thinking about the sixties might be termed the "bifurcation" model. Recalling the sociologist Daniel Bell's claim that different "realms" of American life began moving in very different directions during the 1960s, the bifurcation framework combines stories of *both* decline and transformation within a single narrative. According to this interpretation, which became increasingly popular during the 1980s and 1990s, politics began to move rightward while cultural and social life, particularly on college campuses, tracked leftward during the sixties.

Studies recounting their authors' personal renunciation of a youthful flirtation with political or cultural insurgency often employed the bifurcation framework. Rejecting any claim that the liberals or radicals of the sixties made the United States a better place, conservative stories employing the bifurcation framework highlight many of the same social-cultural changes for which the transformation framework credits the radicals, but from a sharply critical perspective. In this paradigm, the sixties becomes a time of frenzied opposition, simply for the sake of opposition, to worthwhile values: sobriety, hard work, patriotism, and toleration for difference. The insurgents claimed to be opening up political and cultural life, advocates of this interpretation allege, but their programs, such as *affirmative action, "Balkanized" American life and encouraged, in the phrase of conservative critic Allan Bloom, "the closing of the American mind."

Although late twentieth-century conservatives such as Robert Bork and William Bennett employed this framework to vilify the Bill *Clinton presidency, it was not advanced exclusively by the political right or cultural conservatives. A neopopulist variant, for example, praised the sixties for reinvigorating grassroots politics but then chastised it for fracturing the old liberal political coalition without offering any coherent alternative, spreading an avant-garde cultural style that denigrated the tastes of ordinary people, and allowing conservatives such as Nixon and Reagan to seize the mantle of "traditional values" to advance their political agendas.

The All-Inclusive Model. Finally, by the end of the twentieth century, what might be called the "Big-Sixties" interpretive framework was clearly evident. This expansive framework allowed nearly everyone to identify a part of the sixties as his or her own. Challenges to the familiar story of the Vietnam War illustrate the all-inclusive Big-Sixties framework. Histories of the war at home written from this perspective, for instance, find more than a binary struggle between interventionist "hawks" and antiwar "doves." Rather, they find doubts about the war scattered throughout the population, including among the nonwhite, ethnic, and blue-collar families whose sons were more likely to be sent into combat than were those from more affluent families who could gain student deferments or stateside positions in the National Guard. Diverse new narratives told of the young men who fought—willingly or reluctantly—in Southeast Asia or who to avoid fighting in the war simply left the United States, and about the variety of ways the war affected the lives of women. With significant *immigration from Southeast Asia beginning in the late 1970s, the stories of *Asian American families have been added to the Big-Sixties framework in describing "our" involvement in a conflict that was hardly limited to Vietnam.

One can argue that the collection and interpretation of an ever-greater number of primary sources from an ever-expanding number of perspectives should generate "better" historical accounts. Indeed, stories based on the Big-Sixties frame often did expand familiar stories into more complete accounts. Political narratives in the declension mode told from this more nuanced perspective, for instance, debated more precisely when and how liberal politics collapsed. Was it in 1968, when 57 percent of the electorate voted for either Richard Nixon or George Wallace? Or did liberalism remain viable, opposing Nixon's foreign policies and preserving federal spending for social programs, well into the 1970s? Did it disintegrate because of its own limitations, especially on social-economic issues, or its excesses? Or did it fall victim to the machinations of cagy conservatives such as Nixon and Reagan?

In another sense, however, the Big-Sixties framework, by launching a multitude of representations and by segmenting familiar stories into smaller and smaller episodes, threatened the very status of "the Sixties" as a meaningful signifier. The sheer volume of disparate accounts can undermine any coherent meaning to the term. After the 1989 collapse of the Soviet

Union, for example, foreign-policy issues associated with the sixties label, particularly those involving the Vietnam War, though dealing with events that were certainly traumatic for anyone touched by them, increasingly appeared to mark no exceptional juncture in the course of post–World War II. U.S. foreign relations.

Other familiar topics such as the civil rights movement, which had long helped to define the sixties as a unique and coherent period, also began to seem constrained by the sixties label. Many late twentieth-century accounts represented the movement as a long-term, multifronted battle against discrimination and inequality that included many different, not always compatible, impulses shaped by *social class, gender, *religion, region, and ethnicity. Microhistories of the 1940s and early 1950s argued that the intense ethnic-racial ferment associated with the sixties, including struggles to end residential segregation and to maintain the liberal political coalition, actually emerged much earlier. Even the story of the transition from civil rights to Black Power increasingly splintered into a multitude of microaccounts involving a diversity of goals, tactics, and leadership styles.

The use of any historical label, in sum, is not a self-evident proposition. The meaning of the sixties has been fashioned—and continues to be refashioned—through a wide variety of background narratives.

[*See also* African Americans; Antinuclear Protest Movements; Antiwar Movements; Black Nationalism; Civil Rights Legislation; Cold War; Drugs, Illicit; Historiography, American; Kent State and Jackson State; Labor Movements; Music: Popular Music; Popular Culture; Postmodernism; Race and Ethnicity; Riots, Urban; Sexual Morality and Sex Reform; Space Program.]

• Alice Echols, *Dare to Be Bad: Radical Feminism in America, 1967–75,* 1990. Todd Gitlin, *The Sixties: Years of Hope, Days of Rage,* rev. ed., 1993. David Farber, ed., *The Sixties: From Memory to History,* 1994. Alexander Bloom and Wini Breines, *Takin' It to the Streets: A Sixties Reader,* 1995. Alan Nadel, *Containment Culture: American Narrative, Postmodernism, and the Nuclear Age,* 1995. Peter Collier et al., *Destructive Generation: Second Thoughts about the Sixties,* 1996. Gerald Horne, *The Fire This Time: The Watts Uprising and the 1960s,* 1997. Robert D. Schulzinger, *A Time for War: The United States and Vietnam, 1941–1975,* 1997. Arthur Marwick, *The Sixties: Cultural Revolution in Britain, France, Italy, and the United States, c. 1958–c. 1974,* 1998. Maurice Isserman and Michael Kazin, *America Divided: The Civil War of the 1960s,* 1999.

—Norman L. Rosenberg

SKYSCRAPERS. The term "skyscraper" first appeared in *Chicago in the 1880s to denote structures taller than the ten-story "elevator buildings" erected in *New York City and elsewhere after 1870. First built in Chicago and New York, skyscrapers eventually spread worldwide. Initially they were dedicated to a single function—commercial, residential, service, or industrial—but as they grew taller, multiuse skyscrapers emerged.

No "first" skyscraper can be singled out, because elements of the type appeared in many European and American buildings. New York's five-story Haughwout Store (1856) installed the first safety passenger elevators. Changes in foundation technology in the early 1880s liberated cellar areas for ancillary services. The first nonloadbearing curtain-walls were hung on the iron frame of a Liverpool, England, office building in 1864. Chicago's Home Insurance Building (1883) was long considered the world's first skyscraper. However, it had an incomplete wrought- and cast-iron frame and used steel beams only for part of the upper floor framing. Chicago's Rand McNally Building (1890) boasted the first all-steel frame strong enough to resist wind forces on its own. Other notable early skyscrapers included Louis *Sullivan's Wainwright Building in St. Louis (1890–1891) and New York's Flatiron Building (Daniel H. Burnham, 1902), Metropolitan Life Insurance Tower (1909), and the sixty-story Woolworth Building (Cass Gilbert, 1913). Manhattan's 102-story *Empire State Building (1930–1931), a tourist mecca, long ranked as the world's tallest building.

Skyscrapers continued to evolve after *World War II. Ludwig Mies van der Rohe's functionalist Seagram Building in Manhattan (1956–1958) employed reflecting glass to dramatic effect. Frame columns arranged in tubes along the exterior surfaces, introduced in Chicago's Dewitt-Chestnut Building (1964), provided unencumbered interior floor space. Chicago's Sears Tower (1974), at 110 stories, was the world's highest skyscraper until surpassed in 1996 by the Petronas Towers in Kuala Lumpur.

[*See also* Architecture: Public Architecture; Business; Industrialization; Urbanization.]

• Carl W. Condit, *The Rise of the Skyscraper,* 1952. Paul Goldberger, *The Skyscraper,* 1983.

—Tom F. Peters

SLAUGHTERHOUSE CASES (1873), a *Supreme Court ruling interpreting the *Fourteenth Amendment. During the *Reconstruction Era, the Louisiana legislature granted certain business and political interests a monopoly over the butchering of animals in *New Orleans. Before refrigeration technology was developed, private butchering practices created *public-health problems that properly regulated slaughterhouse monopolies helped to remedy. A group of the city's butchers nonetheless sued, contending that the state law prevented them from freely pursuing their trade.

Defeated in state court, the butchers appealed to the U.S. Supreme Court; their lawyer, John A. Campbell, argued that the monopoly violated his clients' rights under the Fourteenth Amendment's privileges and immunities (due-process) clause. The *Slaughterhouse* cases presented the Court with its first chance to define the meaning of the Fourteenth Amendment, which had originated in the *Republican party's post-Emancipation efforts to grant black freedmen full rights of citizenship. Campbell contended, however, that the privileges and immunities clause protected economic as well as *civil rights from state infringement. The Court divided 5–4. Justice Samuel F. Miller's majority opinion sustained the monopoly, interpreting the privileges and immunities clause narrowly as a guarantee of only a few civil rights, such as the right to petition, and not as a broad charter of economic liberty. The dissenters, to the contrary, embraced Campbell's theory that the clause guaranteed the right to pursue economic activity free of government regulation.

By 1890 a new Court majority reversed this position, adopting the view that the Fourteenth Amendment's due-process clause protected individual and corporate economic rights. The Court's expansion of economic due process limited state and federal regulation of business, especially of large corporations. Not until 1937, in the *New Deal Era, did the Court abandon this construction of the Fourteenth Amendment. Meanwhile, Justice Miller's narrow construction of the civil rights amendment guarantee fostered the triumph of racial *segregation. It took the *civil rights movement following *World War II to overcome the consequences of Miller's *Slaughterhouse* decision and other prosegregation judicial rulings.

[*See also* Business; Capitalism; Economic Regulation; Emancipation Proclamation; Gilded Age; Laissez-faire.]

• Charles Fairman, *History of the Supreme Court,* vol. 6, *Reconstruction and Reunion, 1864–1888, Part One,* 1971. Michael Les Benedict, "Preserving Federalism: Reconstruction and the Waite Court," *Supreme Court Review* (1978): 39–79.

—Tony Freyer

SLAVERY

SLAVERY: OVERVIEW

No field of United States history produced a larger body of scholarship in the decades after *World War II, or underwent more substantial revision, than did slavery. We now understand that the Africans who came to the North American mainland formed only a small part of the stream of Atlantic slavery. Indeed, only in North America did the unfree population reproduce itself in substantial numbers. Further, contemporary historians now study North American slavery as part of a larger Atlantic history linking Africa, Europe, and the Americas, and recognize differences related to where slaves originated, the crops that they produced and the scale of plantations on which they labored, and the time period involved. The slave experience of those who arrived in North America early in the period of European colonization differed from those who toiled at the peak of the plantation system in the era of "King Cotton," 1830–1860. On the eve of the *Civil War, slavery remained a dynamic and expanding system, not an antiquated labor system on its way to extinction.

Recent scholarship also demonstrates how slaves maintained their humanity under the most trying circumstances. Historians have done much to uncover the extent to which African cultures survived in the Americas; how slave societies grew more hybrid as Africans adapted to new circumstances and as their offspring became *African Americans; how slaves struggled to maintain families in the face of long-distance migration and slave sales; how *religion, Muslim as well as Christian, buttressed slaves' humanity; and how slaves strained to create for themselves a measure of space and liberty under the most oppressive conditions.

—Melvyn Dubofsky

SLAVERY: THE SLAVE TRADE

The British North American colonies and the United States received about 600,000 slaves in the transatlantic slave trade from Africa, about 6 percent of all slaves arriving in the Americas. Prior to the eighteenth century, some slaves were shipped or transshipped from the British West Indies, but most were sent to the mainland directly from the coastal areas of West Africa, particularly Angola and the Bight of Biafra. The enslaved most often had been captured in warfare or kidnapped within Africa by other Africans, and then marched to the coast for sale to European traders. In addition to the slave trade to the Americas, slaves were also sold for use elsewhere in Africa or in the Arabian world, the direction of movement depending on relative demands for slave labor from different parts of a global trading area.

In the middle passage between Africa and the Americas the ships generally carried more people per ton of carrying capacity than ships carrying free passengers. On slave ships bound for the United States, as on those in other parts of the slave trade, captives' mortality rates averaged about 10 percent over the period, with a decline in shipboard mortality rates over time.

The slave trade peaked just prior to the ending of the international slave trade to the United States in 1808, by act of Congress in accord with a provision of the *Constitution. British traders carried most of the slaves to the colonies, although colonists and later independent Americans, primarily in Rhode Island, also engaged in slave trading. Rum was the major commodity Rhode Islanders used in trading for slaves. Most of the slaves arrived in the southern states, Virginia and South Carolina serving as the major recipients.

Sale of slaves within the colonies began with their arrival. The British placed few restrictions on slave sales within or between colonies, and the U.S. Constitution did not limit such transactions. Slave sales could occur directly between buyer and seller or through a specialized middleman, the slave trader. A distinct occupation within the antebellum *South, slave trading involved purchasing and selling slaves, often by public auction; shipping slaves within the South from buying to selling regions; providing credit for slave sales; and advertising and distributing information sheets about the state of the slave market and the current prices for slaves of different age, sex, and occupational status. Slave trading was a risky but moderately profitable occupation.

Prior to 1790, most internal slave movement covered short distances, generally inland from the initial coastal settlements. After 1790, long-distance movement from the eastern states of the Upper South to western states of the Lower South became more common, as the cotton kingdom spread westward. The interstate movement caused the share of slave population in the earlier-settled parts of the South to fall from over 95 percent of all southern slaves in 1790 to less than 50 percent in 1860. The magnitude of this movement, about one million slaves, is not in dispute; historians, however, still debate what proportion of slaves moved with owners, which meant some prospect of holding families intact, and what proportion involved the slave trade. A related debate concerns the interstate slave trade's contribution to the profitability of slavery in the selling areas of the old South. Although owners moved or sold slaves to areas of higher productivity, the income from the actual numbers of slaves sold was insufficient in itself to ensure either the persistence or profitability of slavery in the older areas.

[*See also* Colonial Era; Cotton Industry.]

• Frederic Bancroft, *Slave-Trading in the Old South,* 1931; reprint 1996. James A. Rawley, *The Transatlantic Slave Trade: A History,* 1981. Michael Tadman, *Speculators and Slaves,* 1989.

—Stanley L. Engerman

SLAVERY: DEVELOPMENT AND EXPANSION OF SLAVERY

In the early eighteenth century, when English authorities in Virginia and South Carolina gathered the disparate laws affecting slavery into comprehensive slave codes, slavery in North America entered a new phase. Although Africans had arrived on the continent with the early Spanish explorers, slavery under English dominion existed as a combination of acquired customs and laws enacted piecemeal to restrict the behavior of Africans and Native Americans. Beginning in Virginia in 1705, however, slavery took on new institutional life. Thenceforward, a class of human beings identifiable merely by their non-European ancestry were held as property and systematically denied the rights and privileges of free persons.

The prime mover behind this transformation was the growth of world trade during the sixteenth and seventeenth centuries, which created unprecedented demand for commodities of every variety. While Europe supplied manufactured goods, the Americas and Africa contributed raw materials and slaves. The English in the northern colonies produced naval stores, fish, animal hides, and cattle. Their counterparts to the south raised tobacco and other plantation staples using slave laborers as well.

The Colonial and Revolutionary Eras. The tobacco-based plantation system that evolved in the area surrounding Chesapeake Bay proved to be the seedbed of slavery in British North America. As early as 1676, *Bacon's Rebellion had demonstrated the settlers' passion for fresh lands on which to grow tobacco. As they pressed westward, white Virginians established satellite "quarters" where newly imported African slaves cleared the land and planted tobacco. Plantation routines, particularly those governing labor, evolved by trial and error. If smallholders often worked side-by-side with their slaves, larger planters embraced a more intense—and more exploitive—system characterized by long hours in the fields under the direction of overseers. Eventually called gang labor, this routine furnished little to the laborers other than food, clothing, and shelter.

Emulating the sugar plantations of the West Indies, the En-

MAP 19: SLAVE POPULATION IN THE SOUTH (1860)

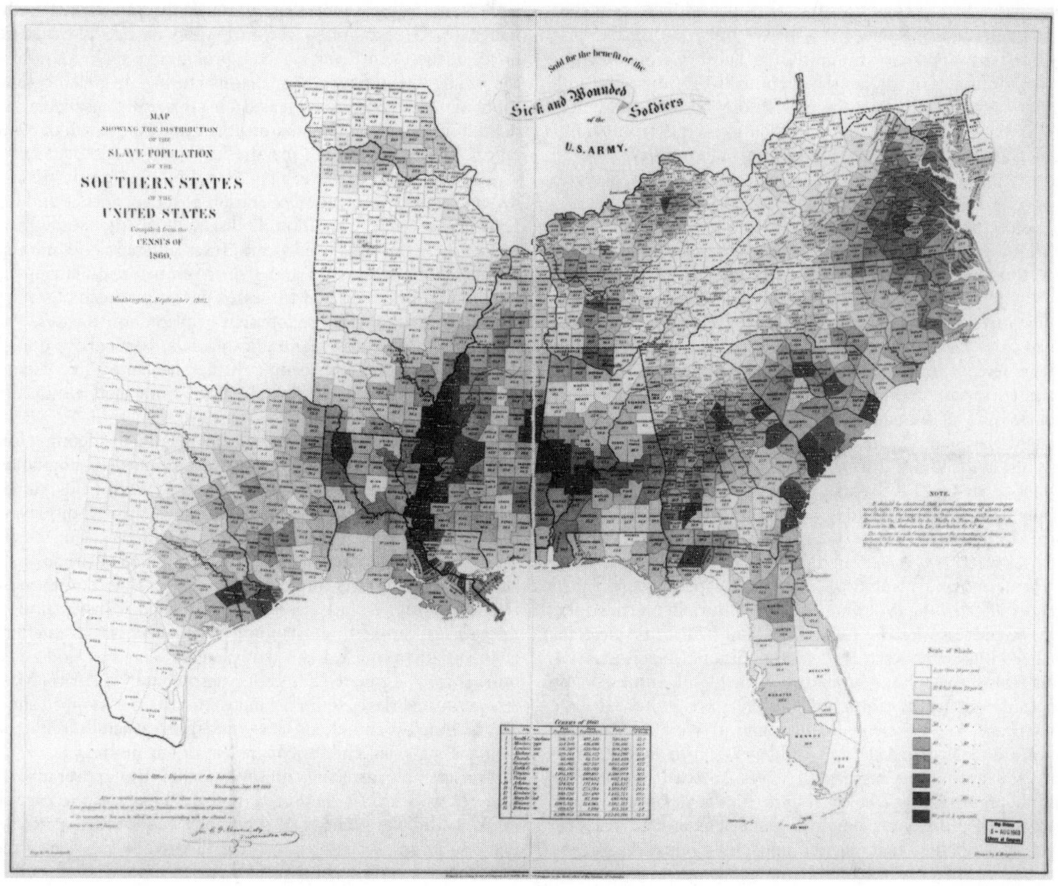

Based on data from the 1860 census and certified as accurate by the Census Bureau, this 1861 map was sold to benefit sick and wounded Union soldiers during the Civil War. The map shows the concentration of slaves along the coastal states southward from Virginia and Maryland, and in the cotton belt westward into Texas.

[*See* Civil War; Cotton Industry; Slavery: Development and Expansion of Slavery; South, The; Tobacco Industry.]

glish built a plantation colony in South Carolina during the last quarter of the seventeenth century. When the colonists realized that the swampy soil favored rice cultivation, they developed a plantation system that, while different from the Chesapeake Bay pattern, nonetheless displayed important similarities. Recognizing their own susceptibility to *malaria and the Africans' apparent immunity, the South Carolinians imported thousands of African slaves annually over the eighteenth century. After 1750, when the new colony of Georgia authorized slavery, Carolina planters pushed rice cultivation southward. They also revolutionized production, using slave labor to reshape the landscape, harnessing the tidal flow of rivers to flood the rice fields. The task system of labor that evolved in this setting rested on the individual laborer's responsibility for performing a fixed amount of work per day. Overseers assigned tasks to individual slaves and inspected the completed work at day's end. Obliged largely to support themselves, rice-plantation slaves also controlled whatever surplus they produced from their allotment gardens.

The new plantation systems of Virginia and South Carolina increased social stratification among Europeans and gave rise to a division of labor among the slaves. Masters increasingly brought slaves into their households as cooks, butlers, maidservants, and carriage drivers. Other slaves, mostly men, began practicing trades. The balance between field and house labor on any particular slaveholding plantation depended on the personal circumstances of specific masters and the economic and political currents prevalent in different places at different times.

The farms and plantations of the Chesapeake region profoundly affected the evolution of slave culture in North America. The process whereby Africans became *African Americans occurred unevenly, as slaves wielded traditional beliefs and customs against the cultural assault unleashed by their masters. By the mid–eighteenth century, however, slave culture in the Chesapeake Bay represented a blending of West African, European, and Native American influences. Even before large-scale conversion to Christianity, slaves imbibed the political culture of the English colonial system. They petitioned and sued for their freedom, employing the language of personal rights and liberties that was gaining public currency. In the Carolina lowcountry, a combination of geographic isolation and the high proportion of Africans in the population accounted for a pronounced African influence on language, folklore, burial customs, medical practices, and crafts that in some respects persisted into the late twentieth century.

The *Revolutionary War shook but did not topple slavery. The Virginia planters who played a major role in crafting the rationale for independence took care that the demand for freedom not reach the slaves. They took equal pains to assure that the new nation's fundamental law favored the property interest of slaveholders over the human rights of slaves. As northern slaveholders embraced gradual emancipation and some of their southern counterparts embraced the African *colonization movement, most southern slaveholders clung ever more firmly to slavery.

Amidst this renewed commitment to human bondage, planters in the Chesapeake Bay region diversified their agriculture by growing wheat and other grains along with tobacco. As a result of declining soil fertility, a slave population growing rapidly through natural increase, and changes in international markets, planters confronted a surplus of slaves. Thus they allied with opponents of the trans-atlantic slave trade to ban the importation of enslaved Africans after 1807. As the plantation system expanded westward with the new nation, the lower *South provided a ready market for the "surplus" slaves of the upper South.

The Slave System Spreads Westward. The South Atlantic states of North Carolina, South Carolina, and Georgia illustrate the post-revolutionary expansion of slavery westward. Opposed to abolishing the slave trade, much less slavery, settlers streamed into the upcountry even before Eli *Whitney's cotton gin made the large-scale cultivation of short-staple cotton profitable. They crossed the Appalachian Mountains into Kentucky and Tennessee, knowing that, although the *Northwest Ordinance (1783) prohibited the formation of new slave states north of the Ohio River, no such prohibition applied south of the Ohio. Expanding cotton manufacturing in England (and soon in *New England) created an apparently insatiable demand for raw cotton that sparked the explosive growth of plantation slavery throughout the South.

The expansion of slavery continued for the four-score and seven years between the *Declaration of Independence and the *Emancipation Proclamation. Louisiana, Alabama, Mississippi, Missouri, Arkansas, Florida, and Texas entered the Union as slave states between 1803 and 1845. Even before qualifying for statehood, these areas had witnessed the rapid spread of slavery and the equally rapid development of plantation clusters. The appropriation of Native American lands, particularly during Andrew *Jackson's presidency, further facilitated this expansion. By 1850, the Black Belt stretched from the Carolinas to eastern Texas.

Gang labor under overseers quickly became the defining feature of the cotton-plantation system. To outsiders, plantation life often appeared unusually monotonous, with fields, buildings, slave quarters, and even the crossroads towns displaying little distinctiveness. Work routines likewise seemed to lack variety: Daily toil began before sunrise and ended at sundown or later. Cultural aspects of the system also became routinized by the 1830s. Masters acquiesced in the religious instruction of their slaves, on the understanding that slavery was a system of labor ordained by God and that planters served as God's custodians for the putatively inferior descendants of Africa. Masters permitted slaves to marry in ceremonies that stopped short of sanction by church or state, and they generally refrained from selling small children apart from their mothers.

Considerable diversity, however, belied the appearance of uniformity. Seasonal rhythms varied the kind and the pace of work, as did the vagaries of geography and weather patterns. Even on large plantations, routines differed by the size of the slave force, the relationship between overseers and slaves, and—most importantly—the personality and beliefs of the master. If few masters renounced the whip, each wielded it with different frequency and intensity. Some offered their slaves such prerogatives as gardening and marketing. On smaller farms, the circumstances in which slaves lived and worked varied widely. Cities and towns offered masters and slaves additional possibilities for experimentation, depending on the size of the city, its racial and ethnic *demography, the nature of its economy, and the local political climate.

A critical element in slavery's westward spread was the growth of a regional market in slaves. Trading houses emerged in areas where slaves were in abundant supply (such as Richmond) and where they were in demand (such as *New Orleans). Between 1800 and 1861, perhaps as many as one million slaves were relocated from the Upper South to the Lower South and from the southeastern to the southwestern slave states. Like other forms of property, slaves were sold to speculators, deeded to heirs, given as wedding presents, and wagered in games of chance. The scant restraints on such exchanges intensified the slaves' most dreaded fate—the breakup of families through sale to strangers—a process intrinsic to the machinery of expansion.

As early as the 1830s, the lands settled in the years after the Revolution had begun to deteriorate under relentless cotton cultivation. In upcountry Georgia, for instance, travelers observed deep gullies where the topsoil had washed from the fields. The Panic of 1837, largely a product of heavy speculation in western lands, temporarily limited slavery expansion but in the long run fostered it. The ensuing contraction depressed cotton prices until after the *Mexican War, but amidst the stagnation, cotton planters studied the prescriptions for agricultural reform that such Upper South figures as Edmund Ruffin of Virginia had long advocated: deep plowing; fertilizers; improved methods, implements, seeds, and work animals; and, most important of all, diversification. They organized agricultural societies to pursue these objectives, circulated tracts on improved farming, and subscribed to reform-minded agricultural journals. If the rising price of cotton by the late 1840s produced some backsliding, the reform cause—and its cardinal tenet of self-sufficiency—gained a new lease on life as the sectional crisis deepened.

The Expansive 1850s. With the return of prosperity in the 1850s, a number of significant changes helped spread cotton cultivation—and slavery—into new areas. Prosperity, for instance, enabled planters to reduce the wild canebrakes of the Yazoo-Mississippi Delta to the plow. Likewise, railroad promoters, perfecting the networks they had been envisioning since the 1820s, convinced cotton planters that *railroads provided the key to the future of marketing their crops. The startling growth in rail mileage across the South generated profound social changes. Railroads sped the movement of goods, people, and ideas, but at a price. For many planters, railroads represented the distilled essence of the market and transportation revolutions that threatened the stability of the region.

The 1850s also witnessed the expansion of cotton cultivation into yeoman-farming areas outside the Black Belt. Not surprisingly, the railroad played a part in this development. Traditionally, yeoman farmers had viewed market production as a supplement to subsistence-oriented production. Railroads introduced an alluring range of consumer goods to which cotton growing promised access. Although the full effects of the yeoman farmers' switch from subsistence to market production did not materialize until after the *Civil War, the numbers of new cotton growers, fresh cotton acres, and additional bales of cotton profoundly affected the institution of slavery on the eve of the Civil War. Cotton mania even gave rise to a short-lived but intense campaign to reopen the transatlantic slave trade. Although the proposal failed, it alerted the North to the growing demand for slaves amid the rising tide of cotton prosperity.

Through the secession crisis and the events leading up to the Civil War, many white southerners became convinced that leaving the Union would not only guarantee their independence, but also improve the prospects for expanding slavery. They looked approvingly on the fact that between 1790 and 1860 the slave population had grown from approximately .7 million to nearly 4 million. On the eve of the Civil War, the two most populous slave states, Virginia and Georgia, alone had more slaves than had been in the entire United States in 1790. Eyeing Central America and the Caribbean (especially Cuba), planters believed that the future of slave expansion looked bright. Beyond generating wealth, they believed, they would also demonstrate to the world slavery's ability to harmonize capital and labor and thereby avoid the class conflicts that threatened to plunge urban, industrial societies into chaos. Not until invading northern armies moved south and by 1863 undertook an all-out war against slavery did planters realize the unreality of that dream.

[*See also* African American Religion; Agriculture: Colonial Era; Agriculture: 1770s to 1890; Antebellum Era; Antislavery; Brown, John; Business Cycle; Calhoun, John C.; Colonial Era; Compromise of 1850; Cotton Industry; Depressions, Economic; Early Republic, Era of the; Expansionism; Foreign Trade, U.S.; Fugitive Slave Act; Indian History and Culture: From 1800 to 1900; Industrialization; Nat Turner's Uprising; Racism; Revolution and Constitution, Era of; *Scott* v. *Sandford;* Slave Uprisings and Resistance; Textile Industry; Tobacco Industry.]

• Kenneth M. Stampp, *The Peculiar Institution,* 1956. Eugene D. Genovese, *Roll, Jordan, Roll: The World the Slaves Made,* 1974. Lawrence W. Levine, *Black Culture and Black Consciousness,* 1977. Albert J. Raboteau, *Slave Religion,* 1978. James Oakes, *The Ruling Race: A History of American Slaveholders,* 1982. Sterling Stuckey, *Slave Culture,* 1987. Michael Tadman, *Speculators and Slaves: Masters, Traders, and Slaves in the Old South,* 1989. Ira Berlin, *Many Thousands Gone: The First Two Centuries of Slavery in North America,* 1998. Philip D. Morgan, *Slave Counterpoint: Black Culture in the Eighteenth-Century Chesapeake and Lowcountry,* 1998.

—Joseph P. Reidy

SLAVERY: SLAVE FAMILIES, COMMUNITIES, AND CULTURE

African enslavement in North America was a deeply isolating experience. After enduring the middle passage, newcomers underwent a brutal "seasoning" process intended to accommodate them to an alien culture and break their independent wills. Torn away from the families, communities, landscapes, and cultures they had known, survivors faced the Herculean task of reconstructing their lives, individually and collectively, within the harsh and hostile confines of the New World slavery system.

The challenge, though enormous for all, differed significantly for each person. Age and sex mattered, as did physical, mental, and spiritual health. So too did the nature of the climate faced, the crops raised, and the master to be endured. Did you arrive earlier, or later? Did fate confine you to a large plantation or a small farm? Did you live in the city, learn languages quickly, work in the big house, or possess special skills of use to your workmates or your owner? All these variables and many more shaped the personal conditions for gradually rebuilding a web of relationships within the system of hereditary, race-based enslavement.

Establishing human ties under inhuman conditions often appeared impossible, and many succumbed to depression, insanity, or suicide. Thousands of newcomers each year found their unpaid work exhausting, their nutrition poor, and their shelter minimal. Violence and abuse proved commonplace, freedom of movement was monitored, and access to *literacy prohibited. Such conditions taxed strength, drained emotion, and left hope in short supply. But slave narratives (and memoirs from slave labor camps in modern times) demonstrate that the need for community and culture is difficult to crush entirely.

Since newcomers found it virtually impossible to retain contact with enslaved members of their African family or village of origin, they established bonds with others who spoke a similar language or had survived the Atlantic passage on the same ship. They also had frequent contacts with European indentured servants and artisans, Native Americans (enslaved and free), and a variety of free blacks and mulattoes. But their most important encounters were with two other groups: recently arrived "saltwater slaves" from different (though frequently similar) African cultures, and "country-born Negroes," with no personal knowledge of Africa, who had adapted to life in the American "gulag."

Out of these contacts, new families took shape in the face of conflicting pressures. Motivated by self-interest, planters encouraged domestic ties. Slave offspring represented added labor and larger profits; *family bonds tempered the desire for escape or rebellion; and conjugal units among slaves suited slave owners' desires to enforce propriety. But owners also frustrated and mocked close slave relationships. Exploiting their nearly absolute power, they frequently raped black women, forced couples to procreate against their will, punished polygamy (acceptable in some African cultures), and discouraged lasting relationships between slaves belonging to different masters.

Even when unused, the legally sanctioned power of any owner to offer large rewards (including freedom itself) and impose stringent punishments (including whipping, maiming, chaining, or castration) affected relations among the enslaved. Planters held, and occasionally used, the legal power to separate husbands from wives and parents from children—suddenly and permanently—by invoking the right to sell human property for profit. Even manumission could have divisive effects, for owners occasionally freed their own mulatto offspring, turncoats who betrayed conspiracies, and elderly or crippled workers who then had to subsist on their own.

A comparison to the West Indies is revealing, for the slave regime in the U.S. *South was less harsh and life expectancy longer than in the sugar islands. Also, child mortality remained lower. Therefore, long before the end of the slave trade in 1807, mainland planters preferred to encourage childbirth and absorb the cost of raising future laborers, rather than working slaves to early deaths and buying costly adult replacements. Since the ratio of women to men was less imbalanced among the enslaved population in North America (in part owing to the importance of African women in Carolina rice production), this population achieved and sustained a positive growth rate much sooner than in the Caribbean.

A further contrast proved significant. By the eighteenth century, Africans vastly outnumbered Europeans on the Caribbean islands, while in most slaveholding areas of North America whites maintained not only legal, but also numerical, domination. Black majorities prevailed in the lowcountry of South Carolina and Georgia, in tidewater counties of Virginia and Maryland, and in the cotton plantation regions of Louisiana and Mississippi. But as the United States expanded while curtailing the African slave trade and absorbing a steady flow of immigrants from Europe, black Americans had fewer contacts with Africans and more with Europeans and Native Americans than did their West Indian counterparts.

Add to this important demographic fact the heavy weight of racist ideology, the brutalizing nature of hereditary slavery, plus its sheer longevity, and the roots and complexities of African-American culture make increasing sense. Though African traditions and practices persisted more strongly under enslavement than many have understood, the above-mentioned factors also help explain why such cultural patterns were less abundant and enduring in the American South than in the Caribbean region.

Given the formidable odds, safe, stable families could not be the norm among enslaved Americans. Yet lasting marriages and wide kin networks emerged, and new lifeways developed. With regard to speech, food, music, dance, dress, body language, religious belief, and most other aspects of life, slaves steadily mixed different African traditions together, while also integrating and absorbing significant aspects of Euro-American and Native American experience. The result of this extended syncretic process was the appearance, even before 1800, of a distinctive and enduring African-American culture, with common strands and numerous regional variations.

Nothing epitomized Afro-America's emergent culture more than the rise of a distinctive black Christianity. Despite efforts by white authorities to preach only submission and conformity to slaves, the *Bible offered precedent and inspiration for a message of triumph over bondage. Its stories, when personalized, provided meaning and hope in the face of deep suffering. More than any other institution created in slave times, the church provided a sanctioned haven for building communities of belief and mutual support.

[*See also* African American Religion; African Americans; Antislavery; Cotton Industry; Douglass, Frederick; Gospel Music, African American; Marriage and Divorce; Racism; Protestantism; Religion; Slave Uprisings and Resistance; Spirituals; Tobacco Industry; *Uncle Tom's Cabin.*]

• John W. Blassingame, *The Slave Community: Plantation Life in the Antebellum South,* 1972. Herbert G. Gutman, *The Black Family in Slavery and Freedom, 1750–1925,* 1976. Sterling Stuckey, *Slave Culture,* 1987. Larry E. Hudson Jr., *To Have and to Hold: Slave Work and Family Life in Antebellum South Carolina,* 1997. Michael A. Gomez, *Exchanging Our Country Marks: The Transformation of African Identities in the Colonial and Antebellum South,* 1998. Ira Berlin, *Many Thousands Gone: The First Two Centuries of Slavery in North America,* 1998.

—Peter H. Wood

SLAVERY: HISTORIANS AND SLAVERY

In *American Negro Slavery* (1918), Ulrich B. Phillips portrayed the institution of slavery as a benign paternalism that ordered relations between docile, childlike slaves and their masters. Though Phillips's knowledge of the plantation economy was not balanced by an understanding of slaves as human beings, his was for decades the most influential text on the subject. Herbert Aptheker's *American Negro Slave Revolts* (1943) represented a sustained response to Phillips, who had labeled slave uprisings as "crimes." Aptheker provided extensive evidence of slave resistance and gave imaginative attention to relevant institutional features of slavery, but not until Kenneth Stampp's *The Peculiar Institution* (1956) was plantation slavery examined in ways that systematically reversed or modified Phillips. For Stampp, slavery as labor system, far more than paternalism, was its defining reality. However, Stanley Elkins in *Slavery: A Problem in American Intellectual and Institutional Life* (1959), drawing upon the analogy of Nazi concentration camps, reintroduced Phillips's serio-comic slave (the so-called Sambo), contending that the totalitarian nature of slavery so battered the slaves' personality that childlike behavior seemed natural to large numbers of slaves in the deep *South.

Eugene Genovese's *Roll, Jordan, Roll* (1972) borrowed Phillips's conception of a benevolent paternalism but stressed a reciprocal, often subtle relationship between master and slave that assumed the humanity of slaves. The slaves' desire for freedom, Genovese argued, stemmed mainly from Christian influence. New lines of investigation, however, soon reconsidered the degree of slave dependence on the master. Peter Wood's *Black Majority* (1974) disclosed that Africans brought work skills with them, including rice cultivation, that greatly benefited the plantation economy of South Carolina. A year later, in *American Slavery, American Freedom,* Edmund Morgan contended that slave labor in tobacco fields, especially in Virginia, was vital to the colonists' Revolutionary struggle against England that led to freedom for white European settlers but, paradoxically, not for slaves. Owing to Morgan's interpretation, Edward McColley's earlier demonstrations, in *Slavery in Jeffersonian Virginia* (1964), of slaves' responsibility for tobacco cultivation and for every aspect of readying it for shipment took on new resonance. Consequently, the significance of slave labor in America's overall *economic development was recast as a vital factor.

Although Lawrence Levine in *Black Culture and Black Consciousness* (1975) credited African influences in slave music and tales, he deflated the question of cultural origins, concluding that by the mid–nineteenth century slaves were mainly Christian. But disagreement among historians of slavery about the degree to which Christianity influenced slave religion and culture remained acute. Leslie Howard Owens's *This Species of Property* (1976), for example, was among the first studies to insist on the centrality of slave reliance on African religious values.

William Piersen's *Black Legacy* (1993) and Sterling Stuckey's *Slave Culture* (1987) offered sustained explorations of the question of origins. Piersen demonstrated that slaves in the West Indies and North America shared numerous African values, while Stuckey contended, contrary to long-held opinion, that specific African cultural elements—Ibo, Bakongo, Mendi, and others—formed the central core of slave culture throughout antebellum America and militated against the possibility of slaves being merely Christian.

[*See also* African American Religion; Antebellum Era; Colonial Era; Cotton Industry; Historiography, American; Racism; Slave Uprising and Resistance; Tobacco Industry.]

• David Brion Davis, *The Problem of Slavery in Western Culture*, 1996.

—Sterling Stuckey

SLAVE UPRISINGS AND RESISTANCE. Slave revolts, conspiracies, and resistance have been problematic for all Americans, and buffeted by emotional and ideological considerations, ever since the beginnings of *slavery in North America in the seventeenth century. Historians agree that far fewer and much smaller actual revolts occurred in North America than in the West Indies, Surinam, and Brazil. The crucial reason for this difference was that the ratio of blacks to whites was much higher in those regions than in most of North America. But historians also emphasize that slaves in North America engaged in a great deal of "day-to-day" resistance that took the form of sabotage, malingering, running away, and creative shamming, as well as acts of individual violence.

At least two outright revolts in the *Colonial Era were organized by specific African ethnic groups—by Akan-speaking people in *New York City in 1712 and by Angolans at Stono, South Carolina, in 1739. Later, after the *Revolutionary War, important conspiracies involved slaves who were culturally much further removed from Africa, such as Gabriel's in Virginia in 1800, Denmark Vesey's in Charleston, South Carolina, in 1822, and *Nat Turner's uprising in Virginia in 1831. During the era of the French Revolution, the massive and successful slave revolt in Haiti profoundly affected both blacks and whites in the United States. It sparked a wave of unrest among American slaves for a generation and an even longer-lasting fear among slaveholders in the *South.

The mere idea of a slave uprising frightened whites, yet over the long term their reactions changed dramatically. In the eighteenth century, slave revolts appeared to northern and southern whites as both natural and nearly inevitable. In the nineteenth century, southern whites came to view such revolts as both improbable and unnaturally fomented by outside agitation. Yet when historians began retrospective discussion about slave revolts in about 1940, they unconsciously reverted to the eighteenth-century view.

Much less is known about how *African Americans reacted to outright revolts, though it is clear that many felt a deep-seated ambiguity because of the vicious suppression they knew would follow. American slaves well understood that even individual acts of defiance almost always had dire consequences.

During the second half of the twentieth century, historians argued about the extent of slave resistance. In general, they stressed the substantial resistance to slavery among American slaves, but they differed about the nature of the myriad forms those activities took, which in fact ranged all the way from killing masters, mistresses, and overseers, through breaking tools, faked pregnancies, and folktales about the clever and resourceful Brer Rabbit.

Long after the end of slavery in the United States, historians still debated questions related to slave uprisings and to what slaves actually felt and did. By the end of the twentieth century, however, a broad consensus had emerged that enslaved African Americans frequently resisted slavery, and that they did so in highly diverse and often creative ways.

• Eugene D. Genovese, *From Rebellion to Revolution: Afro-American Slave Revolts in the Making of the Modern World*, 1979.

—Winthrop D. Jordan

SLOAN, ALFRED P. (1875–1966), businessman, philanthropist. Born in New Haven, Connecticut, and educated at the Massachusetts Institute of Technology (MIT), Sloan entered business as president of his father's Hyatt Roller Bearing Company, which in 1916 became part of the General Motors Corporation (GM). Appointed a GM vice president in 1919, he instituted a management plan involving sophisticated market forecasting and inventory control throughout the unwieldy GM empire. Widely copied by other corporations, his model was adopted in Europe and Japan after *World War II. Business historians view Sloan as the primary architect of the modern corporate structure. Under his leadership as president (1923–1937) and chief executive officer (1923–1946), GM became the world's largest corporation and surpassed Ford as America's leading automaker. What came to be called "Sloanism" entailed centralized financial planning and investment strategies integrated with decentralized production units. Under Sloan, GM produced a car "for every purse and purpose," from Chevrolet to Cadillac. GM's efficiencies of production and shrewd marketing of annual model changes became the standard for mass producers of consumer goods and services.

During the *New Deal Era, Sloan articulated business opposition to unionization and resistance to government intervention in social and economic affairs. Only reluctantly did he recognize the United Auto Workers (UAW) after the 1937 sit-down strikes. In 1950, GM and the UAW signed the "Treaty of Detroit," a labor agreement that enshrined the principle that autoworkers should share in the industry's prosperity but left in place Sloan's principal legacy: management control over production and pricing.

As a philanthropist, Sloan, with his wife Irene, gave away $300 million, including millions to MIT. With his friend Charles F. Kettering (1876–1958), a GM vice president, he endowed the Sloan-Kettering Foundation for the Study of Cancer in 1945. By the end of the century, the Memorial Sloan-Kettering Cancer Center in New York City was a world leader in *cancer research, treatment, and education.

[*See also* Automotive Industry; Business; Ford, Henry; Labor Movements; Laissez-faire; Mass Marketing; Mass Production; Medicine: Since 1945; Philanthropy and Philanthropic Foundations; Reuther, Walter; Sit-down Strike, Flint; Technology.]

• Alfred P. Sloan, *My Years with General Motors*, ed. Catherine Stevens and John McDonald, 1964. Alfred D. Chandler, *The Visible Hand*, 1977.

—Douglas M. Reynolds

SLUMS. The word "slum" originated as an East London slang term, probably in the early nineteenth century. By 1850, in both England and America, "slums" referred to places inhabited by poor people and allegedly characterized by *crime, filth, and immorality. Almost always used by outsiders rather than inhabitants of the communities so labeled, the term connoted (and often confused) both *poverty and deviance.

Two late nineteenth-century developments combined to raise the term from slang usage to a potent and controversial word in the vocabulary of urban reformers. First, the explosive growth of working-class *housing districts of industrial cities, characterized by miles of multifamily housing and occupied by poor immigrants, prompted affluent urbanites to apply the term to huge areas. Second was the rise of a movement for housing regulation. From the 1840s on, sanitary investigations highlighted the link between poor housing and epidemic *diseases. In the late nineteenth century, tenement housing reform became a cause in its own right. Jacob Riis's exposés **How the Other Half Lives* (1890) and *The Battle with the Slum* (1902), fueled pressures for stricter standards of ventilation, density, and plumbing, first in *New York City and then in many other places.

Once slums were defined as a public threat, reformers began to consider their removal. Although British and European authorities had experimented with state-sponsored slum clearance as early as the 1850s, most American tenement reformers initially rejected such use of public authority. But between 1910 and the 1950s, American officials moved at first gingerly and then enthusiastically toward large-scale slum clearance. Planners such as Harland Bartholomew in St. Louis advocated clearance to allow for coherent, neighborhood redevelopment.

Housing reformers such as Edith Elmer Wood of New York became convinced that public, low-income housing could replace slums. Slum clearance moved onto the legislative agenda in a few states in the 1920s, and gained national visibility during the *New Deal Era. The Housing Act of 1937 established the basic structure of a federal subsidy program expanded by the Housing Act of 1949 and the Urban Renewal Program of the 1950s.

Despite its advocates' best intentions, slum clearance became highly controversial. Clearing slums required mapping and defining them, and clearance advocates of the mid–twentieth century moved away from probing the morality of such areas to studying measurable characteristics such as age of housing, density, and adequacy of plumbing. Still, the selection process at the local level frequently and disproportionately targeted areas of minority residence. Moreover, while in some cases low-income housing replaced demolished structures, an increasing number of federally funded projects involved commercial or high-income residential redevelopment.

This trend in turn stoked a backlash, marked by strong protests from *African-American communities and climaxed by the publication of Jane Jacobs's *Death and Life of Great American Cities* in 1961. By the mid–1960s, federal authorities had turned away from large-scale clearance in favor of smaller rehabilitation projects and the word "slum" fell out of favor in policy discussions. Ironically, in the late twentieth century the term was often applied to the federally backed public housing that had been meant to replace older "slums."

[*See also* Great Society; Immigration; Industrialization; Johnson, Lyndon B.; Progressive Era; Public Health; Sixties, The; Urbanization; Urban Renewal.]

• James Ford, *Slums and Housing, with Special Reference to New York City,* 1936. Mark Gelfand, *A Nation of Cities: The Federal Government and Urban America, 1933–1965,* 1975. David Ward, *Poverty, Ethnicity, and the American City, 1840–1925: Changing Conceptions of the Slum and the Ghetto,* 1989.

—Henry C. Binford

SMALLPOX. Smallpox, a highly contagious, often fatal viral *disease marked by high fever and skin eruptions that leave survivors severely disfigured, was one of the most deadly diseases that Europeans unwittingly brought to the Americas. Native Americans, lacking both immunity and experience with its ravages, succumbed quickly when it swept through Mexico and Central America in the 1520s. The first pandemic established a pattern of devastation that persisted into the twentieth century. From *New England to the Pacific, smallpox routinely killed at least 30 percent of the Native Americans exposed to it. Epidemics wiped out villages, uprooted tribes, and undermined resistance to European territorial incursions. In the 1760s, during *Pontiac's Rebellion, the British military commander in America, Sir Jeffrey Amherst, advocated efforts to deliberately spread smallpox among the Indians.

Smallpox epidemics also severely affected English colonists in the eighteenth century, forcing them to develop rules of notification, isolation, and quarantine—the first systems of organized *public-health law in America. Colonists also sought to minimize the virulence of smallpox through the practice of inoculation, a method of inducing mild smallpox that usually left patients alive, unscathed, and immune to further attacks. In 1721, the minister Cotton Mather and the physician Zabdiel Boylston (1679–1766) introduced inoculation in *Boston, but controversy greeted their experiment. Townspeople reasonably feared that uncontrolled inoculation could start epidemics. Further refining their health regulations, most towns allowed inoculation only after an epidemic was already under way. By the late eighteenth century, widespread inoculation had greatly reduced smallpox mortality.

In 1798, the English physician Edward Jenner (1749–1823) announced that vaccination (inoculation with cowpox virus) could prevent smallpox altogether. Benjamin Waterhouse (1754–1846), professor of physic (a branch of medicine) at Harvard, performed the first American vaccination in 1800. American physicians soon were vaccinating routinely. Smallpox did not disappear, however, and vaccination was not risk free. Vaccine purity and technique varied widely and vaccination occasionally led to infection or even death. These hazards convinced some people—antivaccinationists—to avoid it at all cost.

As epidemics periodically erupted throughout the nineteenth century, many cities instituted compulsory vaccination laws. Antivaccinationists refused to comply, arguing that these laws abridged their *civil liberties and endangered their health. Although they won repeal in some states and routed health departments in Milwaukee, Wisconsin, and *New York City in the 1890s, they lost in the *Supreme Court. In *Jacobson* v. *Massachusetts* (1905), Justice John Marshall *Harlan's majority opinion declared compulsory-vaccination statutes constitutional, providing the legal foundation for sweeping twentieth-century state authority over individuals to protect public health. Health departments realized, however, that persuasion was more effective than compulsion. By the early twentieth century, cities, states, and the federal government were addressing objections against vaccination by ensuring its safety. The Biologics Control Act of 1902 set production and quality standards for vaccines that became a model for the world. By 1947, confidence in vaccination was such that more than six million citizens avidly sought it when an epidemic threatened New York City. Smallpox last appeared in the United States in 1949, but the *World Health Organization (WHO) did not declare it eradicated globally until 1980. Two sites currently hold samples of the virus: the *Centers for Disease Control in *Atlanta and the Russian State Research Center of Virology and Biotechnology in Siberia. Although WHO slated these samples for destruction on 30 June 1999, both the American and Russian governments postponed it in order to conduct research on defenses against the disease should it ever be used as a weapon of bioterrorism.

[*See also* Colonial Era; Indian History and Culture: From 1500 to 1800; Mather, Increase and Cotton; Medicine.]

• John B. Blake, *Public Health in the Town of Boston 1630–1822,* 1959. Judith W. Leavitt, " 'Be Safe. Be Sure': New York City's Experience with Epidemic Smallpox," in *Hives of Sickness: Public Health and Epidemics in New York City,* ed. David Rosner, 1995, pp. 95–114.

—Karen Walloch

SMITH, ALFRED E. (1873–1944), governor of New York and Democratic presidential candidate. Smith was born on *New York City's Lower East Side. His father was of German and Italian background; his mother was Irish American. Forced by his father's death to quit school early, he supported his family by working in the Fulton Fish Market. Local leaders of New York City's Democratic organization, Tammany Hall got him a job with the Commissioner of Jurors. Elected to the state assembly in 1903 he served for twelve years, rising to become Speaker. He also cochaired the State Factory Investigating Commission, which was established in response to the *Triangle Shirtwaist Company fire of 1911. The commission sponsored numerous bills regulating factory work and established Smith as a champion of the working class.

Needing more income, Smith, now a father of five, became sheriff of New York County in 1915 and president of the New York City Board of Aldermen two years later. Nominated as the Democratic candidate for governor in 1918 he won easily, serving from 1919 to 1920, and again from 1923 to 1928. His strong legislative record as a progressive reformer expanded his political support. Though Smith lost the Democratic presidential nomination at the party's rancorous 1924 convention, he won in 1928, becoming the first Catholic to run for president on a major party ticket. A number of factors—Smith's religion, his stand against Prohibition, and eight years of Republican prosperity—led to his crushing loss to the Republican candidate, Herbert *Hoover. In New York, Franklin Delano *Roosevelt was narrowly elected governor, winning the post that Smith had vacated.

After losing the 1932 Democratic presidential nomination to Roosevelt, Smith did not seek office again. Embittered by Roosevelt's popularity, he opposed much of the *New Deal and even joined the conservative American Liberty League. He was an active Catholic layman and served as figurehead president of the *Empire State Building Corporation headed by John J. Raskob, a prominent Democrat. Popular with audiences and the press for his affability and oratorical skills, Al Smith remains one of New York's most beloved public figures.

[*See also* Democratic Party; Irish Americans; Progressive Era; Roman Catholicism; Temperance and Prohibition; Twenties, The.]

• Oscar Handlin, *Al Smith and His America,* 1958. Paula Eldot, *Governor Alfred E. Smith: The Politician as Reformer,* 1983.

—Elisabeth Israels Perry

SMITH, JOHN (1580–1631), colonial historian and promoter, governor of Virginia. Captain John Smith, by his own account, saved the *Jamestown colony. The son of a yeoman farmer, he served in the religious wars in Europe, first in France and then against the Turks. In Jamestown, Smith was frustrated by the inept leadership of his social superiors compounded by the Virginia Company's pressure for riches. He explored Chesapeake Bay, of which he produced a remarkably accurate map. He spent three weeks as a captive of *Powhatan, the paramount chief of the region, after which the two men formed a relationship of mutual respect and wariness. His supposed rescue by Powhatan's twelve-year-old daughter, *Pocahontas, would become one of America's most enduring legends.

Elected president of the Virginia Council in September 1608, effectively the colony's governor, Smith set about to assure the floundering colony's survival. Following Indian practice he dispersed the men in small groups to live off the land, and he forced everyone to work. Smith left Virginia in late 1609; he had been severely injured by the explosion of his powder bag, and the Virginia Company's reorganization of the colony's government ended his authority.

Except for a brief trip to *New England, Smith spent the rest of his life publishing his accounts of the colonies. He disliked Virginia's reliance on tobacco, and coined the name "New England" to promote creation there of a truly English American society based on fishing and family farms. His influential *Generall Historie of Virginia, New-England, and the Summer Isles* (1624) was the first comprehensive history of English America written by an eyewitness.

[*See also* Colonial Era; Exploration, Conquest, and Settlement, Era of European; Indian History and Culture: From 1500 to 1800; Tobacco Industry.]

• Alden T. Vaughan, *American Genesis: Captain John Smith and the Founding of Virginia,* 1975. Philip L. Barbour, ed., *The Complete Works of Captain John Smith,* 3 vols., 1986.

—Karen Ordahl Kupperman

SMITH, JOSEPH. *See* Mormonism.

SMITH ACT. In 1940, with war erupting in Europe, radical ideologies winning domestic support, and the *Supreme Court curtailing the government's ability to regulate speech, Congress passed the so-called Smith Act, named for its author, Representative Howard W. Smith of Virginia. This law made it a crime to "advocate, abet, advise, or teach the duty, necessity, desirability or propriety of overthrowing or destroying any government in the United States by force . . ."; to "print, publish, edit, issue, circulate, sell, distribute or publicly display" such ideas; or to organize, belong to, or "affiliate with" any organization espousing such doctrines.

Federal prosecutors first applied the law in 1941 against union activists in Minneapolis, Minnesota, who belonged to the Trotskyite Socialist Workers party. In *Dennis* v. *U.S.* (1951), the Supreme Court upheld the constitutionality of the Smith Act and sent eleven leaders of the U.S. Communist party to prison. Justice Hugo *Black, in dissent, called the law "a virulent form of prior censorship of speech and press, which I believe the First Amendment forbids." In *Yates* v. *U.S.* (1957), also involving Communist party officials, the high court narrowed the law by ruling that the ban on "organizing" a revolutionary group applied to the original founders only, not to later officials. In *Scales* v. *U.S.* (1961), the Supreme Court further limited the Smith Act by distinguishing between "active and purposive" membership as opposed to merely "passive" membership in banned organizations. Congress sought to close these loopholes in a 1962 bill signed by President John F. *Kennedy. Of 141 people indicted under the Smith Act in the 1950s, 29 went to prison. Though prosecutions under the Smith Act largely ended by the early 1960s, the law remains on the books.

[*See also* Anticommunism; Censorship; Communist Party—USA.; Sedition.]

• Michal R. Belknap, *Cold War Political Justice: The Smith Act, the Communist Party and American Civil Liberties,* 1977. Ellen Schrecker, *The Age of McCarthyism: A Brief History with Documents,* 1994.

—Timothy Messer-Kruse

SMITHSONIAN INSTITUTION, chartered by Congress in 1846 to promote "the increase & diffusion of knowledge." Established after more than a decade of debate in Congress about the appropriate disposition of a bequest to the nation from the Englishman James Smithson, the Smithsonian's museums and less-visible research facilities would ultimately dominate the central Mall west of the Capitol in *Washington, D.C. With funding from Smithson's endowment, private gifts, and federal appropriations, the Smithsonian Institution operates, in fact, as the national museum of science, history, and art. It is governed by fourteen trustees who include (ex officio) the U.S. vice president and the chief justice of the *Supreme Court.

Under the first secretary, the physicist Joseph *Henry, who served from 1846 until his death in 1878, the Smithsonian promoted research and publication with emphasis on the sciences. In 1848, for example, Henry published a pioneering archaeological study, *Ancient Monuments of the Mississippi,* launching a monograph series that ran until 1916. He and his staff offered a public lecture series, coordinated meteorological data gathered from around the country, and developed an international exchange that distributed publications from American learned societies worldwide. Henry's successor, the zoologist Spencer F. Baird, used a cadre of explorers and naturalists to build a substantial natural-history collection that, coupled with the specimens and artifacts acquired from other countries after the *Philadelphia Centennial Exposition of 1876, led to the creation of the U.S. National Museum. Under the third secretary, the astrophysicist Samuel Pierpont Langley, the Smithsonian established a research branch, the Astrophysical Laboratory (1890), in Cambridge, Massachusetts, and a National Zoological Park (1891) in Washington, D.C.

The Smithsonian continued to grow in the twentieth century, despite some setbacks, including a failed effort to form a museum of science and industry in the 1920s. The Freer Gallery of Art (1923) became a center for the study and display of Oriental art. What some observers called the "nation's attic" added research branches, new museums on the Mall, and branch museums in Washington and *New York City. Secretary S. Dillon Ripley (1963–1983) provided energy and vision that generated new museum buildings and provided for upgraded older facilities that included more visitor-oriented shops. The National Museum of History and Technology (1965, since transformed into the National Museum of American History) became the preeminent center for research on artifacts and the

MAP 20: JOHN SMITH'S 1614 MAP OF NEW ENGLAND

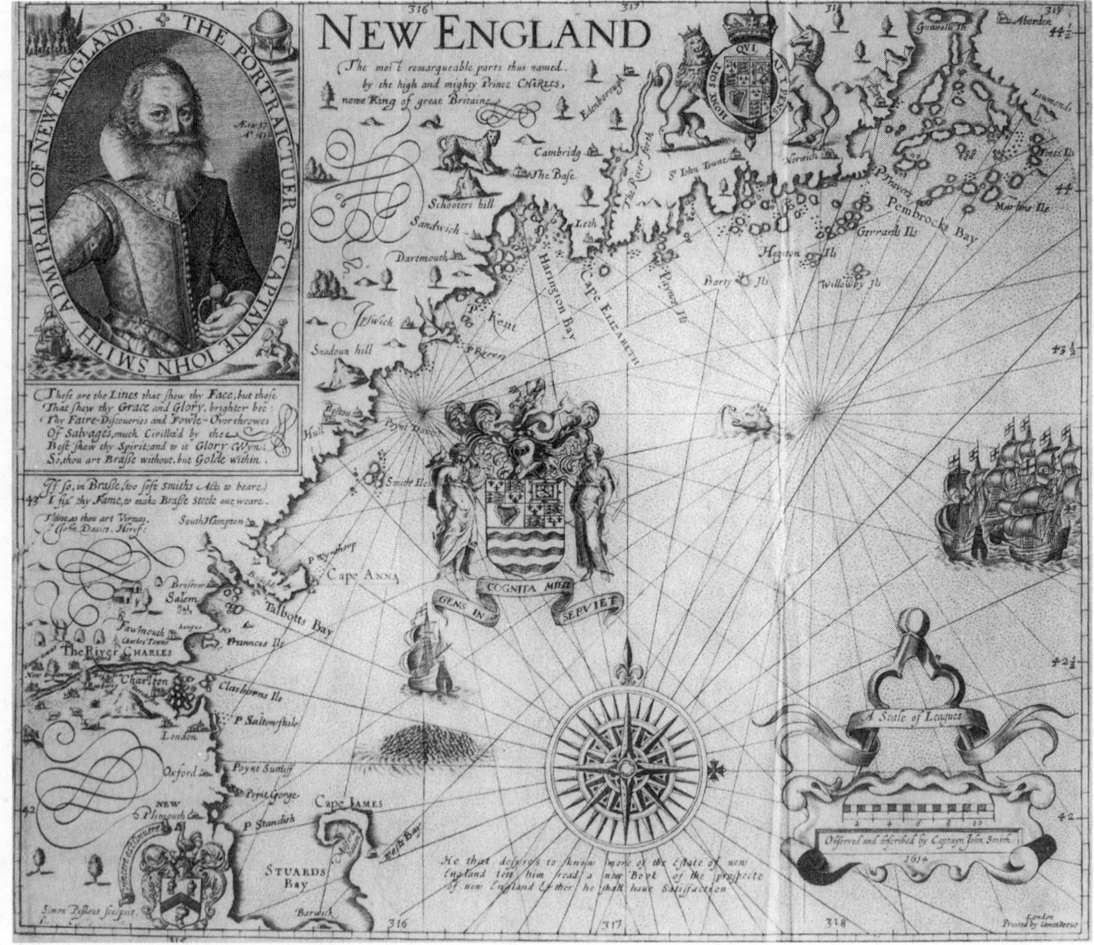

Drawn by Smith on the basis of his 1614 voyage to investigate the region's economic potential, this map first appeared in his book *A Description of New England* (1616). It included such features as Cape James (now Cape Cod), Cape Anna (now Cape Ann), and the Charles River, named by England's Prince Charles (the future Charles I), for his father, James I; his mother Anne of Denmark; and himself. Smith's publications helped fix the name of this region as "New England."

[*See* Colonial Era; Exploration, Conquest, and Settlement, Era of; New England; Smith, John.]

history of *science and *technology. The National Collection of Fine Arts (with holdings dating from 1846) joined the collections of the National Portrait Gallery and has since 1968 been housed in the Old Patent Office Building. The National Air and Space Museum, whose new building opened in 1976, soon became the world's most visited museum. A few facilities, such as the Joseph H. Hirshhorn Museum and Sculpture Garden (1974), are under the Smithsonian's aegis but administered by separate boards of trustees. Together these agencies continued the tradition of encouraging research and, in most cases, furthered the diffusion of knowledge through their publications, public exhibitions, audiovisual materials, educational programs on and off site, and collaboration with other museums. The *Smithsonian* magazine, launched in 1970, provided another popular way to carry out the institution's mandate.

[*See also* Museums.]

• G. Brown Goode, *The Smithsonian Institution, 1846–1896: The History of Its First Half Century*, 1897. Paul H. Oehser, *Sons of Science: The Story of the Smithsonian Institution*, 1949.

—Sally Gregory Kohlstedt

SMOOT-HAWLEY TARIFF. *See* Tariffs.

SOCIAL CLASS. Americans have long cherished a belief in the essential classlessness of their society. While acknowledging large inequalities of wealth and income, they have characteristically attached little significance to social class either as a source of personal identity or as a fundamental aspect of social order, and have insisted upon the instability and permeability of such class boundaries as do exist. Indeed, the practice of egalitarian democracy in an open and "classless" society constitutes the core of American exceptionalism. The reality of American social relations, however, is more complex, combining, in different ways in different eras, both fluidity and egalitarianism on the one hand and structured social hierarchy on the other.

Social Hierarchy in Early America. The process of colonial settlement, and the conditions of the first colonial societies, altered the practice of social hierarchy among Europeans in America. Those who settled in British North America included very few titled aristocrats (those nobles who did migrate to America tended not to remain), relatively few gentry and rich townspeople and an apparently small number of the very poor. Hence, Anglo-American society began with a disproportionately large number of people from the middling ranks of British society, and this flattening of the social structure was quickly reinforced by a rudimentary economy and by the policy, prevalent in all colonies in varying degrees, of distributing land widely among settlers. In their physical isolation from the mother country, moreover, non-noble colonial leaders were able to establish and expand political institutions that enjoyed increasing autonomy from royal and aristocratic authority, thereby loosening a connection between social status and political power that underpinned the English aristocracy.

These conditions reduced social hierarchy, but by no means eliminated it. European settlers in the new world came from highly unequal societies in which social hierarchy was deeply inscribed in culture and daily life, and such patterns of belief and practice were not easily shed. In all the colonies, distinctions between "better sorts," "middling sorts," and "meaner sorts" of people remained central to conceptions of social order, and no colony attempted to place society on a formally egalitarian basis. Social differences, furthermore, did not decrease, but rather increased over time, as a developing economy provided greater opportunities for the accumulation of individual fortunes, and as wars and economic dislocations increased the numbers of Americans who were poor or near the margins of *poverty. (The forced migration of Africans introduced another category of poor Americans, but slaves did not enter society in the same way as the free population, and were considered apart from the developing social system.) Particularly after the middle of the eighteenth century, families controlling the larger southern tobacco and rice plantations, and the more successful merchants of *Boston, *New York City, *Philadelphia, and other port towns, had the means to build and furnish spacious and elegant homes, purchase carriages and fine clothes, commission family portraits, send their children to colleges and on European tours, and in other ways imitate the genteel lifestyle flourishing in Georgian England. Simultaneously, in the larger towns at least, the poor grew more numerous, as did the middling folk, especially small-scale artisans, who were less assured than in former times of a stable subsistence. By the 1760s, in Philadelphia and Boston, the wealthiest tenth owned nearly two-thirds of the assets tabulated on local tax records (their percentage share of untaxed wealth was no doubt higher), while the number qualifying for poor relief could amount to as many as one in six of the population. Poverty among European Americans was probably not as prevalent elsewhere in the colonies, but in the plantation *South the wealth share of large planters was as great as that of the urban merchants.

Increasing inequalities enabled wealthier Americans to claim the deference of "middling" and "meaner" sorts, with respect to both social superiority and political authority. In this sense, American "better sorts" imitated their counterparts in the mother country, who made much of ancient traditions of patronage and clientage between the great and the small. This tradition (in some senses an "invented tradition," less ancient than some gentry tried to assert) was weaker in America, and more vulnerable to popular resistance, but it provided the basic pattern of social and political relations. In face-to-face daily encounters, greater and lesser social worth manifested itself not so much as categorical "classes," horizontally layered according to wealth, lifestyle, social exclusivity, or standing within the agricultural and commercial economy, as vertically understood "ranks" that emphasized the superiority and inferiority of specific persons within known communities. Traditional understandings of hierarchy, and of the rights and responsibilities of superiors and inferiors, underlay the daily intermingling of people of differing ranks. Rank was reinforced by the tacit understanding that these relations would remain in some respects reciprocal, the lesser respecting the status and authority of the greater, the greater respecting and protecting the rights of the lesser.

This system of distinctions worked imperfectly as the imperial crisis evolved into the American struggle for independence. Although wealthy merchants and planters were conspicuous leaders in this struggle, the *Revolutionary War unleashed democratizing forces that eventually destroyed the deferential system of social and political relations. Although the corrosion of deference took a half-century and more, it resulted in a more democratic ideology and political system and a society that Alexis de Tocqueville in **Democracy in America* would characterize as at once massive and boundless, remarkably free from the restraints of the old aristocratic order. It was in the era of so-called "Jacksonian Democracy" that the American self-image of a nation of free and equal strivers was fashioned as a more or less official ideology.

Social Class in the Urban-Industrial Era. Simultaneously, however, new forms of social distinction arose as *industrialization and *urbanization transformed the craft shops of an earlier era into a complex mix of factories, small shops, and domestic sweatshops. As early as the second and third decades of the nineteenth century, some workers complained of new modes of production, identifying themselves (in mechanics' newspapers, at least) as an exploited "working class." This identity, if exaggerated at first for rhetorical effect, was grounded in real changes that continued to alter the economic and social circumstances of workers. The de-skilling subdivision of tasks in many trades, preceding or accompanying the introduction of machinery into the production process, opened many industrial jobs to inexperienced "green hands," and threatened the livelihood and status of skilled craftworkers, driving many into workingmen's organizations that for the first time excluded employing masters. Larger, more heavily capitalized workshops and factories threatened these workers' prospects of ever becoming masters of their own shops, perpetuating their status as wage earners and further loosening the craftsman's claim to middling status. Larger workplaces also loosened the connection between work and domestic life, driving large numbers of workers for the first time into crowded and shabby urban neighborhoods easily perceived as "working class." These neighborhoods reflected the fact that most manual workers were not experiencing the rising per capita incomes that flowed to other groups. By the mid–nineteenth century, the well-grounded perception of an American working class contradicted the ideology of classlessness.

So, too, did the perception of other emerging classes, which in some ways were products of the same forces. As manual work increasingly aligned with wage employment in an industrializing economy, nonmanual work (work with one's "head" rather than with one's "hands") aligned with *business ownership and new forms of salaried employment. By the second half of the century, the distinction between a manual, wage-earning working class and a nonmanual, salaried, and profit-making middle class became quite sharp. Diverging living standards and living spaces underscored the distinction. Workers and the nonmanual middle class had come to live quite different and separate lives, especially in the city, but to some extent also in smaller towns and in the countryside, as middle-class styles spread outward to shape the social aspirations of business and farm proprietors in rural America.

Urban middle-class styles (and what has been called the "vernacular gentility" of rural American middling folk) imitated the more opulent styles and manners of the wealthy, who nonetheless preserved and even enhanced their distinctiveness as an upper class. The latter term, indeed, applies with greater force to later nineteenth-century elites as older personal relationships between social superiors and inferiors dissolved. Just as middle-class businessmen and wage-earning workers separated themselves into class-defined neighborhoods, institutions, and social worlds, so did the wealthy establish exclusive ways of life on fashionable avenues, in elite clubs, and in clearly defined social circles. Deferential relations did not entirely disappear from nineteenth-century America, but they played a smaller role in a society increasingly separated by living standards, institutions, and space. After mid-century, the most significant relation between the wealthy and lesser folk was within an impersonal, mediated, celebrity culture, in which middle- and working-class Americans read and spoke about rich people they would never meet and an exclusive "Society" in which they would never participate. The term "aristocracy" increasingly applied to this upper class was full of irony, since a patronizing aristocracy was exactly what the American upper class had ceased to be.

The late nineteenth century, and perhaps the early years of the twentieth, constitute the high-water mark of class division in the United States. In 1883 the sociologist William Graham Sumner (1840–1910) observed that despite the continuing assertion of classlessness, "we constantly read and hear discussion of social topics in which the existence of social classes is assumed as a simple fact." In a letter written a few years earlier, the reformer Lydia Maria *Child had noted the demarcation of "genteel," "middle," and "laboring" classes that "are as much strangers to each other, as if they live in different countries." Comments such as these summarize the effects of nearly a century of class formation. But changes would soon occur that, while not ending class divisions, would blur the borders between them and give new strength to the idea of a classless America.

The Blurring of Class Lines in the Later Twentieth Century. Three related twentieth-century developments obscured the boundary between the working and middle classes, just as the terms "blue collar" and "white collar" were gaining currency as expressions of that boundary. One was the vast expansion of the ranks of low-level office workers and sales clerks, who earned low salaries (or, in the case of many sales clerks, hourly wages) in jobs that often did not lead to significant promotion or self-employment. This trend had begun earlier when *department stores employed young women as sales clerks, but it expanded significantly after the turn of the century, and extended increasingly to male workers in large stores and corporate offices. Men gained promotion more frequently than women, but no longer was clerkship viewed as an apprenticeship to full-fledged membership in the business world. By mid-century, the Marxist sociologist C. Wright Mills (1916–1962) could write persuasively in his classic text *White Collar* (1951) of American office and store workers as a new proletariat, no less regimented, poorly paid, and declassed than manual workers of the previous century.

A second development was the improvement of industrial wages. These were driven upward by increasingly effective labor unions (whose wage bargaining power was enhanced by federal policy after 1935), by the industrial demands of *World War II, and perhaps too by the "trickle down" rewards of a booming postwar economy. Real wage gains remained modest, but in conjunction with the expansion of poorly paying white-collar jobs, they diminished the income gap between the two employment sectors and permitted many blue-collar workers to live as well as or better than some white-collar employees. In the later twentieth century, the transfer of numerous jobs from industrial production to the service sector further obscured the historic distinction between manual and nonmanual labor by introducing jobs—from fast-food servers to computer technicians—not clearly identifiable as one or the other. Not only did blue-collar and white-collar incomes overlap, but the categories themselves became more difficult to define and hence served less effectively as markers of social class.

The distinction between the middle and upper classes also became less clear as the twentieth century ended, but for different reasons. Once quite open to public view, upper-class institutions and social life retreated to more private spaces, where elite family and club life, and even "society" marriages and charity balls, attracted little attention from most Americans. The celebrity once enjoyed by the upper class was largely supplanted by sports and entertainment figures and tabloid celebrities. As the patrician Cleveland Amory suggested in his 1960 book *Who Killed Society?*, the upper class no longer played a significant role in shaping the aspirations and social perceptions of most Americans.

It might seem, therefore, that by the end of the twentieth century the American social structure had finally confirmed the assertion of classlessness. Public discussion of class during the closing decades of the century commonly distinguished between a broadly inclusive "middle class" and an excluded "underclass" sometimes conflated with racial and ethnic minorities—a distinction perceived more as a failure of public policy than as an integral component of an enduring social class structure. But even apart from the problem of the "underclass," the concept of an all-inclusive "middle class" failed to account for continuing patterns of social differentiation. As a new century began, social classes were not as clearly inscribed in the social order as they once had been, but they had by no means disappeared. The boundaries and criteria of class were less clear, but America remained a society of unequals, and the social styles historically associated with the upper, middle, and working classes continued to shape the lives of most Americans within reasonably distinct social spheres.

[*See also* Antebellum Era; Capitalism; Colonial Era; Economic Development; Factory System; Gilded Age; Immigration; Labor Markets; Labor Movements; Mobility; Race and Ethnicity; Slavery; Sociology; Women in the Labor Force; Working-Class Life and Culture.]

• Robert S. Lynd and Helen Merrell Lynd, *Middletown,* 1929. William Kornblum, *Blue Collar Community,* 1974. Gary B. Nash, *The Urban Crucible,* 1979. Frederic Cople Jaher, *The Urban Establishment,* 1982. Michael H. Frisch and Daniel J. Walkowitz, *Working-Class America,* 1983. Stuart M. Blumin, *The Emergence of the Middle Class,* 1989. Richard L. Bushman, *The Refinement of America,* 1992. Gordon S. Wood, *The Radicalism of the American Revolution,* 1992. Dennis Gilbert and Joseph A. Kahl, *The American Class Structure,* 1993.

—Stuart M. Blumin

SOCIAL DARWINISM. Appearing first in the writings of European socialists about 1880, this term characterized theories that applied to human society Darwinian concepts of selection, struggle, and survival. When the phrase "survival of the fittest," coined by Herbert Spencer, the *laissez-faire theorist, entered American social discourse in the 1880s, social Darwinism came to be associated with references to the social organism, competition, or natural law, whether invoked in support of laissez-faire, governmental controls, or imperialism. Given its negative implications, few theorists defined themselves as social Darwinists. The term nonetheless made its way into common usage to characterize social policies ranging from sociobiology to Reaganomics.

British writers promoted early varieties of social Darwinism: the social evolutionism of Spencer; the hereditarianism of Francis Galton, founder of *eugenics; the conflict theory of journalist Walter Bagehot who, in *Physics and Politics* (1872), described the evolution of groups into nations through struggle. Each had counterparts in the United States. Yale professor William Graham Sumner (1840–1910), the prominent laissez-faire advocate of the 1880s, told audiences that the only alternative to the "survival of the fittest" was "the survival of the unfittest." Eugenics, too, gained support after 1900. Darwinian rhetoric also colored debates over American imperialism, for example, in the writings of historian John Fiske (1842–1901) and naval strategist Alfred Thayer *Mahan.

Darwinism's greatest impact came after 1900, ironically among the reformers and socialists who were the most vocal in denouncing the "social Darwinism" of their opponents. These "reform Darwinists" argued that the evolution of human intelligence demanded conscious control of social policy, a view first presented in Lester *Ward's *Dynamic Sociology* (1884). Some of these reformers and socialists used such reasoning to support racist and sexist ideas that made "reform Darwinism" no more acceptable to later generations than its laissez-faire counterpart.

Biologized social theory declined rapidly after 1914 for reasons that included the spread of the anthropological concept of culture; advances in genetics that undermined eugenics even before Adolf Hitler's programs disgraced the movement entirely; and the rise of fascism, widely viewed as the final logic of social Darwinism. Synthesizing these themes, historian Richard Hofstadter delivered the coup de grâce in *Social Darwinism in American Thought* (1944).

Biological social theory returned in the post–*World War II decades with the successful description of the DNA molecule, containing the basic genetic code of all biological organisms, in 1953; ethnographic studies of the biological basis of human aggression and mate selection in the 1960s; renewed controversy over the biological basis of intelligence; and the publication in 1975 of Edward O. Wilson's *Sociobiology: The New Synthesis.* In the 1980s and beyond, "supply side economics" and the assault on government welfare programs brought charges that social Darwinism had resurfaced in practice as well as theory. Sociobiologists and free-marketeers denied, however, that they advocated a Darwinian struggle of all against all. First introduced in an age that looked to "science" for social salvation, the label "social Darwinism" exaggerated Darwin's influence on social thought and distorted the theories of its advocates. But then as now, the term expressed the recognition that misused "science" may serve as a mask for power and privilege.

[*See also* Biological Sciences; Evolution, Theory of; Science: Revolutionary War to World War I; Socialism; Welfare, Federal.]

• Robert C. Bannister, *Social Darwinism: Science and Myth in Anglo-American Social Thought,* 1988. Carl N. Degler, *In Search of Human Nature: The Decline and Revival of Darwinism in American Social Thought,* 1991.

—Robert C. Bannister

SOCIAL GOSPEL. The Social Gospel, a moderate variety of Protestant "social Christianity," took shape in response to the dislocations produced by *urbanization, *industrialization, and mass *immigration in the late nineteenth century and crested during the *Progressive Era after 1900. In contrast to the root-and-branch approach of socialist Christians, Social Gospel leaders called for reforms in values and institutions. Rejecting the individualistic social ethic of conservatives, they insisted on addressing the structural roots of injustice and distress.

The Social Gospel was heir to a centuries-old Protestant belief in a Christian America with a divine mission in the process of world redemption. More immediately, it had antecedents in pre–*Civil War evangelical reform movements for temperance, peace, women's rights, and the abolition of *slavery. If not entirely novel, however, the Social Gospel had distinctive characteristics. The new urban-industrial order shaped the movement's agenda around such issues as *child labor, the rights of labor unions, factory safety, tenement *housing, *public health, and urban misgovernment. The theological liberalism that emerged out of attempts to reconcile the Christian faith with evolutionary thought, historical-critical analysis of the *Bible, philosophical idealism, and the study of other world religions lent it a distinctively optimistic rationale. This rationale included emphases on the "Fatherhood of God" (and the corollary, the "Brotherhood of Man"); the progressive character of scripture, culminating in the person and teachings of Jesus; and the coming millennial kingdom of God—a perfected society of love, justice, and peace—on earth and within history.

The Social Gospel emerged most strongly in the Congregational, Episcopal, northern *Baptist, Methodist, and Presbyterian denominations. Its leaders were typically prominent urban pastors, denominational publicists and other officials, and professors. Congregationalists Lyman Abbott (1835–1922) of Brooklyn and Washington Gladden (1836–1918) of Columbus, Ohio, utilized long ministries to address virtually all public issues that emerged from the 1870s on. Unitarian social ethicist Francis Greenwood Peabody (1847–1936) at Harvard Divinity School and Baptist theologian and historian Walter *Rauschenbusch at Rochester Theological Seminary combined theoretical and practical interests in their seminary settings.

The Social Gospel was not limited to northern, urban, and liberal sectors of *Protestantism, but where social change was less pronounced, or resistance to theological modernization more intense, it appeared in truncated form. The *South, rural and orthodox, was not fertile ground. Northern conservative evangelicals, whose commitment to biblical inerrancy and premillennialism led eventually to militant fundamentalism, despite their own heritage of social reform, generally rejected the Social Gospel because of its theological liberalism.

As a reform movement, the Social Gospel was first and foremost an effort to reform the churches, so they might advance God's will on earth. To this end, its advocates introduced numerous changes into church life. Their sermons and Sunday-school literature applied Christian ethics to social, political, and economic issues. Social Gospel fiction, exemplified by Charles M. Sheldon's best-seller *In His Steps* (1897), gave an element of fantasy, and even romance, to readers' contemplation of their social responsibilities. A sense of estrangement between middle-class Protestants and the poor crowding into once-genteel neighborhoods led some congregations to open their facilities—or even construct new facilities—for weekday social services to the immigrant newcomers. A few congregations actually established *settlement houses. To train ministers for their widened calling, seminaries added courses in *social science, social ethics, and new forms of parish work.

The problems that Social Gospel leaders addressed often involved some resort to politics, and these leaders endorsed many Progressive Era causes as steps toward the kingdom of God. Urban pastors and their congregants supported municipal-reform crusades to eradicate prostitution, regulate saloons, break the power of political machines, and regulate streetcar and utility companies in the public interest. (A few ministers, like Gladden, ran for and won public office.) Social Gospel principles also led naturally to support for worker-protection laws, the conservation and *consumer movements, and corporate regulation.

If the Social Gospel redirected congregational energies and drew thousands of comfortable churchgoers into reform causes, it also profoundly affected the structure of American Protestantism. Under Social Gospel influence, leading denominations established commissions or agencies for social education and advocacy, and Protestant ecumenicity came to fruition in the Federal (later National) Council of Churches (1908), with its influential "Social Creed of the Churches." Although the Social Gospel lost buoyancy and its theological grounding eroded after *World War I, organized social concern and many of the reforms it inspired in church life remained intact throughout the twentieth century.

[*See also* Conservation Movement; Fundamentalist Movement; Labor Movements; Methodism; Millennialism and Apocalypticism; National Council of Churches; Peace Movements; Prostitution and Antiprostitution; Religion; Socialism; Temperance and Prohibition; Unitarianism and Universalism; Urbanization; Women's Rights Movements.]

• Charles Howard Hopkins, *The Rise of the Social Gospel in American Protestantism, 1865–1915,* 1940. Robert T. Handy, ed., *The Social Gospel in America: Gladden, Ely, Rauschenbusch,* 1966. John P. McDowell, *The Social Gospel in the South: The Woman's Home Mission Movement in the Methodist Episcopal Church, South, 1886–1939,* 1982. Donald K. Gorrell, *The Age of Social Responsibility: The Social Gospel in the Progressive Era, 1900–1920,* 1988. Ralph E. Luker, *The Social Gospel in Black and White: American Racial Reform, 1885–1912,* 1991. Jacob H. Dorn, "Washington Gladden and the Social Gospel," in *American Reform and Reformers: A Biographical Dictionary,* eds. Randall Miller and Paul Cimbala, 1995, pp. 255–69. James H. Moorhead, *World without End: Mainstream American Protestant Visions of the Last Things, 1880–1925,* 2000.

—Jacob H. Dorn

SOCIALISM, a political ideology, rejects the private ownership of land, factories, and other means of production as well as the wage-labor system and the competitive market economy. Socialist beliefs and movements, though dizzyingly varied, have generally fallen into four groups: communitarian, revolutionary socialist, democratic socialist, and syndicalist. Communitarianism, which has the longest pedigree, can be traced to eighteenth-century religious movements such as the Shakers, who reacted to a commercializing society by retreating into rural settlements, holding their property communally, and hoping to reform society by example. As antebellum Americans felt the first shocks of the emerging industrial order, some embraced European alternatives to capitalism, from the paternalistic industrialism of Robert Owen to Charles Fourier's utopian blueprints for communal cooperatives.

By the 1860s, having absorbed the work of Karl Marx, most socialists turned from debating how best to withdraw from capitalist society to arguing over how to revolutionize it. Two major streams of thought emerged, both initially espoused in America mainly by German immigrants, who founded a branch of Marx's Communist International in New York in 1872. Orthodox Marxists, committed to overthrowing capitalism through revolutionary class struggle, concentrated on infiltrating labor unions and mobilizing the masses. Democratic socialists, by contrast, sometimes called "Lassalleans," for the German Ferdinand Lassalle, believed that socialism could be achieved peacefully through electoral politics.

Neither group proved notably successful. The revolutionary Marxists, squandering their energies in factional infighting, were rejected by the trade-union movement they assiduously courted. On the electoral front, the Workingmen's party (1874), renamed the Socialist Labor party (SLP) in 1877 and led after 1890 by Daniel De Leon, fielded a presidential candidate in 1892, but he won only 21,000 votes. Foreign-language socialist newspapers did little to broaden the movement's appeal. The *Socialist party of America (SPA), founded in 1901 by Eugene V. *Debs, Morris Hillquit (1869–1933), Victor Berger (1860–1929), and other defectors from the SLP, never overcame most Americans' tendency to give their racial, ethnic, and religious identity a higher priority than their social class. Neither Debs, the SPA's five-time presidential candidate between 1900 and 1920, nor Norman *Thomas, the party's perennial candidate from the 1920s to the 1960s, seriously challenged the major-party nominees.

The final category of socialism, syndicalism, combined the immigrant Marxists' critique of capitalism with the Abolitionists' suspicion of government. Whereas Marxists sought to transform the labor movement into a revolutionary force to overthrow the government, syndicalists envisioned a new society emerging from workers' control of the mills and factories. Syndicalism flourished in western mining, lumber, and railroad camps with the founding of the *Industrial Workers of the World (IWW, or Wobblies) in 1905. The Wobblies' dramatic strikes; flamboyant leaders; and wealth of songs, lore, and poetry made them a romantic symbol of the syndicalist version of socialism.

Despite its overall failure, American socialism has influenced American thought and culture, particularly in the late nineteenth and early twentieth centuries. Edward Bellamy's novel of evolutionary socialism, **Looking Backward* (1888), which drew upon Laurence Gronlund's *Cooperative Commonwealth* (1884), proved enormously popular. Some prominent *Social Gospel advocates espoused Christian Socialism, and influential reformist works by socialists, or reflecting socialist ideas, included Henry Demarest Lloyd's *Wealth against Commonwealth* (1894); William Dean *Howells's *A Traveler from Alturia* (1894), Upton *Sinclair's *The *Jungle* (1906); and Jack London's *The Iron Heel* (1907). The socialist magazine the *Masses* (founded 1911) enjoyed considerable *Progressive Era influence.

*World War I, which brought repression of the antiwar left and the Bolshevik Revolution in Russia—a revolution celebrated by the American socialist John Reed in *Ten Days That Shook the World* (1919)—redrew the contours of American socialism. The U.S. Communist party (CP), founded in 1919, ceded control of its affairs to Moscow and, like its Marxist forebears, generally favored doctrinal purity over coalition building. Both the CP and the SPA gained ground early in the Great Depression, but both were eclipsed by the popularity of the *New Deal and then by the antiradical climate of the *Cold War.

Socialism's fortunes rose with the emergence of the *New Left in the 1960s. The leading New Left organization, *Students for a Democratic Society, a hybrid of socialist traditions, rejected Marxist dogmatism while it embraced both the communitarian dream and the democratic-socialists' hope for radical social change through a revitalized politics. Socialism's indirect influence resurfaced in the 1960s as well. For example, the socialist Michael Harrington's *The *Other America* (1962) helped inspire President Lyndon B. *Johnson's War on Poverty. Although the New Left soon faded, its blend of communitarian hopes and democratic-socialist goals remained alive in the late twentieth century. The Democratic Socialists of America, founded by Harrington in 1983 to pursue socialist goals within the *Democratic party, was the latest manifestation of socialism's continuing influence in American life.

[*See also* Capitalism; Communist Party—USA; Conservatism; Labor Movements; Liberalism; Radicalism; Shakerism; Utopian and Communitarian Movements.]

• Donald Egbert and Stow Persons, eds., *Socialism and American Life,* 1952. James Weinstein, *The Decline of Socialism in America, 1912–1925,* 1967. Paul Buhle, *Marxism in the U.S.A.: From 1870 to the Present Day,* 1987. Maurice Isserman, *If I Had a Hammer: The Death of the Old Left and the Birth of the New Left,* 1987. John Patrick Diggins, *The Rise and Fall of the American Left,* 1992. Mari Jo Buhle, Paul Buhle, and Dan Georgakas, eds., *Encyclopedia of the American Left,* rev. ed., 1998.

—Timothy Messer-Kruse

SOCIALIST PARTY OF AMERICA. Founded in 1901, the Socialist party of America (SPA) drew on deep roots of dissent within American society, enjoyed its peak influence during the *Progressive Era, and remained a sometimes lively ghost in later years. The Socialist party's precursors—including abolitionists, women's rights campaigners, agrarian radicals, utopian socialists, and trade unionists—had long proposed alternative social arrangements. Small socialist political organizations, led mainly by *German Americans in the post–*Civil War decades, played a crucial role in the formation of the American *labor movement. But the depression of the 1890s, violent labor struggles, the Populist revolt, and the appearance of newer ethnic immigrants (especially East European Jews) with socialist connections all foreshadowed a major reorientation. A split in the sectarian Socialist Labor party of 1899 and the emergence of former railroad-union leader Eugene V. *Debs in 1900 brought unity within sight.

The SPA's founding convention, held at Indianapolis, Indiana, in 1901, included various elements of the socialist movement, especially small-town and rural socialists—native-born, often middle-aged railroad mechanics, teachers, ministers, and farmers—who carried the educational zeal of earlier times into hundreds of local presses, study clubs, and political campaigns. Because these grassroots activists were unimpeachably "American," immigrant socialists usually ceded them leadership in the movement. By 1912, Oklahoma had become the epicenter of socialist influence, more than a thousand socialist candidates had been elected nationwide, and Debs garnered 6 percent of the presidential vote.

The labor movement changed dramatically as well. Beginning in 1909, a wave of strikes by unskilled, foreign-born workers shook the confidence of the business classes. The *Industrial Workers of the World, launched with socialist assistance in 1905, preached "solidarity" among all working people. Even within the staid *American Federation of Labor, headed by antisocialist Samuel *Gompers, a number of member unions turned strongly leftward. Buoyed by this energy, the Socialist party reached a membership of 100,000, including a growing number of foreign-language federations made up of immigrant nationalities.

But the two-party system quickly adjusted itself to the threat of radical outsiders. In many localities where socialists sought election, Republicans and Democrats formed "fusion" tickets with resources beyond the reach of newcomers. Elsewhere, reformers appropriated socialist positions involving municipal issues and honest government. Many disappointed voters fell away from Socialist party ranks. America's entry into *World War I nearly finished off socialism, as the government's crackdown on antiwar activities fell heavily upon socialists and labor radicals.

The Socialist party never fully recovered from the war. Although Debs received a million presidential votes in 1920 while in a federal penitentiary, the party lost more than half of its members. Its remaining appeal owed largely to the charismatic leadership of Norman *Thomas, a former Presbyterian minister from New York. A perennial candidate for local, state, and national office, Thomas garnered 800,000 votes for president in 1932. Yet the party faced an uphill struggle as the *New Deal borrowed socialist planks (as in the *Social Security Act) and won blue-collar workers to the *Democratic party. A shattering division in 1936 between moderates and radicals and the coming of another world war reduced the party to a few thousand members. Nevertheless, loyalists persisted in maintaining a few press organs and running local candidates for office. A handful continued to be elected, generally in nonpartisan races.

[*See also* Capitalism; Depressions, Economic; Labor Movements; Political Parties; Populist Era; Socialism.]

• Richard Judd, *Socialist Cities: Explorations into the Grass Roots of American Socialism,* 1990. Mari Jo Buhle, Paul Buhle, and Dan Georgakas, eds. *Encyclopedia of the American Left,* rev. ed., 1998.

—Paul Buhle

SOCIAL SCIENCE. The history of social science and the American republic are roughly conterminous. Both had their origins in the Enlightenment with its faith in progress and belief in the existence of natural laws. Most historians have maintained that the concept of society itself did not emerge in European thought until the sixteenth century and could not truly develop until the decline of feudalism and the development of *individualism made the recognition of society's impact possible. For the first time, observers could perceive society as a separate structure with particular characteristics that might change over time. By the eighteenth century, figures such as Adam Smith, Montesquieu, and Condorcet were using factual data and scientific reasoning to discover new, empirically verifiable truths to replace the discarded models of the past. They perceived the social sciences as reform instruments that could provide unimpeachable guides to the construction of good societies.

In the United States, various versions of social science emerged in the first half of the nineteenth century. Foremost among these claimants were college professors of moral philosophy and political economy. Primarily clergymen trained in the philosophy of Scottish commonsense realism, they saw existent social and economic conditions as synonymous with moral laws. In the *South, George Fitzhugh (1806–1881) and other proslavery apologists praised Auguste Comte's emphasis upon social stability and portrayed the South as an example of Comte's ideal moral society. Finally, social statisticians sought to tabulate such social problems as *crime and pauperism in order to reform American society with so-called exact knowledge.

Such competition for the true science of society increased in the aftermath of the *Civil War. Just as the Industrial and French revolutions in Europe had led to a questioning of traditional authority, so too did the Civil War in the United States. Consequently, the goal of an empirically valid science of society that all parties would accept became increasingly desirable. In 1865, a group of elite northeastern reformers met to form the American Social Science Association. Its twin goals were discovering what is and promoting what should be. Within the organization, radicals competed with academic specialists for controlling interest. Faced with questions of their expertise and objectivity, the specialists, beginning in the 1870s, gradually broke off to form their own disciplinary organizations.

As numerous scholars have noted, the social sciences have differed from nation to nation. In the United States, these disciplines have traditionally shared an emphasis on empirical quantification and practical research insistence upon scholarly objectivity, and a belief in American exceptionalism. Many of these attributes arose out of the disciplines' late nineteenth-century attempts to achieve public acceptance. Like physicians and lawyers, social scientists sought to win this approval through *professionalization and the subsequent adoption of a regulative code of ethics, common training, and community sanction. Seeking this training and sanction via an alliance with the emerging universities, they found the allegedly objective use of the scientific method to be absolutely necessary within the politics of the universities. Conservative boards of trustees distrusted social scientists and frequently dismissed them for political activism or unpopular conclusions.

By the early twentieth century, individuals in all the social-science disciplines were beginning actually to produce such empirical work rather than merely advocate it. In *economics, young German-trained scholars emphasized specific institutional studies in place of overarching theory. Historians embraced Leopold von Ranke's goal of recovering "Geschichte wie es eigentlich gewesen" (history as it really happened), with J. Franklin Jameson, the founder of the *American Historical Review,* calling for discrete, small-scale studies without concern for overall synthesis. The political scientist Charles Merriam (1874–1953) abandoned the theoretical formalism of his teachers and laid out extensive plans for empirical political research. In *anthropology, Franz *Boas and his students replaced the evolutionary ranking of peoples and societies with concentration upon specific cultures. *Psychology shifted from the introspective study of consciousness to a concern with behavior and applied psychology represented at its most extreme by the *behaviorism of John B. Watson. *Sociology retained both its theoretical and reformist characteristics the longest, but by the 1920s the University of Chicago school of sociology and its careful description of urban America was dominant.

*World War I appeared to validate this approach. When the United States entered the war, the government turned to historians, political scientists, and psychologists to staff its Committee on Public Information and economists and statisticians to run the *War Industries Board. Their success in these agencies led to corporate support for numerous research institutes. Emulation of the natural and physical sciences became a mantra. University of Chicago sociologist William Ogburn happily envisioned the day when journals of physics and sociology would become indistinguishable.

While a number of figures during the 1920s and 1930s demanded a return to theoretical work and personal activism, the opportunity of government service during *World War II aroused American social scientists' traditional interests in quantification and short-term practicality. Becoming convinced that social experts could and should control individuals and societies, many continued after the war to work for government agencies and private corporations without questioning the use of their research. In the well-publicized example of Project Camelot, begun in 1963 and exposed in 1965, a number of prominent social scientists secretly working for the Department of Defense designed specific counterinsurgency plans while relying on the cooperation and hospitality of their unsuspecting Latin American colleagues. Electoral polling and social survey research became two of the largest growth areas.

Simultaneously, however, émigré scholars such as Max Horkheimer (1895–1973) and Theodor Adorno (1903–1969) of the Institute of Social Research at the University of Frankfurt reinvigorated American social science with new methodologies. Disciplines quickly adopted innovations from other fields and nations. The structural social theory of the Harvard sociologist Talcott Parsons became increasingly popular in *political science and anthropology as well as in sociology. The "thick description" of the anthropologist Clifford Geertz (1923–) precipitated a rise in qualitative methods across the disciplines. In history, the "Annales" school of history in France and the neo-Marxism of British historian E. P. Thompson helped lead to a boom in local and social history. By the end of the twentieth century, such interdisciplinary and international perspectives had lessened the distinctive national characteristics of American social science. Qualitative methods rivaled quantitative ones; theoretical work was seen to be as practical as empirical studies; and the belief in a uniquely American social science had become as outmoded as the belief in the exceptionalism of American history.

[*See also* Education: Collegiate Education; Education: The Rise of the University; Historiography, American; Mathematics and Statistics; Philosophy; Progressive Era; Secularization; Slavery.]

• Thomas Haskell, *The Emergence of Professional Social Science: The American Social Science Association and the Nineteenth Century Crisis of Authority,* 1977. Robert C. Bannister, *Sociology and Scientism: The American Quest for Objectivity,* 1987. Peter Novick, *That Noble Dream: The "Objectivity Question" and the American Historical Profession,* 1988. Dorothy Ross, *The Origins of American Social Science,* 1991. Mark C. Smith, *Social Science in the Crucible: The American Debate over Objectivity and Purpose, 1918–1941,* 1994. Ellen Herman, *The Romance of American Psychology: Political Culture in the Age of Experts,* 1995.

—Mark C. Smith

SOCIAL SECURITY. The passage of the *Social Security Act in 1935 launched the federal *welfare state. Without this program, now a central feature of American life, the incomes of most older citizens would fall below the *poverty line. By the 1990s, more than a quarter of all U.S. households received monthly old age, survivors, or disability pensions. The enactment of this historic measure was neither sudden nor inevitable. Lawmakers and critics had been debating for decades whether the United States should borrow European models, modify programs from the *Progressive Era (such as pensions for the aged poor or corporate gratuities), or continue to rely on traditional forms of relief.

In the depths of the Depression of the 1930s, when more than a quarter of all workers were unemployed, large numbers of middle-class Americans faced dependency in their later years. Older workers were among the first fired, and some hard-pressed corporations reneged on pension promises. Struggling with bankruptcy and lost savings, many families could not provide for their elderly relatives. Charities and state welfare boards ran out of money. States with old-age pensions tightened eligibility requirements, and veterans' benefits were cut.

Something had to be done, but President Franklin Delano *Roosevelt, who as governor of New York in 1929 had signed into law the nation's most progressive old-age pension plan, proceeded cautiously. Roosevelt told Congress early in 1934, "I am looking for a sound means which I can recommend to provide at once security against several of the great disturbing factors in life—especially those which relate to unemployment and old age." Building on New Deal strategies, the president wanted to give workers and their families "the security of social insurance." He expected state governments, employers, and workers themselves to join with the federal government in developing a plan built on traditional American practices.

The 1935 act was a complex piece of legislation. Title I provided federal grants to states to pay half the cost of old-age assistance. Titles II and VIII inaugurated an old-age *insurance program, while Titles III and IX launched an *unemployment compensation program. Title IV gave states funds for aid to dependent children. Title V underwrote four different programs for (disabled or not, depending on the program) children and their mothers, especially in rural areas. Title VI increased *public-health services. Title VII created a Social Security Board to oversee programs and to collect data on the program's impact. Title X provided support for the needy blind. Title XI acknowledged Congress's right to "alter, amend, or repeal any provision of this Act."

Congress radically altered the original provisions of Title II before they even went into effect. Whereas the 1935 act had treated benefits based on employees' contributions as if they were annuities, and thus correlated to wages, the 1939 amendments gave lower-income contributors and their surviving families benefits more "adequate" than they had earned. With this change of policy, the system henceforth was tilted toward a welfare model rather than a private-insurance model. Incremental reforms gradually made Social Security broader in coverage and more generous in benefits. Congress increased Title II benefits 77 percent in 1950. Disability provisions were introduced in the mid–1950s. Medicare, which covered hospitalization for Social Security recipients, was added in 1965. Seven years later, Social Security benefits were automatically indexed to reflect changes in the cost of living.

In its formative years, Social Security enjoyed overwhelming popular support. The system ran surpluses as long as the ratio of workers to beneficiaries was high. Republican presidential candidates Alf Landon in 1936 and Barry *Goldwater in 1964 criticized the program, but Republicans generally joined Democrats in supporting reforms recommended by Social Security officials and outside experts. By the mid–1970s, however, support for Social Security had become more problematic. Inflation eroded trust funds. Public confidence was shaken by doomsday scenarios. Some predicted intergenerational warfare: They feared that when the millions of baby-boomers retired, the cost of their Social Security benefits would place a very heavy tax burden on the younger generation. Congress, spurred by President Jimmy *Carter, increased Social Security taxes substantially in 1977. A compromise set of amendments six years later raised the retirement age in the twenty-first century and set a ceiling on benefits not subject to income tax. Such measures were taken to reaffirm the fundamental aims of the original act.

In many ways, Social Security fulfilled Roosevelt's conviction that the measure was "a sound idea—a sound ideal." New Jersey senator Bill Bradley in 1983 called it "the best expression of community that we have in this country today." The value of Social Security benefits in the mid–1990s for an average wage earner who died and left a spouse and two children under eighteen was equivalent to a $322,000 life insurance policy. The program by the mid–1990s paid monthly survivor benefits to 7.4 million Americans, including 2 million children. More than 4 million disabled workers under the age of 65, in addition to 1.7 million of their dependents (including more than a million children), received benefits under Social Security's disability program. Monthly benefits averaged about $680; for a disabled worker, spouse, and two children, roughly $1,100.

For all of its successes, however, Social Security remained under fire as the century ended. Loath to make dramatic changes, politicians were nonetheless frustrated by their inability to reduce the scope of entitlements. Those receiving benefits or who expected to get them shortly were more likely than younger Americans to declare the system financially secure. Many people, moreover, misperceived the program's scope and operations. Some still thought Social Security operated like a private insurance program. Others felt that monthly Social Security checks should be enough to cover basic expenses, obviating the need for private savings or other retirement pensions. As a result, Social Security appeared likely to become even more controversial in the twenty-first century, particularly if Washington's role in delivering human services continued to diminish.

[*See also* Depressions, Economic; Life Stages; Medicare and Medicaid; New Deal Era, The.]

• Alan Pifer and Forrest Chisman, eds., *The Report of the Committee on Economic Security of 1935*, 50th Anniversary ed., 1985. W. Andrew Achenbaum, *Social Security: Visions and Revisions*, 1986. Jill Quadagno, *The Transformation of Old Age Security: Class and Politics in the American Welfare State*, 1988. Edward D. Berkowitz and Kim McQuaid, *Creating the Welfare State: The Political Economy of 20th-Century Reform*, rev. ed., 1992. Carole Haber and Brian Gratton, *Old Age and the Search for Security*, 1994.

—W. Andrew Achenbaum

SOCIAL SECURITY ACT (1935). The Social Security Act of 1935, the foundation for most federal *welfare provisions and one of the most important pieces of legislation in U.S. history, has been widely misunderstood. The title phrase, "*Social Security," came to refer in general usage to only one of the eleven major sections or titles in the act, old-age pensions, the nation's most popular welfare program. The term "welfare" became attached to another of Social Security's titles, Aid to Dependent Children, and few realize that it derived from the same omnibus legislation.

The Depression of the 1930s provided an opportunity, for which social reformers had been agitating since at least 1910, to create a federally sponsored economic security program. Two aspects of the Depression—widespread impoverishment that affected even the middle classes, and powerful social movements demanding economic provision—weakened resistance to government responsibility. President Franklin Delano *Roosevelt supported temporary emergency relief with enthusiasm but at first opposed a permanent federal role. By late 1934, however, the deepening depression led the president to appoint a Committee on Economic Security to draft a bill. Its staff headed by Edwin Witte and his colleagues from Wisconsin's state government and the University of Wisconsin, the committee was dominated by proponents of social *insurance. Their vision, derived from private life-insurance plans, called for government funds to replace wages lost through illness, injury, *unemployment, or retirement. Its advocates sought to serve the prosperous as well as the poor, thereby avoiding the stigma of "poor relief," and to prevent, not simply alleviate, *poverty. The committee adapted social insurance principles in designing three programs—unemployment compensation, old-age pensions, and medical insurance, the last of which died owing to opposition from the organized medical profession.

Meanwhile a separate women's network of welfare reformers, at first unrepresented in discussions of the new bill, observed that social insurance, providing eligibility through the workplace, neglected the substantial number of women and children who had no supporting male breadwinner. They designed several other Social Security proposals, which became known as public assistance as distinct from social insurance. The most prominent of these was Aid to Dependent Children (ADC, forerunner of Aid to Families with Dependent Children, or AFDC). Organized on an entirely different principle, public-assistance programs did not initially vest any entitlement in recipients. They provided states with only one-third of the funding cost and limited eligibility to the needy and the "deserving," which stipulation required means-testing and supervising recipients. The women's network also introduced into the bill several programs to aid the disabled.

Congress radically amended both the social-insurance and public-assistance provisions before passing the Social Security Act. Powerful southern members of Congress forced the elimination of agricultural and domestic workers from the employment-based programs, thus excluding the vast majority of workers of color. With ADC, they insisted on limiting federal oversight, thereby allowing the states to exercise great discretion in determining eligibility for ADC, discretion which notably included race discrimination. The act provided that the social insurance system would be funded by taxes paid partly by employers and partly by funds withheld from workers' paychecks, so as to create the impression that these benefits were earned.

Amendments to Social Security accumulated rapidly. In 1939 Congress added survivors' insurance to old-age pensions and moved their first disbursement from 1942 to 1940. Later changes broadened eligibility, indexed benefits to inflation so as to maintain their real value, and added Medicare, health-care insurance for the eligible elderly. The result was considerable reduction in poverty among the elderly. Unemployment insurance changed less, and as the twentieth century ended, typically offered six months of payments and continued to exclude the majority of the unemployed from coverage.

Public assistance also underwent substantial change over the years. Single parents, as well as their children, became recipients of AFDC in 1950; Supplemental Security Income, adopted in 1972, added assistance for the elderly and disabled poor; the food-stamp system developed in the 1960s and 1970s; Medicaid was added in 1965. In the 1960s organized welfare recipients agitated for and won *Supreme Court rulings guaranteeing several rights, including that to a hearing before being denied benefits. Meanwhile the numbers of AFDC recipients grew rapidly as many single-parent families once excluded, such as unwed mothers and their children, gained access to the program. As a result, poverty in the United States declined substantially through the mid-1970s. But that trend soon reversed itself, as rising prices shrank AFDC benefits and low-paid workers were left without medical insurance and effective unemployment insurance. After 1980, poverty grew, particularly among children, partly as a result of deindustrialization and partly as a result of conservative administrations and Congresses that further reduced benefits out of a conviction that "welfare," as public assistance had come to be called, stimulates poverty by discouraging work and promoting family disintegration. Congress repealed AFDC entirely in 1996.

By contrast, Social Security old-age pensions, not considered "welfare" by most Americans although they disburse more taxpayer money than did AFDC, remained popular and protected from attack until the mid–1990s, when conservative economists and politicians asserted that the system of old-age pensions, coupled with an aging and longer-lived population, threatened to plunge the system into bankruptcy.

[*See also* Depressions, Economic; Medicare and Medicaid; New Deal Era, The.]

• Roy Lubove, *The Struggle for Social Security, 1900–1935,* 1968. W. Andrew Achenbaum, *Social Security: Visions and Revisions,* 1986. Michael B. Katz, *The Undeserving Poor: From the War on Poverty to the War on Welfare,* 1989. Edward D. Berkowitz, *America's Welfare State from Roosevelt to Reagan,* 1991. Linda Gordon, *Pitied but Not Entitled: Single Mothers and the History of Welfare,* 1994. James T. Patterson, *America's Struggle against Poverty 1900–1994,* 1994.

—Linda Gordon

SOCIAL WORK. In antebellum America, before the term "social work" was coined, men and women of the urban elite, acting from religious and humanitarian motives, donated time and resources to helping the poor and distressed, founding *orphanages, *alms houses, and other charitable institutions. For leisured women, excluded from higher education and the professions, such activity provided a vehicle for benevolent work in the public arena. The *Civil War U.S. Sanitary Commission accelerated the organization of private philanthropic efforts, enlisting thousands of volunteers, especially women.

*Gilded Age reformers lobbied against institutionalized, government-funded poor relief (called "outdoor relief") in favor of volunteer assistance to the poor in their own homes. Modern social work thus took shape mainly in the private sector. Beginning in the 1870s, charity-organization societies (COS) in *New York City, *Boston, and other cities sought to coordinate private charities and to curb indiscriminate giving to professional beggars and the "unworthy" poor. Embued with the dogmas of *social Darwinism, leaders of the *charity organization movement saw a close connection between success and virtue, failure and vice. The COS recruited voluntary female "friendly visitors" to investigate the poor in their homes and encourage habits of thrift and sobriety. Eventually some of these became paid district agents or caseworkers, the first social workers. In its casework approach, the COS anticipated later social-work practice. By the 1890s, the National Conference of Charities and Corrections had emerged as a forum for these early social workers.

The social worker entered the twentieth century as part social scientist, part city missionary, and part detective; the 1910 census lumped "social workers" with "religious and charity workers." The *Progressive Era *settlement-house movement embodied new hopes for social betterment in the immigrant city. Living among the poor, settlement workers, often women, encouraged community development, interpreted the poor to middle-class America, and lobbied legislatures on their behalf. They also generated statistics ("social knowledge") about housing, health, and labor conditions, supplying the data for a social work that increasingly saw itself as applied *social science. Also influential in shaping the emerging field were *Social Gospel theologians and the mostly male social scientists at the new research universities such as Johns Hopkins.

Struggles over identity and purpose marked the evolution of social work. Sometimes the conflict was expressed in gendered language, as the advocates of *professionalization represented themselves as champions of a masculinized, scientific objectivity and their opponents as feminized, sentimental do-gooders. But the stereotypes bore little relation to reality. In such a vital figure as Mary Van Kleeck, a social-work leader, industrial investigator, foundation executive, and Christian socialist, for example, scientific ambition coexisted with evangelical purpose. *World War I offered such social experts unprecedented opportunities to put theory into practice in government agencies and private organizations such as the Young Men's Christian Association (YMCA).

Crucially important in social-work history was a semipublic institution, the Russell Sage Foundation (RSF), established in 1907 "for the improvement of the social and living conditions in the United States." Its trustees were drawn from the COS, academic social science, women's associations, and private *philanthropy. Effectively underwriting social work's development as a profession, the RSF funded schools of philanthropy in Boston, St. Louis, New York, and *Chicago; gave over a million dollars to the New York COS between 1907 and 1947; financed the social-work journal *The Survey* (1911); and funded such projects as *tuberculosis prevention, *housing reform, and a pathbreaking survey of social conditions in Pittsburgh. Mary Richmond (1861–1928) of the RSF supplied a handbook of professional practice with her *Social Diagnosis* (1917). In their continuing campaign for professional recognition, social workers compared their diagnostic and prescriptive role to that of the physician. Full professional status proved elusive, however, as such emerging subfields as medical social work, probation work, social work in the schools, and psychiatric social work remained auxiliary to other professions.

As academic social science turned from describing deviance to defining normality, social work redefined its task as one of promoting social adjustment. Therapeutic goals replaced reform and research. At the local level, following a model pioneered by the COS, private social-welfare agencies formed umbrella organizations called Community Chests (later the United Way) for fund-raising purposes. These links to the established order further discouraged social workers from advocating social change. Social workers increasingly found employment in federal, state, and local government agencies; think tanks; and private (including religious) welfare organizations. The quest for professional recognition continued through academic credentialing, notably the Master of Social Work (MSW) degree, and membership in the American Association of Social Work, founded in 1921. Successors to the nineteenth-century genteel volunteers and the Progressive Era activist/investigators, late twentieth-century social workers typically "patrol[ed] the borders of [social] class" (as historian Daniel Walkowitz has put it) as middle-class professionals in hierarchical public or private bureaucracies serving a poor, predominantly nonwhite clientele.

[*See also* Immigration; Poverty; Social Class; Urbanization; Welfare, Federal; YMCA and YWCA.]

• Frank J. Bruno, *Trends in Social Work, 1874–1956,* 1957. Roy Lubove, *The Profesional Altruist: The Emergence of Social Work as a Career,* 1965.

Walter I. Trattner, *From Poor Law to Welfare State: A History of Social Welfare and Social Work in the United States* 1978. Ruth Crocker, *Social Work and Social Order: The Settlement Movement in Two Industrial Cities*, 1992. Regina G. Kunzel, *Fallen Women, Problem Girls: Unmarried Mothers and the Professionalization of Social Work, 1890–1945*, 1993. Nancy Fraser and Linda Gordon, "A Genealogy of Dependency: Tracing a Keyword of the Welfare State," *Signs* 19, 2 (1994): 308–63. Dawn Greeley, "Beyond Benevolence: Gender, Class, and the Development of Scientific Charity in New York City, 1882–1935," Ph.D. diss., SUNY Stony Brook, 1995. Helene Silverberg, ed., *Gender and American Social Science* (1998). Daniel Walkowitz, *Working with Class: Social Workers and the Politics of Middle-Class Identity*, 1999.

—Ruth Crocker

SOCIETY OF FRIENDS (Quakers), a religious organization that began in England in the 1640s, led by George Fox. The first Quakers arrived in North America in 1656. They were distinguished by their silent worship, their belief in the Inward Light of Christ in all people and the spirituality of the sacraments, their refusal to bear arms, their openness to women's preaching, and their antipathy to professional clergy. By 1660, Friends had won converts in *New England, on Long Island, and in the Chesapeake region. They also, as in England, faced persecution, climaxing in the execution of four Friends in *Boston. In the 1670s and 1680s thousands of Friends settled in New Jersey and Pennsylvania, colonies that Quakers established. By 1700, Friends were the third largest denomination in the British colonies.

After 1700, the number of Quakers remained relatively static. Nevertheless, individual Friends like John *Woolman exercised considerable influence as reformers. They were early leaders of *antislavery movements and defenders of the rights of Native Americans and free blacks. Friends dominated the 1848 women's rights convention, Seneca Falls, and Quaker women, notably Lucretia *Mott and Susan B. *Anthony, provided much of the movement's leadership.

After 1820, American Quakerism splintered. In the 1820s, Hicksite Friends, led by Elias Hicks of Long Island, who emphasized the primacy of the Inward Light, separated from Orthodox Friends, who emphasized the divinity of Christ and the authority of scripture. In the 1840s and 1850s the Orthodox further divided into Wilburites, unbending conservatives, and Gurneyites, more open to non-Quaker influences. After 1870 Gurneyite Friends, especially in the *Middle West, gave up most of Quakerism's distinctive features and adopted a pastoral ministry.

Twentieth-century Quakers were most visible as social activists and peace advocates, especially through the *American Friends Service Committee, founded in 1917. At the end of the century, American Quakers ranged from New Age universalists to fundamentalists.

[*See also* Colonial Era; Conscientious Objection; Fundamentalist Movement; Pacifism; Peace Movements; Penn, William; Religion; Seneca Falls Convention; Unitarianism and Universalism.]

• Hugh Barbour and J. William Frost, *The Quakers*, 1988.

—Thomas D. Hamm

SOCIOLOGY. Sociology, the study of society, arose in the United States, as in Europe, in response to the problem of social order in modern society in the wake of the American and French revolutions and the rise of *industrialization and market *capitalism. Whereas Enlightenment theorists viewed society in terms of a "social contract" and a convergence of individual interests, early sociologists sought to identify sources of social order within the forms and structures of society itself.

In the *Antebellum Era, the anomaly of chattel *slavery in a "free" society inspired George Fitzhugh's *Sociology for the South* (1854) and Henry Hughes's *Treatise on Sociology* (1854). These critiques of northern industrial society were the first American works to employ the term "sociology," coined by the Frenchman Auguste Comte a decade earlier. Comte also directly influenced various antebellum Utopian reformers in the North. Sociology reemerged after the *Civil War in response to industrial conflict, *immigration, and *urbanization, drawing again on Comte and on the English social theorist Herbert Spencer. In 1875 Yale professor William Graham Sumner (1840–1910) offered the first course titled "Sociology," assigning Spencer's *Principles of Sociology*, then appearing in installments. In his seminal work *Dynamic Sociology* (1884), a synthesis of Comte and Spencer, Lester *Ward called for the direction of social policy by state-appointed experts. Sociology also built on empirical and survey work supported by census bureaus, state agencies, and reform organizations, a tradition represented by Jane *Addams and others in *Hull House Maps and Papers* (1895) and W. E. B. *Du Bois in *The Philadelphia Negro* (1899).

The first departments of sociology were created at the University of Chicago under Albion W. Small in 1892, and at Columbia University under Franklin Giddings two years later. The most important studies written in this period, however, were by professors at Wisconsin, Michigan, and Yale: Edward A. Ross, *Social Control* (1901); Charles Horton Cooley, *Human Nature and the Social Order* (1902); and Sumner's *Folkways* (1906). In 1895, Small founded the *American Journal of Sociology*, later the official organ of the American Sociological Society (ASS), organized in 1905.

Although prewar sociology was a victim of *World War I, the University of Chicago led a major revival in the interwar years. Initially taking shape around the work of Robert Park (1864–1944) and his students, "Chicago sociology" eventually developed diverse approaches defined by individuals and generation. These included Park's urban ecology as outlined in *An Introduction to the Science of Society* (1921), written with Ernest Burgess; a rigorously quantitative sociology, introduced with the appointment in 1927 of William F. Ogburn, author of *Social Change* (1922) and head investigator for *Recent Social Trends* (1932), a report commissioned by President Herbert *Hoover; and "symbolic interactionism," so named in 1937 by Herbert Blumer, building on the work of Chicago philosopher George Herbert Mead. Symbolic interactionism continued to flourish into the post–*World War II Era, for example, in Erving Goffman's popular study *The Presentation of Self in Everyday Life* (1959).

Although the Columbia sociology department declined during the 1920s, its influence continued through the work of its graduates at Minnesota (F. Stuart Chapin), North Carolina (Howard Odum), Pennsylvania (James Lichtenberger and Stuart Rice), and Wisconsin (John Gillin). With Ogburn, also a Columbia graduate, all played important roles in the educational foundations that funded much of interwar sociology, including Robert and Helen Lynd's **Middletown* (1929), an investigation of Muncie, Indiana, and Gunnar Myrdal and others' *An *American Dilemma* (1944), a classic study of race in America.

The Depression of the 1930s shifted sociologists' focus from the assimilation of immigrants (the Chicago school's specialty) to *unemployment and *poverty. The Depression also caused a decline in academic funding, jobs, and graduate enrollments. A revolt within the ASS in the mid–1930s effectively ended Chicago's domination of the profession, shifting the balance of power to the East. In 1931 Harvard belatedly created a department of sociology, with Pitirim Sorokin as head and Talcott *Parsons as an instructor. In 1941, the arrival at Columbia of Parsons's student Robert Merton and the German émigré Paul Lazarsfeld laid the groundwork for an informal but powerful Harvard-Columbia postwar alliance. Other developments meanwhile sowed the seeds of a revival of sociology under American leadership: increased opportunities for government service; the articulation of the "classical" European sociological tradition in Parsons's *The Structure of Social Action* (1937); and the arrival of many distinguished émigré sociologists.

From 1950 through the mid–1960s, American sociology was dominated by Parsonian functionalism and "systems theory," a modification of Parsons's earlier "action theory" more suited to the consensus mood of the *Cold War. Recognizing the weakness of Parsonianism for practical research, Robert Merton in *Social Theory and Social Structure* (1949) called for theories of "the middle range," effecting an influential theory/method compromise. Issues arising from World War II inspired such collaborative efforts as Dorothy S. Thomas et al., *The Spoilage* (1946), a study of the forced evacuation and detention of West Coast Japanese Americans during the war; Samuel Stouffer et al., *The American Soldier* (1949); and Theodore Adorno et al., *The Authoritarian Personality* (1950). Sociology reached a wide audience in three critical examinations of the postwar social and economic order: David Riesman's *The *Lonely Crowd* (1950), *White Collar* (1951), C. Wright Mills (1916–1962), and William Whyte's *The Organization Man* (1956). As the discipline's influence spread, "status," "norm," "role," and other sociological terms entered the American vocabulary.

Parsonian hegemony, although never unchallenged, was shattered by the mid–1960s as Merton's compromise gave way to a politically charged humanist/positivist divide. Conflict theorists, notably Mills in *The Sociological Imagination* (1959) and Alvin Gouldner in *The Coming Crisis of Western Sociology* (1970) attacked Parsons for ignoring the reality of force and repression. Symbolic interactionists, phenomenologists, and exchange theorists, meanwhile, took aim at Parsons's rigid model of human behavior and his alleged obliviousness to the complexities of cognition and reality construction. A new breed of positivists, armed with *computers and mathematical sophistication, insisted that Parsons's theories be tested empirically—thereby creating new power and influence for themselves. Feminists charged that functionalism reinforced existing *gender roles. Outside sociology, sociobiologists raised a specter of biological determinism that most sociologists believed had expired long before. By the end of the 1970s, many within the profession lamented the fragmentation of sociology and spoke of an "interregnum" in the discipline's development. Despite proposals for a postmodern sociology, for example in Zygmunt Bauman's *Intimations of Postmodernity* (1992), these laments continued two decades later.

[*See also* Anthropology; Boas, Franz; Education: The Rise of the University; Feminism; Fifties, The; Professionalizaton; Sixties, The; Utopian and Communitarian Movements.]

• Nicholas C. Mullins and Carolyn J. Mullins, *Theories and Theory Groups in Contemporary American Sociology*, 1973. Robert Bierstedt, *American Sociological Theory*, 1981. Robert C. Bannister, *Sociology and Scientism*, 1987. Stephen Park Turner and Jonathan H. Turner, *The Impossible Science*, 1990. Dorothy Ross, *The Origins of American Social Science*, 1991.

—Robert C. Bannister

SOJOURNER TRUTH (ca. 1797–1883), abolitionist, feminist, and Pentecostal preacher. Sojourner Truth was born a slave named Isabella in Ulster County in New York's Hudson River valley. During her enslavement, Isabella married and bore five children. Emancipated by a New York State law passed in 1828, she embraced a "perfectionist" (Pentecostal) *Methodism. She also sued successfully for the return of Peter, her young son, who had been illegally sold into *slavery in Alabama.

Moving with Peter to *New York City in 1828, Isabella joined the utopian religious community "Kingdom of the Prophet Matthias (Robert Matthews)" for a time in the early 1830s. On 1 June 1843, Pentecost Sunday, at the height of the Millerite adventist movement, wherein William Miller had predicted Christ's second coming in 1843–1844, the voice of the Holy Spirit told her she was Sojourner Truth, itinerant preacher. That winter, Truth settled in an industrial commune, the Northampton Association in Massachusetts. There she imbibed *feminism and abolitionism, met William Lloyd *Garrison and Frederick *Douglass, and dictated the *Narrative of Sojourner Truth*. Between 1850 and 1864, Truth frequently participated in feminist and *antislavery meetings. She spoke at an Akron, Ohio, women's rights meeting in 1851 but—contrary to later accounts—did *not* ask, "Ar'n't I a woman?"

Truth saw the *Civil War as a kind of Armageddon struggle remaking American society. She embraced political action (which, as a Garrisonian, she had earlier repudiated), and in 1864 campaigned for Abraham *Lincoln's reelection. After the war she championed woman suffrage. Truth died in Battle Creek, Michigan, where she lived with her two surviving daughters.

[*See also* African American Religion; African Americans; Antebellum Era; Millennialism and Apocalypticism; Pentecostalism; Utopian and Communitarian Movements; Woman Suffrage Movement; Women's Rights Movements.]

• Nell Irvin Painter, *Sojourner Truth, A Life, A Symbol*, 1996. Nell Irvin Painter, ed., *Narrative of Sojourner Truth*, 1998.

—Nell Irvin Painter

SONS OF LIBERTY. After the British Parliament passed the *Stamp Act in 1765, small groups in each colony—generally artisans or intercolonial merchants, joined by a few attorneys, doctors, and teachers—became convinced that only large crowds prepared to act violently could successfully resist the tax. Together they had the contacts and expertise to organize townspeople against the tax. Leaders in Connecticut dubbed their followers "Sons of Liberty." The name spread rapidly, soon coming to stand for everyone who participated in the popular resistance to the Stamp Act. Between August and December 1765, the Sons of Liberty forced stamp distributors to resign, governors to withhold stamped paper, and courts to remain open in defiance of the law. Their efforts prevented enforcement of the act and led to its repeal in March 1766.

British politicians and conservative colonists hoped the Sons of Liberty would disband after repeal. Suspicious of British motives and convinced that *liberty was still at risk, however, the Sons remained active, and maintained contact with one another throughout the colonies. While persuading voters to purge conservatives from colonial assemblies and replace them with liberty's friends, they strengthened their own popular base by serving the interests of artisans and small merchants.

In every imperial crisis between 1766 and 1774, the Sons of Liberty called forth crowds to bully British officials and American sympathizers, confident that colonial governments could not respond effectively. In the process, they deepened estrangement between the colonists and their British governors and taught the people that government should rest on popular consent. The collapse of royal authority in 1774–1775 and its swift replacement by local committees and provincial congresses reflected a decade's work by the Sons of Liberty.

[*See also* Adams, Samuel; Boston Tea Party; Colonial Era; Republicanism; Revolution and Constitution, Era of; Revolutionary War.]

• Pauline Maier, *From Resistance to Revolution: Colonial Radicals and the Development of American Opposition to Britain, 1765–1776*, 1972. Edward Countryman, *A People in Revolution: The American Revolution and Political Society in New York, 1760–1790*, 1981.

—John L. Bullion

SOTO, HERNANDO DE (ca. 1500–1542), Spanish conquistador. Hernando De Soto is best known in American history as the leader of the first major Spanish expedition into the present-day southeastern United States. He landed with an army of more than six hundred men near Tampa Bay on the Gulf of Mexico in present-day Florida in May 1539, and died along the *Mississippi River three years later. It was a march of death and devastation that marked the beginning of the end of major American Indian civilizations that flourished during this age of European exploration and conquest.

De Soto was a veteran conquistador by the time he reached North America. His exploits in the conquest of the Inca in Peru had made him rich, and he sought more fortune and fame in North America, hoping to discover native empires as rich as those found by the Spanish in Mexico (the Aztec) and Peru. He was bitterly disappointed as his army of soldiers, horses, Indian captives, equipment, and even a herd of pigs drove across the future states of Florida, Georgia, the Carolinas, Tennessee, Alabama, and Mississippi, and thence across the Mississippi River to Arkansas, Louisiana, and Texas.

*Influenza, *smallpox, and other diseases introduced by De Soto's army decimated the Native Americans already shocked by the ferocity and calculated terror of the Spanish. A century later, other European explorers would find little remnant of the impressive Woodland cultures described by the chroniclers of the De Soto expedition.

[*See also* Columbian Exchange; Exploration, Conquest, and Settlement, Era of European; Indian History and Culture: Distribution of Major Groups, Circa 1500; Indian History and Culture: From 1500 to 1800; Spanish Settlements in North America.]

• Lawrence A. Clayton, Vernon James Knight Jr., and Edward C. Moore, eds., *The De Soto Chronicles: The Expedition of Hernando De Soto to North America in 1539–1543,* 2 vols., 1993. David Ewing Duncan, *Hernando De Soto: A Savage Quest in the Americas,* 1996. Charles Hudson, *Knights of Spain, Warriors of the Sun: Hernando De Soto and the South's Ancient Chiefdoms,* 1997.

—Lawrence A. Clayton

SOUTH, THE, a diverse region including all or parts of the states of Virginia, West Virginia, Maryland, North Carolina, South Carolina, Georgia, Florida, Alabama, Mississippi, Louisiana, Tennessee, Kentucky, Arkansas, Missouri, and Texas. Varying climates, soils, and topography have produced a multiplicity of landscapes: the tidewater plain along the Atlantic coast, the rolling Piedmont of central Virginia and the Carolinas, the Appalachian Mountains ranging down to Georgia and Alabama, the piney woods along the Gulf coast across to East Texas, and the rich soils of the *Mississippi River delta and Alabama Black Belt. The region is defined less by geography than by its history and culture, which, while also diverse, constitute the core of regional identity. The South's population, its economic relationship to the rest of the country, and its particular historical experience have been sufficiently distinctive to shape both its identity and its place in the nation.

The French and Spanish explored and laid claims along the Gulf coast and the Mississippi River, and the Spanish established the earliest permanent European settlement at St. Augustine in 1565. The colony at *Jamestown (1607) led to significant English settlement in the Middle Atlantic region. Later settlements by the Scots-Irish and Germans in the Piedmont, by French Huguenots in South Carolina, and by Acadians, or Cajuns (descendants of French-speaking farmers deported from Canada's maritime provinces by the British in the 1750s), in Louisiana, added variety to the European population. A most significant migration was the forced settlement of enslaved Africans, beginning as early as 1619.

Slaves accounted for as much as a third of the population in some southern colonies by 1750. Their presence, and the predominance of *agriculture—cotton, rice, tobacco, sugar, and indigo—delineated much of the region's character and future. Although at the mercy of their masters, slaves, as well as free blacks, preserved some elements of their cultures and the dignity of work and family life. Most southern whites did not own slaves, but the political and economic influence of large plantation agriculture, and the controls necessary to sustain a system of chattel slavery, permeated southern society by the beginning of the *Antebellum Era.

The indigenous Indian tribes in the region—Cherokee, Choctaw, Chickasaw, Creek, and Seminole—were coerced into treaties relinquishing their lands in Alabama, Florida, Georgia, and Mississippi, and were forcibly removed, over the "Trail of Tears," to Indian Territory in Oklahoma during the 1830s. A Seminole band retreated to the Everglades where they resisted resettlement, but were nearly exterminated by 1845.

Tensions over *slavery and sectional self-determination led to heightened southern nationalism and, eventually, to the *Civil War and the economic dislocation that followed. The *Reconstruction Era and its aftermath laid the foundations for the South's return to the national fold, but did not bring racial reconciliation. The end of slavery provided new opportunities for *African Americans, but the post–Reconstruction Era brought a new system of racial *segregation that insured continued white dominance.

Economic development and urban growth in the late nineteenth and early twentieth centuries inspired talk of a "New South." Ambitious ventures in raw-materials processing, *mining, and manufacturing, and the rapid growth of interior cities like *Atlanta, Birmingham, and Nashville, narrowed the gap between the region and the rest of the country. But the southern economy retained a dependent relationship on the more extensive and sophisticated industries and financial institutions of the Northeast and *Middle West. Consequently, by the Depression of the 1930s, President Franklin Delano *Roosevelt identified the region as "the nation's number one economic problem." In *Let Us Now Praise Famous Men* (1941), writer James Agee and photographer Walker Evans memorably evoked the harsh life of Depression-Era southern sharecroppers.

Even more dramatic social and economic changes after *World War II heralded a revolution in southern race relations that culminated in the *civil rights movement of the 1960s and fractured the infrastructure of white supremacy. These events again underscored the significance of southern history and culture in the national story. The last quarter of the twentieth century witnessed unprecedented demographic, technological, and economic changes in the South, and brought it more within the national mainstream as part of the rapidly developing "Sunbelt." The modern South's interstate *highway system, major businesses, modern communications networks, professional *sports teams, and large numbers of black elected officials all testified to the extent of these changes, as did the fact that this region supplied four U.S. presidents between 1960 and 2000: Lyndon B. *Johnson, Jimmy *Carter, George *Bush, and Bill *Clinton. Despite the transformations, however, the South retained many of its traditional values and burdens. Regional *folklore, traditional *music, and a powerful strain of evangelical *Protestantism all helped shape this legacy.

Southern culture and identity were embedded, too, in a flourishing *literature that included such Antebellum Era writers as Edgar Allan *Poe and reached its heights in such twentieth-century writers and playwrights as William *Faulkner, Tennessee Williams, Richard *Wright, Zora Neale *Hurston, Eudora Welty, and William Styron. From the rich folklore and *humor of the southern frontier in the eighteenth century to the oral traditions of black slaves to the *blues, gospel music, and *jazz, as well as the florid rhetoric of the southern pulpit, the region's literature and *popular culture drew strength from the moral challenges of slavery and the harsh realities of southern poverty. Southern history has been a deep well that replenished the imagination and cast a unique perspective on the nation's experience.

[*See also* African American Religion; Baptists; *Cherokee*

Cases; Cotton Industry; Depressions, Economic; Economic Development; French Settlements in North America; Gospel Music, African American; Indian History and Culture: From 1500 to 1800; Indian History and Culture: From 1800 to 1900; Indian Removal Act; Regionalism; Religion; Seminole Wars; Sharecropping and Tenantry; Spanish Settlements in North America; Tobacco Industry.]

• C. Vann Woodward, *Origins of the New South, 1877–1913,* 1951. Wilbur J. Cash, *The Mind of the South,* 1941. Jack Bass and Thomas Terrill, eds., *The American South Comes of Age,* 1986. Numan V. Bartley, *The New South, 1945–1980,* 1995. Carole E. Hill and Patricia D. Bearer, eds., *Cultural Diversity in the U.S. South: Anthropological Contributions to a Region in Transition,* 1998. Stephen David Kantrowicz, *Ben Tillman and the Reconstruction of White Supremacy,* 2000.

—Blaine A. Brownell

SOUTHERN CHRISTIAN LEADERSHIP CONFERENCE. Created in the wake of the Montgomery Bus Boycott in 1957 by Martin Luther *King Jr. and his followers, the Southern Christian Leadership Conference (SCLC) coordinated and assisted local organizations working for the full equality of *African Americans during the *civil rights movement. Initial organizers included Ella Baker, Ralph Abernathy, Fred Shuttlesworth, Joseph Lowery, C. K. Steele, T. J. Jemison, and Bayard Rustin. Animated by King's philosophy of nonviolent direct action and his vision of a mass movement rooted in Christian love and multiracial democracy, the organization conducted leadership training programs, citizen-education projects, and voter registration drives. Along with the *Student Non-Violent Coordinating Committee, SCLC played an integral role in various southern desegregation and voting-rights campaigns, most notably in Albany, Georgia, and Birmingham and Selma, Alabama. These campaigns spurred the passage of the Civil Rights Act of 1964 and the Voting Rights Act of 1965. In addition, SCLC helped organize the 1963 March on Washington for Jobs and Freedom where King delivered his famous "I Have a Dream" speech.

Following these initial successes, SCLC experienced a series of setbacks. In 1965 and 1966, as Black Power began to eclipse nonviolent direct action among many activists and organizations, King and SCLC embarked on an unsuccessful campaign in *Chicago. In 1968, SCLC planned a Poor People's Campaign to be held in *Washington, D.C., with the hope of uniting poor people from all races, ethnicities, and religions. This effort was cut short by King's assassination in Memphis. Following his death, SCLC maintained its philosophy of nonviolent direct action, but focused on smaller, local efforts. The organization was further weakened by internal schisms, most significantly the 1972 departure of the Reverend Jesse Jackson (1941–) of Chicago and his followers who had staffed Operation Breadbasket, an SCLC effort directed at economic justice for African Americans. Despite these difficulties, SCLC remained active in the struggle for racial, social, and economic justice as the twentieth century ended.

[*See also* African American Religion; Civil Rights Legislation; Racism.]

• David Garrow, *Bearing the Cross: Martin Luther King, Jr., and the Southern Christian Leadership Conference,* 1986. Adam Fairclough, *To Redeem the Soul of America,* 1987.

—Patrick D. Jones

SOUTHERN TENANT FARMERS' UNION AND NATIONAL FARM LABOR UNION. Galvanized by a 1934 visit to northeast Arkansas by the socialist leader Norman *Thomas, local Socialist party members H. L. Mitchell and Clay East helped found the Southern Tenant Farmers' Union (STFU). Initially focused on securing for sharecroppers government payments under the *Agricultural Adjustment Administration's crop-reduction program, the STFU quickly evolved into an interracial social movement that challenged the power wielded by large landholders over indebted sharecroppers, tenants, and small farmers in the rural *South. Led by a coalition of socialists, radical Christians, and African American preachers, the organization by 1936 had enrolled 25,000 members in Arkansas, Missouri, Oklahoma, and Texas, uniting black and white sharecroppers for the first time since the Populist movement of the 1890s.

Appealing to "laborers, share-croppers, renters, or small landowners whose lands are worked by themselves," the STFU organized men and women victimized by the collapse of the cotton economy during the 1930s. The union led a strike of Arkansas cotton pickers in 1936, and it also sought to break the dependency engendered by the crop-lien system, which kept sharecroppers and tenants perpetually in debt to their landlords.

Despite its rapid expansion and early success, the STFU declined by the end of the 1930s. The union's most significant achievement, the creation of an interracial social movement in the segregated South, made it vulnerable to violent repression by planters and their allies. Factional disputes generated by the sharecroppers' uneasy alliance with the *Congress of Industrial Organizations, which was oriented primarily toward industrial workers, weakened the STFU internally. Finally, the later 1930s saw the rapid uprooting from the land of the very people the union sought to organize, thwarting the hopes of the STFU's leadership to remake the rural South by replacing the plantation and crop-lien system with interracial cooperative farms.

Renamed the National Farm Labor Union (NFLU) in 1946, the union affiliated with the *American Federation of Labor. Although in its new incarnation the NFLU recruited farmworkers in California and Louisiana, it never regained its identity as a radical social movement. Nevertheless, the STFU's original vision of an interracial movement of the poor provided an important precedent for the *civil rights movement that would transform the South thirty years later.

[*See also* Agriculture: Since 1920; Cotton Industry; Labor Movements; New Deal Era, The; Sharecropping and Tenantry; Socialism; Socialist Party of America.]

• Howard Kester, *Revolt among the Sharecroppers,* 1936, reprint 1997. Donald H. Grubbs, *Cry from the Cotton Gin: The Southern Tenant Farmers' Union and the New Deal,* 1971.

—Alex Lichtenstein

SOUTHWEST, THE. Definitions of this region vary, but all include present-day New Mexico, Arizona, and the El Paso area of western Texas. Until the twentieth century, physical barriers such as the Mojave and Sonoran deserts, the Llano Estacado (Staked Plains), the southern *Rocky Mountains, and the Colorado Plateau isolated the area and limited contact with outsiders. A sizeable Hispanic population and a variety of Native American groups also distinguished the region. Although both Arizona and New Mexico are large states geographically, they remain lightly populated by national standards. Climatic extremes often appear forbidding; much of the area gets only about ten inches of rainfall annually. The Southwest's distance from most of the nation's major population centers and its abundance of vacant land have helped to shape regional development.

The Southwest's earliest human inhabitants arrived as big-game hunters twelve to fifteen thousand years ago. As the large animals became extinct, the people shifted to hunting small game, gathering, and agriculture. Eventually they developed several distinct cultures, the Mogollon, Anasazi, and Hohokam. Between 1200 and 1400, these peoples disappeared. As raiding Athabascan people—called "Apaches" (enemies) by the settled groups—entered the region, more heavily fortified villages or pueblos developed. At the end of the sixteenth century, perhaps forty thousand Indians lived in at least sixty pueblos, most along the Rio Grande.

In 1598, Juan de Oñate led some four hundred Spaniards north into present-day New Mexico. They brought new diseases, religious disputes, warfare, and destruction to the Indians. During the seventeenth century, Spanish friars and priests strove to discredit native religious beliefs and replace them with *Roman Catholicism. The *Pueblo Revolt of 1680, centered in present-day New Mexico and led by a San Juan pueblo Indian, Popé, drove the invaders south to El Paso. The Spanish returned, however, in 1692. In Arizona, Spanish priests founded modest missions, but few other Spaniards came north to deal with the Indians. A mixed-race culture gradually developed in the eighteenth century, mostly Indian physically, but partly Spanish culturally.

Anglo Americans arrived early in the nineteenth century as part of the Rocky Mountain *fur trade. Following the *Mexican War, the United States in 1848 annexed most of the region, rounding out the border in 1853 with the *Gadsden Purchase. During the next several decades the incoming Anglo Americans and the native peoples, particularly the Apaches, clashed repeatedly. These conflicts ended in 1886 with the surrender and exile of the Apache warrior *Geronimo. In 1880 the Southern Pacific Railroad opened the region to easy settlement by easterners. At first gold and silver *mining attracted most attention, but the later development of copper mining and smelting had more long-range impact. Federal programs to speed western *economic development began with the 1911 Roosevelt Dam in Arizona and the 1916 Elephant Butte Dam in New Mexico. These projects continued into the 1990s with such undertakings as the Central Arizona Project to bring Colorado River water to Phoenix and Tucson.

*World War II changed the Southwest profoundly. Thousands of military personnel trained there, and many returned with their families after the war to settle permanently. *Manhattan Project scientists harnessed atomic power at Alamagordo, New Mexico, during the war, and much of the nation's uranium came from Navajo lands. Both Senator Barry *Goldwater of Arizona, the 1964 Republican candidate for president, and Morris Udall, an Arizona Democratic congressman who focused on environmental matters, heightened national awareness of the Southwest. Beginning in the 1960s, high-technology developments attracted new corporate enterprises with well-paying jobs, while ever-growing sunbelt retirement communities drew thousands of older Americans.

The Southwest has figured prominently in American culture. For nearly a century, writers as diverse as Zane Grey, Mary Austin, D. H. Lawrence, Willa *Cather, and Tony Hillerman have focused attention on the region. *Films and *television programs have presented the Southwest as exotic, alluring, and distinctly American. Those depictions stressed open space, natural beauty, and few people, and offered the allure of an imagined virgin frontier. Mabel Dodge (1879–1962) and her circle helped make Santa Fe, New Mexico, a cultural center as early as the 1920s. Subsequently, Georgia *O'Keeffe and other artists, along with Native American potters, weavers, and jewelry makers, enhanced the community's reputation as an artistic mecca. Nearby Taos and other pueblos became major tourist attractions.

The Southwest includes more prosaic realities as well, however, such as large-scale mining, *lumbering, ranching, *tourism, interstate highways, heavy *urbanization, and a substantial federal presence. Still, for many in the United States and abroad, the Southwest remains the land of the Indian pueblos, saguaro cactus, the *Grand Canyon, and beautiful sunsets—a uniquely American region.

[*See also* Environmentalism; Hispanic Americans; Indian History and Culture; Indian Wars; Literature, Popular; Livestock Industry; Railroads; Regionalism; Spanish Settlements in North America; West, The.]

• W. Eugene Hollon, *The Southwest: Old and New,* 1961. Edward H. Spicer, *Cycles of Conquest: The Impact of Spain, Mexico, and the United States on the Indians of the Southwest,* 1962. Donald W. Meinig, *Southwest: Three Peoples in Geographical Change, 1600–1970,* 1971. Lynn I. Perrigo, *The American Southwest: Its Peoples and Cultures,* 1971. David J. Weber, *Foreigners in Their Native Land: Historical Roots of the Mexican Americans,* 1973. Gerald D. Nash, *The American West in the Twentieth Century: A Short History of an Urban Oasis,* 1977.

—Roger L. Nichols

SPACE PROGRAM. The American space program emerged in large part from the pressures of national defense during the *Cold War. In the late 1940s, eager to assure American leadership in *technology, the Department of Defense began pursuing research in rocketry and upper-atmospheric science. The civilian side of the space effort began in 1952, when the International Council of Scientific Unions began planning for an International Geophysical Year (IGY) for the period 1 July 1957 through December 1958. As part of this effort, the U.S. scientific community in 1955 persuaded President Dwight D. *Eisenhower to approve a plan to orbit a scientific satellite. The Naval Research Laboratory's Project Vanguard was chosen to carry out this mission.

In this context, the Soviet Union's launch of *Sputnik I,* the world's first artificial satellite, on 4 October 1957, had a galvanic effect on American public opinion. *Sputnik* created the illusion of a yawning technological gap between the United States and the Soviet Union, and provided the impetus for a massive increase in American aerospace endeavors. The United States launched its first Earth satellite, Explorer 1, in January 1958 to study radiation zones encircling the earth. In the same year the government created a new agency, the *National Aeronautics and Space Administration (NASA), to manage civilian space operations.

As NASA's program developed over the next four decades, it consisted of several major components:

- Human spaceflight initiatives: Project Mercury's single astronaut program (1961–1963), to ascertain if a human being could survive in space; Project Gemini (1965–1966), with two astronauts practicing space operations; and Project Apollo (1968–1972) to explore the Moon.
- Robotic missions to the Moon (Ranger, Surveyor, and Lunar Orbiter); Venus (Pioneer Venus); Mars (Mariner 4, Viking 1 and 2); and the outer planets (Pioneer 10 and 11, Voyager 1 and 2).
- Orbiting space observatories (the Orbiting Solar Observatory and the Hubble Space Telescope) to view the galaxy from space, beyond Earth's atmospheric clutter.
- Remote-sensing Earth satellites (Landsat) for information gathering.
- Communications satellites (Echo I, TIROS, and Telstar) and weather-monitoring instruments.
- An orbital workshop for astronauts, Skylab.
- A reusable spacecraft, the Space Shuttle.

The capstone of the space program, Project Apollo, the human expedition to the Moon, began with President John F. *Kennedy's 1961 announcement that the United States would land an astronaut on the moon by 1970, as proof of the nation's technological virtuosity. The first major mission, Apollo 8, orbited the moon in December 1968, with astronauts Frank Borman, James A. Lovell Jr., and William A. Anders. The first moon landing came with the Apollo 11 mission in 1969. At 4:18 P.M. EST on 20 July, the lunar module—with astronauts Neil A. Armstrong (1930–) and Edwin E. Aldrin (1930–) aboard—landed on the lunar surface while Michael Collins orbited overhead. As Armstrong set foot on the lunar surface, he intoned to millions listening and watching on earth: "That's one small step for [a] man, one giant leap for mankind." Aldrin soon followed him onto the lunar surface, and the two astronauts planted an American flag, collected soil and rock samples, and set up scientific experiments. Project Apollo cost $25.4 billion, making it (along with the *Panama Canal) one of the two largest nonmilitary technological endeavors ever undertaken by the United States.

After Apollo, the space program went into a holding pattern for nearly a decade before the first flight of the space shuttle, in 1981. In spite of high hopes, the shuttle program provided neither inexpensive nor routine access to space. Although it developed an exceptionally sophisticated vehicle, the shuttle program launched fewer missions and conducted fewer scientific experiments than NASA had publicly predicted.

Criticism of the space program reached a crescendo following the tragic loss of Challenger during a launch on 28 January 1986. This accident was especially poignant because the Challenger crew represented a cross-section of the American population in terms of race, gender, geography, and religion. The explosion became one of the most significant events of the 1980s, watched on television by billions worldwide. After the *Challenger disaster, the shuttle program shut down while NASA redesigned the system. The Space Shuttle returned to flight without incident in 1988. Over the next decade, NASA launched eighty-five shuttle missions, all but one without incident. Each undertook scientific and technological experiments, ranging from the deployment of space probes such as the Magellan radar-mapping mission to Venus in 1989 and the Hubble Space Telescope in 1990. Project Voyager also provided satellite reconnaissance of great importance, exploring the solar system's giant outer planets.

The late 1980s brought a new round of planetary exploration, typified by the successful Magellan mission to Venus and the Galileo mission to Jupiter, which, though plagued by malfunctioning systems, returned useful scientific data. Planetary exploration received a further boost in 1997 when the Mars Pathfinder successfully landed on Mars. Its small, twenty-three pound robotic rover, Sojourner, exited from the lander vehicle and recorded weather patterns, atmospheric opacity, and the chemical composition of rocks. In 1984, seeking to reinvigorate the space program, the Ronald *Reagan administration called for the development of a permanently occupied space station, built cooperatively with other nations interested in space exploration. Almost from the outset, the Freedom program, as it came to be called, proved controversial. The projected cost of eight billion dollars had more than tripled within five years. In 1993 NASA negotiated a landmark agreement to include Russia in the building of the space station.

The uncertain fate of the space-station project, and indeed the checkered history of the entire space program, pointed up the complexities of high-technology policymaking, and the difficulties of building a constituency for expensive science and technology projects in a democracy where politicians must wrestle with competing political agendas.

[*See also* Federal Government, Executive Branch: Department of Defense; Military, The; Physical Sciences; Science: Since 1945.]

• Walter A. McDougall, *The Heavens and the Earth: A Political History of the Space Age,* 1985. William E. Burrows, *Exploring Space,* 1990. Andrew Chaiken, *A Man on the Moon: The Voyages of the Apollo Astronauts,* 1994. Roger D. Launius, *NASA: A History of the U.S. Civil Space Program,* 1994. Roger D. Launius and Howard E. McCurdy, *Spaceflight and the Myth of Presidential Leadership,* 1997. Howard E. McCurdy, *Space and the American Imagination,* 1997.

—Roger D. Launius

SPANISH-AMERICAN WAR, an important episode in America's entry into world politics and abandonment of political isolation. The war's origins lay in Cuba's struggle for independence, which resumed in 1895, when the Cuban General Máximo Gómez adopted guerrilla tactics. Spanish General Valeriano ("Butcher") Weyler ordered civilians into concentration camps, which caused much suffering and aroused U.S. public opinion. Spain's premier Mateo Práxedes Sagasta, responding to a proposal by President William *McKinley, eventually accepted partial home rule, but the Cubans held out for independence. On 15 February 1898, the U.S. battleship *Maine* blew up in Havana harbor, killing 266 American sailors. Inflamed by a jingoistic press, the American public blamed Spain, forcing McKinley to demand Cuban independence. When Sagasta refused, Congress authorized armed intervention. It also enacted the Teller Amendment, forbidding the U.S. annexation of Cuba.

Neither Spain nor the United States had expected war, and both were unprepared. Spain had garrisons in Cuba and the *Philippines, but minuscule naval strength. Although the United States had only 28,000 regular army troops, it possessed a well-trained navy and quickly annexed *Hawai'i to bolster its strategic position.

After mutual declarations of war, Admiral William Sampson blockaded Havana, where Spain's main forces were concentrated. On 1 May, Commodore George Dewey (1837–1917), commanding the U.S. Asiatic Squadron, entered Manila Bay and easily destroyed a weak Spanish squadron. This act stirred public enthusiasm, gave Dewey a base, and precluded Spanish raids on U.S. commerce. On 19 May a small Spanish squadron under Admiral Pascual Cervera arrived at Santiago de Cuba, where it was blockaded. A weak Spanish garrison of ten thousand protected the city. McKinley, ordering the regular army to Cuba along with a few volunteers, also secretly conveyed his war aims to Spain through Great Britain. They included Cuban independence, annexation of *Puerto Rico and Guam, and acquisition of a port in the Philippines. Spain ignored this initiative, sending a naval expedition under Admiral Manuel de la Camara to relieve the Philippines.

On 14 June the Tenth Army Corps commanded by Major General William Shafter, seventeen thousand strong, landed in Cuba. On 1 July, Shafter launched an ill-prepared attack on El Caney and the San Juan hills, guarding Santiago's eastern approach. The Tenth Corps routed some one thousand Spanish defenders after suffering significant losses. Instead of occupying Santiago, as intended, the exhausted attackers fortified the heights and besieged the city. Legends surrounding the mislabeled "Battle of San Juan Hill" contributed to the reputation of Theodore *Roosevelt. Two days later Admiral Cervera sailed from the harbor, but the blockading vessels sank his entire command, with a heavy toll of Spanish lives.

An expedition led by Major General Nelson Miles invaded Puerto Rico on 25 July and raced toward San Juan. Meanwhile Major General Wesley Merritt, commanding troops sent to assist Dewey's operations in the Philippines, prepared to attack Manila. On 13 August, after a mock battle arranged by Dewey to avoid bloodshed and satisfy Spanish honor, the Spanish garrison capitulated.

After the disaster at Santiago, Premier Sagasta ordered Camara's expedition back to Spain, authorized Santiago's surrender, and began peace negotiations. On 12 August Spain suspended hostilities, granted Cuban independence, and ceded Puerto Rico and Guam to the United States. Disposition of the Philippines was left to a peace conference.

Most U.S. casualties in the Spanish-American War were non-combat related, but resulted from food poisoning, *yellow fever, *malaria, and other diseases. Despite segregation and racist abuses, several thousand *African Americans fought with distinction in the conflict.

Amid widespread public enthusiasm for acquiring the Philippines, the hesitant McKinley, citing duty and destiny, ultimately decided on annexation. This provision was included in the Treaty of Paris, signed in December, which formally ended the war. The Senate gave its consent on 6 February 1899, two days after Filipinos under Emilio Aguinaldo (1870–1964) seeking independence, attacked the U.S. garrison at Manila, beginning a long insurgency.

The U.S. army governed Cuba until 1902, when it withdrew under the terms of the Platt Amendment (1901). This measure passed by Congress asserted a U.S. right to future intervention in Cuba, restricted Cuba's treatymaking powers, and provided for a U.S. naval base at Guantánamo Bay. Meanwhile the Filipino insurrection continued until 1902. Of some 125,000 U.S. troops who fought in the Philippines, around 4,000 were killed. An estimated 20,000 Filipino independence fighters died, and civilian casualties were heavy as well. A U.S. Senate committee in 1902 heard testimony of burned villages and Filipino prisoners killed or tortured.

The war that began as a humanitarian crusade on behalf of Cuban independence fostered an imperial spirit that brought the United States a small empire. In the war's aftermath, the *Anti-imperialist League formed, and Americans debated the relationship between *republicanism and empire. Subsequent historians have seen America's involvement in the war as stemming, variously, from the sensationalism of tabloid journalism, the quest for markets, the need for naval coaling stations, a new spirit of aggressive nationalism, and a fear of being left behind in the race for empire.

[*See also* Expansionism; Foreign Relations: U.S. Relations with Asia; Foreign Relations: U.S. Relations with Latin America; Hearst, William Randolph; Journalism; Protectorates and Dependencies; Pulitzer, Joseph.]

• Ernest R. May, *Imperial Democracy: The Emergence of America as a Great Power,* 1961. Graham A. Cosmas, *An Army for Empire: The United States Army in the Spanish-American War,* 1971. David F. Trask, *The War with Spain in 1898,* 1981. John L. Offner, *An Unwanted War: The Diplomacy of the United States and Spain over Cuba, 1895–1898,* 1992. Joseph Smith, *The Spanish-American War,* 1994.

—David F. Trask

SPANISH SETTLEMENTS IN NORTH AMERICA. Spain initially sought to populate its far-flung northern frontier in America less by settling Spanish or mestizo people than by transforming the indigenous population into Hispanicized and loyal subjects of the Spanish Crown. Unlike *New England, where Indians were killed or displaced in order to open lands for European settlement, New Spain (Mexico) sought to use the Catholic church to evangelize the Indians and make them into *gente de razón* ("people of reason"): Spanish-speaking, Catholic, peasant farmers who followed Euro-Christian practices of work and sexual discipline.

To this end, the Spanish settlements in what is now the United States were of three mutually reinforcing types: the mission, the *presidio* (fort), and the *pueblo* (town). The importance of each varied from place to place depending on the terrain; the receptiveness of the Indians; the behavior of the priests and soldiers; and the aggressiveness of the Crown's enemies, whether Indian or European. Ideally, the mission would instruct the Indians in European ways and religious beliefs; the *presidio* would protect priests and the neophyte Christians from adversaries and rebellions; and the Hispanicized Indians would join settlers in the *pueblos.* Although rarely functioning in this ideal fashion, such institutions embodied Spain's strategy for peopling Florida, Texas, New Mexico, southern Arizona, and the *California coast.

Two factors catalyzed missionization: the incursion of rival powers and the zeal of the mission friars. Soon after Spain explored and claimed lands north of Mexico, the Crown experienced threats from other European powers. The first settlements in Florida at Cape Canaveral and San Augustín (St. Augustine) began in 1565 under Don Pedro Menédez de Avilés, who with daring and much bloodshed expelled French claimants. Beginning in 1573, soldiers and Franciscan priests superseded Menédez's warriors and sought to counter England by missionizing and forging alliances with the Indians along the Atlantic coast and, later, in the Florida panhandle.

Meanwhile, further west, Juan de Oñate in 1598 headed north from New Spain to New Mexico with 20 missionaries, 129 soldiers (some with families), and 7,000 head of cattle. With limited success, Franciscans sought to impose Christian beliefs and lifeways upon the corn-farming Pueblo Indians of the Rio Grande valley. The *Pueblo Revolt of 1680 ended both the *encomienda* and *repartimiento* systems of taxation and forced labor, while also dashing Franciscan hopes for establishing a community of believers. But at about the same time, the remarkable Padre Eusebio Kino (ca. 1644–1711) began the missionization of Pimería Alta—present-day southern Arizona and northern Sonora. Here, Jesuits sought to settle, or "reduce," the seminomadic Pima and Papago people to an agropastoralist mode. Tucson's Mission San Javier del Bac (1700) stands as a monument to this effort.

The mixed outcomes of these missionization efforts compelled Spanish authorities to sponsor several forms of secular settlements. After Governor Diego de Vargas led the reconquest of the Rio Grande valley (1693–1696), détente prevailed between the Spaniards and Pueblos, in part because of the Pueblos' fighting ability, but also because of the necessity for a military alliance in the face of constant Apache and Navajo raids and warfare. In the eighteenth century, and especially after 1750, New Spain fostered settlement of New Mexico by a system of *mercedes,* or land grants, given to prestigious individuals and to groups of more humble status. This approach fostered respect for Puebloan lands and also increased tensions with Navajos and Apaches. In these villages, bonds of godparentage, work on the *acéquías* (irrigation ditches), and the Penitentes (a lay Catholic brotherhood) provided social cohesion within a pattern of dispersed settlement.

In the Texas region at the close of the seventeenth century, Spain responded to expanding French settlements in the *Mississippi River valley, and even incursions along the Red River, by establishing two small missions in 1690 and five more in 1716, and then by situating a presidio (1718) at the Río San Antonio. From this emerging center several more missions were founded, and for over a century priests laboriously evangelized the Indians of Texas. In the Texas War for Independence (1836), a Mexican siege of Mission San Antonio de Valero gained enduring fame as Alamo.

Concerned about Russian fur-trapping and raiding settlements along the coast of Alta California in the 1760s, Spanish authorities initiated another program of temporal and spiritual conquest. Under the leadership of José de Gálvez, appointed *visitador general* by King Carlos III, and Father Junípero *Serra, Catalonian soldiers and Franciscan priests founded several presidios and twenty-one missions along the Pacific coast, from San Diego (1769) to Solano (1823). Although some rebellions erupted—at San Diego in 1775, at San Gabriel in 1785, and at Santa Barbara, Santa Inez, and La Purísima in 1824—apathy and *disease (especially syphilis, introduced by the soldiers) mostly reigned at the missions. Argument continues about the priests' treatment of the Indians, responsibility for the precipitous decline in the Indian populations, and the legitimacy of the whole effort to so radically change, often by force, Indian culture and beliefs.

Generally speaking, the mission effort overwhelmingly failed. Disease, indifference, rebellion, and the resilience of Native beliefs meant that most Indian peoples never genuinely converted to Spanish ways. In Texas in 1823–1824 and in California in 1833, Mexico "secularized" the missions, converting them into simple parish churches. The Indians were to have regained lands preempted by the missions, but most settled in towns or returned to their original habitats, and former army personnel occupied the mission lands.

Several settlements in the Spanish borderlands grew into metropolises—especially *Los Angeles (1781) and San Jose (1777)—but Spain founded only *pueblos* (small towns) and several lasting *villas* (large towns), most notably Santa Fe (1610), Albuquerque (1716), and San Antonio. Each city remains a magnet for contemporary Mexican immigrants who move *al norte* (to the north), to places their predecessors founded and named. Although Spain ceded Florida to England in 1763, St. Augustine remains the oldest European-founded city in the United States.

On the California coast only a few Native peoples remained by the close of the twentieth century, and their ceremonies and languages had all but disappeared. In New Mexico and Arizona the ability of the still-vibrant Puebloan peoples to compartmentalize Catholicism and their Native beliefs, to deflect further intrusions into their lifeways, and to adapt to modern politics and work has produced remarkable cultural survival. The California missions, restored with varying regard for historical accuracy, still remain—beautiful and complex emblems of a once-dominant Spanish presence.

[*See also* Alamo, Battle of the; Colonial Era; Exploration, Conquest, and Settlement, Era of European; French Settlements in North America; Hispanic Americans; Indian History and Culture: From 1500 to 1800; Roman Catholicism; Southwest, The; Texas Republic and Annexation.]

• John Francis Bannon, ed., *Bolton and the Spanish Borderlands,* 1964. Douglas Monroy, *Thrown among Strangers: The Making of Mexican Culture in Frontier California,* 1990. Ramón A. Gutiérrez, *When Jesus Came, the Corn Mothers Went Away: Marriage, Sexuality, and Power in New Mexico, 1500–1846,* 1991. David J. Weber, *The Spanish Frontier in North America,* 1992.

—Douglas Monroy

SPELLMAN, FRANCIS CARDINAL (1889–1967), Catholic archbishop of New York. Born in Whitman, Massachusetts, and educated at Fordham University and the American College at Rome, Francis Joseph Spellman entered the priesthood in 1916. After serving in the *Boston diocese and as assistant to the papal secretary of state in the Vatican, he became auxiliary bishop of Boston in 1932, archbishop of New York in 1939, and a cardinal in 1946.

Spellman was one of the most influential leaders of American Catholicism during his nearly thirty years as leader of the New York archdiocese. From his midtown residence, known locally as "the powerhouse," Cardinal Spellman was an aggressive and influential player in *New York City politics who worked to advance the institutional interests of his church. Cardinal Spellman was also a powerful figure in the international life of the Roman Catholic church. Close to both Pope Pius XII and President Franklin Delano *Roosevelt, Spellman played an important role as an intermediary between the Vatican and the White House during *World War II. In fact, Spellman's influential voice in the Vatican earned him the nickname "The American Pope." In terms of internal church politics, he may have been the most powerful prelate in American history.

Francis Spellman embodied American Catholicism's anticommunist zeal and patriotic fervor during the *Cold War. As military vicar, or special bishop to America's armed forces, he outspokenly defended U.S. foreign policy and, near the end of this life, enthusiastically supported the *Vietnam War. In 1965, echoing the early nineteenth-century naval hero Stephen Decatur, Spellman declared, "My country, may it always be right, but right or wrong, my country."

[*See also* Anticommunism; Religion; Roman Catholicism.]

• John Cooney, *The American Pope: The Life and Times of Francis Cardinal Spellman,* 1984. William A. Au, *The Cross, the Flag, and the Bomb: American Catholics Debate War and Peace,* 1985.

—Timothy A. Byrnes

SPIRITUALISM, a quasi-mystical movement that began in Hydesville, New York, on 31 March 1848 when mysterious rapping sounds in the farmhouse of John D. Fox were said by the family to emanate from a spirit communicating with Fox's daughters, Margaret (age thirteen) and Kate (age twelve). The girls were soon taken by their older sister, Leah Fox Fish, to Rochester, which became the center of the new movement. The three Fox sisters, the first "mediums," introduced the major features of subsequent Spiritualism: the séance; the trance of the medium (borrowed from still-novel demonstrations of hypnotism); and the asking of questions through the medium to spirits, who supposedly answered by rapping or by other phenomena such as jiggling the table at which the medium and her clients sat. (Mediums were usually, though not always, women.)

Spiritualism spread quickly through the United States in the 1850s, and into Europe as well. The novelist William D. *Howells reported, with doubtless some exaggeration, that in the Ohio of his boyhood every household had its medium and its tipping table. Séances, as Howells's comment indicates, were conducted by amateur as well as professional mediums, and many occasional practitioners regarded Spiritualism simply as a parlor pastime. The proportions of genuine belief, casual entertainment, and outright fraud in the movement are impossible to assess. Spiritualism waned in the late 1850s, but regained popularity after the *Civil War as bereaved families attempted to communicate with the spirits of lost soldiers.

In 1888 Margaret Fox recanted, explaining how she and her sisters produced the original rapping noises by cracking their toe joints. This date may be considered the effective end of the movement, though mediums continued to practice their craft in the twentieth century.

Spiritualism in its prime had many of the qualities of a *religion, since to believers it offered proof of an afterlife. It was thus to some degree in competition with the older Protestant orthodoxies and profited from their decline. The growth of Spiritualism paralleled for a time that of *Mormonism and *Christian Science, although these others movements had a strength of leadership and coherency of belief that the Rochester movement never attained. The prolific Spiritualist writer Andrew Jackson Davis (1826–1910), among others, did attempt to compose a Spiritualist theology, and the movement established some links with reforms such as *feminism and utopian *socialism. The sex reformer and woman-suffrage advocate Victoria Woodhull (1838–1927) and Robert Dale Owen (1801–1877) of the New Harmony community in Indiana were proponents of Spiritualism, as was, for a time, the Populist writer Hamlin Garland.

[*See also* Antebellum Era; Gilded Age; Protestantism; Utopian and Communitarian Movements.]

• Howard Kerr, *Mediums, and Spirit-Rappers, and Roaring Radicals: Spiritualism in American Literature, 1850–1900,* 1973. Howard Kerr and Charles L. Crow, eds., *The Occult in America: New Historical Perspectives,* 1983.

—Charles L. Crow

SPIRITUALS, an *African-American musical tradition rooted in slave folk songs. Controversy surrounded the Christianization of slaves in the mid–seventeenth century. Many slaveowners argued that slaves did not possess souls and therefore needed no religious instruction; others contended that slaves did possess souls but as long as they were not Christianized they could be held in bondage. Attempting to solve the discrepancy, a Virginia law of 1667 stated, "Baptism doth not alter the condition of the person as to his bondage or freedom." Thereafter slaveowners, with varying degrees of commitment, addressed the religious education of the slaves.

At first attending religious services segregated by race (and gender), slaves gradually accepted Christianity. Not until the middle of the eighteenth century, however, did slaves adopt Christianity in large numbers. This was accomplished initially through the evangelistic efforts of Samuel Davies (1723–1761) and Charles Wesley (1707–1788), and then by other ministers who led a series of camp meetings in the early 1800s. Through the lining hymns of Dr. Isaac Watts (1674–1748) and the more spirited hymns of John (1703–1791) and Charles Wesley, the slaves developed a repertoire of Christian songs that, during the camp meetings, provided the material from which they began to compose their own songs. The "camp meeting spiritual," with texts of praise and thanks, held together by the camp meeting shout "hallelujah," was the first sacred composition of the slaves. By the second quarter of the nineteenth century, a religious folk-song tradition, complete with slave text, melodies, harmony, and performance practices, had been conceived.

Employing themes of suffering and sorrow, hope and affirmation, these folk songs were based on five-note and other gapped melodic scales markedly different from the diatonic scale of Western music. The characteristic "blue" notes in work and play songs of the period were melodic staples of the spiritual as well. Many of the songs, such as "Steal Away" and "Roll, Jordan Roll," were reported to have double meanings, referring to biblical passages while also commenting on the slaves' immediate situation. Harmony, while based on that of Western music, was often in octaves, with intermittent fourths and fifths, unusual in Western music. Rhythm was marked by strongly accented and syncopated pulses and by body movements—swaying, hand clapping, and foot patting—synchronized with the rhythmic beat.

The first publication of spirituals in book form was *Slave Songs of the United States* (1867) by William Francis Allen, Charles Pickard Ware, and Lucy McKim Garrison. Some early scholars, working from manuscripts, argued that the "Negro Spiritual," this slave folk song, was simply an adaptation of white hymns. What these scholars missed, however, was the timbre or "sound" of the singing in actual performance. Producing the sound from the back of the throat and using the fatty tissues of the mouth for resonance, the singers created a sound of great sorrow or joy, but with an earthy character unfamiliar in Western music. Manuscripts could not capture the slides, whoops, microtones, variable pitch, or freely improvised melodies delivered by the leader ("call") or the static, but forceful answer of the congregation ("response"). Nor could manuscripts convey the improvised interjections of the singers or the multilayered rhythm of handclapping.

The Negro spirituals lost popularity as black church music in the 1930s but were featured as concert music by touring university groups such as the Jubilee Singers from Fisk and Hampton universities. Spirituals regained popularity in the 1950s and 1960s when they served as the primary music of the *civil rights movement.

[*See also* African American Religion; Anderson, Marian; Bible, The; Gospel Music, African American; Johnson, James Weldon; Music: Traditional Music; Protestantism; Revivalism; Slavery: Slave Families, Communities, and Culture.]

• T. F. Seward, *Jubilee Songs as Sung by the Jubilee Singers of Fisk University*, 1872. W. E. B. Du Bois, *The Souls of Black Folk*, 1903. James Weldon Johnson and John Rosamond Johnson, *The Book of American Negro Spirituals*, 1925, 1927. John Lovell Jr., *Black Song: The Forge and the Flame—The Story of How the Afro-American Spiritual Was Hammered Out*, 1972.

—Horace Clarence Boyer

SPOCK, BENJAMIN. *See Baby and Child Care.*

SPOILS SYSTEM. *See* Jacksonian Era; Civil Service Reform.

SPORTS

Amateur Sports and Recreation
Professional Sports

SPORTS: AMATEUR SPORTS AND RECREATION

Sports in the *Colonial Era and the early nineteenth century were participatory *leisure activities, based on traditional European folk games. They were enjoyed for their own sake or for the thrill of *gambling, except among Puritans and Quakers who required their recreations to be moral and beneficial to the individual or society. Early American sports were mainly noncompetitive field pursuits like hunting, fishing, and fox hunting, or competitive gambling activities like *horse racing, bowling, and billiards. Leisure sports were first organized by the elite Schuylkill River Fishing Colony of *Philadelphia in 1732. By the 1740s, jockey clubs in *New York City, Williamsburg (Virginia), and Charles Town (now Charleston), South Carolina, were building racetracks and scheduling competitive horse races.

Antebellum sports were dominated by a male bachelor subculture whose favorite diversions such as *boxing, horse racing, and billiards were disdained by the Victorian middle class as dangerous, immoral, or a waste of time. Middle-class resistance to sport ended following the development of a positive sports creed in the 1840s and 1850s by moral reformers and health professionals. This ideology justified participation in such athletic activities as gymnastics, introduced by German immigrants, and the new game of *baseball, which purportedly improved health and strengthened character. Victorians stressed amateurism—participation in sport for its own sake—a concept primarily developed by mid-nineteenth-century elite English sportsmen to avoid competing with athletes from lower social backgrounds. The line dividing amateur and professional was originally status, not cash. In the United States, antebellum amateur and professional cricket players and trackmen competed against each other, and college crews hired professional trainers. Amateurism first became an issue in the 1860s when certain baseball clubs used financial incentives to recruit top players.

Amateur Athletic Clubs. Amateurism was propelled by the rise of status-conscious elite sports clubs that became increasingly fearful of scheduling events with lower-class athletes and worried that full-time professionals, who allegedly did anything necessary to win, would take over their games. In 1876 the New York Athletic Club (NYAC) drew up an amateur code based on English precedents to regulate its competitions, barring anyone who had competed for money, played with professionals, or taught or coached athletics for a living. These rules were adopted by other athletic clubs and, in 1879, by the new National Amateur Athletic Association of America (N4A).

The American amateur code, unlike the English, historian Benjamin Rader points out, did not rest on a body of established customs or the patronage of an aristocracy for whom style transcended victory. Upper-middle-class and elite Americans were accustomed to winning in business at all costs, and their clubs hypocritically skirted N4A rules, recruiting top athletes, regardless of social background, to assure victories and gain prestige. Inducements included free initiation and membership, room and board, employment, and even cash. In 1878 the prestigious Manhattan Athletic Club (MAC) recruited the Jewish athlete Lon Myers, a bookkeeper by profession, who held every American track record from fifty yards to the mile, by hiring him as club secretary. Top performers like Myers further profited by selling their prizes—medals, silverware, gold watches, and so forth—for cash; an 1884 MAC benefit for Myers raised four thousand dollars.

*Gilded Age track-and-field champions were mainly students and clerks, partly because the amateur code discouraged working-class participation. Amateur blue-collar athletes had difficulty training because of long working hours, low wages, and lack of access to equipment, facilities, coaching, and sponsorship. Those who did succeed—typically artisans (especially printers) or municipal workers, like policemen, who had flexible hours and jobs that called for physical fitness and strength—mainly competed at annual picnics sponsored by employers, unions, benevolent societies, ethnic organizations, or political parties.

In the 1880s, emulating the lifestyle of the English country gentry, wealthy Americans established country clubs, beginning with one in Brookline, Massachusetts (1882). Membership in these suburban clubs was more prestigious than in the urban athletic clubs. Their main competitive sports, for men and women, were *golf and tennis. Tennis also became popular with the middle class as courts were laid out in public urban *parks. Middle-class women, already active in such leisure sports as sleighing, ice skating, and croquet, became avid cyclists during the bicycle craze of the 1890s.

In the early 1880s, to attract older, more socially prominent members, the NYAC altered its recruitment policies to emphasize prestige rather than athletic skill. It also campaigned against perceived violators of the amateur code, particularly by the MAC, and fought professionalism by helping to establish the Amateur Athletic Union (AAU) in 1888. The AAU quickly became the dominant organization in amateur sport, disqualifying athletes who violated the amateur codes and erasing their records. By the early 1900s, however, the AAU itself faced criticism for duplicity because favored promoters provided star athletes with "under-the-table" payments, and the practice of redeeming prizes for cash persisted, especially among boxers.

The Olympic Games. The Olympic Games, revived in 1896, became by 1912 the centerpiece of amateur competition in track and field, swimming, and boxing. Historian Steven Pope argues that the Olympics solidified amateurism by linking it to nationalism. Most early Olympic stars were collegians or alumni competing for noted athletic clubs, but a substantial proportion, especially in strength events, were working-class athletes representing less prestigious organizations like New York's Irish-American Athletic Club.

The most infamous amateur controversy involved the *football and track star Jim Thorpe (1888–1953), who won both the pentathlon and decathlon at the 1912 Olympics. When it was revealed several months later that Thorpe had briefly played minor league baseball, and was therefore a "professional," he was forced to return his medals.

Avery Brundage, president of the International Olympic Committee from 1952 to 1972, tried to protect amateurism as the concept came under increasing pressure. After *World War II, the Communist bloc sent to the Olympics state-subsidized athletes Americans considered "professionals." U.S. competitors were typically younger and primarily supported by college athletics scholarships. The purity of Olympic amateurism further waned in the 1960s as athletes, especially Austrian skiers, accepted payments to endorse products. The amateur-professional division largely collapsed in the mid-1970s when the Olympics introduced open competition. The Amateur Sports Act of 1978 enabled American Olympic aspirants to accept appearance payments, earn money on the international track circuit, work as consultants, and do commercials if the funds were placed in trust accounts for living and training expenses. By the 1990s, the distinction between amateur and professional had become virtually meaningless, as evidenced by the *basketball "Dream Team" at the 1992 Olympics.

Intercollegiate Athletics. In addition to voluntary sports clubs, intercollegiate athletics was the other main bastion of amateurism. Even here, however, a win-at-all-costs attitude led to professionalization. As early as 1900, historian Robert Smith points out, sport at elite institutions like Yale had become commercialized and professionalized, providing a model for other colleges.

Rowing, the first male intercollegiate sport, began in 1852 with the Harvard-Yale race. It was followed by cricket, baseball (the main college sport in the 1870s), football, and track. The best college baseball nines periodically played pro teams. From 1865 to 1875, Yale's squad played twice as many professional clubs as college squads. The College Baseball Association (1879), the first intercollegiate baseball league, had little control over player eligibility and could not cope with the problem of summer baseball. Beginning in the 1880s, top collegians played during the summer break, often under pseudonyms, on semipro, resort, and professional teams, either for a salary or other compensation, without losing their amateur standing.

Intercollegiate competition in football, which would soon supplant baseball as the most popular intercollegiate sport, began in 1869. By the 1890s, teams were hiring professional coaches and recruiting athletes with scholarships, easy courses, and high-paying jobs. In 1905, for instance, James J. Hogan, Yale's twenty-seven-year-old football captain, received free tuition, a fancy suite, a vacation in Cuba, and a monopoly of American Tobacco Company products sold on campus.

The *National Collegiate Athletic Association, founded in 1906 to make football safer and reform and enforce eligibility and financial rules, faced a herculean task. Intercollegiate athletes of the 1990s were still ostensibly amateurs who forfeited their eligibility if they received financial compensation in their sport beyond their grants-in-aid, but periodic scandals underscored the difficulty of preserving the distinction.

Women's intercollegiate competition, popular at elite women's colleges at the turn of the century, was halted by physical educators fearful that women were too delicate for vigorous competition and desirous of avoiding the negative consequences of men's sport. They preferred "play days" and intramural activities. Only in the 1970s, owing to the revived *women's rights movement and Title IX of the Educational Amendments Act of 1972, did the emphasis in women's athletics return to competitive sport.

Opportunities for urban immigrant boys to participate in sports expanded during the *Progressive Era, encouraged by YMCAs, *settlement houses, the staffs of inner-city parks, and public schools intent on socializing them and providing an alternative to morally suspect street amusements. Competitive high school sports programs arose in the late nineteenth century, based on the collegiate model, to promote school spirit and community pride and develop athletic skills. By 1923, forty-five states held statewide high school competitions. Working-class adult participation in amateur sports promoted by companies whose welfare-capitalism programs included financing lifelong sports like bowling and softball, and by the New Deal's Public Works Administration, which built and improved thousands of parks and beaches.

Participatory sports grew significantly in the 1980s and 1990s, influenced by middle-class *health and fitness anxieties, concerns about physical appearance, and the women's movement. These years saw a great increase in cycling and jogging, exercising at health clubs, and even marathoning, which was sponsored by hundreds of cities. Entries in the New York City Marathon rose from 126 in 1972 to over 20,000 in the mid-1980s. Despite the perennial intrusions of professionalism, amateur sports remained a vital force as the twentieth century ended.

[*See also* Bicycles and Bicycling; Education: Collegiate Education; Education: The Rise of the University; Feminism; New Deal Era, The; Popular Culture; Social Class; Working-Class Life and Culture; YMCA and YWCA.]

• Ted Vincent, *Mudville's Revenge: The Rise and Fall of American Sport,* 1981. Allen Guttman, *The Olympics: A History of the Modern Games,* 1982. Donald Mrozek, *Sport and American Mentality, 1880–1910,* 1983. Allen Guttman, *The Games Must Go On: Avery Brundage and the Olympic Movement,* 1984. Ronald A. Smith, *Sports and Freedom: The Rise of Big-Time College Athletics,* 1988. Steven A. Riess, *City Games: The Evolution of American Urban Society and the Rise of Sports,* 1989. Benjamin G. Rader, *American Sports: From the Age of Folk Games to the Age of Televised Sports,* 3d ed., 1996. S. W. Pope, *Patriotic Games: Sporting Traditions in the American Imagination, 1876–1926,* 1997. Mark Oyreson, *Making the American Team: Sport, Culture, and the Olympic Experience,* 1998.

—Steven A. Riess

SPORTS: PROFESSIONAL SPORTS

Professional athletes compete for cash or other remuneration. The first professional sportsmen were probably New York oarsmen in the 1810s who competed for prizes in rowing races; long-distance runners, called "pedestrians," in the 1830s and 1840s, who raced for cash purses at enclosed tracks; and pugilists who competed for side bets. Professional sports boomed in the late nineteenth century, as the nation became sufficiently urbanized to support commercial *leisure. During this era, sport became modernized, entrepreneurs marketed quality sports to spectators, and paid athletes worked full time at their craft.

A few professional sports in the *Gilded Age, like track, were carryovers from the *Antebellum Era. The Caledonian games celebrating traditional Scottish highland culture dominated track and field from the early 1850s until the mid–1870s, offering cash prizes of a few hundred dollars for running races and such events as throwing the caber (a long, heavy pole) and pitching the heavy stone. Professional runners also competed at working-class picnics and *amusement parks, often sponsored by saloonkeepers or local politicians who shared their winning wagers with the athletes. Long-distance running at indoor arenas continued to be very popular in the 1870s. In these years, too, a brief fad developed for six-day foot races that covered over five hundred miles. Winners in the prestigious Astley Belt series of 1878–1879 made as much as twenty thousand dollars—the top earnings of professional athletes. But thereafter, amateurs completely dominated track, and pro records went unrecognized. Professional track returned in the 1970s once Olympic athletes were permitted openly to accept appearance fees and prize money. Cycling became a professional sport in the 1890s, with riders often subsidized by manufacturers advertising their product.

*Horse racing was popular as well. Jockeys had little status in the Antebellum Era, when southern riders were usually slaves. The occupation gained stature after the *Civil War, however, as horsemen recognized that good jockeys helped win races, and soon jockeys were among the highest paid athletes. By the early 1900s, a top jockey could make ten thousand dollars a year just from retainer fees. A large portion of riders were *African Americans, including Isaac Murphy, whose career earnings totaled over $250,000. They encountered considerable jealousy and prejudice from white competitors, however, who formed secret unions to force them out of this extremely lucrative occupation.

*Boxing drew tough men from the bottom ranks of society. The pugilist John L. Sullivan (1858–1918) won fame in the late nineteenth century, even though prizefighting was nearly universally barred because of its brutality and corruption. The Irish dominated the sport until the 1920s, and thereafter recruitment followed a pattern of ethnic succession, ending with men of color. New York legitimized prizefighting under a boxing commission in 1920, and by the 1930s there were thousands of professional pugilists.

Professional *golf and tennis developed more slowly. The U.S. Open began in 1894, and the Professional Golfers Association tournament in 1916, but early pros were mainly teachers. Purses were modest until the pro tour became popular in the 1960s, led by Arnold Palmer. The Ladies Professional Golf Association, founded in 1946, received little attention until the emergence of stars like Nancy Lopez in the 1970s. Pro tennis dates to the 1930s, but its period of dramatic growth began with the advent of major international championships, starting with Wimbledon in 1968 and Forest Hills (U.S. Open) a year later. Women's purses, originally 10 percent of men's, eventually achieved near parity through the efforts of pioneers like Billie Jean *King.

The first paid team athletes were antebellum cricketeers, but the model professional team sport was *baseball. In 1860 pitcher James Creighton of the Brooklyn Atlantics became the first compensated ballplayer. Others soon followed, including players for the New York Mutuals, sponsored by Tammany Hall (New York's *Democratic party organization), who held government sinecures. Sporting journals supported professionalization to facilitate working-class participation and improve the quality of play. The first fully professional team was the Cincinnati Red Stockings of 1869, whose players earned from six hundred to two thousand dollars a season. The rise of professional baseball continued with the founding of the National League of Professional Baseball Clubs in 1876, the rival American League in 1901, and their merger in 1903.

Most early pros, typically from skilled, blue-collar backgrounds, had little control over their income or working conditions, and were subjected to the reserve clause, which prevented them from leaving their teams. But competition for players gradually raised salaries, attracted better educated and higher-status athletes, and elevated the occupation's prestige. The early professional ballplayers were mainly urban, white, native-born Americans of English, Irish, or German origins. African Americans were completely excluded from organized professional baseball after 1898, and restricted to their own teams and leagues.

Professional *football and *basketball were originally minor, unstable sports with short-lived professional leagues (1902 and 1898, respectively). The National Football League (NFL) was formed in 1920, but franchises came and went until the early 1930s. The NFL only gained major stature in the 1950s because of *television coverage. The National Basketball Association, founded in 1949, went through a shaky period as smaller cities dropped out or teams relocated. From the mid–1920s on, both sports recruited players overwhelmingly from the college ranks.

As of 1998, there were thirty major league baseball and NFL teams, twenty-nine professional basketball teams, and twenty-six professional hockey teams. As cities competed to gain or protect sports teams that symbolized urban prestige and supposedly promoted economic development, professional franchises became extremely lucrative. In 1994 the average football franchise was worth $129 million; basketball, $114 million; and baseball, $111 million. Players' incomes similarly skyrocketed following the end of reserve clauses. Average baseball and basketball salaries rose from about nineteen thousand dollars in 1967 to over one million dollars by 1993. Buttressed by enthusiastic fans, powerful economic interests, and saturation television coverage, professional sports occupied a secure niche in American *popular culture as the twentieth century ended.

[*See also* Advertising; Automobile Racing; Bicycles and Bicycling; Mass Marketing; Social Class; Urbanization; Working-Class Life and Culture.]

• Harold Seymour, *Baseball,* 3 vols., 1969–1990. Melvin Adelman, *A Sporting Time: New York City and the Rise of Modern Athletics, 1820–70,* 1986. Elliott Gorn, *The Manly Art: Bareknuckle Prize Fighting in Nineteenth Century America,* 1986. Steven A. Riess, *City Games: The Evolution of American Urban Society and the Rise of Sports,* 1989. Stephen Fox, *Big Leagues: Professional Baseball, Football, and Basketball in National Memory,* 1994. Eric M. Leifer, *Making the Majors: The Transformation of Team Sports in America,* 1995. Benjamin G. Rader, *American Sports: From the Age of Folk Games to the Age of Televised Sports,* 1996.

—Steven A. Riess

STAMP ACT (1765). To British politicians seeking new sources of revenue after the *Seven Years' War, the American colonies seemed an ideal source, for both economic and political reasons. Prosperous and lightly taxed, the colonists could afford to help pay for their defense. They had obviously benefited from the expulsion of the French from Canada and should be willing to assist the Mother Country. With the exception of William Pitt, a popular leader of the parliamentary opposition, no prominent British politician questioned Parliament's right to tax colonists. The principal difficulty in planning American taxation was finding self-enforcing duties that were appropriate for a people accustomed to evading British customs duties by smuggling and bribery.

Stamp taxes in England provided a precedent. To be legally binding, a wide range of legal proceedings and commercial agreements had to be recorded on stamped papers. In 1764, George Grenville, first lord of the treasury, announced plans to impose such a tax in America the next year, inviting in the interim colonial suggestions about specific stamp duties or alternative taxes. Instead, colonial assemblies argued that since Americans were not represented in Parliament, that body could not tax them. Grenville countered by arguing that members of Parliament represented all Britons, not just those who actually elected them. This doctrine of virtual representation was not simply the first response in the constitutional debate; it also signaled the ministry's determination to impose the stamp tax. Parliament passed the legislation, by 249–51 in the Commons and unanimously in the Lords. Grenville did agree to the appointment of Americans as stamp distributors, a step he felt would reduce opposition to the tax and encourage ambitious colonists to look to Britain for political jobs and power.

The reaction in America, partially coordinated by resistance groups calling themselves the *Sons of Liberty, was immediate and violent. Rioting crowds forced distributors to resign; colonial assemblies coordinated political resistance through the Stamp Act Congress. Governors could not compel the distribution of stamps, and thus the tax did not enforce itself.

The repeal of the Stamp Act in March 1766 was a major defeat for Britain. George III would subsequently claim that retreat on this issue set the stage for rebellion. Without question the Stamp Act crisis weakened royal authority in the colonies, heightened American suspicions about British policy, and encouraged further resistance.

[*See also* Colonial Era; Revolution and Constitution, Era of; Revolutionary War.]

• P. D. G. Thomas, *British Politics and the Stamp Act Crisis, 1763–1767,* 1975. John L. Bullion, *A Great and Necessary Measure: George Grenville and the Genesis of the Stamp Act, 1763–1765,* 1982. Marc Egnal, *A Mighty Empire: The Origins of the American Revolution,* 1988.

—John L. Bullion

STANDARD OIL CORPORATION. *See* Petroleum Industry; Rockefeller, John D.

STANTON, ELIZABETH CADY (1815–1902), women's rights leader and theorist. A favorite child of a prominent and wealthy New York lawyer, Elizabeth Cady attended Emma Willard's girls' school in Troy, New York, graduating in 1832. In 1840 she married a prominent abolitionist, Henry Stanton. She was inspired to focus on women's rights by her own difficulties as a wife and mother (eventually with seven children), by the serious discriminations against women in U.S. society, and by the reform community around her. In 1848, with Lucretia *Mott and others, she organized America's first woman's rights convention, in Seneca Falls, New York, where she lived with her family. She drafted the convention's Declaration of Sentiments, an assertion of women's rights modeled on the *Declaration of Independence. In 1851, along with Amelia Bloomer, editor of the temperance newspaper the *Lily,* she designed and wore the simplified Bloomer dress. (The opposition was so vehement, however, that they gave it up after several years.) That same year she met her life-long coworker in the women's rights cause, Susan B. *Anthony.

In 1863, after moving to *New York City, she and Anthony founded the Women's Loyal National League. The organization secured over 300,000 signatures to a petition demanding the abolition of *slavery. In 1866 she ran (unsuccessfully) for the House of Representatives, when she discovered that the state's prohibition against women voting did not extend to their holding office. She was the first woman to do so. In 1868 she and Anthony founded a cross-class Workingwoman's Association to improve working conditions for women. That same year they also launched a weekly newspaper, the *Revolution,* which lasted a year and a half. In 1869 they founded the National Woman Suffrage Association, of which Stanton served as president for the next twenty-one years. That same year she began a twelve-year stint as a national lecturer for the New York Lyceum Bureau, becoming one of its most popular speakers.

Stanton was known for her searching intellect, wide-ranging views, and radical positions. Although suffrage and property rights remained central to her women's rights platform, she also favored birth control and liberalized divorce laws—inflammatory issues in her era. She was attracted to communalism, practiced homeopathy and diet reform, critiqued unfair labor practices, and excoriated men for their treatment of women. Far in advance of her times, she saw the abuse of women's bodies in slavery, *rape, and confining fashions as central to men's control of women, under a system she occasionally called "patriarchy." Although Stanton strongly supported woman suffrage—and coedited with Anthony a three-volume *History of Woman Suffrage* (1881–1886)—she rejected Anthony's exclusive focus on this issue. In her final decades, she crusaded against *religion's oppression of women, writing a *Woman's Bible* (2 vols., 1895–1898) in which she reworked *Bible stories according to women's rights principles. In 1888, along with Anthony, she participated in the founding of the International Council of Women. Her memoirs *Eighty Years and More* appeared in 1898. A long-planned systemic treatise on women's rights remained uncompleted, but her output of speeches and articles were sufficient to make her the preeminent women's-rights theorist of nineteenth-century America.

[*See also* Antebellum Era; Antislavery; Birth Control and Family Planning; Clothing and Fashion; Feminism; Marriage and Divorce; National American Woman Suffrage Association; Seneca Falls Convention; Stone, Lucy; Woman Suffrage Movement; Women in the Labor Force; Women's Rights Movements.]

• Lois W. Banner, *Elizabeth Cady Stanton: A Radical for Women's Rights,* 1979. Elizabeth Griffith, *In Her Own Right: The Life of Elizabeth Cady Stanton,* 1984.

—Lois W. Banner

STATE COURTS. *See* Federal Government, Judicial Branch; Municipal Judicial Systems.

STATE DEPARTMENT. *See* Federal Government, Executive Branch: Department of State.

STATE GOVERNMENTS. The American scheme of government is a historical paradox. The federal *Constitution proclaims the supremacy of the *federal government in a theoretically indissoluble Union, but since the inception of the nation, states and cities have performed most of the tasks of day-to-day governance. The states, like the national government, claim their authority based on the will of the people, yet the Constitution is entirely silent on where cities derive their powers. Indeed, the word "city" nowhere appears in the document. Far from being a neat hierarchy of local, state, and national governments, the American scheme of governance has historically mixed and overlapped levels of governmental activity, combined public and private interests, and appealed to often conflicting theories of popular and state sovereignty.

Creating and Defining State Government. Each of the original thirteen states had a colonial antecedent that lacked a well-defined scheme of separation of powers. In most colonies, power rested with the assembly, and the judiciary was often tied to the legislature. The *Revolutionary War, however, transformed these colonial appendages into independent states, each with its own form of government that rested, except for Connecticut and Rhode Island, on a constitution.

These new American states bound themselves into a revolutionary alliance that worked first through the *Continental Congress and then, beginning in 1781, the *Articles of Confederation. Under the Articles, the national government rested upon a compact among the states. The members of the federal Congress were selected by the state legislatures and any amendment to the Articles required the unanimous vote of the states. The Constitution of 1787, however, provided for a popularly based federal republic of enumerated powers in which the nation held sway in a few areas (e.g., making war, controlling commerce, issuing legal tender), but with a high level of dependency on state governments. For example, the framers allotted representatives in Congress based on population, but the state governments were given the task of apportioning these representatives among districts in the states and setting the terms of their election. Each state was guaranteed two senators to be selected (until passage of the Seventeenth Amendment in 1913) by the state legislatures. The president of the United States was elected not by the people but through the states in an *Electoral College. Finally, the Tenth Amendment, ratified in 1791 along with the other *Bill of Rights amendments, reserved to the states all governmental power not delegated to the national government.

Under this arrangement, state and local governments retained significant powers, most notably the police powers. Through these powers the states (and local governments) provided for the health, safety, morals, and welfare of their citizens. Throughout American history, therefore, while the national government has fulfilled high political functions (e.g., national defense, foreign policy, and territorial acquisitions), state and city governments have played decisive roles in matters such as *crime and punishment, marriage, family affairs, contracts, property, and all manner of commercial relations.

When the Constitution was written, no legal distinction existed between cities and other corporations. Gradually, however, American law began to recognize such distinction. In *Dartmouth College* v. *Woodward* (1819), *Supreme Court justice Joseph *Story crafted an important distinction, defining as *public* corporations legal entities such as towns and cities that existed for public political purposes only. As a practical matter, city governments developed as if they were the state itself. In *Hunter* v. *Pittsburgh* (1907), the Supreme Court held that "[m]unicipal corporations are political subdivisions of the State created as convenient agencies for exercising such of the governmental powers of the State as may be entrusted to them." States were free to add, withdraw, and modify at their pleasure the powers exercised by cities. In *Community Communications Co.* v. *City of Boulder* (1982) the high court pithily ruled: "We are a nation not of city-states but of States."

The Evolution of State Government. By the late nineteenth century the states began to develop legal schemes assuring cities a measure of self-government. The Missouri Constitution of 1875, for example, was the first to include a home-rule provision, which was adopted widely. These provisions granted municipalities control over their local affairs in return for a pledge to abide by certain legislative restrictions, the most important of which involved their borrowing power.

Unlike cities, the federal Constitution recognized the states. One of the most profound powers delegated to the national government was the provision in Article IV, section 4, guaranteeing each state a "republican form of government." Since the Supreme Court's decision in *Luther* v. *Borden* (1849), the power to assess either the legitimacy or the republican character of a state government has rested with Congress.

Republican government has meant in concrete terms executive, legislative, and judicial branches. Throughout their history, the legislatures have exercised the greatest authority. In the modern era, except for Nebraska, which has been unicameral since 1934, states have been bicameral, with an upper house composed of members with usually longer terms and larger districts, and a more numerous lower chamber with shorter terms and smaller districts. Today, these legislatures average about 180 total members, with New Hampshire's more than 400 legislators topping the list.

Governors have invariably been popularly elected and generally weaker than their counterparts in the White House. Many states, for example, have an "executive department" of government, of which the governor is one of only several elected officials, such as a treasurer, attorney general, superintendent of public instruction, and secretary, any of whom may be from other than the governor's party. Some states also limit the governor's power to commute sentences and pardon convicted criminals.

Populist forces have similarly shaped state judiciaries. State courts form the largest system of justice in America. Over 97 percent of all judges serve on state or local benches. Each state has a system of trial courts, one or more intermediate courts of appeal, and a final appellate court, usually called a supreme court, to decide matters of state law. These courts exercise the great residue of common law concerning private transactions as well as interpreting state statute and constitutional law. The relationship between state and federal courts is complex. The state courts have some authority to rule on the federal Constitution, but the federal courts, especially the district courts, hold broad powers to adjudicate questions of state law. Most state judges, moreover, exercise their powers on short tethers. For example, federal judges are appointed by the president with the advice and consent of the Senate and serve during good behavior. In the mid-nineteenth century, however, the states began to rein in the judiciary by electing most of them for limited terms of office. The judges of the highest state appellate courts also exercise the power of judicial review, as do federal Supreme Court justices, but in seven states these judges can also render advisory opinions, a practice prohibited to the Supreme Court under the Constitution.

State government differs from the federal government in another important way: the limits placed on the terms of elected public officials. The practice dates to the Louisiana constitution of 1812, which provided that no governor could serve more than two consecutive terms of four years each. Missouri followed suit in 1821, Indiana in 1851. (Indiana did permit a former governor to run again after four years out of office.) By the end of the twentieth century some thirty-eight states limited governors to two four-year terms, and eighteen limited the terms of state legislators, hoping to encourage a citizen legislature free from professional politicians.

The States as Laboratories of Reform. In this and other areas, state governments have been laboratories of the federal system. In fiscal matters, for example, many state governments, unlike the federal government, require a balanced budget and allow the governor a line-item veto. The states are also limited in their authority to tax and to issue bonds. These restrictions reflect the ease with which many state constitutions can be amended. State governments, therefore, have been subjected to direct popular pressures in ways that the federal government has not. For example, the federal *equal rights amendment failed to win ratification, yet at least twelve states have adopted just such a provision. Eight other states have adopted constitutional guarantees of a right to privacy.

The *Progressive Era was a particularly active period of experimentation for, state and municipal governments, with long-lasting consequences. To stem the power of political parties, many states adopted the initiative, referendum, and recall; adopted woman suffrage; established non-partisan elections for city councils, and provided for home rule by municipal governments. The states were the first to prohibit the sale of alcohol and the first to create nature preserves. The Progressives also accelerated the trend toward greater involvement by the states in economic matters, creating new nonpartisan agencies to oversee labor, *business, and *health issues on a scientific basis.

The Shifting Balance of State-Federal Power. Since the *Civil War two broad trends have shaped the fortunes of state government. First, the power balance between, the states and the national government has tilted in favor of the latter. For example, the Civil War Amendments, especially the *Fourteenth Amendment, affirmed in law what the war had made plain on the battlefield: the national government was supreme. The new amendments established the primacy of federal citizenship and introduced the concept of state action, which authorized the federal government to override specific measures taken by the states.

Second, as America became more industrialized and population more mobile, political issues became increasingly national and less susceptible to solution by state and local government. Amidst the Depression of the 1930s, for example, Congress passed a host of legislation, most of it eventually sustained by the Supreme Court, granting Washington broad powers of economic regulation. By the mid-twentieth century, state law in matters involving consumer transactions and civil rights had been replaced in part by federal law and regulation based on a significantly expanded understanding of the power granted the federal government through the commerce clause of the Constitution (Article I, section 8).

The federal government impacted state and local governments in another way as well. Among the powers delegated to the national government was the authority to tax and spend for the general welfare. Beginning in 1921, with the Sheppard-Towner Act, Congress has appropriated federal tax dollars to support national programs carried out at the state level. As the twentieth century wore on, these grants grew in importance, comprising in some instances the largest part of a state's budget. These revenues, however, carried with them restrictions on the ways states and cities could expend them. Moreover, Congress increasingly enacted so-called unfunded mandates that require the states to use their own funds to meet federally imposed guidelines on such matters as *highway construction, health care, *welfare, and *education.

Despite the federal government's broadened powers, the states, and (to a lesser extent) local governments, retain great vitality. State governments have done so not by reclaiming lost autonomy but by carving out new areas of authority. Through this process, state governments remain, as they were at the nation's founding, the most ubiquitous influence on the day-to-day lives of Americans.

[*See also Dartmouth College Case;* Depressions, Economic; Economic Regulation; Federalism; Industrialization; Municipal and County Government; National Civic Federation; New Deal Era, The; Republicanism; Taxation; Temperance and Prohibition; Urbanization.]

• Daniel J. Elazar, *American Federalism: A View from the States,* 1972. Daniel J. Elazar, *Cities of the Prairie: The Metropolitan Frontier and American Politics,* 1984. Gerald E. Frug, "The City as a Legal Concept," *Harvard Law Review* (1980). Kermit L. Hall, "Mostly Anchor and Little Sail: The Evolution of American State Constitutions," in *Toward a Usable Past: Liberty under State Constitutions,* eds. Paul Finkelman and Stephen E. Gottlieb, 1991, pp. 388–417. Hendrik Hartog, *Public Property and Private Power: The Corporation of the City of New York in American Law, 1730–1870,* 1983.

—Kermit L. Hall

STATE JUDICIAL SYSTEM. *See* Federal Government, Judicial Branch; Municipal Judicial Systems.

STATES' RIGHTS. Rooted in the classical republican view that freedom and virtue are incompatible with empire and in antifederalist fears of centralized power, the doctrine of states' rights is enshrined in several parts of the *Constitution, including the guarantee of each state's equal standing in the Senate (the only provision permanently unchangeable by amendment). The most often cited guarantee of states' rights is the Tenth Amendment. To states'-rights supporters, the amendment limits the federal government's powers to those specifically enumerated in the Constitution, and reserves all other powers of government (such as the power to create and tax corporations) to the states.

The first major confrontation between defenders of states' rights and the proponents of centralized power came in response to the *Federalist party's *Alien and Sedition Acts of 1798. Thomas *Jefferson and James *Madison, in the Kentucky and Virginia Resolutions, declared the acts unconstitutional and asserted that states, as parties to the constitutional "compact," had the power to protect the liberties of their citizens and "alien friends" from federal acts that violated the compact. Nationalists on the U.S. *Supreme Court under Chief Justice John *Marshall restricted states' rights (and protected corporations) in such decisions as **Fletcher* v. *Peck* and **McCulloch* v. *Maryland,* but the issue remained unsettled.

In the second major confrontation, during the *War of 1812, commercially minded *New England Federalists convened the 1814 *Hartford Convention, which denounced what they considered the dangerous imperialism of the Republicans in Washington and asserted the rights of states to refuse to authorize the conscription and taxation needed to support "Mr. Madison's War."

In the third major confrontation, the *nullification crisis of 1828–1832, involving the federal *tariff, the doctrine became associated with John C. *Calhoun, who had earlier opposed states' rights. Calhoun's major opponent on nullification, President Andrew *Jackson, was also inconsistent: Like many *Democratic party leaders, Jackson supported states' rights on most matters. Although states' rights doctrine was increasingly tied to the defense of *slavery, some abolitionists invoked it in their efforts to thwart the *Fugitive Slave Act of 1850 (e.g., in *Ableman* v. *Booth,* 1859).

While South Carolina had stood alone on nullification, proslavery politicians espoused other versions of states' rights doctrine, eventually taking the ultimate step of secession. Their advocacy of the doctrine returned to haunt them as the *Confederate States of America struggled for wartime unity and discipline in the fourth major confrontation, the *Civil War. In *State Rights in the Confederacy* (1925), Frank Lawrence Owsley noted the central irony that in order to defend states' rights effectively, the Confederacy's leaders would have had to crush them.

After the Civil War, opponents of *African-American rights embraced states' rights. Although the Supreme Court again restricted state power to regulate corporations in the 1880s and 1890s, it supported broad state power to enforce racial *segregation. The principal twentieth-century uses of the doctrine were to ward off federal anti-*lynching laws and to defend racial *segregation. Opponents of federal *economic regulation sometimes invoked the doctrine as well.

After *World War II, liberals generally condemned states' rights through a kind of guilt-by-association with slavery and segregation. With **Brown* v. *Board of Education* and related decisions, the Supreme Court under Earl *Warren brought civil rights law into line with broader nationalistic trends. After the 1960s, the doctrine moved to the margins of American political culture, although conservatives, including Ronald *Reagan, invoked it occasionally in rhetorical thrusts at "big government" and the massive federal budget. Subsequently, under William Rehnquist's chief justiceship (1986–) a narrow majority on the Court resuscitated states' rights for some purposes, but it was not clear how durable these decisions would be. Curiously, despite its historical roots in the defense of *civil liberties, immigrant rights, and anti-imperialism, late twentieth century nonconservative opponents of centralized power (governmental and corporate) found little merit in the doctrine.

[*See also* Bill of Rights; Conservatism; Early Republic, Era of the; Federalism; Liberalism; Federalism; Republicanism; Revolution and Constitution, Era of; States' Rights Party.]

• Alpheus Thomas Mason, *The States' Rights Debate: Antifederalism and the Constitution,* 1964. Chester James Antineau, *States' Rights under Federal Constitutions,* 1984.

—David L. Chappell

STATES' RIGHTS PARTY. In 1948, disgruntled southern Democrats, nicknamed Dixiecrats, launched the States' Rights party. While conservative, white southern Democrats had for many years decried the *Democratic party's liberal drift and particularly its courting of northern black voters, the support of a moderate *civil rights program by President Harry S. *Truman and national Democratic party leaders provided the immediate impetus for the party bolt.

The Dixiecrats initially tried with limited success to convince southern state Democratic parties to oppose Truman's nomination, but the Democrats' convention, meeting in Philadelphia in July, nominated Truman and adopted a pro–civil rights plank. Two days later, a convention in Birmingham recommended that southern Democratic parties put Governor Strom Thurmond (1902–) of South Carolina on their ballots as the official Democratic presidential candidate, along with Mississippi Governor Fielding Wright as his running mate. Mississippi, Alabama, South Carolina, and Louisiana complied, but when the Dixiecrats proved unable to control other state Democratic parties, they organized a third party and held a convention in Houston that nominated the Thurmond/Wright ticket.

In the fall election, the Dixiecrats failed to garner national support or even regional solidarity for their party, carrying only those four states where the ballots listed Thurmond as the Democratic nominee instead of Truman. Their revolt, however, represented the beginning of the end of the solid Democratic South and revealed the potential divisiveness of the civil rights issue for the New Deal Democratic coalition. Strom Thurmond, rejoining the *Republican party, went on to become one of the longest-serving U.S. senators in American history.

[*See also* New Deal Era, The; Political Parties; Segregation, Racial; States' Rights.]

• Robert A. Garson, *The Democratic Party and the Politics of Sectionalism, 1941–1948,* 1974. Numan V. Bartley, *The New South 1945–1980,* 1995.

—Charles C. Bolton

STATISTICS. *See* Mathematics and Statistics.

STATUE OF LIBERTY. The Statue of Liberty National Monument is situated on Bedloe's (now Liberty) Island in New York harbor. The 151-foot statue (entitled *Liberty Enlightening the World*) of a robed female figure bearing an uplifted torch was designed by the Frenchman Frédéric-Auguste Bartholdi; completed in Paris in 1885 with the aid of Alexandre-Gustave Eiffel, who designed the inner skeleton; and officially presented to the United States by the French government. The huge structure reached *New York City in June 1885, but the base was not ready. A grassroots fundraising campaign suggested by Joseph *Pulitzer, publisher of the *New York World,* quickly raised $100,000—much of it in pennies, nickels, and dimes from schoolchildren, laborers, and others—and the pedestal was completed in April 1886. On 28 October of that year, officially designated as "Bartholdi Day," President Grover *Cleveland, Count Ferdinand de Lesseps, members of the Franco-American Union, and thousands of onlookers, many aboard ships and small craft, gathered for the festive dedication ceremony marked by bands, parades, and cannon salutes. A major restoration in 1984 was followed by a formal rededication precisely a century later, 28 October 1986.

Over the years, the Statue of Liberty greeted millions of immigrants, visitors, and returning troops from two world wars; it remains perhaps the nation's most instantly recognizable symbol. Nearly as well known is the sonnet by Emma Lazarus (1849–1887) inscribed on the pedestal in 1903:

> Give me your tired, your poor,
> Your huddled masses yearning to breathe free,
> The wretched refuse of your teeming shore.
> Send these, the homeless, tempest-tost to me,
> I lift my lamp beside the golden door!

• Oscar Handlin, *Statue of Liberty,* 1971. I. B. Penick, *The Story of the Statue of Liberty,* 1986.

—Leo Hershkowitz

STEAMBOATS. *See* Steam Power.

STEAM POWER. Thomas Newcomen constructed the first commercially useful steam engine in England around 1712 to pump water out of mines. During the 1720s, England exported a number of engines to continental Europe. American intellectuals such as John *Adams and Thomas *Jefferson knew of such engines, but not until 1753 was the first Newcomen engine brought to America, to pump water from the copper mine of Col. John Schuyler, on New Jersey's Passaic River. It was accompanied by Joseph Hornblower, whose family had been installing Newcomen engines in Cornwall. Put into operation in 1755, Schuyler's steam engine burned in 1768 and remained out of commission until 1793. Between 1799 and 1801 the emigrant British engineer Benjamin Henry Latrobe designed and erected two massive engines for the new *Philadelphia waterworks, built at the Soho Works in New Jersey.

These early engines were all used to pump water, a task adapted to their relatively slow reciprocating motion and small horsepower. By the time Robert Fulton (1765–1815) successfully launched his celebrated Hudson River steamboat *Clermont* in 1807 (using an English engine purchased from Boulton and Watt), a dozen other American inventors had already experimented with steamboats. With the exception of John Fitch's boat, which he operated on the Delaware River between Philadelphia and Burlington, New Jersey, during the summer of 1790, none of these worked well and all (including Fitch's) had engines designed by the makers themselves. Fulton's success, coupled with the appearance of boats designed specifically for the western waters by Oliver Evans (1755–1819) and others, launched a steamboat era that greatly improved the nation's transportation on both coasts and in the *Mississippi River watershed. Fulton's Pittsburgh-built *New Orleans,* launched on the Mississippi in 1811, was only the first of a vast fleet that brought improved transportation and fostered *industrialization throughout the interior.

Oliver Evans, whose high-pressure engine dominated the western fleet, built his first engine in 1801. The Newcomen engine had worked at atmospheric pressure (about 16 pounds per square inch [psi]) as had James Watt's improved design of 1763. In such engines, increased power could only be secured by increased size. Evans, a Delaware-born inventor and manufacturer, built his new "Columbian" engine at his Mars Iron Works in Philadelphia to operate on pressures as high as 100 psi. Very powerful for their size, such engines quickly became standard on the western waters as well as in factories.

During the early nineteenth century steam engines gradually replaced water power as the favored source of power for manufacturing, and by 1899 steam engines were producing over eight million horsepower of energy for industrial uses. As coal slowly replaced wood for fuel, new engine designs used steam expansively in more than one cylinder or in the form of turbines. With improved boilers, some of the new engines by the end of the century used steam at 300 psi and produced thousands of horsepower. In this process, George H. Corliss of Providence and Charles T. Porter of Newark were particularly important innovators. Since steam engines were the first large machines made from iron, the spread of steam power stimulated the growth of the iron and machine trades. And by freeing manufacturers from reliance on water power, steam allowed factories to be built in cities, closer to transportation and a labor supply.

Steam was also applied to the operation of *railroads. By the time Robert Stephenson's locomotive *Rocket* won the celebrated Rainhill trials in England in 1829, Americans were already investigating steam propulsion for land transport. In 1829–1830, Americans purchased the *John Bull* from

Stephenson and *The Stourbridge Lion* from another English locomotive maker. The latter became the model for *The Best Friend of Charleston,* the first steam locomotive built in the United States for sale. In 1830, Peter Cooper's *Tom Thumb* raced a horsedrawn train on the new Baltimore and Ohio Railroad, which opened its first line that year. Soon such large manufacturers as Philadelphians William Norris and Matthias Baldwin dominated the American locomotive trade and sold large numbers of engines abroad as well. Steam remained the unchallenged source of power for railroads until 1925, when the Central Railroad of New Jersey introduced the first diesel-electric locomotive. In 1934 the Burlington line used diesel-electric for its streamlined Zephyr passenger trains, and in 1941 the Santa Fe became the first railroad to use that power for freight service. As late as 1945 only 3,800 of 43,500 American locomotives were diesel, but by 1960, diesels accounted for 95 percent of the total.

The use of steam power in American *agriculture began late, proceeded slowly, and never became as widespread as in other sectors of the economy. A federal census of engines in 1838 reported several hundred at work at specialized tasks on farms, especially in grinding sugarcane on Louisiana plantations. The lack of power for fieldwork hampered nineteenth-century agriculture, although the replacement of oxen with horses improved the situation for most farmers. In 1849, however, portable steam engines that could be pulled by horses to a barn, woodlot, or wherever more power for belt work was needed became available. As the nation's wheat acreage doubled between 1866 and 1878, the demand for mechanically powered machines led to efforts to use these portable steam engines to power self-propelled vehicles that could be steered. The first such traction engines were produced in 1882, and in 1910 the horsepower produced by steam used in agriculture peaked at 3.6 million. Some ten thousand traction engines were in use on farms in 1913, but already gasoline-powered tractors were competing with them. By 1925 the manufacture of steam traction engines had largely been abandoned.

A few early automobiles were steam powered, including the Stanley Steamer, built in Massachusetts by the twin brothers Francis and Freelan Stanley from 1897 until 1918. But the gasoline-powered internal combustion engine soon supplanted the steam engine in automotive technology.

Steam power remained of some economic importance as the twentieth century ended. Steam turbines, for example, were widely used to generate electricity. Its ubiquity and dominance as a power source for transportation, manufactures, and agriculture, however, was largely confined to the nineteenth century, after which internal combustion engines burning petroleum products eliminated steam engines from most sectors of the American economy.

[*See also* Antebellum Era; Automotive Industry; Economic Development; Electricity and Electrification; Factory System; Gilded Age; Iron and Steel Industry; Maritime Transport; Motor Vehicles.]

• James Thomas Flexner, *Steamboats Come True,* 1944. Louis C. Hunter, *Steamboats on the Western Rivers,* 1949. Carroll W. Pursell Jr., *Early Stationary Steam Engines in America,* 1969. Louis C. Hunter, *A History of Industrial Power in the United States, 1780–1930, Volume II, Steam Power,* 1985.

—Carroll Pursell

STEAMSHIPS. *See* Maritime Transport.

STEEL INDUSTRY. *See* Iron and Steel Industry.

STEEL STRIKE OF 1919. This strike marked the unsuccessful culmination of efforts to unionize *mass-production workers during *World War I. War production increased steelworker unrest by worsening already poor working conditions. The twelve-hour day and seven-day work week every other week became entrenched, and wages, inadequate prior to the war for most unskilled workers, barely kept pace with inflation. As the war influenced the industry's foreign-born workers to view the United States as their permanent home, they took to heart the wartime propaganda themes and sought to bring industrial democracy to the workplace.

Spurred by its success in unionizing the meatpacking industry, the *American Federation of Labor (AFL) in 1918 launched a steel organizing drive. Ill-organized and inadequately funded, the campaign clashed with the industry's open-shop policy and refusal to negotiate with unions. The strike began on 22 September and proceeded unevenly. Strikers shut down mills in *Chicago, but in the crucial Pittsburgh district—where the union encountered severe repression from state and local authorities—most mills kept operating. Employers and the press effectively used national strike leader William Z. Foster's radical past to portray the strike as a radical insurrection and then Red-bait its leaders. Division among workers also emerged. Foreign-born unskilled workers honored the strike, but most skilled, U.S.–born workers and unskilled blacks did not. In January 1920, the strike ended in complete defeat. The loss revealed management's power in open-shop industries, the inadequate approach of the AFL, and the fragmentation of the workforce. It would take another twenty years to unionize the steel industry.

[*See also* Homestead Lockout; Immigrant Labor; Industrial Relations; Iron and Steel Industry; Meatpacking and Meat Processing Industry; Strikes and Industrial Conflict.]

• David Brody, *Labor in Crisis: The Steel Strike of 1919,* 1982, reprint 1987.

—James D. Rose

STEFFENS, LINCOLN (1866–1936), journalist. Son of a Sacramento banker, Joseph Lincoln Steffens attended the University of California at Berkeley and then studied ethics and philosophy at the University of Berlin, art history at Heidelberg, and psychology at Leipzig. He worked as a reporter and newspaper editor in New York before joining the staff of *McClure's Magazine.* His articles analyzing and documenting municipal corruption were published in book form in 1904 with the memorable title *The Shame of the Cities.* These and subsequent articles established him—along with Ray Stannard Baker, Upton *Sinclair, and Ida M. Tarbell—as a leading practitioner of critical, investigative, adversarial journalism. Charging Steffens and the others with a single-minded focus on the "vile and debasing," President Theodore *Roosevelt branded them "muckrakers," a label they perforce embraced and which has endured.

The conclusions Steffens had reached in *The Shame of the Cities, The Struggle for Self-Government* (1906), and other books concerning the linkage of corruption, *business, and politics drove him leftward. In 1919, with William C. Bullitt, he visited Soviet Russia, then emerging from the chaos of revolution, and returned with the slogan ever after associated with him, "I have seen the future, and it works." Assuming that the absolute dictatorships of Lenin and Stalin were evolutionary stages on the way to true democracy, Steffens never lost faith in that illusory future. His work and career are marked by ethical fervor and good hope. In 1931 he published a classic *Autobiography.*

[*See also* Journalism; Magazines; Muckrakers; Municipal and County Governments; Progressive Era; Radicalism.]

• Louis Filler, *Crusaders for American Liberalism,* 1964. Justin Kaplan, *Lincoln Steffens, A Biography,* 1974.

—Justin Kaplan

STEICHEN, EDWARD JEAN (1879–1973), photographer. Part of the avant-garde modernist circle around Alfred *Stieglitz; a prominent advertising, fashion, and wartime photographer; and director of the Museum of Modern Art's Photography Department (1947–1962), Steichen championed a *photography that could move fluidly between elite museum work and popular, even frankly commercial imagery.

Born in Luxembourg, Steichen came to America with his working-class parents in 1881 and grew up in Michigan and

Wisconsin. Apprenticed to a Milwaukee commercial lithographer, he soon turned to photography. His work, exhibited in Philadelphia in 1899, garnered the attention of major national figures in the arts, including Stieglitz. During two years in Paris (1900–1902), he served as Stieglitz's representative and soaked up the dominant trends in painting and photography. Opening a portrait studio in *New York City in 1902, he photographed many well-known figures of the day while working with Stieglitz to promote photography as an art form. In 1917–1918, he headed the photographic office of the U.S. Army Air Service. By the 1920s, while continuing as a portrait photographer, Steichen was also firmly entrenched in the worlds of commercial photography, practically inventing the genre in the United States with his *advertising and fashion work in such glossy journals as *Vanity Fair* and *Vogue*. Like many others, he was converted in the 1930s to the cause of social documentation and the power of the camera as a persuader of national truths, whether Great Depression Era realities or the *World War II naval conflict in the Pacific—dogma that served him well as curator of nationalistic blockbuster photograph exhibitions at the Museum of Modern Art during and after the war. His most famous endeavor, *The Family of Man* (1955), which toured worldwide and became a best-selling book, brought the layout and rhetorical styles of photojournalism and advertising to the elite museum. As both photographer and curator, Steichen's greatest talent lay in adapting techniques from other media—painting and *journalism—to the realms of high-art photography.

[*See also* Depressions, Economic; Modernist Culture; Museums: Museums of Art.]

• Eric Sandeen, *Picturing an Exhibition: The Family of Man and 1950s America*, 1995. Penelope Niven, *Steichen: A Biography*, 1997. Joel Smith, *Edward Steichen: The Early Years*, 1999.

—Peter Bacon Hales

STEINBECK, JOHN. *See Grapes of Wrath, The;* Literature: Since World War I.

STEVENSON, ADLAI (1900–1965), governor, presidential nominee, ambassador to the *United Nations. A grandson and namesake of Grover *Cleveland's vice president, Adlai E. Stevenson was born in *Los Angeles and reared in Bloomington, Illinois. He graduated from Yale in 1922, received a law degree from Northwestern University in 1926, and worked as an attorney in Chicago until *World War II, when he became a special assistant to the secretary of the Navy. In 1945, Stevenson moved to the State Department where he helped plan the United Nations and participated in its activities for several years.

Elected governor of Illinois in 1948, Stevenson won a national following with his eloquent speech-making and broad public appeal. As the Democratic presidential nominee in 1952 and 1956, he campaigned as a proud disciple of Franklin Delano *Roosevelt and a vigorous opponent of Senator Joseph *McCarthy. Soundly defeated in both races by Dwight D. *Eisenhower, Stevenson half-heartedly sought the Democratic nomination in 1960, losing to John F. *Kennedy.

In 1961, President Kennedy appointed Stevenson ambassador to the United Nations. In that role, he argued strongly against invading Cuba during the 1962 *Cuban Missile Crisis, thereby helping Kennedy guide the United States safely through the most dangerous weeks of the *Cold War. Stevenson remained at the UN until his sudden death in July 1965.

• John Bartlow Martin, *Adlai Stevenson of Illinois*, 1976. John Bartlow Martin, *Adlai Stevenson and the World: The Life of Adlai Stevenson*, 1977.

—William L. O'Neill

STIEGLITZ, ALFRED (1864–1946), photographer. An uncompromising figure in American *photography, Alfred Stieglitz was essential to the import of European modernist ideas and the art that contained them, and the nurturing of American modernism in *painting, photography, *literature, criticism, and culture more broadly. Raised in a prosperous mercantile family in *New York City, Stieglitz left for Berlin in 1882 to study engineering. There he met the German scientist-photographer Hermann W. Vogel, who introduced him to photography within a context of high artistic standards and rigorous technical discipline.

Returning to the United States in 1890, Stieglitz sought to launch an artistic photography movement resembling those he had seen among devoted amateurs in Europe. His increasingly rigorous and solitary understanding of the medium and its possibilities, as well as his continuing connections to modernist Europe, found expression in his founding of the journal *Camera Work* in 1903 and the "Little Galleries of the Photosecession" in New York, made legendary by its address, "291." In these venues he championed both European and American varieties of modernism. At the same time, his own increasingly spare and demanding photography culminated in work that used realist subjects to make images of high abstraction, most notably his Equivalents series, made beginning in the 1920s, using clouds as his sources. Involved with the painter Georgia *O'Keeffe, whom he married in 1924, and a champion of the American modernists John Marin, Marsden Hartley, Paul Strand, and others, Stieglitz figured prominently in American modernist circles until his death.

[*See also* Greenwich Village; Modernist Culture; Twenties, The.]

• Jonathan Green, *Camera Work: A Critical Anthology*, 1973. Sarah Greenough and Juan Hamilton, *Alfred Stieglitz*, 1983. Richard Whelan, *Alfred Stieglitz: A Biography*, 1995.

—Peter Bacon Hales

STILWELL, JOSEPH (1883–1946), *World War II general. Born in Palatka, Florida, and graduating from West Point in 1904, Joseph Warren Stilwell was assigned first to the *Philippines, beginning an army career that would be closely associated with Asia. An intelligence officer during *World War I, Stilwell then assumed a series of assignments in China, including U.S. military attaché (1935–1939) during the Sino-Japanese War. He was promoted to brigadier general in 1939 and general in 1944.

Fluent in Chinese and highly regarded by Army Chief of Staff George *Marshall, Stilwell was appointed commander of the China-Burma-India theater in 1942. Allotted minimal resources, Stilwell pressed Chinese leader Chiang Kai-shek to build an effective military force to counter Japanese advances in China and Burma. His relationship with Chiang soured, however, because of his caustic manner (hence his nickname "Vinegar Joe") and Chiang's unwillingness to reform the corrupt and poorly led Chinese armies. Stilwell proved unable to use Chinese troops to halt the Japanese conquest of northern Burma in 1942, which cut the only viable land link between China and India. Two years later, however, relying largely on American-trained Chinese troops, he recaptured much of northern Burma, making possible the reopening of the Burma Road, constructed under his supervision.

Recalled to Washington by President Franklin Delano *Roosevelt in October 1944 at Chiang's behest, Stilwell became commander of army ground forces. He commanded the U.S. Tenth Army in the final stages of the Okinawa campaign (June 1945) and would have led this force in an invasion of Japan had not the Japanese surrendered in August 1945.

• Barbara W. Tuchman, *Stilwell and the American Experience in China, 1911–1945*, 1970. Eric Larrabee, *Commander in Chief: Franklin Delano Roosevelt, His Lieutenants, and Their War*, 1987.

—G. Kurt Piehler

STIMSON, HENRY (1867–1950), statesman. Born in *New York City and educated at Andover, Yale, and Harvard Law School, Henry L. Stimson became a successful lawyer. He was deeply influenced by Secretary of War (1899–1904) and Secretary of State (1905–1909) Elihu Root and by President Theodore *Roosevelt, who appointed him U.S. attorney for the southern district of New York (1906–1909). After an unsuccessful try for the governorship of New York in 1910, he served as secretary of war (1911–1913), working to bring progressive reform to the army. When war broke out in Europe in 1914 he strongly advocated U.S. preparedness, and when the United States entered the war in 1917, he volunteered and was commissioned a lieutenant colonel. He served as special mediator in the Nicaraguan Civil War in 1927, and the following year was appointed governor-general of the *Philippines.

From 1929 to 1933, Stimson served as secretary of state under President Herbert *Hoover. He enunciated the Stimson Doctrine of nonrecognition of the 1931–1932 Japanese conquest of Manchuria and establishment of the puppet state of Manchukuo. (He personally desired economic sanctions against Japan, but was pressured by President Hoover to settle for nonrecognition instead.) His strong *internationalism led to his appointment as secretary of war in June 1940 within President Franklin Delano *Roosevelt's newly bipartisan cabinet. Remaining in this position throughout *World War II, he worked well with Chief of Staff George *Marshall and played a major role in a host of pivotal wartime issues ranging from aid to England to use of the atomic bomb. He retired in September 1945. Througout his career he embodied the progressive ideal of selfless public service.

[*See also* Federal Government, Executive Branch: Department of Defense; Federal Government, Executive Branch: Department of State; Foreign Relations; Hiroshima and Nagasaki, Atomic Bombing of; Manhattan Project; Military, The; Nuclear Weapons.]

• Elting E. Morison, *Turmoil and Tradition: A Study of the Life and Times of Henry L. Stimson,* 1960. Godfrey Hodgson, *The Colonel: The Life and Wars of Henry Stimson, 1867–1950,* 1990.

—Mark A. Stoler

ST. LAWRENCE SEAWAY PROJECT. *See* Canals and Waterways.

STOCK MARKET. Stock exchanges are places where the investing public buys and sells shares of companies that are listed on the respective markets. The earliest stock exchanges arose in Holland and Britain in the seventeenth century. Originally called "bourses," these exchanges traded shares of companies that had raised money for overseas exploration. In the early years of the Industrial Revolution, banks, *insurance companies, and manufacturers began to sell public securities that were traded on exchanges. Stock exchanges are called secondary markets because they provide a location where buyers and sellers may agree upon a price for securities.

In the nineteenth century, the European bourses, and especially the London stock market, were the largest and most active in the world. Until *World War I London was the world's financial capital, and many companies from around the world had their shares traded there. The *New York Stock Exchange (NYSE), on Wall Street in *New York City, became preeminent after the war because money could flow in and out of the United States without interference. As a result, the American markets boomed during the 1920s—a boom that ended in the *stock market crash of 1929. President Herbert *Hoover accused the stock exchanges of manipulation, especially concerning short selling (selling borrowed stock, hoping to profit as it goes down), and blamed them for the country's economic woes during the early days of the Depression of the 1930s. A congressional investigation of stock market practices led to the Securities Exchange Act (1934), creating the *Securities and Exchange Commission (SEC) and putting the organized U.S. stock exchanges under government regulation for the first time.

In addition to the organized exchanges, where brokers and dealers agreed to quote prices on stocks, an over-the-counter (OTC) market also traded shares of companies without having an organized exchange floor. This market itself became more organized when Congress established the National Association of Securities Dealers (NASD) through the Maloney Act in 1937. This self-regulating association trades the shares of companies not large enough to trade on the NYSE, American Stock Exchange, or one of the regional exchanges. In the 1970s, the NASD market became computerized and, as a result, began to rival the NYSE for business. While many NASD companies remained small, others grew enormously, particularly *computer and Internet companies in the 1990s. Traditionally, the NYSE has been referred to as the first market, the other organized exchanges such as the American Stock Exchange as the second market, and the OTC market or NASD as the third market.

Once the exchanges and NASD came under federal regulation, trading became more orderly and less predatory. In 1937 William McChesney Martin became the president of the NYSE and implemented changes to reform the market according to the spirit of the regulatory legislation passed during President Franklin Delano *Roosevelt's first term. Without major reforms, public confidence in the market would have been seriously undermined, in turn affecting the amount of money that companies could raise from the new-issues market, the part of the market where new stocks are sold, separate from the stock exchanges.

The function of the exchanges and the NASD market is to establish prices at which new stock issues can come to market, and at which buyers and sellers can trade. To facilitate price reporting, the consolidated ticker tape was established in 1975. The smaller exchanges and the NASD also have a centralized quotation system called the Intermarket Trading System (ITS). The consolidated tape, along with other NYSE reforms like negotiated commission rates, which replaced fixed commissions in 1975, helped the markets develop more uniform prices.

Developments in electronic communications in the 1990s added to the volume of shares traded on all the exchanges and NASD. The average volume of shares traded on the NYSE alone was about 400 million per day in 1997, four times that of a decade earlier. In 1997, the NYSE experienced its first billion-share day. The shares of many American companies are now also traded in overseas markets, while the exchanges and NASDAQ (National Association of Securities Dealers Automated Quotations) trade the shares of many foreign companies as well. All these developments made the markets more international than ever as the twentieth century ended.

[*See also* Banking and Finance; Business; Business Cycle; Capitalism; Depressions, Economic; Economic Development; Economic Regulation; Global Economy, America and the; Internet and World Wide Web; New Deal Era, The.]

• Robert Sobel, *The Curbstone Brokers: The Origins of the American Stock Exchange,* 1970. Charles Geisst, *Wall Street: A History,* 1997. Barrie Wigmore, *Securities Markets in the 1980s,* 1997.

—Charles Geisst

STOCK MARKET CRASH OF 1929. On 24 October and again on 29 October 1929, panic selling swept the *New York Stock Exchange. The index of common stocks had peaked in early September; within two months, however, it fell 39 percent, reducing the value of stocks traded on the exchange by $26 billion.

The 1920s brought the great bull market in which the value and quantity of stocks traded soared. Most experts agree that until early 1928, the rise in stock prices was justified. The U.S. economy grew rapidly, productivity soared, and corporate earnings multiplied. Firms sought funds for mergers or for new plants and equipment through the sale of stocks and bonds. More importantly, anticipating large gains, thousands of investors snapped up the new issues and bid up the prices of old issues.

But by 1928 the market had become a bubble—that is, the

prices paid by investors exceeded any reasonable expectation of future earnings. Speculation was particularly rampant in high *technology and utilities stocks such as the Radio Corporation of America, RKO (Radio-Keith-Orpheum), Westinghouse, United Aircraft, and Commonwealth and Southern. Securities affiliates of banks and brokers encouraged speculation by letting investors buy stocks on credit, known as margin accounts. Investors put up as little as 25 percent of the stock's purchase price and borrowed the remainder from their brokers or banks, using the stock purchased as collateral.

By September 1929, the economy was contracting. With corporate earnings down, stock prices began to slip. The crashes of late October reflected panic selling. With millions of shares of stock traded, quotations of stock values fell hours behind. Unable to keep track of their stocks' values, investors dumped them. Those who had bought stocks on margin faced calls from their brokers for more collateral to cover their loans, forcing many of them to liquidate their stock holdings to satisfy their debts. The result was the great stock market crash.

The crash did not cause the Depression of the 1930s. To be sure, the losses sustained by investors and the greater difficulty firms had in floating new issues depressed the economy. But the Federal Reserve stepped in quickly, lending freely to member banks and thereby confining the crash to the financial system. During the 1930s, congressional investigations uncovered a number of unsavory practices by the essentially private, unregulated stock exchanges. In response, Congress passed the Securities Act of 1933 and the Securities and Exchange Act of 1934, inaugurating active federal regulation of the securities markets.

[*See also* Banking and Finance; Business Cycle; Depressions, Economic; Federal Reserve System; Hoover, Herbert; Securities and Exchange Commission; Stock Market; Twenties, The.]

• John Kenneth Galbraith, *The Great Crash*, 1954. Eugene N. White, "The Stock Market Boom and Crash Revisited," *Journal of Economic Perspectives* 4 (Spring 1990): 67–83.

—Diane Lindstrom

STONE, HARLAN FISKE (1872–1946), legal educator, lawyer, associate justice (1925–1941) and chief justice (1941–1946) of the *Supreme Court. To date, Stone remains the sole university professor ever to serve as chief justice and, along with Democrat Edward White, one of only two chief justices appointed by a president from a different party. A Republican and a professor at Columbia Law School, Stone was appointed an associate justice by President Warren *Harding, and Democrat Franklin Delano *Roosevelt elevated him to the chief justiceship. As an associate justice, Stone dissented vigorously against the so-called Four Horsemen, a bloc of justices that routinely objected to Roosevelt's *New Deal measures. Stone insisted that the judiciary should exercise restraint and recognize the need for the legislative and executive branches to respond to the Great Depression. By the late 1930s, with new appointees on the court, this had become the majority view.

During his brief service as chief justice (the shortest since that of Oliver Ellsworth, 1796–1800), Stone moved his colleagues away from issues of economic regulation and toward matters of *civil rights. Stone began the process of developing the implications of footnote four of his most famous opinion, *U.S.* v. *Carolene Products* (1938). This celebrated footnote, while upholding the position that courts should generally defer to legislative bodies on economic matters, suggested that laws restricting the rights of racial or other minorities "may call for a correspondingly more searching judicial inquiry." Stone also led the effort to abolish the all-white primary (*Smith* v. *Allwright*, 1944).

Stone urged the justices to reason cases out at length, a technique markedly different from that of his predecessors. Greater discussion, however, produced more dissent and increased judicial backbiting, neither of which Stone was able to alleviate. Indeed, high levels of dissent on the modern Court date from Stone's tenure as chief justice.

[*See also* Civil Rights Movement; Fourteenth Amendment; Economic Regulation; Laissez-faire; Segregation, Racial; South, The; Suffrage.]

• Alpheus T. Mason, *Harlan Fiske Stone: Pillar of the Law*, 1956. *Public Control of Business: Selected Opinions of Harlan Fiske Stone*, ed. Alfred Lief, 1996.

—Kermit L. Hall

STONE, LUCY (1818–1893), early women's rights advocate. Born in Brookfield, Massachusetts, Lucy Stone gave her first women's rights lecture in 1847 following her graduation from Oberlin College. Prior to the *Civil War, she divided her lecture time between women's rights and *antislavery. She organized the first National Woman's Rights Convention, held in Worcester, Massachusetts, in 1850. A skilled lobbyist and political organizer, Stone addressed legislatures throughout the United States and Canada on behalf of women's legal and political rights. Beginning in the 1840s she set up education committees in cities, towns, and villages, using her lecture fees to print and distribute women's rights propaganda. At her marriage to Henry Blackwell in 1855 she and her husband issued a public protest against women's legal disabilities in marriage; thereafter she retained her birth name, a bold and unusual gesture at the time.

After the Civil War, women's exclusion from the *Fifteenth Amendment caused suffrage advocates Elizabeth Cady *Stanton and Susan B. *Anthony to campaign against its ratification. Stone led the majority of suffragists in resisting these racially divisive tactics. When a schism in the movement developed in 1869, Stone founded the Boston-based American Woman Suffrage Association, the larger and more politically oriented organization to emerge from the break. The Stanton-Anthony wing would write the *History of Woman Suffrage*, however, which marginalized Stone's contribution. In 1870 Stone launched *The Woman's Journal;* for the next sixty years it chronicled women's progress. Reconciliation of the divided movement came in 1890 with the merger of the two rival groups to form the *National American Woman Suffrage Association. Stone continued to lobby, petition, and lecture for woman suffrage until her death.

[*See also* Feminism; Woman Suffrage Movement; Women's Right Movements.]

• Andrea Moore Kerr, *Lucy Stone: Speaking Out for Equality*, 1992. Andrea Moore Kerr, "White Women's Rights, Black Men's Wrongs," in *One Woman, One Vote*, ed. Marjorie Spruill Wheeler, 1995, pp. 61–79.

—Andrea Moore Kerr

STORY, JOSEPH (1779–1845), justice of the U.S. *Supreme Court. Born in Marblehead, Massachusetts, Joseph Story graduated from Harvard in 1798, read law with various jurists, and entered the bar in 1801. A Jeffersonian Republican, he served in the Massachusetts legislature and a term in Congress. Story was appointed to the Supreme Court in 1811 by President James *Madison, after three other individuals had declined. A close ally of Chief Justice John *Marshall, Story became a strong advocate of federal jurisdiction, economic nationalism, and the role of federal law in protecting property rights and the sanctity of contract. His dissent in **Charles River Bridge* v. *Warren Bridge* (1837) invoked the contract clause of the *Constitution in a failed attempt to sustain an implicitly conferred monopoly in a charter the Massachusetts legislature had given the Charles River Bridge Company. The federal government, Story argued, should protect investors in such projects from politicians' whims—in this case the Massachusetts legislators who had authorized a new bridge to compete with the Charles River Bridge.

Story's most important nationalist decisions were *Martin* v. *Hunter's Lessee* (1816) and *Prigg* v. *Pennsylvania* (1841). In the former, he spoke for the Court in ruling constitutional the clause in the Judiciary Act of 1789 allowing the Supreme Court to review state judicial interpretations of the federal *Constitution. In *Prigg,* Story found that state personal-liberty laws guaranteeing escaped slaves their freedom violated the Constitution's pledge that the national government would assist in returning escaped slaves. Faced with denunciations by abolitionists, Story resigned. He hoped to return to scholarly writing and teaching, but died before he could do so.

[*See also* Antislavery; Federalism; Fugitive Slave Act; Jurisprudence; Legal Profession.]

• R. Kent Newmyer, *Supreme Court Justice Joseph Story: Statesman of the Old Republic,* 1985.

—Kermit L. Hall

STOWE, HARRIET BEECHER. *See Uncle Tom's Cabin.*

STRATEGIC ARMS LIMITATION TREATIES (START I, START II). *See* Nuclear Arms Control Treaties.

STRATEGIC DEFENSE INITIATIVE. On 23 March 1983, President Ronald *Reagan called for a missile defense system that would make *nuclear weapons "impotent and obsolete." The president's Strategic Defense Initiative (SDI) was fiercely attacked by those who believed it scientifically impossible, fiscally irresponsible, and strategically dangerous, since it threatened to upset the delicate balance of the nuclear age. It was supported by those who both believed in the limitless potential of American *technology and had never accepted mutual nuclear-age vulnerability as inescapable.

Interest in ballistic missile defense began shortly after the end of *World War II, with controversies over the development and deployment of an antiballistic missile (ABM) system and continuing until the United States and the Soviet Union placed severe restrictions on such work in April 1972. Reagan revived interest in a high-tech shield at the urging of defense enthusiasts such as Edward *Teller; Gen. Daniel O. Graham (ret.), former head of the Defense Intelligence Agency and founder of High Frontier, Inc., a missile defense advocacy group; members of the president's "kitchen cabinet"—brewer Joseph Coors, oilman William Wilson, and businessman Karl Bendetsen; and some members of Congress enthralled by Teller's vision of X-ray laser weapons or chemical lasers. At least one member of the *Joint Chiefs of Staff pronounced missile defense morally superior to deterrence through mutual vulnerability to counterattack, arguing that it is better to save lives than avenge them.

Despite a lavish research budget, SDI—derided by its opponents as "Star Wars," after the 1977 science-fiction movie directed by George Lucas—did not come to fruition during the Reagan presidency. A drum fire of criticism continued, however, including warnings that such a system would violate the 1972 ABM Treaty. A more modest vision of missile defense endured, however, and in 1999, President Bill *Clinton recommended further research into the possibility of defense against missiles from "rogue" nations, a recommendation that reawakened the controversy over the feasibility and strategic advisability of this approach. In September 2000, after several failed tests, Clinton announced that he would leave to his successor the decision on whether to proceed further with a strategic defense system.

[*See also* Cold War; Nuclear Arms Control Treaties; Space Program.]

• "Weapons in Space," *Daedalus* 1 and 2 (Spring and Summer 1985). Edward Tabor Linenthal, *Symbolic Defense: The Cultural Significance of the Strategic Defense Initiative,* 1989. William J. Broad, *Teller's War: The Top-Secret Story behind the Star Wars Deception,* 1992.

—Edward Linenthal

STRAUSS, LEVI (1829–1902), dry-goods merchant. Levi Strauss was the coinventor and manufacturer of the ubiquitous blue denim trousers called "Levis." Born in Bavaria, he emigrated in 1847 to *New York City with part of his family, where they ran a dry-goods shop called Strauss and Brother.

In 1853, Strauss became a U.S. citizen and moved to burgeoning *San Francisco where he established his own dry-goods business, which in 1863 became Strauss and Company. Active in the community, he joined Temple Emanu-El, the city's first synagogue. In 1872, a tailor, Jacob Davis, informed Strauss of the process that led to the production of "Levi's Jeans." In 1873, Strauss and Davis received a patent for "waist overalls," soon to become known as jeans or 'Levis,' made of heavy cotton denim dyed with natural indigo and featuring zinc buttons and copper rivets on pocket corners. Marketed with a small red tag carrying the company name, their product proved an enormous success. As demand increased, the partners opened new factory facilities in San Francisco.

As the company prospered, Strauss pursued other interests. Active on the San Francisco Board of Trade, he was also a director of the Nevada Bank, the San Francisco Gas and Electric Company, and an insurance company. In 1897, he endowed twenty-eight scholarships at the University of California, Berkeley. His estate of six million dollars went mainly to his family, but also included bequests to local orphanages and various religious charities. A century after his death, Levis continued to be marketed throughout the world.

[*See also* Business; Mass Marketing.]

• Isabel Dunwoody, "The Pants with the Small Red Tag," *National Jewish Monthly,* November 1967, pp. 14–15. Lynne Downey, *Levi Strauss, a Biography,* 2000.

—Leo Hershkowitz

STRIKES AND INDUSTRIAL CONFLICT. The strike has been the primary expression of collective action by American workers since the beginning of the *industrialization process. Although strikes occurred prior to the industrial transformation of the United States in the late nineteenth century, they were relatively infrequent and local events initiated by skilled workers belonging to small trade organizations, which rarely survived the frequent economic *depressions that wracked the early national economy.

The Nineteenth Century. By the mid-1800s, as technological innovations eroded the privileged position of many skilled craftsmen, a new era of industrial and labor relations arose. One of the first "industrial strikes" occurred in the textile mills of Lowell, Massachusetts, in 1834 when over eight hundred women walked off the job protesting a reduction in their wages. The strike failed, but two years later an even larger group of women struck and successfully forced employers to restore the wage cuts. The largest pre–*Civil War labor dispute began in February 1860 among the skilled shoemakers of Lynn, Massachusetts. At the peak of the strike, between ten and twenty thousand workers across *New England joined in support of Lynn's men and women shoemakers and helped them win a partial victory.

The Civil War and *Reconstruction years saw relatively few notable strikes. The *Gilded Age, however, witnessed the emergence of massive and sometimes violent labor disputes between a new class of industrial workers and large corporations. Most of these disputes ended peacefully, either in the defeat of one side or in compromise. Violence primarily marked those disputes where employers refused to negotiate, hired strikebreakers, or called in state or federal troops. The first of the great industrial battles began on 16 July 1877 when railroad workers in Martinsburg, West Virginia, struck to protest a reduction in wages. The strike quickly spread as railroad workers around the nation walked out in sympathy. Violence erupted when the governor of Maryland ordered the state militia to restore order in Baltimore, where crowds of strike sympathizers occupied the streets. At the end of the melee, nine workers were dead, most of the railway station was destroyed, and the strike had been dealt a fatal blow.

Despite the unrelenting resistance of most employers, workers continued to strike. One of the most famous "strikes" of the period began in July 1892 when the general manager of Andrew *Carnegie's steel plant in Homestead, Pennsylvania, Henry Clay Frick, locked out the workers in an attempt to break their union. Frick hired operatives from the Pinkerton Agency, a private-detective and security-guard firm, to reopen the plant and provide protection for strikebreakers. The strikers defeated the Pinkertons in a pitched battle, but the strike collapsed when the governor of Pennsylvania dispatched state militia to occupy the town of Homestead. By September the plants were operating normally, without union labor.

Workers also lost the *Pullman strike and boycott of 1894. Unable to defeat George Pullman by themselves, his workers appealed to Eugene V. *Debs, president of the American Railway Union (ARU). ARU members voted to support the strike, which brought out more than 260,000 railroad workers and effectively paralyzed the nation's railroad system. Once again government officials sided with business. Attorney General Richard Olney obtained legal injunctions interdicting union activities, sent federal troops and marshals to enforce the court orders, and had Debs and other ARU leaders arrested for disobeying the injunction. This federal intervention effectively terminated the strike, and by mid-July most of the defeated strikers had returned.

1900 to 1945. Strike activity remained at relatively high levels during the first two decades of the twentieth century. In May 1902, the United Mine Workers of America struck in the anthracite coal fields of Pennsylvania, demanding union recognition and better working conditions. As coal production fell precipitately, President Theodore *Roosevelt pressured the employers to negotiate an agreement meeting many of the union's demands. These years also witnessed a series of strikes by immigrant clothing workers; the most famous of these, "the uprising of 20,000," was a 1909 walkout by women garment workers in *New York City. The syndicalist *Industrial Workers of the World (IWW), which aimed to organize all workers into "One Big Union," also led several mass strikes, the most notable of which occurred in Lawrence, Massachusetts, in January 1912 when roughly twenty thousand textile workers staged a successful walkout. The success of the IWW proved short-lived, as a year later (1913) its members lost a strike by silk workers in Paterson, New Jersey.

The *World War I years were especially strike-ridden. Workers in large numbers voted to strike as their wages failed to keep pace with rapidly rising prices. More strikes occurred in 1915–1916 than in any comparable earlier period. The number of industrial disputes fell slightly in 1917 and 1918, largely owing to the efforts of the National War Labor Board (NWLB), which responded to organized labor's demands in exchange for a no-strike pledge. Nonetheless, well over a million workers walked picket lines in 1918. The cessation of hostilities brought an end to the NWLB and unleashed a tidal wave of industrial unrest. In 1919 over four million workers, including nearly 600,000 coal miners and 300,000 steelworkers, went on strike to preserve their wartime gains. Without government support, however, workers lost the most crucial postwar industrial battles.

The number of strikes steadily declined throughout the 1920s and remained stable during the first years of the depression of the 1930s. Beginning in 1933, however, the number of strikes exploded. Not only did more strikes occur, but the primary reason behind them also shifted. Before the Great Depression, nearly all strikes concerned wages, hours, and working conditions. While these issues remained important, the industrial unrest beginning in 1934, when waterfront workers in San Francisco, teamsters in Minnesota, and 500,000 textile workers across the nation struck, was fueled by the strikers' demand for union recognition. This initial burst of labor activity declined in 1935 and 1936 after the U.S. *Supreme Court declared unconstitutional the National Industrial Recovery Act and its protection of workers' rights to organize. Beginning in late 1936, however, a second wave of industrial strikes spurred by passage of the *National Labor Relations Act (Wagner Act) involved millions of American workers. The *Congress of Industrial Organizations (CIO), which had split from the *American Federation of Labor (AFL), stood at the forefront of the movement, leading walkouts in the unorganized mass production sectors of the economy. The best-known CIO-led work stoppage, the Flint *sit-down strike, began on 30 December 1936 when General Motors (GM) employees in Flint, Michigan, sat down on the job and occupied the company's plants. Their innovative tactics forced GM to recognize and bargain with their union, the United Automobile Workers. By June 1937 nearly 500,000 workers, inspired by the union victory at GM, had participated in sit-down strikes that spread across the nation.

The number of strikes fell between 1938 and 1940 as a return of depression conditions slowed the economy and increased *unemployment. As the war in Europe stimulated the economy and solved the persistent problem of unemployment, however, strike activity intensified. In 1941 two million workers participated in over 4,200 strikes in the auto, coal, textile, and steel industries. Determined to maintain wartime production, President Franklin Delano *Roosevelt appointed a wartime labor board to alleviate the causes of industrial conflict. When the war ended, however, American workers by the millions once again went on strike, demanding the higher wages denied them during the war. In 1946, almost two million workers, including 300,000 meatpackers and 750,000 steelworkers, walked picket lines. This number rose in April when John L. *Lewis, president of the United Mine Workers, called out 400,000 miners. In all, the year following the end of the war witnessed a record number of labor disputes; close to five million workers participated in over 4,600 strikes, and, more importantly, unlike the comparable 1919 strike wave, workers managed to retain and solidify their wartime gains.

1945 to 2000. Although several large walkouts occurred between 1947 and 1951, the overall number of strikes averaged only one-third the number recorded in 1946. One of the largest strikes of this period erupted in 1952 when 560,000 steelworkers threatened to walk out if their wage demands were not met. President Harry S. *Truman's seizure of the steel plants temporarily delayed the strike but when the Supreme Court ruled this action unconstitutional, the workers resumed their walkout. Despite the steel strike, the rest of the decade was marked by the solidification of a relatively peaceful collective bargaining system between well-entrenched unions and large industrial corporations.

Beginning in the late 1950s, the fortunes of organized labor, and the number of strikes began a long decline that continued into the 1990s. By 1965 only 25 percent of the labor force belonged to unions while the numbers of workers outside the labor movement grew rapidly. One of organized labor's few successes during the 1960s and 1970s involved *migratory agricultural workers organized by the Mexican American labor leader César *Chávez in *California's farms and fields. Chávez used innovative consumer boycotts to organize the table grape pickers. As the labor movement entered the 1970s and 1980s, however, successes were few and far between. A moribund economy and the decline of traditionally unionized industries eroded the base of the labor movement. Thus, despite a brief flurry of strike activity in the early 1970s and growth in public-sector unions, by 1978 labor still counted only about a quarter of the workforce in its ranks. Organized labor's rapid decline continued in the last two decades of the century. In 1980, 795,000 workers participated in strikes; by 1988, this number had plummeted to 118,000. Overall, between 1980 and 1997 strike activity fell to the lowest level in American history—lower even than the late 1920s and first years of the Great

Depression. Although labor engaged in a number of large, well-publicized work stoppages in 1997, such as the Teamsters' successful strike against United Parcel Service, the percentage of workers belonging to unions continued to decline as did the number of workers choosing to go on strike.

[*See also* Automotive Industry; Gompers, Samuel; Homestead Lockout; Immigrant Labor; Industrialization; Industrial Relations; Iron and Steel Industry; Labor Markets; Labor Movements; Mining; New Deal Era, The; Railroads; Railroad Strikes of 1877; Reuther, Walter; Textile Industry.]

• Florence Peterson, *Strikes in the United States:1880–1936,* 1939. David Montgomery, "Strikes in Nineteenth-Century America," *Social Science History* 4 (February 1980): 81–103. P. K. Edwards, *Strikes in the United States: 1881–1974,* 1981. H. Gutman, ed., *Who Built America? Working People and the Nation's Economy, Politics, Culture, and Society,* 1992. Walter Licht, *Industrializing America: The Nineteenth Century,* 1995. Melvyn Dubofsky, *Industrialization and the American Worker: 1865–1920,* 1996. Jeremy Brecher, *Strike,* 1997.

—Douglas J. Feeney

STUDENT NON-VIOLENT COORDINATING COMMITTEE (SNCC). This organization was founded at a 1960 conference in Raleigh, North Carolina, to give students a voice in the *civil rights movement. Ella Baker, executive director of the *Southern Christian Leadership Conference, and James Lawson, a divinity student, played key roles. Initially formed to bring student leaders together, to share experiences and discuss future goals and strategies, SNCC quickly evolved into an organization of full-time organizers and protesters. Committed at first to nonviolent direct action, group-centered leadership, and multiracial democracy, SNCC's increasing militancy was mainly shaped by members' direct experiences.

SNCC members reorganized the Freedom Rides in 1961, after the *Congress of Racial Equality (CORE) encountered bus-burnings and beatings. They also organized local *African Americans to register to vote in Selma, Alabama, and Hattiesburg, Mississippi, and to demonstrate against racial *segregation in Albany, Georgia. Early in 1964, SNCC joined with CORE to invite northern white college students to Mississippi that summer to teach in Freedom Schools, help with voter registrations, and bring national attention to racial injustice in the *South. More than one thousand responded. During Freedom Summer, three young activists, Michael Schwerner, Andrew Goodman, and James Chaney, were murdered by white racists. In August 1964, SNCC helped form the integrated Mississippi Freedom Democratic party, which challenged the all-white Mississippi delegation at the national convention in Atlantic City, but was ultimately rebuffed.

In 1966, amid increasing racial violence in U.S. cities, SNCC's new president, Stokely Carmichael (1941–), articulated his vision of Black Power, including black self-reliance, racial exclusivity, and violent self-defense. Under Carmichael's incendiary successor, H. Rap Brown, this increasing spiral of *radicalism and violence caused internal fissures that ultimately led to the disintegration of SNCC in the early 1970s. Despite this downfall, SNCC played a pivotal role in the southern civil rights movement and prefigured later social movements, particularly the student movement and the *women's rights movement of the 1970s.

[*See also* Black Nationalism; King, Martin Luther Jr.; Sixties, The.]

• Clayborne Carson, *In Struggle: SNCC and the Black Awakening of the 1960s,* 1981. Charles Payne, *I've Got the Light of Freedom: The Organizing Tradition and the Mississippi Freedom Struggle,* 1995.

—Patrick D. Jones

STUDENTS FOR A DEMOCRATIC SOCIETY (SDS), the most influential and best-known political organization of the white *New Left during the 1960s. In 1960, SDS emerged from its forerunner, the Student League for Industrial Democracy, a social democratic organization. Inspired by and affiliated with both the *civil rights movement and organized labor, SDS sought to design a political strategy to achieve progressive social change in postwar America. In June 1962, fifty-nine members meeting at a labor-union resort in Michigan drafted *The Port Huron Statement,* a political manifesto critiquing American race relations, the persistence of *poverty, and America's *Cold War role. The principal author was Tom Hayden (1939–), a University of Michigan student. Arguing that these problems reflected the impoverishment of politics, the manifesto called for "participatory democracy," whereby Americans would involve themselves directly in the decisions affecting their lives and communities. The commitment to participatory democracy guided SDS's organizational structure and future political action.

Over the ensuing decade, SDS members participated in civil rights activism, began community organizing in the urban North with the Economic Research and Action Project in 1963–1964, and played a prominent role in the anti–*Vietnam War and student movements. Bringing direct action tactics to these movements, SDS sponsored mass antiwar demonstrations in 1965 in *Washington, D.C., and at the *Democratic party's 1968 national convention in *Chicago, as well as student strikes on college campuses, including a heavily publicized one in 1968 at Columbia University. As protests and media attention intensified, SDS grew to an estimated membership ranging from 30,000 to 100,000. Rapid growth and ideological divisions contributed to conflicts within the organization about strategy and goals. When the fractious 1969 SDS national convention split between the revolutionary Weathermen (a term drawn from a protest song by Bob *Dylan) and the neo-Maoist Progressive Labor party, the organization collapsed. Many former members remained committed to progressive politics, however, through their career choices and participation in later social and community movements.

[*See also* Antiwar Movements; *Other America, The;* Radicalism; Sixties, The; Socialism; Socialist Party of America.]

• James Miller, *"Democracy Is in the Streets": From Port Huron to the Siege of Chicago,* 1987. Alice Echols, "We Gotta Get Out of This Place: Notes toward a Remapping of the Sixties," *Socialist Review* 22 (April–June 1992): 9–33.

—Jennifer Frost

SUBMARINES. Invented by the American David Bushnell in 1773 and later improved by Robert Fulton, submarines were used by the Confederates in several *Civil War naval operations. It was around 1900, however, that submarines became feasible for warfare. Electricity propelled a double-hulled, cigar-shaped boat; compressed air forced ballast out of tanks between the hulls to permit surfacing; and the torpedo served as the main armament. Navies originally intended to use the submarine to scout and screen for the battle fleet.

Both world wars stimulated changes in mission and extensive improvements. German U-boats became successful commerce raiders during *World War I, but antisubmarine tactics, especially the escort of merchant-ship convoys, eventually contained them. During *World War II Germany deployed U-boats equipped with snorkels to increase range and endurance. Wolf-pack tactics were employed against convoys, but sophisticated antisubmarine methods—radar, sonar, and air-sea-ground cooperation—again thwarted German commerce raiding. Meanwhile, during the Pacific war, the United States maneuvered large fleet submarines against Japanese shipping. This effort eventually interdicted Japanese maritime communications and made a vital contribution to victory.

During the *Cold War, the submarine became the most important naval vessel. The use of nuclear power to propel tear-shaped submarines capable of launching nuclear-armed missiles from beneath the surface provided an invulnerable weapon that became the principal instrument of nuclear deterrence in the age of mutual assured destruction. Admiral Hyman Rickover (1900–1986) emerged as a major advocate of nuclear submarines. The USS *Nautilus* (1954), which possessed great range and endurance, presaged the Polaris submarine-launched ballistic missiles (SLBM) of the 1960s. The Poseidon missile entered service in 1970, followed by the Trident intercontinental ballistic missile (ICBM), accurate to 4,600 miles. Meanwhile the Soviet Union achieved comparable advances as the nuclear arms competition continued to escalate.

The end of the Cold War and the consequent decline of international tension increased interest in arms control and disarmament, including nuclear submarines. The nuclear-armed submarine, however, remained a part of the nation's military arsenal. Underwater vessels have also proven useful in scientific research and salvage operations.

[*See also* Federal Government, Executive Branch: Department of Defense; Military, The; Nuclear Strategy; Nuclear Weapons.]

• Norman Friedman, *U.S. Submarines since 1945,* 1994. Norman Friedman, *U.S. Submarines through 1945,* 1995.

—David F. Trask

SUBSIDIES, AGRICULTURAL. The earliest government subsidies for farmers, beginning in 1890, benefited cane-sugar and beet-sugar growers. The first general subsidy program was established in 1933 under the *Agricultural Adjustment Administration, part of the New Deal's economic recovery plan. The government offered cash payments to farmers to reduce their output of such basic commodities as hogs, wheat, corn, cotton, rice, and dairy products. The goal was "parity," by which farmers' purchasing power would match what it had been in the prosperous 1909–1914 years. Taxes on grain mills and other food processors (ultimately passed along to consumers) financed the subsidies. As southern cotton growers reduced production in return for federal payments, sharecroppers and tenant farmers were driven from the land.

Farmers received two forms of subsidies, cash payments for taking land out of production and direct price supports through government purchase, loans, and management of surpluses. The Commodity Credit Corporation (CCC), created by executive order in 1933, lent farmers money with their crops as collateral. If prices held steady or increased, the farmer paid off his loan. If not, the CCC marketed the crop and absorbed the loss. Similar subsidy programs lasted into the 1990s. Government subsidies tended to concentrate production of basic crops in the hands of more efficient, larger owners. In 1970, for example, nine individuals or corporations each received over a million dollars in crop-reduction subsidies.

In 1981, President Ronald *Reagan proposed to end production controls and target prices, the mechanisms that had sustained the agricultural economy since the early *New Deal Era. But huge surpluses and congressional opposition forced the administration to retreat. A 1982 program combined a smaller acreage-allotment program with guaranteed prices. Under it, the Reagan administration paid farmers more not to grow crops than any previous administration. Although the 1995 Freedom to Farm Act officially ended most agricultural subsidies, farmers continued to receive billions of dollars in phase-out payments and "emergency relief" appropriations. An elaborate milk price-support program remained in place as well.

[*See also* Agriculture: Since 1920; Cotton Industry; Dairy Industry; Economic Regulation; Federal Government, Executive Branch: Department of Agriculture; Grain Processing Industry; Sharecropping and Tenantry.]

• Lauren Soth, *An Embarrassment of Plenty,* 1965. Nancy Blanpied, ed., *Farm Policy: The Politics of Soil, Surpluses, and Subsidies,* 1984.

—Richard Lowitt

SUBURBANIZATION, the diffusion of urban life (people, commerce, and industry) from the center of a city to the periphery, also connotes lifestyle differences between those who reside in the suburbs and those who live in cities. Historically, suburbanization has been propelled by technological developments as well as by cultural values that underscore an American penchant for semirural living. Beginning as a distinct movement in the nineteenth century, suburbanization continued throughout the twentieth, making the United States one of the world's most decentralized industrial societies.

In the first half of the nineteenth century, urban life was shaped by the characteristics of the walking city. Residential and commercial space lay within close proximity and, since movement depended on the distance one could comfortably travel by foot, individuals from multiple ethnic and income groups concentrated in the centralized downtown areas. In 1850, *Boston was typical: Its residents lived within two miles of the center of town. The introduction of public transportation, first the omnibus (1830) and eventually the railway, gradually influenced this basic structure and allowed well-to-do residents to move to the city's periphery or beyond. These mid-nineteenth-century suburbs primarily comprised white-collar male workers who commuted to the city, their families, and working-class residents restricted to service employment within the suburbs because of the high cost of rail transportation. Such communities (for example Llewellyn Park, New Jersey, or Riverside, Illinois) expressed ideals popularized through the *Romantic movement, which accentuated the curative powers of nature and stressed the need to preserve preindustrial values threatened by modernization. Homes in these communities were generally situated on large plots of land (up to twenty acres) and connected through curvilinear roads, which, in stark contrast to the gridiron pattern of the city, followed the natural contours of the land.

The expansion of the trolley car in the 1880s ended this era of "romantic" suburbs and ushered in a new period of peripheral growth. Trolleys offered affordable cross-town transportation, allowing middle-class Americans to live on the suburban fringe while continuing to work in the city center. Although plots were smaller and conditions more crowded than in the earlier suburbs, these new communities retained the romantic ideal of semirural living and provided a sense of refuge from a downtown increasingly associated with danger. Labor radicalism, immigrant slums, industrial pollution, black migration, and machine politics associated with the city contrasted sharply with an emerging suburban ideal that emphasized the patriotism of property ownership, the link between democracy and rural life, the sanctity of the family, and, most importantly, the belief that the home should provide a haven from the harshness of the industrial city. By the turn of the century, the suburban, single-family, detached dwelling lay at the heart of the American dream. While this dream was theoretically open to all, in practice the rise of the trolley suburb resulted in a divided city. Between the 1870s and 1900, the middle class increasingly migrated to the suburban residential fringe while immigrants and the working poor stayed behind in the city center. The working class found it economically unfeasible to live in an outlying area of the city and commute to the downtown where most of the commercial and industrial jobs remained.

The automobile had a profound effect on suburbanization. First, it facilitated movement between suburbs and cities to such a degree that, as early as the 1920s, the suburbs grew at a faster rate than the city core. Second, automobiles dramatically changed the nature of retailing. The central business districts had survived the initial waves of suburbanization, but with the automobile, businesses found it necessary and profitable to move to the periphery. Walking cities were not designed to accommodate automobile traffic, nor did they possess adequate parking. Retailers addressed the problem of congestion by moving *department stores and other businesses to fringe areas with more open land. Consequently, suburbs experienced commercial diversification and economic growth as downtown areas declined.

The Depression of the 1930s and *World War II effectively brought the suburbanization process to a halt. It revived dramatically after the war, however, and by 1970 more Americans lived in suburbs than in any other form of community. This process was stimulated by the availability of cheap land, new building techniques, a severe *housing shortage, the baby boom, and a continuing cultural predilection for low-density housing. Postwar suburbanization also received an impetus from governmental policies that favored growth in the suburbs over growth in the city. Some have argued that underlying racial prejudice also encouraged white Americans to flee urban centers that were increasingly populated by minorities. Postwar suburbs were typified by communities like Levittown, New York, composed of hundreds of nearly identical tract homes assembled virtually overnight. According to the conventional view, reinforced by 1950s *television comedies and cultural critics, the residents were typically young, white, middle-class men who commuted to the city; wives who were committed to domesticity; and young children. Such a view defined the suburb as an economically dependent, homogeneous, racially exclusive, manicured bedroom community focused on the family.

This image of suburbia survived into the late twentieth century, even as the relationship between cities and their suburbs underwent tremendous change, and the dependent, commuting, homogeneous residential suburb had all but disappeared. Fringe communities engaged in a variety of industrial and commercial activities. Suburbs could now be characterized variously as working class, Latino, Asian, African American, upper middle class, exclusive, or nonexclusive. To be sure, the poor, racial minorities, and immigrants continued to be concentrated in city centers. Owing to the suburbs' increased diversity, however, historians disagreed over whether they should be considered independent cities in their own right or specialized areas within larger metropolitan wholes—areas that would never replace the traditional city's complexity and cultural diversity.

[*See also* Automotive Industry; Fifties, The; Immigration; Mobility; Motor Vehicles; Racism; Shopping Centers and Malls; Social Class; Urbanization.]

• Sam Bass Warner Jr., *Streetcar Suburbs: The Process of Growth in Boston, 1870–1900,* 1962. Kenneth T. Jackson, *Crabgrass Frontier: The Suburbanization of the United States,* 1985. Robert Fishman, *Bourgeois Utopias,* 1987. Margaret Marsh, *Suburban Lives,* 1990. Joel Garreau, *Edge City: Life on the New Frontier,* 1991. William Sharpe and Leonard Wallock, "Bold New City or Built up Burb?: Redefining Contemporary Suburbia," in *The Making of Urban America,* ed., Raymond A. Mohl, 1997, pp. 309–331.

—Jennifer L. Kalish

SUEZ CRISIS. *See* Foreign Relations: U.S. Relations with the Middle East.

SUFFRAGE. Suffrage, the right or privilege of voting to choose candidates or enact laws in a public election, has been practiced and regulated since classical times. In England, in 1430, Parliament imposed property restrictions that in effect limited those permitted to vote in parliamentary elections to no more than 15 percent of adult males. In the American colonies, land was cheap; rank was fluid; and suffrage restrictions, such as property, civility, and religious qualifications, were casually enforced and easily evaded. Surviving eighteenth-century voting records suggest that most adult white males could vote in local elections.

In the United States, war has often been a catalyst for the extension of suffrage. Religious qualifications were largely abandoned during and after the *Revolutionary War. So were property qualifications, though later and more grudgingly, as landless veterans sought a voice in government, party competition became the rule, and property qualifications proved hard to enforce. Often they were replaced by a poll-tax requirement. Rhode Island became the last state to drop the freehold requirement, following the so-called Dorr Rebellion of 1841. In that year a convention of Rhode Island men led by Thomas W. Dorr proposed a "People's Constitution" granting universal adult male suffrage. This constitution was overwhelmingly approved by popular vote but was not recognized by Rhode Island's conservative legislature. Each side held its own elections and mobilized its own militia. Dorr's side soon lost heart and disbanded, but the victorious charter government in 1843 enacted most of the reforms Dorr had demanded. Women and blacks remained generally unfranchised, though a few free blacks could vote in *New England and New York. Virtually all suffrage disputes before the *Civil War were decided at the state level.

After the Civil War, Radical Republicans in Congress became concerned with suffrage, primarily to block southern Democrats' return to power. With the *Fourteenth Amendment (1868), Radical Republicans attempted to disfranchise southern whites without enfranchising more northern blacks. With the *Fifteenth Amendment (1870), they barred the states from restricting the franchise of U.S. citizens on the basis of race, but they neglected to ban literacy or character tests or registration and poll-tax requirements. These were later used, along with white primaries and grandfather clauses, to keep southern blacks (and poor whites) from the polls.

The greatest single expansion of suffrage came in 1920 with the ratification of the *Nineteenth Amendment, granting women the vote and capping a campaign by women's rights advocates dating from the 1840s. Wyoming was the first state to adopt women's suffrage (1869), and other western states followed suit. A woman-suffrage campaign in New York State succeeded in 1917. The final victory reflected the larger *Progressive Era reform spirit, with a tinge of nativism as well. President Woodrow *Wilson supported the amendment campaign in part because of women's contributions during *World War I.

In the 1940s, suffrage debates shifted from legislatures to the *Supreme Court, with more emphasis on the constitutional rights of the unfranchised and less concern about political results. In *Smith* v. *Allwright* (1944), the Court outlawed white-only primaries. In **Baker* v. *Carr* (1962), it ruled that state legislative districts must be of equal size under the principle of "one person, one vote."

In both cases the Court used novel constitutional doctrines to fill a void left by state and federal legislative inaction. These rulings, together with the Voting Rights Act of 1965 (which suspended literacy tests and was long construed by lower federal courts to require "affirmative action" gerrymandering of electoral districts), fundamentally altered the political landscape. In the *South, black voter registration rose from 5 percent in 1940 to 66 percent in 1969; southern white registration in the same period rose from 15 to 83 percent. Black officeholders, rare in the 1940s, numbered over two thousand by 1970. Blacks in Congress grew from one or two in the 1940s to forty by 1992.

Thanks to *affirmative action gerrymanders, most of these African American members of Congress were Democrats from safe, overwhelmingly black districts, strongly committed to black issues, many with high seniority. The Black Caucus was among the most powerful and united voting blocs in the Democrat-controlled 103d Congress (1992–1994). However, racial gerrymandering also contributed to the Democrats' loss of Congress in 1994, by removing black Democrats from otherwise winnable swing districts and delivering those districts to Republican candidates. The Democrats' loss of Congress gravely diminished the power of the Black Caucus. Some observers argued that partisan and incumbent-serving gerrymandering, which was also indirectly encouraged by "one person, one vote" requirements, diminished competitiveness, lowered turnover, polarized party politics, and helped fuel the movement to impose term limits on legislators.

Other post-1960 suffrage extensions—enfranchising the District of Columbia for presidential elections (1961), abolishing the poll tax (1964), and lowering the voting age to eighteen (1971)—took place through constitutional amendments, not judicial interpretation. None of these had much impact on politics, and they may be the last domestic extensions of the franchise. By the 1970s, only juveniles, noncitizens, convicted felons, and insane persons could not vote in most states. In *California, however, mental patients were inadvertently enfranchised by a 1972 referendum. They voted in every election thereafter, making no discernible difference in the state's politics.

[*See also* African Americans; Civil Rights Legislation; Civil Rights Movements; Constitution; Republicanism; Woman Suffrage Movement.]

• Chilton Williamson, *American Suffrage from Property to Democracy*, 1960. William Gillette, *The Right to Vote: Politics and the Passage of the Fifteenth Amendment*, 1965. J. R. Pole, *Political Representation in England and the Origins of the American Republic*, 1966. Alan P. Grimes, *The Puritan Ethic and Woman Suffrage*, 1967. J. Morgan Kousser, *The Shaping of Southern Politics: Suffrage Restriction and the Establishment of the One-Party South, 1880–1910*, 1974. Ward Elliott, *The Rise of Guardian Democracy: The Supreme Court's Role in Voting Rights Disputes, 1845–1969*, 1975.

—Ward E. Y. Elliot

SULLIVAN, LOUIS (1856–1924), architect. Born in *Boston, Louis Sullivan studied *architecture for a year at the Massachusetts Institute of Technology, after which he worked for Philadelphia architect Frank Furness. In 1873, he moved to *Chicago to work for William Le Baron Jenney and then to Paris, where he attended the École des Beaux-Arts. Returning to Chicago in 1875, Sullivan worked for various architects, the last being Dankmar Adler, with whom, in 1883, he formed the partnership of Adler and Sullivan.

Louis Sullivan's fame rests on the new style of architecture he created in 1890 and developed during the ensuing decade. It was then that Sullivan in the United States and a handful of architects in Europe envolved personal styles no longer based on the classical vocabulary of Greco-Roman buildings, styles that in their opinion expressed mystically the spirit of their own age, and were therefore "modern." When in 1890 Sullivan achieved the kind of originality both in architectural and ornamental design that he sought, he was slightly ahead of most European modernists. His new style first emerged in the Getty Tomb in Chicago and Wainwright Building in St. Louis, where each structure is a simple cube decorated with Sullivan's own floral and geometric ornament.

Between 1888 and 1893 Frank Lloyd *Wright worked for Sullivan. The fruit of this relationship was Wright's acceptance of Sullivan's credo that the modern architect's only worthy goal was to create an original architecture of his own, an ideal that Wright brought to fruition in his own work. After 1895, when the firm of Adler and Sullivan was dissolved, Sullivan garnered only occasional commissions, mostly for small banks.

[*See also* Modernist Culture.]

• Hugh Morrison, *Louis Sullivan*, 1935, reprint 1998. Robert Twombly, *Louis Sullivan*, 1986.

—Paul E. Sprague

SUMNER, WILLIAM GRAHAM. *See* Social Darwinism.

SUNDAY, BILLY (1862–1935), evangelist. William Ashley Sunday was born in Ames, Iowa. His youth was marked by poverty and intermittent education. A gifted athlete, Sunday in 1883 joined the Chicago White Stockings *baseball team. Having converted to Christ in 1886, he left baseball in 1891 to engage in Christian ministry. After assisting two traveling evangelists, Sunday set out on his own in 1896. Ordained as a Presbyterian minister in 1903, he maintained a grueling schedule of revival meetings in small midwestern towns. But by 1910 he was holding huge evangelistic campaigns in major cities throughout America.

Over his lifetime, Sunday preached to and converted more people than any American revivalist before Billy *Graham. He "got results" because of his simple language, physical stunts, and dramatic theatrics. Undergirding Sunday's showmanship was an extraordinary organizational apparatus managed by his wife, Nell Sunday.

Sunday vehemently attacked what he viewed as the evils afflicting modern America, including urban corruption, *immigration, and most important, alcohol—concerns shared by many *Progressive Era reformers. Sunday's solution was appealingly (or appallingly) simple: Conversion to Christ brought with it common decency; if enough people converted, America could be righteous again.

During *World War I, Sunday was a prominent and chauvinistic supporter of the U.S. war effort and vehement in his denunciations of Germany. Soon thereafter his career began to fade, in part because of family and health problems, but he kept preaching until his death. Billy Sunday's legacy includes the estimated one million individuals who came forward in his revivals, and the *Fundamentalist movement that continued his crusade against forces perceived to be turning America into a moral wasteland.

[*See also* Protestantism; Revivalism; Temperance and Prohibition; Twenties, The.]

• William G. McLoughlin Jr., *Billy Sunday Was His Real Name*, 1955. Douglas W. Frank, *Less than Conquerors: How Evangelicals Entered the Twentieth Century*, 1986. Lyle W. Dorsett, *Billy Sunday and the Redemption of Urban America*, 1991.

—William Vance Trollinger Jr.

SUPREME COURT, U.S. Article III of the *Constitution provides that "the judicial Power of the United States, shall be vested in one supreme Court, and in such inferior Courts as Congress may from time to time ordain and establish." The First Congress created a Supreme Court and lower tribunals in the Judiciary Act of 1789; the three-tiered system, with some modification, remains the basis for the modern federal court system.

Overview. The Judiciary Act created a Supreme Court of six judges, a chief justice and five associate justices. It also created thirteen district courts, one for each state, and an intermediate court of appeals, consisting of the judge for the district court and two justices of the Supreme Court riding circuit. In addition, the Act spelled out the jurisdiction of the federal courts, and in the very important Section 25 gave the Supreme Court appellate jurisdiction over federal questions arising in state courts. It is this provision, allowing the Supreme Court to review state court decisions touching on federal questions, that is the key to enforcing Article VI, which makes the Constitution the supreme law of the land.

Since then, the basic structure of the federal judicial system has been modified slightly. Membership of the Supreme Court increased; during the *Civil War it reached ten, but afterward it dropped to nine, where it has remained. Judges are appointed for life, and serve during "good behavior." The only means for removing a judge is through *impeachment. One justice of the Supreme Court, Samuel Chase, was impeached in 1804, but was not convicted.

The Supreme Court hears appeals in cases of original jurisdiction (such as suits between two states) and has appellate jurisdiction from both the state and federal systems. In the federal system, cases usually originate in a district court, and then may be appealed to one of the Circuit Courts of Appeal. From there plaintiffs may appeal to the Supreme Court, but the so-called Judges Bill of 1925 gave the Court almost complete control over its docket as well as the power to limit the number of cases it accepts for review. That number, which ran in the 150 range in the 1970s, was steadily reduced thereafter, so that by the mid-nineties the Court was giving a full hearing to fewer than eighty cases a year.

The Court will also hear appeals of final decisions from the highest state court, if a federal constitutional issue is involved. If the case can be resolved on adequate state statutory or legislative grounds, the Court will not grant review. For a case to be accepted for review, the "rule of four" applies, by which four members of the Court must agree that review is warranted. The Court's caseload consists primarily of two types of litigation, one involving constitutional questions, in which the Court's word is final, and the other involving interpretation of federal legislation, in which Congress can in effect overrule the justices by revising the statute.

The Marshall Court. In its first ten years the Supreme Court enjoyed little popular esteem, and the first Chief Justice, John *Jay, resigned because he believed the court would never become a coequal partner in government with the legislative and executive branches. That began to change with President John *Adams's appointment of John *Marshall as chief justice, a position he held from 1801 to his death in 1835.

Marshall established one of the key powers of the Court in **Marbury* v. *Madison* (1803), in which he ruled a portion of the 1789 Judiciary Act unconstitutional, thus claiming for the Court not only the power of *judicial review over federal legislation, but also establishing the Court as the ultimate interpreter of the Constitution. In a series of decisions over the next three decades, Marshall helped to clothe the new government with extensive powers, carrying out the vision enunciated by the Federalists in the 1790s.

The Court gave a broad reading to the Contracts Clause in **Fletcher* v. *Peck* (1810), and further expanded its reach in *Dartmouth College* v. *Woodward* (1819), thus protecting private property interests against state legislative power. In **McCulloch* v. *Maryland* (1819), Marshall relied on the argument Alexander *Hamilton had made in defense of the first *Bank of the United States and elevated it to a constitutional rule, that federal creations made under a legitimate exercise of constitutional power are immune from state regulation or taxation. Marshall carried the reach of the Commerce Power furthest in *Gibbons* v. *Ogden* (1824), in which he strained the meaning of the federal coastal licensing law to strike down a New York-sponsored steamboat monopoly.

Gibbons marked the high point of the Marshall Court's expansive nationalism. In the next decade the Marshall Court proved more amenable to *states' rights interests, as the Chief Justice fought to blunt growing criticism of the judiciary and moves to restrict its powers over the states. In *Wilson* v. *Blackbird Creek Marsh Co.* (1829) he ceded substantial power to the states over interstate waterways, and in *Barron* v. *Baltimore* (1833) the Court ruled that the *Bill of Rights did not apply to the states. When the Court did try to limit state powers, as in the Cherokee removal cases (1831 and 1832), Georgia ignored the rulings and President Andrew *Jackson supposedly sneered, "The Chief Justice has made his decision; now let him enforce it."

The Taney Court and Beyond. When Jackson named Roger B. *Taney chief justice in 1835, many expected the nationalist tone of the Court to change to a more states' rights orientation, and in some cases it did. Taney and his colleagues proved more sympathetic to local interests, and in the famous case **Charles River Bridge* v. *Warren Bridge* (1837) gave the states extensive leeway over commercial regulation and contracts. This decision also represented a shift in sympathy for new entrepreneurial capital as opposed to the more established *capitalism favored by the Federalists. In *Cooley* v. *Board of Wardens* (1852), the Court pronounced a commonsense rule that, while leaving the federal commerce power supreme, nonetheless gave states far greater leeway to act.

But the Taney Court was in many ways as nationalistic as its predecessor, and in a number of cases reaffirmed or only slightly modified Marshall Court precedents. Moreover, in *Luther* v. *Borden* (1849), Taney introduced the "political question" doctrine, allowing the Court to evade issues that, in its opinion, belonged more to the realm of politics than law.

Unfortunately, Taney's reputation, as well as that of his Court, is so bound up with its decisions on *slavery that much of its other work has been unappreciated. Taney, a firm believer in both slavery and the right of states to protect the institution, went out of his way in **Scott* v. *Sandford* (1857) not only to uphold slavery, but also to deny the federal government any power to regulate or limit it.

That case wounded the prestige of the Court until after the Civil War, a conflict in which the Court played a very limited role. As in most wars, the justices delayed hearing potentially divisive issues until after the fighting had ended. Although in *Ex parte Milligan* (1866) the Court, now headed by Salmon P. Chase (1808–1873, chief justice 1864–1873) ruled that the federal government could not resort to military tribunals in areas where civilian courts remained open, for the most part the Court endorsed nearly all of the actions taken by Congress and the Executive during the war. Fear that the Court might invalidate some of its *Reconstruction measures led Congress to restrict the Court's jurisdiction in some areas, but these restrictions proved temporary and ephemeral. Moreover, in *Texas* v. *White* (1869), the Court put its imprimatur on congressional Reconstruction, and held the secession of the southern states to have been invalid at all times.

The Court as Protector of Property Rights. By then, national attention had shifted to the great postwar economic expansion underway, and the constitutional issues it raised. The Supreme Court is commonly referred to by the name of its chief justice—the Marshall Court, the Taney Court—and in some instances the chief did exert a commanding influence. But the associate justices, the so-called "side judges," also can have great influence—sometimes greater influence than that of the chief. This proved the case in the latter nineteenth century when Chief Justices Morrison R. Waite (1816–1888, chief justice 1874–1888) and Melville W. Fuller (1833–1910, chief justice 1888–1910) were overshadowed by some of their associates, such as John Marshall *Harlan and, above all, Stephen J. Field (1816–1899).

Field and his ideas came to dominate the Court, and his fierce protection of property rights against state regulation of any sort, complete *laissez-faire, strongly influenced the Court until the 1930s. The new industrialists looked to the courts to protect them from reformers who wanted to regulate private property in the name of the public good or to protect labor from the harsh conditions of mine and factory.

In *Munn* v. *Illinois* (1877), over a strong protest from Field, Chief Justice Waite held that states could regulate the rates charged by common carriers. But in the next two decades Field won a majority to his view that states had little or no power to regulate rates or to interfere in any way with vested property rights. The notion of the judiciary as the defender of property as against populist efforts to reform through regulation shaped the Court's decisions from the late nineteenth century until 1937. In a strong dissent in **Lochner* v. *New York* (1905), Oliver Wendell *Holmes Jr. sharply criticized the Supreme Court's hostility to worker-protection legislation in the name of property rights; the Constitution, he insisted, "is not intended to embody a particular economic theory, whether of paternalism . . . or of *laissez faire*." The Court did, in fact, approve some Progressive-era laws protecting women and children, most notably in **Muller* v. *Oregon* (1908), in which attorney Louis *Brandeis, defending Oregon's right to regulate the hours of working women, presented a brief full of sociological data. (Brandeis himself was appointed to the Supreme Court in 1916 by President Woodrow *Wilson, and confirmed despite fierce conservative—and in some cases anti-Semitic—opposition.) Nevertheless, in **Adkins* v. *Children's Hospital* (1923), the high court make clear its position that in all circumstances government regulation of the economy would be the exception, and laissez-faire the rule.

As in the Civil War, *World War I again raised the issue of the government's right to limit First Amendment free-speech protections. Writing for the majority in **Schenck* v. *United States* (1919), Justice Holmes upheld the wartime Espionage Act, but enunciated the principle that only a "clear and present danger" could justify restraints on free speech. In a notable dissent in **Abrams* v. *United States* (1919), involving the wartime Sedition Amendment, Holmes eloquently called for "free trade in ideas."

The Supreme Court in the New Deal and Civil Rights Eras. When Depression struck in 1929, and especially after Franklin Delano *Roosevelt's New Deal began trying to meliorate its effects, reformers hit a stone wall of conservatism on the high court. A bloc of four—Pierce Butler, James McReynolds, George Sutherland, and Willis Van Devanter—opposed any and all reform measures, often securing Owen J. Roberts as their fifth vote.

To remove what he saw as an unwarranted block to popular demands for reform, Roosevelt proposed a bill in February 1937 that would have allowed him to name up to six more justices on the Court. The public reaction to Roosevelt's so-called Court-packing plan eventually led Congress to reject it. But the overwhelmingly negative public response to the Court's reactionary stance hastened the retirement of the conservatives and the appointment of justices thoroughly sympathetic to the New Deal and state efforts to reform the economy. After several decades of a cramped view of the Commerce Clause, Justice Robert Jackson in *Wickard* v. *Filburn* (1942) gave Congress such an expanded view of that power that it would be a half century before the Court would invalidate a federal law as having exceeded the commerce power.

In fact the Court's agenda had begun to change in the 1920s, as more and more cases involving individual rights rather than property rights came up for review. Louis Brandeis had suggested that the *Fourteenth Amendment's Due Process Clause included more than property rights, and by 1926 the incorporation of the protections included in the *Bill of Rights into the Due Process Clause had begun, and in a series of cases that *de facto* overruled *Barron* v. *Baltimore*, the Court applied to the states the Constitution's guarantees of freedom of speech and freedom of the press and criminal-procedure protections.

In 1938, in the otherwise obscure case *United States* v. *Carolene Products*, Justice Harlan Fiske *Stone suggested in footnote four that the Court should apply higher standards of review to those issues involving individual rights or affecting discrete and insular minorities. During the 1940s and 1950s, and especially during the chief justiceship of Earl *Warren, which began in 1953, the Court began to do this in earnest, first elaborating the meaning of the speech clause (despite some set-backs during the *Cold War), and then undertaking to make people of color full citizens. A series of cases led up to the Warren Court's epic decision in **Brown* v. *Board of Education* (1954) that reversed the holding in **Plessy* v. *Ferguson* (1896) and other cases that permitted states to impose an apartheid system separating and humiliating blacks. In the years that followed, the Court upheld one challenge after another to laws and customs that segregated people on the basis of color.

The Warren Court did not invent the rights revolution, but many of the most famous cases expanding the meaning of *civil rights and *civil liberties were decided between 1953 and 1969, when Warren retired. *Mapp* v. *Ohio* (1961) expanded the protections of the Fourth Amendment, while *Gideon* v. *Wainwright* (1963) and **Miranda* v. *Arizona* (1966) ensured that all criminal defendants would have attorneys and protected the rights of persons in police custody. *Griswold* v. *Connecticut* (1965), involving the distribution of birth-control information, established a right to privacy, while *Reynolds* v. *Sims* (1964) transformed the American political scene by requiring states to reapportion their legislatures on the basis of "one person, one vote."

The rights revolution once again underscored the Court's co-equal role alongside the executive and legislative branches. Not all Americans welcomed this judicial activism, and many conservatives believed the Court had gone too far in its solicitude for minorities and accused criminals. Richard M. *Nixon, in the 1968 electoral campaign, promised that if elected he would appoint a "law-and-order" judiciary, and yet the rights revolution continued under Chief Justice Warren Burger (1907–1995, chief justice 1969–1986) thanks in large measure to the skill and influence of Justice William J. Brennan Jr. (1906–1997). The Burger Court handed down one of the most controversial decisions of the twentieth century, **Roe* v. *Wade* (1973), establishing a woman's right to an *abortion, and struck down many legal barriers that had made women second-class citizens. While it modified some Warren Court rulings, the Burger Court generally confirmed the growing rights consciousness in the country.

Recent Trends. That began to change in 1986, when Burger retired and President Ronald *Reagan named William H. Rehnquist (1924–) chief justice, and Antonin Scalia to serve alongside him. These two appointments, as well as three others made by Reagan and his successor George *Bush, gave the Court a more conservative cast than it had had in fifty years. While some conservatives cheered the efforts to cut back on constitutionally protected rights, others were dismayed. Whatever the lasting effect of the Rehnquist era, it seemed probable that just as the pendulum swung away from *conservatism in the 1930s and away from a liberal rights consciousness in the 1970s, this latest effort to push the constitutional balance far in one direction would elicit a countervailing trend in the opposite direction.

For its first 178 years, the Supreme Court consisted exclusively of white males. This changed in 1967 when President Lyndon B. *Johnson elevated the African-American civil-rights leader Thurgood *Marshall to the high court. The first woman justice, Sandra Day *O'Connor, was appointed by President Ronald Reagan in 1981.

[*See also* Birth Control and Family Planning; *Cherokee Cases; Dartmouth College Case;* Federal Government, Judicial Branch; Jurisprudence; Liberalism; Municipal Judicial System; Political Parties; Segregation, Racial; Social Darwinism; States' Rights.]

• Charles Warren, *The Supreme Court in United States History,* 2 vols., 1926. William F. Swindler, *Court and Constitution in the Twentieth Century,* 3 vols., 1969–1974. G. Edward White, *The American Judicial Tradition,* 1988. David P. Currie, *The Constitution in the Supreme Court,* 2 vols., 1985, 1990. Kermit Hall, ed., *The Oxford Companion to the Supreme Court of the United States,* 1992. Bernard Schwartz, *A History of the Supreme Court,* 1993. Melvin I. Urofsky, ed., *The Supreme Court Justices: A Biographical Dictionary,* 1994.

—Melvin I. Urofsky

SURGERY. Surgery in colonial America was taught chiefly by apprenticeship and practiced in the patient's home. Unlike English surgeons, who formed a profession apart from physicians and apothecaries, American surgeons were distinguished from physicians neither by licensure nor societies. The establishment of *hospitals and medical colleges in *Philadelphia and *New York City during the late *Colonial Era and the resumption of European travel after the *Revolutionary War offered surgeons educational options besides apprenticeship. Many prominent late eighteenth- and nineteenth-century American physicians who advanced both the teaching and practice of surgery—such as Philip Syng Physick in Philadelphia, the nation's first professor of surgery; Valentine Mott and David Hosack in New

York City; and *Boston's Oliver Wendell Holmes Sr.—trained in European hospitals and imported European ideas and techniques. American physicians took pride in their surgical skills and in such innovations as Ephraim McDowell's 1809 ovariotomy and J. Marion Sim's 1849 vesicovaginal fistula.

After William T. G. Morton, a dentist, developed sulfuric ether as an anesthetic, John Collins Warren, of a prestigious Boston medical family, and Henry Jacob Bigelow introduced it on 16 October 1845 at the Massachusetts General Hospital. Within ten years, the surgical use of anesthesia had spread around the world, enhancing the prestige of American surgery.

Although anesthesia removed the fear of pain from surgery, surgical infections remained a problem. In 1867 the Scottish surgeon Joseph Lister announced an antiseptic method of treating surgical wounds. That same year, several American surgeons adopted Lister's carbolic acid spray—thereby touching off a twenty-year debate over whether or not Louis Pasteur's and Robert Koch's newly announced germ theory of *disease adequately explained surgical sepsis. By the 1890s aseptic surgery—performed in a germ-free surgical area with sterilized equipment—became the norm in American surgery. William Stewart Halsted's popularization of the surgical rubber glove around 1890 proved a notable American contribution to asepsis.

In the 1870–1920 era, reforms of *medical education at Harvard, the University of Pennsylvania, and especially Baltimore's Johns Hopkins University Medical School and Hospital improved the surgeon's education and professional status. Rigorous and lengthy clinical training replaced the short courses, European *Wanderjahre,* and apprenticeships of antebellum America. Although surgical education remained closely linked to medical education generally, surgeons began to form their own professional societies. The American Surgical Association, founded in 1880, first met in 1882, and launched a journal, the *Transactions of the American Surgical Association,* in 1883. A century later, several specialized associations and journals reflected surgery's diversity.

Throughout the nineteenth century, surgeons continued to operate mostly in the patient's home and limited themselves mainly to such procedures as amputations, hernia repair, and the excision of growths. After 1900, the hospital increasingly became the locus of surgical activity. The evolution of hospitals and operating rooms into complex institutions, technologically and organizationally, gave rise to ancillary disciplines such as surgical *nursing, radiology, and anesthesiology and encouraged the growth of pharmaceutical and surgical-instrument industries. Among the first surgeons to specialize were the pioneering neurosurgeons Harvey Cushing at the Harvard Medical School and the Peter Bent Brigham Hospital and Walter Dandy at the Johns Hopkins Memorial Hospital. In 1902 Alexis Carrel aseptically rejoined severed blood vessels without thrombosis; in 1905 he and Charles Claude Guthrie transplanted a dog's kidney. Although the dog died, the dream did not.

The application of ideas or inventions initially unconnected with surgery often spurred the development of the field. Karl Landsteiner's discovery of blood types in 1901 removed the theoretical barrier to blood transfusions; George Washington Crile performed the first successful transfusion between patients in 1905. When the pharmaceutical and technical problems of blood storage were solved by the end of *World War II, blood loss and shock disappeared as major hurdles to surgical procedures. Advances in immunology, genetics, and pharmacology enabled Joseph Murray to accomplish the first successful kidney transplant in 1954. Thomas Starzl, using cyclosporin, developed the protocols for successful liver transplants, and Francis Moore and Norman Shumway, among others, developed them for heart transplants. Lasers transformed ophthalmic surgery, while CT (computerized tomography) scans and MRIs (magnetic resonance imaging) extended imaging technology far beyond the X ray. Helen Taussig and Alfred *Blalock developed a surgical correction for the tetralogy of Fallot ("blue babies") in 1944, using insights gained from fluoroscope images and advances on Carrel's method. If inventions stimulated surgery, the reverse was likewise true. Difficulties in thoracic and cardiac surgery, for example, motivated John H. Gibbon's invention of the heart-lung machine during the 1940s. This, in turn, made open-heart surgery possible, and prompted Medtronics, Inc., to develop the pacemaker in the 1950s. Orthopedic surgery grew with improvements in prosthetic devices.

The individualism and technical virtuosity of eighteenth- and nineteenth-century surgery gave way in the twentieth to teamwork and a more solid scientific foundation. The *Mayo Clinic in Rochester, Minnesota, for example, gained fame for its advancement of the surgical arts and for being one of the first American medical group practices. William Halsted's importance in the annals of surgery derives not only from his introduction of rubber gloves and improved surgical techniques, but also from his insistence that surgery be pursued collaboratively with the basic clinical sciences. Owen H. Wangensteen of the University of Minnesota Medical School, like Halsted, taught generations of future surgeons that surgery rests on scientific foundations. In 1952 a team at Minnesota headed by C. Walton Lillehei successfully conducted the first open-heart surgery under direct vision, an achievement made possible by collaboration among cardiac physiologists, anatomists, and surgeons.

[*See also* Heart Disease; Medicine; Pharmaceutical Industry.]

• Martin S. Pernick, *A Calculus of Suffering: Pain, Professionalism, and Anesthesia in Nineteenth-Century America,* 1985. Charles E. Rosenberg, *The Care of Strangers: The Rise of America's Hospital System,* 1987. Ira M. Rutkow, *The History of Surgery in the United States 1775–1900,* 2 vols., 1988, 1992. Christopher Lawrence, ed., *Medical Theory, Surgical Practice: Studies in the History of Surgery,* 1992. Joel D. Howell, *Technology in the Hospital: Transforming Patient Care in the Early Twentieth Century,* 1995.

—Thomas P. Gariepy

SWANN* v. *CHARLOTTE-MECKLENBURG BOARD OF EDUCATION (1971), a landmark U.S. *Supreme Court decision, based on a case arising in North Carolina, that extended to large metropolitan school districts the duty to dismantle *de jure* (legally established) *racial segregation. Crafted by Justice Potter Stewart, the unanimous ruling upheld federal district judge James B. McMillan's countywide busing order. According to the Court, busing schoolchildren to achieve greater racial balance in individual schools is a constitutionally proper remedy in districts burdened by the effects of past or present *de jure* segregation. Dismissing the North Carolina school board's argument that Judge McMillan's race-based busing order violated the 1964 Civil Rights Act, the Court sanctioned the use of optimal racial percentages and the involuntary transfer of children to schools outside of their neighborhoods.

Swann placed a heavy burden of proof on any school board attempting to demonstrate that racially imbalanced schools did not reflect official policy, but rather resulted from de facto forces. As a result, it became the touchstone of school desegregation litigation in the 1970s and 1980s mandating the use of court-ordered busing programs in hundreds of American cities. The effects of such programs were mixed, leading to meaningful desegregation in some districts and counterproductive "white flight" in others. In many communities, the dictates of the *Swann* decision triggered widespread opposition to "forced busing" among angry parents who demanded a return to traditional neighborhood schools. The opponents of court-ordered busing received a measure of legal relief in the early 1990s when the Court weakened *Swann* by ruling (in *Board of Education* v. *Dowell,* 1991, and *Freeman* v. *Pitts,* 1992) that lower courts could suspend busing programs in districts that made a good-faith and "reasonable" effort to desegregate.

[*See also* *Brown* v. *Board of Education;* Civil Rights Legislation; Civil Rights Movement; Education: Education in Contemporary America.]

• Bernard Schwartz, *Swann's Way: The School Busing Case and the Supreme Court,* 1986. Bob Woodward and Scott Armstrong, *The Brethren: Inside the Supreme Court,* 1988, pp. 96–112.

—Raymond O. Arsenault

SWEATSHOPS. *See* Domestic Labor; Homework.

SWIFT, GUSTAVUS (1839–1903), meatpacker and corporate innovator. The younger son of a large Cape Cod farm family, Gustavus F. Swift rose from a partnership in a *Boston wholesale meat market to become a legendary captain of the meatpacking industry in *Chicago. The key to Swift's ascendancy was his use of refrigerated railroad cars to ship dressed beef from livestock markets and packing plants in Chicago and other western centers to eastern, urban markets. Employing that technology to integrate the entire production-to-distribution process, Swift undercut eastern centers by as much as 75 cents per hundred weight. By 1886, his Chicago packing plant, Swift and Company, utilized an advanced division of labor to produce three thousand carcasses a week. The company operated a national network of twenty-four refrigerated branch distribution outlets and four hundred refrigerator cars while maintaining an army of traveling salesmen who convinced local retailers of their product's safety and high quality.

Swift's leading Chicago competitors quickly adopted his innovations in distribution and production. By the time of his death, Swift and Company was one of four firms supplying more than half the nation's meat. Collectively keeping labor costs low and pricing their goods on the basis of average costs rather than supply and demand, these firms dominated the industry into the 1950s. Swift was a true entrepreneurial pioneer—an innovator who shook up the established order. He played a key role in the emergence of the modern managerial corporation based on the concentration within a single business enterprise of activities formerly dispersed among multiple small companies.

[*See also* Food and Diet; Gilded Age; Industrialization; Livestock Industry; Mass Production; Meatpacking and Meat Processing Industry; Railroads; Urbanization.]

• Mary Yeager, *Competition and Regulation: The Development of Oligopoly in the Meatpacking Industry,* 1981. Jimmy Skaggs, *Prime Cut: Livestock Raising and Meatpacking in the United States, 1607–1983,* 1986.

—Paul Street

SYPHILIS. *See* Venereal Disease.

T

TAFT, ROBERT (1889–1953), U.S. senator, *Republican party leader, and son of President William Howard *Taft. Born in Cincinnati, Ohio, Taft graduated from Yale University, earned a degree from Harvard Law School in 1913, and married Martha Wheaton Bowers the following year. They had four sons.

Taft got his start in politics by serving in the Ohio House of Representatives (1921–1926) and the Ohio Senate (1931–1932). An arch critic of Franklin Delano *Roosevelt's *New Deal, he won a U.S. Senate seat in 1938 and was reelected in 1944 and 1950. While strongly opposed to FDR's interventionist foreign policy in the later 1930s, Taft supported the war effort after the attack on *Pearl Harbor. Following *World War II, he remained skeptical of the so-called bipartisanship in foreign affairs—voting for American membership in the *United Nations but opposing the *North Atlantic Treaty Organization. Taft also condemned President Harry S. *Truman's commitment of American troops to Korea in 1950 without a formal declaration of war, calling the action unconstitutional. In domestic affairs, he coauthored the *Taft-Hartley Act (1947), which limited the activities of labor unions, and he encouraged the early Red-hunting activities of his junior Republican colleague Senator Joseph *McCarthy of Wisconsin.

Known as "Mr. Republican," Taft was deeply skeptical of federal power, which grew dramatically in the 1930s and after. Running as a conservative, he unsuccessfully sought the Republican presidential nomination in 1940, 1948, and 1952, failing each time to win the support of the more liberal and internationalist Eastern wing of the party. Following President Dwight D. *Eisenhower's inauguration in 1953, Taft enjoyed his greatest political success as an effective Senate majority leader. In June of that year, however, rapidly progressing cancer forced him to relinquish his leadership role.

[*See also* Conservatism; Federal Government, Legislative Branch: Senate; Isolationism; Korean War.]

• James T. Patterson, *Mr. Republican: A Biography of Robert A. Taft*, 1972. Robert Merry, "Robert A. Taft: A Study in the Accumulation of Legislative Power," in *First Among Equals: Outstanding Senate Leaders of the Twentieth Century*, ed. Richard A. Baker and Roger H. Davidson, 1991, pp. 163–98.

—Gary W. Reichard

TAFT, WILLIAM HOWARD (1857–1930), twenty-seventh president of the United States, chief justice of the United States. A native of Cincinnati, Ohio, Taft graduated from Yale and the Cincinnati Law School. He married Helen Herron in 1886. After a legal career in Ohio including three years as a superior court judge, he was named solicitor general of the Justice Department in 1890 and became a federal circuit judge in 1892. President William *McKinley appointed Taft to head the Philippine Commission in 1900, in which capacity he proved an effective colonial administrator. Three years later, President Theodore *Roosevelt appointed him secretary of war. In 1908, having won the Republican nomination for president as Roosevelt's designated successor, Taft defeated the Democratic candidate, William Jennings *Bryan.

The rotund and lawyerlike Taft did not enjoy a happy presidency. Lacking Roosevelt's sure political touch, he had poor press relations and gravitated toward the conservative wing of his party in an era of reform. He proved unable to satisfy Republican Progressives who wanted more of the political and economic reform of the Roosevelt years. His mishandling of the Payne-Aldrich Tariff in 1909 alienated advocates of lower customs duties; the *Ballinger-Pinchot Controversy over conservation strained his friendship with Roosevelt. Republican losses in the 1910 elections reflected voter unhappiness with the administration.

During his last two years in the White House, Taft unsuccessfully pursued a reciprocal trade agreement with Canada and international arbitration treaties. Meanwhile, his relations with Roosevelt deteriorated. By early 1912, the former president was openly maneuvering to supplant Taft as the Republican nominee. A fierce struggle ensued in which Taft's command of the machinery of the *Republican party enabled him to repel Roosevelt's challenge. Bitter over his defeat, Roosevelt bolted the GOP and started a third party. After a desultory campaign against both Roosevelt and the Democratic candidate, Woodrow *Wilson of New Jersey, Taft came in third in the popular vote and won the electoral votes of only Vermont and Utah.

Out of office, Taft taught at Yale Law School and remained active behind the scenes in Republican politics. During *World War I he served on the National War Labor Board. He advocated world organization through the League to Enforce Peace. After the Republicans under Warren G. *Harding regained the White House in 1921, Taft became the chief justice of the United States. Happy at last in a position that suited him, Taft presided over the *Supreme Court in an harmonious fashion, he played a large role in the selection of Supreme Court justices during his tenure and improved many of the Court's working procedures. His votes on particular cases reflected the *conservatism of his later years, especially on such issues as the rights of labor unions and efforts to curb the power of corporations. Taft's presidency had creditable achievements, but his place between Theodore Roosevelt and Woodrow Wilson has consigned him to the ranks of less-than-successful chief executives.

[*See also* Conservation Movement; Federal Government, Executive Branch: The Presidency; Philippines; Progressive Era; Tariffs.]

• Henry F. Pringle, *The Life and Times of William Howard Taft* 2 vols., 1939. Lewis L. Gould, *Reform and Regulation: American Politics from Roosevelt to Wilson*, 3d. ed., 1996.

—Lewis L. Gould

TAFT-HARTLEY ACT, 1947 labor law passed over President Harry S. *Truman's veto. A series of attacks on the *National Labor Relations Board (NLRB), particularly the hostile investigation of the board conducted by the Virginia congressman Howard Smith in 1939–1940, created public distrust of the agency and support for amendments to the 1935 *National Labor Relations (Wagner) Act, to restore a balance of power between labor and management. A series of postwar strikes in basic industries such as coal, steel, automobiles, and railroads reinforced the public view that unions had become "too powerful." Charges of union corruption; racial discrimination; and, in some cases, communist domination heightened the antilabor climate. A Republican victory in the 1946 congressional elections gave critics of the Wagner Act sufficient power to change the nation's labor policy. Senator Robert *Taft, chairman of the Senate Labor Committee, and the New Jersey congressman Fred Hartley, the new chair of the House Committee on Education and Labor, offered separate bills that Senate and House conferees combined into the Taft-Hartley Bill.

Taft-Hartley expanded the NLRB from three members to five and created an independent NLRB general counsel as the agency's prosecuting arm, replacing the general counsel who had functioned as part of the board. It included the Wagner Act's preamble encouraging the practices and procedures of collective bargaining but now emphasized workers' right to refrain from such activities. The bill specified unfair union labor practices, established provisions protecting employers' right of "free speech" to resist unionization, authorized the president to intervene in labor disputes by invoking an eighty-day "national emergency" injunction, and required the NLRB to seek injunctions against unions involved in secondary boycotts or jurisdictional strikes. It also required union officials to sign noncommunist affidavits to obtain the law's protection, outlawed the closed shop, and permitted states to prohibit other forms of compulsory union-membership clauses.

Although Taft-Hartley was hardly the "slave labor law" unions claimed it to be, its emphasis on the right to reject collective bargaining, its protection of employee and employer rights against unions, and its listing of specific unfair labor practices by unions did encourage employers to resist unionization and collective bargaining. Yet the core of the Wagner Act survived in Taft-Hartley, so that interpretations of the law's meaning came to depend primarily on which political party held power. The related *Landrum-Griffin Act of 1959 further restricted certain boycott and picketing practices by organized labor, though it did give workers who lost their jobs in a strike the continued right to vote in union elections.

[*See also* Anticommunism; Industrial Relations; Labor Markets; Labor Movements; Strikes and Industrial Conflict.]

• James A. Gross, *Broken Promise: The Subversion of U.S. Labor Relations Policy, 1947–1994*, 1995.

—James A. Gross

TANEY, ROGER B. (1777–1864), chief justice of the United States from 1836 until his death. Taney's reputation has never recovered from the catastrophe of his majority opinion in the **Scott* v. *Sandford* (Dred Scott) case of 1857. He blighted his considerable accomplishments by his dedication to *slavery, but he made lasting and significant contributions to the law of corporations, federal jurisdiction, and state regulatory power.

Born on a tobacco plantation in southern Maryland and educated at Dickinson College in Pennsylvania, Taney was admitted to the Maryland bar in 1799. He served in the state legislature, became a Jacksonian Democrat, and was attorney general of the United States (1831–1833) and secretary of the treasury (1833–1834) in Andrew *Jackson's cabinet.

Taney's most important opinions include **Charles River Bridge* v. *Warren Bridge* (1837), which refused to read an implied grant of monopoly privileges into a corporate charter; *Propeller Genesee Chief* v. *Fitzhugh* (1851), extending federal admiralty jurisdiction to inland navigable waters; and *Prigg v. Pennsylvania* (1842), a concurrence in which he insisted on complete and exclusive state regulatory authority over all aspects of slavery.

In the Dred Scott ruling, Taney held that no black American descended from slaves could ever be a citizen of the United States and that Congress lacked constitutional power to exclude slavery from the territories. In thus attempting to impose an undemocratic judicial solution on a grave political and moral issue, Taney both degraded the role of the *Supreme Court and besmirched his positive contributions to American public law.

[*See also* Antebellum Era; Civil War: Causes; Democratic Party; Economic Regulation.]

• Carl B. Swisher, *The Taney Period, 1835–64*, 1974.

—William M. Wiecek

TARIFF OF ABOMINATIONS. *See* Tariffs.

TARIFFS. Tariffs have a long premodern history, but in U.S. history they have served two primary purposes: (1) to protect the domestic economy and specific economic sectors from foreign competition and (2) to raise government revenues. Even before the founding of the United States, British attempts to regulate imperial trade through tariffs and taxes precipitated resistance in the American colonies. Hence, the *Constitution of 1789 gave the new federal government control of overseas commerce, and Congress set low tariff rates solely to raise revenue to cover public expenses and obligations. The first secretary of the treasury, Alexander *Hamilton, proposed higher tariffs to promote domestic industry but found scant support in Congress.

Between 1816 and 1820, Congress raised some tariffs to project "infant" industries from British competition, but most imports traded freely. Political party competition and the rise of manufacturing in *New England as shipping declined produced a high tariff in 1828, denounced as the "Tariff of Abominations" by agrarians in the *South and *West who favored a low tariff policy benefiting U.S. agricultural exports. When Congress passed another high tariff in 1832, the South Carolina legislature declared both the 1828 and 1832 tariffs null and void in the state, leading to a *states'-rights confrontation—the so-called *Nullification Crisis—pitting South Carolina and its political leader, John C. *Calhoun, against the Andrew *Jackson administration. Over the next three decades, however, southern and western congressmen, whose constituents depended on agricultural exports, kept tariffs low and promoted free-trade principles.

The federal government's financial needs during the *Civil War and the absence of southern congressmen led to higher tariffs in the 1860s. From the Civil War through the 1920s, the *Republican party advocated high tariffs to favor domestic industry, protect U.S. workers against low-wage foreign labor, and defend the "American standard of living." When the *Democratic party regained national power in 1913, southern leaders through the Underwood-Simmons Tariff lowered average rates to antebellum levels. The return to Republican dominance in the 1920s restored high rates, however, through the Fordney-McCumber (1922) and Smoot-Hawley (1930) tariffs. These high protective tariffs disrupted international trade and contributed to the Great Depression of the 1930s. To reinvigorate international trade and promote U.S. exports, President Franklin Delano *Roosevelt supported the Reciprocal Trade Agreements Act of 1934. This measure authorized the president to negotiate bilateral tariff reductions with America's trading partners. After *World War II, twenty-three industrial nations institutionalized reciprocal-trade principles on a multilateral basis in the *General Agreement on Tariffs and Trade (1948). Lower tariff rates negotiated under GATT laid the foundation for the reconstruction of the international economy on free-trade principles and fueled the postwar growth of the industrial economies. By century's end, 124 nations belonged to GATT, known after 1995 as the World Trade Organization (WTO). In 1960 and 1964, Congress passed Trade Expansion Acts; they set the stage for GATT negotiations in 1967 that lowered tariffs still further and practically eliminated those on machinery, chemicals, and transportation equipment. In the ensuing decade U.S. exports and imports doubled, pushing merchandise trade, as a share of the gross domestic product, to levels not seen since 1913. Multilateral trade liberalization also enabled the United States to strengthen its anti-Soviet *Cold War alliances and bolster its allies' economic health at low political cost.

Because the U.S. economy was the world's most prosperous

and productive from 1945 through 1973, the United States allowed many of its allies, including the member nations of the European Economic Union (EU), launched in 1948, to protect their domestic industries and agriculture. By the mid-1970s, however, as foreign competition increased and the U.S. economy faltered because of rising energy costs, imperiled U.S. industries, especially steel, textiles, and automobiles, petitioned Congress for protection. Textiles obtained the Multi-Fiber Arrangement (1974), by which overseas competitors voluntarily limited their exports. Under pressure, Japan in 1981 "voluntarily" restricted its auto exports to the United States.

Congress also adopted a confrontational strategy to restore "lost competitiveness" and to protect newer American service industries, *agriculture, trade-related investments, and intellectual-property rights. The Omnibus Trade and Competitiveness Act (1988) gave the president an array of coercive powers, including quotas, "voluntary" restraint agreements, and domestic subsidies, to wrest concessions from recalcitrant trading partners who used various nontariff barriers to limit imports. The U.S. also supported the WTO's efforts to combat nontariff barriers to free trade. The 1999 telecommunications agreement between Japan and the United States required the Japanese government to monitor actively Japanese companies that unfairly discriminated against U.S. competition.

The formation of regional preferential tariff systems that discriminated between members and nonmembers challenged GATT's multilateral approach. The EU from the beginning circumvented GATT rules. In 1976, for example, the EU set up a preferential tariff system linking former colonies to the European Common Market. The United States conceded the utility of this approach by emulating it. In 1988, Canada and the United States formed a free-trade zone that became the world's largest when Mexico joined in 1994, through the *North American Free Trade Agreement (NAFTA). Caribbean nations were invited to participate as well. An Asian trading system centered around Japan, though less formally organized, showed similar regional aspects.

As the century ended, the U.S. effort to eliminate nontariff barriers to trade globalization, coupled with the emerging world information network, had profound political and social implications. Critics warned that a supranational trading authority such as the WTO could arouse nationalism or reinforce a tendency toward rival regional systems. Protesters cautioned that global trading arrangements weakened efforts to protect the environment and workers' rights. U.S. efforts in the 1990s to bring the communist People's Republic of China into the WTO proved deeply divisive domestically. Supporters of WTO responded that international political stability would benefit if global economic integration, through the elimination of tariff and nontariff trade barriers, outweighed the attractions of regional trade alliances. Whether the American initiative would lead to a stable and equitable multilateralism in the global environment remained an open question as the twenty-first century began.

[*See also* Automotive Industry; Depressions, Economic; Economic Development; Foreign Relations: The Economic Dimension; Foreign Trade, U.S.; Global Economy, America and the; Iron and Steel Industry; Textile Industry.]

• Harry G. Johnson, *International Trade and Economic Growth*, 1958. John M. Dobson, *Two Centuries of Tariffs: The Background and Emergence of the U.S. International Trade Commission*, 1976. Patrick Low, *Trading Free: The GATT and U.S. Trade Policy*, 1993. Jeffrey E. Garten, "Is America Abandoning Multilateral Trade?" *Foreign Affairs* (Nov.–Dec. 1995): 50–62. Douglas Irwin, *From Smoot-Hawley to Reciprocal Trade Agreements: The Changing Course of U.S. Trade Policy in the 1930's*, 1997.

—Paul P. Abrahams

TAXATION. The fundamental structure of the American tax system emerged from the extended political crisis that led to the formation of the U.S. *Constitution. Its architects struggled with the problems of how to finance the *Revolutionary War debts and establish the nation's credit in international financial markets. Consequently, the Constitution gave the new government clear fiscal authority to establish its sovereignty. In the words of Article I, Section 8, Congress had the general power "to lay and collect taxes, duties, imposts, and excises."

The one tax that the new federal government could not enact was a property tax. Property taxation had been the mainstay of local government in the *Colonial Era, and after 1775 the newly independent states employed it extensively and worried that the proposed national government might preempt its use. Accordingly, Article I, Section 9 required that Congress allocate direct taxes, like property taxes, to the states in proportion to their population, rather than to the value of their property.

Taxation in the Early National Era. The financial program of Alexander *Hamilton, the first secretary of the treasury, established *tariffs, set at low rates, as the major source of the federal government's revenue. Tariff revenues paid off the Revolutionary War debts and financed the *Quasi-War with France in the late 1790s and President Thomas *Jefferson's war against the Barbary pirates. Tariff revenues, in combination with borrowing and land sales, funded the *Louisiana Purchase and allowed presidents from Jefferson through John Quincy *Adams to implement an ambitious program of internal improvements. By 1836, tariff revenues had enabled the federal government to retire its debt, and in 1837 customs duties also enabled President Martin *Van Buren to distribute surplus revenues to the states for internal improvements.

Before the *Civil War, the nation's leaders rarely broke from a reliance on low tariffs. One exception occurred in the early 1790s, when Congress followed the recommendation of President George *Washington and Secretary Hamilton and enacted the nation's first excise taxes. These applied to distilled spirits and touched off the *Whiskey Rebellion of 1794. The revolt ended significant use of excise taxation until the Civil War.

Congress also experimented with high tariffs from the 1820s until the early 1830s. Protective tariffs were imposed to promote *industrialization and to shelter America's high-wage workers and high-cost industries from British competition. But American industries quickly become competitive, and southern planters and western farmers resisted tariffs that increased the price of manufactured goods. Southern politicians, especially in South Carolina, denounced the 1828 tariff legislation as the "Tariff of Abominations" and vowed to overturn it. During the *Nullification Crisis of 1832–1833, high tariffs came to symbolize federal power for South Carolinians worried about the future of *slavery.

Consequently, Congress in 1833 reduced tariffs and in 1846 passed the low Walker Tariff, which paralleled Britain's repeal of the Corn Laws in the same year, another defeat for protectionism. These actions heralded the adoption of free trade throughout the Anglo-American world.

Meanwhile, state and local governments developed revenue systems that relied heavily on property taxes. As the Industrial Revolution gathered force during the 1820s and 1830s, Jacksonian reformers extended property taxation, trying to tax all forms of wealth. By the Civil War, most states had a general property tax designed to reach not only real estate, tools, equipment, and furnishings, but also intangible personal property such as cash, credits, notes, stocks, bonds, and mortgages.

Civil War to World War I. The financial system of the early republic might have remained adequate for at least another generation had not the Civil War created such enormous requirements for capital that Washington had to adopt emergency taxes unprecedented in scale and scope.

The wartime government placed excise taxes on virtually all consumer goods, license taxes on a wide variety of activities (including every profession except the ministry), special taxes on corporations, stamp taxes on legal documents, and taxes on inheritances. Each wartime Congress also raised the tariffs on foreign goods. And, for the first time, the government levied a federal *income tax—a graduated tax reaching a maximum rate of 10 percent.

Republican Congresses phased out most of the excise taxes after the war and in 1872 allowed the income tax to expire. Republicans, however, maintained the consumption basis of the federal tax system by retaining two elements of the Civil War tax system. First, they kept high tariffs. Until the Underwood-Simmons Tariff of 1913 significantly reduced the Civil War rates, the tariff on dutiable goods often approached 50 percent of their value. By 1872, the tariff again supplied most federal revenues. The high-tariff system of the Civil War Era came to be justified as a means of creating a national market and protecting American industries and their workers. Second, Republicans retained the taxes on alcohol and tobacco products. A buoyant demand for both meant that revenues from these levies produced at least one-third of all federal tax revenues. These taxes appealed to moralists as discouragements to, and punishments for, the consumption of commodities they stigmatized as sinful and threatening to a virtuous social order.

Between the Civil War and *World War I, however, the class and sectional tensions created by industrialization increased political pressure for reform of the federal tax system. One result was the enactment in 1894 of a progressive income tax (i.e., rates rose as incomes increased). But in 1895 the *Supreme Court, in *Pollock* v. *Farmers' Loan and Trust Co.*, declared this measure unconstitutional because it was a direct tax not assessed in proportion to population. Popular support for progressive income taxation grew, however, and in 1909 congressional reformers from both parties sent the *Sixteenth Amendment, legalizing a federal income tax, to the states for ratification. It prevailed in 1913, and Congress forthwith passed a modest income tax.

State and local governments, too, gradually transformed their tax systems. With *urbanization, the rising demands for parks, schools, hospitals, transit systems, waterworks, and sewers overwhelmed the long-established system of general property taxation. Traditional self-reporting of property holdings proved especially inadequate for assessing the value of "intangible" property such as stocks and bonds. Accordingly, most local governments focused property taxation on real estate, which they believed could be assessed accurately at relatively low cost. States gradually abandoned property taxation altogether and adopted special taxes to replace the lost revenues. In 1911, Wisconsin adopted the first modern income tax.

World War I expanded the use of income taxation by the federal government. Mobilization required enormous revenue, and President Woodrow *Wilson and other Democratic leaders strongly favored progressive income taxes and opposed the regressive general sales taxes preferred by the *Republican party. To persuade Americans to make financial and human sacrifices for World War I, President Wilson and Congress introduced significant progressive income taxation.

The World War I income tax, enacted in 1916 as a preparedness measure, was an explicit "soak-the-rich" levy. Rejecting an approach that would have fallen most heavily on wages and salaries, it imposed the first significant taxation of corporate profits and personal incomes, and placed a graduated tax on all business profits above a "normal" rate of return. This "excess-profits" tax actually raised most of the federal government's wartime tax revenues.

1920–1940. During the 1920s three successive Republican administrations granted substantial tax reductions to corporations and the wealthiest individuals. Secretary of the Treasury Andrew Mellon (1855–1937) argued that the tax cuts would promote economic *productivity and expansion. In 1921 Republicans abolished the excess-profits tax, dashing Democratic hopes that the tax would become permanent. In addition, Congress made the nominal rate structure of the income tax less burdensome on the wealthy and introduced a wide range of special tax exemptions and deductions, including the preferential taxation of capital gains and oil- and gas-depletion allowances.

Nonetheless, the tax system retained most of its "soak-the-rich" character. Indeed, Secretary Mellon struggled within the Republican party to defend income taxation against those who wanted to replace it with a national sales tax. He helped persuade corporations and the wealthiest individuals to accept some progressive income taxation and the principle of "ability to pay." This approach, Mellon told them, would defuse radical attacks on capitalists.

During the 1920s, state governments faced growing expenses for schools, highways and other needs but were reluctant to compete with the federal government for income-tax revenues. Instead, they expanded their use of sales taxes and of various levies such as vehicle-registration fees, license fees, and gasoline taxes designed to make vehicle users pay the cost of highways. During the 1930s, state governments further increased the scope and rates of their sales taxes until, in 1940, they were raising most of their funds by this means.

The Depression of the 1930s produced a new "soak-the-rich" tax system. Beginning in 1935, President Franklin Delano *Roosevelt and the Democratic Congress responded to threats from the left, particularly Huey *Long's "Share Our Wealth" movement, by increasing the taxes on the wealthiest individuals and corporations while adopting payroll taxes to fund the new *Social Security system. In 1936, Roosevelt and Congress took the radical step of enacting an undistributed-profits tax—a progressive tax on the profits that corporations did not distribute to their stockholders. This innovation, more than any other New Deal measure, aroused fear and hostility among large corporations. Business seized the political opening created by the recession of 1937–1938 and Roosevelt's faltering political power, and in 1938 and 1939 a congressional coalition of Republicans and conservative Democrats eliminated the undistributed-profits tax and halted New Deal tax reform.

World War II through the 1990s. During the mobilization for *World War II, Roosevelt sought to finance the war with substantial taxes on corporations and upper-income groups, but opposition to radical war-tax proposals proved too strong. One source of opposition came from a diverse group of military planners, foreign policy strategists, financial leaders, and economists. To mobilize greater resources than during World War I, and to do so more predictably while also reducing inflationary pressures, they favored a general sales tax or an income tax that would produce most of its revenue from wages and salaries. The second source of opposition to Roosevelt's radical wartime tax proposals came from Democrats in Congress and the administration. They worried that anticorporate taxation could cause a postwar slump and even another major depression.

In October 1942, Roosevelt and Congress finally reached a compromise. They dropped a general sales tax, which Roosevelt opposed, and adopted an income tax that was progressive, although not as progressive as Roosevelt wanted. The act substantially reduced personal exemptions, establishing the means for the federal government to acquire huge revenues from the taxation of middle-class wages and salaries. To make the new individual income tax work, the administration and Congress relied on payroll withholding, deductions that sweetened the tax system for the middle class, a progressive rate structure, and the popularity of the war effort.

Under the new tax system, the number of individual taxpayers soared from 3.9 million in 1939 to 42.6 million in 1945, and federal income-tax collections over the period leaped from $2.2 billion to $35.1 billion. Mass taxation had become more important than class taxation.

Victory in World War II and postwar prosperity produced a popular, bipartisan consensus for maintaining the wartime tax regime. This consensus meant that Republicans accepted levels of taxation on large incomes and corporate profits that were substantially higher than the prewar rates. Democrats, in turn, largely abandoned taxation as an instrument to mobilize class interests. Instead, adopting the principles of *Keynesianism, they used taxation as a means of stabilizing the economy, often giving Keynesian arguments a conservative twist. Presidents John F. *Kennedy and Lyndon B. *Johnson won bipartisan support for major tax cuts, enacted in 1964, by hawking the same growth-promoting, "supply-side" benefits that Andrew Mellon had urged during the 1920s.

The tax system of World War II endured for the rest of the twentieth century. Until the late 1970s, inflation and economic growth extended the system's life by pushing people into higher tax brackets (a process known as "bracket creep") and enlarging the tax base. The federal government could cut taxes while still funding national defense and creating new domestic programs. In the late 1970s, however, a stagnant economy eroded the system's basis. Also, a powerful antigovernment movement emerged. California voters in 1978 passed Proposition 13, which slashed property taxes, encouraging President Ronald *Reagan and Congress to make deep cuts in the federal income tax in 1981. The federal government subsequently ran huge budget deficits until the mid-1990s, when economic revival once again produced abundant income-tax revenues.

At century's end, antigovernment reformers proposed replacing the World War II system with more regressive taxes, such as a national sales tax. To succeed, they would have to persuade Americans to abandon their historic commitment to the progressive principle of taxation according to the "ability to pay."

[*See also* Business; Foreign Trade, U.S.; Laissez-faire; Monetary Policy, Federal; New Deal Era, The.]

• Randolph Paul, *Taxation in the United States,* 1954. Sidney Ratner, *Taxation and Democracy in America,* 1967. Mark Leff, *The Limits of Symbolic Reform: The New Deal and Taxation,* 1984. John Witte, *The Politics and Development of the Federal Income Tax,* 1985. Eugene Steuerle, *The Tax Decade, 1981–1990,* 1992. Ronald Frederick King, *Money, Time and Politics: Investment Tax Subsidies in American Democracy,* 1993. Robert Stanley, *Dimensions of Law in the Service of Order: Origins of the Federal Income Tax, 1861–1913,* 1993. W. Elliot Brownlee, *Federal Taxation in America: A Short History,* 1996. W. Elliot Brownlee, ed., *Funding the Modern American State, 1941–1995: The Rise and Fall of the Era of Easy Finance,* 1996.

—W. Elliot Brownlee

TAYLOR, FREDERICK W. *See* Scientific Management.

TAYLOR, ZACHARY (1784–1850), twelfth president of the United States. Born in Virginia and reared in Kentucky, Taylor acquired plantations and many slaves in Louisiana. Joining the army in 1808, he fought with distinction in the *War of 1812. Placed in command of western forts, he honored Indian treaties; prevented white settlement of Indian lands; and during the *Seminole wars in Florida, refused to return to their owners escaped slaves living with the Seminoles.

Although opposed to Texas annexation, Taylor in January 1846 was ordered by President James Knox *Polk to advance to the Rio Grande River. A Mexican attack on a unit of his army in April led to the *Mexican War. Winning battles against numerical odds, he became a national hero, nicknamed "Old Rough and Ready." As the *Whig party's presidential candidate in 1848, he defeated Democrat Lewis Cass. Although a slaveowner, Taylor as president defended the interests of slavery opponents. He angered fellow southerners by refusing to oppose the Wilmot Proviso banning *slavery from territories acquired from Mexico. He also opposed southern efforts to extend slavery by filibustering expeditions to seize Cuba from Spain. His administration's principal foreign-policy achievement was the *Clayton-Bulwer Treaty.

Seeking to defuse the bitter sectional controversy over the newly acquired territories, he supported statehood for *California and New Mexico on the understanding that they would themselves decide the slavery issue. With his support, California voted to become a free state. Slaveholding Texas, however, claimed most of New Mexico. Taylor's threat of military intervention may have prevented Texas from seizing New Mexico by force. When southern legislators combined Henry *Clay's compromise proposals into a single "Omnibus Bill," Taylor opposed it as an effort to advance Texas's New Mexico claims. The Omnibus Bill eventually failed, and the amended parts that did pass, as the *Compromise of 1850, generally conformed to Taylor's views. He did not live to see this outcome, however, having died on 9 July 1850 after a brief illness caused by gastroenteritis complicated by poor medical treatment. Vice president Millard *Fillmore succeeded him.

[*See also* Antebellum Era; Antislavery; Civil War: Causes; Expansionism; Federal Government, Executive Branch: The Presidency; Military, The; Political Parties; Texas Republic and Annexation.]

• Holman Hamiton, *Zachary Taylor, Soldier of the Republic,* 1941. Holman Hamilton, *Zachary Taylor, Soldier in the White House,* 1951. Elbert B. Smith, *The Presidencies of Zachary Taylor and Millard Fillmore,* 1988.

—Elbert B. Smith

TAYLORISM. *See* Scientific Management.

The **TEAPOT DOME SCANDAL,** one of the most sensational in American political history, took its name from the site of a naval oil reserve in Wyoming that in 1922 was leased by Secretary of the Interior Albert B. Fall to the oilman Harry F. Sinclair. This and a similar lease of the Elk Hills, California, reserve to Edward L. Doheny were possible because Fall, an advocate of private development, had recently persuaded President Warren G. *Harding to give him jurisdiction over the reserves and had won the navy's agreement by stipulating that oil royalties could be used to expand above-ground storage facilities. Conservationists objected strongly, and the secrecy surrounding the deal aroused suspicions of favoritism and bribery, especially when Fall began improvements on his New Mexico Ranch. The Senate voted to investigate, and in late 1923, after Harding's death and Fall's departure from the Cabinet, Senator Thomas J. Walsh began an inquiry.

As the story unfolded in subsequent governmental investigations and court cases, Fall had received $409,000 from the two oilmen, partly as unsecured, interest-free loans and partly through the assignment to him of $233,000 in government bonds. The leases would probably have been made without these incentives, but as the evidence of fraud mounted, they were canceled. Fall, convicted of accepting bribes, was sentenced in 1929 to a year in prison and fined $100,000. Sinclair and Doheny were acquitted of criminal charges, although Sinclair did serve short jail sentences for contempt of Congress and contempt of court.

Teapot Dome entered American political folklore as the symbol and major example of Harding Era corruption, and as late as 1928 revelations about those involved and their connections with *Republican party financing continued. Thanks, however, to Harding's death, President Calvin *Coolidge's success in winning public trust, and revelations connecting leading Democrats to Doheny, the scandal failed to shake Republican dominance. Teapot Dome's long-range significance lay less in its political fallout than in its relationship to conservation policy. Its roots were in the fierce conservation battles of the William Howard *Taft and Woodrow *Wilson administrations, and conservationists made good use of the scandal to overturn the prodevelopment actions of 1921–1922, secure creation of a Federal Oil Conservation Board, and return the oil reserves to naval control.

[*See also* Conservation Movement; Environmentalism; Petroleum Industry; Twenties, The.]

• M. R. Werner and John Starr, *Teapot Dome,* 1959. Burl Noggle, *Teapot Dome: Oil and Politics in the 1920s,* 1962.

—Ellis W. Hawley

TECHNOLOGY. Few forces have more profoundly shaped the American experience than technology. This essay examines historians' shifting understanding of the term, traces the major eras of technological change, and explores some of the factors that have influenced the pace and direction of that change.

Defining the Term. The meaning of "technology" has undergone a revolution over the last two centuries. Although the term was familiar in German (Technologie) in the late *Colonial Era, it came into limited use in English only as the American economy was beginning to industrialize. In 1829 Harvard professor Jacob Bigelow entitled his treatise "on the application of the sciences to the useful arts" *Elements of Technology* because he sought a "sufficiently expressive" word for his subject and "practical men" were employing it. Through 1900, however, its use was confined mainly to technical manuals or to the names of new institutes of technology. Most Americans favored the all-encompassing phrase "the useful arts" or the narrower "mechanical arts."

"Technology" came into currency in its modern sense in the early twentieth century. Popularized by Thorstein *Veblen in the 1920s and in 1930s debates about technological *unemployment, it was understood in an anthropological sense as "useful knowledge" but confined to the largely male preserves of industry and *engineering. Veblen and others also stressed the machine-like, autonomous nature of the emerging "industrial system" (which they believed engineers were uniquely suited to head). As engineers strove to enhance their status, meanwhile, they embraced the term but defined it as "applied science," closely allied with "pure" or "basic" *science. Although these conceptions continued to govern popular thought, a profoundly social understanding of technology took shape among scholars after the 1960s. Historians of technology, organized professionally in the 1950s, disputed the "applied science" definition, stressing instances where useful artifacts or processes were developed without a foundation of scientific understanding. This finding was reinforced by a federal study of weapons development (Project Hindsight, 1966). Also rejecting technological determinism and autonomy, historians explored the role of social choice and human agency in technological change, and inspired by *gender and *race studies, challenged the focus on white-male-dominated industry and engineering that had characterized earlier conceptions of "technology."

The result was a broader view of technology as ways of "making and doing things" that at its most expansive, encompasses all ways of shaping the real world—natural and social—to human ends. Technology so understood signifies a thoroughly social process, which touches all human beings, whose history is inevitably bound up with questions of power and authority.

Overlapping Eras of Change. This definitional transformation reflected momentous changes in ways of shaping the real world, in the role of technology in American life, and in the nature of technological knowledge. Generalizing about these changes is risky, not least because some technologies, periods, and regions are better understood than others. Still, as a first approximation, the history of American technology may be divided into four, broadly overlapping eras.

Colonial Era through the Early 1800s. The first era extends from the establishment of the British colonies through the early 1800s. While conditions differed over this time span and from one colony to another, colonial technology shared certain characteristics. It was small in scale, since most products, if not imported, were produced in limited quantities—in homes, on plantations or farms, or village workshops—and used or consumed locally. Most work was done manually with simple tools rather than by machine. Direct personal relationships, accordingly, marked the social relations of technology: relations among producers, between producers and their work, between producers and consumers. Furthermore, colonial technology was tied closely to nature and its rhythms. Wood, an abundant resource, provided fuel and construction material. Lighting as well as power (stationary and motive) came from natural sources (sun, wind, water, animals). The ebb and flow of daylight and the turning of the seasons shaped all technological activities. Great diversity also marked colonial technology, since goods produced manually for local markets varied widely.

The workings of colonial technology had a certain transparency, since its underlying principles, though seldom understood scientifically, were familiar. Transportation and communication still relied on age-old technologies (turnpikes and *canals), as did even technically complex production sites such as iron "plantations" or water-powered gristmills. Skills passed from individual to individual, learned through hands-on experience rather than from books, reinforcing social intimacy.

Yet colonial technology was not static. Certainly, the technologies that transformed eighteenth-century British industry had little direct impact, for British mercantilism encouraged the colonists to produce raw materials or semi-finished goods (e.g., bar iron), not finished goods such as textiles or machinery. But conquest and settlement depended on the ability to adapt European technologies to a new environment; to develop crops such as rice (first grown successfully in South Carolina by slaves who probably brought the know-how from West Africa), and to adopt Indian techniques for cultivating maize and clearing forests. Indians, too, engaged in selective adaptation, favoring flintlock over matchlock guns, for example. Such accomplishments forged a distinctive American technology, though well within a pre-industrial tradition.

But signs of a break with traditional practice gradually emerged. Adoption of the *Constitution (1789) and a national *patent law (1790) erected a political framework for a national market. Experimentation with steam engines and "automatic" flour milling (Oliver Evans, 1780s), erection of the first spinning mill, based on British know-know (Samuel Slater, 1790), and invention of the cotton gin (Eli *Whitney, 1793) all signaled rising interest in mechanization. But the breakthrough came with the *War of 1812, which stimulated the domestic market by cutting off imports and prompting *tariff increases. As domestic manufacturing surged, Boston merchants built the nation's first large-scale cotton textile factory at Waltham, Massachusetts, in 1813. Integrating all steps of the manufacturing process, it applied waterpower even to weaving (a departure from British practice). Seeking more waterpower, the Boston merchants opened the *Lowell mills in the 1820s. Wartime experience also heightened demand for improved transportation, stimulating the construction of steamboats, roads, canals, and, by the late 1820s *railroads. Under an 1815 congressional, mandate, the War Department pursued "uniformity" in arms production, a project that ultimately led to the "*American System" of interchangeable-parts manufacturing technology, a key to *mass production.

The Later Nineteenth Century: The Industrial Age. As *industrialization unfolded, technology took on very different qualities. *Railroads and *telegraphs opened regional and national markets. Labor-saving farm machinery freed labor for factory work and spurred urban growth. The scale of technology increased dramatically. Although many products continued to be produced by craft methods, others—from cigarettes to petroleum—were manufactured in vast quantities as mechanization and capital-intensive factory production soared after the *Civil War. The social relations of technology grew correspondingly more complex. Production sites became removed from sites of consumption, as even preserved-food production moved out of the household or off the farm. As the division of labor increased and more Americans were employed by large firms, work relations took on a bureaucratic nature; with factory production and mechanization, control of the work process shifted from workers to managers (though not without resistance and seldom completely).

Industrial technology also altered ties to nature and diminished diversity. Railroads and telegraphs, it was said, "annihilated time and space." In both industry and *agriculture, complex machines (sewing machines, machine tools, horse-drawn reapers) lessened dependence on manual skills. While the shift to coal (for fuel) and iron or steel (for construction) proceeded slowly, by 1900 they had replaced wood as the material of choice. Meanwhile, gas *illumination and, later, electrical lighting supplanted natural light, while *steam slowly became the dominant source of stationary and motive power. Daily life was less closely linked to diurnal and seasonal rhythms, and new technologies altered the physical environment on an unprecedented scale. By the 1880s, coal smoke, lumber-mill sawdust, and wastewater from hydraulic mining and urban waterworks generated air and water pollution in many parts of the nation. With the spread of railroads, telegraphs, and mass production, diversity yielded to standardization—not only of products but also of time, news, work and travel schedules, and weights and measures.

Technological knowledge underwent equally dramatic changes. The principles underlying steam power, machine tools, and mass production were less familiar, hence less transparent. Invention by individuals remained the norm—indeed, the post–Civil War years marked the highpoint of independent inventors such as Thomas *Edison. But it was increasingly defined as machine-related and patentable. (The annual number of patents rose from 600 in 1840 to some 26,000 by 1900.) Further, invention was seen as the preserve of white males, despite efforts by *African Americans and white women to defend a broader conception. With the rise of capital-intensive industry, moreover, the ability to profit from invention increasingly depended on access to capital, disadvantaging those without social connections, such as Granville T. Woods, a prolific African American inventor. Book-learning and systematic investigation also began to supplant traditional know-how. From a handful in the *Antebellum Era (notably, Philadelphia's Franklin Institute and the U.S. Military Academy at West Point), institutions of *engineering education multiplied (e.g., Massachusetts Institute of Technology, 1861). As practitioners of the "mechanic arts" evolved into "engineers" distinguished by specialty (e.g., civil, mining, mechanical, or electrical), professional associations proliferated.

The Early Twentieth Century: Technological Systems Take Shape. By 1900 a new era of "technological systems" had arisen. The electrical-power industry, for example, inaugurated by the opening of Edison's generating station in Manhattan (1882), grew from a fragmented collection of local lighting stations into an integrated system of regional power grids by the 1920s. Utility companies transmitted a standardized product (alternating current at sixty cycles per second) over a network of wires to one-third of American households. *Electricity also powered streetcars (pioneered by Frank J. Sprague, 1888) and factory motors (after 1900). By the 1930s, the "system" included those who made and sold household devices such as radios and refrigerators credit companies to finance their purchase, appliances, *advertising to promote electrical use, and sophisticated techniques to manage demand. The two dominant companies, General Electric and Westinghouse, employed many engineers, and in 1901 General Electric opened the nation's first industrial *research laboratory. An array of other system-like technologies emerged from 1880 to 1940; from *telephones, *motor vehicles, and western irrigation projects to motion pictures, commercial broadcasting, and aviation.

The qualities that characterized industrial technology marked American life deeply in the early twentieth century: scale and standardization increased, the lines of mediation between production and (now largely female) consumption became more intricate, and nature grew more remote (though in a sense accessible by automobile). But the era of systems also introduced a new level of social interdependence. Technological systems comprise many interlocking parts—including people—that must function properly and predictably; disruption or change at any one point affects the whole. To be sure, personal interdependence had marked the colonial era, while railroads, telegraph companies, and mass producers had all grappled with organizational complexity in the industrial era, giving rise to managerial hierarchies and Frederick W. Taylor's *scientific management methods in the 1880s. But technological systems brought new, industry-wide hierarchies of social interdependence that linked producers with distant consumers, in some cases shifting the production of services onto the consumer. By 1930 the housewife who drove an automobile and thus provided transportation for the household was embedded in a system that encompassed not only auto manufacturers such as Henry *Ford and his assembly line but also steel, glass, rubber, and upholstery manufacturers, finance companies, gasoline producers and filling stations, garages and mechanics, roads, traffic lights, and self-service "supermarkets." Even farm households, once reliant on nature and neighbors, became dependent on complex systems for everything from gasoline-powered tractors and seed corn (from the 1930s) to entertainment.

Technological knowledge was systematized as well. In a transformation first perceptible in the *electrical and *chemical industries (in what some call the "second industrial revolution"), practical and scientific knowledge became interdependent. Technological knowledge became enmeshed in the corporations that spawned systems, as independent inventors yielded to corporate engineers and industrial scientists. The workings of technology thus grew more opaque, more remote from everyday experience. Technological knowledge, concentrated in engineering schools and professional associations, also became further masculinized. As the percentage of doctoral degrees in science and engineering awarded to women declined from 1920 through the 1960s, and as professional associations excluded women from full membership, the expertise and systems of male engineers came to symbolize "progress."

The 1930s to the Late Twentieth Century: Technology as "Second Nature." In viewing the fourth era in the history of American technology, whose beginnings stretched back to the 1930s, two trends stand out: the extension of ever larger technological systems into virtually every corner of American life, and the reconstitution of nature itself through new technologies. From the 1930s on, technological systems expanded and multiplied, merging into an interlocking national, then global, infrastructure. *New Deal Era programs promoted regional *hydroelectric power systems and encouraged rural electrification and the Rural Telephone Act (1949) brought telephone lines to American farms. Post-war agriculture became "agribusiness": capital-, energy-, and chemical-intensive. In the 1950s and 1960s, the federal government built a nationwide interstate *highway system. Airline passengers carried by a nascent civil *aviation industry increased to nearly thirteen million by 1947, then multiplied as jets were introduced in the 1950s. The first *radio network (National Broadcasting Company, 1926) linked two systems to create a third; partly owned by General Electric and Westinghouse, it distributed radio programs over leased telephone lines. Commercial *television broadcasting, launched in 1939–1940, burgeoned after *World War II. By 1959 Americans owned fifty million TV sets. The major networks dominated programming until the arrival of cable TV (also color television and videotape recorders) in the 1960s. The first commercial communication satellite (Intelstat I) was launched in 1965); by the early 1970s virtually global satellite coverage had been achieved. By the 1990s, satellite transmissions, cable television, digital facsimiles, fiber optics, and the *Internet put the vast majority of Americans within reach of a global network of technological systems.

World War II and the *Cold War yielded other giant technological systems as well, including *nuclear weapons, *nuclear power, the *space program, and the Internet, developed in the late 1950s chiefly through the Pentagon's Advanced Research Projects Agency (ARPA). At the heart of most systems in this era lay electronic devices. Electronic digital (i.e., binary) *computers, developed for military purposes during World War II, became feasible for civilian use after transistors replaced vacuum tubes in the 1950s. Small electronic signal devices made of semiconductors (mainly silicon), transistors were soon integrated with other components into a single silicon chip—the integrated circuit (1960s)—then in large-scale circuits (microprocessors, 1971), and finally in very-large-scale integrated (VLSI) circuits (mid-1980s). These and related advances, most funded by the Pentagon, increased the power of computers dramatically and reduced their size from room-sized mainframes to desktop (1980s) and palm-held (1990s) computers. Thanks to microprocessors, a host of consumer products as well as manufacturing and other business processes were computerized from the 1970s on. Linked in local-area networks (LAN) or through the Internet, microelectronic devices unleashed an "information revolution" that had touched the lives of virtually all Americans by the 1990s. (Actual access remained uneven, however.)

Over the same years, other technologies offered sweeping powers to manipulate nature itself. One line of development centered on molecular manipulation in the manufacture of synthetic materials. An early, widely used *plastic, Bakelite (ca. 1909), was the first in a series of synthetic materials constructed of complex molecules or "polymers." Technical advances during World War II included nylon (a linear polymer), alloys, and composites. The new postwar discipline of "materials science," emerging from chemistry, physics, and metallurgy, was funded after 1960 by the Pentagon's advanced research agency, which was interested in developing high-temperature, high-strength-to-weight materials for military purposes. This culminated in the 1990s in "nanotechnology," the precise positioning of atoms and molecules in what physicist Richard Feynman envisioned in 1959 as "bottom up" manufacturing of materials and microscopic devices.

Another line of research, on the manipulation of reproduction, led from hybrid corn in the 1920s through discovery of the double helical structure of DNA (1952) to recombinant DNA techniques (gene cloning) in the 1970s. The 1980s and 1990s saw the development of genetically altered microorganisms (declared patentable in 1980), plants (1977), and animals (1996) as well as gene therapies for human *diseases (e.g., cystic fibrosis, 1993). Meanwhile, the *birth-control pill was approved for sale in 1960, and the first American in vitro fertilization achieved in 1981. Amidst debates about the ethics of human cloning, the federally funded *Human Genome Project was launched in 1990, and successfully concluded a decade later, as part of a global effort to identify the location and structure of every human gene. By the end of the twentieth century, in short, new technologies offered the possibility of constructing all kinds of matter from the "bottom up."

These two trends combined to give American technology the qualities of "second nature" in the post–World War II years. For a time in the 1970s and 1980s, "quality management" techniques, computerization, flexible methods of production, and niche markets seemed to herald a reversal of the centralization and standardization that marked earlier technological systems. "Lean" production methods such as just-in-time inventory control and subcontracting eased the rigidities inherent in Fordist methods of mass production. The Internet, moreover, retained the decentralization designed into its military progenitor, ARPANET, to withstand a nuclear attack. But, in practice, the hierarchies of interdependence expanded, as interlocking technological systems encompassed not merely those who produced and consumed its products but virtually all Americans. Standardization became pervasive, evident in the rapid spread of commodities (or computer viruses) around the world. Working in concert, systems such as electricity, automobiles, television, and the Internet ordered social life as nature once did. The "24/7 economy" of the 1990s—operating twenty-four hours a day, seven days a week—decoupled daily life from nature. Even environmental problems generated by twentieth-century technologies were addressed largely with new technologies (e.g., air pollution control devices, genetically engineered microorganisms to combat oil spills). Technology had become so deeply woven into American life as to be taken for granted. Nano- and biotechnologies, moreover, permitted nature itself to be constructed anew at the atomic and genetic level.

Technological knowledge became even more opaque and further removed from everyday life. Technology's shift from the mechanical toward the scientific accelerated in these years, with the growing importance of solid-state physics and molecular biology. The locus of technological knowledge moved from corporate research labs to a larger nexus composed of industry, the military, and universities—the "military-industrial complex" whose emergence President Dwight D. *Eisenhower had discerned in 1961. During the Cold War—particularly in response to the Soviet atomic bomb (1949), the *Korean War, and the Soviets' launching of *Sputnik I* (1957)—federal funds poured into *education (National Defense Education Act, 1958) and into industrial research and development (R&D), on the model that had proved so productive during World War II. By 1965, fully two-thirds of American R&D was funded by the federal government. As total R&D spending more than tripled thereafter, the government's share declined, but it still accounted for about one-third in the 1990s. In short, technological knowledge in the era of technology-as-second-nature became increasingly scientific, highly institutionalized, and inflected by government priorities.

Understanding Technological Change. Tracing the evolution of machines once seemed sufficient to explain technological change, but scholars now view it as a multi-layered social process that has not followed a predetermined course. Sorting out the relevant historical forces involves distinguishing between the pace and the particular direction of technological change.

Two factors quickened the *pace* of change over the course of American history. Competition, both capitalist and nationalist, encouraged the search for improved technologies. The pursuit of profits and economic efficiency generated enormous increases in *productivity. Farm productivity more than doubled between 1960 and 1996, for example, while nonfarm labor productivity nearly doubled. Likewise, international competition—economic as well as political—prompted government funding for specific technological advances. The pattern of support established after the *War of 1812—the armories' work on interchangeable parts, the state governments' promotion of canals and railroads—grew more pronounced in the twentieth century, particularly during World War II and the Cold War, when technological innovation appeared critical to national security. Federal funding supported virtually all post-1945 technological breakthroughs.

Technological "borrowing" also hastened the pace of change. Through the 1850s, the United States was a net borrower, adapting European textile and railroad technology to local circumstances, for example. By the Philadelphia Centennial Exhibition of 1876, however, American innovations enjoyed wide recognition in Europe. By 1900, American inventors were drawing from and contributing to an international pool of technical knowledge in the electrical, chemical, and other industries. Twentieth century America became, on balance, a net technology exporter—for example, of mass-production techniques to Europe and the Soviet Union after World War I. Borrowing went on among industries as well. Innovations spread rapidly, for example, within the nineteenth-century machine-tool industry and the twentieth-century electronics industries. The "spinoff" of technologies from the military to the private sector further accelerated the process of technological change.

But the factors that help account for the pace of technological change do not necessarily explain its direction. At critical moments in American history, competing technologies seemed equally viable: canals, railroads, and steam carriages on common roads in the early 1830s; alternating and direct electric current or large-scale mass production and more flexible forms of production in the 1880s; numerical control and record-playback control in computerized manufacturing in the 1950s. While Americans have been portrayed as naturally inventive, enthusiastic about mechanization, and prone to define "progress" in technological terms, throughout the nation's history critics have questioned the direction of technological change. Debates about the social utility of factory labor marked the 1830s and 1840s; intellectuals from Henry David *Thoreau to Lewis *Mumford questioned the movement toward technological systems; the Depression of the 1930s sparked debates about mass production's role in "technological unemployment"; and social protesters in the 1960s challenged technology's social and environmental consequences and launched an "alternative technology" movement. Why some voices or technologies, but not others, achieved dominance requires deeper analysis.

Among the factors that have influenced the direction of technological change, two stand out. The availability of resources created distinctive incentives expressed in relative prices. In the nineteenth century, natural resources such as wood and water were abundant, while capital and labor were comparatively scarce. Thus Americans relied longer on wood and waterpower than did the British. The relative costliness of labor encouraged labor-saving mechanization; the scarcity of capital made it worthwhile to build machines cheaply and use them intensively. But if relative costs biased the direction of technological change, they seldom determined specific technological choices, since costs themselves change during the process of invention, development, and diffusion. Prior technological choices also generated inertia that constrained the direction of change. Existing technologies tended to absorb capital and inventive energy that would otherwise have been directed elsewhere, and, once a set of supporting institutions and behaviors grew up around specific technologies such as the QWERTY keyboard layout or the internal-combustion automobile, fundamental change became more costly.

Within the parameters established by relative prices and existing technologies, other factors tipped the balance toward specific technological solutions. Sometimes, the actions of individuals proved decisive (e.g., Thomas Edison's in the battle between alternating and direct current). Government funding was often critical, especially when it targeted specific technological solutions (e.g., machine tools and transistors better suited to military than to commercial needs). Although the effects of ideologies are difficult to gauge, they have also shaped the direction of technological change. Examples include the "command and control" ideology expressed in military support of computer research, gender or racial ideologies that influenced product design or use, and "progress" ideologies that privileged the use of iron or electricity. Consumers have also had their say, putting technologies to unanticipated uses. The creators of both the telephone and the Internet's predecessor, ARPANET, intended them for business use; it was telephone callers and researchers who turned them into devices for social interaction. The answer to the question of which technology or whose voice prevails often lies immersed in the messy details of history.

[*See also* Atomic Energy Commission; Automation and Computerization; Automotive Industry; Biotechnology Industry; Business; Capitalism; Cotton Industry; Education: The Rise of the University; Education: Education in Contemporary America; Federal Government, Executive Branch: Department of Defense; Iron and Steel Industry; Lumbering; Manhattan Project; Mass Marketing; Petroleum Industry; National Aeronautics and Space Administration; Physical Sciences; Roads and Turnpikes, Early; Tennessee Valley Authority; Textile Industry; Tobacco Industry.]

• David A. Hounshell, *From the American System to Mass Production, 1800–1932: The Development of Manufacturing Technology in the United States,* 1984. David F. Noble, *Forces of Production: A Social History of Industrial Automation,* 1984. Langdon Winner, *The Whale and the Reactor: A Search for Limits in an Age of High Technology,* 1986. Thomas P. Hughes, *American Genesis: A Century of Invention and Technological Enthusiasm,* 1989. David E. Nye, *Electrifying America: Social Meanings of a New Technology,* 1990. Stuart W. Leslie, *The Cold War and American Science: The Military-Industrial-Academic Complex at MIT and Stanford,* 1993. Judith A. McGaw, ed., *Early American Technology: Making and Doing Things from the Colonial Era to 1850,* 1994. Carroll Pursell, *The Machine in America: A Social History of Technology,* 1995. Ruth Schwartz Cowan, *A Social History of Technology,* 1997. Roger Horowitz and Arwen Mohun, eds., *His and Hers: Gender, Consumption, and Technology,* 1998. Merritt Roe Smith and Gregory Clancy, eds., *Major Problems in the History of Technology: Documents and Essays,* 1998. Ruth Oldenziel, *Making Technology Masculine: Men, Women and Modern Machines in America, 1870–1945,* 1999. Eric Schatzberg, *Wings of Wood, Wings of Metal: Culture and Technical Choice in American Airplane Materials, 1914–1945,* 1999.

—Colleen A. Dunlavy

TECUMSEH (1768–1813), Native American leader. Born to a Creek mother and Shawnee father at Old Piqua, a Shawnee village on the Mad River in Ohio, Tecumseh was raised by an older sister and grew to manhood during the border warfare of the Revolutionary Era. He served as a scout for the war party that defeated Arthur St. Clair's army in 1791, and in 1794 he fought at both Fort Recovery and Fallen Timbers. He refused, however, to sign the Treaty of Greenville (1795), which ceded most Indian lands in Ohio to the United States.

In 1805–1806, Tecumseh's younger brother, Tenskwatawa, or the Shawnee Prophet, experienced a series of visions and predicted a solar eclipse. The Prophet then emerged as a holy man who led a multi-tribal religious revitalization movement that spread to tribes throughout the Great Lakes region. In 1808, Tecumseh and the Prophet established Prophetstown, a village near the juncture of the Wabash and Tippecanoe Rivers in Indiana, and Tecumseh traveled to the midwestern tribes, transforming his brother's religious movement into a political confederacy. During 1811, Tecumseh visited the Creeks, Choctaws, and Chickasaws, but in November, while Tecumseh was in the South, William Henry *Harrison and an American army attacked and destroyed Prophetstown, after defeating the Prophet at the Battle of Tippecanoe.

Early in 1812, Tecumseh returned to Indiana and began to rebuild his confederacy. He journeyed to Canada, where he sought British assistance. When the *War of 1812 erupted, Tecumseh and his allies aided the British in the capture of *Detroit and in the unsuccessful campaigns against Fort Meigs and Fort Stephenson, in northern Ohio. In 1813, when American forces invaded Canada, Tecumseh urged the British to stand and fight, but he was killed on 5 October at the Battle of the Thames, when the British army fled from the Americans.

Tecumseh was highly respected during his lifetime; both the British and the Americans admired his bravery and leadership ability. After his death he emerged as an American folk hero, his exploits embellished by myth and legend. Modern Native Americans remember him as a great leader dedicated to his people and to the defense of their homeland.

[*See also* Early Republic, Era of the; Expansionism; Indian History and Culture: From 1800 to 1900; Indian Wars.]

• R. David Edmunds, *Tecumseh and the Quest for Indian Leadership,* 1984. Gregory Evans Dowd, *A Spirited Resistance: The North American Indian Struggle for Unity, 1745–1815,* 1992.

—R. David Edmunds

TELEGRAPH. The United States telegraph industry began in the mid-1840s, following several years of work by the painter

Samuel F. B. *Morse and the mechanic Alfred Vail to develop an electrical telegraph system conceived by Morse in 1832. Congress funded the first line, built between *Washington, D.C., and Baltimore, Maryland, in 1844 but refused to purchase the patent rights or establish a permanent postal telegraph system. As a consequence, private entrepreneurs acquired the rights from Morse and his partners and built lines between major American cities.

By the mid-1850s the many small, regional telegraph companies had been consolidated into a few large ones led by American Telegraph Company and Western Union Telegraph Company. Western Union controlled the most important lines west of *New York City, while American Telegraph, with crucial links to the planned *Atlantic Cable between Great Britain and Nova Scotia, dominated the East Coast market. In 1857, they and four other companies signed a cartel agreement that carved the market into clearly defined territories. Western Union broke ranks in 1860 and won a government subsidy to construct the first transcontinental telegraph. The completion of this line, combined with other government subsidies acquired during the *Civil War, gave Western Union considerable advantage over its rivals, and by 1866 it enjoyed a near monopoly of the industry.

Following the war, Western Union, led by William Orton, consolidated the lines of its main rivals into the first truly national telecommunications network. Orton also undertook an extensive program of line reconstruction and improvement and channeled profits into technical improvements, supporting the work of key telegraph inventors such as Thomas *Edison. Under Orton's direction Western Union focused on meeting the needs of its primary markets, businessmen, whose dependence on the rapid communication of commercial information also led to the development of new telegraph systems such as stock tickers, and new newspapers, which relied on press reports sent by telegraph.

Because government dispatches played a small role in the United States, agitation for a national postal telegraph system failed to result in a government takeover, as occurred throughout Europe. However, new private competitors to Western Union did arise, notably the New York railroad speculator Jay Gould, who combined the telegraph lines of his railroad empire with those of smaller telegraph companies to mount serious challenges to Western Union; this enabled him to take over the company in 1881. Western Union continued to dominate the telecommunications industry until around 1900, when it faced a new challenge from the growing long-distance *telephone network of American Telephone and Telegraph (AT&T), the long-distance arm of the American Bell Telephone Company. By 1909 the telephone had become so important that AT&T briefly took over Western Union before government antitrust action forced their separation. Telegraphy played a declining role in the nation's telecommunications system as the century progressed, and after *World War II it was supplanted by other technologies.

[*See also* Antitrust Legislation; Business; Economic Development; Electricity and Electrification; Gilded Age; Industrialization; Journalism; Technology.]

• William Thompson, *Wiring a Continent: The History of the Telegraph Industry in the United States, 1832–1866,* 1947. Paul Israel, *From the Machine Shop to the Industrial Laboratory: Telegraphy and the Changing Context of American Invention, 1830–1920,* 1992.

—Paul Israel

TELEPHONE. In 1876, Alexander Graham *Bell devised the *technology for the electronic communication of the human voice between two points—a technology involving variations in an electric current responding to the sound waves created by human speech. By 1878, a "switchboard" permitted any telephone user to reach any other user in the same network. Further advances in the nineteenth century extended the effective distance of the telephone to hundreds of miles, reduced electrical interference, simplified the instrument, and expanded the number of telephones that could be connected through one exchange. Early twentieth-century innovations permitted cross-country and global calls, direct customer dialing unassisted by switchboard operators, and a system that allowed many calls to occupy the same wire simultaneously. Later developments liberated long-distance calls from wires, first by microwave transmission and then by *satellite communication. Wireless local calling became common near the end of the twentieth century with cellular telephone systems.

Telephone production and service in the United States, unlike elsewhere, remained in the hands of private companies but under government regulation. Bell and his associates formed the ancestral company of American Telephone and Telegraph (AT&T) immediately after the invention of the telephone. By 1880, AT&T had established a patent-based monopoly. Its Western Electric subsidiary had exclusive rights to manufacture telephones, which AT&T then leased to customers. Only its local subsidiaries could provide telephone service, an expensive luxury used largely by urban businessmen.

In 1893, when AT&T's patents expired, there were four telephones per thousand Americans, with two-thirds of those in businesses. Shortly afterward, thousands of new enterprises, including small cooperatives, formed to provide local telephone service. Prices dropped sharply and telephone subscription expanded rapidly, particularly in rural areas. By 1907, homes with telephones had multiplied about tenfold, but AT&T now served fewer than half the nation's three million customers. Acquired by the financier J. P. *Morgan in 1907, AT&T bought or bankrupted many competitors. To fend off federal antitrust action, the corporation agreed in 1913 to cease aggressive takeovers and to interconnect its lines with those of competitors. Ultimately, a national system emerged, consisting of a dominant AT&T controlling all long-distance service and most local service; many small "independents" providing local service in isolated places; and regulatory agencies, state and federal, charged with keeping telephone rates affordable.

In 1984, new antitrust challenges led a federal court to divide AT&T into separate regional companies. It also introduced competition to telephone manufacturing and long-distance service. Deregulation brought expanded telephone services and reduced the costs of long-distance calling; basic telephone service, however, now less subsidized, increased in cost.

Telephone companies initially promoted their service as an aid to commerce. Phoning saved trips, sped up transactions, and linked field representatives to central offices. Early telephone marketers paid less attention to home subscribers. In 1900, fewer than 10 percent of American families had telephones, but lower prices had raised that figure to almost 40 percent by 1930. The rate of household-telephone subscription dropped during the depression of the 1930s but then rebounded to almost 80 percent in 1960 and 94 percent in 1994.

Some commentators have speculated that the telephone may have changed how Americans think and act. However, the best evidence is that the telephone enabled Americans to pursue their characteristic ways of life more efficiently.

[*See also* Antitrust Legislation; Business; Economic Regulation; Gilded Age; Internet and World Wide Web; Telegraph.]

• John Brooks, *Telephone: The First Hundred Years,* 1976. Claude S. Fischer, *America Calling: A Social History of the Telephone to 1940,* 1992.

—Claude S. Fischer

TELEVANGELISM. Televangelism, the propagation of *religion over the airwaves, extended Evangelicals' long role as pioneers in mass communications: George Whitefield's open-air preaching in the eighteenth century, Charles G. *Finney's use of newspapers in the nineteenth, and the *radio programs of Aimee Semple *McPherson and Charles E. Fuller early in the twentieth. When Billy *Graham emerged at midcentury he turned first to radio and then to *television to reach the masses.

The Roman Catholic bishop Fulton J. Sheen (1895–1979), though not an evangelical, won a vast television audience in the 1950s with his program *Life Is Worth Living.*

Changes in the television industry gave evangelists an even larger influence on the medium in the 1970s. The *Federal Communications Commission (FCC) had mandated that all local stations allocate time to religious broadcasting, but network policy had forbidden affiliates from charging for such programming. With the increased independence of local stations, however, and with the blessings of the FCC, they began charging for religious broadcasts.

Seizing the opportunity, evangelists solicited donations that more than paid for the inexpensive airtime available in the Sunday morning "religious ghetto." Religious programming now changed dramatically. Whereas the liturgies and messages of *Roman Catholicism and mainline *Protestantism had once dominated religious broadcasts, Evangelicals, drawing on a long tradition of mixing religion with entertainment, now translated the Gospel into show business. The "electronic church" took many forms: the Pentecostal and divine healing emphases of Kathryn Kuhlman, Oral Roberts, and Ernest Angley; the positive-thinking, Jesus-will-make-you-rich-and-successful message of Rex Humbard, Robert Schuller, and Robert Tilton; the inimitable theatrics of Jimmy Swaggart; the conservative political cant of James Robison and Jerry Falwell; the talk-show format of Pat Robertson and Jim Bakker.

Televangelism became immensely profitable, with many televangelists drawing in millions of dollars every year, far exceeding the budgets of entire denominations. Robertson's Christian Broadcasting Network (CBN) became a formidable organization, providing the foundation for his 1988 *Republican party presidential campaign and his later conservative political lobby, the *Christian Coalition.

By the mid-1980s, however, scandal enveloped many televangelists. Bakker's flamboyant lifestyle and dreams of empire led to sexual and financial improprieties that eventually sent him to prison, Swaggart was caught in several dalliances with prostitutes, and Roberts declared that God would "take him home" unless God's people ponied up several million dollars to save his flagging empire. Early in the 1990s, Tilton faced an ABC News exposé that questioned his integrity.

The scandals severely reduced ratings and, consequently, revenues. Many of the larger televangelist organizations cut back their operations, but the proliferation of cable television opened doors for new televangelists and new networks as the century ended.

[*See also* Fundamentalist Movement; Missionary Movement; Moral Majority; Pentecostalism; Revivalism.]

• Quentin J. Schultze, *Televangelism and American Culture: The Business of Popular Religion,* 1991. J. Gordon Melton, Phillip Charles Lucas, and Jon R. Stone, eds., *Prime-Time Religion: An Encyclopedia of Religious Broadcasting,* 1997.

—Randall Balmer

TELEVISION. Experiments in the radio transmission of visual images had been conducted for several decades before manufacturers offered the first television receivers for sale in 1939. Consumer indifference and *World War II, however, kept demand slight until 1948 when, soon after the beginning of regular network telecasts, TV sales took off. In 1949, 2.3 percent of homes had televisions; by 1962, 90 percent did. Despite the relatively high costs of the first sets, Americans purchased televisions regardless of income. And television quickly emerged as the most popular mass medium, with more Americans spending more time watching TV than consuming any other mass medium. Television's initial popularity owed much to its convenience. For the post–World War II family, television, compared to moviegoing, was cost-efficient entertainment; parents and children could be entertained at home, without traveling to a theater or buying tickets.

The 1950s: Rise of the Networks. Most TV stations—over 90 percent in the 1950s and early 1960s—signed exclusive "affiliation" agreements with networks. In exchange for compensation, an affiliate agreed to carry network programming at specified hours (usually in the evening). As a result, the networks determined evening viewing, when most Americans watched television.

Two networks, Columbia Broadcasting System (CBS) and the National Broadcasting Company (NBC), initially dominated. Their large lead in *radio gave them clear advantages, including show-business expertise and goodwill with their radio affiliates, many of which acquired TV licenses. Then, too, the number of TV channels was limited to twelve on the very high frequency (VHF) transmitting band. The *Federal Communications Commission (FCC) encouraged rival commercial and noncommercial networks by awarding channels 14 through 81 in the ultra high frequency (UHF) beginning in 1952. In most markets, however, UHF could not compete with VHF outlets. By early 1956, 60 of 159 UHF channels had left the air. UHF's stark disadvantages seriously undercut educational television as well as the third commercial network, the American Broadcasting Company (ABC), which disproportionately relied on UHF channels for affiliates.

Advertisers played a powerful role in early programming. With some advertisers holding back from entering television, the position of those who did was strengthened. Typically sponsoring entire programs, they often insisted on changes in individual productions. In one instance a tobacco company ordered that the Russian villains in a *Cold War drama not be shown smoking cigarettes. Commercials were frequently integrated into shows. In the middle of a program, the leads would suddenly praise (or be shown using) the sponsor's product. Yet some of TV's earliest underwriters championed more diverse programming by sponsoring dramatic and news series targeting smaller, more educated audiences. As viewership increasing and advertising rates rose in the late 1950s and early 1960s, however, advertisers abandoned sole sponsorships, preferring instead to spread their investment, and the networks asserted near total control over programming and scheduling.

The earliest programming appealed to a wide range of tastes. Because the first stations were established in the largest cities, popular shows tended to reflect a big-city sensibility. This included comedy variety hours, notably one starring Milton Berle, as well as original dramas. Nearly all were aired live. As television reached smaller communities in the *South and *West, however, the appeal of such shows faded. Viewers preferred filmed series with a regular cast of characters who were uniformly white, usually middle class, and living in smaller cities or towns. The dominant characters were almost always male.

The 1960s and 1970s: New Technologies and New Challenges. By the late 1950s, network programming had been standardized. Most series were produced in Southern California in assembly-line fashion, by the old *film studios or companies utilizing studio facilities and talent. Reruns of popular series, "syndicated" to TV stations across the countries for fees, and later to cable channels, proved popular and immensely profitable.

The development of videotape in the late 1950s profoundly affected the industry. Until then, the networks had to telecast programs live, across four continental time zones, meaning that a dramatic program aired at 9 PM eastern time was telecast at 6 PM on the West Coast. (Affiliates could carry poor quality "kinescope" recordings, in which motion-picture cameras photographed the images on television picture tubes.) At first, the networks used videotaping largely for time-shifting, to telecast programs later in the Mountain and Pacific time zones. Over time, however, most productions were taped to correct any flaws in a telecast and at the insistence of performers, most of whom preferred not to appear live. Videotape's greatest impact may have been on TV news. Film was expensive and could take hours to develop and edit. Videotape, by comparison, provided quick and cost-efficient TV reporting.

By the late 1960s, television technology changed in another important way. Since the 1950s, the Radio Corporation of America (RCA) and other TV manufacturers had been promoting color television. But consumers were put off by the comparatively high cost. As late as 1965, less than 6 percent of all homes had color receivers. As prices fell, however, more families purchased color TVs, and by 1972 just over half of all households owned them.

News programs appeared on TV from the beginning, but they had almost always lost money, and the networks offered them mainly to placate federal overseers. Resources normally went into fifteen-minute newscasts in the early and late evenings. Gradually, though, TV news gained respect and larger audiences. In 1963, CBS and NBC expanded their nightly newscasts to thirty minutes; ABC followed in 1967. In November 1963, the networks canceled all entertainment programming for four days to cover the assassination and funeral of President John F. *Kennedy. By then most critics agreed that TV news had demonstrated its potential and maturity, and surveys suggested that, for the first time, Americans ranked TV as their main source of information. More important to the networks, advertising on the evening newscasts had become a vital revenue source. Debates between the major party presidential candidates, introduced in 1960, became a quadrennial ritual beginning in 1976.

The *Vietnam War constituted the networks' greatest journalistic challenge in the 1960s. Contrary to a common misperception, TV coverage up to 1968 was, with very few exceptions, supportive of America's intervention and dismissive of the budding antiwar movement. Fearful of upsetting viewers, the networks rarely showed actual combat or bloodshed. To cut costs, the networks did not use satellites to transmit signals to New York, electing instead to fly film, which could take several days. Although the respected CBS news anchor Walter Cronkite (1916–), who declared the war a stalemate early in 1968, has been credited with helping to end U.S. escalation, most studies suggest that President Lyndon B. *Johnson and his advisers were already war weary. Nevertheless, the networks and some writers popularized myths that TV made Vietnam "the living-room war" and that Cronkite forced peace on the government. More likely, the more critical coverage beginning in 1968 prevented Johnson's successor, Richard M. *Nixon, from seriously escalating the fighting.

All told, the influence of network news ought not be overstated. The nightly newscasts never had audiences comparable to the entertainment shows that followed, and local newscasts normally had larger followings. Indeed, local stations in the 1960s had begun pouring resources into their newscasts, which proved their most profitable programming. In time, the drive for profits diluted most local stations' news agenda. Light features and sensational crimes were highlighted to boost ratings.

The 1960s similarly marked the marriage of *sports and television. TV had carried certain sporting events, notably wrestling and *boxing, from the beginning. But in the 1960s, more mobile cameras afforded viewers better angles, while instant replays of controversial calls by referees gave viewers twenty-twenty hindsight. Although every sports league coveted television, none matched the National Football League in making its game a television ritual. ABC's *Wide World of Sports*, meanwhile, introduced Americans to a broad array of sporting events year round. ABC also pioneered in turning the Olympic Games into television spectacles.

Although economics normally shaped television broadcast fare, the FCC in the 1960s took modest steps to change the industry, promoting increased competition by improving UHF reception and fostering noncommercial, educational television stations (ETV), many of which were on the upper frequency. Empowered by Congress to set standards for TV receivers, the commission ruled that all TVs sold after 1 April 1964 must be able to receive both UHF and VHF signals. Over time, this greatly expanded the total audience for the upper-frequency channels. In 1967, with the Public Broadcasting Act, Congress created the Public Broadcasting System (PBS), which displaced the old ETV network. Although chronically underfunded, PBS provided alternatives in cultural and news programming that the commercial networks had largely abandoned.

In the 1960s and 1970s, most Americans most of the time watched network programming, and network TV became more diverse. *African Americans began appearing and even starring in some programs. In series like *The Mary Tyler Moore Show* and *Charlie's Angels,* women played prominent roles. The main character in the most popular sitcom of the 1970s, *All in the Family,* was a working-class bigot.

Ever eager to fill their schedules, the networks in the late 1960s began producing made-for-TV movies. This partly reflected the growing sexual explicitness of theatrical releases as well as Hollywood's over-attention to younger moviegoers. Although most made-for-TV movies were forgettable, some had enormous impact. ABC's *Roots* (1977), a panoramic history of an African American family, based on a book by Alex Haley, helped to move the network for the first time into first-place in ratings and revenues. More often, TV movies consciously appealed to women viewers, who had gained more control over viewing, particularly in homes having second TVs.

The 1970s also brought important shifts in television news. Despite pressure from the Nixon administration, CBS aggressively reported on the *Watergate scandals; NBC and ABC belatedly did so as well. CBS News also scored a ratings coup in the late 1970s and 1980s with its top-rated *60 Minutes,* an hour-long collection of features and interviews dubbed a TV "news magazine." For the first time, a news program successfully competed for audiences in evening prime time. Only after many misfires did imitations by ABC and NBC enjoy comparable success with the "news magazine," which was much less expensive to produce than the typical hour-long entertainment series. Meanwhile, early morning news programs—NBC's *Today* and ABC's *Good Morning, America*—became immensely profitable.

The 1980s and Beyond: Fragmentation of Audience, Consolidation of Ownership. Still, the three-network hold over television came undone in the 1980s. Non-network or independent channels, often airing reruns of network shows, became serious competitors in many larger markets. Between 1979 and 1987, the proportion of stations affiliated with a network dropped from 86 to 61 percent. The Fox network, founded in 1986, lured younger viewers and advertisers. Two more networks, WB and UPN, commenced operations in the early 1990s.

The spread of cable television further undermined the networks. First introduced in the 1950s to improve reception for viewers in mountainous areas, cable burgeoned in the late 1970s and 1980s as Americans started subscribing to increase their programming choices. In many areas, subscribing to cable meant access to as many as thirty-two channels. By the mid-1990s, just over 60 percent of all homes had cable. Channels specializing in sports, the arts, *religion, and other special-interest areas added to cable's allure, as did the programming on "superstations" like Atlanta's WTBS and Chicago's WGN. With so many choices, the networks' viewership fell. Between the 1976–1977 and 1996–1997 TV seasons, the combined network share of evening prime time had dropped by a third, from 93 percent of the audience to 62 percent.

The proliferation of cable prompted a number of responses from the networks. To hold viewers, they tolerated increased sexual explicitness and violence. Spurred by Fox's appeal to younger viewers, they paid more attention to the demographic composition of audiences. Series popular with older viewers were frequently dumped in favor of sitcoms targeting younger adults.

Meanwhile, the networks and many stations underwent changes in ownership. Stations owned by individuals all but vanished in favor of group ownership. This trend was hurried along by the relaxation of long-time FCC rules on multiple ownership. In 1985–1986, new proprietors acquired all three networks. A station group, Capital Cities, purchased ABC; General Electric purchased NBC's parent company, RCA; and Laurence Tisch assumed controlling interest in CBS. Two of the networks were purchased again in 1995, when Westinghouse secured CBS and Disney bought ABC. Four years later, Viacom bought CBS.

Despite such concentration in ownership, the larger development at the end of the twentieth century was the fragmentation of the once gargantuan television audience. Although a few programs, notably the annual NFL Super Bowl and ABC's *Who Wants to be a Millionaire?* had high ratings, the audiences for most TV series dwindled drastically. The new world of choices, combined with greater internet use, was fragmenting society and, by distracting citizens from informational programming, weakening civic bonds.

[*See also* Advertising; Consumerism; Fifties, The; Foreign Relations: The Cultural Dimension; Internet and World Wide Web; Journalism; Mass Marketing; Multinational Enterprises; Murrow, Edward R.; Popular Culture; Public Broadcasting; Sarnoff, David; Satellite Communication; Sixties, The; Televangelism.]

• Daniel Hallin, *The "Uncensored War": The Media and Vietnam*, 1986. Christopher H. Sterling and John Kittross, *Stay Tuned: A Concise History of American Broadcasting*, 2d ed., 1990. James L. Baughman, *Republic of Mass Culture: Journalism, Filmmaking and Broadcasting in America since 1941*, 2d ed., 1997.

—James L. Baughman

TELLER, EDWARD (1908–), theoretical physicist, coinventor of the U.S. hydrogen bomb. Born in Budapest, Hungary, Teller studied physics at the University of Leipzig, receiving his doctorate in 1930. Fleeing Germany because of Nazi persecution, Teller and his wife in 1935 immigrated to the United States, where he taught at George Washington University.

In 1943, Teller joined the *Manhattan Project at Los Alamos, New Mexico, where the atomic bomb was being developed under the direction of the physicist J. Robert *Oppenheimer. There Teller worked on an even more powerful weapon, the hydrogen bomb (H-bomb). His original concept proved unworkable.

After the war, the H-bomb became a near-obsession for Teller, who joined a politically conservative coalition of government and military leaders to lobby for its development. After the Soviet Union tested an atomic bomb in August 1949, President Harry S. *Truman gave a green light to the H-bomb project. In early 1951, Teller and the Los Alamos mathematician Stanislaw Ulam proposed a radically different design for the H-bomb, which was successfully tested the following year. Also in 1952, Teller played an important role in establishing a second weapons-design laboratory, at Livermore, California. In 1954, Teller became a pariah to many in the nation's scientific community for his testimony against Oppenheimer at the latter's security hearing.

As director of the Livermore laboratory from 1958 to 1960 and an outside advocate long after, Teller lobbied for causes he believed in. These included opposition to a nuclear test-ban treaty and support for the civilian *nuclear-power industry. In 1983, as a member of the White House Science Council, Teller played a key role in President Ronald *Reagan's *Strategic Defense Initiative, which envisioned a space-based defense against missile attack.

[*See also* Antinuclear Protest Movements; Cold War; Limited Nuclear Test Ban Treaty; Nuclear Arms Control Treaties; Nuclear Strategy; Nuclear Weapons; Science: Since 1945.]

• Stanley A. Blumberg and Louis G. Panos, *Edward Teller: Giant of the Golden Age of Physics*, 1990. William J. Broad, *Teller's War: The Top-Secret Story behind the Star Wars Deception*, 1992.

—Gregg Herken

TEMPERANCE AND PROHIBITION, two closely related reforms that have figured prominently in U.S. history and influenced American society and politics in significant ways. Temperance reformers sought to reduce Americans' alcoholic intake or, by means of persuasion, to convince drinkers to give up alcohol entirely. Prohibition advocates attempted to eliminate alcoholic beverages from American life by force of law.

Early Temperance and Local Prohibition Movements. The first temperance reformers were Native Americans seeking to free their people from the deadly effects of the liquor trade introduced by European colonists. Among the latter, temperance reform appeared late in the *Colonial Era, when the level of alcohol consumption was high, most people drank, and distilled spirits provided much of the alcohol consumed. The first prominent nonnative voice raised for temperance, in a tract of 1784, was that of the *Philadelphia physician Benjamin *Rush. Medical concerns were reinforced by the spirit of evangelicalism aroused by the Second Great Awakening (1800–1830). The demands of an accelerating capitalist economy also made many Americans receptive to temperance injunctions to self-discipline. The first mass temperance organization, the American Temperance Society (1826), pledged hundreds of thousands of citizens from all social classes and both sexes, primarily in the northeastern states, to total abstinence from distilled spirits. Their efforts helped to bring about a sharp decline in alcohol consumption by the late 1830s.

While consumption declined, the temperance forces were dividing over the new goal of "teetotalism"—total abstinence from all alcoholic beverages—and the value of local political campaigns against licensing the liquor trade. Fresh impetus for the movement appeared in 1840 from working-class drinkers, who mobilized in "Washingtonian" clubs, which focused on the reclamation of drunkards through public meetings featuring personal narratives by the reformed. When the Washingtonian wave receded in the mid-1840s, it left behind new fraternal temperance organizations. These groups supported a shift toward coercive tactics embodied in campaigns for the Maine Law (1846), a state prohibition statute that spread to a dozen other states and territories. The Maine Law provoked opposition from liquor dealers and from ethnic groups whose customs were threatened. Although state and local prohibition laws did reduce drinking when they were enforced, their effect was often negated by the political conflicts they spawned.

Temperance reform was rejuvenated by a grassroots movement, the Women's Crusade of 1873–1874. Spurning the use of law, women in midwestern and northeastern communities marched peacefully on local liquor dealers with prayers and hymns. This transfer of temperance leadership to women led to the formation of the *Woman's Christian Temperance Union (WCTU) in 1874. Under Frances *Willard, the WCTU's agenda broadened to include woman suffrage and a host of other reforms. Willard also allied the WCTU with the Prohibition party (founded 1869). Competing with the Populists for reformers' support, the Prohibition party in 1892 adopted a radical platform that split the party and provoked conservative prohibitionists to form a new, nonpartisan organization, the Anti-Saloon League (ASL), in 1893. Through the ASL, which drew heavily on Protestant clergymen, men regained leadership of the prohibition movement, narrowed its focus to the liquor issue, adopted a corporate model of organization, and employed an incremental strategy of working toward prohibition using pressure-group tactics.

The Era of National Prohibition. The ASL strategy paid off by the early twentieth century, as gradually widening areas adopted local or state prohibition. The ensuing campaign for a constitutional amendment to mandate prohibition had complex sources, among which were Progressive hopes for social betterment; fears of the social effects of rising alcohol consumption; and deepening class and ethnic conflict. The campaign met little effective resistance from a weak and divided liquor industry. Success came with ratification of the *Eighteenth Amendment in January 1919. National prohibition officially began one year later.

Prohibition succeeded in cutting alcohol consumption and the incidence of alcohol-related diseases, although its effects varied by region and among social classes. Working-class drinking was most affected. Middle-class and elite drinkers paid more for inferior or even dangerous liquor manufactured domestically or for bootleg liquor smuggled in from abroad. Taxpayers saw rates increase to make up for lost federal liquor revenues. In *Chicago and other metropolitan areas, gangs waged bloody turf battles for control of the illegal liquor traffic.

Organized opposition soon emerged. Male upper-class leadership launched the Association Against the Prohibition Amendment in 1918 in protest against prohibition's expansion of national authority. Beginning in 1930, upper-class women organized more effectively through the Women's Organization for National Prohibition Reform. Despite these efforts, prohibition enjoyed considerable popular support. After the onset of the Great Depression in 1929, however, prohibition came to be viewed as a hindrance to economic recovery. The Twenty-first Amendment, repealing the Eighteenth, was passed by Congress early in 1933. By December, the required three-fourths of the states having ratified, national prohibition was over.

Recent Trends. After repeal, temperance reform assumed new configurations. In 1935, two habitual drunkards, Bill Wilson and Dr. Robert Smith, formed Alcoholics Anonymous (AA), a self-help organization based on viewing habitual drinking as an addiction and employing a twelve-step program of recovery. Their view of "alcoholism" as a disease was endorsed by academic researchers, led by E. M. Jellinek, and spread by the National Council on Alcoholism (founded 1944). Treatment and research institutions for alcoholism proliferated, especially after a new federal agency, the National Institute on Alcohol Abuse and Alcoholism, was established in 1970. Corporations and government agencies created programs to treat their workers. The disease concept of alcoholism held sway until the 1960s, when sharply rising consumption stimulated consideration of more restrictive alcohol-control measures. These changes tended to place decisions about alcohol control in the hands of elites, in contrast to earlier periods, when temperance conflicts were typically grassroots struggles.

High levels of alcohol-related automobile accidents and fatalities led to a campaign to dissuade drinkers from taking the wheel, and for tougher sentencing of offenders. One organization focused on this issue, Mothers Against Drunk Driving, founded in 1980, claimed 3.2 million members by 2000.

Temperance reform affected American society in numerous ways, not only sensitizing citizens to the dangers of drinking, but also providing a powerful vehicle for women's political mobilization. Numerous imitators adopted the model of pressure-group politics pioneered by the ASL. Through AA and its allies, both the concept of addiction and AA's twelve-step method became widely accepted modes of defining and treating personal problems.

[*See also* Alcohol and Alcohol Abuse; Brewing and Distilling; Capone, Al; Great Awakening, First and Second; Twenties, The; Woman Suffrage Movement; Working-Class Life and Culture.]

• Ernest Kurtz, *Not-God: A History of Alcoholics Anonymous,* 1979. Ian R. Tyrrell, *Sobering Up: From Temperance to Prohibition in Antebellum America,* 1979. Ruth Bordin, *Woman and Temperance,* 1981. K. Austin Kerr, *Organized for Prohibition: A New History of the Anti-Saloon League,* 1985. Jack S. Blocker Jr., *American Temperance Movements: Cycles of Reform,* 1989. Thomas R. Pegram, *Battling Demon Rum: The Struggle for a Dry America, 1800–1933,* 1998.

—Jack S. Blocker Jr.

TENEMENTS. *See* Housing; Slums.

TENNESSEE VALLEY AUTHORITY. Established in May 1933 during the frenzied first one hundred days of the New Deal, the Tennessee Valley Authority (TVA) sought to revitalize one of America's poorest regions. At the time, the farms and small towns in the seven states that bordered the nearly impassable Tennessee River and its tributaries presented a bleak checkerboard of weather-beaten shacks lacking electricity, crumbling churches, and one-room schools.

President Franklin Delano *Roosevelt was not the first public official who sought to harness the Tennessee River's power and address the valley's crippling *poverty, but his vision surpassed anything previously imagined. Proposing the TVA to Congress, Roosevelt declared: "It is time . . . [for] national planning for a complete river watershed involving many States and the future lives and welfare of millions." Under agency heads Arthur E. Morgan (1878–1976) and then the Chicago lawyer David E. Lilienthal (1899–1981), the TVA built sixteen *dams to prevent spring floods and limit soil erosion, supplied the valley with cheap electricity and recreational facilities, provided farmers with inexpensive fertilizer, and established a model community of neatly placed modern homes. Like most TVA programs and, indeed, most New Deal programs, this model community was racially segregated. Indeed, the TVA's insistence on local control, or "grassroots democracy," meant that discriminatory political and social structures often remained in place, even while the agency fought to eradicate poverty.

For supporters and critics, TVA symbolized the best and worst of the New Deal. Roosevelt's opponents saw it as a frightening instance of government excess; some even denounced it as "creeping *socialism." New Dealers, however, pointed to the project as a shining example of government action at its best. For the first time, thanks to TVA, recalled one enthusiast, "the poor and dispossessed of America could imagine a new kind of world, a life based on brotherhood and mutuality." A particularly strong supporter was Senator George W. Norris (1861–1944) of Nebraska, a long-time advocate of public power development. TVA's massive Norris Dam near Knoxville was named in his honor.

The TVA's legacy proved mixed. Within a decade the agency transformed an unpredictable river into a manageable waterway providing vast amounts of *hydroelectric power to thousands of isolated rural homes. *Malaria, once endemic in the area, was virtually eliminated. The TVA's accomplishments, moreover, eventually including *nuclear power, laid the groundwork for industrial development and economic expansion in the Tennessee Valley. But that progress did not end economic inequities or *racism or redistribute political power. As the twentieth century ended, the TVA survived, its spectacular dams a major tourist destination. But it survived simply as another big power company, no longer as a model of visionary government planning.

[*See also* Electrical Industry; Electricity and Electrification; New Deal Era, The; South, The.]

• Thomas McCraw, *TVA and the Power Fight, 1933–1939,* 1971. Erwin C. Hargrove and Paul K. Conkin, eds., *TVA: Fifty Years of Grassroots Bureaucracy,* 1983.

—Bryant Simon

TERRITORIES. *See* Protectorates and Dependencies.

TEST BAN TREATY. *See* Limited Nuclear Test Ban Treaty.

TET OFFENSIVE (1968), a major turning point in the *Vietnam War. In the summer of 1967, North Vietnam and the

MAP 21: TENNESSEE VALLEY AUTHORITY DAMS (1940)

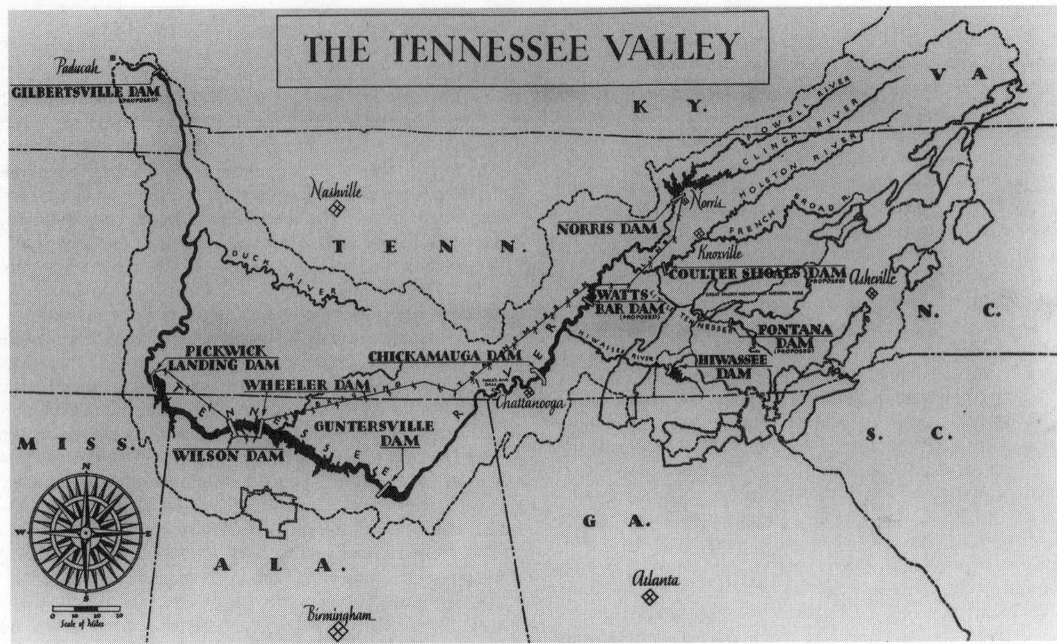

The Tennessee Valley Authority (TVA) was one of the New Deal's most admired projects. Concentrated in Tennessee but extending to adjacent states as well, TVA's hydroelectric-power and flood-control dams (shown in this map), park and recreational facilities, and other development projects transformed life in this region and helped Franklin D. Roosevelt's Democratic party retain its electoral grip on the "Solid South." Norris Dam (center) was named for Senator George W. Norris of Nebraska, long a champion of public-power projects in the region.

[*See* Electricity and Electrification; Hydroelectric Power; New Deal Era, The; Roosevelt, Franklin Delano; South, The; Tennessee Valley Authority.]

National Liberation Front of South Vietnam (NLF) devised a major offensive to break an increasingly costly military stalemate. In late 1967, the North Vietnamese attacked remote outposts in South Vietnam, luring U.S. forces from the cities. During the Tet (lunar new year) holiday of early 1968, the NLF then attacked thirty-six of forty-four provincial capitals, five of South Vietnam's major cities, sixty-four district capitals, and fifty hamlets. In Saigon, they briefly penetrated the U.S. Embassy compound and assaulted the presidential palace. In Hue, they seized the ancient Citadel, the seat of the emperors of Vietnam.

Although caught by surprise, the United States and South Vietnam responded quickly. Within several days, they cleared Saigon. The result was the same elsewhere, except in Hue where it took nearly a month of massive firepower and savage fighting to secure the city.

The impact of Tet remains difficult to assess. The North Vietnamese and NLF did not force the collapse of South Vietnam, as they had hoped. Their battle deaths have been estimated as high as forty thousand. The NLF bore the brunt of the fighting. Its main force units were decimated and would never recover.

But if Tet was a victory for the United States and South Vietnam, it was a very costly and at best a hollow one. South Vietnamese forces had to be withdrawn from the countryside, weakening the government presence there. The massive destruction in the cities brought enormous new problems for an already embattled government. American and South Vietnamese losses were also high. In the first two weeks of the fighting, 1,100 Americans and 2,300 South Vietnamese were killed. There were an estimated 12,500 civilian deaths, and as many as 1 million new refugees. In Hue, 2,800 civilians were massacred and buried in mass graves by NLF "liberators." As with so much of the war, enormous destruction produced no clear winner or loser.

Perhaps the major impact was in the United States. The military insisted that it had the upper hand, but President Lyndon B. *Johnson and his advisers were shocked by the suddenness and magnitude of the offensive. Among the public, Tet brought a mood of gloom, making clear that at best the United States faced a long and costly war. Popular approval of Johnson's handling of the war plummeted, and the Democratic senators Eugene McCarthy and Robert *Kennedy challenged his reelection.

Tet forced major changes in U.S. policy. Rejecting military appeals for thousands of additional troops, and thus ending the process of piecemeal escalation, Johnson initiated a limited cutback of the bombing of North Vietnam, agreed to negotiations, and withdrew from the presidential race.

Tet probably ensured an eventual U.S. withdrawal, but it did not end the war. Negotiations began in Paris in May 1968, but neither side would make the concessions necessary for a settlement, and each sought to apply maximum military pressure. Tet merely hardened the deadlock, and it would take four more years of fighting while negotiating before it would be broken.

[*See also* Antiwar Movements; Military, The; Nixon, Richard M.; Sixties, The.]

• Don Oberdorfer, *Tet!*, 1971. Ronald H. Spector, *After Tet: The Bloodiest Year in Vietnam*, 1993.

—George C. Herring

TEXAS REPUBLIC AND ANNEXATION. The leaders of the Republic of Texas (1836–1845) steered it through a crisis-filled decade before finally achieving their original goal of annexation to the United States. This sprawling nation of limited resources and boundless ambitions was born from rebellion against Mexico. The issues dividing Mexico and Texas, a department of the state of Coahuila, centered on Texas's resistance to firmer control by the central government, in contrast to the weak governance system established by the Constitution of 1824. Residents of Texas—mostly but not exclusively Anglo-Americans—took up arms against the Mexican government in October 1835, fought for five months for the official goal of restoring the older federalist system, and then in March 1836 declared independence. The new nation's prospects appeared bleak as Mexico achieved a series of military successes beginning with the capture of the Alamo in San Antonio and the massacre of its defenders, on 6 March. The outlook brightened on 21 April, however, when Texas forces under Sam *Houston defeated Mexican president Antonio López de Santa Anna at the Battle of San Jacinto.

Independent nationhood posed many problems for Texas. War and diplomacy were foremost because these matters placed heavy demands on the fledgling government's statesmanship and financial resources. Mexico never recognized Texas as independent and, indeed, viewed it as menacing. Disputes over the border proved a further irritant, worsened by Texas's ahistorical claim to the Rio Grande. In practice, Texas never governed any of the territory west or south of the Nueces River. Still, the boundary issue added to the tension, and relations between Mexico and Texas ran the gamut from full-scale war to skirmishes, incursions, and belligerent exchanges. In reality, neither side had the resources to make good on the bluster.

Texas did win recognition from many important nations, led by the United States (March 1837), France (September 1839), and Great Britain (November 1840). European relations were significant as a tool of manipulations skillfully managed by Sam Houston, who served as president in 1836–1838 and again in 1841–1844. Between Houston's two terms, the more decidedly nationalistic and even imperialistic Mirabeau B. Lamar held the presidency. Lamar spurned Houston's diplomatic prudence, military restraint, and fiscal conservatism; his principal legacy was to increase Texas's debt and to found Austin, the future state capital, named for the pioneer settler Stephen F. Austin, in 1834. Lamar's expansionist designs on Santa Fe, New Mexico, ended in the embarrassing surrender of Texas forces on the plains southwest of Santa Fe in 1841. His covert support for rebellious factions in the Yucatan and Mexico's northeastern border states of Coahuila, Nuevo León, and Tamaulipas further exacerbated tensions. Responding to these aggressive moves, Mexico dispatched two expeditions that reached San Antonio in 1842, during Sam Houston's second term. Houston in turn authorized volunteers to move to the Rio Grande. These volunteers sacked one town (Laredo) and were imprisoned after a failed assault against another (Mier). All these expeditions and counter-expeditions served primarily to stimulate mutual bitterness and a desire for revenge.

The Texas Republic also proved inept in its relations with Indians, adding to its insecurity. To the east, Lamar made war on and removed those Indians most amenable to a peaceful and sedentary life, Houston's beloved Cherokees. On the southwestern frontier, neither leader coped adequately with the intractable Comanches, although Houston's policy of negotiation and trade proved more successful than Lamar's focus on military force, retaliation, and destruction.

The greatest success of the Republic of Texas was in attracting emigrants: the population grew from about 40,000 in 1836 to 150,000 in 1845. Most of these newcomers were lured from the United States by liberal land policies; many others—in fact the fastest growing segment—came involuntarily as slaves. The commitment to *slavery by the government and citizens of Texas presented the greatest obstacle to their goal of annexation, which the *Free-Soil party and other northern *antislavery forces vigorously opposed. This opposition was overcome by the expansionist fever manifested in the election of 1844 in the United States, with President Houston shrewdly exploiting the strong Anglophobia of Texans who feared a British protectorate. In 1845, the people of Texas voted overwhelmingly in favor of annexation. The U.S. Congress concurred, and Texas entered the Union as the twenty-eighth state, ending its brief existence as an independent nation. These developments, in turn, laid the groundwork for the *Mexican War.

[*See also* Alamo, Battle of the; Antebellum Era; Cotton Industry; Expansionism; Foreign Relations: U.S. Relations with Latin America; Indian History and Culture: From 1800 to 1900; Manifest Destiny; Slavery: Development and Expansion of; Tyler, John.]

• William C. Binkley, *The Texas Revolution,* 1952. David M. Pletcher, *The Diplomacy of Annexation: Texas, Oregon, and the Mexican War,* 1973. Randolph B. Campbell, *Sam Houston and the American Southwest,* 1993. John Hoyt Williams, *Sam Houston,* 1993. Rupert N. Richardson, et al., *Texas: The Lone Star State,* 7th ed., 1997.

—Paul D. Lack

TEXTILE INDUSTRY. American colonists hand-produced textiles for various purposes. The English first devised textile-manufacturing machinery, and Samuel Slater, an English mill overseer who immigrated to America, successfully produced cotton yarn at a Pawtucket, Rhode Island, mill in 1790. As was to be the case repeatedly, Slater's success rested on the contributions of a community of inventors, machinists, laborers and financial backers. Relying on the employment of families, the "putting-out system" to weave yarn in area homes, and the development of corporate villages, the Slater system spread throughout *New England. Entrepreneurs in *Philadelphia, *New York City, and other cities employed skilled labor to produce short runs of expensive specialty materials such as fashion goods and upholstery, gradually moving from hand to factory production.

A group of merchants known as the Boston Associates created a third style of production, first at Waltham, Massachusetts, in 1814, and then at Lowell, Massachusetts, and other single-purpose industrial cities across New England. Building large, integrated factories and installing water-powered looms that processed raw cotton into vast quantities of coarse cloth, they hired rural young women to tend machines requiring minimal skills. With large-scale capital investment, and aided by state governments, these corporations harnessed major waterpower sites.

Each type of textile production endured decades of strife between management seeking profit and labor attempting to negotiate acceptable terms and conditions for the new ways of work. In mill villages, some accommodation was necessary to maintain production with limited human resources on both sides of the dispute, although the owners' preponderance of power gave them an advantage. Skilled producers of specialty goods and their bosses, sharing the culture and rewards of production, generally adapted pay, hours, and profits to mutually acceptable levels. In the large single-industry cities, employers refused to make concessions, and successive groups of workers—Yankees, Irish, French-Canadians, immigrants from southern and eastern Europe—all rejected conditions and left the mills at the first opportunity, with no reconciliation of conflicting interests.

Though northern textile mills and specialty production survived well into the twentieth century, the New *South desired to industrialize to make both cloth and profits more easily by shifting their investments away from the circumstances and taxes (e.g., workers' compensation and unemployment insurance) their manner of operation had created. By 1900, the capital generated by northern textile workers was financing southern branches of established mills and new mills founded by southerners. Textile-machinery builders and cloth-marketing agents, taking stock instead of cash from southern mills, came to control many of them. American industry thus began its perpetual search for easier, cheaper venues in which to operate.

By the end of the twentieth century, however, the industry faced intense competition from cheaper producers abroad, especially Asia. Total employment in U.S. textile mills fell from 1.2. million in 1950 to under 700,000 in 1990.

[*See also* Clothing and Fashion; Cotton Industry; Factory System; Global Economy, America and the; Immigrant Labor; Industrialization; Labor Movements; Lowell Mills; Strikes and Industrial Conflict; Women in the Labor Force.]

• Philip Scranton, *Figured Tapestry,* 1989. Laurence F. Gross, *The Course of Industrial Decline,* 1993.

—Laurence F. Gross

THEATER. The beginnings of the English-speaking theater in America are dimmer than the candlelit stages of the era. In 1665, the performers, almost certainly amateurs, of a play called *The Bear and the Cub* were prosecuted in Accomac County, Virginia, on charges of public wickedness. The charges were dismissed, but nothing more is known of the play or its actors. However, the incident demonstrates the fanatically moralistic opposition that would plague the arts all through American history. In 1703 or 1704, Anthony Aston, an adventurer turned player, gave performances along the East Coast from Florida to New York. Again, sadly, what roles he played and where are uncertain. The real beginnings of the American stage date to 1752, when Lewis Hallam landed in Yorktown, Virginia, with a small troupe, some scenery, and costumes. On 15 September, having obtained the governor's permission, he staged Shakespeare's *The Merchant of Venice* and Edward Ravenscroft's farce *The Anatomist.* No mid-eighteenth-century American city was large enough to sustain a season-long theatrical program, so Hallam and his band moved on to *New York City, *Philadelphia, and Charleston, offering a broad repertory of works by Shakespeare as well as Restoration and contemporary dramatists. Welcomed by playgoers but denounced by some religious extremists, Hallam and his company left for Jamaica in late 1754 or early 1755. He soon died there, but his son, Lewis, Junior, returned in 1758 with a new company organized with his mother and stepfather, David Douglass. The group became known as the American Company, and, later in its forty-year existence, as the Old American Company. This troupe opened several important early playhouses, such as the John Street Theater in New York, and staged the first professionally mounted American play, Thomas Godfrey's *The Prince of Parthia,* in 1767 in Philadelphia. British theatricals continued to dominate American stages for decades, however. Hallam and his successors were eventually bought out by William Dunlap (1766–1839) a playwright, manager, and first towering figure in American theatrical history. When Dunlap went bankrupt, control of New York's Park Theater, which he had helped build, was assumed by Thomas Abthorpe Cooper (1776–1849), considered by many America's first great tragedian.

Through most of this time, major American cities—all still confined to the East Coast—could each support only a single auditorium, and presentations were offered for only a limited number of performances in repertory. Distances and poor transportation between cities encouraged the development of local stock companies, occasionally joined by a visiting foreign luminary such as George Frederick Cooke. Away from larger eastern cities, smaller troupes circulated or attempted lesser stock companies. As the nation pushed westward, intrepid actors and managers, among them Samuel Drake and Noah Ludlow, cruised the great rivers bringing floating theaters to local audiences. Ludlow afterward combined with Sol Smith to establish permanent playhouses in towns along the *Mississippi River and even inland.

By the early nineteenth century urban growth in the East allowed a second and sometimes a third playhouse to compete. Beginning in 1825, playhouses converted from candlelight to gas. The growth in population also encouraged the notion of "long runs." The three-week stand of Dion Boucicault's *London Assurance* at the Park Theater in 1841 inaugurated the practice in America. The same production also introduced American playgoers to the three-walled box set, although it did not completely replace the meticulously painted wing-and-drop sets for many decades. Pre–*Civil War audiences also applauded a growing roster of immigrant and native-born players such as Junius Brutus Booth (1796–1852), Edwin Forrest (1806–72), and Charlotte Cushman (1816–76).

The Civil War ended the prosperous and often independent theater that had flourished in the antebellum *South, especially in Charleston and Savannah, which had even had their own respected playwrights. Only *New Orleans partially recovered. On the other hand, Civil War–born prosperity helped the North, promoting longer runs, more venues, and more productions. With the wartime growth of *railroads, stars no longer had to endure rough trips between towns to act briefly with an often barely competent stock troupe. Instead, trains allowed a complete and carefully chosen cast, along with excellent scenery and costumes, to move from city to city, giving smaller centers the same polished mountings big cities saw. This competition forced surviving stock companies to raise standards and led to such admired ensembles as Wallack's and Daly's in New York, Mrs. Drew's Arch Street Theater in Philadelphia, and the Boston Museum, whose company was led by two beloved players, William Warren and Mrs. Vincent. By the later nineteenth century, thousands of American cities had some sort of auditorium, enabling players to tour for decades in one play or at least in a limited repertory. Joseph Jefferson (1829–1905) as Rip Van Winkle, Lotta Crabtree (1847–1924) in her little-girl roles, and Edwin Booth (1833–1893) in his mostly Shakespearean repertory exemplified the practice. By the late 1880s, as major theaters began to be electrified, brighter lighting ended the practice of older actors impersonating young lovers, and forced many other changes in acting styles.

In the mid–1890s, a group of New York businessmen formed what became known as the Syndicate to control theaters and productions around the country. They were beaten at their own game, however, by the brothers Lee, Samuel, and Jacob Shubert, Lithuanian Jewish immigrants from Syracuse, New York, who leased New York's Herald Square Theater, in 1900. By the mid–1920s, the Shuberts owned nearly one hundred theaters in major cities in the United States, Canada, and Great Britain, and leased many more in smaller cities. Three-quarters of all theater tickets sold, it was said, were to productions in Shubert theaters.

Meanwhile, the rise of silent *films eroded live theater. After about 1906, the touring companies with their one-night stands declined precipitously. Theater in New York and other major cities flourished through the 1920s, however. In 1927–1928 Broadway (New York's theater district) had more than 70 theaters and a record 264 productions. Philadelphia supported 10 playhouses. But the simultaneous introduction of sound movies and the onset of the Great Depression plunged the stage into a radical decline. The change in urban demographics after *World War II further hurt live theater, as did an alteration in ticket pricing, making the cheapest balcony seats almost as costly as the best orchestra seats. As *television seduced many into remaining at home for their entertainment, miking and amplification, especially of musicals, destroyed the flesh-and-blood reality and intimacy of performances. By the late 1990s only a few dozen plays were produced on Broadway and almost nothing toured. Small off-Broadway houses and regional theaters were more productive, though many tended to be consciously arty and attracted only a limited number of loyalists.

[*See also* Drama; Minstrelsy; Musical Theater; Vaudeville.]

• Burns Mantle *et al*, eds., *The Best Plays*, annual publication, 1920–present. Jack Poggi, *Theater in America: The Impact of Economic Forces. 1870–1967*, 1968. Gerald Bordman, *A Chronicle of Comedy and Drama*, 3 vols., 1994–1996. Mary C. Henderson, *Theater in America: 250 Years of Plays, Players, and Productions*, 1996. Theater histories, of varying quality, exist for nearly all major American cities.

—Gerald Bordman

THEME PARKS. *See* Amusement Parks and Theme Parks.

THEORY OF BUSINESS ENTERPRISE, THE (1904). In this sequel to his better-known **Theory of the Leisure Class* (1899), Thorstein *Veblen painted an unflattering portrait of the *business class. Inverting Horatio *Alger's image of the virtuous, self-sufficient capitalist, Veblen's businessman, far from being a pillar of the community, simply manipulated the capitalist system for personal profit. Veblen described the modern economy as a "concatenation" of interdependent systems. Like the proverbial butterfly whose flapping wings could ultimately cause a typhoon, disturbances in any one industry spread quickly throughout the system. Business managers were best situated to predict and shape market psychology, profit from the boom-bust cycle, and accumulate intangible assets and credit lines. Like the leisure class to which it aspired, the business class with its commitment to *laissez-faire exerted a conservative, even corrupting influence on politics.

As business imperatives (the profit motive) eroded the instincts of industriousness and workmanship (production), he warned, social upheaval became more likely. A predatory, militaristic state, he predicted, would emerge to quell the ensuing unrest. Yet he also envisioned the possibility of a benevolent alliance of workers and engineers, unified by allegience to the "machine discipline," viewing facts in the context of material cause and effect and dedicated to the impartial solution of social problems. Veblen also equated the "machine discipline" with *socialism, interpreting the growth of labor unions as marking the end of outmoded values such as property rights and *religion. Though his darker predictions proved the more prescient, Veblen's vision of an enlightened technocracy resonated with *Progressive Era social theorists, especially Walter *Lippmann, and later with New Dealers like Rexford Tugwell.

[*See also* Capitalism; Economics; Engineering; Industrialization; New Deal Era The; Social Class; Technology.]

• John P. Diggins, *The Bard of Savagery*, 1978. Rich Tilman, *Thorstein Veblen and His Critics*, 1992.

—Andrew Chamberlin Rieser

THEORY OF THE LEISURE CLASS, THE (1899). In his best-known book, the economist Thorstein *Veblen satirized the *Gilded Age moneyed class, deconstructed the "rational man" of neoclassical economics, and redefined *economics as the study of the cultural meanings imputed to material goods. Veblen portrayed an economic order shaped not by Adam Smith's "hidden hand" but by the institutionalization of "barbarian traits" underlying all social conventions. When a "predatory" class of capitalists enshrined private property and enriched itself by controlling society's surplus labor, *work became a badge of low status rather than a source of pride, while the ostentatious avoidance of work signaled higher status. Veblen dissected the leisure class's culture of "wastemanship" in fashion, *architecture, entertainment, *leisure, and many other areas. The elaborate, confining dresses of rich women, for example, indicated their freedom from productive labor. The habit of "conspicuous consumption," he argued, shaped morality, aesthetics, *religion, education, and marital alliances, fortifying a parasitic regime. Inverting a familiar social Darwinist argument, Veblen contended that the leisure class retarded social progress by sheltering itself from the economic forces that encouraged adaption.

Veblen shared Karl Marx's tendency to romanticize preindustrial labor, and his arcane vocabulary obscured his aims and blurred the crucial distinction between biology and culture, leading to specious ethnic and racial generalizations. The relationship between *social class and culture would change dramatically in succeeding decades, as non-elites became consumers of mass-produced goods and the upper class's tastemaking role eroded. Nevertheless, *The Theory of the Leisure Class,* prophetic in its attention to consumerism, remains a penetrating critique of the subtle exercise of power in modern society.

[*See also* Capitalism; Clothing and Fashion; Consumer Culture; Economics; Social Darwinism; Sociology.]

• David Riesman, *Thorstein Veblen: A Critical Interpretation,* 1953. John P. Diggins, *The Bard of Savagery,* 1978. Rick Tilman, *Thorstein Veblen and His Critics,* 1992.

—Andrew Chamberlin Rieser

THOMAS, NORMAN (1884–1968), Socialist party leader and six-time socialist candidate for president (1928–1948). Born in Marion, Ohio, Norman Thomas attended Princeton University and Union Theological Seminary and was ordained as a Presbyterian minister in 1911. He joined the Socialist party after supporting the socialist and labor leader Morris Hillquit for *New York City mayor in 1917.

A spiritual heir to the nineteenth-century moralistic reformers, Thomas derived his appeal from the ethical-moral perspective, and the intense moral revulsion to human suffering that he brought to social, economic, and international problems. A pacifist during *World War I, Thomas dropped his *pacifism during the Spanish Civil War (1936–1939). He continued to find war morally abhorrent, however, a view that led him to oppose aid to the allies before *World War II. This position served him well when he later critically supported that conflict, and also in his postwar efforts for world peace, disarmament, and opposition to the *Vietnam War.

As a socialist, Thomas criticized President Franklin Delano *Roosevelt's policies because Thomas envisioned a cooperative society and not the reformed *capitalism of the New Deal. He edged away from socialist orthodoxy after World War II, but never lost his belief in the incompatibility of a just economy and the profit system.

Thomas's historical importance lies with his moral vision. Achieving no socialist goals, he nevertheless moved masses of people to protest the denial of *civil rights, *civil liberties, and material security to millions of their brothers and sisters.

[*See also* Antiwar Movements; Debs, Eugene V.; New Deal Era, The; Radicalism; Social Gospel; Socialism; Socialist Party of America.]

• Frank A. Warren, *An Alternative Vision: The Socialist Party in the 1930s,* 1974. W. A. Swanberg, *Norman Thomas: The Last Idealist,* 1976.

—Frank A. Warren

THOMAS, THEODORE (1835–1905), conductor. Born in Esens, Germany, Thomas emigrated to *New York City in 1845 with his family. A violin prodigy, he toured the *South on his own in 1850. Back in New York, he formed his own orchestra and, beginning in 1869, toured widely on a core route nicknamed the "Thomas Highway." He led the New York Philharmonic Orchestra in 1877–1878 and again from 1880 to 1891. He also was the founding conductor of the Chicago Orchestra (later the Chicago Symphony), which he led from 1891 until his death.

Thomas is an iconic figure for the late *Gilded Age. Religiously devoted to the German masters and masterworks, he called his concerts "sermons in tones." His melioristic fervor endeared him to moralists of genteel persuasion. His appeal to others depended on his "masculinity," counteracting stereotypes of effete high culture. The embodiment of Theodore *Roosevelt's "strenuous life," he hardened his body with gymnastics and icy baths. A cultural frontiersman, he was sturdy, pragmatic, and dominating, self-educated and self-reliant. He looked like a banker and disapproved of eccentricities of manner or attire. The musician in Thomas was comparably stern and autocratic. Eschewing interpretation, he was a paragon of discipline and integrity. The unified bowings, smooth blends, and perfect intonation of his performances set standards for America and amazed visiting Europeans. His influential credo was "a symphony orchestra shows the culture of the community, not opera." Thanks partly to Thomas, the concert orchestra became an American specialty, in contradistinction to the pit orchestras of Europe. No other individual so potently disseminated symphonic culture in the United States.

[*See also* Music: Classical Music.]

• Ezra Schabas, *Theodore Thomas: America's Conductor and Builder of Orchestras,* 1989. Joseph Horowitz, *Wagner Nights: An American History,* 1994.

—Joseph Horowitz

THOREAU, HENRY DAVID (1817–1862), writer, scientist, transcendentalist. Of the better-known writers of Concord, Massachusetts, only Thoreau was born there. After graduating from Harvard in 1837 he returned home, became friends with Ralph Waldo *Emerson, and embarked on a career of reading, writing, and observing nature. His short stints of gainful employment included work as a day laborer, pencil maker, and surveyor. Except for brief excursions to Staten Island, Cape Cod, Maine, Montreal, New Jersey, and Minnesota, he spent the rest of his life in Concord, where, as he said, he traveled extensively. On 4 July 1845, he began the intermittent stay of just over two years at nearby Walden Pond that is chronicled in his autobiographical and philosophical work *Walden* (1854). Incontestably a masterpiece of American *literature, *Walden,* structured around Thoreau's observations of the changing seasons, has inspired a small library of similar volumes.

The first to call for national parks (in *The Maine Woods,* 1864), Thoreau was also a pioneer ecologist ("The Succession of Forest Trees," 1860, and the posthumous *Faith in a Seed*) and an originator of America's conservation ethic. He understood nature not as an adversary but as the cradle and matrix of human existence, and wilderness not as the antithesis, but as the source, of civilization. "In wildness is the preservation of the world," he wrote. Thoreau crossed the boundaries of literature and science, indeed, his last writings, some still unpublished, are almost purely scientific.

In his nature writing, Thoreau promulgated a gospel of immediate experience and the present moment: "I believe in the forest, and in the meadow, and in the night in which the corn grows." He reminded his own and successive generations of their link to nature. As he wrote in his journal for 17 May 1854: "Who shall distinguish between the *law* by which a brook finds its river, the *instinct* [by which] a bird performs its migrations, and the *knowledge* by which a man steers his ship round the globe?"

Interested in social reform as well as in the environment, Thoreau in July 1846 was jailed overnight for refusing to pay a poll tax as a protest against the *Mexican War and the expansion of *slavery. He supported John *Brown's raids and assisted fugitive slaves fleeing northward. His social thought, akin to that of classical Stoicism, emphasized self-rule and *individualism as the true basis for community. His essay "Civil Disobedience" (1849) asserts the primacy of the individual conscience, declaring: "It is not desirable to cultivate a respect for the law so much as for the right." In such works as *Walden* and *A Week on the Concord and Merrimack Rivers* (1849), Thoreau forged a personal ethic which held that for a guide to life, one must turn not to the state, the gods, society, or even history, but to nature. He recognized, however, that the turn to nature and to the self were merely starting points. With Emerson, Margaret *Fuller, and the other transcendentalists, he understood the social imperatives latent in the insistence on personal worth and autonomy: What applies to the individual applies to everyone; if I wish to be free, all must be free.

[*See also* Antebellum Era; Antislavery; Conservation Movement; Environmentalism; Leopold, Aldo; Muir, John; Romantic Movement; Transcendentalism.]

• Robert D. Richardson Jr., *Henry Thoreau: A Life of the Mind,* 1986. Lawrence Buell, *The Environmental Imagination: Thoreau, Nature Writing and the Formation of American Culture,* 1995.

—Robert D. Richardson Jr.

THREE MILE ISLAND (1979), nuclear power generating station on the Susquehanna River near Harrisburg, Pennsylvania. Three Mile Island first attracted national attention—and precipitated a crisis for commercial *nuclear power in the United States—on 28 March 1979, when a valve for regulating the flow of cooling water to a reactor closed. The malfunctioning of this valve led to a series of mechanical failures and human mistakes that threatened the surrounding area with radioactive contamination. Uncertain about how much radiation had been or would be released beyond the building, experts recommended that children and pregnant women leave the area. On 30 March, amid a glare of worldwide publicity, the governor of Pennsylvania ordered such an evacuation, although by that time engineers had stabilized the reactor. President Jimmy *Carter, wearing protective garb, toured the plant.

The Three Mile Island accident jolted the nuclear-power industry. Utilities shelved plans to build new plants and shut down some already in operation. An antinuclear power movement, already under way, gained momentum. The *Nuclear Regulatory Commission, the federal oversight body, moved aggressively to improve safety in all nuclear plants. The accident also affected research and scholarship. Earlier, engineering studies on reactor safety had typically sought to estimate the likelihood and health impact of specific mishaps. Subsequently, the research explored the interplay of multiple failures and the effect of procedures and training programs on operators' performance. More than a cataclysm for an industry, the Three Mile Island accident also illuminated larger issues on the technological, social, and ideological horizon.

[*See also* Antinuclear Protest Movements; Electrical Industry; Hydroelectric Power; Technology.]

• Charles Perrow, *Normal Accidents: Living with High-Risk Technologies,* 1984. John L. Campbell, *Collapse of an Industry: Nuclear Power and the Contradictions of U.S. Policy,* 1988.

—Cora Bagley Marrett

TOBACCO INDUSTRY. Few commercial enterprises have had more economic, social, and medical impact, and provoked more political and cultural debate than the tobacco industry. Tobacco, long cultivated and cured by North American Indians, was first transported to Europe by Christopher *Columbus. Cultivation by English colonists began in Virginia in 1612, when John Rolfe planted the first crop. Tobacco exports—limited to England or English colonies by the Navigation Act of 1660—proved crucial to the Chesapeake region's economy throughout the *Colonial Era. In 1770, North American growers exported more than £900,000 worth of tobacco to England. The spread of tobacco culture was also intimately linked to the growth and expansion of *slavery.

Tobacco remained vital to the *South's economic well-being in the early national era, as production expanded to supply a growing export market and to meet Americans' own fondness for snuff, pipe tobacco, chewing tobacco, and cigars. As tobacco cultivation spread westward into Kentucky and Tennessee, annual output increased from 110,000 to 160,000 hogsheads in the years 1790–1860.

The origins of the modern tobacco industry, characterized by the *mass production and *mass marketing of *tobacco products—including the increasingly popular cigarettes—dates to 1865, when Washington Duke started a fledgling tobacco manufactory in Durham, North Carolina. Duke's enterprise flourished as a manufacturer of plug and chewing tobacco, but it was his son, James Buchanan Duke (1856–1925), who took over W. Duke and Sons in the 1880s, who built a financial empire that soon dwarfed all other tobacco companies. The pivotal moment came in 1884 when James Duke secured exclusive rights to a machine developed by Virginian James A. Bonsack that could mass-produce cigarettes. While cigarette manufacturing had been an expensive and time-consuming enterprise involving hand rollers, a single Bonsack machine could produce over 100,000 cigarettes a day. In 1889, Duke organized the five largest U.S. tobacco enterprises—W. Duke and Sons, Kinney, Allen and Ginter, William S. Kimball, and Goodwin and Company—into the mammoth American Tobacco Company (ATC), originally capitalized at $25 million. Duke became its first president.

Acquiring or driving out of business over 250 tobacco manufacturers over the next decade, the ATC by 1907 was one of the world's most powerful industrial monopolies, now capitalized at $450 million and producing nearly 80 percent of the world's plug and twist tobacco, 71 percent of smoking tobacco, and over 96 percent of snuff tobacco. Duke pioneered in turning a portion of his profits back into the mass marketing of his major brands. For tobacco farmers, particularly those in Virginia, North Carolina, and Kentucky, Duke's methods and market dominance resulted in prices that were well below the cost of production. Thousands of small family farmers were forced into *poverty and chronic indebtedness. While farmers in central Kentucky organized a successful strike in 1908 against the ATC and ultimately forced Duke to pay higher prices, the ATC's firm control of the entire tobacco industry continued until the U.S. *Supreme Court, in a 1911 *antitrust case, split the tobacco giant into several smaller companies, including Liggett and Myers, Lorillard, and R. J. Reynolds.

Despite periodic reform campaigns to curtail or prohibit cigarettes, smoking by *World War I had become nearly ubiquitous, and its popularity increased as Hollywood began portraying cigarettes as glamorous. Ads even spoke of cigarettes' beneficial health effects in promoting endurance and reducing nervousness and throat irritation. A new generation of industry leaders emerged, such as the ATC's George W. Hill who orchestrated a highly successful marketing campaign for Lucky Strike cigarettes, launched in 1917 to compete with R. J. Reynolds' Camels. While the industry enriched its executives and stockholders, many tobacco growers remained impoverished. Plummeting agricultural prices during the Depression of the 1930s further damaged the tobacco economy of the rural South. In 1933, congressional leaders from tobacco-producing states succeeded in including tobacco in the *Agricultural Adjustment Act, which established a price support system for agricultural commodities in exchange for production limits.

Tobacco use continued to increase after *World War II. By 1964, 42 percent of adult Americans smoked cigarettes. In that year, however, confirming what many had long suspected, a U.S. Surgeon General's report established the relationship between smoking and *cancer. Although the industry strongly denied any such link, health warnings were added to cigarette packages, and cigarette *advertising on *television was halted. Nevertheless, despite the growing concern about cancer and *heart disease risks, the tobacco industry flourished in the 1970s and 1980s. Industry giants such as Philip Morris and R. J. Reynolds promoted their leading brands aggressively and sought new areas of acquisition and market development, particularly in the consumer-friendly food and beverage sector. Shrewd marketing campaigns designed to counter the negative publicity made the rugged "Marlboro Man" and the cartoonish "Joe Camel" cultural icons.

Despite mounting medical and scientific evidence linking tobacco and disease, industry leaders continued to insist that no such link had been positively established. They also denied the additional charge that nicotine (a central component of tobacco) was physically addictive. By the 1990s, however, company insiders released numerous internal documents revealing that major tobacco manufacturers had long been aware of tobacco's *health risks and its addictive nature, and had initiated advertising campaigns to encourage youth smoking. Its credibility severely damaged, the industry moved in the late 1990s to offset further possibly bankrupting legal challenges by agreeing to a settlement with forty-six state attorneys general totaling $206 billion. But many issues remained, such as whether Congress would empower the Food and Drug Administration to regulate nicotine as a drug; whether the controversial tobacco price-support system would survive; and how the numerous existing lawsuits by dying smokers and their families would finally be resolved.

The tobacco industry's devastating toll on countless users of its products, and the grinding long-term poverty of small-scale tobacco farmers, are part of the legacy of America's long love affair with tobacco. But although embattled on many fronts, the industry remained an economic behemoth, and tobacco a vital agricultural commodity, as the twentieth century ended. The leading U.S. tobacco company, Philip Morris, manufacturer of Marlboro cigarettes, enjoyed 1998 revenues of $57.8 billion, and was the nation's eighth largest corporation. (Nontobacco subsidiaries accounted for part of this revenue.) Global markets beckoned as well, especially in poorer nations, and U.S. cigarette exports in 1998 totaled nearly $4.2 billion.

[*See also* Agriculture; Disease; Factory System; Foreign Trade, U.S.; Industrialization; Medicine: Since 1945; Navigation Acts; New Deal Era, The.]

• Nannie May Tilley, *The R. J. Reynolds Tobacco Company,* 1985. Tracy Campbell, *The Politics of Despair: Power and Resistance in the Tobacco Wars,* 1993. Richard Kluger, *Ashes to Ashes: America's Hundred-Year Cigarette War, the Public Health, and the Unabashed Triumph of Philip Morris,* 1996. Jeffrey R. Kerr-Ritchie, *Freedpeople in the Tobacco South: Virginia, 1860–1900,* 1999. Cassandra Tate, *Cigarette Wars: The Triumph of "The Little White Slaver,"* 1999.

—Tracy Campbell

TOBACCO PRODUCTS. Despite official English policies that held tobacco to be harmful, and a denunciatory tract by James I, the plant became colonial Virginia's export staple, and tobacco use was widespread among the colonists. Before 1750, Americans' preferred method of tobacco use was pipe smoking—popularized by the upper classes in Europe. Snuff (ground tobacco mixed with flavorings or scents) next became the style for elite men and women. The nasal inhalation of snuff lost favor after the American Revolution, however, and those who continued to use snuff now placed small quantities between the lip or cheek and the gum. But most early nineteenth-century users switched to chewing tobacco, again a flavored tobacco, or cigars. The latter, varying widely in quality and price to suit all classes, were considered cleaner—and manlier—than chewing-tobacco.

Cigarettes slowly gained popularity in the late nineteenth century. Initially associated with *New York City bohemians, street urchins, and other disreputable characters, cigarettes revived opposition to tobacco on health and moral grounds. Yet by the 1920s, cigarettes dominated tobacco use. Three factors account for this success: increased production of lighter, milder "bright" tobacco; innovations in production technologies, especially the Bonsack cigarette machine; and advances in *advertising and other *mass-marketing techniques such as premiums, price cutting, and rebates. The introduction of safety matches also facilitated the spread of cigarette smoking. Unlike cigars or pipes, a cigarette could be smoked in a few minutes, and it could be enjoyed almost anywhere without the unsightly spitting and plug-disposal problems associated with chewing tobacco.

A new era in tobacco sales and advertising opened in 1914 with the introduction of Camel cigarettes by R. J. Reynolds, a former associate of *tobacco-industry pioneer James B. Duke. Camel was a mild cigarette that allowed deep inhalation of the smoke. Brand loyalty, rather than price competition, now became the key in cigarette marketing. Cigarettes were heavily promoted during both world wars, with free or cut-rate distribution to service personnel, and systematically introduced on college campuses between the wars. By 1927, state legislatures had repealed all laws regulating tobacco-product sales to adults. Advertisers marketed cigarettes to women as sophisticated, romantic, and a badge of emancipation, while simultaneously appealing to men by portraying cigarette smoking as a sign of masculinity. With such promotion, cigarette sales soared from 70 billion in 1925 to 339 billion in 1945 and 640 billion in 1981—the all-time high. Opponents of tobacco use, meanwhile, were increasingly marginalized. Even the few physicians who warned against smoking were dismissed as moralistic zealots.

Change lay ahead, however. In 1948, the makers of Parliament, a filtered cigarette, claimed that physicians recommended them. This innovation gained significance in 1950 when the *Journal of the American Medical Association* suggested, on epidemiological grounds, a possible connection between smoking and lung *cancer. By 1958, filter-tip cigarettes had captured 46 percent of the market.

But the complicated chemistry of tobacco smoke and the uncertain laboratory understanding of cancer made the smoking–lung cancer connection difficult for many researchers to accept, and modern medical epidemiology in fact developed from the attempts to establish the link. As epidemiological evidence accumulated, smoking was linked to other illnesses such as emphysema and *heart disease. But since most physicians were smokers, and good research could be found on both sides of the issue, Americans had difficulty deciding where the truth and the *public-health interest lay. Only under much political and scientific pressure did the U.S. surgeon general in 1964 issue an authoritative report presumptively linking smoking to several specific diseases—as opposed to the general unhealthiness assumed by earlier hygienists and moralists.

Dismissing mere statistical associations as unconvincing, the tobacco industry took the position that until a specific carcinogen could be found in tobacco smoke, it would deny a causal link between smoking and cancer. Through the Tobacco Institute (founded 1958), the industry resisted government regulation of its multibillion dollar business. By the mid–1960s, however, an array of medical and lay groups constituted a strong antismoking lobby dedicated to regulating the marketing and smoking of tobacco products. Seeking protection against legal liability, manufacturers in 1966 added warning labels to cigarette packages and in 1971 stopped advertising cigarettes on *radio and *television and included health warnings in print advertising. In the 1980s, organizations such as GASP (Group against Smokers' Pollution) and ASH (Action on Smoking and Health) publicized research on the hazards of "second-hand smoke" inhaled from cigarettes being smoked by others. By the 1990s, alarmed by increasing tobacco use among young people, smoking opponents focused on nicotine's addictive qualities. The antismoking campaign had its effect: From 1985 to 1998, the percentage of Americans who smoked fell from 38.7 to 27.7. In 1998, the four largest tobacco companies signed a $206 billion agreement with forty-six states to cover public-health costs related to smoking.

As the twentieth century ended, growing evidence of cigarettes' devastating medical toll; litigation by individual smokers and class-action lawsuits; a federal lawsuit for deceptive practices; and smoking bans by local municipalities, airlines, businesses, restaurants, and public institutions all battered the tobacco industry. Strenuous antismoking campaigns continued to target children and young people. Despite declining smoking rates, however, millions of Americans continued to smoke cigarettes or use tobacco in other forms, and U.S.-made cigarettes flooded foreign markets. Ironically, in the prosperous 1990s, expensive cigars enjoyed a resurgence of popularity as a badge of affluence.

[*See also* Agriculture; Antitrust Legislation; Colonial Era;

Foreign Trade, U.S.; Health and Fitness; Mass Production; Medicine: Since 1945; Twenties, The.]

• Nannie May Tilley, *The Bright-Tobacco Industry, 1860–1929,* 1948. Richard B. Tennant, *The American Cigarette Industry: A Study in Economic Analysis and Public Policy,* 1950. Kenneth Michael Friedman, *Public Policy and the Smoking-Health Controversy: A Comparative Study,* 1975. Gideon Doron, *The Smoking Paradox: Public Regulation in the Cigarette Industry,* 1979. John C. Burnham, "American Physicians and Tobacco Use: Two Surgeons General, 1929 and 1964," *Bulletin of the History of Medicine* 63 (1989):1–31. Cassandra Tate, *Cigarette Wars: The Triumph of "The Little White Slaver,"* 1999.

—John E. Sauer and John C. Burnham

TOCQUEVILLE, ALEXIS DE. *See Democracy in America.*

TOMB OF THE UNKNOWNS. Located in *Arlington National Cemetery and originally known as the Tomb of the Unknown Soldier, this memorial contains the graves of three unidentified servicemen who each individually symbolize the sacrifice of all American servicemen who died in the nation's twentieth-century wars. Established under a congressional mandate and patterned after similar memorials in Europe created after *World War I, the first Unknown was entombed on 11 November 1921 after a state funeral stressing the theme of selfless sacrifice of the individual to the nation. This and subsequent ceremonies portrayed the Unknown Soldier as representative of a national vision transcending class, ethnic, racial, regional, and religious differences.

The tomb was originally conceived as a memorial to World War I, once called the "war to end all wars," but events after 1939 required a reinterpretation. In 1950, the Defense Department planned to add a grave for an unidentified serviceman from the *World War II, but the outbreak of the *Korean War interrupted these arrangements. In 1958 the Defense Department entombed Unknown Soldiers for both World War II and Korea. On Memorial Day 1984, an Unknown Serviceman from the *Vietnam War was included.

With advances in genetic testing, Secretary of Defense William S. Cohen in 1998 ordered the exhumation of the Unknown from the Vietnam War to determine whether the body could be identified. Sophisticated DNA testing confirmed that the remains were those of First Lieutenant Michael J. Blassie of the U.S. Air Force, who was then interred privately.

• B. C. Mossman and M. W. Stark, *The Last Salute: Civil and Military Funerals, 1921–1969,* 1971. G. Kurt Piehler, *Remembering War the American Way,* 1995.

—G. Kurt Piehler

TOSCANINI, ARTURO (1867–1957), conductor. From the 1930s to the 1950s, Toscanini was the undisputed symbol of classical music for a generation of Americans; according to *Time* magazine, he was as well-known as Joe *DiMaggio. Born in Italy and trained as a cellist, Toscanini led Milan's La Scala Opera from 1898 to 1908 and again in 1914–1929. In America he was principal conductor of the Metropolitan Opera (1908–1915), the New York Philharmonic (1926–1936), and the NBC Symphony (1937–1954). His performances were acclaimed for their razor precision, superhuman intensity, and (less accurately) objectivity. His repertoire in the United States centered on Beethoven and other European composers as certifiably supreme as Toscanini himself.

The Toscanini phenomenon coincided with the post-*World War I popularization of high culture. In music the popularizing impulse translated into proliferating orchestras, radio concerts, and "music appreciation" books and courses. For a new generation of culture consumers (significantly including the new middle classes), Toscanini's vaunted superiority, and the superiority of his orchestras, validated American achievement vis-à-vis the parent traditions of Europe.

While Toscanini was unquestionably a towering musician, the high praise he engendered also revealed conditions peculiar to the United States. America's impressive symphonic culture had essentially been borrowed from Germany. Self-made, masculine, an instinctive democrat, Toscanini denounced Hitler and Mussolini. His ostensible textual fidelity rebuffed claims that only Germans could conduct Beethoven.

In retrospect, Toscanini's celebrity was cathartic yet problematic. His reputation eclipsed that of the composers he served. That his 1950 transcontinental tour, hailed as a "a lasting monument to American culture," excluded American works, excited little comment. Surveying the American musical scene in 1941, Aaron *Copland pertinently remarked about the cult of "masterpieces" that Toscanini did so much to foster: "When they are used, unwittingly perhaps, to stifle contemporary effort in our own country, then I am almost tempted to take the most extreme view and say that we should be better off without them." Toscanini's American career documents a period of high accomplishment and complex provincialism. Within a decade of his death, America no longer needed to flaunt a "world's greatest conductor."

[*See also* Music: Classical Music; Opera.]

• B. H. Haggin, *The Toscanini Musicians Knew,* 1967. Harvey Sachs, *Toscanini,* 1978. Joseph Horowitz, *Understanding Toscanini—A Social History of American Concert Life,* 1987, reprint 1994.

—Joseph Horowitz

TOURISM. Rooted in the British tradition of spas, seaside resorts, and the "grand tour," tourism in the United States was reenforced by Americans' wanderlust and close connection to the land. As *canals and waterways, steamboats, and *railroads made travel easier, *Niagara Falls; Newport, Rhode Island; Cape May, New Jersey; and the Catskill, Berkshire, White, and Great Smoky Mountains became popular early retreats. Later, hotels developed by major railroads sprang up at desirable tourist locations. The rise of travel agencies (Thomas Cook's, 1865), traveler's checks (American Express, 1891), national parks (starting with Yellowstone in 1872), and the lowly picture postcard all made travel easier or helped spread information about popular destinations. Paintings and photographic images of the *West that circulated widely in the East increased that region's tourist appeal. Henry M. Flagler, a railroad entrepreneur and a founder of the Standard Oil Company, promoted Florida's east coast both economically and as a tourist locale in the late nineteenth century.

Originally a pastime of the well-to-do, tourism became democratized in the twentieth century. The automobile and the national *highway system, as well as the demographic move from farm to city and the spread of paid vacations and increased *leisure time for workers, stimulated tourism. After *World War II, the family vacation became a summer ritual, and travel abroad grew increasingly common for the more affluent. Not only national parks, but also major cities (*New York, *Boston, *San Francisco, *New Orleans, Honolulu), historic sites (Gettysburg, the Alamo, and Colonial Williamsburg, restored by John D. Rockefeller Jr.), and eventually theme parks (starting with Disneyland in 1955) attracted throngs of visitors. *Washington, D.C., has been a perennially popular tourist destination, especially for high-school seniors taking class trips. Gambling meccas such as Las Vegas, Nevada, and Atlantic City, New Jersey, competed for the tourist dollar as well.

By the late twentieth century, with continued prosperity, the promotion of popular locales by entrepreneurs and chambers of commerce, and the spread of standardized motel and fast-food chains, tourism flourished. Involving both Americans and growing numbers of foreign travelers, tourism had become a major sector of the U.S. economy, generating more than six million jobs, over $50 billion in annual taxes, and total expenditures in excess of $400 billion a year.

Tourism has impacted on the landscape, both natural and constructed, in many ways. Deluged by visitors, some popular

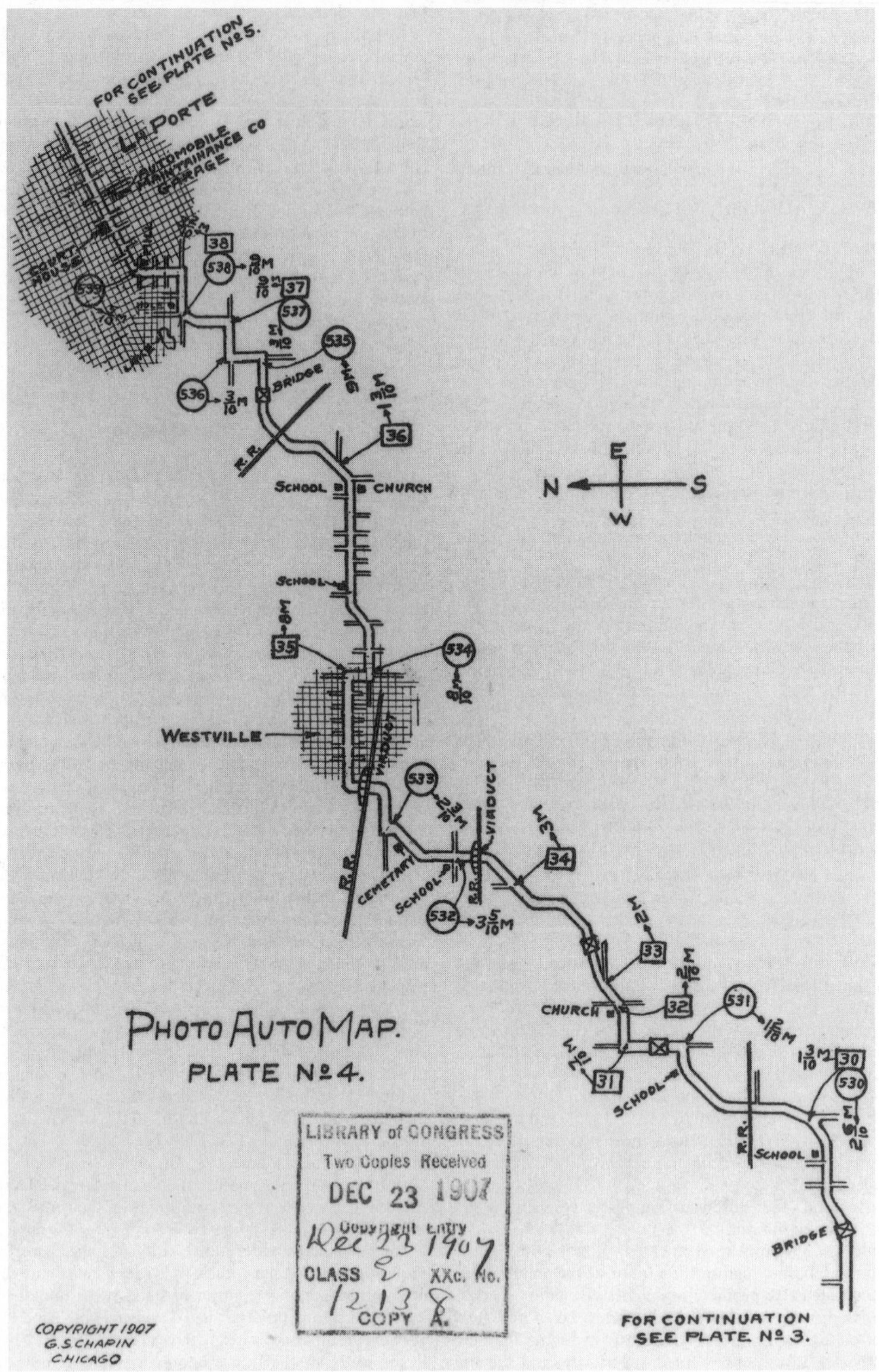

The coming of the automobile introduced a new era in tourism, and cartographers soon published maps to guide drivers to their destinations through a confusing network of local roads. The early maps used schools, barns, churches, cemeteries, and other landmarks to help drivers orient themselves. This map of a section of northwestern Indiana, includes an "automobile maintenance" garage in the town of La Porte.

[*See* Automotive Industry; Progressive Era; Tourism; Twenties, The.]

sites such as Santa Fe, New Mexico, and *Yellowstone National Park suffered from visual pollution and environmental stress, leading to debates over how to preserve America's natural beauty and historic sites while at the same time making them accessible to ever-growing numbers of tourists.

[*See also* Amusement Parks and Theme Parks; Automotive Industry; Environmentalism; Gambling and Lotteries; Motor Vehicles; National Park System; Photography; Popular Culture; Urbanization.]

• John F. Sears, *Sacred Places: American Tourist Attractions in the Nineteenth Century,* 1989. Robert W. McIntosh, Charles R. Goeldner, and J. R. Brent Ritchie, *Tourism Principles, Practices, Philosophies,* 1995.

—Richard V. Smith

TRADE POLICY. *See* Foreign Trade, U.S.; General Agreement on Tariffs and Trade; Global Economy, America and the; North American Free Trade Agreement; Tariffs.

TRADING WITH THE ENEMY ACT (1917). This *World War I measure, passed by Congress on 6 October 1917, aimed to prevent the Central Powers (Germany and its allies) from obtaining supplies and money. Enacted in a time when trade involved not just commodities but credits sent by new technologies such as the *telegraph, the law regulated and punished a range of trade with the enemy. For instance, it authorized the president to supervise foreign exchange, gold, and property in the United States, and defined as an enemy any nation, neutral, or political agent doing business with the Central Powers and their sympathizers. Congressional liberals feared that such sweeping coverage could stigmatize aliens in America as disloyal, but proponents cited English and U.S. case law to validate the comprehensive controls. The act bolstered the wartime British blockade of Germany.

Successive administrations progressively broadened the law's application. A 1933 amendment under the Emergency Banking Act expanded the president's power to impose controls during national domestic crises such as the Great Depression. This led to an open-ended status during subsequent international contests including *World War II, the *Cold War, and the *Persian Gulf War, when the law provided the legal justification for consumer controls, export restrictions, and economic sanctions against designated enemies. The National Emergencies Act of 1977, a post–*Watergate effort to curb executive power, terminated all additions to the act since 1933 and provided for congressional oversight of the measure in the future. Emergencies were more precisely defined to limit the law's scope in domestic policy and diplomacy.

[*See also* Federal Government, Executive Branch: The Presidency; Foreign Trade, U.S.]

• U.S. Congress, House Subcommittee on International Trade and Commerce of the Committee on International Relations, *Trading with the Enemy: Legislative and Executive Documents Concerning Regulation of International Transactions in Time of Declared National Emergency,* 94th Cong., 2d sess., 1976. Richard J. Ellings, *Embargoes and World Power: Lessons from American Foreign Policy,* 1985.

—Thomas W. Zeiler

TRAMPS. *See* Homelessness and Vagrancy.

TRANSCENDENTALISM. "What is popularly called Transcendentalism among us, is Idealism," wrote Ralph Waldo *Emerson in his 1842 essay of the same name. Others have since variously seen the movement as a group of intellectuals sharing a commitment to liberal thought; a largely indigenous school of American *literature and *philosophy; a religious reform and a form of spirituality; or an impetus for social reform and communitarianism. Along with Emerson, those numbered as transcendentalists include Henry David *Thoreau, Margaret *Fuller, Orestes Brownson (1803–1876), George Ripley (1802–1880), Theodore *Parker, and Bronson Alcott (1799–1888). What finally united this diverse group? Their origins in the liberal religionist tradition of Unitarianism, centered in the *Boston area, was one common denominator. So, too, was their adoption of a radically monistic worldview, based in contemporary idealist European philosophy and in some aspects of Asian spirituality. A third commonality was a tendency to criticize contemporary society and to propose the systematic reconfiguration of existing institutions on the basis of standards of judgment and behavior originating in individual moral intuition. The transcendentalists articulated their position through lectures, dialogues, conversations, and works of literature.

The Harvard literary scholar Perry Miller, in his 1950 anthology *The Transcendentalists,* located the first publications consciously influenced by the new idealist philosophy in the early 1830s, with Emerson's 1836 essay "Nature" marking a major watershed. The *Christian Examiner,* a Boston Unitarian periodical, published articles throughout the 1830s debating the new religio-philosophical ideas based largely on the romantic idealism of such German philosophers as Immanuel Kant, Johann Fichte, and Friedrich Schelling, and on their popularizers, William Wordsworth and Samuel Taylor Coleridge in England and Victor Cousin in France. Their chief difference from Lockean materialism, on which the Unitarian worldview was in part based, lay in their insistence that ideas existed independently of sensations and were consonant with the structure of an ideal moral and natural order of which they were a part. Those interested in the new ideas met irregularly beginning in 1836, most often during the Boston visits of liberal minister and moving spirit Frederic Henry Hedge (1805–1890), pastor of the Unitarian church in Bangor, Maine, from 1835 to 1850.

The belief that individuals could have immediate access to moral sentiment opened the proponents of the "new thought," as it was called, to charges of antinomianism. The split between liberal Unitarians influenced by the new German philosophy and those holding to more traditional Lockean premises came to a head with Emerson's Divinity School Address (1838). Theodore Parker, another Unitarian minister, translated the sometimes esoteric language of transcendentalism into sentiments intelligible to a wider audience. Parker's *Discourse of the Transient and Permanent in Christianity* (1841) resulted in his ostracism from most Unitarian pulpits. He subsequently undertook an independent ministry focused heavily on reform causes. *The Dial* (1840–1844), a periodical edited mainly by Fuller and Emerson, provided a venue for transcendental literary expression.

As befitted a movement valuing individual impulses, transcendentalism spawned a variety of experiments. Emerson and Thoreau not only produced the movement's most significant literary expressions, they also self-consciously embodied the transcendentalist vision. The best-known collective effort, Brook Farm in Roxbury, Massachusetts (1841–1847), was a communitarian experiment in individual freedom and economic justice. Margaret Fuller's variegated personality blossomed in educational efforts for women, in writing and criticism, and finally in revolutionary politics in Italy. Bronson Alcott's school experimented with alternative forms of moral education for children, described in his *Conversations with Children on the Gospels* (1836).

As intellectuals, the transcendentalists were probably the first group in America to establish a substantial cultural presence without church or state sponsorship. Although some, like Emerson and George Ripley, began as Unitarian ministers, by the transcendental heyday of the 1840s most had left that calling for lecturing, publishing, freelance teaching and writing, or subsistence pursuits that left time free for philosophizing and writing. Both their insistence on the radical integrity of individual judgment and their reliance on new forms of disseminating their ideas secure their status as the first intellectual flowering of American democratic culture. Not that transcendentalists joined the *Democratic party; most, in fact, to the extent that they were overtly political, supported the *Whig party's moralistic programs of self-culture and reform. Their relationship to the marketplace, moreover, was ambivalent, as they utilized the burgeoning commercial medium of print to criticize the new economic order.

By the late 1850s, transcendentalism as a distinct movement had disbanded. But enough of the transcendental worldview had filtered into the popular imagination that one can say not that the movement collapsed, but rather that the culture absorbed it.

[*See also* Antebellum Era; Religion; Romantic Movement; Unitarianism and Universalism; Utopian and Communitarian Movements.]

• Octavius B. Frothingham, *Transcendentalism in New England: A History,* 1876. Perry Miller, *The Transcendentalists: An Anthology,* 1950. William R. Hutchison, *The Transcendentalist Ministers: Church Reform in the New England Renaissance,* 1959. Anne C. Rose, *Transcendentalism as a Social Movement, 1830–1850,* 1981. Charles Capper, *Margaret Fuller: An American Romantic Life—The Private Years,* 1992. Richard F. Teichgraeber, *Sublime Thoughts/Penny Wisdom: Situating Emerson and Thoreau in the American Market,* 1995.

—Mary Kupiec Cayton

TRANSCONTINENTAL TREATY. *See* Adams-Onís Treaty.

TREASURY DEPARTMENT. *See* Federal Government, Executive Branch: Department of the Treasury.

TRIANGLE SHIRTWAIST COMPANY FIRE. On 25 March 1911, a sunny afternoon in lower Manhattan, fire broke out in the Triangle Shirtwaist Company's factory. Sweeping through the building in minutes, it claimed the lives of 146 young workers, mostly immigrant Jewish and Italian women. The garment shop, occupying the top three floors of a building in *Greenwich Village, employed 800 workers and billed itself as a model operation far better than the stifling sweatshops where many immigrants labored. Yet the company employed children as young as seven years old to trim threads from finished garments. Teenagers and young women worked at sewing machines in crowded rows, the aisles blocked by piles of highly flammable grass linen, a popular fabric for making shirtwaist dresses. The doors to each floor were often kept bolted to prevent theft or "frivolous" bathroom breaks. The fire moved so fast that some women died at their sewing machines. Others collapsed of smoke inhalation, their bodies blocking the building's inner doors.

Thousands of New Yorkers heard the fire engines and gathered on the sidewalks below, watching in horror as the aging, rusted fire escape collapsed, plunging more young women to their deaths. Singly and in pairs, scores of young girls jumped from eight and nine stories up, their bodies striking the pavement with such force that the cement shattered. Alfred E. *Smith, the future governor of New York, and Frances *Perkins, the future secretary of labor, were among the eyewitnesses as grief-stricken families pored over the remains to identify loved ones.

The Triangle Fire shocked the nation, seared the consciences of middle-class reformers, and galvanized public support for effective factory-safety legislation. Al Smith cited the tragedy as a motivating force behind the reforms he enacted as governor. Perkins would later write that her memories of Triangle fueled her life-long commitment to strong regulation of wages, hours, and factory safety. As secretary of labor, Perkins collaborated with Senator Robert F. *Wagner to pass the *National Labor Relations Act and the Fair Labor Standards Act, putting the force of federal law behind her conviction that government had a responsibility to make the workplace safe for all workers.

[*See also* Child Labor; Immigrant Labor; Immigration; New Deal Era, The; New York City; Progressive Era; Strikes and Industrial Conflict; Textile Industry; Women in the Labor Force.]

• Frances Perkins, *The Roosevelt I Knew,* 1946. Leon Stein, *The Triangle Fire,* 1962. Annelise Orleck, *Common Sense and a Little Fire: Women and Working Class Politics in the U.S.,* 1995.

—Annelise Orleck

TRILATERAL COMMISSION, an internationalist policy-planning and advocacy organization comprising several hundred leaders from the private sector, government, academia, and the media. Promoting cooperation among the ruling elements of western Europe, the United States, Canada, and Japan, the commission was founded in 1973 in *New York City by Chase Manhattan Bank chairman David Rockefeller, future National Security Advisor Zbigniew Brzezinski, and other prominent figures.

The commission first focused on providing solutions to destabilizing political and economic problems. These included instabilities in the international monetary system, protectionism and trade issues, barriers to investment, the commercial challenges posed by Japanese efforts, poverty in the developing world, and nuclear arms control. For the long-term, the commission set an ambitious agenda including such diverse topics as demographic growth, exploitation of the sea, educational reform, rules for *multinational enterprises, and U.S. democracy.

Based in New York City, Paris, and Tokyo, the commission is run by an extensive bureaucracy. The leadership represents the apex of global power, including merchants; future and former political leaders; corporate and agribusiness executives; investors and bankers; and, in some European cases, trade unions and leftist politicians.

American membership traditionally has been drawn from an inner core of elites in frequent contact with U.S. officials. The commission thus became a target of criticism in some U.S. circles for underrepresenting Congress, women, labor unions, and the populist left and right. Ronald *Reagan criticized George *Bush's links to the commission in the 1980 Republican presidential primary campaign. Others accused the group of promoting corporate hegemony, one-world government, or elitism. Nevertheless, the commission remained influential. President Jimmy *Carter drew on fellow members to fill administration posts and even Reagan appointed Trilateralists as secretaries of state, treasury, and defense, and as White House advisers.

[*See also* Capitalism; Cold War; Foreign Relations; Global Economy, America and the; Internationalism; Isolationism; Nuclear Arms Control Treaties; Post–Cold War Era.]

• Holly Sklar, ed., *Trilateralism: The Trilateral Commission and Elite Planning for World Management,* 1980. Stephen Gill, *American Hegemony and the Trilateral Commission,* 1990.

—Thomas W. Zeiler

TROTTER, WILLIAM MONROE (1872–1934), *civil rights activist, newspaper editor, integrationist. Born in Ohio, William Monroe Trotter spent most of his life in *Boston. A Phi Beta Kappa graduate of Harvard, he belonged to a class of northern, middle-class *African Americans whose backgrounds included college education and a profession. Along with W. E. B. *Du Bois, Ida B. *Wells-Barnett, and the novelist Charles Chesnutt, he was part of what Du Bois called the "Talented Tenth," which insisted upon equal rights for African Americans and challenged the racial leadership of Booker T. *Washington and his accommodationist platform.

In 1901, Trotter and his wife, Geraldine L. Pindell, founded the *Boston Guardian,* an African American newspaper devoted to the cause of racial integration. Two years later, Trotter gained national attention in the so-called "Boston Riot" by publicly confronting Washington at a local church. Trotter's actions and editorials made him a central figure in the Niagara movement, a series of annual meetings of African-American leaders held at Niagara Falls, New York, beginning in 1905, and Trotter's own National Equal Rights League, which competed unsuccessfully with Du Bois and the *National Association for the

Advancement of Colored People (NAACP) for the allegiance of integrationists, black and white.

Trotter again made headlines by criticizing the racial policies of President Woodrow *Wilson, and by meeting with presidents Warren G. *Harding and Calvin *Coolidge to protest racial segregation in the federal government. In the 1920s, he tried to connect his organization to Marcus *Garvey's movement and the African Blood Brotherhood. The death of his wife, combined with financial problems and waning national influence, shadowed Trotter's final years. He spent his life and fortune pushing the nation to recognize African Americans as full citizens.

[*See also* Civil Rights Movement; Racism.]

• Stephen R. Fox, *The Guardian of Boston: William Monroe Trotter*, 1970. David Levering Lewis, *W. E. B. Du Bois: Biography of a Race*, 1993.

—Gregory Mixon

TRUMAN, HARRY S. (1884–1972), thirty-third president of the United States. Born in the farm village of Lamar, Missouri, 120 miles south of *Kansas City, to John A. and Martha Ellen Truman, the future president spent his earliest years on a succession of farms until 1890, when his family, including a sister and younger brother, moved to Independence. Graduating from high school in 1901, Truman worked in Kansas City banks until 1906 when he became a farmer on his grandmother's land near Grandview, Missouri. With America's entry into *World War I in 1917, he enlisted in a field artillery regiment and saw action in France. Mustered out in 1919, he operated a haberdashery in Kansas City until 1922.

Truman's political career began with his 1922 election to a three-person county court from the rural, eastern part of Jackson County, which included Independence. In effect he was a county commissioner, as the office generally was known in the *Middle West. Defeated in 1924, he was elected presiding judge in 1926, a post he held for eight years. In this position he undertook to construct roads suitable for the automobile era. This led him to encounter the political boss of Kansas City, Thomas J. Pendergast. Truman cooperated in an arrangement whereby Pendergast supporters received county jobs, but the boss allowed Truman to manage the road program without graft.

Elected as a Democrat to the U.S. Senate in 1934 with Pendergast support and tens of thousands of fraudulent votes in Kansas City, Truman at the outset was considered "the senator from Pendergast" and treated as such by President Franklin Delano *Roosevelt. Gradually he made a name for himself as (so he put it) a workhorse and not a show horse; his fellow senators came to admire him. Reelected narrowly in 1940, after Pendergast's imprisonment for income-tax evasion, Truman formed a committee to investigate wartime production. It proved so effective that he was chosen as Roosevelt's running mate in 1944, in place of the sitting vice president, Henry A. Wallace. He became president upon Roosevelt's death on 12 April 1945.

President Roosevelt had not been close to his vice president and had told him almost nothing about *foreign relations. Yet as luck would have it, foreign affairs dominated Truman's presidency. The new president did know about the *nuclear-weapons program, although not in detail. His decision to authorize the atomic bombing of *Hiroshima and Nagasaki (1945) was the most controversial of his presidency. His second major involvement in foreign relations was the series of measures—the *Truman Doctrine (1947), the *Marshall Plan (1947), the *Berlin Blockade and Airlift (1948–1949), and the formation of the *North Atlantic Treaty Organization (1949)—by which the United States strengthened the nations of western Europe against the eastern bloc led by the Soviet Union. These measures, which included declarations of support for nations threatened by communism, economic aid, opposition to a Soviet takeover of the western sectors of Berlin, and a military alliance, strengthened the U.S. position in the *Cold War confrontation with the Soviet Union. After the Soviet Union's successful test of an atomic bomb in 1949, Truman authorized a U.S. program to develop the hydrogen bomb.

Truman's third major action, intervention in the *Korean War on 25 June, 1950 as part of a *United Nations police action, forestalled North Korea's takeover of South Korea. The task proved unexpectedly difficult. When, after an initial retreat before the North Korean attack, the UN forces under General Douglas *MacArthur went on the offensive, crossed the thirty-eighth parallel, and penetrated far into North Korea, the troops of communist China in November 1950 attacked and nearly defeated MacArthur's overextended troops. The Chinese intervention created a military crisis, resolved early the next year by the U.S. Eighth Army under General Matthew B. Ridgway. When MacArthur pushed his own strategic proposals to the point of insubordination, Truman dismissed him in April 1951. After a long stalemate, a truce was signed in Korea in 1953, shortly after Truman left office.

On the domestic front, Truman managed reconversion of the economy after *World War II, despite strikes and inflation. The new president gradually brought the cabinet departments and bureaucracy under his control—a lesson he had learned, albeit on a small scale, in county government. But the Cold War, especially the Korean War, bedeviled his domestic policy. In 1947, as Cold War alarms brought fears of domestic subversion, he initiated a loyalty-review program to ferret out federal workers suspected of disloyalty. It turned up a minuscule number of employees who were alleged security risks.

A bright spot in an otherwise modest domestic record was his championing of *civil rights for *African Americans. When Congress refused to pass civil rights legislation, Truman did what he could by executive action. He created a Fair Employment Board within the U.S. Civil Service Commission and by a historic executive order of July 1948 established procedures for desegregating the *military. The services dragged their feet, but the Korean War crisis sped the process of integration.

In the 1948 election, Truman's civil rights activism gave rise to a third party in the *South, the *States' Rights, or Dixiecrat, party. His electoral chances dimmed further with a challenge on the left from Henry A. Wallace's *Progressive party of 1948. Nevertheless, confounding the experts, Truman and his running mate, Senator Alben Barkley of Kentucky, won one of the great upset victories of American political history, narrowly defeating his Republican challenger, New York governor Thomas E. Dewey (1902–1971).

In 1949, Truman proposed to Congress the Fair Deal, a package of legislative reforms and civil rights proposals designed to continue and extend the New Deal. The Fair Deal got nowhere, and Truman's second term was beset by accusations of corruption, by the bloody conflict in Korea, and by the anticommunist crusade of Senator Joseph *McCarthy. Truman hated McCarthy but did not give sufficient attention to the senator's name-calling and accusations.

Stepping aside in 1952, Truman endorsed the Democratic candidate Adlai *Stevenson, who lost heavily to the Republican Dwight D. *Eisenhower. Returning to Independence, Truman composed his memoirs, arranged construction of a presidential library, and participated in Democratic causes until ill health curtailed his activities in the mid-1960s.

Truman's presidency has come to be seen as highly successful, principally in foreign policy, with domestic policy mostly a holding action. The low points were probably Truman's 1947 loyalty program and his failure to respond forcefully to Senator McCarthy's crusade. But the administration's successes abroad far outweighed the domestic failures. Often underrated in his own day, Truman has become one of the most admired holders of the presidency.

[*See also* Anticommunism; Acheson, Dean; Containment; Democratic Party; Federal Government, Executive Branch: The

Presidency; House Committee on Un-American Activities; Liberalism; Nuclear Strategy; Nuclear Weapons; Strikes and Industrial Conflict.]

• Harry S. Truman, *Memoirs,* 2 vols., 1955–1956. David McCullough, *Truman,* 1992. Robert H. Ferrell, *Harry S. Truman,* 1994. Alonzo L. Hamby, *Man of the People,* 1995

—Robert H. Ferrell

TRUMAN DOCTRINE. On 12 March 1947, President Harry S. *Truman asked Congress for $400 million in economic and military aid to Greece and Turkey. His message was a response to Great Britain's warning that it could no longer underwrite the Greek monarchy, which was embroiled in a civil war against communist rebels supported by Yugoslavia's communist ruler, Josip Broz Tito. Embracing the view of Undersecretary of State Dean *Acheson, Truman insisted that the Soviet Union intended to use the civil war to dominate Greece and then "Europe, the Middle East, and Asia." Every nation, he insisted, must choose between "alternative ways of life": democratic rule or communist terror; the choice in Greece lay between American democracy and Soviet dictatorship. His message largely ignored the complexities of the Greek civil war; the authoritarian, reactionary regimes in Athens and Ankara; and U.S. strategic interests in Turkey. This message, labeled the "Truman Doctrine," was hailed by the press and public, and Congress passed the proposed legislation in May 1947. Convinced by Truman's arguments, one-time Republican isolationists like Senator Arthur Vandenberg of Michigan backed the appropriation.

American aid, plus the fact that the Soviet dictator Joseph Stalin gave very little aid to the Greek communists and did not challenge this aspect of U.S. policy, fostered the Greek government's victory. In July 1949, Yugoslavia—seeking U.S. economic assistance—closed its borders to the Greek rebels. The civil war soon ended, leaving 158,000 dead, 800,000 refugees, and Greece near ruin.

Truman later claimed that his doctrine had marked a turning point in America's commitment to resist "aggression" globally, and many historians agreed that U.S. national interest required sustaining noncommunist governments in the strategically vital eastern Mediterranean. Other scholars, however, argued that Truman's sweeping rhetoric obscured the specifics of the Greek situation, spurred an excessively militaristic response to the Soviet challenge, and gave Truman's successors too much latitude to intervene in conflicts from the Caribbean to Southeast Asia.

[*See also* Cold War; Containment; Foreign Relations: U.S. Relations with Europe.]

• Howard Jones, *"A New Kind of War": America's Global Strategy and the Truman Doctrine in Greece,* 1989. Lawrence S. Wittner, *American Intervention in Greece, 1943–1949,* 1982.

—Arnold A. Offner

TRUST TERRITORY OF THE PACIFIC ISLANDS. *See* Protectorates and Dependencies.

TRUTH, SOJOURNER. *See* Sojourner Truth.

TUBERCULOSIS (TB), a *disease with epidemiologic, socioeconomic, and cultural significance, was long believed to be a wasting condition caused by climate, poor diet, and bad habits, but since 1882, when the German bacteriologist Robert Koch identified the tubercle bacillus, it has been understood as an infectious bacterial disease. Tuberculosis can affect animals (particularly birds and cattle) as well as human beings. It most often attacks the lungs but can also strike bones and soft tissues; though infectious, it is not epidemic.

Tuberculosis, first known as phthisis or consumption, has been recognized as a leading cause of American deaths for as long as records have been kept. Anthropological evidence suggests that it was present in Native American populations before European contact. The missionaries, surveyors, and physicians who catalogued early American disease found it so prevalent that it seemed, as one surveyor wrote, "the direct offspring of the American soil and climate."

Tuberculosis became particularly noteworthy during the nineteenth century, when it accounted for almost a quarter of all North American deaths. Early death from tuberculosis figured prominently in the literature and popular music of the era. The disease struck all classes of Americans, but not equally. Mid-century physicians considered race a major determinant of TB and identified African-American slaves as particularly susceptible. After the *Civil War, TB came to be seen as a particular problem of cities, with "city habits, city houses, city occupations and city life" all cited as causes. Physicians often identified women, particularly millworkers, as especially at risk. In the early twentieth century, immigrants, Native American populations, and the rural poor were thought to be particularly vulnerable. As recently as 1960, the U.S. Public Health Service described tuberculosis as "the costliest of communicable diseases," which reflected not only the expense of screening and treatment, but also the lost wages and dependency.

As late as the mid-twentieth century, tuberculosis was difficult to treat. Late-nineteenth and early-twentieth century physicians commonly advocated the sanatorium treatment, comprising rest, good diet, and exercise that Dr. Edward Livingston Trudeau (1848–1915) pioneered at Adirondack Cottage Sanatorium at Saranac Lake, New York, in 1884. Prevention, through *public-health measures, including antispitting ordinances and the disposal of infected milk and meat, became a first line of defense after Koch identified the tubercle bacillus in 1882. Voluntary associations, especially the National Tuberculosis Association, launched major educational campaigns and funded research.

Koch's identification of the tubercle bacillus inspired hopes for a vaccine, and his highly touted "tuberculin cure" (1890) aroused great optimism. But while tuberculin proved a useful diagnostic agent, it had no curative properties BCG, a vaccine developed in France in 1924, from the bacillus Calmette-Guérin, enjoyed widespread use around the world but not in the United States. Twentieth-century American campaigns against TB relied on public-health measures and the antibiotic streptomycin, developed by Salman Waksman in 1943. Long-term chemoprophylaxis with the combination of bacteriostatic agents isoniazid and PAS (para-aminosalicylic acid) became common after 1952.

After decades of low incidence and declining visibility, tuberculosis reemerged in the 1980s as a public-health problem. This resurgence was variously attributed to *immigration, the *acquired immunodeficiency syndrome (AIDS) epidemic, drug-resistant strains of TB, urban *poverty, and the absence of an adequate health and social services net.

[*See also* Biological Sciences; Medicine: From 1776 to the 1870s; Medicine: From the 1870s to 1945; Medicine: Since 1945; Urbanization]

• Barbara Bates, *Bargaining for Life: A Social History of Tuberculosis, 1876–1938,* 1992. Sheila Rothman, *Living in the Shadow of Death: Tuberculosis and the Social Experience of Illness in American History,* 1994. Georgina Feldberg, *Disease and Class: Tuberculosis and the Shaping of Modern North American Society,* 1995.

—Georgina Feldberg

TUBMAN, HARRIET (1820–1913), abolitionist, *Civil War volunteer, escaped slave who assisted other slaves to freedom. Born into *slavery on Maryland's Eastern Shore, one of eleven children of Benjamin Ross and Harriet Greene, Harriet Ross worked as a field slave, gaining the strength and endurance that would later prove invaluable. About 1844, she married a free black man, John Tubman. In 1849, fearful of being sold into the Deep South, she escaped to *Philadelphia. In 1850–1851, she made three trips back to bring out various of her siblings and their families. As the decade went on, she made some sixteen more trips to Maryland, displaying great courage and ingenuity in assisting other slaves to escape, including, in 1857, her aged parents. Estimates of the number of slaves she helped escape range from sixty to more than three hundred.

Viewing Tubman's activities as a major threat, Maryland slaveowners offered rewards totalling forty thousand dollars for her capture. As her exploits became known, she sometimes spoke at abolitionist rallies. Living at first in St. Catharines, Ontario, she moved to farm near Auburn, New York, around 1858. Here she built a home for her parents and, later, a residence for aged and disabled ex-slaves. A civilian volunteer with the Union Army during and after the Civil War, she worked as a nurse and a cook in military hospitals in South Carolina and Virginia and gathered military intelligence from African-American informants. In 1897, after years of effort by Tubman and her supporters, Congress awarded her a twenty-dollar monthly pension for her wartime service. The subtitle of Sarah Bradford's 1869 biography gave her the epithet often associated with her name: "Moses of Her People."

[*See also* Antislavery; Slave Uprisings and Resistance.]

• Earl Conrad, *Harriet Tubman,* 1974 Benjamin Quarles, "Harriet Tubman's Unlikely Leadership," in *Black Leaders of the Nineteenth Century,* ed. Leon Litwack and August Meier, 1988, pp. 43–57. "Harriet Ross Tubman," in *Black Women in America: An Historical Encyclopedia,* ed. Darlene Clark Hine et al., vol. 2, 1993, pp. 1176–80.

—Theresa D. Napson-Williams

TURNER, FREDERICK JACKSON (1861–1932), historian. Born and reared in Portage, Wisconsin, the son of a newspaper publisher and politician, he was educated at the University of Wisconsin (B.A. 1884, M.A. 1888) and Johns Hopkins University (Ph.D. 1891). Turner taught at Wisconsin, first rhetoric and later history, from 1885 to 1910, at Harvard from 1910 to 1924, and summer sessions at Utah State University (1924 and 1925). He was a senior research associate at the Huntington Library in San Marino, California, from 1927 until his death. Turner played a key role in establishing Wisconsin as a major center for historical studies. His scholarly interests were broad, and he early understood that historians could benefit from cognate disciplines, especially geography and statistics. Although not the originator of this idea, he persistently and ardently advocated it. Active in the profession, his early publications and network of friendships, including Woodrow *Wilson, Yale historian Max Farrand, and J. Franklin Jameson (editor of the *American Historical Review*), gave him positions of leadership. He was president of the American Historical Association (AHA) in 1910.

Turner helped shift the focus of American historical writing from the so-called "germ theory," which traced American institutions to Germanic tribal origins, to the effect of environment and experience in shaping American culture and national character. He strongly believed in "American exceptionalism," the idea that the United States was not only different from other nations but also unique in its social evolution. His first major work, "The Significance of the Frontier in American History" (1893), delivered at the AHA's annual meeting at the World's Columbian Exposition in Chicago, rejected the germ theory and urged the study of the influence of the West and the frontier on American institutions and character. It had an enormous impact on the profession and remains controversial. He proceeded to write a score of essays elaborating this theme. *The Rise of the New West, 1819–1829* (1906), a pioneering analytical study that attempted to correlate and map voting districts and key issues, demonstrated the role of sections (regions) in American history. His essays on sectionalism, published as *The Significance of Sections in American History,* won the *Pulitzer Prize posthumously in 1933. His final work, *The United States, 1830–1850: The Nation and Its Sections* (1935), appeared posthumously. Turner is unique among American historians, both for his frontier and sectional theses and as the founder of a school of scholarship.

[*See also* Historiography, American; West, The.]

• Ray Allen Billington, *Frederick Jackson Turner: Historian, Scholar, Teacher,* 1973. Martin Ridge, "The Life of an Idea: The Significance of Frederick Jackson Turner's Frontier Thesis," *Montana: The Magazine of Western History* 41 (Winter 1991): 2–13. Allan G. Bogue, *Frederick Jackson Turner: Strange Roads Going Down,* 1998.

—Martin Ridge

TURNER, NAT. *See* Nat Turner's Uprising.

TURNPIKES. *See* Roads and Turnpikes, Early.

TUSKEGEE EXPERIMENT. The notorious Tuskegee experiment emerged from a pioneering health program to provide medical care to select groups of desperately poor *African Americans. In the late 1920s and early 1930s the U.S. Public Health Service (USPHS) conducted several studies of syphilis in African Americans from different parts of the *South, hoping to learn what percentage of the populations under study had syphilis and to treat sufferers from the disease. In 1932, the USPHS returned to Tuskegee, Alabama, the site of one of the earlier syphilis-control demonstrations, to conduct a short-term study (six months to a year) of the spontaneous evolution of syphilis in black males.

From the beginning, USPHS officials engaged in willful deceit. Instead of revealing their true purpose, they told African Americans in the community (most of whom were poor and uneducated sharecroppers) that the USPHS was offering free examinations and free treatment for a variety of illnesses. The USPHS did not act alone. Over time it received cooperation in varying degrees from the Alabama State Board of Health, the Macon County Health Department, the Tuskegee Institute, and the Milbank Memorial Fund. At the outset, the Alabama State Board of Health insisted that medical care be given to every man in the study who had syphilis. Grudgingly, the USPHS gave every subject who suffered from syphilis a modicum of treatment—not enough to effect a cure, but more than enough to interfere with the spontaneous evolution of the disease. In short, the study was hopelessly contaminated from the start.

Once launched, the Tuskegee experiment developed a life of its own, as USPHS officials quickly decided to continue the study until all the subjects had died. Subsequent events, such as the development of penicillin, the creation of the post–*World War II Nuremberg codes, regarding human experimentation, and the rise of the *civil rights movement, had little or no impact on the study. In 1972, however, a whistle-blower named Peter Buxtun revealed the story to the press, and the Tuskegee experiment became a national scandal overnight. Faced with public outrage, the USPHS officially ended the study in 1972. In 1974, the Justice Department settled a lawsuit and paid damages to survivors of the experiment and to the estates of the deceased. In 1997, President Bill *Clinton formally apologized to the victims. While this act of atonement helped heal the wounds of those who were wronged, the Tuskegee experiment for many African Americans remained a potent metaphor for white deception and medical neglect. Indeed, it is a primary reason that many African Americans do not trust physicians, refuse to participate in clinical trials, and view health officials with suspicion.

[*See also* Medicine: From the 1870s to 1945; Medicine: Since 1945; Public Health; Racism; Sharecropping and Tenantry; Venereal Disease.]

• James H. Jones, *Bad Blood: The Tuskegee Syphilis Experiment,* rev. ed., 1993.

—James H. Jones

TWAIN, MARK. *See* Clemens, Samuel L.

TWEED, WILLIAM MAGEAR (1823–1878), political leader. Born in *New York City of Scottish ancestry, Tweed worked as a chairmaker and brushmaker. A volunteer fireman, he was elected a Democratic alderman in 1851, and as a member of Tammany Hall, New York City's Democratic organization, he served a term in Congress (1853–1855) and in 1868 went to the New York State Senate, while retaining considerable political control of New York City and the loyalty of a largely immigrant and working-class constituency, including many Irish Catholics.

"Boss" Tweed's political machinations and close ties to the railroad entrepreneurs Jay Gould and James Fisk also brought him increasing criticism. In 1870, he was named a member of a state-mandated "board of audit" intended to oversee bills relating to construction of a new County Court House. In 1871, the Republican *New York Times* headlined "Tweed Ring graft" related to the Court House. Political cartoonist Thomas Nast (1840–1902) relentlessly caricatured him in *Harper's Weekly*. The state Democratic leader, Samuel J. Tilden, alleged that Tweed and his associates had defrauded the city of at least thirty million dollars and engaged in bribery, electoral fraud, and judicial corruption. Tweed was indicted in 1872 for failing to properly audit bills. The first trial resulted in a hung jury, but the second produced a conviction, and Tweed served a year in jail. Upon his release, he was arrested on related charges and imprisoned. Late in 1875, he fled to Spain followed by agents of the U.S. State Department. He was extradicted and in 1876 again convicted on the audit charge. He died in prison.

Politics and prejudice played a major role in the anti-Tweed campaign. Tweed's nemesis Thomas Nast hated Catholics and Irish immigrants. Judge Noah Davis, a partisan Republican politician, presided over Tweed's second trial before a jury handpicked by the state prosecution. Along with his often repeated misdeeds, Tweed accomplished much for New York City. As a state senator he introduced or supported bills that created Riverside Drive; widened Broadway; improved Central Park, Columbus Circle, and Prospect Park; and incorporated the Metropolitan Museum of Art, the New York Stock Exchange, and Lenox Library, forerunner of the present New York Public Library. Little of this is remembered; Nast's cartoons are.

[*See also* Anti-Catholic Movement; Democratic Party; Gilded Age; Immigration; Municipal and County Governments; Nativist Movement.]

• Seymour J. Mandelbaum, *Boss Tweed's New York,* 1965. Leo Hershkowitz, *Tweed's New York: Another Look,* 1977.

—Leo Hershkowitz

TWENTIES, THE. The twenties have spawned an image of bathtub gin, speakeasies, flappers, and decadence: in short, The Jazz Age. This superficial vision masks a far more complex history. In this period Americans grappled with the disruptions of ethnic and cultural conflict, the growth of the mass media and a *consumer culture, and a transformation in women's roles. Acutely conscious of far-reaching social changes, they struggled to interpret and cope with an increasingly modern society.

A Decade of Prosperity. This sense of change was evident in the title *Republican party politicians gave to the period. Calling it "The New Era," presidents Warren G. *Harding (1921–1923), Calvin *Coolidge (1923–1929), and Herbert *Hoover (1929–1933) promoted government-*business cooperation. After decades of reform activity, including efforts to enlarge federal regulation of corporations and the economy, demands for corporate reform receded, as big business enjoyed unprecedented public approval. "The man who builds a factory builds a temple," Coolidge intoned; "The man who works there, worships there."

This apotheosis of business stemmed in part from Americans' delight in widespread prosperity. The affluence of the 1920s, symbolized by a booming *stock market, was rooted in surging industrial *productivity, which rose 64 percent between 1920 and 1930, compared with only 12 percent in 1910–1920. The *automotive industry—a major factor in the boom—increased annual car production from 1.5 million in 1919 to 4.8 million in 1929. Other dynamic economic sectors included the steel, rubber, chemical, and construction industries. The growth derived in part from technological developments, such as the widespread electrification of factory production, as well as from efficient new assembly-line methods. Observers came from all over the world to witness what was called The Ford Miracle, Henry *Ford's plant in River Rouge, Michigan, but Ford's company was only the most famous of the *mass production industries churning out a seemingly limitless array of consumer goods.

The economy of the 1920s also became increasingly concentrated. In manufacturing and *mining, over 1,200 mergers took place; in *banking and finance, by 1929, thanks to consolidations, 1 percent of the banks controlled 46 percent of the country's banking resources. In that same year, 200 corporations owned approximately 20 percent of the nation's wealth. More and more Americans found themselves working for large corporations—either in blue-collar jobs or in the rapidly expanding ranks of white-collar employees necessary to maintain modern business operations. These changes in the nature of *work undoubtedly led to more alienating labor, but there were compensations. Increasingly, Americans could experience the satisfactions of consumption and *leisure.

Contemporary observers rightly viewed the plethora of products—electric toasters and irons, pastel-colored plumbing fixtures and ranges, phonographs and *radios, automobile and sporting goods equipment—as a consumer-goods revolution. Although poorer Americans, especially *African Americans and recent immigrants, could enjoy the new products only sparingly, innovations such as installment buying enhanced working- and middle-class Americans' buying power. A significant portion of their dollars—an increase of 300 percent during the decade—went to leisure-time pursuits. Americans enjoyed vacations, played at amusement parks, patronized sporting events, and idolized sports heroes like George Herman ("Babe") *Ruth and Red *Grange. Above all, they flocked to the movies and worshipped screen stars like Mary Pickford, Rudolph *Valentino, Charlie *Chaplin, and Douglas Fairbanks. An estimated twenty to thirty million patrons a week helped to make the movies a key forum for entertainment and the spread of new cultural values. The growing interest in consumer goods and leisure-time pursuits was stimulated by an increasingly sophisticated *advertising industry, which developed new methods to encourage Americans to derive satisfaction and identity from the products they bought.

Changing Women's Roles and Urbanization. Among the most eager consumers were young women who helped to create the persona most identified with the 1920s: the flapper. The flapper's daring appearance—bobbed hair, cosmetics, short skirts—matched her audacious behavior—smoking, drinking, *jazz dancing, and sexual experimentation. Although the flapper stereotype exaggerates the liberation women enjoyed in the decade, sexual mores were evolving. Between the popularization of Freudian notions about sexuality, the movies' portrayal of highly sexualized relationships, changing notions about equality within marriage, and the increased availability of birth control, new sexual patterns emerged.

Contemporaries observed other changes in women's roles that seemed to augur the New Woman. The *Nineteenth Amendment gave women the vote in 1920. Beginning around 1910, women's participation in the paid workforce grew. In addition, a greater percentage of married women worked for wages and the increased availability of respectable white-collar office and sales work expanded the ranks of employed young, middle-class women. Despite their increased presence in the *labor market, most women encountered discrimination. In general, career women were limited to such "feminized" professions as *nursing, teaching, and *social work, while domestic work remained the only option for most women of color. Although more married women were working, social conventions continued to view *child rearing and and housekeeping as women's most important roles, an idea that profoundly constricted women's opportunities for careers and mobility.

Another important hallmark of social change was the Census Bureau's finding that as of 1920 the nation had become more urban than rural. Although based on a somewhat arbitrary definition of "urban," the bureau's calculations nonetheless, symbolize the way urban life increasingly dominated the American scene. America's cities had been burgeoning for years, augmented not just by rural-to-urban migration, but by massive *immigration as well. Although immigration slowed dramatically during *World War I, it quickly revived after the armistice: In 1921, over 800,000 newcomers entered the United States. Also contributing to *urbanization was the "Great Migration" of over a million African Americans out of the *South. Lured by wartime job opportunities in northern industries, they eagerly fled the South's *poverty and racial caste system. Although most found a better life in the North, here too, African Americans encountered racial *segregation and discrimination.

Cultural Conflict. Many Americans embraced the social changes of the decade—the modern woman, the consumer culture, urban life. Others, however, alarmed at the pace of change, helped make the 1920s a period of deep cultural conflict. The *Fundamentalist movement disrupted many Protestant denominations as its leaders insisted upon their literalistic reading of the Bible. Their aggressive campaign to prohibit the teaching of the theory of *evolution in the public schools, culminating in the *Scopes Trial, thrust religious controversy into the public arena. After decades of agitation, national prohibition went into effect in 1920 with the ratification of the *Eighteenth Amendment, which prohibited the manufacture and sale of alcoholic beverages. Prohibition represented the use of federal law to impose Protestant, old-stock moral values of restraint and sobriety on the rest of the nation, especially immigrants. The movement to repeal Prohibition, which began almost immediately, remained highly controversial throughout the decade. Whether a candidate was "wet" or "dry" loomed large in many political campaigns.

Anti-immigrant sentiment, a factor in the *Sacco and Vanzetti case, permeated American politics in the 1920s. Following on the heels of the Red Scare of 1919–1921, rooted initially in the fear of immigrant radicals, the *immigration laws of 1921 and 1924 established restrictive quotas for southern and eastern Europeans, and excluded Asian immigrants altogether. Immigration restriction proved popular, especially among members of the newly re-constituted *Ku Klux Klan. Claiming over three million members, the Klan at its peak in mid-decade was an especially powerful political force in the South, *Middle West, and *West. Limited to native-born, white, Protestant males (although women could join a female auxiliary), the Klan targeted immigrants, blacks, Jews, and Catholics for failing to live up to its definition of "100% Americanism."

Intellectual and Cultural Creativity. Intellectuals deplored these reactionary movements, or what they called the village mentality. The writers and artists known collectively as the Lost Generation, which included F. Scott *Fitzgerald, Ernest *Hemingway, Gertrude Stein (1874–1946), and William Carlos Williams (1883–1963), articulated a searing critique of the sterility of American culture. Sinclair *Lewis and H. L. *Mencken satirized small-town provinciality and middle-class conformity. These writers also explored the possibilities and dilemmas facing men and women as they encountered the more modern, and often more alienating, world of the early twentieth century.

Another group of intellectuals, African Americans who participated in the *Harlem Renaissance, had different concerns. Writers like Langston *Hughes, Zora Neale *Hurston, and Claude McKay (1890–1948) used their talents to promote black pride and to explore African American culture's distinctive contribution to American society. So, too, did musicians and performers like Edward ("Duke") *Ellington, Louis *Armstrong, and Paul *Robeson. The vitality of their work and the community that nourished their creativity—Harlem—points to the need for a vision of the 1920s that moves beyond stereotypes of flappers and jazzhounds to encompass the full diversity of the American population and its struggles to adapt to a rapidly changing society.

[*See also* Amusement Parks and Theme Parks; Anticommunism; Baseball; Birth Control and Family Planning; Business Cycle; Chemical Industry; Courtship and Dating; Electricity and Electrification; Film; Football; Iron and Steel Industry; Literature: Since World War I; Marriage and Divorce; Motor Vehicles; Nativist Movement; Religion; Science: From 1914 to 1945; Sexual Morality and Sex Reform; Smith, Alfred E.; Sports: Professional Sports; Stock Market Crash of 1929; Temperance and Prohibition.]

• Lawrence W. Levine, *Defender of the Faith, William Jennings Bryan: The Last Decade 1915–1925*, 1965. John Braeman, Robert H. Bremner, and David Brody, eds., *Change and Continuity in Twentieth Century America: The 1920s*, 1968. Lary May, *Screening out the Past: The Birth of Mass Culture and the Motion Picture Industry*, 1980. Roland Marchand, *Advertising the American Dream: Making Way for Modernity, 1920–1940*, 1985. Nancy Cott, *The Grounding of Modern Feminism*, 1987. James R. Grossman, *Land of Hope: Chicago, Black Southerners and the Great Migration*, 1989. Lizabeth Cohen, *Making a New Deal: Industrial Workers in Chicago, 1919–1939*, 1990. Ann Douglas, *Terrible Honesty: Mongrel Manhattan in the 1920s*, 1995. Lynn Dumenil, *The Modern Temper: American Culture and Society in the 1920s*, 1995.

—Lynn Dumenil

TYLER, JOHN (1790–1862), tenth president of the United States. A Virginian, John Tyler attended the College of William and Mary studied law, and served in the House of Burgesses, the U.S. House of Representatives, and as governor of Virginia (1825–1827) before beginning a distinguished career in the U.S. Senate in 1827.

At first, the rising Jacksonians in Congress looked to Tyler as an ally. By the early 1830s, however, antipathy for President Andrew *Jackson's governing style and a strict belief in *states' rights led Tyler to join a handful of discontented Democrats in bolting to the fledgling *Whig party. In 1836 the Democratic controlled Virginia legislature demanded that the maverick Tyler resign his Senate seat.

In 1840, when the Whigs nominated the northerner William Henry *Harrison for president, they sought a southerner with less nationalistic views to balance the ticket. Tyler accepted the vice presidential nod, expecting to play a small role in the administration. Harrison's sudden death one month into his term thrust Tyler into the presidency. Derided as "His Accidency," Tyler found himself adrift politically. His states' rights ideas clashed with the nationalist Whigs in Congress, led by the master politician Henry *Clay, who sent bills to the new president expecting Tyler simply to comply with his wishes. When Tyler issued two successive vetoes, the Whig congressional caucus wrote him out of the party and all but one of his inherited cabinet members resigned.

Tyler then latched onto the Texas annexation issue as a means of resurrecting his career. Although both parties wished to avoid the Texas question and the brewing conflict over *slavery, Tyler saw it as an opportunity to defend both the *South and states' rights. He negotiated an annexation treaty and waited for southern Jacksonians to assist in its ratification. The Democrats heeded the call in 1844 by nominating James Knox *Polk, an ardent annexationist. Bypassing the ratification process that would have required a two-thirds majority for Tyler's treaty, Congress simply admitted Texas by resolution in February 1845, just days before Tyler left office. In 1860, Tyler served on a futile peace commission during the secession crisis. He later supported Virginia's secession and was elected to the Confederate House of Representatives, but died before he could take office.

[*See also* Antebellum Era; Confederate States of America; Democratic Party; Federal Government, Executive Branch: The Presidency; Texas Republic and Annexation.]

• Oliver Perry Chitwood, *John Tyler, Champion of the Old South,* 1939. Robert J. Morgan, *A Whig Embattled: The Presidency under John Tyler,* 1954.

—Eric D. Daniels

TYPEWRITER. *See* Office Technology.

TYPHOID FEVER, a bacterial *disease spread by fecal contamination of food or water. Untreated, its course takes about four weeks, with 10 percent of patients dying. Typhoid has symptoms in common with several other diseases, and only in the 1830s was it distinguished from typhus (a disease of different etiology, but with a similar clinical picture). Historians credit William Wood Gerhard of *Philadelphia with having established typhoid as a specific disease in 1837.

Typhoid has been present in America at least since the early seventeenth century, when it virtually depopulated *Jamestown, Virginia. Nineteenth-century epidemiological studies consistently confirmed the British finding in 1856 that typhoid is waterborne; and years before German bacteriologists identified the pathogen in early 1880s, the experience of several cities demonstrated that water filtration reduced typhoid incidence. By 1920, when almost all American municipal water supplies were filtered, *public-health advocates were pointing to the dramatic decline of typhoid as evidence that governmental action could lessen sickness and reduce mortality.

Typhoid decimated army camps during the *Civil War and again in the *Spanish-American War, when cases were typically misdiagnosed as *malaria and treated futilely with quinine. With death rates in the camps over five times battlefield mortality, the army commissioned an investigation by Walter *Reed, Victor Vaughan, and Edward O. Shakespeare. Concluding that typhoid was responsible, they recommended strict sanitary control of camps—a reform that led to a significantly healthier army in *World War I.

The importance of healthy carriers and of tainted food in the transmission of typhoid was underscored by the case of Mary Mallon ("Typhoid Mary"), a cook in *New York City. First identified as responsible for an outbreak in 1906, Mallon eventually was incarcerated to prevent her from working in the food trades.

Although a vaccine of limited efficacy exists, the principal protection against typhoid remains a pure water supply and stringent enforcement of food-handling regulations. By the late twentieth century, almost all typhoid cases reported in the United States were contracted during visits to less-developed countries. The exceptions, such as the 1973 outbreak in a Florida migrant labor camp, were quickly traced to breakdowns in the separation of sewage from food and water. With antibiotics, recovery takes three or four days and the mortality rate is negligible.

[*See also* Medicine: Colonial Era; Medicine: From 1776 to the 1870s; Medicine: From the 1870s to 1945.]

• Michael P. McCarthy, *Typhoid and the Politics of Public Health in Nineteenth-Century Philadelphia,* 1987. Judith Walzer Leavitt, *Typhoid Mary: Captive to the Public Health,* 1996

—Edward T. Morman

TYPHOID MARY. *See* Typhoid Fever.

U

U-2 INCIDENT (1960). In the 1950s, the specter of Japan's surprise attack on *Pearl Harbor continued to haunt America's security officials. Could the nation's *Cold War adversary, the Soviet Union, similarly strike the United States—this time with *nuclear weapons? Was there a "bomber gap" that favored the USSR? To answer these questions, U.S. officials developed improved methods of intelligence gathering to probe Soviet military capabilities and intentions.

The first breakthrough was the high-altitude U-2 reconnaissance aircraft, the "Black Lady of Espionage," secretly built by the Lockheed Corporation in cooperation with the *Central Intelligence Agency and the U.S. Air Force. The U-2's first flight over the USSR took place on 4 July 1956. Additional flights deep into Soviet territory provided photography clear enough to persuade American leaders that the Soviets had far fewer long-range bombers and missiles than initially feared, although they could not make this information public lest their spying capabilities be compromised.

On 1 May 1960, the Soviets shot down over Sverdlovsk in Russia a U-2 piloted by Frances Gary Powers. The Dwight D. *Eisenhower administration first claimed that a weather plane had veered off course, but Soviet premier Nikita Khrushchev released photos of Powers, who had been captured, and the reconnaissance instruments. The incident embarrassed the United States on the eve of a Paris summit conference. The Soviets withdrew in protest, gaining a propaganda victory and setting back superpower relations. President Eisenhower suspended U-2 missions and promised Khrushchev that he would curb further flights. Instead, the United States increasingly relied upon satellite photography from the more secure confines of space. U-2 flights remained an important intelligence source in the Cold War, however, as the 1962 *Cuban Missile Crisis would demonstrate. The Soviets released Powers in 1962 in exchange for a convicted Russian spy.

[*See also* Intelligence Gathering and Espionage.]

• Michael Beschloss, *Mayday: Eisenhower, Khrushchev, and the U-2 Affair*, 1986. Richard M. Bissell Jr., with Jonathan E. Lewis and Frances T. Pudlo, *Reflections of a Cold Warrior*, 1996.

—Loch K. Johnson

UNCLE TOM'S CABIN (1852), *antislavery novel by Harriet Beecher Stowe (1811–1896). Though Stowe famously said that "God wrote it," she is nonetheless credited with the authorship of this best-selling work that galvanized opposition to *slavery in the 1850s. Written in the aftermath of the *Fugitive Slave Act of 1850, *Uncle Tom's Cabin: or, Life among the Lowly* was first serialized in the *National Era* (June 1851–April 1852) and then published in book form. It sold more than 10,000 copies in the first few weeks after publication and some 300,000 in the first year.

Based on various slave narratives, including those of Henry Bibb and Josiah Henson, the novel primarily focuses on the title character, a slave who is sold by his owner and torn from his home and family. Tom is first purchased at the *New Orleans slave market by Augustine St. Clare as a companion for his daughter Eva, who shares Tom's devotion to Christianity. After Eva and St. Clare tragically die, Tom is sold to a plantation owner who turns him over to a vicious and cruel overseer, Simon Legree. Repelled by Tom's innate goodness and enraged when Tom refuses to reveal the hiding place of two slaves seeking to escape, Legree beats Tom savagely. Tom dies just as his former owner, George Shelby, arrives to purchase him.

Stowe's novelistic blend of history, personal experience, politics, law, and *religion captured the public imagination and moved many northerners to a more vocal opposition to slavery. Even President Abraham *Lincoln acknowledged Stowe's role in escalating tensions that led to the *Civil War, calling her "the little lady who started the big war." Southern whites' response was predictably negative. In the face of southern criticism that she had misrepresented the reality of slavery, Stowe in *A Key to* Uncle Tom's Cabin (1853) collected historical and legal records documenting events similar to those in her novel.

The power and interest of *Uncle Tom's Cabin* endured long after the Civil War ended and the slavery issue was resolved. Uncle Tom, Simon Legree, Little Eva, and Eliza Harris, the courageous slave mother who escapes the slave catchers by jumping across ice floes on the Ohio River, became familiar archetypes. Dramatizations of *Uncle Tom's Cabin* were frequently staged and immensely popular with nineteenth- and early twentieth-century audiences. Always recognized for its political and cultural importance, the novel by the late twentieth century had also come to be recognized as a major literary classic.

[*See also* Civil War: Causes; Literature: Early National and Antebellum Eras.]

• Jane Tompkins, *Sensational Designs: The Cultural Work of American Fiction, 1790–1850*, 1985. Joan D. Hedrick, *Harriet Beecher Stowe: A Life*, 1994.

—Wendy Wagner

UNDERGROUND RAILROAD. *See* Antislavery.

UNEMPLOYMENT. America has always known unemployment although definitions of the term "out of work" have varied, depending on such factors as individual inclination and seasonality, as well as geographical, occupational, and social-mobility considerations. From its colonial origins until the late nineteenth century, when the United States was mainly agricultural, unemployed people generally relied on other resources for sustenance, such as gardening, hunting, or household contract work. Consequently, poor laws, *laissez-faire ideology, and social Darwinist notions all assumed that any individual should and could be able to provide for his or her own living.

The acceleration of *industrialization after the *Civil War rendered this assumption questionable. As wage labor became the predominant form of employment and the labor force swelled through large-scale *immigration, workers thrown out of work in periods of industrial depression could no longer be expected to manage for themselves. But because of the novelty of widespread unemployment and the public's unwillingness to assume an obligation to the jobless, two generations passed before Americans recognized unemployment as a societal responsibility and agreed on remedial responses. The inadequacy of private poor relief induced a growing number of *Progressive Era reformers, especially those in the American Association for Labor Legislation led by William M. Leiserson and John B. Andrews, to call for government involvement. Slowly, several state governments as well as the federal government, drawing on English and German models, began to gather statistics on the out of work, to furnish them with job information through public employment-agencies, to employ them on public works projects, and to debate the merits of unemployment insurance.

The Depression of the 1930s stimulated more substantial initiatives. The *Social Security Act of 1935 established a joint federal-state scheme of unemployment insurance, administered in conjunction with a network of public employment agencies and, as a welcome by-product, at last made available reliable unemployment figures. Other New Deal measures implemented a huge public works program to provide paid work for the masses of unemployed—by some counts up to one-third of the labor force in 1933.

The *Employment Act of 1946 acknowledged the government's obligation to assist job-seekers. By then, also, all states had passed unemployment compensation laws. But the states controlled the tax rates paid by employers to fund insurance, and their programs lacked uniformity. During a recessionary period in 1959, for example, several states had to borrow money from the federal government to make their unemployment payments, whereas other states ran large surpluses. Nonetheless, suggestions that the federal government take full responsibility for the system were rejected. Most people apparently felt that the system satisfactorily fulfilled its twofold task: to alleviate individual need and to soften economic downturns by sustaining purchasing power. Whereas in the worst depression years of 1894 and 1933 an estimated 18 and 25 percent, respectively, of the labor force had been out of work, after 1940 the rate never exceeded 10.8 percent, a high it briefly reached in 1982. The character of unemployment also changed with the composition of the labor force, so that by the end of the twentieth century women as well as men fed the ranks of the out of work.

[*See also* Depressions, Economic; Labor Markets; Labor Movements; New Deal Era, The; Poverty; Social Darwinism; Welfare, Federal; Women in the Labor Force.]

• Edward D. Berkowitz, *America's Welfare State from Roosevelt to Reagan,* 1991. Udo Sautter, *Three Cheers for the Unemployed: Government and Unemployment before the New Deal,* 1991.

—Udo Sautter

UNION OF CONCERNED ATOMIC SCIENTISTS. *See* Peace Movements.

UNITARIANISM AND UNIVERSALISM. The Unitarian Universalist Association was formed in 1961 by the union of the American Unitarian Association and the Universalist Church of America. The two denominations shared a liberal approach to religion and ethics, but each has its own history. Though both originated in *New England, Unitarianism began among the upper and middle classes of urban areas along the seacoast, while early Universalism was more rural and appealed to the common people.

The American Unitarian Association was founded in 1825 as the outcome of prolonged theological controversy within the Congregational church of Massachusetts. Traditionally, the Congregationalists had been Calvinists, endorsing belief in original sin and the predestination of God's elect to salvation. By the mid–eighteenth century, however, a liberal wing of Congregationalism had emerged, affirming the freedom of the will. By the early nineteenth century, these liberals came to reject the deity of Jesus Christ and the doctrine of the Trinity and therefore were called Unitarians. Separation of the Unitarians from the orthodox Calvinists was complicated by the status of Congregationalism as the established church of Massachusetts until 1833. The Unitarians' most prominent leader during this formative era was William Ellery *Channing.

Universalism, also a protest against Calvinism, arose outside the established church. While the Unitarian protest focused on the Calvinist doctrine of original sin, the Universalists objected to the doctrine that some were elected by God to salvation and others to eternal damnation. Universalists acquired their name from their insistence that all people would eventually be saved. Their most important early leader was Hosea Ballou (1771–1852), pastor of the Second Universalist Society in *Boston and editor of the denomination's periodical.

Although both sects remained small, Unitarianism became the more intellectually influential. In the split of the Congregational establishment, the Unitarians had gained control of Harvard University and its divinity school. They counted among their members many leaders of American literature, education, and science. The Universalists founded Tufts University.

In the late twentieth century, while debating the extent to which they should retain their historically Christian identity, Unitarians and Universalists maintained their emphasis on the dignity of humanity and participated prominently in radical and reform politics.

[*See also* Antebellum Era; Emerson, Ralph Waldo; Protestantism; Religion; Romantic Movement; Transcendentalism.]

• David Robinson, *The Unitarians and the Universalists,* 1985.

—Daniel Walker Howe

UNITED AUTOMOBILE WORKERS. *See* Congress of Industrial Organizations; Labor Movements; Reuther, Walter.

UNITED FARM WORKERS OF AMERICA. *See* Chavez, Cesar.

UNITED MINE WORKERS OF AMERICA. *See* Congress of Industrial Organizations; Lewis, John L.; Mining.

UNITED NATIONS. The United Nations (UN) is an international organization of sovereign nations, with headquarters in *New York City, founded in *San Francisco in 1945. Planning for the UN evolved slowly during *World War II. Although its forerunner, the *League of Nations, had failed to preserve peace in the 1930s, Allied leaders had become even more determined to create another, more effective international security organization after the defeat of the Axis. A U.S. State Department subcommittee on postwar planning completed its proposed draft for a new international organization in March 1943. During subsequent weeks the draft was approved by Congress as well as by the governments of Great Britain, the Soviet Union, and China. At Teheran that December, President Franklin Delano *Roosevelt, Soviet premier Joseph Stalin, and British prime minister Winston Churchill committed their countries to the contemplated postwar United Nations organization. The Big Three meeting at Dumbarton Oaks, a Washington mansion (August–October 1944), began the difficult process of formulating the new organization's structure. At the *Yalta Conference of February 1945, the three leaders resumed their quest for agreement, resolving the most contentious issues of veto power and UN membership. Stalin, who earlier insisted on the right to veto any discussion in the Security Council that touched Soviet interests, accepted a proposal that seven of the council's eleven members could bring an issue before the whole council. Roosevelt and Churchill agreed to Stalin's request that Byelorussia and Ukraine receive membership.

At the *San Francisco Conference (April–June 1945), delegates from fifty nations—including the sponsoring countries: the United States, Great Britain, the Soviet Union, France, and China—drafted the official United Nations charter. These states, with the addition of Poland, became the original fifty-one members. The conference established six principal UN organs: the General Assembly, the Security Council, the Economic and Social Council, the Trusteeship Council, the International Court of Justice, and the Secretariat under a secretary-general. The General Assembly, consisting of all UN member states, and the core of the organization, was authorized to "discuss any questions or any matters within the scope of the present charter or relating to the power and functions of any organs provided for in the present charter." The Security Council, consisting of the five sponsoring powers as permanent members and six rotating members, received powers not granted to the former council of the League of Nations on matters of peace and security, notably the authority to "determine the existence of any threat to the peace, breach of the peace, or act of aggression and . . . make recommendations, or decide what measures shall be taken . . . to maintain or restore international peace and security." The council could authorize economic sanctions, the severance of diplomatic relations, and even resort to military force, but was given no power to enforce such decisions. The conference accepted the principle that regional alliances could function when the Security Council failed to act.

Most of the modifications made at San Francisco in the Dumbarton Oaks's draft came in response to smaller countries' demands for a greater voice. The critical issue, however, on which hung approval of the charter, was the role of the veto in the Security Council. To assure their necessary unity, the Yalta Conference had granted the five permanent Security Council members the right to veto a council action. But at San Francisco the Soviets again denied the council the right even to discuss issues that touched the Soviet Union directly. Following direct appeals to Stalin in Moscow, the Kremlin in early June accepted the Yalta formula that retained the power to veto any Security Council *action,* but that no country could use its veto power to prevent council *discussion* of any matter brought before it. Amid a pervasive euphoria, the delegates approved the charter on 25 June 1945, and signed it the following day. In 1946, John D. Rockefeller Jr. contributed land along the East River in New York City for a permanent UN headquarters. The first UN secretary general, Trygve Lie of Norway, was succeeded by Sweden's Dag Hammarskjold (1953–1961), who died in a plane crash on a mission to the Congo, and U Thant of Burma (1962–1971).

If the United Nations charter changed little after 1945, the organization's membership and functioning changed dramatically. With the Soviet Union and its satellites reduced to a small minority of the membership, the United States, beginning with the first session in early 1946, dominated the organization on all security issues. China's seat on the Security Council, for example, was denied to the People's Republic of China, the communist government that came to power in 1949. The veto became the means whereby the Soviet Union prevented unwanted Security Council decisions. The resulting Security Council paralysis prompted the United States, backed by smaller powers as well as America's European allies, to increase the authority of the General Assembly. U.S. influence, however, ultimately diminished, as the United Nations expanded to over 180 members by the 1990s. Reflecting that growth, the Security council grew from eleven to fifteen members, while the Economic and Social Council eventually expanded to fifty-four members. Most of the new additions were Third World states with interests and concerns at odds with those of the major powers. By the 1980s, the United States on many key issues could command only a small minority of voting allies and repeatedly used its Security Council veto power. This loss of control, added to perennial complaints of bureaucratic inefficiency and waste, prompted Congress in 1982 to withhold payment of America's UN dues.

Twice the United Nations supported the United States's recommendations to marshal force to resist external aggression: first to confront North Korea's invasion of South Korea in 1950; then to repel Iraq's occupation of Kuwait in 1990. In 1956, a UN Emergency Force for Palestine played a part in securing and maintaining an armistice after the Suez Crisis of that year. Many UN peacekeeping activities, especially in the *post–Cold War Era, also responded to U.S. and international concerns, but the UN, limited to peacekeeping functions, could succeed only where the contending parties accepted its intervention. UN efforts in Bosnia, Somalia, and Cambodia during the presidency of Bill *Clinton, for example, revealed the organization's limitations in dealing with ongoing civil conflict; UN brokered peace processes, however, helped several Central American countries to end their civil wars and establish more democratic structures during the 1990s.

A significant part of the UN's activities have been carried out by its specialized agencies, including the *World Health Organization (WHO); United Nations International Children's Emergency Fund (UNICEF); and the United Nations Education, Scientific, and Cultural Organization (UNESCO). A temporary organization, the United Nations Relief and Rehabilitation Administration (UNRRA), helped in resettling refugees after World War II. The United Nations Conference on Environment and Development sponsored the international "Earth Summit" held in Rio de Janeiro, Brazil, in 1992.

Although not the prelude to world government that some of the founders had hoped for (and some feared), the UN has played a minor but important role in sustaining world peace.

[*See also* Baruch, Bernard; Foreign Relations; Internationalism; Korean War, Persian Gulf War.]

• Leland M. Goodrich and A. P. Simon, *The United Nations and the Maintenance of International Peace and Security,* 1955. R. B. Russell, *A History of the United Nations Charter: The Role of the United States, 1940–1945,* 1958. Leland M. Goodrich, *The United Nations,* 1959. Lori Fisher Damrosch, ed., *Enforcing Restraint: Collective Intervention in Internal Conflicts,* 1993. Roger A. Coate, *U.S. Policy and the Future of the United Nations,* 1995. Stanley Meisler, *United Nations: The First Fifty Years,* 1995.

—Norman A. Graebner

UNITED STATES INFORMATION AGENCY (USIA), a governmental agency created by President Dwight D. *Eisenhower in 1953 to provide information about the official policies of the United States and its people, values, and institutions. Its predecessors included the Committee for Public Information (created during *World War I), the State Department's Interdepartmental Committee for Scientific and Cultural Cooperation (operating on the eve of *World War II), and the Office of War Information (established during World War II).

In the aftermath of World War II, U.S. officials expressed dismay at international stereotypes of the United States. These concerns, combined with a desire to combat communism, created support for peacetime information activities. In September 1945, President Harry S. *Truman ordered all overseas information and cultural programs consolidated into the State Department. Until 1953, the State Department controlled these activities under a variety of names including the International Information Administration and the Office of International and Educational Exchange.

Throughout its history, the USIA engaged in both overt and covert activities designed to extol the virtues of American democracy and society. At times, domestic political controversies affected the agency's budget and personnel levels. In 1978, President Jimmy *Carter combined USIA and the State Department's Bureau of Educational and Cultural Affairs (including the Fulbright program) into the U.S. International Communications Agency (USICA).

In 1982, President Ronald *Reagan signed legislation readopting the name USIA. In the 1980s, USIA director Charles Wick instituted Spanish broadcasting to Cuba, greater use of *television (Worldnet), and youth exchanges. By the 1990s the

USIA maintained two-hundred offices in 140 countries and supervised a wide array of activities, including the Fulbright scholarships, "Voice of America" radio broadcasts, and cultural exchanges. With the end of the *Cold War, the USIA cut staff and discontinued several publications. The agency was terminated in 1999 as its functions again were incorporated into the State Department.

[*See also* Anticommunism; Federal Government, Executive Branch: Department of State; Foreign Relations: The Cultural Dimension; Propaganda.]

• John Henderson, *The United States Information Agency,* 1969. Walter L. Hixson, *Parting the Curtain: Propaganda, Culture, and Cold War, 1945–1961,* 1997.

—Laura A. Belmonte

UNIVERSITIES. *See* Education: The Rise of the University.

UPDIKE, JOHN (1932–), novelist, essayist, poet, short-story writer. The only child in a relatively poor family, Updike was born in Shillington, Pennsylvania, during the Great Depression. His father, Wesley, taught in the local high school, while his mother, Linda, hoped to make her mark as a writer. The family moved to an isolated farm in Plowville, Pennsylvania, when Updike was thirteen, a move he resented as later recounted in "Flight" (*Pigeon Feathers,* 1962), "The Dogwood Tree: A Boyhood" (*Assorted Prose,* 1965), and *Of the Farm* (1965). Updike won a scholarship to Harvard, from which he graduated summa cum laude in 1954 after majoring in English. He then studied art at the Ruskin School in Oxford before returning to the United States in 1955 to work for two years at the *New Yorker* magazine. Updike's decades-long association with the *New Yorker* had begun on 30 October 1954, when the magazine published his first professional short story, "Friends from Philadelphia" (reprinted in *The Same Door,* 1959).

After moving to Massachusetts in 1957, he launched the career that would make him a leading writer of his generation. Twice winner of the National Book Award (*The Centaur,* 1963; *Hugging the Shore,* 1983) and of the *Pulitzer Prize (*Rabbit Is Rich,* 1981; *Rabbit at Rest,* 1990), he was honored for his meticulously detailed depiction of the American middle class. The four so-called Rabbit novels (including *Rabbit, Run,* 1960, and *Rabbit Redux,* 1971) trace the decline of religious surety and social cohesiveness in America after 1950 and illustrate Updike's skill at evoking specific historical and cultural contexts. By the end of the twentieth century he had published more than forty books.

[*See also* Literature: Since World War I.]

• Donald J. Greiner, *John Updike's Novels,* 1984. Donald J. Greiner, "John Updike," in *Dictionary of Literary Biography: American Novelists since World War II,* eds. James R. and Wanda H. Giles, 3d series, vol. 143, 1994, pp. 250–76.

—Donald J. Greiner

URBANIZATION. Over four centuries, the United States gradually emerged as a predominantly urban nation. Since 1920, a majority of Americans have lived in urban places. The process of urbanization—the growth and settlement of cities—has been the result of interactions among technological and economic change and such social processes as population growth, *immigration, and internal migration. Public policy has also played a decisive role in the transformation of urban areas. The physical form and social structure of cities have reflected conscious choices by political officials, planners, and ordinary citizens.

Until the mid–eighteenth century, not many settlements in North America could properly be called cities. Prior to contact with European colonists, few Native Americans lived in urban settlements. With a small number of noteworthy exceptions, such as pueblo villages of the Anasazi people of the *Southwest and the thirteenth-century city of Cahokia, near the *Mississipi River in what is now East St. Louis, Illinois, most American Indians lived in traveling bands or in small, often seasonal villages.

The Colonial Era. Early European settlers imposed European models of urbanism on the North American landscape. Spanish colonists along the Gulf of Mexico and the Atlantic imported traditional Roman designs for their settlements, although most of their North American settlements were small fortifications. English-born city-builders often imitated the commercial and residential layouts of their native towns and cities. Some farsighted planners, such as William *Penn, the proprietor of Pennsylvania and founder of *Philadelphia, attempted to build utopian cities. Penn hoped that Philadelphia, with its grid of streets, public squares, and large lots, would offer an alternative to the crowded, disorderly streets that characterized many British and colonial towns. Although Penn's vision of a "Greene Countrie Town" remained unfulfilled, his grid plan became a nearly universal feature of later North American city-building. The easily replicated grid promoted real-estate development and the flow of people and traffic.

Urbanization proceeded at different paces, but followed a distinct pattern. Primarily commercial in origin, most colonial cities functioned as local and regional marketplaces. The four largest cities in British North America (Philadelphia, *New York, *Boston, and Charleston, South Carolina) had deepwater ports that allowed them to serve as entrepôts for intercolonial and international trade. These commercial cities had sizable populations of merchants, artisans, and other craftspeople. But even these colonial cities were small by later standards. In 1775, Philadelphia had about 25,000 residents; New York, 18,000; Boston, 16,000; and Charleston, 12,000. Commercial cities tended to be undifferentiated spatially by economic status, race, or ethnicity. Wealthy urban residents usually lived in close proximity to artisans, laborers, and poor people. In addition, working people usually lived near their places of employment; many artisans and shopkeepers lived above their shops.

Urbanization in the Industrial Age. With the rise of *industrialization in the late eighteenth and early nineteenth centuries, cities expanded and took on new forms. Early manufacturing cities, such as Lowell, Massachusetts, emerged in places with waterpower, abundant cheap labor, and well-heeled investors. The expansion of canals such as New York's *Erie Canal and the introduction of *steam power propelled urban growth inland. By the mid–nineteenth century, *railroads also spurred urbanization, bringing industry, migrants and immigrants, and commercial goods to places as diverse as Wheeling, in present-day in West Virginia; *Chicago; Omaha, Nebraska; and Butte, Montana. These cities grew in tandem with the commercial expansion of their hinterlands. Pittsburgh, Pennsylvania; Wheeling; and Butte rose because of their proximity to rich mineral and ore deposits; Chicago depended on the lumber and agricultural goods from its hinterland; Omaha on its access to the cattle and grain produced on the Great Plains.

Industrial cities attracted newcomers from declining agricultural regions who sought employment in factories and other commercial enterprises. Port cities and places easily accessible by rail attracted the lion's share of immigrants from abroad. Immigration and rural-to-urban migration significantly increased the proportion of Americans living in cities, from 5.1 percent in 1790 to 25.7 percent in 1870.

In contrast to *Colonial Era "walking cities," industrial cities were more diverse but more segregated by *social class. Workers clustered in neighborhoods abutting industrial districts while well-to-do urbanites began to settle in more homogeneous neighborhoods distant from immigrants and industry. Innovations in urban transportation, particularly commuter railways and streetcars, facilitated an upper- and middle-class exodus from center cities and encouraged early *suburbanization.

From the 1870s through the 1920s, American cities underwent dramatic growth and change. The advent of affordable public transportation and the coming of the automobile drew urban populations outward. The process of residential segre-

MAP 23: BIRD'S EYE VIEW OF COUNCIL BLUFFS, IOWA (1868)

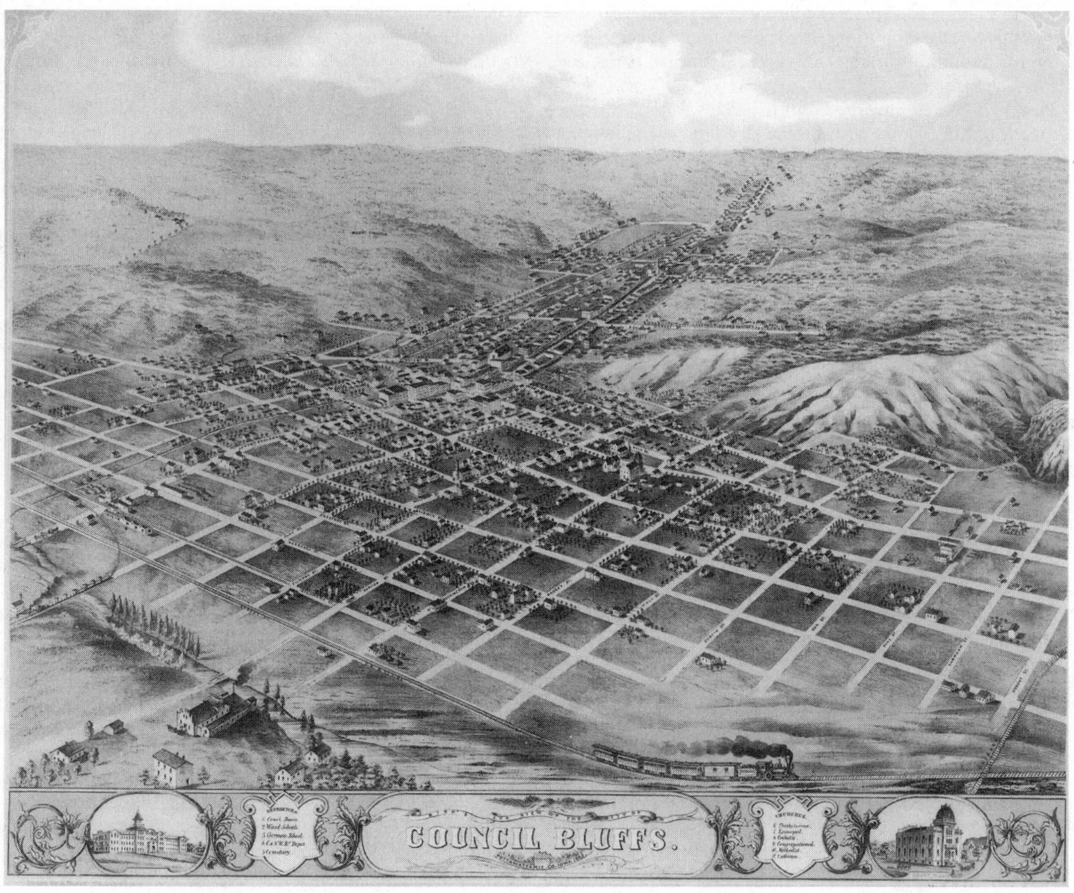

As urbanization burgeoned in the later nineteenth century, local promoters frequently commissioned "bird's eye" maps like this to publicize their town's growth and attractive setting. Sketches of local factories, churches, public institutions, and points of interest typically adorned the maps. In some of these representations, wishful thinking and boosterism triumphed over absolute accuracy, and they portrayed vistas that no bird had ever seen.

[*See* Gilded Age; Urbanization.]

gation by class accelerated. At the same time, cities reached their industrial and commercial zenith. By the early twentieth century, downtowns hummed with corporate and retail activity and new forms of mass entertainment, including *vaudeville, movie theaters, and *sports stadiums. The period also witnessed the construction of a remarkable variety of centralized urban institutions, including *museums, municipal parks, and *department stores.

Post-1920 Developments. From the 1920s through the late twentieth century, urban growth and development followed a new course. Most older industrial cities in the Northeast and *Middle West lost population while new cities, largely in the *South and *West (the Sun Belt), grew rapidly. The nonwhite populations of cities also expanded rapidly during the two great migrations of *African Americans from the rural South (1914–1929 and 1941–1968). The urbanization of black Americans was extraordinarily rapid: in 1920, more than 90 percent lived in rural areas; by 1990, more than 90 percent lived in cities. The ethnic composition of many cities also changed with the migration of Caribbean, Latin American, and Asians, particularly after the 1965 immigration reforms. As the central cities became more heterogeneous, Americans of European descent migrated en masse from cities to suburbs. By 1980, a plurality of Americans, most of them white, lived in suburban areas.

Government policies played a crucial role in shaping the twentieth-century metropolis. In the *New Deal Era, the federal government funneled massive economic assistance to the South. *World War II and *Cold War military spending fueled the rise of Sun Belt cities. At the same time, government subsidies for road construction, especially the interstate *highway system, spurred metropolitan decentralization and encouraged the flight of population and jobs to suburban and rural areas. Persistent racial *segregation, coupled with the high-rise *housing projects associated with postwar *urban-renewal programs, also shattered many older inner-city neighborhoods and contributed to the isolation and marginalization of the urban poor and the concentration of crime and other social problems in the inner city.

The federal government also underwrote suburbanization through generous mortgage programs and loan guarantees by the Home Owners Loan Corporation, the Federal Housing Administration, and the *Veterans Administration. Federal housing subsidies exacerbated class and racial segregation by requiring that new developments be economically and racially homogeneous. With federally backed loans and mortgages seldom available to racial minorities, most suburbs remained overwhelmingly white. State laws also encouraged the proliferation of separate municipalities in metropolitan areas, most with their own tax bases, social services, and school districts.

By the end of the twentieth century, America had become a metropolitan nation. Whereas the nineteenth-century central cities witnessed rapid population growth and economic development, the highest rates of population and economic growth in the late twentieth century occurred in suburban areas. By 1980, a plurality of the nation's population lived in suburbs, not in central cities. Central-city downtowns no longer held a monopoly over business and commercial activity. Suburban office and industrial parks and *shopping centers competed successfully with central business districts, dispersing economic activity over wide areas. Metropolitan areas remained deeply segregated by race, despite an increase in minority suburbanization and a reverse flow of affluent whites back to the inner cities, sometimes called gentrification. Fragmentation and multiplication of local governmental jurisdictions characterized the late twentieth-century metropolis. At century's end, some cities, notably Portland, Oregon, and Minneapolis, Minnesota, experimented with new forms of metropolitan government and enacted policies to discourage suburban sprawl. But these initiatives remained exceptions to the prevailing pattern of demographic and economic decentralization.

[*See also* Agriculture: Since 1920; Architecture: Public Architecture; Asian Americans; Automotive Industry; Canals and Waterways; Detroit; Factory System; Hispanic Americans; Immigrant Labor; Immigration Law; Los Angeles; Lowell Mills; Mobility; Motor Vehicles; Muckrakers; Municipal and County Government; New Orleans; Parks, Urban; Popular Culture; Poverty; Race and Ethnicity; San Francisco; Spanish Settlements in North American; Steffens, Lincoln; Tweed, William Magear; Working-Class Life and Culture.]

• Gary Nash, *The Urban Crucible: Social Change, Political Consciousness, and the Origins of the American Revolution,* 1979. Kenneth T. Jackson, *Crabgrass Frontier: The Suburbanization of the United States,* 1985. Carl Abbott, *The New Urban America: Growth and Politics in Sunbelt Cities,* 1987. Sam Bass Warner, *The Private City: Philadelphia in Three Periods of Its Growth,* 2d ed., 1987. Eric Monkkonen, *America Becomes Urban: The Development of U.S. Cities and Towns, 1790–1980,* 1988. William Cronon, *Nature's Metropolis: Chicago and the Great West,* 1991. Michael B. Katz, ed., *The "Underclass" Debate: Views from History,* 1993. Howard Chudacoff, with Judith E. Smith, *The Evolution of American Urban Society,* 1994. Thomas J. Sugrue, *The Origins of the Urban Crisis: Race and Inequality in Postwar Detroit,* 1996.

—Thomas J. Sugrue

URBAN LEAGUE, NATIONAL. A growing awareness of problems facing African American migrants to urban centers in the North at the turn of the twentieth century led to the founding of three organizations in *New York City: the National League for the Protection of Colored Women (1905), the Committee for Improving the Industrial Conditions of Negroes in New York (1906), and the Committee on Urban Conditions among Negroes in New York (1910). In 1911, these three organizations merged to form the National League on Urban Conditions among Negroes. The name was soon changed to the National Urban League (NUL). Addressing the problems facing urban migrants, the NUL's national leaders and local Urban Leagues relied upon persuasion and winning the cooperation of white elites who were most likely to support improved economic opportunities for *African Americans. Throughout its history, the NUL pursued the goals established by the founders: merging the black elite's objective of racial uplift with northern business leaders' hopes of integrating African Americans into the corporate culture. A nonpolitical, interracial community-planning agency, the NUL was committed to the expansion of equality of opportunity for African Americans in all phases of the national economy.

Successive NUP leaders adopted differing strategies for achieving the goal of closing the socioeconomic gap between African Americans and whites. The first chief executive officer, George E. Haynes, challenged the interracial status quo, establishing a social-work program at Fisk University to train African American social workers. His successor, Eugene K. Jones, promoted the idea of vocational education and secured financial support for local Urban Leagues from the Community Chest. Lester B. Granger promoted the integration of the urban newcomers into an orderly multiracial society by involving the NUL in *civil rights causes. Whitney M. Young Jr., executive director from 1961 to 1971, more than any other NUL chief executive, informed white business leaders, foundation executives, and public officials—the traditional power base of the NUL—of African Americans' aspirations and of their frustration at being denied equal rights. Vernon E. Jordan Jr. (1971–1981) promoted *cultural pluralism as a goal for American society, backing voting and desegregation initiatives and improved health care for the poor. John E. Jacob explored ways of resolving racial tension in urban America. Hugh B. Price, NUL's president in the 1990s, called for a rethinking of community development and more public attention to education, welfare issues, and equal justice before the law.

[*See also* Civil Rights Movement; Labor Markets; National Association for the Advancement of Colored People; Racism; Segregation, Racial; Urbanization; Welfare, Federal.]

• Nancy J. Weiss, *The National Urban League, 1910–1940,* 1974. Jesse T. Moore Jr., *A Search for Equality: The National Urban League, 1910–60,* 1918.

—Jesse T. Moore Jr.

URBAN RENEWAL. Arising from more than a half-century of slum clearance and urban *housing reform campaigns, "Urban Renewal" was a federally sponsored and largely federally financed program that altered the physical landscapes of many American cities between the mid-1950s and the early 1970s. Proponents promised to provide cities with funds and legal powers to tear down slums, sell the land to private developers at reduced cost, relocate slum-dwellers in decent, safe housing, stimulate large-scale private construction of new housing, revitalize decaying urban downtowns by eliminating "blight" (economically unprofitable districts), and add new property-tax revenues to shrinking city budgets. Urban renewal, proponents argued, would also slow the departure of middle- and upper-income whites for the suburbs.

Program implementation proved costly, complex, and controversial, and generally failed to accomplish the often contradictory goals. There were some success stories: the soaring "Gateway to the West" arch in St. Louis, Missouri, that supplanted blocks of dilapidated riverfront buildings, gleaming office towers and apartment buildings that replaced the slums bordering Yale University in New Haven, Connecticut; a "renaissance" construction of offices, luxury apartments, and a civic arena that restored the luster of downtown Pittsburgh's "Golden Triangle." Such successes, however, often masked failures inherent in the legislation that established the program.

Title I of the Housing Act of 1949 defined "redevelopment" as encouraging private enterprise to meet public housing needs. It required local governments eager to acquire and refurbish slum neighborhoods to submit plans that focused on "predominantly residential" areas in order to qualify for federal assistance. The law did not, however, include any relocation provisions for dispossessed slum-dwellers. Limited private-enterprise participation, plus harsh criticism from housing advocates, led Congress to revisions in the Housing Act of 1954. "Redevelopment" gave way to "renewal," with the focus shifting from housing toward the rescue of business districts. The 1954 act enhanced profitability for private investors by specifying that 10 percent of federal funds (expanded under continuing business pressures in 1961 to 30 percent) could go to projects in "nonresidential" areas while also calling on communities to submit a "workable program" of relocating the displaced population—a provision rarely enforced by any level of government. Between 1949 and 1970, some 500,000 more housing units fell to the renewal wrecking balls than government subsequently rebuilt. In *Chicago and other cities, the stark high-rise housing that was built for citizens displaced by urban renewal often became centers of crime, drug abuse, and other social ills. That low-income minorities occupied most of the destroyed units lent weight to critics' fears that "urban renewal" meant "Negro removal." Although well intentioned, urban renewal often caused more problems than it solved.

[*See also* Cold War; Fifties, The; Poverty; Sixties, The; Slums; Urbanization.]

• Jewel Bellush and Murray Hausknecht, eds., *Urban Renewal: People, Politics, and Planning,* 1967. Mark I. Gelfand, *A Nation of Cities: The Federal Government and Urban America, 1933–1965,* 1975.

—Stanley K. Schultz

UREY, HAROLD C. (1893–1981), chemist, Nobel laureate. Born in Walkerton, Indiana, Urey received his B.A. in zoology with a minor in chemistry from Montana State University (1917) and his Ph.D. in chemistry from the University of California, Berkeley, in 1923. He taught first at Johns Hopkins (1925–1928) and then at Columbia University (1929–1945). He won the Nobel Prize in chemistry in 1934 for the discovery of deuterium (the rare "heavy" isotope of hydrogen), the first isotope tracer used in biomedical research.

During *World War II, Urey directed one of the groups involved in the *Manhattan Project, which built the atomic bomb. Raised in a church with a pacifist tradition (The Church of the Brethren), he opposed dropping the bomb on Japan and throughout his career promoted the peaceful uses of atomic energy. Following the war, while teaching at the University of Chicago (1945–1958) and the University of California, San Diego (1958–1981), he turned to the uses of isotopes in studying the geochemistry of terrestrial and extraterrestrial planetary materials. He developed a means of inferring marine paleotemperatures over geologic time by measuring the oxygen isotope ratios of carbonates in marine sediments. Urey's interest in the origins of life gave rise to a famous experiment in which electric discharges through a mixture of gases produced amino acids. An active supporter of the U.S. *space program, he served on the Space Board of the *National Academy of Sciences.

[*See also* Hiroshima and Nagasaki, Atomic Bombing of; Nuclear Power; Nuclear Weapons; Physicial Sciences; Science: From 1914 to 1945; Science: Since 1945.]

• Harold Urey, *The Planets: Their Origin and Development,* 1952. Joseph N. Tatarewicz, "Urey, Harold," *Dictionary of Scientific Biography,* vol. 18, 1990, pp. 943–48.

—R. E. Taylor

U.S. PUBLIC HEALTH SERVICE. *See* Public Health.

U.S. VIRGIN ISLANDS. *See* Protectorates and Dependencies.

UTOPIAN AND COMMUNITARIAN MOVEMENTS. The quest for the perfect society arose in Western thought in ancient tales of a Golden Age, Greek theories of the perfect city-state, and early Christians' anticipation of Christ's second coming. With European colonization of the New World, such hopes took on the enticing aura of possibility. The very name "America" became a metaphor for perfectionist longings, as in Thomas More's *Utopia* (1516), describing an ideal community on an island off the South American coast. Beginning with a party of Dutch Mennonites who settled in Delaware in 1663 and French Labadists (followers of the mystic Jean de Labadie) who came to Maryland in 1684, a succession of radical Protestant sects looked to the British colonies for refuge from persecution and the opportunity to build a godly society in miniature.

After the *Revolutionary War, these expectations were heightened by the new nation's prosperity and expansionism, its religious freedom, and its openness to *immigration and social experiment. The Shakers, a celibate sect led to America in 1776 by the English mystic Ann Lee, established nearly twenty tidy villages of American converts whose prosperity proved that economic "communism" was possible. The Harmonists, followers of the German pietist George Rapp, arriving in 1804, established communities in Pennsylvania, southern Indiana, and again in Pennsylvania.

Secular utopian socialists, such as the Owenites and the Icarians, founded communal ventures as well. Robert Owen, a wealthy Scottish mill-owner and philanthropist, established a colony called New Harmony in Indiana in 1825, on a site along the Wabash River purchased from the Harmonists. Although it eventually failed as a cooperative venture, New Harmony became a major center of culture, intellectual life, and educational innovation on the frontier. The French Icarians, utopian socialists led by Etienne Cabet, founded communities in Illinois, Iowa, Missouri, and California from the 1840s through the 1880s.

These humanitarian idealists saw in America's cheap land and republican institutions a hospitable environment for their goal of replacing competitive *capitalism with cooperative "social science." By the 1840s, communitarianism—the idea that successful pilot communities could revolutionize society—had become a major expression of American reform, influencing some *labor movements and spawning dozens of immigrant colonies and home-grown experiments that attracted more than twenty thousand Americans. The Latter-day Saints (Mormons) under Joseph Smith shared land and property in Ohio and Illinois before trekking to Utah in 1846. In 1841, New England transcendentalists, led by the Reverend George Ripley (1802–1880) and influenced by the ideas of Ralph Waldo *Emerson, established a communal society at Brook Farm near *Boston. Nathaniel *Hawthorne offered a skeptical view of the venture in his 1852 novel *The Blithedale Romance.* The Oneida Community (1848–1881), formed in western New York by the Perfectionist preacher John Humphrey *Noyes (and patterned on Noyes's earlier communal experiment in Putney, Vermont), sanctioned a controlled and theologically based practice of multiple sexual relationships called "complex marriage." German pietists led by Christian Metz founded Amana, a highly successful communitarian venture, in Iowa in 1855.

The most influential utopians of the *Antebellum Era were the Fourierists, followers of the French utopian writer Charles Fourier (1772–1837), whose ideas were publicized in America by Albert Brisbane's *Social Destiny of Man* (1840). The Fourierists set up nearly thirty communes (or "phalanxes") and induced thousands of workers to form producer and consumer cooperatives. Brook Farm became a Fourierite phalanx in 1845, shortly before its demise. But this loose communal movement, which had been confined to the northern states, faded when its experimental communities either collapsed or conformed to the values of the mainstream culture, and when the North's victory in the *Civil War ensured that individualist capitalism would become the American way.

After 1880 the rise of Karl Marx's "scientific" (as contrasted to "utopian") *socialism, coupled with massive urban-industrial development, seemed to render anachronistic the strategy of social reconstruction through ideal communal ventures. Some workers and middle-class reformers still harbored utopian aspirations, but these typically found expression in political schemes such as Henry George's *single-tax movement; Edward Bellamy's Nationalist program, set forth in his utopian novel **Looking Backward* (1888); or radical political parties such as Eugene V. *Debs's *Socialist party of America.

Nevertheless, communal experiments, although no longer in the center of the debate over social change, continued to crop up in varied forms. The Hutterites, followers of the sixteenth-century Anabaptist martyr Jacob Hutter, settled in South Dakota in 1874, where their communal agricultural colonies continue to flourish. Western colonies of radical workers sprang up in the 1880s and 1890s. Julius Wayland's Ruskin Cooperative Association in Tennessee (1894–1899) drew Depression-battered workers with its communal values and pooled resources. Sex radicals established "Spirit Fruit," a homoerotic community, in Lisbon, Ohio, in 1899.

The *Progressive Era brought *Social Gospel enclaves and other communal ventures. Upton *Sinclair started a short-lived cooperative colony in Edgewood, New Jersey, in 1906. The anarchist Home Colony in Washington State (1896–1921) and Ferrer Colony in New Jersey (1915–1956) emphasized individual rights within a cooperative community. Job Harriman's Llano del Rio colony in *California (1914–1918) espoused socialism, agrarianism, and resistance to established authority.

Traditional cloistered Roman Catholic orders, introduced to America by Augustinian monks who reached *Philadelphia in the 1790s, and perpetuated in the twentieth century by Trappists, Benedictines, and other orders, represented a different form of the communitarian vision. So, too, did colonies embracing *Spiritualism or Theosophy; gender-based settlements such as the Women's Commonwealth in Texas and *Washington, D.C. (1874–1906), and ashrams established by Asian-influenced mystics in Massachusetts and California in the 1920s. In the Depression-wracked 1930s, Catholic renewalists started a communitarian religious retreat, "The Grail," in Ohio; conservative Protestants founded communities in Texas and Arkansas to promote fundamentalist religious beliefs; and radical Jews formed socialist colonies in Michigan.

Communal living reemerged during the countercultural revolt of the late 1960s and its aftermath. More than three-thousand small, rural communes were established by disaffected young people seeking a return to nature and the simple life. Some experimented with drugs or sexually free lifestyles, or explored alternative religious traditions. Less clearly committed to social reconstruction than their nineteenth-century predecessors, some of these groups espoused anarchistic "do you own thing" values that challenged the established social order and sought to maximize individual freedom. Opposition from neighbors and the public at large—a chronic problem for utopian groups—doomed some of these ventures, but others endured. Communes such as The Farm in Tennessee, Padanaram in Indiana, and Ananda Cooperative Village in California survived into the 1980s and 1990s. By then, however, the communal torch had been taken up by hundreds of new religious sects such as the Korean-based Unification Church (whose followers some called "Moonies" after its founder, the Reverend Sun Myung Moon), the Family, and the Children of God. These groups aggressively recruited stray individuals and adopted communal living less on philosophical grounds than as a mechanism to maintain unity and enforce members' isolation from nonbelievers and the authorities.

Noyes and other nineteenth-century observers had noted that religious communities tended to cohere better and last longer than secular ones. In *Commitment and Community* (1972), sociologist Rosabeth Moss Kanter argued that not religion per se but the "commitment mechanisms" employed by religious communes—charismatic and authoritarian leadership, an ascetic lifestyle, restricted outside contact, and so forth—enhanced their longevity. Yet these bonding techniques often appeared antithetical to mainstream American notions of individual freedom. Charges that communities destroyed families, oppressed women, and "brainwashed" disciples, hurled against many nineteenth-century religious groups including the Shakers and Mormons, were voiced against religious "cults" of the 1980s and 1990s, with some justification in both cases. Utopian enthusiasm promises enlightenment and community but it also risks exploitation, depersonalization, and megalomania. Indeed, the public's perception of such dangers increased following the 1978 mass suicide of the Reverend Jim Jones' People's Temple followers at Jonestown, Guyana, to which Jones had moved from San Francisco, and the tragic 1993 standoff between federal authorities and members of David Koresh's Branch Davidian religious movement at Waco, Texas. More than seventy Davidians died when their compound burned down as the authorities moved in. Whether the fire was caused by the attack, or was set by the Davidians themselves, remained a matter of intense debate. Another mass suicide by the Heaven's Gate commune of computer programmers in San Diego in 1997 underscored the self-destructive potential in some communal sects' apocalyptic and millennialist preoccupations.

Although the utopian and communitarian groups that have emerged throughout American history appeared deviant and lived separately from outsiders, they have also been inextricably bound to the larger culture. They have offered new combinations or exaggerated versions of beliefs shared by many Americans, such as faith in a national mission; the myth of new beginnings; the promise of self-realization; and the expectation of impending salvation, often after a time of trial and suffering.

As long as these generative ingredients permeate the subsoil of American culture, utopian experiments and movements appear likely to continue sprouting from it.

[*See also* Anarchism; Individualism; Industrialization; Mennonites and Amish; Millennialism and Apocalypticism; Mormonism; New Age Movement; Protestantism; Republicanism; Roman Catholicism; Sexual Morality and Sex Reform; Shakerism; Sixties, The; Transcendentalism; Urbanization.]

• Arthur Bestor, *Backwoods Utopias: The Sectarian Origins and the Owenite Phase of Communitarian Socialism in America, 1663–1829,* 2d ed., 1970. Iacov Oved, *Two Hundred Years of American Communes,* 1988. Robert S. Fogarty, *All Things New: American Communes and Utopian Movements, 1860–1914,* 1990. Carl J. Guarneri, *The Utopian Alternative: Fourierism in Nineteenth-Century America,* 1991. Stephen J. Stein, *The Shaker Experience in America,* 1993. Donald E. Pitzer, ed., *America's Communal Utopias,* 1997.

—Carl J. Guarneri

V

VACATIONS. *See* Leisure.

VACCINATIONS. *See* Smallpox.

VALENTINO, RUDOLPH (1895–1926), silent-era motion picture star. Born in Italy, the son of an army veterinarian, Rudolph Valentino emigrated to New York in 1913 to find work. After a series of odd jobs, he became a taxi dancer and then an exhibition dancer in *New York City. Moving to Hollywood in 1917, he landed small roles in several *films. His big break came in 1921, when screenwriter June Mathis insisted that he play the lead in *The Four Horsemen of the Apocalypse,* about a South American playboy who becomes a hero in France during *World War I. A huge hit, the film catapulted Valentino to stardom and established his status as Hollywood's first male sex symbol. Before Valentino, popular male stars like Douglas Fairbanks were more action- than romance-oriented. But with his lithe body, dark features, and passionate gaze, Valentino had a more explicitly sexual charisma.

In 1921, he consolidated his popularity with *The Sheik,* playing an Arab chieftain who abducts an English lady only to reveal his true identity as a British aristocrat. Between 1921 and 1926 he starred in more than a dozen films, the best known of which are *Blood and Sand* (1922), *Monsieur Beaucaire* (1924), and *The Eagle* (1925). His movies typically featured torrid romances, weak narratives, exotic locales, and elaborate costumes that appealed to female viewers while angering male critics, who considered him effeminate. Promoted as "every woman's dream," Valentino provided the inspiration for several "Latin lovers" in Hollywood. He died at the age of 31, soon after his hospitalization for a perforated ulcer. His sudden death prompted an outpouring of grief from his fans. He remains an enduring Hollywood legend.

[*See also* Popular Culture; Twenties, The.]

• Alexander Walker, *Rudolph Valentino,* 1976.

—Cynthia Lee Felando

VALLEY FORGE. Having failed to prevent the British general William Howe from occupying *Philadelphia during the autumn of 1777, George *Washington made the tactical decision that the main Continental Army should winter on high ground at Valley Forge, Pennsylvania, a small community of farms, dwellings, and workshops (including an iron forge) about eighteen miles northwest of the city. From a position too distant to invite British attack, where local resources would provide food and shelter, the soldiers could be drilled and detachments could interfere with British foraging parties.

From December 1777 until June 1778, the army camped on approximately two thousand acres bounded by the Schuykill River, Valley Creek, and a natural ridge. Approximately twelve thousand men lived in huts, and an outer and inner line of defensive earthworks were built. Although no battles were fought at Valley Forge, bitter cold and shortages of provisions plagued the army, while poor sanitation contributed to significant losses of men to *disease.

Valley Forge has been described as a turning point in the *Revolutionary War, since its privations helped Washington convince Congress that victory depended on an improved supply system. Acting as inspector general, Friedrich von Steuben drafted a training manual and initiated a system of standardized military training so that the army could be further honed as a fighting force.

In the nineteenth century, Valley Forge came to symbolize the suffering, perseverance, and sacrifice that won American independence. In 1893, the Valley Forge Park Commission was established to create Pennsylvania's first state park at Valley Forge. President Gerald *Ford signed legislation on 4 July 1976 making Valley Forge a national historic park.

[*See also* National Park System.]

• John B. B. Trussell, *Birthplace of an Army: A Study of the Valley Forge Encampment,* 1983. Lorett Trese, *Valley Forge: Making and Remaking a National Symbol,* 1995.

—Lorett Treese

VAN BUREN, MARTIN (1782–1862), eighth president of the United States. Born in Kinderhook in New York's Hudson Valley, Martin Van Buren attended the local school and took a traditional path into public life, clerking for a judge. While he worked as a lawyer, his true profession became politics. By his early thirties he had twice won election to the state senate.

Settling in Albany, Van Buren zestfully joined the factional battles that marked New York politics in the 1820s. Active in the so-called Albany Regency opposed to Governor DeWitt *Clinton, he won election to the U.S. Senate in 1821 and reelection in 1828. In the Senate he supported state-financed improvements and opposed the Bank of the United States, positions consistent with Andrew *Jackson's politics. In a rapid series of changes he resigned his Senate seat, was elected governor of New York (1828), but resigned in 1829 to become Jackson's secretary of state, a post he filled successfully. In 1831 Jackson appointed him ambassador to Great Britain, but the Senate failed to confirm him. He was elected vice president in 1832, replacing John C. *Calhoun, who had resigned amid political and personal differences with Jackson. A master of the spoils system in New York, he urged the patronage system on Jackson as well. Winning the 1836 Democratic presidential nomination, he defeated the Whig William Henry *Harrison and three other Whig candidates.

As president, Van Buren sought to keep the *Democratic party's northern and southern wings united amid rising *antislavery agitation. He opposed ending *slavery in the District of Columbia and any federal interference with slavery in the territories. Despite the clamor of southerners, however, he opposed the annexation of Texas, fearing war with Mexico. His wife Hannah having died in 1819, his daughter-in-law Angelica Van Buren served as *White House hostess.

The severe depression of 1837 defined Van Buren's presidency. Rather than proposing public relief measures or increasing the money supply, Van Buren sought to protect government deposits from unstable and speculative state banks. His independent treasury bill proposed to create a central repository for federal funds and the government's financial transactions. Congress did not pass this bill until 1840, however, and repealed it in 1841.

Ridiculed as "Martin Van Ruin" and "Van, Van, a used-up man," Van Buren lost the 1840 election to Harrison and retired to New York. He reemerged in 1848, however, as the presidential candidate of the *Free Soil party, pledged to "free soil, free labor, free speech [an allusion to congressional efforts to block antislavery petititons], and free men." He came in a distant third behind the Whig Zachary *Taylor and the Democrat Lewis Cass. Witty and charming, Van Buren also had a reputation for political manipulation captured in his nickname, "the Sly Fox." He understood the importance of organized *political parties and pursued politics as a career, not simply an avocation.

[*See also* Antebellum Era; Bank of the United States, First and Second; Civil Service Reform; Depressions, Economic; Federal Government, Executive Branch: The Presidency; Fillmore, Millard; Texas Republic and Annexation.]

• Robert Remini, *Martin Van Buren and the Making of the Democratic Party,* 1959. Richard P. McCormick, *The Second American Party System,* 1966. Donald B. Cole, *Martin Van Buren and the American Political System,* 1984.

—Jean Harvey Baker

VANDERBILT, CORNELIUS (1794–1877), shipping and railroad tycoon, financier. Born on Staten Island, New York, to poor Dutch parents, Cornelius Vanderbilt in 1810 borrowed a small sum from his family to begin a ferry service to Manhattan. He soon expanded into maritime trade, with shipping interests that included a steamship line that dominated East Coast shipping, and service to *San Francisco with an overland segment through Nicaragua.

After the *Civil War, Vanderbilt moved into *railroads, acquiring the Hudson River line. Through further acquisitions, including the New York Central line, he created a system that extended past Buffalo to the Great Lakes. His reputation suffered, however, because he often bribed legislatures to insure their compliance. During the depression of 1873, he built Grand Central Station in *New York City to provide a terminus for his railroads. His legend grew when he became embroiled in the bitter "Erie wars" with his former protégées Jay Gould and James Fisk for control of the Erie Railroad.

An avid *stock market speculator, Vanderbilt often used the market to break his competitors financially. His fortune of over $100 million, left primarily to his son William, made him the wealthiest American of his day. Despite his reputation as a "robber baron," Vanderbilt played a major role in consolidating steamship and rail transportation into systems that extended nationally and internationally.

[*See also* Depressions, Economic; Gilded Age; Industrialization; Maritime Transport.]

• Wheaton J. Lane, *Commodore Vanderbilt: An Epic of the Steam Age,* 1942. Edwin P. Hoyt, *Commodore Vanderbilt,* 1962.

—Charles Geisst

VAUDEVILLE, the most popular form of American theatrical entertainment between 1900 and 1920. Typically a series of variety acts ranging from trained animals, sports heroes, and exotic dancers to magicians, blackface comics, and shortened versions of full dramas, vaudeville played before elite and poor spectators, at sumptuous and austere theaters, in small towns and major cities. Its entertainments helped "Americanize" immigrant populations, instructed rural folks in city ways, and taught middle-class consumers the latest fashions in clothes, humor, and songs. A significant commercial force in the modernization of American culture, vaudeville also perpetuated and intensified racist practices and beliefs.

Despite its modernizing influence, vaudeville began in an attempt to capture a middle-class Victorian audience for variety theater in the 1870s and '80s. For respectable Victorians after 1870, variety shows—typically presented in "concert saloons" and featuring dancing girls for working-class spectators—were taboo. To attract female shoppers and office workers, the variety impresario and songwriter Tony Pastor offered family entertainment and banned alcohol and tobacco from his New York theater in the 1880s. The businessmen B. F. Keith and Edward F. Albee improved on Pastor's formula by running their shows continuously from midmorning until midnight. By 1900, these two moguls had monopolized vaudeville in the East through their theater ownership (more than four hundred by 1920) and booking practices. In the *West, the Orpheum circuit cooperated with the Keith-Albee monopoly to control "Big Time" vaudeville nationally. Similar booking circuits dominated "Small Time" vaudeville, which played at lower prices in hundreds of theaters to mostly working-class spectators.

But while Keith and Albee advertised the moral purity of their shows, they and other vaudeville promoters appealed to their spectators' desire for sensual and irreverent entertainment that undercut Victorian sentimentality and respectability. The vaudeville stage featured *ragtime, slapstick comedy, suggestive dancing, and comic and acrobatic routines that challenged conventional gender roles. It also manufactured ethnic stereotypes—"the Mick" (Irish), "the Dutch" (German), and "the Heb" (Jewish) among them—that softened as these immigrant groups gained in social status and economic success. By 1920, Big Time Vaudeville had boosted hundreds of formerly working-class performers, including Eva Tanguay, W. C. Fields, Sophie Tucker, Eddie Cantor, and Will *Rogers, to wealth and stardom. Like the minstrel show before it, however, vaudeville constructed "whiteness" so as to degrade *African Americans. Blacks were segregated in the worst seats (if admitted at all) and denigrated on stage as knife-wielding or watermelon-eating "coons." The African American comic Bert Williams, who had to "black up" to portray a convincing Negro for white audiences, recognized that his comic effects depended on his character's humiliation.

In competition with musical comedy, burlesque houses, nightclubs, and especially the movies, vaudeville declined in the 1920s. By mid-decade, nearly all vaudeville theaters were "combination" houses, interspersing films with live entertainment. The 1932 closing of The Palace, the New York hub of the Keith-Albee empire, marked the symbolic end of American vaudeville. As many big time performers shifted to *film and *radio in the 1930s, small time vaudeville struggled on through the decade before it, too, faded away.

[*See also* Gilded Age; Immigration; Leisure; Minstrelsy; Music: Popular Music; Musical Theater; Popular Culture; Progressive Era; Race and Ethnicity; Racism; Twenties, The; Urbanization; Working-Class Life and Culture.]

• Charles W. Stein, ed., *American Vaudeville as Seen by Its Contemporaries,* 1984. Robert W. Snyder, *The Voice of the City: Vaudeville and Popular Culture in New York,* 1989.

—Bruce McConachie

VEBLEN, THORSTEIN (1857–1929), sociologist, economist, social critic. Raised by frugal Norwegian parents on the Wisconsin frontier, Thorstein Veblen graduated from Carleton College in Minnesota and studied *philosophy at Johns Hopkins and Yale universities (with the sociologist and champion of *social Darwinism William Graham Sumner). Although educated and socialized to middle-class norms, Veblen remained a perpetual outsider. He dressed eccentrically, spoke with a difficult accent, and wrote about American customs in the manner of an anthropologist researching an alien culture. Witty and erudite yet often aloof from colleagues and students, he had a well-deserved reputation as a womanizer that contributed to his dismissal from academic posts at Chicago, Stanford, Harvard, and Missouri. Veblen died alone in a mountain cabin above Palo Alto, California.

Veblen's most significant contribution to American social thought lay in redefining *economics as the study of cultural meanings imputed to material goods. Classical economics, which he rejected, reduced human behavior to an idealized model of rational economic calculation in which the inexorable laws of commerce and Adam Smith's "invisible hand" combined to assure social progress. For Veblen, the prototypical rational man of classical economics did not exist. In *The *Theory of the Leisure Class* (1899), he traced the corruption of the instinct for "workmanship" in a commercial society. *Work, originally a source of pride, became irksome by its association with lower status. To flaunt its privileged avoidance of labor, the "leisure class" developed an elaborate hierarchy of "wastemanship" involving the ostentatious display of surplus wealth and the virtual ownership of women. Through patterns of intermarriage and emulation, "conspicuous consumption" saturated morality, aesthetics, *religion, and education, thus fortifying a "pecuniary" social order.

Although primarily a critique of the subtle exercise of power, Veblen's book gained popularity as a biting satire of upper-class pretensions. Turning to the political implications of his theory, Veblen in *The *Theory of Business Enterprise* (1904), *The Instinct of Workmanship* (1914), and *Engineers and the Price System* (1921) issued dire warnings and tentative solutions. As the profit motive eroded the instinct for industry, he argued, a conservative regime of business managers was increasingly corrupting the democratic process. Expanding the Darwinian theme of his first book—in which workers forced to adapt to the changing economic environment were the fittest to survive and progress—Veblen saw hope in an alliance of workers and engineers dedicated to the rational and systematic solution of social problems. A reluctant reformer at best, Veblen moved to *Washington, D.C., in 1917 to support the war effort and then to *New York City, where radical postwar intellectuals enlisted him in the revolt against the Victorian establishment.

Subsequent scholars who braved Veblen's turgid prose found him a compelling yet puzzling thinker. Some wondered if his legendary sense of irony hinted at radical thoughts he dared not express directly. But Veblen resisted easy categorization: He was critical of mass culture but too irreverent to be a conservative; hostile to big *business but too pessimistic to be a liberal; insightful about capitalist hegemony but too skeptical to be a Marxist. Feminists applauded his insights into patriarchy and his support of woman suffrage, but questioned his personal behavior. In the 1930s, New Dealers posthumously adopted him as a theoretician of government intervention. Critics continue to debate his historical significance, admiring his prophetic attention to *consumer culture but finding his biological determinism problematic.

[*See also* Engineering; Gilded Age; Progressive Era; Social Class; Social Science; Sociology; Twenties, The.]

• Joseph Dorfman, *Thorstein Veblen and His America, With New Appendices,* 1966. John P. Diggins, *The Bard of Savagery,* 1978. Rick Tilman, *Thorstein Veblen and His Critics,* 1992.

—Andrew Chamberlin Rieser

VENEREAL DISEASE. Although gonorrhea, syphilis, and other sexually transmitted diseases existed in colonial America, considerable confusion surrounded the distinctions among them, their causes, and their effects. Sexual activity itself was often blamed for symptoms now recognized as third-stage syphilis. The Revolutionary Era physician Benjamin *Rush popularized such causal explanations, focusing especially on masturbation. The linking of masturbation and venereal disease continued through the nineteenth century. Medical knowledge about these diseases gradually increased, however. In *A Practical Treatise on Venereal Diseases* (1842), the American-born French researcher Philippe Ricord identified syphilis's three stages and the tertiary stage's devastating effects.

Increasingly, researchers focused on prostitution as a means of transmission. In *History of Prostitution: Its Extent, Causes, and Effects throughout the World* (1858), the *New York City physician William W. Sanger estimated that at least 40 percent of the prostitutes he interviewed in New York's Indigent and Convict Hospital in the mid-1850s had syphilis or gonorrhea. At New York Hospital, the city's preeminent nineteenth-century medical institution, syphilis and gonorrhea were the most often treated diseases. This connection gave rise in the late nineteenth and early twentieth centuries to a concentrated attack on prostitution, or "the social evil." The influential *American Medical Association actively supported this campaign. The New York City dermatologist Prince A. Morrow (1846–1914), a prominent figure in the venereal-disease field in the later part of his life, worked to dispel the silence surrounding these diseases and their spread. Only the elimination of prostitution, not just its regulation, Morrow insisted, would suffice. Because of the reformers' emphasis on sexual self-control, the U.S. Army during *World War I resisted issuing prophylactics to the troops, a decision that resulted in such rapid spread of venereal disease among U.S. soldiers in France that American military officers at the front were forced to ignore the government's policy.

Despite the public-education efforts of Morrow and others, venereal disease remained a generally taboo subject until the later 1930s, when the U.S. surgeon general, Thomas Parran, mounted a campaign to increase awareness of how these infections spread and how they could be prevented. The result was a dramatic decrease in venereal disease in the United States, even during *World War II, when the government required that all cases be reported and assigned investigative teams to trace the source. The postwar development of penicillin, tetracycline, and other antibiotics provided powerful new weapons against venereal diseases, although some strains proved resistant. Nevertheless, infection rates began to rise in the 1950s, especially among teenagers and young people, with changing patterns of sexual behavior. The public paid little attention until the early 1980s, however, when the advent of *acquired immunodeficiency syndrome (AIDS) reinvigorated the campaign to eradicate these ancient scourges, now renamed sexually transmitted diseases.

[*See also* Disease; Medicine; Prostitution and Antiprostitution; Public Health; Sexual Morality and Sex Reform.]

• Alan M. Brandt, *No Magic Bullet; A Social History of Venereal Disease in the United States Since 1880,* 1985.

—Vern L. Bullough

VERSAILLES, TREATY OF (1919). The Treaty of Versailles ended *World War I between Germany and the Allied powers. On 6 October 1918, Chancellor Max von Baden appealed to President Woodrow *Wilson to facilitate an armistice based on Wilson's *Fourteen Points. The Allies had never endorsed this progressive set of war aims, but they now acceded to most of it because, in the armistice negotiations with Wilson, Germany had agreed to the confiscation or internment of virtually all of its machines of war.

At the 1919 Paris peace conference, the president's highest priority was the inclusion of the Covenant of the *League of Nations. Despite grave reservations, the other Allied leaders—David Lloyd George of Great Britain, Georges Clemenceau of France, and Vittorio Orlando of Italy—bowed to the massive public support that Wilson's proposal enjoyed throughout Europe. But the peacemakers used their acceptance as a lever to gain concessions on other issues. For example, Australia, New Zealand, and South Africa coveted the captured colonies of (respectively) New Guinea, Samoa, and German Southwest Africa, which they occupied. Wilson favored making these territories League "mandates" (the League's arrangement for assisting ex-colonial areas to self-government). In the end, the territories were designated as mandates, but their administration was assigned to the occupying countries, an arrangement that critics charged perpetuated colonialism.

Clemenceau, implying that he might withdraw his endorsement of the League, demanded for France the coal-rich Saar basin and military occupation of the Rhineland. Orlando claimed for Italy the Yugoslav port city of Fiume and stormed out of the conference when Wilson refused to indulge him. Japan, too, threatened to bolt as it insisted on retaining exploitative economic control over Shantung. Wilson succeeded in moderating some of these demands, but often in ways that opened him to criticism for compromising too much. From Japan he wrung a pledge (honored in 1922) to restore Chinese sovereignty in Shantung through mediation by the League. On the Rhineland issue, Wilson and Clemenceau settled on a fifteen-year occupation. The crisis over Fiume was never resolved.

The acrimony deepened when Lloyd George added military pensions to the already astronomical reparations bill that France had presented against Germany. On the verge of physical collapse, Wilson eventually capitulated. Then came Article 231—a declaration saddling Germany with moral responsibility for the war. The reparations section and the "war-guilt" clause would spark unending controversy, eventually helping to ignite a resentful nationalism in Germany. Throughout, Wilson hoped that, once wartime passions had cooled, the League would redress the injustices.

Ironically, the peace that Wilson worked so hard to shape was never ratified by the U.S. Senate. Some opponents charged that it did not keep faith with the spirit of the Fourteen Points; many others opposed the Leagues of Nations provision. Wilson, in his own day and in history, would bear the main burden for the shortcomings of the treaty and for the failure to steer some acceptable version through the Senate. Yet many subsequent scholars contend that the territorial provisions were not as bad as disillusioned contemporaries and later revisionist historians of the interwar period contended, and that, without the president's exertions, the document would have been far more severe than it was. Nevertheless, it remains the most controversial peace treaty of the twentieth century.

[*See also* Foreign Relations: U.S. Relations with Europe; World War II: Causes.]

• Thomas A. Bailey, *Woodrow Wilson and the Lost Peace*, 1944. Arno J. Mayer, *Politics and Diplomacy of Peacemaking: Containment and Counterrevolution at Versailles, 1918–1919*, 1967. Arthur Walworth, *Wilson and His Peacemakers*, 1986.

—Thomas J. Knock

VETERANS ADMINISTRATION. Congress established the cabinet-status Department of Veteran Affairs (VA) in 1989 as a successor to the Veterans Administration. The VA represents the most recent in a long series of government agencies concerned with veterans, a legacy from the *Colonial Era. The type and extent of veteran benefits and their administration also have changed over time.

Initially, Congress and then the War Department administered pensions to disabled veterans and their dependents. In 1849 Congress transferred pension jurisdiction to the newly formed Department of the Interior. After the *Civil War, Congress established the National Home for Disabled Volunteer Soldiers, actually a number of facilities in various states, to provide care to indigent and disabled veterans. Following *World War I, Congress formed the U.S. Veterans Bureau (VB) to consolidate several federal agencies that administered veteran benefits. In 1930 Congress merged the VB, the National Homes, and the Bureau of Pensions into the Veterans Administration. Frank T. Hines, director of the VB since 1923, continued as VA director until 1945.

*World War II vastly increased the VA's duties, including administration of the home-loan guarantees and programs for education and training established by the *Servicemen's Readjustment Act (the so-called G.I. Bill of Rights). Subsequent legislation extended these responsibilities still further. In 1973 the army transferred to the VA oversight of the national military cemetery system, except for *Arlington National Cemetery. By 2000, the VA, serving almost 25 million veterans and millions more dependents of veterans, employed approximately 220,000 persons, managed the nation's fourth largest insurance program, and operated the country's largest medical system, including 173 hospitals.

[*See also* American Legion; Federal Government, Executive Branch: Other Departments; Military, The; Welfare, Federal.]

• Keith W. Olson, "Veterans Administration," in *Government Agencies*, ed. Donald R. Whitnah, 1983, pp. 598–602.

—Keith W. Olson

VETERINARY MEDICINE. This branch of *medicine, which derives its name from the Latin root for "beast of burden," has existed in some form in North America for eons. Folk care of sick animals antedated the arrival of Europeans and continued to flourish even after the veterinary profession began to develop. Unlike physicians, who primarily emphasize their patients' needs, veterinarians have based their practice almost exclusively on the value of animals to human society and culture—whether economic, scientific, nutritional, or sentimental.

The idea of an American veterinary profession won early support from agricultural societies, such as the Philadelphia and Massachusetts Societies for Promoting Agriculture, and from physicians, such as Benjamin *Rush and Andrew Stone. Before the 1880s most school-trained veterinarians, and most of the profession's leaders, had been trained in Europe. The development of veterinary schools in the United States arose from a general interest in scientific *agriculture (signaled by the *Morrill Land Grant Act of 1862) and concern over animal-*disease epidemics following the *Civil War. Taking advantage of federal funding under the Morrill Act, Iowa State College (now University) established the first college-affiliated veterinary school in 1879.

By the late nineteenth century, a web of institutions, organizations, and periodicals united veterinarians. Among the most important were the U.S. Veterinary Medical Association (founded in 1863 and renamed the American Veterinary Medical Association in 1898); the Bureau of Animal Industry, or BAI (created in 1884 in the U.S. Department of Agriculture and headed until 1905 by veterinarian Daniel E. Salmon); and the *American Veterinary Review* (begun in 1877 and renamed the *Journal of the American Veterinary Medical Association* in 1914–1915). BAI veterinarians Fred L. Kilbourne and Cooper Curtice and physician Theobald Smith first demonstrated the role of vectors (such as insects) in the transmission of animal diseases. The BAI also certified and employed veterinarians in food inspection and influenced veterinary school curricula. The late nineteenth-century *professionalization of veterinary medicine stemmed from veterinarians' ability to control animal epidemics and from the expertise that came with their adoption of bacteriology and the germ theory of disease developed by Louis Pasteur and Robert Koch—expertise that most lay "animal doctors" lacked. Between the 1880s and 1925, graduate veterinarians sponsored state laws creating examining boards and setting graduation and licensing requirements, thus excluding most laypersons from practicing veterinary medicine.

By the early 1900s veterinary practice included large numbers of pets, which drew the profession into debates with animal-protection organizations such as the American Humane Association. During *World War I, veterinarians won commissions to manage the large population of horses used by the military, and to inspect military food rations. In late nineteenth and early twentieth centuries, Leonard Pearson, a bovine tuberculosis expert, directed veterinarians' attention to the relationship between animal and human health. The profession also became more diversified. Although *African Americans had been admitted to veterinary schools in small numbers since the 1890s, the first veterinary school devoted primarily to educating African Americans, at the Tuskegee Institute in Alabama, did not open until 1945. In 1903 the McKillip Veterinary College in Chicago graduated the first woman veterinarian. The early twentieth century also brought several challenges, including protests against exclusionary veterinary-practice laws, the replacement of the horse (veterinarians' most valuable patient) by the internal combustion engine, and the interwar agricultural depression.

The availability of antibacterial drugs and other new scientific tools after *World War II radically changed veterinary practice. Pet practice increased exponentially, and new methods of raising livestock in confinement, called "factory farming," proliferated. Veterinarians worked increasingly with zoo and exotic animals, poultry, fish, and wildlife, as well as on a nationwide hog-cholera eradication campaign.

As the twentieth century ended, veterinary medicine was shaped by such developments as the unrestrained admission of women into veterinary schools; growing specialization that reflected new technologies and clients' increasing willingness to pay for expensive treatments; ethical discussions of the human-animal bond, factory farming, and animal pain, stimulated by the animal-welfare and animal-rights movements; and new *public-health concerns, including possible links between antibiotic residues in milk and meats and resistant bacterial superinfections in human consumers. Meanwhile, new tools (such as the genetic manipulation of animals) and new discoveries (including diseases such as bovine spongiform encephalopathy [BSE], or mad-cow disease) continued to transform veterinarians' role as medical experts.

[*See also* Agricultural Education and Extension; Agricultural Experiment Stations; Education: The Rise of the University.]

• Bert W. Bierer, *American Veterinary History,* 1940. Bert W. Bierer, *A Short History of Veterinary Medicine in America,* 1955. J. F. Smithcors, *The American Veterinary Profession,* 1963. J. F. Smithcors, *The Veterinarian in America, 1625–1975,* 1975. O. H. V. Stalheim, *The Winning of Animal Health,* 1994. Susan D. Jones, "Animal Value, Veterinary Medicine, and the Domestic Animal Economy in the United States, 1890–1930," Ph.D. diss., University of Pennsylvania, 1997.

—Susan D. Jones

VETO POWER. Derived from the Latin term meaning "I forbid," the veto traces back to the Roman Republic of the sixth century B.C. British monarchs long exercised an absolute veto over acts of Parliament, but waning monarchical authority eroded this power. The last royal veto over a parliamentary act occurred in 1707. The Crown continued to veto colonial legislation in America, however, and the first two complaints lodged against George III in the *Declaration of Independence were his arbitrary vetoes of American laws.

Experimentation with allowing vetoes by governors in South Carolina (1776) and New York (1777) opened the door to a presidential veto, provided for in Article I, section 7 of the *Constitution. This qualified power, reversible by a two-thirds vote in both houses of Congress, significantly enhanced presidents' roles in the legislative process. The pocket veto, not subject to override, is used when congressional adjournment prevents a bill's return.

The years down to 1865 saw only fifty-nine presidential vetoes, but they exploded thereafter, owing to escalating executive involvement in legislative matters, as well as presidential opposition to runaway *Civil War pensions and other private-benefits legislation. President Grover *Cleveland was especially prolific in vetoing private pension bills.

The veto remained a highly effective power in the late twentieth century, with only about 7 percent of all vetoes successfully overridden by Congress. Modern presidents who relied too heavily on a veto strategy, however, such as Gerald *Ford and George *Bush, suffered politically for what was seen as an overly negative and reactive approach in dealing with Congress.

[*See also* Federal Government, Executive Branch: The Presidency.]

• Robert J. Spitzer, *The Presidential Veto: Touchstone of the American Presidency,* 1988. Richard A. Watson, *Presidential Vetoes and Public Policy,* 1993.

—Robert J. Spitzer

VICKSBURG, SIEGE OF (1863). The fall of *New Orleans to Union forces during the *Civil War in April 1862 made the bluff city of Vicksburg, Mississippi, the key to control of the *Mississippi River. That summer, Union naval forces under Flag Officer David *Farragut failed to reduce the bastion. Union army efforts to dig a bypass canal also proved unsuccessful. In December, a two-pronged Union advance failed when Confederate cavalry destroyed Major General Ulysses S. *Grant's supply base at Holly Springs and members of Vicksburg's garrison under Major General John C. Pemberton repulsed Major General William T. *Sherman's assault at Chickasaw Bayou. On 1 May 1863, after several unsuccessful efforts, Grant finally managed to position most of his army southeast of Vicksburg. Union Colonel Benjamin H. Grierson's cavalry raid, together with conflicting orders from Confederate General Joseph E. Johnston and Confederate President Jefferson *Davis, disconcerted Pemberton. His failure to lead his forces out of Vicksburg and join Johnston enabled Grant to defeat Confederate forces in a series of encounters at Port Gibson, Grand Gulf, Raymond, Jackson, Champion Hill, and, on 17 May, Big Black River. Grant assaulted Vicksburg's main defenses on 19 and 22 May. Bloodily repulsed both times, Grant then resorted to a siege that brought terrible suffering to the people of Vicksburg. On 4 July 1863, Grant accepted Pemberton's surrender of 2,166 officers, 27,230 enlisted men, 172 cannons, and 60,000 rifles. Grant's tenacity, substantial Union reinforcements, and Johnston's negligible efforts to relieve the garrison ensured Vicksburg's capitulation. This victory marked the beginning of Grant's rise to overall command of the Union army and ultimately to his ascent to the presidency. For the Confederacy, it was a severe psychological blow. The surrender of Port Hudson on 9 July split the Confederacy and brought the entire Mississippi River under Union control. The citizens of Vicksburg long remembered the round-the-clock bombardment, the starvation, and their diet of rats. Not until 1945 did the town again celebrate the Fourth of July, because of the date's grim associations.

• Edwin C. Bearss, *The Vicksburg Campaign,* 3 vols., 1985–1986.

—Lawrence Lee Hewitt

VIETNAM VETERANS MEMORIAL. First proposed in 1979 by the *Vietnam War veteran Jan Scruggs, this memorial, despite initial controversy, emerged soon after its completion in 1982 as one of the most visited and culturally influential public monuments of the late twentieth century. In 1980, Congress authorized the Vietnam Veterans Memorial Fund, headed by Scruggs, to raise the necessary funds and oversee the construction on the Mall in *Washington, D.C., of a memorial that incorporated the name of every U.S. serviceperson killed during the war. The fund soon raised the ten million dollars needed for a monument but encountered opposition over its choice of design. Maya Lin, a Yale architectural student who won an open competition, proposed a memorial consisting of two stark black marble walls that touched at a 125-degree angle and sloped into the ground. Many political conservatives denounced the proposal as an antimonument and demanded a "traditional" statue and flagpole. James Watt, secretary of the interior in the Ronald *Reagan administration, initially refused to authorize construction of the memorial but eventually compromised, accepting Lin's monument after the fund agreed to

MAP 24: MILITARY MAP OF VICKSBURG, MISSISSIPPI (1863)

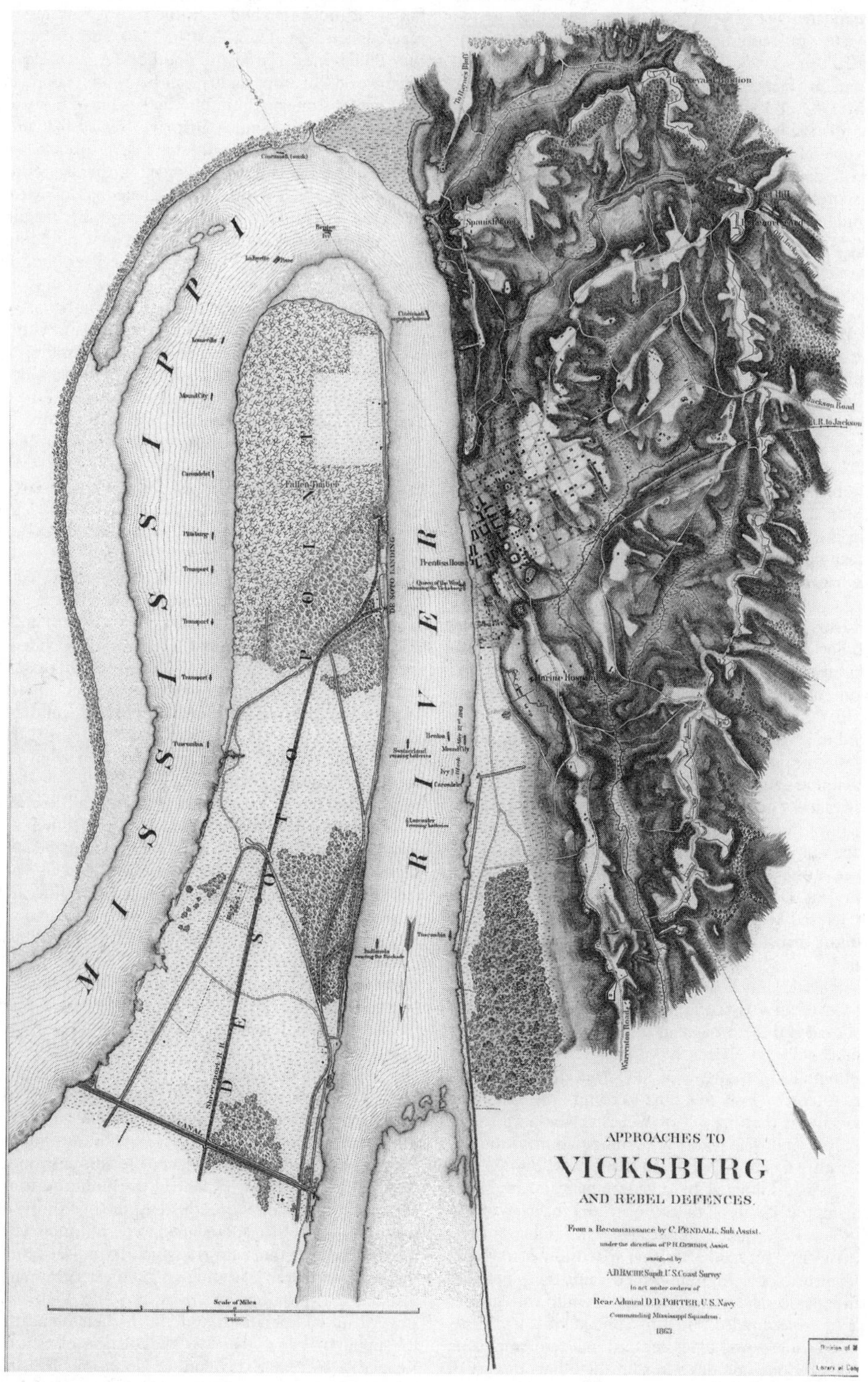

Vicksburg's surrender on 4 July 1863, gave the Union forces full control of the Mississippi. This 1863 U.S. Coast Survey map shows the siege of Vicksburg, a shipping center vital to the Confederacy. The map shows the position of some twenty Union vessels, many identified by name. De Soto Point and De Soto Landing, on the spit of land formed by the oxbow curve of the river, commemorate the Spanish explorer Hernando de Soto, probably the first European to see and cross the Mississippi.

[*See* Civil War: Military and Diplomatic Course; Coast and Geodetic Survey, U.S.; Soto, Hernando de; Grant, Ulysses S.; Mississippi River.]

add a flagpole and a statue. Frederick Hart's more traditional statue of three soldiers was unveiled in 1984. In 1989, responding to demands by female veterans and women's organizations, Congress mandated that a sculptural figure be added to the memorial site to commemorate the contribution of servicewomen.

Many Vietnam veterans attended ceremonies dedicating the memorial in 1982 and embraced the memorial as a site for emotional catharsis. In the 1980s and 1990s, many visitors left letters and objects mourning the dead named on the walls. Hailed as an aesthetic triumph, the Vietnam Veterans Memorial influenced scores of local and state war memorials erected in the 1980s and 1990s.

• Jan C. Scruggs and Joel L. Swerdlow, *To Heal a Nation: The Vietnam Veterans Memorial,* 1985. G. Kurt Piehler, *Remembering War the American Way,* 1995.

—G. Kurt Piehler

VIETNAM WAR. In its entirety, the Vietnam War lasted for nearly three decades (1946–1975), and its American phase, officially dated from 1964 to 1973, was longer and more divisive than any other war in which the United States has participated. Enormously costly and destructive, the war had a profound impact in very different ways on the nations that waged it.

Causes. The conflict originated from the interaction of two major phenomena of the post–*World War II Era: the dissolution of colonial empires and the *Cold War. The rise of nationalism in the colonial areas and the weakness of the war-torn European powers in 1945 combined to destroy a colonial system that had been an established feature of world politics for centuries.

In some areas this transformation occurred peacefully, but in French Indochina it provoked war. Since the late nineteenth century, Vietnam, Laos, and Cambodia had comprised the French colony of Indochina. After the fall of France to Germany in 1940, the Japanese had established a protectorate over Vietnam, and in a March 1945 coup d'état they assumed direct control. In the meantime, a veteran communist agitator and ardent Vietnamese nationalist named Ho Chi Minh capitalized on French weakness and the rising nationalism of his people to launch a revolution. Exploiting the vacuum left by the surrender of Japan in August 1945, Ho's Vietminh (League for the Independence of Vietnam) on 2 September 1945 declared Vietnam independent. Determined to retain their overseas empire, the French refused to relinquish their colony. In November 1946, after more than a year of futile negotiations, the two sides went to war.

As the Vietminh launched a bloody anticolonial war with France, the Cold War was taking form, and at least from 1949 on, Americans viewed the struggle in Indochina largely in terms of their conflict with the Soviet Union. They saw Ho Chi Minh and the Vietminh as instruments of the Soviet drive for world domination. After the "loss" of China to communism in 1949, they also concluded that the fall of Vietnam would endanger interests deemed vital. The Harry S. *Truman administration's *National Security Council Document #68 (1950) posited that the Soviet Union, "animated by a new fanatical faith," was "seeking to impose its absolute authority on the rest of the world." In the frantic milieu of the day, U.S. policy-makers concluded that any "substantial further extension of the area under the control of the Kremlin would raise the possibility that no coalition adequate to confront the Kremlin with greater strength could be assembled." In this context of a world divided into two hostile power blocs engaged in a zero-sum game in which a gain for one side was a loss for the other, areas such as Vietnam, previously of marginal importance, took on great significance. The Truman administration thus extended to East Asia a policy of *containment originally applied in Europe. The first commitment to Vietnam, designed to assist the French in putting down the Vietminh revolution, was part of a broader effort to contain communist expansion in Asia.

There were other reasons why Americans after 1950 attached growing significance to Vietnam. The first, usually called the domino theory, held that the fall of Vietnam could cause the fall of all Indochina and then the rest of Southeast Asia, with repercussions extending west to India and east to Japan and the *Philippines. The loss of Southeast Asia would deprive the "free world" of important naval bases and raw materials and threaten its strategic position. The lessons of history, in particular the so-called Munich analogy, stressed that the failure of the Western democracies to stand firm against German and Japanese aggression had encouraged further aggression, leading to World War II. The rancorous debate that followed the "loss" of China in 1949 and the *Republican party's exploitation of it at the polls led to the conclusion that no administration, especially a Democratic one, could survive politically the loss of Vietnam.

Operating on the basis of these assumptions, Washington gradually expanded the U.S. stake in Vietnam. Until 1950, the United States maintained a pro-French "neutrality" in the First Indochina War. After 1950, the United States supported France, eventually paying up to 80 percent of the cost of the war. When France was defeated in 1954 following the climatic battle of Dien Bien Phu and agreed to negotiations at Geneva, Switzerland, the United States first sought to keep the war going and then to limit Vietminh gains at the conference table. The Geneva Accords, to which the United States was not a party, called for the temporary division of Vietnam at the seventeenth parallel pending national elections.

Between 1954 and 1961, the First Indochina War gave way to the Second. In the aftermath of the Geneva Accords, the United States eased the French out of Vietnam and set out to build in the southern half of a temporarily divided nation an independent, noncommunist government that could stand as a bulwark against further communist gains in the region. Washington provided billions of dollars in military and economic aid and sent hundreds of advisers to assist the fledgling government of South Vietnam under Ngo Dinh Diem. With American support, Diem refused to conduct the national elections called for by the Geneva Accords and launched a campaign to eliminate those Vietminh who remained in the South. Frustrated by their failure to establish an independent, unified Vietnam, despite their victory over the French, southern Vietminh began a revolt against the Diem regime in 1957. The communist government of North Vietnam came to their aid with men and supplies in May 1959. The United States in turn increased its aid to South Vietnam.

Between 1961 and 1965, the insurgency against Diem grew into full-scale war. Exploiting growing discontent with the authoritarian Diem regime, the National Liberation Front of South Vietnam (NLF) combined political agitation, terrorism, and military operations to threaten the increasingly embattled Saigon government. North Vietnam expanded its support, sending thousands of soldiers and supplies down the Ho Chi Minh trail through Laos and Cambodia into South Vietnam. Frustrated with its ally in Saigon, the administration of President John F. *Kennedy expanded the number and role of U.S. advisers and in late 1963 authorized the overthrow of Diem by dissident army officers. Designed to permit more effective conduct of the war, the coup (in which Diem was murdered) had the opposite results, leading to political decay and rampant instability. Exploiting the chaos in South Vietnam, the NLF stepped up its operations and North Vietnam again expanded its support. Facing the possible collapse of South Vietnam, Kennedy's successor, Lyndon B. *Johnson, in February 1965 initiated the bombing of North Vietnam and in July 1965 committed U.S. combat troops to the war.

The open-ended *Gulf of Tonkin Resolution, passed by Congress by an 88–2 vote in the Senate and a unanimous vote in the House in August 1964 at the request of the Johnson administration after a supposed North Vietnamese attack on a

U.S. gunboat, authorized "all necessary measures to repel any armed attack against the armed forces of the United States and to prevent further aggression" and thus provided the sole legal foundation for the conflict; there was never a formal declaration of war. Among the war's chief architects were Secretary of State Dean Rusk; Secretary of Defense Robert McNamara; national security advisers McGeorge Bundy (1961–1966) and Walt W. Rostow (1966–1969); and the "Wise Men," an informal advisory group headed unofficially by Dean *Acheson that Johnson assembled periodically.

Course of the War, 1965–1972. After July 1965, the war escalated into a major international conflict. Thousands of North Vietnamese regulars supported NLF main-force units estimated at 80,000. American forces expanded incrementally from around 6,000 in June 1965 to more than 536,000 in 1968 and were supplemented by 800,000 South Vietnamese troops and 68,000 provided by other countries.

Each side's strategy sought to capitalize on its strengths. America possessed great national wealth, modern weaponry, and a highly professional military force under the command of General William C. Westmoreland (1914–). It sought through gradually expanded and tightly controlled bombing of North Vietnam and through "search and destroy" operations in South Vietnam to inflict sufficiently heavy losses to compel the North Vietnamese and NLF to stop trying to destroy the Saigon government. It did not seek to defeat North Vietnam militarily. Remembering the "lessons" of the *Korean War, it scrupulously avoided any step that might provoke war with the Soviet Union or China.

In contrast, the NLF and North Vietnam, under the overall direction of Defense Minister Vo Nguyen Giap, pursued a defensive strategy. Lightly armed and equipped, their forces relied on stealth and mobility. Recognizing that as long as they did not lose, they won, they avoided set-piece battles where America's superior firepower could be decisive. They sought to wear down the adversary through harassing actions and protracted conflict. They had the advantages of infinite patience, the strategic initiative, a seemingly inexhaustible reservoir of manpower, knowledge of the terrain, and support from the Soviet Union and China.

Between 1965 and 1967, the two sides fought to a bloody stalemate. The United States expanded the bombing of North Vietnam from 63,000 tons in 1965 to 226,000 in 1967, inflicting an estimated $600 million damage on a still primitive economy. But the North Vietnamese successfully dispersed and concealed their most vital resources, and aid from their allies helped make up the losses. As a result, the bombing did not decisively affect North Vietnam's will to resist or its capacity to move men and supplies into South Vietnam. The American ground strategy also failed to produce clear-cut results. When the U.S. Army or Marines actually engaged enemy forces in battle, they usually prevailed. But North Vietnam could replace its losses and to some extent control them by retreating into sanctuaries in Laos, Cambodia, and across the demilitarized zone dividing North and South Vietnam. The Americanization of the war proved counterproductive in terms of building a stable government in South Vietnam. The South Vietnamese army (ARVN), relegated to pacification duty, did not receive the training or experience to prepare it to assume the burden of the fighting. The firepower unleashed by the United States devastated much of the South Vietnamese countryside and made refugees of as many as one-third of the population. The infusion of hundreds of thousands of men and billions of dollars into a small, backward country had a profoundly destabilizing effect, and corruption flourished.

As the war dragged on, opposition in the United States increased dramatically. While "hawks" protested Johnson's policy of gradual escalation, urging full mobilization and a knockout blow against North Vietnam, a diverse and heterogeneous group of "doves" increasingly questioned the war's wisdom and morality. Antiwar activists conducted teach-ins on college campuses and organized mass protests in Washington and other major cities. They openly encouraged draft resistance and sponsored efforts to disrupt the war effort. In October 1967, some fifty-thousand opponents of the war marched on the Pentagon. Nonetheless, the war's mounting cost was probably more important than the antiwar movement in generating public uneasiness. Increased casualties, indications that more troops might be required, and Johnson's request for new taxes combined in late 1967 to produce growing signs of impatience. Polls indicated a sharp decline in support for the war and Johnson's handling of it. The press increasingly questioned America's goals and methods in Vietnam, and leading Democratic and Republican members of Congress abandoned the president. Doubts arose even within Johnson's inner circle. Defense Secretary McNamara, deeply disillusioned by the war, departed in February 1968. A major public-relations campaign by the administration in late 1967 reversed the trend only temporarily.

The North Vietnamese–NLF *Tet Offensive of 1968 initiated a new phase of the war. In late 1967, the North Vietnamese launched operations in remote areas, drawing U.S. forces away from the cities. On 31 January 1968, the NLF launched massive attacks on previously secure urban areas, striking thirty-six provincial capitals, five of South Vietnam's six major cities, and sixty-four district capitals. The NLF besieged the U.S. embassy in Saigon for a time and held the imperial city of Hue for several weeks. In a strictly military sense, the Tet Offensive failed. The United States and South Vietnam quickly recovered from the initial shock and inflicted huge casualties on exposed enemy forces. But the offensive had a profound psychological impact domestically. Coming in the wake of official year-end reports of progress, it further undermined the administration's credibility and raised even more urgent questions as to whether the mounting toll in Vietnam was worth the cost. In Washington, Tet forced basic changes in policy. Johnson rejected the military's request for 206,000 additional forces and for expansion of the war, thus terminating the policy of gradual escalation. He cut back the bombing of North Vietnam to the area below the twentieth parallel (and subsequently stopped it entirely); offered another plea for negotiations; and, most dramatically, withdrew from the 1968 presidential race. Bloodied from the battles of Tet and anxious for some relief from the bombing, North Vietnam agreed to negotiate, and peace talks opened in Paris in May 1968.

Neither side had entirely abandoned its goals, however, and when the peace talks failed to produce a settlement, Johnson's successor, the Republican Richard M. *Nixon, proclaimed a new policy called Vietnamization. Recognizing that public impatience required a scaled-down American involvement, Nixon initiated the phased withdrawal of U.S. combat troops. At the same time, he expanded assistance to the South Vietnamese government of Nguyen Van Thieu and enlarged training programs for its army in the expectation that it would take over the fighting.

To disrupt North Vietnam's offensive capabilities until Vietnamization could progress further, Nixon expanded the war into neutral Cambodia. In early 1969, he ordered the bombing of North Vietnamese base areas in Cambodia, keeping the decision secret from the press and indeed from much of his own government. Going public in the spring of 1970, he ordered U.S. and South Vietnamese troops to invade enemy sanctuaries in Cambodia. Significant stocks of weapons were captured, and the enemy's timetable for a new offensive may have been set back, but the Cambodian incursion also aroused a storm of protest at home. The domestic backlash assumed ominous and unprecedented proportions when National Guardsmen and police killed six students during protests at Kent State University in Ohio and Jackson State in Mississippi. Congress responded by setting a date for the removal of U.S. troops from Cambodia.

Domestic opposition to the war escalated in the Nixon years. After the Cambodian "incursion," Congress repealed the Tonkin Gulf resolution and debated proposals setting strict timetables for ending military operations. A huge demonstration in the spring of 1971 produced momentary chaos in Washington, D.C. The trial of Lieutenant William Calley, commander of a unit that carried out the 1968 murder of some 500 South Vietnamese civilians at *My Lai, raised in the starkest form the fundamental moral issues of the war. Publication of the so-called *Pentagon Papers by the *New York Times* and other newspapers in the summer of 1971 deepened public distrust in the government. By 1971, more than 70 percent of those polled thought the United States had erred in sending troops to Vietnam.

During 1972–1973, the American phase of the war ended. In the spring of 1972, North Vietnam launched a massive, conventional invasion of South Vietnam, hoping to exploit the obvious weaknesses of Vietnamization and, as in 1968, take advantage of the presidential election in the United States. To Hanoi's surprise, Nixon responded forcefully, resuming the bombing of North Vietnam, mining Haiphong harbor, and unleashing U.S. airpower against enemy forces in the South. Nixon's moves blunted a North Vietnamese drive that had penetrated deep into South Vietnam. The failure of the so-called Easter Offensive, along with a major American concession to permit North Vietnamese forces to remain in the South after a cease-fire, led to the negotiation in October 1972 of preliminary peace terms. South Vietnamese president Thieu rejected the agreement Nixon's national security adviser Henry *Kissinger had negotiated with Le Duc Tho, and when Nixon agreed to some of Thieu's reservations, the North Vietnamese issued new demands. Final agreement was reached only in January 1973, and only after American B-52s, in what became known as the Christmas Bombing, unleashed a final attack on North Vietnam, producing pressures on both sides to end the war.

Outcome and Significance. The agreement signed in Paris on 27 January 1973 fell short of the peace with honor that Nixon had promised. It permitted the extrication of U.S. military forces from Vietnam and provided for the return of American prisoners of war, but left unresolved the fundamental issues over which the conflict had been fought. North Vietnam was permitted to leave some 150,000 troops in the South, and the Provisional Revolutionary Government (PRG) that had been formed by the NLF was accorded a measure of political status. The future of South Vietnam was to be determined by political mechanisms that were never established and likely would not have worked.

Predictably, the issues were resolved by force. Negotiations between the two sides in Vietnam quickly broke down. The Thieu government and the PRG, each supported by its allies, launched land-grabbing operations to improve their positions. Nixon apparently hoped to enforce the peace agreement by keeping alive the threat of U.S. military intervention, but his ability to do so was increasingly limited. In 1973, a war-weary Congress, reflecting the mood of the nation, cut off funds for air operations in Indochina. A year later, Congress drastically reduced military and economic aid to South Vietnam. Nixon, increasingly paralyzed by the *Watergate investigations of abuses of power in the executive branch, resigned in August 1974.

Ever diminishing American support demoralized South Vietnam and encouraged North Vietnam to challenge a precarious status quo. In late 1974, the North Vietnamese seized Phuoc Long northeast of Saigon. Encouraged by this success and America's failure to respond, they struck the Central Highlands in March 1975. When Thieu ordered an ill-considered withdrawal, panic ensued. Much of the South Vietnamese army was captured or destroyed, and thousands of civilians perished in what became known as the "convoy of tears." Hanoi next struck Hue and Danang, duplicating its smashing success in the Highlands. Congress rejected President Gerald *Ford's request for $722 million in aid for South Vietnam, providing only $300 million in emergency aid to evacuate the remaining American personnel and some 150,000 South Vietnamese supporters. This was narrowly accomplished, concluding with panicky helicopter evacuations from the embassy roof, as Saigon fell on 1 May 1975.

The war's human and material costs were huge. South Vietnamese battle deaths exceeded 350,000, and estimates of North Vietnamese losses range between 500,000 and 1 million. Civilian deaths ran into the millions. The bombing destroyed much of North Vietnam's rudimentary industrial base and infrastructure. In the South, bombing and artillery fire destroyed an area roughly the size of Massachusetts and left an estimated 21 million craters. Unexploded bombs and mines remained a hazard to Vietnamese peasants for years. The use of defoliants such as Agent Orange and various herbicides scarred the landscape and caused untold human costs.

Although the United States emerged from the war physically unscathed, it, too, paid a heavy cost. The *Vietnam Veterans Memorial in *Washington, D.C., records the names of more than 58,000 American dead or missing. Some 300,00 U.S. troops were injured. The estimated economic cost, in excess of $167 billion, does not begin to measure the full impact. The war triggered inflation that at least temporarily undermined America's position in the world. Along with Watergate, it deepened popular suspicion of government, leaders, and institutions. It discredited the military, at least for a time, and estranged the United States from much of the rest of the world.

The war also destroyed the foreign-policy consensus that had existed since the late 1940s, leaving Americans confused and deeply divided on the goals to be pursued and the methods used. From the Angolan crisis of the mid-1970s through the *Persian Gulf War of 1991 and the Balkan and Somalian interventions of the 1990s, foreign policy issues were debated in the context of the Vietnam trauma.

Much like *World War I for the Europeans, Vietnam's greatest impact in the United States was in the realm of the spirit. As no other event in the nation's history, it challenged some of Americans' most basic beliefs about themselves, including the conviction of their generally benevolent relations with other peoples and the idea that nothing the nation sought to achieve was beyond reach. The war played a fundamental role in a larger crisis of the spirit that began in the 1970s, raising profound questions about America's history and its values. Its deep wounds festered for decades among some of its 2.7 million veterans.

By the turn of the century, the United States had recovered from the tangible effects of Vietnam, emerging in the *post–Cold War Era as the world's greatest economic and military power. The Vietnam War was the defining event for a generation of Americans, however, and its psychological effects seemed likely to persist, its scars remaining until the passing of the generation that fought the war and protested against it.

[*See also* Antiwar Movements; Democratic Party; Federal Government, Executive Branch: The Presidency; Federal Government, Executive Branch: Department of State; Federal Government, Executive Branch: Department of Defense; Foreign Relations; Kent State and Jackson State; Military, The; National Security Council; Sixties, The; Students for a Democratic Society.]

• Larry Berman, *Planning a Tragedy*, 1983. Bruce Palmer, *The Twenty-five Year War*, 1984. George McT. Kahin, *Intervention: How America Became Involved in Vietnam*, 1986. Gabriel Kolko, *Anatomy of a War*, 1986. Lloyd C. Gardner, *Approaching Vietnam: From World War II to Dienbienphu*, 1988. Mark Clodfelter, *The Limits of Air Power*, 1989. Eric Bergerud, *The Dynamics of Defeat: The Vietnam War in Hau Nghia Province*, 1991. David Levy, *The Debate over Vietnam*, 1991. Ronald Spector,

After Tet: The Bloodiest Year in Vietnam, 1993. Tom Wells, *The War Within: America's Battle over Vietnam,* 1994. Lloyd C. Gardner, *Pay Any Price: Lyndon Johnson and the Wars for Vietnam,* 1995. George C. Herring, *America's Longest War: The United States and Vietnam, 1950–1975,* 1996.

—George C. Herring

VIRGINIA DECLARATION OF RIGHTS (1776), the first written enumeration of the rights of citizens and the fundamental principles of government in the newly independent United States. In May 1776, the acting revolutionary government of Virginia officially dissolved the colony's former royal government and created a committee to draw up a declaration of rights and a constitution for the new state. The Virginia Declaration of Rights, passed on 12 June 1776, profoundly influenced other state declarations of rights and the federal *Bill of Rights.

Drafted by George Mason (1725–1792), a wealthy planter and political leader, the declaration set forth principles such as popular sovereignty, the separation of powers, freedom of the press, freedom of religion, trial by jury, and security from unreasonable searches and unjust punishments. Most importantly, the declaration grounded these rights not in the traditional liberties of British citizens or in the common law, but in a conception of natural law and social contract. The first article stated "that all men are by nature equally free and independent, and have certain inherent rights, of which, when they enter into a state of society, they cannot, by any compact, deprive or divest their posterity," including life, liberty, property, the pursuit of happiness, and safety.

While this language echoed that of John Locke and prefigured that of Thomas *Jefferson's *Declaration of Independence, it was also designed to meet the exigencies of eighteenth-century Virginia. The convention added the phrase "when they enter into a state of society" to insure that the promises of *equality and right contained in the declaration did not apply to slaves, who were not considered party to a social contract reserved for politically enfranchised male citizens. Thus, in addition to establishing the supremacy of natural law and popular sovereignty in American political thought, the Virginia Declaration of Rights also foreshadowed the compromises on *slavery embodied in the Declaration of Independence and the federal *Constitution.

[*See also* Republicanism; Revolution and Constitution, Era of.]

• Warren Billings, " 'That All Men Are Born Equally Free and Independent': Virginians and the Origins of the Bill of Rights," in *The Bill of Rights and the States: The Colonial and Revolutionary Origins of American Liberties,* eds. Patrick T. Conley and John P. Kaminski, 1992, pp. 335–69. Jack N. Rakove, *Declaring Rights: A Brief History with Documents,* 1998.

—Randolph Scully

VIROLOGY. *See* Biological Sciences.

VOICE OF AMERICA (VOA), the official broadcasting service of the United States, provides news and information in fifty-two languages to approximately 92 million people worldwide. Each week, VOA airs more than nine hundred hours of programming. Its chief aims are to serve as a reliable and objective news source; to represent all aspects of American society; and to present the policies of the United States.

On 24 February 1942, the Foreign Information Service began shortwave broadcasts as "Voices of America," soon changed to "Voice of America." Throughout *World War II, conservatives accused VOA of liberal bias and severely cut its budget. But the *Cold War rescued it from oblivion. In 1947, VOA began transmitting anticommunist propaganda, news, and cultural shows to international audiences. In 1953, VOA survived a demoralizing investigation by Senator Joseph *McCarthy. Shortly thereafter, it was incorporated into the *United States Information Agency (USIA).

From its inception, VOA supported democratic ideals and informed millions about American culture and policies. The results were mixed. Although Willis Conover's "Music USA" popularized *jazz abroad, VOA's coverage of such topic as the *Vietnam War and *Watergate drew criticism. In 1985, Congress established "Radio Martí," operating under the standards of the VOA charter, to broadcast to Cuba. VOA was beset by budgetary problems, political interference, and foreign censorship from the first, and the end of the Cold War did not diminish these difficulties. The International Broadcasting Act of 1994 placed VOA under the control of a board of governors. Despite problems and constraints, however, VOA remained the official voice of the U.S. government to the world as the twentieth century ended.

[*See also* Foreign Relations: The Cultural Dimension; Propaganda.]

• Laurien Alexandre, *The Voice of America: From Détente to the Reagan Doctrine,* 1988. Holly Cowan Schulman, *The Voice of America: Propaganda and Democracy, 1941–1945,* 1990.

—Laura A. Belmonte

VOLUNTARISM. This concept is identified with the early *American Federation of Labor (AFL), when Samuel *Gompers dominated the organization. First used by Gompers to summarize his view of the AFL's goals, voluntarism stressed the importance of freely chosen and noncompulsory relationships within the union movement. Subsequently, historians adopted the term to describe the AFL's early emphasis on the trade union as central to workers' lives, its focus on economic objectives, and its rejection of most forms of government intervention.

The trade unionists who created the AFL in 1886 wanted the resources and strength of a federation, but they refused to sacrifice the power or autonomy of their individual unions. Thus the federation emerged structurally as a fairly weak and decentralized organization. Gompers celebrated this decentralization and from this emerged his emphasis on the "voluntary coming together of unions with common needs and common aims."

Gompers's emphasis on voluntary cooperation was linked to his political attitudes. Workers, he believed, should rely primarily on their union and its economic activities for assistance and resources, rejecting the government intervention and partisan alliances that would limit their independence. While espousing these notions ideologically, Gompers and other AFL leaders in practice largely ignored them. In the early twentieth century, the federation entered wholeheartedly into politics, including lobbying campaigns and electoral mobilization. By 1908 this strategy had resulted in a de facto alliance with the *Democratic party. The AFL worked closely with the Woodrow *Wilson administration to pursue its legislative agenda. During *World War I, AFL leaders even accepted government intervention into *industrial relations. Meanwhile, local trade unionists also ignored the voluntarist principle, working during the *Progressive Era for legislation benefiting workers and forming partisan alliances toward that end. Despite this gap between ideology and political reality, voluntarism remained central to the AFL perspective, and historians have continued to rely upon the concept in interpreting the federation's history.

[*See also* Labor Movements.]

• Michael Rogin, "Voluntarism: The Political Functions of an Antipolitical Doctrine," *Industrial and Labor Relations Review* 15, no. 4 (July 1962): 521–35. Julie Greene, *Pure and Simple Politics: The American Federation of Labor and Political Activism, 1881 to 1917,* 1998.

—Julie Greene

VON NEUMANN, JOHN (1903–1957), *computer pioneer, mathematician, government consultant. Born in Budapest,

John von Neumann received his doctorate in mathematics with minors in experimental physics and chemistry from the University of Budapest in 1926. He came to Princeton University as a visiting lecturer in 1930 and three years later became professor of mathematics at the Institute for Advanced Study in Princeton. His *Theory of Games and Economic Behavior* (with Oskar Morgenstern) appeared in 1944 and the English translation of a work published earlier in Europe, *Mathematical Foundations of Quantum Mechanics*, in 1955. Active in government service, he worked at Los Alamos on the *Manhattan Project (1943–1945); consulted with the army's Ballistic Research Laboratory at Aberdeen, Maryland; and served on the *Atomic Energy Commission (1954–1957).

Von Neumann also participated in numerous discussions with the staff of the Electronic Numeric Integrator and Computer (ENIAC) project at the University of Pennsylvania, and in 1945 drafted a report on this project defining the key elements of a digital computer and introducing the "stored-program" concept used by ENIAC's successor, the Electronic Discrete Variable Computer (EDVAC). Although not intended for distribution, this document circulated widely, touching off an early controversy in the fledgling computer-science field, since it bore only von Neumann's name. A computer von Neumann built at the Institute for Advanced Study, called the Mathematical Analyzer, Numerical Integrator, and Computer (MANIAC), served as a prototype for many early computers and supplied computations crucial to the development of the hydrogen bomb. A brilliant theoretician, he also wrote two posthumously published works, *The Computer and the Brain* (1958) and, with Arthur Burks, *Theory of Self-Reproducing Automata* (1966).

[*See also* Mathematics and Statistics; Nuclear Weapons; Physical Science; Science: From 1914 to 1945; Science: Since 1945.]

• A. H. Taub, ed., *John von Neumann: Collected Works*, 6 vols., 1960–1963. William Aspray, *John von Neumann and the Origins of Modern Computing*, 1990.

—Thomas J. Bergin

W

WAGNER, ROBERT F. (1877–1953), U.S. senator. Born in Germany, Wagner immigrated with his family to *New York City at the age of nine. After graduating from the City College of New York (1898) and New York Law School (1900), Wagner practiced law and entered ward-level politics, where he attracted the attention of the Tammany Hall leadership of the *Democratic party. Elected to the state assembly in 1904 and the state senate in 1908, he became that body's youngest president pro tempore in 1911. There he teamed with his assembly counterpart Alfred E. *Smith to enact an impressive body of labor and welfare legislation, including fifty-six factory safety laws passed after the tragic *Triangle Shirtwaist Company fire in 1911. Widowed with a young son (the future New York mayor Robert F. Wagner Jr.), in 1919, he was appointed to the state supreme court, where he championed consumers, labor unions, and government economic legislation.

Elected to the U.S. Senate in 1926, Wagner compiled an unparalleled body of social legislation before his resignation owing to ill health in 1949. Known as the "Legislative Pilot of the New Deal," he was instrumental in the enactment of the National Industrial Recovery Act, the *National Labor Relations (Wagner) Act, the *Social Security Act, and the Wagner-Steagall Housing Act. Wagner also crusaded for national *health insurance, veterans' benefits, and a federal antilynching law. At his death, the *New York Times* lauded Wagner's "deep-seated humanitarianism" and "sympathy for those handicapped in the race for life." Pick any law designed to help common people, the *Times* proclaimed, "and the chances are that Bob Wagner's name is attached to it."

[*See also* Federal Government, Legislative Branch: Senate; Housing; Lynching; National Recovery Administration; New Deal Era, The; Progressive Era; Roosevelt, Franklin Delano.]

• Joseph Huthmacher, *Senator Robert F. Wagner and the Rise of Urban Liberalism*, 1968.

—John D. Buenker

WAGNER ACT. *See* National Labor Relations Act.

WALKER, DAVID. *See David Walker's Appeal.*

WALKER, MADAME C. J. (1867–1919), African American entrepreneur, philanthropist, activist. Born on a Louisiana cotton plantation shortly after the end of *slavery, Sarah Breedlove was orphaned at the age of seven. At ten she became a domestic worker, and at fourteen, living in Vicksburg, Mississippi, she married Moses McWilliams. He died in 1887, leaving her with a two-year-old daughter, Lelia (latter known as A'Lelia). Moving to St. Louis, she eked out a living as a washerwoman. Using available products, she also developed hair-care treatments for black women, including remedies for baldness and other scalp conditions brought on by poor diet, stress, and damaging hair treatments.

Recognizing a lucrative market, she developed her own line of products for a growing clientele. She moved to Denver in 1905 and in 1906 married Charles Joseph Walker, a journalist who became her business partner and promoter. They marketed their products and the "Walker System" through door-to-door sales and promotional tours. In 1910 the Walkers moved the business and manufacturing enterprise to Indianapolis, Indiana, where they employed a large workforce, including women who demonstrated her products in homes. After Walker and her husband divorced, she and her daughter ran the business.

In 1914 she moved to *New York City where, now a wealthy woman, she became a philanthropist and outspoken political activist. A successful entrepreneur and advocate of black women's economic independence, she often declared: "I got myself a start by giving myself a start." She bequeathed substantial sums to black schools, organizations, and institutions. Her daughter conducted a salon that became a gathering place for the writers, artists, and musicians of the *Harlem Renaissance.

[*See also* African Americans.]

• Walter Fisher, "Walker, Sarah Breedlove," in Edward T. James et al., eds., *Notable American Women, 1607–1950,* III, pp. 533–535, 1971. A'Lelia P. Bundles, "Madam C. J. Walker—Cosmetics Tycoon" *Ms.* (July 1983). A'Lelia P. Bundles, *Madam C. J. Walker—Entrepreneur*, 1991.

—Tiffany Ruby Patterson

WALLACE, DEWITT (1889–1981), magazine editor and publisher, philanthropist, and **WALLACE, LILA** (1888–1984), philanthropist. Born in St. Paul, Minnesota, DeWitt Wallace proved an indifferent student. Expelled from Macalester College (where his father taught religion, Greek, and political science), he later dropped out of the University of California, Berkeley. After apprenticing at a St. Paul publishing firm, he joined the army. Wounded during *World War I in the Meuse-Argonne offensive, he perfected his idea for the *Reader's Digest* in a military hospital. On his return, he courted Lila Bell Acheson, a social worker. Born in Virden, Manitoba, Lila shared with DeWitt both a strict Presbyterian upbringing and a rebellious individualism. Married in October 1921, they published the first issue of *Reader's Digest* in *New York City the following February, with Lila nominally listed as an editor to attract women readers. Later they transferred the headquarters of the Reader's Digest Association to Pleasantville, New York.

The *Digest*'s emphasis on brevity, spiritual uplift, confidence-building, real-life dramas, and homey humor found a ready market. The editorial formula was later broadened to include original material in addition to condensed reprints from other magazines. From its inception, the magazine also reflected DeWitt's pronounced conservative views and nostalgic yearning for an idealized America. With government help, the first foreign editions appeared during and after *World War II to counter Axis and communist propaganda. The immensely successful Condensed Books Division was launched in 1950. In 1955, to keep the cover price low, the *Digest* began accepting *advertising.

In later years the childless Wallaces turned increasingly to *philanthropy, particularly the arts and education. The Reader's Digest Association, worth three billion dollars, was bequeathed to seven major charities, with Macalester College as a major beneficiary. By the end of the twentieth century, published in nineteen languages, with a combined circulation above 27 million, the *Reader's Digest* remained the world's largest-circulation magazine.

[*See also* Journalism; Magazines; Popular Culture; Twenties, The.]

• John Heidenry, *Theirs Was the Kingdom: Lila and DeWitt Wallace and the Story of the* Reader's Digest, 1993. Peter Canning, *American Dreamers: The Wallaces and* Reader's Digest: *An Insider's Story,* 1996.

—John Heidenry

WALLACE, GEORGE C. (1919–1998), Alabama governor, presidential candidate. A 1942 graduate of the University of Alabama Law School, Wallace was elected to the Alabama House of Representatives in 1946 and elected a circuit judge in 1953. A racial moderate until he lost a 1958 gubernatorial bid to an ultrasegregationist, Wallace vowed that he would "never be out-niggered again." Elected governor in 1962 as the *civil rights movement gained momentum, he pledged "Segregation now! Segregation tomorrow! Segregation forever!" In 1963, however, after fulfilling a pledge to "stand in the schoolhouse door" at the University of Alabama, he stepped aside to allow the enrollment of black students. His segregationist stance won strong support among whites in his state and beyond. In 1964 he challenged Lyndon B. *Johnson in the *Democratic party's Wisconsin, Indiana, and Maryland presidential primaries, winning more than a third of the votes. Barred from a further consecutive gubernatorial term in 1966, he was succeeded by his wife, Lurleen.

As the presidential candidate of his American Independent party in 1968, Wallace drew ten million votes, half from outside the *South, and carried five states. His running mate was the retired air force general Curtis LeMay, former head of the Strategic Air Command. Regaining the Alabama governorship in 1970, he entered the Democratic presidential primaries in 1972 (with President Richard M. *Nixon's secret support), pledging to restore law and order, end court-ordered school busing, and "get tough with protesters." He made strong showings throughout the South and Midwest, including victories on 16 May in Michigan and Maryland.

The day before, however, an unemployed drifter shot and critically wounded Wallace at a rally in Maryland, leaving him permanently paralyzed below the waist. He retired in 1979 but regained the governorship in 1982, winning significant black support after repudiating his earlier *racism. A major political figure of the 1960s and 1970s, Wallace helped shape the agenda of social *conservatism and white blacklash that would dominate the politics of the 1980s.

[*See also* Segregation, Racial; Sixties, The.]

• Marshall Frady, *Wallace,* 1968. Dan T. Carter, *The Politics of Rage: George Wallace, the Origins of the New Conservatism, and the Transformation of American Politics,* 1995.

—Dan T. Carter

WALLACE, HENRY A. *See* Federal Government, Executive Branch: Department of Agriculture; Progressive Party of 1948.

WALL STREET. *See* Banking and Finance; New York Stock Exchange; Stock Market.

WALTON, SAM (1918–1992), merchant, founder of Wal-Mart Stores. Sam Walton was born near Kingfisher, Oklahoma. Graduating from the University of Missouri in 1940, he became a management trainee with J. C. Penney Company in Des Moines, Iowa. After *World War II military service, Walton in 1945 opened a Ben Franklin variety store in Newport, Arkansas. In 1950, having lost his lease in Newport, and assisted by a loan from his wealthy father-in-law, Walton opened his own store in Bentonville, Arkansas. There his talents as a retailer blossomed, and, by the early 1960s, in partnership with his brother, he had built a chain of sixteen variety stores.

Meantime, the growth of discount retailing threatened the survival of variety stores, so Walton entered the new field, opening the first Wal-Mart Discount City store in Rogers, Arkansas, in 1962, the same year the retailing giant Kresge launched its K-mart chain. In 1970, with thirty-two retail outlets, Walton incorporated the firm and offered stock to the public. Ten years later, Wal-Mart was the leading southern discounter with 276 stores and a net income of $41 million. Observers credited the firm's success to superior management and to Walton's personality, while critics complained that Wal-Mart was destroying small-town merchants.

In the 1980s and 1990s, Wal-Mart expanded nationwide and turned to new retailing formats, including Sam's Wholesale Clubs and Supercenters. By the time of Walton's death, he had ranked for several years as "the richest man in America," and Wal-Mart with its 1,928 outlets and net income of $1.6 billion had surpassed Sears and K-mart as the nation's leading retailer.

[*See also* Consumer Culture; Mass Marketing; Shopping Centers and Malls.]

• Sam Walton with John Huey, *Sam Walton, Made in America: My Story,* 1992. Sandra S. Vance and Roy V. Scott, *Wal-Mart: A History of Sam Walton's Retail Phenomenon,* 1994.

—Roy V. Scott

WANAMAKER, JOHN (1838–1922), department-store merchant. The eldest son of a *Philadelphia brick-maker, Wanamaker was largely self-educated. In 1871 he opened in Philadelphia what he called a "New Kind of Store" named for himself. As a leader in *department-store retailing for over five decades, Wanamaker pioneered the use of *technology, from pneumatic tubes to escalators; personnel policies that included employee training and paid summer vacations; and such marketing techniques as frequent sales and full-page illustrated newspaper ads. His innovations in customer service included restaurants, reading and restrooms, and home delivery. Wanamaker's was known for its stained-glass windows, elaborate store displays, and spectacles including organ concerts, pageants, and storybook characters in show windows. In 1896, Wanamaker expanded from Philadelphia to *New York City. Other merchants such as Rowland Macy in New York, Marshall Field in *Chicago, and the Filenes in *Boston adapted Wanamaker's retailing innovations, but none matched his level of self-promotion or so enthusiastically incorporated the golden rule into retailing through the maxim that the customer is always right.

A paragon of the Victorian Christian gentleman in business, Wanamker amassed a vast furtune while spurning the crasser aspects of the commercial world. He devoted time and money to the Young Men's Christian Association, the *Civil War Christian Commission, the *Red Cross, the Salvation Army, Sunday schools, and the revivals of Dwight L. *Moody and Billy *Sunday. As postmaster general in the Benjamin *Harrison administration (1889–1893), he championed such Populist policies as parcel post, rural free delivery, and postal savings banks.

[*See also* Advertising; Consumer Culture; Gilded Age; Mass Marketing; Protestantism; Revivalism; YMCA and YWCA.]

• Joseph H. Appel, *The Business Biography of John Wanamaker, Founder and Builder,* 1930. William Leach, *Land of Desire: Merchants, Power, and the Rise of a New American Culture,* 1993.

—Susan Porter Benson

WAR CRIMES TRIALS, NUREMBERG AND TOKYO (1945–1948). The experience of allowing Germany to try its own war criminals after *World War I, which involved farcical trials, led the Allies in Janaury 1942 to announce their intention of trying enemy war criminals. In the Declaration on German Atrocities in Occupied Europe (1 November 1943), the Allies asserted that those accused of general crimes would be tried by an international tribunal, while those charged with local crimes would be tried at the scene. The Japanese received similar warnings. The British favored summary execution of war criminals, but the American preference for trials prevailed. The London Conference of June 1945 developed a charter for the international tribunal, and President Harry S. *Truman appointed *Supreme Court Justice Robert Jackson as the U.S. representative.

After formal opening proceedings in Berlin, the German trials were held in Nuremberg from November 1945 to October 1946 before a tribunal of U.S., British, French, and Russian judges. The twenty-four individuals indicted included German foreign ministers and Adolf Hitler's top military advisers and commanders; six organizations were indicted as well. The charges included conspiracy to wage aggressive war, the mistreatment of civilians and prisoners of war, and crimes against humanity (particularly the campaign to exterminate the Jews). The defendants were provided with lawyers; the prosecution depended primarily on documents written or received by the defendants. Of the nineteen individuals found guilty, twelve were sentenced to death, including the top Nazis Hermann Göring (who committed suicide in prison) and Joachim von Ribbentrop, and the remainder were given prison sentences from ten years to life. Acting under the London Charter and authority granted by the Allied Control Council, the United States conducted twelve additional trials at Nuremberg; the French held one at Rastatt.

The International Tribunal for the Far East, established in April 1946 with an eleven-nation panel of judges, was restricted to trying persons charged with the crime of aggressive war. The twenty-eight Japanese officials indicted included four prime ministers, four foreign ministers, and five war and two navy ministers. Emperor Hirohito was not tried. Of twenty-five found guilty in April 1948, seven received death sentences, including Prime Minister Hideki Tōjō, and the others, prison sentences. Hundreds of local trials were held in Europe and the Pacific. Beginning in the late 1950s, the Germans conducted war crime trials of their own. In 1961–1962, the Nazi official Adolf Eichmann was extradicted, tried, and executed by Israel for his role in the wartime campaign to exterminate the Jews.

The trials proved significant, especially in Germany, for the records and testimony about wartime events they made available. Furthermore, they established mechanisms and precedents for dealing with war crimes by formal proceedings rather than by acts of vengeance. The *Cold War prevented the subsequent application of these precedents except in isolated cases, such as the conviction of William Calley for his role in the *My Lai massacre, but they remained available. In the 1990s several persons involved in atrocities associated with ethnic conflict in former Yugoslavia were charged as war criminals by the International Court of Justice at the Hague, Netherlands, and some were apprehended and tried.

[*See also* International Law; World War II.]

• Whitney R. Harris, *Tyranny on Trial: The Evidence at Nuremberg,* 1954. Richard H. Minear, *Victor's Justice: The Tokyo War Crimes Trial,* 1971. Philip R. Piccigallo, *The Japanese on Trial: Allied War Crimes Operations in the East, 1945–1951,* 1979.

—Gerhard L. Weinberg

WARD, LESTER FRANK (1841–1913), sociologist. The end of the *Civil War found Ward, a sparsely educated but ambitious army veteran from rural Illinois, seeking a clerkship in *Washington, D.C. He took night courses, earned a master's degree in science, and flourished as a paleobotanist in John Wesley *Powell's U.S. Geological Survey. With the publication of *Dynamic Sociology* (1883), and later *The Psychic Factors of Civilization* (1893) and *Applied Sociology* (1906), he emerged as one of America's foremost critics of the *laissez-faire *individualism of Herbert Spencer and William Graham Sumner. Ward cautioned against applying scientific principles to politics. Rejecting the belief that any interference in the market economy jeopardized social progress by elevating the unfit, Ward stressed the power of human intellect as expressed through art, science, and institutions. Far from being helpless before immutable natural laws, human beings could master nature and achieve progress through the collective exercise of intelligence. Ward also criticized *eugenics as scientifically flawed and antidemocratic. He envisioned a future "Sociocracy" in which social problems would be solved by a government of disinterested experts.

His faith in science, efficiency, democracy, and especially education as agents of social change appealed to *Progressive Era activists seeking a scientific foundation for reform and to sociologists aspiring to social relevance. But when Brown University hired him in 1906, he was sixty-five and in intellectual decline. A philosopher by temperament, Ward seemed out of step as *sociology grew more technical and specialized. His work enjoyed a renaissance in the mid–twentieth century, however, among intellectuals seeking the philosophical roots of the welfare state.

[*See also* Gilded Age; Social Darwinism; Welfare, Federal.]

• Henry Steele Commager, *Lester Ward and the Welfare State,* 1967. Clifford H. Scott, *Lester Frank Ward,* 1976.

—Andrew Chamberlin Rieser

WAR DEPARTMENT. *See* Federal Government, Executive Branch: Department of Defense.

WARHOL, ANDY (1928–1987), artist. Born Andrew Warhola in McKeesport, Pennsylvania, Warhol earned a B.A. in pictorial design at Pittsburgh's Carnegie Institute of Technology and became a commercial artist in *New York City. He designed book jackets, magazine illustrations, greeting cards, and award-winning shoe advertisements. In 1962 he created his first silk-screen paintings of mechanically processed subject matter from newspapers and pulp tabloids. These ranged from serial images of Marilyn *Monroe and Campbell Soup cans to contiguous repetitions of body-strewn car wrecks. His choice of synthetic polymer paint for these canvases enhanced their reference to pop art's mass-media sources. Warhol's calculated quest of celebrity peaked in the mid-1960s. His Forty-seventh Street studio, painted silver from floor to ceiling and dubbed the Factory, became the most notorious art-world hot spot for camp fashion, underground film, rock music, hallucinatory drug culture, self-dramatization, and multimedia spectacles. His films, a form of pop phenomenalism, explored "what things really are" by featuring such subjects as six hours of a man sleeping, eight hours of the *Empire State Building, and shorter reels of various sex acts.

After his near-fatal 1968 shooting by a woman who wanted him to produce a pornographic film she had written, Warhol recovered to start a superstar magazine, *Interview.* He also produced silk-screen portraits of celebrities, including Mao Tsetung. Debate over whether Warhol's art should be viewed as cool detachment or as critical commentary extended his celebrity well beyond his often-quoted wish of fifteen minutes of fame for everyone. The Andy Warhol Museum in Pittsburgh displays many of his works.

[*See also* Consumer Culture; Painting: Since 1945; Popular Culture; Postmodernism.]

• Andy Warhol, *The Philosophy of Andy Warhol (from A to B and Back Again),* 1975. Carter Ratcliff, *Andy Warhol,* 1983.

—James M. Dennis

WAR INDUSTRIES BOARD. The War Industries Board (WIB) was formed in July 1917 by the Council of National Defense, a wartime agency set up by President Woodrow *Wilson, to assure the availability of vital raw materials and resources for war production. The WIB fell short of its goals, however, and in March 1918 Wilson appointed the Wall Street financier Bernard *Baruch to reorganize and head it. Although it was a new departure in executive authority, the WIB lacked compulsory power, even with the addition of a price-fixing committee in March 1918. Making matters worse was industry's hostile reaction to Baruch's appointment. Such heads of the major auto and steel corporations as John Dodge, Henry *Ford, and Elbert H. Gary did not disguise their disdain for Baruch. While the hostility stemmed in part from business's fear that it could not control the tough and fiercely independent Baruch, *anti-Semitism played a role as well. With powers more illusory than real, Baruch relied on persuasion to gain the voluntary cooperation of business and labor. Even so, profit-oriented manufacturers often resisted his patriotic appeals to invoke modest wartime price controls. Only after he threatened to marshal the entire force of the federal government against the titans of industry did they capitulate. Still, guided by Baruch, the WIB did keep inflation in check while providing the War Department with needed resources. The WIB was dismantled in 1918, a few weeks after the war ended.

During the Great Depression of the 1930s, the WIB served as a model for the Franklin Delano *Roosevelt administration's efforts to rework the economic forces of supply and demand. In 1939, it was resurrected in modified form when President Roosevelt established the short-lived War Resources Board. When the United States entered *World War II, Roosevelt again turned to the WIB precedent and drew upon many of Baruch's ideas about managing a war economy.

[*See also* Economic Regulation; New Deal Era, The; World War I.]

• Bernard Baruch, *My Own Story*, 1957. Jordan A. Schwarz, *The Speculator: Bernard M. Baruch in Washington, 1917–1965*, 1981. William O'Neill, *A Democracy at War: America's Fight at Home and Abroad in World War II*, 1993.

—Anthony Troncone

WAR OF 1812. The War of 1812 between the United States and Great Britain, also known as the Second Anglo-American War, was caused primarily by the United States' desire to defend its presumed right as a neutral state to trade freely with other nations even in wartime. Great Britain's determination to prevent America from trading with France during the wars of the French Revolution (1792–1815) eventually resulted in open warfare.

The road to war began in 1794 when the British navy seized more than 250 American merchant vessels trading with the French West Indies. Although the French had also attacked U.S. shipping, American anger focused on the British because of the number of ships they had seized and their policy of capturing sailors suspected of desertion (known as impressment) from the decks of American ships on the high seas. Amid fears of resubjugation by their former colonial masters, many Americans (among them Thomas *Jefferson and James *Madison) called for strong action, including war if necessary, to halt the British attacks.

To head off this sentiment, President George *Washington sent John *Jay to London to negotiate a settlement. *Jay's Treaty (1794), while it prevented war, did little to protect American maritime rights and proved politically divisive. The Jeffersonian faction, attacking the treaty as pro-British, urged closer friendship with France; the *Federalist party, fearing an alliance with revolutionary France, defended the treaty.

In early 1807, responding to Napoleon's blockade of the British Isles, the British government issued two Admiralty decrees, or orders in council, that effectively forbade neutral vessels (including those of the United States) from entering any French-controlled port. Later that year, the seizure by the HMS *Leopard* of five alleged deserters from the USS *Chesapeake* in international waters near the Cheaspeake Bay provoked calls for war, especially from the western states. President Jefferson, seeking to "peaceably coerce" Great Britain and France into respecting neutral rights, imposed a nationwide embargo on all *foreign trade. The *Embargo Act and two subsequent modifications of it not only failed to budge either Britain or France, but precipitated an economic *depression, as farmers found themselves barred from world markets by their own government.

In 1808–1811, the British navy, desperate for able-bodied seamen, impressed more than six thousand Americans. Angry over this state of affairs, Americans elected to Congress in 1810 a fiery group of expansionists, mostly from the western states. These "War Hawks," as they were known, including Henry *Clay of Kentucky and John C. *Calhoun of South Carolina, pushed for the conquest of British Canada as a means of compelling London to alter its policy.

Responding to this pressure, President James Madison on 1 June 1812, citing impressment, ship seizures, and Britain's alleged incitement of Native Americans on the western frontier, called for a declaration of war against Great Britain. After heated debate, Congress passed the measure on votes of 79–49 in the House and 19–13 in the Senate. A clear partisan division emerged: Republicans voted for war 98–23 and Federalists opposed it 39–0.

The nation, like the Congress, divided sharply over the conflict. New York and *New England shipping interests that might have been expected to support retaliation against Great Britain recognized that while the harassment of American trade hurt their business, war would stop it entirely. As a result, the war began with powerful economic interests firmly opposed to it. Throughout the war, trading with the enemy flourished, particularly along the Canadian frontier.

Militarily the war did not go well. Invasions of Canada in 1812 and 1813 (whose conquest Jefferson predicted would be "a mere matter of marching") resulted in humiliating defeats. In August 1814, British forces captured and briefly occupied *Washington, D.C., burning the Capitol, the *White House, and other government buildings. These setbacks were somewhat offset by victories at sea, including the destruction of the British frigate *Guerrière* by the U.S. frigate *Constitution* ("Old Ironsides," now preserved in Boston Harbor) off Nova Scotia in August 1812 and Oliver Hazard Perry's triumph at the Battle of Lake Erie (September 1813). In September 1814, British expeditions were repulsed at Lake Champlain and at Fort McHenry in Baltimore, Maryland, whose survival amid an all-night bombardment prompted Francis Scott Key to write "The Star-Spangled Banner."

The war's cost resulted in the most extensive system of internal *taxation prior to the *Civil War. By 1814, however, the nation verged on financial collapse. War loans were undersubscribed and the closing of the First Bank of the United States in 1811 meant that no central bank could stabilize the currency. In November 1814 the federal government defaulted on its bond payments and was effectively bankrupt.

Only Great Britain's precarious situation in Europe in late 1814, combined with the defeat of its invasion forces in the United States, prompted the government of Lord Liverpool to compromise. On 24 December 1814, American and British negotiators meeting at Ghent, Belgium, signed a treaty reestablishing the prewar status quo. Although the pact left unsettled the maritime issues that had caused the conflict, the end of the Napoleonic wars in 1815 rendered them moot. The war enhanced American power vis-à-vis Indian tribes in the *West and *South and thus set the stage for westward expansion after 1815.

The war also boosted American nationalism, especially Andrew *Jackson's smashing victory at the Battle of *New Orleans on 8 January 1815. Even though better political leadership and more astute diplomacy could probably have avoided it, the War of 1812 was long seen by Americans as a vindication of their courage and patriotism.

The war resulted in 2,500 American combat-related deaths and as many as 20,000 U.S. deaths from all causes. Its direct costs totaled $158 million including benefits that continued until the last pensioner (the dependent of a veteran) died in 1946.

[*See also* Bank of the United States, First and Second; Early Republic, Era of the Expansionism; Foreign Relations: U.S. Relations with Europe; Ghent, Treaty of; Indian History and Culture: From 1800 to 1900; Perry, Oliver Hazard and Matthew; Quasi-War with France.]

• Julius Pratt, *Expansionists of 1812*, 1925. Roger H. Brown, *The Republic in Peril: 1812*, 1964. Reginald Horsman, *The War of 1812*, 1964. J. C. A. Stagg, *Mr. Madison's War: Politics, Diplomacy, and Warfare in the Early American Republic, 1783–1830*, 1983. Steven Watts, *The Republic Reborn: War and the Making of Liberal America, 1790–1820*, 1987. Donald R. Hickey, *The War of 1812: A Forgotten Conflict*, 1989.

—William Earl Weeks

WAR ON POVERTY. *See* Great Society; Johnson, Lyndon B.; Poverty.

WAR POWERS ACT. Adopted by Congress in 1973 over President Richard M. *Nixon's veto, this resolution stemmed from legislators' perception that Presidents Lyndon B. *Johnson and Nixon had abused the *Constitution's war-making powers during the *Vietnam War. The act required the president to consult with Congress "in every possible instance" before introducing armed forces "into hostilities or into situations where imminent involvement in hostilities is clearly indicated by the circumstances." It also required the president to report any such deployments to Congress within forty-eight hours, and stipulated that if within sixty days Congress refused to endorse the president's use of force, the troops must return home—with a thirty-day extension to assure a safe withdrawal. The resolution also permitted Congress to force the withdrawal of U.S. troops from a region at any time by majority vote, without presidential recourse to a veto. In 1983 the *Supreme Court invalidated this provision, ruling that only a congressional joint resolution, subject to a presidential veto, could force a withdrawal.

The War Powers Act did not work as its proponents anticipated, since presidents failed to notify Congress of troop deployments that would start the sixty-day clock. Yet it remained in force, a potential check on the president's authority to deploy U.S. military force abroad.

[*See also* Federal Government, Executive Branch: The Presidency; Federal Government, Legislative Branch.]

• Michael J. Glennon, *Constitutional Diplomacy*, 1990. Louis Fisher, *Presidential War Power*, 1995.

—Loch K. Johnson

WARREN, EARL (1891–1974), governor of *California, chief justice of the U.S. *Supreme Court. Reared in Bakersfield, California, Warren received his undergraduate and law degrees from the University of California at Berkeley. In 1925, he married Nina Meyers; the couple had six children. Warren slowly ascended the political ladder in California—as district attorney of Alameda County (1920–1938), attorney general (1938–1942), and governor (1943–1953). During *World War II, he actively supported the *incarceration of Japanese Americans in detention camps. Known as a political moderate, Warren ran as the *Republican party's candidate for vice president in 1948, on a ticket headed by Thomas E. Dewey, and then sought the Republican presidential nomination in 1952, losing to Dwight D. *Eisenhower. The following year, President Eisenhower appointed him chief justice of the United States.

As chief justice, Warren was less concerned with technical constitutional issues than with the ethical imperatives of the *Constitution—*equality, procedural fairness, and a broad range of rights associated with American citizenship. In **Brown* v. *Board of Education* (1954), the Supreme Court overruled **Plessy* v. *Ferguson* (1896) and unanimously held that segregated public schools deprived black students of the equal protection of the laws. In **Baker* v. *Carr* (1962), the Court, overruling earlier precedent, rejected the doctrine that the apportionment of legislative districts was beyond the scope of *judicial review. In *Griswold* v. *Connecticut* (1965), ruling unconstitutional a Connecticut statute banning the use of contraceptives, the Court discovered a "right of privacy" in the Constitution, despite the absence of any textual language codifying such a right. In **Miranda* v. *Arizona* (1966), the Court held that the Fifth Amendment's protection against self-incrimination required *police to give a precise set of warnings to suspects being interrogated in their custody. Warren was in the majority in all of these decisions, writing both *Brown* and *Miranda*.

Some commentators have celebrated Earl Warren's judicial activism, while others have viewed it with alarm. Few, however, have doubted his enormous impact upon some of the most important social and political issues of his time.

[*See also* Civil Rights; *Engel* v. *Vitale*; Jurisprudence.]

• G. Edward White, *Earl Warren: A Public Life*, 1982. Bernard Schwartz, *The Unpublished Opinions of the Warren Court*, 1987.

—G. Edward White

WARREN MERCY OTIS (1728–1814), poet, political pamphleteer, historian. Born in Barnstable, Massachusetts, married to James Warren, and the mother of five sons, Mercy Otis Warren in her writings captured the political ideology of the "old republican" elite that played a leading role in the struggle for independence. This point of view came naturally to her: The Otis and Warren families were among the most influential in Revolutionary Massachusetts. In 1788, Warren published "Observations on the New Constitution," an important pamphlet opposing ratification of the federal *Constitution. Although she was strongly anti-Federalist, her pseudonym, "A Columbian Patriot," reflected her commitment to the ideal of an American nation. The new nation would be destroyed, Warren contended, if a powerful central government were allowed to trample the rights of the states and the people. Warren spoke for a small but powerful group of elite anti-Federalists who embraced a more traditional republican view of politics and believed that individuals of their own class could be trusted to guide the ship of state safely through the troubled times of the post-Revolutionary Era. This vision was most fully elaborated in her three-volume *History of the Rise, Progress, and Termination of the American Revolution* (1805). In this republican jeremiad, Warren argued that the extraordinary display of virtue during the Revolution had given way to a speculative frenzy and a lust for aristocratic titles. Warren urged Americans to restore the pure republican principles of the Revolution.

[*See also* Articles of Confederation; Early Republic, Era of the; Gender; Republicanism; Revolution and Constitution, Era of; Revolutionary War.]

• Mercy Otis Warren, *History of the Rise, Progress, and Termination of the American Revolution: Interspersed with Biographical, Political, and Moral Observations*, ed. Lester H. Cohen, 1988. Rosemarie Zagarri, *A Woman's Dilemma: Mercy Otis Warren and the American Revolution*, 1995.

—Saul Cornell

WASHINGTON, BOOKER T. (1856–1915), African-American educator and leader. Born into *slavery in Hale's Ford, Virginia, Washington was nine years old at the conclusion of the *Civil War when he walked with his mother, brother, and sister from Virginia to Malden, West Virginia, to join his stepfather. There he worked as a child laborer in a salt-processing operation and in a coal mine, escaping that work eventually to become a houseboy for his employer's wife, Mrs. Viola Ruffin, who encouraged his educational aspirations. At sixteen he made his way from Malden to Hampton, Virginia, a distance of five hundred miles, and was admitted to Hampton Institute, a training school for former slaves, founded and led by Samuel Chapman Armstrong of Massachusetts. He graduated in 1875.

When Armstrong, his lifetime mentor and adviser, was asked by officials at Tuskegee, Alabama, to suggest someone who could establish another school for former slaves, Armstrong recommended Washington, who in 1881 founded Tuskegee Normal and Industrial Institute, modeling it closely on his alma mater.

Washington built the school by tirelessly seeking funds from northern philanthropists introduced to him by Armstrong. In 1895, the year of the death of the first widely recognized leader of *African Americans, Frederick *Douglass, Washington was invited to deliver an address at the so-called Atlanta Exposition, a project designed to encourage northern investment in southern commerce. The invitation reflected the recognition that black labor must play a key role in any scheme to rebuild the *South's economy after the devastation of the Civil War. Washington's position made him a perfect mediator among southern and northern white entrepreneurs and former slaves. In the speech (sometimes called the "Atlanta Compromise"), Washington pledged that blacks in the South would be faithful laborers, would oppose unions, and would eschew political and social *equality, even to the extent of surrendering the newly won right to vote and accepting racial *segregation. Supported by powerful whites both north and south, and pledged not to oppose the racial status quo, Washington became the recognized leader of black America.

Washington's most fervent opponent, W. E. B. *Du Bois, called in no uncertain terms for the vote, the immediate end of segregation, adequate education for black children, and full equality. But though Washington's power and influence waned in his later years, he was never entirely displaced as a prominent and powerful figure in national politics and African-American affairs generally. The mechanism through which he exercised his power has been called "the Tuskegee machine," and indeed his social and political role did resemble that of a political boss. A wide network of correspondents regularly reported to him on the activities of his critics, rivals, and enemies; he controlled or influenced a number of African American newspapers throughout the country; and he carried on many of his activities surreptitiously, even his attempts to fight *racism, *lynching, and segregation. His widely read autobiography, *Up from Slavery,* appeared in 1901.

[*See also* Gilded Age; Trotter, William Monroe.]

• Louis R. Harlan, *Booker T. Washington: The Making of a Black Leader, 1856–1910,* 1972. Louis R. Harlan, *Booker T. Washington: The Wizard of Tuskegee, 1901–1915,* 1983.

—Donald B. Gibson

WASHINGTON, GEORGE (1732–1799), commander in chief of the Continental army during the American Revolution, first president of the United States. He was born at his father's estate, Wakefield, in Westmoreland County, Virginia, the eldest son of Augustine Washington and his second wife, Mary Ball Washington. Coming from a family of middling rank, he received little formal education, but soon developed a penchant for self-improvement and an ambition to better himself. During his early youth his greatest influence was his older half brother Lawrence Washington, the master of *Mount Vernon, whose marriage into the influential Fairfax family brought him into the first rank of Virginia society. The time young George spent with his brother and his brother's friends fueled his ambition and brought him a coterie of influential friends. By the time he was twenty he had become surveyor for Culpeper County, traveled with his ailing brother to Barbados and, after Lawrence's death in 1752, succeeded not only to his estate at Mount Vernon but to his brother's position as adjutant of the Northern Neck and Eastern Shore of Virginia.

Washington chose the military as his route to advancement, and the encroachment of the French on Virginia's frontiers provided the opportunity. He acted as emissary to the French forces for Governor Robert Dinwiddie in 1753, served as lieutenant colonel of Virginia's military forces during the unsuccessful Fort Necessity campaign in 1754, and as a volunteer aide-de-camp with General Edward Braddock's disastrous 1755 campaign against the French at Fort Duquesne. Assuming command of the Virginia Regiment in the fall of 1755, he spent the next four years defending Virginia's western frontier, constructing forts, making military and financial arrangements with the colonial government in Williamsburg, negotiating with England's allies among the Indian tribes, and gaining invaluable experience in command. Eager for promotion, greedy for land, and often critical of his superiors to the point of insubordination, the brash young Washington little resembled the later mature statesman.

Retiring from the regiment in December 1759, he married the wealthy young widow Martha Custis (1731–1802), and established himself as a squire at Mount Vernon. They had no children. Backed by Martha's great personal fortune, he managed his plantation and its slave laborers, served on local vestries and in the House of Burgesses, and acquired substantial land holdings. With other Virginia planters he engaged in land speculation on the Virginia-North Carolina frontier and in the Ohio Country. He also gradually rectified the character defects he had displayed as a young regimental commander. By the time he was elected to the First *Continental Congress in 1774, he had already become a prominent figure in Virginia and a leader in the political activities that would lead to the break with England. Both because of his previous military experience and the delegates' wish to draw Virginia into the war, Congress appointed Washington commander in chief of the American army in June 1775.

Throughout the *Revolutionary War he struggled with a lack of supplies, men, support from Congress and state governments, and his own lack of military genius. The *Boston siege of 1775–1776 was successful, owing in part to Washington's administrative ability, but in 1776 he faced what was probably the insurmountable challenge of defending New York against British attack. Unable to hold the city, he managed the evacuation adroitly, regrouping his forces at White Plains. While not a master tactician, he occasionally displayed flashes of brilliance. Among his successes were the battles of Trenton and Princeton at the end of the New Jersey campaign, 1776–1777, and his ability to hold his small rag-tag army together through the Philadelphia campaign and the winter of 1777–1778 at *Valley Forge. After the Monmouth campaign, June-July 1778, Washington's role in military operations took second place to the war in the South until, in the spring and summer of 1781, in collaboration with the French, he embarked on the southern campaign that culminated in the surrender of General Cornwallis at Yorktown. At the end of 1783 he gave up his commission to Congress and returned to Mount Vernon, where he hoped to retire. Instead Mount Vernon became a mecca for Americans honoring the military leader who had become an icon of integrity and patriotism. Swarms of visitors sought Washington's opinion on every conceivable subject. Both at home and abroad he symbolized the new republic. In 1787 he served as president of the *Constitutional Convention.

Although he accepted the office with considerable misgivings, George Washington was elected president of the United States in February 1789 and reelected in 1792. In office, Washington used his extraordinary administrative abilities to construct an efficient civil service, and under his leadership, the fiscal policies of Treasury secretary Alexander *Hamilton brought financial stability to the new nation. Asserting the power of the new federal government, he mobilized and personally led a militia force tax-resisting frontiersmen during the 1794 against *Whiskey Rebellion. In foreign affairs his administration succeeded in maintaining United States neutrality as war erupted between France and England in 1793 and in normalizing diplomatic relations with England by means of *Jay's

Treaty (1794). A combination of negotiations and military operations brought peace to the country's frontiers. By the end of his second administration his political faith in the new nation was shaken by the growing factional disputes between the *Federalist party, which Washington supported, and Democratic Republicans led by Thomas *Jefferson and James *Madison. Always obsessive concerning his reputation, he left office embittered by attacks on his policies. In a precedent-setting farewell address (September 1796) he deplored the rise of *political parties, explained his decision not to seek a third term, and warned against "permanent alliances" with other nations.

Whatever the criticism of his administration, George Washington's contributions to the creation and development of the new republic were indispensable and unparalleled, a fact the American public clearly understood. His place as an American icon was secure. Retiring to Mount Vernon in March 1797, he resumed the life of a Virginia planter, returning to public life briefly as lieutenant general and commander of the army during the *Quasi-War with France in 1798–1799. Washington died at Mount Vernon, 14 December 1799, and was buried on the estate.

[*See also* Adams, John; Colonial Era; Early Republic, Era of the; Federal Government, Executive Branch: The Presidency; Foreign Relations: U.S. Relations with Europe; Revolution and Constitution, Era of; Seven Years' War; Washington's Farewell Address.]

• James T. Flexner, *George Washington,* 4 vols., 1965–1972. W. W. Abbot, Dorothy Twohig, Philander D. Chase, Beverly H. Runge, eds., *The Papers of George Washington,* 45 vols. to date, 1982–. Barry Schwartz, *George Washington: The Making of An American Symbol,* 1987. John Ferling, *The First of Men: A Life of George Washington,* 1988. Paul K. Longmore, *The Invention of George Washington,* 1988. Richard Norton Smith, *Patriarch,* 1993.

—Dorothy Twohig

WASHINGTON, D.C. Tourist mecca and home of the federal government, Washington, D.C. (District of Columbia), contains many of the nation's most revered sites, including the Capitol, the *White House, the Supreme Court Building, the *Lincoln Memorial, the Washington Monument (completed 1885), and others. The site on the Potomac River was chosen in a 1790 compromise that resolved a dispute not only over the new government's location but also over Alexander *Hamilton's economic program. Construction went forward, and in 1800, President John *Adams occupied the White House and Congress moved to the new city from *Philadelphia.

As both a city and a national capital, Washington, D.C., functions like other urban areas even as its governance remains under federal supervision. This special relationship, assured by a clause in the U.S. *Constitution, has brought the city parks, *museums, and a stable source of employment. But federal restrictions both fiscal and political have hampered Washington's development and prevented it from becoming the model its founders envisioned.

From the outset of the federal government's relocation to the District of Columbia, local concerns were subordinated to national business. Funds to develop the urban infrastructure lagged behind those designated for federal functions. Washington's designers anticipated that trade, more than the government's presence, would stimulate development, but when Congress failed to fund the canals, and later the *railroads necessary for commerce, Washington fell behind its competitors, most notably Baltimore, Maryland. The *Civil War vastly expanded the federal presence in Washington without bringing additional attention to the city's physical needs. Consolidation of the different district jurisdictions under a territorial government in 1871 sparked the city's modernization, but in 1874, after local officials greatly exceeded their spending authority, Congress imposed a presidentially appointed commission to govern the district. As compensation for the loss of popular sovereignty, and as payment in lieu of taxes on federal properties. Congress promised an annual appropriation to cover half the local expenses. This practice continued although by the 1990s, Congress's contribution to Washington's operating budget was closer to 15 percent.

To mark the centennial of the federal presence, the U.S. Senate in 1900 chartered a commission to develop a new plan for government buildings and parks. The commission's plan, based on a 1791 design by Pierre L'Enfant, concentrated government facilities at the heart of the city and connected them by a system of parks. Over the next quarter century the plan materialized, but in the process the federal government set itself apart both physically and symbolically from the city around it.

By 1950, Washington, D.C.'s population approached 800,000. The *Cold War further stimulated government expansion, and the area grew rapidly. Much of the growth was in the suburbs, however, and by 1957, when Washington became the nation's first majority black city, it represented a greatly diminished portion of the metropolitan area. Although a national civil rights campaign helped the city secure the right to elect local officials in 1974, Congress continued to withhold national representation and prohibited Washington from taxing either government property or workers living outside the city. With its growing importance as a world capital, Washington thrived during the real-estate boom of the 1980s but in the early 1990s declined under the combined burdens of poor management and insufficient funds. The population dropped precipitously to under 600,000, and revenues fell correspondingly. In 1995, Congress placed the city in virtual receivership, further compromising home rule. Washington's residents protested federal interference in local affairs, but until the city's finances could be stabilized, the nation's capital was destined to see its fate largely dictated by federal authorities.

[*See also* Arlington National Cemetery; Canals and Waterways; Federal Government; Library of Congress; Smithsonian Institution; Vietnam Veterans Memorial; War of 1812.]

• Howard Gillette Jr., *Between Justice and Beauty: Race, Planning, and the Failure of Urban Policy in Washington, D.C.,* 1995. Carol O' Cleireacain, *The Orphaned Capital,* 1997.

—Howard Gillette Jr.

WASHINGTON NAVAL ARMS CONFERENCE, THE (1921–1922), produced three treaties affecting the power balance in the western Pacific. The United States, seeking to ameliorate its potential post–*World War I isolation as diplomacy shifted to the new *League of Nations in Geneva, Switzerland, called the conference.

Secretary of State Charles Evans *Hughes electrified the delegates at the opening session on 12 November 1921 by proposing a ten-year naval building "holiday," along with scrapping existing ships and others planned or under construction. The goal, he announced, was to prevent a naval arms race in the Pacific. Serving the cause of both peace and budgetary restraint, Hughes's plan was incorporated into the Five-Power Naval Limitation Treaty (often called the Washington Treaty). It mandated strict limits on capital-ship (battleships and aircraft carriers) construction and set a capital-ship ratio among the five signatories: United States and Great Britain, 5; Japan, 3; France and Italy, 1.75. The treaty did not restrict the tonnage, weight, or gun size of capital ships or substantially limit the construction of other ships. This treaty ostensibly favored the United States and Great Britain, but since each had a two-ocean fleet, it in fact gave Japan, a single-ocean power, naval dominance in the western Pacific. This was accentuated when the United States agreed not to fortify its bases in the *Philippines.

By augmenting Japan's naval influence, the Five-Power Naval Limitation Treaty subtly undermined the objectives of the two other treaties. The Four-Power Pact, which superseded the 1902 Anglo-Japanese alliance, pledged the United States, Great Britain, Japan, and France to respect each other's "rights" in the Pacific, but lacked enforcement provisions. The Nine-Power Pact, signed by the five naval powers plus China, Bel-

MAP 25: WASHINGTON, D.C., AS ENVISIONED IN 1792

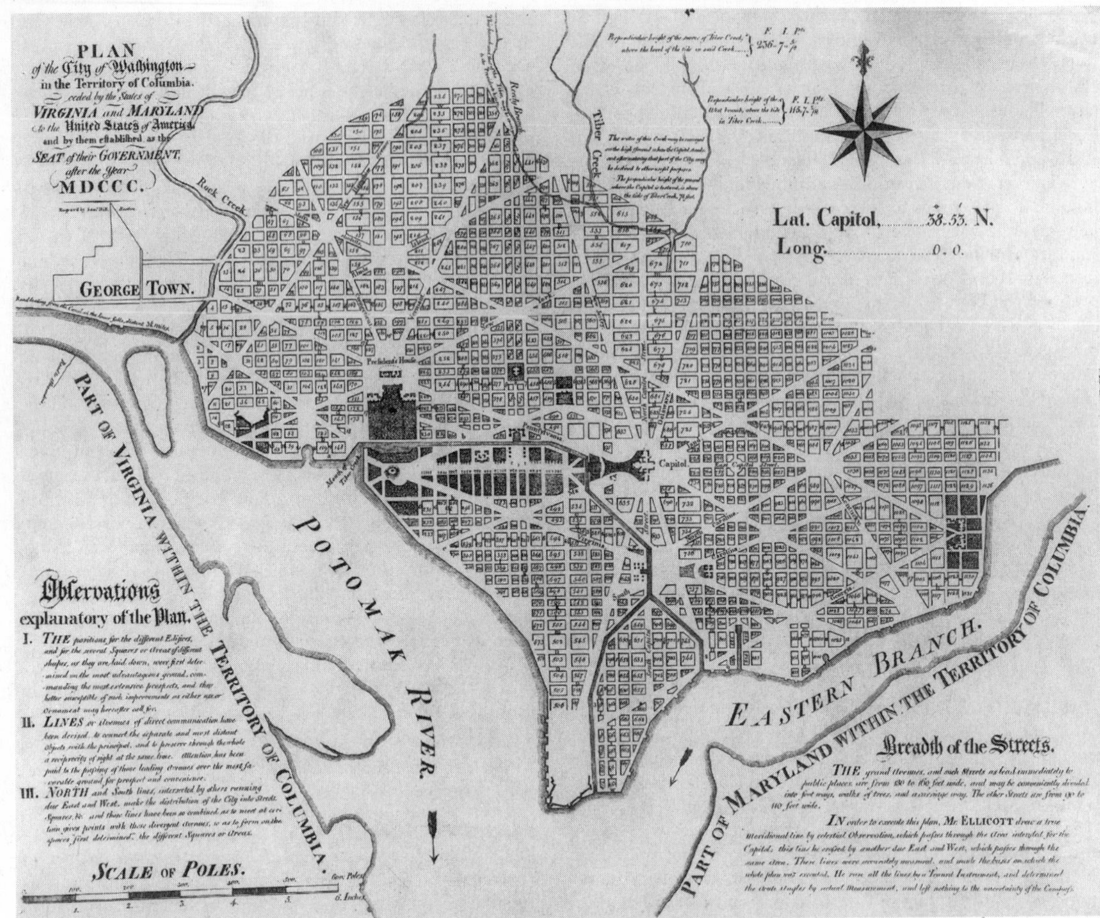

This 1792 map was prepared by the Pennsylvania surveyor Andrew Ellicott (1754–1820). After the 1790 compromise by which Virginia and Maryland jointly contributed a ten-mile-square tract of land along the Potomac River as the site of the federal government, Ellicott surveyed the site and proposed this layout of the city of Washington, based on a plan drafted the year before by the Frenchman Pierre L'Enfant. The siting of Pennsylvania Avenue, the Capitol, and the "President's House" (later called the White House) followed this layout, but not until 1901 did L'Enfant's plan become the basis of Washington, D.C.'s urban redevelopment.

[*See* Early Republic, Era of the; City Planning; Washington, D.C.; White House.]

gium, the Netherlands, and Portugal, sanctioned the *Open-Door Policy in China. Ostensibly denying any nation the right to exclude the commerce of others by abridging China's sovereignty and territorial integrity, it, too, had no enforcement procedures. Nine years later, ignoring the Four-Power Pact and taking advantage of U.S. naval weakness in the western Pacific, Japan occupied Manchuria.

[*See also* Foreign Relations: U.S. Relations with Europe; Foreign Relations: U.S. Relations with Asia: Harding, Warren G.; World War II: Causes.]

• Thomas A. Buckley, *The Washington Conference, 1921–1922,* 1970. Roger Dingman, *Power in the Pacific: The Origins of Naval Arms Limitations, 1914–1922,* 1976.

—Gary B. Ostrower

WASHINGTON'S FAREWELL ADDRESS. Published on 19 September 1796 in Claypoole's *American Daily Advertiser,* George *Washington's Farewell Address to the nation quickly came to be regarded as the first president's legacy to the American political system. Conceived by Washington partly to answer critics of his presidential policies and partly as a means of deflecting public pressure for a third term, the address often reveals Washington's dismay at the charges of partisanship leveled against him by political opponents during his second term. But the valedictory address that closed his public career also gave him an opportunity to express his own blueprint for the new nation's future. Drawing upon his stature as Revolutionary leader and as president, he counseled unity among the states and among citizens, advised against partisan politics, expressed his support for public education, and emphasized the importance of maintaining the government's public credit. In the part of the address that would have a lasting impact on American *foreign relations, he advised the nation to pursue a policy of neutrality, have as little political connection as possible with foreign nations, and steer clear of "permanent alliances with any portion of the foreign world." In drawing up the address, Washington relied on advice and drafts that he requested from James *Madison, Alexander *Hamilton, John *Jay, and others, but the ideas contained in the message were his own.

Although viewed by many of Washington's contemporary critics and some subsequent historians as a partisan political statement reflecting the *Federalist party policy of opposing any alliance with Republican France, the widely published address was lauded by the American public and has had a lasting influence on American political thought. Emulating Washington, other presidents have issued farewell messages, most notably Dwight D. *Eisenhower in 1961.

[*See also* Early Republic, Era of the; Federal Government, Executive Branch: The Presidency; Political Parties.]

• Felix Gilbert, *To the Farewell Address: Ideas of Early American Foreign Policy,* 1961. Matthew Spalding and Patrick J. Garrity, *A Sacred Union of Citizens: George Washington's Farewell Address and the American Character,* 1996.

—Dorothy Twohig

WATCHTOWER BIBLE AND TRACT SOCIETY. *See* Jehovah's Witnesses.

WATERGATE, a political espionage and cover-up case that began during the 1972 presidential campaign and eventually caused President Richard M *Nixon's resignation. The name derives from the *Washington, D.C., residential and office complex that was the site of the break-in that triggered the entire episode.

Nixon Administration Illegalities. The constitutional crisis known as "Watergate" resulted from President Nixon's obsession with his political "enemies" and his resolve to win reelection by the largest possible margin. In 1970, amid massive protests against the *Vietnam War, Nixon authorized extensive surveillance of antiwar groups by the *Central Intelligence Agency (CIA), the *Federal Bureau of Investigation (FBI), the National Security Agency, and even the Internal Revenue Service. In 1971, Nixon staff members recruited a team of ex-FBI and CIA sleuths, nicknamed "the Plumbers," to trace the leaks that had led to the publication of the *Pentagon Papers, a hoard of government documents detailing Vietnam War planning. Among other illegal activities, the Plumbers stole the confidential psychiatric records of Daniel Ellsberg, the Pentagon staff member who had released the documents, in an effort to discredit him.

As a natural extension of these tactics, Nixon's reelection campaign manager (and head of "CREEP," the Committee to Re-Elect the President), the former attorney general John Mitchell, in March 1972 approved "Operation Gemstone," a blueprint for "dirty tricks" aimed at undermining potential Democratic nominees. The break-in at the headquarters of the Democratic National Committee (DNC) in the Watergate building on the night of 17 June 1972 was part of Gemstone; its objective was to plant wiretaps on DNC telephones. Those who staged the break-in made crucial mistakes, however, and were arrested by municipal police. Apprehended were four Cuban nationals and a former CIA employee, James McCord, whose address book implicated G. Gordon Liddy and E. Howard Hunt of the Plumbers' unit.

Journalistic, Judicial, and Legislative Inquiries. Although Democratic nominee George McGovern tried to make the break-in a campaign issue, the media dismissed it as a mere "caper," and it did not impede Nixon's landslide victory in November. Two *Washington Post* reporters, Robert Woodward and Carl Bernstein, continued to probe the case, however. They later revealed that an unidentified source they labeled "Deep Throat" told them early on that Mitchell and top White House aides John Ehrlichman and H. R. Haldeman were involved not only in the break-in but in a subsequent cover-up operation as well. In January 1973, Federal District Judge John Sirica convicted the four Cuban defendants, along with McCord and White House operatives Liddy and Hunt, and ominously suggested that Congress investigate further. In fact, McCord had revealed to Sirica details of the conspiracy, including large payoffs from White House sources to the Watergate defendants to buy their silence. In February, the Senate established the Select Committee on Presidential Campaign Activities, whose charge included investigation of the break-in. Democrat Sam Ervin of North Carolina was appointed chair, with Republican Minority Leader Howard Baker of Tennessee serving as vice chair.

The administration's denials of any involvement began to unravel in March, when White House Counsel John Dean III testified in court that Ehrlichman and Haldeman, and perhaps Nixon himself, had ordered a cover-up of the White House connection with the break-in. In late April, Nixon announced the resignations of Ehrlichman, Haldeman, and Dean, further fanning public suspicions. Within weeks, the president yielded to pressures for a neutral investigator to conduct a nonpolitical inquiry, permitting the Justice Department to appoint the Harvard law professor Archibald Cox as special prosecutor. Cox launched his investigation just as the Senate committee's hearing got under way in mid-May. The "Watergate hearings," televised over fifty-three days extending into November, attracted enormous public and media attention.

A major breakthrough in the Senate investigation occurred on 16 July 1973, when White House assistant Alexander Butterfield revealed the existence of a system for tape-recording conversation in the president's Oval Office. Both Cox and the Senate committee pressed Nixon to release tapes of several key conversations, but he refused, invoking "executive privilege." On 20 October 1973, Nixon ordered Attorney General Elliott Richardson to fire Cox. After Richardson and Deputy Attorney General William Ruckelshaus both refused the order and resigned, Solicitor General Robert Bork ousted Cox. This episode, dubbed the "Saturday Night Massacre," escalated the worsening crisis. In August and October, respectively, CREEP official Jeb

Magruder and John Dean had pleaded guilty to obstruction of justice and other charges. The resignation of Vice President Spiro Agnew on 10 October (after pleading no contest to tax evasion charges unrelated to Watergate) added to the sense of constitutional crisis. The Senate committee concluded its hearings in November (though its final report did not appear until mid-1974), but the drama continued in the courts.

Impeachment Hearings, Nixon's Resignation, and Aftereffects. Throughout early 1974, Nixon continued to resist subpoenas for the tapes. In March, a federal grand jury indicted seven more administration figures for conspiracy, obstruction of justice, perjury, and other charges. Those indicted included Mitchell, Ehrlichman, Haldeman, and White House Special Counsel Charles Colson, with the president named an "unindicted co-conspirator." Nixon agreed in late April to release edited transcripts, but his strategy backfired as even the sanitized transcripts increased public outrage. On 24 July 1974, the U.S. *Supreme Court ruled unanimously that Nixon must release the relevant tapes. The tapes revealed Nixon's intimate involvement in all phases of the cover-up and provided the "smoking gun" that investigators had been seeking. The Judiciary Committee of the House of Representatives had already commenced *impeachment hearings. After the panel voted positively on four articles, impeachment was inevitable and a Senate vote for the president's removal seemed likely. Facing defeat, Nixon resigned on 9 August 1974; he was succeeded by Gerald *Ford, Agnew's replacement as vice president. Ford's pardon in September saved the former president from prosecution but also contributed to Ford's defeat in the 1976 election.

Except for Nixon himself, nearly all the major figures implicated in the break-in and cover-up eventually served prison sentences. Mitchell, Ehrlichman, and Haldeman each served terms of eighteen months or more—among the longest of any of the conspirators. Most of the highest-profile figures in the case, however, later earned substantial royalties from books about their involvement and commanded large fees on the lecture circuit. Watergate-related legal skirmishes continued for more than two decades, as Nixon and the executors of his estate battled to prevent public release of all the White House tapes.

Conventional wisdom both at the time and later held that the outcome of Watergate proved that the "system works." Yet, had it not been for the persistence of Woodward and Bernstein, the determination of Judge Sirica, and the disclosure of the White House tapes, attempts to conceal official involvement in the break-in might have gone undetected. Historians continue to debate whether the episode was a bizarre aberration or a logical outgrowth of the massive expansion of presidential power and the official preoccupation with secrecy and "national security" in *Cold War America. The institutional impacts of the crisis—in addition to Nixon's resignation—were obvious and significant: The *War Powers Act (1973), the Federal Election Campaign Amendments (1974), the Ethics in Government Act (1978), and the Presidential Records Act (1978) all grew directly out of the unraveling of the Watergate conspiracy.

[*See also* Democratic Party; Federal Government, Executive Branch: The Presidency; Federal Government, Judicial Branch; Republican Party.]

• J. Anthony Lukas, *Nightmare: The Underside of the Nixon Years,* 1976. Bob Woodward and Carl Bernstein, *The Final Days,* 1976. Stanley Kutler, *The Wars of Watergate: The Last Crisis of Richard Nixon,* 1990. Michael Schudson, *Watergate in American Memory: How We Remember, Forget, and Reconstruct the Past,* 1992. Barry Sussman, *The Great Cover-Up: Nixon and the Scandal of Watergate,* 1992. Fred Emery, *Watergate: The Corruption and Fall of Richard Nixon,* 1994.

—Gary W. Reichard

WATSON, JAMES D. (1928–), molecular biologist. A native of *Chicago, Watson earned a B.S. degree in zoology from the University of Chicago (1947) and a Ph.D. from Indiana University (1950), at age twenty-two, before going to Copenhagen and Cambridge, England, on postdoctoral fellowships. He joined the Harvard University faculty in 1955 and remained there until 1976, when he became director of the Cold Spring Harbor Laboratory, a research and educational institution on Long Island, New York. From 1988 to 1992 he directed the National Center for Human Genome Research at the *National Institutes of Health. In 1994 he became president of the Cold Spring Harbor Laboratory, which he turned into what some called "DNA University."

Watson first rose to scientific prominence as the coauthor (with the Cambridge University scientist Francis Crick) of four papers in 1953–1954 that established the double helical structure of deoxyribonucleic acid (DNA), a megamolecule that is a key substance in the process of genetic replication. This work won Watson and Crick (along with Maurice Wilkins) the 1962 Nobel Prize in physiology or medicine. Beginning in the 1960s, Watson also won fame as a science writer, first for his textbook *Molecular Biology of the Gene* (1965), later for his best-selling autobiographical book *The Double Helix* (1968), which revealed the sometimes unseemly behind-the-scenes behavior of scientists involved in making (or missing) a great discovery. Watson used his post-1968 celebrity to become a leading voice in the management of American science. More than any other American scientist, Watson epitomized the revolution in twentieth-century science brought about the rise of molecular biology and its two applied offshoots, biotechnology and the *Human Genome Project.

[*See also* Biological Sciences; Biotechnology Industry; Genetics and Genetic Engineering; Science: 1914 to 1945; Science: Since 1945.]

• James D. Watson, "Growing Up in the Phage Group," in *Phage and the Origins of Molecular Biology,* ed. John Cairns, Gunther S. Stent, and James D. Watson, 1966, 141–7. James D. Watson, *The Double Helix: A Personal Account of the Discovery of the Structure of DNA,* 1968. James D. Watson with John Tooze, *The DNA Story,* 1981.

—Pnina G. Abir-Am

WATSON, THOMAS, SR. (1874–1956), business executive, head of the International Business Machines (IBM) Company. Watson was born and raised in rural upstate New York, near Corning. Educated as an accountant, he chose instead to become a traveling salesman, at first for a firm that sold pianos and eventually for the National Cash Register (NCR) Company, which he joined in 1895. He moved up quickly at NCR, and in 1907 its president, John Henry Patterson, named Watson the firm's sales manager.

When Patterson, fearful of creating a rival, fired him in 1913, Watson joined, as CEO, a New York State firm called the Computing-Tabulating-Recording Company (CTR), where he applied the salesmanship and management skills he had learned at NCR. Identifying the firm's tabulating machines as the key to future success, Watson promoted internal product research in that area. By 1919, CTR (which he renamed the International Business Machines Company in 1924) had emerged as the leading American firm in that field, an advantage the company consolidated over the next decade. IBM grew rapidly thanks to rising demand for business machines both from companies seeking to cut labor costs and from the federal government, which required ever more record-keeping equipment to implement New Deal measures and, later, military expansion. The creator of an unusually generous pay-and-benefits system at IBM, introduced during the 1930s, Watson also distinguished himself by becoming a leader in national and world business organizations.

[*See also* Automation and Computerization; Business; Computers; New Deal Era, The; Technology.]

• Thomas Graham Belden and Marva Robins Belden, *The Lengthening Shadow: The Life of Thomas J. Watson,* 1962. William Rodgers, *Think: A*

Biography of the Watsons and IBM, 1969. Thomas J. Watson Jr. and Peter Petre, *Father, Son and Co.: My Life at IBM and Beyond,* 1990.

—David L. Stebenne

WATTS RIOT. *See* Riots, Urban.

WEAPONRY, NONNUCLEAR. The history of English conquest in America began with five native bowmen ambushing a scouting party of prospective *Jamestown settlers, armed with matchlock muskets. Wounding two settlers before the scouting party could fire a single shot, the native warriors faded into the forest. This encounter symbolized the almost three-hundred-year war between Europeans and Amerindians.

Colonial Era through the Civil War. The first colonists arrived in America during the seventeenth-century European revival of the integrated system of heavy and light infantry and cavalry. But cavalry was useless in the forests, and the early militia manuals neglected the skirmish tactics of light infantry and instead emphasized line tactics with pike and musket. Matchlock muskets proved inferior, in a skirmish, to the Stone Age bows and arrows of native adversaries, and pikes were discarded in the absence of cavalry. With the introduction of flintlocks at the end of the seventeenth century, Native American fighters gave up bows and adopted the weapons of their European foes. The subsequent stages of the conquest of the Amerindian saw the introduction on both sides of rifled weapons, beginning with the adaptation of the Alpine hunting rifle as the "Pennsylvania" rifle.

In the *Revolutionary War, the Continental Army regulars fought as light infantry armed with flintlock muskets and bayonets in skirmishing and line encounters, while in the *South and on the western frontier, irregulars exploited the Pennsylvania rifle in stealth and skirmishing tactics. Though the *War of 1812 saw no appreciable change in land weapons, it did witness developments in naval weaponry. Adapting the classic strategy of weaker powers, the United States opted for a navy of commerce raiders rather than capital ships of the line to blockade or to break a blockade. The feats of American frigates such as the *Constitution*—larger, more heavily armed, and built with heavier timber than their counterparts—helped counterbalance the fact that by the end of the war Britain's ships of the line had bottled up in port most American warships and privateers. The first *submarine, invented by the American David Bushnell, saw action in the Revolutionary War.

By the mid-nineteenth century, advances in physics, chemistry, metallurgy, and ballistics were influencing the manufacture of weapons. Shortly after the Russians introduced land and water mines in the Crimean War (1853–1856), the Confederate army in the American *Civil War improved on them with a sensitive contact fuse for percussion-type mines. These mines could also serve as torpedoes, to be delivered by being secretly attached to hulls or by ramming at the end of a spar. The infantry of both armies in the Civil War for the first time used muzzle-loading rifled muskets, while cavalry with breech-loading carbines fought dismounted. New rifled artillery, though present, was not sufficiently developed to make a significant impact on Civil War battlefields, nor did the machine gun, invented by the American Richard Gatling in 1862, play any role.

Through the mid- and late-nineteenth century, the combined impact of the steam engine, the screw propeller, and metallurgical developments in iron and steel on both armament and armor revolutionized naval war. The American Robert Fulton built the first steam warship (1814) and the first screw-driven vessel of substantial size (1839). The first screw-propeller warship was the American *Princeton,* launched in 1843. Meanwhile, stronger hooped guns (built-up rifled artillery) gradually replaced cast-iron guns. Hooped guns designed and built by the American Robert Parrott saw action in the Civil War, which also witnessed the first battle between ironclads in the famous *Merrimac* and *Monitor* duel off Hampton Roads, Virginia, in 1861. Building on French and British precedents, the U.S. Navy's monitor class of ironclads, armed with advanced American-designed Dahlgren guns, figured prominently in the river and coastal conflicts of the Civil War. By the mid-1860s the era of iron was giving way to that of steel, as lighter and stronger steel plates became cheap enough to compete with iron in ship design.

Late Nineteenth Century through World War I. Naval and coastal gunnery, which had benefited from the development of the shell gun in the late eighteenth and early nineteenth centuries, improved even more with the rifled breech-loading steel gun and slow-burning powders, introduced between 1860 and 1885. Firing enormous shells with great velocity, range, and penetration, naval guns combined with increasingly thick steel armor to produce the modern heavily armored big-gun battleship, first represented by the British-built *Dreadnought* in 1906. The development of the "director" system of fire, involving electrical controls and mechanical computers, greatly improved accuracy. Meanwhile, beneath the sea, the Confederate submarine *Hunley* was the first to sink an enemy warship, delivering a spar topedo.

Turn-of-the-century American politicians, followed the lead of naval theorist Alfred Thayer *Mahan. Spurred on by the American destruction of two Spanish fleets in the *Spanish-American War, they moved toward a modern battleship navy supported by cruisers that could challenge for control of the sea. In 1900 the U.S. Navy acquired its first modern submarine, fitted with torpedo tubes and running submerged on electricity from storage batteries.

In *World War I, U.S. infantrymen fought with magazine rifles, light and heavy machine guns, mortars, grenades, and sometimes, flame throwers. They were supported by bombardment from modern artillery equipped with indirect ranging and firing devices, shooting shrapnel shells that exploded over entrenched defenders. Early in the war, assaulting infantry forces were often pinned down by artillery and machine gun fire; later, and increased complement of light machine guns, combined with tanks and *airplanes (a recent invention), restored the offensive. The widespread use of poison gas in the 1914–1918 conflict resulted in the founding of the U.S. Army's Chemical Warfare Service in 1917.

On the eve of World War I, Germany put gyroscopic compasses on its U-boat (submarine) fleet and introduced engine improvements that extended their range from 1,000 to 5,000 miles, making them deadly commerce raiders and a threat to the anchorage of the British fleet. The Allies' development of the convoy system, with destroyer escorts using new hydrophones for detection and newly invented depth charges, restored the balance of power and avoided disaster.

World War II. During *World War II, aircraft carriers and landing aircraft dominated American fighting in the Pacific. Marines and infantry went ashore in landing craft, supported by the guns and rockets of surface vessels and land- and carrier-based aircraft. Meanwhile, the submarine fleet devastated enemy shipping, while Army Air Force bombers destroyed Japan's cities. In the Pacific as in Europe, Americans fought with greatly improved airplanes, bombs, automatic guns, tanks, surface ships, submarines, torpedoes, rockets, and mines. All sides developed chemical and biological weapons, but except for Japanese experimentation against the Chinese army and civilians, refrained from using them. The largest U.S. weapons development program during the war after the *Manhattan Project that created the atomic bomb was the 4,000-person program to develop biological weapons.

World War II saw the development of motorized and armored divisions combining infantry, artillery, tanks, and air support. It also witnessed the introduction of radar and electronic *computers, allowing for the precise detection of submarines and antiaircraft batteries, as well as the development of fire-control systems. Toward the end of the war, electronic bombsights, which could aim through clouds, gave American bombers some precision-bombing capability. The proximity fuse, a small radar set that detonated a shell in proximity to its target, eliminated the necessity of computing the time of flight and presetting the fuse. Invented by the British and developed by the Americans, this fuse proved to be a devastating antiaircraft weapon. World War II also saw the debut of an old invention, the rocket, as an effective weapon. The American invention of napalm, a jellied incendiary, provided the means for firebombing enemy cities and for designing an improved flame thrower, which American troops used extensively in the Pacific.

Korean War through the Persian Gulf War. Postwar weapons development concentrated on improving World War II systems. The *Korean War (1950–1953) was fought largely with World War II–type weapons and systems, the major innovation being the widespread use of jet aircraft. Later in the 1950s, aircraft, warships, armored vehicles, guns, and rockets all benefited from improvements in propulsion, radar, and computers. Bacteriological and chemical weapons development flourished along with *nuclear weapons. During the Korean War period, the United States included biological warfare in its emergency plan for general war against the Soviet Union and China, thus becoming the first nation to incorporate biological weapons in offensive military doctrine. There is evidence that U.S. forces experimented with these weapons during the Korean War.

The U.S. phase of the protracted *Vietnam War (1961–1975) combined existing weapons systems with the maturation of the helicopter. Armed with heavy machine guns and rockets and carrying a dozen or so soldiers, helicopters were used in a search-and-destroy strategy against elusive enemy units. Their weakness was their vulnerability to antiaircraft fire. The major technical innovation in the Vietnam conflict was the guided bomb. Developed in the 1960s, the "smart bomb" used a sensor to lock onto an image or respond to reflected laser-beam radiation. The United States also used "Agent Orange," to defoliate and uncover enemy supply routes.

By the early 1970s the growing use of nuclear-powered engines was revolutionizing conventional as well as nuclear naval warfare. The threat of the attack submarine as a weapon against surface ships was increased by its ability to stay submerged and undetected while traveling at high speeds for long periods of time. Nuclear-powered surface ships could spend almost unlimited time away from base.

In the *Persian Gulf War of 1990–1991, the United States introduced the Stealth bomber, which did not reflect radar signals, and a missile that honed in on enemy radar. The power of the Iraqi army's ground weapons system matched that of the United States, but a combination of the U.S.-led coalition's superiority in air power, antiradar missiles, and electronic technology proved decisive. The Gulf War (like the Egyptian-Israeli War of 1973) emphasized the importance of weighing up offensively and defensively with state-of-the-art technology in a modern conventional war, just as Vietnam displayed the limitations of modern weapons systems against guerrilla warfare fought from a pre-modern logistical base—a lesson that brought the American way of war full circle from its conquest of the native peoples, though with a different outcome.

[See also Chemical Industry; Federal Government, Executive Branch: Department of Defense; Indian Wars; Iron and Steel Industry; Military, The; Pharmaceutical Industry; Steam Power.]

• Bernard and Fawn Brodie, *From Crossbow to H-Bomb,* rev. ed., 1973. Merritt Roe Smith, ed., *Military Enterprise and Technological Change: Perspectives on the American Experience,* 1985. Archer Jones, *The Art of War in the Western World,* 1987. Edward Hagerman, *The American Civil War and the Origins of Modern Warfare,* 1988. Paddy Griffith, *Battle Tactics of the Civil War,* 1989. Perry D. Jamieson, *Crossing the Deadly Ground: U.S. Army Tactics, 1865–1899,* 1994. Robert A. Doughty, et al., *American Military History and the Evolution of Warfare in the Western World,* 1996. Archer Jones, *Elements of Military Strategy,* 1996. Stephen Endicott and Edward Hagerman, *The United States and Biological Warfare: Secrets from the Early Cold War and Korea,* 1998.

—Edward Hagerman

WEBSTER, DANIEL (1782–1852), lawyer, politician, orator, secretary of state. Born in Salisbury, New Hampshire, Webster graduated from Dartmouth College (1801), entered the bar in 1805, and practiced law in Portsmouth, New Hampshire. Gaining national recognition for his argument before the U.S. *Supreme Court in *Dartmouth College* v. *Woodward* (1818), he eventually argued more than 170 cases before the high court, including such landmarks as **Gibbons* v. *Ogden* (1824). He helped determine the nation's constitutional and economic direction by upholding property rights and the federal government's authority over interstate commerce.

A celebrated public speaker, he established the tradition of commemorative oratory in the United States. Active in the *Federalist and later the *Whig party, Webster served in Congress as a representative from New Hampshire (1813–1817) and Massachusetts (1823–1827) and then as senator from Massachusetts (1827–1841, 1845–1850). A conservative, he spoke for his *business constituents. Like *New England's merchants and shippers, he initially supported low *tariffs and opposed the *Embargo Act and the *War of 1812 for disrupting trade. By the 1820s, however, as mills and factories arose in the region, he advocated high protective tariffs. In 1830 he engaged in a notable series of debates with the South Carolina senator Robert Y. Hayne, who, in opposition to the high tariff of 1828, championed *states' rights and *nullification. On the contrary, said Webster, the *Constitution had created a perpetual union of one people: "Liberty *and* union, now and forever, one and inseparable!" In 1850, however, he outraged abolitionists by endorsing the *Fugitive Slave Act as part of a sectional compromise.

Webster served two noteworthy terms as secretary of state (1841–1843 and 1850–1852). In 1842 he negotiated the *Webster-Ashburton Treaty, which improved relations with Great Britain. He fashioned U.S. policy toward Asia by formulating a statement of America's position toward *Hawai'i (1842), inaugurating the first diplomatic mission to China (1843), and initiating Matthew C. Perry's 1851–1852 voyage to Japan.

[*See also* Antislavery; Compromise of 1850; *Dartmouth College* Case; Factory System; Federal Government, Executive Branch: Department of State; Federal Government, Legislative Branch: Senate; Foreign Relations; Perry, Matthew and Oliver Hazard.]

• Maurice G. Baxter, *One and Inseparable: Daniel Webster and the Union,* 1984. Kenneth E. Shewmaker, ed., *Daniel Webster: "The Completest Man,"* 1990.

—Kenneth E. Shewmaker

WEBSTER, NOAH (1758–1843), lexicographer, journalist, educator. Born in West Hartford, Connecticut, Webster grew up on a small *New England farm. His father made great sacrifices to send Noah to Yale, from which he graduated in 1778. Failing to establish himself as a teacher or lawyer, Webster turned to writing. From 1783 to his death, he produced school books, political essays, scientific research, and dictionaries.

Webster's reputation as "the schoolmaster of America" rests primarily on his *Spelling Book* (1783), which enjoyed huge sales. He also produced a grammar and a reader that were sold as a set with the speller. Between 1785 and 1806, Webster wrote incessantly—on politics, language, and *science, and also edited two influential periodicals, the *American Magazine* and the *Minerva,* which provided further outlets for his decidedly Federalist political opinions. His *conservatism was particularly apparent in his essay *The Revolution in France* (1794).

After 1806, when Webster published his *Compendious Dictionary of the English Language,* he focused his energies on language theory and dictionaries. His much expanded *Ameri-*

can Dictionary of the English Language (1828) made the words "Webster" and "dictionary" virtually synonymous.

Webster's impact on American thought and culture was broad and long-lasting. Once considered primarily a literary nationalist intent on limiting the influence of English books on Americans, he is better understood as a conservative force and partisan of New England habits and values. Increasingly alarmed by the growth of democracy and the decline of deference to the Federalist elite, Webster sought to use language to defend the virtues of a Calvinist, rural New England that was in nearly full retreat as America became more heterogeneous and cosmopolitan.

[*See also* Antebellum Era; Early Republic, Era of the; Education: The Public School Movement; Federalist Party; Language, American; Nationalism; Whig Party.]

• Richard M. Rollins, *The Long Journey of Noah Webster,* 1980. Richard J. Moss, *Noah Webster,* 1984.

—Richard J. Moss

WEBSTER-ASHBURTON TREATY (1842). This treaty settled many long-standing issues between the United States and England that by 1842 had become acute. These included U.S.-Canadian boundary disputes; the 1837 burning by Canadians of a U.S. steamship, the *Caroline,* in the Niagara River, with the death of a crewman; the 1840 arrest in New York State of a Canadian, Alexander McLeod, accused of involvement in the *Caroline* affair; and the refusal of British authorities to return to the United States the African-American slaves who in 1841 had seized and diverted to the Bahamas a U.S. brig, the *Creole,* transporting them from Virginia to *New Orleans.

To resolve these issues, the British government appointed Lord Ashburton (Alexander Baring) to meet Secretary of State Daniel *Webster in Washington. The resulting treaty, concluded in August 1842, resolved the boundary disputes, incorporated an extradition agreement, and provided for joint U.S.-British squadrons to halt the African slave trade. Other issues, including the McLeod and *Creole* matters, were resolved by an exchange of notes included in the treaty package. To facilitate the final boundary settlement between Maine and New Brunswick, President John *Tyler authorized Webster to draw from the president's Secret Service fund. In 1846, when Webster stood accused of wrongdoing related to the negotiations, Tyler defended his secretary of state's actions before a congressional committee, helping to exonerate him.

The Webster-Ashburton Treaty granted the United States nearly 60 percent of the disputed area in the Northeast, including a strategic military location at the top of Lake Champlain, along with a region west of Lake Superior, Minnesota's Mesabi Range, that later proved rich in iron ore. It also allowed Americans to turn westward and encouraged what proved to be an enduring Anglo-American rapprochement.

[*See also* Antebellum Era; Expansionism; Foreign Relations: U.S. Relations with Europe; Foreign Relations: U.S. Relations with Canada; Slavery: The Slave Trade.]

• Howard Jones, *To the Webster-Ashburton Treaty: A Study in Anglo-American Relations, 1783–1843,* 1977. Howard Jones and Donald A. Rakestraw, *Prologue to Manifest Destiny: Anglo-American Relations in the 1840s,* 1997.

—Howard Jones

WELCH, WILLIAM H. (1850–1934), pathologist, bacteriologist, first dean of the Johns Hopkins University Medical School. Welch was born in Norfolk, Connecticut, to William Wickham Welch, a physician, and Emiline Collin. He graduated from Yale College in 1870. Failing to secure a teaching position in classics, he turned to medicine, receiving his M.D. degree in 1875 from the College of Physicians and Surgeons in *New York City (now part of Columbia University). He studied experimental pathology in Europe for a year before returning to establish America's first pathology teaching laboratory, at Bellevue Hospital Medical College, in 1878. In 1884 he became chairman of the Department of Pathology at the Johns Hopkins University in Baltimore, the first American university to make scientific research central to its curriculum. As first dean of its school of medicine, which opened in 1893, he made the scientific laboratory essential to the training of physicians and helped create a medical school widely regarded as a model. Among the first Americans to introduce bacteriology into medicine, he identified *Clostridium perfringens,* the bacillus of gas gangrene, in 1892, and used the success of bacteriology to promote laboratory research nationwide. Welch founded the *Journal of Experimental Medicine* (1895); the Johns Hopkins School of Public Health (1918); and the Institute for the History of Medicine, which he headed after his retirement in 1925.

A man of diplomacy and charisma, Welch became the premier national spokesman for scientific medicine. He presided over numerous medical and scientific societies, including the *American Medical Association (1910–1911) and the *National Academy of Sciences (1913–1916). He influenced the funding of scientific research by serving on the boards of various philanthropic organizations, including several financed by the Rockefeller and Carnegie foundations.

[*See also* Biological Sciences; Medical Education; Medicine: From the 1870s to 1945; Philanthropy and Philanthropic Foundations; Public Health.]

• Simon Flexner and James Thomas Flexner, *William Henry Welch and the Heroic Age of American Medicine,* 1941; reprint 1993. Donald H. Fleming, *William H. Welch and the Rise of Modern Medicine,* 1954.

—Patricia Peck Gossel

WELFARE, FEDERAL. The term "welfare" has been radically transformed in the last half century, narrowing from its original generic meaning to refer mainly to one disadvantaged program, Aid to Families with Dependent Children (AFDC).

Colonial and Antebellum Eras. Early American poor relief was guided by two principles that would long continue to shape the U.S. welfare system. One emphasized distinguishing the "deserving" from the "undeserving" poor, providing relief only to the former, and keeping relief penurious enough that it would discourage laziness and immorality. These moral distinctions heightened discrimination against women, especially since women's sexual activity outside marriage, and lone motherhood in general, were morally suspect. A second principle insisted that public assistance provide less than the lowest local wages. Poor-law authorities believed that aid should not interfere with employers' access to labor; the effect was that relief often drove down wages by pressuring workers to accept what they were offered.

In the North American colonies, local governments provided both "indoor" (institutional) and "outdoor" (in-home) assistance. Kin were expected to care for relatives; those among the needy who lacked helpful kin and could not care for themselves were often placed in the households of unrelated women who, for a small stipend, provided caretaking services. The Tenth Amendment to the U.S. *Constitution upheld state and local responsibility for the public welfare, a provision that would later create legal and ideological obstacles to the development of a national welfare state.

In the nineteenth century *industrialization, *urbanization and *immigration worsened some aspects of *poverty and made it more visible. As town and counties proved unable to provide for the needy, states introduced welfare budgets. As early as the 1820s, states established institutions for "dependent" children (i.e., those whose parents could not support them), the deaf, blind, insane, and retarded. "Private" charities multiplied, although many were actually quasi-public, receiving substantial government grants. The stigma of relief intensified, fueled and rationalized by the Horatio-Alger mythology that hard work would assure success and that poverty was in itself a sign of defective character. These attitudes stimulated institutionalizing the needy in poorhouses where their characters could be reformed.

Civil War through the 1920s. Despite the Tenth Amendment, two federal welfare programs arose in the mid-nineteenth century. The *Freedmen's Bureau after the *Civil War provided help for former slaves, but with the defeat of *Reconstruction its work ended. Civil War *pensions for Union veterans, by contrast, became the most massive federal program before the New Deal; by the 1890s 40 percent of the federal budget went to veterans or their dependents. Recipients were not screened for need or morality. Political patronage shaped the administration of the pensions, however, leading many reformers to conclude that all government provision would necessarily be corrupt.

By the 1890s the problems of poverty and the horrors of under-funded asylums had become so visible that a renewed campaign for public "outdoor" aid developed. Its first victory was won by organized women who designed state aid programs for lone mothers, primarily widows, these Mothers' Aid laws passed in forty-one states between 1911 and 1920. These reformers' objectives were to prevent children from being separated from their mothers, to stop *child labor, and to demonstrate that public aid could be administered efficiently and cleanly. The reformers tried to free recipients from the stigma of poor relief by helping only the "deserving," screening applicants for their moral and domestic rectitude, and the program also discriminated against immigrants, minorities, and lone mothers other than widows. At the same time a group of male reformers launched workmen's compensation laws in twenty-one states between 1911 and 1913, providing benefits to workers injured on the job.

*Progressive-Era women reformers then created the first federal welfare programs beyond veterans' pensions. In 1912, even before women could vote, they succeeded in establishing the Children's Bureau in the Department of Labor, which collected social welfare data and provided a governmental base for a welfare state; another part of this reform network established the Women's Bureau in 1919. After ratification of the woman suffrage amendment in 1920, the women's welfare coalition pushed the Sheppard-Towner Act through Congress (1921), providing *public health nursing to poor mothers and children in rural areas; although repealed seven years later in response to a campaign by the *American Medical Association, Sheppard-Towner reduced infant mortality considerably in those few years.

The New Deal Era to the End of the Twentieth Century. Resistance to a federal welfare role continued until the Depression of the 1930s. With one-third of the nation in poverty, the conservative, corporate, labor-union and states'-rights opposition to public welfare were temporarily weakened, enabling President Franklin Delano *Roosevelt to lay the foundations of a national welfare system. The most dramatic New Deal initiatives provided emergency aid and public jobs through programs such as the *Works Progress Administration, the *Civilian Conservation Corps, and the Federal Emergency Relief Administration. Although these programs discriminated against women and minorities, they relieved suffering among millions and were extremely popular. Roosevelt was nevertheless reluctant to accept an enduring federal role in welfare until the Depression continued to worsen and social movements demanding welfare provision continued to grow.

Roosevelt's response was the *Social Security Act of 1935. Its centerpiece was two social-insurance programs—old-age insurance and *unemployment compensation—designed to prevent (not ameliorate) poverty by compensating unemployed men for lost wages, thus also providing for their dependents. The designers of these programs sought to avoid the stigma of poor relief by creating universal programs, not means-tested or morals-tested; by funding them through special taxes rather than general revenue; and by a public-relations campaign to convince Americans that these programs offered "earned" benefits, not relief. Old-age pensions thus became an honored and beloved program. Deriving *Social Security's entitlements from employment, however, reinforced women's status as "dependents" by offering them pensions only as wives and daughters, devaluing women's unpaid labor and disadvantaging women and children without male breadwinners. Congressional amendments to Social Security further excluded so many minorities and white women that it did not cover a majority of Americans for several decades. Several other parts of the New Deal welfare agenda, such as medical insurance and public jobs, failed to materialize.

Female welfare advocates tried to compensate for one aspect of Social Security's limitations by adding federal money to existing state mothers'-aid programs. They envisioned this program, Aid to Dependent Children (ADC), as small and temporary because they believed that single motherhood would decline as an expanding welfare state reduced poverty. In contrast to the social-insurance programs, ADC (called AFDC after 1950) was means-tested and morals-tested; its benefits were below the lowest prevailing minimum wages; it was funded primarily by the states through property and sales taxes; and it was not an entitlement but a public charity.

Ultimately, the New Deal could end neither the Depression—only the massive public spending engendered by *World War II did that—nor poverty. In the early 1960s, largely as a result of a renewed *civil rights movement, influential whites "rediscovered" poverty in the United States and stimulated the War on Poverty. Food stamps were created in 1964. Federal funds supported community action programs and services for the poor including legal aid, Head Start preschool education, medical clinics, and birth control. *Medicare was added for those receiving Social Security pensions and Medicaid for those receiving public assistance. Supplemental Security Income (SSI) expanded benefits to the needy aged, blind, and disabled, and their survivors.

Meanwhile, in the late 1950s many poor mothers previously excluded from AFDC, notably women of color and never-married women, began successfully to demand inclusion. The increase in the "welfare" rolls did not at first indicate an increase in poverty, but a growing civil rights consciousness. AFDC served many women as a route to upward mobility for themselves or, more often, their children. In the 1960s welfare-rights campaigns yielded several *Supreme Court decisions that guaranteed due process rights to recipients. But public assistance benefit levels declined, in contrast to those of old-age pensions, which rose along with inflation. Similarly, as Social Security old-age pensions grew ever more respected and its recipients more politically powerful, AFDC became more stigmatized and its recipients increasingly politically powerless. By the 1970s the term "welfare" had become pejorative and was applied exclusively to AFDC (and sometimes to general relief).

The fact that AFDC benefits were never high enough to bring poor families out of poverty served, along with de-industrialization and rising unemployment, to trap many in the welfare system. This in turn stimulated anti-welfare sentiment. In the 1970s and 1980s, attempts to cut back welfare by requiring mothers' employment foundered, largely because poor mothers usually could not support children on the low wages and absence of benefits in the jobs they could get.

A conservative anti-welfare campaign reached victory in 1996 with the repeal of AFDC. In its place was put Temporary Assistance to Needy Families (TANF), a system of block grants to the states without any guarantee of aid to poor children and their needy parents.

[*See also* Alms Houses; Birth Control and Family Planning; Depressions, Economic; Mental Health Institutions; New Deal Era, The; Orphanages; Social Darwinism; Woman Suffrage Movement.]

• Michael B. Katz, *In the Shadow of the Poorhouse: A Social History of Welfare in America,* 1986. Margaret Weir, Ann Shola Orloff, and Theda Skocpol, eds., *The Politics of Social Policy in the United States,* 1988. Michael B. Katz, *The Undeserving Poor: From the War on Poverty to the War on Welfare,* 1989. Linda Gordon, ed., *Women, the State and Welfare,* 1990. Alan Dawley, *Struggles for Justice: Social Responsibility and the Liberal State,* 1991. Edward D. Berkowitz and Kim McQuaid, *Creating the Welfare State: The Political Economy of 20th-century Reform,* rev. ed., 1992. Theda Skocpol, *Protecting Soldiers and Mothers: The Political Origins of Social Policy in the United States,* 1993. Linda Gordon, *Pitied but Not Entitled: Single Mothers and the History of Welfare,* 1994. James T. Patterson, *America's Struggle against Poverty 1900–1994,* rev. ed., 1994. Gwendolyn Mink, *The Wages of Motherhood: Inequality in the Welfare State, 1917–1942,* 1995.

—Linda Gordon

WELLS-BARNETT, IDA B. (1862–1931), African-American journalist and activist. Born in Holly Springs, Mississippi, and educated in a local freedmen's school, Ida Wells moved to Memphis, Tennessee, in 1884. Her activist career began in 1883, when she refused to leave a first-class car on the Chesapeake, Southwestern and Ohio Railway. Her account of her lawsuit against the railway led to a journalistic career and co-ownership of The *Memphis Free Speech,* a black newspaper. Her editorials against three Memphis *lynchings in 1892 launched her lifelong antilynching campaign. When a mob destroyed the *Free Speech* offices soon after the editorials ran, she shifted her campaign to *New York City. In 1893–1894 she toured Great Britain, where such dignitaries as the archbishop of Canterbury publicized her cause. In such works as *The Red Record* (1895), Wells unmasked the racial and *gender stereotypes underlying the rape-lynch syndrome.

Marrying the *Chicago lawyer and newspaper publisher Ferdinand L. Barnett in 1895, Wells continued her activism while rearing four children. Her antilynching crusade inspired the formation of the National Association of Colored Women (1896), the first secular national black women's organization. One of two black women to sign the call for the formation of the *National Association for the Advancement of Colored People (1909), she also founded the Negro Fellowship League (1910), a *settlement house, and the Alpha Suffrage Club (1913). She led local black and interracial women's organizations; worked with the African-American leaders William Monroe *Trotter and Marcus *Garvey; and organized support for victims of racial violence in Chicago and elsewhere. In 1930 she ran unsuccessfully for the Illinois State Senate.

[*See also* African Americans; Civil Rights; Civil Rights Movement; Racism; Segregation, Racial; Woman Suffrage Movement.]

• Alfreda M. Duster, ed., *Crusade for Justice: The Autobiography of Ida B. Wells,* 1970. Henry Louis Gates Jr., ed., *Selected Works of Ida B. Wells-Barnett,* comp. and with an introduction by Trudier Harris, 1991.

—Paula Giddings

WEST, THE. The American West is both a place and a state of mind, and the two are not easily disentangled, since no agreement exists about either its geographic boundaries or its cultural meaning. Perhaps no region of the United States has inspired so many novels, *films, *television programs, and *advertising images. Even the modern built environment is often tailored to fit popular stereotypes of the West as it "ought to be," to evoke dramatic nineteenth-century events rather than the more prosaic present, or to attract tourist dollars—a major source of income in many western states. Despite a prevailing association of the West with rugged *individualism, the region has long depended on the federal government for public-land management, *railroad subsidies, *hydroelectric power projects, and billions in *Cold War defense appropriations.

Geographically, the West begins at the *Mississippi River—or perhaps at the ninety-eighth meridian, which bisects Oklahoma, Kansas, and the Dakotas and marks the point at which the average annual rainfall drops below twenty inches, the minimum necessary to sustain crop *agriculture. It ends at the Pacific coast—or perhaps it also encompasses *Alaska and *Hawai'i. Along with *California and the noncontinguous Alaska and Hawai'i, the land west of the ninety-eighth meridian includes the Pacific Northwest (Oregon, Washington, Idaho); the *Rocky Mountains (Montana, Wyoming, Colorado); the Great Basin (Nevada, Utah); the *Southwest (Arizona, New Mexico, Texas, Oklahoma); and the Great Plains (North and South Dakota, Nebraska, Kansas). Encompassing nearly 2.5 million square miles, this region in 1990 was home to some eighty million people, about a third of the total U.S. population.

A common attribute of much of the West is its aridity, and it is the arid West that figures most prominently in fictional descriptions. The sagebrush and imposing mesas and buttes of the Great Basin and the giant saguaro cacti of the Sonoran Desert define the West of countless Hollywood films and the novels of Zane Grey, Louis L'Amour, and others. Most arid of all is California's bone-dry Death Valley. Other parts of the West are wet and even lush, however. These include—in addition to Alaska and Hawai'i—Northern California, the western slopes of Oregon and Washington, and various high mountain ranges. Parts of Washington's soggy Olympia Peninsula sometimes receive in excess of 180 inches of rain annually.

Nor does uniform population density characterize the West. To be sure, the region includes sparsely populated Wyoming and Montana, which conform to popular frontier stereotypes, and some western counties still tally fewer than two persons per square mile. But the West also includes California and Texas, the nation's two most populous states, and some of America's largest cities, including *Los Angeles, *San Francisco, Portland, Seattle, Phoenix, Las Vegas, Salt Lake City, Denver, Dallas, and Houston.

Certainly this is a region of scenic beauty, including Oregon's Mount Hood; Washington's Mount Rainier and Puget Sound; and the stark beauty of New Mexico, a mecca for artists. Here is the world's oldest national park, *Yellowstone (mostly in Wyoming), as well as the *Grand Canyon (Arizona), *Yosemite (California), and Glacier (Montana).

Historically, the West has been a crossroads of cultures. Numerous Native American nations were already in place when Spanish explorers and settlers arrived from Mexico. From the east came peoples from the empires of England and France and, after the 1780s, from the new United States. From Asia arrived Chinese and later Japanese, eventually followed by Filipinos, Koreans, and Vietnamese. *African Americans came as *cowboys and soldiers in the nineteenth century and as urban-industrial workers in the twentieth. Heavy and sustained *immigration from Mexico and Central America made *Hispanic Americans a substantial component of the population in many parts of the West by the late twentieth century. The encounters of ethnic and racial groups were not always harmonious, as *Indian wars, racial violence, and Euro-American hostility to Hispanics and Asians attest. But ethnic diversity has unquestionably shaped the region's distinctive social and cultural flavor.

The West and its peoples have frequently been transformed into commodities in films and as names of trucks, automobiles, and other products. The cigarette industry's "Marlboro Man" is a hard-bitten Western cowboy. Commodities of a more traditional sort—grain, fruit, lumber, minerals, livestock, dairy products, fisheries, and wine—formed the backbone of the western economy for two centuries and remain important. The twentieth century brought a multibillion-dollar film and entertainment industry in Southern California; giant aircraft and aerospace industries in California, Washington, and Texas; a *gambling empire in Nevada; oil and natural-gas production in Oklahoma and Texas; and the electronics and computer giants of California's Silicon Valley as well as Washington, Colorado, and Texas. Higher education, including major research universities and networks of community colleges, characterizes the twentieth-century West as well. Indeed, it is perhaps no single characteristic, but rather its startling divergences and juxtapositions—geographic, demographic, cultural, and economic—that best define the modern West.

[*See also* Agriculture; Airplanes and Air Transport; Asian Americans; Computers; Gold Rushes; Incarceration of Japanese Americans; Indian History and Culture; Literature, Popular; Lumbering; Mining; Petroleum Industry; Spanish Settlements in North America; Tourism.]

• Henry Nash Smith, *Virgin Land: The American West as Symbol and Myth,* 1940. Michael P. Malone and Richard W. Etulain, *The American West: A Twentieth-Century History,* 1989. Richard White, *"It's Your Misfortune and None of My Own": A New History of the American West,* 1991. Clyde A. Milner II, Carol A. O'Connor, and Martha A. Sandweiss, eds., *The Oxford History of the American West,* 1994. William E. Riebsame, ed., *Atlas of the New West: Portrait of a Changing Region,* 1997. Howard R. Lamar, ed., *The New Encyclopedia of the American West,* 1998.

—Carlos Arnaldo Schwantes

WEST COAST HOTEL COMPANY* v. *PARRISH (1937), *Supreme Court case reversing a series of anti–New Deal decisions and upholding the constitutionality of legislation regulating the economy. The case involved a 1913 Washington State statute establishing a minimum wage of $14.50 for a forty-eight-hour week. A chambermaid, Elsie Parrish, who had been paid $12 weekly by the West Coast Hotel in Seattle, Washington, sued her employer for the difference. The case was argued before the Supreme Court in December 1936. Parrish's attorneys asked the Court to overrule precedents, such as **Adkins* v. *Children's Hospital* (1923), that had held minimum-wage laws unconstitutional. In his 5–4 majority opinion, Chief Justice Charles Evans *Hughes dismissed the notion of freedom of contract, holding that under their constitutional police powers, states had the authority to regulate wages and hours in the public interest. Despite a spirited dissent by Justice George Sutherland on behalf of the conservative justices, a thirty-year era of conservative, antireform judicial activism—going back to **Lochner* v. *New York* (1905), which struck down a New York law regulating the maximum hours of bakery workers—had come to an end. Not for many decades would the Supreme Court again overturn either a federal or a state law regulating the economy.

The *West Coast Hotel* decision has sometimes been seen as the Court's efforts to forestall President Franklin Delano *Roosevelt's 1937 "court packing" plan. The chronology of the case, however, makes clear that although the decision was not announced until late March 1937, after FDR had publicized his scheme, the justices' vote on the case antedated Roosevelt's announcement.

[*See also* Economic Regulation; Laissez-faire; *Muller* v. *Oregon*; New Deal Era, The.]

• Charles A. Leonard, *A Search for a Judicial Philosophy: Mr. Justice Roberts and the Constitutional Revolution of 1937,* 1971. Judith Bauer, *The Chains of Protection: The Judicial Response to Women's Labor Legislation,* 1978.

—Melvin I. Urofsky

WESTINGHOUSE, GEORGE (1846–1914), inventor, industrialist. Born in Central Bridge, New York, Westinghouse worked as an apprentice in his father's machine shop. During the *Civil War, he served as an engineering officer in the U.S. Navy. After the war, Westinghouse devoted himself to invention, and in 1869 he patented the railroad air brake. Until then, brakemen stopped trains by manually applying brakes in each car. Westinghouse perfected a compressed air system; by operating a valve in the locomotive, the engineer could now brake all cars simultaneously. To manufacture and market this invention, Westinghouse moved to Pittsburgh where, over the next four decades, he became a major industrialist, establishing sixty firms that produced railway signals and heavy machinery.

Westinghouse entered the electrical field in 1884. Because the *electrical industry was dominated by Thomas *Edison's direct-current (DC) system, Westinghouse focused on alternating current (AC). Employing a transformer designed by William Stanley and a motor invented by the Croatian immigrant Nikola Tesla (1856–1943), the Westinghouse system enabled utilities to serve more customers over a wider area and hence lowered the cost of electricity. Threatened by AC, the Edison company attacked Westinghouse's system, claiming that high-voltage AC would electrocute people. Insisting that AC was safe, Westinghouse used it at the 1893 Chicago World's Fair to power 100,000 electric lights. AC ultimately prevailed when Westinghouse engineers employed it to transmit power from *Niagara Falls in 1896. Thanks to Westinghouse's vision, America enjoyed the benefits of low-cost electric power and he grew wealthy as the founder of one of the nation's great industrial corporations.

[*See also* Electricity and Electrification; Illumination; Industrialization; Railroads; World's Fairs and Expositions.]

• Henry G. Leupp, *A Life of George Westinghouse,* 1922; Thomas P. Hughes, *Networks of Power: Electrification in Western Society, 1880–1930,* 1982.

—W. Bernard Carlson

WEST POINT. *See* Military, The.

WHARTON, EDITH (1862–1937), novelist, feminist. Born in *New York City to socially prominent parents who expected her only to marry and entertain, Edith even as a child announced her determination to write. She married the banker Edward Wharton in 1885. They lived in Manhattan and traveled widely, but Wharton chafed at this "comfortable" life: Men could use their intelligence, pursue careers, even create art; women were confined to the domestic realm and, even worse, stifled by sexual ignorance and the notion that no "decent" woman could enjoy sex.

Longing for escape, Wharton resumed writing and studied decorative arts and landscape architecture. *The Decoration of Houses,* coauthored with the architect Ogden Codman, appeared in 1897. Persevering despite a disabling emotional crisis in 1898, she designed and built The Mount, an estate in Lenox, Massachusetts, in 1901–1902. *The House of Mirth,* a brilliant novel examining contemporary New York society, appeared in 1905.

Settling in Paris, Wharton found a friend and mentor in Henry *James and in 1908 had a brief but intense relationship with the American journalist Morton Fullerton. She divorced her husband in 1913. These years brought a dazzling series of novels: *Ethan Frome* (1911), a stark tale of thwarted love in backwoods New England; *The Reef* (1912); and *The Custom of the Country* (1913). Marshaling her considerable organizational skills during *World War I, Wharton raised and disbursed money as head of a vast relief agency and wrote journalistic accounts of the conflict, urging America to join the Allied cause. France awarded her the Legion of Honor in 1916. Her novel *Summer* (1917) was followed in 1920 by the *Pulitzer Prize–winning *Age of Innocence,* a somewhat elegiac story of New York society in the 1870s. Never explicitly autobiographical, her work nonetheless drew powerfully upon her own stifling upbringing and unhappy marriage to a chronically unfaithful husband in portraying society's mutilation of women's lives. Moving to Pavillon Colombe, an eighteenth-century estate outside Paris, she continued to write until her death, exploring taboo sexual themes in some late, unpublished work.

[*See also* Feminism; Gilded Age; Literature: Civil War to World War I; Sexual Morality and Sex Reform.]

• R. W. B. Lewis, *Edith Wharton: A Biography,* 1975. Cynthia Griffin Wolff, *A Feast of Words: The Triumph of Edith Wharton,* 1995.

—Cynthia Griffin Wolff

WHEATLEY, PHILLIS (ca. 1753–1784), African-American poet. Born in West Africa, Wheatley as a child of about eight was kidnapped and brought to *Boston, where she was purchased by John Wheatley, a prosperous tailor, to be a servant for his wife, Susanna. In the pious household she was given the name Phillis and tutored in both English and Latin as well as the *Bible. Admiring the English poets John Milton and Thomas Gray, Alexander Pope's translation of Homer, and the Latin poets Virgil and Ovid, she began to write verse very early; her first poem appeared in a newspaper in 1767. In the early 1770s, having published several of her poems as broadsides that were widely reprinted, she became something of a local celebrity. In 1773 she traveled to London to seek support of her poetry, and while there she met many notables, including Benjamin *Franklin. Her forty *Poems on Various Subjects, Religious and Moral* (1773) was published there, accompanied by an engraved portrait of the poet, the first book published by an African American. Returning to America to care for Susanna Wheatley, she was manumitted. In 1778, following the deaths of both Wheatleys, she married John Peters, an impoverished freedman, by whom she had three children, none of whom survived her. In 1779 she sought unsuccessfully to publish a volume of thirty-three poems and thirteen letters. She died when she was said to be thirty-one and was buried in an unmarked grave.

Her mostly impersonal, deeply religious poetry is marked by neoclassicism, a style in which she felt at ease. A few of her writings reflect her status, such as the poem "On Being Brought from Africa to America," a poem written to the earl of Dartmouth, and her letter on the natural rights of Negroes. In the later twentieth century, her writings received wide attention.

[*See also* African Americans; Literature: Colonial Era; Poetry; Slavery.]

• William Henry Robinson, *Phillis Wheatley and Her Writings,* 1984. Phillis Wheatley, *The Collected Works,* ed. John Shields, 1988. Wheatley, Phillis, *The Poems,* ed. Julian Mason, 1989.

—Everett Emerson

WHEELER, EARLE G. (1908–1975), chairman of the *Joint Chiefs of Staff during the *Vietnam War. A 1932 graduate of the U.S. Military Academy, Wheeler spent most of *World War II training troops in the United States. In the postwar years he earned a reputation as a skilled staff officer sensitive to the politics of military policy. His intelligence, gentlemanly style, and adaptability as a "team player" appealed to his civilian superiors, leading to his appointment in 1964 as chairman of the Joint Chiefs of Staff.

Wheeler initially supported President Lyndon B. *Johnson's gradualist approach in Vietnam, although he was privately convinced that only the swift application of full military power could achieve victory. Increasingly frustrated by Johnson's restrictions, Wheeler attempted to chip away at them so that the *military could wage war as it saw fit. These efforts culminated in 1968 when he tried to use the *Tet Offensive to pressure Johnson into mobilizing the reserves. Wheeler's gambit had the opposite effect, however, for Johnson chose instead to cap America's commitment to the war. Convinced that the nation's Vietnam strategy would not succeed, Wheeler nevertheless remained as chairman until his retirement in 1970.

• H. R. McMaster, *Dereliction of Duty: Lyndon Johnson, Robert McNamara, the Joint Chiefs of Staff, and the Lies That Led to Vietnam,* 1997. Frank E. Vandiver, *Shadows of Vietnam: Lyndon Johnson's Wars,* 1997.

—John Kennedy Ohl

WHIG PARTY. When President Andrew *Jackson won reelection in 1832, soundly defeating a divided field of challengers, anti-administration leaders recognized the need for a new opposition party to challenge the Democrats. The National Republican party, represented by Henry *Clay of Kentucky and Daniel *Webster of Massachusetts, no longer garnered widespread support. The newly formed *Anti-Masonic party, led by Thurlow Weed and William *Seward in New York and Thaddeus Stevens in Pennsylvania, represented an organized but narrowly focused group. Coming together in 1834, the founders of the new party dubbed themselves the Whigs, opposing "King Andrew" as the English Whig party had opposed James II in the *Glorious Revolution, and later George III.

Born of political opposition to Jackson, the early Whigs struggled to define a more positive party platform. The Democrat Martin *Van Buren's presidential victory in 1836 gave them ample time to consolidate their party. With the Panic of 1837 as a backdrop, they articulated a program for economic recovery. Most Whigs embraced Clay's American System, calling for high protective *tariffs, federally subsidized internal improvements, and a national bank. (Despite Clay's prominence as a Whig congressional leader, he never managed to win the presidency.) Though accused of being the party of elite businessmen, Whig candidates in fact won votes among all economic groups, giving them a rough parity of electoral power with the *Democratic party.

Whigs criticized the growth of executive power, a development they associated with Jackson's use of civil-service patronage. Many who came from an evangelical Protestant background encouraged groups fostering moral reform. Whigs also vehemently opposed U.S. territorial expansion during and after the *Mexican War. What brought Whigs together, however, was not a rigid set of policies. Indeed, when they won the presidency in 1840 and 1848, electing the military heroes William Henry *Harrison and Zachary *Taylor (both of whom died soon after taking office), their candidates had run without a formal platform. Rather, party members united around a common worldview and a shared vision of the nation's future. Their conservative temperament emphasized individual self-control and the harmony of collective interests. So long as the populace preserved republican virtues, Whigs saw hope in an emerging industrial nation.

Whatever their foresight, the Whigs ran aground in the 1850s when they confronted the divisive *slavery issue. Though Whigs had previously bridged northern and southern interests, differences over the *Compromise of 1850 tore the party asunder as many of its supporters defected to the recently formed nativist *Know-Nothing party. Despite their collapse as an electoral force in 1854, Whigs and Whig ideas continued to influence American politics through the emergent *Republican party. Indeed, the first Republican president, Abraham *Lincoln, like many others in the new party, had spent much of his career as a Whig.

[*See also* Antebellum Era; Bank of the United States, First and Second; Conservatism; Depressions, Economic; Individualism; Industrialization; Political Parties; Protestantism; Republicanism.]

• Daniel Walker Howe, *The Political Culture of the American Whigs,* 1979. Michael F. Holt, *The Rise and Fall of the American Whig Party,* 1999.

—Eric D. Daniels

WHISKEY REBELLION, 1794 uprising in western Pennsylvania by settlers protesting a federal excise tax on distilled whiskey. Although similar protests erupted elsewhere, western Pennsylvania became the flash point because it was where the federal government tried to enforce the tax by legal coercion and military intimidation.

A tax on whiskey at the still was part of Secretary of the Treasury Alexander *Hamilton's program, enacted in 1790–1791, to fund federal and state debt. But the excise measure roused anger in the cash-poor backcountry, particularly because it taxed large distillers at a lower rate, forcing small, seasonal distillers either to absorb the added cost or charge more to their customers, many of whom were small farmers and rural laborers. As backcountry protests, intimidations, and stonewalling erupted from Georgia to Pennsylvania, halting tax collections, President George *Washington and Hamilton, mindful of *Shays's Rebellion of 1786, decided in the summer of 1794 on a forceful response. Because of western Pennsylvania's proximity to the federal capital at *Philadelphia, it was selected as a test case. As federal marshals served court orders requiring noncomplying distillers to appear in federal district court in Philadelphia, several thousand armed men defiantly gathered near Pittsburgh. In August and September, Washington called up thirteen thousand militia and ordered them into western Pennsylvania. With Washington and Hamilton personally leading the troops, along with the *Revolutionary War hero Henry Lee, organized resistance collapsed. Two ringleaders convicted of treason were pardoned by Washington.

For the first time under the new *Constitution, the central government had marshaled impressive power to uphold federal authority. Although the government in fact never effectively collected the whiskey tax, which was repealed in 1802, Federalists could nevertheless plausibly claim that the new nation had demonstrated its determination to enforce the law against defiant citizens. This display of Federalist power, however, also stirred resentments that helped elect Thomas *Jefferson president in 1800.

[*See also* Early Republic, Era of the; Federalist Party; Taxation.]

• Thomas P. Slaughter, *The Whiskey Rebellion: Frontier Epilogue to the American Revolution,* 1986. Stanley Elkins and Eric McKitrick, *The Age of Federalism,* 1993, Chapter 10, pp. 451–488.

—Roger H. Brown

WHISTLER, JAMES MCNEILL (1834–1903), artist. Although James Whistler lived abroad his entire adult life, he became well-known in the United States as a publicist for the Aesthetic movement. Born in Lowell, Massachusetts, Whistler entered West Point Military Academy in 1851. At age twenty-one, he left to study art in Paris. Moving to London in 1859, he settled in Chelsea, an artists' enclave, in 1863. *The White Girl* (1862), rejected by the French Salon and shown instead in the scandalous Salon des Refusés, established Whistler's avant-garde reputation.

Whistler called his paintings "arrangements" and "harmonies" to highlight their abstract qualities; like music, his compositions omit subject and moral judgment. *Arrangement in Gray & Black No. 1: Portrait of the Artist's Mother* (1871) thus reminds the viewer that the subject is Whistler's aesthetic sensibility. Critic John Ruskin attacked *Nocturne in Black & Gold: The Falling Rocket* (1875), inspired by fireworks at Cremorne Gardens, for precisely this lack of an intelligible subject. Whistler's libel suit against Ruskin netted only a farthing in damages, but his account of the trial, *Art and Art Critics* (1878), enhanced his fame.

In his "Ten o'clock Lecture" at the Royal Academy in 1885, Whistler presented his controversial view that the only purpose of art is to create beauty. He expressed this philosophy by borrowing from Japanese art simple, asymmetrical design; shallow space; and bright pattern. In 1876, Liverpool shipowner Frederick Leyland commissioned him to design his London dining room as a showcase for Leyland's collection of Asian porcelain and Whistler's paintings. The resulting *Harmony in Blue and Gold: The Peacock Room,* filled with blue and white porcelain as well as blue, green, and gold pattern on all surfaces, possessed a unified aesthetic achieved through the artist's complete control of an environment. By 1890, Whistler and his ideas had won wide acceptance in Europe and America. In 1904, the *Peacock Room* was bought by American railroad supplier Charles Freer, a connoisseur of Asian art whose collection, donated to the nation, is displayed at Washington's Freer Gallery.

[*See also* Painting: To 1945.]

• Ronald Anderson, *James McNeill Whistler: Beyond the Myth,* 1994. Richard Dorment and M. F. MacDonald, *James McNeill Whistler,* 1994.

—Wendy J. Katz

WHITE HOUSE, the president's official residence in *Washington, D.C. In 1792, Irish architect James Hoban won a competition for the design of a president's house. Hoban's Anglo-Palladian design was at least partly patterned on Dublin's Lenster House. Construction began in 1792 on a site selected by Pierre Charles L'Enfant, and in 1800 John *Adams occupied the unfinished mansion on Pennsylvania Avenue in view of the unfinished Capitol. British troops burned the house in 1814, leaving only the outer shell intact. During the *Civil War, Abraham *Lincoln established this residence as a visible center of national policy-making, rather than simply the president's home.

The popular name "The White House," some sources maintain, derived from the whitewash applied in the post–1812 restoration; others date it to Thomas *Jefferson's presidency. Through the nineteenth century, it was more properly called the Executive Mansion or the President's House. In 1902 Theodore *Roosevelt first used the name "The White House" on official papers and correspondence. That same year, Roosevelt added the West Wing, where, in 1909, William Howard *Taft built the first Oval Office. Franklin Delano *Roosevelt built the present Oval Office in 1934. In 1948–1952, Harry S. *Truman remodeled the interior and added the Truman Balcony and a bomb shelter. The East Room and the elliptical Blue Room are used for receptions and public events. Landscape architect Andrew Jackson Downing designed the grounds.

National icon and symbol of presidential power, the White House has been the focus of national mourning, such as followed John F. *Kennedy's assassination; a center of crisis, as during the *Watergate scandal; and a target of protest, as during the *Vietnam War.

[*See also* Architecture: Public Architecture; Early Republic, Era of the; Federal Government, Executive Branch: The Presidency; War of 1812.]

• Esther Singleton, *The Story of the White House,* 1907, reprint 1969. Wendell Garrett, ed., *Our Changing White House,* 1995.

—Kenneth Franklin Kurz

WHITE SLAVERY. *See* Prostitution and Antiprostitution.

WHITMAN, WALT (1819–1892), poet. Walt Whitman revolutionized *poetry by replacing conventional rhyme and meter with a free-flowing, proselike poetic form that followed the natural rhythms of voice and feeling. Announcing himself as the representative American "bard," he brought a new democratic inclusiveness to poetry, opening the way for later writers by his experimentation with novel social and sexual themes.

The third of seven children of Walter and Louisa Van Velsor Whitman, he was born in West Hills, Long Island. In 1823, the Whitmans moved to Brooklyn, where his carpenter father barely kept the family above the poverty level. His mother was an unlearned but imaginative woman with a gift for storytelling. Whitman left school at eleven to help support the family, working as a lawyer's assistant and then as a printer's apprentice for Brooklyn newspapers. In 1836 he began a five-year stint as an itinerant teacher in rural Long Island. In 1838 he founded and briefly edited a newspaper, *The Long Islander.*

He moved in 1841 to Manhattan to pursue a career in journalism, contributing fiction, poetry, and nonfiction prose—most of it derivative and conventional—to local newspapers. From 1846 to early 1848 he edited the *Brooklyn Daily Eagle,* after which he spent three months in the *South writing for the *New Orleans Daily Crescent.* Upon returning to Brooklyn, he worked as a freelance journalist, variety-store manager, and carpenter.

Alarmed by intensifying sectional controversies, Whitman offered poetic healing to a nation on the verge of unraveling. "The proof of the poet," he wrote, "is that his country absorbs him as affectionately as he has absorbed it." In the twelve poems of the first edition of *Leaves of Grass* (1855), particularly the first one (later entitled "Song of Myself"), he evoked nearly every cultural and social strand of the *Antebellum Era: Emersonian *transcendentalism; techniques of *photography and genre *painting; images from *spiritualism and pseudoscience; devices from popular *music and *opera; inflections from oratory; and the radical spirit of the *antislavery and *women's rights movements.

Although *Leaves of Grass* was well received by Ralph Waldo *Emerson, who called it "the most extraordinary piece of wit and wisdom that America has yet contributed," and by most early reviewers, sales were slow, and objections were aired against its stylistic unconventionality and sexual frankness, including homoerotic allusions. He regularly added new poems to *Leaves of Grass,* which appeared in five more editions in his lifetime.

In the late 1850s Whitman hobnobbed with bohemian artists and writers in Charles Pfaff's Broadway restaurant. During the *Civil War he moved to *Washington, D.C., where he became a government clerk and a volunteer nurse in military hospitals. His collection *Drum Taps* (1865) included two well-known poems honoring the assassinated Abraham *Lincoln, "O Captain! My Captain!" and the elegiac "When Lilacs Last in the Dooryard Bloom'd." His prose essay *Democratic Vistas* (1871) lamented the debasement of democratic ideals amid the crass materialism of post–Civil War America.

Partially paralyzed by a stroke in 1873, he moved from Washington to Camden, New Jersey, where he lived first with his brother George and then in his own home. Increasingly famous, he lectured widely in the United States and Canada until further strokes in the late 1880s left him confined to a wheelchair.

[*See also* Literature: Early National and Antebellum Eras.]

• Gay Wilson Allen, *The Solitary Singer: A Critical Biography of Walt Whitman,* 1955. David S. Reynolds, *Walt Whitman's America: A Cultural Biography,* 1995.

—David S. Reynolds

WHITNEY, ELI (1765–1825), inventor and arms manufacturer. Born in Westboro, Massachusetts, the eldest son of farmer Eli Whitney and Elizabeth Fay Whitney, Eli Whitney demonstrated mechanical talent earlier than scholarship, but belatedly graduated from Yale in 1792. Upon graduation Whitney accepted a position as a tutor in Georgia, travelling with Yale alumnus Phineas Miller and Miller's employer, Catherine Greene, the widow of *Revolutionary War general Nathanael Greene. When the expected tutorship fell through, Greene invited Whitney to remain at her plantation near Savannah.

There he learned of the urgent need for an improved cotton gin (short for "engine"). The grooved roller gin used for removing the black seeds from the bolls of the long-staple cotton grown in coastal Georgia failed to dislodge with equal ease the tenacious green seeds of the upland short-staple cotton. With Greene's encouragement, workshop, and materials, Whitney constructed a model in which a hook-studded rotating cylinder pulled cotton fiber through slots in a metal barrier, leaving seeds behind. Powered by horse or waterwheel, Whitney's gin could clean as much cotton as fifty people working by hand.

Backed by Greene, Phineas Miller and Eli Whitney formed a partnership to build and operate such gins. In 1793 Whitney obtained a patent and began gin production in New Haven, Connecticut. Southern plantations vastly expanded their acreages of cotton for export to England's textile factories. As cotton harvests outstripped Miller and Whitney's capacity to meet the demand for ginning, southern blacksmiths made gins without paying for the patent, embroiling Miller and Whitney in costly and prolonged lawsuits. Whitney's patent, although finally upheld in southern courts before expiring in 1807, garnered him small reward.

Meanwhile, deep in debt from the cotton-gin venture, Whitney won a contract from the U.S. government in 1798 to produce ten thousand muskets in an incredibly short two years. Responding to the desire of French-influenced U.S. Ordnance officers for uniform military muskets, Whitney propounded the elusive goal of interchangeable parts. He built a water-powered factory outside New Haven, and trained unskilled workers to specialize in using different "molds and patterns" to standardize filling and drilling. They produced quantities of individual parts before fitting them together into complete muskets. With contract extensions, they completed the ten thousand muskets in ten years. By modern standards, their parts were not interchangeable, nor were those made then at other armories.

Through technological exchange among private arms contractors and the federal armories, however, such methods spread, along with gauges intended to induce uniformity. With subsequent inventions such as Thomas Blanchard's gunstock lathe and the milling machines of Simeon North and John Hall, arms makers were producing standard military muskets with interchangeable parts by the late 1840s. Over the next half-century, other manufacturers adapted armory methods for high-volume production of sewing machines, typewriters, watches, bicycles, and, in the early twentieth century, automobiles.

Eli Whitney married Henrietta Edwards in 1817 and began a family before prostate cancer ended his life at age sixty. Posthumous heroic stories credited Whitney with inventing both the cotton gin and interchangeable parts. Historians of *technology have debunked this oversimplification, which lingers even into the twenty-first century.

[*See also* Cotton Industry; Factory System; Industrialization; Mass Production; Military, The; Slavery: Development and Expansion of Slavery; Weaponry, Nonnuclear.]

• Constance McLaughlin Green, *Eli Whitney and the Birth of American Technology,* 1956. Merritt Roe Smith, *Harpers Ferry Armory and the New Technology,* 1977.

—Carolyn C. Cooper

WIENER, NORBERT (1894–1964), mathematician and computer theorist. Norbert Wiener's father, a professor of Slavonic languages at Harvard, supervised his early education. A child prodigy, Wiener began to read at four, graduated from Tufts College at fourteen, and received his Ph.D. in mathematics from Harvard at eighteen. During a Harvard-sponsored trip to Europe, he consulted with such eminent mathematicians as Bertrand Russell, David Hilbert, and G. H. Hardy. In 1918, as a mathematician at the U.S. Army's Aberdeen Proving Grounds, he worked on ballistics. In 1919, he became a mathematics instructor at the Massachusetts Institute of Technology where he remained until he retired in 1960, having become one of MIT's best-known faculty members and the subject of many affectionate stories about his legendary absent-mindedness.

Wiener's *World War II work on fire-control systems turned his attention to theories of man-machine communications. His *Cybernetics; or, Control and Communication in the Animal and Machine* (1948), discussing control and automation theory, ranks as a classic anticipation of the computer revolution. In *The Human Uses of Human Beings* (1950), directed to general readers, Wiener discussed both the promise and the potential hazards of automation—the application of *computers to information processing. His essay "Some Moral and Technical Consequences of Automation" (*Science,* 6 May 1960) conveyed his deepening pessimism about the computer's social implications. In 1964, shortly before his death, Wiener was awarded the National Medal of Science by President Lyndon B. *Johnson. He wrote two autobiographies: *I Am a Mathematician* (1956) and *Ex-Prodigy: My Childhood and Youth* (1979).

[*See also* Automation and Computerization; Mathematics and Statistics.]

• Pesi Masani, ed., *Norbert Wiener: Collected Works,* 4 vols., 1976–1986. Pesi Masani, *Norbert Wiener, 1894–1964,* 1992.

—Thomas J. Bergin

WIGNER, EUGENE (1902–1995), physicist. Born and reared in a Hungarian-Jewish milieu that included three other great scientists—Edward *Teller, John *von Neumann, and Leo Szilard (1898–1964)—Eugene Wigner was a brilliant theoretical physicist and first-rate engineer who advanced the study of physics in ways various and profound. In the late 1920s, Wigner laid the groundwork for the theory of symmetries in quantum mechanics. In the 1930s, he showed that the essential properties of nuclei, including the behavior of protons and neutrons, follow the well-known symmetries of the laws of motion.

Trained largely in Germany, Wigner emigrated to the United States in 1933 as Adolf Hitler came to power in that country, invited by Princeton University. In 1939, with Szilard and Teller, he was part of a small group of scientists who persuaded Albert *Einstein to alert President Franklin Delano *Roosevelt that nuclear chain reaction could produce an atomic bomb of almost unimaginable power. During *World War II, while working on the *Manhattan Project in the Metallurgical Laboratory at the University of Chicago, Wigner helped produce such a bomb. Bent on defeating Nazi Germany, Wigner worked on plutonium production and made superb engineering designs for the air-cooled atomic pile built by the DuPont Corporation.

For his work on the mechanics of nuclear protons and neutrons, and for his symmetry principles of nuclear particles, Wigner shared the 1963 Nobel Prize in Physics. In the 1960s, he staunchly advocated national *civil-defense programs. Becoming more philosophical in his later years, Wigner explored the paradox of consciousness, the unnatural quality of fame, and the mystery of life itself.

[*See also* Hiroshima and Nagasaki, Atomic Bombing of; Nuclear Weapons; Physical Sciences; Science: From 1914 to 1945; Science: Since 1945.]

• Eugene P. Wigner and Andrew Szanton, *The Recollections of Eugene P. Wigner*, 1992.

—Andrew Szanton

WILDERNESS MOVEMENT. *See* Environmentalism.

WILKES EXPEDITION (1838–1842). Beginning in the 1820s, *New England merchants seeking new regions in which to hunt seals and whales, and U.S. Navy officers hoping to extend the reach of American naval influence, joined with American scientists to persuade Congress to authorize a naval exploration of the South Seas. In 1836 Congress appropriated funds for an expedition, known officially as the U.S. South Seas Exploring Expedition and informally as the Wilkes Expedition after its commanding officer, U.S. Navy lieutenant Charles Wilkes (1798–1877). Mandated to explore the Antarctic and Pacific to gain information that would aid commerce, the expedition was instructed to make hydrographic surveys and astronomical observations, chart navigational hazards, and collect natural history specimens. This, the U.S. Navy's first large-scale scientific exploring mission, served as a model for subsequent expeditions. The nine civilians on the expedition included two artists, two botanists, a conchologist, a geologist, two naturalists, and a philologist.

In 1838 six naval vessels—the largest of which was the sloop-of-war USS *Vincennes,* weighing only seven hundred tons—set out from Norfolk, Virginia. By the time the squadron returned in 1842, it had traversed 85,000 miles of ocean; surveyed 280 islands, including the Tuamotu, Society, Samoan, and Fiji islands; charted 800 miles of rivers and coastline in Oregon Territory and 1,500 miles of coastal Antarctica; and established that Antarctica is a continent. The ensuing nineteen scientific reports, including Wilkes's own five-volume narrative, recording findings on the botany, crustacea, ethnography, geology, hydrography, meteorology, and zoophytes of the South Seas, enhanced the stature of the United States in the international scientific community. Among the major scientific contributions resulting from the expedition were James Dwight Dana's trenchant observations on volcanic island chains. The tens of thousands of natural history specimens and ethnographic objects collected by the expedition became the basis of the *Smithsonian Institution's National Museum of the United States in 1858.

[*See also* Antebellum Era; Coast and Geodetic Survey, U.S.; Geological Surveys; Military, The; Physical Sciences.]

• William Stanton, *The Great United States Exploring Expedition,* 1975.

—Michael J. Crawford

WILLARD, FRANCES (1839–1898), temperance leader, reformer. Born in Churchville, New York, and reared on a Wisconsin farm, "Frank" (her preferred name as a child) graduated from North Western Female College in Evanston, Illinois, in 1859, taught school, toured Europe (1868–1870) with a wealthy female friend, and in 1871 became president of the Evanston College for Ladies. When it merged with Northwestern University in 1873 she became dean of women.

Willard resigned in 1874 to become corresponding secretary of the *Woman's Christian Temperance Union (WCTU). She was elected president of the Illinois WCTU in 1878, and of the national organization in 1879. Under Willard, the WCTU advocated not only prohibition, but also woman suffrage, *public health, penal reform, labor unions, kindergardens, higher standards of sexual morality, and other reforms. However, her 1892 effort to weld the WCTU, the *Populist party, and the *Knights of Labor into a reform party proved unsuccessful. Living mostly in England in 1892–1896, on the estate of Lady Somerset, a temperance leader, she embraced Christian *socialism. She died in *New York City of chronic anemia at the age of fifty-eight. Her funerals, in New York and *Chicago, were notable public events. In 1905, Illinois placed her statue in the U.S. Capitol Statuary Hall, making Willard the only woman so honored.

As leader of America's first mass organization of women, Willard mobilized conservative support for reform causes. A powerful speaker, she lectured tirelessly, drawing women into political life by using social conventions about the purity and sanctity of the Victorian home as justifications for action on many fronts.

[*See also* Alcohol and Alcohol Abuse; Gilded Age; Prostitution and Antiprostitution; Sexual Morality and Sex Reform; Temperance and Prohibition; Woman Suffrage Movement.]

• Mary Earhart, *Frances Willard,* 1944. Ruth Bordin, *Frances Willard: A Biography,* 1986.

—Peter C. Holloran

WILLIAMS, DANIEL HALE (1856–1931), surgeon and educator, pioneer in both surgical technique and race relations. Born in Hollidaysburg, Pennsylvania, Williams possessed a mixed racial ancestry, with Caucasian, Native American, and African-American antecedents on both sides of his family. Williams considered himself a "Negro," and it was as a Negro that he moved to Janesville, Wisconsin, where at the age of seventeen he worked as a barber while attending a local academy and later reading law at night. Deciding against a career in law, he apprenticed with a local physician and then attended Chicago Medical College.

Williams evinced great skill as a surgeon and clinician. His most noteworthy contribution to medical practice came in 1893, when he performed the first successful open-heart surgery. He helped found both the American College of Surgeons and the *National Medical Association (1895), the black equivalent of the the all-white *American Medical Association. He also was the prime mover behind the Provident Hospital and Training School in *Chicago, the nation's first interracial hospital, founded in 1891.

Williams achieved renown as an educator, both at Provident Hospital and at Freedmen's Hospital, an institution attached to Howard University in *Washington, D.C. Appointed chief surgeon at Freedmen's in the mid-1890s, William worked to improve its clinical program. Although his later years were mired in political controversy, Williams remains a major figure in African-American medicine and in American medical history.

[*See also* African Americans; Heart Disease; Hospitals; Medicine: From the 1870s to 1945; Surgery.]

• Helen Buckler, *Daniel Hale Williams: Negro Surgeon,* 1968. Vanessa Northington Gamble, "The Provident Hospital Project: An Experiment in Race Relations and Medical Education," *Bulletin of the History of Medicine* 65 (1991): 457–75.

—Robert Oliver

WILLIAMS, ROGER (1603?–1683), founder of Rhode Island, advocate of religious liberty. Educated for the ministry at Pembroke College, Cambridge, Williams became a Puritan and immigrated to Massachusetts Bay in 1631. During pastorates at Plymouth and Salem, Williams advocated the separatist view that congregations must purify themselves by severing all connections with the Church of England, and this antagonized the colony's nonseparatist leadership. In 1635 the General Court of Massachusetts found his opinions dangerously disruptive. He fled to land purchased from the Narragansett Indians and in 1636 established Rhode Island's first town, Providence. Williams's religious ideas continued their radical trajectory, and by 1639 he had concluded that Christian institutions were so thoroughly corrupted that the true church no longer existed and would not be reestablished until authoritative new apostles arrived at the millennium.

Although he remained an admiring friend of the Massachusetts governor John *Winthrop, Williams believed that Massachusetts had persecuted him for following his conscience. In response, during trips to England in 1643–1644 and 1651–1654, Williams published several polemics, including *The Bloudy Tenent of Persecution* (1644), that advocated liberty of conscience and attacked such Massachusetts clergy as John Cotton for favoring state regulation of religion. Since Rhode Island followed Williams's principles of religious freedom, the colony became a haven for diverse beliefs. In this, Williams steadfastly supported the colony, but, because he continued to hope for a purified Christianity, he also denounced error where he saw it and, late in his career, engaged the Quakers in a public debate, published as *George Fox Digg'd out of His Burrowes* (1676).

[*See also* Baptists; Colonial Era; Puritanism; Religion.]

• Roger Williams, *The Complete Writings of Roger Williams,* 7 vols. 1963. Edmund S. Morgan, *Roger Williams: The Church and the State,* 1967.

—W. Clark Gilpin

WILSON, WOODROW (1856–1924), twenty-eighth president of the United States. Thomas Woodrow Wilson, the son of a Presbyterian clergyman, was born in Staunton, Virginia; raised in Georgia and South Carolina; and educated at Davidson College (1873–1874) and the College of New Jersey, later Princeton University (1875–1879). He attended the University of Virginia Law School, was admitted to the Georgia bar in 1882, and practiced law briefly in Atlanta. In 1883 he began graduate study in history and *political science at Johns Hopkins University, receiving his Ph.D. in 1886. His first book, *Congressional Government* (1885), served as his dissertation.

In 1885 Wilson married Ellen Axson (1860–1914); they had three daughters. Wilson taught at Bryn Mawr College and Wesleyan University, and in 1890, having published a second book, *The State,* returned to Princeton as a professor. His work on public administration, begun in the late 1880s, opened a new field of study. In 1902 he was named president of Princeton.

In that position, Wilson implemented reforms to strengthen the institution academically and proposed to abolish private eating clubs on campus. The suggestion angered alumni but earned Wilson praise as an opponent of privilege. In 1910 New Jersey's *Democratic party bosses invited him to run for governor, believing that his reputation as a reformer would make him popular but that his political inexperience would enable them to control him. They were wrong on the second count. Winning the election, Wilson worked closely with both Democratic and Republican reformers to change state laws in ways that helped bring New Jersey into the mainstream of the national Progressive movement.

The Early Presidential Years. On the strength of his New Jersey record, Wilson captured the 1912 Democratic presidential nomination and, thanks in part to Theodore *Roosevelt's Progressive party insurgency, won the election. Again he moved quickly, calling Congress into special session to consider his program. In 1913 he signed into law the Underwood Act reducing the *tariff and implementing the first federal *income tax under the *Sixteenth Amendment to the *Constitution. He played a key role in shaping the *Federal Reserve Act, which reformed the banking and currency systems. In 1914 he signed the *Federal Trade Commission Act and the Clayton Antitrust Act to regulate big business practices and encourage competition. Over the next two years, among other reforms, Wilson supported legislation to promote agricultural education, extend credit to farmers, begin a federal *highway system, curtail *child labor, and establish the eight-hour day for railroad workers. On racial matters, Wilson shared the prejudices of his time and region, and racial *segregation intensified during his administration.

In *foreign relations, Wilson at first tried to apply the same principles that shaped his domestic program. Just as he hoped to free Americans from domination by powerful corporations, he envisioned liberating Mexico and the Caribbean from military tyrants and foreign economic domination. His efforts proved largely unsuccessful, however. Well-intended interventions in Mexico, the Dominican Republic, and Haiti aroused anti-Americanism and often substituted one form of military government for another.

World War I. The outbreak of *World War I in Europe in August 1914 confronted Wilson with his greatest challenge. Both the Allies and the Central Powers tried to cut off the flow of American products to the other side. The British blockade of Germany, enforced with surface vessels, cost Americans money, but the German blockade, implemented by U-boats (submarines), killed innocent people. On 7 May 1915, 128 Americans died when a U-boat torpedoed the British liner *Lusitania* off the Irish coast. Wilson demanded that the Germans change their policy. Early in 1916, after sinking another passenger vessel, Germany agreed to halt such attacks. On the strength of this pledge and his strong domestic record, Wilson won reelection in November 1916, running on the slogan "He Kept Us Out of War."

As the situation grew more dangerous, Wilson proposed on 22 January 1917 that the belligerents accept a "peace without victory" restoring the prewar status quo. Neither side proved interested, and the Germans, having earlier decided on a last great effort to win, now announced a policy of unrestricted U-boat warfare. Wilson broke off diplomatic relations with Germany on 3 February, and on 2 April asked Congress for a declaration of war.

As the administration struggled with the task of military mobilization and production, it also rallied homefront support for the war through posters, speeches, and bond drives, and suppressed dissident voices by means of postal *censorship and the Espionage Act (1917) and Sedition Amendment (1918). A wave of intolerance swept the nation and *German Americans were harassed and antiwar activists arrested. Socialist Eugene V. *Debs and others went to jail for writing and speaking against the war.

Addressing postwar issues, Wilson in January 1918 proposed a statement of Allied war aims, the so-called *Fourteen Points. With the signing of an armistice on 11 November 1918, the president announced that he would personally head the American delegation to the peace conference in Paris.

The Versailles Treaty and the League Fight. Hailed by ordinary Europeans as a savior, Wilson found the Allied leaders tough negotiators. He proposed self-determination for European minorities, freedom of trade, and an international organization to keep the peace. They wanted security and revenge. Although the Treaty of *Versailles (signed in June 1919) was criticized by the Germans as too severe and by the Allies as too lenient, it did create the *League of Nations, which Wilson hoped would secure permanent peace.

When Wilson presented the treaty to the Senate in July 1919 he faced an even tougher fight. Many senators feared that League membership would force the United States to put its armed forces under international command. Wilson argued that the universal nature of the organization would make war impossible, but although he received the 1919 Nobel Peace Prize for his work on the League, he could not win Senate ratification, in part because he adamantly rejected any changes in the League covenant. After an exhausting and futile speaking trip on behalf of the treaty, Wilson suffered a massive stroke on 2 October 1919. A few weeks later the Senate rejected the treaty. Paralyzed and embittered, Wilson served out the remainder of his term as an invalid. Increasingly querulous and emotionally fragile, he was largely isolated from outside contact by his second wife, Edith Galt, whom he had married in December 1915. In late 1919 and early 1920, Wilson's attorney general, A. Mitchell Palmer, and young J. Edgar *Hoover of the Justice Department's countersubversion division, exploiting a Red Scare that swept America after the 1917 Bolshevik Revolution in Russia, organized a series of raids and deportations of alleged radicals and communists, including Emma *Goldman. Wilson, leaving the White House in March 1921 as Republican Warren G. *Harding took office, lived in seclusion in Washington until his death in 1924.

Assessment. Wilson followed in Theodore Roosevelt's footsteps in enlarging the power of the presidency in an urban-industrial age. His domestic record exemplified the emergence of an activist federal government and dramatically demonstrated of how much a president, by focusing public opinion on issues and working closely with Congress, can accomplish. In foreign policy he wielded America's immense economic and military might and served notice that the United States had arrived as a major power with a distinctive global vision. Many Americans shared that vision even if they were not yet ready to accept permanent obligations to achieve it. Wilson's tragedy was that his own intransigence played a major role in his failure to achieve his loftiest vision, American membership in the new world organization for which he had labored so tirelessly

[See also Anticommunism; Antitrust Legislation; Antiwar Movements; Banking and Finance; Baruch, Bernard; Economic Regulation; Education: Rise of the University; Federal Government, Executive Branch: The Presidency; Federal Government, Legislative Branch: Senate; Federal Regulatory Agencies; Foreign Relations; Internationalism; Isolationism; Political Parties; Progressive Era; Progressive Party of 1912–1924; Racism; War Industries Board.]

• Ray Stannard Baker, *Woodrow Wilson: Life and Letters,* 8 vols., 1927–1939. Arthur S. Link, *Wilson,* 5 vols., 1947–1965. John M. Blum, *Woodrow Wilson and the Politics of Morality,* 1956. *The Papers of Woodrow Wilson,* eds., Arthur S. Link, et al., 69 vols., 1966–1993. August Heckscher, *Woodrow Wilson,* 1991. Kendrick A. Clements, *The Presidency of Woodrow Wilson,* 1992.

—Kendrick A. Clements

WINTHROP, JOHN (1588–1649), leader of the Puritan settlement in *New England and first governor of the Massachusetts Bay Colony. Between 1602 and 1620, John Winthrop attended Trinity College, Cambridge; studied law; was married three times and widowed twice; took over his father's estate at Groton Manor; served as justice of the peace; and became an acknowledged Puritan. Throughout the 1620s, economic pressures, political crises, and his intensifying engagement with *Puritanism led Winthrop to despair of England's future and to join other Puritans planning an escape to America. As governor of the newly formed Massachusetts Bay Company, his sermon in 1630 on board the *Arbella*—"A Modell of Christian Charity"—defined the Puritans' mission to create a biblical commonwealth in covenant with God that would "be as a Citty upon a hill."

Winthrop's *Journal* documents his skillful guidance and leadership during the first two decades of settlement. A generally moderate man, he tried to balance the authority of the governors with the liberties and interests of the governed, seeking harmony in the face of conflicts and emphasizing communal over private interests. Deeply religious, he endeavored also to balance his lifelong quest for assurance of grace with an appreciation of life's pleasures, opposing Anne *Hutchinson's claims to absolute spiritual assurance and Roger *Williams's perfectionism. His wisdom, intelligence, and political acumen helped insure the survival and success of the Puritan experiment in America.

[*See also* Colonial Era; Exploration, Conquest, and Settlement, Era of European; Religion.]

• Edmund S. Morgan, *The Puritan Dilemma: The Story of John Winthrop,* 1958. James G. Moseley, *John Winthrop's World: History as a Story; The Story as History,* 1992.

—Philip Greven

WISE, ISAAC MAYER (1819–1900), rabbi and leader of Reform *Judaism. Born in Steingrub, Bohemia (present day Kamenny Ovu, Czech Republic), Wise officiated in Radnitz, near Prague, before immigrating to America in 1846. He then served as the rabbi of Albany's Congregation Beth El. His ritual innovations aimed at improving decorum proved divisive, and in 1850, following a fracas in the synagogue, his followers formed Congregation Anshe Emeth around him. In 1854 he moved to Cincinnati, Ohio, accepting a life contract from Congregation Bene Yeshurun.

Wise sought to unite American Jews around a modernized form of Judaism. He established and edited two national Jewish newspapers to promote his ideas, the English-language *Israelite* (later *American Israelite*) and the German *Die Deborah.* He also produced an influential new prayer book (1857), *Minhag America* (The American rite). In a dramatic symbol of Judaism's rising status, he moved his congregation in 1866 into a palatial synagogue ("the Plum Street Temple") across from Cincinnati's city hall. In 1873, his lay leaders founded the Union of American Hebrew Congregations, and two years later at his urging it established in Cincinnati what was then America's only rabbinical seminary, Hebrew Union College. Presiding over this school until his death, he trained legions of rabbis who followed in his footsteps. In 1889, he helped to organize the school's graduates and rabbinic supporters into the Central Conference of American Rabbis.

Usually an advocate of moderate as opposed to radical reforms within Judaism, Wise was a pragmatist rather than a systematic or consistent thinker. The institutions he created remain central to American Reform Judaism.

[*See also* Religion.]

• James G. Heller, *Isaac M. Wise: His Life, Work and Thought,* 1965. Sefton D. Temkin, *Isaac Mayer Wise: Shaping American Judaism,* 1992.

—Jonathan D. Sarna

WISE, STEPHEN S. (1874–1949), rabbi, reformer, Zionist leader. Born in Hungary, Wise came to America as an infant with his family. He graduated from the College of the City of New York in 1891 and received a Ph.D. in Semitic Studies from Columbia in 1901. Ordained as a rabbi, he held pulpits in New York and Oregon before establishing the Free Synagogue in *New York City in 1907. Nominally a part of the Reform movement, the Free Synagogue stood for absolute freedom of the pulpit, a radical notion at a time when many synagogue trustees essentially told their rabbis what to preach. A great pulpit orator, Wise preached nearly every Sunday morning for more than forty years to packed audiences in Carnegie Hall, often dealing with the burning issues of the day.

Wise sought to make so-called classic Reform Judaism more responsive to modern Jewish needs. He founded the Jewish Institute of Religion in 1923 as a liberal seminary emphasizing *social work as well as religious training. It was the first rabbinical seminary to admit women. By the end of his life, Wise had seen his ideas triumph within the Reform movement.

An early recruit to Zionism (the drive to re-create a Jewish homeland in Palestine), Wise dropped out of the movement to concentrate on his Free Synagogue but returned during *World War I as an aide to Louis *Brandeis. He remained an active Zionist leader thereafter.

Embracing a Jewish version of the *Social Gospel, Wise played a leading role in reform politics in Portland and in New York, where he tackled the corrupt Tammany Hall machine, New York City's Democratic organization. After opposing Franklin Delano *Roosevelt when he ran for governor of New York, Wise became one of President Roosevelt's most vocal supporters. Wise has been criticized because, not wishing to embarrass Roosevelt, he did not push for greater American resistance to Nazi Germany and the Holocaust.

[*See also* Judaism; Religion.]

• Melvin I. Urofsky, *A Voice that Spoke for Justice: The Life and Times of Stephen S. Wise,* 1982.

—Melvin I. Urofsky

WOMAN'S CHRISTIAN TEMPERANCE UNION. The national Woman's Christian Temperance Union (WCTU), founded in Cincinnati in 1874, emerged from a grassroots movement, the so-called Woman's Crusade, against the consumption of alcoholic beverages. At first the organization focused on temperance, but under Frances *Willard, president from 1879 to her death in 1898, the agenda broadened to include a variety of causes, from peace and missions to kindergartens. Willard's "do-everything" policy gave rise to a series of WCTU "departments" in line with the principle of bureaucratic specializations; state and local affiliates arose as well. The WCTU flourished in the *Middle West and Northeast but lagged in the *South. A campaign for "scientific temperance-instruction" laws achieved great success. Becoming more radical after 1886, the WCTU advocated the eight-hour work day and equal wages for men and women workers, and courted the *Knights of Labor and the *Populist party. A small minority became socialists, their beliefs deriving not from Marxism but from the *Social Gospel, which enjoyed broad support among temperance women. Willard and the WCTU also embraced the *woman suffrage movement, advocating votes for women as a means of protecting the home and strengthening family values.

From 1884 to 1889 the WCTU split over whether to endorse the Prohibition party and criticize *Republican party inaction, but the breakaway Non-Partisan WCTU, which sided with the Republican party, never became a serious rival. Through the efforts of Willard and her lieutenants, the WCTU attracted 150,000 members by 1890. Aside from the *women's club movement, this made it the nation's largest and most significant women's organization. After 1883 WCTU missionaries spread the movement internationally. Within the United States, Matilda Carse's Woman's Temperance Publishing Association promoted the WCTU's arguments. The depression of the 1890s took its toll, however, and WCTU membership stagnated. Willard now faced criticism over her absences abroad and her friendship with Isabel Somerset, an English aristocrat and the World WCTU's vice president. Somerset's support of state-regulated prostitution in the British Empire and her reputed hostility to prohibition added to the friction. After Willard's death, the WCTU returned to a more conservative stance but never fully abandoned the do-everything policy.

After 1898 the Anti-Saloon League, led by Protestant ministers, emerged as the leader of a resurgent and narrowly focused prohibition movement, but the WCTU provided grassroots back-up. With ratification of the *Eighteenth Amendment (prohibition) in 1919 the WCTU's membership rose again, reaching over 300,000 in the 1920s under presidents Anna Gordon and Ella Boole, giving the organization considerable lobbying power for enforcement of the Volstead Act. Repeal of the Eighteenth Amendment in 1933 proved a terminal setback to national prohibition, but the WCTU, based in Evanston, Illinois, continued to defend state and local liquor laws and to campaign for social welfare and world peace.

[*See also* Alcohol and Alcohol Abuse; Feminism; Labor Movements; Methodism; Peace Movements; Prostitution and Antiprostitution; Temperance and Prohibition.]

• Ruth Bordin, *Woman and Temperance: The Quest for Power and Liberty, 1873–1900,* 1980. Ian Tyrrell, *Woman's World/Woman's Empire: The Woman's Christian Temperance Union in International Perspective, 1880–1930,* 1991.

—Ian Tyrrell

WOMAN SUFFRAGE MOVEMENT. The first formal demand for equal political rights for women was made by Elizabeth Cady *Stanton at the 1848 Seneca Falls, New York, Women's Rights Convention. Woman *suffrage was initially controversial, even among the radical pioneers of the *women's rights movement, because electoral politics was held in low repute and partisanship was considered fundamentally male. The *Civil War and the abolition of *slavery, however, moved questions of citizenship and enfranchisement to the forefront of the national political agenda. By 1866, suffrage had become the foremost demand among women's rights activists.

At war's end, Stanton, Susan B. *Anthony, Lucy *Stone, and other woman suffrage leaders expected that white women would win the vote along with freedmen and freedwomen in a single, comprehensive act of universal enfranchisement. Yet the Republican authors of the *Fifteenth Amendment refused to include "sex" along with "race, color, or previous condition of servitude" as federally prohibited grounds for disfranchisement. Disagreeing over how to proceed, the woman suffrage forces in 1869 formed two rival organizations, the National and the American woman suffrage associations. In a final effort to secure the vote as part of postwar *Reconstruction, the National Woman Suffrage Association, led by Stanton and Anthony, advanced a daring constitutional argument, claiming that because women had been made national citizens by the *Fourteenth Amendment, they already possessed the franchise, the defining right of citizenship. The U.S. *Supreme Court in *Minor* v. *Happersett* (1875) rejected this argument: While women were indeed citizens, the Court declared, voting was a privilege, not a right.

Although stalled constitutionally, the movement gained many adherents. In the 1880s, Frances *Willard's *Woman's Christian Temperance Union endorsed woman suffrage as the best means to control liquor and protect the home. By 1890, woman suffrage, originally a radical demand among a small group of reformers, had gained respectability among middle-class American women. That year, the two rival organizations merged, forming the *National American Woman Suffrage Association (NAWSA). With respectability, however, the suffrage movement, forged in the fires of the *antislavery crusade, became increasingly conservative and racist in its arguments. African-American women, who well knew the power of the vote, formed their own woman suffrage societies.

The constitutional upheavals of the Reconstruction Era had left unresolved the question of whether the states or the federal government controlled the right to vote. Through the late nineteenth and early twentieth centuries, woman suffrage advocates concentrated on particular states. The first breakthroughs came in the *West where the democratic politics of radical populism opened up political space for the enfranchisement of women. In 1869 and 1870, the territorial legislatures of Wyoming and Utah respectively enacted woman suffrage provisions and retained these provisions through the process of becoming states (although Congress, reflecting anti-Mormon sentiment, objected strongly in the case of Utah). In 1893, a majority of Colorado's male voters approved a woman suffrage provision to their state constitution; Idaho (1896), Washington (1910), and *California (1911) followed. By 1912, women had full voting rights in ten states, all west of the *Mississippi River. But in 1915, voters in four heavily urbanized eastern states with large immigrant populations—New Jersey, New York, Pennsylvania, and Massachusetts—decisively defeated woman suffrage referenda. At this point, suffrage strategy shifted back to amending the federal *Constitution.

By the first decade of the twentieth century, as the Progressive reform movement flourished, the suffrage movement itself was also changing. Heavy *immigration, *urbanization, an expanding female labor force, and rising numbers of college-educated women altered both the composition and the tactics of suffragism. New organizations oriented toward wage-earning women arose in New York and San Francisco. Women college graduates also flooded into the movement. These new suffragists took to the streets, organizing mass parades, automobile caravans, and soapbox speaking. Carrie Chapman *Catt, alert to new trends but cautious about innovations, consolidated these changes within NAWSA.

In 1913, Alice Paul formed a second national organization, the Congressional Union, to pursue more aggressively a woman suffrage constitutional amendment. Determined to use the voting women of the ten "suffrage states" as a lever in national politics, these militants in 1916 urged western women to vote against President Woodrow *Wilson on the grounds that he was antisuffrage. After the United States entered *World War I in April 1917, the Congressional Union switched to tactics of public protest. They picketed the *White House carrying signs denouncing Wilson. When many were arrested, they insisted that they were political prisoners and engaged in civil disobedience. Meanwhile, the moderates of the NAWSA concentrated on Congressional lobbying. In 1920, the combination of approaches, and the transformations of World War I, finally led to the passage and ratification of the *Nineteenth Amendment to the Constitution. Seventy-two years after Seneca Falls, national woman suffrage had been achieved.

[*See also* Feminism; League of Women Voters; Mormonism; Populist Era; Progressive Era; Seneca Falls Convention; Women in the Labor Force; Women's Club Movement; Women's Rights Movements.]

• Aileen Kraditor, *Ideas of the Woman Suffrage Movement, 1890–1920,* 1965. Ellen Carol DuBois, *Feminism and Suffrage: The Emergence of an Independent Women's Movement in America, 1848–1869,* 1978. Marjorie Spruill Wheeler, ed., *One Woman, One Vote: Rediscovering the Suffrage Movement,* 1995. Eleanor Flexner with Ellen Fitzpatrick, *Century of Struggle: The Woman's Rights Movement in the United States,* enlarged ed., 1996.

—Ellen C. DuBois

WOMEN IN THE LABOR FORCE. The history of women in the American labor force has been shaped by diverse cultural, legal, demographic, and ethno-racial influences. Like men, women in preindustrial America contributed to their household and community economies through paid and unpaid labor, but the material rewards of their labor were limited by cultural beliefs, social practices, and laws that subordinated women to men. Except by special legal arrangement, married women could not sign labor contracts, own property, or claim their own wages. Some women did work for wages, but those who did, even unmarried women and widows, clustered in lower-paying occupations and earned lower wages than men.

Initially, these conditions were reproduced, and even accentuated, as the industrial economy developed. As families became more dependent on cash for survival, free women (as well as free men) increased their participation in the paid labor force. Especially numerous as seamstresses in the needle trades and in domestic work, women were also essential to the emerging factories. As textile-mill operatives, rural *New England daughters became the first regular factory labor force. Other women worked as members of "family" production units (in shoemaking or retail shops, for example) and as homeworkers in textiles, shoes, or other products—patterns of work that still persist.

Law and social convention obscured the extent and importance of women's labor to families and to the developing national economy. Laws granting married women legal rights to their wages and to property became common only in the late nineteenth century. These reforms sought to preserve households in an industrializing society, rather than arising from an impulse toward equal labor rights for women. The growing identification of men as "breadwinners" and the rise of an urban middle class (with its status-conscious emphasis on the "lady of leisure" further reinforced the tendency to view women as secondary wage-earners, regardless of their actual contributions to family survival.

*African-American women, most of whom arrived in North America as enslaved laborers, constitute the telling exception to this pattern. *Slavery, the labor system that built the *South and spurred *industrialization in the North, starkly illustrates not only women's employment in hard manual labor, but also the importance of unpaid labor to regional and national economic growth. Enslaved women regularly engaged in heavy field labor, as well as performing most of the *domestic labor of cooking, cleaning, and raising children. Since the late nineteenth century, African-American women have participated in the labor force at a rate higher than that of any other group of American women. As late as 1997, 51 percent of black women worked full time, compared to 42 percent of white women and 35 percent of Hispanic women. Not until *World War II did African-American women make significant headway in industrial jobs, however, and only in the late twentieth century did they make important progress in professional occupations other than teaching.

The labor force participation of immigrant women (first from Europe and later from Latin America and Asia) was constrained by employer discrimination; *immigration policies that made employment status uncertain; and attitudes within their own cultures that restricted some married immigrant women to home-based outwork, family-operated enterprises, or industries that employed family-based groups. *Poverty and discrimination combined to concentrate immigrant women in particularly exploitative jobs in domestic work, migrant agricultural labor, and low-wage manufacturing. By the early twentieth century, for example, women from southern and eastern Europe dominated the garment industry, laboring for low pay in factories, sweatshops, or crowded, urban workplaces like the notorious Triangle Shirtwaist Company in *New York City, where 146 women died in a 1911 fire. In the twentieth century, a growing Latina workforce, both U.S.-born and immigrant, was concentrated in migrant labor, food processing, industrial sweatshops, and homework.

From the late nineteenth century onward, U.S.-born white women enjoyed steadily expanding access to nonagricultural and nonindustrial occupations. They increasingly found jobs as office clerks and secretaries and in retailing. Benefiting from expanded educational opportunities, white, middle-class women in the late nineteenth century entered the professions in growing numbers, initially as teachers, librarians, social workers, and nurses, and later in a variety of career paths, from firefighting and police work to the law, medicine, the ministry, higher education, and in the corporate world.

Historically, patterns of participation in the paid labor force have varied dramatically by marital status as well as by ethnicity and nativity. Until the 1930s, most wage-earning women were unmarried. As late as 1960, only one-third of married women were gainfully employed—a figure that obscures a common pattern of irregular yet continuing labor-force participation. Only in the late twentieth century did that pattern decisively shift. In 1997, 61.3 percent of married women were in the labor force.

Although only in the late twentieth century did most labor unions show an interest in organizing female workers, women in the paid labor force long constituted an aggressive force for reform. In the 1830s, women were among the first American workers to strike for higher wages. A strike of some twenty thousand New York shirtwaist workers in 1909–1910, the largest women's strike up to that time, helped turn the International Ladies Garment Workers Union into one of the nation's largest unions. Early twentieth-century protective work legislation for women proved the precursor to similar reforms for male workers. In the post–*World War II era, married women and African-American women (who had taken advantage of wartime mobilization to gain footholds in higher paying jobs) fought efforts to return them to prewar status. In the late twentieth century, women fought for better jobs and better working conditions through the *civil rights movement and second-wave *feminism.

With some notable cross-class and multiracial exceptions (for example, the *Women's Trade Union League of the early twentieth century), racial, ethnic, and class divisions continued throughout the century to impede efforts at labor equity. Meanwhile, the steady growth of the two-wage-earner family created a form of women's work some analysts called "the second shift": Even as they engaged in paid labor, married women still performed most of the unpaid family labor. This was true even for mothers of young children: Roughly two-thirds of women with children under six years of age held paid jobs in 1997. Despite federal and state efforts to provide women with job protection during pregnancy and the early childhood years, women remained especially vulnerable to low wages and job insecurity. Although women had made occupational gains as the century ended, they continued in many cases to earn less than comparably educated and experienced men. Even economically successful professional and managerial women often found their progress impeded by the nebulous pattern of biases sometimes called "the glass ceiling."

[*See also* Asian Americans; Factory System; Hispanic Americans; Immigrant Labor; Labor Markets; Labor Movements; Legal Profession; Libraries; Marriage and Divorce; Migratory Agricultural Workers; Nursing; Race and Ethnicity; Social Class; Social Work; Strikes and Industrial Conflict; Textile Industry; Triangle Shirtwaist Company Fire; Women's Rights Movements; Working-Class Life and Culture.]

• Philip Sheldon Foner, *Women and the American Labor Movement: From the First Trade Unions to the Present,* 1982. Alice Kessler-Harris, *Out to Work: a History of Wage-Earning Women in the United States,* 1982. Jacqueline Jones, *Labor of Love, Labor of Sorrow: Black Women, Work, and the Family from Slavery to the Present,* 1985. Jeanne Boydston, *Home and Work: Housework, Wages, and the Ideology of Labor in the Early American Republic,* 1990. Alice Kessler-Harris, *A Woman's Wage: Historical Meanings and Social Consequences,* 1990. Ava Baron, ed., *Work Engendered: Toward a New History of American Labor,* 1991. Vicki L. Ruiz, *From Out of the Shadow: Mexican American Women in Twentieth-Century America,* 1998. Deborah Gray White, *Ar'n't I a Woman?: Female Slaves in the Plantation South,* rev. ed., 1999.

—Jeanne Boydston

WOMEN'S CLUB MOVEMENT. As social conventions prescribed increasingly separate roles for men and women in early and mid-nineteenth-century America, middle-class women often found themselves isolated in the home, excluded from the civic arena. Rather than acquiesce, many women won a voice in the public sphere by forming societies and clubs for self-improvement and community reform. In the early 1800s, women organized to address church, temperance, missionary, benevolence, *antislavery, and even voting issues. During the *Civil War, both Union and Confederate women created associations to support the soldiers and facilitate patriotic activities. In the *Gilded Age, women established local groups devoted to family, health, educational, and municipal concerns. Clubwomen organized study groups, raised funds, and focused public attention on such diverse issues as collegiate education for women; homes for unwed mothers; pensions for widows with dependents; protection of industrial workers; *child-labor laws; maternal and infant-care clinics; and such civic projects as *libraries, streetlights, parks and playgrounds, services for immigrants, and *housing reform.

The club movement attracted mainly white, Protestant, middle-class wives of successful professional and businessmen, although career women, especially educators, writers, physicians, and other professionals also joined. *African-American women, unwelcome in most clubs, formed separate societies to pursue similar projects. Many local groups united with the *Woman's Christian Temperance Union (1873), the General Federation of Women's Clubs (1890), and the National Association of Colored Women's Clubs (1896). Among the early leaders of women's voluntary activism were Frances *Willard, Mary McLeod *Bethune, Jane Cunningham Croly in *New York City, Julia Ward Howe of *Boston, and Caroline Severance of Boston and *Los Angeles. By the turn of the century, specialized clubs in many towns and cities were linking up with like-minded groups in other cities through such national associations as the National Council of Jewish Women, Drama League of America, National Federation of Music Clubs, National Congress of Mothers (later the Parent-Teacher Association), Association of Collegiate Alumnae (later the *American Association of University Women), the National Federation of Business and Professional Women, National Consumers' League, League of Women Voters, Junior League of America, Daughters of the American Revolution, *National American Woman Suffrage Association, Women's International League for Peace and Freedom, Garden Club of America, and women's auxiliaries to masonic orders and other *fraternal organizations.

The women's club movement, threatening the social convention that "women's place is in the home," initially engendered criticism. Newspaper editorials deplored clubwomen's intrusion into the public sphere and their alleged neglect of child care and household responsibilities. Members persevered, however, and by the first decade of the twentieth century, over a million clubwomen had won respect for their tenacity in demanding needed reforms. The enfranchisement of women in 1920, coupled with increasing opportunities for modern women, drained the club movement of members and resources. While many clubs survived into the late twentieth century, the movement lacked the size or influence it had enjoyed in its heyday.

[*See also* Consumer Movement; Feminism; Gender; Missionary Movement; Parks, Urban; Progressive Era; Temperance and Prohibition; Woman Suffrage Movement.]

• Anne Firor Scott, *Natural Allies: Women's Associations in American History,* 1991. Anne Ruggles Gere, *Intimate Practices: Literacy and Cultural Work in U.S. Women's Clubs, 1880–1920,* 1997.

—Karen J. Blair

WOMEN'S INTERNATIONAL LEAGUE FOR PEACE AND FREEDOM. *See* Pacifism; Peace Movements.

WOMEN'S RIGHTS MOVEMENTS. The American women's rights movement is usually dated from the convention held in Seneca Falls, New York, in 1848 to discuss the "Social, Civil, and Religious Condition of Woman." This meeting gathered activists from a wide range of political and reform concerns: *antislavery, *Free-Soil party supporters, temperance advocates, and Congregational Friends—a dissident religious group that had recently separated from the Hicksite Quakers. Lucretia

*Mott, the only nationally known woman speaker at the meeting, gained recognition as the convention's moving "spirit." Elizabeth Cady *Stanton drafted the "Declaration of Sentiments," a document read and revised during the proceedings. This treatise called not only for women's right to vote, but insisted that women be granted "immediate admission to all the rights and privileges which belong to them as citizens of the United States."

The Antebellum Era. Yet the women's rights movement did not begin in a single place nor did it focus exclusively on the vote. The process of mobilizing a women's rights movement was, in fact, far more complex. Before the *Civil War, activists organized local and national women's rights conventions in Indiana, Massachusetts, New York, Ohio, and Pennsylvania. The national conventions were most vociferously promoted by Paulina Wright Davis (1813–1876), of Providence, Rhode Island, who also edited *The Una* (1853–1855), the first periodical devoted exclusively to the movement. These national gatherings occurred annually from 1850 to 1860 in Worcester, Syracuse, Cleveland, Cincinnati, *Philadelphia, and *New York City.

In each state, coalitions of activists used this symbolic public forum to draft resolutions, make speeches, and organize petition campaigns that helped create a "critical public" and establish a "community discourse" about a wide range of issues. Holding a convention for open discussion of women's status as "rights-bearers" demonstrated that women constituted a portion of "the people" capable of shaping public opinion and stimulating political action. This goal was made clear at the 1850 Woman's Rights Convention in Salem, Ohio, where only women were permitted to participate in the deliberations, while males were relegated to the role of silent spectators, the traditional place of women in *Antebellum Era politics.

In an era of avid constitutional revision, eleven states called conventions between 1846 and 1851 to redraft their original compacts. The early women's rights conventions organized in response to these state constitutional conventions. The 1848 Seneca Falls and Rochester women's rights meetings occurred two years after a New York constitutional convention, and the local delegate to the state constitutional deliberations, Ansel Bascom, attended the Seneca Falls meeting. Similarly, the early women's rights conventions in Ohio were responses to the Ohio state constitutional convention of 1850–1851. Activists held a convention in Indiana while that state revised its constitution. And the first two national conventions in Worcester, Massachusetts, were held in anticipation of an 1853 state constitutional convention.

Through this process, women's rights activists generated a coherent critique of women's position in society. They framed their arguments not only in natural-rights terms, but according to current understandings of the right of protection, due process, and personal *liberty. They developed a sophisticated theoretical perspective on *equality, consent, representation, and national citizenship. Supporters of women's rights also shaped their view of democratic polity through their earlier involvement in campaigns protesting black codes, fugitive slave laws, prostitution, capital punishment, and the *Mexican War. All of these constituted a critique of the state's power to vest and divest rights, create "disabled castes," and undermine women's equal protection before the law.

Recognizing the link between women's family status and their political and civil standing, activists campaigned for married women's property rights, equal custody rights, a wife's contractual right to keep her wages, and, by 1860, women's right to divorce. This last issue proved divisive, however: Proponents such as Stanton argued that divorce required state protection, while some, like Antoinette Brown Blackwell (1825–1921), called for separation rather than divorce as a solution to unfit marriages.

The church provided another arena of political struggle because, in the language of representation, the dual images of the husband as head of the family and the minister as head of the congregation, reinforced the dominant political justification for women's exclusion from the political domain—namely, that all women were represented by proxy through men. Most supporters of the women's rights movement were also active in radical religious groups such as the Progressive Friends, evangelical and transcendentalist free churches, or the Religious Union of Associationists. These dissident religious groups created a public forum that acknowledged the "coequal representation" of the sexes.

From the Civil Wart to 1890. The Civil War curtailed the women's rights conventions. Nevertheless, during the war Susan B. *Anthony and other politically active reformers organized the Women's National Loyal League in New York to collect signatures on petitions urging the emancipation of slaves, which was achieved in 1865 with ratification of the Thirteenth Amendment.

By 1869 the women's rights movement had split into two factions: the National Woman Suffrage Association (NWSA), led by Stanton and Anthony, and the American Woman Suffrage Association (AWSA), supported by Lucy *Stone and Antoinette Brown Blackwell. The NWSA, headquartered in New York, published *The Revolution* (1868–1872); the Boston-based AWSA, which emerged from the American Equal Rights Association and the New England Woman's Suffrage Association, published *Woman's Journal* (1870–). The division resulted from the *Republican party's readiness, by means of the *Fourteenth and *Fifteenth Amendments, to grant equal protection and *suffrage to African-American men while excluding women from these same rights. The NWSA, refusing to postpone women's claims, explicitly asserted white women's superiority over black men as potential voters. The AWSA took a more qualified position on this issue, reaffirming the prewar alliance between the antislavery and women's rights movements. Further, while the NWSA was run exclusively by women, the AWSA included men and indeed granted them leadership positions. While the AWSA was linked to the Republican party, the Stanton-Anthony organization joined forces with *Democratic party supporters of the cause. Beginning in the volatile Kansas woman suffrage campaign of 1867, Stanton and Anthony collaborated with George Francis Train, who celebrated the superiority of white, middle-class, educated women over the newly freed, black male population.

In the following decades, the AWSA encouraged the formation of woman suffrage associations at the state and local level. The NWSA used more confrontational tactics, promoting efforts of women to vote illegally. This strategy of storming the polls began in 1870, resulting in Anthony's arrest and prosecution in 1872–1873. The NWSA focus on constitutional rights led to its involvement in two important if unsuccessful *Supreme Court cases. *Bradwell* v. *Illinois* (1873) denied Myra Bradwell the right to practice law, restricted women's rights to engage in other professions or public pursuits, and reaffirmed the distinction between women's basic *civil rights and their political rights. In *Minor* v. *Happersett* (1875), the Court ruled that although women were "citizens" and "persons," this did not guarantee them the privilege of voting. These two cases made clear that state-level campaigns to secure the rights of citizenship held more promise than national campaigns. Even state-level campaigns, however, required long-term plans for changing public opinion and working with partisan politicians.

During the 1870s and 1880s, the demands for "equal rights" or "women's rights" faced competition from a new political ideology, "Home Protection," advocated by Frances *Willard of the *Woman's Christian Temperance Union (WCTU). This new wave of reform emphasized certain traditional values, particularly the ideal of women's vital domestic role, and stressed women's moral distinctiveness rather than their political equality. Under Willard's leadership, the WCTU gained over 200,000 members in the 1880s, built a national grassroots organization, and established local alliances with state politicians. The WCTU did not escape *racism, especially as it organized in southern states. By playing upon fears of sexual assault by drunken men, the WCTU contributed to the "southern *rape complex" that southern white politicians used to justify the *lynching of black men.

From 1890 to 1920. State campaigns brought some success. Women won the right to vote in Colorado in 1893, relying on support from the WCTU, the *Populist party, and the Colorado State Equal Suffrage League. In 1890, the two wings of the movement joined to form the *National American Woman Suffrage Association (NAWSA), a union long pursued by Susan B. Anthony, the first president of the new organization. Race remained divisive, however, as the NAWSA excluded black women in an attempt to retain support from southern white women. But in 1906, NAWSA president Anna Howard Shaw (1847–1919) refused to endorse the racist campaigns in the *South, arguing that woman suffrage should not promote racial exploitation.

Dramatic changes came around 1910, as the woman suffrage campaign emerged as a "feminist" movement. A new cadre of leaders, including Harriet Stanton Blatch (daughter of Elizabeth Cady Stanton), Carrie Chapman *Catt, Jane *Addams, and Alice Paul (1885–1977), argued for suffrage not only as a matter of justice, but also as a solution to such political and social problems as prostitution, labor exploitation, and municipal corruption, thus linking it to the powerful wave of Progressive political reform. Distancing themselves from the nativist and racist agendas of the late nineteenth century, the new leaders even attempted to form alliances with immigrant men through their support for *child-labor laws and literacy campaigns. By linking suffrage to social policy at the state level, the NAWSA laid the foundation for a larger national campaign to amend the federal *Constitution. This final push for suffrage, initiated in 1914, culminated in 1920 with ratification of the *Nineteenth Amendment, guaranteeing women's right to vote.

[*See also* Civil Rights; Feminism; Marriage and Divorce; Progressive Era; Prostitution and Antiprostitution; Rape; Religion; Seneca Falls Convention; Society of Friends; State Governments; Temperance and Prohibition; Transcendentalism; Woman Suffrage Movement.]

• Ellen Carol DuBois, *Feminism and Suffrage: The Emergence of an Independent Women's Movement in America, 1848–1869,* 1978. Nancy F. Cott, *The Grounding of Modern Feminism,* 1987. Nancy Caraway, *Segregated Sisterhood: Racism and the Politics of American Feminism,* 1991. Joan Hoff, *Law, Gender and Injustice: A Legal History of U.S. Women,* 1991. Judy Wellman, "The Seneca Falls Women's Rights Convention: A Study of Social Networks," *Journal of Women's History* 3 (Spring 1991): 9–37. Ellen Carol DuBois, "Taking the Law into Our Own Hands: *Bradwell, Minor,* and Suffrage Militance in the 1870s," in *Visible Women: New Essays on American Activism,* eds. Nancy A. Hewitt and Suzanne Lebsock, 1993, pp. 19–40. Suzanne M. Marilley, *Woman Suffrage and the Origins of Liberal Feminism in the United States, 1820–1920,* 1996. Ellen Carol DuBois, *Harriot Stanton Blatch and the Winning of Woman Suffrage,* 1997. Nancy Isenberg, *Sex and Citizenship in Antebellum America,* 1998.

—Nancy Isenberg

WOMEN'S STRIKE FOR PEACE. *See* Antinucler Protest Movements; Pacificism; Peace Movements.

WOMEN'S TRADE UNION LEAGUE. Founded in 1903 as an alliance of working women with middle- and upper-class reformers, the National Women's Trade Union League (NWTUL) wedded *feminism with class concerns to create the *Progressive Era's most effective voice for working-class women. The league was a unique blend of reform unionism and social feminism in which Swedish bootmakers, Italian candymakers, and Jewish seamstresses, among others, joined forces with former debutantes and heiresses.

The league's emblem embodied its mission: Minerva, the Roman goddess of wisdom and war, reached over the rising sun and the league's motto—"The Eight Hour Day, A Living Wage, To Guard the Home"—to clasp the hand of a young mother, babe in arms, standing before the smokestacks of a factory. In serving this mission, the NWTUL organized women into trade unions; secured protective legislation, especially minimum wages and maximum hours for women; and educated the public to the needs of working-class women. At its peak, the organization had twenty-two branches, with its strength concentrated in *New York City, *Chicago, and *Boston.

The league's most notable achievements, during the presidency of Margaret Dreier Robins from 1907 to 1922, include its support of major garment-workers' strikes in New York and Chicago in 1909–1911. Robins and the WTUL played a central role in the development of arbitration mechanisms at Chicago's Hart, Schaffner and Marx men's clothing company, a landmark in labor history that introduced a measure of industrial democracy for workers. The organization published its own journal, *Life and Labor,* and trained working women as union organizers. Robins recruited as members both reform-minded women of wealth and poor, young working women like Rose Schneiderman of New York, who became an influential labor organizer and social reformer in her own right.

Never warmly embraced by the *American Federation of Labor, the league nevertheless worked effectively in the *South during the 1920s. Its role diminished in the 1930s, however, and it ceased to exist in 1950. In its heyday, the WTUL achieved considerable success in pursuing its three-pronged goal of labor organization, legislation, and education. The league championed the cause of working women at a time when both the industrial workforce and the labor movement were overwhelmingly male-dominated.

[*See also* Labor Movements; Strikes and Industrial Conflict; Triangle Shirtwaist Company Fire; Women in the Labor Force.]

• Nancy Schrom Dye, *As Equals and as Sisters: Feminism, the Labor Movement, and the Women's Trade Union League of New York,* 1980. Elizabeth Anne Payne, *Reform, Labor, and Feminism: Margaret Dreier Robins and the Women's Trade Union League,* 1988.

—Elizabeth Anne Payne

WOOLMAN, JOHN (1720–1772), Quaker minister, *antislavery activist, essayist. Born in West Jersey (now part of New Jersey) and married in 1749, he gave up his successful tailor shop in order to simplify his life. He became convinced that, in their pursuit of wealth, the rich exploit the labor of the poor and cultivate an unhealthy appetite for idleness and luxury. Such a system, he noted in the posthumously published *A Plea for the Poor* (1793), sacrifices all lives to spiritually debilitating activities. Avoiding business entanglements, he earned enough to live on by tailoring, school teaching, and drafting wills and bills of sale.

Woolman examined the most heinous form of that acquisitive system in his two-part essay, *Some Considerations on the Keeping of Negroes* (1754, 1762), which denounced the institution of *slavery as inconsistent with the ideal of human brotherhood and the "natural Right of Freedom." Yet, as detailed in his *Journal* (1774), a spiritual autobiography, his most effective antislavery work took place during extensive travels throughout British North America, where he spoke with people in meetings, in taverns, and in homes. Believing that "conduct is more convincing than language," he strove to make his life consistent with his principles. He declined to write bills of sale or wills for the transfer of slaves, and he eschewed the use of rum, sugar, molasses, and dyed clothes, all products of West Indian slave labor. A moving example of the peace born of a simplified life, the *Journal* also reveals how, for Woolman, spiritual development was inextricably intertwined with social responsibility. Praised by such writers as Samuel Taylor Coleridge and Charles Lamb, the *Journal* secured Woolman's status as one of the *Colonial Era's major essayists and opponents of slavery.

[*See also* Religion; Society of Friends.]

• Janet Whitney, *John Woolman: American Quaker,* 1942. Paul Rosenblatt, *John Woolman,* 1969.

—Emily Schiller

WORK. Apart from the occupations of a comparatively small proportion of the population who were ministers, teachers, lawyers, merchants, or shopkeepers, farm work was the chief occupation in early America. Tobacco growing, the main activity in the seventeenth-century Chesapeake region, was labor intensive. Planting, hoeing, cutting, and drying was done by farmers and a larger indentured labor force. Indentured servants financed their passage to America by contracting to labor for four to seven years. Many eventually acquired their own farms.

Enslaved Africans began to replace indentured servants by the 1690s. Even though most tobacco farmers never owned slaves, *slavery grew enormously in the eighteenth century. By 1770, 40 percent of the southern population, or 400,000 people, was enslaved. Eighty percent of these lived in the Chesapeake region and the rest in South Carolina, where they grew indigo and rice. Slave labor became even more important with the growth of the nineteenth century *cotton industry. Of the four million slaves in 1860—one in three southerners—most worked in cotton fields, as far west as east Texas, while others worked on tobacco farms or on Louisiana sugar plantations. Once slavery ended in 1865, many former slaves became sharecroppers. Planters rented their land in parcels for usually half of the crop. As southern *agriculture declined, many white farmers also became sharecroppers.

It was small yeoman farmers, however, who dominated American agriculture from the *Colonial Era through the nineteenth century. Even in the antebellum *South, 75 percent of white southern farmers had owned no slaves. Male farmers and their sons from Maine to Florida cleared land, plowed, planted, and cultivated primarily food crops such as corn and wheat. Wives and daughters contributed to the household economy by cooking, spinning, weaving, preserving foods, growing vegetable gardens, tending cows, chickens, and hogs, and working in the fields during harvest time. *New England farmers also engaged in *lumbering and raising livestock. Fishing, especially for cod, was another important activity. Farmers in the middle colonies led the way in developing commercial agriculture in wheat and other grains.

Wheat farming expanded into the *Middle West after 1830. Farmers cultivated prairie lands with new steel plows, and harvested three-quarters of an acre a day with hand-held scythes. By the 1880s, however, steam-powered harvesters reaped 20 acres a day, and a combine did the work of 20 men. Two men could cultivate 250 acres. Although the number of farms rose from 2 million in 1869 to over 5.7 million by 1900, mechanization freed many for work in industry and commerce. A surplus rural population, combined with increased *immigration supplied the workforce for the factories and shops of what had been a labor-starved industrial sector.

*Industrialization, which would fundamentally change work habits, grew slowly in America, but by 1860 almost 20 percent of all laborers worked in factories. Among the earliest were the Massachusetts textile-mill hands, farm girls and women aged sixteen to twenty-three who after 1814 worked twelve hours a day, six days a week on mechanized carders, spinners, and looms. Women, mostly young and single, continued to work in textile mills through the early twentieth century; others found employment as domestics. Immigrant and poor married women worked at home in low-paying industries like the needle trades, made more efficient by the sewing machine.

Immigrant Irish and Chinese men worked as day laborers building the transcontinental *railroads. Immigrant and native-born men also worked in *mining, in the *iron and steel industry, and in all kinds of manufacturing. By 1900, 48.3 percent of all male workers had industrial jobs. Factory discipline, which had begun with the time clock, intensified with the introduction of assembly-line work. Time-and-motion studies, developed by the *scientific-management pioneer Frederick W. Taylor, threatened to rob workers of all autonomy in the workplace. Children, who had long worked at home and on the farm, now were also employed in coal mines, textile mills, and factories. By 1900, children aged ten to fifteen made up 18 percent (or 1.7 million operatives) of the entire labor force, and 7 percent of non-agricultural workers.

Industrialization and the growth of retailing also produced many new white-collar jobs, not only for managers, but also for secretaries and shop clerks; by the beginning of the twentieth century many of these positions were held by women. Along with corporate managers and specialists in business-related fields such as accounting, banking, *insurance, and *advertising, the white-collar workforce also included ministers and growing numbers of professionals in such fields as *journalism, publishing, *education, *medicine, and the law.

Labor patterns changed again during the Depression of the 1930s and *World War II. *Child labor declined sharply during the 1930s. World War II brought many women into skilled factory jobs formerly reserved for men. By 1944, eighteen million women had jobs, 50 percent more than in 1939, many in well-paid industries like ship-, automobile-, and machine manufacturing. After a decline in female employment in the immediate postwar period, women by 1960 again held more than one-third of all jobs. More married women worked than ever before, and by the 1980s they were well represented in all the professions. Agricultural employment decreased dramatically in the same period (the farm population fell from thirty to thirteen million between 1940 and 1964) owing to increased mechanization and large-scale commercial farming. The economy also shifted from production to services. By 1960, blue-collar workers constituted just 40 percent of the total workforce, as more workers were employed in goods distribution and services. The dramatic decline of manufacturing in the 1970s and 1980s furthered this trend, as the number of well-paid factory jobs diminished while lower-paying service jobs increased.

American attitudes toward work underwent changes as well. New England Puritans had seen work as a secular calling, with deep religious meaning. Although assembly-line work could be deadening, as late as the mid-twentieth century many blue-collar workers still felt strong ties to the companies that employed them, while white-collar company men felt a loyalty to their employers that was frequently reciprocated. By the 1980s, downsizing had changed these attitudes. Work had become for many simply a means of income, and early retirement a pervasive goal.

[*See also* Banking and Finance; Depressions, Economic; Factory System; Fisheries; Immigrant Labor; Indentured Servitude; Labor Markets; Labor Movements; Legal Profession; Leisure; Mass Production; Professionalization; Sharecropping and Tenantry; Social Class; Strikes and Industrial Conflict; Tobacco Industry; Unemployment; Women in the Labor Force.]

• Paul W. Gates, *The Farmer's Age: Agriculture, 1815–1860,* 1960. Daniel T. Rodgers, *The Work Ethic in Industrial America, 1850–1920,* 1978. David W. Galenson, *White Servitude in Colonial America: An Economic Analysis,* 1981. David A. Hounshell, *From the American System to Mass Production, 1800–1932,* 1984. W. J. Rorabaugh, *The Craft Apprentice: From Franklin to the Machine Age in America,* 1986. Peter Kolchin, *American Slavery, 1619–1877,* 1993. Kathryn Marie Dudley, *The End of the Line: Lost Jobs, New Lives in Postindustrial America,* 1994.

—David M. Gordon

WORKING-CLASS LIFE AND CULTURE. In his landmark study *Work, Culture and Society in Industrializing America*

(1976), historian Herbert Gutman drew upon the work of anthropologist Sidney Mintz to define working-class culture as a "kind of resource" for workers in their daily lives and struggles. Much recent scholarship has focused on interpreting working-class culture, from its origins in *Colonial-Era artisanal life through the immigrant-industrial era of the nineteenth century to the diverse and complex patterns of the twentieth century. There is, in fact, no single working-class culture, but a shifting kaleidoscope of subcultures, in which *race and ethnicity, *gender, *religion, region, and type of employment all play a part.

The Late Colonial and Antebellum Eras. Distinct urban working classes first emerged in the cities of mid-eighteenth century America. With craft work the predominant way of producing goods, artisans occupied an important, if subordinate, place in the cultural life of the late Colonial Era. The closely linked values of craft work and "manliness" influenced both revolutionary and class politics, as artisans, inspired by Thomas *Paine, adopted the banner of *republicanism. The artisanal culture spawned by the *Revolutionary War and its aftermath found expression in the politics of the early republic.

As the economic and cultural gap separating the social classes widened in the *Antebellum Era, the urban working class was characterized by fear of dependence, loss of political status, and racial and ethnic fissures. While immigrants fleeing Ireland's potato famine flooded into seaboard cities, white migrants arrived from rural America and the poverty-stricken free black population also increased. Employed largely as day laborers in construction and transportation, these new workers drew upon agrarian traditions to create their own rough culture. U.S.-born and immigrant white craftsmen, meanwhile, differed from both the emerging middle classes and the laboring poor. Reacting against the threat of their own transformation into wage laborers, craftsmen adopted artisanal republicanism and its labor theory of value to proclaim productive labor of the kind they themselves performed as the moral grounding of republican democracy, even as they distanced themselves from the unskilled masses and the dependent poor by celebrating their autonomy and respectability. Among printers, builders, shoemakers, tailors, and other artisans and mechanics, a sense of solidarity and pride in shared skills generated the first working-class trade associations and, later, the first labor unions.

Economic dependency and political disfranchisement lowered the status of working-class women. Politically and economically, men were the principal public actors in the working class. With a few exceptions, such as the early *New England textile mills, women were denied employment in either skilled or unskilled occupations. Although most working-class families required an economic contribution from wives and daughters, fathers and older sons were the principal wage-earners and authority figures. For some workers, manliness expressed itself in dress, sporting competitions, braggadocio about drinking and sexual prowess, and the equation of masculinity with whiteness. Volunteer fire brigades and political clubs welded younger working men into ethnically defined solidarities. In *New York and other cities, an urban subculture of native-born and immigrant workingmen, typified by New York's "Bowery B'hoys," glorified drinking, street fighting, and dandified clothes. If this expressed one facet of antebellum working-class culture, another was revealed in the behavior of respectable artisans whose evangelical *Protestantism extolled piety and sobriety.

The Urban-Industrial Age. Post-*Civil War working-class culture assumed new forms in the growing cities of the North and *Middle West. Racial divisions and differences among various ethnic immigrant groups, as well as membership in cross-class organizations such as the *Grand Army of the Republic and *fraternal organizations like the *Masonic Order and Odd Fellows, often undercut working-class solidarity. For a time in the late 1870s and 1880s, however, the *Knights of Labor became the dominant institutional expression of working-class political culture. Dedicated to improving social conditions and educating and organizing the producing classes, the Knights recruited skilled craftsmen, unskilled laborers, industrial workers, and—with less success—small businessmen. Under the banner of worker republicanism, the Knights espoused a radical working-class political sensibility and adopted innovative forms of working-class protest. The order also fostered a vibrant working-class culture through political clubs, newspapers, songs, and literature, as well as land-reform and home-ownership associations and trade and industrial unions. The Knights supported women's rights and racial equality as well, rhetorically if not always in practice, as part of the effort to recruit all working people. But the Knights at their peak represented no more than 10 percent of all workers. Most politically active workers remained in the *Republican or *Democratic parties.

The Knights declined in the early 1890s as the bitter *Homestead lockout and *Pullman strike (1892 and 1894 respectively) thrust class conflict into national politics and as continued *industrialization and *immigration contributed to a shifting class terrain and intensified conflicts among workers of different ethnic and racial backgrounds. With *racism and Jim Crow practices at a peak in America, the hostility of white workers toward the small but growing number of *African-American wage earners and, on the West Coast, Chinese immigrant workers, was particularly intense. With the new immigrants lacking labor-market power and therefore proving difficult to organize, the railroad brotherhoods and the craft unions of the *American Federation of Labor concentrated on advancing their own economic interests, and some actively supported immigration restriction.

Religious differences within the working class also intensified in the late nineteenth and early twentieth centuries. Earlier waves of *immigration had brought religious diversity to the U.S. working class. German immigrants had been both Catholic and Protestant, and the influx of Irish Catholic newcomers in a predominantly Protestant nation had stirred protests and riots. The religious divisions now deepened as Catholic, Eastern Orthodox, and Jewish immigrants arrived in great numbers from southern and eastern Europe. Immigration peaked at about 1 million people a year between 1900 and *World War I. While divergent religious loyalties reinforced ethnic and skill-based differences among workers, they also encouraged new forms of working-class organization. Immigrant fraternal organizations and mutual-aid societies provided insurance benefits and enlivened community life with dances, fairs and holidays, and political activities. Ethnic parishes, publications, shops, taverns, athletic clubs, and cultural societies broadened and nourished working-class culture. The preservation of Yiddish, Italian, Czech, Polish, and other immigrant languages in newspapers, religious services, and popular entertainments further cemented the solidarity of these immigrant working-class enclaves.

Russian Jewish radicals, Italian anarchists, and eastern European socialists expanded working-class political culture. While only a minority of immigrant workers were politically active, these enclaves did generate inclusive forms of worker protest and association. The *Industrial Workers of the World (IWW), founded in 1905 to spread industrial unionism, organized immigrant and native-born workers. Emphasizing class unity, the IWW promoted a vibrant working-class culture through songs, poetry, and cartoons.

From World War I to the Late Twentieth Century. Nevertheless, the culture of both immigrant and U.S.-born workers was inexorably changing. Mass-market fiction, dime novels, and the popular press increasingly appealed to a broad, cross-class audience with stories tailored to the language skills and educational levels of working-class readers. Music halls, *vaudeville, *amusement parks, professional *sports, dance pavilions, and the songs of Tin Pan Alley all attracted working-class consumers. Vaudevillians, sheet-music publishers, and early filmmakers appropriated themes from immigrant and working-class culture while tailoring their products to a mass audience. The immigrant working-class cultural enclaves remained strong through the 1920s, but thereafter the new mass culture steadily undermined the ethnic associations and businesses that had dominanted the immigrants' social and cultural life. One result of this process was to make *social class more salient than ethnicity and to encourage the formation of a working-class consciousness. The hard times of the 1930s and the patriotism of *World War II contributed to this process as well, as did the decline of immigration caused by World War I and the restrictive immigration laws of the 1920s. Working-class life and culture was further transformed as increasing numbers of native-born women and southern black and white migrants replaced European immigrants in the labor force. Southern whites introduced country music and the "hillbilly" culture of *Appalachia to northern cities, even as African Americans brought *gospel music and the *blues.

As the economic crisis of the 1930s bankrupted ethnic fraternal unions, banks, and businesses, the specter of *unemployment, and the continued influence of *popular culture, united workers across ethnic and occupational lines. The shift found expression in the political culture of the *New Deal. The labor movement of the 1930s, encouraged by the *National Labor Relations Act and led by the *Congress of Industrial Organizations and a revitalized American Federation of Labor, transformed working-class culture. Labor newspapers, radical theater, union-sponsored recreational events, and workers'-education programs underscored how far many workers had moved toward broad-based class solidarity. The new language of working-class unity did not always match its practice, as racial and gender discrimination and conflict continued to roil working-class life, but World War II furthered racial integration, drew millions of women at least temporarily into the labor force, and encouraged pluralistic values in culture and society.

In the prosperous 1950s, working-class culture became almost indistinguishable from mass culture. *Television, movies, mass *magazines, paperback books, chain stores, fast-food outlets, and the popular music promoted by the recording industry and radio disk jockeys all relied heavily on working-class consumers. While mass culture producers sometimes employed class themes, they sought to build a consumer market that transcended class. For example, while African-American music retained its distinctivenes, the blues evolved into rock-and-roll, which expressed a youth culture more than a class culture. Its wide acceptance among young people of differing ethnic, racial, and class origins blunted its political edge.

Working-Class Culture? A Summing Up. As the twentieth century ended, the question of whether one could even speak of an American working-class culture remained unresolved. In any simple sense, the answer was probably no. In many respects that had always been true. Throughout the nation's history, the working class had been characterized by its fragmentation, even though class-defined political movements in the workplace and the electoral arena had sometimes opened a common ground for broad working-class constituencies. Ironically, the moments of exceptional class solidarity had often come at times of national cultural unity, as in the early national era, the New Deal period, and World War II. The rise of a mass culture and other pressures countering class consciousness did not, therefore, preempt and undermine working-class culture so much as exist in dynamic relationship with it. Similarly, competing racial, ethnic, religious, and gender identities did not erode working-class culture but rather vastly complicated it, posing major hurdles to efforts to discover and define it. As a new century dawned, the task of understanding both the contradictions and the strengths of America's working-class culture seemed as challenging as ever.

[*See also* Anarchism; Asian Americans; Consumer Culture; Depressions, Economic; Film; German Americans; Immigrant Labor; Immigration Law; Industrial Relations; Irish Americans; Judaism; Labor Markets; Labor Movements; Lowell Mills; Mobility; Radicalism; Railroads; Roman Catholicism; Socialism; Strikes and Industrial Conflict; Urbanization; Women in the Labor Force; Women's Rights Movements.]

• Kathy Peiss, *Cheap Amusements: Working Women and Leisure in Turn of the Century New York,* 1986. Christine Stansell, *City of Women: Sex and Class in New York, 1789–1860,* 1986. Herbert Gutman, *Power and Culture: Essays on the American Working Class,* ed. Ira Berlin, 1987. Jacquelyn Dowd Hall, James Leloudis, Robert Korstad, Mary Murphy, Lu Ann Jones, and Christopher B. Daly, *Like a Family: The Making of the Cotton Mill World* 1987. David Montgomery, *The Fall of the House of Labor: The Workplace, the State, and American Labor Activism, 1865–1925,* 1987. Lizabeth Cohen, *Making a New Deal: Industrial Workers in Chicago, 1919–1939,* 1990. Elizabeth Faue, *Community of Suffering and Struggle: Women, Men, and the Labor Movement in Minneapolis, 1915–1945,* 1991. Leon Fink, *In Search of the Working Class: Essays in American Labor History and Political Culture,* 1994. Robin D. G. Kelley, *Race Rebels: Culture, Politics and the Black Working Class,* 1994.

—Elizabeth Faue

WORKS PROGRESS ADMINISTRATION. One of the most prominent of the New Deal agencies, the Works Progress Administration (WPA) was established in 1935 as an ambitious and wide-ranging federal jobs program. Harry *Hopkins, an advocate of federally funded employment for the jobless, was appointed by President Franklin Delano *Roosevelt in 1934 to head the WPA's immediate predecessor, the Civil Works Administration (CWA), a limited work-relief program operating under the Federal Emergency Relief Administration. Its funds exhausted, the CWA ceased operations after only a few months.

The WPA, funded under the 1935 Emergency Relief Appropriations Act, differed from the CWA by seeking to provide employment on necessary projects rather than merely make-work tasks—to replace relief with real jobs. WPA undertakings included such diverse activities as building and road construction, day-nursery work, bookbinding, a federal theater project, a writers' project, research for the *Library of Congress, the creation and maintenance of parks and recreational facilities, and many other forms of blue- and white-collar employment. Jobs were of limited duration and usually paid prevailing wages. All told, the WPA employed some 8.5 million people.

The WPA—along with the entire New Deal—encountered considerable opposition from conservatives in Congress. In 1939 the Dies Committee, headed by Congressman Martin Dies of Texas, investigated alleged communist influence in the agency, focusing on the Federal Theater Project, which was terminated that year.

Renamed the Work Projects Administration in 1939, the WPA became increasingly involved in defense work; by late 1941, 40 percent of its workers were employed in defense projects. After the United States entered *World War II, war work and military service drastically reduced unemployment and in 1942, Roosevelt declared that the WPA had "earned an honorable discharge." It was disbanded on 30 June 1943.

[*See also* Depressions, Economic; New Deal Era, The; Unemployment.]

• Paul S. Kurzman, *Harry Hopkins and the New Deal,* 1974. Anthony J. Badger, *The New Deal,* 1989.

—Kenneth Franklin Kurz

WORLD BANK. Delegates to the *Bretton Woods Conference of 1944 understood that creating a lending institution devoted to extending credit for postwar rebuilding and development was essential to reviving the economy of a war-ravaged world. The result was the International Bank for Reconstruction and Development (IBRD), or World Bank. As with the simultaneously created *International Monetary Fund, the IBRD primarily reflected American ideas. Since the size of a country's voting rights depended on the amount of its capital subscription, the United States as the largest contributor has had the biggest say in selecting the president, who has usually been an American. The American determination to keep the initial subscription low, however, rendered the World Bank unable to cope with the economic crises of the immediate postwar period. Instead, ad hoc American loans and the U.S.-funded *Marshall Plan paid for the recovery of western Europe.

In the decade after 1946, major World Bank loans went to war-devastated industrial countries; thereafter the proportion of credits devoted to reconstruction plummeted. Under the presidency of Robert McNamara (1968–1981), the World Bank devoted itself to assisting the developing world, which generally lacked both internal and external private sources for development. Having initially concentrated on large-scale infrastructure, such as dams and ports, the World Bank increasingly funded "soft projects" such as agricultural development, population control, urban sewage supply, and educational endeavors. At the end of the 1970s the World Bank Group (consisting of the IBRD, the International Finance Corporation, and the Multilateral Investment Guaranty Corporation) also began lending for some nondevelopment purposes, such as bridging a balance-of-payments problem. With the American electorate largely oblivious to the World Bank's activities, U.S. presidents found it highly convenient to channel increasingly unpopular *foreign aid projects through this multilateral organization, thereby avoiding serious congressional or public scrutiny.

[*See also* Foreign Relations: The Economic Dimension; Global Economy, America and the; Internationalism; World War II: Postwar Impact.]

• Devesh Kapur, John P. Lewis, and Richard Webb, *The World Bank: Its First Half Century,* 1997.

—Diane B. Kunz

WORLD COURT. *See* Permanent Court of International Justice.

WORLD HEALTH ORGANIZATION (WHO), specialized organization of the *United Nations (UN). Headquartered in Geneva, the WHO was founded in 1948. Its constitution, adopted in 1946 by a UN-sponsored World Health Assembly, envisioned an ambitious effort to raise health standards worldwide. The WHO's antecedents included a series of international sanitary conferences beginning in 1851; an International Bureau of Public Hygiene created in Paris in 1907; and an International Health Organization established by the *League of Nations in 1921. Governed by a World Health Assembly that meets annually, and financed by assessments on member states, the WHO has focused on combating such diseases as *poliomyelitis, *cholera, leprosy, *malaria, and *tuberculosis. A global program to combat *acquired immunodeficiency syndrome (AIDS) was launched in 1987.

From the beginning, U.S. diplomats and *public-health experts played key roles in planning and implementing the WHO's program. The WHO subsumed tasks earlier performed by other international organizations, including the Washington-based Pan American Sanitary Bureau (PASB). With U.S. diplomatic support, the PASB joined the WHO, while preserving its own budget and other autonomous powers. Designated the WHO's "regional office in the Western Hemisphere" in 1949, the PASB was renamed the Pan American Health Organization (PAHO).

In the spirit of postwar *internationalism, Congress in 1948 agreed to underwrite approximately 35 percent of WHO's budget. The organization soon became enmeshed in *Cold War politics, however. In 1955, President Dwight D. *Eisenhower urged support for international health programs because *disease contributed to "the spread of communism." The Soviet Union, for its part, brought such contentious issues as the *Vietnam War before the WHO. During intervals of détente, however, the superpowers cooperated on major WHO initiatives. A Soviet proposal for eradicating *smallpox, for example, was brought to fruition by epidemiologists from the *Centers for Disease Control, and in 1979 a global commission declared smallpox eradicated. In the later twentieth century, U.S. policy toward the WHO remained ambivalent. While supporting programs to eradicate diseases such as polio, and to reduce infant mortality through immunization, nutritional supplements, and control of diarrheal diseases, Washington balked at diffuse and expensive efforts to transform global health through long-term infrastructural change. An ambitious WHO program entitled "Health for All by the Year 2000" won little support in Washington. Nevertheless, thousands of Americans continued to staff WHO and PAHO programs with passion and commitment.

[*See also* Medicine: Since 1945.]

• Pan American Health Organization, *Pro Salute Novi Mundi: A History of the Pan American Health Organization,* 1992. Javed Siddiqi, *World Health and World Politics: The WHO and the UN System,* 1995.

—Paul R. Greenough

WORLD'S COLUMBIAN EXPOSITION. *See* World's Fairs and Expositions.

WORLD'S FAIRS AND EXPOSITIONS. The era of modern world's fairs began with the 1851 Crystal Palace Exhibition in London. Housed in Joseph Paxton's stunning glass and iron structure, this fair attracted over six million visitors and served as a model for many subsequent fairs. In the United States, *New York City hosted its own Crystal Palace exhibition, complete with an iron and glass building, in 1853–1854; President Franklin *Pierce attended the opening ceremonies. But attendance was disappointing, and fair managers reported a loss of $300,000.

The New York exposition, as well as more successful fairs in Europe, perpetuated the legacy, however, and in 1876, *Philadelphia celebrated the centennial of U.S. independence with an elaborate world's fair called the Centennial International Exhibition. Situated in Fairmount Park, it included several large thematic exhibition halls and many small pavilions. Richard Wagner composed a march for the opening ceremonies. The most spectacular exhibit, the 700-ton Corliss steam engine, dominated Machinery Hall. The Centennial Exhibition attracted nearly 10 million visitors; garnered much favorable publicity; and although it lost money, spawned more fairs and expositions over the next thirty years. In the *South, seven fairs were held in various cities between 1881 and 1907. Initially intended to revitalize the southern economy after the *Civil War, these southern fairs eventually returned to the more traditional practice of celebrating anniversaries. Thus the *Jamestown (Virginia) Exposition of 1907 commemorated the tercentenary of the first permanent English settlement in North America.

The Philadelphia exhibition also convinced those looking forward to the four hundredth anniversary of Christopher *Columbus's voyage to America that a world's fair should be part of the festivities. The World's Columbian Exposition, held in *Chicago in 1893, arguably the most influential exposition in American history, featured a lagoon, statuary, electric illumination, and a dazzling display of white-painted neoclassical architecture. Under Chicago architect Daniel H. Burnham (1846–1912), many of the nation's leading architects and architectural firms, including Richard Morris Hunt; McKim, Mead, and White; and Adler and Sullivan, designed a fair that would long influence American *city planning and public *architecture.

The Chicago fair also featured the first entertainment center, the Midway Plaisance, offering rides (including the world's first Ferris wheel, invented by engineer George Ferris); circus sideshow features; and anthropological exhibits calculated to convince mainly Anglo-Saxon visitors that they were indeed members of the most advanced race. Following this exposition, the midway became a popular feature at world's fairs. Over 27 million visitors came to Chicago for the fair.

The 1901 Pan American Exposition in Buffalo, New York, intended to encourage trade between the United States and Latin America, was an aesthetic success, making good use of color and electric lighting. Its reputation was forever sullied, however, when on 6 September 1901, an anarchist shot President William *McKinley during a reception in the Temple of Music.

Three years later, in St. Louis, the Louisiana Purchase International Exposition commemorated the centennial of the *Louisiana Purchase. Spread over 1,271 acres in Forest Park, the St. Louis exposition covered nearly twice the area of the 1893 Columbian exposition. It attracted 20 million visitors (some drawn by a popular song of the day, "Meet Me in St. Louie, Louie"), earned a modest profit, and hosted the 1904 Summer Olympics.

The completion of the *Panama Canal and *San Francisco's recovery from the 1906 earthquake and fire provided the rationale for the Panama Pacific International Exposition of 1915. This, the largest of several fairs held on the West Coast, featured neoclassical buildings constructed around three courtyards, with the fair's signature building, Bernard Maybeck's Palace of Fine Arts, situated across a lagoon. Signaling the advent of the automobile, a miniature assembly line in the Palace of Transportation produced eighteen Model T Fords daily.

Post–*World War I political *isolationism dampened American enthusiasm for world's fairs. Philadelphia's 1926 effort to mark the nation's sesquicentennial with a world's fair was a aesthetic and commercial disappointment. By the late 1920s, however, a committee was planning a gala fair for Chicago's centennial in 1933, and despite the onset of the Great Depression, the Century of Progress Exposition proved a success. Adopting a geometric Art Deco architectural style, the planners minimized construction costs by reliance on bright colors and creative lighting for aesthetic effect. The fair exhibits focused on the progress and promise of *science.

The 1939–1940 New York World's Fair, celebrating the sesquicentennial of George *Washington's inauguration, offered another wonderland of Art Deco architecture and exhibits of scientific and technological marvels, including *television and limited-access superhighways. Robert Moses, the city's parks commissioner, saw the fair as a way to replace a large ash dump in the Flushing Meadows area with a park. Unfortunately, the fair, caught on the cusp of *World War II, failed to earn the profit that Moses had envisioned.

Perhaps because of *Cold War tensions, few fairs were held in the years immediately after World War II. The first large postwar fair, in Brussels in 1958, was full of Cold War symbolism. America's first postwar fair was the Century 21 Exposition in Seattle, Washington, in 1962. Prompted by concern over U.S. prestige following the 1957 Soviet *Sputnik* flight and a desire to promote *urban renewal in Seattle, it highlighted the theme of science education and featured a flashy U.S. pavilion funded by the federal government. The signature structure, a 605-foot Space Needle, continued to dominate Seattle's landscape a generation later. The success of the Seattle fair inspired smaller fairs in San Antonio, Texas (1968), Spokane, Washington (1974), Knoxville, Tennessee (1982), and *New Orleans (1984). Each was thematic rather than universal, and each focused on the redevelopment of a neglected part of its host city. While San Antonio and Spokane did well, the Knoxville fair was plagued by corrupt management and the New Orleans fair by financial disaster, leaving a dubious legacy for the future. Indeed, the rise of theme parks like Florida's Walt Disney World (1971) seemed in some ways to have preempted the whole idea of world's fairs.

[*See also* Amusement Parks and Theme Parks; Circuses; Disney, Walt; Popular Culture; Urbanization.]

• Robert C. Post, ed., *1876: A Centennial Exhibition*, 1976. Burton Benedict, et al., *The Anthropology of World's Fairs*, 1983. Robert W. Rydell, *All the World's a Fair: Visions of Empire at America's International Expositions, 1876–1916*, 1984. John E. Findling and Kimberly D. Pelle, eds., *Historical Dictionary of World's Fairs and Expositions, 1851–1988*, 1990. Robert W. Rydell, *World's Fairs: The Century-of-Progress Expositions*, 1993. John E. Findling, *Chicago's Great World's Fairs*, 1994. Robert W. Rydell, John E. Findling, and Kimberly D. Pelle, *Fair America: World's Fairs in the United States*, 2000.

—John Findling

WORLD TRADE ORGANIZATION. *See* General Agreement on Tariffs and Trade.

WORLD WAR I. In August 1914, nobody living anywhere in the world could imagine a spectacle as violent as the one into which humanity was about to be plunged. The magnitude of the destruction in World War I (1914–1918) strained human comprehension. Yet the conflict proved only a prelude to an even more horrendous tragedy, *World War II. The United States, after an initial period of neutrality, entered the war in April 1917 and played a decisive role in the final outcome and the peace settlement that followed.

Early Stages. On 28 June 1914, a young Serbian nationalist shot and killed the Archduke Franz Ferdinand, heir to the throne of Austria-Hungary, and his wife Sophie, as they paid a state visit to Sarajevo, capital of the restive Balkan province of Bosnia. The assassination set in motion a complicated chain reaction. Austria-Hungary declared war on Serbia on 28 July, which precipitated Russia's decision to mobilize on 30 July. In turn, Germany declared war on Russia on 1 August and on France, the latter's ally, two days later. Great Britain entered the war against Germany on 4 August, and against Austria-Hungary the following week.

Few Americans understood the origins or implications of these catalytic events, but they did not come "as lightning out of a clear sky," as one U.S. politician wrote. To the contrary, in the years before 1914, European diplomats had constructed a precarious balance of power—the Triple Alliance (Germany, Austria-Hungary, and Italy) on one side and the Triple Entente (France, Russia, and Great Britain) on the other—resting on a complex set of secret treaties. This division was rendered potentially calamitous by intense nationalism; by long-standing imperial rivalries over Africa, Asia, and the Middle East; by a massive military and naval build-up forged by rapid industrialization; and by unstable domestic environments, especially in capitals where reactionary governments confronted rising vanguards of liberals and socialists. Ultraconservatives in Germany and Russia, in particular, seized upon the Balkan crisis and exploited patriotic fervor to subdue domestic political challenges.

Once the titanic struggle was underway, it did not take long for the human toll to mount. In September, during the first Battle of the Marne, the Allies and the Central Powers together sustained more than a million casualties. By the end of 1914, France alone counted 900,000 dead, wounded, or missing. In 1915, 330,000 French soldiers were killed and another million wounded. The corresponding figures for Germany were 170,000 and 680,000, and for Great Britain 73,000 and 240,000. The carnage resulting from the five-month clash in 1916 between the French and the Germans over a single strategic objective (two forts near Verdun, France) equalled that of the entire American *Civil War, or some 600,000 killed. By the time the Russian czar abdicated in March 1917, his country had suffered 3.6 million dead or otherwise incapacitated. Recent innovations in warfare—including machine guns, poison gas, *submarines, and tanks—only added to the horror and outran the strategic calculations of elderly generals whose experience of war bore little relationship to the realities of the new technological age. In all, at least ten million people—mainly Europeans, but also hundreds of thousands of Asians and Americans—would go to their deaths as a consequence of the "Great War."

The American Response: From Neutrality to Intervention. When the war began, President Woodrow *Wilson issued a proclamation of neutrality, and his fellow citizens thanked heaven for the Atlantic Ocean. But geographic remoteness alone did not determine America's neutrality. A century-long tradition of noninvolvement in European affairs and the self-serving nature of the belligerents' war aims were equally important. Demography may have been even more decisive: according to the 1910 census, one-third of the U.S. population consisted of immigrants and their children. This ethnic diversity, and particularly the large numbers of *German Americans and *Irish Americans, precluded an overwhelming national consensus one way or the other, notwithstanding a somewhat vague pro-British sympathy felt by perhaps a majority of Americans.

The attempt to preserve neutrality posed innumerable problems for the Wilson administration. Great Britain imposed a naval blockade of the Atlantic and the North Sea to deprive the Central Powers of vital supplies, and the Royal Navy began to stop American merchant ships suspected of carrying contraband. In March 1915, a British Order in Council authorized the interdiction of all neutral commerce bound for Germany. The Wilson administration protested, invoking the principle of freedom of the seas. But the British were undeterred; subsequently, they went so far as to seize American parcels and mail on the Atlantic and to publish a "blacklist" of hundreds of U.S. businesses that allegedly traded with the Central Powers. By the summer of 1916, Anglo-American relations had fallen to their lowest ebb since the British burned *Washington, D.C., during the *War of 1812.

For all of its severity, Allied economic warfare was more than matched by the German government's novel method of retribution. On 4 February 1915, Berlin commenced submarine (U-boat) warfare against all enemy vessels, a policy that also imperiled American lives and commerce. Wilson's vow to hold Germany to "strict accountability" was soon put to the test. On 7 May 1915, a submarine sank the British passenger liner *Lusitania* without warning, off the southern coast of Ireland, drowning 1,198 men, women, and children—civilians all, among them 128 Americans. (Later research revealed that the *Lusitania* was also carrying a small cache of munitions bound for Britain.) With this seemingly wanton murder of innocents, in tandem with their trampling of neutral Belgium in their drive toward Paris, the Germans forfeited the contest for American public favor. Even so, the vast majority of Americans expected Wilson to keep them out of the war.

The U-boat issue came to a tentative resolution in the spring of 1916, in the wake of another torpedo that severely damaged the unarmed French steamer *Sussex* in the English Channel. Four Americans were among the eighty casualties, and Wilson demanded that the Germans henceforth observe the rules of cruiser warfare—to "visit and search" enemy vessels before sinking them and to provide for the safety of noncombatants. Because Wilson did not insist that Germany abandon submarine warfare altogether, and because its fleet of twenty-one U-boats was not yet large enough to justify the risk of a diplomatic break, Germany, in the so-called *Sussex* pledge of 4 May 1916, acceded to the ultimatum. For the rest of the year German-American relations stayed on a relatively even keel. This unexpected accord outraged the British, especially when, in two days during October 1916, a long-range German U-boat sank nine Allied merchant ships off Nantucket while American destroyers looked on and then picked up the crews.

Nonetheless, the Central Powers continued to complain bitterly that the Wilson administration was pro-British, citing America's economic ties with the Allies. Owing mainly to the British blockade, U.S. exports to Germany had plummeted from $345 million in 1914 to barely $2 million by 1916. During the same period, exports to England and France had shot up from $754 million to $2.75 billion. The administration also allowed American banks to finance this commerce through loans to the Allies. Yet, for the United States to have curtailed trade with (and loans to) the belligerent that enjoyed the advantage on the high seas would have been, under *international law, an unneutral act in favor of the belligerent that did not. But those who doubted the commitment to neutrality, especially activists in the peace movement, complained of the policy's one-sided effects and pointed to Wilson's endorsement of a military "Preparedness" campaign, which was led by large industrialists and bankers who stood to profit from increased spending on munitions.

In any event, neither the Central Powers nor the Allies wanted to provoke the world's most powerful neutral to armed retaliation. As each side made aggressive moves and well-calculated concessions at critical moments, Wilson, for some thirty months, alternately protested and accommodated the belligerents' conduct, while striving to preserve American neutral rights and public sensibilities.

Wilson's adroit diplomacy enabled him to campaign for a second term in 1916 on the slogan, "He Kept Us Out Of War!" He could boast, as well, of recently having pushed through Congress an array of social justice legislation—the eight-hour day for railroad workers, restrictions on *child labor, and a progressive *income tax weighted against corporations and the wealthy to pay for the military preparedness program. During the campaign he also championed American membership in a future association of nations, a theme that complemented his peace platform. On election day, a coalition of liberal reformers, progressive internationalists, and socialists swelled the normal Democratic vote. By a narrow margin Wilson prevailed over his Republican challenger, Charles Evans *Hughes.

Although the election may have constituted a referendum on progressivism and peace, American neutrality remained fragile. The best way to avoid war, Wilson reasoned, was to bring about a negotiated settlement between the warring alliances. Twice, in 1915 and 1916, he had sent his emissary, Colonel Edward M. House, to Europe for direct (albeit futile) parlays with the belligerent governments. Successful at the polls, Wilson now decided on a bold stratagem for ending the conflict. On 22 January 1917, he went before the Senate and called for "peace without victory." In this manifesto, the president offered a penetrating critique of European imperialism, militarism, and balance-of-power politics—the root causes of the war, he said. In their place, he advanced the vision of a new world order sustained by procedures for the arbitration of disputes between nations, a dramatic reduction of armaments, freedom of the seas, self-determination, and security against aggression. The chief instrumentality of this sweeping program would be a league of nations.

But events were rushing forward with grim indifference to Wilson's interposition. One week later, Germany resumed unrestricted submarine warfare against all flags. With their U-boats now numbering over 100, the German High Command gambled that the Allies would founder within a few months—before the United States could bring to bear sufficient force to tip the scales. In March, German submarines sank 600,000 tons of Allied and neutral shipping. Public opinion shifted markedly after three American vessels were sunk without warning and the Zimmermann Note (a sensational German plan to induce Mexico to invade Texas) came to light. By then, Wilson had reluctantly concluded that belligerency had been "thrust upon" the United States. In his war message to Congress, on 2 April 1917, he declared, "The world must be made safe for democracy." Americans, he went on, would be fighting "for a universal dominion of right by such a concert of free peoples as shall bring peace and safety to all nations and the world itself at last free"—a program attainable, apparently, only through the crucible of war. By a vote of 82 to 6 in the Senate and 378 to 50 in the House, Congress approved the call to arms.

America at War. The United States mounted a mobilization effort of phenomenal proportions. Newly created federal agencies coordinated every sector of the economy to harness America's agricultural and industrial might for military purposes. The *War Industries Board, though shunning full-scale state control, exercised unprecedented powers in organizing and stimulating production and superintended remarkable feats of miltary-industrial output. The Railroad Administration took over and modernized the country's transportation system. The Fuel Administration regulated coal production and consumption to assure that the needs of the *military and war plants were met. (Daylight saving time was introduced in March 1918 to conserve fuel.) The National War Labor Board, in order both to spur output and to avoid strikes, established a minimum wage and the eight-hour day in most industries, and settled labor disputes almost always in favor of workers. The Food Administration, headed by Herbert *Hoover, exhorted American families to observe "Meatless Mondays" and "Wheatless Wednesdays" and guaranteed farmers high prices for their commodities so that foodstuffs could be shipped to the Allies. Under the Selective Service Act, the size of the armed forces grew from 100,000 to five million within a year. Draftees and volunteers were hastily prepared in army training camps across the nation, and, in an innovation of great significance for the future, the War Department introduced large-scale intelligence testing of recruits.

Any undertaking so enormous could not help but strain the nation's social and political fabric. Fifty-six members of Congress had voted against the war resolution. Countless other Americans, many with ethnic roots in central Europe, had grave doubts about the crusade, while leading progressives and socialists divided up into pro- and anti-war factions. To build support for the war and to discredit all things German, the administration created the Committee on Public Information, chaired by George Creel, to inaugurate an extraordinary *propaganda campaign. An estimated 75 million pieces of pamphlet literature spread the official line on the war. Stirring poster art to encourage enlistments and homefront patriotism appeared everywhere; 75,000 "Four Minute Men" made speeches that were heard by tens of millions of people in theaters and other public gatherings. Movie stars such as Charlie *Chaplain, Douglas Fairbanks, and Mary Pickford appeared at rallies to urge citizens to buy "Liberty Bonds."

As a result, a tidal wave of anti-German hysteria and superpatriotism known as "One Hundred Percent Americanism" swept the country. Local ordinances banned Brahms and Beethoven from concert halls and prohibited the teaching of the German language. Acts of political repression and violence, abetted by federal legislation such as the Espionage Act of 1917 and the Sedition Act of 1918, were committed against pacifists and radicals as well as German-Americans. Dissenters expressed their views in public only at great risk. For example, for speaking against the war, the socialist leader Eugene V. *Debs was sentenced to ten years in prison. Postmaster General Albert S. Burleson denied second-class mailing privileges to left-wing publications such as the *Appeal to Reason, The Masses,* and the *Milwaukee Leader,* virtually shutting them down.

For some, however, the war brought unaccustomed opportunity. The prohibition movement gained momentum in part because of the prominence of German-Americans in the brewing industry. Anti-prostitution crusaders succeeded in closing red-light districts near military installations, including New Orleans' famed Storyville. The *woman suffrage movement won its century-long struggle for the right to vote, in part by invoking Wilson's rhetoric about democracy. At least one million women streamed into the workplace, augmenting the female labor force and taking all kinds of jobs traditionally reserved for men. Thousands of other women served in noncombatant roles in the military and in voluntary agencies such as the *Red Cross in both Europe and America. As many as 500,000 *African Americans left the *South to find employment in northern industrial centers. But this migration into predominantly white communities such as St. Louis and *Chicago spawned the worst outbursts of racial violence since *Reconstruction. A similar blend of hope and humiliation awaited the 400,000 blacks who joined the military. Whereas France awarded the *Croix de Guerre* medal to many African Americans for courage under fire, the United States maintained a strictly segregated army and handed three out of four black servicemen a shovel or a potato peeler instead of a gun. Yet African Americans played a vital part, albeit in a segregated capacity, in unloading U.S. supply convoys at the French port of Le Havre.

As for the fighting itself, before American troops had begun to arrive in prodigious numbers, the Allied military position had been dealt a potentially mortal blow. In late 1917, the Bolsheviks, led by Vladimir Lenin and Leon Trotsky, seized power in Russia and pulled their ravaged nation out of the war, thus enabling the Germans to transfer an additional forty divisions to the Western Front. Because the Bolsheviks challenged both the Allies and the Central Powers to repudiate plans for conquest and imperial expansion, the military crisis also carried serious political overtones. It fell to Wilson to respond. In his celebrated *Fourteen Points address of 8 January 1918, the president reiterated much of his anti-imperialist "peace without victory" formula, once again making the League of Nations the capstone. Greeted by near universal acclaim, this statement of progressive war aims reassured doubters that their cause was just and their sacrifices worthwhile. The Fourteen Points became the ideological cement that held the Allied coalition together during exceedingly ominous days.

In March and April the Germans mounted a ferocious spring offensive across northeastern France. By May, as the Germans advanced westward several miles a day, the French government prepared to evacuate Paris. Just then, sizeable contingents of the American Expeditionary Force, which totaled some two million by summer's end, at last reached France. The American commander, General John J. *Pershing, ordered his troops—untested, but fresh and well-equipped—into action at Cantigny in May and at Chateau-Thierry and Belleau Wood in June. Pershing later endured criticism for hurling masses of soldiers into combat and incurring very heavy casualties, especially at Belleau Wood; but, butchery or no, the Americans fought bravely and effectively. In an independent operation in September, the doughboys completely wiped out the salient at St. Mihiel, bringing the German assault to a standstill. By the end of the month, Pershing had amassed 1,200,000 men and hundreds of heavy guns and tanks along a two-hundred-mile-long front in preparation for a climactic joint counteroffensive with the Allies. Pounding the Hindenburg Line, the combined armies pushed the enemy out of the Argonne Forest, across the Meuse River, and back toward Belgium and Germany. On 6 October 1918, the German government appealed to Wilson to facilitate an armistice based on the Fourteen Points. Although the Allied governments had previously declined to endorse the president's progressive peace program, they now assented. At 5 A.M. on 11 November, in a railroad car in the Compiègne forest, the Armistice was signed. Six hours later the guns fell silent.

Aftermath. Deciding to take part personally in the Paris Peace Conference, Wilson seemed on the threshold of achieving his supreme ambition. In the meantime, however, a crucial mid-term congressional election had taken place. The Republicans had mounted a fiercely partisan campaign against the Democrats, denouncing the Wilsonian peace plan as pacifistic and socialistic. The president answered by imploring the public to keep his party in power. When the Republicans captured both houses of Congress, they claimed that the voters had repudiated him.

In contrast to his domestic troubles, Wilson's arrival in France was triumphal. In Paris, London, Rome, and Milan, millions turned out to hail "the Savior of Humanity." These extraordinary demonstrations strengthened his hand and helped to ensure the inclusion of the *League of Nations Covenant (its drafting supervised by Wilson himself) as an integral part of the peace treaty. But "the Moses from across the Atlantic" paid a heavy price. His fellow peacemakers—Britain's David Lloyd George, France's Georges Clemenceau, and Italy's Vittorio Orlando—held grave doubts about "the New Diplomacy." ("God gave us the Ten Commandments, and we broke them," Clemenceau quipped. "Wilson gives us the Fourteen Points. We shall see.") The statesmen of Europe exploited their acceptance of the Covenant to gain concessions on other contentious issues. During six months of acrimonious negotiations, the president was able to moderate some of the Allies' more extreme territorial and other punitive demands against Germany, but he was just as often compelled to compromise his principles. On the verge of physical collapse, he permitted the Allies to impose upon Germany an exorbitant reparations burden as well as a "war guilt" clause, saddling it with the moral responsibility for having started the war. Wilson's hope was that eventually the League would rectify the injustices contained in the Treaty of *Versailles itself.

When he returned home in July 1919, the vast majority of Americans seemed to favor both the treaty and League membership. But an untoward combination of factors—ideological and partisan opposition in the Republican-controlled Senate, a debilitating stroke that Wilson suffered, and the unraveling of his progressive coalition—dashed the president's great hope. Three times, in November 1919 and March 1920, the Senate voted on and rejected the treaty. The United States would never join the League of Nations, the capstone of Wilson's idealistic war aims. In the summer of 1921, the Republican administration of Warren G. *Harding ratified a new peace treaty with Germany that embraced all the terms of Versailles, minus the League. For the United States the war at last officially came to an end.

Some 113,000 American soldiers died in the First World War—51,000 in battle, 62,000 from disease. The direct financial costs to the United States totaled $33 billion—one-third raised by taxes, the rest by loans (mainly in the form of bonds). But the overall impact could not be calibrated in blood and treasure alone. Although the network of wartime agencies was quickly dismantled, the government's experiment in managing the economy provided important models that the New Deal would later adapt in combatting the Depression of the 1930s. Belligerency also released forces of intolerance and political reaction, including a postwar "Red Scare" that choked off the progressive reform impulse. In reaction to Wilsonian idealism, the country embraced a policy of noninvolvement in European politics during the 1920s and 1930s. Nevertheless, the war had thrust the United States upon the world stage, transformed the nation into the world's leading creditor, and propelled it into a period of unprecedented overseas economic expansion—from Latin America to the Middle East to Asia.

The war and its aftermath profoundly affected American intellectual life as well. During the months of belligerency, most ministers, journalists, poets, and reformers had echoed Wilson's interpretation of the conflict as "the culminating and final war for human liberty." But when it ended, the mood quickly gave way to disillusionment. In *The Enormous Room* (1922), the poet e. e. cummings captured the absurdity of bureaucratic officialdom in wartime, recounting his experiences in a French military prison on unfounded charges of espionage. Ernest *Hemingway's *A Farewell to Arms* (1929) presented a searing indictment of the war's ultimate futility and of the emptiness of wartime propaganda. World War I remains a watershed in American cultural history, separating the optimism and reformist energy of the *Progressive Era from the alienation of many young writers and intellectuals in the 1920s.

Neither the Great War nor the twenty years' truce that followed remedied the deeper sources of Europe's political, economic, and social ills. Indeed, the death toll and destruction and the vindictive aspects of the Versailles Treaty helped create the conditions that led to an even more disastrous conflict in 1939. In retrospect, the ordeal was only the first terrible phase of a protracted struggle that would culminate in World War II, the Nazi Holocaust, and the advent of the nuclear age.

[*See also* Antiwar Movements; Economic Regulation; Federal Government, Executive Branch: The Presidency; Department of Defense; Federal Government, Legislative Branch: Senate; Foreign Relations: The Economic Dimension; Foreign Relations: U.S. Relations with Europe; Isolationism; Literature: Since World War I; Nativism; Pacifism; Peace Movements; Prostitution and Anti-Prostitution; Socialism; Socialist Party; Temperance and Prohibition; Racism; Twenties, The.]

• Arthur S. Link, *Wilson,* vols. III-V, 1960–1966. Arno J. Mayer, *Politics and Diplomacy of Peacemaking: Containment and Counterrevolution at Versailles,* 1967. Edward M. Coffman, *The War to End All Wars: The American Military Experience in World War I,* 1968. N. Gordon Levin, *Woodrow Wilson and World Politics,* 1968. Patrick Devlin, *Too Proud to Fight: Woodrow Wilson's Neutrality,* 1974. Robert Ferrell, *Woodrow Wilson and World War I,* 1985. Paul Fussell, *The Great War in Modern Memory,* 1975. David M. Kennedy, *Over Here: The First World War and American Society,* 1980. Thomas J. Knock, *To End All Wars: Woodrow Wilson and the Quest for a New World Order,* 1992. Stephen Vaughn, *Holding Fast the Inner Lines: Democracy, Nationalism, and the Committee on Public Information,* 1980. Lloyd E. Ambrosius, *Woodrow Wilson and the American Diplomatic Tradition: The Treaty Fight in Perspective,* 1987. Kendrick A. Clements, *Woodrow Wilson: World Statesman,* 1987. David Stevenson, *The First World War and International Politics,* 1988. Ronald Schaffer, *America in the Great War: The Rise of the War Welfare State,* 1991.

—Thomas J. Knock

WORLD WAR II

WORLD WAR II: CAUSES

Japan's attack on *Pearl Harbor in *Hawai'i on 7 December 1941 belatedly catapulted the United States into war, four years after Japan's full-scale invasion of China and more than two years after Nazi Germany's invasion of Poland on 1 September 1939 led to declarations of war by Great Britain and France two days later—the official beginning of World War II. Only gradually had Americans come to view Japanese and German aggression as a threat to their economic and strategic interests and as an affront to a humane world order.

Isolationist attitudes also shaped U.S. diplomacy prior to the war. In the mid-1930s, as Germany, Italy, and Japan expanded, Congress passed *neutrality legislation designed to prevent the kind of entanglements that had drawn the United States into *World War I. These laws abandoned the claim that Americans had the right to travel on belligerent ships like the *Lusitania,* which had been sunk by a German U-boat in 1915 with heavy loss of U.S. lives. The neutrality laws also banned loans to belligerents and the sale abroad of arms and munitions, put all other trade on a cash-and-carry basis, and barred American ships from war zones. These restrictions applied to the civil war in Spain, where fascists under General Francisco Franco triumphed by 1939. With public opinion strongly against U.S. involvement, President Franklin Delano *Roosevelt acquiesced, needing isolationists' votes for his domestic legislation.

The spring and summer of 1940 changed American politics

decisively. Adolf Hitler won quick blitzkrieg victories over Denmark, Norway, the Netherlands, Belgium, and France; the British evacuated thousands of troops from Dunkirk (26 May–4 June); and Hitler launched massive bombing raids on England (the Battle of Britain). These developments created grave insecurities in America, including fears of a direct attack on the United States if Germany captured or destroyed the British navy.

Roosevelt responded by transferring to England fifty old destroyers in exchange for long-term leases on eight British bases from Newfoundland to the Caribbean; in mid-September he obtained passage of the Selective Service Act of 1940, the first peacetime draft in American history. Reelected to a third term after promising not to send American boys into foreign wars, FDR nonetheless inched toward intervention by "steps short of war," including U.S. occupation of Greenland and Iceland in the name of hemispheric defense; secret contingency military plans with British and Canadians; Lend-Lease aid to Britain, China, and Soviet Russia; and naval patrols, convoys, and economic embargoes. He gradually secured repeal of the neutrality legislation. According to British Prime Minister Winston Churchill, Roosevelt promised to "wage war" against Germany, "but not declare it," and to do "everything" to "force an incident."

Despite clashes between American destroyers and German submarines in the Atlantic, war came via the Pacific. When Japan occupied French Indochina in July 1941, in apparent concert with Germany's invasion of Russian in June, Roosevelt froze all Japanese funds in the United States. U.S. officials also stopped all trade with Japan, including oil, of which Japan required twelve thousand tons each day. Viewing U.S. pressure as provocative and life-strangling, Japan's military leaders formulated plans to attack the U.S. fleet and seize oil-rich Dutch and British colonies unless Washington lifted its embargo. Negotiations between Japanese diplomats and Secretary of State Cordell *Hull proved ineffective, in part because key U.S. officials, having cracked Tokyo's diplomatic code, knew that Japanese forces were massing to strike southward after mid-November. Americans did not, however, learn about the huge Japanese task force, including six carriers, sailing westward across the Pacific toward Pearl Harbor. After Congress declared war against Japan on 8 December, Hitler mistakenly believed that American forces would be preoccupied in the Pacific, and thus declared war against the United States, whereupon Congress voted unanimously for war against Germany. Pearl Harbor had "ended isolationism for any realist" (as Senator Arthur Vandenberg put it) and galvanized the country for a war against fascist and aggressive states.

[*See also* Foreign Relations: U.S. Relations with Europe; Foreign Relations U.S. Relations with Asia; Isolationism; New Deal Era, The.]

• Waldo Heinrichs, *Threshold of War,* 1988. Jonathan Utley, *Going to War with Japan, 1937–1941,* 1985.

—J. Garry Clifford

WORLD WAR II: MILITARY AND DIPLOMATIC COURSE

Japan's surprise attack on *Pearl Harbor in December 1941 plunged America into a global conflict that had been raging since 1937 in Asia and since 1939 in Europe. Until final victory came in August 1945, World War II dominated all aspects of American life. While the United States and its allies pursued the war militarily in Asia, North Africa, and Europe, U.S. leaders also participated in a series of high-level diplomatic conferences that had profound implications not only for the conduct of the war but for the shape of the postwar order.

Military Course of the War. Following blitzkrieg victories over Poland, Denmark, Norway, the Benelux countries (Belgium, Luxembourg, and the Netherlands), France, Yugoslavia, and Greece, German armies had reached the outskirts of Moscow and Leningrad by December 1941 and threatened the Suez Canal and Mideast oil fields; Nazi submarines ravaged the Atlantic, sinking 2.6 million tons of merchant shipping off American shores in the first four months of 1942. Meanwhile, Japan's destruction of U.S. battleships in *Hawai'i enabled Japanese forces, over the next six months, to move beyond their four-year war with China. Advancing into Southeast Asia, the Japanese occupied Thailand, Malaya, and Burma; seized the Dutch East Indies; conquered the *Philippines, Wake Island, and Guam; invaded New Guinea; and threatened both India and Australia. Only American naval victories at the Coral Sea and Midway in May–June 1942 halted the Japanese juggernaut.

U.S. and Soviet Feats of Production. Two factors eventually tipped the scales in favor of the Allies: the enormous speed and scale of American rearmament, surpassing anything the Germans and Japanese had envisioned; and the unexpected revival of Soviet strength after its initial devastation in 1941. By 1943, America was outproducing the Axis powers combined, 47,000 planes to 27,000, 24,000 tanks to 11,000, and six times more heavy guns. U.S. shipyards turned out 8,000 warships and 87,000 landing craft in four years; for every naval vessel produced in Japan, the United States constructed sixteen. Similarly, the relocation of Russian factories and workers beyond the Ural Mountains enabled the Soviets, with only one-fourth the steel available to Germany, to turn out more guns, planes, and tanks (including the famed T–34) than their enemy. Such production, augmented by $11 billion in Lend-Lease materials from the United States, undergirded the great Russian counteroffensives that bled the *Wehrmacht* in 1943 and 1944.

Superior organization and *technology also won the war at sea and in the air. By mid-1943, through increased construction of merchant ships and escort carriers, as well as intelligence breakthroughs, the Anglo-American struggle against nazi U-boats turned in the Allies' favor. By war's end, some 29,000 German submarine crewmembers had been killed, almost three-fourths of those who fought. Similarly, U.S. airmen, beginning in the summer of 1942, joined the Royal Air Force in strategic bombing raids against European targets. By 1944 the air offensive had disrupted Hitler's economy and worn down the German *Luftwaffe* sufficiently to permit the cross-Channel invasion of France. By the spring of 1945, despite the loss of 21,000 bombers and 140,000 British and American air deaths, Allied bombs had pounded German industry into rubble. Firestorms caused by saturation bombing raids obliterated Hamburg, Dresden, and other German cities, causing massive civilian casualties.

German technology posed formidable threats, as evidenced by the deployment of jet fighter planes and long-range V-1 and V-2 rockets, but intra-service rivalries and misjudgments by Hitler prevented the decisive application of these new weapons. Ironically, it was a feat of German science that prompted the British and Americans to pool their scientific resources in a race to build atomic weapons. The *Manhattan Project achieved success too late for the European war but in time to help end the Pacific war.

The War in North Africa and Europe. The first major land offensive in the Atlantic theater began in November 1942 when Anglo-American forces under General Dwight D. *Eisenhower invaded French North Africa. After belated assistance from Vichy French authorities, Eisenhower's forces moved eastward to link up with British armies pursuing General Erwin Rommel's *Afrika Korps* after the British victory at El Alamein in Egypt. German counterattacks in Tunisia, however, delayed Allied victory in North Africa until May 1943.

At the Casablanca Conference in January 1943, Anglo-American planners agreed to invade Sicily and the Italian mainland and promised a second front in Europe that would engage enemy forces "as heavily as possible." President Franklin Delano *Roosevelt also announced the Allied decision to demand the Axis forces' "unconditional surrender." After U.S. and British troops assaulted Sicily in July, Italian officials ousted Benito

Mussolini, formally surrendered on 8 September, and declared war against Germany, whose forces quickly occupied Italy. The ensuing Anglo-American advance up the Italian boot proved slow and costly. Not until the eve of the invasion of France did Allied soldiers liberate Rome.

The cross-Channel attack (*D-Day) came on 6 June 1944, under the overall command of General Eisenhower. Within six weeks, more than a million allied soldiers were fighting in Brittany and Normandy. Paris was liberated on 23–24 August and by October German forces had completely evacuated France. Meanwhile, after victories at Stalingrad (January 1943) and Kursk (July–August 1943), Soviet armies had pushed into Eastern Europe and occupied most of Poland and East Prussia. Hopes for early surrender faded, however, after a failed assassination plot by German dissidents against Hitler in July 1944 and the desperate German counteroffensive in Belgium (the Battle of the *Bulge) in December. Finally, Anglo-American armies crossed the Rhine in March 1945. A month later, G.I.s shook hands with Russian soldiers at the Elbe. Hitler committed suicide on 30 April and Germany surrendered on 7 May, celebrated as V-E (victory in Europe) Day.

The War in the Pacific. The U.S. counterattack in the Pacific had commenced in August 1942 with the invasion of Guadalcanal in the Solomon Islands. The ensuing struggle for the island climaxed in a major American naval victory in mid-November, after which Japanese units quietly evacuated. The route to Tokyo now involved a vast network of fortified islands and atolls, bristling with air fields, stretching some 14,200 miles from the Dutch Indies across Micronesia to the Aleutians. Eventually a two-prong strategy emerged: while U.S. Army and Australian forces under General Douglas *MacArthur advanced northward from New Guinea to the Philippines, U.S. sailors and marines under Admiral Chester *Nimitz "leap-frogged" across the central Pacific by seizing key islands in the Gilbert, Marshall, and Mariana archipelagoes, thereby neutralizing or bypassing Japanese strongholds. President Roosevelt's expectation that China would figure decisively in defeating Japan and policing postwar Asia was undermined by China's military ineffectiveness and internal bickering between Nationalists and Communists.

The Battle of the Philippine Sea (June 1944), which cost Japan three aircraft carriers and 345 planes, and an even more devastating defeat at *Leyte Gulf in October, reduced the Japanese navy to impotence. MacArthur's troops liberated Luzon in February 1945; *Iwo Jima fell in march; and Okinawa surrendered in June, after 12,500 American battle deaths. Meanwhile, B-29 "Superfortresses" based in the Marianas blasted Japan's cities, killing as many as 100,000 in the fire-bombing of Tokyo on 9–10 March. Allied leaders at the *Potsdam Conference in July warned the Japanese to surrender or face "prompt and utter destruction." U.S. authorities, having broken the Japanese diplomatic code, were aware of behind-the-scenes maneuvers within the Japanese government to end the war. But with no clear response from Tokyo to the Potsdam ultimatum, President Harry S. *Truman (who had succeeded to the presidency upon Roosevelt's death on 12 April 1945), ordered an atomic bomb dropped on *Hiroshima on 6 August. Two days later the Soviet Union, fulfilling a pledge by Premier Josef Stalin at the *Yalta Conference, declared war against Japan and invaded Manchuria. A second atomic bomb immolated Nagasaki on 9 August. The Japanese inquired about peace terms, received assurance that the emperor would retain his throne, formally capitulated on 14 August triggering joyous V-J Day celebrations across America. Formal surrender ceremonies took place on 2 September board the *USS Missouri* in Tokyo harbor, with General MacArthur presiding.

U.S. battle deaths in World War II, as later tallied by the Department of Defense, totaled 292,131, with an additional 115,185 deaths from other causes. High as these numbers were, they were far surpassed by those of other nations. Total military and civilian deaths in the conflict have been estimated at fifty million

Diplomatic Course of the War. America's wartime diplomacy had two main objectives: maintaining the Grand Alliance necessary to winning the war, and planning the postwar international order. President Roosevelt signaled his intentions early when he met with British Prime Minister Winston Churchill off Newfoundland in August 1941; proclaimed the Allied war aims in the *Atlantic Charter; and affirmed Woodrow *Wilson's principles of *collective security, national self-determination, freedom of the seas, and liberal trading practices.

Wilsonian Visions and Wartime Realities. Indeed, a Wilsonian outlook, tempered by a pragmatic determination to avoid Wilson's errors during *World War I, infused American diplomacy during World War II. Germany would have to surrender unconditionally; no debts-reparations tangle would arise, because Lend-Lease would "eliminate the dollar sign"; and the United States would join a postwar international organization to maintain peace, even if it meant wooing isolationist Republican senators. Prominent, too, was the State Department's desire to promote American economic and commercial influence through multilateral economic arrangements. Reflecting Secretary of State Cordell *Hull's Wilsonian belief that trade restrictions were the principal cause of wars, the effort led to the 1944 *Bretton Woods Conference, which created the *World Bank and the *International Monetary Fund. So strong was Hull's Wilsonian faith that he could report after the Moscow Conference of 1943: "[T]here will no longer be need for spheres of influence, for alliances, for balance of power, or any other . . . special arrangements through which, in the unhappy past, the nations strove to safeguard their security or to promote their interests."

If total war inspired visions of total peace, military expediency sometimes required compromises that violated Wilsonian principles. Working arrangements with Vichy French collaborators in North Africa, peace negotiations with Mussolini's successors in Italy, support of Chiang Kai-shek's authoritarian regime in China, even the failure to rescue victims of the Holocaust—all resulted from the effort to win the war quickly with the fewest possible casualties. With Roosevelt proclaiming that America's principal contribution to the war would be as the "Arsenal of Democracy," the administration never fully mobilized the population for actual military service. With no threat of invasion and the bulk of Axis forces engaged in Russia and China, Roosevelt gambled that "an air war plus the Russians" would require only ninety U.S. divisions to achieve victory.

Such calculations increased allied dependence on the Soviet Union. With the Red Army "killing more Axis . . . than all other twenty-five United Nations put together" (as Roosevelt announced in November 1943 speech), Roosevelt gave the Soviets billions in Lend-Lease assistance and placed a high priority on maintaining good relations with the Soviets at the wartime conferences at Tehran (November 1943) and Yalta (February 1945). The "Unconditional Surrender" demand assured Stalin that there would be no separate peace with Hitler or his underlings.

The insistence of unconditional surrender also underscored Roosevelt's determination to punish Germany for Hitler's crimes by such means as permanent partition, demilitarization, and dismantling of heavy industry, the president's postwar vision anticipated a disarmed, decentralized, and decolonized Europe policed by British and Soviet armies, while U.S. forces patrolled the Western Hemisphere and replaced Japanese power in the Pacific. Because Red Army victories guaranteed Soviet dominance in Eastern Europe, Roosevelt urged "open" spheres and free elections in this region and hoped that increased contacts with the West would make the Russians "less barbarian." Roosevelt's tactic of wooing the Soviets also reflected the view of his military advisers. The *Joint Chiefs of

Staff invariably opposed "get-tough" policies toward Moscow on military grounds, including the need for Soviet help against Japan. "[I]n the big military matters," insisted Secretary of War Henry L. *Stimson in 1945, "the Soviet Government have kept their word." Only after the war did the military's perception of the Soviet Union become more hostile.

Roosevelt pursued his goals through summit diplomacy. Meeting with Churchill at Cairo, Casablanca, Quebec, and other venues produced unprecedented Anglo-American cooperation but also disagreement over how best to defeat Hitler and over the postwar disposition of colonial empires. Roosevelt's military advisers suspected that Churchill's insistence on Mediterranean priorities indicated a desire to shore up Britain's imperial lifelines, and not, as the British claimed, a coherent strategy to weaken Germany on the periphery before launching a full-scale invasion of France. Not until the Tehran Conference did the British finally commit to opening a cross-Channel second front in 1944. As for decolonization, "hands off the British Empire" remained Churchill's maxim as he resisted Roosevelt's advice about independence for India and new arrangements for Hong Kong, Indochina, and other colonies overrun by Japan. Unwilling to jeopardize Great Power cooperation, Roosevelt eventually compromised by allowing the Europeans to reclaim their Asian empires but envisioned their becoming only trustees under *United Nations auspices. He correctly anticipated that postwar momentum toward self-determination would become irresistible.

The Tehran and Yalta Conferences. The Big Three summits at Tehran, Iran, and Yalta, in the Crimea were the high points of wartime diplomacy. The former prefigured the more controversial results of the latter. At Tehran, Roosevelt, Churchill, and Stalin tentatively agreed on a peace dictated by the great powers, an international organization dominated the victorious Allies, and a territorial settlement that partitioned Germany and conceded Soviet hegemony over Eastern Europe. Stalin also promised Soviet help against Japan after Hitler's defeat. Although Roosevelt had previously refused to recognize prewar Soviet boundaries, Churchill proposed moving Poland's boundaries a considerable distance to the west, incorporating German lands. Polish territory in the east would be transferred to the Soviets to secure their western frontier. While avoiding formal endorsement of this arrangement lest he lose Polish-American votes in the 1944 elections, Roosevelt indicated his general approval.

At Yalta the president compromised again on Poland by accepting a "more broadly based" version of the Soviet-sponsored Communist Lublin Polish government, to be followed by "free and unfettered elections" as soon as possible. A "Declaration for Liberated Europe" called for similar elections in other countries occupied by Allied armies. Negotiations at Yalta over the United Nations organization also involved compromise. Because China and France had previously been added as permanent members of the Security Council, each possessing a veto, Stalin demanded membership for all sixteen Soviet republics in the General Assembly and insisted on an absolute veto in the Security Council on all issues, procedural and substantive. The Soviets eventually received three seats in the General Assembly, and Stalin agreed to limit the veto to substantive issues only. In a secret protocol at Yalta, Stalin reiterated his pledge to enter the war against Japan three months after Germany's surrender. He also agreed to sign a pact of friendship and alliance with Chiang Kai-shek's Kuomintang regime, not with Mao Tse-tung's rival communists. In return, the Soviet Union obtained the Kurile islands, southern Sakhalin, Dairen as a free port, Port Arthur as a naval base, and joint operation (with China) of Manchurian railroads.

Strains in the Wartime Alliance. Notwithstanding claims that Yalta marked the "dawn of a new day," the Grand Alliance barely survived long enough to defeat Germany and Japan. Allied victories brought recriminations over the German surrender in northern Italy, quarrels over Poland, the abrupt cutoff of U.S. Lend-Lease supplies to the Allies after Germany's surrender, peppery lectures to Soviet diplomats from President Truman, postponement of contentious issues at the Potsdam Conference in July 1945, and even the belief among some U.S. officials that using atomic bombs against Japan might not only hasten the war's end, but also make the Russians more manageable in Europe. Such developments accelerated changes in American goals and attitudes. Still strong, especially in the public mind, was the Rooseveltian view that the postwar world would be Wilsonian: the United Nations would maintain collective security; that the most likely dangers would come from a defeated Japan or Germany and that America, while remaining militarily powerful, would confine itself to protecting the Western Hemisphere. However, a second worldview, held by those officials most familiar with the Soviets, pictured the postwar world more in terms of power, placed less faith in the United Nations, feared Soviet encroachments in Eastern Europe and Asia, and saw Moscow as the primary threat to peace. This viewpoint gained more adherents as the contradiction between "free elections" in Eastern Europe and Soviet security objectives became apparent. In short, the end of World War II ushered in the beginning of the *Cold War.

[*See also* Federal Government, Executive Branch: Department of Defense; Federal Government, Executive Branch: Department of State; Foreign Relations: U.S. Relations with Europe; Foreign Relations: U.S. Relations with Asia; Hopkins, Harry; King, Ernest J.; Marshall, George C.; Midway, Battle of; Military, The; Nuclear Weapons; Leahy, William D.; Patton, George S., Jr.; Stilwell, Joseph; Weaponry, Nonnuclear.]

• Samuel Eliot Morison, *Strategy and Compromise,* 1958. Eric Larrabee, *Commander in Chief: Franklin Delano Roosevelt, His Lieutenants and Their War,* 1987. Paul Fussell, *Wartime,* 1989. Frank Freidel, *Franklin D. Roosevelt: A Rendezvous with Destiny,* 1990. Lloyd Gardner, *Spheres of Influence,* 1993. Gerhard Weinberg, *A World at Arms,* 1994. Irwin Gellman, *Secret Affairs,* 1995. Richard Overy, *Why the Allies Won,* 1995. Warren F. Kimball, *Forged in War: Roosevelt, Churchill, and the Second World War,* 1997.

—J. Garry Clifford

WORLD WAR II: DOMESTIC EFFECTS

World War II had a large and lasting impact on the United States. But whether and in what ways the war's domestic effects amounted to a transformative historical "watershed" continues to be debated, especially since in many cases the war continued or reinforced long-existing trends.

Perhaps the war's most obvious domestic impact was to restore prosperity after the Depression of the 1930s. As wartime mobilization made the United States the world's dominant economic power, the gross national product soared from $91 billion in 1939 to $214 billion in 1945, and unemployment plummeted from 15 percent in 1940 to just 1 percent by 1944. National income more than doubled, and both consumer spending and personal savings reached record levels. Although little income redistribution occurred, a general rise in living standards produced an inspiriting sense of personal and national possibilities.

Mobilizing for war had important consequences for the political economy as well. The federal government grew enormously in size, power, and cost as it oversaw production and labor, rationed goods and set prices, and taxed and spent at unprecedented levels. The evident connection between wartime deficit spending and the dramatic economic recovery confirmed Keynesian economics and made the use of fiscal policy to promote full-employment prosperity central to liberal policy prescriptions for the postwar era. The government also sponsored major scientific, technological, and medical advances, not only in atomic energy but also in such areas as *computers, synthetic materials, insecticides, and drugs.

Even after postwar retrenchment, the federal government remained significantly larger and more powerful than it had been before the war. So, too, did big *business, which won a heavy share of defense contracts and rebuilt goodwill and political power lost in the Depression decade. Organized labor also grew—union membership rose by about 50 percent—but its power was secondary to that of business (and the military) in government councils. Continuing a pattern long in the making, the American political economy by 1945 was characterized by the "countervailing" powers of big government, big business, big labor, and big *agriculture.

American politics changed surprisingly little in the new and much different circumstances of global war and domestic prosperity. President Franklin Delano *Roosevelt won decisive reelection victories in 1940 and 1944, and salient issues and voting patterns continued much as in the 1930s. Democrats remained the majority party, and the core of the New Deal remained essentially intact, though Republicans reduced Democratic control of Congress, and the wartime Congresses, dominated by Republicans and conservative Democrats, opposed new social programs (with the signal exception of the *Servicemen's Readjustment Act, or G.I. Bill of Rights). But this conservative trend, too, had started in the late 1930s.

The war had important and complex effects on American society. Wartime mobilization produced extraordinary geographic *mobility; one of every five Americans made a significant move, as people headed to military bases and war plants especially in the *West, *South, and suburban areas of the large industrial centers. Yet the migration to the Sun Belt and the suburbs had begun well before the war and would vastly increase afterwards. In bringing a variety of people into contact, wartime mobility, paradoxically, both contributed to a sense of common cause and also produced tension and conflict, especially along longstanding class, racial, and cultural lines.

Ethnic groups generally experienced enhanced economic opportunity and increased social acceptance. Time and generational succession were already bringing such change, but especially for the "new immigrant" groups from southern and eastern Europe, the war's impact proved important. Prejudice nonetheless persisted against *Italian Americans early in the war, for example, and against such other groups as Jews and Mexican Americans, target of the "zoot suit" riots in *Los Angeles in 1943. In by far the worst wartime violation of civil liberties, Japanese Americans, citizens and non-citizens alike, were removed from their homes and placed in internment camps.

*African Americans encountered familiar prejudice and discrimination in the armed forces, employment, housing, and other aspects of life. On the home front, racial tensions exploded in violence in Harlem and *Detroit in the summer of 1943. Yet the war also laid the groundwork for an end to racial segregation and sped black migration from the rural South to Northern cities, bringing gains in employment and income. The war years brought increased black activism and, with such initiatives as the 1941 *Fair Employment Practice Committee, new attention from the federal government. Although gains were limited, World War II meant geographic and social *mobility for many African Americans and helped catalyze the postwar *civil rights movement.

The war's impact on American women was even more ambiguous. Employment increased by 50 percent, with particularly noticeable gains in the number and range of blue-collar jobs, and many women emerged from their wartime experiences with increased self-confidence and changed expectations. Policies barring married women from white-collar employment were largely eliminated, an especially important development since by war's end more married than single women were working. But war work for women was cast as a temporary expedient to help win the war, and the wartime experience did not change the prevailing cultural norm, held by women as well as men, that women's primary roles should be as wives and homemakers. Partly because of layoffs among women factory workers resulting from re-employment preferences given veterans, many women with industrial jobs returned, some willingly and some not, to more traditional employment or to the home after the war. In the long run, World War II made much less difference in changing gender roles and norms and in producing postwar *feminism than did long-term economic, social, and demographic trends.

While World War II clearly had a major impact on the United States prewar trends, values, and patterns of life and politics, it also continued to shape the postwar nation. The war's impact on the American home front, moreover, was relatively small compared to its consequences for other nations involved in the conflict. Depending upon their focus and angle of vision, historians will surely continue to reach diverse conclusions about the domestic effect of World War II.

[*See also* Democratic Party; Depression, Economic; Hispanic Americans; Housing; Incarceration of Japanese Americans; Keynesianism; Labor Movements; New Deal Era, The; Productivity; Republican Party; Taxation; Women in the Labor Force.]

• John Morton Blum, *V Was for Victory: Politics and American Culture During World War II*, 1976. Susan M. Hartmann, *The Home Front and Beyond: American Women in the 1940s*, 1982. Harold G. Vatter, *The U.S. Economy in World War II*, 1985. Neil A. Wynn, *The Afro-American and the Second World War*, rev. ed., 1993. Alan Brinkley, *The End of Reform: New Deal Liberalism in Recession and War*, 1995. John W. Jeffries, *Wartime America: The World War II Home Front*, 1996.

—John W. Jeffries

WORLD WAR II: POSTWAR IMPACT

World War II left the international system in complete disarray. Some 50 million people died during the conflict, and hungry, homeless survivors ("displaced persons") struggled to live in the rubble. The war so weakened the French, British, and Dutch that they could no longer manage their colonies and traditional spheres of interest. In their retreat from empire, the British granted independence to India in 1947 and to Burma in 1948; the Dutch relinquished Indonesia the following year; and the French fought unsuccessfully to maintain their hold over Indochina and Algeria. Issues related to decolonization would dominate international politics for decades.

Prosperous America, untouched by enemy bombs or marauding armies, stood in stark contrast to Europe's receding power. The United States became a full-fledged global power for the first time. The Gross National Product leaped from $90.5 billion in 1939 to $211.9 billion in 1945. Having produced fewer than 6,000 military and civilian aircraft in 1939, American factories turned out 300,000 military planes during the war, including 95,000 in 1944. By V-J Day, U.S. forces controlled over 434 bases throughout the world, nearly half of them in Asia. Retained as trusteeships under *United Nations auspices, some of these Pacific bases, together with the United States' position in occupied Japan, transformed the Pacific into an American lake. With a booming economy, the world's largest navy and air force, and a monopoly of *nuclear weapons until 1949, Washington commanded first rank in world affairs.

The war began what historian Michael Sherry has labeled the "age of militarization" for Americans. Government agencies dealing with national security ballooned in size. The *military establishment, symbolized by the new Pentagon building in *Washington, D.C., grew in influence as the State Department, frequently bypassed by President Franklin Delano *Roosevelt, lost status. Roosevelt centralized decision-making in the White House, while Congress relinquished its prerogatives in the name of bipartisanship. A vast espionage establishment arose, beginning with the *Office of Strategic Services (OSS) in 1942, succeeded by the *Central Intelligence Agency (CIA) five years later. Prewar American *business executives had looked askance at full mobilization, fearing excess capacities, obsolete plants, and overexpansion. General Motors wanted to make cars, not tanks. By 1944, however, with war contracts flowing to the biggest corporations, the president of General Electric proposed a "permanent war economy" in which war production would assure prosperity as well as buttress military preparedness. Most notably in the *Manhattan Project, academic experts also enlisted against the Axis; universities, once mobilized, were as reluctant to give up government contracts as the Navy was to scrap aircraft carriers after the war. These new arrangements would prompt President Dwight D. *Eisenhower to warn in his 1961 farewell message against "the acquisition of unwarranted influence . . . by the military-industrial complex."

Indeed, the war reshaped broad areas of American life, from politics to *popular culture, *economics to social relations. For example, wartime exigencies accelerated the government's impact on social change, as increased participation by women and *African Americans in the armed services and war industries enhanced the status of both groups, although most women war workers were quickly displaced from the labor force once the war ended. Claims of equal rights, underscored by wartime service and rhetoric, spurred antidiscrimination and *civil rights movements in the postwar decades. For sixteen million veterans, the *Servicemen's Readjustment Act, the "G.I. Bill of Rights" (1944), offered unemployment benefits, job preference, tuition and living expenses for education, and low-interest housing loans. Memories of wartime sacrifices would long provide a metaphor for later "wars" against *poliomyelitis, *cancer, *poverty, illicit *drugs, *crime, and other ills.

Internationally, World War II gave rise to a new global monetary system, hammered out at the 1944 *Bretton Woods Conference, and a new international organization, the *United Nations, crafted by the Allied leaders at a series of wartime conferences. But hopes for a more peaceful and cooperative world order were soon dashed by the war's most conspicuous legacy: the *Cold War. In filling the vacuum created by the defeat of the Axis and a weakened colonial system, victorious America soon confronted its erstwhile ally, the Soviet Union, whose ghastly wartime losses included at least twenty million military and civilian deaths. In driving back the invading Nazi hordes, Russian troops had occupied Eastern Europe and thrust deep into Germany's heartland, and Soviet premier Josef Stalin had no intention of relinquishing power in this realm. Motivated by traditional Russian nationalism, communist ideology, and fears of a revived Germany, the Kremlin made the most of its limited power. Often cruel and ruthless, yet cautious and realistic, Stalin vowed that his country would never again be invaded through Eastern Europe. Rooted in World War II, the ensuing confrontation emerged from the different interests, ideologies, style, power, and historical experience of the two antagonists. Each saw the other, in mirror image, as the world's bully; each charged the other with perpetuating Adolf Hitler's aggressive designs. Characterized by a costly arms race, proxy wars, and military alliances and interventions, the Cold War lasted nearly fifty years, eventually ending in the Soviet Union's collapse.

[*See also* Aviation Industry; Business Cycle; Foreign Relations; Global Economy, America and the; Nuclear Weapons; Productivity; Women in the Labor Force.]

• John M. Blum, *V Was for Victory*, 1976. Thomas McCormick, *America's Half-Century*, 1989. Thomas G. Paterson, *On Every Front: The Making and Unmaking of the Cold War*, 1992. Michael S. Sherry, *In the Shadow of War: The United States Since the 1930s*, 1995. Donald W. White, *The American Century: The Rise and Decline of the United States as a World Power*, 1996.

—J. Garry Clifford

WORLD WAR II: CHANGING INTERPRETATIONS

Controversies surrounding World War II have involved the attack on *Pearl Harbor, President Franklin Delano *Roosevelt's policies toward the Soviet Union, the administration's response to the Holocaust, and President Harry S. *Truman's atomic-bomb decision.

Some isolationists contended that Roosevelt deliberately provoked Japan's attack on Pearl Harbor to silence domestic opponents of intervention and plunge America into the war. Most scholars, however, agree that while Washington knew in general of Japan's aggressive moves, the assault at Pearl Harbor was a surprise.

Some *Cold War critics argued that Roosevelt naively relied on the Soviet Union to defeat Adolf Hitler, conceded too much to Stalin at the *Yalta Conference to gain Soviet cooperation against Japan, and needlessly prolonged the war with his unconditional-surrender policy, thus ensuring postwar communist control of eastern Europe. Most historians, however, emphasize the narrow choices available to U.S. planners. Not naïveté but necessity, including the Allies' reliance on the Russians to engage Hitler's *Wehrmacht* until the 1944 cross-Channel invasion, they contend, dictated U.S. policy toward the Soviets.

On the U.S. response to the Holocaust, the Nazi extermination campaign against Jews and other groups, some historians underscore the sketchy nature of wartime information about the extermination program and contend that the administration rightly gave highest priority to winning the war. The historian David Wyman and others, however, fault the administration for failing to admit more Jewish refugees in the 1930s and for not bombing the Nazi concentration camps and railroad lines leading to them during the war. *Anti-Semitism, they contend, influenced Washington's failure to act more aggressively to aid the victims of Nazi genocide.

On the atomic-bomb decision, most historians, like most Americans, initially accepted Truman's explanation that the bombs were dropped solely to end the war and avoid an invasion of Japan. In the 1960s, however, Gar Alperovitz and other revisionist scholars argued that power calculations vis-à-vis the Soviet Union also influenced Truman's decision.

[*See also* Hiroshima and Nagasaki, Atomic Bombing of.]

• David S. Wyman, *The Abandonment of the Jews: America and the Holocaust*, 1985. Warren F. Kimball, *The Juggler*, 1991. J. Samuel Walker, *Prompt and Utter Destruction: Truman and the Use of the Atomic Bombs against Japan*, 1997.

—J. Garry Clifford

WORLD WIDE WEB. *See* Internet and World Wide Web.

WOUNDED KNEE TRAGEDY (29 December 1890), bloodbath that engulfed Chief Big Foot's band of Miniconjou Lakota Sioux by the U.S. Army. The slaughter grew out of a revitalization movement known as the Ghost Dance, which swept western Indian reservations in 1889–1890. Prescribed dances and rituals promised the eradication of white people, a return to the old way of life, and reunion with ancestors long dead. On the impoverished and demoralized Sioux reservations in the Dakotas, people embraced the new religion with fervor. Fearful of violence, Indian agents called for military assistance. Strong forces occupied the Pine Ridge and Rosebud agencies.

The overall commander, Major General Nelson A. Miles, sought to end the confrontation peacefully. At the same time, he pressed for the imprisonment of such "troublemakers" as *Sitting Bull and Big Foot. Sitting Bull was killed on 15 December 1890 while resisting arrest by Indian policemen on the Standing Rock Reservation. Big Foot eluded arrest and led his people in a trek toward Pine Ridge. His intent was not hostile, as the military assumed, but peaceful. Cavalry intercepted the band and escorted it to Wounded Knee Creek on the Pine Ridge Reservation to be disarmed. Big Foot lay in his wagon, ill with pneumonia.

Colonel James W. Forsyth and the Seventh Cavalry, about 500 strong and bolstered by four small-caliber cannon, surrounded the Indian encampment of about 350 people. Neither side intended a fight, but the Indians resisted disarming, and the search for weapons built tension and suspicion. A rifle accidentally discharged and touched off battle. After a brief exchange of close-range fire and hand-to-hand fighting in which Big Foot was killed, the Indians scattered and the artillery opened fire. The village was flattened and knots of Indians fleeing in all directions were cut down. Nearly two-thirds of Big Foot's people, including women and children, were killed or wounded, while the troops lost twenty-five killed and thirty-nine wounded. After Wounded Knee, General Miles maneuvered his forces in such fashion as to bring about the surrender of the Ghost Dancers.

The Indians and even General Miles accused the troops of indiscriminate massacre. Although few such incidents can be documented, Wounded Knee poisoned relations between whites and Indians and still symbolizes the wrongs inflicted by one people upon another. In 1973, 200 members of the *American Indian Movement chose the site of the Wounded Knee conflict to protest conditions of Indians, a symbolic act that again resulted in violence.

[*See also* Indian History and Culture: From 1800 to 1900; Indian Wars.]

• Robert M. Utley, *The Last Days of the Sioux Nation,* 1963. Richard E. Jensen, R. Eli Paul, and John E. Carter, *Eyewitness at Wounded Knee,* 1991.

—Robert M. Utley

WOVOKA (ca. 1856–1932), Paiute religious leader. Born in western Nevada, Wovoka was the son of Tavibo, a Paiute religious leader from the Walker Lake region. As a young man he worked for Mormon ranchers and also as an agricultural laborer in Washington and Oregon, where he was influenced by Smoholla and the Dreamers, a messianic movement among the Northwest tribes. In the late 1880s, while suffering from *smallpox, he experienced visions of dances, songs, and other ceremonies that would bring dead Native Americans back to life, restore game to the plains and forests, re-create a traditional Indian way of life, and cause all non-Indians to disappear.

Wovoka's new religion, called the Ghost Dance, rapidly spread onto the northern plains. Like other Native American revitalization movements that arose during periods of socioeconomic stress, it found ready recipients among impoverished and demoralized Indian communities. Combining elements of traditional tribal religion with Christianity, it offered Native Americans an escape from the desperation and hopelessness of reservation existence.

Although Wovoka espoused nonviolence, in the Dakotas the Sioux dressed in what one observer called "ghost shirts or dresses" that were supposedly impregnable to bullets and sometimes carried arms during their ceremonies. U.S. Army efforts to suppress the Ghost Dance movement led directly to the killing of the Sioux leader *Sitting Bull and to the *Wounded Knee Tragedy in December 1890. Although the Ghost Dance declined after Wounded Knee, Wovoka remained an influential spiritual leader among the Walker Valley Paiutes until his death.

[*See also* Indian History and Culture: From 1800 to 1900.]

• James Mooney, *The Ghost-Dance Religion and the Sioux Outbreak of 1890; Fourteenth Annual Report, Bureau of American Ethnography, Part 2, 1892–1893,* 1896. Michael Hittman, *Wovoka and the Ghost Dance: A Sourcebook,* 1990.

—R. David Edmunds

WPA. *See* Works Progress Administration.

WRIGHT, FRANK LLOYD (1867–1959), architect. Born in Richland Center, Wisconsin, Wright at age twenty withdrew from his first year of engineering studies at the University of Wisconsin and moved to *Chicago, where he worked for architects Dankmar Adler and Louis *Sullivan. Opening his own practice in 1893, Wright in 1900 developed his "Prairie House," the first truly American mode of dwelling appropriate to the emerging suburban residential communities. During this prolific period, Wright also redefined workplace and church architecture with the Larkin Building (1902), and the Unity Temple (1905). In 1889 Wright married Catherine Tobin; they had six children. In 1909 he left his family, traveling to Europe with Mamah Cheney, the wife of a client. In 1911, they moved to Taliesin, the home and studio he built at Spring Green, Wisconsin.

By 1910, Wright's work was being hailed in Europe as a revolutionary, truly modern way of building appropriate to life in the twentieth century. Yet Wright's single important work built abroad, Tokyo's Imperial Hotel (1914–1922), was followed by a twenty-year period of relative inactivity, during which he realized only a series of concrete-block houses and the Aline Barnsdall "Hollyhock" House in Los Angeles (1917). Personal tragedy also contributed to this long hiatus. In 1914, an insane employee burned Taliesen and murdered seven people, including Mamah Cheney and her children. In 1924, after a brief second marriage, Wright began a relationship with Olgivanna Lazovich, who survived him. In 1932, amid the Depression of the 1930s, Wright established the Taliesin Fellowship, a school and apprenticeship program at his rebuilt home and studio.

Almost forgotten at age seventy, Wright re-emerged to dominate the American architectural scene with his three great works of the late 1930s, the Edgar Kaufmann "Fallingwater" House in Pennsylvania, the Johnson Wax Building in Racine, Wisconsin, and the first "Usonian," the Herbert Jacobs House, in Madison, Wisconsin. Like the early Prairie House, the Usonian House was Wright's answer to the housing needs of a new generation. Over the next twenty years Wright built hundreds of these low-cost dwellings for America's rapidly expanding middle class. The Broadacre City project of 1932, an idealized community composed of these individual houses, was Wright's visionary counterproposal to suburban sprawl.

In his final two decades, Wright built numerous internationally acclaimed works, including Taliesin West (1937) in Scottsdale, Arizona; Florida Southern College (1938) in Lakeland, Florida; the Price Tower (1952) in Bartlesville, Oklahoma; the Beth Sholom Synagogue (1954) in Elkins Park, Pennsylvania; the Marin County Civic Center (1957) in San Rafael, California; and New York's Guggenheim Museum, designed in 1943 but not completed until after Wright's death. It is the hundreds of modest Usonian Houses, however, affordable to the middle class yet offering a quality of sun-filled space unmatched even today, which stand as Wright's greatest achievement and most important legacy.

At the end of the twentieth century, Frank Lloyd Wright remained America's most influential and most famous architect. His buildings of the Prairie Period, an indigenous alternative to the dominant classical style imported from Europe, not only founded the "organic" tradition in American architecture, but also directly inspired the beginning of modern architecture in Europe. Wright established by example the fundamental attributes of a modern American architecture shaped by the landscape, the materials of its construction, and the daily lives that take place within its spaces.

[*See also* Architecture: Public Architecture; Architecture: Domestic Architecture; Suburbanization.]

• Meryle Secrest, *Frank Lloyd Wright,* 1992. Robert McCarter, *Frank Lloyd Wright,* 1997.

—Robert McCarter

WRIGHT, RICHARD (1908–1960), writer. Wright was born near Natchez, Mississippi, to Nathan and Ella Wright, he a sharecropper and she a deeply religious schoolteacher. Nathan deserted the family when Richard was five years old. The resulting hardship emerges in Wright's autobiography, *Black Boy* (1945), with its descriptions of childhood hunger and family disruption. In 1925, Wright moved to Memphis, Tennessee, where he read widely among contemporary American writers. In 1927 he migrated to *Chicago's South Side where, his reading told him, he could live in freedom and dignity. There he held odd jobs and was aided by the John Reed Club, the Communist party's organization for young writers. He joined the party in 1934, both to further his literary ambitions and because of its acceptance and support. He published widely, both poetry and prose, in leftist journals. The New Deal's Federal Writers' Project provided support as well.

Breaking with the Chicago party in 1937, Wright moved to *New York City and became Harlem editor of the party's newspaper, The *Daily Worker. Uncle Tom's Children* (1938), four novellas about southern *racism, won wide acclaim. His best-known novel, *Native Son* (1940), enjoyed even broader acclaim as a *Book-of-the-Month Club selection. Set in Chicago, it told the searing story of an uneducated young black slum dweller, Bigger Thomas, who becomes a murderer and rapist. Arrested after a massive manhunt, he is tried and executed. Like no previous novel, *Native Son* evoked the realities of black oppression and racism in the urban North. Increasingly disillusioned with *communism, Wright publicly broke with the party in the 1944 *Atlantic Monthly* essay "I Tried to be a Communist," reprinted in the influential anticommunist manifesto *The God that Failed* (1950).

In 1947 he moved to France to escape the racial hostility he and his family confronted in New York. His writings from this period include *The Outsider* (1953), a philosophical novel influenced by Existentialism, and the autobiographical *The Long Dream* (1958). Active on many fronts, he nurtured in his writing and speaking a growing interest in Africa and in the Third World. A figure of international prominence, he lived in Paris until his death.

Richard Wright brought to literature contemporary understandings of human nature and social relations. His knowledge of society derived not only from experience, but also from the insights of sociologists and social psychologists. Discarding older modes of thinking about the African American experience and U.S. race relations, he blazed new paths of understanding. Many have seen his work as a harbinger of the *civil rights movement and as the fountainhead of subsequent African American literature.

[*See also* African Americans; Communist Party—USA; Literature: Since World War I; New Deal Era, The.]

• Michel Fabre, *The Unfinished Quest of Richard Wright,* 1973. Henry Louis Gates Jr. and K. A. Appiah, eds., *Richard Wright: Critical Perspectives Past and Present,* 1993. Richard Wright, *Native Son and How "Bigger" Was Born,* with an introduction by Arnold Rampersad, 1993.

—Donald B. Gibson

WRIGHT, WILBUR (1867–1912) and **ORVILLE** (1871–1948), inventors of the airplane. The Wright brothers operated a bicycle shop in Dayton, Ohio, in the 1890s. As expert mechanics, they became avidly interested in the problem of human flight. They designed and flew three gliders in the years 1900–1902. In the course of these gliding experiments, they perfected (and in 1906 patented) the most efficient method of controlling an aircraft in the air. In 1903, using data derived from a series of model airfoil tests in their bicycle-shop wind tunnel, they constructed a propeller-driven flying machine, powered by a homemade motor.

In this machine, the Wright brothers made the world's first man-carrying airplane flights on 17 December 1903, above the sands of the Outer Banks near Kitty Hawk, North Carolina.

They continued experimenting in relative secrecy until October 1905, when their long circling flights over a pasture near Dayton attracted attention. Afraid that others might copy their invention, they dismantled their flying machine and spent two years trying to interest the governments of the United States, England, France, and Germany in purchasing a Wright airplane.

In February 1908, the U.S. War Department finally agreed to consider a purchase. In March the Wrights signed a contract with the French. By that summer, French aviators were making flights of up to twenty minutes. Europe seemed poised to take the lead in aviation development, but when Wilbur made his first flights in France in August 1908, they created a sensation. Wilbur's smooth banked turns convinced the world that the Wrights were far ahead of their competitors. In September, Orville astounded Americans with flights of more than an hour near *Washington, D.C.

In November 1909, the brothers established the Wright Company and went into business. They could now afford to sue infringers of their basic 1906 patent, which was not for the airplane itself, but for the means of controlling an airplane—any airplane—in flight. They therefore felt justified in suing anyone who manufactured or flew airplanes for profit and refused to pay royalties to the Wright Company. Warned that the patent suits were hampering the development of aviation, they protested that they merely sought a fair return for having spent their own money and risked their lives while inventing the airplane and learning to fly it.

Wilbur died in 1912. In 1914, Orville locked horns with the *Smithsonian Institution over former Smithsonian Secretary Samuel Langley's unflyable airplane, the *Aerodrome,* which had crashed into the Potomac River on 8 December 1903. The new Secretary authorized the rebuilding of the *Aerodrome* with many modifications. After the plane made a few brief hops, the Smithsonian claimed that had it been properly launched in 1903, it would have flown, nine days before the Wrights' airplane, the *Kitty Hawk.* The *Aerodrome* was later displayed in the Smithsonian's National Museum, as the first airplane "capable of sustained free flight." Orville retaliated by exiling the *Kitty Hawk* to England for display in London's Science Museum. The feud was settled in 1942, but not until December 1948—eleven months after Orville's death—was the *Kitty Hawk* installed as the National Museum's prized centerpiece.

[*See also* Airplanes and Air Transport; Aviation Industry.]

• Fred Howard, *Wilbur and Orville,* 1987. Tom D. Crouch, *The Bishop's Boys,* 1989.

—Fred Howard

X

XYZ AFFAIR. *Jay's Treaty of 1794 with Great Britain, concluded during the war between Britain and revolutionary France, failed to secure the neutral rights of American ships against British searches and seizures. The French were enraged because, after the superior British navy had swept French merchant ships from the sea, France depended on neutral American ships to carry the trade of the French empire. In retaliation, the French began to seize American ships and cargoes. They also refused to receive the new American minister, Charles Cotesworth Pinckney.

Seeking to avoid war, President John *Adams sent John *Marshall and Elbridge Gerry to join Pinckney in Paris to settle the dispute. The French foreign minister, Talleyrand, believing that the Republicans in the U.S. Congress were gaining ground against Adams's less friendly Federalists, tried to stall the negotiations. He sent three messengers to tell the Americans that before he would receive them, they would have to pay him a $250,000 bribe, loan France $12 million, and apologize for America's supposedly anti-French policies. Marshall and Pinckney, the two Federalists on the delegation, rejected the demands and left Paris. Gerry, the lone Republican, refused to leave, fearing that a complete break would mean war.

Since Gerry had not left Paris, his Republican colleagues in Congress refused to believe President Adams's report that France had made outrageous demands. They insisted on seeing the letters sent home by the delegation to prove Adams's charges. Adams turned over the correspondence but substituted the letters *X*, *Y*, and *Z* for the names of Talleyrand's messengers. Thus, the episode was dubbed the XYZ Affair. With the Republicans shocked into silence by the proof of French perfidy, Adams in 1798 authorized American ships to protect themselves from French abuse and secured an appropriation to prepare for war. The *Quasi-War with France was under way.

[*See also* Early Republic, Era of the; Federalist Party; Foreign Relations: U.S. Relations with Europe.]

• Alexander DeConde, *The Quasi-War*, 1966. William Stinchcombe, *The XYZ Affair*, 1980.

—Jerald A. Combs

Y

YALTA CONFERENCE. The *World War II conference of top Allied leaders held at the Black Sea resort of Yalta in the Crimea on 3–12 February 1945 developed from an Anglo-American perception that, with their own and Soviet forces rapidly converging on Berlin, postwar political issues needed urgent attention. Two potentially incompatible views of the postwar world order had already appeared: the American conception of a universalistic *United Nations, and the scenario defined by British Prime Minister Winston Churchill and Soviet leader Josef Stalin at Moscow in October 1944 envisioning British (or Western) and Soviet spheres in postwar Europe. President Franklin Delano *Roosevelt, alarmed by growing domestic criticism of British and Soviet conduct as they consolidated power in their respective spheres, pressed for a meeting. He hoped to bind the Allies to the United Nations framework and also win Soviet agreement to enter the Pacific war. In preliminary diplomatic maneuvering, Stalin made clear that he in return wanted territorial acquisitions in East Asia, recognition of Soviet paramountcy in eastern Europe, and substantial reconstruction aid.

At Yalta, Roosevelt found Stalin determined to dominate eastern and central Europe, already largely under Soviet military control. On the crucial Polish issue, discussed at seven of the eight plenary sessions, Roosevelt and Churchill conceded much of prewar eastern Poland to the Soviets with territorial compensation envisaged for Poland at Germany's expense. Stalin refused a freely elected Polish government, though he accepted a tripartite commission to facilitate the addition of non-communists to the pro-Soviet Lublin regime. In other significant agreements, Stalin accepted the American United Nations formula and promised, in return for territorial concessions at Chinese expense, to declare war on Japan within three months of Germany's surrender. Churchill won an enhanced role for postwar France.

In retrospect, however, the real drama lay elsewhere, in Roosevelt's casual introduction of an ostensibly cosmetic Declaration on Liberated Europe promising "free and unfettered elections" and "democratic institutions" in eastern Europe. Stalin, characteristically insensitive to Western public opinion and/or relying on the political ambiguity of these phrases in the existing context, signed it. He was doubtless upset to find Roosevelt emphasizing it after the conference as the centerpiece of a stunning American diplomatic success.

Stalin reacted angrily to this image-making. He frustrated the operation of the tripartite commission in Poland, arrested Polish resistance leaders, mounted a procommunist coup in Rumania, and refused to send Soviet foreign minister Vyacheslav Molotov to the founding conference of the United Nations. Roosevelt and Churchill, and especially President Harry S. *Truman after taking office on 12 April, responded with increasing vigor. The crisis dragged on until late May when Roosevelt's former aide, Harry *Hopkins, sent by Truman on a conciliatory mission to Moscow, settled the Polish government issue on Stalin's terms.

Yalta long remained deeply controversial. Many Europeans and American conservatives saw the conference as a "betrayal"of Poland, eastern Europe, and China. This image, notwithstanding Roosevelt's spirited liberal defenders, helped stimulate the excesses of the McCarthy era. Later revisionists portrayed a successful negotiation subsequently undermined by Truman's belligerence. Yalta marks the first full American political engagement with Europe's postwar problems. Although some saw it as the high-water mark of American-Soviet cooperation, it also began a process that by stages led to the *Cold War. In retrospect, it appears to have ended the "Grand Alliance" and any prospect of a consensual, cooperative approach to postwar issues.

[*See also* Foreign Relations: U.S. Relations with Europe; World War II: Postwar Impact.]

• John Snell ed., *The Meaning of Yalta,* 1956. Diane S. Clemens, *Yalta,* 1970.

—Fraser J. Harbutt

YAMASEE WAR (1715–1717). Ecological and economic forces precipitated this intertribal war against South Carolina. Cattle owned by South Carolina settlers had destroyed the habitat of the deer on which the Yamasee Indians' hunting-for-trade economy depended. The increasingly debt-ridden Indians complained of trading abuses, including the enslavement of Yamasees, by British trader-creditors. Erstwhile allies of the colony, Yamasees struck its outlying settlements on 15 April 1715, killing more than 160 people in succeeding weeks. Indians of the Piedmont and numerous Creeks joined the low-country Yamasees.

In April and June, Governor Charles Craven and Captain George Chicken counterattacked, driving the Yamasees toward Florida and pacifying the Piedmont Indians. But Creek hostilities persisted. Cherokees rescued the embattled colony by opening hostilities with the Creeks, killing Creek ambassadors at the Cherokee town of Tugaloo in January 1716. Creeks turned for aid to the French and Spanish while also reopening discussions with the English. In 1717, while one group of the Creeks allowed France to erect Fort Toulouse in their country, another group made formal peace with the English settlers of South Carolina.

In the war's aftermath, Creeks emerged as a neutral power courted by three empires; both the Creeks and the Catawbas of the Piedmont gained numerical strength by absorbing Indians displaced by the war; Cherokees intensified their dealings with South Carolina; and while South Carolina survived, the Crown took the weakened colony from its proprietors in 1720. The Yamasees' deerskin trade recovered by the early 1720s, but the trade in Indian slaves never recovered. The Yamasees never made formal peace with their adversaries.

[*See also* Colonial Era; French Settlements in North America; Indian History and Culture: 1500 to 1800; Indian Wars; Spanish Settlements in North America.]

• Verner Crane, *The Southern Frontier, 1670–1732,* 1929. Richard L. Haan, " 'The Trade Do's Not Flourish as Formerly': The Ecological Origins of the Yamasee War of 1715," *Ethnohistory* 38 (1981): 341–58.

—Gregory Evans Dowd

YANKEES. *See* New England.

YELLOW FEVER. Yellow fever, a virus-based infectious *disease transmitted by female mosquitoes that breed in stagnant water, was long endemic in the tropics and in temperate regions during warm seasons. Depending on the severity, its effects range from fever and headache to chills, nausea, hemorrhage, and death. Although scattered outbreaks occurred earlier, the first major yellow fever epidemics in America broke out during the 1790s. Following outbreaks in the Caribbean, the disease flared in *Philadelphia in 1793, disrupting the new federal government and engendering the first major controversy over the etiology (cause) of epidemic disease in the United States. One side argued that the disease arose spontaneously from the filth coating the streets and docks; others claimed it was an imported pestilence. Arguments about *public-health policy flowed from these theories, with one side promoting sanitation, and the other, quarantine. All segments of the population were affected, although the affluent found some protection in flight and *African Americans appeared to suffer less than others.

By the mid-nineteenth century, yellow fever had become principally a disease of southern ports, especially *New Orleans. The argument over transmission and prevention continued, but with a new twist. Southern physicians practicing in rural areas became increasingly convinced that yellow fever could be transported, since they were able to tie rare outbreaks in their areas to contacts with epidemic centers. Physicians voiced a compromise "seed-soil" theory, which held that "seeds" of the disease had to be imported but only thrived in the sort of welcoming environment provided by poor sanitation. Hence, both quarantine *and* sanitation should help prevent yellow fever.

The century's worst yellow fever outbreak struck the *South in 1878, taking an estimated 10,000 lives. Its severity, and impact on trade, led directly to the formation of the first federal public-health agency, the National Board of Health. This foray into national health policy ended in the early 1880s, but the standard was taken up again in the late 1880s by the Marine Hospital Service. This federal organization, previously charged with providing hospital care for sailors, assumed responsibility for yellow fever prevention after 1888 and in the early twentieth century evolved into the U.S. Public Health Service (USPHS). Both state and federal authorities built disinfecting quarantine stations in the 1880s and 1890s to kill the suspected yellow fever "germ," although its identity eluded investigators.

After the U.S. occupation of Cuba in the *Spanish-American War, Surgeon General George Sternberg sent Walter *Reed there as the head of a commission to study yellow fever. He and his colleagues established that the disease was caused by a virus and that it was spread by mosquitoes. In 1905 the USPHS used this knowledge to terminate the last U.S. yellow fever epidemic when it broke out in New Orleans.

[*See also* Medicine: From 1776 to the 1870s; Medicine; From the 1870s to 1945.]

• Margaret Humphreys, *Yellow Fever and the South,* 1992.

—Margaret Humphreys

YELLOWSTONE NATIONAL PARK. Yellowstone, the world's first national park, is situated mainly in Wyoming and extends into Montana and Idaho. It was established in 1872 by Congress, primarily because of its geysers, but also because of its remarkable assemblage of wildlife and unusual natural features. The "national park idea" pioneered at Yellowstone eventually spread worldwide. In the United States, Mackinac Island National Park (now a Michigan state park) was established in 1875 and Sequoia and Yosemite National Parks in 1890. (Yosemite had been a *California state park since 1864.) Yellowstone remains the "mother park" in the U.S. *national park system, which by the 1990s included 376 sites.

Boasting about three-quarters of the world's geysers (of which Old Faithful is the most famous) and over half of the thermal features, it also has one of the globe's most spectacular canyons, one of North America's most celebrated waterfalls, and more than 225 permanent waterfalls higher than fifteen feet. It has the premier wildlife sanctuary (and the top three trout-fishing streams) in the continental United States. Unmatched in the variety and number of its megafauna, the park shelters the world's largest concentration of elk and is one of the last remaining strongholds of the grizzly bear in the coterminous states. It is the only site in the United States (and one of only two in the world) where a wild bison herd has survived continuously since ancient times. At the center of the largest relatively intact ecosystem in the North Temperate Zone, its hundreds of lakes, creeks, mountains, and valleys survive in essentially pristine condition. As in all major parks, Yellowstone's administrators debate the appropriate forms of intervention to protect this delicate ecosystem and strive to balance the competing claims of public access and wilderness preservation.

[*See also* Environmentalism; Tourism; West, The.]

• Aubrey L. Haines, *The Yellowstone Story,* 1996. James Pritchard, *Preserving Yellowstone's Natural Conditions: Science and the Perception of Nature,* 1999.

—Lee H. Whittlesey

YMCA AND YWCA. The Young Men's Christian Association (YMCA) and Young Women's Christian Association (YWCA) are service organizations that arose as part of evangelical *Protestantism's response to *urbanization and *industrialization.

The YMCA movement began in London in 1844; the first American YMCA started in *Boston in 1851. YMCAs were subsequently established for *African-Americans (1853), students (1856), railroad workers (1872), and Native Americans (1879). The National Council of Young Men's Christian Associations (or YMCA of the USA) was founded in 1854. Early Ys were "fellowships" of young men seeking "spiritual and mental improvement" through prayer, *Bible study, lectures, and good works. During the *Civil War, the YMCA-led Christian Commission provided social services for Union soldiers. After the war the YMCA added "social" and "physical" to its statements of purpose while limiting full participation to active members of certain evangelical churches. YMCA staff members invented *basketball (Springfield, Massachusetts, 1891) and volleyball (Holyoke, Massachusetts, 1895).

Eventually abandoning its evangelical membership test, the YMCA gradually expanded its services to boys, women and girls, families, and seniors, while still emphasizing character-building and youth work. The YMCA pioneered in nontraditional education, residential camping, teaching English as a second language, ecumenical relations, and more. The autonomy of local Ys and the involvement of community members guaranteed diversity of membership and a range of programs responsive to local needs. In 1999, with 971 separately-incorporated branches nationwide, the YMCA of the USA was part of an international association representing YMCAs in 120 countries.

The YWCA, America's "largest and oldest women's organization," originated with a "Ladies Christian Association" founded in *New York City in 1858. The YMCA name originated in Boston in 1859. The early YWCA opened a boarding house for young women (1860); a day-nursery (1864), and a student branch (Normal, Illinois, 1873). Based in New York, the YWCA by 2000 had 326 local associations in every state and was affiliated with the World YWCA operating in 101 countries. Focusing on female empowerment, it addressed many social issues including *racism, peace, and voter education. In 1941, the YWCA, the YMCA, and other groups formed the United Service Organizations (USO) which provides social services to soldiers.

Two related organizations, the Young Men's Hebrew Asso-

MAP 26: HOT SPRINGS AND GEYSERS IN YELLOWSTONE NATIONAL PARK (1937)

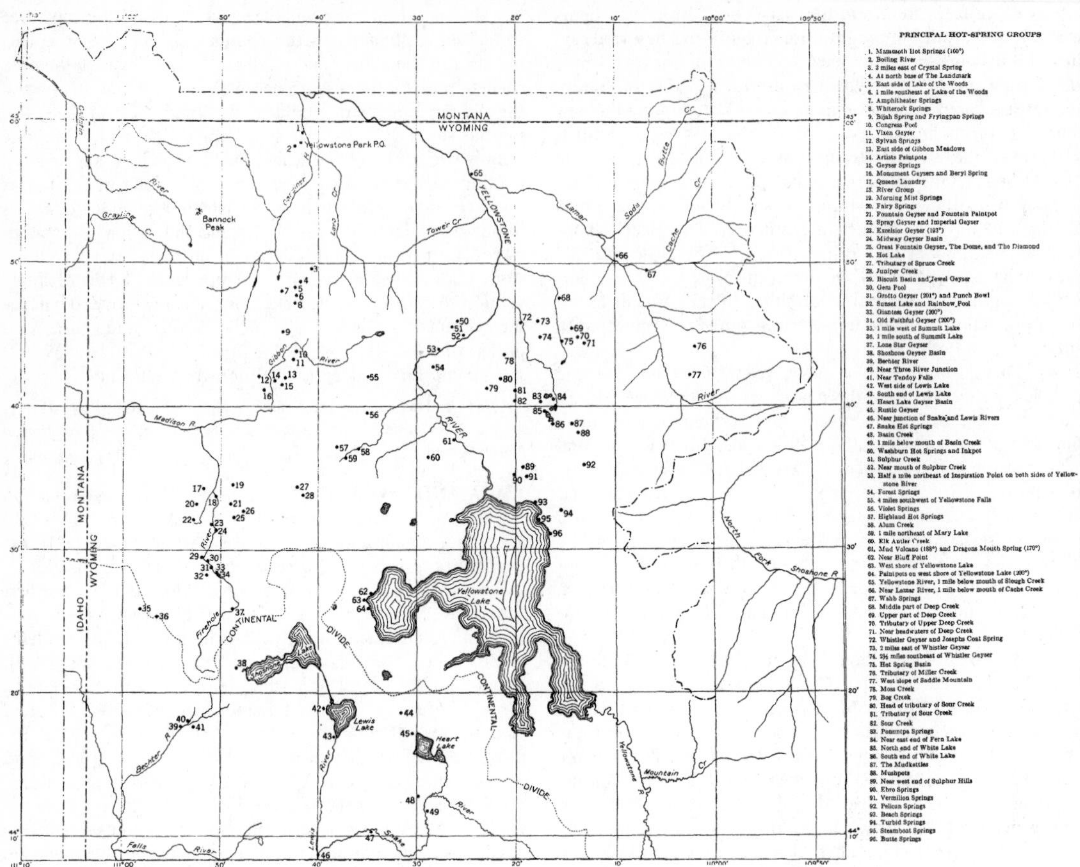

As part of the New Deal's inventory of natural resources, in 1937 the U.S. Geological Survey prepared this map of the hot springs and geysers to be found in Yellowstone National Park, the nation's oldest national park.

[*See* Conservation Movement; National Park System; New Deal Era, The; West, The; Yellowstone National Park.]

ciation (YMHA) and Young Women's Hebrew Association (YWHA) provide lectures, discussion groups, and other activities for their members.

[See also Feminism; Religion; Sports: Amateur Sports and Recreation.]

• C. Howard Hopkins, *History of the YMCA in North America,* 1951. Nina Mjagkij and Margaret Spratt, eds., *Men and Women Adrift: The YMCA and YWCA in the City,* 1997.

—Andrea Hinding

YORKTOWN, BATTLE OF. The Franco-American victory at Yorktown, Virginia, over 8,000 British and Hessian troops on 19 October 1781 ended the *Revolutionary War and secured American independence. The victory arose from France's crucial 1781 decision to send a strong force to aid the Americans.

General George *Washington had planned to attack the British stronghold at *New York City, but finding its defenses too strong, he shifted the campaign to Virginia. A nucleus of 2,500 of Washington's best troops, supplemented by French forces under the Comte de Rochambeau, moved south on 20 August. After overcoming transport problems on Chesapeake Bay, the force reached the Yorktown area on 26 September. Here the British field commander, Charles, Earl Cornwallis, having received conflicting orders from his superior, Sir Henry Clinton, had led his army into a cul-de-sac to await a British fleet that would transport it back to New York. At full strength, the allied force consisted of over 11,000 Americans (roughly 8,000 Continental Army troops and 3,000 militiamen) and nearly 9,000 French soldiers. Another 15,000 French sailors manned the fleet that was crucial to victory.

Washington gambled on a two-part plan that required luck and perfect timing. First, the French naval force under the Comte de Grasse had to prevent the British fleet from reaching Yorktown and evacuating Cornwallis's troops. Second, French siege artillery, too heavy for land transport, had to arrive safely by sea from Newport, Rhode Island. Both parts of the plan succeeded.

The siege at Yorktown, the last major operation of the war, was the only one in which Washington directly commanded the American army. At dusk on 14 October, two 400-man columns, one French grenadiers and chasseurs, the other American light infantry under Alexander *Hamilton, attacked two redoubts in advance of the main British line. Cornwallis, after failing in a half-hearted attempt to dislodge the allies from their advanced positions, opened negotiations on 17 October. Stalling for two days in hopes that the British fleet might appear, he formally surrendered on 19 October. The Battle of Yorktown destroyed Britain's political will to continue the war. Having failed to achieve a military solution to a political crisis, British leaders opened negotiations to end the fighting, a decision that implied recognition of American independence.

[See also Revolution and Constitution, Era of.]

• Henry P. Johnston, *The Yorktown Campaign and the Surrender of Cornwallis, 1781,* 1881; repr. 1979. Douglas S. Freeman, *George Washington: Victory with the Help of France,* 1955. William B. Wilcox, *Portrait of a General: Sir Henry Clinton in the War of Independence,* 1964. Theodore Thayer, *Yorktown: A Campaign of Strategic Options,* 1975. Edward Countryman, *The American Revolution,* 1985.

—Harold E. Selesky

YOSEMITE NATIONAL PARK. Located on the western slope of *California's Sierra Nevada, Yosemite National Park contains over 761,000 acres of protected land, including sequoia groves and expanses of alpine wilderness. The main attraction is Yosemite Valley, where the Merced River winds through meadows in a dramatic rock-walled canyon. Yosemite's cliffs and waterfalls form a monumental landscape that has long been a sacred national icon, a tourist mecca, and a focal point for conservation efforts.

U.S. troops drove out Yosemite's Ahwahneechee Indians in 1853, and *tourism began two years later. The painters Albert Bierstadt and Thomas Hill and the photographer Carleton Watkins soon immortalized Yosemite as a sacred space. In 1864, Congress granted Yosemite Valley to California as a state park. Although *Yellowstone became America's first national park in 1872, the wildland park concept originated in Yosemite. John *Muir, Yosemite's greatest advocate, arrived in 1868, and he fought to protect and expand Yosemite until his death. In 1890, Yosemite National Park was formed from lands surrounding California's small park, and in 1906, Muir and the *Sierra Club convinced California to return Yosemite Valley to the nation.

Muir's final campaign was a decade-long struggle to stop San Francisco from damming and flooding the park's Hetch Hetchy Valley. His effort failed in 1913, but the national debate spurred wilderness preservation and the National Park Service was created three years later. At the end of the twentieth century, Yosemite remained a jewel in the national park system, but its pollution and overcrowding kept it at the center of debates on wilderness use.

[*See also* Environmentalism; National Park System; West, The.]

• Roderick Nash, *Wilderness and the American Mind,* 3rd ed., 1982. Alfred Runte, *Yosemite: The Embattled Wilderness,* 1990.

—William C. Barnett

YOUNG, BRIGHAM. *See* Mormonism.

YOUNG MEN'S CHRISTIAN ASSOCIATION. *See* YMCA and YWCA.

YOUNG WOMEN'S CHRISTIAN ASSOCIATION. *See* YMCA and YWCA.

Z

ZAHARIAS, MILDRED DIDRIKSON ("Babe") (1911–1956), athlete. Considered the most versatile female athlete of the twentieth century, she began her sports career as an industrial-league *basketball player in her hometown, Beaumont, Texas, leading her team to national championships. In the 1932 track and field Olympic trials, she won six gold medals and set four world records in one afternoon. At the Olympic Games in Los Angeles, she set world records in the javelin and 80-meter hurdles (winning two gold medals) and she gained a silver medal in the high jump. At *baseball she once hit seven home runs in seven times at bat, pitched exhibition innings with major league teams, and was nicknamed "the Babe" (after Babe *Ruth). She won tennis and bowling tournaments and toured the United States giving billiards exhibitions and in 1938 married the wrestler George Zaharias. Her greatest fame came in the sport of *golf where she revolutionized the game, won a record eighty-two tournaments, and helped create the Ladies Professional Golfers' Association. The Associated Press named her "Female Athlete of the Year" six times and "Best Female Athlete of the First Half Century" in 1951. She received numerous other honors and awards and appeared on a commemorative U.S. stamp in 1981.

Zaharias defied convention, and manipulated the media image to enhance her celebrity. Crude, crass, and controversial, she created a persona that both captivated the public and perpetuated the stereotype of female athletes as "unnatural" in a period when delicacy and femininity were revered. A sports legend and role model, "the Babe" symbolized pure athleticism, and she lived for competition. She died at forty-five of cancer.

[*See also* Gender; Popular Culture; Sports: Amateur Sports and Recreation; Sports: Professional Sports.]

• Betty Hicks, "The Legendary Babe Didrikson Zaharias" in *Women in Sport: Issues and Controversies,* ed. Greta L. Cohen, 1993, pp. 38–48. Susan E. Cayleff, *Babe: The Life and Legend of Babe Didrikson Zaharias,* 1995.

—Greta Laquia Cohen

ZAKRZEWSKA, MARIE (1829–1902), midwife, physician, founder of the New England Hospital for Women and Children. Born in Berlin, Zakrzewska (pronounced Zak-shef'-ska) studied midwifery in Germany before coming to America in 1853 to pursue a *medical education. Earning her M.D. from Western Reserve College in Cleveland, Ohio, in 1856, she first practiced at the New York Infirmary for Indigent Women and Children. In 1859, she moved to *Boston to teach at the New England Female Medical College, but soon clashed with the College's founder, Samuel Gregory, over her desire to instruct students in such new scientific techniques as microscopy and thermometry. In 1862, with the support of several of Boston's leading liberal reformers, including Caroline Severance and William Lloyd *Garrison, Zakrzewska founded the New England Hospital for Women and Children, where she worked until her retirement in 1899. This institution provided women an opportunity to receive clinical training at a time when most hospital positions were closed to them.

Zakrzewska's strong commitment to scientific medicine was unusual among her contemporaries. At a time when most women physicians justified their entry into the medical profession by emphasizing their caring and sympathetic natures, she insisted that women physicians, like their male counterparts, must develop their scientific investigative skills. Zakrzewska's battles to help women gain entry into the medical profession earned her a reputation as one of the leading women physicians of the nineteenth century.

[*See also* Hospitals; Medicine: From 1776 to the 1870s; Medicine: From the 1870s to 1945.]

• Agnes Vietor, *A Woman's Quest: The Life of Marie E. Zakrzewska, M.D.,* 1924, reprint 1972. Virginia G. Drachman, *Hospital with a Heart. Women Doctors and the Paradox of Separatism at the New England Hospital, 1862–1969,* 1984.

—Arleen Marcia Tuchman

ZENGER TRIAL. In 1733, John Peter Zenger, a German immigrant, launched the first opposition newspaper in the American colonies. His *New York Weekly Journal* vigorously attacked New York's royal governor William Cosby. Among the chief backers of this paper were Lewis Morris, whom Cosby had recently removed as chief justice of the colony. Zenger's paper relentlessly attacked Cosby, using sarcasm, innuendo, and allegory to ridicule the overbearing, greedy, and politically inept governor and his chief advisers. The *Weekly Journal* was also the first American publication to reprint numerous essays by the leading English libertarian philosophers of the period, including *Cato's Letters,* essays written by John Trenchard and Thomas Gordon that would heavily influence the ideology of the American Revolution a generation later.

After several futile attempts to persuade a grand jury to indict Zenger, Governor Cosby arranged for his arrest in November 1734. When the grand jury once again refused to indict Zenger, the colony's attorney general, Richard Bradley, charged the printer with seditious libel. Zenger was initially represented by James Alexander and William Smith, two prominent New York attorneys who were also among the chief backers of the *Weekly Journal,* but the new chief justice, James DeLancey, disbarred them when they challenged the legitimacy of his appointment. DeLancey then selected a pro-Cosby lawyer, John Chambers, to defend Zenger. Chambers planned a traditional defense, in which Zenger would have denied publishing the allegedly libelous newspapers. When the case came to trial, however, Zenger was represented by Andrew Hamilton of Philadelphia, the most prominent attorney in British America. Defying the prevailing rules of libel law, Hamilton argued that his client should be acquitted because what he had published about the governor was, in fact, true. Although apparently guilty under the accepted understanding of libel law, Zenger was acquitted by the jury in August 1735.

Zenger's acquittal did not change the common law of libel, but it did set a powerful political precedent: Zenger was the last colonial printer prosecuted by royal authorities. In 1736 Zenger published *A Brief Narrative of the Case and Tryal of John Peter Zenger,* in which Hamilton, writing anonymously, recounted the events of his famous libel trial and reiterated his argument that newspapers should be free to criticize the government so long as what they wrote was true. Frequently reprinted in England and America, the *Brief Narrative* helped shape the political culture that led to the *Revolutionary War and the subsequent adoption of the *Bill of Rights.

[*See also* Censorship; Civil Liberties; Colonial Era; Journalism; Revolution and Constitution, Era of.]

• Vincent Buranelli, ed., *The Trial of John Peter Zenger,* 1957, reprint 1985. Paul Finkelman, ed., *A Brief Narrative of the Case and Tryal of John Peter Zenger, Printer of the New York Weekly Journal,* 2000.

—Paul Finkelman

ZONING. *See* City Planning.

ZOOLOGY. *See* Biological Sciences.

ILLUSTRATION CREDITS

National Archives: 13; Courtesy of Map Collection, Yale Library: 83; Map Division, New York Public Library, Astor, Lenox and Tilden Foundations: 99; Library of Congress (G3861.E1 1884.R6 TIL): 114; Library of Congress (G159.B7PI Rare Book Division): 180; Library of Congress (F229.H27 1972): 236; Courtesy, American Antiquarian Society: 303; Library of Congress (G3701.E27 1853.Z5 TIL): 306; Library of Congress (G3701.E27 1853.Z5 TIL): 360; Library of Congress (Collection: United States Northeast Region-Industries-Iron & Steel): 395; National Archives: 432; Library of Congress (G4125 1807.F Vault): 440; Courtesy of the Bancroft Library, University of California, Berkeley (G4352 C65 1878 R6 Case XD): 505; Library of Congress (G3804.N4:2M3P3 1881.L3 RR.454): 552; Library of Congress (G4127.O7 1846.F7 TIL Vault): 571; By Permission of the British Library (Maps.K.Top.118.49.b): 580; Library of Congress (G4051.P3 1884.P6 RR.323): 649; Boston Public Library/Rare Books Department. Courtesy of the Trustees (map): 663; National Archives (engraving): 663; Library of Congress (G3861.E9 1860.H4 CW13.2): 715; Courtesy of the Osher Map Library, University of Southern Maine: 722; Courtesy of the Franklin D. Roosevelt Library: 774; Library of Congress (G3711.P2 svar.C4): 782; Library of Congress (G4154.C8A3 1868.R8 Rug 52): 795; Library of Congress (G3984.V855 1863.F4 CW.278): 805; Library of Congress (G3850 1792.E41 Vault): 818; Library of Congress (G4262.Y4 1937.G4 TIL): 856.

INDEX

Note: Pages numbers in **boldface** indicate a major discussion of the topic.